THE
LATER
RENAISSANCE
IN
ENGLAND

THE LATER RENAISSANCE IN ENGLAND

Nondramatic Verse and Prose, 1600-1660

Herschel Baker

Harvard University

WAVELAND

PRESS, INC.

Prospect Heights, Illinois

For information about this book, write or call:

Waveland Press, Inc.
P.O. Box 400
Prospect Heights, Illinois 60070
(847) 634-0081

Copyright © 1975 by Herschel Baker
1996 reissued with changes by Waveland Press, Inc.

ISBN 0-88133-842-7

Printed in the United States of America

7 6 5 4 3 2 1

Preface

With this anthology I complete a project started many years ago when the late Hyder Edward Rollins and I published *The Renaissance in England: Non-dramatic Prose and Verse of the Sixteenth Century* in 1954 (reissued in 1990 by Waveland Press, Inc.). Here, as there, the intention was to provide reliable texts for a generous sampling of the nondramatic literary activity of a period rich in writers great and small. However, the area of the present book—roughly, from the accession of James I in 1603 to the restoration of his grandson Charles II in 1660, or from the death of Spenser to Dryden's emergence as a writer—is made so exciting and important by the literary expression of political, theological, philosophical, and other extra-literary concerns that I have gone beyond the merely belletristic. Thus one will find here not only books and writers never staled by repetition but others hitherto neglected in works like this. It may be argued that such men as Lewis Bayly, John Speed, and Alexander Ross should be allowed to slumber in oblivion, but to represent the theology of this momentous period only by such giants as Andrewes, Donne, and Taylor, the historical writing only by Clarendon, the philosophical speculation only by Bacon and Hobbes is to give a very partial view of an age conspicuous for its conflict and diversity.

In a further effort to avoid a partial view I have tried, whenever possible, to represent both sides of the incessant controversies of this crucial epoch, and so to give a fairer picture of what Milton called its wars of truth. Camden's great *Britannia* is of course of more importance than the waspish criticism of his rival Brooke, but each contributes to our understanding of historiography at a time of rapid change. And so it is with Hakewill and Goodman on the doctrine of decay, Browne and Digby on the problems of philosophy, Chillingworth and Cheynell on latitudinarian theology, Milton and Hall on the roles of church and state, Clarendon and May on the causes of the civil war.

Seeking to impose some sort of order on the sometimes confusing interactions of this age of splendid amateurs—when doctors wrote about religion, politicians doubled as historians, divines were men of letters, and everybody had his say on politics—I have arranged the prose by rubrics that, though arbitrary, help us to discern the major topics of discussion and bring the many forms of prose discourse into alignment. The poets, on the other hand, are presented chronologically. Those who, in defiance of our pigeonholes and labels, turned Jacobean only in their middle years or who wrote on into the Restoration are represented mainly by those works that fall within the limits of our period. This means, for instance, that Drayton's early works and Milton's later ones have been excluded, but at least it serves to keep the focus clear.

As with its predecessor, great care has been expended on the texts, which, with negligible exceptions duly noted in the introductions, are based upon a fresh examination of the earliest printed or manuscript sources. For printed works these sources are identified by the corresponding entry numbers in A. W. Pollard and G. R. Redgrave's *Short-title Catalogue . . . 1475–1640* (STC) or in Donald Wing's *Short-title Catalogue . . . 1641–1700* (Wing). Although I have modernized the spelling and the punctuation, I have generally retained (especially in the poetry) those forms whose obsolete orthography presumably corresponded to pronunciation or preserved the meter and the rime in verse. Whereas this principle permits the modernization of such distracting forms as *anker* (anchor) and *leitourgie* (liturgy) it requires the retention (and glossing) of such uncurrent spellings as *accompt* (account), *acron* (acorn), *bin* (been) *breath* (breathe), *Cales* (Calais), *champion* (*champaign*), *chuse* (*choose*), *delphin* (*dolphin*), *drest* (*dressed*), *ey(e)n* (*eyes*), *interessed* (*interested*), *percullies* (*portcullises*), *salvage* (*savage*), *sixt* (*sixth*), and *wrack* (*wreck*). Two exceptions are *than* (*then*) and *whan* (*when*), which are modernized except where the early spelling preserves a rime. The distinction between -*'d* and -*ed* (where -*ed* represents an additional syllable) has been retained in verse, but -*'d* has been changed to -*ed* in prose; similarly, contracted forms like *ling'ring* and *pow'r* have been retained in verse but expanded in prose. Generally, initials, dates, and contractions (titular and other) have been silently expanded, most marginal glosses have been omitted, and the frequently capricious use of roman and arabic numerals has been normalized.

Following the text there is a short Glossary of frequently cited proper nouns and of words whose change of meaning since Milton's time may be perplexing or misleading to the modern reader. A General Bibliography, divided into five sections to match the major divisions of the texts, has been designed to supplement the more specific items in the introductions that precede each writer's work.

I am grateful to the Delegates of the Clarendon Press for permission to use the late H. M. Margoliouth's transcriptions of Traherne's manuscripts in his edition of the *Centuries, Poems, and Thanksgivings* (2 vols., 1965) and to the staff of the Houghton Library of Harvard University for their patience and cooperation. The almost bottomless resources of that great library have supplied not only the manuscript of part of Milton's *History of Britain* but also the printed texts of almost every other writer included in this book.

H. B.

Harvard University
November 1974

Contents

William Habington 233

Thomas Randolph 239

Henry Vaughan   367

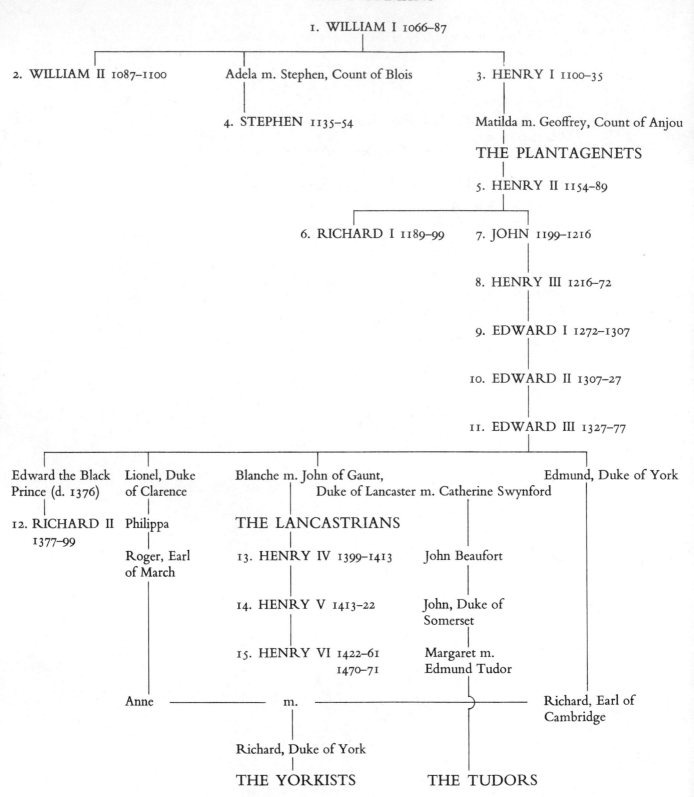

THE NORMANS

I. WILLIAM I 1066–87

2. WILLIAM II 1087–1100   Adela m. Stephen, Count of Blois   3. HENRY I 1100–35

4. STEPHEN 1135–54

Matilda m. Geoffrey, Count of Anjou

THE PLANTAGENETS

5. HENRY II 1154–89

6. RICHARD I 1189–99   7. JOHN 1199–1216

8. HENRY III 1216–72

9. EDWARD I 1272–1307

10. EDWARD II 1307–27

11. EDWARD III 1327–77

Edward the Black Prince (d. 1376)   Lionel, Duke of Clarence   Blanche m. John of Gaunt, Duke of Lancaster m. Catherine Swynford   Edmund, Duke of York

12. RICHARD II 1377–99   Philippa

THE LANCASTRIANS

Roger, Earl of March

13. HENRY IV 1399–1413   John Beaufort

14. HENRY V 1413–22   John, Duke of Somerset

15. HENRY VI 1422–61 1470–71   Margaret m. Edmund Tudor

Anne ——— m. ——— Richard, Earl of Cambridge

Richard, Duke of York

THE YORKISTS   THE TUDORS

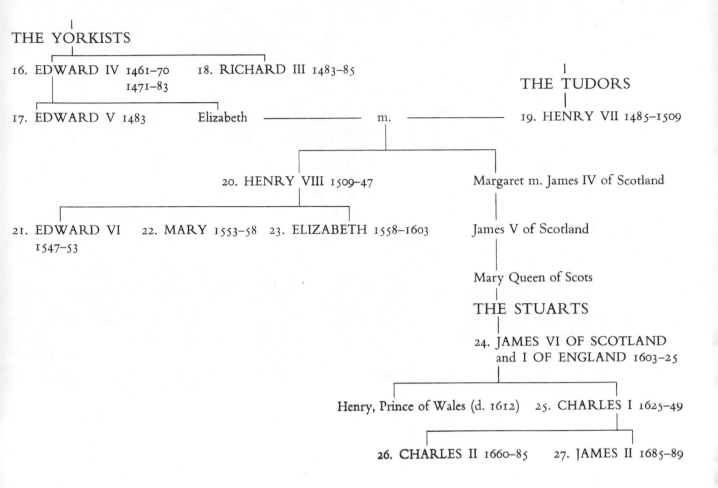

THE YORKISTS

16. EDWARD IV 1461–70
        1471–83

18. RICHARD III 1483–85

THE TUDORS

17. EDWARD V 1483   Elizabeth ————————— m. ————————— 19. HENRY VII 1485–1509

20. HENRY VIII 1509–47

Margaret m. James IV of Scotland

21. EDWARD VI   22. MARY 1553–58   23. ELIZABETH 1558–1603
    1547–53

James V of Scotland

Mary Queen of Scots

THE STUARTS

24. JAMES VI OF SCOTLAND
    and I OF ENGLAND 1603–25

Henry, Prince of Wales (d. 1612)   25. CHARLES I 1625–49

26. CHARLES II 1660–85   27. JAMES II 1685–89

The Kings of England
from William I to James II

The dates are regnal
m. = married
d. = died

POETRY I

Fulke Greville, Baron Brooke[1] [1554-1628]

Although urbanely chided by George Puttenham as early as 1589 for refusing to permit his "excellently" written poems to be "found out and made public," Fulke Greville so resolutely kept his political and literary lives apart that not until 1633, five years after his death, did *Certain Learned and Elegant Works* of this grandee appear. Such reticence was of course obligatory for the scion of a great Warwickshire family made greater by dynastic marriage and by royal bounty from the spoliated monasteries. Greville's gilded youth led through Shrewsbury School and Jesus College, Cambridge, to service with the father of his schoolmate, Sir Philip Sidney, and then to court, where he so much pleased Queen Elizabeth that he enjoyed "the longest lease and the smoothest time without rub of any of her favorites." Like that of many Elizabethan politicians, in the early reign of James I his position was for several years imperiled; but eventually his offices, honors, and emoluments led him to the peerage (as Baron Brooke) in 1621, and when he died in 1628, of wounds inflicted by a disaffected servant, he had long since climbed what his friend Bacon called the winding stair to power. His epitaph in St. Mary's Church at Warwick, which he himself composed, is terse but comprehensive: "Fulke Greville, servant to Queen Elizabeth, councillor to King James, and friend to Sir Philip Sidney. *Trophaeum peccati.*"

Through all this long career of public service and mounting recognition he had also been a somewhat furtive man of letters. From the day in 1564 when they entered Shrewsbury School together he had "observed, honored, and loved" Sir Philip Sidney, and it was as a member of Sir Philip's coterie that he had made his first attempts in verse. Then and later he declined to publish, but he assisted other, needier writers—including Daniel, Camden, Giordano Bruno, John Speed, and Davenant—and he himself continued writing (and revising) almost until his death. Apart from some of the early amatory poems preserved in *Caelica*, however, he eschewed the facile, standard themes. Perhaps in the shock of Sidney's early death (1586), perhaps as a consequence of his unbending Calvinism, he turned to deeper, darker themes. According to Daniel, who dedicated *Musophilus* to him in 1599, Greville thought a poet should "discourse," and in the later parts of *Caelica*, as well as in the frigid closet dramas and the poetical treatises on public affairs that occupied his middle years, he discoursed relentlessly on man's divided soul, his public gains and private desolations, his moral imperatives and social necessities. As a mature poet his aim was not to titillate and please, but to examine and record his own hard-bought convictions in a style as flinty and unyielding as his thinking.

Apart from a few lyrics in poetical miscellanies and an unauthorized edition of the closet drama *Mustapha* in 1609, all of Greville's works were published posthumously, and therefore they are very hard to date. Most of the contents of the 1633 edition are preserved in six manuscript volumes at Warwick Castle (which Greville lavishly restored after the king presented it to him in 1605), and although these show that the author, at intervals of years, continued to revise and tinker with the scribal copies, they tell us nothing of the dates of composition. A few inferences are, however, possible. One of the manuscript volumes contains *Caelica*, and the bewildering diversity in style and form and subject of its 110 "sonnets" suggests an extended span of composition, from perhaps the later 1570's (when Greville was strongly under Sidney's sway) until after 1600. Another of the manuscript volumes is devoted to the treatises on *Human Learning, Religion, Fame and Honor,* and

[1]For other work of Greville, see Books and Men, pp. 689 ff.

Wars; and if the first of these was intended, as Mr. Bullough argues it may have been, as an answer to Bacon's *Advancement of Learning* (1605)—and more remotely to *Musophilus*—it should be assigned to Greville's middle years. The two extant closet dramas *Mustapha* and *Alaham*—together with a third on Antony and Cleopatra that the author prudently destroyed at the time of Essex' fall (1601) lest its politics be misconstrued—were probably linked to such coterie productions as the countess of Pembroke's version of Garnier's *Marc Antoine* (1592) and Daniel's *Cleopatra* (1594). "As inexplicable as the riddles of the Sphinx," in Hazlitt's view, these plays were not intended for the stage; their purpose, as the author said, was "to trace out the high ways of ambitious governors, and to show in the practice that the more audacity, advantage, and good success such sovereignties have, the more they hasten to their own desolation and ruin."

The graceless life of Sidney (1610?–?12), which in manuscript is called "A Dedication," was perhaps intended, as an *apologia* for the author, to introduce the posthumous edition of his own works that Greville must have had in mind. However, the editor of the 1633 collection excluded it, perhaps because of its excessive length. On the other hand, his exclusion of the treatises on *Monarchy* (also among the Warwick Castle manuscripts) and *Religion* should no doubt be attributed to the state of politics in the troubled 1630's. In any event, the life of Sidney (pp. 689 ff.) first appeared in 1652 and the two treatises as part of Greville's literary *Remains* in 1670.

My texts are based upon the posthumous *Certaine Learned and Elegant Workes*, 1633 (STC 12361) and *The Life of the Renowned Sr. Philip Sidney*, 1652 (Wing B–4899). There are editions of the complete works by A. B. Grosart (4 vols., 1870), of *Caelica* by Una Ellis-Fermon (1936), of the *Poems and Dramas* by Geoffrey Bullough (2 vols., 1939), of the *Life* of Sidney by Nowell Smith (1907), and of the 1670 *Remains* by G. A. Wilkes (1965). In addition to M. M. Croll's old but still useful book on Greville (1903) there are recent studies by Joan Rees (1971), Ronald A. Rebholz (1971), and Richard Waswo (1972). Wilkes has bravely undertaken to trace the chronology of the major works (*N & Q*, V, 1958; *SP*, LVI, 1959), as has Rebholz, and William Frost has written a monograph on *Caelica* (privately printed, 1942).

from Certain Learned and Elegant Works (1633)

A TREATY[1] OF HUMAN LEARNING

1

The mind of man is this world's true dimension,[2]
And knowledge is the measure of the mind;
And as the mind, in her vast comprehension,
Contains more worlds than all the world can find,
  So knowledge doth itself far more extend
  Than all the minds of men can comprehend.

2

A climbing height it is without a head,
Depth without bottom, way without an end,
A circle with no line environed;
Not comprehended, all it comprehends:
  Worth infinite, yet satisfies no mind
  Till it that infinite of the Godhead find.

3

This knowledge is the same forbidden tree
Which man lusts after to be made his Maker,
For knowledge is of Power's eternity
And perfect Glory the true image-taker,
  So as[3] what doth the infinite contain
  Must be as infinite as it again.

4

No marvel, then, if proud desire's reflection
By gazing on this sun do make us blind,
Nor if our lust, our centaur-like affection,
Instead of nature fadom[4] clouds and wind,
  So adding to original defection

A TREATY OF HUMAN LEARNING [1]Treatise. [2]Measurement.
[3]So that (a frequent usage in this poem: cf. "such as"="such that" in st. 19). [4]Fathom.

As no man knows his own unknowing mind,
  And our Egyptian darkness[5] grows so gross
  As we may easily in it feel our loss.

5

For our defects in nature who sees not?
We enter, first, things present not conceiving,
Not knowing future, what is past forgot;
All other creatures instant power receiving
  To help themselves, man only bringeth sense[6]
  To feel and wail his native impotence.

6

Which sense, man's first instructor, while it shows[7]
To free him from deceit, deceives him most,
And from this false root that mistaking grows
Which truth in human knowledges hath lost,
  So that by judging sense herein perfection,
  Man must deny his nature's imperfection;

7

Which to be false, even sense itself doth prove,
Since every beast in it doth us exceed;
Besides, these senses which we thus approve,
In us as many divers likings breed
  As there be different tempers in complexions,[8]
  Degrees in healths, or age's imperfections.

8

Again, change from without no less deceives
Than do our own debilities within,
For th' object which in gross our flesh conceives
After a sort, yet when light doth begin
These to retail[9] and subdivide, or sleaves
Into more minutes,[10] then grows sense so thin
  As none can so refine the sense of man
  That two or three agree in any can.

9

Yet these, rack'd up by wit[11] excessively,
Make fancy think she such gradations finds
Of heat, cold, colors, such variety
Of smells and tastes, of tunes such divers kinds,
As that brave Scythian[12] never could descry
  Who found more sweetness in his horse's neighing
  Than all the Phrygian, Dorian, Lydian[13] playing.

10

Knowledge's next organ is imagination,
A glass wherein the object of our sense
Ought to reflect true height or declination
For understanding's clear intelligence;
But this power also hath her variation,
Fixed[14] in some, in some with difference,[15]
In all so shadowed with self-application[16]
  As makes her pictures still too foul or fair,
  Not like the life in lineament or air.

11

This power, besides, always cannot receive
What sense reports, but what th' affections please

To admit; and as those princes that do leave
Their state in trust to men corrupt with ease,
  False in their faith, or but to faction friend,
  The truth of things can scarcely comprehend,

12

So must th' imagination from the sense
Be misinform'd while our affections cast
False shapes and forms on their intelligence,
And to keep out true intromissions thence
  Abstracts the imagination, or distastes
  With images preoccupately plac'd.[17]

13

Hence our desires, fears, hopes, love, hate, and sorrow
In fancy make us hear, feel, see impressions
Such as out of our sense they do not borrow,
And are the efficient cause, the true progression,[18]
  Of sleeping visions, idle phantasms waking,
  Life dreams and knowledge apparitions making.[19]

14

Again, our memory, register of sense
And mold of arts, as mother of induction,
Corrupted with disguis'd intelligence,
Can yield no images for man's instruction
  But as from stained wombs abortive birth
  Of strange opinions to confound the earth.

15

The last chief oracle of what man knows
Is understanding, which though it contain
Some ruinous notions which our nature shows
Of general truths, yet have they such a stain
From our corruption as all light they lose
  Save to convince[20] of ignorance and sin,
  Which where they reign let no perfection in.

16

Hence weak and few those dazzled[21] notions be
Which our frail understanding doth retain,
So as man's bankrupt nature is not free
By any arts to raise itself again,
  Or to those notions which do in us live
  Confus'd, a well-fram'd art-like state to give.

17

Nor in a right line can her eyes ascend
To view the things that immaterial are,

[5]Referring to the plague of darkness that God visited on Egypt (Exodus 10.21–29).   [6]Sense perception, the five senses.   [7]Appears.   [8]Temperaments.   [9]Reveal in detail.
[10]*Sleaves...minutes*: separates (like filaments of silk) into smaller parts.   [11] *Racked...wit*: Stretched by the mind.
[12]Tamerlane, the Mongol conqueror (d. 1405)?
[13]*Phrygian...Lydian*: three modes in Greek music.   [14]Stable.
[15]Variable.   [16]Subjectivism, self-interest.
[17]*To keep...plac'd*: i.e., in order to prevent the admittance of true reports diverts the imagination or offends it with images prejudicially placed.   [18]Process, succession.
[19]*Life...making*: i.e., turning dreams into reality and apparitions into knowledge.   [20]Convict.   [21]Dim, confused.

For as the sun doth, while his beams descend,
Lighten the earth but shadow every star,
  So reason, stooping to attend the sense,
  Darkens the spirit's clear intelligence.

18
Besides, these faculties of apprehension—
Admit they were as in the soul's creation
All perfect here (which blessed large dimension,
As none denies, so, but by imagination
Only, none knows), yet in that comprehension,
  Even through those instruments whereby she works,
  Debility, misprision,[22] imperfection lurks,

19
As many as there be within the brain
Distempers, frenzies, or indispositions;
Yea, of our fall'n estate the fatal stain
Is such as in our youth, while compositions[23]
  And spirits are strong, conception[24] then is weak,
  And faculties in years of understanding break.

20
Again, we see the best complexions vain,
And in the worst more nimble subtilty,
From whence wit a distemper of the brain
The schools conclude;[25] and our capacity,
  How much more sharp, the more it apprehends
  Still to distract, and less truth comprehends.

21
But all these natural defects perchance
May be supplied by sciences and art,
Which we thirst after, study, admire, advance
As if restore our fall, recure our smarts
  They could, bring in perfection, burn our rods,
  With Demades[26] to make us like our gods.

22
Indeed, to teach they confident pretend[27]
All general, uniform axioms scientifical
Of truth that want beginning, have no end:
Demonstrative, infallible, only essential;
  But if these arts contain this mystery,
  It proves them proper to the Deity,

23
Who only is eternal, infinite, all-seeing
Even to the abstract essences of creatures,
Which pure transcendent power can have no being
Within man's finite, frail, imperfect features.[28]
  For proof, what grounds so general and known
  But are with many exceptions overthrown?

24
So that where our philosophers confess
That we a knowledge universal have,
Our ignorance in particulars we express.
Of perfect demonstration who yet[29] gave
  One clear example? Or since time began
  What one true form found out by wit of man?

Having thus exposed man's feeble faculties of knowledge, Greville turns to a conventionally disheartening analysis of man's achievements in the arts and sciences. With arguments drawn from a long line of skeptics he asserts that the principal disciplines are frivolous because they lack "the power to make us better" (st. 35); indeed, we are so deeply "stain'd" by sin that everything we know is built upon the "false foundation" of our guilt (st. 55). Thus our highest wisdom is to recognize our own infirmity, for only by such humbling self-awareness may we see the world for what it is and so "refine" (but not "cure") its stupidity and "ostentation" (st. 63). In the final section of his treatise Greville tries to show how this is done. Like Bacon in *The Advancement of Learning*—but with a very different tone and manner —he calls for a general reformation of the arts and sciences. Although he surveys a wide terrain—theology, law, medicine, philosophy, politics, and logic among others— his comments on poetry and music may serve to represent his values, which are generally empirical, utilitarian, and anti-humanistic.

107
Rhetoric, to this[30] a sister and a twin,
Is grown a siren in the forms of pleading,
Captiving reason with the painted skin
Of many words, with empty sounds misleading
  Us to false ends by these false forms' abuse,
  Brings never forth that truth whose name they use.

108
Besides, this art, where scarcity of words
Forc'd her, at first, to metaphoric wings,
Because no language in the earth affords
Sufficient characters to express all things,
  Yet, since, she plays the wanton with this need,
  And stains the matron with the harlot's weed,[31]

109
Whereas those words in every tongue are best
Which do most properly express the thought,
For as of pictures, which should manifest
The life, we say not that is fineliest wrought
  Which fairest simply shows, but fair and like,
  So words must sparks be of those fires they strike.

110
For the true art of eloquence indeed
Is not this craft of words, but forms of speech
Such as from living wisdoms do proceed,
Whose ends are not to flatter or beseech,
  Insinuate or persuade, but to declare
  What things in nature good or evil are.

[22]Mistaking one thing for another.
[23]Physical and mental constitutions.   [24]Power of conceiving ideas.
[25]*From whence...conclude*: from whence the schools conclude wit to be a distemper of the brain.
[26]Unscrupulous Athenian politician (d. 319 B.C.) who, to curry favor with the conquering Macedonians, procured the deification of Alexander the Great.   [27]Profess, claim.   [28]Forms.
[29]Text *it*, but the Warwick manuscript supports the emendation.
[30]i.e., logic.   [31]Apparel.

111

Poesy and music, arts of recreation,
Succeed (esteem'd as idle men's profession)
Because their scope, being merely contentation,[32]
Can move, but not remove or make impression
 Really, either to enrich the wit
 Or (which is less) to mend our states by it.

112

This makes the solid judgments give them place
Only as pleasing sauce to dainty food,
Fine foils[33] for jewels' or enamels' grace,
Cast upon things which in themselves are good,
 Since if the matter be in nature vile,
 How can it be made precious by a style?

113

Yet in this life both these play noble parts:
The one to outward church-rites if applied
Helps to move thoughts while God may touch the hearts
With goodness, wherein He is magnified;
 And if to Mars we dedicate this art,
 It raiseth passions which enlarge the mind
 And keeps down passions of the baser kind.

114

The other twin,[34] if to describe or praise
Goodness or God she her ideas frame,
And like a maker her creations raise
On lines of truth, it beautifies the same;
 And while it seemeth only but to please,
 Teacheth us order under pleasure's name,
 Which in a glass shows Nature how to fashion
 Herself again, by balancing of passion.

115

Let therefore human wisdom use both these
As things not precious in their proper kind:[35]
The one a harmony to move and please,
If studied for itself, disease of mind;
The next, like Nature, doth ideas raise,
Teaches and makes, but hath no power to bind;
 Both, ornaments to life and other arts
 Whiles they do serve and not possess our hearts.

As Greville, with characteristic discursiveness, approaches his conclusion he reasserts his major themes: the infinite goodness of God and the infinite depravity of man. Since these polarities cannot be reconciled, it remains for us to recognize our narrow limits and to use our faulty knowledge for the common good.

143

The chief use, then, in man of that he knows
Is his painstaking for the good of all:
Not fleshly weeping for our own-made woes,
Not laughing from a melancholy gall,
Not hating from a soul that overflows
With bitterness, breath'd out from inward thrall,[36]
 But sweetly rather to ease, loose, or bind,
 As need requires, this frail, fall'n humankind.

144

Yet some seek knowledge merely but to know,[37]
And idle curiosity that is;
Some but to sell, not freely to bestow;
These gain and spend both time and wealth amiss,
Embasing[38] arts by basely deeming so;
Some to be known, and vanity is this;[39]
 Some to build others, which is charity;
 But these to build themselves,[40] who wise men be.

145

And to conclude: whether we would erect
Ourselves or others by this choice of arts,
Our chief endeavor must be to effect
A sound foundation, not on sandy parts
 Of light opinion, selfness, words of men,
 But that sure rock of truth: God's word or pen.

146

Next, that we do not overbuild our states
In searching secrets of the Deity,
Obscurities of nature, casualty of fates;
But measure first our own humanity,
Then on our gifts impose an equal rate,[41]
And so seek wisdom with sobriety:
 Not curious what our fellows ought to do,
 But what our own creation binds us to.

147

Lastly, we must not to the world erect
Theaters, nor plant our paradise in dust,
Nor build up Babels for the devil's elect;
Make temples of our hearts to God we must,
 And then, as godless wisdoms follies be,
 So are His lights our true philosophy.

148

With which fair cautions man may well profess
To study God, whom he is born to serve;
Nature, t' admire the greater in the less;
Time, but to learn; ourselves we may observe
 To humble us; others, to exercise
 Our love and patience, wherein duty lies;

149

Lastly, the truth and good, to love and do them;
The error, only to destroy and shun it;
Our hearts in general will lead us to them
When gifts of grace and faith have once begun it,
 For without these the mind of man grows numb,
 The body darkness, to the soul a tomb.

[32]Contentment, pleasure. [33]Settings for gems. [34]I.e., music.
[35]Own nature. [36]Distress.
[37]Text *to be knowne*. The emendation is supported by the Warwick manuscript. [38]Debasing.
[39]*Some...this*: This line, missing in the text, is supplied by the Warwick manuscript. [40]I.e., seek their own salvation.
[41]Proportionate levy.

150

Thus are true learnings in the humble heart
A spiritual work, raising God's image razed
By our transgression, a well-framed art
At which the world and error stand amazed,
A light divine where man sees joy and smart[42]
Immortal in this mortal body blazed,[43]
  A wisdom which the Wisdom us assureth
  With hers even to the sight of God endureth.

151

Hard characters,[44] I grant, to flesh and blood,
Which in the first perfection of creation
Freely resign'd the state of being good
To know the evil where it found privation,
And lost her being ere she understood
Depth of this fall, pain of regeneration:
  By which she yet must raise herself again
  Ere she can judge all other knowledge vain.

MUSTAPHA

CHORUS SACERDOTUM[1]

O wearisome condition of humanity!
Born under one law, to another bound,
Vainly[2] begot, and yet forbidden vanity,
Created sick, commanded to be sound!
What meaneth Nature by these diverse laws?   5
Passion and reason self-division cause.
Is it the mark or majesty of Pow'r
To make offenses that it may forgive?
Nature herself doth her own self deflow'r
To hate[3] those errors she herself doth give.   10
For how should man think that[4] he may not do
If Nature did not fail[5] and punish too?
Tyrant to others, to herself unjust,
Only commands things difficult and hard;
Forbids us all things which it knows is lust,[6]   15
Makes easy pains, unpossible reward.[7]
If Nature did not take delight in blood
She would have made more easy ways to good.
We that are bound by vows and by promotion[8]
With pomp of holy sacrifice and rites   20
To teach belief in good and still devotion,
To preach of heaven's wonders and delights,
Yet when each of us in his own heart looks
He finds the God there far unlike his books.

CAELICA

SONNET 85[1]

Love is the peace whereto all thoughts do strive,
Done and begun with all our pow'rs in one,
The first and last in us that is alive,
End of the good, and therewith pleas'd alone.
Perfection's spirit, goddess of the mind,   5

Passed through hope, desire, grief, and fear,
A simple goodness in the flesh refin'd,
Which of the joys to come doth witness bear.

Constant because it sees no cause to vary,
A quintessence of passions overthrown,   10
Rais'd above all that change of objects carry,
A Nature by no other nature known,
  For glories of eternity a frame
  That by all bodies else obscures her name.

SONNET 86

The earth with thunder torn, with fire blasted,
With waters drown'd, with windy palsy shaken
Cannot for this with heaven be distasted,[1]
Since thunder, rain, and winds from earth are taken.
Man torn with Love, with inward furies blasted,   5
Drown'd with despair, with fleshly lustings shaken
Cannot for this with heaven be distasted:
Love, fury, lustings out of man are taken.
Then, Man, endure thyself! Those clouds will vanish;
Life is a top which whipping Sorrow driveth;[2]   10
Wisdom must bear what our flesh cannot banish:
The humble lead, the stubborn bootless striveth.
  Or, Man, forsake thyself! To heaven turn thee!
  Her flames enlighten Nature, never burn thee.

SONNET 88

Man, dream no more of curious mysteries,
As what was here before the world was made,
The first man's life, the state of paradise,
Where heaven is or hell's eternal shade,
  For God's works are like Him, all infinite,   5
  And curious search but crafty Sin's delight.

The flood that did and dreadful fire that shall
Drown and burn up the malice[1] of the earth,
The divers tongues and Babylon's[2] downfall
Are nothing to the man's renewed birth: 10
  First let the Law plow up thy wicked heart,
  That Christ may come, and all these types[3] depart.
When thou hast swept the house that all is clear,

[42]Pain. [43]Blazoned, proclaimed. [44]Characteristics.
CHORUS SACERDOTUM [1]Chorus of priests.
[2]In vanity, i.e., idly, thoughtlessly. [3]Manifest hatred for.
[4]Form ideas of that which. [5]Err, fall short. [6]Pleasure.
[7]*Makes...reward*: i.e., makes punishment easy to incur, reward impossible to achieve.
[8]Preferments, i.e., the priestly office to which we have been preferred.
SONNET 85 [1]Text *84*. The misnumbering of No. 28 (as 27) is continued through the sequence.
SONNET 86 [1]Offended. [2]Spins, whips. SONNET 88 [1]Wickedness.
[2]Referring to the tower of Babel whereby Noah's descendants tried to climb to heaven but failed when God confused the language of the builders (Genesis 11.1–10).
[3]Personages or events in the Old Testament that prefigure something in the New.

When thou the dust hast shaken from thy feet,
When God's All-might doth in thy flesh appear,   15
Then seas with streams above thy sky do meet;
    For goodness only doth God comprehend,
    Knows what was first and what shall be the end.

SONNET 98

Wrapp'd up, O Lord, in man's degeneration,
The glories of Thy truth, Thy joys eternal
Reflect upon my soul dark desolation,
And ugly prospects o'er the sp'rits[1] infernal.
    Lord, I have sinn'd, and mine iniquity
    Deserves this hell—yet, Lord, deliver me!   5

Thy pow'r and mercy, never comprehended,
Rest lively imag'd in my conscience wounded,
Mercy to grace and pow'r to fear extended,
Both infinite, and I in both confounded.[2]   10
    Lord, I have sinn'd, and mine iniquity
    Deserves this hell—yet, Lord, deliver me!

If from this depth of sin, this hellish grave
And fatal absence from my Saviour's glory,
I could implore His mercy who can save,   15
And for my sins, not pains of sin, be sorry,
    Lord, from this horror of iniquity
    And hellish grave Thou wouldst deliver me.

SONNET 99

Down in the depth of mine iniquity,
That ugly center of infernal spirits
Where each sin feels her own deformity
In these peculiar torments she inherits,
    Depriv'd of human graces and divine,   5
    Even there appears this saving God of mine.

And in this fatal mirror of transgression
Shows man as fruit of his degeneration,
The errors' ugly, infinite impression
Which bears the faithless down to desperation,   10
    Depriv'd of human graces and divine,
    Even there appears this saving God of mine.

In power and truth, almighty and eternal,
Which on the sin reflects strange desolation,
With glory scourging all the sp'rits infernal,   15
And uncreated hell with unprivation,[1]

Depriv'd of human graces, not divine,
    Even there appears this saving God of mine.

For on this sp'ritual cross condemned lying
To pains infernal by eternal doom,[2]   20
I see my Saviour for the same sins dying,
And from that hell I fear'd, to free me come;
    Depriv'd of human graces, not divine,
    Thus hath His death rais'd up this soul of mine.

SONNET 109

Sion lies waste, and Thy Jerusalem,
O Lord, is fall'n to utter desolation;
Against Thy prophets and Thy holy men
The sin hath wrought a fatal combination,
    Profan'd Thy name, Thy worship overthrown,   5
    And made Thee, living Lord, a god unknown.

Thy powerful laws, Thy wonders of creation,
Thy Word incarnate, glorious heaven, dark hell
Lie shadowed under man's degeneration,
Thy Christ still crucified for doing well;   10
    Impiety, O Lord, sits on Thy throne,
    Which makes Thee, living Light, a god unknown.

Man's superstition hath Thy truths entomb'd;
His atheism again her pomps defaceth;
That sensual, unsatiable, vast womb   15
Of Thy seen church Thy unseen church disgraceth.
    There lives no truth with them that seem Thine own,
    Which makes Thee, living Lord, a god unknown.

Yet unto Thee, Lord (mirror of transgression),
We who for earthly idols have forsaken   20
Thy heavenly image (sinless pure impression),
And so in nets of vanity lie taken,
    All desolate implore that to Thine own,
    Lord, Thou no longer live a god unknown.

Yet, Lord, let Israel's plagues not be eternal,   25
Nor sin forever cloud Thy sacred mountains,
Nor with false flames, spiritual but infernal,
Dry up Thy mercy's ever-springing fountains;
    Rather, sweet Jesus, fill up time and come
    To yield the sin her everlasting doom.   30

SONNET 98   [1]Spirits.   [2]Abashed.
SONNET 99   [1]I.e., God's goodness (reflecting the Augustinian notion that evil is merely *privatio boni*, "the absence of good").
[2]Judgment.

George Chapman [1559?-1634]

Whereas the theory and practice of most great men of letters—Jonson, Keats, and Eliot, for example—reinforce and exemplify each other, Chapman's often seem to draw apart. To be sure, his noble translations of the *Iliad* and the *Odyssey* capture some of Homer's surging power and illustrate the moral force of Chapman's own conception of his art, but these translations are so hard to represent by short selections that their author must be sampled in this book by his own gnarled and knotty verse and by his prose pronouncements on poetry as a kind of knowledge. In the dedication to his first published work—the notoriously obscure *Skia Nuktos, The Shadow of Night* (1594)—he adumbrated a theory of literature that he maintained, with damnable iteration, to the end of his career. Compounded of neoplatonic metaphysics and neo-Stoic ethics, and resting on an angry disesteem for merely pleasant, facile writing, this theory holds that since literature is, or ought to be, inspired, it conveys to certain men a special kind of knowledge. One corollary of this proposition is that because the true poet deals in sacred things, he serves a priestly function; another is that conventional men of letters, whose "benumbing ignorance" turns art into a "pretty toy," cannot even comprehend the "rapture" that they have no right to share. Warming to the subject in the dedication of his second publication (*Ovid's Banquet of Sense*, 1595), Chapman propounded an esthetic of such systematic obfuscation that it seems to hold the reader in defiance. "Obscurity in affection of words and indigested conceits is pedantical and childish," he concedes,

> but where it shroudeth itself in the heart of his subject, uttered with fitness of figures and expressive epithets, with that darkness will I still labor to be shadowed.

Stated baldly, Chapman's view of literature as a form of lofty knowledge (a view that looks back to Sidney and ahead to Milton) may be regarded as a commonplace of Christian humanism, and in the poet's more successful statements of this notion—for example, the epistle to Thomas Harriot in *Achilles' Shield* and the dedication to Prince Henry of *The Iliads of Homer*—it acquires an almost Miltonic ardor and conviction. Elsewhere, however, his moralizing deteriorates into strident or querulous complaint, murkily expressed, and the poet-priest becomes almost a bore. But however prolix and cloudy Chapman's precepts often are, they convey intense conviction. The following excerpts fairly represent his thought and style, and taken all together they reveal an attitude toward art that in its weight and intellectual poise can still command attention.

Although Chapman was almost middle-aged before he began to publish, his corpus is substantial. By the time the old queen died in 1603 he had produced, in addition to *The Shadow of Night* and *Ovid's Banquet of Sense*, half a dozen plays, the completion of Marlowe's *Hero and Leander* (1598), and—most important in his own opinion—the first installments of his Homer. Inevitably for a work of such majestic scope, the Homer was to be his main concern for many years. In 1598 there appeared, with a dedication to the earl of Essex, both *Seven Books of the Iliads of Homer* and *Achilles' Shield*, the first a translation in septenary couplets of Books I–II and VII–XI, the second a partial translation in heroic couplets of Book XVIII. The excerpt below from the preliminary matter of *Achilles' Shield* shows something of Chapman's truculence and pride as he began his massive undertaking, and also, in the address to Harriot, of his conception of poetry as the product of celestial inspiration. In 1609, he published his translation of the first twelve books of the *Iliad*; about the same time *Euthymiae Raptus or the Tears of Peace* enabled him to comment on contemporary affairs while expounding his own view of "learning" as essential to "good life and true humanity." Two years later the complete *Iliads of Homer* appeared, buttressed with an eloquent dedication to Prince Henry and an important "Preface to the Reader."

Along with free translations and paraphrases of Petrarch, Vergil, and Epictetus, *Petrarch's Seven Penitential Psalms* (1612) also contains "A Hymn to Our Saviour on the Cross," Chapman's most extended statement of his Christian faith. Prince Henry's early death—which to Chapman, as to Raleigh and to many other men of letters, was a real disaster—was duly mourned in a turgid *Epicede or Funeral Song* (1613), which was quickly followed by two other occasional poems: *Eugenia*, a formidably tedious elegy on William, Lord Russell, and *Andromeda Liberata*, an allegory designed to celebrate the marriage of the author's new patron, Robert Carr, earl of Somerset, with the divorced and profligate Frances Howard, countess of Essex. Despite its almost impenetrable obscurity the latter work gave such offense, owing to the scandal of the marriage, that it required a labored *Justification* (1614) for the poet to clarify his own intentions.

These regrettable distractions no doubt delayed but did not stop his work on Homer. In 1614 he published the first twelve books of the *Odyssey* in the heroic couplets first tested in *Achilles' Shield*, and two years later he crowned his long devotion to the god of his idolatry with *The Whole Works of Homer*. Although the aging poet had eighteen years to live, the work that he was born to do was done, and the sporadic labors of his later life—including versions of Musaeus (1616), Hesiod (1618), and the minor Homerica (1624)—could not diminish or enlarge his solid reputation.

My texts are based on *Achilles Shield. Translated as the other seuen Bookes of Homer, out of his eighteenth booke of Iliades*, 1598 (STC 13635), *Euthymiae Raptus; or The Teares of Peace: With Interlocutions*, 1609 (STC 4976), *The Iliads of Homer Prince of Poets. Neuer before in any languag truely translated*, 1611 (STC 13634), *Petrarchs Seven Penitentiall Psalms, Paraphrastically Translated: With other Philosophicall Poems, and a Hymne to Christ vpon the Crosse*, 1612 (STC 19810), and *The Whole Works of Homer in His Iliads and Odysses*, 1616 (STC 13624).

Phyllis B. Bartlett's edition of the *Poems* (1941) replaces the unsatisfactory *Poems and Minor Translations* (for which Swinburne supplied a strenuous introduction, 1875), and Allardyce Nicoll's admirable edition of the serial translation of Homer (2 vols., 1956) supersedes all its predecessors. F. A. Schoell has studied some of Chapman's sources (*Études sur l'humanisme continental en Angleterre*, 1926), Jean Jacquot *Sa vie, sa poésie, son théâtre, sa pensée* (1951), Ennis Rees his ethics (*The Tragedies of George Chapman*, 1954), and George de F. Lord one of his principal achievements in *Homeric Renaissance: The Odyssey of George Chapman* (1956). Chapman appears importantly in M. C. Bradbrook's *School of Night* (1936) and E. A. Strathman's *Sir Walter Raleigh* (1951). There are more comprehensive studies by Millar MacLure (1966) and Charlotte Spivack (1967), and a *Concise Bibliography* by S. A. Tannenbaum (1938), subsequently expanded with a *Supplement* (1946).

from Dedications and Prefaces to Homer

ACHILLES' SHIELD (1598)

TO MY ADMIRED AND SOUL-LOVED FRIEND, MASTER OF
ALL ESSENTIAL AND TRUE KNOWLEDGE,
MASTER HARRIOTS[1]

To you whose depth of soul measures the height
And all dimensions of all works of weight,
Reason being ground, structure, and ornament
To all inventions grave and permanent,
And your clear eyes the spheres where reason moves,   5
This artisan, this god of rational loves,
Blind Homer, in this shield, and in the rest
Of his seven books which my hard hand hath dress'd
In rough integuments, I send for censure,
That my long time and labor's deep extensure[2]   10
Spent to conduct him to our envious light,
In your allowance may receive some right
To their endeavors, and take virtuous heart
From your applause, crown'd with their own desert.
Such crowns suffice the free and royal mind,   15
But these subjected hangbys[3] of our kind,
These children that will never stand alone,
But must be nourish'd with corruption,

Which are our bodies, that are traitors born
To their own crowns, their souls, betray'd to scorn,   20
To gaudy insolence and ignorance,
By their base flesh's frailties, that must dance
Profane attendance at their states and birth,
That are mere servants to this servile earth,
These must have other crowns for meeds than merits,   25
Or starve themselves and quench their fiery spirits.
Thus as the soul upon the flesh depends,
Virtue must wait on wealth; we must make friends
Of the unrighteous Mammon,[4] and our sleights
Must bear the forms of fools or parasites.   30
Rich mine of knowledge, O that my strange Muse
Without this body's nourishment could use
Her zealous faculties only t' aspire[5]
Instructive light from your whole sphere of fire!
But woe is me, what zeal or pow'r soever   35
My free soul hath, my body will be never

TO MASTER HARRIOTS   [1]Thomas Harriot (1560–1621), distinguished astronomer and mathematician, and a valued member of the coterie of freethinkers around Sir Walter Raleigh.   [2]Extent.   [3]Dependents, hangers-on.
[4]Personification of covetousness (from the Aramaic word for "riches" in the Bible).   [5]Attain.

Able t' attend: never shall I enjoy
Th' end of my hapless birth, never employ
That smother'd fervor that in loathed embers
Lies swept from light, and no clear hour remembers.   40
O had your perfect eye[6] organs to pierce
Into that chaos whence this stifled verse
By violence breaks, where glowworm-like doth shine
In nights of sorrow this hid soul of mine,
And how her genuine forms struggle for birth   45
Under the claws of this foul panther earth,
Then under all those forms you should discern
My love to you in my desire to learn.

.   .   .   .   .   .

Continue then your sweet, judicial kindness   111
To your true friend, that though this lump of blindness,
This scornful, this despis'd, inverted world,
Whose head is Fury-like with adders curl'd,
And all her bulk a poisoned porcupine,   115
Her stings and quills darting at worths divine,
Keep under my estate[7] with all contempt
And make me live even from myself exempt,[8]
Yet if you see some gleams of wrastling[9] fire
Break from my spirit's oppression, showing desire   120
To become worthy to partake your skill
(Since virtue's first and chief step is to will),
Comfort me with it and prove you affect me,
Though all the rotten spawn of earth reject me.
For though I now consume in poesy,   125
Yet Homer being my root I cannot die.
But lest to use all poesy in the sight
Of grave Philosophy show brains too light
To comprehend her depth of mystery,
I vow 'tis only strong necessity   130
Governs my pains herein, which yet may use
A man's whole life without the least abuse.
And though to rhyme and give a verse smooth feet,
Uttering to vulgar palates passions[10] sweet,
Chance often in such weak, capricious spirits   135
As in nought else have tolerable merits,
Yet where high Poesy's native habit shines,
From whose reflections flow eternal lines,
Philosophy retir'd to darkest caves
She can discover, and the proud world's braves[11]   140
Answer in anything but impudence
With circle of her general excellence....

THE ILIADS OF HOMER, PRINCE OF POETS (1611)

TO THE HIGH-BORN PRINCE OF MEN, HENRY,
THRICE-ROYAL INHERITOR TO THE UNITED KINGDOMS
OF GREAT BRITAIN, ETC.[1]

Since perfect happiness, by princes sought,
Is not with birth born nor exchequers bought,
Nor follows in great trains, nor is possess'd
With any outward state,[2] but makes him blest

That governs inward and beholdeth there   5
All his affections stand about him bare,
That by his power can send to Tow'r and death
All trait'rous passions, marshaling beneath
His justice his mere will, and in his mind
Holds such a scepter as can keep confin'd   10
His whole life's actions in the royal bounds
Of virtue and religion, and their grounds
Takes in to sow his honors, his delights,
And complete empire; you should learn these rights,
Great Prince of men, by princely precedents,   15
Which here, in all kinds, my true zeal presents
To furnish your youth's groundwork and first state,
And let you see one godlike man create
All sorts of worthiest men, to be contriv'd
In your worth only, giving him[3] reviv'd   20
For whose life Alexander would have given
One of his kingdoms; who (as sent from heaven[4]
And thinking well that so divine a creature
Would never more enrich the race of nature)
Kept as his crown his works, and thought them still   25
His angels, in all power to rule his will;
And would affirm that Homer's poesy
Did more advance his Asian victory
Than all his armies. O, 'tis wondrous much
(Though nothing priz'd) that the right virtuous touch   30
Of a well written soul to virtue moves.
Nor have we souls to purpose if their loves
Of fitting objects be not so inflam'd.
How much, then, were this kingdom's main soul maim'd
To want this great inflamer of all powers   35
That move in human souls! All realms but yours
Are honor'd with him, and hold bless'd that state
That have his works to read and contemplate,
In which humanity to her height is rais'd,
Which all the world—yet none enough—hath prais'd.   40
Seas, earth, and heaven he did in verse comprise,
Outsung the Muses, and did equalize[5]
Their king Apollo, being so far from cause
Of princes' light thoughts that their gravest laws
May find stuff to be fashion'd by his lines.   45
Through all the pomp of kingdoms still he shines,
And graceth all his gracers. Then let lie
Your lutes and viols, and more loftily
Make the heroics of your Homer sung,
To drums and trumpets set his angel's tongue;   50
And with the princely sport of hawks[6] you use,
Behold the kingly flight of his high Muse;

[6]I.e., Harriot's telescope?   [7]Keep my position low.   [8]Removed.
[9]Wrestling, i.e., struggling.   [10]Love poems.   [11]Bullies.
TO THE HIGH-BORN PRINCE   [1]*Henry . . . Britain:* Henry Frederick,
prince of Wales (1594–1612), eldest son of James I. When Chapman published his completed translations of *The Whole Works of Homer* (1616) he included some memorial verses "To the Immortal Memory of the Incomparable Hero, Henry, Prince of Wales."
[2]Splendor.   [3]I.e., Homer.
[4]Following his conquest of Egypt, Alexander was saluted by the priests of the temple of Jupiter Ammon as the son of the god whom they worshiped.   [5]Equal.   [6]I.e., falconry.

And see how like the phoenix she renews
Her age and starry feathers in your sun,
Thousands of years attending, every one   55
Blowing the holy fire and throwing in
Their seasons, kingdoms, nations that have been
Subverted in them, laws, religions, all
Offer'd to Change and greedy Funeral;
Yet still your Homer lasting, living, reigning,   60
And proves how firm Truth builds in poets' feigning.

    A prince's statue, or in marble carv'd
Or steel or gold, and shrin'd (to be preserv'd)
Aloft on pillars or pyramides,
Time into lowest ruins may depress;   65
But drawn with all his virtues in learn'd verse,
Fame shall resound them on Oblivion's hearse,
Till graves gasp with her blasts, and dead men rise.
No gold can follow where true Poesy flies.

    Then let not this divinity in earth,   70
Dear Prince, be slighted as[7] she were the birth
Of idle Fancy, since she works so high,
Nor let her poor disposer, Learning, lie
Still bedrid; both which, being in men defac'd,
In men (with them) is God's bright image rac'd.[8]   75
For as the sun and moon are figures given
Of His refulgent deity in heaven,
So Learning and her light'ner, Poesy,
In earth present His fiery majesty.
Nor are kings like Him since[9] their diadems   80
Thunder and lighten and project brave beams,
But since they His clear virtues emulate,
In truth and justice imaging His state,
In bounty and humanity since they shine,
Than which is nothing (like Him) more divine: 85
Not fire, not light, the sun's admired course,
The rise nor set of stars, nor all their force
In us and all this cope beneath the sky,
Nor great Existence, term'd His treasury;
Since not for being greatest He is blest,   90
But being just, and in all virtues best.

    What sets His justice and His truth best forth,
Best Prince, then use best, which is Poesy's worth.
For as great princes, well inform'd and deck'd
With gracious virtue, give more sure effect   95
To her persuasions, pleasures, real worth
Than all th' inferior subjects she sets forth,
Since there she shines at full, hath birth, wealth, state,
Power, fortune, honor fit to elevate
Her heavenly merits, and so fit they are,   100
Since she was made for them and they for her;
So Truth with Poesy grac'd is fairer far,
More proper, moving, chaste, and regular,
Than when she runs away with untruss'd[10] Prose:
Proportion, that doth orderly dispose   105
Her virtuous treasure and is queen of graces
In Poesy, decking her with choicest phrases,
Figures, and numbers; when loose Prose puts on

Plain letter-habits, makes her trot upon
Dull earthly business (she being mere divine),   110
Holds her to homely cates and harsh hedge-wine[11]
That should drink Poesy's nectar, every way
One made for other as the sun and day,
Princes and virtues. And as in a spring
The pliant water, mov'd with anything   115
Let fall into it, puts her motion out
In perfect circles that move round about
The gentle fountain, one another raising,
So Truth and Poesy work; so Poesy, blazing[12]
All subjects fall'n in her exhaustless fount,   120
Works most exactly, makes a true account
Of all things to her high discharges given,
Till all be circular, and round as heaven.

    And lastly, great Prince, mark and pardon me:
As in a flourishing and ripe fruit tree   125
Nature hath made the bark to save the bole,
The bole the sap, the sap to deck the whole
With leaves and branches, they to bear and shield
The useful fruit, the fruit itself to yield
Guard to the kernel, and for that all those[13]   130
(Since out of that again the whole tree grows);
So in our tree of man, whose nervy root
Springs in his top, from thence even to his foot
There runs a mutual aid through all his parts,
All join'd in one to serve his queen of arts;[14]   135
In which doth Poesy like the kernel lie
Obscur'd, though her Promethean faculty[15]
Can create men and make even death to live;
For which she should live honor'd: kings should give
Comfort and help to her, that she might still   140
Hold up their spirits in virtue, make the will
That governs in them, to the power conform'd,
The power to justice; that the scandals storm'd
Against the poor dame, clear'd by your fair grace,
Your Grace may shine the clearer. Her low place,   145
Not showing her, the highest leaves obscure.
Who raise her, raise themselves; and he sits sure
Whom her wing'd hand advanceth, since on it
Eternity doth (crowning Virtue) sit.
All whose poor seed, like violets in their beds,   150
Now grow with bosom-hung and hidden heads;
For whom I must speak (though their fate convinces[16]
Me, worst of poets) to you, best of princes.

> *By the most humble and faithful*
> *implorer for all the graces to*
> *Your Highness eternized by your*
> *divine Homer,*
> *Geo. Chapman*

[7]As if.   [8]Erased, destroyed.   [9]Because.
[10]Unbridled, undisciplined.
[11]*Homely cates . . . hedge-wine*: plain food and cheap wine (instead
of nectar).   [12]Heralding, proclaiming.
[13]The aforementioned parts.   [14]"The soul" (Chapman's gloss).
[15]Creative force. See Prometheus in Glossary.   [16]Convicts.

THE PREFACE TO THE READER

Of all books extant in all kinds, Homer is the first and best. No one before his, Josephus[1] affirms; nor before him, saith Velleius Paterculus,[2] was there any whom he imitated, nor after him any that could imitate him. And that Poesy may be no cause of detraction from all the eminence we give him, Spondanus[3] (preferring it to all arts and sciences) unanswerably argues and proves; for to the glory of God, and the singing of His glories, no man dares deny, man was chiefly made. And what art performs this chief end of man with so much excitation and expression as Poesy, 10 Moses, David, Solomon, Job, Esay, Jeremy, etc. chiefly using that to the end abovesaid? And since the excellence of it cannot be obtained by the labor and art of man, as all easily confess it, it must needs be acknowledged a divine infusion. To prove which in a word, this distich, in my estimation, serves something nearly:

> Great Poesy, blind Homer, makes all see
> Thee capable of all arts, none of thee.

For out of him, according to our most grave and judicial Plutarch,[4] are all arts deduced, confirmed, or illustrated. 20 It is not therefore the world's vilifying of it that can make it vile; for so we might argue, and blaspheme the most incomparably sacred. It is not of the world indeed, but, like truth, hides itself from it. Nor is there any such reality of wisdom's truth in all human excellence as in ₁ oets' fictions. That most vulgar and foolish receipt of poetical license, being of all knowing men to be exploded, accepting it, as if poets had a tale-telling privilege above others, no artist being so strictly and inextricably confined to all the laws of learning, wisdom, and truth as a poet. For were not his 30 fictions composed of the sinews and souls of all those, how could they defy fire, iron,[5] and be combined with eternity? To all sciences, therefore, I must still, with our learned and ingenious Spondanus, prefer it, as having a perpetual commerce with the Divine Majesty, embracing and illustrating all His most holy precepts, and enjoying continual discourse with His thrice-perfect and most comfortable[6] Spirit. And as the contemplative life is most worthily and divinely preferred by Plato to the active, as much as the head to the foot, the eye to the hand, reason to sense, the 40 soul to the body, the end itself to all things directed to the end, quiet to motion, and eternity to time, so much prefer I divine Poesy to all worldly wisdom. To the only shadow of whose worth, yet, I entitle not the bold rhymes of every apish and impudent braggart, though he dares assume anything; such I turn over to the weaving of cobwebs, and shall but chatter on molehills (far under the hill of the Muses) when their fortunatest self-love and ambition hath advanced them highest. Poesy is the flower of the sun, and disdains to open to the eye of a candle. So kings hide their 50 treasures and counsels from the vulgar, *ne evilescant*[7] (saith our Spondanus). We have example sacred enough that true Poesy's humility, poverty, and contempt are badges of divinity, not vanity. Bray then, and bark against it, ye wolf-faced wordlings, that nothing but honors, riches, and magistracy, *nescio quos turgide spiratis* (that I may use the words of our friend still) *qui solas leges Justinianas crepatis; paragraphum unum aut alterum, pluris quam vos ipsos facitis,* etc.[8] I (for my part) shall ever esteem it much more manly and sacred, in this harmless and pious study, to sit till I sink into my grave than shine in your vainglorious bubbles and impieties; all your poor policies, wisdoms, and their trappings at no more valuing than a musty nut. And much less I weigh the frontless detractions of some stupid ignorants, that, no more knowing me than their own beastly ends, and I ever (to my knowledge) blessed from their sight, whisper behind me vilifyings of my translation, out of the French[9] affirming them, when both in French and all other languages but his own our with-all-skill-enriched poet is so poor and unpleasing that no man can discern from whence flowed his so generally given eminence and admiration. And therefore (by any reasonable creature's conference of my slight comment and conversion)[10] it will easily appear how I shun them, and whether the original be my rule or not. In which he shall easily see, I understand the understandings of all other interpreters and commentors in places of his most depth, importance, and rapture. In whose exposition and illustration, if I abhor[11] from the sense that others wrest and wrack out of him, let my best detractor examine how the Greek word warrants me. For my other fresh fry,[12] let them fry in their foolish galls, nothing so much weighed as the barkings of puppies or foisting[13] hounds, too vile to think of our sacred Homer, or set their profane feet within their lives' lengths of his thresholds. If I fail in something, let my full performance in other some[14] restore me, haste spurring me on with other

THE PREFACE TO THE READER ¹Flavius Josephus (37?–100), Jewish historian.
²Roman statesman (ca. 19 B.C.–A.D. 30) who wrote an abridgment of Roman history from the fall of Troy to his own time.
³Jean de Sponde (1557–95), French scholar whose notable edition of Homer's works appeared, with an elaborate commentary, in 1583. The accompanying Latin translation by Andreas Divus was thought by Chapman to be the work of Spondanus.
⁴Greek biographer and moralist (46?–?120).
⁵*Defy fire, iron*: text *differ far from*. According to Richard Hooper, whose edition of Chapman's Homer appeared in 1857, the emendation was made by Chapman in his own copy of the 1611 *Iliads*. ⁶Comforting. ⁷"Lest they become worthless."
⁸*That nothing . . ipsos facitis*: This passage, itself a loose rendition of Spondanus' original (to which Chapman is heavily indebted throughout this preface) might be paraphrased as follows: who are full of bursting enthusiasm for honors, riches, and offices (I know not which), who prattle only of the laws of Justinian and esteem one paragraph or another more than themselves.
⁹*Out of the French*: i.e., the French translation (1555) by Hagues Salel (which had been used by Arthur Hall for his clumsy *Ten Books of Homer's Iliads*, 1581).
¹⁰*Conference...conversion*: comparison of my brief commentary and translation. ¹¹Shrink (a Latinism).
¹²Young fish, i.e., paltry critics. ¹³Evil-smelling.
¹⁴In some other.

necessities. For as at my conclusion I protest,[15] so here at my entrance, less than fifteen weeks was the time in which all the last twelve books were entirely new translated. No conference had with anyone living in all the novelties I presume I have found. Only some one or two places I have showed to my worthy and most learned friend Master Harriots,[16] for his censure how much mine own weighed; whose judgment and knowledge in all kinds I know to be incomparable and bottomless, yea, to be admired as much as his most blameless life and the right sacred expense of his time is to be honored and reverenced. Which affirmation of his clear unmatchedness in all manner of learning I make in contempt of that nasty objection often thrust upon me— that he that will judge must know more than he of whom he judgeth; for so a man should know neither God nor himself. Another right learned, honest, and entirely loved friend of mine, Master Robert Hews,[17] I must needs put into my confessed conference[18] touching Homer, though very little more than that I had with Master Harriots. Which two, I protest, are all, and preferred to all. Nor charge I their authorities with any allowance of my general labor, but only of those one or two places which, for instances of my innovation and how it showed to them, I imparted. If any tax me for too much periphrasis or circumlocution in some places, let them read Laurentius Valla and Eobanus Hessus,[19] who either use such shortness as cometh nothing home to Homer, or, where they shun that fault, are ten parts more paraphrastical than I. As for example, one place I will trouble you (if you please) to confer with the original, and one interpreter for all. . . .

> Chapman then proceeds to document the point by citing Valla's translation of the *Iliad,* III.403 ff., "which (besides his superfluity) is utterly false."

This one example I thought necessary to insert here to show my detractors that they have no reason to vilify my circumlocution sometimes, when their most approved Grecians, Homer's interpreters generally, hold him fit to be so converted. Yet how much I differ, and with what authority, let my impartial and judicial reader judge. Always conceiving how pedantical and absurd an affectation it is in the interpretation of any author (much more of Homer) to turn him word for word, when (according to Horace[20] and other best lawgivers to translators) it is the part of every knowing and judicial interpreter not to follow the number and order of words, but the material things themselves, and sentences[21] to weigh diligently, and to clothe and adorn them with words, and such a style and form of oration as are most apt for the language into which they are converted. If I have not turned him in any place falsely (as all other his interpreters have in many, and most of his chief places), if I have not left behind me any of his sentence,[22] elegancy, height, intention, and invention, if in some few places (especially in my first edition,[23] being done so long since, and following the common tract)[24] I be something paraphrastical and faulty, is it justice in that poor fault (if they will needs have it so) to drown all the rest of my labor? But there is a certain envious windfucker[25] that hovers up and down, laboriously engrossing[26] all the air with his luxurious [27]ambition, and buzzing into every ear my detraction, affirming I turn Homer out of the Latin only, etc., that sets all his associates and the whole rabble of my maligners on their wings with him to bear about my impair and poison my reputation. One that, as he thinks, whatsoever he gives to others, he takes from himself; so whatsoever he takes from others, he adds to himself. One that in this kind of robbery doth like Mercury,[28] that stole good and supplied it with counterfeit bad still. One like the two gluttons, Philoxenus and Gnatho,[29] that would still empty their noses in the dishes they loved, that no man might eat but themselves. For so this castrill,[30] with too hot a liver and lust after his own glory, and to devour all himself, discourageth all appetites to the fame of another. I have stricken, single[31] him as you can. Nor note I this to cast any rubs or plashes[32] out of the particular way of mine own estimation with the world; for I resolve this with the willfully obscure:

Sine honore vivam, nulloque numero ero.

Without men's honors I will live, and make
No number in the manless course they take.

But, to discourage (if it might be) the general detraction of industrious and well-meaning virtue, I know I cannot too much diminish and deject[33] myself; yet that passing little that I am, God only knows, to whose ever-implored respect and comfort I only submit me. If any further edition of these my silly endeavors shall chance, I will mend what is amiss (God assisting me) and amplify my harsh[34] comment to Homer's far more right, and mine own earnest and ingenious[35] love of him. Notwithstanding, I know the curious and envious will never sit down satisfied. A man may go over and over, till he come over and over, and his pains be only

[15]Affirm. See Chapman's epilogue, p. 17 below. [16]See p. 12, n. 1.
[17]Unidentified.
[18]*Put . . . conference*: i.e., acknowledge as one whom I consulted.
[19]*Valla . . . Hessus*: authors respectively of a Latin prose (1474) and Latin verse (1540) translation of Homer.
[20]*Ars poetica*, ll. 125–34, where Horace advises writers to adapt rather than translate their Greek originals. Opposite this passage in his own copy of *The Whole Works of Homer* (1616) Ben Jonson, here as elsewhere in his marginalia severely critical of Chapman's learning, wrote (in Latin): "To say the least, Chapman, you have badly misunderstood Horace. Read him again." See *Ben Jonson* (ed. C. H. Herford and Percy and Evelyn Simpson), XI (1952), 593. [21]Thoughts, ideas [22]Sententiousness.
[23]Between publishing his *Seven Books of the Iliads* (1598), his first attempt at translating Homer, and the complete *Iliads* of 1611, Chapman entirely reworked his versions of books I–II.
[24]Usual course. [25]Windhover or kestrel, a small hawk.
[26]Monopolizing. [27]Excessive.
[28]In Roman myth, the messenger of the gods, and himself the god of thieves.
[29]Respectively a notorious glutton and voluptuary of Leucadia and a parasite in Terence's *Eunuchus*. [30]Kestrel, falcon.
[31]Identify. The detractor is unknown, but Jonson is a likely candidate.
[32]Obstacles or obstructions. Text *plasters*. According to Richard Hooper (see p. 15, n. 5) the emendation is Chapman's own.
[33]Abase. [34]Rough, unpolished. [35]Sincere, unfeigned.

his recompense, every man is so loaded with his particular head, and nothing in all respects perfect but what is perceived by few. Homer himself hath met with my fortune in many maligners, and therefore may my poor self put up without motion.[36] And so little I will respect malignity, and so much encourage myself with mine own known strength, and what I find within me of comfort and confirmance examining myself throughout with a far more jealous and severe eye than my greatest enemy, imitating this:

> *Judex ipse sui totum se explorat ad unguem,*[37] etc.

that after these *Iliads*, I will (God lending me life and any meanest means) with more labor than I have lost here, and all unchecked alacrity, dive through his *Odysseys*. Nor can I forget here (but with all hearty gratitude remember) my most ancient, learned, and right noble friend Master Richard Stapleton,[38] first most desertful mover in the frame of our Homer. For which (and much other most ingenious and utterly undeserved desert) God make me amply his requiter, and be his honorable family's speedy and full restorer. In the mean space, I entreat my impartial and judicial reader that all things to the quick he will not pare, but humanely and nobly pardon defects, and, if he find anything perfect, receive it unenvied.

[CHAPMAN'S EPILOGUE TO THE ILIADS]

Thus far the Ilian ruins I have laid
Open to English eyes, in which (repaid
With thine own value) go, unvalu'd[1] book,
Live and be lov'd. If any envious look
Hurt thy clear fame, learn that no state more high
Attends on virtue than pin'd Envy's eye.
Would thou wert worth it, that the best doth wound
Which this age feeds, and which the last shall bound.[2]

Thus with labor enough, though with more comfort in the merits of my divine author, I have brought my translation of his *Iliads* to an end. If either therein, or in the harsh utterance or matter of my comment before, I have, for haste, scattered with my burthen (less than fifteen weeks being the whole time that the last twelve books' translation stood me in),[3] I desire my present will and (I doubt not) hability[4] (if God give life) to reform and perfect all hereafter may be ingenuously accepted for the absolute work—the rather, considering the most learned, with all their helps and time, have been so often and unanswerably miserably taken halting. In the meantime, that most assistful and unspeakable[5] Spirit by whose thrice-sacred conduct[6] and inspiration I have finished this labor diffuse the fruitful horn of His blessings through these goodness-thirsting watchings, without which, utterly dry and bloodless is whatsoever Mortality soweth. But where our most diligent Spondanus ends his work with a prayer to be taken out of these Meanders and Euripian rivers[7] (as he terms them) of ethnic[8] and profane writers (being quite contrary to himself at the beginning),[9] I thrice-humbly beseech the most dear and divine Mercy—ever most incomparably preferring the great light of His truth in His direct and infallible Scriptures—I may ever be enabled, by

resting wondering in His right comfortable shadows in these,[10] to magnify the clearness of His almighty appearance in the other.[11] . . .

THE WHOLE WORKS OF HOMER, PRINCE OF POETS, IN HIS ILIADS AND ODYSSES (1616)

To THE MOST WORTHILY HONORED, MY SINGULAR GOOD LORD, ROBERT, EARL OF SOMERSET,[1] LORD CHAMBERLAIN, ETC.

. . . That Your Lordship may in his[2] face take view of his mind, the first word of his *Iliads* is μῆνιν, "wrath"; the first word of his *Odysses*, ἄνδρα, "man"—contracting in either word his each work's proposition. In one, predominant perturbation; in the other, overruling wisdom; in one, the body's fervor and fashion of outward fortitude to all possible height of heroical action; in the other, the mind's inward, constant, and unconquered empire, unbroken, unaltered with any most insolent and tyrannous infliction. To many most sovereign praises is this poem[3] entitled, but to that grace in chief which sets on the crown both of poets and orators, . . . that is, *parva magne dicere, pervulgata nove, jejuna plene*: "to speak things little greatly, things common rarely, things barren and empty fruitfully and fully." The return of a man into his country is his whole scope and object, which in itself, Your Lordship may well say, is jejune and fruitless enough, affording nothing feastful, nothing magnificent. And yet even this doth the divine inspiration render vast, illustrious, and of miraculous composure.[4] And for this, my Lord, is this poem preferred to his *Iliads*, for therein much magnificence, both of person and action, gives great aid to his industry, but in this are these helps exceeding sparing or nothing; and yet is the structure so elaborate and pompous[5] that the poor plain groundwork,

---

[36]Without commotion. Text *with motion.* According to Hooper, the emendation is Chapman's own.
[37]"The judge examines himself even to his fingernail."
[38]The subject of one of the commendatory sonnets in Chapman's sonnet sequence *Ovid's Banquet of Sense* (1595) and perhaps the "R. S." who edited *The Phoenix Nest* (1593), one of the most distinguished of Elizabethan poetical miscellanies.
CHAPMAN'S EPILOGUE [1]Inestimable.
[2]*Would . . . bound:* i.e., since Envy attacks the best and will do so as long as the world lasts, I hope that my translation is worthy of Envy by being in the category of the best.   [3]Cost me.
[4]Ability.   [5]Inexpressible.   [6]Guidance.
[7]*Meanders . . . rivers:* i.e., pagan sources. Meander was the ancient name of Menderes, a river in Asia Minor, and Euripus is the strait between the island of Euboea and the Greek mainland.
[8]Pagan.
[9]In his elaborate "Prolegomena" (*Homeri quae exstant omnia*, 1583, sig. β6r) Spondanus had invoked divine assistance in terms that Chapman translated almost word for word in the previous paragraph ("In the meantime," etc.).   [10]I.e., the Homeric poems.
[11]I.e., the Scriptures.
TO THE EARL OF SOMERSET [1]See p. 715   [2]I.e., Homer's.
[3]I.e., the *Odyssey.*   [4]Composition.   [5]Splendid.

considered together, may seem the naturally rich womb to it, and produce it needfully.

Much wondered at, therefore, is the censure of Dionysius Longinus[6] (a man otherwise affirmed grave[7] and of elegant judgment) comparing Homer in his *Iliads* to the sun rising, in his *Odysses* to his descent or setting; or to the ocean robbed of his aesture,[8] many tributory[9] floods and rivers of excellent ornament withheld from their observance; when this his work so far exceeds the ocean, with all his court and concourse, that all his sea is only a serviceable stream to it.[10] Nor can it be compared to any one power to be named in nature, being an entirely well-sorted and digested confluence of all, where the most solid and grave is made as nimble and fluent as the most airy and fiery, the nimble and fluent as firm and well-bounded as the most grave and solid, and—taking all together—of so tender impression, and of such command to the voice of the Muse, that they knock heaven with her breath and discover their foundations as low as hell.

Nor is this all-comprising poesy fantastic or mere fictive, but the most material and doctrinal illations[11] of truth, both for all manly information[12] of manners in the young, all prescription of justice and even Christian piety in the most grave and high-governed. To illustrate both which in both kinds, with all height of expression, the poet creates both a body and a soul in them, wherein if the body (being the letter, or history) seems fictive and beyond possibility to bring into act, the sense, then, and allegory (which is the soul) is to be sought: which intends a more eminent expressure of virtue for her loveliness and of vice for her ugliness, in their several effects going beyond the life, than any art within life can possibly delineate.

Why, then, is fiction to this end so hateful to our true ignorants? Or why should a poor chronicler of a Lord Mayor's naked truth[13] (that peradventure will last his year) include more worth with our modern wizards than Homer for his naked Ulysses, clad in eternal fiction? But this proser[14] Dionysius and the rest of these grave and reputatively[15] learned—that dare undertake for their gravities the headstrong censure of all things, and challenge the understanding

of these toys in their childhoods when even these childish vanities retain deep and most necessary learning enough in them to make them children in their ages and teach them while they live—are not in these absolutely divine infusions allowed either voice or relish. For *qui poeticas ad fores accedit,* etc., says the divine philosopher:[16] "he that knocks at the gates of the Muses *sine Musarum furore*"[17] is neither to be admitted entry nor a touch at their thresholds, his opinion[18] of entry ridiculous and his presumption impious.

Nor must poets themselves—might I a little insist on these contempts,[19] not tempting too far Your Lordship's Ulyssean patience—presume to these doors without the truly genuine and peculiar induction, there being in poesy a twofold rapture (or alienation of soul, as the abovesaid teacher terms it): one *insania,* a disease of the mind and a mere madness, by which the infected is thrust beneath all the degrees of humanity *et ex homine brutum quodammodo redditur*[20] (for which poor Poesy in this diseased and imposturous age is so barbarously vilified); the other is *divinus furor,* by which the sound and divinely healthful *supra hominis naturam erigitur, et in Deum transit:*[21] one a perfection directly infused from God, the other an infection obliquely and degenerately proceeding from man. Of the divine fury, my Lord, your Homer hath ever been both first and last instance. . . .

[6]Text *Longimus.* A Greek rhetorician of the third century A.D., reputed author of the famous critical treatise *On the Sublime.* The passage that Chapman found so offensive is in Chapter IX, which Edward Gibbon later called "one of the finest monuments of antiquity." [7]Weighty, of great authority.
[8]Boiling. Chapman apparently coined the word. [9]Tributary.
[10]In comparison with it. [11]Deductions, conclusions.
[12]Inculcation.
[13]*Chronicler. . . truth:* i.e., a hack annalist who records humdrum events factually. [14]I.e., tiresome writer. [15]Reputedly.
[16]Plato? The comments on poetic inspiration seem to be based on *Ion,* Sect. 533–34. [17]*Sine . . . furore:* i.e., uninspired by the Muses.
[18]Expectation. [19]Objects of contempt.
[20]"And after a fashion is reduced from man to brute."
[21]"Is raised above the nature of man and becomes a god."

from Euthymiae Raptus[1], or the Tears of Peace (1609)

TO THE HIGH-BORN PRINCE OF MEN, HENRY,[2]
THRICE-ROYAL INHERITOR TO THE
UNITED KINGDOMS OF GREAT BRITAIN

INDUCTIO[3]

Now that our sovereign, the great king of Peace,[4]
Hath (in her[5] grace) outlabor'd Hercules
And past his pillars[6] stretch'd her victories,

EUTHYMIAE RAPTUS [1]"The Ravishing of Peace." Although εὐθυμία is normally defined as "cheerfulness" Chapman characteristically expands its meaning to mean "contentment" or even "peace of soul." [2]See p. 13, n. 1. [3]Introduction.
[4]Partly through the mediation of James I, in 1609 the so-called Twelve Years' Truce was arranged to end the long hostilities between Spain and the northern provinces of the Low Countries.
[5]I.e., Peace's.
[6]The Pillars of Hercules, i.e, the Rock of Gibraltar and the cor-

Since (as he were sole soul t' all royalties)
He moves all kings in this vast universe   5
To cast chaste nets on th' impious lust of Mars,[7]
See, all, and imitate his goodness still;
That (having clear'd so well war's outward ill)
He, godlike, still employs his firm desires
To cast learn'd ink upon those inward fires   10
That kindle worse war in the minds of men,
Like to incense the outward war again:[8]
Self-love inflaming so men's sensual blood
That all good, public, drowns in private good,
And that sinks under his own overfreight,   15
Men's reasons and their learnings shipwrack'd quite,
And their religion, that should still be one,
Takes shapes so many that most know't in none.
Which I admiring[9] (since in each man shin'd
A light so clear that by it all might find,   20
Being well inform'd, their object, perfect peace,
Which keeps the narrow path to happiness),
In that discourse[10] I shunn'd (as is my use)
The jarring press[11] and all their time's abuse
T' enjoy least trodden fields and freest shades,   25
Wherein (of all the pleasure that invades
The life of man and flies all vulgar feet,
Since silent meditation is most sweet),
I sat to it, discoursing what main want[12]
So ransack'd man that it did quite supplant   30
The inward peace I spake of, letting in
(At his loose veins) sad war and all his sin.
When suddenly a comfortable[13] light
Brake through the shade, and, after it, the sight
Of a most grave and goodly person shin'd,   35
With eyes turn'd upwards, and was outward blind,
But, inward, past and future things he saw,
And was to both and present times their law.
His sacred bosom was so full of fire
That 'twas transparent, and made him expire   40
His breath in flames that did instruct (methought),
And (as my soul were then at full) they wrought.[14]

> This "grave and goodly person" is the "Elysian" shade of
> Homer, who, as the symbol of poetic truth and inspiration,
> presents a mournful pageant: the sad and stately matron
> Peace as she conducts the funeral rites of Love. In the en-
> suing dialogue between her and the poet or "Interlocutor"
> (which constitutes the body of the work) she explains the
> sorry state of things as a consequence of ignorance, for since
> only "learning" enables man to know God and live virtu-
> ously, his neglect of it inexorably leads not only to un-
> reason, brutality, and war but also to the loss of inward peace
> and of the soul's control over passion. The following ex-
> cerpt constitutes a central statement of Chapman's Christian
> humanism.

Peace

To prove that learning—the soul's actual frame,
Without which 'tis a blank, a smoke-hid flame—
Should sit great arbitress of all things done,
And in your souls, like gnomons[15] in the sun,   355
Give rules to all the circles of your lives,

I prove it by the regiment[16] God gives
To man, of all things; to the soul, of man;
To learning, of the soul. If then it can
Rule, live, of all things best is it not best?   360
O who what God makes greatest dares make least?
But to use their terms: life is root and crest
To all man's coat of noblesse; his soul is
Field to that coat; and learning differences
All his degrees in honor, being the coat.[17]   365
And as a statuary,[18] having got
An alablaster[19] big enough to cut
A human image in, till he hath put
His tools and art to it—hewn, form'd, left none
Of the redundant matter in the stone—   370
It bears the image of a man no more
Than of a wolf, a camel, or a boar:
So when the soul is to the body given—
Being substance of God's image sent from heaven—
It is not His true image till it take   375
Into the substance those fit forms that make
His perfect image; which are then impress'd
By learning and impulsion,[20] that invest
Man with God's form in living holiness,
By cutting from his body the excess   380
Of humors, perturbations, and affects,
Which nature without art no more ejects
Than without tools a naked artisan
Can in rude stone cut th' image of a man.

Interlocutor

How, then, do ignorants,[21] who oft, we try,[22]   385
Rule perturbations, live more humanely
Than men held learn'd?

Peace

Who are not learn'd indeed,
More than a house fram'd loose, that still doth need
The haling up and joining, is a house.
Nor can you call men mere religious   390

---

responding promontory on the African side of the Strait of
Gibraltar.
[7]The Roman god of war. The image alludes to the classical story
that Mars and Venus, while making love, were immobilized in
a net cast over them by Venus' husband Vulcan.
[8]*He, godlike...war again*: Chapman is perhaps thinking of *The
True Law of Free Monarchies* (1603), one of King James's several
essays on political theory. See p. 683, n. 3   [9]Wondering at.
[10]Pondering. [11]Throng. [12]Powerful need. [13]Comforting.
[14]*And...wrought*: i.e., in this beatific vision the *flames* of Homer's
inspiration worked upon (*wrought*) and transformed the poet's
soul.
[15]Pointers to indicate time by the shadows that they cast, as on a
sundial. [16]Rule, control.
[17]*But to use...coat*: In heraldic terms, the quality of life is both the
lineage (*root*) and outward sign (*crest*) of man's nobility (*noblesse*);
his soul is the surface (*field*) of his *coat* of arms, and his learning
distinguishes (*differences*) his proper rank. [18]Sculptor.
[19]Alabaster, i.e., block of marble.
[20]Impelling cause. [21]Ignorant persons.
[22]Learn from experience, observe.

That have good wills to knowledge, ignorant;[23]
For virtuous knowledge hath two ways to plant—
By power infus'd and acquisition:
The first of which those good men graft upon,
For good life is th' effect of learning's act,   395
Which th' action of the mind did first compact[24]
By infus'd love to learning 'gainst all ill.
Conquest's first step is, to all good the will.

Interlocutor

If learning, then, in love or act, must be
Mean[25] to good life and true humanity,   400
Where are our scarecrows now, or men of rags,
Of titles merely, places, fortunes, brags,
That want and scorn both? those inverted men,
Those dungeons whose souls no more contain
The actual light of reason than dark beasts?   405
Those clouds driven still 'twixt God's beam and their
      breasts?
Those giants[26] throwing golden hills 'gainst heaven,
To no one spice[27] of true humanity given?

Peace

Of men there are three sorts that most foes be
To Learning and her love, themselves, and me: 410
Active, passive, and *intellective* men,
Whose self-loves Learning and her love disdain.
Your *active* men consume their whole life's fire
In thirst of state-height,[28] higher still and higher,
Like seeled pigeons[29] mounting to make sport   415
To lower lookers-on, in seeing how short
They come of that they seek, and with what trouble;
Lamely, and far from nature, they redouble
Their pains in flying, more than humbler wits,
To reach death more direct. For Death, that sits   420
Upon the fist of Fate, past highest air,
Since she commands all lives within that sphere,
The higher men advance, the nearer finds
Her seeled quarries, when, in bitterest winds,
Lightnings, and thunders, and in sharpest hails,   425
Fate casts her off at states,[30] when lower sails[31]
Slide calmly to their ends. Your *passive* men—
So call'd of only passing time in vain—
Pass it in no good exercise, but are
In meats and cups laborious, and take care   430
To lose without all care their soul-spent time.
And since they have no means nor spirits to climb,
Like fowls of prey, in any high affair,
See how like kites they bangle[32] in the air
To stoop[33] at scraps and garbage in respect   435
Of that which men of true peace should select,
And how they trot out, in their lives, the ring
With idly iterating oft one thing—
A new-fought combat, an affair at sea,
A marriage or a progress[34] or a plea.[35]   440
No news but fits them as if made for them,
Though it be forg'd but of a woman's dream;

And stuff with such stol'n ends their manless breasts—
Sticks, rags, and mud—they seem mere puttocks'[36] nests,
Curious in all men's actions but their own,   445
All men and all things censure, though know none.
Your *intellective* men, they study hard
Not to get knowledge, but for mere reward:
And therefore that true Knowledge that should be
Their studies' end, and is in nature free,   450
Will not be made their broker, having pow'r
With her sole self to bring both bride and dow'r.
They have some shadows of her (as of me,
Adulterate, outward peace) but never see
Her true and heavenly face. Yet those shades serve   455
(Like errant-knights that by enchantments swerve
From their true lady's being, and embrace
An ugly witch with her fantastic face)
To make them think Truth's substance in their arms;
Which that they have not, but her shadow's charms,   460
See if my proofs be like their arguments,
That leave Opinion still her free dissents.
They have not me with them, that all men know
The highest fruit that doth of knowledge grow,
The bound of all true forms, and only act;   465
If they be true, they rest, nor can be rack'd
Out of their posture by Time's utmost strength,
But last, the more of force, the more of length;
For they become one substance with the soul,
Which Time with all his adjuncts shall control.   470
But since men willful may believe perchance
(In part of Error's twofold ignorance,
Ill disposition)[37] their skills look as high,
And rest in that divine security,
See if their lives make proof of such a peace;   475
For learning's truth makes all life's vain war cease,
It making peace with God, and joins to God,
Whose information drives her period[38]
Through all the body's passive instruments,
And by reflection gives them soul-contents.   480
Besides, from perfect learning you can never
Wisdom with her fair reign[39] of passions sever.
For wisdom is nought else than learning fin'd[40]
And with the understanding pow'r combin'd;

---

[23]*Nor can...ignorant*: i.e., nor can you call men ignorant who, from simple piety, aspire to knowledge. [24]Join. [25]Means.
[26]Monstrous sons of Ge (Earth) who used huge rocks and trunks of trees in their futile war against the gods on Mt. Olympus.
[27]Trace. [28]I.e., political power.
[29]Pigeons with eyelids stitched together, the prey or *quarries* of line 424. The whole passage is built upon terms from falconry.
[30]I.e., those in high position.
[31]Lower wings, those who do not fly so high. [32]Flap.
[33]Swoop down. [34]State journey. [35]Lawsuit.
[36]Birds of prey, kites.
[37]I.e., partaking of Envy's two qualities, ignorance and aversion to learning. [38]Terminates (and transcends).
[39]Rule, mastery. [40]Refined.

That is, a habit of both habits standing,[41] 485
The blood's vain humors ever countermanding.
But if these show more humor than th' unlearn'd—
If in them more vain passion be discern'd,
More mad ambition, more lust, more deceit,
More show of gold than gold, than dross less weight, 490
If flattery, avarice have their souls so given,
Headlong and with such devilish furies driven
That fools may laugh at their imprudency
And villains blush at their dishonesty,
Where is true learning, prov'd to separate[42] these, 495
And seat all forms in her soul's height, in peace?
Raging Euripus,[43] that in all their pride
Drives ships 'gainst roughest winds with his fierce tide,
And ebbs and flows seven times in every day,
Toils not on earth with more irregular sway, 500
Nor is more turbulent and mad than they,
And shine like gold-worms,[44] whom you hardly find
By their own light, not seen, but heard like wind.
But this is learning: to have skill to throw
Reins on your body's pow'rs, that nothing know, 505
And fill the soul's powers so with act and art
That she can curb the body's angry part:
All perturbations, all affects that stray
From their one object, which is to obey
Her sovereign empire, as herself should force 510
Their functions only to serve her discourse:[45]
And that, to beat the straight path of one end,
Which is to make her substance still contend
To be God's image, in informing it
With knowledge, holy thoughts and all forms fit 515
For that eternity ye seek in way
Of His sole imitation; and to sway
Your life's love so that He may still be center
To all your pleasures, and you here may enter
The next life's peace, in governing so well 520
Your sensual parts that you as free may dwell
Of vulgar raptures here as when calm death
Dissolves that learned empire with your breath.
To teach and live thus is the only use
And end of learning. Skill that doth produce 525
But terms and tongues and parroting of art,
Without that pow'r to rule the errant part,
Is that which some call learned ignorance:
A serious trifle, error in a trance;
And let a scholar all earth's volumes carry, 530
He will be but a walking dictionary,
A mere articulate clock that doth but speak
By others' arts. When wheels wear or springs break
Or any fault is in him, he can mend
No more than clocks; but at set hours must spend 535
His mouth[46] as clocks do. If too fast speech go,
He cannot stay it, nor haste if too slow:
So that as travelers seek their peace through storms,
In passing many seas for many forms
Of foreign government, endure the pain 540

Of many faces seeing and the gain
That strangers make of their strange-loving humors,
Learn tongues, keep notebooks—all to feed the tumors
Of vain discourse at home, or serve the course
Of state employment, never having force 545
T' employ themselves, but idle compliments
Must pay their pains, costs, slaveries, all their rents;[47]
And though they many men know, get few friends:
So covetous readers, setting many ends
To their much skill to talk, studiers of phrase, 550
Shifters in art, to flutter in the blaze
Of ignorant count'nance,[48] to obtain degrees
And lie in learning's bottom like the lees,
To be accounted deep by shallow men,
And carve all language in one glorious pen, 555
May have much fame for learning, but th' effect
Proper to perfect learning—to direct
Reason in such an art as that it can
Turn blood to soul and make both one calm man,
So making peace with God—doth differ far 560
From clerks that go with God and man to war.

Interlocutor
But may this peace and man's true empire then
By learning be obtain'd and taught to men?

Peace
Let all men judge; who is it can deny
That the rich crown of old humanity 565
Is still your birthright, and was ne'er let down
From heaven for rule of beasts' lives, but your own?
You learn the depth of arts, and, curious, dare
By them (in Nature's counterfeits) compare
Almost with God: to make perpetually 570
Motion like heaven's, to hang sad rivers by
The air in air, and earth 'twixt earth and heaven
By his own paise.[49] And are these virtues given
To pow'rful art, and virtue's self denied?
This proves the other vain and falsified. 575
Wealth, honor, and the rule of realms doth fall
In less than reason's compass; yet what all
Those things are given for (which is living well)
Wants discipline and reason to compel.
O foolish men! How many ways ye vex 580
Your lives with pleasing them, and still perplex
Your liberties with license, every way
Casting your eyes and faculties astray
From their sole object!

. . . . . .

[41]Consisting. [42]Distinguish.
[43]A strait separating Euboea from Boeotia, noted for its heavy tides. [44]Glowworms. [45]Operation.
[46]Give voice. [47]Expenses. [48]Repute.
[49]Peise, poise, i.e., weight.

from Petrarch's Seven Penitential Psalms (1612)

A HYMN TO OUR SAVIOUR ON THE CROSS

Hail, great Redeemer, man and God, all hail!
Whose fervent agony tore the temple's veil,
Let sacrifices out, dark prophecies
And miracles;[1] and let in, for all these,
A simple piety, a naked heart,   5
And humble spirit, that no less impart
And prove Thy Godhead to us, being as rare,
And in all sacred pow'r as circular.[2]
Water and blood mix'd were not sweat from Thee
With deadlier hardness, more divinity   10
Of supportation, than through flesh and blood
Good doctrine is diffus'd, and life as good.[3]
O open to me then, like Thy spread arms
That east and west reach, all those mystic charms
That hold us in Thy life and discipline,   15
Thy merits in Thy love so thrice divine
It made Thee, being our God, assume our man,
And like our champion Olympian
Come to the field 'gainst Sathan and our sin,
Wrastle[4] with torments, and the garland win   20
From death and hell, which cannot crown our brows
But blood must follow; thorns mix'd[5] with Thy boughs
Of conquering laurel, fast nail'd to Thy cross,
Are all the glories we can here engross.[6]
Prove then to those that in vain glories place   25
Their happiness here, they hold not by Thy grace;
To those whose pow'rs proudly oppose Thy laws,
Oppressing virtue, giving vice applause,
They never manage just authority,
But Thee in Thy dear members crucify.   30
    Thou couldst have come in glory past them all,
With pow'r to force Thy pleasure and empale
Thy church with brass and adamant, that no swine
Nor thieves nor hypocrites nor fiends divine[7]
Could have broke in or rooted or put on   35
Vestments of piety when their hearts had none,
Or rapt[8] to ruin with pretext to save;
Would pomp and radiance[9] rather not outbrave
Thy naked truth than clothe or count'nance it
With grace, and such sincereness as is fit.   40
But since true piety wears her pearls within,
And outward paintings only prank up[10] sin,
Since bodies strength'ned, souls go to the wall,[11]
Since God we cannot serve and Belial,[12]
Therefore Thou putst on earth's most abject plight,   45
Hidst Thee in humblesse, underwentst despite,
Mockery, detraction, shame, blows, vilest death.
These Thou Thy soldiers taughtst to fight beneath,
Madst a commanding precedent of these,
Perfect, perpetual, bearing all the keys   50
To holiness and heaven. To these such laws

Thou in Thy blood writst that were no more cause
T' inflame our loves and fervent faiths in Thee
Than in them Truth's divine simplicity,
'Twere full enough; for therein we may well   55
See Thy white[13] finger furrowing blackest hell,
In turning up the errors that our sense
And sensual pow'rs incur by negligence
Of our eternal, truth-exploring soul. . . .

[Man's sinfulness and pride, says Chapman, are reflected in]
[the sects and schisms of the church.]

    Since truth and real worth men seldom seize,
Impostors most, and slightest learnings please.
And where the true church like the nest should be   95
Of chaste and provident Alcione[14]
(To which is only one strait[15] orifice,
Which is so strictly fitted to her size
That no bird bigger than her self, or less,[16]
Can pierce and keep it or discern th' access,   100
Nor which the sea itself, on which 'tis made,
Can ever overflow or once invade),
Now ways so many to her altars are,
So easy, so profane, and popular,
That torrents charg'd with weeds and sin-drown'd beasts 105
Break in, load, crack them: sensual joys and feasts
Corrupt their pure fumes, and the slend'rest flash
Of lust or profit makes a standing plash
Of sin about them, which men will not pass.
Look, Lord, upon them! Build them walls of brass   110
To keep profane feet off. Do not Thou
In wounds and anguish ever overflow,
And suffer such, in ease and sensuality,
Dare to reject Thy rules of humble life,
The mind's true peace, and turn their zeals to strife   115

A HYMN TO OUR SAVIOUR   [1]*Whose fervent...miracles*: When Christ
died, reports Matthew (27.51–53), "the veil of the temple was
rent in twain from the top to the bottom; and the earth did quake,
and the rocks rent; and the graves were opened; and many bodies
of the saints that slept arose, and came out of the graves after his
resurrection, and went into the holy city, and appeared unto
many."   [2]The circle was a traditional symbol of God's perfection.
[3]*More divinity...life as good*: "Simplicity of piety and good
life, answerable to such doctrine in men; now as rare as miracles in
other times, and require as much divinity of supportation" (Chap-
man's gloss).   [4]Wrestle.   [5]Text *mixe*.   [6]Amass.
[7]"Such as are divines in profession, and in fact devils, or wolves in
sheep's clothing" (Chapman's gloss).   [8]Carried by force.
[9]"Outward glory" (Chapman's gloss).
[10]Bedeck, adorn.   [11]*Go . . . wall*: give way, succumb.
[12]In the New Testament, the spirit of evil, i.e., Satan. See 2 Cor-
inthians 6.15.   [13]Pure, precious.
[14]The halcyon, a bird fabled to breed in a nest floating on the sea.
[15]Narrow. Text *straight*.
[16]"If the bird be less, the sea will get in" (Chapman's gloss).

For objects earthly and corporeal.
A trick of humblesse[17] now they practice all,
Confess their no deserts, habilities[18] none,
Profess all frailties and amend not one,
As if a privilege they meant to claim   120
In sinning by acknowledging the maim
Sin gave in Adam; nor the surplusage
Of Thy redemption seem to put in gage
For his transgression, that Thy virtuous pains,
Dear Lord, have eat out all their former stains,   125
That Thy most mighty innocence had pow'r
To cleanse their guilts, that the unvalued[19] dow'r
Thou madst the church, Thy spouse, in piety
And (to endure pains impious) constancy,
Will and alacrity (if they invoke)   130
To bear the sweet load and the easy yoke
Of Thy injunctions, in diffusing these
(In Thy perfection) through her faculties;
In every fiber[20] suffering to her use,
And perfecting the form Thou didst infuse   135
In man's creation: made him clear as then
Of all the frailties since defiling men.

. . . .

Didst Thou not offer, to restore our fall,   190
Thy sacrifice, full, once, and one for all?
If we be still down, how then can we rise
Again with Thee, and seek crowns in the skies?
But we excuse this, saying we are but men
And must err, must fall; what Thou didst sustain   195
To free our beastly frailties never can,
With all Thy grace, by any pow'r in man
Make good Thy rise to us: O blasphemy
In hypocritical humility!
As we are men, we death and hell control,   200
Since thou createdst man a living soul;
As every hour we sin, we do like beasts,
Heedless and willful, murthering in our breasts
Thy saved image, out of which one calls
Our human souls, mortal celestials,   205
When, casting off a good life's godlike grace,
We fall from God; and then make good our place
When we return to Him; and so are said
To live when life like His true form we lead,
And die (as much as can immortal creature):[21]   210
Not that we utterly can cease to be,
But that we fall from life's best quality.
   But we are toss'd out of our human throne
By pied and protean opinion;
We vouch Thee only for pretext and fashion,   215
And are not inward with Thy death and passion.
We slavishly renounce Thy royalty
With which Thou crownst us in Thy victory,
Spend all our manhood in the fiend's defense,
And drown Thy right in beastly negligence.   220
      God never is deceiv'd so to respect
His shade[22] in angels' beauties to[23] neglect
His own most clear and rapting[24] loveliness;

Nor angels dote so on the species[25]
And grace given to our soul (which is their shade)   225
That therefore they will let their own forms fade.
And yet our soul (which most deserves our woe,
And that from which our whole mishap doth flow)
So soft'n'd is and rapt (as with a storm)
With flatteries of our base corporeal form   230
(Which is her shadow) that she quite forsakes
Her proper noblesse,[26] and for nothing takes
The beauties that for her love Thou putst on,
In torments rarefied far past the sun.
      Hence came the cruel fate that Orpheus   235
Sings of Narcissus, who, being amorous
Of his shade in the water (which denotes
Beauty in bodies, that like water floats),
Despis'd himself, his soul, and so let fade
His substance for a never-purchas'd[27] shade.   240
Since souls of their use ignorant are still,
With this vile body's use men never fill.[28]
      And as the sun's light in streams ne'er so fair
Is but a shadow to[29] his light in air,
His splendor that in air we so admire   245
Is but a shadow to his beams in fire,
In fire his brightness but a shadow is
To radiance fir'd in that pure breast of his:
So as the subject on which Thy grace shines
Is thick or clear, to earth or heaven inclines,   250
So that Truth's light shows, so Thy passion takes;
With which who inward is and thy breast makes
Bulwark to his breast against all the darts
The foe still shoots more, more his late blow smarts,
And sea-like raves most where 'tis most withstood.   255
He tastes the strength and virtue of Thy blood;
He knows that when flesh is most sooth'd and grac'd,
Admir'd and magnified, ador'd and plac'd
In height of all the blood's idolatry,
And fed with all the spirits of luxury,[30]   260
One thought of joy, in any soul that knows
Her own true strength and thereon doth repose,
Bringing her body's organs to attend
Chiefly her pow'rs to her eternal end,
Makes all things outward, and the sweetest sin   265
That ravisheth the beastly flesh within,
All but a fiend, prank'd in an angel's plume,
A shade, a fraud, before the wind a fume.
      Hail then, divine Redeemer, still all hail!
All glory, gratitude, and all avail   270
Be given Thy all-deserving agony,
Whose vinegar Thou nectar makst in me,
Whose goodness freely all my ill turns good:
Since Thou being crush'd and strain'd through flesh
      and blood,

[17]Humbleness. [18]Abilities. [19]Supremely valuable.
[20]Text *fiuer.*
[21]*And . . . creature:* A line is apparently missing following this one.
[22]Reflection. [23]As to. [24]Enrapturing. [25]Appearance.
[26]Nobility. [27]Never-attained. [28]Are satisfied.
[29]In comparison with. [30]Lust.

Each nerve and artere[31] needs must taste of Thee.   275
What odor[32] burn'd in airs that noisome be
Leaves not his[33] scent there? O then how much more
Must Thou whose sweetness sweat eternal odor
Stick where it breath'd, and for whom Thy sweet breath
Thou freely gavst up to revive his death?   280
Let those that shrink then as their conscience loads,

That fight in Sathan's right and faint in God's,
Still count them slaves to Sathan. I am none:
Thy fight hath freed me, Thine Thou mak'st mine own.

. . . . . .

[31]Artery.   [32]Fragrant substance.   [33]Its.

Samuel Daniel[1]   [1563?-1619]

Unlike his contemporary Michael Drayton, "well-languaged" Daniel—the famous epithet is William Browne's—reveals no sharp distinction between the Elizabethan and the Jacobean phases of his work. A member of the literary coterie around the countess of Pembroke, Sir Philip Sidney's sister, he served as tutor to her sons at Wilton House when, as Aubrey later said, that stately seat in Wiltshire "was like a college." Thrust into the posture of a published poet when twenty-seven of his sonnets were included in an unauthorized edition of Sidney's *Astrophil and Stella* in 1591, he complained of his betrayal "by the indiscretion of a greedy printer," explained that he was "forced" to supervise a new edition, and therefore promptly published *Delia*, together with *The Complaint of Rosamond*, in 1592. The little volume made his reputation. It was probably about this time that Spenser, in *Colin Clout's Come Home Again*, did the reluctant young poet the signal honor of praising him by name and urging him to "rouse [his] feathers" in a more ambitious work. Daniel followed the advice. In addition to composing a Senecan play called *Cleopatra* (1594), presumably written to gratify the countess' taste for closet drama, he found a major subject in fifteenth-century English history and duly published four books about *The Civil Wars* in 1595. Book V must have followed soon thereafter, for it was bound in with the unsold sheets of the first edition. This broad-scaled, serious poem, an attempt to trace the moral and dynastic consequences of Richard II's deposition, was to be the work of many years. Although Jonson complained to Drummond that its author—"a good, honest man," but "no poet"—wrote about the civil wars without a single battle, the work made Daniel famous and earned for him the sobriquet of "the English Lucan," a tag that underscored his debt to the Latin poet's *Pharsalia*. Book VI was published in 1601 in a "newly augmented" collection of the author's *Works*, but before the poem assumed its final form Daniel reconstructed it by splitting Book III in two, renumbering the three succeeding books, and adding a new Book VIII that ended—or broke off—with Edward IV's imprudent marriage. The completed work, which reached more than 7,000 lines of ottava rima, was published with a dedication to the countess of Pembroke in 1609.

Meanwhile Daniel had been writing other things both in drama and in the smaller forms of verse. His *Poetical Essays* of 1599 contained revisions of his early poems—his incessant tinkering with his works makes a jungle of his bibliography—and also the splendid *Musophilus* and *A Letter from Octavia*. His growing popularity was attested two years later by his expanded *Works* in folio, and then in 1603 by *A Panegyric Congratulatory* to celebrate the King's accession. The latter poem appeared together with several stately verse epistles to his titled friends and patrons and with the fine *Defense of Rhyme* (see pp. 683 ff.), an answer to Thomas Campion's plea for quantitative meters in his *Observations in the Art of English Poetry* (1602).

For a scholarly, retiring man Daniel was extraordinarily appealing to the rich and famous.

[1]For other works of Daniel, see Books and Men, pp. 683 ff., and History and Historiography, pp. 847 ff.

Toward the end of the 1590's he joined the household of Lady Margaret, countess of Cumberland, as tutor to her daughter Anne; Fulke Greville consented to receive the dedication of *Musophilus*; both the lord keeper (Sir Thomas Egerton) and the Queen herself conferred on him their patronage; and he was on such cordial terms with Essex that his second play, *Philotas* (begun in 1600 and printed five years later in *Certain Small Poems*), was thought by some important people to be a veiled defense of that overreaching peer. As a result Daniel not only had to justify the work before the Privy Council but also felt obliged to add a long apology in its next edition (1607). Already, however, the new reign had brought him new responsibilities with his appointment (1604) as licenser for the children of the queen's revels, a post that led to his composing, within the next decade, some half a dozen masques and plays for presentation at the court.

Although at the outset of *The Civil Wars* he said that he aspired "to versify the truth, not poetize," by 1609 Daniel came to think that history ought to be in prose. "For mine own part," he told the countess of Pembroke in the dedication of *The Civil Wars*, "I am not so far in love with this form of writing (nor have I sworn fealty only to rhyme) but that I may serve in any other state of invention with what weapon of utterance I will; and, so it may make good my mind, I care not." Therefore he decided to become a prose historian, and in 1612 he inaugurated this final phase of his career with *The First Part of the History of England* (see pp. 847 f.). In a long epistle to Sir Robert Carr, Viscount Rochester (and soon to be the powerful earl of Somerset) he announced that to do his country the "best service" he could he had blocked out the project in three main parts. The first would trace the history of the realm from the invasion of the Romans to King Stephen's death in 1154 ("and this part I have here done"); the second would begin with Henry II and go to Richard III; the third, starting with the advent of the Tudors in 1485, would bring the story down to modern times. This ambitious scheme was not to be fulfilled. When, just a year before his death, the former poet published his *Collection of the History of England* (see pp. 849 ff.), he confessed that age and disability had thwarted his intention, and so he had had to stop with Edward III, it being "more than the work of one man (were he of never so strong forces) to compose a passable contexture of the whole history of England." Since, as Thomas Fuller later said, Daniel had "the happiness to reconcile brevity and clearness, qualities of great distance in other writers," it is all the more to be regretted that he was forced to leave his final work unfinished.

My texts are based on *A Panegyrike Congratulatory Deliuered to the Kings most excellent maiesty . . . Also certaine Epistles. With a Defence of Ryme, heeretofore written, and now published by the Author*, 1603 (STC 6258), *Certaine Small Poems Lately Printed*, 1605 (STC 6239), *The Civile Wares betweene the Howses of Lancaster and Yorke corrected and continued by Samuel Daniel one of the Groomes of hir Maiesties most honorable Priuie Chamber*, 1609 (STC 6245), *The First Part of the Historie of England*, 1613 (STC 6247), and *The Collection of the Historie of England*, 1618 (STC 6248).

A. B. Grosart's unsatisfactory edition of the *Complete Works in Verse and Prose* (5 vols., 1885–96) still has no successor, but there are editions of *The Tragedy of Cleopatra* by Max Lederer (1911), of *Philotas* and *The Civil Wars* by Laurence Michel (1949, 1958), and of a good selection from the poems and *A Defense of Rhyme* by A. C. Sprague (1930). Although G. K. Brady's old book on Daniel (1923) is still useful, it has in certain aspects been susperseded by the more recent general studies by Joan Rees (1964) and Cecil Seronsy (1967). John Buxton's *Sir Philip Sidney and the English Renaissance* (1954) is good on Daniel's early poetry and Frances A. Yates's *John Florio* (1934) on some of his literary associations. Among the many shorter studies Mark Eccles has investigated Daniel's early travels on the Continent (*SP*, XXXIV, 1937, M. H. Shackford his epistles (*SP*, XLV, 1948, and J. I. M. Stewart his borrowings from Montaigne (*RES*, IX, 1933). His historical works have been studied by May McKisack (*RES*, XXIII, 1947), Rudolf B. Gottfried (*Studies in the Renaissance*, III, 1956), W. Blisset (*English Studies*, XXXVIII, 1957), W. L. Godshalk (*JEGP*, LXIII, 1964), and Arthur Ferguson (*JHI*, XXXII, 1971). There are bibliographies by Harry Sellers (*Oxford Bibliographical Society Proceedings and Papers*, II, 1927) and S. A. Tannenbaum (1942).

from A Panegyric Congratulatory (1603)

TO THE LADY MARGARET, COUNTESS OF CUMBERLAND[1]

He that of such a height hath built his mind,
And rear'd the dwelling of his thoughts so strong
As neither fear nor hope can shake the frame
Of his resolved pow'rs, nor all the wind
Of vanity or malice pierce to wrong   5
His settled peace, or to disturb the same,
What a fair seat hath he, from whence he may
The boundless wastes and wilds of man survey.

And with how free an eye doth he look down
Upon these lower regions of turmoil   10
Where all the storms of passions mainly beat
On flesh and blood; where honor, power, renown,
Are only gay afflictions, golden toil,
Where greatness stands upon as feeble feet
As frailty doth, and only great doth seem   15
To little minds, who do it so esteem.

He looks upon the mightiest monarchs' wars
But only as on stately robberies,
Where evermore the fortune that prevails
Must be the right, the ill-succeeding mars   20
The fairest and the best-fac'd enterprise;
The great pirate, Pompey,[2] lesser pirates quails.
Justice, he sees, as if seduced, still
Conspires with pow'r, whose cause must not be ill.

He sees the face of right t' appear as manifold   25
As are the passions of uncertain man,
Who puts it in all colors, all attires,
To serve his ends and make his courses hold;
He sees that let deceit work what it can,
Plot and contrive base ways to high desires,   30
That the all-guiding Providence doth yet
All disappoint, and mocks this smoke of wit.

Nor is he mov'd with all the thunder-cracks
Of tyrants' threats, or with the surly brow
Of power, that proudly sits on others' crimes,   35
Charg'd with more crying sins than those he checks;
The storms of sad confusion that may grow
Up in the present, for the coming times,
Appal not him, that hath no side at all
But of himself, and knows the worst can fall.   40

Although his heart, so near allied to earth,
Cannot but pity the perplexed state
Of troublous and distress'd mortality,
That thus make way unto the ugly birth
Of their own sorrows, and do still beget   45
Affliction upon imbecility;
Yet seeing thus the course of things must run,
He looks thereon, not strange, but as foredone.

And whilst distraught ambition compasses
And is encompass'd, whilst as craft deceives   50
And is deceiv'd, whilst man doth ransack man,
And builds on blood, and rises by distress,
And th' inheritance of desolation leaves
To great-expecting hopes, he looks thereon
As from the shore of peace with unwet eye,   55
And bears no venture in impiety.

Thus, Madam, fares that man that hath prepar'd
A rest for his desires, and sees all things
Beneath him, and hath learn'd this book of man,
Full of the notes of frailty, and compar'd   60
The best of glory with her sufferings,
By whom I see you labor all you can
To plant your heart, and set your thoughts as near
His glorious mansion as your pow'rs can bear;

Which, Madam, are so soundly fashioned   65
By that clear judgment that hath carried you
Beyond the feeble limits of your kind
As they can stand against the strongest head[3]
Passion can make, inur'd to any hue
The world can cast, that cannot cast that mind   70
Out of her form of goodness, that doth see
Both what the best and worst of earth can be.

Which makes that, whatsoever here befalls,
You in the region of yourself remain,
Where no vain breath of th' impudent molests;   75
That hath secur'd within the brazen walls
Of a clear conscience that without all stain
Rises in peace, in innocency rests,
Whilst all what malice from without procures
Shows her own ugly heart, but hurts not yours.   80

And whereas none rejoice more in revenge
Than women use to do, yet you well know
That wrong is better check'd by being contemn'd
Than being pursu'd, leaving to him t' avenge
To whom it appertains; wherein you show   85
How worthily your clearness hath condemn'd
Base malediction, living in the dark,
That at the rays of goodness still doth bark.

Kno..ing the heart of man is set to be
The center[4] of this world, about the which   90
These revolutions of disturbances

TO THE LADY MARGARET [1]Margaret Clifford (1560?–1616), coun-
tess of Cumberland, for whose daughter Anne Daniel was a tutor.
The countess, a dowager formidably given to litigation, had
(with her sister) received the dedication of Spenser's *Four Hymns*.
[2]Pompey the Great (106–48 B.C.), a founder, with Caesar and
Crassus, of the first triumvirate (60 B.C.), whose dissolution led
to civil war and ultimately to Pompey's defeat at the great battle
of Pharsalia.
[3]Attack.
[4]See the General Glossary for this and the other astronomical terms
in thi stanza.

Still roll, where all th' aspects of misery
Predominate, whose strong effects are such
As he must bear, being pow'rless to redress;
And that unless above himself he can   95
Erect himself, how poor a thing is man!

And how turmoil'd they are that level lie
With earth, and cannot lift themselves from thence;
That never are at peace with their desires,
But work beyond their years, and even deny   100
Dotage her rest, and hardly will dispense⁵
With death; that when ability expires,
Desire lives still, so much delight they have
To carry toil and travail to the grave.

Whose ends you see, and what can be the best   105
They reach unto, when they have cast the sum
And reck'nings of their glory, and you know
This floating life hath but this port of rest—
A heart prepar'd, that fears no ill to come.
And that man's greatness rests but in his show,   110

The best of all whose days consumed are
Either in war, or peace conceiving war.

This concord, Madam, of a well-tun'd mind
Hath been so set by that all-working hand
Of heaven, that though the world hath done his worst   115
To put it out by discords most unkind,
Yet doth it still in perfect union stand
With God and man, nor ever will be forc'd
From that most sweet accord, but still agree,
Equal in fortune's inequality.   120

And this note, Madam, of your worthiness
Remains recorded in so many hearts
As time nor malice cannot wrong your right
In th' inheritance of fame you must possess;
You that have built you by your great deserts,   125
Out of small means, a far more exquisite
And glorious dwelling for your honored name
Than all the gold that leaden minds can frame.

⁵Put up (with).

from Certain Small Poems Lately Printed (1605)

ULYSSES AND THE SIREN

Siren: Come, worthy Greek, Ulysses, come,
Possess these shores with me!
The winds and seas are troublesome,
And here we may be free.
    Here may we sit and view their toil   5
That travail in the deep,
And joy the day in mirth the while,
And spend the night in sleep.

Ulysses: Fair nymph, if fame or honor were
To be attain'd with ease,   10
Then would I come and rest with thee,
And leave such toils as these.
    But here it dwells, and here must I
With danger seek it forth;
To spend the time luxuriously   15
Becomes not men of worth.

Siren: Ulysses, O be not deceiv'd
With that unreal name;
This honor is a thing conceiv'd,¹
And rests on others' fame²   20
    Begotten only to molest
Our peace, and to beguile
The best thing of our life, our rest,
And give us up to toil.

Ulysses: Delicious nymph, suppose there were   25
Nor honor nor report,
Yet manliness would scorn to wear

The time in idle sport.
    For toil doth give a better touch³
To make us feel our joy;   30
And ease finds tediousness, as much
As labor yields annoy.

Siren: Then pleasure likewise seems the shore
Whereto tends all your toil.
Which you forgo to make it more,   35
And perish oft the while.
    Who may disport them diversly,
Find never tedious day,
And ease may have variety
As well as action may.   40

Ulysses: But natures of the noblest frame
These toils and dangers please,
And they take comfort in the same
As much as you in ease,
    And with the thoughts of actions past   45
Are recreated still
When pleasure leaves a touch at last
To show that it was ill.

Siren: That doth opinion only cause
That's out of custom bred,   50
Which makes us many other laws
Than ever nature did.
    No widows wail for our delights,
Our sports are without blood;

ULYSSES AND THE SIREN   ¹Imagined, existing only in the mind.
²Report.   ³Capacity to feel.

The world, we see, by warlike wights   55
Receives more hurt than good.

   Ulysses: But yet the state of things require
These motions of unrest,
And these great spirits of high desire
Seem born to turn them best,   60
   To purge the mischiefs that increase
And all good order mar;
For oft we see a wicked peace
To be well chang'd for war.

   Siren: Well, well, Ulysses, then I see   65
I shall not have thee here,
And therefore I will come to thee,
And take my fortunes there.
   I must be won that cannot win,
Yet lost were I not won;   70
For beauty hath created been
T' undo or be undone.

from The Civil Wars (1609)

To the Right Noble Lady, the Lady Mary,
Countess Dowager of Pembroke[1]

Madam,

This poem of our last civil wars of England (whereof the
many editions show what kind of entertainment it hath had
with the world) I have now again sent forth with the ad-
dition of two books: the one continuing the course of the
history, the other making up a part which (for haste) was
left unfurnished in the former impressions.[2] And having
nothing else to do with my life but to work whilst I have it,
I held it my part to adorn, the best I could, this province
Nature hath allotted to my charge; and which I desire to
leave after my death in the best form I may, seeing I can
erect no other pillars to sustain my memory but my lines,
nor otherwise pay my debts and the reckonings of my
gratitude to their honor who have done me good and fur-
thered this work.

   And whereas this argument was long since undertaken (in
a time which was not so well secured of the future as, God be
blessed, it is) with a purpose to show the deformities of civil
dissension and the miserable events of rebellions, conspiracies,
and bloody revengements, which followed (as in a circle)
upon that breach of the due course of succession by the
usurpation of Henry IV, and thereby to make the blessings
of peace and the happiness of an established government
(in a direct line) the better to appear, I trust I shall do a
grateful work to my country to continue the same unto the
glorious union of Henry VII,[3] from whence is descended our
present happiness.

   In which work I have carefully followed that truth which
is delivered in the history without adding to or substracting
from the general received opinion of things as we find them
in our common annals, holding it an impiety to violate the
public testimony we have without more evident proof, or
to introduce fictions of our own imagination in things of this
nature. . . . I have only used that poetical license of framing
speeches to the persons of men according to their occasions,
as Gaius Sallustius and Titus Livius[4] (though writers in prose,
yet in that kind poets) have, with divers other ancient and
modern writers, done before me. Wherein, though they

have encroached upon others' rights and usurped a part
that was not properly theirs, yet, seeing they hold so just
a proportion with the nature of men and the course of
affairs, they pass as the parts of the actor (not the writer),
and are received with great approbation.

   And although many of these images are drawn with the
pencil of mine own conceiving, yet I know they are ac-
cording to the portraiture of Nature, and carry a resemblance
to the life of action and their complexions whom they rep-
resent. For I see ambition, faction, and affections speak
ever one language, wear like colors (though in several
fashions), feed and are fed with the same nutriments, and
only vary but in time.

   Man is a creature of the same dimension he was, and how
great and eminent soever he be, his measure and height is
easy to be taken. And all these great actions are openly
presented on the stage of the world, where there are ever
spectators who will judge and censure[5] how men personate
those parts which they are set to perform, and so enter them
in the records of memory. . . .

   Setting aside those ornaments proper to this kind of writ-
ing, I have faithfully observed the history, wherein such as

To the lady mary [1]As Sir Philip Sidney's sister and, according
to John Aubrey, "the greatest patroness of wit and learning of any
lady of her time," Mary Herbert, countess of Pembroke, had long
been on friendly terms with Daniel. In the early 1590's he seems to
have served as tutor to her sons, and to one of them—William,
third earl of Pembroke—he dedicated his *Defense of Rhyme*
(see p. 683).
[2]In the 1609 edition Daniel added Book VIII and expanded the
earlier Book III into Books III and IV.
[3]*Union . . . Henry VII:* i.e., the marriage (1486) between Henry
and Elizabeth, daughter of Edward IV, which united the great
rival houses of Lancaster and York. Daniel did not take his poem
to this intended consummation and conclusion.
[4]*As Gaius Salustius . . . Livius:* Sallust (86–44 b.c.) wrote the histories
of the Jugurthine war and Catiline's conspiracy, Livy (59 b.c.–
a.d. 17) *The Annals of the Roman People* (not all of which survives).
Their precedent for injecting fabricated speeches into the narrative
was Thucydides (d. 400 b.c.), whose *History of the Peloponnesian
War* was immensely influential. [5]*Judge and censure:* synonyms.

love this harmony of words may find that a subject of the greatest gravity will be aptly expressed, howsoever others (seeing in what sort verse hath been idly abused) hold it but as a language fitting lightness and vanity.

For mine own part I am not so far in love with this form of writing (nor have I sworn fealty only to rhyme) but that I may serve in any other state of invention with what weapon of utterance I will, and so it may make good my mind I care not. For I see judgment and discretion (with whatsoever is worthy) carry their own ornaments and are graced with their own beauties, be they appareled in what fashion they will. And because I find the common tongue of the world is prose, I purpose in that kind to write the history of England from the Conquest,[6] being encouraged thereunto by many noble and worthy spirits. Although, Madam, I must not neglect to prosecute the other part of this work, being thus revived by your goodness, to whom and to whose noble family I hold myself ever bound, and will labor to do you all the honor and service I can.

Sam. Daniel

THE EIGHTH BOOK

THE ARGUMENT

King Edward pow'r against King Henry led,
And hath at Towton field the victory;[1]
From whence King Henry into Scotland fled,
Where he attempts his state's recovery;
Steals into England, is discovered,
Brought prisoner to the Tow'r disgracefully;
And Edward, whiles great Warwick doth assay
A match in France, marries the Lady Grey.

1

On yet, sad verse, though those bright stars[2] from whence
Thou hadst thy light are set for evermore,
And that these times do not like grace dispense
To our endeavors as those did before,
Yet on, since she[3] whose beams do reincense
This sacred fire seems as reserv'd in store[4]
To raise this work, and here to have my last
Who had the first of all my labors past.

2

On (with her blessed favor) and relate
With what new bloodshed this new-chosen lord[5]
Made his first entry to th' afflicted state,
Pass'd his first act of public with the sword,
Ingor'd his new-worn crown; and how he gat[6]
Possession of affliction, and restor'd
His right unto a royal misery,
Maintained with as bloody dignity.

3

Show how our great Pharsalian field[7] was fought
At Towton in the north, the greatest day
Of ruin that dissension ever brought
Unto this kingdom; where two crowns did sway
The work of slaughter, two kings' causes wrought
Destruction to one people by the way

Of their affections and their loyalties,
As if one for these ills could not suffice.[8]

4

Where Lancaster and that courageous side
(That noble, constant part) came furnished
With such a pow'r as might have terrified
And overrun the earth, had they been led
The way of glory where they might have tried
For th' empire of all Europe, as those did
The Macedonian[9] led into the east,
Their number being double at the least.

5

And where brave York comes as completely mann'd
With courage, valor, and with equal might,
Prepar'd to try with a resolved hand
The metal of his crown and of his right,
Attended with his fatal firebrand
Of war, Warwick,[10] that blazing star of fight,
The comet of destruction that portends
Confusion[11] and distress what way he tends.

6

What rage, what madness, England, do we see,
That this brave people in such multitude

[6]For Daniel's later prose history of England, the first installment of which appeared in 1612, see p. 847

THE EIGHTH BOOK [1]*King Edward...victory*: The two kings are Henry VI (1421–71) and Edward IV (1442–83), leaders respectively of the Lancastrians and the Yorkists, whose bloody competition for the throne had kept England in a state of intermittent civil war since 1455. The battle of Towton was fought in 1461.
[2]The famous Robert Devereux, earl of Essex (p. 843) and Charles Blount, Lord Mountjoy and later earl of Devonshire (d. 1606), both powerful patrons of Daniel at the start of his career.
[3]The countess of Pembroke, to whom Daniel had dedicated *Delia*, his first volume of poetry, in 1592.
[4]As a stock for future use. [5]Edward IV. [6]Got.
[7]At the battle of Pharsalia (48 B.C.) in northern Greece, Julius Caesar defeated his mighty rival Pompey, thus ending a protracted civil war and securing his control of Rome. These events are treated in the epic poem *Pharsalia* by Marcus Annaeus Lucanus (39–65), a work which in theme and style was such a useful model that Daniel was often called the English Lucan.
[8]"Edward being proclaimed and acknowledged for king, presently sets forward towards the North to encounter with King Henry VI, who in Yorkshire had assembled a puissant army of near 60,000 men; and at a place called Towton, about four miles from York, both their powers met, where was fought the greatest battail our stories mention in all these civil wars, where both the armies consisted of above 100,000 men, and all of our own nation" (Daniel's gloss).
[9]I.e., Alexander the Great.
[10]Richard Neville (1428–71), earl of Warwick and of Salisbury, "the kingmaker," a central figure in the savage political jockeying of the mid-fifteenth century. Long a stalwart of the Yorkists, he was virtually the uncrowned king of England after young Edward IV's accession in 1461, but mutual irritations and suspicions soon drove the two apart, whereupon Warwick threw his support to the dispossessed Lancastrians and engineered Henry VI's brief return to power in 1470. The following year he perished with his new-found cause at the battle of Barnet. [11]Destruction.

Run to confound themselves, and all to be
Thus mad for lords and for mere servitude?
What might have been if (Roman-like and free)
These gallant spirits had nobler ends pursu'd,
And strain'd to points of glory and renown
For good of the republic and their own?

7

But here no Cato[12] with a senate stood
For commonwealth, nor here were any sought
T' emancipate the state for public good,
But only headlong for their faction wrought.
Here every man runs on to spend his blood
To get but what he had already got,
For whether Pompey or a Caesar won,
Their state was ever sure to be all one.

> There follows a long account of the battle, which left the
> Yorkists in control of England and the Lancastrians dis-
> persed and leaderless after Henry VI fled to Scotland in
> despair.

34[13]

Thus, England, didst thou see the mightiest king
Thou ever hadst[14] (in power and majesty
Of state and of dominions, governing
A most magnificent nobility,
With an advent'rous people flourishing
In all the glories of felicity)
Chas'd from his kingdom, forc'd to seek redress
In parts remote, distress'd and succorless.

35

Now, Bolingbroke,[15] these miseries, here shown,
Do much unload thy sin; make thy ill, good.
For if thou didst by wrong attain the crown,
'Twas without cries: it cost but little blood.
But York by his attempt hath overthrown
All the best glory wherein England stood,
And did his state by her undoing win,
And was, though white without, yet red within.

> The remainder of Book VIII—with which the work abrupt-
> ly ends—is concerned with the attempts of Henry's formi-
> dable consort Margaret to rally the Lancastrians and with
> Edward's protracted wooing of Elizabeth Woodville and
> his marriage to her—a match that left the king's once power-
> ful supporter Warwick humiliated and exposed. In the final
> stanzas of the book we see Warwick, temporarily retired
> to his estate, being instructed by his confessor to forget
> about the court, put aside ambition, and cultivate his soul.

102

Thus the good father, with an humble thought
(Bred in a cellulary low retire)[16]
According to his quiet humor, sought
T' avert him from his turbulent desire,
When the great earl began: "Father, I note
What you with zeal advise, with love require,
And I must thank you for this care you have
And for those good advertisements[17] you gave.

103

"And truly, Father, could I but get free
(Without being rent)[18] and hold my dignity,
That sheepcote which in yonder vale you see
(Beset with groves and those sweet springs hard by)
I rather would my palace wish to be
Than any roof of proudest majesty,
But that I cannot do: I have my part,
And I must live in one house with my heart.

104

"I know that I am fix'd unto a sphere
That is ordain'd to move. It is the place
My fate appoints me, and the region where
I must whatever happens there embrace.
Disturbance, travail, labor, hope, and fear
Are of that clime, engend'red in that place;
And action best, I see, becomes the best:
The stars that have most glory have no rest.

105

"Besides, it were a coward's part to fly
Now from my hold,[19] that have held out so well,
It being the station of my life where I
Am set to serve and stand as sentinel,
And must, of force, make good the place or die
When Fate and Fortune (those great states) compel.
And then we lords in such case ever are
As peace can cut our throats as well as war;

106

"And hath her griefs and her encumbrances,
And doth with idle rest deform us more
Than any magha[20] can, or sorceress,
With basely wasting all the martial store
Of heat and spirit (which graceth manliness),
And makes us still false images adore,
Besides profusion[21] of our faculties
In gross, dull glutt'ny, vap'rous gourmandise.

107

"And therefore since I am the man I am,
I must not give a foot, lest I give all.
Nor is this bird within my breast so tame
As to be fed at hand and mock'd withal.

[12]Cato the Censor (d. 149 B.C.), a Roman statesman noted for his unflinching probity and patriotism.
[13]Text *33*. Subsequent misnumbering of the stanzas is silently corrected.
[14]Actually Henry VI was egregiously incompetent.
[15]I.e., Henry IV, whose sinful usurpation (1399) of his cousin Richard II's throne led to the "deformities" of dissension that are the subject of *The Civil Wars*. He is, of course, a central figure in the earlier books.   [16]Humble monastic retreat.   [17]Admonitions.
[18]Torn, i.e., destroyed.
[19]Fortress (with perhaps a pun on *hold* meaning "struggle" or "resistance").
[20]Sorceress. The *OED* cites this passage as the only example of the word, which is apparently a misspelling of *maga* (feminine of *magus*).   [21]Pouring out, i.e., wasting.

I rather would my state were out of frame
Than my renown should come to get a fall.
No, no! Th' ungrateful boy[22] shall never think
That I, who him enlarg'd to pow'r, will shrink.

108

"What is our life without our dignity,
Which oft, we see, comes[23] less by living long.
Who ever was there worth the memory,
And eminent indeed, but still died young?
As if Worth had agreed with Destiny
That time, which rights them, should not do them wrong.
Besides, old age doth give, by too long space,
Our souls as many wrinkles as our face.

109

"And as for my inheritance and state
(Whatever happen) I will so provide
That law shall, with what strength it hath, collate[24]
The same on mine and those to mine allied,
Although I know she serves a present state,
And can undo again what she hath tied;
But that we leave to Him who points out heirs,
And howsoever, yet the world is theirs,

110

"Where they must work it out, as born to run
Those fortunes, which as mighty families
(As ever they could be) before have done.
Nor shall they gain by mine indignities
Who may without my courses[25] be undone.
And whoso makes his state and life his ties

To do unworthily is born a slave,
And let him with that brand go to his grave!"

111

Here would the reverend father have replied
That it were far more magnanimity
T' endure than to resist, that we are tied
As well to bear the inconveniency[26]
And strains of kings and states as to abide
Untimely rains, tempests, sterility,[27]
And other ills of nature that befall,
Which we of force must be content withal;

112

But that a speedy messenger was sent
To show the duke of Clarence[28] was hard by,
And thereupon Warwick breaks off, and went
(With all his train attending formally)
To entertain him with fit compliment,[29]
As glad of such an opportunity
To work upon for those high purposes
He had conceiv'd in discontentedness.

The End of the Eighth Book

[22]I.e., Edward IV, who was fourteen years younger than Warwick.
[23]Becomes. [24]Bestow. [25]I.e., personal actions.
[26]Harm, injury. [27]Drought.
[28]George, duke of Clarence, the king's faithless brother and Warwick's son-in-law, who, although a party to the latter's conspiracy, at the decisive battle of Barnet (1471) shifted his allegiance to the victorious Edward. [29]Ceremony.

Michael Drayton [1563-1631]

Like many writers of his splendid generation, Drayton spanned the Elizabethan and Jacobean periods, but unlike some of his contemporaries he showed a steady growth for almost forty years. Beginning in the 1590's as one who followed all the fashions, he worked with some success in such current forms of verse as biblical paraphrase, drama, pastoral, sonnet, heroic epistle, Ovidian narrative, and historical poems; but when the last of the Tudors died and he was disappointed in his hope of favors from King James, he liked to think that his merits were ignored and he himself was "trodden lower than the dust." Thereafter he assumed the posture of the cantankerous and superannuated man. When, well into his middle years, he predicted that "this lunatic age" would deride his *Poly-Olbion* as a quaint anachronism, or complained in the preface to his 1619 *Poems* that the "world's coldness" had "nipped our flowery Tempe," or remarked to William Browne that everything was "arsy-versy," he expressed a disaffection that both nettled him for some thirty years and inspired his greatest work. In various ways—as satirist, pastoralist, and celebrant of his country's fading glory—Drayton voiced his discontent with Jacobean England, and in doing so he found his proper stance and style. For this disgruntled old Elizabethan who died a subject of the second Stuart king improved in ease and strength as he grew older; and when, as Fuller said, "he changed his laurel for a crown of glory" in 1631, his burial in Westminster Abbey was a tribute to his supple, lasting power.

In his Jacobean phase, with which we are concerned, that power reveals itself in various ways: in an extraordinary capacity for revising (and generally improving) his earlier pieces; in a willingness to experiment with new modes of composition; in a persistent affection for such obsolescent forms as the pastoral and the heroic verse epistle, which he continued to invest with new vitality; in an exuberant if old-fashioned kind of patriotism that he converted into art. By progressive changes in his work—notably in the big retrospective collections of his poems published in 1605, 1608, 1619, and 1630—Drayton logged his own advance. Consequently, to study the successive versions of his poems is to trace the evolution of a most uncommon writer.

Perhaps the best example of Drayton's technique of revision is provided by the sequential alterations of his sonnets, from the languid affectations of *Idea's Mirror* in 1594 to the wit and passion of his 1619 *Poems*. Through five editions he corrected, rearranged, and added to these poems until, altered almost out of recognition, they reveal a Shakespearian strength and candor. A similar if less striking progression is discernible in the movement from the conventionally Spenserian pastorals of *The Shepherd's Garland* (1593) through the eclogues of the 1606 edition to the "nymphals" in *The Muses' Elysium*, which appeared in 1630, a year before his death. In these late pastorals (as in the famous mock-heroic *Nymphidia* of 1627) Drayton fuses lyric grace and irony in a way that marks them as his own. Progress of a somewhat different kind is shown in the transformation of the historical poem *Mortimeriados* (1596) to *The Barons' Wars* (1603), an undertaking that involved not only extensive stylistic and structural alterations but also—and with even more imposing effect—a shift from rhyme royal to ottava rima in an effort to achieve, as the intrepid author said, the "majesty, perfection, and solidity" demanded by the subject. Indefatigably, he reworked *The Barons' Wars* for the 1619 *Poems*. Revision of still another kind, which may be called thematic, is that whereby the platonic idealism of *Endymion and Phoebe* (1595) became the knotty and abrasive satire of *The Man in the Moon* (1606).

If Drayton's bent for innovation appears to disadvantage in a satire like *The Owl* (1604), which was no doubt prompted by his recent disappointment, it triumphed in his celebrated *Odes* of 1606, which stylistically and metrically are among his most virile and attractive poems. "New they are, and the work of playing hours," he said by way of introduction, "but what other commendation is theirs, and whether inherent in the subject, must be thine to judge." Two of them, at least ("To the Virginian Voyage" and "His Battle of Agincourt"), have become the common property of English-speaking people, whereas such additions to the 1619 *Poems* as "To His Valentine" and "To His Coy Love" are so fresh and debonair that they suggest the flippant charm of Herrick. Of the twelve elegies published in 1627 only five are funeral poems, the others being Horatian epistles of the sort that Jonson, Donne, and many other poets were writing. But here, as elsewhere, Drayton stamps his signature. If their topicality, their extended range of reference, and their colloquial vigor show him as the easy master of his craft, their sorrow and their mounting indignation at "these slothful times" express his favorite theme:

> Dear friend, be silent and with patience see
> What this mad time's catastrophe will be.

Another mark of Drayton's growing alienation from Jacobean England is his imaginative reconstruction of glories that had faded. The many editions of *A Mirror for Magistrates* (1559 ff.), William Warner's *Albion's England* (1586 ff.), the second book of Spenser's *Faerie Queene*, Shakespeare's history plays, Daniel's *Civil Wars* (p. 24), and dozens of other works suggest how enthusiastically Elizabethan writers turned history into literature; and it was inevitable that the patriotic Drayton, who experimented with so many forms of writing, should draw upon the treasures of his nation's past. Beginning in 1594 with a brace of "legends" (on Piers Gaveston and Queen Matilda), he moved on to the ambitious quasi-epic *Mortimeriados* (1596) and then, in the late nineties, to the most successful of his many works, *England's Heroical Epistles* (1597 ff.), which, characteristically, he altered and expanded for more than thirty years. But his major undertaking of this kind was the gigantic *Poly-Olbion* ("land of many blessings"). This "chorographical description of tracts, rivers, mountains, forests, and other parts of this renowned isle of Great Britain"

—a sort of poetical equivalent, in hexameter couplets, of Camden's great *Britannia* (p. 816), to which, in fact, it is indebted—so relentlessly records the flora, fauna, topography, mythology, history, and quasi-history of the realm that it had to be the work of many years. Although he had started "penning" it by 1598, as Francis Meres reported, it was not until 1612 that the first install-ment, containing eighteen "songs," appeared; and by then, as Drayton grumpily conceded, the market for such old-fashioned works was gone. But he himself was adamant:

> And to any that shall demand wherefore, having promised this poem of the general island so many years, I now publish only this part of it, I plainly answer that many times I had deter-mined with myself to have left it off, and have neglected my papers sometimes two years together, finding the times since his Majesty's happy coming-in to fall so heavily upon my distressed fortunes after my zealous soul had labored so long in that which, with the general happiness of the kingdom, seemed not then impossible somewhat also to have advanced me. But I instantly saw all my long-nourished hopes even buried alive before my face, so uncertain, in this world, be the ends of our clearest endeavors. . . . Sundry other songs I have also, though yet not so perfect that I dare commit them to public censure; and the rest I determine to go forward with, God enabling me, may I find means to assist my endeavor.

Drayton persisted in the "herculean labor" until 1622, when the last twelve songs appeared. Although he asserted that neither the scurrility of printers (interested in nothing but "beastly and abominable trash") nor the indifference of the public could deter him "from going on with Scotland," he finally had to stop after 15,000 lines. It was just as well, no doubt: *Poly-Olbion* is full of splendid things, as I hope my excerpts show, but there are many *longueurs* too. As Johnson said of *Paradise Lost,* none ever wished it longer than it is.

My texts are based on *Poly-Olbion. Or A Chorographicall Description of Tracts, Rivers, Mountaines, Forests, and other Parts of this renowned Isle of Great Britaine . . . Digested in a Poem,* 1612 (STC 7226), *The Second Part, or A Continuance of Poly-Olbion From the Eighteenth Song,* 1622 (STC 7229), *Poems by Michael Drayton Esquyer. Collected into one Volume, With sondry Peeces inserted neuer before Im-printed,* 1619 (STC 7222), *The Battaile of Agincourt . . . Elegies vpon sundry occasions,* 1631 (STC 7191), and *The Muses Elizium, Lately discouered, By A New Way Over Parnassus. The passages therein, being the subiect of ten sundry Nymphalls,* 1630 (STC 7210). It will be noted that I have used the second (1631) edition of *The Battaile of Agincourt,* since Harvard's copy of the first (1627) edition is without the *Elegies.*

The edition of Drayton's *Works* by J. W. Hebel, Kathleen Tillotson, and Bernard H. Newdigate (5 vols., 1931–41), a triumph of modern scholarship, has of course supplanted such predecessors as the first collected *Works* (1748, 1753), J. P. Collier's *Poems* (1856), and Richard Hooper's curiously entitled *Complete Works* (3 vols., 1876). There are useful selections in Cyril Brett's *Minor Poems* (1907) and John Buxton's *Poems* (2 vols., 1953). Newdigate's biography (1941) has superseded Oliver Elton's (1905), but there is a more recent general study by J. A. Berthelot (1967). Drayton is of course discussed in most of the accounts of Elizabethan and Jacobean poetry listed in the General Bibliography, Section I, and the complicated bibliography has been treated by B. Juel-Jensen (*Library,* VIII, 1953) and S. A. Tannenbaum (1941).

from Poly-Olbion (1612)

To the General Reader

In publishing this essay[1] of my poem there is this great disadvantage against me: that it cometh out at this time when verses are wholly deduced[2] to chambers, and nothing esteemed in this lunatic age but what is kept in cabinets[3] and must only pass by transcription. In such a season, when the idle, humorous world must hear of nothing that either savors of antiquity or may awake it to seek after more than

TO THE GENERAL READER [1]I.e., first installment. [2]Diverted.
[3]Private rooms, boudoirs.

dull and slothful ignorance may easily reach unto, these, I say, make much against me, and especially in a poem from[4] any example, either of ancient or modern, that have proved in this kind, whose unusual tract[5] may perhaps seem difficult to the female sex, yea, and I fear, to some that think themselves not meanly learned, being not rightly inspired by the Muses. Such I mean as had rather read the fantasies of foreign inventions than to see the rarities and history of their own country delivered by a true native Muse. Then, whosoever thou be, possessed with such stupidity and dullness that, rather than thou wilt take pains to search into ancient and noble things, choosest to remain in the thick fogs and mists of ignorance, as near the common laystall[6] of a city, refusing to walk forth into the Tempe[7] and fields of the Muses, where, through most delightful groves, the angelic harmony of birds shall steal thee to the top of an easy hill; where, in artificial caves cut out of the most natural rock, thou shalt see the ancient people of this isle delivered[8] thee in their lively images; from whose height thou mayst behold both the old and later times, as in thy prospect, lying far under thee, then conveying thee down by a soul-pleasing descent through delicate embroidered meadows, often veined with gentle gliding brooks in which thou mayst fully view the dainty nymphs in their simple, naked beauties bathing them in crystalline streams, which shall lead thee to most pleasant downs where harmless shepherds are, some exercising their pipes, some singing roundelays to their gazing flocks. If, as I say, thou hadst rather (because it asks thy labor) remain where thou wert than strain thyself to walk forth with the Muses, the fault proceeds from thy idleness, not from any want in my industry. And to any that shall demand wherefore, having promised this poem of the general island so many years, I now publish only this part of it, I plainly answer that many times I had determined with myself to have left it off, and have neglected my papers sometimes two years together, finding the times since His Majesty's happy coming-in[9] to fall so heavily upon my distressed fortunes after my zealous soul had labored so long in that which, with the general happiness of the kingdom, seemed not then impossible somewhat also to have advanced me. But I instantly saw all my long-nourished hopes even buried alive before my face, so uncertain, in this world, be the ends of our clearest endeavors. And whatever is herein that tastes of a free spirit, I thankfully confess it to proceed from the continual bounty of my truly noble friend Sir Walter Aston,[10] which hath given me the best of those hours whose leisure hath effected this which I now publish. Sundry other songs I have also, though yet not so perfect that I dare commit them to public censure; and the rest I determine to go forward with, God enabling me, may I find means to assist my endeavor. Now, reader, for the further understanding of my poem thou hast three especial helps: first, the argument to direct thee still where thou art and through what shires the Muse makes her journey and what she chiefly handles in the song thereto belonging; next, the map,[11] lively delineating to thee every mountain, forest, river, and valley, expressing in their sundry postures their loves, delights, and natural situations; then hast thou

the illustration of this learned gentleman [John Selden], my friend, to explain every hard matter of history that, lying far from the way of common reading, may, without question, seem difficult unto thee.[12] Thus wishing thee thy heart's desire and committing my poem to thy charitable censure, I take my leave.

Thine as thou art mine,
Michael Drayton

THE FOURTH SONG

In order to determine whether the Isle of Lundy in the Bristol Channel should belong to England or to Wales, the nymphs of the tributary streams hold a singing contest. The Welsh rivers tell of British Arthur's triumphs and of Merlin's feats of magic, and the English rivers of the Saxon and the Norman kings of England. When, finally, the Welsh mountains frown and threaten war, the Severn River brings the contest to a close. Illustrating Drayton's blend of "history" and topography, this fourth song of *Poly-Olbion* presents the natural features of several Welsh and English counties (Monmouth, Glamorgan, Brecknock, Somerset, and Devon) together with the stories of a region rich in legend.

THE ARGUMENT

England and Wales strive, in this song,
To whether[1] Lundy doth belong,
When either's nymphs, to clear the doubt,
By music mean to try it out.
Of mighty Neptune leave they ask.
Each one betakes her to her task,
The Britons with the harp and crowd,[2]
The English both with still and loud.[3]
The Britons chant King Arthur's glory,
The English sing their Saxons' story.
The hills of Wales their weapons take
And are an uproar like to make
To keep the English part in awe.
There's heave and shove and hold and draw,
That Severn can them scarce divide
Till judgment may the cause decide.

. . . . . .

---

[4]Different from. [5]Scope. [6]Dumping ground.
[7]A lovely valley in Thessaly frequented by Apollo.
[8]I.e., represented.
[9]Drayton was disappointed in his hope of royal patronage after James I's accession in 1603.
[10]Sir Walter Aston, Baron Aston of Forfar (1584–1639), an immensely wealthy courtier and diplomat who befriended Drayton.
[11]*Poly-Olbion* was sumptuously adorned with the series of maps of Great Britain engraved by Christopher Saxton (p. 841) between 1574 and 1579.
[12]For John Selden's "Illustrations" or commentaries see p. 854.
THE FOURTH SONG [1]Which of the two.
[2]Ancient musical instrument resembling the violin.
[3]Soft and loud instruments.

Thus either, well prepar'd the other's power before,   235
Conveniently being plac'd upon their equal[4] shore,
The Britons, to whose lot the onset doth belong,
Give signal to the foe for silence to their song.
    To tell each various strain and turning of
        their rhymes—
How this in compass falls or that in sharpness climbs   240
(As where they rest and rise, how take it one from one,
As every several chord hath a peculiar tone)—
Even Memory herself, though striving, would come short,
But the material things, Muse, help me to report.
    At first, t' affront[5] the foe in th' ancient
        Britons' right,   245
With Arthur they begin,[6] their most renowned knight:
The richness of the arms their well-made Worthy[7] wore,
The temper of his sword (the tried Escalabore),
The bigness and the length of Rone, his noble spear,
With Pridwin, his great shield, and what the proof
        could bear,   250
His baudrick[8] how adorn'd with stones of wondrous price,
The sacred Virgin's shape he bore for his device—
These monuments of worth the ancient Britons song.[9]
    Now, doubting lest these things might hold them but
        too long,
His wars they took to task:[10] the land then overlaid   255
With those proud German powers, when, calling to his aid
His kinsman Howell, brought from Brittany the Less,[11]
Their armies they unite, both swearing to suppress
The Saxon here that sought through conquest all to gain.
On whom he chanc'd to light at Lincoln, where
        the plain   260
Eachwhere[12] from side to side lay scatter'd with the dead,
And when the conquer'd foe that from the conflict fled
Betook them to the woods, he never left them there
Until the British earth he forc'd them to forswear.
And as his actions rose, so raise they still their vein   265
In words whose weight best suit a sublimated strain.
    They sung how he himself at Badon bore that day
When at the glorious goal[13] his British scepter lay:
Two days together how the battle strongly stood;
Pendragon's worthy son,[14] who waded there in blood,   270
Three hundred Saxons slew with his own valiant hand.
    And after, call'd the Pict and Irish to withstand,
How he by force of arms Albania[15] overran,
Pursuing of the Pict beyond Mount Calidon,
There strongly shut them up whom stoutly he subdu'd.   275
    How Gillamore again to Ireland he pursu'd
So oft as he presum'd the envious Pict to aid,
And having slain the king, the country waste he laid.
    To Gothland how again this conqueror maketh forth
With his so prosp'rous powers into the farthest north,   280
Where Iceland first he won, and Orkney after got.
    To Norway sailing next with his dear nephew Lot,
By deadly dint of sword did Ricoll there defeat,
And having plac'd the prince on that Norwegian seat
How this courageous king did Denmark then control,   285
That scarcely there was found a country to the pole
That dreaded not his deeds, too long that were to tell.

And after these, in France th' adventures him befell
At Paris in the lists, where he with Flollio fought,
The Emperor Leon's power to raise his siege
        that brought.   290
    Then bravely set they forth in combat how
        these knights
On horseback and on foot perform'd their several fights:
As with what marvelous force each other they assail'd,
How might Flollio first, how Arthur then prevail'd,
For best advantage how they traversed their grounds,   295
The horrid blows they lent, the world-amazing wounds,
Until the tribune, tir'd, sank under Arthur's sword.
    Then sing they how he first ordain'd the circled board,
The knights whose martial deeds far fam'd that
        Table Round,
Which truest in their loves, which most in
        arms renown'd.   300
The laws which long upheld that Order they report,
The Pentecosts prepar'd at Carleon in his court,
That Table's ancient seat: her temples and her groves,
Her palaces, her walks, baths, theaters, and stoves;
Her academy, then, as likewise they prefer;   305
Of Camelot they sing and then of Winchester,
The feasts that underground the faery did him make,
And there how he enjoy'd the Lady of the Lake.
    Then told they how himself great Arthur did advance
To meet, with his allies, that puissant force in France   310
By Lucius thither led, those armies that whilere[16]
Affrighted all the world, by him strook[17] dead with fear;
Th' report of his great acts that over Europe ran
In that most famous field he with the emperor wan;[18]
As how great Rython's self he slew in his repair,   315
Who ravish'd Howell's niece, young Helena the fair,
And for a trophy brought the giant's coat away
Made of the beards of kings. Then bravely chanted they
The several twelve pitch'd fields he with the
        Saxons fought;
The certain day and place to memory they brought.   320

[4]Level.   [5]Confront.
[6]*With Arthur they begin*: Drayton's account of Arthur's exploits is based mainly on Geoffrey of Monmouth's *Historia regum Britanniae*, IX.i–XI.ii.
[7]The Nine Worthies of the World included three pagans (Hector of Troy, Alexander, Julius Caesar), three Jews (Joshua, David, Judas Maccabaeus), and three Christians (Arthur, Charlemagne, Godfrey of Bouillon). For Shakespeare's rather different list see *Love's Labors Lost*, V.ii.   [8]Baldric, ornamental belt.   [9]Sung.
[10]*Took to task*: took up.
[11]*Brittany the Less*: Brittany (French *Bretagne*) was known as Britannia Minor to distinguish it from Britannia Major or Great Britain.   [12]Everywhere.
[13]Text *Gole*, apparently Drayton's misinterpretation of Geoffrey of Monmouth's *cacumen* ("peak"), referring to Mt. Badon. Drayton understood the word in its derived sense "highest point, utmost limit" (as in "the peak of one's ambition").
[14]*Pendragon's worthy son*: Arthur.   [15]Albion, i.e., England.
[16]Formerly.   [17]Struck.
[18]Won.

Then by false Mordred's hand how last he chanc'd to fall,
The hour of his decease, his place of burial.
   When out the English cried to interrupt their song,
But they, which knew to this more matter must belong,
Not out at all for that, nor any whit dismay'd,   325
But to their well-tun'd harps their fingers closely laid,
'Twixt every one of which they plac'd their
      country's crowd,
And with courageous spirits thus boldly sang aloud:
How Merlin by his skill and magic's wondrous might
From Ireland hither brought the Ston'enge in a night,   330
And for Carmarden's sake would fain have brought
      to pass
About it to have built a wall of solid brass;
And set his fiends to work upon the mighty frame,
Some to the anvil, some that still enforc'd the flame,
But whilst it was in hand, by loving of an elf,[19]   335
For all his wondrous skill, was coz'ned[20] by himself,
For, walking with his fay, her to the rock he brought
In which he oft before his nigromancies[21] wrought,
And going in thereat his magics to have shown,
She stopp'd the cavern's mouth with an
      enchanted stone;   340
Whose cunning strongly cross'd, amaz'd whilst he
      did stand,
She captive him convey'd unto the Fairy Land.
   Then how the laboring spirits, to rocks by fetters bound,
With bellows' rumbling groans and hammers'
      thund'ring sound
A fearful horrid din still in the earth do keep,   345
Their master to awake, suppos'd by them to sleep,
As at their work how still the grieved spirits repine,
Tormented in the fire and tired at the mine.
   When now the British side scarce finished their song
But th' English, that repin'd to be delay'd so long,   350
All quickly at the hint, as with one free consent,
Strook up at once and sung each to the instrument....
   Of Germany they sung the long and ancient fame,
From whence their noble sires, the valiant Saxons, came,

Who sought by sea and land adventures far and near,   370
And seizing at the last upon the Britons here,
Surpris'd the spacious isle, which still for theirs
      they hold. . . .
They Saxons first were call'd whose far-extended fame
For hardiness in war, whom danger never fray'd,
Allur'd the Britons here to call them to their aid,   390
From whom they after reft Loëgria[22] as their own,
Brut's[23] offspring then too weak to keep it being grown.
   This told, the nymphs again, in nimbler strains of wit,
Next neatly come about the Englishmen to quit
Of that inglorious blot by Bastard William[24] brought   395
Upon this conquered isle, than which Fate never wrought
A fitter mean, say they, great Germany to grace:
To graft again in one two remnants of her race,
Upon their several ways two several times that went
To forage for themselves. The first of which she sent   400
To get their seat in Gaul, which on Nuestria[25] light
And in a famous war the Frenchmen put to flight,
Possess'd that fruitful place, where only from their name
(Call'd Northmen, from the north of Germany that came,
Who thence expell'd the Gauls and did their
      rooms supply)   405
This, first Nuestria nam'd, was then call'd Normandy;
That by this means the less, in conquering of the great,
Being drawn from their late home unto this ampler seat,
Residing here, resign'd what they before had won,
That as the conquerors' blood did to the conquered run,   410
So kindly being mix'd and up together grown,
As, severed, they were hers; united, still her own.

. . . . . .

[19]Fairy (so also "Fay," two lines below).   [20]Duped.
[21]Necromancies, i.e., enchantments.
[22] England (after Logrin or Locrine, the eldest son of Brut).
[23]Referring to the legendary founder of Britain and progenitor of a line of kings. See p. 808, n. 3.   [24]William the Conqueror.
[25]Neustria, i.e., Normandy.

from The Second Part or a Continuance of Poly-Olbion from the Eighteenth Song (1622)

To Any That Will Read It

When I first undertook this poem or (as some very skillful in this kind have pleased to term it) this herculean labor, I was by some virtuous friends persuaded that I should receive much comfort and encouragement therein, and for these reasons: first, that it was a new, clear way, never before gone by any; then, that it contained all the delicacies, delights, and rarities of this renowned isle interwoven with the histories of the Britons, Saxons, Normans, and the later

English; and, further, that there is scarcely any of the nobility or gentry of this land but that he is some way or other by his blood interested[1] therein. But it hath fallen out otherwise; for instead of that comfort which my noble friends, from the freedom of their spirits, proposed as my due, I have met with barbarous ignorance and base detraction; such a cloud hath the devil drawn over the world's judgment, whose opinion is in few years fallen so far below

TO ANY THAT WILL READ IT   [1]Interested.

all ballatry[2] that the lethargy is incurable. Nay, some of the stationers that had the selling of the first part of this poem, because it went not so fast away in the sale as some of their beastly and abominable trash (a shame both to our language and nation), have either despitefully left out or at least carelessly neglected the epistles to the readers and so have cozened the buyers with unperfected books; which these that have undertaken the second part have been forced to amend in the first for the small number that are yet remaining in their hands. And some of our outlandish, unnatural English (I know not how otherwise to express them) stick not to say that there is nothing in this island worthy studying for, and take a great pride to be ignorant in anything thereof. For these, since they delight in their folly, I wish it may be hereditary from them to their posterity that their children may be begged for[3] fools to the fift[4] generation, until it may be beyond the memory of man to know that there was ever any other of their families. Neither can this deter me from going on with Scotland, if means and time do not hinder me, to perform as much as I have promised in my first Song:

> Till to the sleepy main, to Thuly I have gone
> And seen the frozen isles, the cold Deucalidon,[5]
> Amongst whose iron rocks grim Saturn yet remains,
> Bound in those gloomy caves with adamantine chains.

And as for those cattle whereof I spake before, *odi profanum vulgus et arceo*,[6] of which I account them, be they never so great; and so I leave them. To my friends and the lovers of my labors I wish all happiness.

Michael Drayton

THE TWO AND TWENTIETH SONG
[The Battle of Shrewsbury]

I choose the battle next of Shrewsbury[1] to chant, 425
Betwixt Henry the Fourth, the son of John of Gant,[2]
And the stout Percies, Henry Hotspur and his eam[3]
The Earl of Wor'ster, who the rightful diadem
Had from King Richard reft and heav'd up to his seat
This Henry, whom (too soon) they found to be too great. 430
Him seeking to depose and to the rule prefer
Richard's proclaimed heir, their cousin Mortimer,
Whom Owen Glendour[4] then in Wales a prisoner stay'd,
Whom to their part[5] they won and thus their plot they laid:
That Glendour should have Wales along as Severn went, 435
The Percies all the north that lay beyond the Trent,
And Mortimer from thence the south to be his share.
Which Henry having heard doth for the war prepare
And down to Cheshire makes (where gathering powers
    they were)
At Shrewsbury to meet, and doth affront them there. 440
With him his peerless son, the princely Henry, came
With th' Earl of Stafford and of gentlemen of name
Blunt, Shirley, Clifton, men that very powerful were,
With Cokayne, Calverly, Massie, and Mortimer,
Gausell and Wendsley, all in friends and tenants strong, 445
Reporting to the King still as he pass'd along,
Which[6] in the open field before the ranged fights[7]

He, with his warlike son, there dubb'd his maiden knights.
    Th' Earl Douglas for this day doth with the
        Percies stand,
To whom they Berwick gave, and in Northumberland 450
Some seigniories and holds,[8] if they the battle got,
Who brought with him to field full many an angry Scot
At Holmdon battle late that being overthrown
Now on the King and Prince hop'd to regain their own,
With almost all the power of Cheshire got together 455
By Venables (there great) and Vernon must'red thether.[9]
The vaward[10] of the King great Stafford took to guide;
The vaward of the lords upon the other side
Consisted most of Scots, which joining made such spoil
As at the first constrain'd the English to recoil 460
And almost brake their ranks, which when King
        Henry found,
Bringing his battle[11] up to reinforce the ground,
The Percies bring up theirs again to make it good.
Thus whilst the either host in opposition stood,
Brave Douglas with his spurs his furious courser strake,[12] 465
His lance set in his rest, when desperately he brake
In where his eye beheld th' imperial ensign pight,[13]
Where soon it was his chance upon the King to light,
Which in his full career he from his courser threw;
The next Sir Walter Blunt he with three other slew, 470
All armed like the King, which he dead sure accounted,
But after, when he saw the King himself remounted,
"This hand of mine," quoth he, "four kings this day
        hath slain,"
And swore out of the earth he thought they sprang again
Or Fate did him defend at whom he only aim'd. 475
When Henry Hotspur, so with his high deeds inflam'd,
Doth second him again and through such dangers press
That Douglas' valiant deeds he made to seem the less,
As still the people cried a Percy *"Esperance!"*[14]
The King, which saw then time or never to advance 480
His battle in the field, which near from him was won,
Aided by that brave prince, his most courageous son,
Who bravely coming on in hope to give them chase,
It chanc'd he with a shaft was wounded in the face;
Whom when out of the fight his friends would
        bear away, 485
He strongly it refus'd, and thus was heard to say:

[2]Balladry. [3]*begged for*: set down as [4]Fifth.
[5]*Till to . . . Deucalidon*: i.e., the northernmost parts of the habitable world. Thule (*Thuly*) was usually identified by the ancients as Iceland or Norway, Ducalidon (*Deucalidon*) as the sea to the north of Scotland.
[6]*Odi . . . arceo*: "I hate the ignorant herd and keep them at a distance" (Horace, *Odes*, III.i.1).
TWO AND TWENTIETH SONG [1]A battle (1403) in which the rebellious northern nobles led by Sir Henry Percy ("Hotspur") were defeated by the forces of Henry IV. For another account of this event see Shakespeare's *1 Henry IV*, Acts IV–V.
[2]Gaunt, i.e., Ghent. [3]Uncle. [4]Glendower.
[5]Party, i.e., conspiracy. [6]Whom. [7]Battalions.
[8]Fortresses. [9]Thither. [10]Vanguard. [11]Army.
[12]Streaked (with the rowels of his spurs). [13]Pitched.
[14]"Hope!" (the motto of the Percies).

"Time never shall report Prince Henry left the field
When Harry Percy stay'd, his trait'rous sword to wield."
Now rage and equal wounds alike inflame their bloods,
And the main battles join as do two adverse floods   490
Met in some narrow arm, should'ring as they
    would shove
Each other from their path, or would their banks remove.
The King his trait'rous foes before him down doth hew,
And with his hands that day near forty persons slew,

When conquest wholly turns to his victorious side,   495
His power surrounding all like to a furious tide,
That Henry Hotspur dead upon the cold earth lies,
Stout Wor'ster taken was, and doughty Douglas flies.
Five thousand from both parts left dead upon the ground,
'Mongst whom the King's fast friend, great Stafford's
    corse was found,   500
And all the knights there dubb'd the morning but before
The evening's sun beheld there swelt'red in their gore.

from Poems (1619)

IDEA, IN SIXTY-THREE SONNETS

TO THE READER OF THESE SONNETS

Into these loves who but for passion looks,
At this first sight here let him lay them by
And seek elsewhere in turning other books
Which better may his labor satisfy.
No far-fetch'd sigh shall ever wound my breast;
Love from mine eye a tear shall never wring;
Nor in "Ah me's" my whining sonnets drest.
A libertine, fantastic'ly I sing.
My verse is the true image of my mind,
Ever in motion, still desiring change;
And as thus to variety inclin'd,
So in all humors sportively I range.
    My Muse is rightly of the English strain,
    That cannot long one fashion entertain.

1.

Like an adventurous seafarer am I,
Who hath some long and dang'rous voyage been,
And call'd to tell of his discovery,
How far he sail'd, what countries he had seen,
Proceeding from the port whence he put forth,
Shows by his compass how his course he steer'd,
When east, when west, when south, and when by north,
As how the pole to ev'ry place was rear'd,[1]
What capes he doubled, of what continent,
The gulfs and straits that strangely[2] he had pass'd,
Where most becalm'd, where with foul weather spent,
And on what rocks in peril to be cast.
    Thus in my love Time calls me to relate
    My tedious travels and oft-varying fate.

6.

How many paltry, foolish, painted things
That now in coaches trouble ev'ry street
Shall be forgotten, whom no poet sings,
Ere they be well wrapp'd in their winding sheet!

Where I to thee eternity shall give
When nothing else remaineth of these days,
And queens hereafter shall be glad to live
Upon the alms of thy superfluous praise.
Virgins and matrons reading these my rhymes
Shall be so much delighted with thy story
That they shall grieve they liv'd not in these times,
To have seen thee, their sex's only glory.
    So shalt thou fly above the vulgar throng,
    Still to survive in my immortal song.

8.

There's nothing grieves me but that age should haste
That in my days I may not see thee old,
That where those two clear sparkling eyes are plac'd,
Only two loop-holes then I might behold;
That lovely, arched, ivory, polish'd brow
Defac'd with wrinkles that I might but see,
Thy dainty hair, so curl'd and crisped now,
Like grizzled moss upon some aged tree;
Thy cheek, now flush with roses, sunk and lean,
Thy lips, with age, as any wafer thin,
Thy pearly teeth out of thy head so clean
That when thou feed'st, thy nose shall touch thy chin.
    These lines that now thou[1] scorn'st, which should
      delight thee,
    Then would I make thee read but to despite thee.

15. HIS REMEDY FOR LOVE

Since to obtain thee nothing me will stead,
I have a med'cine that shall cure my love:
The powder of her heart, dried when she is dead,
That[1] gold nor honor ne'er had pow'r to move;
Mix'd with her tears that ne'er her true love cross'd

1. LIKE A SEAFARER [1]*How the pole...rear'd*: i.e., the altitude of the polestar in each case (from which the latitude can be reckoned). [2]In strange manner (or circumstances).
8. THERE'S NOTHING GRIEVES ME [1]Omitted in text, supplied from the 1637 edition.
15. HIS REMEDY FOR LOVE [1]Referring to *thee* of line one.

Nor at fifteen ne'er long'd to be a bride;
Boil'd with her sighs in giving up the ghost
That for her late-deceased husband died;
Into the same then let a woman breathe
That being chid did never word reply,
With one thrice-married's pray'rs that did bequeathe
A legacy to stale virginity.
  If this receipt have not the pow'r to win me,
  Little I'll say, but think the devil's in me.

21.

A witless gallant a young wench that woo'd
(Yet his dull spirit her not one jot could move)
Entreated me, as e'er I wish'd his good,
To write him but one sonnet to his love;
When[1] I, as fast as e'er my pen could trot,
Pour'd out what first from quick invention came,
Nor never stood one word thereof to blot,
Much like his wit that was to use the same.
But with my verses he his mistress won,
Who doted on the dolt beyond all measure.
But see, for you to heav'n for phrase I run,
And ransack all Apollo's golden treasure,
  Yet by my froth this fool his love obtains,
  And I lose you for all my wit and pains.

61.

Since there's no help, come, let us kiss and part.
Nay, I have done: you get no more of me,
And I am glad, yea, glad with all my heart
That thus so cleanly I myself can free.
Shake hands for ever, cancel all our vows,
And when we meet at any time again
Be it not seen in either of our brows
That we one jot of former love retain.
Now at the last gasp of Love's latest breath,
When, his pulse failing, Passion speechless lies,
When Faith is kneeling by his bed of death,
And Innocence is closing up his eyes,
  Now if thou wouldst, when all have given him over,
  From death to life thou mightst him yet recover.

ODES, WITH OTHER LYRIC POESIES

TO THE READER[1]

Odes I have called these my few poems, which how happy soever they prove, yet criticism itself cannot say that the name is wrongfully usurped; for (not to begin with definitions against the rule of oratory, nor *ab ovo*[2] against the prescript[3] rule of poetry in a poetical argument, but somewhat only to season thy palate with a slight description) an ode is known to have been properly a song moduled[4] to the ancient harp, and neither too short-breathed, as hasting to the end, nor composed of the longest verses, as unfit for the sudden turns and lofty tricks with which

Apollo used to manage it. They are, as the learned say, divers: some transcendently lofty and far more high than the epic (commonly called the heroic poem), witness those of the inimitable Pindarus,[5] consecrated to the glory and renown of such as returned in triumph from Olympus, Elis, Isthmus, or the like; others among the Greeks are amorous, soft, and made for chambers, as others for theaters; as were Anacreon's,[6] the very delicacies of the Grecian Erato,[7] which Muse seemed to have been the minion of that Teian old man which composed them. Of a mixed kind were Horace's,[8] and may truly therefore be called his mixed. Whatsoever else are mine, little partaking of the high dialect of the first—

> Though we be all to seek
> Of Pindar, that great Greek—

nor altogether of Anacreon, the arguments being amorous, moral, or what else the Muse pleaseth. To write much in this kind, neither know I how it will relish, nor in so doing can I but injuriously presuppose ignorance or sloth in thee, or draw censure upon myself for sinning against the decorum of a preface by reading a lecture where it is enough to sum the points. New they are, and the work of playing hours, but what other commendation is theirs, and whether inherent in the subject, must be thine to judge. But to act the go-between of my poems and thy applause is neither my modesty nor confidence,[9] that oftener than once have acknowledged thee kind, and do not doubt hereafter to do somewhat in which I shall not fear thee just. And would at this time also gladly let thee understand what I think above the rest, of the last ode[10] of this number—or if thou wilt, ballad—in my book; for both the great master of Italian rhymes, Petrarch, and our Chaucer and other of the upper house of the Muses have thought their canzons honored in the title of a ballad; which, for that I labor to meet truly therein with the old English garb, I hope as able to justify as the learned Colin Clout his roundelay.[11] Thus requesting thee, in thy better judgment, to correct such faults as have escaped in the printing, I bid thee farewell.

M. Drayton

21. A WITLESS GALLANT [1]Whereupon.

TO THE READER [1]Drayton's comments on the history of the ode should be compared with those of Cowley, p. 328.
[2]"From the egg," i.e., at the beginning [3]Prescribed.
[4]I.e., contrived to be sung.
[5]Pindar (522?–443 B.C.), Greek lyric poet whose forty-four extant odes (*Epinicia*) celebrating the Olympian, Isthmian, Nemean, and Pythian games are notable for their density and power.
[6]Greek lyric poet (6th cent. B.C.), born at Teos in Ionia (hence *Teian*), whose works, surviving only in fragments, are mainly light songs about the pleasures of love and wine. Poems of this sort, like Cowley's (p. 334), were popular in the seventeenth century. [7]The Muse of lyric poetry.
[8]Roman poet (65–8 B.C.) whose four books of odes were immensely popular in the Renaissance. [9]Boldness.
[10]I.e., "To the Cambro-Britons and Their Harp, the Ballad of Agincourt" (see pp. 41–43).
[11]I.e., Edmund Spenser, who in the "June" eclogue (line 49) of *The Shepherds' Calendar* (1579) used the new word *roundelay*.

TO HIS VALENTINE

Muse, bid the morn awake:
  Sad winter now declines,
Each bird doth choose a make,[1]
  This day's Saint Valentine's.
For that good bishop's[2] sake   5
Get up and let us see
What beauty it shall be
  That Fortune us assigns.

But lo, in happy hour,
  The place wherein she lies,   10
In yonder climbing tow'r,
  Gilt by the glitt'ring rise.
O Jove! that in a show'r,
As once that Thund'rer[3] did
When he in drops lay hid,   15
  That I could her surprise!

Her canopy[4] I'll draw,
  With spangled plumes bedight;
No mortal ever saw
  So ravishing a sight,   20
That it the gods might awe,
And pow'rfully transpierce
The globy universe,
  Outshooting ev'ry light.

My lips I'll softly lay   25
  Upon her heav'nly cheek,
Dy'd like the dawning day,
  As polish'd ivory sleek;
And in her ear I'll say,
"O thou bright morning star,   30
'Tis I that come so far,
  My Valentine to seek."

Each little bird this tide
  Doth choose her loved fere,[5]
Which constantly abide   35
  In wedlock all the year;
As Nature is their guide,
So may we two be true
This year, nor change for new,
  As turtles[6] coupled were.   40

The sparrow, swan, the dove,
  Though Venus' birds they be,
Yet are they not for love
  So absolute[7] as we;
For reason us doth move,   45
They but by billing woo,
Then try what we can do,
  To whom each sense is free.

Which we have more than they,
  By livelier organs sway'd,   50
Our appetite each way
  More by our sense obey'd;
Our passions to display
This season us doth fit;

Then let us follow it,   55
  As Nature us doth lead.

One kiss in two let's break,
  Confounded with the touch;
But half-words let us speak,
  Our lips employ'd so much   60
Until we both grow weak
With sweetness of thy breath;
O smother me to death!
  Long let our joys be such!

Let's laugh at them that choose   65
  Their Valentines by lot,
To wear their names that use
  Whom idly they have got.
Such poor choice we refuse;
Saint Valentine befriend,   70
We thus this morn may spend;
  Else, Muse, awake her not.

TO THE VIRGINIAN VOYAGE[1]

You brave heroic minds,
Worthy your country's name,
  That honor still pursue,
  Go, and subdue,
Whilst loit'ring hinds
Lurk here at home with shame.   5

Britons, you stay too long;
Quickly aboard bestow you,
  And with a merry gale
  Swell your stretch'd sail,   10
With vows as strong
As the winds that blow you.

Your course securely steer,
West and by south forth keep,
  Rocks, lee shores, nor shoals,   15
  When Aeolus scowls.
You need not fear,
So absolute[2] the deep.

And cheerfully at sea,
Success you still entice,   20
  To get the pearl and gold,
  And ours to hold
Virginia,
Earth's only paradise,

TO HIS VALENTINE [1]Mate.
[2]St. Valentine's Day was named after a quasi-legendary Christian
martyr of the third century.
[3]I.e., Jove, who descended to Danaë in a shower of gold.
[4]I.e., bed-curtains. [5]Companion.
[6]Turtledoves, proverbially constant in love.
[7]I.e., totally committed.
TO THE VIRGINIAN VOYAGE [1]This famous ode, first published
(with its companion piece, "The Battle of Agincourt") in *Poems
Lyric and Pastoral* of 1606, was probably inspired by preparations
for the expedition that sailed in December of that year.
[2]I.e., profound.

Where Nature hath in store   25
Fowl, venison, and fish,
  And the fruitful'st soil
  Without your toil
Three harvests more,
All greater than your wish.   30

And the ambitious vine
Crowns with his purple mass,
  The cedar reaching high
  To kiss the sky,
The cypress, pine,   35
And useful sassafras.

To whose the golden age
Still Nature's laws doth give,
  No other cares that tend
  But them to defend   40
From winter's age,
That long there doth not live.

Whenas the luscious smell
Of that delicious land,
  Above the seas that flows,   45
  The clear wind throws,
Your hearts to swell
Approaching the dear strand,

In kenning of the shore,
Thanks to God first given,   50
  O you, the happi'st men,
  Be frolic then,
Let cannons roar,
Frighting the wide heaven.

And in regions far   55
Such heroes bring ye forth
  As those from whom we came,
  And plant our name
Under that star
Not known unto our north.   60

And as there plenty grows
Of laurel everywhere,
  Apollo's sacred tree,
  You it may see
A poet's brows   65
To crown, that may sing there.

Thy voyages attend,
Industrious Hakluyt,[3]
  Whose reading shall enflame
  Men to seek fame,   70
And much commend
To aftertimes thy wit.

TO HIS COY LOVE
A Canzonet

I pray thee leave,[1] love me no more,
  Call home the heart you gave me.
I but in vain that saint adore

That can but will not save me:
These poor half-kisses kill me quite.   5
  Was ever man thus served,
Amidst an ocean of delight
  For pleasure to be sterved?[2]

Show me no more those snowy breasts
  With azure riverets branched,   10
Where whilst mine eye with plenty feasts
  Yet is my thirst not stanched.
O Tantalus,[3] thy pains ne'er tell;
  By me thou art prevented;
'Tis nothing to be plagu'd in hell,   15
  But thus in heaven tormented.

Clip[4] me no more in those dear arms,
  Nor thy life's comfort call me;
O, these are but too pow'rful charms
  And do but more enthrall me.   20
But see how patient I am grown
  In all this coil[5] about thee:
Come, nice thing, let thy heart alone,
  I cannot live without thee.

TO THE CAMBRO-BRITONS[1] AND THEIR HARP, HIS BALLAD OF AGINCOURT

Fair stood the wind for France,
When we our sails advance,
Nor now to prove our chance
  Longer will tarry;
But putting to the main,   5
At Caux,[2] the mouth of Seine,
With all his martial train,
  Landed King Harry.

And taking many a fort,
Furnish'd in warlike sort,   10
Marcheth tow'rds Agincourt
  In happy hour;
Skirmishing day by day
With those that stopp'd his way,
Where the French gen'ral lay   15
  With all his power.

Which in his height of pride,
King Henry to deride,
His ransom to provide

[3]Richard Hakluyt (1552?–1616), geographer and propagandist for colonial exploration whose famous *Principal Navigations... of the English Nation* (1589) was a powerful stimulus to overseas expansion.
TO HIS COY LOVE [1]Leave off, cease. [2]Starved.
[3]A son of Zeus condemned in Hades to stand in water that receded as he tried to drink and under branches laden with fruit that he could not reach. [4]Embrace. [5]Fuss.
TO THE CAMBRO-BRITONS [1]I.e., the Welsh and English soldiers whom Henry V (*Harry*) led to a great victory at the French village of Agincourt on 25 October 1415.
[2]District in Normandy on the estuary of the Seine.

To the King sending;   20
Which he neglects the while
As from a nation vile,
Yet with an angry smile
  Their fall portending.

And turning to his men,   25
Quoth our brave Henry then:
  "Though they to one be ten,
  Be not amazed.
Yet have we well begun,
Battles so bravely won   30
Have ever to the sun
  By fame been raised.

"And for myself," quoth he,
  "This my full rest shall be;
England ne'er mourn for me,   35
  Nor more esteem me:
Victor I will remain
Or on this earth lie slain,
Never shall she sustain
  Loss to redeem me.   40

"Poiters and Cressy[3] tell,
When most their pride did swell,
Under our swords they fell;
  No less our skill is
Than when our grandsire[4] great,   45
Claiming the regal seat,
By many a warlike feat
  Lopp'd the French lilies."

The Duke of York[5] so dread
The eager vaward[6] led;   50
With the main[7] Henry sped
  Amongst his henchmen.
Excester[8] had the rear,
A braver man not there,
O Lord, how hot they were   55
  On the false Frenchmen!

They now to fight are gone,
Armor on armor shone,
Drum now to drum did groan,
  To hear was wonder,   60
That with cries they make
The very earth did shake,
Trumpet to trumpet spake,
  Thunder to thunder.

Well it thine age became,   65
O noble Erpingham,[9]
Which didst the signal aim
  To our hid forces;
When from a meadow by,
Like a storm suddenly,   70
The English archery
  Stuck the French horses,

With Spanish yew so strong,
Arrows a cloth-yard long,

That like to serpents stung,   75
  Piercing the weather;
None from his fellow starts,
But playing manly parts,
And like true English hearts,
  Stuck close together.   80

When down their bows they threw,
And forth their bilboes[10] drew,
And on the French they flew,
  Not one was tardy;
Arms were from shoulders sent,   85
Scalps to the teeth were rent,
Down the French peasants went;
  Our men were hardy.

This while our noble King,
His broadsword brandishing,   90
Down the French host did ding,[11]
  As to o'erwhelm it;
And many a deep wound lent,
His arms with blood besprent,
And many a cruel dent   95
  Bruised his helmet.

Gloster,[12] that duke so good,
Next of the royal blood,
For famous England stood
  With his brave brother;   100
Clarence,[13] in steel so bright,
Though but a maiden knight,
Yet in that furious fight
  Scarce such another.

Warwick[14] in blood did wade,   105
Oxford the foe invade,
And cruel slaughter made
  Still as they ran up;
Suffolk his ax did ply,
Beaumont and Willoughby   110
Bare them right doughtily,
  Ferrers and Fanhope.

[3]Poitiers and Crécy, French villages where the English decisively defeated the French in 1356 and 1346 respectively.
[4]King Edward III of England, Henry V's grandfather.
[5]Edward of Norwich, second duke of York, who commanded the English right wing at Agincourt and was killed in the battle.
[6]Vanguard.   [7]I.e., the body of the army.
[8]Thomas Beaufort, duke of Exeter. There is some doubt that he was actually at Agincourt.
[9]Sir Thomas Erpingham, commander of the English battleline at Agincourt.
[10]Swords (from Bilboa, Spain).   [11]Strike.
[12]Humphrey, duke of Gloucester, youngest brother of Henry V.
[13]Thomas, duke of Clarence, another brother of Henry V.
[14]Like the other historical details, the names of the English leaders in this stanza are derived from Raphael Holinshed's *Chronicles* second ed., 1586), which was also used by Shakespeare for his history plays.

Upon Saint Crispin's day[15]
Fought was this noble fray,
Which fame did not delay   115
   To England to carry;
O, when shall English men

With such acts fill a pen,
Or England breed again
   Such a King Harry?   120

[15]I.e., October 25. Crispinus and Crispianus, who suffered martyrdom in 287, became the patron saints of shoe-makers.

from Elegies upon Sundry Occasions (1627)

TO MASTER GEORGE SANDYS,[1] TREASURER FOR THE ENGLISH COLONY IN VIRGINIA

Friend, if you think my papers may supply
You with some strange omitted novelty
Which others' letters yet have left untold,
You take me off before I can take hold
Of you at all. I put not thus to sea   5
For two months' voyage to Virginia
With news which now a little something here,
But will be nothing ere it can come there.
   I fear as I do stabbing this word *state*:[2]
I dare not speak of the Palatinate,   10
Although some men make it[3] their hourly theme,
And talk what's done in Austria and in Beame,
I may not so; what Spinola intends,
Nor with his Dutch which way Prince Maurice bends,
To other men although these things be free,   15
Yet, George, they must be mysteries to me.
   I scarce dare praise a virtuous friend that's dead,
Lest for my lines he should be censured.[4]
It was my hap before all other men
To suffer shipwrack by my forward pen   20
When King James ent'red; at which joyful time
I taught his title to this isle in rhyme,
And to my part[5] did all the Muses win
With high-pitch paeans to applaud him in;[6]
When cowardice had tied up every tongue   25
And all stood silent, yet for him I sung;
And when before by Danger I was dar'd,
I kick'd her from me, nor a jot I spar'd.
Yet had not my clear spirit in Fortune's scorn
Me above earth and her afflictions borne,   30
He next my God on whom I built my trust
Had left me trodden lower than the dust.
But let this pass: in the extremest ill
Apollo's brood must be courageous still.
Let pies[7] and daws sit dumb before their death;   35
Only the swan sings at the parting breath.
   And, worthy George, by industry and use
Let's see what lines Virginia will produce.
Go on with Ovid as you have begun
With the first five books;[8] let your numbers run   40
Glib[9] as the former, so shall it live long,
And do much honor to the English tongue.
Entice the Muses thither to repair,

Entreat them gently, train them to that air,
For they from hence may thither hap to fly   45
T'wards[10] the sad time which but too fast doth hie;
For Poesy is followed with such spite
By groveling drones that never raught[11] her height
That she must hence: she may no longer stay.
The driery[12] Fates prefixed have the day   50
Of her departure, which is now come on.
And they command her straightway to be gone.
That bestial herd so hotly her pursue,
And to her succor there be very few,
Nay, none at all, her wrongs that will redress;   55
But she must wander in the wilderness
Like to the woman which that holy John
Beheld in Patmos in his vision.[13]
   As th' English now, so did the stiff-neck'd Jews
Their noble prophets utterly refuse,   60
And of those men such poor opinions had,
They counted Esay and Ezekiel mad;
When Jeremy his Lamentations writ,
They thought the wizard quite out of his wit;
Such sots they were as worthily to lie   65
Lock'd in the chains of their captivity.
Knowledge hath still her eddy in her flow;
So it hath been, and it will still be so.
   That famous Greece where learning flourish'd most
Hath of her Muses long since left to boast;   70
Th' unletter'd Turk and rude barbarian trades
Where Homer sang his lofty Iliads,
And this vast volume of the world hath taught;

TO MASTER GEORGE SANDYS [1]For George Sandys see pp. 104 ff.
[2]I.e., politics and foreign policy, discussion of which had been forbidden in a royal proclamation of 1620. The Palatinate, Austria, and Bohemia (*Beame*) were regions of great political sensitivity in the Thirty Years' War (which had begun two years before), and its leading generals—Ambrogio Spinola for the Spanish forces and Maurice of Nassau for the Dutch—were personages of large importance.
[3]Text *in*. [4]Regarded unfavorably. [5]Cause.
[6]Drayton's "To the Majesty of King James," which he wrote in 1603 to celebrate the new monarch's accession, did not bring him the patronage for which he hoped. [7]Magpies.
[8]Although Sandys' translation of the first five books of Ovid's *Metamorphoses* was apparently published in 1621, no copy of the work is known to survive. See p. 105. [9]Smoothly flowing.
[10]At the approach of. [11]Reached. [12]Dreary.
[13]Revelation 12.1–6.

Much may to pass in little time be brought.

As if to symptoms we may credit give,   75
This very time wherein we two now live
Shall in the compass[14] wound the Muses more
Than all the old English ignorance before.
Base ballatry[15] is so belov'd and sought,
And those brave numbers are put by for nought   80
Which, rarely read, were able to awake
Bodies from graves and to the ground to shake
The wand'ring clouds, and to our men-at-arms
'Gainst pikes and muskets were most powerful charms,
That, but[16] I know ensuing ages shall   85
Raise her again who now is in her fall,
And out of dust reduce[17] our scattered rhymes,
Th' rejected jewels of these slothful times,
Who with the Muses would misspend an hour,
But let blind Gothish barbarism devour   90
These feverous dog days, blest by no record,
But to be everlastingly abhorr'd.

If you vouchsafe rescription,[18] stuff your quill
With natural bounties and impart your skill
In the description of the place, that I   95
May become learned in the soil thereby;
Of noble Wyatt's[19] health and let me hear,
The governor, and how our people there
Increase and labor; what supplies are sent;
Which I confess shall give me much content.   100
But you may save your labor if you please
To write to me aught of your savages:
As savage slaves be in Great Britain here
As any one that you can show me there.
And though for this I'll say I do not thirst,   105
Yet I should like it well to be the first
Whose numbers hence into Virginia flew.
So, noble Sandys, for this time adieu.

TO MY NOBLE FRIEND MASTER WILLIAM BROWNE[1], OF THE EVIL TIME

Dear friend, be silent and with patience see
What this mad time's catastrophe[2] will be.
The world's first wise men certainly mistook
Themselves, and spoke things quite beside the book,
And that which they have said of God, untrue—   5
Or else expect strange judgment to ensue.[3]

This isle is a mere bedlam, and therein
We all lie raving mad in every sin,
And him the wisest most men use to call
Who doth, alone, the maddest thing of all.   10
He whom the master of all wisdom found
For a mark'd fool and so did him propound,
The time we live in to that pass is brought
That only he a censor[4] now is thought;
And that base villain, not an age yet gone   15
Which a good man would not have look'd upon,
Now like a god with divine worship follow'd,
And all his actions are accounted hollow'd.[5]

This world of ours thus runneth upon wheels,[6]

Set on the head, bolt upright with her heels,   20
Which makes me think of what the ethnics[7] told,
Th' opinion the Pythagorists uphold,
That the immortal soul doth transmigrate.
Then I suppose by the strong power of fate
That those which at confused Babel were,   25
And since that time now many a lingering year
Through fools and beasts and lunatics have pass'd,
Are here embodied[8] in this age at last;
And though so long we from that time be gone,
Yet taste we still of that confusion.   30

For certainly there's scarce one found that now
Knows what t' approve or what to disallow:
All arsy-versy,[9] nothing is its own,
But to our proverb all turn'd upside down.
To do in time is to do out of season,   35
And that speeds best that's done the farth'st from reason.
He's high'st that's low'st, he's surest in that's out,
He hits the next[10] way that goes farth'st about,
He getteth up unlike to rise at all,
He slips to ground as much unlike to fall;   40
Which doth enforce me partly to prefer
The opinion of that mad philosopher[11]
Who taught that those all-framing powers above
(As 'tis suppos'd) made man not out of love
To him at all, but only as a thing   45
To make them sport with, which they use to bring
As men do monkeys, puppets, and such tools
Of laughter: so men are but the gods of fools.
Such are by titles lifted to the sky
As wherefore no man knows, God scarcely why: 50
The virtuous man depressed like a stone
For that dull sot to raise himself upon;
He who ne'er thing yet worthy man durst do,
Never durst look upon his country's foe,
Nor durst attempt that action which might get   55
Him fame with men, or higher might him set
Than the base beggar (rightly if compar'd),
This drone yet never brave attempt that dar'd
Yet dares be knighted, and from thence dares grow
To any title empire can bestow.   60
For this believe: that impudence is now
A cardinal virtue, and men it allow
Reverence—nay more, men study and invent
New ways, nay, glory to be impudent.

Into the clouds the devil lately got,   65

[14]Course. [15]Balladry. [16]Except that. [17]Bring back.
[18]I.e., condescend to answer this epistle.
[19]Sir Francis Wyatt (1575?–1644), governor of the Virginia Company.
TO MASTER WILLIAM BROWNE [1]For William Browne see pp. 164 ff.
[2]Conclusion.
[3]*The world's...ensue*: i.e., the Hebrews were wrong (*beside the book*) when they said that God would permit sin—if some extraordinary punishment does not befall this age shortly.
[4]Arbiter of manners and morals. [5]Hallowed.
[6]Makes good progress. [7]Pagans. [8]Reincarnated [9]Backside foremost. [10]Nearest. [11]Zeno (Drayton's gloss).

And by the moisture doubting[12] much the rot,
A medicine took to make him purge and cast,[13]
Which in short time began to work so fast
That he fell to't, and from his backside flew
A rout of rascal,[14] a rude ribald crew   70
Of base plebeians, which no sooner light
Upon the earth but with a sudden flight
They spread this isle; and as Deucalion[15] once
Over his shoulder back by throwing stones
They became men, even so these beasts became   75
Owners of titles, from an obscure name.

    He that by riot,[16] of a mighty rent,[17]
Hath his late goodly patrimony spent
And into base and willful beggary run,
This man as[18] he some glorious act had done   80
With some great pension or rich gift reliev'd,
When he that hath by industry achiev'd
Some noble thing, contemned and disgrac'd
In the forlorn hope[19] of the times is plac'd,
As though that God had carelessly left all   85
That being hath on this terrestial[20] ball
To Fortune's guiding, nor would have to do
With man nor aught that doth belong him to;
Or at the least God having given more
Power to the devil than He did of yore   90
Over this world, the fiend as he doth hate
The virtuous man, maligning his estate,
All noble things, and would have by his will
To be damn'd with him, using all his skill
By his black hellish ministers to vex   95
All worthy men, and strangely to perplex
Their constancy, thereby them so to fright
That they should yield them wholly to his might.
But of these things I vainly do but tell,
Where hell is heaven and heav'n is now turn'd hell,   100
Where that which lately blasphemy hath been,
Now godliness, much less accounted sin;
And a long while I greatly marvel'd why
Buffoons and bawds should hourly multiply,
Till that of late I construed it that they   105
To present thrift[21] had got the perfect way,

When I concluded by their odious crimes,
It was for us no thriving in these times.
    As men oft laugh at little babes when they
Hap to behold some strange thing in their play,   110
To see them on the sudden strucken sad,
As in their fancy some strange forms they had,
Which they by pointing with their fingers show,
Angry at our capacities so slow,
That by their countenance we no sooner learn   115
To see the wonder which they so discern;
So the celestial powers do sit and smile
At innocent and virtuous men the while
They stand amazed at the world o'ergone
So far beyond imagination   120
With slavish baseness that they[22] silent sit,
Pointing like children in describing[23] it.
    Then, noble friend, the next[24] way to control
These worldly crosses is to arm thy soul
With constant patience, and with thoughts as high   125
As these below, and poor, winged to fly
To that exalted stand whether[25] yet they
Are got with pain that sit out of the way
Of this ignoble age, which raiseth none
But such as think their black damnation   130
To be a trifle, such so ill that when
They are advanc'd, those few poor honest men
That yet are living, into search do run
To find what mischief they have lately done
Which so prefers[26] them. Say thou he doth rise   135
That maketh virtue his chief exercise,
And in this base world, come whatever shall,
He's worth lamenting that for her doth fall.

[12]Fearing. [13]Void. [14]Rabble.
[15]This son of Prometheus and his wife Pyrrha were the only survivors of a deluge sent by Zeus to punish the wicked world.
[16]Dissipation. [17]Income. [18]As if.
[19]Originally, a picked body of men detached to the front to begin the attack; hence a desperate or reckless position.
[20]Terrestrial. [21]Thriving, prosperity. [22]Text *the*.
[23]Descrying, pointing out. [24]Nearest, i.e., best. [25]Whither.
[26]Advances.

from The Muses' Elysium (1630)

THE DESCRIPTION OF ELYSIUM

A paradise on earth is found,
Though far from vulgar sight,
Which with those pleasures doth abound
That it Elysium hight.[1]

Where in delights that never fade   5
The Muses lulled be,

And sit at pleasure in the shade
Of many a stately tree,

Which no rough tempest makes to reel
Nor their straight bodies bows;   10
Their lofty tops do never feel
The weight of winter's snows;

THE DESCRIPTION OF ELYSIUM   [1]Is called.

In groves that evermore are green;
No falling leaf is there,
But Philomel,[2] of birds the queen,   15
In music spends the year.

The merle[3] upon her myrtle perch,
Thereto the mavis[4] sings,
Who from the top of some curl'd birch
Those notes redoubled rings.   20

There daisies damask every place,
Nor once their beauties lose,
That when proud Phoebus hides his face
Themselves they scorn to close.

The pansy and the violet here,   25
As seeming to descend
Both from one root, a very pair,
For sweetness yet contend;

And pointing to a pink, to tell
Which bears it,[5] it is loath   30
To judge it; but replies, for smell
That it excels them both.

Wherewith displeas'd, they hang their heads,
So angry soon they grow,
And from their odoriferous beds   35
Their sweets at it they throw.

The winter here a summer is,
No waste is made by time,
Nor doth the autumn ever miss
The blossoms of the prime.[6]   40

The flower that July forth doth bring,
In April here is seen;
The primrose that puts on[7] the spring,
In July decks each green.

The sweets for sovereignty contend,   45
And so abundant be
That to the very earth they lend
And bark of every tree.

Rills rising out of every bank
In wild meanders strain,   50
And playing many a wanton prank
Upon the speckled plain,

In gambols and lascivious gyres
Their time they still bestow,
Nor to their fountains[8] none retires,   55
Nor on their course will go.

Those brooks with lilies bravely deck'd,
So proud and wanton made
That they their courses quite neglect,
And seem as though they stay'd   60

Fair Flora[9] in her state to view,
Which through those lilies looks;
Or as those lilies lean'd to shew
Their beauties to the brooks,

That Phoebus in his lofty race   65
Oft lays aside his beams,
And comes to cool his glowing face
In these delicious streams.

Oft spreading vines climb up the clives,[10]
Whose ripen'd clusters there   70
Their liquid purple drop, which drives
A vintage through the year,

Those clives whose craggy sides are clad
With trees of sundry suits,
Which make continual summer glad,   75
Even bending with their fruits,

Some ripening, ready some to fall,
Some blossom'd, some to bloom,
Like gorgeous hangings on the wall
Of some rich princely room.   80

Pomegranates, lemons, citrons so
Their laded branches bow,
Their leaves in number that outgo
Nor roomth[11] will them allow.

There in perpetual summer's shade   85
Apollo's prophets sit
Among the flow'rs that never fade,
But flourish like their wit;

To whom the nymphs upon their lyres
Tune many a curious lay,   90
And with their most melodious choirs
Make short the longest day.

The thrice three virgins[12] heavenly clear
Their trembling timbrels sound,
Whilst the three comely Graces there   95
Dance many a dainty round.

Decay nor age there nothing knows,
There is continual youth,
As time on plant or creatures grows,
So still their strength renew'th.   100

The poets' paradise this is,
To which but few can come,
The Muses' only bower of bliss,
Their dear Elysium;

Here happy souls, their blessed bowers   105
Free from the rude resort
Of beastly people, spend the hours
In harmless mirth and sport.

Then on to the Elysian plains
Appollo doth invite you,   110
Where he provides with pastoral strains
In nymphals to delight you.

[2]The nightingale. [3]Blackbird. [4]Thrush. [5]Is the victor.
[6]Spring. [7]Imitates. [8]Springs, sources. [9]Goddess of flowers.
[10]Cliffs. [11]Space. [12]Muses.

THE FOURTH NYMPHAL
Cloris and Mertilla

Chaste Cloris doth disclose the shames
Of the Felician frantic dames;[1]
Mertilla strives t' appease her woe;
To golden wishes then they go.

Mertilla:

Why, how now, Cloris! What, thy head
Bound with forsaken willow?
Is the cold ground become thy bed,
The grass become thy pillow?
O let not those life-lightning eyes   5
In this sad veil be shrouded,
Which into mourning puts the skies,
To see them overclouded.

Cloris:

O my Mertilla, do not praise
These lamps so dimly burning;   10
Such sad and sullen lights as these
Were only made for mourning.
Their objects are the barren rocks
With aged moss o'ershaded,
Now whilst the spring lays forth her locks   15
With blossoms bravely braided.

Mertilla:

O Cloris, can there be a spring?
O my dear nymph, there[2] may not,
Wanting thine eyes it forth to bring,
Without which Nature cannot.   20
Say what it is that troubleth thee,
Increas'd by thy concealing;
Speak; sorrows many times, we see,
Are less'ned by revealing.

Cloris:

Being of late too vainly bent,   25
And but at too much leisure,
Not with our groves and downs content,
But surfeiting in pleasure,
Felicia's fields I would go see,
Where Fame[3] to me reported   30
The choice nymphs of the world to be
From meaner beauties sorted;
Hoping that I from them might draw
Some graces to delight me,
But there such monstrous shapes I saw   35
That to this hour affright me.
Through the thick hair that thatch'd their brows
Their eyes upon me stared,
Like to those raging frantic froes[4]
For Bacchus' feasts prepared.   40
Their bodies, although straight by kind,
Yet they so monstrous make them
That for huge bags blown up with wind
You very well may take them.

Their bowels in their elbows are,   45
Whereon depend their paunches,
And their deformed arms by far
Made larger than their haunches.
For their behavior and their grace,
Which likewise should have priz'd them,   50
Their manners were as beastly base
As th' rags that so disguis'd them:
All antics,[5] all so impudent,
So fashion'd out of fashion,
As black Cocytus[6] up had sent   55
Her fry into this nation,
Whose monstrousness doth so perplex
Of reason and deprives me
That for their sakes I loathe my sex,
Which to this sadness drives me.   60

Mertilla:

O my dear Cloris, be not sad,
Nor with these Furies danted,[7]
But let these female fools be mad,
With hellish pride enchanted.
Let not thy noble thoughts descend   65
So low as their affections,
Whom neither counsel can amend
Nor yet the gods' corrections.
Such mad folks ne'er let us bemoan,
But rather scorn their folly,   70
And since we two are here alone,
To banish melancholy
Leave we this lowly creeping vein,
Not worthy admiration,
And in a brave and lofty strain   75
Let's exercise our passion
With wishes of each other's good
From our abundant treasures,
And in this jocund, sprightly mood
Thus alter we our measures.   80

Mertilla:

O I could wish this place were strew'd with roses,
And that this bank were thickly thrumm'd[8] with grass
As soft as sleave[9] or sarcenet[10] ever was,
Whereon my Cloris her sweet self reposes.

Cloris:

O that these dews rosewater were for thee,   85
These mists perfumes that hang upon these thicks,[11]
And that the winds were all aromatics,
Which if my wish could make them, they should be.

Mertilla:

O that my bottle one whole diamond were,
So fill'd with nectar that a fly might sup,   90

THE FOURTH NYMPHAL [1]I.e., human women as they appear to
their "Elysian" counterparts. [2]Text *they*. [3]Rumor.
[4]Bacchantes, frenzied followers of Bacchus, the god of wine and
revelry. [5]Clowns. [6]One of the rivers of Hades. [7]Daunted.
[8]Adorned. [9]Filament of silk. [10]Fine silk. [11]Thickets.

And at one draft that thou mightst drink it up—
Yet a carouse[12] not good enough, I fear.

Cloris:
That all the pearl the seas or Indias have
Were well dissolv'd and thereof made a lake,
Thou therein bathing, and I by to take   95
Pleasure to see thee clearer than the wave.

Mertilla:
O that the horns of all the herds we see
Were of fine gold, or else that every horn
Were like to that one of the unicorn,
And of all these not one but were thy fee.   100

Cloris:
O that their hooves were ivory, or some thing
Than the pur'st ivory far more crystalline,
Fill'd with the food wherewith the gods do dine,
To keep thy youth in a continual spring.

Mertilla:
O that the sweets of all the flowers that grow   105
The laboring air would gather into one,
In gardens, fields, nor meadows leaving none,
And all their sweetness upon thee would throw.

Cloris:
Nay, that those sweet harmonious strains we hear
Amongst the lively birds' melodious lays   110

As they recording[13] sit upon the sprays
Were hovering still for music at thine ear.

Mertilla:
O that thy name were carv'd on every tree,
That as these plants still great and greater grow,
Thy name, dear nymph, might be enlarged so   115
That every grove and coppice might speak thee.

Cloris:
Nay, would thy name upon their rinds[14] were set,
And by the nymphs so oft and loudly spoken
As that the echoes, to that language broken,
Thy happy name might hourly counterfeit.   120

Mertilla:
O let the spring still put stern winter by,
And in rich damask let her revel still,
As it should do if I might have my will,
That thou mightst still walk on her tapestry;
And thus since Fate no longer time allows   125
Under this broad and shady sycamore
Where now we sit, as we have oft before,
Those yet unborn shall offer up their vows.

[12]Full bumper. [13]Practicing (songs). [14]Barks.

Joshua Sylvester [1563-1618]

The scriptural epics of the Huguenot soldier-poet Guillaume de Salluste, seigneur du Bartas (1544–90) are hardly staple items nowadays, but they were very widely read and praised for several generations, and their enormous popularity tells us a good deal of what Milton's contemporaries thought about didactic poetry. Resolved to prove that art could serve the interests of religion, in 1578 Du Bartas published *La Semaine, ou création du monde*, a paraphrase, in seven books or "days," of the opening chapters of Genesis. Spurred on, no doubt, by its success, in 1584 he began to publish its even more ambitious sequel as *La Seconde semaine, ou enfance du monde*. In this second gigantic but unfinished undertaking, Du Bartas, tracing sacred history from the creation to the birth of Christ, could not encompass his material in only seven "days." Each book or "day" therefore had to be divided into parts, and each part was made to represent an epoch in the history of the Jews. Before he died in 1590 (of wounds received in fighting for his patron Henri IV) Du Bartas had finished only two "days" of this second week, but from fragments posthumously recovered two more "days" were stitched together. Of the four "days" that thus compose the work, the first (entitled "Adam") runs from prelapsarian bliss to the consequences of the fall; the second ("Noah") takes us from the Flood to the dim beginnings of recorded history; the third ("Abraham") gives the record of the Jews down to Samuel's choice of Saul as King of Israel; the fourth ("David") carries on the story to Nebuchadnezzar's capture of Jerusalem.

This huge mass of piety and instruction—which Douglas Bush has called a kind of Albert Memorial of encyclopedic fundamentalism—mingles an orthodox account of providential history with enough geographical, astronomical, and quasi-scientific lore to confirm its author's zeal, and it was so successful that more than a hundred editions (in collected versions, separate parts, fragments, and translations) appeared in northern Europe by the 1630's. In England, where Du Bartas' assertive Protestantism compounded his appeal, many poets and poetasters (including Spenser, Sidney, and James VI of Scotland) extolled his genius and translated portions of his work; but it remained for Joshua Sylvester, a Kentish wool-merchant who used his French for both literature and trade, to preempt the undertaking.

Starting as early as 1584 by turning some of Du Bartas' lesser pieces into English, he was soon busy converting the fourteen thousand alexandrines of the two *Semaines* into his own heroic couplets. As the years went by, Sylvester slowly gained upon his goal. Following the appearance of separate parts in 1595 and 1598, by 1605 he was ready with most of what Du Bartas had written in his major epics plus such "fragments and other small works" as poems on Abraham and Jonah, *Urania* (which James VI had earlier attempted), a panegyric called *The Triumph of Faith*, and assorted pieces of Sylvester's own composing. But still the work went on—through bibliographical complexities needless to rehearse—as Sylvester added to the bulk. He issued new editions and additions in 1608, 1611, and 1613; and there were others, after he himself had died, in 1621 and 1633 (the last announced as a "complete collection of all the other most delightful works" of Du Bartas). In 1641 a final gathering comprised not only all Sylvester's versions of Du Bartas but also such original and translated pieces as his own hymns and odes and sonnets, an elaborate funeral poem for Prince Henry (1612), *Tobacco Battered and the Pipes Shattered* (1614?), *The Maiden's Blush, or Joseph, Mirror of Modesty, Map of Piety, Maze of Destiny* (1620), *Automachia, or the Self-Conflict of a Christian* (1607), and *A Glimpse of Heavenly Joys* (1617?). Any reader of this 1641 edition can sympathize with Michael Drayton's observation: if Sylvester had "stay'd" with *La Semaine*, he said,

> He had done well, and never had bewray'd
> His own invention to have been so poor,
> Who still wrote less in striving to write more.

Despite such strictures on his own productions, Sylvester's version of Du Bartas met with almost universal approbation. Daniel praised it in a eulogistic sonnet; Drayton predicted that "wrackful Time" would never injure it; Jonson (before he himself learned French) extolled its accuracy; Milton aped its mannerisms as a boy and borrowed lines from it when old (*Paradise Lost*, III.373, XII.266). But by Milton's time the tides of taste were turning. Dryden, who when young was dazzled by Sylvester's moral grandeur, eventually came to sneer at such "abominable fustian," and the shift in his position may be said to mark a downward turn in Sylvester's reputation that has never been reversed.

My text is based upon *Bartas: His Deuine weekes and workes Translated: & Dedicated to the Kings most excellent Maiestie, by Iosuah Sylvester*, 1605 (STC 21649). There is an edition of Sylvester's *Complete Works* by A. B. Grosart (2 vols., 1880), an abridgment of his once admired translation by T. W. Haight (1908), and a Scholars' Facsimile & Reprints edition of the 1605 *Bartas* (1965). Du Bartas himself has been authoritatively edited by U. T. Homes, J. C. Lyons, and R. W. Linker (3 vols., 1935–40). H. Ashton has written on *Du Bartas en Angleterre* (1908), G. C. Taylor on *Milton's Use of Du Bartas* (1934); and there are shorter studies on the religious epic by Lily B. Campbell ("The Christian Muse," *Huntington Library Bulletin*, 1935) and E. M. W. Tillyard (*The English Epic*, 1954), on Sylvester's prosody by W. B. Hunter (*PQ*, XXVIII, 1949), and on "The Reception of Du Bartas in England" by Anne Lake Prescott (*Studies in the Renaissance*, XV, 1968).

from Bartas, His Divine Weeks and Works (1605)

<small>TO MY GOOD FRIEND MASTER SYLVESTER
IN HONOR OF THIS SACRED WORK</small>

Thus to adventure forth and reconvey[1]
  The best of treasures from a foreign coast,
  And take that wealth wherein they gloried most,
And make it ours by such a gallant prey,
And that without injustice, doth bewray
  The glory of the work, that we may boast
  Much to have won, and others nothing lost
By taking such a famous prize away,
As thou, industrious Sylvester, hast wrought,
  And here enrich'd us with th' immortal store
  Of others' sacred lines, which from them brought
Comes[2] by thy taking greater than before.
  So hast thou lighted from a flame devout
  As great a flame, that never shall go out.

Samuel Daniel[3]

THE FIRST WEEK, OR BIRTH OF THE WORLD, OF THE NOBLE, LEARNED, AND DIVINE SALUSTIUS, LORD OF BARTAS

THE FIRST DAY OF THE FIRST WEEK

<small>THE ARGUMENT</small>
  God's aid implor'd, the sum of all propos'd;
  World not eternal, nor by chance compos'd,
  But of mere nothing God it essence gave;
  It had beginning and an end shall have;
  Curs'd atheists quipp'd,[1] the heathen clerks controll'd;[2]
  Doom's glorious day, star-doctors[3] blam'd for bold;
  The matter form'd, creation of the light,
  Alternate changes of the day and night,
  The birth of angels, some for pride dejected,[4]
  The rest persist in grace and guard th' elected.

Thou glorious Guide of heav'ns star-glist'ring motion,
Thou, Thou (true Neptune), tamer of the ocean,
Thou earth's dread shaker, at whose only word
Th' Eolian scouts[5] are quickly still'd and stirr'd,
Lift up my soul, my drossy spirits refine,   5
With learned art enrich this work of mine!
O Father, grant I sweetly warble forth
Unto our seed the world's renowned birth;
Grant, gracious God, that I record in verse
The rarest beauties of this universe,   10
And grant therein Thy power I may discern,
That, teaching others, I myself may learn.
  And also grant, great Architect of wonders,
  Whose mighty voice speaks in the midst of thunders,

Causing the rocks to rock and hills to tear,   15
Calling the things that are not as they were,
Confounding mighty things by means of weak,
Teaching dumb infants Thy dread praise to speak,
Inspiring wisdom into those that want
  And giving knowledge to the ignorant,   20
Grant me, good Lord (as Thou hast giv'n me heart
To undertake so excellent a part),
Grant me such judgment, grace, and eloquence,
So correspondent to that excellence,
  That in some measure I may seem t' inherit   25
  (Elisha-like) my dear Elias' spirit.[6]
Clear fire forever hath not air embrac'd,
Nor aye[7] the air environ'd waters vaste,[8]
Nor waters always wrapp'd the earth therein,
But all this all did once (of nought) begin.   30
Once all was made not by the hand of Fortune
(As fond Democritus[9] did yerst importune)[10]
With jarring concords making motes to meet,
Invisible, immortal, infinite.
  Th' immutable divine decree, which shall   35
Cause the world's end, caus'd his original:[11]
Neither in time, nor yet before the same,
But in the instant when Time first became.
I mean a time confused; for the course
Of years, of months, of weeks, of days, of hours,   40
Of ages, times, and seasons is confin'd
By th' ord'red dance unto the stars assign'd.
  Before all time, all matter, form, and place,
God all in all and all in God it was:
Immutable, immortal, infinite,   45
Incomprehensible, all spirit, all light,
All majesty, all self-omnipotent,
Invisible, impassive, excellent,
Pure, wise, just, good, God reign'd alone at rest,   50

<small>TO MASTER SYLVESTER   [1]Bring back.   [2]Becomes.
[3]Daniel's sonnet to Sylvester—one of some dozen commendatory poems, in Latin and English, prefixed to the 1605 edition of this work—is reciprocated by a sonnet of Sylvester's in *The Second Week*, where he implies that Daniel, then busy with his *Civil Wars*, will perhaps turn next to a heroic poem on the career of the famous soldier Charles Blount, earl of Devonshire.
THE FIRST WEEK   [1]Scoffed at wittily.   [2]Scholars rebuked.
[3]Astrologers.   [4]Thrown down (from heaven).
[5]The winds (which in Greek mythology were thought to be controlled by Aeolus).
[6]*And also grant...spirit*: This, the first of Sylvester's many additions and interpolations, is explained in a marginal gloss as the translator's acknowledgment of his "insufficiency" for such an exalted undertaking. Elisha, the appointed successor to Elijah (*Elias*), asked that he might inherit a "double portion" of his predecessor's spirit (2 Kings 2.9).   [7]Always.   [8]Waste.
[9]Greek philosopher (b. ca. 460 B.C.) who taught that the universe is made up of indestructible particles of matter.
[10]Argued of old.   [11]Origin, beginning.</small>

Himself alone self's palace, host, and guest.
    Thou scoffing atheist that inquirest what
Th' Almighty did before He framed that,
What weighty work His mind was busied on
Eternally before this world begun   55
(Sith[12] so deep wisdom and omnipotence
Nought worse beseems than sloth and negligence),
Know, bold blasphemer, that before He built
A hell to punish the presumptuous guilt
Of those ungodly whose proud sense dares cite   60
And censure too His wisdom infinite.

. . . . . .

[THE END OF THE WORLD]

    One day the rocks from top to toe shall quiver,
The mountains melt and all in sunder shiver;
The heav'ns shall rent for fear; the lowly fields,
Puff'd up, shall swell to huge and mighty hills;
Rivers shall dry, or if in any flood   385
Rest any liquor,[13] it shall all be blood;
The sea shall all be fire, and on the shore
The thirsty whales with horrid noise shall roar;
The sun shall seize the black coach of the moon,
And make it midnight when it should be noon;   390
With rusty mask the heav'ns shall hide their face,
The stars shall fall, and all away shall pass.
Disorder, dread, horror, and death shall come,
Noise, storms, and darkness shall usurp the room.
And then the chief chief-justice, venging Wrath   395
(Which here already often threat'ned hath),
Shall make a bonfire of this mighty ball,
As once He made it a vast ocean all.

. . . . . .

[THE CREATION OF THE ANGELS AND THEIR REBELLION]

    Whether this day[14] God made you, angels bright,
Under the name of heav'n or of the light,   590
Whether you were, after, in th' instant born
With those bright spangles that the heav'ns adorn,
Whether you do derive your high descent
Long time before the world and firmament—
For I nill[15] stiffly argue to and fro   595
In nice opinions, whether so or so,
Especially where curious search, perchance,
Is not so safe as humble ignorance—
I am resolv'd that once th' Omnipotent
Created you immortal, innocent,   600
Good, fair, and free: in brief, of essence such
As from His own differ'd not very much.
    But even as those whom princes' favor oft
Above the rest have rais'd and set aloft
Are oft the first that (without right or reason)   605
Attempt rebellion and do practice treason,
And so at length are justly tumbled down
Beneath the foot, that raught[16] above the crown,

Even so some legions of those lofty spirits
(Envy'ng the glory of their Maker's merits)   610
Conspir'd together, strove against the stream
T' usurp His scepter and His diadem.
But He whose hands do never lightnings lack
Proud, sacrilegious mutiners[17] to wrack,[18]
Hurl'd them in th' air or in some lower cell,   615
For where God is not, everywhere is hell.
    This cursed crew, with pride and fury fraught,
Of us at least have this advantage got,
That by experience they can truly tell
How far it is from highest heav'n to hell,   620
For by a proud leap they have ta'en the measure
When headlong thence they tumbled in displeasure.
    These fiends are so far off from bett'ring them
By this hard judgment that still more extreme,
The more their plague, the more their pride increases,   625
The more their rage: as lizards cut in pieces
Threat with more malice though with lesser might,
And even in dying show their living spite.·
For ever since, against the King of Heav'n
Th' apostate prince of darkness still hath striven,   630
Striv'n to deprave[19] His deeds, t' inter their story,
T' undo His church, to undermine His glory,
To reave[20] this world's great body, ship, and state
Of head, of master,[21] and of magistrate.[22]

. . . . . .

THE SECOND WEEK, OR CHILDHOOD OF THE WORLD[1]

The Deceit

THE SECOND BOOK OF THE
FIRST DAY OF THE SECOND WEEK

TO THE . . . RIGHT HONORABLE EARL OF DEVONSHIRE

A Sonnet

Though in thy brook, great Charles, there swim a swan[2]
    Whose happy, sweet, immortal tunes can raise

---

[12]Since. [13]Remain any liquid. [14]I.e., the first day of creation.
[15]Will not, i.e., am unwilling to. [16]Reached, aspired.
[17]Mutineers, rebels. [18]Destroy. [19]Pervert. [20]Plunder.
[21]Shipmaster.
[22]Text *Maiestrate*, i.e., Majestrate (a form not recorded in the *Oxford English Dictionary*).
THE SECOND WEEK [1]*The Second...World*: This section of the work is prefaced by a dedicatory epistle (dated 11 May 1598) and a eulogistic sonnet addressed to Robert Devereux, earl of Essex (see p. 843).
[2]I.e., Samuel Daniel, commonly known as "the English Lucan" because his *Civil Wars* was modeled on the Latin poet's *Pharsalia*. In the dedicatory epistle preceding this sonnet Devonshire is addressed as "Lieutenant General of Ireland," a title he acquired in 1601 following his friend Essex' disastrous Irish expedition of 1599, the prologue to his rebellion and execution (1601).

The virtuous greatness of thy noble praise
 To higher notes than my faint numbers can;
Yet while thy Lucan doth in silence scan   5
 Unto himself new-meditated lays
 To finish up his sad Pharsalian frays,
Lend ear to Bartas (now our countryman),
For though his English be not yet so good
 (As Frenchmen hardly[3] do our tongue attain), 10
He hopeth yet to be well understood;
The rather if you, worthy Lord, shall deign
 His bashfulness a little to advance
 With the mild favors of your countenance.
Joshua Sylvester

THE ARGUMENT

Justice and mercy model'd in their kind;[4]
Sathan's proud hate and envy to mankind,
His many engines[5] and malicious wiles
Whereby the best he many times beguiles;
Why he assum'd a body and began
With Eve, by her to undermine her man;
Their dreadfall fall, their drowsy conscience;
God's righteous sentence, for their foul offense,
On them and theirs; their exile; Eden barr'd
With flaming sword, and seraphin[6] for guard.

> Having been seduced by Satan in the form of a serpent and
> eaten of the forbidden "sharp-sweet fruit," Adam and Eve,
> like a man after "much drink," are racked by "raving
> fancies" when God suddenly appears in the garden to pass
> judgment on their "self-doom'd" souls.

"Adam," quoth God with thundering majesty,
"Where art thou, wretch? What dost thou? Answer me,
Thy God and Father, from whose hand thy health 390
Thou hold'st, thine honor, and all sorts of wealth."
 At this sad summons woeful man resembles
A bearded rush that in a river trembles.
His rosy cheeks are chang'd to earthen hue;
His dying body drops an icy dew;   395
His tear-drown'd eyes a night of clouds bedims;
About his ears a buzzing horror swims;
His fainting knees with feebleness are humble;
His foult'ring[7] feet do slide away and stumble; 400
He hath not now his free, bold, stately port,[8]
But downward looks in fearful slavish sort.
Now nought of Adam doth in Adam rest;
He feels his senses pain'd, his soul oppress'd;
A confus'd host of violent passions jar;   405
His flesh and spirit are in continual war;
And now no more, through conscience[9] of his error,
He hears or sees th' Almighty but with terror;
And loath he answers, as with tongue distraught,
Confessing thus his fear, but not his fault: 410
 "O Lord, Thy voice, Thy dreadful voice, hath made
Me, fearful, hide me in this covert shade,
For naked as I am, O most of might,
I dare not come before Thine awful sight."
 "Naked!" quoth God. "Why, faithless renegade, 415

Apostate pagan, who hath told thee that?
Whence springs thy shame? What makes thee thus to run
From shade to shade, my presence still to shun?
Hast thou not tasted of the learned tree
Whereof, on pain of death, I warned thee?" 420
 "O righteous God," quoth Adam, "I am free
From this offense! The wife Thou gavest me
For my companion and my comforter,
She made me eat that deadly meat with her."
 "And thou," quoth God, "O thou frail,
  treacherous bride,   425
Why with thyself hast thou seduc'd thy guide?"
 "Lord," answers Eve, "the serpent did entice
My simple frailty to this sinful vice."
 Mark here how He, who fears not who reform
His high decrees, not subject unto form   430
Or style of court, who (all-wise) hath no need
T' examine proof or witness of the deed,
Who for sustaining of unequal scale
Dreads not the doom of a Mercurial,
Yer sentence pass doth publicly convent,   435
Confront, and hear with ear indifferent
Th' offenders sad, then with just indignation
Pronounceth thus their dreadful condemnation;[10]
 "Ah, cursed serpent, which my fingers made
To serve mankind, th' hast made thyself a blade 440
Wherewith vain man and his inveigled wife,
Self-parricides, have reft their proper[11] life.
For this thy fault, true fountain[12] of all ill,
Thou shalt be hateful 'mong all creatures still.
Groveling in dust, of dust thou aye shalt feed. 445
I'll kindle war between the woman's seed
And thy fell race: hers on the head shall ding[13]
Thine, thine again[14] hers in the heel shall sting.
 "Rebel to me, unto thy kindred curst,
False to thy husband, to thyself the worst,   450
Hope not thy fruit so eas'ly to bring forth
As now thou flay'st it. Henceforth, every birth

---

[3]Not easily.
[4]*Model'd...kind*: i.e., portrayed according to their nature.
[5]Contrivances, snares.
[6]Seraph, one of the seraphim (or seraphin), the highest of the
nine angelic orders. Sylvester was presumably unaware that he
was using a plural form. [7]Faltering. [8]Bearing.
[9]Inner knowledge, consciousness.
[10]*Mark...condemnation*: This passage may be paraphrased as fol-
lows: Observe that He, who need not fear that any higher court
will overturn His decisions, who is bound by no legal technicalities,
who in His omniscience has no need to examine evidence or hear
witnesses, who need not fear official censure for upholding unfair
decisions—that He nevertheless, before (*yer*) sentence is passed,
summons, confronts, and with impartial ear listens to the wretched
offenders. *Mercurial* was the name given to a weekly assembly of
French judicial personnel at which a minister of state critically
reviewed the administration of justice during the preceding week;
it was so called because it took place every Wednesday (French
mercredi, "Mercury's day"). [11]Own. [12]Spring, source.
[13]Hammer. [14]In return.

Shall torture thee with thousand sorts of pain;
Each artire,[15] sinew, muscle, joint, and vein
Shall feel his part, besides foul vomitings,   455
Prodigious longings, thoughtful[16] languishings,
With change of choler,[17] swouns,[18] and many others,
Eternal fellows of all future mothers.
Under his yoke thy husband thee shall have,
Tyrant, by thee made the arch-tyrant's slave!   460
    "And thou, disloyal, which hast hark'ned more
To a wanton fondling than my sacred lore,
Henceforth the sweat shall bubble on thy brow;
Thy hands shall blister and thy back shall bow;
Ne'er shalt thou send into thy branchy veins   465
A bit but bought with price of thousand pains.
For the earth, feeling even in her th' effect
Of the doom thund'red 'gainst thy foul defect,
Instead of sweet fruits which she selfly[19] yields
Seedless and artless over all thy fields,   470
With thorns and burrs shall bristle up her breast.
In short, thou shalt not taste the sweets of rest
Till ruthless Death by his extremest pain
Thy dust-born body turn to dust again."
    Here I conceive that flesh and blood will brangle,[20]   475
And murmuring Reason with th' Almighty wrangle,
Who did our parents with free will endue,
Though He foresaw that that would be the clue[21]
Should lead their steps into the woeful way
Where life is death ten thousand times a day.   480
Now all that He foresees befalls, and, further,
He all events by His free power doth order.
Man taxeth God of too unjust severity
For plaguing Adam's sin in his posterity,
So that th' old years' renewed generations   485
Cannot assuage His venging indignations,
Which have no other ground to prosecute
But the miseating of a certain fruit.
    O dusty wormling! Dar'st thou strive and stand
With heav'n's high Monarch? Wilt thou,
        wretch, demand   490
Count[22] of His deeds? Ah, shall the potter make
His clay such fashion as him list[23] to take,
And shall not God—world's founder, nature's father—
Dispose of man, his own mere creature, rather?
The supreme king who, judge of greatest kings,   495
By number, weight, and measure acts[24] all things,
Vice-loathing Lord, pure Justice' patron strong,
Law's life, Right's rule, will He do any wrong?
    Man, holdest thou of God thy frank free will,
But free t'obey His sacred goodness still?   500
Freely to follow Him and do His hest,
Not philter-charm'd, nor by Busiris press'd[25]
God arms thee with discourse,[26] but thou, O wretch,
By the keen edge the wound-soul sword dost catch,
Killing thyself and in thy loins thy line.   505
O baneful spider, weaving woeful twine,
All heaven's pure flowers thou turnest into poison.
Thy sense reaves sense, thy reason robs thy reason;

For thou complainest of God's grace, whose still[27]
Extracts from dross of thine audacious ill   510
Three unexpected goods: praise for His name;
Bliss for thyself; for Sathan, endless shame,
Sith but for sin justice and mercy were
But idle names, and but that thou didst err,
Christ had not come to conquer and to quell   515
Upon the cross sin, sathan, death, and hell,
Making thee blessed more since thine offense
Than in thy primer[28] happy innocence.
    Then mightst thou die, now death thou dost not doubt[29]
Now in the hav'n, then didst thou ride without;   520
In earth thou liv'dst then, now in heav'n thou beest;
Then thou didst hear God's word, it now thou seest;
Then pleasant fruits, now Christ is thy repast;
Then mightst thou fall, but now thou standest fast.

.   .   .   .   .   .

Man's seed, then, justly by succession
Bears the hard penance of his high transgression,
And Adam, here from Eden banished,   605
As first offender is first punished.
    "Hence," quoth the Lord, "hence, hence, accursed race!
Out of my garden! Quick, avoid[30] the place,
This beauteous place, pride of this universe,
A house unworthy masters so perverse.   610

.   .   .   .   .   .

Those well may guess the bitter agonies
And lukewarm rivers gushing down the eyes
Of our first parents, out of Eden driven
(Of repeal hopeless) by the hand of heaven,
For the Almighty set before the door   635
Of th' holy park a seraphin that bore
A waving sword, whose body shined bright
Like flaming comet in the midst of night,
A body merely metaphysical,[31]
Which (differing little from th' One unical,[32]   640
Th' Act simply pure, the only Being being)
Approacheth matter ne'ertheless, not being
Of matter mix'd; or rather is so made
So merely spirit that not the murdering blade
His joined quantity can part in two,   645
For (pure) it cannot suffer aught,[33] but do.[34]

[15]Artery. [16]Melancholy. [17]Bilious spells. [18]Swoons.
[19]Spontaneously. [20]Wrangle.
[21]A ball of twine which leads through a maze. [22]Accounting.
[23]It pleases him. [24]Does.
[25]*By Busiris press'd*: i.e., tyranically compelled. Busiris was a
legendary king of Egypt notorious for his cruelty. [26]Reason.
[27]The operation of God's grace is likened to distillation.
[28]I.e., pristine (comparative of *prime*, "early"). [29]Fear.
[30]Depart from. [31]Immaterial. [32]Unique.
[33]Be acted upon by anything. [34]Act.

Sir Henry Wotton [1568-1639]

Wotton, who started his career in politics as secretary and agent for the earl of Essex, spent his middle years as a diplomat at Venice and elsewhere on the Continent, and ended as provost of Eton College (1624–39), was at best a dilettante of literature. But this graceful writer in both verse and prose, the cherished friend of Donne and other men of letters, was the author of "You Meaner Beauties of the Night," the subject of one of Izaak Walton's *Lives*, and an admirer of young Milton, and so he has a claim on our attention. Although he published a trivial little book on architecture in 1624, his projected history of England got no further than some random jottings. When the life of Donne that he had promised as an introduction for that famous preacher's *LXXX Sermons* (1640) also remained unwritten at his death, it was Walton who rather diffidently acted as his surrogate—and thus produced one of the great short biographies in the language. In 1651 Walton also put together the collection of his old friend's literary remains entitled *Reliquiae Wottonianae*, whereon his small but tidy reputation rests. The book was republished and enlarged in 1654, 1672, and 1685.

My text is based on *Reliquiae Wottonianae. Or A Collection of Lives, Letters, Poems; With Characters of Sundry Personages: And other Incomparable Pieces of Language and Art. By the curious Pensil of the Ever Memorable Sr Henry Wotton Kt, Late Provost of Eton Colledg*, 1651 (Wing W-3648). Logan P. Smith's *Life and Letters* (2 vols., 1097) is authoritative. There are editions of the poems by Alexander Dyce (1842) and John Hannah (1845); J. B. Leishman has explored the enormous popularity of "You Meaner Beauties of the Night" (*Library*, XXVI, 1945–46); and David Novarr has studied Walton's biography in *The Making of Walton's Lives* (1958). For Wotton's famous "Character of a Happy Life," which was included in the fourth (1614) edition of *Sir Thomas Overbury His Wife. With Additions of New Characters*, see p. 719.

from Reliquiae Wottonianae (1651)

A HYMN TO MY GOD, IN A NIGHT OF MY LATE SICKNESS[1]

O thou great Power in whom I move,
  For whom I live, to whom I die,
Behold me through Thy beams of love
  Whilst on this couch of tears I lie,
And cleanse my sordid soul within   5
By Thy Christ's blood, the bath of sin.

No hallowed oils, no grains[2] I need,
  No rags of saints, no purging fire;
One rosy drop from David's seed[3]
  Was worlds of seas to quench Thine ire.   10

O precious ransom, which once paid,
That *consummatum est*[4] was said!

And said by Him that said no more,
  But seal'd it with His sacred breath.

A HYMN TO MY GOD   [1]In the text this poem is printed between the "Letters" and the "Poems." Writing to Izaak Walton not long before his death, Wotton explained that the hymn had been prompted by a quotidian fever ("of more contumacy than malignity") that recurred with an attack of "splenetic vapors." [2]Beads (of a rosary). [3]I.e., Christ, whose father Joseph was descended from King David (Matthew 1.16). [4]"It is finished," Christ's last words on the cross (John 19.30).

Thou, then, that hast dispung'd my score,[5]   15
  And dying wast the death of Death,
Be to me now, on Thee I call,
My life, my strength, my joy, my all!

ON HIS MISTRESS, THE QUEEN OF BOHEMIA[1]

You meaner beauties of the night,
  That poorly satisfy our eyes
More by your number than your light,
  You common people of the skies
  What are you when the sun shall rise?   5

You curious chanters of the wood
  That warble forth Dame Nature's lays,
Thinking your voices understood
  By your weak accents, what's your praise
  When Philomel[2] her voice shall raise?   10

You violets that first appear,
  By your pure purple mantles known
Like the proud virgins of the year,
  As if the spring were all your own
  What are you when the rose is blown?[3]   15

So, when my mistress shall be seen
  In form and beauty of her mind,
By virtue first, then choice, a queen,
  Tell me if she were not design'd
  Th' eclipse and glory of her kind?   20

UPON THE SUDDEN RESTRAINT OF THE EARL OF SOMERSET,[1] THEN FALLING FROM FAVOR

Dazzled thus with height of place,
  Whilst our hopes our wits beguile,
No man marks the narrow space
  'Twixt a prison and a smile.

Then, since Fortune's favors fade,   5
  You, that in her arms do sleep,
Learn to swim and not to wade,
  For the hearts of kings are deep.

But if greatness be so blind
  As to trust in towers of air,   10
Let it be with goodness lin'd,[2]
  That at least the fall be fair.

Then, though dark'ned, you shall say,
  When friends fail and princes frown,
Virtue is the roughest way   15
  But proves at night a bed of down.

ON A BANK AS I SAT A-FISHING, A DESCRIPTION OF THE SPRING[1]

And now all Nature seem'd in love;
The lusty sap began to move;
New juice did stir th' embracing vines,
And birds had drawn their valentines;

The jealous trout, that low did lie,   5
Rose at a well-dissembled fly;
There stood my friend, with patient skill
Attending of his trembling quill.[2]
Already were the eaves possess'd
With the swift pilgrim's daubed nest;   10
The groves already did rejoice
In Philomel's triumphing voice.
The showers were short, the weather mild,
The morning fresh, the evening smil'd.
Joan takes her neat-rubb'd pail, and now   15
She trips to milk the sand-red cow;
Where for some sturdy football[3] swain
Joan strokes a sillabub[4] or twain.
The fields and gardens were beset
With tulip, crocus, violet;   20
And now, though late, the modest rose
Did more than half a blush disclose.
Thus all looked gay, all full of cheer,
To welcome the new-liveried year.

TEARS AT THE GRAVE OF SIR ALBERTUS MORTON[1] (WHO WAS BURIED AT SOUTHAMPTON) WEPT BY SIR H. WOTTON

Silence, in truth, would speak my sorrow best,
For deepest wounds can least their feelings tell;
Yet let me borrow from mine own unrest
But time to bid him, whom I lov'd, farewell.

O my unhappy lines! You that before   5
Have serv'd my youth to vent some wanton cries,
And now, congeal'd with grief, can scarce implore
Strength to accent, here my Albertus lies,

[5] Wiped out my debt.
ON HIS MISTRESS [1] Elizabeth (1596–1662), daughter of James I, married (1613) Frederick V, the Elector Palatine, six years before he, a leading Protestant, was chosen king of Bohemia. Their brief reign crushed in the opening phases of the Thirty Years' War, the "Winter King" and his "Queen of Hearts" spent their later years in exile and futility. Although Elizabeth survived her husband by thirty years to die a pensioner of her nephew Charles II, her daughter Sophia became the mother of George I, the first Hanoverian king of England [2] The nightingale.
[3] Blossomed.
UPON THE SUDDEN RESTRAINT [1] James Carr, earl of Somerset (d. 1645), powerful favorite of James I whose part in the murder (1613) of Sir Thomas Overbury was one of the great scandals of the century. See p. 715. [2] Fortified.
ON A BANK AS I SAT A-FISHING [1] Izaak Walton, who includes this poem in his *Compleat Angler* (1653), said that Wotton, then "beyond seventy years of age," wrote it as he "sat quietly in a summer's evening on a bank afishing."
[2] Reed, i.e., fishing pole. [3] I.e., athletic, muscular.
[4] *strokes a sillabub*: whips up a drink of milk and wine.
TEARS AT THE GRAVE [1] A nephew (d. 1625) of Wotton's whose distinguished career as diplomat included service with his uncle in Venice. According to Walton, the old man's grief, as expressed in this famous elegy, was "too hearty to be dissembled."

This is the sable stone, this is the cave
And womb of earth that doth his corpse embrace: 10
While others sing his praise, let me engrave
These bleeding numbers to adorn the place.

Here will I paint the characters of woe,
Here will I pay my tribute to the dead,
And here my faithful tears in show'rs shall flow   15
To humanize the flints whereon I tread.

Where though I mourn my matchless loss alone,
And none between my weakness judge and me,
Yet even these gentle walls allow my moan,
Whose doleful echoes to my plaints agree.   20

But is he gone? And live I rhyming here
As if some Muse would listen to my lay,
When all distun'd sit waiting for their dear,
And bathe the banks where he was wont to play?

Dwell thou in endless light, discharged soul,   25
Freed now from Nature's and from Fortune's trust,
While on this fluent[2] globe my glass[3] shall roll,
And run the rest of my remaining dust.

UPON THE DEATH OF SIR ALBERT MORTON'S WIFE

He first decʼas'd; she for a little tried
To live without him, lik'd it not, and died.

[2]Unstable. [3]Hourglass.

John Donne[1] [1572-1631]

Since for several generations Donne has had so much attention and even adulation, it is fortunate that we possess in Izaak Walton's famous life of this courtier, poet, and divine (pp. 758 ff.) a more or less contemporary account of his extraordinary career. Despite its distortions, errors, and omissions Walton's work remains a primary source for much of what we know or may conjecture about one of the most influential writers of his time, and so the following comments on those works of Donne that are included in this book are intended merely to supplement Walton's flawed but basic sketch of his career.

Like Paul's and Augustine's, that career was almost archetypal in its main configuration: a brilliant worldling is with difficulty brought to God, whereupon his life is altered in the service of the church and his enormous talents find a new expression in devotion. Donne's licentious youth (whose wickedness both he and Walton may have overemphasized) embraced his "first breeding and conversation" in the Roman Catholic Church, perhaps several years (1584 ff.) at Oxford and Cambridge (where his religion barred him from degrees), study of the law (with excursions into literature) at the Inns of Court (1591–94?), a fashionable taste of military action in Essex' Cadiz and Islands expeditions (1596–97), and appointment (1597–98) as secretary to Sir Thomas Egerton, the lord keeper. But then, on the threshold of what promised to be a glittering career, Donne ruined his prospects by a secret marriage that alienated his patron (1601). There followed almost fifteen years of increasing domestic obligations, shabby gentility, political jockeying, hack writing, and intellectual malaise. But at last, and because he had reluctantly concluded that a career in politics was closed to him, the disappointed politician agreed to enter Holy Orders, and so, at forty-three, began a new career. Thereafter he enjoyed a rising spiral of appointments and successes, climaxed by the deanship of St. Paul's (1621) and a dazzling reputation as a preacher. His later years, as Walton shows them, were an exercise in piety that was itself the final triumph of the priest and man of letters.

The fact that Donne's poetry has come down to us in some forty manuscript collections and in more than a hundred poetical miscellanies containing his and other writers' work means that any modern text is bound to be eclectic. He started writing poetry in the early 1590's and continued, off and on, almost until he died in 1631; but apart from the commendatory and elegiac verses in

[1]For other works of Donne, see Religion and Politics, pp. 544 ff., and Books and Men, pp. 680 ff., 717 f.

Thomas Coryate's *Crudities* (1611) and in an obituary volume for Prince Henry entitled *Lacrymae lacrymarum* (1612) he published almost none of his own poetry except *An Anatomy of the World* (i.e., "The First Anniversary") in 1611 and *The First and Second Anniversaries* in the following year. Thus it is that the first edition of his *Poems* was the very imperfect little volume put together by the printer John Marriot in 1633, two years after the author's death. As if conceding its deficiencies, a preface "to the understander" explained that the compiler "could add hereto a promise of more correctness or enlargement of the next edition if you shall in the meantime content you with this." Subsequent editions—by Marriott in 1635, 1639, and 1649, by Donne's own wayward son and namesake in 1650 and 1654, and by the printer Henry Herringman in 1669—reveal progressive deterioration of the text together with some additions to the canon.

Therefore, and for want of something better, the 1633 *Poems, By J. D. With Elegies On the Author's Death* (STC 7045) has been adopted as the basis of the present text, but with these clear-cut exceptions: from the 1635 and subsequent editions I have borrowed the grouping of the poems as "Songs and Sonnets," "Elegies," "Satires," and the like, whereby some sort of order was imposed upon the chaos of the 1633 edition; as indicated in the notes, I have sometimes accepted readings from the manuscripts as well as some modern conjectural emendations; I have based my text of "The Second Anniversary" on the 1612 edition (STC 7023); for "On His Mistress", "I am a little world," and "Hymn to God My God In My Sickness" I have followed the 1635 edition (STC 7046) and for "To His Mistress Going to Bed" the 1669 edition (Wing D–1871), where these poems first appeared; following Miss Helen Gardner's precedent, I have moved "To E. of D. with Six Holy Sonnets" from the verse epistles in the 1633 edition to let it serve as introduction (which Donne presumably intended) for the first six Holy Sonnets; and I have based my texts of "She whom I lov'd" and "O, to vex me" on Miss Gardner's transcription (*The Divine Poems*, pp. 14–16) of their unique source, the Westmoreland manuscript in the Berg Collection of the New York Public Library.

For obvious reasons the dean of St. Paul's did not himself arrange the publication of the flippant, frisky little essays (pp. 680–82) that he had written in his wanton youth, and that, in a letter to a friend in 1600, he described as "nothings." In Donne's own coterie, however, these iconoclastic witticisms must have found admiring readers, and eventually a manuscript fell into the hands of Henry Seyle, who had it duly licensed in 1632 and printed it the following year as Donne's *Juvenilia, or Certain Paradoxes and Problems* (STC 7043, on which my text is based). Consisting of eleven paradoxes and ten problems, the little book sold well enough to justify a "corrected" new edition within a year of publication (this time without the benefit of license).

In 1637 Donne's son was enough disturbed by these and similar publications (including Marriott's editions of the *Poems* in 1633 and 1635) to protest to Archbishop Laud the printing of the poems as well as such allegedly spurious bagatelles as the *Juvenilia* and the anti-Jesuit *Ignatius His Conclave* (which since its first English version in 1611 had been reissued in 1626 and again in 1634 and 1635). Although Laud duly issued an injunction against the petitioner's enterprising rivals, it did not prevent Marriott from printing a third unauthorized edition of the *Poems* in 1639. About this time, however, the younger Donne, in ways not altogether clear, at last gained some control of his father's literary remains and promptly undertook their publication. In 1640 he brought out *LXXX Sermons*, in 1647 *Biathanatos* (a treatise justifying suicide that Donne wrote about 1608, long before his ordination), in 1649 *Fifty Sermons* and the *Poems*, in 1651 *Letters to Several Persons of Honor* (supplemented nine years later with *A Collection of Letters Made by Sir Tobie Mathews* [sic], *Knight*), and in 1652 a miscellaneous gathering of "things of the least and greatest weight that ever fell from my father's pen," including the *Juvenilia* (expanded by one new paradox and seven problems), "The True Character of a Dunce" that had first appeared anonymously in the 1622 edition of the Overburian *Characters* (p. 717), "A Sheaf of Miscellany Epigrams" and even lesser things, a reprint of *Ignatius His Conclave*, and the hitherto unpublished *Essays in Divinity*. As noted earlier, the *Poems* appeared again in 1654, and the badly edited *XXVI Sermons* (which is so disordered that it prints two sermons twice) followed in 1660, two years before the younger Donne's death at fifty-eight.

The *Essays in Divinity* (pp. 544 ff.)—which in the 1652 composite volume have a separate title page dated 1651—were presented by the younger Donne as his father's "voluntary sacrifices of several hours when he had many debates betwixt God and himself whether he were worthy and competently learned to enter into Holy Orders." They were almost surely written about 1614, when, as Walton says, Donne in preparing for his ordination "applied himself to an incessant study of textual divinity." Though with little of the stylistic splendor of the sermons and *Devotions*, these knotty disquisitions are none the less important as a sort of theological compendium or reservoir of the doctrines, themes, and motifs that Donne embellished in his later work. Ostensibly an exposition of the opening verses of Genesis and Exodus, they are in fact a set of complex, interlocking meditations that reveal their author's tough but subtle mind, his uncommon erudition, and the depth of his commitment to religion. Except for such occasional passages as the sonorous meditation on time (p. 546), it is mainly in the prayers with which each section ends that Donne anticipates the beauty of his later prose. My text is based upon the 1651 edition (Wing D 1861).

A different and a more attractive kind of meditation appears in the volume of *Devotions* (pp. 548 ff.) where Donne logged, with a characteristic blend of clinical precision, curiosity, and emotion, the stages of his serious illness in 1623. Here, as Walton says, we see "the most secret thoughts that then possessed his soul paraphrased and made public, a book that may not unfitly be called a sacred picture of spiritual ecstasies occasioned and appliable to the emergencies of that sickness." On one level these twenty-three devotions (each comprising a meditation, expostulation, and prayer) trace Donne's nearly fatal illness from his first malaise to his convalescence and "the fearful danger of relapsing;" on another and a higher level they display the virtuoso stylist as he manipulates the themes of man's fragility and God's omnipotence, of sin and mercy, time and eternity, death and resurrection. The work appeared early in 1624 as *Devotions upon Emergent Occasions* (STC 7033, on which my text is based) and was so successful that it was reissued later in the same year and again in 1626/7, 1634, and 1638.

There are many testimonials, poetical and other, to Donne's enormous power as a preacher. Walton (who was one of his parishioners at St. Dunstan's in the West) compared him to "an angel from a cloud" who transported some in "holy raptures" and led others "by a sacred art and courtship to amend their lives." Thomas Carew, who is not remembered for his piety, spoke (p. 230) about the flame of his

> brave soul, that shot such heat and light
> As burnt our earth and made our darkness bright,
> Committed holy rapes upon our will,
> Did through the eye the melting heart distill,
> And the deep knowledge of dark truths so teach
> As sense might judge what fancy could not reach.

The celebrated Lucius Cary, later Lord Falkland, could not forget "that heavenly eloquence/With which he did the bread of life dispense," nor could Richard Busby, the famous, long-lived master of Westminster School:

> Methinks I see him in the pulpit standing,
> Not ears or eyes but all men's hearts commanding,
> Where we that heard him to ourselves did feign
> Golden Chrysostom was alive again.

Donne did not trust to luck in working such effects upon his listeners. Extemporaneous preaching, so much favored by the Puritans, was, he thought, both vulgar and impertinent, for the Holy Ghost would have his ministers approach their sacred function "with consideration, with meditation, with preparation; and not barbarously, not suddenly, not occasionally, not extemporarily, which might derogate from the dignity of so great a service." Therefore, although he usually preached from notes or memory, he made such a thorough preparation that when he later came to write a sermon down he could reconstruct it almost as he had delivered it. Thus it was, according to Walton, that he left "sixscore sermons all written with his own hand."

Although apparently none of Donne's own manuscripts are extant, his practice of recording and preserving his old sermons no doubt accounts for the treasure trove that somehow—perhaps with Walton's aid—eventually passed from his executors to his son. Of these manuscripts the most important was a big collection of his sermons that he had "exscribed" in 1625 at Chelsea, where he had been driven by the plague. "I have revised as many of my sermons as I have kept any note of," he informed an unnamed correspondent, "and I have written out a great many, and hope to do more. I have already come to the number of eighty, of which my son, who, I hope, will take the same profession, or some other in the world of understanding, may hereafter make some use." Whether or not the younger Donne, as he said later, was "commanded by the king and encouraged by most of the chief men in the kingdom to recollect and print my father's sermons," he set to work at once. As a result, the six sermons printed between 1622 and 1627 and the seven already printed posthumously were augmented by the bounty of *LXXX Sermons* in 1640, *Fifty Sermons* in 1649, and *XXVI Sermons* in 1660.

This vast collection of sermons, together with fifteen others whose attribution seems to be secure, fill ten stately volumes in the authoritative Simpson and Potter edition. Since they range in time from Donne's first attempt at preaching in 1615 to his lurid valediction with "Death's Duel" in 1631, and in style from relentless exegesis to almost mystic rapture, it is hard to represent them with only one selection. The one that I have chosen, which is stylistically and thematically characteristic of his best exertions, is from the famous set of five that he delivered as a prebend of St. Paul's at the very height of his career. All five of these so-called prebend sermons were included in the folio of 1640 (STC 7038), which is the basis of my text (pp. 553 ff.).

Although there were editions of the poetry by A. B. Grosart (2 vols., 1872–73), J. R. Lowell and C. E. Norton (2 vols., 1895), and E. K. Chambers (2 vols., 1896), and of the *Works* (including the sermons) by Henry Alford (6 vols., 1839), Donne's extraordinary revival may be said to have begun in the present century with Sir Herbert Grierson's great edition of the *Poetical Works* (2 vols., 1912). This revival—which shows no signs of diminution—has been marked by Grierson's own one-volume recension (1929), R. E. Bennett's edition of the poems (1942), Helen Gardner's of *The Divine Poems* (1952) and *The Elegies and the Songs and Sonnets* (1965), Theodore Redpath's of the *Songs and Sonnets* (1956), Frank Manley's of the *Anniversaries* (1963), Wesley Milgate's of *The Satires, Epigrams and Verse Letters* (1967), John T. Shawcross's of *The Complete Poetry* (1967), and A. J. Smith's of the English poems (1971). There are editions of the poetry and selections from the prose by John Hayward (rev. 1962), C. M. Coffin (1952), and F. J. Warnke (1967), and one of selected poems and critical studies by A. L. Clements (1966). In addition to the edition of the sermons by G. R. Potter and Evelyn M. Simpson (10 vols., 1953–62), which has superseded Alford's, there is a facsimile of *Five Sermons upon Special Occasions* (1626) from the Scolar Press (1970), an edition of the *Prebend Sermons* by Janel M. Mueller (1971, volumes of selections by L. P. Smith (1919), Sir Geoffrey Keynes (1923), and T. A. Gill (1958), and a useful compilation of *Selected Prose* by Mrs. Simpson, Miss Gardner, and Timothy Healy (1967). C. E. Merrill has edited the *Letters to Several Persons of Honor* (1910), Keynes the *Paradoxes and Problems* (1923), John Sparrow (1923) and W. H. Draper (1925) the *Devotions*, Mrs. Simpson the *Essays in Divinity* (1952), and Healy *Ignatius His Conclave* (1970). *In A Study of the Prose Works* (rev. 1948) Mrs. Simpson has admirably surveyed these and other things. Keynes's standard *Bibliography*, which has now attained a third edition (1958), may be supplemented by William White's listing (1942) of periodical articles since 1900.

The biographies of course begin with the one that Walton supplied for *LXXX Sermons* in 1640 and subsequently enlarged; this (with Walton's other lives) has been discussed by David Novarr in *The Making of Walton's "Lives"* (1958). Edmund Gosse's *Life and Letters* (2 vols., 1889), long the standard work despite its imperfections, has been superseded by R. C. Bald's authoritative biography (1970). Edward Le Compte's *Grace for a Witty Sinner* (1965) and Richard E. Hughes' *The Progress of the Soul: The Interior Career of John Donne* (1968), are on a smaller scale.

Even apart from the innumerable articles and explications of individual poems the commentary on Donne is so extensive that it cannot be fairly represented in a note like this. In addition to the broader studies cited in the General Bibliography, Section III, however, certain things stand out as deserving of special mention: M. P. Ramsay's *Doctrines médiévales chez Donne* (rev. 1924), Pierre Legouis' *Donne the Craftsman* (1928), George Williamson's *The Donne Tradition* (1930), the stimulating essays edited by Theodore Spencer in *A Garland for John Donne* (1931), T. S. Eliot's extremely influential pieces assembled in his *Selected Essays* (1932), M. A. Rugoff's *Donne's Imagery* (1939), Leonard Unger's *Donne's Poetry and Modern Criticism* (1950), J. B. Leishman's *Monarch of Wit* (1951, rev. 1962), Doniphan Louthan's *Poetry of Donne* (1951), Clay Hunt's *Donne's Poetry: Essays in Literary Analysis* (1954), K. W. Grandsen's *John Donne* (1954), Robert Ellrodt's *Les Poètes métaphysiques anglais* (2 vols., 1960), and Frank Kermode's monograph (rev. 1961). There are full-length studies of the poetry by D. L. Guss (*John Donne, Petrarchist*, 1966), N. J. C. Andreasen (1967), and Judah Stampfer (1970); and of the sermons by William R. Mueller (*John Donne: Preacher*, 1962), Winfried Schleiner (*The Imagery of Donne's Sermons*, 1970), and Gale H. Carrithers, Jr. (*Donne at Sermons*, 1972). Miss Gardner (1962) and Kermode (1962) have assembled some of the more important essays on Donne's work, and A. J. Smith has recently compiled a volume of interesting studies in *Essays of Celebration* (1972).

from Poems (1633)

THE PRINTER TO THE UNDERSTANDERS

. . . If you look for an epistle as you have before ordinary publications, I am sorry that I must deceive you, but you will not lay it to my charge when you shall consider that this is not ordinary; for if I should say it were the best in this kind that ever this kingdom hath yet seen, he that would doubt of it must go out of the kingdom to inform himself, for the best judgments within it take it for granted.

You may imagine, if it please you, that I could endear it unto you by saying that importunity drew it on, that had it not been presented here it would have come to us from beyond the seas (which perhaps is true enough), that my charge and pains in procuring of it hath been such and such. I could add hereto a promise of more correctness or enlargement of the next edition if you shall in the meantime content you with this. But these things are so common as that I should profane this piece by applying them to it. . . .

Howsoever it may appear to you, it shall suffice me to inform you that it hath the best warrant that can be: public authority and private friends.

There is one thing more wherein I will make you of my counsel, and that is that whereas it hath pleased some who had studied and did admire him to offer to the memory of the author, I have thought I should do you service in presenting them unto you now; only whereas had I placed them

in the beginning they might have served for so many encomiums of the author (as is usual in other works where, perhaps, there is need of it to prepare men to digest such stuff as follows after), you shall here find them in the end, for whosoever read the rest so far shall perceive that there is no occasion to use them to that purpose.[1] Yet there they are as an attestation for their sakes that knew not so much before, to let them see how much honor was attributed to this worthy man by those that are capable to give it. Farewell.

> In 1650, when the disreputable younger John Donne finally secured at least partial control over the publication of his father's poetry, there appeared an edition entitled *Poems, By J. D. With Elegies on the Authors Death. To Which Is added divers Copies under his own hand never before in print.* In this edition the introductory "Printer to the Understanders" was replaced by the following dedicatory epistle.

THE PRINTER TO THE UNDERSTANDERS [1]At the end of the 1633 *Poems* are thirteen "elegies upon the author." In addition to famous pieces by Henry King and Thomas Carew (see pp. 193, 230 f.) there are contributions by the royalist divine (not the famous statesman) Edward Hyde, Thomas Browne (apparently his earliest published work), Sir Lucius Cary, Bishop Richard Corbet, Henry Valentine, Izaak Walton, Jaspar Mayne, Endymion Porter, and others.

To the Right Honorable William, Lord Craven, Baron of Hamsted–Marsham[1]

My Lord,

Many of these poems have, for several impressions, wandered up and down, trusting (as well they might) upon the author's reputation; neither do they now complain of any injury but what may proceed either from the kindness of the printer or the courtesy of the reader, the one by adding something too much lest any spark of this sacred fire might perish undiscerned, the other by putting such an estimation upon the wit and fancy they find here that they are content to use it as their own: as if a man should dig out the stones of a royal amphitheater to build a stage for a country show. Amongst all the monsters this unlucky age has teemed with, I find none so prodigious as the poets of these later times, wherein men, as if they would level[2] understandings too as well as estates, acknowledging no inequality of parts and judgments, pretend as indifferently to the chair of wit as to the pulpit, and conceive themselves no less inspired with the spirit of poetry than with that of religion: so it is not only the noise of drums and trumpets which have drowned the Muses' harmony, or the fear that the church's ruin will destroy their priests likewise, that now frights them from this country, where they have been so ingenuously received, but these rude pretenders to excellencies they unjustly own who, profanely rushing into Minerva's temple, with noisome airs blast the laurel which thunder cannot hurt. In this sad condition these learned sisters are fled to beg Your Lordship's protection, who have been so certain a patron both to arts and arms, and who in this general confusion have so entirely preserved your honor that in Your Lordship we may still read a most perfect character of what England was in all her pomp and greatness; so that although these poems were formerly written upon several occasions and to several persons, they now unite themselves, and are become one pyramid to set Your Lordship's statue upon, where you may stand like armed Apollo, the defender of the Muses, encouraging the poets now alive to celebrate your great acts by affording your countenance to his poems that wanted only so noble a subject.

My Lord,
Your most humble servant,
John Donne[3]

Songs and Sonnets

THE GOOD MORROW

I wonder, by my troth, what thou and I
   Did till we lov'd? Were we not wean'd till then,
But suck'd on country[1] pleasures childishly?
   Or snorted we in the Seven Sleepers' den?[2]
'Twas so; but[3] this, all pleasures fancies be.   5
   If ever any beauty I did see
Which I desir'd, and got, 'twas but a dream of thee.

And now good morrow to our waking souls,
   Which watch not one another out of fear;
For love all love of other sights controls,   10
   And makes one little room an everywhere.
Let[4] sea-discoverers to new worlds have gone,
Let maps to other,[5] worlds on worlds have shown,
Let us possess one world: each hath one, and is one.

My face in thine eye, thine in mine appears,   15
   And true plain hearts do in the faces rest.
Where can we find two better hemispheres
   Without sharp north, without declining west?
Whatever dies was not mix'd equally;[6]
   If our two loves be one, or thou and I   20
Love so alike that none do slacken, none can die.

SONG

Go and catch a falling star,
   Get with child a mandrake[1] root,
Tell me where all past years are,
   Or who cleft the devil's foot,
Teach me to hear mermaids singing,   5
Or to keep off envy's stinging,
      And find
      What wind
Serves to advance an honest mind.

If thou bee'st born to strange sights,   10
   Things invisible to see,
Ride ten thousand days and nights
   Till age snow white hairs on thee;
Thou, when thou return'st, wilt tell me
All strange wonders that befell thee,   15
      And swear
      Nowhere
Lives a woman true and fair.

TO WILLIAM, LORD CRAVEN [1]A soldier (1606–97) who served on the Continent with Maurice of Nassau, Gustavus Adolphus of Sweden, and Elizabeth of Bohemia, the unfortunate daughter of James I whose marriage (1613) to Frederick V, Elector Palatine, had been commemorated by Donne with a stately epithalamion. [2]Make level, equalize. [3]The younger Donne (1604–62) was a highly educated reprobate whose checkered career included the petulant murder of a little boy (1633), much foreign travel, ordination in the church of England, and (just before his death) the publication of a grossly indecent volume entitled *Donne's Satyr.* He was described by Anthony Wood as a man of "vile" character who "proved no better all his lifetime than an atheistical buffoon, a banterer, and a person of overfree thoughts."

THE GOOD MORROW [1]Rustic, i.e., simple. [2]*Seven Sleepers' den*: According to an ancient legend, seven Christian youths of Ephesus, walled up in a cave by the Emperor Decius, miraculously slept for two hundred years and emerged to find that Christianity had triumphed over paganism.   [3]Except for. [4]I.e., concede that. [5]Other people. [6]*Whatever . . . equally*: Mixtures of contrary elements were thought liable to decay.

SONG [1]A plant whose forked root resembles the human body.

If thou find'st one, let me know;
  Such a pilgrimage were sweet—   20
Yet do not; I would not go
  Though at next door we might meet.
Though she were true when you met her,
And last till you write your letter,
    Yet she   25
    Will be
False, ere I come, to two or three.

WOMAN'S CONSTANCY

Now thou hast lov'd me one whole day,
Tomorrow when thou leav'st,[1] what wilt thou say?
Wilt thou then antedate some new-made vow?
    Or say that now
We are not just those persons which we were?   5
Or that oaths made in reverential fear
Of Love and his wrath any may forswear?
Or as true deaths true marriages untie,
So lovers' contracts, images of those,
Bind but till sleep, death's image, them unloose?   10
    Or, your own end to justify,
For having purpos'd change and falsehood, you
Can have no way but falsehood to be true?
Vain lunatic, against these scapes[2] I could
    Dispute and conquer, if I would,   15
    Which I abstain to do,
For by tomorrow I may think so too.

THE SUN RISING

    Busy[1] old fool, unruly sun,
      Why dost thou thus
Through windows and through curtains call on us?
Must to thy motions lovers' seasons run?
    Saucy, pedantic wretch, go chide   5
    Late schoolboys and sour prentices,
  Go tell court huntsmen that the king will ride,
  Call country ants to harvest offices.[2]
Love, all alike, no season knows, nor clime,
Nor hours, days, months, which are the rags of time.   10

    Thy beams, so reverend and strong
      Why shouldst thou think?
I could eclipse and cloud them with a wink,
But that I would not lose her sight so long.
    If her eyes have not blinded thine,   15
    Look, and tomorrow late tell me
  Whether both th' Indias[3] of spice and mine
  Be where thou left'st them, or lie here with me;
Ask for those kings whom thou saw'st yesterday,
And thou shalt hear: All here in one bed lay.   20

    She's all states, and all princes I;
      Nothing else is.
Princes do but play us; compar'd to this,
All honor's mimic, all wealth alchemy.[4]
    Thou, sun, art half as happy's we   25

In that the world's contracted thus.
  Thine age asks ease, and since thy duties be
  To warm the world, that's done in warming us.
Shine here to us, and thou art everywhere;
This bed thy center[5] is, these walls thy sphere.   30

THE INDIFFERENT

    I can love both fair and brown,[1]
Her whom abundance melts, and her whom
    want betrays,
Her who loves loneness best, and her who masks
    and plays,
  Her whom the country form'd, and whom
    the town,
    Her who believes, and her who tries,[2]   5
    Her who still weeps with spongy eyes,
    And her who is dry cork and never cries;
I can love her, and her, and you, and you;
I can love any, so she be not true.

    Will no other vice content you?   10
Will it not serve your turn to do as did your mothers?
Or have you all old vices spent, and now would find
    out others?
  Or doth a fear that men are true torment you?
    O, we are not. Be not you so.
    Let me, and do you, twenty know.   15
    Rob me, but bind me not, and let me go.
Must I, who came to travail thorough[3] you,
Grow your fix'd subject because you are true?

    Venus heard me sigh this song,
And by love's sweetest part, variety, she swore   20
She heard not this till now, and that it should be so
    no more.
  She went, examin'd, and return'd ere long,
    And said, "Alas, some two or three
    Poor heretics in love there be,
    Which think to 'stablish dangerous constancy,   25
But I have told them, 'Since you will be[4] true,
You shall be true to them who're false to you.' "

THE CANONIZATION

For God's sake hold your tongue and let me love!
  Or chide my palsy or my gout,
My five gray hairs or ruin'd fortune flout;
With wealth your state, your mind with arts improve,

WOMAN'S CONSTANCY   [1]I.e., stop loving. [2]Tricks, wiles.
THE SUN RISING   [1]Officious [2]Duties, tasks.
[3]I.e., the East and West Indies. Text *th' Indias*. Such elisions, which
are very common in the text, have normally been indicated, as in
this instance, by substituting an apostrophe for the elided vowel.
[4]Imitation gold.
[5]In Ptolemaic astronomy, the earth (around which the sun revolves
in its *sphere*).
THE INDIFFERENT   [1]*Fair and brown*: Blonde and brunette.
[2]Tests. [3]Through. [4]*Will be*: insist on being.

Take you a course,[1] get you a place,[2]   5
  Observe[3] His Honor or His Grace,
Or the King's real or his stamped face[4]
  Contemplate; what you will, approve,[5]
    So you will let me love.

Alas, alas, who's injur'd by my love?   10
  What merchant's ships have my sighs drown'd?
Who says my tears have overflow'd his ground?
When did my colds a forward[6] spring remove?
  When did the heats which my veins fill
    Add one more[7] to the plaguy bill?[8]   15
Soldiers find wars, and lawyers find out still
  Litigious men which quarrels move,[9]
    Though she and I do love.

Call us what you will, we are made such by love.
  Call her one, me another fly,[10]   20
We're tapers too, and at our own cost die;
And we in us find th' eagle and the dove.[11]
  The phoenix riddle hath more wit,
  By us; we two, being one, are it.
So to one neutral thing both sexes fit;   25
  We die and rise the same, and prove
    Mysterious by this love.[12]

We can die by it, if not live by love,
  And if unfit for tombs and hearse[13]
Our legend be, it will be fit for verse;   30
And if no piece of chronicle we prove,
  We'll build in sonnets pretty rooms[14]
(As well a well-wrought urn becomes
The greatest ashes, as half-acre tombs),
  And by these hymns all shall approve   35
    Us canoniz'd for love,

And thus invoke us: "You whom reverend love
  Made one another's hermitage,
You to whom love was peace, that now is rage,
Who did the whole world's soul extract,[15] and drove   40
  Into the glasses of your eyes
  (So made such mirrors and such spies
That they did all to you epitomize)
  Countries, towns, courts: beg from above
    A pattern of your[16] love!"   45

THE TRIPLE FOOL

  I am two fools, I know,
    For loving, and for saying so
      In whining poetry.
  (But where's that wise man that would not be I
    If she would not deny?)   5
  Then as th' earth's inward, narrow, crooked lanes
  Do purge sea water's fretful salt away,
    I thought if I could draw my pains
  Through rhyme's vexation, I should them allay.
  Grief brought to numbers cannot be so fierce, 10
  For he tames it that fetters it in verse.

  But when I have done so,
    Some man, his art and voice to show,
      Doth set[1] and sing my pain,
  And by delighting many, frees again   15
    Grief, which verse did restrain.
  To love and grief tribute of verse belongs,
  But not of such as pleases when 'tis read;
    Both are increased by such songs,
  For both their triumphs so are published,   20
  And I, which was two fools, do so grow three.
  Who are a little wise, the best fools be.

SONG

  Sweetest love, I do not go
    For weariness of thee,
  Nor in hope the world can show
    A fitter love for me;
      But since that I   5
  Must die at last, 'tis best
  To use myself in jest
    Thus by feign'd deaths to die.

  Yesternight the sun went hence,
    And yet is here today;   10
  He hath no desire nor sense,
    Nor half so short a way.
      Then fear not me,
  But believe that I shall make
  Speedier journeys, since I take   15
    More wings and spurs than he.

  O how feeble is man's power,
    That if good fortune fall,
  Cannot add another hour,
    Nor a lost hour recall!   20
      But come bad chance,
  And we join to it our strength,

THE CANONIZATION [1]Career? Course of action leading to profit? [2]Appointment. [3]Be attentive to. [4]I.e., on a coin. [5]Try. [6]Early. [7]Most manuscripts and some editors read *man*. [8]A published list of deaths from the plague. [9]*Which...move*: Who stir up disputes. [10]Butterfly (which is attracted to its death by the flame of a candle). [11]*Eagle...dove*: traditional emblems of the powerful and the gentle. [12]*The phoenix...love*: i.e., the problem of how the phoenix achieves immortality (by rising from its own ashes) is better understood by our example, for though we "die" (in sexual intercourse) we revive to "die" again. See *phoenix* and *die* in Glossary. [13]Wooden framework or catafalque to cover or support a coffin. On such structures friends of the deceased often affixed poems or epitaphs. [14]*Sonnets...rooms*: There is perhaps a bilingual pun on Italian *stanza*: "room." [15]Text *contract*, but most manuscripts read *extract*: in alchemy, extraction is the process of distillation and sublimation. [16]Text *our*.
THE TRIPLE FOOL [1]I.e., set to music.

And we teach it art and length,
 Itself o'er us t' advance.

When thou sigh'st, thou sigh'st not wind,   25
 But sigh'st my soul away;
When thou weep'st, unkindly kind,
 My life's blood doth decay.
  It cannot be
That thou lov'st me as thou say'st,   30
If in thine my life thou waste.
  Thou art the best of me.

Let not thy divining[1] heart
 Forethink me any ill;
Destiny may take thy part,   35
 And may thy fears fulfill;
  But think that we
Are but turn'd aside to sleep.
They who one another keep
 Alive, ne'er parted be.   40

AIR AND ANGELS

 Twice or thrice had I loved thee
 Before I knew thy face or name
(So in a voice, so in a shapeless flame
Angels affect us oft, and worshipp'd be);
 Still when to where thou wert I came,   5
Some lovely glorious nothing I did see.
 But since my soul, whose child love is,
Takes limbs of flesh (and else could nothing do),
 More subtile[1] than the parent is
Love must not be, but take a body too;   10
 And therefore what thou wert, and who,
  I bid love ask, and now
That it assume thy body I allow,
And fix itself in thy lip, eye, and brow.

 Whilst thus to ballast love I thought,   15
 And so more steadily to have gone,
With wares which would sink admiration,
I saw I had love's pinnace overfraught.[2]
 Ev'ry thy hair for love to work upon
Is much too much; some fitter must be sought.   20
 For nor in nothing nor in things
Extreme and scatt'ring bright can love inhere.
 Then, as an angel face and wings
Of air—not pure as it, yet pure—doth wear,[3]
 So thy love may be my love's sphere.   25
  Just such disparity
As is 'twixt air and angels' purity,
'Twixt women's love and men's will ever be.

THE ANNIVERSARY

 All kings, and all their favorites,
 All glory of honors, beauties, wits,
The sun itself, which makes times, as they[1] pass,
Is elder by a year now than it was.

When thou and I first one another saw.   5
All other things to their destruction draw;
 Only our love hath no decay;
This, no tomorrow hath nor yesterday;
Running, it never runs from us away,
But truly keeps his first, last, everlasting day.   10

 Two graves must hide thine and my corse.[2]
 If one might, death were no divorce.
Alas, as well as other princes, we
(Who prince enough in one another be)
Must leave at last in death these eyes and ears,   15
Oft fed with true oaths and with sweet salt tears;
 But souls where' nothing dwells[3] but love
(All other thoughts being inmates)[4] then shall prove
This,[5] or a love increased there above,
When bodies to their graves, souls from their
   graves, remove.   20

 And then we shall be throughly[6] blest,
 But we[7] no more than all the rest.
Here upon earth we're kings, and none but we
Can be such kings, nor of such, subjects be.
Who is so safe as we, where none can do   25
Treason to us except one of us two?
 True and false fears let us refrain,
 Let us love nobly, and live, and add again
Years and years unto years till we attain
To write threescore. This is the second of our reign. 30

TWICKENHAM GARDEN[1]

Blasted with sighs and surrounded[2] with tears,
 Hither I come to seek the spring,
 And at mine eyes and at mine ears
Receive such balms as else cure everything;
 But O, self-traitor, I do bring   5
 The spider love, which transubstantiates all,
  And can convert manna to gall;[3]
And that this place may thoroughly be thought
True paradise, I have the serpent brought.

'Twere wholesomer for me that winter did   10
 Benight the glory of this place,
 And that a grave[4] frost did forbid
These trees to laugh and mock me to my face;
 But that I may not this disgrace

SONG   [1]Prophetic.

AIR AND ANGELS   [1]Rarefied.   [2]Overloaded.
[3]*Then as an angel...wear*: It was long believed that angels (who are normally immaterial) could assume rarefied bodies of air or mist.

THE ANNIVERSARY   [1]I.e., kings, favorites, etc.   [2]Corpse.
[3]Has permanent residence.   [4]Sojourners, temporary lodgers.
[5]I.e., that death is no divorce.   [6]Thoroughly   [7]Text *now*.

TWICKENHAM GARDEN   [1]Between 1608 and 1617 Twickenham Park, on the Thames west of London, was the seat of Donne's friend and patroness, Lucy, countess of Bedford.   [2]Inundated.
[3]*Convert manna to gall*: i.e., reverse the Eucharistic miracle by making sweet and wholesome things bitter.   [4]Heavy.

Endure, nor leave this garden,[5] Love, let me 15
  Some senseless piece of this place be:
Make me a mandrake so I may grow[6] here,
Or a stone fountain weeping out my year.

Hither with crystal vials, lovers, come,
  And take my tears, which are love's wine, 20
  And try[7] your mistress' tears at home,
For all are false that taste not just like mine.
  Alas! hearts do not in eyes shine,
Nor can you more judge woman's thoughts by tears,
  Than by her shadow what she wears. 25
O perverse sex, where none is true but she,
Who's therefore true because her truth kills me.

THE DREAM

  Dear love, for nothing less than thee
  Would I have broke this happy dream.
    It was a theme
For reason, much too strong for fantasy;
  Therefore thou wak'dst me wisely. Yet 5
My dream thou brok'st not, but continuedst it;
Thou art so[1] Truth that thoughts of thee suffice
To make dreams truths, and fables histories.
Enter these arms, for since thou thoughtst it best
Not to dream all my dream, let's act the rest. 10

  As lightning or a taper's light,
  Thine eyes and not thy noise wak'd me.
    Yet I thought thee
(For thou lov'st truth) an angel at first sight;
  But when I saw thou saw'st my heart, 15
And knew'st my thoughts (beyond an angel's art),[2]
When thou knew'st what I dreamt, when thou
    knew'st when
Excess of joy would wake me, and cam'st then,
I must confess it could not choose but be
Profane to think thee anything but thee. 20

  Coming and staying show'd thee thee,
  But rising makes me doubt[3] that now
    Thou art not thou.
That love is weak where fear's as strong as he.
  'Tis not all spirit, pure and brave, 25
If mixture it of fear, shame, honor have.
Perchance as torches which must ready be
Men light and put out, so thou deal'st with me:
Thou cam'st to kindle, go'st to come; then I
Will dream that hope again, but else would die. 30

A VALEDICTION: OF WEEPING

  Let me pour forth
My tears before thy face whilst I stay here,
For thy face coins them, and thy stamp they bear,
And by this mintage they are something worth,
    For thus they be 5
    Pregnant[1] of thee;

Fruits of much grief they are, emblems of more:
  When a tear falls, that *thou* falls[2] which it bore;
So thou and I are nothing then, when on a
    divers shore.[3]

    On a round ball 10
A workman that hath copies by, can lay
An Europe, Afric, and an Asia,
And quickly make that which was nothing all;
    So doth each tear
    Which *thee* doth wear 15
A globe, yea world, by that impression grow,
Till thy tears mix'd with mine do overflow
This world: by waters sent from thee, my heaven
    dissolved so.

    O more than moon,
Draw not up seas to drown me in thy sphere, 20
Weep me not dead in thine arms, but forbear
To teach the sea what it may do too soon;
    Let not the wind
    Example find
To do me more harm than it purposeth; 25
Since thou and I sigh one another's breath,
Whoe'er sighs most is cruelest, and hastes the
    other's death.

THE FLEA

  Mark but this flea, and mark in this
How little that which thou deny'st me is;
  It suck'd me first, and now sucks thee,
And in this flea our two bloods mingled be.
  Thou know'st that this cannot be said 5
A sin, nor shame, nor loss of maidenhead,
  Yet this enjoys before it woo,
And, pamper'd, swells with one blood made of two,
And this, alas, is more than we would do.

  O stay, three lives in one flea spare, 10
Where we almost, yea more than married are.
  This flea is you and I, and this
Our marriage bed and marriage temple is;
  Though parents grudge, and you, we're met
And cloister'd in these living walls of jet. 15
  Though use make you apt to kill me,
Let not to that, self-murder added be,
And sacrilege: three sins in killing three.[1]

---

[5]*Nor leave this garden*: text *nor yet leave loving.*
[6]Some manuscripts read *groane*, a variant no doubt associated with the fact that the mandrake, a plant with a forked root resembling the figure of a man, was thought to groan when uprooted. [7]Test.
THE DREAM [1]To such a degree. [2]Capacity. [3]Suspect.
OF WEEPING [1]Quickened by. [2]Text *falst.*
[3]I.e., in different countries separated by the sea.
THE FLEA [1]I.e., the sin of murder in killing her lover, of suicide in killing herself, and of sacrilege in killing the flea (because she will be destroying the *temple* of line 13).

Cruel and sudden, hast thou since
Purpled thy nail in blood of innocence?   20
   Wherein could this flea guilty be,
Except in that drop which it suck'd from thee?
    Yet thou triumph'st, and say'st that thou
Find'st not thyself nor me the weaker now.
    'Tis true. Then learn how false fears be: 25
Just so much honor, when thou yield'st to me,
Will waste, as this flea's death took life from thee.

A NOCTURNAL UPON ST. LUCY'S DAY[1]
BEING THE SHORTEST DAY

'Tis the year's midnight, and it is the day's,
Lucy's, who scarce seven hours herself unmasks.
   The sun is spent, and now his flasks[2]
   Send forth light squibs,[3] no constant rays;
    The world's whole sap is sunk;   5
The general balm th' hydroptic earth hath drunk,[4]
Whither, as to the bed's feet, life is shrunk,
Dead and interr'd; yet all these seem to laugh
Compar'd with me, who am their epitaph.

Study me, then, you who shall lovers be   10
At the next world (that is, at the next spring),
   For I am every dead thing
   In whom Love wrought new alchemy;
    For his art did express[5]
A quintessence even from nothingness,   15
From dull privations and lean emptiness.
He ruin'd me, and I am re-begot
Of absence, darkness, death: things which are not.

All others from all things draw all that's good:
Life, soul, form, spirit, whence they being have;   20
   I, by love's limbec,[6] am the grave
   Of all that's nothing. Oft a flood
    Have we two wept, and so
Drown'd the whole world—us two. Oft did we grow
To be two chaoses when we did show   25
Care to aught else; and often absences
Withdrew our souls and made us carcasses.

But I am by her death (which word wrongs her)
Of the first nothing the elixir[7] grown;
   Were I a man, that I were one   30
   I needs must know; I should prefer,
    If I were any beast,
Some ends, some means; yea plants, yea stones detest
And love; all, all some properties invest;[8]
If I an ordinary nothing were,   35
As shadow, a light and body must be here.

But I am none, nor will my sun renew.
You lovers, for whose sake the lesser sun
   At this time to the Goat[9] is run
   To fetch new lust and give it you,
    Enjoy your summer all.   40
Since she enjoys her long night's festival,
Let me prepare towards her, and let me call

This hour her vigil and her eve, since this
Both the year's and the day's deep midnight is.   45

THE BAIT[1]

Come live with me and be my love,
And we will some new pleasures prove
Of golden sands and crystal brooks,
With silken lines and silver hooks.

There will the river whispering run,   5
Warm'd by thy eyes more than the sun,
And there th' enamor'd fish will stay,
Begging themselves they may betray.

When thou wilt swim in that live bath,
Each fish which every channel hath   10
Will amorously to thee swim,
Gladder to catch thee than thou him.

If thou to be so seen be'st loath,
By sun or moon, thou dark'nest both,
And if myself have leave to see,   15
I need not their light, having thee.

Let others freeze with angling reeds,[2]
And cut their legs with[3] shells and weeds,
Or treacherously poor fish beset
With strangling snare or windowy net;   20

Let coarse bold hands from slimy nest
The bedded fish in banks outwrest,
Or curious traitors, sleavesilk[4] flies,
Bewitch poor fishes' wand'ring eyes.

For thee, thou need'st no such deceit,   25
For thou thyself art thine own bait;
That fish that is not catch'd thereby,
Alas, is wiser far than I.

A NOCTURNAL [1]December 13, which in the Julian or Old Style calendar was conventionally regarded as the shortest day of the year.
[2]I.e., the stars, which were thought to store up sunlight and then to emit it.
[3]Small charges of gunpowder, i.e., intermittent gleams of starlight. The figure is suggested by a more specialized sense of *flasks*, "containers for gunpowder."
[4]*The general balm...drunk*: i.e., the earth, with the insatiable thirst of one suffering from dropsy, has drunk all the life-preserving rainwater (*balm*), so that the world is desiccated. [5]Squeeze out.
[6]Alembic, a retort used by alchemists.
[7]The *quintessence* of line 15, i.e., utter nothingness.
[8]*Some properties invest*: i.e., are endowed with attributes or qualities.
[9]The zodiacal sign of Capricorn (and also a traditional symbol of lechery).
THE BAIT [1]This title was added in the 1635 edition. According to Izaak Walton, Donne wrote this reply to Marlowe's "Passionate Shepherd to His Love" in order "to show the world that he could make soft and smooth verses when he thought them fit and worth his labor." [2]Rods. [3]Text *which*.
[4]Text *sleavesicke*. Sleavesilk is a silken thread capable of being separated into smaller filaments.

THE APPARITION

When by thy scorn, O murd'ress, I am dead,
　　And that thou think'st thee free
From all solicitation from me,
Then shall my ghost come to thy bed,
And thee, feign'd vestal, in worse arms shall see.　　5
Then thy sick taper will begin to wink,[1]
And he whose thou art then, being tir'd before,
Will, if thou stir or pinch to wake him, think
　　Thou call'st for more,
And in false sleep will from thee shrink,　　10
And then, poor aspen[2] wretch, neglected, thou
Bath'd in a cold, quicksilver sweat wilt lie
　　A verier ghost than I.
What I will say I will not tell thee now,
Lest that preserve thee; and since my love is spent,　　15
I'd rather thou shouldst painfully repent
Than by my threat'nings rest still innocent.

A VALEDICTION: FORBIDDING MOURNING

As virtuous men pass mildly away,
　　And whisper to their souls to go,
Whilst some of their sad friends do say,
　　"The breath goes now," and some say, "No,"

So let us melt and make no noise,　　5
　　No tear-floods nor sigh-tempests move;
'Twere profanation of our joys
　　To tell the laity our love.

Moving of th' earth[1] brings harms and fears;
　　Men reckon what it did and meant;　　10
But trepidation of the spheres,[2]
　　Though greater far, is innocent.[3]

Dull sublunary[4] lovers' love,
　　Whose soul is sense,[5] cannot admit[6]
Absence, because it doth remove　　15
　　Those things which elemented[7] it.

But we by a love so much refin'd
　　That ourselves know not what it is,
Interassured of the mind,
　　Care less eyes, lips, and hands to miss.　　20

Our two souls, therefore, which are one,
　　Though I must go, endure not yet
A breach, but an expansion,
　　Like gold to airy thinness beat.

If they be two, they are two so　　25
　　As stiff twin compasses are two;
Thy soul, the fix'd foot, makes no show
　　To move, but doth if th' other do.

And though it in the center sit,
　　Yet when the other far doth roam,　　30
It leans and hearkens after it
　　And grows erect as that[8] comes home.

Such wilt thou be to me, who must,
　　Like th' other foot, obliquely run;
Thy firmness makes my circle just,　　35
　　And makes me end where I begun.

THE ECSTASY[1]

Where, like a pillow on a bed,
　　A pregnant bank swell'd up to rest
The violet's reclining head,
　　Sat we two, one another's best.[2]

Our hands were firmly cemented　　5
　　With a fast balm which thence did spring,
Our eye-beams twisted, and did thread
　　Our eyes upon one double string;

So t' intergraft our hands, as yet
　　Was all the means to make us one,　　10
And pictures in our eyes to get[3]
　　Was all our propagation.

As 'twixt two equal armies fate
　　Suspends uncertain victory,
Our souls, which to advance their state　　15
　　Were gone out, hung 'twixt her and me.

And whilst our souls negotiate there,
　　We like sepulchral statues lay;
All day the same our postures were,
　　And we said nothing all the day.　　20

If any (so by love refin'd
　　That he soul's language understood,
And by good love were grown all mind)
　　Within convenient distance stood,

He (though he knew[4] not which soul spake,　　25
　　Because both meant, both spake the same)
Might thence a new concoction[5] take,
　　And part far purer than he came.

This ecstasy doth unperplex,
　　We said, and tell us what we love;　　30

THE APPARITION　[1]Flicker (in the presence of a ghost).
[2]Quivering.

FORBIDDING MOURNING　[1]*Moving...earth*: i.e., earthquakes.
[2]*Trepidation...spheres:* In Ptolemaic astronomy the libration or oscillation of the ninth sphere was thought to account for certain phenomena throughout the universe. See *sphere* in Glossary.
[3]Harmless
[4]Earthly, i.e., below the sphere of the moon and therefore subject to change.　[5]Sensuality.　[6]Permit, endure.　[7]Composed.
[8]I.e., the other foot of the compass.

THE ECSTASY　[1]Greek *extasis* ("stepping out"), the mystical rapture in which the soul, released from its bodily prison, contemplates divine truth or enjoys a direct union with God.
[2]Unlike many of the manuscripts, the 1633 edition does not divide the poem into quatrain stanzas.
[3]Beget. The reflection (*picture*) of oneself in the pupils of another person's eyes was sometimes called a baby.　[4]Text *knowes.*
[5]A process of purification by heat.

We see by this it was not sex,
  We see we saw not what did move;

But as all several souls contain
  Mixture of things, they know not what,
Love these mix'd souls doth mix again   35
And makes both one, each this and that.

A single violet transplant,
  The strength, the color, and the size
(All which before was poor and scant)
  Redoubles still and multiplies.   40

When love with one another so
  Interinanimates two souls,
That abler soul which thence doth flow
  Defects of loneliness controls.[6]

We then, who are this new soul, know   45
  Of what we are compos'd and made,
For th' atomies[7] of which we grow
  Are souls whom no change can invade.

But O, alas, so long, so far
  Our bodies why do we forbear?   50
They are ours, though they are not we;[8] we are
  The intelligences,[9] they the spheres.[10]

We owe them thanks because they thus
  Did us to us at first convey.
Yielded their forces, sense,[11] to us,   55
  Nor are dross to us, but allay.[12]

On man heaven's influence works not so,
  But that it first imprints the air;
So soul into the soul may flow
  Though it to body first repair.   60

As our blood labors to beget
  Spirits[13] as like souls as it can,
Because such fingers need[14] to knit
  That subtile knot which makes us man,

So must pure lovers' souls descend   65
  T' affections and to faculties
Which sense may reach and apprehend;
  Else a great prince in prison lies.

T' our bodies turn we then, that so
  Weak men on love reveal'd may look;   70
Love's mysteries in souls do grow,
  But yet the body is his book.

And if some lover, such as we,
  Have heard this dialogue of one,
Let him still mark us; he shall see   75
  Small change when we're to bodies gone.

LOVE'S DEITY

I long to talk with some old lover's ghost
  Who died before the god of love was born.
I cannot think that he who then lov'd most
  Sunk so low as to love one which did scorn.

But since this god produc'd a destiny,   5
And that vice-nature, custom, lets it be,
  I must love her that loves not me.

Sure they which made him god meant not so much,
  Nor he in his young godhead practic'd it.
But when an even[1] flame two hearts did touch,   10
  His office was indulgently to fit
Actives to passives. Correspondency
Only his subject was. It cannot be
  Love till I love her that loves me.

But every modern god will now extend   15
  His vast prerogative as far as Jove.
To rage, to lust, to write to, to commend,
  All is the purlieu of the god of love.
O were we waken'd by this tyranny
T' ungod this child again, it could not be 20
  I should love her who loves not me.

Rebel and atheist too, why murmur I
  As though I felt the worst that Love could do?
Love might make me leave loving, or might try
  A deeper plague, to make her love me too, 25
Which, since she loves before,[2] I'm loath to see.
Falsehood is worse than hate, and that must be
  If she whom I love should love me.

THE FUNERAL

Whoever comes to shroud me, do not harm
    Nor question much
That subtle wreath of hair which crowns mine arm;
The mystery, the sign, you must not touch,
    For 'tis my outward soul,   5
Viceroy to that, which, then to heav'n being gone,
    Will leave this to control
And keep these limbs, her provinces, from dissolution.

For if the sinewy thread[1] my brain lets fall
    Through every part   10
Can tie those parts and make me one of all,
These hairs, which upward grew, and strength and art
    Have from a better brain,
Can better do't; except she meant that I
    By this should know my pain,   15
As prisoners then are manacled when they're condemn'd
    to die.

[6]*Defects...controls*: corrects the imperfections of singleness.
[7]Atoms. [8]*Though...we*: text *though not we*.
[9]In Ptolemaic astronomy, each sphere (see Glossary) was thought to be controlled by its appropriate angel or spirit. See "Good Friday, 1613, Riding Westward" (p. 84) for an elaborate development of this idea.
[10]Most manuscripts read *sphere* (i.e., the heavens).
[11]*Forces, sense*: text *senses force*. [12]Alloy.
[13]In Elizabethan physiology, the vapors or rarefied liquids rising from the blood which were thought to link the soul and body.
[14]Are necessary.
LOVE'S DEITY [1]Equal. [2]I.e., loves someone else.
THE FUNERAL [1]Network of nerves.

Whate'er she meant by't, bury it with me,
    For since I am
Love's martyr, it might breed idolatry
If into others' hands these relics came.   20
    As 'twas humility
T' afford to it all that a soul can do,
    So 'tis some bravery
That since you would save none of me, I bury some of you.

THE BLOSSOM

    Little think'st thou, poor flower,
      Whom I've watch'd six or seven days,
And seen thy birth, and seen what every hour
Gave to thy growth, thee to this height to raise,
And now dost laugh and triumph on this bough: 5
      Little think'st thou
That it will freeze anon, and that I shall
Tomorrow find thee fall'n, or not at all.

    Little think'st thou, poor heart,
      That labor'st[1] yet to nestle thee,   10
And think'st by hovering here to get a part
In a forbidden or forbidding tree,
And hop'st her stiffness by long siege to bow:
      Little think'st thou
That thou tomorrow, ere that sun[2] doth wake,   15
Must with this sun and me a journey take.

    But thou,[3] which lov'st to be
      Subtile to plague thyself, wilt say,
"Alas, if you must go, what's that to me?
Here lies my business, and here I will stay.   20
You go to friends whose love and means present
      Various content
To your eyes, ears, and tongue,[4] and every part.
If then your body go, what need you a[5] heart?"

    Well then, stay here; but know,   25
      When thou hast stay'd and done thy most,
A naked, thinking heart that makes no show
Is to a woman but a kind of ghost.
How shall she know my heart, or, having none,
      Know thee for one?   30
Practice may make her know some other part,
But take my word, she doth not know a heart.

    Meet me at London, then,
      Twenty days hence, and thou shalt see
Me fresher and more fat by being with men   35
Than if I had stay'd still with her and thee.
For God's sake, if you can, be you so too.
      I would[6] give you
There to another friend, whom we shall find
As glad to have my body as my mind.   40

THE RELIC

    When my grave is broke up again
      Some second guest to entertain

    (For graves have learn'd that womanhead[1]
      To be to more than one a bed)
      And he that digs it spies   5
A bracelet of bright hair about the bone,
      Will he not let us alone,
And think that there a loving couple lies,
Who thought that this device might be some way
To make their souls at the last busy day[2]
Meet at this grave, and make a little stay?   10

    If this fall in a time or land
      Where misdevotion[3] doth command,
      Then he that digs us up will bring
      Us to the bishop and the king   15
      To make us relics; then
Thou shalt be a Mary Magdalen,[4] and I
      A something else[5] thereby.
All women shall adore us, and some men;
And since at such time miracles are sought,[6]   20
I would have that age by this paper[7] taught
What miracles we harmless[8] lovers wrought:

    First, we lov'd well and faithfully,
      Yet knew not what we lov'd, nor why;
      Difference of sex no more we knew   25
      Than our guardian angels do;
      Coming and going, we
Perchance might kiss, but not between those meals;[9]
      Our hands ne'er touch'd the seals
Which nature, injur'd by late law, sets free.[10]   30
These miracles we did, but now, alas,
All measure and all language I should pass
Should I tell what a miracle she was.

THE PROHIBITION

    Take heed of loving me;
At least remember I forbid it thee;
    Not that I shall repair my unthrifty waste
Of breath and blood upon[1] thy sighs and tears
    By being to thee then what to me[2] thou wast;   5
But so great joy[3] our life at once outwears.
    Then, lest thy love by my death frustrate be,
    If thou love me, take heed of loving me.

THE BLOSSOM [1]Text *labours*. [2]I.e., the poet's beloved.
[3]I.e., the poet's heart. [4]Text *tast*. [5]Text *your*. [6]Will
THE RELIC [1]Feminine characteristic. [2]The day of judgment.
[3]Idolatry (probably referring to Roman Catholicism, whose
veneration of relics was widely denounced by Protestants).
[4]The woman taken in adultery whom Jesus forgave (Luke 7.36–
50); traditionally a name for a penitent harlot.
[5]I.e., some other spurious relic.
[6]*At such...sought*: Because relics need to be authenticated by
miracles. [7]I.e., this poem. [8]Innocent.
[9]*Coming...meals*: i.e., only in greeting and leavetaking would we
engage in kissing, which is the food of the soul.
[10]*Our hands...free*: i.e., we did not indulge in physical love, which
law (but not nature) restrains.
THE PROHIBITION [1]With. [2]*What to me*: text *that which*.
[3]I.e., of mutual love.

Take heed of hating me,
Or too much triumph in the victory;[4]   10
   Not that I shall be mine own officer,[5]
And hate with hate again retaliate,
   But thou wilt lose the style[6] of conqueror
If I, thy conquest, perish by thy hate.
   Then, lest my being nothing lessen thee,   15
   If thou hate me, take heed of hating me.

     Yet love and hate me too,
So these extremes shall neither[7] office do;
   Love me, that I may die the gentler way;
Hate me, because thy love's too great for me;   20
   Or let these two themselves, not me, decay;
So shall I live thy stage,[8] not triumph be.[9]
   Then, lest thy love, hate, and me thou undo,
   O let me live, yet love and hate me too.[10]

ELEGIES

[ELEGY IX] THE AUTUMNAL[1]

No spring nor summer beauty hath such grace
As I have seen in one autumnal face.
Young beauties force our love, and that's a rape;
This doth but counsel, yet you cannot 'scape.
If 'twere a shame to love, here 'twere no shame;   5
Affection[2] here takes reverence's name.
Were her first years the Golden Age? That's true,
But now she's[3] gold oft tried[4] and ever new.
That was her torrid and inflaming time;
This is her tolerable tropic clime.   10
Fair eyes! Who asks more heat than comes from hence,
He in a fever wishes pestilence.
Call not these wrinkles graves.[5] If graves they were,
They were Love's graves, for else he is nowhere.
Yet lies not Love dead here, but here doth sit   15
Vow'd to this trench like an anachorit;[6]
And here, till hers, which must be his death, come,
He doth not dig a grave, but build a tomb.
Here dwells he; though he sojourn ev'rywhere
In progress, yet his standing-house[7] is here,   20
Here, where still evening is, not noon nor night,
Where no voluptuousness, yet all delight.
In all her words, unto all hearers fit,
You may at revels, you at council, sit.
This is Love's timber, youth his underwood;   25
There[8] he, as wine in June, enrages blood,
Which then comes seasonabliest when our taste
And appetite to other things is past.
Xerxes' strange Lydian love, the platan tree,[9]
Was lov'd for age, none being so large as she,   30
Or else because, being young, nature did bless
Her youth with age's glory, barrenness.
If we love things long sought, age is a thing
Which we are fifty years in compassing;
If transitory things, which soon decay,   35
Age must be loveliest at the latest day.

But name not winter faces, whose skin's slack,
Lank as an unthrift's purse, but a soul's sack,
Whose eyes seek light within, for all here's shade,
Whose mouths are holes, rather worn out than made,   40
Whose every tooth to a several place is gone
To vex their souls at resurrection;
Name not these living death's-heads unto me,
For these not ancient, but antique[10] be.
I hate extremes; yet I had rather stay   45
With tombs than cradles, to wear out a day.
Since such love's natural lation is,[11] may still
My love descend and journey down the hill,
Not panting after growing beauties. So
I shall ebb on[12] with them who homeward go.   50

[ELEGY XVI] ON HIS MISTRESS[1]

By our first strange and fatal[2] interview,
By all desires which thereof did ensue,
By our long starving hopes, by that remorse[3]
Which my words' masculine, persuasive force
Begot in thee, and by the memory   5
Of hurts which spies and rivals threaten'd me,
I calmly beg; but by thy father's wrath,
By all pains which want and divorcement hath,
I conjure thee; and all the oaths which I
And thou have sworn to seal joint constancy,   10
Here I unswear, and overswear them thus:
Thou shalt not love by ways[4] so dangerous.[5]

[4]I.e., the victory of gaining his love without granting hers.
[5]Legal officer, who exacts retribution and executes punishment?
[6]Title. [7]Text *ne'r their*. [8]Text *stay*.
[9]*So shall...be*: i.e., alive, I shall be the stage of your continuing triumph; otherwise, your dead victim (as in a Roman triumph).
[10]*Then, lest...too*: text *Lest thou thy love and hate and me undoe, | To let mee live, Oh love and hate mee too.*
THE AUTUMNAL [1]Although Miss Gardner, for various reasons, has reduced the twenty "Elegies" brought together by Grierson to thirteen, I have retained his numbering for the three reprinted here. "The Autumnal" first appeared in 1633, "On His Mistress" in 1635, and "To His Mistress Going to Bed" in 1669. My texts are based upon these first editions. [2]Text *Affections*.
[3]Text *they'are*. [4]Tested. [5]Trenches, furrows (i.e., wrinkles). [6]Anchorite.
[7]Permanent dwelling (as opposed to places where he stays on a *progress* or official visitation.) [8]I.e., in youth.
[9]*Xerxes'...tree*: According to Herodotus, Xerxes, king of Persia, was so much attracted to an ancient plane tree (*platan*) in Lydia that he had it decked with golden ornaments.
[10]Antic, grotesque. Miss Gardner follows some of the manuscripts in reading *Antiques*.
[11]*Natural...lation*: text *motion natural*. Lation is an astronomical term for the movement of a body from one place to another.
[12]Text *out*.
ON HIS MISTRESS [1]At its first appearance in 1635 this poem was printed with the "Funeral Elegies." [2]Fated, predetermined.
[3]Pity. [4]Most manuscripts read *means*.
[5]The "dangerous" situation is made clear by the title in some manuscripts: "On His Mistress' Desire To Be Disguised and To Go Like a Page with Him."

Temper, O fair love, love's impetuous rage;
Be my true mistress still, not my feign'd page.
I'll go, and by thy kind leave, leave behind   15
Thee, only worthy to nurse in my mind
Thirst to come back. O, if thou die before,
My soul from other lands to thee shall soar.
Thy (else almighty) beauty cannot move
Rage from the seas, nor thy love teach them love,   20
Nor tame wild Boreas' harshness.[6] Thou hast read
How roughly he in pieces shivered
Fair Orithyia, whom he swore he lov'd.
Fall ill or good, 'tis madness to have prov'd[7]
Dangers unurg'd. Feed on this flattery: 25
That absent lovers one in th' other be.
Dissemble nothing, not a boy,[8] nor change
Thy body's habit,[9] nor mind's; be not strange
To thyself only; all will spy in thy face
A blushing, womanly, discovering grace.   30
Richly cloth'd apes are call'd apes, and as soon
Eclips'd as bright, we call the moon the moon.
Men of France, changeable chameleons,
Spitals[10] of diseases, shops of fashions,
Love's fuelers,[11] and the rightest company   35
Of players which upon the world's stage be,
Will quickly know thee, and know thee, and alas![12]
Th' indifferent Italian, as we pass
His warm land, well content to think thee page,
Will hunt[13] thee with such lust and hideous rage   40
As Lot's fair guests[14] were vex'd. But none of these,
Nor spongy, hydroptic[15] Dutch shall thee displease
If thou stay here. O stay here! for, for thee
England is only a worthy gallery[16]
To walk in expectation, till from thence   45
Our great King call thee into his presence.
When I am gone, dream me some happiness,
Nor let thy looks our long-hid love confess,
Nor praise nor dispraise me, nor bless nor curse
Openly love's force, nor in bed fright thy nurse   50
With midnight's startings, crying out, "O! O!
Nurse! O! my love is slain! I saw him go
O'er the white Alps alone; I saw him, I,
Assail'd, fight, taken, stabb'd, bleed, fall, and die."
Augur[17] me better chance, except dread Jove   55
Think it enough for me to have had thy love.

[ELEGY XIX] TO HIS MISTRESS GOING TO BED

Come, Madam, come, all rest my powers defy;
Until I labor, I in labor lie.
The foe ofttimes, having the foe in sight,
Is tir'd with standing though he never fight.
Off with that girdle, like heaven's zone[1] glittering,   5
But a far fairer world encompassing.
Unpin that spangled breastplate,[2] which you wear
That th' eyes of busy fools may be stopp'd there.
Unlace yourself, for that harmonious chime
Tells me from you that now it is bedtime.   10
Off with that happy busk,[3] which I envy,

That still can be, and still can stand so nigh.
Your gown going off such beauteous state reveals
As when from[4] flow'ry meads th' hill's shadow[5] steals.
Off with that wiry coronet, and show   15
The hairy diadem which on you[6] doth grow.
Now off with those shoes and then safely[7] tread
In this, Love's hallow'd temple, this soft bed.
In such white robes heaven's angels us'd to be
Receiv'd by[8] men; thou, angel, bring'st with thee   20
A heaven like Mahomet's paradise.[9] And though
Ill spirits walk in white, we eas'ly know
By this these angels from an evil sprite:
Those set our hairs, but these our flesh upright.
License my roving hands and let them go   25
Before, behind, between, above, below.
O my America, my new-found land!
My kingdom, safeliest[10] when with one man mann'd,
My mine of precious stones, my empery,[11]
How blest am I in this[12] discovering thee!   30
To enter in these bonds is to be free;
Then where my hand is set, my seal shall be.
Full nakedness, all joys are due to thee!
As souls unbodied, bodies uncloth'd must be
To taste whole joys. Gems which you women use   35
Are like Atalanta's balls,[13] cast in men's views
That when a fool's eye lighteth on a gem,
His earthly soul may covet theirs,[14] not them.
Like pictures, or like books' gay coverings made
For laymen, are all women thus arrayed;   40
Themselves are mystic books, which only we[15]

[6]In Greek mythology, Boreas, the north wind, boisterously wooed and then abducted Orithyia, an Athenian princess. The destruction of the woman appears to be Donne's addition.
[7]Endured, tried, exposed oneself to.
[8]*Dissemble . . . boy*: i.e., hide nothing, and do not impersonate a boy.
[9]1. clothing; 2. constitution. [10]Leper lazar houses.
[11]I.e., inflamers.
[12]*Will quickly . . . alas!*: text *Will quickly know thee, and no lease, alas!* The emendation, which has strong manuscript support, preserves the pun on *know*: 1) recognize, 2) have carnal knowledge of.
[13]Most manuscripts read *haunt*.
[14]I.e., the two angels who visited Lot in Sodom (Genesis 19).
[15]Insatiably thirsty. [16]Corridor, anteroom. [17]Prophesy for.
TO HIS MISTRESS GOING TO BED [1]The belt or girdle on the constellation Orion, or perhaps the outermost sphere of the universe wherein the fixed stars wheel.
[2]Stomacher, an ornamental covering for the chest, worn under the bodice lacing. [3]Corset. [4]Text *through*. [5]Text *shadows*.
[6]Text *your head*. [7]Text *softly*. [8]Text *Reveal'd to*.
[9]I.e., a place of sensual delights. [10]Text *My Kingdom's safest*.
[11]Domain of an emperor.
[12]*How blest am I in this*: text *How am I blest in thus*.
[13]Text *ball*. In Greek legend, the fleet Atalanta was defeated in a footrace when Hippomenes distracted her by throwing three golden apples in her path.   [14]*Covet theirs*: text *court that*.
[15]*Themselves . . . we*: text *Themselves are only mystick books, which we*.

(Whom their imputed grace will dignify)[16]
Must see revealed. Then, since that I may know,
As liberally as to a[17] midwife show
Thyself. Cast all, yea, this white linen hence; 45
Here is no penance, much less innocence.[18]
To teach thee, I am naked first. Why then,
What need'st thou have more covering than a man?

SATIRES

SATIRE III

Kind pity chokes my spleen[1]; brave scorn forbids
Those tears to issue which swell my eyelids;
I must not laugh, nor weep[2] sins and be wise.
Can railing, then, cure these worn maladies?
Is not our mistress, fair Religion, 5
As worthy of all our souls' devotion
As virtue was in[3] the first, blinded[4] age?
Are not heaven's joys as valiant to assuage
Lusts as earth's honor was to them? Alas,
As we do them in means, shall they surpass 10
Us in the end? and shall thy father's spirit
Meet blind philosophers in heaven, whose merit
Of strict life may be imputed faith,[5] and hear
Thee, whom he taught so easy ways and near
To follow, damn'd? O, if thou dar'st, fear this; 15
This fear great courage and high valor is.
Dar'st thou aid mutinous Dutch, and dar'st thou lay
Thee in ships, wooden sepulchers, a prey
To leaders' rage, to storms, to shot, to dearth?
Dar'st thou dive seas, and dungeons[6] of the earth? 20
Hast thou courageous fire to thaw the ice
Of frozen north discoveries? And thrice
Colder than salamanders,[7] like divine
Children in th' oven,[8] fires of Spain and the Line.[9]
Whose countries limbecs[10] to our bodies be, 25
Canst thou for gain bear? and must every he
Which cries not "Goddess!" to thy mistress, draw,
Or eat thy poisonous words? Courage of straw!
O desperate coward, wilt thou seem bold, and
To thy foes and His (who made thee to stand 30
Soldier in His world's garrison) thus yield,
And for forbidden wars leave th' appointed field?
Know thy foes; the foul devil, whom[11] thou
Strivest to please, for hate, not love, would allow
Thee fain his whole realm, to be quit[12], and as 35
The world's all parts wither away and pass,
So the world's self, thy other lov'd foe, is
In her decrepit wane, and thou, loving this,
Dost love a withered and worn strumpet; last,
Flesh (itself death) and joys which flesh can taste 40
Thou lovest, and thy fair, goodly soul, which doth
Give this flesh power to taste joy, thou dost loathe.
Seek true Religion. O where? Mirreus,
Thinking her unhous'd here[13] and fled from us,
Seeks her at Rome—there, because he doth know 45

That she was there a thousand years ago;
He loves her rags so as[14] we here obey[15]
The state-cloth[16] where the prince sat yesterday.
Crants to such brave loves will not be enthrall'd,
But loves her only who at Geneva is call'd 50
Religion, plain, simple, sullen, young,
Contemptuous, yet unhandsome; as among
Lecherous humors there is one that judges
No wenches wholesome but coarse country drudges.
Graius stays still at home here, and because 55
Some preachers (vile, ambitious bawds) and laws,
Still new[17] like fashions, bid[18] him think that she
Which dwells with us is only perfect, he
Embraceth her whom his godfathers will
Tender to him, being tender,[19] as wards still 60
Take such wives as their guardians offer, or
Pay values.[20] Careless Phrygius doth abhor
All, because all cannot be good, as one,
Knowing some women whores, dares marry none.
Graccus loves all as one,[21] and thinks that so 65
As women do in divers countries go
In divers habits, yet are still one kind,
So doth, so is Religion; and this blind-
ness too much light breeds. But unmoved thou
Of force must one, and, forc'd, but one allow, 70
And the right. Ask thy father which is she.
Let him ask his. Though Truth and Falsehood be
Near twins, yet Truth a little elder is.
Be busy to seek her; believe me this:
He's not of none, nor worst, that seeks the best. 75
To adore or scorn an image, or protest[22]

[16]*Whom...dignify*: i.e., who are ennobled, like the Christian faithful made worthy of salvation (*dignified*) by the *imputed grace* of Christ. [17]Text *thy*.
[18]*Here is...innocence*: text *There is no pennance due to innocence*.
SATIRE III [1]*Kind...spleen*: Natural (*kind*) compassion tempers my ridicule and laughter. [2]Lament.
[3]Some manuscripts and editors read *to*.
[4]I.e., deprived of Christian revelation.
[5]*Whose merit...faith*: i.e., whose good works may be as efficacious as the "imputed faith" that most Protestants thought essential for salvation. [6]Caves and mines.
[7]Salamanders were thought to be so cold that they could extinguish fire on contact.
[8]*Children...oven*: Shadrach, Meshach, and Abednego, servants of God who survived the fiery furnace into which King Nebuchadnezzar cast them (Daniel 3.8–30).
[9]*Fires...Line*: i.e., the torrid regions held by Spain along the Equator (*Line*). Donne is perhaps thinking also of the fires of the Spanish Inquisition. [10]Alembics, stills.
[11]*Know...whom*: text *Know thy foe, the foule devil h' is, whom*.
[12]*The foul devil...quit*: i.e., moved by hatred rather than by love, the devil, whom you strive to please, would gladly (*fain*) give you all of hell to be rid (*quit*) of you. [13]Text *her*.
[14]I.e., in the same way that. [15]Do obeisance to.
[16]Canopy over a throne. [17]Continually changing. [18]Text *bids*.
[19]Young, compliant.
[20]A ward refusing a marriage arranged by his guardian was obliged to pay a fine (*values*); an Englishman paid a fine for nonattendance at an Anglican church. [21]All alike. [22]I.e., be a Protestant.

May all be bad. Doubt wisely: in strange way
To stand inquiring right is not to stray;
To sleep or run wrong is. On a huge hill,
Cragged[23] and steep, Truth stands, and he that will   80
Reach[24] her, about must and about must go,
And what the hill's suddenness resists, win so.[25]
Yet strive so that before age, death's twilight,
Thy soul rest, for none can work in that night.
To will implies delay; therefore now do.   85
Hard deeds the body's pains, hard knowledge too[26]
The mind's endeavors reach; and mysteries
Are like the sun, dazzling, yet plain to all eyes.
Keep the truth which thou hast found; men do not stand
In so ill case that God hath with His hand   90
Sign'd kings blank charters to kill whom they hate,
Nor are they vicars, but hangmen to Fate.
Fool and wretch, wilt thou let thy soul be tied
To men's laws, by which she shall not be tried
At the last day? Will it then boot[27] thee   95
To say a Philip or a Gregory,
A Harry or a Martin[28] taught thee this?
Is not this excuse for mere[29] contraries,
Equally strong? Cannot both sides say so?
That thou mayest rightly obey power, her   100
   bounds know;
Those pass'd, her nature and name is chang'd; to be
Then humble to her is idolatry.
As streams are, power is; those blest flowers that dwell
At the rough stream's calm head thrive and do well,   105
But having left their roots and themselves given
To the stream's tyrannous rage, alas, are driven
Through mills and rocks and woods, and at last, almost
Consum'd in going, in the sea are lost.
So perish souls which more choose men's unjust   110
Power from God claim'd than God himself to trust.

LETTERS TO SEVERAL PERSONAGES

THE STORM. TO MASTER CHRISTOPHER BROOKE[1]

Thou which art I ('tis nothing to be so),
Thou which art still thyself, by these shalt know
Part of our passage; and a hand or eye
By Hilliard[2] drawn is worth an history
By a worse painter made; and (without pride)   5
When by thy judgment they are dignified,
My lines are such. 'Tis the preeminence
Of friendship only to impute excellence.

England, to whom we owe what we be and have,
Sad that her sons did seek a foreign grave   10
(For fate's or fortune's drifts none can soothsay;[3]
Honor and misery have one face and way),
From out her pregnant entrails sigh'd a wind
Which at th' air's middle, marble room[4] did find
Such strong resistance that itself it threw   15
Downward again, and so when it did view

How in the port our fleet dear time did leese,[5]
Withering like prisoners which lie but for fees,[6]
Mildly it kiss'd our sails, and fresh and sweet,
As to a stomach starv'd, whose insides meet,   20
Meat comes, it came and swole our sails, when we
So joy'd as Sarah her swelling joy'd to see.[7]
But 'twas but so kind as our countrymen
Which bring friends one day's way[8] and leave them then.
Then, like two mighty kings which, dwelling far   25
Asunder, meet against a third to war,
The south and west winds join'd, and as they blew,
Waves like a rolling trench before them threw.
Sooner than you read this line did the gale,
Like shot not fear'd till felt, our sails assail,   30
And what at first was call'd a gust, the same
Hath now a storm's, anon a tempest's name.
Jonas, I pity thee, and curse those men
Who when the storm rag'd most, did wake thee then;[9]
Sleep is pain's easiest salve, and doth fulfill   35
All offices of death except to kill.
But when I wak'd, I saw that I saw not;
I and the sun which should teach me had forgot
East, west, day, night; and I could only say
If the world had lasted, now it had been day.   40
Thousands our noises were; yet we 'mongst all
Could none by his right name, but thunder, call.
Lightning was all our light, and it rain'd more
Than if the sun had drunk the sea before.
Some coffin'd in their cabins lie, equally   45

[23]Many manuscripts read *Ragged*.   [24]Achieve.
[25]*And what...win so*: i.e., attain the summit, despite the steepness (*suddenness*) of the hill, by only one means—going about and about.
[26]*Text to*   [27]Profit
[28]*Philip...Martin*: Philip II of Spain, Pope Gregory, Henry VIII, and Martin Luther.   [29]Absolute.
TO MASTER CHRISTOPHER BROOKE [1]A close friend of Donne at Lincoln's Inn who was subsequently imprisoned for his part in Donne's clandestine marriage to Ann More (see p. 56). This verse letter, together with its companion piece "The Calm," was written while Donne was with the so-called Islands Expedition led by the earl of Essex to divert Philip II's threatened invasion of England in 1597. Soon after setting sail for the Azores in July the fleet of sixty ships was so severely buffeted by a storm that it put back to Plymouth for repairs.
[2]Nicholas Hilliard (1547-1619), a painter and jeweler especially admired for his miniatures.   [3]Predict truly.
[4]*Th' air's middle, marble room*: The intensely cold "middle air" above the earth was regarded as the seat of hail and snow. In calling it *marble* Donne is perhaps alluding to its whiteness.   [5]Lose.
[6]*Which lie...fees*: i.e., who are held in prison after serving their terms because they lack money to pay the jailer's fees.
[7]*Sarah...see*: When the aged Sarah realized that she was going to bear a child to Abraham she "laughed within herself" (Genesis 18.12).
[8]*Bring...way*: i.e., accompany departing guests on their first day's journey.
[9]*Jonas...then*: As Jonah lay sleeping through a fearful storm at sea, the shipmaster said to him, "What meanest thou, O sleeper? Arise, call upon thy God, if so be that God will think upon us, that we perish not" (Jonah 1.6).

Griev'd that they are not dead and yet must die;
And as sin-burd'ned souls from graves[10] will creep
At the last day, some forth their cabins peep
And tremblingly ask what news, and do hear so,
Like jealous husbands, what they would not know.   50
Some, sitting on the hatches, would seem there
With hideous gazing to fear[11] away fear.
Then note they the ship's sicknesses, the mast
Shak'd with this ague, and the hold and waist[12]
With salt dropsy clogg'd, and all our tacklings   55
Snapping like too high-stretched treble strings.
And from our totter'd[13] sails rags drop down so
As from one hang'd in chains a year ago.
Even our ordnance, plac'd for our defense,
Strive to break loose and 'scape away from thence.   60
Pumping hath tir'd our men, and what's the gain?
Seas into seas thrown we suck in again;
Hearing hath deaf'd our sailors, and if they
Knew how to hear, there's none knows what to say.
Compar'd to these storms, death is but a qualm,   65
Hell somewhat lightsome, and the Bermuda calm.[14]
Darkness, Light's eldest brother, his birthright
Claims o'er this world, and to heaven hath chas'd Light.
All things are one, and that one none can be,
Since all forms, uniform deformity   70
Doth cover so that we, except God say
Another *Fiat,* shall have no more day.[15]
So violent, yet long, these furies be
That though thine absence starve[16] me, I wish not thee.

TO SIR EDWARD HERBERT AT JULIERS[1]

Man is a lump where all beasts kneaded be;
Wisdom makes him an ark where all agree.
The fool, in whom these beasts do live at jar,
Is sport to others and a theater;
Nor 'scapes he so, but is himself their prey;   5
All which was man in him is eat away,
And now his beasts on one another feed,
Yet couple in anger and new monsters breed.
How happy is he which hath due place assign'd
To his beasts, and disafforested[2] his mind!   10
Empal'd[3] himself to keep them out, not in,
Can sow, and dares trust corn where they have been,
Can use his horse, goat, wolf, and every beast,
And is not ass himself to all the rest!
Else man not only is the herd of swine,   15
But he's those devils too which did incline
Them to a headlong rage and made them worse;[4]
For man can add weight to heaven's heaviest curse.
As souls (they say) by our first touch[5] take in
The poisonous tincture of original sin,   20
So to the punishments which God doth fling,
Our apprehension contributes the sting.
To us as to His chickens He doth cast
Hemlock, and we, as men, His hemlock taste;[6]
We do infuse to what He meant for meat   25
Corrosiveness, or intense cold or heat;[7]
For God no such specific poison hath

As kills we know not how; His fiercest wrath
Hath no antipathy, but may be good
At least for physic, if not for our food.   30
Thus man, that might be his pleasure, is his rod,
And is his devil that might be his God.
Since, then, our business is to rectify
Nature to what she was,[8] we are led awry
By them who man to us in little show.[9]   35
Greater than due, no form we can bestow
On him, for man into himself can draw
All, all his faith can swallow or reason chaw,
All that is fill'd and all that which doth fill,
All the round world to man is but a pill;   40
In all it works not, but it is in all
Poisonous or purgative or cordial;[10]
For knowledge kindles calentures[11] in some,
And is to others icy opium.
As brave[12] as true is that profession[13] than   45
Which you do use to make—that you know man.
This makes it credible: you have dwelt upon
All worthy books, and now are such an one.
Actions are authors, and of those, in you
Your friends find every day a mart[14] of new.   50

TO THE COUNTESS OF SALISBURY.[1]
AUGUST 1614

Fair, great, and good, since seeing you we see
What heaven can do and what any earth can be;

[10]Text *grave.* [11]Frighten [12]Midships. [13]Tattered.
[14]*Compar'd...calm*: i.e., compared to these savage storms death is a mere fit of giddiness, hell is entertaining, and the notoriously stormy Bermuda is tranquil.
[15]*All things...day*: i.e., everything has been reduced to nothing (*none*) by darkness, and this general nothingness (*uniform deformity*), like primeval chaos, is so profound that it will take another *Fiat lux* ("Let there be light") from God to illuminate the darkened world. [16]Kill.

TO SIR EDWARD HERBERT [1]In 1610 Sir Edward Herbert (later Lord Herbert of Cherbury) had joined the Protestant forces commanded by the prince of Orange at Juliers in the Low Countries, where the Catholics were besieged. According to Herbert's characteristically immodest account in his *Autobiography*, he was the "first of all the nations there" to penetrate the barricades. For Herbert's "The State Progress of Ill," which presumably prompted Donne's epistle, see p. 118.
[2]In English law, land converted from woodland used for hunting to land used for grazing and agriculture, i.e., civilized. [3]Fenced.
[4]*Those devils...worse*: When two demons, exorcised by Jesus, entered a herd of Gadarene swine, "the whole herd of swine ran violently down a steep place into the sea, and perished in the waters" (Matthew 8.32). [5]I.e., at first contact with the body.
[6]*Hemlock...taste*: The ancients thought that hemlock, which was fatal to men, was nutritious for fowls.
[7]*Corrosiveness...heat*: effects by which various poisons were thought to kill. Hemlock was "cold"; cf. "icy opium," line 44.
[8]I.e., before the fall.
[9]*We are...show*: i.e., we are misled by those who describe men as a microcosm. [10]Invigorating. [11]Fevers. [12]Splendid.
[13]Assertion. [14]Large and varied supply.
TO THE COUNTESS OF SALISBURY [1]Catherine Howard, youngest daughter of Thomas, first earl of Suffolk, was the wife of William

Since now your beauty shines, now, when the sun,
Grown stale, is to so low a value run
That his dishevel'd beams and scattered fires   5
Serve but for ladies' periwigs and tires[2]
In lovers' sonnets—you come to repair
God's book of creatures,[3] teaching what is fair;
Since now, when all is withered, shrunk, and dried,
All virtues ebb'd out to a dead low tide,   10
All the world's frame being crumbled into sand
Where every man thinks by himself to stand,
Integrity, friendship, and confidence
(Cements of greatness) being vapor'd hence,
And narrow man being fill'd with little shares   15
(Court, city, church are all shops of small wares,
All having blown to sparks their noble fire
And drawn their sound gold ingot into wire,
All trying by a love of littleness
To make abridgments and to draw to less   20
Even that nothing which at first we were),
Since in these times your greatness doth appear,
And that we learn by it that man to get
Towards Him that's infinite must first be great;
Since in an age so ill, as none is fit   25
So much as to accuse, much less mend it—
For who can judge or witness of those times
Where all alike are guilty of the crimes?
Where he that would be good is thought by all
A monster, or at best fantastical?—   30
Since now you durst be good, and that I do
Discern by daring to contemplate you
That there may be degrees of fair, great, good,
Through your light, largeness, virtue understood:
If in this sacrifice[4] of mine be shown   35
Any small spark of these, call it your own.
And if things like these have been said by me
Of others, call not that idolatry,
For had God made man first, and man had seen
The third day's fruits and flowers and various green, 40
He might have said the best that he could say
Of those fair creatures which were made that day,
And when next day he had admir'd the birth
Of sun, moon, stars, fairer than late-prais'd earth,
He might have said the best that he could say,   45
And not be chid for praising yesterday;
So though some things are not together true,
As that another is worthiest, and that you,[5]
Yet to say so doth not condemn a man
If when he spoke them, they were both true than.[6]   50
How fair a proof of this in our soul grows!
We first have souls of growth and sense, and those,
When our last soul, our soul immortal, came,[7]
Were swallowed into it, and have no name.
Nor doth he injure those souls which[8] doth cast   55
The power and praise of both them on the last.
No more do I wrong any; I adore
The same things now which I ador'd before,
The subject chang'd and measure; the same thing
In a low constable and in the king   60
I reverence: his power to work on me.

So did I humbly reverence each degree
Of fair, great, good; but more, now I am come
From having found their *walks* to find their *home*.
And as I owe my first souls thanks that they   65
For my last soul did fit and mold my clay,
So am I debtor unto them whose worth
Enabled me to profit, and take forth
This new great lesson, thus to study you,
Which none, not reading others first, could do.   70
Nor lack I light to read this book, though I
In a dark cave, yea, in a grave do lie,
For as your fellow angels, so you do
Illustrate[9] them who come to study you.
The first whom we in histories do find   75
To have profess'd all arts was one born blind.[10]
He lack'd those eyes beasts have as well as we,
Not those by which angels are seen and see;
So though I'm born without those eyes to live
Which Fortune, who hath none herself, doth give,   80
Which are fit means to see bright courts and you,
Yet, may I see you thus as now I do,
I shall by that all goodness have discern'd,
And though I burn my library, be learn'd.

THE SECOND ANNIVERSARY.[1] OF THE
PROGRESS[2] OF THE SOUL. WHEREIN BY
OCCASION OF THE RELIGIOUS DEATH OF
MISTRESS ELIZABETH DRURY THE INCOMMODITIES
OF THE SOUL IN THIS LIFE AND HER
EXALTATION IN THE NEXT ARE CONTEMPLATED

Nothing could make me sooner to confess   *The*
That this world had an everlastingness   *entrance*
Than to consider that a year is run
Since both this lower world's and the sun's sun,
The luster and the vigor of this all,   5
Did set—'twere blasphemy to say "did fall."
But as a ship which hath stroock sail doth run
By force of that force which before it won,
Or as sometimes in a beheaded man,

Cecil, second earl of Salisbury, and sister of the notorious Frances Howard, countess of Essex, whose second marriage to Robert Carr, earl of Somerset, led to the murder of Sir Thomas Overbury and thus to one of the greatest scandals of the age.   [2]Headdresses.
[3]*God's...creatures*: For Donne's own elaborate explanation of the *liber creaturarum* see his *Essays in Divinity*, p. 545.
[4]Votive offering.   [5]I.e., that you are the worthiest.
[6]*If...than*: if each was true at the time it was spoken.
[7] *We first...came*: for another of Donne's many allusions to Aristotle's doctrine of man's tripartite soul (vegetative, sensory, and rational) see p. 77, l. 162.   [8]Who.   [9]Illuminate.
[10]Tiresias, a blind soothsayer of Greek mythology? Homer?
THE SECOND ANNIVERSARY   [1]This and its companion piece "The First Anniversary," two annual commemorations of the death (1610) of Elizabeth Drury, the fourteen-year-old daughter of Sir Robert Drury, were the only important poems that Donne himself published. The text is based upon the first edition of 1612.
[2]Royal journey.

Though[3] at those two Red Seas which freely ran,   10
One from the trunk, another from the head,
His soul be sail'd to her eternal bed,
His eyes will twinkle,[4] and his tongue will roll,
As though he beckon'd and call'd back his soul,
He grasps his hands, and he pulls up his feet,   15
And seems to reach, and to step forth to meet
His soul when all these motions which we saw
Are but as ice which crackles at a thaw,
Or as a lute which in moist weather rings
Her knell alone by cracking of her strings,   20
So struggles this dead world now she is gone;
For there is motion in corruption.
As some days are at the creation nam'd
Before the sun, the which fram'd days, was fram'd.[5]
So after this sun's set some show appears,   25
And orderly vicissitude[6] of years.
Yet a new Deluge, and of Lethe[7] flood,
Hath drown'd us all: all have forgot all good,
Forgetting her, the main reserve of all.
Yet in this deluge, gross and general,   30
Thou seest me strive for life. My life shall be
To be hereafter prais'd for praising thee,
Immortal maid, who, though thou wouldst refuse
The name of mother, be unto my Muse
A father, since her chaste ambition is   35
Yearly to bring forth such a child as this.
These hymns may work on future wits, and so
May great-grandchildren of thy praises grow,
And so, though not revive, embalm and spice
The world, which else would putrefy with vice;   40
For thus man may extend thy progeny
Until man do but vanish, and not die.[8]
These hymns thy issue may increase so long
As till God's great *Venite*[9] change the song.
Thirst for that time, O my insatiate soul,   *A just disesti-* 45
And serve thy thirst with God's safe-   *mation of this*
      sealing[10] bowl.   *world*
Be thirsty still and drink still till thou go;
'Tis[11] th' only health, to be hydropic[12] so.
Forget this rotten world, and unto thee
Let thine own times as an old story be.   50
Be not concern'd. Study not why nor whan;
Do not so much as not believe a man,
For though to err be worst, to try truths forth[13]
Is far more business than this world is worth.
The world is but a carcass; thou art fed   55
By it but as a worm that[14] carcass bred.
And why shouldst thou, poor worm, consider more
When this world will grow better than before
Than those thy fellow-worms do think upon
That carcass's last resurrection?   60
Forget this world, and scarce think of it so
As of old clothes cast off a year ago.
To be thus stupid[15] is alacrity;
Men thus lethargic[16] have best memory.
Look upward; that's towards her whose happy state   65
We now lament not, but congratulate.[17]

She to whom all this world was[18] but a stage
Where all sat heark'ning how her youthful age
Should be employ'd, because in all she did
Some figure[19] of the golden times was hid,   70
Who could not lack whate'er this world could give,
Because she was the form[20] that made it live,
Nor could complain that this world was unfit
To be stay'd in, then when she was in it;
She that first tried[21] indifferent desires   75
By virtue, and virtue by religious fires;
She to whose person paradise adher'd
As courts to princes; she whose eyes enspher'd
Star-light enough t' have made the south control
(Had she been there) the star-full northern pole[22]   80
She, she is gone. She is gone. When thou knowest this,
What fragmentary rubbidge[23] this world is
Thou knowest, and that it is not worth a thought,
He honors it too much that thinks   *Contemplation*
   it nought.   *of our state in*
Think then, my soul, that Death is but   *our death-bed*
   a groom   85
Which brings a taper to the outward room,
Whence thou spiest first a little, glimmering light,
And after brings it nearer to thy sight;
For such approaches doth heaven make in death.
Think thyself laboring now with broken breath,   90
And think those broken and soft notes to be
Division[24] and thy happiest harmony.
Think thee laid on thy death-bed, loose and slack,
And think that but unbinding of a pack
To take one precious thing, thy soul, from thence.   95
Think thyself parch'd with fever's violence;
Anger thine ague more by calling it
Thy physic;[25] chide the slackness of the fit.

---

[3]Text *Through*. This is one of several emendations authorized by an errata slip pasted into a copy of the 1612 edition and discovered only in 1946. [4]Blink.

[5]*As some days...fram'd*: The sun, the moon, and the stars were not created until the fourth day (Genesis 1.14–19).

[6]Changes, i.e., succession.

[7]River in Hades, a drink from which produced oblivion.

[8]*Until...die*: i.e., until the Day of Judgment, when those who are then alive will proceed directly from this world to the next. See Luke 9.27, 1 Corinthians 15.51–52.

[9]"Come" (the first word of Psalm 95).

[10]The Eucharistic cup, giving assurance of saving grace, like the seals that marked the servants of God mentioned in Revelation 7.3–4. The text reads *safe-fealing*.

[11]Text *T'o*, corrected in the errata slip.

[12]Dropsical (and hence continually thirsty). Text *Hydroptique*, corrected in the errata slip. [13]*Try...forth*: test thoroughly.

[14]Maggot that. [15]Stupefied. [16]Forgetful. [17]Rejoice with.

[18]Text *twas*, corrected in the errata slip. [19]Likeness.

[20]In Scholastic philosophy, the soul, conceived as the essential and defining principle of man. [21]Refined, purified.

[22]It was long believed that the northern sky had many more stars than the southern. [23]Rubbish.

[24]In music, a rapid run of notes embellishing a melodic line. [25]Medicine, remedy.

Think that thou hear'st thy knell, and think no more
But that as bells call'd thee to church before,   100
So this to the Triumphant Church[26] calls thee.
Think Satan's sergeants round about thee be,
And think that but for legacies they thrust;
Give one thy pride, to another give thy lust;
Give them those sins which they gave thee before,   105
And trust th' immaculate blood to wash thy score.[27]
Think thy friends weeping round, and think that they
Weep but because they go not yet thy way.
Think that they close thine eyes, and think in this
That they confess much in the world amiss,   110
Who dare not trust a dead man's eye with that
Which they from God and angels cover not.
Think that they shroud thee up, and think from thence
They reinvest[28] thee in white innocence.
Think that thy body rots, and (if so low,   115
Thy soul exalted so, thy thoughts can go)
Think thee a prince, who of themselves create
Worms which insensibly devour their state.
Think that they bury thee, and think that rite
Lays thee to sleep but a Saint Lucy's night.[29]   120
Think these things cheerfully, and if thou be
Drowsy or slack, remember then that she,
She whose complexion[30] was so even made
That which of her ingredients should invade
The other three no fear, no art[31] could guess,   125
So far were all remov'd from more or less;
But as in mithridate[32] or just[33] perfumes,
Where, all good things being met, no one presumes
To govern or to triumph on[34] the rest,
Only because all were, no part was best,   130
And as, though all do know that quantities
Are made of lines, and lines from points arise,
None can these lines or quantities unjoint
And say this is a line, or this a point,
So, though the elements and humors were   135
In her, one could not say, this governs there;
Whose even constitution might have won[35]
Any disease to venter[36] on the sun
Rather than her, and make a spirit fear
That he to disuniting subject were;[37]   140
To whose proportions if we would compare
Cubes, they're unstable, circles angular;
She who was such a chain[38] as Fate employs
To bring mankind all fortunes it enjoys,
So fast, so even wrought, as one would think   145
No accident could threaten any link—
She, she embrac'd a sickness, gave it meat,[39]
The purest blood and breath that e'er it eat,
And hath taught us that though a good man hath
Title to heaven, and plead it by his faith,   150
And though he may pretend[40] a conquest (since
Heaven was content to suffer violence),[41]
Yea, though he plead a long possession too
(For they are in heaven on earth who heaven's works do),
Though he had right and power and place before,   155
Yet death must usher, and unlock the door.

Think further on thyself, my soul, and think   *Incommodi-*
How thou at first wast made but in a sink;[42]   *ties of the soul*
Think that it argued some infirmity   *in the body*
That those two souls which then thou foundst in me   160
Thou fed'st upon and drew'st into thee, both
My second soul of sense and first of growth.[43]
Think but how poor thou wast, how obnoxious,[44]
Whom a small lump of flesh could poison thus.
This curded milk, this poor unlittered[45] whelp,   165
My body, could, beyond escape or help,
Infect thee with original sin, and thou
Couldst neither then refuse, nor leave it now.
Think that no stubborn, sullen anchorit
Which fix'd to a pillar or a grave doth sit,   170
Bedded and bath'd in all his ordures, dwells
So foully as our souls in their first-built cells.
Think in how poor a prison thou didst lie
After, enabled but to suck and cry.
Think, when 'twas grown to most, 'twas a poor inn,   175
A province pack'd up in two yards of skin,
And that usurped or threat'ned with the rage
Of sicknesses or their true mother, age.
But think that death hath now enfranchis'd[46]
   thee;   *Her liberty*
Thou hast thy expansion[47] now, and liberty.   *by death*   180
Think that a rusty piece,[48] discharg'd, is flown
In pieces, and the bullet is his own[49]
And freely flies. This to thy soul allow:
Think thy sheel[50] broke, think thy soul hatch'd but now,
And think this slow-pac'd soul, which late did cleave   185

[26]The church in heaven, victorious over evil, as distinguished from the Church Militant on earth.
[27]Debt (continuing the figure introduced by *Satan's sergeants*, i.e., bailiffs or officers, in line 102). [28]Reclothe.
[29]December 13, in the Julian or Old Style calendar, generally regarded as the longest night of the year. See "A Nocturnal upon St. Lucy's Day," p. 66.
[30]In Elizabethan psychology, the mixture of the four *humors* (see Glossary) that determines personality.
[31]I.e., no anxious or skilled observer; neither her family and friends' physicians.
[32]An antidote against poison and infection (attributed to Mithridates VI, king of Pontus (d. 63 B.C.) that was composed of many ingredients. [33]I.e., carefully blended. [34]Text *no*.
[35]Text *worne*, corrected in the errata slip. [36]Venture against, attack.
[37]*A spirit fear...were*: Any spirit (i.e., souls, angels, or devils) was thought to be a simple, non-compounded being and therefore incapable of division (*disuniting*) into constituent elements.
[38]The *aurea catena Homeri* or golden chain of Homer (*Iliad*, VIII.19), from antiquity allegorized as the unalterable sequence of cause and effect that governs all earthly things. [39]Food. [40]Claim.
[41]"And from the days of John the Baptist until now the kingdom of heaven suffereth violence, and the violent take it by force" (Matthew 11.12). [42]Sewer.
[43]*My second soul...growth*: On the basis of Aristotle's *De anima* most of Donne's contemporaries recognized three kinds of soul: one of growth or vegetation (as in plants), one of sense perception and motion (as in animals), and one of reason and understanding (as in man). [44]Exposed to injury. [45]Unborn. [46]Liberated.
[47]Text *expausion*. [48]Firearm. [49]Under its own power. [50]Shell.

To a body, and went but by the body's leave,
Twenty, perchance, or thirty mile a day,
Dispatches in a minute all the way
'Twixt heaven and earth.[51] She stays not in the air
To look what meteors there themselves prepare;   190
She carries no desire to know, nor sense,
Whether th' air's middle region be intense;[52]
For th' element of fire, she doth not know
Whether she pass'd by such a place or no;
She baits[53] not at the moon, nor cares to try[54]   195
Whether in that new world men live and die;
Venus retards her not to inquire how she
Can (being one star) Hesper and Vesper[55] be.
He that charm'd Argus' eyes, sweet Mercury,[56]
Works not on her, who now is grown all eye,   200
Who, if she meet the body of the sun,
Goes through, not staying till his course be run,
Who finds in Mars his camp no corps of guard,
Nor is by Jove nor by his father[57] barr'd,
But ere she can consider how she went,   205
At once is at and through the firmament,
And as[58] these stars were but so many beads
Strung on one string, speed undistinguish'd leads
Her through those spheres as through the beads a string,
Whose quick succession makes it still one thing.   210
As doth the pith, which, lest our bodies slack,
Strings fast the little bones of neck and back,
So by the soul doth death string heaven and earth,
For when our soul enjoys this her third birth
(Creation gave her one, a second, grace),   215
Heaven is as near and present to her face
As colors are, and objects, in a room
Where darkness was before, when tapers come.
This must, my soul, thy long-short progress be.
To advance these thoughts remember then that she,   220
She, whose fair body no such prison was
But that a soul might well be pleas'd to pass
An age in her, she whose rich beauty lent
Mintage to others' beauties, for they went[59]
But for so much as they were like to her,   225
She, in whose body (if we dare prefer[60]
This low world to so high a mark as she)
The western treasure, eastern spicery,
Europe and Afric and the unknown rest
Were easily found, or what in them was best;   230
And when w'have made this large discovery
Of all in her some one part, there[61] will be
Twenty such parts, whose plenty and riches is
Enough to make twenty such worlds as this,
She, whom had they known, who did first betroth   235
The tutelar[62] angels, and assigned one both
To nations, cities, and to companies,
To functions, offices, and dignities,
And to each several man, to him, and him,
They would have given her one for every limb,   240
She, of whose soul, if we may say 'twas gold,
Her body was th' electrum,[63] and did hold
Many degrees of that; we understood

Her by her sight; her pure and eloquent blood
Spoke in her cheeks, and so distinctly wrought[64]   245
That one might almost say her body thought—
She, she, thus richly and largely hous'd, is gone,
And chides us slow-pac'd snails who crawl upon
Our prison's prison, earth, nor think us well
Longer than whilst we bear our brittle shell.   250
But 'twere but little to have chang'd our room   *Her ignorance*
If, as we were in this our living tomb   *in this life and*
Oppress'd with ignorance, we still were so.   *knowledge in*
Poor soul, in this thy flesh what dost thou know? *the next*
Thou know'st thyself so little as thou know'st not   255
How thou didst die nor how thou wast begot.
Thou neither know'st how thou at first camest in
Nor how thou took'st the poison of man's sin.
Nor dost thou (though thou know'st that thou art so)
By what way thou art made immortal know.   260
Thou art too narrow, wretch, to comprehend
Even thyself, yea, though thou wouldst but bend
To know thy body. Have not all souls thought
For many ages that our body is wrought
Of air and fire and other elements?   265
And now they think of new ingredients,[65]
And one soul thinks one, and another way
Another thinks, and 'tis an even lay.[66]
Know'st thou but how the stone doth enter in
The bladder's cave and never break the skin?   270
Know'st thou how blood which to the heart doth flow
Doth from one ventricle to th' other go?
And for the putrid stuff which thou dost spit,
Know'st thou how thy lungs have attracted it?
There are no passages; so that there is   275
(For aught thou know'st) piercing of substances.
And of those many opinions which men raise
Of nails and hairs,[67] dost thou know which to praise?

[51]In the following passage (lines 189–206) concerning the ascent of the soul from earth to heaven Donne traces its "progress" through the Ptolemaic universe: from the terrestrial region of the warring elements (earth, water, air, fire) through the spheres of the seven planets to the firmament of the fixed stars. Here the order of Venus and Mercury is reversed.   [52]Turbulent.   [53]Pauses. [54]Ascertain.
[55]I.e., Venus, which was both the morning and the evening star.
[56]*He...Mercury*: Mercury had killed the hundred-headed herdsman Argus whom Juno had set to guard Io, a maiden whom Jove had turned into a heifer.   [57]*Jove...Father*: i.e., Jupiter and Saturn. [58]As if.
[59]Went current, had value (as a coin is accepted as currency because it bears the likeness of the sovereign).   [60]Advance, elevate.
[61]Text *then*, corrected in the errata slip.
[62]Tutelary. Donne is glancing critically at the Roman Catholic practice of assigning patron (*tutelar*) saints to specific places.
[63]An alloy of gold and silver.   [64]Worked.
[65]The innovative physician Paracelsus (d. 1541) had suggested that sickness and health depend on the proportions of salt, sulphur, and mercury in the human body.   [66]Wager.
[67]*Many opinions...hairs*: i.e., how nails and hair should be classified among parts of the body, or if indeed they should be considered parts of the body at all.

What hope have we to know ourselves, when we
Know not the least things which for our use be?   280
We see in authors, too stiff to recant,
A hundred controversies of an ant,
And yet one watches,[68] starves, freezes, and sweats
To know but catechisms and alphabets[69]
Of unconcerning[70] things, matters of fact;   285
How others on our stage their parts did act,
What Caesar did, yea, and what Cicero said.
Why grass is green, or why our blood is red
Are mysteries which none have reach'd unto.
In this low form,[71] poor soul, what wilt thou do?   290
When wilt thou shake off this pedantry[72]
Of being taught[73] by sense and fantasy?[74]
Thou look'st through spectacles; small things seem great
Below; but up unto the watch-tow'r get,
And see all things despoil'd of fallacies.   295
Thou shalt not peep through lattices of eyes,
Nor hear through labyrinths of ears, nor learn
By circuit or collections[75] to discern.
In heaven thou straight know'st all concerning it,
And what concerns it not, shall straight forget.   300
There thou (but in no other school) mayst be,
Perchance, as learned and as full as she,
She who all libraries had throughly read
At home, in her own thoughts, and practiced
So much good as would make as many more;   305
She whose example they must all implore
Who would or[76] do or think well, and confess
That aye[77] the virtuous actions they express
Are but a new and worse edition
Of her some one thought or one action;   310
She who in th' art of knowing heaven was grown
Here upon earth to such perfection
That she hath, ever since to heaven she came
(In a far fairer print)[78] but read the same—
She, she, not satisfied with all this weight   315
(For so much knowledge as would overfreight
Another did but ballast her), is gone
As well t' enjoy as get perfection,
And calls us after her in that she took
(Taking herself) our best and worthiest book.   320
Return not, my soul, from this ecstasy   *Of our com-*
And meditation of what thou shalt be,   *pany in this*
To earthly thoughts till it to thee appear   *life and in*
With whom thy conversation[79] must be there. *the next*
With whom wilt thou converse? what station   325
Canst thou choose out, free from infection,
That will nor give thee theirs nor drink in thine?
Shalt thou not find a spongy, slack divine
Drink and suck in th' instructions of great men,
And for the word of God vent them again?   330
Are there not some courts (and then, no things be
So like as courts) which in this let us see
That wits and tongues of libelers are weak,
Because they do more ill than these can speak?
The poison is gone through all; poisons affect   335
Chiefly the chiefest parts, but some effect

In nails and hairs, yea excrements,[80] will show;
So will[81] the poison of sin in the most low.
Up, up, my drowsy soul, where thy new ear
Shall in the angels' songs no discord hear;   340
Where thou shalt see the blessed Mother-maid
Joy in not being that which men have said,[82]
Where she is exalted more for being good
Than for her interest of motherhood.
Up to those patriarchs, which did longer sit   345
Expecting[83] Christ than they have enjoy'd Him yet.
Up to those prophets, which now gladly see
Their prophecies grown to be history.
Up to th' apostles, who did bravely run
All the sun's course with more light than the sun.   350
Up to those martyrs, who did calmly bleed
Oil to th' apostles' lamps, dew to their seed.
Up to those virgins, who thought[84] that almost
They made joint-tenants with the Holy Ghost
If they to any should His temple give.   355
Up, up! for in that squadron there doth live
She who hath carried thither new degrees
(As to their number) to their dignities,
She who, being to herself a state, enjoy'd
All royalties[85] which any state employ'd,   360
For she made wars and triumph'd—reason still
Did not overthrow but rectify her will;
And she made peace, for no peace is like this,
That beauty and chastity together kiss;
She did high justice, for she crucified   365
Every first motion of rebellious pride;
And she gave pardons and was liberal,
For, only herself except, she pardon'd all;
She coin'd, in this, that her impressions gave
To all our actions all the worth they have;   370
She gave protections: the thoughts of her breast
Satan's rude officers could ne'er arrest.
As these prerogatives, being met in one,
Made her a sovereign state, religion
Made her a church; and these two made her all.   375
She who was all this all, and could not fall
To worse by company (for she was still
More antidote than all the world was ill),

[68]Stays up late. [69]I.e., the bare rudiments. [70]Inconsequential
[71]1) Shape, body; 2) class in school. [72]Pedantry
[73]Text *thought*, corrected in the errata slip.
[74]In Elizabethan psychology, the mental faculty that synthesizes
sense into images of the objects perceived and presents them to the
understanding; i.e., the imagination. [75]Accumulations of data.
[76]Either. [77]Ever, always. [78]Text *point*, corrected in the errata slip.
[79]Association.
[80]Donne plays here on two distinct words, one meaning "excreted
matter" (from Latin *excernere*, to sift out), the other meaning
"outgrowth, excrescence (from Latin *excrescere*);" the latter was
frequently used of the nails and hair. Shakespeare depends on the
two senses for the comic effect of Armado's "dally with my
excrement, with my mustachio" (*Love's Labor's Lost*, V.i.104).
[81]Text *wise*, corrected in the errata slip. [82]I.e., that she was sinless.
[83]Awaiting. [84]Text *thoughts*, corrected in the errata slip.
[85]Royal prerogatives.

She, she doth leave it, and by death survive
All this in heaven, whither[86] who doth not strive   380
The more because she is there, he doth not know
That accidental[87] joys in heaven do grow.
But pause, my soul, and study, ere thou fall   *Of essential joy*
On accidental joys, th' essential.   *in this life and*
Still before accessories do abide   *in the next*   385
A trial, must the principal be tried.
And what essential joy canst thou expect
Here upon earth? what permanent effect
Of transitory causes? Dost thou love
Beauty? (And beauty worthiest is to move.)[88]   390
Poor coz'ned coz'ner, that she and that thou
Which did begin to love are neither now.
You are both fluid, chang'd since yesterday;
Next day repairs (but ill) last day's decay.
Nor are (although the river keep the name)   395
Yesterday's waters and today's the same.
So flows her face and thine eyes; neither now
That saint nor pilgrim which your loving vow[89]
Concern'd remains, but whilst you think you be
Constant, you are hourly in inconstancy.   400
Honor may have pretense unto our love,
Because that God did live so long above
Without this honor and then lov'd it so
That He at last made creatures to bestow
Honor on Him, not that He needed it,   405
But that to His hands man might grow more fit.
But since all honors from inferiors flow
(For they do give it; princes do but show
Whom they would have so honor'd) and that this
On such opinions and capacities   410
Is built as rise and fall to more and less,
Alas, 'tis but a casual[90] happiness.
Hath ever any man to himself assign'd[91]
This or that happiness to arrest his mind
But that another man, which takes a worse,   415
Thinks[92] him a fool for having ta'en that course?
They who did labor Babel's tower[93] t' erect[94]
Might have consider'd that for that effect
All this whole solid earth could not allow
Nor furnish forth materials enow,[95]   420
And that this center,[96] to raise such a place,
Was far too little to have been the base.
No more affords this world[97] foundation
To erect true joy, were all the means in one.
But as the heathen made them several gods   425
Of all God's benefits and all His rods[98]
(For as the wine and corn and onions are
Gods unto them, so agues be, and war),
And as, by changing that whole, precious gold
To such small copper coins, they lost the old,   430
And lost their only God, who ever must
Be sought alone, and not in such a thrust,[99]
So much mankind true happiness mistakes:
No joy enjoys that man that many makes.
Then, soul, to thy first pitch[1] work up[2] again;   435
Know that all lines which circles do contain,

For once that they the center touch, do touch
Twice the circumference; and be thou such:
Double on heaven thy thoughts on earth employ'd.
All will not serve. Only who have enjoy'd   440
The sight of God in fullness can think it,
For it is both the object and the wit.
This is essential joy, where neither He
Can suffer diminution, nor we.
'Tis such a full and such a filling good,   445
Had th' angels[3] once look'd on him, they had stood.
To fill the place of one of them, or more,
She whom we celebrate is gone before,
She, who had here so much essential joy
As no chance could distract, much less destroy;   450
Who with God's presence was acquainted so
(Hearing and speaking to Him) as to know
His face in any natural stone or tree
Better than when in images they be;
Who kept by diligent devotion   455
God's image in such reparation
Within her heart that what decay was grown
Was her first parents' fault, and not her own;
Who, being solicited to any act,
Still heard God pleading His safe precontract;   460
Who by a faithful confidence was here
Betroth'd to God, and now is married there;
Whose twilights were more clear than our midday,
Who dreamt devoutlier than most use to pray,
Who, being here fill'd with grace, yet strove to be   465
Both where more grace and more capacity
At once is given—she to heaven is gone,
Who made this world in some proportion
A heaven, and here became unto us all
Joy (as our joys admit)[4] essential.   470
But could this low world joys essential touch,   *Of acci-*
Heaven's accidental joys would pass them much.   *dental joys*
How poor and lame must then our casual be?[5]   *in both*
If thy prince will his subjects to call thee   *places*
"My Lord," and this do swell thee, thou art than,   475
By being a greater, grown to be less man.
When no physician of redress[6] can speak,
A joyful, casual violence may break
A dangerous apostem[7] in thy breast,

[86]Text *whether*, corrected in the errata slip.
[87]Incidental, i.e., not deriving from the essence of something.
[88]Arouse.   [89]Text *row*, corrected in the errata slip.
[90]Nonessential, accidental, therefore temporary.   [91]Text *assigned*.
[92]Text *Thinke*.   [93]See Genesis 11.1–9.
[94]Text *to'rect*, corrected in the errata slip.   [95]Enough.
[96]In Ptolemaic astronomy, the earth.   [97]Text *worlds*.
[98]I.e., afflictions.   [99]Throng.   [1]Greatest height.   [2]Text *upon*.
[3]I.e., the angels who subsequently rebelled and were cast out of heaven.
[4]*As. . .admit*: so far as our joys can be.
[5]*But could. . .casual be*: i.e., since the earth's essential joys are so far inferior to heaven's accidental joys, the earth's accidental joys must be indeed contemptible.
[6]Remedy, relief. Text *Reders*, corrected in the errata slip.
[7]Imposthume, abscess.

And whilst thou joyest in this, the dangerous rest, 480
The bag, may rise up, and so strangle thee.
What aye was casual[8] may ever be.
What should the nature change? or make the same
Certain, which was but casual when it came?
All casual joy doth loud and plainly say 485
Only by coming that it can away.
Only in heaven joy's strength is never spent,
And accidental things are permanent.
Joy of a soul's arrival ne'er decays,
For that soul ever joys and ever stays; 490
Joy that their last great consummation
Approaches in the resurrection,
When earthly bodies more celestial
Shall be than angels were (for they could fall)—
This kind of joy doth every day admit 495
Degrees of growth, but none of losing it.
In this fresh joy 'tis no small part that she,
She, in whose goodness he that names degree
Doth injure her ('tis loss to be call'd best
There where the stuff is not such as the rest), 500
She, who left such a body as even she
Only in heaven could learn how it can be
Made better (for she rather was two souls,
Or like to full, on-both-sides-written rolls,
Where eyes might read upon the outward skin 505
As strong records for God, as minds within),
She, who by making full perfection grow,
Pieces[9] a circle and still keeps it so—
Long'd for, and longing for it, to heaven is gone,
Where she receives and gives addition. 510
Here[10] in a place where misdevotion frames *Conclusion*
A thousand prayers to saints whose very names
The ancient church knew not—heaven knows not yet—
And where what laws of poetry admit,
Laws of religion have at least the same,[11] 515
Immortal maid, I might invoke[12] thy name.
Could any saint provoke that appetite,
Thou here shouldst make me a French convertite,
But thou wouldst not, nor wouldst thou be content
To take this for my second year's true rent, 520
Did this coin bear any other stamp than His
That gave thee power to do, me to say this.
Since His will is that to posterity
Thou shouldst for life and death a pattern be,
And that the world should notice have of this, 525
The purpose and th' authority is His.
Thou art the proclamation, and I am
The trumpet at whose voice the people came.

DIVINE POEMS

LA CORONA[1]

Deign[2] at my hands this crown of prayer and praise,
Weav'd in my low, devout melancholy,
Thou, which of good hast, yea, art treasury,

All-changing, unchang'd Ancient of Days,
But do not with a vile crown of frail bays
Reward my Muse's white sincerity,
But what thy thorny crown gain'd, that give me,
A crown of glory which doth flower always.
The ends crown our works, but thou crown'st
        our ends,
For at our end begins our endless rest.
The first last end, now zealously possess'd
With a strong sober thirst, my soul attends.[3]
'Tis time that heart and voice be lifted high,
Salvation to all that will is nigh.

2. ANNUNCIATION[4]

Salvation to all that will is nigh:
That All which always is all everywhere,
Which cannot sin, and yet all sins must bear,
Which cannot die, yet cannot choose but die,
Lo, faithful Virgin, yields Himself to lie
In prison in thy womb; and though He there
Can take no sin, nor thou give, yet He'll wear,
Taken from thence, flesh, which death's force may try.[5]
Ere by the spheres time was created, thou
Wast in His mind, who is thy son and brother,
Whom thou conceiv'st, conceiv'd; yea, thou art now
Thy Maker's maker and thy Father's mother;
Thou hast light in dark, and shutt'st in little room
Immensity, cloister'd in thy dear womb.

3. NATIVITY

Immensity, cloister'd in thy dear womb,
Now leaves His well-belov'd imprisonment.
There He hath made himself to His intent
Weak enough now into our world to come;
But O, for thee, for Him, hath th' inn no room?
Yet lay him in this stall, and from the orient
Stars and wise men will travel to prevent
Th' effects of Herod's jealous, general doom.[6]
Seest thou, my soul, with thy faith's eyes how He

[8]*What...casual*: What was always subject
to chance. [9]Adds to (a circle, the symbol of perfection).
[10]I.e., France, where Donne composed the poem in the winter of
1611–12 while accompanying Sir Robert Drury on an extended
Continental junket.
[11]*What laws...same*: i.e., invocations (to the Muses in poetry and
to saints in Roman Catholicism).
[12]Text *iuoque*, corrected in the errata slip.
LA CORONA [1]"The Crown," signifying both Christ's crown of
thorns and a kind of rosary of "prayer and praise" whose seven
parts are laced together by the repetition of the last line of each
sonnet as the first line of the next. [2]I.e., deign to accept.
[3]Awaits.
[4]I.e., the archangel Gabriel's announcement to Mary that she was
blessed among women and would bear a child (Luke 1.26–35).
In the text the arabic numbering of each sonnet precedes the first
line, not the title. [5]Test.
[6]I.e., the decree that all the children of Bethlehem be slaughtered,
which prompted the Holy Family's flight into Egypt (Matthew
2.13–16).

Which fills all place, yet none holds Him, doth lie?
Was not His pity towards thee wondrous high,
That would have need to be pitied by thee?
Kiss Him and with Him into Egypt go,
With His kind mother, who partakes thy woe.

4. TEMPLE[7]

With His kind mother, who partakes thy woe,
Joseph, turn back; see where your child doth sit,
Blowing, yea blowing out those sparks of wit
Which himself on those doctors did bestow.
The Word[8] but lately could not speak, and lo!
It suddenly speaks wonders. Whence comes it
That all which was, and all which should be writ,
A shallow-seeming child should deeply know?
His godhead was not soul to His manhood,
Nor had time mellow'd Him to this ripeness,
But as for one which hath a long task 'tis good
With the sun to begin his business,
He in His age's morning thus began
By miracles exceeding power of man.

5. CRUCIFYING

By miracles exceeding power of man
He faith in some, envy[9] in some begat,
For what meek spirits admire, ambitious hate;
In both affections many to Him ran,
But O! the worst are most; they will and can,
Alas, and do unto the Immaculate,
Whose creature fate is, now prescribe a fate,
Measuring self-life's infinity to a span,[10]
Nay, to an inch. Lo, where, condemned, He
Bears His own cross with pain, yet by and by
When it bears Him, He must bear more and die.
Now Thou art lifted up, draw me to Thee,[11]
And at Thy death, giving such liberal dole,[12]
Moist with one drop of Thy blood my dry soul.

6. RESURRECTION

Moist with one drop of Thy blood, my dry soul
Shall (though she now be in extreme degree
Too stony-hard, and yet too fleshly) be
Freed by that drop from being starv'd,[13] hard, or foul;
And life, by this death abled,[14] shall control
Death, whom Thy death slew; nor shall to me
Fear of first or last death[15] bring misery
If in thy little book[16] my name thou enroll.
Flesh in that long sleep is not putrefied,
But made that there of which and for which 'twas;
Nor can by other means be glorified.
May then sin's sleep, and death's, soon from me pass,
That, wak'd from both, I again risen may
Salute the last and everlasting day.

7. ASCENSION

Salute the last and everlasting day,
Joy at th' uprising of this Sun and Son,
Ye whose just tears or tribulation
Have purely wash'd or burnt your drossy clay;

Behold the Highest, parting hence away,
Lightens the dark clouds which He treads upon;
Nor doth He by ascending show alone,
But first He, and He first, enters the way.
O strong Ram,[17] which hast batter'd heaven for me,
Mild Lamb, which with Thy blood hast mark'd the path,
Bright Torch, which shin'st that I the way may see,
O, with Thine own blood quench Thine[18] own just wrath,
And if Thy Holy Spirit my Muse did raise,
Deign at my hands this crown of prayer and praise.

TO E. OF D.[1] WITH SIX HOLY SONNETS

See, Sir, how as the sun's hot masculine flame
Begets strange creatures on Nile's dirty slime,[2]
In me your fatherly yet lusty[3] rhyme
(For these songs are their fruits) have wrought the same.
But though the engend'ring force from whence they came
Be strong enough, and nature do admit
Seven to be born at once,[4] I send as yet
But six (they[5] say the seventh hath still some maim).
I choose your judgment—which the same degree
Doth with her sister, your invention, hold—

[7]For the youthful Jesus' conversation with the doctors in the temple see Luke 2.46–47.
[8]The logos or eternal Word made incarnate in Jesus (John 1.1–5).
[9]Malice.
[10]Measure of nine inches (giving rise to "Nay, to an inch" in line 9).
[11]*Now...Thee*: "And I, if I be lifted up from the earth, will draw all men unto me" (John 12.32).
[12]1) Distribution of charitable gifts; 2) grief. [13]Withered.
[14]Strengthened.
[15]I.e., the "second death" or eternal punishment cited in Revelation 2.11, 20.14.
[16]Perhaps the "Book of Life" of Revelation 3.5. Miss Gardner tentatively advanced but did not herself adopt the emendation *title-book*, i.e., the book recording one's title or claim to heaven. Some manuscripts read *life-booke*.
[17]1) battering ram; 2) the sacrificial ram in the thicket of Genesis 22.13, which was identified with Christ.
[18]*Thine...thine*: text *thy...thy*.
TO E. OF D. [1]Probably Richard Sackville (1589–1624), who became the third earl of Dorset in February 1609, just two days after his marriage to the Lady Anne Clifford. As a member of a literary family he may have done some writing, but probably of insufficient merit to justify Donne's flattery. First printed in the 1633 *Poems* among the verse epistles, this sonnet was placed in A. B. Grosart's edition (1872) at the head of the La Corona sequence. Miss Helen Gardner, in her edition of *The Divine Poems* (1952), has moved it once again on the ground that it serves better as an introduction to the first six of the twelve Holy Sonnets as printed in the 1633 *Poems*. She has persuasively argued that these six sonnets, which form a sort of sequence on the eschatological themes of death, judgment, hell, and heaven, were (like many of Donne's religious poems) written long before his ordination (1615), and not in his last years, as Walton had assumed. These six sonnets, for example, she assigns to 1609, about the same time as the La Corona sequence.
[2]The fertility of the slime in the Nile is recorded by Pliny, *Natural History*, IX. 1xxxiv. [3]Pleasing.
[4]Pliny (VII.iii) records among other examples of fecundity that of an Egyptian woman who produced seven children at a birth (*uno utero*). [5]I.e., those who have seen them?

As fire these drossy rhymes to purify,
Or as elixir to change them to gold:
You are that alchemist which always had
Wit whose one spark could make good things of bad.

HOLY SONNETS

1.[1] [As Due by Many Titles]

As due by many titles I resign
Myself to thee, O God; first I was made
By Thee and for Thee, and when I was decay'd,
Thy blood bought that the which before was Thine.
I am Thy son, made with Thyself to shine,
Thy servant, whose pains Thou hast still repaid,
Thy sheep, Thine image, and till I betray'd
Myself, a temple of Thy Spirit divine.
Why doth the devil then usurp on me?
Why doth he steal, nay ravish that's[2] Thy right?
Except Thou rise and for Thine own work fight,
O, I shall soon despair when I do see
That Thou lov'st mankind well, yet wilt not choose me,
And Satan hates me, yet is loath to lose me.

2. [O My Black Soul]

O my black soul! now thou art summoned
By sickness, death's herald and champion,
Thou'rt like a pilgrim which abroad hath done
Treason and durst not turn to whence he is fled,
Or like a thief which, till death's doom[1] be read,
Wisheth himself delivered from prison,
But damn'd and hal'd to execution,
Wisheth that still he might be imprisoned.
Yet grace, if thou repent, thou canst not lack;
But who shall give thee that grace to begin?
O, make thyself with holy mourning black,
And red with blushing, as thou art with sin;
Or wash thee in Christ's blood, which hath this might,
That being red, it dyes red souls to white.

3. [This is My Play's Last Scene]

This is my play's last scene; here heavens appoint
My pilgrimage's last mile; and my race,
Idly yet quickly run, hath this last pace,
My span's last inch, my minute's latest point;
And gluttonous death will instantly unjoint
My body and my soul, and I shall sleep a space,
But my ever-waking part shall see that face
Whose fear already shakes my every joint:
Then, as my soul to heaven, her first seat, takes flight,
And earth-born body in the earth shall dwell,
So fall my sins, that all may have their right,
To where they are bred, and would press me—to hell.
Impute me righteous, thus purg'd of evil,
For thus I leave the world, the flesh, the devil.

4. [At The Round Earth's]

At the round earth's imagin'd corners[1] blow
Your trumpets, angels, and arise, arise

From death, you numberless infinities
Of souls, and to your scatter'd bodies go
All whom the flood did, and fire[2] shall o'erthrow,
All whom war, dearth,[3] age, agues, tyrannies,
Despair, law, chance hath slain, and you whose eyes
Shall behold God and never taste death's woe.[4]
But let them sleep, Lord, and me mourn a space,
For if above all these my sins abound,
'Tis late to ask abundance of Thy grace
When we are there; here on this lowly ground
Teach me how to repent, for that's as good
As if Thou hadst seal'd my pardon with Thy blood.

5. [If Poisonous Minerals]

If poisonous minerals, and if that tree
Whose fruit threw death on else immortal us,
If lecherous goats, if serpents envious
Cannot be damn'd, alas, why should I be?
Why should intent or reason, born in me,
Make sins, else equal, in me more heinous?
And mercy being easy and glorious
To God, in His stern wrath why threatens He?
But who am I that dare dispute with Thee?
O God, O! of Thine only worthy blood
And my tears make a heavenly Lethean[1] flood,
And drown in it my sins' black memory.
That Thou remember them, some claim as debt;
I think it mercy if Thou wilt forget.

6. [Death, Be Not Proud]

Death, be not proud, though some have called thee
Mighty and dreadful, for thou art not so;
For those whom thou think'st thou dost overthrow
Die not, poor Death, nor yet canst thou kill me.
From rest and sleep, which but thy pictures be,
Much pleasure, then from thee much more must flow;
And soonest our best men with thee do go,
Rest of their bones and soul's delivery.[1]
Thou art slave to fate, chance, kings, and desperate men,
And dost[2] with poison, war, and sickness dwell;
And poppy or charms can make us sleep as well,
And better than thy stroke. Why swell'st thou then?
One short sleep pass'd, we wake eternally,
And death shall be no more. Death, thou shalt die.

AS DUE BY MANY TITLES [1]Grierson's numbering of the sonnets is indicated by the figures in parentheses: 1 (II), 2 (IV), 3 (VI), 4 (VII), 5 (IX), 6 (X), 10 (XIV). [2]That which is.
O MY BLACK SOUL [1]Decree, judgment.
AT THE ROUND EARTH'S [1]"And after these things I saw four angels standing on the four corners of the earth" (Revelation 7.1). [2]The final conflagration when "the elements shall melt with fervent heat; the earth also, and the work that are in it, shall be burned up" (2 Peter 3.10). [3]Text *death*.
[4]*Never taste death's woe*: See Luke 9.27, 1 Corinthians 15.51–52.
IF POISONOUS MINERALS [1]Referring to Lethe, the river of forgetfulness in the underworld.
DEATH, BE NOT PROUD [1]Liberation (from the prison of the body). [2]Text *doth*.

10. [BATTER MY HEART]

Batter my heart, three-person'd God,[1] for You
As yet but knock, breathe, shine, and seek to mend.
That I may rise and stand, o'erthrow me and bend
Your force to break, blow, burn, and make me new.
I, like an usurp'd town to another due,
Labor to admit You, but O, to no end!
Reason, Your viceroy in me, me should defend,
But is captiv'd, and proves weak or untrue.
Yet dearly I love You and would be loved[2] fain,
But am betroth'd unto Your enemy.
Divorce me, untie, or break that knot again,
Take me to You, imprison me, for I,
Except You enthrall me, never shall be free,
Nor ever chaste except You ravish me.

[FROM THE 1635 *Poems*]

[I AM A LITTLE WORLD]

I am a little world made cunningly
Of elements and an angelic sprite,[1]
But black sin hath betray'd to endless night
My world's both parts, and O, both parts must die.
You which beyond that heaven which was most high
Have found new spheres, and of new lands can write,[2]
Pour new seas in mine eyes that so I might
Drown my world with my weeping earnestly,
Or wash it, if it must be drown'd no more.[3]
But O, it must be burnt! Alas, the fire
Of lust and envy have[4] burnt it heretofore
And made it fouler. Let their flames retire,
And burn me, O Lord, with a fiery zeal
Of Thee and Thy house, which doth in eating heal.[5]

[FROM THE WESTMORELAND MANUSCRIPT]

[SINCE SHE WHOM I LOV'D]

Since she whom I lov'd[1] hath paid her last debt
To nature, and to hers,[2] and my good is dead,
And her soul early into heaven ravished,
Wholly in heavenly things my mind is set.
Here, the admiring her my mind did whet
To seek Thee, God; so streams do show the head;
But though I have found Thee, and Thou my thirst
   hast fed,
A holy, thirsty dropsy melts me yet.
But why should I beg more love, whenas Thou
Dost woo my soul, for hers off'ring all Thine,
And dost not only fear lest I allow
My love to saints and angels, things divine,
But in Thy tender jealousy dost doubt[3]
Lest the world, flesh, yea, devil put Thee out.

[O, TO VEX ME]

O, to vex me contraries meet in one;
Inconstancy unnaturally hath begot

A constant habit, that when I would not,
I change in vows and in devotion.
As humorous is my contrition
As my profane love, and as soon forgot,
As riddlingly distemper'd,[1] cold and hot;
As praying as mute; as infinite as none.
I durst not view heaven yesterday, and today
In prayers and flattering speeches I court God;
Tomorrow I quake with true fear of His rod.
So my devout fits come and go away
Like a fantastic ague, save that here
Those are my best days when I shake with fear.

GOOD FRIDAY, 1613, RIDING WESTWARD[1]

Let man's soul be a sphere, and then in this
The intelligence that moves, devotion is;
And as the other spheres, by being grown
Subject to foreign motions,[2] lose their own,
And, being by others hurried every day,   5
Scarce in a year their natural form obey,
Pleasure or business, so, our souls admit
For their first mover, and are whirl'd by it.[3]
Hence is't that I am carried towards the west
This day when my soul's form bends toward the east.   10
There I should see a sun by rising set,
And by that setting endless day beget;
But that Christ on this cross did rise and fall,
Sin had eternally benighted all.
Yet dare I almost be glad I do not see   15
That spectacle of too much weight for me.

---

10 BATTER MY HEART [1]Father, Son, and Holy Spirit.
[2]Text *lov'd*, but most manuscripts support the emendation.
I AM A LITTLE WORLD [1]Spirit.
[2]*You which...can write*: Although this has been seen as a reference to the "new lands" of the moon as revealed through Galileo's telescope and announced in his *Sidereus Nuncius* (1610), it could also refer both to the recently postulated eleventh sphere of Ptolemaic astronomers and to the terrestrial discoveries of maritime explorers. *Lands*: text *land*.
[3]After the flood God made a covenant with Noah that never again would the earth be inundated (Genesis 9.11). [4]Text *hath*.
[5]Cf. Psalms 69.9, "For the zeal of thy house hath eaten me up."
SINCE SHE WHOM I LOV'D [1]Donne's wife died 15 August 1617 following the birth of her twelfth child.
[2]I.e., her own mortal nature?
[3]*In Thy...doubt*: i.e., in Thy solicitude dost fear.
O, TO VEX ME [1]Disturbingly confused.
GOOD FRIDAY, 1613 [1]In one manuscript the title is expanded to "Riding to Sir Edward Herbert in Wales." For Donne's exchange of verse epistles with Herbert see pp. 74, 118. [2]Text *motion*.
[3]Just as each of the ten *spheres* (see Glossary) of the Ptolemaic system was thought to be directed by an angel (*intelligence*) that controlled and synchronized its *motions*, so man's soul, conceived of as a sphere, should have religious devotion as its angel, *natural form*, and guiding principle. But just as the harmonious motion of the spheres is disturbed by the pull of *foreign* forces, so man's soul is *whirl'd* from its proper course when *pleasure or business* displaces *devotion* as its *primum mobile* or *first mover*.

Who sees God's face, that is self life,[4] must die;[5]
What a death were it then to see God die!
It made His own lieutenant, Nature, shrink;
It made His footstool crack, and the sun wink.[6]   20
Could I behold those hands which span the poles
And tune[7] all spheres at once, pierc'd with those holes?
Could I behold that endless height, which is
Zenith to us and our antipodes,
Humbled below us? or that blood which is   25
The seat of all our souls, if not of His,
Make[8] dirt of dust, or that flesh which was worn
By God for His apparel, ragg'd and torn?
If on these things I durst not look, durst I
Upon His miserable mother cast mine eye,   30
Who was God's partner here, and furnish'd thus
Half of that sacrifice which ransom'd us?
Though these things as I ride be from[9] mine eye,
They are present yet unto my memory,
For that looks towards them; and Thou look'st
    towards me,   35
O Saviour, as Thou hang'st upon the tree.
I turn my back to Thee but to receive
Corrections till Thy mercies bid Thee leave.[10]
O think me worth Thine anger, punish me,
Burn off my rusts and my deformity,
Restore Thine image so much by Thy grace   40
That Thou mayst know me, and I'll turn my face.

A HYMN TO CHRIST, AT THE AUTHOR'S LAST GOING INTO GERMANY[1]

In what torn ship soever I embark,
That ship shall be my emblem of Thy ark;
What sea soever swallow me, that flood
Shall be to me an emblem of Thy blood.
Though Thou with clouds of anger do disguise   5
Thy face, yet through that mask I know those eyes,
    Which, though they turn away sometimes,
      They never will despise.

I sacrifice this island unto Thee,
And all whom I lov'd there, and who lov'd me;   10
When I have put our seas 'twixt them and me,
Put thou Thy sea[2] betwixt my sins and thee.
As the tree's sap doth seek the root below
In winter, in my winter now I go
    Where none but Thee, th' eternal root   15
      Of true love, I may know.

Nor Thou nor Thy religion dost control[3]
The amorousness of an harmonious soul,
But Thou wouldst have that love thyself. As Thou
Art jealous,[4] Lord, so am I jealous now.   20
Thou lov'st not, till from loving more[5] Thou free
My soul. Whoever gives, takes liberty.
    O, if Thou car'st not whom I love,
      Alas, Thou lov'st not me.

Seal then this bill of my divorce to all   25
On whom those fainter beams of love did fall;

Marry those loves which in youth scattered be
On fame, wit, hopes (false mistresses), to Thee.
Churches are best for prayer that have least light;
To see God only, I go out of sight,   30
    And to 'scape stormy days, I choose
      An everlasting night.

HYMN TO GOD MY GOD IN MY SICKNESS[1]

Since I am coming to that holy room
    Where with Thy choir of saints for evermore
I shall be made Thy music, as I come
    I tune the instrument here at the door,
    And what I must do then, think now[2] before.   5

Whilst my physicians by their love are grown
    Cosmographers, and I their map, who lie
Flat on this bed, that by them may be shown
    That this is my southwest discovery
    Per fretum febris, by these straits to die,[3]   10

I joy that in these straits I see my west.
    For though their[4] currents yield return to none,
What shall my west hurt me? As west and east
    In all flat maps (and I am one) are one
    So death doth touch the resurrection.[5]   15

Is the Pacific Sea my home? Or are
    The eastern riches? Is Jerusalem?
Anyan and Magellan and Gibraltar,
    All straits, and none but straits, are ways to them,
    Whether where Japhet dwelt, or Cham, or Shem.[6]   20

[4]Life itself.
[5]"Thou canst not see my face; for there shall no man see me, and live" (Exodus 33.20).   [6]Close its eyes, i.e., grow dark.
[7]Some manuscripts read *turne* (which Grierson adopted).
[8]Text *Made*. "Make dirt of dust" seems to mean "make the vile even viler."   [9]Absent from.   [10]Desist.
A HYMN TO CHRIST: [1]Between May 1619 and the following January Donne served as chaplain to Lord Doncaster on a diplomatic mission to Germany.   [2]Text *seas*.   [3]Prohibit, censure.
[4]Insistent on complete devotion. "Thou shalt not bow down thyself to them, nor serve them; for I, the Lord thy God, am a jealous God" (Exodus 20.5).   [5]Others.
HYMN TO GOD MY GOD [1]Although Izaak Walton firmly dated this hymn only eight days before Donne's death on 31 March 1631, the eminent jurist Sir Julius Caesar noted on a manuscript copy in his possession that it was written in Donne's "greate" illness of December 1623 (which also prompted the *Devotions*, p. 548). The hymn was first printed in the 1635 *Poems*.   [2]Text *here*.
[3]*That this...die*: i.e., that through the raging heat of fever (*per fretum febris*) I pass through the dangerous straits (*fretum*) that bring me to my goal.   [4]Text *those*.
[5]*As east...resurrection*: i.e., death and resurrection are like the right (*east*) and left (*west*) sides of a *flat map* because they actually *touch* each other.
[6]*Is the Pacific...Shem*: Through the wealth of geographical allusion in this stanza Donne seems to be saying that no matter where paradise is in the whole known world—in Europe or Africa or Asia (the inheritances respectively of *Japhet*, *Cham*, and *Shem*, who were the sons of Noah), in the Southern Ocean or amid the *eastern riches* of China and Japan, in the Bering Strait (*Anyan*)

We think that paradise and Calvary,
Christ's cross and Adam's tree, stood in one place.[7]
Look, Lord, and find both Adams[8] met in me;
As the first Adam's sweat surrounds my face,
May the last Adam's blood my soul embrace.

So in his purple wrapp'd, receive me, Lord,
By these His thorns give me His other crown;
And as to others' souls I preach'd Thy word,
Be this my text, my sermon to mine own:
Therefore that He may raise, the Lord throws down.

A HYMN TO GOD THE FATHER

1

Wilt Thou forgive that sin where I begun,
Which is[1] my sin though it were done before?
Wilt Thou forgive those sins[2] through which I run,
And do them[3] still, though still I do deplore?
When Thou hast done, Thou hast not done,
For I have more.

2

Wilt Thou forgive that sin by which I won[4]
Others to sin, and made my sin their door?

Wilt Thou forgive that sin which I did shun
A year or two, but wallowed in a score?
When Thou hast done, Thou hast not done,
For I have more.

3

I have a sin of fear, that when I have spun
My last thread, I shall perish on the shore;
Swear[5] by thyself that at my death Thy Sun[6]
Shall shine as it[7] shines now, and heretofore;
And having done that, Thou hast[8] done.
I have[9] no more.

---

or the Straits of *Magellan*—our way to it involves a perilous passage.
[7]Since there was apparently no authority for Donne's suggestion that the Forbidden Tree and Christ's cross stood on the same spot, Miss Gardner suggests that *place* here means "region," i.e., the vicinity of Jerusalem, the city of peace which is every Christian's goal.
[8]Adam (through whom all men sinned) and Christ (through whom all men are saved).
TO GOD THE FATHER   [1]Text *was.*   [2]Text *that sin.*   [3]Text *do run.*
[4]Text *which I have won.*   [5]Text *But sweare.*   [6]Text *sonne.*
[7]Text *he.*   [8]Text *haste.*   [9]Text *feare.*

Ben Jonson[1] [1572/3-1637]

By authoritative precept and masterful example Jonson so much impressed his own contemporaries that he acquired (and to some extent retains) the status of an institution. Armed with his dominating, sometimes domineering force of mind and character and with a vast prestige as artist, he was cherished by his so-called "sons" as both a mentor and a boon companion, and as a person he is more alive for us, warts and all, than any other writer of the age. As with his eighteenth-century namesake, however, we are sometimes so much taken by the Jonson of the tavern—convivial but crotchety, immensely learned but burly and opinionated—that we almost forget the writer. Yet Jonson was first and foremost a man of letters, and it was as a disciplined professional who revered his craft and exulted in its "offices and function" that he made his moral and artistic presence felt. His name, said Clarendon, "can never be forgotten," for "surely as he did exceedingly exalt the English language in eloquence, propriety, and masculine expression, so he was the best judge of and fittest to prescribe rules to poetry and poets of any man who had lived with or before him." Jonson's credo in the preface to *Volpone* (p. 709), like young Milton's in *The Reason of Church Government* (p. 772), still enables us at least in part to understand the Renaissance conception of the civic and the civilizing force of art that they exemplified:

For if men will impartially, and not asquint, look toward the offices and function of a poet, they will easily conclude to themselves the impossibility of any man's being the good poet without first being a good man. He that is said to be able to inform young men to all good disciplines, inflame grown men to all great virtues, keep old men in their best and supreme

[1]For other works of Jonson, see Books and Men, pp. 693 ff.

state (or, as they decline to childhood, recover them to their first strength), that comes forth the interpreter and arbiter of nature, a teacher of things divine no less than human, a master in manners, and can alone (or with a few) effect the business of mankind—this, I take him, is no subject for pride and ignorance to exercise their railing rhetoric upon.

As the contemporary accounts of Jonson by Drummond, Clarendon, and Fuller show (see pp. 693, 754, 795), the man who wrote these stirring words was vain, bibulous, and quarrelsome. The grandson (by his own account) of a "gentleman" of Annandale, posthumous son of a needy clergyman, and stepson of a bricklayer, he was, though "brought up poorly," a student at Westminster School long enough to revere the memory of its second master, William Camden,

> to whom I owe
> All that I am in arts, all that I know.

Leaving school about 1589, he worked briefly at his stepfather's trade, soldiered in the Low Countries (where, as he told Drummond proudly, he killed a man and seized his spoils), returned to England where he married, and drifted into acting before he started writing plays about 1597. In 1598 he killed his second man—this one a fellow-actor—and during his subsequent imprisonment, when he was "almost at the gallows," he became a Roman Catholic.

Happily for English literature, he escaped the scaffold by pleading self-defense and claiming benefit of clergy, and with *Every Man in His Humor*, which was presented by the lord Chamberlain's company (with Shakespeare in the cast) that same year, he began a decade and a half of extraordinary production that included not only such equivocal successes as *Cynthia's Revels* (1600), *Poetaster* (1601), *Sejanus* (1603), and *Catiline* (1611) but such authentic comic masterpieces as *Volpone* (1606), *Epicoene* (1609), *The Alchemist* (1610), and *Bartholomew Fair* (1614). Moreover, on James' accession in 1603 he launched a collateral career by writing the first of his nearly thirty masques and entertainments for the court.

In 1616 a royal pension and the publication of his collected *Works* in folio—an act of unprecedented authorial presumption that in certain quarters was greeted with derision—stamped the seal of his success, and thereafter Jonson was a public character. The famous pedestrian tour to Scotland (1618–19) that has been immortalized by Drummond, an honorary degree from Oxford (1619), the friendship of many powerful men and women whom he celebrated in encomiastic poems, repeated signs of royal favor, wide if unofficial recognition as the poet laureate of the realm, perhaps a deputy professorship at Gresham College (1619 ff.), and certainly the adulation of his "sons" who caroused with him at the Mermaid, "the Sun, the Dog, the Triple Tun" were the smiling aspects of a life that also knew misfortune: the loss by fire of his beloved books and manuscripts in 1623, a paralyzing stroke in 1628, financial insecurity, and the beginning of the so-called "dotage" with the disastrous failure of *The New Inn* in 1629. Although not spared the indignities of a querulous old age, Jonson earned the honor of a funeral in Westminster Abbey and the praise of almost every leading poet of the day in *Jonsonus Virbius*, a volume of commendatory verses that appeared in 1638. In 1640–41 his old friend Sir Kenelm Digby, carrying on a project that Jonson had begun some half a dozen years before his death, supervised the publication of many of his later pieces as the second volume of his *Works*.

Although Jonson called his *Epigrams* "the ripest of my studies," they were licensed for the press in 1612, when he was only forty. Like the small but splendid group of occasional and commendatory poems that he subsequently brought together as *The Forest*, they first appeared in the 1616 folio edition of his *Workes* (STC 14751), on which my texts are based. The so-called second folio of 1640–41 (STC 14754) supplies the texts for the larger and more miscellaneous group of "lesser poems of later growth" that he called *Underwoods*, as he explained, "out of the analogy they hold to the 'forest' in my former book." The texts of the "Uncollected Verse"—some of them lyrics from his plays and some encomiastic pieces supplied for the publications of his friends and colleagues—are indicated in the notes.

As for Jonson's prose in Section IV, the sources of the "Dedications and Addresses" are also indicated in the notes. "Conversations with Drummond" is based upon Sir Robert Sibbald's transcription (ca. 1710) of Drummond's now lost manuscript as presented in the first volume (1925) of the great Herford and Simpson edition of Jonson's works, pp. 132–51. The text for *Timber or Discoveries*—a gathering of 171 detached paragraphs consisting chiefly of translated excerpts from Seneca, Quintilian, Juan Luis Vives, and others—is the folio of 1640–41, where it first appeared.

One of the unquestioned monuments of modern scholarship is the edition of Jonson's works by C. H. Herford and Percy and Evelyn Simpson (11 vols., 1925–52), which of course supersedes William Gifford's (9 vols., 1816), Francis Cunningham's revision of Gifford (9 vols., 1875), and F. E. Schelling's edition of the plays (2 vols., 1910). There are more or less complete editions of the poetry by B. H. Newdigate (1936), G. B. Johnston (1954), and W. B. Hunter (1963), a volume of selections by John Hollander (1961), and a useful facsimile edition of *Epigrammes, The Forrest,* and *Under-wood* by H. H. Hudson (1936). *Timber* has been edited by Schelling (1892), Sir Israel Gollancz (1898), Maurice Chastelain (1906), G. B. Harrison (1923), and Ralph Walker (1953), and there is a wide selection from the plays and nondramatic works by Harry Levin (1938).

The biographies, which of course begin with Drummond's "Conversations," include those by Castelain (in French, 1907), G. G. Smith (1919), Herford and Simpson (Vols. I–II, 1925), John Palmer (1934), and Marchette Chute (1953). From the mass of critical studies—most of them centered on the plays—one might mention those by J. A. Symonds (1886), Swinburne (1889), and Schelling (*Ben Jonson and the Classical School*, 1898). The poetry has been treated by E. C. Dunn (1925), G. B. Johnston (1945), Wesley Trimpi (1962), and J. G. Nichols (1969). J. D. Redwine has studied Jonson as a critic (1970). Samuel Tannenbaum has followed his bibliography (1938) with a supplement (1947); and some of the fiendish bibliographical complexities of the folios have been explored by H. L. Ford (1942). Although concerned mainly with the plays, A. H. Sackton's study of Jonson's rhetoric (1948) and Jonas Barish's of his language as a comic dramatist (1960) are not unrelated to his performance as a poet.

from The Works (1616)

EPIGRAMS

TO THE GREAT EXAMPLE OF HONOR AND VIRTUE, THE MOST NOBLE WILLIAM, EARL OF PEMBROKE, LORD CHAMBERLAIN, ETC.[1]

My Lord, while you cannot change your merit I dare not change your title: it was that made it,[2] and not I. Under which name I here offer to Your Lordship the ripest of my studies, my *Epigrams*, which though they carry danger in the sound do not therefore seek your shelter. For when I made them I had nothing in my conscience to expressing of which I did need a cipher. But if I be fallen into those times wherein, for the likeness of vice and facts,[3] everyone thinks another's ill deeds object to him, and that in their ignorant and guilty mouths the common voice is (for their security) "Beware the poet," confessing therein so much love to their diseases as they would rather make a party for[4] them than be either rid or told of them, I must expect at Your Lordship's hand the protection of truth and liberty while you are constant to your own goodness. In thanks whereof I return you the

honor of leading forth so many good and great names (as my verses mention on the better part) to their remembrance with posterity.[5] Amongst whom if I have praised unfortunately[6] anyone that doth not deserve, or if all answer not in all numbers the pictures I have made of them, I hope it will be forgiven me that they are no ill pieces, though they be not like the persons. But I foresee a nearer[7] fate to my book than this, that the vices therein will be owned before the virtues (though there I have avoided all particulars, as I have done names), and that some will be so ready to discredit me as they will have the impudence to belie themselves. For if I meant them not, it is so. Nor can I hope otherwise, for why should they remit anything of their riot,[8] their

TO WILLIAM, EARL OF PEMBROKE [1]On William Herbert (1580–1630), third earl of Pembroke, see pp. 683, 697.
[2]That (i.e., your merit) that made it.   [3]Crimes (a Latinism).
[4]*Make . . . for*: Band together in defense of.
[5]Most of the 133 poems in *Epigrams* are addressed to noble or distinguished persons, whose merits they applaud.   [6]Unaptly.
[7]More immediate.   [8]Dissipation.

pride, their self-love, and other inherent graces to consider truth or virtue? But with the trade of the world lend their long ears against men they love not,[9] and hold their dear mountebank or jester in far better condition than all the study or studiers of humanity. For such, I would rather know them by their vizards still than they should publish their faces[10] at their peril in my theater, where Cato,[11] if he lived, might enter without scandal.[12]

> Your Lordship's most faithful honorer,
> *Ben Jonson*

1. TO THE READER

Pray thee, take care, that tak'st my book in hand,
To read it well: that is, to understand.

2. TO MY BOOK

It will be look'd for, book, when some but see
Thy title, *Epigrams*, and nam'd of me,
Thou shouldst be bold, licentious, full of gall,
Wormwood, and sulphur, sharp and tooth'd withal,
Become a petulant thing, hurl ink and wit,   5
As madmen stones, not caring whom they hit.
Deceive[1] their malice who could wish it so,
And by thy wiser temper let men know
Thou art not covetous of least self-fame
Made from the hazard of another's shame,   10
Much less with lewd, profane, and beastly phrase
To catch the world's loose laughter or vain gaze.
He that departs[2] with his own honesty
For vulgar praise doth it too dearly buy.

3. TO MY BOOKSELLER

Thou that mak'st gain thy end and, wisely well,
Call'st a book good or bad as it doth sell,
Use mine so too; I give thee leave, but crave,
For the luck's sake, it thus much favor have,
To lie upon thy stall, till it be sought,   5
Not offer'd as[1] it made suit to be bought;
Nor have my title-leaf on posts or walls,
Or in cleft sticks, advanc'd to make calls
For termers,[2] or some clerk-like servingman
Who scarce can spell th' hard names, whose knight
   less can.   10
If without those vile arts, it will not sell,
Send it to Bucklersbury:[3] there 'twill well.

4. TO KING JAMES

How, best of kings, dost thou a scepter bear?
How, best of poets, dost thou laurel wear?[1]
But two things rare the Fates had in their store,
And gave thee both, to show they could no more.
For such a poet, while thy days were green,   5
Thou wert, as chief of them are said t' have been.

And such a prince thou art, we daily see,
As chief of those still promise they will be.
Whom should my Muse then fly to, but the best
Of kings for grace, of poets for my test?   10

14. TO WILLIAM CAMDEN[1]

Camden! most reverend head, to whom I owe
All that I am in arts, all that I know—
How nothing's that! to whom my country owes
The great renown and name wherewith she goes!
Than thee the age sees not that thing more grave,   5
More high, more holy, that she more would crave.
What name, what skill, what faith hast thou in things!
What sight in searching the most antique springs!
What weight and what authority in thy speech!
Men scarce can make that doubt, but thou canst teach.[2]   10
Pardon free truth, and let thy modesty,
Which conquers all, be once o'ercome by thee.
Many of thine, this better could than I;
But for their powers, accept my piety.

45. ON MY FIRST SON[1]

Farewell, thou child of my right hand and joy!
My sin was too much hope of thee, lov'd boy;
Seven years tho'[2] wert lent to me, and I thee pay,
Exacted by thy fate, on the just day.[3]
O could I lose all father now! For why   5
Will man lament the state he should envy?
To have so soon 'scap'd world's and flesh's rage,
And, if no other misery, yet age!

[9]*But with…love not*: i.e., that will rather, after the manner of the world, listen avidly to slander about men whom they dislike.
[10]*Know…faces*: i.e., remove their masks (*vizards*) and make their identity publicly known.
[11]Cato the Censor (234–149 B.C.), Roman statesman notable for his zeal as a reformer of manners and morals.
[12]Without finding anything to take offense at.
TO MY BOOK [1]Frustrate. [2]Parts.
TO MY BOOKSELLER [1]As if.
[2]*Nor have…termers*: i.e., do not exhibit the title page like a poster in order to attract purchasers from the swarm of London visitors during term time of the courts of law.
[3]London street chiefly inhabited by grocers (who used pages of unsold books for wrapping paper).
TO KING JAMES [1]King James, whose modest poetical talent Jonson egregiously overrates, had published *Essays of a Prentice in the Divine Art of Poetry* in 1584 (when he was only eighteen) and a volume of *Poetical Exercises* in 1591.
TO WILLIAM CAMDEN [1]Jonson's former master at Westminster. The publication, in 1586, of his *Britannia* (see p. 817) had made him the most esteemed antiquarian of his generation. In the 1616 Folio his former student dedicated to him *Every Man in His Humor*.
[2]*Men…teach*: i.e., whatever men wonder about can be taught by you.
ON MY FIRST SON [1]For Jonson's account to Drummond of his son Benjamin's early death see p. 696. [2]Thou.
[3]*On…day*: precisely when due.

Rest in soft peace, and ask'd, say here doth lie
Ben Jonson his best piece of poetry.   10
For whose sake, henceforth, all his vows be such
As what he loves may never like too much.

76. ON LUCY, COUNTESS OF BEDFORD[1]

This morning, timely rapt with holy fire,
    I thought to form unto my zealous Muse
What kind of creature I could most desire
    To honor, serve, and love, as poets use.
I meant to make her fair and free and wise.   5
    Of greatest blood, and yet more good than great;
I meant the daystar should not brighter rise,
    Nor lend like influence from his lucent seat.
I meant she should be courteous, facile,[2] sweet,
    Hating that solemn vice of greatness, pride;   10
I meant each softest virtue there should meet,
    Fit in that softer bosom to reside.
Only a learned and a manly soul
    I purpos'd her, that should, with even powers,
The rock, the spindle, and the shears[3] control   15
    Of destiny, and spin her own free hours.
Such when I meant to feign, and wish'd to see,
My Muse bade, "Bedford write"—and that was she!

79. TO ELIZABETH, COUNTESS OF RUTLAND[1]

That poets are far rarer births than kings,
    Your noblest father proved; like whom, before
Or then or since, about our Muses' springs
    Came not that soul exhausted so their store.
Hence was it that the Destinies decreed   5
    (Save that most masculine issue of his brain)[2]
No male unto him: who could so exceed
    Nature, they thought, in all that he would feign.
At which, she[3] happily displeas'd, made you,
    On whom if he were living now to look,   10
He should those rare and absolute numbers view
    As he would burn, or better far his book.

88. ON ENGLISH MONSIEUR

Would you believe, when you this Monsieur see,
That his whole body should speak French, not he?
That so much scarf of France, and hat, and feather,
And shoe, and tie, and garter should come hither,
And land on one whose face durst never be   5
Toward the sea farther than half-way tree?[1]
That he, untravel'd, should be French so much
As Frenchmen in his company should seem Dutch?
Or had his father, when he did him get,[2]
The French disease,[3] with which he labors yet?   10
Or hung some Monsieur's picture on the wall,
By which his dam conceiv'd him, clothes and all?
Or is it some French statue? No; 't doth move,
And stoop, and cringe. O then it needs must prove

The new French tailor's motion, monthly made,   15
Daily to turn in Paul's, and help the trade.[4]

89. TO EDWARD ALLEN[1]

If Rome so great, and in her wisest age,
Fear'd not to boast the glories of her stage,
As skillful Roscius and grave Aesop,[2] men
Yet crown'd with honors as with riches then,
Who had no less a trumpet of their name   5
Than Cicero, whose every breath was fame,
How can so great example die in me
That, Allen, I should pause to publish[3] thee?
Who both their graces in thyself hast more
Outstripp'd than they did all that went before,   10
And present worth in all dost so contract
As others speak but only thou dost act.
Wear this renown. 'Tis just that who did give
So many poets life, by one should live.

95. TO SIR HENRY SAVILE[1]

If, my religion safe, I durst embrace
That stranger doctrine of Pythagoras,[2]
I should believe the soul of Tacitus
In thee, most weighty Saville, liv'd to us:
So hast thou rend'red him in all his bounds   5
And all his numbers, both of sense and sounds.
But when I read that special piece, restor'd,

ON LUCY, COUNTESS OF BEDFORD   [1]Daughter (d. 1627) of Baron Harington of Exton (and thus niece of the translator of Ariosto), Lucy married Edward, third earl of Bedford in 1594. She was an adornment of the Jacobean court and both friend and patron to such distinguished men of letters as Jonson, Daniel, Drayton, and Donne.   [2]Affable.

[3]*Rock...shears*: emblems respectively of the three fates—Clotho (who spins the thread of life on her *rock* or spindle), Lachesis (who measures it), and Atropos (who cuts it).

TO ELIZABETH, COUNTESS OF RUTLAUD   [1]Daughter (d. 1612) of Sir Philip Sidney and wife of Roger Manners, fifth earl of Rutland, Elizabeth was herself a poet of distinction.

[2]I.e., the *Arcadia*, Sidney's famous novel (see p.691).   [3]I.e., Nature.

ON ENGLISH MONSIEUR   [1]Presumably a landmark between London and Dover.   [2]Beget   [3]The pox or syphilis.

[4]*Motion...trade*: presumably a puppet used for advertising in St. Paul's Cathedral, in Jonson's time a center of trade.

TO EDWARD ALLEN   [1]Edward Alleyn (1566–1626), famous Elizabethan actor who created most of Marlowe's tragic heroes, with his father-in-law Philip Henslowe built the Fortune theater, amassed a fortune in real estate, and founded Dulwich College. His second wife was Donne's daughter (see p. 764).

[2]*Roscius...Aesop*: Quintus Roscius (d. 62 B.C.) and his contemporary Clodius Aesopus were the most celebrated Roman actors of comedy and tragedy respectively. Both were praised by Cicero.   [3]Make known.

TO SIR HENRY SAVILE   [1]Scholar and historian (1549–1622) who translated parts of Tacitus (1591) and edited the works of Chrysostom (1610–13). As provost of Eton (1596) he was famous for his erudition.

[2]*Doctrine of Pythagoras*: i.e., the transmigration of souls.

Where Nero falls and Galba is ador'd,[3]
To thine own proper[4] I ascribe then more,
And gratulate the breach I griev'd before;[5]   10
Which fate, it seems, caus'd in the history
Only to boast thy merit in supply.
O, wouldst thou add like hand to all the rest!
Or—better work!—were thy glad country blest
To have her story woven in thy thread,   15
Minerva's loom[6] was never richer spread.
For who can master those great parts like thee,
That liv'st from hope, from fear, from faction free?
Thou hast thy breast so clear of present crimes,
Thou need'st not shrink at voice of aftertimes;   20
Whose knowledge claimeth at the helm to stand,
But wisely thrusts not forth a forward hand.
No more than Sallust in the Roman state:[7]
As, then, his cause, his glory emulate.
Although to write be lesser than to do,   25
It is the next deed, and a great one too.
We need a man that knows the several graces
Of history, and how to apt their places;[8]
Where brevity, where splendor, and where height,
Where sweetness is required, and where weight;   30
We need a man can speak of the intents,
The councils, actions, orders, and events
Of states, and censure[9] them; we need his pen
Can write the things, the causes, and the men;
But most we need his faith (and all have you)   35
That dares not write things false, nor hide things true.

96. TO JOHN DONNE

Who shall doubt, Donne, whe'r[1] I a poet be,
When I dare send my *Epigrams* to thee,
That so alone canst judge, so alone dost make,
And in thy censures evenly dost take
As free simplicity to disavow   5
As thou hast best authority t' allow?
Read all I send; and if I find but one
Mark'd by thy hand, and with the better stone,[2]
My title's seal'd. Those that for claps do write,
Let pui'ness',[3] porters', players' praise delight,   10
And, till they burst, their backs, like asses, load:
A man should seek great glory, and not broad.

101. INVITING A FRIEND TO SUPPER

Tonight, grave Sir, both my poor house and I
Do equally desire your company;
Not that we think us worthy such a guest,
But that your worth will dignify our feast
With those that come; whose grace may make that seem   5
Something, which else could hope for no esteem.
It is the fair acceptance, Sir, creates
The entertainment perfect, not the cates.[1]
Yet shall you have, to rectify your palate,
An olive, capers, or some bitter salad[2]   10
Ush'ring the mutton; with a short-legg'd hen,

If we can get her, full of eggs, and then
Lemons and wine for sauce; to these, a coney[3]
Is not to be despair'd of for our money;
And though fowl now be scarce, yet there are clarks,[4]   15
The sky not falling, think we may have larks.[5]
I'll tell you of more, and lie so you will come,
Of partrich,[6] pheasant, woodcock, of which some
May yet be there; and godwit if we can,
Knat, rail, and ruff,[7] too. Howsoe'er, my man   20
Shall read a piece of Vergil, Tacitus,
Livy, or of some better book to us,
Of which we'll speak our minds, amidst our meat,
And I'll profess[8] no verses to repeat:
To this if aught appear, which I not know of,   25
That will the pastry, not my paper, show of.[9]
Digestive cheese and fruit there sure will be;
But that which most doth take my Muse and me
Is a pure cup of rich Canary wine,
Which is the Mermaid's[10] now, but shall be mine: 30
Of which had Horace or Anacreon tasted,
Their lives, as do their lines, till now had lasted.
Tobacco, nectar, or the Thespian spring[11]
Are all but Luther's beer[12] to this I sing.
Of this we will sup free, but moderately,   35
And we will have no Pooly or Parrot[13] by;
Nor shall our cups make any guilty men,
But at our parting we will be as when
We innocently met. No simple word
That shall be utter'd at our mirthful board,   40
Shall make us sad next morning, or affright
The liberty that we'll enjoy tonight.

[3]*Where Nero...ador'd*: Savile affixed to his translation of Tacitus an account of *The End of Nero and Beginning of Galba*.
[4]Personal ability.
[5]*Gratulate...before*: i.e., rejoice in the omission from Tacitus' history that I had earlier deplored (before you supplied it).
[6]Minerva was the goddess of weaving.
[7]Gaius Sallustius Crispus (d. 34 B.C.), the eminent historian of the Catiline conspiracy and the Jugurthine war, turned to literature after a distinguished military career.
[8]Adapt to their subjects or topics.   [9]Judge.
TO JOHN DONNE   [1]Whether.
[2]The Romans used a white stone to signify fortunate days.
[3]Puisnees', i.e., juniors' or inferiors'.
INVITING A FRIEND TO SUPPER   [1]Delicacies.
[2]The word was pronounced (and often written) *sallat*.   [3]Rabbit.
[4]Clerks, learned men.
[5]It was proverbial that when the sky falls we shall have larks.
[6]Partridge.   [7]*Godwit...ruff*: varieties of edible birds.
[8]Declare my intention.
[9]*To this...show of*: i.e., if, after my promise not to read my poetry aloud, any paper should be seen, it will be wrapped around the pastry and not scribbled with verses.
[10]The Mermaid, in Bread Street, just east of St. Paul's, was Jonson's favorite tavern.
[11]A spring on Mt. Helicon frequented by the Muses.
[12]I.e., inferior German beer.
[13]Perhaps the government spies Robert Poley (or Poole) and Henry Parrot, who gathered incriminating evidence against their victims by posing as their friends.

102. TO WILLIAM, EARL OF PEMBROKE[1]

I do but name thee, Pembroke, and I find
It is an epigram on all mankind,
Against the bad, but of and to the good,
Both which are ask'd to have thee understood.
Nor could the age have miss'd thee in this strife   5
Of vice and virtue, wherein all great life
Almost is exercis'd; and scarce one knows
To which, yet, of the sides he owes.
They follow virtue for reward today;
Tomorrow vice, if she give better pay;   10
And are so good, and bad, just at a price,
As nothing else discerns the virtue or vice.
But thou, whose noblesse keeps one stature still,
And one true posture, though besieg'd with ill
Of what ambition, faction, pride can raise;   15
Whose life ev'n they that envy it must praise;
That art so reverenc'd as thy coming in,
But in the view, doth interrupt their sin;[2]
Thou must draw more, and they that hope to see
The commonwealth still safe must study thee.   20

120. EPITAPH ON S[ALOMON] P[AVY],[1] A CHILD OF QUEEN ELIZABETH'S CHAPEL

Weep with me, all you that read
    This little story,
And know for whom a tear you shed
    Death's self is sorry.
'Twas a child that so did thrive   5
    In grace and feature
As heaven and nature seem'd to strive
    Which own'd the creature.
Years he numb'red scarce thirteen
    When Fates turn'd cruel,   10
Yet three fill'd zodiacs[2] had he been
    The stage's jewel,
And did act, what now we moan,
    Old men so duly
As, sooth, the Parcae[3] thought him one,   15
    He play'd so truly.
So, by error, to his fate
    They all consented,
But viewing him since—alas, too late—
    They have repented,   20
And have sought (to give new birth),
    In baths to steep him,
But, being so much too good for earth,
    Heaven vows to keep him.

128. TO WILLIAM ROE[1]

Roe, and my joy to name, th' art now to go
Countries and climes, manners and men, to know,
T' extract and choose the best of all these known,
And those to turn to blood, and make thine own.
May winds as soft as breath of kissing friends   5

Attend thee hence; and there may all thy ends,
As the beginning here, prove purely sweet,
And perfect in a circle always meet!
So when we, bless'd with thy return, shall see
Thyself, with thy first thoughts brought home by thee,   10
We each to other may this voice inspire:[2]
"This is that good Aeneas[3], pass'd through fire,
Through seas, storms, tempest; and, embark'd for hell,
Came back untouch'd. This man hath travel'd[4] well."

132. TO MASTER JOSHUA SYLVESTER[1]

If to admire were to commend, my praise
Might then both thee, thy work, and merit raise;
But as it is, the child of ignorance
And utter stranger to all air of France,
How can I speak of thy great pains but err,   5
Since they can only judge that can confer?[2]
Behold, the reverend shade of Bartas stands
Before my thought and, in thy right, commands
That to the world I publish, for him, this:
"Bartas doth wish thy English now were his."   10
So well in that are his inventions wrought
As his will now be the translation thought,
Thine the original; and France shall boast
No more those maiden glories she hath lost.

THE FOREST[1]

1. WHY I WRITE NOT OF LOVE

Some act of Love's bound to rehearse,
I thought to bind him in my verse;
Which when he felt, "Away!" quoth he,
"Can poets hope to fetter me?"

TO WILLIAM, EARL OF PEMBROKE [1]The nobleman to whom Jonson dedicated his *Epigrams*. See p. 683, n, 4.
[2]*That are . . . sin*: i.e., you are held in such esteem that even the sight of you deters wrongdoers.
EPITAPH ON SALOMON PAVY [1]A boy actor (d. 1602) in Jonson's plays which were performed before the court by the troop of boy actors known as Children of the Chapel. [2]I.e., years. [3]The Fates.
TO WILLIAM ROE [1]Younger son (b. 1585) in a prominent London family, to various members of which Jonson addressed no less than seven of his *Epigrams*. In 1610 the poet appeared in his behalf in an action in the High Court of Chancery.
[2]*This voice inspire*: express this judgment.
[3]The hero of Vergil's *Aeneid*, who survived many dangerous adventures, including a visit to Hades, to fulfill his destiny of founding the Roman Empire.
[4]Text *travail'd*. The two words were originally not distinguished, and perhaps the sense here is both "journeyed" and "labored."
TO MASTER JOSHUA SYLVESTER [1]See p. 49.
[2]I.e., compare the translation with the original. As Jonson later told Drummond (p. 694), when he learned French he thought less well of Sylvester's work.
THE FOREST [1]The title translates Latin *silva*, a common name for collections of occasional verse. For Jonson's own comment on the title see his prefatory note to *Underwoods*, p. 96.

It is enough they once did get
Mars and my mother in their net;[1] 5
I wear not these my wings in vain."
With which he fled me; and again
Into my rhymes could ne'er be got
By any art. Then wonder not 10
That, since, my numbers are so cold,
When Love is fled, and I grow old.

2. TO PENSHURST[1]

Thou art not, Penshurst, built to envious show
Of touch[2] or marble, nor canst boast a row
Of polish'd pillars or a roof of gold;
Thou hast no lantern[3] whereof tales are told,
Or stair, or courts; but stand'st an ancient pile, 5
And these grudg'd at, art reverenc'd the while.[4]
Thou joy'st in better marks of soil, of air,
Of wood, of water; therein thou art fair.
Thou hast thy walks for health as well as sport;
Thy mount, to which the Dryads do resort, 10
Where Pan and Bacchus their high feasts have made
Beneath the broad beech and the chestnut shade;
That taller tree, which of a nut was set
At his great birth[5] where all the Muses met.
There in the writhed[6] bark are cut the names 15
Of many a sylvan taken with his flames;[7]
And thence the ruddy satyrs oft provoke
The lighter fauns to reach thy lady's oak.[8]
Thy copps,[9] too, nam'd of Gamage,[10] thou hast there,
That never fails to serve thee season'd deer 20
When thou wouldst feast or exercise thy friends.
The lower land, that to the river bends,
Thy sheep, thy bullocks, kine, and calves do feed;
The middle grounds thy mares and horses breed;
Each bank doth yield thee conies,[11] and the tops 25
Fertile of wood, Ashore and Sidney's copps,
To crown thy open table doth provide
The purpled pheasant with the speckled side;
The painted partrich[12] lies in every field,
And for thy mess[13] is willing to be kill'd; 30
And if the high-swoln Medway[14] fail thy dish,
Thou hast thy ponds that pay thee tribute fish,
Fat aged carps that run into thy net,
And pikes, now weary their own kind to eat,
As loth the second draught or cast to stay,[15] 35
Officiously[16] at first themselves betray;
Bright eels that emulate them and leap on land
Before the fisher, or into his hand.
Then hath thy orchard fruit, thy garden flowers,
Fresh as the air and new as are the hours: 40
The early cherry, with the later plum,
Fig, grape, and quince, each in his time doth come;
The blushing apricot and woolly peach
Hang on thy walls, that every child may reach.
And though thy walls be of the country stone, 45
They are rear'd with no man's ruin, no man's groan;
There's none that dwell about them wish them down,

But all come in, the farmer and the clown,
And no one empty-handed, to salute
Thy lord and lady, though they have no suit. 50
Some bring a capon, some a rural cake,
Some nuts, some apples; some that think they make
The better cheeses, bring 'em; or else send
By their ripe daughters, whom they would commend
This way to husbands, and whose baskets bear 55
An emblem of themselves in plum or pear.
But what can this (more than express their love)
Add to thy free provisions, far above
The need of such? whose liberal board doth flow
With all that hospitality doth know! 60
Where comes no guest but is allow'd to eat,
Without his fear, and of thy lord's own meat;
Where the same beer and bread, and selfsame wine
That is His Lordship's shall be also mine.
And I not fain to sit, as some this day 65
At great men's tables, and yet dine away.
Here no man tells[17] my cups nor, standing by,
A waiter doth my gluttony envy,
But gives me what I call, and lets me eat;
He knows below[18] he shall find plenty of meat; 70
Thy tables hoard not up for the next day,
Nor, when I take my lodging, need I pray
For fire or lights or livery;[19] all is there,
As if thou then wert mine, or I reign'd here;
There's nothing I can wish for which I stay. 75
That found King James, when hunting late this way,
With his brave son, the prince, they saw thy fires
Shine bright on every hearth, as the desires
Of thy Penates had been set on flame
To entertain them; or the country came, 80
With all their zeal, to warm their welcome here.
What (great, I will not say, but) sudden cheer
Didst thou then make 'em! and what praise was heap'd

WHY I WRITE NOT OF LOVE   [1]Vulcan's trapping of Mars and Venus in a net while they were making love was long a favorite subject for poets and painters.

TO PENSHURST   [1]The seat of the Sidney family in Kent. When Jonson wrote about this famous house its master was Sir Robert Sidney (1563–1626), the younger brother of Sir Philip, who, after distinguished military and political services to the crown, was created earl of Leicester in 1618.
[2]Touchstone, i.e., black marble or basalt.
[3]Glazed structure atop a tower, dome, or upper room to admit light.
[4]*And these...while*: i.e., whereas elaborate houses are envied, Penshurst is admired.
[5]Sir Philip Sidney was born at Penshurst 30 November 1554.
[6]Gnarled. [7]*Of many...flames*: i.e., of many a rustic lover.
[8]According to a family tradition, Lady Sidney was seized with labor pains under an ancient oak in Penshurst Park.
[9]Copse, thicket.
[10]The family name of Sir Robert Sidney's wife.
[11]Rabbits. [12]Partridge. [13]Meal.
[14]A river in Kent, tributary to the Thames. [15]Wait for.
[16]Dutifully. [17]Counts. [18]I.e., in the servants' quarters.
[19]Provision.

On thy good lady then! who therein reap'd
The just reward of all her huswifery;[20]   85
To have her linen, plate, and all things nigh
When she was far and not a room but dress'd
As if it had expected such a guest!
These, Penshurst, are thy praise, and yet not all.
Thy lady's noble, fruitful, chaste withal.   90
His children thy great lord may call his own,
A fortune in this age but rarely known.
They are, and have been, taught religion; thence
Their gentler spirits have suck'd innocence.
Each morn and even they are taught to pray   95
With the whole household, and may, every day,
Read in their virtuous parents' noble parts[21]
The mysteries[22] of manners, arms, and arts.
Now, Penshurst, they that will proportion[23] thee
With other edifices, when they see   100
Those proud, ambitious heaps and nothing else,
May say, "Their lords have built, but thy lord dwells."

5. SONG TO CELIA[1]

Come, my Celia, let us prove,[2]
While we may, the sports of love;
Time will not be ours forever:
He at length our good will sever.
Spend not, then, his gifts in vain: 5
Suns that set may rise again,
But if once we lose this light,
'Tis with us perpetual night.
Why should we defer our joys?
Fame and rumor are but toys.   10
Cannot we delude the eyes
Of a few poor household spies?
Or his[3] easier ears beguile,
So removed by our wile?
'Tis no sin love's fruit to steal,   15
But the sweet theft to reveal,
To be taken, to be seen,
These have crimes[4] accounted been.

7. SONG
That Women Are But Men's Shadows[1]

Follow a shadow, it still flies you;
   Seem to fly it, it will pursue:
So court a mistress, she denies you;
   Let her alone, she will court you.
Say, are not women truly, then,   5
Styl'd but the shadows of us men?

At morn and even shades are longest;
   At noon they are or short or none:
So men at weakest, they are strongest,
   But grant us perfect, they're not known.   10
Say, are not women truly, then,
Styl'd but the shadows of us men?

9. SONG TO CELIA[1]

Drink to me only with thine eyes,
   And I will pledge[2] with mine;
Or leave a kiss but in the cup,
   And I'll not look for wine.
The thirst that from the soul doth rise   5
   Doth ask a drink divine,
But might I of Jove's nectar sup
   I would not change for thine.
I sent thee late a rosy wreath,
   Not so much honoring thee   10
As giving it a hope that there
   It could not withered be.
But thou thereon didst only breathe
   And sent'st it back to me,
Since when it grows and smells, I swear,   15
   Not of itself, but thee.

10. [AND MUST I SING?][1]

And must I sing? What subject shall I choose,
Or whose great name in poets' heaven use
For the more countenance[2] to my active Muse?

Hercules? Alas, his bones are yet sore
With his old earthly labors; t' exact more   5
Of his dull godhead were sin. I'll implore

Phoebus. No, tend thy cart[3] still. Envious day
Shall not give out that I have made thee stay,
And found'red thy hot team, to tune my lay.

[20]Housekeeping. [21]Qualities, endowments. [22]Skills.
[23]Compare.
5. SONG [1]This song is from Jonson's great comedy *Volpone* (1605), III.vii, where Volpone sings it to the virtuous Celia in an effort to seduce her. [2]Experience.
[3]Referring to Celia's husband Corvino. [4]Sins.
7. SONG [1]Adapted from a Latin poem by Barthélemi Aneau (d. 1565), a professor of rhetoric at Lyons.
9. SONG [1]This famous song, which survives in several differing manuscript versions, is based upon passages from the *Epistles* attributed to the Greek poet Flavius Philostratus (b. ca. 182). [2]Drink a toast.
10. AND MUST I SING? [1]This and the following poem, together with two other pieces ("The Phoenix Analyzed" and "Ode ἐνθουσιασ-τική") that Jonson did not include in *The Forest*, first appeared among a set of "Diverse Poetical Essaies" appended to Robert Chester's *Love's Martyr* (1601). This appendix to Chester's little book—itself a rambling platonic allegory on the phoenix as the ideal woman and the turtledove as her faithful lover—contains, among others, signed poems by Shakespeare, Marston, Chapman, and Jonson; but the circumstances that led these distinguished writers into this loose collaboration are unknown. Despite the burly humor of the "Proludium" (as No. 10 is labeled in *Love's Martyr*), the "Epode" that it introduces is one of Jonson's noblest ethical pronouncements.
[2]*For...countenance*: to give greater authority.
[3]The chariot of the sun.

Nor will I beg of thee, lord of the vine,[4]   10
To raise my spirits with thy conjuring wine,
In the green circle of thy ivy twine.

Pallas, nor thee I call on, mankind maid,[5]
That at thy birth mad'st the poor smith afraid,
Who with his ax thy father's midwife play'd.[6]   15

Go, cramp dull Mars, light Venus, when he snorts,[7]
Or with thy tribade trine[8] invent new sports;
Thou nor thy looseness with my making sorts.[9]

Let the old boy, your son,[10] ply his old task,
Turn the stale prologue to some painted mask;   20
His absence in my verse is all I ask.

Hermes, the cheater, shall not mix with us,
Though he would steal his sisters' Pegasus,
And rifle him; or pawn his petasus.[11]

Nor all the ladies of the Thespian lake,[12]   25
Though they were crush'd into one form, could make
A beauty of that merit that should take

My Muse up by commission.[13] No, I bring
My own true fire: now my thought takes wing,
And now an Epode to deep ears I sing.   30

11. EPODE

Not to know vice at all, and keep true state,
  Is virtue and not fate:
Next to that virtue is to know vice well,
  And her black spite expel,
Which to effect (since no breast is so sure   5
  Or safe but she'll procure
Some way of entrance) we must plant a guard
  Of thoughts to watch and ward
At th' eye and ear, the ports[1] unto the mind,
  That no strange or unkind[2]   10
Object arrive there, but the heart, our spy,
  Give knowledge instantly
To wakeful reason, our affections' king,
  Who, in th' examining,
Will quickly taste the treason, and commit   15
  Close, the close cause of it.[3]
'Tis the securest policy we have,
  To make our sense our slave.
But this true course is not embrac'd by many:
  By many! scarce by any.   20
For either our affections do rebel,
  Or else the sentinel
That should ring 'larum[4] to the heart doth sleep;
  Or some great thought doth keep
Back the intelligence, and falsely swears   25
  Th' are base and idle fears
Whereof the loyal conscience so complains.
  Thus, by these subtle trains,[5]
Do several passions invade the mind,
  And strike our reason blind: 30

Of which usurping rank, some have thought love
  The first, as prone to move
Most frequent tumults, horrors, and unrests
  In our inflamed breasts;
But this doth from the cloud of error grow,   35
  Which thus we overblow.[6]
The thing they here call love is blind desire,
  Arm'd with bow, shafts, and fire;
Inconstant like the sea, of whence 'tis born,
  Rough, swelling, like a storm;   40
With whom who sails rides on the surge of fear,
  And boils as if he were
In a continual tempest. Now, true love
  No such effects doth prove;
That is an essence far more gentle, fine,   45
  Pure, perfect, nay, divine;
It is a golden chain[7] let down from heaven,
  Whose links are bright and even;
That falls like sleep on lovers, and combines
  The soft and sweetest minds   50
In equal[8] knots. This bears no brands nor darts
  To murder different hearts,
But, in a calm and godlike unity,
  Preserves community.
O, who is he that, in this peace, enjoys   55
  Th' elixir of all joys?
A form more fresh than are the Eden bowers,
  And lasting as her flowers;
Richer than Time, and as Time's virtue[9] rare;
  Sober as saddest[10] care;   60
A fixed thought, an eye untaught to glance:
  Who, blest with such high chance,
Would, at suggestion[11] of a steep desire,

[4]Bacchus. [5]Mannish woman.
[6]Pallas Athene sprung from Zeus's head after Hephaestus or Vulcan (*the poor smith*) had cleft it with an ax.
[7]*Go...snorts*: i.e., wanton Venus, pinch your lover Mars when he snores.
[8]I.e., your homosexual companions, the three Graces.
[9]*Thou...sorts*: neither you nor your lasciviousness suits my poetizing. [10]Cupid.
[11]*Hermes...petasus*: i.e., Mercury, the god of thieves, is unsuitable for invocation in elevated poetry because he would carry off as booty (*rifle*) the Muses' winged horse Pegasus or pawn his own winged hat (*petasus*).
[12]*Ladies...lake*: i.e., the Muses of the Thespian spring on Mt. Helicon. [13]On command.
EPODE [1]Gates. [2]Unnatural.
[3]*Taste...cause of it*: i.e., recognize the treason and restrain the secret (*close*) cause of it. [4]Alarm. [5]Tricks, wiles.
[6]Rise above, overcome.
[7]In his masque *Hymenaei* (1606) Jonson, citing the Roman commentator Macrobius as his source, allegorized Homer's golden chain (*Iliad*, VIII.19–22) attached to Zeus' throne as the "soul" that emanates from the mind of God and binds the universe together. [8]Free from variation.
[9]I.e., truth, which is proverbially known as the daughter of Time. [10]Most steadfast. [11]Temptation.

Cast himself from the spire
Of all his happiness? But soft, I hear   65
  Some vicious fool draw near
That cries we dream, and swears there's no such thing
  As this chaste love we sing.
Peace, Luxury![12] thou art like one of those
  Who, being at sea, suppose,   70
Because they move, the continent doth so.
  No, Vice, we let thee know
Though thy wild thoughts with sparrows' wings do fly,
  Turtles can chastely die;[13]
And yet (in this t' express ourselves more clear)   75
  We do not number here
Such spirits as are only continent
  Because lust's means are spent,
Or those who doubt[14] the common mouth of fame,
  And for their place and name,   80
Cannot so safely sin: their chastity
  Is mere necessity;
Nor mean we those whom vows and conscience
  Have fill'd with abstinence,
Though we acknowledge who can so abstain   85
  Makes a most blessed gain;
He that for love of goodness hateth ill,
  Is more crown-worthy still
Than he which for sin's penalty forbears:
  His heart sins, though he fears.   90
But we propose a person like our Dove,
  Grac'd with a Phoenix' love;
A beauty of that clear and sparkling light

Would make a day of night,
And turn the blackest sorrows to bright joys: 95
  Whose odorous breath destroys
All taste of bitterness, and makes the air
  As sweet as she is fair.
A body so harmoniously compos'd
  As if nature disclos'd   100
All her best symmetry in that one feature!
  O, so divine a creature
Who could be false to? chiefly, when he knows
  How only she bestows
The wealthy treasure of her love on him,   105
  Making his fortunes swim
In the full flood of her admir'd perfection?
  What savage, brute affection,
Would not be fearful to offend a dame
  Of this excelling frame?   110
Much more a noble and right generous mind
  To virtuous moods inclin'd,
That knows the weight of guilt: he will refrain
  From thoughts of such a strain,
And to his sense object[15] this sentence ever,   115
  "Man may securely[16] sin, but safely never."

[12]Lust.
[13]*Though thy...die*: Sparrows were traditional symbols of lechery, turtledoves (*turtles*) of constancy. Jonson is perhaps punning, as Donne frequently does, on *die* as a euphemism for sexual intercourse. [14]Fear. [15]Adduce as a reason.
[16]Carelessly, without anxiety.

from The Works (1640-1641)

UNDERWOODS CONSISTING OF
DIVERS POEMS

TO THE READER

With the same leave the ancients called that kind of body *silva* or ὕλη in which there were works of divers nature and manner congested, as the multitude call timber trees promiscuously growing a wood or forest, so am I bold to entitle these lesser poems of later growth by this of "underwood" out of the analogy they hold to the "forest" in my former book, and no otherwise.

Ben Jonson

POEMS OF DEVOTION

A HYMN TO GOD THE FATHER

Hear me, O God!
  A broken heart
  Is my best part:

Use still Thy rod,
  That I may prove   5
  Therein thy love.

If thou hadst not
  Been stern to me,
  But left me free,
I had forgot   10
  Myself and Thee.

For sin's so sweet
  As minds ill bent
  Rarely repent
Until they meet   15
  Their punishment.

Who more can crave
  Than Thou hast done,
  That gav'st a Son
To free a slave,   20
  First made of nought,
  With all since bought?

Sin, Death, and Hell
  His glorious name
  Quite overcame,   25
Yet I rebel,
  And slight the same.

But I'll come in
  Before my loss,
  Me farther toss,   30
As sure to win
  Under His cross.

A HYMN ON THE NATIVITY OF MY SAVIOUR

I sing the birth was born tonight,
The author both of life and light;
        The angels so did sound it,
And like the ravish'd[1] shepherds said,
Who saw the light and were afraid,   5
        Yet search'd, and true they found it.

The Son of God, th' Eternal King,
That did us all salvation bring,
        And freed the soul from danger,
He whom the whole world could not take,[2]   10
The Word,[3] which heaven and earth did make,
        Was now laid in a manger.

The Father's wisdom will'd it so,
The Son's obedience knew no No,
        Both wills were in one stature;   15
And as that wisdom had decreed,
The Word was now made flesh indeed,
        And took on Him our nature.

What comfort by Him do we win,
Who made himself the price of sin,   20
        To make us heirs of glory!
To see this Babe, all innocence,
A martyr born in our defense;
        Can man forget this story?

A Celebration of Charis in Ten Lyric Pieces

1. HIS EXCUSE FOR LOVING

Let it not your wonder move,
Less your laughter, that I love.
Though I now write fifty years,
I have had, and have, my peers;
Poets, though divine, are men;   5
Some have lov'd as old again.
And it is not always·face,
Clothes, or fortune gives the grace,
Or the feature, or the youth;
But the language and the truth,   10
With the ardor and the passion,
Gives the lover weight and fashion.
If you, then, will read the story,
First prepare you to be sorry
That you never knew till now   15

Either whom to love, or how;
But be glad, as soon with me,
When you know that this is she
Of whose beauty it was sung
She shall make the old man young.   20
Keep the middle age at stay
And let nothing high decay
Till she be the reason why
All the world for love may die.

4. HER TRIUMPH

See the chariot at hand here of Love,
  Wherein my lady rideth!
Each that draws is a swan or a dove,
  And well the car Love guideth.
As she goes, all hearts do duty
        Unto her beauty;   5
And, enamor'd, do wish so they might
        But enjoy such a sight
That they still were to run by her side
Through swords, through[1] seas, whether[2] she
  would ride.   10

Do but look on her eyes, they do light
  All that Love's world compriseth.
Do but look on her hair, it is bright
  As Love's star[3] when it riseth.
Do but mark, her forehead's smoother   15
        Than words that soothe her.
And from her arched brows such a grace
        Sheds itself through the face
As alone there triumphs to the life
All the gain, all the good, of the elements' strife.[4]   20

Have you seen but a bright lily grow
  Before rude hands have touch'd it?
Have you mark'd but the fall o' the snow
  Before the soil hath smutch'd it?
Have you felt the wool o' the beaver?   25
        Or swan's down ever?
Or have smelt o' the bud o' the brier?
        Or the nard[5] i' the fire:
Or have tasted the bag o' the bee?
O so white, O so soft, O so sweet is she!   30

A SONG

O do not wanton with those eyes,
  Lest I be sick with seeing;
Nor cast them down, but let them rise,
  Lest shame destroy their being.

A HYMN ON THE NATIVITY [1]Enraptured. [2]Contain.
[3]The Logos or second member of the Trinity, which became in-carnate in Christ (John 1.14).
HER TRIUMPH [1]Here pronounced thorough (and often so spelled).
[2]Whither. [3]Venus.
[4]The elements of air, earth, fire, and water were thought to be continually at war until order was imposed on them. See Spenser's *Hymn in Honor of Love*, lines 78–91. [5]An aromatic plant.

O be not angry with those fires,   5
   For then their threats will kill me;
Nor look too kind on my desires,
   For then my hopes will spill[1] me.

O do not steep them in thy tears,
   For so will sorrow slay me;   10
Nor spread them as distract with fears:
   Mine own enough betray me.

THE HOUR-GLASS

Do but consider this small dust
   Here running in the glass
      By atoms mov'd.
Could you believe that this
   The body was   5
      Of one that lov'd,
And in his mistress' flame playing like a fly,[1]
   Turn'd to cinders by her eye?
   Yes, and in death as life unblest,
      To have't express'd: 10
Even ashes of lovers find no rest.

A FIT OF RHYME AGAINST RHYME

Rhyme, the rack of finest wits,
That expresseth but by fits
      True conceit,
Spoiling senses of their treasure,
Cozening judgment with a measure,   5
      But false weight;
Wresting words from their true calling;
Propping verse for fear of falling
      To the ground;
Jointing syllabes,[1] drowning letters,   10
Fast'ning vowels, as with fetters
      They were bound!
Soon as lazy thou wert known,
All good poetry hence was flown,
      And art banish'd;   15
For a thousand years together.
All Parnassus' green[2] did wither,
      And wit vanish'd!
Pegasus[3] did fly away;
At the well[4] no Muse did stay,   20
      But bewail'd,
So to see the fountain dry,
And Apollo's music die,
      All light fail'd!
Starveling rhymes did fill the stage,   25
Not a poet in an age,
      Worth crowning;
Not a work deserving bays,
Nor a line deserving praise,
      Pallas frowning.   30
Greek was free from rhyme's infection,
Happy Greek, by this protection,
      Was not spoiled;

Whilst the Latin, queen of tongues,
Is not yet free from rhyme's wrongs,   35
      But rests foiled.
Scarce the hill again doth flourish,
Scarce the world a wit doth nourish,
      To restore
Phoebus to his crown again,   40
And the Muses to their brain
      As before.
Vulgar languages that want
Words, and sweetness, and be scant
      Of true measure,[5]   45
Tyran[6] rhyme hath so abused,
That they long since have refused
      Other cesure.[7]
He that first invented thee,
May his joints tormented be,   50
      Cramp'd for ever;
Still may syllabes jar with time,
Still may reason war with rhyme,
      Resting never!
May his sense when it would meet   55
The cold tumor in his feet,[8]
      Grow unsounder;
And his title be long fool,
That in rearing such a school
      Was the founder!   60

AN EPIGRAM ON WILLIAM, LORD BURLEIGH, LORD HIGH TREASURER OF ENGLAND[1]

If thou wouldst know the virtues of mankind,
Read here in one what thou in all canst find,
And go no further: let this circle be
Thy universe, though his epitome.[2]
Cecil, the grave, the wise, the great, the good,   5

A SONG [1]Destroy.

THE HOUR-GLASS [1]Butterfly, moth.

A FIT OF RHYME AGAINST RHYME [1]Dismembering syllables.
[2]The bays and laurels on Mt. Parnassus, sacred to Apollo and the Muses. Greek poetry was unrhymed.
[3]The winged steed of poetic inspiration.
[4]The fountain of Hippocrene on Mt. Helicon.
[5]I.e., the prosodic refinements of classical poetry, which was quantitative rather than accentual. [6]Tyrant.
[7]Caesura, in classical prosody the break occurring when a word ends within a metrical foot. In modern accentual verse the caesura is a pause that usually occurs near the middle of the line.
[3]Jonson is punning on the *feet* or prosodic units of accentual verse.
AN EPIGRAM ON WILLIAM, LORD BURLEIGH [1]William Cecil (1521–98), Queen Elizabeth's most trusted adviser through almost her entire reign, was created baron of Burleigh in 1571. In a note Jonson explains that this epigram was "presented upon a plate of gold to his [Burleigh's] son Robert, earl of Salisbury, when he was also treasurer." The presentation, otherwise unrecorded, may have occurred when Robert Cecil was raised to his father's former post of lord high treasurer in 1608.
[2]I.e., the circular plate as the symbol of perfection.

What is there more that can ennoble blood?
The orphan's pillar, the true subject's shield,
The poor's full storehouse, and just servant's field;
The only faithful watchman for the realm,
That in all tempests never quit the helm,   10
But stood unshaken in his deeds and name,
And labor'd in the work, not with the fame;
That still was good for goodness' sake, nor thought
Upon reward till the reward him sought;
Whose offices and honors did surprise   15
Rather than meet him; and, before his eyes
Clos'd to their peace, he saw his branches shoot,
And in the noblest families took root
Of all the land. Who now, at such a rate
Of divine blessing, would not serve a state?   20

A SONG

Lover
Come, let us here enjoy the shade,
For love in shadow best is made.
Though Envy oft his shadow be,
None brooks the sunlight worse than he.

Mistress
Where love doth shine there needs no sun;   5
All lights into his one doth run,
Without which all the world were dark,
Yet he himself is but a spark.

Arbiter
A spark to set whole worlds[1] afire,
Who more they burn, they more desire,   10
And have their being their waste to see,
And waste still, that they still might be.[2]

Chorus
Such are his powers whom time hath still'd,
Now swift, now slow, now tame, now wild,
Now hot, now cold, now fierce, now mild: 15
The eldest god,[3] yet still a child.

LORD BACON'S BIRTHDAY[1]

Hail, happy genius of this ancient pile![2]
How comes it all things so about thee smile?
The fire, the wine, the men—and in the midst
Thou stand'st as if some mystery[3] thou didst.
Pardon, I read it in thy face, the day   5
For whose returns, and many, all these pray,
And so do I. This is the sixtieth year
Since Bacon, and thy lord, was born, and here,
Son to the grave wise keeper of the seal,[4]
Fame and foundation of the English weal.   10
What then his father was, that since is he,
Now with a title more to the degree:
England's high chancellor, the destin'd heir
In his soft cradle to his father's chair,
Whose even thread the Fates spin round and full   15

Out of their choicest and their whitest wool.
'Tis a brave cause of joy, let it be known,
For 'twere a narrow gladness, kept thine own.
Give me a deep-crown'd bowl, that I may sing,
In raising him, the wisdom of my king.   20

TO THE IMMORTAL MEMORY AND FRIENDSHIP OF THAT NOBLE PAIR, SIR LUCIUS CARY AND SIR H. MORISON[1]

THE TURN[2]

Brave infant of Saguntum, clear
Thy coming forth in that great year,
When the prodigious Hannibal did crown
His rage with razing your immortal town.
Thou, looking then about,   5
Ere thou wert half got out,
Wise child, didst hastily return,
And mad'st thy mother's womb thine urn.[3]
How summ'd a circle didst thou leave mankind
Of deepest lore, could we the center find!   10

THE COUNTER-TURN

Did wiser nature draw thee back,
From out the horror of that sack,
Where shame, faith, honor, and regard of right
Lay trampled on? The deeds of death and night
Urg'd, hurried forth, and hurl'd   15
Upon th' affrighted world;
Sword, fire, and famine with fell fury met,
And all on utmost ruin set;
As, could they but life's miseries foresee,
No doubt all infants would return like thee.   20

A SONG [1]Text *world.*
[2]*And waste...be*: i.e., fire must destroy in order to exist. [3]Cupid.
LORD BACON'S BIRTHDAY [1]Written for Bacon's sixtieth birthday (26 January 1621), this eulogistic poem preceded by only a few weeks the start (March 14) of the parliamentary investigation into the lord chancellor's misconduct that led to his conviction and disgrace (May 3).
[2]York House in the Strand, where Bacon had been born, was presented to him by the King on his appointment as lord chancellor in 1618. [3]Religious ceremony.
[4]Bacon's father Sir Nicholas (1509–79), one of Queen Elizabeth's most trusted ministers. The younger Bacon succeeded to his father's former post as keeper of the seal in 1617.
TO SIR LUCIUS CARY AND SIR HENRY MORISON [1]On Sir Lucius Cary (1610?–43), second Viscount Falkland, see Clarendon's moving tribute on pp. 797–800. Sir Henry Morison, Cary's brother-in-law, died (1629) at about twenty-one before fulfilling his great promise.
[2]As a strict Pindaric ode this noble eulogy is built upon the ancient tripartite choric movement to the left (the *strophe* or "turn") and to the right (the *antistrophe* or "counterturn"), followed by the *epode* or "stand."
[3]*Brave infant...urn*: According to Pliny (*Natural History*, VII.iii), an infant born at Saguntum in the year that Hannibal took and razed that ancient Spanish city (218 B.C.) at once (*protinus*) went back into its mother's womb.

THE STAND

For what is life if measur'd by the space,
    Not by the act?
Or masked man if valu'd by his face
    Above his fact?[4]
    Here's one outliv'd his peers,   25
    And told forth fourscore years;
He vexed time and busied the whole state,
    Troubled both foes and friends,
    But ever to no ends:
What did this stirrer but die late?   30
How well at twenty had he fall'n or stood!
For three of his fourscore he did no good.

2. THE TURN

    He ent'red well, by virtuous parts,[5]
    Got up, and thriv'd with honest arts;
He purchas'd friends, and fame, and honors then,   35
And had his noble name advanc'd with men:
    But weary of that flight,
    He stoop'd[6] in all men's sight
To sordid flatteries, acts of strife,
And sunk in that dead sea of life   40
So deep as he did then death's waters sup,
But that the cork of title buoy'd him up.

THE COUNTER TURN

    Alas! but Morison fell young:
    He never fell—thou fall'st, my tongue.
He stood a soldier to the last right end,
A perfect patriot and a noble friend,   45
    But most a virtuous son.
    All offices[7] were done
By him so ample, full, and round,
In weight, in measure, number, sound   50
As, though his age imperfect might appear,
His life was of humanity the sphere.[8]

THE STAND

Go now, and tell out days summ'd up with fears,
    And make them years;
Produce thy mass of miseries on the stage   55
    To swell thine age;
    Repeat of things a throng
    To show thou hast been long,
Not liv'd; for life doth her great actions spell[9]
    By what was done and wrought   60
    In season, and so brought
To light: her measures are, how well
Each syllabe[10] answer'd, and was form'd how fair;
These make the lines of life, and that's her air![11]

3. THE TURN

    It is not growing like a tree   65
    In bulk doth make men better be;
Or standing long an oak, three hundred year,
To fall a log at last, dry, bald, and sear:

    A lily of a day
    Is fairer far in May   70
Although it fall and die that night;
It was the plant and flow'r of light.
In small proportions we just beauties see,
And in short measures life may perfect be.

THE COUNTER TURN

    Call, noble Lucius, then for wine,   75
    And let thy looks with gladness shine:
Accept this garland, plant it on thy head.
And think, nay know, thy Morison's not dead.
    He leap'd the present age,
    Possess'd with holy rage[12]   80
    To see that bright eternal day
    Of which we priests and poets say
Such truths as we expect for happy men;
And there he lives with memory and Ben.

THE STAND

Jonson, who sung this of him ere he went,   85
    Himself, to rest,
Or taste a part of that full joy he meant
    To have express'd
    In this bright asterism[13]
    Where it were friendship's schism   90
    (Were not his Lucius long with us to tarry)
    To separate these twi-
    Lights, the Dioscuri,[14]
    And keep the one half from his Harry.
But fate doth so alternate the design,   95
Whilst that in heav'n, this light on earth must shine—

4. THE TURN

    And shine as you exalted are,
    Two names of friendship but one star:
Of hearts the union, and those not by chance
Made, or indentur'd or leas'd out t'advance   100
    The profits for a time.
    No pleasures vain did chime
    Of rhymes or riots at your feasts,
    Orgies of drink, or feign'd protests:[15]
But simple love of greatness and of good,   105
That knits brave minds and manners more than blood.

THE COUNTER TURN

    This made you first to know the why
    You lik'd, then after to apply
    That liking; and approach so one the tother,[16]

[4]Deed.   [5]Strong natural endowments.
[6]Descended quickly from a height (a term from falconry).
[7]Duties, moral obligations (a Latinism).
[8]Like the circle, an emblem of completion and perfection.
[9]Declare.   [10]Syllable, i.e., part.
[11]*These make...air*: i.e., these *measures* (line 63) determine the proper length of a man's life and reveal its proper style and manner?   [12]Impassioned desire.   [13]Constellation.
[14]Castor and Pollux, sons of Leda whom Zeus set among the stars as the constellation Gemini ("Twins").   [15]Protestations.   [16]Other.

Till either grew a portion of the other: 110
 Each styled by his end
 The copy of his friend
 You lived to be the great surnames
 And titles by which all made claims
Unto the virtue: nothing perfect done 115
But as a Cary or a Morison.

THE STAND

 And such a force the fair example had
  As they that saw
The good, and durst not practice it, were glad
  That such a law 120
  Was left yet to mankind;
  Where they might read and find
Friendship in deed was written, not in words;
  And with the heart, not pen,
  Of two so early men, 125
  Whose lines her rolls were, and records;
Who, ere the first down bloom'd upon the chin,
Had sow'd these fruits, and got the harvest in.

TO THE RIGHT HONORABLE, THE LORD
HIGH TREASURER OF ENGLAND[1] AN
EPISTLE MENDICANT 3 1631

My Lord,
Poor wretched states, press'd by extremities,
Are fain to seek for succors and supplies
Of princes' aids or good men's charities.

Disease, the enemy, and his engineers,
Want, with the rest of his conceal'd compeers, 5
Have cast a trench about me, now five years,[2]

And made those strong approaches by false brays,
Reduicts, half-moons, horn-works,[3] and such close[4] ways,
The Muse not peeps out one of hundred days,

But lies block'd up and strait'ned, narrow'd in, 10
Fix'd to the bed and boards, unlike to win
Health, or scarce breath, as she had never been,

Unless some saving honor of the Crown
Dare think it to relieve no less renown
A bedrid wit than a besieged town. 15

TO THE KING, ON HIS BIRTHDAY
An Epigram Anniversary[1]

This is King Charles his day. Speak it, thou Tower,
 Unto the ships, and they, from tier to tier,[2]
Discharge it 'bout the island in an hour,
 As loud as thunder, and as swift as fire.
Let Ireland meet it out at sea, half way, 5
 Repeating all Great Britain's joy, and more,
Adding her own glad accents to this day,
 Like Echo playing from the other shore.
What drums or trumpets, or great ordnance can,
 The poetry of steeples, with the bells, 10

Three kingdoms' mirth, in light and aery man,
 Made lighter with the wine. All noises else,
At bonefires,[3] rockets, fireworks, with the shouts
 That cry that gladness which their hearts would pray,
Had they but grace of thinking, at these routs, 15
 On th' often coming of this holiday:
And ever close the burden of the song,
Still to have such a Charles, but this Charles long.
The wish is great; but where the prince is such,
What prayers, people, can you think too much! 20

UNCOLLECTED VERSE

SONG[1]

Slow, slow, fresh fount, keep time with my salt tears;
 Yet slower, yet, O faintly, gentle springs;
List to the heavy part the music bears:
 "Woe weeps out her division[2] when she sings.
  Droop, herbs and flow'rs; 5
  Fall, grief, in show'rs:
  Our beauties are not ours."
   O I could still,
Like melting snow upon some craggy hill,
  Drop, drop, drop, drop, 10
Since nature's pride is now a wither'd daffodil.

THE HYMN[1]

Queen and huntress,[2] chaste and fair,
 Now the sun is laid to sleep,
Seated in thy silver chair,
 State in wonted manner keep.
Hesperus[3] entreats thy light, 5
Goddess, excellently bright.

TO THE LORD HIGH TREASURER [1]Richard, Lord Western (1577–1635), having served as chancellor and under-treasurer of the exchequer since 1621, was named lord high treasurer in 1628. For his political services to the crown Charles created him earl of Portland in 1632.
[2]Jonson suffered a paralytic stroke in 1628. Thus the date of this supplication must be 1633, not 1631 as noted at the start.
[3]*False brays...horn-works:* i.e., military devices and procedures. Faussebraies (*false brays*) are artificial defensive walls erected in front of a main rampart; redoubts (*reducts*) are secondary strongholds within a ring of outworks; demilunes (*half-moons*) are defensive lines in the shape of a crescent; and *horn-works* are fortified positions outside the main ramparts of a garrison.
[4]Restricting.
TO THE KING [1]A marginal note dates this epigram 19 November 1632. [2]I.e., of guns. [3]Bonfires.
SONG [1]From *Cynthia's Revels* (1600), I.ii. The text is that of the 1616 Folio.
[2]In music, the dividing of a succession of long notes into shorter ones. Jonson exemplified the metrical effect in the lines that follow.
THE HYMN [1]From *Cynthia's Revels* (1600), V.vi. The text is that of the 1616 Folio.
[2]The chaste Diana (or Cynthia), goddess of the moon and of the hunt. [3]The evening star.

Earth, let not thy envious shade
  Dare itself to interpose;
Cynthia's shining orb was made
  Heaven to clear[4] when day did close.   10
Bless us, then, with wished sight,
Goddess, excellently bright.

Lay thy bow of pearl apart,
  And thy crystal-shining quiver;
Give unto the flying hart   15
  Space to breathe, how short soever,
Thou that mak'st a day of night,
Goddess, excellently bright.

TO THE WORTHY AUTHOR, MASTER JOHN FLETCHER[1]

The wise and many-headed bench[2] that sits
Upon the life and death of plays and wits
(Compos'd of gamester, captain, knight, knight's man,
Lady or pusil[3] that wears mask or fan,
Velvet or taffeta cap, rank'd[4] in the dark   5
With the shop's foreman or some such brave spark
That may judge for his sixpence) had, before
They saw it half, damn'd thy whole play, and more.
Their motives were, since it had not to do
With vices, which they look'd for and came to.   10
I, that am glad thy innocence was thy guilt,
And wish that all the Muses' blood were spilt
In such a martyrdom, to vex their eyes
Do crown thy murd'red poem, which shall rise
A glorified work to Time when fire   15
Or moths shall eat what all these fools admire.

SONG[1]

Still to be neat,[2] still to be drest
As[3] you were going to a feast,
Still to be powd'red, still perfum'd,
Lady, it is to be presum'd,
Though art's[4] hid causes are not found,   5
All is not sweet, all is not sound.

Give me a look, give me a face,
That makes simplicity a grace:
Robes loosely flowing, hair as free;
Such sweet neglect more taketh[5] me   10
Than all th' adulteries[6] of art.
They[7] strike mine eyes, but not my heart.

TO MY WORTHY AND HONORED FRIEND, MASTER GEORGE CHAPMAN, ON HIS TRANSLATION OF HESIOD'S WORKS AND DAYS[1]

Whose work could this be, Chapman, to refine
Old Hesiod's ore and give it thus, but thine,
Who hadst before wrought in rich Homer's mine?[2]

What treasure hast thou brought us! And what store
Still, still dost thou arrive with at our shore   5
To make thy honor and our wealth the more!

If all the vulgar tongues that speak this day
Were ask'd of thy discoveries, they must say,
To the Greek coast thine only knew the way.

Such passage hast thou found, such returns made,   10
As now, of[3] all men, it is call'd thy trade,[4]
And who make thither else, rob or invade.

TO THE MEMORY OF MY BELOVED, THE AUTHOR, MASTER WILLIAM SHAKESPEARE, AND WHAT HE HATH LEFT US[1]

To draw no envy, Shakespeare, on thy name,
Am I thus ample[2] to thy book and fame,
While I confess thy writings to be such
As neither man nor Muse can praise too much.
'Tis true, and all men's suffrage.[3] But these ways   5
Were not the paths I meant unto thy praise;
For seeliest[4] Ignorance on these may light,
Which, when it sounds at best, but echoes right;
Or blind Affection, which doth ne'er advance
The truth, but gropes, and urgeth all by chance;   10
Or crafty Malice might pretend this praise,
And think to ruin where it seem'd to raise.
These are as[5] some infamous bawd or whore
Should praise a matron: what would hurt her more?
But thou art proof against them, and indeed   15
Above th' ill fortune of them, or the need.
I therefore will begin: Soul of the age!
The applause! delight! the wonder of our stage!
My Shakespeare, rise! I will not lodge thee by
Chaucer, or Spenser, or bid Beaumont lie   20
A little further to make thee a room:[6]
Thou art a monument without a tomb,
And art alive still while thy book doth live
And we have wits to read and praise to give.
That I not mix thee so, my brain excuses—   25
I mean with great but disproportion'd Muses;

[4]Make bright

TO MASTER JOHN FLETCHER [1]From a set of commendatory verses prefixed to John Fletcher's *The Faithful Sheperdess* (1610? STC 11068), a pastoral drama that despite its unfavorable reception in the theater was published to applause. For William Cartwright's use of this poem see p. 298. [2]I.e., bench of judges. [3]Pucelle, i.e., harlot. [4]Seated in rows.

SONG [1]From *Epicoene, or the Silent Woman* (acted 1609), I.i. The text is that of the 1616 Folio. [2]Elegantly appareled. [3]As if. [4]Artifice's. [5]Captives, charms. [6]Adulterations. [7]Text *Thy.*

TO MASTER GEORGE CHAPMAN [1]From *The Georgicks of Hesiod, By George Chapman; Translated Elaborately out of the Greek* (1618 STC 13249). [2]On the long history of Chapman's translation of Homer see pp. 11–12. [3]By. [4]I.e., trading monopoly.

TO MASTER WILLIAM SHAKESPEARE [1]From *Mr. William Shakespeares Comedies, Histories, & Tragedies* (1623, STC 22273). [2]Liberal, unstinted. [3]Consent. [4]Silliest, i.e., simplest, most innocent. [5]As if. [6]*I will not...room:* Chaucer, Spenser, and Beaumont lie close together on the north side of the nave (in the so-called Poets' Corner) of Westminster Abbey, where Jonson himself joined them in 1637. Shakespeare was buried in Holy Trinity Church at Stratford-upon-Avon.

For if I thought my judgment were of years,
I should commit thee surely with thy peers,
And tell how far thou didst our Lyly outshine,
Or sporting Kyd, or Marlowe's mighty line.[7]   30
And though thou hadst small Latin and less Greek,
From thence to honor thee I would not seek
For names: but call forth thundring Aeschylus,
Euripides, and Sophocles to us,
Pacuvius, Accius, him of Cordova dead,[8]   35
To life again, to hear thy buskin tread
And shake a stage; or, when thy socks[9] were on,
Leave thee alone for the comparison
Of all that insolent Greece or haughty Rome
Sent forth, or since did from their ashes come.   40
Triumph, my Britain, thou hast one to show
To whom all scenes[10] of Europe homage owe.
He was not of an age, but for all time!
And all the Muses still were in their prime
When like Apollo he came forth to warm   45
Our ears, or like a Mercury to charm!
Nature herself was proud of his designs,
And joy'd to wear the dressing of his lines!
Which were so richly spun, and woven so fit,
As, since, she will vouchsafe no other wit.   50
The merry Greek, tart Aristophanes,
Neat[11] Terence, witty Plautus now not please,
But antiquated and deserted lie
As they were not of Nature's family.
Yet must I not give Nature all; thy art,   55
My gentle Shakespeare, must enjoy a part.
For though the poet's matter Nature be,
His art doth give the fashion; and that he[12]
Who casts to write a living line must sweat
(Such as thine are) and strike the second heat   60
Upon the Muse's anvil; turn the same,
And himself with it, that he thinks to frame;
Or for[13] the laurel he may gain a scorn,
For a good poet's made as well as born.
And such wert thou. Look how[14] the father's face   65
Lives in his issue, even so the race
Of Shakespeare's mind and manners brightly shines
In his well-turned and true-filed lines;
In each of which he seems to shake a lance,[15]
As brandish'd at the eyes of Ignorance.   70
Sweet Swan of Avon! what a sight it were
To see thee in our waters yet appear,
And make those flights upon the banks of Thames
That so did take[16] Eliza and our James![17]
But stay, I see thee in the hemisphere   75
Advanc'd, and made a constellation there!
Shine forth, thou star of poets, and with rage
Or influence[18] chide or cheer the drooping stage,
Which, since thy flight from hence, hath mourn'd
    like night,
And despairs day, but for thy volume's light.   80

[IT WAS A BEAUTY THAT I SAW][1]

It was a beauty that I saw,
So pure, so perfect as the frame

Of all the universe was lame
To that one figure, could I draw
Or give least line of it a law.   5

A skein of silk without a knot,
A fair march made without a halt,
A curious form without a fault,
A printed book without a blot,
All beauty, and without a spot.   10

THE JUST INDIGNATION THE AUTHOR TOOK AT
THE VULGAR CENSURE OF HIS PLAY BY SOME
MALICIOUS SPECTATORS BEGAT
THIS FOLLOWING ODE TO HIMSELF[1]

    Come, leave the loathed stage
    And the more loathsome age,
Where Pride and Impudence, in faction knit,
    Usurp the chair of Wit,
Indicting and arraigning every day   5
    Something they call a play.
    Let their fastidious,[2] vain
    Commission of the brain
Run on, and rage, sweat, censure, and condemn:
They were not made for thee, less thou for them.   10

    Say that thou pour'st them wheat.
    And they would acorns eat:
'Twere simple[3] fury still thyself to waste
    On such as have no taste,
To offer them a surfeit of pure bread   15
    Whose appetites are dead.

[7]*For if I thought...line:* i.e., if I were to take a long view (*of years*) I would rank (*commit*) you with your peers among ancient writers, not with your immediate predecessors like John Lyly, Thomas Kyd, and Christopher Marlowe, whom, despite their merits, you easily surpassed.
[8]*Pacuvius...dead:* The works of the Latin tragedians Marcus Pacuvius (d. ca. 130 B.C.) and Lucius Accius or Attius (d. ca. 86 B.C.) survive only in fragments, but the nine extant tragedies of Lucius Annaeus Seneca (who was born at Corduba or *Cordova* in Spain) were widely admired and very influential in the sixteenth century. Horace (*Epistles*, II.i.56) named Pacuvius and Accius as preeminent among "old" writers.
[9]*Buskin...sock:* Respectively, the boot (*cothurnus*) and light shoe worn by ancient actors of tragedy and comedy. [10]Stages.
[11]Elegant. [12]Man. [13]In place of. [14]Just as.
[15]Jonson is punning on Shakespeare's name. [16]Charm.
[17]Queen Elizabeth and James I.
[18]*With...influence:* i.e., with malign or benign effect (a figure from astrology).
IT WAS A BEAUTY THAT I SAW   [1]*It was...I saw:* From *The New Inn* 1631, STC 14780), IV.iv.
THE JUST INDIGNATION   [1]*The just...himself:* Printed as a kind of afterpiece to *The New Inn*, a comedy that had been hissed from the stage in 1629 and that Jonson published two years later with this compendious and excoriating explanation on the title page: "As it was never acted, but most negligently played, by some, the King's Servants. And more squeamishly beheld and censured by others, the King's Subjects, 1629. Now, at last, set at liberty to the readers, his Majesty's Servants and Subjects, to be judged, 1631. By the author, B. Jonson." [2]Disdainful. [3]Foolish.

No, give them grains[4] their fill,
  Husks, draff,[5] to drink and swill;
If they love lees, and leave the lusty[6] wine,
Envy them not: their palate's with the swine.   20

  No doubt a moldy tale
  Like *Pericles*,[7] and stale
As the shrieve's[8] crusts and nasty as his fish—
  Scraps out of every dish,
Thrown forth and rak'd into the common tub,   25
  May keep up the play club.[9]
  There sweepings do as well
  As the best-order'd meal,
For who the relish of these guests will fit
Needs set them but the alms-basket of wit.   30

  And much good do't ye then,
  Brave plush-and-velvet men,
Can feed on orts, and safe in your stage-clothes
  Dare quit, upon your oaths,
The stagers and the stage-wrights too, your peers,   35
  Of larding your large ears
  With their foul comic socks,
  Wrought upon twenty blocks;
Which if they are torn and turn'd and patch'd enough,
The gamesters share your guilt, and you their stuff.[10]   40

  Leave things so prostitute
  And take the Alcaic lute,
Or thine own Horace's or Anacreon's lyre;
  Warm thee by Pindar's fire;[11]
And though thy nerves[12] be shrunk and blood be cold   45
  Ere years have made thee old,
  Strike that[13] disdainful heat
  Throughout, to their defeat,
As curious fools, and envious of thy strain,
May, blushing, swear no palsy's in thy brain.   50

  But when they hear thee sing
  The glories of thy king,
His zeal to God and his just awe o'er men,
  They may, blood-shaken, then
Feel such a flesh-quake to possess[14] their powers   55
  As they shall cry, "Like ours,
  In sound of peace or wars,
  No harp e'er hit the stars[15]
In tuning forth the acts of his sweet reign
And raising Charles his chariot 'bove his Wain."[16]   60

[THOUGH I AM YOUNG, AND CANNOT TELL][1]

Though I am young, and cannot tell
  Either that Death or Love is well,
Yet I have heard they both bear darts,
  And both do aim at human hearts.
And then again I have been told   5
  Love wounds with heat,[2] as Death with cold,
So that I fear they do but bring
  Extremes to touch, and mean one thing.

As in a ruin we it call
  One thing to be blown up or fall,   10
Or to our end like way may have
  By a flash of lightning or a wave,
So Love's inflamed shaft or brand
  May kill as soon as Death's cold hand,
Except Love's fires the virtue[3] have   15
  To fright the frost out of the grave.

[4]Refuse malt. [5]Dregs. [6]Powerful.
[7]Shakespeare's play (first printed in 1609) apparently retained its popularity despite its loose construction and sensational plotting. [8]Sheriff's. The basket kept outside a jail to receive gifts of food (often left-over scraps) for impoverished prisoners was called the sheriff's tub. [9]I.e., regular playgoers.
[10]*Brave plush...stuff*: This complicated stanza may be roughly paraphrased as follows: The theater is generally corrupt. The play-going gentry in their fine clothes (*brave plush-and-velvet men*) are content with trash and scraps (*orts*); they absolve (*quit*) the players and the playwrights (*stagers and the stage-wrights*) of using stale devices (*foul comic socks*) to please an undiscriminating public; everyone is party to the fraud.
[11]*Alcaic...Pindar's fire*: i.e., return to classical propriety as represented by such renowned lyric poets as Alcaeus of Lesbos (inventor of the Alcaic meter), Horace, Anacreon, and Pindar. For Jonson' own notable attempt to produce a Pindaric ode see "To the Immortal Memory and Friendship of That Noble Pair," pp. 99–101. [12]Sinews (Latin *nervi*). In 1628, a year before the production of *The New Inn*, Jonson had suffered a stroke that disabled him for the rest of his life. [13]Such. [14]Take possession of.
[15]I.e., write great poetry. The phrase—which Herrick uses too (p. 184)—is Horace's (*Odes*, I.x.41).
[16]Charles' Wain (i.e., Charlemagne's chariot), the Big Dipper.
THOUGH I AM YOUNG [1]*Though...tell*: from *The Sad Shepherd, or A Tale of Robin Hood*, I.v. This last, unfinished play of Jonson's was published in the 1640 Folio with a title page dated 1641. [2]Text *heart*. [3]Power.

George Sandys [1578–1644]

George Sandys was one of those Elizabethans who combined literature and action. Like Thomas Lodge's *Rosalynde* ("hatched in the storms of the ocean and feathered in the surges of many perilous seas") and Sir Walter Raleigh's *History of the World* (the trophy of his long incarceration in the Tower while awaiting execution), his translation of Ovid's *Metamorphoses* was not written in a cloistered academic study: it was put together amid the hazards and the tedium of the Virginian wilderness where Sandys, a colonial entrepreneur, was seeking fame and fortune.

Sandys' thirst for travel and adventure had early shown itself when this seventh and youngest son of an archbishop of York left Oxford without taking a degree and embarked upon the travels that took him as far as Palestine and Egypt. His adventures were recorded in *The Relation of a Journey*, a work so popular that it went through eight editions between 1615 and 1673. In the light of his experiences it was only natural that he should be infected with the contemporary fever for colonial exploration. Although one of the "undertakers" of the Virginia charter as early as 1611 and then a shareholder of the Bermudas Company, not until 1621 did he finally reach America. There he stayed for ten years, first as treasurer of the Virginian Company and then, after the crown assumed the governance of the colony in 1624, as a somewhat quarrelsome member of the council. However, his duties as administrator and landowner (for he of course acquired his own "plantation") did not stop his work on Ovid's *Metamorphoses*, five books of which had appeared in 1621 on the eve of his departure. It was then that Drayton urged him, in a cantankerous epistle (see p. 43), to see the undertaking through despite the hazards of Virginia:

> And, worthy George, by industry and use
> Let's see what lines Virginia will produce.
> Go on with Ovid as you have begun
> With the first five books; let your numbers run
> Glib as the former, so shall it live long,
> And do much honor to the English tongue.

By 1626 the job was done and duly published. It was a work "sprung from the stock of the ancient Romans," Sandys explained in the dedication to the king, "but bred in the New World, of the rudeness whereof it cannot but participate, especially having wars and tumults to bring it to light instead of the Muses." In 1632, after Sandys, denied the post of secretary, had returned to England in disgust, his work attained its final sumptuous form with such embellishments as a life of Ovid, engraved title pages, erudite allegorical commentaries for all the fifteen books, and an appended English version of the first book of the *Aeneid* (which was never carried further). Despite the occasional strain (and even obscurity) of a literal line-for-line rendition of the compact Latin into English, Sandys' trim pentameter couplets with their artfully varied caesuras became a model for Augustan poets. However questionable his unyielding literalism, the "ingenious and learned" Sandys was, said Dryden flatly, "the best versifier of the former age."

With his return to England in 1631 Sandys' travels were completed, and apart from a brief and unsuccessful appointment (1638) as London agent for the Virginian legislative assembly he gave his final years to literature. As a gentleman of the privy chamber to Charles I (to whom all his books were dedicated) and an honored member of Lord Falkland's remarkable coterie at Great Tew that Clarendon has immortalized (see pp. 799–800), his position in society was secure. His *Paraphrase upon the Psalms and upon the Hymns Dispersed throughout the Old and New Testaments*, reinforced by a dedication to the king and queen and by commendatory verses of Falkland and Dudley Digges, appeared in 1636 and again in 1638 as a lavish folio with new poetical tributes from many men of letters. His final works were a translation (1640) in heroic couplets of Hugo Grotius' tragedy *Christus patiens* and a paraphrase (1641) in octosyllabic couplets of the Song of Solomon. Even as "a very aged man," according to Thomas Fuller, he retained "a youthful soul in a decayed body" until his death in 1644.

My texts are based on *Ovid's Metamorphosis Englished, Mythologiz'd, And Represented in Figures. An Essay to the Translation of Virgil's Aeneis*, 1632 (STC 18966), *A Paraphrase vpon the Psalmes of David. And vpon the Hymnes Dispersed throughout the Old and New Testaments*, 1636 (STC 21724), and *A Paraphrase vpon the Divine Poems*, 1638 (STC 21725). There are editions of the *Poetical*

Works—i.e., the paraphrases and *Christ's Passion*—by Richard Hooper (2 vols., 1872), of *Selections from the Paraphrases* by H. J. Todd (1839), and of the 1632 Ovid by K. K. Hulley and S. T. Vandersall (1970). The standard life is that by R. B. Davis (1955). The articles include a study of Sandys' metrics by Ruth C. Wallerstein (*PMLA*, L, 1935), of his translation of the *Metamorphoses* by Davis (*Papers of the Bibliographical Society of America*, XXXV, 1941) and J. G. McManaway (*Bibliographical Society: University of Virginia*, I, 1948–49), and of early editions of the works by Fredson Bowers and Davis (*Bulletin of the New York Public Library*, LIV, 1950).

from Ovid's Metamorphoses (1632)

To the Reader

Since it should be the principal end in publishing of books to inform the understanding, direct the will, and temper the affections, in this second edition[1] of my translation I have attempted (with what success I submit to the reader) to collect out of sundry authors the philosophical sense of these fables of Ovid—if I may call them his when most of them are more ancient than any extant author, or perhaps than letters themselves; before which, as they expressed their conceptions in hieroglyphics, so did they their philosophy and divinity under fables and parables: a way not untrod by the sacred penmen, as by the prudent lawgivers in their reducing[2] of the old world to civility, leaving behind a deeper impression than can be made by the liveless precepts of philosophy. Plato in his imaginary commonwealth ordaineth that mothers and nurses should season the tender minds of their children with these instructive fables,[3] wherein the wisdom of the ancient was involved, some under allegories expressing the wonderful works of nature, some administering comfort in calamity, others expelling the terrors and perturbations of the mind, some inflaming by noble examples with an honest emulation and leading, as it were, by the hand to the temple of honor and virtue. For the poet not only renders things as they are, but what are not as if they were, or rather as they should be, agreeable to the high affections of the soul and more conducing to magnanimity, juster than either men or Fortune in the exalting of virtue and suppressing of vice, by showing the beauty of the one and deformity of the other, pursued by the divine vengeance, by inbred terrors, and infernal torments. For apparent it is that they among the heathen preserved that truth of the immortality of the soul; and therefore Epicurus,[4] who maintained the contrary, dehorted[5] his scholars from the reading of poetry. In the mythology[6] I have rather followed (as fuller of delight and more useful) the variety of men's several conceptions (where they are not overstrained) than curiously examined their exact propriety, which is to be borne with in fables and allegories, so as the principal parts of application resemble the groundwork.

I have also endeavored to clear the historical part by tracing the almost worn-out steps of antiquity, wherein the sacred stories afford the clearest direction. For the first period from the creation to the flood, which the ethnics[7] called the "Obscure" (some the "Empty Times"), and the ages next following, which were styled the "Heroical" because the after[8] deified heroes then flourished; as also the "Fabulous," in that those stories conveyed by tradition in loose and broken fragments were by the poets interwoven with instructing mythologies, are most obscurely and perplexedly delivered by all but the supernaturally inspired Moses. Wherefore not without authority have I here and there given a touch of the relation which those fabulous traditions have to the divine history, which the Fathers have observed and made use of in convincing the heathen. By this and the rest it may appear that our subject, however slight in appearance, is nothing less both in use and substance, wherein if my intentions fail not, the matter and delivery is so tempered that the ordinary reader need not reject it as too difficult nor the learned as too obvious.

To the translation I have given what perfection my pen could bestow by polishing, altering, or restoring the harsh, improper, or mistaken with a nicer exactness than perhaps is required in so long a labor. I have also added marginal notes for illustration and ease of the mere English reader, since divers places in our author are otherwise impossible to be understood but by those who are well versed in the ancient poets and historians. . . .

Lastly, since I cannot but doubt that my errors in so various a subject require a favorable connivence,[9] I am to desire that the printer's may not be added to mine. The literal will easily pass without rubs in the reading; the gross ones correct themselves; but by those between both, the sense is in greatest danger to suffer. However, I have sifted out all, or the most material, and exposed them in the end of the volume.

TO THE READER   [1]For the history of the publication of Sandys' Ovid see the headnote.   [2]Leading (a Latinism).
[3]*Plato . . . fables: The Republic*, II.377. However, Plato goes on to say that "we must reject" most of the fables told to children.   [4]Greek materialist philosopher (342?–270 B.C.).   [5]Advised.
[6]I.e., the elaborate commentary accompanying Sandys' translation.   [7]Pagans.   [8]Subsequently.
[9]Literally, winking at, i.e., indulgence.

THE FIRST BOOK

> No sooner had the world been created out of primordial chaos, Ovid relates, than it began an accelerating decline from the Age of Gold to the Age of Iron. It was then, when Astraea had left "the blood-defiled earth" and the Giants had waged their savage, futile war on heaven, that Zeus, in a council of the gods, declared that man should be destroyed.

Jove's words a part approve and his intent
Exasperate;[1] the rest give their consent.
Yet all for man's destruction griev'd appear,
And ask what form the widowed earth shall bear.
Who shall with odors their cold altars feast?[2]
Must earth be only by wild beasts possess'd?
The king of gods recomforts[3] their despair,
And biddeth them impose on him that care,
Who promis'd, by a strange original[4]
Of better people, to supply their fall.
And now, about to let his lightning fly,
He fear'd lest so much flame should catch the sky
And burn heaven's axletree. Besides, by doom[5]
Of certain Fate[6] he knew the time should come
When sea, earth, ravish'd heaven, the curious frame
Of this world's mass should shrink in purging flame.
He therefore those Cyclopean darts[7] rejects,
And different-natur'd punishments elects:[8]
To open all the flood-gates of the sky
And man by inundation to destroy.
   Rough Boreas in Aeolian prison laid,
And those dry blasts which gathered clouds invade,
Out flies the south[9] with drooping wings,[10] who shrouds
His terrible aspect in pitchy clouds.
His white hair streams, his beard big-swoll'n with show'rs,
Mists bind his brows, rain from his bosom pours,
As [11]with his hands the hanging clouds he crush'd,
They roar'd, and down in show'rs together rush'd.
All-color'd Iris,[12] Juno's messenger,
To weeping clouds doth nourishment confer.[13]
The corn is lodg'd,[14] the husbandmen despair,
Their long year's labor lost with all their care.
Jove, not content with his ethereal rages,[15]
His brother's[16] auxil'ary floods engages.
The streams convented,[17] " 'Tis too late to use
Much speech," said Neptune. "All your pow'rs effuse,[18]
Your doors unbar, remove whate'er restrains
Your liberal waves, and give them the full reins."
Thus charged, they return, their springs unfold,
And to the sea with headlong fury roll'd.
He[19] with his trident strikes the earth; she shakes,
And way for water by her motion makes.
Through open fields now rush the spreading floods,
And hurry with them cattle, people, woods,
Houses, and temples with their gods enclos'd.
What such a force unoverthrown oppos'd,
The higher-swelling water quite devours,
Which hides th' aspiring[20] tops of swallowed tow'rs,
Now land and sea no different visage bore,

For all was sea, nor had the sea a shore.
One takes a hill; one in a boat deplores,
And where he lately plow'd now strikes his oars:
O'er corn, o'er drowned villages he sails;
This[21] from high elms entangled fishes hales.
In fields they anchor cast, as chance did guide,
And ships the underlying vineyards hide.
Where mountain-loving goats did lately graze,
The sea-calf[22] now his ugly body lays.
Groves, cities, temples cover'd by the deep
The nymphs admire; in woods the delphins[23] keep
And chase about the boughs; the wolf doth swim
Amongst the sheep;[24] the lion (now not grim)
And tigers tread the waves. Swift feet no more
Avail the hart, nor wounding tusks the boar.
The wand'ring birds, hid earth long sought in vain,
With weary wings descend into the main.
Licentious[25] seas o'er drowned hills now fret,
And unknown surges airy mountains beat.
The waves the greater part devour; the rest,
Death, with long-wanted sustenance, oppress'd. . . .

UPON THE FIRST BOOK OF OVID'S "METAMORPHOSES"

   . . . The gods in this council are chiefly solicitous about the preservation of the divine worship; to inform how religion should be the chief and first care in all consultations, the world being made for man, and man for God's service, as the divine philosopher[1] could instruct us.
   Jupiter, intending to burn the earth, is restrained by that remembered destiny, how not only earth but heaven itself should one day by fire be consumed. This is held to be but once revealed in the scriptures, and that by St. Peter.[2] How came it, then, to the knowledge of Ovid, who was dead

THE FIRST BOOK [1]I.e., intensify his purpose (to act even more harshly). [2]Regale. [3]Consoles. [4]I.e., fresh creation. [5]Decree.
[6]"Concurring which [i.e., with?] the sacred scripture" (Sandys' gloss).
[7]"Lightning forged by the Cyclops" (Sandys' gloss).
[8]*Different...elects*: i.e., chooses another kind of punishment.
[9]South wind (associated with rain and fog).
[10]*Rough Boreas...wings*: i.e., the blustery north wind (*Boreas*) and all the cloud-scattering dry winds being confined in the cave of Aeolus, god of the winds. [11]As if.
[12]"A name for the rainbow" (Sandys' gloss).
[13]*To weeping...confer*: i.e., she draws up the water again to replenish the clouds. [14]The grain is beaten down (by rain).
[15]I.e., disturbances from the sky.
[16]"Neptune, the god of waters" (Sandys' gloss).
[17]Convoked, assembled. [18]Pour out (a Latinism).
[19]I.e., Neptune. [20]Rising, thrusting upward. [21]I.e., another.
[22]Seal. [23]Dolphins.
[24]*The wolf...sheep*: "Seneca reproves this part of the description as too light for so sad an argument, herein perhaps a better philosopher than a poet" (Sandys' gloss). [25]Unrestrained.
UPON THE FIRST BOOK [1]Plato?
[2]"But the day of the Lord will come as a thief in the night, in which the heavens shall pass away with a great noise, and the elements shall melt with fervent heat; the earth also, and the works that are in it, shall be burned up" (2 Peter 3.10).

before that epistle was written? It may be out of the proph-
ecies of the Sibyls, as in this:

> These signs the world's combustion shall forerun:
> Arms clashing, trumpets, from the rising sun
> Horrible fragors[3] heard by all; this frame
> Of nature then shall feed the greedy flame.
> Men, cities, floods, and seas by rav'nous lust
> Of fire devour'd, all shall resolve to dust.[4]

From hence, perhaps, the ancient philosophers derived their
opinions, as Seneca a latter:[5] "The stars shall encounter one
another, and whatsoever now shines so orderly shall burn
in one fire." Who presume to ascribe it to a natural cause
that the sun and the stars, being fed by watery vapors,
shall set the world on a conflagration as soon as that nourish-
ment is exhausted, whenas the stars are not fiery in their
proper nature, and no vapors ascend above the middle
region of the air. Besides, what sustenance can they receive
from the humidity of the earth when the least fixed star
which is observed is eighteen and the sun one hundred sixty
and seven times bigger than the earth itself? But the im-
mediate hand of God shall effect it, as it did this deluge,
although this also the naturalists impute to watery constella-
tions.

The sins of men drew on (in which our poet concurs with
Moses) the general deluge, although he transfer it to Deu-
calion's,[6] wherein most of Greece was surrounded, which
happened seven hundred and fourscore years after the other;
yet in this he describeth the former, as appears by many
particulars which may serve to reconcile his chronology, for
many of these following stories were before the days of
Deucalion. There is no nation so barbarous—no, not the
salvage Virginians[7]—but have some notion of so great a ruin.
The natural causes he allégeth of these accumulated waters.
The north winds are shut up, the south set at liberty; the
clouds descend in showers which are nourished by the rain-
bow because the rain is increased by that dissolving vapor
wherein it appeareth. . . . To confirm what hath been al-
leged by a known experiment: if with a scoop[8] against the
setting sun you cast water circularly into the air, a rainbow
will appear therein. This is called Iris, the daughter of Thau-
mas, or "Wonder." Iris imports a message because it pre-
sageth fair or foul weather, as it followeth the contrary, and
therefore the messenger of Juno, who is taken for the air
where clouds are engendered. Moreover, Neptune lifts up
his floods, the commanded rivers unlock their fountains;
he strikes the earth with his trident, which is said to shake
in that the land which borders on the sea is most subject
unto earthquakes, whose breaches give new ascents to sub-
terrene[9] waters, or let in those of the ocean. . . .

THE TENTH BOOK

[Orpheus and Eurydice]

Hence to the Cicones[1] through boundless skies
In saffron mantle Hymenaeus flies,
By Orpheus call'd, but neither usual words
Nor cheerful looks nor happy signs affords.

The torch his hand sustain'd, still sputtering, rais'd
A sullen smoke; nor yet, though shaken, blaz'd.
Th' event[2] worse than the omen; as his bride
Troops with the Naiades by Hebrus' side
A serpent bit her by the heel, which forc'd
Life from her hold and nuptial ties divorc'd.[3]
Whom when the Thracian poet had above[4]
Enough bewail'd that his complaints might move
The under shades by Tenarus[5] descends
To Stygian floods; and his bold steps extends,
By airy shapes and fleeting souls that boast
Of sepulture,[6] through that unpleasant coast
To Pluto's court; when, having tun'd his strings,
Thus to his harp the godlike poet sings:
  "You pow'rs that sway the world beneath the earth,
The last abode of all our human birth,
If we the truth without offense may tell,
I come not hither to discover[7] hell,
Nor bind that scowling cur[8] who barking shakes
About his triple brows Medusa's snakes.
My wife this journey urg'd,[9] who by the tooth
Of trod-on viper perish'd in her youth.
I would, and strove t' have borne her loss;[10] but Love
Won in that strife—a god well known above,
Nor here perhaps unknown. If truly fame
Report old rapes, you also felt his flame.
By these obscure abodes so full of dread,
By this huge chaos and deep silence spread
Through your vast empire, by these prayers of mine,
Eurydice's too-hasty fate untwine.
We all are yours, and after a short stay,
Early or late we all must run one way.
Hither we throng for our last home assign'd,
Th' eternal habitation of mankind.
She, when her time by nature shall expire,

[3]Harsh noises.
[4]Sandys quotes from the so-called *Sibylline Books* (*Sibyllini libri* or *Libri fatales*), a collection of prophecies compiled after the ut-
terances of the Cumaean Sibyl, whom Aeneas had allegedly consulted, were lost when fire destroyed the temple of Jupiter (82 B.C.).
[5]I.e., as the Stoic philosopher Lucius Annaeus Seneca (d. 65) subsequently derived.
[6]A virtuous son of Prometheus who, on the advice of his father, built a ship in which he and his wife Pyrrha safely rode out the nine-day flood. They were the only mortals spared.
[7]I.e., savages of the New World.   [8]Ladle.   [9]Subterranean.
THE TENTH BOOK   [1]"A people of Thrace, by the River Hebrus" (Sandys' gloss).   [2]Outcome.
[3]*A serpent...divorc'd*: In a later version of the myth Eurydice is bitten by a serpent while trying to escape the lustful Aristaeus.
[4]In the upper world.
[5]"A promontory of Laconia, wherein a cave, as they held, de-
scended to hell." (Sandys' gloss)
[6]Only the souls of those who had received proper burial were admitted to Hades.   [7]Attain knowledge of.
[8]Cerberus, a three-headed dog who guarded the portals of Hades.
[9]Prompted, motivated.
[10]*I...loss*: I wanted to be strong enough to endure her loss, and strove to do so.

Again is yours; I but the use desire.
If Fate deny me this, my second choice
Is here t' abide: in both our deaths rejoice."
　　While thus he sung and struck the quavering strings,
The bloodless shadows wept; nor flattering springs
Tempt Tantalus, Ixion's wheel stood still,
Their urn the Belides no longer fill,
The vultures feed not, Tityus left[11] to groan,
And Sisyphus sat list'ning on his stone.[12]
The Furies, vanquish'd by his verse, were seen
To weep, that never wept before. Hell's Queen,
The King of Darkness[13] yield t' his pow'rful plea.
Among the late-come souls Eurydice
They call; she came, yet halting[14] of her wound;
Given Orpheus with this law: "Till thou the bound
Of pale Avernus pass, if back thou cast
Thy careful[15] eyes thou losest what thou hast."
A steep ascent, dark, thick with fogs, they climb
Through everlasting silence; by this time
Approach the confines of illustrious[16] light.
Fearing to lose and longing for a sight,
His eyes th' impatient lover backward threw,
When she, back-sliding, presently withdrew.
He catches at her, in his wits distraught,
And yielding air for her (unhappy!) caught.[17]
Nor did she, dying twice, her spouse reprove,
For what could she complain of but his love?
Who takes her last farewell—her parting breath
Scarce reach'd his ears—and so revolves[18] to death. . . .

Upon the Tenth Book of Ovid's "Metamorphoses"

Invoked Hymen repairs to the nuptials of Orpheus and Eurydice, but with unusual silence and an ominous sadness. He is said to be clothed in a mantle of a saffron dye in that brides accustomed to cover their faces with veils of that color, not only for modesty and to conceal their resembled[1] blushes, but as a happy presage, since continually worn by the wives of the flamens,[2] between whom and their husbands there could be no divorcement. The nuptial torches among the Romans were borne by five comely youths of her kindred, pretending[3] concord by that uneven number which cannot be divided into an equal fraction, but one will remain to compose the difference; and declaring by their light how the wife is the splendor and glory of her husband. But among the Grecians they used only a single torch, and that carried by one who represented Hymen, which if it burnt not clearly (as here), but crackled and cast up a black and cloudy vapor, was held to prognosticate infelicity; and therefore they not seldom made the staff of whitethorn, which afforded but a little light, yet free from smoke or ill savor. But truer presages they are of the weather: if the lights burn bright, of fair; if blue, of frosty; if obscurely and with spongeous wicks, of foul and rainy.

> Night-working spinsters know, when they
> 　　behold
> Oil sputter in the blazing lamp or view
> The spongy wick, foul weather will ensue.[4]

So the trembling and flexuous[5] burning of the flame prognosticates winds and a troubled sky, because no wind, till it hath driven the air, is apparent to the sense, the flame than the air more easily shaken. These omens forerun the death of Eurydice, bit on the heel by a serpent as she sported with the Naiads; and followed by her husband to the infernal kingdom.

> To hell descends an easy way;
> Black Pluto's gates stand open night and day.
> But to retire to that pure light above,
> Most hard! A few belov'd by equal Jove,
> By ardent virtue rais'd to bless'd abodes,
> Could this achieve, the sons of powerful gods.[6]

Such was our Orpheus, the son of Apollo and Calliope, one of the Muses; who with the sweetness of his music and sad lamentations draws tears from the eyes of the remorseless Furies and a consent from Pluto and Proserpina of his wife's restitution, provided that he looked not back to behold her before they had passed the confines of the Stygian empire. But

> True love detests and no delay can brook:[7]
> Hasting to see, he lost her with a look.[8]

I have heard a fable, sayeth Sabinus,[9] not unlike unto this, if it be to be reputed a fable which the testimonies of many affirm for a history. A gentleman in Bavaria, of a noble family, so extremely grieved for the death of his wife that he abandoned all the comforts of life and fed his constant sorrow with solitariness, until at length he regained her; who told him how she had finished the time prescribed by nature, but by his importunate prayers was restored to life and commanded by God to accompany him longer. Upon these conditions, that their matrimony, dissolved by death, should be again solemnized, and withal that he should abstain from his former blasphemous execrations, for which he lost and should lose her again upon the like commission. This said, she followed her household affairs as before, and bare him some children; but was ever pensive and of a pale complexion. Divers years after, the gentleman, heated with wine and choler, rapped out horrible oaths and bitterly cursed his

[11]Ceased.
[12]*Tantalus...stone*: Unfortunates who for their crimes on earth were condemned to endless torments in the underworld: *Tantalus* to stand in water that receded as he tried to drink, *Ixion* to be tied to a perpetually revolving wheel, the *Belides* (the fifty granddaughters of Belus, king of Egypt) to fill a bottomless cistern with water carried in sieves, *Tityus* to lie outstretched on the ground while vultures and snakes gnawed at his liver, and *Sisyphus* to push uphill a huge stone that always rolled down again.
[13]*Hell's...darkness*: i.e., Proserpine and Pluto.　[14]Still limping.
[15]Anxious, solicitous.　[16]Shining.
[17]*And yielding...caught*: i.e., in place of her, Orpheus (unfortunate man) caught only empty air.　[18]Returns.
Upon the tenth book　[1]Similar?
[2]In ancient Rome, priests who served one particular deity.
[3]Signifying.　[4]Vergil, *Georgics*, I.390–92.
[5]Undulating, waving to and fro.　[6]Vergil, *Aeneid*. VI.126–31.
[7]*True...brook*: i.e., true love detests delay and can endure none.
[8]Seneca, *Hercules Furens*, lines 588–89.　[9]Georg Schüler (1508–60), a German scholar noted for his Latin poetry.

servants; when his wife, withdrawing into another room, was never more heard of, her apparel, without her body, standing upright as if an apparition. This, sayeth he, have I heard from many credible persons, who affirm that the Duke of Bavaria told it for a certain truth to the Duke of Saxony. . . .

from A Paraphrase upon the Psalms of David (1636)

PSALM 23

The Lord my shepherd, me His sheep
Will from consuming famine keep.
He fosters me in fragrant meads,
By softly sliding waters leads,
My soul refresh'd with pleasant juice,   5
And lest they should His name traduce,
Then when I wander in the maze
Of tempting sin, informs my ways.
No terror can my courage quail,
Though shaded in death's gloomy veil;   10
By Thy protection fortified,
Thy staff my stay, Thy rod my guide.
My table Thou hast furnished,
Pour'd precious odors on my head;
My mazer[1] flows with pleasant wine,   15
While all my foes with envy pine.
Thy mercy and beneficence
Shall ever join in my defense;
Who in Thy house will sacrifice,
Till aged Time close up mine eyes.   20

PSALM 63[1]

To Thee, O God, my God, I pray
Before the dawning of the day.
      My soul and wasting flesh
With thirsty ardor Thee desire,

In soils scorch'd with aetherial fire,   5
      Whose drought no show'rs refresh.
That in Thy sanctuary I
May see Thy power and majesty
      Once more with ravish'd eyes,
My lips shall celebrate Thy praise,   10
Thy goodness more than length of days
      Or life itself I prize.

Extoll'd while I have utterance,
To Thee will I my palms advance,
      That wilt with marrow feast.   15
My verse Thy wonders shall recite,
Remember'd in the silent night,
      As on my bed I rest.

Secur'd beneath Thy shady wing,
I will in sacred raptures sing,   20
      And to Thy promise cleave.
Thy Hand upholds; but who with hate
My soul seek to precipitate
      Hell's entrails shall receive.

The raging sword shall shed their blood,   25
A prey for wolves, for foxes food.
      Yet God His king shall bless,
And such as swear by His great Name;
But those whose tongues the just defame
      Confusion shall suppress.   30

PSALM 23   [1]Wooden cup or drinking bowl.
PSALM 63   [1]For Donne's sermon on this Psalm see p. 553.

from A Paraphrase upon the Divine Poems (1638)

A PARAPHRASE UPON ECCLESIASTES
Chapter 3

Lo, all things have their times, by God decreed
In nature's changes; all things which proceed
From man's intentions under the vast sky.

A time when to be born, a time to die;
A time to plant, to extirp; to kill, to cure;   5
A time to batter down, a time to immure;
A time of laughter, and a time to turn
Our smiles to tears; a time to dance, to mourn;
To scatter stones, to gather them again;

A time to embrace, embraces to refrain;　10
A time to get, to lose; to save, to spend;
To tear asunder, and the torn to mend;
A time to speak, from speaking to surcease;
A time for love, for hate; for war, for peace.
What good can human industry obtain　15
When all things are so changeable and vain?
For God on man these various labors throws.
To afflict him with variety of woes.
He in their times all beautiful hath made,
The world into our narrow hearts convey'd,　20
Yet cannot they the causes apprehend
Of His great works, the original nor end.
What other good can man from these produce
But to take pleasure in their present use?
To eat, to drink, t' enjoy what is our own　25
Is such a gift as God bestows alone.
His purpose is eternal; nor can we
Add or subtract from His divine decree:
That mortals might their bold attempts forbear,
And curb their wild affections by His fear.　30
What hath been, is; what shall be, was before;
And what is past, the Almighty will restore.
Besides, the seats of justice I survey'd,

There saw how favor and corruption sway'd.
Then said I in my heart, God surely shall　35
Reward the just, the unjust to judgment call.
All purposes and actions have their times;
A time for vengeance to pursue our crimes.
As much as sense concerns, God manifests
To men how little they dissent from beasts:[1]　40
One end to both befalls; to equal death
Are liable, and breathe the self-same breath.
Then what preheminence hath man above
A beast, since both so transitory prove?
Both travel to one home, are earth, and must　45
Return to their originary dust.[2]
Who knows that souls of men ascend the sky?
That those of beasts with their frail bodies die?
What mortal then can make so good a choice
As[3] in his own acquirements to rejoice?　50
This is his portion: for of things to come,
None can inform him in the grave's dark womb.

[1]*As much as...beasts*: i.e., physically, men do not differ (*dissent*) from the lower animals, for all are mortals.
[2]The dust from which they took their origin.
[3]*So...as*: i.e., a better choice than.

Richard Corbett [1582-1635]

Like Joseph Hall and Henry King, Richard Corbett was both a minor poet and a bishop of the Church of England, but there resemblance ends. Whereas Hall's verse satires were the product of his formidably moral youth and the best of King's occasional poems were elegiac tributes to his friends and members of his family, Corbett's work may be regarded as a sort of raffish commentary on the personalities, scandals, and private jokes of Jacobean Oxford. However, he deserves to be remembered not merely as the author of the famous "Fairies' Farewell" but also as a jolly, worldly churchman for whom, even in the age of Donne and Herbert, religion was distinct from art.

The son of a Surrey gardener, Corbett was so engaging, venal, and ambitious that, in this golden age of pluralism, he was bound to fix his hopes upon the Church of England. At Westminster School, according to John Aubrey, he was "something apt to abuse, and a coward," but at Christ Church, Oxford (M. A. 1605) his "poems, jests, fancies, and exploits," as Anthony Wood reported, secured his local reputation. A skilled and indefatigable place-hunter, by 1612 he was junior proctor of the university and, with his unerring eye for the main chance, a supporter of the rising William Laud, then president of St. John's. His ordination as deacon and priest in 1613 led to a doctorate of divinity four years later and then, by easy stages, to the clerical emoluments that a loyal Jacobean churchman had every reason to expect. Through the good offices of the powerful duke of Buckingham, whom he had flattered with untiring zeal, in 1620 Corbett was named dean of Christ Church, a post to which in time were added various vicarages, a prebendary at Salisbury, a royal chaplaincy, and finally (1628) the bishopric of Oxford. In 1632 he was moved to Norwich, where, convivial to the end, he died in 1635.

Although Corbett's works had been widely (and often anonymously) circulated in manuscript collections and printed miscellanies, he himself made no attempt to publish them. It was not until 1647 that John Donne's disreputable son and namesake brought some of them together as *Certain Elegant Poems, Written by Dr. Corbet, Bishop of Norwich*, a slovenly little book that despite its imperfections went through two impressions in a year. *Poëtica Stromata*, a corrected and enlarged edition, was printed on the Continent (perhaps in Holland) in 1648, and sometime thereafter a third impression of *Certain Elegant Poems* (dated 1647) annexed its additions. A generation later, in 1672, this work was carelessly reprinted as "the third edition, corrected and enlarged," of *Poems Written by the Right Reverend Dr. Richard Corbet*. Thereafter the bishop's reputation slumbered until Thomas Percy, in 1765, included "The Fairies' Farewell" in his influential *Reliques of Antient English Poetry*, thus inaugurating a revival that eventuated in Octavius Gilchrist's still useful edition of Corbett's works in 1807.

My text is based on *Certain Elegant Poems, Written by Dr. Corbet, Bishop of Norwich*, 1647 (Wing C-6270). The scattered poetical works have been expertly edited by J. A. W. Bennett and H. R. Trevor-Roper (1955), and J. E. V. Crofts has written an assessment of Corbett's life and works in *Essays and Studies by Members of the English Association*, X (1924).

from Certain Elegant Poems (1647)

ON DOCTOR CORBETT'S FATHER

Vincent Corbett,[1] farther known
By Poynter's name than by his own,
Here lies engaged till the day
Of raising bones and quick'ning clay.
No wonder, reader, that he hath
Two surnames in one epitaph,   5
For this one[2] doth comprehend
All that both families could lend.
And if to know more art than any
Could multiply one into many,   10
Here a colony lies, then,
Both of qualities and men.
Years he liv'd were near four-score,
But count his virtues, he liv'd more;
And number him by doing good,   15
He liv'd the age before the flood.
Should we undertake his story,
Truth would seem feign'd and plainess[3] glory;
Besides, the tablet were too small,
Adding the pillars and the wall.   20
Yet of this volume much is[4] found
Writ in many a fertile ground,
Where the printer thee affords
Earth for paper, trees for words.
He was Nature's factor[5] here   25
And leiger-large[6] for every shire
To supply the ingenious[7] wants
Of some spring fruits and foreign plants.
Simple he was, and withal
His purse not base nor prodigal;   30

Poorer in substance than in friends,
Future and public were his ends;
His conscience, like his diet, such
As neither took nor left too much,
So the made laws needless grown   35
To him, he needed but his own.
Did he his neighbor bid[8] like those
That feast them only to enclose,[9]
Or with their roast meat rack[10] their rents,
And cozen them with their fed consents?   40
No: the free meeting of his board
Did but one liberal sense afford;
No close[11] or acre understood,
But only love and neighborhood.
His alms were such as Paul defines:[12]   45
Not[13] causes to be sav'd,[14] but signs;
Which alms, by faith, hope, love laid down,

ON DOCTOR CORBETT'S FATHER [1]The elder Corbett (d. 1619), who for some reason adopted the name Poynter, was a well-known gardener. In an affectionate "Epitaph" in *Underwoods* his son's friend Ben Jonson said that his mind was

> as pure and neatly kept
> As were his nurseries, and swept
> So of uncleanness or offense
> That never came ill odor thence.

[2]I.e., this man. [3]Text *feignednesse*. The emendation is authorized by the 1648 *Poëtica Stromata*. [4]Text *if*. [5]Agent, manager. [6]Ledger-large, i.e., general agent. [7]Indigenous. [8]Invite. [9]Appropriate arable land for pasturage. [10]Raise excessively. [11]Enclosure. [12]1 Corinthians 13.3, 13. [13]Text *Nor*. [14]Text *said*, but the emendation is supported by several manuscripts.

Laid up what now he wears, a crown.
Besides his fame, his goods, his life,
He left a griev'd son and wife: 50
Strange sorrow scarce to be believ'd,
Whenas a son and heir is griev'd.[15]

TO HIS SON, VINCENT CORBET[1]

What I shall leave thee none can tell,
But all shall say I wish thee well:
I wish thee, Vin, before all wealth,
Both bodily and ghostly health;
Nor too much wealth, not wit, come to thee,   5
So much of either may undo thee.
I wish thee learning, not for show,
Enough for to instruct and know,
Not such as gentlemen require
To prate at table or at fire.   10
I wish thee all thy mother's graces,
Thy father's fortunes, and his places.
I wish thee friends, and one at court,
Not to build on, but support,
To keep thee, not in doing many   15
Oppressions, but from suffering any.
I wish thee peace in all thy ways,
Nor lazy nor contentious days;
And when thy soul and body part,
As innocent as now thou art.   20

AN EPITAPH ON DOCTOR DONNE, DEAN OF PAUL'S[1]

He that would write an epitaph for thee,
And do it well, must first begin to be
Such as thou wert, for none can truly know
Thy worth, thy life, but he that hath liv'd so.
He must have wit to spare, and to hurl down   5
Enough to keep the gallants of the town.
He must have learning plenty, both the laws,
Civil and common, to judge any cause;
Divinity great store above the rest,
Not of the last edition, but the best.   10
He must have language, travel, all the arts,
Judgment to use, or else he wants thy parts.
He must have friends the highest able to do,
Such as Maecenas and Augustus[2] too.
He must have such a sickness, such a death,   15
Or else his vain descriptions come beneath.
Who then shall write an epitaph for thee,
He must be dead first. Let 't alone for me.

A PROPER NEW BALLAD ENTITLED "THE FAIRIES' FAREWELL, OR GOD–A–MERCY WILL"[1]

To Be Sung or Whistled to the Tune of "The Meadow Brow"
by the Learned, by the Unlearned to the Tune of "Fortune"[2]

Farewell, rewards and fairies,
   Good housewives now may say,
For now foul sluts in dairies

Do fare as well as they.
And though they sweep their hearths no less   5
   Than maids were wont to do,
Yet who of late for cleanliness
   Finds sixpence in her shoe?

Lament, lament, old abbeys,
   The fairies lost command;   10
They did but change priests' babies,
   But some have chang'd your land,
And all your children stol'n from thence
   Are now grown Puritans;
Who live as changelings ever since,   15
   For love of your demains.[3]

At morning and at evening both
   You merry were and glad,
So little care of sleep or sloth
   These pretty ladies had;   20
When Tom came home from labor,
   Or Ciss to milking rose,
Then merrily went their tabor,
   And nimbly went their toes.

Witness those rings and roundelays   25
   Of theirs, which yet remain,

[15]The 1672 edition and several manuscripts supply a brace of couplets in conclusion:

> Read, then, and mourn, whate'er thou art
> That dost hope to have a part
> In honest epitaphs, lest, being dead,
> Thy life be written and not read.

TO HIS SON, VINCENT CORBET [1]According to John Aubrey the younger Corbett (b. 1627), though "a very handsome youth" who was educated at Westminster, came to a bad end, for "he is run out of all, and goes begging up and down to gentlemen."

AN EPITAPH ON DOCTOR DONNE [1]Like the elegies by Carew (p. 230) and King (p. 193), this poem was first printed in the 1633 edition of Donne's *Poems*.
[2]The statesman Gaius Cilnius Maecenas and the Emperor Augustus were both notable patrons of writers.

A PROPER NEW BALLAD [1]This poem, which attained great popularity through its inclusion in Thomas Percy's *Reliques of Antient English Poetry* (1765), is based on the common Protestant notion that Roman Catholicism or the "old religion" was connected with superstitious belief in fairies. In a famous passage of *Leviathan* (IV. xlvii) Hobbes remarks that "from the time that the Bishop of Rome had gotten to be acknowledged for bishop universal, by pretense of succession to St. Peter, their whole hierarchy, or kingdom of darkness, may be compared not unfitly to the kingdom of fairies; that is, to the old wives' fables in England concerning ghosts and spirits, and the feats they play in the night. And if a man consider the original of this great ecclesiastical dominion, he will easily perceive that the papacy is no other than the ghost of the deceased Roman Empire sitting crowned upon the grave thereof. For so did the papacy start up on a sudden out of the ruins of that heathen power."
[2]Although "ballads" like Corbett's were normally written to be sung to well-known tunes, neither of the two recommended (of which the second, "Fortune My Foe," was extremely popular) fits the meter of the poem.
[3]Estates (most of which had been confiscated during Henry VIII's spoliation of the monasteries).

Were footed in Queen Mary's days
  On many a grassy plain;
But since of late, Elizabeth,
  And later James came in,   30
They never danc'd on any heath
  As when the time hath been.[4]

By which we note the fairies
  Were of the old profession;[5]
Their songs were Ave Maries,   35
  Their dances were procession;
But now, alas, they all are dead,
  Or gone beyond the seas,
Or further from religion fled,
  Or else they take their ease.   40

A tell-tale in their company
  They never could endure,
And whoso kept not secretly
  Their mirth was punish'd sure;
It was a just and Christian deed   45
  To pinch such black and blue;
O how the commonwealth doth need
  Such justices as you!

Now they have left our quarters,
  A register[6] they have,   50

Who can preserve their charters,
  A man both wise and grave;
A hundred of their merry pranks
  By one that I could name
Are kept in store; con[7] twenty thanks   55
  To William for the same.

To William Chourne of Staffordshire
  Give laud and praises due,
Who every meal can mend your cheer
  With tales both old and true;   60
To William all give audience,
  And pray ye for his noddle,
For all the fairies' evidence
  Were lost if it were addle.

---

[4] *When...been*: in times past. [5] Faith.
[6] Registrar, i.e., William Chourne (a servant of Corbett's friend and future father-in-law Doctor Leonard Hutten of Christ Church), who was noted for his antiquarian lore. In "Iter Boreale," a poem by Corbett about his expedition through the Midlands with Hutten and other cronies, Chourne is affectionately remembered; and in the 1648 edition an entire additional stanza (following line 56 in the present text) expatiates affectionately upon the erudition of "old William Chourne." [7] Offer.

Edward, Lord Herbert of Cherbury[1] [1582-1648]

Lord Herbert's versatile achievements as a soldier, diplomat, amorist, duelist, adventurer, philosopher, historian, and poet almost qualify him as a universal man. As the product of an ancient Welsh family of Norman descent that in its various branches came to be honored with a marquisate, seven earldoms, two viscountcies, fourteen baronies, seven baronetcies, and seven belts of the Order of the Garter, he was so haughty, vain, and captious that in his own account of his exploits he sometimes cuts a comic figure; but his ample self-esteem was equaled by his valor, and his crotchets and caprices did not impede the workings of a strong and supple mind. He was often foolish and eccentric, but he was seldom dull.

The eldest child of Richard and Magdalen Herbert of Montgomery Castle, he was born to wealth and power, and almost to literary distinction. His mother, a friend of Donne's for twenty years and the subject of his grave "Autumnal" (p. 70) and a famous funeral sermon, bore seven sons and three daughters—"Job's number and Job's distribution," as Donne recalled her saying—who included George (pp. 201 ff.), the greatest poet of his church, and Sir Henry, who was, implausibly, both the patron of young Richard Baxter and the master of the revels for three Stuart kings. A more distant kinsman was William Herbert, third earl of Pembroke (see p. 683), the nephew of Sir Philip Sidney, perhaps the "Mr. W. H." of Shakespeare's *Sonnets*, and assuredly the dedicatee (together with his brother Philip) of the first folio edition of Shakespeare's plays in 1623.

Young Herbert himself—tall, dark, and strikingly good-looking—was extreme in everything he did. As a gentleman commoner at University College, Oxford, at sixteen he married his own

---

[1] For another work of Lord Herbert, see History and Historiography, pp. 917 ff.

cousin and then pursued his education while living with his bride, his widowed mother, and his siblings. "I remember little more of myself but that from that time until King James' coming to the crown I had a son which died shortly afterwards and that I attended my studies seriously, the more I learnt out of my books adding still a desire to know more." Although created a knight of the Bath when King James was on his way to London in 1603, he refused to be distracted by the heady joys of court. By 1608, however, he thought it time to see the outer world, and so he left his wife and family for an extended stay in France. There, as he himself relates, he made a great impression on everybody from King Henri IV and the Grand Constable Montmorency to the ladies of the court, engaged in many duels, and consulted with the noted Isaac Casaubon and other men of learning. If he himself may be believed, this visit set the pattern for a string of amatory and military adventures that included—to take a random sampling from his autobiography— valiant service with the prince of Orange in his wars against the Spanish (1610), a visit with the Elector Palatine at Heidelberg, an almost royal triumph through the chief Italian cities, capture and incarceration by the French (1615), and a second warm reception by the prince of Orange before he went back to his patient wife and family after more than seven years abroad. "If men get name for some one virtue," his friend Jonson wrote in salutation,

> then
> What man art thou, that art so many men,
> All-virtuous Herbert, on whose every part
> Truth might spend all her voice, Fame all her art.

Still youthfully ambitious, Herbert soon returned to action. Through Buckingham's good offices, in 1619 he was named ambassador to France, where (with an interruption in 1621 as a consequence of one of his incessant brawls) he served until King James, rejecting his advice on foreign policy, recalled him five years later.

This long sojourn in France marked the apex of his public service, and thereafter he turned from politics and derring-do to speculation and research. As early as 1622 he had finished, and dedicated to his brother George, *De veritate* (Paris, 1624), a work that has been called the first purely meta-physical treatise written by an Englishman and one that accredited its author as the "father of deism." Though he received various new distinctions after his return to England—an Irish peerage in 1624, the barony of Cherbury in 1629, a place in the council of war in 1632—his repeated pleas for the arrears of withheld salary and for more substantial recognition by the crown were un-successful. Not even a laborious vindication of Buckingham's conduct at La Rochelle, which he wrote and spread abroad in manuscript in 1630, could move the unaccommodating Charles.

And so, assisted by the "vast scholar" Thomas Master of New College, Oxford, in 1632 he began his long exertions on a life of Henry VIII, a work whose only rival in the period is Bacon's slighter book on Henry VII (pp. 882–91). Only from a sense of painful duty, it would seem, did he obey King Charles' command to join the court at York in 1639 and again in 1640, and when his advice to prosecute the war against the Scots was put aside he retreated to Montgomery Castle and never saw his luckless king again. Despite his desire to remain neutral in the civil war, the aging, ailing peer was, by parliamentary order, imprisoned briefly in the Tower in 1642. In an effort to save his books and papers from threatened destruction, in 1643 he admitted a parliamentary garrison into Montgomery Castle, an act that made him odious to his peers and threw him on the mercy of their parliamentary foes. Taking a last farewell of his beloved castle in 1644—five years before its demolition—he made his way to London, and there, assisted by a modest grant from Parliament, he spent his final years.

The famous autobiography, begun when he was "past three-score," was undertaken, he ex-plained,

> to recollect my former actions and examine what had been done well or ill to the intent I may both reform that which was amiss and so make my peace with God, as also comfort myself in

those things which, through God's great grace and favor, have been done according to the rules of conscience, virtue, and honor.

Despite these high intentions, Herbert stopped the story of his life with the events of 1624. More important than this record of his own adventures, he no doubt thought, were the philosophical works that he published or prepared for publication not long before he died: a new edition of *De veritate* (1645), a treatise on logic (*De causis errorum*, 1645) that also contained two essays on religion (*De religione laici* and *Ad sacerdotes de religio laici*) as well as a group of Latin poems, and an ambitious study of comparative religion (*De religione gentilium*) that appeared in Amsterdam in 1663. Apart from his appointment as steward of the duchy of Cornwell in 1646 and a brief trip to Paris the following year (when he visited the philosopher Gassendi), the old man's final phase was uneventful. According to John Aubrey, as he lay dying in August 1648 he sent for Archbishop Ussher to administer the sacrament, but when he remarked indifferently that "if there was good in anything, 'twas in that," adding that "if it did no good, 'twould do no hurt," Ussher was dismayed and refused to give the rites upon such terms, whereupon Herbert turned away his head and then "serenely" died.

By his own directions he was buried at midnight in St. Giles in the Fields, near his house in London, but the elaborate monument that he designed to be erected at Montgomery or Cherbury was never built. In 1649, however, there appeared *The Life and Reign of King Henry VIII*, prefaced by a dedication to the monarch who had so long ignored his pleas for money and attention, and who a few months later followed him in death. Sixteen years went by before his brother Henry supervised the publication of his *Occasional Verses*, but the uncompleted autobiography remained in manuscript until 1764, when Horace Walpole, at Strawberry Hill, printed it for private circulation.

My texts are based upon *Occasional Verses of Edward Lord Herbert, Baron of Cherbery and Castle-Island. Deceased in August, 1648*, 1665 (Wing H-1508) and *The Life and Raigne of King Henry the Eighth. Written By the Right Honourable Edward Lord Herbert of Cherbury*, 1649 (Wing H-1504). The unsatisfactory edition of *Occasional Verses* by J. C. Collins (1881) has been superseded by that of G. C. M. Smith (1923), and the English poems are included in R. G. Howarth's *Minor Poets of the 17th Century* (rev. 1953). The popular autobiography, which went through seven editions between 1764 and 1826, was edited by Sir Sidney Lee (1886, rev. 1910), but the life of Henry VIII, after appearing in 1649, 1672, 1682, and 1706 (in White Kennett's *Complete History of England*), has found no modern editor. *De veritate* was translated and edited by M. H. Carré (1937), *De religione laici* by H. R. Hutcheson (1944), and *De religione gentilium* by William Lewis (1705). An English manuscript in Herbert's hand entitled *Religio laici*, which differs from the Latin work, was edited by H. G. Wright (*MLR*, XXVIII, 1933). The standard study of Herbert's life and works is by Mario M. Rossi (in Italian, 3 vols., 1947), and James H. Hanford has written interestingly on his later years in *HLQ*, V (1941–42).

from Occasional Verses (1665)

TO HIS WATCH, WHEN HE COULD NOT SLEEP

Uncessant minutes, whilst you move you tell
   The time that tells our life, which though it run
Never so fast or far, your new begun
   Short steps shall overtake; for though life well
May 'scape his own account,[1] it shall not yours: 5

You are Death's auditors, that both divide
And sum whate'er that life inspir'd endures
   Past a beginning;[2] and through you we bide[3]

TO HIS WATCH [1]Accounting.
[2]*Whate'er...beginning*: i.e., whatever, once life has begun, lasts beyond its beginning. [3]Encounter.

The doom[4] of Fate, whose unrecall'd[5] decree
   You date, bring, execute, making what's new— 10
Ill and good—old;[6] for as we die in you,
   You die in Time, Time in Eternity.

A DESCRIPTION

I sing her worth and praises high[1]
Of whom a poet cannot lie.
The little world the great shall blaze:[2]
Sea, earth her body; heaven her face;
Her hair sunbeams, whose[3] every part   5
Lightens, inflames each lover's heart,
That thus you prove the axiom[4] true,
Whilst[5] the sun help'd nature in you.
   Her front[6] the white and azure sky,
In light and glory raised high;   10
Being o'ercast by a cloudy frown,
All hearts and eyes dejecteth down.
   Her each brow a celestial bow,
Which through this sky her light doth show,
Which doubled, if it strange appear,   15
The sun's likewise is doubled there.[7]
   Her either cheek a blushing morn
Which, on the wings of beauty borne,
Doth never set, but only fair
Shineth, exalted in her hair.   20
   Within her mouth, heaven's heav'n, reside
Her words: the soul's there glorified.
   Her nose th' equator of this globe,[8]
Where nakedness, beauty's best robe,
Presents a form all hearts to win.   25
   Last, Nature made that dainty chin
Which, that it might in every fashion
Answer the rest, a constellation,[9]
Like to a desk, she there did place
To write the wonders of her face.   30
   In this celestial frontispiece,
Where happiness eternal lies,
First arranged stand three senses,
This heaven's intelligences,
Whose several motions, sweet combin'd,   35
Come from the first mover, her mind.[10]
   The weight of this harmonic sphere
The Atlas of her neck doth bear,
Whose favors day to us imparts,[11]
When frowns make night in lovers' hearts.   40
   Two foaming billows are her breasts,
That carry, rais'd upon their crests,
The Tyrian fish:[12] more white's their foam
Than that whence Venus once did come.[13]
   Here take her by the hand, my Muse,   45
With that sweet foe to make my truce,
To compact manna best compar'd,
Whose dewy inside's not full hard.
   Her waist's an invers'd pyramis,[14]
Upon whose cone love's trophy is.   50
Her belly is that magazine[15]

At whose peep[16] nature did resign
That precious mold by which alone
There can be framed such a one.
   At th' entrance of which hidden treasure,   55
Happy making above measure,
Two alabaster pillars stand,
To warn all passage from that land;
At foot whereof engraved is
The sad *non ultra*[17] of man's bliss.   60
   The back of this most precious frame
Holds up in majesty the same,
Where, to make music to all hearts,
Love bound the descant[18] of her parts.
   Though all this Beauty's temple be,   65
There's known within no deity
Save virtues shrin'd within her will.
As I began, so say I still,
I sing her worth and praises high
Of whom a poet cannot lie.   70

TO HER FACE

Fatal aspect, that hast an influence
   More powerful far than those immortal fires[1]
That but incline the will and move the sense,
   Which thou alone constrain'st, kindling desires
   Of such an holy force as more inspires   5
The soul with knowledge than experience
   Or revelation can do with all
Their borrow'd helps: sacred astonishment
   Sits on thy brow, threat'ning a sudden fall

[4]Sentence. [5]Unrecallable, irrevocable.
[6]*Making...old*: i.e., making old that which is new, either good or bad.
A DESCRIPTION [1]Text *praises, Ey.* G. C. Moore Smith, Lord Herbert's most authoritative editor, attributes the mistake (which recurs in lines 10 and 69 below and elsewhere in *Occasional Verses*) to the printer's misreading the old written *H* as *E.*
[2]Portray, set forth. [3]I.e., the woman's.
[4]A side gloss supplies the saying: *Sol et homo generant hominem,* i.e., the sun and a man engender a man.
[5]At one time, on one occasion. [6]Forehead.
[7]I.e., if it seems strange that there are two rainbows in the heaven of her face, the explanation is that there are two suns (her eyes) there. [8]Her head. [9]I.e., a dimple or a group of dimples?
[10]*This heaven's...mind*: See *sphere* in the Glossary.
[11]Modern usage would require *impart.*
[12]The murex, a fish valued in antiquity as a source of purple dye; here, the lady's nipples.
[13]*Foam...come*: Venus (or Aphrodite), goddess of love, was often represented (as in Botticelli's famous *Venus Anadyomene*) as springing from the foam of the sea. [14]Inverted pyramid.
[15]Repository.
[16]At sight of which. One contemporary manuscript supplies the preferable reading *To whose keep.* [17]"No farther."
[18]Harmony.
TO HER FACE [1]I.e., stars, which by their position (*aspect*) were thought to exert control (*influence*) on human behavior. See *aspect* and *influence* in the Glossary.

To all those thoughts that are not lowly[2] sent,   10
In wonder and amaze; dazzling[3] that eye
  Which on those mysteries doth rudely gaze,
Vow'd only unto Love's divinity:
  Sure Adam sinn'd not in that spotless face.

[THUS ENDS MY LOVE][1]

Thus ends my love, but this doth grieve me most,
  That so it ends, but that ends too; this yet—
Besides the wishes, hopes, and time I lost—
  Troubles my mind awhile, that I am set
Free, worse than denied: I can neither boast   5
  Choice nor success, as my case is, nor get
Pardon from myself, that I loved not
  A better mistress, or her worse. This debt
Only's her due still, that she be forgot
Ere chang'd, lest I love none; this done, the taint   10
  Of foul inconstancy is clear'd at least
In me; there only rests but to unpaint
  Her form in my mind, that, so dispossess'd,
It be a temple, but without a saint.

DITTY IN IMITATION OF THE SPANISH
Entre tanto que l'Avril.[1]

Now that the April of your youth adorns
  The garden of your face,
Now that for you each knowing lover mourns,
  And all seek to your grace,
Do not repay affection with scorns.   5

What though you may a matchless beauty vaunt,
  And that all hearts can move
By such a power as seemeth to enchant,
  Yet, without help of love,
Beauty no pleasure to itself can grant.   10

Then think each minute that you lose, a day;
  The longest youth is short,
The shortest age is long; Time flies away,
  And makes us but his sport,
And that which is not Youth's is Age's prey.   15

See but the bravest[2] horse that prideth most.
  Though he escape the war,
Either from master to the man[3] is lost,
  Or turn'd unto the car;
Or else must die with being ridden post.[4]   20

Then lose not beauty, lovers, time, and all;
  Too late your fault you see,
When that in vain you would these days recall;
  Nor can you virtuous be,
When, without these, you have not wherewithal.   25

THE STATE PROGRESS OF ILL[1]

I say, 'tis hard to write satires. Though Ill,
Great'ned in his[2] long course, and swelling still,

Be now like to a deluge, yet, as[3] Nile,
'Tis doubtful in his original;[4] this while,[5]
We may thus much on either part[6] presume,   5
That what so universal are must come
From causes great and far. Now in this state
Of things, what is least like Good, men hate,
Since 'twill be the less sin. I do see
Some ill requir'd, that one poison might free   10
The other; so states[7] to their greatness find
No faults requir'd but their own, and bind
The rest. And though this be mysterious, still,
Why should we not examine how this Ill[8]
Did come at first, how 't keeps his greatness[9] here.   15
When 'tis disguis'd, and when it doth appear?[10]
This Ill, having some attributes of God—
As, to have made itself, and bear the rod
Of all our punishments as it seems — came
Into the world to rule it, and to tame—   20
The pride of Goodness; and though his reign
Great in the hearts of men he doth maintain
By love, not right, he, yet[11] the tyrant here
(Though it be him we love, and God we fear),
Pretense yet wants not that it was before   25
Some part of Godhead, as mercy, that store
For souls grown bankrupt[12] their first stock of grace,
And that which the sinner of the last place
Shall number out, unless th' Highest will show
Some power not yet reveal'd to man below.   30

But that I may proceed, and so go on
To trace Ill in his first progression,
And through his secret'st ways, and where that he
Had left his nakedness as well as we,
And did appear himself: I note that in   35
The yet infant world how Mischief and Sin,
His agents here on earth, and easy known,
Are now conceal'd intelligencers[13] grown;
For since that as a guard th' Highest at once
Put Fear t' attend their private actions,   40

[2]Humbly. [3]Confusing with excessive brightness.
THUS ENDS MY LOVE [1]By its position in the 1665 volume this untitled poem seems to be the conclusion of the three preceding pieces: "To Her Face," "To Her Body," and "To Her Mind."
DITTY IN IMITATION [1]"Now that April." The song has not been identified. [2]Most splendid. [3]Servant.
[4]*Turn'd...post*: i.e., used as a workhorse or ridden so hard and fast that it will die. The sexual innuendoes are apparent.
THE STATE PROGRESS OF ILL [1]This difficult poem, which traces the origin and development of evil conceived of as the royal journey (*progress*) of a monarch, was presumably the verse epistle that Donne responded to in "To Sir Edward Herbert at Juliers" (p. 74). Herbert had gone with Lord Chandos to the duchy of Juliers in the Low Countries to assist the Protestant forces besieging the Catholic stronghold there.
[2]Its. "Ill" is referred to as "it" until line 22. [3]Like. [4]Source.
[5]For the present. [6]In both cases. [7]Monarchs.
[8]I.e., this Ill we are talking about. [9]Maintains its state.
[10]Show itself without disguise. [11]Always. [12]I.e., bankrupt of.
[13]Spies.

And Shame their public (other means being fail'd),
Mischief under doing of good was veil'd,
And Sin of pleasure; though in this disguise
They only hide themselves from mortal eyes,
Sins, those that both com- and o-mitted be,   45
Once hot and cold but in a third[14] degree,
Are now such poisons that though they may lurk
In secret parts awhile, yet they will work
Though after death; nor ever come alone,
But sudden-fruitful multiply ere done;   50
While in this monstrous birth, they only die
Whom we confess, those live which we deny.
Mischiefs, like fatal constellations,
Appear unto the ignorant at once
In glory and in hurt, while th' unseen part   55
Of the great cause may be perchance the art
Of th' Ill, and hiding it; which that I may
Ev'n in his first original display
And best example, sure amongst kings he
Who first wanted succession, to be   60
A tyrant, was wise enough to have chose
An honest man for king, which should dispose
Those beasts; which, being so tame, yet otherwise,[15]
As it seems, could not herd; and with advice[16]
Somewhat indifferent for both, he might   65
Yet have provided for their children's right,
If they grew wiser,[17] not his own, that so
They might repent, yet under treason, who
Ne'er promis'd faith;[18] though now we cannot spare
(And not be worse) kings on those terms they are.   70
No more than we could spare (and have been sav'd)
Original sin. So then those priests that rav'd
And prophesied, they did a kind of good
They knew not of by whom the choice first stood.

Since, then, we may consider now, as fit,   75
State government and all the arts of it,
That we may know them yet, let us see how,
They were deriv'd, done, and are maintain'd now,
That princes may by this yet understand
Why we obey, as well as they command.   80

State a proportion'd color'd table[19] is;
Nobility, the masterpiece, in this
Serves to show distances, while being put
'Twixt sight and vastness they seem higher but
As they're further off; yet, as those blue hills   85
Which th' utmost border of a region fills,
They are great and worse parts, while in the steep
Of this great prospective[20] they seem to keep
Further absent from those below. Though this
Exalted spirit, that's sure a free soul is   90
A greater privilege than to be born
At Venice, although he seek not rule, doth scorn
Subjection but as he is flesh—and so
He is to dullness, shame, and many mo[21]
Such properties—knows (but the painter's art)   95
All in the frame is equal; that desert
Is a more living thing, and doth obey,
As he gives poor,[22] for God's sake (though they

And kings ask it not so[23]; thinks honors are
Figures compos'd of lines irregular;   100
And, happy-high, knows no election[24]
Raiseth man to true greatness but his own.
Meanwhile sug'red divines, next place to this,
Tells us humility and patience is
The way to heaven, and that we must there   105
Look for our kingdom; that the great'st rule here
Is for to rule ourselves; and that they might
Say this the better, they to no place have right
B' inheritance, while whom ambition sways,
Their office is to turn it other ways.   110
     Those yet whose harder minds religion
Cannot invade, nor turn from thinking on
A present greatness, that combin'd curse of law,
Of officers, and neighbors' spite doth draw
Within such whirlpools that till they be drown'd   115
They ne'er get out, but only swim them round.
     Thus brief, since that the infinite of Ill
Is neither easy told nor safe, I will
But only note how free-born man, subdu'd
By his own choice, that was at first indu'd   120
With equal power over all, doth now submit
That infinite of number, spirit, wit,
To some eight monarchs. Then why wonder men
Their rule of horses?
The world, as in the Ark of Noah, rests,
Compos'd as then: few men and many beasts.[25]   125

AUGUST 1608[1] AT MERLOU[2] IN FRANCE
Madrigal

How should I love my best?
What though my love unto that height be grown
     That, taking joy in you alone,
          I utterly this world detest,
Should I not love it yet as th' only place   5
     Where beauty hath his perfect grace,
          And is possest?

     But I beauties despise;
You, universal Beauty seem to me,

[14]I.e., moderate. Some poisons were thought to kill by inducing extreme heat or extreme cold.   [15]I.e., without a king.
[16]Judgment.   [17]I.e., able to *herd* without a king.
[18]*They...faith*: i.e., they could abolish kingship without being guilty of treason since they had never sworn loyalty to a hereditary monarchy.
[19]A picture painted according to the rules of perspective.
[20]Perspective view.   [21]More.   [22]Gives to the poor.
[23]For that reason.
[24]1) advancement; 2) salvation by God's predestination, a Calvinist doctrine.
[25]Donne opens his reply to Herbert by picking up this allusion to the beasts in the Ark.
AUGUST 1608   [1]Text 1668.
[2]The Castle of Merlou (or Mello), the seat of the duke of Montmorency near Clermont, where Herbert stayed for several months in 1608–09.

Giving and showing form and degree   10
  To all the rest in your fair eyes;
Yet should I not love them as parts whereon
    Your beauty, their perfection
      And top, doth rise?

    But ev'n myself I hate: 15
So far my love is from the least delight
    That at my very self I spite,[3]
      Senseless[4] of any happy state.
Yet may I not with justest reason fear[5]
    How, hating hers, I truly her   20
      Can celebrate?

    Thus unresolved still,
Although world, life, nay what is fair beside
    I cannot for your sake abide,
      Methinks I love not to my fill;   25
Yet if a greater love you can devise,
    In loving you some other wise,
      Believe 't, I will.

EPITAPH OF KING JAMES[1]

Here lies King James, who did so propagate
Unto the world that bless'd and quiet state
Wherein his subjects liv'd, he seem'd to give
That peace which Christ did·leave, and so did live
As once that king[2] and shepherd of his sheep,   5
That whom God saved, here he seem'd to keep,
Till with that innocent and single heart
With which he first was crown'd he did depart
To better life. Great Britain, so lament
That[3] strangers more than thou may yet resent[4]   10
The sad effects, and while they feel the harm
They must endure from the victorious arm
Of our King Charles, may they so long complain[5]
That tears in them force thee to weep again.

A VISION[1]

Within an *open curled sea of gold,*[2]
  A *bark of ivory*[3] one day I saw,
  Which, striking with his *oars,*[4] did seem to draw
Towards a fair *coast*[5] which I then did behold.

A lady held the stern, while her white hand,   5
  Whiter than either ivory or *sail,*[6]
  Over the surging waves did so prevail,
That she had now approached near the *land.*[7]

When suddenly, as if she feared some wrack
  (And yet the sky was fair, and air was clear,   10
  And neither *rock*[8] nor *monster*[9] did appear),
Doubting the point,[10] which spied, she turned back.

Then with a *second course*[11] I saw her steer
  As if she meant to reach some other bay,
  Where being approach'd she likewise turn'd away,   15
Though in the bark some *waves*[12] now ent'red were.

Thus varying oft her course, at last I found,
  While I in quest of the adventure go,
  The sail took down, and oars had ceas'd to row,
And that the bark itself was run aground.[13]   20

Wherewith *earth's fairest creature*[14] I behold,[15]
  For which both *bork and sea I gladly lost.*[16]
  Let no philosopher of knowledge boast,
Unless that he my vision can unfold.

EPITAPH ON SIR FRANCIS VERE[1]

Reader,
    If thou appear
  Before this tomb, attention give
    And do not fear
    Unless it be to live,
  For dead is great Sir Francis Vere.   5

Of whom this might be said: should God ordain
  One to destroy all sinners whom that One[2]
  Redeem'd not there, that so He might atone[3]
His chosen flock and take from earth that stain
  That spots it still, he worthy were alone   10
  To finish it, and have, when they were gone,
This world for him made paradise again.

TO MRS.[1] DIANA CECIL[2]

Diana Cecil, that rare beauty thou dost show
  Is not of milk or snow,
  Or such as pale and whitely things do owe,[3]
But an illustrious oriental bright,[4]
Like to the diamond's refracted light,   5
Or early morning breaking from the night.

Nor is thy hair and eyes made of that ruddy beam
  Or golden-sanded stream

[3]Am annoyed. [4]Insensible. [5]Doubt, question.
EPITAPH OF KING JAMES [1]James I died 27 March 1625.
[2]David, king of Israel. [3]So that. [4]Feel keenly, regret.
[5]Lament.
A VISION [1]"A lady combing her hair." The glosses to this poem
are Cherbury's. Editor's notes are so indicated.
[2]*Open...gold:* "The hair."
[3]*Bark...ivory:* "The comb." [4]"The teeth of the comb."
[5]"Her side." [6]"The cuff or smock sleeve." [7]"Her shoulder."
[8]"Wart." [9]"Lice." [10]Fearing the promontory (ed.'s note).
[11]"Combing in another place." [12]"Hairs in the comb."
[13]*The...aground:* "She had given over combing."
[14]"Her face." [15]Text *beheld* (ed.'s note).
[16]*Bark...lost:* "Her hair put up and comb cast away."
EPITAPH ON SIR FRANCIS VERE [1]An English commander (1560–
1609) noted for his services to the Protestants in the Low Coun-
tries. [2]I.e., Christ. [3]Reconcile to himself.
TO MRS. DIANA CECIL [1]Mistress, a title given to unmarried as well
as to married women.
[2]The beautiful daughter and heiress (d. 1654) of William Cecil,
second earl of Exeter, and successively the wife of the earl of Ox-
ford and the earl of Elgin. [3]Possess.
[4]Shining, lustrous brightness.

Which we find still the vulgar poets' theme,
But reverend black, and such as you would say   10
Light did but serve it, and did show the way
By which at first night did precede the day.

Nor is that symmetry of parts and form divine
    Made of one vulgar line,
    Or such as any know how to define,   15
But of proportions new, so well express'd.
That the perfections in each part confess'd
Are beauties to themselves and to the rest.

Wonder of all thy sex! let none henceforth inquire
    Why they so much admire,   20
    Since they that know thee best ascend no higher;
Only, be not with common praises woo'd,
Since admiration were no longer good
When men might hope more than they understood.

TO HER EYES

    Black eyes, if you seem dark,
    It is because your beams are deep,
    And with your soul united keep.
        Who could discern
    Enough into them, there might learn   5
        Whence they derive that mark,
        And how their power is such
That all the wonders which proceed from thence,
        Affecting more the mind than sense,
        Are not so much   10
        The works of light as influence.

    As you then joined are
    Unto the soul, so it again
    By its connection doth pertain
        To that First Cause,   15
    Who, giving all their proper laws,
        By you doth best declare
        How He at first b'ing hid
Within the veil of an eternal night,
        Did frame for us a second light,   20
        And after bid
        It serve for ordinary sight.

    His image then you are.
    If there be any yet who doubt
    What power it is that doth look out   25
        Through that your black,
    He will not an example lack,
        If he suppose that there
        Were gray or hazel glass,
And that through them though sight or soul might shine, 30
        He must yet at the last define[1]
        That beams which pass
        Through black cannot but be divine.

SONNET OF BLACK[1] BEAUTY

Black beauty, which above that common light
    Whose power can no colors here renew

But those which darkness can again subdue,
Dost still remain unvaried to the sight,
    And like an object equal to the view,   5
Art[2] neither chang'd with day, nor hid with night;
When all these colors which the world call bright,
    And which old poetry doth so pursue,
Are with the night so perished and gone
    That of their being there remains no mark,   10
Thou still abidest so entirely one,[3]
    That we may know thy blackness is a spark
Of light inaccessible, and alone
    Our darkness which can make us think it dark.

THE THOUGHT

1
If you do love as well as I,
Then every minute from your heart
    A thought doth part;
And winged with desire doth fly
Till it hath met in a straight line   5
    A thought of mine
So like to yours, we cannot know
Whether of both[1] doth come, or go,
    Till we define
Which of us two that thought doth owe.[2]   10

2
I say, then, that your thoughts which pass
Are not so much the thoughts you meant
    As those I sent:
For as my image in a glass
Belongs not to the glass you see,   15
    But unto me,
So when your fancy is so clear
That you would think you saw me there,
    It needs must be
That it was I did first appear.   20

3
Likewise, when I send forth a thought,
My reason tells me 'tis the same
    Which from you came,
And which your beauteous image wrought.
Thus while our thoughts by turns do lead   25
    None can precede;
And thus while in each other's mind
Such interchanged forms we find,
    Our loves may plead
To be of more than vulgar kind.   30

4
May you then often think on me,
And by that thinking know 'tis true

TO HER EYES [1]Decide.
SONNET OF BLACK BEAUTY [1]Brunette. [2]Text *And.*
[3]Uniform, unchanging.
THE THOUGHT [1]*Whether of both*: which of the two. [2]Own.

I thought on you;
I in the same belief will be,
While by this mutual address   35
  We will possess
A love must[3] live when we do die;
Which rare and secret property
  You will confess,
If you do love as well as I.   40

TO HIS MISTRESS FOR HER TRUE PICTURE

Death, my life's mistress, and the sovereign queen
Of all that ever breath'd, though yet unseen,
My heart doth love you best; yet I confess,
Your picture I beheld, which doth express
No such eye-taking beauty; you seem lean,   5
Unless you're mended since. Sure he did mean
No honor to you that did draw you so;
Therefore I think it false. Besides, I know
The picture Nature drew (which sure's the best)
Doth figure[1] you by sleep and sweetest rest: 10
Sleep, nurse of our life, care's best reposer,
Nature's high'st rapture, and the vision-giver;
Sleep, which when it doth seize us, souls go play,
And make man equal[2] as he was first day.
Yet some will say, Can pictures have more life   15
Than the original? To end this strife,
Sweet mistress, come, and show yourself to me
In your true form, while then I think to see
Some beauty angelic[3] that comes t' unlock
My body's prison, and from life unyoke   20
My well-divorced soul, and set it free
To liberty eternal. Thus you see
I find the painter's error, and protect
Your absent beauties, ill drawn, by the effect.
For grant it were your work, and not the grave's,   25
Draw love by madness then, tyrants by slaves,
Because they make men such. Dear mistress, then,
If you would not be seen by owl-ey'd men,
Appear at noon i' th' air, with so much light
The sun may be a moon, the day a night;   30
Clear to my soul, but dark'ning the weak sense
Of those the other world's Cimmerians;[4]
And in your fatal robe, embroidered
With star-characters, teaching me to read
The destiny of mortals, while your clear brow   35
Presents a majesty to instruct me how
To love or dread nought else. May your bright hair,
Which are the threads of life, fair crown'd appear
With that your crown of immortality:
In your right and the keys of heaven be;   40
In th' other those of the infernal pit,
Whence none retires if once he enter it.
And here let me complain how few are those
Whose souls you shall from earth's vast dungeon loose
To endless happiness! few that attend   45
You, the true guide, unto their journey's end;
And if of old[5] virtue's way narrow were,

'Tis rugged now, having no passenger.[6]
Our life is but a dark and stormy night,
To which sense yields a weak and glimmering light,   50
While wand'ring man thinks he discerneth all
By that which makes him but mistake and fall.
He sees enough who doth his darkness see;
These are great lights, by which less[7] dark'ned be.
Shine then sun-brighter[8] through my sense's veil,   55
A day-star of the light doth[9] never fail;
Show me that goodness which compounds the strife
'Twixt a long sickness and a weary life;
Set forth that justice which keeps all in awe,
Certain and equal more than any law;   60
Figure that happy and eternal rest
Which till man do enjoy he is not blest.
Come and appear then, dear soul-ravisher,
Heaven's-light-usher,[10] man's deliverer,
And do not think, when I new beauties see,   65
They can withdraw my settled love from thee.
Flesh-beauty strikes me not at all: I know,
When thou dost leave them to the grave, they show
Worse than they now show thee: they shall not move
In me the least part of delight or love   70
But as they teach your power. Be she[11] nut-brown,
The loveliest color which the flesh doth crown,
I'll think her like a nut, a fair outside,
Within which worms and rottenness abide;
If fair, then like the worm itself to be;   75
If painted, like their slime and sluttery.
If any yet will think their beauties best,
And will against you, spite of all, contest,
Seize them with age: so in themselves they'll hate
What they scorn'd in your picture, and too late   80
See their fault and the painter's. Yet if this,
Which their great'st plague and wrinkled torture is,
Please not, you may to the more wicked sort,
Or such as of your praises make a sport,
Denounce[12] an open war, send chosen bands   85
Of worms, your soldiers, to their fairest hands,
And make them leprous-scabb'd; upon their face
Let those your pioneers,[13] ring-worms, take their place,
And safely near with strong approaches got,
Entrench it round, while their teeth's rampire,[14] rot[15] 90
With other worms, may with a damp inbred
Stink[16] to their senses, which they shall not, dead:
And thus may all that ere they prided in
Confound them now. As for the parts within,
Send gut-worms, which may undermine a way   95

---

[3]That must.
TO HIS MISTRESS [1]Represent. [2]Exactly.
[3]Accented on the first syllable.
[4]I.e., dwellers in darkness (from the mythical people mentioned by
Homer, *Odyssey*, XI.14–19).
[5]*If of old*: text *if old*. The emendation has manuscript support.
[6]Traveler. [7]Lesser lights. [8]Text *Sun-bright, or.* [9]That doth.
[10]Text *Heav'ns lightest Usher.* [11]Text *the.* [12]Proclaim.
[13]Soldiers whose duty it was to dig trenches and mines.
[14]Rampart. [15]Rotted. [16]Text *Sink.*

Unto their vital parts, and so display
That your pale ensign on the walls; then let
Those worms, your veterans, which never yet
Did fail, enter pell-mell and ransack all,
Just as they see the well-rais'd building fall;   100
While they do this, your foragers command,
The caterpillars, to devour their land,
And with them wasps, your wing'd-worm-horsemen,
    bring,
To charge, in troop, those rebels with their sting:
All this, unless your beauty they confess.[17]   105

And now, sweet mistress, let me a while digress,
T' admire these noble worms whom I invoke,
And not the Muses. You that eat through oak
And bark, will you spare paper and my verse,
Because your praises they do here rehearse?   110

Brave legions then, sprung from the mighty race
Of man corrupted, and which hold the place
Of his undoubted issue; you that are
Brain-born, Minerva-like, and like her war,
Well arm'd complete mail-jointed[18] soldiers,   115
Whose force herculean links in pieces tears;
To you the vengeance of all spill-bloods falls,
Beast-eating men, men-eating cannibals.
Death-privileg'd, were you in sunder smit
You do not lose your life but double it: 120
Best-framed types of the immortal soul,
Which in yourselves and in each part are whole;
Last-living creatures, heirs of all the earth,
For when all men are dead, it is your birth;
When you die, your brave, self-kill'd general   125
(For nothing else can kill him) doth end all.
What vermin-breeding body then thinks scorn
His flesh should be by your brave fury torn?

Willing[19] to you this carcase I submit,
A gift so free I do not care for it;   130
Which yet you shall not take until I see
My mistress first reveal herself to me.

Meanwhile, great mistress whom my soul admires,
Grant me your true picture who it desires,
That he your matchless beauty might maintain   135
'Gainst all men that will quarrels entertain[20]
For a flesh-mistress; the worst I can do[21]
Is but to keep the way that leads to you,
And howsoever the event doth prove,
To have revenge below, reward above;   140
Hear, from my body's prison, this my call,
Who from my mouth-grate and eye-window bawl.

EPITAPH FOR HIMSELF

Reader,
The monument which thou beholdest here
    Presents Edward Lord Herbert to thy sight,
A man who was so free from either hope or fear
    To have or lose this ordinary light

That when to elements his body turned were,   5
    He knew that as those elements would fight,
So his immortal soul should find above,
    With his Creator, peace, joy, truth, and love.

AN ODE UPON A QUESTION MOVED,
WHETHER LOVE SHOULD CONTINUE FOREVER

Having interr'd her infant birth,
    The wat'ry ground, that late did mourn,
    Was strew'd with flow'rs for the return
Of the wish'd bridegroom of the earth.

The well-accorded birds did sing   5
    Their hymns unto the pleasant time,
    And in a sweet consorted[1] chime
Did welcome in the cheerful spring;

To which soft whistles of the wind,
    And warbling murmurs of a brook,   10
    And varied notes of leaves that shook,
An harmony of parts did bind,

While, doubling joy unto each other,
    All in so rare concent[2] was shown,
    No happiness that came alone,   15
Nor pleasure that was not another;

When with a love none can express,
    That mutually happy pair,
    Melander and Celinda fair,
The season with their loves did bless.   20

Walking thus towards a pleasant grove,
    Which did, it seem'd, in new delight
    The pleasures of the time unite,
To give a triumph to their love,

They stay'd at last, and on the grass   25
    Reposed so, as o'er his breast
    She bow'd her gracious head to rest,
Such a weight as no burden was.

While over either's compass'd waist
    Their folded arms were so compos'd   30
    As if, in straitest bonds enclos'd,
They suffer'd for joys they did taste.

Long their fix'd eyes to heaven bent
    Unchanged, they did never move,
    As if so great and pure a love   35
No glass but it could represent.

When with a sweet though troubled look,
    She first brake silence, saying, "Dear friend,
    O that our love might take no end,
Or never had beginning took!   40

[17]Acknowledge. [18]Text *compleat-mail'd-jointed.*
[19]Willingly, freely. [20]Fight duels.
[21]The worst that can befall me (in such a duel).
AN ODE UPON A QUESTION [1]Harmonious. [2]Harmony.

"I speak not this with a false heart—"
   Wherewith his hand she gently strain'd—
   "Or that would change a love maintain'd
With so much faith on either part.

"Nay, I protest, though Death with his   45
   Worst counsel should divide us here,
   His terrors could not make me fear
To come where your lov'd presence is.

"Only if love's fire with the breath
   Of life be kindled, I doubt[3]   50
   With our last air 'twill be breath'd out,
And quenched with the cold of death.

"That if affection be a line
   Which is clos'd up in our last hour,
   O how 'twould grieve me any pow'r   55
Could force so dear a love as mine!"

She scarce had done, when his shut eyes
   An inward joy did represent,
   To hear Celinda thus intent
To a love he so much did prize.   60

Then with a look, it seem'd, deni'd
   All earthly pow'r but hers, yet so
   As if to her breath he did owe
This borrow'd life, he thus replied:

"O you wherein, they say, souls rest   65
   Till they descend pure heavenly fires,
   Shall lustful and corrupt desires
With your immortal seed be blest,

"And shall our love, so far beyond
   That low and dying appetite,   70
   And which so chaste desires unite,
Not hold in an eternal bond?

"Is it because we should decline,[4]
   And wholly from our thoughts exclude,
   Objects that may the sense delude,   75
And study only the divine?

"No, sure, for if none can ascend
   Ev'n to the visible degree
   Of things created, how should we
The invisible comprehend?   80

"O rather since that Pow'r express'd
   His greatness in His works alone,
   Being here best in 's creatures known,
Why is He not lov'd in them best?

"But is't not true, which you pretend,   85
   That since our love and knowledge here
   Only as parts of life appear,
So they with it should take their end.

"O no, beloved, I am most sure
   Those virtuous habits we acquire,   90
   As being with the soul entire,
Must with it evermore endure.

"For if where sins and vice reside
   We find so foul a guilt remain,
   As never dying in his stain   95
Still punish'd in the soul doth bide,

"Much more that true and real joy
   Which in a virtuous love is found
   Must be more solid in its ground
Than Fate or Death can e'er destroy.   100

"Else should our souls in vain elect,
   And vainer yet were heaven's laws,
   When to an everlasting cause
They gave a perishing effect.

"Nor here on earth then, nor above.   105
   Our good affection can impair,[5]
   For where God doth admit the fair,
Think you that he excludeth love?

"These eyes again, then, eyes shall see,
   And hands again these hands enfold,   110
   And all chaste pleasures, can[6] be told
Shall with us everlasting be.

"For if no use of sense remain,
   When bodies once this life forsake,
   Or they could no delight partake,   115
Why should they ever rise again?

"And if every imperfect mind
   Made love the end of knowledge here,
   How perfect will our love be, where
All imperfection is refin'd!   120

"Let then no doubt, Celinda, touch,
   Much less your fairest mind invade;
   Were not our souls immortal made,
Our equal loves can make them such.

"So when one wing can make no way,   125
   Two joined can themselves dilate,
   So can two persons propagate,
When singly either would decay.

So when from hence we shall be gone,
   And be no more, nor you, nor I,   130
   As one another's mystery,
Each shall be both, yet both but one."

This said, in her uplifted face,
   Her eyes, which did that beauty crown,
   Were like two stars, that having fall'n down,   135
Look up again to find their place;

While such a moveless, silent peace
   Did seize on their becalmed sense,
   One would have thought some influence
Their ravish'd[7] spirits did possess.   140

---

[3]Fear. [4]Repudiate. [5]Deteriorate. [6]That can. [7]Enraptured.

PLATONIC LOVE (I)

1

Madam, your beauty and your lovely parts
Would scarce admit poetic praise and arts,
As they are Love's most sharp and piercing darts,
   Though, as again they only wound and kill
   The more deprav'd affections of our will,
   You claim a right to commendation still.

2

For as you can unto that height refine
All Love's delights, as while they do incline
Unto no vice, they so become divine,
   We may as well attain your excellence
   As without help of any outward sense
   Would make us grow a pure intelligence.

3

And as a soul, thus being quite abstract,
Complies not properly[1] with any act,
Which from its better being may detract,
   So through the virtuous habits you infuse
   It is enough that we may like and choose
   Without presuming yet to take or use.

4

Thus angels in their starry orbs proceed
Unto affection without other need
Than that they still on contemplation feed;
   Though as they may unto this orb descend,
   You can, when you would so much lower bend,
   Give joys beyond what man can comprehend.

5

Do not refuse then, Madam, to appear,
Since every radiant beam comes[2] from your sphere
Can so much more than any else endear,
As while through them we do discern each grace,
The multiplied lights from every place
Will turn and circle, with their rays, your face.

OCTOBER 14, 1644[1]

Enraging griefs, though you most divers be
In your first causes, you may yet agree
   To take an equal share within my heart,
   Since if each grief strive for the greatest part,
You needs must vex yourselves as well as me.   5

For your own sakes and mind, then, make an end
In vain you do about a heart contend
   Which, though it seem in greatness to dilate,
   Is but a tumor, which in this its state
The choicest remedies would but offend.   10

Then storm't at once: I neither feel constraint,
Scorning your worst, nor suffer any taint,
   Dying by multitudes;[2] though if you strive,
   I fear my heart may thus be kept alive
Until it under its own burden faint.   15

What, is't not done? Why, then my God, I find,
Would have me use you to reform my mind,
   Since through His help I may from you extract
   An essence pure, so spriteful[3] and compact
As it will be from grosser parts refin'd.   20

Which b'ing again converted by His grace
To godly sorrow, I may both efface
   Those sins first[4] caus'd you and together have
   Your pow'r to kill turn'd to a power to save,
And bring my soul to its desired place.   25

PLATONIC LOVE I   [1]By its own nature. [2]That comes.
OCTOBER 14, 1644   [1]Text *1664*. The emendation is conjectural.
[2]I.e., as the victim of many enemies. [3]Spiritual. [4]That first.

Phineas Fletcher [1582-1650] and Giles Fletcher [1585/6-1623]

Though hardly Tweedledum and Tweedledee, Phineas and Giles Fletcher were so near allied, genetically and otherwise, that they have long been paired by literary historians. As sons of the distinguished Giles Fletcher the Elder (1549?-1611)—whose career of public service was embellished by such excursions into literature as a useful book on Russia (1591) and a sonnet sequence entitled *Licia* (1593)—and as cousins of John Fletcher the dramatist, they were members of a bookish family and were early drawn to writing. Although Phineas went from Eton to King's College, Cambridge (B.A. 1604, M.A. 1608) and Giles from Westminster to Trinity (B.A. 1606, B.D. 1619), their association was so close, according to the elder brother, that they "seem'd two join'd in one, or one disjoin'd in two."

This affinity revealed itself not only in their poetry, which was their avocation, but also in their academic and clerical careers. Giles had progressed from a minor fellowship of his college (1608) to a readership in Greek grammar (1615) and then in literature when he at last secured—perhaps through the good offices of Francis Bacon—a college living that he exchanged in 1619 for the rectory at Alderton in Suffolk. There, according to Thomas Fuller, the bad air and the rudeness of his "clownish and low-parted parishioners" conspired to make him melancholy and so brought on his early "dissolution" in 1623. Following Phineas' service as a fellow at King's (1611–16) and then a five-year stint as chaplain to Sir Henry Willoughby, in 1621 he was appointed to the rectory at Hilgay in Norfolk, which he occupied until his death in 1650.

Although both the Fletchers contributed to *Sorrow's Joy* (1603), a Cambridge miscellany that thriftily combined lamentation for Elizabeth and rejoicing at her heir's accession, it was Giles, the younger and the shorter-lived, who first established his credentials as a poet with *Christ's Victory and Triumph* (1610). Its preface, which eruditely argues that since the spirit of God breathes "through what pipe it please," poetry may be made to serve the uses of religion, is at best a graceful commonplace, but the poem itself (which Milton long remembered) generates uncommon power. Citing the "thrice-honored Bartas" and Spenser (along with King James) as his immediate exemplars and inspirations, Fletcher depicts in four cantos the birth, temptation, crucifixion, and resurrection of Christ with a fusion of biblical imagery, Spenserian allegory, pictorialism, and contemporary "wit" so complex as to justify that much used term *baroque*. Giles' own admission of defeat in the final section of his work—"impotent words," he says, can only strive "In vain, alas, to tell so heav'nly sight"—perhaps explains why he abandoned poetry at the age of twenty-four. His piety thereafter found expression in the prose of *The Reward of the Faithful*, which appeared the year he died.

Phineas, though in his later years reluctant to recognize his early sportive work, was more prolific than his younger brother. *Venus and Anchises* (which, after its belated publication in six voluptuous cantos as *Brittain's Ida* in 1628, was long ascribed to Spenser) was no doubt a product of his Cambridge years, as was *Sicelides* (1631), a "piscatory" play in blank and rhymed verse that was acted at King's College in 1615. More edifying, or at any rate more lurid, was the sternly anti-Catholic *Locustae vel pietas Jesuitica*, whose Latin hexameters were translated and expanded into five cantos (each, except the third, of forty nine-line stanzas) as *The Locusts or Apollyonists* in 1627. Also to this early period must be assigned the notorious *Purple Island*, which through twelve cantos exhaustively and implausibly expounds human physiology with a blend of Spenserian pastoralism and relentless allegory. On consenting to its publication in 1633, Fletcher, then entering the "winter" of his life, accurately predicted that these "raw essays" of his "very unripe years" and "blooms" of his first spring would, in certain quarters, be greeted with derision. By this time, however, he too had gone beyond such youthful indiscretions, and apart from *Sylva Poetica* (1633) and *A Father's Testament*, a melange of prose and verse published posthumously in 1670, such later treatises as *The Way to Blessedness* (1632) and *Joy in Tribulation* (1632) were unabashedly devotional.

My texts are based on *Christs Victorie, and Triumph in Heauen, and Earth, ouer, and after death*, 1610 (STC 11058), *The Locusts, or Apollyonists*, 1627 (STC 11081), and *The Purple Island, or the Isle of Man: Together with Piscatorie Eclogs and other Poeticall Miscellanies*, 1633 (STC 11082). There is an edition of a manuscript of Phineas' *Venus and Anchises* (*Brittain's Ida*) by Ethel Seaton (1926). K. Waibel has studied the Spenserian elements in *The Purple Island* (*Englische Studien*, LVIII, 1924), Arno Esch the baroque elements in *Christ's Victory and Triumph* (1937), and H. E. Cory the brothers' relation to Spenser and Milton (*University of California Publications in Modern Philology*, II, 1912). The most substantial monograph is Abram B. Langdale's *Phineas Fletcher, Man of Letters, Science and Divinity* (1937).

from The Locusts, or Apollyonists[1] (1627)

CANTO I

1

Of men, nay beasts; worse, monsters; worst of all,
Incarnate fiends, English Italianate,
Of priests, O no, mass-priests,[2] priests-cannibal,
Who make their Maker, chew, grind, feed, grow fat
With flesh divine; of that great city's[3] fall,
Which, born, nurs'd, grown with blood, th' earth's
      empress sat,
  Cleans'd, spous'd to Christ, yet back to whoredom
    fell,
  None can enough, something I fain would tell.
How black are quenched lights! Fall'n heaven's
    a double hell.

    . . . . . .

3

Thou world's sole Pilot, who in this poor isle[4]
(So small a bottom) hast embark'd Thy light
And glorious self, and steer'st it safe the while
Hoarse-drumming seas and winds' loud trumpets fight,
Who causest stormy heavens here only smile,
Steer me, poor ship-boy, steer my course aright;
  Breathe, gracious Spirit, breathe gently on
      these lays,
  Be Thou my compass, needle to my ways:
Thy glorious work's my fraught,[5] my haven is Thy praise.

4

Thou purple whore,[6] mounted on scarlet beast,
Gorg'd with the flesh, drunk with the blood of saints,
Whose amorous golden cup and charmed feast
All earthly kings, all earthly men attaints;
See thy live pictures, see thine own, thy best,
Thy dearest sons, and cheer thy heart that faints.
  Hark, thou sav'd island, hark, and never cease
  To praise that hand which held thy head in peace,
Else hadst thou swum as deep in blood as now in seas.

> His subject stated and his plea for God's assistance made,
> Fletcher begins the action with Pluto's summoning an in-
> fernal council to plot the destruction of Protestant England.
> It is night, when the world is drowned in sleep and "the
> laborer snorteth fast," but Pluto's gloomy kingdom is alive
> with action. While "hell's pursuivants" are rounding up
> the demons, and Sin—"a shapeless shape, a foul deformed
> thing"—stands guard before the gate, those who "burn, fry,
> hiss" within moan in unremitting grief.

17

And now th' infernal powers, through th' air driving,
For speed their leather pinions broad display;
Now at eternal Death's wide gate arriving,
Sin gives them passage; still they cut their way,
Till to the bottom of hell's palace diving,
They enter Dis'[7] deep conclave; there they stay,
  Waiting the rest, and now they all are met,
  A full foul senate, now they all are set,
The horrid court, big swoll'n with th' hideous
    council sweat.

18

The midst but lowest (in hell's heraldry
The deepest is the highest room) in state
Sat lordly Lucifer; his fiery eye,
Much swoll'n with pride, but more with rage and hate,
As censor muster'd all his company,
Who round about with awful silence sate.
  This do, this let rebellious spirits gain,
  Change God for Satan, heaven's for hell's sov'reign;
O let him serve in hell, who scorns in heaven to reign!

19

Ah, wretch, who with ambitious cares opprest,
Long'st still for future, feel'st no present good,
Despising to be better, wouldst be best,
Good never, who wilt serve thy lusting mood,
Yet all command; not he who rais'd his crest,
But pull'd it down, hath high and firmly stood.
  Fool, serve thy tow'ring lusts, grow still, still crave,
  Rule, reign, this comfort from thy greatness have,
Now at thy top, thou art a great commanding slave.

20

Thus fell this prince of darkness, once a bright
And glorious star; he willful turn'd away
His borrowed globe from that eternal light;
Himself he sought, so lost himself; his ray
Vanish'd to smoke, his morning sunk in night
And never more shall see the springing day.
  To be in heaven the second he disdains,
  So now the first in hell and flames he reigns,
Crown'd once with joy and light, crown'd now with fire
    and pains.

21

As where the warlike Dane the scepter sways
They crown usurpers with a wreath of lead,
And with hot steel, while loud the traitor brays,
They melt and drop it down into his head—
Crown'd he would live, and crown'd he ends his days;
All so in heaven's courts this traitor sped,[8]
  Who now, when he had overlook'd his train,[9]

THE LOCUSTS   [1]In Revelation 9.11 Apollyon ("the destroyer") is
identified as "the angel of the bottomless pit."
[2]In sixteenth- and seventeenth-century England a highly pejorative
term for Roman Catholic clergy.   [3]Rome.   [4]England.   [5]Cargo.
[6]The Roman Catholic Church. For the origin of the term (and
of Fletcher's lurid description) see Revelation 17.2–6.
[7]The god of the underworld.   [8]Fared.   [9]Surveyed his followers.

Rising upon his throne, with bitter strain
Thus gan to whet their rage and chide their frustrate pain:

22

"See, see, you spirits, I know not whether more
Hated or hating heaven, ah, see the earth
Smiling in quiet peace and plenteous store.
Men fearless live in ease, in love, and mirth;
Where arms did rage, the drum and cannon roar,
Where hate, strife, envy reign'd, and meager dearth,
    Now lutes and viols charm the ravish'd ear;
    Men plow with swords, horse-heels their armors wear;
Ah, shortly scarce they'll know what war and armors were.

23

"Under their sprouting vines they sporting sit.
Th' old tell of evils past; youth laugh and play,
And to their wanton heads sweet garlands fit,
Roses with lilies, myrtles weav'd with bay;
The world's at rest; Erinnys,[10] forced to quit
Her strongest holds, from earth is driven away.
    Even Turks forget their empire to increase;
    War's self is slain and whips of fury cease.
We, we ourselves, I fear, will shortly live in peace.

24

"Meantime (I burn, I broil, I burst with spite)
In midst of peace that sharp two-edged sword
Cuts through our darkness, cleaves the misty night,
Discovers all our snares; that sacred word,
Lock'd up by Rome, breaks prison, spreads the light,
Speaks every tongue, paints, and points out the Lord,
    His birth, life, death, and cross; our gilded stocks,[11]
    Our laymen's books, the boy and woman mocks;
They laugh, they fleer,[12] and say, Blocks[13] teach and
    worship blocks.

25

"Springtides of light divine the air surround,
And bring down heaven to earth; deaf Ignorance,
Vex'd with the day, her head in hell hath drown'd;
Fond Superstition, frighted with the glance
Of sudden beams, in vain hath cross'd her round.
Truth and Religion everywhere advance
    Their conq'ring standards; Error's lost and fled;
    Earth burns in love to heaven; heaven yields her bed
To earth, and common grown, smiles to be ravished.

26

"That little swimming isle above the rest,
Spite of our spite and all our plots, remains
And grows in happiness; but late our nest,
Where we and Rome and blood and all our trains,
Monks, nuns, dead and live idols, safe did rest;
Now there (next th' oath of God) that wrastler[14] reigns
    Who fills the land and world with peace; his spear
    Is but a pen, with which he down doth bear
Blind ignorance, false gods, and superstitious fear.

27

"There God hath fram'd another paradise,
Fat olives dropping peace, victorious palms,

Nor in the midst, but everywhere doth rise
That hated tree of life, whose precious balms
Cure every sinful wound, give light to th' eyes,
Unlock the ear, recover fainting qualms.
    There richly grows what makes a people blest,
    A garden planted by Himself and drest,
Where He himself doth walk, where He himself doth rest.

28

"There every star sheds his sweet influence
And radiant beams; great, little, old, and new,
Their glittering rays and frequent confluence
The milky path to God's high palace strew;
Th' unwearied pastors with steel'd confidence,
Conquer'd and conquering fresh, their fight renew.
    Our strongest holds that thund'ring ordinance
    Beats down, and makes our proudest turrets dance,
Yoking men's iron necks in His sweet governance.

29

"Nor can th' old world content ambitious light,
Virginia, our soil, our seat, and throne,
To which so long possession gives us right,
As long as hell's, Virginia's self is gone;
That stormy isle which th' Isle of Devils[15] hight,
Peopled with faith, truth, grace, religion.
    What's next but hell? That now alone remains,
    And that subdu'd, even here He rules and reigns,
And mortals gin to dream of long but endless pains.

30

"While we, good harmless creatures, sleep or play,
Forget our former loss and following pain,
Earth sweats for heaven, but hell keeps holy-day.
Shall we repent, good souls, or shall we plain?
Shall we groan, sigh, weep, mourn, for mercy pray?
Lay down our spite, wash out our sinful stain?
    Maybe He'll yield, forget, and use us well,
    Forgive, join hands, restore us whence we fell;
Maybe He'll yield us heaven, and fall himself to hell.

31

"But me, O never let me, spirits, forget
That glorious day when I your standard bore,
And scorning in the second place to sit,
With you assaulted heaven, His yoke forswore.
My dauntless heart yet longs to bleed and sweat
In such a fray; the more I burn, the more
    I hate; should He yet offer grace and ease,
    If subject we our arms and spite surcease,
Such offer should I hate, and scorn so base a peace.

32

"Where are those spirits? Where that haughty rage
That durst with me invade eternal light?
What? Are our hearts fall'n too? Droop we with age?
Can we yet fall from hell and hellish spite?
Can smart our wrath, can grief our hate assuage?

[10]Erinyes, the Furies. Fletcher apparently construes the word as
singular. [11]Wooden images. [12]Deride. [13]Blockheads.
[14]James I. [15]Bermuda

Dare we with heaven and not with earth to fight?
  Your arms, allies, yourselves as strong as ever;
  Your foes, their weapons, numbers weaker never.
For shame, tread down this earth! What wants but
    your endeavor?

33

"Now by yourselves and thunder-daunted arms,
But never-daunted hate, I you implore,
Command, adjure, reinforce your fierce alarms;
Kindle, I pray, who never prayed before,
Kindle your darts, treble repay our harms.
O, our short time, too short, stands at the door,
  Double your rage; if now we do not ply,
  We lone in hell, without due company,
And worse, without desert, without revenge shall lie.

34

"He, spirits (ah that, that's our main torment), He
Can feel no wounds, laughs at the sword and dart,
Himself from grief, from suff'ring wholly free;
His simple nature cannot taste of smart,
Yet in His members we Him grieved see,
For and in them He suffers; where His heart
  Lies bare and nak'd, there dart your fiery steel,
  Cut, wound, burn, sear, if not the head, the heel;
Let him in every part some pain and torment feel.

35

"That light comes posting on, that cursed light,
When they as He, all glorious, all divine,
Their flesh cloth'd with the sun, and much more bright,
Yet brighter spirits, shall in His image shine,
And see Him as He is; there no despite,
No force, no art their state can undermine,
  Full of unmeasur'd bliss, yet still receiving,
  Their souls still childing joy, yet still conceiving
Delights beyond the wish, beyond quick thoughts
    perceiving.

36

"But we fast pinion'd with dark fiery chains
Shall suffer every ill, but do no more;
The guilty spirit there feels extremest pains,
Yet fears worse than it feels, and finding store
Of present deaths, death's absence sore complains;
Oceans of ills without or ebb or shore,
  A life that ever dies, a death that lives,

And, worst of all, God's absent presence gives
A thousand living woes, a thousand dying griefs.

37

"But when He sums his time and turns his eye
First to the past, then future pangs, past days
(And every day's an age of misery)
In torment spent, by thousands down he lays,
Future by millions, yet eternity
Grows nothing less, nor past to come allays.
  Through every pang and grief he wild doth run,
  And challenge coward death, doth nothing shun,
That he may nothing be, does all to be undone.

38

"O let our work equal our wages, let
Our judge fall short, and when His plagues are spent,
Owe more than He hath paid, live in our debt;
Let heaven want vengeance, hell want punishment
To give our dues; when we with flames beset
Still dying live in endless languishment,
  This be our comfort, we did get and win
  The fires and tortures we are whelmed in;
We have kept pace, outrun His justice with our sin.

39

"And now, you states of hell, give your advice,
And to these ruins lend your helping hand."
This said, and ceas'd; straight humming murmurs rise;
Some chafe, some fret, some sad and thoughtful stand,
Some chat, and some new stratagems devise,
And everyone heaven's stronger power bann'd,[16]
  And tear for madness their uncombed snakes,
  And everyone his fiery weapon shakes,
And everyone expects[17] who first the answer makes.

40

So when the falling sun hangs o'er the main,
Ready to drop into the western wave,
By yellow Cam,[18] where all the Muses reign,
And with their tow'rs his reedy head embrave,[19]
The warlike gnat their flutt'ring armies train—
All have sharp spears, and all shrill trumpets have;
  Their files they double, loud their cornets sound;
  Now march at length, their troops now gather round;
The banks, the broken noise, and turrets fair rebound.

[16]Cursed.   [17]Waits to see.
[18]The river that flows through Cambridge.   [19]Adorn splendidly.

from The Purple Island[1], or the Isle of Man (1633)

TO MY MOST WORTHY AND LEARNED FRIEND
EDWARD BENLOWES,[2] ESQUIRE

Sir,
As some optic glasses,[3] if we look one way, increase the

THE PURPLE ISLAND [1]I.e., the human body. Purple was the color associated not only with the blood but also with regality and power.
[2]A poet (1602–76), who was patron of such men of letters as Fletcher, Quarles, James Howell, and Fuller. His *Theophilia*, a lavish allegory of the soul's ascent to heaven, appeared in 1652.

object, if the other, lessen the quantity, such is an eye that looks through affection: it doubles any good and extenuates what is amiss. Pardon me, Sir, for speaking plain truth; such is that eye whereby you have viewed these raw essays of my very unripe years, and almost childhood. How unseasonable are blossoms in autumn, unless perhaps in this age where are more flowers than fruit. I am entering upon my winter, and yet these blooms of my first spring must now show themselves to our ripe wits, which will certainly give them no other entertainment[4] but derision. For myself, I cannot account that worthy of your patronage which comes forth so short of my desires, thereby meriting no other light than the fire. But since you please to have them see more day than their credit can well endure, marvel not if they fly under your shadow to cover them from the piercing eye of this very curious (yet more censorious) age. In letting them go abroad I desire only to testify how much I prefer your desires before mine own, and how much I owe to you more than any other. This if they witness for me, it is all the service I require. Sir, I leave them to your tuition,[5] and entreat you to love him who will contend with you in nothing but to outlove you, and would be known to the world by no other name than

> *Your true friend,*
> *Phineas Fletcher*
> *Hilgay,[6] May 1, 1633*

CANTO I

> In May, when "the shepherd boys who with the Muses dwell" gather on the river bank in Cambridge to celebrate the spring, there are among them two brothers—Giles and Phineas Fletcher—who in their affection "seem'd two join'd in one, or one disjoin'd in two." When the elder is urged to "wake thy long, thy too long sleeping Muse" with an appropriate ditty, he protests that all the good subjects have been used:
>
>> Tell me, ye Muses, what our father-ages
>>   Have left succeeding times to play upon.
>> What now remains unthought on by those sages
>>   Where a new Muse may try her pinion?
>
> But after a long survey of ancient and modern poetry from Homer to Spenser, he at last agrees to sing.

34

Hark then, ah, hark! you gentle shepherd crew;
  An isle I fain would sing, an island fair;
A place too seldom view'd, yet still in view;
  Near as ourselves, yet farthest from our care;
    Which we by leaving find, by seeking lost;
    A foreign home; a strange, though native coast;
Most obvious to all, yet most unknown to most.

35

Coeval with the world in her nativity;
  Which though it now hath pass'd through many ages,
And still retain'd a natural proclivity
  To ruin, compass'd with a thousand rages
    Of foemen's spite, which still this island tosses,

Yet ever grows more prosp'rous by her crosses,[1]
By with'ring, springing fresh, and rich by often losses.

36

Vain men! too fondly wise, who plow the seas,
  With dangerous pains another earth to find;
Adding new worlds to th' old, and scorning ease,
  The earth's vast limits daily more unbind!
    The aged world, though now it falling shows
    And hastes to set, yet still in dying grows:
Whole lives are spent to win what one death's hour
    must lose.

37

How like's the world unto a tragic stage!
  Where every changing scene the actors change;
Some, subject, crouch and fawn; some reign and rage;
  And new strange plots bring scenes as new and strange,
    Till most are slain; the rest their parts have done.
    So here, some laugh and play, some weep and groan,
Till all put off their robes, and stage and actors gone.

38

Yet this fair isle, sited so nearly near
  That from our sides nor place nor time may sever,
Though to yourselves yourselves are not more dear,
  Yet with strange carelessness you travel never:
    Thus while, yourselves and native home forgetting,
    You search far distant worlds with needless sweating,
You never find yourselves; so lose ye more by getting.

39

When that great Power, that All, far more than all,
  (When now His time foreset was fully come)
Brought into act this indigested ball,
  Which in Himself till then had only room,
    He labor'd not, nor suffer'd pain or ill,
    But bid each kind their several places fill:
He bid and they obey'd: their action was His will.

. . . . . .

43

Now when the first week's life was almost spent,
  And this world built and richly furnished,
To store heav'n's courts and steer earth's regiment,
  He cast to frame an isle, the heart and head
    Of all His works, compos'd with curious art;
    Which like an index briefly should impart
The sum of all: the whole, yet of the whole a part.

44

That Trine-One with Himself in council sits,
  And purple dust takes from the new-born earth;

---

[3] I.e., telescopes.
[4] *Which will...entertainment*: i.e., who will certainly give them no other reception.   [5] Protection.
[6] A town in Norfolk where Fletcher lived after 1621.
CANTO I [1] Adversities.

Part circular and part triang'lar fits;
  Endows it largely at the unborn birth;
    Deputes his favorite viceroy; doth invest
    With aptness thereunto, as seem'd Him best;
      And lov'd it more than all, and more than all it blest.

45

Then plac'd it in the calm, pacific seas,
  And bid nor waves nor troublous winds offend it;
Then peopled it with subjects apt to please
  So wise a prince, made able to defend it
    Against all outward force or inward spite:
    Him framing like Himself, all shining bright;
A little living sun, son of the living *Light.*

46

Nor made He this like other isles; but gave it
  Vigor, sense, reason, and a perfect motion
To move itself whither itself would have it,
  And know what falls within the verge of notion:
    No time might change it, but as ages went,
    So still return'd; still spending, never spent;
More rising in their fall, more rich in detriment.

47

So once the cradle of that double light[2]
  Whereof one rules the night, the other day
(Till sad Latona, flying Juno's spite,
  Her double burden there did safely lay),
    Nor rooted yet, in every sea was roving,
    With every wave and every wind removing;
But since, to those fair twins hath left her ever moving.[3]

48

Look: as a scholar who doth closely gather
  Many large volumes in a narrow place,
So that great Wisdom all this all together
  Confin'd unto this island's little space;
    And being one, soon into two he fram'd it;
    And now made two, to one again reclaim'd it;[4]
The little Isle of Man or Purple Island nam'd it.

> Though happy in "the world's first infancy," this isle was
> not immune to danger, for the "sly old serpent," vexed by
> its felicity, "allures it subtly from the peaceful shore" and
> would have sunk it in a "deathful lake" had God not "Se-
> cured" it in a "new recover'd seat."

CANTO II

> In the second canto Fletcher can proceed, therefore, to his
> description of "this isle pull'd from that horrid main/
> Which bears the fearful looks and name of Death." The
> following account of the approaches to its "belly" (which,
> like the "breast" and "head," is one of its main regions) is
> fairly representative.

27

Six goodly cities,[1] built with suburbs round,
  Do fair adorn this lower region;
The first Koilia,[2] whose extremest bound
  On this side border'd by the Splenion,[3]

On that by sovereign Hepar's[4] large commands,
  The merry Diazome[5] above it stands,
To both these join'd in league and never-failing bands.[6]

28

The form (as when with breath the bagpipes rise
  And swell) roundwise and long, yet longwise more,
Fram'd to the most capacious figure's guise;
  For 'tis the Island's garner; here its store
    Lies treasur'd up, which, well prepar'd, it sends
    By secret path that to th' arch-city bends;
Which, making it more fit, to all the Isle dispends.

29

Far hence at foot of rocky Cephal's hills,
  This city's steward[7] dwells in vaulted stone;
And twice a day Koilia's storehouse fills
  With certain rent and due provision:
    Aloft he fitly dwells in arched cave,
    Which to describe I better time shall have,
When that fair mount I sing, and his white curdy wave.

30

At that cave's mouth, twice sixteen porters[8] stand,
  Receivers of the customary rent;
On each side four (the foremost of the band)
  Whose office to divide what in is sent;
    Straight other four break it in pieces small;
    And at each hand twice five, which, grinding all,
Fit it for convoy and this city's arsenal.

31

From thence a groom[9] of wondrous volubility
  Delivers all unto near officers,
Of nature like himself and like agility;
  At each side four, that are the governors,[10]
    To see the victuals shipp'd at fittest tide;
    Which straight from thence with prosp'rous
      channel slide,
And in Koilia's port with nimble oars glide.

32

The haven, fram'd with wondrous sense and art,
  Opens itself to all that entrance seek,

---

[2]*Cradle...light*: In Greek myth, the floating island of Delos, which Zeus anchored in the Aegean Sea so that Leto (*Latona*) might bear in security his children Apollo and Artemis (later identified with the sun-god and the moon-goddess). [3]Constant motion.
[4]*Soon into two...reclaim'd it*: i.e., Zeus made the two sexes distinct but both are subsumed in the notion of mankind?
CANTO II [1]"Beside the bladder there are six special parts contained in this lower region: the liver, stomach (with the guts), the gall, the spleen or milt, the kidneys, and parts for generation" (Fletcher's gloss). [2]Koilia: κοιλία, "stomach." [3]Splenion: σπλήν, "spleen."
[4]Hepar: ἧπαρ, "liver." [5]Diazome: διαξῶμα, "girdle, diaphragm." [6]Bonds, ties.
[7]"Gustus, the taste, is the caterer or steward to the stomach, which hath his place in Cephal, that is, the head" (Fletcher's gloss).
[8]"In each jaw are sixteen teeth, four cutters, two dog-teeth or breakers, and ten grinders" (Fletcher's gloss). [9]The tongue.
[10]Muscles for swallowing.

Yet if aught back would turn, and thence depart,
  With thousand wrinkles shuts the ready creek:
    But when the rent is slack, it rages rife,
    And mutines[11] in itself with civil strife:
Thereto a little groom[12] eggs it with sharpest knife.

33

Below dwells in this city's market-place.
  The Island's common cook, Concoction;[13]
Common to all, therefore in middle space
  Is quarter'd fit in just proportion:
    Whence never from his labor he retires;
    No rest he asks, or better change requires:
Both night and day he works, ne'er sleeps nor sleep
    desires.

34

That heat which in his furnace ever fumeth
  Is nothing like to our hot parching fire,
Which, all consuming, self at length consumeth;
  But moist'ning flames a gentle heat inspire,
    Which sure some inborn neighbor to him lendeth;
    And oft the bord'ring coast fit fuel sendeth,
And oft the rising fume, which down again descendeth.

35

Like to a pot, where, under hovering,
  Divided flames the iron sides entwining,
Above is stopp'd with close lid covering,
  Exhaling fumes to narrow straits confining;
    So doubling heat, his duty doubly speedeth;
    Such is the fire Concoction's vessel needeth,
Who daily all the Isle with fit provision feedeth.

36

There many a groom the busy cook attends
  In under-offices and several place:
This gathers up the scum, and thence it sends
  To be cast out; another, liquors base;
    Another, garbage, which the kitchen cloys,
    And divers filth, whose scent the place annoys,
By divers secret ways in under-sinks[14] convoys.

. . . . . .

[11]Mutines.
[12]"*Vas breve* or the short vessel, which, sending in a melancholic humor, sharpens the appetite" (Fletcher's gloss). [13]Digestion.
[14]Sewers.

from Christ's Victory and Triumph in Heaven and Earth, Over and After Death (1610)

To the Reader

There are but few of many that can rightly judge of poetry, and yet there are many of those few that carry so left-handed an opinion of it as some of them think it half sacrilege for profane poetry to deal with divine and heavenly matters, as though David were to be sentenced by them for uttering his grave matter upon the harp. Others, something more violent in their censure but sure less reasonable (as though poetry corrupted all good wits when, indeed, bad wits corrupt poetry), banish it with Plato out of all well-ordered commonwealths.[1] Both these I will strive rather to satisfy than refute.

And of the first I would gladly know whether they suppose it fitter that the sacred songs in the Scripture of those heroical saints, Moses, Deborah, Jeremy, Mary, Simeon, David, Solomon (the wisest schoolman and wittiest poet) should be ejected from the canon for want of gravity, or rather this error erased out of their minds for want of truth. But it may be they will give the Spirit of God leave to breathe through what pipe it please, and will confess, because they must needs, that all the songs dittied by Him must needs be, as their fountain is, most holy. But their common clamor

is, Who may compare[2] with God? True, and yet as none may compare without presumption, so all may imitate, and not without commendation. . . .

[To buttress his contention that poetry and piety are not incompatible Fletcher presents a formidable list of Greek and Latin writers who combined the two (Gregory Nazianzen, Juvencus, Prudentius, Sedulius, and others) and then moves on to modern instances.]

Thrice-honored Bartas[3] and our (I know no other name more glorious than his own) Master Edmund Spenser (two blessed souls) not thinking ten years enough, laying out their whole lives upon this one study. Nay, I may justly say that the princely father of our country[4] (though, in my conscience, God hath made him of all the learned princes that ever were the most religious and of all the religious princes the most learned, that so by the one he might oppose him against the Pope, the pest of all religion, and by the other against Bellarmine,[5] the abuser of all good learning)

TO THE READER [1]*Banish...commonwealths*: Plato, *Republic*, Sect. 606–07. [2]Vie, enter into rivalry. [3]See p. 48
[4]James I, for whose literary productions see p. 683, n. 3
[5]Roberto Cardinal Bellarmino (1543–1621), noted Jesuit contro-

is yet so far enamored with this celestial Muse that it shall never repent me *calamo trivisse labellum* whensoever I shall remember *haec eadem ut sciret quid non faciebat Amyntas*.[6] To name no more in such plenty, where I may find how to begin sooner than to end: St. Paul, by the example of Christ, that went singing to Mount Olivet with His disciples after His last supper, exciteth the Christians to solace themselves with hymns and psalms and spiritual songs;[7] and therefore, by their leaves, be it an error for poets to be divines, I had rather err with the scripture than be rectified by them; I had rather adore the steps of Nazianzen, Prudentius, Sedulius than follow their steps to be misguided; I had rather be the devout admirer of Nonnius,[8] Bartas, my sacred sovereign, and others (the miracles of our latter age) than the false sectary of these that have nothing at all to follow but their own naked opinions. To conclude, I had rather with my Lord and His most divine apostle[9] sing (though I sing sorrily) the love of heaven and earth than praise God (as they do) with the worthy gift of silence and sitting still, or think I dispraised Him with this poetical discourse. . . .

For the second sort therefore, that eliminate poets out of their city gates as though they were now grown so bad as they could neither grow worse nor better, though it be somewhat hard for those to be the only men should want cities that were the only causers of the building of them, and somewhat inhumane to thrust them into the woods to live among the beasts who were the first that called men out of the woods from their beastly and wild life, yet since they will needs shoulder them out for the only firebrands to inflame lust (the fault of earthly men, not heavenly poetry), I would gladly learn what kind of professions these men would be entreated to entertain that so deride and disaffect poesy. . . . If philosophers please them, who is it that knows not that all the lights of example to clear[10] their precepts are borrowed by philosophers from poets—that without Homer's examples Aristotle would be as blind as Homer? If they retain musicians, who ever doubted but that poets infused the very soul into the inarticulate sounds of music—that without Pindar and Horace the lyrics had been silenced forever? If they must needs entertain soldiers, who can but confess that poets restore again that life to soldiers which they before lost for the safety of their country —that without Vergil, Aeneas had never been so much as heard of. How then can they for shame deny commonwealths to them who were the first authors of them? How can they deny the blind philosopher that teaches them, his light; the empty musician that delights them, his soul; the dying soldier that defends their life, immortality after his own death? Let philosophy, let ethics, let all the arts bestow upon us this gift, that we be not thought dead men whilest we remain among the living. It is only poetry that can make us be thought living men when we lie among the dead, and therefore I think it unequal[11] to thrust them out of our cities that call us out of our graves, to think so hardly of them that make us to be so well thought of, to deny them to live a while among us that make us live forever among our posterity.

So being now weary in persuading those that hate, I commend myself to those that love such poets as Plato speaks of, that sing divine and heroical matters,[12] . . . recommending[13] these my idle hours, not idly spent, to good scholars and good Christians that have overcome their ignorance with reason, and their reason with religion.

CHRIST'S VICTORY IN HEAVEN

1

The birth of Him that no beginning knew,
Yet gives beginning to all that are born,
And how the Infinite far greater grew
By growing less, and how the rising Morn
That shot from heav'n did back to heaven return,
  The obsequies of Him that could not die,
  And death of life, end of eternity,
How worthily He died that died unworthily;

2

How God and man did both embrace each other,
Met in one person, heav'n and earth did kiss,
And how a virgin did become a mother
And bare[1] that Son who the world's Father is
And Maker of His mother, and how bliss
  Descended from the bosom of the High
  To clothe himself in naked misery,
Sailing at length to heav'n, in earth triumphantly;

3

Is the first flame wherewith my whiter[2] Muse
Doth burn in heavenly love, such love to tell.
O Thou that didst this holy fire infuse,
And taughtst this breast, but late the grave of hell
Wherein a blind and dead heart liv'd, to swell
  With better thoughts, send down those lights that lend
  Knowledge how to begin and how to end,
The love that never was, nor ever can be penn'd.

4

Ye sacred writings in whose antique leaves
The memories of heav'n entreasur'd lie,
Say what might be the cause that Mercy heaves
The dust of sin above th' industrious[3] sky
And lets it not to dust and ashes fly.

versialist, who defended the temporal power of the pope against James I.
[6]*Calamo . . . amyntas*: "[Nor would you be sorry] to have chafed your lips with a reed; to learn this same art, what did not Amyntas do?" (Vergil, *Eclogues*, I.34–35).
[7]"Let the word of Christ dwell in you richly, in all wisdom teaching and admonishing one another, in psalms and hymns and spiritual songs singing with grace in your hearts to the Lord" (Colossians 3.16).
[8]Fletcher is presumably thinking of Nonnus (ca. 400), a Greek poet who wrote a paraphrase of the Gospel of St. John. [9]John.
[10]Illuminate. [11]Unfair. [12]*Ion*, Sect. 533–34.
[13]Commending, i.e., committing, offering.
CHRIST'S VICTORY IN HEAVEN [1]Bore. [2]More innocent.
[3]Designed, purposed (with perhaps a play on *dust*).

Could Justice be of sin so overwooed,
Or so great ill because of so great good,
That, bloody man to save, man's Saviour shed His blood?

5

Or did the lips of Mercy drop soft speech
For trait'rous man when at th' Eternal's throne
Incensed Nemesis[4] did heav'n beseech
With thund'ring voice that justice might be shown
Against the rebels that from God were flown?
 O say, say how could Mercy plead for those
 That, scarcely made, against their Maker rose?
Will any slay his friend that he may spare his foes?

6

There is a place beyond that flaming hill
From whence the stars their thin apparance[5] shed,
A place beyond all place where never ill
Nor impure thought was every harbored,
But saintly heroes are forever s'ed[6]
 To keep an everlasting sabbath's rest,
 Still wishing that of what th' are still possest,
Enjoying but one joy, but one of all joys best.

7

Here, when the ruin of that beauteous frame
Whose golden building shin'd with every star
Of excellence, deform'd with age became,
Mercy, rememb'ring peace in midst of war,
Lift up the music of her voice to bar
 Eternal fate, lest it should quite erase
 That from the world which was the first world's grace,
And all again into their nothing, Chaos, chase.

8

For what had all this all, which man in one
Did not unite? The earth, air, water, fire,
Life, sense, and spirit, nay the pow'rful throne
Of the divinest Essence did retire
And His own image into clay inspire,
 So that this creature well might called be
 Of the great world the small epitome,
Of the dead world, the live and quick anatomy.[7]

9

But Justice had no sooner Mercy seen
Smoothing the wrinkles of her Father's brow
But up she starts and throws herself between:
As when a vapor from a moory slough,
Meeting with fresh Eous[8] that but now
 Open'd the world which all in darkness lay,
 Doth heav'n's bright face of his rays disarray,[9]
And sads the smiling orient of the springing day.

10

She was a virgin of austere regard,
Not, as the world esteems her, deaf and blind,
But as the eagle that hath oft compar'd
Her eye with heav'n's;[10] so, and more brightly, shin'd
Her lamping[11] sight; for she the same could wind

Into the solid heart, and with her ears
The silence of the thought loud speaking hears,
And in one hand a pair of even scoals[12] she wears.

> Standing majestically before the throne of God, Justice rehearses the iniquity and ingratitude of "that wretch, beast, caitive, monster" man, and she closes with a call for his destruction.

40

She ended, and the heav'nly hierarchies,
Burning in zeal, thickly imbranded[13] were:
Like to an army that alarum cries,
And everyone shakes his ydraded[14] spear,
And the Almighty's self, as He would tear
 The earth and her firm basis quite in sunder,
 Flam'd all in just revenge, and mighty thunder
Heav'n stole itself from earth by clouds that
 moistur'd under.

41

As when the cheerful sun, elamping[15] wide,
Glads all the world with his uprising ray,
And woos the widow'd earth afresh to pride,
And paints her bosom with the flow'ry May,
His silent sister steals him quite away,
 Wrapp'd in a sable cloud from mortal eyes,
 The hasty stars at noon begin to rise,
And headlong to his early roost the sparrow flies.

42

But soon as he again disshadowed is,
Restoring the blind world his blemish'd sight,
As though another day were newly ris,[16]
The cozen'd birds busily take their flight
And wonder at the shortness of the night,
 So Mercy once again herself displays,
 Out from her sister's cloud, and open lays
Those sunshine looks whose beams would dim a
 thousand days.

43

How may a worm that crawls along the dust
Clamber the azure mountains thrown so high,
And fetch from thence thy fair idea just,
That in those sunny courts doth hidden lie,
Cloth'd with such light as blinds the angel's eye?
 How may weak mortal ever hope to file
 His unsmooth tongue and his deprostrate[17] style?
O raise thou from his corse[18] thy now entomb'd exile.

44

One touch would rouse me from my sluggish hearse,
One word would call me to my wished home,

[4]Goddess of retributive justice or vengeance. [5]Appearance.
[6]Sued, paid homage? [7]Skeleton, i.e., framework.
[8]Eos or Aurora, the goddess of dawn. [9]Despoil.
[10]*Compar'd...heav'n's*: put her eye into competition with the sun. The ancients believed that only the eagle could gaze into the sun unblinded. [11]Resplendent. [12]Scales.
[13]Armed with brands or swords. [14]Dreaded. [15]Shining forth.
[16]Risen. [17]Extremely prostrate. [18]Corpse.

One look would polish my afflicted verse,
One thought would steal my soul from her thick loam
And force it, wand'ring, up to heav'n to come,
  There to importune and to beg apace
  One happy favor of thy sacred grace,
To see (what though it lose her eyes?), to see thy face.

45

If any ask why roses please the sight,
Because[19] their leaves upon thy cheeks do bow'r;
If any ask why lilies are so white,
Because their blossoms in thy hand do flow'r;
Or why sweet plants so grateful odors show'r,
  It is because thy breath so like they be;
  Or why the orient sun so bright we see,
What reason can we give, but from thine eyes and thee?

46

Ros'd all in lively crimson are thy cheeks,
Where beauties indeflourishing[20] abide;
And as to pass his fellow either seeks,
Seems both do blush at one another's pride;
And on thine eyelids, waiting thee beside,
  Ten thousand graces sit, and when they move
  To earth their amorous belgards[21] from above,
They fly from heav'n, and on their wings convey thy love.

> After many stanzas in which her beauty, power, and good-
> ness are the theme, Mercy is finally permitted to plead for
> sinful man's redemption. Although the devil was the culprit,
> she tells God, "Thy thrice-honor'd Son that now beneath
> doth stray" can undo the devil's work and expiate man's
> crime.

75

"But if or He or I may live and speak,
And heav'n can joy to see a sinner weep,
O let not Justice' iron scepter break
A heart already broke, that low doth creep,
And with prone humblesse her feet's dust doth sweep.
  Must all go by desert? Is nothing free?
  Ah, if, but[22] those that only worthy be,
None should Thee ever see, none should Thee ever see.

76

"What hath man done that man shall not undo,
Since God to him is grown so near a kin?
Did his foe slay him? He shall slay his foe.
Hath he lost all? He all again shall win.
Is sin his master? He shall master sin.
  Too hardy soul with sin the field to try,
  The only way to conquer was to fly;
But thus long Death hath liv'd, and now Death's self
    shall die.

77

"He is a path, if any be misled;
He is a robe, if any naked be;
If any chance to hunger, he is bread;
If any be a bondman, he is free;

If any be but weak, how strong is he:
  To dead men life He is, to sick men health,
  To blind men sight, and to the needy wealth:
A pleasure without loss, a treasure without stealth.[23]

78

"Who can forget, never to be forgot,
The time that all the world in slumber lies,
When, like the stars, the singing angels shot
To earth, and heav'n awaked all his eyes
To see another Sun at midnight rise?
  On earth was never sight of pareil fame,
  For God before man like himself did frame,
But God Himself now like a mortal man became.

79

"A child He was and had not learn'd to speak
That with His Word the world before did make;
His mother's arms Him bore, He was so weak
That with one hand the vaults of heav'n could shake.
See how small room my infant[24] Lord doth take,
  Whom all the world is not enough to hold.
  Who of His years or of His age hath told?
Never such age so young, never a child so old.

80

"And yet but newly He was infanted,[25]
And yet already He was sought to die;
Yet scarcely born, already banished,
Not able yet to go, and forc'd to fly;
  But scarcely fled away when by and by
    The tyran's[26] sword with blood is all defil'd,
    And Rachel, for her sons with fury wild,
Cries, 'O thou cruel king' and 'O my sweetest child.'[27]

81

"Egypt his nurse became, where Nilus springs,
Who straight to entertain the rising sun
The hasty harvest in his bosom brings;
But now for drieth[28] the fields were all undone,
And now with waters all is overrun,
  So fast the Cynthian[29] mountains pour'd their snow
  When once they felt the sun so near them glow
That Nilus Egypt lost, and to a sea did grow.

82

"The angels carol'd loud their song of peace;
The cursed oracles were strucken dumb;

[19]It is because. [20]Unfading [21]Loving looks. [22]Except.
[23]*Without loss...without stealth*: that cannot be lost...that cannot be stolen.
[24]Like Milton in "On the Morning of Christ's Nativity," line 16, Fletcher is perhaps punning on Latin *infans* ("speechless").
[25]Brought forth.
[26]Tyrant's, i.e., King Herod's, referring to the slaughter of the infants (Matthew 2.16).
[27]*Rachel...child*: "In Ramah was there a voice heard, lamentation, and weeping, and great mourning, Rachel weeping for her children, and would not be comforted, because they are not" (Matthew 2.18). [28]Drought.
[29]Referring to Cynthia, the moon goddess. Fletcher is perhaps

To see their Shepherd the poor shepherds press;
To see their King the kingly sophies[30] come;
And them to guide unto his Master's home
    A star comes dancing up the orient,
    That springs for joy over the strawy tent,
Where gold, to make their Prince a crown,
        they all present.

        83

"Young John, glad child, before he could be born
Leapt in the womb, his joy to prophesy;[31]
Old Anna, though with age all spent and worn,
Proclaims her Saviour to posterity;[32]
And Simeon fast his dying notes doth ply.[33]
    O how the blessed souls about him trace:
    It is the fire of heav'n thou dost embrace.
Sing, Simeon, sing! sing, Simeon, sing apace!"

        84

With that the mighty thunder dropp'd away
From God's unwary arm, now milder grown
And melted into tears, as if to pray
For pardon and for pity it had known,

That should have been for sacred vengeance thrown.
    Thereto the armies angelic devow'd[34]
    Their former rage, and all to Mercy bow'd;
Their broken weapons at her feet they gladly strow'd.[35]

        85

Bring, bring, ye Graces, all your silver flaskets,
Painted with every choicest flow'r that grows,
That I may soon unflow'r your fragrant baskets
To strow the fields with odors where He goes;
Let whatsoe'er He treads on be a rose.
    So down she let her eyelids fall, to shine
    Upon the rivers of bright Palestine,
Whose woods drop honey, and her rivers skip
        with wine.[36]

---

thinking of Ptolemy's "Mountains of the Moon" as the supposed source of the Nile.   [30]Rulers, i.e., the three Magi.   [31]Luke 1.41.
[32]*Old Anna...posterity*: Luke 2.36–38.
[33]*And Simeon...ply*: Luke 2.25–32.   [34]Disavowed.
[35]Strewed
[36]*Bring...Wine*: In a marginal note Fletcher explains that this stanza is "a transition to Christ's second victory," i.e., His temptation by Satan in the wilderness, which is the subject of Canto II.

Sir John Beaumont [1583?-1627]

Thanks to his social and financial status, to say nothing of his stalwart Roman Catholic faith, Beaumont was not a public man of letters, but his work was praised by famous poets, and it still deserves attention for its unobtrusive skill. In particular, his adroit manipulation of the couplet exemplifies the grace that he himself admired in art:

        Pure phrase, fit epithets, a sober care
        Of metaphors, descriptions clear yet rare,
        Similitudes contracted smooth and round,
        Not vex'd by learning, but with nature crown'd.

The scion of a distinguished family of Leicestershire recusants, Beaumont, like his brothers (one of them the playwright), attended Broadgates Hall at Oxford before going to the Inner Temple in 1597. The mock-heroic *Metamorphosis of Tobacco*, which appeared anonymously in 1602 with a dedication to Michael Drayton, was no doubt his first attempt at verse, and although he wrote no more for publication after succeeding to Gracedieu Priory, the family seat in Leicestershire, on his elder brother's death in 1605, he was an amateur of letters all his life. Much of his later work is occasional and elegiac, much of it religious (like the elaborate *Crown of Thorns* that occupied him off and on for twenty years or so), but *Bosworth Field*, his best known and most important poem, is a stirring quasi-epic in the mode of Drayton and Daniel. Intermittent harassments like an indictment for recusancy in 1606 and litigation of his estate in 1611 ended with the rise to power of George Villiers, duke of Buckingham, a kinsman of his mother. This great favorite exposed the retiring country gentleman to the glitter of the court, and in 1627 obtained for him a baronetcy. One result of Beaumont's new exposure was a group of poems prompted by or written for the royal family; another was *The Theater of Apollo*, an entertainment for the anniversary in 1625 of James' coronation that was canceled when the sovereign died. Anthony Wood asserted that had not death "untimely" cut the poet off (only three months after he attained his title), "he might have proved a patriot, being accounted in his time a person of great knowledge, gravity, and worth." In 1629, two years after his burial in Westminster Abbey, his son and heir published, with a dedication to King Charles and a cluster of commendatory poems by Jonson and Drayton and others, his father's *Bosworth Field* and a generous sampling of the shorter pieces. But the manuscript of the ambitious *Crown of Thorns*, in twelve books, remains unpublished in the British Museum, where it was belatedly discovered by Bernard H. Newdigate (*RES*, XVIII, 1942).

My text is based upon *Bosworth-field: With A Taste of the Variety of Other Poems, Left by Sir John Beaumont, Baronet, deceased: Set forth by His Sonne, Sir John Beaumont, Baronet; And dedicated to the Kings most Excellent Maiestie*, 1629 (STC 1694). *Bosworth-field* has been edited (with additions) by A. B. Grosart (1869), *The Metamorphosis of Tabacco* by J. P. Collier (*Illustrations of Early English Popular Literature*, I, 1863), and the previously unprinted *Theatre of Apollo* by Sir W. W. Greg (1926). There is an account of Beaumont's life by Mark Eccles (*HLQ*, V, 1941–42), a study of the recently exhumed *Crown of Thorns* by Ruth C. Wallerstein (*JEGP*, LIII, 1954), and a critical assessment by George Williamson (*MP*, XXXIII, 1935–36).

from Bosworth Field, with a Taste of the Variety of Other Poems (1629)

BOSWORTH FIELD

The winter's storm of civil war[1] I sing,
Whose end is crown'd with our eternal spring,
Where roses join'd, their colors mix in one,
And armies fight no more for England's throne.
Thou gracious Lord, direct my feeble pen,   5
Who from the actions of ambitious men
Hast by Thy goodness drawn our joyful good,
And made sweet flow'rs and olives grow from blood,
While we, delighted with this fair release,
May climb Parnassus in the days of peace.   10
   The King—whose eyes were never fully clos'd,
Whose mind, oppress'd with fearful dreams, suppos'd
That he in blood had wallow'd all the night—
Leaps from his restless bed before the light.
Accursed Tyrell[2] is the first he spies,   15
Whom threat'ning with his dagger, thus he cries:
"How dar'st thou, villain, so disturb my sleep?
Were not the smother'd children buried deep?
And hath the ground again been ripp'd by thee
That I their rotten carcases might see?"   20
The wretch, astonish'd, hastes away to slide
(As damned ghosts themselves in darkness hide)
And calls up three[3] whose counsels could assuage
The sudden swellings of the prince's rage:
Ambitious Lovell, who to gain his grace   25
Had stain'd the honor of his noble race;

Perfidious Catesby, by whose curious skill
The law was taught to speak his master's will;
And Ratcliffe, deeply learn'd in courtly art,
Who best could search into his sov'reign's heart.   30
Affrighted Richard labors to relate
His hideous dreams as signs of hapless fate.
"Alas," said they, "such fictions children fear.
These are not terrors showing danger near,
But motives sent by some propitious power   35
To make you watchful[4] at this early hour;
These prove that your victorious care prevents[5]
Your slothful foes that slumber in their tents;
This precious time must not in vain be spent
Which God, your help, by heav'nly means hath lent."   40

BOSWORTH FIELD [1]When the Lancastrian pretender Henry, earl of Richmond, defeated the Yorkist Richard III at Bosworth Field in Leicestershire (22 August 1485) and mounted the throne as Henry VII he ended the Wars of the Roses that had distracted England since 1455. In 1486 Henry's marriage with Elizabeth, daughter of Edward IV, finally united the white rose of York and the red of Lancaster. For other treatments of the same large subject—or parts of it—see Daniel's *Civil Wars* (pp. 28 ff.) and Bacon's life of Henry VII (pp. 882 ff.).
[2]Sir James Tyrell (d. 1502), a Yorkist stalwart who, in the hostile view of most Tudor historians, murdered at Richard's instigation the two young sons of Edward IV in the Tower of London.
[3]Francis, Viscount Lovell, William Catesby, and Sir Richard Ratcliffe, three unscrupulous confidants of Richard III whose fortunes rose and fell with their master's. [4]Wakeful. [5]Forestalls.

He by these false conjectures much appeas'd,
Contemning fancies which his mind diseas'd,[6]
Replies: "I should have been asham'd to tell
Fond dreams to wise men. Whether heav'n or hell
Or troubled nature these effects hath wrought,   45
I know this day requires another thought.
If some resistless strength my cause should cross,
Fear will increase and not redeem the loss.
All dangers, clouded with the mist of fear,
Seem great far off, but lessen coming near.   50
Away, ye black illusions of the night!
If ye, combin'd with Fortune, have the might
To hinder my designs, ye shall not bar
My courage, seeking glorious death in war."
Thus being cheer'd, he calls aloud for arms,   55
And bids that all should rise whom Morpheus[7] charms.

. . . . . .

[THE DEATH OF RICHARD III]

But at th' approach of Stanley's fresh supply[8]
The king's side droops: so gen'rous[9] horses lie
Unapt to stir or make their courage known
Which under cruel masters sink and groan.
There at his prince's foot stout Ratcliffe dies;   720
Not fearing, but despairing, Lovell flies,
For he shall after end his weary life
In not so fair but yet as bold a strife.[10]
The King maintains the fight, though left alone: 725
For Henry's life he fain would change[11] his own,
And as a lioness which, compass'd round
With troops of men, receives a smarting wound
By some bold hand, though hinder'd and opprest
With other spears, yet slighting all the rest   730
Will follow him alone that wrong'd her first:
So Richard, pressing with revengeful thirst,
Admits no shape but Richmond's to his eye,
And would in triumph on his carcase die;
But that great God to whom all creatures yield   735
Protects His servant with a heav'nly shield;
His pow'r, in which the Earl securely trusts,
Rebates[12] the blows and falsifies[13] the thrusts.
The King grows weary and begins to faint;
It grieves him that his foes perceive the taint.   740
Some strike him that till then durst not come near;
With weight and number they to ground him bear,
Where, trampled down and hew'd with many swords,
He softly utter'd these, his dying words:
"Now strength no longer Fortune can withstand: 745
I perish in the center of my land."
His hand he then with wreaths of grass enfolds
And bites the earth, which he so strictly holds
As if he would have borne it with him hence,
So loth he was to lose his right's pretense.   750

OF TRUE LIBERTY

He that from dust of worldly tumults flies
May boldly open his undazzled eyes

To read wise Nature's book, and with delight
Surveys the plants by day and stars by night.
We need not travail, seeking ways to bliss;   5
He that desires contentment cannot miss.
No garden walls this precious flow'r embrace;
It common grows in ev'ry desert[1] place.
Large scope of pleasure drowns us like a flood;
To rest in little is our greatest good.   10
Learn ye that climb the top of Fortune's wheel
That dang'rous state which ye disdain to feel.
Your highness puts your happiness to flight;
Your inward comforts fade with outward light;
Unless it be a blessing not to know   15
This certain truth, lest ye should pine for woe
To see inferiors so divinely blest
With freedom and yourselves with fetters prest;
Ye sit like pris'ners barr'd with doors and chains,
And yet no care perpetual care restrains.   20
Ye strive to mix your sad conceits with joys,
By curious pictures and by glitt'ring toys,
While others are not hind'red from their ends,
Delighting to converse with books or friends,
And living thus retir'd obtain the pow'r   25
To reign as kings of every sliding hour.
They walk by Cynthia's[2] light, and lift their eyes
To view the ord'red armies in the skies.
The heav'ns they measure with imagin'd lines,
And when the northern hemisphere declines,   30
New constellations in the south they find,
Whose rising may refresh the studious mind.
In these delights, though freedom show more high,
Few can to things above their thoughts apply.
But who is he that cannot cast his look   35
On earth and read the beauty of that book?
A bed of smiling flow'rs, a trickling spring,
A swelling river more contentment bring
Than can be shadow'd by the best of art:
Thus still the poor man hath the better part.   40

TO HIS LATE MAJESTY[1] CONCERNING THE TRUE FORM OF ENGLISH POETRY

Great king, the sov'reign ruler of this land,
By whose grave care our hopes securely stand,

[6]Made uneasy. [7]The god of sleep.
[8]At Bosworth Field Thomas Stanley, earl of Derby, and his brother Sir William, although nominally followers of Richard III, threw their support to Henry and so assured his victory.
[9]Thoroughbred.
[10]Ratcliffe died in battle, Catesby was captured and beheaded, but Lovell escaped from Bosworth to die two years later (allegedly of starvation) after the failure of a plot to dislodge Henry VII.
[11]Give in exchange. [12]Reduces the effect of.
[13]Prevents the fulfillment of.
OF TRUE LIBERTY [1]Solitary, retired. [2]The moon goddess.
TO HIS LATE MAJESTY [1]James I, who had expounded his "judicious rules" (line 11) for writing verse in *Ane Schort Treatise Conteining Some Reulis and Cautelis to Be Observit and Eschewit in Scottis Poesy* and exemplified them in *The Essays of a Prentice in the Divine Art of Poetry* (1584).

Since you, descending from that spacious reach,
Vouchsafe to be our master, and to teach
Your English poets to direct their lines, 5
To mix their colors, and express their signs;
Forgive my boldness that I here present
The life of Muses yielding true content
In ponder'd numbers, which with ease I tried
When your judicious rules have been my guide. 10

   He makes sweet music who, in serious lines,
Light dancing tunes and heavy prose declines;
When verses like a milky torrent flow,
They equal temper in the poet show.
He paints true forms who with a modest heart 15
Gives luster to his work, yet covers[2] art.
Uneven swelling is no way to fame,
But solid joining of the perfect frame,
So that no curious finger there can find
The former chinks, or nails that fastly bind; 20
Yet most would have the knots of stitches seen,
And holes where men may thrust their hands between.
On halting feet the ragged poem goes
With accents neither fitting verse nor prose;
The style mine ear with more contentment fills 25
In lawyers' pleadings or physicians' bills,
For though in terms of art their skill they close,[3]
And joy in darksome words as well as those,
They yet have perfect sense more pure and clear
Than envious Muses which sad garlands wear 30
Of dusky clouds, their strange conceits to hide
From human eyes; and, lest they should be spied
By some sharp Oedipus,[4] the English tongue
For this their poor ambition suffers wrong.
In ev'ry language now in Europe spoke 35
By nations which the Roman Empire broke,
The relish of the Muse consists in rhyme;
One verse must meet another like a chime.
Our Saxon shortness hath peculiar grace
In choice of words fit for the ending place, 40
Which leave impression in the mind as well
As closing sounds of some delightful bell.
These must not be with disproportion lame,
Nor should an echo still repeat the same.
In many changes these may be exprest 45
But those that join most simply run the best;
Their form, surpassing far the fetter'd staves,[5]
Vain care and needless repetition saves.

These outward ashes keep those inward fires
Whose heat the Greek and Roman works inspires; 50
Pure phrase, fit epithets, a sober care
Of metaphors, descriptions clear yet rare,
Similitudes contracted smooth and round,
Not vex'd by learning, but with nature crown'd;
Strong figures drawn from deep invention's springs, 55
Consisting less in words and more in things;
A language not affecting ancient times,
Nor Latin shreds, by which the pedant climbs;
A noble subject which the mind may lift
To easy use of that peculiar gift 60
Which poets in their raptures hold most dear,
When actions by the lively sound appear:
Give me such helps, I never will despair
But that our heads which suck the freezing air,
As well as hotter brains, may verse adorn, 65
And be their wonder, as we were their scorn.

OF MY DEAR SON, GERVASE BEAUMONT[1]

Can I, who have for others oft compil'd
The songs of death, forget my sweetest child,
Which like a flow'r crush'd with a blast is dead,
And ere full time hangs down his smiling head,
Expecting with clear hope to live anew 5
Among the angels fed with heav'nly dew?
We have this sign of joy: that many days
While on the earth his struggling spirit stays,
The name of Jesus in his mouth contains
His only food, his sleep, his ease from pains. 10
O may that sound be rooted in my mind,
Of which in him such strong effect I find.
Dear Lord, receive my son, whose winning love
To me was like a friendship far above
The course of nature or his tender age, 15
Whose looks could all my bitter griefs assuage;
Let his pure soul, ordain'd sev'n years to be
In that frail body which was part of me,
Remain my pledge in heav'n, as sent to show
How to this port at ev'ry step I go. 20

[2]Conceals.   [3]Enclose, conceal.
[4]Oedipus secured the throne of Thebes by solving the riddle of the Sphinx.   [5]Intricate stanzas.
OF MY DEAR SON   [1]This moving little poem for one of the younger of Beaumont's eleven children was written about 1621.

Aurelian Townshend [1583?-?1651]

The fact that Townshend, the record of whose life is nearly blank, wrote little and published almost nothing makes a long account of his career unnecessary, not to say impossible. Born in Norfolk not later than 1583, by his later teens he had somehow acquired enough facility in foreign languages to secure appointment by the great Sir Robert Cecil, first earl of Salisbury, as a servant (or perhaps companion) for his son, then a student at the university. Although Cecil arranged for him to live abroad, presumably to improve his skill in languages, by 1603 Townshend's careless way with money may have led to his dismissal; at any rate, he disappears for several years. As one who spoke French, Italian, and Spanish "in great perfection," in 1608 he went as a "companion" on Sir Edward Herbert's Continental tour (see p. 115), but in 1609 the curtain drops again. After 1622 he was living in the parish of St. Giles, Cripplegate, with his wife and several children, and in 1632 he enjoyed an hour of glory when he collaborated with Inigo Jones on a pair of masques— *Albion's Triumph* and *Tempe Restored*—for presentation at court. Presumably it was his success on these occasions that secured for him admission to the fellowship of Gray's Inn and the friendship of such wits as Digby, Suckling, and Carew. When we hear of him a decade later, however, it is in a note by Philip Herbert, earl of Pembroke and Montgomery, wherein he is described as a "poor and pocky poet" who "would be glad to sell an hundred verses not at sixpence apiece, fifty shillings an hundred verses." Forced by either debt or poverty, in 1643 he petitioned Parliament for protection against arrest by a silkman with the lilting name of Isaac Tulley. He presumably lived to see his rather wanton daughter Mary married to George Kirke, a groom of the king's bedchamer, in 1646, but like almost everything about his later years his death went unrecorded.

Apart from the two masques of 1632 Townshend's work survived only in manuscript collections until it started to appear in songbooks and miscellanies in the early 1650's. This work, and almost everything that is known or may be plausibly inferred about his life, has been brought together by E. K. Chambers in *Aurelian Townshend's Poems and Masks* (1912), on which my texts are based. Despite Chambers' assiduity, G. C. M. Smith supplemented some of his bibliographical data in *MLR*, XII (1917) and the (London) *Times Literary Supplement*, 23 October 1924.

UNCOLLECTED VERSE

[LET NOT THY BEAUTY][1]

Let not thy beauty make thee proud,
  Though princes do adore thee,
Since time and sickness were allow'd
  To mow such flowers before thee.

Nor be not shy to that degree   5
  Thy friends may hardly know thee,
Nor yet so coming or so free
  That every fly may blow thee.

A state[2] in every princely brow
  As decent is requir'd,   10
Much more in thine, to whom they bow
  By Beauty's lightnings fir'd,

And yet a state so sweetly mixt
  With an attractive mildness
It may like Virtue sit betwixt   15
  The extremes of pride and vileness.

Then every eye that sees thy face
  Will in thy beauty glory,
And every tongue that wags[3] will grace
  Thy virtue with a story.   20

[VICTORIOUS BEAUTY][1]

Victorious beauty, though your eyes
  Are able to subdue an host,

And therefore are unlike to boast
The taking of a little prize,
Do not a single heart despise.   5

It came alone, but yet so arm'd
  With former love, I durst have sworn
  That as that privy coat[2] was worn
With characters of beauty charm'd,[3]
Thereby it might have 'scap'd unharm'd.   10

But neither steel nor stony breast
  Are proof against those looks of thine,
  Nor can a beauty less divine
Of any heart be long possest
Where thou pretend'st[4] an interest.   15

The conquest in regard of me,
  Alas, is small, but in respect
  Of her that did my love protect,[5]
Were it divulg'd, deserv'd to be
Recorded for a victory;   20

LET NOT THY BEAUTY [1]Printed without ascription to Townshend in John Playford's *Select Musical Ayres* (1652). [2]Dignity. [3]Moves, speaks.

VICTORIOUS BEAUTY [1]Printed without ascription to Townshend in Playford's *Select Musical Ayres* (1652). Entitled "To the Countess of Salisbury" in other contemporary recensions, this famous poem was perhaps inspired by Catherine Howard, a sister of the notorious countess of Essex (see p. 715), who in 1608 married William Cecil, a grandson of Elizabeth's great minister, who became the second earl of Salisbury in 1612.
[2]I.e., secret protection (*coat*: coat of mail). [3]Fortified. [4]Claims.
[5]*Her...protect*: i.e., of his "former love," who had been displaced.

And such a one as some that view
  Her lovely face perhaps may say,
  Though you have stolen my heart away,
If all your servants[6] prove not true,
May steal a heart or two from you.   25

YOUTH AND BEAUTY[1]

Thou art so fair and young withal,
  Thou kindlest young desires in me,
Restoring life to leaves that fall
  And sight to eyes that hardly see
  Half those fresh beauties bloom[2] in thee.   5

Those, under sev'ral herbs and flow'rs
  Disguis'd, were all Medea gave
When she recall'd Time's flying hours
  And aged Aeson[3] from his grave,
  For Beauty can both kill and save.   10

Youth it inflames, but age it cheers.
  I would go back, but not return
To twenty but to twice those years,
  Not blaze, but ever constant burn,
  For fear my cradle prove my urn.   15

A DIALOGUE BETWIXT TIME AND A PILGRIM[1]

Pilgrim: Aged man that mows these fields—
Time: Pilgrim, speak! What is thy will?
Pilgrim: Whose soil is this that such sweet pasture yields?
  Or who art thou whose foot stands never still?
  Or where am I?   *Time*: In love.   5
Pilgrim: His Lordship lies above.
Time: Yes, and below, and round about,
  Wherein all sorts of flow'rs are growing,
  Which as the early spring puts out,
  Time falls as fast amowing.   10
Pilgrim: If thou art Time, these flow'rs have lives,
  And then I fear
  Under[2] some lily she I love
  May now be growing there.
Time: And in some thistle or some spire of grass   15
  My scythe thy stalk, before hers come, may pass.
Pilgrim: Wilt thou provide it may? *Time*: No.
Pilgrim: Allege the cause.
Time: Because Time cannot alter, but obey, Fate's laws.
Chorus: Then happy those whom Fate, that is the
    stronger,   20
  Together twists their threads, and yet draws hers the
    longer.

AN ELEGY MADE BY MASTER AURELIAN TOWNSHEND IN REMEMBRANCE OF THE LADY VENETIA DIGBY[1]

What travelers of matchless Venice say
Is true of thee, admir'd Venetia:
He that ne'er saw thee wants belief to reach
Half those perfections thy first sight could teach.
Imagination can no shape create   5

Airy enough thy form to imitate,
Nor beds of roses, damask, red, and white,
Render like thee a sweetness to the sight.
Thou wert eye-music, and no single part,   10
But Beauty's concert; not one only dart,
But Love's whole quiver; no provincial face,
But universal, best in every place.
Thou wert not born, as other women be,
To need the help of height'ning poesy,
But to make poets. He that could present   15
Thee like thy glass were superexcellent.
Witness that pen[2] which, prompted by thy parts
Of mind and body, caught as many hearts
With every line as thou with every look,
Which we conceive was both his bait and hook.   20
His style before, though it were perfect steel,
Strong, smooth, and sharp, and so could make us feel
His love or anger, witnesses agree,
Could not attract till it was touch'd by thee.
Magnetic then, he was for heighth[3] of style   25
Suppos'd in heaven, and so he was, the while
He sat and drew thy beauties by the life,
Visible angel, both as maid and wife.
In which estate thou didst so little stay
Thy noon and morning made but half a day,   30
Or half a year, or half of such an age
As thy complexion sweetly did presage
An hour before those cheerful beams were set,
Made all men losers to pay Nature's debt,
And him[4] the greatest that had most to do,   35
Thy friend, companion, and co-partner too,
Whose head, since hanging on his pensive breast,
Makes him look just like one had been possest
Of the whole world, and now hath lost it all.
Doctors to cordials,[5] friends to counsel fall.   40
He that all med'cines can exactly make
And freely give them, wanting power to take,
Sits and such doses hourly doth dispense,
A man unlearn'd may rise a doctor thence.

[6]Lovers.
YOUTH AND BEAUTY [1]Printed and ascribed to Townshend in Henry Lawes's *Ayres and Dialogues*, Book I (1653). [2]That bloom. [3]*Medea...Aeson*: According to Ovid (*Metamorphoses*, VII.162 ff.), the sorceress Medea, wife of Jason, leader of the Argonauts, restored her father-in-law Aeson to youth by the somewhat strenuous procedure of cutting the old man's throat and then giving him a transfusion made of magic herbs.
TIME AND A PILGRIM [1]Printed and ascribed to Townshend in Henry Lawes' *Ayres and Dialogues*, Book I (1653). [2]In the form of.
AN ELEGY [1]*An elegy...Digby*: This poem, which is preserved in a collection of elegies (British Museum Add. MS 30259) on the celebrated Venetia, wife of Sir Kenelm Digby (see p. 486), was first printed in *Poems from Sir Kenelm Digby's Papers* (ed. H. A. Bright, 1877), which supplies the last two lines. [2]I.e., Ben Jonson, whose "Eupheme" (*Underwoods*, No. 84), a set of linked elegies on Lady Venetia Digby, is one of his most elaborate commendatory poems. [3]Height. [4]Sir Kenelm Digby. [5]Medical stimulants.

I that delight most in unusual ways   45
Seek to assuage his sorrow with thy praise,
Which if at first it swell him up with grief,
At last may draw[6] and minister relief,
Or at the least, attempting it, express
For an old debt a friendly thankfulness.   50
I am no herald, so ye can expect
From me no crests or scutcheons[7] that reflect
With brave memorials on her great allies;[8]
Out of my reach that tree would quickly rise.
I only strive to do her fame some right,   55
And walk her mourner in this black and white.[9]

UPON KIND AND TRUE LOVE[1]

'Tis not how witty, nor how free,
Nor yet how beautiful she be,
But how much kind and true to me.
Freedom and wit none can confine,

And beauty like the sun doth shine,   5
But kind and true are only mine.

Let others with attention sit
To listen and amire her wit:
That is a rock where I'll not split.
Let others dote upon her eyes   10
And burn their hearts for sacrifice:
Beauty's a calm where danger lies.

But kind and true have been long tried
A harbor where we may confide[2]
And safely there at anchor ride.   15
From change of winds there we are free,
And need not fear storm's tyranny,
Nor pirate, though a prince he be.

[6]Drain, promote suppuration.   [7]Escutcheons, armorial bearings.
[8]Relatives, family.   [9]I.e., ink and paper.
UPON KIND AND TRUE LOVE   [1]Printed without ascription to Townshend in *Choice Drollery* (1656). E. K. Chambers groups it among the "Doubtful Poems."   [2]Trust, feel confident.

William Drummond of Hawthornden[1] [1585-1649]

Jonson, who was not noted for his tact, told William Drummond that he thought his "verses" good, "save that they smelled too much of the schools and were not after the fancy of the time." Although Drummond did not record his own response it is unlikely that this leisured, moneyed amateur of letters bridled at the censure, for he was, as Jonson also pointed out to him, "good and simple" to a fault. A well-born Scot (and distant kinsman of the king), he took his M.A. degree at Edinburgh in 1605, studied law at Bourges and Paris, and dabbled in ancient and contemporary authors before succeeding his distinguished father in 1610 as laird of his ancestral acres at Hawthornden, not far from Edinburgh. Thereafter he gave himself to literature, reading widely in half a dozen languages, collecting a remarkable library, and drifting gently into authorship with *Tears on the Death of Meliades* (1613) in commemoration of Prince Henry. The first edition of his *Poems*, which included both the elegy and a group of "madrigals and epigrams," followed soon thereafter (1614?), and in 1616, not long after the death of his fiancée, the little book appeared again with extensive changes and mortuary additions. The next year Drummond, always a loyal Scot, celebrated James I's visit to his homeland with *Forth Feasting*, a strenuously patriotic poem that attests its author's loyalty rather than his frankness and discernment. "Eye of our western world," he salutes the foolish James,

> Mars-daunting king,
> With whose renown the earth's seven climates ring,
> Thy deeds not only claim these diadems
> To which Thames, Liffey, Tay subject their streams,
> But to thy virtues rare and gifts is due
> All that the planet of the year doth view;
> Sure if the world above did want a prince,
> The world above to it would take thee hence.

And so on for more than four hundred lines.

In 1618–19 Drummond's placid, bookish life must have been enlivened, not to say disrupted, when Jonson, then on his well-publicized pedestrian tour of Scotland, paid a visit to Hawthornden.

[1] For Drummond's record of his conversations with Jonson see *Books and Men*, pp. 693 ff.

Although his bibulous, crotchety guest was, as Drummond noted, "a great lover and praiser of himself, a contemner and scorner of others," he was also the most influential writer of the day; and since his talk was almost entirely of literature, Drummond's artless record of their conversation (see pp. 693 ff.), from which he modestly almost eliminates himself, is of very large importance to the literary historian. Moreover, it presents the burly Jonson with matchless candor and precision. No other writer of the age, not even Izaak Walton, enables us to hear and see a man so clearly.

Drummond's Muse was never very jocund, but a serious illness in 1620 and then a fire and famine that ravaged Edinburgh made her almost morbid. What Burton would call the "religious melancholy" of *Flowers of Sion* is given full, sonorous reinforcement in *A Cypress Grove*, a prose meditation on death that was "adjoined" and printed with those lugubrious poems in 1623 and again in 1630. (*A Midnight Trance*, an earlier version of *A Cypress Grove* that was presumably written about 1612–14 and published in 1619, survives in a recently discovered and apparently unique copy in the Bodleian Library at Oxford.) Although Drummond lived long enough to be dismayed by the mounting troubles of the House of Stuart—rumor had it that he died of grief at Charles' execution—his later works (which include a history of Scotland and various political tracts) do not belong to literature.

For all his polyglot erudition Drummond was a writer whose graceful talent matched his modest aspirations and whose production in both prose and verse was mainly quarried from the works of other men. Traces of Desportes, Ronsard, Guarini, Sannazaro, Marino, Sidney, Shakespeare, and a dozen lesser poets have been detected in his verse; and *A Cypress Grove* shows pilferings from Pico della Mirandola, Charron, Montaigne, Ringhieri, Guevara, Donne, Sir John Hayward, and —of all men—Francis Bacon. In introducing the first collected edition of Drummond's poems in 1656 Milton's nephew Edward Phillips said that his "genius" was "polite and verdant." If the epithets are guarded, they at any rate are apt.

My texts are based on *Poems: By William Drummond, of Hawthorne-denne. The second Impression*, 1616 (STC 7255), *Flowres of Sion: By William Drummond of Hawthorne-denne. To Which Is Adjoyned His Cypress Grove*, 1630 (STC 7250), and Sir Robert Sibbald's transcription (ca. 1710) of Drummond's now lost manuscript of the "Conversations" between Jonson and Drummond as presented in C. H. Herford and Percy Simpson's *Ben Jonson*, I (1925), 132–51. As noted above, Drummond's *Poems* were first assembled by Edward Phillips in 1656 and his *Works* (including the "Conversations") by Bishop John Sage and Thomas Ruddiman in 1711. The poems were edited by Thomas Maitland and D. Irving (1832), Peter Cunningham (1833), W. B. Turnbull (1856, 1890), and W. C. Ward (2 vols., 1894) before L. E. Kastner achieved the definitive edition (2 vols., 1913). Ward and Kastner include *A Cypress Grove*, which was printed separately by Samuel Clegg in 1919; *A Midnight Trance*, its near relation, was edited by its discoverer Robert Ellrodt in 1951. David Masson's biography (1873) has been superseded by A. Joly's (in French, 1934), which itself has been supplemented by F. R. Fogle's *Critical Study* (1952). The breadth of Drummond's reading is suggested by Robert H. McDonald (ed.), *The Library of Drummond of Hawthornden* (1971).

from Poems (1616)

THE FIRST PART

SONNET [2]

I know that all beneath the moon decays,
And what by mortals in this world is brought

In time's great periods shall return to nought,
That fairest states have fatal nights and days.
I know how all the Muses' heavenly lays,　　　　5
With toil of sprite[1] which are so dearly bought,
As idle sounds of few or none are sought,

SONNET [2]　[1]Spirit.

And that nought lighter is than airy praise.
I know frail beauty, like the purple flow'r
To which one morn oft² birth and death affords;   10
That love a jarring is of minds' accords,
Where sense and will³ invassal reason's power;
  Know what I list, this all can not me move,
  But that, oh me, I both must write and love!

SONNET [6]¹

Vaunt not, fair heavens, of your two glorious lights,
Which though most bright yet see not when they shine,
And shining cannot show their beams divine
Both in one place, but part by days and nights.
Earth, vaunt not of those treasures ye enshrine,   5
Held only dear because hid from our sights,
Your pure and burnish'd gold, your diamonds fine,
Snow-passing ivory that the eye delights.
Nor, seas, of those dear wares are² in you found
Vaunt not, rich pearl, red coral, which do stir   10
A fond desire in fools to plunge your ground.³
Those all (more fair) are to be had in her:
  Pearl, ivory, coral, diamond, suns, gold,
  Teeth, neck, lips, heart, eyes, hair are to behold.

SONNET [7]¹

That learned Grecian² who did so excel
In knowledge passing sense that he is nam'd
Of all the after-worlds divine, doth tell
That at the time when first our souls are fram'd,
Ere in these mansions blind they come to dwell,   5
They live bright rays of that eternal light,
And others see, know, love, in heaven's great height,
Not toiled with aught to reason doth rebel.³
Most true it is, for straight at the first sight
My mind me told that in some other place   10
It elsewhere saw the idea of that face,
And lov'd a love of heavenly pure delight.
  No wonder now I feel so fair a flame,
  Sith I her lov'd ere on this earth she came.

SONNET [9]¹

Sleep, Silence' child, sweet father of soft rest,
Prince whose approach peace to all mortals brings,
Indifferent host to shepherds and to kings,
Sole comforter of minds with grief opprest,
Lo, by thy charming rod all breathing things   5
Lie slumb'ring, with forgetfulness possest;
And yet o'er me to spread thy drowsy wings
Thou spares, alas, who cannot be thy guest.
Since I am thine, O come, but with that face
To inward light which thou art wont to show,   10
With feigned solace ease a true-felt woe;
Or if, deaf god, thou do deny that grace,
  Come as thou wilt, and what thou wilt bequeath;
  I long to kiss the image of my death.²

MADRIGAL [1]¹

A Daedal² of my death,
Now I resemble that subtile worm on earth
Which prone to its own evil can take not rest,
For with strange thoughts possest
I feed on fading leaves   5
Of Hope, which me deceives,
And thousand webs doth warp within my breast.
And thus in end unto myself I weave
A fast-shut prison, no, but even a grave.

SONNET [23]

Then is she gone? O fool and coward, I!
O good occasion lost, ne'er to be found!
What fatal chains have my dull senses bound,
When best they may, that they not Fortune try?
Here is the flow'ry bed where she did lie;   5
With roses here she stellified the ground;
She fix'd her eyes on this (yet smiling) pond,
Nor time nor courteous place seem'd aught deny.
Too long, too long, Respect, I do embrace
Your counsel, full of threats and sharp disdain;   10
Disdain in her sweet heart can have no place,
And though come there, must straight retire again.
  Henceforth, Respect, farewell! I oft hear told
  Who lives in love can never be too bold.

SONNET [27]

That I so slenderly set forth my mind,
Writing I wot not what in ragged rhymes,
And, charg'd with brass into these golden times,¹
When others tow'r² so high, am left behind,
I crave not Phoebus leave his sacred cell   5
To bind my brows with fresh Aonian³ bays;
Let them have that who tuning sweetest lays
By Tempe⁴ sit, or Aganippe well.⁵

²Text *of*. ³*Sense and will*: sensuality and carnal desire.
SONNET [6] ¹Freely adapted from a sonnet by the Italian poet and
playwright Luigi Groto (1541–85). ²I.e., that are.
³I.e., plunder your depths.
SONNET [7] ¹This sonnet is perhaps based upon, and certainly
influenced by, Sir Philip Sidney's *Astrophil and Stella*, No. 25.
²Plato.
³*Not toil'd...rebel*: not entangled, ensnared (*toil'd*) by anything
that rebels against reason; i.e., living by pure intellect.
SONNET [9] ¹Although sonnets on sleep were extremely common
in the Renaissance, Drummond's immediate source was probably
a sonnet by the Neapolitan poet Giovanni Battista Marino (1569–
1625) that begins *O del Silentio figlio*. ²I.e., sleep.
MADRIGAL [1] ¹Based on a madrigal by Marino that begins *Fabro
dela mia morte*.
²Contriver (from Daedalus, the cunning artificer of Greek myth).
SONNET [27] ¹*Charg'd...times*: weighted down with brass in these
golden times. ²Soar (a term from hawking).
³Referring to Mt. Helicon, home of the Muses.
⁴A lovely vale in Thessaly, a favorite haunt of Apollo.
⁵A fountain of poetical inspiration on Mt. Helicon.

Nor yet to Venus' tree[6] do I aspire,
Sith[7] she for whom I might affect that praise   10
My best attempts with cruel words gainsays;
And I seek not that others me admire.
   Of weeping myrrh the crown is which I crave,
   With a sad cypress to adorn my grave.

SONNET [28]

Sound hoarse, sad lute, true witness of my woe,
And strive no more to ease self-chosen pain
With soul-enchanting sounds; your accents strain
Unto these tears uncessantly which flow;
Shrill treble, weep; and you dull basses show   5
Your master's sorrow in a deadly vein;
Let never joyful hand upon you go,
Nor consort keep but when you do complain;
Fly Phoebus' rays, nay, hate the irksome light—
Woods' solitary shades for thee are best,   10
Or the black horrors of the blackest night,
When all the world, save thou and I, doth rest.
   Then sound, sad lute, and bear a mourning part;
   Thou hell mayst move, though not a woman's heart.

SONG [2]

Phoebus, arise,
And paint the sable skies
With azure, white, and red;
Rouse Memnon's mother[1] from her Tithon's bed
That she thy career[2] may with roses spread;   5
The nightingales thy coming each where sing;
Make an eternal spring;
Give life to this dark world which lieth dead.
Spread forth thy golden hair
In larger locks than thou wast wont before,   10
And emperor-like, decore[3]
With diadem of pearl thy temples fair.
Chase hence the ugly night,
Which serves but to make dear thy glorious light.
This is that happy morn,   15
That day, long-wished day
Of all my life so dark
(If cruel stars have not my ruin sworn,
And fates not hope betray),
Which, only white,[4] deserves   20
A diamond forever should it mark;
This is the morn should bring unto this grove
My love, to hear and recompense my love.
Fair king, who all preserves,
But show thy blushing beams,   25
And thou two sweeter eyes
Shalt see than those which by Peneus'[5] streams
Did once thy heart surprise;
Nay, suns, which shine as clear
As thou when two thou did to Rome appear.[6]   30
Now Flora,[7] deck thyself in fairest guise;
If that ye, winds, would hear

A voice surpassing far Amphion's lyre,[8]
Your stormy chiding stay;
Let Zephyr[9] only breathe   35
And with her tresses play,
Kissing sometimes these purple ports of death.
The winds all silent are,
And Phoebus in his chair,[10]
Ensaffroning[11] sea and air,   40
Makes vanish every star;
Night like a drunkard reels
Beyond the hills to shun his flaming wheels;[12]
The fields with flow'rs are deck'd in every hue,
The clouds bespangle with bright gold their blue;   45
Here is the pleasant place,
And ev'ry thing save she, who all should grace.

SONNET [45][1]

Are these the flow'ry banks? Is this the mead
Where she was wont to pass the pleasant hours?
Did here her eyes exhale mine eyes' salt show'rs
When on her lap I laid my weary head?
Is this the goodly elm did us o'erspread,   5
Whose tender rine[2] cut out in curious flow'rs
By that white hand contains those flames of ours?
Is this the rustling spring us music made?
Deflourish'd mead,[3] where is your heavenly hue?
Bank, where that arras did you late adorn?   10
How look ye, elm, all withered and forlorn?
Only, sweet spring, nought altered seems in you,
   But while here chang'd each other thing appears,
   To sour your streams take of mine eyes these tears.

MADRIGAL [8]

I fear not henceforth death,
Sith after this departure yet I breath.[1]
Let rocks and seas and wind
Their highest treasons show!
Let sky and earth combin'd   5

[6]The myrtle. [7]Since.
SONG [2] [1]I.e., Eos or Aurora, the goddess of the dawn, whose husband was Tithonus. [2]Course. [3]Decorate.
[4]Auspicious.
[5]A river god whose daughter Daphne was loved by Apollo.
[6]*When two...appear*: According to legend, two suns were seen at Rome when Scipio Africanus (d. ca. 183 B.C.) was named leader of the successful war against Carthage.
[7]Goddess of vegetation.
[8]A son of Zeus who with his twin brother Zethus raised the walls of Thebes by the music of his lyre. [9]The west wind.
[10]Chariot. [11]Making yellow (with sunlight).
[12]*Night...wheels*: Drummond remembers *Romeo and Juliet*, II.iii. 3-4: "And flecked darkness like a drunkard reels / From forth day's path and Titan's fiery wheels."
SONNET [45] [1]Adapted from a sonnet in *Erreurs Amoreuse* by the French poet Pontus de Tyard (1521-1605). [2]Rind, bark.
[3]Deflowered meadow.
MADRIGAL [8] [1]Breathe.

Strive, if they can, to end my life and woe!
Sith grief cannot, me nothing can o'erthrow,
　Or if that aught can cause my fatal lot,
　It will be when I hear I am forgot.

THE SECOND PART

SONNET [4][1]

O woeful life! Life, no, but living death,
Frail boat of crystal in a rocky sea,
A sport expos'd to Fortune's stormy breath,
Which kept with pain, with terror doth decay.
The false delights, true woes thou dost bequeath　　　5
Mine all-appalled mind do so affray[2]
That I those envy who are laid in earth,
And pity them that run thy dreadful way.
When did mine eyes behold one cheerful morn?
When had my tossed soul one night of rest?　　　10
When did not hateful stars my projects scorn?
O now I find for mortals what is best:
　Even, sith our voyage shameful is and short,
　Soon to strike sail, and perish in the port.

MADRIGAL [1][1]

This life which seems so fair
Is like a bubble blown up in the air
By sporting children's breath,
Who chase it everywhere,
And strive who can most motion it bequeath;　　　5
And though it sometime seem of its own might,
Like to an eye of gold, to be fix'd there,
And firm to hover in that empty height,
That only is because it is so light;
But in that pomp it doth not long appear　　　10
　For even when most admir'd, it in a thought
　As swell'd from nothing, doth dissolve in nought.

SONNET [12][1]

As in a dusky and tempestuous night
A star is wont to spread her locks of gold,
And while her pleasant rays abroad are roll'd
Some spiteful cloud doth rob us of her sight;
Fair soul, in this black age so shin'd thou bright,　　　5
And made all eyes with wonder thee behold,
Till ugly Death, depriving us of light,
In his grim misty arms thee did enfold.
Who more shall vaunt true beauty here to see?
What hope doth more in any heart remain　　　10
That such perfections shall his reason reign?
If Beauty, with thee born, too died with thee,
　World, plain[2] no more of Love nor count his harms:
　With his pale trophies Death hath hung his arms.

URANIA, OR SPIRITUAL POEMS

[2][1]

Too long I follow'd have my fond desire,
And too long painted on the ocean streams;
Too long refreshment sought amidst the fire,
And hunted joys which to my soul were blames.
Ah! when I had what most I did admire,　　　5
And seen of life's delights the last extremes,
I found all but a rose hedg'd with a brier,
A nought, a thought, a show of mocking dreams.
Henceforth on Thee mine only good I'll think,
For only Thou canst grant what I do crave;　　　10
Thy nail my pen shall be, Thy blood mine ink,
Thy winding sheet my paper, study grave;
　And till that soul forth of this body fly,
　No hope I'll have but only only Thee.

[4][1]

Come forth, come forth, ye bless'd triumphing bands,
Fair citizens of that immortal town!
Come see that King, who all this all commands,
Now (overcharg'd with love) die for His own.
Look on those nails which pierce His feet and hands!　　　5
What a strange diadem His brows doth crown!
Behold His pallid face, His eyes which sown,[2]
And what a throng of thieves Him mocking stands.
Come forth, ye empyrean troops, come forth!
Preserve this sacred blood which earth adorns;　　　10
Gather those liquid roses from His thorns:
O, to be lost they be of too much worth,

　　　1　　2　　3　　　　　1
For streams, juice, balm they are, which quench,
　　　2　　3
kills, charms:
　1　　2　　3　　　1　　2　　3
Of God, death, hell the wrath, the life, the harms.

SONNET [4] [1]The first twelve lines of this sonnet are translated from one by the Neapolitan poet Jacopo Sannazaro (1458–1530) that begins *O vita, vita no, ma vivo affanno*; the concluding couplet derives from another sonnet by the same author. [2]Disturb, set in turmoil.

MADRIGAL [1] [1]Translated from a madrigal by the Italian poet Giovanni Battista Guarini (1537–1612) that begins *Questa vita mortale,/ Che par si bella, è quasi piume al vento.*

SONNET [12] [1]The first eight lines are translated from a sonnet by the Italian poet Torquato Tasso (1544–95) that begins *Come in turbato Ciel lucida stella*; the last six lines derive from another sonnet by the same author. [2]Complain.

[2] [1]The last six lines of this sonnet are translated from one of the *Sonnets spirituels* by the French poet Philippe Desportes (1546–1606).

[4] [1]Translated from one of Marino's sonnets that begins *Uscite, uscite a rimirar pietose.* [2]Are sunken.

[7][1]

Thrice happy he who by some shady grove
Far from the clamorous world doth live his own;
Though solitaire, yet who is not alone,
But doth converse with that eternal love.
O how more sweet is birds' harmonious moan,   5
Or the soft sobbings of the widow'd dove,
Than those smooth whisp'rings near a prince's throne,

Which good make doubtful, do the evil approve!
O how more sweet is Zephyr's wholesome breath,
And sighs perfum'd, which do the flowers unfold,   10
Than that applause vain honor doth bequeath!
How sweet are streams to poison drunk in gold!
   The world is full of horrors, falsehoods, slights,
   Woods' silent shades have only true delights.

[7] [1]Translated from one of Marino's sonnets that begins *Felice
è ben chi selva ombroso e folta.*

from Flow'rs of Sion by William Drummond of Hawthornden, To Which Is Adjoined His Cypress Grove (1630)

FLOW'RS OF SION, OR SPIRITUAL POEMS BY W. D.

[2]

A good that never satisfies the mind,
A beauty fading like the April flow'rs,
A sweet with floods of gall that runs combin'd,
A pleasure passing ere in thought made ours,
A honor that more fickle is than wind,   5
A glory at Opinion's frown that lours,
A treasury which bankrupt Time devours,
A knowledge than grave Ignorance more blind,
A vain delight our equals to command,
A style of greatness, in effect a dream,   10
A fabulous thought of holding sea and land,
A servile lot, deck'd with a pompous name
   Are the strange ends we toil for here below,
   Till wisest Death make us our errors know.

[11]

The last and greatest herald[1] of heaven's King,
Girt with rough skins, hies to the deserts wild,
Among that savage brood the woods forth bring,
Which he than man more harmless found and mild;
His food was blossoms and what young doth spring,   5
With honey that from virgin hives distill'd;
Parch'd body, hollow eyes, some uncouth thing
Made him appear, long since from earth exil'd.
There burst he forth: all ye whose hopes rely
On God, with me amidst these deserts mourn,   10
Repent, repent, and from old errors turn.
Who listen'd to his voice? obey'd his cry?

Only the echoes which he made relent,
Rung from their marble caves, "Repent, repent!"

[25]

More oft than once Death whisper'd in mine ear:
"Grave[1] what thou hears in diamond and gold.
I am that monarch whom all monarchs fear,
Who hath in dust their far-stretch'd pride uproll'd.
All, all is mine beneath moon's silver sphere,   5
And nought save virtue can my power withhold.
This, not believ'd, experience true thee told
By danger late when I to thee came near.
As bugbear then my visage I did show,
That of my horrors thou right use mightst make,   10
And a more sacred path of living take,
Now still walk armed for my ruthless blow;
   Trust flattering life no more, redeem time past,
   And live each day as if it were thy last."

A CYPRESS GROVE

Though it hath been doubted if there be in the soul such imperious and super-excellent power as that it can, by the vehement and earnest working of it, deliver knowledge to another without bodily organs, and by only conceptions and ideas produce real effects; yet it hath been ever, and of all, held as infallible and most certain that it often (either by outward inspiration or some secret motion in itself) is augur of its own misfortunes, and hath shadows of approaching dangers presented unto it before they fall forth. Hence

[11] [1]John the Baptist.
[25] [1]Engrave.

so many strange apparitions and signs, true visions, uncouth[1] heaviness, and causeless languishings: of which to seek a reason, unless from the sparkling of God in the soul, or from the God-like sparkles of the soul, were to make reason unreasonable, by reasoning of things transcending her reach.

Having, when I had given myself to rest in the quiet solitariness of the night, found often my imagination troubled with a confused fear, no, sorrow or horror, which, interrupting sleep, did astonish my senses, and rouse me, all appalled and transported, in a sudden agony and amazedness; of such an unaccustomed perturbation, not knowing nor being able to dive into any apparent cause, carried away with the stream of my (then doubting) thoughts, I began to ascribe it to that secret foreknowledge and presaging power of the prophetic mind, and to interpret such an agony to be to the spirit, as a sudden faintness and universal weariness useth to be to the body, a sign of following sickness; or as winter lightnings, earthquakes, and monsters prove to commonwealths and great cities harbingers of wretched events, and emblems of their hidden destinies.

Hereupon, not thinking it strange if whatsoever is human should befall me, knowing how Providence overcometh grief and discountenances crosses, and that as we should not despair in evils which may happen us, we should not be too confident nor too much lean to those goods we enjoy, I began to turn over in my remembrance all that could afflict miserable mortality, and to forecast every accident which could beget gloomy and sad apprehensions, and with a mask of horror show itself to human eyes. Till in the end (as by unities and points mathematicians are brought to great numbers, and huge greatness), after many fantastical glances of the woes of mankind, and those encumbrances which follow upon life, I was brought to think, and with amazement, on the last of human terrors, or, as one termed it, the last of all dreadful and terrible evils—Death. . . .

Death is the sad estranger of acquaintance, the eternal divorcer of marriage, the ravisher of the children from their parents, the stealer of parents from the children, the interrer of fame, the sole cause of forgetfulness, by which the living talk of those gone away as of so many shadows, or fabulous paladins. All strength by it is enfeebled, beauty turned in deformity and rottenness, honor in contempt, glory into baseness: it is the unreasonable breaker-off of all the actions of virtue; by which we enjoy no more the sweet pleasures on earth, neither contemplate the stately revolutions of the heavens; sun perpetually setteth, stars never rise unto us. It in one moment depriveth us of what with so great toil and care in many years we have heaped together. By this are successions of lineages cut short, kingdoms left heirless, and greatest states orphaned. It is not overcome by pride, smoothed by gaudy flattery, tamed by entreaties, bribed by benefits, softened by lamentations, diverted by time. Wisdom, save this, can alter and help anything. By death we are exiled from this fair city of the world; it is no more a world unto us, nor we any more people into it. The ruins of fanes, palaces, and other magnificent frames yield a sad prospect to the soul, and how should it consider the wrack of such a wonderful masterpiece as is the body, without horror?

Though it cannot well and altogether be denied but that death naturally is terrible and to be abhorred, it being a privation of life, and a not being, and every privation being abhorred of nature and evil in itself, the fear of it too being ingenerate[2] universally in all creatures; yet I have often thought that even naturally, to a mind by only nature resolved and prepared, it is more terrible in conceit than in verity, and at the first glance than when well pried into; and that rather by the weakness of our fantasy than by what is in it; and that the marble colors of obsequies, weeping, and funeral pomp (with which we ourselves limn it forth) did add much more ghastliness unto it than otherwise it hath. To aver which conclusion, when I had recollected my overcharged spirits, I began thus with myself:

If on the great theater of this earth, amongst the numberless number of men, to die were only proper to thee and thine, then undoubtedly thou hadst reason to grudge at so severe and partial a law. But since it is a necessity, from the which never an age by-past hath been exempted, and unto which these which be, and so many as are to come, are thralled[3] (no consequent of life being more common and familiar), why shouldst thou, with unprofitable and nothing-availing stubbornness, oppose to so unevitable and necessary a condition? This is the highway of mortality, our general home: behold, what millions have trod it before thee, what multitudes shall after thee, with them which at that same instant run! In so universal a calamity, if death be one, private complaints cannot be heard: with so many royal palaces, it is small loss to see thy poor cabin burn. Shall the heavens stay their ever-rolling wheels (for what is the motion of them but the motion of a swift and ever-whirling wheel, which twinneth[4] forth and again up-windeth our life?) and hold still time, to prolong thy miserable days, as if the highest of their working were to do homage unto thee? Thy death is a piece of the order of this All, a part of the life of this world; for while the world is the world, some creatures must die, and others take life. Eternal things are raised far above this orb of generation and corruption, where the first matter, like a still flowing and ebbing sea, with diverse waves but the same water, keepeth a restless and never tiring current. What is below, in the universality of the kind,[5] not in itself, doth abide; *Man* a long line of years hath continued, *this man* every hundredth is swept away. This air-encircled globe is the sole region of death, the grave, where everything that taketh life must rot, the lists of fortune and change, only glorious in the inconstancy and varying alterations of it; which, though many, seem yet to abide one, and being a certain entire one, are ever many. The never-agreeing bodies of the elemental brethren turn one in another: the earth changeth her countenance with the seasons, sometimes looking cold and naked, other times hot and flowery: nay, I can not tell how, but even the lowest of those celestial bodies,[6] that mother of months, and empress of seas and moisture, as if she were a mirror of our constant mutability, appeareth (by her great nearness unto

A CYPRESS GROVE   [1]Unusual, strange.   [2]Innate.   [3]Enslaved.
[4]Twines, i.e., spins?   [5]Species.   [6]*Lowest...bodies*: i.e., the moon.

us) to participate of our alterations, never seeing us twice with that same face, now looking black, then pale and wan, sometimes again in the perfection and fullness of her beauty shining over us. Death here no less than life doth act a part; the taking away of what is old being the making way for what is young. . . .

If thou dost complain that there shall be a time in the which thou shalt not be, why dost thou not too grieve that there was a time in the which thou wast not, and so that thou art not as old as that enlifening planet of time?[7] For not to have been a thousand years before this moment is as much to be deplored as not to be a thousand after it, the effect of them both being one: that will be after us which long long ere we were was. Our children's children have that same reason to murmur that they were not young men in our days which we now to complain that we shall not be old in theirs. The violets have their time, though they empurple not the winter, and the roses keep their season, though they discover not their beauty in the spring.

Empires, states, kingdoms have, by the doom of the supreme Providence, their fatal periods; great cities lie sadly buried in their dust; arts and sciences have not only their eclipses but their wanings and deaths; the ghastly wonders of the world, raised by the ambition of ages, are overthrown and trampled; some lights above, deserving to be entitled stars, are loosed and never more seen of us; the excellent fabric of this universe itself shall one day suffer ruin, or a change like a ruin; and poor earthlings thus to be handled complain! . . .

> Following a long section on the miseries of man's existence—"Is not the entering into life weakness? the continuing, sorrow?"—Drummond suggests that death is not an anguish but a solace.

If death be good, why should it be feared, and if it be the work of nature, how should it not be good? For nature is an ordinance, disposition, and rule which God hath established in creating this universe, as is the law of a king which can not err. For how should the maker of that ordinance err, sith in Him there is no impotency and weakness, by the which He might bring forth what is unperfect, no perverseness of will, of which might proceed any vicious action, no ignorance, by the which He might go wrong in working; being most powerful, most good, most wise, nay, all-wise, all-good, all-powerful? He is the first orderer; and marshaleth every other order; the highest essence, giving essence to all other things; of all causes the cause. He worketh powerfully, bounteously, wisely, and maketh nature, his artificial organ, do the same. How is not death of nature, sith what is naturally generate[8] is subject to corruption, and sith such an harmony, which is life, arising of the mixture of the four elements, which are the ingredients of our bodies, can not ever endure; the contrarieties of their qualities, as a consuming rust in the baser metals, being an inward cause of a necessary dissolution? O of frail and instable things the constant, firm, and eternal order! For even in their changes they keep ever universal, ancient, and uncorruptible laws.

Again, how can death be evil, sith it is the thaw of all these vanities which the frost of life bindeth together? If there be a satiety in life, then must there not be a sweetness in death? Man were an intolerable thing were he not mortal; the earth were not ample enough to contain her offspring if none died. In two or three ages, without death, what an unpleasant and lamentable spectacle were the most flourishing cities! For, what should there be to be seen in them save bodies languishing and courbing[9] again into[10] the earth, pale disfigured faces, skeletons instead of men? And what to be heard but the exclamations of the young, complaints of the old, with the pitiful cries of sick and pining persons? There is almost no infirmity worse than age. . . .

Life is a journey in a dusty way, the furthest rest is death; in this some go more heavily burdened than others: swift and active pilgrims come to the end of it in the morning, or at noon, which tortoise-paced wretches, clogged with the fragmentary rubbish of this world, scarce with great travail crawl unto at midnight. Days are not to be esteemed after the number of them, but after the goodness: more compass maketh not a sphere more complete, but as round is a little as a large ring; nor is that musician most praiseworthy who hath longest played, but he in measured accents who hath made sweetest melody; to live long hath often been a let[11] to live well. Muse not how many years thou mightst have enjoyed life, but how sooner thou mightst have lost it; neither grudge so much that it is no better, as comfort thyself that it hath been no worse: let it suffice that thou hast lived till this day, and (after the course of this world) not for nought; thou hast had some smiles of fortune, favors of the worthiest, some friends, and thou hast never been disfavored of the heaven. . . .

> It is indeed a "poor ambition" to hope that monuments—mortuary, literary, or other—will keep our names alive. "What can it avail thee to be talked of whilst thou art not? Consider in what bounds our fame is confined, how narrow the lists are of human glory, and the furthest she can stretch her wings. This globe of the earth and water, which seemeth huge to us in respect of the universe, compared with that wide, wide pavilion of heaven is less than little, of no sensible quantity, and but as a point." If flesh is frail and fame is fleeting, we should think upon our souls, for there our true distinction lies. It is through our souls, and not our bodies, that we shall pass from time into eternity, and come to know the "all-sufficient" peace of God.

Bedded and bathed in these earthly ordures, thou canst not come near this sovereign good, nor have any glimpse of the far-off dawning of His unaccessible brightness, no, not so much as the eyes of the birds of the night have of the sun. Think, then, by death that thy shell is broken, and thou then but even hatched; that thou art a pearl raised from thy mother, to be enchased in gold; and that the deathday of thy body is thy birthday to eternity. . . .

But it is not of death, perhaps, that we complain, but of time, under the fatal shadow of whose wings all things decay and wither. This is that tyrant which, executing against us his diamantine[12] laws, altereth the harmonious constitution of our bodies, benumbing the organs of our knowledge,

---

[7]I.e., the sun. [8]Born. [9]Curving, stooping. [10]Unto, toward. [11]Hindrance. [12]Adamantine.

turneth our best senses senseless, makes us loathsome to others and a burden to ourselves; of which evils death relieveth us. So that, if we could be transported (O happy colony!) to a place exempted from the laws and conditions of time, where neither change, motion, nor other affection of material and corruptible things were, but an immortal, unchangeable, impassible, all-sufficient kind of life, it were the last[13] of things wishable, the term[14] and center of all our desires. Death maketh this transplantation; for the last instant of corruption, or leaving-off of anything to be what it was, is the first of generation, or being of that which succeedeth. Death then, being the end of this miserable transitory life, of necessity must be the beginning of that other all-excellent and eternal: and so causelessly of a virtuous soul it is either feared or complained on. . . .

> In the final section of his treatise Drummond, enraptured by these contemplations, sees or thinks he sees a "comely" and "majestic" man—perhaps the late Prince Henry—who, in a kind of Boethian colloquy, confirms these transcendental notions. They are fools, the heavenly visitor says, who think that God "doth no otherways regard this His work than as a theater raised for bloody sword-players, wrastlers, chasers of timorous and combaters of terrible beasts, delighting in the daily torments, sorrows, distress, and misery of mankind. No, no, the eternal Wisdom created man an excellent creature, though he fain would unmake himself and return into nothing: and though he seek his felicity among the reasonless wights, He hath fixed it above. He brought him into this world as a master to a sumptuous, well-ordered, and furnished inn, a prince to a populous and rich empery,[15] a pilgrim and spectator to a stage full of delightful wonders and wonderful delights." Mired in flesh and time, man may sometimes lose his sense of glory, but when, through death, his soul regains the realm of spirit and is reunited with his risen body, he will know the "termless joys" of heaven.

"All pleasure, paragoned with what is here, is pain, all mirth mourning, all beauty deformity: here one day's abiding is above the continuing in the most fortunate estate on the earth many years, and sufficient to countervail the extremest torments of life. But although this bliss of souls be great, and their joys many, yet shall they admit addition, and be more full and perfect, at that longwished and general reunion with their bodies."

"Amongst all the wonders of the great Creator, not one appeareth to be more wonderful, nor more dazzle the eye of reason," replied I, "than that our bodies should arise, having suffered so many changes, and Nature denying a return from privation to a habit."[16]

"Such power", said he, "being above all that that the understanding of man can conceive, may well work such wonders; for if man's understanding could comprehend all the secrets and counsels of that eternal Majesty, it would of necessity be equal unto it. The Author of nature is not thralled to the laws of nature, but worketh with them, or contrary to them, as it pleaseth Him: what He hath a will to do, He hath power to perform. To that power which brought all this round All from nought, to bring again in one instant any substance which ever was into it unto what it was once

should not be thought impossible, for who can do more can do less; and His power is no less, after that which was by Him brought forth is decayed and vanished, than it was before it was produced; being neither restrained to certain limits or instruments, or to any determinate and definite manner of working: where the power is without restraint, the work admitteth no other limits than the worker's will. This world is as a cabinet[17] to God, in which the small things (however to us hid and secret) are nothing less kept than the great. For as He was wise and powerful to create, so doth His knowledge comprehend His own creation; yea, every change and variety in it, of which it is the very source. Not any atom of the scattered dust of mankind, though daily flowing under new forms, is to Him unknown; and His knowledge doth distinguish and discern what once[18] His power shall awake and raise up. Why may not the arts-master[19] of the world, like a molder, what He hath framed in divers shapes, confound in one mass, and then severally fashion them again out of the same? Can the spagyric[20] by his art restore for a space to the dry and withered rose the natural purple and blush, and cannot the Almighty raise and refine the body of man after never so many alterations in the earth? Reason herself finds it more possible for infinite power to cast out from itself a finite world, and restore anything in it, though decayed and dissolved, to what it was first than for man, a finite piece of reasonable misery, to change the form of matter made to his hand: the power of God never brought forth all that it can, for then were it bounded, and no more infinite. That time doth approach (O haste, ye times, away!) in which the dead shall live, and the living be changed,[21] and of all actions the guerdon is at hand: then shall there be an end without an end, time shall finish, and place shall be altered, motion yielding unto rest, and another world of an age eternal and unchangeable shall arise." Which when he had said, methought he vanished, and I all astonished did awake.

TO SIR W. A.[1]

Though I have twice been at the doors of death,
And twice found shut those gates which ever mourn,
This but a lightning is, truce ta'en to breath,
For late-born sorrows augur fleet return.

Amidst thy sacred cares and courtly toils,   5
Alexis, when thou shalt hear wand'ring fame
Tell Death hath triumph'd o'er my mortal spoils,
And that on earth I am but a sad name,

If thou e'er held me dear, by all our love,
By all that bliss, those joys heaven here us gave,   10

[13]Utmost. [14]Goal, objective. [15]Wide dominion.
[16]Having, possession. [17]Small room. [18]At some future time.
[19]Chief artificer. [20]Alchemist.
[21]"Behold, I show you a mystery: We shall not all sleep, but we shall all be changed" (1 Corinthians 15.51).
TO SIR W. A. [1]Sir William Alexander, earl of Stirling (1567?–1640), statesman and poet who enjoyed a long friendship with Drummond.

I conjure thee, and by the maids of Jove,[2]
To grave this short remembrance on my grave:

Here Damon lies, whose songs did sometime grace
The murmuring Esk[3]—may roses shade the place!

[2]I.e., the Muses.　[3]A river in Scotland.

George Wither [1588-1667]

In the course of his long career George Wither wrote so many books—something like a hundred —that his work was bound to be uneven. It is also fatiguingly prolix. After some five hundred lines of airy fluting to his ideal lady in *Fair Virtue* he announces,

> If I please I'll end it here;
> If I list I'll sing this year.

And then the poem ripples on another four thousand lines. Comprising limpid pastorals in the mode of Spenser, abrasive prose satire, amatory lyrics, manuals of instruction, emblematic poetry, political diatribes, moral tracts, and hymns, his corpus is extraordinary in its range of style and form, but most of it is beyond all hope of resurrection. Nonetheless, his early work retains a certain fluent charm, and even his later sermonizing (in both prose and verse) reminds us that Milton was not the only writer of his age who thought that poets "are of power beside the office of a pulpit" to serve the highest moral function.

We may infer from this immense production that Wither lisped in numbers and wrote until the day he died. As the scion of an ancient Hampshire family he was duly sent to Magdalen College, Oxford, where, says Anthony Wood, he "made some proficiency with much ado in academical learning," but "his geny being addicted to things more trivial," about 1605 he abandoned higher education in order to devote himself to writing. In his *Juvenilia* (1622) he concedes, with some complacency, his indifferent preparation as a man of letters:

> Among the learn'd this author had no name,
> Nor did he think this way to purchase fame;
> For when he this composed it was more
> Than he had read in twice-twelve months before.

By 1615, when he had studied law enough to be entered at Lincoln's Inn, he was already well established as a writer. Although the doings of the royal family prompted his first books—*Prince Henry's Obsequies* in 1612, followed quickly by a set of *Epithalamia* in honor of Princess Elizabeth's wedding (1613)—he gained more attention by *Abuses Stript and Whipt* (1613), a group of twenty "satirical essays" on such edifying topics as revenge and lust, which went through at least four editions in the year of publication. They seem tame enough today, but in 1614 they landed him in prison, where, characteristically, he beguiled the time by writing. Having already contributed two eclogues to William Browne's *Shepherd's Pipe* (1614), where he appeared as a rustic named "Roget," Wither was inspired to produce a sort of sequel in *The Shepherd's Hunting* (1615), where Browne appeared as "Willy" and Wither again as "Roget" (later changed to "Philarete").

A catalogue of Wither's works would be exhausting, but mention should be made of *Wither's Motto* (1621), which, according to the writer, sold 30,000 copies and earned for him a second term in prison because it spoke with too much candor about some powerful politicians. *Fair Virtue* (1622), which is an endless but engaging book, reprints several earlier pieces (like the famous "Shall I Wasting in Despair" from the 1619 edition of a love poem called *Fidelia*), and it also closes Wither's first and most attractive phase.

In his subsequent work, which was heralded by the dreary but instructive prose of *A Preparation for the Psalter* (1619), he turned from pastoral song to religious fervor and moral castigation. This phase is represented in our excerpts by *Britain's Remembrancer* (1628), whose eight cantos of heroic couplets commemorate the plague of 1625. Its assertive piety also informed a version of the Psalms, each accompanied by a "meditation" (1632), and *A Collection of Emblems* (1635), a work commissioned by a thrifty London printer who wished to use a set of plates that he had bought abroad. As Wither rather primly pointed out, although this book displayed the grace of art and even artifice, it was not to be confused with literature, for its purpose was instruction.

> I . . . have always intermingled sports with seriousness in my inventions, and taken in verbal conceits, as they came to hand, without affectation; but having ever aimed rather to profit my readers than to gain their praise, I never pump for those things; and am otherwhile contented to seem foolish (yea, and perhaps more foolish than I am) to the overweening wise, that I may make others wiser than they were. . . . Nevertheless, if some have said and thought truly, my poems have instructed and rectified many people in the course of honest living, which is the best wisdom, much more than the austerer volumes of some critical authors, who are by the common sort therefore only judged wise because they composed books which few understand, save they who need them not.

In his preface to *Hallelujah, or Britain's Second Remembrancer* (1641), Wither seems to summarize his own progression from a jejune delight in verbal artifice, through "the delivery of necessary truths" embellished only with "such flowers of rhetoric" as are useful to the pious reader, to the summit of his craft: that "plain and profitable poesy" which conveys "commodious truths and things really necessary in as plain and in as universal terms as it can possibly devise." Was it bravado, or serene assurance, or merely literary convention that led him to assert, at the conclusion of this book, that his fame had been secured?

> The work is finish'd which nor human pow'r,
> Nor flames, nor Time, nor Envy shall devour,
> But with devotion to God's praise be sung
> As long as Britain speaks her English tongue.

Wither's later years, which of course included many books, brought to him a variety of military and political assignments in opposition to the crown, and they also produced one famous anecdote: when captured by a troop of royalists in 1642 his life was spared through Sir John Denham's intercession with the plea "that so long as Wither lived, Denham would not be accounted the worst poet in England." Although imprisoned at the Restoration (1660–63), the old man did not slacken his production. Indeed, the publication of his final book—*Fragmenta Poetica* (1666)—almost coincided with his death.

My texts are based upon *The Shepheardes Hunting: Being certaine Eclogues written during the time of the Authors Imprisonment in the Marshalsey*, 1622, which was printed (with a separate title page), in *Juvenilia. A Collection of those Poemes which were heretofore imprinted, and written by George Wither*, 1622 (STC 25911), *Faire-Virtue, the Mistresse of Phil'arete. Written by Him-selfe*, 1622 (STC 25903), *Britain's Remembrancer Containing A Narration of the Plague lately past; A Declaration of the Mischiefs present; and a Prediction of Iudgments to come; (If Repentance prevent not.)*, 1628 (STC 25899), *A Collection of Emblemes, Ancient and Moderne: Quickened With Metricall Illustrations, both Morall and Divine*, 1635 (STC 25900), and *Haleluiah or, Britans Second Remembrancer*, 1641 (Wing W-3162).

In addition to the extensive *Miscellaneous Works* issued by the Spenser Society (6 vols., 1872–73) there are editions of *Select Lyrical Passages* by Sir Egerton Brydges (1815), of *Juvenila* by J. M. Gutch (4 vols., 1820), and of *Poems* by Henry Morley (1891). Frank Sidgwick's edition of the (chiefly pastoral) *Poetry* (2 vols., 1902) has a useful introduction. Sir Charles Firth has written an evaluation (*RES*, II, 1926); J. M. French has investigated Wither's life in prison (*PMLA*, XLV,

1930) and edited his *History of the Pestilence* (1932); and Percy Simpson and L. Kirschbaum have published studies of the complicated bibliography (*Library*, VI, 1925–26; XIX, 1938–39). C. S. Hensley's *Late Career of George Wither* (1969) does not exhaust the subject.

from The Shepherd's Hunting (1622)

THE FOURTH ECLOGUE[1]

THE ARGUMENT

Philarete on Willy calls
To sing out his pastorals,
Warrants Fame shall grace his rhymes
Spite of Envy and the times,
And shows how in care he uses
To take comfort from his Muses.

[In the opening section of the eclogue Philarete tries to learn from Willy why he, "once the blithest lad," has become so sad and silent, as if neglected by his former friends.]

Philarete:
What's the wrong?

Willy:
A slight offense
Wherewithal I can dispense[2]
But hereafter for their sake[3]   195
To myself I'll music make.

Philarete:
What, because some clown offends,
Wilt thou punish all thy friends?

Willy:
Do not, Phil, misunderstand me,
Those that love me may command me;   200
But, thou know'st, I am but young,
And the pastoral I sung
Is by some suppos'd to be
By a strain too high for me:
So they kindly let me gain   205
Not my labor for my pain.
Trust me, I do wonder why
They should me my own deny.
Though I'm young, I scorn to flit
On the wings of borrow'd wit.   210
I'll make my own feathers rear me
Whither others cannot bear me.
Yet I'll keep my skill in store
Till I've seen some winters more.

Philarete:
But, in earnest, mean'st thou so?   215
Then thou art not wise, I trow:

Better shall advise thee Pan,
For thou dost not rightly than;[4]
That's the ready way to blot
All the credit thou hast got.   220
Rather in thy age's prime
Get another start of Time,
And make those that so fond be,
Spite of their own dullness see
That the sacred Muses can   225
Make a child in years a man.
It is known what thou canst do,
For it is not long ago
When that Cuddy, thou, and I,
Each the others' skill to try,   230
At Saint Dunstan's charmed well,
As some present there can tell,
Sang upon a sudden[5] theme,
Sitting by the crimson stream;
Where if thou didst well or no   235
Yet remains the song to show.
Much experience more I've had,
Of thy skill, thou happy lad,
And would make the world to know it,
But that time will further show it.   240
Envy makes their tongues now run
More than doubt of what is done.
For that needs must be thy own,
Or to be some other's known:
But how then will't suit unto   245
What thou shalt hereafter do?
Or, I wonder, where is he
Would with that song part to thee?
Nay, were there so mad a swain
Could such glory sell for gain,   250
Phoebus would not have combin'd
That gift with so base a mind.
Never did the Nine[6] impart
The sweet secrets of their art
Unto any that did scorn   255
We should see their favors worn.
Therefore unto those that say,

THE SHEPHERD'S HUNTING [1]In the 1615 edition this eclogue is dedicated "to his truly beloved loving friend, Mr. William Browne of the Inner Temple."
[2]*Wherewithal...dispense*: which I can put up with.
[3]On their account. [4]Then. [5]Impromptu. [6]The nine Muses.

Were they pleas'd to sing a lay,
They could do't, and will not though,
This I speak, for this I know;   260
None e'er drunk the Thespian spring,[7]
And knew how, but he did sing.
For that, once infus'd in man,
Makes him show't, do what he can.
Nay, those that do only sip,   265
Or but ev'n their fingers dip
In that sacred fount, poor elves,
Of that brood will show themselves.
Yea, in hope to get them fame,
They will speak, though to their shame.   270
Let those then at thee repine
That by their wits measure thine;
Needs those songs must be thine own,
And that one day will be known.
That poor imputation too   275
I myself do undergo;
But it will appear ere long
That 'twas envy sought our wrong,
Who at twice-ten have sung more
Than some will do at fourscore.   280
Cheer thee, honest Willy, then,
And begin thy song again.

Willy:
Fain I would, but I do fear
When again my lines they hear,
If they yield[8] they are my rhymes,   285
They will feign some other crimes;
And 'tis no safe vent'ring by
Where we see Detraction lie.
For do what I can, I doubt[9]
She will pick some quarrel out;   290
And I oft have heard defended
"Little said is soon amended."

Philarete:
Seest thou not in clearest days
Oft thick fogs cloud heaven's rays,
And that vapors which do breathe   295
From the earth's gross womb beneath
Seem not to us with black steams
To pollute the sun's bright beams,
And yet vanish into air,
Leaving it unblemish'd fair?   300
So, my Willy, shall it be
With Detraction's breath on thee.
It shall never rise so high
As to stain thy poesy.
As that sun doth oft exhale[10]   305
Vapors from each rotten vale,
Poesy so sometimes drains
Gross conceits from muddy brains,
Mists of envy, fogs of spite,
'Twixt men's judgments and her light: 310
But so much her power may do,

That she can dissolve them too.
If thy verse do bravely tower,[11]
As she makes wing, she gets power:
Yet the higher she doth soar,   315
She's affronted still the more:
Till she to the high'st hath past,
Then she rests with fame at last.
Let nought therefore thee affright,
But make forward in thy flight;   320
For if I could match thy rhyme,
To the very stars I'd climb,
There begin again, and fly
Till I reach'd eternity.
But, alas, my Muse is slow;   325
For thy pace she flags too low:
Yea, the more's her hapless fate,
Her short wings were clipp'd of late,
And poor I, her fortune ruing,
Am myself put up amewing.[12]   330
But if I my cage can rid,
I'll fly where I never did.
And though for her sake I'm crost,[13]
Though my best hopes I have lost,
And knew she would make my trouble   335
Ten times more than ten times double,
I would love and keep her too
Spite of all the world could do.
For though banish'd from my flocks,
And, confin'd within these rocks,   340
Here I waste away the light
And consume the sullen night,
She doth for my comfort stay,
And keeps many cares away.
Though I miss the flow'ry fields,   345
With those sweets the springtide yields,
Though I may not see those groves
Where the shepherds chant their loves,
And the lasses more excel
Than the sweet-voic'd Philomel,[14]   350
Though of all those pleasures past
Nothing now remains at last
But remembrance, poor relief,
That more makes than mends my grief;
She's my mind's companion still,   355
Maugre[15] Envy's evil will,
Whence she should be driven too,
Were't in mortal's power to do.
She doth tell me where to borrow
Comfort in the midst of sorrow,   360
Makes the desolatest place
To her presence be a grace,
And the blackest discontents

---

[7]I.e., a spring of poetic inspiration? Thespis was a semi-legendary poet thought to be the founder of Greek tragic drama.
[8]Concede. [9]Fear. [10]Draw up.
[11]Soar aloft (a term from falconry). [12]Molting.
[13]Crossed, i.e., thwarted. [14]The nightingale. [15]Despite.

To be pleasing ornaments.
In my former days of bliss   365
Her divine skill taught me this,
That from everything I saw
I could some invention draw,
And raise pleasure to her height
Through the meanest object's sight.   370
By the murmur of a spring,
Or the least bough's rusteling,[16]
By a daisy whose leaves spread
Shut when Titan goes to bed,
Or a shady bush or tree,   375
She could more infuse in me
Than all Nature's beauties can
In some other wiser man.
By her help I also now
Make this churlish place allow   380
Some things that may sweeten gladness
In the very gall of sadness.
The dull loneness, the black shade
That these hanging vaults have made,
The strange music of the waves   385
Beating on these hollow caves,
This black den which rocks emboss
Overgrown with eldest moss,
The rude portals that give light
More to terror than delight,   390
This my chamber of neglect,
Wall'd about with disrespect;
From all these and this dull air,
A fit object for despair,
She hath taught me by her might   395
To draw comfort and delight.
Therefore, thou best earthly bliss,
I will cherish thee for this.
Poesy, thou sweet'st content
That e'er heav'n to mortals lent,   400
Though they as a trifle leave thee
Whose dull thoughts cannot conceive thee,
Though thou be to them a scorn
That to nought but earth are born,
Let my life no longer be   405
Than I am love with thee.
Though our wise ones call thee madness,
Let me never taste of gladness
If I love not thy madd'st fits
More than all their greatest wits.   410
And though some too seeming holy
Do account thy raptures folly,
Thou dost teach me to contemn
What makes knaves and fools of them.
O high power! that oft doth carry   415
Men above—

Willy:
 Good Philarete, tarry,
I do fear thou wilt be gone

Quite above my reach anon.
The kind flames of poesy
Have now borne thy thoughts so high   420
That they up in heaven be
And have quite forgotten me.
Call thyself to mind again;
Are these raptures for a swain
That attends on lowly sheep   425
And with simple herds doth keep?

Philarete:
 Thanks, my Willy; I had run
Till that time had lodg'd the sun,[17]
If thou hadst not made me stay;
But thy pardon here I pray.   430
Lov'd Apollo's sacred sire
Had rais'd up my spirits higher
Through the love of poesy
Than indeed they use to fly.
But as I said, I say still,   435
If that I had Willy's skill,
Envy nor Detraction's tongue
Should e'er make me leave my song,
But I'd sing it every day
Till they pin'd themselves away.   440
Be thou then advis'd in this
Which both just and fitting is;
Finish what thou hast begun,
Or at least still forward run.
Hail and thunder ill he'll bear   445
That a blast of wind doth fear;
And if words will thus affray thee,
Prithee how will deeds dismay thee?
Do not think so rathe[18] a song
Can pass through the vulgar throng   450
And escape without a touch,
Or that they can hurt it much:
Frosts we see do nip that thing
Which is forward'st in the spring:
Yet at last for all such lets[19]   455
Somewhat of the rest it gets.
And I'm sure that so mayst thou.
Therefore, my kind Willy, now,
Since thy folding time[20] draws on
And I see thou must be gone,   460
Thee I earnestly beseech
To remember this my speech,
And some little counsel take
For Philarete his sake:
And I more of this will say   465
If thou come next holiday.

[16]Rustling. [17]*Till...sun*: i.e., until sunset.
[18]Early, i.e., precocious. [19]Hindrances.
[20]I.e., time for enclosing the sheep at dusk.

from Fair Virtue, the Mistress of Philarete (1622)

SONNET 4

Shall I, wasting in despair,
Die because a woman's fair?
Or make pale my cheeks with care
'Cause another's rosy are?
Be she fairer than the day,   5
Or the flow'ry meads in May,
    If she be not so to me,
    What care I how fair she be?

Shall my heart be griev'd or pin'd
'Cause I see a woman kind?   10
Or a well-disposed nature
Joined with a lovely feature?
Be she meeker, kinder, than
Turtledove or pelican,[1]
    If she be not so to me,   15
    What care I how kind she be?

Shall a woman's virtues move
Me to perish for her love?
Or her well-deserving known
Make me quite forget mine own?   20
Be she with that goodness blest
Which may gain her name of best,
    If she be not such to me,
    What care I how good she be?

'Cause her fortune seems too high,   25
Shall I play the fool and die?
Those that bear a noble mind,
Where they want of riches find,
Think what with them they would do
That without them dare to woo;   30
    And unless that mind I see,
    What care I how great she be?

Great, or good, or kind, or fair,
I will ne'er the more despair;
If she love me, this believe,   35
I will die ere she shall grieve;
If she slight me when I woo,
I can scorn and let her go;
    For if she be not for me,
    What care I for whom she be?   40

SONNET 5

I wander'd out a while agone,[1]
And went I know not whither;
But there do beauties many a one
Resort and meet together,
And Cupid's power will there be shown   5

If ever you come thither.
For like two suns, two beauties bright
I shining saw together,
And tempted by their double light
My eyes I fix'd on either;   10
Till both at once so thrall'd my sight,
I lov'd, and knew not whether.[2]

Such equal sweet Venus gave
That I preferr'd not either;
And when for love I thought to crave,   15
I knew not well of whether,
For one while this I wish'd to have,
And then I that had liefer.

A lover of the curious't eye
Might have been pleas'd in either;   20
And so, I must confess, might I,
Had they not been together.
Now both must love or both deny,
In one enjoy I neither.

But yet at last I 'scaped the smart   25
I fear'd at coming hither;
For seeing my divided heart—
I, choosing, knew not whether—
Love angry grew and did depart,
And now I care for neither.   30

A POSTSCRIPT

If any carp for that my younger times
Brought forth such idle fruit as these slight rhymes,
It is no matter so they do not swear
That they so ill-employed never were.
Whilst their desires perhaps they looselier spent,
I gave my heats of youth this better vent,
And oft by writing thus the blood have tam'd
Which some with reading wanton lays enflam'd.
    Nor care I, though their censure some have past
Because my songs exceed the fiddler's last.
For do they think that I will make my measures
The longer or the shorter for their pleasures?
Or maim or curtalize[1] my free invention
Because fools weary are of their attention?
No, let them know who do their length contemn,
I make to please myself, and not for them.

SONNET 4 [1]The pelican, who was thought to wound her own
breast in order to feed her young with the flowing blood, was
a common symbol of devotion.
SONNET 5 [1]Ago. [2]Which of the two.
A POSTSCRIPT [1]Curtail.

A MISCELLANY OF EPIGRAMS,
SONNETS, EPITAPHS, AND SUCH
OTHER VERSES AS WERE FOUND

WRITTEN WITH THE POEM AFOREGOING

A SONNET UPON A STOL'N KISS

Now gentle sleep hath closed up those eyes
Which waking kept my boldest thoughts in awe,
And free access unto that sweet lip lies
From whence I long the rosy breath to draw;
Methinks no wrong it were if I should steal   5
From those two melting rubies one poor kiss;
None sees the theft that would the thief reveal,
Nor rob I her of aught which she can miss;
Nay, should I twenty kisses take away,

There would be little sign I had done so;   10
Why then should I this robbery delay?
O, she may wake, and therewith angry grow.
  Well, if she do, I'll back restore that one,
  And twenty hundred thousand more for loan.

AN EPITAPH UPON A GENTLEWOMAN WHO HAD
FORETOLD THE TIME OF HER DEATH

Her who beneath this stone consuming lies
For many virtues we might memorize.[1]
But most of all the praise deserveth she
In making of her words and deeds agree.
For she so truly kept the word she spake   5
As that with Death she promise would not break.
"I shall," quoth she, "be dead before the mid
Of such a month." And as she said, she did.

AN EPITAPH UPON A GENTLEWOMAN   [1]Preserve the memory of.

from Britain's Remembrancer (1628)

CANTO THE FIRST

  Our author first with God begins,
Describes His anger for our sins,
Of all His judgments muster makes,
Declares how Mercy undertakes
The pleading of this kingdom's cause
To bring God's wrath unto a pause,
And (for the common reader) suits
High things with lowly attributes.
    Then steps into a praiseful strain
Of Charles his new-beginning reign,
Implores that well succeed he may,
And for his weal makes Mercy pray.
    He Justice also introduces,
Complaining on our gross abuses,
Who proveth so our sinful nation
To merit utter desolation
That all God's plagues had us enclosed
If Mercy had not interposed.
But after pleading of the case,
With Justice Mercy doth embrace,
Who, that our sins may punish'd be,
To send the pestilence agree,
Their other plagues a while suspending
To prove how that will work amending.

One storm[1] is past, and though some clouds appear,
A peaceful air becalms our hemisphere.
That frighting angel whose devouring blade
Among the people such a havoc made

Is now departed, and hath took from hence   5
His poison'd arrows of the pestilence.
God smooths His brow, and lo, we now obtain
The cheerful brightness of His face again.
O boundless Mercy, what a change is this!   10
And what a joy unto my heart it is!
Run quickly, Muse, to carry my oblation,
And 'twixt that angel and the congregation
Some sweet perfume to our Preserver burn
Before that bloody messenger return.   15
    Let all affairs keep off and give thee way,
For though my fairest outward fortunes lay
This hour at spoil, I would not be advis'd
To speak for them till I had sacrific'd;
Nor will I to the world one line allow   20
Till I have made performance of my vow.
    Most awful Power, by whom hath formed bin[2]
The globe of heav'n and earth and all therein,
Thou Alpha and Omega of my songs
To whom all glory and all fame belongs,   25
To Thee, thrice holy and almighty King,
Of Judgment and of Mercy now I sing.
Thou hast unclos'd my lips, and I will raise
My thankful voice in setting out Thy praise;
Thou hast preserv'd Thy children in the flame,   30
And we ascribe the glory to Thy name;
Thou saved hast Thy people from their crimes,
And here I publish unto future times

BRITAIN'S REMEMBRANCER   [1]I.e., the great plague of 1625, in which it was estimated that some 35,000 persons perished.   [2]Been.

What I have seen. O let my poem be
A sanctified sacrifice to Thee!　　　　　　　　　35
Accept this poor oblation I prefer;
These drams of incense and these drops of myrrh
(Which, fired in affliction's flame, perfume
Thy sacred altars) graciously assume;
And give my lines a date to last as long　　　　40
As there are speakers of our English tongue,
That children yet unborn may read the story
Which now I sing to Thy perpetual glory.

　　And hark, ye people, hearken you, I pray,
That were preserv'd with me to see this day;　　45
And listen you, that shall be brought upon
This stage of action when our scene is done;
Come hearken all, and let no soul refrain
To hear, nor let it hear my words in vain.
For from the slaughter-house of death and from　50
The habitations of the dead I come.
I am escaped from the greedy jaws
Of hell, and from the furious lion's paws;
With sorrows I have lodged, and I have
Experience in the horrors of the grave,　　　　55
In those discomforts which by day assail,
And those black terrors which by night prevail.
Despair, with her grim furies, I have seen;
Spectator of God's justice I have been;
And passing through God's judgments had a sight　60
Of those His mercies, which are infinite;
And here I tell the world what I observ'd,
For to this purpose is my soul preserv'd....

THE SECOND CANTO

Let no fantastic reader now condemn
Our homely Muse for stooping unto them

In plain expressions and in words that show
We love not in affected paths to go.
For to be understood is language used,　　　　5
And speech to other ends as much abused.
Lines therefore overdark or overtrimm'd
Are like a picture with a visor limn'd;
Or like pomanders of a curious scent
Within a painted box that hath no vent;　　　10
Or like peach-kernels which, to get them forth,
Require more cracking than the fruit is worth.
Let no man guess my measures framed be
That wiser men my little wit may see,
Or that I do not hold the matter good　　　　15
Which is not more admir'd than understood;
For chiefly such a subject I desire
And such a plain expression to acquire
That ev'ryone my meaning may discern,
And they be taught that have most need to learn.　20
It is the useful matter of my rhymes
Shall make them live; words alter as the times,
And soonest their fantastic rhetorics
Who trim their poesies with schoolboy tricks.
That which this age affects as grave and wise,　25
The following generation may despise.
Greene and Lyly's language were in fashion,[3]
And had among the wits much commendation,
But now another garb of speech with us
Is priz'd, and theirs is thought ridiculous,　　30
As ours perchance will be when Time, who changeth
Things changeable, the present phrase estrangeth.[4]...

[3]Following the enormous success of John Lyly's highly wrought
novel *Euphues, the Anatomy of Wit* (1579), its stylistic affectations
(or euphuisms) were imitated by Robert Greene (d. 1592) and
many other writers.　[4]Makes strange.

from A Collection of Emblems, Ancient and Modern (1633)

TO THE READER

　If there had not been some books conceitedly composed, and suitable to mean capacities, I am doubtful whether I had ever been so delighted in reading as thereby to attain to the little knowledge I have; for I do yet remember that things honestly pleasant brought me by degrees to love that which is truly profitable. . . .

　I take little pleasures in rhymes, fictions, or conceited compositions for their own sakes; neither could I ever take so much pains as to spend time to put my meanings into other words than such as flowed forth without study: partly because I delight more in matter than in wordy flourishes, but chiefly because those verbal conceits which by some are accounted most elegant are not only for the greater part empty sounds and impertinent clinches[1] in themselves, but such inventions as do sometime also obscure the sense to common readers and serve to little other purpose but for witty men to show tricks one to another; for the ignorant understand them not, and the wise need them not.

　So much of them as (without darkening the matter to them who most need instruction) may be made use of to stir up the affections, win attention, or help the memory, I approve and make use of to those good purposes, ac-

TO THE READER　[1]Puns.

cording as my leisure and the measure of my faculty will permit, that Vanity might not to worse ends get them wholly into her possession. For I know that the meanest of such conceits are as pertinent to some as rattles and hobbyhorses to children, or as the ABC and spelling were at first to those readers who are now past them. And indeed, to despise mean inventions, pleasant compositions, and verbal elegancies (being qualified as is aforesaid) or to banish them out of the world because there be other things of more excellency were as absurd as to neglect and root out all herbs which are less beautiful than the tulip or less sweet than the rose.

I, that was never so sullenly wise, have always intermingled sports with seriousness in my inventions, and taken in verbal conceits, as they came to hand, without affectation; but having ever aimed rather to profit my readers than to gain their praise, I never pump for those things; and am otherwhile contented to seem foolish (yea, and perhaps more foolish than I am) to the overweening wise, that I may make others wiser than they were; and (as I do now) am not ashamed to set forth a game at lots[2] or, as it were, a puppet-play in pictures to allure men to the more serious observation of the profitable morals couched in these emblems. Nevertheless, if some have said and thought truly, my poems have instructed and rectified many people in the course of honest living, which is the best wisdom, much more than the austerer volumes of some critical authors, who are by the common sort therefore only judged wise because they composed books which few understand, save they who need them not. . . .

⌈ Whatever the merits of the pictorial emblems, Wither ⌉
  insists that they acquire new value from the verses he had
⌊ fitted to them. ⌋

If they were worthy of the graver's and printer's cost,[3] being only dumb figures little useful to any but to young gravers or painters, and as little delightful except to children and childish gazers, they may now be much more worthy, seeing the life of speech being added unto them may make them teachers and remembrancers of profitable things.

I do not arrogate so much unto my illustrations as to think they will be able to teach anything to the learned, yet if they cast their eyes upon them perhaps these emblems and their morals may remember[4] them either of some duty which they might else forget or mind them to beware of some danger which they might otherwise be unheedful to prevent. But sure I am, the vulgar capacities may from them be many ways both instructed and remembered; yea, they that most need to be instructed and remembered, and they who are most backward to listen to instructions and remembrances by the common course of teaching and admonishing shall be hereby informed of their dangers or duties by the way of an honest recreation, before they be aware.

For when levity or a childish delight in trifling objects hath allured them to look on the pictures, curiosity may urge them to peep further, that they might seek out also their meanings in our annexed illustrations, in which may lurk some sentence or expression so evidently pertinent to

their estates, persons, or affections as will (at that instant or afterward) make way for those considerations which will at last wholly change them, or much better them in their conversation. . . .

When some in former ages had a meaning
An emblem of mortality to make,
They form'd an infant on a death's head leaning,
And round about encircled with a snake.
The child so pictur'd was to signify   5
That from our very birth our dying springs;
The snake her tail devouring doth imply

[2]Having announced on the title page that his "metrical illustrations" would be "disposed into lotteries," Wither ends each of the four books of his *Emblems* with a "lottery," that is, a sort of versified riddle on each of the foregoing emblems. For I.45, which is reprinted below, the lottery is as follows:

When thou hast changes, good or bad,
O'erjoyd thou art or oversad,
As if it seemed very strange
To see the wind or weather change.
Lo, therefore to remember thee
How changeable things mortal be
Thou art assisted by this lot;
Now let it be no more forgot.
See Emblem 45

[3]The pictorial emblems for which Wither supplied "metrical illustrations" had been engraved by the Dutch artist Crispin van Pass for an emblem book (1613) by the German didactic poet Georg Rollenhagen and subsequently purchased by the London printer Henry Taunton, who commissioned Wither's undertaking.
[4]Remind.

The revolution of all earthly things.
For whatsoever hath beginning here
Begins immediately to vary from   10
The same it was, and doth at last appear
What very few did think it should become.
The solid stone doth molder into earth;
That earth ere long to water rarefies;
That water gives an airy vapor birth,   15
And thence a fiery comet doth arise,
That moves until itself it so impair
That from a burning meteor back again
It sinketh down and thickens into air;
That air becomes a cloud, then drops of rain;   20
Those drops, descending on a rocky ground,
There settle into earth, which more and more
Doth harden still; so, running out the round,
It grows to be the stone it was before.
Thus all things wheel about, and each beginning   25
Made entrance to its own destruction hath.
The life of nature ent'reth in with sinning,
And is forever waited on by death;
The life of grace is form'd by death to sin,
And there doth life eternal straight begin.   30
When with a serious musing I behold
The grateful and obsequious[1] marigold,
How duly ev'ry morning she displays
Her open breast when Titan spreads his rays,
How she observes him in his daily walk,   5

Still bending towards him her tender stalk,
How when he down declines, she droops and mourns,
Bedew'd as 'twere with tears till he returns,
And how she veils her flow'rs when he is gone,
As if she scorned to be looked on   10
By an inferior eye, or did contemn
To wait upon a meaner light than him.
When this I meditate, methinks the flowers
Have spirits far more generous than ours,
And give us fair examples to despise   15
The servile fawnings and idolatries,
Wherewith we court these earthly things below
Which merit not the service we bestow.
But, O my God, though groveling I appear
Upon the ground, and have a rooting here   20
Which hales me downward, yet in my desire
To that which is above me I aspire,
And all my best affections I profess
To Him that is the sun of righteousness.
O keep the morning of His incarnation,   25
The burning noontide of His bitter passion,
The night of His descending, and the height
Of His ascension ever in my sight,
    That imitating Him in what I may,
    I never follow an inferior way.   30

BOOK IV, EMBLEM 1   [1]Dutiful, attentive.

from Hallelujah, or Britain's Second Remembrancer (1641)

TO THE THRICE HONORABLE, THE HIGH COURTS OF
PARLIAMENT, NOW ASSEMBLED IN THE TRIPLE EMPIRE
OF THE BRITISH ISLES: GEO. WITHER HUMBLY
TENDERS THIS HIS HALLELUJAH,
OR SECOND REMEMBRANCER.

Fifteen years now past, I was in some things of moment
a remembrancer to these islands,[1] which have in many
particulars so punctually and so evidently succeeded ac-
cording to my predictions that not a few have acknowledged
they were not published so long before they came to pass
without the special providence and mercy of God to these
kingdoms; and some who scornfully jeered and maliciously

TO THE PARLIAMENT   [1]Wither is alluding, of course, to his *Britain's
Remembrancer* (1628), for which see p. 157.

persecuted me for that book, almost to my utter undoing, have lived to see much of that fulfilled which they derided, and to feel that which they would not believe. . . .

For though it were but a bush which burned, God was the inflamer of that shrub; and, as it now seemeth, it was a beacon warrantably fired to give true alarums to prevent those dangers and innovations[2] which then to me appeared near at hand: yea, though my first and these my second remembrances may have some passages and expressions in them savoring so much of my natural infirmities as may make them distasteful to a proud knowledge, and perhaps exercise the humility of a sanctified wisdom, yet I am confident that God hath been pleased to accompany my imperfect musings with some notions pertinent to these times, and proceeding from himself, which I desire may be considered of as they shall deserve, and no otherwise.

I arrogate no more than Balaam's ass[3] might have done: God opened mine eyes to see dangers which neither my most prudent masters, nor men as cunning as Balaam, seemed to behold. God opened my mouth also, and compelled me, beyond my natural abilities, to speak of that which I foresaw would come to pass; and men's eyes are now so cleared, excepting theirs who are willfully blind, that most of us behold the angel of the Lord, which stood in our way with a drawn sword; and we have lately obtained also, partly in hope and partly in possession, such public and private deliverances that both private oblations of thanksgiving and general sacrifices of praise are now and everlastingly due from these islands.

For the better performance of which duty I do now execute the office of a remembrancer in another manner than heretofore; and have directed unto you, the most honorable representative bodies of these kingdoms, the sweet perfume of pious praises, compounded according to the art of the spiritual apothecary to further the performance of thankful devotions, hoping that by your authorities they shall, if they so merit, be recommended unto them for whose use they are prepared. And there will be need both of God's extraordinary blessing and of your grave assistance herein.

For so innumerable are the foolish and profane songs now delighted in, to the dishonor of our language and religion, that hallelujahs and pious meditations are almost out of use and fashion; yea, not in private only, but at our public feasts and civil meetings also, scurrilous and obscene songs are impudently sung without respecting the reverend presence of matrons, virgins, magistrates, or divines. Nay, sometimes in their despite they are called for, sung and acted with such abominable gesticulations as are very offensive to all modest hearers and beholders and fitting only to be exhibited at the diabolical solemnities of Bacchus, Venus, or Priapus.[4]

For prevention whereof I am an humble petitioner that some order may be provided by the wisdom and piety of your assemblies, seeing upon due examination of this abuse it may soon be discovered that as well *Censores Canticorum* as *Librorum*[5] will be necessary in these times; and I am confident your zeal and prudence will provide as you see cause, and accept these endeavors of your humble suppliant and servant, who submitting himself and his remembrances to your grave censures, submissively takes his leave, and

beseecheth God's blessing upon your honorable designs and consultations.

To The Reader.

I was wont to feign myself a shepherd,[1] but now I have really a flock and many other suchlike rural negotiations to oversee;[2] among which I do now and then intermingle employments of this nature, that I might not muddle altogether in dirt and dung, but leave behind me some testimonials that while I labored for the maintenance of my body I was not without meditations pertinent to the wellbeing of my soul, though the affairs which necessity compels me to follow are no little hinderances to the Muses which I affect.

I have observed three sorts of poesy now in fashion: one consisteth merely of rhymes, clinches, anagrammatical fanies, or suchlike verbal or literal conceits as delight schoolboys and pedantical wits, having nothing in them either to better the understanding or stir up good affections.

These rattles of the brain are much admired by those who, being men in years, continue children in understanding, and those chats of wit may well be resembled to the fantastical suits made of taffeties and sarcenets, cut out in slashes,[3] which are neither comely nor commodious for sober men to wear, nor very useful for anything, being out of fashion, but to be cast on the dunghill.

Another sort of poesy is the delivery of necessary truths and wholesome documents couched in significant parables and illustrated by such flowers of rhetoric as are helpful to work upon the affections and to insinuate into apprehensive[4] readers a liking of those truths and instructions which they express.

These inventions are most acceptable to those who have ascended the middle region of knowledge, for though the wisest men make use of them in their writings, yet they are not the wisest men for whose sake they are used. This poesy is frequently varied according to the several growths, ages, and alterations of that language wherein it is worded; and that which this day is approved of as an elegancy may seem less facetious[5] in another age; for which cause such compositions may be resembled to garments of whole silk adorned with gold lace; for while the stuff, shape, and trimming are in fashion, they are a fit wearing for princes; and the materials, being unmangled,[6] may continue useful

[2]The political upheavals of the early 1640's
[3]Although the prophet Balaam had been hired to curse the Israelites, he blessed them after his donkey, at God's command, had spoken to deter him from the sinful deed (Numbers 22).
[4]*Bacchus...Priapus*: pagan deities of wine, love, and sexuality.
[5]*Censores...librorum*: "censors of songs and books." It was to protest the threat of such censorship that Milton, three years later, wrote his *Areopagitica* (pp. 603 ff.).
TO THE READER [1]For a specimen of Wither's early pastoral eclogues see *The Shepherd's Hunting* (1615), pp. 153 ff.
[2]For several years after about 1636 Wither lived in a cottage at Farnham in Surrey.
[3]*Taffeties and...slashes*: garments of taffeta and fine silks cut so as to expose lining of a different color.
[4]Perceptive, understanding.   [5]Polished.
[6]I.e., if they are in good condition.

to some purposes for some other persons.

A third poesy there is which delivers commodious truths and things really necessary in as plain and in as universal terms as it can possibly devise; so contriving also what is intended, that the wisest, having no cause to contemn it, may be profitably remembered of what they know, and the ignorant become informed of what is convenient to be known.

This is not so plausible[7] among the witty as acceptable to the wise, because it regardeth not so much to seem elegant as to be useful for all persons in all times; which it endeavoreth by using a phrase and method neither unpleasing to the time present nor likely to grow altogether out of use in future ages; and if it make use of enigmatical expressions, it is to prevent the profanation of some truths or the oppressing of their professors. The commendation of this poesy is not improperly set forth by a mantle, or suchlike upper garment, of the best English cloth; for that continueth indifferently serviceable for all seasons, and may be usefully and commendably worn by men of every degree.

To this plain and profitable poesy I have humbly aspired, and especially in this book, imitating therein, though coming infinitely behind them, no worse patterns than the most holy prophets; and by this means, I hope the memorial of God's mercies shall be the better preserved in our hearts, and things pertinent to our happiness be the more frequently presented to a due consideration. . . .

Childhood and youth are almost generally so seduced and bewitched with vain (if not wicked) songs and poems that holy and pious meditations are tedious and unwelcome to most men all their life long. Nay, poesy hath been so profaned by unhallowed suggestions—inspirations I will not call them—and by having been long time the bawd to lust and abused to other improper ends that some good men (though therein not very wise men) have affirmed poesy to be the language and invention of the devil.

To prevent these errors and offenses, Mr. Sandys, Mr. Herbert, Mr. Quarles,[8] and some others have lately, to their great commendations, seriously endeavored by turning their Muses to divine strains and by employing them in their proper work. For the like prevention I have also labored according to my talent, and am desirous both to help restore the Muses to their ancient honor and to become a means by the pleasingness of song to season childhood and young persons with more virtue and piety. . . .

As in the language, so in the sorts of verse, I have affected plainness, that I might the more profit them who need such helps. This I have done also that they may be sung to the common tunes of the Psalms and such other as are well known, to which I have directed my reader, not to confine him to such tunes but that he may have those until he be provided of such as may be more proper, which perchance may by some devout musician be hereafter prepared.

In all these compositions I have made use of no man's method or meditations but mine own. Not that I despised good helps, but partly because my fortunes and my employments compelled me to spin them out of my own bowels

as occasions were presented unto me, and chiefly because I thought by searching mine own heart I should the better find out those musings and expressions which would flow with least harshness and be most suitable to their capacities whom I desire to profit.

All these things considered, I hope I shall be judged excusable though I attained not to perfection in my pious endeavors; and I am hopeful also, considering how many songs I have now prepared to advance a Christian rejoicing, that it will not be thought altogether my fault if there follow not a merry time.

Without more words I commit these my humble devotions to their use who shall approve and accept of them, and the event[9] of my studies and desires to God's gracious providence, whom I beseech to sanctify them to His glory.

June 1, 1641

THE FIRST PART, CONSISTING OF HYMNS OCCASIONAL[1]

HYMN XIX
When We Put Off Our Apparel

Whilst we are putting off our apparel, the singing of this brief hymn will be neither tedious nor unprofitable, seeing we may thereby prepare as well our minds as our bodies for the better enjoying of a comfortable rest. Sing this as the 33 or 34 Psalms.

As ere I down am couched there
  Where now I hope to rest,
I first from what I daily wear
  Begin to be undrest;
So in my grave ere I shall be   5
  In blest repoosure laid,
Of many rags yet worn by me
  I must be disarray'd.
2 My fruitless hopes, my foolish fears,
  My lust, my lofty pride;   10
My fleshly joys, my needless cares,
  Must quite be laid aside.
Yea, that self-love which yet I wear
  More near me than my skin
Must off be pluck'd ere I shall dare   15
  My last long sleep begin.
3 Of these and all such rags as these
  When I am disarray'd,
My soul and body shall have ease,
  Wherever I am laid: 20

[7]Pleasing.
[8]*Sandys...Quarles*: For the religious poetry of these contemporary writers see pp. 110 f., 201 ff., 193 ff. [9]Outcome.

THE FIRST PART [1]Wither classifies his hymns as Occasional, Temporary, and Personal. The first and third kinds are represented in these excerpts; the second kind comprised such events as birthdays, Guy Fawkes Day, wedding anniversaries, Christmas, Palm Sunday, Easter, and the like.

Nor fears of death, nor cares of life,
   Shall then disquiet me;
Nor dreaming joys, nor waking grief,
   My sleep's disturbance be.
4 Therefore instruct Thou me, O God!   25
   And give me grace to heed
With what vain things ourselves we load,
   And what we rather need.
O help me tear those clouts[2] away,
   And let them so be loath'd   30
That I on my last rising day
   With glory may be cloth'd.
5 And now when I am naked laid,
   Vouchsafe me so to arm
That nothing make my heart afraid,   35
   Or do my body harm.
And guard me so when down I lie,
   And when I rise again,
That sleep or wake or live or die,
   I still may safe remain.   40

HYMN XX
When We Cannot Sleep

When we cannot sleep at seasonable times, vain musings and want of right meditating on God is frequently chief cause of unrest. Therefore this meditation directeth to the remedy of such untimely watchfulness. Sing this as the former hymn.

What ails my heart, that in my breast
   It thus unquiet lies,
And that it now of needful rest
   Deprives my tired eyes?
Let not vain hopes, griefs, doubts, or fears   5
   Distemper so my mind;
But cast on God thy thoughtful cares,
   And comfort thou shalt find.
2 In vain that soul attempteth aught,
   And spends her thoughts in vain,   10
Who by or in herself hath sought
   Desired peace to gain.
In vain as rising in the morn
   Before the day appear;
In vain to bed we late return,   15
   And lie unquiet there.
3 For when of rest our sin deprives,
   When cares do waking keep,
'Tis God, and He alone, that gives
   To His beloved sleep.   20
On Thee, O Lord! on Thee therefore,
   My musings now I place:
Thy free remission I implore,
   And Thy refreshing grace.
4   Forgive Thou me, that when my mind   25
   Oppress'd begun to be,
I sought elsewhere my peace to find,
   Before I came to Thee.

And, gracious God! vouchsafe to grant,
   Unworthy though I am,   30
The needful rest which now I want,
   That I may praise Thy name.

THE THIRD PART, CONTAINING HYMNS PERSONAL

HYMN XX
For Lovers Tempted by Carnal Desires[1]

From those carnal suggestions whereby wantons are encouraged to fulfill unchaste longings, occasion is here taken to cherish in true lovers rather such affections as beget and continue an everlasting love.

Come, sweet heart, come, let us prove,
   Whilst we may, the joys of love;
To each other let us give
   All our longings whilst we live;
For what most we fear to lose   5
   Slowly comes and swiftly goes;
And the pleasure we delay
   May be lost anon for aye.
2 Those fair lamps which trim the skies
   Daily set and daily rise,   10
But when we have lost our light,
   Everlasting is our night;
We shall see nor torch nor star
   To inform us where we are;
Therefore, come, come, let us prove,   15
   While we may, the joys of love.
3 Thus the carnal dotard sings,
   Wooing shades as real things;
All his hopes and all his joys
   Sickness, age, or death destroys;   20
Fancies vain and foolish fires
   Are the guides of his desires,
And his bliss and chiefest good
   Builded is on flesh and blood.
4 But my dear and I do climb   25
   To affections more sublime,
Neither welfare nor distress
   Makes our love the more or less,
Nor have outward things the pow'r
   To mislead such love as our;   30
And it still abides the same,
   Whether praise it hath or blame.
5 When the beauties which adorn
   Flesh and blood away are worn
From those ruins which will raise   35
   Objects worth more love and praise:

[2]Clothes.

THE THIRD PART [1]The first sixteen lines of this "hymn" are translated from Catullus, Carmen V (*Vivamus, mea Lesbia, atque amemus*). For Crashaw's version of the same famous poem see pp. 312–13.

Yea, when sickness, age, or death
Shall deprive of health and breath,
Youthful strength could never yet
Gain the bliss we then shall get.   40
6 Therefore, stars, and moon, and sun,
Unenvied your courses run;
We, without distrust or fear,
Keep our motions in our sphere;
For we know we shall arise   45
After death puts out our eyes,
And obtain a light divine
Which will moon and sun outshine.

[POSTSCRIPT]

Although my Muse flies yet far short of those
Who perfect hallelujahs can compose,
Here to affirm I am not now afraid
What once, in part, a heathen prophet[1] said,

With slighter warrant, when to end was brought   5
What he for meaner purposes had wrought.
The work is finish'd which nor human pow'r,
Nor flames, nor Time, nor Envy shall devour;
But with devotion to God's praise be sung
As long as Britain speaks her English tongue,   10
Or shall that Christian saving faith profess
Which will preserve these isles in happiness;
And, if conjectures fail not, some that speak
In other languages shall notice take
Of what my humble musings have compos'd   15
And by these helps more often be dispos'd
To celebrate His praises in their songs
To whom all honor and all praise belongs.

POSTSCRIPT   [1]I.e., Horace. In lines 7-8 Wither paraphrases *Odes*,
III.xxx (*Exegi monumentum aere perennius*).

William Browne [1590/1?-?1643/5]

When, at the start of his career, Brown announced that he would sing the beauties and the glories of his native Devon, he hit upon a theme that he sustained, sometimes with slumberous prolixity, through a larger number of gently flowing couplets than perhaps the subject needed. Denying any wish to "tune the swains" of Thessaly or Arcadia, he fixed his eye on things at hand:

> My Muse for lofty pitches shall not roam,
> But homely pipen of her native home,
> And to the swains, Love's rural minstrelsy,
> Thus, dear Britannia, will I sing of thee.

If his blend of discursive pastoralism, topography, patriotism, and rather fuzzy allegory seems old fashioned in the age of Donne and Jonson, it shows at least the force of Spenser's great example, and thanks to Brown's own lyric gift, it also shows the power of song.

Like his friend George Wither (see p. 151), Browne left Exeter College, Oxford, without taking a degree, then read law at Clifford's Inn before entering the Inner Temple, and (again like Wither) became a published poet with an elegy on Prince Henry (which was paired with one by Donne's friend Christopher Brooke in *Two Elegies*, 1613). With that, the floodgates opened. In 1613 there also appeared the first book of *Britannia's Pastorals*, which Browne, though only twenty-two, must have been at work upon for several years. This first installment of his *magnum opus*, didicated to Edward, Baron Zouche, and buttressed by commendatory verses (in three languages) by young John Selden, as well as accolades by Drayton and half a dozen others, enjoyed a prompt success. We should expect Browne's friends to say kind things about the work, but according to Anthony Wood, writing several generations later, others also liked the little book, it being "esteemed then by judicious persons to be written in a sublime strain, and for subject very amorous and pleasing."

This strain promptly showed itself again in *The Shepherd's Pipe* (1614), a kind of coterie anthology containing seven eclogues by Browne, one each by Brooke and John Davies of Hereford, and two by young George Wither. Working with uncommon speed, by January 1615 Browne was ready with *The Inner Temple Masque* (on Circe and Ulysses), which, for reasons not entirely clear, was apparently not presented—nor indeed even published until 1772. In 1616 there appeared the second book of *Britannia's Pastorals*, with a dedication to William Herbert, earl of Pembroke, and another set of commendatory poems by another set of friends (who by now included, in addition to Davies and Wither, the celebrated Jonson). A third, and markedly inferior, book of pastorals, which Browne presumably did not revise for publication, remained in manuscript until 1852.

After 1616 Browne's torrent of production diminished to a trickle. The death of his first wife about 1614 may have prompted the splendid epitaph "In Obitum M. S.," and it certainly made possible the protracted wooing that seems to be recorded in the fourteen sonnets written for his "Caelia," who at last became his bride in 1628. These sonnets, as well as various shorter pieces like the justly famous epitaph on "Sidney's sister, Pembroke's mother" that was once ascribed to Jonson, are preserved in a British Museum manuscript first published in 1815. Apart from a few commendatory poems and epistles Browne's later years were silent. In 1624 he returned to his old college as tutor to the future earl of Carnarvon, and before the year was out his associates, who clearly held him in esteem, conferred on him the M.A. degree. At some later date, according to the questionable assertion of Anthony Wood, he "got wealth" in the service of the Herbert's at Wilton House and "purchased an estate." Tradition has it that he spent his final years at Dorking, Surrey, far from his beloved Devon, but where and when he died are matters of conjecture.

My texts are based on *Britannia's Pastorals*, [1613]–1616 (STC 3915, in which the remainder of the 1613 edition of Book I was bound in with Book II), W. C. Hazlitt's transcriptions of the British Museum Lansdowne MS 777 in his edition of the *Whole Works* (2 vols., 1868–69), and (for "To My Honored Friend Mr. Drayton") Michael Drayton's *Poly-Olbion*, 1622 (STC 7228). Although Browne's *Works* were edited by W. Thompson and T. Davis (3 vols., 1772), the *Whole Works* by W. C. Hazlitt (in the edition cited just above), and the *Poetical Works* by Gordon Goodwin (2 vols., 1894), an authoritative text is needed. The *Inner Temple Masque*, first published in the *Works* of 1772, was edited by Gwyn Jones in 1954. In addition to F. W. Moorman's general account of Browne's career (1897) there are studies of the famous epitaph on the countess of Pembroke by Philip Sidney (1907) and A. Holaday (*PQ*, XXVIII, 1949), as well as bibliographical essays by H. C. H. Candy (*Library*, IX, 1918) and Geoffrey Tillotson (*RES*, VI and VII, 1930, 1931; *Library*, XI, 1930), and a survey of recent work on Browne by Dennis G. Donovan, *ELR*, II (1972).

from Britannia's Pastorals (1613-1616)

To the Reader

The times are swoll'n so big with nicer wits
That nought sounds good but what Opinion strikes;
Censure with Judgment seld[1] together sits
And now the man more than the matter likes.

The great rewardress of a poet's pen,　　　　　　5
Fame, is by those so clogg'd she seldom flies;
The Muses, sitting on the graves of men,
Singing that Virtue lives and never dies,

Are chas'd away by the malignant tongues
Of such by whom Detraction is ador'd:　　　　　10
Hence grows the want of ever-living songs
With which our isle was whilom[2] bravely stor'd.

If such a basilisk[3] dart down his eye
(Imposion'd with the dregs of utmost hate)
To kill the first blooms of my poesy,　　　　　　15
It is his worst, and makes me fortunate.
　　Kind wits I vail to, but to fools precise
　　I am as confident as they are nice.[4]

　　　　　　　　　　　　　　W. B.
　　　　　　　　From the Inner Temple,
　　　　　　　　　June the 18th, 1613

To the Reader [1]Seldom. Many words used by Browne were archaisms in his own time. [2]Formerly.
[3]A fabled reptile whose look was thought to kill.
[4]*Kind wits...nice*: i.e., I defer to men of generous intelligence, but with fastidious, carping fools I am as boldly self-assured as they are.

THE FIRST BOOK

THE FIRST SONG

I that whilere[1] near Tavy's[2] straggling spring
Unto my seely[3] sheep did use to sing,
And play'd to please myself on rustic reed,
Nor sought for bay (the learned shepherd's meed),
But as a swain unkent[4] fed on the plains,   5
And made the echo umpire of my strains,
Am drawn by time (although the weak'st of many)
To sing those lays as yet unsung of any.
What need I tune the swains of Thessaly,
Or, bootless, add to them of Arcady?[5]   10
No, fair Arcadia cannot be completer:
My praise may lessen, but not make thee greater.
My Muse for lofty pitches[6] shall not roam,
But homely pipen[7] of her native home,
And to the swains, Love's[8] rural minstrelsy,   15
Thus, dear Britannia, will I sing of thee. . . .

THE FOURTH SONG
[THE PROGRESS OF LOVE]

Happy ye days of old, when every waste
Was like a sanctuary to the chaste;[1]
When incests, rapes, adulteries were not known;
All pure as blossoms which are newly blown.[2]
Maids were then as free from spots and soils within   5
As most unblemish'd in the outward skin.
Men every plain and cottage did afford
As smooth in deeds as they were fair of word.
Maidens with men as sisters with their brothers,
And men with maids convers'd as with their mothers,   10
Free from suspicion or the rage of blood.
Strife only reign'd, for all striv'd to be good.
  But then as little wrens but newly fledge[3]
First by their nests hop up and down the hedge,
Then one from bough to bough gets up a tree,   15
His fellow, noting his agility,
Thinks he as well may venture as the other;
So flushing[4] from one spray unto another
Gets to the top, and then embolden'd flies
Unto an height past ken of human eyes: 20
So time brought worse. Men first desir'd to talk;
Then came suspect,[5] and then a private walk;
Then by consent appointed times of meeting,
Where most securely each might kiss his sweeting;[6]
Lastly with lusts their panting breasts so swell   25
They came to——but to what I blush to tell.
And ent'red thus, rapes used were of all;
Incest, adultery held as venial.
The certainty in doubtful balance rests
If beasts did learn of men, or men of beasts.   30
Had they not learn'd of man, who was their king,
So to insult upon an underling,

They civilly had spent their lives' gradation
As meek and mild as in their first creation;
Nor had th' infections of infected minds   35
So alter'd nature and disorder'd kinds;[7]
Fida[8] had been less wretched, I more glad
That so true love so true a progress had. . . .

THE SECOND BOOK

THE FIRST SONG

Glide soft, ye silver floods
    And every spring;
Within the shady woods
    Let no bird sing,
Nor from the grove a turtledove   5
Be seen to couple with her love,
But silence on each dale and mountain dwell
Whilst Willy bids his friend and joy farewell.

But (of great Thetis'[1] train)
    Ye mermaids fair,   10
That on the shores do plain[2]
    Your sea-green hair,
As ye in trammels knit your locks,
Weep ye, and so enforce the rocks
In heavy murmurs through the broad shores tell   15
How Willy bade his friend and joy farewell.

Cease, cease, ye murd'ring winds,
    To move a wave;
But if with troubled minds
    You seek his grave,
Know 'tis as various as yourselves,
Now in the deep, then on the shelves,
His coffin toss'd by fish and surges fell,[3]
Whilst Willy weeps and bids all joy farewell.

Had he, Arion-like,[4]   25
    Been judg'd to drown,

THE FIRST SONG [1]Formerly. [2]A river in Devon. [3]Silly, innocent. [4]Unknown, obscure.
[5]*Thessaly . . . Arcady*: regions in Greece associated with pastoral poetry in antiquity. [6]Heights (a term from falconry). [7]Pipe. [8]Text *Loue*.
THE FOURTH SONG [1]*When every . . . Chaste*: time was when one did not need to be in a crowd to feel secure. *Waste*: sparsely inhabited or desolate spot. [2]Bloomed, opened. [3]Feathered, i.e., fit to fly. [4]Flitting. [5]Suspicion, expectation (of something evil?). [6]Sweetheart. [7]Natural classes.
[8]A maiden deserted by her fickle lover.
THE FIRST SONG [1]In Greek myth, a Nereid or sea-maiden who became the mother of Achilles. In *Britannia's Pastorals* she serves as a rather fuzzy symbol for poetical inspiration, specifically of pastoral poetry. [2]Plane, smoothe. [3]Cruel, dire (so also in l. 31). [4]According to legend, when the 7th-century Greek poet Arion flung himself into the sea in order to escape a crew of murderous sailors, a dolphin, charmed by his singing, carried him to safety.

He on his lute could strike
   So rare a sown,[5]
A thousand dolphins would have come
And jointly strive[6] to bring him home.   30
But he on shipboard died, by sickness fell,
Since when his Willy bade all joy farewell.

   Great Neptune, hear a swain!
     His coffin take,
   And with a golden chain   35
     For pity make
It fast unto a rock near land!
Where ev'ry calmy morn I'll stand,
And ere one sheep out of my fold I tell,[7]
Sad Willy's pipe shall bid his friend farewell.   40

[At the end of the First Song we are shown the silver-footed sea-nymph Thetis as she drives her silver throne from Greece to Italy, and then to France and finally England. In this splendid panoramic view of European literature Browne pays homage to Vergil, Ovid, "holy Petrarch," Ariosto, Tasso, "divinest Bartas," Ronsard, and the rest, but he saves his last and highest praise for Spenser.]

But let us leave, fair Muse, the banks of Po;[8]   955
Thetis forsook his brave stream long ago,
And we must after. See, in haste she sweeps
Along the Celtic shores; th' Armoric[9] deeps
She now is ent'ring: bear up, then, ahead,
And by that time she hath discovered   960
Our alablaster[10] rocks we may descry
And stem[11] with her the coasts of Britany.[12]
There will she anchor cast to hear the songs
Of English shepherds, whose all-tuneful tongues
So pleas'd the Naiades[13] they did report   965
Their songs' perfection in great Nereus' court;
Which Thetis hearing, did appoint a day
When she would meet them in the British Sea,
And thither for each swain a dolphin bring
To ride with her whilst she would hear him sing.   970
The time prefix'd was come, and now the star
Of blissful light appear'd, when she her car
Stay'd in the Narrow Seas.[14] At Thames' fair port
The nymphs and shepherds of the isle resort,
And thence did put to sea with mirthful rounds,   975
Whereat the billows dance above their bounds,
And bearded goats that on the clouded head
Of any sea-surveying mountain fed,
Leaving to crop the ivy, list'ning stood
At those sweet airs which did entrance the flood.   980
In jocund sort the goddess thus they met,
And after rev'rence done, all being set
Upon their finny coursers round her throne,
And she prepar'd to cut the wat'ry zone[15]
Engirting Albion,[16] all their pipes were still,   985
And Colin Clout[17] began to tune his quill
With such deep art that everyone was given
To think Apollo, newly slid from heav'n,
Had ta'en a human shape to win his love,
Or with the western swains for glory strove.   990

He sung th' heroic knights of fairyland
In lines so elegant, of such command,
That had the Thracian[18] play'd but half so well
He had not left Eurydice in hell.
But ere he ended his melodious song   995
An host of angels flew the clouds among,
And rapt this swan from his attentive mates
To make him one of their associates
In heaven's fair chair, where now he sings the praise
Of Him that is the first and last of days.   1000
Divinest Spenser, heav'n-bred, happy Muse!
Would any power into my brain infuse
Thy worth, or all that poets had before,
I could not praise till thou deserv'st no more.
   A damp of wonder and amazement strook   1005
Thetis' attendants; many a heavy look
Follow'd sweet Spenser, till the thick'ning air
Sight's further passage stopp'd. A passionate tear
Fell from each nymph; no shepherd's cheek was dry;
A doleful dirge and mournful elegy   1010
Flew to the shore, when mighty Nereus' queen,
In memory of what was heard and seen,
Employ'd a factor[19] fitted well with store
Of richest gems, refined Indian ore,
To raise in honor of his worthy name   1015
A pyramis[20] whose head, like winged Fame,
Should pierce the clouds, yea, seem the stars to kiss,
And Mausolus'[21] great tomb might shroud in his.
Her will had been performance had not Fate,
That never knew how to commiserate,   1020
Suborn'd curs'd Avarice to lie in wait
For that rich prey—gold is a taking bait!—
Who, closely lurking like a subtile snake
Under the covert of a thorny brake,
Seiz'd on the factor by fair Thetis sent,   1025
And robb'd our Colin of his monument.
   Ye English shepherds, sons of Memory,
For satires change your pleasing melody:
Scourge, rail, and curse that sacrilegious hand,
That more than fiend of hell, that Stygian brand,[22]   1030
All-guilty Avarice, that worse of evil,
That gulf-devouring offspring of a devil!
Heap curse on curse so direful and so fell
Their weight may press his damned soul to hell!

[5]Sound. [6]Striven. [7]Count. [8]A river in northern Italy. [9]The sea adjoining Armorica, i.e., Brittany. [10]Alabaster. [11]Sail. [12]Britain. [13]Water-nymphs, daughters of Nereus, the Old Man of the Sea [14]The English Channel. [15]Girdle, belt. [16]England. [17]Edmund Spenser, who had adopted the sobriquet in *The Shepherd's Calendar* (1579). [18]Orpheus, who by his music almost succeeded in rescuing his wife Eurydice from Hades. For Ovid's account of this famous episode, as translated by George Sandys, see p. 108. [19]Agent. [20]Pyramid. [21]A king of Caria (d. ca. 353 B.C.) in Asia Minor whose massive tomb at Halicarnassus was one of the Seven Wonders of the Ancient World. [22]Hellish mark of infamy.

Is there a spirit so gentle can refrain   1035
To torture such? O let a satyr's vein
Mix with that man to lash this hellish limb,[23]
Or all our curses will descend on him.
    For mine own part, although I now commerce[24]
With lowly shepherds in as low a verse,   1040
If of my days I shall not see an end
Till more years press me, some few hours I'll spend
In rough-hewn satires, and my busied pen
Shall jerk[25] to death this infamy of men,
And like a Fury glowing coulters[26] bear   1045

With which—but see how yonder fondlings[27] tear
Their fleeces in the brakes. I must go free
Them of their bonds. Rest you here merrily
Till my return, when I will touch a string
Shall make the rivers dance and valleys ring.   1050

THE SECOND SONG
[THE ENGLISH POETS]

Th' admired mirror,[1] glory of our isle,
Thou far-far-more than mortal man, whose style   250
Struck more men dumb to hearken to thy song
Than Orpheus' harp or Tully's[2] golden tongue,
To him (as right) for wit's deep quintessence,
For honor, valor, virtue, excellence
Be all the garlands, crown his tomb with bay,   255
Who spake as much as e'er our tongue can say.
    Happy Arcadia! While such lovely strains
Sung of thy valleys, rivers, hills, and plains,
Yet most unhappy, other joys among,
That never heardst his music nor his song.   260
Deaf men are happy so whose virtues' praise
(Unheard of them) are sung in tuneful lays.
And pardon me, ye sisters of the mountain
Who wail his loss from the Pegasian fountain,[3]
If, like a man for portraiture unable,   265
I set my pencil to Apelles' table,[4]
Or dare to draw his curtain with a will
To show his true worth, when the artist's skill
Within that curtain fully doth express
His own art's mast'ry, my unableness.   270
    He sweetly touched what I harshly hit,[5]
Yet thus I glory in what I have writ:
Sidney began and (if a wit so mean
May taste with him the dews of Hippocrene)
I sung the past'ral next, his Muse my mover;   275
And on the plains full many a pensive lover
Shall sing us to their loves, and praising be
My humble lines the more for praising thee.
Thus we shall live with them by rocks, by springs,
As well as Homer by the death of kings.   280
    Then in a strain beyond an oaten quill[6]
The learned shepherd of fair Hitchin Hill[7]
Sung the heroic deeds of Greece and Troy
In lines so worthy life that I employ
My reed in vain to overtake his fame.   285
All praiseful tongues do wait upon that name.

Our second Ovid, the most pleasing Muse
That heav'n did e'er in mortal's brain infuse,
All-loved Drayton[8] in soul-raping[9] strains
A genuine note of all the nymphish trains   290
Began to tune; on it all ears were hung,
As sometime Dido's on Aeneas' tongue.[10]
    Jonson, whose full of merit[11] to rehearse
Too copious is to be confin'd in verse,
Yet therein only fittest to be known,   295
Could any write a line which he might own.
One so judicious, so well knowing, and
A man whose least worth is to understand;
One so exact in all he doth prefer
To able censure, for the theater   300
Not Seneca transcends his worth of praise;
Who writes him well shall well deserve the bays.[12]
    Well-languag'd Daniel![13] Brooke,[14] whose polish'd lines
Are fittest to accomplish high designs,
Whose pen (it seems) still young Apollo guides;   305
Worthy the forked hill,[15] forever glides
Streams from thy brain, so fair that time shall see
Thee honor'd by thy verse, and it by thee;
And when thy temple's well-deserving bays
Might imp[16] a pride in thee to reach thy praise,   310
As in a crystal glass fill'd to the ring
With the clear water of as clear a spring,
A steady hand may very safely drop

[23]Agent (i.e., of Satan). [24]Associate. [25]Beat. [26]Plowshares.
[27]Lambs.

THE SECOND SONG [1]Sir Philip Sidney, for whom see pp. 689 ff.
[2]Cicero's. [3]Hippocrene, the fountain of poetic inspiration on
Mt. Helicon, which was formed by a blow from the hoof of the
winged horse Pegasus.
[4]*If...table*: i.e., if, like a man with no talent whatever, I try to
match the greatest painter of antiquity. *Table*: canvas.
[5]*He...hit*: Sidney's *Arcadia* (1590), which contains much pastoral
poetry, was one of the most successful and influential novels of the
Renaissance. [6]Pipe made of straw.
[7]I.e., George Chapman, the translator of Homer (pp. 10 ff.),
who was born at Hitchin in Hertfordshire.
[8]Michael Drayton (pp. 31 ff.), for whose exchange of poetical
compliments with Browne see pp. 44 and 173. [9]Soul-ravishing.
[10]In the *Aeneid*, Book IV, Aeneas wins the love of Dido, queen of
Carthage, by telling her of his misfortunes.
[11]The full extent of whose merit.
[12]*One so exact...bays*: i.e., a man so discriminating and precise
that in the theater not even Seneca surpasses him in merit; anyone
who describes him accurately deserves the poet's wreath.
[13]Samuel Daniel (p. 24), for whom Browne's epithet has become
almost proverbial.
[14]Christopher Brooke (d. 1628), member of Lincoln's Inn and close
friend of Donne's (p. 73), who was himself a minor poet much
praised by his contemporaries. His elegy on Prince Henry was
published with one by Browne in 1613, and one of his eclogues
was printed as an appendix to Browne's *Shepherd's Pipe* a year
later. To his *Ghost of Richard the Third* (1614), a long historical
poem, Browne, Jonson, Chapman, Wither, and others contrib-
uted commendatory verses, but he never achieved the fame that
Browne, here and elsewhere, prophesied for him.
[15]The twin-peaked Mt. Parnassus?
[16]Engraft (a term from falconry).

Some quantity of gold, yet o'er the top
Not force the liquor run, although before   315
The glass of water could contain no more:
Yet so, all-worthy Brooke, though all men sound[17]
With plummets of just praise thy skill profound,
Thou in thy verse those attributes canst take,
And not apparent ostentation make,   320
That any second can thy virtues raise,
Striving as much to hide as merit praise.
    Davies[18] and Wither,[19] by whose Muses' power
A natural day to me seems but an hour,
And could I ever hear their learned lays,   325
Ages would turn to artificial[20] days.
These sweetly chanted to the Queen of Waves;[21]
She prais'd, and what she prais'd, no tongue depraves.[22]
Then base Contempt, unworthy our report,
Fly from the Muses and their fair resort,   330
And exercise thy spleen on men like thee:
Such are more fit to be contemn'd than we.
'Tis not the rancor of a cank'red heart
That can debase the excellence of art,
Nor great in titles make our worth obey,   335
Since we have lines far more esteem'd than they.
For there is hidden in a poet's name
A spell that can command the wings of Fame,
And maugre[23] all Oblivion's hated birth
Begin their immortality on earth;   340
When he that 'gainst a Muse with hate combines
May raise his tomb in vain to reach our lines.

THE THIRD SONG
[THE GOLDEN AGE]

        O the golden age
Met all contentment in no surplusage
Of dainty vands, but, as we do still,   225
Drank the pure water of the crystal rill,
Fed on no other meats than those they fed,
Labor the salad that their stomachs bred.[1]
Nor sought they for the down of silver swans,
Nor those sow-thistle locks each small gale fans,   230
But hides of beasts, which when they liv'd they kept,
Serv'd them for bed and cov'ring when they slept.
If any softer lay, 'twas (by the loss
Of some rock's warmth) on thick and spongy moss,
Or on the ground, some simple wall of clay   235
Parting their beds from where their cattle lay;
And on such pallets one man clipp'd[2] then
More golden slumbers than this age again.
That time, physicians thriv'd not; or if any,
I dare say all; yet then were thrice as many   240
As now profess'd, and more, for every man
Was his own patient and physician.

        . . . . . .

    Happier those times were when the flaxen clue[3]
By fair Archne's hand the Lydians knew,[4]

And sought not to the worm for silken threads
To roll their bodies in or dress their heads.   290
When wise Minerva did th' Athenians learn[5]
To draw their milk-white fleeces into yarn,
And knowing not the mixtures which began,
Of colors, from the Babylonian,
Nor wool in Sardis dy'd, more various known   295
By hues than Iris[6] to the world hath shown;
The bowels of our mother were not ripp'd
For madder-pits,[7] nor the sweet meadows stripp'd
Of their choice beauties, nor for Ceres'[8] load
The fertile lands burd'ned with needless woad.[9]   300
Through the wide seas no winged pine[10] did go
To lands unknown for staining indigo,
Nor men in scorching climates moored their keel
To traffic for the costly cochineal.
Unknown was then the Phrygian broidery,   305
The Tyrian purple, and the scarlet dye.
Such as their sheep clad, such they wove and wore,
Russet or white, or those mix'd, and no more;
Except sometimes, to bravery inclin'd,
They dyed them yellow caps with alder rind.   310
The Grecian mantle, Tuscan robes of state,
Tissue[11] nor cloth of gold of highest rate
They never saw; only in plesant woods,
Or by th' embroider'd margin of the floods,[12]
The dainty nymphs they often did behold   315
Clad in their light silk robes, stitch'd oft with gold.

        . . . . . .

The daisy scatt'red on each mead and down,
A gloden tuft within a silver crown
(Fair fall[13] that dainty flower, and may there be
No shepherd grac'd that doth not honor thee!);
The primrose, when with six leaves gotten grace,[14] 355
Maids as a true-love in their bosoms place;
The spotless lily, by whose pure leaves be
Noted the chaste thoughts of virginity;

[17]Gauge the depth of.
[18]John Davies (1565?–1618) of Hereford, a prolific but undistinguished poet best known for his *Microcosmus* (1603) and *The Scourge of Folly* (1611).
[19]George Wither (p. 151), like Brooke and Davies a contributor to Browne's *Shepherd's Pipe* (1614).   [20]Made by art.   [21]Thetis.
[22]Disparages.   [23]Despite.

THE THIRD SONG   [1]*Labor...bred*: i.e., work was the relish that quickened their appetites (*stomachs*).   [2]Embraced.   [3]Ball of thread.
[4]For her skill at weaving, Arachne, a woman of Lydia, was transformed into a spider by the jealous Athene (*Minerva*).   [5]Teach.
[6]Goddess of the rainbow.
[7]Beds of madder, a herbaceous plant whose roots were a source of red dye.
[8]In Roman mythology, the goddess of grains and harvests.
[9]An herb used for blue dye.   [10]Sailing ships made of pine.
[11]Rich cloth of gauzy texture.
[12]*Margin...floods*: shores of the streams.
[13]May good befall.
[14]*With six...grace*: i.e., when mature and most beautiful.

Carnations sweet with color like the fire,
The fit impress[15] for inflam'd desire;   360
The harebell for her stainless azur'd hue
Claims to be worn of none but those are[16] true;
The rose, like ready, youth, enticing stands,
And would be cropp'd if it might choose the hands;
The yellow kingcup[17] Flora[18] them assign'd   365
To be the badges of a jealous mind;
The orange-tawny marigold, the night
Hides not her color from a searching sight.
(To thee, then, dearest friend,[19] my song's chief mate,
This color chiefly I appropriate,   370
That spite of all the mists Oblivion can,[20]
Or envious frettings of a guilty man,
Retain'st thy worth, nay, mak'st it more in price,
Like tennis balls, thrown down hard, highest rise);
The columbine in tawny often taken   375
Is then ascrib'd to such as are forsaken;
Flora's choice buttons of a russet dye
Is hope even in the depth of misery;
The pansy, thistle, all with prickles set,
The cowslip, honeysuckle, violet,   380
And many hundreds more that grac'd the meads,
Gardens and groves, where beauteous Flora treads,
Were by the shepherds' daughters, as yet are
Us'd in our cotes,[21] brought home with special care,
For bruising them, they not alone would quell[22]   385
But rot the rest and spoil their pleasing smell,
Much like a lad who in his tender prime
Sent from his friends to learn the use of time,
As are his mates or good or bad, so he
Thrives to the world, and such his actions be.   390

. . . . . .

Then with those flow'rs they most of all did prize,
With all their skill, and in most curious wise,
On tufts of herbs or rushes, would they frame   415
A dainty border round their shepherd's name;
Or posies make, so quaint, so apt, so rare,
As if the Muses only lived there;
And that the after world should strive in vain
What they then did to counterfeit again,   420
Nor will the needle nor the loom e'er be
So perfect in their best embroidery,
Nor such composures make of silk and gold
As theirs, when nature all her cunning told.
The word of *mine* did no man then bewitch;   425
They thought none could be fortunate if rich,
And to the covetous did wish no wrong
But what himself desir'd, to live here long.
As of their songs, so of their lives they deem'd,
Not of the long'st, but best perform'd, esteem'd.   430
They thought that heaven to him no life did give
Who only thought upon the means to live,
Nor wish'd they 'twere ordain'd to live here ever,
But as life was ordain'd they might persever.[23]
O happy men! you ever did posses   435

No wisdom but was mix'd with simpleness;[24]
So wanting[25] malice and from folly free,
Since reason went with your simplicity,
You search'd yourselves if all within were fair
And did not learn of others what you were.   440
Your lives the patterns of those virtues gave
Which adulation tells men now they have.
With poverty in love we only close,
Because our lovers it most truly shows,
When they who in that blessed age did move   445
Knew neither poverty nor want of love.
The hatred which they bore was only this,
That everyone did hate to do amiss.
Their fortune still was subject to their will;
Their want, O happy, was the want of ill!   450
Ye truest, fairest, loveliest nymphs that can
Out of your eyes lend fire Promethean,
All-beauteous ladies, love-alluring dames,
That on the banks of Isca, Humber, Thames,[26]
By your encouragement can make a swain   455
Climb by his song where none but souls attain,
And by the graceful reading of our lines
Renew our heat to further brave designs;
You, by whose means my Muse thus boldly says:
Though she do sing of shepherd's loves and lays,   460
And flagging weakly low, gets not on wing
To second that of Helen's ravishing,[27]
Nor hath the love nor beauty of a queen
My subject grac'd, as other works have been;
Yet not to do their age nor ours a wrong,   465
Though queens, nay goddesses, fam'd Homer's song,
Mine hath been tun'd and heard by beauties more
Than all the poets that have liv'd before,
Not 'cause it is more worth, but it doth fall
That Nature now is turn'd a prodigal,   470
And on this age so much perfection spends
That to her last of treasure it extends;
For all the ages that are slid away
Had not so many beauties as this day.
O what a rapture have I gotten now!   475
That age of gold, this of the lovely brow,
Have drawn me from my song! I onward run
Clean from the end to which I first begun.
But ye, the heavenly creatures of the west,
In whom the virtues and the graces rest,   480
Pardon that I have run astray so long
And grown so tedious in so rude a song. . . .

---

[15]Emblem.   [16]Those who are.   [17]Buttercup.
[18]Roman goddess of flowers and fertility.
[19]George Wither? George Chapman?   [20]Is capable of.
[21]Cottages.   [22]Die.   [23]Continue.   [24]Innocence.   [25]Lacking.
[26]*Isca . . . Thames:* rivers in Wales, northern England, and southern England respectively. *Isca:* the River Usk (which is itself the subject of a poem by Henry Vaughan, pp. 380 f.).
[27]The abduction by Paris of Helen, wife of Menelaus, the immediate cause of the Trojan war.

THE FOURTH SONG

[At the start of the Fourth Song Browne, preparing to shift
the scene away from his beloved Devon, recalls the stirring
days when Plymouth stood like a sentinel against the power
of Spain and her Armada.]

Though I awhile must leave this happy soil
And follow Thetis in a pleasing toil,
Yet when I shall return I'll strive to draw   35
The nymphs by Tamar, Tavy, Exe, and Taw,
By Turridge, Otter, Ock, by Dart and Plym,[1]
With all the Naiades that fish and swim
In their clear streams, to these our rising downs,
Where while they make us chaplets, wreaths, and
       crowns,   40
I'll tune my reed unto a higher key,
And have already conn'd some of the lay
Wherein, as Mantua by her Vergil's birth,
And Thames by him[2] that sung her nuptial mirth,
You may be known, though not in equal pride,   45
As far as Tiber throws his swelling tide,
And by a shepherd, feeding on your plains,
In humble, lowly, plain, and ruder strains
Hear your worths challenge other floods among,
To have a period[3] equal with their song.   50
   Where Plym and Tamar with embraces meet,[4]
Thetis weighs anchor now, and all her fleet,
Leaving that spacious sound within whose arms
I have those vessels seen whose hot alarms
Have made Iberia[5] tremble, and her tow'rs[6]   55
Prostrate themselves before our iron show'rs,
While their proud builders' hearts have been inclin'd
To shake, as our brave ensigns,[7] with the wind.
For as an aerie[8] from their siege's wood[9]
Led o'er the plains and taught to get their food   60
By seeing how their breeder takes his prey,
Now from an orchard do they scare the jay,
Then o'er the cornfields as they swiftly fly
Where many thousand hurtful sparrows lie
Beating the ripe grain from the bearded[10] ear,   65
At their approach all (overgone with fear)
Seek for their safety: some into the dike,
Some in the hedges drop, and others like
The thick-grown corn as for their hiding best,
And under turfs or grass most of the rest,   70
That of a flight which cover'd all the grain
Not one appears, but all or hid or slain:
So by heroes were we led of yore,
And by our drums that thund'r'd on each shore
Stroke[11] with amazement countries far and near,   75
Whilst their inhabitants, like herds of deer
By kingly lions chas'd, fled from our arms.
If any did oppose instructed swarms
Of men immail'd,[12] Fate drew them on to be
A greater fame to our got victory.   80
   But now our leaders want;[13] those vessels lie
Rotting like houses through ill husbandry,
And on their masts, where oft the ship-boy stood

Or silver trumpets charm'd the brackish flood,
Some wearied crow is set; and daily seen   85
Their sides instead of pitch caulk'd o'er with green.[14]
Ill hap, alas, have you that once were known
By reaping what was by Iberia sown,
By bringing yellow sheaves from out their plain,
Making our barns the storehouse for their grain,   90
When now as if we wanted land to till
Wherewith we might our useless soldiers fill,
Upon their hatches where half-pikes[15] were borne,
In every chink rise stems of bearded corn,
Mocking our idle times that so have wrought us,   95
Or putting us in mind what once they brought us.
Bear with me, shepherds, if I do digress
And speak of what ourselves do not profess.
Can I behold a man that in the field
Or at a breach hath taken on his shield   100
More darts than ever Roman;[16] that hath spent
Many a cold December in no tent
But such as earth and heaven make; that hath been
Except in iron plates not long time seen;
Upon whose body may be plainly told   105
More wounds than his lank purse doth alms-deeds hold;
O can I see this man, advent'ring all,
Be only grac'd with some poor hospital,[17]
Or maybe worse, entreating at his door
For some relief whom he secur'd before,   110
And yet not show my grief?

MISCELLANEOUS POEMS FROM
THE LANSDOWNE MANUSCRIPT

AN ODE

1
Awake, fair Muse, for I intend
   These everlasting lines to thee,
And, honor'd Drayton,[1] come and lend
   An ear to this sweet melody;

THE FOURTH SONG [1]*Tamar...Plym*: rivers in Devon.
[2]Spenser, who in *The Faerie Queene* (IV. xi) describes the marriage
of the Thames and Medway. [3]Consummation, conclusion.
[4]*Where Plym...meet*: the Plym and Tamar both flow into Ply-
mouth Sound. [5]Spain.
[6]The superstructures of the Spanish galleons. [7]Banners.
[8]Brood of young birds.
[9]Station for a flock of herons on the watch for prey. [10]Tasseled.
[11]Struck. [12]Clad in armor. [13]Are lacking. [14]Barnacles.
[15]Short pikes or spears used in boarding ships.
[16]Browne himself glosses this as "M. Scaeva," i.e., Mucius Scaevola,
an early Roman distinguished by his bravery in resisting Lars
Porsena, king of Etruria.
[17]An institution for housing the needy and the aged. Browne is
protesting the indigence and neglect of those brave men who had
turned back the Armada in 1588.

AN ODE [1]For Drayton's epistle to Browne see p. 44.

For on my harp's most high and silver string   5
To those Nine Sisters[2] whom I love, I sing.

2

This man through death and horror seeks
   Honor by the victorious steel;
Another in unmapped creeks
   For jewels moors his winged keel;   10
The clam'rous bar wins some, and others bite
At looks thrown from a mushroom[3] favorite.

3

But I, that serve the lovely Graces,
   Spurn at that dross which most adore,
And titles hate like painted faces,   15
   And heart-fed care for evermore.
Those pleasures I disdain which are pursu'd
With praise and wishes by the multitude.

4

The bays which deathless Learning crowns
   Me of Apollo's troop installs;   20
The satyrs following o'er the downs
   Fair nymphs to rustic festivals
Make me affect[4] (where men no traffic have)
The holy horror of a savage cave.

5

Through the fair skies I thence intend   25
   With an unus'd and powerful wing
To bear me to my journey's end;
   And those that taste the Muses' spring
Too much celestial fire have at their birth
To live long time like common souls in earth.   30

6

From fair Aurora will I rear
   Myself unto the source of floods,
And from the Ethiopian[5] bear
   To him as white as snowy woods;
Nor shall I fear (from this day taking flight)   35
To be wound up in any veil of night.

7

Of Death I may not fear the dart,
   As is the use of human state,
For well I know my better part
   Dreads not the hand of Time or Fate.   40
Tremble at Death, Envy, and Fortune who
Have but one life: heaven gives a poet two.

8

All costly obsequies inveigh,[6]
   Marble and painting too, as vain;
My ashes shall not meet with clay   45
   As those do of the vulgar[7] train.
And if my Muse to Spenser's glory come,
No king shall own my verses for his tomb.

CAELIA[1]

Sonnets

4.

So sat the Muses on the banks of Thames,
And pleas'd to sing our heavenly Spenser's wit,
Inspiring almost trees with pow'rful flames,
As Caelia when she sings what I have writ.
Methinks there is a spirit more divine,   5
An elegance more rare when aught is sung
By her sweet voice, in every verse of mine
Than I conceive by any other tongue.
So a musician sets what someone plays
With better relish, sweeter stroke, than he   10
That first compos'd; nay, oft the maker weighs
If what he hears his own or other's be.
   Such are my lines: the highest, best of choice,
   Become more gracious by her sweetest voice.

5.

Were't not for you, here should my pen have rest
And take a long leave of sweet poesy;
Britannia's swains and rivers far by west
Should hear no more mine oaten melody;
Yet shall the song I sung of them awhile   5
Unperfect lie, and make no further known
The happy loves of this our pleasant isle
Till I have left some record of mine own.
You are the subject now, and, writing you,
I well may versify, not poetize: 10
Here needs no fiction, for the graces true
And virtues clip not with base flatteries.
   Here could I write what you deserve of praise,
   Others might wear, but I should win, the bays.

IN OBITUM M. S., X⁰ MAII 1614[1]

May, be thou never grac'd with birds that sing,
   Nor Flora's pride!
In thee all flowers and roses spring;
   Mine only died.

ON THE COUNTESS DOWAGER OF PEMBROKE[1]

Underneath this sable hearse
Lies the subject of all verse:
Sidney's sister, Pembroke's mother.
Death, ere thou hast slain another

[2]The Muses. See the Glossary. [3]Upstart. [4]Desire. [5]Black.
[6]Denounce, repudiate. [7]Common, ordinary.
CAELICA [1]The name given to a sequence of fourteen sonnets in the British Museum Lansdowne MS 777.
IN OBITUM [1]"On the Death of M. S., 10 May 1614." It has been conjectured that the initials stand for *Maritae Suae* ("his wife").
ON THE COUNTESS DOWAGER [1]Apparently first printed anonymously in the 1623 edition of William Camden's *Remains Con-*

Fair and learn'd and good as she,   5
Time shall throw a dart at thee.

Marble piles let no man raise
To her name, for after days
Some kind woman born as she,
Reading this, like Niobe[2]   10
Shall turn marble, and become
Both her mourner and her tomb.

ON THE RIGHT HONORABLE SUSAN, COUNTESS OF MONTGOMERY[1]

Though we trust the earth with thee,
We will not with thy memory;
Mines of brass or marble shall
Speak nought of thy funeral;
They are verier dust than we,   5
And do beg a history:
In thy name there is a tomb,
If the world can give it room,
   For a Vere and Herbert's wife
   Outspeaks all tombs, outlives all life.   10

TO MY HONORED FRIEND MASTER DRAYTON[1] FROM MICHAEL DRAYTON, *Poly-Olbion* (1622)

England's brave genius, raise thy head and see
We have a Muse, in this mortality
Of virtue, yet survives; all met not death
When we entomb'd our dear Elizabeth.[2]
Immortal Sidney, honored Colin Clout,   5
Presaging what we feel, went timely out.[3]
Then why lives Drayton when the times refuse
Both means to live and matter for a Muse?
Only without excuse to leave us quite,
And tell us, durst we act, he durst to write.[4]   10
   Now, as the people of a famish'd town,
Receiving no supply, seek up and down
For moldy corn and bones long cast aside
Wherewith their hunger may be satisfied

(Small store now left), we are enforc'd to pry   15
And search the dark leaves of antiquity
For some good name to raise our Muse again
In this her crisis, whose harmonious strain
Was of such compass that no other nation
Durst ever venture on a sole translation,   20
Whilst our full language, musical and high,
Speaks as themselves their best of poesy.
   Drayton, amongst the worthi'st of all those
The glorious laurel or the Cyprian[5] rose
Have ever crown'd, doth claim in every line   25
An equal honor from the sacred Nine;
For if old Time could, like the restless main,
Roll himself back into his spring again,
And on his wings bear this admired Muse
For Ovid, Vergil, Homer to peruse,   30
They would confess that never happier pen
Sung of his loves, his country, and the men.

cerning Britain, this famous elegy on Mary Herbert, countess of Pembroke (d. 1621), was once assigned to Jonson, but the evidence of several contemporary manuscripts (in the British Museum, the Bodleian, and the library of Trinity College, Dublin) seems to make Browne's authorship secure. The last six lines have sometimes been attributed to the countess' son William, third earl of Pembroke (see p. 683), to whom (as "Mr. W. H.") Shakespeare's *Sonnets* (1609) may have been dedicated and to whom (with his brother Philip, earl of Montgomery) the first folio of Shakespeare's plays (1623) assuredly was.
[2]When Niobe, a mother weeping inconsolably for her dead children, was turned into stone by Zeus, her tears continued to flow. Inevitably, she became a favorite subject for statuary fountains.

ON THE COUNTESS OF MONTGOMERY [1]The daughter (d. 1628) of Edward Vere, seventeenth earl of Oxford (whom some believe to be the author of Shakespeare's plays), and the wife of Philip Herbert, earl of Montgomery and fourth earl of Pembroke.

TO MY HONORED FRIEND [1]For Drayton's verse epistle to Browne see p. 44. [2]Queen Elizabeth (d. 1603).
[3]*Immortal...out:* Sir Philip Sidney died in battle in 1586 and Spenser (*Colin Clout*) in 1599. *Timely:* betimes, early.
[4]For Drayton's own bleak view of the *lunatic age* in which he published *Poly-Olbion* see pp. 33 f., 36f.
[5]Referring to the island of Cyprus, sacred to Aphrodite (whose relevance to Drayton's work is anything but clear).

Robert Herrick [1591-1674]

The known facts about Robert Herrick's life are sparse out of all proportion to his very high position among the English lyric poets. The seventh child and fourth son of a prosperous London goldsmith, he was an infant of only fourteen months (and his younger brother not yet born) when his father died in suspicious circumstances by falling from a window in his house and shop on Goldsmiths' Row in Cheapside. Although the resulting investigation did not lead to a finding of suicide and therefore to the confiscation by the crown of the elder Herrick's sizable estate, the scar left by the ancient scandal is evident in "To the Reverend Shade of His Religious Father" (p. 177), and its consequences are apparent in the little that is known of the poet's early life. There is no record of his elementary education, but at sixteen he was apprenticed to his guardian and uncle William Herrick, whose success in the family trade of goldsmithery had earned for him a knighthood. In 1613, however, well before the expiration of the customary ten-year term of an apprenticeship, Robert was enrolled at St. John's College, Cambridge. That Sir William, as guardian, kept a wary eye upon his nephew's money is apparent from Robert's wheedling letters to that rich and frugal merchant. Although the youth confessed, soon after his arrival at St. John's, that 'I still run headlong into Your Worship's debt," the rhetoric of his pleas for money mounted as his debts increased. "Sir." he wrote to his "most careful uncle,"

> understand that my heart (more fervently than my pen can express) speaks my devout thanks, and joys in no greater thing than this, that it can see some sparks of your concealed affection. I have not as hitherto acquainted you with the charge I live in, but yourself can judge by my often (as now at this time) writing for money, which when I do, it is for no impertinent expense, but for constrained necessity.

It was in an effort to reduce his debts, as Herrick told his uncle in what appears to be the last surviving letter of the series, that he finally moved to Trinity Hall in Cambridge, "where I purpose to live recluse till time contract me to some other calling, striving now with myself (retaining upright thoughts) both sparingly to live, thereby to shun the current of expense."

With the ending of this correspondence we have our last clear view of Herrick, whose biography thereafter consists only of some widely separated dates. We know that he managed to survive at Trinity Hall until he took his two degrees (A.B. 1617, M.A. 1620), that he was ordained a deacon and a priest in 1623, that four years later he accompanied the all-powerful duke of Buckingham as chaplain on his abortive expedition to raise the siege of La Rochelle, and that in 1630 he was installed as vicar of Dean Prior, a village on the verge of Dartmoor in the wilds of Devonshire. In that remote exile, as he regarded it, his subsequent career was almost unrecorded.

In 1640 the projected publication of his "several poems" was announced in the Stationers' Register, and it is possible that Herrick was in London at or near this time. For some reason, however, the appearance of *Hesperides*—his only book-length publication—was delayed until 1648, a year after his stubborn royalism had led to his ejection from Dean Prior. It is likely that he returned to London and stayed there until the Restoration, but apart from a commendatory poem in the 1647 folio of Beaumont and Fletcher's works and an elegy on Henry, Lord Hastings in *Lacrymae Musarum* (1649)—to which funereal volume Marvell and Dryden also made their contributions— he apparently wrote no more for publication. In 1674, fourteen years after reclaiming his vicarage at Dean Prior, he was buried in an unmarked grave by his parishioners,

> A people currish, churlish as the seas,
> And rude (almost) as rudest salvages.

Herrick must have started writing verses at a fairly early age and must have gained a certain recognition. As early as 1625 one Richard James, in a threnody for James I called *The Muses' Dirge*, listed him with Jonson and Drayton as the triad of England's leading poets. Since only about ten of his lyrics had been printed (mainly in poetical miscellanies) before the appearance of *Hesperides* in 1648, his contemporary reputation must have rested largely on the circulation of his works in manuscript; and in fact about forty of his poems turn up in some 140 manuscript collections of the period, suggesting a fairly wide renown. In "The Argument of His Book" at the beginning of *Hesperides* he summarizes, with consummate tact, the topics of his art and proclaims his dual purpose: to record his pleasure in man's fleeting joys that must yield to "time's trans-shifting" and to proclaim his hope of heaven. This intention also shows itself in the arrangement of the book. Of the more than 1,400 poems in the 1648 edition, the first 1,130 celebrate his secular concerns, and the rest reveal him in his priestly function.

My text is based upon *Hesperides: Or, The Works Both Humane & Divine of Robert Herrick Esq.,* 1648 (Wing H-1595), which includes (with a separate title page and pagination) a short section of religious poems entitled *His Noble Numbers,* 1647. John Nott's edition of *Select Poems from Hesperides* (1810)—the first reprinting of Herrick's poetry in book form in more than a century and a half—was followed by Thomas Maitland's edition of the *Works* (2 vols., 1823), W. C. Hazlitt's of a larger collection that included additional poems and the letters (2 vols., 1869), and the indefatigable A. B. Grosart's *Complete Poems* (3 vols., 1876). Subsequent editions by A. W. Pollard (2 vols., 1891, rev. 1898, with a eulogistic preface by Swinburne), George Saintsbury (2 vols., 1893), and F. W. Moorman (1915) were superseded by L. C. Martin's definitive *Poetical Works* (1956), which adds many poems (some of questionable authenticity). J. Max Patrick's edition of the *Complete Poetry* appeared in 1963.

The little that is known of Herrick's life has been told by Moorman (1910), Floris Delattre (in French, 1912), E. I. M. Easton (1934), and Marchette Chute (*Two Gentle Men,* 1959). K. A. McEuen's *Classical Influence on the Tribe of Ben* (1939) is much concerned with Herrick. There is a discussion of his work by Sydney Musgrove (1950), a monograph by John Press (1961), a concordance by Malcolm MacLeod (1936), and a *Concise Bibliography* by S. A. and D. R. Tannenbaum (1949).

from Hesperides[1], or the Works, Both Human and Divine, of Robert Herrick (1648)

THE ARGUMENT[2] OF HIS BOOK

I sing of brooks, of blossoms, birds, and bowers;
Of April, May, of June, and July flowers.
I sing of Maypoles, hock-carts,[3] wassails, wakes,
Of bridegrooms, brides, and of their bridal cakes.
I write of youth, of love, and have access   5
By these, to sing of cleanly wantonness.[4]
I sing of dews, of rains, and piece by piece
Of balm, of oil, of spice, and ambergris.
I sing of time's trans-shifting;[5] and I write
How roses first came red, and lilies white.   10
I write of groves, of twilights, and I sing
The court of Mab, and of the fairy king.[6]
I write of hell; I sing (and ever shall)
Of heaven, and hope to have it after all.

TO THE SOUR READER

If thou dislik'st the piece thou light'st on first,
Think that of all that I have writ the worst;
But if thou read'st my book unto the end,
And still dost this and that verse reprehend,
O perverse man, if all disgustful be,   5
The extreme scab[1] take thee and thine for me.

WHEN HE WOULD HAVE HIS VERSES READ

In sober mornings do not thou rehearse
The holy incantation of a verse;
But when that men have both well drunk and fed,
Let my enchantments then be sung or read.
When laurel spirts i' th' fire, and when the hearth   5
Smiles to itself and gilds the roof with mirth;
When up the thyrse[1] is rais'd, and when the sound
Of sacred orgies[2] flies, a round a round!
When the rose reigns, and locks with ointments shine,
Let rigid Cato read these lines of mine.   10

HESPERIDES [1]The "western maidens" (notable for their power of song) who were the guardians of the golden apples that Ge (Earth) presented to Hera when she married Zeus. [2]Theme. [3]The carts carrying home the last load of the harvest. See "The Hock-Cart," p. 181 f. [4]Innocent gaiety. [5]Impermanence. [6]*Mab...king:* the queen of the fairies and her consort Oberon.

TO THE SOUR READER [1]Intolerable itch, i.e., extreme discomfort.

HIS VERSES READ [1]Thyrsus, "a javelin twined with ivy" (Herrick's gloss) that was carried by Dionysus (Bacchus). [2]"Songs to Bacchus" (Herrick's gloss).

TO PERILLA

Ah, my Perilla, dost thou grieve to see
Me, day by day, to steal away from thee?
Age calls me hence, and my gray hairs bid come
And haste away to mine eternal home.
'Twill not be long, Perilla, after this   5
That I must give thee the supremest[1] kiss.
Dead when I am, first cast in salt, and bring
Part of the cream from that religious spring,[2]
With which, Perilla, wash my hands and feet;
That done, then wind me in that very sheet   10
Which wrapp'd thy smooth limbs (when thou didst
    implore
The god's protection but the night before)
Follow me weeping to my turf, and there
Let fall a primrose, and with it a tear;
Then, lastly, let some weekly strewings[3] be   15
Devoted to the memory of me.
Then shall my ghost not walk about, but keep
Still in the cool and silent shades of sleep.

NO LOATHSOMENESS IN LOVE

What I fancy, I approve:
No dislike there is in love.
Be my mistress short or tall,
And distorted therewithal,
Be she likewise one of those   5
That an acre hath of nose,
Be her forehead and her eyes
Full of incongruities,
Be her cheeks so shallow too
As to show her tongue wag through,   10
Be her lips ill hung or set,
And her grinders black as jet,
Has she thin hair, hath she none,
She's to me a paragon.

THE WEEPING CHERRY

I saw a cherry weep, and why?
    Why wept it but for shame?
Because my Julia's lip was by,
    And did out red the same.

But, pretty fondling,[1] let not fall   5
    A tear at all for that
Which rubies, corals, scarlets, all
    For tincture wonder at.

LOVE, WHAT IT IS

Love is a circle that doth restless move
In the same sweet eternity of love.

UPON THE LOSS OF HIS MISTRESSES

I have lost, and lately, these
Many dainty mistresses:

Stately Julia, prime[1] of all;
Sappho next, a principal;
Smooth Anthea, for a skin   5
White, and heaven-like crystalline;
Sweet Electra, and the choice
Myrrha, for the lute and voice;
Next, Corinna, for her wit,
And the graceful use of it;   10
With Perilla: all are gone;
Only Herrick's left alone,
For to number sorrow by
Their departures hence, and die.

DISCONTENTS IN DEVON

More discontents I never had
    Since I was born than here,
Where I have been, and still am, sad,
    In this dull Devonshire;
Yet justly too I must confess;   5
    I ne'er invented such
Ennobled numbers for the press
    Than where I loath'd so much.

THE VISION TO ELECTRA

I dream'd we both were in a bed
Of roses, almost smothered;
The warmth and sweetness had me there
Made lovingly familiar,
But that I heard thy sweet breath say,   5
"Faults done by night will blush by day."
I kiss'd thee, panting, and I call
Night to the record, that was all.
But ah, if empty dreams so please,
Love, give me more such nights as these!   10

HIS REQUEST TO JULIA

Julia, if I chance to die
Ere I print my poetry,
I most humbly thee desire
To commit it to the fire:
Better 'twere my book were dead   5
Than to live not perfected.

UPON JULIA'S VOICE

So smooth, so sweet, so silv'ry is thy voice
As, could they hear, the damn'd would make no noise,
But listen to thee, walking in thy chamber,
Melting melodious words to lutes of amber.

TO PERILLA [1]Final. [2]*Cream...spring*: i.e., tears from her eyes.
[3]Of flowers for his grave.
THE WEEPING CHERRY [1]Lovable little thing.
UPON THE LOSS [1]First.

ALL THINGS DECAY AND DIE

All things decay with time; the forest sees
The growth and downfall of her aged trees.
That timber tall, which threescore lusters[1] stood
The proud dictator of the state-like wood,
I mean (the sovereign of all plants) the oak, 5
Droops, dies, and falls without the cleaver's stroke.

TO THE KING UPON HIS COMING
WITH HIS ARMY INTO THE WEST[1]

Welcome, most welcome to our vows and us,
Most great and universal genius![2]
The drooping west, which hitherto has stood
As one in long-lamented widowhood,
Looks like a bride now, or a bed of flowers, 5
Newly refresh'd both by the sun and showers.
War, which before was horrid, now appears
Lovely in you, brave prince of cavaliers!
A deal of courage in each bosom springs
By your access, O you, the best of kings! 10
Ride on with all white omens,[3] so that where
Your standard's[4] up, we fix a conquest there.

TO THE REVEREND SHADE
OF HIS RELIGIOUS[1] FATHER

That for seven lusters I did never come
To do the rites to thy religious tomb,
That neither hair was cut[2] or true tears shed
By me o'er thee as justments[3] to the dead,
Forgive, forgive me, since I did not know 5
Whether thy bones had here their rest or no.[4]
But now 'tis known, behold, behold I bring
Unto thy ghost th' effused[5] offering;
And look what smallage,[6] nightshade, cypress, yew
Unto the shades have been or now are due, 10
Here I devote;[7] and something more than so,
I come to pay a debt of birth I owe.
Thou gav'st me life (but mortal); for that one
Favor I'll make full satisfaction:
For my life mortal, rise from out thy hearse[8] 15
And take a life immortal from my verse.

DELIGHT IN DISORDER

A sweet disorder in the dress
Kindles in clothes a wantonness:
A lawn[1] about the shoulders thrown
Into a fine distraction;
An erring lace, which here and there 5
Enthralls the crimson stomacher;[2]
A cuff neglectful, and thereby
Ribands to flow confusedly;
A winning wave (deserving note)
In the tempestuous petticoat; 10

A careless shoestring, in whose tie
I see a wild civility,
Do more bewitch me than when art
Is too precise in every part.

DEAN-BOURN, A RUDE RIVER IN DEVON,
BY WHICH SOMETIMES HE LIVED

Dean-bourn, farewell; I never look to see
Dean or thy warty incivility.
Thy rocky bottom that doth tear thy streams,
And makes them frantic, ev'n to all extremes,
To my content, I never should behold, 5
Were thy streams silver or thy rocks all gold.
Rocky thou art; and rocky we discover
Thy men; and rocky are thy ways all over.
O men, O manners, now[1] and ever known
To be a rocky generation! 10
A people currish, churlish as the seas,
And rude (almost) as rudest salvages
With whom I did and may re-sojourn when
Rocks turn to rivers, rivers turn to men.

TO ANTHEA LYING IN BED

So looks Anthea, when in bed she lies,
O'ercome or half betray'd by tiffanies,[1]
Like to a twilight or that simp'ring dawn
That roses show when misted o'er with lawn.
Twilight is yet till that her lawns give way, 5
Which done, that dawn turns then to perfect day.

ALL THINGS DECAY [1]A luster is a period of five years.

TO THE KING [1]In the late summer of 1644 Charles I passed several weeks at Exeter, where Princess Henrietta Anne, his fifth daughter, had been born on June 16. See p. 748, n. 1.
[2]Tutelary deity who protects a place or region.
[3]Propitious auguries.
[4]Royal ensign. Charles's raising his standard at Nottingham on 22 August 1642 signalized the opening of the Civil War.

TO THE REVEREND SHADE [1]Revered.
[2]A customary sign of mourning in antiquity.
[3]Appropriate formalities, obsequies. The word is apparently Herrick's own coinage from Latin *justa*.
[4]*Forgive...or no*: Nicholas Herrick died (1592), perhaps a suicide, of a fall from a window when Robert, the seventh of his eight children, was fourteen months old. The precise location of his grave at St. Vedast's in Cheapside had perhaps been kept secret lest a legal finding of suicide lead to the disinterment of his body and the confiscation of his estate.
[5]Poured out (a Latinism).
[6]A variety of celery or parsley (which, like the other plants that Herrick mentions, was traditionally associated with mourning).
[7]Vow, consecrate (a Latinism). [8]Tomb, grave.

DELIGHT IN DISORDER [1]Piece of fine linen.
[2]A covering, often ornamented, for the breast.

DEAN-BOURN [1]Text *there*, but the page with this reading was canceled in later issues of the first edition.

TO ANTHEA [1]Fine, transparent fabrics, usually of linen.

A COUNTRY LIFE: TO HIS BROTHER, MASTER THOMAS HERRICK[1]

Thrice and above bless'd (my soul's half) art thou
    In thy both last and better vow:
Couldst leave the City, for exchange, to see
    The country's sweet simplicity,
And it to know and practice, with intent   5
    To grow the sooner innocent:
By studying to know virtue, and to aim
    More at her nature than her name:
The last is but the least; the first doth tell
    Ways less to live than to live well: 10
And both are known to thee, who now canst live,
    Led by thy conscience, to give
Justice to soon-pleas'd nature; and to show
    Wisdom and she together go,
And keep one center; this with that conspires,   15
    To teach man to confine desires,
And know that riches have their proper stint[2]
    In the contented mind, not mint.
And canst instruct that those who have the itch
    Of craving more are never rich.   20
These things thou know'st to th' height, and dost prevent
    That plague, because thou are content
With that[3] heav'n gave thee with a wary hand
    (More blessed in thy brass[4] than land),
To keep cheap nature even and upright;   25
    To cool, not cocker[5] appetite.
Thus thou canst tersely[6] live to satisfy
    The belly chiefly, not the eye;
Keeping the barking stomach wisely quiet,
    Less with a neat[7] than needful diet.   30
But that which most makes sweet thy country life
    Is the fruition of a wife:
Whom (stars consenting with thy fate) thou hast
    Got, not so beautiful as chaste:
By whose warm side thou dost securely sleep   35
    (While Love the sentinel doth keep)
With those deeds done by day which ne'er affright
    Thy silken slumbers in the night.
Nor has the darkness power to usher in
    Fear to those sheets that know no sin,   40
But still thy wife, by chaste intentions led,
    Gives thee each night a maidenhead.
The damask'd meadows and the pebbly streams
    Sweeten and make soft your dreams:
The purling springs, groves, birds, and well-weav'd
        bow'rs,   45
    With fields enameled with flow'rs,
Present their shapes, while fantasy discloses
    Millions of lilies mix'd with roses.
Then dream ye hear the lamb by many a bleat
    Woo'd to come suck the milky teat,   50
While Faunus[8] in the vision comes to keep,
    From rav'ning wolves, the fleecy sheep,
With thousand such enchanting dreams that meet
    To make sleep not so sound as sweet.

Nor can these figures so thy rest endear   55
    As not to rise when chanticleer
Warns the last watch, but with the dawn dost rise
    To work, but first to sacrifice,
Making thy peace with heav'n, for some late fault,
    With holy-meal and spirting-salt.[9]   60
Which done, thy painful[10] thumb this sentence[11] tells us,
    Jove for our labor all things sells us.
Nor are thy daily and devout affairs
    Attended with those desp'rate cares
Th'industrious merchant has, who for to find   65
    Gold runneth to the western Inde.
And back again (tortur'd with fears), doth fly,
    Untaught, to suffer poverty.
But thou at home, bless'd with securest ease,
    Sitt'st and believ'st that there be seas   70
And wat'ry dangers, while thy whiter hap[12]
    But sees these things within thy map.
And viewing them with a more safe survey,
    Mak'st easy fear unto thee say,
A heart thrice wall'd with oak and brass that man   75
    Had first[13] durst plow the ocean.
But thou at home without or tide or gale
    Canst in thy map securely sail,
Seeing those painted countries; and so guess
    By those fine shades their substances;   80
And from thy compass taking small advice,
    Buy'st travel at the lowest price.
Nor are thine ears so deaf but thou canst hear
    (Far more with wonder than with fear)
Fame tell of states, of countries, courts, and kings;   85
    And believe there be such things,
When of these truths thy happier knowledge lies
    More in thine ears than in thine eyes.
And when thou hear'st by that too-true report,
    Vice rules the most or all at court,   90
Thy pious wishes are (though thou not there),
    Virtue had and mov'd her sphere.
But thou liv'st fearless, and thy face ne'er shows
    Fortune when she comes or goes.
But with thy equal[14] thoughts, prepar'd dost stand   95
    To take her by the either hand,
Nor car'st which comes the first, the foul or fair.
    A wise man ev'ry way lies square,
And like a surly oak with storms perplex'd,
    Grows still the stronger, strongly vex'd.   100
Be so, bold spirit! Stand center-like, unmov'd;
    And be not only thought but prov'd
To be what I report thee; and inure

A COUNTRY LIFE [1]The poet's elder brother (b. 1588), a prosperous London merchant, retired to a small farm about 1610. [2]Limit. [3]That which. [4]Monetary resources? [5]Pamper. [6]Temperately. [7]Elaborate. [8]Roman god of fields and shepherds. [9]Customary sacrificial offerings. *Spirting*: sprinkling. [10]Hardworked. [11]Gnomic saying (Latin *sententia*). [12]More fortunate circumstances. [13]Who first. [14]Equable, serene.

Thyself, if want comes, to endure.
And so thou dost, for thy desires are   105
    Confin'd to live with private lar,[15]
Not curious whether appetite be fed
    Or with the first or second bread.
Who keep'st no proud mouth for delicious cates:[16]
    Hunger makes coarse meats delicates.   110
Canst, and unurg'd, forsake the larded fare
    Which art, not nature, makes so rare;
To taste boil'd nettles, coleworts,[17] beets, and eat
    These and sour herbs as dainty meat,
While soft opinion makes thy genius[18] say,   115
    Content makes all ambrosia.
Nor is it that thou keep'st this stricter size[19]
    So much for want, as exercise;
To numb the sense of dearth, which should sin haste it,
    Thou mightst but only see't, not taste it.   120
Yet can thy humble roof maintain a quire
    Of singing crickets by thy fire,
And the brisk mouse may feast herself with crumbs
    Till that the green-ey'd kitling comes,
Then to her cabin, bless'd she can escape   125
    The sudden danger of a rape.
And thus thy little well-kept stock doth prove,
    Wealth cannot make a life, but Love.
Nor art thou so close-handed but canst spend
    (Counsel concurring with the end)   130
As well as spare, still conning o'er this theme,
    To shun the first and last extreme.
Ordaining that thy small stock find no breach,
    Or to exceed thy tether's reach,
But to live round and close,[20] and wisely true   135
    To thine own self, and known to few.
Thus let thy rural sanctuary be
    Elysium to thy wife and thee,
There to disport yourselves with golden measure,
    For seldom use commends the pleasure.   140
Live, and live bless'd, thrice happy pair! Let breath
    But lost to one be the other's death.
And as there is one love, one faith, one troth,
    Be so one death, one grave to both.
Till then in such assurance live, ye may   145
    Nor fear or wish your dying day.

HIS FAREWELL TO SACK[1]

Farewell, thou thing, time-past so known, so dear
To me as blood to life and spirit.[2] Near,
Nay, thou more near than kindred, friend, man, wife,
Male to the female, soul to body, life
To quick action, or the warm soft side   5
Of the resigning yet resisting bride,
The kiss of virgins, first-fruits of the bed,
Soft speech, smooth touch, the lips, the maidenhead:
These, and a thousand sweets, could never be
So near or dear as thou wast once to me.   10
O thou the drink of gods and angels! Wine
That scatter'st spirit and lust;[3] whose purest shine,

More radiant than the summer's sunbeams shows;
Each way illustrious,[4] brave, and like to those
Comets we see by night, whose shagg'd[5] portents   15
Foretell the coming of some dire events;
Or some full flame which with a pride aspires,[6]
Throwing about his wild and active fires.
'Tis thou, above nectar, O divinest soul!
(Eternal in thyself) that canst control   20
That which subverts whole nature, grief and care,
Vexation of the mind, and damn'd despair.
'Tis thou, alone, who with thy mystic fan,[7]
Work'st more than wisdom, art, or nature can
To rouse the sacred madness, and awake   25
The frost-bound blood and spirits, and to make
Them frantic with thy raptures, flashing through
The soul like lightning, and as active too.
'Tis not Apollo can, or those thrice three
Castalian sisters,[8] sing, if wanting thee.   30
Horace, Anacreon[9] both had lost their fame
Hadst thou not filled them with thy fire and flame.
Phoebean[10] splendor! and thou Thespian[11] spring!
Of which sweet swans must drink before they sing
Their true-pac'd numbers and their holy lays,   35
Which makes them worthy cedar and the bays.
But why? why longer do I gaze upon
Thee with the eye of admiration?
Since I must leave thee and, enforced, must say
To all thy witching beauties, "Go! Away!"   40
But if thy whimp'ring looks do ask me why,
Then know that Nature bids thee go, not I.
'Tis her erroneous self has made a brain
Uncapable of such a sovereign
As is thy powerful self. Prithee not smile,   45
Or smile more inly, lest thy looks beguile
My vows denounc'd[12] in zeal, which thus much show thee,
That I have sworn but by thy looks to know thee.
Let others drink thee freely, and desire
Thee and their lips espous'd, while I admire   50
And love thee, but not taste thee. Let my Muse
Fail of thy former helps, and only use
Her inadult'rate strength: what's done by me
Hereafter shall smell of the lamp, not thee.

[15]Roman household god.   [16]Delicacies.   [17]Cabbages.
[18]The *lar* of l.106.   [19]Standard.   [20]Fully, liberally, and privately.
HIS FAREWELL TO SACK [1]A kind of dry white wine.
[2]In contemporary physiology, the vital spirit carried by the blood
from the heart to the brain, where it was rarefied into the animal
spirit that linked the soul (*anima*) and body. [3]Pleasure.
[4]Bright. Brave: showy, handsome.
[5]Shaggy (referring to the tail of a comet).
[6]*With...aspires*: i.e., mounts splendidly.
[7]The thyrsus or vine-covered staff (originally used for winnowing
grain) associated with Bacchus.
[8]The nine Muses, to whom the Castalian spring on Mt. Parnassus
was sacred. [9]Lyric poets who celebrated the joys of wine.
[10]Referring to Phoebus ("bright") Apollo.
[11]Referring to Thespis, the legendary founder of Greek drama.
[12]Formally sworn (a Latinism).

TO DIANEME

Sweet, be not proud of those two eyes
Which star-like sparkle in their skies;
Nor be you proud that you can see
All hearts your captives, yours yet free;
Be you not proud of that rich hair   5
Which wantons with the love-sick air:
Whenas that ruby which you wear,
Sunk from the tip of your soft ear,
Will last to be a precious stone
When all your world of beauty's gone.   10

TO A GENTLEWOMAN OBJECTING
TO HIM HIS GRAY HAIRS

Am I despis'd because you say—
And I dare swear—that I am gray?
Know, Lady, you have but your day,
And time will come when you shall wear
Such frost and snow upon your hair,   5
And when (though long it comes to pass)
You question with your looking glass,
And in that sincere crystal seek
But find no rosebud in your cheek,
Nor any bed to give the shew   10
Where such a rare carnation grew.
Ah, then too late, close in your chamber keeping,
            It will be told
            That you are old
By those true tears y' are weeping.   15

JULIA'S PETTICOAT

Thy azure robe I did behold,
As airy as the leaves of gold,
Which, erring here and wand'ring there,
Pleas'd with transgression ev'rywhere.
Sometimes 'twould pant and sigh and heave   5
As if to stir it scarce had leave,
But having got it, thereupon
'Twould make a brave expansion.
And pounc'd[1] with stars, it show'd to me
Like a celestial canopy.   10
Sometimes 'twould blaze and then abate,
Like to a flame grown moderate;
Sometimes away 'twould wildly fling,
Then to thy thighs so closely cling
That some conceit did melt me down,   15
As lovers fall into a swoon;
And all confus'd, I there did lie
Drown'd in delights, but could not die.
That leading cloud[2] I follow'd still,
Hoping t'ave seen of it my fill,   20
But ah, I could not: should it move
To life eternal, I could love.

CORINNA'S GOING A-MAYING

Get up, get up for shame! The blooming morn
Upon her wings presents the god unshorn.[1]
         See how Aurora throws her fair
         Fresh-quilted colors through the air.
         Get up, sweet slug-a-bed, and see   5
         The dew bespangling herb and tree.
Each flower has wept, and bow'd toward the east
Above an hour since, yet you not drest,
         Nay! not so much as out of bed?
         When all the birds have matins said,   10
         And sung their thankful hymns, 'tis sin,
         Nay, profanation, to keep in,
Whenas a thousand virgins on this day
Spring, sooner than the lark, to fetch in May.[2]

Rise, and put on your foliage, and be seen   15
To come forth, like the springtime, fresh and green,
         And sweet as Flora.[3] Take no care
         For jewels for your gown or hair.
         Fear not; the leaves will strew
         Gems in abundance upon you.   20
Besides, the childhood of the day has kept,
Against you come, some orient[4] pearls unwept.
         Come, and receive them while the light
         Hangs on the dew-locks of the night.
         And Titan[5] on the eastern hill   25
         Retires himself, or else stands still
Till you come forth. Wash, dress, be brief in praying:
Few beads[6] are best when once we go a-Maying.

Come, my Corinna, come; and coming, mark
How each field turns a street, each street a park   30
         Made green, and trimm'd with trees: see how
         Devotion gives each house a bough
         Or branch: each porch, each door, ere this,
         An ark, a tabernacle is,
Made up of white-thorn neatly interwove,   35
As if here were those cooler shades of love.
         Can such delights be in the street
         And open fields, and we not see't?
         Come, we'll abroad; and let's obey
         The proclamation made for May.   40
And sin no more, as we have done, by staying;
But, my Corinna, come, let's go a-Maying.

There's not a budding boy or girl this day
But is got up, and gone to bring in May.
         A deal of youth, ere this, is come   45

JULIA'S PETTICOAT [1]Sprinkled.
[2]"And the Lord went before them by day in a pillar of a cloud, to lead them the way" (Exodus 13.21).
CORINNA'S GOING A-MAYING [1]A conventional epithet for Apollo.
[2]To collect the hawthorn (*white-thorn*) blossoms (ll. 35, 46) that symbolized marriage and fertility.
[3]In Roman mythology, the goddess of flowers.
[4]Eastern, i.e., radiant, lustrous (like the rising sun). [5]The sun.
[6]Prayers (said to the beads of a rosary).

Back, and with white-thorn laden home.
Some have dispatch'd their cakes and cream
Before that we have left to dream;
And some have wept, and woo'd, and plighted troth,
And chose their priest, ere we can cast off sloth: 50
    Many a green-gown has been given;[7]
    Many a kiss, both odd and even:
    Many a glance too has been sent
    From out the eye, love's firmament:
Many a jest told of the keys betraying   55
This night, and locks pick'd, yet w' are not a-Maying.

Come, let us go while we are in our prime;
And take the harmless folly of the time.
    We shall grow old apace, and die
    Before we know our liberty.   60
    Our life is short, and our days run
    As fast away as does the sun:
And as a vapor, or a drop of rain
Once lost, can ne'er be found again,
    So when or you or I are made   65
    A fable, song, or fleeting shade,
    All love, all liking, all delight
    Lies drown'd with us in endless night.
Then while time serves, and we are but decaying;
Come, my Corinna, come, let's go a-Maying.   70

TO THE VIRGINS, TO MAKE MUCH OF TIME

Gather ye rosebuds while ye may,
    Old time is still a-flying:
And this same flower that smiles today,
    Tomorrow will be dying.

The glorious lamp of heaven, the sun,   5
    The higher he's a-getting,
The sooner will his race be run,
    And nearer he's to setting.

That age is best which is the first,
    When youth and blood are warmer,   10
But being spent, the worse, and worst
    Times still succeed the former.

Then be not coy, but use your time,
    And while ye may, go marry:
For having lost but once your prime,   15
    You may forever tarry.

HIS POETRY HIS PILLAR

Only a little more
    I have to write,
    Then I'll give o'er,
And bid the world goodnight.

'Tis but a flying minute   5
    That I must stay,
    Or linger in it,
And then I must away.

O Time that cut'st down all!
    And scarce leav'st here   10
    Memorial
Of any men that were.

How many lie forgot
    In vaults beneath?
    And piecemeal rot   15
Without a fame in death?

Behold this living stone
    I rear for me,
    Ne'er to be thrown
Down, envious Time, by thee.   20

Pillars let some set up
    (If so they please);
    Here is my hope
And my pyramides.[1]

THE HOCK-CART, OR HARVEST HOME:[1]
TO THE RIGHT HONORABLE MILDMAY,
EARL OF WESTMORLAND[2]

Come, sons of summer, by whose toil
We are the lords of wine and oil,
By whose tough labors and rough hands
We rip up first, then reap our lands;
Crown'd with the ears of corn, now come,   5
And, to the pipe, sing harvest home.
Come forth, my Lord, and see the cart
Dress'd up with all the country art.
See here a maukin,[3] there a sheet,
As spotless pure as it is sweet;   10
The horses, mares, and frisking fillies
Clad, all, in linen white as lilies.
The harvest swains and wenches bound
For joy to see the hock-cart crown'd.
About the cart, hear how the rout   15
Of rural younglings raise the shout;
Pressing before, some coming after,
Those with a shout, and these with laughter.
Some bless the cart; some kiss the sheaves;
Some prank[4] them up with oaken leaves;   20
Some cross the fill-horse;[5] some, with great
Devotion, stroke the home-borne wheat;
While other rustics, less attent[6]

[7]*Many . . . given*: i.e., by rolling in the grass.
HIS POETRY HIS PILLAR   [1]An obsolete form of *pyramids,* accented on
the second syllable.
THE HOCK-CART   [1]Formerly an annual festival to celebrate the
completion of the harvest.
[2]Mildmay Fane (d. 1666), second earl of Westmorland, a minor
poet and major landholder who owned the great estate of Apthorpe
in Northamptonshire.
[3]Malkin, a pole draped with a sheet to make a scarecrow.
[4]Adorn.   [5]*Some . . . fill-horse*: some straddle the shaft-horse.
[6]Attentive.

To prayers than to merriment,
Run after with their breeches rent.   25
Well, on, brave boys, to your Lord's hearth,
Glitt'ring with fire, where, for your mirth,
Ye shall see first the large and chief
Foundation of your feast, fat beef,
With upper stories, mutton, veal,   30
And bacon,[7] which makes full the meal,
With sev'ral dishes standing by,
As here a custard, there a pie,
And here all-tempting frumenty,[8]
And for to make the merry cheer,   35
If smirking wine be wanting here,
There's that which drowns all care, stout beer;
Which freely drink to your Lord's health,
Then to the plow (the commonwealth),
Next to your flails, your fanes,[9] your fats;[10]   40
Then to the maids with wheaten hats;
To the rough sickle and crook'd scythe,
Drink, frolic boys, till all be blithe.
Feed, and grow fat; and as ye eat,
Be mindful that the lab'ring neat,   45
As you, may have their fill of meat.
And know, besides, ye must revoke[11]
The patient ox unto the yoke,
And all go back unto the plow
And harrow (though they're hang'd up now).   50
And, you must know, your Lord's word's true,
Feed him ye must, whose food fills you;
And that this pleasure is like rain,
Not sent ye for to drown your pain,[12]
But for to make it spring again.   55

TO ANTHEA, WHO MAY COMMAND HIM ANYTHING

Bid me to live, and I will live
   Thy protestant[1] to be,
Or bid me love, and I will give
   A loving heart to thee.

A heart as soft, a heart as kind,   5
   A heart as sound and free
As in the whole world thou canst find,
   That heart I'll give to thee.

Bid that heart stay, and it will stay
   To honor thy decree,   10
Or bid it languish quite away,
   And't shall do so for thee.

Bid me to weep, and I will weep
   While I have eyes to see,
And having none, yet I will keep   15
   A heart to weep for thee.

Bid me despair, and I'll despair
   Under that cypress tree,
Or bid me die, and I will dare
   E'en Death, to die for thee.   20

Thou art my life, my love, my heart,
   The very eyes of me,
And hast command of every part,
   To live and die for thee.

UPON BROCK
Epigram

To cleanse his eyes Tom Brock makes much ado,
But not his mouth (the fouler of the two).
A clammy rheum makes loathsome both his eyes:
His mouth worse furr'd with oaths and blasphemies.

TO MEADOWS

Ye have been fresh and green,
   Ye have been fill'd with flowers,
And ye the walks have been
   Where maids have spent their hours.

You have beheld how they   5
   With wicker arks did come
To kiss and bear away
   The richer couslips[1] home.

Y'ave heard them sweetly sing,
   And seen them in a round: 10
Each virgin, like a spring,
   With honeysuckles crown'd.

But now we see none here
   Whose silv'ry feet did tread,
And with dishevel'd hair   15
   Adorn'd this smoother mead.

Like unthrifts, having spent
   Your stock, and needy grown,
Y' are left here to lament
   Your poor estates, alone.   20

TO DAFFODILS

Fair daffodils, we weep to see
   You haste away so soon:
As yet the early-rising sun
   Has not attain'd his noon.
     Stay, stay,   5
   Until the hasting day
     Has run
   But to the evensong,
And, having pray'd together, we
   Will go with you along.   10
We have short time to stay as you,
   We have as short a spring,
As quick a growth to meet decay

[7]Pork. [8]Spiced pudding made of wheat. [9]Winnowing fans.
[10]Vats. [11]Recall (a Latinism). [12]Labor.
TO ANTHEA [1]Suitor (who protests, i.e., avows, his love).
TO MEADOWS [1]Cowslips, a wild flower of the primrose family.

As you, or anything.
　　We die　　　　　　　　　　　　15
As your hours do, and dry
　　Away
Like to the summer's rain,
Or as the pearls of morning's dew,
　　Ne'er to be found again.　　　　20

HIS EMBALMING TO JULIA

For my embalming, Julia, do but this:
Give thou my lips but their supremest[1] kiss;
Or else transfuse thy breath into the chest
Where my small relics must forever rest:
That breath the balm, the myrrh, the nard shall be　　5
To give an incorruption unto me.

UPON HIS JULIA

Will ye hear what I can say
Briefly of my Julia?
Black and rolling is her eye,
Double chinn'd, and forehead high;
Lips she has all ruby red,　　　　5
Cheeks like cream enclarited,[1]
And a nose that is the grace
And proscenium[2] of her face.
So that[3] we may guess by these,
The other parts will richly please.　　10

TO THE MOST LEARNED, WISE, AND ARCH[1] ANTIQUARY, MASTER JOHN SELDEN[2]

I, who have favor'd many, come to be
Grac'd, now at last, or glorified by thee.
Lo, I, the lyric prophet, who have set
On many a head the Delphic coronet,[3]
Come unto thee for laurel, having spent　　5
My wreaths on those who little gave or lent.
Give me the daphne,[4] that the world may know it:
Whom they neglected, thou hast crown'd a poet.
A city here of heroes I have made
Upon the rock, whose firm foundation laid　　10
Shall never shrink, where making thine abode,
Live thou a Selden, that's a demi-god!

UPON MASTER BEN JONSON
Epigram

After the rare arch-poet Jonson died,
The sock grew loathsome, and the buskin's pride,[1]
Together with the stage's glory, stood
Each like a poor and pitied widowhood.
The cirque[2] profan'd was, and all postures rack'd,　　5
For men did strut and stride and stare, not act.
Then temper flew from words, and men did squeak,
Look red and blow and bluster, but not speak.
No holy rage or frantic fires did stir

Or flash about the spacious theater.　　　10
No clap of hands or shout or praises' proof
Did crack the playhouse sides or cleave her roof.
Artless the scene was, and that monstrous sin
Of deep and arrant ignorance came in:
Such ignorance as theirs was who once hiss'd　　15
At thy unequal'd play, *The Alchemist*.[3]
O fie upon 'em! Lastly too, all wit
In utter darkness did and still will sit,
Sleeping the luckless age out, till that she
Her resurrection has again with thee.

THE WILLOW GARLAND[1]

A willow garland thou didst send
　　Perfum'd (last day) to me,
Which did but only this portend,
　　I was forsook by thee.

Since so it is, I'll tell thee what,　　　5
　　Tomorrow thou shalt see
Me wear the willow; after that,
　　To die upon the tree.

As beasts unto the altars go
　　With garlands dress'd, so I　　　10
Will, with my willow-wreath also,
　　Come forth and sweetly die.

PUTREFACTION

Putrefaction is the end
Of all that Nature doth intend.

TO BLOSSOMS

Fair pledges of a fruitful tree,
　　Why do ye fall so fast?
　　Your date is not so past
But you may stay yet here a while,
　　To blush and gently smile,　　　5
　　　　And go at last.

What, were ye born to be
　　An hour or half's delight,
　　And so to bid goodnight?

HIS EMBALMING　[1]Very last.
UPON HIS JULIA　[1]Tinged with claret, i.e., rosy.
[2]Foremost feature.　[3]If.
TO JOHN SELDEN　[1]Pre-eminent.
[2]On John Selden (1584–1654), the noted antiquarian, see pp. 852 ff.
[3]*Have set...coronet*: i.e., praised in poetry. *Delphic*: pertaining to Delphi, sacred to Apollo, god of music and poetry.
[4]The laurel, a symbol of praise. (The nymph Daphne, pursued by Apollo was transformed into a laurel tree.)
UPON MASTER BEN JONSON　[1]*Sock...buskin*: symbol of comedy and tragedy respectively.　[2]Circus, theater.
[3]One of Jonson's greatest comedies, first acted in 1610 and printed two years later.
THE WILLOW GARLAND　[1]Traditional symbol of unrequited love.

'Twas pity Nature brought ye forth   10
  Merely to show your worth,
      And lose you quite.

But you are lovely leaves where we
  May read how soon things have
      Their end, though ne'er so brave,   15
And after they have shown their pride
  Like you a while, they glide
      Into the grave.

KISSING AND BUSSING

Kissing and bussing differ both in this:
We buss our wantons, but our wives we kiss.

ANACREONTIC[1]

Born I was to be old,
  And for to die here;
After that, in the mold
  Long for to lie here.
But before that day comes,   5
  Still I be bousing,[2]
For I know in the tombs
  There's no carousing.

HIS CONTENT IN THE COUNTRY

Here, here I live with what my board
Can with the smallest cost afford.
Though ne'er so mean the viands be,
They well content my Prue[1] and me.
Or pea, or bean, or wort,[2] or beet,   5
Whatever comes, content makes sweet.
Here we rejoice because no rent
We pay for our poor tenement[3]
Wherein we rest, and never fear
The landlord or the usurer.   10
The quarter-day[4] does ne'er affright
Our peaceful slumbers in the night.
We eat our own, and batten[5] more
Because we feed on no man's score,[6]
But pity those whose flanks grow great,   15
Swell'd with the lard of others' meat.
We bless our fortunes when we see
Our own beloved privacy,
And like our living, where we are known
To very few, or else to none.   20

ON HIMSELF

Live by thy Muse thou shalt when others die,
Leaving no fame to long posterity:
When monarchies tran-shifted are, and gone.
Here shall endure thy vast dominion.

HIS PRAYER TO BEN JONSON

When I a verse shall make,
Know I have pray'd thee,
For old religion's sake,
Saint Ben, to aid me.

Make the way smooth for me,   5
When I, thy Herrick,
Honoring thee, on my knee
Offer my lyric.

Candles I'll give to thee,
And a new altar;   10
And thou, Saint Ben, shalt be
Writ in my psalter.

THE BAD SEASON MAKES THE POET SAD

Dull to myself, and almost dead to these
My many fresh and fragrant mistresses,
Lost to all music now, since everything
Puts on the semblance here of sorrowing:
Sick is the land to th' heart, and doth endure   5
More dangerous faintings by her desp'rate cure.
But if that golden age would come again,
And Charles here rule as he before did reign,
If smooth and unperplex'd the seasons were
As when the sweet Maria[1] lived here,   10
I should delight to have my curls half drown'd
In Tyrian dews, and head with roses crown'd,
And once more yet, ere I am laid out dead,
Knock at a star with my exalted head.[2]

THE NIGHT-PIECE, TO JULIA

Her eyes the glowworm lend thee,
  The shooting stars attend thee;
      And the elves also
      Whose little eyes glow
Like the sparks of fire, befriend thee.   5

No will-o'-the-wisp mislight thee,
  Nor snake or slowworm[1] bite thee:
      But on, on thy way,

ANACREONTIC [1]Drinking song (after Anacreon, a Greek lyric poet
who wrote of love and wine). See Cowley's anacreontics, p. 334.
[2]Overdrinking.
HIS CONTENT [1]Prudence Baldwin, Herrick's housekeeper at Dean
Prior. See p. 185.
[2]Colewort, cabbage.   [3]Dwelling.
[4]The day when the quarterly payment of rent was due.   [5]Thrive.
[6]Record of debt.
THE BAD SEASON [1]Queen Henrietta Maria, consort of Charles I.
For her stay in Devon see p. 748, n. 1.
[2]*Knock...head*: i.e., write great poetry (as Horace, *Odes,* I.x.41,
had promised he would do with Maecenas' patronage).
THE NIGHT-PIECE [1]Lizard.

Not making a stay,
Since ghost there's none to affright thee.   10

Let not the dark thee cumber;[2]
What though the moon does slumber?
The stars of the night
Will lend thee their light,
Like tapers clear without number.   15

Then, Julia, let me woo thee,
Thus, thus to come unto me:
And when I shall meet
Thy silv'ry feet,
My soul I'll pour into thee.   20

ON HIMSELF

I'll sing no more, nor will I longer write
Of that sweet lady or that gallant knight.
I'll sing no more of frosts, snows, dews, and showers,
No more of groves, meads, springs, and wreaths of
      flowers.
I'll write no more, nor will I tell or sing   5
Of Cupid and his witty cozening.
I'll sing no more of death, or shall the grave
No more my dirges and my trentals[1] have.

HIS RETURN TO LONDON[1]

From the dull confines of the drooping west,
To see the day spring from the pregnant east,
Ravish'd in spirit, I come, nay more, I fly
To thee, bless'd place of my nativity!
Thus, thus with hallowed foot I touch the ground,   5
With thousand blessings by thy fortune crown'd.
O fruitful genius! that bestowest here
An everlasting plenty, year by year.
O Place! O People! Manners! fram'd to please
All nations, customs, kindreds, languages!   10
I am a free-born Roman; suffer then
That I amongst you live a citizen.
London my home is: though by hard fate sent
Into a long and irksome banishment,
Yet since call'd back; henceforward let me be,   15
O native country, repossess'd by thee!
For rather than I'll to the west return,
I'll beg of thee first here to have mine urn.
Weak I am grown, and must in short time fall;
Give thou my sacred relics burial.

TO PRINCE CHARLES UPON
HIS COMING TO EXETER[1]

What Fate decreed, Time now has made us see,
A renovation of the west by thee.
That preternatural fever which did threat
Death to our country now hath lost his heat,
And calms succeeding, we perceive no more   5

Th' unequal pulse to beat as heretofore.
Something there yet remains for thee to do,
Then reach those ends that thou wast destin'd to.
Go on with Sylla's fortune;[2] let thy fate
Make thee like him, this, that way fortunate!   10
Apollo's image side with thee to bless
Thy war, discreetly made, with white[3] success!
Meantime thy prophets watch by watch shall pray
While young Charles fights, and fighting wins the day.
That done, our smooth-pac'd poems all shall be   15
Sung in the high doxology of thee.
Then maids shall strew thee, and thy curls from them
Receive, with songs, a flow'ry diadem.

UPON JULIA'S CLOTHES

Whenas in silks my Julia goes,
Then, then, methinks, how sweetly flows
That liquefaction of her clothes.

Next, when I cast mine eyes and see
That brave vibration each way free,   5
O how that glittering taketh me!

UPON PRUE HIS MAID[1]

In this little urn is laid
Prudence Baldwin, once my maid,
From whose happy spark here let
Spring the purple violet.

UPON BEN JONSON

Here lies Jonson with the rest
Of the poets, but the best.
Reader, wouldst thou more have known?
Ask his story,[1] not this stone.
That will speak what this can't tell   5
Of his glory. So farewell.

[2]Hinder.

ON HIMSELF [1]Elegies, dirges. Literally, a set of thirty requiem masses.

HIS RETURN TO LONDON [1]Presumably written about 1647, when Herrick returned to London on being ejected from his parish in Devon.

TO PRINCE CHARLES [1]According to Clarendon (*History*, Bk. IX), Prince Charles, in a vain attempt to hold Devon and Cornwall against the Parliamentary army under Fairfax, entered Exeter on 29 August 1645.
[2]For his military success against his rival Gaius Marius, the Roman general and politician Lucius Cornelius Sulla (or *Sylla*, 138–78 B.C.) acquired the sobriquet *Felix* ("fortunate").
[3]Exemplary, auspicious.

UPON PRUE [1]See p. 184.

UPON BEN JONSON [1]History.

AN ODE FOR HIM

          Ah, Ben,
       Say how or when
       Shall we thy guests
    Meet at those lyric feasts
       Made at the Sun,   5
    The Dog, the Triple Tun![1]
    Where we such clusters had
    As made us nobly wild, not mad;
    And yet each verse of thine
    Outdid the meat, outdid the frolic wine.   10
          My Ben,
       Or come again
       Or send to us
       Thy wit's great overplus;
       But teach us yet   15
       Wisely to husband it,
    Lest we that talent spend,
    And, having once brought to an end
       That precious stock, the store
    Of such a wit the world should have no more. 20

THE PILLAR OF FAME

    Fame's pillar here, at last, we set,
    Outduring[1] marble, brass, or jet,
       Charm'd and enchanted so
       As to withstand the blow
          Of overthrow;   5
       Nor shall the seas
       Or OUTRAGES
       Of storms o'erbear
       What we uprear;
       Tho' kingdoms fall,   10
       This pillar never shall
       Decline or waste at all;
    But stand forever by his own
    Firm and well-fix'd foundation.

His Noble Numbers or His Pious Pieces (1647)

HIS PRAYER FOR ABSOLUTION

    For those my unbaptized rhymes,
    Writ in my wild, unhallowed times;
    For every sentence, clause, and word
    That's not inlaid with Thee (my Lord),
    Forgive me, God, and blot each line   5
    Out of my book, that is not Thine.
    But if, 'mongst all, Thou find'st here one
    Worthy Thy benediction,
    That one of all the rest shall be
    The glory of my work and me.   10

WHAT GOD IS

    God is above the sphere of our esteem,
    And is the best known, not defining Him.

TO GOD

    Do with me, God, as Thou didst deal with John
    (Who writ that heavenly Revelation).
    Let me, like him, first cracks of thunder hear,[1]
    Then let the harp's enchantments strike mine ear;[2]
    Here give me thorns; there, in Thy kingdom, set   5
    Upon my head the golden coronet.
    There give me day, but here my dreadful night;
    My sackcloth here, but there my stole of white.

AN ODE OF THE BIRTH OF OUR SAVIOUR

    In numbers, and but these few,
    I sing Thy birth, O Jesu!
    Thou pretty baby, born here,
    With sup'rabundant scorn here,
    Who for Thy princely port here   5
       Hadst for Thy place
       Of birth a base
    Out-stable for Thy court here.

    Instead of neat enclosures
    Of interwoven osiers,   10
    Instead of fragrant posies
    Of daffodils and roses,
    Thy cradle, kingly Stranger,
       As Gospel tells,
       Was nothing else   15
    But, here, a homely manger.

    But we with silks (not crewels),[1]
    With sundry precious jewels
    And lily-work will dress Thee;
    And as we dispossess Thee   20
    Of clouts[2] we'll make a chamber,
       Sweet Babe, for Thee
       Of ivory,
    And plaister'd[3] round with amber.

    The Jews they did disdain Thee,   25
    But we will entertain Thee
    With glories to await here
    Upon Thy princely state here,
    And more for love than pity.
       From year to year   30

AN ODE FOR HIM   [1]*Sun . . . Tun*: famous London taverns.
THE PILLAR OF FAME   [1]Surviving.
TO GOD   [1]See Revelation 6.1.
[2]*Harp's . . . ear*: see Revelation 14.2.
AN ODE OF THE BIRTH   [1]Worsted garments.
[2]Swaddling clothes.   [3]Plastered, overlaid.

We'll make Thee, here,
A free-born[4] of our city.

HIS LITANY TO THE HOLY SPIRIT

In the hour of my distress,
When temptations me oppress,
And when I my sins confess,
    Sweet Spirit, comfort me!

When I lie within my bed,   5
Sick in heart and sick in head,
And with doubts discomforted,
    Sweet Spirit, comfort me!

When the house doth sigh and weep,
And the world is drown'd in sleep,   10
Yet mine eyes the watch do keep,
    Sweet Spirit, comfort me!

When the artless doctor sees
No one hope but of his fees,
And his skill runs on the lees,[1]   15
    Sweet Spirit, comfort me!

When his potion and his pill,
His or none[2] or little skill,
Meet for nothing but to kill,
    Sweet Spirit, comfort me!   20

When the passing bell doth toll,
And the Furies in a shoal[3]
Come to fright a parting soul,
    Sweet Spirit, comfort me!

When the tapers now burn blue,[4]   25
And the comforters are few,
And that number more than true,
    Sweet Spirit, comfort me!

When the priest his last hath pray'd,
And I nod to what is said,   30
'Cause my speech is now decay'd,
    Sweet Spirit, comfort me!

When, God knows, I'm toss'd about
Either with despair or doubt,
Yet before the glass be out,   35
    Sweet Spirit, comfort me!

When the Tempter me pursu'th
With the sins of all my youth,
And half damns me with untruth,
    Sweet Spirit, comfort me!   40

When the flames and hellish cries
Fright mine ears and fright mine eyes,
And all terrors me surprise,
    Sweet Spirit, comfort me!

When the judgment is reveal'd,   45
And that open'd which was seal'd,

When to Thee I have appeal'd,
    Sweet Spirit, comfort me!

TO HIS ANGRY GOD

    Through all the night
    Thou dost me fright,
And hold'st mine eyes from sleeping;
    And day by day
    My cup can say,   5
"My wine is mix'd with weeping."

    Thou dost my bread
    With ashes knead
Each evening and each morrow;
    Mine eye and ear   10
    Do see and hear
The coming in of sorrow.

    Thy scourge of steel,
    Ay me, I feel
Upon me beating ever,   15
    While my sick heart
    With dismal smart
Is disacquainted never.

    Long, long, I'm sure,
    This can't endure;   20
But in short time 'twill please Thee,
    My gentle God,
    To burn the rod,
Or strike so as to ease me.

HIS CREED

I do believe that die I must.
And be return'd from out my dust;
I do believe that when I rise,
Christ I shall see with these same eyes;
I do believe that I must come   5
With others to the dreadful doom;
I do believe the bad must go
From thence to everlasting woe;
I do believe the good, and I,
Shall live with Him eternally;   10
I do believe I shall inherit
Heaven by Christ's mercies, not my merit;
I do believe the One in Three.
And Three in perfect Unity;
Lastly, that Jesus is a deed   15
Of gift from God. *And here's my Creed.*

[4]With the privileges of a citizen.
HIS LITANY [1]*Runs...lees*: i.e., is exhausted.
[2]Either no (skill). [3]Troop, crowd.
[4]Traditionally a sign that evil spirits are present.

THE WHITE ISLAND, OR
PLACE OF THE BLESS'D

In this world (the isle of dreams)
While we sit by sorrow's streams,
Tears and terrors are our themes
   Reciting;

But when once from hence we fly,   5
More and more approaching nigh,
Unto young eternity
   Uniting

In that whiter island where
Things are evermore sincere,   10
Candor here and luster there
   Delighting;

There no monstrous fancies shall
Out of hell an horror call
To create (or cause at all)   15
   Affrighting.

There in calm and cooling sleep
We our eyes shall never steep,
But eternal watch shall keep,
   Attending   20

Pleasures such as shall pursue
Me immortaliz'd, and you,
And fresh joys as never too
   Have ending.

THE VIRGIN MARY

The Virgin Mary was, as I have read,
The house of God, by Christ inhabited,
Into the which He enter'd, but the door,
Once shut, was never to be open'd more.

PREDESTINATION

Predestination is the cause alone
Of many standing, but of fall to none.

HIS COMING TO THE SEPULCHER

Hence they have borne my Lord. Behold, the stone
Is roll'd away, and my sweet Saviour's gone!
Tell me, white angel, what is now become
Of Him we lately seal'd up in this tomb.

Is He from hence gone to the shades beneath   5
To vanquish hell, as here He conquer'd Death?
If so, I'll thither follow without fear,
And live in hell if that my Christ stays there.

[THIS CROSS-TREE HERE]

   This Cross-Tree here
   Doth Jesus bear,
   Who sweet'ned first
   The Death accurst.
Here all things ready are, make haste, make haste away;
For long this work will be, and very short this day.
Why then, go on to act: here's wonders to be done
Before the last least sand of Thy ninth hour[1] be run,
Or ere dark clouds do dull or dead the midday's sun.
   Act when Thou wilt,   10
   Blood will be spilt,
   Pure balm that shall
   Bring health to all.
   Why then, begin
   To pour first in   15
   Some drops of wine,
   Instead of brine,
   To search the wound,
   So long unsound:
   And when that's done,   20
   Let oil, next, run,
   To cure the sore
   Sin made before.
   And O! dear Christ,
   E'en as Thou di'st,   25
   Look down, and see
   Us weep for Thee.
   And tho' (love knows)
   Thy dreadful woes
   We cannot ease,   30
   Yet do Thou please,
   Who mercy art,
   T' accept each heart
   That gladly would
   Help, if it could.   35
   Meanwhile, let me,
   Beneath this tree,
   This honor have,
   To make my grave.

[THIS CROSS-TREE HERE]   [1]According to Matthew (27.50), the hour at which Christ "yielded up the ghost."

Henry King [1592-1669]

Bishop King's contemporaries would have found it odd that this proud prelate, a scion of one of the great ecclesiastical dynasties of Elizabethan and Jacobean England, should be remembered chiefly for his "Exequy," a moving tribute to his wife. As the son of a bishop of London and vice-chancellor of Oxford who was himself the nephew of a bishop of Oxford in the days of Henry

VIII, young King was almost doomed to be important in the church; it is fortunate that he was able to adorn the many prosperous posts that came his way. A product of such splendid institutions as Westminster School and Christ Church, Oxford (B.A. 1611, M.A. 1614), he began his rapid rise as a prebend of St. Paul's and rector of an Essex parish. Other benefactions from his thrifty father followed—the archdiaconate of Colchester, a sinecure at Fulham, a royal chaplaincy (1617), and the canonry of Christ Church (1623)—and though he suffered severe domestic sorrows in the loss of several of his children and then of his beloved wife (1624), his career continued its ascent until he reached the deanship of Rochester (1638) and at last, in 1641, the bishop's throne at Chichester. No sooner had he gained this height, however, than in the tumult of the civil war he fell. Following the occupation of his palace, the seizure of his books and household goods, and the desecration of his cathedral in 1643, his ruin was completed by the sequestration of his large estates. Reduced to living on the bounty of his friends and relatives, he versified the Psalms (1651) and managed to survive until the Restoration, when, at sixty-eight, he reclaimed his vacant see. There in 1669 he died and was entombed in his cathedral.

Owing partly, no doubt, to his close friendship with Donne (whose love for Bishop John King, according to Izaak Walton, was "doubled upon his heir") and to his wide acquaintance with other men of letters, he early turned to writing. The sermons that from time to time he published were such as might have been expected from a churchman of the period, but poetry was his special gift and lifelong avocation. In 1657 the publishers of his collected poems, acknowledging in an epistle to the author that they had "trespassed" his "consent," disingenuously called his verses "juvenilia" and implied that he himself, "long engaged on better contemplations," had put aside such youthful toys. Similarly, Thomas Fuller, in the interests of propriety, professed to find a steady upward progress from the music and the poetry that had enchanted King when young to the oratory and philosophy that occupied his middle years and finally ("in his reduced age") to the mysteries of divinity. Such comments were misleading, for King's poetical career in fact extended from at least 1612, when he, like almost every poet and poetaster in the kingdom, mourned Prince Henry's death, to 1657, when, in "An Elegy upon My Best Friend L. K. C.," he made his formal valediction to the art of poetry and flung away his "now loathed pen." Through almost half a century, then, he had continued writing verse.

Many of his poems (like the famous "Exequy") were commendatory or elegiac, prompted by such occasions as Sir Walter Raleigh's execution, the birth of the future Charles II, the deaths of Donne and Jonson, and the publication of George Sandys's scriptural *Paraphrase*. But he also wrote many songs and sonnets of uncertain date, and he thought well enough of them to oversee the making of a transcript of his verses which is preserved in the Bodleian Library at Oxford. There also survive two other such collections, showing some variation in content and arrangement, that were probably based upon the first. The 1657 edition of his poems, three of whose seventy-two pieces do not occur in the manuscripts, was reissued in 1664 (with four thitherto unpublished poems), and again in 1700 with the catchy but deceptive title *Ben Jonson's Poems, Elegies, Paradoxes, and Sonnets*.

My text is based on *Poems, Elegies, Paradoxes, and Sonnets*, 1657 (Wing K-501). *The Psalms of David* (1651), whose contemporary esteem is hard to understand, was expanded and reissued in 1654 and 1671. John Hannah's editions of the *Poems and Psalms* appeared in 1843, after which King's poetry slumbered until Lawrence Mason's edition of the *English Poems* in 1914. This was followed by the editions of George Saintsbury (*Minor Poets of the Caroline Period*, 3 vols., 1921), John Sparrow (1925), J. R. Baker (1960), and Margaret Crum (1965), the last of which is definitive. Mason's account of the life and works in *Transactions of the Connecticut Academy of Arts and Sciences*, XVIII (1913) has now been supplemented by Ronald Berman's *Henry King & the Seventeenth Century* (1964). The Bodleian manuscript has been described by Percy Simpson in the *Bodleian Quarterly Record*, V (1929) and the *Bodleian Library Record*, IV (1952–53).

from Poems, Elegies, Paradoxes, and Sonnets (1657)

THE PUBLISHERS TO THE AUTHOR

Sir,

It is the common fashion to make some address to the readers, but we are bold to direct ours to you, who will look on this publication with anger which others must welcome into the world with joy.

The Lord Verulam, comparing ingenious authors to those who had orchards ill neighbored, advised them to publish their own labors lest other might steal the fruit.[1] Had you followed his example, or liked the advice, we had not thus trespassed against your consent, or been forced to an apology, which cannot but imply a fault committed. The best we can say for ourselves is that if we have injured you, it is merely in your own defense, preventing the present attempts[2] of others, who to their theft would, by their false copies of these poems, have added violence, and some way have wounded your reputation.

Having been long engaged on better contemplations, you may perhaps look down on these juvenilia, most of them the issues of your youthful Muse, with some disdain; and yet the courteous reader may tell you with thanks that they are not to be despised, being far from abortive, nor to be disowned, because they are both modest and legitimate. And thus if we have offered you a view of your younger face, our hope is you will behold it with an unwrinkled brow, though we have presented the mirror against your will.

We confess our design hath been set forward by friends that honor you, who lest the ill publishing might disfigure these things from whence you never expected addition to your credit (sundry times endeavored and by them defeated) furnished us with some papers which they thought authentic; we may not turn their favor into an accusation, and therefore give no intimation of their names, but wholly take the blame of this hasty and immethodical impression[3] upon ourselves, being persons at a distance, who are fitter to bear it than those who are nearer related. In hope of your pardon we remain,

> *Your most devoted servants,*
> *Richard Marriot*
> *Henry Herringman*

TO THE SAME LADY UPON
MASTER BURTON'S MELANCHOLY[1]

If in this glass of humors you do find
The passions or diseases of your mind,
Here without pain you safely may endure,
Though not to suffer, yet to read your cure.
But if you nothing meet you can apply,   5
Then ere you need, you have a remedy.

And I do wish you never may have cause
To be adjudg'd by these fanatic laws,
But that this book's example may be known
By others' melancholy, not your own.   10

SONNET

Tell me no more how fair she is,
  I have no mind to hear
The story of that distant bliss
  I never shall come near;
By sad experience I have found   5
That her perfection is my wound.

And tell me not how fond I am
  To tempt a daring fate,
From whence no triumph ever came
  But to repent too late;   10
There is some hope ere long I may
In silence dote myself away.

I ask no pity, Love, from thee,
  Nor will thy justice blame,
So that thou wilt not envy me   15
  The glory of my flame,
Which crowns my heart whene'er it dies,
In that it falls her sacrifice.

LOVE'S HARVEST

Fond lunatic, forbear! Why dost thou sue
For thy affection's pay ere it is due?
Love's fruits are legal use, and therefore may
Be only taken on the marriage day.
  Who for this interest too early call,   5
  By that exaction lose the principal.

Then gather not those immature delights
Until their riper autumn thee invites.
He that abortive corn cuts off his ground,
No husband but a ravisher is found.   10
  So those that reap their love before they wed
  Do in effect but cuckold their own bed.

TO THE AUTHOR [1]In dedicating the first (1597) edition of his *Essays* to his brother Anthony, Francis Bacon said: "I do now like some that have an orchard ill neighbored, that gather their fruit before it is ripe, to prevent stealing."
[2]*Preventing...attempts*: anticipating the imminent attempts.
[3]I.e., irregular printing.
TO THE SAME LADY [1]I.e., the unidentified lady to whom was addressed the preceding poem in the 1657 volume. *Melancholy*: For Robert Burton's famous *Anatomy of Melancholy*—a book so popular that it went through six editions between 1621 and 1651— see pp. 428 ff.

THE RETREAT

Pursue no more, my thoughts, that false unkind;
You may as soon imprison the north wind,
Or catch the lightning as it leaps, or reach
The leading billow first ran down the breach,
Or undertake the flying clouds to track   5
In the same path they yesterday did rack.
  Then like a torch turn'd downward, let the same
  Desire which nourish'd it put out your flame.

Lo, thus I do divorce thee from my breast,
False to thy vow, and traitor to my rest!   10
Henceforth thy tears shall be, though thou repent,
Like pardons after execution sent.
Nor shalt thou ever my love's story read,
But as some epitaph of what is dead.
  So may my hope on future blessings dwell,   15
  As 'tis my firm resolve and last farewell.

THE SURRENDER

My once dear love, hapless that I no more
Must call thee so, the rich affection's store
That fed our hopes lies now exhaust and spent,
Like sums of treasure unto bankrupts lent.

We that did nothing study but the way   5
To love each other, with which thoughts the day
Rose with delight to us, and with them set,
Must learn the hateful art how to forget.

We that did nothing wish that heav'n could give
Beyond ourselves, nor did desire to live   10
Beyond that wish, all these now cancel must
As if not writ in faith, but words and dust.

Yet witness those clear vows which lovers make,
Witness the chaste desires that never brake
Into unruly heats; witness that breast   15
Which in thy bosom anchor'd his whole rest;
'Tis no default in us, I dare acquite
Thy maiden faith, thy purpose fair and white[1]
As thy pure self. Cross planets did envy
Us to each other, and heaven did untie   20
Faster than vows could bind. O, that the stars,
When lovers meet, sould stand oppos'd in wars!

Since, then, some higher destinies command,
Let us not strive, nor labor to withstand
What is past help. The longest date of grief   25
Can never yield a hope of our relief;
And though we waste ourselves in moist laments,
Tears may drown us, but not our discontents.

Fold back our arms, take home our fruitless loves,
That must new fortunes try, like turtle doves   30
Dislodged from their haunts. We must in tears
Unwind a love knit up in many years.
In this last kiss I here surrender thee
Back to thyself, so thou again art free;

Thou in another, sad as that, resend   35
The truest heart that lover e'er did lend.

Now turn from each. So fare our sever'd hearts
As the divorc'd soul from her body parts.

THE EXEQUY[1]

Accept, thou shrine of my dead saint,
Instead of dirges, this complaint;
And for sweet flow'rs to crown thy hearse,
Receive a strew of weeping verse
From thy griev'd friend, whom thou mightst see   5
Quite melted into tears for thee.

Dear loss! since thy untimely fate
My task hath been to meditate
On thee, on thee; thou art the book,
The library whereon I look,   10
Though almost blind. For thee, lov'd clay,
I languish out, not live, the day,
Using no other exercise
But what I practice with mine eyes;
By which wet glasses I find out   15
How lazily time creeps about
To one that mourns; this, only this,
My exercise and bus'ness is.
So I compute the weary hours
With sighs dissolved into show'rs.   20

Nor wonder if my time go thus
Backward and most preposterous;
Thou hast benighted me; thy set[2]
This eve of blackness did beget,
Who wast my day, though overcast   25
Before thou hadst thy noontide past;
And I remember must in tears,
Thou scarce hadst seen so many years
As day tells hours. By thy clear sun
My love and fortune first did run;   30
But thou wilt never more appear
Folded within my hemisphere,
Since both thy light and motion
Like a fled star is fall'n and gone;
And 'twixt me and my soul's dear wish   35
An earth now interposed is,
Which such a strange eclipse doth make
As ne'er was read in almanac.

I could allow thee for a time
To darken me and my sad clime;   40
Were it a month, a year, or ten,
I would thy exile live till then,
And all that space my mirth adjourn,

THE SURRENDER [1]Stainless, innocent.
THE EXEQUY [1]I.e., funeral rites. This, King's most famous poem, was prompted by the death of his wife Anne Berkeley in 1624. Although only about twenty-four herself, she had borne her husband six children.
[2]Setting.

So thou wouldst promise to return,
And putting off thy ashy shroud, 45
At length disperse this sorrow's cloud.
But woe is me! the longest date
Too narrow is to calculate
These empty hopes; never shall I
Be so much blest as to descry 50
A glimpse of thee, till that day come
Which shall the earth to cinders doom,
And a fierce fever must calcine[3]
The body of this world like thine,
My little world. That fit of fire 55
Once off, our bodies shall aspire
To our souls' bliss; then we shall rise
And view ourselves with clearer eyes
In that calm region where no night
Can hide us from each other's sight. 60

Meantime, thou hast her, earth; much good
May my harm do thee. Since it stood
With heaven's will I might not call
Her longer mine, I give thee all
My short-liv'd right and interest 65
In her whom living I lov'd best;
With a most free and bounteous grief,
I give thee what I could not keep.
Be kind to her, and prithee look
Thou write into thy doomsday book 70
Each parcel of this rarity
Which in thy casket shrin'd doth lie.
See that thou make thy reck'ning straight,
And yield her back again by weight;
For thou must audit on thy trust 75
Each grain and atom of this dust,
As thou wilt answer Him that lent,
Not gave thee, my dear monument.

So close the ground, and 'bout her shade
Black curtains draw, my bride is laid. 80
Sleep on, my love, in thy cold bed,
Never·to be disquieted!
My last goodnight! Thou wilt not wake
Till I thy fate shall overtake;
Till age, or grief, or sickness must 85
Marry my body to that dust
It so much loves, and fill the room
My heart keeps empty in thy tomb.
Stay for me there, I will not fail
To meet thee in that hollow[4] vale. 90
And think not much of my delay;
I am already on the way,
And follow thee with all the speed
Desire can make, or sorrows breed.
Each minute is a short degree, 95
And ev'ry hour a step towards thee.
At night when I betake to rest,
Next morn I rise nearer my west
Of life, almost by eight hours' sail,
Than when sleep breath'd his drowsy gale. 100

Thus from the sun my bottom steers,
And my day's compass downward bears;
Nor labor I to stem the tide
Through which to thee I swiftly glide.

'Tis true, with shame and grief I yield, 105
Thou like the van first took'st the field,
And gotten hath the victory
In thus adventuring to die
Before me, whose more years might crave
A just precedence in the grave.[5] 110
But hark! my pulse like a soft drum
Beats my approach, tells thee I come;
And slow howe'er my marches be,
I shall at last sit down by thee.

The thought of this bids me go on, 115
And wait my dissolution
With hope and comfort. Dear, forgive
The crime, I am content to live
Divided, with but half a heart,
Till we shall meet and never part. 120

THE ANNIVERSE:[1] AN ELEGY

So soon grown old! Hast thou been six years dead,
Poor earth, once by my love inhabited?
And must I live to calculate the time
To which thy blooming youth could never climb,
But fell in the ascent? Yet have not I 5
Studied enough thy loss's history?

How happy were mankind if Death's strict laws
Consum'd our lamentations like the cause!
Or that our grief, turning to dust, might end
With the dissolved body of a friend! 10

But sacred heaven, O how just thou art
In stamping Death's impression on that heart
Which through thy favors would grow insolent
Were it not physick'd by sharp discontent.
If, then, it stand resolv'd in thy decree 15
That still I must doom'd to a desert be
Sprung out of my lone thoughts, which know no path
But what my own misfortune beaten hath;
If thou wilt bind me living to a corse
And I must slowly waste, I then of force 20
Stoop to thy great appointment, and obey
That will which nought avail me to gainsay.

For whilst in sorrow's maze I wander on,
I do but follow life's vocation.
Sure we were made to grieve: at our first birth 25
With cries we took possession of the earth;
And though the lucky man reputed be
Fortune's adopted son, yet only he

[3]Burn to dust. [4]Text *hallow*.
[5]King, who was some eight years older than his wife, survived her by almost half a century.
THE ANNIVERSE [1]Anniversary (of Anne King's death).

Is Nature's true-born child who sums his years
(Like me) with no arithmetic but tears.   30

UPON THE DEATH OF MY EVER DESIRED FRIEND, DOCTOR DONNE, DEAN OF PAUL'S[1]

To have liv'd eminent in a degree
Beyond our lofti'st flights (that is, like thee),
Or t' have had too much merit is not safe,
For such excesses find no epitaph.
At common graves we have poetic eyes   5
Can melt themselves in easy elegies;
Each quill can drop his tributary verse
And pin it with the hatchments to the hearse;[2]
But at thine, poem or inscription
(Rich soul of wit and language) we have none;   10
Indeed, a silence does that tomb befit
Where is no herald left to blazon[3] it.
Widow'd invention justly doth forbear
To come abroad, knowing thou art not here,
Late her great patron, whose prerogative   15
Maintain'd and cloth'd her so as none alive
Must now presume to keep her at thy rate,
Though he the Indies for her dow'r estate.[4]
Or else that awful fire which once did burn
In thy clear brain, now fall'n into thy urn,   20
Lives there to fright rude empirics[5] from thence,
Which might profane thee by their ignorance
Whoever writes of thee, and in a style
Unworthy such a theme, does but revile
Thy precious dust and wake a learned spirit   25
Which may revenge his rapes upon thy merit.
For all a low-pitch'd fancy can devise
Will prove at best but hallow'd injuries.

Thou, like the dying swan, didst lately sing
Thy mournful dirge in audience of the King,   30
When pale looks and faint accents of thy breath
Presented so to life that piece of death
That it was fear'd, and prophesied by all,
Thou thither cam'st to preach thy funeral.[6]

O hadst thou in an elegiac knell   35
Rung out unto the world thine own farewell,
And in thy high victorious numbers beat
The solemn measure of thy griev'd retreat,
Thou mightst the poet's service now have miss'd

As well as then thou didst prevent[7] the priest,   40
And never to the world beholden be
So much as for an epitaph for thee.

I do not like the office, nor is't fit
Thou, who didst lend our age such sums of wit,
Shouldst now reborrow from her bankrupt mine   45
That ore to bury thee which once was thine.
Rather still leave us in thy debt, and know
(Exalted soul) more glory 'tis to owe
Unto thy hearse what we can never pay
Than with embased[8] coin those rites defray.   50

Commit we then thee to thyself, nor blame
Our drooping loves which thus to thine own fame
Leave thee executor, since but thy own
No pen could do thee justice, nor bays crown
Thy vast desert, save that we nothing can   55
Depute to be thy ashes' guardian.

So jewelers no art or metal trust
To form the diamond but the diamond's dust.

SIC VITA[1]

Like to the falling of a star,
Or as the flights of eagles are,
Or like the fresh spring's gaudy hue,
Or silver drops of morning dew,
Or like a wind that chafes the flood,   5
Or bubbles which on water stood:
Even such is man, whose borrow'd light
Is straight call'd in, and paid to night.
The wind blows out, the bubble dies;
The spring entomb'd in autumn lies;   10
The dew dries up, the star is shot;
The flight is past, and man forgot.

UPON THE DEATH OF DONNE [1]Like Thomas Carew's famous tribute (p. 230), this poem was one of the large group of "Elegies on the Author's Death" included in the 1633 edition of Donne's *Poems*.
[2]*And pin...hearse*: It was customary to attach mortuary verses and armorial bearings or *hatchments* to the framework (*hearse*) over the bier of distinguished persons.
[3]Adorn with heraldic devices. [4]Endow. [5]Charlatans.
[6]*Thou...funeral*: For the circumstances of Donne's delivering his own funeral sermon ("Death's Duel") before the King in January 1631 see p. 767. [7]Anticipate. [8]Debased.
SIC VITA [1]"Such is life."

Francis Quarles [1592-1644]

Today, after Quarles has suffered generations of derision and neglect, it is useful to remember that his *Emblems* was the most popular book of poetry of its century and that, as Horace Walpole said, "Milton was forced to wait till the world had done admiring Quarles." In his own time his blend of facile versifying and assertive piety was bound to be successful; and the fact that, as

Thomas Fuller put it, he drank of Jordan instead of Helicon was sufficient to secure his reputation with readers whom *Comus* would have baffled.

If his appeal was to the proletariat his birth and training were patrician. The third son of a surveyor-general of victualing for the Elizabethan navy, himself descended from an ancient Essex family, Quarles received his education at Christ's College, Cambridge (B.A. 1608) and then at Lincoln's Inn. Although he studied law, his widow said, not to "benefit" himself but to help preserve the peace among his litigious friends and neighbors, he did not follow that profession very long, for in 1613 we find him in the train of the earl of Arundel as he escorted the Princess Elizabeth, bride of the Elector Palatine, to her new court in Heidelberg. A second stay abroad (1615–17) was followed by his marriage (1618) and then by the advent of a new career. In 1620 he published (as "the first fruits of an abortive birth") *A Feast for Worms*, a lurid metrical paraphrase of Jonah so copiously eked out with pious meditations and severely moral poems that the poetry almost sinks beneath its mournful freight.

Having found his style and subject, he continued quarrying scripture with dismaying ease. A paraphrase of the Book of Esther (1621) led him briskly on to others (each with its own dedication to a royal or a noble person): of Job (1624), Jeremiah (1624), the Psalms (1625), and finally the career of Samson as recorded in Judges (1631). One comment on the paraphrase of Job may be adapted to the others: Quarles depicts his hero's sufferings so precisely, Thomas Fuller said, "that the reader may see his sores, and through them the anguish of his soul." Throughout the later 1620's Quarles's extended stay in Ireland as secretary to the fabulously erudite Archbishop Ussher produced not only *Argalus and Parthenia* (1629), a poetic romance based on an episode in Sir Philip Sidney's *Arcadia*, but also a collected edition of the paraphrases entitled *Divine Poems* (1630) and a stream of elegiac and edifying verses brought together as *Divine Fancies* in 1632.

Early in the 1630's Quarles, retiring to his native Essex, embarked upon his best known work, the hugely popular *Emblems*, which appeared in 1635. Arranged in five books and lavishly illustrated with plates from a pair of Jesuit publications, each of Quarles's poems is prefaced by an emblem and a scriptural motto and followed by a quoted commentary and an instructive epigram. They were intended for both the reader's eye and ear, the author said, for since "an emblem is but a silent parable," he implies that to versify the hieroglyph is to invest it with a double force. A century later Pope had a different explanation of the *Emblems*,

> where the pictures for the page atone,
> And Quarles is saved by beauties not his own.

Whatever the theory behind its composition, Quarles's book was so successful that it was followed three years later with *Hieroglyphics of the Life of Man*, a work so similar in plan that in subsequent editions it was printed with the *Emblems*.

Like almost everyone in England Quarles reacted strongly to the civil war. Although he produced nothing as chronologer (i.e., chronicler) of the City of London, a post to which he was appointed in 1639 and which he held until his death, he devoted himself almost entirely in his later years to controversial prose. A loyal Church of England man and royalist despite his vast appeal for Puritans, Quarles throughout his final troubled years turned more and more to politics, which for him were tightly laced with morals. Following the highly successful *Enchiridion, Containing Institutions Divine and Moral* in 1640, he worked so strongly for the king's defense in *The Loyal Convert, The Whipper Whipt*, and *Barnabas and Boanerges* (all of 1644) that his house was searched and his manuscripts were burned by Parliamentary order.

When he died in 1644 he had produced, in addition to eighteen sons and daughters and the books already noted, various works of prose and verse in manuscript that, posthumously published by his widow, continued to sustain his reputation. Beginning a year after his death with *Solomon's Recantation* (to which his "sorrowful widow" contributed as "the last duty I can perform to a loving husband" an affectionate biographical sketch), these included *The Shepherd's Oracles, Deliv-*

ered in *Certain Eclogues* (1646), a second part of the widely admired *Barnabas and Boanerges* entitled *Judgment and Mercy for Afflicted Souls* (1646), and *The Virgin Widow* (1649), a dramatic allegory about the troubles of the Church of England. New editions of the poems that had made him famous and that, according to Milton's nephew Edward Phillips a generation later, were held "in wonderful veneration among the vulgar" continued to appear until the middle of the eighteenth century.

My texts are based on *A Feast for Wormes. Set Forth In A Poeme Of The History of Jonah*, 1626 (STC 20545), *Divine Fancies: Digested into Epigrammes, Meditations, and Observations*, 1632 (STC 20529), and *Emblemes*, 1635 (STC 20540). A. B. Grosart's collected edition (3 vols., 1880–81) has had no successor. Quarles' most successful poetry is discussed by Edith James (*University of Texas Studies in English*, 1943) as well as by Rosemary Freeman, Mario Praz (*Studies in Seventeenth-Century Imagery*), and other students of emblem literature listed in the General Bibliography, Section I; his biblical narratives by B. O. Kurth, *Milton and Christian Heroism* (1959); his reputation by A. H. Nethercot, *MP*, XX (1922–23); and his bibliography by J. Horden, *Oxford Bibliographical Society Proceedings & Papers*, New Series, II (1948).

from A Feast for Worms, Set Forth in a Poem on the History of Jonah (1626)

TO THE READER

Reader, I fairly salute thee:

I list not to tire thy patient ears with unnecessary language (the abuse of compliment). My mouth's no dictionary: it only serves as the needful interpreter of my heart. I have here sent thee the first fruits of an abortive birth. It is a dainty subject, not fabulous, but Truth itself. Wonder not at the title (*A Feast for Worms*), for it is a song of mercy: what greater feast than mercy? and what are men but worms? Moreover, I have gleaned some few meditations obvious[1] to the history. Let me advise thee to keep the taste of the history whilst thou readest the meditations, and that will make thee relish both the better. Understanding reader, favor me; gently expound what it is too late to correct. *He levado le golpe; Dios sea con ella.*[2] Farewell.

THE ARGUMENT

    The word of God to Jonah came,
    Commanded Jonah to proclaim
    The vengeance of His Majesty
    Against the sins of Ninevy.[3]

SECTION 1

Th' eternal word of God, whose high decree
Admits no change and cannot frustrate be,
Came down to Johan from the heavens above,
Came down to Jonah, heaven's anointed dove,[4]

Jonah, the flow'r of old Amitta's[5] youth,   5
Jonah, the prophet, son, and heir to Truth,
The blessed type[6] of Him that ransom'd us,
That word came to him and bespake him thus:
   "Arise, truss up thy loins, make all things meet,
And put thy sandals on thy hasty feet;   10
Gird up thy reins[7] and take thy staff in hand,
Make no delay, but go where I command.
Me pleases not to send thee, Jonah, down
To sweet Gath-hepher, thy dear native town
Whose tender paps with plenty overflow,   15
Nor yet unto thy brethren shalt thou go
Amongst the Hebrews, where thy spreaden[8] fame
Foreruns the welcome of thine honor'd name.
No, I'll not send thee thither. Up, arise,
And go to Nineveh, where no allies   20
Nor consanguinity preserves thy blood;
To Nineveh, where strangers are withstood;

[1] Lying or standing in the way of.
[2] *He levado...ella:* Quarles's badly garbled Spanish may be translated as "I have thwarted the blow. May God be with it!"
[3] Nineveh, capital of ancient Assyria.
[4] *Jonah* means "dove" in Hebrew.
[5] Amittai, a citizen of Gath-hepher, a town near Bethlehem (Joshua 19.13).
[6] One who prefigures or represents in prophetic similitude. Typologically, many characters and events of the Old Testament are thus construed with reference to the New.
[7] Loins.   [8] Extended.

To Nineveh, a city far remov'd
From thine acquaintance, where th' art not belov'd.
I send thee to Mount Sinai, not Mount Sion,[9]   25
Not to a gentle lamb but to a lion,
Ne yet to Lydia but to bloody Passur,[10]
Not to the land of Canaan but of Assur,[11]
Whose language will be riddles to thine ears,
And thine again will be as strange to theirs.   30
I say, to Nineveh, the world's great hall,
The monarch's seat, high court imperial.
    "But terrible Mount Sinai will affright thee,
Passur's heavy hand is bent to smite thee;
The lions roar, the people's strong and stout,   35
The bulwarks stand afront to keep thee out.
Great Assur menaces with whip in hand
To entertain[12] thee (welcome) to his land.
    "What then? Arise, be gone, stay not to think!
Bad is the cloth that will in wetting shrink.   40
What then if cruel Passur heap on strokes,
Or Sinai blast thee with her sulph'rous smokes,
Or Assur whip thee, or the lions rent[13] thee?
Push[14] on with courage: I, the Lord, have sent thee.
Away, away! Lay by thy foolish pity,   45
And go to Nineveh, that mighty city.
Cry loud against it, let thy dreadful voice
Make all the city echo with the noise.
Not like a dove, but like a dragon go;
Pronounce my judgment and denounce[15] my woe.   50

. . . . . .

The fatness of their fornication fries
On coals of raging lust, and upward flies,
And makes me sick. I hear the mournful groans   70
And heavy sighs of such whose aching bones
Th' oppressor grinds. Alas, their griefs implore me;
Their pray'rs, preferr'd[16] with tears, plead loud before me;
Behold, my sons they have oppress'd and kill'd,   75
And bath'd their hands within the blood they spill'd.
The steam of guiltless blood makes suit unto me,
The voice of many bloods is mounted to me.
    "The vile profaner of my sacred names,
He tears my titles and mine honor maims;   80
Makes rhet'ric of an oath, swears and forswears,
Recks[17] not my mercy nor my judgment fears.
They eat, they drink, they sleep, they tire the night
In wanton dalliance and unclean delight.
    "Heaven's winged herald, Jonas, up and go   85
To mighty Nineveh! Denounce my woe!
Advance thy voice, and when thou hast advanc't,
Spare shrub nor cedar, but cry out against it.
Hold out thy trumpet, and with louder breath
Proclaim my sudden coming, and their death."   90

APOLOGIA AUTHORIS[18]

It was my morning[19] Muse, a Muse whose spirit
Transcends (I fear) the fortunes of her merit:
Too bold a Muse, whose feathers (yet in blood)[20]
She never bath'd in the Pyrenean[21] flood,

A Muse unbreath'd,[22] unlikely to obtain   95
An easy honor by so stout a train.[23]
Expect no lofty haggard that shall fly
A less'ning pitch to the deceived eye.[24]
If in her downy sorage[25] she but ruff[26]
So strong a dove, may it be thought enough.   100
    Bear with her: Time and Fortune may requite
    Your patient sufference with a fairer flight.

APPLICATIO

To thee, Malfido,[27] now I turn my quill,
That God is still that God, and will be still.
The painful pastors take up Jonah's room,   105
And thou the Ninevite to whom they come.

MEDITATIO PRIMA[28]

How great's the love of God unto His creature!
Or is His wisdom or His mercy greater?
I know not whether.[29] O, th' exceeding love
Of highest God, that from His throne above   110
Will send the brightness of His grace to those
That grope in darkness, and His grace oppose.
He helps, provides, inspires, and freely gives,
As pleas'd to see us ravel out our lives.

. . . . . .

Ay, there is care in heaven,[30] and heavenly sprights[31]   120
That guides the world and guards poor mortal wights,
There is; else were the miserable state
Of man more wretched and unfortunate
Than savage beasts'. But O, th' abounding love
Of highest God, whose angels from above   125
Dismount the tow'r of bliss, fly to and fro,
Assisting wretched man, their deadly foe.

[9]*Mount Sinai...Sion*: i.e., to a place of terror, not one of spiritual serenity. Sinai was where Moses received the Ten Commandments (Exodus 19–20), Sion (or Zion) one of the holy hills in Jerusalem.
[10]Pashhur, "chief governor in the house of the Lord," who "smote Jeremiah, the prophet, and put him in the stocks that were in the high gate of Benjamin" (Jeremiah 20.1–2).
[11]The deity of the Assyrians. [12]Receive. [13]Rend, tear.
[14]Text *P'sh.* [15]Proclaim. [16]Offered. [17]Heeds, regards.
[18]"The apology of the author."
[19]Early, i.e., young, untested. *A Feast for Worms* (1620) was Quarles' first published work. [20]Immature?
[21]Quarles is apparently confusing the Pierian spring of poetic inspiration in Thessaly with the Pyrenean mountains (Pyrenees) between France and Spain. [22]Untrained.
[23]Tail (a term from falconry).
[24]*No lofty...eye*: i.e., no adult hawk in full plumage that shall drop from the height of her soaring (*fly a less'ning pitch*) on her unsuspecting prey.
[25]The first year of a hawk.
[26]In falconry, to strike (the quarry) without securing.
[27]One of bad faith, Quarles' label for his sinful reader.
[28]"The first meditation." [29]Which of the two.
[30]*Ay...heaven*: Perhaps Quarles is remembering the beautiful passage in Spenser (*The Faerie Queene*, II.viii.1) that begins "And is there care in heaven?" [31]Spirits.

What thing is man, that God's regard is such?
Or Why should heaven love retchless[32] man so much?
　Why? What are men but quicken'd lumps of
　　earth?　　　　　　　　　　　　　　　　130
A FEAST FOR WORMS, a bubble full of mirth,
A looking glass for grief, a flash, a minute,
A painted tomb with putrefaction in it,
A map of death, a burthen of a song,
A winter's dust, a worm of five foot long;　　135
Begot in sin, in darkness nourish'd, born
In sorrow: naked, shiftless, and forlorn;
His first voice (heard) is crying for relief;
Alas, he comes into a world of grief.
His age is sinful and his youth is vain;　　140
His life's a punishment, his death's a pain;
His life's an hour of joy, a world of sorrow;
His death's a winter's night that finds no morrow.
Man's life's an hourglass which, being run,
Concludes that hour of joy, and so is done.　　145
Jonah must go, nor is this charge confin'd

To Jonah, but to all the world enjoin'd.
You magistrates, arise and take delight
In dealing justice and maintaining right;
There lies your Nineveh. Merchants, arise　　150
And mingle conscience with your merchandise.
Lawyers, arise; make not your righteous laws
A stale[33] for bribes; let justice rule the cause.
Tradesmen, arise and ply your thriving shops
With truer hands, and eat your meat with drops.[34]　155
Paul, to thy tents; and Peter, to thy net;[35]
And all must go that course which God hath set.
　Great God, awake us in these drowsy times,
Lest vengeance finds us sleeping in our crimes.
Increase succession in Thy prophet's lieu,　　160
For lo, Thy harvest's great, and workmen few.

[32]Reckless, heedless. [33]Lure, bait.
[34]Sweat (alluding to Genesis 3.19: "In the sweat of thy face shalt thou eat bread").
[35]*Paul...net*: Before their apostolic missions Paul was a tentmaker (Acts 18.3) and Peter a fisherman (Matthew 4.18).

from Divine Fancies, Digested into Epigrams, Meditations, and Observations (1632)

[THE FIRST BOOK]

6. ON THE LIFE AND DEATH OF MAN

The world's a theater; the earth, a stage
Plac'd in the midst, whereon both prince and page,
Both rich and poor, fool, wise man, base and high
All act their parts in life's short tragedy.
Our life's a tragedy: those secret rooms　　5
Wherein we tire[1] us are our mothers' wombs;
The music ush'ring in the play is mirth
To see a man child brought upon the earth;
That fainting gasp of breath which first we vent
Is a dumb show, presents the argument;　　10
Our new-born cries that new-born griefs bewray
Is the sad prologue of th' ensuing play;
False hopes, true fears, vain joys, and fierce distracts[2]
Are like the music that divides the acts;
Time holds the glass, and when the hour's outrun,　　15
Death strikes the epilogue, and the play is done.

[THE SECOND BOOK]

66.[1] ON RAYMOND SEBUND[2]

I wonder, Raymond, thy illustrious wit,
Strength'ned with so much learning, could commit
So great a folly as to go about
By Nature's feeble light to blazon[3] out

Such heav'n-bred myst'ries, which the heart of men　　5
Cannot conceive, much less the dark'ned pen
Express: such secrets at whose depth the quire[4]
Of blessed angels tremble and admire.
Could thy vainglory lend no easier task
To thy sublime attempt than to unmask　　10
The glorious Trinity, whose triune face
Was ne'er discovered by the eye of Grace,
Much less by th' eye of Nature, being a story
Objected[5] only to the eye of Glory?
Put out thy light, bold Raymond, and be wise:　　15
Silence thy tongue, and close thy ambitious eyes.
Such heights as these are subjects far more fit
For holy admiration than for wit.

78.[1] ON PLAYERS AND BALLAD-MONGERS

Our merry ballads and lascivious plays
Are much alike: to common censure both

ON THE LIFE AND DEATH [1]Dress. [2]Distractions.

ON RAYMOND SEBUND [1]Text *65* (a misnumbering).
[2]Raymond de Sebonde or Sabunde (d. ca. 1432), a Spanish physician and theologian whose *Theologia naturalis* (which attempted to demonstrate the truths of Christianity through natural phenomena) was translated and then, ironically, attacked by Montaigne in the longest and most elaborate of his *Essays*.
[3]Publish. [4]Choir. [5]Presented, exhibited.
ON PLAYERS AND BALLAD-MONGERS [1]Text 77.

Do stand or fall. T' one sings, the other says,
And both are fripp'ries of another's froth.
    In short, they're priest and clerk of Belial's[2] altar: 5
    T' one makes the sermon, t' other tunes the psalter.

[THE THIRD BOOK]

37. ON A TENNIS COURT

Man is a tennis court: his flesh the wall,
The gamesters God and Sathan, th' heart's the ball.
The higher and the lower hazards are
Too bold presumption and too base despair;
The rackets, which our restless balls make fly,   5
Adversity and sweet prosperity.
The angels keep the court and mark the place
Where the ball falls, and chalks out ev'ry chase.[1]

The line's a civil life we often cross,
O'er which the ball not flying makes a loss.   10
Detractors are like standers-by that bet
With charitable men; our life's the set.[2]
Lord, in this conflict, in these fierce assaults,
Laborious Sathan makes a world of faults.[3]
Forgive them, Lord, although he ne'er implore   15
For favor: they'll be set upon our score.
O take the ball before it come to th' ground,
For this base court has many a false rebound.
Strike, and strike hard, but strike above the line:
Strike where Thou please, so as the set be Thine.   20

[2]In Christian tradition, a personification of wickedness.
ON A TENNIS COURT [1]In tennis, the second impact on the court of
a ball that the opponent has not returned.
[2]Contest.
[3]In tennis, strokes that fail to make the ball fall within prescribed
limits.

from Emblems (1635)

TO THE READER

An emblem is but a silent parable. Let not the tender eye
check to see the allusion to our blessed Saviour figured in
these types.[1] In Holy Scripture He is sometimes called a
sower, sometimes a fisher, sometimes a physician. And why
not presented so as well to the eye as to the ear? Before the
knowledge of letters God was known by hieroglyphics, and
indeed what are the heavens, the earth, nay, every creature
but hieroglyphics and emblems of His glory? I have no
more to say. I wish thee as much pleasure in the reading as
I had in the writing. Farewell, reader.

THE THIRD BOOK

12. JOB 14.13
*O that Thou wouldst hide me in the grave, that Thou
wouldst keep me in secret until Thy wrath be past!*

    O whither shall I flee? what path untrod
    Shall I seek out to 'scape the flaming rod
Of my offended, of my angry God?

Where shall I sojourn? what kind sea will hide
My head from thunder? where shall I abide   5
Until His flames be quench'd or laid aside?

What if my feet should take their hasty flight,
And seek protection in the shades of night?
Alas! no shades can blind the God of light.

TO THE READER [1]Symbolic prefigurations. See p. 195, n. 6.

What if my soul should take the wings of day,　　　　10
And find some desert? If she spring away,
The wings of vengeance clip[1] as fast as they.

What if some solid rock should entertain
My frighted soul? Can solid rocks restrain
The stroke of Justice and not cleave in twain?　　　　15

Nor sea, nor shade, nor shield, nor rock, nor cave,
Nor silent deserts, nor the sullen grave,
What flame-ey'd Fury means to smite, can save.

The seas will part, graves open, rocks will split;
The shield will cleave; the frighted shadows flit;　　　　20
Where Justice aims, her fiery darts must hit.

No, no, if stern-brow'd Vengeance means to thunder,
There is no place above, beneath, nor under,
So close but will unlock, or rive in sunder.

'Tis vain to flee; 'tis neither here nor there　　　　25
Can 'scape that hand, until that hand forbear;
Ah me! where is He not, that's everywhere?

'Tis vain to flee till gentle Mercy show
Her better eye; the farther off we go,
The swing[2] of Justice deals the mightier blow.　　　　30

Th'ingenious child, corrected, does not fly
His angry mother's hand, but clings more nigh,
And quenches with his tears her flaming eye.

Shadows are faithless, and the rocks are false;
No trust in brass, no trust in marble walls;　　　　35
Poor cots are e'en as safe as princes' halls.

Great God! there is no safety here below;
Thou art my fortress, though Thou seem'st my foe;
'Tis Thou, that strikest the stroke, must guard the blow.

Thou art my God, by Thee I fall or stand;　　　　40
Thy grace hath giv'n me courage to withstand
All tortures but my conscience and Thy hand.

I know Thy justice is Thyself; I know,
Just God, Thy very self is mercy too;
If not to Thee, where, whither shall I go?　　　　45

Then work Thy will; if passion bid me flee,
My reason shall obey; my wings shall be
Stretch'd out no further than from Thee to Thee.[1]

EPIGRAM 12

Hath vengeance found thee? can thy fears command
No rocks to shield thee from her thund'ring hand?
Know'st thou not where to 'scape? I'll tell thee where:
My soul, make clean thy conscience; hide thee there.

THE FIFT[1] BOOK

4. CANTICLES[2] 7.10

I am my beloved's, and his desire is towards me.

1

Like to the arctic needle that doth guide
　　The wand'ring shade by his magnetic pow'r,

And leaves his silken gnomon[3] to decide
　　The question of the controverted hour,
First frantics up and down from side to side,　　　　5

And restless beats his crystal'd iv'ry case
　　With vain impatience, jets[4] from place to place,
And seeks the bosom of his frozen bride;
　　At length he slacks his motions, and does rest
His trembling point at his bright pole's beloved breast.　　10

2

Ev'n so my soul, being hurried here and there
　　By ev'ry object that presents delight,
Fain would be settled, but she knows not where;
　　She likes at morning what she loathes at night:
She bows to honor; then she lends an ear　　　　15
　　To that sweet swan-like voice of dying pleasure,
　　Then tumbles in the scatter'd heaps of treasure;
Now flatter'd with false hope; now foil'd with fear:

12. JOB 　[1]Flap. 　[2]Stroke.

THE THIRD BOOK 　[1]To reinforce his moral purpose Quarles inserts between each emblem and its epigram a brief patristic commentary on the biblical text that had inspired his poem.

THE FIFT BOOK 　[1]Fifth. 　[2]Song of Solomon.
[3]A pointer whose shadow indicates the time of day, as on a sundial. 　[4]Hops.

Thus finding all the world's delight to be
But empty toys, good God, she points alone to thee.   20

3

But has the virtu'd⁵ steel a pow'r to move?
  Or can the untouch'd needle point aright?
Or can my wand'ring thought forbear to rove,
  Unguided by the virtue of Thy spirit?
O has my leaden soul the art t' improve   25
    Her wasted talent, and, unrais'd, aspire
    In this sad molting time of her desire?
Not first belov'd, have I the pow'r to love?
    I cannot stir but as Thou please to move me,
Nor can my heart return Thee love until Thou love me.   30

4

The still commandress of the silent night⁶
  Borrows her beams from her bright brother's eye;
His fair aspect⁷ fills her sharp horns with light,
  If he withdraw, her flames are quench'd and die:
E'en so the beams of Thy enlight'ning sp'rit,   35
    Infus'd and shot into my dark desire,
    Inflame my thoughts, and fill my soul with fire,
That I am ravish'd with a new delight;
    But if Thou shroud Thy face, my glory fades,
And I remain a nothing, all compos'd of shades.   40

5

Eternal God! O Thou that only art
  The sacred fountain of eternal light
And blessed loadstone of my better part,
  O Thou, my heart's desire, my soul's delight!
Reflect upon my soul, and touch my heart,   45
    And then my heart shall prize no good above Thee;
    And then my soul shall know Thee; knowing, love
    Thee;
And then my trembling thoughts shall never start
    From Thy commands, or swerve the least degree,
Or once presume to move but as they move in Thee.   50

Epigram 4

My soul, thy love is dear: 'twas thought a good
And easy penn' worth of thy Saviour's blood:
But be not proud; all matters rightly scann'd,
'Twas over-bought: 'twas sold at second hand.

15. canticles 8.14

*Make haste, my beloved, and be like the roe, or the young
hart upon the mountains of spices.*

Go, gentle tyrant, go; Thy flames do pierce
My soul too deep; Thy flames are too, too fierce;
My marrow melts, my fainting spirits fry
In th' torrid zone of Thy meridian eye:
Away, away, Thy sweets are too perfuming: 5
Turn, turn Thy face, Thy fires are too consuming:

Haste hence, and let Thy winged steps outgo
  The frighted roebuck and his flying roe.
But wilt Thou leave me, then? O Thou, that art
Life of my soul, soul of my dying heart,   10
Without the sweet aspect of whose fair eyes
My soul does languish, and her solace dies?
Art Thou so easily woo'd? so apt to hear
The frantic language of Thy foolish fear?
  Leave, leave, me not, nor turn Thy beauty from me;   15
  Look, look upon me, though Thine eyes o'ercome me.

O how they wound! but how my wounds content me!
How sweetly these delightful pains torment me!
How am I tortur'd in excessive measure
Of pleasing cruelties! too cruel pleasure!   20
Turn, turn away, remove Thy scorching beams;
I languish with these bitter-sweet extremes:
  Haste, then, and let Thy winged steps outgo
  The flying roebuck and his frighted roe.

Turn back, my dear! O let my ravish'd eye   25
Once more behold Thy face before Thou fly!
What, shall we part without a mutual kiss?
O who can leave so sweet a face as this?
Look full upon me; for my soul desires
To turn a holy martyr in those fires: 30
  O leave me not, nor turn Thy beauty from me;
  Look, look upon me, though Thy flames o'ercome me.

If Thou becloud the sunshine of Thine eye,
I freeze to death; and if it shine, I fry;
Which, like a fever that my soul hath got,   35
Makes me to burn too cold or freeze too hot:
Alas! I cannot bear so sweet a smart,
Nor canst Thou be less glorious than Thou art.
  Haste, then, and let Thy winged steps outgo
  The frighted roebuck and his flying roe.   40

But go not far beyond the reach of breath;
Too large a distance makes another death:
My youth is in her spring; autumnal vows
Will make me riper for so sweet a spouse;
When aftertimes have burnish'd my desire,   45
I'll shoot Thee flames for flames, and fire for fire.
  O leave me not, nor turn Thy beauty from me;
  Look, look upon me, through Thy flames o'ercome me!

epigram 15

My soul, Sin's monster, whom with greater ease
Ten thousandfold thy God could make than please,
What wouldst thou have? Nor pleas'd with sun nor
  shade?
Heav'n knows not what to make of what He made.

---

⁵Strengthened, i.e., magnetized.
⁶*Commandress...night*: i.e., the moon.
⁷ 1) position in the sky;   2) glance.

George Herbert [1593-1633]

Thanks to Edward, Lord Herbert's spirited autobiography (see p. 115) and to Izaak Walton's moving if perhaps misleading account of Herbert's younger brother George, the annals of English literature do not record another pair of kinsmen whose shape and pressure seem to be so well preserved. One has come down to us as a swashbuckling adventurer of such varied tastes and talents (running from metaphysics to dueling) that he defies a neat description, the other as a gentle cleric of the Church of England who renounced his own worldly ambitions in order to secure a "perfect freedom" in the service of his Master, and thus attained the status of a saint. But if George's life, compared with his flamboyant brother's, seems almost uneventful, one should not forget the "many spiritual conflicts" that, converted into art, finally yielded to repose. Something of the strain between the placid surface and the inner drama of this life is indicated by his elder brother's thumb-nail sketch:

My brother George was so excellent a scholar that he was made the public orator of the university in Cambridge, some of whose English works are extant, which, though they be rare in their kind, yet are far short of expressing those rare perfections he had in the Greek and Latin tongue and all divine and human literature. His life was most holy and exemplary, insomuch that about Salisbury, where he lived beneficed for many years, he was little less than sainted. He was not exempt from passion and choler, being infirmities to which all our race is subject, but that excepted, without reproach in his actions.

Although this incisive sketch would seem to be substantially correct, it leaves much unsaid. George, the fifth son of Richard and Magdalen Herbert, was born in 1593, three years before his father's early death. When he was about twelve his remarkable mother sent him to Westminster School, from which the mighty William Camden (see pp. 816 ff.) had not long before retired as master, and which then as now was noted for its excellence in the classics. There his intellectual gifts were soon apparent. Named a king's scholar after only a year, he was duly elected to Trinity College, Cambridge, in 1608 and matriculated there in 1609. A pair of sonnets (p. 204) then written for his mother shows that his thoughts already turned to poetry and religion, and also to their interaction, whereby art could serve devotion; but his many years at Cambridge, thickly strewn with academic honors, reflected other and more worldly aspirations.

Granted his B.A. degree in 1612, he was elected first a minor and then a major fellow of his college before proceeding to his next degree four years later. By 1618 he had been appointed sublector and then praelector or reader in rhetoric, and his success was such that when the university orator was granted leave of absence, Herbert acted as his surrogate (1619). As he told his stepfather, Sir John Danvers (see p. 935), the post was one of great prestige. As holder of "the finest place in the university, though not the gainfulest," he explained with boyish pride, the incumbent "writes all the university letters, makes all the orations, be it to king, prince, or whatever comes to the university," and with his social and other perquisites enjoys "suchlike gaynesses which will please a young man well." There can be no doubt that Herbert used all his charm and influence to secure his title to the post, and that he was much elated when, in 1620, his efforts were successful.

The next few years were gay and busy and productive. As early as 1612 he had shown his prowess as a Latinist in a brace of elegiac poems on Prince Henry, but as university orator he produced a string of Latin letters and orations, as well as a quantity of commendatory and funereal verse and two substantial poems, *Passio discerpta* (on the Crucifixion) and *Lucus* (a set of epigrams, interspersed with pieces on religion, politics, and morals). Also, he assisted in the translation of Bacon's *Advancement of Learning* for its inclusion in *De augmentis scientiae*. Moreover, if Walton is to be believed, his social and intellectual attractions promptly brought him to the notice of King James and to "a desired friendship" with various political and ecclesiastical grandees. Throughout these dizzy years, adds Walton drily, he "seldom looked towards Cambridge unless the king were there, but then he never failed."

About 1623 the bustling young academic politician turned his hopes to higher, more uncertain things. It was no doubt through the influence of his kinsmen William and Philip Herbert, earls of Pembroke and Montgomery respectively, that he was elected to Parliament as a member from Montgomery in 1624 and again in 1625, almost coincidentally with being granted (1624) a share of the living at Llandinam, Montgomeryshire, by John Williams, the politically astute bishop of Lincoln. But what Walton calls Herbert's "court hopes" fluttered and failed with the old king's death in 1625. Two years before, as university orator, he had been imprudent enough to express his disapproval of Prince Charles' abortive Spanish match and also of his warlike views on foreign policy, and for this and other reasons—including, perhaps, the recent fall from favor of his elder brother Edward—he could look for little from the proud young king.

Thus blocked in politics, he had no place to turn to except the church. Sometime before July 1626—when Bishop Williams bestowed on him a sinecure at Leighton Bromswold, not far from a quasi-monastic community founded by Nicholas Ferrar at Little Gidding in Huntingdonshire—he was ordained a deacon in the Church of England; but perhaps because of his bad health, or doubts about his true vocation, or lack of friends at court, he did not at once proceed to the priesthood. Indeed, for a couple of years (1627–29) he seems almost to have disappeared. In the summer of 1627 he lovingly commemorated his mother's recent death with a group of Greek and Latin poems entitled *Memoriae matris sacrum*, and a few months later (January 1628) he at last resigned the university oratorship that, though once the summit of his hopes, had claimed nothing of his time for several years. It was in this troubled phase, no doubt, that his "many spiritual conflicts" found expression in the anguished lyrics to be included later in *The Temple*. Not even his marriage (March 1629) to Jane Danvers, a relation of his stepfather, seemed to make for any quick improvement, or to ease his doubts and indecision; and so another year went by before there came to him, through the efforts of the fourth earl of Pembroke, the offer of the living of Bemerton St. Andrew and Fuggleston St. Peter just a mile or so from Salisbury. It was in the great cathedral there that Bishop John Davenant (who, incidentally, was Thomas Fuller's uncle and benefactor) presided at his installation on 26 April 1630, and that very night, according to Walton, Herbert told a friend that his satisfaction was complete. "I now look back upon my aspiring thoughts and think myself more happy than if I had attained what then I so ambitiously thirsted for."

In September he was ordained a priest. Thus, as an obscure country parson, Herbert finally found the serenity that he had sought so long in vain. In contrast to his early quick successes that ended in despair, these later years were filled with gentle satisfactions. In Walton's hagiography he is shown to be so punctual in his pastoral duties, so busy with improvements in his little church and rectory, so tireless in good works, and so ceaseless in devotion that, as Walton says, it would require Chrysostom's "eloquence" to describe his holy life. Herbert's new vocation also found expression in his writing. It was in these final years that he translated Luigi Cornaro's *Treatise of Temperance and Sobriety* (1634), supplied a set of annotations for Ferrar's version of the Spanish reformer Juan Valdesso's *Considerations* (1638), collected more than a thousand "Outlandish Proverbs" (which, through devious means, were printed as a part of *Wit's Recreation* in 1640), and wrote *A Priest to the Temple* (1652) wherein, as he himself explained, he tried "to set down the form and character of a true pastor, that I may have a mark to aim at."

But by far the most important labor of these closing years was the completion, revision, and arrangement of the 164 poems (in some 140 different stanzaic patterns) that in 1633 were published as *The Temple*. Herbert's final disposition of these famous lyrics, as Walton tells the story, was itself a votive gesture. Although long plagued by failing health, he himself had made no plans for publication. At last, as he lay dying he handed them to Edmund Duncon, an associate of Ferrar's at Little Gidding. "Sir," he told his visitor,

> I pray deliver this little book to my dear brother Ferrar, and tell him he shall find in it a picture of the many spiritual conflicts that have passed betwixt God and my soul before I could subject mine to the will of Jesus my Master, in whose service I have now found perfect freedom. Desire him to read it; and then, if he can think it may turn to the advantage of any dejected poor soul, let it be made public; if not, let him burn it, for I and it are less than the least of God's mercies.

A few weeks later (1 March 1633) he was dead at thirty-nine.

The "little book" that Herbert sent to Ferrar is probably a small manuscript (MS Jones B 62) now preserved in Dr. Williams' Library, Gordon Square, London. Written by an amanuensis but containing a great many authorial corrections in Herbert's own distinguished hand, it no doubt formed the basis of the handsome fair copy (MS Tanner 307) in the Bodleian Library that Ferrar presumably submitted to the licensers. Although Jones B 62 provides less than half the poems in Tanner 307, it contains five pieces not included in the latter or in the first edition. *The Temple* itself, beautifully produced by Thomas Buck, the printer of Herbert's university, and introduced by Ferrar's affecting tribute to his friend and coreligionist, appeared in 1633. One of the most successful (and influential) books of poetry of the century, it went through thirteen editions by 1709. In 1652 *Herbert's Remains*, with an important biography by Barnabas Oley, provided *A Priest to the Temple* and an enlarged version of "Outlandish Proverbs" entitled *Jacula Prudentum*.

My texts are based (for Herbert's two sonnets to his mother) on Izaak Walton's *Lives*, 1675 (Wing W-672) and (for everything else) on *The Temple. Sacred Poems and Private Ejaculations*, 1633 (STC 13183). Neglected through the eighteenth century, *The Temple* was reprinted at Bristol in 1799. A generation later the collected *Works* appeared (2 vols., 1835–36), but another generation passed before A. B. Grosart published a critical edition (3 vols., 1874). This led on to G. H. Palmer's elaborate but eccentric edition (3 vols., 1905, rev. 1907) and then to F. E. Hutchinson's authoritative *Works* (1941, rev. 1945). Among more recent editions are Helen Gardner's recension of Hutchinson (1961), Mark McCloskey and Paul R. Murphy's *Latin Poetry* (1965), and Joseph H. Summers' *Selected Poetry* (1967). Walton's is, of course, the primary life; it has been supplemented by A. G. Hyde's (1906) and Marchette Chute's (*Two Gentle Men*, 1959). In addition to the standard books on metaphysical poetry listed in the General Bibliography, Section I, which accord Herbert much attention, recent studies include those by Austin Warren (*Rage for Order*, 1948), L. C. Knights (*Explorations*, 1946), and M. M. Mahood (*Poetry and Humanism*, 1950). There are full-length studies by Rosemond Tuve (1952), Summers (1954), Margaret Bottrall (1954), Mary Ellen Rickey (*Utmost Art*, 1966), Arnold Stein (1968), and Freer Coburn (*Music for a King: George Herbert's Style and the Metrical Psalms,* 1972).

FROM IZAAK WALTON'S "LIFE OF HERBERT"

[In 1610, shortly after matriculating at Trinity College, Cambridge, the seventeen-year-old Herbert wrote the following letter to his mother, Lady Danvers]

I fear the heat of my late ague hath dried up those springs by which, scholars say, the Muses use to take up their habitations. However, I need not their help to reprove the vanity of those many love poems that are daily writ and consecrated to Venus, nor to bewail that so few are writ that look towards God and heaven. For my own part, my meaning, dear mother, is in these sonnets to declare my resolution to be that my poor abilities in poetry shall be all and ever consecrated to God's glory. And—

My God, where is that ancient heat towards Thee
  Wherewith whole shoals of martyrs once did burn,
Besides their other flames? Doth poetry
  Wear Venus' livery? only serve her turn?
Why are not sonnets made of Thee, and lays   5
  Upon Thine altar burnt? Cannot Thy love
Heighten a spirit to sound out Thy praise
  As well as any she? Cannot Thy Dove[1]

Outstrip their Cupid easily in flight?
  Or, since Thy ways are deep and still the same,   10
  Will not a verse run smooth that bears Thy name?
Why doth that fire, which by Thy power and might
  Each breast does feel, no braver fuel choose
  Than that which one day worms may chance refuse?

Sure, Lord, there is enough in Thee to dry
  Oceans of ink, for as the Deluge did
Cover the earth, so doth Thy majesty:
  Each cloud distills Thy praise, and doth forbid
Poets to turn it to another use.   5
  Roses and lilies speak Thee, and to make
A pair of cheeks of them is Thy abuse.
  Why should I women's eyes for crystal take?
Such poor invention burns in their low mind
  Whose fire is wild, and doth not upward go   10
  To praise, and on Thee, Lord, some ink bestow.
Open the bones, and you shall nothing find
  In the best face but filth, when, Lord, in Thee
  The beauty lies in the discovery.

WALTON'S LIFE   [1]The Holy Spirit.

from The Temple: Sacred Poems and Private Ejaculations (1633)

THE PRINTERS TO THE READER[1]

The dedication of this work having been made by the author to the Divine Majesty only, how should we now presume to interest any mortal man in the patronage of it? Much less think we it meet to seek the recommendation of the Muses for that which himself was confident to have been inspired by a diviner breath than flows from Helicon. The world therefore shall receive it in that naked simplicity with which he left it, without any addition either of support or ornament, more than is included in itself. We leave it free and unforestalled to every man's judgment, and to the benefit that he shall find by perusal. Only for the clearing of some passages, we have thought it not unfit to make the common reader privy to some few particularities of the condition and disposition of the person.

Being nobly born, and as eminently endued with gifts of the mind, and having by industry and happy education perfected them to that great height of excellency whereof his fellowship of Trinity College in Cambridge and his oratorship in the University, together with that knowledge which the King's court had taken of him, could make relation far above ordinary. Quitting both his deserts and all the opportunities that he had for worldly preferment, he betook himself to the sanctuary and temple of God, choosing rather to serve at God's altar than to seek the honor of state employments. As for those inward enforcements to this course (for outward there was none), which many of these

ensuing verses bear witness of, they detract not from the freedom, but add to the honor of this resolution in him. As God had enabled him, so He accounted him meet not only to be called, but to be compelled to this service; wherein his faithful discharge was such as may make him justly a companion to the primitive saints and a pattern or more for the age he lived in.

To testify his independency upon all others, and to quicken his diligence in this kind, he used in his ordinary speech, when he made mention of the blessed name of our Lord and Saviour, Jesus Christ, to add, "My Master."

Next God, he loved that which God himself hath magnified above all things, that is, His Word: so as he hath been heard to make solemn protestation that he would not part with one leaf thereof for the whole world, if it were offered him in exchange.

His obedience and conformity to the church and the discipline thereof was singularly remarkable. Though he abounded in private devotions, yet went he every morning

TO THE READER   [1]Izaak Walton ascribes this preface to Nicholas Ferrar (1592–1637), the spiritual leader of an austere conventual community at Little Gidding in Huntingdonshire that was known derisively as the Protestant Nunnery. It was to Ferrar that the dying Herbert sent the manuscript of *The Temple* with the request that he read it, "and then, if he can think it may turn to the advantage of any dejected poor soul, let it be made public; if not, let him burn it, for I and it are less than the least of God's mercies."

and evening with his family to the church; and by his example, exhortations, and encouragements drew the greater part of his parishioners to accompany him daily in the public celebration of divine service.

As for worldly matters, his love and esteem to them was so little as no man can more ambitiously seek than he did earnestly endeavor the resignation of an eccelesiastical dignity which he was possessor of. But God permitted not the accomplishment of this desire, having ordained him His instrument for re-edifying of the church belonging there-unto, that had lain ruinated almost twenty years.[2] The reparation whereof, having been uneffectually attempted by public collections, was in the end by his own and some few others' private free-will offerings successfully effected. With the remembrance whereof, as of an especial good work, when a friend went about to comfort him on his deathbed, he made answer, "It is a good work if it be sprinkled with the blood of Christ." Otherwise than in this respect he could find nothing to glory or comfort himself with, neither in this nor in any other thing.

And these are but a few of many that might be said, which we have chosen to premise as a glance to some parts of the ensuing book, and for an example to the reader. We conclude all with his own motto, with which he used to conclude all things that might seem to tend any way to his own honor:

"Less than the least of God's mercies."

The Church Porch

PERIRRHANTERIUM[1]

Thou, whose sweet youth and early hopes enhance
Thy rate and price, and mark thee for a treasure,
Harken unto a verser who may chance
Rhyme thee to good and make a bait of pleasure.
   A verse may find him who a sermon flies,   5
   And turn delight into a sacrifice.

Beware of lust: it doth pollute and foul
Whom God in baptism wash'd with His own blood.
It blots thy lesson written in thy soul;
The holy lines cannot be understood.   10
   How dare those eyes upon a Bible look,
   Much less towards God, whose lust is all their book?

Abstain wholly, or wed. Thy bounteous Lord
Allows thee choice of paths: take no byways,
But gladly welcome what He doth afford,   15
Not grudging that thy lust hath bounds and stays.
   Continence hath his joy: weigh both, and so
   If rottenness have more, let heaven go.

    . . . . .

Drink not the third glass, which thou canst not tame   25
When once it is within thee; but before
Mayst rule it as thou list, and pour the shame

Which it would pour on thee upon the floor.
   It is most just to throw that on the ground
   Which would throw me there if I keep the round.[2]   30

    . . . . .

Lie not, but let thy heart be true to God,
Thy mouth to it, thy actions to them both:
Cowards tell lies, and those that fear the rod;   75
The stormy-working soul spits lies and froth.
   Dare to be true. Nothing can need a lie:
   A fault which needs it most grows two thereby.

Fly idleness, which yet thou canst not fly
By dressing, mistressing, and compliment.[3]   80
If those take up thy day, the sun will cry
Against thee, for his light was only lent.
   God gave thy soul brave wings; put not those feathers
   Into a bed to sleep out all ill weathers.

Art thou a magistrate? then be severe;   85
If studious, copy fair what time hath blurr'd;
Redeem truth from his jaws; if soldier,
Chase brave employments with a naked sword
   Throughout the world. Fool not, for all may have,
   If they dare try, a glorious life or grave.   90

O England, full of sin but most of sloth,
Spit out thy phlegm and fill thy breast with glory:
Thy gentry bleats as if thy native cloth
Transfus'd a sheepishness into thy story:
   Not that they all are so, but that the most   95
   Are gone to grass, and in the pasture lost.

This loss springs chiefly from our education.
Some till their ground but let weeds choke their son;
Some mark a partridge, never their child's fashion;[4]
Some ship them over,[5] and the thing is done.   100
   Study this art, make it thy great design,
   And if God's image move thee not, let thine.

    . . . . .

In conversation[6] boldness now bears sway;   205
But know that nothing can so foolish be
As empty boldness; therefore first assay
To stuff thy mind with solid bravery,[7]
   Then march on gallant: get substantial worth.
   Boldness gilds finely, and will set it forth.   210

---

[2]*As for worldly...years*: Unable to transfer to Ferrar his lucrative "ecclesiastical dignity" as prebendary of Leighton Ecclesia in Lincoln Cathedral, Herbert used the proceeds to assist in the restoration of the dilapidated church at Leighton Bromswold, not far from Little Gidding.

PERIRRHANTERIUM [1]An instrument for sprinkling holy water (Latin *aspergillum*).
[2]*Keep the round*: refill my glass when the bottle is passed.
[3]*Dressing...compliment*: fine clothes, courtship, and flattery. Herbert borrowed this line (slightly altered) from Donne's "To Mr. Tilman after He Had Taken Orders." [4]Behavior.
[5]Send them abroad. [6]Demeanor, social behavior.
[7]Things of genuine worth.

Be sweet to all. Is thy complexion sour?
Then keep such company; make them thy allay.[8]
Get a sharp wife, a servant that will lour.
A stumbler stumbles least in rugged way.
   Command thyself in chief. He life's war knows   215
   Whom all his passions follow as he goes.

Catch not at quarrels. He that dares not speak
Plainly and home[9] is coward of the two.
Think not thy fame at ev'ry twitch will break;
By great deeds show that thou canst little[10] do,   220
   And do them not: that shall thy wisdom be,
   And change thy temperance into bravery.

. . . . . .

Wit's an unruly engine,[11] wildly striking   241
Sometimes a friend, sometimes the engineer.
Hast thou the knack? Pamper it not with liking;
But if thou want it, buy it not too dear.
   Many, affecting wit beyond their power,   245
   Have got to be a dear fool for an hour.

A sad,[12] wise valor is the brave complexion
That leads the van and swallows up the cities.
The giggler is a milkmaid whom infection
Or a fir'd beacon frighteth from his ditties.   250
   Then he's the sport; the mirth then in him rests,
   And the sad man is cock of all his jests.

. . . . . .

Though private prayer be a brave design,   397
Yet public hath more promises, more love,
And love's a weight to hearts, to eyes a sign.
We all are but cold suitors; let us move   400
   Where it is warmest. Leave thy six and seven;
   Pray with the most, for where most pray is heaven.

When once thy foot enters the church, be bare.
God is more there than thou, for thou art there
Only by His permission. Then beware,   405
And make thyself all reverence and fear.
   Kneeling ne'er spoiled silk stockings; quit thy state.
   All equal are within the church's gate.

Resort to sermons, but to prayers most:
Praying's the end of preaching. O be drest;   410
Stay not for th' other pin: why, thou hast lost
A joy for it worth worlds. Thus hell doth jest
   Away thy blessings, and extremely flout thee,
   Thy clothes being fast, but thy soul loose about thee.

. . . . . .

Sum up at night what thou hast done by day,   451
And in the morning what thou hast to do.
Dress and undress thy soul: mark the decay
And growth of it. If with thy watch that too
   Be down, then wind up both; since we shall be   455
   Most surely judged, make thy accounts agree.

In brief, acquit thee bravely; play the man.
Look not on pleasures as they come, but go.
Defer not the least virtue: life's poor span
Make not an ell by trifling in thy woe.   460
   If thou do ill, the joy fades, not the pains;
   If well, the pain doth fade, the joy remains.

SUPERLIMINARE[1]

Thou whom the former precepts have
Sprinkled[2] and taught how to behave
Thyself in church, approach and taste
The church's mystical repast.

●

Avoid, Profaneness! Come not here!
Nothing but holy, pure, and clear,
Or that which groaneth to be so,
May at his peril further go.

THE CHURCH

THE ALTAR

   A broken ALTAR, Lord, thy servant rears,
   Made of a heart and cemented[1] with tears,
     Whose parts are as Thy hand did frame:
     No workman's tool hath touch'd the same.
       A HEART alone   5
       Is such a stone
       As nothing but
       Thy pow'r doth cut.
       Wherefore each part
       Of my hard heart   10
       Meets in this frame
       To praise Thy name,
    That if I chance to hold my peace
    These stones to praise Thee may not cease.
   O let Thy blessed SACRIFICE be mine,   15
   And sanctify this ALTAR to be thine.

THE REPRISAL

   I have consider'd it, and find
There is no dealing with Thy mighty passion,
For though I die for Thee, I am behind:
   My sins deserve the condemnation.

[8]Abatement, alleviation (i.e., if you are with sour people your own sourness will be less apparent.)
[9]Directly to the point aimed at.   [10]Lesser deeds.
[11]Product of ingenuity.   [12]Sober.
SUPERLIMINARE [1]"Threshold." In the 1633 edition the two quatrains that follow are separated by a heavy line to make graphic the separation between those admitted and those refused.
[2]*Thou whom...sprinkled*: i.e., you who have been purified (*sprinkled*) by reading "The Church Porch."
THE ALTAR [1]Accented on the first syllable.

O make me innocent, that I
May give a disentangled state and free;
And yet Thy wounds still my attempts defy,
   For by Thy death I die for Thee.   5

Ah! was it not enough that Thou
By Thy eternal glory didst outgo me?   10
Couldst Thou not grief's sad conquests me allow,
   But in all vict'ries overthrow me?

Yet by confession will I come
Into Thy[1] conquest. Though I can do nought
Against Thee, in Thee I will overcome   15
   The man who once against Thee fought.

THE AGONY

Philosophers have measur'd mountains,
Fathom'd the depths of seas, of states, and kings,
Walk'd with a staff[1] to heav'n, and traced fountains;[2]
   But there are two vast, spacious things,
The which to measure it doth more behove,   5
Yet few there are that sound them: Sin and Love.

Who would know Sin, let him repair
Unto Mount Olivet;[3] there shall he see
A man so wrung with pains that all his hair,
   His skin, his garments bloody be.   10
Sin is that press and vise which forceth pain
To hunt his cruel food through ev'ry vein.

Who knows not Love, let him assay
And taste that juice which on the cross a pike
Did set again abroach; then let him say   15
   If ever he did taste the like.
Love is that liquor sweet and most divine
Which my God feels as blood, but I as wine.

REDEMPTION

Having been tenant long to a rich Lord,
   Not thriving, I resolved to be bold
   And make a suit unto Him, to afford
A new small-rented lease, and cancel th' old.
In heaven at His manor I him sought: 5
   They told me there that He was lately gone
   About some land which He had dearly bought
Long since on earth, to take possession.
I straight return'd and knowing His great birth,
   Sought Him accordingly in great resorts,   10
   In cities, theaters, gardens, parks, and courts.
At length I heard a ragged noise and mirth
   Of thieves and murderers: there I Him espied,
   Who straight "Your suit is granted" said, and died.

SEPULCHER

O blessed body! Whither art Thou thrown?
No lodging for Thee but a cold hard stone?

So many hearts on earth, and yet not one
          Receive Thee?
Sure there is room within our hearts good store,   5
For they can lodge transgressions by the score;
Thousands of toys dwell there, yet out of door
          They leave Thee.

But that which shows them large shows them unfit.
Whatever sin did this pure rock commit   10
Which holds Thee now? Who hath indicted it
          Of murder?

Where our hard hearts have took up stones to brain Thee,
And, missing this, most falsely did arraign Thee;
Only these stones in quiet entertain Thee,   15
          And order.

And as of old the Law by heav'nly art
Was writ in stone, so Thou, which also art
The letter of the Word,[1] find'st no fit heart
          To hold Thee.   20

Yet do we still persist as we began,
And so should perish, but that nothing can,
Though it be cold, hard, foul, from loving man
          Withhold Thee.

EASTER

Rise, heart; thy Lord is risen. Sing His praise
          Without delays,
Who takes thee by the hand, that thou likewise
          With Him mayst rise:
That, as His death calcined[1] thee to dust,   5
His life may make thee gold, and, much more, just.

Awake, my lute, and struggle for thy part
          With all thy art.
The cross taught all wood to resound His name
          Who bore the same.   10
His stretch'd sinews taught all strings what key
Is best to celebrate this most high day.

Consort both heart and lute, and twist a song
          Pleasant and long;
Or since all music is but three parts vied   15
          And multiplied,[2]
O let Thy blessed Spirit bear a part,
And make up our defects with His sweet art.

      I got me flowers to straw[3] Thy way;
      I got me boughs off many'a tree;   20

THE REPRISAL [1]Text *the*. The emendation is supported by both the
Bodleian and Williams manuscripts.
THE AGONY [1]1. Stick; 2. measuring rod.
[2]I.e., followed water-courses.
[3]The Mount of Olives, scene of Christ's agony.
SEPULCHER [1]*And as of old . . . word*: Paul (2 Corinthians 3.3) says
that the epistle of Christ is written "not in tables of stone but in
the fleshy tables of the heart."
EASTER [1]Reduced by fire to powder.
[2]*Three parts vied and multiplied*: i.e., constructed on the triad.
[3]Strew.

But Thou wast up by break of day,
And broughtst Thy sweets along with Thee.

The sun arising in the east,
Though he give light, and th' east perfume,
If they should offer to contest   25
With Thy arising, they presume.

Can there be any day but this,
Though many suns to shine endeavor?
We count three hundred,[4] but we miss:
There is but one, and that one ever.   30

EASTER WINGS

Lord, who createdst man in wealth and store,
  Though foolishly he lost the same,
    Decaying more and more
      Till he became
        Most poor: 5
        With Thee
      O let me rise
    As larks, harmoniously,
  And sing this day Thy victories:
Then shall the fall further the flight in me.   10

My tender age in sorrow did begin,
  And still with sickness and shame
    Thou didst so punish sin
      That I became
        Most thin.   15
        With Thee
      Let me combine,
    And feel this day Thy victory:
  For if I imp[1] my wing on thine,
Affliction shall advance the flight in me.   20

SIN (I)

Lord, with what care hast thou begirt us round!
  Parents first season us; then schoolmasters
  Deliver us to laws; they send us bound
To rules of reason, holy messengers,
Pulpits and Sundays, sorrow dogging sin,   5
Afflictions sorted, anguish of all sizes,
Fine nets and stratagems to catch us in,
Bibles laid open, millions of surprises,
Blessings beforehand, ties of gratefulness,
  The sound of glory ringing in our ears: 10
  Without, our shame; within, our consciences;
Angels and grace, eternal hopes and fears.
  Yet all these fences and their whole array
  One cunning bosom[1] sin blows quite away.

AFFLICTION (I)

When first Thou didst entice to Thee my heart,
              I thought the service brave;
So many joys I writ down for my part,
              Besides what I might have

Out of my stock of natural delights,   5
Augmented with Thy gracious benefits.

I looked on Thy furniture so fine,
              And made it fine to me;
Thy glorious household-stuff did me entwine,
              And 'tice me unto Thee.   10
Such stars I counted mine: both heav'n and earth
Paid me my wages in a world of mirth.

What pleasures could I want whose King I served?
              Where joys my fellows were?
Thus argu'd into hopes, my thoughts reserved   15
              No place for grief or fear.
Therefore my sudden soul caught at the place,
And made her youth and fierceness seek Thy face.

At first Thou gav'st me milk and sweetnesses;
              I had my wish and way: 20
My days were straw'd with flow'rs and happiness;
              There was no month but May.
But with my years sorrow did twist and grow,
And made a party unawares for woe.

My flesh began[1] unto my soul in pain,   25
              "Sicknesses cleave my bones;
Consuming agues dwell in ev'ry vein,
              And tune my breath to groans."
Sorrow was all my soul; I scarce believed,
Till grief did tell me roundly, that I lived.   30

When I got health, Thou took'st away my life,
              And more, for my friends die;
My mirth and edge was lost; a blunted knife
              Was of more use than I.
Thus thin and lean, without a fence or friend,   35
I was blown through with ev'ry storm and wind.

Whereas my birth and spirit rather took
              The way that takes the town,
Thou didst betray me to a ling'ring book,
              And wrap me in a gown.   40
I was entangled in the world of strife,
Before I had the power to change my life.

Yet for I threat'ned oft the siege to raise,
              Not simp'ring all mine age,
Thou often didst with academic praise   45
              Melt and dissolve my rage.
I took Thy sweet'ned pill, till I came where[2]
I could not go away, nor persevere.

Yet lest perchance I should too happy be
              In my unhappiness,   50

[4]The days of the year in round numbers.
EASTER WINGS [1]Regraft the feathers in a damaged wing (a term
from falconry).
SIN(I) [1]Secret.
AFFLICTION(I) [1]I.e., began to complain.
[2]Text *neare*, but the emendation is supported by the Williams
manuscript and by an ambiguous correction of *neare* to *where* in
the Bodleian manuscript.

Turning my purge to food, Thou throwest me
    Into more sicknesses.
Thus doth Thy power cross-bias me,[3] not making
Thine own gift good, yet me from my ways taking.

Now I am here, what Thou wilt do with me   55
    None of my books will show:
I read, and sigh, and wish I were a tree;
    For sure then I should grow
To fruit or shade: at least some bird would trust
Her household to me, and I should be just.[4]   60

Yet, though Thou troublest me, I must be meek;
    In weakness must be stout.
Well, I will change the service, and go seek
    Some other master out.
Ah, my dear God! though I am clean forgot,   65
Let me not love Thee if I love Thee not.

PRAYER (I)

Prayer: the church's banquet, angels' age,[1]
    God's breath in man returning to his birth,[2]
    The soul in paraphrase,[3] heart in pilgrimage,
The Christian plummet sounding heav'n and earth;
Engine against th' Almighty, sinners' tow'r,   5
    Reversed thunder, Christ-side-piercing spear,
    The six-days world transposing[4] in an hour,
A kind of tune which all things hear and fear;
Softness and peace and joy and love and bliss,
    Exalted manna, gladness of the best,   10
    Heaven in ordinary,[5] man well drest,
The milky way, the bird of paradise,
    Church bells beyond the stars heard, the soul's blood.
    The land of spices: something understood.

THE HOLY COMMUNION

Not in rich furniture or fine array,
    Nor in a wedge of gold,
    Thou, who for[1] me wast sold,
To me dost now Thyself convey;
For so Thou shouldst without me still have been,   5
    Leaving within me sin:

But by the way of nourishment and strength
    Thou creep'st into my breast;
    Making Thy way my rest,
And Thy small quantities my length: 10
Which spread their forces into every part,
    Meeting sin's force and art,

Yet can these not get over to my soul,
    Leaping the wall that parts
    Our souls and fleshly hearts;   15
But as th' outworks, they may control
My rebel flesh and, carrying Thy name,
    Affright both sin and shame.

Only Thy grace, which with these elements[2] comes,
    Knoweth the ready way,   20

And hath the privy key,
    Op'ning the soul's most subtile rooms;
While those[3] to spirits refin'd, at door attend
    Dispatches from their friend.

Give me my captive soul, or take   25
    My body also thither.
Another lift like this will make
    Them both to be together.

Before that sin turn'd flesh to stone
    And all our lump to leaven,   30
A fervent sigh might well have blown
    Our innocent earth to heaven.

For sure when Adam did not know
    To sin, or sin to smother,
He might to heav'n from paradise go   35
    As from one room t' another.

Thou hast restor'd us to this ease
    By this Thy heav'nly blood,
Which I can go to, when I please,
    And leave th' earth to their food.   40

LOVE

I

Immortal Love, author of this great frame,
    Sprung from that beauty which can never fade,
    How hath man parcel'd out thy glorious name,
And thrown it on that dust which thou hast made,
While mortal love doth all the title gain!   5
    Which siding with invention, they together
    Bear all the sway, possessing heart and brain
(Thy workmanship), and give thee share in neither.
    Wit fancies beauty, beauty raiseth wit:
    The world is theirs; they two play out the game,   10
    Thou standing by: and though thy glorious name
Wrought our deliverance from th' infernal pit,
    Who sings thy praise? only a scarf or glove
    Doth warm our hands, and make them write of love.

II

Immortal Heat, O let thy greater flame
    Attract the lesser to it: let those fires,
    Which shall consume the world, first make it tame;
And kindle in our hearts such true desires
As may consume our lusts, and make thee way.   5
    Then shall our hearts pant thee; then shall our brain

[3]Deflect me from my natural bent (a term from bowls).
[4]Faithful.
PRAYER(I) [1]I.e., eternity (for angels are immortal).
[2]Its source. [3]I.e., amplified and explained. [4]Changing.
[5]I.e., regular. An *ordinary* was a public meal accessible to anybody
at a fixed price.
THE HOLY COMMUNION [1]Text *from*, but the emendation is supported by the Bodleian manuscript.
[2]The bread and wine of the communion service.
[3]Those elements.

All her invention on thine altar lay,
And there in hymns send back thy fire again.
Our eyes shall see thee, which before saw dust,
    Dust blown by wit till that they both were blind.   10
Thou shalt recover all thy goods in kind,
Who wert disseized[1] by usurping lust.
All knees shall bow to thee; all wits shall rise,
    And praise Him who did make and mend our eyes.

THE TEMPER (I)[1]

How should I praise thee, Lord! how should my rhymes
    Gladly engrave Thy love in steel,
If what my soul doth feel sometimes,
    My soul might ever feel!

Although there were some forty heav'ns, or more,   5
    Sometimes I peer above them all;
Sometimes I hardly reach a score,
    Sometimes to hell I fall.

O rack me not to such a vast extent;
    Those distances belong to Thee: 10
The world's too little for Thy tent,
    A grave too big for me.

Wilt Thou meet arms with man, that Thou dost stretch
    A crumb of dust from heav'n to hell?
Will great God measure with a wretch?   15
    Shall he Thy stature spell?[2]

O let me, when Thy roof my soul hath hid,
    O let me roost and nestle there:
Then of a sinner Thou art rid,
    And I of hope and fear.   20

Yet take Thy way, for sure Thy way is best:
    Stretch or contract me, Thy poor debtor:
This is but tuning of my breast
    To make the music better.

Whether I fly with angels, fall with dust,   25
    Thy hands made both, and I am there:
Thy power and love, my love and trust
    Make one place ev'rywhere.

THE TEMPER (II)

It cannot be. Where is that mighty joy
    Which just now took up all my heart?
Lord, if Thou must needs use Thy dart,
Save that[1] and me, or sin for both destroy.

The grosser world stands to Thy word and art,   5
    But Thy diviner world of grace
Thou suddenly dost raise and race,[2]
And ev'ry day a new Creator art.

O fix Thy chair of grace,[3] that all my powers
    May also fix their reverence: 10
For when Thou dost depart from hence,
They grow unruly, and sit in Thy bowers.

Scatter or bind them all to bend to Thee:
    Though elements change, and heaven move,
    Let not Thy higher court remove,   15
But keep a standing majesty in me.

JORDAN (I)[1]

Who says that fictions only and false hair
Become a verse? Is there in truth no beauty?
Is all good structure in a winding stair?
May no lines pass except they do their duty
    Not to a true but painted chair?[2]   5

Is it no verse except "enchanted groves"
And "sudden arbors" shadow coarse-spun lines?
Must "purling streams" refresh a lover's loves?[3]
Must all be veil'd, while he that reads, divines,
    Catching the sense at two removes?   10

Shepherds are honest people; let them sing:
Riddle who list, for me, and pull for prime:[4]
I envy no man's nightingale or spring,
Nor let them punish me with loss of rhyme,
    Who plainly say, My God, My King.   15

GRACE

My stock[1] lies dead, and no increase
Doth my dull husbandry improve.
O let Thy graces without cease
    Drop from above!

If still the sun should hide his face,   5
Thy house would but a dungeon prove,
Thy works night's captives. O let grace
    Drop from above!

The dew doth ev'ry morning fall,
And shall the dew outstrip Thy Dove?   10
The dew, for which grass cannot call,
    Drop from above.

LOVE II [1]Dispossessed (a legal term).
THE TEMPER(I) [1]The title of this and the following poem (both of them prayers) perhaps refers to the suppliant's wished-for spiritual poise between the extremes of exaltation and despair.
[2]Comprehend.
THE TEMPER(II) [1]I.e., "that mighty joy."
[2]Raze. [3]*Chair of grace*: throne.
JORDAN (I) [1]The ambiguous title is perhaps intended to contrast the River Jordan (where Jesus was baptized) as the symbol of religious poetry with the springs of Helicon as the symbol of secular poetry.
[2]Herbert is perhaps thinking of the "chair of grace" in "The Temper (II)," which he had presented as a symbol of divine and therefore authentic regality.
[3]*Is it...loves*: Herbert is parodying the clichés of amatory verse.
[4]*Riddle...Prime*: i.e., let other poets seek success with artifice and verbal ingenuity. To *pull for prime* was to draw for a winning hand in the card game of primero.
GRACE [1]The trunk of a tree. Herbert is perhaps remembering Job 14.7–9.

Death is still working like a mole,
And digs my grave at each remove.
Let grace work too, and on my soul   15
    Drop from above.

Sin is still hammering my heart
Unto a hardness, void of love.
Let suppling grace, to cross his art,[2]
    Drop from above.   20

O come! for Thou dost know the way;
Or if to me Thou wilt not move,
Remove me where I need not say,
    "Drop from above."

CHURCH MONUMENTS

While that my soul repairs to her devotion,
Here I intomb my flesh, that it betimes
May take acquaintance of this heap of dust,
To which the blast of death's incessant motion,
Fed with the exhalation of our crimes,   5
Drives all at last. Therefore I gladly trust

My body to this school, that it may learn
To spell his elements,[1] and find his birth
Written in dusty heraldry and lines,
Which dissolution sure doth best discern,   10
Comparing dust with dust, and earth with earth.
These laugh at jet and marble put for signs,

To sever the good fellowship of dust,
And spoil the meeting. What shall point out them
When they shall bow, and kneel, and fall down flat   15
To kiss those heaps, which now they have in trust?
Dear flesh, while I do pray, learn here thy stem
And true descent, that when thou shalt grow fat

And wanton in thy cravings, thou may'st know
That flesh is but the glass which holds the dust   20
That measures all our time, which also shall
Be crumbled into dust. Mark here below
How tame these ashes are, how free from lust,
That thou may'st fit thyself against thy fall.

CHURCH MUSIC

Sweetest of sweets, I thank you: when displeasure
    Did through my body wound my mind,
You took me thence, and in your house of pleasure
    A dainty lodging me assign'd.

Now I in you without a body move,   5
    Rising and falling with your wings:
We both together sweetly live and love,
    Yet say sometimes, "God help poor kings."
Comfort, I'll die; for if you post from me,
    Sure I shall do so, and much more;   10
But if I travel in your company,
    You know the way to heaven's door.

THE CHURCH FLOOR

Mark you the floor? that square and speckled stone,
    Which looks so firm and strong,
        Is *Patience;*

And th' other black and grave, wherewith each one
    Is checker'd all along,   5
        Humility;

The gentle rising, which on either hand
    Leads to the choir above,
        Is *Confidence;*

But the sweet cement, which in one sure band   10
    Ties the whole frame, is *Love*
        And *Charity*.

    Hither sometimes Sin steals, and stains
    The marble's neat and curious veins;
But all is cleansed when the marble weeps.   15
    Sometimes Death, puffing at the door,
    Blows all the dust about the floor;
But while he thinks to spoil the room, he sweeps.
    Bless'd be the Architect, whose art
    Could build so strong in a weak heart.   20

THE WINDOWS

Lord, how can man preach Thy eternal word?
    He is a brittle, crazy[1] glass;
Yet in Thy temple Thou dost him afford
    This glorious and transcendent place,
    To be a window, through Thy grace.   5

But when Thou dost anneal[2] in glass Thy story,
    Making Thy life to shine within
The holy preacher's, then the light and glory
    More rev'rend grows, and more doth win,
    Which else shows wat'rish, bleak, and thin.   10

Doctrine and life, colors and light, in one
    When they combine and mingle, bring
A strong regard and awe; but speech alone
    Doth vanish like a flaring thing,
    And in the ear, not conscience, ring.   15

TRINITY SUNDAY

Lord, who hast form'd me out of mud,
    And hast redeem'd me through Thy blood,
    And sanctifi'd me to do good,

Purge all my sins done heretofore:
    For I confess my heavy score,[1]   5
    And I will strive to sin no more.

[2]*Cross his art*: thwart the stratagems of Sin.
CHURCH MONUMENTS [1]*Spell his elements*: i.e., learn his rules.
THE WINDOWS [1]Cracked, flawed.
[2]Set the colors in glass by heat.
TRINITY SUNDAY [1]Record of indebtedness.

Enrich my heart, mouth, hands in me,
    With faith, with hope, with charity;
    That I may run, rise, rest with Thee.

SUNDAY

O day most calm, most bright,
The fruit of this, the next world's bud,
Th' indorsement of supreme delight,
Writ by a friend, and with his blood;
The couch of time; care's balm and bay:[1]   5
    The week were dark but for thy light:
    Thy torch doth show the way.

The other days and thou
Make up one man, whose face thou art,
Knocking at heaven with thy brow;   10
The worky-days are the back part:
The burden of the week lies there,
Making the whole to stoop and bow,
    Till thy release appear.

Man had straight forward gone   15
To endless death, but thou dost pull
And turn us round to look on one,
Whom, if we were not very dull,
We could not choose but look on still;
Since there is no place so alone,   20
    The which He doth not fill.

Sundays the pillars are
On which heav'n's palace arched lies;
The other days fill up the spare
And hollow room with vanities.   25
They are the fruitful beds and borders
In God's rich garden: that is bare,
    Which parts their ranks and orders.[2]

The Sundays of man's life,
Threaded together on time's string,   30
Make bracelets to adorn the wife
Of the eternal glorious King.
On Sunday heaven's gate stands ope;
Blessings are plentiful and rife,
    More plentiful than hope.[3]   35

This day my Saviour rose,
And did enclose this light for His,
That, as each beast his manger knows,
Man might not of his fodder miss.
Christ hath took in[4] this piece of ground,   40
And made a garden there for those
    Who want herbs for their wound.

The rest of our creation[5]
Our great Redeemer did remove
With the same shake[6] which at His passion   45
Did th' earth and all things with it move.
As Samson bore the doors away,[7]
Christ's hands, though nail'd, wrought our salvation,
    And did unhinge that day.

The brightness of that day   50
We sullied by our foul offense,
Wherefore that robe we cast away,
Having a new at His expense,
Whose drops of blood paid the full price
That was requir'd to make us gay   55
    And fit for paradise.

Thou art a day of mirth,
And where the weekdays trail on ground,
Thy flight is higher, as thy birth.
O let me take thee at the bound,   60
Leaping with thee from sev'n to sev'n,
Till that we both, being toss'd from earth,
    Fly hand in hand to heav'n!

DENIAL

When my devotions could not pierce
        Thy silent ears,
Then was my heart broken, as was my verse;
    My breast was full of fears
            And disorder.   5

My bent thoughts, like a brittle bow,
        Did fly asunder:
Each took his way; some would to pleasures go,
    Some to the wars and thunder
            Of alarms.   10

"As good go any where," they say,
        "As to benumb
Both knees and heart in crying night and day,
    'Come, come, my God, O come,'
            But no hearing."   15

O that Thou shouldst give dust a tongue
        To cry to Thee,
And then not hear it crying! All day long
    My heart was in my knee,
            But no hearing.   20

Therefore my soul lay out of sight,
        Untuned, unstrung;
My feeble spirit, unable to look right,
    Like a nipp'd blossom, hung
            Discontented.   25

O cheer and tune my heartless breast,
        Defer no time;

SUNDAY   [1] I.e., cure.
[2] *They are...orders*: in "God's rich garden" Sundays are the "fruitful beds and borders" separated by the bare spaces of the weekdays.
[3] *The Sundays...hope*: according to Walton, on the Sunday before his death Herbert "rose suddenly from his bed or couch, called for one of his instruments," and sang this stanza.
[4] Enclosed (for cultivation).
[5] *The rest...creation*: i.e., the Jewish sabbath, commemorating God's resting on the seventh day of the creation.   [6] Earthquake.
[7] *As...away*: for Samson's removal of the city gates of Gaza see Judges 16.1–3.

That so Thy favors granting my request,
    They and my mind may chime,
              And mend my rime.   30

COLOSSIANS 3.3. OUR LIFE IS HID WITH CHRIST IN GOD

My words and thoughts do both express this notion,
That *Life* hath with the sun a double motion.[1]
The first *Is* straight, and our diurnal friend,
The other *Hid*, and doth obliquely[2] bend.
One life is wrapt *In* flesh, and tends to earth;   5
The other winds towards *Him* whose happy birth
Taught me to live here so *That* still one eye
Should aim and shoot at that which *Is* on high,
Quitting with daily labor all *My* pleasure,   10
To gain at harvest an eternal *Treasure*.

VANITY (I)

      The fleet astronomer can bore
And thread the spheres with his quick-piercing mind:
He views their stations, walks from door to door,
      Surveys, as if he had design'd
To make a purchase there: he sees their dances,   5
      And knoweth long before
Both their full-ey'd aspects[1] and secret glances.

      The nimble diver with his side
Cuts through the working waves that he may fetch
His dearly-earned pearl, which God did hide   10
      On purpose from the vent'rous wretch,
That he might save his life and also hers,
      Who with excessive pride
Her own destruction and his danger wears.

      The subtle chymic can devest   15
And strip the creature naked, till he find
The callow principles within their nest:[2]
      There he imparts to them his mind,
Admitted to their bedchamber, before
      They appear trim and drest   20
To ordinary suitors at the door.

      What hath not man sought out and found,
But his dear God? who yet His glorious law
Embosoms in us, mellowing the ground
      With show'rs and frosts, with love and awe,   25
So that we need not say, "Where's this command?"
      Poor man, thou searchest round
To find out *death*, but missest *life* at hand.

VIRTUE

Sweet day, so cool, so calm, so bright,
    The bridal of the earth and sky:
The dew shall weep thy fall tonight,
      For thou must die.

Sweet rose, whose hue angry and brave[1]   5
Bids the rash gazer wipe his eye:

Thy root is ever in its grave,
      And thou must die.

Sweet spring, full of sweet days and roses,
A box where sweets[2] compacted lie;
My music shows ye have your closes,[3]
      And all must die.

Only a sweet and virtuous soul,
Like seasoned timber, never gives;
But though the whole world turn to coal,[4]   15
      Then chiefly lives.

MATTHEW 13.[45]. THE PEARL

I know the ways of learning: both the head
And pipes that feed the press,[1] and make it run;
What reason hath from nature borrowed,
Or of itself, like a good huswife, spun
In laws and policy; what the stars conspire,   5
What willing nature speaks, what forc'd by fire;
Both th' old discoveries and the new-found seas,
The stock and surplus, cause and history:
All these stand open, or I have the keys—
      Yet I love Thee.   10

I know the ways of honor: what maintains
The quick returns of courtesy and wit;
In vies of favors whether[2] party gains,
When glory swells the heart, and moldeth it
To all expressions both of hand and eye,   15
Which on the world a true-love-knot may tie,
And bear the bundle, wheresoe'er it goes;[3]
How many drams of spirit there must be
To sell my life unto my friends or foes—
      Yet I love Thee.   20

I know the ways of pleasure: the sweet strains,
The lullings and the relishes of it;
The propositions of hot blood and brains;
What mirth and music mean; what love and wit
Have done these twenty hundred years, and more;   25

COLOSSIANS 3.3 [1]I.e., the *diurnal* motion from east to west and the annual motion from west to east.
[2]It will be noted that the hidden message (in italics) runs *obliquely* through the poem.

VANITY (I) [1]In astronomy, the relative positions of the planets, which were thought to determine their influence on terrestrial matters. Here the word is accented on the second syllable.
[2]*The subtle...nest*: the chemist (*chymic*) can unclothe (*devest*) an object of its outward traits and then, through study and analysis, comprehend its naked (*callow* = featherless) essence.

VIRTUE [1]*Angry and brave*: red (flushed) and splendid.
[2]Perfumes. [3]Musical cadences.
[4]*But though...coal*: i.e., although everything will be reduced to ashes in the final conflagration.

THE PEARL [1]*Head...press*: it has been variously suggested that this puzzling figure refers to an olive press and to a printing press.
[2]Which of two.
[3]*Which...goes*: who for reasons of ambition and self-interest caters to the fashionable world, which he follows like a servant.

I know the projects of unbridled store:
My stuff is flesh, not brass; my senses live,
And grumble oft that they have more in me
Than he[4] that curbs them, being but one to five—
        Yet I love Thee.   30

I know all these, and have them in my hand:
Therefore not seeled,[5] but with open eyes
I fly to Thee, and fully understand
Both the main sale and the commodities,
And at what rate and price I have Thy love,   35
With all the circumstances that may move;
Yet through these labyrinths, not my groveling wit,
But Thy silk twist let down from heav'n to me
Did both conduct and teach me how by it
        To climb to Thee.   40

AFFLICTION (IV)

Broken in pieces all asunder,
  Lord, hunt me not,
  A thing forgot,
Once a poor creature, now a wonder,
  A wonder tortur'd in the space   5
  Betwixt this world and that of grace.

My thoughts are all a case of knives,
  Wounding my heart
  With scatter'd smart,
As wat'ring pots give flowers their lives.   10
  Nothing their fury can control
  While they do wound and pink[1] my soul.

All my attendants are at strife,
  Quitting their place
  Unto[2] my face: 15
Nothing performs the task of life:
  The elements are let loose to fight,
  And while I live, try out their right.

O help, my God! let not their plot
  Kill them and me,   20
  And also Thee,
Who art my life: dissolve the knot,
  As the sun scatters by his light
  All the rebellions of the night.

Then shall those powers, which work for grief,   25
  Enter Thy pay,
  And day by day
Labor Thy praise and my relief,
  With care and courage building me
  Till I reach heav'n and, much more, Thee.   30

LIFE

I made a posy while the day ran by:
Here will I smell my remnant out, and tie
  My life within this band.
But Time did beckon to the flowers, and they

By noon most cunningly did steal away,   5
  And wither'd in my hand.

My hand was next to them, and then my heart:
I took, without more thinking, in good part
  Time's gentle admonition,
Who did so sweetly death's sad taste convey,   10
Making my mind to smell my fatal day,
  Yet sug'ring the suspicion.

Farewell, dear flowers, sweetly your time ye spent,
Fit, while ye liv'd, for smell or ornament,
  And after death for cures.   15
I follow straight without complaints or grief,
Since, if my scent be good, I care not if
  It be as short as yours.

DECAY

Sweet were the days when Thou didst lodge with Lot,
Struggle with Jacob, sit with Gideon,
Advise with Abraham,[1] when Thy power could not
Encounter Mose's strong complaints and moan:
  Thy words were then, "Let me alone."[2]   5

One might have sought and found Thee presently
At some fair oak, or bush, or cave, or well.
"Is my God this way?" "No," they would reply;
"He is to Sinai gone, as we heard tell.
  List, ye may hear great Aaron's bell."[3]   10

But now Thou dost thyself immure and close
In some one corner of a feeble heart,
Where yet both Sin and Satan, Thy old foes,
Do pinch and straiten[4] Thee, and use much art
  To gain Thy thirds[5] and little part.   15

I see the world grows old whenas the heat
Of Thy great love, once spread, as in an urn
Doth closet up itself and still retreat,

[4]I.e., the will, that curbs the promptings of the five senses.
[5]With eyelids sewn together (a term from falconry).
AFFLICTION (IV) [1]Pierce. Text *prick*, but the emendation is supported by both the Bodleian and Williams manuscripts.
[2]Before.
DECAY [1]*Lodge with lot...Advise with Abraham*: these episodes are related respectively at Genesis 19.3, 32.24, Judges 6.11, and Genesis 18.23-33.
[2]When Moses sought to mollify God's wrath against the "stiff-necked" Jews, the Lord at first replied, "Let me alone," but eventually He was persuaded to forgive His sinful people (Exodus 32.9-14).
[3]Moses' brother Aaron, who became the first high priest of Israel, wore golden bells on the rich robes with which he was adorned when he went "into the holy place before the Lord" (Exodus 28.33-35).
[4]Confine.
[5]In English law, the third part of a deceased husband's real property to which his widow was entitled; here, the *little part* remaining of the *feeble heart* after the depredations of Sin and Satan.

Cold Sin still forcing it, till it return
   And, calling "Justice," all things burn.   20

JORDAN (II)

When first my lines of heav'nly joys made mention,
Such was their luster, they did so excel,
That I sought out quaint words and trim invention;[1]
My thoughts began to burnish,[2] sprout, and swell,
Curling with metaphors a plain intention,   5
Decking the sense as if it were to sell.

Thousands of notions in my brain did run,
Off'ring their service if I were not sped,
I often blotted[3] what I had begun:
This was not quick enough, and that was dead;   10
Nothing could seem too rich to clothe the sun,
Much less those joys which trample on his head.

As flames do work and wind when they ascend,
So did I weave myself into the sense;
But while I bustled, I might hear a friend   15
Whisper, "How wide[4] is all this long pretense!
There is in love a sweetness ready penn'd:
Copy out only that, and save expense."

CONSCIENCE

   Peace, prattler, do not lour:
Not a fair look but thou dost call it foul,
Not a sweet dish but thou dost call it sour;
   Music to thee doth howl.
 By list'ning to thy chatting[1] fears   5
 I have both lost mine eyes and ears

   Prattler, no more, I say;
My thoughts must work, but like a noiseless sphere;
Harmonious peace must rock them all the day;
   No room for prattlers there.   10
 If thou persistest, I will tell thee
 That I have physic to expel thee.

   And the receipt shall be
My Saviour's blood: whenever at His board
I do but taste it, straight it cleanseth me,   15
   And leaves thee not a word;
 No, not a tooth or nail to scratch,
 And at my actions carp or catch.

   Yet if thou talkest still,
Besides my physic, know there's some for thee: 20
Some wood and nails to make a staff or bill[2]
   For those that trouble me:
 The bloody cross of my dear Lord
 Is both my physic and my sword.

SION

Lord, with what glory wast Thou serv'd of old,
When Solomon's temple stood and flourished!
   Where most things were of purest gold;

The wood was all embellished
With flowers and carvings, mystical and rare: 5
All show'd the builder's, crav'd the seer's,[1] care.

Yet all this glory, all this pomp and state,
Did not affect Thee much, was not Thy aim;
   Something there was that sow'd debate:
   Wherefore Thou quittst Thy ancient claim;   10
And now Thy architecture meets with sin,
For all Thy frame and fabric is within.

There Thou art struggling with a peevish heart,
Which sometimes crosseth Thee, Thou sometimes it:
   The fight is hard on either part.   15
   Great God doth fight, He doth submit.
All Solomon's sea of brass and world of stone
Is not so dear to Thee as one good groan.

And truly brass and stone are heavy things,
Tombs for the dead, not temples fit for Thee: 20
   But groans are quick, and full of wings,
   And all their motions upward be;
And ever as they mount, like larks they sing;
The note is sad, yet music for a king.

THE BRITISH CHURCH

I joy, dear Mother, when I view
Thy perfect lineaments and hue
       Both sweet and bright.
Beauty in thee takes up her place,
And dates her letters[1] from thy face   5
       When she doth write.

A fine aspect in fit array,
Neither too mean nor yet too gay,
       Shows who is best.
Outlandish[2] looks may not compare,   10
For all they either painted are,
       Or else undrest.

She on the hills,[3] which wantonly
Allureth all in hope to be
       By her preferr'd,   15
Hath kiss'd so long her painted shrines
That ev'n her face by kissing shines
       For her reward.

She in the valley[4] is so shy
Of dressing that her hair doth lie   20
       About her ears;

JORDAN (II) [1]In rhetoric, the selection (literally "finding") of topics
and arguments.
[2]1. Expand; 2. shine. [3]Crossed out.
[4]I.e., wide of the mark, irrelevant.
CONSCIENCE [1]Chattering.
[2]Halberd, i.e., a broad hooked blade on a long wooden handle.
SION [1]Beholder's.
THE BRITISH CHURCH [1]*Dates her letters*: In England, until the
middle of the eighteenth century, Lady Day or the Feast of the
Annunciation (March 25) marked the beginning of the year.
[2]Foreign. [3]Rome. [4]Geneva, the center of Calvinism.

While she avoids her neighbor's pride,
She wholly goes on th' other side,
    And nothing wears.

But, dearest Mother (what those miss)   25
The mean thy praise and glory is,
    And long may be.
Blessed be God, whose love it was
To double-moat[5] thee with His grace,
    And none but thee.   30

THE QUIP

The merry World did on a day
With his trainbands[1] and mates agree
To meet together where I lay,
And all in sport to jeer at me.

First, Beauty crept into a rose,   5
Which when I pluck'd not, "Sir," said she,
"Tell me, I pray, whose hands are those?"
But thou shalt answer, Lord, for me.

Then Money came and, chinking still,
"What tune is this, poor man?" said he;   10
"I heard in music you had skill."
But thou shalt answer, Lord, for me.

Then came brave Glory puffing by
In silks that whistled, who but he?
He scarce allow'd me half an eye.   15
But thou shalt answer, Lord, for me.

Then came quick Wit and Conversation,
And he would needs a comfort be,
And, to be short, make an oration.   20
But thou shalt answer, Lord, for me.

Yet when the hour of Thy design
To answer these fine things shall come,
Speak not at large: say I am thine,
And then they have their answer home.[2]

DULLNESS

Why do I languish thus, drooping and dull,
    As if I were all earth?
O give me quickness, that I may with mirth
    Praise Thee brimful!   5

The wanton lover in a curious strain
    Can praise his fairest fair,
And with quaint metaphors her curled hair
    Curl o'er again.

Thou art my loveliness, my life, my light,
    Beauty alone to me: 10
Thy bloody death and undeserv'd makes thee
    Pure red and white.

When all perfections as but one appear,
    That those Thy form doth show,

The very dust where Thou dost tread and go   15
    Makes beauties here.

Where are my lines then? my approaches? views?
    Where are my window-songs?[1]
Lovers are still pretending,[2] and ev'n wrongs
    Sharpen their Muse: 20

But I am lost in flesh, whose sug'red lies
    Still mock me, and grow bold;
Sure Thou didst put a mind there, if I could
    Find where it lies.

Lord, clear Thy gift, that with a constant wit   25
    I may but look towards thee:
Look only, for to *love* Thee, who can be,
    What angel, fit?

SIN'S ROUND

Sorry I am, my God, sorry I am,
That my offenses course it in a ring.
My thoughts are working like a busy flame
Until their cockatrice[1] they hatch and bring,
And when they once have perfected their draughts,   5
My words take fire from my inflamed thoughts.

My words take fire from my inflamed thoughts,
Which spit it forth like the Sicilian hill.[2]
They vent[3] the wares, and pass them with their faults,
And by their breathing ventilate[4] the ill.   10
But words suffice not where are lewd intentions:
My hands do join to finish the inventions.

My hands do join to finish the inventions,
And so my sins ascend three stories high,
As Babel grew, before there were dissensions.   15
Yet ill deeds loiter not, for they supply
New thoughts of sinning: wherefore, to my shame,
Sorry I am, my God, sorry I am.

TIME

Meeting with Time, "Slack thing," said I,
"Thy scythe is dull; whet it for shame."
"No marvel, Sir," he did reply,
"If it at length deserve some blame:
    But where one man would have me grind it,   5
    Twenty for one too sharp do find it."

"Perhaps some such of old did pass,[1]
Who above all things lov'd this life;
To whom thy scythe a hatchet was,

[5]I.e., protect impregnably.
THE QUIP [1]Militia. [2]Thoroughly, directly.
DULLNESS [1]Serenades. [2]Always wooing.
SIN'S ROUND [1]A fabulous and deadly creature hatched from a cock's egg by a serpent.
[2]Mt. Etna. [3]1. Discharge; 2. vend, sell.
[4]I.e., make the fire burn hotter by giving it more air.
TIME [1]Die.

Which now is but a pruning-knife.   10
   Christ's coming hath made man thy debtor,
   Since by thy cutting he grows better.

"And in his blessing thou art blest,
For where thou only wert before
An executioner at best,   15
Thou art a gard'ner now, and more,
   An usher to convey our souls
   Beyond the utmost stars and poles.

"And this is that[2] makes life so long,
While it detains us from our God.   20
Ev'n pleasures here increase the wrong,
And length of days lengthen the rod.
   Who wants[3] the place where God doth dwell
   Partakes already half of hell.

"Of what strange length must that needs be,   25
Which ev'n eternity excludes!"
Thus far Time heard me patiently,
Then chafing said, "This man deludes!
   What do I here before his door?
   He doth not crave less time, but more."   30

ARTILLERY

As I one ev'ning sat before my cell,
Methoughts a star did shoot into my lap.
I rose and shook my clothes, as knowing well
That from small fires comes oft no small mishap.
When suddenly I heard one say,   5
"Do as thou usest, disobey,
Expel good motions from thy breast,
Which have the face of fire, but end in rest."

I, who had heard of music in the spheres
But not of speech in stars, began to muse;   10
But turning to my God, whose ministers
The stars and all things are, "If I refuse,
   Dread Lord," said I, "so oft my good,
   Then I refuse not ev'n with blood
   To wash away my stubborn thought,   15
For I will do or suffer what I ought.

"But I have also stars and shooters[1] too,
Born where Thy servants both artilleries use.
My tears and prayers night and day do woo
And work up to Thee, yet Thou dost refuse.   20
   Not but I am (I must say still)
   Much more oblig'd to do Thy will
   Than Thou to grant mine, but because
Thy promise now hath ev'n set Thee Thy laws.

"Then we are shooters both, and Thou dost deign   25
To enter combat with us, and contest
With Thine own clay. But I would parley fain:
Shun not my arrows, and behold my breast.
   Yet if thou shunnest, I am Thine:
   I must be so, if I am mine.   30

   There is no articling[2] with Thee:
I am but finite, yet Thine infinitely."

THE COLLAR[1]

   I struck the board and cried, "No more!
      I will abroad.
   What? shall I ever sigh and pine?
My lines and life are free; free as the road,
Loose as the wind, as large as store.[2]   5
      Shall I be still in suit?
   Have I no harvest but a thorn
   To let me blood, and not restore
What I have lost with cordial fruit?
      Sure there was wine   10
Before my sighs did dry it: there was corn
      Before my tears did drown it.
   Is the year only lost to me?
      Have I no bays to crown it?
No flowers, no garlands gay? all blasted?   15
      All wasted?
   Not so, my heart: but there is fruit,
      And thou hast hands.
   Recover all thy sigh-blown age
On double pleasures: leave thy cold dispute   20
Of what is fit and not. Forsake thy cage,
      Thy rope of sands,
Which petty thoughts have made, and made to thee
   Good cable, to enforce and draw,
      And be thy law,   25
While thou didst wink and wouldst not see.
      Away! Take heed!
      I will abroad.
Call in thy death's head[3] there: tie up thy fears.
      He that forbears   30
     To suit and serve his need,
      Deserves his load."
But as I rav'd and grew more fierce and wild
      At every word,
Methoughts I heard one calling, "Child!"   35
     And I repli'd, "My Lord."[4]

THE PULLEY

   When God at first made man,
Having a glass of blessings standing by,
"Let us," said He, "pour on him all we can:
Let the world's riches, which dispersed lie,
   Contract into a span."   5

   So strength first made a way;
Then beauty flow'd, then wisdom, honor, pleasure:

[2]What. [3]Lacks.
ARTILLERY [1]Shooting stars. [2]Making stipulations.
THE COLLAR [1]The title perhaps puns upon the *collar* or yoke of
discipline and *choler*. [2]Plenty, abundance.
[3]The human skull, conceived of as an emblem of mortality.
[4]*Methoughts...Lord*: Herbert is perhaps echoing the account of
the Lord's calling the child Samuel (1 Samuel 3.1–8).

When almost all was out, God made a stay,
Perceiving that alone of all His treasure
   Rest in the bottom lay.   10

   "For if I should," said He,
"Bestow this jewel also on my creature,
He would adore my gifts instead of me,
   And rest in nature, not the God of nature:
   So both should losers be.   15

   "Yet let him keep the rest,
But keep them with repining restlessness:
Let him be rich and weary, that at least
If goodness lead him not, yet weariness
   May toss him to my breast."   20

THE FLOWER

   How fresh, O Lord, how sweet and clean
Are Thy returns! ev'n as the flowers in spring,
   To which, besides their own demean,[1]
The late-past frosts tributes of pleasure bring.
      Grief melts away   5
      Like snow in May,
   As if there were no such cold thing.

   Who would have thought my shrivel'd heart
Could have recover'd greenness? It was gone
   Quite under ground as flowers depart   10
To see their mother-root when they have blown;
      Where they together
      All the hard weather,
   Dead to the world, keep house unknown.

   These are Thy wonders, Lord of power,   15
Killing and quick'ning, bringing down to hell
   And up to heaven in an hour,
Making a chiming of a passing-bell.
      We say amiss,
      This or that is: 20
   Thy word is all, if we could spell.

   O that I once past changing were,
Fast in Thy paradise, where no flower can wither!
   Many a spring I shoot up fair,
Off'ring[2] at heav'n, growing and groaning thither: 25
      Nor doth my flow'r
      Want a spring-show'r,
   My sins and I joining together.

   But while I grow in a straight line,
Still upwards bent as if heav'n were mine own,   30
   Thy anger comes, and I decline:
What frost to[3] that? what pole is not the zone
      Where all things burn,
      When Thou dost turn,
   And the least frown of Thine is shown?   35

   And now in age I bud again,
After so many deaths I live and write;
   I once more smell the dew and rain,
And relish versing: O my only Light,

      It cannot be   40
      That I am he
   On whom Thy tempests fell all night.

   These are Thy wonders, Lord of love,
To make us see we are but flowers that glide:
   Which when we once can find and prove,   45
Thou hast a garden for us where to bide.
      Who[4] would be more,
      Swelling through store,
   Forfeit their paradise by their pride.

THE FORERUNNERS

The harbingers are come. See, see their mark;
White is their color—and behold my head.
But must they have my brain? must they dispark
Those sparkling notions which therein were bred?
   Must dullness turn me to a clod?   5
Yet have they left me, *Thou art still my God.*[1]

Good men ye be to leave me my best room,
Ev'n all my heart, and what is lodged there;
I pass[2] not, I, what of the rest become,
So *Thou art still my God* be out of fear.[3]   10
   He will be pleased with that ditty;
And if I please Him, I write fine and witty.

Farewell, sweet phrases, lovely metaphors.
But will ye leave me thus? when ye before
Of stews and brothels only knew the doors,   15
Then did I wash you with my tears, and more,
   Brought you to church well dress'd and clad:
My God must have my best, ev'n all I had.

Lovely enchanting language, sugar cane,
Honey of roses, whither wilt thou fly?   20
Hath some fond lover 'ticed thee to thy bane?
And wilt thou leave the Church, and love a sty?
   Fie, thou wilt soil thy broider'd coat,
And hurt thyself, and him that sings the note.

Let foolish lovers, if they will love dung,   25
With canvas, not with arras,[4] clothe their shame:
Let folly speak in her own native tongue.
True beauty dwells on high: ours is a flame
   But borrow'd thence to light us thither.
Beauty and beauteous words should go together.   30

Yet if you go, I pass not; take your way:
For *Thou art still my God* is all that ye
Perhaps with more embellishment can say.

THE FLOWER [1]1. Demeanor; 2. demesne (estate).
[2]Aiming. [3]Compared with. [4]Those who.

THE FORERUNNERS [1]*The harbingers...God:* Just as the couriers (*harbingers*) who ride before a royal progress and arrange for lodging by making a chalk *mark* on the doors, the poet's whitening hairs announce the advent of old age. Despite his anxieties, however, he, like the Psalmist (31.14), can still assert his faith in God.
[2]Care. [3]I.e., safe. [4]Rich tapestry fabric.

Go, birds of spring: let winter have his fee;
Let a bleak paleness chalk the door,   35
So all within be livelier than before.

DISCIPLINE

Throw away Thy rod,
Throw away Thy wrath:
    O my God,
Take the gentle path.

For my heart's desire   5
Unto Thine is bent:
    I aspire
To a full consent.

Not a word or look
I affect to own,   10
    But by book,
And Thy book alone.

Though I fail, I weep;
Though I halt in pace,
    Yet I creep   15
To the throne of grace.

Then let wrath remove;
Love will do the deed,
    For with love
Stony hearts will bleed.   20

Love is swift of foot;
Love's a man of war,
    And can shoot,
And can hit from far.

Who can 'scape his bow?   25
That which wrought on Thee,
    Brought Thee low,
Needs must work on me.

Throw away Thy rod;
Though man frailties hath,   30
    Thou art God:
Throw away Thy wrath.

A WREATH

A wreathèd garland of deservèd praise,
Of praise deserved, unto Thee I give,
I give to Thee, who knowest all my ways,
My crooked winding ways, wherein I live,
Wherein I die, not live: for life is straight,   5
Straight as a line, and ever tends to Thee,
To Thee, who art more far above deceit
Than deceit seems above simplicity.
Give me simplicity, that I may live,
So live and like, that I may know Thy ways,   10
Know them and practice them: then shall I give
For this poor wreath, give Thee a crown of praise.

DEATH

Death, thou wast once an uncouth, hideous thing,
                Nothing but bones,
        The sad effect of sadder groans:
Thy mouth was open, but thou couldst not sing.

For we consider'd thee as at some six   5
                Or ten years hence,
        After the loss of life and sense,
Flesh being turned to dust, and bones to sticks.

We look'd on this side of thee, shooting short;
                Where we did find   10
        The shells of fledge souls[1] left behind,
Dry dust, which sheds no tears, but may extort.

But since our Saviour's death did put some blood
                Into thy face,
        Thou art grown fair and full of grace,   15
Much in request, much sought for as a good.

For we do now behold thee gay and glad,
                As at doomsday,
        When souls shall wear their new array,
And all thy bones with beauty shall be clad.   20

Therefore we can go die as sleep, and trust
                Half that we have
        Unto an honest faithful grave,
Making our pillows either down or dust.

DOOMSDAY

                Come away,
            Make no delay.
Summon all the dust to rise,
Till it stir and rub the eyes,
While this member jogs the other,   5
Each one whisp'ring, "Live you, brother?"

                Come away,
            Make this the day.
Dust, alas, no music feels
But Thy trumpet; then it kneels,   10
As peculiar notes and strains
Cure tarantulae's raging pains.[1]

                Come away,
            O make no stay!
Let the graves make their confession,   15
Lest at length they plead possession:[2]
Flesh's stubbornness may have
Read that lesson to the grave.

DEATH [1] I.e., fledgling souls who have cast off their bodily *shells* before their flight to heaven.

DOOMSDAY [1] *Raging pains*: tarantism, a form of hysteria allegedly caused by the tarantula's sting and characterized by a mad impulse to dance.
[2] *Let the graves...possession*: Let the graves concede that they have no lasting claim upon the bodies they contain.

Come away,
   Thy flock doth stray.   20
Some to winds their body lend,
And in them may drown a friend:
Some in noisome vapors grow
To a plague and public woe.

     Come away,   25
   Help our decay.
Man is out of order hurl'd,
Parcel'd out to all the world.
Lord, Thy broken consort[3] raise,
And the music shall be praise.   30

JUDGMENT

Almighty Judge, how shall poor wretches brook
     Thy dreadful look,
Able a heart of iron to appall,
     When Thou shalt call
For ev'ry man's peculiar book?   5

What others mean to do, I know not well;
     Yet I hear tell,
That some will turn Thee to some leaves therein
     So void of sin
That they in merit shall excel.   10

But I resolve, when Thou shalt call for mine,
     That to decline,
And thrust a Testament into Thy hand:
     Let that be scann'd.
There Thou shalt find my faults are Thine.   15

HEAVEN

O who will show me those delights on high?
     Echo: I.
Thou Echo, thou art mortal, all men know.
     Echo: No.
Wert thou not born among the trees and leaves?   5
     Echo: Leaves.
And are there any leaves that still abide?
     Echo: Bide.

What leaves are they? impart the matter wholly.
     Echo: Holy.   10
Are holy leaves the Echo then of bliss?
     Echo: Yes.
Then tell me, what is that supreme delight?
     Echo: Light.
Light to the mind: what shall the will enjoy?   15
     Echo: Joy.
But are there cares and business with the pleasure?
     Echo: Leisure.
Light, joy, and leisure; but shall they persever?
     Echo: Ever.   20

LOVE (III)

Love bade me welcome, yet my soul drew back,
     Guilty of dust and sin.
But quick-ey'd Love, observing me grow slack
     From my first entrance in,
Drew nearer to me, sweetly questioning,   5
     If I lack'd any thing.

"A guest," I answer'd, "worthy to be here."
     Love said, "You shall be he."
"I, the unkind, ungrateful? Ah, my dear,
     I cannot look on thee."   10
Love took my hand, and smiling did reply,
     "Who made the eyes but I?"

"Truth, Lord, but I have marred them: let my shame
     Go where it doth deserve."
"And know you not," says Love, "who bore
     the blame?"   15
     "My dear, then I will serve."
"You must sit down," says Love, "and taste my meat":
     So I did sit and eat.

FINIS

Glory be to God *on high,*
   And on earth peace,
   Good will towards men.

[3]A combination of various types of musical instruments (e.g., strings, woodwinds, brasses, etc.).

Thomas Carew [1594/5-1640]

In any list of those graceful minor poets whom Pope disparaged as

     the wits of either Charles's days,
The mob of gentlemen who wrote with ease,

Thomas Carew's high position is secure. The wayward second son of the aged and distinguished Sir Matthew Carew (d. 1618), who was a master in chancery for almost forty years, he attended

Merton College, Oxford (B.A. 1611), before proceeding to the Middle Temple. But the law was not for him, and when his own frivolity and his father's precarious financial situation forced him out into the world it must have been regarded as a sign of providential intervention that his kinsman Sir Dudley Carleton, the king's ambassador at Venice, provided him a post. But he bungled this career just as he had bungled legal studies, for after several years abroad (1613–16) in Sir Dudley's entourage he was sent back to England for slandering his patron and his wife. When the elder Carew finally learned the facts about his son's return (which Carleton belatedly and reluctantly revealed), his reaction was intense. "At the reading of your letter," Carleton's emissary reported to his chief,

> I did observe this passage from him, that when he came to that part which did make known his son's foul offense, he burst out into these words, "God's body!" And no sooner had he ended your letter but Mr. Carew came into his study, whom presently he reviled before me, and told him he had utterly overthrown his fortune; who, seeming to make strange at that speech of his father's, as being ignorant of the matter, Sir Matthew gave him Your Lordship's letter to read, which in a manner he slighted as holding the offense no way worthy of blame, being a thing done by him not in dishonor of Your Lordship or my Lady, nor intended ever to be divulged, but only (as his own words were) "for his private ends and direction."

In his last year or so of life, therefore, Sir Matthew took small comfort in his younger son, who, as he observed, "having given over all study here either of law or other learning, vagrantly and debauchedly taketh no manner of good, but all lewd courses, with the which he will weary me and all his other friends, and run himself into utter ruin."

Although the subject of these not overharsh remarks was unemployed and for a period ill with what was probably the first of his recurrent bouts of syphilis, he was hardly moping in disgrace. Not only was he writing verse (including, it would seem, metrical paraphrases of certain of the Psalms that long remained in manuscript), he was also launching a career at court by serving, very elegantly, at the investiture of Prince Charles as Prince of Wales (November 1616). His return to foreign service (1619) as a member of the ambassadorial suite of the flamboyant Edward Herbert, later Lord Herbert of Cherbury (see p. 114), was perhaps an indication of his rising fortunes. The record of the next few years is sparse, but by the later 1620's, as Clarendon recalled (see p. 797), he was one of that coterie of writers, wits, and scholars (including Jonson, Selden, and Sir Kenelm Digby) of which the then young Edward Hyde was proud to be a member.

Thereafter things went very well for Carew. Already noted for his verses (which, said Clarendon, "for the sharpness of the fancy and the elegancy of the language in which that fancy was spread were at least equal, if not superior, to any of that time"), he was so "very much esteemed" at court that in 1630 he was named a gentleman of the privy chamber, and not long after sewer (i.e., server) to the king. His distinction was confirmed when, in 1634, Charles himself agreed to take a part in *Coelum Britannicum*, a masque that Carew wrote for production at the court. Apart from such a mark of royal favor his reputation as a poet was attested by his intimacy—frequently expressed in elegiac or commendatory verses—with Jonson, Donne, Aurelian Townshend, Suckling, Davenant, George Sandys, and others. Most of the products of this social and literary camaraderie are witty, slick, and debonair, but one of them—the stately piece on Donne (p. 230)—superbly fuses criticism and sustained emotion.

But age and maybe dissipation began to take their toll. In the early summer of 1639 Carew— like Suckling, Lovelace, and many of their kind—went with Charles to Berwick in the abortive Bishops' War, and it was perhaps his last exertion. Although Clarendon said it was his "glory" that despite a life "spent with less severity or exactness than it ought to have been" he died a Christian, and repentant, Izaak Walton, not unnaturally, took a sterner view of Carew's final phase. He relates that the aging, ailing courtier, having requested and received spiritual consolation from the godly John Hales, then reverted to his sinful ways; but when his illness came again and he again requested aid, "Mr. Hales told him he should have his prayers, but would by no means give him then either the sacrament or absolution." But if Carew died unhouseled, disappointed, unaneled, he had a sumptuous funeral at St. Dunstan's in the West (23 March 1640), and the collection of his *Poems* that appeared a few months later went through five editions by 1671.

My texts are based upon the *Poems*, 1640 (STC 4620) and *Poems . . . The second Edition revised and enlarged*, 1642 (Wing C-564). The older editions by Thomas Maitland (1824), W. C. Hazlitt (1870), J. W. Ebsworth (1893), Arthur Vincent (1899), and George Saintsbury (*Minor Poets of the Caroline Period*, 3 vols., 1905–21) have been superseded by Rhodes Dunlap's *Poems of Thomas Carew with His Masque "Coelum Britannicum"* (1949), which also treats the poet's life in some detail. Edward I. Selig has discussed Carew at length (*The Flourishing Wreath*, 1957), Louis L. Martz more briefly in *The Wit of Love* (1970), and he is generously reprinted by R. G. Howarth in *Minor Poets of the 17th Century* (rev. 1953).

from Poems (1640)

THE SPRING

Now that the winter's gone, the earth hath lost
Her snow-white robes, and now no more the frost
Candies[1] the grass, or casts an icy cream
Upon the silver lake or crystal stream;
But the warm sun thaws the benumbed earth   5
And makes it tender, gives a sacred birth
To the dead swallow, wakes in hollow tree
The drowsy cuckoo and the humble bee.
Now do a choir of chirping minstrels bring
In triumph to the world the youthful spring.   10
The valleys, hills, and woods in rich array
Welcome the coming of the long'd-for May.
Now all things smile: only my love doth lour,
Nor hath the scalding noonday sun the power
To melt that marble ice which still doth hold   15
Her heart congeal'd, and makes her pity cold.
The ox, which lately did for shelter fly
Into the stall, doth now securely lie
In open fields; and love no more is made
By the fireside, but in the cooler shade: 20
Amyntas now doth with his Chloris sleep
Under a sycamore, and all things keep
Time with the season. Only she doth carry
June in her eyes, in her heart January.

TO A.L.[1] PERSUASIONS TO LOVE

Think not, 'cause men flatt'ring say
Y'are fresh as April, sweet as May,
Bright as is the morning star,
That you are so; or, though you are,
Be not therefore proud, and deem   5
All men unworthy your esteem:
For, being so, you lose the pleasure

Of being fair, since that rich treasure
Of rare beauty and sweet feature
Was bestow'd on you by Nature   10
To be enjoy'd, and 'twere a sin
There to be scarce where she hath bin[2]
So prodigal of her best graces;
Thus common beauties and mean faces
Shall have more pastime, and enjoy   15
The sport you lose by being coy.
Did the thing for which I sue
Only concern myself, not you;
Were men so fram'd as they alone
Reap'd all the pleasure, women none: 20
Then had you reason to be scant;
But 'twere a madness not to grant
That which affords (if you consent)
To you, the giver, more content
Than me, the beggar. O, then be   25
Kind to yourself, if not to me.
Starve not yourself, because you may
Thereby make me pine away;
Nor let brittle beauty make
You your wiser thoughts forsake;   30
For that lovely face will fail:
Beauty's sweet, but beauty's frail;
'Tis sooner past, 'tis sooner done,
Than summer's rain or winter's sun;
Most fleeting when it is most dear,   35
'Tis gone while we but say 'tis here.
These curious locks, so aptly twin'd,
Whose every hair a soul doth bind,
Will change their abroun[3] hue, and grow
White and cold as winter's snow.   40

THE SPRING   [1]Ices.
TO A.L.   [1]Unidentified.   [2]Been.   [3]Auburn.

That eye, which now is Cupid's nest,
Will prove his grave, and all the rest
Will follow; in the cheek, chin, nose
Nor lily shall be found nor rose.
And what will then become of all   45
Those whom now you servants call?
Like swallows, when your[4] summer's done,
They'll fly and seek some warmer sun.
Then wisely choose one to your friend
Whose love may, when your beauties end,   50
Remain still firm: be provident,
And think, before the summer's spent,
Of following winter; like the ant,
In plenty hoard for time of scant.
Cull out, amongst the multitude   55
Of lovers that seek to intrude
Into your favor, one that may
Love for an age, not for a day;
One that will quench your youthful fires,
And feed in age your hot desires.   60
For when the storms of time have mov'd
Waves on that cheek which was belov'd,
When a fair lady's face is pin'd,
And yellow spread where red once shin'd;
When beauty, youth, and all sweets leave her,   65
Love may return, but lover never;
And old folks say there are no pains
Like itch of love in aged veins.
O love me, then, and now begin it,
Let us not lose this present minute;   70
For time and age will work that wrack[5]
Which time or age shall ne'er call back.
The snake each year fresh skin resumes,
And eagles change their aged plumes;
The faded rose each spring receives   75
A fresh red tincture on her leaves:
But if your beauties once decay,
You never know a second May.
O then, be wise, and whilst your season
Affords you days for sport, do reason;   80
Spend not in vain your life's short hour,
But crop in time your beauty's flower,
Which will away, and doth together
Both bud and fade, both blow and wither.

A DIVINE MISTRESS

In Nature's pieces still I see
Some error that might mended be;
Something my wish could still remove,
Alter, or add; but my fair love
Was fram'd by hands far more divine,   5
For she hath every beauteous line;
Yet I had been far happier
Had Nature, that made me, made her.
Then likeness might (that love creates)
Have made her love what now she hates;   10
Yet, I confess, I cannot spare

From her just[1] shape the smallest hair;
Nor need I beg from all the store
Of heaven for her one beauty more.
She hath too much divinity for me: 15
You gods, teach her some more humanity.

A CRUEL MISTRESS

We read of kings and gods that kindly took
A pitcher fill'd with water from the brook;
But I have daily tend'red without thanks
Rivers of tears that overflow their banks.
A slaughter'd bull will appease angry Jove,   5
A horse the sun, a lamb the God of Love;
But she disdains the spotless sacrifice
Of a pure heart, that at her altar lies.
Vesta[1] is not displeas'd if her chaste urn
Do with repaired[2] fuel ever burn;   10
But my saint frowns though to her honor'd name
I consecrate a never-dying flame.
Th' Assyrian king[3] did none i' th' furnace throw
But those that to his image did not bow;
With bended knees I daily worship her,   15
Yet she consumes her own idolater.
Of such a goddess no times leave record,
That burnt the temple where she was ador'd.

SONG. MURD'RING BEAUTY

I'll gaze no more on her bewitching face,
Since ruin harbors there in every place,
For my enchanted soul alike she drowns
With calms and tempests of her smiles and frowns.
I'll love no more those cruel eyes of hers,   5
Which, pleas'd or anger'd, still are murderers,
For if she dart, like lightning, through the air
Her beams of wrath, she kills me with despair.
If she behold me with a pleasing eye,
I surfeit with excess of joy, and die.   10

SECRECY PROTESTED

Fear not, dear love, that I'll reveal
Those hours of pleasure we two steal;
No eye shall see, nor yet the sun
Descry, what thou and I have done;
No ear shall hear our love, but we   5
Silent as the night will be.
The God of Love himself (whose dart
Did first wound mine and then thy heart)
Shall never know that we can tell

[4]Text *their,* corrected in Errata. [5]Destruction.
A DIVINE MISTRESS [1]I.e., flawless.
A CRUEL MISTRESS [1]Roman goddess of the hearth and custodian
of the sacred fire that was tended by the vestal virgins.
[2]Renewed, replaced.
[3]Nebuchadnezzar, king of Babylonia (not Assyria), the story of
whose fiery furnace is related in Daniel 3.10–26.

What sweets in stol'n embraces dwell.   10
This only means may find it out:
If, when I die, physicians doubt
What caus'd my death, and there to view
Of all their judgments which was true,
Rip up my heart, O then, I fear,   15
The world will see thy picture there.

SONG. MEDIOCRITY[1] IN LOVE REJECTED

Give me more love or more disdain;
    The torrid or the frozen zone
Bring equal ease unto my pain,
    The temperate affords me none:
Either extreme of love or hate   5
Is sweeter than a calm estate.

Give me a storm; if it be love,
    Like Danaë[2] in that golden shower,
I swim in pleasure; if it prove
    Disdain, that torrent will devour   10
My vulture-hopes; and he's possess'd
Of heaven, that's but from hell releas'd.
    Then crown my joys, or cure my pain;
    Give me more love, or more disdain.

TO MY MISTRESS SITTING BY A RIVER'S SIDE
An Eddy

Mark how yon eddy steals away
From the rude stream into the bay;
There, lock'd up safe, she doth divorce
Her waters from the channel's course,
And scorns the torrent that did bring   5
Her headlong from her native spring.
Now doth she with her new love play,
Whilst he runs murmuring away.
Mark how she courts the banks, whilst they
As amorously their arms display,   10
T' embrace and clip her silver waves:
See how she strokes their sides, and craves
An entrance there, which they deny;
Whereat she frowns, threat'ning to fly
Home to her stream, and gins to swim   15
Backward, but from the channel's brim
Smiling returns into the creek,
With thousand dimples on her cheek.
    Be thou this eddy, and I'll make
My breast thy shore, where thou shalt take   20
Secure repose, and never dream
Of the quite forsaken stream;
Let him to the wide ocean haste,
There lose his color, name, and taste:
Thou shalt save all, and, safe from him,   25
Within these arms forever swim.

SONG. TO MY INCONSTANT MISTRESS

When thou, poor excommunicate
    From all the joys of love, shalt see

The full reward and glorious fate
    Which my strong faith shall purchase me,
Then curse thine own inconstancy.   5

A fairer hand than thine shall cure
    That heart which thy false oaths did wound,
And to my soul a soul more pure
    Than thine shall by Love's hand be bound,
And both with equal glory crown'd.   10

Then shalt thou weep, entreat, complain
    To Love, as I did once to thee;
When all thy tears shall be as vain
    As mine were then, for thou shalt be
Damn'd for thy false apostasy.   15

SONG. PERSUASIONS TO ENJOY

If the quick spirits in your eye
Now languish, and anon must die;
If every sweet, and every grace
Must fly from that forsaken face:
    Then, Celia, let us reap our joys   5
    Ere Time such goodly fruit destroys.

Or if that golden fleece must grow
Forever free from aged snow;
If those bright suns must know no shade,
Nor your fresh beauties ever fade;   10
Then fear not, Celia, to bestow
What, still being gather'd, still must grow.
    Thus, either Time his sickle brings
    In vain, or else in vain his wings.

A LOOKING GLASS

That flatt'ring glass whose smooth face wears
Your shadow, which a sun appears,
Was once a river of my tears.

About your cold heart they did make
A circle, where the briny lake   5
Congeal'd into a crystal cake.

Gaze no more on that killing eye,
For fear the native cruelty
Doom you, as it doth all, to die.

For fear lest the fair object move   10
Your froward[1] heart to fall in love,
Then you yourself my rival prove.

Look rather on my pale cheeks pin'd:
There view your beauties. There you'll find
A fair face but a cruel mind.   15

Be not forever frozen, coy;
One beam of love will soon destroy
And melt that ice to floods of joy.

MEDIOCRITY [1]Temperance.
[2]A maiden loved by Zeus, to whom he descended in a shower of gold.
A LOOKING GLASS [1]Intractable.

TO MY MISTRESS IN ABSENCE

Though I must live here, and by force
Of your command suffer divorce;
Though I am parted, yet my mind,
That's more myself, still stays behind.
I breathe in you, you keep my heart,   5
'Twas but a carcass that did part.
Then though our bodies are disjoin'd,
As things that are to place confin'd,
Yet let our boundless spirits meet,
And in love's sphere each other greet;   10
There let us work a mystic wreath,
Unknown unto the world beneath;
There let us clasp'd loves sweetly twin,
There let our secret thoughts unseen
Like nets be weav'd and intertwin'd,   15
Wherewith we'll catch each other's mind.
There whilst our souls do sit and kiss,
Tasting a sweet and subtle bliss
(Such as gross lovers cannot know,
Whose hands and lips meet here below),   20
Let us look down and mark what pain
Our absent bodies here sustain,
And smile to see how far away
The one doth from the other stray;
Yet burn and languish with desire   25
To join, and quench their mutual fire;
There let us joy to see from far
Our emulous flames at loving war,
Whilst both with equal luster shine,
Mine bright as yours, yours bright as mine.   30
There seated in those heavenly bowers,
We'll cheat the lag[1] and ling'ring hours,
Making our bitter absence sweet,
Till souls and bodies both may meet.

CELIA BLEEDING, TO THE SURGEON

Fond man, that canst believe her blood
  Will from those purple channels flow,
Or that the pure, untainted flood
  Can any foul distemper know,
Or that thy weak steel can incise   5
The crystal case wherein it lies,

Know, her quick blood, proud of his seat,
  Runs dancing through her azure veins,
Whose harmony no cold nor heat
  Disturbs, whose hue no tincture stains;   10
And the hard rock wherein it dwells
The keenest darts of Love repels.

But thou repli'st, "Behold, she bleeds."
  Fool, thou'rt deceiv'd, and dost not know
The mystic knot whence this proceeds,   15
  How lovers in each other grow;
Thou struck'st her arm, but 'twas my heart
Shed all the blood, felt all the smart.

TO SAXHAM[1]

Though frost and snow lock'd from mine eyes
That beauty which without door lies,
Thy gardens, orchards, walks, that so
I might not all thy pleasures know,
Yet, Saxham, thou within thy gate   5
Art of thyself so delicate,
So full of native sweets that bless
Thy roof with inward happiness,
As neither from nor to thy store
Winter takes aught, or spring adds more.   10
The cold and frozen air had sterv'd[2]
Much poor, if not by thee preserv'd,
Whose prayers have made thy table blest
With plenty, far above the rest.
The season hardly did afford   15
Coarse cates[3] unto thy neighbors' board,
Yet thou hadst dainties, as the sky
Had only been thy volary;[4]
Or else the birds, fearing the snow
Might to another Deluge grow,   20
The pheasant, partridge, and the lark
Flew to thy house, as to the Ark.
The willing ox of himself came
Home to the slaughter, with the lamb,
And every beast did thither bring   25
Himself, to be an offering.
The scaly herd more pleasure took,
Bath'd in thy dish, than in the brook;
Water, earth, air did all conspire
To pay their tributes to thy fire,   30
Whose cherishing flames themselves divide
Through every room, where they deride
The night and cold abroad, whilst they,
Like suns within, keep endless day.
Those cheerful beams send forth their light   35
To all that wander in the night,
And seem to beckon from aloof
The weary pilgrim to thy roof;
Where if, refresh'd, he will away,
He's fairly[5] welcome; or if stay,   40
Far more; which he shall hearty find
Both from the master and the hind.[6]
The stranger's welcome each man there
Stamp'd on his cheerful brow doth wear
Nor doth this welcome or his cheer   45
Grow less 'cause he stays longer here:
There's none observes, much less repines,
How often this man sups or dines.
Thou hast no porter at the door
T' examine or keep back the poor;   50
Nor locks nor bolts: thy gates have bin
Made only to let strangers in;

TO MY MISTRESS IN ABSENCE [1]Tardy.

TO SAXHAM [1]Little Saxham, the country seat of the Croft family
near Bury in Lancashire.
[2]Starved, destroyed. [3]Victuals.
[4]Aviary, large bird cage. [5]Courteously. [6]Servant.

Untaught to shut, they do not fear
To stand wide open all the year,
Careless who enters, for they know   55
Thou never didst deserve a foe,
And as for thieves, thy bounty's such,
They cannot steal, thou giv'st so much.

UPON A RIBAND

This silken wreath, which circles in mine arm,
Is but an emblem of that mystic charm
Wherewith the magic of your beauties binds
My captive soul, and round about it winds
Fetters of lasting love. This hath entwin'd   5
My flesh alone; that hath impal'd[1] my mind.
Time may wear out these soft weak bands, but those
Strong chains of brass, Fate shall not discompose.
This holy relic may preserve my wrist,
But my whole frame doth by that power subsist: 10
To that, my prayers and sacrifice; to this
I only pay a superstitious kiss.
This but the idol, that's the deity;
Religion there is due, here ceremony.
That I receive by faith, this but in trust;   15
Here I may tender duty, there I must.
This order as a layman I may bear,
But I become Love's priest when that I wear.
This moves like air; that as the center stands;
That knot your virtue tied, this but your hands.   20
That Nature fram'd, but this was made by art;
This makes my arm your prisoner, that my heart.

SONG. TO MY MISTRESS, I BURNING IN LOVE

I burn, and cruel you in vain
Hope to quench me with disdain;
If from your eyes those sparkles came
That have kindled all this flame,
What boots[1] it me, though now you shroud   5
Those fierce comets in a cloud?
Since all the flames that I have felt
Could your snow yet never melt,
Nor can your snow, though you should take
Alps into your bosom, slake   10
The heat of my enamor'd heart.
But, with wonder, learn Love's art:
No seas of ice can cool desire,
Equal flames must quench Love's fire.
Then think not that my heat can die,   15
Till you burn as well as I.

SONG. TO HER AGAIN, SHE BURNING IN A FEVER

Now she burns as well as I,
Yet my heat can never die;
She burns that never knew desire,
She that was ice, she now is[1] fire,
She whose cold heart chaste thoughts did arm   5

So as Love's flames could never warm
The frozen bosom where it dwelt,
She burns, and all her beauties melt.
She burns, and cries, "Love's fires are mild;
Fevers are God's; and[2] he's a child."   10
Love, let her know the difference
'Twixt the heat of soul and sense:
Touch her with thy flames divine,
So shalt thou quench her fire, and mine.

A FLY THAT FLEW INTO
MY MISTRESS HER EYE

When this fly liv'd, she us'd to play
In the sunshine all the day,
Till coming near my Celia's sight,
She found a new and unknown light
So full of glory as it made   5
The noonday sun a gloomy shade;
Then this amorous fly became
My rival, and did court my flame.
She did from hand to bosom skip,
And from her breath, her cheek, and lip   10
Suck'd all the incense and the spice,
And grew a bird of paradise.
At last into her eye she flew;
There, scorch'd in flames and drown'd in dew,
Like Phaeton[1] from the sun's sphere   15
She fell, and with her dropp'd a tear,
Of which a pearl was straight compos'd,
Wherein her ashes lie enclos'd.
Thus she receiv'd from Celia's eye
Funeral flame, tomb, obsequy.   20

BOLDNESS IN LOVE

Mark how the bashful morn in vain
    Courts the amorous marigold
With sighing blasts and weeping rain,
    Yet she refuses to unfold.
But when the planet of the day   5
Approacheth with his powerful ray,
Then she spreads, then she receives
His warmer beams into her virgin leaves.

So shalt thou thrive in love, fond boy:
    If thy tears and sighs discover   10
Thy grief, thou never shalt enjoy
    The just reward of a bold lover;
But when, with moving accents, thou

UPON A RIBAND [1]Fenced, enclosed.

TO MY MISTRESS [1]Avails.

TO HER AGAIN [1]*Now is*: Text *that was*, but the emendation is
supported by a contemporary manuscript.
[2]Not in the text, but the emendation (which the meter requires) is
supported by all the manuscripts.

A FLY THAT FLEW [1]Son of Helios who drove his father's chariot
of the sun so recklessly that Zeus destroyed him with a thunder-
bolt.

Shalt constant fair and service vow,
Thy Celia shall receive those charms   15
With open ears and with unfolded arms.

A PASTORAL DIALOGUE
Shepherd   Nymph   Chorus

Shepherd: This mossy bank they press'd. *Nymph*: That
        aged oak
    Did canopy the happy pair
        All night from the damp[1] air.
Chorus: Here let us sit and sing the words they spoke,
Till the day, breaking, their embraces broke.   5

Shepherd:
See, love, the blushes of the morn appear,
    And now she hangs her pearly store
        (Robb'd from the eastern shore)
I' th' cowslip's bell and rose's ear:[2]
Sweet, I must stay no longer here.   10

Nymph:
Those streaks of doubtful light usher not day,
    But show my sun must set; no morn
        Shall shine till thou return.
The yellow planets and the gray
Dawn shall attend thee on thy way.   15

Shepherd:
If thine eyes gild my paths, they may forbear
    Their useless shine. *Nymph*: My tears will quite
        Extinguish their faint light.
Shepherd: Those drops will make their beams more clear:
Love's flames will shine in every tear.   20

Chorus:
They kiss'd and wept, and from their lips and eyes
    In a mix'd dew of briny sweet
        Their joys and sorrows meet,
But she cries out. *Nymph*: Shepherd, arise!
The sun betrays us else to spies.   25

Shepherd:
The winged hours fly fast whilst we embrace,
    But when we want their help to meet,
        They move with leaden feet.
Nymph: Then let us pinion Time, and chase
The day forever from this place.   30

Shepherd:
Hark! *Nymph*: Ay me, stay! *Shepherd*: Forever. *Nymph*:
        No, arise;
    We must be gone. *Shepherd*: My nest of spice!
        Nymph: My soul! *Shepherd*: My paradise!
Chorus: Neither could say farewell, but through their eyes
Grief interrupted speech with tears supplies.   35

A RAPTURE

I will enjoy thee now, my Celia, come,
And fly with me to Love's elysium.

The giant, Honor, that keeps cowards out,
Is but a masquer, and the servile rout
Of baser subjects only bend in vain   5
To the vast idol, whilst the nobler train
Of valiant lovers[1] daily sail between
The huge Colossus' legs,[2] and pass unseen
Unto the blissful shore. Be bold and wise,
And we shall enter: the grim Swiss[3] denies   10
Only tame[4] fools a passage, that not know
He is but form, and only frights in show
The duller eyes that look from far; draw near,
And thou shalt scorn what we were wont to fear.
We shall see how the stalking pageant[5] goes[6]   15
With borrowed legs, a heavy load to those
That made and bear him: not, as we once thought,
The seed of gods, but a weak model wrought
By greedy men, that seek to enclose the common[7]
And within private arms impale[8] free woman.   20
    Come, then, and mounted on the wings of Love
We'll cut the flitting air, and soar above
The monster's[9] head, and in the noblest seats
Of those bless'd shades quench and renew our heats.
There shall the Queens[10] of Love and Innocence,   25
Beauty and Nature, banish all offense
From our close ivy-twines; there I'll behold
Thy bared snow and thy unbraided gold;
There my enfranchis'd[11] hand on every side
Shall o'er thy naked polish'd ivory slide.   30
No curtain there, though of transparent lawn,[12]
Shall be before thy virgin-treasure drawn;
But the rich mine, to the inquiring eye
Expos'd, shall ready still for mintage lie,
And we will coin young Cupids. There a bed   35
Of roses and fresh myrtles shall be spread
Under the cooler shade of cypress groves;
Our pillows of the down of Venus' doves,
Whereon our panting limbs we'll gently lay
In the faint respites of our active play;   40
That so our slumbers may in dreams have leisure
To tell the nimble fancy our past pleasure,
And so our souls, that cannot be embrac'd,
Shall the embraces of our bodies taste.
Meanwhile the bubbling stream shall court the shore,   45

A PASTORAL DIALOGUE [1]Text *danke,* corrected in Errata.
[2]Text *rare,* but all manuscripts support the emendation.
A RAPTURE [1]Text *soldiers,* corrected in Errata.
[2]The Colossus of Rhodes, a gigantic bronze statue of Apollo
bestriding the entrance to the harbor of that port, was one of the
Seven Wonders of the Ancient World.
[3]Carew is perhaps thinking of the Swiss Guards in the Vatican.
[4]*Only tame*: Text *Only to tame,* but all manuscripts support the
emendation.
[5]I.e., the *masquer* Honor (ll. 3–4), conceived of as an elaborate
property to be carried in a procession or masque. [6]Walks.
[7]A tract of land considered as the property of the community and
therefore for the use of everyone.
[8]Fence, enclose (with a phallic pun). [9]I.e., Honor's.
[10]Most manuscripts read *Queene.* [11]Unrestricted. [12]Fine linen.

Th' enamored chirping wood-choir shall adore
In varied tunes the Deity of Love;
The gentle blasts of western winds shall move
The trembling leaves, and through their close
    boughs breathe   50
Still music, whilst we rest ourselves beneath
Their dancing shade; till a soft murmur, sent
From souls entranc'd in amorous languishment,
Rouse us, and shoot into our veins fresh fire,
Till we in their sweet ecstasy expire.

    Then, as the empty bee, that lately bore   55
Into the common treasure all her store,
Flies 'bout the painted field with nimble wing,
Deflowering the fresh virgins[13] of the spring,
So will I rifle all the sweets that dwell
In my delicious paradise, and swell   60
My bag with honey, drawn forth by the power
Of fervent kisses from each spicy flower.
I'll seize the rosebuds in their perfum'd bed,
The violet knots,[14] like curious mazes spread
O'er all the garden, taste the rip'ned cherry,   65
The warm firm apple, tipp'd with coral berry;
Then will I visit with a wandering kiss
The vale of lilies and the bower of bliss:
And where the beauteous region doth divide
Into two milky ways, my lips shall slide   70
Down those smooth alleys, wearing[15] as I go
A tract[16] for lovers on the printed snow;
Thence climbing o'er the swelling Apennine,
Retire into thy grove of eglantine,
Where I will all those ravish'd sweets distill   75
Through Love's alembic, and with chemic[17] skill
From the mix'd mass one sovereign balm derive,
Then bring that great elixir to thy hive.

    Now in more subtile wreaths I will entwine
My sinewy thighs, my legs and arms with thine;   80
Thou like a sea of milk shalt lie display'd,
Whilst I the smooth, calm ocean invade
With such a tempest, as when Jove of old
Fell down on Danaë in a storm of gold;
Yet my tall pine shall in the Cyprian[18] strait   85
Ride safe at anchor, and unlade her freight:
My rudder with thy bold hand, like a tried
And skillful pilot, thou shalt steer, and guide
My bark into love's channel, where it shall
Dance, as the bounding waves do rise or fall.   90
Then shall thy circling arms embrace and clip
My willing[19] body, and thy balmy lip
Bathe me in juice of kisses, whose perfume
Like a religious incense shall consume,
And send up holy vapors to those pow'rs   95
That bless our loves and crown our sportful hours,
That with such halcyon calmness fix our souls
In steadfast peace as no affright controls.
There no rude sounds shake us with sudden starts;
No jealous ears, when we unrip[20] our hearts,   100
Suck our discourse in; no observing spies
This blush, that glance traduce;[21] no envious eyes

Watch our close[22] meetings; nor are we betray'd
To rivals by the bribed chambermaid.
No wedlock bonds unwreathe our twisted loves;   105
We seek no midnight arbor, no dark groves
To hide our kisses: there the hated name
Of husband, wife, lust, modest, chaste, or shame
Are vain and empty words, whose very sound
Was never heard in the elysian ground.   110
All things are lawful there that may delight
Nature or unrestrained appetite;
Like and enjoy, to will and act is one:
We only sin when Love's rites are not done.

    The Roman Lucrece[23] there reads the divine   115
Lectures[24] of Love's great master, Aretine,[25]
And knows as well as Lais[26] how to move
Her pliant body in the act of love.
To quench the burning ravisher, she hurls
Her limbs into a thousand winding curls,   120
And studies artful postures, such as be
Carv'd on the bark of every neighboring tree
By learned hands, that so adorn'd the rind
Of those fair plants, which, as they lay entwined,
Have fann'd their glowing fires. The Grecian dame,[27]   125
That in her endless web toil'd for a name
As fruitless as her work, doth there display
Herself before the youth of Ithaca,
And th' amorous sport of gamesome nights prefer
Before dull dreams of the lost traveler.   130
Daphne[28] hath broke her bark, and that swift foot
Which th' angry gods had fastened with a root
To the fix'd earth doth now unfetter'd run
To meet th' embraces of the youthful Sun.[29]
She hangs upon him like his Delphic[30] lyre;   135
Her kisses blow[31] the old and breathe new fire;
Full of her god, she sings inspired lays,
Sweet odes of love, such as deserve the bays,[32]

[13]I.e., blossoms. [14]Clusters. [15]I.e., making. [16]Track.
[17]Alchemic.
[18]Pertaining to Venus, the goddess of love, to whom Cyprus was a sacred island. [19]Most manuscripts read *naked*.
[20]I.e., lay bare in mutual love. [21]Betray, i.e., reveal.
[22]1. Secret; 2. near.
[23]Lucretia, the virtuous wife of Collatinus, who killed herself after being raped by Sextus Tarquinius; hence a paragon of matrons. [24]Writings.
[25]Pietro Aretino (1492–1556), Italian satirist and pornographer. Carew is perhaps alluding to Aretino's sonnets written to accompany sixteen indecent engravings made by Mercantonio Raimondi for Giulio Romano.
[26]The name of two famous Greek heterae or courtesans, one of Corinth and the other of Phryne.
[27]The faithful Penelope, wife of Ulysses, who in her husband's long absence postponed a choice among her suitors until she had finished work upon a piece of cloth that she wove by day and unraveled by night.
[28]A chaste nymph who by her own entreaty was changed into a laurel tree rather than yield to the persistent Apollo.
[29]I.e., Apollo.
[30]Pertaining to Delphi, a shrine sacred to Apollo. [31]Fan.
[32]Laurels.

Which she herself was. Next her, Laura[33] lies
In Petrarch's learned arms, drying those eyes   140
That did in such sweet, smooth-pac'd numbers flow
As made the world enamor'd of his woe.
These, and ten thousand beauties more, that died
Slave to the tyrant,[34] now enlarg'd[35] deride
His cancel'd laws, and for their time misspent   145
Pay into Love's exchequer double rent.
    Come then, my Celia, we'll no more forbear
To taste our joys, struck with a panic fear,
But will depose from his imperious sway
This proud usurper, and walk free as they,   150
With necks unyok'd; nor is it just that he
Should fetter your soft sex with chastity,
Which Nature made unapt for abstinence;
When yet this false imposter can dispense
With human justice and with sacred right,   155
And, maugre[36] both their laws, command me fight
With rivals or with emulous loves that dare
Equal with thine their mistress' eyes or hair.
If thou complain of wrong, and call my sword
To carve out thy revenge, upon that word   160
He bids me fight and kill, or else he brands
With marks of infamy my coward hands,
And yet religion bids from bloodshed fly,
And damns me for that act. Then tell me why
This goblin Honor, which the world adores,   165
Should make men atheists, and not women whores.

EPITAPH ON THE LADY MARY VILLERS[1]

The Lady Mary Villers lies
Under this stone. With weeping eyes
The parents that first gave her birth,
And their sad friends, laid her in earth.
If any of them, reader, were   5
Known unto thee, shed a tear;
Or if thyself possess a gem
As dear to thee as this to them,
Though a stranger to this place,
Bewail in theirs thine own hard case;   10
For thou perhaps at thy return
Mayest find thy darling in an urn.

ANOTHER

This little vault, this narrow room,
Of Love and Beauty is the tomb.
The dawning beam that gan to clear
Our clouded sky lies dark'ned here,
Forever set to us by death,   5
Sent to enflame the world beneath.
'Twas but a bud, yet did contain
More sweetness than shall spring again;
A budding star that might have grown
Into a sun when it had blown.[1]   10
This hopeful beauty did create

New life in Love's declining state;
But now his empire ends, and we
From fire and wounding darts are free:
His brand, his bow let no man fear;   15
The flames, the arrows all lie here.

TO BEN JONSON
UPON OCCASION OF HIS ODE
OF DEFIANCE ANNEXED TO
HIS PLAY OF "THE NEW INN"[1]

'Tis true, dear Ben, thy just chastising hand
Hath fix'd upon the sotted age a brand,
To their swoll'n pride and empty scribbling due;
It can nor judge nor write, and yet 'tis true
Thy comic Muse, from the exalted line   5
Touch'd by thy *Alchemist*,[2] doth since decline
From that her zenith, and foretells a red
And blushing evening, when she goes to bed;
Yet such as shall outshine the glimmering light
With which all stars shall gild the following night.   10
Nor think it much, since all thy eaglets may
Endure the sunny trial,[3] if we say
This hath the stronger wing, or that doth shine
Trick'd up in fairer plumes, since all are thine.
Who hath his flock of cackling geese compar'd   15
With thy tun'd choir of swans, or else who dar'd
To call thy births deform'd? But if thou bind
By City custom or by gavelkind[4]
In equal shares thy love on all thy race,[5]
We may distinguish of their sex and place;   20
Though one hand form them, and though one brain strike
Souls into all, they are not all alike.
Why should the follies, then, of this dull age
Draw from thy pen such an immodest[6] rage
As seems to blast thy (else immortal) bays,   25

[33]The unattainable beloved of Franceso Petrarch (1304–74), who described his hopeless passion in his sonnets. [34]I.e., Honor. [35]Liberated. [36]Despite.
EPITAPH [1]Presumably the young daughter of Christopher Villiers, first earl of Anglesey, and his wife Elizabeth, who were Carew's patrons. But since the parish register of St. Martin's in the Fields records the date of the child's burial as 4 August 1630, some five months after her father's death, the assertion in lines 3–4 is puzzling.
ANOTHER [1]Blossomed.
TO BEN JONSON [1]One of several contemporary responses to Jonson's "Ode to Himself" (p. 103) that he published (1631) with *The New Inn*, a play that had been hissed from the stage in 1629. [2]One of Jonson's greatest comedies, first acted in 1610. [3]*Sunny trial*: Only eagles, birds traditionally associated with deity and royalty, were thought capable of gazing into the sun unblinded. [4]*City custom...gavelkind*: Respectively, the requirement that a London citizen divide his estate between his wife, children, and executors; a system of land tenure (peculiar to Kent) whereby a deceased person's estate is divided equally among his sons. [5]I.e. the "Sons of Ben," the poet's literary heirs and disciples. [6]Immoderate.

When thine own tongue proclaims thy itch of praise?
Such thirst will argue drought. No, let be hurl'd
Upon thy works by the detracting world
What malice can suggest: let the rout[7] say,
The running sands[8] that, ere thou make a play,   30
Count the slow minutes, might a Goodwin frame,[9]
To swallow, when th' hast done, thy shipwrack'd name.[10]
Let them the dear expense of oil upbraid,
Suck'd by thy watchful lamp, that hath betray'd
To theft the blood of martyr'd authors, spilt   35
Into thy ink, whilst thou growest pale with guilt.
Repine not at the taper's thrifty waste
That sleeks[11] thy terser poems: nor is haste
Praise, but excuse: and if thou overcome
A knotty writer, bring the booty home;   40
Nor think it theft if the rich spoils so torn
From conquered authors be as trophies worn.
Let others glut on the extorted praise
Of vulgar breath; trust thou to after days:
Thy labor'd works shall live when Time devours   45
Th' abortive offspring of their hasty hours.
Thou art not of their rank; the quarrel lies
Within thine own verge.[12] Then let this suffice:
The wiser world doth greater thee confess
Than all men else, than thyself only less.   50

AN ELEGY UPON THE DEATH OF THE DEAN OF PAUL'S, DR. JOHN DONNE[1]

Can we not force from widowed poetry,
Now thou art dead, great Donne, one elegy
To crown thy hearse? Why yet dare we not trust,
Though with unkneaded, dough-bak'd prose,[2] thy dust,
Such as the unscissor'd[3] churchman, from the flower   5
Of fading rhetoric, short-liv'd as his hour,
Dry as the sand that measures it, should lay
Upon thy ashes on the funeral day?
Have we no voice, no tune? Didst thou dispense
Through all our language both the words and sense?   10
'Tis a sad truth. The pulpit may her plain
And sober Christian precepts still retain;
Doctrines it may, and wholesome uses, frame,
Grave homilies and lectures, but the flame
Of thy brave soul, that shot such heat and light   15
As burnt our earth, and made our darkness bright,
Committed holy rapes[4] upon our will,
Did through the eye the melting heart distill,
And the deep knowledge of dark truths so teach
As sense might judge what fancy could not reach,   20
Must be desir'd forever. So the fire
That fills with spirit and heat the Delphic quire,
Which, kindled first by thy Promethean[5] breath,
Glow'd here awhile, lies quench'd now in thy death.
The Muses' garden, with pedantic weeds   25
O'erspread, was purg'd by thee; the lazy seeds
Of servile imitation thrown away,
And fresh invention planted; thou didst pay
The debts of our penurious bankrupt age,

Licentious thefts, that make poetic rage   30
A mimic fury, when our souls must be
Possess'd or with Anacreon's ecstasy
Or Pindar's,[6] not their own; the subtle cheat
Of sly exchanges and the juggling feat
Of two-edg'd words,[7] or whatsoever wrong   35
By ours was done the Greek or Latin tongue,
Thou hast redeem'd, and open'd us a mine
Of rich and pregnant fancy: drawn a line
Of masculine expression, which had good
Old Orpheus[8] seen, or all the ancient brood   40
Our superstitious fools admire, and hold
Their lead more precious than thy burnish'd gold,
Thou hadst been their exchequer, and no more
They each in other's dust had rak'd for ore.
Thou shalt yield no precedence but of time   45
And the blind fate of language, whose tun'd chime
More charms the outward sense. Yet thou may'st claim
From so great disadvantage greater fame,
Since to the awe of thy imperious wit
Our stubborn language bends, made only fit   50
With her tough thick-ribb'd hoops to gird about
Thy giant fancy, which had prov'd too stout
For their soft melting phrases. As in time
They had the start, so did they cull the prime
Buds of invention many a hundred year,   55
And left the rifled fields, besides the fear
To touch their harvest; yet from those bare lands
Of what is purely thine, thy only hands
(And that thy smallest work) have gleaned more
Than all those times and tongues could reap before.   60
    But thou art gone, and thy strict laws will be
Too hard for libertines in poetry.
They will repeal[9] the goodly exil'd train
Of gods and goddesses, which in thy just reign
Were banish'd nobler poems; now, with these,   65
The silenc'd tales o' th' *Metamorphoses*[10]

[7]I.e., the uninformed and prejudiced public.
[8]I.e., of an hourglass. Jonson was a notoriously slow writer.
[9]*A Goodwin frame*: i.e., supply the treacherous Goodwin Sands, a shifting reef off the coast of Kent.
[10]*Done...name*: i.e., to swallow your ruined name when you have finished your play. [11]Smooths, refines.
[12]Domain. Literally, an area twelve miles wide around the royal court, regarded as subject to the jurisdiction of the Lord High Steward.
AN ELEGY [1]I follow the text as printed in the first (1633) edition of Donne's *Poems,* which is markedly superior to that in the 1640 edition of Carew's *Poems.*
[2]I.e., a funeral sermon as delivered by a clergyman.
[3]I.e., with a full beard. [4]Seizures, ravishments.
[5]Referring to the fire that Prometheus stole from heaven and bestowed upon mankind.
[6]*Anacreon's...Pindar's*: i.e., poetic styles plagiarized from ancient writers. [7]Puns.
[8]In Greek myth, the divinely inspired poet-priest whose singing could charm the beasts and rocks and trees. [9]Call back.
[10]Ovid's enormously popular collection of versified tales about pagan deities. For the contemporary translation by George Sandys (whose metrical versions of the Psalms Carew praises in the follow-

Shall stuff their lines and swell the windy page,
Till verse, refin'd by thee, in this last age
Turn ballad-rhyme,[11] or those old idols be
Ador'd again with new apostasy.   70
   O pardon me, that break with untun'd verse
The reverend silence that attends thy hearse,
Whose awful, solemn murmurs were to thee,
More than these faint lines, a loud elegy,
That did proclaim in a dumb eloquence   75
The death of all the arts, whose influence,
Grown feeble, in these panting numbers lies
Gasping short-winded accents, and so dies.
So doth the swiftly turning wheel not stand
In th' instant we withdraw the moving hand,   80
But some small time maintain a faint, weak course
By virtue of the first impulsive force;
And so, whilst I cast on thy funeral pile
Thy crown of bays,[12] O let it crack[13] awhile,
And spit disdain, till the devouring flashes   85
Suck all the moisture up, then turn to ashes.
   I will not draw thee envy, to engross[14]
All thy perfections or weep all our loss;
Those are too numerous for an elegy,
And this too great to be express'd by me.   90
Though every pen should share a distinct part,
Yet art thou theme enough to 'tire[15] all art;
Let others carve the rest; it shall suffice
I on thy tomb this epitaph incise:
   Here lies a king that rul'd as he thought fit   95
   The universal monarchy of wit;
   Here lie two flamens,[16] and both those the best:
   Apollo's first, at last the true God's priest.

TO MY WORTHY FRIEND MASTER GEO. SANDYS, ON HIS TRANSLATION OF THE PSALMS[1]

I press not to the choir, nor dare I greet
The holy place with my unhallowed feet;
My unwash'd[2] Muse pollutes not things divine,
Nor mingles her profaner notes with thine;
Here humbly at the porch she list'ning[3] stays,   5
And with glad ears sucks in thy sacred lays.
So devout penitents of old were wont,
Some without door and some beneath the font,
To stand and hear the church's liturgies,
Yet not assist the solemn exercise: 10
Sufficeth her that she a lay-place gain,
To trim thy vestments, or but bear thy train;
Though nor in tune nor wing she reach[4] thy lark,
Her lyric feet may dance before the Ark.
Who knows but that her wand'ring eyes, that run   15
Now hunting glowworms, may adore the sun?
A pure flame may, shot by Almighty Power
Into her breast, the earthy flame devour;
My eyes in penitential dew may steep
That brine which they for sensual love did weep: 20
So, though 'gainst Nature's course, fire may be quench'd
With fire, and water be with water drench'd.

Perhaps my restless soul, tir'd with pursuit
Of mortal beauty, seeking without fruit
Contentment there, which hath not, when enjoy'd,   25
Quench'd all her thirst, nor satisfied, though cloy'd,
Weary of her vain search below, above
In the first Fair[5] may find th' immortal love.
Prompted by thy example, then, no more
In molds of clay will I my God adore;   30
But tear those idols from my heart, and write
What His bless'd Sp'rit, not fond[6] love, shall indite.
Then I no more shall court the verdant bay,
But the dry leafless trunk on Golgotha,[7]
And rather strive to gain from thence one thorn   35
Than all the flourishing wreaths by laureates worn.

THE COMPARISON

Dearest, thy tresses are not threads of gold,
Thy eyes of diamonds, nor do I hold
Thy lips for rubies, thy fair cheeks to be
Fresh roses, or thy teeth of ivory;
Thy skin that doth thy dainty body sheathe   5
Not alabaster is, nor dost thou breathe
Arabian odors; those the earth brings forth
Compar'd with which would but impair thy worth.
Such may be others' mistresses, but mine
Holds nothing earthly, but is all divine.   10
Thy tresses are those rays that do arise
Not from one sun, but two: such are thy eyes;
Thy lips congealed nectar are, and such
As, but a deity, there's none dare touch.
The perfect crimson that thy cheek doth clothe   15
(But only that it far exceeds them both),
Aurora's blush resembles, or that red
That Iris struts in[1] when her mantle's spread.
Thy teeth in white do Leda's swan[2] exceed;
Thy skin's a heavenly and immortal weed;   20
And when thou breath'st, the winds are ready straight
To filch it from thee, and do therefore wait
Close at thy lips, and snatching it from thence,
Bear it to heaven, where 'tis Jove's frankincense.

---

ing poem) see p. 106.
[11]The most common English stanza, quatrains (rhyming abcb) of alternate four- and three-stress lines. [12]Laurels. [13]Crackle.
[14]Write in large letters, i.e., assert boldly.
[15]Attire, i.e., adorn (with perhaps a pun on *tire*: exhaust).
[16]Priests.
TO MY WORTHY FRIEND [1]On Sandys and his work see pp. 104 ff.
Carew's poem, together with other commendatory verses, first appeared in the second (1638) edition of Sandys' *Paraphrase upon the Divine Poems.*
[2]I.e., not purified by the proper rites, hence poetically unworthy.
[3]*She list'ning stays:* Text *she stays,* but the emendation is supported by the 1638 edition of Sandys' *Paraphrase.* [4]Equal. [5]I.e., God.
[6]Foolish.
[7]*Trunk on Golgotha:* i.e., the cross whereon Christ was crucified.
THE COMPARISON [1]*Iris struts in:* Text *frisketh in,* corrected in Errata.
[2]I.e., Zeus, who embraced Leda in the form of a swan.

Fair goddess, since thy feature³ makes thee one,   25
Yet be not such for these respects alone;
But as you are divine in outward view,
So be within as fair, as good, as true.

A SONG

Ask me no more where Jove bestows,
When June is past, the fading rose,
For in your beauty's orient deep
These flowers, as in their causes, sleep.¹

Ask me no more whither doth stray   5
The golden atoms of the day,
For in pure love heaven did prepare
Those powders to enrich your hair.

Ask me no more whither doth haste
The nightingale when May is past,   10

For in your sweet dividing² throat
She winters, and keeps warm her note.

Ask me no more where those stars light
That downwards fall in dead of night,
For in your eyes they sit, and there   15
Fixed become as in their sphere.

Ask me no more if east or west
The phoenix builds her spicy nest,
For unto you at last she flies,
And in your fragrant bosom dies.   20

³Form, shape, proportions.
A SONG   ¹*For in...sleep*: i.e., just as an object is shaped by and
exemplifies the ideal in what Aristotle called its formal cause, so
the beauty of the rose reflects the radiant depth (*orient deep*) of your
own beauty.
²Performing musical divisions or rapid melodic passages, i.e.,
singing.

from Poems (1642)

AN HYMENEAL SONG ON THE NUPTIALS
OF THE LADY ANN WENTWORTH
AND THE LORD LOVELACE¹

Break not the slumbers of the bride,
But let the sun in triumph ride,
  Scattering his beamy light;

When she awakes, he shall resign
His rays, and she alone shall shine   5
  In glory all the night.

For she, till day return, must keep
An amorous vigil, and not steep
Her fair eyes in the dew of sleep.

Yet gently whisper as she lies,   10
And say her lord waits her uprise,
  The priests at the altar stay,

With flow'ry wreathes the virgin crew
Attend while some with roses strew,
  And myrtles trim the way.   15

Now to the temple and the priest
See her convey'd, thence to the feast,²
Then back to bed, though not to rest!

For now to crown his faith and truth
We must admit the noble youth   20
  To revel in Love's sphere,

To rule as chief intelligence
That orb, and happy time dispense
  To wretched lovers here.³

For they're exalted far above   25
All hope, fear, change; or they do⁴ move
The wheel that spins the fates of Love.

They know no night nor glaring noon,
Measure no hours of sun or moon,
  Nor mark Time's restless glass.   30

Their kisses measure as they flow
Minutes, and their embraces show
  The hours as they pass.

Their motions the year's circle make,
And we from their conjunctions take   35
Rules to make love an almanac.

LOVE'S FORCE

In the first ruder age when Love was wild,
Not yet by laws reclaim'd, not reconcil'd
To order, nor by Reason mann'd,¹ but flew,
Full-summ'd² by Nature, on the instant view,
Upon the wings of Appetite, at all   5
The eye could fair or sense delightful call,

AN HYMENEAL SONG   ¹Ann Wentworth and John Lovelace, second
Baron Lovelace of Hurley, were married in 1638.
²Text *fast,* corrected in the 1651 edition of Carew's *Poems.*
³*To rule...here*: i.e., to act as the governing force (*intelligence*) in
the sphere of Venus, through which, Renaissance Neoplatonists
believed, the ordering of the intelligible realm of ideas was trans-
mitted to the world of sense, so that Venus "spins the fates" (l. 27).
⁴Text *to.*
LOVE'S FORCE   ¹Tamed (a term from falconry).   ²Full-feathered.

Election³ was not yet; but as their cheap
Food from the oak or the next acorn-heap,
As water from the nearest spring or brook,
So men their undistinguish'd⁴ females took   10
By chance, not choice; but soon the heavenly spark

That in man's bosom lurk'd broke through this dark
Confusion: then the noblest breast first felt
Itself for its own proper object melt.

³Choice, discrimination.   ⁴Undifferentiated.

William Habington [1605-1654]

As an amatory poet Habington may be distinguished from the Carews and the Herricks of his day by both his chaste intentions and his rather languid verse. "In all those flames in which I burnt," he insisted in the preface to *Castara*, "I never felt a wanton heat, nor was my intention ever sinister from the strait way of chastity." Although he rejoiced that his "fortune" was "not so high as to be wondered at nor so low as to be contemned," this scion of a landed Roman Catholic family in Worcestershire must have early learned that his religion had its perils and conferred a bad distinction. Long before his birth, both his uncle Edward and his father Thomas Habington (1560–1647) had been condemned to death for their alleged connection with the Babington conspiracy (1586) in support of Mary Queen of Scots, and although his father's life was spared, Elizabeth kept him six years in the Tower before permitting his return to his estate near Worcester. There, while continuing the antiquarian researches that he had started in the Tower, he kept his hand in politics by providing shelter and concealment for persecuted Catholics. Just before his son was born he got into serious trouble for the second time by granting refuge to the elusive Jesuit Henry Garnett after the failure of the Gunpowder Plot in 1605. He again escaped the scaffold, but for the rest of his long life he was confined to Worcestershire and forbidden any role in politics.

Following the younger Habington's education with the Jesuits at St. Omer in the Low Countries (1618–23?) and then a stay in Paris, he returned to England, where, no doubt encouraged by his father, he began the historical researches that eventuated in the publication of *The History of Edward the Fourth, King of England* (1640) and a group of essays entitled *Observations upon History* (1641). It was apparently in the early 1630's that he fell in love with the aristocratic Lucy Herbert, daughter of the first Baron Powis and granddaughter of the eighth earl of Northumberland, and began to write the verses for which, as he explained, "love stole some hours from business and my more serious study."

Despite the difficulties raised by Lucy's father the chaste young lovers married, perhaps in the early spring of 1633, and in March 1634 *Castara*—an altar "both to chastity and love"—was licensed for the press and then anonymously published later in that year. Its two parts, the first on Castara's wooing and the second on her marriage, were republished under the author's name in 1635 with the addition of three prose characters ("A Mistress," "A Wife," and "A Friend") and twenty-six new poems, including eight elegies in honor of the "funerals" of the poet's friend and kinsman George Talbot. The third and last edition of the work in 1640 was again expanded, this time by a third section consisting of a character of "The Holy Man" and twenty-two devotional or meditative poems.

In addition to the two historical works already noted Habington also wrote *The Queen of Aragon*, a tragi-comedy that according to Anthony Wood was produced both at court and at Blackfriars and then published (1640) "against the author's will." When this "old Blackfriars play" was revived in 1668 it proved to be "so good," said Pepys, that he was "astonished at it" and wondered that it had "lain asleep" so long. Although Wood cryptically asserted that during the forties Habington "did then run with the times, and was not unknown to Oliver the usurper," it is unlikely that this gentle Catholic royalist would have sided with King Charles' foes. But his later years, before his death at forty-nine, are almost unrecorded.

My text is based on *Castara:—Carmina non prius Audita, Musarum sacerdos Virginibus.—The third Edition. Corrected and augmented*, 1640 (STC 12585). Kenneth Allot's edition of the poems (1948) supersedes those by C. A. Elton (1812) and Edward Arber (1870), and also gives a full account of Habington's rather uneventful life.

from Castara (1640)

THE AUTHOR

The press hath gathered into one what fancy had scattered in many loose papers. To write this, love stole some hours from business and my more serious study. For though poetry may challenge, if not priority, yet equality with the best sciences, both for antiquity and worth, I never set so high a rate upon it as to give myself entirely up to its devotion. It hath too much air, and (if without offense to our next transmarine neighbor) wantons too much according to the French garb. And when it is wholly employed in the soft strains of love, his soul who entertains it loseth much of that strength which should confirm him man. The nerves of judgment are weakened most by its dalliance, and when woman (I mean only as she is externally fair) is the supreme object of wit, we soon degenerate into effeminacy. For the religion of fancy declines into a mad superstition when it adores that idol which is not secure from age and sickness. Of such heathens our times afford us a pitied multitude, who can give no nobler testimony of twenty years' employment than some loose copies of lust happily expressed.[1] Yet these the common people of wit blow up with their breath of praise, and honor with the sacred name of poets; to which, as I believe they can never have any just claim, so shall I not dare by this essay to lay any title, since more sweat and oil he must spend who shall arrogate so excellent an attribute. Yet if the innocency of a chaste Muse shall be more acceptable and weigh heavier in the balance of esteem than a fame begot in adultery of study, I doubt I shall leave them no hope of competition. For how unhappy soever I may be in the elocution, I am sure the theme is worthy enough. In all those flames in which I burnt, I never felt a wanton heat, nor was my invention ever sinister[2] from the strait way of chastity. And when love builds upon that rock, it may safely contemn the battery of the waves and threatenings of the wind, since time, that makes a mockery of the firmest structures, shall itself be ruinated[3] before that be demolished. Thus was the foundation laid. . . .

[Conceding that he appears "to strive against the stream of best wits in erecting the selfsame altar both to chastity and love," Habington asserts that his lady's perfection justifies the innovation.]

But what malice, begot in the country upon ignorance or in the City upon criticism, shall prepare against me, I am armed to endure. For as the face of virtue looks fair without the adultery of art, so fame needs no aid from rumor to strengthen herself. If these lines want that courtship—I will not say flattery—which insinuates itself into the favor of great men best, they partake of my modesty; if satire to win applause with the envious multitude, they express my content, which maliceth[4] none the fruition of that they esteem happy. And if not too indulgent to what is my own, I think even these verses will have that proportion in the world's opinion that heaven hath allotted me in fortune: not so high as to be wondered at nor so low as to be contemned.

A MISTRESS

Is the fairest treasure the avarice of Love can covet and the only white[5] at which he shoots his arrows, nor while his aim is noble can he ever hit upon repentance. She is chaste, for the devil enters the idol and gives the oracle when wantonness possesseth beauty and wit maintains it lawful. She is as fair as Nature intended her, helped perhaps to a more pleasing grace by the sweetness of education, not by the sleight of art. She is young, for a woman past the delicacy of her spring may well move by virtue to respect, never by beauty to affection. She is innocent even from the knowledge of sin, for vice is too strong to be wrastled[6] with, and gives her frailty the soil.[7] . . . She never understood the language of a kiss but at salutation, nor dares the courtier use so much of his practiced impudence as to offer the rape[8] of it from her, because chastity hath writ it unlawful, and her behavior proclaims it unwelcome. She is never sad[9] and yet not jiggish;[10] her conscience is clear from guilt, and that secures her from sorrow. She is not passionately in love with poetry, because it softens the

---

THE AUTHOR [1] *Of such heathens...expressed*: For a similar view of contemporary love poetry see Vaughan's preface to *Silex Scintillans* (1655), p. 382.
[2] Prejudicial to. [3] Destroyed. [4] Envies, begrudges.
[5] Center of a target. [6] Wrestled. [7] Moral taint. [8] Forcing.
[9] Serious. [10] Frivolous.

heart too much to love, but she likes the harmony in the composition, and the brave examples of virtue celebrated by it she proposeth to her imitation. She is not vain in the history of her gay kindred or acquaintance, since virtue is often tenant to a cottage, and familiarity with greatness (if worth be not transcendent above the title) is but a glorious servitude fools only are willing to suffer. She is not ambitious to be praised, and yet values death beneath infamy. And I'll conclude (though the next synod of ladies condemn this character as an heresy broached by a Precisian)[11] that only she who hath as great a share in virtue as in beauty deserves a noble love to serve her, and a free poesy to speak her.

TO CASTARA, A SACRIFICE

Let the chaste phoenix from the flow'ry east
Bring the sweet treasure of her perfum'd nest
As incense to this altar, where the name
Of my Castara's grav'd[1] by th' hand of Fame.
Let purer virgins, to redeem the air   5
From loose infection, bring their zealous prayer
T' assist at this great feast, where they shall see
What rites Love offers up to Chastity.
Let all the amorous youth whose fair desire
Felt never warmth but from a noble fire   10
Bring hither their bright flames, which here shall shine
As tapers fix'd about Castara's shrine.
    While I the priest my untam'd heart surprise,
    And in this temple make't her sacrifice.

TO ROSES IN THE BOSOM OF CASTARA

Ye blushing virgins happy are
In the chaste nunn'ry of her breasts,
For he'd profane so chaste a fair,
Whoe'er should call them Cupid's nests.

Transplanted thus, how bright ye grow,   5
How rich a perfume do ye yield!
In some close garden cowslips so
Are sweeter than i' th' open field.

In those white cloisters live secure
From the rude blasts of wanton breath,   10
Each hour more innocent and pure,
Till you shall wither into death.

Then that which living gave you room,
Your glorious sepulcher shall be;
There wants no marble for a tomb,   15
Whose breast hath marble been to me.

TO A WANTON

In vain, fair sorceress, thy eyes speak charms;
In vain thou mak'st loose circles with thy arms.
I'm 'bove thy spells. No magic him can move
In whom Castara hath inspir'd her love.
As she, keep thou strict sent'nel o'er thy ear,   5
Lest it the whispers of soft courtiers hear;

Read not his raptures whose invention must
Write journey-work both for his patron's lust
And his own plush.[1] Let no admirer feast
His eye o' th' naked banquet of thy breast.   10
If this fair precedent, nor yet my want
Of love to answer thine, make thee recant
Thy sorc'ries, pity shall to justice turn
And judge thee, witch, in thy own flames to burn.

TO THE WORLD: THE PERFECTION OF LOVE

You who are earth and cannot rise
    Above your sense,
Boasting the envied wealth which lies
Bright in your mistress' lips or eyes,
Betray a pitied eloquence.   5
That which doth join our souls, so light
    And quick doth move
That like the eagle in his flight
It doth transcend all human sight,
Lost in the element[1] of love.   10

You poets reach not this who sing
    The praise of dust
But kneaded, when by theft you bring
The rose and lily from the spring
T' adorn the wrinkled face of lust.   15

When we speak love, nor art nor wit
    We gloss upon;
Our souls engender and beget
Ideas, which you counterfeit
In your dull propagation.   20

While Time seven ages shall disperse
    We'll talk of love,
And when our tongues hold no commerce
Our thoughts shall mutually converse,
And yet the blood[2] no rebel prove.   25

And though we be of several kind
    Fit for offense,
Yet we are so by love refin'd,
From impure dross we are all mind;
Death could not more have conquer'd sense.   30

How suddenly those flames expire
    Which scorch our clay;
Prometheus-like, when we steal fire
From heaven, 'tis endless and entire;
It may know age, but not decay.   35

TO CASTARA, OF THE CHASTITY OF HIS LOVE

Why would you blush, Castara, when the name
Of love you hear? Who never felt his flame

[11]Puritan.
A SACRIFICE [1]Engraved.
TO A WANTON [1]Advantage? The *OED* does not recognize the word as Habington seems to use it.
TO THE WORLD [1]Sky. [2]Sexual passion.

I' th' shade of melancholy night doth stray,
A blind Cimmerian[1] banish'd from the day.
Let's chastely love, Castara, and not soil   5
This virgin lamp by pouring in the oil
Of impure thoughts. O let us sympathize,[2]
And only talk i' th' language of our eyes,
Like two stars in conjunction. But beware
Lest th' angels, who of love compacted are,   10
Viewing how chastely burns thy zealous fire,
Should snatch thee hence to join thee to their quire.[3]
Yet take thy flight: on earth for surely we
So join'd, in heaven cannot divided be.

THE DESCRIPTION OF CASTARA

Like the violet which alone
Prospers in some happy shade,
My Castara lives unknown,
To no looser eye betray'd.
  For she's to herself untrue   5
  Who delights i' th' public view.

Such is her beauty as no arts
Have enrich'd with borrowed grace.
Her high birth no pride imparts,
For she blushes in her place;   10
  Folly boasts a glorious blood,
  She is noblest being good.

Cautious, she knew never yet
What a wanton courtship meant;
Not speaks loud to boast her wit,   15
In her silence eloquent.
  Of herself survey she takes,
  But 'tween men no difference makes.

She obeys with speedy will
Her grave parents' wise commands;   20
And so innocent that ill
She nor acts nor understands.
  Women's feet run still astray
  If once to ill they know the way.

She sails by that rock, the court,   25
Where oft honor splits her mast;
And retir'dness thinks the port
Where her fame may anchor cast.
  Virtue safely cannot fit
  Where vice is enthron'd for wit.   30

She holds that day's pleasure best
Where sin waits not on delight;
Without mask, or ball, or feast,
Sweetly spends a winter's night:
  O'er that darkness whence 'tis thrust,   35
  Prayer and sleep oft governs lust.

She her throne makes reason climb,
While wild passions captive lie;
And each article of time
Her pure thoughts to heaven fly;   40

All her vows religious be,
And her love she vows to me.

THE SECOND PART

A WIFE

Is the sweetest part in the harmony of our being. To the love of which, as the charms of nature enchant us, so the law of grace by special privilege invites us. . . . She is colleague with him in the empire of prosperity, and a safe retiring place when adversity exiles him from the world. She is so chaste she never understood the language lust speaks in, nor with a smile applauds it, although there appear wit in the metaphor. . . . She is inquisitive only of new ways to please him, and her wit sails by no other compass than that of his direction. She looks upon him as conjurers upon the circle, beyond which there is nothing but death and hell, and in him she believes paradise circumscribed. His virtues are her wonder and imitation, and his errors her credulity thinks no more frailty than makes him descend to the title of man. In a word, she so lives that she may die and leave no cloud upon her memory, but have her character nobly mentioned, while the bad wife is flattered into infamy, and buys pleasure at too dear a rate if she only pays for it repentance.

TO CASTARA, NOW POSSESS'D
OF HER IN MARRIAGE

This day is ours. The marriage angel now
Sees th' altar in the odor of our vow
Yield a more precious breath than that which moves
The whisp'ring leaves in the Panchaian[1] groves.
View how his temples shine, on which he wears   5
A wreath of pearl, made of those precious tears
Thou weptst[2] a virgin when cross winds bid blow,
Our hopes disturbing in their quiet flow.
But now, Castara, smile! No envious night
Dares interpose itself t' eclipse the light   10
Of our clear joys. For even the laws divine
Permit our mutual loves so to entwine
That kings, to balance true content, shall say,
Would they were great as we, we blest as they.

TO CASTARA UPON THOUGHT
OF AGE AND DEATH

The breath of Time shall blast the flow'ry spring
Which so perfumes thy cheek, and with it bring

OF THE CHASTITY [1]Referring to a fabulous race in Homer whose land, on the limits of the world, was shrouded in perpetual mist. [2]Enjoy a (spiritual) affinity. [3]Choir.
NOW POSSESS'D [1]Referring to Panchaia, a region in Arabia noted for its precious stones and incenses. [2]Best *wepst*.

So dark a mist as shall eclipse the light
Of thy fair eyes in an eternal night.
Some melancholy chamber of the earth 5
(For that, like Time, devours whom it gave breath)
Thy beauties shall entomb, while all who ere
Lov'd nobly offer up their sorrows there.
But I, whose grief no formal limits bound,
Beholding the dark cavern of that ground 10
Will there immure myself. And thus I shall
Thy mourner be, and my own funeral.
   Else by the weeping magic of my verse
   Thou hadst reviv'd to triumph o'er thy hearse.

LOVE'S ANNIVERSARY. TO THE SUN

Thou art return'd, great light, to that blest hour
In which I first by marriage, sacred power,
Join'd with Castara hearts; and as the same
Thy luster is as then, so is our flame,
Which had increas'd but that by Love's decree 5
'Twas such at first it ne'er could greater be.
But tell me, glorious lamp, in thy survey
Of things below thee, what did not decay
By age to weakness? I since that have seen
The rose bud forth and fade, the tree grow green 10
And wither, and the beauty of the field
With winter wrinkled. Even thyself dost yield
   Something to time, and to thy grave fall nigher.
   But virtuous love is one sweet endless fire.

THE FUNERALS OF THE HONORABLE,
MY BEST FRIEND AND KINSMAN,
GEORGE TALBOT, ESQUIRE[1]
Elegy 8

Boast not the rev'rend Vatican, nor all
The cunning pomp of the Escurial:[2]
Though there both th' Indies[3] met in each small room,
Th' are short in treasure of this precious tomb.
Here is th' epitome of wealth; this chest 5
Is Nature's chief exchequer; hence the east,
When it is purified by th' general fire,
Shall see these now pale ashes sparkle higher
Than all the gems she vaunts, transcending far
In fragrant luster the bright morning star. 10
'Tis true, they now seem dark, but rather we
Have by a cataract lost sight than he,
Though dead his glory. So to us black night
Brings darkness when the sun retains his light.
Thou eclips'd dust, expecting break of day 15
From the thick mists about thy tomb, I'll pay,
Like the just lark, the tribute of my verse.
I will invite thee from thy envious[4] hearse
To rise and 'bout the world thy beams to spread,
That we may see there's brightness in the dead. 20
My zeal deludes me not. What perfumes come

From th' happy vault? In her sweet martyrdom
The nard breathes never so, nor so the rose
When the enamor'd spring by kissing blows
Soft blushes on her cheek, nor th' early east 25
Vying with paradise i' th' phoenix nest.
These gentle perfumes usher in the day
Which from the night of his discolor'd clay
Breaks on the sudden, for a soul so bright
Of force must to her earth contribute light. 30
But if w' are so far blind we cannot see
The wonder of this truth, yet let us be
Not infidels, nor like dull atheists give
Ourselves so long to lust till we believe
(T' allay the grief of sin) that we shall fall 35
To a loath'd nothing in our funeral.
   The bad man's death is horror, but the just
   Keeps something of his glory in his dust.

THE THIRD PART

"SOLUM MIHI SUPEREST SEPULCHRUM." JOB[1]

Welcome, thou safe retreat
Where th' injured man may fortify
'Gainst the invasions of the great,
Where the lean slave who th' oar doth ply
Soft as his admiral may lie. 5

Great statist,[2] 'tis your doom,
Though your designs swell high and wide,
To be contracted in a tomb,
And all your happy cares provide
But for your heir authorized pride. 10

Nor shall your shade delight
I' th' pomp of your proud obsequies;
And should the present flattery write
A glorious epitaph, the wise
Will say, "The poet's wit here lies." 15

How reconcil'd to fate
Will grow the aged villager
When he shall see your funeral state,

THE FUNERALS [1]George Talbot (d. ca. 1634), a younger brother of
John, tenth earl of Shrewsbury, wrote some commendatory
verses for the 1635 edition of *Castara* where, addressing "His Best
Friend and Kinsman," he said that he and Habington
                  are known
   To th' world, as to ourselves, to be but one
   In blood and study.
In the moving character of "A Friend" that stands as a sort of
preface to the eight elegies for Talbot in the 1635 edition, Habing-
ton remarked that "in life he is the most amiable object to the
soul, in death the most deplorable [i.e., to be deplored]."
[2]The Escorial, the huge royal residence built by Philip II near
Madrid. [3]*Both th' Indies*: i.e., the East and West. [4]Odious.
SOLUM MIHI [1]"The grave is ready for me" (Job 17.1).
[2]Statesman, politician.

Since Death will him as warm inter
As you in your gay[3] sepulcher?   20

    The great decree of God
Makes every path of mortals lead
To this dark common period,
For what byways soe'er we tread,
We end our journey 'mong the dead.   25

    Even I, while humble zeal
Makes Fancy a sad truth indite,
Insensible away do steal,
And when I'm lost in Death's cold night,
Who will remember now I write?   30

"NOX NOCTI INDICAT SCIENTIAM." DAVID[1]

When I survey the bright
   Celestial sphere,
So rich with jewels hung that night
Doth like an Ethiop bride appear,

My soul her wings doth spread   5
   And heavenward flies,
Th' Almighty's mysteries to read
In the large volumes of the skies.

For the bright firmament
   Shoots forth no flame   10
So silent, but is eloquent
In speaking the Creator's name.

No unregarded star
   Contracts its light
Into so small a character,[2]   15
Remov'd far from our human sight,

But if we steadfast look,
   We shall discern
In it, as in some holy book,
How man may heavenly knowledge learn.   20

It tells the conqueror
   That far-stretch'd pow'r
Which his proud dangers traffic for,
Is but the triumph of an hour;

That from the farthest north   25
   Some nation may,
Yet undiscovered, issue forth
And o'er his new-got conquest sway.

Some nation yet shut in
   With hills of ice   30
May be let out to scourge his sin
Till they shall equal him in vice.

And then they likewise shall
   Their ruin have;
For as yourselves, your empires fall,   35
And every kingdom hath a grave.

Thus those celestial fires,
   Though seeming mute,

The fallacy of our desires
And all the pride of life confute.   40

For they have watch'd since first
   The world had birth;
And found sin in itself accurst,
And nothing permanent on earth.

"RECOGITABO TIBI OMNES ANNOS MEOS." ISAY[1]

Time, where didst thou those years inter
   Which I have seen decease?
My soul's at war, and Truth bids her
Find out their hidden sepulcher
   To give her troubles peace.   5

Pregnant with flowers, doth not the Spring
   Like a late bride appear,
Whose feather'd music[2] only bring
Caresses, and no requiem sing
   On the departed year?   10

The earth, like some rich wanton heir
   Whose parents coffin'd lie,
Forgets it once look'd pale and bare,
And doth for vanities prepare
   As[3] the Spring ne'er should die.   15

The present hour, flattered by all,
   Reflects not on the last,
But I, like a sad factor,[4] shall
T' account my life each moment call,
   And only weep the past.   20

My mem'ry tracks each several way
   Since Reason did begin
Over my actions her first sway,
And teacheth me that each new day
   Did only vary sin.   25

Poor bankrout[5] Conscience, where are those
   Rich hours but farm'd[6] to thee?
How carelessly I some did lose,
And other to my lust dispose
   As no rent day[7] should be!   30

I have infected with impure
   Disorders my past years,
But I'll to penitence inure
Those that succeed: there is no cure
   Nor antidote but tears.   35

[3]Showy.

NOX NOCTI [1]"[Day unto day uttereth speech, and] night unto night showeth knowledge" (Psalms 19.2).
[2]Sign, emblem.

RECOGITABO TIBI [1]Isaiah 38.15. The translation in the Geneva Bible ("I shall walk weakly all my years") seems to be more appropriate in this context than that of the Authorized Version ("I shall go softly all my years").
[2]Company of musicians. [3]As if. [4]Agent. [5]Bankrupt.
[6]Granted for a term at a fixed payment, i.e., leased.
[7]Stipulated time for payment of rents and other charges.

Thomas Randolph [1605-1635]

Like Chatterton and Rupert Brooke and certain other poets who died untimely, Randolph became the center of a cult that the merits of his work could not long sustain. To read his admirers' lachrymose and absurdly eulogistic poems included in the posthumous edition of his works is to be reminded that affection often stifles criticism. A man is not upon his oath, said Johnson, in lapidary inscriptions.

Although we may question the accuracy of one of these admirers who, anticipating Pope's remark about himself, reported that Randolph "lisp'd wit worthy th' press," we have John Aubrey's word for it that he had seen a versified "History of the Incarnation of Our Saviour" that Randolph composed as a little boy of nine. Fortunately, this prodigy of piety was also bright and able. The son of an estate steward in Northamptonshire, he went as a king's scholar to the great Westminster School and then, in 1624, to Trinity College, Cambridge. Unlike Milton, who entered Christ's the following year, Randolph was such a gregarious and successful undergraduate that after his B.A. in 1628 he was named a minor fellow of his college, and on taking his M.A. in 1632 he was promoted to the rank of major fellow. These academic triumphs were capped not long after by his incorporation for the M.A. degree at Oxford.

Like Cowley's somewhat later, Randolph's years at Trinity were filled with literature. A fluent versifier in both Latin and English, he was, as one of Jonson's young admirers, also warmly drawn to drama. In 1630 his "Entertainment" (subsequently rewritten as *The Muses' Looking-glass*) was licensed, and it was followed by his *Aristippus, or the Jovial Philosopher . . . to Which Is Added the Conceited Peddler*, the first a dramatic sketch in prose and verse and the second a sprightly monologue in prose. Two years later his blank verse comedy *The Jealous Lovers* was presented before King Charles and his consort at Cambridge and then published by the printer to the university.

Already, with the closing of the university in 1630 by an epidemic of the plague, Randolph had very likely tasted the dissipations and delights of London, and in 1632 he went to be among the Sons of Ben and lead the raffish life reflected in his poems. The production, perhaps in 1632/33, of his pastoral play *Amyntas* before the court at Whitehall suggests that he enjoyed a quick success, but it was soon cut short when, on a visit to Northamptonshire for rest and recreation, he came "untimely to his end" at only thirty, the victim, Anthony Wood explained, of "indulging himself too much with the liberal conversation of his admirers (a thing incident to poets)." In his elaborate tomb at Blatherwick, Northamptonshire, according to its mortuary inscription, are sleeping all the Muses and the Graces,

> Who, having wept their fountains dry
> Through the conduit of the eye
> For their friend who here does lie,
> Crept into his grave and died.

A different kind of testimonial was provided by his brother Robert, who supervised the publication of his works in 1638. In thirty years it went through eight editions.

My text is based on *Poems with the Muses Looking-glasse: and Amyntas. By Thomas Randolph Master of Arts and late Fellow of Trinity Colledge in Cambridge*, 1638 (STC 20694). W. C. Hazlitt's edition of Randolph's works (2 vols., 1875), like other things he did, has failed to stand the test of time and now has been supplanted by J. J. Parry's *Poems and Amyntas* (1917) and George Thorn-Drury's *Poems* (1929). Some additions to the canon were reported by C. L. Day, *RES*, VIII (1932).

from Poems, with the Muses' Looking-glass and Amyntas (1638)

A GRATULATORY TO MASTER BEN JONSON FOR HIS ADOPTING OF HIM TO BE HIS SON[1]

I was not born to Helicon, nor dare
Presume to think myself a Muse's heir.
I have no title to Parnassus hill,
Nor any acre of it by the will
Of a dead ancestor, nor could I be   5
Aught but a tenant unto poetry.
But thy adoption quits me of all fear,
And makes me challenge a child's portion[2] there.
I am akin to heroes, being thine,
And part of my alliance is divine.   10
Orpheus, Musaeus, Homer too, beside
Thy brothers by the Roman mother's side,
As Ovid, Vergil, and the Latin lyre
That is so like thy Horace—the whole quire[3]
Of poets are by thy adoption all   15
My uncles; thou hast given me pow'r to call
Phoebus himself my grandsire; by this grant
Each sister of the Nine[4] is made my aunt.
Go, you that reckon from a large descent
Your lineal honors, and are well content   20
To glory in the age of your great name,
Though on a herald's faith[5] you build the same,
I do not envy you, nor think you blest
Though you may bear a Gorgon on your crest
By direct line from Perseus;[6] I will boast   25
No farther than my father; that's the most
I can or should be proud of, and I were
Unworthy his adoption if that here
I should be dully modest; boast I must,
Being son of his adoption, not his lust.   30
And to say truth, that which is best in me
May call you father, 'twas begot by thee.
Have I a spark of that celestial flame
Within me, I confess I stole the same,
Prometheus-like,[7] from thee; and may I feed   35
His vulture when I dare deny the deed.
Many more moons thou hast that shine by night,
All bankrups,[8] were't not for a borrow'd light,
Yet can forswear it; I the debt confess
And think my reputation ne'er the less.   40
For father, let me be resolv'd by you:
Is't a disparagement from rich Peru
To ravish gold, or theft, for wealthy ore
To ransack Tagus' or Pactolus'[9] shore?
Or does he wrong Alcinous,[10] that for want   45

Doth take from him a sprig or two to plant
A lesser orchard? Sure it cannot be;
Nor is it theft to steal some flames from thee.
Grant this, and I'll cry "Guilty," as I am,
And pay a filial reverence to thy name.   50
For when my Muse upon obedient knees
Asks not a father's blessing, let her leese[11]
The fame of this adoption; 'tis a curse
I wish her, 'cause I cannot think a worse.
And here, as piety bids me, I entreat   55
Phoebus to lend thee some of his own heat
To cure thy palsy,[12] else I will complain
He has no skill in herbs; poets in vain
Make him the god of physic. 'Twere his praise
To make thee as immortal as thy bays,   60
As his own Daphne;[13] 'twere a shame to see
The god not love his priest more than his tree.
  But if heaven take thee, envying us thy lyre,
  'Tis to pen anthems for an angels' quire.

AN ELEGY UPON THE LADY VENETIA DIGBY[1]

Death, who'ld not change prerogatives with thee,
That dost such rapes, yet mayst not question'd be?
Here cease thy wanton lust, be satisfied;
Hope not a second and so fair a bride.

A GRATULATORY [1]According to a contemporary account, Randolph, then a Cambridge undergraduate, was adopted by Jonson as his "son" and literary heir after he had improvised some verses during a bibulous meeting in a tavern. *Gratulatory*: a work expressing gratitude.
[2]*Makes...portion*: i.e., makes me claim a son's legal share   [3]Choir.
[4]I.e., the Nine Muses.
[5]I.e., the certification of one's genealogy by the Heralds' College (for whose functions see pp. 821 f.).
[6]*Gorgon...Perseus*: Perseus, the son of Zeus and Danae, won renown by decapitating Medusa, one of three monstrous sisters known as Gorgons.
[7]For stealing fire from heaven and giving it to man the Titan Prometheus was chained to a rock where he was gnawed daily by an eagle.   [8]Bankrupts.
[9]*Tagus...Pactolus*: rivers in the Iberian peninsula and Lydia respectively, noted for their yellow sands.
[10]In the *Odyssey*, the king of the Phaeacians on the island of Scheria (Corfu?), which was noted for its vegetation.   [11]Lose.
[12]During his last ten years of life Jonson (d. 1637) was almost immobilized by palsy.
[13]A maiden who, when pursued by Apollo, was turned into a laurel.

AN ELEGY [1]After a tempestuous courtship the famous beauty

Where was her Mars,[2] whose valiant arms did hold 5
This Venus once, that thou durst be so bold
By thy too nimble theft? I know 'twas fear
Lest he should come that would have rescu'd her.
Monster, confess, didst thou not blushing stand,
And thy pale cheek turn red to touch her hand? 10
Did she not lightning-like strike sudden heat
Through thy cold limbs, and thaw thy frost to sweat?
Well, since thou hast her, use her gently, Death,
And in requital of such precious breath
Watch sentinel to guard her; do not see 15
The worms thy rivals, for the gods will be.
Remember Paris, for whose pettier sin
The Trojan gates let the stout Grecians in;
So when Time ceases (whose unthrifty hand
Has now almost consum'd his stock of sand) 20
Myriads of angels shall in armies come,
And fetch, proud ravisher, their[3] Helen home.
And to revenge this rape, thy other store
Thou shalt resign too, and shalt steal no more.
Till then, fair ladies (for you now are fair, 25
But till her death I fear'd your just despair),
Fetch all the spices that Arabia yields,
Distill the choicest flowers of the fields,
And when in one their best perfections meet,
Embalm her corse, that she may make them sweet, 30
Whilst for an epitaph upon her stone
I cannot write, but I must weep her one.

Epitaph

Beauty itself lies here, in whom alone
Each part enjoy'd the same perfection.
In some the eyes we praise, in some the hair; 35
In her the lips, in her[4] the cheeks are fair;
That nymph's fine feet, her hands we beauteous call;
But in this form we praise no part, but all.
The ages past have many beauties shown,
And I more plenty in our time have known, 40
But in the age to come I look for none:
Nature despairs because her pattern's gone.

AN EPITHALAMIUM

Muse, be a bride-maid! Dost not hear
How honored Hunt and his fair Dear
This day prepare their wedding cheer?

The swiftest of thy pinions take,
And hence a sudden journey make 5
To help 'em break their bridal cake.

Haste 'em to church, tell 'em Love says
Religion breeds but fond[1] delays
To lengthen out the tedious days.

Chide the slow priest, that so goes on 10
As if he fear'd he should have done
His sermon ere the glass be run.

Bid him post o'er his words as fast
As if himself were not to taste
The pleasure of so fair a waste. 15

Now lead the blessed couple home
And serve a dinner up for some:
Their banquet is as yet to come.

Maids dance as nimbly as your blood,
Which I see swell a purple flood 20
In emulation of that good

The bride possesseth, for I deem
What she enjoys will be the theme
This night of every virgin's dream.

But envy not their bless'd content: 25
The hasty night is almost spent,
And they of Cupid will be shent.[2]

The sun is now ready to ride;
Sure 'twas the morning I espied,
Or 'twas the blushing of the bride. 30

See how the lusty bridegroom's veins
Swell till the active torrent strains
To break those o'erstretch'd azure chains.

And the fair bride, ready to cry
To see her pleasant loss so nigh, 35
Pants like the seeled[3] pigeon's eye.

Put out the torch; Love loves no lights.
Those that perform his mystic rites
Must pay their orisons by nights.

Nor can that sacrifice be done 40
By any priest or nun alone,
But when they both are met in one.

Now you that taste of Hymen's cheer,
See that your lips do meet so near
That cockles might be tutor'd there;[4] 45

And let the whisp'rings of your love
Such short and gentle murmurs prove
As they were lectures to the dove.

And in such strict embraces twine
As if you read unto the vine, 50
The ivy, and the columbine.

Then let your mutual bosoms beat
Till they create by virtual heat
Myrrh, balm, and spikenard in a sweat.

Venetia Stanley (d. 1633) secretly married the swashbuckling Sir
Kenelm Digby (see p. 486) in 1625. Her death was commemorated
by Jonson, Habington, and many other poets.
[2]I.e., Sir Kenelm Digby, on whose military exploits see p. 796.
[3]Text *there*.
[4]*In her…in her*: in one woman…in another.
AN EPITHALAMIUM [1] Foolish. [2]Free, exempt.
[3]I.e., with eyelids sewn together (a term from falconry).
[4]*That cockles…there*: i.e., that even the bivalve mollusks may
learn from you to keep their shells tightly closed?

Thence may there spring many a pair 55
Of sons and daughters strong and fair.
How soon the gods have heard my prayer!

Methinks already I espy
The cradles rock, the babies cry,
And drowsy nurses lullaby.[5] 60

UPON HIS PICTURE

When age hath made me what I am not now,
And every wrinkle tells me where the plow
Of Time hath furrowed, when an ice shall flow
Through every vein, and all my head wear snow;
When Death displays his coldness in my cheek, 5
And I myself in my own picture seek,
Not finding what I am, but what I was,
In doubt which to believe, this or my glass:
Yet though I alter, this remains the same
As it was drawn, retains the primitive[1] frame 10
And first complexion; here will still be seen
Blood on the cheek and down upon the chin;
Here the smooth brow will stay, the lively eye,
The ruddy lip, and hair of youthful dye.
Behold what frailty we in man may see, 15
Whose shadow[2] is less given to change than he.

AN ODE TO MASTER ANTHONY STAFFORD[1]
TO HASTEN HIM INTO THE COUNTRY

Come, spur away,
I have no patience for a longer stay,
But must go down
And leave the chargeable[2] noise of this great town.
I will the country see, 5
Where old simplicity
Though hid in gray
Doth look more gay
Than foppery in plush and scarlet clad.
Farewell, you City wits that are 10
Almost at civil war;
'Tis time that I grow wise, when all the world grows mad.

More of my days
I will not spend to gain an idiot's praise,
Or to make sport 15
For some slight puny[3] of the Inns of Court.
Then, worthy Stafford, say
How shall we spend the day;
With what delights
Shorten the nights? 20
When from this tumult we are got secure
Where mirth with all her freedom goes,
Yet shall no finger lose,[4]
Where every word is thought, and every thought is pure.

There from the tree 25
We'll cherries pluck, and pick the strawberry.
And every day

Go see the wholesome country girls make hay,
Whose brown hath lovelier grace
Than any painted face 30
That I do know
Hyde Park can show;
Where I had rather gain a kiss than meet
(Though some of them in greater state
Might court my love with plate)[5] 35
The beauties of the Cheap,[6] and wives of Lombard Street.

But think upon
Some other pleasures; these to me are none.
Why do I prate
Of women, that are things against my fate? 40
I never mean to wed
That torture to my bed;
My Muse is she
My love shall be.
Let clowns get wealth and heirs; when I am gone, 45
And the great bugbear, grisly Death,
Shall take this idle breath,
If I a poem leave, that poem is my son.

Of this, no more;
We'll rather taste the bright Pomona's[7] store 50
No fruit shall 'scape
Our palates, from the damson to the grape.
Then full we'll seek a shade,
And hear what music's made:
How Philomel[8] 55
Her tale doth tell,
And how the other birds do fill the quire;
The thrush and blackbird lend their throats,
Warbling melodious notes.
We will all sports enjoy, which others but desire. 60

Ours is the sky,
Where at what fowl we please our hawk shall fly;
Nor will we spare
To hunt the crafty fox or timorous hare;
But let our hounds run loose 65
In any ground they'll choose;
The buck shall fall,
The stag and all.
Our pleasures must from their own warrants be,
For to my Muse, if not to me, 70

[5]A verb: sing to sleep.
UPON HIS PICTURE [1]Original. [2]I.e., picture.
AN ODE TO MASTER STAFFORD [1]An uncle to the William Stafford
in whose house at Blatherwick, Northamptonshire, Randolph
died in 1635. [2]Burdensome. [3]Student.
[4]Having lost a finger in a fight following a drinking bout, Ran-
dolph promptly wrote a poem on the "departed joint."
[5]I.e., gold or silver plate, part of the customary dowry of a rich
merchant's daughter.
[6]Cheapside, a London thoroughfare noted for its goldsmiths' shops,
as Lombard Street was for commercial establishments.
[7]The Roman goddess of orchards.
[8]Philomela, a maiden who was turned into a nightingale following
her rape and mutilation.

I'm sure all game is free;
Heaven, earth, are all but parts of her great royalty.

And when we mean
To taste of Bacchus' blessings now and then,
    And drink by stealth   75
A cup or two to noble Berkeley's[9] health,
    I'll take my pipe and try
    The Phrygian[10] melody,
      Which he that hears
      Lets through his ears   80
A madness to distemper all the brain.
    Then I another pipe will take
    And Doric music make,
To civilize with graver notes our wits again.

AN ANSWER TO MASTER BEN JONSON'S ODE, TO PERSUADE HIM NOT TO LEAVE THE STAGE[1]

Ben, do not leave the stage
  'Cause 'tis a loathsome age,
For Pride and Impudence will grow too bold
  When they shall hear it told
They frighted thee. Stand high as is thy cause;   5
  Their hiss is thy applause;
  More just were thy disdain
  Had they approv'd thy vein.
So thou for them and they for thee were born:
They to incense and thou as much to scorn.   10

Wilt thou engross[2] thy store
  Of wheat, and pour no more
Because their bacon-brains have such a taste
  As more delight in mast?[3]
No, set 'em forth a board of dainties, full   15
  As thy best Muse can cull,
  While they the while do pine
  And thirst midst all their wine.
What greater plague can hell itself devise
Than to be willing thus to tantalize?   20

Thou canst not find them stuff
  That will be bad enough
To please their palates. Let 'em thine refuse
  For some Pie Corner[4] Muse;
She is too fair an hostess; 'twere a sin   25
  For them to like thine *Inn*:
  'Twas made to entertain
  Guests of a nobler strain,
Yet if they will have any of thy store,
Give 'em some scraps and send them from thy door.   30

And let those things in plush,[5]
  Till they be taught to blush,
Like what they will, and more contented be
  With what Broome[6] swept from thee.
I know thy worth, and that thy lofty strains   35
  Write not to clothes, but brains;
  But thy great spleen doth rise
  'Cause moles will have no eyes.

This only in my Ben I faulty find:
He's angry they'll not see him that are blind.   40

Why should the scene be mute
  'Cause thou canst touch a lute
And string[7] thy Horace? Let each Muse of nine
  Claim thee and say, "Thou art mine."
'Twere fond to let all other flames expire   45
  To sit by Pindar's fire,
  For by so strange neglect
  I should myself suspect
The palsy were as well thy brain's disease
If they could shake thy Muse which way they please.   50

And though thou well canst sing
  The glories of thy king,[8]
And on the wings of verse his chariot bear
  To heaven, and fix it there,
Yet let thy Muse as well some raptures raise   55
  To please him as to praise.
  I would not have thee choose
  Only a treble[9] Muse,
But have this envious, ignorant age to know
Thou that canst sing so high canst reach as low.   60

ON THE DEATH OF A NIGHTINGALE

Go, solitary wood, and henceforth be
Acquainted with no other harmony
Than the pies' chattering, or the shrieking note
Of boding owls, and fatal raven's throat.
Thy sweetest chanter's dead, that warbled forth   5
Lays that might tempests calm, and still the north,
And call down angels from their glorious sphere
To hear her songs, and learn new anthems there.
That soul is fled and to Elysium gone;
Thou a poor desert left; go then and run,   10
Beg there to stand a grove, and if she please
To sing again beneath thy shadowy trees,
The souls of happy lovers crown'd with blisses
Shall flock about thee, and keep time with kisses.

[9]George, Baron Berkeley (1601–58), a nobleman to whom Burton dedicated (1621) *The Anatomy of Melancholy*.
[10]A Greek mode generally used for soft and sensual music, whereas the more severe Doric (line 83) was reserved for martial songs.
AN ANSWER [1]One of several answers to Jonson's "Come, leave the loathed stage" (p. 103), which the old man wrote on the failure of his play *The New Inn* (1629). For Carew's poem on the subject see p. 229. [2]Monopolize, reserve only for yourself.
[3]Food for swine (carrying on the figure in *bacon-brains* in the line above).
[4]A locality in Smithfield, the market district of London, noted for its cookshops.
[5]*Things in plush*: i.e., richly dressed men of fashion (who had joined in damning Jonson's play).
[6]Richard Brome (d. 1652?), a servant (or perhaps secretary) of Jonson's whose own vigorous comedies (e.g., *The Jovial Crew*, 1641) show his master's strong influence. [7]Tune.
[8]Randolph is gently parodying the last stanza of Jonson's poem (see p. 104). [9]Soprano, i.e., thin-voiced.

A MASK FOR LYDIA

Sweet Lydia, take this mask and shroud
Thy face within the silken cloud,
  And veil those powerful skies;
For he whose gazing dares so high aspire
  Makes burning glasses of his eyes,   5
And sets his heart on fire.

Veil, Lydia, veil, for unto me
There is no basilisk[1] but thee;
  Thy very looks do kill.
Yet in those looks so fix'd is my delight,   10
  Poor soul, alas, I languish still
In absence of thy sight.

Close up those eyes, or we shall find
Too great a luster strike us blind.
  Or if a ray so good   15
Ought to be seen, let it but then appear
  When eagles do produce their brood,
To try their young ones there.[2]

Or if thou wouldst have me to know
How great a brightness thou canst show   20
  When they have lost the sun,
Then do thou rise and give the world this theme:
  Sol from th' Hesperides is run,[3]
And back hath whipp'd his team.

Yet through the Goat when he shall stray,   25
Thou through the Crab must take thy way,[4]

For should you both shine bright
In the same tropic, we poor moles should get
  Not so much comfort by the light
As torment by the heat.   30

Where's Lydia now? Where shall I seek
Her charming lip, her tempting cheek,
  That my affections bow'd?
So dark a sable hath eclips'd my fair
  That I can gaze upon the cloud   35
That durst not see the star.

But yet methinks my thoughts begin
To say there lies a white within,
  Though black her pride control.[5]
And what care I how black a face I see   40
  So there be whiteness in the soul?
Still such an Ethiope be!

A MASK [1]A fabled reptile whose look was thought to kill.
[2]*To...there*: Only eagles were thought capable of gazing at the sun unblinded.
[3]*Sol...run*: The sun has returned from the west. The garden of the Hesperides, where the golden apples of the sun were guarded by a group of maidens and a dragon, was in Greek myth located far to the west.
[4]*Yet...way*: You and the other sun must keep always to different hemispheres: thus in midwinter when he is in the zodiacal sign of Capricorn or the Goat, you must be at the opposite extreme, in Cancer or the Crab (which he occupies in midsummer).
[5]*Her pride control*: overpower her outward splendor.

Edmund Waller [1606-1687]

When we recall that Thomas Rymer, in funerary Latin, commemorated Waller as *inter poetas sui temporis facile princeps* ("easily first among the poets of his time") and that Waller's time was also that of Milton, Marvell, and Dryden, we tend to smile at Rymer's bad mistake. However, we condescend toward Dryden at our peril, and Dryden tersely stated, as the received opinion of his day, that the "excellence and dignity" of English rhyme "were never known till Mr. Waller taught it." Since Waller, as has long been recognized, is a very minor poet, the collapse of his enormous reputation serves to warn us that our own cocksure critical assessments are liable to the same reversal and decay.

Like his reception as a poet, Waller's life, except for one imprudent episode, was a series of successes. The eldest son of an extremely wealthy father who died when his heir was only ten, he survived his faulty elementary schooling and finally got to Eton. From there he gained admission (1620) to King's College, Cambridge, and then, in 1622, to Lincoln's Inn. By this time, at the implausibly early age of sixteen or thereabout, he had entered public service by election (or appointment) to the House of Commons. Already rich, he grew even richer through his marriage (1631) to an heiress of the City. Her death in 1634 released him, as it were, for the stylized flirtation reflected in the poems that he wrote for "Sacharissa," his insipid sobriquet for the celebrated Lady

Dorothy Sidney, later countess of Sunderland. These artful tributes to her wit and beauty made Sacharissa famous, but (perhaps as Waller wished) they did not win the lady. (Johnson tells the story of the aged woman asking her old suitor "when he would again write such verses upon her. 'When you are as young, Madam,' said he, 'and as handsome as you were then.' ") It was in the flaring sunset of the second Stuart's reign that Waller, sponsored by George Morley (later bishop of Winchester and grandee of another Stuart's reign), adorned Lord Falkland's circle at Great Tew (see p. 799). In that highly cultivated coterie, said Clarendon (who detested him in later years), Waller had a great success—and "he was not the less esteemed for being very rich."

In the gathering darkness of the early forties Waller, who as a member of the Long Parliament spoke and worked for moderation, made the almost fatal error of participating in the plot to which his name is still attached. Fortunately for English liberties, the plot—to seize London for the King and thus at one stroke end the civil war—was exposed before its preparation was completed, and Waller, together with some of his associates, was at once arrested (May 1643). Although the details of what then happened have remained obscure, it is known that he, no doubt to save his life, informed against his co-conspirators, some of whom were promptly tried and hanged, whereas he was merely barred from ever serving in the House again, fined £10,000, and banished from the realm (November 1644). Waller's base behavior, Clarendon later wrote in icy indignation, "preserved and won his life from those who were most resolved to take it, and in an occasion in which he ought to have been ambitious to have lost it."

But as usual Waller landed on his feet. His French exile was solaced by the wife he married, it appears, on the eve of his departure and by such distinguished refugees as Henry Jermyn, Hobbes, and Evelyn. After he had spent seven years abroad, the House, perhaps at the intervention of his distant kinsman Cromwell, permitted his return and pardoned him. In 1655 the Lord Protector arranged for his return to public service by appointing him a commissioner of trade, and on his benefactor's death Waller wrote the splendid panegyric (p. 251) wherein, as Johnson tersely noted, there is "no mention of the rebel or the regicide."

With Charles' restoration in 1660 (which Waller duly celebrated in heroic couplets) the poet's own recovery was complete, and for almost another generation he enjoyed, and even added to, the perquisites—political, social, and literary—that he had known before. To this later phase of his career belong such once admired productions as his *Instructions to a Painter* (1665) and the six cantos of religious verse (1685) that prompted Johnson's famous strictures on poetry as an instrument of "contemplative piety." No man's "conversation" was more esteemed at court than Waller's, according to John Aubrey, for even in his final feeble years he retained his "intellectuals" unimpaired, and was noted for his "florid" wit. Johnson tells that when the old man found his legs becoming "tumid" he set forth at once for Windsor to consult the king's physician and ask him what the swelling meant. " 'Sir,' answered Scarborough, 'your blood will run no longer.' Waller repeated some lines of Vergil, and went home to die."

Although the first edition of Waller's *Poems* (1645) was perhaps unauthorized, he himself, it seems, was involved in its second issue and in two new editions of 1645. Nonetheless, according to the printer, it was only with extreme reluctance that the poet assented to a "new and well corrected" edition in 1664. Others duly followed in 1668, 1682, and 1686; and in 1690 the later work was brought together as *The Second Part of Mr. Waller's Poems*, a book whose reader, said the eulogistic preface, "needs be told no more in commendation of these poems than that they are Mr. Waller's, a name that carries everything in it that is either great or graceful in poetry."

My texts are based on *Poems, &c. Written Upon Several Occasions, And To Several Persons . . . Never till now Corrected and Published with the approbation of the Author*, 1664 (Wing W-514) and *Three Poems Upon the Death of his late Highness Oliver Lord Protector of England, Scotland, and Ireland. Written By Mr Edm. Waller. Mr Jo. Dryden. Mr Sprat, of Oxford*, 1659 (Wing W-526). Although Elijah Fenton's sumptuous presentation of *The Works in Verse and Prose* (1729) reached a third edition in a generation and was followed by Percival Stockdale's elaborate new edition (with a life) in 1772, the decline in Waller's reputation was reflected by his relative neglect throughout the last two centuries. Indeed, George Thorn-Drury's edition of 1893 (2 vols., 1905) was the first for many decades, and it remains the latest. In addition to Stockdale's life and Johnson's famous piece on Waller there is an old biography of "Sacharissa" by Julia Cartwright (1893) and a new account of Waller's work by W. L. Chernaik (*The Poetry of Limitation*, 1968). Two important articles in which Waller figures are Ruth Wallerstein's on the heroic couplet (*PMLA*, L, 1935) and George Williamson's on the rhetorical pattern of neoclassical wit (*MP*, XXXIII, 1935–36).

from Poems, etc. Written upon Several Occasions and to Several Persons (1664)

THE PRINTER TO THE READER

When the author of these verses (written only to please himself and such particular persons to whom they were directed) returned from abroad some years since, he was troubled to find his name in print but somewhat satisfied to see his lines so ill rendered that he might justly disown them, and say to a mistaking printer, as one did to an ill reciter, *Male dum recitas, incipit esse tuum.*[1]

Having been ever since pressed to correct the many and gross faults (such as use to be[2] in impressions wholly neglected by the authors), his answer was that he made these when ill verses had more favor and escaped better than good ones do in this age, the severity whereof he thought not unhappily diverted by those faults in the impression which hitherto have hung upon his book as the Turks hang old rags (or suchlike ugly things) upon their fairest horses and other goodly creatures to secure them against fascination.[3] And for those of a more confined understanding (who pretend not to censure),[4] as they admire most what they least comprehend, so his verses (maimed to that degree that himself scarce knew what to make of many of them) might that way at least have a title to some admiration, which is no small matter if what an old author observes be true: that the aim of orators is victory; of historians, truth; and of poets, admiration. He had reason, therefore, to indulge those faults in his book whereby it might be reconciled to some and commended to others.

The printer also, he thought, would fare the worse if those faults were amended, for we see maimed statues sell better than whole ones, and clipped and washed money[5] go about when the entire and weighty lies hoarded up. These are the reasons which for above twelve years past he has opposed to our request; to which it was replied that as it would be too late to recall that which had so long been made public, so might it find excuse from his youth (the season it was produced in). And for what had been done since

and now added, if it commend not his poetry it might his philosophy, which teaches him so cheerfully to bear so great a calamity as the loss of the best part of his fortune (torn from him in prison, in which and in banishment the best portion of his life hath also been spent)[6] that he can still sing under the burden. . . .

Not so much moved with these reasons of ours . . . as wearied with our importunity, he has at last given us leave to assure the reader that the poems which have been so long and so ill set forth under his name are here to be found as he first writ them, as also to add some others which have since been composed by him. And though his advice to the contrary might have discouraged us, yet observing how often they have been reprinted, what price they have borne, and how earnestly they have been always inquired after, but especially of late, making good that of Horace, *Meliora dies, ut vina, poemata reddit,*[7] some verses being (like some wines) recommended to our taste by time and age, we have ventured upon this new and well corrected edition, which for our own sakes as well as thine we hope will succeed better than he apprehended.

Vivitur ingenio, caetera mortis erunt.[8]

THE PRINTER TO THE READER   [1]*Male . . . tuum:* "When you speak badly you begin to be yourself."
[2]Are customarily.
[3]I.e., being irresistibly attractive (to thieves).
[4]Do not claim to judge.
[5]*Clipped . . . money:* coins that had been trimmed and "sweated" (i.e., lightened by attrition).
[6]Following the discovery of his royalist plot (see headnote), reported John Aubrey, Waller, already imprisoned, "had much ado then to save his life, and in order to do it, sold his estate in Bedfordshire . . . for about 10,000 pounds (much under value), which was procured in twenty-four hours' time or else he had been hanged; with which money he bribed the whole House, which was the first time a House of Commons was ever bribed."
[7]*Meliora . . . reddit: Epistles,* II.i.34.
[8]*Vivitur . . . erunt:* From an anonymous tag about the great literary

OF HIS MAJESTY'S RECEIVING THE NEWS
OF THE DUKE OF BUCKINGHAM'S DEATH[1]

So earnest with thy God, can no new care,
No sense of danger, interrupt thy prayer?
The sacred wrestler till a blessing given
Quits not his hold, but, halting, conquers heaven;[2]
Nor was the stream of thy devotion stopp'd   5
When from the body such a limb was lopp'd,
As to thy present state was no less maim,
Though thy wise choice has since repair'd the same.[3]
Bold Homer durst not so great virtue feign
In his best pattern of Patroclus slain;   10
With such amazement as weak mothers use
And frantic gesture he receives the news;[4]
Yet fell his darling by th' impartial chance
Of war, impos'd by royal Hector's lance;
Thine in full peace, and by a vulgar hand   15
Torn from thy bosom, left his high command.

The famous painter could allow no place
For private sorrow in a prince's face;
Yet that his piece might not exceed belief
He cast a veil upon supposed grief.[5]   20
'Twas want of such a president[6] as this
Made the old heathen frame their gods amiss.
Their Phoebus should not act a fonder part
For the fair boy than he did for his hart,
Nor blame for Hyacinthus' fate his own,   25
That kept from him wish'd death,[7] hadst thou been known.

He that with thine shall weigh good David's deeds
Shall find his passion, not his love, exceeds;
He curs'd the mountains where his brave friend died,
But let false Ziba with his heir divide [8]   30
Where thy immortal love to thy best friends,
Like that of heaven, upon their seed descends;
Such huge extremes inhabit thy great mind,
Godlike unmov'd and yet like woman kind.
Which of the ancient poets had not brought   35
Our Charles his pedigree from heaven, and taught
How some bright dame, compress'd[9] by mighty Jove,
Produc'd this mix'd divinity and love?

ON MY LADY DOROTHY SIDNEY'S PICTURE[1]

Such was Philoclea, such Musidorus' flame:[2]
The matchless Sidney that immortal frame
Of perfect beauty on two pillars plac'd;
Not his high fancy could one pattern grac'd
With such extremes of excellence compose,   5
Wonder so distant in one face disclose.
Such cheerful modesty, such humble state,
Moves certain love, but with as doubtful fate
As when beyond our greedy reach we see
Inviting fruit on too sublime a tree.   10
All the rich flowers through his Arcadia found
Amaz'd we see in this one garland bound.
Had but this copy which the artist took
From the fair picture of that noble book

Stood at Kalander's, the brave friends had jarr'd   15
And rivals made, th' ensuing story marr'd.
Just Nature, first instructed by his thought,
In his own house thus practiced what he taught.
This glorious piece transcends what he could think,
So much his blood is nobler than his ink.   20

SONG

Go, lovely rose!
Tell her that wastes her time and me
That now she knows
When I resemble her to thee
How sweet and fair she seems to be.   5

Tell her that's young
And shuns to have her graces spied,
That hadst thou sprung

patron Maecenas: *Marmora Moeonii vincunt monumenta libelli: vivitur ingenio, caetera mortis erunt* ("the poet's scrolls will outlive marble monuments; genius survives, but all else will be claimed by death"). The second line was used also by Edmund Spenser for Colin Clout's emblem in the "December" eclogue of *The Shepherds' Calendar* (1579).

BUCKINGHAM'S DEATH [1]Clarendon reports that when Charles I received the news of his powerful favorite's assassination (23 August 1628) at the hands of John Felton, an officer whose promotion the duke had blocked, the king was at his devotions, in which he "continued unmoved and without the least change of his countenance till prayers were ended." For other accounts of Buckingham's extraordinary career and violent end see pp. 754, 791f. [2]*The sacred wrestler...heaven*: Jacob, wrestling with an invincible angel of God, said he would not let his adversary go "except thou bless me" (Genesis 32.26). [3]Immediately after Buckingham's death the king named Robert Bertie, first earl of Lindsey, to succeed him as commander of the naval expedition for the relief of La Rochelle. [4]*Bold Homer...news*: Learning of the death in battle of his friend Patroclus, Achilles was incapacitated by unmanly grief (*Iliad*, Bk. XVIII). [5]*The famous painter...grief*: The Greek artist Timanthes (fl. 400 B.C.), painting the sacrifice of Iphigenia, represented Agamemnon with his face hidden in his mantle.   [6]Precedent. [7]*Their Phoebus...death*: Zephyrus, mad with unrequited love for Hyacinthus, blew a quoit that Apollo had playfully thrown at the boy so that the lovely youth was killed. [8]*He curs'd...divide*: Grief-stricken by the death of his friend and ally Jonathan, eldest son of King Saul, David cursed the mountains of Gilboa (2 Samuel 1.21). For David's transaction with Ziba, a crafty, self-seeking follower of Saul, see 2 Samuel 19.17–29. [9]Embraced.

ON MY LADY [1]Dorothy Sidney (1617–84), granddaughter of Sir Philip Sidney's younger brother Robert, was poetically extolled and wooed as "Sacharissa" by Waller for many years before and after her marriage (1639) to Henry, Lord Spencer, earl of Sunderland. A famous beauty, she was painted at least three times by Anthony Vandyck, and it is probably to one of these portraits that the present poem alludes. [2]*Such...flame*: In Sir Philip Sidney's famous romance *Arcadia* (see p. 691) the shipwrecked princes Pyrocles and Musidorus, while being entertained at Kalander's house, see the portraits of the princesses Philoclea and Pamela, with whom they fall in love.

In deserts where no men abide,
  Thou must have uncommended died. 10

  Small is the worth
Of beauty from the light retir'd;
  Bid her come forth,
Suffer herself to be desir'd,
  And not blush so to be admir'd. 15

  Then die, that she
The common fate of all things rare
  May read in thee
How small a part of time they share
  That are so wondrous sweet and fair. 20

THE BATTLE OF THE SUMMER ISLANDS[1]

CANTO I

*What fruits they have, and how heaven smiles
Upon those late-discovered isles.*

Aid me, Bellona,[2] while the dreadful fight
Betwixt a nation and two whales I write.
Seas stain'd with gore I sing, advent'rous toil,
And how these monsters did disarm an isle.
  Bermudas, wall'd with rocks, who does not know? 5
That happy island where huge lemons grow,
And orange trees, which golden fruit do bear,
Th' Hesperian garden[3] boasts of none so fair;
Where shining pearl, coral, and many a pound,
On the rich shore, of ambergris is found. 10
The lofty cedar, which to heaven aspires,
The prince of trees, is fuel for their fires;
The smoke by which their loaded spits do turn,
For incense might on sacred altars burn;
Their private roofs on od'rous timber borne, 15
Such as might palaces for kings adorn.
The sweet palmettos a new Bacchus yield,
With leaves as ample as the broadest shield,
Under the shadow of whose friendly boughs
They sit, carousing where their liquor grows. 20
Figs there unplanted through the fields do grow,
Such as fierce Cato did the Romans show,
With the rare fruit inviting them to spoil
Carthage, the mistress of so rich a soil.[4]
The naked rocks are not unfruitful there, 25
But at some constant seasons, every year,
Their barren tops with luscious food abound,
And with the eggs of various fowls are crown'd.
Tobacco is the worst of things which they
To English landlords, as their tribute, pay; 30
Such is the mold that the blest tenant feeds
On precious fruits, and pays his rent in weeds.
With candid[5] plantains and the juicy pine,
On choicest melons and sweet grapes they dine,
And with potatoes fat their wanton swine. 35
Nature these cates[6] with such a lavish hand
Pours out among them, that our coarser land
Tastes of that bounty, and does cloth return,
Which not for warmth but ornament is worn;
For the kind spring, which but salutes us here, 40

Inhabits there, and courts them all the year.
Ripe fruits and blossoms on the same trees live;
At once they promise what at once they give.
So sweet the air, so moderate the clime,
None sickly lives, or dies before his time. 45
Heaven sure has kept this spot of earth uncurst,
To show how all things were created first.
The tardy plants in our cold orchards plac'd
Reserve their fruit for the next age's taste;
There a small grain in some few months will be 50
A firm, a lofty, and a spacious tree.
The palma Christi,[7] and the fair papaw,
Now but a seed, preventing[8] Nature's law,
In half a circle of the hasty year
Project a shade, and lovely fruits do wear. 55
And as their trees, in our dull region set,
But faintly grow and no perfection get,
So in this northern tract our hoarser throats
Utter unripe and ill-constrained notes,
Where the supporter of the poets' style, 60
Phoebus, on them eternally does smile.
O how I long my careless limbs to[9] lay
Under the plantain's shade, and all the day
With am'rous airs my fancy entertain,
Invoke the Muses, and improve my vein! 65
No passion there in my free breast should move,
None but the sweet and best of passions, love.
There while I sing, if gentle love be by,
That tunes my lute and winds the strings so high,
With the sweet sound of Sacharissa's name[10] 70
I'll make the list'ning savages grow tame.
  But while I do these pleasing dreams indite,
  I am diverted from the promis'd fight.

TO PHILLIS

Phillis, why should we delay
Pleasures shorter than the day?
Could we (which we never can)
Stretch our lives beyond their span,
Beauty like a shadow flies, 5
And our youth before us dies;
Or would youth and beauty stay,

THE BATTLE OF THE SUMMER ISLANDS [1]The Bermudas, discovered by the Spaniard Juan Bermudez in 1515, were settled in 1612 by the English, who called them the Somers (or *Summer*) Islands after the colonial administrator Sir George Somers. Although Waller's account of the Bermudians' futile effort to capture two stranded whales may be based on fact, there is no evidence that he had visited the islands. Indeed, John Aubrey, writing in 1680, said that the poet had written this work "fifty years since upon the information of one who had been there; walking in his fine woods, the poetic spirit came upon him."
[2]The Roman goddess of war. [3]See p. 175, n. 1.
[4]*Such as...soil:* The treatise on farming known as *De re rustica* by Cato the Censor (234–149 B.C.)—the inveterate foe of Carthage —is the oldest extant literary prose in Latin.
[5]Splendid (with perhaps a pun on *candied*). [6]Delicacies.
[7]The castor-oil plant. [8]Anticipating. [9]Text *do.*
[10]See p. 247, *On My Lady*, n. 1.

Love hath wings and will away.
Love hath swifter wings than Time;
Change in love to heaven does climb.   10
Gods that never change their state
Vary oft their love and hate.
Phillis, to this truth we owe
All the love betwixt us two;
Let not you and I require   15
What has been our past desire,
On what shepherds you have smil'd
Or what nymphs I have beguil'd;
Leave it to the planets too
What we shall hereafter do;   20
For the joys we now may prove,
Take advice of present love.

SONG

Stay, Phoebus, stay!
The world to which you fly so fast,
Conveying day
From us to them, can pay your haste
With no such object, nor salute your rise   5
With no such wonder, as De Mornay's[1] eyes.

Well does this prove
The error of those antique books,
Which made you move
About the world; her charming looks   10
Would fix your beams, and make it ever day,
Did not the rolling earth snatch her away.

ON A GIRDLE

That which her slender waist confin'd
Shall now my joyful temples bind;
No monarch but would give his crown
His arms might do what this has done.

It was my heaven's extremest sphere,   5
The pale which held that lovely deer.
My joy, my grief, my hope, my love,
Did all within this circle move!

A narrow compass, and yet there
Dwelt all that's good and all that's fair;   10
Give me but what this riband bound,
Take all the rest the sun goes round.

AT PENSHURST[1]

Had Sacharissa lived when mortals made
Choice of their deities, this sacred shade
Had held an altar to her power, that gave
The peace and glory which these alleys have;
Embroid'red so with flowers where she stood,   5
That it became a garden of a wood.
Her presence has such more than human grace
That it can civilize the rudest place;
And beauty too, and order, can impart
Where Nature ne'er intended it, nor art.   10

The plants acknowledge this, and her admire
No less than those of old did Orpheus' lyre;
If she sit down, with tops all towards her bow'd,
They round about her into arbors crowd;
Or if she walk, in even ranks they stand   15
Like some well-marshal'd and obsequious[2] band.
Amphion so made stones and timber leap
Into fair figures from a confus'd heap;
And in the symmetry of her parts is found
A power like that of harmony in sound.   20
   Ye lofty beeches, tell this matchless dame
That if together ye fed all one flame
It could not equalize[3] the hundredth part
Of what her eyes have kindled in my heart!
Go, boy, and carve this passion on the bark   25
Of yonder tree, which stands the sacred mark
Of noble Sidney's birth;[4] when such benign,
Such more than mortal-making stars did shine,
That there they cannot but forever prove
The monument and pledge of humble love;   30
His humble love whose hope shall ne'er rise higher
Than for a pardon that he dares admire.

SONG

Behold the brand of beauty tost!
See how the motion does dilate the flame!
Delighted Love his spoils does boast
   And triumph in this game.
Fire to no place confin'd.   5
Is both our wonder and our fear,
   Moving the mind
As lightning hurled through the air

High heaven the glory does increase
Of all her shining lamps this artful way;   10
The sun in figures such as these
   Joys with the moon to play.
To the sweet strains they advance,
Which do result from their own spheres
   As this nymph's dance   15
Moves with the numbers which she hears.

UPON BEN JONSON[1]

Mirror of poets! mirror of our age!
Which her whole face beholding on thy stage,
Pleas'd and displeas'd with her own faults, endures
A remedy like those whom music cures.

SONG [1]Unidentified, but the allusion is perhaps to a beautiful French woman in attendance on Queen Henrietta Maria.
AT PENSHURST [1]Text *Another*. This is the second of two consecutive poems, entitled "At Penshurst," celebrating the Kentish seat of the Sidney family. For Jonson's famous poem on the same place see p. 93. [2]Dutiful. [3]Equal.
[4]*Of yonder tree...birth*: For Jonson's comment on the same tree see "To Penshurst," 11.13–16.
UPON BEN JONSON [1]First printed in *Jonsonus Virbius,* (1638) a collection of poems commemorating Jonson's recent death. Waller told Aubrey that he was "not acquainted" with the older poet.

Thou hast alone those various inclinations   5
Which Nature gives to ages, sexes, nations
So traced with thy all-resembling pen
That whate'er custom has impos'd on men,
Or ill-got habit (which deforms them so
That scarce a brother can his brother know),   10
Is represented to the wond'ring eyes
Of all that see or read thy comedies.
Whoever in those glasses[2] looks may find
The spots return'd or graces of his mind;
And by the help of so divine an art   15
At leisure view and dress his nobler part.
Narcissus, cozened by that flatt'ring well
Which nothing could but of his beauty tell,
Had here, discovering the deform'd estate
Of his fond mind, preserv'd himself with hate.   20
But virtue too, as well as vice, is clad
In flesh and blood so well that Plato had
Beheld what his high fancy once embrac'd,
Virtue with colors, speech, and motion grac'd.
The sundry postures of thy copious Muse   25
Who would express, a thousand tongues must use,
Whose fate's no less peculiar[3] than thy art;
For as thou couldst all characters impart,
So none could render thine, which still escapes,
Like Proteus,[4] in variety of shapes;   30
Who was nor this, nor that, but all we find,
And all we can imagine, in mankind.

TO MASTER GEORGE SANDYS ON HIS TRANSLATION OF SOME PARTS OF THE BIBLE[1]

How bold a work attempts that pen
Which would enrich our vulgar tongue
With the high raptures of those men
Who, here, with the same spirit sung
    Wherewith they now assist the quire   5
    Of angels, who their songs admire!

Whatever those inspired souls
Were urged to express did shake
The aged deep and both the poles;
Their num'rous thunder could awake   10
    Dull earth, which does with heaven consent
    To all they wrote, and all they meant.

Say, sacred bard, what could bestow
Courage on thee to soar so high?
Tell me, brave friend, what help'd thee so   15
To shake off all mortality?
    To light this torch, thou hast climb'd higher
    Than he who stole celestial fire.[2]

TO SIR WILLIAM DAVENANT UPON HIS TWO FIRST BOOKS OF "GONDIBERT" WRITTEN IN FRANCE[1]

Thus the wise nightingale that leaves her home,
Her native wood, when storms and winter come,
Pursuing constantly the cheerful spring,
To foreign groves does her old music bring.
    The drooping Hebrews' banish'd harps, unstrung   5
At Babylon upon the willows hung:[2]
Yours sounds aloud, and tells us you excel
No less in courage than in singing well;
Whilst, unconcern'd, you let your country know
They have impov'rished themselves, not you;   10
Who, with the Muses' help, can mock those fates
Which threaten kingdoms and disorder states.
So Ovid, when from Caesar's rage he fled,
The Roman Muse to Pontus with him led;
Where he so sung that we, through Pity's glass,   15
See Nero milder than Augustus was.[3]
Hereafter such, in thy behalf, shall be
Th' indulgent censure of posterity.
To banish those who with such art can sing
Is a rude crime, which its own curse does bring;   20
Ages to come shall ne'er know how they fought,
Nor how to love their present youth be taught.
This to thyself.—Now to thy matchless book,
Wherein those few that can with judgment look
May find old love in pure, fresh language told,   25
Like new-stamp'd coin made out of angel[4] gold;
Such truth in love as th' antique world did know,
In such a style as courts may boast of now;
Which no bold tales of gods or monsters swell,
But human passions, such as with us dwell.   30
Man is thy theme; his virtue or his rage
Drawn to the life in each elaborate page.
Mars nor Bellona[5] are not named here,
But such a Gondibert as both might fear;
Venus had here, and Hebe[6] been outshin'd   35
By thy bright Birtha and thy Rhodalind.
Such is thy happy skill, and such the odds
Betwixt thy worthies and the Grecian gods!
Whose deities in vain had her come down,
Where mortal beauty wears the sovereign crown;   40
Such as of flesh compos'd, by flesh and blood,
Though not resisted, may be understood.

[2]Mirrors. [3]Distinctive.
[4]Greek sea-god who was able to assume various shapes.
TO MASTER GEORGE SANDYS [1]For Sandys' biblical paraphrases see pp. 110 ff. [2]*He...Fire* Prometheus.
TO SIR WILLIAM DAVENANT [1]For Davenant's *Gondibert* see pp. 254 ff.
[2]*The drooping...hung*: "By the rivers of Babylon, there we sat down, yea, we wept, when we remembered Zion. We hanged our harps upon the willows in the midst thereof" (Psalms 137.1–2).
[3]*So Ovid...was*: Banished (A.D. 8) to the Black Sea by the Emperor Augustus, Ovid described his grief and homesickness in *Tristia* and *Epistulae ex Ponto*. Waller implies that these poignant poems about exile lead us to regard the wise, benign Augustus as crueler than the infamous Nero.
[4]An old English gold coin (originally called the angel-noble) stamped with a figure of St. George and the dragon.
[5]The Roman god and goddess of war. [6]Goddess of youth.

from Three Poems upon the Death of His Late Highness Oliver, Lord Protector of England, Scotland, and Ireland (1659)

UPON THE LATE STORM AND DEATH OF HIS
HIGHNESS ENSUING THE SAME[1]
By Master Waller

We must resign! Heav'n his great soul[2] does claim
In storms[3] as loud as his immortal fame;
His dying groans, his last breath shakes our isle,
And trees uncut fall for his funeral pile;
About his palace their broad roots are tost   5
Into the air: So Romulus was lost.[4]
New Rome in such a tempest miss'd her king,
And from obeying fell to worshipping.
On Oeta's top thus Hercules lay dead,[5]
With ruin'd oaks and pines about him spread;   10
The poplar, too, whose bough he wont to wear
On his victorious head, lay prostrate there.
Those his last fury from the mountain rent;
Our dying hero from the continent
Ravish'd whole towns, and forts from Spaniards reft   15
As his last legacy to Britain left.
The ocean, which so long our hopes confin'd,
Could give no limits to his vaster mind;
Our bound's enlargement was his latest toil,
Nor hath he left us prisoners to our isle.   20
Under the tropic is our language spoke,
And part of Flanders hath receiv'd our yoke.[6]
From civil broils he did us disengage,

Found nobler objects for our martial rage:
And, with wise conduct, to his country show'd   25
Their ancient way of conquering abroad.
Ungrateful, then, if we no tears allow
To him that gave us peace and empire too.
Princes that fear'd him grieve, concern'd to see
No pitch of glory from the grave is free.   30
Nature herself took notice of his death,
And, sighing, swell'd the sea with such a breath
That to remotest shores her billows roll'd,
Th' approaching fate of her great ruler told.

UPON THE LATE STORM   [1]This eulogistic poem, first printed as a broadside soon after Cromwell's death and then included in a volume (1659) with similar things by Dryden and Thomas Sprat, was so embarrassing to Waller after the Restoration that it was not reprinted until 1682.   [2]Text *Sold.*
[3]According to Clarendon, Cromwell died (3 September 1658) on a day "very memorable for the greatest storm of wind that had been ever known."
[4]Livy (I.xvi) records that after reigning thirty-seven years Romulus, the legendary king of Rome, was snatched away to heaven in a thunderstorm.
[5]*On Oeta's...dead*: Knowing that his end was near, Hercules ascended Mt. Oeta in Thessaly, raised a funeral pyre, and ordered it to be ignited. But as it burned he was transported in clouds and thunder to Olympus, where the gods made him immortal.
[6]*Part of Flanders...yoke*: i.e., Dunkirk, ceded to England after an English and French victory over Spain in June 1658.

Sir William Davenant[1] [1606-1668]

In sharp contrast to Milton, his contemporary and counterpart, Davenant enjoyed the sort of literary acclaim that was marked by his succeeding Jonson in the laureateship, by a royal patent to "erect" one of the two authorized companies of actors at Charles' restoration, by his junior colleague Dryden's "veneration," and by a splendid funeral in Westminster Abbey. If now he seems, perhaps, unworthy of these high distinctions, his achievements as a playwright, poet, literary theorist, courtier, soldier, and theatrical producer help us understand why he was famous in his time, and they still serve to keep his name alive.

Contemporary gossip, as reported by John Aubrey, had it that the laureate—one of seven

[1]For other works of Davenant, see Books and Men, pp. 780 ff.

children of a prosperous vintner of Oxford who rose to be the mayor of that city—was in fact an illegitimate son of Shakespeare, and moreover that when "pleasant over a glass of wine" be even boasted of the fact, despite the damage to his mother's reputation. Even if such gossip could be converted into fact it would merely prove that Shakespeare's kind of genius is not transmitted by the genes. The boy had solid schooling, but his education at Lincoln College, Oxford, was abruptly ended by his father's death in 1621. In his will the vintner gave his son, then in his middle teens, a modest sum of money, two changes of apparel, and firm instructions to seek a suitable apprentice-ship with some worthy London merchant. As the spotty record of his next few years reveals, however, he ignored his father's wishes, for instead of starting his career in trade he opted for a more exciting life among the grandees of the realm, beginning as a page in the great London household of Frances, duchess of Richmond (newly married to Lodowick Stuart, a kinsman of the King), and then moving on to Sidney's famous friend, the aging Fulke Greville, Baron Brooke (see pp. 4 f.). These employments were prophetic of his success in Caroline society, his long attachment to the court, and his devotion to the House of Stuart. Similarly, the production (1627) of *The Cruel Brother*—the first of almost thirty masques and plays that include *The Wits* (1633), *The Platonic Lovers* (1636), and the epoch-making *Siege of Rhodes* (1656)—presaged a lasting interest in the stage that would lead him, after thirty years, to a dominating role in early Restoration drama.

It is not, however, for his success at court or for his contributions to the stage that he is represented in this book, but for his fragmentary epic *Gondibert* and its preface, which he himself regarded as his most important work. In 1638 he established his credentials as a poet—or at least as a poet in the little world of Charles' court—by publishing *Madagascar, with Other Poems,* a flimsy, graceful gathering of commendatory verses made socially important by the array of royal or distinguished persons—the King and Queen, their nephew Rupert, and assorted belted earls—for whom these bagatelles were written. Complimentary verses by the powerful Endymion Porter (through whose good offices Davenant had entered into service with the Queen in 1635), Suckling, Carew, and Habington suggest how far the former page had come in the decade since his patron Greville's death.

For a royalist and activist like Davenant the troubled 1640's afforded little time for writing. It was only after he had been arrested and then freed on bail (1641) for plotting to assist the King, accompanied his beloved Queen Henrietta Maria to Holland, returned to fight for Charles, earned a knighthood for his valor at the siege of Gloucester (1643), smuggled arms and ammunition for the hard-pressed royal troops, and finally joined the Queen in exile at her little court at St. Germain near Paris (1645), that he at last returned to literature by starting work on *Gondibert*. Using the heroic quatrain that Dryden later would adopt, he wrote the first two books in 1649, and by 2 January 1650 he was ready with an important prefatory epistle addressed to his fellow-exile Thomas Hobbes, who had "daily" read the work in progress. Hobbes at once supplied a highly complimentary answer, and the subsequent publication (in both Paris and London) of this penetrating correspondence (see pp. 780 ff.) at once assumed a large importance in the history of neoclassic criticism.

Further work on *Gondibert* was interrupted by a new assignment from the queen to transport a colony of "artificers" to Virginia in order to suppress the Parliamentary faction there. This "ingeniose design," as Aubrey called it, was blocked almost before it started when Davenant's ship was intercepted off the coast of France (May 1650) and he himself was taken as a prisoner to Cowes Castle on the Isle of Wight. With more compulsory leisure than he wanted he had started work again on *Gondibert* when he learned that he would be removed to London and there stand trial for treason. It was in these sobering circumstances that on 22 October 1650 he penned a post-script "To the Reader" of his uncompleted epic. Pointing out that he had written only half the poem, he announced that he would do no more.

> 'Tis high time to strike sail and cast anchor (though I have run but half my course), when at the helm I am threatened with death; who, though he can visit us but once, seems troublesome, and even in the innocent may beget such a gravity as diverts the music of verse. And I beseech

thee, if thou art so civil as to be pleased with what is written, not to take ill that I run not on to my last gasp. For though I intended in this poem to strip Nature naked and clothe her again in the perfect shape of Virtue, yet even in so worthy a design I shall ask leave to desist when I am interrupted by so great an experiment as dying.

His failure to complete the work, he added, was a consequence of his involvement in the struggles of his time, but he had no regrets:

Nor could I sit idle, and sigh with such as mourn to hear the drum; for if this age be not quiet enough to be taught virtue a pleasant way, the next may be at leisure; nor could I (like men that have civilly slept till they are old in dark cities) think war a novelty, for we have all heard that Alexander walked after the drum from Macedon into India, and I tell thee, reader, he carried Homer in his pocket.

It is pleasant to record that despite his justified forebodings Davenant was saved from execution (perhaps by Milton's intervention), that during his subsequent incarceration in the Tower (1650–52) the unfinished *Gondibert* appeared (in three books) in 1651, that five years later he produced the famous *Siege of Rhodes,* and that with the Restoration his service to the Stuarts was rewarded with the royal patent which made his later years secure. "I was at his funeral," Aubrey wrote;

He had a coffin of walnut tree; Sir John Denham said 'twas the finest coffin that ever he saw. His body was carried in a hearse from the playhouse to Westminster Abbey, where at the great west door he was received by the singing men and choristers, who sang the service of the church ("I am the resurrection, etc.") to his grave, which is in the south cross aisle, on which, on a paving stone of marble, is writ, in imitation of that on Ben Jonson: "O rare Sir Will. Davenant."

But methought it had been proper that a laurel should have been sit on his coffin—which was not done.

My texts are based on *Madagascar; With Other Poems,* 1638 (STC 6304), *A Discourse upon Gondibert. An Heroick Poem Written by Sr. William D'Avenant. With an Answer to It by Mr. Hobbes,* Paris, 1650 (Wing D-322), and *Gondibert: An Heroic Poem, Written by Sr. William D'Avenant,* 1651 (Wing D-324). Although Davenant's *Works* were collected into a folio within five years of his death, his stage pieces had to wait two centuries for their next edition by James Maidment and W. H. Logan (5 vols., 1872-74), and *Gondibert* did not achieve an authoritative edition until D. F. Gladish's appeared in 1971. The important exchange with Hobbes was included in J. E. Spingarn's *Critical Essays of the Seventeenth Century* (3 vols., 1908–09); *Selected Poems* was privately printed by Geoffrey Bush in 1943; an unused canto of *Gondibert* first printed in 1785 has been edited by J. G. McManaway in *MLQ,* I (1940); and A. M. Gibbs has supplied an authoritative edition of the shorter poems and the songs from Davenant's productions for the stage (1972). There are biographies by Alfred Harbage (1935) and A. H. Nethercot (1938), monographs on *Gondibert* by G. Gronauer (1911) and C. M. Dowlin (1934), and a study of the comedies by H. S. Collins (1965). A facsimile of the 1673 *Works* appeared in 1968.

from Madagascar, with Other Poems (1638)

TO THE QUEEN, ENTERTAIN'D AT NIGHT
BY THE COUNTESS OF ANGLESEY

Fair as unshaded light or as the day
In its first birth, when all the year was May;
Sweet as the altar's smoke or as the new
Unfolded bud, swell'd by the early dew;

Smooth as the face of waters first appear'd, 5
Ere tides began to strive or winds were heard;
Kind as the willing saints, and calmer far
Than in their sleeps forgiven hermits are:
You that are more than our discreeter fear
Dares praise with such dull art, what make you here? 10
Here where the summer is so little seen

That leaves (her cheapest wealth) scarce reach at green,
You come as if the silver planet were
Misled a while from her much injur'd sphere,
And t' ease the travails of her beams tonight   15
In this small lanthorn would contract her light.

IN REMEMBRANCE OF MASTER WILLIAM SHAKESPEARE[1]
Ode

1
Beware, delighted poets, when you sing
To welcome Nature in the early spring,
   Your num'rous[2] feet not tread
The banks of Avon, for each flow'r
(As it ne'er knew a sun or show'r)   5
   Hangs there the pensive head.

2
Each tree whose thick and spreading growth hath made
Rather a night beneath the boughs than shade,
   Unwilling now to grow,
Looks like the plume a captive wears   10
Whose rifled[3] falls are steep'd i' th' tears
   Which from his last rage flow.

3
The piteous river wept itself away
Long since, alas, to such a swift decay
   That reach the map, and look   15
If you a river there can spy,
And for a river your mock'd eye
   Will find a shallow brook.

ON THE DEATH OF THE LADY MARQUESS OF WINCHESTER[1]

In care lest some advent'rous lover may
(T' increase his love) cast his own stock away,
I (that find th' use of grief is to grow wise)
Forbid all traffic now 'tween hearts and eyes.
Our remnant[2] love let us discreetly save,   5
Since not augment, for Love lies in the grave.
Lest men whose patience is their senses' sloth,
That only live t' expect the tedious growth
Of what the following summer slowly yields,
Whose fair elysium is their furrow'd fields,   10
Lest these should so much prize mortality

They ne'er would reach the wit or faith to die,
Know, summer comes no more; to the dark bed
Our sun is gone; the hopeful spring is dead.
And lest kind poets, that delight to raise   15
(With their just truths, not ecstasy of praise)
Beauty to fame, should rashly overthrow
The credit of their songs, I let them know
Their theme is lost—so lost that I have griev'd
They never more can praise and be believ'd.   20

TO THOMAS CAREW[1]

1
Upon my conscience, when soe'er thou di'st
   (Though in the black, the mourning time of Lent)
There will be seen in King's Street,[2] where thou li'st,
   More triumphs than in days of Parl'ament.

2
How glad and gaudy then will lovers be!   5
   For ev'ry lover that can verses read
Hath been so injur'd by thy Muse and thee,
   Ten thousand thousand times he wish'd thee dead.

3
Not but thy verses are as smooth and high
   As glory, love, or wine from wit can raise;   10
But now the devil take such destiny:
   What should commend them turns to their dispraise.

4
Thy wit's chief virtue is become its vice,
   For ev'ry beauty thou hast rais'd so high
That now coarse[3] faces carry such a price   15
   As must undo a lover if he buy.

5
Scarce any of the sex admits commerce;
   It shames me much to urge this in a friend,
But more that they should so mistake thy verse,
   Which meant to conquer whom it did commend.   20

IN REMEMBRANCE [1]Davenant was said to have written this poem when he was only twelve. [2]Rhythmical. [3]Disordered, disheveled.

ON THE DEATH OF LADY WINCHESTER [1]Jane Paulet (d. 1631), wife of the fifth marquis of Winchester, whose untimely death was commemorated also by Jonson and young Milton. [2]Remaining.

TO THOMAS CAREW [1]See p. 220. [2]King Street, a thoroughfare, now destroyed, between Charing Cross and Westminster. [3]Text *course*.

from Gondibert (1651)

THE SECOND BOOK

CANTO THE SEVENTH

[After Gondibert (whom the Princess Rhodalind loves) has killed the ambitious Oswald in a duel, he is taken to the palace of the philosopher Astragon to recover from his] [wounds. In the following passage—which Hobbes (p. 787), regarded as unmatched in any literature—Davenant tells how the pure and lovely Birtha falls in love with her father's noble guest.]

28

She, full of inward questions, walks alone
   To take her heart aside in secret shade;   110
But knocking at her breast, it seem'd, or gone
   Or[1] by confed'racy[2] was useless made;

29

Or else some stranger did usurp its room,
   One so remote and new in ev'ry thought
As his behavior shows him not at home,   115
   Nor the guide sober that him thither brought.

30

Yet with his foreign heart she does begin
   To treat of love, her most unstudied theme,
And, like young-conscienc'd casuists, thinks that sin[3]
   Which will by talk and practice lawful seem.   120

31

With open ears and ever-waking eyes
   And flying feet, love's fire she from the sight
Of all her maids does carry, as from spies,
   Jealous that what burns her might give them light.

32

Beneath a myrtle covert she does spend,   125
   In maid's weak wishes, her whole stock of thought;
Fond maids, who love with mind's fine stuff would mend,
   Which Nature purposely of body's wrought.

33

She fashions him she lov'd of angels' kind,
   Such as in holy story were employ'd   130
To the first fathers from th' Eternal Mind,
   And in short vision only are enjoy'd

34

As eagles then, when nearest heav'n they fly,
   Of wild impossibles soon weary grow,
Feeling their bodies find no rest so high,   135
   And therefore perch on earthly things below,

35

So now she yields: him she an angel deem'd
   Shall be a man, the name which virgins fear;
Yet the most harmless to a maid he seem'd
   That ever yet that fatal name did bear.   140

36

Soon her opinion of his hurtless heart
   Affection turns to faith; and love's fire
To heav'n, though bashfully, she does impart,
   And to her mother in the heav'nly quire.

37

"If I do love," said she, "that love, O heav'n,   145
   Your own disciple, Nature, bred in me!
Why should I hide the passion you have given,
   Or blush to show effects which you decree?

38

"And you, my alter'd mother (grown above
   Great Nature, which you read and rev'renc'd here),   150

Chide not such kindness as you once call'd love,
   When you as mortal as my father were."

39

This said, her soul into her breast retires;
   With love's vain diligence of heart she dreams
Herself into possession of desires,   155
   And trusts unanchor'd hope in fleeting streams.

40

Already thinks the duke her own spous'd lord,
   Cur'd, and again from bloody battle brought,
Where all false lovers perish'd by his sword,
   The true to her for his protection sought.   160

41

She thinks how her imagin'd spouse and she
   So much from heav'n may by her virtues gain
That they by Time shall ne'er o'ertaken be,
   No more than Time himself is overta'en.

42

Or should he touch them as he by does pass,   165
   Heav'n's favor may repay their summers gone,
And he so mix their sand in a slow glass
   That they shall live, and not as two but one.

43

She thinks of Eden-life, and no rough wind
   In their pacific sea shall wrinkles make,   170
That still her lowliness shall keep him kind,
   Her cares keep him asleep, her voice awake.

44

She thinks if ever anger in him sway
   (The youthful warrior's most excus'd disease),
Such chance her tears shall calm, as show'rs allay   175
   The accidental rage of winds and seas.

45

She thinks that babes proceed from mingling eyes,
   Or heav'n from neighborhood increase allows,
As palm and the mamora[4] fructifies,
   Or they are got by close exchanging vows.   180

46

But come they[5] (as she hears) from mother's pain
   (Which by th' unlucky first maid's[6] longing proves
A lasting curse), yet that she will sustain,
   So they be like this heav'nly man she loves.

47

Thus to herself in daydreams Birtha talks.   185
   The duke (whose wounds of war are healthful grown),
To cure Love's wounds, seeks Birtha where she walks,
   Whose wand'ring soul seeks him to cure her own.

CANTO THE SEVENTH [1]*Or...or*: either...or. [2]Conspiracy.
[3]*Like...sin*: like inexperienced casuists, thinks that to be a sin.
[4]Presumably the cork tree, which grows profusely in the Mamore
forest in Morocco. [5]If they come.
[6]Eve, whose *lasting curse* is pronounced in Genesis 3.16.

48
Yet when her solitude he did invade,
  Shame (which in maids is unexperienc'd fear)   190
Taught her to wish night's help to make more shade,
  That love (which maids think guilt) might not appear.

49
And she had fled him now but that he came
  So like an aw'd and conquer'd enemy
That he did seem offenseless as her shame,   195
  As if he but advanc'd for leave to fly.

John Milton[1] [1608-1674]

It is significant that of the three contemporary accounts of the three most important writers represented in this book only one was written by the man himself. For Jonson we must go to Drummond's "Conversations" and for Donne to Walton's almost hagiographic life, but for Milton we have the extraordinary *apologia pro vita sua* inserted in *The Second Defense of the English People* (pp. 776 ff.), where we see the aging revolutionist, in a characteristic posture of defiance, as he relates the facts of his career and justifies his own convictions. If to this uniquely valuable document we add the four contemporary accounts of Milton by his nephew Edward Phillips, John Aubrey, Anthony Wood, and an anonymous biographer (whose manuscript was found in 1889), his own substantial correspondence, and the digressions scattered thick throughout his prose and verse wherein he talks about his motives, aspirations, and achievements, it is clear that we know more about his life than that of any other writer of the period.

Partly by design and partly owing to the pressures of the age, his life reveals three neatly portioned segments: a long youth (1608–39) of intensive education that embraced St. Paul's School (1620?–25), Christ's College, Cambridge (B.A. 1629, M.A. 1632), and six years of rigorous private study climaxed by an extended Continental tour (1638–39); two decades (1640–60) of deepening involvement in the political and religious struggles of the time, when the young schoolmaster progressed from Presbyterian to Independent, from royalist to republican, from pamphleteer to public servant as secretary and propagandist for Cromwell's Council of State (1649–59); and then the long, autumnal close (1660–74), when the blind and superannuated writer, his hopes blasted by the Restoration, at last fulfilled his boyish ambition to "leave something to aftertimes as they should not willingly let it die" with *Paradise Lost* (1667), *Paradise Regained* (1671), and *Samson Agonistes* (1671).

Although Milton's final phase and its majestic artifacts lie beyond the limits of this book, it will perhaps be useful to sketch his emergence as a writer and to put his early verse and prose into a somewhat fuller context than he himself provides. He started writing poetry as a boy, and some of it appealed to him enough in his old age to be exhumed for publication in the last edition of his *Poems* a year before he died. To represent this very early work—metrical paraphrases of the Psalms, Greek and Latin epigrams, and other things that may have been composed as academic exercises— I have chosen "On the Death of a Fair Infant Dying of a Cough," an elegy for his niece that he himself, in the *Poems* of 1673, perhaps inaccurately assigned to 1626, when he was seventeen. Although his Cambridge years produced a substantial group of works in Latin prose and verse— seven biographically interesting *Prolusiones* or orations that were published as a sort of coda to a late (1674) collection of his letters, seven poetical elegies, and *In quintum Novembris*, a lurid small-scale epic on the Gunpowder Plot—his first authentic masterpiece was the astonishing "On the Morning of Christ's Nativity," which he composed on Christmas 1629, when he had just turned

[1]For other works of Milton, see Religion and Politics, pp. 599 ff.; Books and Men, pp. 769 ff.; and History and Historiography, pp. 921 ff.

twenty-one. Of much less certain date are his first six sonnets, five of which were written in Italian (1628–30?), the famous twin poems "L'Allegro" and "Il Penseroso" (1631–32?), the charming little mask *Arcades* (1632?), and such lesser but prophetic things as "On Time" and "On the Circumcision" (1632–33?), whose convoluted verse-paragraphs anticipate the texture of the later epics. Some of these (together with later, more important works like *Comus* and *Lycidas*) were transcribed in the so-called Trinity (or Cambridge) Manuscript, a workbook, much of it in Milton's hand, discovered in the eighteenth century, and all of them were printed in the first edition of his *Poems* in 1645.

With *A Mask Presented at Ludlow Castle* (or *Comus*, to use the title it was given in the eighteenth century), we are on firmer ground. This ambitious undertaking (Milton's first and last attempt at blank verse before *Paradise Lost*) may have been composed at the invitation of Henry Lawes, who supplied the music and acted the Attendant Spirit, and it was certainly designed for presentation at Ludlow Castle on 29 September 1634 to celebrate the appointment (1631) of John Egerton, first earl of Bridgewater, as president of the Council of Wales, with the earl's own children in the leading roles. It survives in various forms: the original acting version still in the possession of the Egerton family; a heavily reworked draft in the Trinity Manuscript; an anonymous first edition that Lawes prepared in 1637 because, as he explained, "the often copying of it hath tired my pen to give my several friends satisfaction"; Milton's own authoritative and enlarged recension (the basis of the present text) in the 1645 edition of the *Poems*; and a negligibly altered version in the *Poems* of 1673.

Because *Lycidas*, like *Comus*, was an occasional work, it may be dated with precision. Its occasion was the death by drowning (10 August 1637) of Edward King, a younger contemporary of Milton who had achieved a local reputation as fellow, tutor, and prelector of Christ's College. Dated November 1637 in the Trinity Manuscript, it was published in a commemorative volume (1638) entitled *Justa Eduardo King*, a collection of twenty-three Greek and Latin and thirteen English poems by the victim's various Cambridge friends. If not formal valedictions to his youth, *Lycidas* and its companion piece *Epitaphium Damonis*, a stately Latin elegy for his former schoolmate Charles Diodati, who died untimely in 1638, were the last and most accomplished works of Milton's long apprenticeship.

Apart from "O nightingale, that on yon bloomy spray" and the five Italian sonnets noted earlier, all of Milton's twenty-three sonnets are topical, recording his response either to such public or private events as his birthday (7), the reception of his controversial pamphlets (11, 12), the Piedmont massacre in 1655 (18), and his blindness (19), or to personages or friends like the valiant Fairfax (15), Cromwell (16), and Cyriac Skinner (21). The first ten of them were printed in the 1645 *Poems*, and again in 1673 with the addition of all the others except 15–17 and 22, which were so politically explosive that they awaited posthumous publication in Edward Phillips' edition of his uncle's *Letters of State* in 1694. Except for the so-called *sonetto caudato*, or tailed sonnet, "On the New Forcers of Conscience" (first published in the 1673 *Poems*) all of them are in the pure Italian or Petrarchan form, with an octave of two enclosed quatrains (abba abba and a sestet of two variously rhyming tercets (cde cde, cdc dcd, etc.).

As he entered his third decade Milton, compared with such Cambridge contemporaries as Thomas Randolph (p. 239) and John Cleveland (pp. 316 f.), was almost an unknown poet. But he had read voraciously, he had acquired his own poetic voice and manner, he had evolved a lofty notion of his function as an artist, and he at last was poised (as he said in *Epitaphium Damonis* and elsewhere) for what he thought would be a major work. Then came the civil war.

In 1654, rehearsing his own contributions to the promotion of that "real and substantial liberty" which he took to be the great achievement of his generation, Milton perhaps found more system, long-range purpose, and progression in his almost fifteen years of pamphleteering than his work in fact reveals. In his own view this torrential production constituted a three-pronged advance upon the "three species of liberty which are essential to the happiness of social life—religious, domestic, and civil." While no doubt simplistic, this comment at least supplies us with some useful rubrics for dealing with these works of his left hand, as he himself described his prose.

His five contributions to the acrimonious religio-political controversies that soon ignited in a civil war—or, as he preferred to put it, to "religious" liberty—were all written, in a sense, to expose the errors of Joseph Hall (p. 526 f.) and James Ussher, "two bishops of superior distinction" who had become the leading spokesmen for the Anglicans against their Presbyterian opponents. Following Hall's publication of *Episcopacy by Divine Right* (1640) and *An Humble Remonstrance to the High Court of Parliament* (1641), he was answered by "Smectymnuus," a syndicate of five Puritan ministers (including Milton's former private tutor Thomas Young) with *An Answer to a Book Entitled "An Humble Remonstrance"* (March 1641), which promptly sparked replies by both Hall and Ussher.

At this juncture, when, as Milton later said, he saw "a way was opening for the establishment of real liberty," the obscure young schoolmaster "determined to relinquish the other pursuits in which I was engaged, and to transfer the whole force of my talents and my industry to this one important object." In the late spring of 1641, therefore, Milton joined the fray, smiting Hall with *Of Reformation in England* (May 1641) and Ussher with *Of Prelatical Episcopacy* (June–July 1641). Already, however, Hall had answered the Smectymnuans with a stirring *Defense of the Humble Remonstrance* (April 1641), and to this the embattled new recruit, seeing that the five ministers were "hardly a match for the eloquence of their opponents," at once replied with the slashing *Animadversions upon the Remonstrant's Defense* (July? 1641). Such thrusts and parries must have been exciting, but Milton clearly thought them less important than the work to which he addressed himself throughout the later summer and the fall of 1641, the spacious *Reason of Church Government*, which appeared in the early months of 1642. This, the most thoughtful and elaborate of his five anti-prelatical pamphlets, was followed (April 1642) by the final item in the series, a small work with such a big title—*An Apology against a Pamphlet Called "A Modest Confutation of the Animadversions upon the Remonstrant against Smectymnuus"*—that it is generally called merely *An Apology for Smectymnuus.*

To represent these dusty verbal skirmishes—in which important issues were often muffled by vituperation—I have chosen, in addition to Bishop Hall's quasi-official statement of the Anglican position in *An Humble Remonstrance* (pp. 530 ff.), Milton's throbbing conclusion to *Of Reformation* (pp. 599 f.) and a couple of excerpts from *The Reason of Church Government* (pp. 600 ff.) that reveal not only his position on the issues but also something of his ardor. The well-known autobiographical digressions in *The Reason of Church Government* (pp. 769 ff.) and *An Apology for Smectymnuus* (pp. 772 ff.)—which tell us much about the youth who, eight years earlier, had written *Comus*—have been put with other statements of his own conception of his function as a writer.

Having thus done his bit for "religious" liberty, in the late spring of 1642 Milton, at the age of thirty-three, took a bride of seventeen. A few weeks later, Mary Powell Milton went to Oxford-shire on a visit to her parents which lasted, to her husband's mounting irritation, until 1645. Whatever bearing these facts had on Milton's keen desire to liberalize the laws on divorce, his second major block of pamphlets were the four he wrote between 1643 and 1645 on the subject of "domestic" liberty: *The Doctrine and Discipline of Divorce* (August 1643), *The Judgment of Martin Bucer Concerning Divorce* (August 1644), *Tetrachordon*, and *Colasterion* (the last two published simultaneously in March 1645). Although I have chosen nothing from these tracts for inclusion in this book, their hostile reception helps us understand their author's rapid progress from the orthodox young Presbyterian of 1641–42 to the impassioned Independent of 1644–45. This hostility, itself a gauge of the repressive climate of Presbyterian opinion that inspired "On the New Forcers of Conscience," showed itself in two petitions of the Stationers' Company for punishing the authors of such scandalous publications as Milton's, in direct attacks on the divorce tracts by several Presbyterian divines, and in the notorious Parliamentary statute of 14 June 1643, which revived the censorship struck down in 1640 as an instrument of Stuart tyranny. It was against this background of triumphant bigotry that Milton published in November 1644—and, significantly, without license—his *Areopa-*

gitica (pp. 603 ff.). Although this noble plea for freedom of the press is the only one of all his controversial tracts whose survival seems to be assured, it went unnoticed at the time. Nonetheless, the soaring eloquence which has kept the work alive will not be obsolete until men can fight their wars of truth without the aid of censors.

Although *Of Education* (pp. 774 ff.) does not fit any of the rubrics under which Milton said he organized his pamphleteering in the forties, both in date of publication (June 1644) and in theme it stands as a companion piece to *Areopagitica*. Its formidable pedagogical proposals may constitute, as its author said, only a "summary" prescription for the "complete and generous education" that "fits a man to perform justly, skilfully, and magnanimously all the offices, both private and public, of peace and war," but its demonstration of the link between informed intelligence and liberty is "sufficiently copious" to underscore a major theme that runs through all of Milton's work.

Apart from such sonnets as those on the hostile reception of his pamphlets (11, 12), "On the New Forcers of Conscience," and on Fairfax (15), Cromwell (16), and Sir Henry Vane (17), Milton refrained from politics and controversy from 1645 to 1649. It was then, "bent upon retiring again to his private studies," as Edward Phillips said, that he began *De doctrina Christiana*, an elaborate treatise on theology that, though probably finished in the later fifties, remained unpublished until 1825. Another major project was *The History of Britain* (pp. 921 ff.), for which (as his commonplace book now in the British Museum shows) he had been collecting data for more than twenty years. By 1649, when he returned to pamphleteering, he had done the first four books, and sometime after 1655, when his official duties slackened, he added V and VI, which ended with the conquest of the Normans. Perhaps hoping to bring his history down to modern times, he kept the work in manuscript until 1670, when it was finally published. The so-called digression in Book III, comparing the disorder in Britain when the Romans left with that in the final stages of the civil war, apparently fell afoul the censor, but it belatedly appeared in 1681 as *Mr. John Milton's Character of the Long Parliament and the Assembly of Divines in MDCXLI.*

It was only in the later forties, after these ambitious projects were begun (and left unfinished), that Milton returned to pamphleteering with a string of contributions to the cause of "civil" liberty. His return to the arena was prompted, as he tells us, by the strenuous opposition of certain Presbyterians to Charles' trial and execution after he had been "voted an enemy by the Parliament and vanquished in the field." In point of fact *The Tenure of Kings and Magistrates*, which he later described as "an abstract consideration of the question, what might lawfully be done against tyrants," was almost surely put together during Charles' trial and published some two weeks after he had stepped upon the scaffold on 30 January 1649. Challenging the "double tyranny of custom from without and blind affections from within," Milton invoked the common theory of contract to argue that sovereignty is delegated by the people to the king, who, if he is wicked or inept, is "as subject to the reach of justice and arraignment as any other transgressors." Although built upon a set of commonplaces dear to generations of political theorists, this tract was so successful, as Milton's nephew later said, that he was "courted" into public service as secretary for foreign tongues to the Council of State (March 1649). It was in this new capacity that he was instructed to counter the extraordinary success of that masterpiece of royalist propaganda *Eikon Basilike* (pp. 614 ff.) with his own *Eikonoklastes* (pp. 609 ff.), which appeared the following fall. "I did not insult over fallen majesty as is pretended," Milton wrote in retrospect: "I only preferred Queen Truth to King Charles."

Milton's later prose as an apologist for the Cromwellian revolution and then, with the triumph of the Restoration, as a defiant anti-royalist is represented in this book only by the autobiographical digression in *Pro populo Anglicano defensio secunda* (1654). The modern reader may admire the stubborn valor and deplore the brutalities with which this "surly republican," as Johnson called him in contempt, tried to save the revolution and prevent his countrymen from "basely and besottedly" running "their necks again into the yoke which they have broken," but he can hardly be unmoved by the stirring valediction of *The Second Defense*. There, where Milton assumes the posture of an "epic poet" to rejoice in battles fought and won and to warn of other battles yet to come, he exemplifies what he had called "the trial of virtue and the exercise of truth"; and this, as he would later show in truly epic terms, is man's most fearful, splendid burden.

For my texts of Milton's verse I have used the 1645 and 1673 editions of the *Poems* (Wing M–2160 and M–2161) and for the prose the following: *Of Reformation* (1641), Wing M–2134; *The Reason of Church Government* (1642), Wing M–2175; *An Apology for Smectymnuus* (1642), Wing M–2090; *Of Education* (1644), Wing M–2132; *Areopagitica* (1644), Wing M–2092; *Eikonoklastes* (2d ed., 1650), Wing M–2113; *The Second Defense of the People of England* (*Pro populo Anglicano defensio secunda*, 1654), translated by Robert Fellows for Charles Symmons' edition of Milton's *Prose Works* (7 vols., 1806) and reprinted in J. H. St. John's edition of the *Prose Works* (Bohn's Library, 5 vols., 1848–53).

Scholarship on Milton, the most learned of the English poets, began as early as 1695 with Patrick Hume's "Annotations" on *Paradise Lost,* and it has now grown so immense that the most recent installment of Calvin Huckabay's *Annotated Bibliography* (1969) lists almost 4,000 items between 1929 and 1968. Such a note as this, even though it ignores the enormous mass of articles, must therefore be regarded as an ineffectual gesture toward a subject that could fill a book. In addition to Huckabay's there are bibliographical guides through the jungle by D. H. Stevens (1930), Harris Fletcher (1931), and J. H. Hanford (1966). Formerly, new items were listed annually in the April number of *Studies in Philology.*

The most important recent edition of the works, both verse and prose, is that by F. A. Patterson and others which was issued by Columbia University in twenty volumes between 1931 and 1940. There are smaller editions of the verse and selections from the prose by Professor Patterson (*The Student's Milton,* revised ed., 1933), E. H. Visiak (1938), and Merritt Hughes (1957); of the poetry alone by David Masson (3 vols., 1890), A. W. Verity (10 vols., 1891–96), H. C. Beeching (1900), W. A. Wright (1903), H. J. C. Grierson (2 vols., 1925), Harris Fletcher (1941), Helen Darbishire (2 vols., 1952–55), J. H. Hanford (revised ed., 1953), B. A. Wright (1956), John Shawcross (1963), Douglas Bush (1965), and John Carey and Alastair Fowler (1968). The Latin poems have been edited by Walter MacKellar (1930), the *Private Correspondence and Academic Exercises* by P. B. and E. M. W. Tillyard (1932), *Lycidas* by Scott Elledge (1966), the sonnets by J. S. Smart (1921) and E. A. J. Honigman (1966), and the 1645 *Poems* by Cleanth Brooks and John E. Hardy (1951). Harris Fletcher has edited the *Complete Poetical Works, Reproduced in Photographic Facsimile* (4 vols., 1943–48), and the long-awaited Milton Variorum has been inaugurated (1970) by Douglas Bush (for the Greek and Latin poems) and J. E. Shaw and A. B. Giamatti (for the Italian poems). In the same series Bush has subsequently supplied a variorum commentary for the *Minor English Poems* (3 vols., 1972). Some of the predecessors of these modern works are described by Ants Oras in *Milton's Editors and Commentators . . . (1695–1801)* (1931). There are selections from the prose by M. W. Wallace (1925), C. E. Vaughan (1927), Merritt Hughes (1947), K. M. Burton (1958), J. Max Patrick (1968), and C.A. Patrides (1974), but these and various separate editions of the principal tracts will be superseded by the Yale edition of the *Complete Prose Works* under the general editorship of Don M. Wolfe (1953 ff.), which has now reached Volume VI (1973), containing *Christian Doctrine.*

As noted earlier, Milton attracted much attention from contemporary biographers, whose works have been assembled by Helen Darbishire in *Early Lives of Milton* (1932). J. S. Diekhoff's *Milton on Himself* (1939) brings together the many personal digressions scattered through the works, and J. Milton French has edited the *Life Records* (5 vols., 1949–58), essential for a study of the poet's life. Not unnaturally, the life itself has been given much attention. David Masson's great but dated work (6 vols., 1859–80, revised ed. of Vols. I–III and an Index, 1881–96) has finally been succeeded by W. R. Parker's major biography (2 vols., 1968). Among scores of smaller biographical or interpretative studies are those by Walter Raleigh (1900), E. M. W. Tillyard (1930),

A. E. Barker (*Milton and the Puritan Dilemma, 1641–1660,* 1942), Denis Saurat (rev. 1944), J. H. Hanford (1949), Kenneth Muir (1955), David Daiches (1957), Douglas Bush (1964), and John Carey (1969). Special mention should be made of J. H. Hanford's classic *Milton Handbook,* which has now, with the assistance of J. G. Taaffe, attained its fifth edition (1970).

In addition to collections of Milton criticism and scholarship by James Thorpe (1950), C. A. Patrides (on *Lycidas,* 1961), A. E. Barker (1965), J. S. Diekhoff (on *Comus,* 1968), and Arnold Stein (1970), there are many separate studies touching on the minor poems: John Arthos, *On a Mask Presented at Ludlow-Castle* (1954), F. T. Prince, *The Italian Element in Milton's Verse* (1954), R. M. Adams, *Ikon: John Milton and the Modern Critics* (1955), Rosemond Tuve, *Images & Themes in Five Poems by Milton* (1957) and a posthumous gathering of *Essays* on Spenser, Herbert, and Milton (ed. Thomas P. Roche, 1970), Joseph H. Summers (ed.), *The Lyric and Dramatic Milton* (1965), John Reesing, *Milton's Poetic Art* (1968), John G. Demaray, *Milton and the Masque Tradition* (1968), J. B. Leishman, *Milton's Minor Poems* (1969), and Mindele Treip, *Milton's Punctuation* (1970). Since 1967 the *Milton Quarterly* (formerly the *Milton Newsletter*) has tried to keep abreast of current publications.

from Poems (1645)

THE STATIONER TO THE READER

It is not any private respect of gain, gentle reader—for the slightest pamphlet is nowadays more vendible[1] than the works of learnedest men—but it is the love I have to our own language that hath made me diligent to collect and set forth such pieces both in prose and verse as may renew the wonted honor and esteem of our English tongue; and it's the worth of these both English and Latin poems, not the flourish of any prefixed encomiums,[2] that can invite thee to buy them, though these are not without the highest commendations and applause of the learned'st academics, both domestic and foreign; and amongst those of our own country, the unparalleled attestation of that renowned Provost of Eton, Sir Henry Wotton.[3] I know not thy palate how it relishes such dainties, nor how harmonious thy soul is; perhaps more trivial airs may please thee better. But howsoever thy opinion is spent upon these, that encouragement I have already received from the most ingenious men in their clear and courteous entertainment of Mr. Waller's late choice pieces[4] hath once more made me adventure into the world, presenting it with these ever green and not-to-be-blasted[5] laurels. The author's more peculiar excellency in these studies was too well known to conceal his papers or to keep me from attempting to solicit them from him. Let the event[6] guide itself which way it will, I shall deserve of the age by bringing into the light as true a birth as the Muses have brought forth since our famous Spenser[7] wrote, whose poems in these English ones are as rarely[8] imitated as sweetly excelled. Reader, if thou art eagle-eyed to censure[9] their worth, I am not fearful to expose them to thy exactest perusal.

Thine to command,
Humph. Moseley

ON THE MORNING OF CHRIST'S NATIVITY
Composed 1629[1]

1

This is the month, and this the happy morn,
Wherein the Son of heav'n's eternal King,
Of wedded Maid and Virgin Mother born,
Our great redemption from above did bring;
For so the holy sages[2] once did sing,

THE STATIONER TO THE READER   [1]Salable. [2]Encomiums.
[3]Standing as a sort of preface to *A Mask* (i.e., *Comus*) in the 1645 *Poems* is "The Copy of a Letter Written by Sir Henry Wotton to the Author upon the Following Poem." Here Wotton (see p. 54), under the date of 13 April 1638, charmingly acknowledges the "dainty piece of entertainment" that Milton had recently sent to him and reciprocates with advice and letters of introduction for the young poet's projected Continental tour. As for *Comus,* Wotton says, "I should much commend the tragical part if the lyrical did not ravish me with a certain Doric delicacy in your songs and odes, whereunto I must plainly confess to have seen yet nothing parallel in our language."
[4]Humphrey Moseley, the writer of this preface and publisher of the 1645 *Poems,* had recently enjoyed a great success with Edmund Waller's *Poems,* which went through three editions in 1645. See p. 245. [5]*Blasted:* withered. [6]Outcome.
[7]Just a year before the publication of his *Poems,* Milton, in *Areopagitica* (p. 605), had praised the "sage and serious" Edmund Spenser (1552?–99) as "a better teacher than Scotus or Aquinas."
[8]Splendidly. [9]Judge, evaluate.
CHRIST'S NATIVITY   [1]In his *Elegia Sexta,* a Latin verse epistle addressed to his former schoolmate Charles Diodati in December 1629, Milton announces the recent composition of this poem as a Christmas offering to the "heaven-descended King."
[2]I.e., Hebrew prophets who allegedly foretold the birth of Christ.

That he our deadly forfeit should release,
And with his Father work us a perpetual peace.

2

That glorious form, that light unsufferable,
And that far-beaming blaze of majesty,
Wherewith he wont at heav'n's high council-table
To sit the midst of Trinal Unity,
He laid aside; and here with us to be
    Forsook the courts of everlasting day,
And chose with us a darksome house of mortal clay.

3

Say, heav'nly Muse,[3] shall not thy sacred vein
Afford a present to the infant[4] God?
Hast thou no verse, no hymn, or solemn strain,
To welcome Him to this His new abode,
Now while the heav'n, by the sun's team untrod,
    Hath took no print of the approaching light,
And all the spangled host keep watch in squadrons bright?

4

See how from far upon the eastern road
The star-led wizards[5] haste with odors sweet!
O run, prevent[6] them with thy humble ode,
And lay it lowly at His blessed feet;
Have thou the honor first thy Lord to greet,
    And join thy voice unto the angel quire
From out His secret altar toucht with hallow'd fire.[7]

THE HYMN

1

It was the winter wild
While the heav'n-born child
    All meanly wrapp'd in the rude manger lies;
Nature in awe to Him
Had doff'd her gaudy trim,
    With her great Master so to sympathize;
It was no season then for her
To wanton with the sun, her lusty paramour.

2

Only with speeches fair
She woos the gentle air
    To hide her guilty front with innocent snow,
And on her naked shame,
Pollute with sinful blame,[8]
    The saintly veil of maiden white to throw,
Confounded that her Maker's eyes
Should look so near upon her foul deformities.

3

But he her fears to cease,
Sent down the meek-eyed Peace;
    She, crown'd with olive green, came softly sliding
Down through the turning sphere,
His ready harbinger,
    With turtle[9] wing the amorous[10] clouds dividing,
And waving wide her myrtle wand,
She strikes a universal peace through sea and land.

4

No war or battle's sound
Was heard the world around:
    The idle spear and shield were high uphung;
The hooked[11] chariot stood
Unstain'd with hostile blood;
    The trumpet spake not to the armed throng;
And kings sat still with awful[12] eye,
As if they surely knew their sovran Lord was by.

5

But peaceful was the night
Wherein the Prince of Light
    His reign of peace upon the earth began:
The winds with wonder whist,[13]
Smoothly the waters kist,
    Whispering new joys to the mild ocean,
Who now hath quite forgot to rave,
While birds of calm[14] sit brooding on the charmed wave.

6

The stars with deep amaze[15]
Stand fix'd in steadfast gaze,
    Bending one way their precious influence,[16]
And will not take their flight
For all the morning light,
    Or Lucifer[17] that often warn'd them thence;
But in their glimmering orbs[18] did glow,
Until their Lord himself bespake, and bid them go.

7

And though the shady gloom
Had given day her room,
    The sun himself withheld his wonted speed,
And hid his head for shame,
As his inferior flame
    The new-enlighten'd world no more should need;
He saw a greater sun appear
Than his bright throne or burning axletree could bear.

8

The shepherds on the lawn,
Or ere the point of dawn,

[3]Urania, in classical mythology, the Muse of astronomy, but here (as earlier in Du Bartas) the Muse of celestial inspiration. In *Paradise Lost* (VII.1–12) Milton invokes her directly and explains, "The meaning, not the name I call."
[4]Milton is perhaps punning on the Latin *infans*, "not speaking."
[5]The "wise men of the east" who, according to Matthew (2.1), brought gifts for the infant Christ.
[6]Anticipate, forestall.
[7]Isaiah (6.6–7) tells how his lips were touched with a live coal that one of the seraphim took from the altar.
[8]*Pollute...blame*: i.e., made sinful by the fall.   [9]Turtle dove.
[10]I.e., clinging.
[11]I.e., with blades projecting from the wheels.   [12]Reverent.
[13]Hushed, silent.
[14]The fabled halcyons, during whose brooding periods in their floating nests the seas were alleged to remain calm.
[15]Amazement.
[16]Power exerted on humans by the heavenly bodies.
[17]The morning star.   [18]Spheres.

Sat simply chatting in a rustic row;
Full little thought they than[19]
That the mighty Pan[20]
   Was kindly[21] come to live with them below;
Perhaps their loves, or else their sheep,
Was all that did their silly[22] thoughts so busy keep.

9
When such music sweet
Their hearts and ears did greet,
   As never was by mortal finger strook,[23]
Divinely warbled voice
Answering the stringed noise,
   As all their souls in blissful rapture took;
The air, such pleasure loth to lose,
With thousand echoes still prolongs each
      heav'nly close.[24]

10
Nature that heard such sound
Beneath the hollow round
   Of Cynthia's seat,[25] the airy region thrilling,[26]
Now was almost won
To think her part was done,
   And that her reign had here its last fulfilling;
She knew such harmony alone
Could hold all heav'n and earth in happier union.

11
At last surrounds their sight
A globe[27] of circular light,
   That with long beams the shamefac'd Night array'd;
The helmed Cherubim
And sworded Seraphim
   Are seen in glittering ranks with wings display'd,
Harping in loud and solemn quire,
With unexpressive[28] notes to heav'n's new-born heir.

12
Such music (as 'tis said)
Before was never made,
   But when of old the sons of morning sung,[29]
While the Creator great
His constellations set,
   And the well-balanc'd world on hinges hung,
And cast the dark foundations deep,
And bid the welt'ring[30] waves their oozy channel keep.

13
Ring out, ye crystal spheres,[31]
Once bless our human ears
   (If ye have power to touch our senses so),
And let your silver chime
Move in melodious time
   And let the base[32] of heav'n's deep organ blow;
And with your ninefold harmony
Make up full consort to th' angelic symphony.

14
For if such holy song
Enwrap our fancy long,

Time will run back and fetch the age of gold,[33]
And speckl'd Vanity
Will sicken soon and die,
   And leprous Sin will melt from earthly mold,
And hell itself will pass away,
And leave her dolorous mansions to the peering day.

15
Yea, Truth and Justice then
Will down return to men,
   Th' enamel'd arras of the rainbow wearing,
And Mercy set between,[34]
Thron'd in celestial sheen,
   With radiant feet the tissued[35] clouds down steering;
And heav'n, as at some festival,
Will open wide the gates of her high palace hall.

16
But wisest Fate says no,
This must not yet be so;
   The Babe lies yet in smiling infancy,
That on the bitter cross
Must redeem our loss,
   So both himself and us to glorify;
Yet first to those ychain'd[36] in sleep,
The wakeful trump of doom must thunder through
      the deep,

17
With such a horrid clang
As on Mount Sinai rang
   While the red fire and smold'ring clouds outbrake:
The aged earth, aghast

[19]Then. Milton's spelling, which in the seventeenth century was interchangeable with *then*, has been retained to save the rhyme.
[20]The pagan god of shepherds, whom Spenser and others identified with Christ as the good shepherd.
[21]1. According to his nature; 2. gently.
[22]Innocent, unsophisticated.   [23]Struck.   [24]Cadence.
[25]The moon (whose orbit is the *hollow round*).
[26]Penetrating, piercing.   [27]Troop (a Latinism).
[28]Inexpressible.   [29]*When of old...sung*: "Where wast thou when I laid the foundations of the earth?... When the morning stars sang together, and all the songs of God shouted with joy?" (Job 38.4–7)   [30]Heaving.
[31]*Ring...spheres*: According to Pythagorean and Platonic doctrine each of the planets, moving in its proper orbit, sounds its characteristic note, which by *ninefold harmony* makes the music of the spheres.
[32]The earth, excluded since the fall from participating in the music of the spheres, will with its regeneration at the birth of Christ join its bass (*base*) to the *ninefold harmony* of the other planets to make a *full consort*.
[33]*Age of gold*: In Ovid (*Metamorphoses*, Book I), the primal era of innocence and happiness, often associated by early Christian writers with paradise before the fall.
[34]*Th' enamel'd...between*: In the 1673 edition of his *Poems* Milton changed these lines to "Orb'd in a Rainbow; and like glories wearing / Mercy will sit between."
[35]Woven with gold or silver threads; i.e., streaked with light.
[36]Chained (a Spenserian archaism).

With terror of that blast,
　Shall from the surface to the center shake,
When at the world's last session
The dreadful Judge in middle air shall spread
　His throne.[37]

18

And then at last our bliss
Full and perfect is,
　But now begins; for from this happy day
Th' old dragon[38] under ground,
In straiter limits bound,
　Not half so far casts his usurped sway,
And, wrath[39] to see his kingdom fail,
Swinges[40] the scaly horror of his folded tail.

19

The oracles are dumb,
No voice or hideous hum
　Runs through the arched roof in words deceiving.
Apollo from his shrine
Can no more divine,
　With hollow shriek the steep of Delphos[41] leaving.
No nightly trance or breathed spell
Inspires the pale-ey'd priest from the prophetic cell.

20

The lonely mountains o'er,
And the resounding shore,
　A voice of weeping heard, and loud lament;
From haunted spring and dale,
Edg'd with poplar pale,
　The parting genius[42] is with sighing sent;
With flow'r-inwoven tresses torn
The nymphs in twilight shade of tangled thickets mourn.

21

In consecrated earth
And on the holy hearth,
　The lars and lemures[43] moan with midnight plaint;
In urns and altars round,
A drear and dying sound
　Affrights the flamens[44] at their service quaint;[45]
And the chill marble seems to sweat,
While each peculiar[46] power forgoes his wonted seat.

22

Peor and Baalim[47]
Forsake their temples dim,
　With that twice-batter'd god[48] of Palestine;
And mooned Ashtaroth,[49]
Heav'n's queen and mother both,
　Now sits not girt with tapers' holy shine;
The Libyc Hammon[50] shrinks his horn,
In vain the Tyrian maids their wounded
　Thammuz[51] mourn.

23

And sullen Moloch,[52] fled,
Hath left in shadows dread
　His burning idol all of blackest hue;

In vain with cymbals' ring
They call the grisly king,
　In dismal dance about the furnace blue;
The brutish gods of Nile[53] as fast,
Isis and Orus, and the dog Anubis, haste.

24

Nor is Osiris[54] seen
In Memphian grove or green,
　Trampling the unshower'd grass with lowings loud;
Nor can he be at rest
Within his sacred chest,
　Nought but profoundest Hell can be his shroud;
In vain with timbrel'd anthems dark
The sable-stoled sorcerers bear his worship'd ark.

25

He feels from Juda's land
The dreaded Infant's hand,
　The rays of Bethlehem blind his dusky eyne;[55]
Nor all the gods beside
Longer dare abide,
　Not Typhon[56] huge ending in snaky twine:
Our Babe, to show His Godhead true,
Can in His swaddling bands control the damned crew.

26

So when the sun in bed,
Curtain'd with cloudy red,

[37]*With such...throne*: The thunder and lightning that accompanied Moses' receiving the Ten Commandments on Mount Sinai (Exodus 19.16) anticipate the Last Judgment as prophesied by Matthew (24.30). *Session*: sitting of a court.
[38]Satan, "that old serpent" of Revelation 20.2. [39]Wroth. [40]Singes, scorches.
[41]Delphi, a shrine on the slopes of Mt. Parnassus in Greece, site of a famous oracle of Apollo. [42]Local tutelary spirit.
[43]*Lars and lemures*: in Roman mythology, deities of cities or houses. [44]Roman priests. [45]Crafty, elaborate. [46]Particular.
[47]Respectively, the Phoenician deity Baal and his various manifestations or local titles like Baal-Berith and Baal-Zebub.
[48]Dagon, whose image, according to 1 Samuel 5.3-4, was overturned twice.
[49]A Phoenician moon goddess who was commonly depicted as horned (*mooned*). She corresponds to Venus and Astarte.
[50]Ammon, an Egyptian god (the manifestation of Jove) who was worshiped in Libya in the form of a ram.
[51]A god of vegetation (identical with the Greek Adonis) whose death by a boar was annually commemorated in Phoenicia, of which Tyre was the principal city.
[52]A sun god (2 Kings 23.10) to whom the Ammonites offered human sacrifice. In *Paradise Lost* (II.43 ff.) he is one of Satan's lieutenants—"the fiercest spirit / That fought in heav'n"—who urges "open war" on God.
[53]Egyptian deities who were commonly depicted with the heads of various animals, for example, Isis with a cow, Orus (or Horus) with a hawk, and Anubis with a jackal.
[54]A powerful Egyptian deity worshiped in the form of Apis, a black bull whose image was kept in an ark or *sacred chest* at Memphis. [55]Archaic plural of *eye*.
[56]Either a hundred-headed monster of Greek mythology that was killed by Zeus or the evil Egyptian deity who slew Osiris.

Pillows his chin upon an orient[57] wave,
The flocking shadows pale
Troop to th' infernal jail;[58]
  Each fetter'd ghost slips to his several[59] grave,
  And the yellow-skirted fays[60]
Fly after the night-steeds, leaving their moon-lov'd maze.

            27
But see, the Virgin blest
Hath laid her Babe to rest.
  Time is our tedious song should here have ending;
Heav'n's youngest-teemed[61] star
Hath fix'd her polish'd car,
  Her sleeping Lord with handmaid lamp attending;
  And all about the courtly stable
Bright-harness'd[62] angels sit in order serviceable.

ON TIME[1]

Fly, envious Time, till thou run out thy race,
Call on the lazy leaden-stepping hours,
Whose speed is but the heavy plummet's pace;[2]
And glut thyself with what thy womb[3] devours,
Which is no more than what is false and vain,   5
And merely mortal dross,
So little is our loss,
So little is thy gain.
For whenas each thing bad thou hast entomb'd,
And last of all thy greedy self consum'd,[4]   10
Then long Eternity shall greet our bliss
With an individual[5] kiss;
And Joy shall overtake us as a flood,
When everything that is sincerely good
And perfectly divine,   15
With Truth, and Peace, and Love shall ever shine
About the supreme throne
Of Him, t'whose happy-making sight alone,
When once our heav'nly-guided soul shall climb,
Then all this earthy grossness quit,   20
Attir'd with stars, we shall forever sit,
  Triumphing over Death, and Chance, and thee
    O Time.

UPON THE CIRCUMCISION

Ye flaming powers,[1] and winged warriors bright,
That erst[2] with music, and triumphant song
First heard by happy watchful shepherd's ear,
So sweetly sung your joy the clouds along
Through the soft silence of the list'ning night;   5
Now mourn, and if·sad share with us to bear
Your fiery essence can distill no tear,
Burn in your sighs, and borrow
Seas wept from our deep sorrow,
He who with all heav'ns heraldry whilere[3]   10
Enter'd the world, now bleeds to give us ease;
Alas, how soon our sin
  Sore doth begin
    His Infancy to seize!

O more exceeding love or law more just?   15
Just law indeed, but more exceeding love!
For we by rightful doom[4] remediless
Were lost in death till He that dwelt above,
High thron'd in secret bliss, for us frail dust
Emptied his glory, ev'n to nakedness;   20
And that great cov'nant[5] which we still transgress
Entirely satisfi'd,
And the full wrath beside
Of vengeful justice bore for our excess,
And seals obedience first with wounding smart   25
This day; but O ere long
Huge pangs and strong
  Will pierce more near His heart.

ON SHAKESPEARE, 1630[1]

What needs my Shakespeare for his honor'd bones
The labor of an age in piled stones,
Or that his hallow'd relics should be hid
Under a star-ypointing[2] pyramid?
Dear son of Memory, great heir of Fame,   5
What need'st thou such weak witness of thy name?
Thou in our wonder and astonishment
Hast built thyself a livelong monument.
For whilst to the shame of slow-endeavoring art
Thy easy numbers[3] flow, and that each heart   10
Hath from the leaves of thy unvalu'd[4] book

[57]Eastern, hence lustrous, shining.
[58]*The flocking...jail*: referring to the ancient belief that ghosts (*shadows*) had to return to the underworld at dawn.
[59]Separate. [60]Fairies. [61]Latest born. [62]Clad in shining armor.
ON TIME [1]In the so-called Trinity Manuscript at Trinity College, Cambridge—a workbook, much of it in Milton's hand, containing drafts of *Comus*, *Lycidas*, and various shorter poems, as well as a list of subjects and other notes for a projected epic poem or drama—this piece has the subtitle (subsequently deleted) "to be set on a clock case." It was probably written about 1633.
[2]*Plummet's pace*: referring to the weights in the mechanism of the clock? [3]Belly.
[4]For Sir Walter Raleigh's extended treatment of the common notion that, as Shakespeare said, "Time must have a stop" in the final conflagration, see pp. 870 ff.
[5]Undividable, hence perpetual.
UPON THE CIRCUMCISION [1]Sixth of the nine orders of angels in the celestial hierarchy that Milton elsewhere (*Paradise Lost*, V.772) lists partially as "thrones, dominations, princedoms, virtues, powers." See *hierarchy* in the Glossary. [2]I.e., at the Nativity. [3]Previously. [4]Judgment.
[5]The pact between God and Abraham (Genesis 17.7–11) that was signalized by circumcision, the *wounding smart* (l. 25) whereby man *seals* his obedience to God.
ON SHAKESPEARE [1]This poem—Milton's first published work—appeared in the second folio of Shakespeare's plays in 1632. Milton's date has led some to think that he perhaps wrote it to accompany a picture of the Stratford monument rather than the Droeshout portrait.
[2]The *y* prefix of the archaic past participle that Milton borrowed from Spenser is here used ungrammatically with the present participle. [3]Verses. [4]Invaluable.

Those Delphic[5] lines with deep impression took,
Then thou, our fancy of itself bereaving,
Dost make us marble with too much conceiving,
And so sepúlchr'd in such pomp dost lie,   15
That kings for such a tomb would wish to die.

L'ALLEGRO[1]

Hence, loathed Melancholy,
  Of Cerberus[2] and blackest Midnight born,
In Stygian[3] cave forlorn
  'Mongst horrid shapes, and shrieks, and sights unholy,
Find out some uncouth[4] cell,   5
  Where brooding darkness spreads his jealous wings,
And the night-raven sings;
  There under ebon[5] shades and low-brow'd rocks,
As ragged as thy locks,
  In dark Cimmerian[6] desert ever dwell.   10

But come, thou goddess fair and free,
In heav'n yclept[7] Euphrosyne,[8]
And by men, heart-easing Mirth,
Whom lovely Venus, at a birth,
With two sister Graces more,   15
To ivy-crowned Bacchus bore;
Or whether (as some sager sing[9])
The frolic wind that breathes the spring,
Zephyr, with Aurora playing,
As he met her once a-Maying,   20
There on beds of violets blue,
And fresh-blown roses wash'd in dew,
Fill'd her with thee, a daughter fair,
So buxom, blithe, and debonair.
Haste thee, Nymph, and bring with thee   25
Jest and youthful Jollity,
Quips and Cranks[10] and wanton Wiles,
Nods, and Becks, and wreathed Smiles,
Such as hang on Hebe's[11] cheek,
And love to live in dimple sleek;   30
Sport that wrinkled Care derides,
And Laughter holding both his sides.
Come, and trip it as ye go
On the light fantastic toe,
And in thy right hand lead with thee   35
The mountain nymph, sweet Liberty;
And if I give thee honor due,
Mirth, admit me of thy crew,
To live with her, and live with thee,
In unreproved pleasures free;   40
To hear the lark begin his flight,
And singing startle the dull night,
From his watch-tow'r[12] in the skies,
Till the dappled dawn doth rise;
Then to come, in spite of sorrow,   45
And at my window bid good-morrow
Through the sweet-briar, or the vine,
Or the twisted eglantine;
While the cock, with lively din
Scatters the rear[13] of darkness thin,   50

And to the stack or the barn door
Stoutly struts his dames before;
Oft list'ning how the hounds and horn
Cheerly rouse the slumb'ring morn,
From the side of some hoar hill,   55
Through the high wood echoing shrill.
Sometime walking, not unseen,
By hedgerow elms, on hillocks green,
Right against[14] the eastern gate,
Where the great sun begins his state,[15]   60
Rob'd in flames and amber light,
The clouds in thousand liveries dight;[16]
While the ploughman, near at hand,
Whistles o'er the furrow'd land,
And the milkmaid singeth blithe,   65
And the mower whets his scythe,
And every shepherd tells his tale[17]
Under the hawthorn in the dale.
Straight mine eye hath caught new pleasures,
Whilst the landskip round it measures: 70
Russet lawns and fallows gray,
Where the nibbling flocks do stray,
Mountains on whose barren breast
The laboring clouds do often rest,
Meadows trim with daisies pi'd,[18]   75
Shallow brooks and rivers wide;
Towers and battlements it sees
Bosom'd high in tufted trees,
Where perhaps some beauty lies,
The cynosure[19] of neighboring eyes.   80
Hard by, a cottage chimney smokes
From betwixt two aged oaks,
Where Corydon and Thyrsis[20] met
Are at their savory dinner set

[5]Inspired by Apollo, who had a famous shrine at Delphos; hence poetical.
L'ALLEGRO   [1]"The happy man."
[2]In Greek mythology, the three-headed watchdog of the underworld.
[3]Referring to the river Styx, which flows through hell.
[4]Unknown, unfrequented.   [5]Ebony, i.e., black.
[6]Dark (from the Cimmerians who, says Homer, lived in a land of perpetual darkness).   [7]Called (a Spenserian archaism).
[8]Mirth, one of the three Graces, sister to Aglaia (Brightness) and Thalia (Bloom). They were usually thought to be the daughters of Zeus and Hera, not (as Milton says) of Bacchus and Venus.
[9]There is no classical authority for this alternative genealogy that makes Zephyr (the West Wind) and Aurora (goddess of the dawn) the parents of the Graces.   [10]Jokes.
[11]Youthful daughter of Jove and cupbearer of the gods.
[12]Milton is perhaps punning on *tower*, a term in falconry referring to the height of a bird's ascent.   [13]Rear guard.   [14]Opposite.
[15]Royal procession.   [16]Clothed, arrayed.
[17]*Tells his tale*: counts his sheep with a *tale* or tally? tells his story (of love)?   [18]Dappled, spotted.
[19]Literally, "dog's tail," name of the constellation Ursa Minor or the Little Bear, which contains the North Star; hence, a center of attention.
[20]Conventional names for rustics in pastoral poetry (like *Phillis* and *Thestylis* below).

Of herbs and other country messes,²¹
Which the neat-handed Phillis dresses;
And then in haste her bow'r she leaves,
With Thestylis to bind the sheaves;
Or if the earlier season lead,
To the tann'd haycock in the mead.   90
Sometimes with secure²² delight
The upland hamlets will invite,
When the merry bells ring round,
And the jocund rebecks²³ sound
To many a youth and many a maid   95
Dancing in the chequer'd shade;
And young and old come forth to play
On a sunshine holiday,
Till the livelong daylight fail;
Then to the spicy nut-brown ale,   100
With stories told of many a feat,
How fairy Mab²⁴ the junkets²⁵ eat;
She²⁶ was pinch'd and pull'd, she said,
And he, by friar's lanthorn²⁷ led,
Tells how the drudging goblin²⁸ sweat   105
To earn his cream-bowl duly set,
When in one night, ere glimpse of morn,
His shadowy flail hath thresh'd the corn
That ten day-laborers could not end;
Then lies him down the lubber fiend,   110
And stretch'd out all the chimney's²⁹ length,
Basks at the fire his hairy strength;
And cropfull out of doors he flings,
Ere the first cock his matin rings.
Thus done the tales, to bed they creep,   115
By whispering winds soon lull'd asleep.
Tow'red cities please us then,
And the busy hum of men,
Where throngs of knights and barons bold
In weeds of peace high triumphs³⁰ hold,   120
With store of ladies, whose bright eyes
Rain influence,³¹ and judge the prize
Of wit or arms, while both contend
To win her grace whom all commend.
There let Hymen³² oft appear   125
In saffron robe, with taper clear,
And pomp, and feast, and revelry,
With mask and antique pageantry;
Such sights as youthful poets dream
On summer eves by haunted stream.   130
Then to the well-trod stage anon,
If Jonson's learned sock³³ be on,
Or sweetest Shakespeare, Fancy's child,
Warble his native wood-notes wild;
And ever against eating cares,   135
Lap me in soft Lydian³⁴ airs,
Married to immortal verse,
Such as the meeting soul may pierce
In notes with many a winding bout³⁵
Of linked sweetness long drawn out,   140
With wanton heed and giddy cunning,
The melting voice through mazes running,

Untwisting all the chains that tie   85
The hidden soul of harmony;
That Orpheus'³⁶ self may heave his head   145
From golden slumber on a bed
Of heap'd Elysian flowers, and hear
Such strains as would have won the ear
Of Pluto, to have quite set free
His half-regain'd Eurydice.   150
These delights if thou canst give,
Mirth, with thee I mean to live.

IL PENSEROSO¹

Hence, vain deluding Joys,
    The brood of Folly without father bred,
How little you bestead,²
    Or fill the fixed mind with all your toys;
Dwell in some idle brain,   5
    And fancies fond with gaudy shapes possess,
As thick and numberless
    As the gay motes that people the sunbeams,
Or likest hovering dreams,
    The fickle pensioners of Morpheus'³ train.   10

But hail, thou goddess sage and holy,
Hail, divinest Melancholy,
Whose saintly visage is too bright
To hit the sense of human sight,
And therefore to our weaker view   15
O'erlaid with black, staid Wisdom's hue;
Black, but such as in esteem
Prince Memnon's sister⁴ might beseem,
Or that starr'd Ethiop queen⁵ that strove

²¹Dishes. ²²Carefree (a Latinism). ²³Three-stringed fiddles.
²⁴The queen of the fairies. ²⁵Cakes or confections.
²⁶I.e., the teller of the story (like *he* in the next line).
²⁷Friar's lantern, the *ignis fatuus* or will-o'-the-wisp.
²⁸The mischievous fairy Robin Goodfellow or Puck (sometimes called Lobbin, hence the *lubber fiend* of l. 110). ²⁹Fireplace.
³⁰Festivals.
³¹Power exerted by the stars (here conventionally associated with the ladies' eyes). ³²God of marriage.
³³Low shoe or slipper worn by actors in Greek comedies (an allusion to the classical element in Jonson's plays, in contrast to the *native wood-notes wild* in Shakespeare's).
³⁴A mode of Greek music especially appropriate for soft, lulling tunes. ³⁵Circuit.
³⁶Legendary Greek poet who by his music persuaded Pluto to release his dead wife Eurydice from the underworld. When Orpheus, ignoring Pluto's warning, looked back upon his wife as she followed him from Hades she was snatched away again, and so he lost his *half-regain'd* wife. For Ovid's version of this story as translated by George Sandys see pp. 107 ff.
IL PENSEROSO ¹"The contemplative man." ²Help.
³God of dreams, which are his *fickle pensioners* or attendants.
⁴According to Homer (*Odyssey*, XI), Himera, the beautiful sister of the valiant Ethiopian, Prince Memnon.
⁵Cassiopeia, who was turned into a constellation (*starr'd*) by the sea nymphs when she boasted of the beauty of her daughter Andromeda.

To set her beauty's praise above   20
The sea nymphs, and their powers offended.
Yet thou art higher far descended:
Thee bright-hair'd Vesta long of yore
To solitary Saturn bore;[6]
His daughter she (in Saturn's reign   25
Such mixture was not held a stain).
Oft in glimmering bow'rs and glades
He met her, and in secret shades
Of woody Ida's inmost grove,
While yet there was no fear of Jove.   30
Come, pensive Nun, devout and pure,
Sober, steadfast, and demure,
All in a robe of darkest grain,[7]
Flowing with majestic train,
And sable stole of cypress lawn[8]   35
Over thy decent[9] shoulders drawn.
Come, but keep thy wonted state,[10]
With ev'n step and musing gait,
And looks commercing with the skies,
Thy rapt soul sitting in thine eyes;   40
There held in holy passion still,
Forget thyself to marble,[11] till
With a sad[12] leaden downward cast
Thou fix them on the earth as fast.
And join with thee calm Peace and Quiet,   45
Spare Fast, that oft with gods doth diet,
And hears the Muses in a ring
Aye round about Jove's altar sing;
And add to these retired Leisure,
That in trim gardens takes his pleasure;   50
But first, and chiefest, with thee bring
Him that yon soars on golden wing,
Guiding the fiery-wheeled throne,
The cherub[13] Contemplation;
And the mute Silence hist[14] along,   55
'Less Philomel[15] will deign a song,
In[16] her sweetest, saddest plight,
Smoothing the rugged brow of Night,
While Cynthia[17] checks her dragon yoke
Gently o'er the accustom'd oak.   60
Sweet bird, that shunn'st the noise of folly,
Most musical, most melancholy!
Thee, chauntress, oft the woods among
I woo to hear thy even-song;
And missing thee, I walk unseen   65
On the dry smooth-shaven green,
To behold the wand'ring moon,
Riding near her highest noon,
Like one that had been led astray
Through the heav'n's wide pathless way;   70
And oft, as if her head she bow'd,
Stooping through a fleecy cloud.
Oft on a plat[18] of rising ground
I hear the far-off curfew sound
Over some wide-water'd shore,   75
Swinging slow with sullen roar;

Or if the air will not permit,
Some still removed place will fit,
Where glowing embers through the room
Teach light to counterfeit a gloom,   80
Far from all resort of mirth,
Save the cricket on the hearth,
Or the bellman's drowsy charm,[19]
To bless the doors from nightly harm.
Or let my lamp at midnight hour   85
Be seen in some high lonely tow'r,
Where I may oft outwatch the Bear,[20]
With thrice great Hermes,[21] or unsphere
The spirit of Plato to unfold
What worlds or what vast regions hold   90
The immortal mind that hath forsook
Her mansion in this fleshly nook;
And of those daemons[22] that are found
In fire, air, flood, or under ground,
Whose power hath a true consent   95
With planet or with element.
Sometime let gorgeous Tragedy
In scepter'd pall[23] come sweeping by,
Presenting Thebes, or Pelops' line,
Or the tale of Troy divine,   100
Or what (though rare) of later age
Ennobled hath the buskin'd[24] stage,
But, O sad Virgin, that thy power

[6]Milton's genealogy for Melancholy is apparently his own invention. Vesta, daughter of Saturn, was the Roman goddess of the household fire; her father was the god who from his throne on Mt. Ida in Crete ruled during the early Golden Age of natural innocence before he was displaced by his son Jove.
[7]Dye, color. [8]*Sable...lawn*: garment of fine black linen.
[9]Comely (a Latinism).
[10]*Wonted state*: customary dignified behavior.
[11]*Forget...marble*: When the soul is rapt in mystic contemplation its neglected and forgotten body becomes immobile like a marble statue. [12]Serious.
[13]In the celestial hierarchy, one of the cherubim, whose special function is the contemplation of God.
[14]Summon, draw. Here the verb is in the imperative mode (like *bring* in line 51).
[15]A maiden transformed into a nightingale after she had been ravished by her brother-in-law Tereus. [16]Text *Id*.
[17]The moon goddess, whose chariot was drawn by dragons.
[18]Plot.
[19]The night watchman's sleepy chant or song (*charm*) as he makes his rounds.
[20]I.e., stay awake all night (for the constellation of the Great Bear or Ursa Major never sets).
[21]Hermes Trismegisthus, a quasi-legendary Egyptian sage and thaumaturge to whom were attributed various works of magic and mysticism.
[22]Spirits who preside over the four elements named in l. 94, and who share the "influences" or powers of celestial bodies.
[23]Regal robes appropriate for the elevated personages of Greek tragic drama, like those of the royal houses of *Thebes* (Oedipus) and of Pelops' line (Agamemnon, Orestes, and Electra).
[24]Equipped with buskins, the high shoes worn by actors in Greek tragic drama.

Might raise Musaeus[25] from his bower,
Or bid the soul of Orpheus sing 105
Such notes as, warbled to the string,
Drew iron tears down Pluto's cheek,
And made hell grant what love did seek;
Or call up him that left half told
The story of Cambuscan bold, 110
Of Camball, and of Algarsife,
And who had Canace to wife,[26]
That own'd the virtuous[27] ring and glass,
And of the wondrous horse of brass,
On which the Tartar king did ride; 115
And if aught else great bards[28] beside
In sage and solemn tunes have sung,
Of tourneys and of trophies hung,
Of forests and enchantments drear,
Where more is meant than meets the ear. 120
Thus, Night, oft see me in thy pale career,
Till civil-suited[29] Morn appear,
Not trick'd and frounc'd[30] as she was wont
With the Attic boy[31] to hunt,
But kerchief'd in a comely cloud, 125
While rocking winds are piping loud,
Or usher'd with a shower still,
When the gust hath blown his[32] fill,
Ending on the rustling leaves,
With minute[33] drops from off the eaves. 130
And when the sun begins to fling
His flaring beams, me, Goddess, bring
To arched walks of twilight groves,
And shadows brown that Sylvan[34] loves,
Of pine or monumental oak, 135
Where the rude axe with heaved stroke
Was never heard the nymphs to daunt,
Or fright them from their hallow'd haunt.
There in close covert by some brook,
Where no profaner eye may look, 140
Hide me from Day's garish eye,
While the bee with honied thigh,
That at her flow'ry work doth sing,
And the waters murmuring
With such consort[35] as they keep, 145
Entice the dewy-feather'd Sleep;
And let some strange mysterious dream
Wave at his wings in airy stream
Of lively portraiture display'd,
Softly on my eyelids laid. 150
And as I wake, sweet music breathe
Above, about, or underneath,
Sent by some spirit to mortals good,
Or the unseen genius[36] of the wood.
But let my due feet never fail 155
To walk the studious cloister's pale,[37]
And love the high embowed roof,
With antic[38] pillars massy proof,[39]
And storied[40] windows richly dight,
Casting a dim religious light. 160

There let the pealing organ blow
To the full-voic'd choir below,
In service high and anthems clear,
As may with sweetness, through mine ear,
Dissolve me into ecstasies, 165
And bring all heav'n before mine eyes.
And may at last my weary age
Find out the peaceful hermitage,
The hairy gown and mossy cell,
Where I may sit and rightly spell[41] 170
Of every star that heav'n doth show,
And every herb that sips the dew,
Till old experience do attain
To something like prophetic strain.
These pleasures, Melancholy, give, 175
And I with thee will choose to live.

SONNETS

1. [O NIGHTINGALE]

O nightingale, that on yon bloomy[1] spray
  Warbl'st at eve, when all the woods are still,
  Thou with fresh hope the lover's heart dost fill,
  While the jolly hours[2] lead on propitious May,
Thy liquid notes that close the eye of day, 5
  First heard before the shallow cuckoo's bill,
  Portend success in love;[3] O, if Jove's will
  Have link'd that amorous power to thy soft lay,
Now timely sing, ere the rude bird of hate
  Foretell my hopeless doom in some grove nigh: 10
  As thou from year to year hast sung too late
For my relief, yet hadst no reason why.
  Whether the Muse or Love call thee his mate,
  Both them I serve, and of their train am I.

[25]Legendary Greek poet, allegedly the disciple of Orpheus.
[26]*The story...wife*: The "story" alluded to, and in part summarized, is that begun but *left half told* by Chaucer in "The Squire's Tale" of *The Canterbury Tales*.
[27]Endowed with special power.
[28]The allusion seems to be to such poets of romance as Ludovico Ariosto (1474–1533) and Edmund Spenser (1552?–99).
[29]Sedately attired.
[30]I.e., with elaborate array and curled hair.
[31]Cephalus, beloved of Eos, daughter of the dawn, who accidentally killed his jealous wife Procris with a magic spear.
[32]Its. The neuter possessive was not established in Milton's time.
[33]Falling at intervals of a minute. [34]God of forests.
[35]Harmony. [36]Local god or tutelary spirit. [37]Enclosure.
[38]Quaint.
[39]I.e., built so massively that they will never fall.
[40]I.e., representing persons and events in stained glass.
[41]Meditate, speculate.
1. O NIGHTINGALE [1]Blossoming.
[2]The Horae, daughters of Jupiter and Themis, often associated with love and spring.
[3]*Thy liquid notes...success in love*: It was believed that a lover who heard the nightingale before the cuckoo (*the rude bird of hate* of l. 9) would have *success in love*.

7. [HOW SOON HATH TIME][1]

How soon hath Time, the subtle thief of youth,
  Stol'n on his wing my three and twentieth year!
  My hasting days fly on with full career,[2]
  But my late spring no bud or blossom show'th.
Perhaps my semblance might deceive the truth,   5
  That I to manhood am arriv'd so near,
  And inward ripeness doth much less appear,
  That some more timely-happy spirits[3] endu'th.[4]
Yet be it less or more, or soon or slow,
  It shall be still[5] in strictest measure ev'n   10
  To that same lot, however mean or high,
Toward which Time leads me, and the will of heav'n;
  All is, if I have grace to use it so,
  As ever in my great Task-Master's eye.

LYCIDAS[1]

In this monody[2] the author bewails a learned friend, un-
fortunately drowned in his passage from Chester on the
Irish Seas, 1637. And by occasion foretells the ruin of our
corrupted clergy, then in their height.

Yet once more, O ye laurels, and once more,
Ye myrtles brown, with ivy never sere,[3]
I come to pluck your berries harsh and crude,[4]
And with forc'd fingers rude
Shatter your leaves before the mellowing year.   5
Bitter constraint, and sad occasion dear,
Compels me to disturb your season due;
For Lycidas is dead, dead ere his prime,
Young Lycidas, and hath not left his peer.
Who would not sing for Lycidas? he knew   10
Himself to sing, and build the lofty rhyme.
He must not float upon his wat'ry bier
Unwept, and welter[5] to the parching wind,
Without the meed[6] of some melodious tear.
  Begin then, Sisters of the sacred well   15
That from beneath the seat of Jove doth spring,[7]
Begin, and somewhat loudly sweep the string.
Hence with denial vain, and coy excuse;
So may some gentle Muse
With lucky words favor my destin'd urn,   20
And as he passes turn,
And bid fair peace be to my sable shroud.
For we were nurs'd upon the selfsame hill,
Fed the same flock, by fountain, shade, and rill.
  Together both, ere the high lawns[8] appear'd   25
Under the opening eyelids of the morn,
We drove afield, and both together heard
What time the gray-fly winds her sultry horn,[9]
Batt'ning[10] our flocks with the fresh dews of night,
Oft till the star[11] that rose, at ev'ning, bright   30
Toward heav'n's descent had slop'd his westering[12] wheel.
Meanwhile the rural ditties were not mute:
Temper'd to th' oaten flute,
Rough Satyrs danc'd, and Fauns with clov'n heel

From the glad sound would not be absent long,   35
And old Damaetas[13] loved to hear our song.
  But O the heavy change, now thou art gone,
Now thou art gone, and never must return!
Thee, Shepherd, thee the woods and desert caves,
With wild thyme and the gadding[14] vine o'ergrown,   40
And all their echoes mourn.
The willows and the hazel copses green
Shall now no more be seen
Fanning their joyous leaves to thy soft lays.
As killing as the canker[15] to the rose,   45
Or taint-worm to the weanling herds that graze,
Or frost to flowers, that their gay wardrobe wear,
When first the white thorn blows;
Such, Lycidas, thy loss to shepherd's ear.
  Where were ye, Nymphs, when the remorseless deep   50
Clos'd o'er the head of your lov'd Lycidas?
For neither were ye playing on the steep
Where your old bards, the famous Druids, lie,
Nor on the shaggy top of Mona high,
Nor yet where Deva spreads her wizard stream.[16]   55
Ay me, I fondly[17] dream,
Had ye been there!—for what could that have done?
What could the Muse herself that Orpheus bore,
The Muse herself, for her enchanting son,

7. HOW SOON [1]This sonnet, probably written on Milton's twenty-
fourth birthday(9 December 1632), was enclosed in a letter (perhaps
for his former tutor, Thomas Young) on his somewhat ambiguous
situation and his apparent "belatedness" in choosing a career.
[2]*With full career*: with speedy progress.
[3]One of these "timely-happy spirits," it has been suggested, may
have been Milton's Cambridge contemporary Thomas Randolph
(see pp. 239 ff.), whose early success—both social and literary—
was in marked contrast to Milton's own. [4]Endow. [5]Always.
LYCIDAS [1]Milton wrote *Lycidas* in the early fall of 1637 for
Justa Edouardo King naufrago ab amicis maerentibus ("rites for
Edward King, drowned by shipwreck, from his grieving friends"),
a collection of twenty-three Greek and Latin and thirteen English
elegies by various Cambridge poets in memory of a young tutor
and fellow of Christ's College who was drowned on 10 August
1637 when his ship capsized on a voyage from Chester to Dublin.
As contemporaries at Christ's College, Milton and King must have
known each other, but there is no evidence of an intimate friend-
ship.
[2]A dirge spoken by one voice (the *uncouth swain* of l. 186).
[3]*Yet once more...sere*: The three evergreens (from which poets'
laurels were made) were associated with Apollo, Venus, and
Bacchus respectively. [4]Unripe. [5]Be tossed. [6]Gift, tribute.
[7]*Sisters...spring*: the Muses, whose *sacred well* was Aganippe on
Mr. Helicon, site of an altar to Jove. [8]Upland glades.
[9]*What time...horn*: i.e., mid-day. [10]Feeding. [11]Hesperus.
[12]Substituted for *burnished* in the Trinity Manuscript.
[13]Probably referring to a Cambridge tutor. Milton could have
got the name from Vergil's third eclogue or from Sir Philip Sid-
ney's *Arcadia* (where it is given to a rustic clown).
[14]Wandering. [15]Cankerworm.
[16]*Nor yet...wizard stream*: The isle of Anglesey (*Mona*) off the
coast of northern Wales and the wandering (*wizard*) river Dee
(*Deva*), on which Chester stands, were both associated with the
Irish Sea, where Edward King was drowned.
[17]Foolishly.

Whom universal nature did lament, 60
When by the rout that made the hideous roar
His gory visage down the stream was sent,
Down the swift Hebrus to the Lesbian shore?[18]
    Alas! what boots[19] it with uncessant care
To tend the homely slighted shepherd's trade,[20] 65
And strictly meditate the thankless Muse?
Were it not better done as others use,
To sport with Amaryllis in the shade,
Or with the tangles of Neaera's hair?[21]
Fame is the spur that the clear spirit doth raise 70
(That last infirmity of noble mind)
To scorn delights, and live laborious days;
But the fair guerdon[22] when we hope to find,
And think to burst out into sudden blaze,
Comes the blind Fury[23] with th' abhorred shears, 75
And slits the thin-spun life. "But not the praise,"
Phoebus[24] repli'd, and touch'd my trembling ears:
"Fame is no plant that grows on mortal soil,
Nor in the glistering foil[25]
Set off to th' world, nor in broad rumor lies, 80
But lives and spreads aloft by those pure eyes
And perfect witness of all-judging Jove;
As he pronounces lastly on each deed,
Of so much fame in heav'n expect thy meed."[26]
    O fountain Arethuse, and thou honor'd flood, 85
Smooth-sliding Mincius,[27] crown'd with vocal reeds,
That strain I heard was of a higher mood.
But now my oat proceeds,[28]
And listens to the Herald of the Sea,
That came in Neptune's plea.[29] 90
He ask'd the waves, and ask'd the felon winds,
What hard mishap hath doom'd this gentle swain?
And question'd every gust of rugged wings
That blows from off each beaked promontory;
They knew not of his story, 95
And sage Hippotades[30] their answer brings,
That not a blast was from his dungeon stray'd;
The air was calm, and on the level brine
Sleek Panope[31] with all her sisters play'd.
It was that fatal and perfidious bark, 100
Built in th' eclipse,[32] and rigged with curses dark,
That sunk so low that sacred head of thine.
    Next Camus,[33] reverend sire, went footing slow,
His mantle hairy, and his bonnet sedge,
Inwrought with figures dim, and on the edge 105
Like to that sanguine flower inscrib'd with woe.[34]
"Ah, who hath reft," quoth he, "my dearest pledge?"[35]
Last came, and last did go,
The Pilot of the Galilean Lake;[36]
Two massy keys[37] he bore of metals twain 110
(The golden opes, the iron shuts amain[38]).
He shook his miter'd[39] locks, and stern bespake:
"How well could I have spar'd for thee, young swain,
Enow[40] of such as for their bellies' sake
Creep and intrude and climb into the fold![41] 115
Of other care they little reck'ning make
Than how to scramble at the shearer's feast,

And shove away the worthy bidden guest.
Blind mouths! that scarce themselves know how to hold
A sheep-hook, or have learn'd aught else the least 120
That to the faithful herdmans' art belongs!
What recks it them? What need they? They are sped;[42]
And when they list, their lean and flashy songs
Grate on their scrannel[43] pipes of wretched straw;
The hungry sheep look up, and are not fed, 125
But swoln with wind and the rank mist they draw,[44]
Rot inwardly, and foul contagion spread;
Besides what the grim wolf with privy paw[45]
Daily devours apace, and nothing said;
But that two-handed engine[46] at the door 130
Stands ready to smite once, and smite no more."
    Return, Alpheus,[47] the dread voice is past

[18]*What could...Lesbian shore*: After the mythical poet Orpheus, son of the Muse Calliope, had been torn to pieces by a crowd (*rout*) of frenzied Bacchantes in Thrace, his severed head was cast into the river Hebrus and thus borne to the island of Lesbos in the Aegean Sea. [19]Profits. [20]I.e., poetry.
[21]*To sport...Neaera's hair*: The names *Amaryllis* and *Neaera*, both of which occur in Vergil's *Eclogues*, became conventional names for girls in pastoral poetry. [22]Prize, reward.
[23]Actually, Atropos, who with her *abhorred shears* cuts the thread of life, was one of the Fates. [24]Apollo, god of poetry.
[25]Thin leaf of gold or silver set under a gem to increase its brilliance. [26]Reward.
[27]*O fountain...Mincius*: When the nymph Arethuse, terrified by the pursuit of the river god Alpheus, was turned into a fountain at Syracuse in Sicily, her lover came through the sea as an underground river to unite with her. The Mincius is a river in northern Italy near Mantua, Vergil's birthplace. Milton's dual allusion (recalling, respectively, the Sicilian Theocritus and Vergil) enables him to return to his proper pastoral mode and theme.
[28]I.e., my song, played on an oaten pipe, continues.
[29]*Herald...plea*: I.e., Triton comes to defend Neptune, god of the sea, against the charge of causing Lycidas' death.
[30]Aeolus, god of the winds, who, according to Vergil, normally confined the savage (*felon*) winds in a cavern (*dungeon*).
[31]One of the Nereids or sea nymphs, daughters of Nereus, the Old Man of the Sea. [32]I.e., at an unlucky time.
[33]The river Cam, which flows through Cambridge. His furred (*hairy*) academic gown and his bonnet of reeds (*sedge*) identify him with the university.
[34]*Sanguine...woe*: the hyacinth, which is *sanguine* (red) because it sprang from the blood of the beautiful youth Hyacinthus, whom Apollo loved and accidentally killed, and *inscrib'd with woe* because the blood stains formed the Greek letters AI, "alas." [35]Child.
[36]*Pilot...Lake*: St. Peter. See Luke 5.2–9.
[37]*Keys*: "And I will give unto thee the keys of the kingdom of heaven" (Matthew 16.19). [38]With force.
[39]I.e., with a bishop's crown or miter. [40]Enough. Text *Anow*.
[41]Sheepfold. [42]Successful. [43]Feeble, thin. [44]Inhale.
[45]*Grim...paw*: the "corrupted clergy" of the Anglican Church under Archbishop Laud? the proselytizing Roman Catholic Church? The second possibility gains support from the two grey wolves in the coat of arms of St. Ignatius Loyola, founder of the Jesuits.
[46]*Two-handed engine*: Of the scores of attempted explanations of this phrase none has gained complete acceptance. *Engine*: instrument (which many commentators take to be a sword).
[47]See n. 27

That shrunk thy streams; return, Sicilian Muse,
And call the vales, and bid them hither cast
Their bells and flow'rets of a thousand hues. 135
Ye valleys low where the mild whispers use
Of shades and wanton winds and gushing brooks.
On whose fresh lap the swart star[48] sparely looks,
Throw hither all your quaint enamel'd eyes,
That on the green turf suck the honied show'rs, 140
And purple all the ground with vernal flow'rs.
Bring the rathe[49] primrose that forsaken dies,
The tufted crow-toe, and pale jessamine,[50]
The white pink, and the pansy freak'd[51] with jet,
The glowing violet, 145
The musk-rose, and the well-attir'd woodbine,
With cowslips wan that hang the pensive head,
And every flower that sad embroidery wears.
Bid amaranthus[52] all his beauty shed,
And daffadillies fill their cups with tears, 150
To strew the laureate hearse[53] where Lycid lies.
For so to interpose a little ease,
Let our frail thoughts dally with false surmise;
Ay me! whilst thee the shores and sounding seas
Wash far away, where'er thy bones are hurl'd, 155
Whether beyond the stormy Hebrides,[54]
Where thou perhaps under the whelming[55] tide
Visit'st the bottom of the monstrous world;
Or whether thou, to our moist vows[56] deni'd,
Sleep'st by the fable of Bellerus[57] old. 160
Where the great vision of the guarded mount
Looks toward Namancos and Bayona's hold;
Look homeward, Angel,[58] now, and melt with ruth;
And, O ye dolphins, waft the hapless youth.
    Weep no more, woeful shepherds, weep no more, 165
For Lycidas, your sorrow, is not dead,
Sunk though he be beneath the wat'ry floor;
So sinks the day-star[59] in the ocean bed,
And yet anon repairs his drooping head,
And tricks[60] his beams, and with new-spangled ore[61] 170
Flames in the forehead of the morning sky:
So Lycidas sunk low, but mounted high,
Through the dear might of Him that walk'd the waves,[62]
Where, other groves and other streams along,
With nectar pure his oozy locks he laves, 175
And hears the unexpressive nuptial song,[63]
In the blest kingdoms meek of joy and love.
There entertain him all the saints above,
In solemn troops and sweet societies
That sing, and singing in their glory move, 180
And wipe the tears forever from his eyes.[64]
Now, Lycidas, the shepherds weep no more;
Henceforth thou art the genius[65] of the shore,
In thy large recompense, and shalt be good
To all that wander in that perilous flood. 185
    Thus sang the uncouth[66] swain to th' oaks and rills,
While the still morn went out with sandals gray;
He touch'd the tender stops of various quills,[67]
With eager thought warbling his Doric[68] lay.
And now the sun had stretch'd out all the hills,[69] 190

And now was dropp'd into the western bay;
At last he rose, and twitch'd his mantle blue:
Tomorrow to fresh woods and pastures new.

A MASK OF THE SAME AUTHOR PRESENTED AT LUDLOW CASTLE, 1634, BEFORE THE EARL OF BRIDGEWATER, THEN PRESIDENT OF WALES COMUS

TO THE RIGHT HONORABLE JOHN, LORD VISCOUNT BRACKLEY, SON AND HEIR APPARENT TO THE EARL OF BRIDGEWATER, &C.

My Lord,

    This poem, which received its first occasion of birth from yourself and others of your noble family,[1] and much honor from your own person in the performance, now returns again to make a final dedication of itself to you. Although not openly acknowledged by the author, yet it is a legitimate offspring, so lovely and so much desired that the often copying of it hath tired my pen to give my several friends satisfaction, and brought me to a necessity of producing it to the public view; and now to offer it up in all rightful devotion to those fair hopes and rare endowments of your much-promising youth, which give a full assurance

[48]Sirius, the Dog Star, darkened (*swart*) by the heat of summer.
[49]Early. [50]Jasmine. [51]Spotted.
[52]The flower of paradise, thought to be immortal.
[53]The bier or tomb of Lycidas—itself a *false surmise* (l. 153) because the drowned shepherd's body was not recovered.
[54]Islands off the western coast of Scotland.
[55]The Trinity manuscript reads "humming." [56]Tearful prayers.
[57]A fabled giant of southern Britain? The name was apparently Milton's own invention, referring to Bellerium or Land's End in Cornwall, where St. Michael's *guarded mount* faces outward across the Bay of Biscay to the (Roman Catholic) strongholds of Namancos and Bayona in northern Spain.
[58]St. Michael, conceived as facing southward on his mountain on the Cornish coast, is implored to turn his gaze to England (*homeward*) and show pity (*ruth*) for the death of Lycidas.
[59]The sun. [60]Trims, adorns. [61]Gold.
[62]*Him...waves*: i.e., Christ. See Matthew 14.25–26.
[63]The unutterable song that is sung at the "marriage supper of the Lamb" (Revelation 19.9), i.e., the saved soul's union with God.
[64]*Wipe...eyes*: "And God shall wipe away all tears from their eyes" (Revelation 7.17). [65]Local tutelary deity.
[66]Unlearned, unknown. [67]Reeds.
[68]The Greek rustic dialect used by the eminent pastoral poets Theocritus, Moschus, and Bion.
[69]*Had stretch'd...hills*: i.e., had lengthened the shadows.

A MASK [1]At its first production the principal parts in *Comus* had been taken by the children of the earl of Bridgewater, the Lady by his daughter Anne (aged fifteen) and the two brothers by his sons John and Thomas (aged eleven and nine respectively). The composer Henry Lawes (1596–1662) played the part of the attendant Spirit, but who played Comus and Sabrina is not known.

to all that know you of a future excellence. Live, sweet Lord, to be the honor of your name, and receive this as your own from the hands of him who hath by many favors been long obliged to your most honored parents, and as in this representation your attendant Thyrsis, so now in all real expression

Your faithful and most humble servant, H. Lawes

The Persons

The Attendant Spirit, afterwards
  in the habit of Thyrsis
Comus, with his crew
The Lady
First Brother
Second Brother
Sabrina, the Nymph

The chief persons which presented were

The Lord Brackley
Mr. Thomas Egerton, his brother
The Lady Alice Egerton

The first scene discovers[2] *a wild wood. The Attendant Spirit descends or enters.*

Before the starry threshold of Jove's court
My mansion is, where those immortal shapes
Of bright aerial spirits live inspher'd
In regions mild of calm and serene air,
Above the smoke and stir of this dim spot   5
Which men call earth, and with low-thoughted care,
Confin'd and pester'd in this pinfold[0] here,
Strive to keep up a frail and feverish being,
Unmindful of the crown that Virtue gives,
After this mortal change,[4] to her true servants   10
Amongst the enthron'd gods on sainted seats.
Yet some there be that by due steps aspire
To lay their just hands on that golden key
That opes the palace of eternity.
To such my errand is, and but for such,   15
I would not soil these pure ambrosial weeds[5]
With the rank vapors of this sin-worn mold.
    But to my task. Neptune, besides the sway
Of every salt flood and each ebbing stream,
Took in by lot 'twixt high and nether Jove[6]   20
Imperial rule of all the sea-girt isles
That like to rich and various gems inlay
The unadorned bosom of the deep,
Which he, to grace his tributary gods,
By course commits to several[7] government,   25
And gives them leave to wear their sapphire crowns
And wield their little tridents. But this isle,[8]
The greatest and the best of all the main,
He quarters[9] to his blue-hair'd deities;
And all this tract[10] that fronts the falling sun   30
A noble peer[11] of mickle[12] trust and power

Has in his charge, with temper'd awe to guide
An old and haughty nation proud in arms;
Where his fair offspring, nurs'd in princely lore,
Are coming to attend their father's state[13]   35
And new-entrusted scepter; but their way
Lies through the perplex'd[14] paths of this drear wood,
The nodding horror of whose shady brows
Threats the forlorn and wand'ring passenger.
And here their tender age might suffer peril,   40
But that by quick command from soveran Jove
I was despatch'd for their defense and guard;
And listen why, for I will tell ye now
What never yet was heard in tale or song
From old or modern bard in hall or bow'r.   45
    Bacchus, that first from out the purple grape
Crush'd the sweet poison of misused wine,
After the Tuscan mariners transform'd,
Coasting the Tyrrhene shore, as the winds listed,
On Circe's island fell. (Who knows not Circe,   50
The daughter of the Sun? whose charmed cup
Whoever tasted, lost his upright shape,
And downward fell into a groveling swine.)[15]
This nymph that gaz'd upon his clust'ring locks,
With ivy berries wreath'd, and his blithe youth,   55
Had by him, ere he parted thence, a son
Much like his father, but his mother more,
Whom therefore she brought up and Comus nam'd;
Who, ripe and frolic of his full-grown age,
Roving the Celtic and Iberian fields,[16]   60
At last betakes him to this ominous wood,
And, in thick shelter of black shades imbow'red,
Excels his mother at her mighty art,
Off'ring to every weary traveler
His orient[17] liquor in a crystal glass,   65
To quench the drouth of Phoebus[18] which as they taste
(For most do taste through fond[19] intemperate thirst),
Soon as the potion works, their human count'nance,
Th' express resemblance of the gods, is chang'd
Into some brutish form of wolf, or bear,   70
Or ounce,[20] or tiger, hog, or bearded goat,
All other parts remaining as they were.

[2]Reveals. [3]Pound. [4]I.e., death. [5]Immortal garments.
[6]*Took in...Jove*: i.e., annexed (*took in*) by Jove (who rules the upper regions) and by his brother Pluto (who rules the *nether*). Thus to the third brother, Neptune, was allotted *sway* over the rivers, seas, and islands.
[7]Separate (by assignment to the *tributary gods* of l. 24).
[8]Britain. [9]Assigns. [10]Wales and the Welsh Marches.
[11]The earl of Bridgewater. [12]Great.
[13]Ceremonial installation. [14]Intricate.
[15]*Bacchus...swine*: Bacchus, god of wine, when taken by Italian (*Tuscan*) pirates, turned his captors into dolphins. Later, sailing in the *Tyrrhene* Sea off the western coast of Italy, he came to the island of Circe, an enchantress who with her magic potion (*charmed cup*) transformed men to beasts. Their son Comus inherited his father's taste for dissipation and his mother's gift for magic. [16]France and Spain. [17]Shining.
[18]*Drouth of Phoebus*: drought or thirst caused by the sun's heat.
[19]Foolish. [20]Lynx.

And they, so perfect is their misery,
Not once perceive their foul disfigurement,
But boast themselves more comely than before   75
And all their friends and native home forget
To roll with pleasure in a sensual sty.
Therefore when any favor'd of high Jove
Chances to pass through this advent'rous glade,
Swift as the sparkle of a glancing star   80
I shoot from heav'n to give him safe convoy,
As now I do. But first I must put off
These my sky-robes, spun out of Iris' woof,[21]
And take the weeds and likeness of a swain[22]
That to the service of this house belongs,   85
Who with his soft pipe and smooth-dittied song
Well knows to still the wild winds when they roar,
And hush the waving woods;[23] nor of less faith,[24]
And in this office of his mountain watch
Likeliest, and nearest to the present aid   90
Of this occasion. But I hear the tread
Of hateful steps: I must be viewless[25] now.

*Comus enters, with a charming-rod in one hand, his glass in the
other; with him a rout[26] of monsters, headed like sundry sorts of
wild beasts, but otherwise like men and women, their apparel
glistering. They come in making a riotous and unruly noise,
with torches in their hands.*

Comus: The star[27] that bids the shepherd fold
Now the top of heav'n doth hold,
And the gilded car of day[28]   95
His glowing axle doth allay[29]
In the steep Atlantic stream;
And the slope[30] sun his upward beam
Shoots against the dusky pole,[31]
Pacing toward the other goal   100
Of his chamber in the east.
Meanwhile welcome joy and feast,
Midnight shout and revelry,
Tipsy dance and jollity.
Braid your locks with rosy twine,   105
Dropping odors, dropping wine.
Rigor now is gone to bed,
And Advice with scrupulous head,
Strict Age and sour Severity
With their grave saws[32] in slumber lie.   110
We that are of purer fire
Imitate the starry quire,
Who in their nightly watchful spheres
Lead in swift round the months and years.
The sounds and seas with all their finny drove[33]
Now to the moon in wavering morris[34] move,   115
And on the tawny sands and shelves
Trip the pert fairies and the dapper elves;
By dimpled brook and fountain brim,
The wood-nymphs, deck'd with daisies trim,   120
Their merry wakes[35] and pastimes keep:
What hath night to do with sleep?

Night hath better sweets to prove,
Venus now wakes, and wak'ns Love.
Come, let us our rites begin;   125
'Tis only daylight that makes sin,
Which these dun shades will ne'er report.
Hail, goddess of nocturnal sport,
Dark-veil'd Cotytto,[36] t' whom the secret flame
Of midnight torches burns; mysterious dame,   130
That ne'er art called but when the dragon womb
Of Stygian[37] darkness spets her thickest gloom,
And makes one blot of all the air,
Stay thy cloudy ebon[38] chair
Wherein thou rid'st with Hecat',[39] and befriend   135
Us thy vow'd priests, till utmost end
Of all thy dues[40] be done, and none left out,
Ere the blabbing eastern scout,
The nice[41] Morn on th' Indian steep,
From her cabin'd loophole[42] peep,   140
And to the tell-tale Sun descry[43]
Our conceal'd solemnity.[44]
Come, knit hands, and beat the ground,
In a light fantastic round.

The Measure[45]

Break off, break off, I feel the different pace   145
Of some chaste footing near about this ground.
Run to your shrouds[46] within these brakes and trees;
Our number may affright. Some virgin sure
(For so I can distinguish by mine art)
Benighted in these woods. Now to my charms,   150
And to my wily trains; I shall ere long
Be well stock'd with as fair a herd as graz'd
About my mother Circe. Thus I hurl
My dazzling spells into the spongy air,
Of power to cheat the eye with blear[47] illusion,   155
And give it false presentments,[48] lest the place
And my quaint habits[49] breed astonishment,
And put the damsel to suspicious flight,
Which must not be, for that's against my course;
I, under fair pretence of friendly ends,   160

[21]*Sky-robes...woof*: i.e., the Spirit's multicolored robes, woven by the rainbow.   [22]Countryman.
[23]*That to the service...woods*: A compliment to Henry Lawes, who played the Attendant Spirit and who, in the *service* of Bridgewater's *house* was valued for his music (*smooth-dittied song*).
[24]*Nor of less faith*: i.e., no less trustworthy (than skilled in music).
[25]Invisible.   [26]Crowd.   [27]Hesperus, the evening star.
[28]*Car of day*: chariot of the sun.   [29]Cool.   [30]Descending.
[31]Sky.   [32]Maxims.   [33]Schools of fish.
[34]Morris (i.e., Moorish) dance.   [35]Nighttime revels.
[36]Thracian goddess whose furtive and licentious rites were held in darkness.   [37]Referring to the river Styx in Hades.
[38]Ebony, black.
[39]Hecate, baleful goddess of witches and sorcerers.
[40]Requisite ceremonies.   [41]Prudish.
[42]*Cabin'd loophole*: little window.   [43]Reveal.   [44]Celebration.
[45]Dance (described in the Trinity Manuscript as a "wild, rude, and wanton antic").   [46]Hiding places.   [47]Misty.
[48]*False presentments*: hallucinations.   [49]*Quaint habits*: strange attire.

And well-plac'd words of glozing[50] courtesy,
Baited with reasons not unplausible,
Wind me into the easy-hearted man,
And hug him into snares. When once her eye
Hath met the virtue[51] of this magic dust,   165
I shall appear some harmless villager
Whom thrift keeps up about his country gear.[52]
But here she comes; I fairly[53] step aside,
And hearken, if I may, her business here.

The Lady enters.

Lady: This way the noise was, if mine ear be true,   170
My best guide now. Methought it was the sound
Of riot and ill-manag'd merriment,
Such as the jocund flute or gamesome pipe
Stirs up among the loose unletter'd hinds,[54]
When for their teeming[55] flocks and granges full   175
In wanton dance they praise the bounteous Pan,[56]
And thank the gods amiss. I should be loth
To meet the rudeness and swill'd[57] insolence
Of such late wassailers;[58] yet O where else
Shall I inform[59] my unacquainted feet   180
In the blind mazes of this tangl'd wood?
My brothers, when they saw me wearied out
With this long way, resolving here to lodge
Under the spreading favor of these pines,
Stepp'd as they said to the next thicket side   185
To bring me berries, or such cooling fruit
As the kind hospitable woods provide.
They left me then when the gray-hooded Ev'n,
Like a sad votarist in palmer's weed,
Rose from the hindmost wheels of Phœbus' wain.[60] 190
But where they are, and why they came not back,
Is now the labor of my thoughts; 'tis likeliest
They had engag'd their wand'ring steps too far,
And envious[61] darkness, ere they could return,
Had stole them from me. Else, O thievish Night,   195
Why shouldst thou, but for some felonious end,
In thy dark lantern thus close up the stars
That Nature hung in heaven, and fill'd their lamps
With everlasting oil, to give due light
To the misled and lonely traveler?   200
This is the place, as well as I may guess,
Whence ev'n now the tumult of loud mirth
Was rife and perfet[62] in my list'ning ear,
Yet nought but single[63] darkness do I find.
What might this be? A thousand fantasies   205
Begin to throng into my memory,
Of calling shapes, and beck'ning shadows dire,
And airy tongues that syllable men's names
On sands and shores and desert wildernesses.
These thoughts may startle well, but not astound   210
The virtuous mind, that ever walks attended
By a strong siding[64] champion, Conscience.
O welcome, pure-eyed Faith, white-handed Hope,
Thou hovering angel girt with golden wings,
And thou unblemish'd form of Chastity,   215

I see ye visibly, and now believe
That He, the Supreme Good, t' whom all things ill
Are but as slavish officers of vengeance,
Would send a glist'ring guardian, if need were,
To keep my life and honor unassail'd.   220
Was I deceiv'd, or did a sable cloud
Turn forth her silver lining on the night?
I did not err, there does a sable cloud
Turn forth her silver lining on the night,
And casts a gleam over this tufted grove.   225
I cannot hallo to my brothers, but
Such noise as I can make to be heard farthest
I'll venter,[65] for my new-enliv'n'd spirits
Prompt me; and they perhaps are not far off.

SONG

Sweet Echo,[66] sweetest nymph, that liv'st unseen   230
     Within thy airy shell
     By slow Meander's margent green,
And in the violet-embroider'd vale
     Where the love-lorn nightingale
Nightly to thee her sad song mourneth well: 235
Canst thou not tell me of a gentle pair
     That likest thy Narcissus are?
          O if thou have
     Hid them in some flow'ry cave,
          Tell me but where,   240
     Sweet queen of parley,[67] daughter of the sphere;
     So may'st thou be translated to the skies,
And give resounding grace to all heav'n's harmonies.

Comus: Can any mortal mixture of earth's mold
Breathe such divine enchanting ravishment?   245
Sure something holy lodges in that breast,
And with these raptures moves the vocal air
To testify his[68] hidd'n residence;
How sweetly did they float upon the wings
Of silence, through the empty-vaulted night,   250
At every fall[69] smoothing the raven down
Of darkness till it smil'd. I have oft heard
My mother Circe with the Sirens three,
Amidst the flowery-kirtl'd Naiades,[70]
Culling their potent herbs and baleful drugs,   255
Who, as they sung, would take the prison'd soul

---

[50]Flattering. [51]Power.
[52]Occupation. This line was omitted in the 1673 *Poems*.
[53]Softly. [54]Farm workers. [55]Fertile, productive.
[56]God of shepherds. [57]Drunken. [58]Revelers, drinkers of ale.
[59]Direct. [60]Wagon. [61]Malicious.
[62]*Rife and perfet*: loud and distinct. *Perfet*: perfect. [63]Total.
[64]Taking the side of, defending. [65]Venture.
[66]A water nymph, vainly in love with *Narcissus*, who wandered
far and wide, from the sinuous river *Meander* in Phrygia to the
violet-embroider'd vale near Athens where the *love-lorn nightingale*
nightly sings her grief. When finally changed into an echoing
voice she lived in the *airy shell* or vault of heaven (which was also
the Attendant Spirit's home). [67]Speech.
[68]Its (referring to *something holy* of l. 246). [69]Cadence.
[70]*Flowery-kirtl'd Naiades*: water nymphs with flowered garments.

And lap it in Elysium; Scylla[71] wept,
And chid her barking waves into attention,
And fell Charybdis murmur'd soft applause.
Yet they in pleasing slumber lull'd the sense,   260
And in sweet madness robb'd it of itself;
But such a sacred and home-felt[72] delight,
Such sober certainty of waking bliss,
I never heard till now. I'll speak to her,
And she shall be my queen. Hail, foreign wonder,   265
Whom certain these rough shades did never breed,
Unless the goddess that in rural shrine
Dwell'st here with Pan or Sylvan,[73] by blest song
Forbidding every bleak unkindly fog
To touch the prosperous growth of this tall wood.   270
Lady: Nay, gentle shepherd, ill is lost that praise
That is address'd to unattending ears.
Not any boast of skill, but extreme shift[74]
How to regain my sever'd company
Compell'd me to awake the courteous Echo   275
To give me answer from her mossy couch.

Comus: What chance, good lady, hath bereft you thus?

Lady: Dim darkness and this leavy labyrinth.

Comus: Could that divide you from near-ushering guides?

Lady: They left me weary on a grassy turf.   280

Comus: By falsehood, or discourtesy, or why?

Lady: To seek i' the valley some cool friendly spring.

Comus: And left your fair side all unguarded, lady?

Lady: They were but twain, and purpos'd quick return.

Comus: Perhaps forestalling night prevented them.   285

Lady: How easy my misfortune is to hit![75]

Comus: Imports their loss,[76] beside the present need?

Lady: No less than if I should my brothers lose.

Comus: Were they of manly prime, or youthful bloom?

Lady: As smooth as Hebe's[77] their unrazor'd lips.   290

Comus: Two such I saw, what time the labor'd ox
In his loose traces from the furrow came,
And the swink'd[78] hedger at his supper sat;
I saw them under a green mantling[79] vine
That crawls along the side of yon small hill.   295
Plucking ripe clusters from the tender shoots;
Their port[80] was more than human, as they stood.
I took it for a fairy vision
Of some gay creatures of the element,[81]
That in the colors of the rainbow live,   300
And play i' the plighted[82] clouds. I was awe-strook,
And as I passed, I worship'd; if those you seek,
It were a journey like the path to heav'n
To help you find them.
Lady: Gentle villager,
What readiest way would bring me to that place?   305

Comus: Due west it rises from this shrubby point.
Lady: To find out that, good shepherd, I suppose,
In such a scant allowance of star-light,
Would overtask the best land-pilot's art,
Without the sure guess of well-practis'd feet.   310

Comus: I know each lane and every alley green,
Dingle[83] or bushy dell, of this wild wood,
And every bosky bourn[84] from side to side,
My daily walks and ancient[85] neighborhood,
And if your stray attendance[86] be yet lodg'd,   315
Or shroud[87] within these limits, I shall know
Ere morrow wake or the low-roosted lark
From her thatch'd pallet[88] rouse; if otherwise,
I can conduct you, lady, to a low
But loyal cottage, where you may be safe   320
Till further quest.

Lady: Shepherd, I take thy word,
And trust thy honest-offer'd courtesy,
Which oft is sooner found in lowly sheds
With smoky rafters, than in tap'stry[89] halls
And courts of princes, where it first was nam'd,   325
And yet is most pretended. In a place
Less warranted[90] than this, or less secure,
I cannot be, that I should fear to change it.
Eye me, blest Providence, and square[91] my trial
To my proportion'd strength. Shepherd, lead on.   330
                                                      [*Exeunt*]

[*Enter*] *the Two Brothers.*

Elder Brother: Unmuffle, ye faint stars, and thou, fair moon,
That wont'st to love the traveler's benison,[92]
Stoop thy pale visage through an amber cloud,
And disinherit Chaos, that reigns here
In double night of darkness and of shades;   335
Or if your influence be quite damm'd up
With black usurping mists, some gentle taper,
Though a rush-candle from the wicker hole
Of some clay habitation,[93] visit us
With thy long level'd rule of streaming light,   340
And thou shalt be our star of Arcady,
Or Tyrian cynosure.[94]

[71]A nymph whom Circe transformed into a monster girded
with barking dogs and confined to a rock across the Sicilian
Straits from the whirlpool *Charybdis* (l. 259).   [72]Keenly felt.
[73]Wood gods.   [74]Urgent expedients.   [75]Guess at.
[76]*Imports their loss*: Is their loss important?
[77]Cupbearer to the gods.   [78]Wearied.   [79]Covering.
[80]Deportment.   [81]Sky.   [82]Folded.   [83]Little valley.
[84]Tree-arched brook.   [85]Familiar.   [86]Attendants.   [87]Seek shelter.
[88]Bed or nest of straw.   [89]Adorned with tapestry.
[90]Guaranteed safe.   [91]Adjust.
[92]*That wont'st...benison*: that usually loves the traveler's blessing.
[93]*Wicker hole...habitation*: wicker-latticed window in a house of
clay.
[94]*Star of Arcady or Tyrian cynosure*: i.e., the North Star (by which
Phoenician or *Tyrian* mariners steered) was the tip of the tail in
the constellation of the Little Bear into which Jove transformed
Arcas, his son by the Arcadian Princess Callisto.

Second Brother: Or if our eyes
Be barr'd that happiness, might we but hear
The folded flocks penn'd in their wattled cotes,[95]
Or sound of pastoral reed with oaten stops,   345
Or whistle from the lodge, or village cock
Count the night-watches to his feathery dames,
'Twould be some solace yet, some little cheering,
In this close dungeon of innumerous[96] boughs.
But O that hapless virgin, our lost sister,   350
Where may she wander now, whither betake her
From the chill dew, amongst rude burs and thistles?
Perhaps some cold bank is her bolster now,
Or 'gainst the rugged bark of some broad elm
Leans her unpillow'd head, fraught with sad fears.   355
What if in wild amazement and affright,
Or, while we speak, within the direful grasp
Of savage hunger or of savage heat?

Elder Brother: Peace, brother, be not over-exquisite
To cast[97] the fashion of uncertain evils;   360
For grant they be so, while they rest unknown,
What need a man forestall[98] his date of grief,
And run to meet what he would most avoid?
Or if they be but false alarms of fear,
How bitter is such self-delusion?   365
I do not think my sister so to seek,[99]
Or so unprincipl'd in virtue's book,
And the sweet peace that goodness bosoms[1] ever,
As that the single[2] want of light and noise
(Not being in danger, as I trust she is not)   370
Could stir the constant mood of her calm thoughts,
And put them into misbecoming plight.
Virtue could see to do what Virtue would
By her own radiant light, though sun and moon
Were in the flat sea sunk. And Wisdom's self   375
Oft seeks to sweet retired solitude,
Where with her best nurse, Contemplation,
She plumes[3] her feathers, and lets grow her wings,
That in the various bustle of resort
Were all to-ruffl'd,[4] and sometimes impair'd.   380
He that has light within his own clear breast
May sit i' th' center,[5] and enjoy bright day,
But he that hides a dark soul and foul thoughts
Benighted walks under the midday sun;
Himself is his own dungeon.

Second Brother: 'Tis most true   385
That musing meditation most affects
The pensive secrecy of desert cell,
Far from the cheerful haunt of men and herds,
And sits as safe as in a senate house;
For who would rob a hermit of his weeds,   390
His few books, or his beads, or maple dish,
Or do his gray hairs any violence?
But Beauty, like the fair Hesperian tree[6]
Laden with blooming gold, had need the guard
Of dragon-watch with unenchanted eye,   395
To save her blossoms, and defend her fruit
From the rash hand of bold Incontinence.

You may as well spread out the unsunn'd heaps
Of miser's treasure by an outlaw's den,
And tell me it is safe, as bid me hope   400
Danger will wink on[7] opportunity,
And let a single helpless maiden pass
Uninjur'd in this wild surrounding waste.
Of night or loneliness it recks me not;[8]
I fear the dread events that dog them both,   405
Lest some ill-greeting touch [9]attempt the person
Of our unowned[10] sister.

Elder Brother: I do not, brother,
Infer as if I thought my sister's state
Secure without all doubt or controversy;
Yet where an equal poise of hope and fear   410
Does arbitrate th' event,[11] my nature is
That I incline to hope, rather than fear,
And gladly banish squint[12] suspicion.
My sister is not so defenceless left
As you imagine; she has a hidden strength   415
Which you remember not.

Second Brother: What hidden strength,
Unless the strength of heaven, if you mean that?

Elder Brother: I mean that too, but yet a
    hidden strength
Which, if heav'n gave it, may be term'd her own:
'Tis chastity, my brother, chastity.   420
She that has that is clad in complete steel,
And, like a quiver'd nymph[13] with arrows keen,
May trace huge forests and unharbor'd[14] heaths,
Infamous hills and sandy perilous wilds,
Where, through the sacred rays of chastity,   425
No savage fierce, bandit, or mountaineer
Will dare to soil her virgin purity.
Yea, there where very desolation dwells,
By grots and caverns shagg'd[15] with horrid shades,
She may pass on with unblench'd[16] majesty,   430
Be it not done in pride or in presumption.
Some say no evil thing that walks by night,
In fog or fire, by lake or moorish fen,
Blue meager hag, or stubborn unlaid ghost,
That breaks his magic chains at curfew time,[17]   435
No goblin or swart[18] fairy of the mine,
Hath hurtful power o'er true virginity.

[95]*Folded...cotes*: flocks enclosed in wicker pens.   [96]Innumerable.
[97]Foretell.   [98]Anticipate.   [99]*So to seek*: so lacking.
[1]Encloses.   [2]Mere.   [3]Preens.   [4]Bedraggled.
[5]*Sit...center*: i.e., rest upon his own integrity.
[6]Fabulous tree that grew golden fruit in the Hesperides, islands
guarded by ever-watchful (*unenchanted*) dragons.
[7]Close the eye.   [8]*It recks me not*: i.e., I do not mind.
[9]Offensive approach.   [10]Unprotected.
[11]*Where an equal...event*: where the outcome (*event*) is deter
mined by the balance (*equal poise*) of hope and fear.
[12]Jealous.
[13]A nymph armed with arrows (like the chaste huntress Diana).
[14]Unsheltered.   [15]Made rough.   [16]Undismayed.
[17]*That breaks...time*: Ghosts were free to leave their graves only
at night (after *curfew time*).   [18]Blackened, sooty.

Do ye believe me yet, or shall I call
Antiquity from the old schools of Greece
To testify the arms[19] of chastity? 440
Hence had the huntress Dian[20] her dread bow,
Fair silver-shafted queen for ever chaste,
Wherewith she tam'd the brinded[21] lioness
And spotted mountain pard,[22] but set at nought
The frivolous bolt of Cupid; gods and men 445
Fear'd her stern frown, and she was queen o' th' woods.
What was that snaky-headed Gorgon shield
That wise Minerva[23] wore, unconquer'd virgin.
Wherewith she freez'd her foes to congeal'd stone,
But rigid looks of chaste austerity, 450
And noble grace that dash'd brute violence
With sudden adoration and blank awe?
So dear to heav'n is saintly chastity
That when a soul is found sincerely so,
A thousand liveried angels lackey[24] her, 455
Driving far off each thing of sin and guilt,
And in clear dream and solemn vision
Tell her of things that no gross ear can hear,
Till oft converse[25] with heav'nly habitants
Begin to cast a beam on th' outward shape, 460
The unpolluted temple of the mind,
And turns it by degrees to the soul's essence,
Till all be made immortal. But when lust,
By unchaste looks, loose gestures, and foul talk,
But most by lewd and lavish act of sin, 465
Lets in defilement to the inward parts,
The soul grows clotted by contagion,
Imbodies and imbrutes,[26] till she quite lose
The divine property of her first being.
Such are those thick and gloomy shadows[27] damp 470
Oft seen in charnel vaults and sepulchers,
Lingering, and sitting by a new-made grave,
As loth to leave the body that it lov'd,
And link'd itself by carnal sensualty
To a degenerate and degraded state. 475

Second Brother: How charming is divine philosophy!
Not harsh and crabbed, as dull fools suppose,
But musical as is Apollo's lute,
And a perpetual feast of nectar'd sweets,
Where no crude[28] surfeit reigns. 480

Elder Brother: List, list, I hear
Some far-off hallo break the silent air.

Second Brother: Methought so too; what should it be?

Elder Brother: For certain,
Either some one, like us, night-founder'd[29] here,
Or else some neighbor woodman, or at worst
Some roving robber calling to his fellow. 485

Second Brother: Heaven keep my sister! Again, again,
   and near!
Best draw, and stand upon our guard.

Elder Brother: I'll hallo;
If he be friendly, he comes well; if not,
Defence is a good cause, and heav'n be for us,

[Enter] the Attendant Spirit, habited like a shepherd.

That hallo I should know. What are you? Speak. 490
Come not too near, you fall on iron stakes[30] else.

Spirit: What voice is that? My young lord? Speak again.

Second Brother: O brother, 'tis my father's shepherd, sure.

Elder Brother: Thyrsis,[31] whose artful strains have
   oft delayed
The huddling[32] brook to hear his madrigal, 495
And sweeten'd every musk rose of the dale,
How cam'st thou here, good swain? Hath any ram
Slipp'd from the fold, or young kid lost his dam,
Or straggling wether the pent flock forsook?
How couldst thou find this dark sequester'd nook? 500

Spirit: O my lov'd master's heir, and his next[33] joy,
I came not here on such a trivial toy
As a stray'd ewe, or to pursue the stealth
Of pilfering wolf; not all the fleecy wealth
That doth enrich these downs is worth a thought 505
To this my errand, and the care it brought.
But O my virgin lady, where is she?
How chance she is not in your company?

Elder Brother: To tell thee sadly,[34] shepherd, without blame
Or our neglect, we lost her as we came. 510

Spirit: Ay me unhappy, then my fears are true.

Elder Brother: What fears, good Thyrsis? Prithee
   briefly shew.

Spirit: I'll tell ye. 'Tis not vain or fabulous
(Though so esteem'd by shallow ignorance)
What the sage poets, taught by th' heav'nly Muse, 515
Storied of old in high immortal verse
Of dire chimeras[35] and enchanted isles,
And rifted rocks whose entrance leads to hell;
For such there be, but unbelief is blind.
Within the navel[36] of this hideous wood, 520
Immur'd in cypress shades, a sorcerer dwells,
Of Bacchus and of Circe born, great Comus,
Deep skill'd in all his mother's witcheries,
And here to every thirsty wanderer
By sly enticement gives his baneful cup, 525
With many murmurs[37] mix'd, whose pleasing poison
The visage quite transforms of him that drinks,

[19]Might.
[20]Diana, the chaste huntress whose bow and silver arrows made her invulnerable to bestial passions. [21]Striped. [22]Leopard.
[23]Goddess whose shield, bearing the head of the *snaky-headed Gorgon* Medusa, turned her foes to *congeal'd stone.* [24]Serve.
[25]Frequent intercourse.
[26]*Imbodies and imbrutes*: i.e., becomes carnal and bestial. This is the first recorded occurrence of these two words. [27]Ghosts.
[28]Indigestible. [29]Sunk in night. [30]Swords.
[31]A pastoral name used by both Theocritus and Vergil.
[32]Hurrying.
[33]Nearest. *Next* is the superlative degree of the positive *nigh* and the comparative *near.* [34]Seriously.
[35]Monsters formed of parts of various animals. [36]Center.
[37]Incantations.

And the inglorious likeness of a beast
Fixes instead, unmolding reason's mintage
Character'd[38] in the face; this have I learnt   530
Tending my flocks hard by i' th' hilly crofts[39]
That brow[40] this bottom glade, whence night by night
He and his monstrous rout are heard to howl
Like stabl'd wolves, or tigers at their prey,
Doing abhorred rites to Hecate   535
In their obscured haunts of inmost bow'rs.
Yet have they many baits and guileful spells
To inveigle and invite th' unwary sense
Of them that pass unweeting[41] by the way.
This evening late, by then the chewing flocks   540
Had ta'en their supper on the savory herb
Of knot-grass dew-besprent,[42] and were in fold,
I sat me down to watch upon a bank
With ivy canopied, and interwove
With flaunting honeysuckle, and began,   545
Wrapp'd in a pleasing fit of melancholy,
To meditate my rural minstrelsy,[43]
Till fancy had her fill. But ere a close[44]
The wonted roar was up amidst the woods,
And fill'd the air with barbarous dissonance,   550
At which I ceas'd, and listen'd them awhile,
Till an unusual stop of sudden silence
Gave respite to the drowsy frighted[45] steeds
That draw the litter of close-curtain'd Sleep.
At last a soft and solemn-breathing sound   555
Rose like a steam of rich distill'd perfumes,
And stole upon the air, that even Silence
Was took[46] ere she was ware, and wish'd she might
Deny her nature and be never more,
Still to be so displac'd. I was all ear,   560
And took in strains that might create a soul
Under the ribs of Death, but O ere long
Too well I did perceive it was the voice
Of my most honor'd lady, your dear sister.
Amaz'd I stood, harrow'd[47] with grief and fear,   565
And "O poor hapless nightingale," thought I,
"How sweet thou sing'st, how near the deadly snare!"
Then down the lawns I ran with headlong haste
Through paths and turnings oft'n trod by day,
Till guided by mine ear I found the place   570
Where that damn'd wizard, hid in sly disguise
(For so by certain signs I knew), had met
Already, ere my best speed could prevent,
The aidless innocent lady, his wish'd prey,
Who gently ask'd if he had seen such two,   575
Supposing him some neighbor villager;
Longer I durst not stay, but soon I guess'd
Ye were the two she meant; with that I sprung
Into swift flight, till I had found you here;
But further know I not.

Second Brother: O night and shades,   580
How are ye join'd with hell in triple knot
Against th' unarmed weakness of one virgin,
Alone and helpless! Is this the confidence
You gave me, brother?

Elder Brother: Yes, and keep it still,
Lean on it safely; not a period[48]   585
Shall be unsaid for me. Against the threats
Of malice or of sorcery, or that power
Which erring men call Chance, this I hold firm:
Virtue may be assail'd, but never hurt,
Surpris'd by unjust force, but not enthrall'd;[49]   590
Yea, even that which Mischief meant most harm
Shall in the happy trial prove most glory.
But evil on itself shall back recoil,
And mix no more with goodness, when at last,
Gather'd like scum, and settl'd to itself.   595
It shall be in eternal restless change
Self-fed and self-consum'd; if this fail,
The pillar'd firmament is rott'nness,
And earth's base built on stubble. But come, let's on.
Against th' opposing will and arm of heav'n   600
May never this just sword be lifted up;
But for that damn'd magician, let him be girt[50]
With all the grisly legions that troop
Under the sooty flag of Acheron,[51]
Harpies and Hydras,[52] or all the monstrous forms   605
'Twixt Africa and Ind, I'll find him out
And force him to return his purchase[53] back,
Or drag him by the curls to a foul death,
Curs'd as his life.

Spirit: Alas, good vent'rous youth,
I love thy courage yet, and bold emprise,[54]   610
But here thy sword can do thee little stead;[55]
Far other arms and other weapons must
Be those that quell the might of hellish charms.
He with his bare wand can unthread thy joints,
And crumble all thy sinews.

Elder Brother: Why, prithee, shepherd,   615
How durst thou then thyself approach so near
As to make this relation?

Spirit: Care and utmost shifts[56]
How to secure the lady from surprisal
Brought to my mind a certain shepherd lad,
Of small regard to see to, yet well skill'd   620
In every virtuous[57] plant and healing herb
That spreads her verdant leaf to th' morning ray.
He lov'd me well, and oft would beg me sing;
Which when I did, he on the tender grass
Would sit, and hearken even to ecstasy,   625
And in requital ope his leathern scrip,[58]

[38]Engraved. [39]Fields. [40]Top, overlook. [41]Heedless.
[42]Sprinkled.
[43]*Meditate...minstrelsy*: i.e., play my shepherd's pipe.
[44]Before reaching the end of the ditty.
[45]Many editors prefer the Trinity Manuscript reading *flighted*.
[46]Captivated, charmed. [47]Anguished. [48]Sentence.
[49]Imprisoned. [50]Surrounded.
[51]One of the four rivers of hell. Here it stands for hell itself.
[52]*Harpies and Hydras*: infernal creatures in Greek mythology.
[53]Prey, i.e., the Lady. [54]Chivalric prowess. [55]Benefit.
[56]I.e., precaution. [57]Powerful. [58]Bag.

And show me simples[59] of a thousand names,
Telling their strange and vigorous faculties;
Amongst the rest a small unsightly root,
But of divine effect, he cull'd me out;   630
 Theleaf was darkish, and had prickles on it,
But in another country, as he said,
Bore a bright golden flower, but not in this soil;
Unknown, and like esteem'd, and the dull swain
Treads on it daily with his clouted shoon;[60]   635
And yet more med'cinal is it than that moly[61]
That Hermes once to wise Ulysses gave;
He call'd it haemony,[62] and gave it me,
And bade me keep it as of sovran use
'Gainst all enchantments, mildew blast, or damp,   640
Or ghastly Furies' apparition;
I purs'd it up, but little reck'ning made,
Till now that this extremity compell'd,
But now I find it true; for by this means
I knew the foul enchanter though disguis'd,   645
Enter'd the very lime-twigs[63] of his spells,
And yet came off. If you have this about you
(As I will give you when we go), you may
Boldly assault the necromancer's hall;
Where if he be, with dauntless hardihood   650
And brandish'd blade rush on him, break his glass,
And shed the luscious liquor on the ground,
But seize his wand. Though he and his curst crew
Fierce sign of battle make, and menace high,
Or like the sons of Vulcan[64] vomit smoke,   655
Yet will they soon retire, if he but shrink.

Elder Brother: Thyrsis, lead on apace, I'll follow thee,
And some good angel bear a shield before us.

*The scene changes to a stately palace, set out with all manner
of deliciousness: soft music, tables spread with all dainties.
Comus appears with his rabble, and the Lady set in an enchanted
chair, to whom he offers his glass, which she puts by, and goes
about to rise.[65]*

Comus: Nay, lady, sit; if I but wave this wand,
Your nerves are all chain'd up in alabaster,   660
And you a statue, or as Daphne[66] was,
Root-bound, that fled Apollo.

Lady: Fool, do not boast;
Thou canst not touch the freedom of my mind
With all thy charms, although this corporal rind[67]
Thou hast immanacl'd, while heav'n sees good.   665

Comus: Why are you vex'd, lady? why do you frown?
Here dwell no frowns, nor anger; from these gates
Sorrow flies far. See, here be all the pleasures
That fancy can beget on youthful thoughts,
When the fresh blood grows lively, and returns   670
Brisk as the April buds in primrose season.
And first behold this cordial julep[68] here
That flames and dances in his crystal bounds,
With spirits of balm and fragrant syrups mix'd.
Not that nepenthes[69] which the wife of Thone   675

In Egypt gave to Jove-born Helena
Is of such power to stir up joy as this,
To life so friendly, or so cool to thirst.
Why should you be so cruel to yourself,
And to those dainty limbs which Nature lent   680
For gentle usage and soft delicacy?
But you invert the cov'nants of her trust,
And harshly deal like an ill borrower
With that which you receiv'd on other terms,
Scorning the unexempt condition[70]   685
By which all mortal frailty must subsist,
Refreshment after toil, ease after pain,
That have been tir'd all day without repast,
And timely rest have wanted; but, fair virgin,
This will restore all soon.   690

Lady: 'Twill not, false traitor,
'Twill not restore the truth and honesty
That thou hast banish'd from thy tongue with lies.
Was this the cottage and the safe abode
Thou told'st me of? What grim aspects are these,
These ugly-headed monsters? Mercy guard me!   695
Hence with thy brew'd enchantments, foul deceiver;
Hast thou betray'd my credulous innocence
With vizor'd[71] falsehood and base forgery,[72]
And wouldst thou seek again to trap me here
With lickerish[73] baits fit to ensnare a brute?   700
Were it a draught for Juno when she banquets,
I would not taste thy treasonous offer; none
But such as are good men can give good things,
And that which is not good is not delicious
To a well-goven'd and wise appetite.   705

Comus: O foolishness of men! that lend their ears
To those budge doctors of the Stoic fur,
And fetch their precepts from the Cynic tub,[74]
Praising the lean and sallow Abstinence.
Wherefore did Nature pour her bounties forth   710
With such a full and unwithdrawing hand,
Covering the earth with odors, fruits, and flocks,

[59]Medicinal herbs.   [60]Studded boots.
[61]Magic herb that Hermes gave to Ulysses to protect him from
the charms of Circe (*Odyssey* X).
[62]Another magic plant (like moly), named perhaps for Haemonia
(i.e., Thessaly), a land of witchcraft. Both moly and haemony are
probably intended as symbols of Christian temperance.
[63]Twigs coated with sticky lime, used for catching birds.
[64]Volcanic monsters, sons of the fire god.
[65]*Puts by...rise*: rejects and tries to rise.
[66]A nymph turned into a laurel tree when Apollo tried to seize her.
[67]The body, conceived as the fleshy shell of the soul.
[68]Inspiriting sweet drink.
[69]A drug, procured in Egypt from Polydamna, wife of Thone,
whereby Helen, daughter of Jove, tried to ease the grief of Mene-
laus (*Odyssey* IV).   [70]Necessary limitations.
[71]Concealed, masked.   [72]Deception.   [73]Tempting.
[74]*To those...tub*: Comus is ridiculing the pompous academic
doctors with furred (*budge*) hoods whose austerities recall those of
the ancient *Stoic* moralists and of Diogenes, the famed Cynic
philosopher who lived in a *tub*.

Thronging the seas with spawn innumerable,
But all to please and sate the curious[75] taste?
And set to work millions of spinning worms, 715
That in their green shops[76] weave the smooth-hair'd silk
To deck her sons; and that no corner might
Be vacant of her plenty, in her own loins
She hutch'd[77] th' all-worship'd ore[78] and precious gems
To store her children with. If all the world 720
Should in a pet of temperance feed on pulse,[79]
Drink the clear stream, and nothing wear but frieze,[80]
Th' All-giver would be unthank'd, would be unprais'd,
Not half his riches known, and yet despis'd,
And we should serve him as a grudging master, 725
As a penurious niggard of his wealth,
And live like Nature's bastards, not her sons,
Who would be quite surcharg'd[81] with her own weight,
And strangl'd with her waste fertility:
Th' earth cumber'd, and the wing'd air dark'd
    with plumes, 730
The herds would over-multitude their lords,
The sea o'erfraught would swell, and th'
    unsought diamonds
Would so emblaze the forehead of the deep,
And so bestud with stars, that they below
Would grow inur'd to light, and come at last 735
To gaze upon the sun with shameless brows.[82]
List, lady,[83] be not coy,[84] and be not cozen'd
With that same vaunted name Virginity;
Beauty is Nature's coin, must not be hoarded,
But must be current, and the good thereof 740
Consists in mutual and partak'n[85] bliss,
Unsavory in th' enjoyment of itself.
If you let slip time, like a neglected rose
It withers on the stalk with languish'd head.
Beauty is Nature's brag,[86] and must be shown 745
In courts, at feasts, and high solemnities[87]
Where most may wonder at the workmanship;
It is for homely features to keep home,
They had their name thence; coarse complexions
And cheeks of sorry grain[88] will serve to ply[89] 750
The sampler, and to tease[90] the huswife's wool.
What need a vermeil'-tinctur'd[91] lip for that,
Love-darting eyes, or tresses like the Morn?[92]
There was another meaning in these gifts,
Think what, and be advis'd; you are but young yet. 755

Lady: I had not thought to have unlock'd my lips
In this unhallow'd air, but that this juggler
Would think to charm my judgment, as mine eyes,
Obtruding false rules prank'd[93] in reason's garb.
I hate when vice can bolt[94] her arguments, 760
And virtue has no tongue to check her pride.
Impostor, do not charge most innocent Nature,
As if she would her children should be riotous
With her abundance; she, good cateress,[95]
Means her provision only to the good, 765
That live according to her sober laws
And holy dictate of spare[96] Temperance.
If every just man that now pines with want

Had but a moderate and beseeming share
Of that which lewdly-pamper'd luxury 770
Now heaps upon some few with vast excess,
Nature's full blessings would be well dispens'd
In unsuperfluous even proportion,
And she no whit encumber'd with her store;
And then the Giver would be better thank'd, 775
His praise due paid, for swinish gluttony
Ne'er looks to heav'n amidst his gorgeous feast,
But with besotted base ingratitude
Crams, and blasphemes his Feeder. Shall I go on?
Or have I said enough? To him that dares 780
Arm his profane tongue with contemptuous words
Against the sun-clad power of Chastity,
Fain would I something say, yet to what end?
Thou hast nor ear nor soul to apprehend
The sublime notion and high mystery[97] 785
That must be utter'd to unfold the sage
And serious doctrine of virginity,
And thou art worthy[98] that thou shouldst not know
More happiness than this thy present lot.
Enjoy your dear wit and gay rhetoric 790
That hath so well been taught her dazzling fence,[99]
Thou art not fit to hear thyself convinc'd;
Yet should I try, the uncontrolled worth
Of this pure cause[1] would kindle my rapt spirits
To such a flame of sacred vehemence 795
That dumb things would be mov'd to sympathize,
And the brute Earth would lend her nerves,[2] and shake,
Till all thy magic structures, rear'd so high,
Were shatter'd into heaps o'er thy false head.

Comus: She fables not, I feel that I do fear 800
Her words set off by some superior power;
And though not mortal, yet a cold shudd'ring dew
Dips me all o'er, as when the wrath of Jove
Speaks thunder and the chains of Erebus[3]
To some of Saturn's crew. I must dissemble, 805
And try her yet more strongly. Come, no more,

[75]Fastidious.
[76]Leaves that silkworms feed on. [77]Enclosed. [78]Gold.
[79]Peas and beans. [80]Coarse woolen cloth. [81]Overloaded.
[82]*Th' unsought diamonds...shameless brows:* The subterranean inhabitants of the earth (*they below*) would be so conditioned by the unmined gems in the hollow interior of the earth (*the forehead of the deep*) that they, *inur'd to light,* would ascend to the surface and *gaze upon the sun.*
[83]*List lady...young yet:* Comus' extended attack upon chastity (ll. 737–55), like the Lady's defense (ll. 779–806), are not included in the acting version of the mask in the Bridgewater Manuscript.
[84]Reserved. [85]Shared. [86]Display. [87]Ceremonies.
[88]Dull color. [89]Work. [90]Comb. [91]Vermilion colors.
[92]I.e., Aurora, goddess of the dawn. [93]Dressed. [94]Sift.
[95]Provider. [96]Frugal.
[97]A religious truth not verifiable by sensory experience.
[98]Deserve. [99]Art of fencing.
[1]I.e., "the sage and serious doctrine of virginity."
[2]Sinews, i.e., force.
[3]Hell, to which the *thunder* of Jove's voice assigns the adversaries (*Saturn's crew*) whom he had overthrown.

This is mere moral babble, and direct
Against the canon laws of our foundation:[4]
I must not suffer this, yet 'tis but the lees
And settlings of a melancholy blood;   810
But this will cure all straight; one sip of this
Will bathe the drooping spirits in delight
Beyond the bliss of dreams. Be wise, and taste.

*The Brothers rush in with swords drawn, wrest his glass out
of his hand, and break it against the ground; his rout make sign
of resistance, but are all driven in; the Attendant Spirit comes
in.*

Spirit. What, have you let the false enchanter 'scape?
O ye mistook, ye should have snatch'd his wand   815
And bound him fast; without his rod revers'd,
And backward mutters of dissevering power,[5]
We cannot free the lady that sits here
In stony fetters fix'd and motionless;
Yet stay, be not disturb'd; now I bethink me,   820
Some other means I have which may be us'd,
Which once of Meliboeus[6] old I learnt,
The soothest[7] shepherd that e'er pip'd on plains.
    There is a gentle Nymph not far from hence,
That with moist curb sways the smooth
        Severn stream;   825
Sabrina[8] is her name, a virgin pure;
Whilom she was the daughter of Locrine,
That had the scepter from his father Brut.
She, guiltless damsel, flying the mad pursuit
Of her enraged stepdame Guendolen,   830
Commended her fair innocence to the flood
That stay'd her flight with his cross-flowing course;
The water-nymphs that in the bottom play'd
Held up their pearled wrists and took her in,
Bearing her straight to aged Nereus'[9] hall,   835
Who, piteous of her woes, rear'd her lank[10] head,
And gave her to his daughters to imbathe
In nectar'd lavers strew'd with asphodel,[11]
And through the porch and inlet of each sense
Dropp'd in ambrosial oils, till she reviv'd   840
And underwent a quick immortal change,
Made goddess of the river. Still she retains
Her maid'n gentleness, and oft at eve
Visits the herds along the twilight meadows,
Helping all urchin blasts,[12] and ill-luck signs   845
That the shrewd meddling elf delights to make,
Which she with precious vial'd liquors heals;
For which the shepherds at their festivals
Carol her goodness loud in rustic lays,
And throw sweet garland wreaths into her stream   850
Of pansies, pinks, and gaudy daffodils.
And, as the old swain[13] said, she can unlock
The clasping charm and thaw the numbing spell,
If she be right invok'd in warbled song;
For maid'nhood she loves, and will be swift   855
To aid a virgin such as was herself
In hard-besetting need. This will I try,
And add the power of some adjuring verse.

SONG

Sabrina fair,
    Listen where thou art sitting
Under the glassy, cool, translucent wave,   860
    In twisted braids of lilies knitting
The loose train of thy amber-dropping hair;
    Listen for dear honor's sake,
    Goddess of the silver lake,
        Listen and save.

Listen and appear to us   865
In name of great Oceanus,
By the earth-shaking Neptune's mace,
And Tethys' grave majestic pace,
By hoary Nereus' wrinkled look,
And the Carpathian wizard's hook,   870
By scaly Triton's winding shell,
And old soothsaying Glaucus' spell,
By Leucothea's lovely hands,
And her son that rules the strands,
By Thetis' tinsel-slipper'd feet,   875
And the songs of Sirens sweet,
By dead Parthenope's dear tomb,
And fair Ligea's golden comb,
Wherewith she sit on diamond rocks
Sleeking her soft alluring locks;[14]   880

[4]*Direct against . . . foundation*: absolutely opposed to the regulations of our community.
[5]*Rod revers'd . . . power*: It was thought that magic spells could be undone by reversing the charms and incantations by which they are achieved.
[6]Conventional pastoral name for a wise old shepherd; here, perhaps Milton's source and model Edmund Spenser, who relates the story of Sabrina (*The Faerie Queene*, II.x).   [7]Truest.
[8]In Geoffrey of Monmouth's *Historia Britonum*—the ultimate source of much of Milton's and other poets' lore about the legendary history of Britain—Sabrina is the daughter of Estrildis (or Astrild), queen of King Humber, by her lover Locrine (a son of Brut, the founder of Britain). Although Geoffrey—and, with certain variations, Spenser (*The Faerie Queene*, II.x) and Drayton (*Poly-Olbion*, Song VI)—tells how both sinful mother and daughter were drowned in the river Severn by Locrine's jealous wife Guendolen, Milton, suppressing some of the ugly aspects of the story, relates that Sabrina, fleeing from the *enraged* Guendolen, *commended her fair innocence to the flood* and by *a quick immortal change* was transformed into a *goddess* of the river Severn (to which she gave her name.) See *Brut* in the Glossary.
[9]The Old Man of the Sea, father of the Nereids.   [10]Drooping.
[11]Immortal flower of paradise.
[12]Blights caused by mischievous fairies. *Urchin*: hedgehog.
[13]Meliboeus.
[14]*In the name of great Oceanus . . . alluring locks*: Oceanus and the other water gods and nymphs invoked constitute a pantheon of the beneficent deities appropriate for the situation: *Oceanus* as the god of the ocean stream, *Neptune* with his trident (*mace*), *Thetys* as the wife of Oceanus, *Nereus* as the Old Man of the Sea, Proteus as the Shepherd of the Ocean with his *hook* (whereby, like a *Carpathian wizard*, he could change his shape), *Triton* as Neptune's herald, *Glaucus* as a Boeotian fisherman transformed into a sea god, *Leucothea* as a sea nymph who befriended Ulysses, her *son* Melicertes as one who *rules the strands*, *Thetis* (mother of

By all the nymphs that nightly dance
Upon thy streams with wily glance,
Rise, rise, and heave thy rosy head
From thy coral-pav'n bed,
And bridle in thy headlong wave, 885
Till thou our summons answer'd have.
        Listen and save.

Sabrina rises, attended by water-nymphs, and sings.

By the rushy-fringed bank,
Where grows the willow and the osier dank,
    My sliding chariot stays,
Thick set with agate, and the azurn sheen 890
Of turquoise blue, and emerald green,
    That in the channel strays,
Whilst from off the waters fleet
Thus I set my printless feet
O'er the cowslip's velvet head, 895
    That bends not as I tread.
Gentle swain, at thy request
        I am here.

Spirit: Goddess dear,
We implore thy powerful hand
To undo the charmed band 900
Of true virgin here distress'd,
Through the force and through the wile
Of unblest enchanter vile.

Sabrina: Shepherd, 'tis my office[15] best
To help ensnared chastity. 905
Brightest lady, look on me;
Thus I sprinkle on thy breast
Drops that from my fountain pure
I have kept of precious cure,
Thrice upon thy finger's tip, 910
Thrice upon thy rubied lip;
Next this marble venom'd[16] seat,
Smear'd with gums of glutinous[17] heat,
I touch with chaste palms moist and cold.
Now the spell hath lost his hold; 915
And I must haste ere morning hour
To wait in Amphitrite's[18] bow'r.

Sabrina descends, and the Lady rises out of her seat.

Spirit: Virgin, daughter of Locrine,
Sprung of old Anchises' line,[19]
May thy brimmed waves for this 920
Their full tribute never miss
From a thousand petty rills,
That tumble down the snowy hills;
Summer drouth or singed air
Never scorch thy tresses fair, 925
Nor wet October's torrent flood
Thy molten crystal fill with mud;
May thy billows roll ashore
The beryl and the golden ore;

May thy lofty head be crown'd 930
With many a tower and terrace round,
And here and there thy banks upon
With groves of myrrh and cinnamon.
    Come, lady, while heaven lends us grace,
Let us fly this cursed place, 935
Lest the sorcerer us entice
With some other new device.
Not a waste or needless sound
Till we come to holier ground;
I shall be your faithful guide 940
Through this gloomy covert wide,
And not many furlongs thence
Is your father's residence,
Where this night are met in state
Many a friend to gratulate 945
His wish'd presence, and beside
All the swains that there abide
With jigs and rural dance resort;
We shall catch them at their sport,
And our sudden coming there 950
Will double all their mirth and cheer.
Come, let us haste, the stars grow high,
But Night sits monarch yet in the mid sky.

The scene changes, presenting Ludlow Town, and the President's Castle; then come in country dancers, after them the Attendant Spirit, with the two Brothers and the Lady.

SONG

Spirit: Back, shepherds, back, enough your play
Till next sunshine holiday; 955
Here be without duck[20] or nod
Other trippings to be trod
Of lighter toes,[21] and such court guise[22]
As Mercury did first devise
With the mincing Dryades[23] 960
On the lawns and on the leas.

This second Song presents them to their father and mother.

    Noble Lord, and Lady bright,
I have brought ye new delight.
Here behold so goodly grown
Three fair branches of your own; 965
Heav'n hath timely[24] tri'd their youth,
Their faith, their patience, and their truth,

Achilles) as a Nereid, *Parthenope* (whose *dear tomb* was near Naples) as a Siren, and *Ligea*, another Siren whose "shining tresses" Vergil mentions in his *Georgics* (IV.336). [15]Duty, function. [16]Poisoned. [17]Sticky. [18]Wife of Neptune. [19]Anchises was the father of Aeneas, from whom descended (*sprung*) Brutus and his son Locrine, father of Sabrina. [20]Curtsy. [21]*Other trippings...toes*: i.e., the rustic dances will be followed by the *lighter toes* of the aristocrats. [22]Behavior. [23]Wood nymphs. [24]Early.

And sent them here through hard assays
With a crown of deathless praise,
To triumph in victorious dance   970
O'er sensual folly and intemperance.

The dances ended, the Spirit epiloguizes.

Spirit: To the ocean[25] now I fly,
And those happy climes that lie
Where day never shuts his eye,
Up in the broad fields of the sky.   975
There I suck the liquid[26] air
All amidst the gardens fair
Of Hesperus, and his daughters three
That sing about the golden tree.
Along the crisped[27] shades and bow'rs   980
Revels the spruce and jocund Spring;
The Graces and the rosy-bosom'd Hours
Thither all their bounties bring,
That there eternal summer dwells,
And west winds with musky wing   985
About the cedarn alleys fling
Nard and cassia's balmy smells.[28]
Iris there with humid bow
Waters the odorous banks that blow
Flowers of more mingled hue   990
Than her purfl'd scarf[29] can show,
And drenches with Elysian dew
(List, mortals, if your ears be true)
Beds of hyacinth and roses,
Where young Adonis[30] oft reposes,   995
Waxing well of his deep wound
In slumber soft, and on the ground

Sadly sits th' Assyrian queen;
But far above in spangled sheen
Celestial Cupid,[31] her fam'd son, advanc'd,   1000
Holds his dear Psyche, sweet entranc'd
After her wand'ring labors long,
Till free consent the gods among
Make her his eternal bride,
And from her fair unspotted side   1005
Two blissful twins are to be born,
Youth and Joy; so Jove hath sworn.
    But now my task is smoothly done,
I can fly, or I can run
Quickly to the green earth's end,   1010
Where the bow'd welkin[32] slow doth bend,
And from thence can soar as soon
To the corners of the moon.
    Mortals that would follow me,
Love Virtue, she alone is free;   1015
She can teach ye how to clime
Higher than the sphery chime;
Or if Virtue feeble were,
Heav'n itself would stoop to her.

[25]The celestial sphere. [26]Clear. [27]Curled?
[28]*Nard...smells*: the spicy odors of spikenard and cinnamon.
[29]The rainbow fringed (*purfl'd*) with various colors.
[30]A youth, beloved by Venus (the *Assyrian queen* of l. 1002) who, though killed by a boar (i.e., winter), returned from death each spring.
[31]Son of Venus whose love for and eventual union with Psyche was allegorically interpreted as man's heavenly aspirations and also as Christ's love for man's soul. Their children *Youth* and *Joy* denote the bliss of heaven. [32]Sky.

from Poems, etc. upon Several Occasions (1673)

ON THE DEATH OF A FAIR INFANT
DYING OF A COUGH.
Anno aetatis 17[1]

1
O fairest flower no sooner blown but blasted,
Soft silken primrose fading timelessly,[2]
Summer's chief honor if thou hadst outlasted
Bleak Winter's force that made thy blossom dry;
For he being amorous on that lovely dye   5
    That did thy cheek envermeil,[3] thought to kiss
But kill'd alas, and then bewail'd his fatal bliss.

2
For since grim Aquilo[4] his charioteer
By boist'rous rape th' Athenian damsel got,
He thought it toucht his deity full near,   10
If likewise he some fair one wedded not,

Thereby to wipe away th' infamous blot
    Of long uncoupled bed and childless eld,[5]
Which 'mongst the wanton gods a foul reproach was held.

3
So mounting up in icy-pearled car   15
Through middle empire of the freezing air[6]

ON THE DEATH OF AN INFANT   [1]"[Written] at the age of seventeen." Either Milton erred in assigning this poem to 1626 (when he was seventeen) or it was written for someone other than his little niece Anne Phillips (1625–28), who is usually assumed to be the *fair infant* of the title. Milton's nephew Edward Phillips records merely that the poem was prompted by "the death of one of his sister's children (a daughter) who died in her infancy."
[2]Untimely. [3]Make rosy.
[4]The North Wind, who, says Ovid, snatched away the *Athenian damsel* Orithyia, daughter of King Erectheus. [5]Old age.
[6]*Middle...air*: Habitat of destructive spirits.

He wander'd long, till thee he spi'd from far,
There ended was his quest, there ceas'd his care.
Down he descended from his snow-soft chair,
  But all unwares with his cold-kind embrace   20
Unhous'd thy Virgin Soul from her fair biding place.

4

Yet art thou not inglorious in thy fate;
For so Apollo, with unweeting[7] hand
Whilom[8] did slay his dearly loved mate
Young Hyacinth born on Eurotas' strand,   25
Young Hyacinth the pride of Spartan land;
  But then transform'd him to a purple flower;[9]
Alack that so to change thee winter had no power.

5

Yet can I not persuade me thou art dead
Or that thy corse corrupts in earth's dark womb,   30
Or that thy beauties lie in wormy bed,
Hid from the world in a low delved tomb;
Could heav'n for pity thee so strictly doom?
  Oh no! for something in thy face did shine
Above mortality that show'd thou wast divine.   35

6

Resolve me then, O soul most surely blest
(If so it be that thou these plaints dost hear),
Tell me, bright Spirit, where'er thou hoverest
Whether above that high first-moving sphere[10]
Or in the Elysian fields[11] (if such there were),   40
  O say me true if thou wert mortal wight[12]
And why from us so quickly thou didst take thy flight.

7

Wert thou some star which from the ruin'd roof
Of shak'd Olympus by mischance didst fall;[13]
Which careful Jove in nature's true behoof[14]   45
Took up, and in fit place did reinstall?
Or did of late earth's sons[15] besiege the wall
  Of sheeny[16] heav'n, and thou some goddess fled
Amongst us here below to hide thy nectar'd head?

8

Or wert thou that just maid[17] who once before   50
Forsook the hated earth, O tell me sooth,
And cam'st again to visit us once more?
Or wert thou that sweet smiling youth?[18]
Or that crown'd matron, sage white-robed Truth?
  Or any other of that heav'nly brood   55
Let down in cloudy throne to do the world some good?

9

Or wert thou of the golden-winged host,[19]
Who having clad thyself in human weed,[20]
To earth from thy prefixed[21] seat didst post,[22]
And after short abode fly back with speed,   60
As if to show what creatures heav'n doth breed,
  Thereby to set the hearts of men on fire
To scorn the sordid world, and unto heav'n aspire?

10

But O why didst thou not stay here below
To bless us with thy heav'n-lov'd innocence,   65
To slake his[23] wrath whom sin hath made our foe
To turn swift-rushing black perdition hence,
Or drive away the slaughtering pestilence,[24]
  To stand 'twixt us and our deserved smart?[25]
But thou canst best perform that office[26] where   70
  thou art.

11

Then thou, the mother[27] of so sweet a child,
Her false imagin'd loss cease to lament,
And wisely learn to curb thy sorrows wild;
Think what a present thou to God hast sent,
And render Him with patience what He lent;   75
  This if thou do He will an offspring[28] give,
That till the world's last end shall make thy name to live.

SONNETS

12. [I DID BUT PROMPT THE AGE][1]

I did but prompt the age to quit their clogs[2]
  By the known rules of ancient liberty,

[7]Unknowing. [8]Once upon a time.
[9]Hyacinth(us), a beautiful youth of Amyclae on the river Eurotas near Sparta, was accidentally killed by the infatuated Apollo. In *Lycidas* (l. 106) Milton again alludes to the *purple flower* that sprung from his blood and that therefore bears his name.
[10]*First-moving sphere*: the *primum mobile* or outermost sphere of the universe, which puts the other spheres in motion. See *Sphere* in the Glossary.
[11]In classical mythology, the realm of the blest, paradise.
[12]Creature.
[13]Jove *shak'd* Mt. Olympus, home of the gods, when he seized power from his father Saturn. [14]Interest.
[15]The giants, son of Ge (Earth), who waged unsuccessful war against the gods on Mt. Olympus. [16]Shining.
[17]Astraea, the virgin goddess of Justice, who *forsook the hated earth* when the Golden Age ended.
[18]*Or wert...youth*: The line is metrically defective by two syllables, which some editors supply by inserting *Mercy* after *thou*. The *youth* is perhaps Peace, which Milton elsewhere (*Prolusion* IV) associates with Justice (or Astraea). But see "On the Morning of Christ's Nativity", Stanza 15, where Milton depicts Mercy *thron'd in celestial sheen* between Truth and Justice.
[19]I.e., host of angels. [20]I.e., the body. [21]Destined. [22]Hasten.
[23]Satan's.
[24]This apparent reference to the great plague of 1625 perhaps supports a date of 1626 for the composition of the poem.
[25]Suffering (for sin). [26]Duty, function.
[27]I.e., Milton's sister Anne, who married Edward Phillips in 1623.
[28]Another infant? the enduring fame of the infant who died?
12.[I DID BUT PROMPT] [1]In the text this sonnet, which follows No. 11 ("A book was writ of late call'd *Tetrachordon*") is entitled "On the Same." Both sonnets were prompted by the hostile reception of the divorce pamphlets that Milton wrote between 1643 and 1645. For another statement of his motives in opening up the subject of "domestic" liberty see pp. 778 f. [2]Shackles.

When straight a barbarous noise environs me
Of owls and cuckoos, asses, apes, and dogs;
As when those hinds that were transform'd to frogs   5
Railed at Latona's twin-born progeny,
Which after held the sun and moon in fee.[3]
But this is got by casting pearl to hogs,
That bawl for freedom in their senseless mood,
And still revolt when truth would set them free.   10
License they mean when they cry liberty;
For who loves that must first be wise and good:
But from that mark how far they rove we see,
For all this waste of wealth and loss of blood.

18. ON THE LATE MASSACRE IN PIEMONT[1]

Avenge, O Lord, thy slaughter'd saints, whose bones
Lie scatter'd on the Alpine mountains cold,
Ev'n them who kept Thy truth so pure of old
When all our fathers worship'd stocks and stones,
Forget not; in Thy book record their groans   5
Who were Thy sheep and in their ancient fold
Slain by the bloody Piemontese, that roll'd
Mother with infant down the rocks. Their moans
The vales redoubl'd to the hills, and they
To heav'n. Their martyr'd blood and ashes sow   10
O'er all th' Italian fields where still doth sway
The triple tyrant,[2] that from these may grow
A hunder'dfold,[3] who, having learnt Thy way
Early may fly the Babylonian woe.[4]

19. [WHEN I CONSIDER HOW MY LIGHT IS SPENT][1]

When I consider how my light is spent
Ere half my days in this dark world and wide,
And that one talent[2] which is death to hide
Lodg'd with me useless, though my soul more bent
To serve therewith my Maker, and present   5
My true account, lest He returning chide,
"Doth God exact day-labor, light denied?"
I fondly[3] ask. But Patience, to prevent
That murmur, soon replies, "God doth not need
Either man's work or his own gifts; who best   10
Bear His mild yoke, they serve Him best. His state
Is kingly: thousands at His bidding speed,
And post[4] o'er land and ocean without rest.
They also serve who only stand and wait.

23. [METHOUGHT I SAW MY LATE ESPOUSED SAINT][1]

Methought I saw my late espoused saint
Brought to me like Alcestis[2] from the grave,
Whom Jove's great son to her glad husband gave,
Rescu'd from death by force, though pale and faint.
Mine, as whom wash'd from spot of child-bed taint   5
Purification in the Old Law[3] did save,

And such as yet once more I trust to have
Full sight of her in heaven without restraint,
Came vested[4] all in white, pure as her mind.
Her face was veil'd, yet to my fancied sight   10
Love, sweetness, goodness in her person shin'd
So clear as in no face with more delight.
But O, as to embrace me she inclin'd,
I wak'd, she fled, and day brought back my night.

ON THE NEW FORCERS OF CONSCIENCE UNDER THE LONG PARLIAMENT[1]

Because you have thrown off your prelate lord,
And with stiff vows renounc'd his liturgy
To seize the widow'd whore, Plurality,[2]

[3]Possession. When some crude rustics (*hinds*) insulted the goddess Latona and her *progeny* Apollo and Artemis—who later ruled the sun and moon respectively—Jove turned them into frogs.

18. ON THE LATE MASSACRE [1]This famous sonnet—numbered 15 in the 1673 *Poems* but here renumbered in conformity with Milton's own presumed intentions as revealed in the Trinity Manuscript—was occasioned by a Catholic massacre (24 April 1655) of a group of Waldensian "heretics" in Piedmont, a mountainous region of northern Italy. [2]The pope, whose three-tiered (*triple*) crown symbolizes the pontiff's alleged temporal, spiritual, and purgatorial sovereignty. [3]Hundredfold. [4]I.e., Papal tyranny, which Protestants thought to be predicted by the desolating account of Babylon in Revelation 18.

19. [WHEN I CONSIDER] [1]Numbered 16 in the 1673 *Poems*. This sonnet was probably written some three years after Milton became totally blind in 1652. [2]Gift (with a reference to the Parable of the Talents, Matthew 25). [3]Foolishly [4]Hasten.

23. [METHOUGHT I SAW] [1]Numbered 19 in the 1673 *Poems*. Although the subject of this sonnet has prompted much discussion, it is not yet clear whether Milton wrote it to commemorate his first wife, Mary Powell, who died 2 May 1652, three days after the birth of her daughter Deborah, or his second wife, Katharine Woodcock, who died 3 February 1658, two years after her marriage and four months after the birth of her daughter Katharine (who herself died in the following March). [2]Wife of Admetus, King of Pherae in Thessaly, who, having consented to an early death in order that her husband might be spared, was returned to life by *Jove's great son* Hercules. [3]The Mosaic law, which required (Leviticus 12.4–5) a period of thirty-three days for the "purifying" of a woman after the birth of a son and sixty-six days after the birth of a daughter. [4]Clothed.

ON THE NEW FORCERS [1]This sonnet—a twenty-line *sonetto caudato* or "tailed sonnet" which to the customary fourteen lines adds two tails or tercets, each comprising a trimeter and a pentameter couplet—is Milton's savage commentary on the reactionary Presbyterians in the Long Parliament and their fellow bigots in the Westminster Assembly. It was Milton's view that these men, having abolished episcopacy (1643) and outlawed the Book of Common Prayer (1645), were trying to suppress the Independents. It was probably written in 1646, and reflects the mounting anger that Milton revealed about this time in the so-called "Digression" in his *History of Britain* (pp. 925 ff.). [2]The holding of more than one clerical benefice, a practice for which Presbyterians in Parliament had bitterly assailed their Anglican opponents but which, to Milton's vast disgust, they themselves subsequently adopted.

From them whose sin ye envi'd, not abhorr'd,
Dare ye for this adjure the civil sword   5
  To force our consciences that Christ set free,
  And ride us with a classic hierarchy[3]
  Taught ye by mere A. S. and Rutherford?[4]
Men whose life, learning, faith, and pure intent
  Would have been held in high esteem with Paul   10
  Must now be nam'd and printed heretics
By shallow Edwards and Scotch what-d'ye-call[5]
  But we do hope to find out all your tricks,
  Your plots and packing, worse than those of Trent,[6]
            That so the Parliament   15
May with their wholesome and preventive shears
Clip your phylacteries,[7] though baulk[8] your ears,
            And succor our just fears,
When they shall read this clearly in your charge:
New Presbyter is but old priest writ large.[9]   20

[3]Referring to the Presbyterian (and Scottish) system of organizing the reformed national church into classes (i.e., governing bodies consisting of ministers and elders) to replace the Anglican system of bishops in their dioceses. Milton implies that there was little difference between the two kinds of ecclesiastical discipline, for both rested on compulsory conformity and thus force the consciences of the more liberal Independents.
[4]Adam Stewart and Samuel Rutherford, two advocates of rigid Presbyterianism.
[5]Thomas Edwards and Robert Baillie, vehement opponents of the Independents.
[6]The Council of Trent (1545–63), which codified the doctrine and set the course of the Counter-Reformation, and so was detested by the Puritans.
[7]Little boxes containing quotations from the Mosaic law that devout Jews wore on their foreheads; thus symbols of legalism and hypocrisy.
[8]Avoid, miss. Text bauk. For an account of the clipping of the Presbyterian William Prynne's ears, see pp. 580 f.
[9]The words presbyter and priest are etymologically related, the latter being a contracted form that when expanded (writ large) is indistinguishable from the former.

Sir John Suckling [1609-1642]

Although the printer Humphrey Moseley, in introducing Suckling's Last Remains (1659), wrote about "this gentle and princely poet" in terms of florid adulation, Congreve's Millamant (in The Way of the World) was speaking with her customary precision when she called him "natural, easy Suckling." This hard-drinking, hard-gambling cavalier, an offspring of an influential Norfolk family, was the son of King James' secretary of state and the nephew of a dean of Norwich. He may have gone to Westminster, and he was certainly an undergraduate at Trinity College, Cambridge, before his admittance to Gray's Inn in 1627; but with his father's death a few weeks later he came into a rich estate that released him from the perils of further education. Following a brief sojourn at court, he set forth in 1628 to join a troop of English volunteers who were fighting with the Dutch. During a year or so abroad he saw no military action, but when he returned to England he was knighted by the king, and then (1631) embarked upon another expedition, this time in the entourage of Sir Henry Vane, ambassador extraordinary to the headquarters of King Gustavus Adolphus of Sweden, the Protestant champion of the Thirty Years' War, who was sweeping northern Europe by his dazzling feats of arms. His letters from this German expedition provide a vivid picture not only of the writer but also of important men and actions, which he wrote about with gusto and perception.

The decade that was left to him on his return to England in 1632 was divided mainly, it appears, between a life of letters and prodigious dissipation. "He was the greatest gallant of his time," reported Aubrey, "and the greatest gamester, both for bowling and cards, so that no shopkeeper would trust him for 6 d., as today, for instance, he might, by winning, be worth 200 pounds and the next day he might be worth half so much, or perhaps sometimes be minus nihilo." Despite such diversions and distractions—including a celebrated fracas with Sir Kenelm Digby's younger brother in which the warlike Suckling was made to seem a coward and a fool—there was also time for literature. In addition to his famous lyrics it was in the 1630's that "A Sessions of the Poets" was written. With its intimacies and topicalities it reveals its author's close familiarity with a rowdy literary society quite remote from that of Lord Falkland and his circle, whose philosophical discussions supplied a model for the sober prose of his *Account of Religion by Reason*. Concurrently he was much attracted by the drama. In 1638 a lavish production of *Aglaura* (which was also published in that year) set some sort of record for expense; it was followed by the lively *Goblins* (1638) and by *The Discontented Colonel* (1640), which, expanded and revised, appeared as *Brennoralt* in 1646. *The Sad One*, another tragedy that Suckling never finished, was published posthumously in 1659.

In 1639 the dashing cavalier (like young Richard Lovelace) went at vast expense to Scotland with the King, and in 1641, as Charles' parliamentary opposition mounted, he (like Edmund Waller later) was implicated in a daring, unsuccessful plot to gain the mastery of the army and free the earl of Strafford from the Tower. With the exposure of the plot (May 1641) Suckling fled abroad, where he died in 1642 in circumstances not altogether clear. According to Aubrey (whose account is perhaps substantially correct), he was a desperate man.

> Being come to the bottom of his found, reflecting on the miserable and despicable condition he should be reduced to, having nothing left to maintain him, he (having a convenience for that purpose lying at an apothecary's house in Paris) took poison, which killed him miserably with vomiting.

In 1646 and again in 1648 Moseley published as *Fragmenta Aurea* (i.e., golden fragments) a collection of his "incomparable pieces" consisting of the poems, letters, plays, and *An Account of Religion by Reason*. "They that conversed with him alive and truly," the printer told the reader,

> under which notion I comprehend only knowing gentlemen, his soul being transcendent and incommunicable to others but by reflection, will honor these posthume ideas of their friend; and if any have lived in so much darkness as not to have known so great an ornament to our age, by looking upon these remains with civility and understanding they may timely yet repent and be forgiven.

In 1659 the collection, which had reached a third edition (1658) was expanded and reprinted as *The Last Remains*. By 1770 the honorific *Works* (1676) had gone through six editions.

My texts are based on *Fragmenta Aurea. A Collection of all the Incomparable Peeces, Written by Sir John Suckling. And published by a Friend to perpetuate his memory. Printed by his owne Copies*, 1646 (Wing S-6126) and *The Last Remains of Sir John Suckling. Being a Full Collection Of all his Poems and Letters Which have been so long Expected, and never till now Published. With The License and Approbation of his Noble and Dearest Friends*, 1659 (Wing S-6130). Although A. H. Thompson's edition of the works (1910) superseded the unsatisfactory *Selections* by the Rev. Alfred Suckling (1836) and *The Poems, Plays and Other Remains* by W. C. Hazlitt (2 vols., 1874, rev. 1892), L. A. Beaurline's recent edition of the plays (1971) and Thomas Clayton's of the nondramatic works (1971) supply a longfelt need. Herbert Berry's *Sir John Suckling's Poems and Letters from Manuscript* (1960) clarifies some details about his soldiering on the Continent, and Beaurline's examination of the canon (*SP*, LVII, 1960) has whittled down the *Last Remains*. Suckling is included in R. G. Howarth's *Minor Poets of the 17th Century* (rev. 1953).

from Fragmenta Aurea (1646)

TO THE READER

While Suckling's name is in the forehead of this book these poems can want no preparation. It had been a prejudice to posterity they should have slept longer, and an injury to his own ashes. They that conversed with him alive and truly (under which notion I comprehend only knowing gentlemen, his soul being transcendent and incommunicable to others but by reflection) will honor these posthume[1] ideas of their friend; and if any have lived in so much darkness as

TO THE READER   [1]Posthumous.

not to have known so great an ornament to our age, by look-ing upon these remains with civility and understanding they may timely yet repent and be forgiven.

In this age of paper-prostitutions a man may buy the rep-utation of some authors into the price of their volume; but know, the name that leadeth into this Elysium is sacred to art and honor, and no man that is not excellent in both is qualified a competent judge. For when knowledge is allow-ed, yet education in the censure of a gentleman requires as many descents[2] as goes to make one, and he that is bold upon his unequal stock to traduce[3] this name, or learning, will deserve to be condemned again into ignorance (his original sin), and die in it.

But I keep back the ingenuous reader by my unworthy preface. The gate is open, and thy soul invited to a garden of ravishing variety. Admire his wit that created these for thy delight, while I withdraw into a shade and contemplate who must follow.[4]

A SESSIONS[1] OF THE POETS

A session was held the other day,
And Apollo[2] himself was at it, they say;
The laurel that had been so long reserv'd
Was now to be given to him best deserv'd.
          And
Therefore the wits of the town came thither;   5
'Twas strange to see how they flocked together,
Each strongly confident of his own way,
Thought to gain the laurel away that day.

There was Selden,[3] and he sat hard by the chair;
Weniman[4] not far off, which was very fair;   10
Sandys with Townshend,[5] for they kept no order;
Digby and Chillingworth[6] a little further.
          And
There was Lucan's translator[7] too, and he
That makes God speak so big in 's poetry;
Selwin and Walter, and Bartlets both the brothers;[8]   15
Jack Vaughan and Porter,[9] and divers others.

The first that broke silence was good old Ben,
Prepar'd before with Canary wine,
And he told them plainly he deserv'd the bays,
For his were called *Works*,[10] where others were but
    plays.   20
          And
Bid them remember how he had purg'd the stage
Of errors that had lasted many an age;
And he hoped they did not think the *Silent Woman*,
The *Fox*, and the *Alchemist* outdone by no man.

Apollo stopp'd him there, and bade him not go on,   25
'Twas merit, he said, and not presumption
Must carry 't, at which Ben turned about,
And in great choler offer'd to go out;
          But
Those that were there thought it not fit
To discontent so ancient a wit;   30

And therefore Apollo call'd him back again,
And made him mine host of his own *New Inn*.[11]

Tom Carew[12] was next, but he had a fault
That would not well stand with a laureate;
His Muse was hard-bound, and th' issue of 's brain   35
Was seldom brought forth but with trouble and pain.
          And
All that were present there did agree,
A laureate Muse should be easy and free;
Yet sure 'twas not that, but 'twas thought that, his grace
Consider'd, he was well he had a cup-bearer's place.   40

Will Davenant,[13] asham'd of a foolish mischance
That he had got lately traveling in France,
Modestly hoped the handsomeness of 's Muse
Might any deformity about him excuse.
          And
Surely the company would have been content,   45
If they could have found any president;[14]
But in all their records, either in verse or prose,
There was not one laureate without a nose.[15]

To Will Bartlet sure all the wits meant well,
But first they would see how his snow would sell;   50
Will smil'd and swore in their judgments they went less
That concluded of merit upon success.

Suddenly taking his place again,
He gave way to Selwin, who straight stepp'd in;
But alas! he had been so lately a wit   55
That Apollo hardly knew him yet.

Toby Mathews[16] (pox on him, how came he there?)
Was whispering nothing in somebody's ear,

[2]As long a lineage. [3]Usurp.
[4]I.e., which author I shall publish next. This preface was probably the work of Humphrey Moseley (d. 1661), the publisher of the first collected edition of Milton's poems (1645) as well as works by Waller, Crashaw, Davenant, Donne, and others.
A SESSIONS OF THE POETS [1]Judicial sitting.
[2]The god of song and poetry. [3]See pp. 852 ff.
[4]Probably Sir Francis Wenman, a member of Lord Falkland's circle that Clarendon so movingly described (pp. 797 ff.).
[5]George Sandys (pp. 104 ff.) and Aurelian Townshend (pp. 139 ff.).
[6]Sir Kenelm Digby (p. 486) and William Chillingworth (pp. 561 ff.). Text *Shillingsworth*. [7]Thomas May (pp. 912 f.).
[8]*Selwin...brothers*: Unidentified. In later editions *Walter* is changed to *Waller*.
[9]Perhaps John Vaughan of the Inner Temple and Endymion Porter (1587–1649), a courtier and patron of poets.
[10]The publication of Jonson's collected *Works* (1616) in a sumptu-ous folio was a topic of much comment, some of it unflattering.
[11]Jonson's last play (1629), which had been a failure. For the author's own comment on his humiliation see "Come, leave the loathed stage" (p. 103). [12]See pp. 220 ff. [13]See pp. 251 ff.
[14]Precedent. [15]Davenant's nose was disfigured by syphilis.
[16]Sir Tobie Matthew (1577–1655), courtier, wit, and friend of many writers (notably Bacon) who, after his conversion to Roman Catholicism (1606) was active both in England and on the Continent in behalf of his coreligionists.

When he had the honor to be nam'd in court;
But sir, you may thank my Lady Carlisle[17] for 't,   60

For had not her care furnish'd you out
With something of handsome, without all doubt
You and your sorry lady Muse had been
In the number of those that were not let in.

In haste from the court two or three came in,   65
And they brought letters, forsooth, from the queen;
'Twas discreetly done, too, for if th' had come
Without them, th' had scarce been let into the room.

Suckling next was called, but did not appear,
But straight one whispered Apollo i' th' ear,   70
That of all men living he cared not for 't;
He loved not the Muses so well as his sport,

And prized black eyes, or a lucky hit
At bowls above all the trophies of wit;
But Apollo was angry, and publicly said,   75
'Twere fit that a fine were set upon 's head.

Wat Montagu[18] now stood forth to his trial,
And did not so much as suspect a denial;
But witty Apollo asked him first of all
If he understood his own pastoral.   80

For if he could do it, 'twould plainly appear
He understood more than any man there,
And did merit the bays above all the rest;
But the Monsieur was modest, and silence confest.

During these troubles in the court was hid   85
One that Apollo soon miss'd, little Sid;[19]
And having spied him, call'd him out of the throng,
And advis'd him in his ear not to write so strong.

Then Murray[20] was summon'd, but 'twas urg'd that he
Was chief already of another company.   90

Hales,[21] set by himself, most gravely did smile
To see them about nothing keep such a coil;
Apollo had spied him, but knowing his mind,
Pass'd by, and call'd Falkland that sat just behind.
                                But
He was of late so gone with divinity,   95
That he had almost forgot his poetry;
Though to say the truth, and Apollo did know it,
He might have been both his priest and his poet.

At length who but an alderman did appear,
At which Will Davenant began to swear;   100
But wiser Apollo bade him draw nigher,
And when he was mounted a little higher,

Openly declared that it was the best sign
Of good store of wit's to have good store of coin;
And without a syllable more or less said,   105
He put the laurel on the alderman's head.

At this all the wits were in such a maze
That for a good while they did nothing but gaze
One upon another; not a man in the place
But had discontent writ in great[22] in his face.   110

Only the small poets clear'd up again,
Out of hope, as 'twas thought, of borrowing;
But sure they were out, for he forfeits his crown
When he lends any poets about the town.

SONG

Why so pale and wan, fond lover?
    Prithee, why so pale?
Will, when looking well can't move her,
    Looking ill prevail?
    Prithee, why so pale?   5

Why so dull and mute, young sinner?
    Prithee, why so mute?
Will, when speaking well can't win her,
    Saying nothing do 't?
    Prithee, why so mute?   10

Quit, quit, for shame, this will not move,
    This cannot take her.
If of herself she will not love,
    Nothing can make her.
    The devil take her!   15

SONNET I

1

Dost see how unregarded now
    That piece of beauty passes?
There was a time when I did vow
    To that alone;
    But mark the fate of faces,
That red and white works now no more on me
Than if it could not charm, or I not see.

2

And yet the face continues good,
    And I have still desires,
Am still the selfsame flesh and blood,

[17]Lucy, countess of Carlisle (1599–1660), a famous beauty, wit, and (in her later years) political manipulator whose charms were sung by Carew, Herrick, Suckling, Waller, Davenant, and others.
[18]Walter Montagu (1603?–77), courtier, poet, and Catholic convert who (following his banishment in 1649) became abbot of St. Martin near Pontoise. Queen Henrietta Maria's participation in the lavish court performance of his frigid pastoral comedy *The Shepherd's Paradise* almost coincided with the publication of William Prynne's *Histriomastix* (1632), a virulent attack upon the stage for which the author was savagely punished (p. 578).
[19]Sidney Godolphin (1610–43), a minor poet who, like many of Lord Falkland's circle, met an early death in battle. According to Clarendon, "there was never so great a mind and spirit contained in so little room; so large an understanding and so unrestrained a fancy in so very small a body."
[20]Perhaps William Murray (1600?–51), an early friend of Charles I who became first earl of Drysart.
[21]John Hales (1584–1656), one of the most esteemed members of Lord Falkland's circle. For Clarendon's affectionate memorial to him see pp. 800 ff.   [22]In large letters.

As apt to melt
And suffer from those fires;
O some kind power unriddle where it lies,
Whether my heart be faulty, or her eyes!

3

She every day her man does kill,
  And I as often die;
Neither her power, then, nor my will
    Can question'd be.
    What is the mystery?
Sure beauty's empires, like to greater states,
Have certain periods set, and hidden fates.

SONNET II

1

Of thee, kind boy, I ask no red and white,
  To make up my delight;
    No odd becoming graces,
Black eyes, or little know-not-whats in faces;
Make me but mad enough, give me good store
Of love for her I court;
    I ask no more,
'Tis love in love that makes the sport.

2

There's no such thing as that we beauty call,
  It is mere cozenage all;
    For though some, long ago,
Lik'd certain colors mingled so and so,
That doth not tie me now from choosing new;
If I a fancy take
    To black and blue,
That fancy doth it beauty make.

3

'Tis not the meat, but 'tis the appetite
  Makes eating a delight,
    And if I like one dish
More than another, that a pheasant is;
What in our watches, that in us is found,
So to the height and nick
    We up be wound,
No matter by what hand or trick.

SONNET III

1

O! for some honest lover's ghost,
  Some kind unbodied post[1]
    Sent from the shades below!
    I strangely long to know
Whether the nobler chaplets wear,
Those that their mistress' scorn did bear,
    Or those that were us'd kindly.

2

For whatsoe'er they tell us here
  To make those sufferings dear,

'Twill there, I fear, be found
That to the being crown'd
T' have lov'd alone will not suffice,
Unless we also have been wise
  And have our loves enjoy'd.

3

What posture can we think him in,
  That here unlov'd again
    Departs, and 's thither gone
    Where each sits by his own?
Or how can that Elysium be,
Where I my mistress still must see
    Circled in other's arms?

4

For there the judges all are just,
  And Sophonisba must
    Be his whom she held dear,
    Not his who lov'd her here;[2]
The sweet Philoclea, since she died,
Lies by her Pyrocles his side,
    Not by Amphialus.[3]

5

Some bays, perchance, or myrtle bough,
  For difference crowns the brow
    Of those kind souls that were
    The noble martyrs here;
And if that be the only odds,
(As who can tell?) ye kinder gods,
    Give me the woman here.

SONG

1

No, no, fair heretic, it needs must be
  But an ill love in me,
    And worse for thee.
For were it in my power
To love thee now this hour
    More than I did the last,
I would then so fall,
    I might not love at all.
Love that can flow, and can admit increase,
Admits as well an ebb, and may grow less.

2

True love is still the same; the torrid zones,
  And those more frigid ones,
    It must not know;

SONNET III   [1]Messenger.
[2]*Sophonisba...here:* Sophonisba, (daughter of the Carthaginian general Hasdrubal) committed suicide (ca. 204 B.C.) when she was taken from her Numidian husband Masinissa by the victorious Roman Scipio Africanus.
[3]*Philoclea...Amphialus:* In Sir Philip Sidney's *Arcadia* (see. p. 690) the cruel Cecropia, having captured the sisters Pamela and Philoclea together with the latter's faithful lover Pyrocles, tried to force one of the girls to marry her son Amphialus.

For love, grown cold or hot,
Is lust or friendship, not
  The thing we have;
For that's a flame would die,
  Held down or up too high.
Then think I love more than I can express,
And would love more, could I but love thee less.

TO MY FRIEND WILL. DAVENANT ON HIS OTHER POEMS[1]

Thou hast redeem'd us, Will, and future times
Shall not account unto the age's crimes
Dearth of pure wit. Since the great lord of it
(Donne) parted hence, no man has ever writ
So near him in's own way. I would commend   5
Particulars, but then, how should I end
Without a volume? Ev'ry line of thine
Would ask (to praise it right) twenty of mine.

['TIS NOW SINCE I SAT DOWN]

1

'Tis now, since I sat down before
  That foolish fort, a heart,
(Time strangely spent) a year and more,
  And still I did my part.

2

Made my approaches, from her hand
  Unto her lip did rise,
And did already understand
  The language of her eyes;

3

Proceeded on with no less art,
  My tongue was engineer;
I thought to undermine the heart
  By whispering in the ear.

4

When this did nothing, I brought down
  Great cannon-oaths, and shot
A thousand thousand to the town;
  And still it yielded not.

5

I then resolv'd to starve the place
  By cutting off all kisses,
Praising and gazing on her face,
  And all such little blisses.

6

To draw her out and from her strength,
  I drew all batteries in,
And brought myself to lie at length
  As if no siege had been.

7

When I had done what man could do,
  And thought the place mine own,

The enemy lay quiet too,
  And smil'd at all was done.

8

I sent to know from whence and where
  These hopes and this relief:
A spy inform'd, Honor was there,
  And did command in chief.

9

March, march, quoth I, the word straight give,
  Let's lose no time, but leave her;
That giant upon air will live,
  And hold it out forever.

10

To such a place our camp remove,
  As will no siege abide;
I hate a fool that starves her love,
  Only to feed her pride.

A BALLADE UPON A WEDDING[1]

I tell thee, Dick, where I have been,
Where I the rarest things have seen,
  Oh, things without compare!
Such sights again cannot be found
In any place on English ground,   5
  Be it at wake or fair.

At Charing Cross,[2] hard by the way
Where we, thou know'st, do sell our hay,
  There is a house with stairs;
And there did I see coming down   10
Such folk as are not in our town,
  Vorty[3] at least, in pairs.

Amongst the rest, one pest'lent fine
(His beard no bigger though than thine)
  Walk'd on before the rest;   15
Our landlord looks like nothing to him,
The King, God bless him, 'twould undo him
  Should he go still so dress'd.

At course-a-park,[4] without all doubt,
He should have first been taken out   20
  By all the maids i' th' town;
Though lusty Roger there had been,
Or little George upon the Green,
  Or Vincent of the Crown.

But wot you what? the youth was going   25
To make an end of all his wooing,
  The parson for him stay'd;

TO MY FRIEND WILL DAVENANT [1]In the text this poem is preceded by one concerned with Davenant's *Madagascar* (pp. 253 ff.).
A BALLADE UPON A WEDDING [1]Perhaps written for the wedding of Roger Boyle, Baron Broghill, and Lady Margaret Howard in 1641.
[2]A thoroughfare in Westminster. [3]Rustic dialect for "forty."
[4]A country kissing-game.

Yet by his leave, for all his haste,
He did not so much wish all past,
  Perchance, as did the maid.

The maid—and thereby hangs a tale:
For such a maid no Whitsun ale
  Could ever yet produce;
No grape that's kindly[5] ripe could be
So round, so plump, so soft as she,
  Nor half so full of juice.

Her finger was so small the ring
Would not stay on, which they did bring,
  It was too wide a peck;[6]
And to say truth (for out it must)
It looked like the great collar, just,
  About our young colt's neck.

Her feet beneath her petticoat,
Like little mice, stole in and out,
  As if they fear'd the light;
But oh, she dances such a way!
No sun upon an Easter day
  Is half so fine a sight.

He would have kissed her once or twice,
But she would not, she was nice,
  She would not do't in sight;
And then she look'd as who should say,
I will do what I list to-day,
  And you shall do't at night.

Her cheeks so rare a white was on,
No daisy makes comparison,
  Who sees them is undone;
For streaks of red were mingled there,
Such as are on a Katherne pear,
  The side that's next the sun.

Her lips were red, and one was thin,
Compar'd to that was next her chin,
  Some bee had stung it newly;
But Dick, her eyes so guard her face
I durst no more upon them gaze
  Than on the sun in July.

Her mouth so small, when she does speak
Thou'dst swear her teeth her words did break,
  That they might passage get;
But she so handled still the matter,
They came as good as ours, or better,
  And are not spent a whit.

If wishing should be any sin,
The parson himself had guilty bin,
  She look'd that day so purely;
And did the youth so oft the feat
At night, as some did in conceit,[7]
  It would have spoil'd him surely.

Just in the nick the cook knock'd thrice,
And all the waiters in a trice
  His summons did obey;

Each serving-man, with dish in hand,
March'd boldly up like our train'd band,[8]
  Presented, and away.

When all the meat was on the table,
What man of knife or teeth was able
  To stay to be entreated?
And this the very reason was—
Before the parson could say grace,
  The company was seated.

The bus'ness of the kitchen's great,
For it is fit that men should eat,
  Nor was it there denied.
Passion o' me, how I run on!
There's that that would be thought upon
  (I trow) besides the bride.

Now hats fly off, and youths carouse,
Healths first go round, and then the house,
  The bride's came thick and thick;
And when 'twas nam'd another's health,
Perhaps he made it hers by stealth,
  And who could help it, Dick?

O' th' sudden up they rise and dance,
Then sit again and sigh and glance,
  Then dance again, and kiss;
Thus sev'ral ways the time did pass,
Till ev'ry woman wish'd her place,
  And ev'ry man wish'd his.

By this time all were stol'n aside
To counsel and undress the bride,
  But that he must not know;
But yet 'twas thought he guess'd her mind,
And did not mean to stay behind
  Above an hour or so.

When in he came, Dick, there she lay
Lake new-fall'n snow melting away
  ('Twas time, I trow, to part);
Kisses were now the only stay,
Which soon she gave, as who would say
  Good boy! with all my heart.

But just as heav'ns would have, to cross it,
In came the bridesmaids with the posset;[9]
  The bridegroom eat in spite,
For, had he left the women to 't,
It would have cost two hours to do 't,
  Which were too much that night.

At length the candle's out, and now
All that they had not done they do 't[10]
  What that is, who can tell?
But I believe it was no more
Than thou and I have done before
  With Bridget and with Nell.

[5]Naturally. [6]I.e., by a great deal. [7]Imagination [8]Local militia.
[9]A spiced hot drink of wine or ale and milk.
[10]*At length . . . they do:* Text *At length the candles out and out, | All that they had not done, they do 't.*

from The Last Remains of Sir John Suckling (1659)

THE STATIONER TO THE READER.

Among the highest and most refined wits of the nation, this gentle and princely poet took his generous[1] rise from the court, where, having flourished with splendor and reputation, he lived only long enough to see the sunset of that majesty from whose auspicious beams he derived his luster, and with whose declining state his own loyal fortunes were obscured. But after the several changes of those times, being sequestered from the more serene contentments of his native country, he first took care to secure the dearest and choicest of his papers in the several cabinets of his noble and faithful friends; and among other testimonies of his worth, these elegant and florid pieces of his fancy were preserved in the custody of his truly honorable and virtuous sister, with whose free permission they were transcribed, and now published exactly according to the original.

This might be sufficient to make you acknowledge that these are the real and genuine works of Sir John Suckling; but if you can yet doubt, let any judicious soul seriously consider the freedom of the fancy, richness of the conceit, proper expression, with that air and spirit diffused through every part, and he will find such a perfect resemblance with what hath been formerly known that he cannot with modesty doubt them to be his.

I could tell you further (for I myself am the best witness of it) what a thirst and general inquiry hath been after what I here present you, by all that hath either seen or heard of them. And by that time you have read them, you will believe me, who have, now for many years, annually published the productions of the best wits of our own and foreign nations.

H.M.[2]

[OUT UPON IT, I HAVE LOVED]

1

Out upon it! I have lov'd
  Three whole days together;
And am like to love three more,
  If it prove fair weather.

2

Time shall moult away his wings,
  Ere he shall discover
In the whole wide world again
  Such a constant lover.

3

But the spite on 't is, no praise
  Is due at all to me;
Love with me had made no stays,
  Had it any been but she.

4

Had it any been but she,
  And that very face,
There had been at least ere this
  A dozen dozen in her place.

LOVE AND DEBT ALIKE TROUBLESOME

This one request I make to him that sits the clouds above,
That I were freely out of debt as I am out of love.
Then for to dance, to drink, and sing I should be very willing;
I should not owe one lass a kiss, nor ne'er a knave a shilling.
'Tis only being in love and debt that breaks us of our rest, 5
And he that is quite out of both, of all the world is blest;
He sees the golden age, wherein all things were free and common;
He eats, he drinks, he takes his rest, he fears no man nor woman.
Though Croesus compassed great wealth, yet he still craved more,
He was as needy a beggar still as goes from door to door. 10
Though Ovid were a merry man, love ever kept him sad;
He was as far from happiness as one that is stark mad.
Our merchant, he in goods is rich, and full of gold and treasure;
But when he thinks upon his debts, that thought destroys his pleasure.
Our courtier thinks that he's preferr'd, whom every man 15 envies;
When love so rumbles in his pate, no sleep comes in his eyes.
Our gallant's case is worst of all, he lies so just betwixt them;
For he's in love and he's in debt, and knows not which most vex him.
But he that can eat beef, and feed on bread which is so brown,
May satisfy his appetite, and owe no man a crown; 20
And he that is content with lasses clothëd in plain woolen,
May cool his heat in every place; he need not to be sullen,
Nor sigh for love of lady fair, for this each wise man knows—
As good stuff under flannel lies, as under silken clothes.

SONG

I prithee send me back my heart,
  Since I cannot have thine;

THE STATIONER TO THE READER [1]Text *gerous*.
[2]Humphrey Moseley (see p. 289, n. 4.).

For if from yours you will not part,
  Why then shouldst thou have mine?

Yet now I think on 't, let it lie,　　　5
  To find it were in vain;
For th' hast a thief in either eye
  Would steal it back again.

Why should two hearts in one breast lie,
  And yet not lodge together?　　　10
O love, where is thy sympathy,
  If thus our breasts thou sever?

But love is such a mystery,
  I cannot find it out;
For when I think I'm best resolv'd,　　　15
  I then am most in doubt.

Then farewell care, and farewell woe,
  I will no longer pine;
For I'll believe I have her heart
  As much as she hath mine.　　　20

PROFFER'D LOVE REJECTED

It is not four years ago
I offered forty crowns
To lie with her a night or so;
She answer'd me in frowns.

Not two years since, she meeting me　　　5
Did whisper in my ear
That she would at my service be
If I contented were.

I told her I was cold as snow
And had no great desire,　　　10
But should be well content to go
To twenty, but no higher.

Some three months since or thereabout,
She that so coy had bin
Bethought herself and found me out,　　　15
And was content to sin.

I smil'd at that and told her I
Did think it something late,
And that I'd not repentance buy
At above half the rate.　　　20

This present morning early she
Forsooth came to my bed,
And gratis there she offered me
Her high-priz'd maidenhead.

I told her that I thought it then　　　25
Far dearer than I did
When I at first the forty crowns
For one night's lodging bid.

A SONG[1]

Hast thou seen the down i' th' air
  When wanton blasts have toss'd it,

Or the ship on the sea
  When ruder waves have cross'd it?
Hast thou mark'd the crocodile's weeping,　　　5
  Or the fox's sleeping?
Or hast viewed the peacock in his pride,
  Or the dove by his bride
  When he courts for his lechery?
O so fickle, O so vain, O so false, so false is she!　　　10

UPON A. M.

Yield all, my love, but be withal as coy
As if thou knew'st not how to sport and toy.
The forts resign'd with ease, men cowards prove
And lazy grow. Let me besiege my love;
Let me despair at least three times a day,　　　5
And take repulses upon each essay.
If I but ask a kiss, straight blush as red
As if I tempted for thy maidenhead.
Contract thy smiles if that they go too far,
And let thy frowns be such as threaten war.　　　10
That face which Nature sure never intended
Should e'er be marr'd because 't could ne'er be mended.
Take no corruption from thy grandam Eve;
Rather want faith to save thee than believe
Too soon: for, credit me, 'tis true,　　　15
Men most of all enjoy when least they do.

AN ANSWER TO SOME VERSES MADE IN HIS PRAISE

The ancient poets and their learned rhymes
We still admire in these our later times,
And celebrate their fames. Thus though they die,
Their names can never taste mortality.
Blind Homer's Muse and Vergil's stately verse,　　　5
While any live, shall never need a hearse.
Since, then, to these such praise was justly due
For what they did, what shall be said to you?
These had their helps: they writ of gods and kings,
Of temples, battles, and such gallant things,　　　10
But you of nothing. How could you have writ
Had you but chose a subject to your wit?
To praise Achilles or the Trojan crew
Showed little art, for praise was but their due.
To say she's fair that's fair, this is no pains:　　　15
He shows himself most poet that most feigns.
To find out virtues strangely hid in me,
Aye, there's the art and learned poetry:
To make one striding of a barbed steed,
Prancing a stately round. I use indeed　　　20
To ride Bat Jewel's jade:[1] this is the skill,
This shows the poet wants not wit at will.
  I must admire aloof, and for my part
  Be well contented, since you do 't with art.

A SONG　[1]A parody of Jonson's "Her Triumph" (p. 97).
AN ANSWER TO SOME VERSES　[1]The passage (which seems to be corrupt) perhaps refers to a well-known whore or bawd. A *bat* is a horse used for carrying baggage or supplies.

William Cartwright [1611-1643]

William Cartwright was so highly overrated by his friends and coreligionists that his real but minor talent has not yet recovered from their suffocating adulation. Like Thomas Randolph (see pp. 239 ff.), who has languished from the same affliction, he was a poor boy whose merit won for him a scholarship at Westminster. From there he went to Christ Church, Oxford (B.A. 1632, M.A. 1635), where, though working "sixteen hours a day at all manner of knowledge," he gained a local fame for poetry. Some of this, according to Humphrey Moseley, the publisher of his collected works in 1651, was written "before he was twenty years old, scarce any after five and twenty; never his business, only to sweeten and relieve deeper thoughts." As early as 1634, it seems, he wrote *The Ordinary*, a satirical comedy that perhaps was followed by *The Lady-Errant*; and then, in 1636, there was the dizzy triumph of *The Royal Slave*, a tragi-comedy so successfully produced at Christ Church for a royal visitation that the Queen herself, a few months later, ordered it to be performed again at Hampton Court. *The Siege, or Love's Convert*, his fourth and final play that may have been composed about this time, was widely read in manuscript, but there is no record of production.

If, as Moseley said, Cartwright virtually abandoned literature following his ordination in 1638—"here is but one sheet was written after he entered holy orders"—he did not slip into obscurity. On the contrary, as Anthony Wood reported, he at once acquired new fame as "the most florid and seraphical preacher in the university." For the rest of his short life his interests focused on his church and university. In 1642, for instance, he was named a reader in philosophy, awarded the succentorship of Salisbury Cathedral, honored by the King's command to preach a sermon of thanksgiving after the battle of Edgehill, and nominated to the so-called council of war through which the various colleges were enlisted in defense of Oxford. His exertions must have been intense, for in November 1643—six months after his appointment as junior proctor of the university—he succumbed to a malignant fever called the camp disease and was buried in Christ Church Cathedral.

The King himself, said Aubrey, was observed to drop a tear at the news of his untimely death, and he was so widely mourned that more than fifty eulogistic poems were collected for the memorial edition of his works that Moseley published eight years later. "If the wits read his poems," Wood assured a younger generation, "divines his sermons, and philosophers his lectures on Aristotle's metaphysics, they would scarce believe that he died at a little above thirty years of age."

My texts are based on *Comedies, Tragi-Comedies, With other Poems, By Mr William Cartwright, late Student of Christ-Church in Oxford, and Proctor of the University. The Ayres and Songs set by Mr Henry Lawes, Servant to His late Majesty in His publick and Private Musick*, 1651 (Wing C–709); for "A Song of Dalliance" on *Sportive Wit*, 1656 (Wing P–2113); and for "To Philip, Earl of Pembroke . . ." on the transcription of a contemporary broadside by G. Blakemore Evans in his authoritative edition of *The Plays and Poems of William Cartwright* (1951).

from Comedies, Tragi-Comedies, With Other Poems (1651)

THE DREAM

I dream'd I saw myself lie dead,
    And that my bed my coffin grew;
Silence and Sleep this strange sight bred,
    But wak'd, I found I liv'd anew.
Looking next morn on your bright face,   5
    Mine eyes bequeath'd mine heart fresh pain:
A dart rush'd in with every grace,
    And so I kill'd myself again.
O eyes, what shall distressed lovers do
If open you can kill, if shut you view?   10

A SONG OF DALLIANCE[1]

Hark, my Flora, Love doth call us
To that strife that must befall us.
He has robb'd his mother's myrtles
And hath pull'd her downy turtles.[2]
See, our genial[3] posts are crown'd,   5
And our beds like billows rise:
Softer combat's nowhere found,
And who loses wins the prize.

Let not dark nor shadows fright thee;
Thy limbs of luster[4] they will light thee.   10
Fear not any can surprise us;
Love himself doth now disguise us.
From thy waist thy girdle throw;
Night and darkness both dwell here.
Words or actions who can know,   15
Where there's neither eye nor ear?

Show thy bosom and then hide it;
License touching and then chide it.
Give a grant and then forbear it;
Offer something and forswear it.   20
Ask where all our shame is gone;
Call us wicked, wanton men.
Do as turtles, kiss and groan;
Say we ne'er shall meet again.

I can hear thee curse, yet chase thee;   25
Drink thy tears, yet still embrace thee.
Easy riches is no treasure;
She that's willing spoils the pleasure.
Love bids learn the restless fight;
Pull and struggle whilst ye twine;   30
Let me use my force tonight,
The next conquest shall be thine.

TO CHLOE, WHO WISH'D HERSELF YOUNG ENOUGH FOR ME

Chloe, why wish you that your years
    Would backwards run till they meet mine,
That perfect likeness, which endears
    Things unto things, might us combine?
Our ages so in date agree   5
That twins do differ more than we.

There are two births: the one when light
    First strikes the new awaken'd sense;
The other when two souls unite,
    And we must count our life from thence.   10
When you lov'd me and I lov'd you,
Then both of us were born anew.

Love then to us did new souls give,
    And in those souls did plant new pow'rs;
Since when another life we live,   15
    The breath we breathe is his, not ours;
Love makes those young whom age doth chill,
And whom he finds young, keeps young still.

Love, like that angel that shall call
    Our bodies from the silent grave,
Unto one age doth raise us all,   20
    None too much, none too little have;
Nay, that the difference may be none,
He makes two not alike, but one.

And now since you and I are such,   25
    Tell me what's yours and what is mine?
Ours eyes, our ears, our taste, smell, touch,
    Do, like our souls, in one combine;
So by this, I as well may be
Too old for you, as you for me.   30

A VALEDICTION

Bid me not go where neither suns nor show'rs
    Do make or cherish flow'rs,
Where discontented things in sadness lie,
    And Nature grieves as I;
When I am parted from those eyes   5
From which my better day doth rise,
    Though some propitious pow'r
    Should plant me in a bow'r,
Where amongst happy lovers I might see
    How showers and sunbeams bring   10
    One everlasting spring,
Nor would those fall, nor these shine forth to me;
    Nature herself to him is lost

A SONG OF DALLIANCE [1]This famous poem—which Sir Herbert Grierson regarded as the "nearest rival" to Carew's "A Rapture" (pp. 227 ff.)—first appeared in the miscellany *Sportive Wit* (1656), upon which I base my text.
[2]Turtledoves, which, like *myrtles* (line 3), were traditionally associated with Venus, the goddess of love. [3]Nuptial.
[4]Shining flesh.

Who loseth her he honors most.
Then fairest to my parting view display   15
　Your graces all in one full day,
Whose blessed shapes I'll snatch and keep till when
　I do return and view again;
So by this art Fancy shall fortune cross,[1]
And lovers live by thinking on their loss.   20

NO PLATONIC LOVE

Tell me no more of minds embracing minds,
　And hearts exchang'd for hearts;
That spirits spirits meet as winds do winds,
　And mix their subtlest parts;
That two unbodied essences may kiss,   5
And then like angels, twist and feel one bliss.

I was that silly thing that once was wrought
　To practise this thin love;
I climb'd from sex to soul, from soul to thought;
　But thinking there to move,   10
Headlong I roll'd from thought to soul, and then
From soul I lighted at the sex again.

As some strict down-look'd,[1] men pretend to fast
　Who yet in closets eat,
So lovers who profess they spirits taste,   15
　Feed yet on grosser meat;
I know they boast they souls to souls convey,
Howe'er they meet, the body is the way.

Come, I will undeceive thee: they that tread
　Those vain aerial ways   20
Are like young heirs and alchemists, misled
　To waste their wealth and days;
For searching thus to be forever rich,
They only find a med'cine for the itch.

UPON THE DRAMATIC POEMS OF
MASTER JOHN FLETCHER[1]

Though when all Fletcher writ, and the entire
Man was indulg'd unto that sacred fire,[2]
His thoughts and his thought's dress appear'd both such
That 'twas his happy fault to do too much,
Who therefore wisely did submit each birth   5
To knowing Beaumont ere it did come forth,
Working again until he said 'twas fit,
And made him the sobriety of his wit;[3]
Though thus he call'd his judge into his fame,
And for that aid allow'd him half the name,   10
'Tis known that sometimes he did stand alone,
That both the sponge and pencil were his own,
That himself judg'd himself, could singly do,
And was at last Beaumont and Fletcher too;
　Else we had lost his *Shepherdess*,[4] a piece   15
Even and smooth, spun from a finer fleece,
Where softness reigns, where passions passions greet,
Gentle and high, as floods of balsam meet;

Where, dress'd in white[5] expressions, sit bright loves,
Drawn, like their fairest queen, by milky doves,   20
A piece which Jonson in a rapture bid
Come up a glorified work, and so it did.[6]
　Else had his Muse set with his friend; the stage
Had miss'd those poems, which yet take the age;
The world had lost those rich exemplars, where   25
Art, learning, wit sit ruling in one sphere,
Where the fresh matters soar above old themes
As prophets' raptures do above our dreams,
Where in a worthy scorn he dares refuse
All other gods, and makes the thing his Muse;   30
Where he calls passions forth and lays them so
As spirits, aw'd by him to come and go;
Where the free author did whate'er he would,
And nothing will'd but what a poet should.
　No vast, uncivil bulk swells any scene: 35
The strength's ingenuous[7] and the vigor clean;
None can prevent[8] the fancy, and see through
At the first opening; all stand wond'ring how
The thing will be until it is, which thence
With fresh delights still cheats, still takes the sense,   40
The whole design, the shadows, the lights such
That none can say he shows or hides too much.
Business grows up, ripened by just increase,
And by as just degrees again doth cease;
The heats and minutes[9] of affairs are watcht,   45
And the nice points of time are met and snatcht;
Nought later than it should, nought comes before;
Chemists and calculators do err more;
Sex, age, degree, affections, country, place,
The inward substance and the outward face   50
All kept precisely, all exactly fit;
What he would write he was before he writ.
'Twixt Jonson's grave and Shakespeare's lighter sound
His Muse so steer'd that something still was found:
Nor this, nor that, nor both, but so his own   55
That 'twas his mark, and he was by it known.
Hence did he take true judgments, hence did strike

A VALEDICTION [1]Thwart.

NO PLATONIC LOVE [1]With downcast eyes, demure.

UPON THE DRAMATIC POEMS [1]This piece, together with another
on the same subject by Cartwright, was first printed with a group
of commendatory poems in the 1647 folio of Beaumont and
Fletcher's *Comedies and Tragedies.*
[2]*Indulg'd . . . fire:* seized by poetic inspiration.
[3]The notion that Beaumont was merely a prudent editor who
curbed his collaborator's flowing inspiration has been long dis-
carded.
[4]*The Faithful Shepherdess* (ca. 1608), a pastoral play by Fletcher that,
though not initially a success, came to be greatly admired by
Jonson, Milton, and others.   [5]Pure.
[6]In his commendatory poem "To Mr. John Fletcher" (p. 102)
Jonson predicted that despite its failure to please vulgar playgoers
The Faithful Shepherdess would rise
　　　A glorified work to Time when fire
　　　Or moths shall eat what all these fools admire.
[7]Noble, generous.   [8]Anticipate.
[9]Large passions and trivial details?

All palates some way, though not all alike.
The god of numbers might his numbers crown,
And, list'ning to them, wish they were his own.   60
   Thus welcome forth what ease or wine or wit
   Durst yet produce: that is, what Flecther writ.

TO PHILIP, EARL OF PEMBROKE,[1] UPON HIS LORDSHIP'S ELECTION OF CHANCELLOR OF THE UNIVERSITY OF OXFORD[2]

My Lord,
   When studies now are blasted, and the times
Place us in false lights, and see arts as crimes,
When to heap knowledge is but thought to fill
The mind with more advantage to do ill,   5
When all your honor'd brother's[3] choice and store
Of learn'd remains with sweat and charge fetch'd o'er
Are thought but useless pieces, and some trust
To see our schools mingled with abbey dust,
That now you dare receive us, and profess   10
Yourself our patron, makes you come no less
Than a new founder, whilst we all allow
What was defense before is building now;
And this you were reserv'd for, set apart
For times of hazard as the shield and dart   15
Laid up in store to be extracted thence
When serious need shall ask some tried defense;
And who more fit to manage the gown's cause
Than you, whose even[4] life may dare the laws
And the law-makers too, in whom the great   20
Is twisted with the good as light with heat.

What though your sadder[5] cares do not profess
To find the circle's squaring or to guess
How many sands within a grain or two
Will fill the world: these speculations do   25
Steal man from man. You're he that can suggest
True rules, and fashion manners to the best;
You can preserve our charters from the wrongs
Of the untaught town, as far as now the tongue
Doth from their understanding; you can give   30
Freedom to men, and make that freedom live,
And divert hate from the now hated arts.
These are your great endowments, these your parts,
And 'tis our honest boast, when this we scan,
We give a title but receive a man.   35
       Your Lordship's most honored,
          humble servant,
           William Cartwright

TO PHILIP, EARL OF PEMBROKE [1]Philip Herbert (1584–1650), earl of Montgomery and fourth earl of Pembroke. A strenuous Parliamentarian in his later years, he succeeded Archbishop Laud (then a prisoner in the Tower) as vice-chancellor of Oxford in 1641 and eventually superintended a vigorous visitation of the colleges that led to the harassment and ejection of many royalists.
[2]I base my text on two contemporary broadsides as transcribed by G. Blakemore Evans in his edition of *The Plays and Poems of William Cartwright* (1951), which are markedly superior to the version in the 1651 *Poems.*
[3]The fourth earl's elder brother William, third earl of Pembroke (d. 1630), the friend and patron of many men of letters (see p. 683, n. 4), had been named chancellor of Oxford in 1617. Unlike his younger brother, he was such a generous benefactor of the university that Broadgates Hall was named for him.
[4]Just.   [5]More serious.

Richard Crashaw [1612/13-1649]

It is ironical that William Crashaw (d. 1626), an eminent Anglican divine noted for his relentless opposition to the Roman Catholic Church, should have sired England's great poetic exemplar and spokesman of the Counter-Reformation. Despite the loss of his mother, then his stepmother, and finally his father when he was still a boy, the younger Crashaw was not left unprovided for, and he received an excellent education. Going from the Charterhouse in London to Pembroke College, Cambridge, in 1631, he wrote so much—and such accomplished—Greek and Latin poetry in order to satisfy the requirements of a scholarship he held that by 1634, when he was not yet twenty-two, he was encouraged to publish most of it as *Epigrammatum sacrorum liber,* i.e., a book of epigrams on scriptural topics. Following his B.A. in that same year he was elected to a fellowship at Peterhouse, and there, in the very citadel of Laud's High-Church Anglicanism, he no doubt thought that he had found his proper place.

    Proceeding to his M.A. in 1638, he then or shortly later was ordained and appointed curate of Little St. Mary's, a parish church adjacent to and serving as the chapel of his college. In this attractive setting, where "he made his nest more gladly than David's swallow near the house of God," and at nearby Little Gidding, a quasi-monastic community in Huntingdonshire founded by George Herbert's friend and literary executor Nicholas Ferrar, his love of ritual was so deeply gratified and so openly expressed that in 1641 it was duly censured by a parliamentary visitation. As England in the early forties moved toward civil war, Crashaw's notorious inclinations as an Anglo-Catholic and a royalist made his situation hopeless long before his ejection from his fellowship in 1644. It is unlikely that he remained in Cambridge long enough to watch Cromwell and his troops, under parliamentary orders to demolish "monuments of superstition and idolatry," late in 1643 deface his college and his little church with its "sixty superstitious pictures" and other papist baubles.

His movements then and later are extremely hard to follow, but Anthony Wood's telescoped and imprecise account of these uncertain matters gives at least the contour of events:

> at length, upon an infallible foresight that the Church of England would be quite ruined by the unlimited fury of the Presbyterians, he changed his religion and went beyond the seas and took up his abode for a time in the great city of Paris.

It seems likely that on leaving Cambridge Crashaw went to Little Gidding and then to Lincolnshire, where he left his poems in manuscript with the unknown friend who supervised their publication in 1646. By February 1644 the refugee had somehow got to Holland, where, as his one surviving letter indicates, he perhaps went over to the Roman Catholic Church.

If, as some believe, he returned to England in the spring of 1644 to seek the protection of Queen Henrietta Maria at her little court in Oxford, he could there have formed the friendships reflected in his proselytizing epistle to the Countess of Denbigh (see p. 314) and in Cowley's moving tribute to the poet (see p. 333). At any rate it is certain that by 7 September 1646 he had joined the Queen in Paris (where she herself had fled two years before), for on that date she recommended Crashaw to the Pope as a needy member of her entourage whose talents, she implied, the pontiff should reward. Armed with this endorsement, Crashaw went at once to Rome, but it was not until a year or more had passed that a second supplication from the Queen brought him to the notice and protection of Cardinal Palotto. In the court of this great prelate, according to one contemporary account, the English convert was so censorious of and unpopular with his colleagues that the cardinal, "to secure his life," arranged for him a "small employ" in Loretto at the Santa Casa, allegedly the house in which Jesus had lived and which angels had brought from Nazareth. Beleaguered to the very end, however, he had scarcely reached this haven when he died (21 August 1649), perhaps of a fever contracted on the road from Rome or perhaps, as some believed, of poison.

Apart from the little book of epigrams of 1634, Crashaw apparently had no part in the publication of any of his works. In 1646 there appeared (with an important preface by an unknown friend) *Steps to the Temple*, whose fifteen long religious poems as well as translations of nearly fifty of his early epigrams were juxtaposed with *The Delights of the Muses*, a gathering of his earlier occasional, secular, and academic pieces. A second and significantly revised edition of this work, "wherein are added divers pieces not before extant," followed two years later. In 1652 the posthumous *Carmen Deo Nostro* provided not only the ultimate revisions of thirty-two previously published poems but also the famous verse epistle "To the Noblest and Best of Ladies the Countess of Denbigh." According to the title page it was to this great and kindly woman—herself a convert to the Roman Church in 1651—that the book was dedicated by "her most devoted servant R. C. in hearty acknowledgment of his immortal obligation to her goodness and charity." In a tortuous "Anagram" that serves as preface to the little book one Thomas Car, an ardent coreligionist whom Crashaw knew in Paris, almost canonized his late friend in bidding him farewell:

> Nor would he give nor take offense; befall
> What might, he would possess himself, and live
> As dead (devoid of interest) t' all might give
> Disease t' his well composed mind, forestall'd
> With heavenly riches which had wholly call'd
> His thoughts from earth to live above in th' air,
> A very bird of paradise.

Mᴛ texts are based upon *Steps to the Temple, Sacred Poems. With The Delights of the Muses. By Richard Crashaw . . . The second Edition wherein are added divers pieces not before extant*, 1648 (Wing C–6837), and *Carmen Deo Nostro, Te Decet Hymnus Sacred Poems, Collected, Corrected, Augmented, Most humbly Presented. To My Lady The Countesse of Denbigh By Her most devoted Seruant. R. C. In heaty acknowledgment of his immortall obligation to her Goodness & Charity. At Paris*, 1652 (Wing C–6830). Editions of the poems by A. B. Grosart (2 vols., 1872–73, supplement 1887–88), A. R. Waller (1904), and J. R. Tutin (1905) have been superseded by L. C. Martin's (2d ed., 1957). George W. Williams' edition of the *Complete Poetry* (1970) separates the secular and sacred poems. Crashaw receives attention in all the discussions of metaphysical poetry listed in the General Bibliography, Section I, and there are important full-length studies by Ruth Wallerstein (1935), Austin Warren (1939), Mario Praz (1945), George W. Williams (*Image and Symbol in the Sacred Poetry of Richard Crashaw*, 1963), and Marc F. Bertonosco (*Crashaw and the Baroque*, 1971). Basil Willey has supplied a perceptive tercentenary lecture (1949) and Robert T. Petersson an interesting account of St. Teresa, Bernini, and Crashaw in *The Art of Ecstasy* (1970). Margaret Willey's brochure *Three Metaphysical Poets* (1961) treats Crashaw as well as Vaughan and Traherne.

from Steps to the Temple (1648)

Learned Reader,

The author's friend will not usurp much upon thy eye. This is only for those whom the name of our divine poet hath not yet seized into admiration. I dare undertake that what Iambilicus (in *Vita Pythagorae*) affirmeth of his master at his contemplations, these poems can, viz., they shall lift thee, reader, some yards above the ground;[1] and as in Pythagoras' school every temper was first tuned into a height by several proportions[2] of music and spiritualized for one of his weighty lectures, so mayest thou take a poem hence and tune thy soul by it into a heavenly pitch; and thus refined and borne up upon the wings of meditation, in these poems thou mayest talk freely of God and of that other state.

Here's Herbert's[3] second but equal, who hath retrieved poetry of late and returned it up to its primitive use. Let it bound back to heaven gates, whence it came! Think ye St. Augustine would have stained his graver learning with a book of poetry had he fancied its dearest end to be the vanity of love sonnets and epithalamiums?[4] No, no! He thought with this our poet that every foot in a high-borne verse might help to measure the soul into that better world. Divine poetry! I dare hold it, in position against Suarez[5] on the subject, to be the language of the angels; it is the quintessence of fantasy and discourse centered in heaven; 'tis the very outgoings of the soul; 'tis what alone our author is able to tell you, and that in his own verse.

It were profane but to mention here in the preface those underheaded poets, retainers to seven shares and a half,[6] madrigal fellows, whose only business in verse it to rhyme a poor, six-penny soul, a suburb sinner, into hell. May such

arrogant pretenders to poetry vanish with their prodigious issue of tumorous heats and flashes of their adulterate brains, and forever after may this our poet fill up the better room of men. O, when the general arraignment of poets shall be to give an account of their higher souls, with what a triumphant brow shall our divine poet sit above and look down upon poor Homer, Vergil, Horace, Claudian, etc., who had amongst them the ill luck to talk out a great part of their gallant genius upon bees, dung, frogs, and gnats, etc., and not as himself here upon scriptures, divine graces, martyrs, and angels.[7]

STEPS TO THE TEMPLE   [1]*I dare…ground*: According to L. C. Martin, the power of levitation was not attributed to Pythagoras by the Neoplatonist Iambilicus (d. ca. 333) but to Iambilicus by the Greek sophist Eunapius (b. 347).
[2]Harmonies.   [3]George Herbert's (see pp. 201 ff).
[4]*Think ye…epithalamiums*: Although Augustine, when old, deplored his youthful enthusiasm for pagan poetry as an example of his "vanity" (*Confessions*, I.xiii.22), there is no record of his composing verse himself.
[5]*In position against Saurez*: contrary to the opinion of Francesco Suarez (1548–1617), famed Spanish Jesuit controversialist and casuist.
[6]Playwrights whose income derived from their *shares* of the receipts in popular theaters.
[7]*Homer…angels*: In addition to the *Batrachomyomachia* or "Battle of Frogs and Mice" traditionally attributed to Homer and the *Culex* or "Gnat" assigned to Vergil, the writer is perhaps thinking of Vergil's *Georgics* (which is in part concerned with bee-keeping),

Reader, we style his sacred poems "Steps to the Temple," and aptly, for in the temple of God, under His wing, he led his life in St. Mary's Church near St. Peter's College.[8] There he lodged under Tertullian's roof of angels;[9] there he made his nest more gladly than David's swallow near the house of God,[10] where, like a primitive saint, he offered more prayers in the night than others usually offer in the day; there he penned these poems, steps for happy souls to climb heaven by.

And those other of his pieces entitled "The Delights of the Muses," though of a more human mixture, are as sweet as they are innocent.

The praises that follow are but few of many that might be conferred on him: he was excellent in five languages (besides his mother tongue), vid. Hebrew, Greek, Latin, Italian, Spanish (the two last whereof he had little help in: they were of his own acquisition).

Amongst his other accomplishments in academic (as well pious as harmless) arts he made his skill in poetry, music, drawing, limning, graving—exercises of his curious invention and sudden fancy—to be but his subservient recreations for vacant hours, not the grand business of his soul.

To the former qualifications I might add that which would crown them all: his rare moderation in diet (almost Lessian[11] temperance). He never created a Muse out of distempers nor (with our canary[12] scribblers) cast any strange mists of surfeits before the intellectual beams of his mind or memory, the latter of which he was so much a master of that he had there, under lock and key in readiness, the richest treasures of the best Greek and Latin poets, some of which authors he had more at his command by heart than others that only read their works to retain little and understand less.

Enough, reader! I intend not a volume of praises larger than his book, nor need I longer transport thee to think over his vast perfections. I will conclude all that I have impartially writ of this learned young gentlemen—now dead to us[13]—as he himself doth, with the last line of his poem upon Bishop Andrewes' picture before his sermons:[14]

Verte paginas!
Look on his following leaves and see him breathe!

THE WEEPER[1]

Lo where a wounded heart with bleeding eyes conspire! Is she a flaming fountain or a weeping fire?

1
Hail, sister springs!
Parents of silver-forded[2] rills!
Ever bubbling things!
Thawing crystal! snowy hills,
Still spending, never spent! I mean
Thy fair eyes, sweet Magdalen!

2
Heavens thy fair eyes be;
Heavens of ever-falling stars.
'Tis seed-time still with thee,
And stars thou sow'st, whose harvest dares
Promise the earth to countershine[3]
Whatever makes heav'n's forehead fine.

3
But we are deceived all.
Stars indeed they are too true,
For they but seem to fall
As heav'n's other spangles do.
It is not for our earth and us
To shine in things so precious.

4
Upwards thou dost weep.
Heav'n's bosom drinks the gentle stream.
Where th' milky rivers creep,
Thine floats above and is the cream.
Waters above the heav'ns, what they be
We are taught best by thy tears and thee.

5
Every morn from hence
A brisk cherub something sips
Whose sacred influence
Adds sweetness to his sweetest lips.
Then to his music. And his song
Tastes of this breakfast all day long.

6
Not in the evening's eyes
When they red with weeping are
For the sun that dies,
Sits sorrow with a face so fair;
Nowhere but here did ever meet
Sweetness so sad, sadness so sweet.

---

some of Horace's satires, and the fragmentary *Gigantomachia* of Claudian.
[8]Little St. Mary's, a church adjoining Peterhouse, was used as the college chapel during part of Crashaw's time at Cambridge.
[9]The early Christian apologist Tertullian (160?–?230) speaks several times of angels in the church.
[10]*David's swallow...god*: "Yea, the sparrow hath found an house, and the swallow a nest for herself, where she may lay her young, even thine altars, O Lord of hosts, my king and my God" (Psalms 84.3).
[11]Referring to Léonard Leys or Lessius (d. 1623), a Dutch Jesuit whose treatise on health and continence (*Hygiasticon, seu vera ratio valetudinis bonae et vitae*) prompted Crashaw to write a poem entitled "In Praise of Lessius His Rule of Health."
[12]A sweet white wine from the Canary Islands.
[13]The fact that Crashaw did not die until 1649, three years after the first (1646) edition of *Steps to the Temple,* suggests that the unknown author of this preface was without certain knowledge of the poet's movements after his departure from England.
[14]*Poem...sermons*: For the text of this poem see p. 312.

THE WEEPER [1]I. e., Mary Magdalene, the penitent sinner of Luke 7.36–50, who became a devoted follower of Jesus, witnessed His crucifixion (Mark 15.40), and discovered His resurrection (Mark 16.1–11). My text is based on *Carmen Deo Nostro.*
[2]1652 reads *syluer-footed.* [3]Shine with equal brilliance.

7

When Sorrow would be seen
In her brightest majesty
(For she is a queen)
Then is she dress'd by none but thee.
Then, and only then, she wears
Her proudest pearls; I mean thy tears.

8

The dew no more will weep
The primrose's pale cheek to deck,
The dew no more will sleep
Nuzzl'd in the lily's neck;
Much rather would it be thy tear,
And leave them both to tremble here.

9

There's no need at all
That the balsam-sweating bough
So coyly should let fall
His med'cinable tears; for now
Nature hath learnt t' extract a dew
More sovereign[4] and sweet from you.

10

Yet let the poor drops weep,
(Weeping is the ease of woe)
Softly let them creep,
Sad that they are vanquish'd so.
They, though to others no relief,
Balsam may be for their own grief.

11

Such the maiden gem
By the purpling vine put on,
Peeps from her parent stem
And blushes at the bridegroom sun.
This wat'ry blossom of thy ey'n,[5]
Ripe, will make the richer wine.

12

When some new bright guest
Takes up among the stars a room,
And heav'n will make a feast,
Angels with crystal vials come
And draw from these full eyes of thine
Their master's water, their own wine.

13

Golden though he be,
Golden Tagus[6] murmurs though;
Were his way by thee,
Content and quiet he would go;
So much more rich would he esteem
Thy silver than his golden stream.

14

Well does the May that lies
Smiling in thy cheeks confess
The April in thine eyes.
Mutual sweetness they express:

No April e'er lent kinder show'rs.
Nor May returned more faithful[7] flow'rs.

15

O cheeks! Beds of chaste loves,
By your own showers seasonably dash'd,
Eyes! nests of milky doves
In your own wells decently wash'd,
O wit of love! that thus could place
Fountain and garden in one face.

16

O sweet contest of woes
With loves and tears and smiles disputing!
O fair and friendly foes,
Each other kissing and confuting!
While rain and sunshine, cheeks and eyes,
Close in kind contrarieties.

17

But can these fair floods be
Friends with the bosom[8] fires that fill thee?
Can so[9] great flames agree
Eternal tears should thus distill thee?
O floods, O fires! O suns, O show'rs!
Mixed and made friends by Love's sweet pow'rs.

18

'Twas his well-pointed dart
That digg'd these wells and dress'd this vine,
And taught that wounded heart
The way into these weeping ey'n.
Vain loves avaunt! bold hands forbear!
The lamb hath dipp'd his white foot here.

19

And now where'er he strays
Among the Galilean mountains
Or more unwelcome ways,
He's followed by two faithful fountains,
Two walking baths, two weeping motions,
Portable and compendious oceans.

20

O thou, thy Lord's fair store![10]
In thy so rich and large expenses,
Even when he show'd most poor,
He might provoke the wrath of princes.
What prince's wanton'st pride e'er could
Wash with silver, wipe with gold?

21

Who is that king but he
Who calls't[11] his crown to be call'd thine,
That thus can boast to be
Waited on by a wand'ring mine,

---

[4]Efficacious.   [5]Eyes.   [6]A river in Spain and Portugal.
[7]1646 reads *fairer*.   [8]Text *balsome*, but 1652 reads *bosom*.
[9]Text *Cause*, but 1652 reads *Can so*.   [10]Wealth.
[11]The text has a blank space here, but 1652 reads *calls't*.

A voluntary mint, that strows[12]
Warm silver showers where'er he goes!

22
O precious prodigal!
Fair spendthrift of thyself! thy measure
(Merciless love!) is all,
Even to thy last pearl in thy treasure.
All places, times, and objects be
Thy tear's sweet opportunity.

23
Does the day star rise?
Still thy stars do fall and fall.
Does day close his eyes?
Still the fountain weeps for all.
Let night or day do what they will,
Thou hast thy task; thou weepest still.

24
Does thy song lull the air?
Thy falling tears keep faithful time.
Does thy sweet-breath'd prayer
Up in clouds of incense climb?
Still at each sigh, that is, each stop,
A bead, that is, a tear, does drop.

25
At these thy weeping gates
(Watching their wat'ry motion),
Each winged moment waits,
Takes his tear, and gets him gone.
By thine eye's tinct ennobled thus,
Time lays him up; he's precious.

26
Not so long she lived,
Shall thy tomb report of thee;
But, so long she grieved:
Thus must we date thy memory.
Others by moments, months, and years
Measure their ages; thou, by tears.

27
So do perfumes expire,
So sigh tormented sweets, oppress'd
With proud unpitying fire.
Such tears the suff'ring rose that's vex'd
With ungentle flames does shed,
Sweating in a too warm bed.

28
Say, ye bright brothers,
The fugitive sons of those fair eyes,
Your fruitful mother's!
What make you here? what hopes can 'tice
You to be born? what cause can borrow
You from those nests of noble sorrow?

29
Whither away so fast?
For sure the sordid earth
Your sweetness cannot taste,
Nor does the dust deserve your birth.
Sweet, whither haste you then? O say
Why you trip so fast away?

30
We go not to seek
The darlings of Aurora's bed,
The rose's modest cheek,
Nor the violet's humble head,
Though the field's eyes too weepers be
Because they want such tears as we.

31
Much less mean we to trace
The fortune of inferior gems,
Preferr'd to some proud face
Or perch'd upon fear'd diadems.
Crown'd heads are toys. We go to meet
A worthy object, our Lord's feet.

THE TEAR

1
What bright soft thing is this,
Sweet Mary, thy fair eyes' expense?
A moist spark it is,
A wat'ry diamond; from whence
The very term, I think, was found,
The water of a diamond.

2
O 'tis not a tear,
'Tis a star about to drop
From thine eye its sphere;
The sun will stoop and take it up.
Proud will his sister[1] be to wear
This thine eyes' jewel in her ear.

3
O 'tis a tear,
Too true a tear; for no sad ey'n,
How sad soe'er,
Rain so true a tear as thine;
Each drop leaving a place so dear
Weeps for itself, is its own tear.

4
Such a pearl as this is
(Slipp'd from Aurora's dewy breast),
The rosebud's sweet lip kisses;
And such the rose itself when vex'd
With ungentle flames does shed,
Sweating in too warm a bed.

5
Such the maiden gem,[2]
By the wanton spring put on,

[12]Strews.
THE TEAR   [1]I.e., the sun.
[2]Presumably a flower, although the *Oxford English Dictionary* defines it only as "virginity."

Peeps from her parent stem
And blushes on the wat'ry sun:
This wat'ry blossom of thy ey'n,
Ripe, will make the richer wine.

6

Fair drop, why quak'st thou so?
'Cause thou straight must lay thy head
In the dust? O no!
The dust shall never be thy bed:
A pillow for thee will I bring,
Stuff'd with down of angel's wing.

7

Thus carried up on high,
(For to heaven thou must go)
Sweetly shalt thou lie,
And in soft slumbers bathe thy woe;
Till the singing orbs awake thee,
And one of their bright chorus make thee.

8

There thyself shalt be
An eye, but not a weeping one,
Yet I doubt of thee
Whether th' hadst rather there have shone
An eye of Heaven; or still shine here
In th' heaven of Marie's eye, a tear.

DIVINE EPIGRAMS

ON THE WATER OF OUR LORD'S BAPTISM

Each blest drop on each blest limb
Is wash'd itself in washing Him:
'Tis a gem while it stays here;
While it falls hence, 'tis a tear.

ACTS 8. ON THE BAPTIZED ETHIOPIAN.[1]

Let it no longer be a forlorn hope
  To wash an Ethiope:
He's wash'd: his gloomy skin a peaceful shade
  For his white soul is made;
And now, I doubt not, the eternal Dove   5
  A black-fac'd house will love.

ON THE STILL SURVIVING MARKS
OF OUR SAVIOUR'S WOUNDS

Whatever story of their cruelty,
Or nail or thorn or spear have writ in Thee
  Are in another sense
    Still legible;
Sweet is the difference: 5
  Once I did spell
Every red letter
  A wound of Thine,

Now (what is better)
  Balsam for mine.   10

TO PONTIUS WASHING HIS HANDS[2]

Why hands are wash'd, but O the water's spilt
  That labor'd to have wash'd thy guilt:
The flood, if any can, that can suffice
  Must have its fountain in thine eyes.

TO THE INFANT MARTYRS[3]

Go, smiling souls, your new-built cages break:
In heav'n you'll learn to sing ere here to speak,
Nor let the milky fonts that bathe your thirst
  Be your delay;
The place that calls you hence is at the worst   5
  Milk all the way.

ON THE MIRACLE OF THE LOAVES[4]

Now, Lord, or never they'll believe on Thee:
Thou to their teeth hast prov'd Thy deity.

UPON LAZARUS HIS TEARS[5]

Rich Lazarus! Richer in those gems, thy tears,
  Than Dives in the robes he wears:
He scorns them now, but O they'll suit full well
  With th' purple he must wear in hell.

TO OUR LORD UPON THE WATER MADE WINE[6]

Thou water turn'st to wine, fair friend of life;
  Thy foe, to cross the sweet arts of Thy reign,
Distills from thence the tears of wrath and strife,
  And so turns wine to water back again.

LUKE 11. BLESSED BE THE PAPS WHICH
THOU HAST SUCKED[7]

Suppose He had been tabled at thy teats,
  Thy hunger feels not what He eats.
He'll have His teat ere long (a bloody one);
  The mother then must suck the Son.

DIVINE EPIGRAMS [1]The story of the Apostle Philip and "a man of
Ethiopia" whom he baptized is related in Acts 8.26–39.
[2]Matthew 27.24.
[3]For Herod's slaughter of the innocents see Matthew 2.16.
[4]Matthew 14.15–21.
[5]For the parable of Dives and Lazarus see Luke 16.19–31.
[6]For the miracle of the wedding feast at Cana see John 2.1–11.
[7]"And it came to pass, as he spoke these things, a certain woman of
the company lifted up her voice, and said unto him, Blessed is the
womb that bore thee, and the paps which thou hast sucked. But
he said, Yea rather, blessed are they that hear the word of God,
and keep it" (Luke 11.27–28).

UPON THE INFANT MARTYRS

To see both blended in one flood,
The mother's milk, the children's blood,
Makes me doubt if heav'n will gather
Roses hence, or lilies rather.

LUKE 16. DIVES ASKING A DROP

A drop, one drop, how sweetly one fair drop
  Would tremble on my pearl-tipp'd fingers' top!
My wealth is gone, O go it where it will,
  Spare this one jewel, I'll be Dives still.

LUKE 7. SHE BEGAN TO WASH HIS FEET WITH TEARS AND WIPE THEM WITH THE HAIRS OF HER HEAD[8]

Her eyes' flood licks His feet's fair stain,
Her hair's flame licks up that again.
This flame thus quench'd hath brighter beams,
This flood thus stained, fairer streams.

ON OUR CRUCIFIED LORD, NAKED AND BLOODY

They have left Thee naked, Lord, O that they had!
  This garment too I would they had deni'd.
  Thee with thyself they have too richly clad,
  Opening the purple wardrobe of Thy side.
  O never could there be garment too good   5
  For Thee to wear but this of Thine own blood.

UPON EASTER DAY

1

Rise, heir of fresh eternity,
  From thy virgin tomb!
Rise, mighty man of wonders, and Thy world with Thee,
  Thy tomb, the universal east,
  Nature's new womb,
Thy tomb, fair immortality's perfumed nest.

2

Of all the glories make[1] noon gay
  This is the morn:
This rock buds forth the fountain of the streams of day.
  In joy's white annals lives this hour
  When life was born.
No cloud scowl on His radiant lids, no tempest low'r!

3

Life by this light's nativity
  All creatures have.
Death only by this day's just doom is forc'd to die;
  Nor is Death forc'd, for may he lie
  Thron'd in Thy grave:
Death will on this condition be content to die.

ON MASTER GEORGE HERBERT'S BOOK ENTITLED THE TEMPLE OF SACRED POEMS, SENT TO A GENTLEWOMAN

Know you, fair, on what you look;
Divinest love lies in this book:
Expecting fire from your eyes
To kindle this his sacrifice.
When your hands untie these strings,   5
Think you have an angel by the wings.
One that gladly will be nigh
To wait upon each morning sigh,
To flutter in the balmy air
Of your well-perfumed prayer.   10
These white plumes of his he'll lend you,
Which every day to Heaven will send you:
To take acquaintance of the sphere,
And all the smooth-fac'd kindred there.
And though Herbert's name do owe[1]   15
These devotions, fairest, know
That while I lay them on the shrine
Of your white hand, they are mine.

IN MEMORY OF THE VIRTUOUS AND LEARNED LADY MADRE DE TERESA, THAT SOUGHT AN EARLY MARTYRDOM[1]

Love, thou art absolute sole lord
Of life and death. To prove the word,
We'll now appeal to none of all
Those thy old soldiers, great and tall,
Ripe men of martyrdom, that could reach down   5
With strong arms their triumphant crown;
Such as could with lusty breath
Speak loud into the face of death
Their great Lord's glorious name; to none
Of those whose spacious bosoms spread a throne 10
For Love at large to fill: spare blood and sweat,
And see him take a private seat,
Making his mansion in the mild
And milky soul of a soft child.
  Scarce has she learnt to lisp the name   15
Of martyr, yet she thinks it shame
Life should so long play with that breath
Which, spent, can buy so brave a death.
She never undertook to know
What death with love should have to do;   20
Nor has she e'er yet understood
Why to show love, she should shed blood.
Yet though she cannot tell you why,

[8]Luke 7.38.
UPON EASTER DAY [1]That make.
HERBERT'S BOOK [1]Own
IN MEMORY [1]This poem and "The Flaming Heart" (p. 308),
Crashaw's two famous works on the Spanish mystic St. Theresa
(1515–1582), were inspired by *The Flaming Heart or the Life of the
Glorious S. Theresa* (1642), a translation of her autobiography.

She can love, and she can die.
    Scarce hath she blood enough to make   25
A guilty sword blush for her sake;
Yet hath she a heart dares hope to prove
How much less strong is death than love.
    Be love but there; let poor six years
Be pos'd with maturest fears   30
Man trembles at, you straight shall find
Love knows no nonage, nor the mind.
'Tis love, not years or limbs that can
Make the martyr or the man.
    Love touch'd her heart, and lo it beats   35
High and burns with such brave heats,
Such thirsts to die as dares drink up
A thousand cold deaths in one cup.
Good reason. For she breathes all fire.
Her weak breast heaves with strong desire   40
Of what she may with fruitless wishes
Seek for amongst her mother's kisses.
    Since 'tis not to be had at home
She'll travail for[2] a martyrdom.
No home for her confesses she   45
But where she may a martyr be.
    She'll to the Moors and try[3] with them
For this unvalued[4] diadem.
She'll offer them her dearest breath,
With Christ's name in't, in change for death.   50
She'll bargain with them; and will give
Them God; teach them how to live
In Him: or, if they this deny,
For Him she'll teach them how to die.
So shall she leave amongst them sown   55
Her Lord's blood; or at least her own.
    Farewell then, all the world! Adieu.
Teresa is no more for you.
Farewell all pleasures, sports, and joys
(Never till now esteemed toys),   60
Farewell whatever dear may be,
Mother's arms or father's knee;
Farewell house, and farewell home!
She's for the Moors, and martyrdom.
    Sweet, not so fast! Lo thy fair spouse   65
Whom thou seek'st with so swift vows,
Calls thee back, and bids thee come
T'embrace a milder martyrdom.
    Blest powers forbid thy tender life
Should bleed upon a barbarous knife;   70
Or some base hand have power to rase[5]
Thy breast's soft[6] cabinet, and uncase
A soul kept there so sweet, O no;
Wise Heaven will never have it so.
Thou art Love's victim; and must die   75
A death more mystical and high.
Into Love's arms thou shalt let fall
A still-surviving funeral.
His is the dart must make the death
Whose stroke shall taste thy hallow'd breath;[7]   80
A dart thrice dipp'd in that rich flame

Which writes thy spouse's radiant name
Upon the roof of heaven, where aye[8]
It shines, and with a sovereign ray
Beats bright upon the burning faces   85
Of souls which in that name's sweet graces
Find everlasting smiles. So rare,
So spiritual, pure, and fair
Must be th' immortal instrument
Upon whose choice point shall be sent   90
A life so lov'd; and that there be
Fit executioners for thee,
The fair'st and first-born sons of fire,
Blest seraphims, shall leave their choir
And turn Love's soldiers, upon thee   95
To exercise their archery.
    O how oft shalt thou complain
Of a sweet and subtile pain?
Of intolerable joys;
Of a death, in which who dies,   100
Loves his death, and dies again,
And would forever so be slain?
And lives, and dies; and knows not why
To live, but that he thus may never leave to die?
    How kindly will thy gentle heart   105
Kiss the sweetly-killing dart!
And close in thine[9] embraces keep
Those delicious wounds that weep
Balsam to heal themselves with. Thus
When these thy deaths, so numerous,   110
Shall all at last die into one,
And melt thy soul's sweet mansion;
Like a soft lump of incense, hasted
By too hot a fire, and wasted
Into perfuming clouds, so fast   115
Shalt thou exhale to heav'n at last
In a resolving sigh, and then,
O what? Ask not the tongues of men.
Angels cannot tell. Suffice,
Thyself shall feel thine own full joys   120
And hold them fast forever. There

[2]Both 1646 and 1652 read *to*.   [3]Both 1646 and 1652 read *trade*.
[4]Of inestimable value.   [5]Cut, slash.
[6]Both 1646 and 1652 read *chast*.
[7]*His is the dart . . . breathe*: In her autobiography, St. Theresa relates that in one of her mystic raptures she was visited by an angel ("not great, but rather little") who "had a long dart of gold in his hand; and at the end of the iron below methought there was a little fire; and I conceived that he thrust it some several times through my very heart after such a manner as that it passed the very inwards of my bowels; and when he drew it back methought it carried away as much as it had touched within me, and left all that which remained wholly inflamed with a great love of Almighty God. The pain of it was so excessive that it forced me to utter those groans; and the suavity which that extremity of pain gave was also so very excessive that there was no desiring at all to be rid of it; nor can the soul then receive any contentment at all in less than God Almighty himself." This famous episode is treated more fully in "The Flaming Heart" (p. 308).   [8]Always.
[9]Both 1646 and 1652 read *his*.

So soon as thou shalt first appear,
The moon of maiden stars, thy white
Mistress, attended by such bright
Souls as thy shining self, shall come   125
And in her first ranks make thee room,
Where 'mongst her snowy family
Immortal welcomes wait for thee.
    O what delight, when reveal'd life shall stand
And teach thy lips heav'n with her[10] hand;   130
On which thou now may'st to thy wishes
Heap up thy consecrated kisses.
What joys shall seize thy soul, when she,
Bending her blessed eyes on thee
(Those second smiles of heaven), shall dart   135
Her mild rays through thy melting heart!
    Angels, thy old friends, there shall greet thee,
Glad at their own home now to meet thee.
    All thy good works which went before
And waited for thee at the door,   140
Shall own thee there; and all in one
Weave a constellation
Of crowns, with which the King thy Spouse
Shall build up thy triumphant brows.
    All thy old woes shall now smile on thee   145
And thy pains sit bright upon thee.
All thy sorrows here shall shine,
All thy suff'rings be divine.
Tears shall take comfort and turn gems,
And wrongs repent to diadems.   150
Ev'n thy deaths shall live and new
Dress the soul that erst they slew.
Thy wounds shall blush to such bright scars
As keep account of the Lamb's wars.
    Those rare works where thou shalt leave writ 155
Love's noble history, with wit
Taught thee by none but Him, while here
They feed our souls, shall clothe thine there.
Each heav'nly word by whose hid flame
Our hard hearts shall strike fire, the same   160
Shall flourish on thy brows, and be
Both fire to us and flame to thee;
Whose light shall live bright in thy face
By glory, in our hearts by grace.
    Thou shalt look round about, and see   165
Thousands of crown'd souls throng to be
Themselves thy crown. Sons of thy vows,
The virgin-births with which thy sovereign Spouse
Made fruitful thy fair soul, go now
And with them all about thee bow   170
To Him. "Put on" (He'll say), "put on
(My rosy love) that, thy rich zone,[11]
Sparkling with sacred flames
Of thousand souls, whose happy names
Heaven keeps upon thy score." Thy bright   175
Life brought them first to kiss the light
That kindled them to stars, and so
Thou with the Lamb, thy Lord, shalt go;
And wheresoe'er He sets His white

Steps, walk with Him those ways of light   180
Which who in death would live to see,
Must learn in life to die like thee.

THE FLAMING HEART[1]
Upon the Book and Picture of Teresa as She Is
Usually Expressed with a Seraphim beside Her

Well-meaning readers, you that come as friends
And catch the precious name this piece pretends,[2]
Make not too much haste to admire
That fair-cheek'd fallacy of fire.
That is a seraphim, they say,   5
And this the great Teresia.
Readers, be rul'd by me, and make
Here a well-plac'd and wise mistake;
You must transpose the picture quite,
And spell it wrong to read it right;   10
Read *him* for *her* and *her* for *him*;
And call the *saint* the *seraphim*.
    Painter, what didst thou understand,
To put her dart into his hand?
See, even the years and size of him   15
Shows this the mother seraphim.
This is the mistress-flame; and duteous he
Her happy fireworks, here, comes down to see.
O most poor-spirited of men!
Had thy cold pencil kiss'd her pen,   20
Thou couldst not so unkindly err
To show us this faint shade for her.
Why man, this speaks pure mortal frame;
And mocks with female frost love's manly flame.
One would suspect thou meant'st to paint   25
Some weak, inferior, woman saint.
But had thy pale-fac'd purple took
Fire from the burning cheeks of that bright book,
Thou wouldst on her have heap'd up all
That could be form'd[3] seraphical;   30
Whate'er[4] this youth of fire wears fair,
Rosy fingers, radiant hair,
Glowing cheek, and glist'ring wings,
All those fair and flagrant[5] things,
But before all that fiery dart   35
Had fill'd the hand of this great heart.
    Do then as equal right requires,
Since his the blushes be, and hers the fires,
Resume and rectify thy rude design;
Undress thy seraphim into mine.   40
Redeem this injury of thy art;
Give him the veil, give her the dart.
    Give him the veil, that he may cover
The red cheeks of a rival'd lover,
Asham'd that our world now can show   45

---

[10]1652 reads *his*. [11]Belt, girdle.
THE FLAMING HEART [1]For the significance of the title see p. 307,
n. 7. *Expressed*: portrayed. [2]Presents. [3]1652 reads *found*.
[4]Text *But e're*, but 1652 reads *What e're*. [5]Flaming.

Nests of new seraphims here below.
    Give her the dart, for it is she
(Fair youth) shoots both thy shaft and thee.
Say, all ye wise and well-pierc'd hearts
That live and die amidst her darts,   50
What is 't your tasteful spirits do prove
In that rare life of her, and love?
Say and bear witness. Sends she not
A seraphim at every shot?
What magazines[6] of immortal arms there shine!   55
Heav'n's great artillery in each love-spun line.
Give, then, the dart to her who gives the flame;
Give him the veil, who kindly takes the shame.
    But if it be the frequent fate
Of worse faults to be fortunate;   60
If all's prescription;[7] and proud wrong
Harkens not to an humble song;
For all the gallantry of him,
Give me the suff'ring seraphim.
His be the bravery[8] of all those bright things,   65
The glowing cheeks, the glittering[9] wings;
The rosy hand, the radiant dart;
Leave her alone the flaming heart.
    Leave her that; and thou shalt leave her
Not one loose shaft, but love's whole quiver.   70
For in love's field was never found
A nobler weapon than a wound.
Love's passives are his activ'st part.
The wounded is the wounding heart.
O heart! the equal poise[10] of love's both parts,   75
Big alike with wounds and darts,
Live in these conquering leaves; live all the same,
And walk through all tongues one triumphant flame;
Live here, great heart, and love and die and kill.
And bleed and wound, and yield and conquer still.   80
Let this immortal life, where'er it comes,
Walk in a crowd of loves and martyrdoms.
Let mystic deaths wait on 't, and wise souls be
The love-slain witnesses of this life of thee.
O sweet incendiary! show here thy art,   85
Upon this carcass of a hard, cold heart;
Let all thy scatter'd shafts of light, that play
Among the leaves of thy large books of day,
Combin'd against this breast, at once break in
And take away from me myself and sin!   90
This gracious robbery shall thy bounty be,
And my best fortunes such fair spoils of me.
O thou undaunted daughter of desires!
By all thy dow'r of lights and fires;
By all the eagle in thee, all the dove;   95
By all thy lives and deaths of love;
By thy large draughts of intellectual day,
And by thy thrists[11] of love more large than they;
By all thy brim-fill'd bowls of fierce desire,
By thy last morning's draught of liquid fire;   100
By the full kingdom of that final kiss
That seiz'd thy parting soul, and seal'd thee His;
By all the heav'ns thou hast in Him,

Fair sister of the seraphim,
By all of Him we have in thee,   105
Leave nothing of myself in me!
Let me so read thy life that I
Unto all life of mine may die![12]

AN APOLOGY FOR THE PRECEDENT
HYMNS ON TERESA[1]

Thus have I back again to thy bright name,
Fair flood of holy fires, transfus'd the flame
I took from reading thee. 'Tis to thy wrong,
I know, that in my weak and worthless song
Thou here art set to shine where thy full day   5
Scarce dawns. O pardon if I dare to say
Thine own dear books are guilty, for from thence
I learn'd to know that love is eloquence.
That hopeful maxim gave me heart to try
If—what to other tongues is tun'd so high—   10
Thy praise might not speak English too. Forbid,
By all thy mysteries that here lie hid,
Forbid it, mighty Love! Let no fond[2] hate
Of names and words so far prejudicate.[3]
Souls are not Spaniards too: one friendly flood   15
Of baptism blends them all into a blood.
Christ's faith makes but one body of all souls,
And Love's that body's soul. No law controls
Our free traffic for heav'n: we may maintain
Peace, sure, with piety, though it come from Spain.   20
What souls soe'er, in any language, can
Speak heav'n like hers is my soul's countryman.
O 'tis not Spanish, but 'tis heav'n she speaks!
'Tis heav'n that lies in ambush there, and breaks
From thence into the wond'ring reader's breast,   25
Who feels his warm heart hatch'd into a nest
Of little eagles and young loves, whose high
Flights scorn the lazy dust, and things that die.
There are enow whose draughts (as deep as hell)
Drink up all Spain in sack.[4] Let my soul swell   30
With thee, strong wine of love! Let others swim
In puddles: we will pledge this seraphim
Bowls full of richer blood than blush of grape
Was ever guilty of. Change we too our shape,

[6]Armories.
[7]I.e., a title or right sanctioned by custom and convention.
[8]Splendor. [9]1652 reads *glistering*. [10]Weight, balance.
[11]Thirsts.
[12]*O sweet incendiary...may die*: This coda—the most famous passage in Crashaw's works—was added in 1652.
AN APOLOGY [1]First printed in 1646 following "In Memory of the Virtuous and Learned Lady Madre de Theresa" (p. 306) as "An Apology for the Precedent Hymn," this poem was reprinted in 1648 following both works on St. Theresa (with the necessary change from "Hymne" to "Hymnes"). In 1652 it was again affixed to the first hymn with the title "An Apologie. For the Foregoing Hymne as having been writt when the author was yet among the protestantes."
[2]Foolish. [3]Prejudice in advance. [4]A Spanish wine.

My soul! Some drink from men to beasts; O then   35
Drink we till we prove more, not less, than men,
And turn not beasts, but angels. Let the king
Me ever into these his cellars bring
Where flows such wine as we can have of none
But Him who trod the wine-press all alone:⁵   40
Wine of youth, life, and the sweet deaths of love,
Wine of immortal mixture which can prove
Its tincture from the rosy nectar, wine
That can exalt weak earth, and so refine
Our dust that at one draught mortality   45
May drink itself up, and forget to die.

CHARITAS NIMIA,¹ OR THE DEAR BARGAIN

    Lord, what is man?² why should he cost thee
So dear? what had his ruin lost thee?
Lord, what is man that Thou hast overbought
       So much a thing of nought?

    Love is too kind, I see, and can   5
Make but a simple merchant man.
'Twas for such sorry merchandise
Bold painters have put out his eyes.³

    Alas, sweet lord, what wer't to Thee
If there were no such worms as we?   10
Heav'n ne'er the less still heav'n would be,
       Should mankind dwell
       In the deep hell.
What have his woes to do with Thee?

       Let him go weep   15
       O'er his own wounds;
       Seraphims will not sleep
Nor spheres let fall their faithful rounds.

    Still would the youthful spirits sing;
And still Thy spacious palace ring.   20
Still would those beauteous ministers of light
       Burn all as bright,

    And bow their flaming heads before Thee;
Still thrones and dominations⁴ would adore Thee,
Still would those ever-wakeful sons of fire   25
       Keep warm Thy praise
       Both nights and days,
And teach Thy lov'd name to their noble lyre.

    Let froward⁵ dust, then, do its kind,⁶
And give itself for sport to the proud wind.   30
Why should a piece of peevish clay plead shares
In the eternity of Thy old cares?

Why shouldst Thou bow Thy awful breast to see
What mine own madnesses have done with me?

    Should not the king still keep his throne   35
Because some desperate fool's undone?
Or will the world's illustrious⁷ eyes
Weep for every worm that dies?

       Will the gallant sun
       E'er the less glorious run?   40
Will he hang down his golden head
Or e'er the sooner seek his western bed
       Because some foolish fly
       Grows wanton, and will die?

    If I was lost in misery,   45
What was it to thy heav'n and Thee?
What was it to thy precious blood
If my foul heart call'd for a flood?

    What if my faithless soul and I
       Would needs fall in   50
       With guilt and sin,
What did the Lamb, that He should die?
What did the Lamb, that He should need,
When the wolf sins, himself to bleed?

       If my base lust   55
Bargain'd with death and well-beseeming dust
       Why should the white
       Lamb's bosom write
       The purple name
       Of my sin's shame?   60

    Why should His unstain'd breast make good
My blushes with his own heart-blood?

    O my Saviour, make me see
How dearly Thou hast paid for me,

    That lost again, my life may prove   65
As then in death, so now in love.

THE DELIGHTS OF THE MUSES

MUSIC'S DUEL

Now westward Sol¹ had spent the richest beams
Of noon's high glory, when hard by the streams
Of Tiber,² on the scene of a green plat,³
Under protection of an oak, there sat
A sweet lute's-master in whose gentle airs   5
He lost the day's heat and his own hot cares.
    Close in the covert of the leaves there stood
A nightingale, come from the neighboring wood:
(The sweet inhabitant of each glad tree,
Their muse, their siren, harmless siren she)   10

⁵*But him...alone*: "I have trodden the winepress alone" (Isaiah 63.3).
CHARITAS NIMIA   ¹"Excessive love."
²*Lord...man*: "What is man, that thou art mindful of him? And the son of man, that thou visitest him?" (Psalms 8.4).
³Love (or Cupid) is often depicted as blind.
⁴*Thrones and dominations*: Two of the nine orders of angels (lower in rank than seraphim and cherubim).   ⁵Refractory.
⁶Fulfill its natural function.   ⁷1) Luminous; 2) distinguished.
MUSIC'S DUEL   ¹The sun.
²A river in Italy that flows through Rome.   ³Level place.

There stood she list'ning, and did entertain
The music's soft report and mold the same
In her own murmurs, that whatever mood
His curious fingers lent, her voice made good.
The man perceiv'd his rival and her art,   15
Dispos'd to give the light-foot lady sport
Awakes his lute, and 'gainst the fight to come
Informs it, in a sweet *praeludium*,[4]
Of closer strains, and ere the war begin,
He lightly skirmishes on every string   20
Charg'd with a flying touch; and straightway she
Carves out her dainty voice as readily
Into a thousand sweet distinguish'd tones.
And reckons up in soft divisions
Quick volumes of wild notes to let him know,   25
By that shrill taste, she could do something too.
  His nimble hands instinct[5] then taught each string
A cap'ring cheerfulness and made them sing
To their own dance; now negligently rash
He throws his arm, and with a long drawn dash   30
Blends all together, then distinctly trips
From this to that, then quick returning skips
And snatches this again, and pauses there.
She measures every measure, everywhere
Meets art with art; sometimes as if in doubt   35
Not perfect yet, and fearing to be out,[6]
Trails her plain ditty in one long-spun note
Through the sleek passage of her open throat:
A clear, unwrinkled song, then doth she point it
With tender accents, and severely joint it   40
By short diminutives, that being rear'd
In controverting warbles evenly shar'd,
With her sweet self she wrangles; he, amazed
That from so small a channel should be rais'd
The torrent of a voice, whose melody   45
Could melt into such sweet variety,
Strains higher yet; that, tickled with rare art,
The tattling strings (each breathing in his part)
Most kindly do fall out: the grumbling bass
In surly groans disdains the treble's grace.   50
The high-perch'd treble chirps at this and chides
Until his finger (moderator)[7] hides
And closes the sweet quarrel, rousing all
Hoarse, shrill, at once; as when the trumpets call
Hot Mars to th' harvest of death's field, and woo   55
Men's hearts into their hands; this lesson too
She gives him back; her supple breast thrills out
Sharp airs, and staggers in a warbling doubt
Of dallying sweetness, hovers o'er her skill,
And folds in wav'd notes with a trembling bill,   60
The pliant series of her slippery song.
Then starts she suddenly into a throng
Of short thick sobs, whose thund'ring volleys float
And roll themselves over her lubric[8] throat
In panting murmurs, still'd[9] out of her breast,   65
That ever-bubbling spring; the sug'red nest
Of her delicious soul, that there does lie
Bathing in streams of liquid melody;

Music's best seed plot, when in ripen'd airs
A gold-headed harvest fairly rears   70
His honey-dropping tops, plow'd by her breath
Which there reciprocally laboreth
In that sweet soil. It seems a holy quire[10]
Founded to th' name of great Apollo's lyre.
Whose silver roof rings with the sprightly notes   75
Of sweet-lipp'd angel imps, that swill their throats
In cream of morning Helicon, and then
Prefer[11] soft anthems to the ears of men,
To woo them from their beds, still murmuring
That men can sleep while they their matins sing   80
(Most divine service), whose so early lay
Prevents the eyelids of the blushing day.
There you might hear her kindle her soft voice
In the close murmur of a sparkling noise,
And lay the groundwork of her hopeful song,   85
Still keeping in the forward stream so long
Till a sweet whirlwind (striving to get out)
Heaves her soft bosom, wanders round about,
And makes a pretty earthquake in her breast,
Till the fledg'd[12] notes at length forsake their nest;   90
Fluttering in wanton shoals, and to the sky,
Wing'd with their own wild echoes, prattling fly.
She opes the floodgate, and lets loose a tide
Of streaming sweetness, which in state doth ride
On the wav'd back of every swelling strain,   95
Rising and falling in a pompous train.
And while she thus discharges a shrill peal
Of flashing airs, she qualifies their zeal
With the cool epode of a graver note,
Thus high, thus low, as if her silver throat   100
Would reach the brazen voice of war's hoarse bird;
Her little soul is ravish'd: and so pour'd
Into loose ecstasies that she is plac'd
Above herself, music's enthusiast.[13]
  Shame now and anger mix'd a double stain   105
In the musician's face. "Yet once again,
Mistress, I come; now reach a strain, my lute,
Above her mock, or be forever mute.
Or tune a song of victory to me,
Or to thyself sing thine own obsequy."   110
So said, his hands sprightly as fire he flings,
And with a quavering coyness tastes the strings.
The sweet-lipp'd sisters[14] musically frighted,
Singing their fears are fearfully delighted.
Trembling as when Apollo's golden hairs   115
Are fann'd and frizzled in the wanton airs
Of his own breath: which, married to his lyre,
Doth tune the spheres, and make heaven's self look higher.
From this to that, from that to this he flies,
Feels Music's pulse in all her arteries,   120
Caught in a net which there Apollo spreads,

[4]Musical introduction. [5]Impelled, excited. [6]At fault.
[7]Conductor (of the music). [8]Slippery. [9]Distilled. [10]Choir.
[11]Present. [12]Feathered, i.e., fully formed. [13]Text *Enthusiasts*.
[14]I.e., Polyhymnia and Euterpe, the Muses of sacred lyric and music
respectively.

His fingers struggle with the vocal threads.
Following those little rills, he sinks into
A sea of Helicon; his hand does go
Those parts of sweetness, which with nectar drop,   125
Softer than that which pants in Hebe's cup.
The humorous strings expound his learned touch
By various glosses; now they seem to grutch[15]
And murmur in a buzzing din, then jingle
In shrill-tongu'd accents: striving to be single.   130
Every smooth turn, every delicious stroke
Gives life to some new grace; thus doth h' invoke
Sweetness by all her names; thus, bravely thus
(Fraught with a fury so harmonious),
The lute's light genius now does proudly rise,   135
Heav'd on the surges of swoll'n rhapsodies.
Whose flourish (meteor-like) doth curl the air
With flash of high-borne fancies: here and there
Dancing in lofty measures, and anon
Creeps on the soft touch of a tender tone,   140
Whose trembling murmurs, melting in wild airs,
Runs to and fro, complaining his sweet cares
Because those precious mysteries that dwell
In music's ravish'd soul he dare not tell,
But whisper to the world: thus do they vary   145
Each string his note, as if they meant to carry
Their master's blest soul (snatch'd out at his ears
By a strong ecstasy) through all the spheres
Of Music's heaven; and seat it there on high
In th' empyreum of pure harmony.   150
At length (after so long, so loud a strife
Of all the strings, still breathing the best life
Of blest variety attending on
His finger's fairest revolution
In many a sweet rise, many as sweet a fall)   155
A full-mouth diapason swallows all.
  This done, he lists what she would say to this,
And she although her breath's late exercise
Had dealt too roughly with her tender throat,
Yet summons all her sweet powers for a note   160
Alas! in vain! for while (sweet soul) she tries
To measure all those wild diversities
Of chatt'ring strings by the small size of one
Poor simple voice, rais'd in a natural tone,
She fails, and failing grieves, and grieving dies.   165
She dies; and leaves her life the victor's prize,
Falling upon his lute. O fit to have
(That liv'd so sweetly) dead, so sweet a grave!

UPON BISHOP ANDREWES HIS PICTURE
BEFORE HIS SERMONS[1]

This reverend shadow cast that setting sun
Whose glorious course, through our horizon run,
Left the dim face of this dull hemisphere
All one great eye, all drown'd in one great tear,
Whose fair, illustrious soul led his free thought   5
Through learning's universe and vainly sought

Room for her spacious self, until at length
She found the way home, with an holy strength
Snatch'd herself hence to heaven, fill'd a bright place
'Mongst those immortal fires, and on the face   10
Of her great Maker fix'd her flaming eye,
There still to read true, pure divinity.
And now that grave aspect hath design'd to shrink
Into this less appearance. If you think
'Tis but a dead face art doth here bequeath,   15
Look on the following leaves, and see him breathe.

AN EPITAPH UPON A YOUNG MARRIED COUPLE,
DEAD AND BURIED TOGETHER

To these, whom Death again did wed,
This grave's their second marriage bed,
For though the hand of fate could force
'Twixt soul and body a divorce
It could not sunder man and wife,   5
'Cause they both lived but one life.
Peace, good reader, do not weep;
Peace, the lovers are asleep.
They, sweet turtles,[1] folded lie
In the last knot Love could tie;   10
And though they lie as they were dead,
Their pillow stone, their sheets of lead
(Pillow hard and sheets not warm),
Love made the bed: they'll take no harm.
Let them sleep, let them sleep on,   15
Till this stormy night be gone,
And the eternal morrow dawn;
Then the curtains will be drawn
And they wake into that light
Whose day shall never die in night.   20

UPON FORD'S TWO TRAGEDIES, "LOVE'S
SACRIFICE" AND "THE BROKEN HEART"[1]

Thou cheat'st us, Ford, mak'st one seem two by art:
What is *Love's Sacrifice* but *The Broken Heart?*

ON MARRIAGE

I would be married, but I'd have no wife:
I would be married to a single life.

OUT OF CATULLUS[1]

Come and let us live, my dear,
Let us love and never fear

[15]Grumble.

UPON BISHOP ANDREWES [1]This eulogy of Lancelot Andrewes (1555–1626), bishop of Winchester and formerly master of Pembroke College, was first printed in the second (1631) edition of that famous preacher's *XCVI Sermons* (for which see pp. 518 ff.).
AN EPITAPH [1]Turtledoves.
UPON FORD'S TRAGEDIES [1]The two famous tragedies of John Ford were published in 1633.
OUT OF CATULLUS [1]Catullus, Carmen V (*Vivamus, mea Lesbia,*

What the sourest fathers say.
Brightest Sol, that dies Today,
Lives again as blithe tomorrow,   5
But if we, dark sons of sorrow,
Set, O then how long a night
Shuts the eyes of our short light!
Then let amorous kisses dwell
On our lips! Begin and tell   10
A thousand and a hundred score,
An hundred and a thousand more,
Till another thousand smother
That, and that wipe off another.
Thus at last when we have numb'red   15
Many a thousand, many a hundred,
We'll confound the reckoning quite,
And lose ourselves in wild delight,
While our joys so multiply
As shall mock the envious eye.   20

WISHES TO HIS (SUPPOSED)[1] MISTRESS

Whoe'er she be,
That not impossible she
That shall command my heart and me;

Where'er she lie,
Lock'd up from mortal eye,   5
In shady leaves of destiny;

Till that ripe birth
Of studied fate stand forth,
And teach her fair steps to our earth;

Till that divine   10
Idea[2] take a shrine
Of crystal flesh through which to shine,

Meet you her, my wishes,
Bespeak her to my blisses,
And be ye call'd my absent kisses.   15

I wish her beauty
That owes not all his duty
To gaudy tire[3] or glist'ring shoe-tie.

Something more than
Taffeta or tissue can,   20
Or rampant feather, or rich fan.

More than the spoil
Of shop or silkworm's toil
Or a bought blush or a set smile.

A face that's best   25
By its own beauty drest
And can alone command the rest.

A face made up
Out of no other shop
Than what Nature's white hand sets ope.   30

A cheek where youth
And blood, with pen of truth,
Write what the reader sweetly ru'th.

A cheek where grows
More than a morning rose: 35
Which to no box[4] his being owes.

Lips where all day
A lover's kiss may play,
Yet carry nothing thence away.

Looks that oppress   40
Their richest tires, but dress
And clothe their simplest nakedness.

Eyes that displaces
The neighbor diamond, and outfaces
That sunshine by their own sweet graces.   45

Tresses that wear
Jewels but to declare
How much themselves more precious are,

Whose native ray
Can tame the wanton day   50
Of gems that in their bright shades play.

Each ruby there,
Or pearl that dare appear,
Be its own blush, be its own tear.

A well-tam'd heart,   55
For whose more noble smart
Love may be long choosing a dart.

Eyes that bestow
Full quivers on Love's bow,
Yet pay less arrows than they owe.   60

Smiles that can warm
The blood, yet teach a charm,
That Chastity shall take no harm.

Blushes that bin[5]
The burnish of no sin,   65
Nor flames of ought too hot within.

Joys that confess
Virtue their mistress,
And have no other head to dress.

Fears fond and flight[6]   70
As the coy bride's when night
First does the longing lover right.[7]

Tears quickly fled
And vain as those are[8] shed
For a dying maidenhead.   75

Days that need borrow
No part of their good morrow
From a forespent night of sorrow.

atque amemus).
WISHES TO HIS MISTRESS [1]Imagined.
[2]The Platonic idea of womanhood (which is imperfectly represented by actual women). [3]Attire. [4]I.e., box of cosmetics.
[5]Been, i.e., are. [6]Foolish and volatile. [7]Sanction.
[8]Those that are.

Days that in spite
Of darkness, by the light   80
Of a clear mind are day all night.

Nights, sweet as they,
Made short by lovers' play
Yet long by th' absence of the day.

Life that dares send   85
A challenge to his end,
And when it comes say, "Welcome friend."

Sydnean[9] showers
Of sweet discourse, whose powers
Can crown old Winter's head with flowers,   90

Soft silken hours,
Open suns, shady bowers;
'Bove all, nothing within that lowers.

Whate'er delight
Can make day's forehead bright,   95
Or give down to the wings of night.

In her whose frame,
Have Nature all the name,
Art and ornament the shame.

Her flattery,   100
Picture and poesy,
Her counsel her own virtue be.

I wish her store
Of worth may leave her poor
Of wishes; and I wish—no more.   105

Now if Time knows
That her whose radiant brows
Weave them a garland of my vows;

Her whose just bays
My future hopes can raise   110
A trophy to her present praise;

Her that dares be
What these lines wish to see:
I seek no further: it is she.

'Tis she, and here   115
Lo! I unclothe and clear
My wishes' cloudy character.[10]

May she enjoy it
Whose merit dare apply it
But modesty dares still deny it.   120

Such worth as this is
Shall fix my flying wishes,
And determine them to kisses.

Let her full glory,
My fancies, fly before ye.   125
Be ye my fictions, but her story.

[9]In the style of Sir Philip Sidney.
[10]Indistinct and imperfect depiction.

from Carmen Deo Nostro (1652)

TO THE NOBLEST AND BEST OF LADIES
THE COUNTESS OF DENBIGH[1]
*Persuading her to Resolution in Religion, and to
Render Herself without Further Delay into the
Communion of the Catholic Church*

What heav'n-entreated heart[2] is this
Stands trembling at the gate of bliss?
Holds fast the door, yet dares not venture
Fairly to open it, and enter?
Whose definition is a doubt   5
'Twixt life and death, 'twixt in and out?
Say, lingering fair, why comes the birth
Of your brave soul so slowly forth?
Plead your pretenses (O you strong
In weakness!) why you choose so long   10
In labor of yourself to lie,
Nor daring quite to live nor die.
Ah linger not, lov'd soul! A slow
And late consent was a long *no,*
Who grants at last, long time tri'd   15

And did his best to have deni'd.
What magic bolts, what mystic bars
Maintain the will in these strange wars!
What fatal yet fantastic bands
Keep the free heart from its own hands!   20
So when the year takes cold, we see
Poor waters their own prisoners be.
Fetter'd and lock'd up fast they lie
In a sad self-captivity.
Th'astonish'd nymphs their flood's strange fate deplore,   25

TO THE NOBLEST [1]Susan Villiers, a sister of the powerful duke of
Buckingham (see p. 754) who married William Feilding (d. 1643),
first earl of Denbigh. As first lady of the bedchamber to Queen
Henrietta Maria, she accompanied her royal mistress to France,
where she was converted to Roman Catholicism and as a con-
sequence suffered the sequestration of her property (1651) by
Cromwell's Council of State. *Carmen Deo Nostro,* the posthumous
collection of her protégé Crashaw's religious poetry, was dedicated
to her in 1652.
[2]In the 1652 edition this poem was preceded by an emblem of a
padlocked heart.

To see themselves their own severer shore.
Thou that alone canst thaw this cold
And fetch the heart from its stronghold,
Almighty Love! end this long war,
And of a meteor make a star.   30
O fix this fair indefinite,
And 'mongst thy shafts of sovereign light
Choose out that sure decisive dart
Which has the key of this close heart,
Knows all the corners of't, and can control   35
The self-shut cabinet[3] of an unsearch'd soul.
O let it be at last love's hour.
Raise this tall trophy of thy pow'r;
Come once the conquering way, not to confute
But kill this rebel-word, *irresolute,*   40
That so, in spite of all this peevish strength
Of weakness, she may write *Resolv'd at length.*
Unfold at length, unfold, fair flow'r
And use the season of love's show'r,
Meet his well-meaning wounds, wise heart!   45
And haste to drink the wholesome dart,
That healing shaft, which heaven till now
Hath in love's quiver hid for you.
O, dart of love! Arrow of light!
O happy you, if it hit right;   50
It must not fall in vain: it must
Not mark the dry, regardless dust.
Fair one, it is your fate; and brings
Eternal worlds upon its wings.
Meet it with widespread arms, and see   55
Its seat your soul's just center be.
Disband dull fears; give faith the day.
To save your life, kill your delay.
It is love's siege; and sure to be
Your triumph, though his victory.   60
'Tis cowardice that keeps this field
And want of courage not to yield.
Yield then, O yield, that love may win
The fort at last, and let life in.
Yield quickly, lest perhaps you prove   65
Death's prey before the prize of love.
This fort of your fair self, if't be not won,
He is repuls'd indeed; but you are undone.

IN THE HOLY NATIVITY OF OUR LORD GOD
A Hymn Sung as by the Shepherds[1]

Chorus:
Come, we shepherds whose blest sight
Hath met love's noon in nature's night;
Come, lift we up our loftier song
And wake the sun that lies too long.

To all our world of well-stol'n joy   5
    He slept, and drempt of no such thing,
While we found out heav'n's fairer eye,
    And kiss'd the cradle of our King.
Tell him he rises now too late
To show us aught worth looking at.   10

Tell him we now can show him more
    Than he e'er show'd to mortal sight,
Than he himself e'er saw before,
    Which to be seen needs not his light.
Tell him, Tityrus, where th' hast been;   15
Tell him, Thyrsis, what th' hast seen.

Tityrus:
Gloomy night embrac'd the place
    Where the noble Infant lay;
The Babe look'd up and show'd His face:
    In spite of darkness, it was day.   20
It was Thy day, Sweet, and did rise
Not from the east, but from Thine eyes.

    Chorus: It was Thy day, Sweet, [etc.]

Thyrsis:
Winter chid aloud, and sent
    The angry north to wage his wars;   25
The north forgot his fierce intent,
    And left perfumes instead of scars.
By those sweet eyes' persuasive pow'rs,
Where he meant frost, he scatter'd flow'rs.

    Chorus: By those sweet eyes' [etc.]   30

Both:
We saw Thee in Thy balmy nest,
    Young Dawn of our eternal day!
We saw Thine eyes break from their east
    And chase the trembling shades away.
We saw Thee, and we bless'd the sight;   35
We saw Thee by Thine own sweet light.

Tityrus:
"Poor world," said I, "what wilt thou do
    To entertain this starry stranger?
Is this the best thou canst bestow,
    A cold and not too cleanly manger?   40
Contend, the powers of heav'n and earth,
To fit a bed for this huge birth!"

    Chorus: Contend, the powers [etc.]

Thyrsis:
"Proud world," said I, "cease your contest,
    And let the mighty Babe alone—   45
The phoenix builds the phoenix' nest,
    Love's architecture is His own;
The Babe whose birth embraves[2] this morn
Made His own bed ere He was born."

    Chorus: The Babe whose [etc.]   50

[3]Private room.

IN THE HOLY NATIVITY   [1]Accompanying the final (1652) version of
this poem (which had been included in the 1646 and 1648 editions)
is a woodcut depicting the shepherds' adoration of the new-born
Christ.   [2]Adorns.

Tityrus:
I saw the curl'd drops, soft and slow,
   Come hovering o'er the place's head,
Off'ring their whitest sheets of snow
   To furnish the fair Infant's bed.
"Forbear," said I, "be not too bold;   55
Your fleece is white, but 'tis too cold."

   Chorus: "Forbear," said I, [etc.]

Thyrsis:
I saw the obsequious[3] seraphims
   Their rosy fleece of fire bestow;
For well they now can spare their wings,   60
   Since heav'n itself lies here below.
"Well done," said I, "but are you sure
Your down so warm will pass for pure?"

   Chorus: "Well done," said I, [etc.]

Tityrus:
No, no, your King's not yet to seek   65
   Where to repose His royal head;
See, see, how soon His new-bloom'd cheek
   'Twixt mother's breasts is gone to bed.
"Sweet choice!" said we, "no way but so,
Not to lie cold, yet sleep in snow."   70

   Chorus: "Sweet choice!" said we, [etc.]

Both:
We saw Thee in Thy balmy nest,
   Bright Dawn of our eternal day!
We saw Thine eyes break from Their east,
   And chase the trembling shades away.
We saw Thee, and we bless'd the sight;   75
We saw Thee by Thine own sweet light.

   Chorus: We saw Thee, [etc.]

Full Chorus:
Welcome, all wonders in one sight!
   Eternity shut in a span,   80
Summer in winter, day in night,
   Heaven in earth, and God in man!
Great little One, whose all-embracing birth
Lifts earth to Heaven, stoops Heav'n to earth.

Welcome, though nor to gold nor silk,   85
   To more than Caesar's birthright is;
Two sister-seas of virgin-milk,
   With many a rarely temper'd kiss,
That breathes at once both maid and mother,
Warms in the one, cools in the other.   90

Welcome, though not to those gay flies
   Gilded i' th' beams of earthly kings,
Slippery souls in smiling eyes,
   But to poor shepherds, homespun things,
Whose wealth's their flock, whose wit, to be   95
   Well read in their simplicity.
Yet when young April's husband-show'rs
   Shall bless the fruitful Maia's bed,
We'll bring the first-born of her flowers
   To kiss Thy feet and crown Thy head.   100
To Thee, dread Lamb, whose love must keep
   The shepherds more than they the sheep;
To Thee, meek Majesty! soft King
   Of simple graces and sweet loves,
Each of us his lamb will bring,   105
   Each his pair of silver doves;
Till burnt at last in fire of Thy fair eyes,
   Ourselves become our own best sacrifice.

[3]Dutiful.

John Cleveland [1613-1658]

The some twenty-five editions of Cleveland's poems between 1647 and 1700 certify an enormous reputation that has almost disappeared. Noted or notorious in his time for his assertive royalism and famous for his wit, Cleveland, according to his editors in 1677, was "the wonder of his own and the pattern of succeeding ages." But the context of this bold assertion is both querulous and defensive about the poet's obsolescence, and the "lofty fancy" that, as Thomas Fuller said, seemed "to stride from the top of one mountain to the top of another" was clearly not to be the mode of Restoration verse.

Cleveland, the son of a Yorkshire clergyman of unyielding royalist conviction, was born in Leicestershire, where he received an excellent elementary education. In 1627 he entered Christ's

College, Cambridge (where Milton was an undergraduate), and for almost twenty years thereafter he adorned the Cambridge scene. Even before the second of his two degrees (B.A. 1631, M.A. 1635), he was named (1634) a fellow of St. John's and began to build the glittering reputation—as rhetoric reader (1635–37), tutor, wit, and satirist—that enabled Milton's nephew Edward Phillips to recall him (with a certain condescension) as "a notable, high-soaring, witty loyalist of Cambridge." It was in these golden years that Cleveland wrote many of those occasional eulogistic or vituperative poems whose bristling topicalities delighted his contemporaries and dismay the modern annotator.

As one who had wittily expressed his devotion to the King and just as wittily excoriated his opponents, Cleveland could and would not long remain in Cambridge after war had been declared. Anticipating his ejection (which occurred in 1645), in about 1643 he joined the King at Oxford, where he continued writing verse and started writing prose ("The Character of a London Diurnal") against seditious Scots, Presbyterians, Parliamentarians, and other caterpillars of the troubled realm. Two years later we have a glimpse of him as judge advocate to the royalist garrison at Newark, a post from which he simply disappeared when Charles surrendered to the Scots in 1646. For almost ten years thereafter Cleveland's record is a blank, and when, in 1655, he briefly reappeared, it was as a prisoner in Yarmouth on such unsubstantial charges that by his own petition they were finally dropped. According to John Aubrey he at last found repose and fellowship at Gray's Inn in London, where he "died of the scurvy" in 1658.

During these obscure and furtive years Cleveland's real or supposititious works were so frequently and so confusingly reprinted that what George Saintsbury called the "terrible tangle" of his bibliography can hardly be unraveled. Although he himself apparently had no part in the publication of his poems, the floodgates burst in 1647 when seventeen of them were included in *The Character of a London Diurnal, with Several Select Poems by the Same Author.* Within a year this had gone through six editions and two re-issues, some of them with spurious additions. In 1651 *Poems by J. C.* presented an independent collection of twenty-two reprinted pieces and four new ones, which by 1669 had attained its seventeenth edition. While this series was progressing and expanding, *Cleaveland Revived* (1659) appeared and reached its fourth edition within a decade of its author's death. Constantly expanded to include new pieces, in a little more than twenty years these three collections had presented to the public almost 150 poems allegedly by Cleveland. It was no doubt partly in an effort to ascertain and straighten out the canon that John Lake and Samuel Drake, two of Cleveland's former students, published in 1677 *Clievelandi Vindiciae,* which added two new poems to the only twenty-nine that they retained from the earlier collections. Finally, in 1687 *The Works of Mr. John Cleveland,* ignoring Lake and Drake's exclusions, uncritically reprinted almost everything that had been ascribed to Cleveland and even added one new piece of prose. The third and last edition of this omnium-gatherum appeared in 1742, by which time its author had become—as he has ever since remained—a flawed but gifted writer whom the changing tides of taste had turned into a freak.

My text is based on *Clievelandi Vindiciae; or Clieveland's Genuine Poems, Orations, Epistles, &c. Purged from the many False & Spurious Ones Which had usurped his Name, and from innumerable Errours and Corruptions in the True. To which are added many never Printed before. Published according to the Author's own Copies,* 1677 (Wing C–4669). Editions of the poems by J. M. Berdan (1903) and George Saintsbury (*Minor Poets of the Caroline Period,* 3 vols., 1921) have been superseded by that of Brian Morris and Eleanor Withington (1967), who include thirty poems as surely Cleveland's and thirteen more as "probably" from his pen. Cleveland's prose characters have been treated by Benjamin Boyce (*The Polemic Character 1640–1661,* 1955), his obscure biography by S. V. Gapp (*PMLA,* XLVI, 1931), and his stylistic mannerisms by most of the students of metaphysical poetry listed in the General Bibliography, Section I.

from Clievelandi Vindiciae, or Clieveland's Genuine Poems (1677)

TO THE RIGHT WORSHIPFUL AND REVEREND
FRANCIS TURNER,[1] D.D., MASTER OF ST. JOHN'S
COLLEGE IN CAMBRIDGE, AND TO THE
WORTHY FELLOWS OF THE SAME COLLEGE

Gentlemen,

That we interrupt your more serious studies with the offer of this piece, the injury that hath been and is done to the deceased author's ashes not only pleadeth our excuse but engageth you (whose once he was, and within whose walls this standard of wit was first set up) in the same quarrel with us.

Whilst Randolph and Cowley[2] lie embalmed in their own native wax, how is the name and memory of Cleveland equally profaned by those that usurp and those that blaspheme it? By those that are ambitious to lay their cuckoo's eggs in his nest and those that think to raise up phenixes of wit by firing his spicy bed about him? . . .

Some of these grand sophys will not allow him the reputation of wit at all, yet how many such authors must be creamed and spirited to make up his "Fuscara"?[3] And how many of their slight productions may be gigged[4] out of one of his pregnant words? There perhaps you may find some leaf-gold, here massy wedges, there some scattered rays, here a galaxy, there some loose fancy frisking in the air, here wit's zodiac.

The quarrel in all this is upbraiding merit, and eminence his crime.[5] His touring fancy soareth so high a pitch that they fly like shades below him. The torrent thereof (which riseth far above their high water mark) drowneth their levels. Usurping upon the state poetic of the time, he hath brought in such insolent measures of wit and language that, despairing to imitate, they must study to understand. That alone is wit with them to which they are commensurate, and what exceedeth their scantling is monstrous.

Thus they deify his wit and fancy as the clown the plump oyster when he could not crack it. And now instead of that strenuous masculine style which breatheth in this author we have only an enervous,[6] effeminate froth offered, as if they had taken the salivating pill before they set pen to paper. You must hold your breath in the perusal lest the jest vanish by blowing on.

Another blemish in this monster of perfection is the exuberance of his fancy. His manna lieth so thick upon the ground they loathe it. When he should only fan, he with hurricanoes[7] of wit stormeth the sense, and doth not so much delight his reader as oppress and overwhelm him.

To cure this excess, their frugal wit hath reduced the world to a Lessian diet.[8] If perhaps they entertain their reader with one good thought (as these new dictators affect to speak), he may sit down and say grace of it. The rest is words and nothing else. . . .

From these unequal[9] censures we appeal to such competent judges as yourselves, in whose just value of him Clieveland shall live the wonder of his own and the pattern of succeeding ages. And although we might (upon several accounts) bespeak your affections, yet (abstracting[10] from these) we submit him to your severer judgments, and doubt not but he will find that patronage from you which is desired and expected by

Your humble servants,
J.L. S.D.[11]

CLEVELAND'S POEMS DIGESTED IN ORDER

Section I, Containing Love Poems

FUSCARA, OR THE BEE ERRANT

Nature's confectioner, the bee
(Whose suckets[1] are moist alchemy,
The still of his refining mold
Minting the garden into gold),
Having rifled all the fields   5
Of what dainties Flora yields,
Ambitious now to take excise
Of a more fragrant paradise,
At my Fuscara's sleeve arriv'd,
Where all delicious sweets are hiv'd.   10
The airy freebooter distrains[2]
First on the violets of her veins,
Whose tincture,[3] could it be more pure,
His ravenous kiss had made it bluer.
Here did he sit and essence quaff   15
Till her coy pulse had beat him off,
That pulse which he that feels may know
Whether the world's long-liv'd or no.
The next he preys on is her palm
(That alm'ner of transpiring[4] balm),   20

TO THE RIGHT WORSHIPFUL [1]Francis Turner (1638?–1700), master of St. John's from 1670 to 1679, and subsequently bishop of Rochester and then Ely, was deprived of his episcopal office when he refused to take the oath of allegiance to William and Mary. [2]Thomas Randolph (pp. 239 ff.) and Abraham Cowley (pp. 234 ff., popular poets whose reputations, it is implied, exceeded their merits. [3]Cleveland's most famous poem, in which he tells how a bee committed "parricide" by feasting on the sweet Fuscara. [4]Whipped up. [5]*The quarrel . . . crime*: i.e., we protest those who carp at excellence and make eminence a crime. [6]Powerless. [7]Hurricanes. [8]See p. 302, n. 11. [9]Unjust. [10]Withdrawing. [11]John Lake and Samuel Drake, former students of Cleveland's at St. John's College, where the poet had been named a fellow in 1634.

FUSCARA, OR THE BEE ERRANT [1]Sweetmeats. [2]Seizes for debt. [3]Hue. [4]Exhaling.

So soft, 'tis air but once remov'd,
Tender as 'twere a jelly glov'd.
Here, while his canting dronepipe scann'd
The mystic figures of her hand,
He tipples palmistry and dines   25
On all her fortune-telling lines.
He bathes in bliss and finds no odds
Betwixt this nectar and the gods';
He perches now upon her wrist,
A proper hawk for such a fist,   30
Making that flesh his bill of fare
Which hungry cannibals would spare;
Where lilies in a lovely brown
Inoculate[5] carnation,
Her *argent* skin with *or* so stream'd   35
As if the milky-way were cream'd.[6]
From hence he to the woodbine bends
That quivers at her finger's ends,
That runs division on the tree
Like a thick-branching pedigree.   40
So 'tis not her the bee devours,
It is a pretty maze of flowers;
It is the rose that bleeds when he
Nibbles his nice phlebotomy.
About her finger he doth cling   45
I' th' fashion of a wedding ring,
And bids his comrades of the swarm
Crawl like a bracelet 'bout her arm.
Thus when the hovering publican
Had suck'd the toll of all her span,[7]   50
Tuning his draughts with drowsy hums
As Danes carouse by kettle-drums,[8]
It was decreed, that posy glean'd,
The small familiar[9] should be wean'd.
At this the errant's courage quails,   55
Yet aided by his native sails
The bold Columbus still designs
To find her undiscover'd mines.
To th' Indies of her arm he flies,
Fraught both with east and western prize;   60
Which when he had in vain essay'd,
Armed like a dapper lancepresade[10]
With Spanish pike, he broach'd a pore
And so both made and heal'd the sore;
For as in gummy trees there's found   65
A salve to issue at the wound,
Of this her breach the like was true,
Hence trickled out a balsam, too.
But on, what wasp was 't that could prove
Ravaillac[11] to my Queen of Love?   70
The King of Bees now jealous grown
Lest her beams should melt his throne,
And finding that his tribute slacks,
His burgesses and state of wax
Turn'd to an hospital, the combs   75
Built rank and file like beadsmen's rooms,
And what they bleed but tart and sour
Match'd with my Danaë's golden show'r,[12]

Live honey all—the envious elf
Stung her, 'cause sweeter than himself.   80
   Sweetness and she are so alli'd
    The bee committed parricide.

THE SENSES' FESTIVAL

I saw a vision yesternight
Enough to sate a Seeker's sight.
I wish'd myself a Shaker[1] there,
And her quick pants my trembling sphere.
It was a she so glittering bright   5
You'd think her soul an Adamite,[2]
A person of so rare a frame,
Her body might be lin'd with th' same.
Beauty's chiefest maid of honor,
You may break Lent with looking on her.   10
   Not the fair abbess of the skies
    With all her nunnery of eyes[3]
    Can show me such a glorious prize.

And yet because 'tis more renown
To make a shadow shine, she's brown;   15
A brown for which heaven would disband
The galaxy and stars be tann'd.
Brown by reflection, as her eye
Deals out the summer's livery,
Old dormant[4] windows must confess   20
Her beams; their glimmering spectacles,
Struck with the splendor of her face,
Do th' office of a burning-glass.
   Now where such radiant lights have shown,
    No wonder if her cheeks be grown   25
    Sunburnt with luster of her own.

My sight took pay,[5] but (thank my charms)
I now impale her in mine arms
(Love's compass), confining you,
Good angles, to a circle too.   30
Is not the universe strait-lac't
When I can clasp it in the waist?
My amorous folds about thee hurl'd,
With Drake[6] I girdle in the world.

[5]Engraft.
[6]*Her argent... cream'd*: The mingling of silver (*argent*) and gold (*or*)
perhaps refers to the freckles on the lady's wrist.
[7]I.e., hand. [8]*As Danes... drums*: See *Hamlet*, I.iv.10–12.
[9]Household spirit, i.e., the bee.
[10]Lancepesade, i.e., a noncommissioned officer of the lowest grade.
[11]François Ravaillac, the assassin of Henri IV of France.
[12]The shower of gold in which Zeus visited Danae, thus siring
Perseus. The shower of gold was produced by Zeus, not (as
Cleveland implies) by the girl.
THE SENSES' FESTIVAL [1]*Seeker... Shaker*: seventeenth-century
sectaries, the latter notorious for the shaking or convulsions that
accompanied their devotions.
[2]Another kind of sectary who advocated nudity.
[3]*Fair abbess... eyes*: i.e., the moon and stars. [4]Dormer.
[5]Satisfaction.
[6]Sir Francis Drake led the first English circumnavigation of the
globe, 1577–80.

I hoop the firmament, and make   35
This my embrace the zodiac.
  How would thy center take my sense
  When admiration doth commence
  At the extreme circumference?

Now to the melting kiss that sips   40
The jelli'd philter of her lips,
So sweet there is not tongue can phrase 't
Till transubstantiate with a taste.
Inspir'd like Mahomet from above
By th' billing of my heav'nly dove,[7]   45
Love prints his signets in her smacks,
Those ruddy droops of squeezing[8] wax,
Which, wheresoever she imparts,
They're privy seals to take up hearts.
  Our mouths encountering at the sport,   50
  My slippery soul had quit the fort
  But that she stopp'd the sally port.

Next to those sweets, her lips dispense
(As twin conserves[9] of eloquence)
The sweet perfume her breath afford,   55
Incorporating with her words.
No rosary this vot'ress needs:
Her very syllables are beads.
No sooner 'twixt those rubies born,
But jewels are in earrings worn.[10]   60
With what delight her speech doth enter,
It is a kiss o' th' second venter,[11]
  And I dissolve at what I hear
  As if another Rosomond were
  Couch'd in the labyrinth of my ear.[12]   65

Yet that's but a preludious bliss,
Two souls pickeering[13] in a kiss.
Embraces do but draw the line,
'Tis storming that must take her in.
When bodies join and victory hovers   70
'Twixt the equal fluttering lovers,
This is the game. Make stakes, my dear,
Hark how the sprightly chanticlere,
That Baron Tell-clock[14] of the night,
Sounds boot-esel[15] to Cupid's knight.   75
  Then have at all, the pass is got!
  For coming off, O name it not!
  Who would not die upon the spot?

THE ANTI-PLATONIC

For shame, thou everlasting wooer,
Still saying grace and ne'er fall to her!
Love that's in contemplation plac'd
Is Venus drawn but to the waist.
Unless your flame confess its gender   5
And your parley cause surrender,
Y' are salamanders of a cold desire,
That live untouch'd amid the hottest fire.

What though she be a dame of stone,
The widow of Pygmalion?[1]   10

As hard and unrelenting she
As the new-crusted Niobe?[2]
Or (what doth more of statue carry)
A nun of the Platonic quarry?
Love melts the rigor which the rocks have bred;   15
A flint will break upon a featherbed.

For shame, you pretty female elves!
Cease thus to candy[3] up yourselves!
No more, you sectaries of the game,[4]
No more of your calcining[5] flame.   20
Women commence by Cupid's dart
As a king's hunting dubs a hart.[6]
Love's votaries enthrall each other's soul
Till both of them live but upon parole.[7]

Virtue's no more in womankind   25
But the greensickness of the mind:
Philosophy, their new delight,
A kind of charcoal appetite;
There is no sophistry prevails
Where all-convincing Love assails,   30
But the disputing petticoat will warp
As skillful gamesters are to seek at sharp.[8]

The soldier, that man of iron
Whom ribs of horror all environ,
That's strung with wire instead of veins,   35
In whose embraces you're in chains,
Let a magnetic girl appear,
Straight he turns Cupid's cuirassier:[9]

[7]*Inspir'd...dove*: Mohammed (*Mahomet*) was allegedly inspired by a dove that, trained to sit on his shoulder, seemed to whisper in his ear. [8]I.e., sealing. [9]Stores.
[10]*No sooner...worn*: i.e., no sooner do her words issue from her ruby lips than they become jewels in the ears of her suitor.
[11]*It is...venter*: i.e., the lady's words fall upon her lover's ears like an ardent kiss? *Venter*, which means womb and is normally used (in English law) for a spouse who is a mother, here seems to imply merely something deep and inward.
[12]*As if another...ear*: King Henry II constructed a labyrinth or maze at Woodstock to conceal his mistress Rosamond (*Rosomond*) Clifford from the jealous Queen Eleanor.
[13]Scouting, reconnoitering (with a pun on *ear*).
[14]I.e., officious timekeeper. In the seventeenth century *baron* was a title commonly used for freemen and burgesses in London, York, and certain other towns.
[15]French *boute-selle*: "place the saddle," i.e., a trumpet call.
THE ANTI-PLATONIC [1]Pygmalion was so much infatuated with the statue he had made of a beautiful woman that Aphrodite gave it life so that they could marry. The notion that she survived her husband appears to be Cleveland's own addition to the myth.
[2]A woman so grief-stricken for the death of her children that Zeus turned her into a weeping statue.
[3]I.e., preserve and protect as in a syrup? [4]I.e., heretics of love.
[5]Reduced to powder by fire.
[6]*As a...hart*: Merely by hunting the hart the king invests (*dubs*) it with dignity. [7]Pledged word.
[8]*There is...sharp*: Philosophy is no protection: when passion strikes, the stiffest petticoat will yield (*warp*) just as surely as skillful fencers will avoid (*are to seek*) a dangerous bout with rapiers.
[9]A cavalryman with an armored breastplate.

Love storms his lips and takes the fortress in
For all the bristl'd turnpikes[10] of his chin.   40

Since Love's artillery then checks
The breastworks of the firmest sex,
Come, let us in affections riot:
Th' are sickly pleasures keep a diet.
Give me a lover bold and free,   45
Not eunuch'd with formality,
Like an ambassador that beds a queen
With the nice caution of a sword between.

Section II, Containing Poems Which Relate to State Affairs

UPON THE KING'S RETURN FROM SCOTLAND[1]

Return'd? I'll ne'er believe 't. First prove him hence.
Kings travel by their beams and influence.
Who says the soul gives out her gests,[2] or goes
A flitting progress 'twixt the head and toes?
She rules by omnipresence, and shall we   5
Deny a prince the same ubiquity?
Or grant he went and, 'cause the knot was slack,
Girt both the nations with his zodiac;
Yet as the tree at once both upward shoots
And just as much grows downward to the roots,   10
So at the same time that he posted thither,
By counter-stages he rebounded hither.
Hither and hence at once: thus every sphere
Doth by a double motion interfere,
And when his native form inclines him east,   15
By the first mover he is ravish'd west.[3]
Have you not seen how the divided dam
Runs to the summons of her hungry lamb,
But when the twin cries halves,[4] she quits the first?
Nature's *commendam*[5] must be likewise nurst!   20
So were his journeys, like the spider's, spun
Out of his bowels of compassion.
Two realms, like Caecus, so his steps transpose,
His feet still contradict him as he goes:[6]
England's return'd, that was a banish'd soil: 25
The bullet flying makes the gun recoil.
Death's but a separation, though endors'd
With spade and javelin; we were thus divorc'd.
Our soul hath taken wing, while we express
The corpse, returning to our[7] principles.   30
But the Crab tropic[8] must not now prevail;
Islands go back but when you're under sail.
So his retreat hath rectified that wrong:
Backward is forward in the Hebrew tongue.[9]
Now the church militant in plenty rests,   35
Nor fears, like th' Amazon, to lose her breasts.[10]
Her means are safe, not squeez'd until the blood
Mix with the milk and choke the tender brood.
She that hath been the floating Ark is that
She that's now seated on Mount Ararat.[11]   40
Quits Charles; our souls did guard him northward thus,
Now he, the counterpart,[12] comes south to us.

THE HUE AND CRY AFTER SIR JOHN PRESBYTER

With hair in character and lugs in text,[1]
With a splay[2] mouth and a nose circumflext,[3]
With a set ruff of musket-bore that wears,
Like cartridge or linen bandeliers
Exhausted of their sulphurous contents   5
In pulpit fireworks which the bomb-all vents;[4]
The Negative and Covenanting Oath,[5]
Like two mustachos, issuing from his mouth;
The bush upon his chin like a carv'd story
In a box-knot cut by the *Directory*:[6]   10
Madam's confession[7] hanging at his ear,
Wire-drawn through all the questions, "How"
   and "Where,"

[10]Pikes set to form a barrier in a road.

UPON THE KING'S RETURN [1]Cleveland contributed this poem to *Irenodia Cantabrigiensis* (1641), a Cambridge miscellany celebrating Charles I's return to London on 25 November 1641 after an abortive effort to pacify the dissatified Scots. [2]Stages of a journey. [3]*Thus every sphere...ravish'd west*: by their own motion the planetary spheres move from west to east, but by the motion of the primum mobile (*first mover*) they are pulled (*ravish'd*) from east to west. See *sphere* in Glossary and Donne's "Good Friday, 1613. Riding Westward," pp. 84 f. [4]Claims a half-share. [5]An office bestowed or "commended" to a surrogate in its incumbent's absence. Thus when the king is in either England or Scotland the other country is held by Nature *in commendam*. [6]*Two realms...goes*: No matter which way Charles' footprints seem to point (whether toward Scotland or England), they are in fact reversed, for he belongs to either realm. The giant Cacus (*Caecus*) tried to conceal the movement of Hercules' stolen cattle by dragging them backward and thus confusing their tracks. [7]*Text their* [8]The northern Tropic of Cancer, i.e., Scotland. [9]*Backward...tongue*: Hebrew is read from right to left, and therefore *backward* to an Englishman. [10]*Now the church...breasts*: I.e., the church in England and Scotland remains unmutilated unlike the Amazons who removed their right breasts for better handling of their bows. [11]The mountain range in Armenia where Noah's ark came to rest after the flood (Genesis 8.4). [12]Earlier editions read *counterpane*, which in English law means the *counterpart* or second of two parts of an indenture, both of which should match.

THE HUE AND CRY [1]*With hair...text*: i.e., with short hair and long ears (*lugs*). *Characters* and *text* are kinds of writing, the former shorthand and the latter text-hand or longhand. [2]Widespread. [3]Bent, i.e., hooked. [4]*With a set...vents*: On his scrawny (*musket-bore*) neck he wears a wide ruff or collar like a cartridge-belt or bandolier whose ammunition has been discharged in the *pulpit fireworks* of his fire-and-brimstone sermons. [5]*The Negative...Oath*: Respectively, an oath not to support the king against Parliament and to uphold the Solemn League and Covenant (on which see p. 937, n.46.) [6]*The bush...Directory*: i.e., Sir John's beard was trimmed as formally as a box hedge made to represent the persons in a story. In 1645 Parliament replaced the outlawed Book of Common Prayer with the rigorously prescriptive *Directory for the Public Worship of God*. [7]Presbyterians advocated both public and private confession of sin as a sign of true repentance.

Each circumstance so in the hearing felt
Then when his ears are cropp'd he'll count them gelt;[8]
The weeping cassock scar'd into a jump,[9]   15
A sign the Presbyter's worn to the stump,
The Presbyter, though charm'd against mischance
With the divine right of an ordinance:[10]
    If you meet any that do thus attire 'em,
    Stop them: they are the tribe of Adoniram.[11]   20
What zealous frenzy did the senate seize
That tare the rochet[12] to such rags as these?
Episcopacy minc'd, reforming Tweed
Hath sent us runts even of her church's breed,
Lay, interlining clergy, a device   25
That's nickname to the stuff call'd lops and lice:[13]
The beast at wrong end branded, you may trace
The devil's footsteps in his cloven face:
A face of several parishes and sorts,
Like to sergeant shav'd at Inns of Court.   30
What mean the elders else, those kirk dragoons,[14]
Made up of ears and ruffs like ducatoons,[15]
That hierarchy of handicrafts begun,
Those New Exchange men of religion?[16]
Sure, they're the antic heads[17] which, plac'd without   35
The church, do gape and disembogue[18] a spout;
Like them above the Commons House t' have been
So long without, now both are gotten in.
    Then what imperious in the bishop sounds,
    The same the Scotch executor rebounds—[19]   40
This stating prelacy, the classic[20] rout
That speak it often ere it spake it out.
    So by an abbey's skeleton of late
    I heard an echo supererogate
    Through imperfection, and the voice restore   45
    As if she had the hiccup o'er and o'er.[21]
Since they our mix'd diocesans[22] combine
Thus to ride double in their discipline,
That Paul's shall to the consistory call
A dean and chapter out of Weaver's Hall,   50
Each at the ordinance for to assist
With the five thumbs of his groat-changing fist.[23]
    Down, Dagon[24] synod, with thy motley ware,
    Whilst we are champions for the Common Prayer
(That dove-like embassy that wings our sense   55
To heaven's gate in shape of innocence),
Pray for the mit'red[25] authors, and defy
Those demicasters of divinity.[26]
    For when Sir John with Jack of all trades joins,
    His finger's thicker than the prelate's loins.[27]   60

THE GENERAL ECLIPSE[1]

Ladies that gild the glittering noon,
And by reflection mend[2] his ray,
Whose beauty makes the sprightly sun
To dance as upon Easter day,
    What are you now the queen's away?   5

Courageous eagles who have whet[3]
Your eyes upon majestic light,
And thence deriv'd such martial heat
That still your looks maintain the fight,
    What are you since the king's goodnight?[4]   10

Cavalier-buds whom Nature teems[5]
As a reserve for England's throne,
Spirits whose double edge redeems
The last age and adorns your own,
    What are you now the prince is gone?   15

[8]Gelded.
[9]*The weeping...jump*: Most Presbyterian ministers preferred a short coat (*jump*) to the long Anglican cassock.
[10]Before 1641, a royal declaration, with the force of law, not requiring the concurrence of Parliament; thereafter a Parliamentary declaration not requiring the king's approval.
[11]I.e., tax collectors. One of the eleven princes under King Solomon was Adoniram, who served a fiscal function (1 Kings 4.6).
[12]Tore the clerical vestments.
[13]*Episcopacy minc'd...lice*: i.e., with the Anglican Church abolished, the Scots have sent us their unqualified (*lay*) Presbyterian clergy who are as intent upon protecting their position as upon reinforcing (*interlining*) their coarse, flea-bitten clothing. *Lops* means "fleas," but the phrase *lops and lice* seems to indicate some sort of sleazy fabric (*stuff*).   [14]Presbyterian warriors.
[15]Silver coins.
[16]*That hierarchy...religion*: i.e., the Anglican hierarchy (of archbishops, bishops, priests) has been replaced by businessmen and merchants. *The New Exchange* was a bazaar and place of commercial resort on the south side of the Strand.   [17]Gargoyles.
[18]Flow out at the mouth.
[19]*Then what...rebounds*: i.e., the Scottish preachers are as overbearing as the bishops were alleged to be.
[20]Referring to the classes or subdivisions of provinces into which the Presbyterian church was organized.
[21]*So by...o'er*: Perhaps Cleveland is alluding to the Westminster Assembly (which held its meetings in the Abbey) and its protracted attempts (1643–49) to formulate the doctrine and discipline of a national Presbyterian church.
[22]The Westminster Assembly consisted of 10 peers, 20 members of the House of Commons, 121 divines, and 6 deputies from Scotland.
[23]*That Paul's...fist*: Cleveland is ridiculing the Presbyterians' confusion of religion and business (*groat-changing*), leading to the clerics of St. Paul's being recruited from artisans and merchants. *Weavers' Hall*, the seat of the Weavers' Company or guild, seems to have been used as a Presbyterian meetinghouse before its destruction in the Great Fire of 1666.
[24]I.e., heathen. Dagon was the Philistine god whose temple was destroyed by Samson (Judges 16.23–31).   [25]Episcopal.
[26]I.e., clerical frauds with their merchants' hats (instead of bishops' miters). *Demicasters* were hats made of inferior felt.
[27]*His finger's...loins*: King Solomon's foolish son and successor Rehoboam was urged to tell the Israelites, pleading for a gentle reign, that whereas his father was a stern monarch, "my little finger shall be thicker than my father's loins" (2 Chronicles 10.10).
THE GENERAL ECLIPSE [1]This is one of many seventeenth-century poems modeled on Sir Henry Wotton's "On His Mistress, the Queen of Bohemia" (p. 55).   [2]Supplement.
[3]Sharpened. On the eagle's alleged ability to stare into the sun unblinded see p. 229, n.3
[4]Charles' surrender to the Scots (1646)? His execution (1649)?
[5]Gives birth to.

As an obstructed fountain's head
Cuts the entail off from the streams,
And brooks are disinherited,
Honor and beauty are mere dreams
   Since Charles and Mary lost their beams.   20

Criminal valors, who commit
Your gallantry, whose paean brings
A psalm of mercy after it,[6]
In this sad solstice of the king's
   Your victory hath mew'd[7] her wings.   25

See how your soldier wears his cage
Of iron like the captive Turk[8]
And as the guerdon of his rage!
See how your glimmering peers do lurk,
   Or at the best work journey-work!   30

Thus 'tis a general eclipse,
And the whole world is all amort;[9]
Only the House of Commons trips
The stage in a triumphant sort.
   Now e'en John Lilburn[10] take 'em for't!   35

Section III, Containing Miscellanies

ON THE MEMORY OF MASTER EDWARD KING DROWN'D IN THE IRISH SEAS[1]

I like not tears in tune, nor do I prize
His artificial grief who scans his eyes.
Mine weep down pious beads, but why should I
Confine them to the Muse's rosary?
I am no poet here: my pen's the spout   5
Where the rainwater of mine eyes run out
In pity of that name whose fate we see
Thus copied out in grief's hydrography.
The Muses are not mermaids, though upon
His death the ocean might turn Helicon.[2]   10
The sea's too rough for verse; who rhymes upon 't
With Xerxes strives to fetter th' Hellespont.[3]
My tears will keep no channel, know no laws
To guide their streams, but like the waves, their cause,
Run with disturbance till they swallow me   15
As a description of his misery.
But can his spacious virtue find a grave
Within the impostum'd[4] bubble of a wave,
Whose learning if we sound, we must confess
The sea but shallow, and him bottomless.   20
Could not the winds to countermand thy death
With their whole card of lungs[5] redeem thy breath?
Or some new island in thy rescue peep
To heave thy resurrection from the deep,
That so the world might see thy safety wrought   25
With no less wonder than thyself was thought?
The famous Sagirite (who in his life
Had Nature as familiar as his wife)
Bequeath'd his widow to survive with thee
Queen Dowager of all philosophy—   30

An ominous legacy, that did portend
Thy fate and predecessor's second end.[6]
Some have affirm'd that what on earth we find,
The sea can parallel for shape and kind.[7]
Books, arts, and tongues were wanting, but in thee   35
Neptune hath got an university
   We'll dive no more for pearls; the hope to see
Thy sacred relics of mortality
Shall welcome storms and make the seaman prize
His shipwrack now more than his merchandise.   40
He shall embrace the waves, and to thy tomb,
As to a royaler Exchange,[8] shall come.
What can we now expect? Water and fire,
Both elements our ruin do conspire;
And that dissolves us which doth us compound: 45
One Vatican was burnt, another drown'd.[9]
We of the gown our libraries must toss
To understand the greatness of our loss;
Be pupils to our grief, and so much grow
In learning as our sorrows overflow.   50
When we have fill'd the rundlets[10] of our eyes
We'll issue 't forth, and vent such elegies,
As that our tears shall seem the Irish Seas,
We floating islands, living Hebrides.

AN ELEGY UPON THE ARCHBISHOP OF CANTERBURY[1]

I need no Muse to give my passion vent;
He brews his tears that studies to lament.

[6]*Criminal valors...after it*: i.e., the victorious Parliamentarians who hypocritically follow their triumphal *paean* with pleas of mercy for their victim's soul. [7]Shed, molted.
[8]The captured Emperor Bajazet, who in Marlowe's *Tamburlaine* dashes out his brains on the bars of the cage where he had been confined. [9]Inanimate, dispirited.
[10]A political agitator (1614?–57) who in the late forties became increasingly hostile and embarrassing to Parliamentarians. See pp. 583 f.
ON THE MEMORY [1]This elegy, like Milton's *Lycidas* (p. 240), was contributed to *Justa Eduardo King* (1638), a collection of poems in Latin, Greek, and English commemorating the death by shipwreck (10 August 1637) of Edward King, a fellow of Christ's College, Cambridge.
[2]Cleveland confuses Mt. Helicon with Aganippe and Hippocrene, the fountains of poetic inspiration that flow from it.
[3]*With Xerxes...Hellespont*: In his unsuccessful attempt to subdue Greece Xerxes (d. 645 B.C.), King of Persia, threw a bridge of boats across the Hellespont. [4]Swollen, puffed up.
[5]A map (*card*) whose corners were adorned with pictures of the four winds (*lungs*).
[6]According to legend, Aristotle drowned himself in the Strait of Euripus because he was unable to explain the movement of its tides.
[7]*Some have...kind*: For another statement of this ancient notion see p. 259, n.8   [8]See p. 322, n. 16.
[9]*One...drown'd*: Cleveland implies the loss to learning by King's drowning was comparable to the destruction of the Vatican library by fire (of which there is no record).
[10]Runlets, i.e., casks or barrels.
UPON THE ARCHBISHOP [1]For a famous account of the execution

Verse chemically[2] weeps: that pious rain
Distill'd with art is but the sweat o' th' brain.
Who ever sobb'd in numbers? Can a groan   5
Be quaver'd out by soft division?[3]
'Tis true, for common formal elegies
Not Bushell's wells[4] can match a poet's eyes
In wanton waterworks; he'll tune his tears
From a Geneva jig[5] up to the spheres.   10
But then he mourns at distance, weeps aloof,
Now that the conduit-head is our own roof,
Now that the fate is public—we may call
It Britain's vespers, England's funeral—
Who hath a pencil to express the saint,   15
But he hath eyes too, washing off the paint?
There is no learning but what tears surround,
Like to Seth's pillars[6] in the deluge drown'd.
There is no church: religion is grown[7]
So much of late that she's increas'd to none, 20
Like an hydropic body full of rheums
First swells into a bubble, then consumes.
The law is dead or cast into a trance,
And by a law dough-bak'd,[8] an ordinance.[9]
The liturgy, whose doom was voted next,[10]   25
Died as a comment upon him, the text.
There's nothing lives: life is, since he is gone,
But a nocturnal lucubration.
Thus you have seen death's inventory read
In the sum total—Canterbury's dead.   30
A sight would make a pagan to baptize
Himself a convert in his bleeding eyes;
Would thaw the rabble, that fierce beast of ours
(That which, hyena-like, weeps and devours)
Tears that flow brackish from their souls within, 35
Not to repent, but pickle up their sin.

Meantime no squalid grief his look defiles:
He gilds his sadder fate with nobler smiles.
Thus the world's eye with reconciled streams
Shines in his showers as if he wept his beams. 40
How could success such villainies applaud?
The state in Strafford[11] fell, the church in Laud:
The twins of public rage adjudg'd to die
For treasons they should act by prophecy.
The facts were done before the laws were made; 45
The trump turn'd up after the game was play'd.
Be dull, great spirits, and forbear to climb,
For worth is sin and eminence a crime.
    No churchman can be innocent and high:
    'Tis height makes Grantham steeple stand awry.[12] 50

---

of William Laud, archbishop of Canterbury, on 10 January 1646
see p. 931f.
[2]By alchemy.   [3]Gentle melody.
[4]Thomas Bushell (d. 1674) was an engineer noted for a grotto with
elaborate waterworks that he built near Woodstock.
[5]Frisky dance?
[6]According to the Jewish historian Josephus, the descendants of
Seth, third son of Adam, recorded their discoveries and achieve-
ments on two pillars, one of stone and the other of brick (which
was destroyed in the flood).
[7]I.e., through the exfoliation of sects following the abolition of
the Anglican Church.   [8]Half-baked.
[9]See p. 322, n. 10.
[10]*The liturgy...next*: In 1645 Parliament replaced the Anglican
Book of Common Prayer with the Presbyterian *Directory for the
Public Worship of God.*
[11]Thomas Wentworth, first earl of Strafford, one of Charles' most
powerful (and detested) ministers, was executed in 1641.
[12] *'Tis height...awry*: A widely current proverb about the graceful
280-foot spire of St. Wulfram's in Grantham, a town in Lincoln-
shire.

Abraham Cowley [1618-1667]

The history of Cowley's reputation is instructive but depressing. When the "Muses' Hannibal," as he described himself, was buried in Westminster Abbey, a eulogist explained that "it was fit/ Amongst our kings to lay the King of Wit." A year later Cowley's literary executor Thomas Sprat—historian of the Royal Society and later bishop of Rochester—contributed to a handsome collected edition of his works a sort of saint's life of unrelieved encomium. The aging Milton, according to his widow, ranked Cowley with Shakespeare and Spenser as his favorite English poets. But within a generation the tide began to turn. Whereas young Dryden had asserted that the authority of "the darling of my youth, the famous Cowley," was "almost sacred," an older Dryden, in the preface to the *Fables* (1700), said with some exaggeration that Cowley was so "sunk" in reputation that his sales had dwindled from ten editions in a decade to a hundred copies in a year. About the same time, rising wits like Addison and Congreve implied, respectively, that Cowley's celebrated wit was sometimes in "excess" and that his loose Pindaric odes were very loose indeed.

A further stage of this decline was marked by Pope in 1737 ("Who now reads Cowley?"), and a generation later Johnson, in one of the most famous of his *Lives*, undertook a reassessment that in fact destroyed the once-proud reputation. It has never been restored.

The subject of this excessive praise and disesteem was a prodigy who not only lisped in numbers but saw his lispings attain the dignity of print while he was still a boy at school. If what Johnson called the "learned puerilities" of his *Poetical Blossoms* (1633) may be fairly said to match the title, they at any rate were well enough received to justify a new, enlarged edition three years later and a third in 1637. By this time the precocious author had progressed from Westminster School to Trinity College, Cambridge, where he took his B.A. in 1639 and was duly made a fellow. It was then, no doubt, that he wrote much of the lyric poetry later brought together as *The Mistress* in 1647; composed, for undergraduate production, the Latin comedy *Naufragium Joculare* in 1638 and *The Guardian* in 1641 (which would one day be reworked and produced as *The Cutter of Coleman Street* in 1661); and, according to Sprat, "laid the design" for several larger works that were reserved for future publication. Chief among these were the once-famed Pindaric odes and the ambitious biblical epic *Davideis*, of which a Vergilian twelve books were planned and only four were written. As an attempt to restore the art of poetry to "the service of the Deity" *Davideis* was, as Johnson demonstrated with severe precision, a lavish impertinence; "still, however," he concluded, "it is the work of Cowley, of a mind capacious by nature and replenished by study."

To Cowley, as to his friend Crashaw, the war brought drastic changes. Ejected from his fellowship in 1644, he joined the court at Oxford in the service of Henry Jermyn, secretary to the Queen, and for almost a decade thereafter he was so deep in her employment, at Paris and elsewhere, as courier, spy, and confidential scribe, that it is hard to trace his movements. Like this phase of his career, the circumstances of his return to England in 1654, his subsequent arrest, and his eventual retirement are extremely murky; and although Sprat was careful to exonerate him of disloyalty to the Stuarts or submission to their foes, Johnson indicted him of "cowardice."

Following the hugger-mugger of these middle years he reverted to the ease of literature and learning. In 1656 he collected and revised the verse he wished to save (which did not include the juvenilia) and published it as *Poems* with an important introduction. Although he there expressed the weary wish "to retire myself to some of our American plantations," where, in an "obscure retreat," he could "forsake this world forever," he in fact resumed a life of letters within easy reach of London. Although he failed to gain a sinecure from Charles II at the Restoration he was, as Sprat reports, "sufficiently furnished" by bounty from the queen and Henry Jermyn (now earl of St. Albans) and the duke of Buckingham to live as quietly as he wished. A new interest in botany had led to a degree in medicine from Oxford in 1657 and resulted in the publication (1662) of a poetical treatise entitled *Planatarum libri duo* (later expanded to six books) whose Latin Johnson highly praised. To these last years must also be assigned his interest in the newly founded Royal Society (for which he wrote a famous ode), his researches into ecclesiastical history, and his engaging *Discourses by Way of Essays in Verse and Prose*—"Of Solitude," "The Country Life," "Of Myself," and so on—that were published posthumously by Sprat in the collected *Works* of 1668. When this famous poet died, at only forty-nine, he was mourned as one

> Who like a lightning to our eyes was shown,
> So bright he shin'd, and was so quickly gone.

My texts are based on *Poeticall Blossoms. The third Edition. Enlarged by the Author*, 1637 (STC 5908)—which includes, with a separate title page, *Sylva, or, Divers Copies of Verses, Made upon sundry occasions by A. C.*—and *Poems: Viz. I. Miscellanies. II. The Mistress, or, Love Verses. III. Pindarique Odes. And IV. Davideis, or, A Sacred Poem of the Troubles of David. Written by A. Cowley*, 1656 (Wing C-6683). Sprat's incomplete edition of the *Works* (1668)—which contains his eulogistic life—reached a twelfth edition by 1721; a *Second Part* (1681) contains the works of Cowley's "younger years" and a *Third Part* (1689) "his six books of plants now made English." A. B.

Grosart's was the first critical edition (2 vols. 1881), but it was superseded by A. R. Waller's of the English works (2 vols., 1905–6). There are editions of the *Prose Works* by J. R. Lumby (1887, rev. Arthur Tilley, 1923), of the *Essays and Other Prose Writings* by A. B. Gough (1915), of *The Mistress with Other Select Poems* by John Sparrow (1926), and of selections from the prose and verse by James G. Taffe (1970). The two standard biographies—by A. H. Nethercot and Jean Loiseau (in French)—appeared almost simultaneously in 1931, R. B. Hinman's important study of his thought (*Abraham Cowley's Word of Order*), in 1960, Taafe's short but useful life in 1972, and Allan D. Pritchard's first complete edition of Cowley's polemical poem called *The Civil War* in 1973. The decline in Cowley's reputation has been traced by Nethercot in *PMLA*, XXXVIII (1923).

from Poetical Blossoms (1637)

TO THE READER

1

I call'd the buskin'd Muse Melpomene,[1]
And told her what sad story I would write.
She wept at hearing such a tragedy,
Though wont in mournful ditties to delight.
 If thou dislike these sorrowful lines, then know
 My Muse with tears, not with conceits, did flow.

2

And as she my unabler quill did guide,
Her briny tears did on the paper fall.
If, then, unequal numbers be espied,
O reader, do not that my error call,
 But think her tears defac'd, and blame then
 My Muse's grief, and not my missing pen.

CONSTANTIA AND PHILETUS
The Song

1

Time, fly with greater speed away,
 Add feathers to thy wings,
 Till thy haste in flying brings
That wish'd for and expected day.

2

Comfort's sun we then shall see,
Though at first it dark'ned be
With dangers, yet those clouds being gone,
Our day will put his luster on.

3

Then though death's sad night do come,
 And we in silence sleep,
 Lasting day again will greet
Our ravish'd souls, and then there's none

4

Can part us more. No death nor friends,
Being dead, their power o'er us ends.

Thus there's nothing can dissever
Hearts which Love hath join'd together.

THE TRAGICAL HISTORY OF PYRAMUS AND THISBE

TO THE RIGHT WORSHIPFUL, MY VERY LOVING MASTER,
MASTER LAMBERT OSBOLSTON,[2] CHIEF
SCHOOLMASTER OF WESTMINSTER SCHOOL

Sir,
My childish Muse is in her spring, and yet
Can only show some budding of her wit.
One frown upon her work, learn'd Sir, from you,
Like some unkinder storm shot from your brow,
Would turn her spring to withering autumn's time,
And make her blossoms perish ere their prime.
But if you smile, if in your gracious eye
She an auspicious alpha[3] can descry,
How soon will they grow fruit? How will they flourish
That had such beams their infancy to nourish?
 Which being sprung to ripeness, expect then
 The best and first fruits of her grateful pen.
              Your most dutiful scholar,
              Abraham Cowley

SYLVA, OR DIVERS COPIES OF VERSES[4]

AN ELEGY ON THE DEATH OF
MISTRESS ANNE WHITFIELD[5]

She's dead, and like the hour that stole her hence
With as much quietness and innocence.
And 'tis as difficult a task to win

POETICAL BLOSSOMS [1]The Muse of tragedy.
[2]Lambert Osbolston or Osbaldston (1594–1659), master of Westminster School from 1625 to 1639.
[3]I.e., beginning (*alpha* being the first letter of the Greek alphabet).
[4]*Sylva . . . Verses*: This section was added to the second (1636) edition of *Poetical Blossoms*. [5]Unidentified.

Her traveling soul back to its former inn
As force that hour, fled without tract[6] away,   5
To turn and stop the current of the day.
What, shall we weep for this, and clothe our eye
With sorrow, the grave's mourning livery?
Or shall we sigh, and with that pious wind
Drive faster on what we already find   10
Too swift for us, her soul? No, she who died,
Like the sick sun when Night entombs his pride,
Or trees in autumn when unseen decay
And slow consumption steals the leaves away,
Without one murmur shows that she did see   15
Death as a good, not as a misery.

    And so she went to undiscovered fields,
From whence no path hope of returning yields
To any traveler, and it must be
Our solace now to court her memory.   20

We'll tell how love was dandled in her eye,
Yet curb'd with a beseeming gravity,
And how (believe it you that hear or read)
Beauty and chastity met and agreed
In her, although a courtier. We will tell   25
How far her noble spirit did excel
Hers—nay, our—sex. We will repeat her name,
And force the letters to an anagram.
Whitfield we'll cry, and amorous winds shall be
Ready to snatch that word's sweet harmony   30
Ere 'tis spoke out. Thus we must dull grief's sting
And cheat the sorrow that her loss would bring;
Thus in our hearts we'll bury her, and there
We'll write: "Here lies Whitfield the chaste and fair."
    Art may no doubt a statelier tomb invent,   35
    But not, like this, a living monument.

[6]Trace.

from Poems (1656)

THE PREFACE

Urbanely vexed to discover that during his absence abroad a worthless book had been published in his name and that his early play *The Guardian* had been printed in a "mangled and imperfect" form, Cowley has resolved to gather such of his work as he wishes to preserve and to present it to the world while he himself is still alive to supervise the publication. To do so exposes him to "some raillery," he concedes, but he has been persuaded to overcome the "just repugnances" of his own modesty by the thought that he has in fact already ended his career as poet, and is thus assisting at the funeral of his Muse.   10

For to make myself absolutely dead in a poetical capacity, my resolution at present is never to exercise any more that faculty. It is, I confess, but seldom seen that the poet dies before the man, for when we once fall in love with that bewitching art we do not use it to court it as a mistress but marry it as a wife, and take it for better or worse as an inseparable companion for our whole life. But as the marriages of infants do but rarely prosper, so no man ought to wonder at the diminution or decay of my affection to 20 poesy, to which I had contracted myself so much under age, and so much to my own prejudice in regard of those more profitable matches which I might have made among the richer sciences. As for the portion which brings of fame, it is an estate (if it be any, for men are not oft'ner deceived in their hopes of widows than in their opinion of *Exegi monumentum aere perennius*)[1] that hardly ever comes in whilst we are living to enjoy it, but is a fantastical kind of reversion to our own selves; neither ought any man to envy poets this posthumous and imaginary happiness, since they find 30 commonly so little in present that it may be truly applied to them which St. Paul speaks of the first Christians: "If

their reward be in this life, they are of all men the most miserable."[2]

And if in quiet and flourishing times they meet with so small encouragement, what are they to expect in rough and troubled ones? If wit be such a plant that it scarce receives heat enough to preserve it alive even in the summer of our cold climate, how can it choose but wither in a long and a sharp winter? A warlike, various, and a tragical age is best to write of, but worst to write in. And I may, though in a very unequal proportion, assume that to myself which was spoken by Tully to a much better person upon occasion of the civil wars and revolutions in his time: *Sed in te intuens, Brute, doleo, cuius in adolescentiam per 'medias laudes quasi quadrigis vehentem transversa incurrit misera fortuna Reipublicae.*[3]

Neither is the present constitution of my mind more proper than that of the times for this exercise, or rather divertisement. There is nothing that requires so much serenity and cheerfulness of spirit; it must not be either overwhelmed with the cares of life, or overcast with the clouds of melancholy, or shaken and disturbed with the storms of injurious fortune; it must, like the halcyon, have fair weather to breed in. . . . The truth is, for a man to write well it is necessary to be in good humor; neither is wit less eclipsed with the unquietness of mind than beauty with the indisposition of body. So that it is almost as hard a thing to be a poet in despite of fortune as it is in despite of nature. . . .

PREFACE [1]*Exegi . . . perennius:* "I have built a monument more enduring than bronze" (Horace, *Odes*, III.xxx).
[2]Paraphrased from 1 Corinthians 15.19.
[3]*Sed in te . . . Reipublicae:* i.e., looking on you, my Brutus, I grieve that one whose youthful career, which had moved so swiftly to applause, should be blasted by the miseries of the time (Cicero, *Brutus* or *De claris oratoribus*, Sect. xcvii).

And this resolution of mine does the more befit me because my desire has been for some years past (though the execution has been accidentally diverted), and does still vehemently continue, to retire myself to some of our American plantations, not to seek for gold or enrich myself with the traffic of those parts (which is the end of most men that travel thither), . . . but to forsake this world forever, with all the vanities and vexations of it, and to bury myself in some obscure retreat there (but not without the consolation of letters and philosophy). . . .

Having been forced, for my own necessary justification, to trouble the reader with this long discourse of the reasons why I trouble him also with all the rest of the book, I shall only add somewhat concern the several parts of it and some other pieces which I have thought fit to reject in this publication, as, first, all those which I wrote at school from the age of ten years till after fifteen;[4] for even so far backward there remain yet some traces of me in the little footsteps of a child, which, though they were then looked upon as commendable extravagances in a boy (men setting a value upon any kind of fruit before the usual season of it), yet I would be loath to be bound now to read them all over myself, and therefore should do ill to expect that patience from others. Besides, they have already passed through several editions, which is a longer life than used to be enjoyed by infants that are born before the ordinary terms. . . .

As for the ensuing book, it consists of four parts. The first is a miscellany of several subjects, and some of them made when I was very young, which it is perhaps superfluous to tell the reader. I know not by what chance I have kept copies of them; for they are but a very few in comparison of those which I have lost, and I think they have no extraordinary virtue in them to deserve more care in preservation than was bestowed upon their brethren, for which I am so little concerned that I am ashamed of the arrogancy of the word when I said I had "lost" them.

The second is called "The Mistress, or Love Verses," for so it is that poets are scarce thought freemen of their company without paying some duties and obliging themselves to be true to love. Sooner or later they must all pass through that trial, like some Mahometan monks that are bound by their order, once at least in their life, to make a pilgrimage to Mecca:

In furias ignemque ruunt: amor omnibus idem.[5]

But we must not always make a judgment of their manners from their writings of this kind, as the Romanists uncharitably do of Beza for a few lascivious sonnets composed by him in his youth.[6] It is not in this sense that poesy is said to be a kind of painting; it is not the picture of the poet, but of things and persons imagined by him. . . . I speak it to excuse some expressions (if such there be) which may happen to offend the severity of supercilious[7] readers, for much excess is to be allowed in love, and even more in poetry, so we avoid the two unpardonable vices in both, which are obscenity and profaneness, of which I am sure if my words be ever guilty they have ill represented my thoughts and intentions. . . .

As for the "Pindaric Odes" (which is the third part), I am in great doubt whether they will be understood by most readers, nay, even by very many who are well enough acquainted with the common roads and ordinary tracks of poesy. They either are, or at least were meant to be, of that kind of style which Dion Halicarnasseus calls μεγα-λοφνὲς καὶ ἡδὺ μετὰ δεινότητος and which he attributes to Alcaeus.[8] The digressions are many and sudden and sometimes long, according to the fashion of all lyrics and of Pindar above all men living. The figures are unusual and bold, even to temerity, and such as I durst not have to do withal in any other kind of poetry; the numbers[9] are various and irregular, and sometimes (especially some of the long ones) seem harsh and uncouth if the just measures and cadencies[10] be not observed in the pronunciation. So that almost all their sweetness and numerosity[11] (which is to be found, if I mistake not, in the roughest, if rightly repeated) lies in a manner wholly at the mercy of the reader. I have briefly described the nature of these verses in the ode entitled "The Resurrection,"[12] and though the liberty of them may incline a man to believe them easy to be composed, yet the undertaker will find it otherwise:

> *Ut sibi quivis*
> *Speret idem, sudet multum frustraque laboret*
> *Ausus idem.*[13]

I come now to the last part, which is "Davideis, or An Heroical Poem of the Troubles of David," which I designed into twelve books, not for the tribes' sake[14] but after the pattern of our master Vergil, and intended to close all with that most poetical and excellent elegy of David on the death of Saul and Jonathan;[15] for I had no mind to carry him quite on to his anointing at Hebron because it is the custom of heroic poets (as we see by the examples of Homer and Vergil, whom we should do ill to forsake to imitate others) never to come to the full end of their story, but only so near that everyone may see it, as men commonly play not out the game when it is evident that they can win it, but lay down their cards and take up what they have won. This,

[4]*Those which . . . fifteen:* Cowley refers to the juvenilia published as *Poetical Blossoms* (see p. 326), which went through three editions between 1633 and 1637.
[5]*In furias . . . idem:* "[They] rush into the fire of passion: all are caught by love" (Vergil, *Georgics*, III.244).
[6]Théodore de Bèze (1519–1608), a leader of the Reformation who succeeded Calvin in Geneva, published (1548) a volume of his early poetry that he tried later to suppress.
[7]Censorious.
[8]Greek lyric poet (fl. 600 B.C.) whose work, according to Dionysius of Halicarnassus (*De priscis scriptoribus censura*, II.8), combined grandeur with sweetness and terror.
[9]Lines, verses.
[10]Cadences.
[11]Rhythmic quality.
[12]See p. 336.
[13]*Ut . . . idem:* i.e., whoever hopes for the same success must sweat and toil in vain (Horace, *Art of Poetry*, ll. 240–42).
[14]According to Genesis 49.1–28, the twelve tribes of Israel descended from the twelve sons of Jacob.
[15]*Elegy . . . Jonathan:* 2 Samuel 1.19–27.

I say, was the whole design, in which there are many noble and fertile arguments behind, as the barbarous cruelty of Saul to the priests at Nob, the several flights and escapes of David, with the manner of his living in the wilderness, the funeral of Samuel, the love of Abigal, the sacking of Ziglag, the loss and recovery of David's wives from the Amalekites, the witch of Endor, the war with the Philistines, and the battle of Gilboa;[16] all which I meant to interweave, upon several occasions, with most of the illustrious stories of the Old Testament, and to embellish with the most remarkable 10 antiquities of the Jews and of other nations before or at that age.

But I have had neither leisure hitherto nor have appetite at present to finish the work, or so much as to revise that part which is done with that care which I resolved to bestow upon it and which the dignity of the matter well deserves. For what worthier subject could have been chosen among all the treasuries of past times than the life of this young prince; who from so small beginnings, through such infinite troubles and oppositions, by such miraculous virtues and 20 excellencies, and with such incomparable variety of wonderful actions and accidents became the greatest monarch that ever sat on the most famous throne of the whole earth? Whom should a poet more justly seek to honor than the highest person who ever honored his profession? Whom a Christian poet rather than the man after God's own heart, and the man who had that sacred preeminence above all other princes, to be the best and mightiest of that royal race from whence Christ himself, according to the flesh, disdained not to descend? 30

When I consider this, and how many other bright and magnificent subjects of the like nature the holy scripture affords and proffers, as it were, to poesy, in the wise managing and illustrating whereof the glory of God Almighty might be joined with the singular utility and noblest delight of mankind, it is not without grief and indignation that I behold that divine science employing all her inexhaustible riches of wit and eloquence either in the wicked and beggarly flattery of great persons, or the unmanly idolizing of foolish women, or the wretched affectation of scurrile 40 laughter, or at best on the confused, antiquated dreams of senseless fables and metamorphoses. Amongst all holy and consecrated things which the devil ever stole and alienated from the service of the Deity—as altars, temples, sacrifices, prayers, and the like—there is none that he so universally and so long usurped as poetry. It is time to recover it out of the tyrant's hands and to restore it to the kingdom of God, who is the father of it. . . .

There is not so great a lie to be found in any poet as the vulgar conceit of men that lying is essential to good poetry.[17] 50 Were there never so wholesome nourishment to be had (but alas, it breeds nothing but diseases) out of these boasted feasts of love and fables, yet, methinks, the unalterable continuance of the diet should make us nauseate it, for it is almost impossible to serve up any new dish of that kind. They are all but the cold meats of the ancients, new heated and new set forth. I do not at all wonder that the old poets made some rich crops out of these grounds: the heart of the soil was not then wrought out with continual tillage; but what can we expect now, who come agleaning, not after the first reapers, but after the very beggars? Besides, though those mad stories of the gods and heroes seem in themselves so ridiculous, yet they were then the whole body (or rather chaos) of the theology of those times. They were believed by all but a few philosophers and perhaps some atheists, and served to good purpose among the vulgar (as pitiful things as they are) in strengthening the authority of law with the terrors of conscience and expectation of certain rewards and unavoidable punishments. There was no other religion, and therefore that was better than none at all. But to us who have no need of them, to us who deride their folly and are wearied with their impertinencies, they ought to appear no better arguments for verse than those of their worthy successors, the knights errant. What can we imagine more proper for the ornaments of wit or learning in the story of Deucalion than in that of Noah? Why will not the actions of Samson afford as plentiful matter as the labors of Hercules? Why is not Jeptha's daughter as good a woman as Iphigenia, and the friendship of David and Jonathan more worth celebration than that of Theseus and Pirithous?[18] . . . What do I instance in these few particulars? All the books of the Bible are either already most admirable and exalted pieces of poesy, or are the best materials in the world for it.

Yet though they be in themselves so proper to be made use of for this purpose, none but a good artist will know how to do it; neither must we think to cut and polish diamonds with so little pains and skill as we do marble. For if any man design to compose a sacred poem by only turning a story of the scripture (like Mr. Quarles) or some other godly matter (like Mr. Heywood of angels) into rhyme,[19] he is so far from elevating of poesy that he only abases divinity. In brief, he who can write a profane well may write a divine one better, but he who can do that but ill will do this much worse. The same fertility of invention, the same wisdom of disposition, the same judgment in observance of decencies, the same luster and vigor of elocution, the same modesty and majesty of number, briefly, the same kind of habit is required to both; only this latter allows better stuff, and therefore would look more deformedly if ill dressed in it. I am far from assuming to myself to have fulfilled the duty of this weighty undertaking, but sure I am there is nothing yet in our language (nor perhaps in any) that is in any degree answerable to the idea that I conceive of it. And I shall be ambitious of no other fruit from this weak and imperfect attempt of

[16]*This, I say . . . Gilboa:* The main events of David's tumultuous career in his progress from shepherd boy to King of Israel are recorded in 1 Samuel 16–31, 2 Samuel, 1 Kings 1–2, and 1 Chronicles 11–29.

[17]*Lying . . . poetry:* For Bacon's statement of this Renaissance commonplace see *The Advancement of Learning,* pp. 667f.

[18]*What can we imagine . . . Pirithous:* Cowley is juxtaposing pagan and biblical versions of such common themes as the flood, the legendary strong man, human sacrifice, and friendship.

[19]*For if any man . . . rhyme:* Cowley is alluding derisively to earlier poetical recensions of biblical materials like Francis Quarles' *Feast of Worms* (1620), a paraphrase of Jonah, and Thomas Heywood's *Hierarchy of the Blessed Angels* (1635).

mine but the opening of a way to the courage and industry of some other persons who may be better able to perform it throughly[20] and successfully.

MISCELLANIES

THE MOTTO
Tentanda via est, etc.[1]

What shall I do to be forever known,
  And make the age to come my own?
I shall, like beasts or common people, die
  Unless you write my elegy,
Whilst others great, by being born, are grown: 5
  Their mother's labor, not their own.
In this scale gold, in th' other fame does lie:
  The weight of *that* mounts *this* so high.
These men are Fortune's jewels, molded bright,
  Brought forth with their own fire and light.   10
If I, her vulgar stone, for either look,
  Out of myself it must be strook,[2]
Yet I must on. What sound is't strikes mine ear?
  Sure I Fame's trumpet hear.
It sounds like the last trumpet, for it can   15
  Raise up the buried man.
Unpass'd Alps stop me, but I'll cut through all,
  And march, the Muses' Hannibal.[3]
Hence all the flattering vanities that lay
  Nets of roses in the way.   20
Hence the desire of honors or estate,
  And all that is not above Fate!
Hence Love himself, that tyrant of my days,
  Which intercepts my coming praise!
Come, my best friends, my books, and lead me on;   25
  'Tis time that I were gone.
Welcome, great Stagirite,[4] and teach me now
  All I was born to know.
Thy scholar's vict'ries[5] thou dost far outdo:
  He conquer'd the earth, the whole world you.   30
Welcome, learn'd Cicero, whose blest tongue and wit
  Preserves Rome's greatness yet.
Thou art the first of or'tors; only he
  Who best can praise thee, next must be.
Welcome the Mantuan swan,[6] Vergil the wise,   35
  Whose verse walks highest, but not flies,
Who brought green poesy to her perfect age,
  And made that art which was a rage.
Tell me, ye mighty three, what shall I do
  To be like one of you.   40
But you have climb'd the mountain's top, there sit
  On the calm flour'shing head of it,
And whilst with wearied steps we upward go
  See us and clouds below.

ODE OF WIT

1

Tell me, O tell, what kind of thing is wit,
  Thou[1] who master art of it.

For the first matter[2] loves variety less:
Less women love't either in love or dress.
  A thousand different shapes it bears,
  Comely in thousand shapes appears.
Yonder we saw it plain, and here 'tis now,
Like spirits in a place, we know not how.

2

London, that vents of false ware so much store,
  In no more ware deceives us more.
For men led by the color and the shape,
Like Zeuxis' birds fly to the painted grape;[3]
  Some things do through our judgment pass
  As through a multiplying[4] glass.
And sometimes, if the object be too far,
We take a falling meteor for a star.

3

Hence 'tis a wit, that greatest word of fame,
  Grows such a common name,
And wits by our creation they become,
Just so, as tit'lar bishops made at Rome.[5]
  'Tis not a tale, 'tis not a jest
  Admir'd with laughter at a feast,
Nor florid talk, which can that title gain;
The proofs of wit forever must remain.

4

'Tis not to force some lifeless verses meet
  With their five gouty feet.
All ev'rywhere, like man's, must be the soul,
And reason the inferior powers control.
  Such were the numbers which could call
  The stones into the Theban wall.[6]
Such miracles are ceas'd; and now we see
No towns or houses rais'd by poetry.

5

Yet 'tis not to adorn and gild each part
  That shows more cost than art.

[20]Thoroughly.
THE MOTTO [1]*Tentanda . . . etc.*: "I must essay a path whereby I too may rise from earth and fly victorious on the lips of men" (Vergil, *Georgics*, III.8–9).
[2]Struck.
[3]Carthaginian general who invaded Italy by crossing the Alps in 218 B.C.
[4]Aristotle, who was born (384 B.C.) at Stagira, a Greek colony on the northwestern shore of the Aegean Sea.
[5]I.e., the conquests of Alexander the Great (356–323 B.C.), who had been Aristotle's pupil.
[6]Vergil, who was born at Pietola, a village near Mantua in northern Italy.
ODE OF WIT [1]Presumably, Cowley is addressing not an actual person but his poetical ideal.
[2]Primordial chaos.
[3]*Like Zeuxis' birds . . . grape*: The fifth-century Athenian painter Zeuxis allegedly painted a bunch of grapes so realistically that birds tried to eat them.
[4]Magnifying.
[5]Titular bishops are those who bear a title but do not hold a see.
[6]*Such were . . . wall*: According to legend, Amphion caused the stones of Thebes to leap into place by the power of his music.

Jewels at nose and lips but ill appear;
Rather than all thing wit, let none be there.
  Several lights will not be seen
  If there be nothing else between.
Men doubt, because they stand so thick i' th' sky,
If those be stars which paint the galaxy.

6

'Tis not when two like words make up one noise,
  Jests for Dutch men and English boys,
In which who finds out wit, the same may see
In an'grams and acrostic poetry.
  Much less can that have any place
  At which a virgin hides her face.
Such dross the fire must purge away; 'tis just
The author blush, there where the reader must.

7

'Tis not such lines as almost crack the stage
  When Bajazet begins to rage.[7]
Nor a tall[8] metaphor in th' Oxford[9] way,
Nor the dry chips of short-lung'd Seneca.[10]
  Nor upon all things to obtrude,
  And force some odd similltude.
What is it then, which like the Power Divine
We only can by negatives define?[11]

8

In a true piece of wit all things must be,
  Yet all things there agree,
As in the ark, join'd without force or strife,
All creatures dwelt, all creatures that had life;
  Or as the primitive forms of all
  (If we compare great things with small)
Which without discord or confusion lie,
In that strange mirror of the Deity.[12]

9

But Love, that molds one man up out of two,
  Makes me forget and injure you.
I took you for myself, sure, when I thought
That you in anything were to be taught.
  Correct my error with thy pen;
  And if any ask me then,
What thing right wit and height of genius is,
I'll only show your lines, and say," 'Tis this."

THE CHRONICLE
A Ballad

1

Margarita first possess'd,
  If I remember well, my breast,
  Margarita first of all;
But when a while the wanton maid
With my restless heart had play'd,
  Martha took the flying ball.

2

Martha soon did it resign
  To the beauteous Catharine.

Beauteous Catharine gave place
(Though loath and angry she to part
With the possession of my heart)
  To Elisa's conquering face.

3

Elisa till this hour might reign
  Had she not evil counsels ta'en.
  Fundamental laws she broke,
And still new favorites she chose,
Till up in arms my passions rose,
  And cast away her yoke.

4

Mary then and gentle Ann
  Both to reign at once began.
  Alternately they sway'd,
And sometimes Mary was the fair,
And sometimes Ann the crown did wear,
  And sometimes both I obey'd.

5

Another Mary then arose
  And did rigorous laws impose.
  A mighty tyrant she!
Long, alas, should I have been
Under that iron-scepter'd queen
  Had not Rebecca set me free.

6

When fair Rebecca set me free,
  'Twas then a golden time with me.
  But soon those pleasures fled,
For the gracious princess died
In her youth and beauty's pride,
  And Judith reigned in her stead.

7

One month, three days, and half an hour
  Judith held the sovereign power.
  Wondrous beautiful her face,
But so weak and small her wit
That she to govern was unfit,
  And so Susanna took her place.

8

But when Isabella came
  Arm'd with a resistless flame
  And th' artillery of her eye,

Numbers: verses.
[7]*Bajazet...rage:* The role of the Turkish sultan Bajazet in Christopher Marlowe's *Tamburlaine* was notorious for its theatricality and rant. [8]Grandiloquent.
[9]In the 1668 folio the word is changed to *Bombast*.
[10]An allusion to the notably curt, sententious style of Lucius Annaeus Seneca (d. 65), whose tragedies and philosophical treatises were widely read and imitated in the seventeenth century.
[11]I.e., God is unknowable, His ways are unsearchable, His power and goodness are illimitable, etc.
[12]"And before the throne there was a sea of glass like crystal; and in the midst of the throne, and round about the throne, were four living creatures full of eyes in front and behind" (Revelation 4.6).

Whilst she proudly march'd about
Great conquests to find out,
  She beat out Susan by the by.

9

But in her place I then obey'd
  Black-ey'd Bess, her viceroy maid,
  To whom ensu'd a vacancy.
Thousand worse passions then possess'd
The interregnum of my breast.
  Bless me from such an anarchy!

10

Gentle Henriette than
  And a third Mary next began,
  Then Joan and Jane and Audria,
And then a pretty Thomasine,
And then another Katharine,
  And then a long et cetera.

11

But should I now to you relate
  The strength and riches of their state,
  The powder, patches, and the pins,
The ribbons, jewels, and the rings,
The lace, the paint, and warlike things
  That make up all their magazines,[1]

12

If I should tell the politic arts
  To take and keep men's hearts,
  The letters, embassies, and spies,
The frowns and smiles and flatteries,
The quarrels, tears, and perjuries,
  Numberless, nameless mysteries!

13

And all the little lime-twigs[2] laid
  By Matchavil[3] the waiting maid,
  I more voluminous should grow
(Chiefly if I, like them, should tell
All change of weathers that befell)
  Than Holinshed or Stow.[4]

14

But I will briefer with them be,
  Since few of them were long with me.
  An higher and a nobler strain
My present emperess[5] does claim,
Heleonora, first o' th' name,
  Whom God grant long to reign!

TO SIR WILLIAM DAVENANT UPON HIS TWO FIRST BOOKS OF "GONDIBERT," FINISHED BEFORE HIS VOYAGE TO AMERICA[1]

Methinks heroic poesy till now
Like some fantastic fairyland did show:
Gods, devils, nymphs, witches, and giants' race,
And all but man in man's chief work had place.
Thou like some worthy knight with sacred arms   5

Dost drive the monsters thence and end the charms.
Instead of those dost men and manners plant,
The things which that rich soil did chiefly want.
Yet ev'n thy mortals do their gods excell,
Taught by thy Muse to fight and love so well.   10
  By fatal hands whilst present empires fall,
Thine from the grave past monarchies recall.
So much more thanks from humankind does merit
The poet's fury than the zealot's spirit.[2]
And from the grave thou mak'st this empire rise,   15
Not like some dreadful ghost t' affright our eyes,
But with more luster and triumphant state
Than when it crown'd at proud Verona[3] sate.
So will our God rebuild man's perish'd frame
And raise him up much better, yet the same.   20
So godlike poets do past things rehearse,
Not change but heighten nature by their verse.
  With shame, methinks, great Italy must see
Her conqu'rors raised to life again by thee.
Rais'd by such pow'rful verse that ancient Rome   25
May blush no less to see her wit o'ercome.
Some men their fancies[4] like their faith derive,
And think all ill but that which Rome does give,
The marks of old and Catholic would find,
To the same chair would truth and fiction bind.   30
Thou in those beaten paths disdain'st to tread,
And scorn'st to live by robbing of the dead.
Since time does all things change, thou think'st not fit
This latter age should see all new but wit.
Thy fancy, like a flame, its way does make,   35
And leave bright tracks for following pens to take.
Sure 'twas this noble boldness of the Muse
Did thy desire to seek new worlds infuse,
And ne'er did heav'n so much a voyage bless,
If thou canst plant but there[5] with like success. 40

THE TREE OF KNOWLEDGE
That There Is No Knowledge Against the Dogmatists

1

The sacred tree 'midst the fair orchard grew;
  The phoenix[1] truth did on it rest

THE CHRONICLE   [1]I.e., stores of arms, ammunition, etc.
[2]Twigs smeared with bird-lime for catching birds, i.e., snares.
[3]Alluding to Machiavelli as a master of deceit and trickery.
[4]Raphael Holinshed (d. ca. 1580) and John Stow (d. 1605), old-fashioned Elizabethan chroniclers noted for their prolixity.
[5]Empress.
TO SIR WILLIAM DAVENANT   [1]When Davenant set sail for America, following the publication of his unfinished epic *Gondibert* (1651) he was captured and imprisoned. See p. 252.
[2]*By fatal hands...spirit:* Cowley is alluding to the recent civil war and the execution of Charles I. His own sympathies were strongly royalist.
[3]The action of Gondibert concerns amatory and political intrigue in medieval Lombardy, whose capital was Verona.
[4]Poetical imaginings.
[5]I.e., America, where Davenant, as a political refugee, proposed to emigrate.
THE TREE OF KNOWLEDGE   [1]Perennial. See *Phoenix* in the Glossary.

And built his perfum'd nest:
That right Porphyrian[2] tree which did true logic show,
  Each leaf did learned notions give,
  And th' apples were demonstrative.
  So clear their color and divine,
The very shade they cast did other lights outshine.

2

"Taste not," said God; "'tis mine and angels' meat;
  A certain death does sit
  Like an ill worm i' th' core of it.
Ye cannot know and live, nor live or know and eat."
  Thus spoke God, yet man did go
  Ignorantly on to know,
Grew so more blind, and she[3]
Who tempted him to this grew yet more blind than he.

3

The only science man by this did get
  Was but to know he nothing knew;
  He straight his nakedness did view,
His ign'rant, poor estate, and was asham'd of it;
  Yet searches probabilities
  And rhetoric and fallacies,
  And seeks by useless pride
With slight and withering leaves that nakedness to hide.

4

"Henceforth," said God, "the wretched sons of earth
  Shall sweat for food in vain
  That will not long sustain,
And bring with labor forth each fond abortive birth.
  That serpent too, their pride,
  Which aims at things denied,
  That learn'd and eloquent lust,
Instead of mounting high, shall creep upon the dust."

ON THE DEATH OF MR. CRASHAW[1]

Poet and saint! to thee alone are given
The two most sacred names of earth and heaven,
The hard and rarest union which can be,
Next that of Godhead with humanity.
Long did the Muse's banish'd slaves abide,   5
And built vain pyramids to mortal pride;
Like Moses thou (though spells and charms withstand)
Hast brought them nobly home back to their Holy Land.
  Ah, wretched we, poets of earth! but thou
Wert living the same poet which thou'rt now   10
Whilst angels sing to thee their airs divine,
And joy in an applause so great as thine.
Equal society with them to hold,
Thou need'st not make new songs, but say the old.
And they (kind spirits!) shall all rejoice to see   15
How little less than they exalted man may be.
Still the old heathen gods in numbers dwell,
The heav'nliest thing on earth still keeps up hell.
Nor have we yet quite purg'd the Christian land;
Still idols here like calves at Bethel stand.[2]   20
And though Pan's death long since all oracles breaks,

Yet still in rhyme the fiend Apollo speaks:[3]
Nay, with the worst of heathen dotage we
(Vain men!) the monster woman[4] deify;
Find stars and tie our fates there in a face,   25
And paradise in them by whom we lost it, place.
What different faults corrupt our Muses thus?
Wanton as girls, as old wives, fabulous?
  Thy spotless muse, like Mary, did contain
The boundless Godhead; she did well disdain   30
That her eternal verse employ'd should be
On a less subject than eternity;
And for a sacred Mistress scorn'd to take
But her whom God himself scorn'd not His spouse
  to make.
It (in a kind) her miracle did do;   35
A fruitful mother was, and virgin too.
  How well, blest swan, did Fate contrive thy death,[5]
And made thee render up thy tuneful breath
In thy great Mistress' arms? thou most divine
And richest off'ring of Loreto's shrine!   40
Where like some holy sacrifice t' expire,
A fever burns thee, and love lights the fire.
Angels (they say) brought the fam'd chapel there,
And bore the sacred load in triumph through the air.
'Tis surer much they brought thee there, and they   45
And thou, their charge, went singing all the way.
  Pardon, my Mother Church,[6] if I consent
That angels led him when from thee he went,
For even in error, sure, no danger is
When join'd with so much piety as his.   50
Ah, mighty God, with shame I speak't, and grief,
Ah, that our greatest faults were in belief!
And our weak reason were ev'n weaker yet,
Rather than thus our wills too strong for it.
His faith perhaps in some nice tenents[7] might   55
Be wrong; his life, I'm sure, was in the right.
And I myself a Catholic will be,
So far, at least, great saint, to pray to thee.
  Hail bard triumphant! and some care bestow
On us, the poets militant below!   60
Oppos'd by our old en'my, adverse chance,
Attack'd by envy and by ignorance,

---

[2]Referring to the neoplatonic philosopher Porphyry (232?–?304), who depicted all created things, including man, as branches of a genealogical chart or tree, the trunk of which was the primal genus substance.   [3]I.e., Eve.

ON THE DEATH OF MR. CRASHAW   [1]For Richard Crashaw's life see pp. 299 ff.

[2]Having made two golden calves, the idolatrous King Jereboam "set the one in Bethel, and the other put he in Dan" (1 Kings 12.28–29).

[3]*And though Pan's death...speaks*: See Cowley's "Preface" (p. 329) for a fuller statement of the notion that despite the rout of the pagan gods at the birth of Christ, they continued to exert their power in certain kinds of poetry.   [4]I.e., the Sphinx.

[5]"Mr. Crashaw died of a fever at Loreto, being newly chosen canon of that church" (Cowley's marginal gloss).

[6]I.e., the Church of England, which Crashaw had rejected in order to become a Roman Catholic.

[7]I.e., minute points of theology.

Enchain'd by beauty, tortur'd by desires,
Expos'd by tyrant love to savage beasts and fires,
Thou from low earth in nobler flames didst rise,   65
And like Elijah, mount alive the skies.
Elisha-like (but with a wish much less,
More fit thy greatness, and my littleness)
Lo here I beg (I whom thou once didst prove
So humble to esteem, so good to love)   70
Not that thy spirit might on me doubled be,[8]
I ask but half thy mighty spirit for me.
And when my Muse soars with so strong a wing,
'Twill learn of things divine, and first of thee to sing.

ANACREONTICS, OR SOME COPIES OF VERSES TRANSLATED PARAPHRASTICALLY OUT OF ANACREON[1]

2. DRINKING

The thirsty earth soaks up the rain,
And drinks and gapes for drink again.
The plants suck in the earth and are
With constant drinking fresh and fair.
The sea itself, which one would think   5
Should have but little need of drink,
Drinks ten thousand rivers up,
So fill'd that they o'erflow the cup.
The busy sun (and one would guess
By's drunken fiery face no less)   10
Drinks up the sea, and when has[2] done,
The moon and stars drink up the sun.
They drink and dance by their own light,
They drink and revel all the night.
Nothing in Nature's sober found,   15
But an eternal health goes round.
Fill up the bowl, then, fill it high,
Fill all the glasses there, for why
Should every creature drink but I,
Why, man of morals, tell me why?   20

5. AGE

Oft am I by the women told,
"Poor Anacreon, thou grow'st old.
Look how thy hairs are falling all:
Poor Anacreon, how they fall!"
Whether I grow old or no,   5
By th' effects I do not know.
This I know without being told;
'Tis time to live if I grow old;
'Tis time short pleasures now to take,
Of little life the best to make,   10
And manage wisely the last stake.

8. THE EPICURE

Fill the bowl with rosy wine,
Around our temples roses twine,
And let us cheerfully awhile

Like the wine and roses smile.
Crown'd with roses, we contemn   5
Gyges'[3] wealthy diadem.
Today is ours, what do we fear?
Today is ours, we have it here!
Let's treat it kindly, that it may
Wish, at least, with us to stay.   10
Let's banish business, banish sorrow:
To the gods belongs tomorrow.

THE MISTRESS, OR SEVERAL COPIES OF LOVE POEMS

INCONSTANCY

Five years ago (says story) I lov'd you,
For which you call me most inconstant now;
Pardon me, Madam, you mistake the man,
For I am not the same that I was than.[1]
No flesh is now the same 'twas then in me,   5
And that my mind is chang'd, yourself may see.
The same thoughts to retain still, and intents,
Were more inconstant far; for accidents
Must of all things most strangely inconstant prove
If from one subject they t' another move.   10
My members then the father members were,
From whence these take their birth which now are here.
If, then, this body love what th' other did,
'Twere incest, which by nature is forbid.
You might as well this day inconstant name   15
Because the weather is not still the same
That it was yesterday, or blame the year
'Cause the spring, flowers, and autumn, fruit, does bear.
The world's a scene of changes, and to be
Constant, in nature were inconstancy,   20
For 'twere to break the laws herself has made.
Our substances themselves do fleet and fade;
The most fix'd being still does move and fly,
Swift as the wings of Time 'tis measur'd by.
T' imagine, then, that love should never cease   25
(Love which is but the ornament of these)
Were quite as senseless as to wonder why
Beauty and color stays not when we die.

[8]*And like Elijah...doubled be*: As the prophet Elijah and his appointed successor Elisha walked together, the latter requested that "a double portion of thy spirit be upon me. . . . And it came to pass, as they still went on and talked, that, behold, there appeared a chariot of fire, and horses of fire, and parted them asunder, and Elijah went up by a whirlwind into heaven" (2 Kings 2.9–11).

ANACREONTICS [1]Greek lyric poet (572?–?488 B.C.) whose celebrations of wine and love supplied a generic label for poetry on these topics.
[2]Text *'has*, presumably to indicate the omission of *he*.
[3]Gyges (c.685–652 B.C.) was a king of Lydia proverbial for his wealth.
INCONSTANCY [1]Then

PLATONIC LOVE

1

Indeed I must confess,
  When souls mix 'tis an happiness,
But not complete till bodies too do join,
And both our wholes into one whole combine;[1]
But half of heaven the souls in glory taste
  Till by love in heaven at last
  Their bodies too are plac'd.

2

In thy immortal part
  Man, as well as I, thou art.
But something 'tis that differs thee and me,
And we must one even in that difference be.
I thee both as a man and woman prize,
  For a perfect love implies
  Love in all capacities.

3

Can that for true love pass
  When a fair woman courts her glass?
Something unlike must in love's likeness be:
His wonder is one and variety.
For he whose soul nought but a soul can move
  Does a new Narcissus prove,
  And his own image love.

4

That souls do beauty know
  'Tis to the body's help they owe;
If when they know't they straight abuse that trust
And shut the body from't, 'tis as unjust
As if I brought my dearest friend to see
  My mistress and at th' instant he
  Should steal her quite from me.

COLDNESS

1

As water fluid is till it do grow
  Solid and fix'd by cold,
So in warm seasons love does loosely flow;
  Frost only can it hold.
A woman's rigor and disdain
Does his swift course restrain.

2

Though constant and consistent now it be,
  Yet when kind beams appear
It melts and glides apace into the sea,
  And loses itself there.
So the sun's amorous play
Kisses the ice away.

3

You may in vulgar loves find always this,
  But my substantial love

Of a more firm and perfect nature is;
  No weathers can it move:
Though heat dissolve the ice again,
The crystal solid does remain.

COUNSEL

1

Ah, what advice can I receive?
  No, satisfy me first,
For who would physic-potions give
  To one that dies with thirst?

2

A little puff of breath, we find,
  Small fires can quench and kill;
But when they're great, the adverse wind
  Does make them greater still.

3

Now whilst you speak it moves me much,
  But straight I'm just the same;
Alas, th' effect must needs be such
  Of cutting through a flame.

PINDARIC ODES IN THE STYLE AND MANNER OF THE ODES OF PINDAR

THE PRAISE OF PINDAR
IN IMITATION OF HORACE HIS SECOND ODE, BOOK IV
Pindarum quisquis student aemulari, etc.[1]

1

Pindar is imitable by none;
The phoenix Pindar is a vast species alone.
Whoe'er but Daedalus with waxen wings could fly
And neither sink too low nor soar too high?
  What could he who follow'd claim
But of vain boldness the unhappy fame,
  And by his fall a sea to name?[2]
  Pindar's unnavigable song
Like a swoll'n flood from some steep mountain pours along.
  The ocean meets with such a voice
From his enlarged mouth as drowns the ocean's noise.

PLATONIC LOVE [1]*too do...combine*: In the 1668 folio this couplet is changed to "too combine/And closely as our minds together join."
PINDARIC ODES [1]*Pindarum...etc.*: i.e., whoever tries to rival Pindar is, like Daedalus with his waxen wings, attempting the impossible (Horace, *Odes*, IV.ii). Cowley picks up the analogy in the first stanza of his ode. Among the extant works of Pindar (522?–443 B.C.) are four books of odes celebrating victories in the Olympian, Pythian, Nemean, and Isthmian games.
[2]*What could he...name* When on their escape from Crete Daedalus' son Icarius flew too near the sun, his waxen wings were melted and he fell into the sea that thenceforth bore his name (Icarian).

2

So Pindar does new words and figures roll
Down his impetuous dithyrambic tide,
    Which in no channel deigns t' abide,
    Which neither banks nor dikes control.
      Whether th' immortal gods he sings
      In a no less immortal strain,
Or the great acts of god-descended kings,
Who in his numbers still survive and reign.
      Each rich embroidered line,
Which their triumphant brows around
      By his sacred hand is bound,
Does all their starry diadems outshine.

3

Whether at Pisa's race he please
To carve in polish'd verse the conqu'rors' images,[3]
Whether the swift, the skillful, or the strong
Be crowned in his nimble, artful, vigorous song.
Whether some brave young man's untimely fate
In words worth dying for he celebrate,
    Such mournful and pleasing words
As joy t' his mother's and his mistress' grief affords:
    He bids him live and grow in fame,
    Among the stars he sticks his name:
The grave can but the dross of him devour,
So small is death's, so great the poet's power.

4

Lo, how th' obsequious wind and swelling air
    The Theban swan does upwards bear
Into the walks of clouds, where he does play,
And with extended wings opens his liquid[4] way,
    Whilst alas, my tim'rous Muse
    Unambitious tracks pursues;
    Does with weak, unballast[5] wings,
    About the mossy brooks and springs,
    About the trees' new-blossom'd heads,
    About the gardens' painted beds,
    About the fields and flowery meads.
    And all inferior beauteous things
      Like the laborious bee,
      For little drops of honey flee,
And there with humble sweets contents her industry.

THE RESURRECTION[1]

1

Not winds to voyagers at sea
Nor showers to earth more necessary be
(Heav'n's vital seed cast on the womb of earth
    To give the fruitful year a birth)
    Than verse to virtue, which can do
The midwife's office and the nurse's too;
It feeds it strongly, and it clothes it gay,
    And when it dies, with comely pride
Embalms it, and erects a pyramid
    That never will decay
    Till heaven itself shall melt away,
    And nought behind it stay.

2

Begin the song and strike the living lyre!
Lo how the years to come, a numerous and
      well-fitted quire,[2]
All hand in hand do decently advance,
And to my song with smooth and equal measures dance.
Whilst the dance lasts, how long soe'er it be,
My music's voice shall bear it company,
    Till all gentle notes be drown'd
    In the last trumpet's dreadful sound.
That to the spheres themselves shall silence bring,
    Untune the universal string.
    Then all the wide extended sky
    And all th' harmonious worlds on high
    And Vergil's sacred work shall die.
And he himself shall see in one fire shine
Rich nature's ancient Troy, though built by hands divine.[3]

3

    Whom[4] thunder's dismal noise
And all that prophets and apostles louder spake,
And all the creatures' plain conspiring voice
    Could not, whilst they liv'd, awake,
    This mightier sound shall make,
      When dead, t' arise,
    And open tombs and open eyes:
To the long sluggards of five thousand years,
This mightier sound shall make[5] its hearers' ears.
Then shall the scatter'd atoms crowding come
    Back to their ancient home,
    Some from birds, from fishes some,
    Some from earth and some from seas,
    Some from beasts and some from trees.
    Some descend from clouds on high,
    Some from metals upwards fly,
And where th' attending soul naked and shivering stands,
    Meet, salute, and join their hands.
As dispers'd soldiers at the trumpet's call
    Haste to their colors all.
    Unhappy most, like tortur'd men,
Their joints new set to be new rack'd again.
    To mountains they for shelter pray;

[3] *Whether...images:* "The conquerors in the Olympic games were not only crowned with a garland of wild olive but also had a statue erected to them" (Cowley's note). *Pisa* was a town near the site of the famous games at Olympia in the Peloponnesus.
[4] Unconstrained, i.e., unchallenged.   [5] Unbalanced.

THE RESURRECTION   [1] "This ode is truly Pindarical, falling from one thing into another after his enthusiastical manner" (Cowley's note).
[2] *Numerous...quire:* rhythmical and well-appointed choir.
[3] *And he...divine:* "Shall see the whole world burnt to ashes like Troy, the destruction of which was so excellently written by him, though it was built like Troy too by divine hands. The walls of Troy were said to be built by Apollo and Neptune" (Cowley's note).
[4] Those whom, i.e., the dead or *long sluggards of five thousand years* who will be aroused for the last judgment.   [5] Reach.

The mountains shake, and run about no less confus'd
    than they.

4

Stop, stop, my Muse, allay thy vig'rous heat,
  Kindled at a hint so great.
Hold thy Pindaric Pegasus[6] closely in,
    Which does to rage begin,
And this steep hill would gallop up with violent course:
'Tis an unruly and a hard-mouth'd horse,
    Fierce and unbroken yet,
    Impatient of the spur or bit.
Now prances stately, and anon flies o'er the place,
Disdains the servile law of any settled pace,
Conscious and proud of his own natural force.
    'Twill no unskilful touch endure,
But flings writer and reader too that sits not sure.

TO MR. HOBBES

1

Vast bodies of philosophy
    I oft have seen and read,
    But all are bodies dead,
    Or bodies by art fashioned;
I never yet the living soul could see
    But in thy books and thee.
    'Tis only God can know
Whether the fair idea thou dost show
Agree entirely with His own or no.
    This I dare boldly tell,
'Tis so like truth 'twill serve our turn as well.
Just, as in Nature thy proportions be,
As full of concord their variety,
As firm the parts upon their center rest,
And all so solid are that they at least
As much as Nature emptiness detest.

2

Long did the mighty Stagirite[1] retain
The universal intellectual reign,
Saw his own country's short-liv'd leopard slain,[2]
The stronger Roman eagle did outfly,
Oft'ner renewed his age, and saw that die.
Mecca itself in spite of Mahomet possess'd,
And chas'd by a wild deluge from the east,
His monarchy new planted in the west.
But as in time each great imperial race
Degenerates, and gives some new one place,
    So did this noble empire waste,
    Sunk by degrees from glories past
And in the Schoolmen's hands it perish'd quite at last.
    Then nought but words it grew,
    And those all barb'rous too.
    It perish'd and it vanish'd there,
The life and soul breath'd out, became but empty air.[3]

3

The fields which answer'd well the ancients' plow,
Spent and outworn, return no harvest now,

In barren age wild and unglorious lie,
    And boast of past fertility,
The poor relief of present poverty.[4]
    Food and fruit we now must want
    Unless new lands we plant.
We break up tombs with sacrilegious hands;
    Old rubbish we remove;
To walk in ruins, like vain ghosts, we love,
    And with fond divining wands
      We search among the dead
      For treasures buried,
    Whilst still the liberal earth does hold
So many virgin mines of undiscover'd gold.

4

The Baltic, Euxin, and the Caspian,
And slender-limb'd Mediterranean,[5]
Seem narrow creeks to thee, and only fit
For the poor wretched fisher boats of wit.
Thy nobler vessel the vast ocean tries,
    And nothing sees but seas and skies,
    Till unknown regions it descries,
Thou great Columbus of the golden lands of
    new philosophies.
    Thy task was harder much than his,
    For thy learn'd America is
    Not only found out first by thee,
And rudely left to future industry,
    But thy eloquence and thy wit
Has planted, peopled, built, and civilized it.

5

    I little thought before
    (Nor being my own self so poor,
    Could comprehend so vast a store)
That all the wardrobe of rich eloquence
    Could have afforded half enough
    Of bright, of new, and lasting stuff[6]
To clothe the mighty limbs of thy gigantic sense:
Thy solid reason, like the shield from heaven
    To the Trojan hero given,[7]
Too strong to take a mark from any mortal dart,

[6]In Greek mythology, the winged horse of poetic inspiration.
TO MR. HOBBES [1]Aristotle, from his birthplace at Stagira in Macedonia.
[2]*Saw...slain*: "Outlasted the Grecian Empire, which in the Visions of Daniel is represented by a leopard with four wings upon the back and four heads, Chapter 7, Verse 6" (Cowley's note).
[3]*And in the Schoolmen's...air*: For an earlier but equally vehement attack on the Schoolmen, see Bacon's *Advancement of Learning*, p. 402.
[4]*The fields...poverty*: Cowley develops the same metaphor in his "Preface," p. 329.
[5]*The Baltic...Mediterranean*: "All the navigation of the ancients was in these seas; they seldom ventured into the ocean, and when they did, did only *littus legere*, coast about near the shore"(Cowley's note). [6]Fabric.
[7]*Like the shield...given*: The shield, given to Aeneas by his mother Venus, on which Vulcan had embossed the whole of Roman history (Vergil, *Aeneid*, VIII.626–728).

Yet shines with gold and gems in every part,
And wonders on it grav'd by the learn'd hand of art;
  A shield that gives delight
  Even to the enemies' sight,
Then when they're sure to lose the combat by 't.

   6
Nor can the snow which now cold age does shed
  Upon thy reverend head[8]
Quench or allay the noble fires within,
  But all which thou hast been,
  And all that youth can be, thou'rt yet,
  So fully still dost thou
Enjoy the manhood and the bloom of wit,
And all the natural heat, but not the fever too.
So contraries on Etna's top conspire,
Here hoary frosts, and by them breaks out fire,
A secure peace the faithful neighbors keep,
Th' emboldened snow next to the flame does sleep.
  And if we weigh, like thee,
  Nature and causes, we shall see
  That thus it needs must be:
To things immortal Time can do no wrong,
And that which never is to die, forever must be young.

DAVIDEIS

THE FIRST BOOK

I sing the man who Judah's scepter bore
In that right hand which held the crook before,
Whom from best poet, best of kings did grow,
The two chief gifts heav'n could on man bestow.
Much danger first, much toil did he sustain,   5
Whilst Saul and hell cross'd his strong fate in vain.
Nor did his crown less painful work afford,
Less exercise his patience or his sword
So long her conqu'ror Fortune's spite pursu'd,
Till with unwearied virtue he subdu'd   10
All homebred malice and all foreign boasts:
Their strength was armies, his the Lord of Hosts.[1]
 Thou[2] who didst David's royal stem adorn,
And gav'st him birth from whom thyself wast born,
Who didst in triumph at Death's court appear,   15
And slew'st him with Thy nails, Thy cross and spear,
Whilst hell's black tyrant trembled to behold
The glorious light he forfeited of old,
Who heav'n's glad burden now, and justest pride,
Sit'st high enthron'd next Thy great Father's side   20
(Where hallowed flames help to adorn that head
Which once the blushing thorns environed
Till crimson drops of precious blood hung down
Like rubies to enrich Thine humble crown),
Even Thou my breast with such blest rage inspire   25
As moved the tuneful strings of David's lyre,
Guide my bold steps with Thine old trav'ling flame[3] ·
In these untrodden paths to sacred fame.

Lo, with pure hands Thy heav'nly fires to take,
My well chang'd Muse I a chaste vestal make.[4]   30
From earth's vain joys and love's soft witchcraft free,
I consecrate my Magdalene[5] to Thee!
Lo, this great work, a temple to Thy praise,
On polish'd pillars of strong verse I raise!
A temple where if Thou vouchsafe to dwell   35
It Solomon's and Herod's shall excel.
Too long the Muses' lands have heathen been;
Their gods too long were de'ils, and virtues sin.
But Thou, Eternal Word, hast call'd forth me,
Th' apostle to convert that world to Thee,   40
T' unbind the charms that in slight fables lie,
And teach that truth is truest poesy.

> Following a lavish display of epic machinery—the statement of the theme, the invocation, a scene in hell to explain King Saul's envy of young David, and a scene in heaven to explain God's choice of David as the future King of Israel—the narrative begins with David's being summoned to appease the raging monarch with his lyre. The action yields at once, however, to "a digression concerning music."

 Tell me, O Muse (for thou or none canst tell
The mystic pow'rs that in blest numbers dwell,
Thou their great nature know'st, nor is it fit
This noblest gem of thine own crown t' omit),
Tell me from whence these heav'nly charms arise: 445
Teach the dull world t' admire what they despise.
 As first a various unform'd hint we find
Rise in some godlike poet's fertile mind
Till all the parts and words their places take,
And with just marches verse and music make,   450
Such was God's poem, this world's new essay.[6]
So wild and rude in its first draft it lay;
Th' ungovern'd parts no correspondence knew;
An artless war from thwarting motions grew
Till they to number and fix'd rules were brought   455
By the eternal Mind's poetic thought.

[8]Hobbes, born in 1588, was in his mid-sixties when Cowley wrote this ode to celebrate the publication of *Leviathan* (1651).
DAVIDEIS [1]*I sing...Hosts:* For a more prosaic statement of Cowley's subject and intentions see his "Preface," pp. 328 f.
[2]Christ, who as a mortal was descended from the royal House of David (Matthew 1.17, Luke 3.31).
[3]"And the Lord went before them by day in a pillar of a cloud, to lead them the way; and by night in a pillar of fire, to give them light; to go by day and night" (Exodus 13.21).
[4]*Lo...make:* "I hope this kind of boast (which I have been taught by almost all the old poets) will not seem immodest; for though some in other languages have attempted the writing a divine poem, yet none, that I know of, has in English" (Cowley's note).
[5]I.e., the poet's penitent Muse, conceived of as a reformed harlot like Mary Magdalene (Luke 8.36–50).
[6]*As first...new essay:* "This order and proportion of things is the true music of the world, and not that which Pythagoras, Plato, Tully, Macrobius, and many of the Fathers imagined, to arise audibly from the circumvolution of the heavens. This is their musical and loud voice, of which David speaks, Psalm 19" (Cowley's note).

Water and air He for the tenor chose,
Earth made the bass, the treble flame arose;
To th' active moon a quick, brisk stroke He gave,
To Saturn's string a touch more soft and grave.[7] 460
The motions straight and round and swift and slow
And short and long were mix'd and woven so,
Did in such artful figures smoothly fall,
As made this decent, measur'd dance of all.
And this is music: sounds that charm our ears 465
Is[8] but one dressing that rich science wears.
Though no man hear 't, though no man it rehearse,
Yet will there still be music in my verse.
In this great world so much of it we see:
The lesser, man, is all o'er harmony. 470
Storehouse of all proportions, single quire,[9]
Which first God's breath did tunefully inspire!
From hence blest music's heav'nly charms arise,
From sympathy which them and man allies.
Thus they our souls, thus they our bodies win, 475
Not by their force but party that's within.
Thus the strange cure on our spilt blood appli'd
Sympathy to the distant wound does guide.
Thus when two brethren strings are set alike,
To move them both, but one of them we strike. 480
Thus David's lyre did Saul's wide rage control,
And tun'd the harsh disorders of his soul.

THE SECOND BOOK

Fleeing from the jealous wrath of Saul, David falls asleep and, aided by an angelic visitation, dreams of the future glory of the royal line that he himself will found. The vision reaches its climax in a rather tinsel version of the Annunciation and Christ's nativity.

With sober pace an heav'nly Maid walks in,
Her looks all fair, no sign of native sin
Through her whole body writ;[10] immod'rate grace
Spoke things far more than human in her face. 745
It casts a dusky gloom o'er all the flow'rs,
And with full beams their mingled light devours.
An angel straight broke from a shining cloud,
And press'd his wings, and with much reverence bow'd.
Again he bow'd, and grave approach he made, 750
And thus his sacred message sweetly said:

"Hail, full of grace, thee the whole world shall call
Above all blest—thee who shalt bless them all.
Thy virgin womb in wondrous sort shall shroud
Jesus the God"—and then again he bow'd. 755
"Conception the great Spirit shall breathe on thee;
Hail thou, who must God's wife,[11] God's mother be!"
With that, his seeming form to heav'n he rear'd;
She low obeisance made, and disappear'd.
Lo, a new star three eastern sages see 760
(For why should only earth a gainer be?):
They saw this Phosphor's[12] infant light, and knew
It bravely usher'd in a sun as new.
They hasted all this rising sun t' adore;
With them rich myrrh and early spices bore. 765
Wise men, no fitter gift your zeal could bring:
You'll in a noisome stable find your king.
Anon a thousand devils run roaring in;
Some with a dreadful smile deform'dly grin,
Some stamp their cloven paws, some frown and tear 770
The gaping snakes from their black-knotted hair,
As if all grief and all the rage of hell
Were doubled now, or that just now they fell.
But when the dreaded Maid they ent'ring saw,
All fled with trembling fear and silent awe. 775
In her chaste arms th' eternal Infant lies,
Th' almighty voice chang'd into feeble cries.
Heav'n contain'd virgins oft, and will do more:
Never did virgin contain heav'n before.
Angels peep round to view this mystic thing, 780
And hallelujah round, all hallelujah sing.

[7]*To th' active moon...grave:* "Because the moon is but 28 days and Saturn above 29 years in finishing his course" (Cowley's note).
[8]Corrected to *Are* in the 1668 folio. [9]Choir.
[10]*Her looks...writ:* "I do not mean that she was without original sin, as her Roman adorers hold very temerariously, but that neither disease nor imperfection, which are the effects and footsteps, as it were, of sin, were to be seen in her body" (Cowley's note).
[11]"Though the word seem bold, I know no hurt in the figure. And *spouse* is not an heroical word. The church is called 'Christ's spouse' because whilst it is *militant* it is only, as it were, contracted, not married, till it becomes *triumphant*: but here is not the same reason" (Cowley's note). [12]The morning star's, i.e., Venus'.

Richard Lovelace [1618-1656/57]

Richard Lovelace has come down to us as the ideal cavalier, *sans peur et sans reproche*, who in the strength and plumage of his youth exemplified and gave expression to a way of life whose destruction he could not survive. Sprung from an ancient and distinguished Kentish family with a valiant military tradition, he went to the Charterhouse (when Richard Crashaw was a student there) and then, in 1634, to Gloucester Hall (now Worcester College), Oxford, where, according to Anthony Wood, he was accounted "the most amiable and beautiful person that ever eye beheld." Already, in 1631, Charles had signalized his royal approbation by naming him a gentleman waiter extraordinary, and in 1636, on a royal visit to the university, the archbishop of Canterbury, as chancellor, honored him still further with the M.A. degree—a tribute, one supposes, to his youth and beauty rather than his erudition. Already he had gained a local reputation with *The Scholars*, a comedy that, though never printed, was acted with success at Gloucester Hall and at the Whitefriars, Salisbury Court. A few months' stay in Cambridge, where he enrolled in 1637, was productive mainly, it would seem, of young Andrew Marvell's friendship, which found expression later in some commendatory verses for *Lucasta*.

In 1638 this admired of all admirers came to Charles' splendid court, where his social and amatory successes were obviously compatible with (and perhaps essential to) the poetry with which he quickly gained attention. In 1639 he flew, if not to war and arms, to the first of Charles' two abortive Scottish expeditions, but since these led only to the inglorious Treaty of Ripon (1640) and the weakening of the royal cause, it is not at all unlikely that he expressed his haughty disappointment in *The Soldier*, a now-lost play that he wrote about this time. At any rate he soon retired to Kent, where, at twenty-one, he took possession of his large estate to become a country gentleman and serve as justice of the peace. It was in this capacity that he was chosen (April 1642) by a group of disaffected royalists to present to Parliament a petition calling for the retention of episcopacy and the restoration of the King's eroded power. The Presbyterians in Parliament, having ordered a similar royalist petition to be burned not long before, were not amused by such intransigence, and so Lovelace promptly went to prison. When, several weeks later, he petitioned for release, he was freed on heavy bail, but with the condition that he refrain from any military action and not leave London without permission from the Speaker of the House.

Thus blocked from going to Charles' aid when the civil war began, he nonetheless, says Wood, sold most of his estates to raise money for the King, helped his younger brothers in their military careers, and perhaps went back and forth for several years to Holland on furtive missions for the royal cause. It was in these troubled times, presumably, that he wrote much of the poetry—to the still-unidentified Lucasta and to other, perhaps imaginary, ladies—on which his reputation rests. In 1648, however, Lovelace (who must long have been an object of suspicion) was again arrested and imprisoned just before his royal master's "martyrdom"—that is, his trial and execution. He probably spent his six-month term readying his *Lucasta* for the press, for the publication of the book almost coincided with his own release from prison in the spring of 1649. Thereafter Lovelace almost fades from view. If Wood may be believed (which Lovelace's most authoritative editor thinks unlikely), the prematurely aged poet, broken both in health and spirit, lived in destitution and died a pauper in "a very mean lodging in Gunpowder Alley near Shoe Lane." In 1660 the appearance of *Lucasta. Posthume Poems* (dated 1659), a collection of his later verses that the poet may have started and that his brother Dudley finished, did little to augment his reputation, which languished until Bishop Percy, recovering "To Althea from Prison" and "To Lucasta, Going to the Wars" for his *Reliques* (1765), inaugurated a revival.

My texts are based on *Lucasta: Epodes, Odes, Sonnets, Songs, &c. To Which Is Added Aramantha, a Pastorall*, 1649 (Wing L–3240) and *Lucasta. Posthume Poems*, 1659 (Wing L–3241). Virtually ignored throughout the eighteenth century, Lovelace was belatedly honored with a new edition of his poems by S. W. Singer (2 vols., 1817–18). Singer's unsatisfactory work was not markedly improved by W. C. Hazlitt (1864, rev. 1897), Harold Child (1904), and W. L. Phelps (2 vols., 1921), but at last C. H. Wilkinson produced the definitive edition (2 vols., 1925; 1 vol., 1930). The most substantial treatments of Lovelace's life and works are by C. H. Hartman (1925) and Manfred Weidhorn (1970), and he is represented in R. G. Howarth's *Minor Poets of the 17th Century* (rev. 1953).

from Lucasta: Epodes, Odes, Sonnets, Songs, etc. (1649)

TO HIS NOBLE FRIEND, MR. RICHARD
LOVELACE, UPON HIS POEMS

Sir,
Our times are much degenerate from those
Which your sweet Muse, which your fair fortune chose,
And as complexions alter with the climes,
Our wits have drawn th' infection of our times.
That candid age no other way could tell   5
To be ingenious but by speaking well.
Who best could praise had then the greatest praise:
'Twas more esteem'd to give than wear the bays.
Modest ambition studi'd only then
To honor not herself but worthy men.   10
These virtues now are banish'd out of town:
Our civil wars have lost the civic crown;
He highest builds who with most art destroys,
And against others' fame his own employs.
I see the envious caterpillar sit   15
On the fair blossom of each growing wit.
    The air's already tainted with the swarms
Of insects which against you rise in arms:
Word-peckers, paper-rats, book-scorpions,
Of wit corrupted the unfashion'd[1] sons.   20
The barbed censurers begin to look
Like the grim consistory on thy book,
And on each line cast a reforming eye,
Severer than the young presbytery.
Till when, in vain, they have thee all perus'd   25
You shall for being faultless be accus'd.
Some, reading your *Lucasta*, will allege
You wrong'd in her the House's privilege;
Some that you under sequestration are
Because you write when going to the war;[2]   30
And one the book prohibits because Kent
Their first petition by the author sent.[3]
    But when the beauteous ladies came to know
That their dear Lovelace was endanger'd so—
Lovelace that thaw'd the most congealed breast,   35
He who lov'd best and them defended best,
Whose hand so rudely grasps the steely brand,
Whose hand so gently melts the lady's hand—
They all in mutiny, though yet undrest,
Salli'd, and would in his defence contest.   40
And one, the loveliest that was yet e'er seen,
Thinking that I too of the rout had been,
Mine eyes invaded with a female spite
(She knew what pain t'would be to lose that sight).
"O no, mistake not," I repli'd, "for I   45
In your defence or in his cause would die."
But he, secure of glory and of time,
Above their envy or mine aid doth clime.
Him valian'st men and fairest nymphs approve:

His book in them finds judgment, with you, love.   50
            Andrew Marvell[4]

SONG, SET BY MR. HENRY LAWES:[1]
TO LUCASTA, GOING BEYOND THE SEAS

            1
If to be absent were to be
            Away from thee,
        Or that when I am gone,
        You or I were alone,
Then, my Lucasta, might I crave
Pity from blust'ring wind or swallowing wave.

            2
But I'll not sigh one blast or gale
            To swell my sail,
        Or pay a tear to 'suage[2]
        The foaming blew god's rage;[3]
For whether he will let me pass
Or no, I'm still as happy as I was.

            3
Though seas and land betwixt us both,
            Our faith and troth,
        Like separated souls,
        All time and space controls;
Above the highest sphere we meet,
Unseen, unknown, and greet as angels greet.

            4
So then we do anticipate
            Our after-fate,
        And are alive i' the skies,
        If thus our lips and eyes
Can speak like spirits unconfin'd
In heaven, their earthy bodies left behind.

TO HIS NOBLE FRIEND   [1]Misshapen, unrefined.
[2]*The barbed censurers...war*: Marvell seems to be repudiating all
varieties of censorship, whether imposed by the Roman Catholics'
dread *consistory* or by their Puritan adversaries' machinery of
Parliamentary acts. For a classical statement of this libertarian
theme see Milton's *Areopagitica*, pp. 603 ff.
[3]*And one the book...sent*: In April 1642, when Lovelace and Sir
William Boteler (or Butler), acting on behalf of their neighboring
gentry in Kent, audaciously presented a strongly royalist petition
to the House of Commons both men were sent to prison.
[4]For Andrew Marvell, whose earliest published work is this con-
tribution to *Lucasta*, see pp. 348 ff.

GOING BEYOND THE SEAS   [1]Prominent composer (1596–1662)
whose many works include the music for Thomas Carew's
Coelum Britannicum (1633) and Milton's *Comus* (1634).
[2]Assuage.
[3]Lovelace is apparently thinking of Aeolus, the god of the winds.
Some editors emend to *blue*, a conventional epithet for Neptune,
god of the sea.

SONG, SET BY MR. JOHN LANIERE:[1]
TO LUCASTA, GOING TO THE WARS

1

Tell me not, sweet, I am unkind,[2]
  That from the nunnery
Of thy chaste breast and quiet mind
  To war and arms I fly.

2

True, a new mistress now I chase,
  The first foe in the field;
And with a stronger faith embrace
  A sword, a horse, a shield.

3

Yet this inconstancy is such
  As you too shall adore;
I could not love thee, dear, so much,
  Lov'd I not honor more.

A PARADOX

1

'Tis true the beauteous star
  To which I first did bow
Burnt quicker, brighter far
  Than that which leads me now,
    Which shines with more delight;
    For gazing on that light
    So long near lost my sight.

2

Through foul we follow fair,
  For had the world one face
And earth been bright as air,
  We had known neither place;
    Indians smell not their nest;
    A Swiss or Finn tastes best
    The spices of the east.

3

So from the glorious sun,
  Who to his height hath got,
With what delight we run
  To some black cave or grot.
    And heav'nly Sidney[1] you
    Twice read, had rather view
    Some odd romance so new.

4

The god that constant keeps
  Unto his deities
Is poor in joys, and sleeps
  Imprison'd in the skies:
    This knew the wisest,[2] who
    From Juno stole below
    To love a bear or cow.

SONG, SET BY MR. HENRY LAWES:
TO ARAMANTHA, THAT SHE WOULD
DISHEVEL HER HAIR

1

Aramantha, sweet and fair,
Ah, braid no more that shining hair!
  As my curious hand or eye,
Hovering round thee, let it fly.

2

Let it fly as unconfin'd
As its calm ravisher, the wind,
  Who hath left his darling, th' east,
To wanton o'er that spicy nest.

3

Every tress must be confest,[1]
But neatly tangled at the best,
  Like a clue[2] of golden thread,
Most excellently ravelled.

4

Do not, then, wind up that light
In ribands and o'ercloud in night
  Like the sun in's early ray,
But shake your head and scatter day.

5

See, 'tis broke! Within this grove,
The bower and the walks of love,
  Weary lie we down and rest,
And fan each other's panting breast.

6

Here we'll strip and cool our fire
In cream below, in milk-baths higher;
  And when all wells are drawn dry,
I'll drink a tear out of thine eye,

7

Which our very joys shall leave,
That sorrows thus we can deceive;
  Or our very sorrows weep,
That joys so ripe, so little keep.

GRATIANA DANCING AND SINGING

1

See! with what constant motion,
Even and glorious as the sun,

GOING TO THE WARS [1]Son (d. 1650) of Nicholas Laniere (1588–1666), a court musician who supplied music for the masques of Jonson and Campion. [2]*Unkind*: (1) unnatural; (2) harsh.
A PARADOX [1]Sir Philip Sidney's *Arcadia* (1590) was popular throughout the seventeenth century.
[2]I.e., Zeus, whose infidelity to Hera (not Juno) was notorious. Among his many amorous escapades was one with Io (whom he transformed into a heifer), but there is no record of his alliance with a bear.
TO ARAMANTHA [1]Disclosed. [2]A ball of thread or twine.

Gratiana steers that noble frame,
Soft as her breast, sweet as her voice,
  That gave each winding law and poise,
    And swifter than the wings of Fame.

2

She beat the happy pavement
By such a star-made firmament,
  Which now no more the roof envies,
But swells up high with Atlas[1] ev'n,
Bearing the brighter, nobler heav'n,
  And in her all the deities.

3

Each step trod out a lover's thought
And the ambitious hopes he brought;
  Chain'd to her brave feet with such arts,
Such sweet command and gentle awe,
As when she ceas'd, we sighing saw
  The floor lay pav'd with broken hearts,

4

So did she move, so did she sing
Like the harmonious spheres that bring
  Unto their rounds their music's aid;
Which she performed such a way
As all th' enamor'd world will say
  The Graces danced, and Apollo play'd.

THE SCRUTINY. SONG: SET BY MR. THOMAS CHARLES[1]

1

Why should you swear I am forsworn,
  Since thine I vow'd to be?
Lady, it is already morn,
  And 'twas last night I swore to thee
That fond impossibility.

2

Have I not lov'd thee much and long,
  A tedious twelve hours' space?
I must all other beauties wrong
  And rob thee of a new embrace,
Could I still dote upon thy face.

3

Not but all joy in thy brown hair
  By others may be found;
But I must search the black and fair,
  Like skillful mineralists that sound[2]
For treasure in unplow'd-up ground.

4

Then, if when I have lov'd my round,
  Thou prov'st the pleasant she,
With spoils of meaner beauties crowned
  I laden will return to thee,
Ev'n sated with variety.

ORPHEUS TO WOODS

SONG: SET BY MR. CURTES[1]
Hark, O hark, you guilty trees,
In whose gloomy galleries
Was the cruel'st murder[2] done
That e'er yet eclips'd the sun.
Be, then, henceforth in your twigs
Blasted e'er you sprout to sprigs.
Feel no season of the year
But what shaves off all your hair,
Nor carve any from your wombs
Ought but coffins and their tombs.

THE GRASSHOPPER
To My Noble Friend, Mr. Charles Cotton[1]

ODE

1
O thou that swing'st upon the waving hair
  Of some well-filled oaten beard,
Drunk every night with a delicious tear
  Dropp'd thee from heav'n, where now th'art rear'd;

2
The joys of earth and air are thine entire,
  That with thy feet and wings dost hop and fly;
And, when thy poppy works, thou dost retire
  To thy carv'd acron[2] bed to lie.

3
Up with the day, the sun thou welcom'st then,
  Sport'st in the gilt plats[3] of his beams,
And all these merry days mak'st merry men,
  Thyself, and melancholy streams.[4]

4
But ah, the sickle! Golden ears are cropp'd;
  Ceres and Bacchus bid good night;
Sharp, frosty fingers all your flowers have topp'd,[5]
  And what scythes spar'd, winds shave off quite,

GRATIANA [1]In Greek mythology, a Titan who supported the heavens on his shoulders.
THE SCRUTINY [1]Although the composer has not been identified this popular song was included in several contemporary collections. [2]Dig.
ORPHEUS TO WOODS [1]Unidentified.
[2]Lovelace is perhaps alluding to Orpheus' wife Eurydice, a dryad or tree-nymph who died when she had stepped upon a snake while fleeing from the lustful Aristaeus.
THE GRASSHOPPER [1]A friend (d. 1658) of many men of letters whom Clarendon called "the greatest ornament of the town, in the esteem of those who had been best bred," and to whom Herrick, in a poem addressed to him, said that "it is my pride to be/Not so much known as to be lov'd of thee." He was father of the minor poet (1630–87) now chiefly remembered as the translator of Montaigne.
[2]Acorn. [3]Golden rays.
[4]*And all these . . . streams*: i.e., you make merry not only other men but also yourself and the melancholy streams.
[5]Sheared the tops from.

5

Poor verdant fool! and now green ice! thy joys,
  Large and as lasting as thy perch of grass,
Bid us lay in 'gainst winter rain, and poise[6]
  Their floods with an o'erflowing glass.

6

Thou best of men and friends! we will create
  A genuine summer in each other's breast,
And spite of this cold time and frozen fate,
  Thaw us a warm seat to our rest.

7

Our sacred hearths shall burn eternally
  As vestal flames; the north wind, he
Shall strike[7] his frost-stretch'd wings, dissolve, and fly
  This Etna in epitome.

8

Dropping December shall come weeping in,
  Bewail th' usurping of his reign;[8]
But when in show'rs of old Greek[9] we begin,
  Shall cry he hath his crown again.

9

Night as clear Hesper[10] shall our tapers whip
  From the light casements where we play,
And the dark hag from her black mantle strip,
  And stick there everlasting day.

10

Thus richer than untempted kings are we,
  That, asking nothing, nothing need;
Though lord of all what seas embrace, yet he
  That wants himself is poor indeed.

TO LUCASTA FROM PRISON
An Epode

1

Long in thy shackles, liberty
  I ask, not from these walls but thee[1]
(Left for awhile another's bride),
  To fancy all the world beside.

2

Yet ere I do begin to love,
  See! how I all my objects prove;
Then my free soul to that confine
  'Twere possible I might call mine.

3

First I would be in love with Peace,
  And her rich swelling breasts' increase;
But how, alas! how may that be,
  Despising earth, she will love me?

4

Fain would I be in love with War,
  As my dear, just, avenging star;

But War is lov'd so everywhere,
  Ev'n he disdains a lodging here.

5

Thee and thy wounds I would bemoan,
  Fair, thorough-shot Religion;
But he lives only that kills thee,
  And whoso binds thy hands is free.

6

I would love a Parliament
  As a main prop from Heav'n sent;
But ah! who's he that would be wedded
  To th' fairest body that's beheaded?[2]

7

Next would I court my liberty,
  And then my birthright, property;
But can that be, when it is known
  There's nothing you can call your own?

8

A reformation I would have,
  As for our griefs a sov'reign salve;[3]
That is, a cleansing of each wheel
  Of state that yet some rust doth feel;

9

But not a reformation so
  As to reform were to o'erthrow;
Like watches by unskillful men
  Disjointed, and set ill again.

10

The "public faith" I would adore,[4]
  But she is bankrupt of her store;[5]
Nor how to trust her can I see,
  For she that cozens all, must me.

11

Since, then, none of these can be
  Fit objects for my love and me,
What then remains but th' only spring[6]
  Of all our loves and joys, the king?

12

He who, being the whole ball[7]
  Of day on earth, lends it to all;
When seeking to eclipse his right,
  Blinded, we stand in our own light.

[6]Balance, i.e. counteract.   [7]Spread.
[8]In 1644 Parliament forbad the traditional celebration of Christmas as a pagan holiday.
[9]Copious drafts of hippocras, a cordial made of spiced wine?
[10]Venus, the evening star.
TO LUCASTA FROM PRISON   [1]I.e., Lucasta.
[2]I.e., Parliament without the king as sovereign head of state.
[3]Efficacious cure.
[4]Monies borrowed by Parliament without proper collateral.
[5]Wealth.   [6]Source.   [7]Globe, i.e., the sun.

13

And now an universal mist
    Of error is spread o'er each breast,
With such a fury edg'd as is
    Not found in th' inwards of th' abyss.

14

Oh, from thy glorious starry wain,
    Dispense on me one sacred beam,
To light me where I soon may see
    How to serve you, and you trust me.

LUCASTA PAYING HER OBSEQUIES TO THE CHASTE MEMORY OF MY DEAREST COUSIN, MRS. BOWES BARNE[1]

1

See, what an undisturbed tear
She weeps for her last sleep,
But viewing her, straight wak'd, a star,
She weeps that she did weep.

2

Grief ne'er before did tyrannize
    On th' honor of that brow,
And at the wheels of her brave eyes
    Was captive led till now.

3

Thus for a saint's apostasy,
    The unimagin'd woes
And sorrows of the hierarchy,
    None but an angel knows.

4

Thus for lost souls' recovery,
    The clapping of all wings
And triumphs of this victory,
    None but an angel sings.

5

So none but she knows to bemoan
    This equal[2] virgin's fate:
None but Lucasta can her crown
    Of glory celebrate.

6

Then dart on me, chaste light, one ray
    By which I may descry
Thy joy clear through this cloudy day
    To dress my sorrow by.

TO ALTHEA FROM PRISON
Song Set by Dr. John Wilson[1]

1

When Love with unconfined wings
    Hovers within my gates,

And my divine Althea brings
    To whisper at the grates;[2]
When I lie tangled in her hair
    And fetter'd to her eye,
The gods that wanton in the air
    Know no such liberty.

2

When flowing cups run swiftly round,
    With no allaying Thames,[3]
Our careless heads with roses bound,
    Our hearts with loyal flames;
When thirsty grief in wine we steep,
    When healths and draughts go free,
Fishes that tipple in the deep
    Know no such liberty.

3

When, like committed linnets, I
    With shriller throat shall sing
The sweetness, mercy, majesty,
    And glories of my king;
When I shall voice aloud how good
    He is, how great should be,
Enlarged winds that curl the flood
    Know no such liberty.

4

Stone walls do not a prison make,
    Nor iron bars a cage:
Minds innocent and quiet take
    That for an hermitage.
If I have freedom in my love,
    And in my soul am free,
Angels alone, that soar above,
    Enjoy such liberty.

LUCASTA'S WORLD
Epode

1

Cold as the breath of winds that blow
To silver shot descending snow,

    Lucasta sigh'd[1] when she did close
      The world in frosty chains!
    And then a frown to rubies froze
      The blood boil'd in our veins:

Yet cooled not the heat her sphere
Of beauties first had kindled there.

TO THE CHASTE MEMORY [1]Presumably an unmarried relative of Lovelace's mother (née Anne Barne). Mrs.: Mistress, i.e., Miss. [2]Comparable (to Lucasta herself).
TO ALTHEA FROM PRISON [1]The composer (1595–1674) of the musical setting of this famous poem, himself a noted lutenist at the court of Charles I, was identified on the title page of his *Cheerful Ayres or Ballads* (1660) as "Music Professor" at Oxford. [2]Bars. [3]I.e., no water (to dilute the wine).
LUCASTA'S WORLD [1]Text *sight.*

2

Then mov'd and with a sudden flame
Impatient to melt all again,

Straight from her eyes she lightning hurl'd,
And earth in ashes mourns;
The sun his blaze denies the world,
And in her luster burns:

Yet warmed not the hearts her nice
Disdain had first congeal'd to ice.

3

And now her tears nor griev'd desire
Can quench this raging, pleasing fire;

Fate but one way allows; behold
Her smiles' divinity!
They fann'd this heat, and thaw'd that cold,
So fram'd up a new sky.

Thus earth from flames and ice repriev'd,
E'er since hath in her sunshine liv'd.

[LA BELLA BONA ROBA][1]

1

I cannot tell who loves the skeleton
Of a poor marmoset,[2] nought but bone, bone.
Give me a nakedness with her clothes[3] on.

2

Such whose white satin upper coat of skin,
Cut upon velvet rich incarnadin,[4]
Has yet a body (and of flesh) within.

3

Sure it is meant good husbandry in men
Who do incorporate with airy lean,
T' repair their sides and get their rib again.[5]

4

Hard hap unto that huntsman that decrees
Fat joys for all his sweat, whenas he sees,
After his 'say, nought but his keeper's fees.[6]

5

Then, Love, I beg, when next thou tak'st thy bow,
Thy angry shafts, and dost heart-chasing go,
Pass rascal[7] deer, strike me the largest doe.

LA BELLA BONA ROBA [1]Owing presumably to a printer's error, the title of this poem (which means "harlot") was affixed, most inappropriately, to the poem that precedes it in the text, an "Ode" addressed to "My Lady H."
[2]Prostitute. [3]I.e., skin and flesh.
[4]Incarnadine, i.e., pink or flesh-colored.
[5]*Sure it is...again*: i.e., men who copulate with thin harlots (*incorporate with airy lean*) are perhaps thriftily trying to regain the rib that Adam lost at Eve's creation (Genesis 2.21). Their: text *they*.
[6]*Hard hap...fees*: i.e., it is unfair (*hard hap*) that at the assay (*'say*) or dismemberment of the deer the hunter should get only a meager portion of the carcass. Keeper's fees: the (usually undesirable) parts of the deer given to the gamekeeper. [7]Lean, inferior.

from Lucasta: Posthume[1] Poems of Richard Lovelace, Esq. (1660)

TO LUCASTA, HER RESERVED LOOKS

Lucasta, frown and let me die,
But smile and see I live;
The sad indifference of your eye
Both kills and doth reprieve.
You hide our fate within its screen,   5
We feel our judgment ere we hear:
So in one picture I have seen
An angel here, the devil there.

A BLACK PATCH[1] ON LUCASTA'S FACE

Dull as I was, to think that a court fly
Presum'd so near her eye,
When 'twas th' industrious bee
Mistook her glorious face for paradise.

To sum up all his chemistry of spice,   5
With a brave pride and honor led,
Near both her suns[2] he makes his bed,
And though a spark struggles to rise as red,
Then emulates the gay
Daughter of day,   10
Acts the romantic phoenix' fate:
When now with all his sweets laid out in state,
Lucasta scatters but one heat,
And all the aromatic pills do sweat,
And gums calcin'd[3] themselves to powder beat;   15
Which a fresh gale of air
Conveys into her hair.
Then, chaste, he's set on fire,

LUCASTA: POSTHUME POEMS [1]Posthumous.
A BLACK PATCH [1]Beauty patch. [2]I.e., eyes.
[3]Reduced by fire to powder.

And in these holy flames doth glad expire;
　　And that black marble tablet there
　　　So near her either sphere
　　　Was plac'd, nor foil nor ornament,
But the sweet little bee's large monument.

TO LUCASTA

1

Like to the sent'nel stars I watch all night,
　　For still the grand round of your light
　　　And glorious breast
　　　Awakes in me an east,
Nor will my rolling eyes e'er know a west.

2

Now on my down I'm toss'd as on a wave,
　　And my repose is made my grave;
　　　Fluttering I lie,
　　　Do beat myself and die
But for a resurrection from your eye.

3

Ah, my fair murd'ress, dost thou cruelly heal
　　With various pains to make me well?
　　　Then let me be
　　　Thy cut anatomy,[1]
And in each mangled part my heart you'll see.

THE SNAIL

Wise emblem of our politic world,
Sage snail, within thine own self curl'd,
Instruct me softly to make haste,
Whilst these my feet go slowly fast.
　Compendious snail! thou seem'st to me　　　　5
Large Euclid's strict epitome,
And in each diagram dost fling
Thee from the point unto the ring:
A figure now triangular,
An oval now, and now a square;　　　　10
And then a serpentine dost crawl,
Now a straight line, now crook'd, now all.
　Preventing[1] rival of the day,
Th'art up and openest thy ray,
And ere the morn cradles the moon　　　　15
Th' art broke into a beauteous noon.
Then when the sun sups in the deep,
Thy silver horns ere Cynthia's[2] peep;
And thou from thine own liquid bed,
New Phoebus,[3] heav'st thy pleasant head.　　　　20
　Who shall a name for thee create,
Deep riddle of mysterious state?
Bold Nature, that gives common birth
To all products of seas and earth,
Of thee, as earthquakes, is afraid,　　　　25
Nor will thy dire deliv'ry aid.

Thou thine own daughter then, and sire,
That son and mother art entire,
That big still with thyself dost go,
And liv'st an aged embryo;　　　　30
That like the cubs of India,[4]
Thou from thyself a while dost play;
But frightened with a dog or gun,
In thine own belly thou dost run,
And as thy house was thine own womb,　　　　35
So thine own womb concludes thy tomb.
　But now I must (analyz'd king)
Thy economic[5] virtues sing;
Thou great staid husband still within,
Thou thee, that's thine, dost discipline;[6]　　　　40
And when thou art to progress bent,
Thou mov'st thyself and tenement;[7]
As warlike Scythians travel'd, you
Remove your men and city too;[8]
Then after a sad dearth and rain,　　　　45
Thou scatterest thy silver train;
And when the trees grow nak'd and old,
Thou clothest them with cloth of gold,
Which from thy bowels thou dost spin,
And draw from the rich mines within.　　　　50
　Now hast thou chang'd thee, saint, and made
Thyself a fane[9] that's cupola'd
And in thy wreathed cloister thou
Walkest thine own gray friar too;
Strict and lock'd up, th'art hood all o'er　　　　55
And ne'er eliminat'st[10] thy door.
On salads thou dost feed severe,
And 'stead of beads thou dropp'st a tear,
And when to rest, each calls the bell,
Thou sleep'st within thy marble cell,　　　　60
Where in dark contemplation plac'd
The sweets of nature thou dost taste;
And now with time thy days resolve,
And in a jelly thee dissolve
Like a shot star, which doth repair　　　　65
Upward, and rarefy the air.

TO LUCASTA 　[1]A subject for dissection.

THE SNAIL 　[1]Anticipating, i.e., early.
[2]The moon goddess. 　[3]The sun god.
[4]Lovelace is perhaps thinking of the su (or sue), an exotic creature described by the contemporary lexicographer Henry Cockeram as "a most cruel, fierce beast" that carries its young upon its back "to shadow them from the heat with her huge tail."
[5]I.e., pertaining to household management.
[6]*Thou great...discipline:* i.e., the snail, like the stately (*staid*) master of a household (*husband*), is always at home (*still within*), presiding over both himself and his residence, which are identical (*thee, that's thine*). 　[7]Habitation, residence.
[8]*As warlike...too:* "Having neither cities nor forts, and carrying their dwellings with them wherever they go," Herodotus said (IV.46), the ancient Scythians were almost invulnerable. 　[9]Temple.
[10]Pass the threshold of.

Andrew Marvell [1621-1678]

Although literary history is strewn with the wrecks of once-proud reputations, the slow, corrective work of time occasionally produces astonishing reversals and recoveries. A case in point is Andrew Marvell, whose enthronement as a major lyric poet after some two centuries of neglect reinforces Hazlitt's contention that the judgment of posterity, on which a writer's fame must finally rest, can be neither bargained for nor hurried.

Certainly Marvell did little to secure his own renown. Even if we did not know, on Aubrey's testimony, that he was an intensely private man of such "very modest conversation" that he had no "general acquaintance," we might infer from the blend of reticence and hauteur apparent in his work that conventional authorial egotism would have been repugnant to him. His lyric poems, most of them presumably written in his youth, remained in manuscript until his death, and he was so discreet—not to say evasive—about the publication of the politically explosive satires of his later years that it is hard to ascertain the canon. Virtually unknown as a poet in his own time and thereafter remembered, if at all, as a hard-working member of Parliament and a political pamphleteer who throughout the early Restoration sought to check the crown's encroachments, he hardly had a place in literature until his rediscovery in the later nineteenth century. Despite his enormous current reputation, as certified by bales of scholarship and exegesis, he remains a somewhat hooded, enigmatic figure: a Puritan whose verses were as witty as Donne's and as debonair as Herrick's, a protégé of Milton's and a eulogist of Cromwell's who sat for almost twenty years in Charles II's House of Commons, a man of fastidious intellect and far-ranging erudition who flung himself into the swamp of Restoration politics, a poet who abandoned lyric charm for the brutalities and topicalities of partisan satire, a writer whose artful ambiguities both challenge and repel our efforts to ascertain what sort of man he was really or to trace, with professorial precision, the links between his life and works.

Although spottily recorded, it was not an uneventful life. The fourth child and only son of an Anglican clergyman whom Fuller described as "most facetious in his discourse, yet grave in his carriage," Marvell went at twelve from the Grammar School at Hull to Trinity College, Cambridge. There he showed his youthful royalism by contributing (along with Crashaw, Cowley, Edward King, and others) Greek and Latin verses to a congratulatory volume (1637) on the birth of Princess Anne; also, he alarmed his aging father by a brief conversion to the Roman Catholic Church. After receiving his B.A. degree in 1638 he stayed on in Cambridge as a scholar of his college until 1641, when, shortly after his father's death by drowning, he embarked upon a different kind of education by going abroad for several years of travel and of learning foreign languages. It was at about this time, presumably, that he began to write. By 1645 his "Dialogue between Thyrsis and Dorinda" had been set to music by Milton's friend William Lawes; in 1649 (when he was back in England) he contributed a commendatory poem to Richard Lovelace's *Lucasta* (see p. 341) and (together with Herrick and Dryden) poetically mourned Henry, Lord Hasting's untimely death by smallpox in the lugubrious *Lacrymae Musarum*. Although here as elsewhere conjecture must take the place of knowledge, we may assume that his appointment as tutor to Mary, daughter of the great Thomas Fairfax, who had recently resigned as commander-in-chief of the parliamentary forces to live in cultivated ease at Nun Appleton in Yorkshire, gave him leisure for the composition of those lyric poems on which his reputation rests. By 1653, having missed appointment (despite Milton's strong endorsement) as assistant secretary to the Council of State, he became the tutor of Cromwell's ward William Dutton at Eton, and thereafter, despite his earlier dubieties, he followed Cromwell's star, duly publicizing his attachment in a string of panegyrics in both Latin and English and finally (1657) attaining the reward of Milton's former post as Latin secretary to the Council of State.

The final and most public phase of his career, which began in 1659 with his election as a member of Parliament for Hull, lies beyond our limits. It was marked not only by zealous and devoted service in the House of Commons until he died and by at least two extended stays (for espionage or diplomacy or both) in Holland and in Russia, but also by a stream of satire and anti-royalist propaganda in prose and verse. For some of this material—like the anonymous *Rehearsal Transprosed* (1672–73) and *An Account of the Growth of Popery and Arbitrary Government in England* (1677)—Marvell was remembered as a champion of dissent and toleration; but most of the verse satires, which mercilessly attacked Charles II and his ministers, were published so furtively that their authorship is still a matter of dispute despite their attribution to Marvell "and other eminent wits" in the posthumous *Collection of Poems on Affairs of State* (1689). Even the presumably authoritative *Miscellaneous Poems*, which were published three years after Marvell's death by one Mary Palmer, a fortune-hunter posing as his widow, by no means fixed the canon. Although this volume finally made public the great lyric and reflective poems of his early years, it was stripped (after printing and before publication) of such politically dangerous pieces as the famous "Horatian Ode," "The First Anniversary of the Government under O.C.," and "A Poem upon the Death of O.C." A British Museum copy of the 1681 *Miscellaneous Poems* that somehow escaped the censor's hand long supplied the only texts of these three canceled poems, but in 1946 the Bodleian Library acquired another copy that contained manuscript additions (perhaps by the poet's nephew William Popple) of seventeen verse satires of the reign of Charles II as well as the three deleted poems (one of them—the elegy on Cromwell—with a previously unrecorded conclusion of some 300 lines). It is hard to think of another major English poet whose works have so narrowly escaped oblivion.

For everything except "An Horatian Ode" (pp. 365 f.) I have based my text upon the Harvard copy of *Miscellaneous Poems*, 1681 (Wing M–872), and for "An Horatian Ode" on the Scolar Press facsimile (1969) of the unique British Museum copy of *Miscellaneous Poems* (shelfmark C. 59. i.8). There were editions of what purported to be the collected works by Thomas Cooke (2 vols., 1726), Edward Thompson (3 vols., 1776), and A. B. Grosart (4 vols., 1872–75). The last remains the only available collection of Marvell's complete prose (Vols. III-IV), but H. M. Margoliouth's edition of the *Poems and Letters* as revised and enlarged by Pierre Legouis and E. E. Duncan-Jones (3d ed., 2 vols., 1971) is authoritative. More modest editions of the poems are those by G. A. Aitken (2 vols., 1892), Edward Wright (1904), Hugh Macdonald (1952), Joseph Summers (1961), James Winny (1962), Frank Kermode (1967), George de F. Lord (1968), James Reeves and Martin Seymour-Smith (1969), and Elizabeth Donno (1972); of selections from the prose and poetry by Dennis Davison (1952); and of the Latin poems alone by W. A. McQueen and K. A. Rockwell (1964). There is an excellent edition of both parts of *The Rehearsal Transprosed* by D. I. B. Smith (1971).

The standard life is Pierre Legouis' masterly *André Marvell, poète, puritain, patriote* (1928) which is now available in English (2d ed., 1968). Still of great importance is T. S. Eliot's influential tercentenary tribute of 1921 (*Selected Essays*, 1932), and from the many subsequent critical assessments one may mention M. C. Bradbrook and M. G. Lloyd Thomas' stimulating *Andrew Marvell* (1940, corrected reprint 1962), J. B. Leishman's explication of the poems (1965), Harold E. Toliver's *Marvell's Ironic Vision* (1965), John M. Wallace's important *Destiny His Choice: The Loyalism of Andrew Marvell* (1968), Donald Friedman's *Marvell's Pastoral Art* (1970), Rosalie L. Colie's *"My Echoing Song": Andrew Marvell's Poetry of Criticism* (1970), and Ann E. Berthoff's *Resolved Soul: A Study of Marvell's Major Poems* (1970). Something of the enormous range of smaller critical commentary on Marvell is suggested by the recent anthologies of George de F. Lord (1968), John Carey (1969), and Michael Wilding (1969). Thomas Clayton has discussed some of the texual problems (particularly the notorious "morning glew" in "To His Coy Mistress") in *ELR*, III (1972). There is a short bibliography by John Peter in his recent monograph (1958) and a longer one by Dennis G. Donnovan (1969). The Scolar Press facsimile cited earlier includes the manuscript additions in the Bodleian copy of *Miscellaneous Poems*.

from Miscellaneous Poems (1681)

TO THE READER

These are to certify every ingenious reader that all these poems, as also the other things in this book contained, are printed according to the exact copies of my late dear husband under his own handwriting, being found since his death among his other papers, witness my hand this fifteenth day of October, 1680.

Mary Marvell[1]

A DIALOGUE BETWEEN THE RESOLVED SOUL AND CREATED PLEASURE

Courage, my soul, now learn to wield
The weight of thine immortal shield.[1]
Close on thy head thy helmet bright;
Balance thy sword against the fight;
See where an army, strong as fair,   5
With silken banners spreads the air.
Now, if thou be'st that thing divine,
In this day's combat let it shine,
And show that nature wants an art
To conquer one resolved heart.   10

Pleasure:
Welcome the creation's guest,
Lord of earth and heaven's heir.
Lay aside that warlike crest,
And of nature's banquet share.
Where the souls of fruits and flow'rs   15
Stand prepar'd to heighten yours.

Soul:
I sup above, and cannot stay
To bait[2] so long upon the way.

Pleasure:
On these downy pillows lie,
Whose soft plumes will thither fly   20
On these roses strow'd so plain
Lest one leaf thy side should strain.[3]

Soul:
My gentler rest is on a thought,
Conscious of doing what I ought.

Pleasure:
If thou be'st with perfumes pleas'd,   25
Such as oft the gods appeas'd,
Thou in fragrant clouds shalt show
Like another god below.

Soul:
A soul that knows not to presume
Is heaven's and its own perfume.   30

Pleasure:
Everything does seem to vie
Which should first attract thine eye,
But since none deserves that grace,
In this crystal[4] view thy face.

Soul:
When the Creator's skill is priz'd,   35
The rest is all but earth disguis'd.

Pleasure:
Hark how music then prepares
For thy stay these charming airs,
Which the posting[5] winds recall,
And suspend the river's fall.   40

Soul:
Had I but any time to lose,
On this I would it all dispose
Cease, tempter! None can chain a mind
Whom this sweet chordage[6] cannot bind.

Chorus:
Earth cannot show so brave a sight   45
As when a single soul does fence
The batteries of alluring sense,
And heaven views it with delight.

TO THE READER [1]Actually Mary Palmer, an impostor who claimed to be Marvell's widow in order to inherit part of his estate.
A DIALOGUE [1]The imagery derives from Paul's injunction (Ephesians 6.17) to the Christian warrior to "take the helmet of salvation, and the sword of the spirit, which is the word of God." [2]Pause for refreshment.
[3]*Strow'd...strain*: strewn so flat (*plain*) that there would not be a single crumpled petal. [4]Mirror. [5]Rushing.
[6]With a pun on *cord* and *chord*.

Then persevere, for still new charges sound,
And if thou overcom'st thou shalt be crown'd.　　50

Pleasure:
All this fair and soft⁷ and sweet,
　Which scatteringly doth shine,
Shall within one beauty meet,
　And she be only thine.

Soul:
If things of sight such heavens be,　　55
What heavens are those we cannot see?

Pleasure:
Wheresoe'er thy foot shall go,
　The minted gold shall lie,
Till thou purchase all below,
　And want new worlds to buy.　　60

Soul:
Were't not a price⁸ who'ld value gold?
And that's worth nought that can be sold.

Pleasure:
Wilt thou all the glory have
　That war or peace commend?
Half the world shall be thy slave,　　65
　The other half thy friend.

Soul:
What friends, if to myself untrue?
What slaves, unless I captive you?

Pleasure:
Thou shalt know each hidden cause,
　And see the future time;　　70
Try what depth the center⁹ draws,
　And then to heaven climb.

Soul:
None thither mounts by the degree
Of knowledge, but humility.

Chorus:
Triumph, triumph, victorious soul!　　75
The world has not one pleasure more.
The rest does lie beyond the pole,
And is thine everlasting store.

ON A DROP OF DEW

See how the orient¹ dew,
Shed from the bosom of the morn
　Into the blowing² roses,
Yet careless of its mansion new,
For³ the clear region where 'twas born　　5
　Round in itself incloses,
　And in its little globe's extent
Frames as it can its native element;⁴
　How it the purple flow'r does slight,
　Scarce touching where it lies,　　10

But gazing back upon the skies,
　Shines with a mournful light
　　Like its own tear,
Because so long divided from the sphere.
　Restless it rolls and unsecure,　　15
　　Trembling lest it grow impure,
　Till the warm sun pity its pain,
And to the skies exhale it back again.
　So the soul, that drop, that ray
Of the clear fountain of eternal day,　　20
　Could it within the human flow'r be seen,
　　Rememb'ring still its former height,
　Shuns the sweet leaves and blossoms green;
　　And recollecting⁵ its own light,
Does, in its pure and circling thoughts, express　　25
The greater heaven in an heaven less.
　　In how coy a figure wound,
　　Every way it turns away;
　So the world excluding round,⁶
　　Yet receiving in the day;　　30
　Dark beneath but bright above,
　　Here disdaining, there in love;
　How loose and easy hence to go,
　　How girt and ready to ascend;
　　Moving but on a point below,　　35
　　It all about does upwards bend.
Such did the manna's sacred dew distill,
White and entire, though congeal'd and chill;⁷
Congeal'd on earth, but does, dissolving, run
Into the glories of th' almighty sun.　　40

THE CORONET

When for the thorns with which I long, too long,
　With many a piercing wound
　My Saviour's head have crown'd,
I seek with garlands to redress that wrong;
　Through every garden, every mead　　5
I gather flow'rs (my fruits are only flowers)
　Dismantling all the fragrant towers¹
That once adorn'd my shepherdess' head.
And now when I have summ'd up all my store,
　Thinking (so I myself deceive)　　10
　So rich a chaplet thence to weave
As never yet the king of glory wore;
　Alas I find the serpent old
　That, twining in his speckled breast,

⁷Text *cost*. The emendation is supported by the Bodleian copy of the *Poems*. ⁸Valuable commodity in terms of money. ⁹Center of the earth, which in the Ptolemaic system is itself the center of the universe.
ON A DROP OF DEW ¹Pearlike, lustrous.
²Blooming. ³On account of. ⁴The sky, i.e., heaven.
⁵Gathering, concentrating. ⁶Around about.
⁷*Dew...chill*: "And they gathered it [i.e., manna] every morning, every man according to his eating; and when the sun waxed hot, it melted" (Exodus 16.21).
THE CORONET ¹Floral headdresses.

About the flow'rs disguis'd does fold, 15
  With wreaths of fame and interest.
Ah, foolish man, that wouldst debase with them,
  And mortal glory, heaven's diadem!
  But Thou who only couldst the serpent tame,
Either his slipp'ry knots at once untie, 20
  And disentangle all his winding snare;
Or shatter too with him my curious frame,[2]
And let these wither, so that he may die,
Though set with skill and chosen out with care,
That they, while Thou on both their spoils dost tread, 25
May crown Thy feet, that could not crown Thy head.

BERMUDAS[1]

Where the remote Bermudas ride
In th' ocean's bosom unespi'd,
From a small boat that row'd along,
The listening winds receiv'd this song:
  "What should we do but sing His praise 5
That led us through the wat'ry maze
Unto an isle so long unknown,
And yet far kinder than our own?
Where He the huge sea-monsters[2] wracks,
That lift the deep upon their backs; 10
He lands us on a grassy stage,
Safe from the storms' and prelates' rage.[3]
He gave us this eternal spring
Which here enamels everything,
And sends the fowls to us in care, 15
On daily visits through the air;
He hangs in shades the orange bright,
Like golden lamps in a green night,
And does in the pom'granates close
Jewels more rich than Ormus[4] shows; 20
He makes the figs our mouths to meet,
And throws the melons at our feet;
But apples[5] plants of such a price,
No tree could ever bear them twice;
With cedars, chosen by His hand, 25
From Lebanon, He stores the land;
And makes the hollow seas, that roar,
Proclaim[6] the ambergris on shore;
He cast (of which we rather boast)
The gospel's pearl upon our coast, 30
And in these rocks for us did frame
A temple, where to sound His name.
O! let our voice His praise exalt,
Till it arrive at heaven's vault,
Which thence (perhaps) rebounding, may 35
Echo beyond the Mexique Bay."
  Thus sung they in the English boat,
An holy and a cheerful note;
And all the way, to guide their chime,
With falling oars they kept the time. 40

CLORINDA AND DAMON

C: Damon, come drive thy flocks this way.
D: No, 'tis too late[1] they went astray.

C: I have a grassy scutcheon spi'd
    Where Flora blazons[2] all her pride.
    The grass I aim to feast thy sheep; 5
    The flow'rs I for thy temples keep.
D: Grass withers, and the flow'rs too fade.
C: Seize the short joys, then, ere they vade.[3]
    Seest thou that unfrequented cave?
D: That den? C: Love's shrine. D: But Virtue's grave. 10
C: In whose cool bosom we may lie
    Safe from the sun. D: Not heaven's eye.
C: Near this, a fountain's liquid bell
    Tinkles within the concave shell.
D: Might a soul bathe there and be clean, 15
    Or slake its drought? C: What is't you mean?
D: These once had been enticing things,
    Clorinda: pastures, caves, and springs.
C: And what late change? D: The other day
    Pan[4] met me. C: What did great Pan say? 20
D: Words that transcend poor shepherds' skill,
    But He e'er since my songs does fill,
    And His name swells my slender oat.
C: Sweet must Pan sound in Damon's note.
D: Clorinda's voice might make it sweet. 25
C: Who would not in Pan's praises meet?

Chorus:
    Of Pan the flow'ry pastures sing,
    Caves echo, and the fountains ring.
    Sing, then, while He doth us inspire,
    For all the world is our Pan's quire.[5] 30

A DIALOGUE BETWEEN THE SOUL AND BODY

Soul:
Oh, who shall from this dungeon raise
A soul enslav'd so many ways?
With bolts of bones that fetter'd stands
In feet and manacled in hands;
Here blinded with an eye, and there 5
Deaf with the drumming of an ear;
A soul hung up, as 'twere, in chains
Of nerves and arteries and veins;
Tortur'd, besides each other part,
In a vain head and double heart. 10

[2]Elaborate construction (of the poetry).
BERMUDAS [1]Discovered by the Spaniards in 1515, the Bermudas
were first colonized in 1612 by the English (who named them
the Somers or Summer Islands). See p. 248, n.1.
[2]I.e., stranded whales.
[3]Much of the emigration to America in the earlier seventeenth
century was prompted by the Anglican bishops' (*prelates'*) strenuous
efforts to secure religious conformity.
[4]Hormuz, a city at the mouth of the Persian Gulf notable for its
wealth. [5]Pineapples. [6]Reveal, exhibit.
CLORINDA AND DAMON [1]Lately. [2]Exhibits splendidly.
[3]Pass away.
[4]In pastoral poetry, Pan, the pagan god of shepherds, was often
made into a symbol of Christ, the good shepherd. Thus the gloss
to "May" in Spenser's *Shepherds' Calendar* explains that "Great
Pan is Christ, the very God of all shepherds." [5]Choir.

Body:
Oh, who shall me deliver whole
From bonds of this tyrannic soul?
Which, stretch'd upright, impales me so
That mine own precipice I go;[1]
And warms and moves this needless[2] frame   15
(A fever could but do the same).
And, wanting where its spite to try,
Has made me live to let me die.
A body that could never rest
Since this ill spirit it possess'd.   20

Soul:
What magic could me thus confine
Within another's grief to pine?
Where whatsoever it[3] complain,
I feel, that cannot feel, the pain.
And all my care itself employs   25
That to preserve which me destroys.
Constrain'd not only to endure
Diseases, but, what's worse, the cure;
And ready oft the port[4] to gain,
Am shipwrack'd into health again.   30

Body:
But physic[5] yet could never reach
The maladies[6] thou me dost teach:
Whom first the cramp of hope does tear,
And then the palsy shakes of fear;
The pestilence of love does heat,   35
Or hatred's hidden ulcer eat.
Joy's cheerful madness does perplex,
Or sorrow's other madness vex;
Which knowledge forces me to know,
And memory will not forgo.   40
What but a soul could have the wit
To build me up for sin so fit?
So architects do square and hew
Green trees that in the forest grew.

THE NYMPH COMPLAINING FOR
THE DEATH OF HER FAWN

The wanton troopers[1] riding by
Have shot my fawn, and it will die.
Ungentle men! They cannot thrive
To kill thee.[2] Thou ne'er didst alive
Them any harm, alas, nor cou'd   5
Thy death yet do them any good.
I'm sure I never wish'd them ill,
Nor do I for all this, nor will;
But if my simple pray'rs may yet
Prevail with heaven to forget   10
Thy murder, I will join my tears
Rather than fail. But oh, my fears!
It cannot die so. Heaven's King
Keeps register of everything,
And nothing may we use in vain.   15
Ev'n beasts must be with justice slain,

Else men are made their deodands.[3]
Though they should wash their guilty hands
In this warm life-blood which doth part
From thine, and wound me to the heart,   20
Yet could they not be clean, their stain
Is dy'd in such a purple grain.
There is not such another in
The world to offer for their sin.
    Unconstant Sylvio, when yet   25
I had not found him counterfeit,
One morning (I remember well)
Ti'd in this silver chain and bell,
Gave it to me: nay, and I know
What he said then; I'm sure I do: 30
Said he, "Look how your huntsman here
Hath taught a fawn to hunt his dear."
But Sylvio soon had me beguil'd;
This waxed tame, while he grew wild,
And quite regardless of my smart,   35
Left me his fawn, but took his heart.
    Thenceforth I set myself to play
My solitary time away
With this, and very well content,
Could so mine idle life have spent;   40
For it was full of sport, and light
Of foot and heart, and did invite
Me to its game: it seem'd to bless
Itself in me; how could I less
Than love it? Oh, I cannot be   45
Unkind t' a beast that loveth me.
    Had it liv'd long, I do not know
Whether it too might have done so
As Sylvio did; his gifts might be
Perhaps as false, or more, than he;   50
But I am sure, for ought that I
Could in so short a time espy,
Thy love was far more better then[4]
The love of false and cruel men.
    With sweetest milk and sugar, first   55
I it at mine own fingers nurs'd;
And as it grew, so every day
It wax'd more white and sweet than they.
It had so sweet a breath! And oft
I blush'd to see its foot more soft   60
And white, shall I say than my hand?
Nay, any lady's of the land.

A DIALOGUE [1]*That mine...go*: As H. M. Margoliouth has noted,
a passage in *The Rehearsal Transprosed* (1672), one of Marvell's
pamphlets in support of religious toleration, explains this brilliant
image: "After he was stretch'd to such an height in his own fancy,
that he could not look down from top to toe but his Eyes dazzled
at the precipice of his Stature." [2]Unneeded.
[3]The body, whose afflictions are felt by the incorporeal soul.
[4]Death, the liberation of the soul from the body. [5]Medicine.
[6]Spiritual afflictions.
THE NYMPH [1]Undisciplined cavalrymen.
[2]*They cannot...thee*: i.e., having killed you, they cannot thrive.
[3]Literally, things to be given to God. In English law, a personal
chattel that had been the immediate cause of a person's death was
forfeited to the crown for pious uses. [4]Than.

It is a wondrous thing how fleet
'Twas on those little silver feet;
With what a pretty skipping grace   65
It oft would challenge me the race;
And when 't had left me far away,
'Twould stay, and run again, and stay;
For it was nimbler much than hinds,
And trod as if on the four[5] winds.   70

I have a garden of my own,
But so with roses overgrown,
And lilies, that you would it guess
To be a little wilderness;
And all the springtime of the year   75
It only loved to be there.
Among the beds of lilies I
Have sought it oft, where it should lie,
Yet could not, till itself would rise,
Find it, although before mine eyes;   80
For, in the flaxen lilies' shade,
It like a bank of lilies laid.
Upon the roses it would feed,
Until its lips ev'n seem'd to bleed;
And then to me 'twould boldly trip,   85
And print those roses on my lip.
But all its chief delight was still
On roses thus itself to fill,
And its pure virgin limbs to fold
In whitest sheets of lilies cold: 90
Had it liv'd long, it would have been
Lilies without, roses within.

O help! O help! I see it faint
And die as calmly as a saint!
See how it weeps! the tears do come   95
Sad, slowly dropping like a gum.
So weeps the wounded balsam; so
The holy frankincense doth flow;
The brotherless Heliades[6]
Melt in such amber tears as these.   100
I in a golden vial will
Keep these two crystal tears, and fill
It till it do o'erflow with mine;
Then place it in Diana's shrine.

Now my sweet fawn is vanish'd to   105
Whither the swans and turtles[7] go,
In fair Elysium to endure,
With milk-white lambs and ermines pure.
O do not run too fast, for I
Will but bespeak thy grave, and die.   110

First, my unhappy statue shall
Be cut in marble; and withal
Let it be weeping, too; but there
Th'engraver sure his art may spare;
For I so truly thee bemoan   115
That I shall weep, though I be stone,[8]
Until my tears, still dropping, wear
My breast, themselves engraving there.
There at my feet shalt thou be laid,
Of purest alabaster made;   120

For I would have thine image be
White as I can, though not as thee.

TO HIS COY MISTRESS

Had we but world enough and time,
This coyness, Lady, were no crime.
We would sit down, and think which way
To walk, and pass our long love's day.
Thou by the Indian Ganges' side   5
Shouldst rubies find; I by the tide
Of Humber[1] would complain. I would
Love you ten years before the Flood,
And you should, if you please, refuse
Till the conversion of the Jews.   10
My vegetable[2] love should grow
Vaster than empires and more slow;
An hundred years should go to praise
Thine eyes, and on thy forehead gaze;
Two hundred to adore each breast,   15
But thirty thousand to the rest;
An age at least to every part,
And the last age should show your heart.
For, Lady, you deserve this state,
Nor would I love at lower rate.   20

But at my back I always hear
Time's winged chariot hurrying near,
And yonder all before us lie
Deserts of vast eternity.
Thy beauty shall no more be found,   25
Nor, in thy marble vault, shall sound
My echoing song; then worms shall try
That long-preserv'd virginity,
And your quaint[3] honor turn to dust,[4]
And into ashes all my lust: 30
The grave's a fine and private place,
But none, I think, do there embrace.

Now therefore, while the youthful hue
Sits on thy skin like morning dew,[5]
And while thy willing soul transpires   35
At every pore with instant fires,[6]

[5]Pronounced as a dissyllable.
[6]The three sorrowful daughters of Helios, the sun god, who were transformed into amber-dropping trees following the death of their brother Phaeton.   [7]Turtledoves.
[8]Niobe, who was turned to stone for incessantly lamenting the death of her children, was a favorite subject for statuary fountains.
TO HIS COY MISTRESS   [1]A river in the north of England.
[2]I.e., slowly growing.
[3]Prim, fastidious. It has been suggested that Marvell was perhaps punning on both *quaint* and *honor* as seventeenth-century euphemisms for the female genitalia.   [4]Text *durst.*
[5]Text *glew.* This notorious crux has been the subject of much controversy and conjecture. Following Thomas Cooke's edition of Marvell's *Works* (1720) editors have generally adopted *dew*: but H. M. Margoliouth proposed (and subsequently abandoned) *lew* (warmth), and more recent commentators have argued for the retention of *glew* as a northern dialectal form of *glow.*
[6]*Transpires...fires:* i.e., in your own erotic excitement you are flushed with desire. *Transpires:* breathes forth. *Instant:* urgent.

Now let us sport us while we may,
And now, like am'rous birds of prey,
Rather at once our time devour
Than languish in his slow-chapp'd⁷ pow'r.   40
Let us roll all our strength and all
Our sweetness up into one ball,
And tear our pleasures with rough strife
Through the iron gates of life.
Thus, though we cannot make our sun   45
Stand still, yet we will make him run.

THE GALLERY

1

Clora, come view my soul, and tell
Whether I have contriv'd it well.
Now all its several lodgings lie
Compos'd into one gallery.
And the great arras-hangings, made
Of various faces, by are laid,
That, for all furniture,¹ you'll find
Only your picture in my mind.

2

Here thou art painted in the dress
Of an inhuman murderess;
Examining² upon our hearts
Thy fertile shop³ of cruel arts,
Engines more keen than ever yet
Adorned tyrant's cabinet,⁴
Of which the most tormenting are
Black eyes, red lips, and curled hair.

3

But, on the other side, th' art drawn.
Like to Aurora in the dawn,
When in the east she slumb'ring lies,
And stretches out her milky thighs,
While all the morning choir does sing,
And manna falls and roses spring,
And at thy feet the wooing doves
Sit perfecting⁵ their harmless loves.

4

Like an enchantress here thou show'st,
Vexing thy restless lover's ghost;
And, by a light obscure, dost rave
Over his entrails in the cave,
Divining thence with horrid care
How long thou shalt continue fair;
And (when inform'd) them throw'st away
To be the greedy vulture's prey.

5

But, against that, thou sitt'st afloat,
Like Venus in her pearly boat;
The halcyons, calming all that's nigh,
Betwixt the air and water fly;
Or if some rolling wave appears,
A mass of ambergris it bears,

Nor blows more wind than what may well
Convoy the perfume to the smell.

6

These pictures, and a thousand more,
Of thee my gallery do⁶ store,
In all the forms thou canst invent
Either to please me or torment;
For thou alone, to people me,
Art grown a num'rous colony,
And a collection choicer far
Than or Whitehall's or Mantua's⁷ were.

7

But of these pictures, and the rest,
That at the entrance likes me best,
Where the same posture and the look
Remains with which I first was took:
A tender shepherdess, whose hair
Hangs loosely playing in the air,
Transplanting flow'rs from the green hill
To crown her head and bosom fill.

THE FAIR SINGER

1

To make a final conquest of all me,
Love did compose so sweet an enemy,
In whom both beauties to my death agree,
Joining themselves in fatal harmony,
That while she with her eyes my heart does bind,
She with her voice might captivate my mind.

2

I could have fled from one but singly fair;
My disentangled soul itself might save,
Breaking the curled trammels of her hair.
But how should I avoid to be her slave
Whose subtile art invisibly can wreathe
My fetters of the very air I breathe?

3

It had been easy fighting in some plain,
Where victory might hang in equal choice,
But all resistance against her is vain
Who has th' advantage both of eyes and voice;
And all my forces needs must be undone,
She having gained both the wind and sun.

THE DEFINITION OF LOVE

1

My love is of a birth as rare
As 'tis, for object, strange and high;

⁷Slow jawed, i.e., slowly devouring.
THE GALLERY ¹Furnishings.
²Testing. ³I.e., copious array. ⁴Private room.
⁵Accented on the first syllable.
⁶Text *dost*. Some editors emend to *does*, thus making *gallery* the subject.
⁷Charles I's great collection of art at Whitehall contained many

It was begotten by Despair
Upon Impossibility.

2

Magnanimous Despair alone
Could show me so divine a thing,
Where feeble Hope could ne'er have flown,
But vainly flapped its tinsel wing.

3

And yet I quickly might arrive
Where my extended soul is fixt;
But Fate does iron wedges drive,
And always crowds itself betwixt.

4

For Fate with jealous eyes does see
Two perfect loves, nor lets them close;[1]
Their union would her ruin be,
And her tyrannic pow'r depose.

5

And therefore her decrees of steel
Us as the distant poles have plac'd
(Though Love's whole world on us doth wheel),
Not by themselves to be embrac'd;

6

Unless the giddy heaven fall,
And earth some new convulsion tear,
And, us to join, the world should all
Be cramp'd into a planisphere.[2]

7

As lines, so loves, oblique may well
Themselves in every angle greet;
But ours, so truly parallel,
Though infinite, can never meet.

8

Therefore the love which us doth bind,
But Fate so enviously debars,
Is the conjunction of the mind,
And opposition of the stars.[3]

THE PICTURE OF LITTLE T. C.[1]
IN A PROSPECT OF FLOWERS

1

See with what simplicity
This nymph begins her golden days!
In the green grass she loves to lie,
And there with her fair aspect tames
The wilder flow'rs, and gives them names;[2]
But only with the roses plays,
    And them does tell
What color best becomes them, and what smell.

2

Who can foretell for what high cause
This darling of the gods was born?
Yet this is she whose chaster laws

The wanton Love shall one day fear,
And under her command severe
See his bow broke and ensigns torn.
    Happy, who can
Appease this virtuous enemy of man!

3

O then let me in time compound,[3]
And parley with those conquering eyes,
Ere they have tri'd their force to wound;
Ere with their glancing wheels they drive
In triumph over hearts that strive,
And them that yield but more despise.
    Let me be laid
Where I may see thy glories from some shade.

4

Meantime, whilst every verdant thing
Itself does at thy beauty charm,
Reform the errors of the spring:
Make that the tulips may have share
Of sweetness, seeing they are fair;
And roses of their thorns disarm;
    But most procure
That violets may a longer age endure.

5

But, O young beauty of the woods
Whom nature courts with fruits and flow'rs,
Gather the flow'rs but spare the buds,
Lest Flora, angry at thy crime,
To kill her infants in their prime,
Do quickly make th' example yours,
    And, ere we see,
Nip in the blossom all our hopes and thee.

THE MOWER AGAINST GARDENS

Luxurious[1] man, to bring his vice in use,[2]
    Did after him the world seduce,
And from the fields the flow'rs and plants allure,
    Where Nature was most plain and pure.
He first enclos'd within the gardens square
    A dead and standing pool of air,
And a more luscious earth for them did knead,
    Which stupefi'd them while it fed.
The pink grew then as double as his mind;

---

pieces purchased from Vincenzo Gonzaga, Duke of Mantua.
THE DEFINITION OF LOVE [1]Come together.
[2]A chart for observing the positions of the heavenly bodies by means of projecting the celestial sphere on a plane.
[3]*Conjunction...stars*: i.e., the spiritual union of the lovers and their fated physical alienation. The terms are astronomical.
THE PICTURE OF LITTLE T.C. [1]H. M. Margoliouth has tentatively identified the subject as Theophila Cornewall (b. 1644), whose parents were the poet's friends.
[2]Similarly, Adam, before the fall, had named the beasts and fowls (Genesis 2.19–20). [3]Come to terms with.
THE MOWER AGAINST GARDENS [1]Lecherous, voluptuous.
[2]*To bring...use*: i.e., to make his vice popular and profitable.

The nutriment did change the kind.
With strange perfumes he did the roses taint;
   And flow'rs themselves were taught to paint.
The tulip white did for complexion seek,
   And learn'd to interline its cheek;
Its onion root they then so high did hold
   That one was for a meadow sold:[3]
Another world was search'd through oceans new,
   To find the Marvel of Peru:[4]
And yet these rarities might be allow'd
   To man, that sov'reign thing and proud,
Had he not dealt between the bark and tree,
   Forbidden mixtures there to see.
No plant now knew the stock from which it came;
   He grafts upon the wild the tame
That the uncertain and adult'rate fruit
   Might put the palate in dispute.
His green seraglio has its eunuchs too,
   Lest any tyrant him outdo;
And in the cherry he does Nature vex,
   To procreate without a sex.[5]
'Tis all enforc'd, the fountain and the grot,
   While the sweet fields do lie forgot,
Where willing Nature does to all dispense
   A wild and fragrant innocence,
And fauns and fairies do the meadows till
   More by their presence than their skill.
Their statues, polish'd by some ancient hand,
   May to adorn the gardens stand;
But, howsoe'er the figures do excel,
   The Gods themselves with us do dwell.

DAMON THE MOWER

1

Hark how the mower Damon sung,
With love of Juliana stung,
While ev'rything did seem to paint
The scene more fit for his complaint.
Like her fair eyes the day was fair,
But scorching like his am'rous care.
Sharp like his scythe his sorrow was,
And wither'd like his hopes the grass.

2

"O what unusual heats are here,
Which thus our sunburn'd meadows fear!
The grasshopper its pipe gives o'er,
And hamstring'd[1] frogs can dance no more.
But in the brook the green frog wades,
And grasshoppers seek out the shades.
Only the snake, that kept within,
Now glitters in its second skin.

3

"This heat the sun could never raise,
Nor Dog Star so inflames the days.
It from an higher beauty grow'th,
Which burns the fields and mower both,
Which mads[2] the dog, and makes the sun

Hotter than his own Phaëton.[3]
Not July causeth these extremes,
But Juliana's scorching beams.

4

"Tell me where I may pass the fires
Of the hot day or hot desires.
To what cool cave shall I descend,
Or to what gelid fountain bend?
Alas, I look for ease in vain
When remedies themselves complain.
No moisture but my tears do rest,
Nor cold but in her icy breast.

5

"How long wilt thou, fair shepherdess,
Esteem me and my presents less?
To thee the harmless snake I bring,
Disarmed of its teeth and sting,
To thee chameleons changing hue,
And oak leaves tipp'd with honeydew,
Yet thou, ungrateful, hast not sought
Nor what they are nor who them brought.

6

"I am the mower Damon, known
Through all the meadows I have mown.
On me the morn her dew distills
Before her darling daffodils.
And if at noon my toil me heat,
The sun himself licks off my sweat,
While, going home, the ev'ning sweet
In cowslip water[4] bathes my feet.

7

"What though the piping shepherd stock
The plains with an unnumber'd flock?
This scythe of mine discovers wide
More ground than all his sheep do hide.
With this the golden fleece I shear
Of all these closes[5] ev'ry year,
And though in wool more poor than they,
Yet am I richer far in hay.

8

"Nor am I so deform'd to sight
If in my scythe I looked right,
In which I see my picture done
As in a crescent moon the sun.

[3]*Its onion...sold*: Marvell is alluding to the great cost of rare Dutch tulip bulbs.
[4]A plant (*Mirabilis Jalapa*) that the botanist and herbalist John Parkinson (d. 1650) termed *Mirabilia Peruviana*.
[5]*To procreate...sex*: Marvell is perhaps alluding to the process of propagation by grafting, or to the cultivation of stoneless (i.e., sexless) cherries.
DAMON THE MOWER [1]Rendered inert (through excessive heat).
[2]Text *made*, but the emendation is supported by the Bodleian copy of the *Poems*.
[3]The son of Helios whose reckless use of his father's chariot of the sun threatened the earth with a conflagration.
[4]A lotion for cleansing the skin.   [5]Enclosed fields.

The deathless fairies take me oft
To lead them in their dances soft,
And when I tune myself to sing,
About me they contract their ring.

9

"How happy might I still have mow'd
Had not Love here his thistles sow'd!
But now I all the day complain,
Joining my labor to my pain,
And with my scythe cut down the grass,
Yet still my grief is where it was;
But when the iron blunter grows,
Sighing I whet my scythe and woes."

10

While thus he threw his elbow round,
Depopulating all the ground,
And with his whistling scythe does cut
Each stroke between the earth and root,
The edged steel, by careless chance,
Did into his own ankle glance,
And there among the grass fell down,
By his own scythe the mower mown.

11

"Alas," said he, "these hurts are slight
To those that die by Love's despite.
With shepherd's purse and clown's all-heal[6]
The blood I stanch and wound I seal.
Only for him no cure is found
Whom Juliana's eyes do wound.
'Tis Death alone that this must do,
For, Death, thou art a mower too."

THE MOWER TO THE GLOWWORMS

1

Ye living lamps, by whose dear light
The nightingale does sit so late,
And studying all the summer night,
Her matchless songs does meditate;

2

Ye country comets, that portend
No war nor prince's funeral,
Shining unto no higher end
Than to presage the grass' fall;

3

Ye glowworms, whose officious[1] flame
To wand'ring mowers shows the way,
That in the night have lost their aim,
And after foolish fires[2] do stray;

4

Your courteous lights in vain you waste,
Since Juliana here is come,
For she my mind hath so displac'd
That I shall never find my home.

THE MOWER'S SONG

1

My mind was once the true survey[1]
Of all these meadows fresh and gay,
And in the greenness of the grass
Did see its hopes as in a glass,
When Juliana came, and she,
What I do to the grass, does to my thoughts and me.

2

But these, while I with sorrow pine,
Grew more luxuriant still and fine,
That not one blade of grass you spi'd
But had a flower on either side,
When Juliana came, and she,
What I do to the grass, does to my thoughts and me.

3

Unthankful meadows, could you so
A fellowship so true forgo,
And in your gaudy May-games meet,
While I lay trodden under feet?
When Juliana came, and she,
What I do to the grass, does to my thoughts and me.

4

But what you in compassion ought
Shall now by my revenge be wrought;
And flow'rs, and grass, and I, and all
Will in one common ruin fall;
For Juliana comes, and she,
What I do to the grass, does to my thoughts and me.

5

And thus, ye meadows, which have been
Companions of my thoughts more green,
Shall now the heraldry become
With which I shall adorn my tomb;
For Juliana comes, and she,
What I do to the grass, does to my thoughts and me.

THE GARDEN

1

How vainly men themselves amaze
To win the palm, the oak, or bays,[1]
And their uncessant labors see
Crown'd from some single herb or tree,
Whose short and narrow-vergèd shade
Does prudently their toils upbraid,
While all flow'rs and all trees do close[2]
To weave the garlands of repose.

---

[6]Plants thought to stop bleeding and to heal wounds.
THE MOWER TO THE GLOWWORMS [1]Dutiful, attentive.
[2]*Ignis fatuus,* the will-o'-the-wisp.
THE MOWER'S SONG [1]Surveyor's inventory of an estate.
THE GARDEN [1]*Palm...bays:* respectively, rewards for distinction
in war, politics, and poetry. [2]Unite.

2

Fair Quiet, have I found thee here,
And Innocence, thy sister dear?
Mistaken long, I sought you then
In busy companies of men.
Your sacred plants, if here below,
Only among the plants will grow;
Society is all but rude
To this delicious solitude.

3

No white nor red[3] was ever seen
So am'rous as this lovely green.
Fond lovers, cruel as their flame,
Cut in these trees their mistress' name:
Little, alas, they know or heed
How far these beauties hers exceed!
Fair trees, wheres'e'er your[4] barks I wound,
No name shall but your own be found.

4

When we have run our passion's heat,
Love hither makes his best retreat.
The gods, that mortal beauty chase,
Still in a tree did end their race;
Apollo hunted Daphne so,
Only that she might laurel grow;
And Pan did after Syrinx speed,
Not as a nymph, but for a reed.[5]

5

What wondrous life in this I lead!
Ripe apples drop about my head;
The luscious clusters of the vine
Upon my mouth do crush their wine;
The nectarine and curious[6] peach
Into my hands themselves do reach;
Stumbling on melons as I pass,
Ensnar'd with flow'rs, I fall on grass.

6

Meanwhile the mind from pleasure less[7]
Withdraws into its happiness;
The mind, that ocean where each kind
Does straight its own resemblance find,[8]
Yet it creates, transcending these,
Far other worlds and other seas,
Annihilating all that's made
To a green thought in a green shade.[9]

7

Here at the fountain's sliding foot,
Or at some fruit-tree's mossy root,
Casting the body's vest aside,
My soul into the boughs does glide:
There, like a bird, it sits and sings,
Then whets[10] and combs its silver wings,
And, till prepar'd for longer flight,
Waves in its plumes the various light.

8

Such was that happy garden-state,
While man there walk'd without a mate:
After a place so pure and sweet,
What other help could yet be meet!
But 'twas beyond a mortal's share
To wander solitary there:
Two paradises 'twere in one
To live in paradise alone.

9

How well the skillful gardener drew,
Of flow'rs and herbs, this dial[11] new,
Where, from above, the milder sun
Does through a fragrant zodiac run;
And, as it works, th' industrious bee
Computes its time[12] as well as we!
How could such sweet and wholesome hours
Be reckon'd but with herbs and flow'rs?

AT EPITAPH UPON ———[1]

Enough—and leave the rest to fame.
'Tis to commend her but to name.
Courtship, which living she declin'd,
When dead to offer were unkind.
Where never any could speak ill,   5
Who would officious praises spill?
Nor can the truest wit or friend,
Without detracting, her commend.
To say she liv'd a virgin chaste
In this age loose and all unlac'd,   10
Nor was (when vice is so allow'd)
Of virtue or asham'd or proud,
That her soul was on heaven so bent
No minute but it came and went,[2]
That ready her last debt to pay   15
She summ'd her life up ev'ry day,
Modest as morn, as midday bright,
Gentle as ev'ning, cool as night—
'Tis true, but all so weakly said,
'Twere more significant, *She's dead.*   20

3*White...red*: colors traditionally associated with female beauty.
4Text *you.*
5*Apollo hunted...reed*: When pursued by Apollo and Pan respectively, Daphne was changed into a laurel and Syrinx into a reed.
6Choice, exquisite.
7The inferior gratification afforded by the body (as contrasted with those of the mind and soul)?
8*The mind...find*: It was popularly believed that the sea contained a marine creature corresponding to each land animal.
9*Annihilating...shade*: i.e., reducing the material world to nothing in comparison to the products of man's powerful creative imagination. 10Preens. 11Sundial made of plants and flowers.
12Marvell is punning on *time* (as recorded by the floral sundial) and *thyme* (which, growing in the *fragrant zodiac*, supplies its nectar to the bee).
AN EPITAPH UPON ——— 1The subject is unknown.
2I.e., in the course of her devotions.

UPON THE HILL AND GROVE AT BILBROUGH[1]
To the Lord Fairfax

1

See how the arched earth does here
Rise in a perfect hemisphere!
The stiffest compass could not strike
A line more circular and like,[2]
Nor softest pencil draw a brow
So equal as this hill does bow.
It seems as for a model[3] laid,
And that the world by it was made.

2

Here learn, ye mountains more unjust,
Which to abrupter greatness thrust,
That do with your hook-shoulder'd height
The earth deform and heaven fright,
For whose excrescence ill design'd
Nature must a new center[4] find,
Learn here those humble steps to tread
Which to securer glory lead.

3

See what a soft access and wide
Lies open to its grassy side,
Nor with the rugged path deters
The feet of breathless travelers.
See then how courteous it ascends,
And all the way it rises bends:
Not for itself the height does gain,
But only strives to raise the plain.

4

Yet thus it all the field commands,
And in unenvi'd greatness stands,
Discerning further than the cliff
Of heaven-daring Teneriff.[5]
How glad the weary seamen hast[6]
When they salute it from the mast!
By night the Northern Star their way
Directs, and this no less by day.

5

Upon its crest this mountain grave
A plump[7] of aged trees does wave.
No hostile hand durst e'er invade
With impious steel the sacred shade,
For something always did appear
Of the great master's[8] terror there,
And men could hear his armor still
Rattling through all the grove and hill.

6

Fear of the master and respect
Of the great nymph did it protect:
Vera[9] the nymph that him inspir'd,
To whom he often here retir'd,
And on these oaks engrav'd her name.
Such wounds alone these woods became,

But e'er he well the barks could part,
'Twas writ already in their heart.

7

For they ('tis credible) have sense,
As we, of love and reverence,
And underneath the coarser rind
The genius of the house do bind.
Hence they successes seem to know,
And in their lord's advancement grow,
But in no memory were seen
As under this[10] so straight and green,

8

Yet now no further strive to shoot,
Contented if they fix their root,
Nor to the wind's uncertain gust
Their prudent heads too far entrust.
Only sometimes a flutt'ring breeze
Discourses with the breathing trees,
Which in their modest whispers name
Those acts that swell'd the cheek of Fame.

9

"Much other groves," say they, "than these
And other hills him once did please.
Through groves of pikes he thunder'd then,
And mountains rais'd of dying men.
For all the civic garlands due
To him our branches are but few,
Nor are our trunks enow to bear
The trophies of one fertile year."

10

'Tis true, ye[11] trees, nor ever spoke
More certain oracles in oak,[12]
But peace if you his favor prize:
That courage its own praises flies.
Therefore to your obscurer seats
From his own brightness he retreats,
Nor he the hills without the groves
Nor height but with retirement loves.

UPON THE HILL [1]A manor near the great estate of Nun Appleton in Yorkshire to which Thomas Fairfax (1612–71), third Baron Fairfax of Cameron, retired upon relinquishing his post as commander-in-chief of the parliamentary forces (1650) in opposition to the projected invasion of Scotland that Cromwell subsequently conducted. In 1651 Fairfax and his wife (the former Ann Vere, daughter of the distinguished commander Sir Horace Vere) appointed Marvell as tutor to their daughter Mary (b. 1638). Bilbrough Hill, with its crowning tuft of trees, was a landmark for ships in the estuary of the River Wharfe.
[2]Even. [3]I.e., a model of circularity and thus perfection.
[4]Center of the earth.
[5]Teneriffe, a volcanic peak in the Canary Islands. [6]Haste.
[7]Clump. Text *plum.* [8]I.e., Fairfax's.
[9]Lady Fairfax, née Ann Vere. [10]I.e., this master, Lord Fairfax.
[11]Text *the.*
[12]At Dodona in Epirus, a famous shrine to Zeus, the responses of the oracle were thought to come from the rustling in the sacred oaks.

UPON APPLETON HOUSE
TO MY LORD FAIRFAX[1]

1

Within this sober frame expect
Work of no foreign architect
That unto caves the quarries drew,
And forests did to pastures hew;
Who, of his great design in pain,
Did for a model vault his brain;
Whose columns should so high be rais'd,
To arch the brows which on them gaz'd.

2

Why should, of all things, man, unrul'd,
Such unproportion'd dwellings build?
The beasts are by their dens exprest
And birds contrive an equal[2] nest;
The low-roof'd tortoises do dwell
In cases fit of tortoise-shell;
No creature loves an empty space;
Their bodies measure out their place.

3

But he, superfluously spread,
Demands more room alive than dead;
And in his hollow palace goes
Where winds, as he, themselves may lose,
What need of all this marble crust
T' impark the wanton mote[3] of dust,
That thinks by breadth the world t' unite,
Though the first builders[4] fail'd in height?

4

But all things are composed here,
Like nature, orderly and near;
In which we the dimensions find
Of that more sober age and mind,
When larger-sized men did stoop
To enter at a narrow loop,
As practicing, in doors so strait,
To strain themselves through heaven's gate.

5

And surely, when the after-age
Shall hither come in pilgrimage,
These sacred places to adore,
By Vere[5] and Fairfax trod before,
Men will dispute how their extent
Within such dwarfish confines went;
And some will smile at this, as well
As Romulus his bee-like cell.[6]

6

Humility alone designs
Those short but admirable lines
By which, ungirt and unconstrain'd,
Things greater are in less contain'd.
Let others vainly strive t' immure
The circle in the quadrature![7]

These holy mathematics can
In ev'ry figure equal man.

7

Yet thus the laden house does sweat,
And scarce endures the master great;
But where he comes, the swelling hall
Stirs, and the square grows spherical:[8]
More by his magnitude distrest
Than he is by its straitness prest
And too officiously it slights
That[9] in itself, which him delights.

8

So honor better lowness bears
Than that unwonted greatness wears;
Height with a certain grace does bend,
But low things clownishly ascend.
And yet what needs there here excuse,
Where everything does answer use?
Where neatness nothing can condemn,
Nor pride invent what to contemn?

9

A stately frontispiece of poor
Adorns without the open door,
Nor less the rooms within commends[10]
Daily new furniture[11] of friends.
The house was built upon the place
Only as for a mark of grace,
And for an inn to entertain
Its lord a while, but not remain.

10

Him Bishop's Hill or Denton may,
Or Bilbrough,[12] better hold than they,
But Nature here hath been so free
As if she said, "Leave this to me."
Art would more neatly have defac'd
What she had laid so sweetly waste
In fragrant gardens, shady woods,
Deep meadows, and transparent floods.

UPON APPLETON HOUSE [1]See the first note to the previous poem.
[2]Suitable to their size, appropriate.
[3]Text *mose*. The emendation is supported by the Bodleian copy of
the *Poems*. [4]The builders of the Tower of Babel (Genesis 11.1–9).
[5]Ann Vere, Lady Fairfax.
[6]On the Palatine Hill the Romans long preserved the thatched
casa Romuli, traditionally associated with the legendary founder
of the city.
[7]*Let others...quadrature*: i.e., let others waste their time in such
notoriously profitless pursuits as trying to square the circle.
[8]As rebuilt by Fairfax following his marriage (1637) to Ann Vere
Appleton House consisted of a long main hall that was surmounted
by a cupola and joined by two wings, the whole forming three
sides of a square. [9]I.e., its unpretentiousness. [10]Adorns.
[11]Furnishings.
[12]*Bishop's Hill...Bilbrough*: three Fairfax holdings in the vicinity
of Nun Appleton. The first was a house in York, the second an
estate upstream on the River Wharfe, and the third (the subject
of the previous poem) a manor not far from Appleton House.

> There follows a long passage (Stanzas 11–35) on the history
> of the Fairfax family in which Marvell tells how the heiress
> Isabel Thwaites, the beloved of William Fairfax of Steeton,
> was immured by her guardian the Lady Anna Langton,
> prioress of the ancient nunnery of Nun Appleton, and
> finally released by force so that she could marry (1518) her
> suitor. Upon the dissolution of the monasteries under Henry
> VIII, Appleton House in 1542 was surrendered to their sons,
> and so descended to its present master, whose virtues
> Marvell celebrates.

36

From that blest bed the hero[13] came
Whom France and Poland yet does fame,
Who, when retired here to peace,
His warlike studies could not cease,
But laid these gardens out in sport
In the just figure of a fort,
And with five bastions it did fence,
As aiming one for ev'ry sense.[14]

37

When in the east the morning ray
Hangs out the colors of the day,
The bee through these known allies hums,
Beating the dian[15] with its drums.
Then flow'rs their drowsy eyelids raise,
Their silken ensigns each displays,
And dries its pan yet dank with dew,
And fills its flask[16] with odors new.

> Enchanted by the serenity of Fairfax's pastoral retreat and
> dismayed by the desolation of England in time of civil war,
> Marvell wonders if such a prince of men should not have
> tried to revive the withered "gardens" of the fallen world.

41

O thou, that dear and happy isle,
The garden of the world erewhile,
Thou paradise[17] of four seas
Which Heaven planted us to please,
But, to exclude the world, did guard
With wat'ry if not flaming sword,
What luckless apple did we taste,
To make us mortal, and thee waste?

42

Unhappy! shall we never more
That sweet militia restore,
When gardens only had their tow'rs
And all the garrisons were flow'rs;
When roses only arms might bear,
And men did rosy garlands wear?
Tulips, in several colors barr'd,
Were then the Switzers[18] of our guard;

43

The gardener had the soldier's place,
And his more gentle forts did trace;
The nursery of all things green
Was then the only magazine;
The winter quarters were the stoves,

Where he the tender plants removes.
But war all this doth overgrow:
We ordnance plant, and powder sow.

44

And yet there walks one on the sod.
Who, had it pleased him and God,
Might once have made our gardens spring
Fresh as his own, and flourishing.
But he preferr'd to the Cinque Ports[19]
These five imaginary forts,
And, in those half-dry trenches, spann'd[20]
Pow'r which the ocean might command.

45

For he did, with his utmost skill,
Ambition weed, but conscience till;
Conscience, that heaven-nursed plant,
Which most our earthly gardens want.
A prickling leaf it bears, and such
As that which shrinks at ev'ry touch,
But flow'rs eternal and divine,
That in the crowns of saints do shine.

> But the pastoral calm of Appleton House cannot obliterate
> the poet's memory of the outer world. For him, even the
> "tawny mowers" in the meadow acquire a sinister em-
> blematic significance as agents of destruction.

47

And now to the abyss I pass
Of that unfathomable grass,
Where men like grasshoppers appear,
But grasshoppers are giants there;[21]
They, in their squeaking laugh, contemn
Us as we walk more low than them,
And from the precipices tall
Of the green spires to us do call.

48

To see men through this meadow dive,
We wonder how they rise alive,
As under water none does know

[13]It is not clear whether Marvell means the Thomas Fairfax (d. 1599) who fought with much distinction on the Continent or the present Thomas Fairfax, who was the poet's patron.
[14]*But laid...sense*: The flower beds at Appleton House were presumably laid out to resemble five-sided fortifications. [15]Reveille.
[16]*Pan...flask*: the firing-pan and powder-flask used by musketeers (whom the flowers are represented as resembling).
[17]Text *Puradise*.
[18]The uniforms designed by Michelangelo for the Papal Swiss Guard were (and are) conspicuous for their black, yellow, and red stripes.
[19]The five ancient ports (Hastings, Sandwich, Down, etc.) on the Channel coast of England whose prestigious wardenship was usually bestowed upon a distinguished military man. It is not entirely clear that Fairfax ever held the post.
[20]Encompassed, contained.
[21]*Grasshoppers...there*: "And there we saw the giants, the sons of Anak, who come of the giants; and we were in our own sight as grasshoppers, and so we were in their sight" (Numbers 13.33).

Whether he fall through it or go.
But, as the mariners that sound,
And show upon their lead the ground,
They bring up flow'rs so to be seen,
And prove they've at the bottom been.

49
No scene that turns with engines strange[22]
Does oftener than these meadows change.
For when the sun the grass hath vex'd,
The tawny mowers enter next;
Who seem like Israelites[23] to be,
Walking on foot through a green sea.[24]
To them the grassy deeps divide,
And crowd a lane to either side.

50
With whistling scythe and elbow strong
These massacre the grass along,
While one, unknowing, carves the rail[25]
Whose yet unfeather'd quills her fail.
The edge all bloody from its breast
He draws, and does his stroke detest,
Fearing the flesh untimely mow'd
To him a fate as black forebode.

51
But bloody Thestylis, that waits
To bring the mowing camp their cates,[26]
Greedy as kites has truss'd it up,
And forthwith means on it to sup,
When on another quick she lights,
And cries, "He call'd us Israelites,
But now, to make his saying true,
Rails rain for quails, for manna dew."[27]

52
Unhappy birds, what does it boot
To build below the grasses' root,
When lowness is unsafe as height,
And Chance o'ertakes what 'scapeth Spite?
And now your orphan parents' call
Sounds your untimely funeral;
Death-trumpets creak in such a note,
And 'tis the sourdine[28] in their throat.

53
Or sooner hatch or higher build:
The mower now commands the field,
In whose new traverse[29] seemeth wrought
A camp of battle newly fought,
Where, as the meads with hay, the plain
Lies quilted o'er with bodies slain:
The women that with forks it fling
Do represent the pillaging.

54
And now the careless victors play,
Dancing the triumphs of the hay,[30]
Where every mower's wholesome heat
Smells like an Alexander's sweat.

Their females, fragrant as the mead
Which they in fairy circles tread,
When at their dance's end they kiss,
Their new-made hay not sweeter is.

> [Recoiling from such imagined horrors—even the opening
> of the sluices in the meadow reminds him of the flood with
> which an angry God had punished sinful man—the poet
> seeks a more remote retreat.]

61
But I, retiring from the flood,
Take sanctuary in the wood,
And while it lasts myself embark
In this yet green, yet growing ark,
Where the first carpenter might best
Fit timber for his keel have prest,[31]
And where all creatures might have shares,
Although in armies, not in pairs.

. . . . . .

65
The nightingale does here make choice
To sing the trials of her voice.
Low shrubs she sits in, and adorns
With music high the squatted thorns.
But highest oaks stoop down to hear,
And list'ning elders prick the ear.
The thorn, lest it should hurt her, draws
Within the skin its shrunken claws.

66
But I have for my music found
A sadder yet more pleasing sound:
The stock doves, whose fair necks are grac'd
With nuptial rings, their ensigns chaste,
Yet always, for some cause unknown,
Sad pair unto the elms they moan.
O why should such a couple mourn,
That in so equal flames do burn!

. . . . . .

71
Thus I, easy philosopher,
Among the birds and trees confer,

[22]*No scene...strange*: Marvell is thinking of the elaborate scenic devices of the Jacobean and Caroline stage.   [23]Text *Israaliies*.
[24]"And the children of Israel went into the midst of the sea upon the dry ground; and the waters were a well unto them on their right hand, and on their left" (Exodus 14.22).
[25]The landrail or corncrake, a bird that frequents grain fields.
[26]*But bloody...cates*: The *mowing camp* is accompanied by a woman (*bloody Thestylis*) who prepares their food (*cates*).
[27]*Rails...dew*: "And it came to pass that at evening the quails came up, and covered the camp; and in the morning the dew lay round about the host" (Exodus 16.13).   [28]Low-voiced trumpet.
[29]I.e., newly cut path.
[30]1) the new-mown hay; 2) a country dance.
[31]*Where the first...prest*: i.e., where Noah might have commandeered (*prest*) the timber for his ark.

And little now to make me wants
Or of the fowls or of the plants:
Give me but wings as they, and I
Straight floating on the air shall fly;
Or turn me but and you shall see
I was but an inverted tree.

72

Already I begin to call
In their most learned original,
And, where I language want my signs
The bird upon the bough divines,
And more attentive there doth sit
Than if she were with lime-twigs knit.
No leaf does tremble in the wind,
Which I returning cannot find.

73

Out of these scatter'd Sibyl's leaves,[32]
Strange prophecies my fancy weaves,
And in one history consumes,
Like Mexique painting,[33] all the plumes;
What Rome, Greece, Palestine e'er said,
I in this light mosaic read.
Thrice happy he, who, not mistook,
Hath read in nature's mystic book!

74

And see how chance's better wit
Could with a mask my studies hit!
The oak-leaves me embroider all,
Between which caterpillars crawl;
And ivy, with familiar trails,
Me licks and clasps and curls and hales.
Under this antic cope I move,
Like some great prelate of the grove.

75

Then, languishing with ease, I toss
On pallets swol'n of velvet moss,
While the wind, cooling through the boughs,
Flatters with air my panting brows.
Thanks for my rest, ye mossy banks,
And unto you, cool zephyrs, thanks,
Who, as my hair, my thoughts too shed,[34]
And winnow from the chaff my head!

76

How safe, methinks, and strong behind
These trees, have I encamp'd my mind
Where Beauty, aiming at the heart,
Bends in some tree its useless dart,
And where the world no certain shot
Can make, or me it toucheth not,
But I on it securely play,
And gall its horsemen all the day.

77

Bind me, ye woodbines, in your twines;
Curl me about, ye gadding vines;

And O, so close your circles lace
That I may never leave this place!
But lest your fetters prove too weak,
Ere I your silken bondage break,
Do you, O brambles, chain me too,
And, courteous briars, nail me through!

Recalled from these transports by the sight of young Maria Fairfax emerging for her evening walk, Marvell leaves his lovely "sanctuary" of nature, but he does so with a new and healing knowledge: that the beauty, fecundity, and "decent order" of nature persist despite the brutalities of history and the moral ambiguities of a fallen world. Embodied in the queenly little Maria, these are the values that justify the present and will perhaps redeem the future.

82

But now away my hooks, my quills,
And angles, idle utensils!
The young Maria walks tonight:
Hide, trifling youth, thy pleasures slight;
'Twere shame that such judicious eyes
Should with such toys a man surprise;
She that already is the law
Of all her sex, her age's awe.

83

See how loose Nature, in respect
To her, itself doth recollect,
And everything so whisht[35] and fine
Starts forthwith to its *bonne mine.*[36]
The sun himself of her aware,
Seems to descend with greater care,
And, lest she see him go to bed,
In blushing clouds conceals his head.

. . . . . .

87

'Tis she that to these gardens gave
That wondrous beauty which they have;
She straightness on the woods bestows;
To her the meadow sweetness owes;
Nothing could make the river be
So crystal pure, but only she;
She yet more pure, sweet, straight, and fair
Than gardens, woods, meads, rivers are.

88

Therefore what first she on them spent,
They gratefully again present;
The meadow carpets where to tread,
The garden flow'rs to crown her head,
And for a glass the limpid brook,
Where she may all her beauties look;

[32]The leaves upon which in Roman legend, the Sibyl of Cumae wrote her oracular utterances.
[33]A picture made by sewing and pasting feathers together.
[34]Separate. [35]Hushed.
[36]"Best appearance." *Bonne* is here disyllabic.

But, since she would not have them seen,
The wood about her draws a screen.

. . . . . .

93

Hence she with graces more divine
Supplies beyond her sex the line,[37]
And like a sprig of mistletoe
On the Fairfacian oak does grow,
Whence, for some universal good,
The priest shall cut the sacred bud
While her glad parents most rejoice,
And make their destiny their choice.[38]

94

Meantime, ye fields, springs, bushes, flow'rs,
Where yet she leads her studious hours,
(Till Fate her worthily translates,
And find a Fairfax for our Thwaites)[39]
Employ the means you have by her,
And in your kind yourselves prefer,
That as all virgins she precedes,
So you all woods, streams, gardens, meads.

95

For you, Thessalian Tempe's seat
Shall now be scorn'd as obsolete;
Aranjuez, as less, disdain'd;
The Bel-Retiro, as constrain'd;
But name not the Idalian grove,[40]
For 'twas the seat of wanton love;
Much less the dead's Elysian fields;
Yet nor to them your beauty yields.

96

'Tis not, what once it was, the world,
But a rude heap together hurl'd,
All negligently overthrown,
Gulfs, deserts, precipices, stone;
Your lesser world contains the same,
But in more decent order tame;
You, heaven's center, nature's lap,
And paradise's only map.

97

But now the salmon-fishers moist
Their leathern boats begin to hoist,
And, like Antipodes[41] in shoes.
Have shod their heads in their canoes.
How tortoise-like, but not so slow,
These rational amphibii go!
Let's in, for the dark hemisphere
Does now like one of them appear.[42]

AN HORATIAN ODE UPON CROMWELL'S RETURN FROM IRELAND[1]

The forward youth that would appear[2]
Must now forsake his Muses dear,

Nor in the shadows sing
  His numbers languishing:
'Tis time to leave the books in dust,
And oil th' unused armor's rust,
  Removing from the wall
  The corslet of the hall.
So restless Cromwell could not cease
In the inglorious arts of peace,
  But through advent'rous war
  Urged his active star;
And like the three-fork'd lightning, first
Breaking the clouds where it was nurst,
  Did thorough[3] his own side[4]
  His fiery way divide.
For 'tis all one to courage high,
The emulous or enemy;
  And with such to inclose
  Is more than to oppose.
Then burning through the air he went,
And palaces and temples rent;
  And Caesar's head[5] at last
  Did through his laurels blast.
'Tis madness to resist or blame
The force of angry heaven's flame;
  And, if we would speak true,

[37] *Supplies...line*: i.e., establishes a standard of excellence beyond the reach of ordinary women.
[38] *When, for...choice*: In the light of this apocalyptic vision of little Mary Fairfax's wedding day it is ironical that her marriage (1657) to the profligate George Villiers, second Duke of Buckingham, was wretchedly unhappy and that she herself died childless in 1704.
[39] It was through the marriage (1518) of the heiress Isabel Thwaits to William Fairfax of Steeton that Appleton House, which had formerly been a nunnery, came into the possession of the Fairfax family in 1542.
[40] *Thessalian...grove*: Marvell cites as symbols of an earthly paradise the Vale of Tempe in Thessaly; some lavish royal gardens near Madrid; Buen-Retiro, a royal palace near Madrid; and the garden of Aphrodite at Idalium in Cyprus. *Aranjuez*: text *Aranjuez*.
[41] People who dwell on the other side of the earth (so that they are upside-down to us).
[42] *The dark...appear*: i.e., the hemisphere of darkness covers the earth like the inverted boat that the salmon-fisher carries on his head.
AN HORATIAN ODE [1] This famous poem was apparently written in the early summer of 1650, between Cromwell's return in May from his brutally effective campaign against the Irish and his start in July of his equally decisive campaign against the Scots. It was Lord Fairfax's opposition to the projected invasion of Scotland that had prompted his resignation as commander-in-chief and his retirement to Appleton House, which is so notably treated in the preceding poem.
[2] *The forward...appear*: i.e., the eager young man who wants to make his reputation. [3] Thorough. Text *through*.
[4] 1) Side of the cloud; 2) party, faction.
[5] Marvell is of course alluding to Charles I, whose trial and execution had been strongly urged by Cromwell. Laurels were thought to be immune to lightning.

Much to the man is due,
Who, from his private gardens, where
He liv'd reserved and austere
  (As if his highest plot
  To plant the bergamot),[6]
Could by industrious valor climb
To ruin the great work of time,
  And cast the kingdom old
  Into another mold
Though Justice against Fate complain,
And plead the ancient rights in vain.
  But those do hold or break
  As men are strong or weak.
Nature, that hateth emptiness,
Allows of penetration[7] less,
  And therefore must make room
  Where greater spirits come.
What field of all the civil wars
Where his were not the deepest scars?
  And Hampton shows what part
  He had of wiser art;
Where, twining subtile fears with hope,
He wove a net of such a scope
  That Charles himself might chase
  To Carisbrooke's narrow case,
That thence the royal actor born
The tragic scaffold might adorn;
  While round the armed bands
  Did clap their bloody hands.[8]
He nothing common did, or mean,
Upon that memorable scene,
  But with his keener eye
  The axe's edge did try;[9]
Nor call'd the gods with vulgar spite
To vindicate his helpless right;
  But bow'd his comely head
  Down, as upon a bed.
This was that memorable hour
Which first assur'd the forced pow'r.
  So, when they did design
  The Capitol's first line,
A bleeding head, where they begun,
Did fright the architects to run;
  And yet in that the state
  Foresaw its happy fate.[10]
And now the Irish are asham'd
To see themselves in one year tam'd;
  So much one man can do
  That does both act and know.
They[11] can affirm his praises best,
And have, though overcome, confest
  How good he is, how just,
  And fit for highest trust,
Nor yet grown stiffer with command,
But still in the republic's hand.
  How fit is he to sway
  That can so well obey!

He to the Commons'[12] feet presents
A kingdom for his first year's rents;
  And, what he may, forbears
  His fame to make it theirs;
And has his sword and spoils ungirt,
To lay them at the public's skirt:
  So when the falcon high
  Falls heavy from the sky,
She, having kill'd, no more does search
But on the next green bough to perch;
  Where, when he first does lure,
  The falc'ner has her sure.
What may not, then, our isle presume,
While victory his crest does plume?
  What may not others fear,
  If thus he crown each year?
A Caesar he, ere long, to Gaul,
To Italy an Hannibal,
  And to all states not free
  Shall climacteric[13] be.
The Pict[14] no shelter now shall find
Within his parti-color'd[15] mind,
  But from this valor sad[16]
  Shrink underneath the plaid;
Happy if in the tufted brake
The English hunter him mistake,
  Nor lay his hounds in near
  The Caledonian[17] deer.
But thou, the war's and Fortune's son,
March indefatigably on!
  And for the last effect,
  Still keep thy sword erect;
Besides the force it has to fright
The spirits of the shady night,[18]
  The same arts that did gain
  A pow'r must it maintain.

---

[6]A variety of pear.
[7]The simultaneous occupation of a space by two bodies.
[8]*And Hampton...bloody hands*: Following his capture by parliamentary troops in June 1647, Charles was confined in Hampton Court until November, when he fled to Carisbrooke Castle on the Isle of Wight. After more than a year of incessant plots and stratagems on Charles' part, he was returned to London (January 1649) for his speedy trial and execution. Marvell's implication that Cromwell had engineered the King's flight in order to advance his own designs is not supported by the known facts. For another famous account of these events see pp. 933 ff. [9]Test.
[10]*So, when...fate*: According to Pliny, *Natural History*, xxviii.2, the unearthing of a human head at the site of the Temple of Jupiter on the Capitoline Hill was interpreted as a good omen.
[11]I.e., the Irish (who, of all people, would in fact be the least likely to *affirm* Cromwell's merits). [12]Text *Common*.
[13]Pivotal, decisive.
[14]Celt, i.e., Scot (from Latin *pictus*, "painted").
[15]Variously colored (in plaids and tartans), fickle.
[16]Steadfast, austere. [17]Scottish.
[18]*Besides the force...night*: a cross (such as that formed by the hilt and blade of a sword) was thought to ward off evil spirits.

Henry Vaughan [1621/2-1695]

In 1673, when the antiquarian John Aubrey asked Vaughan for information about himself and his brother, that obscure country physician and occasional poet professed to be astonished that anyone should take an interest in such "low and forgotten things." His answer could not have been entirely disingenuous, for although a modest man, Vaughan had a good deal to be modest about. A Welshman who practiced his vocation and pursued his avocation with such a singular lack of recognition that he lived and died almost unknown beyond his native village, Vaughan—like Marvell and Traherne—has had to wait for his renown. Now, however, it seems to be secure.

Not unnaturally, his life was ill recorded. Born in Newton, Breconshire, in 1621/22, he, like his twin brother Thomas, was probably admitted to Jesus College, Oxford, in 1638. Although Thomas stayed on at Oxford, as Henry dimly recollected, for "ten or twelve years," he himself, "being then designed by my father for the study of the law," in about 1640 went to London to prepare for his career—and incidentally to enjoy, however briefly, the frolicsome literary life reflected in his early poems. Brought back to Wales by the outbreak of the war in 1642, within the next four years he seems to have served as a secretary to the chief justice of the Brecon circuit and as a soldier for the King, but in 1646 or thereabout he apparently married and settled in the town where he was born and where, almost half a century later, he would also die.

It was in 1646 that a volume entitled *Poems, with the Tenth Satire of Juvenal Englished* marked his debut as a writer intent on pleasing those "ingenious lovers of poesy . . . whose more refined spirits outwing these dull times and soar above the drudgery of dirty intelligence." A year later, according to its dated preface, he was ready with *Olar Iscanus* ("the swan of Usk"), but when this little book of poems and translations from Ovid, Boethius, and others finally appeared in 1651 it had most likely been altered and revised. Meanwhile the death of his younger brother William in 1648, the darkening political situation of the later forties, and the posthumous influence of George Herbert seem to have conspired to bring about the change that Vaughan himself acknowledged in the second (1655) section of *Silex Scintillans* ("sparkling flint"). There he repudiated the flashy poetical "wits" with whom "this kingdom hath abounded" and whom he himself had in his youth admired, proclaimed his reformation and repentance, and enlisted himself among Herbert's many converts to the "true, practic piety" which alone inspires great literature.

However unctuous and assertive this belated explanation of his literary development, the fact of Vaughan's conversion was at once apparent in the first installment of *Silex Scintillans* (1650), where the themes of God's immanence in nature and of man's thirst for spiritual illumination find intense expression. It also showed itself in his response to his twin brother's theosophical speculations and in his own prose writings, which included a devotional manual called *The Mount o Olives* (1652) and a group of translations published two years later as *Flores Solitudinis* ("flowers of solitude"). The so-called "second edition" of *Silex Scintillans* of 1655 was a reprint of the work of 1650, enlarged by its important preface already cited and by a group of hitherto unpublished poems. It may have been about this time that Vaughan married his late wife's sister and began the study of "physic" that, as he told Aubrey in 1673, he had "practised now for many years with good success (I thank God)." But his important work was done. The long evening of his life included more translations (of Henricus Nollius' mystical *Hermetical Physic* in 1655 and *The Chemist's Key* in 1657) and a scrappy collection of his and his late brother's poems entitled *Thalia Rediviva*

(1678), but his medical practice and protracted litigation with the children of his first marriage apparently killed the spark of literature. Apart from the inscription on his tombstone, his death in 1695 went almost unrecorded.

My texts are based upon *Poems, With The tenth Satyre of Juvenal Englished. By Henry Vaughan, Gent.,* 1646 (Wing V–124), *Silex Scintillans: Or Sacred Poems and Private Ejaculations. By Henry Vaughan Silurist,* 1650 (Wing V–125), *Olor Iscanus. A Collection of Some Select Poems, and Translations, Formerly written by Mr. Henry Vaughan, Silurist,* 1651 (Wing V–123), and *Silex Scintillans . . . The second Edition, In two Books; By Henry Vaughan, Silurist,* 1655 (Wing V–126).

A. B. Grosart edited *The Works in Verse and Prose Complete* (4 vols., 1871), E. K. Chambers the *Poems* (2 vols., 1896), L. C. Martin the *Works* (2 vols., 1914; rev. and enlarged, 1957), E. L. Marilla the *Secular Poems* (1958), and French Fogle the *Complete Poetry* (1964). On a smaller scale are L. I. Guiney's edition of *The Mount of Olives* (1902), W. A. L. Bettany's of *Silex Scintillans* (1905), and Christopher Dixon's of *A Selection from Henry Vaughan* (1967). In addition to F. E. Hutchinson's standard biography (1947) there are critical studies by Edmund Blunden (1927), Ross Garner (1959), E. C. Pettet (*Of Paradise and Light: A Study of Vaughan's Silex Scintillans,* 1960), R. A. Durr (*On the Mystical Poetry of Henry Vaughan,* 1962), and James D. Simmonds (*Masques of God: Form and Theme in the Poetry of Henry Vaughan,* 1972). Elizabeth Holmes has written on Vaughan's hermetic philosophy (1932), Marilla has supplied a *Comprehensive Bibliography* (1948), and Margaret Willey has treated Vaughan as well as Crashaw and Traherne in her brochure *Three Metaphysical Poets* (1961).

from Poems, With the Tenth Satire of Juvenal Englished (1646)

TO ALL INGENIOUS LOVERS OF POESY

Gentlemen,

To you alone, whose more refined spirits outwing these dull times and soar above the drudgery of dirty intelligence, have I made sacred these fancies. I know the years and what coarse entertainment they afford poetry. If any shall question that courage that durst send me abroad so late and revel it thus in the dregs of an age, they have my silence. Only

Languescente seculo, liceat aegrotari.[1]

My more calm ambition, amidst the common noise, hath thus exposed me to the world. You have here a flame, bright only in its own innocence, that kindles nothing but a generous thought, which though it may warm the blood, the fire at highest is but Platonic, and the commotion within these limits excludes danger . . . . It is for you only that I have adventured thus far and invaded the press with verse, to whose more noble indulgence I shall now leave it, and so am gone.

H. V.

A SONG TO AMORET

If I were dead, and in my place
  Some fresher youth design'd

To warm thee with new fires, and grace
  Those arms I left behind,

Were he as faithful as the sun   5
  That's wedded to the sphere,
His blood as chaste and temp'rate run
  As April's mildest tear,

Or were he rich, and with his heaps
  And spacious share of earth   10
Could make divine affection cheap
  And court his golden birth,

For all these arts I'd not believe
  (No, though he should be thine)
The mighty amorist could give   15
  So rich a heart as mine.

Fortune and beauty thou mightst find,
  And greater men than I,
But my true resolved mind
  They never shall come nigh.   20

For I not an hour did love,
  Or for a day desire,

TO ALL INGENIOUS [1]"When the whole age is ailing, one may be permitted to languish."

But with my soul had from above
  This endless holy fire.

A RHAPSODY[1]

Occasionally written upon[2] a meeting with some of his
friends at the Glove Tavern[3] in a chamber painted overhead
with a cloudy sky and some few dispersed stars, and on the
sides with landscapes, hills, shepherds, and sheep.

Darkness and stars i' th' midday! They invite
Our active fancies to believe it night,
For taverns need no sun, but for a sign,
Where rich tobacco and quick tapers shine,
And royal, witty sack, the poet's soul,   5
With brighter suns than he doth gild the bowl,
As though the pot and poet did agree
Sack should to both illuminator be.
That artificial cloud with its curl'd brow
Tells us 'tis late; and that blue space below   10
Is fir'd with many stars. Mark how they break
In silent glances o'er the hills, and speak
The evening to the plains, where, shot from far,
They meet in dumb salutes as one great star.
    The room, methinks, grows darker, and the air   15
Contracts a sadder[4] color, and less fair.
Or is't the drawer's skill? Hath he no arts
To blind us so we can't know pints from quarts?

    .   .   .   .   .   .

But see, the moon is up! View where she stands
Sentinel o'er the door, drawn by the hands   25
Of some base painter that for gain hath made
Her face the landmark to the tippling trade.
This cup to her, that to Endymion[5] give;
'Twas wit at first and wine that made them live.
Choke may the painter, and his box disclose   30
No other colors than his fiery nose,
And may we no more of his pencil see
Than two churchwardens and mortality.
    Should we go now awand'ring, we should meet
With catchpoles,[6] whores, and carts in ev'ry street. 35
Now when each narrow lane, each nook and cave,
Signposts and shopdoors, pimp for ev'ry knave;
When riotous, sinful plush and telltale spurs
Walk Fleet Street and the Strand;[7] when the soft stirs
Of bawdy, ruffled silks turn night to day,   40
And the loud whip and coach scolds all the way;
When lust of all sorts, and each itchy blood
From the Tower Wharf to Cymbeline and Lud,[8]
Hunts for a mate, and the tir'd footman reels
'Twixt chairmen, torches, and the hackney wheels. 45

    .   .   .   .   .   .

Drink deep! This cup be pregnant, and the wine,
Spirit of wit, to make us all divine,
That, big with sack and mirth, we may retire   65
Possessors of more souls and nobler fire,

And by the influx of this painted sky
And labor'd forms to higher matters fly.
So, if a nap shall take us, we shall all,
After full cups, have dreams poetical.   70

Let's laugh now, and the press'd grape drink
Till the drowsy Day Star wink,
And in our merry, mad mirth run
Faster and further than the sun;
And let none his cup forsake   75
Till that star again doth wake.
So we men below shall move
Equally with the gods above.

TO AMORET, OF THE DIFFERENCE 'TWIXT HIM AND OTHER LOVERS, AND WHAT TRUE LOVE IS

Mark, when the evening's cooler wings
  Fan the afflicted air, how the faint sun,
    Leaving undone
    What he begun,
Those spurious flames suck'd up from slime and earth   5
    To their first low birth
    Resigns and brings.

They shoot their tinsel beams and vanities,
  Threading with those false fires their way;
    But as you stay   10
    And see them stray,
You lose the flaming track, and subtly they
    Languish away,
    And cheat your eyes.

Just so base, sublunary[1] lovers' hearts,   15
  Fed on loose, profane desires,
    May for an eye
    Or face comply;
But those removed, they will as soon depart,
    And show their art   20
    And painted fires.

Whilst I, by pow'rful love so much refin'd
  That my absent soul the same is,
    Careless to miss
    A glance or kiss,   25
Can with those elements of lust and sense
    Freely dispense,
    And court the mind.

A RHAPSODY [1]Text *Rhapsodis*.
[2]Written on the occasion of.
[3]Presumably the Globe in Fleet Street. [4]Darker.
[5]A shepherd boy of Mt. Latmos whom the moon goddess Diana,
enamored of his beauty, caused to sleep forever.
[6]Petty officers of the law.
[7]*Fleet Street...Strand*: principal thoroughfares of London.
[8]*Tower Wharf...Lud*: i.e., from the eastern to the western side of
London. Statues of Lud and Cymbeline, legendary kings of the
ancient Britons, adorned Ludgate, near St. Paul's Cathedral.
TO AMORET [1]The epithet, like *refin'd* in the following stanza,
obviously derives from Donne's "Valediction: Forbidding
Mourning" (p. 67).

Thus to the north the loadstones move,
  And thus to them th' enamor'd steel aspires.   30
    Thus, Amoret,
    I do affect,

And thus by winged beams and mutual fire
  Spirits and stars conspire,
  And this is LOVE.   35

from Silex Scintillans (1650)

THE DEDICATION

My God, Thou that didst die for me,
These Thy death's fruits I offer Thee;
Death that to me was life and light,
But dark and deep pangs to Thy sight.
Some drops of Thy all-quick'ning blood
Fell on my heart; these made it bud,
And put forth thus, though, Lord, before
The ground was curs'd and void of store.[1]
Indeed I had some here to hire
Which long resisted Thy desire,
That ston'd Thy servants, and did move
To have Thee murd'red for Thy love;
But, Lord, I have expell'd them, and so bent,
Beg Thou wouldst take Thy tenant's rent.

REGENERATION

[1]

A ward, and still in bonds, one day
    I stole abroad:
It was high spring, and all the way
  Primros'd, and hung with shade:
    Yet was it frost within;
      And surly winds
Blasted my infant buds, and sin
    Like clouds eclips'd my mind.

2

Storm'd thus, I straight perceiv'd my spring
    Mere stage and show,
My walk a monstrous, mountain'd thing.
    Rough-cast with rocks and snow
      And as a pilgrim's eye,
        Far from relief,
Measures the melancholy sky,
    Then drops and rains for grief,

3

So sigh'd I upward still; at last,
    'Twixt steps and falls,
I reach'd the pinnacle, where plac'd
    I found a pair of scales;
    I took them up, and laid
      In th'one late pains;
The other smoke and pleasures weighed,
    But prov'd the heavier grains.[1]

4

With that, some cried "Away!" Straight I
    Obey'd, and led
Full east, a fair, fresh field could spy;
    Some call'd it Jacob's Bed,[2]
    A virgin soil which no
    Rude feet e'er trod;
Where—since He stepp'd there—only go
    Prophets, and friends of God.

5

Here I repos'd; but scarce well set,
    A grove descried
Of stately height, whose branches met
    And mix'd on every side;
    I ent'red, and once in,
      Amaz'd to see't,
Found all was chang'd, and a new spring
    Did all my senses greet.

6

The unthrift[3] sun shot vital gold,
    A thousand pieces,
And heaven its azure did unfold
    Checker'd with snowy fleeces;
    The air was all in spice,
      And every bush
A garland wore: thus fed my eyes,
    But all the ear[4] lay hush.

[7]

Only a little fountain lent
    Some use for ears,
And on the dumb shades language spent
    The music of her tears;
    I drew her near, and found
      The cistern full
Of divers stones, some bright and round,
    Others ill-shap'd and dull.

8

The first, pray mark, as quick as light
    Danc'd through the flood;
But th' last, more heavy than the night,

DEDICATION [1]Fertility.

REGENERATION [1]Units of weight.
[2]Jacob himself called the place Bethel (Genesis 28. 19).
[3]Spendthrift. [4]Some editors emend to *earth*.

Nail'd to the center[5] stood;
  I wonder'd much, but tir'd
    At last with thought,
My restless eye, that still desir'd,
  As strange an object brought.

9

It was a bank of flowers, where I descried,
  Though 'twas midday,
Some fast asleep, others broad-eyed
  And taking in the ray;
    Here musing long, I heard
    A rushing wind,
Which still increas'd, but whence it stirr'd,
  Nowhere I could not find.

10

I turn'd me round, and to each shade
  Dispatch'd an eye
To see if any leaf had made
  Least motion or reply;
    But while I list'ning sought
    My mind to ease
By knowing where 'twas or where not,
  It whisper'd, "Where I please."
"Lord," then said I, "on me one breath,
  And let me die before my death!"

Canticles[6] Cap. 4, Ver. 16[7]
Arise, O North, and come thou South wind, and blow
upon my garden, that the spices thereof may flow out.

DAY OF JUDGMENT

When through the north a fire shall rush
  And roll into the east,
And like a fiery torrent brush
  And sweep up south and west,

When all shall stream and lighten round,   5
  And with surprising flames
Both stars and elements confound
  And quite blot out their names,

When Thou shalt spend Thy sacred store
  Of thunders in that heat,   10
And low as e'er they lay before
  Thy six-days' buildings beat,

When like a scroll the heavens shall pass
  And vanish clean away,
And nought must stand of that vast space   15
  Which held up night and day,

When one loud blast shall rend the deep,
  And from the womb of Earth
Summon up all that are asleep
  Unto a second birth,   20

When Thou shalt make the clouds Thy seat,
  And in the open air

The quick and dead, both small and great,
  Must to Thy bar repair;

O then it will be all too late   25
  To say, "What shall I do?"
Repentance there is out of date,
  And so is Mercy too.

Prepare, prepare me then, O God!
  And let me now begin   30
To feel my loving Father's rod
  Killing the man of sin!

Give me, O give me crosses here,
  Still more afflictions lend;
That pill, though bitter, is most dear   35
  That brings health in the end.

Lord God, I beg nor friends nor wealth,
  But pray against them both;
Three things I'd have, my soul's chief health,
  And one of these same[1] loathe;   40

A living faith, a heart of flesh,
  The world an enemy;
This last will keep the first two fresh,
  And bring me where I'd be.

1 Peter 4.7.
Now the end of all things is at hand; be you therefore
sober, and watching in prayer.[2]   45

RELIGION[1]

My God, when I walk in those groves
  And leaves Thy Spirit doth still fan,
I see in each shade that there grows
  An angel talking with a man.

Under a juniper, some house,   5
  Or the cool myrtle's canopy;
Others beneath an oak's green boughs,
  Or at some fountain's bubbling eye.[2]

Here Jacob dreams, and wrestles; there
  Elias by a raven is fed;   10
Another time by th' angel, where
  He brings him water with his bread.

In Abr'ham's tent the winged guests
  (Oh how familiar then was heaven!)
Eat, drink, discourse, sit down, and rest,   15
  Until the cool and shady even.

[5]Earth.   [6]I.e., The Song of Solomon.   [7]Text *Cap. 5. Ver. 17.*
DAY OF JUDGMENT [1]Text *seme.*
[2]*Now...prayer*: Here, as often elsewhere, Vaughan quotes the Geneva Bible (1560).
RELIGION [1]This is one of the many poems in *Silex Scintillans* inspired by George Herbert. See "Decay" (p. 214).
[2]*Under a juniper...eye*: The juniper, myrtle, oak, and fountain are all biblical (1 Kings 19.4, Zecheriah 1.11, Judges 6.11, Genesis 16.7).

Nay Thou thyself, my God, in fire,
  Whirlwinds, and clouds, and the soft voice,
Speak'st there so much, that I admire
  We have no conf'rence in these days.[3]   20

Is the truce broke? or 'cause we have
  A Mediator now with Thee,
Dost Thou therefore old treaties waive,
  And by appeals from Him decree?

Or is't so, as some green heads say,   25
  That now all miracles must cease?
Though Thou has promis'd they should stay
  The tokens of the church and peace.

No, no, Religion is a spring
  That from some secret, golden mine   30
Derives her birth, and thence doth bring
  Cordials in every drop, and wine.

But in her long and hidden course,
  Passing through the earth's dark veins,
Grows still from better unto worse,   35
  And both her taste and color stains;

Then, drilling[4] on, learns to increase
  False echoes and confused sounds,
And unawares doth often seize
  On veins of sulphur underground;   40

So poison'd, breaks forth in some clime,
  And at first sight doth many please;
But drunk, is puddle or mere slime,
  And, stead of physic, a disease.

Just such a tainted sink we have,   45
  Like that Samaritan's dead well;[5]
Nor must we for the kernel crave
  Because most voices like the shell.

Heal, then, these waters, Lord; or bring Thy flock,
Since these are troubled, to the springing rock;   50
Look down, Great Master of the feast; O shine,
And turn once more our water into wine!

Canticles Cap. 4, Ver. 12
My sister, my spouse is as a garden enclosed, as a spring
shut up, and a fountain sealed up.

THE LAMP

'Tis dead night round about: horror doth creep
And move on with the shades; stars nod and sleep,
And through the dark air spin a fiery thread
Such as doth gild the lazy glowworm's bed.
    Yet burn'st thou here a full day while I spend   5
My rest in cares, and to the dark world lend
These flames as thou dost thine to me. I watch
That hour which must thy life and mine dispatch,
But still thou dost outgo me. I can see,
Met in thy flames, all acts of piety: 10

Thy light is charity; thy heat is zeal;
And thy aspiring, active fires reveal
Devotion still on wing. Then as thou dost weep
Still as thou burn'st, and the warm droppings creep
To measure out thy length, as if thou'dst know   15
What stock and how much time were left thee now.
Nor dost thou spend one tear in vain, for still,
As thou dissolv'st to them and they distill,
They're stor'd up in the socket where they lie,
When all is spent, thy last and sure supply,   20
And such is true repentance: ev'ry breath
We spend in sighs is treasure after death.
Only one point escapes thee: that thy oil
Is still out[1] with thy flame, and so both fail;
But whensoe'er I'm out, both shall be in,   25
And where thou mad'st an end, there I'll begin.

Mark Cap. 13, Ver. 35
Watch you, therefore, for you know not when the master
of the house cometh, at evening, or at midnight, or at the
cock-crowing, or in the morning.

THE SHOWER

[1]
'Twas so I saw thy birth: that drowsy lake
From her faint bosom breath'd thee, the disease
Of her sick waters and infectious ease.
    But now at even,
    Too gross for heaven,
Thou fall'st in tears, and weep'st for thy mistake.

2
Ah, it is so with me. Oft have I prest[1]
Heaven with a lazy breath, but fruitless this
Pierc'd not. Love only can with quick access
    Unlock the way
    When all else stray—
The smoke and exhalations of the breast.

3
Yet if, as thou dost melt and with thy train
Of drops make soft the earth, my eyes could weep
O'er my hard heart, that's bound up and asleep,
    Perhaps at last
    (Some such show'rs past)
My God would give a sunshine after rain.

[3]*Here Jacob...days*: The various incidents of deific intervention
in human affairs are related respectively at Genesis 28.11–12,
32.24–30 (Jacob's dream and his struggle with God), 1 Kings
17.6, 19.5–8 (Elijah's being given food and water), Genesis 18.1–8
(Abraham's angelic visitors), Exodus 3.2–6, Job 38.1, Exodus
24.16, 1 Kings 19.12 (God's speaking from fire, a whirlwind, etc.).
[4]Trickling.
[5]See John 4.6–26 for Jesus' encounter with the woman of Samaria
at the well.
THE LAMP [1]Exhausted.
THE SHOWER [1]Pressed, i.e., importuned.

DISTRACTION

O knit me, that am crumbled dust! The heap
  Is all dispers'd and cheap;
  Give for a handful but a thought,
    And it is bought;
      Hadst Thou   5
Made me a star, a pearl, or a rainbow,
  The beams I then had shot
  My light had lessen'd not;
    But now
I find myself the less, the more I grow.   10
    The world
Is full of voices; man is call'd and hurl'd
  By each; he answers all,
  Knows every note and call;
    Hence, still   15
Fresh dotage tempts, or old usurps his will.
Yet hadst Thou clipp'd my wings, when coffin'd in
  This quicken'd mass of sin,
  And saved that light, which freely Thou
    Didst then bestow,   20
    I fear
I should have spurn'd, and said Thou didst forbear,
  Or that Thy store was less.
  But now since Thou didst bless
    So much,   25
I grieve, my God, that Thou hast made me such.
    I grieve?
O, yes! Thou know'st I do; come, and relieve,
  And tame, and keep down with Thy light
  Dust that would rise and dim my sight!   30
    Lest left alone too long
    Amidst the noise and throng,
    Oppressed I,
Striving to save the whole, by parcels die.

THE PURSUIT

Lord, what a busy, restless thing
  Hast Thou made man!
Each day and hour he is on wing,
  Rests not a span;[1]
Then having lost the sun and light,   5
  By clouds surpris'd,
He keeps a commerce in the night
  With air disguis'd.
Hadst Thou given to this active dust
  A state untir'd,   10
The lost son had not left the husk,
  Nor home desir'd.[2]
That was Thy secret, and it is
  Thy mercy too,
For when all fails to bring to bliss,   15
  Then this must do.
Ah, Lord, and what a purchase will that be,
To take us sick that sound would not take Thee!

[THOU THAT KNOW'ST FOR WHOM I MOURN]

Thou that know'st for whom I mourn,[1]
  And why these tears appear,
That keep'st account till he return
  Of all his dust left here;
As easily Thou might'st prevent   5
  As now produce these tears,
And add unto that day he went
  A fair supply of years.
But 'twas my sin that forc'd Thy hand
  To cull this primrose out,   10
That by Thy early choice forewarn'd
  My soul might look about.
Oh what a vanity is man!
  How like the eye's quick wink
His cottage[2] fails, whose narrow span   15
  Begins even at the brink!
Nine months Thy hands are fashioning us,
  And many years, alas,
Ere we can lisp, or ought discuss
  Concerning Thee, must pass;   20
Yet have I known Thy slightest things—
  A feather or a shell,
A stick or rod which some chance brings—
  The best of us excel:
Yea, I have known these shreds outlast   25
  A fair-compacted frame,
And for one twenty we have past
  Almost outlive our name.[3]
Thus hast Thou plac'd in man's outside
  Death to the common eye,   30
That heaven within him might abide,
  And close[4] eternity,
Hence youth and folly, man's first shame,
  Are put unto the slaughter,
And serious thoughts begin to tame   35
  The wise man's madness, laughter.
Dull, wretched worms! that would not keep
  Within our first fair bed,
But out of paradise must creep
  For ev'ry foot to tread!   40
Yet had our pilgrimage been free,
  And smooth without a thorn,
Pleasures had foil'd eternity,
  And tares had chok'd the corn.
Thus by the Cross salvation runs;   45
  Affliction is a mother
Whose painful throes yield many sons,

THE PURSUIT [1]A fragment of time.
[2]*The lost son...desir'd*: The Prodigal Son, in his distress, "would fain have filled his belly with the husks that the swine did eat" (Luke 15.16).
[THOU THAT KNOW'ST] [1]I.e., Vaughan's brother William, who died in 1648. [2]I.e., body.
[3]*For one twenty...name*: i.e., despite our own protracted lives such *shreds* will outlast the memory of our names. [4]Enclose.

Each fairer than the other.
A silent tear can pierce Thy throne
When loud joys want a wing,   50
And sweeter airs stream from a groan
Than any arted[5] string.
Thus, Lord, I see my gain is great,
My loss but little to it;
Yet something more I must entreat,   55
And only Thou canst do it.
O let me—like Him—know my end
And be as glad to find it!
And whatsoe'er Thou shalt commend,
Still let Thy servant mind it!   60
Then make my soul white as His own,
My faith as pure and steady,
And deck me, Lord, with the same crown
Thou hast crown'd Him already!

THE RETREAT

Happy those early days when I
Shin'd in my angel-infancy,
Before I understood this place
Appointed for my second race.
Or taught my soul to fancy ought   5
But a white, celestial thought;
When yet I had not walk'd above
A mile or two from my first love,
And looking back—at that short space—
Could see a glimpse of His bright face;   10
When on some gilded cloud, or flower,
My gazing soul would dwell an hour,
And in those weaker glories spy
Some shadows of eternity;
Before I taught my tongue to wound   15
My conscience with a sinful sound,
Or had the black art to dispense
A sev'ral sin to ev'ry sense,
But felt through all this fleshly dress
Bright shoots of everlastingness.   20
    Oh how I long to travel back,
And tread again that ancient track!
That I might once more reach that plain,
Where first I left my glorious train;
From whence th' enlightened spirit sees   25
That shady city of palm trees.[1]
But ah! my soul with too much stay
Is drunk, and staggers in the way!
Some men a forward motion love.
But I by backward steps would move   30
And when this dust falls to the urn,
In that state I came, return.

[COME, COME, WHAT DO I HERE?]

[1]

Come, come, what do I here?
    Since he[1] is gone

Each day is grown a dozen year,
    And each hour, one.
        Come, come!
    Cut off the sum
By these soil'd tears
(Which only Thou
Know'st to be true).
Days are my fears.

2

There's not a wind can stir,
    Or beam pass by,
But straight I think (though far)
    Thy hand is nigh.
        Come, come!
    Strike these lips dumb.
This restless breath
That soils Thy name
Will ne'er be tame
Until in death.

3

Perhaps some think a tomb
    No house of store,[2]
But a dark and seal'd-up womb
    Which ne'er breeds more.
        Come, come!
    Such thoughts benumb,
But I would be
With him I weep,
Abed and sleep,
To wake in Thee.

MIDNIGHT

[1]

    When to my eyes
(Whilst deep sleep others catches)
    Thine host of spies,
The stars, shine in their watches,
    I do survey
    Each busy ray,
And how they work and wind,
    And wish each beam
    My soul doth stream
With the like ardor shin'd.
    What emanations,
    Quick vibrations,
And bright stirs are there!
    What thin ejections,
    Cold affections,
And slow motions here!

[5]I.e., contrived, artful.
THE RETREAT [1]I.e., the sight afforded Moses as he looked into the promised land from the top of Mt. Pisgah (Deuteronomy 34.3).
COME, COME [1]Probably Vaughan's younger brother William (d. 1648). [2]I.e., a dwelling amply supplied.

2

Thy heav'ns (some say)
Are a firey-liquid light
  Which mingling aye[1]
Streams and flames thus to the sight.
  Come then, my God!
  Shine on this blood
And water in one beam,
  And Thou shalt see
  Kindled by Thee
Both liquors burn and stream.
  O what bright quickness,
  Active brightness,
And celestial flows
  Will follow after
  On that water
Which Thy spirit blows!

Matthew Cap. 3, Ver. 11

I indeed baptize you with water unto repentance, but he
that cometh after me is mightier than I, whose shoes I am
not worthy to bear; he shall baptize you with the Holy
Ghost and with fire.

CONTENT

[1]

Peace, peace! I know 'twas brave,
  But this coarse fleece
I shelter in is slave
  To no such peace.[1]
  When I am gone
I shall no wardrobes leave
  To friend or son
But what their own homes weave.

2

Such, though not proud nor full,
  May make them weep
And mourn to see the wool
  Outlast the sheep.
  Poor, pious wear!
Hadst thou been rich or fine
  Perhaps that tear
Had mourn'd thy loss, not mine.

3

Why, then, these curl'd, puff'd points,[2]
  Or a laced story?
Death sets all out of joint
  And scorns their glory.
  Some love a rose
In hand, some in the skin,
  But, cross[3] to those,
I would have mine within.

[JOY OF MY LIFE WHILE LEFT ME HERE]

[1]

Joy of my life[1] while left me here,
      And still my love!

How in thy absence thou dost steer
      Me from above!
      A life well led
      This truth commends,
      With quick or dead
      It never ends.

2

Stars are of mighty use; the night
      Is dark and long,
The road foul; and where one goes right,
      Six may go wrong.
      One twinkling ray
      Shot o'er some cloud
      May clear much way
      And guide a crowd.

3

God's saints are shining lights; who stays
      Here long must pass
O'er dark hills, swift streams, and steep ways
      As smooth as glass;
      But these all night,
      Like candles, shed
      Their beams, and light
      Us into bed.

4

They are, indeed, our pillar fires,
      Seen as we go;
They are that city's shining spires
      We travel to:
      A swordlike gleam
      Kept man for[2] sin
      First out; this beam
      Will guide him in.

THE MORNING-WATCH[1]

O joys! infinite sweetness! with what flow'rs
And shoots of glory my soul breaks and buds!
    All the long hours
    Of night and rest.
    Through the still shrouds   5
    Of sleep, and clouds,
  This dew fell on my breast;
    O how it bloods
And spirits all my earth![2] hark! in what rings
And hymning circulations the quick world   10
    Awakes and sings!

MIDNIGHT [1]Always.
CONTENT [1]With a pun on *piece* (of fabric). [2]Tagged laces or
cords for attaching the hose to the doublet. [3]Contrary to.
JOY OF MY LIFE [1]Perhaps Vaughan's first wife Catherine (d. ca.
1653) or perhaps his brother William. [2]Because of.
THE MORNING WATCH [1]Religious service, i.e., prayer.
[2]*Bloods and spirits all my earth*: i.e, invigorates and animates my
body.

The rising winds
And falling springs,
Birds, beasts, all things
Adore Him in their kinds.   15
Thus all is hurl'd
In sacred hymns and order: the great chime
And symphony of Nature. Prayer is
The world in tune,
A spirit-voice,
And vocal joys,   20
Whose echo is heav'n's bliss.
O let me climb[3]
When I lie down! The pious soul by night
Is like a clouded star, whose beams, though said   25
To shed their light
Under some cloud,
Yet are above,
And shine and move
Beyond that misty shroud.   30
So in my bed,
That curtain'd grave, though sleep, like ashes, hide
My lamp and life, both shall in Thee abide.

[SILENCE AND STEALTH OF DAYS, 'TIS NOW]

Silence and stealth of days, 'tis now,
Since thou[1] art gone,
Twelve hundred hours, and not a brow
But clouds hang on.
As he that in some cave's thick damp,   5
Lock'd from the light,
Fixeth a solitary lamp
To brave the night,
And walking from his sun, when past
That glimm'ring ray,   10
Cuts through the heavy mists in haste
Back to his day;
So o'er fled minutes I retreat
Unto that hour
Which show'd thee last, but did defeat   15
Thy light and pow'r.
I search; and rack my soul to see
Those beams again;
But nothing but the snuff[2] to me
Appeareth plain,   20
That, dark and dead, sleeps in its unknown
And common urn;
But those, fled to their Maker's throne,
There shine and burn:
O could I track them! but souls must   25
Track one the other;
And now the spirit, not the dust,
Must be my brother.
But I have one pearl,[3] by whose light
All things I see;   30
And in the heart of earth and night
Find heaven, and Thee.

CHEERFULNESS

[1]

Lord, with what courage and delight
I do each thing
When Thy least breath sustains my wing!
I shine and move
Like those above,
And (with much gladness
Quitting sadness)
Make me fair days of every night.

2

Affliction thus mere pleasure is,
And hap what will,
If Thou be in't, 'tis welcome still;
But since Thy rays
In sunny days
Thou dost thus lend
And freely spend,
Ah, what shall I return for this?

3

O that I were all soul! That Thou
Wouldst make each part
Of this poor, sinful frame pure heart!
Then would I drown
My single one,
And to Thy praise
A consort raise
Of hallelujahs here below.

PEACE

My soul, there is a country
Far beyond the stars,
Where stands a winged sentry
All skillful in the wars:
There, above noise and danger,   5
Sweet Peace sits crown'd with smiles,
And One born in a manger
Commands the beauteous files.
He is thy gracious friend.
And—O my soul awake!—   10
Did in pure love descend,
To die here for thy sake.
If thou canst get but thither,
There grows the flower of Peace,
The rose that cannot wither,   15
Thy fortress and thy ease.
Leave, then, thy foolish ranges,[1]
For none can thee secure,
But One who never changes,
Thy God, thy life, thy cure.   20

[3]I.e., mount to heaven (through prayer).
SILENCE AND STEALTH [1]Vaughan's brother William?
[2]Burned wick. [3]I.e., religious faith?
PEACE [1]Wanderings.

ROMANS CAP. 8, VER. 19

Etenim res Creatae exerto Capite observantes
expectant revelationem Filiorum Dei.[1]

[1]

And do they so? Have they a sense
　　Of ought but influence?
Can they their heads lift, and expect,
　　And groan[2] too? Why, th' elect
Can do no more; my volumes said
　　They were all dull and dead;
They judg'd them senseless, and their state
　　Wholly inanimate.
　　　Go, go; seal up thy looks,
　　　　And burn thy books!

2

I would I were a stone or tree
　　Or flow'r by pedigree,
Or some poor highway herb, or spring
　　To flow, or bird to sing!
Then should I—tied to one sure state—
　　All day expect my date;
But I am sadly loose, and stray
　　A giddy blast each way;
　　　O let me not thus range!
　　　　Thou canst not change.

3

Sometimes I sit with Thee and tarry
　　An hour or so, then vary.
Thy other creatures in this scene
　　Thee only aim and mean;
Some rise to seek Thee, and with heads
　　Erect, peep from their beds;
Others, whose birth is in the tomb,
　　And cannot quit the womb,
Sigh there and groan for Thee,
　　　Their liberty.

4

O let not me do less! Shall they
　　Watch while I sleep or play?
Shall I Thy mercies still abuse
　　With fancies, friends, or news?
O brook it not! Thy blood is mine,
　　And my soul should be Thine;
O brook it not! Why wilt Thou stop,
　　After whole show'rs, one drop?
　　　Sure, Thou wilt joy to see
　　　　Thy sheep with Thee.

THE RELAPSE

My God, how gracious art Thou! I had slipt
　　Almost to hell,
And on the verge of that dark, dreadful pit

Did hear them yell,
But O Thy love, Thy rich, almighty love　　　　5
　　That sav'd my soul,
And check'd their fury when I saw them move
　　And heard them howl!
O my sole comfort, take no more these ways,
　　This hideous path,　　　　10
And I will mend my own without delays.
　　Cease Thou Thy wrath!
I have deserv'd a thick, Egyptian damp,
　　Dark as my deeds,
Should mist within me and put out that lamp　　15
　　Thy spirit feeds;
A darting conscience full of stabs and fears,
　　No shade but yew.
Sullen and sad eclipses, cloudy spheres,
　　These are my due.　　　　20
But He that with His blood (a price too dear)
　　My scores did pay
Bid me, by virtue from Him, challenge here
　　The brightest day.
Sweet, downy thoughts, soft lily-shades, calm streams,　25
　　Joys full and true,
Fresh, spicy mornings and eternal beams—
　　These are His due.

UNPROFITABLENESS

How rich, O Lord, how fresh Thy visits are!
'Twas but just now my bleak leaves hopeless hung,
　　Sullied with dust and mud;
Each snarling blast shot through me and did share[1]
　　Their youth and beauty, cold show'rs nipp'd and wrung　5
　　Their spiciness and blood.
But since Thou didst in one sweet glance survey
Their sad decays, I flourish, and once more
　　Breathe all perfumes and spice.
I smell a dew like myrrh, and all the day　　　　10
Wear in my bosom a full sun, such store
　　Hath one beam from Thy eyes.
But ah, my God, what fruit hast Thou of this?
What one poor leaf did ever I yet[2] fall
　　To wait upon Thy wreath?　　　　15
Thus Thou all day a thankless weed dost dress,
And when Th' hast done, a stench or fog is all
　　The odor I bequeath.

IDLE VERSE

Go, go, quaint follies, sug'red sin,
　　Shadow no more my door!

ROMANS [1]*Etenim...Dei*: "For the earnest expectation of the creature waiteth for the manifestation of the sons of God."
[2]"For we know that the whole creation groaneth and travaileth in pain together until now" (Romans 8.22).
UNPROFITABLENESS [1]Shear. [2]Some editors emend to *let*.

I will no longer cobwebs spin;
    I'm too much on the score.[1]

For since amidst my youth and night   5
    My great Preserver smiles,
We'll make a match, my only light,
    And join against their wiles.

Blind, desp'rate fits, that study how
    To dress and trim our shame;   10
That gild rank poison, and allow
    Vice in a fairer name;

The purls[2] of youthful blood and bowels,
    Lust in the robes of Love,
The idle talk of fev'rish souls   15
    Sick with a scarf or glove;

Let it suffice my warmer days
    Simper'd and shin'd on you;
Twist not my cypress with your bays,
    Or roses with my yew.   20

Go, go, seek out some greener thing,
    It snows and freezeth here;
Let nightingales attend[3] the spring;
    Winter is all my year.

SUNDAYS

[1]

Bright shadows of true rest, some shoots of bliss,
        Heaven once a week,
The next world's gladness prepossess'd in this,
        A day to seek
Eternity in time, the steps by which
We climb above all ages, lamps that light
Man through his heap of dark days, and the rich
And full redemption of the whole week's flight.

2

The pulleys unto headlong man, time's bower,
        The narrow way,
Transplanted paradise, God's walking hour,
        The cool o' th' day,
The creatures' jubilee, God's parle with dust,
Heaven here, man on those hills of myrrh and flow'rs,
Angels descending, the returns of trust,
A gleam of glory after six days' show'rs.

3

The church's love-feasts, time's prerogative[1]
        and interest
Deducted from the whole, the combs and hive
        And home of rest,
The Milky Way chalk'd out with suns, a clue[2]
That guides through erring hours, and in full story
A taste of heav'n on earth, the pledge and cue
Of a full feast, and the outcourts of glory.

THE PILGRIMAGE

As travelers, when the twilight's come,
And in the sky the stars appear,

The past day's accidents[1] do sum
With, "Thus we saw there, and thus here,"

Then, Jacob-like, lodge in a place[2]   5
(A place, and no more, is set down)
Where till the day restore the race
They rest and dream homes of their own.

So for this night I linger here,
And full of tossings to and fro   10
Expect[3] still when Thou wilt appear,
That I may get me up and go.

I long and groan and grieve for Thee,
For Thee my words, my tears do gush,
"O that I were but where I see"   15
Is all the note within my bush.

As birds robb'd of their native wood,
Although their diet may be fine,
Yet neither sing nor like their food,
But with the thought of home do pine,   20

So do I mourn and hang my head,
And though Thou dost me fullness give,
Yet look I for far better bread,
Because by this man cannot live.

O feed me then, and since I may   25
Have yet more days, more nights to count,
So strengthen me, Lord, all the way,
That I may travel to Thy mount.

Hebrews Cap. 11, Ver. 13
And they confessed that they were strangers, and pilgrims
        on the earth.

THE WORLD [I]

[1]

I saw Eternity the other night,
Like a great ring of pure and endless light,
    All calm as it was bright;
And round beneath it, Time in hours, days, years,
    Driv'n by the spheres
Like a vast shadow moved; in which the world
    And all her train were hurl'd.
The doting lover in his quaintest strain
    Did there complain;
Near him, his lute, his fancy, and his flights,
    Wit's sour delights;
With gloves and knots, the silly snares of pleasure,
    Yet his dear treasure,
All scatter'd lay while he his eyes did pour
    Upon a flow'r.

IDLE VERSE [1]In debt. [2]Purlings. [3]Await.
SUNDAYS [1]Priority (as the first day of the week).
[2]A ball of twine (that guides through a maze).
THE PILGRIMAGE [1]Events.
[2]I.e., Bethel, where Jacob dreamed of a ladder reaching up to heaven (Genesis 28.11–22). [3]Await

2

The darksome statesman, hung with weights and woe
Like a thick midnight fog, mov'd there so slow.
  He did nor stay nor go;
Condemning thoughts—like sad eclipses—scowl
  Upon his soul,
And clouds of crying witnesses without
  Pursued him with one shout.
Yet digg'd the mole, and lest his ways be found,
  Work'd under ground,
Where he did clutch his prey, but one did see
  That policy.[1]
Churches and altars fed him; perjuries
  Were gnats and flies;
It rain'd about him blood and tears, but he
  Drank them as free.

3

The fearful miser on a heap of rust
Sat pining all his life there, did scarce trust
  His own hands with the dust,
Yet would not place one piece above, but lives
  In fear of thieves.
Thousands there were as frantic as himself,
  And hugged each one his pelf;[2]
The downright epicure plac'd heav'n in sense,
  And scorn'd pretense;
While others, slipp'd into a wide excess,
  Said little less;
The weaker sort slight, trivial wares enslave,
  Who think them brave;
And poor, despised Truth sat counting by
  Their victory.

4

Yet some, who all this while did weep and sing,
And sing and weep, soar'd up into the ring:
  But most would use no wing.
"O fools," said I, "thus to prefer dark night
  Before true light!
To live in grots and caves, and hate the day
  Because it shows the way,
The way which from this dead and dark abode
  Leads up to God;
A way where you might tread the sun, and be
  More bright than he!"
But as I did their madness so discuss,
  One whisper'd thus,
"This ring the Bridegroom did for none provide,
  But for His bride."

John Cap. 2, Ver. 16–17
All that is in the world, the lust of the flesh, the lust of
the eyes, and the pride of life, is not of the Father, but is of
the world.

And the world passeth away, and the lusts thereof; but he
that doeth the will of God abideth for ever.

MOUNT OF OLIVES [II]

When I first saw true beauty, and Thy joys,
Active as light and calm without all noise,
Shin'd on my soul, I felt through all my pow'rs
Such a rich air of sweets, as evening show'rs
Fann'd by a gentle gale convey, and breathe
On some parch'd bank, crown'd with a flow'ry wreath;
Odors and myrrh and balm in one rich flood
O'erran my heart, and spirited my blood;
My thoughts did swim in comforts, and mine eye
Confess'd the world did only paint and lie.
And where before I did no safe course steer,
But wander'd under tempests all the year;
Went bleak and bare in body as in mind,
And was blown through by every storm and wind,
I am so warm'd now by this glance on me
That midst all storms I feel a ray of Thee.
So have I known some beauteous *paysage*[1] rise
In sudden flow'rs and arbors to my eyes,
And in the depth and dead of winter bring
To my cold thoughts a lively sense of spring.
  Thus fed by Thee, who dost all beings nourish,
My wither'd leaves again look green and flourish;
I shine and shelter underneath Thy wing,
Where sick with love I strive Thy name to sing,
Thy glorious name! which grant I may so do
That these may be Thy praise, and my joy too!

MAN

[1]
  Weighing the steadfastness and state
Of some mean things which here below reside,
Where birds, like watchful clocks, the noiseless date
  And intercourse of times divide,
Where bees at night get home and hive, and flow'rs,
    Early as well as late,
Rise with the sun and set in the same bow'rs;[1]

2
  I would, said I, my God would give
The staidness of these things to man; for these
To His divine appointments ever cleave,
  And no new business breaks their peace;
The birds nor sow nor reap, yet sup and dine;
    The flow'rs without clothes live,
Yet Solomon was never dress'd so fine.[2]

3
  Man hath still either toys or care;
He hath no root, nor to one place is ti'd,
But ever restless and irregular

THE WORLD [1]Crafty device, stratagem.   [2]Riches.
MOUNT OF OLIVES [1]Rural scene.
MAN [1]Some editors emend to *hours*.
[2]*Solomon...fine*: "Consider the lilies of the field, how they grow;
they toil not, neither do they spin, and yet I say unto you that even
Solomon, in all his glory, was not arrayed like one of these"
(Matthew 6.28–29).

About this earth doth run and ride.
He knows he hath a home, but scarce knows where;
   He says it is so far
That he hath quite forgot how to go there.

     4
   He knocks at all doors, strays and roams,
Nay, hath not so much wit as some stones have,

Which in the darkest nights point to their homes
   By some hid sense their Maker gave;
Man is the shuttle, to whose winding quest
   And passage through these looms
God order'd motion, but ordain'd no rest.

from Olor Iscanus (1651)

TO THE RIVER ISCA[1]

When Daphne's lover here first wore the bays,
Eurotas' secret streams heard all his lays,
And holy Orpheus, Nature's busy child,
By headlong Hebrus his deep hymns compil'd;
Soft Petrarch, thaw'd by Laura's flames, did weep   5
On Tiber's banks, when she, proud fair, could sleep;
Mosella boasts Ausonius, and the Thames
Doth murmur Sidney's Stella to her streams;
While Severn, swoll'n with joy and sorrow, wears
Castara's smiles mixed with fair Sabrin's tears.[2]   10
Thus poets—like the nymphs, their pleasing themes—
Haunted the bubbling springs and gliding streams
And happy banks, whence such fair flow'rs have sprung,
But happier those were where they have sat and sung!
Poets, like angels, where they once appear,   15
Hallow the place, and each succeeding year
Adds rev'rence to 't, such as at length doth give
This aged faith, that there their genii live.
Hence th' ancients say that from this sickly air
They pass to regions more refin'd and fair,   20
To meadows str'w'd with lilies and the rose,
And shades whose youthful green no old age knows;
Where all in white they walk, discourse, and sing
Like bees' soft murmurs, or a chiding spring.
   But Isca, whensoe'er those shades I see,   25
And thy lov'd arbors must no more know me.
When I am laid to rest hard by thy streams,[3]
And my sun sets where first it sprang in beams,
I'll leave behind me such a large, kind light
As shall redeem thee from oblivious night,   30
And in these vows which, living yet, I pay,
Shed such a previous and enduring ray
As shall from age to age thy fair name lead,
'Till rivers leave to run, and men to read.
   First, may all bards born after me,   35
   When I am ashes, sing of thee!
   May thy green banks or streams, or none,
   Be both their hill and Helicon!
   May vocal groves grow there, and all
   The shades in them prophetical,   40
   Where, laid, men shall more fair truths see
   Than fictions were of Thessaly!

May thy gentle swains, like flow'rs,
Sweetly spend their youthful hours;
And thy beauteous nymphs, like doves,   45
Be kind and faithful to their loves!
Garlands and songs and roundelays,
Mild, dewy nights, and sunshine days,
The turtle's[4] voice, joy without fear,
Dwell on thy bosom all the year!   50
May the evet[5] and the toad
Within thy banks have no abode,
Nor the wily, winding snake
Her voyage through thy waters make!
In all thy journey to the main,   55
No nitrous clay nor brimstone vein
Mix with thy streams, but may they pass
Fresh as the air and clear as glass,
And where the wand'ring crystal treads
Roses shall kiss and couple heads!   60
The factor-wind[6] from far shall bring
The odors of the scatter'd spring,
And loaden with the rich arrear,[7]
Spend it in spicy whispers there.
No sullen heats, nor flames that are   65
Offensive and canicular,[8]

TO THE RIVER   [1]The River Usk in Wales.
[2]*When Daphne...Sabrin's tears*: This catalogue of rivers made famous by poets comprises the Eurotas in Greece, where Daphne, pursued by Apollo, was turned into a laurel; the Hebrus in Thrace, on whose banks the poet Orpheus was dismembered by the local women in their Bacchanalian orgies; the Arno (not the Tiber) in Tuscany, where Petrarch loved but did not win his Laura; the Moselle in Germany, which Decimus Magnus Ausohius (b. ca. 310) celebrated in one of his *Idyllia*; the Thames, which Vaughan associates with the love affair described in Sir Philip Sidney's *Astrophel and Stella* (1591); and the Severn in Wales, scene of the wooing described in William Habington's *Castara* (1634) and of the untimely death of the unfortunate Sabrina that Spenser melodiously relates in *The Faerie Queene* (II.x). *Proud*: text *prou'd. Swoll'n*: text *sworn* (corrected in the Errata).
[3]*When I...streams*: Vaughan lies buried in Llansantffread churchyard, Breconshire, on the banks of the Usk.   [4]Turtledove's.
[5]Salamander.
[6]I.e., the wind in its capacity as a business agent (*factor*) assembling merchandise (*the odors of the scatter'd spring*).   [7]Array.
[8]Pertaining to Sirius, the Dog Star, which rises and sets with the

Shine on thy sands, nor pry to see
Thy scaly, shading family,
But noons as mild as Hesper's rays,
Or the first blushes of fair days!   70
What gifts more heav'n or earth can add,
With all those blessings be thou clad!
        Honor, beauty,
        Faith and duty,
        Delight and truth,   75
        With love and youth
Crown all about thee! and whatever fate
Impose elsewhere, whether the graver state
Or some toy else, may those loud, anxious cares
For dead and dying things, the common wares   80
And shows of Time, ne'er break thy peace, nor make
Thy repos'd arms to a new war awake!
But freedom, safety, joy and bliss,
United in one loving kiss,
Surround thee quite, and style thy borders   85
The land redeem'd from all disorders!

TO MY WORTHY FRIEND MASTER T. LEWES[1]

Sees not my friend what a deep snow
Candies our country's woody brow?
The yielding branch his load scarce bears,
Oppress'd with snow and frozen tears,
While the dumb rivers slowly float,   5
All bound up in an icy coat.
  Let us meet, then, and while this world
In wild eccentrics[2] now is hurl'd,
Keep we, like nature, the same key
And walk in our forefathers' way.   10
Why any more cast we an eye
On what may come, not what is nigh?
Why vex ourselves with fear or hope
And care beyond our horoscope?
Who into future times would peer   15
Looks oft beyond his term set here,
And cannot go into those grounds
But through a churchyard which them bounds.
Sorrows and sighs and searches spend
And draw our bottom to an end,   20
But discreet joys lengthen the lease
Without which life were a disease;
And who this age a mourner goes
Doth with his tears but feed his foes.

BOETHIUS, LIBER I, METRUM I[1]

I whose first year flourish'd with youthful verse,
In slow, sad numbers now my grief rehearse;
A broken style my sickly lines afford,
And only tears give weight unto my words;
Yet neither fate[2] nor force my Muse could fright,   5
The only faithful consort of my flight;
Thus what was once my green years' greatest glory
Is now my comfort, grown decay'd and hoary,

For killing cares th' effects of age spurr'd on,
That grief might find a fitting mansion;   10
O'er my young head runs an untimely gray,
And my loose skin shrinks at my blood's decay.
Happy the man whose death in prosp'rous years
Strikes not nor shuns him in his age and tears.
But O how deaf is she to hear the cry   15
Of th' oppress'd soul, or shut the weeping eye!
While treacherous Fortune with slight honors fed
My first estate, she almost drown'd my head,
But now since (clouded thus) she hides those rays,
Life adds unwelcom'd length unto my days.   20
Why then, my friends, judg'd you my state so good?
He that may fall once never firmly stood.

[LIBER II,] METRUM V

Happy that first white age when we
Lived by the earth's mere charity!
No soft, luxurious diet then
Had effeminated men;
No other meat nor wine had any   5
Than the coarse mast or simple honey,
And by the parents' care laid up,
Cheap berries did the children sup.
No pompous wear was in those days
Of gummy[1] silks or scarlet bays;[2]   10
Their beds were on some flow'ry brink,
And clear spring water was their drink.
The shady pine in the sun's heat
Was their cool and known retreat,
For then 'twas not cut down, but stood   15
The youth and glory of the wood.
The daring sailor with his slaves
Then had not cut the swelling waves,
Nor for desire of foreign store
Seen any but his native shore.   20
No stirring drum had scar'd that age,
Nor the shrill trumpet's active rage;
No wounds by bitter hatred made
With warm blood soil'd the shining blade,
For how could hostile madness arm   25
An age of love to public harm?
When common justice none withstood,
Nor sought rewards for spilling blood.
  O that at length our age would raise
Into the temper of those days!   30

---

sun in July and August and is therefore associated with hot weather.
TO MASTER LEWES [1]Thomas Lewes, rector of Llanfigan, a village on the Usk near Vaughan's home at Newton.
[2]I.e., irregular courses. In Ptolemaic astronomy, an *eccentric* was the supposed orbit of a planet around the sun or earth, but with the sun or earth not in its center.
BOETHIUS [1]This and the following poem are loose translations of interpolated lyrics in Boethius' *De consolatione philosophiae.* [2]Text *faith.* [1]I.e., stiffened? [2]Baize.

But—worse than Etna's fires!—debate
And avarice inflame our state.
Alas, who was it that first found

Gold hid of purpose under ground,
That sought out pearls, and div'd to find   35
Such precious perils for mankind!

from Silex Scintillans (1655)

THE AUTHOR'S PREFACE TO THE FOLLOWING HYMNS

That this kingdom hath abounded with those ingenious persons which in the late notion are termed "wits" is too well known. Many of them having cast away all their fair portion of time in no better employments than a deliberate search or excogitation of idle words and a most vain, insatiable desire to be reputed poets, leaving behind them no other monuments of those excellent abilities conferred upon them but such as they may (with a predecessor of theirs) term parricides and a soul-killing issue; for that is the βραβεῖον[1] and laureate crown which idle poems will certainly bring to their unrelenting authors. . . .

To continue (after years of discretion) in this vanity is an inexcusable desertion of pious sobriety; and to persist so to the end is a wilful despising of God's sacred exhortations by a constant, sensual volutation or wallowing in impure thoughts and scurrilous conceits, which both defile their authors and as many more as they are communicated to. If "every idle world shall be accounted for"[2] and if "no corrupt communication should proceed out of our mouths,"[3] how desperate (I beseech you) is their condition who, all their lifetime, and out of mere design, study lascivious fictions, then carefully record and publish them, that instead of grace and life they may minister sin and death unto their readers? . . .

And here, because I would prevent a just censure by my free confession, I must remember that I myself have for many years together languished of this very sickness, and it is no long time since I have recovered. But—blessed be God for it!—I have by His saving assistance suppressed my greatest follies, and those which escaped from me are (I think) as innoxious[4] as most of that vein use to be; besides, they are interlined with many virtuous and some pious mixtures. What I speak of them is truth, but let no man mistake it for an extenuation of faults, as if I intended an apology for them or myself, who am conscious of so much guilt in both as can never be expiated without special sorrows, and that cleansing and precious effusion of my Almighty Redeemer; and if the world will be so charitable as to grant my request I do here most humbly and earnestly beg that none would read them. . . .

The first that with any effectual success attempted a diversion of this foul and overflowing stream was the blessed man, Mr. George Herbert, whose holy life and verse gained many pious converts (of whom I am the least) and gave the first check to a most flourishing and admired wit of his time.

After him followed divers, *sed non passibus aequis:*[5] they had more of fashion than force. And the reason of their so vast distance from him, besides differing spirits and qualifications (for his measure was eminent), I suspect to be because they aimed more at verse than perfection, as may be easily gathered by their frequent impressions and numerous pages. Hence sprang those wide, those weak and lean conceptions which in the most inclinable[6] reader will scarce give any nourishment or help to devotion; for not flowing from a true, practic[7] piety, it was impossible they should effect those things abroad which they never had acquaintance with at home, being only the productions of a common spirit and the obvious ebullitions of that light humor which takes the pen in hand out of no other consideration than to be seen in print. . . .

> Despite a recent illness that brought him "nigh unto death" Vaughan, providentially restored to health, had resolved to devote his art to "devotion and sanctity."

The God of the spirits of all flesh hath granted me a further use of mine than I did look for in the body, and when I expected and had (by His assistance) prepared for a message of death, then did He answer me with life—I hope to His glory and my great advantage, that I may flourish not with leaf only but with some fruit also, which hope and earnest desire of His poor creature I humbly beseech Him to perfect and fulfil for His dear Son's sake, unto whom, with Him and the most holy and loving Spirit, be ascribed by angels, by men, and by all His works all glory and wisdom and dominion in this the temporal and in the Eternal Being. Amen.

Newton by Usk, near
Skethrock,[8] September 30
1654

[THEY ARE ALL GONE INTO THE WORLD OF LIGHT]

They are all gone into the world of light!
    And I alone sit ling'ring here;
Their very memory is fair and bright
    And my sad thoughts doth clear.

THE AUTHOR'S PREFACE   [1]The prize in the Greek games.
[2]Matthew 12.36. [3]Ephesians 4.29. [4]Harmless.
[5]"But with unequal steps" (Vergil, *Aeneid*, II.724).
[6]Favorably disposed. [7]Experienced, practised.
[8]Scethrog, a town on the Usk near Brecon.

It glows and glitters in my cloudy breast 5
  Like stars upon some gloomy grove,
Or those faint beams in which this hill is dress'd
  After the sun's remove.

I see them walking in an air of glory,
  Whose light doth trample on my days: 10
My days, which are at best but dull and hoary,
  Mere glimmering and decays.

O holy hope and high humility,
  High as the heavens above!
These are your walks, and you have show'd them me 15
  To kindle my cold love.

Dear, beauteous Death! the jewel of the just,
  Shining nowhere but in the dark,
What mysteries do lie beyond thy dust,
  Could man outlook that mark! 20

He that hath found some fledg'd[1] bird's nest, may know
  At first sight if the bird be flown;
But what fair well or grove he sings in now,
  That is to him unknown.

And yet, as angels in some brighter dreams 25
  Call to the soul when man doth sleep,
So some strange thoughts transcend our wonted themes,
  And into glory peep.

If a star were confin'd into a tomb,
  Her captive flames must needs burn there; 30
But when the hand that lock'd her up gives room,
  She'll shine through all the sphere.

O Father of eternal life, and all
  Created glories under Thee!
Resume[2] Thy spirit from this world of thrall 35
  Into true liberty.

Either disperse these mists, which blot and fill
  My perspective[3] still as they pass,
Or else remove me hence unto that hill
  Where I shall need no glass. 40

COCKCROWING

Father of lights,[1] what sunny seed,
What glance of day has Thou confin'd
Into this bird? To all the breed
This busy ray Thou hast assign'd;
  Their magnetism works all night, 5
  And dreams of paradise and light.

Their eyes watch for the morning hue;
Their little grain, expelling night,
So shines and sings as if it knew
The path unto the house of light. 10
  It seems their candle, howe'er done,
  Was tinn'd[2] and lighted at the sun.

If such a tincture,[3] such a touch,
So firm a longing can impow'r,[4]

Shall Thy own image think it much 15
To watch for Thy appearing hour?
  If a mere blast so fill the sail,
  Shall not the breath of God prevail?

O thou immortal light and heat
Whose hand so shines through all this frame 20
That by the beauty of the seat
We plainly see who made the same,
  Seeing Thy seed abides in me,
  Dwell Thou in it and I in Thee!

To sleep without Thee is to die; 25
Yea, 'tis a death partakes of hell,
For where Thou dost not close the eye,
It never opens, I can tell.
  In such a dark, Egyptian border
  The shades of death dwell, and disorder.[5] 30

If joys and hopes and earnest throws[6]
And hearts, whose pulse beats still for light,
Are given to birds, who, but Thee, knows
A lovesick soul's exalted flight?
  Can souls be track'd by any eye 35
  But His who gave them wings to fly?

Only this veil which Thou hast broke,[7]
And must be broken yet in me,
This veil, I say, is all the cloak
And cloud which shadows Thee from me. 40
  This veil Thy full-ey'd love denies,
  And only gleams and fractions spies.

O take it off! Make no delay,
But brush me with Thy light, that I
May shine into a perfect day 45
And warm me at Thy glorious eye!
  O take it off, or till it flee,
  Though with no lily, stay with me!

[THEY ARE ALL GONE]   [1]Feathered, i.e., mature.   [2]Take back.
[3]Perspective glass, i.e., telescope.

COCKCROWING   [1]*Father of lights, seed, glance of day,* and (in the second stanza) *grain* are all conventional terms for spiritual illumination in seventeenth-century hermetical writing. A passage cited by L. C. Martin from *Anima Magica Abscondita* (1650) by the poet's brother Thomas Vaughan illustrates their use: "For she [the *anima* or soul] is guided in her Operations by a *Spirituall Metaphysicall Graine,* a seed or Glance of *Light,* simple, and without any Mixture, descending from the *first Father of Lights.*"
[2]Lighted.
[3]I.e., hue or tint of the spiritual principle of things.
[4]Glossed by some editors as *in-pour.*
[5]*In such...disorder:* "And the Lord said unto Moses, Stretch out thine hand toward heaven, that there may be darkness over the land of Egypt, even darkness which may be felt" (Exodus 10.21)   [6]Throes.
[7]*Only...broke:* According to St. Paul (2 Corinthians 3.13–18), the "veil" with which Moses had concealed the meaning of the Old Testament and which Christ had "done away" will finally be removed so that we may behold God's glory unobstructed.

THE STAR

Whatever 'tis whose beauty here below
Attracts thee thus and makes thee stream and flow,
    And wind and curl and wink and smile,
        Shifting Thy gait and guile,

Though thy close[1] commerce nought at all imbars   5
My present search for eagle's eye, not stars,
    And still the lesser by the best
        And highest good is blest,

Yet, seeing all things that subsist and be
Have their commissions from divinity,   10
    And teach us duty, I will see
        What man may learn from thee.

First, I am sure, the subject so respected
Is well disposed, for bodies once infected,
    Deprav'd or dead, can have with thee   15
        No hold nor sympathy.

Next, there's in it a restless, pure desire
And longing for thy bright and vital fire,
    Desire that never will be quench'd,
        Nor can be writh'd nor wrench'd.   20

These are the magnets which so strongly move
And work all night upon thy light and love,
    As beauteous shapes, we know not why,
        Command and guide the eye.

For where desire—celestial, pure desire—   25
Hath taken root and grows and doth not tire,
    There God a commerce states, and sheds
        His secret on their heads.

This is the heart He craves, and whoso will
But give it Him, and grudge not, he shall feel   30
    That God is true, as herbs unseen
        Put on their youth and green.

CHILDHOOD

I cannot reach it, and my striving eye
Dazzles at it, as at eternity.

    Were now that chronicle alive,
Those white designs which children drive,
And the thoughts of each harmless hour,   5
With their content too in my pow'r,
Quickly would I make my path even,
And by mere playing go to heaven.

    Why should men love
A wolf more than a lamb or dove?   10
Or choose hell-fire and brimstone streams
Before bright stars and God's own beams?
Who kisseth thorns will hurt his face,
But flowers do both refresh and grace;
And sweetly living—fie on men!—   15

Are, when dead, medicinal then;
If seeing much should make staid eyes,
And long experience should make wise;
Since all that age doth teach is ill,
Why should I not love childhood still?   20
Why, if I see a rock or shelf,
Shall I from thence cast down myself?
Or by complying with the world,
From the same precipice be hurl'd?
Those observations are but foul   25
Which make me wise to love my soul.

And yet the practice worldlings call
Business, and weighty action all,
Checking the poor child for his play.
But gravely cast themselves away.   30

    Dear harmless age! the short, swift span
Where weeping Virtue parts with man;
Where love without lust dwells, and bends
What way we please without self-ends.

An age of mysteries which he   35
Must live twice that would God's face see,
Which angels guard, and with it play,
Angels which foul men drive away.

How do I study now, and scan
Thee more than e'er I studied man,   40
And only see through a long night
Thy edges and thy bordering light!
O for thy center and midday!
For sure that is the narrow way!

THE NIGHT
John 3.2[1]

    Through that pure virgin shrine,
That sacred veil drawn o'er Thy glorious noon,
That men might look and live, as glow-worms shine,
        And face the moon,
        Wise Nicodemus saw such light   5
        As made him know his God by night.

    Most blest believer he!
Who in that land of darkness and blind eyes
Thy long-expected healing wings could see
        When Thou didst rise!   10
        And, what can never more be done,
        Did at midnight speak with the Sun!

    O who will tell me where
He found Thee at that dead and silent hour?
What hallow'd, solitary ground did bear   15
        So rare a flower,
        Within whose sacred leaves did lie
        The fulness of the Deity?

THE STAR   [1]Secret.
THE NIGHT   [1]Text *2.3*. The reference is to Nicodemus' coming to
Jesus "by night" to inquire about spiritual rebirth.

No mercy seat of gold,
No dead and dusty cherub, nor carv'd stone,
But His own living works did my Lord hold
        And lodge alone;
    Where trees and herbs did watch and peep
    And wonder, while the Jews did sleep.

        Dear Night! this world's defeat,   25
The stop to busy fools, care's check and curb,
The day of spirits, my soul's calm retreat
        Which none disturb!
    Christ's progress² and His prayer time,
    The hours to which high Heaven doth chime.   30

        God's silent, searching flight;
When my Lord's head is fill'd with dew, and all
His looks are wet with the clear drops of night;³
        His still, soft call;
    His knocking-time; the soul's dumb watch,   35
    When spirits their fair kindred catch.

        Were all my loud, evil days
Calm and unhaunted as is thy dark tent,
Whose peace but by some angel's wing or voice
        Is seldom rent;   40
    Then I in heaven all the long year
    Would keep, and never wander here.

        But living where the sun
Doth all things wake, and where all mix and tire
Themselves and others, I consent and run   45
        To every mire,
    And by this world's ill-guiding light,
    Err more than I can do by night.

        There is in God, some say,
A deep but dazzling darkness; as men here   50
Say it is late and dusky, because they
        See not all clear.
    O for that night! where I in Him
    Might live invisible and dim!

THE WATERFALL

With what deep murmurs through time's silent stealth
Doth thy transparent, cool, and wat'ry wealth
        Here flowing fall
        And chide and call,
As if his liquid, loose retinue stay'd
Ling'ring, and were of this steep place afraid,
        The common pass
        Where, clear as glass,
        All must descend,
        Not to an end
But, quick'ned by this deep and rocky grave,
Rise to a longer course more bright and brave.

Dear stream, dear bank, where often I
Have sat and pleas'd my pensive eye,
Why, since each drop of thy quick¹ store

Runs thither, whence it flow'd before,
Should poor souls fear a shade or night,
Who came, sure, from a sea of light?
Or since those drops are all sent back
So sure to Thee, that none doth lack,
Why should frail flesh doubt anymore
That what God takes, He'll not restore?
O useful element and clear!
My sacred wash and cleanser here,
My first consigner unto those
Fountains of life where the Lamb goes!²
What sublime truths and wholesome themes
Lodge in thy mystical, deep streams,
Such as dull man can never find
Unless that Spirit lead his mind
Which first upon thy face did move,
And hatch'd all with His quick'ning love.
As this loud brook's incessant fall
In streaming rings restagnates³ all
Which reach by course the bank and then
Are no more seen, just so pass men.
O my invisible estate,
My glorious liberty, still late!
Thou art the channel my soul seeks,
Not this with cataracts and creeks.

QUICKNESS

False life, a foil and no more, when
        Wilt thou be gone?
Thou foul deception of all Men
That would not have the true come on!

Thou art a moonlike toil, a blind,
        Self-posing state,
A dark contest of waves and wind,
A mere tempestuous debate.

Life is a fix'd, discerning light,
        A knowing joy;
No chance or fit, but ever bright
And calm and full, yet doth not cloy.

'Tis such a blissful thing that still
        Doth vivify,
And shine and smile, and hath the skill
To please without eternity.

Thou art a toilsome mole or less,
        A moving mist;
But life is—what none can express—
A quickness which my God hath kist.

²Vaughan, in a note, supplies a reference to Mark 1.35 and Luke
21.37.
³*His locks...night*: The line echoes the Song of Solomon 5.2.
THE WATERFALL   ¹Living
²*Fountains...goes*: The Lamb "shall lead them unto living fountains
of waters" (Revelation 7.17).   ³Becomes stagnant

Thomas Traherne [1637-1674]

Although Traherne himself, in the third book of his *Centuries*, minutely traces his spiritual progress from infant bliss to the contagion of the world's slow stain and then to the recovery of that "felicity" which is the theme of all his major works, the known facts of his external life are few and quickly stated. The son of a shoemaker of Hereford (to whose "poor house" he makes allusion), he was born in 1637 and apparently lost his parents at a very early age. Although there is no record of his schooling, it is likely that he and his elder brother Philip were adopted by a Philip Traherne, innkeeper and prosperous citizen of Hereford, who could have been related to the boys. At any rate, in 1652-53 Thomas was enrolled at Brasenose College, Oxford, where, as he recorded later (*Centuries*, III.36), he came to understand that "logic, ethics, physics, metaphysics, geometry, astronomy, poesy, medicine, grammar, music, rhetoric, all kind of arts, trades, and mechanicisms that adorned the world pertained to felicity." Since, however, he could not take all knowledge as his province, it was probably inevitable that his interests centered on divinity.

Following his B.A. in 1656 and then perhaps a period spent away from Oxford, in 1661 he was made M.A. by decree and thereupon appointed rector of Credenhill, a village near his native Hereford. With perhaps occasional junkets back to Oxford for research on *Roman Forgeries*, a learned exposé of Catholic propaganda and deceptions that may have been submitted for his B.D. degree in 1669, he remained at Credenhill until he secured a post (perhaps in 1669) as chaplain to Sir Orlando Bridgeman, a leader of the bar who was ending his career as Lord Keeper of the Great Seal. His last five years, which were no doubt filled with writing, were spent at London and at Teddington, a village on the Thames near Hampton Court, where he died in 1674 and thus, as one of his admirers said, "got early to those blissful mansions to which he at all times aspired."

Ironically, the things that Traherne himself arranged for publication—*Roman Forgeries* (1673) and a rather ponderous work entitled *Christian Ethics* (1675)—have been dwarfed by those that stayed in manuscript two hundred years or more. It was in the winter of 1896-97 that one W. T. Brooke picked up for a few pence on a London bookstall two anonymous manuscripts (now in the Bodleian at Oxford) that were thought by A. B. Grosart to be the work of Henry Vaughan but that Bertram Dobell subsequently ascertained to be Traherne's. One contains *The Centuries,* i.e., four books (of a hundred items each) made up of meditations and interpolated poems on those "profitable wonders" whereby the author hoped to help an unnamed friend (now known to have been Mrs. Susanna Hopton) attain "felicity." The untitled work breaks off abruptly with the tenth section of the fifth century. The second manuscript comprises fair copies of a group of poems followed by such miscellaneous items as alphabetically arranged extracts and reading notes, expense accounts, and even remedies for deafness and toothache.

After Traherne's death his brother Philip drew upon this second manuscript in assembling the sixty-one "Poems of Felicity" that, though acquired by the British Museum in 1818, went unnoticed until it was exhumed and published in 1910, seven years after Dobell had made his findings known. Philip's manuscript supplies highly edited versions of the first twenty-two poems and part of the twenty-third in the so-called Dobell manuscript, but it excludes fourteen and part of the fifteenth as well as adding thirty-nine new poems for which no other source exists. In addition to these two collections—the Dobell manuscript and Philip's "Poems of Felicity"—other items have been added to the canon from Traherne's *Christian Ethics* (1675), *Hexameron or Meditations on the*

Six Days of Creation (which, like *Meditations and Devotions of the Life of Christ*, was published in 1717 from manuscripts that Traherne left with Mrs. Hopton, for whom he wrote the *Centuries*), and a Bodleian manuscript of meditations, prayers, and poems that Dobell called "The Book of Private Devotions." In 1699 the Reverend George Hicks published ("at the request of a friend of the author's") *A Serious and Pathetical Contemplation of the Mercies of God in Several Most Devout and Sublime Thanksgivings for the Same,* a group of poems now known as the *Thanksgivings.*

With the permission of the Delegates of the Clarendon Press I have based my text upon H. M. Margoliouth's transcriptions of the Traherne manuscripts in his edition of *Centuries, Poems, and Thanksgivings* (2 vols., 1965). Dobell's pioneer editions of the *Poems* (1903) and of *Centuries of Meditations* (1908, rev. 1928), H. I. Bell's of *Poems of Felicity* (1910), and Gladys I. Wade's of *The Poetical Works* (1932) have been superseded by Margoliouth. There are editions of the *Centuries* by John Hayward (1950) and John Farrar (1960), of *Poems, Centuries and Three Thanksgivings* by Anne Ridler (1966), of *A Serious and Pathetical Contemplation* by R. Daniells (1941), and of *Christian Ethics* by Margaret Bottrall (1962) and Carol L. Marks (1968). A hitherto unknown manuscript of "Select Meditations" now at Yale has been described by James Osborn in the (London) *Times Literary Supplement,* 8 October 1964, p. 928.

Miss Wade's biography (1944) is authoritative, and among longer critical studies are those by Queenie Iredale (1935), K. W. Salter (1964), A. L. Clements (1969), and Stanley Stewart (*The Expanded Voice: The Art of Thomas Traherne,* 1970). Margaret Willy's *Three Metaphysical Poets* (1961) treats Traherne as well as Crashaw and Vaughan.

THE POEMS

THE SALUTATION

1

These little limbs,
These eyes and hands which here I find,
These rosy cheeks wherewith my life begins,
Where have ye been? Behind
What curtain were ye from me hid so long?
Where was, in what abyss, my speaking tongue?

2

When silent I
So many thousand, thousand years
Beneath the dust did in a chaos lie,
How could I smiles or tears
Or lips or hands or eyes or ears perceive?
Welcome ye treasures which I now receive!

3

I that so long
Was nothing from eternity,
Did little think such joys as ear or tongue
To celebrate or see:
Such sounds to hear, such hands to feel, such feet,
Beneath the skies on such a ground to meet.

4

New burnish'd joys,
Which yellow gold and pearl excel!
Such sacred treasures are the limbs in boys,
In which a soul doth dwell;

Their organized joints and azure veins
More wealth include than all the world contains.

5

From dust I rise,
And out of nothing now awake;
These brighter regions which salute mine eyes,
A gift from GOD I take.
The earth, the seas, the light, the day, the skies,
The sun and stars are mine if those I prize.

6

Long time before
I in my mother's womb was born,
A GOD, preparing, did this glorious store,
The world, for me adorn.
Into this Eden so divine and fair,
So wide and bright, I come His son and heir.

7

A stranger here
Strange things doth meet, strange glories see;
Strange treasures lodg'd in this fair world appear,
Strange all, and new to me;
But that they mine should be, who nothing was,
That strangest is of all, yet brought to pass.

WONDER

1

How like an angel came I down!
How bright are all things here!
When first among His works I did appear

O how their GLORY me did crown!
The world resembled His eternity,
    In which my soul did walk;
And ev'rything that I did see
        Did with me talk.

2

The skies in their magnificence,
    The lively, lovely air,
O how divine, how soft, how sweet, how fair!
The stars did entertain my sense,
And all the works of GOD, so bright and pure,
    So rich and great did seem
As if they must endure
        In my esteem.

3

A native health and innocence
    Within my bones did grow;
And while my GOD did all His glories show,
I felt a vigor in my sense
That was all SPIRIT. I within did flow
    With seas of life, like wine;
I nothing in the world did know
        But 'twas divine.

4

Harsh ragged objects were conceal'd;
    Oppressions, tears, and cries,
Sins, griefs, complaints, dissensions, weeping eyes
Were hid, and only things reveal'd
Which heav'nly spirits and the angels prize.
    The state of innocence
And bliss, not trades and poverties,
        Did fill my sense.

5

The streets were paved with golden stones,
    The boys and girls were mine,
O how did all their lovely faces shine!
The sons of men were holy ones,
Joy, beauty, welfare did appear to me,
    And ev'rything which here I found,
While like an angel I did see,
        Adorn'd the ground.

6

Rich diamond and pearl and gold
    In ev'ry place was seen;
Rare splendors, yellow, blue, red, white, and green,
Mine eyes did ev'rywhere behold.
Great wonders cloth'd with glory did appear,
    Amazement was my bliss,
That and my wealth was ev'rywhere;
        No joy to this!

7

Curs'd and devis'd proprieties,[1]
    With envy, avarice,
And fraud, those fiends that spoil even paradise,

Flew from the splendor of mine eyes;
And so did hedges, ditches, limits, bounds:
    I dream'd not ought of those,
But wander'd over all men's grounds,
        And found repose.

8

Proprieties themselves were mine,
    And hedges ornaments;
Walls, boxes, coffers, and their rich contents
Did not divide my joys, but shine.
Clothes, ribbons, jewels, laces, I esteem'd
    My joys by others worn:
For me they all to wear them seem'd
        When I was born.

EDEN

1

A learned and a happy ignorance
    Divided me
    From all the vanity,
From all the sloth, care, pain, and sorrow that advance
    The madness and the misery
Of men. No error, no distraction I
Saw soil the earth or overcloud the sky.

2

I knew not that there was a serpent's sting
    Whose poison, shed
    On men, did overspread
The world, nor did I dream of such a thing
    As sin, in which mankind lay dead.
They all were brisk and living wights[1] to me,
Yea, pure and full of immortality.

3

Joy, pleasure, beauty, kindness, glory, love,
    Sleep, day, life, light,
    Peace, melody, my sight,
My ears and heart did fill and freely move.
    All that I saw did me delight.
The universe was then a world of treasure,
To me an universal world of pleasure.

4

Unwelcome penitence was then unknown;
    Vain costly toys,
    Swearing and roaring boys,
Shops, markets, taverns, coaches were unshown;
    So all things were that drown'd my joys.
No briers choak'd up my path, nor hid the face
Of bliss and beauty, nor eclips'd the place.

5

Only what Adam in his first estate
    Did I behold;

WONDER [1]Bequeathed properties.
EDEN [1]Text *Weights*.

Hard silver and dry gold
As yet lay underground; my blessed fate
  Was more acquainted with the old
And innocent delights, which he did see
In his original simplicity.

6

Those things which first his Eden did adorn,
    My infancy
    Did crown. Simplicity
Was my protection when I first was born.
  Mine eyes those treasures first did see
Which God first made. The first effects of love
My first enjoyments upon earth did prove;

7

And were so great and so divine, so pure,
    So fair and sweet,
    So true when I did meet
Them here at first, they did my soul allure,
  And drew away my infant feet
Quite from the works of men, that I might see
The glorious wonders of the DEITY.

INNOCENCE

1

But that which most I wonder at, which most
I did esteem my bliss, which most I boast,
And ever shall enjoy, is that within
    I felt no stain nor spot of sin.

  No darkness then did overshade,
  But all within was pure and bright;
  No guilt did crush nor fear invade,
  But all my soul was full of light.

  A joyful sense and purity
    Is all I can remember;
  The very night to me was bright,
    'Twas summer in December.

2

A serious meditation did employ
My soul within, which, taken up with joy,
Did seem no outward thing to note, but fly
    All objects that do feed the eye,

  While it those very objects did
  Admire and prize and praise and love,
  Which in their glory most are hid,
  Which presence only doth remove.

  Their constant daily presence I,
    Rejoicing at, did see,
  And that which takes them from the eye
  Of others offer'd them to me.

3

No inward inclination did I feel
To avarice or pride; my soul did kneel
In admiration all the day. No lust, nor strife,
    Polluted then my infant life.

No fraud nor anger in me mov'd,
No malice, jealousy, or spite;
All that I saw I truly lov'd:
Contentment only and delight

  Were in my soul. O heav'n! what bliss
    Did I enjoy and feel!
  What powerful delight did this
  Inspire! For this I daily kneel.

4

Whether it be that nature is so pure,
And custom only vicious; or that sure
God did by miracle the guilt remove,
    And made my soul to feel His love

  So early; or that 'twas one day,
  Wherein this happiness I found,
  Whose strength and brightness so do ray,
  That still it seemeth to surround.

  Whate'er it is, it is a light
    So endless unto me
  That I a world of true delight
  Did then and to this day do see.

5

That prospect was the gate of heav'n, that day
The ancient light of Eden did convey
Into my soul: I was an Adam there,
    A little Adam in a sphere

  Of joys! O there my ravish'd sense
  Was entertain'd in paradise,
  And had a sight of innocence,
  Which was beyond all bound and price.

  An antepast[1] of heaven sure!
    I on the earth did reign;
  Within, without me, all was pure:
  I must become a child again.

THE INSTRUCTION

1

Spew out thy filth, thy flesh abjure;
Let not contingents[1] thee defile.
For transients only are impure,
And airy things alone beguile.

2

Unfelt, unseen let those things be
Which to thy spirit were unknown
When to thy blessed infancy
The world, thyself, thy God was shown.

3

All that is great and stable stood
Before thy purer eyes at first:
All that in visibles is good
Or pure or fair or unaccurst.

INNOCENCE   [1]Foretaste.
THE INSTRUCTION   [1]Trivial things.

4

Whatever else thou now dost see
In custom, action, or desire,
'Tis but a part of misery,
In which all men on earth conspire.

THE RAPTURE

1

Sweet infancy!
O fire of heaven! O sacred light!
How fair and bright!
How great am I,
Whom all the world doth magnify!

2

O heavenly joy!
O great and sacred blessedness
Which I possess!
So great a joy
Who did into my arms convey!

3

From GOD above
Being sent, the heavens me inflame
To praise His name.
The stars do move![1]
The burning sun doth show His love.

4

O how divine
Am I! To all this sacred wealth,
This life and health,
Who rais'd? Who mine
Did make the same? What hand divine?

THE RECOVERY[1]

1

To see us but receive is such a sight
As makes His treasures infinite!
Because His goodness doth possess
In us His own and our own blessedness.
Yea more, His love doth take delight
To make our glory infinite;
Our blessedness to see
Is even to the Deity
A beatific vision! He attains
His ends while we enjoy. In us He reigns.

2

For God enjoy'd is all His end.[2]
Himself He then doth comprehend
When He is blessed, magnified,
Extoll'd, exalted, prais'd, and glorified,
Honor'd, esteem'd, belov'd, enjoy'd,
Admired, sanctified, obey'd,
That is receiv'd. For He
Doth place His whole felicity
In that: who is despised and defied,
Undeified almost if once denied.

3

In all His works, in all His ways,
We must His glory see and praise;
And since our pleasure is the end,
We must His goodness and His love attend.
If we despise His glorious works,
Such sin and mischief in it lurks
That they are all made vain;
And this is even endless pain
To Him that sees it, whose diviner grief
Is hereupon (ah me!) without relief.

4

We please His goodness that receive;
Refusers Him of all bereave,
As bridegrooms know full well that build
A palace for their bride. It will not yield
Any delight to him at all
If she for whom he made the hall
Refuse to dwell in it,
Or plainly scorn the benefit.
Her act that's wooed yields more delight and pleasure
If she receives, than all the pile of treasure.

5

But we have hands, and lips, and eyes,
And hearts and souls can sacrifice;
And souls themselves are made in vain
If we our evil stubbornness retain.
Affections, praises, are the things
For which He gave us all these springs;
They are the very fruits
Of all those trees and roots,
The fruits and ends of all His great endeavors,
Which he abolisheth whoever severs.

6

'Tis not alone a lively sense,
A clear and quick intelligence,
A free, profound, and full esteem;
Though these elixirs all and ends do seem:
But gratitude, thanksgiving, praise,
A heart return'd for all those joys,
These are the things admir'd,
These are the things by Him desir'd:
These are the nectar and the quintessence,
The cream and flower that most affect His sense.

7

The voluntary act whereby
These are repaid is in His eye
More precious than the very sky.
All gold and silver is but empty dross;
Rubies and sapphires are but loss;
The very sun and stars and seas
Far less His spirit please:
One voluntary act of love

THE RAPTURE   [1]Prompt (the poet to praise God's name).
THE RECOVERY   [1]I.e., God's compensation for His love.
[2]Intention, purpose.

Far more delightful to His soul doth prove,
And is above all these as far as love.

DESIRE

1

For giving me desire,
An eager thirst, a burning, ardent fire,
A virgin, infant flame,
A love with which into the world I came,
An inward, hidden, heavenly love
Which in my soul did work and move
And ever, ever me inflame
With restless, longing, heavenly avarice
That never could be satisfied,
That did incessantly a paradise
Unknown suggest, and something undescried
Discern, and bear me to it—be
Thy name forever prais'd by me!

2

Parched my wither'd bones
And eyes did seem; my soul was full of groans;
My thoughts extensions[1] were:
Like steps and paces they did still appear;
They somewhat hotly did pursue,
Knew that they had not all their due,
Nor ever quiet were,
But made my flesh like hungry, thirsty ground,
My heart a deep, profound abyss,
And ev'ry joy and pleasure but a wound,
So long as I my blessedness did miss.
O happiness! A famine burns,
And all my life to anguish turns!

3

Where are the silent streams,
The living waters and the glorious beams,
The sweet, reviving bowers,
The shady groves, the sweet and curious flowers,
The springs and trees, the heavenly days,
The flow'ry meads, the glorious rays,
The gold and silver towers?
Alas, all these are poor and empty things:
Trees, waters, days, and shining beams,
Fruits, flowers, bowers, shady groves, and springs
No joy will yield, no more than silent streams.
These are but dead material toys,
And cannot make my heavenly joys.

4

O love! Ye amities
And friendships that appear above the skies,
Ye feasts and living pleasures,
Ye senses, honors, and imperial treasures,
Ye bridal joys, ye high delights
That satisfy all appetites!
Ye sweet affections and
Ye high respects! Whatever joys there be
In triumphs, whatsoever stand
In amicable, sweet society,

Whatever pleasures are at His right hand,
Ye must, before I am divine,
In full propriety be mine.

5

This soaring, sacred thirst,
Ambassador of bliss approached first,
Making a place in me
That made me apt to prize and taste and see
For not the objects but the sense,
Of things, doth bliss to souls dispense,
And makes it Lord like Thee.
Sense, feeling, taste, complacency,[2] and sight:
These are the true and real joys,
The living, flowing, inward, melting, bright
And heavenly pleasures; all the rest are toys:
All which are founded in desire,
As light in flame and heat in fire.

THE CENTURIES

THE FIRST CENTURY

1

An empty book is like an infant's soul, in which anything may be written. It is capable of all things, but containeth nothing. I have a mind to fill this with profitable wonders. And since Love made you put it into my hands I will fill it with those truths you love without knowing them and with those things which, if it be possible, shall show my love: to you, in communicating most enriching truths; to Truth, in exalting her beauties in such a Soul.

2

Do not wonder that I promise to fill it with those truths you love, but know not; for though it be a maxim in the schools that there is no love of a thing unknown, yet I have found that things unknown have a secret influence on the soul, and like the center of the earth unseen violently attract it. We love we know not what, and therefore everything allures us. As iron at a distance is drawn by the lodestone, there being some invisible communications between them: so is there in us a world of love to somewhat, though we know not what in the world that should be. There are invisible ways of conveyance by which some great thing doth touch our souls, and by which we tend to it. Do you not feel yourself drawn with the expectation and desire of some great thing?

THE SECOND CENTURY

92

As it becometh you to retain a glorious sense of the world, because the earth and the heavens and the heaven of heavens are the magnificent and glorious territories of God's kingdom, so are you to remember always the unsearchable extent and illimited greatness of your own soul; the length

DESIRE [1]I.e., extensions of the poet's physical misery.
[2]Tranquillity

and breadth and depth, and height of your own understanding. Because it is the House of God, a living temple, and a glorious throne of the Blessed Trinity, far more magnificent and great than the Heavens; yea a person that in union and communion with God is to see eternity, to fill His omnipresence, to possess His greatness, to admire His love; to receive His gifts, to enjoy the world, and to live in His image. Let all your actions proceed from a sense of this greatness, let all your affections extend to this endless wideness, let all your prayers be animated by this spirit and let all your praises arise and ascend from this fountain. For you are never your true self till you live by your soul more than by your body, and you never live by your soul till you feel its incomparable excellency, and rest satisfied and delighted in the unsearchable greatness of its comprehension.

THE THIRD CENTURY

1

Will you see the infancy of this sublime and celestial greatness? Those pure and virgin apprehensions I had from the womb, and that divine light wherewith I was born are the best unto this day wherein I can see the universe. By the gift of God they attended me into the world, and by His special favor I remember them till now. Verily they seem the greatest gifts His wisdom could bestow, for without them all other gifts had been dead and vain. They are unattainable by book, and therefore I will teach them by experience. Pray for them earnestly, for they will make you angelical, and wholly celestial. Certainly Adam in paradise had not more sweet and curious apprehensions of the world than I when I was a child.

2

All appeared new, and strange at first, inexpressibly rare and delightful and beautiful. I was a little stranger, which at my entrance into the world was saluted and surrounded with innumerable joys. My knowledge was divine. I knew by intuition those things which since my apostasy I collected again by the highest reason. My very ignorance was advantageous. I seemed as one brought into the estate of innocence. All things were spotless and pure and glorious: yea, and infinitely mine, and joyful and precious. I knew not that there were any sins or complaints or laws. I dreamed not of poverties, contentions, or vices. All tears and quarrels were hidden from mine eyes. Everything was at rest, free and immortal. I knew nothing of sickness or death or rents or exaction. In the absence of these I was entertained like an angel with the works of God in their splendor and glory; I saw all in the peace of Eden; heaven and earth did sing my Creator's praises, and could not make more melody to Adam than to me. All time was eternity, and a perpetual sabbath. Is it not strange that an infant should be heir of the whole world, and see those mysteries which the books of the learned never unfold?

16

Once I remember (I think I was about four years old) when I thus reasoned with myself, sitting in a little obscure room in my father's poor house: If there be a God, certainly

He must be infinite in goodness; and that I was prompted to by a real whispering instinct of Nature. And if He be infinite in goodness, and a perfect Being in wisdom and love, certainly He must do most glorious things, and give us infinite riches. How comes it to pass, therefore, that I am so poor? Of so scanty and narrow a fortune, enjoying few and obscure comforts? I thought I could not believe Him a God to me unless all His power were employed to glorify me. I knew not then my soul or body; nor did I think of the heavens and the earth, the rivers and the stars, the sun or the seas: all those were lost, and absent from me. But when I found them made out of nothing for me, then I had a God indeed, whom I could praise, and rejoice in.

17

Sometimes I should be alone, and without employment, when suddenly my soul would return to itself, and forgetting all things in the whole world which mine eyes had seen, would be carried away to the ends of the earth, and my thoughts would be deeply engaged with enquiries: how the earth did end? Whether walls did bound it, or sudden precipices? Or whether the Heavens by degrees did come to touch it, so that the face of the earth and heaven were so near that a man with difficulty could creep under? Whatever I could imagine was inconvenient, and my reason, being posed, was quickly wearied. What also upheld the earth (because it was heavy) and kept it from falling; whether pillars, or dark waters? And if any of these, what then upheld those, and what again those, of which I saw there would be no end? Little did I think that the earth was round, and the world so full of beauty, light, and wisdom. When I saw that, I knew by the perfection of the work there was a God, and was satisfied, and rejoiced. People underneath, and fields and flowers, with another sun and another day, pleased me mightily: but more when I knew it was the same sun that served them by night, that served us by day.

25

When I heard any news I received it with greediness and delight, because my expectation was awakened with some hope that my happiness and the thing I wanted was concealed in it. Glad tidings, you know, from a far country brings us our salvation: and I was not deceived. In Jewry[1] was Jesus killed, and from Jerusalem the gospel came. Which when I once knew, I was very confident that every kingdom contained like wonders and causes of joy, though that was the fountain of them. As it was the first fruits, so was it the pledge of what I shall receive in other countries. Thus also when any curious cabinet, or secret in chemistry, geometry, or physic was offered to me, I diligently looked in it, but when I saw it to the bottom and not my happiness I despised it. These imaginations and this thirst of news occasioned these reflections.

26. ON NEWS

1

News from a foreign country came,
As if my treasure and my wealth lay there:
So much it did my heart enflame

THE THIRD CENTURY   [1]The land of the Jews, Judea.

'Twas wont to call my soul into mine ear!
  Which thither went to meet
    The approaching sweet:
And on the threshold stood,
To entertain the unknown good.
    It hover'd there,
  As if 'twould leave mine ear,
And was so eager to embrace
The joyful tidings as they came,
'Twould almost leave its dwelling place,
  To entertain the same.

      2

  As if the tidings were the things,
My very joys themselves, my foreign treasure,
  Or else did bear them on their wings;
With so much joy they came, with so much pleasure.
    My soul stood at the gate
      To recreate
    Itself with bliss, and to
    Be pleas'd with speed. A fuller view
      It fain would take
      Yet journeys back would make
Unto my heart: as if 'twould fain
Go out to meet, yet stay within
  To fit a place, to entertain,
    And bring the tidings in.

      3

  What sacred instinct did inspire
My soul in childhood with a hope so strong?
  What secret force mov'd my desire,
To expect my joys beyond the seas, so young?
    Felicity I knew
      Was out of view:
    And being here alone,
I saw that happiness was gone
      From me! For this
    I thirsted absent bliss,
And thought that sure beyond the seas,
Or else in something near at hand
I knew not yet: since nought did please
  I knew, my bliss did stand.

      4

  But little did the infant dream
That all the treasures of the world were by,

And that himself was so the cream
And crown of all, which round about did lie:
    Yet thus it was. The gem,
      The diadem,
    The ring enclosing all
That stood upon this earthly ball;
    The heavenly eye,
  Much wider than the sky,
Wherein they all included were
10 The glorious soul that was the king
Made to possess them, did appear
    A small and little thing!

THE FIFTH CENTURY

      4

Were it not for this infinity, God's bounty would of
necessity be limited. His goodness would want a receptacle
for its effusions. His gifts would be confined into narrow
room, and His Almighty Power for lack of a theater magnif-
20 icent enough, a storehouse large enough, be straitened. But
Almighty Power includes infinity in its own existence. For
because God is infinitely able to do all things, there must of
necessity be an infinite capacity to answer that power,
because nothing itself is an obedient subject to work upon;
and the eternal privation of infinite perfections is to Al-
mighty Power a Being capable of all. As sure as there is a
space infinite, there is a power, a bounty, a goodness, a wis-
dom infinite: a treasure, a blessedness, a glory.

      7

Eternity is a mysterious absence of times and ages: an
30 endless length of ages always present, and forever perfect.
For as there is an immovable space wherein all infinite spaces
are enclosed, and all motions carried on and performed, so
is there an immovable duration that contains and measures
all moving durations. Without which first the last could not
be, no more than finite places, and bodies moving without
infinite space. All ages being but successions correspondent
to those parts of the eternity wherein they abide, and filling
no more of it than ages can do. Whether they are com-
mensurate with it or no is difficult to determine. But the
infinite immovable duration is eternity, the place and dura-
40 tion of all things, even of infinite space itself: the cause and
end, the author and beautifier, the life and perfection of all.

PHILOSOPHY AND SPECULATION III

Francis Bacon[1] [1561-1626]

To recall Jonson's comment on Bacon as the triumphant politician (p. 99), William Rawley's as "the glory of his age and nation" (p. 669), Cowley's as the Moses who "from the mountain's top of his exalted wit" viewed the promised land of modern thought, and Pope's as "the wisest, brightest, meanest of mankind" is to be reminded of the accomplishments and ambiguities of this extraordinary man. Elsewhere in this book (pp. 669 ff.) the facts of his career are given (albeit with some charitable omissions) by one who knew him well; in the selections from his works that follow he himself reveals the vigor of his mind and style.

Although they were by-products of his winding search for fame and fortune, the *Essays* (pp. 661 ff.) were, as he himself observed, the "most current" of his works because "they come home to men's business and bosoms." Modeled on Montaigne, but with nothing of Montaigne's easy charm and candor, ten of them appeared in 1597, together with a set of Latin *meditationes sacrae* and some pungent observations on "The Colors of Good and Evil" (or "places of persuasion and dissuasion," as the title page described them). These trenchant little essays on such topics as study, followers and friends, faction, and negotiating are swift and lean in style, and packed with worldly wisdom. Shrewd and steely in their absence of emotion, they are prescriptions for success; and they reveal an author who, while slowly gaining recognition at the age of thirty-six, was determined to succeed. They themselves were so successful that there were new editions (some of them un-authorized) in 1598 and 1616, and two in 1612. In 1612 Bacon—who then could sign himself as "Knight" and "the King's Attorney-General"—expanded most of those already published and added twenty-nine new pieces. The third and last edition, which Bacon put together just a year before he died, runs to fifty-eight items, thirty-eight of them altered and enlarged from the 1612 edition and twenty of them new. The *Essays* quickly gained a fame that they have never lost. They were translated into Italian as early as 1617, into French two years later, into Latin in 1638, and they have been reprinted countless times in English. In bulk they constitute a little book; in wisdom, style, and intellectual poise they constitute a lasting triumph.

When James succeeded to the throne in 1603, Bacon, still inching up the winding stair to power, apparently set to work at once on a book expressly written for the king and designed to bring its author into notice. As a bid for royal favor *The Advancement of Learning* (pp. 399 ff., 667 ff., 878 ff.) was only moderately successful. Bacon, together with three hundred other aspiring politicians, had been already knighted (1603), and the appearance of his book in 1605, coinciding as it did with the discovery of the Gunpowder Plot, created no sensation. But books, like men, take time to work their way. As both a prolegomenon to his more mature productions and as a paradigm of his intellectual procedures, *The Advancement of Learning* is one of Bacon's most sug-gestive works, and it remains a landmark in the intellectual history of the age. In its stirring affirma-tion of the power and force of knowledge, its analysis of the impediments—traditional and acquired—to its accelerating progress, and its statement of the method of induction whereby that progress was to be secured, Bacon's book epitomizes his own ebullient hopes and the temper of the time.

Two years after its appearance Bacon was named solicitor general, and then, in quick succession, there followed a string of more important posts that in 1618 brought him to the woolsack and the

[1]For other works of Bacon, see Books and Men, pp. 661 ff. and History and Historiography, pp. 878 ff.

peerage. It was in 1620, at the height of his success and just a year before his fall, that the publication (in Latin) of *Novum organum* or *The New Organon* enabled him to clock his intellectual advance, to align the parts and fragments of his system, and to speculate about the outcome of his long endeavors. Although the 1620 publication consists mainly of *The New Organon,* the title page proclaims the splendid caption *Magna instauratio* or the great renewal (pp. 406 ff.), and in the prefatory material the author makes his large intentions clear. By kindling a "new light in the darkness of philosophy," he told King James, he hoped to "be the means of making this age famous to posterity," and in "The Plan of the Work" (*Distributio operis*), he showed how this would be effected. There would be six major parts of the massive undertaking: the first—presumably an expanded version of the *Advancement*—on "the divisions of the sciences"; the second, on his methodology, was *The New Organon*; the third, a treatise on "natural and experimental history for the foundation of philosophy"; the fourth, the "ladder of the intellect"; the fifth, "anticipations of the new philosophy"; the sixth—the crown and summit of the enterprise that would remain the work of future generations—would be "the new philosophy, or active science."

Not even a Bacon could hope to see this scheme perfected. Even though his "learned chaplain" Rawley said that his master had revised *The New Organon* twelve times in twelve successive years, it was published as a fragment. In 1623 *De augmentis scientiarum* provided a Latin version of the *Advancement,* expanded to nine books. But the other bits and pieces that survive—*De sapientia veterum* (1609, trans. 1619), *Historia densi et rari* (1622), *Sylva sylvarum* (1627), *De fluxu et refluxu maris* (1653), *Valerius Terminus of the Interpretation of Nature* (1734), and so on—can be only conjecturally positioned within the vast design. The utopian *New Atlantis,* a graceful by-product of the sage's later years, was written before 1617 and published as an uncompleted *jeu d'esprit* in 1627.

As the *Advancement* shows (pp. 878 ff.), Bacon had firm convictions on historiography, and since he held most modern histories to be "beneath mediocrity" it is not surprising that he should try to blaze the path of reformation. As he told James, he thought that a proper history of England "from the uniting of the Roses to the uniting of the kingdoms" would be a service to the nation, and it is probable that his various fragments on Henry VIII, Elizabeth, and James himself were drafts and studies for such an enterprise. All that he completed of what would have been a major undertaking, however, was his famous life of Henry VII (pp. 882 ff.). Supplied with data from Sir Robert Cotton's library, and working at uncommon speed (an anodyne, no doubt, to his disgrace the spring before), he began and finished it in the summer and the early fall of 1621; on 8 October he sent the manuscript to James for his approval; and the book itself, with a dedication to Prince Charles, appeared the following March. Scorning both the "dispersed report" and the "barren elogies" that most biographers were content to write, Bacon, as he warned Prince Charles, merely tried to tell the truth about King Henry and his parlous situation. "I have not flattered him, but took him to life as well as I could, sitting so far off and having no better light." His brilliant portrait of this "most sufficient" monarch is a gauge of his success.

Although my selections from the *Essays* represent the three main stages of their growth (1597, 1612, and 1625), I have based my text upon the 1625 edition (STC 1147), which contains the author's final changes and expansions. Excerpts from the *Advancement* are based upon the 1605 edition (STC 1164), those from *The Great Instauration* upon the translation in the Spedding, Ellis, and Heath edition of the *Works,* and from *The History of the Reign of King Henry the Seventh* on the 1622 edition (STC 1159).

Basil Montagu's ambitious edition of the collected works (16 vols., 1825–36) has long been superseded by that of James Spedding, R. L. Ellis, and D. D. Heath (7 vols., 1857–59), a monument of Victorian scholarship that Spedding supplemented with *The Letters and the Life* (7 vols., 1861–74) and that J. S. Robertson drew upon for his copious gathering of *The Philosophical Works* (1905). More recent volumes of selections from the principal works are those by R. F. Jones (1937), H. G.

Dick (1955), and Sidney Warhaft (1965). There are editions of the *Essays* by W. A. Wright (1862), E. A. Abbot (2 vols., 1876), S. H. Reynolds (1890), M. A. Scott (1908), and Geoffrey Grigson (1937); of the *Advancement* by W. A. Wright (1868) and F. G. Selby (2 vols., 1892–95); of *Novum organum* by Thomas Fowler (1889); and of the life of Henry VII by J. R. Lumby (1876) and F. J. Levy (1972). Edward Arber's *Harmony of the Essays* (1871) enables one to trace their changes and expansions, and J. Kemp Houck's bibliography (1968) to get some notion of the complex history of the canon.

All subsequent lives of Bacon have been built upon the affectionate memoir that his "learned chaplain" and secretary William Rawley published in 1657 (see pp. 669 ff.), but Spedding's great *Letters and the Life* (which he himself abridged in 1878) has been essential to such later biographers as R. W. Church (1884), E. A. Abbot (1885), John Nichol (2 vols., 1888–89), G. W. Steeves (1910), Mary Sturt (1932), Charles Williams (1933), A. W. Green (1948), J. G. Crowther (1960), J. Max Patrick (1961), F. H. Anderson (1962), Catherine Drinker Bowen (1963), and A. W. Green (1966). Macaulay's famous essay first appeared in the *Edinburgh Review* in 1837.

Of the small library of books about various aspects of Bacon's thought and influence mention might be made of those by Thomas Fowler (1881), C. D. Broad (1926), F. H. Anderson (1948), Benjamin Farrington (1949), Loren Eiseley (1962), and V. K. Whitaker (1962). Of special interest to students of literature are M. W. Croll, "Attic Prose: Lipsius, Montaigne, Bacon," *Schelling Anniversary Papers* (1932) and reprinted in "*Attic and Baroque Prose Style* (ed. J. Max Patrick *et al.*, 1969), Jacob Zeitlin, "The Development of Bacon's Essays," *JEGP*, XXVII (1928), M. W. Bundy, "Bacon's True Opinion of Poetry," *SP*, XXVII (1930), Karl R. Wallace, *Francis Bacon on Communication and Rhetoric* (1943) and *Francis Bacon on the Nature of Man* (1967), and Brian Vickers, *Francis Bacon and Renaissance Prose* (1968). For more general studies see the General Bibliography, Sections II and V.

from Of the Proficience and Advancement of Learning, Divine and Human (1605)

[THE FIRST BOOK]

[THE STATE OF MODERN KNOWLEDGE]

Since *The Advancement of Learning* was, among other things, a bid for royal favor, it was addressed directly to the king. Assuming a deferential posture at the start of his iconoclastic little book, Bacon tells his vain and rather foolish sovereign that not since Christ has there been such a paragon of intellect, of moral grandeur, and of erudition. Combining "the power and fortune of a king, the knowledge and illumination of a priest, and the learning and universality of a philosopher," James is a monarch of such uncommon merit that he requires a votive offering in the form of "some solid work, fixed memorial, and immortal monument," which Bacon, happily, is ready to supply.

. . . Therefore I did conclude with myself that I could not make unto Your Majesty a better oblation than of some treatise tending to that end, whereof the sum will consist

of these two parts: the former concerning the excellency of learning and knowledge, and the excellency of the merit and true glory in the augmentation and propagation thereof; the latter, what the particular acts and works are which have been embraced and undertaken for the advancement of learning, and again what defects and undervalues[1] I find in such particular acts; to the end that though I cannot positively or affirmatively advise Your Majesty or propound unto you framed particulars, yet I may excite your princely cogitations to visit the excellent treasure of your own mind, and thence to extract particulars for this purpose agreeable to your magnanimity and wisdom.

In the entrance to the former of these—to clear the way and, as it were, to make silence to have the true testimonies concerning the dignity of learning to be better heard without the interruption of tacit objections—I think good to deliver

THE ADVANCEMENT OF LEARNING [1]Deficiencies.

it from the discredits and disgraces which it hath received, all from ignorance, but ignorance severally disguised, appearing sometimes in the zeal and jealousy of divines, sometimes in the severity and arrogancy of politiques,[2] and sometimes in the errors and imperfections of learned men themselves.

I hear the former sort say that knowledge is of those things which are to be accepted of with great limitation and caution; that the aspiring to overmuch knowledge was the original temptation and sin, whereupon ensued the fall of man; that knowledge hath in it somewhat of the serpent, and therefore where it entereth into a man it makes him swell;—*Scientia inflat:*[3]—that Solomon gives a censure "that there is no end of making books, and that much reading is weariness of the flesh;"[4] and again in another place "that in spacious knowledge there is much contristation, and that he that increaseth knowledge increaseth anxiety;"[5] that St. Paul gives a caveat that we be not spoiled through vain philosophy;"[6] that experience demonstrates how learned men have been arch-heretics, how learned times have been inclined to atheism, and how the contemplation of second causes doth derogate from our dependence upon God, who is the first cause.

To discover, then, the ignorance and error of this opinion and the misunderstanding in the grounds thereof, it may well appear these men do not observe or consider that it was not the pure knowledge of nature and universality, a knowledge by the light whereof man did give names unto other creatures in paradise as they were brought before him, according unto their proprieties,[7] which gave the occasion to the fall, but it was the proud knowledge of good and evil, with an intent in man to give law unto himself and to depend no more upon God's commandments, which was the form of the temptation. Neither is it any quantity of knowledge how great soever that can make the mind of man to swell, for nothing can fill, much less extend, the soul of man but God and the contemplation of God; and therefore Solomon, speaking of the two principal senses of inquisition, the eye and the ear, affirmeth that the eye is never satisfied with seeing, nor the ear with hearing, and if there be no fulness, then is the continent[8] greater than the content; so of knowledge itself and the mind of man, whereto the senses are but reporters, he defineth likewise in these words, placed after that calendar or ephemerides which he maketh of the diversities of times and seasons for all actions and purposes, and concludeth thus: "God hath made all things beautiful, or decent in the true return of their seasons. Also He hath placed the world in man's heart, yet cannot man find out the work which God worketh from the beginning to end,"[9] declaring not obscurely that God hath framed the mind of man as a mirror or glass capable of[10] the image of the universal world, and joyful to receive the impression thereof as the eye joyeth to receive light; and not only delighted in beholding the variety of things and vicissitude of times, but raised[11] also to find out and discern the ordinances and decrees which throughout all those changes are infallibly observed. And although he doth insinuate that the supreme or summary law of nature,

which he calleth "the work which God worketh from the beginning to the end," is not possible to be found out by man, yet that doth not derogate from the capacity of the mind, but may be referred to the impediments, as of shortness of life, ill conjunction[12] of labors, ill tradition of knowledge over from hand to hand, and many other inconveniences whereunto the condition of man is subject. For that nothing parcel[13] of the world is denied to man's inquiry and invention he doth in another place rule over when he saith, "The spirit of man is as the lamp of God, wherewith he searcheth the inwardness of all secrets."[14] If, then, such be the capacity and receit[15] of the mind of man, it is manifest that there is no danger at all in the proportion or quantity of knowledge, how large soever, lest it should make it swell or outcompass itself; no, but it is merely the quality of knowledge, which be it in quantity more or less, if it be taken without the true corrective thereof, hath in it some nature of venom or malignity, and some effects of that venom, which is ventosity[16] or swelling. This corrective spice, the mixture whereof maketh knowledge so sovereign, is charity, which the apostle immediately addeth to the former clause, for so he saith, "knowledge bloweth up, but charity buildeth up;"[17] not unlike unto that which he delivereth in another place: "If I spake" (saith he) "with the tongues of men and angels, and had not charity, it were but as a tinkling cymbal;"[18] not but that it is an excellent thing to speak with the tongues of men and angels, but because if it be severed from charity, and not referred to the good of men and mankind, it hath rather a sounding and unworthy glory than a meriting and substantial virtue. And as for that censure of Solomon concerning the excess of writing and reading books and the anxiety of spirit which redoundeth from knowledge, and that admonition of St. Paul "that we be not seduced by vain philosophy," let those places be rightly understood and they do indeed excellently set forth the true bounds and limitations whereby human knowledge is confined and circumscribed, and yet without any such contracting or coarctation[19] but that it may comprehend all the universal nature of things. For these limitations are three. The first, "that we do not so place our felicity in knowledge as we forget our mortality." The second, "that we make application of our knowledge to give ourselves repose and contentment, and not distaste or repining." The third, "that we do not presume by the contemplation of nature to attain to the mysteries of God." For as touching the first of these, Solomon doth excellently expound himself in another place of the same book where he saith, "I saw well that knowledge recedeth as far from

---

[2]Politicians. [3]"Knowledge puffeth up" (1 Corinthians 8.1).
[4]Ecclesiastes 12.1. [5]Ecclesiastes 1.18 (*contristation:* sadness).
[6]Colossians 2.8. [7]Properties, characteristics.
[8]Container. [9]Ecclesiastes 3.11 (*Decent:* suitable, comely).
[10]Capable of receiving. [11]Incited, inspired. [12]Coordination.
[13]No part.
[14]Proverbs 20.27. This was to be the central text of Benjamin Whichcote (see p. 617) and the Cambridge Platonists.
[15]Power of receiving. [16]Windiness. [17]1 Corinthians 8.1.
[18]1 Corinthians 13.1. [19]Restraint.

ignorance as light doth from darkness, and that the wise man's eyes keep watch in his head, whereas the fool roundeth about in darkness: but withal I learned that the same mortality involveth them both."[20] And for the second, certain it is there is no vexation or anxiety of mind which resulteth from knowledge otherwise than merely by accident, for all knowledge and wonder (which is the seed of knowledge) is an impression of pleasure in itself; but when men fall to framing conclusions out of their knowledge, applying it to their particular,[21] and ministering to themselves thereby weak fears or vast desires, there groweth that carefulness[22] and trouble of mind which is spoken of, for then knowledge is no more *lumen siccum*, whereof Heraclitus[23] the profound said, *lumen siccum optima anima*,[24] but it becometh *lumen madidum* or *maceratum*,[25] being steeped and infused in the humors of the affections. And as for the third point, it deserveth to be a little stood[26] upon and not to be lightly passed over, for if any man shall think by view and inquiry into these sensible and material things to attain that light whereby he may reveal unto himself the nature or will of God, then indeed is he spoiled by vain philosophy, for the contemplation of God's creatures and works produceth (having regard to the works and creatures themselves) knowledge, but having regard to God, no perfect knowledge, but wonder, which is broken knowledge. And therefore it was most aptly said by one of Plato's school "that the sense of man carrieth a resemblance with the sun, which (as we see) openeth and revealeth all the terrestrial globe; but then again it obscureth and concealeth the stars and celestial globe; so doth the sense discover natural things, but it darkeneth and shutteth up divine."[27] And hence it is true that it hath proceeded that divers great learned men have been heretical whilst they have sought to fly up to the secrets of the deity by the waxen wings of the senses. And as for the conceit that too much knowledge should incline a man to atheism, and that the ignorance of second causes should make a more devout dependence upon God which is the first cause, first, it is good to ask the question which Job asked of his friends, "Will you lie for God, as one man will do for another, to gratify him?"[28] For certain it is that God worketh nothing in nature but by second causes; and if they would have it otherwise believed, it is mere imposture, as it were, in favor towards God, and nothing else but to offer to the author of truth the unclean sacrifice of a lie. But farther, it is an assured truth and a conclusion of experience that a little or superficial knowledge of philosophy may incline the mind of man to atheism, but a farther proceeding therein doth bring the mind back again to religion; for in the entrance of philosophy, when the second causes, which are next unto the senses, do offer themselves to the mind of man, if it dwell and stay there it may induce some oblivion of the highest cause, but when a man passeth on farther, and seeth the dependence of causes and the works of providence, then, according to the allegory of the poets, he will easily believe that the highest link of nature's chain must needs be tied to the foot of Jupiter's chair.[29] To conclude therefore, let no man, upon a weak conceit of sobriety or an ill-applied moderation, think or maintain that a man can search too far or be too well studied in the book of God's word or in the book of God's works, divinity or philosophy, but rather let men endeavor an endless progress or proficience[30] in both; only let men beware that they apply both to charity and not to swelling; to use, and not to ostentation; and again, that they do not unwisely mingle or confound these learnings together. . . .

> Having defended the advancement of learning from the "zeal and jealousy of divines," Bacon proceeds to exonerate it from the "discredits and disgraces" of shortsighted politicians. Whereas its detractors charge that the pursuit of knowledge makes men effeminate or intractable or irresolute, Bacon claims for it a social purpose: to convert the "churlish, thwart, and mutinous" into citizens who are "gentle, generous, maniable,[31] and pliant to government."

Now I proceed to those errors and vanities which have intervened amongst the studies themselves of the learned, which is that which is principal and proper to the present argument, wherein my purpose is not to make a justification of the errors but by a censure and separation of the errors to make a justification of that which is good and sound, and to deliver that from the aspersion of the other. For we see that it is the manner of men to scandalize and deprave[32] that which retaineth the state and virtue by taking advantage upon that which is corrupt and degenerate, as the heathens in the primitive church used to blemish and taint the Christians with the faults and corruptions of heretics. But nevertheless I have no meaning at this time to make any exact animadversion of the errors and impediments in matters of learning which are more secret and remote from vulgar opinion, but only to speak unto such as do fall under, or near unto, a popular observation.

There are therefore chiefly three vanities in studies whereby learning hath been most traduced. For those things we do esteem vain which are either false or frivolous, those which either have no truth or no use, and those persons we esteem vain which are either credulous or curious; and curiosity is either in matter or words, so that in reason as well as in experience there fall out to be these three distempers (as I may term them) of learning: the first, fantastical learning; the second, contentious learning; and the last, delicate learning: vain imaginations, vain altercations, and vain affectations, and with the last I will begin. Martin Luther, conducted (no doubt) by an higher providence but in discourse of reason finding what a province he had undertaken against the Bishop of Rome and the degenerate traditions of the church, and finding his own solitude[33] being no ways aided by the

[20]Ecclesiastes 2.13 (*roundeth*: strays). [21]Themselves.
[22]Anxiety. [23]Greek philosopher of the sixth and fifth cent. B.C.
[24]Bacon cites and translates this comment in his essay "Of Friendship": "Heraclitus sayeth well in one of his enigmas, 'Dry light is ever the best.' " [25]"Moist." [26]Pondered.
[27]Philo Judaeus, *De somnis*, I.83–84. [28]A paraphrase of Job 13.7, 9.
[29]In Homer's *Iliad* (VIII.19 ff.) Zeus (*Jupiter*) tells the gods on Olympus that they could not drag him from his throne with a golden chain. [30]Improvement. [31]Manageable. [32]Deprecate.
[33]His lonely and exposed posture of dissent.

opinions of his own time, was enforced to awake all antiquity and to call former times to his succors to make a party against the present time, so that the ancient authors, both in divinity and in humanity, which had long time slept in libraries, began generally to be read and revolved. This by consequence did draw on a necessity of a more exquisite[34] travail in the languages original wherein those authors did write, for the better understanding of those authors and the better advantage of pressing and applying their words. And thereof grew again a delight in their manner of style and phrase, and an admiration of that kind of writing, which was much furthered and precipitated by the enmity and opposition that the propounders of those (primitive but seeming new) opinions had against the Schoolmen, who were generally of the contrary part, and whose writings were altogether in a differing style and form, taking liberty to coin and frame new terms of art to express their own sense and to avoid circuit of speech without regard to the pureness, pleasantness, and (as I may call it) lawfulness of the phrase or word. And again, because the great labor then was with the people (of whom the Pharisees were wont to say, *Execrabilis ista turba, quae non novit legem*),[35] for the winning and persuading of them there grew of necessity in chief price and request eloquence and variety of discourse, as the fittest and forciblest access into the capacity of the vulgar sort. So that these four causes concurring—the admiration of ancient authors, the hate of the Schoolmen, the exact study of languages, and the efficacy of preaching—did bring in an affectionate study of eloquence and copy[36] of speech, which then began to flourish. This grew speedily to an excess, for men began to hunt more after words than matter, and more after the choiceness of the phrase, and the round and clean composition of the sentence, and the sweet falling of the clauses, and the varying and illustration of their works with tropes and figures than after the weight of matter, worth of subject, soundness of argument, life of invention,[37] or depth of judgment. Then grew the flowing and watery vein of Osorius, the Portugal bishop, to be in price. Then did Sturmius spend such infinite and curious pains upon Cicero the orator and Hermogenes the rhetorician, besides his own books of periods and imitation and the like. Then did Car of Cambridge and Ascham, with their lectures and writings, almost deify Cicero and Demosthenes, and allure all young men that were studious unto that delicate and polished kind of learning.[38] Then did Erasmus take occasion to make the scoffing echo, *Decem annos consumpsi in legendo Cicerone,* and the echo answered in Greek, *"Ονε,* Asine.[39] Then grew the learning of the Schoolmen to be utterly despised as barbarous. In sum, the whole inclination and bent of those times was rather towards copy than weight.

Here, therefore, is the first distemper of learning, when men study words and not matter, whereof though I have represented an example of late times, yet it hath been and will be *secundum majus et minus*[40] in all time. And how is it possible but this should have an operation to discredit learning, even with vulgar capacities, when they see learned men's works like the first letter of a patent or limned book,[41] which though it hath large flourishes, yet it is but a letter? It seems to me that Pygmalion's frenzy[42] is a good emblem or portraiture of this vanity, for words are but the images of matter, and except they have life of reason and invention, to fall in love with them is all one as to fall in love with a picture. . . .

The second, which followeth, is in nature worse than the former, for as substance of matter is better than beauty of words, so contrariwise vain matter is worse than vain words; wherein it seemeth the reprehension of St. Paul was not only proper for those times but prophetical for the times following, and not only respective to divinity but extensive[43] to all knowledge: *"Devita profanas vocum novitates, et oppositiones falsi nominis scientiae."*[44] For he assigneth two marks and badges of suspected and falsified science: the one, the novelty and strangeness of terms; the other, the strictness of positions,[45] which of necessity doth induce oppositions, and so questions and altercations. Surely, like as many substances in nature which are solid do putrefy and corrupt into worms, so it is the property of good and sound knowledge to putrefy and dissolve into a number of subtile, idle, unwholesome, and (as I may term them) vermiculate questions, which have indeed a kind of quickness[46] and life of spirit, but no soundness of matter or goodness of quality. This kind of degenerate learning did chiefly reign amongst the Schoolmen, who having sharp and strong wits and abundance of leisure and small variety of reading, but their wits being shut up in the cells of a few authors (chiefly Aristotle their dictator) as their persons were shut up in the cells of monasteries and colleges, and knowing little history, either of nature or time, did out of no great quantity of

[34]Painstaking.
[35]"This accursed mob, ignorant of the law" (see John 7.49).
[36]Abundance, fluency (Latin *copia*).
[37]In rhetoric, the selection of topics or arguments.
[38]*Then grew...learning*: Bacon is, of course, deprecating the ancient and modern humanists who, as he thought, were more concerned with "words" than "matter." Jeronymo Osorio (1506–1580), bishop of Silves, wrote on Portuguese history; Johann Sturm (1507–1589) was a German scholar who edited the works of Cicero; in the Renaissance Cicero himself was the most esteemed of Latin prose stylists; Hermogenes was an influential rhetorician of the second century A.D.; Nicholas Car (1524–1568) was a professor of Greek at Cambridge who published Latin versions of Eusebius and Demosthenes; Roger Ascham (1515–1568), tutor of Princess Elizabeth and Lady Jane Grey and Latin secretary to Queen Mary, was the author of the celebrated *Schoolmaster* (1570). Many of these same names are cited with a much more favorable intention by Henry Peacham in *The Complete Gentleman* (see p. 732).
[39]*Decem...asine*: the foolish boast "I have spent ten years in reading Cicero" returns the echo (of the last three letters) of the Greek word for "ass." [40]"More or less."
[41]A book of elaborate design, adorned with illuminated capitals and ornaments.
[42]In Greek mythology, the sculptor Pygmalion fell so ardently in love with his statue of Galatea that Aphrodite brought the work to life. [43]*Respective...extensive*: regarding...applicable.
[44]"Avoiding profane and vain babblings, and oppositions of science falsely so called" (1 Timothy 6.20).
[45]Rigidity of principles. [46]Vitality.

matter and infinite agitation of wit spin out unto us those laborious webs of learning which are extant in their books. For the wit and mind of man, if it work upon matter, which is the contemplation of the creatures of God, worketh according to the stuff, and is limited thereby, but if it work upon itself, as the spider worketh his web, then it is endless, and brings forth indeed copwebs[47] of learning, admirable for the fineness of thread and work but of no substance or profit.

This same unprofitable subtility or curiosity is of two sorts: either in the subject itself that they handle, when it is a fruitless speculation or controversy (whereof there are no small number both in divinity and philosophy), or in the manner or method of handling of a knowledge, which amongst them was this: upon every particular position or assertion to frame objections, and to those objections, solutions; which solutions were for the most part not confutations but distinctions; whereas indeed the strength of all sciences is, as the strength of the old man's faggot, in the bond.[48] For the harmony of a science, supporting each part the other, is and ought to be the true and brief confutation and suppression of all the smaller sort of objections, but on the other side, if you take out every axiom, as the sticks of the faggot, one by one, you may quarrel with them and bend them and break them at your pleasure; so that as was said of Seneca, *Verborum minutiis rerum frangit pondera*,[49] so a man may truly say of the Schoolmen, *Quaestionum minutiis scientiarum frangunt soliditatem*.[50] For were it not better for a man in a fair room to set up one great light or branching candlestick of lights than to go about with a small watch candle[51] into every corner? And such is their method, that rests not so much upon evidence of truth proved by arguments, authorities, similitudes, examples, as upon particular confutations and solutions of every scruple, cavillation,[52] and objection, breeding for the most part one question as fast it solveth another, even as in the former resemblance, when you carry the light into one corner you darken the rest; so that the fable and fiction of Scylla[53] seemeth to be a lively image of this kind of philosophy or knowledge, which was transformed into a comely virgin for the upper parts, but then *Candida succinctan latrantibus inguina monstris;*[54] so the generalities of the Schoolmen are for a while good and proportionable,[55] but then when you descend into their distinctions and decisions, instead of a fruitful womb for the use and benefit of man's life, they end in monstrous altercations and barking questions. So as it is not possible but this quality of knowledge must fall under popular contempt, the people being apt to contemn truth upon occasion of controversies and altercations, and to think they are all out of their way which never meet, and when they see such digladiation[56] about subtilties and matter of no use nor moment, they easily fall upon that judgment of Dionysius of Syracusa, *Verba ista sunt senum otiosorum*.[57]

Notwithstanding, certain it is that if those Schoolmen to their great thirst of truth and unwearied travail of wit had joined variety and universality of reading and contemplation, they had proved excellent lights to the great advancement of all learning and knowledge. But as they are, they are great undertakers[58] indeed, and fierce with dark keeping;[59] but as in the inquiry of the divine truth their pride inclined to leave the oracle of God's word and to vanish in the mixture of their own inventions, so in the inquisition of nature they ever left the oracle of God's works and adored the deceiving and deformed images which the unequal[60] mirror of their own minds or a few received authors or principles did represent unto them. And thus much for the second disease of learning.

For the third vice or disease of learning, which concerneth deceit or untruth, it is of all the rest the foulest as that which doth destroy the essential form of knowledge, which is nothing but a representation of truth, for the truth of being and the truth of knowing are one, differing no more than the direct beam and the beam reflected. This vice therefore brancheth itself into two sorts: delight in deceiving and aptness to be deceived, imposture and credulity; which, although they appear to be of a diverse nature, the one seeming to proceed of cunning and the other of simplicity, yet certainly they do for the most part concur, for as the verse noteth,

Percontatorem fugito, nam garrulus idem est,[61]

an inquisitive man is a prattler; so upon the like reason a credulous man is a deceiver, as we see it in fame,[62] that he that will easily believe rumors will as easily augment rumors and add somewhat to them of his own, which Tacitus wisely noteth when he saith, *Fingunt simul creduntque*,[63] so great an affinity hath fiction and belief.

This facility of credit and accepting or admitting things weakly authorized or warranted is of two kinds, according to the subject: for it is either a belief of history (as the lawyers speak, matter of fact) or else of matter of art and opinion. As to the former, we see the experience and inconvenience of this error in ecclesiastical history, which hath too easily received and registered reports and narrations of miracles wrought by martyrs, hermits, or monks of the desert and other holy men, and their[64] relics, shrines, chapels, and

[47]Cobwebs.
[48]According to one of the fables attributed to Aesop, a single stick is easily broken, but when tied with other sticks into a bundle (*faggot*) it acquires new strength.
[49]"He breaks up the weighty matter with quibbles." Bacon uses the same phrase in his essay "Of Seeming Wise."
[50]"They break up solid sciences with petty questions."
[51]Night light. [52]Quibbling.
[53]In Greek mythology, a monster who dwelt in a cave on the Italian coast opposite the whirlpool Charybdis.
[54]"Her white waist encircled with howling monsters" (Vergil, *Eclogues*, VI.75). [55]Sufficient.
[56]Sword play, i.e., contention.
[57]"Those are the words of idle old men." [58]Innovators.
[59]Close restraint. [60]Uneven, distorting.
[61]"Avoid a questioner, for he is a babbler" (Horace, *Epistles*, I.xviii.69). [62]Rumor.
[63]"They believe whatever they invent" (adapted from Tacitus, *Histories*, I.51). [64]Text *there*.

images, which though they had a passage[65] for a time by the ignorance of the people, the superstitious simplicity of some, and the politic toleration of others, holding them but as divine poesies, yet after a period of time, when the mist began to clear up, they grew to be esteemed but as old wives' fables, impostures of the clergy, illusions of spirits, and badges of antichrist, to the great scandal and detriment of religion. . . .

[Similarly, natural history has been "fraught" with so much "fabulous matter, a great part not only untried but notoriously untrue," that it disgusts "the grave and sober kind of wits." However worthy their intentions, says Bacon, such pseudosciences as astrology, natural magic, and alchemy are so full of "error and vanity" that their professors have resorted to fraud and obfuscation "to save the credit of impostures."]

Thus have I gone over these three diseases of learning, besides the which there are some other rather peccant[66] humors than formed diseases, which nevertheless are not so secret and intrinsic[67] but that they fall under a popular observation and traducement,[68] and therefore are not to be passed over.

The first of these is the extreme affecting of two extremities, the one antiquity, the other novelty, wherein it seemeth the children of time do take after the nature and malice of the father. For as he devoureth his children,[69] so one of them seeketh to devour and suppress the other, while antiquity envieth there should be new additions, and novelty cannot be content to add but it must deface. Surely the advice of the prophet is the true direction in this matter, "*State super vias antiquas, et videte quaenam sit via recta et bona, et ambulate in ea.*"[70] Antiquity deserveth that reverence, that men should make a stand thereupon and discover what is the best way, but when the discovery is well taken, then to make progression. And to speak truly, *Antiquitas saeculi juventus mundi.*[71] These times are the ancient times, when the world is ancient, and not those which we account ancient *ordine retrogrado,* by a computation backward from ourselves.

Another error induced by the former is a distrust that anything should be now to be found out which the world should have missed and passed over so long time, as if the same objection were to be made to time that Lucian maketh to Jupiter and other the heathen gods, of which he wondereth that they begot so many children in old time and begot none in his time, and asketh whether they were become septuagenary, or whether the law *Pappia,* made against old men's marriages, had restrained them.[72] So it seemeth men doubt lest time is become past children and generation, wherein contrariwise we see commonly the levity and unconstancy of men's judgments, which, till a matter be done, wonder that it can be done, and as soon as it is done, wonder again that it was no sooner done; as we see in the expedition of Alexander into Asia, which at first was prejudged as a vast and impossible enterprise, and yet afterwards it pleaseth Livy to make no more of it than this, "*Nil aliud quam bene ausus vana contemnere.*"[73] And the same happened to Columbus in the western navigation. But in intellectual matters it is much more common, as may be seen in most of the propositions of Euclid, which till they be demonstrate,[74] they seem strange to our assent,[75] but being demonstrate, our mind accepteth of them by a kind of relation[76] (as the lawyers speak) as if we had known them before.

Another error, that hath also some affinity with the former, is a conceit that of former opinions or sects, after variety and examination,[77] the best hath still prevailed and suppressed the rest, so as if a man should begin the labor of a new search, he were but like to light upon somewhat formerly rejected and by rejection brought into oblivion, as if the multitude or the wisest for the multitude's sake were not ready to give passage rather to that which is popular and superficial than to that which is substantial and profound; for the truth is that time seemeth to be of the nature of a river or stream, which carrieth down to us that which is light and blown up, and sinketh and drowneth that which is weighty and solid.

Another error, of a diverse nature from all the former, is the overearly and peremptory reduction of knowledge into arts and methods from which time commonly sciences receive small or no augmentation. But as young men, when they knit and shape perfectly[78] do seldom grow to a further stature, so knowledge, while it is in aphorisms and observations, it is in growth, but when it once is comprehended in exact methods,[79] it may perchance be further polished and illustrate,[80] and accommodated for use and practice, but it increaseth no more in bulk and substance.

Another error, which doth succeed that which we last mentioned, is that after the distribution of particular arts and sciences men have abandoned universality, or *philosophia prima,* which cannot but cease and stop all progression. For no perfect discovery can be made upon a flat or a level; neither is it possible to discover the more remote and deeper parts of any science if you stand but upon the level of the same science and ascend not to a higher science.

Another error hath proceeded from too great a reverence and a kind of adoration of the mind and understanding of man, by means whereof men have withdrawn themselves

[65]Acceptance. [66]Morbid, unhealthy. [67]Hidden.
[68]Misrepresentation.
[69]In Greek mythology, Time (Chronos) devoured his children as soon as they were born.
[70]"Stand in the old ways, and see, and ask for the old paths, where is the good way, and walk in it" (Jeremiah 6.16).
[71]"Antiquity was the youth of the world."
[72]*Lucian . . . restrained them:* According to Lactantius, *Divine Institutes,* I.16 (*De falsa religione*), it was Seneca, not Lucian, who raised the question. *Septuagenary:* seventy years old (and therefore too old to beget children). *Law Pappia:* a Roman law that granted certain privileges for those who married young.
[73]"It was nothing but the audacity to ignore groundless fears" (Livy, IX.17). [74]Demonstrated.
[75]*Strange . . . assent:* they seem too novel for us to assent to them.
[76]In law, an action made effective from a date earlier than the time of its occurrence.
[77]After various possibilities have been canvassed.
[78]*When . . . perfectly:* when physically mature. [79]Systems.
[80]Illustrated.

too much from the contemplation of nature and the observations of experience, and have tumbled up and down in their own reason and conceits. Upon these intellectualists, which are notwithstanding commonly taken for the most sublime and divine philosophers, Heraclitus gave a just censure, saying, "Men sought truth in their own little worlds, and not in the great and common world," for they disdain to spell and so by degrees to read in the volume of God's works; and contrariwise by continual meditation and agitation of wit do urge and as it were invocate[81] their own spirits to divine and give oracles unto them, whereby they are deservedly deluded.

Another error that hath some connexion with this latter is that men have used[82] to infect their meditations, opinions, and doctrines with some conceits which they have most admired, or some sciences which they have most applied,[83] and given all things else a tincture according to them utterly untrue and unproper. So hath Plato intermingled his philosophy with theology, and Aristotle with logic, and the second school of Plato,[84] Proclus and the rest with the mathematics. For these were the arts which had a kind of primogeniture with them severally. So have the alchemists made a philosophy out of a few experiments of the furnace, and Gilbertus,[85] our countryman, hath made a philosophy out of the observations of a stone. So Cicero, when, reciting the several opinions of the nature of the soul, he found a musician that held the soul was but a harmony, sayeth pleasantly, *"Hic ab arte sua non recessit, etc."*[86] But of these conceits Aristotle speaketh seriously and wisely when he sayeth, *"Qui respiciunt ad pauca de facili pronunciant."*[87]

Another error is an impatience of doubt and haste to assertion without due and mature suspension of judgment. For the two ways of contemplation are not unlike the two ways of action commonly spoken of by the ancients: the one plain and smooth in the beginning, and in the end impassable; the other rough and troublesome in the entrance, but after a while fair and even. So it is in contemplation: if a man will begin with certainties, he shall end in doubts, but if he will be content to begin with doubts, he shall end in certainties.

Another error is in the manner of the tradition[88] and delivery of knowledge, which is for the most part magistral and peremptory and not ingenuous and faithful, in a sort as may be soonest believed and not easiliest examined. It is true that in compendious treatises for practice that form is not to be disallowed. But in the true handling of knowledge men ought not to fall either on the one side into the vein of Velleius the Epicurean (*Nil tam metuens, quam ne dubitare aliqua de re videretur*)[89] nor on the other side into Socrates his ironical doubting of all things, but to propound things sincerely, with more or less asseveration, as they stand in a man's own judgment proved more or less.

Other errors there are in the scope[90] that men propound to themselves, whereunto they bend their endeavors, for whereas the more constant and devote kind of professors of any science ought to propound to themselves to make some additions to their science, they convert their labors to aspire to certain second prizes, as to be a profound interpreter or commenter, to be a sharp champion or defender, to be a methodical compounder or abridger; and so the patrimony of knowledge cometh to be sometimes improved but seldom augmented.

But the greatest error of all the rest is the mistaking or misplacing of the last or furthest end of knowledge. For men have entered into a desire of learning and knowledge, sometimes upon a natural curiosity and inquisitive appetite; sometimes to entertain their minds with variety and delight; sometimes for ornament and reputation; and sometimes to enable them to victory of wit and contradiction; and most times for lucre and profession;[91] and seldom sincerely to give a true account of their gift of reason to the benefit and use of men; as if there were sought in knowledge a couch whereupon to rest a searching and restless spirit, or a terrace for a wandering and variable mind to walk up and down with a fair prospect or a tower of state, for a proud mind to raise itself upon, or a fort or commanding ground, for strife and contention, or a shop for profit or sale, and not a rich storehouse for the glory of the creator and the relief of man's estate.[92] But this is that which will indeed dignify and exalt knowledge: if contemplation and action may be more nearly and straitly conjoined and united together than they have been, a conjunction like unto that of the two highest planets, Saturn, the planet of rest and contemplation, and Jupiter, the planet of civil society and action. Howbeit, I do not mean, when I speak of use and action, that end before mentioned of the applying of knowledge to lucre and profession; for I am not ignorant how much that diverteth and interrupteth the prosecution and advancement of knowledge, like unto the golden ball thrown before Atalanta, which while she goeth aside and stoopeth to take up, the race is hindered,

Declinat cursus, aurumque volubile tollit.[93]

Neither is my meaning, as was spoken of Socrates, to call philosophy down from heaven to converse upon the earth; that is, to leave natural philosophy aside, and to apply knowledge only to manners and policy.[94] But as both heaven

[81]Invoke. [82]Been accustomed. [83]Cultivated.
[84]*Second...Plato*: the Neoplatonists.
[85]William Gilbert (1540–1603), English physician whose experiments in magnetism and electricity led to the publication of his epoch-making *De magnete* (1600).
[86]"He has not gone beyond the limits of his art" (*Tusculan Disputations*, I.x.20). Cicero has *artificio*, not *arte*.
[87]"It is easy for those who consider only a few things to make sweeping generalizations." [88]Transmission, handing on.
[89]"Fearing nothing so much as to seem uncertain about anything."
[90]Goal. [91]Livelihood. [92]State, condition.
[93]"She leaves the course to pick up the golden ball" (Ovid, *Metamorphoses*, X.667). When racing her unwelcome suitor Hippomenes (who would win her if he won the race), the fleet Atalanta, unable to resist three golden apples that he dropped along the course, stooped to get the baubles and therefore lost the victory that she would otherwise have gained.
[94]Morals and politics.

and earth do conspire and contribute to the use and benefit of man, so the end ought to be from both philosophies to separate and reject vain speculations and whatsoever is empty and void, and to preserve and augment whatsoever is solid and fruitful, that knowledge may not be as a courtesan, for pleasure and vanity only, or as a bond-woman, to acquire and gain to her master's use, but as a spouse, for generation, fruit, and comfort.

Thus have I described and opened, as by a kind of dissection, those peccant humors (the principal of them) which have not only given impediment to the proficience of learning, but have given also occasion to the traducement thereof, wherein if I have been too plain, it must be remembered, *Fidelia vulnera amantis, sed dolosa oscula malignantis.*[95] This I

think I have gained, that I ought to be the better believed in that which I shall say pertaining to commendation because I have proceeded so freely in that which concerneth censure. And yet I have no purpose to enter into a laudative[96] of learning, or to make a hymn to the Muses (though I am of opinion that it is long since their rites were duly celebrated), but my intent is, without varnish or amplification, justly to weigh the dignity of knowledge in the balance with other things, and to take the true value thereof by testimonies and arguments divine and human. . . .

[95]"Faithful are the wounds of a friend, but the kisses of an enemy are deceitful" (Proverbs 27.6).   [96]Encomium.

from The Great Instauration (1620)

PROEMIUM

Francis of Verulam reasoned thus with himself and judged it to be the interest of the present and future generations that they should be made acquainted with his thoughts.

Being convinced that the human intellect makes its own difficulties, not using the true helps which are at man's disposal soberly and judiciously, whence follows manifest ignorance of things, and by reason of that ignorance mischiefs innumerable, he thought all trial should be made whether that commerce between the mind of man and the nature of things, which is more precious than anything on earth, or at least than anything that is of the earth, might by any means be restored to its perfect and original condition, or if that may not be, yet reduced to a better condition than that in which it now is. Now that the errors which have hitherto prevailed, and which will prevail forever, should (if the mind be left to go its own way) either by the natural force of the understanding or by help of the aids and instruments of logic one by one correct themselves was a thing not to be hoped for, because the primary notions of things which the mind readily and passively imbibes, stores up, and accumulates (and it is from them that all the rest flow) are false, confused, and overhastily abstracted from the facts; nor are the secondary and subsequent notions less arbitrary and inconstant; whence it follows that the entire fabric of human reason which we employ in the inquisition of nature is badly put together and built up, and like some magnificent structure without any foundation. For while men are occupied in admiring and applauding the false powers of the mind, they pass by and throw away those true powers which, if it be supplied with the proper aids and can itself be content to wait upon nature instead of vainly affecting to overrule her, are within its reach. There

was but one course left, therefore—to try the whole thing anew upon a better plan, and to commence a total reconstruction of sciences, arts, and all human knowledge, raised upon the proper foundations. And this, though in the project and undertaking it may seem a thing infinite and beyond the powers of man, yet when it comes to be dealt with it will be found sound and sober, more so than what has been done hitherto. For of this there is some issue, whereas in what is now done in the matter of science there is only a whirling round about and perpetual agitation, ending where it began. And although he was well aware how solitary an enterprise it is, and how hard a thing to win faith and credit for, nevertheless he was resolved not to abandon either it or himself, nor to be deterred from trying and entering upon that one path which is alone open to the human mind. For better it is to make a beginning of that which may lead to something than to engage in a perpetual struggle and pursuit in courses which have no exit. And certainly the two ways of contemplation are much like those two ways of action, so much celebrated, in this: that the one, arduous and difficult in the beginning, leads out at last into the open country; while the other, seeming at first sight easy and free from obstruction, leads to pathless and precipitous places.

Moreover, because he knew not how long it might be before these things would occur to any one else, judging especially from this, that he has found no man hitherto who has applied his mind to the like, he resolved to publish at once so much as he has been able to complete. The cause of which haste was not ambition for himself but solicitude for the work; that in case of his death there might remain some outline and project of that which he had conceived, and some evidence likewise of his honest mind and inclination towards the benefit of the human race. Certain it is that all other ambition whatsoever seemed poor in his eyes compared with the work which he had in hand, seeing that the matter at issue is either nothing or a thing so great that it may well be content with its own merit, without seeking other recompense.

EPISTLE DEDICATORY
To Our Most Gracious and Mighty Prince and Lord James,
by the Grace of God of Great Britain, France, and Ireland
King, Defender of the Faith, Etc.

Most Gracious and Mighty King,
Your Majesty may perhaps accuse me of larceny, having stolen from your affairs so much time as was required for this work. I know not what to say for myself. For of time there can be no restitution unless it be that what has been abstracted from your business may perhaps go to the memory of your name and the honor of your age, if these things are indeed worth anything. Certainly they are quite new, totally new in their very kind; and yet they are copied from a very ancient model, even the world itself and the nature of things and of the mind. And to say truth, I am wont for my own part to regard this work as a child of time rather than of wit, the only wonder being that the first notion of the thing and such great suspicions concerning matters long established should have come into any man's mind. All the rest follows readily enough. And no doubt there is something of ac-cident (as we call it) and luck as well in what men think as in what they do or say. But for this accident which I speak of, I wish that if there be any good in what I have to offer it may be ascribed to the infinite mercy and goodness of God, and to the felicity of Your Majesty's times, to which as I have been an honest and affectionate servant in my life, so after my death I may yet perhaps, through the kindling of this new light in the darkness of philosophy, be the means of making this age famous to posterity; and surely to the times of the wisest and most learned of kings belongs of right the regeneration and restoration of the sciences. Lastly, I have a request to make, a request no way unworthy of Your Majesty and which especially concerns the work in hand; namely, that you who resemble Solomon in so many things—in the gravity of your judgments, in the peace-fulness of your reign, in the largeness of your heart, in the noble variety of the books which you have composed—would further follow his example in taking order[1] for the collecting and perfecting of a natural and experimental history true and severe (unincumbered with literature and book-learning), such as philosophy may be built upon, such, in fact, as I shall in its proper place describe, that so at length, after the lapse of so many ages, philosophy and the sciences may no longer float in air, but rest on the solid foundation of experience of every kind, and the same well examined and weighed. I have provided the machine, but the stuff must be gathered from the facts of nature. May God Al-mighty long preserve Your Majesty!

Your Majesty's most bounden and devoted servant,
Francis Verulam,
Chancellor

[Following this dedication to the king, Bacon, in a sub-stantial "Preface," tries to explain his purposes in undertak-ing a reconstruction of human knowledge. Something of the scope of his vast design may be inferred from the bare list of books that he intends to write.]

THE PLAN OF THE WORK
The work is in six parts:
1. The Divisions of the Sciences
2. The New Organon, or Directions Concerning the Interpretation of Nature
3. The Phenomena of the Universe, or a Natural and Experimental History for the Foundation of Philosophy
4. The Ladder of the Intellect
5. The Forerunners, or Anticipations of the New Philosophy
6. The New Philosophy, or Active Science

[Having commented as "plainly and perspicuously" as pos-sible on each of these six "parts," Bacon is finally ready to present (if only in a tentative and aphoristic form) a portion of the work itself. Although Part I ("The Divisions of the Sciences") "is wanting," he explains that "some account of them will be found in the second book of *The Proficience and Advancement of Learning, Divine and Human.*" However, he is ready with Part II.]

THE SECOND PART OF THE WORK, WHICH IS CALLED THE NEW ORGANON, OR TRUE DIRECTIONS CONCERNING THE INTERPRETATION OF NATURE

PREFACE

Those who have taken upon them to lay down the law of nature as a thing already searched out and understood, whether they have spoken in simple assurance or profes-sional affectation, have therein done philosophy and the sciences great injury. For as they have been successful in inducing belief, so they have been effective in quenching and stopping inquiry, and have done more harm by spoiling and putting an end to other men's efforts than good by their own. Those on the other hand who have taken a contrary course, and asserted that absolutely nothing can be known—whether it were from hatred of the ancient Sophists,[2] or from uncertainty and fluctuation of mind, or even from a kind of fullness of learning, that they fell upon this opinion—have certainly advanced reasons for it that are not to be despised; but yet they have neither started from true principles nor rested in the just conclusion, zeal and affectation having carried them much too far. The more ancient of the Greeks (whose writings are lost)[3] took up with better judgment a

THE GREAT INSTAURATION [1]Making arrangements.
[2]In ancient Greece, teachers of rhetoric, philosophy, and conduct who were noted (and criticized by Plato) for their vaunted ability to argue fluently and speciously on any side of any question.
[3]Bacon probably has in mind such early thinkers as Pythagoras

position between these two extremes—between the presumption of pronouncing on everything and the despair of comprehending anything; and though frequently and bitterly complaining of the difficulty of inquiry and the obscurity of things, and like impatient horses champing the bit, they did not the less follow up their object and engage with nature, thinking (it seems) that this very question, viz., whether or no anything can be known, was to be settled not by arguing, but by trying. And yet they too, trusting entirely to the force of their understanding, applied no rule, but made every-10 thing turn upon hard thinking and perpetual working and exercise of the mind.

Now my method, though hard to practise, is easy to explain, and it is this. I propose to establish progressive stages of certainty. The evidence of the sense, helped and guarded by a certain process of correction, I retain. But the mental operation which follows the act of sense I for the most part reject; and instead of it I open and lay out a new and certain path for the mind to proceed in, starting directly from the simple sensuous perception. The necessity of this was felt 20 no doubt by those who attributed so much importance to logic, showing thereby that they were in search of helps for the understanding, and had no confidence in the native and spontaneous process of the mind. But this remedy comes too late to do any good, when the mind is already, through the daily intercourse and conversation of life, occupied with unsound doctrines and beset on all sides by vain imaginations. And therefore that art of logic coming (as I said) too late to the rescue, and no way able to set matters right again, has had the effect of fixing errors rather than disclosing truth. There 30 remains but one course for the recovery of a sound and healthy condition, namely, that the entire work of the understanding be commenced afresh, and the mind itself be from the very outset not left to take its own course, but guided at every step, and the business be done as if by machinery. Certainly if in things mechanical men had set to work with their naked hands, without help or force of instruments, just as in things intellectual they have set to work with little else than the naked forces of the understanding, very small would the matters have been which, even with their best 40 efforts applied in conjunction, they could have attempted or accomplished. Now (to pause awhile upon this example and look in it as in a glass) let us suppose that some vast obelisk were (for the decoration of a triumph[4] or some such magnificence) to be removed from its place, and that men should set to work upon it with their naked hands, would not any sober spectator think them mad? And if they should then send for more people, thinking that in that way they might manage it, would he not think them all the madder? And if they then proceed to make a selection, putting away the 50 weaker hands and using only the strong and vigorous, would he not think them madder than ever? And if lastly, not content with this, they resolved to call in aid the art of athletics, and required all their men to come with hands, arms, and sinews well anointed and medicated according to the rules of art, would he not cry out that they were only taking pains to show a kind of method and discretion in their madness?

Yet just so it is that men proceed in matters intellectual—with just the same kind of mad effort and useless combination of forces—when they hope great things either from the number and cooperation or from the excellency and acuteness of individual wits; yea, and when they endeavor by logic (which may be considered as a kind of athletic art) to strengthen the sinews of the understanding, and yet with all this study and endeavor it is apparent to any true judgment that they are but applying the naked intellect all the time; whereas in every great work to be done by the hand of man it is manifestly impossible, without instruments and machinery, either for the strength of each to be exerted or the strength of all to be united.

Upon these premises two things occur to me of which, that they may not be overlooked, I would have men reminded. First, it falls out fortunately, as I think, for the allaying of contradictions and heart-burnings that the honor and reverence due to the ancients remains untouched and undiminished, while I may carry out my designs and at the same time reap the fruit of my modesty. For if I should profess that I, going the same road as the ancients, have something better to produce, there must needs have been some comparison or rivalry between us (not to be avoided by any art of words) in respect of excellency or ability of wit; and though in this there would be nothing unlawful or new (for if there be anything misapprehended by them, or falsely laid down, why may not I, using a liberty common to all, take exception to it?) yet the contest, however just and allowable, would have been an unequal one, perhaps, in respect of the measure of my own powers. As it is, however, (my object being to open a new way for the understanding, a way by them untried and unknown) the case is altered; party zeal and emulation are at an end, and I appear merely as a guide to point out the road, an office of small authority, and depending more upon a kind of luck than upon any ability or excellency. And thus much relates to the persons only. The other point of which I would have men reminded relates to the matter itself.

Be it remembered then that I am far from wishing to interfere with the philosophy which now flourishes, or with any other philosophy more correct and complete than this which has been or may hereafter be propounded. For I do not object to the use of this received philosophy, or others like it, for supplying matter for disputations or ornaments for discourse, for the professor's lecture and for the business of life. Nay more, I declare openly that for these uses the philosophy which I bring forward will not be much available. It does not lie in the way. It cannot be caught up in passage. It does not flatter the understanding by conformity with preconceived notions. Nor will it come down to the apprehension of the vulgar except by its utility and effects.

Let there be, therefore, (and may it be for the benefit of both) two streams and two dispensations of knowledge, and in like manner two tribes or kindreds of students in philos-

----

and Heraclitus (whose work, if it survives at all, survives only in fragments).   [4]Pageant.

ophy, tribes not hostile or alien to each other, but bound together by mutual services; let there in short be one method for the cultivation, another for the invention, of knowledge.

And for those who prefer the former, either from hurry or from considerations of business or for want of mental power to take in and embrace the other (which must needs be most men's case), I wish that they may succeed to their desire in what they are about, and obtain what they are pursuing. But if any man there be who, not content to rest in and use the knowledge which has already been discovered, aspires to penetrate further; to overcome not an adversary in argument, but nature in action; to seek not pretty and probable conjectures, but certain and demonstrable knowledge—I invite all such to join themselves, as true sons of knowledge, with me, that passing by the outer courts of nature, which numbers have trodden, we may find a way at length into her inner chambers. And to make my meaning clearer and to familiarize the thing by giving it a name, I have chosen to call one of these methods or ways *Anticipation of the Mind,* the other *Interpretation of Nature.*

Moreover I have one request to make. I have on my own part made it my care and study that the things which I shall propound should not only be true, but should also be presented to men's minds, how strangely soever preoccupied and obstructed, in a manner not harsh or unpleasant. It is but reasonable however (especially in so great a restoration of learning and knowledge) that I should claim of men one favor in return, which is this: if any one would form an opinion or judgment either out of his own observation, or out of the crowd of authorities, or out of the forms of demonstration (which have now acquired a sanction like that of judicial laws) concerning these speculations of mine, let him not hope that he can do it in passage or by the by, but let him examine the thing thoroughly; let him make some little trial for himself of the way which I describe and lay out; let him familiarize his thoughts with that subtlety of nature to which experience bears witness; let him correct by seasonable patience and due delay the depraved and deep-rooted habits of his mind; and when all this is done and he has begun to be his own master, let him (if he will) use his own judgment.

[BOOK I]

APHORISMS CONCERNING THE INTERPRETATION OF NATURE AND THE KINGDOM OF MAN

38[5]

The idols and false notions which are now in possession of the human understanding, and have taken deep root therein, not only so beset men's minds that truth can hardly find entrance, but even after entrance obtained, they will again in the very instauration of the sciences meet and trouble us unless men, being forewarned of the danger, fortify themselves as far as may be against their assaults.

39

There are four classes of idols which beset men's minds. To these for distinction's sake I have assigned names, calling the first class *Idols of the Tribe,* the second *Idols of the Cave,* the third *Idols of the Market Place,* the fourth *Idols of the Theater.*

40

The formation of ideas and axioms by true induction is no doubt the proper remedy to be applied for the keeping off and clearing away of idols. To point them out, however, is of great use, for the doctrine of idols is to the interpretation of nature what the doctrine of the refutation of sophisms is to common logic.

41

The Idols of the Tribe have their foundation in human nature itself and in the tribe or race of men. For it is a false assertion that the sense of man is the measure of things.[6] On the contrary, all perceptions as well of the sense as of the mind are according to the measure of the individual and not according to the measure of the universe. And the human understanding is like a false mirror, which, receiving rays irregularly, distorts and discolors the nature of things by mingling its own nature with it.

42

The Idols of the Cave are the idols of the individual man. For every one (besides the errors common to human nature in general) has a cave or den of his own, which refracts and discolors the light of nature, owing either to his own proper and peculiar nature, or to his education and conversation with others, or to the reading of books and the authority of those whom he esteems and admires, or to the differences of impressions accordingly as they take place in a mind preoccupied and predisposed or in a mind indifferent and settled, or the like. So that the spirit of man (according as it is meted out to different individuals) is in fact a thing variable and full of perturbation, and governed as it were by chance. Whence it was well observed by Heraclitus that men look for sciences in their own lesser worlds and not in the greater or common world.

43

There are also Idols formed by the intercourse and association of men with each other, which I call Idols of the Market Place on account of the commerce and consort of men there. For it is by discourse that men associate, and words are imposed according to the apprehension of the vulgar. And therefore the ill and unfit choice of words wonderfully obstructs the understanding. Nor do the definitions or explanation where-

[5]Text *XXXVIII.* The aphorisms are given roman numerals throughout.
[6]A notion traditionally attributed to the fifth-century Greek philosopher Protagoras, who was known as the first of the Sophists.

with in some things learned men are wont to guard and defend themselves by any means set the matter right. But words plainly force and overrule the understanding, and throw all into confusion, and lead men away into numberless empty controversies and idle fancies.

44

Lastly, there are Idols which have immigrated into men's minds from the various dogmas of philosophies and also from wrong laws of demonstration. These I call Idols of the Theater, because in my judgment all the received systems are but so many stage plays, representing worlds of their own 10 creation after an unreal and scenic fashion. Nor is it only of the systems now in vogue or only of the ancient sects and philosophies that I speak, for many more plays of the same kind may yet be composed and in like artificial manner set forth, seeing that errors the most widely different have nevertheless causes for the most part alike. Neither again do I mean this only of entire systems, but also of many principles and axioms in science, which by tradition, credulity, and negligence have come to be received.

But of these several kinds of Idols I must speak more largely 20 and exactly, that the understanding may be duly cautioned.

[Following a long discussion of man's congenital infirmities,]
[Bacon summarizes his conclusions in Aphorism 52.]

52

Such then are the idols which I call Idols of the Tribe, and which take their rise either from the homogeneity of the substance of the human spirit,[7] or from its preoccupation, or from its narrowness, or from its restless motion, or from an infusion of the affections, or from the incompetency of the senses, or from the mode of impression.

53

The Idols of the Cave take their rise in the peculiar constitu- 30 tion, mental or bodily, of each individual, and also in education, habit, and accident. Of this kind there is a great number and variety, but I will instance those the pointing out of which contains the most important caution, and which have most effect in disturbing the clearness of the understanding.

54

Men become attached to certain particular sciences and speculations either because they fancy themselves the authors and inventors thereof or because they have bestowed the greatest pains upon them and become most habituated to them. But men of this kind, if they betake themselves to 40 philosophy and contemplations of a general character, distort and color them in obedience to their former fancies, a thing especially to be noticed in Aristotle, who made his natural philosophy a mere bondservant to his logic, thereby rendering it contentious and well nigh useless. . . .

58

Let such then be our provision and contemplative prudence for keeping off and dislodging the Idols of the Cave, which grow for the most part either out of the predominance of a favorite subject, or out of an excessive tendency to compare or to distinguish, or out of partiality for particular ages, or out of the largeness or minuteness of the objects contemplated. And generally let every student of nature take this as a rule, that whatever his mind seizes and dwells upon with peculiar satisfaction is to be held in suspicion, and that so much the more care is to be taken in dealing with such questions to keep the understanding even and clear.

59

But the Idols of the Market Place are the most troublesome of all—idols which have crept into the understanding through the alliances of words and names. For men believe that their reason governs words, but it is also true that words react on the understanding, and this it is that has rendered philosophy and the sciences sophistical and inactive. Now words, being commonly framed and applied according to the capacity of the vulgar, follow those lines of division which are most obvious to the vulgar understanding. And whenever an understanding of greater acuteness or a more diligent observation would alter those lines to suit the true divisions of nature, words stand in the way and resist the change. Whence it comes to pass that the high and formal discussions of learned men end oftentimes in disputes about words and names, with which (according to the use and wisdom of the mathematicians) it would be more prudent to begin, and so by means of definitions reduce them to order. Yet even definitions cannot cure this evil in dealing with natural and material things, since the definitions themselves consist of words, and those words beget others, so that it is necessary to recur to individual instances, and those in due series and order, as I shall say presently when I come to the method and scheme for the formation of notions and axioms.

60

The idols imposed by words on the understanding are of two kinds. They are either names of things which do not exist (for as there are things left unnamed through lack of observation, so likewise are there names which result from fantastic suppositions and to which nothing in reality corresponds), or they are names of things which exist, but yet confused and ill defined and hastily and irregularly derived from realities. Of the former kind are *fortune, the prime mover,*[8] *planetary orbits,*[9] *element of fire,* and like fictions which owe their origin to false and idle theories. And this class of

---

[7]In Axiom 45 Bacon observed that "the human understanding is of its own nature prone to suppose the existence of more order and regularity in the world than it finds."

[8]The *primum mobile,* for which see *sphere* in the Glossary.

[9]In Ptolemaic astronomy, the spheres of the planets. See *sphere* in the Glossary.

idols is more easily expelled, because to get rid of them it is only necessary that all theories should be steadily rejected and dismissed as obsolete.

But the other class, which springs out of a faulty and unskilful abstraction, is intricate and deeply rooted. Let us take for example such a word as *humid,* and see how far the several things which the word is used to signify agree with each other; and we shall find the word *humid* to be nothing else than a mark loosely and confusedly applied to denote a variety of actions which will not bear to be reduced to any 10 constant meaning. For it both signifies that which easily spreads itself round any other body, and that which in itself is indeterminate and cannot solidize, and that which readily yields in every direction, and that which easily divides and scatters itself, and that which easily unites and collects itself, and that which readily flows and is put in motion, and that which readily clings to another body and wets it, and that which is easily reduced to a liquid, or being solid easily melts. Accordingly, when you come to apply the word, if you take it in one sense, flame is humid; if in another, air is not 20 humid; if in another, fine dust is humid; if in another, glass is humid. So that it is easy to see that the notion is taken by abstraction only from water and common and ordinary liquids without any due verification.

There are, however, in words certain degrees of distortion and error. One of the least faulty kinds is that of names of substances, especially of lowest species and well deduced (for the notion of *chalk* and of *mud* is good, of *earth* bad); a more faulty kind is that of actions, as *to generate, to corrupt, to alter;* the most faulty is of qualities (except such as are the immedi- 30 ate objects of the sense) as *heavy, light, rare, dense,* and the like. Yet in all these cases some notions are of necessity a little better than others in proportion to the greater variety of subjects that fall within the range of the human sense.

61

But the Idols of the Theater are not innate, nor do they steal into the understanding secretly, but are plainly impressed and received into the mind from the playbooks of philosophical systems and the perverted rules of demonstration. To attempt refutations in this case would be merely inconsistent with what I have already said, for since we agree neither upon 40 principles nor upon demonstrations there is no place for argument. And this is so far well, inasmuch as it leaves the honor of the ancients untouched. For they are no wise disparaged, the question between them and me being only as to the way. For as the saying is, the lame man who keeps the right road outstrips the runner who takes a wrong one. Nay, it is obvious that when a man runs the wrong way, the more active and swift he is the further he will go astray.

But the course I propose for the discovery of sciences is such as leaves but little to the acuteness and strength of wits, 50 but places all wits and understandings nearly on a level. For as in the drawing of a straight line or a perfect circle much depends on the steadiness and practice of the hand, if it be done by aim of hand only, but if with the aid of rule or

compass, little or nothing; so is it exactly with my plan. But though particular confutations would be of no avail, yet touching the sects and general divisions of such systems I must say something; something also touching the external signs which show that they are unsound; and finally something touching the causes of such great infelicity and of such lasting and general agreement in error: that so the access to truth may be made less difficult, and the human understanding may the more willingly submit to its purgation and dismiss its idols.

62

Idols of the Theater, or of systems, are many, and there can be and perhaps will be yet many more. For were it not that now for many ages men's minds have been busied with religion and theology, and were it not that civil governments, especially monarchies, have been averse to such novelties, even in matters speculative, so that men labor therein to the peril and harming of their fortunes, not only unrewarded but exposed also to contempt and envy, doubtless there would have arisen many other philosophical sects like to those which in great variety flourished once among the Greeks. For as on the phenomena of the heavens many hypotheses may be constructed, so likewise (and more also) many various dogmas may be set up and established on the phenomena of philosophy. And in the plays of this philosophical theater you may observe the same thing which is found in the theater of the poets, that stories invented for the stage are more compact and elegant, and more as one would wish them to be than true stories out of history.

In general, however, there is taken for the material of philosophy either a great deal out of a few things, or a very little out of many things, so that on both sides philosophy is based on too narrow a foundation of experiment and natural history, and decides on the authority of too few cases. For the rational school of philosophers[10] snatches from experience a variety of common instances, neither duly ascertained nor diligently examined and weighed, and leaves all the rest to meditation and agitation of wit.

There is also another class[11] of philosophers who, having bestowed much diligent and careful labor on a few experiments, have thence made bold to educe and construct systems, wresting all other facts in a strange fashion to conformity therewith.

And there is yet a third class[12] consisting of those who out of faith and veneration mix their philosophy with theology and traditions, among whom the vanity of some has gone so far aside as to seek the origin of sciences among spirits and genii. So that this parent stock of errors—this false philosophy—is of three kinds: the sophistical, the empirical, and the superstitious.

[10]*Rational...philosophers*: Aristotle and his followers.
[11]The alchemists and such alleged empiricists as William Gilbert, who tried to explain everything (including gravity) by the principles of magnetism.
[12]Rational theologians like St. Thomas Aquinas.

The Goodman–Hakewill Controversy

When the psalmist predicted (102.26) that the heavens would grow old like a garment and perish, he was lending his prestige to a theme almost as old as human utterance. In man's most rudimentary perception all things exemplify the fact of change: the turn from day to night, the sequence of the seasons, the decay of youth and beauty, the rise and fall of institutions, the very pulse of life itself attests to mutability. It is not surprising, therefore, that what Herrick calls "time's trans-shifting" has been a major theme in literature, religion, and philosophy from Homer to Dylan Thomas, from Augustine to Barth, from Parmenides to Russell.

In the later Renaissance, however, it had a special vogue and special terror. For one thing, the revival, by the great reformers, of Augustine's theology powerfully reinforced his linear view of history as a steady downward movement from primal bliss to sin, and then to apocalyptic retribution. For another, the rediscovery of pagan antiquity had underscored—or so it seemed to many learned men—a sad decline from the serenity and poise and radiance of classic art to the stylistic, formal, and thematic imprecision of its modern counterpart. But there were other reasons to support the widely shared conviction that the changes wrought by time involved not merely alteration but decay. It was poignant to observe that golden lads and girls must come to dust and that mighty states and institutions sink from splendor to extinction, but it was terrifying to be instructed by Copernicus and his fellows that the universe itself was prey to alteration and disorder. Donne (in his *First Anniversary*) and Burton (in his "Digression of the Air," pp. 447 ff.) record the impact of this "new philosophy" on certain special minds; and Gloucester, in *King Lear* (I. ii.112 ff.) may be regarded as a spokesman for the average man when he inferred from terrifying portents in the sky the dissolution of those political and familial ties that bind our moral universe. As the world wagged on, new prophets of disaster rose. Sir Thomas Browne asserted that " 'tis too late to be ambitious" (p. 483), and Owen Felltham thought that "in reason and nature" all signs pointed to the final conflagration: "we have seen the infancy, the youth, the virility all past. Nay, we have seen it well stept into years and declination, the most infallible premonitors of a dissolution" (p. 730). Similar remarks, ranging from querulous complaint to majestic threnody, are scattered thick through Jacobean literature.

But if many men were haunted by the specter of devouring Time and mutability, there were others, like Bacon and his intellectual progeny, who saw change as progress rather than decay, and who therefore viewed the future with elation. Truth is the daughter of Time, these meliorists asserted, and man's progressive gains on truth record the stages of his triumph over fear and superstition.

These conflicting responses to the fact of change—despair and cheerful zeal—are shown in an almost emblematic fashion by the two once famous books represented here. Godfrey Goodman's *Fall of Man* is a relentless recapitulation of the ancient *de contemptu mundi* theme; George Hakewill's *Apology*—a kind of gigantic footnote to Bacon's *Advancement of Learning*—marshals all the culture of the Renaissance to redeem the "captivated truth" of human progress. That these two Jacobean divines could expend such learning and self-intoxicating zeal in defending such extreme positions helps us understand the intellectual legacy and the ferment of the age.

Passing briskly from Westminster School (where he studied under Camden) to Trinity College,

Cambridge, and then to ordination (1603), Goodman was clearly bent upon success. Indeed, it is odd that the author of *The Fall of Man*, who so much despised the world, was so zealous to advance his own career. It was as vicar of Stapleford Abbots, Essex, that he preached the sermon which, with immense proliferation, became the gloomy book on which his reputation rests; but well before its publication in 1616 he had begun collecting the offices, emoluments, and sinecures that led him to the bishop's throne at Gloucester in 1625. Thereafter he began a long decline. Although his later theological and political differences with a string of strong opponents—including the king, Archbishop Laud, and the Puritans in Parliament—need not be rehearsed, it perhaps should be recorded that his affection for the Church of Rome became clear enough for Lord Falkland to assert in 1641 that bishops like him were "so absolutely, directly, and cordially papists" that only their emoluments could keep them in the Church of England. Such comments were a portent of disaster. In 1641 Goodman, with eleven other bishops, was charged with treason and imprisoned in the Tower (where Laud refused to speak to him); after his release he returned to Gloucester in 1643 to find his palace sacked and his books and papers scattered; and he spent his later years in London in apparent destitution. Although Goodman died a "professed Romanist," Thomas Fuller said that he should not be too severely censured, being just a "harmless man, hurtful to none but himself." In addition to *The Fall of Man*, Goodman wrote, among other things, *The Creatures Praising God, or the Religion of Dumb Creatures* (1622) and *A Large Discourse* on the Trinity and the Incarnation (1653). *The Court of James the First*, a sympathetic record of a subject near and dear to him, remained in manuscript until 1839, but a history of the English church that he said he wrote before the outbreak of the war has disappeared.

George Hakewill was a more attractive person and a more accomplished writer. Going from the grammar school in his native Exeter to Oxford, he earned two degrees (B.A. 1599, M.A. 1602) from Exeter College before taking holy orders and then living abroad for several years. Two more degrees (B.D. 1610, D.D. 1611) certified his reputation as an erudite divine, and his appointment (1612) as a chaplain to Prince Charles would no doubt have led to better things had not his opposition to the Prince's projected Spanish marriage blasted his career at court. It was just as well, perhaps, for with sufficient means to become a benefactor of his college and sufficient leisure to compose the book that made him famous, Hakewill lived an honest, useful life. His election in 1642 to the rectorship of Exeter College—a post that he retained, despite the upheavals of the war, until his death in 1649—was in fitting recognition of his merits. Although he published some dozen devotional and theological works between 1608 (when his *Vanity of the Eye* appeared) and 1641 (when he undertook to challenge Peter Heylyn's views about the Eucharist), it is the famous *Apology or Declaration of the Power and Providence of God*, a rebuttal of Goodman's *Fall of Man*, that keeps his name alive. First published (in four books) in 1627, revised in 1630, and enlarged with "two entire books" in 1635, it is at once a strong attack on Goodman, a lavish demonstration of God's benign control of His creation, a compendium of universal knowledge, and a program for man's accelerated progress.

Writing on the same gigantic scale as Goodman, but with a firmer style and structure, Hakewill devotes Book I (whose five chapters, each with five or six big sections, runs to some 600 pages) to an attack upon the doctrine of decay "in general"; Book II narrows the discussion to the heavens, the elements, and the "elementary bodies, man only excepted"; Book III (a long essay on ancients vs. moderns) challenges man's alleged decay in longevity, in strength, and in production of the arts and sciences; Book IV extends the discussion to morals and manners, and ends, in Christian orthodoxy, with an apocalyptic vision of the Last Judgment and the eventual (but conveniently remote) destruction of the world. Of the two new books added to the 1635 edition (with separate pagination), the first (i.e., Book V) is a string of long excerpts from Goodman with Hakewill's refutation; the second (i.e., Book VI) is a general recapitulation in response to certain objections that had been lodged against the first edition.

My texts are based upon the first and only edition (1616) of Goodman's *Fall of Man* (STC 12023) and on the third (1635) of Hakewill's *Apology* (STC 12613). There is a life of Goodman by G. I. Soden (1953), but none of his more engaging adversary. However, their controversy has been fully treated by Victor Harris in *All Coherence Gone* (1949) and summarized by R. H. Hepburn in *JHI*, XVI (1955). There are important articles on the doctrine of decay by George Williamson (ELH, II, 1935) and D. C. Allen (*SP*, XXXV, 1938), and the subject is discussed by R. F. Jones and others listed in the General Bibliography, Section II.

Godfrey Goodman [1583-1656]

from The Fall of Man (1616)

[THE FIRST PART]

[THE DEPRAVITY OF MAN]

Having opened his gigantic threnody on fallen man with a grossly flattering dedication to Queen Anne, Goodman, in a murky address "To the Reader," explains the circumstances under which the book was written. He had begun, he says, by blocking out a sermon (on 1 Corinthians 2.14) that he thought to have finished "within the compass of an hour," but as the subject grew he decided, almost against his will, to convert the sermon to a treatise. It is a decision that any but the most resolute reader will deplore, for it leads to an immense, and immensely prolix, demonstration of a theme grown stale by repetition. Like Lancelot Andrewes' great sermon on Epiphany (pp. 520 ff.), the first of the three long sections begins as a celebration of the journey of the Magi, through whom the newborn Christ was manifested to the Gentiles, but it soon declines into a discussion of the Fall, its consequences, and the sorry plight of the natural man. The following excerpt, a sort of recapitulation midway through Part I, suggests something of Goodman's theme and scope and style.

To conclude this one point: considering, first, that nature so much aboundeth in evil; secondly, and is so much inclined unto evil; thirdly, considering how the heavens stand affected to the earth; fourthly, how elements amongst themselves; fifthly, how mixed creatures one to another; sixthly, and in themselves what defects and imperfections there are; seventhly, how art serves like a cobbler or tinker to piece up the walls and to repair the ruins of nature, I hope it will sufficiently appear that she is corrupted and much declined from her first perfection, which certainly was intended by the Founder and by all probable conjecture was imparted to her in her first institution. I could be infinite in this point, but indeed it is not so pertinent, nor doth it so nearly concern my text. I have already alleged seven arguments to this purpose; seven is a perfect number; as I challenge a rest on the seventh day, so here I will rest in my seventh argument.

Now in this great uproar and tumult of nature, when heaven and earth seem to threaten a final destruction, give me leave, with the mariners of Jonah's ship, to cast lots and search out the first occasion of this evil.[1] Alas, alas, the lot falls upon man—man alone of all other creatures, in regard of the freedom of his will and the choice of his own actions, being only capable of the transgression, the rest of the creatures are wholly excluded from the offense. The punishment, I confess, appears in them, but chiefly and principally in man. I will therefore descend from the great world to this little world[2] which first set on fire and inflamed the whole, for I should greatly wrong myself if I should lose so much time as to take a general survey of nature, to wander in the deserts and caves of the creatures to search out their imperfections. I will therefore tie myself to man, and by man alone the fall and corruption shall manifestly appear. My proofs and arguments I will dispose into three several ranks: first, for such things which seem to be proper and peculiar to man in regard of his constitution, whereof all nature cannot furnish us with the like example and president,[3] and therefore we may well suppose that they are peculiar punishments of man's sin. Secondly, I will speak of man's condition in general and compare man with the beast of the field, whereby it shall appear that our misery is far greater than theirs, contrary to the first intent and institution of nature, wherein she gave us a greater dignity and so consequently should impart a greater measure of happiness. Thirdly, I will insist in those

THE FALL OF MAN   [1]Jonah 1.7.
[2]*Great...world*: from the macrocosm to the microcosm.
[3]Precedent.

particular punishments of sin which are related in Scripture to be the punishments of the first sin, where·n I will show the truth, the certainty, and I will examine them by the touchstone and light of our natural reason.

> The remainder of Part I—a grim account of the exacerbating conflicts between man's soul and body, reason and will, mortal and immortal elements—concludes with the following arraignment.

I could be infinite in these points, but calling to mind that I have proceeded in a legal course according to the form of law, I have impaneled my jury consisting of twelve reasons; I will use no shifts or delays, but refer myself to their verdict. I will here only rehearse and briefly recapitulate the sum of my proofs, considering that in the very constitution of man many things happen beyond the common course of nature, without president or pattern, such as could not stand with the divine providence were it not that they are the particular punishments of man's sin.

> Goodman then rehearses twelve proofs of man's desolating natural state: for example, that "the spirit with the flesh, mortal with immortal, should together subsist," that "the soul, being coupled, should find such mean and base entertainment," "that the body should hinder every action of the soul, the senses falsely informing and distracting the understanding," that there should be such a gross discrepancy between the "gifts" of the body and those of the mind.

Let these allegations be duly examined, and I do not fear to come to a trial, for I do here call heaven and earth to witness that these things cannot stand with the wisdom of nature, the goodness of nature; neither have they conformity to the rest of the works of nature; and therefore they serve as an extraordinary punishment for some offence undoubtedly signifying the fall and corruption of man. And thus much for the very person of man, together with his parts and constitution.

THE SECOND PART

> Warming to his subject, in Part II Goodman relentlessly describes man's misery both "in himself" and "in comparison with the rest of the creatures." It is a topic, as he himself concedes, that has a bad effect upon the style and structure of his treatise.

I pray pardon me if I be not overstrict and curious in my method, though I speak promiscuously[4] and confound them together, for misery betokens confusion. A confused style and a disturbed method is fittest to discourse of our misery, which cannot consist with the right use of our reason or understanding. Instead of an eloquent phrase or a learned discourse, if I shall use sighs, tears, sobs, and complaints, thereby to move · your compassion, this would prove the best lecture[5] of misery. And if I shall lay open yourselves to yourselves, and that my tongue shall serve as a glass to discover your misery, instead of the foot and burthen of my speech at the clause of a sentence, I pray use this short ejacula-

tion and prayer: "*Jesu, fili David, miserere nostri*:[6] according to our misery, extend Thy mercy, sweet Jesu, clothe our nakedness, cover our shame, heal our infirmities; for Thou art our house of defence and our castle."

> Goodman finds that man, compared with other creatures, is a mass of evils and afflictions that must derive from primal sin. In respect of odor, for example, he is a noisome thing.

Many herbs, many beasts, many trees are in themselves odoriferous and yield a sweet savor, for God hath ordained them to be nature's sacrifice to himself. But I think if men were thoroughly searched, search the very entrails and bowels and you shall hardly endure the scent. I will not speak of his filth issuing from his ears, his eyes, nostrils, mouth, navel, and the unclean parts; take his very flesh, his bones, and his sinews; burn and consume them with fire. O the sweet smelling sacrifice, as loathed of God, so hateful and distasteful to man himself! For what should we expect of flesh and blood but corruption [The very elements are hostile to this sinful spawn of Adam.]

First for the contagious air: no creature is so subject to a general infection and pestilence as is man. In this one city we have buried three thousand a week, and so for many weeks together much about that number when the plague hath continued within the kingdom for many years. This plague, it doth not arise from the food or any distemper of our bodies, but from the air: it is a poison which works upon the vital spirits, and seeming to neglect other baser and inferior parts first sets upon the heart, striking at the root of life, and suddenly in a moment it brings us to ruin. If the party himself shall happily escape, yet still the infection continueth though the garment be worn out with use, consumed with the moth, yet in the bare threads the poison will privily lurk. The open air cannot sufficiently pierce, the fire cannot cleanse, man's providence cannot prevent; but it finds out some lurking hole, some shelter or covering to hide itself until at length it bursts into vengeance, to the wonder and astonishment of nature. Summer and winter both serve alike to harbor such an unkind guest; it will inhabit the bare walls rather than it will be excluded; the dumb creatures, the dogs and the mice shall serve to scatter it; especially fruit shall nourish it, for it was the forbidden fruit which gave it the first entrance and occasion. Marvel not how man's sin, like an hereditary disease, should be together propagated with his seed when the breath of his nostrils may thus work upon thousands at once, upon the strongest and ablest bodies to their utter dissolution and ruin. . . .

Leaving the elements, let us come to our bodies consisting of elements. Why should man be more subject to disease than all other creatures? Not any part of man without several and special diseases, not any moment of his age wherein sicknesses and infirmities do not watch and attend their opportunity arising from the very constitution of his body. The smallpox and the measles creep in his cradle; the worms, the scabs,

---

[4]Confusedly. [5]Lesson.
[6]*Jesu...nostri*: "Jesus, Son of David, have pity on us!"

and the botches[7] attend him to school; in his youth, hot agues and plurisies, like burning seas with their ebbings and flowings, going and returning according to their fits and their seasons, to the wonder of nature and the astonishment of the physician; in his elder years, the stone, the gout, the strangullion,[8] then ruptures, aches, and coughs; at length the dead palsy, the apoplexy, the lethargy gives him his deadly wound. Thus man stands to be baited, while all the diseases, like so many furies, some gnaw at his throat, others thrust at his liver, some dart at the kidneys, others aim at the heart. All nature cannot supply the like president, and therefore give me leave (though I offend much against the rules of art) to compare man to man himself, the general state of man to the picture of that man which stands in the forefront of an almanac:[9] the Lion strikes at the heart and the back while Cancer nips the breast and the stomach, Sagittarius shoots at the thighs, Capricorn butts at the knees, and here you have the lively representation of man.

[THE FALLEN WORLD]

Toiling and panting after Goodman as he wanders through the trackless wastes of Part II, we confront (and often linger on) a bewildering variety of topics; but however loose his method, his intent is fairly clear: by forcing us to stare on our corruption—sexual, social, medical, political, pedagogical, and other—to make us fix our hopes on God. "I thought fit to set our own tents and tabernacles on fire," he explains with some complacency, "to make our homebred joys and delights vanish in smoke," for only through the knowledge of our own corruption can we attain the higher knowledge of contrition, and thereby qualify for mercy. In the third and final section of his book, however, Goodman does not celebrate God's mercy; he writes instead of justice, and this requires a lurid treatment of man's progressive deterioration and of the decay of nature as punishment for sin.

I forget myself, I forget myself! For, speaking of man's corruption, I am so far entangled that I cannot easily release myself: being corrupted as well as others, methinks whatsoever I see, whatsoever I hear, all things seem to sound[10] corruption. But recalling myself, I cannot forget that I have allotted this third part to treat only of those punishments which are generally related in Scripture to be the punishments of the first sin; neither can I speak of all the punishments, for so I should undertake an infinite task. I must therefore tie myself to a certain number; and, considering that the state of this life is a sinful state, I will resemble it to the state of the Israelites in Egypt, where they were borne in slavery and could not be delivered but by their passage through the Red Sea, which is a figure[11] either of our baptism by water or of our baptism by blood, either of our entrance to grace or of our entrance to glory. Now, answerable to the plagues of Egypt, I will proportion the number of our punishments: ten plagues of Egypt according to the breach of God's Ten Commandments. This number of ten, being the most perfect number observed in our punishments, shall sufficiently argue the perfection of God's justice and our imperfection in sin.

THE THIRD PART

[THE DOWNWARD COURSE OF HISTORY]

Like the final books of *Paradise Lost,* but on a grotesquely distended scale, Part III of Goodman's treatise presents the history of the race after the fall. Needless to say, it makes for very sober reading, as the following account of the Flood suggests.

As man was corrupted and all the creatures, forsaking their first and natural use, did serve for man's punishment and rebelled against him, so it stood with the uniformity of God's judgments that nothing should remain untouched— no, not the elements themselves, being the first principles, seeds, and foundations of nature; for as man was totally defaced and had lost the image of God, so this world, though coming far short of that most excellent state of Paradise, yet being God's own immediate workmanship and so still continuing, God at length in His wisdom for our sins thought fit to deface it; and behold the rule of His justice: whenas the children of God were mixed with the children of men, God sends a deluge of waters to confound them together. Death is the punishment of sin: that we might herein acknowledge God's own handiwork, the judgment fell from above, their graves were fashioned in the clouds, and the elements did for a time change their situation and these were likewise confounded together; and as in the creation the waters did flow upon the face of the earth, so now again the whole world did seem to go backward and to return to the first nothing. Hence began a great alteration in nature, and all things were changed to the worst; the earth did decay in plenty and goodness of fruits, for immediately after the deluge God did enlarge Noah's commission and gave him free power to feed on the flesh of the creatures;[12] the water likewise lost her natural property of goodness, and therefore Noah immediately began to plant a vineyard. The air was more subject to vapors, foggy mists, and dark clouds; the fire with hot fumes and exhalations, ascending and turning to meteors, was made more imperfect and impure; the heavens themselves have not freely escaped: though these sublunary contagions could not infect the stars, yet were they able much to hinder the goodness of their actions and operations, as likewise to eclipse and obscure their beauty, some of them never appearing unto us (as are those stars *in via lactea*),[13] others seem twinkling *titillantes*[14] through the thickness, opacity, and gloominess of our air not giving passage to their beams, and all of them appear short in beauty, less in quantity than

---

[7]Boils.

[8]A disease of horses characterized by swelling of the glands of the throat. Goodman perhaps means *stranguary*, a disease of the urinary organs in man.

[9]*Picture...almanac*: the chart of the zodiac, in which the twelve parts are named for various constellations (Leo the Lion, Cancer, the Archer or Sagittarius, the Goat or Capricorn, etc.).

[10]Have a tendency toward.   [11]Emblem, symbol, representation.

[12]*Noah's...creatures*: Genesis 9.2–3.

[13]"In the Milky Way."   [14]"Ticklings."

indeed they are, and assuredly are much hindered in their operations.

So that this general deluge was indeed the general confusion of nature; and as it was the death of nature, so nature herself could neither hinder nor hasten her own death; and being once fallen, she could not raise herself by her own natural power, for howsoever the God of nature might well use natural means (the watery constellations) for the effecting of His good will and purpose, yet surely these in themselves were not sufficient unless you will thereunto add God's 10 infinite power and His absolute authority.

⌐ Finally, after more than a hundred pages of such serpentine ¬
  digressions, Goodman admits that he has wandered far
  afield, and he tries to regain control of the discussion by
⌐ restating and returning to his theme. ⌐

I will not stay my time and in the latter end of my speech crave pardon for all my offences; here, rather, I will now snatch at the present occasion so fitly offered: if I have spoken anything, or shall hereafter speak in this pamphlet, unadvisedly, illiterately, without good order or method, acknowl- 20 edge (I beseech thee) the general punishment of whole mankind, which more especially discovers itself in my weakness, the confusion of tongues. I am confounded, I am confounded, poor silly wretch that I am; I am confounded. My mind is distracted, my tongue is confounded, and my whole nature corrupted. In me, in me alone, see the punishment of whole mankind! Learn now to be compassionate and pitiful, for I cannot altogether excuse thee. *Nihil humani a te alienum putes.*[15] Here is thy benefit indeed: my weakness appears, the press hath proclaimed it, this pamphlet can witness it, and 30 thine is yet undiscovered.

Now in this general confusion I know not where to betake myself or what to speak in the next place, for my tongue is confounded. I will therefore suppose myself to be lost in the woods, and that at length, after much wandering, I should recall myself; and finding no way for my passage I should have recourse to my card and consider the intended scope of my journey: from whence I came (*natus ex muliere*[16]), my present state and condition (I am a sojourner and stranger, as all my forefathers were), the scope and end of my travel 40 (*pulvis in pulverem,* from dust to dust), that so at length I might safely arrive to mine own native country (*a statu via ad statum patria*). Now, certainly, right reason would thus inform and instruct me *ut secundum rectam lineam incedam,* that born of the dust and tending to the dust, I should keep my straight way, neither puffed up with pride above my natural state nor sinking down with despair beneath my condition; that I should not upon any occasion start out of the way, but remembering my beginning, remembering my end, I should square out my course and travel accordingly. Intend- 50 ing, therefore, to speak of the fall of man, the corruption of nature, and the punishment of the first sin, I will lay aside all other slighter punishments, all chastisements and corrections of sin (which were infinite to repeat), and I will only insist in those two general judgments, being indeed the extremes, the first and the last, including all other punishments within their bounds: 1) *in dolore paries,* thou shalt

bring forth with pain and sorrow, being spoken to the woman; 2) *morte morieris,* thou shalt die the death, pronounced indifferently against both. And thus his corruption shall appear by his first welcome and salutation into this world and by his last adieu and farewell out of his world. You shall better judge of the whole course of his entertainment in this world.

⌐ Skipping the great mass of obstetrical and mortuary detail ¬
  with which Goodman embellishes his discussion of these
  two terminal punishments, we approach the apocalyptic
  theme that since nature is corrupted by man's sin, it too
⌐ must "die the death" that God had promised him. ⌐

Give me leave to compare myself, that am the meanest of all men, to Alexander the Great, and this my present treatise, wherein I labor to show the fall and corruption of man, to the conquest of nature. Methinks I have subdued the little world and brought man as a captive or slave, through much misery and sorrow, at length to the place of his execution; and having now possessed myself of the fairest fortress or tower in nature (man, that is a little world), I cannot here content myself, but I begin to inquire whether there are as yet more worlds to be conquered. And behold, in the second place I will fall upon the great world, and I will attempt, with Archimedes,[17] to shake her foundations, to threaten her ruin, in this general corruption and dissolution of man. For this punishment—*morte morieris*—though it principally concerns man, yet the whole world cannot be exempted from it, being directed and ordained only for man's use, containing in itself the very same seeds and causes of death and destruction, and as it is most fit and agreeable to our present condition, that being corruptible in ourselves we should likewise dwell in houses of corruption.

For proof and demonstration whereof I must ascend from the individuals and singulars to the species and kinds of the creatures; and among all other kinds, assuredly man is the most noble and therefore best deserves to be the subject of our knowledge. We should be best acquainted with ourselves, which makes for the certainty of our knowledge; and speaking of things which so nearly concern ourselves, we should much desire to be better informed in our own state and condition. Now if the whole kind and species of man seems daily to decline and decay—which shall appear by the comparison of times past with times present, of ourselves with our ancestors—then assuredly the whole world cannot be excused from corruption, but as it dies daily in the singulars, so at length it shall fail in the universals and in the kinds of the creatures.

This truth seems to rely upon these three foundations: 1) Man, as all other creatures, being immediately created by God, as he comes nearer and nearer the first mold, so is he more and more perfect; and according to the degrees of his

---

[15]"Regard nothing human as indifferent to you" (adapted from Terence, *Heauton Timorumenos,* I.i.25). [16]"Born of woman."
[17]Greek mathematician (d. 212 B.C.) reported to have remarked of his discovery of the lever or fulcrum, "Give me where I may stand and I will move the world."

distance, so he incurs the more imperfection and weakness, as the streams of a fountain, the further they run through unclean passages the more they contract the corruption. 2) It would imply a contradiction in nature if the parts and the whole were not of like condition—but how wonderful is the difference if you will suppose a corruption of the singulars and an eternity of the kind! For whereas the recompence should be made by succession or equivalency, we must consider that succession may well prolong the corruption—adding more degrees, proceeding more leisurely—but cannot wholly exclude the corruption. 3) The general intent and scope of nature wholly tends to corruption, for I would gladly ask why should not nature either renew man's age or preserve him in a state of consistency? The answer is, because the juice and sap which we receive from our food or our nourishment is not so agreeable to the state of our bodies as is that humor *et calor radicalis*[18] which we receive from our first birth. Here I will reply, "How falls it out that our bodies should impart *semen ad procreandum*[19] wherein that radical humor is resident?" And both seed and humor arising from our food and our nourishment, yet nature should seem in the preservation of our bodies to refuse the best, making it an excrement of the third concoction[20] and taking for her own food and sustenance the worst part of the substance. See, then, the general intent and scope of nature, tending to corruption, must likewise argue that nature herself in general shall at length be tainted with the same corruption.

> It is in the development of this broad theme that Goodman brings his "pamphlet" to a close. A few of his many examples of the progressive deterioration of both man and nature will exemplify his method.

It should seem that death is not only competent to every person in particular, but even the whole world, and all the several kinds of creatures, tend to confusion. There is a great decay in every species; men come not to that strength nor to that growth nor to that ripeness of wit nor to that fullness of years which they did in former times. The world hath his period[21] and his determinate course of years; now is the old age or decay of this world. The growth and strength of men seem to proceed from the same causes and to rely upon the same foundation—the bones—which, according to their massiness,[22] their weight, or their length, give the proportion and strength to the whole body. These bones are yet extant and are daily taken up in sepulchers, whereof I have often been an eyewitness, and having duly considered them according to measure and weight, I find by most undoubted experience that they did far exceed ours. Their weapons will likewise testify as much, for these are yet extant and are reserved as relics and trophies of their valor, which the strength of man in these days cannot manage or rule. Many things there are likewise wherein I could instance, which were in former times trials for their strength, but now seem very impossible to our weakness. Consider all their actions which they did undertake, for therein they did as far exceed us as their strength did exceed ours; observe their attempts in erecting stately cathedral churches for the exercise of religion,

in building huge castles for defence of their people, in contriving highways, causeways, bridges, and suchlike, which well betoken noble and brave spirits; whereas our wits in these days make their employments in things of less moment, some pretty toys and trifles, some new fashion and attire; our buildings are paper buildings, made only to serve the present use and occasion. I am ashamed of ourselves. We dote, we dote, though herein I do acknowledge a wonderful providence of God, while the world had some time of continuance, when the years were not fully expired, then God gave man a mind and disposition to intend the good of posterity; but now in these latter days, when the world is almost come to an upshot,[23] when the period[24] of time is now approaching, no marvel if God leave man to himself, that out of his own immoderate love of himself, neglecting the common good and the good of succession, he should only intend, in his buildings, in the waste of his woods, and in all other of his actions his own private and present commodity. . . .

For the wits of former times, certainly they did far exceed ours; their bodies were better tempered as being nearer the first mold, and the mind follows the temper and disposition of the body; though I confess that this our age, being most proud, arrogant, and vainglorious, doth most unjustly claim unto itself the name and title of the learned age. Shall we ascribe no more to the first founders and inventors of arts? Was it a work of small difficulty to hew and square out nature, allotting to every science her proper subject, her due limitation? To reduce all the several stars into constellations, to observe their motion, their quality, their influence? Grammar, which is the first entrance and the meanest of all arts, seems to be most excellent in her invention, that all the several words, how different soever in sound and signification, should be comprehended in an alphabet of four and twenty letters; that cases, declensions, numbers, tenses, and the like should figure out the variety of nature. For all arts whatsoever, the best authors are the most ancient, even unto this day. I could instance in every one in particular, though we, building upon their foundations, have added some ornaments, yet such as are not necessary to perfit the art. And generally for the ancients, whatsoever you shall observe in practice amongst them, you shall find that it stood with great wisdom and providence, if you please to have relation to the times and occasions. And wherein they seem to be defective, you may ascribe it to the happiness of their times, for their plenty was such as that they were not inforced to try all conclusions in husbandry, whereas our wants seem to require our best inventions; their honest plain and charitable meaning was such as that they were unacquainted, or at least thought it not fit, to discover the guile and subtlety of a serpentine generation, the hardness of their

[18]"And vital heat."   [19]"Seed for reproduction."
[20]Secretion (as distinguished from the first concoction, which is digestion in the stomach, and the second concoction, which is the process whereby chyle is changed into blood).
[21]Time of duration.   [22]Solidity.   [23]Termination.   [24]End.

bodies, their fear of God, and the joy of his service was such as that utterly destesting all carnality (fearing lest the glory and pomp of this world might steal away themselves from themselves, and that they might be carried with an immoderate love to the creatures) they thought it fitter to prevent this mischief in the root, to profess a more homely and strict kind of life, and therein to give themselves contentment, that so their time and leisure might better serve them for the practice of zeal and devotion. . . .

Now since the fruitfulness or barrenness of the earth pro- 10 ceeds from the influence and disposition of the heavens, in the last place I dare accuse the material heavens as being guilty, conspiring, and together jointly tending to corruption. Scripture shall warrant me: "The heavens shall wax old as doth a garment" (Psalm 102, Verse 26). Reason and all human learning shall back me, for certain it is that the sun hath descended much lower by many degrees than he was in the time of King Ptolemy.[25] The same mathematical instruments, which agree together in all other dimensions, do undoubtedly prove the diversity. By virtue of perspective 20 glasses we have lately discerned spots and shadows in the moon;[26] and within our memory, in the year 1572, a true comet did appear in the eighth heaven,[27] which as it had a time of beginning, so had it a period and time of dissolving. And thus being mortal of ourselves, we dwell in houses of clay, the roof of this world as well as the foundations shall together be moved; for wherefore serves the diversity of seasons, the day and the night succeeding each other, summer and winter, the rising and setting of stars, the different and contrary motions, the various aspects and oppositions, but 30 that in some sort they partake of our nature, and shall have their part and portion with ours? . . .

⸢ From these and many other signs of universal decay, says Goodman, we must conclude that the world is near its end and that the final judgment is at hand. ⸣

I cannot nor dare not prescribe the day and hour of that judgment. Rather with patience I will wait on God's leisure, and with my assured hope will expect to see my Redeemer in His flesh, and in my flesh, so descending as He ascended; for herein we have the testimony of angels: "This Jesus which 40 is taken up from you into heaven shall so come as you have seen him go into heaven" (Acts 1.11), the same in nature, the same in power, the same in mercy, the same in true love and affection—Jesus the son of David, Jesus the son of Marie, who was the propitiation for our sins and shall come again in glory to judge both the quick and the dead. Yet sure I am that the time cannot be long absent, for all the signs of His coming do already appear. When the hangings and furniture are taken down it is a token that the king and the court are removing: nature, now beginning to decay, 50 seems to hasten Christ's coming. To let pass many strong presumptions of our divines concerning the approach of that day, these three proofs, drawn from natural reason, do easily induce me to believe it.

First, looking to the general decay of this world, which argues the approach of this judgment; secondly, to the great

preparation for fire, which must then serve for the execution of God's wrath; thirdly, the fit occasions seeming to hasten this judgment, etc. Most certain it is that if the world should continue many thousand years, and that we should suppose that nature would decay in such sort as we are able to prove by demonstrative evidence already she hath done, assuredly nature of herself, through her own weakness, would come to nothing and the world should not be able to supply men's necessities. Suppose this one kingdom, besides the general barrenness which hath befallen us, whereof we may justly complain, if we should commit the like waste in our woods as formerly we have done in this last forepassed age, assuredly we should be left so destitute of fuel, of houses, of shipping that within a short time our land would prove almost inhabitable; for such things as require a great growth wherein man cannot see the present fruits of his providence, husbandry, and labor for the most part, they are always neglected, and it lies not in the power of one age to recover herself. Thus out of the decay of nature we may almost expect a dissolution, as by the signs and symptoms we judge of a dangerous and desperate disease. Thus you may observe almost a like distance from the creation to the deluge, from the deluge to Christ, from Christ unto us, as God ordains everything according to rule, order, and measure. After fifteen generations expired, you shall always note in Scripture some great alteration and change.[28] St. Matthew was therefore called from the receipt of custom[29] to cast up this account in the genealogy of Christ, as it appears in his first chapter. Now at length in God's name what may we expect should befall us? Whatsoever concerns the kingdom of Shilo, *consummatum est*: it is already perfited.[30] We must not look for any further addition. That which remains, it is the sound of the trumpet, *ut consummetur seculum*: that the world may be destroyed by fire.

Secondly, fire shall be the second overthrow, this Scripture and reason confirms. Now certain it is that God, who hath

[25]Second-century astronomer and geographer of Alexandria whose hypothesis of a geocentric universe was being gradually displaced in Goodman's time by the Copernican system. Ptolemy was unrelated to the dynasty of Egyptian kings who bore the name.
[26]Learning of the primitive telescopes (*perspective glasses*) constructed by the Dutch opticians Jan Lippershey and Jacobus Melius, Galileo in 1609 contrived an instrument of his own that (with subsequent improvements) enabled him to see and report such marvels as the mountains of the moon and the satellites of Jupiter in *The Sidereal Messenger* (1610), a book that enjoyed immense success throughout western Europe.
[27]In 1572 the Danish astronomer Tycho Brahe discovered a new star in the constellation Cassiopeia and announced the event, with great effect, in his *De nova stella*. On the *eighth heaven* see *sphere* in the Glossary.
[28]Matthew (1.17), whose periodic chronology was influentially endorsed by St. Augustine (*The City of God*, XXII.30), separates such great pivotal events as Abraham's migration, the reign of David, the Babylonian captivity, and the birth of Christ by *fourteen* generations. [29]*Receipt of custom*: Matthew 9.9.
[30]Perfected, consummated.

first instituted nature, hath so ordained her as she may best serve to be an instrument to work His own ends and purposes, to show a conformity of the effects with the cause, thereby to manifest His own empire and rule which still He retains in the creatures; as likewise the obediential power whereunto the creatures are subject, that so may appear how absolute and powerful He is first to appoint the creatures, then how gracious and merciful He is to impart himself and to join with the creatures in the same action. Thus the watery constellations did then govern and rule when the world was overwhelmed with waters; now at this time and for a few hundred years yet to continue the fiery constellations shall have the predominancy; and therefore credible it is that within the compass of this time there shall happen the general combustion.

Thirdly, the dissolution of this world betokens a general punishment; the judgment accompanying hath reference to our transgressions, as in the first permission of sin appears the goodness of God (who can turn our sins to His glory, either for the manifestation of His mercy or justice), so in this great tolerating of sin appears God's patience and long suffering. But now our sins are come to a full ripeness; now is the harvest, and the weeds choke up the wheat, and therefore necessity seems to inforce and to hasten the approach of this judgment, that at length there might be a separation of both, though hitherto they have grown up together. Thus Christ's first coming in the flesh was to restore the decayed state of the Jews, for then He was born into this world when charity

was grown cold, the priesthood bought and sold for a price, the King's office extinguished, the tribe of Judah neglected, the synagogue divided into sects and schisms. And this is in some sort resembled by the barrenness of the earth, for He came in the winter season and He was born at midnight to argue the world's universal darkness and ignorance. So must it be for His second coming: He hath given us a watchword "that the Son of Man will come at an hour when He is not expected" (Luke 12, Verse 40). Now is that time when we do not expect Him; we never think of judgment, of hell, of fire, of damnation. Religion hath taken up wings and is returned to heaven from whence she descended. Men are now grown careless in their profession and live after a sensual manner like beasts; we are now grown to the height and top of all sin; our sins, our crying sins, now cry for vengeance, and therefore the time of His coming cannot be far absent. He will take the best opportunity, like a thief in the night. We may, then, expect Him when we do least expect Him. But I will leave this as being not so pertinent to my purpose, and grounded only upon conjectures, etc.

It is perhaps appropriate to leave Goodman dangling on his own "etc." As if reluctant to abandon such a cheerful theme, in the "Corollary" or coda of his book he rambles on for many pages more, but he has already "buried" man and nature, as he himself concedes, and his work is really done. "I have cast the heavens and the earth upon him, and together with man intombed the whole world."

George Hakewill [1578-1649]

from An Apology or Declaration of the Power and Providence of God in the Government of the World (1635)

THE PREFACE

Truth it is that this ensuing treatise was long since in my younger years begun by me for mine own private exercise and satisfaction, but afterward, considering not only the rarity of the subject and variety of the matter but withal that it made for the redeeming of a captivated truth, the vindicating of God's glory, the advancement of learning, and the honor of the Christian and reformed religion, by the advice and with the approbation and encouragement of such special friends whose piety, learning, and wisdom I well know and much reverence, I resolved (*permissu superiorum*[1] and none

otherwise) to make it public for the public good and the encountering of a public error, which may in some sort be equalled, if not preferred, before the quelling of some great monster. Neither do I take it to lie out of my profession, the principal mark which I aim at throughout the whole body of the discourse being an apologetical defence of the power and providence of God, His wisdom, His truth, His justice, His goodness and mercy; and besides, a great part of the book itself is spent in pressing theological reasons, in clearing doubts

AN APOLOGY...IN THE GOVERNMENT OF THE WORLD   [1]"With the permission of superiors."

arising from thence, in producing frequent testimonies from Scriptures, Fathers, Schoolmen, and modern divines in proving that Antichrist[2] is already come (from the writings of the Romanists themselves), in confirming the article of our faith touching the world's future and total consummation by fire and a day of final judgment from discourse of reason and the writings of the Gentiles,[3] and lastly by concluding the whole work with a pious meditation touching the uses which we may and should make of the consideration thereof, serving for a terror to some, for comfort to others, for admonition to all. And how other men may stand affected in reading I know not; sure I am that in writing, it often lifted up my soul in admiring and praising the infinite wisdom and bounty of the Creator in maintaining and managing His own work, in the government and preservation of the universe, which in truth is nothing else but (as the Schools speak) *continuata productio,* a continuated production; and often did it call to my mind those holy raptures of the Psalmist: "O Lord our Governor, how excellent is Thy name in all the world. . . ."[4]

He that shall narrowly observe the prints of the Almighty's footsteps, traced throughout this ensuing discourse, may not unjustly from thence collect both comfort and assurance, that as the heavens remain unchangeable, so doth the Church Triumphant in heaven; and as all things under the cope of heaven vary and change, so doth the Militant[5] here on earth: it hath its times and turns, sometimes flowing and again ebbing with the sea, sometimes waxing and again waning with the moon; which great light, it seems, the Almighty therefore set the lowest in the heavens and nearest the earth that it might daily put us in mind of the constancy of the one and inconstancy of the other, herself in some sort partaking of both, though in a different manner: of the one in her substance, of the other in the copy of her visage.

And if the moon thus change, and all things under the moon, why should we wonder at the change of monarchies and kingdoms, much less petty states and private families? They rise and fall and rise again and fall again, that no man might either too confidently presume because they are subject to continual alteration, or cast away all hope and fall to despair because they have their seasons and appointed times of returning again. . . .

I must confess that sometimes, looking steadfastly upon the present face of things both at home and abroad, I have often been put to a stand,[6] and staggered in mine opinion whether I were in the right or no; and perchance the state of my body and present condition in regard of those fair hopes I sometimes had served as false perspective glasses[7] to look through, but when again I abstracted[8] and raised my thoughts to an higher pitch and as from a vantage ground took a larger view, comparing time with time and things with thing and place with place, and considered myself as a member of the universe and a citizen of the world, I found that what was lost to one part was gained to another, and what was lost in one time was to the same part recovered in another; and so the balance by the divine providence overruling all kept upright. . . . O that men would therefore

praise the Lord for His goodness, and declare the wonders that He hath done for the children of men! Or at leastwise cry out in admiration with the Apostle, "O the depth of the riches both of the wisdom and knowledge of our God! How unsearchable are His paths, and His ways past finding out!"[9]

Yet the next way, in some measure, to find them out—so far as is possible for us poor worms here crawling in a mist upon the face of the earth—is, next the sacred oracles of supernatural and revealed truth, to study the great volume of the creatures[10] and the histories not only of our own but of foreign countries, and those not only of the present but more ancient times. . . . If, then, to make my party good and to wait upon divinity I have called in subsidiary aids from philosophers, historiographers, mathematicians, grammarians, logicians, poets, orators, soldiers, travelers, lawyers, physicians; and if I have in imitation of Tertullian, Cyprian, Eusebius, Augustine, Lactantius, Arnobius, Minutius[11] endeavored to cut the throats of the paynims[12] with their own swords and pierce them with their own quills, I hope no learned man or lover of learning will censure me for this. Philosophy and the arts I must account a part of mine own profession; and for physic and the laws, I have therein consulted the chief as well in this university[13] as out of it, of mine own acquaintance; nay, in history, the mathematics, and divinity itself I have not only had the approbation of the public professors therein for the main points in my book which concern their several professions, but some pieces I must acknowledge as received from them, which I have made bold to insert into the body of my discourse. Let no man think, then, that I maintain a paradox for ostentation of wit, or have written out of spleen, to gall any man in particular, nor yet to humor the present times. The times themselves, mine indisposition that way, and resolution to sit down content with my present fortunes, if they serve not to give others satisfaction therein yet do they fully to clear me to myself from any such aspersion. Yet thus much I hope I safely may say without suspicion of flattery, that by the goodness of God and our gracious sovereign under God we yet enjoy many great blessings which former ages did not; and were we thankful for these as we ought, and truly penitent for our excess in all kind of monstrous sins—which, above all, threatens our ruin—I nothing doubt but upon our return to our God by humiliation and newness of life He would soon dissolve the cloud which hangs

[2]The great antagonist (predicted in 2 John 2.18, 22) who, near the end of time, would appear and fill the world with wickedness until Christ's second coming, when he would be suppressed forever. [3]Pagans. [4]Psalm 8.1.
[5]*Church Triumphant. . .Militant:* see p. 555, n.36. [6]Baffled.
[7]Optical instruments. [8]Withdrew. [9]Romans 11.33.
[10]Text *creature.*
[11]*Tertullian. . .Minutius:* early Christian apologists who used their pagan learning to refute the enemies of the church. [12]Pagans.
[13]Oxford, from which Hakewill held four degrees (B.A. 1599, M.A. 1602, B.D. 1610, D.D. 1611). Hakewill's own college was Exeter, of which he was a fellow and a generous benefactor.

over us, and return unto us with the comfortable beams of His favor, and make us to return each to other with mutual embracements of affection and duty, and our armies and fleets to return with spoil and victory, and reduce again as golden and happy times as ever we or our forefathers saw. But if we still go on with an high hand and a stiff neck in our profaneness, our pride, our luxury, our uncharitableness, our unnatural divisions in Church and commonwealth, there needs no prophetical spirit to divine what will shortly become of us. . . . 10

If, then, we come short of that courage and valor which made our ancestors so renowned by sea and land, not only in France and Spain and the Netherlands, but in Palestina itself, sure it is not because the world declines but because our luxury increases, the most evident symptom of a declining state; for as all empires have risen to their greatness by virtue, and specially by sobriety and frugality, so is it clear that by vice, and specially by luxury (which of necessity draws on softness and cowardice) they have all again declined and come to nothing; and out of their ashes have others sprung 20 up, which likewise within a while—such a circulation there is in all things—have been turned into ashes again. . . .

Again, for matter of learning and knowledge if we come short of the ancients we need not impute it to Nature's decay: our own riot,[14] our idleness and negligence in regard of them will sufficiently discharge Nature and justly cast back the blame upon ourselves. . . . For a false and fond similitude it is of some, which they take up as a most witty and proper one, that we, being compared to the ancients, are as dwarfs upon the shoulders of giants. It is not so: 30 neither are we dwarfs nor they giants, but we are all of one stature save that we are lifted up somewhat higher by their means, conditionally there be found in us the same studiousness, watchfulness, and love of truth as was in them; which if they be wanting, then are we not dwarfs nor set on the shoulders of giants, but men of a competent stature groveling on the earth. . . .[15]

The common complaint is that we want time, but the truth is, *Non parum habemus temporis, sed multum perdimus:* we do not so much want as waste it, either *male agendo* or 40 *nihil agendo* or *aliud agendo*; either in doing naughtiness or nothing or impertinencies we do *bonas horas male collocare,* trifle out our precious hours in eating and drinking and sleeping and sporting and gaming and dressing our bodies, and then give out and persuade ourselves that Nature forsooth is decayed, that our bodies cannot endure that study which our predecessors did. And truly I think many justly complain of weak and crazy bodies, but withal that more have made them so by intemperance than study, or found them so by nature. Let us, then, lay the fault where it is, and accuse 50 ourselves, not Nature, or rather God under that name. . . .

Now for the work itself, I am well assured (as all other books and actions) it will be diversely censured as men stand diversely affected. If but three guests meet at a feast they will hardly accord in one dish, and truly I think that as men's fancies (could they be seen) would be found to differ more than their faces, so are their judgments more different than their tastes. But this common courtesy (due by the laws of civility and humanity) I shall crave (which I hope no ingenuous mind will deny me) that I be not condemned before I be understood. . . .

I have walked, I confess, in an untrodden path, neither can I trace the prints of any footsteps that have gone before me but only as it led them to some other way, thwarting and upon the by,[16] not directly. Some parts belonging to this discourse some have slightly handled, none thoroughly considered of the whole; which I speak not to derogate from their worth—it being *puerilis jactantiae accusando illustres viros suo nomini famam quaerere,* a childish kind of bragging to hunt after applause by contradicting famous men—but only to show that whiles they intended another thing they might happily in this be carried away with the common stream; for surely such a sweet harmony there is between all the members of this body,[17] such a coherence and mutual dependance betwixt all the links of this chain, that he who takes a view of the whole will easily grant that he might he deceived by looking upon some parts thereof.

Yet some perhance will conceive I might have delivered my mind with less expense of words and time; and truly I must acknowledge that *in multiloqui non deerit peccatum*: it cannot be but in speaking so much, somewhat should be spoken amiss. Yet withal it must be remembered that being to grapple with such a giantlike monster, I could not think him dead till I had his head off; and that which to some may seem superfluous or impertinent will happily by others be thought not unprofitable or unpleasant. The pains is mine, and if it be overdone, done I am sure it is; if I have said more than enough, enough is said to serve the turn.

And if any shall have a mind to publish anything against that I have written I shall desire it may be done fairly, not by sucking of the sores and flying over the sound parts, nor by nibbling upon the twigs and utmost branches, but by striking at the root or body of the tree, or at leastwise some of the principal limbs thereof; and in the mean season I say with St. Augustine, *Quisquis haec legit, ubi pariter certus est, pergat mecum; ubi periter haesitat, quaerat mecum; ubi errorem suum cognoscit, redeat ad me; ubi meum, revocet me:* whosoever thou art that reads this discourse, where thou art assured, go on with me; where thou art in doubt, search with me; where thou dost acknowledge thine error, return to me; where thou findest mine, recall me. And conclude with Lactantius: *Etiamsi nulli alii, nobis certe proderit, delectabit se conscientia, gaudebitque mens in veritatis se luce versari, quod est anima pabulum incredibili quadam jacunditate perfusum*: if this treatise profit none else, yet shall it me; my conscience shall comfort itself and my mind be refreshed in the light of truth, which is the food of the soul mixed with delight incredible.

[14]Dissipation.
[15]*For a false . . . earth*: Hakewill's translation of a long Latin passage (here omitted) from *De causis corruptarum artium* by the Spanish humanist Juan Luis Vives (1492–1540), a work anticipating Bacon's *Advancement of Learning* (1605).
[16]*Thwarting . . . by*: obliquely and accidentally. [17]The universe.

LIBER I. WHICH TREATS OF THIS PRETENDED
DECAY IN GENERAL, TOGETHER WITH SOME
PREPARATIVES THEREUNTO

CHAPTER II. OF THE REASONS INDUCING THE AUTHOR TO
THE WRITING AND PUBLISHING OF THIS DISCOURSE

SECTION 2. THE SECOND IS THE VINDICATING OF THE
CREATOR'S HONOR

As my first reason for the writing and publishing this discourse was for the redeeming of a captivated truth, so my second is for the vindicating of the Creator's honor, the reputation of His wisdom, His justice, His goodness, and His power, being all of them in my judgment by the opinion of Nature's decay not a little impeached and blemished. His wisdom for that[18] intending (as by the sacred oracles of His word He hath in sundry passages clearly manifested it) to put an end to the world by fire, it cannot, I think, be well conceived why he should ordain or admit such a daily, universal, and irrecoverable consumption in all the parts of Nature, which without fire or any other outward means would undoubtedly bring it to that final period.

His justice for that withdrawing from later ages that strength and ability of performing religious duties and practicing moral virtues which to the former He granted, yet to demand and expect no less from the later than He did from the former, what is it but to reap where He sowed not, to require as much of him that hath but five talents as of him that had ten, or to deal as Pharaoh did with the Israelites, still to exact the same task of brick and yet to withhold the wonted allowance of straw?[19] Neither can we with that confidence reprehend the reigning vices of the times if we cast the reason thereof not so much upon the voluntary malice and depravation of men's wills as upon the necessity of the times preordained by God; which upon the matter what is it but to lay the burden upon God, and to accuse Him that so we may free and excuse ourselves?

His bounty and goodness as if out of a niggardly and sparing disposition He envied the succeeding generations of the world that happiness which upon the preceding He freely and richly conferred; whereas I am rather of opinion that as in Holy Scripture, for the most part, He accepted and preferred the younger brother before the elder, and as Christ our Saviour turned the water into wine towards the end of the feast,[20] which far excelled that in the beginning; so the gifts and graces of God have been more plentifully poured out upon mankind in this later age of the world than ever since the first creation thereof. As was foretold by the prophet in the Old Testament[21] and remember by the apostle in the New: "And it shall come to pass in the last days," saith God, "I will pour out of my Spirit upon all flesh."[22]

Lastly, the reputation of His power is thereby most of all stained and wounded as if His treasury could at any time be emptied and drawn dry, as if He had but one blessing in store, or were forced to say with old Isaac when he had

blessed Jacob, "With corn and wine have I blessed him, and what shall I do now to thee, my son?"[23] No, no, His arm is not shortened, neither is His mighty power any way abated; yet they who thus complain of Nature's decay, what do they but implicitly impeach and accuse His power? Which indeed is nothing else but *Natura naturans* (as the School phrase is), active Nature, and the creature the workmanship thereof, *Natura naturata*, Nature passive. That which the Samaritans ignorantly and blasphemously spake of Simon Magus[24] may properly and truly be spoken of Nature, that it is "the great power of God" or "the power of the great God," as is divinely observed by the witty Scaliger against Cardan in that exercitation which in its front bears this inscription opposed to Cardan's assertion[25]: *Non ex fatigatione mundum solutum iri,* that the world shall not dissolve by being tired, *quasi Natura* (saith he) *sit asinus ad molas, non autem Dei Optimi Maximi potesta, quae eodem nata gubernat infinito quo creavit:* we may not conceive that Nature is as an ass wasted and wearied out at the mill, but the power of the mighty God which governs all things with the same infinite command wherewith they were created. And with him accords Valesius,[26] discoursing of the world's end towards the end of his book *De sacra philosophia: Quae a Deo ipso per se ac sine causa secunda compacta sunt, non possunt ab alia causa solvi, sed solum ab eo ipso aquo unt coagmentata:* those things which are made of God himself immediately by himself without the concurrence of second causes cannot be unmade by any inferior cause, but by Him alone by whom they were first made. And again, *Certe ita est, virtutem divinam apponi necesse est ut deleatur quod Deus ipse fecit:* there needs no less than a divine power for the abolishing of that which the Deity itself hath wrought; which he seems to have borrowed from Plato *In Timaeo,* where he thus speaks of the world: *Ita apte cohaeret ut dissolvi nullo modo queat, nisi ab eodem a quo est colligatus:* so proportionably doth each part answer other that it is indissoluble, but only from His hands who first framed it.[27] As, then, Almighty God created all things of nothing by the power of His word, so doth He still uphold them, and will till the dissolution of all things in their essences, faculties, and operations by the "word of His power, reaching from one end to the other mightily, and disposing all things sweetly."[28] Indeed, with the works of man it is not so: when he hath employed about them all the cunning and cost and care that may be, he can neither preserve them

18Because. 19Exodus 5.7–8. 20John 2.1–10. 21Joel 2.19.
22Acts 2.17. 23Genesis 27.37.
24"This man is the great power of God" (Acts 8.10).
25Hakewill refers to the *Exercitationes* wherein the great Italian humanist Julius Caesar Scaliger (1485–1558) commented on *De subtilitate rerum* (1551), a treatise on scientific speculation by the skeptical Jerome Cardan (1501–76).
26The allusion is probably to Henri de Valois, seigneur d'Orcé (1603–76), an eminent French scholar who edited Eusebius and other ecclesiastical historians.
27The reference seems to be to Plato's *Timaeus,* Sect. 31–32.
28*As, then...sweetly:* a conflation of Hebrews 1.3 and the Apocryphal Wisdom of Solomon 8.1.

nor himself; both they and he molder away and return to their dust. "But I know," saith the Preacher, "that whatsoever God doth, it shall be forever; nothing can be put to it, nor anything taken from it."[29] And the Son of Sirach: "He garnished His works forever, and in His hand are the chief of them unto all generations; they neither labor nor are weary, nor cease from their works; none of them hindereth another, and they shall never disobey His word."[30]

CHAPTER III. THE CONTROVERSY TOUCHING THE WORLD'S DECAY STATED, AND THE METHOD HELD THROUGH THIS ENSUING TREATISE PROPOSED

SECTION 6. THE PRECEDENTS OF THIS CHAPTER SUMMARILY RECOLLECTED, AND THE METHOD OBSERVED IN THE ENSUING TREATISE PROPOSED

Now briefly and summarily to recollect and as it were to wind up into one clew or bottom[31] what hath more largely 10 been discoursed through this chapter, I hold, first, that the heavenly bodies are not at all, either in regard of their substance, motion, light, warmth, or influence, in the course of Nature impaired or subject to any impairing or decay. Secondly, that all individuals under the cope of heaven, mixed of the elements, are subject to a natural declination and dissolution. Thirdly, that the quantity of the elements themselves is subject to impairing in regard of their parts, though not of their entire bodies. Fourthly, that the air and earth and water are at diverse seasons diversely affected, sometimes for 20 the better, sometimes for the worse, and that either by some special favor or judgment of God or by some cause in nature, secret or apparent. Fiftly, that the several kinds of beasts, of plants, of fishes, of birds, of stones, of metals are as many in number as at the creation, and every way in Nature as vigorous as at any time since the flood. Sixthly and lastly, that the manners, the wits, the health, the age, the strength, and stature of men do daily vary, but so as by a vicissitude and revolution they return again to their former points from which they declined, and again decline and again return by 30 alternative and interchangeable course. *Eat hic rerum in se remeantium orbis, quamdiu erit ipse orbis*:[32] this circle and ring of things returning always to their principles will never cease as long as the world lasts.

> *Repetunt proprios quaeque recursus*
> *Redituque suo singula gaudent;*
> *Nec manet ulli traditus ordo*
> *Nisi quod fini junxerit ortum*
> *Stabilemque sui fecerit orbem.*[33]

> To their first spring all things are backward bound, 40
> And everything in it return delighteth;
> Th' order once settled can in naught be found
> But what the end unto the birth united,
> And of itself doth make a constant round.

And consequently there is no such universal and perpetual decay in the frame of the creatures as is commonly imagined, and by some strongly maintained.

The method which I propose is first to treat hereof in general, that so a clear way and easier passage may be opened to the particulars; then of the heavens, as being highest in situation and the noblest in outward glory and duration, as also in their efficacy and universality of operation, and therefore doth the prophet rightly place them next God himself in the order of causes: "It shall come to pass in that day, saith the Lord, that I will hear the heavens, and they shall hear the earth, and the earth shall hear the corn and the wine and the oil, and they shall hear Jezreel."[34] From that we may descend to the four elements, which as a musical instrument of four strings is both tuned and touched by the hand of heaven; and in the next place those bodies which are mixed and tempered of these elements offer themselves to our consideration, whether they be without life (as stones and metals), or have the life of vegetation only (as plants), or both of vegetation and sense (as beasts and birds and fishes); and in the last place man presents himself upon this theater as being created last, though first intended, the master of the whole family and chief commander in this great house, nay the masterpiece, the abridgment, the map, and model of the universe. And in him we will examine this pretended decay first in regard of age and length of years, secondly in regard of strength and stature, thirdly in regard of wits and arts, and fourthly and lastly in regard of manners and conditions, to which all that is in man is or should be finally referred, as all that is in the world is, under God, finally referred to man. And because it is not sufficient to possess our own fort without the dismantling and demolishing of our enemies, a principal care is to be had throughout the whole work to answer, if not all, at least the principal of those objections which I have found to weigh most with the adverse part. And in the last place, lest I should any way be suspected to shake or undermine the ground of our Christian religion, or to weaken the article of our belief touching the consummation of the world by teaching that it decays not, to wipe off that aspersion I will endeavor to prove the certainty thereof, not so much by Scripture (which no Christian can be ignorant of) as by force of reason and the testimony of heathen writers; and finally I will conclude with an exhortation grounded thereupon for the stirring of men up to a preparation of themselves against that day which shall not only end the world but judge their actions and dispose of the everlasting estate of their persons.

CHAPTER IV. TOUCHING THE WORLD'S DECAY IN GENERAL

SECTION 5. THE SEVENTH AND LAST GENERAL ARGUMENT THAT THE SEEDS OF DECAY WERE NOT INFUSED INTO THE WORLD BEFORE THE FALL, NOR AFTER IT, AND CONSEQUENTLY NOT AT ALL

If the decay of the world be an effect of the fall of man and a punishment of sin, as some would have it, it could not be created subject to decay except we should make the effect

---

[29]Ecclesiastes 3.14.
[30]The Apocryphal Book of Sirach 16.27–28.   [31]Ball or skein.
[32]*Eat...orbis:* Justus Lipsius, *De constantia,* I.xvi. *Eat:* text *Erit.*
[33]*Repetunt...orbem:* Boethius, *Philosophiae consolationis,* III.ii. *Quaeque:* text *cuncta.*   [34]Joel 2.21–22. *Jezreel:* text *Israel.*

before the cause and the punishment before the offence, inasmuch as the world was built and furnished before man was made, and consequently before he had sinned, by which means it cannot be but that even in the state of integrity before his fall he must of necessity actually suffer as a sinner; which how it can stand with the justice of the Creator I must profess that for mine own part I cannot understand. Besides, when Almighty God had finished the work of the creation, He saw and pronounced both the whole and all the parts thereof to be exceeding good, which could not be 10 if He had originally sown in it the seeds and principles of corruption. For as St. Augustine speaks in his book *De natura boni* (*Caput*[35] iv), *Ipsa corrupta in quantum natura est, bona est; in quantum corrupta est, mala est.*[36] And if it be evil as it is corrupted and cannot be from God as it is evil, neither can it be from Him as it is corrupted, from whom, being goodness itself, nothing can flow but what is good. He being most pure and incorruptible in himself can no more be the author of corruption than He can of sin; both which He permitted, and according to His excellent wisdom and power 20 ordereth both, but directly and for themselves ordained neither; He being so good and so just as He would not so much as have permitted either had He not withal been so wise and so powerful as out of both to draw some good for the advancement of His own glory, the advantage of His children that serve Him, and the confusion of such as rebel against Him. . . .

Now for the second opinion, which is that this decay came in after the fall by making it the just punishment of sin: it cannot stand with the former position of the inbred and nat- 30 ural principles of corruption, nor yet with that other assertion that it happens not from any foreign or accidental cause, inasmuch as sin in regard of the world (men and angels only excepted) can be none other than a foreign cause, nor yet other than accidental as it is opposed to necessary; and if, then, this decay be not introduced by any foreign or accidental cause, how can sin be the cause thereof? Or if it be only occasioned by sin, what other cause shall we find out of power sufficient to alter and deprave those principles of Nature which the Author of her had planted in her? 40

Here the Manichees[37] would have recourse to their idol, the god of evil; but the truth is that no created power (as all power is created save only that of the Creator himself), were all the power of men and devils and angels combined in one, is of force sufficient any way to change or alter, much less to abolish or utterly corrupt, the principles of Nature. True it is that men and angels being the only rational creatures that God made, inbued with understanding and freedom of will, have both corrupted their own ways and feel the smart thereof, and the other creatures by the abuse of them; but 50 neither of them have or possibly can alter the fundamental laws of Nature in themselves, much less in the other creatures; from whence it inevitably follows that if upon the fall of man the principles of Nature be corrupted, they are undoubtedly corrupted by the Author of them, there being none other power of sufficient ability to produce such an effect. . . .

LIBER III. OF THE PRETENDED DECAY OF MANKIND IN REGARD OF AGE AND DURATION, OF STRENGTH AND STATURE, OF ARTS AND WITS[38]

CHAPTER VI. CONTAINING A DISCOURSE IN GENERAL THAT THERE IS NO SUCH UNIVERSAL AND PERPETUAL DECAY IN THE POWERS OF THE MIND OR IN THE ARTS AND SCIENCES AS IS PRETENDED

SECTION 2. THAT THERE IS BOTH IN WITS AND ARTS, AS IN ALL THINGS BESIDES, A KIND OF CIRCULAR PROGRESS AS WELL IN REGARD OF PLACES AS TIMES

There is, it seems, both in wits and arts, as in all things besides, a kind of circular progress: they have their birth, their growth, their flourishing, their failing, their fading, and within a while after their resurrection and reflourishing again. The arts flourished for a long time among the Persians, the Chaldeans, the Egyptians; and therefore is Moses said to be learned in all the wisdom of the Egyptians,[39] who, well knowing their own strength, were bold to object to the Grecians that they were still children, as neither having the knowledge of antiquity nor the antiquity of knowledge. But afterwards the Grecians got the start of them and grew so excellent in all kind of learning that the rest of the world in regard of them were reputed barbarians, which reputation of wisdom they held even to the Apostles' times. "I am a debtor," saith St. Paul, "both to the Grecians and to the barbarians, both to the wise and to the unwise."[40] And again: "The Jews require a sign, and the Grecians seek after wisdom."[41] By reason whereof they relished not the simplicity of the Gospel, it seeming foolishness unto them; and in the seventeenth of the Acts the philosophers of Athens (sometimes held the most famous university in the world) out of an opinion of their own great learning scorned St. Paul and his doctrine, terming him a sower of words, a very babbler, trifler;[42] yet not long after this these very Grecians declined much, and themselves (whether through their own inclination or by reason of their bondage under the Turk,[43] the common enemy both of religion and learning, I cannot determine) are now become so strangely barbarous that their knowledge is converted into a kind of affected ignorance, as is their liberty into contented slavery; yet after the loss both of their empire and learning they still

[35]Chapter.

[36]*Ipsa...est*: although corruption is evil in itself, it is good insofar as it pertains to nature (for nature is the work of God).

[37]Members of a heretical sect founded by the Persian prophet Manes (ca. 215–75), who taught a rigid dualism of good and evil.

[38]Mental prowess, intelligence.

[39]Acts 7.22. Like most such panoramic views of history in the Renaissance, Hakewill's survey of the progress of civilization derives ultimately from the vision of the four great empires—Babylonian (Chaldean), Assyrian (Persian), Grecian, and Roman—as expounded in Daniel 7.4–7.   [40]Romans 1.14.

[41]1 Corinthians 1.22.   [42]Acts 17.32.

[43]The Ottoman empire. See pp. 837 ff. for Richard Knolles' assessment of the Turkish peril.

retained some spark of their former wit and industry.

> *Ingenium velox, audacia perdita, sermo*
> *Promptus et Isaeo torrentior. Ede quid illum*
> *Esse putas, quemvis hominem secum attulit ad nos:*
> *Grammaticus, rhetor, geometres, pictor, aliptes,*
> *Augur, schoenobates, medicus, magus; omnia novit*
> *Graeculus esuriens; in coelum iusseris, ibit.*[44]

> Quick witted, wondrous bold, well spoken, than
> Isaeus fluenter, tell who all men
> Brought with himself: a soothsayer, a physician,
> Magician, rhetorician, geometrician,
> Grammarian, painter, ropewalker, all knows
> The needy Greek. Bid go to heaven, he goes.

But now they wholly delight in ease, in shades, in dancing, in drinking, and for the most part no farther endeavor the enriching either of their minds or purses than their bellies compel them.

The lamp of learning being thus near extinguished in Greek,

> *In Latium spretis Academic migrat Athenis.*

> Athens forsaken by philosophy,
> She forthwith traveled into Italy.

It began to shine afresh in Italy near about the time of the birth of Christ, there being a general peace through the world, and the Roman Empire being fully settled and established, poets, orators, philosophers, historians never more excellent. From thence this light spread itself over Christendom and continued bright till the inundation of the Goths and Huns and Vandals, who ransacked libraries and defaced almost all the monuments of antiquity, insomuch as that lamp seemed again to be put out by the space of almost a thousand years; and had longer so continued had not first Mensor,[45] King of Africa and Spain, raised up and spurred forward the Arabian wits to the restauration of good letters by proposing great rewards and encouragements unto them. And afterwards Petrarch, a man of a singular wit and rare natural endowments, opened such libraries as were left undemolished, beat off the dust from the motheaten books, and drew into the light the best authors. *Literas a multo aevo misere sepultas e Gothicis sepulchris excitavit:* he raised up to life good learning from the sepulchers of the Goths, having been buried by the space of many ages.

He was seconded by Boccace and John of Ravenna, and soon after by Aretine, Philephus, Valla, Poggius, Omnibonus, Vergerius, Blondus, and others. And those again were followed by Aeneas Silvius, Angelus Politianus, Hermolaus Barbarus, Marsilius Ficinus, and that Phoenix of learning, Johannes Picus, Earl of Mirandula;[46] who, as appears in the entrance of his *Apology,* proposed openly at Rome nine hundred questions in all kind of faculties to be disputed,[47] inviting all strangers thither from any part of the known world, and offering himself to bear the charge of their travel both coming and going and during their abode there. So as he deservedly received that epitaph which after his death was bestowed on him:

> *Iohannes jacet hic Mirandula, caetera norunt*
> *Et Tagus et Ganges forsan et antipodes.*

Here lies Mirandula; Tagus the rest doth know,
And Ganges and perhaps th' antipodes also.

And rightly might that be verified of him which Lucretius sometimes wrote of Epicurus, his master:

> *Hic genus humanum ingenio superavit, et omnes*
> *Praestrinxit stellas, exortus ut aethereus sol.*

> In wit all men he hath far overgone,
> Eclipsing them like to the rising sun.

Yet himself, in one of his epistles, gives this testimony to Angelus Politianus, his contemporary: *Quod si plures essent tales, non haberent haec saecula cur inviderent antiquitati:* had we some more such, these times need not envy antiquity.

This path being thus beaten out by these heroical spirits, they were backed by Rodolphus Agricola, Reuchlin, Melanchthon, Joachimus Camerarius, Wolphangus Lazius, Beatus Rhenanus (Almains);[48] the great Erasmus (a Netherlander); Ludovicus Vives (a Spaniard); Bembus, Sadoletus,

[44]*Ingenium...ibit:* Juvenal, *Satires,* III.73–78.

[45]Mansur (712?–75), enlightened caliph of Baghdad who sponsored the translation of Greek and Latin classics into Arabic.

[46]*Boccace...Mirandula:* Apart from such authentic luminaries as Petrarch, Boccaccio, Erasmus, and More, Hakewill's helter-skelter lists of Renaissance notables commemorate worthy but mainly forgotten men. John of Ravenna was probably Giovanni de Malpaghinsis (d. 1417), a pupil of Petrarch who became a professor of rhetoric at Florence; Aretine was not the notorious satirist Pietro Aretino but Leonardo Aretino (Leonardo Bruni, d. 1444), who was famous for his Latin translations of Plutarch, Plato, Aristotle, and other Greek writers; Philephus (Francesco Felelfo, d. 1481) taught Greek at Florence and Milan; Lorenzo Valla (d. 1457) translated Homer and the Greek historians into Latin; Poggius (Braccolini Poggio, d. 1459) was a papal secretary indefatigable in searching out ancient manuscripts; Leonicenus Omnibonus (b. ca. 1420) produced treatises on rhetoric and grammar and also elaborate commentaries on many Latin writers; Vergerius (Pietro Vergerio, d. ca. 1420) taught at Padua and wrote a life of Petrarch; Blondus (Flavio Biondo, d. 1463) was another papal secretary noted for his erudition as a historian; Aeneas Silvius (Enea Silvio de Piccolomini, d. 1464), was an accomplished ecclesiastical politician and man of letters who died as Pope Pius II; Angelus Politianus (Angelo Poliziano, d. 1494) enjoyed immense prestige as a sort of writer in residence at the court of Lorenzo de' Medici; Hermolaus Barbarus (Ermalao Barbaro, d. 1471) was a belletristic bishop of Treviso; Marsilius Ficinus (Marsilio Ficino, d. 1499), head of the Florentine Academy founded by the elder Cosimo de' Medici, influentially translated Plato and the Neoplatonists; and his famous protégé Johannes Picus (Count Giovanni Pico della Mirandola, d. 1494) was a prodigy and polymath who dazzled his contemporaries.

[47]In 1486 Pico posted a list of nine hundred questions (in logic, ethics, theology, mathematics, etc.) that he undertook to defend publicly against all adversaries.

[48]*Rodolphus...(Almains):* Hakewill's list of northern humanists (*Almains,* Germans) includes Rodolphus Agricola (Roelof Huysman, d. 1485), a Dutch scholar who taught Greek at Heidelberg; Johann Reuchlin (d. 1522), the most eminent Hebraist of his generation; Melanchthon (Philipp Schwarzert, d. 1560), a humanist and reformer closely associated with Luther; Joachim Camerarius (d. 1574), a reformer whose *Epistolae familiares* vividly describe his troubled times; Wolfgang Lazius (d. 1565), a learned physician

Eugubinus[49] (Italians); Turnebus, Muretus, Ramus, Pythaeus, Budaeus, Amyot, Scaliger[50] (Frenchmen); Sir Thomas More and Linacre[51] (Englishmen). . . . And it is worth the observing that about this time the slumbering drowsy spirit of the Grecians began again to be revived and awakened in Bessarion, Gemistus, Trapezontius, Gaza, Argyropylus, Calcondilas,[52] and others. Nay, those very northern nations which before had given the greatest wound to learning began now, as by way of recompence, to advance the honor of it by the fame of their studies, as Olaus Magnus, Holsterus, Tycho Brahe, Hemingius[53] (Danes); Hosius, Frixius, Crummerus (Polonians).[54] But the number of those worthies who, like so many sparkling stars, have since through all Christendom succeeded and some of them exceeded these in learning and knowledge is so infinite that the very recital of their names were enough to fill whole volumes. And if we descend to a particular examination of the several professions, arts, sciences, and manufactures we shall surely find the prediction of the divine Seneca accomplished: *Multa venientis aevi populus ignota nobis sciet:*[55] the people of future ages shall come to the knowledge of many things unknown to us. And that of Tacitus most true: *nec omnia apud priores meliora, imitanda posteris tulit sed nostra quoque aetas multa laudis et artium imitanda posteris tulit:*[56] neither were all things in ancient times better than ours, but our age hath left unto posterity many things worthy praise and imitation. Ramus goes further, and perchance warrantably enough: *majorem doctorum hominum et operum proventum saeculo uno vidimus, quam totis antea quotuordecim seculis majores nostri viderant:*[57] we have seen within the space of one age a more plentiful crop of learned men and works than our predecessors saw in fourteen next going before.

I will conclude this section with the memorable words of Sir Thomas Bodley, my honored kinsman, and the renowned founder of our public library, taken from a letter of his to Sir Francis Bacon upon occasion of his *Advancement of Learning,* sent by Sir Francis to Sir Thomas to be perused and censured by him before it was published[58]: "I do not hold it an erroneous conceit to think of every science that as now they are professed, so they have been before in all precedent ages, though not in all places alike nor at all times alike in one and the same, but according to the changes and turnings of times with a more exact and plain or with a more rude and obscure kind of teaching. And if the question should be asked what proof I have of it, I have the doctrine of Aristotle and of the deepest learned clerks of whom we have any means to have any notice, that as there is of every other thing, so there is of sciences *ortus et interitus.*[59] Which is also the meaning, if I should expound it, of *nihil novum est sub sole;*[60] and is as well to be applied to *facta* as *dicta, ut nihil neque dictum neque factum quod non et dictum et factum prius.*[61] I have farther for my warrant that famous complaint of Solomon to his son against the infinite making of books in his time,[62] or which in all congruity it must needs be understood that a very great part were observations and instructions in all kind of literature, and of those there is not so much as one petty pamphlet (only some parcels of the Bible excepted) remaining to posterity. As, then, there was

not in like manner any footing to be found of millions of authors that were long before Solomon, and yet we must give credit to that which he affirmed; that whatsoever was then or had been before, it could never be truly pronounced of it, 'Behold, this is new!' "[63]

best known for his massive study of the migrations of nations and origin of languages (1557); and Beatus Rhenanus (d. 1547), a close friend of Erasmus whose *Rerum Germanicarum libri tres* (1531) is a monument of German historiography.

[49]*Bembus. . . Eugubinus*: Bembus (Pietro Bembo, d. 1547), a fastidious writer in both Latin and Italian (*Gli Asolani* and *Prose della Volgar Lingua*), was created a cardinal in 1529; Sadoletus (Jacopo Sadoleto, d. 1547) was an erudite cardinal active at the Council of Trent; Eugubinus (Girolamo Accoramboni, d. 1537)—called Eugubio or Gubio from his birthplace—was an eminent writer on medical subjects who served as private physician to Pope Leo X.

[50]*Turnebus. . . Scaliger*: Adrianus Turnebus (Adrian Turnèbe, d. 1565) was a prolific Hellenist praised by Montaigne as "the most polished soul in the world"; Muretus (Marc Antoine Muret, d. 1585) was a French scholar who became professor of civil law in Rome and wrote commentaries on many classical authors; Pythaeus (Pierre Pithou, d. 1596) was a jurist and scholar who edited Juvenal and Persius as well as *Leges Visigothorum* (1579) and the *Capitula* of Charlemagne; Budaeus (Guillaume Budé, d. 1540) was a friend of Erasmus instrumental in founding the Collège de France; Jacques Amyot (d. 1593), whose great translation of Plutarch's *Lives* (1559) was the basis of Sir Thomas North's even greater English version (1579), was bishop of Auxerre; Julius Caesar Scaliger (d. 1558) and his son Joseph Justus (d. 1609) were both internationally famed for their many works of scholarship.

[51]*Linacre*: Sir Thomas Linacre (d. 1524), an influential spokesman for the so-called New Learning in early Tudor England, was a founder of the College of Physicians (1518) and a translator of Galen.

[52]*Bessarion. . . Calcondilas*: Johannes Bessarion (d. 1472), a Greek archbishop who became a cardinal in the Roman Catholic Church, translated Aristotle; Georgius Gemistus Pletho (d. ca. 1450), a Greek ecclesiastic who attended the Council of Florence (1438), advanced the knowledge of Plato's work in Italy; Trapezontius (George of Trebizond, d. 1486) taught Greek at Venice and translated many Greek classics into Latin; Theodore Gaza (d. ca. 1478), a refugee Greek scholar in Italy, wrote a grammar of his language; Joannes Argyropylus (d. ca. 1490) taught Greek at Florence and Rome and translated Aristotle into Latin; Calcondilas (Demetrius Chalcondyles, d. 1511) was a protégé of Cardinal Bessarion who taught at Padua, Florence, and Milan.

[53]*Olaus. . . Hemingius*: Nicolas Olahus or Olaus (d. 1568), a Hungarian scholar who became archbishop of Strigonia, wrote a history of Attila the Hun; Gaspar Holsterus was the editor of a treatise on prosody (1544) by Johann van der Varen; Tycho Brahe (d. 1601) was a celebrated Danish astronomer; Hemingius (Niels Hemmingsen) was a prolific writer on theological subjects, several of whose biblical commentaries (for example, *A Postil or Exposition of the Gospels,* 1569) were translated into English.

[54]*Hosius. . . (Polonians)*: Hakewill's list of learned Poles (*Polonians*) makes problems for the annotator. Stanilaus Hosius or Hozjusz (d. 1579), author of *Confessio fidei Christianae Catholicae* (1551), was a Polish cardinal who served as delegate to the Council of Trent; Frixius was probably Johann Fries (or Frisini, d. 1565) once remembered as author of a Latin-German dictionary (1541) and a translation of Hesiod (1548); but Crummerus must be assigned to the illustrious unknown.

LIBER IV. OF THE PRETENDED DECAY IN MATTER OF MANNERS, TOGETHER WITH A LARGE PROOF OF THE FUTURE CONSUMMATION OF THE WORLD, FROM THE TESTIMONIES OF THE GENTILES, AND THE USES WHICH WE ARE TO DRAW FROM THE CONSIDERATION THEREOF

CHAPTER XIII. THAT THE WORLD SHALL HAVE AN END BY FIRE AND BY IT BE ENTIRELY CONSUMED

SECTION 1. THAT THE WORLD SHALL HAVE AN END IS A POINT SO CLEAR IN CHRISTIAN RELIGION THAT IT NEEDETH NOT TO BE PROVED FROM THE PRINCIPLES THEREOF, NEITHER IS HE WORTHY THE NAME OF A CHRISTIAN WHO MAKETH ANY DOUBT OF IT

Having now by God's assistance done with mine *Apology* of His providence in the preservation of the world, lest I should seem thereby to undermine or weaken the article of our faith touching the world's end, it remains that according to promise I endeavor to confirm it, not so much from Scriptures which no true Christian can doubt of; and besides the passages thereof to this purpose, specially in the New Testament, are so many and clear as to be ignorant of them were stupidity no less gross than to deny them profane impiety. In this chapter, then, I will propose three things to 10 myself: first, to prove by the testimony of the Gentiles that the world shall have an end. Secondly, that it shall have an end by fire. Thirdly and lastly, that it shall by fire be totally and entirely consumed. That the world shall have an end is as clear in Christianity as that there is a sun in the firmament; and therefore, whereas there can hardly be named any other article of our faith which some heretics have not presumed to impugn or call into question, yet to my remembrance I never met with any who questioned this; and though at this day many and eager be the differences 20 among Christians in other points of religion, yet in this they all agree and ever did, that the world shall have an end, and that there shall be a resurrection from the dead, and a day of judgment. And surely as by the event of many things already fallen out we are sure that was true which the prophets and apostles foretold of them, so are we as certain that all other

things and this in particular shall come to pass which they have likewise foretold, though happily we cannot set down the time or manner of their event.[64] And inasmuch as we who now live have seen the accomplishment of many prophesies foretold by the penmen of Holy Writ which our forefathers saw not, if we steadfastly believe not the fulfilling of those which are yet to come in their due time we shall thereby be made the more guilty and the less excusable before God. Howsoever, if we believe (as we all pretend) the Scriptures to be the lively oracles of God and to have been indited by the divine and sacred inspiration of the Holy Ghost, we cannot but withal believe that the consummation of the world shall most undoubtedly in due time, though to us most uncertain, be accomplished. Now as the clear light of this truth hath by God's grace so brightly shined among Christians that except they wilfully shut their eyes against it they cannot but apprehend and embrace it, so did it appear to the Jews, though not in so conspicuous a manner; yea, some sparks of this truth have been scattered even among the Gentiles themselves, so as it was a shame unpardonable for us Christians not to acknowledge it, or so much as once to doubt of it.

[55]*Multa . . . sciet*: Naturalium quaestionum, VII.31.
[56]*Nec . . . tulit*: Annals, III.55. *Multa* and *posteris* are omitted in the text.
[57]*Majorem . . . viderant*: Scholarum mathematicarum libri unus et trigenta, "Prefatio." Quatuordecim seculis: text *14*.
[58]Sir Thomas Bodley (1545–1613)—whose precise relationship with Hakewill is uncertain—was an English diplomat and scholar who began the formation of the famous Bodleian Library at Oxford in 1598 and endowed it in 1611. In sending Sir Thomas the second copy of his *Advancement of Learning* (see p. 389)—the first having gone to King James, to whom the work was dedicated—Bacon said that "you, having built an ark to save learning from deluge, deserve propriety in any new instrument or engine whereby learning should be improved or advanced."
[59]"Rise and fall."
[60]"There is no new thing under the sun" (Ecclesiastes 1.9).
[61]*Facta . . . prius*: it is as applicable to things done as to things spoken, for there is nothing said or done that has not been said or done before.
[62]*Complaint . . . time*: "Of making many books there is no end; and much study is a weariness of the flesh" (Ecclesiastes 12.12).
[63]*Behold . . . new*: Ecclesiastes 1.10. [64]Outcome.

Robert Burton [1577-1640]

Burton said he "never traveled but in map and card," but his reading took him through a universe of books. The fourth of nine children of an "ancient" Leicestershire family, he matriculated at Brasenose College, Oxford, in 1593, but not long after, it would seem, he fell a victim to the malady that became his lifelong study. By 1599 he was sufficiently recovered to transfer to Christ

Church College, where he finally took his first degree at the age of twenty-five. The "silent, sedentary, solitary, private" life of Oxford was clearly what he needed. Having proceeded to the M.A. degree in 1605 and the B.D. in 1614, he was perhaps unable and almost surely unwilling to confront the outer world, and so he stayed at Christ Church, as tutor and librarian, for the remainder of his life.

It was a life so uneventful that most of it is unrecorded. In 1605 he had a hand in *Alba*, a lost pastoral play which when performed before King James at Oxford almost drove the guest of honor from the room, and the next year he wrote the lively *Philosophaster*, which in 1618 was revised for presentation at his college. Such widely spaced events tell us nothing of the man, if course, but we know by his own testimony that he was proud of his connection with such a "royal and ample foundation" as Christ Church College, that he read omnivorously "but to little purpose for want of a good method," that although he thought but poorly of his major work (" 'tis not worth the reading") he was pleased by its success, and that he looked upon himself as a "mere spectator" in a world beset by "fools and madmen." He must have been eccentric, but he was not a misanthrope. There were some who thought him very odd, said Anthony Wood, but those "who knew him well" admired his candor and his wit.

His later years were no doubt given to revising and expanding the *Anatomy* that had first appeared in 1621, but he was not entirely cut off from the world. In 1616 the dean and chapter of Christ Church named him to the nearby vicarage of St. Thomas; between 1624 and 1631 Frances, Countess Dowager of Essex, bestowed on him the living of Waleby in his native Leicestershire; and sometime after 1630 George Lord Berkeley (to whom, as *honoratissimo domino*, Burton had inscribed his *magnum opus*) gave him yet another benefice. According to Wood, Burton's death was not without a trace of scandal, for he "paid his last debt to nature" so near the time he had predicted that certain Oxford scholars said "rather than there should be a mistake in the calculation he sent up his soul to heaven thro' a slip about his neck." Appropriately, neither he nor his beloved books left Oxford: he was buried in the cathedral of his college, and most of the books were given to the Bodleian.

Although Burton as a writer was a late beginner, having found his proper subject he stayed with it until the end. First published as an anonymous octavo in 1621, *The Anatomy of Melancholy* was so successful that, as Thomas Fuller said, "scarce any book of philology in our land hath in so short a time passed so many impressions." It was greatly enlarged and reissued as a folio in 1624, and new editions—each of them expanded—followed in 1628, 1632, and 1638. The fifth edition of 1638 was, of course, the last that Burton supervised, but he left an annotated copy whose "several considerable additions by his own hand" were duly worked into the sixth (1651).

Despite its staggering dimensions, the *Anatomy* reveals a careful structure. Of its three "partitions" (each of which is organized into "sections," "members," and "subsections"), the first explores the causes, symptoms, and prognostics of melancholy; the second its cure; and the third (on love and religion) the two main forms of the disease. Moreover, there are now and then "digressions" that serve as vast appoggiaturas to the major theme.

The work bristles with editorial problems, one of which is textual. Although Burton said from time to time—for example, in the preface to the third (1628) edition—that his book had reached its final form, he not only persisted with his alterations and expansions through the fifth (1638) but, as we have noted, left others for the sixth. "Although this be a sixth edition," he conceded in the posthumous printing of 1651,

> in which I should have been more accurate, corrected all those former escapes, yet it was *magni laboris opus*, so difficult and tedious, that as carpenters do find out of experience, 'tis much better build anew sometimes than repair an old house; I could as soon write as much more as alter that which is written.

The Anatomy of Melancholy was, in fact, a work of serial composition with an estimated increment between 1621 and 1651 of some sixty percent, or from about 300,000 to almost half a million words. About all that a modern editor can do is to follow, with misgivings, the 1651 edition, even though he knows it swarms with errors. The verification and annotation of Burton's numberless quotations and allusions present another set of problems, some of which remain unsolved despite the heroic exertions of A. R. Shilleto and Edward Bensly. A really satisfactory edition of the *Anatomy* —that is, one with an appropriate textual apparatus and complete glossarial notes—would require a syndicate of dedicated editors not restricted to the normal terms of life expectancy.

It is therefore obvious that the mere anthologist, who cannot entertain such grandiose ambitions, is obliged to make concessions in dealing with this famous book. Thus my annotations, though numerous, are confined almost entirely to rendering Burton's Latin tags in English. To identify, however briefly, all the books and things and persons that he mentions would result in a thin trickle of text winding through a vast terrain of annotations. Moreover, since the *Anatomy*, like the *Encyclopaedia Britannica*, cannot be fairly represented by selections, the following excerpts were chosen not to epitomize the book but to illustrate at least a part of its enormous range in subject, style, and manner. "Democritus Junior to the Reader," which serves the function of a preface, is of course essential as Burton's fullest explanation of himself and of his purpose. The excerpt on "Man's Excellency, Fall, Miseries, Infirmities," from the opening pages of the first partition, reminds us that, as Burton said, he was by "profession" a divine and by "inclination" a physician. It was in the latter capacity that he summarized (I.ii.1 ff.) with almost clinical coldness and precision the received opinions of his day on physiology and psychology. The famous digression on "Air Rectified" from the second partition records with prodigal erudition the impact of the new science on an age of changing values. The selections from the third partition—on the tyranny of love and on religious melancholy—not only show the protean author in the roles of historian, moralist, and satirist, they also show the supple strength and richness of his style. These selections may not make the modern reader understand why Johnson said that the *Anatomy* was the "only book that ever took him out of bed two hours sooner than he wished to rise," but they should enable him to sample one of the authentic masterpieces of the later Renaissance in England.

Although the text of the *Anatomy* presents, if possible, greater problems than its jungle of allusions, they yield but slowly to solution. A. R. Shilleto, who performed a notable service in tracing Burton's sources, unfortunately based his text (3 vols., 1893) upon the seventh (1660) edition, which of course has no authority. There is an unsatisfactory edition from the Nonesuch Press (2 vols., 1925) and better ones by Floyd Dell and Paul Jordan-Smith (2 vols., 1927, reissued in one volume in 1929) and by Holbrook Jackson (3 vols., 1932), who used the sixth (1651) edition. Edward Bensly has valiantly worked upon the text and the allusions in *Notes & Queries* (Series 9, Vols. XI and XII; Series 10, Vols. I–VII and X); Falconer Madan and others helped to shed more light in *Oxford Bibliography Society Proceedings & Papers*, I (1925); and E. C. Duff has made a study of the fifth (1638) edition in the *Library*, IV (1923–24). *Philosophaster*, which was first printed in 1862, has been translated by Paul Jordan-Smith (1931), who has also elucidated textual and other problems in *Bibliographia Burtoniana* (1931) and (with Margaret Mulhauser) compiled the useful *Burton's Anatomy of Melancholy and Burtoniana* (1959). Among other modern studies are S. B. Ewing's *Burtonian Melancholy in the Plays of John Ford* (1940), H. J. Gottlieb's *Robert Burton's Knowledge of English Poetry* (1937), Bergen Evans' *Psychiatry of Robert Burton* (1944), Lawrence Babb's *Elizabethan Malady* (1951) and *Sanity in Bedlam* (1959), and W. R. Mueller's *Anatomy of Robert Burton's England* (1952), a perceptive discussion of his social and religious thinking. Burton's style, or lack thereof, receives attention in several of the books cited in the General Bibliography, Section IV, and recent work on him has been surveyed by Dennis G. Donovan in *ELR*, I (1971).

from The Anatomy of Melancholy (1651)

THE AUTHOR'S ABSTRACT OF MELANCHOLY

Διαλογῶς[1]

When I go musing all alone,
Thinking of divers things foreknown,
When I build castles in the air,
Void of sorrow and void of fear,
Pleasing myself with phantasms sweet,
Methinks the time runs very fleet.
    All my joys to this are folly.
    Naught so sweet as melancholy.
When I lie waking[2] all alone
Recounting what I have ill done,
My thoughts on me then tyrannize,
Fear and sorrow me surprise,
Whether I tarry still or go,
Methinks the time moves very slow.
    All my griefs to this are jolly,
    Naught so sad as melancholy.
When to myself I act and smile,
With pleasing thoughts the time beguile,
By a brookside or wood so green,
Unheard, unsought for, or unseen,
A thousand pleasures do me bless
And crown my soul with happiness.
    All my joys besides are folly,
    None so sweet as melancholy.
When I lie, sit, or walk alone,
I sigh, I grieve, making great moan
In a dark grove or irksome den,
With discontents and Furies then
A thousand miseries at once
Mine heavy heart and soul ensconce.
    All my griefs to this are jolly,
    None so sour as melancholy.
Methinks I hear, methinks I see
Sweet music, wondrous melody,
Towns, palaces,[3] and cities fine;
Here now, then there; the world is mine;
Rare beauties, gallant ladies shine,
Whate'er is lovely or divine,
    All other joys to this are folly,
    None so sweet as melancholy.
Methinks I hear, methinks I see
Ghosts, goblins, fiends; my fantasy
Presents a thousand ugly shapes,
Headless bears, black men, and apes,
Doleful outcries and fearful sights
My sad and dismal soul affrights.
    All my griefs to this are jolly.
    None so damn'd as melancholy.
Methinks I court, methinks I kiss,
Methinks I now embrace my mistress.

O blessed days! O sweet content!
In paradise my time is spent.
Such thoughts may still my fancy move,
So may I ever be in love.
    All my joys to this are folly,
    Naught so sweet as melancholy.
When I recount love's many frights,
My sighs and tears, my waking nights,
My jealous fits, O mine hard fate
I now repent, but 'tis too late.
No torment is so bad as love,
So bitter to my soul can prove.
    All my griefs to this are jolly,
    Naught so harsh as melancholy.
Friends and companions, get you gone,
'Tis my desire to be alone;
Ne'er well but when my thoughts and I
Do domineer in privacy.
No gem, no treasure like to this,
'Tis my delight, my crown, my bliss.
    All my joys to this are folly,
    Naught so sweet as melancholy.
'Tis my sole plague to be alone,
I am a beast, a monster grown,
I will no light nor company;
I find it now my misery.
The scene is turned, my joys are gone;
Fear, discontent, and sorrows come.
    All my griefs to this are jolly,
    Naught so fierce as melancholy.
I'll not change life with any king,
I ravished am. Can the world bring
More joy than still to laugh and smile,
In pleasant toys time to beguile?
Do not, O do not trouble me!
So sweet content I feel and see.
    All my joys to this are folly,
    None so divine as melancholy.
I'll change my state with any wretch
Thou canst from gaol or dunghill fetch.
My pain past cure, another hell,
I may not in this torment dwell.
Now desperate I hate my life,
Lend me a halter or a knife.
    All my griefs to this are jolly,
    Naught so damn'd as melancholy.

DEMOCRITUS JUNIOR TO THE READER

Gentle reader, I presume thou wilt be very inquisitive to know what antic or personate[4] actor this is that so insolently

ANATOMY OF MELANCHOLY   [1]"Conversation."   [2]Text *walking.*
[3]Text *places.*   [4]Masked.

intrudes upon this common theater to the world's view, arrogating another man's name, whence he is, why he doth it, and what he hath to say. Although as he said, *Primum si noluero, non respondebo, quis coacturus est?*—I am a free man born and may choose whether I will tell, who can compel me? If I be urged, I will as readily reply as that Egyptian in Plutarch when a curious fellow would needs know what he had in his basket, *Quam vides velatim, quid inquiris in rem absconditam?*[5] It was therefore covered because he should not know what was in it. Seek not after that which is hid. If the contents please thee and be for thy use, suppose the man in the moon or whom thou wilt to be the author. I would not willingly be known. Yet in some sort to give thee satisfaction, which is more than I need, I will show a reason both of this usurped name, title, and subject. And first of the name of Democritus, lest any man by reason of it should be deceived, expecting a pasquil,[6] a satire, some ridiculous treatise—as I myself should have done—some prodigious tenent or paradox of the earth's motion, of infinite worlds, *in infinito vacuo, ex fortuita atomorum collisione*, in an infinite waste, so caused by an accidental collision of motes in the sun, all which Democritus held, Epicurus and their master Leucippus[7] of old maintained, and are lately revived by Copernicus, Brunus,[8] and some others. Besides it hath been always an ordinary custom, as Gellius observes, "for later writers and impostors to broach many absurd and insolent fictions under the name of so noble a philosopher as Democritus to get themselves credit and by that means the more to be respected," as artificers usually do, *Novo qui marmori ascribunt Praxitelem suo.*[9] 'Tis not so with me.

> *Non hic Centauros, non Gorgonas, Harpyasque*
> *Invenies, hominem pagina nostra sapit.*

> No centaurs here or gorgons look to find,
> My subject is of man and humankind.

Thou thyself art the subject of my discourse.

> *Quicquid agunt homines, votum, timor, ira, voluptas,*
> *Gaudia, discursus, nostri farrago libelli.*

> Whate'er men do, vows, fears, in ire, in sport,
> Joys, wanderings are the sum of my report.

My intent is no otherwise to use his name than Mercurius Gallobelgicus, Mercurius Britannicus use the name of Mercury, Democritus Christianus, etc. Although there be some other circumstances for which I have masked myself under this vizard and some peculiar respects which I cannot so well express until I have set down a brief character of this our Democritus, what he was, with an epitome of his life.

Democritus, as he is described by Hippocrates and Laertius, was a little wearish[10] old man, very melancholy by nature, averse from company in his latter days, and much given to solitariness, a famous philosopher in his age, *coaevus*[11] with Socrates, wholly addicted to his studies at the last and to a private life, writ many excellent works, a great divine according to the divinity of those times, an expert physician, a politician, an excellent mathematician, as *Diacosmus* and the rest of his works do witness. He was much delighted with the studies of husbandry, saith Columella, and often

I find him cited by Constantinus and others treating of that subject. He knew the natures, differences of all beasts, plants, fishes, birds, and as some say, could understand the tunes and voices of them. In a word, he was *omnifariam doctus*, a general scholar, a great student; and to the intent he might better contemplate, I find it related by some that he put out his eyes and was in his old age voluntarily blind, yet saw more than all Greece besides, and writ of every subject, *Nihil in toto opificio naturae de quo non scripsit.*[12] A man of an excellent wit, profound conceit; and to attain knowledge the better in his younger years, he travelled to Egypt and Athens to confer with learned men, "admired of some, despised of others." After a wandering life, he settled at Abdera, a town in Thrace, and was sent for thither to be their law-maker, recorder, or town-clerk, as some will, or as others, he was there bred and born. Howsoever it was, there he lived at last in a garden in the suburbs wholly betaking himself to his studies and a private life, "saving that sometimes he would walk down to the haven and laugh heartily at such variety of ridiculous objects which there he saw." Such a one was Democritus.

But in the meantime, how doth this concern me or upon what reference do I usurp his habit?[13] I confess indeed that to compare myself unto him for aught I have yet said were both impudency and arrogancy. I do not presume to make any parallel, *Antistat mihi millibus trecentis, parvus sum, nullus sum, altum nec spiro, nec spero.*[14] Yet thus much I will say of myself, and that I hope without all suspicion of pride or self-conceit: I have lived a silent, sedentary, solitary, private life *mihi et Musis*,[15] in the university as long almost as Xenocrates in Athens, *ad senectam fere*,[16] to learn wisdom as he did, penned up most part in my study. For I have been brought up a student in the most flourishing college of Europe, *augustissimo collegio*[17] and can brag with Jovius, almost, *in ea luce domicilii Vaticani, totius orbis celeberrimi, per 37 annos nulta opportunaque didici;*[18] for thirty years I have continued, having the use of as good libraries as ever he had, a scholar, and would be therefore loth, either by living as a drone to be an unprofitable or unworthy a member of so learned and noble a society or to write that which should be any way

[5]"Seeing the cover, why do you ask what is concealed?"
[6]Lampoon.
[7]*Democritus...Leucippus*: Leucippus of Miletus (fl. ca. 440 B.C.) was with Democritus of Abdera (ca. 460–ca. 370 B.C.) the founder of the atomistic philosophy that Epicurus (342?–?270 B.C.) adopted and taught at Athens. Only fragments of their works survive.
[8]Giordano Bruno (1548?–1600), Italian priest and free thinker who was executed for his advocacy of Copernican astronomy and other advanced opinions.
[9]"Who sign their own new statues with the name of Praxiteles" (a famous sculptor). [10]Wizened. [11]"Coeval."
[12]"There is nothing in nature's works about which he has not written." [13]Apparel.
[14]"He is incalculably superior to me—an insignificant person who neither aspires to nor hopes for distinction."
[15]"For myself and my studies." [16]"Virtually to old age."
[17]Christ's Church, Oxford.
[18]"In the splendor of my Vatican retreat, the most famous in the world, I have lived thirty-seven full, productive years."

dishonorable to such a royal and ample foundation. Something I have done, though by my profession a divine; yet *turbine raptus ingenii,* as he said, out of a running wit, an unconstant, unsettled mind I had a great desire (not able to attain to a superficial skill in any) to have some smattering in all, to be *aliquis in omnibus, nullus in singulis;*[19] which Plato commends, out of him Lipsius approves and furthers "as fit to be imprinted in all curious wits, not be a slave of one science or dwell altogether in one subject as most do, but to rove abroad, *centum puer artium,*[20] to have an oar in every man's boat, to taste of every dish, and sip of every cup," which, saith Montaigne, was well performed by Aristotle and his learned countryman Adrian Turnebus.

This roving humor—though not with like success—I have ever had, and like a ranging spaniel that barks at every bird he sees, leaving his game, I have followed all saving that which I should, and may justly complain and truly *qui ubique est, nusquam est,*[21] which Gesner did in modesty, that I have read many books, but to little purpose for want of good method; I have confusedly tumbled over divers authors in our libraries with small profit for want of art, order, memory, judgment. I never travelled but in map or card[22] in which my unconfined thoughts have freely expatiated as having ever been especially delighted with the study of cosmography. Saturn was lord of my geniture, culminating, etc., and Mars, principal *significator* of manners in partile conjunction with mine ascendant, both fortunate in their houses, etc.[23] I am not poor, I am not rich; *nihil est, nihil deest,* I have little, I want nothing. All my treasure is in Minerva's tower. Greater preferment as I could never get, so am I not in debt for it. I have a competency, *laus Deo,*[24] from my noble and munificent patrons, though I live still a collegiate student as Democritus in his garden and lead a monastic life, *ipse mihi theatrum,*[25] sequestered from those tumults and troubles of the world, *et tanquam in specula positus,* as he said, in some high place above you all like *Stoicus sapiens, omnia saecula, praeterita, praesentiaque videns, uno velut intuitu.*[26]

I hear and see what is done abroad, how others run, ride, turmoil, and macerate themselves in court and country, far from those wrangling lawsuits, *aulae vanitatem, fori ambitionem, ridere mecum soleo.*[27] I laugh at all, "only secure lest my suit go amiss, my ships perish," corn and cattle miscarry, trade decay; "I have no wife nor children good or bad to provide for." A mere spectator of other men's fortunes and adventures and how they act their parts, which methinks are diversely presented unto me as from a common theater or scene. I hear new news every day and those ordinary rumors of war, plagues, fires, inundations, thefts, murders, massacres, meteors, comets, spectrums, prodigies, apparitions, of towns taken, cities besieged in France, Germany, Turkey, Persia, Poland, etc., daily musters and preparations and such like which these tempestuous times afford, battles fought, so many men slain, monomachies,[28] shipwrecks, piracies and seafights, peace, leagues, stratagems, and fresh alarums. A vast confusion of vows, wishes, actions, edicts, petitions, lawsuits, pleas, laws, proclamations, complaints, grievances are daily brought to our ears. New books every day, pamphlets, corantos,[29] stories, whole catalogues of volumes of all

sorts, new paradoxes, opinions, schisms, heresies, controversies in philosophy, religion, etc. Now come tidings of weddings, maskings, mummeries, entertainments, jubilees, embassies, tilts and tournaments, trophies, triumphs, revels, sports, plays. Then again, as in a new-shifted scene, treasons, cheating tricks, robberies, enormous villainies in all kinds, funerals, burials, deaths of princes, new discoveries, expeditions; now comical, then tragical matters. Today we hear of new lords and officers created, tomorrow of some great men deposed, and then again of fresh honors conferred; one is let loose, another imprisoned; one purchaseth, another breaketh; he thrives, his neighbor turns bankrupt; now plenty, then again dearth and famine; one runs, another rides, wrangles, laughs, weeps, etc. Thus I daily hear, and such like, both private and public news amidst the gallantry and misery of the world; jollity, pride, perplexities and cares, simplicity and villainy, subtlety, knavery, candor and integrity mutually mixed and offering themselves.

I rub on *privus privatus;*[30] as I have still lived so I now continue *statu quo prius,*[31] left to a solitary life and mine own domestic discontents; saving that sometimes, *ne quid mentiar,*[32] as Diogenes went into the city and Democritus to the haven to see fashions, I did for my recreation now and then walk abroad, look into the world, and could not choose but make some little observation, *non tam sagax observator ac simplex recitator,*[33] not as they did to scoff or laugh at all but with a mixed passion.

Bilem saepe, jocum vestri movere tumultus.[34]

I did sometime laugh and scoff with Lucian and satirically tax with Menippus, lament with Heraclitus, sometimes again I was *petulanti splene cachinno,* and then again, *urere bilis jecur,*[35] I was much moved to see that abuse which I could not amend. In which passion howsoever I may sympathize with him or them, 'tis for no such respect I shroud myself under his name, but either in an unknown habit to assume a little more liberty and freedom of speech, or if you will needs know, for that reason and only respect which Hippocrates relates at large in his epistle to Damagetus, wherein he doth express how coming to visit him one day, he found Democ-

[19]Competent in all, eminent in none.
[20]"The servant of a hundred arts."
[21]"Who is everywhere is nowhere." [22]Chart.
[23]*Saturn...etc.*: I was born and attained my maturity under the sign of the gloomy planet Saturn, whose influence was somewhat modified by that of the more fiery and energetic Mars. *Houses*: in astrology, the twelve parts of the heavens occupied by the various planets, each with special significance for the characters of those persons born in its *ascendant.* [24]"Praise be to God."
[25]"A theater to myself."
[26]"The Stoic sage seeing past and present simultaneously, and at a single glance."
[27]"I laugh to myself at the vanities of the court and the chicanery of public life." [28]Single combats. [29]Newspapers.
[30]"In complete privacy." [31]"In the same condition as before."
[32]"Not to conceal anything."
[33]"Not so much as a sage observer as a mere reporter."
[34]"Your passions have often stirred my wrath or anger."
[35]*Sometimes again...jecur*: I was sometimes bitterly amused and sometimes boiling with rage.

ritus in his garden at Abdera in the suburbs under a shady bower with a book on his knees, busy at his study, sometimes writing, sometimes walking. The subject of his book was melancholy and madness. About him lay the carcasses of many several beasts newly by him cut up and anatomized, not that he did contemn God's creatures, as he told Hippocrates, but to find out the seat of this *atra bilis* or melancholy, whence it proceeds and how it was engendered in men's bodies, to the intent he might better cure it in himself, by his writings and observations teach others how to prevent and avoid it. Which good intent of his Hippocrates highly commended. Democritus Junior is therefore bold to imitate, and because he left it imperfect and it is now lost, *quasi succenturiator Democriti,*[36] to revive again, prosecute, and finish in this treatise.

You have had a reason of the name. If the title and inscription offend your gravity, were it a sufficient justification to accuse others, I could produce many sober treatises, even sermons themselves, which in their fronts carry more fantastical names. Howsoever it is kind of policy in these days to prefix a fantastical title to a book which is to be sold. For as larks come down to a day-net,[37] many vain readers will tarry and stand gazing like silly passengers at an antic picture in a painter's shop that will not look at a judicious piece. And indeed, as Scaliger observes, "nothing more invites a reader than an argument unlooked for, unthought of, and sells better than a scurril pamphlet, *tum maxime cum novitas excitat palatum.*"[38] Many men, saith Gellius, "are very conceited in their inscriptions," and able, as Pliny quotes out of Seneca, to make him loiter by the way "that went in haste to fetch a midwife for his daughter now ready to lie down." For my part, I have honorable precedents for this, which I have done. I will cite one for all, Anthony Zara, *Pap. Episc.,*[39] his Anatomy of Wit, in four sections, members, subsections, etc., to be read in our libraries.[40]

If any man except against the matter or manner of treating of this my subject and will demand a reason of it, I can allege more than one. I write of melancholy, by being busy to avoid melancholy. There is no greater cause of melancholy than idleness, "no better cure than business," as Rhasis holds. And howbeit *stultus labor est ineptiarum,* to be busied in toys is to small purpose, yet hear that divine Seneca, better *aliud agere quam nihil,* better do to no end than nothing. I writ therefore and busied myself in this playing labor, *otiosaque diligentia ut vitarem torporem feriandi,*[41] with Vectius in Macrobius, *atque otium in utile verterem negotium.*

> *Simul et iucunda et idonea dicere vitae,*
> *Lectorem delectando simul atque momendo.*[42]

. . . .

As already, we shall have a vast chaos and confusion of books; we are oppressed with them, our eyes ache with reading, our fingers with turning. For my part, I am one of the number, *nos numerus sumus,* I do not deny it. I have only this of Macrobius to say for myself, *Omne meum, nihil meum,* 'tis all mine and none mine. As a good housewife out of divers fleeces weaves one piece of cloth, a bee gathers wax and honey out of many flowers and makes a new bundle of all,

> *Floriferis ut apes in saltibus omnia libant,*

I have laboriously collected this cento out of divers writers and that *sine iniuria;*[43] I have wronged no authors, but given every man his own; which Jerome so much commends in Nepotian, he stole not whole verses, pages, tracts, as some do nowadays, concealing their authors' names, but still said this was Cyprian's, that Lactantius', that Hilarius', so said Minutius Felix, so Victorinus, thus far Arnobius. I cite and quote mine authors—which, howsoever some illiterate scribblers account pedantical, as a cloak of ignorance, and opposite to their affected fine style, I must and will use—*sumsi, non surripui;*[44] and what Varro, *lib. 6, De re rust.,* speaks of bees, *minime maleficae, nullius opus vellicantes faciunt deterius,*[45] I can say of myself, whom have I injured? The matter is theirs most part and yet mine, *apparet unde sumptum sit,*[46] which Seneca approves, *aliud tamen quam quam sumptum sit unde apparet,*[47] which nature doth with the aliment of our bodies, incorporate, digest, assimilate, I do *concoquere quod hausi,* dispose of what I take. I make them pay tribute to set out this my *macaronicon.*[48] The method only is mine own. I must usurp that of Wecker *e Ter., nihil dictum quod non dictum prius, methodus sola artificem ostendit.* We can say nothing but what hath been said, the composition and method is ours only and shows a scholar. Oribasius, Aetius, Avicenna, have all out of Galen, but to their own method, *diverso stilo, non diversa fide;*[49] our poets steal from Homer, he spews, saith Aelian, they lick it up. Divines use Austin's words verbatim still, and our story-dressers do as much. He that comes last is commonly best,

> *donec quid grandius aetas*
> *Postera sorsque ferat melior.*[50]

Though there were many giants of old in physic and philosophy, yet I say with Didacus Stella, "A dwarf standing on the shoulders of a giant may see farther than a giant himself"; I may likely add, alter, and see farther than my predecessors; and it is no greater prejudice for me to endite after others than for Aelianus Montaltus, the famous physician, to write *de morbis capitis*[51] after Jason Pratensis, Heurnius, Hildesheim,

---

[36] "As successor to Democritus." [37] Net for catching small birds.
[38] "Especially if it tickles the palate with novelty."
[39] A bishop of the Roman church.
[40] Burton refers to Antonio Zara, bishop of Petina, whose *Anatomia ingeniorum et scientiarum* (1615) is an encyclopedic analysis of "anatomy" of man's physical and mental functions, his achievements in various arts and sciences, his institutions, and his history.
[41] "To avoid the boredom of idleness with leisurely activity."
[42] *Atque...momendo*: "turn my leisure to employment so as to teach and please mankind, and both instruct and delight my reader." [43] "Without injury." [44] "I have borrowed, not stolen."
[45] "They do no wrong because they hurt nothing that they take honey from." [46] "It is clear whence it came."
[47] "It seems to be something different from its source."
[48] Polyglot pastiche.
[49] With distinctives styles, not distinctive doctrines.
[50] "Until a later and more accomplished age produces something better." [51] "About diseases of the head."

etc. Many horses to run in a race; one logician, one rhetorician, after another. Oppose then what thou wilt,

> *Allatres licet usque nos et usque,*
> *Et gannitibus improbis lacessas.*[52]

I solve it thus. And for those other faults of barbarism, Doric dialect, extemporanean style, tautologies, apish imitation, a rhapsody of rags gathered together from several dung-hills, excrements of authors, toys and fopperies confusedly tumbled out without art, invention, judgment, wit, learning, harsh, raw, rude, fantastical, absurd, insolent, indiscreet, ill-composed, undigested, vain, scurril, idle, dull and dry; I confess all ('tis partly affected). Thou canst not think worse of me than I do of myself, 'Tis not worth the reading, I yield it, I desire thee not to lose time in perusing so vain a subject; I should be peradventure loth myself to read him or thee so writing, 'tis not *operae pretium.*[53] All I say is this, that I have precedents for it, which Isocrates calls *perfugium iis qui peccant,*[54] others as absurd, vain, idle, illiterate, etc. *Nonnulli alii idem fecerunt,* others have done as much, it may be more, and perhaps thou thyself, *Novimus et qui te,*[55] etc., we have all our faults; *scimus, et hanc veniam,*[56] etc., thou censurest me, so have I done others and may do thee, *Cedimus inque vicem,* etc., 'tis *lex talionis, quid pro quo.*[57] Go now censure, criticize, scoff and rail!

> *Nasutus sis usque licet, sis denique nasus,*
> *Non potes in nugas dicere plura meas,*
> *Ipse ego quam dixi, etc.*

> Wer'st thou all scoffs and flouts, a very Momus,
> Than we ourselves, thou canst not say worse of us.

· · · · · ·

As a Dutch host, if you come to an inn in Germany and dislike your fare, diet, lodging, etc., replies in a surly tone, *aliud tibi quaeras diversorium,* if you like not this, get you to another inn; I resolve, if you like not my writing, go read something else. I do not much esteem thy censure, take thy course, 'tis not as thou wilt, nor as I will. But when we have both done, that of Plinius Secundus to Trajan will prove true, "Every man's witty labor takes not, except the matter, subject, occasion, and some commending favorite happen to it." If I be taxed, exploded by thee and some such, I shall haply be approved and commended by others, and so have been; *expertus loquor,*[58] and may truly say with Jovius in like case—*absit verbo jactantia—heroum quorundam, pontificum, et virorum nobilium familiaritatem et amicitiam, gratasque gratias, et multorum bene laudatorum laudes sum inde promeritus,*[59] as I have been honored by some worthy men, so have I been vilified by others, and shall be. At the first publishing of this book, which Probus said of Persius' satires, *editum librum continuo mirari homines, atque avide deripere coeperunt,*[60] I may in some sort apply to this my work. The first, second, and third edition were suddenly gone, eagerly read, and, as I have said, not so much approved by some as scornfully rejected by others. But it was Democritus his fortune, *idem admirationi et irrisioni habitus.*[61] 'Twas Seneca's fate, that superintendent of wit, learning, judgment, *ad stuporem doctus,*[62] the best of

Greek and Latin writers, in Plutarch's opinion, that "renowned corrector of vice,"as Fabius terms him, "and painful omniscient philosopher, that writ so excellently and admirably well," could not please all parties or escape censure. How is he vilified by Caligula, Agellius, Fabius, and Lipsius himself, his chief propugner![63] . . . If Seneca be thus lashed, and many famous men that I could name, what shall I expect? How shall I that am *vix umbra tanti philosophi*[64] hope to please! "No man so absolute," Erasmus holds, "to satisfy all, except antiquity, prescription, etc., set a bar." But as I have proved in Seneca, this will not always take place, how shall I evade! 'Tis the common doom of all writers, I must, I say, abide it; I seek not applause; *Non ego ventosae venor suffragia plebis;* again, *non sum adeo informis,*[65] I would not be vilified.

> *Laudatus abunde,*
> *Non fastiditus si tibi, lector, ero.*[66]

I fear good men's censures and to their favorable acceptance I submit my labors,

> *et linguas mancipiorum*
> *Contemno.*[67]

As the barking of a dog, I securely contemn those malicious and scurril obloquies, flouts, calumnies of railers and detractors; I scorn the rest. What therefore said I have *pro tenuitate mea*[68] I have said.

One or two things yet I was desirous to have amended if I could concerning the manner of handling this my subject, for which I must apologize, *deprecari,* and upon better advice give the friendly reader notice. It was not mine intent to prostitute my Muse in English or to divulge *secreta Minervae,*[69] but to have exposed this more contract[70] in Latin, if I could have got it printed. Any scurril pamphlet is welcome to our mercenary stationers in English, they print all,

> *cuduntque libellos*
> *In quorum foliis vix simia nuda cacaret;*[71]

but in Latin they will not deal; which is one of the reasons

[52]Although you bark and growl at me relentlessly.
[53]Worth the reading. [54]"A refuge for sinners."
[55]We know about you and your faults.
[56]We acknowledge our faults and claim our pardon.
[57]"We strike, and in turn (we are struck again). It is the law of retaliation: one thing for another." [58]"I speak from experience."
[59]"May I say it without boasting, I have enjoyed the friendship and favor of some distinguished people—warriors, pontiffs, and noblemen—and have won their esteem together with the praises of many famous men."
[60]"At the appearance of this book men opened their eyes and eagerly began to rip it apart."
[61]"He was accustomed to both admiration and derision."
[62]"Marvelously erudite." [63]Advocate, champion.
[64]"Scarcely the shadow of such a philosopher."
[65]"I do not seek the approval of the mob; again, I am not so homely."
[66]"I shall be praised enough, O discriminating reader, if you do not disdain me." [67]"I scorn the talk of slaves."
[68]"To the best of my poor ability. [69]"The secrets of Minerva."
[70]Contracted, i.e., orderly and shapely.
[71]Turn out things that a monkey would not use for toilet paper.

Nicholas Carr[72] in his oration of the paucity of English writers gives that so many flourishing wits are smothered in oblivion, lie dead and buried in this our nation. Another main fault is that I have not revised the copy and amended the style, which now flows remissly as it was first conceived; but my leisure would not permit, *Feci nec quod potui, nec quod volui*,[73] I confess it is neither as I would or as it should be.

> *Cum relego scripsisse pudet, quia plurima cerno*
> *Me quoque quae fuerunt iudice digna lini.*
>
> When I peruse this tract which I have writ,   10
> I am abashed and much I hold unfit.

Et *quod gravissimum*,[74] in the matter itself many things I disallow at this present which when I writ, *Non eadem est aetas, non mens;*[75] I would willingly retract much, etc., but 'tis too late, I can only crave pardon now for what is amiss.

I might indeed—had I wisely done—observed that precept of the poet,

> *nonumque prematur in annum,*[76]

and have taken more care. Or as Alexander the physician would have done by lapis lazuli, fifty times washed before it   20 be used, I should have revised, corrected and amended this tract; but I had not, as I said, that happy leisure, no *amanuenses* or assistants. Pancrates in Lucian, wanting a servant as he went from Memphis to Coptus in Egypt, took a door bar and after some superstitious words pronounced—Eucrates the relator was then present—made it stand up like a servingman, fetch him water, turn the spit, serve him supper, and what work he would besides; and when he had done that service he desired, turned his man to a stick again. I have no such skill to make new men at my pleasure or means to hire   30 them, no whistle to call like the master of a ship and bid them run, etc. I have no such authority, no such benefactors as that noble Ambrosius was to Origen, allowing him six or seven *amanuenses* to write out his dictates. I must for that cause do my business myself, and was therefore enforced, as a bear doth her whelps, to bring forth this confused lump; I had not time to lick it into form, as she doth her young ones, but even so to publish it as it was first written, *quicquid in buccam venit*,[77] in an extemporean style, as I do commonly all other exercises, *effudi quicquid dictavit genius meus*,[78] out of a confused com-   40 pany of notes and writ with as small deliberation as I do ordinarily speak, without all affectation of big words, fustian phrases, jingling terms, tropes, strong lines, that like Acestes' arrows caught fire as they flew, strains of wit, brave heats, eulogies, hyperbolical exornations, elegancies, etc., which many so much affect. I am *aquae potor*, drink no wine at all, which so much improves our modern wits, a loose, plain, rude writer, *ficum voco ficum, et ligonem ligonem*,[79] and as free as loose, *idem calamo quod in mente*,[80] call a spade a spade, *enimis haec scribo, non auribus*,[81] I respect matter, not words,   50 remembering that of Cardan, *verba propter res, non res propter verba*,[82] and seeking with Seneca, *quid scribam, non quemadmodum*, rather what than how to write. For as Philo thinks, "He that is conversant about matter neglects words, and those that excel in this art of speaking have no profound learning."

Verba nitent phaleris, at nullus verba medullas
Intus habent.[83]

Besides, it was the observation of that wise Seneca, "when you see a fellow careful about his words and neat in his speech, know this for a certainty, that man's mind is busied about toys, there's no solidity in him." *Non est ornamentum virile concinnitas:*[84] as he said of a nightingale,

> *vox es, praeterea nihil, etc.*[85]

I am therefore in this point a professed disciple of Apollonius, a scholar of Socrates: I neglect phrases and labor wholly to inform my reader's understanding, not to please his ears; 'tis not my study or intent to compose neatly, which an orator requires, but to express myself readily and plainly as it happens. So that, as a river runs sometimes precipitate and swift, then dull and slow, now direct, then *per ambages*,[86] now deep, then shallow, now muddy, then clear, now broad, then narrow, doth my style flow; now serious, then light, now comical, then satirical, now more elaborate, then remiss, as the present subject required or as at that time I was affected. And if thou vouchsafe to read this treatise, it shall seem no otherwise to thee than the way to an ordinary traveler, sometimes fair, sometimes foul, here champion,[87] there enclosed, barren in one place, better soil in another. By woods, groves, hills, dales, plains, etc., I shall lead thee *per ardua montium et lubrica vollium et roscida cespitum et glebosa camporum*,[88] through variety of objects, that which thou shalt like and surely dislike.

. . . . . .

If I be convict of an error, I will yield, I will amend. *Si quid bonis moribus, si quid veritati dissentaneum, in sacris vel humananis literis a me dictum sit, id nec dictum esto.*[89] In the meantime I require a favorable censure of all faults omitted, harsh compositions, pleonasms of words, tautological rep-

---

[72]Noted Hellenist (1524–68) and Regius Professor of Greek at Cambridge whose *De scriptorum Britannicorum paucitate* appeared posthumously in 1576.
[73]"I have done what I could, not what I wished."
[74]"What is more serious."
[75]I was not so old and wise as I am now.
[76]Withheld (and polished) it for nine years.
[77]"Whatever came first to my mouth."
[78]I spouted out whatever occurred to me.
[79]"I call a fig a fig, and a mattock a mattock."
[80]What my mind thinks my pen writes.
[81]"I write for the mind, not the ear."
[82]"The words should be suited to the matter, not the matter to the words."
[83]Words richly adorned but containing nothing.
[84]"Mere prettiness is not a manly distinction."
[85]"You are a voice and nothing more."   [86]Winding.
[87]Champaign, i.e., open country.
[88]Over steep mountains, slippery slopes, wet grass, and muddy fields.
[89]"If I have said anything opposed to good morals or truth, as expressed in either sacred or profane literature, may it be regarded as not said."

etitions—though Seneca bear me out, *munquam nimis dicitur quod nunquam satis dicitur*[90]—perturbations of tenses, numbers, printer's faults, etc. My translations are sometimes rather paraphrases than interpretations, *non ad verbum,* but as an author I use more liberty; and that's only taken which was to my purpose. Quotations are often inserted in the text, which makes the style more harsh, or in the margin as it happened. Greek authors, Plato, Plutarch, Athenaeus, etc., I have cited out of their interpreters, because the original was not so ready. I have mingled *sacra profanis*[91] but I hope not profaned, and in repetition of authors' names ranked them *per accidens,* not according to chronology; sometimes neoterics[92] before ancients, as my memory suggested. Some things are here altered, expunged in this sixth edition, others amended, much added, because many good authors in all kinds are come to my hands since, and 'tis no prejudice, no such indecorum, or oversight.

> *Nunquam ita quicquam bene subducta ratione ad vitam fuit,*
> *Quin res, aetas, usus, semper aliquid apportent novi,*
> *Aliquid moneant, ut illa quae scire te credas, nescias,*
> *Et quae tibi putaris prima, in experiundo ut repudies.*

> Ne'er was aught yet at first contrived so fit
> But use, age, or something would alter it,
> Advise thee better, and upon peruse
> Make thee not say, and what thou tak'st, refuse.

But I am now resolved never to put this treatise out again; *ne quid nimis,*[93] I will not hereafter add, alter, or retract. I have done.

The last and greatest exception is that I being a divine have meddled with physic.

> *Tantumne est ab re tua otii tibi,*
> *Aliena ut cures, eaque nihil quae ad te attinent?*

which Menedemus objected to Chremes. Have I so much leisure or little business of mine own as to look after other men's matters which concern me not? What have I to do with physic! *Quod medicorum est promittamt medici.*[94] The Lacedemonians were once in council about state matters; a debauched fellow spake excellent well and to the purpose; his speech was generally approved. A grave senator steps up and by all means would have it repealed, though good, because *dehonestabatur pessimo auctore,* it had no better an author; let some good man relate the same, and then it should pass. This counsel was embraced, *factum est,* and it was registered forthwith, *et sic bona sententia mansit, malus auctor mutatus est.*[95] Thou sayest as much of me, *stomachosus*[96] as thou art, and grantest peradventure this which I have written in physic not to be amiss, had another done it, a professed physician, or so; but why should I meddle with this tract! Hear me speak. There be many other subjects, I do easily grant, both in humanity and divinity, fit to be treated of, of which, had I written *ad ostentationem* only, to show myself, I should have rather chosen and in which I have been more conversant; I could have more willingly luxuriated and better satisfied myself and others; but that at this time I was fatally driven upon this rock of melancholy and carried away by this bystream which as a rillet is de-

ducted from the main channel of my studies; in which I have pleased and busied myself at idle hours as a subject most necessary and commodious. Not that I prefer it before divinity, which I do acknowledge to be the queen of professions and to which all the rest are as handmaids, but that in divinity I saw no such great need. For had I written positively, there be so many books in that kind, so many commentators, treatises, pamphlets, expositions, sermons that whole teams of oxen cannot draw them; and had I been as forward and ambitious as some others I might have haply printed a sermon at Paul's Cross, a sermon in St. Mary's *Oxon.,* a sermon in Christ Church, or a sermon before the right honorable, right reverend, a sermon before the right worshipful, a sermon in Latin, in English, a sermon with a name, a sermon without, a sermon, a sermon, etc. But I have been ever as desirous to suppress my labors in this kind as others have been to press and publish theirs. To have written in controversy had been to cut off an hydra's head; *lis litem, generat,*[97] one begets another, so many duplications, triplications, and swarms of questions *in sacro bello hoc quod stili mucrone agitur*[98] that having once begun I should never make an end. One had much better, as Alexander the Sixth, pope, long since observed, provoke a great prince than a begging friar, a Jesuit or a seminary priest I will add, for *inexpugnabile genus hoc hominum,* they are an irrefragable society, they must and will have the last word; and that with such eagerness, impudence, abominable lying, falsifying, and bitterness in their questions they proceed that as he said, *furone caecus, an rapit vis acrior, an culpa? responsum date.*[99] Blind fury or error or rashness or what it is that eggs them I know not, I am sure many times, which Austin perceived long since, *tempestate contentionis serenitas caritatis obnubilatur,* with this tempest of contention the serenity of charity is overclouded, and there be too many spirits conjured up already in this kind in all sciences and more than we can tell how to lay which do so furiously rage and keep such a racket that as Fabius said, "It had been much better for some of them to have been born dumb and altogether illiterate than so far to dote to their own destruction."

> *At melius fuerat non scribere, namque tacere*
> *Tutum semper erit.*[1]

'Tis a general fault, so Severinus the Dane complains in physic, "unhappy men as we are we spend our days in unprofitable questions and disputations," intricate subtleties, *de lana caprina*[2] about moonshine in the water, "leaving in

[90]That cannot be too often repeated which cannot be said often enough. [91]"Sacred with profane." [92]Moderns.
[93]"Not too much of anything."
[94]Let doctors concern themselves with medicine.
[95]And so the good advice was followed whereas its evil sponsor was rejected. [96]"Truculent."
[97]One lawsuit produces another.
[98]"In this sacred war fought with the point of a pen."
[99]"Is it blind rage, irresistible force, or error that prompts you? Answer me!"
[1]"It had been better not to write at all, for safety always lies in silence." [2]"About a goat's fleece."

the meantime those chiefest treasures of nature untouched wherein the best medicines for all manner of diseases are to be found and do not only neglect them ourselves but hinder, condemn, forbid, and scoff at others that are willing to inquire after them." These motives at this present have induced me to make choice of this medicinal subject.

. . . . . .

Never so much cause of laughter as now, never so many fools and madmen. 'Tis not one Democritus will serve turn to laugh in these days, we have now need of a "Democritus to laugh at Democritus," one jester to flout at another, one 10 fool to fleer at another. A great stentorian Democritus as big as that Rhodian Colossus. For now, as Salisburiensis said in his time, *totus mundus histrionem agit,* the whole world plays the fool; we have a new theater, a new scene, a new comedy of errors, a new company of personate actors, *volupiae sacra,*[3] as Calcagninus wittily feigns in his *Apologues,* are celebrated all the world over, where all the actors were madmen and fools and every hour changed habits or took that which came next. He that was a mariner today is an apothecary tomorrow; a smith one while, a philosopher 20 another, in his *volupiae ludis;*[4] a king now with his crown, robes, scepter, attendants, by and by drove a loaded ass before him like a carter, etc. If Democritus were alive now, he should see strange alterations, a new company of counterfeit vizards, whistlers, Cuman asses, maskers, mummers, painted puppets, outsides, fantastic shadows, gulls, monsters, giddy-heads, butterflies. And so many of them are indeed, if all be true that I have read. For when Jupiter and Juno's wedding was solemnized of old, the gods were all invited to the feast and many noblemen besides. Amongst the rest 30 came Chrysalus, a Persian prince, bravely attended, rich in golden attires, in gay robes, with a majestical presence, but otherwise an ass. The gods seeing him come in such pomp and state rose up to give him place *ex habitu hominem metientes;*[5] but Jupiter perceiving what he was, a light, fantastic, idle fellow, turned him and his proud followers into butterflies. And so they continue still, for aught I know to the contrary, roving about in pied coats and are called *chrysalides* by the wiser sort of men; that is, golden outsides, drones, flies, and things of no worth. Multitudes of such, etc., 40

ubique invenies
Stultos avaros, sycophantas prodigos.[6]

Many additions, much increase of madness, folly, vanity, should Democritus observe, were he now to travel or could get leave of Pluto to come see fashions, as Charon did in Lucian, to visit our cities of Moronia Pia, and Moronia Felix; sure I think he would break the rim of his belly with laughing.

Si foret in terris rideret Democritus, seu, etc.[7]

A satirical Roman in his time thought all vice, folly, and 50 madness were all at full sea,

Omne in praecipiti vitium stetit.[8]

Josephus the historian taxeth his countrymen Jews for bragging of their vices, publishing their follies, and that

they did contend amongst themselves who should be most notorious in villainies; but we flow higher in madness, far beyond them,

Mox daturi progeniem vitiosiorem,[9]

and the latter end—you know whose oracle it is—is like to be worst. 'Tis not to be denied, the world alters every day, *Ruunt urbes, regna transferuntur,*[10] etc., *variantur habitus, leges innovantur,* as Petrarch observes, we change language, habits, laws, customs, manner, but not vices, not diseases, not the symptoms of folly and madness; they are still the same. And as a river we see keeps the like name and place but not water and yet ever runs,

Labitur et labetur in omne volubilis aevum;

our times and persons alter, vices are the same, and ever will be; look how nightingales sang of old, cocks crowed, kine lowed, sheep bleated, sparrows chirped, dogs barked, so they do still; we keep our madness still, play the fools still, *nec dum finitus Orestes,*[11] we are of the same humors and inclinations as our predecessors were, you shall find us all alike, much at one, we and our sons,

Et nati natorum, et qui nascuntur ab illis,[12]

and so shall our posterity continue to the last. But to speak of times present.

If Democritus were alive now and should but see the superstition of our age, our religious madness, as Meteran calls it, *religiosam insaniam,* so many professed Christians yet so few imitators of Christ, so much talk of religion, so much science, so little conscience, so much knowledge, so many preachers, so little practice, such variety of sects, such have and hold of all sides,

obvia signis signa, etc.,[13]

such absurd and ridiculous traditions and ceremonies; if he should meet a Capuchin, a Franciscan, a pharisaical Jesuit, a man-serpent, a shave-crowned monk in his robes, a begging friar, or see their three-crowned sovereign lord the pope, poor Peter's successor, *servus servorum Dei,*[14] to depose kings with his foot, to tread on emperors' necks, make them stand barefoot and barelegged at his gates, hold his bridle and stirrup, etc.,—O that Peter and Paul were alive to see this!—if he should observe a prince creep so devoutly to kiss his toe, and those red-cap cardinals, poor parish priests of old, now princes' companions; what would he say? *Coelum ipsum petitur stultitia.*[15] Had he met some of our devout pilgrims going barefoot to Jerusalem, our lady of Loretto, Rome, St. Iago, St. Thomas' shrine, to creep to

[3]Voluptuous rites. [4]Voluptuous sport.
[5]"Judging the man by his garments."
[6]"You will find greedy fools and wasteful sycophants everywhere."
[7]"How Democritus would live if he were on earth again!"
[8]Every vice unreined.
[9]"Soon destined to produce a worse offspring."
[10]"Cities fall, kingdoms are dislodged."
[11]"Nor is the play (about Orestes) finished."
[12]"The sons of our sons and those born of them."
[13]Banners ranged in opposition.
[14]"The servant of the servants of God."
[15]"Folly seeks entrance even into heaven."

those counterfeit and maggot-eaten relics. Had he been present at a mass and seen such kissing of paxes, crucifixes, cringes, duckings, their several attires and ceremonies, pictures of saints, indulgences, pardons, vigils, fasting, feasts, crossing, knocking, kneeling at *Ave Marias,* bells, with many such,

jucunda rudi spectacula plebi,[16]

praying in gibberish, and mumbling of beads. Had he heard an old woman say her prayers in Latin, their sprinkling of holy water, and going a procession,

Incedunt monachorum agmina mille,
Quid memorem vexilla, cruces, idolaque culta, etc.[17]

their breviaries, bulls, hallowed beads,[18] exorcisms, pictures, curious crosses, fables, and baubles. Had he read the Golden Legend, the Turks' Alcoran, or Jews' Talmud, the Rabbins' Comments, what would he have thought? How dost thou think he might have been affected? Had he more particularly examined a Jesuit's life amongst the rest, he should have seen an hypocrite profess poverty and yet possess more goods and lands than many princes, to have infinite treasures and revenues, teach others to fast, and play the gluttons themselves, like watermen that row one way and look another. Vow virginity, talk of holiness, and yet indeed a notorious bawd and famous fornicator, *lascivum pecus,*[19] a very goat. Monks by profession, such as give over the world and the vanities of it, and yet a Machiavellian rout interested in all manner of state. Holy men, peace-makers, and yet composed of envy, lust, ambition, hatred and malice, firebrands, *adulta patriae pestis,*[20] traitors, assassins, *hac itur ad astra,*[21] and this is to supererogate and merit heaven for themselves and others! Had he seen on the adverse side some of our nice and curious schismatics in another extreme abhor all ceremonies and rather lose their lives and livings than do or admit anything Papists have formerly used though in things indifferent—they alone are the true church, *sal terrae, cum sint omnium insulsissimi.*[22] Formalists, out of fear and base flattery like so many weathercocks turn round, a rout of temporizers, ready to embrace and maintain all that is or shall be proposed in hope of preferment. Another Epicurean company, lying at lurch as so many vultures, watching for a prey of church goods, and ready to rise by the downfall of any. As Lucian said in like case, what dost thou think Democritus would have done, had he been spectator of these things?

Or had he but observed the common people follow like so many sheep one of their fellows drawn by the horns over a gap, some for zeal, some for fear, *quo se cunque rapit tempestas,*[23] to credit all, examine nothing, and yet ready to die before they will abjure any of those ceremonies to which they have been accustomed; others out of hypocrisy frequent sermons, knock their breasts, turn up their eyes, pretend zeal, desire reformation, and yet professed usurers, gripers, monsters of men, harpies, devils in their lives, to express nothing less?

What would he have said to see, hear, and read so many bloody battles, so many thousands slain at once, such streams of blood able to turn mills, *unius ob noxam furiasque,*[24] or to make sport for princes, without any just cause, "for vain titles," saith Austin, "precedency, some wench, or such like toy, or out of desire of domineering, vainglory, malice, revenge, folly, madness," goodly causes all, *ob quas universus orbis bellis et caedibus misceatur,*[25] whilst statesmen themselves in the meantime are secure at home, pampered with all delights and pleasures, take their ease, and follow their lusts, not considering what intolerable misery poor soldiers endure, their often wounds, hunger, thirst, etc.; the lamentable cares, torments, calamities, and oppressions that accompany such proceedings, they feel not, take no notice of it. "So wars are begun by the persuasion of a few debauched, harebrain, poor, dissolute, hungry captains, parasitical fawners, unquiet Hotspurs, restless innovators, green-heads, to satisfy one man's private spleen, lust, ambition, avarice," etc., *tales rapiunt scelerata in proelia causae.*[26] *Flos hominum,*[27] proper men, well proportioned, carefully brought up, able both in body and mind, sound, led like so many beasts to the slaughter in the flower of their years, pride, and full strength, without all remorse and pity sacrificed to Pluto, killed up as so many sheep for devils' food, 40,000 at once. At once, said I?—that were tolerable, but these wars last always and for many ages; nothing so familiar as this hacking and hewing, massacres, murders, desolations,

ignoto coelum clangore remugit.[28]

They care not what mischief they procure so that they may enrich themselves for the present; they will so long blow the coals of contention till all the world be consumed with fire. The siege of Troy lasted ten years, eight months, there died 870,000 Grecians, 670,000 Trojans at the taking of the city, and after were slain 276,000 men, women, and children, of all sorts. Caesar killed a million, Mahomet the second Turk 300,000 persons. Sicinius Dentatus fought in an hundred battles, eight times in single combat he overcame, had forty wounds before, was rewarded with 140 crowns, triumphed nine times for his good service. M. Sergius had thirty-two wounds; Scaeva the centurion I know not how many; every nation hath their Hectors, Scipios, Caesars and Alexanders. Our Edward the Fourth was in twenty-six battles afoot. And as they do all, he glories in it, 'tis related to his honor. At the siege of Jerusalem 1,100,000 died with sword and famine. At the battle of Cannae 70,000 men were slain as Polybius records, and as many at Battle Abbey[29] with us. And 'tis no news to fight from sun to sun as they did, as Constantine and Licinius, etc. At the siege of Ostend, the Devil's Academy, a poor town in respect, a small fort, but a great grave, 120,000 men lost their lives, besides whole

---

16"Costly spectacles for the common herd."
17"With a thousand groups of monks marching in procession why should one recall banners, crosses, idols, and the like?"
18Text *beans.*   19"A lustful beast."
20"A major menace to the realm."   21"This is the road to heaven."
22"The salt of the earth, though the most insipid of people."
23Wherever they are whirled.
24"Through the deadly fury of a single person."
25"For which the whole world should heave with war and slaughter."   26Such intensify the evils of war.
27"Flower of humanity."
28"The sky re-echoes with the strange noise."
29The battle of Hastings.

towns, dorps,[30] and hospitals full of maimed soldiers; there were engines, fireworks, and whatsoever the Devil could invent to do mischief with 2,500,000 iron bullets shot of forty pound weight, three or four millions of gold consumed. "Who," saith mine author, "can be sufficiently amazed at their flinty hearts, obstinacy, fury, blindness, who without any likelihood of good success hazard poor soldiers and lead them without pity to the slaughter, which may justly be called the rage of furious beasts that run without reason upon their own deaths."   10

. . . . . .

To see so many lawyers, advocates, so many tribunals, so little justice; so many magistrates, so little care of common good; so many laws, yet never more disorders; *tribunal litium segetem*,[31] the tribunal a labyrinth, so many thousand suits in one court sometimes, so violently followed! To see *iniustissimum saepe iuri praesidentem, impium religioni, imperitissimum eruditioni, otiosissimum labori, monstrosum humanitati!*[32] To see a lamb executed, a wolf pronounce sentence, *latro*[33] arraigned, and *fur*[34] sit on the bench, the judge severely punish others and do worse himself, *eundem furtum facere et* [20] *punire, rapinam plectere, quum sit ipse raptor!*[35] Laws altered, misconstrued, interpreted *pro* and *con*, as the judge is made by friends, bribed, or otherwise affected as a nose of wax, good today, none tomorrow; or firm in his opinion, cast in his! Sentence prolonged, changed *ad arbitrium iudicis*,[36] still the same case, "one thrust out of his inheritance, another falsely put in by favor, false forged deeds or wills." *Incisae leges negliguntur*,[37] laws are made and not kept; or if put in execution, they be some silly ones that are punished. As put case it be fornication, the father will disinherit or abdicate [30] his child, quite cashier him (out! villain, begone! come no more in my sight), a poor man is miserably tormented with loss of his estate perhaps, goods, fortunes, good name, forever disgraced, forsaken, and must do penance to the utmost; a mortal sin, and yet make the worst of it, *Nunquid aliud fecit*, saith Tranio in the poet, *nisi quod faciunt summis nati generibus?* he hath done no more than what gentlemen usually do.

Neque novum, neque mirum, neque secus quam alii solent.[38]

For in a great person, right worshipful sir, a right honorable [40] grandee, 'tis not a venial sin, no, not a *peccadillo*, 'tis no offense at all, a common and ordinary thing, no man takes notice of it; he justifies it in public and peradventure brags of it.

Nam quod turpe bonis, Titio, Seioque, decebat Crispinum.[39]

Many poor men, younger brothers, etc., by reason of bad policy and idle education—for they are likely brought up in no calling—are compelled to beg or steal, and then hanged for theft; than which what can be more ignominious! [50] *Non minus enim turpe principi multa supplicia quam medico multa funera*,[40] 'tis the governor's fault. *Libentius verberant quam docent*, as schoolmasters do rather correct their pupils than teach them when they do amiss. "They had more need

provide there should be no more thieves and beggars, as they ought with good policy, and take away the occasions than let them run on as they do to their own destruction," root out likewise those causes of wrangling, a multitude of lawyers, and compose controversies, *lites lustrales et seculares*,[41] by some more compendious means. Whereas now for every toy and trifle they go to law, *Mugit litibus insanum forum, et saevit invicem discordantium rabies*,[42] they are ready to pull out one another's throats; and for commodity "to squeeze blood," saith Jerome, "out of their brother's heart," defame, lie, disgrace, backbite, rail, bear false witness, swear, forswear, fight and wrangle, spend their goods, lives, fortunes, friends, undo one another, to enrich an harpy advocate that preys upon them both and cries, *Eia, Socrates! Eia, Xantippe!* or some corrupt judge that like the kite in Aesop, while the mouse and frog fought, carried both away. Generally they prey one upon another as so many ravenous birds, brute beasts, devouring fishes. . . .

Our *summum bonum* is commodity, and the goddess we adore *Dea Moneta*, Queen Money, to whom we daily offer sacrifice, which steers our hearts, hands, affections, all, that most powerful goddess, by whom we are reared, depressed, elevated, esteemed the sole commandress of our actions, for which we pray, run, ride, go, come, labor, and contend as fishes do for a crumb that falleth into the water. It's not worth, virtue (that's *bonum theatrale*),[43] wisdom, valor, learning, honesty, religion, or any sufficiency for which we are respected, but money, greatness, office, honor, authority; honesty is accounted folly; knavery, policy; men admired out of opinion, not as they are but as they seem to be. Such shifting, lying, cogging, plotting, counterplotting, temporizing, flattering, cozening, dissembling "that of necessity one must highly offend God if he be conformable to the world, *Cretizare cum Crete*[44] or else live in contempt, disgrace and misery." One takes upon him temperance, holiness, another austerity, a third an affected kind of simplicity, when as indeed he and he and he and the rest are hypocrites, ambodexters,[45] outsides, so many turning pictures, a lion on the one side, a lamb on the other. How would Democritus have been affected to see these things!

To see a man turn himself into all shapes like a chameleon

---

[30]Villages. [31]"The court is a crop of lawsuits."
[32]"The worst rogue presiding over justice, the sinner over religion, the dunce over learning, the idler over working men, the moral monster over acts of charity." [33]"Robber." [34]"Thief."
[35]"The same person both to commit and punish theft, he himself a robber to condemn robbery."
[36]"At the discretion of the judge." [37]"Engraven laws ignored."
[38]"It is not novel or remarkable, or even different from what others do."
[39]"For what is reprehensible for good men like Titus and Seius is suitable for Crispinus."
[40]Frequent punishments are no less discreditable for a ruler than frequent funerals for a doctor. [41]Interminable lawsuits.
[42]The court bellows with angry litigation and rages with noisy strife. [43]"A theatrical good."
[44]To behave like a Cretan in Crete.
[45]Ambodexters, i.e., double-dealers.

or as Proteus, *omnia transformans sese in miracula rerum*,[46] to act twenty parts and persons at once for his advantage, to temporize and vary like Mercury the planet, good with good, bad with bad; having a several face, garb, and character for everyone he meets; of all religions, humors, inclinations; to fawn like a spaniel, *mentitis et mimicis obsequiis*,[47] rage like a lion, bark like a cur, fight like a dragon, sting like a serpent, as meek as a lamb, and yet again grin like a tiger, weep like a crocodile, insult over some, and yet others domineer over him, here command, there crouch, tyrannize in one place, be baffled in another, a wise man at home, a fool abroad to make others merry.

To see so much different betwixt words and deeds, so many parasangs betwixt tongue and heart, men like stage-players act variety of parts, give good precepts to others, soar aloft, whilst they themselves grovel on the ground.

To see a man protest friendship, kiss his hand, *quem mallet truncatum videre*,[48] smile with an intent to do mischief, or cozen him whom he salutes, magnify his friend unworthy with hyperbolical eulogies; his enemy, albeit a good man, to vilify and disgrace him, yea, all his actions, with the utmost livor and malice can invent.

To see a servant able to buy out his master, him that carries the mace more worth than the magistrate, which Plato, *lib*. 11, *De leg*., absolutely forbids, Epictetus abhors. An horse that tills the land fed with chaff, an idle jade have provender in abundance; him that makes shoes go barefoot himself, him that sells meat almost pined; a toiling drudge starve, a drone flourish.

To see men buy smoke for wares, castles built with fools' heads, men like apes follow the fashions in tires, gestures, actions. If the king laugh, all laugh;

Rides? majore cachinno
Concutitur, flet si lachrymas conspexit amici.[49]

Alexander stooped, so did his courtiers; Alphonsus turned his head, and so did his parasites. Sabina Poppea, Nero's wife, wore amber-colored hair, so did all the Roman ladies in an instant, her fashion was theirs.

To see men wholly led by affection, admired and censured out of opinion without judgment; an inconsiderate multitude, like so many dogs in a village, if one bark, all bark without a cause; as fortune's fan turns, if a man be in favor or commended by some great one, all the world applauds him; if in disgrace, in an instant all hate him, and as at the sun when he is eclipsed, that erst took no notice now gaze and stare upon him.

To see a man wear his brains in his belly, his guts in his head, an hundred oaks on his back, to devour 100 oxen at a meal, nay, more, to devour houses and towns, or as those *anthropophagi*,[50] to eat one another.

To see a man roll himself up like a snowball, from base baggary to right worshipful and right honorable titles, unjustly to screw himself into honors and offices; another to starve his genius, damn his soul to gather wealth, which he shall not enjoy, which his prodigal son melts and consumes in an instant.

To see the καοζηλίαν[51] of our times, a man bend all his forces, means, time, fortunes, to be a favorite's favorite's favorite, etc., a parasite's parasite's parasite that may scorn the servile world as having enough already.

To see an hirsute beggar's brat that lately fed on scraps, crept, and whined, crying to all and for an old jerkin ran on[52] errands, now ruffle in silk and satin, bravely mounted, jovial and polite, now scorn his old friends and familiars, neglect his kindred, insult over his betters, domineer over all.

To see a scholar crouch and creep to an illiterate peasant for a meal's meat; a scrivener better paid for an obligation; a falconer receive greater wages than a student; a lawyer get more in a day than a philosopher in a year, better reward for an hour than a scholar for a twelvemonth's study; him that can paint Thais, play on a fiddle, curl hair, etc., sooner get preferment than a philologer or a poet.

To see a fond mother like Aesop's ape, hug her child to death, a wittol wink at his wife's honesty and too perspicacious in all other affairs; one stumble at a straw, and leap over a block; rob Peter, and pay Paul; scrape unjust sums with one hand, purchase great manors by corruption, fraud, and cozenage, and liberally to distribute to the poor with the other, give a remnant to pious uses, etc. Penny wise, pound foolish; blind men judge of colors; wise men silent, fools talk; find fault with others, and do worse themselves; denounce that in public which he doth in secret; and which Aurelius Victor gives out of Augustus, severely censure that in a third, of which he is most guilty himself.

To see a poor fellow or an hired servant venture his life for his new master that will scarce give him his wages at year's end; a country colone toil and moil, till and drudge for a prodigal idle drone that devours all the gain or lasciviously consumes with fantastical expenses; a noble man in a bravado to encounter death and for a small flash of honor to cast away himself; a worldling tremble at an executor[53] and yet not fear hell-fire; to wish and hope for immortality, desire to be happy, and yet by all means avoid death, a necessary passage to bring him to it.

To see a foolhardy fellow like those old Danes, *qui decollari malunt quam verberari*, die rather than be punished, in a sottish humor embrace death with alacrity yet scorn to lament his own sins and miseries or his dearest friend's departures.

To see wise men degraded, fools preferred, one govern towns and cities, and yet a silly woman overrules him at home; command a province, and yet his own servants or children prescribe laws to him, as Themistocles' son did in Greece: "what I will," said he, "my mother will, and what my mother will my father doth." To see horses ride in a coach, men draw it; dogs devour their masters; towers

---

[46]"Change himself into astonishing shapes."
[47]"With deceitful and contrived formality."
[48]"Whom he would like to see cut down."
[49]When you laugh he laughs even more, and when you weep he weeps. [50]"Cannibals." [51]"Evil rivalry." [52]Text *of*.
[53]Executioner.

build masons; children rule; old men go to school; women wear the breeches; sheep demolish towns, devour men, etc. And in a word, the world turned upside downward. *O viveret Democritus!*[54]

. . . . .

I may not deny but that this nation of ours doth *bene audire apud exteros*,[55] is a most noble, a most flourishing kingdom; by common consent of all geographers, historians, politicians 'tis *unica velut arx*;[56] and which Quintius in Livy said of the inhabitants of Peloponnesus may be well applied to us: we are *testudines testa sua inclusi*, like so many tortoises in our shells, safely defended by an angry sea as a wall on all sides. Our island hath many such honorable elogiums; and as a learned countryman of ours right well hath it, "Ever since the Normans' first coming into England, this country, both for military matters and all other of civility, hath been paralleled with the most flourishing kingdoms of Europe and our Christian world," a blessed, a rich country, and one of the Fortunate Isles; and for some things preferred before other countries: for expert seamen, our laborious discoveries, art of navigation, true merchants: they carry the bell away from all other nations, even the Portugals and Hollanders themselves, "without all fear," saith Boterus, "furrowing the ocean winter and summer, and two of their captains, with no less valor than fortune, have sailed round about the world." We have besides many particular blessings which our neighbors want: the gospel truly preached, church discipline established, long peace and quietness, free from exactions, foreign fears, invasions, domestical seditions, well manured, fortified by art and nature, and now most happy in that fortunate union of England and Scotland which our forefathers have labored to effect and desired to see. But in which we excel all others, a wise, learned, religious king, another Numa, a second Augustus, a true Josiah; most worthy senators, a learned clergy, an obedient commonalty, etc.

Yet amongst many roses some thistles grow, some bad weeds and enormities, which much disturb the peace of this body politic, eclipse the honor and glory of it, fit to be rooted out, and with all speed to be reformed. The first is idleness, by reason of which we have many swarms of rogues and beggars, thieves, drunkards, and discontented persons (whom Lycurgus in Plutarch calls *morbos reipublicae*, the boils of the commonwealth), many poor people in all our towns, *civitates ignobiles*, as Polydore calls them, base-built cities, inglorious, poor, small, rare in sight, ruinous, and thin of inhabitants. Our land is fertile, we may not deny, full of all good things, and why doth it not then abound with cities as well as Italy, France, Germany, the Low Countries? Because their policy hath been otherwise, and we are not so thrifty, circumspect, industrious. Idleness is the *malus genius*[57] of our nation. . . . Amongst our towns there is only London that bears the face of a city, *epitome Britanniae*,[58] a famous emporium, second to none beyond seas, a noble mart. But *sola crescit decrescentibus aliis*,[59] and yet, in my slender judgment, defective in many things. The rest (some few excepted) are in mean estate, ruinous most part, poor and full of beggars by reason of their decayed trades, neglected or bad policy, idleness of their inhabitants, riot, which had rather beg or loiter, and be ready to starve, than work.

. . . . .

To conclude, this being granted, that all the world is melancholy or mad, dotes, and every member of it, I have ended my task, and sufficiently illustrated that which I took upon me to demonstrate at first. At this present I have no more to say. *His sanam mentem Democritus*;[60] I can but wish myself and them a good physician, and all of us a better mind. . . . If I have overshot myself in this which hath been hitherto said, or that it is (which I am sure some will object) too fantastical, "too light and comical for a divine, too satirical for one of my profession," I will presume to answer with Erasmus in like case: 'Tis not I but Democritus; *Democritus dixit*.[61] You must consider what it is to speak in one's own or another's person, an assumed habit and name—a difference betwixt him that affects or acts a prince's, a philosopher's, a magistrate's, a fool's part and him that is so indeed—and what liberty those old satirists have had. It is a cento collected from others, not I but they that say it.

> *Dixero si quid forte jocosius, hoc mihi juris*
> *Cum venia dabis.*[62]

Take heed you mistake me not. If I do a little forget myself, I hope you will pardon it. And to say truth, why should any man be offended, or take exceptions at it?

> *Licuit, semperque licebit,*
> *Parcere personis, dicere de vitiis.*

> It lawful was of old, and still will be,
> To speak of vice, but let the name go free.

I hate their vices, not their persons. . . . If any man take exceptions let him turn the buckle of his girdle. I care not. I owe thee nothing, reader; I look for no favor at thy hands; I am independent; I fear not.

No, I recant, I will not, I care, I fear, I confess my fault, acknowledge a great offense.

> *Motos praestat componere fluctus.*[63]

I have overshot myself, I have spoken foolishly, rashly, unadvisedly, absurdly; I have anatomized mine own folly. And now methinks upon a sudden I am awaked, as it were, out of a dream; I have had a raving fit, fantastical fit, ranged up and down, in and out; I have insulted over most kind of men, abused some, offended others, wronged myself; and now being recovered, and perceiving mine error, cry with Orlando, *Solvite me*, pardon, *O boni*,[64] that which is past, and

54"O that Democritus were alive again!"
55"Well esteemed abroad." 56"A formidable citadel."
57"Evil genius." 58"The abridgment of England."
59It flourishes at the expense of others.
60"Democritus wishes them sane." 61"Democritus said it."
62"If I speak too freely, grant me your favor and forgiveness."
63"It is necessary to calm the troubled waters." 64"Good friends."

I will make you amends in that which is to come. I promise you a more sober discourse in my following treatise.

If through weakness, folly, passion, discontent, ignorance, I have said amisss, let it be forgotten and forgiven. I acknowledge that of Tacitus to be true, *Asperae facetiae, ubi nimis ex vero traxere, acrem sui memoriam relinquunt*: a bitter jest leaves a sting behind it; and as an honorable man observes, "They fear a satirist's wit, he their memories." I may justly suspect the worst, and though I hope I have wronged no man, yet in Medea's words I will crave pardon.

> *Illud jam voce extrema peto,*
> *Ne si qua noster dubius effudit dolor,*
> *Maneant in animo verba, sed melior tibi*
> *Memoria nostri subeat, haec irae data*
> *Obliterentur.*

> And in my last words this I do desire,
> That what in passion I have said, or ire,
> May be forgotten, and a better mind
> Be had of us, hereafter as you find.

I earnestly request every private man, as Scaliger did Cardan, not to take offense. I will conclude in his lines: *si me cognitum haberes, non solum donares nobis has facetias nostras, sed etiam indignum duceres, tam humanum animum, lene ingenium, vel minimam suspicionem deprecari oportere.* If thou knewest my modesty and simplicity thou wouldst easily pardon and forgive what is here amiss, or by thee misconceived. If hereafter, anatomizing this surly humor, my hand slip, as an unskillful prentice I lance too deep, and cut through skin and all at unawares, make it smart, or cut awry, pardon a rude hand, an unskillful knife; 'tis a most difficult thing to keep an even tone, a perpetual tenor, and not sometimes to lash out; *difficile est satiram non scribere;*[65] there be so many objects to divert, inward perturbations to molest, and the very best may sometimes err; *aliquando bonus dormitat Homerus;*[66] it is impossible not in so much to overshoot; *opere in longo fas est obrepere somnum.*[67] But what needs all this? I hope there will be no such cause of offense be given; if there be, *Nemo aliquid recognoscat, nos mentimur omnia.*[68] I'll deny all (my last refuge), recant all, renounce all I have said, if any man except, and with as much facility excuse as he can accuse; but I presume of thy good favor and gracious acceptance, gentle reader. Out of an assured hope and confidence thereof, I will begin.

THE FIRST PARTITION

THE FIRST SECTION, MEMBER, SUBSECTION
MAN'S EXCELLENCY, FALL, MISERIES, INFIRMITIES. THE CAUSES OF THEM

Man, the most excellent and noble creature of the world, "the principal and mighty work of God, wonder of nature," as Zoroaster calls him; *audacis naturae miraculum,*[69] "the marvel of marvels," as Plato; "the abridgment and epitome of the world," as Pliny; *microcosmus*, a little world, a model of the world, sovereign lord of the earth, viceroy of the world, sole commander and governor of all the creatures in it, to whose empire they are subject in particular, and yield obedience; for surpassing all the rest, not in body only but in soul, *imaginis imago,*[70] created to God's own image, to that immortal and incorporeal substance, with all the faculties and powers belonging unto it; was at first pure, divine, perfect happy, "created after God in true holiness and righteousness"; *Deo congruens,*[71] free from all manner of infirmities, and put in paradise to know God, to praise and glorify Him, to do His will, *ut diis consimiles parturiat deos*[72] (as an old poet saith), to propagate the church.

But this most noble creature, *heu tristis et lachrymosa commutatio* (one exclaims)—O pitiful change!—is fallen from that he was and forfeited his estate, become *miserabilis homuncio,*[73] a castaway, a caitiff, one of the most miserable creatures of the world, if he be considered in his own nature, an unregenerate man, and so much obscured by his fall that (some few relics excepted) he is inferior to a beast. "Man in honor that understandeth not is like unto beasts that perish," so David esteems him: a monster by stupend[74] metamorphoses, a fox, a dog, a hog, what not? *Quantum mutatus ab illo!* How much altered from that he was! Before blessed and happy, now miserable and accursed, "he must eat his meat in sorrow," subject to death and all manner of infirmities, all kind of calamities. "Great travail is created for all men, and an heavy yoke on the sons of Adam, from the day that they go out of their mother's womb unto that day they return to the mother of all things. Namely, their thoughts and fear of their hearts, and their imagination of things they wait for, and the day of death; from him that sitteth in the glorious throne to him that sitteth beneath in the earth and ashes; from him that is clothed in blue silk and weareth a crown to him that is clothed in simple linen. Wrath, envy, trouble, and unquietness, and fear of death, and rigor, and strife, and such things come to both man and beast, but sevenfold to the ungodly." All this befalls him in this life, and peradventure eternal misery in the life to come.

The impulsive cause of these miseries in man, this privation or destruction of God's image, the cause of death and diseases, of all temporal and eternal punishments, was the sin of our first parent Adam, in eating of the forbidden fruit, by the devil's instigation and allurement. His disobedience, pride, ambition, intemperance, incredulity, curiosity, from whence proceeded original sin and that general corruption of mankind, as from a fountain flowed all bad inclinations and actual transgressions, which cause our several calamities inflicted upon us for our sins. And this, belike, is that which our fabulous poets have shadowed unto us in the tale of Pandora's box, which, being opened through her curiosity, filled the world full of all manner of diseases. It is not curiosity alone, but those other crying sins of ours, which pull these several plagues and miseries upon our heads. For *ubi peccatum,*

---

[65]"It is hard not to write satire." [66]Sometimes even Homer nods.
[67]In such a long work it is permissible for sleep to steal upon us.
[68]No one should take this seriously, for it is all a lie.
[69]"A daring miracle of nature."
[70]"Image of the image (of God)."
[71]"Corresponding to God himself."
[72]"That like a god he may produce more gods."
[73]"A miserable dwarf." [74]Stupendous.

ibi procella,[75] as Chrysostom well observes. "Fools, by reason of their transgression, and because of their iniquities, are afflicted." "Fear cometh like sudden desolation, and destruction like a whirlwind, affliction and anguish," because they did not fear God. "Are you shaken with wars," as Cyprian well urgeth to Demetrius, "are you molested with death and famine, is your health crushed with raging diseases, is mankind generally tormented with epidemical maladies? 'Tis all for your sins" (Haggai 1. 9–10, Amos 1, Jeremiah 7) God is angry, punisheth and threateneth, because of their obstinacy and stubbornness they will not turn unto Him. "If the earth be barren then for want of rain, if, dry and squalid, it yield no fruit, if your fountains be dried up, your wine, corn, and oil blasted, if the air be corrupted, and men troubled with diseases, 'tis by reason of their sins": which like the blood of Abel cry loud to heaven for vengeance. Lamentations 5.15: "That we have sinned, therefore our hearts are heavy." Isaiah 59.11–12: "We roar like bears, and mourn like doves, and want health, etc., for our sins and trespasses." But this we cannot endure to hear or to take notice of. Jeremiah 2.30: We are smitten in vain and receive no correction;" and Chapter 5.3: "Thou has stricken them, but they have not sorrowed; they have refused to receive correction; they have not returned." "Pestilence He hath sent, but they have not turned to Him" (Amos 4). Herod could not abide John Baptist, nor Domitian endure Apollonius to tell the causes of the plague at Ephesus, his injustice, incest, adultery, and the like. . . .

Now the instrumental causes of these our infirmities are as diverse as the infirmities themselves: stars, heavens, elements, etc. and all those creatures which God hath made are armed against sinners. They were indeed once good in themselves, and that they are now many of them pernicious unto us is not in their nature but our corruption, which hath caused it. For from the fall of our first parent Adam they have been changed, the earth accursed, the influence of stars altered, the four elements, beasts, birds, plants are now ready to offend us. "The principal things for the use of man are water, fire, iron, salt, meal, wheat, honey, milk, oil, wine, clothing, good to the godly, to the sinners turned to evil" (Ecclesiasticus 39.26). "Fire and hail and famine and dearth, all these are created for vengeance" (Ecclesiasticus 39.29). The heavens threaten us with their comets, stars, planets, with their great conjunctions, eclipses, oppositions, quartiles[76] and such unfriendly aspects; the air with his meteors, thunder and lightning, intemperate heat and cold, mighty winds, tempests, unseasonable weather; from which proceed dearth, famine, plague, and all sorts of epidemical diseases consuming infinite myriads of men. At Cairo in Egypt, every third year (as it is related by Boterus and others) 300,000 die of the plague, and 200,000 in Constantinople every fifth or seventh at the utmost. How doth the earth terrify and oppress us with terrible earthquakes, which are most frequent in China, Japan, and those eastern climes, swallowing up sometimes six cities at once! How doth the water rage with his inundations, irruptions, flinging down towns, cities, villages, bridges, etc., besides shipwrecks! Whole islands are sometimes suddenly overwhelmed with all their inhabitants in

Zeeland, Holland, and many parts of the continent drowned, as the Lake Erne in Ireland. *Nihilque praeter arcium cadavera patenti cernimus freto.*[77] In the fens of Friesland, 1230, by reason of tempests, the sea drowned *multa hominum millia, et jumenta sine numero,*[78] all the country almost, men and cattle in it. How doth the fire rage, that merciless element, consuming in an instant whole cities! What town of any antiquity or note hath not been once, again, and again by the fury of this merciless element defaced, ruinated, and left desolate? In a word,

> *Ignis pepercit, unda mergit, aeris*
> *Vis pestilentis aequori ereptum necat,*
> *Bello superstes, tabidus morbo perit.*

> Whom fire spares, sea doth drown; whom sea,
> Pestilent air doth send to clay;
> Whom war 'scapes, sickness takes away.

. . . . . .

To come nearer yet, our own parents by their offenses, indiscretion, and intemperance are our mortal enemies. "The fathers have eaten sour grapes, and the children's teeth are set on edge." They cause our grief many times, and put upon us hereditary diseases, inevitable infirmities: they torment us, and we are ready to injure our posterity:

> *mox daturi progeniem vitiosiorem,*[79]

and the latter end of the world, as Paul foretold, is still like to be the worst. We are thus bad by nature, bad by kind, but far worse by art, every man the greatest enemy unto himself. We study many times to undo ourselves, abusing those good gifts which God hath bestowed upon us, health, wealth, strength, wit, learning, art, memory to our own destruction: *Perditio tua ex te.*[80] As Judas Maccabaeus killed Apollonius with his own weapons, we arm ourselves to our own overthrows; and use reason, art, judgment, all that should help us, as so many instruments to undo us. Hector gave Ajax a sword, which, so long as he fought against enemies, served for his help and defense; but after he began to hurt harmless creatures with it, turned to his own hurtless bowels. Those excellent means God hath bestowed on us, well employed, cannot but much avail us; but if otherwise perverted, they ruin and confound us: and so by reason of our indiscretion and weakness they commonly do, we have too many instances. This St. Austin acknowledgeth of himself in his humble *Confessions*: "Promptness of wit, memory, eloquence, they were God's good gifts, but he did not use them to His glory." If you will particularly know how, and by what means, consult physicians, and they will tell you that it is in offending in some of those six non-natural things,

---

[75]"Where is sin there is also a tempest."
[76]Aspects of two heavenly bodies 90 degrees distant from each other.
[77]"And we discern nothing but the remains of cities in the open sea." [78]"Many thousands of men and countless animals."
[79]"Soon to produce a worse offspring."
[80]"You are your own destroyer."

of which I shall after dilate more at large;[81] they are the causes of our infirmities, our surfeiting and drunkenness, our immoderate, insatiable lust and prodigious riot. *Plures crapula quam gladius* is a true saying, the board consumes more than the sword. Our intemperance it is that pulls so many several incurable diseases upon our heads, that hastens old age, perverts our temperature, and brings upon us sudden death. And last of all, that which crucifies us most, is our own folly, madness (*quos Jupiter perdit, dementat*,[82] by subtraction of His assisting grace God permits it), weakness, want of government, our facility and proneness in yielding to several lusts, in giving way to every passion and perturbation of the mind: by which means we metamorphose ourselves and degenerate into beasts. All which that prince of poets observed of Agamemnon, that when he was well pleased, and could moderate his passion, he was *os oculosque Jovi par*: like Jupiter in feature, Mars in valour, Pallas in wisdom, another god; but when he became angry, he was a lion, a tiger, a dog, etc., there appeared no sign or likeness of Jupiter in him; so we, as long as we are ruled by reason, correct our inordinate appetite, and conform ourselves to God's word, are as so many living saints; but if we give reins to lust, anger, ambition, pride, and follow our own ways, we degenerate into beasts, transform ourselves, overthrow our constitutions, provoke God to anger, and heap upon us this of melancholy, and all kinds of incurable diseases, as a just and deserved punishment of our sins.

SECTION I, MEMBER II

SUBSECTION 1. DIGRESSION OF ANATOMY

Before I proceed to define the disease of melancholy, what it is, or to discourse farther of it, I hold it not impertinent to make a brief digression of the anatomy of the body and faculties of the soul, for the better understanding of that which is to follow; because many hard words will often occur, as mirach[83] hypochondries,[84] hemrods,[85] etc., imagination, reason, humors, spirits, vital, natural, animal, nerves, veins, arteries, chylus,[86] pituita;[87] which of the vulgar will not so easily be perceived, what they are, how cited, and to what end they serve. And besides, it may peradventure give occasion to some men to examine more accurately, search farther into this most excellent subject, and thereupon with that royal prophet to praise God ("for a man is fearfully and wonderfully made, and curiously wrought"), that have time and leisure enough, and are sufficiently informed in all other worldly businesses as to make a good bargain, buy and sell, to keep and make choice of a fair hawk, hound, horse, etc. But for such matters as concern the knowledge of themselves, they are wholly ignorant and careless; they know not what this body and soul are, how combined, of what parts and faculties they consist, or how a man differs from a dog. And what can be more ignominious and filthy (as Melancthon well inveighs) "than for a man not to know the structure and composition of his own body, especially since the knowledge of it tends so much to the preservation of his health and information of his manners?" To stir them up therefore to this study,

to peruse those elaborate works of Galen, Bauhinus, Plater, Vesalius, Fallopius, Laurentius, Remelinus, etc., which have written copiously in Latin; or that which some of our industrious countrymen have done in our mother tongue, not long since, as that translation of Columbus, and *Microcosmographia*, in thirteen books, I have made this brief digression. Also because Wecker, Melancthon, Fernelius, Fuchsius, and those tedious tracts *De anima* (which have more compendiously handled and written of this matter) are not at all times ready to be had, to give them some small taste, or notice of the rest, let this epitome suffice.

SUBSECTION 2. DIVISION OF THE BODY, HUMORS, SPIRITS

Of the parts of the body there be many divisions; the most approved is that of Laurentius, out of Hippocrates, which is into parts contained or containing. Contained are either humors or spirits.

A humor is a liquid or fluent part of the body, comprehended in it, for the preservation of it; and is either innate or born with us, or adventitious and acquisite.[88] The radical or innate is daily supplied by nourishment, which some call cambium, and make those secondary humors of ros and gluten to maintain it: or acquisite, to maintain these four first primary humors, coming and proceeding from the first concoction[89] in the liver, by which means chylus is excluded. Some divide them into profitable and excrementitious. But Crato, out of Hippocrates, will have all four to be juice, and not excrements, without which no living creature can be sustained; which four, though they be comprehended in the mass of blood, yet they have their several affections, by which they are distinguished from one another, and from those adventitious, peccant, or diseased humors, as Melancthon calls them.

Blood is a hot, sweet, temperate, red humour, prepared in the meseraic[90] veins, and made of the most temperate parts of the chylus in the liver, whose office is to nourish the whole body, to give it strength and colour, being dispersed by the veins through every part of it. And from it spirits are first begotten in the heart, which afterwards by the arteries are communicated to the other parts.

Pituita, or phlegm, is a cold and moist humor, begotten of the colder part of the chylus (or white juice coming out of the meat digested in the stomach) in the liver; his office is to nourish and moisten the members of the body which, as the tongue, are moved, that they be not overdry.

Choler is hot and dry, bitter, begotten of the hotter parts of the chylus, and gathered to the gall; it helps the natural

[81]In Partition I, Section ii, Member 2, Burton discusses such "non-natural" causes of melancholy as bad diet, "retention and evacuation," air, etc.
[82]"Jupiter maddens those whom he destroys." [83]Abdomen.
[84]Hypochondria. [85]Hemorrhoids.
[86]Chyle, a milky fluid secreted in the process of digestion.
[87]Phlegm, mucus. [88]Acquired.
[89]The first part of the digestive process in the stomach and intestines. The second concoction is the process whereby the resulting chyme is converted into blood, and the third is secretion.
[90]Mesaraic, pertaining to the veins of the peritoneum.

heat and senses, and serves to the expelling of excrements.

Melancholy, cold and dry, thick, black, and sour, begotten of the more feculent part of nourishment, and purged from the spleen, is a bridle to the other two hot humors, blood and choler, preserving them in the blood, and nourishing the bones. These four humors have some analogy with the four elements, and to the four ages in man.   10

To these humors you may add serum, which is the matter of urine, and those excrementitious humours of the third concoction, sweat and tears.

Spirit is a most subtle vapor, which is expressed from the blood, and the instrument of the soul, to perform all his actions; a common tie or medium betwixt the body and the soul, as some will have it; or, as Paracelsus, a fourth soul of itself. Melancthon holds the fountain of these spirits to be the heart; begotten there and afterward conveyed to the brain, they take another nature to them. Of these spirits there be three kinds, according to the three principal parts, brain, heart, liver; natural, vital, animal. The natural are begotten 20 in the liver, and thence dispersed through the veins to perform those natural actions. The vital spirits are made in the heart of the natural, which by the arteries are transported to all the other parts; if these spirits cease, then life ceaseth, as in a syncope or swooning. The animal spirits, formed of the vital, brought up to the brain, and diffused by the nerves to the subordinate members, give sense and motion to them all.

SUBSECTION 10. OF THE UNDERSTANDING

"Understanding is a power of the soul by which we perceive, know, remember, and judge, as well singulars as universals, having certain innate notices or beginnings of arts, a re- 30 flecting action, by which it judgeth of his own doings and examines them." Out of this definition (besides his chief office, which is to apprehend, judge all that he performs, without the help of any instruments or organs) three differences appear betwixt a man and a beast. As first, the sense only comprehends singularities, the understanding universalities. Secondly, the sense hath no innate notions. Thirdly, brutes cannot reflect upon themselves. Bees indeed make neat and curious works, and many other creatures besides; but when they have done, they cannot judge of them. His 40 object is God, *Ens,* all nature, and whatsoever is to be understood, which successively it apprehends. The object first moving the understanding is some sensible thing; after, by discoursing, the mind finds out the corporeal substance, and from thence the spiritual. His actions (some say) are apprehension, composition, division, discoursing, reasoning, memory, which some include in invention, and judgment. The common divisions are, of the understanding: agent and patient, speculative and practic,[91] in habit or in act, simple or compound. The agent is that which is called the wit of man, 50 acumen or subtlety, sharpness of invention, when he doth invent of himself without a teacher, or learns anew, which abstracts those intelligible species from the fantasy and transfers them to the passive understanding, "because there is nothing in the understanding which was not first in the sense." That which the imagination hath taken from the sense this agent judgeth of, whether it be true or false; and being so judged he commits it to the passible to be kept. The agent is a doctor or teacher, the passive a scholar; and his office is to keep and farther judge of such things as are committed to his charge; as a bare and razed table[92] at first, capable of all forms and notions. Now these notions are twofold, actions or habits: actions, by which we take notions of and perceive things; habits, which are durable lights and notions, which we may use when we will. Some reckon up eight kinds of them: sense, experience, intelligence, faith, suspicion, error, opinion, science; to which are added art, prudency, wisdom; as also synteresis, *dictamen rationis*[93] conscience; so that in all there be fourteen species of the understanding, of which some are innate, as the three last mentioned; the other are gotten by doctrine, learning, and use. Plato will have all to be innate; Aristotle reckons up but five intellectual habits: two practic, as prudency, whose end is to practise, art to fabricate; wisdom to comprehend the use and experiments of all notions and habits whatsoever.[94] Which division of Aristotle (if it be considered aright) is all one with the precedent; for three being innate, and five acquisite, the rest are improper imperfect, and in a more strict examination excluded. Of all these I should more amply dilate, but my subject will not permit. Three of them I will only point at, as more necessary to my following discourse.

Synteresis, or the purer part of the conscience, is an innate habit, and doth signify "a conservation of the knowledge of the law of God and Nature, to know good or evil." And (as our divines hold) it is rather in the understanding than in the will. This makes the major proposition in a practic syllogism. The *dictamen rationis* is that which doth admonish us to do good or evil, and is the minor in the syllogism. The conscience is that which approves good or evil, justifying or condemning our actions, and is the conclusion of the syllogism: as in that familiar example of Regulus the Roman, taken prisoner by the Carthaginians, and suffered to go to Rome, on that condition he should return again or pay so much for his ransom. The synteresis proposeth the question; his word, oath, promise, is to be religiously kept, although to his enemy, and that by the law of nature. "Do not that to another which thou wouldest not have done to thyself." *Dictamen* applies it to him, and dictates this or the like: "Regulus, thou wouldst not another man should falsify his oath, or break promise with thee;" conscience concludes, "Therefore, Regulus, thou dost well to perform thy promise, and oughtest to keep thine oath." More of this in Religious Melancholy.[95]

---

[91]Practical.   [92]Blank tablet (*tabula rasa*).
[93]"The dictate of reason."
[94]*Aristotle reckons...whatsoever*: In the *Nicomachean Ethics* (VI.iii) Aristotle lists what Burton calls the "intellectual habits" as art, scientific knowledge, practical wisdom, philosophic wisdom, and intuitive reason. It will be observed that Burton omits three of these.
[95]Partition III, Sect. iii-iv. For excerpts from this part of the *Anatomy* see below, pp. 453 ff.

SUBSECTION 11. OF THE WILL

Will is the other power of the rational soul, "which covets or avoids such things as have been before judged and apprehended by the understanding." If good, it approves; if evil, it abhors it: so that his object is either good or evil. Aristotle calls this our rational appetite; for as, in the sensitive, we are moved to good or bad by our appetite, ruled and directed by sense, so in this we are carried by reason. Besides, the sensitive appetite hath a particular object, good or bad; this an universal, immaterial: that respects only things delectable and pleasant; this honest. Again, they differ in liberty. The sensual appetite seeing an object, if it be a convenient good, cannot but desire it; if evil, avoid it; but this is free in his essence, "much now depraved, obscured, and fallen from his first perfection; yet in some of his operations still free," as to go, walk, move at his pleasure, and to choose whether it will do or not do, steal or not steal. Otherwise, in vain were laws, deliberations, exhortations, counsels, precepts, rewards, promises, threats and punishments: and God should be the author of sin. But in spiritual things we will no good, prone to evil (except we be regenerate, and led by the spirit), we are egged on by our natural concupiscence, and there is ἀταξία, a confusion in our powers, "our whole will is averse from God and His law," not in natural things only, as to eat and drink, lust, to which we are led headlong by our temperature and inordinate appetite,

*Nec nos obniti contra, nec tendere tantum
Sufficimus,*[96]

we cannot resist, our concupiscence is originally bad, our heart evil, the seat of our affections captivates and enforceth our will, so that in voluntary things we are averse from God and goodness, bad by nature, by ignorance worse, by art, discipline, custom, we get many bad habits, suffering them to domineer and tyrannize over us; and the devil is still ready at hand with his evil suggestions, to tempt our depraved will to some ill-disposed action, to precipitate us to destruction, except our will be swayed and counterpoised again with some divine precepts and good motions of the spirit, which many times restrain, hinder, and check us, when we are in the full career of our dissolute courses. So David corrected himself, when he had Saul at a vantage. Revenge and malice were as two violent oppugners on the one side; but honesty, religion, fear of God, withheld him on the other.

The actions of the will are *velle* and *nolle,* to will and nill: which two words comprehend all, and they are good or bad, accordingly as they are directed, and some of them freely performed by himself; although the Stoics absolutely deny it, and will have all things inevitably done by destiny, imposing a fatal necessity upon us, which we may not resist; yet we say that our will is free in respect of us, and things contingent, howsoever (in respect of God's determinate counsel) they are inevitable and necessary. Some other actions of the will are performed by the inferior powers which obey him, as the sensitive and moving appetite; as to open our eyes, to go hither and thither, not to touch a book, to speak fair or foul; but this appetite is many times rebellious in us, and will not be contained within the lists of sobriety and temperance. It was (as I said) once well agreeing with reason, and there was an excellent consent and harmony betwixt them, but that is now dissolved, they often jar, reason is overborne by passion: *Fertur equis auriga, nec audit currus habenas,* as so many wild horses run away with a chariot, and will not be curbed. We know many times what is good, but will not do it, as she[97] said:

*Trahit invitam nova vis, aliudque cupido,
Mens aliud suadet.*[98]

Lust counsels one thing, reason another; there is a new reluctancy in men.

Odi, nec possum cupiens non esse quod odi.[99]

We cannot resist, but as Phaedra confessed to her nurse, *quae loqueris, vera sunt, sed furor suggerit sequi pejora:*[1] she said well and true, she did acknowledge it, but headstrong passion and fury made her to do that which was opposite. So David knew the filthiness of his fact,[2] what a loathsome, foul crying sin adultery was, yet notwithstanding he would commit murder, and take away another man's wife, enforced against reason, religion, to follow his appetite.

Those natural and vegetal powers are not commanded by will at all, for "who can add one cubit to his stature?" These other may, but are not; and thence come all those headstrong passions, violent perturbations of the mind; and many times vicious habits, customs, feral diseases because we give so much way to our appetite and follow our inclination, like so many beasts. The principal habits are two in number, virtue and vice, whose peculiar definitions, descriptions, differences, and kinds are handled at large in the ethics, and are, indeed, the subject of moral philosophy.

THE SECOND PARTITION. THE CURE OF MELANCHOLY

SECTION II, MEMBER III. AIR RECTIFIED, WITH A DIGRESSION OF THE AIR

As a long-winged hawk when he is first whistled off the fist mounts aloft, and for his pleasure fetcheth many a circuit in the air, still soaring higher and higher till he be come to his full pitch, and in the end, when the game is sprung, comes down amain and stoops upon a sudden, so will I, having come at last into these ample fields of air wherein I may freely expatiate and exercise myself for my recreation, a while rove, wander round about the world,

[96]We can neither resist or stand firm against them.
[97]Medea in Ovid's *Metamorphoses,* VII.19020 (which Burton characteristically misquotes).
[98]A new force drives me on: I am pushed one way by desire and another by discretion.
[99]"I hate, yet am unable not to be the thing I hate."
[1]What you say is true, but fury makes me do what is wrong.
[2]Deed, crime (i.e., in committing adultery with Bathsheba, wife of Uriah the Hittite). See 2 Samuel 11–12.

mount aloft to those etherial orbs and celestial spheres, and so descend to my former elements again.

In which progress I will first see whether that relation of the friar of Oxford be true concerning those northern parts under the Pole—if I meet *obiter*[3] with the Wandering Jew, Elias Artifex, or Lucian's Icaromenippus, they shall be my guides—whether there be such four Euripes and a great rock of loadstones which may cause the needle in the compass still to bend that way, and what should be the true cause of the variation of the compass. Is it a magnetical rock, or the Pole [10] Star, as Cardan will, or some other star in the Bear, as Marsilius Ficinus, or a magnetical meridian, as Maurolicus, *vel situs in vena terrae,*[4] as Agricola, or the nearness of the next continent, as Cabeus will, or some other cause, as Scaliger, Cortesius, Conimbricenses, Peregrinus contend; why at the Azores it looks directly north, otherwise not? In the Mediterranean or Levant, as some observe, it varies 7 *grad.*[5] by and by 12 and then 22. In the Baltic Seas, near Rasceburg in Finland, the needle runs round if any ships come that way, though Martin Ridley write otherwise, that the needle near [20] the pole will hardly be forced from his direction. 'Tis fit to be inquired whether certain rules may be made of it, as 11 *grad. Lond. variat. alibi* 36,[6] etc.; and that which is more prodigious, the variation varies in the same place, now taken accurately 'tis so much after a few years quite altered from that it was. Till we have better intelligence, let our Dr. Gilbert and Nicholas Cabeus the Jesuit, that have both written great volumes of this subject, satisfy these inquisitors.

Whether the sea be open and navigable by the Pole Arctic, [30] and which is the likeliest way, that of Bartison the Hollander, under the pole itself, which for some reasons I hold best, or by *Fretum* Davis,[7] or Nova Zembla. Whether Hudson's discovery be true of a new-found ocean, any likelihood of Button's Bay in 50 degrees, Hubberd's Hope in 60, that of *ut ultra* near Sir Thomas Roe's welcome in Northwest Fox, being that the sea ebbs and flows constantly there 15 foot in 12 hours, as our new cards[8] inform us that California is not a cape but an island, and the west winds make the neap[9] tides equal to the spring, or that there be any probability to [40] pass by the Straits of Anian to China by the Promontory of Tabin. If there be, I shall soon perceive whether Marcus Polus[10] the Venetian's narration be true or false of that great City of Quinsay and Cambalu; whether there be any such places, or that, as Matth. Riccius the Jesuit hath written, China and Cataia be all one, the great Cham of Tartary and the King of China be the same, Xuntain and Quinsay and the City of Cambalu be that new Peking, or such a wall 400 leagues long to part China from Tartary; whether Presbyter John be in Asia or Africa; M. Polus Venetus puts him in [50] Asia; the most received opinion is that he is emperor of the *Abissines,* which of old was Ethiopia, now Nubia, under the equator in Africa. Whether Guinea be an island or part of the continent, or that hungry Spaniard's discovery of *Terra Australis Incognita,*[11] or *Magellanica,* be as true as that of Mercurius Britannicus, or his of Utopia, or his of Lusinia.[12] And yet in likelihood it may be so, for without all question it, being extended from the Tropic of Capricorn to the Circle

Antarctic and lying as it doth in the temperate zone, cannot choose but yield in time some flourishing kingdoms to succeeding ages, as America did unto the Spaniards. Shouten and Le Meir have done well in the discovery of the Straits of Magellan, in finding a more convenient passage to *Mare Pacificum.*[13] Methinks some of our modern Argonauts should prosecute the rest.

.   .   .   .   .

In the meantime let us consider of that which is *sub dio*[14] and find out a true cause, if it be possible, of such accidents, meteors, alterations as happen above ground. Whence proceed that variety of manners and a distinct character, as it were, to several nations? Some are wise, subtle, witty; others dull, sad and heavy; some big, some little, as Tully, *De fato,* Plato in *Timaeo,* Vegetius and Bodin proves at large, *method., cap.* 5; some soft and some hardy, barbarous, civil, black, dun, white—is it from the air, from the soil, influence of stars, or some other secret cause? Why doth Africa breed so many venomous beasts, Ireland none? Athens owls, Crete none? Why hath Daulis and Thebes no swallows—so Pausanias informeth us—as well as the rest of Greece, Ithaca no hares, Pontus asses, Scythia swine? Whence come this variety of complexions, colors, plants, birds, beasts, metals, peculiar almost to every place? Why so many thousand strange birds and beasts proper to America alone, as Acosta demands, *lib.* 4, *cap.* 36; were they created in the six days, or ever in Noah's ark? If there, why are they not dispersed and found in other countries? It is a thing, saith he, hath long held me in suspense; no Greek, Latin, Hebrew ever heard of them before, and yet as differing from our European animals as an egg and a chestnut; and which is more, kine, horses, sheep, etc., till the Spaniards brought them, were never heard of in those parts.

How comes it to pass that in the same site, in one latitude, to such as are *perioeci,*[15] there should be such difference of soil, complexion, color, metal, air, etc.? The Spaniards are white, and so are Italians, whenas the inhabitants about *Caput Bonae Spei*[16] are blackamoors, and yet both alike distant from the equator; nay, they that dwell in the same parallel line with these Negroes, as about the Straits of Magellan, are white colored, and yet some in Presbyter John's country in Ethiopia are dun; they in Zeilan and Malabar, parallel with them again, black. Manamotapa in

[3]"On the way."   [4]"Or placed in the middle of the earth."
[5]"Degrees."
[6]With a variation from 11 degrees at London to 36 elsewhere.
[7]Davis Strait, between Greenland and Baffin Island.   [8]Maps.
[9]Low.
[10]Marco Polo (1254?–?1324), Italian traveler who wrote a famous account of his adventures.   [11]"The unknown land of the south."
[12]*Mercurius Britannicus...Lucinia*: i.e., authors of three fanciful narrations. "Mercurius Britannicus" was the pseudonym used by Joseph Hall for his *Mundus alter et idem* (1605); Sir Thomas More published his famous *Utopia* in 1516; Lusinia was an imaginary country depicted in John Barclay's *Euphormionis satyricon* (1605).
[13]The Pacific Ocean.   [14]"Under the sky," i.e., in the open.
[15]"Neighbors."   [16]The Cape of Good Hope.

Africa and St. Thomas' Isle are extreme hot, both under the line, coal-black their inhabitants; whereas in Peru they are quite opposite in color, very temperate, or rather cold, and yet both alike elevated. Moscow in 53 degrees of latitude extreme cold, as those northern countries usually are, having one perpetual hard frost all winter long; and in 52 deg. lat. sometimes hard frost and snow all summer, as in Button's Bay, etc., or by fits; and yet England near the same latitude and Ireland, very moist, warm, and more temperate in winter than Spain, Italy, or France. Is it the sea that causeth this difference and the air that comes from it? Why then is Ister so cold near the Euxine, Pontus, Bithynia, and all Thrace? *Frigidas regiones*[17] Maginus calls them, and yet their latitude is but 42, which should be hot. Quevira, or Nova Albion, in America, bordering on the sea, was so cold in July that our Englishmen could hardly endure it. At Norembega in 45 lat. all the sea is frozen ice, and yet in a more southern latitude than ours. New England and the Island of Cambrial Colchos, which that noble gentleman, Mr. Vaughan, or Orpheus Junior, describes in his Golden Fleece, is in the same latitude with Little Britain in France, and yet their winter begins not till January, their spring till May; which search he accounts worthy of an astrologer. Is this from the easterly winds, or melting of ice and snow dissolved within the Circle Arctic? Or that the air, being thick, is longer before it be warm by the sunbeams, and once heated like an oven will keep itself from cold? Our climes breed lice. Hungary and Ireland *male audiunt*[18] in this kind; come to the Azores, by a secret virtue of that air they are instantly consumed, and all our European vermin almost, saith Ortelius. Egypt is watered with Nilus not far from the sea, and yet there it seldom or never rains. Rhodes, an island of the same nature, yields not a cloud, and yet our islands ever dropping and inclining to rain. The Atlantic Ocean is still subject to storms, but in Del Zur, or *Mari Pacifico,* seldom or never any. Is it from tropic stars, *apertio portarum,*[19] in the dodecatemories or constellations, the moon's mansions, such aspects of planets, such winds, or dissolving air, or thick air, which causeth this and the like differences of heat and cold?

. . . . .

Examine likewise *an coelum sit coloratum?*[20] Whether the stars be of that bigness, distance, as astronomers relate, so many in number, 1,026 or 1,725, as I. Bayerus; or as some rabbins, 29,000 myriads; or as Galileo discovers by his glasses,[21] infinite, and that *via lactea*[22] a confused light of small stars like so many nails in a door, or all in a row like those 12,000 isles of the Maldives in the Indian Ocean? Whether the least visible star in the eighth sphere be 18 times bigger than the earth, and as Tycho calculates, 14,000 semidiameters distant from it? Whether they be thicker parts of the orbs, as Aristotle delivers, or so many habitable worlds, as Democritus? Whether they have light of their own, or from the sun, or give light round, as Patricius discourseth? *An aeque distent a centro mundi?*[23] Whether light be of their essence; and that light be a substance or an accident? Whether they be hot by themselves, or by ac-

cident cause heat? Whether there be such a precession of the equinoxes as Copernicus holds, or that the eighth sphere move? *An bene philosophentur R. Bacon et. J. Dee, Aphorism de multiplicatione specierum?*[24] Whether there be any such images ascending with each degree of the zodiac in the east, as Aliacensis feigns? *An aqua super coelum?*[25] as Patricius and the Schoolmen will, a crystalline watery heaven, which is certainly to be understood of that in the middle region? For otherwise, if at Noah's flood the water came from thence, it must be above an hundred years falling down to us, as some calculate. Besides, *an terra sit animata?*[26] which some so confidently believe with Orpheus, Hermes, Averroes, from which all other souls of men, beasts, devils, plants, fishes, etc., are derived and into which again, after some revolutions, as Plato in his *Timaeus,* Plotinus in his *Enneades* more largely discuss, they return (see Chalcidius and Bennius, Plato's commentators) as all philosophical matter *in materiam primam.*[27] Keplerus, Patricius, and some other neoterics[28] have in part revived this opinion, and that every star in heaven hath a soul, angel, or intelligence to animate or move it, etc.

Or to omit all smaller controversies as matters of less moment and examine that main paradox of the earth's motion now so much in question. Aristarchus Samius, Pythagoras maintained it of old, Democritus and many of their scholars. Didacus Astunica, Anthony Fascarinus, a Carmelite, and some other commentators will have Job to insinuate as much, *cap. 9, ver. 6, qui commovet terram de loco suo,*[29] etc., and that this one place of Scripture makes more for the earth's motion than all the other prove against it; whom Pineda confutes, most contradict. Howsoever, it is revived since by Copernicus, not as a truth but a supposition, as he confesseth himself in the preface to Pope Nicholas, but now maintained in good earnest by Calcagninus, Telesius, Kepler, Rotman, Gilbert, Digges, Galileus, Campanella, and especially by Lansbergius, *naturae, rationi, et veritati consentaneum,*[30] by Origanus, and some others of his followers. For if the earth be the center of the world, stand still, and the heavens move, as the most received opinion is, which they call *inordinatam coeli dispositionem,*[31] though stiffly maintained by Tycho, Ptolemeus, and their adherents, *quis ille furor?* etc., what fury is that, saith Dr. Gilbert, *satis animose,*[32] as Cabeus notes, that shall drive the heavens about with such incomprehensible celerity in 24 hours, whenas every point of the firmament and in the equator must needs move, so

[17]"Cold regions." [18]Have an evil reputation.
[19]"The opening of the gates." [20]"Whether the sky be colored."
[21]Telescope. [22]The Milky Way.
[23]"Whether they are equidistant from the center of the earth."
[24]"Whether Roger Bacon and John Dee philosophized wisely in their aphorisms on the multiplication of images."
[25]"Whether there is water above the sky."
[26]"Whether the earth is animated."
[27]"To the first or original matter." [28]Moderns.
[29]"Who shaketh the earth out of its place."
[30]"As harmonious with nature, reason, and truth."
[31]"A disordered arrangement of the heavens."
[32]With considerable vehemence.

Clavius calculates, 176,660 in one 246th part of an hour; and an arrow out of a bow must go seven times about the earth whilst a man can say an *Ave Maria* if it keep the same space or compass the earth 1,884 times in an hour, which is *supra humanam cogitationem,* beyond human conceit, *ocior et jaculo, et ventos, aequante sagitta.*[33] A man could not ride so much ground, going 40 miles a day, in 2,904 years as the firmament goes in 24 hours; or so much in 203 years as the said firmament in one minute; *quod incredible videtur.*[34]

. . . . . .

And 'tis true, they say, according to optic principles, the visible appearances of the planets do so indeed answer to their magnitudes and orbs and come nearest to mathematical observations and precedent calculations; there is no repugnancy to physical axioms because no penetration of orbs. But then between the sphere of Saturn and the firmament there is such an incredible and vast space of distance—7,000,000 semidiameters of the earth, as Tycho calculates—void of stars. And besides, they do so enhance the bigness of the stars, enlarge their circuit to solve those ordinary objections of parallaxes and retrogradations of the fixed stars, that alteration of the poles, elevation in several places or latitude of cities here on earth; for, say they, if a man's eye were in the firmament, he should not at all discern that great annual motion of the earth, but it would still appear *punctum indivisible*[35] and seem to be fixed in one place, of the same bigness; that it is quite opposite to reason, to natural philosophy, and all out as absurd as disproportional, so some will, as prodigious as that of the sun's swift motion of heavens. But *hoc posito,* to grant this their tenet of the earth's motion, if the earth move, it is a planet and shines to them in the moon and to the other planetary inhabitants as the moon and they do to us upon the earth. But shine she doth, as Galileo, Kepler, and others prove, and then *per consequens* the rest of the planets are inhabited as well as the moon, which he grants in his dissertation with Galileo's *Nuncius Sidereus,* "that there be Jovial and Saturn inhabitants," etc., and those several planets have their several moons about them as the earth hath hers, as Galileus hath already evinced by his glasses, four about Jupiter, two about Saturn (though Sitius the Florentine, Fortunius Licetus, and Julius Caesar le Galla cavil at it), yet Kepler, the emperor's mathematician, confirms out of his experience that he saw as much by the same help and more about Mars, Venus; and the rest they hope to find out peradventure even amongst the fixed stars, which Brunus and Brutius have already averred.

Then, I say, the earth and they be planets alike, inhabited alike, moved about the sun, the common center of the world alike, and it may be those two green children which Nubrigensis speaks of in his time, that fell from heaven, came from thence; and that famous stone that fell from heaven in Aristotle's time, Olymp. 84, *anno tertio, ad Capuoe Fluenta,*[36] recorded by Laertius and others, or *ancile* or buckler in Numa's time, recorded by Festus. We may likewise insert with Campanella and Brunus that which Pythagoras, Aristarchus Samius, Heraclitus, Epicurus, Melissus, De-

mocritus, Leucippus maintained in their ages, there be infinite worlds and infinite earths or systems *in infinito aethere,*[37] which Eusebius collects out of their tenets, because infinite stars and planets like unto this of ours, which some stick not still to maintain and publicly defend, *sperabundus expecto innumerabilium mundorum in aeternitate perambulationem,*[38] etc. (Nic. Hill, *Londinensis, Philos. Epicur.*) For if the firmament be of such an incomparable bigness as these Copernical giants will have it, *infinitum, aut infinito proximum,*[39] so vast and full of innumerable stars, as being infinite in extent, one above another, some higher, some lower, some nearer, some farther off, and so far asunder, and those so huge and great, insomuch, that if the whole sphere of Saturn and all that is included in it, *totum aggregatum,* as Fromundus of Louvain in his tract *De immobilitate terrae* argues, *evehatur inter stellas, videri a nobis non poterat, tam immanis est distantia inter tellurem et fixas, sed instar puncti,*[40] etc.

If our world be small in respect, why may we not suppose a plurality of worlds, those infinite stars visible in the firmament to be so many suns with particular fixed centers, to have likewise their subordinate planets, as the sun hath his dancing still round him? Which Cardinal Cusanus, Walkarinus, Brunus, and some others have held, and some still maintain, *animae Aristotelismo innutritae, et minutis speculationibus assuetae, secus forsan,*[41] etc. Though they seem close to us, they are infinitely distant, and so *per consequens* there are infinite habitable worlds; what hinders? Why should not an infinite cause, as God is, produce infinite effects? as Nic. Hill, *Democrit. philos.,* disputes. Kepler, I confess, will by no means admit of Brunus' infinite worlds or that the fixed stars should be so many suns with their compassing planets, yet the said Kepler betwixt jest and earnest in his perspectives, lunar geography, *et somnio suo, dissertat. cum nunc. sider.,*[42] seems in part to agree with this and partly to contradict; for the planets, he yields them to be inhabited, he doubts of the stars; and so doth Tycho in his astronomical epistles out of a consideration of their vastity and greatness break out into some suchlike speeches, that he will never believe those great and huge bodies were made to no other use than this that we perceive, to illuminate the earth, a point insensible in respect of the whole. But who shall dwell in these vast bodies, earths, worlds "if they be inhabited? Rational creatures?" as Kepler demands, "or have they souls to be saved? Or do they inhabit a better part of the world than we do? Are we

---

[33]"Quicker than a spear or arrow flying like the wind."
[34]"Which seems incredible."   [35]"An indivisible point."
[36]"In the third year (of the 84th Olympiad) in the Capuan stream."
[37]"In the infinite heavens."
[38]"I confidently maintain the eternal movement of innumerable worlds."   [39]Infinite or nearly so.
[40]Owing to the immense distance between the earth and the fixed stars, if the whole mass were carried to the stars we would see it only as a point.
[41]"Minds nourished on Aristotle and used to refined speculation (understand these things) perhaps differently."
[42]The fanciful speculations in Kepler's *Dissertatio* affixed to Galileo's *Sidereus Nuncius* ("heavenly messenger"), wherein the great Italian reported some of his discoveries with the telescope. Burton cites the same work two paragraphs above.

or they lords of the world? And how are all things made for man?" *Difficile est nodum hunc expedire, eo quod nondum omnia quae huc pertinent explorata habemus;*[43] 'tis hard to determine; this only he proves, that we are in *praecipuo mundi sinu,* in the best place, best world, nearest the heart of the sun. Thomas Campanella, a Calabrian monk, in his second book *De sensu rerum, Cap.* 4, subscribes to this of Keplerus; that they are inhabited he certainly supposeth, but with what kind of creatures he cannot say, he labors to prove it by all means, and that there are infinite worlds, having made an apology for Galileus, and dedicates this tenet of his to Cardinal Cajetanus. Others freely speak, mutter, and would persuade the world, as Marinus Marcenus complains, that our modern divines are too severe and rigid against mathematicians, ignorant and peevish in not admitting their true demonstrations and certain observations, that they tyrannize over art, science, and all philosophy in suppressing their labors, saith Pomponatius, forbidding them to write, to speak a truth, all to maintain their superstition and for their profit's sake. As for those places of Scripture which oppugn it, they will have spoken *ad captum vulgi,*[44] and if rightly understood and favorably interpreted, not at all against it, and as Otho Casman, *Astrol., cap.* 1, *part.* 1, notes, many great divines, besides Porphyrius, Proclus, Simplicius, and those heathen philosophers, *doctrina et aetate venerandi, Mosis Genesin mundanam popularis nescio cuius ruditatis, quae longa absit a vera philosophorum eruditione, insimulant;*[45] for Moses makes mention but of two planets, . . . [the sun and the moon], no four elements, etc. Read more in him, in Grossius and Junius.

But to proceed, these and such like insolent and bold attempts, prodigious paradoxes, inferences must needs follow if it once be granted which Rotman, Kepler, Gilbert, Diggeus, Origanus, Galileus, and others maintain of the earth's motion, that 'tis a planet and shines as the moon doth, which contains in it "both land and sea as the moon doth;" for so they find by their glasses that *maculae in facie lunae,*[46] "the brighter parts are earth, the dusky sea," which Thales, Plutarch, and Pythagoras formerly taught, and manifestly discern hills and dales and such like concavities, if we may subscribe to and believe Galileo's observations. But to avoid these paradoxes of the earth's motion, which the Church of Rome hath lately condemned as heretical, as appears by Blancanus' and Fromundus' writings, our latter mathematicians have rolled all the stones that may be stirred; and to solve all appearances and objections have invented new hypotheses and fabricated new systems of the world out of their own Daedalean[47] heads. Fracastorius will have the earth stand still as before; and to avoid that supposition of eccentrics and epicycles, he hath coined 72 homocentrics to solve all appearances. Nicholas Ramerus will have the earth the center of the world, but movable, and the eighth sphere immovable, the five upper planets to move about the sun, the sun and moon about the earth. Of which orbs, Tycho Brahe puts the earth the center immovable, the stars immovable, the rest with Ramerus, the planets without orbs to wander in the air, keep time and distance, true motion, according to that virtue which God hath given them. Heliseus Roeslin censureth both, with Copernicus (whose hypothesis *de terrae*

motu[48] Philippus Lansbergius hath lately vindicated and demonstrated with solid arguments in a just volume, Jansonius Caesius hath illustrated in a sphere).[49] . . .

But why should the sun and moon be angry or take exceptions at mathematicians and philosophers whenas the like measure is offered unto God himself by a company of theologasters?[50] They are not contented to see the sun and moon, measure their site and biggest distance in a glass, calculate their motions, or visit the moon in a poetical fiction or a dream, as he saith, *Audax facinus et memorabile nunc incipiam, neque hoc saeculo usurpatum prius, quid in lunae regno hac nocte gestum sit exponam, et quo nemo unquam nisi somniando pervenit,*[51] but he and Menippus, or as Peter Cuneus, *Bona fide agam, nihil eorum quae scripturus sum, verum esse scitote,* etc., *quae nec facta, nec futura sunt, dicam, stili tantum et ingenii causa,*[52] not in jest but in good earnest these gigantical Cyclopes will transcend spheres, heaven, stars into that empyrean heaven, soar higher yet, and see what God himself doth. The Jewish Talmudists take upon them to determine how God spends His whole time, sometimes playing with Leviathan, sometimes overseeing the world, etc., like Lucian's Jupiter, that spent much of the year in painting butterflies' wings and seeing who offered sacrifice, telling the hours when it should rain, how much snow should fall in such a place, which way the wind should stand in Greece, which way in Africa. In the Turks' Alcoran Mahomet is taken up to heaven upon a Pegasus sent a purpose from him[53] as he lay in bed with his wife, and after some conference with God is set on ground again. The pagans paint him and mangle him after a thousand fashions; our heretics, schismatics, and some Schoolmen come not far behind; some paint him in the habit of an old man and make maps of heaven, number the angels, tell their several names, offices; some deny God and His providence, some take his office out of his hand, will bind and loose in heaven, release, pardon, forgive, and be quartermaster with him; some call his Godhead in question, His power and attributes, His mercy, justice, providence; they will know with Cecilius why good and bad are punished together, war, fires, plagues infest all alike, why wicked men flourish, good are poor, in prison, sick, and ill at ease. Why doth He suffer so much mischief and evil to be done if He be able to help? why doth He not assist good or resist bad, reform our wills, if He be not the author of sin, and let such enormities be committed unworthy of His knowledge, wisdom, government, mercy, and providence, why lets He all things be

[43]It is hard to account for this because we lack the pertinent information.   [44]For the common man.
[45]"Venerable for age and knowledge, charge the Mosaic account in Genesis with being crude and vulgar, and far from true philosophical refinement."   [46]"The spots on the face of the moon."
[47]Inventive.   [48]"Concerning the motion of the earth."   [49]Globe.
[50]Dabblers in theology.
[51]"I now begin the bold and notable undertaking—as yet unattempted in this age—of explaining what has happened tonight in the kingdom of the moon, where no one has been except in a dream."
[52]Candidly, nothing that I have written is true, for I tell of things that have not happened and that will not happen merely to display my witty style.   [53]Jupiter.

done by fortune and chance? Others as prodigiously inquire after His omnipotency, *an possit plures similes creare deos? an ex scarabaeo deum? etc., et quo demum ruetis sacrificuli?*[54]

Some by visions and revelations take upon them to be familiar with God and to be of privy council with Him; they will tell how many and who shall be saved, when the world shall come to an end, what year, what month, and whatsoever else God hath reserved unto himself and to His angels. Some again, curious fantastics, will know more than this, and inquire with Epicurus what God did before the world was made? Was He idle? Where did He bide? What did He make the world of? Why did He then make it and not before? If He made it new, or to have an end, how is He unchangeable, infinite, etc.? Some will dispute, cavil, and object, as Julian did of old, whom Cyril confutes, as Simon Magus is feigned to do in that dialogue betwixt him and Peter; and Ammonius the philosopher in that dialogical disputation with Zacharias the Christian. If God be infinitely and only good, why should He alter or destroy the world? If He confound that which is good, how shall himself continue good? If He pull it down because evil, how shall He be free from the evil that made it evil? etc. With many such absurd and brainsick questions, intricacies, froth of human wit, and excrements of curiosity, etc., which, as our Saviour told His inquisitive disciples, are not fit for them to know.

But hoo! I am now gone quite out of sight, I am almost giddy with roving about. I could have ranged farther yet, but I am an infant and not able to dive into these profundities or sound these depths; not able to understand, much less to discuss. I leave the contemplation of these things to stronger wits, that have better ability and happier leisure to wade into such philosophical mysteries. For put case I were as able as willing, yet what can one man do? . . . When God sees His time, He will reveal these mysteries to mortal men and show that to some few at last which He hath concealed so long. For I am of his mind that Columbus did not find out America by chance but God directed him at that time to discover it; it was contingent to him, but necessary to God; He reveals and conceals to whom and when He will. And which one said of histories and records of former times, "God in His providence to check our presumptuous inquisition wraps up all things in uncertainty, bars us from long antiquity, and bounds our search within the compass of some few ages." Many good things are lost which our predecessors made use of, as Pancirola will better inform you; many new things are daily invented to the public good; so kingdoms, men, and knowledge ebb and flow, are hid and revealed, and when you have all done, as the Preacher concluded, *Nihil est sub sole novum.*[55] But my melancholy spaniel's quest, my game, is sprung, and I must suddenly come down and follow. . . .

THE THIRD PARTITION. LOVE MELANCHOLY

SECTION II, MEMBER I

SUBSECTION 2. HOW LOVE TYRANNIZETH OVER MEN. LOVE OR HEROICAL MELANCHOLY, HIS DEFINITION, PART AFFECTED

. . . This love of ours is immoderate, inordinate, and not to be comprehended in any bounds. It will not contain itself within the union of marriage, or apply to one object, but is a wandering, extravagant, a domineering, a boundless, an irrefragable, a destructive passion: sometimes this burning lust rageth after marriage, and then it is properly called jealousy; sometimes before, and then it is called heroical melancholy; it extends sometimes to corrivals, etc., begets rapes, incests, murders: *Marcus Antonius compressit Faustinam sororem, Caracalla Juliam novercam, Nero matrem, Caligula sorores, Cinyras Myrrham filiam, etc.*[56] But it is confined within no terms of blood, years, sex, or whatsoever else. Some furiously rage before they come to discretion or age. Quartilla in Petronius never remembered she was a maid; and the Wife of Bath, in Chaucer, cracks,

> Since I was twelve years old, believe,
> Husbands at kirk-door had I five.[57]

Aretine's[58] Lucretia sold her maidenhead a thousand times before she was twenty-four years old, *plus millies vendideram virginitatem, etc., neque te celabo, non deerant qui ut integram ambirent.*[59] Rahab, that harlot, began to be a professed quean at ten years of age, and was but fifteen when she hid the spies, as Hugh Broughton proves, to whom Serrarius the Jesuit, *quaest. 6 in cap. 2 Josue,* subscribes. Generally women begin *pubescere,*[60] as they call it, or *catulire,*[61] as Julius Pollux cites, *lib. 2, cap. 3, Onomast.* out of Aristophanes, at fourteen years old, then they do offer themselves, and some plainly rage. Leo Afer saith that in Africa a man shall scarce find a maid at fourteen years of age, they are so forward, and many amongst us after they come into the teens do not live without husbands, but linger. What pranks in this kind the middle age have played is not to be recorded, *Si mihi sint centum linguae, sint oraque centum,*[62] no tongue can sufficiently declare, every story is full of men and women's insatiable lust, Neros, Heliogabali, Bonosi, etc. *Coelius Aufilenum, sed Quintius Aufilenam depereunt, etc.*[63] They neigh after other men's wives (as Jeremy, *cap.* v, 8, complaineth) like fed horses, or range like town bulls, *raptores virginum et viduarum,*[64] as many of our great ones do. Solomon's wisdom was extinguished in this fire of lust, Samson's strength enervated, piety in Lot's daughters quite forgot, gravity of priesthood in Eli's sons, reverend old age in the elders that would violate Susanna, filial duty in Absalom to his stepmother, brotherly love in Amnon towards his sister. Human, divine laws, precepts, exhortations, fear of God and men, fair, foul means, fame, fortunes, shame, disgrace, honor cannot oppose, stave off, or withstand the fury of it, *omnia vincit amor,*[65] etc. No cord nor cable can so forcibly draw, or hold so fast,

[54]"Is He able to make other gods? A god from a scarab? If so, where will you sacrificing priests collapse?"
[55]"There is no new thing under the sun" (Ecclesiastes 1.9).
[56]"Mark Antony embraced his sister Faustina, Caracalla his stepmother Julia, Nero his mother, Caligula his sisters, Cinyras his daughter Myrrha."
[57]*Had I five*: Here, as often elsewhere, Burton quotes inaccurately from memory. [58]Text *Aretine.*
[59]Moreover, there were those who could restore it.
[60]"To grow pubic hair." [61]"To desire a male."
[62]"If I had a hundred tongues and mouths."
[63]"Coelius burned with lust for Aufilenus, Quinctius for Aufilena."
[64]"Ravishers of maids and widows." [65]"Love conquers all."

as love can do with a twined thread. The scorching beams under the equinoctial, or extremity of cold within the circle arctic, where the very seas are frozen, cold or torrid zone cannot avoid or expel this heat, fury, and rage of mortal men.

> *Quo fugis? ah, demens! nulla est fuga, tu licet usque*
> *Ad Tanaim fugias, usque sequetur amor.*[66]

Of women's unnatural, unsatiable lust, what country, what village doth not complain? Mother and daughter sometimes dote on the same man; father and son, master and servant on one woman.

> *Sed amor, sed ineffrenata libido,*
> *Quid castum in terris intentatumque reliquit?*[67]

What breach of vows and oaths, fury, dotage, madness, might I reckon up! Yet this is more tolerable in youth, and such as are still in their hot blood; but for an old fool to dote, to see an old lecher, what more odious, what can be more absurd? and yet what so common? Who so furious? *Amare ea aetate si occeperint, multo insaniunt acrius.*[68] Some dote then more than ever they did in their youth. How many decrepit, hoary, harsh, writhen, bursten-bellied, crooked, toothless, bald, blear-eyed, impotent, rotten old men shall you see flickering still in every place? One gets him a young wife, another a courtesan, and when he can scarce lift his leg over a sill, and hath one foot already in Charon's boat, when he hath the trembling in his joints, the gout in his feet, a perpetual rheum in his head, a continuate cough, "his sight fails him, thick of hearing, his breath stinks," all his moisture is dried up and gone, may not spit from him, a very child again, that cannot dress himself, or cut his own meat, yet he will be dreaming of, and honing after wenches; what can be more unseemly? Worse it is in women than in men; when she is *aetate declivis, diu vidua, mater olim, parum decore matrimonium sequi videtur*, an old widow, a mother so long since (in Pliny's opinion), she doth very unseemly seek to marry; yet whilst she is so old a crone, a beldam, she can neither see nor hear, go nor stand, a mere carcass, a witch, and scarce feel, she caterwauls, and must have a stallion, a champion, she must and will marry again, and betroth herself to some young man, that hates to look on [her] but for her goods, abhors the sight of her; to the prejudice of her good name, her own undoing, grief of friends, and ruin of her children.

But to enlarge or illustrate this power and effects of love is to set a candle in the sun. It rageth with all sorts and conditions of men, yet is most evident among such as are young and lusty, in the flower of their years, nobly descended, high fed, such as live idly and at ease; and for that cause (which our divines call burning lust) this *ferinus insanus amor*, this mad and beastly passion, as I have said, is named by our physicians heroical love, and a more honorable title put upon it, *amor nobilis*, as Savonarola styles it, because noble men and women make a common practice of it, and are so ordinarily affected with it. Avicenna, *lib. 3, fen. 1, tract. 4, cap.* 23, calleth this passion *Ilishi*, and defines it to be "a disease or melancholy vexation, or anguish of mind, in which a man continually meditates of the beauty, gesture, manners of his mistress, and troubles himself about it"; "desiring"

(as Savonarola adds) "with all intentions and eagerness of mind to compass or enjoy her; as commonly hunters trouble themselves about their sports, the covetous about their gold and goods, so is he tormented still about his mistress." Arnoldus Villanovanus, in his book of heroical love, defines it "a continual cogitation of that which he desires, with a confidence or hope of compassing it"; which definition his commentator cavils at. For continual cogitation is not the *genus*, but a symptom of love; we continually think of that which we hate and abhor, as well as that which we love; and many things we covet and desire, without all hope of attaining. Carolus à Lorme, in his *Questions*, makes a doubt *an amor sit morbus*, whether this heroical love be a disease: Julius Pollux, *Onomast. lib.* 6, *cap.* 44, determines it. They that are in love are likewise sick; *lascivus, salax, lasciviens, et qui in venerem furit, vere est aegrotus.*[69] Arnoldus will have it improperly so called, and a malady rather of the body than mind. Tully, in his *Tusculans*, defines it a furious disease of the mind; Plato, madness itself; Ficinus, his commentator, *cap.* 12, a species of madness, "for many have run mad for women" (1 Esdras); but Rhasis, "a melancholy passion"; and most physicians make it a species or kind of melancholy (as will appear by the symptoms), and treat of it apart; whom I mean to imitate, and to discuss it in all his kinds, to examine his several causes, to show his symptoms, indications, prognostics, effect, that so it may be with more facility cured. . . .

SECTION IV, MEMBER 1

SUBSECTION 2. CAUSES OF RELIGIOUS MELANCHOLY . . .

. . . What power of prince or penal law, be it never so strict, could enforce men to do that which for conscience' sake they will voluntarily undergo? As to fast from all flesh, abstain from marriage, rise to their prayers at midnight, whip themselves, with stupend fasting and penance, abandon the world, wilful poverty, perform canonical and blind obedience, to prostrate their goods, fortunes, bodies, lives, and offer up themselves at their superior's feet at his command? What so powerful an engine as superstition? Which they, right well perceiving, are of no religion at all themselves: *Primum enim* (as Calvin rightly suspects, the tenor and practice of their life proves) *arcanae illius theologiae, quod apud eos regnat, caput est, nullum esse deum,*[70] they hold there is no God, as Leo X did, Hildebrand the magician, Alexander VI, Julius II, mere atheists, and which the common proverb amongst them approves: "The worst Christians of Italy are the Romans, of the Romans the priests are wildest, the lewdest priests are preferred to be cardinals, and the baddest man amongst the cardinals is chosen to be Pope," that is an epicure, as most part the popes are, infidels and Lucianists, for

---

[66]"Where will you flee? Ah, you madman, there is no escape. If you fly as far as the River Tanais, love will follow you."
[67]"Whom have love and ungovernable desire left pure and untouched in all the world?"
[68]"If they begin to love at that age their madness is all the worse."
[69]"He who is lustful, lecherous, and lascivious, and who rages with desire, is truly sick."
[70]"For indeed the main secret of these theologians, which is dominant among them, is that there is no god."

so they think and believe; and what is said of Christ to be fables and impostures, of heaven and hell, day of judgment, paradise, immortality of the soul, are all

> *Rumores vacui, verbaque inania,*
> *Et par sollicito fabula somnio,*

dreams, toys, and old wives' tales. Yet as so many whetstones to make other tools cut, but cut not themselves, though they be of no religion at all, they will make others most devout and superstitious, by promises and threats compel, enforce from, and lead them by the nose like so 10 many bears in a line; whenas their end is not to propagate the church, advance God's kingdom, seek His glory or common good, but to enrich themselves, to enlarge their territories, to domineer and compel them to stand in awe, to live in subjection to the See of Rome. For what otherwise care they? *Si mundus vult decipi, decipiatur,*[71] 'tis fit it should be so. And [that] for which Austin cites Varro to maintain his Roman religion, we may better apply to them: *Multa vera, quae vulgus scire non est utile; pleraque falsa, quae tamen aliter existimare populum expedit;* some things are true, some 20 false, which for their own ends they will not have the gullish commonalty take notice of. As well may witness their intolerable covetousness, strange forgeries, fopperies, fooleries, unrighteous subtleties, impostures, illusions, new doctrines, paradoxes, traditions, false miracles, which they have still forged to enthrall, circumvent, and subjugate them, to maintain their own estates. One while by bulls, pardons, indulgences, and their doctrine of good works, that they be meritorious, hope of heaven, by that means they have so fleeced the commonalty, and spurred on this free superstitious 30 horse, that he runs himself blind, and is an ass to carry burdens. They have so amplified Peter's patrimony that from a poor bishop he is become *Rex regum, Dominus dominantium*[72] a demigod, as his canonists make him (Felinus and the rest), above God himself; and for his wealth and temporalties is not inferior to many kings; his cardinals, princes' companions; and in every kingdom almost, abbots, priors, monks, friars, etc., and his clergy, have engrossed a third part, half, in some places all, into their hands. Three princes electors in Germany, bishops; besides Magdeburg, Spires, 40 Salzburg, Bremen, Bamberg, etc. In France, as Bodine, *Lib. de repub.,* gives us to understand, their revenues are twelve millions and three hundred thousand livres; and of twelve parts of the revenues in France the church possesseth seven. The Jesuits, a new sect begun in this age, have, as Middendorpius and Pelargus reckon up, three or four hundred colleges in Europe, and more revenues than many princes. In France, as Arnoldus proves, in thirty years they have got *bis centum librarum millia annua,*[73] £200,000. I say nothing of the rest of their orders. We have had in England, 50 as Armachanus demonstrates, above thirty thousand friars at once, and as Speed collects out of Leland and others, almost six hundred religious houses, and near £200,000 in revenues of the old rent belonging to them, besides images of gold, silver plate, furniture, goods and ornaments, as Weever calculates, and esteems them, at the dissolution of abbeys, worth a million of gold.

How many towns in every kingdom hath superstition enriched! What a deal of money by musty relics, images, idolatry, have their mass priests engrossed, and what sums have they scraped by their other tricks, Loretto in Italy, Walsingham in England, in those days, *ubi omnia auro nitent,*[74] saith Erasmus, St. Thomas' shrine, etc., may witness. Delphi, so renowned of old in Greece for Apollo's oracle; Delos, *commune conciliabulum et emporium sola religione munitum;*[75] Dodona, whose fame and wealth were sustained by religion, were not so rich, so famous. If they can get but a relic of some saint, the Virgin Mary's picture, idols or the like, that city is forever made, it needs no other maintenance. Now if any of these their impostures or juggling tricks be controverted, or called in question; if a magnanimous or zealous Luther, an heroical Luther, as Dithmarus calls him, dare touch the monks' bellies, all is in a combustion, all is in an uproar: Demetrius and his associates are ready to pull him in pieces to keep up their trades. "Great is Diana of the Ephesians": with a mighty shout of two hours long they will roar and not be pacified.

Now for their authority, what by auricular confession, satisfaction, penance, Peter's keys, thunderings, excommunications, etc., roaring bulls, this high priest of Rome, shaking his Gorgon's head, hath so terrified the soul of many a silly man, insulted over majesty itself, and swaggered generally over all Europe for many ages, and still doth to some, holding them as yet in slavish subjection, as never tyrannizing Spaniards did by their poor Negroes, or Turks by their galley-slaves. "The Bishop of Rome" (saith Stapleton, a parasite of his, *De mag. Eccles. lib. 2, cap.* 1) "hath done that without arms, which those Roman emperors could never achieve with forty legions of soldiers," deposed kings, and crowned them again with his foot, made friends, and corrected at his pleasure, etc. " 'Tis a wonder," saith Machiavel, *Florentinae hist. lib.* 1, "what slavery King Henry the Second endured for the death of Th. Becket, what things he was enjoined by the Pope, and how he submitted himself to do that which in our times a private man would not endure," and all through superstition. Henry the Fourth, deposed of his empire, stood barefooted with his wife at the gates of Canossa. Frederick the Emperor was trodden on by Alexander the Third; another held Adrian's stirrup; King John kissed the knees of Pandulph the pope's legate, etc. What made so many thousand Christians travel from France, Britain, etc., into the Holy Land, spend such huge sums of money, go a pilgrimage so familiarly to Jerusalem, to creep and crouch,[76] but slavish superstition? What makes them so freely venture their lives, to leave their native countries, to go seek martyrdom in the Indies, but superstition? to be assassinates,[77] to meet death, murder kings, but a false persuasion of merit, of canonical or blind obedience which they instill into them, and animate them by strange illusions, hope

---

[71]"If the world wishes to be deceived, let it be deceived."
[72]"King of kings, lord of lords."
[73]"Two hundred thousand pounds annually."
[74]"Where everything glistens with gold."
[75]"A combined social and commercial center fortified only by religion." [76]Text *couch.* [77]Assassins.

of being martyrs and saints? Such pretty feats can the devil work by priests, and so well for their own advantage can they play their parts. And if it were not yet enough by priests and politicians to delude mankind and crucify the souls of men, he hath more actors in his tragedy, more irons in the fire, another scene of heretics, factious, ambitious wits, insolent spirits, schismatics, impostors, false prophets, blind guides, that out of pride, singularity, vainglory, blind zeal, cause much more madness yet, set all in an uproar by their new doctrines, paradoxes, figments, crotchets, make new divisions, subdivisions, new sects, oppose one superstition to another, one kingdom to another, commit prince and subjects, brother against brother, father against son, to the ruin and destruction of a commonwealth, to the disturbance of peace, and to make a general confusion of all estates.

How did those Arians rage of old! How many did they circumvent! Those Pelagians, Manichees, etc.! their names alone would make a just volume. How many silly souls have impostors still deluded, drawn away, and quite alienated from Christ! Lucian's Alexander; Simon Magus, whose statue was to be seen and adored in Rome, saith Justin Martyr, *Simoni deo sancto,* etc., after his decease; Apollonius Tyanaeus, Cynops, Eumo, who, by counterfeiting some new ceremonies and juggling tricks of that *Dea Syria,*[78] by spitting fire, and the like, got an army together of forty thousand men, and did much harm: with Eudo de Stellis, of whom Nubrigensis speaks, *lib.* 1, *cap.* 19, that in King Stephen's days imitated most of Christ's miracles, fed I know not how many people in the wilderness, and built castles in the air, etc., to the seducing of multitudes of poor souls. In Franconia, 1476, a base illiterate fellow took upon him to be a prophet and preach, John Beheim by name, a neatherd at Nichollausen; he seduced thirty thousand persons, and was taken by the commonalty to be a most holy man, come from heaven. "Tradesmen left their shops, women their distaffs, servants ran from their masters, children from their parents, scholars left their tutors, all to hear him, some for novelty, some for zeal. He was burnt at last by the Bishop of Wurtzburg, and so he and his heresy vanished together." How many such impostors, false prophets, have lived in every king's reign! What chronicle will not afford such examples, that as so many *ignes fatui,* have led men out of the way, terrified some, deluded others, that are apt to be carried about with the blast of every wind, a rude inconstant multitude, a silly company of poor souls, that follow all, and are cluttered together like so many pebbles in a tide. What prodigious follies, madness, vexations, persecutions, absurdities, impossibilities, these impostors, heretics, etc., have thrust upon the world, what strange effects, shall be showed in the Symptoms.

SUBSECTION 3. SYMPTOMS GENERAL . . .

[To show that superstition, credulity, and religious frenzy are not confined to Roman Catholics, Burton also treats the knaves and fools who have vulgarized the pure truth of reformed theology.]

Thus they continued in such error, blindness, decrees, sophisms, superstitions; idle ceremonies and traditions were the sum of their new-coined holiness and religion, and by these knaveries and stratagems they were able to involve multitudes, to deceive the most sanctified souls, and, if it were possible, the very elect. In the meantime the true church, as wine and water mixed, lay hid and obscure to speak of till Luther's time, who began upon a sudden to defecate,[79] and as another sun to drive away those foggy mists of superstition, to restore it to that purity of the primitive church. And after him many good and godly men, divine spirits, have done their endeavours, and still do.

> And what their ignorance esteemed so holy,
> Our wiser ages do accompt as folly.

But see the devil, that will never suffer the church to be quiet or at rest: no garden so well tilled but some noxious weeds grow up in it, no wheat but it hath some tares: we have a mad giddy company of precisians, schismatics, and some heretics, even in our own bosoms in another extreme (*Dum vitant stulti vitia in contraria currunt*);[80] that out of too much zeal in opposition to Antichrist, human traditions, those Romish rites and superstitions, will quite demolish all, they will admit of no ceremonies at all, no fasting days, no cross in baptism, kneeling at communion, no church music, etc., no bishops' courts, no church government, rail at all our church discipline, will not hold their tongues, and all for the peace of thee, O Sion! No, not so much as degrees some of them will tolerate, or universities; all human learning ('tis *cloaca diaboli*),[81] hoods, habits, cap and surplice, such as are things indifferent in themselves, and wholly for ornament, decency, or distinction sake, they abhor, hate, and snuff at, as a stone-horse[82] when he meets a bear: they make matters of conscience of them, and will rather forsake their livings than subscribe to them. They will admit of no holidays, or honest recreations, as of hawking, hunting, etc., no churches, no bells some of them, because papists use them; no discipline, no ceremonies but what they invent themselves; no interpretations of Scriptures, no comments of Fathers, no councils, but such as their own phantastical spirits dictate, or *recta ratio,* as Socinians; by which spirit misled, many times they broach as prodigious paradoxes as papists themselves. Some of them turn prophets, have secret revelations, will be of privy council with God Himself, and know all His secrets, *per capillos Spiritum Sanctum tenent, et omnia sciunt cum sint asini omnium obstinatissimi.*[83] A company of giddy heads will take upon them to define how many shall be saved and who damned in a parish, where they shall sit in heaven, interpret apocalypses (*commentatores praecipites et vertiginosos,*[84] one calls them, as well he might) and those hidden mysteries to private persons, times, places, as their own spirit informs them, private revelations shall suggest, and precisely set down when the world shall come to an end, what year, what month, what day. Some of them again

---

78"Syrian goddess."
79Purify. 80Fools rush from one extreme to the other.
81"The devil's sewer." 82Stallion.
83"Grasp the Holy Ghost by the hair, and know everything even though they are the most obstinate of all asses."
84"Rash and dizzy-minded commentators."

have such strong faith, so presumptuous, they will go into infected houses, expel devils, and fast forty days, as Christ himself did; some call God and His attributes into question, as Vorstius and Socinus; some princes, civil magistrates, and their authorities, as Anabaptists, will do all their own private spirit dictates, and nothing else. Brownists, Barrowists, Familists, and those Amsterdamian sects and sectaries are led all by so many private spirits. It is a wonder to reveal what passages Sleidan relates in his *Commentaries* of Cretink, Knipperdoling, and their associates, those madmen of Munster in Germany; what strange enthusiasms, 'sottish revelations they had, how absurdly they carried themselves, deluded others; and as profane Machiavel in his *Political Disputations* holds of Christian religion, in general it doth enervate, debilitate, take away men's spirits and courage from them, *simpliciores reddit homines,*[85] breeds nothing so courageous soldiers as that Roman: we may say of these peculiar sects, their religion takes away not spirits only, but wit and judgment, and deprives them of their understanding; for some of them are so far gone with their private enthusiasms and revelations that they are quite mad, out of their wits.

What greater madness can there be than for a man to take upon him to be God, as some do? to be the Holy Ghost, Elias, and what not? In Poland, 1518, in the reign of King Sigismund, one said he was Christ, and got him twelve apostles, came to judge the world, and strangely deluded the commons. One David George, an illiterate painter, not many years since, did as much in Holland, took upon him to be the Messias, and had many followers. Benedictus Victorinus Faventinus, *Consil.* 15, writes as much of one Honorius, that though he was not only inspired as a prophet, but that

he was a god himself, and had familiar conference with God and His angels. Lavater, *De spect. cap.* 2, *part.* 8, hath a story of one John Sartorius that thought he was the prophet Elias, and, *cap.* 7, of divers others that had conference with angels, were saints, prophets. Wierus, *lib.* 3 *De lamiis, cap.* 7, makes mention of a prophet of Groningen that said he was God the Father; of an Italian and Spanish prophet that held as much. We need not rove so far abroad, we have familiar examples at home: Hacket that said he was Christ; Coppinger and Arthington his disciples; Burchet and Hovatus, burned at Norwich. We are never likely seven years together without some such new prophets that have several inspirations, some to convert the Jews, some fast forty days, go with Daniel to the lions' den; some foretell strange things, some for one thing, some for another. Great precisians[86] of mean conditions and very illiterate, most part by a preposterous zeal, fasting, meditation, melancholy, are brought into those gross errors and inconveniences. Of those men I may conclude generally that howsoever they may seem to be discreet, and men of understanding in other matters, discourse well, *laesam habent imaginationem,*[87] they are like comets, round in all places but only where they blaze, *caetera sani,*[88] they have impregnable wits many of them, and discreet otherwise, but in this their madness and folly breaks out beyond measure, *in infinitum erumpit stultitia.* They are certainly far gone with melancholy, if not quite mad, and have more need of physic than many a man that keeps his bed, more need of hellebore[89] than those that are in Bedlam.

[85]"Makes men even simpler."   [86]Puritans.
[87]"They have diseased imaginations."   [88]"Otherwise sane."
[89]An herb prescribed for mental disorders.

Sir Thomas Browne [1605-1682]

Although Browne called his early life "a miracle of thirty years, which to relate were not a history but a piece of poetry," Johnson, with characteristic bluntness, pointed out that the facts did not support this high-flown notion. "A scholastic and academical life is very uniform," he said, "and has, indeed, more safety than pleasure. . . . Surely a man may visit France and Italy, reside at Montpellier and Padua, and at last take his degree at Leiden without anything miraculous." It would seem that Johnson was, as usual, right. The son of a prosperous mercer who left him well endowed with money, Browne, like Keats, was harried by rapacious guardians, but unlike Keats he received an excellent education, first at Winchester (1616–23) and then at Broadgate Hall (the present Pembroke College), Oxford, where he took two degrees (B.A. 1626, A.M. 1629). Four more years of study on the Continent (1629–33)—mainly, it would seem, at Montpellier—led to the M.D. degree from Leiden and the completion of his formal education.

It was presumably after his return to England and certainly not long before his thirtieth year that he wrote his first and best-known book (as well as other pieces "of affinity thereto") for his "private exercise and satisfaction." *Religio Medici* was "penned," he later said," in such a place, and with such disadvantage, that (I protest) from the first setting of pen unto paper I had not the assistance of any good book whereby to promote my invention or relieve my memory"; but despite these disabilities it was passed among Browne's friends in manuscripts (at least eight of which survive) until its publication in two unauthorized editions in 1642. Except for the "importunity" of those whose opinion he respected and his own "allegiance" unto truth he would have let the matter rest, he said,

> but because things evidently false are not only printed, but many things of truth most falsely set forth, in this latter I could not but think myself engaged. For though we have no power to redress the former, yet in the other, reparation being within ourselves, I have at present represented unto the world a full and intended copy of that piece which was most imperfectly and surreptitiously published before.

And so in 1643 there appeared an authorized edition, which, incidentally, was printed by the same Andrew Crooke who had "most imperfectly and surreptitiously" produced the work in 1642.

Religio Medici at once achieved the fame, or notoriety, that it has never lost. Sir Kenelm Digby promptly registered some of his objections to the 1642 edition (see pp. 486 ff.), and in 1645 the incorrigible Alexander Ross (see p. 501) impartially exposed the errors of both Browne and Digby in his *Medicus Medicatus*; but meanwhile a Latin translation by one James Merryweather, which had appeared at Leiden in 1644, gave the work a Continental reputation that was in time attested by versions in Dutch, French, and German, as well as by its listing, with other dangerous books, in the Catholic *Index librorum prohibitorum*. It has been said that *Religio Medici* was the first literary (as distinct from learned) English work to enjoy such a European success since Sir Thomas More's *Utopia*.

Between the composition and the publication of his famous book Browne had established a successful medical practice in Norwich, married (1641), and—despite his earlier wish that "we might procreate like trees, without conjunction"—begun to sire a family of twelve children, to whom, as his charming letters show, he was a most devoted parent. In 1646 his *Pseudodoxia Epidemica* (or *Vulgar Errors*) secured his reputation as a scholar immensely erudite about "the America and untraveled parts of Truth." Enlarged in 1650, this extraordinary book was so successful that by 1672 it had reached a sixth edition. It was followed in 1658 by the joint publication of *Hydriotaphia* (or *Urn Burial*) and *The Garden of Cyrus*, treatises respectively on funerary customs and on the quincunx. Although these were the last works that Browne himself prepared for publication, he continued his career in Norwich as a doctor, savant, and virtuoso of international repute. The knighthood that Charles II bestowed on him during a state visit to the town in 1671 may have cost that fickle monarch nothing, as Johnson brusquely noted, but it confirmed the wide esteem of one whose epitaph described him truly as *vir prudentissimus, integerrimus, doctissimus*.

Although Browne had declared "diuturnity" to be "a dream and folly of expectation," the record of his posthumous publications tends to jeopardize his own prediction. In 1683 Thomas Tenison, later archbishop of Canterbury, brought together some of his late friend's "disordered" papers—most of them apparently drafts of letters to his learned correspondents—as *Certain Miscellany Tracts* on such subjects as plants mentioned in the Bible, falconry, the Delphic oracle, and "the fishes eaten by our Saviour with His disciples after His resurrection from the dead." Although the so-called collected *Works* appeared in folio in 1686, the canon was enlarged in 1690 with *A Letter to a Friend* (a consolatory and clinical report on the terminal illness of one of Browne's own patients), in 1712 by the *Posthumous Works* (which include, among other oddments, an account of the tombs and monuments in Norwich Cathedral), and in 1716 by a string of rather disconnected essays entitled *Christian Morals* (for the second edition of which Johnson wrote his famous life of Browne in 1756). Many other tracts and letters are preserved among the Sloan Manuscripts in the British Museum.

I have based my text of *Religio Medici* on the second, authorized edition of 1643 (Wing B-5169), of *Pseudodoxia Epidemica* on the second (1650) edition (Wing B-5160), and of *Hydriotaphia* on the

1658 edition (Wing B-5154). Browne was fortunate in his first editor, the indefatigable Simon Wilkins (4 vols., 1835-36; Bohn Library, 3 vols., 1852), whose work is still of value despite later editions by Charles Sayle (3 vols., 1904–07) and Sir Geoffrey Keynes (6 vols., 1928–31; rev., 4 vols., 1961). There are editions of *Religio Medici* by W. A. Greenhill (1881), W. Murison (1922), and J. J. Denonain (2d ed., 1955), and of *Hydriotaphia* by Sir John Evans (1893), Greenhill (1896), Murison (1922), and John Carter (2d ed., 1958)—the last of great importance for its attention to the text. Keynes' volume of selections (1968) is less useful than Norman Endicott's (1968), which has an excellent apparatus. Keynes' standard *Bibliography* (2d ed., 1958) has been in no way superseded by Denis Donovan's (1968), which should be used with caution.

Johnson's life of Browne (1756) is still important, but Edmund Gosse's (1905) has in various ways been superseded by Olivier Leroy's (in French, 1931), F. L. Huntley's (1962), and Joan Bennett's (1962). J. S. Finch's biography (1950) is of less importance. Browne is properly given much attention by the students of seventeenth-century philosophy and of prose style listed in the General Bibliography, Sections I and IV, but there are more special studies (in addition to Sir Kenelm Digby's) by W. P. Dunn (2d ed., 1950), Robert Sencourt (*Outflying Philosophy*, 1924), D. K. Ziegler (*In Divided and Distinguished Worlds*, 1943), C. E. Raven (*English Naturalists*, 1947), E. S. Merton (*Science and Imagination in Sir Thomas Browne*, 1949), and Leonard Nathanson (*The Strategy of Truth: A Study of Sir Thomas Browne*, 1967).

from Religio Medici (1643)

To The Reader

Certainly that man were greedy of life who should desire to live when all the world were at an end, and he must needs be very impatient who would repine at death in the society of all things that suffer under it. Had not almost every man suffered by the press or were not the tyranny thereof become universal,[1] I had not wanted reason for complaint; but in times wherein I have lived to behold the highest perversion of that excellent invention, the name of His Majesty defamed, the honor of Parliament depraved, the writings of both depravedly, anticipatively, counterfeitly imprinted, [10] complaints may seem ridiculous in private persons; and men of my condition may be as incapable of affronts as hopeless of their reparations. And truly had not the duty I owe unto the importunity of friends and the allegiance I must ever acknowledge unto truth prevailed with me, the inactivity of my disposition might have made these sufferings continual, and time, that brings other things to light, should have satisfied me in the remedy of its oblivion. But because things evidently false are not only printed, but many things of truth most falsely set forth, in this latter I could not but think [20] myself engaged. For though we have no power to redress the former, yet in the other, reparation being within ourselves, I have at present represented unto the world a full and intended copy of that piece which was most imperfectly and surreptitiously published before.

This, I confess, about seven years past, with some others of affinity thereto, for my private exercise and satisfaction, I had at leisurable hours composed; which being communicated unto one, it became common unto many, and

was by transcription successively corrupted, until it arrived in a most depraved copy at the press. He that shall peruse that work, and shall take notice of sundry particularities and personal expressions therein, will easily discern the intention was not public; and being a private exercise directed to myself, what is delivered therein was rather a memorial unto me than an example or rule unto any other; and therefore if there be any singularity therein correspondent unto the private conceptions of any man, it doth not advantage them; or if dissentaneous[2] thereunto, it no way overthrows them. It was penned in such a place, and with such disadvantage, that (I protest) from the first setting of pen unto paper I had not the assistance of any good book whereby to promote my invention or relieve my memory; and therefore there might be many real lapses therein which others might take notice of, and more than I suspected myself. It was set down many years past, and was the sense of my conception at that time, not an immutable law unto my advancing judgement at all times; and therefore there might be many things therein plausible unto my passed apprehension which are not agreeable unto my present self. There are many things delivered rhetorically, many expressions therein meerly tropical,[3] and as they best illustrate my intention; and therefore also there are many things to be

RELIGIO MEDICI   [1]After 1640, when the Long Parliament relaxed the rigid censorship that had been a formidable instrument of terror in the hands of Charles and Archbishop Laud and the Star Chamber, there was a flood of books and pamphlets on controversial questions of politics and religion.   [2]At variance.   [3]Metaphorical.

taken in a soft and flexible sense, and not to be called unto the rigid test of reason. Lastly, all that is contained therein is in submission unto maturer discernments and, as I have declared, shall no further father them than the best and learned judgments shall authorize them, under favor of which considerations I have made its secrecy public, and committed the truth thereof to every ingenuous reader.

Tho. Browne

[THE FIRST PART]

SECTION 1

For my religion, though there be several circumstances that might persuade the world I have none at all, as the general scandal of my profession,[4] the natural course of my studies, the indifferency[5] of my behavior and discourse in matters of religion, neither violently defending one nor with that common ardor and contention opposing another, yet, in despite hereof I dare, without usurpation, assume the honorable style of a Christian. Not that I merely owe this title to the font, my education, or clime wherein I was born, as being bred up either to confirm those principles my parents instilled into my understanding, or by a general consent proceed in the religion of my country, but having in my riper years and confirmed judgment seen and examined all, I find myself obliged by the principles of grace and the law of mine own reason to embrace no other name but this. Neither doth herein my zeal so far make me forget the general charity I owe unto humanity, as rather to hate than pity Turks, infidels, and (what is worse) Jews, rather contenting myself to enjoy that happy style than maligning those who refuse so glorious a title.

SECTION 2

But because the name of a Christian is become too general to express our faith, there being a geography of religion as well as lands, and every clime distinguished not only by their laws and limits but circumscribed by their doctrines and rules of faith; to be particular, I am of that reformed new-cast religion, wherein I dislike nothing but the name;[6] of the same belief our Saviour taught, the apostles disseminated, the fathers authorized, and the martyrs confirmed, but by the sinister ends of princes, the ambition and avarice of prelates, and the fatal corruption of times so decayed, impaired, and fallen from its native beauty that it required the careful and charitable hands of these times to restore it to its primitive integrity. Now the accidental occasion whereon, the slender means whereby the low and abject condition of the person[7] by whom so good a work was set on foot, which in our adversaries beget contempt and scorn, fills me with wonder, and is the very same objection the insolent pagans first cast at Christ and his disciples.

SECTION 3

Yet have I not so shaken hands with those desperate resolutions who had rather venture at large their decayed bottom[8] than bring her in to be new trimmed in the dock, who had rather promiscuously retain all than abridge any, and obstinately be what they are than what they have been,

as to stand in diameter and sword's point with them. We have reformed from them, not against them; for omitting those improperations[9] and terms of scurrility betwixt us, which only difference[10] our affections and not our cause, there is between us one common name and appellation, one faith and necessary body of principles common to us both; and therefore I am not scrupulous to converse and live with them, to enter their churches in defect of ours, and either pray with them or for them. I could never perceive any rational consequence from those many texts which prohibit the children of Israel to pollute themselves with the temples of the heathens, we being all Christians, and not divided by such detested impieties as might profane our prayers or the place wherein we make them; or that a resolved conscience may not adore her Creator anywhere, especially in places devoted to His Service; where if their devotions offend Him, mine may please Him; if theirs profane it, mine may hallow it. Holy water and crucifix (dangerous to the common people) deceive not my judgment nor abuse my devotion at all. I am, I confess, naturally inclined to that which misguided zeal terms superstition. My common conversation I do acknowledge austere, my behaviour full of rigor, sometimes not without morosity; yet at my devotion I love to use the civility of my knee, my hat, and hand, with all those outward and sensible motions which may express or promote my invisible devotion. I should violate my own arm rather than a church, nor willingly deface the memory of saint or martyr. At the sight of a cross or crucifix I can dispense with my hat, but scarce with the thought or memory of my Saviour. I cannot laugh at, but rather pity, the fruitless journeys of pilgrims, or contemn the miserable condition of friars, for though misplaced in circumstances there is something in it of devotion. I could never hear the Ave Mary Bell without an elevation, or think it a sufficient warrant, because they erred in one circumstance, for me to err in all, that is, in silence and dumb contempt; whilst therefore they directed their devotions to her, I offered mine to God, and rectify the errors of their prayers by rightly ordering mine own. At a solemn procession I have wept abundantly while my consorts, blind with opposition and prejudice, have fallen into an excess of scorn and laughter. There are questionless both in Greek, Roman, and African churches solemnities and ceremonies whereof the wiser zeals do make a Christian use, and stand condemned by us, not as evil in themselves, but as allurements and baits of superstition to those vulgar heads that look asquint on the face of truth, and those unstable judgments that cannot consist in the narrow point and center of virtue without a reel or stagger to the circumference.

SECTION 4

As there were many reformers, so likewise many reformations, every country proceeding in a particular way and method according as their national interest, together with

---

[4]Medicine (whose practitioners were notoriously irreligious).
[5]Impartiality, objectivity.
[6]Protestant (which had combative implications).
[7]Martin Luther, who was born of humble parents.   [8]Vessel.
[9]Reproaches. [10]Differentiate.

their constitution and clime, inclined them; some angrily, and with extremity; others calmly and with mediocrity;[11] not rending but easily dividing the community, and leaving an honest possibility of a reconciliation; which though peaceable spirits do desire, and may conceive that revolution of time and the mercies of God may effect, yet that judgment that shall continue the present antipathies between the two extremes, their contrarieties in condition, affection, and opinion, may with the same hopes expect an union in the poles of heaven.

Section 5

But to difference myself nearer, and draw into a lesser circle, there is no church whose every part so squares unto my conscience, whose articles, constitutions, and customs seem so consonant unto reason, and as it were framed to my particular devotion as this whereof I hold my belief, the Church of England, to whose faith I am a sworn subject; and therefore in a double obligation subscribe unto her articles, and endeavor to observe her constitutions. Whatsoever is beyond, as points indifferent, I observe according to the rules of my private reason, or the humor and fashion of my devotion, neither believing this because Luther affirmed it, or disproving that because Calvin hath disavouched it. I condemn not all things in the Council of Trent, nor approve all in the Synod of Dort.[12] In brief, where the Scripture is silent, the church is my text; where that speaks, 'tis but my comment; where there is a joint silence of both I borrow not the rules of my religion from Rome or Geneva, but the dictates of my own reason. It is an unjust scandal of our adversaries, and a gross error in ourselves, to compute the nativity of our religion from Henry the Eighth, who, though he rejected the pope, refused not the faith of Rome, and effected no more than what his own predecessors desired and assayed in ages past, and was conceived the State of Venice would have attempted in our days.[13] It is as uncharitable a point in us to fall upon those popular scurrilities and opprobrious scoffs of the Bishop of Rome, whom as a temporal prince we owe the duty of good language. I confess there is cause of passion between us; by his sentence I stand excommunicated; heretic is the best language he affords me;[14] yet can no ear witness I ever returned him the name of Antichrist, Man of Sin, or Whore of Babylon. It is the method of charity to suffer without reaction. Those usual satires and invectives of the pulpit may perchance produce a good effect on the vulgar, whose ears are opener to rhetoric than logic; yet do they in no wise confirm the faith of wiser believers, who know that a good cause needs not to be patroned[15] by passion, but can sustain itself upon a temperate dispute.

Section 6

I could never divide myself from any man upon the difference of an opinion, or be angry with his judgment for not agreeing with me in that from which perhaps within a few days I should dissent myself. I have no genius to disputes in religion, and have often thought it wisdom to decline them, especial-

ly upon a disadvantage, or when the cause of truth might suffer in the weakness of my patronage. Where we desire to be informed, 'tis good to contest with men above ourselves; but to confirm and establish our opinions, 'tis best to argue with judgments below our own, that the frequent spoils and victories over their reasons may settle in ourselves an esteem and confirmed opinion of our own. Every man is not a proper champion for truth, nor fit to take up the gauntlet in the cause of verity. Many, from the ignorance of these maxims and an inconsiderate zeal unto truth, have too rashly charged the troops of error, and remain as trophies unto the enemies of truth. A man may be in as just possession of truth as of a city, and yet be forced to surrender; 'tis therefore far better to enjoy her with peace than to hazard her on a battle. If therefore there rise any doubts in my way, I do forget them, or at least defer them till my better settled judgement and more manly reason be able to resolve them; for I perceive every man's own reason is his best Oedipus,[16] and will upon a reasonable truce find a way to loose those bonds wherewith the subtleties of error have enchained our more flexible and tender judgements. In philosophy, where truth seems double-faced, there is no man more paradoxical than myself; but in divinity I love to keep the road; and, though not in an implicit yet an humble faith, follow the great wheel of the church by which I move, not reserving any proper poles or motion from the epicycle of my own brain;[17] by this means I leave no gap for heresies, schisms, or errors, of which at present I hope I shall not injure truth to say I have no taint or tincture. I must confess my greener studies have been polluted with two or three, not any begotten in the latter centuries, but old and obsolete, such as could never have been revived but by such extravagant and irregular heads as mine; for indeed heresies perish not with their authors, but, like the river Arethusa,[18] though they lose their currents in one place, they rise up again in another. One general council is not able to extirpate one single heresy; it may be canceled for the present, but revolution of time and the like aspects from heaven will restore it, when it will flourish till it be condemned again. For as though there were a metempsychosis, and the soul of one man passed into another, opinions do find, after certain

[11]Moderation.
[12]*Trent...Dort*: Respectively, the two great councils where the doctrinal fundamentals of the Roman Catholic and the Calvinistic churches were reaffirmed. The first met at Trent in Italy at intervals between 1545 and 1563, the second at Dordrect in Holland in 1618–19. See p. 800, n. 31.
[13]When the Venetians were excommunicated in 1606, they threatened to leave the Roman Catholic Church.
[14]In 1570 Pius V had excommunicated Queen Elizabeth and released her subjects from their allegiance.   [15]Defended.
[16]In Greek mythology, the hero who gained the throne of Thebes by solving the riddle of the sphinx.
[17]Without any private reservations. In Ptolemaic astronomy an epicycle was a small circle centered on the circumference of a large circle.
[18]A fountain in Sicily that the ancients thought was fed by a subterranean river rising in Greece.

revolutions, men and minds like those that first begat them. To see ourselves again we need not look for Plato's year:[19] every man is not only himself; there hath been many Diogenes, and as many Timons,[20] though but few of that name; men are lived over again; the world is now as it was in ages past; there was none then, but there hath been some one since that parallels him, and is, as it were, his revived self.

SECTION 9

As for those wingy mysteries in divinity and airy subtleties in religion which have unhinged the brains of better heads, they never stretched the *pia mater* of mine. Methinks there be not impossibilities enough in religion for an active faith; the deepest mysteries ours contains have not only been illustrated but maintained by syllogism and the rule of reason. I love to lose my self in a mystery, to pursue my reason to an *O altitudo!*[21] 'Tis my solitary recreation to pose my apprehension with those involved enigmas and riddles of the Trinity, with Incarnation and Resurrection. I can answer all the objections of Satan and my rebellious reason with that odd resolution I learned of Tertullian, *Certum est quia impossibile est.*[22] I desire to exercise my faith in the difficultest point, for to credit ordinary and visible objects is not faith, but persuasion. Some believe the better for seeing Christ His sepulcher, and when they have seen the Red Sea, doubt not of the miracle.[23] Now contrarily, I bless myself and am thankful that I lived not in the days of miracles, that I never saw Christ nor His disciples; I would not have been one of those Israelites that passed the Red Sea, nor one of Christ's patients on whom He wrought His wonders; then had my faith been thrust upon me, nor should I enjoy that greater blessing pronounced to all that believe and saw not.[24] 'Tis an easy and necessary belief, to credit what our eye and sense hath examined. I believe He was dead and buried and rose again, and desire to see Him in His glory rather than to contemplate Him in his cenotaph or sepulcher. Nor is this much to believe; as we have reason, we owe this faith unto history. They only had the advantage of a bold and noble faith who lived before His coming, who upon obscure prophesies and mystical types[25] could raise a belief, and expect apparent impossibilities.

SECTION 10

'Tis true, there is an edge in all firm belief, and with an easy metaphor we may say the sword of faith; but in these obscurities I rather use it in the adjunct the apostle gives it, a buckler;[26] under which I conceive a wary combatant may lie invulnerable. Since I was of understanding to know we knew nothing, my reason hath been more pliable to the will of faith; I am now content to understand a mystery without a rigid definition, in an easy and platonic description. That allegorical description of Hermes[27] pleaseth me beyond all the metaphysical definitions of divines; where I cannot satisfy my reason, I love to humor my fancy: I had as lieve you tell me that *anima est angelus hominis, est Corpus Dei,* as *entelechia; Lux est umbra Dei,* as *actus perspicui.*[28] Where there is an obscurity too deep for our reason, 'tis good to sit down

with a description, periphrasis, or adumbration; for by acquainting our reason how unable it is to display the visible and obvious effects of nature, it becomes more humble and submissive unto the subtleties of faith; and thus I teach my haggard and unreclaimed reason to stoop unto the lure of faith.[29] I believe there was already a tree whose fruit our unhappy parents tasted, though in the same chapter when God forbids it,[30] 'tis positively said, the plants of the field were not yet grown, for God had not caused it to rain upon the earth. I believe that the serpent (if we shall literally understand it) from his proper form and figure made his motion on his belly before the curse. I find the trial of the pucellage[31] and virginity of women, which God ordained the Jews,[32] is very fallible. Experience and history informs me that not only many particular women but likewise whole nations have escaped the curse of childbirth, which God seems to pronounce upon the whole sex; yet do I believe that all this is true, which indeed my reason would persuade me to be false; and this I think is no vulgar part of faith to believe a thing not only above but contrary to reason, and against the arguments of our proper senses.

SECTION 11

In my solitary and retired imagination (*Neque enim cum porticus aut me lectulus accepit, desum mihi*)[33] I remember I am not alone, and therefore forget not to contemplate Him and His attributes who is ever with me, especially those two

[19]"A revolution of certain thousand years when all things should return to their former estate and he be teaching again in his school as when he delivered this opinion" (Browne's gloss).
[20]Diogenes was a Cynic philosopher and Timon (the hero of Shakespeare's *Timon of Athens*) a notorious misanthrope who shunned their fellow men.
[21]*O altitudo divitiarum sapientiae, et scientiae Dei:* "O the depth of the riches both of the wisdom and knowledge of God" (Romans 11.33).
[22]Tertullian (d. 230?), a father of the African church, speaking of the Resurrection: "It is certain because it is impossible."
[23]Of the Israelites crossing the Red Sea (Exodus 14.21–31).
[24]John 20.29.
[25]Symbolic prefiguring of events in the New Testament by events in the Old Testament (for example, the sacrifice of Christ by the sacrifice of the paschal lamb). This branch of theology, much cultivated in the Middle Ages, is called *typology,* on which see the Glossary.
[26]Perhaps referring to Ephesians 6.16–17, where St. Paul speaks of the "shield of faith, . . . the helmet of salvation, and the sword of the Spirit."
[27]"[*Deus est*] *sphaera cuius centrum utique, circumferentia nullibi*": God is a circle whose center is everywhere and whose circumference is nowhere (Browne's gloss).
[28]That the soul is the angel of man and the body of God rather than its guiding principle (*entelechia*); that light is the shadow of God rather than perceptible action.
[29]Thus I subject an undisciplined bird (i.e., reason) to training and restraint (i.e., faith). The image is from falconry. [30]Genesis 2.5.
[31]Virginity (French *pucelle:* maiden). [32]Deuteronomy 22.13–17.
[33]Not even in my moments of leisure and relaxation do I forget myself (adapted from Horace, *Satires,* I.iv.133–134).

mighty ones, His wisdom and eternity; with the one I recreate, with the other I confound my understanding; for who can speak of eternity without a solecism, or think thereof without an ecstasy? Time we may comprehend; 'tis but five days elder then ourselves,[34] and hath the same horoscope with the world; but to retire so far back as to apprehend a beginning, to give such an infinite start forwards as to conceive an end in an essence that we affirm hath neither the one nor the other, it puts my reason to St. Paul's sanctuary:[35] my philosophy dares not say the angels can do it: God hath not made a creature that can comprehend Him; 'tis a privilege of His own nature. "I am that I am" was His own definition unto Moses;[36] and 'twas a short one, to confound mortality, that durst question God, or ask Him what He was; indeed He onely is; all others have and shall be; but in eternity there is no distinction of tenses; and therefore that terrible term *predestination,* which hath troubled so many weak heads to conceive, and the wisest to explain, is in respect to God no prescious determination of our estates to come, but a definitive blast of His will already fulfilled, and at the instant that He first decreed it; for to His eternity, which is indivisible and all together, the last trump is already sounded, the reprobates in the flame, and the blessed in Abraham's bosom. St. Peter speaks modestly when he saith a thousand years to God are but as one day;[37] for to speak like a philosopher, those continued instances of time which flow into [a] thousand years make not to Him one moment; what to us is to come, to His eternity is present, His whole duration being but one permanent point without succession, parts, flux, or division.

SECTION 12

There is no attribute that adds more difficulty to the mystery of the Trinity, where, though in a relative way of Father and Son, we must deny a priority. I wonder how Aristotle could conceive the world eternal,[38] or how he could make good two eternities. His similitude of a triangle comprehended in a square[39] doth somewhat illustrate the trinity of our souls, and that the triple unity of God; for there is in us not three, but a trinity of souls,[40] because there is in us, if not three distinct souls, yet differing faculties that can and do subsist apart in different subjects, and yet in us are so united as to make but one soul and substance. If one soul were so perfect as to inform three distinct bodies, that were a pretty trinity: conceive the distinct number of three, not divided nor separated by the intellect but actually comprehended in its unity, and that is a perfect trinity. I have often admired the mystical way of Pythagoras and the secret magic of numbers. "Beware of philosophy"[41] is a precept not to be received in too large a sense, for in this mass of nature there is a set of things that carry in their front, though not in capital letters yet in stenography and short characters, something of divinity, which to wiser reasons serve as luminaries in the abyss of knowledge, and to judicious beliefs as scales and roundles[42] to mount the pinnacles and highest places of divinity. The severe schools[43] shall never laugh me out of the philosophy of Hermes, that this visible world is but a picture of the invisible, wherein, as in a pourtract,[44] things are not truly but in equivocal shapes, and as they counterfeit some more real substance in that invisible fabric.

SECTION 14

There is but one first cause and four second causes[45] of all things; some are without efficient, as God; others without matter, as angels; some without form, as the first matter;[46] but every essence, created or uncreated, hath its final cause, and some positive end both of its essence and operation. This is the cause I grope after in the works of nature; on this hangs the providence of God: to raise so beauteous a structure as the world and the creatures thereof was but His art, but their sundry and divided operations, with their predestinated ends, are from the treasure of His wisdom. In the causes, nature, and affections of the eclipses of the sun and moon there is most excellent speculation; but to profound[47] farther, and to contemplate a reason why His providence hath so disposed and ordered their motions in that vast circle as to conjoin and obscure each other is a sweeter piece of reason and a diviner point of philosophy; therefore sometimes, and in some things, there appears to me as much divinity in Galen his books *De usu partium* as in Suarez'[48] metaphysics. Had Aristotle been as curious in the inquiry of this cause as he was of the other, he had not left behind him an imperfect piece of philosophy, but an absolute tract of divinity.

SECTION 15

Natura *nihil agit frustra*[49] is the only indisputed axiom in philosophy; there are no grotesques in nature, nor anything framed to fill up empty cantons[50] and unnecessary spaces: in the most imperfect creatures, and such as were not preserved in the ark, but having their seeds and principles in the womb of nature, are everywhere where the power of the sun is; in these is the wisdom of His hand discovered. Out

[34]Man was created on the sixth day (Genesis 1.26).
[35]Romans 11.33 (to which Browne had alluded earlier in saying he loved to lose himself in a mystery and pursue his reason to an *O altitudo*). [36]Exodus 3.14. [37]2 Peter 3.8.
[38]The Christian doctrine of creation *ex nihilo* (see p. 871) was of course incompatible with Aristotle's assertion that the world was eternal.
[39]*Comprehended in a square:* that a square implies a triangle. It is likely that Browne is alluding, with faulty memory, to Aristotle's comment (*De anima,* Sect. 413a) about squaring a rectangle.
[40]Vegetative, animal, and rational.
[41]"Beware lest any man spoil you through philosophy and vain deceit" (Colossians 2.8). [42]Steps and rungs of a ladder.
[43]Aristotelian naturalists (as opposed to Platonic idealists, who thought that material things were imperfect shadows of a transcendental spiritual reality). [44]Portrait.
[45]The Aristotelian doctrine that all things have an efficient, formal, material, and final cause. [46]Primordial matter without form.
[47]Plunge.
[48]The Jesuit Francisco de Suarez' *Disputationes metaphysicae* (1597) was an influential essay in theology and philosophy.
[49]"Nature does nothing in vain." [50]Corners, angles.

of this rank Solomon chose the object of his admiration;[51] indeed what reason may not go to school to the wisdom of bees, ants, and spiders? What wise hand teacheth them to do what reason cannot teach us? Ruder heads stand amazed at those prodigious pieces of nature, whales, elephants, dromidaries and camels; these, I confess, are the colossus and majestic pieces of her hand; but in these narrow engines there is more curious mathematics; and the civility of these little citizens more neatly sets forth the wisdom of their maker. Who admires not Regiomontanus his fly beyond his eagle,[52] or wonders not more at the operation of two souls in those little bodies than but one in the trunk of a cedar?[53] I could never content my contemplation with those general pieces of wonder, the flux and reflux of the sea, the increase of Nile, the conversion of the needle to the north; and have studied to match and parallel those in the more obvious and neglected pieces of nature, which without further travel I can do in the cosmography of myself; we carry with us the wonders we seek without us. There is all Africa and her prodigies in us; we are that bold and adventurous piece of nature, which he that studies wisely learns in a compendium what others labor at in a divided piece and endless volume.

Section 16

Thus there are two books from which I collect my divinity: besides that written one of God, another of His servant nature, that universal and public Manuscript that lies expansed[54] unto the eyes of all; those that never saw Him in the one have discovered Him in the other. This was the scripture and theology of the heathens. The natural motion of the sun made them more admire Him than its supernatural station did the children of Israel;[55] the ordinary effects of nature wrought more admiration in them than in the other all His miracles; surely the heathens knew better how to join and read these mystical letters than we Christians, who cast a more careless eye on these common hieroglyphics, and disdain to suck divinity from the flowers of nature. Nor do I so forget God as to adore the name of nature; which I define not with the schools the principle of motion and rest, but that straight and regular line, that settled and constant course the wisdom of God hath ordained the actions of His creatures, according to their several kinds. To make a revolution every day is the nature of the sun because of that necessary course which God hath ordained it, from which it cannot swerve [but] by a faculty[56] from that voice which first did give it motion. Now this course of nature God seldom alters or perverts, but like an excellent artist hath so contrived His work that with the selfsame instrument, without a new creation, He may effect His obscurest designs. Thus He sweetneth the water with a wood,[57] preserveth the creatures in the ark, which the blast of His mouth might have as easily created; for God is like a skilful geometrician, who when more easily and with one stroke of His compass He might describe or divide a right line had yet rather do this in a circle or longer way, according to the constituted and forelaid principles of His art. Yet this rule of His He doth sometimes pervert to acquaint the world with His prerog-

ative, lest the arrogancy of our reason should question His power, and conclude He could not; and thus I call the effects of nature the works of God, whose hand and instrument she only is; and therefore to ascribe His actions unto her is to devolve the honor of the principal agent upon the instrument, which if with reason we may do, then let our hammers rise up and boast they have built our houses, and our pens receive the honor of our writings. I hold there is a general beauty in the works of God, and therefore no deformity in any kind or species of creature whatsoever. I cannot tell by what Logic we call a toad, a bear, or an elephant ugly, they being created in those outward shapes and figures which best express the actions of their inward forms. And having passed that general visitation of God, who saw that all that He had made was good,[58] that is, conformable to His will, which abhors deformity, and is the rule of order and beauty. There is no deformity but in monstrosity, wherein, notwithstanding, there is a kind of beauty, nature so ingeniously contriving the irregular parts as they become sometimes more remarkable than the principal fabric. To speak yet more narrowly, there was never anything ugly or misshapen but the chaos; wherein, notwithstanding, to speak strictly, there was no deformity because no form, nor was it yet impregnate[59] by the voice of God. Now nature is not at variance with art, nor art with nature, they being both servants of His providence. Art is the perfection of nature; were the world now as it was the sixt day, there were yet a chaos. Nature hath made one world, and art another. In brief, all things are artificial,[60] for nature is the art of God.

Section 17

This is the ordinary and open way of His providence, which art and industry have in a good part discovered, whose effects we may foretell without an oracle; to foreshow these is not prophesy, but prognostication. There is another way, full of meanders and labyrinths, whereof the devil and spirits have no exact ephemerides,[61] and that is a more particular and obscure method of His providence, directing the operations of individuals and single essences. This we call fortune, that serpentine and crooked line, whereby he draws those actions His wisdom intends in a more unknown

[51]Proverbs 6.6–8.
[52]Johann Müller (1436–76) or Regiomontanus (the Latin version of Konigsberg, his birthplace), a German mathematician and astronomer, allegedly constructed an iron fly and a wooden eagle capable of flight.
[53]Such "little bodies" as ants and bees contain a vegetative and a sensitive soul, whereas a majestic cedar exhibits only the function of vegetation.   [54]Spread out.
[55]When God caused the sun to stand still so that the Israelites would have time to slaughter more of their enemies (Joshua 10.12–13).   [56]Authority.
[57]"And he cried unto the Lord; and the Lord showed him a tree, which when he had cast into the waters, the waters were made sweet" (Exodus 15.25).   [58]Genesis 1.31.   [59]Impregnated.
[60]The result of art or artifice. With this passage should be compared Hobbes' introduction to his *Leviathan* (p. 493).   [61]Almanacs.

and secret way. This cryptic and involved method of His providence have I ever admired, nor can I relate the history of my life, the occurrences of my days, the escapes of dangers, and hits of chance with a *bezo las manos*[62] to fortune, or a bare gramercy to my good stars. Abraham might have thought the ram in the thicket came thither by accident;[63] human reason would have said that mere chance conveyed Moses in the ark to the sight of Pharaoh's daughter.[64] What a labyrinth is there in the story of Joseph,[65] able to convert a Stoic? Surely there are in every man's life certain rubs, doublings, and wrenches, which pass a while under the effects of chance, but at the last, well examined, prove the mere[66] hand of God. 'Twas not dumb chance that, to discover the fougade or powder-plot, contrived a miscarriage in the letter.[67] I like the victory of '88[68] the better for that one occurrence, which our enemies imputed to our dishonor and the partiality of fortune, to wit, the tempests and contrariety of winds. King Philip did not detract from the nation when he said he sent his Armado to fight with men, and not to combat with the winds. Where there is a manifest disproportion between the powers and forces of two several agents, upon a maxim of reason we may promise the victory to the superior; but when unexpected accidents slip in, and unthought of occurrences intervene, these must proceed from a power that owes no obedience to those axioms: where, as in the writing upon the wall,[69] we may behold the hand but see not the spring that moves it. . . .

SECTION 27

That miracles are ceased I can neither prove nor absolutely deny, much less define the time and period of their cessation. That they survived Christ is manifest upon the record of Scripture; that they outlived the apostles also and were revived at the conversion of nations, many years after, we cannot deny if we shall not question those writers whose testimonies we do not controvert in points that make for our own opinions; therefore that may have some truth in it that is reported by the Jesuits of their miracles in the Indies: I could wish it were true, or had any other testimony than their own pens. They may easily believe those miracles abroad who daily conceive a greater at home, the transmutation of those visible elements into the body and blood of our Saviour. For the conversion of water into wine, which he wrought in Cana,[70] or what the devil would have had him done in the wilderness, of stones into bread,[71] compared to this, will scarce deserve the name of a miracle. Though indeed to speak properly, there is not one miracle greater than another, they being the extraordinary effects of the hand of God, to which all things are of an equal facility; and to create the world as easy as one single creature. For this is also a miracle, not onely to produce effects against or above nature, but before nature, and to create nature as great a miracle as to contradict or transcend her. We do too narrowly define the power of God, restraining it to our capacities. I hold that God can do all things; how He should work contradictions I do not understand, yet dare not therefore deny. I cannot see why the angel of God should question Esdras to recall the time past[72] if it were beyond his own

power; or that God should pose[73] mortality in that which He was not able to perform himself. I will not say God cannot, but He will not perform many things which we plainly affirm He cannot. This, I am sure, is the mannerliest[74] proposition, wherein, notwithstanding, I hold no paradox. For strictly His power is the same with His will, and they both with all the rest do make but one God.

SECTION 28

Therefore that miracles have been I do believe; that they may yet be wrought by the living I do not deny, but have no confidence in those which are fathered on the dead; and this hath ever made me suspect the efficacy of relics, to examine the bones, question the habits and appurtenances of saints, and even of Christ himself. I cannot conceive why the cross that Helena found,[75] and whereon Christ himself died, should have power to restore others unto life. I excuse not Constantine[76] from a fall off his horse, or a mischief from his enemies, upon the wearing those nails on his bridle which our Savior bore upon the cross in His hands. I compute among your *Piae fraudes*,[77] nor many degrees before consecrated swords and roses, that which Baldwin, King of Jerusalem, returned the Genovese for their cost and pains in his war, to wit, the ashes of John the Baptist.[78] Those that hold the sanctity of their souls doth leave behind a tincture and sacred faculty on their bodies speak naturally of miracles, and do not salve the doubt.[79] Now one reason I tender so little devotion unto relics, is, I think, the slender and doubtful respect I have always held unto antiquities; for that indeed which I admire is far before antiquity, that is, eternity; and that is, God himself, who, though he be styled the Ancient of Days,[80] cannot receive the adjunct of antiquity who was before the world, and shall be after it, yet is not older than it; for in His years there is no climacter:[81] his duration is eternity, and far more venerable than antiquity.

SECTION 30

It is a riddle to me, how this story of oracles[82] hath not wormed out of the world that doubtful conceit of spirits

---

[62]"Kiss the hands," an expression of gratitude.   [63]Genesis 22.13.
[64]Exodus 2.3–10.   [65]Genesis 37–48.   [66]Absolute.
[67]The Gunpowder Plot (1605) was accidentally revealed when one of the conspirators wrote to Lord Monteagle to warn him against taking his seat in Parliament.
[68]The defeat of the Spanish Armada in 1588.   [69]Daniel 5.5.
[70]John 2.1–10.   [71]Matthew 4.3, Luke 4.3.
[72]The Apocryphal 2 Esdras 4.5.   [73]Puzzle.   [74]Most seemly.
[75]St. Helena, mother of the Emperor Constantine, allegedly found Christ's cross in 326.
[76]I do not believe that Constantine was miraculously prevented, etc.   [77]"Pious frauds."
[78]Baldwin I, king of Jerusalem (1100–18) was, with his famous brother Godfrey of Bouillon, a leader of the First Crusade.
[79]Resolve the problem.   [80]Daniel 7.9.
[81]Climacteric, i.e., any critical year or period.
[82]The ancient belief (treated by Milton in his hymn "On the Morning of Christ's Nativity") that the pagan gods were routed at the birth of Christ. Browne had registered his own belief in this "great and indisputable miracle" in Section 29.

and witches; how so many learned heads should so far forget their metaphysics, and destroy the ladder and scale of creatures, as to question the existence of spirits. For my part, I have ever believed, and do now know, that there are witches.[83] They that doubt of these do not only deny them, but spirits; and are obliquely and upon consequence a sort not of infidels, but atheists. Those that, to confute their incredulity, desire to see apparitions shall questionless never behold any, nor have the power to be so much as witches; the devil hath them already in a heresy as capital as witch-craft; and to appear to them were but to convert them. Of all the delusions wherewith he deceives mortality, there is not any that puzzleth me more than the legerdemain of changelings; I do not credit those transformations of reasonable creatures into beasts, or that the devil hath a power to transpeciate[84] a man into a horse, who tempted Christ (as a trial of His divinity) to convert but stones into bread. I could believe that spirits use with man the act of carnality, and that in both sexes; I conceive they may assume, steal, or contrive a body wherein there may be action enough to content decrepit lust or passion to satisfy more active veneries,[85] yet in both without a possibility of generation. And therefore that opinion that Antichrist should be born of the Tribe of Dan,[86] by conjunction with the devil, is ridiculous, and a conceit fitter for a rabbin than a Christian. I hold that the devil doth really possess some men, the spirit of melancholy others, the spirit of delusion others; that as the devil is concealed and denied by some, so God and good angels are pretended by others, whereof the late defection of the Maid of Germany[87] hath left a pregnant example.

Section 33

Therefore for spirits, I am so far from denying their existence that I could easily believe that not only whole countries but particular persons have their tutelary and guardian angels. It is not a new opinion of the Church of Rome, but an old one of Pythagoras and Plato; there is no heresy in it, and if not manifestly defined in Scripture, yet is it an opinion of a good and wholesome use in the course and actions of a man's life, and would serve as an hypothesis to salve many doubts, whereof common philosophy affordeth no solution. Now if you demand my opinion and metaphysics of their natures, I confess them very shallow, most of them in a negative way,[88] like that of God; or in a comparative, between ourselves and fellow creatures; for there is in this universe a stair or manifest scale of creatures, rising not disorderly or in confusion, but with a comely method and proportion. Between creatures of mere existence and things of life there is a large disproportion of nature; between plants and animals or creatures of sense, a wider difference; between them and man, a far greater; and if the proportion hold on, between man and angels there should be yet a greater. We do not comprehend their natures who retain the first definition of Porphyry,[89] and distinguish them from ourselves by immortality; for before his fall man also was immortal: yet must we needs affirm that he had a different essence from the angels. Having therefore no certain knowledge of their natures, 'tis no bad method of the schools,

whatsoever perfection we find obscurely in our selves, in a more complete and absolute way to ascribe unto them. I believe they have an extemporary knowledge, and upon the first motion of their reason do what we cannot without study or deliberation; that they know things by their forms, and define by specifical[90] difference what we describe by accidents and properties; and therefore probabilities to us may be demonstrations unto them; that they have knowledge not only of the specifical but numerical[91] forms of individuals, and understand by what reserved difference each single hypostasis (besides the relation to its species) becomes its numerical self. That as the soul hath a power to move the body it informs, so there's a faculty to move any, though inform none; ours upon restraint of time, place, and distance; but that invisible hand that conveyed Habakkuk to the lion's den,[92] or Philip to Azotus,[93] infringeth this rule, and hath a secret conveyance wherewith mortality is not acquainted. If they have that intuitive knowledge whereby as in reflexion they behold the thoughts of one another, I cannot peremptorily deny but they know a great part of ours. They that to refute the invocation of saints have denied that they have any knowledge of our affairs below have proceeded too far, and must pardon my opinion till I can thoroughly answer that piece of Scripture, "At the conversion of a sinner the Angels in Heaven rejoice."[94] I cannot with those in that great father securely interpret the work of the first day, *Fiat lux*, to the creation of angels,[95] though I confess there is not any creature that hath so near a glimpse of their nature as light in the sun and elements. We style it a bare accident, but where it subsists alone, 'tis a spiritual substance, and may be an angel. In brief, conceive light invisible, and that is a spirit.

Section 34

These are certainly the magisterial and master pieces of the Creator, the flower or (as we may say) the best part of nothing actually existing, what we are but in hopes and probability; we are only that amphibious piece between a corporal and spiritual essence, that middle form that links those two together and makes good the method of God and nature, that

[83]In a trial where two alleged witches were found guilty and executed at Bury St. Edmunds in 1664 Browne gave evidence against the accused.

[84]Change into a different species.   [85]Sexual desires.

[86]A Hebrew tribe descended from Dan, son of Jacob, by Rachel's handmaiden Bilhah (Genesis 30.6).

[87]"That lived without meat upon the smell of a rose" (Browne's gloss). The allusion is probably to one Eva Flegan, who allegedly stopped eating after 1597. By 1628 she had been exposed as a fraud and imprisoned.

[88]In the sense that God is defined by such negatives as incomprehensible, illimitable, infinite, etc.

[89]*"Essentia rationalis immortalis"*: an essence rational and immortal (Browne's gloss). Porphyry was a Neoplatonist of the third century.   [90]Generic?   [91]Individual.

[92]The Apocryphal Bel and the Dragon, v. 33–39.   [93]Acts 8.40.
[94]Luke 15.10.

[95]St. Augustine, *Confessions*, xiii.3. *Fiat lux:* "Let there be light" (Genesis 1.3).

jumps not from extremes, but unites the incompatible distances by some middle and participating nature. That we are the breath and similitude of God, it is indisputable, and upon record of holy Scripture;[96] but to call ourselves a microcosm, or little world, I thought it only a pleasant trope of rhetoric till my near judgement and second thoughts told me there was a real truth therein. For first we are a rude mass, and in the rank of creatures which only are, and have a dull kind of being not yet privileged with life, or preferred to sense or reason; next we live the life of plants, the life of animals, the life of men, and at last the life of spirits, running on in one mysterious nature those five kinds of existences which comprehend the creatures not only of the world but of the universe; thus is man that great and true amphibium, whose nature is disposed to live not only like other creatures in divers elements, but in divided and distinguished worlds; for though there be but one to sense, there are two to reason, the one visible, the other invisible, whereof Moses seems to have left [no] description, and of the other[97] so obscurely that some parts thereof are yet in controversy. And truly for the first chapters of Genesis I must confess a great deal of obscurity; though divines have to the power of human reason endeavored to make all go in a literal meaning, yet those allegorical interpretations are also probable, and perhaps the mystical method of Moses bred up in the hieroglyphical schools of the Eygptians.

Section 37[98]

Now for these walls of flesh wherein the soul doth seem to be immured before the resurrection, it is nothing but an elemental composition, and a fabric that must fall to ashes. "All flesh is grass" is not only metaphorically but literally true; for all those creatures we behold are but the herbs of the field, digested into flesh in them, or more remotely carnified[99] in ourselves. Nay further, we are what we all abhor, anthropophagi[1] and cannibals, devourers not only of men, but of ourselves; and that not in an allegory but a positive truth. For all this mass of flesh which we behold came in at our mouths; this frame we look upon hath been upon our trenchers; in brief, we have devoured ourselves. I cannot believe the wisdom of Pythagoras did ever positively and in a literal sense affirm his metempsychosis, or impossible transmigration of the souls of men into beasts. Of all metamorphoses or transmigrations. I believe only one, that is of Lot's wife;[2] for that of Nebuchodonosor proceeded not so far;[3] in all others I conceive there is no further verity than is contained in their implicit sense and morality. I believe that the whole frame of a beast doth perish, and is left in the same state after death as before it was materialed[4] unto life; that the souls of men know neither contrary nor corruption; that they subsist beyond the body, and outlive death by the privilege of their proper natures, and without a miracle; that the souls of the faithful, as they leave earth, take possession of heaven; that those apparitions and ghosts of departed persons are not the wandering souls of men, but the unquiet walks of devils, prompting and suggesting[5] us unto mischief, blood, and villainy; instilling and stealing into our hearts

that the blessed spirits are not at rest in their graves, but wander solicitous of the affairs of the world; that those[6] phantasms appear often, and do frequent cemeteries, charnel houses, and churches, it is because those are the dormitories of the dead, where the devil, like an insolent champion, beholds with pride the spoils and trophies of his victory in Adam.

Section 38

This is that dismal conquest we all deplore, that makes us so often cry *O Adam, quid fecisti?*[7] I thank God I have not those strait ligaments, or narrow obligations to the world, as to dote on life, or be convulsed and tremble at the name of death. Not that I am insensible of the dread and horror thereof, or by raking into the bowels of the deceased, continual sight of anatomies,[8] skeletons, or cadaverous relics, like vespillos[9] or gravemakers, I am become stupid, or have forgot the apprehension of mortality; but that marshaling all the horrors, and contemplating the extremities thereof, I find not anything therein able to daunt the courage of a man, much less a well-resolved Christian; and therefore am not angry at the error of our first parents, or unwilling to bear a part of this common fate, and like the best of them to die, that is, to cease to breathe, to take a farewell of the elements, to be a kind of nothing for a moment, to be within one instant of a spirit. When I take a full view and circle of myself, without this reasonable moderator and equal piece of justice, death, I do conceive myself the miserablest person extant; were there not another life that I hope for, all the vanities of this world should not intreat a moment's breath from me. Could the devil work my belief to imagine I could never die, I would not outlive that very thought; I have so abject a conceit of this common way of existence, this retaining to the sun and elements, I cannot think this is to be a man, or to live according to the dignity of humanity. In expectation of a better I can with patience embrace this life, yet in my best meditations do often defy death. I honor any man that contemns it, nor can I highly love any that is afraid of it. This makes me naturally love a soldier, and honor those tattered and contemptible regiments that will die at the command of a sergeant. For a pagan there may be some motives to be in love with life; but for a Christian to be amazed at death, I see not how he

[96]Genesis 2.7.   [97]The visible.
[98]Text *36*. Since Sections 36 and 37 bear the same number, the numbering of the following sections is confused, and the confusion is twice confounded by identical numbers for Sections 46 and 47.
[99]Converted into flesh.
[1]"Man-eaters."
[2]Who was turned into a pillar of salt (Genesis 19.26).
[3]According to Daniel (4.33), King Nebuchadnezzar of Babylonia "did eat grass like oxen, and his body was wet with the dew of heaven till his hairs were grown like eagles' feathers, and his nails like birds' claws."   [4]Given material form.   [5]Tempting.
[6]Text *but that those,* corrected in the "Errata."
[7]"What hast thou done?" (Genesis 3.13).   [8]Dissected cadavers.
[9]Those who bury victims of plague.

can escape this dilemma: that he is too sensible of this life, or hopeless of the life to come.

SECTION 40

I am naturally bashful, nor hath conversation, age, or travel been able to effront[10] or enharden me; yet I have one part of modesty which I have seldom discovered in another, that is (to speak truly) I am not so much afraid of death as ashamed thereof; 'tis the very disgrace and ignominy of our natures that in a moment can so disfigure us that our nearest friends, wife, and children stand afraid and start at us. The birds and beasts of the field, that before in a natural fear obeyed us, forgetting all allegiance, begin to prey upon us. This very conceit hath in a tempest disposed and left me willing to be swallowed up in the abyss of waters, wherein I had perished unseen, unpitied, without wondering eyes, tears of pity, lectures of mortality, and none had said, *Quantum mutatus ab illo!*[11] Not that I am ashamed of the anatomy of my parts, or can accuse nature for playing the bungler in any part of me, or my own vicious life for contracting any shameful disease upon me, whereby I might not call myself as wholesome a morsel for the worms as any.

SECTION 41

Some upon the courage[12] of a fruitful issue, wherein, as in the truest chronicle they seem to outlive themselves, can with greater patience away with death. This conceit[13] and counterfeit subsisting in our progenies seems to me a mere fallacy, unworthy the desires of a man that can but conceive a thought of the next world; who, in a nobler ambition, should desire to live in his substance in heaven rather than his name and shadow in the earth. And therefore at my death I mean to take a total adieu of the world, not caring for a monument, history, or epitaph, not so much as the bare memory of my name to be found anywhere but in the universal register of God. I am not yet so cynical as to approve the testament of Diogenes,[14] nor do I altogether allow that *rodomontado*[15] of Lucan:

> *Caelo tegitur, qui non habet urnma.*[16]
>
> He that unburied lies wants not his herse,
> For unto him a tomb's the universe

But commend in my calmer judgement those ingenuous intentions that desire to sleep by the urns of their fathers, and strive to go the nearest way unto corruption. I do not envy the temper of crows and daws,[17] nor the numerous and weary days of our fathers before the flood. If there be any truth in astrology, I may outlive a jubilee;[18] as yet I have not seen one revolution of Saturn,[19] nor hath my pulse beat thirty years; and yet, and excepting one, have seen the ashes, and left under ground all the kings of Europe; have been contemporary to three emperors, four Grand Signiors, and as many popes. Methinks I have outlived myself, and begin to be weary of the sun; I have shaken hands with delight in my warm blood and canicular days.[20] I perceive I do anticipate the vices of age. The world to me is but a dream

or mock-show, and we all therein but pantaloons and antics,[21] to my severer contemplations.

SECTION 45

Now besides the literal and positive kind of death there are others whereof divines make mention, and those I think not merely metaphorical, as mortification, dying unto sin and the world; therefore, I say, every man hath a double horoscope, one of his humanity, his birth; another of his Christianity, his baptism, and from this do I compute or calculate my nativity, not reckoning those *horae combustae*[22] and odd days, or esteeming myself anything before I was my Saviour's, and enrolled in the register of Christ. Whosoever enjoys not this life, I count him but an apparition, though he wear about him the sensible affections of flesh. In these moral acceptions, the way to be immortal is to die daily; nor can I think I have the true theory of death when I contemplate a skull or behold a skeleton with those vulgar imaginations it casts upon us; I have therefore enlarged that common *Memento mori*[23] into a more Christian memorandum, *Memento quatuor novissima*,[24] those four inevitable points of us all: death, judgement, heaven, and hell. Neither did the contemplations of the heathens rest in their graves, without a further thought of Rhadamanth[25] or some judicial proceeding after death, though in another way, and upon suggestion of their natural reasons. I cannot but marvail from what sibyl or oracle they stole the prophesy of the word's destruction by fire, or whence Lucan learned to say,

> *Communis mundo superest rogus ossibus astra*
> *   Misturus.*[26]
>
> There yet remains to th' world one common fire,
> Wherein our bones with stars shall make one pyre.

I believe the world grows near its end, yet is neither old nor decayed, nor shall ever perish upon the ruins of its own principles.[27] As the work of creation was above nature, so is its adversary[28] annihilation, without which the world hath

[10]Free from bashfulness.
[11]"How much changed from what he was!" (Vergil, *Aeneid*, II.274).   [12]Confidence.   [13]Conceited, i.e., fanciful.
[14]"Who willed his friends not to bury him, but to hang him up with a staff in his hand to fright away the crows" (Browne's gloss).
[15]"Rodomontade," bluster.   [16]*Pharsalia*, VI. 819
[17]Creatures allegedly of long lives.
[18]Fiftieth year. Browne lived to the age of seventy-seven.
[19]Almost thirty years.
[20]The dog-days of summer; here, the years of early manhood, when passions are most heated.   [21]Fools and clowns.
[22]"That time when the moon is in conjunction, and obscured by the sun, the astrologers call *horae combustae* [burning period]" (Browne's gloss). Here, of course, the phrase refers to the interval between birth and baptism.   [23]"Remember you must die."
[24]"Remember the four last things."
[25]In Greek mythology, a judge of the underworld.
[26]*Pharsalia*, VII.814–15.
[27]The world is approaching the end of its appointed cycle (of six thousand years), but not decaying from senility or exhaustion of its vital processes.   [28]Reciprocal.

not its end but its mutation. Now what force should be able to consume it thus far without the breath of God, which is the truest consuming flame, my philosophy cannot inform me. Some believe there went not a minute to the world's creation, nor shall there go to its destruction; those six days, so punctually described, make not to them one moment, but rather seem to manifest the method and idea of the great work of the intellect of God than the manner how He proceeded in its operation. I cannot dream that there should be at the last day any such judicial proceeding, or calling to the bar, as indeed the Scripture seems to imply and the literal commentators do conceive; for unspeakable mysteries in the Scriptures are often delivered in a vulgar and illustrative way, and being written unto man are delivered, not as they truly are, but as they may be understood; wherein notwithstanding the different interpretations according to different capacities may stand firm with our devotion, nor be any way prejudicial to each single edification.

Section 46

Now to determine the day and year of this inevitable time is not only convincible and statute madness,[29] but also manifest impiety. How shall we interpret Elias' 6000 years,[30] or imagine the secret communicated to a rabbi, which God hath denied unto His angels? It had been an excellent quaere to have posed the devil of Delphos,[31] and must needs have forced him to some strange amphibology;[32] it hath not only mocked the predictions of sundry astrologers in ages past, but the prophecies of many melancholy heads in these present, who, neither understanding reasonably things past or present, pretend a knowledge of things to come; heads ordained only to manifest the incredible effects of melancholy, and to fulfill old prophecies rather than be the authors of new. In those days there shall come "wars and rumors of wars"[33] to me seems no prophecy, but a constant truth, in all times verified since it was pronounced. "There shall be signs in the moon and stars";[34] how comes He then "like a thief in the night,"[35] when He gives an item[36] of His coming? That common sign drawn from the revelation of Antichrist is as obscure as any: in our common compute he hath been come these many years; but for my own part to speak freely, I am half of opinion that Antichrist is the philosopher's stone in divinity, for the discovery and invention thereof, though there be prescribed rules and probable inductions, yet hath hardly any man attained the perfect discovery thereof. That general opinion that the world grows near its end hath possessed all ages past as nearly as ours; I am afraid that the souls that now depart cannot escape that lingering expostulation of the saints under the altar, *Quousque, Domine?* "How long, O Lord?"[37] and groan in the expectation of that great jubilee.

Section 52

I thank God, and with joy I mention it, I was never afraid of hell nor never grew pale at the description of that place. I have so fixed my contemplations on heaven that I had almost forgot the idea of hell, and am afraid rather to lose the joys of the one than endure the misery of the other. To be deprived of them is a perfect hell, and needs, methinks, no addition to complete our afflictions. That terrible term hath never detained me from sin, nor do I owe any good action to the name thereof. I fear God, yet am not afraid of Him; His mercies make me ashamed of my sins before His judgments afraid thereof. These are the forced and secondary method of His wisdom, which He useth but as the last remedy, and upon provocation: a course rather to deter the wicked than incite the virtuous to His worship. I can hardly think there was ever any scared into heaven; they go the fairest way to heaven that would serve God without a hell. Other mercenaries that crouch into Him in fear of hell, though they term themselves the servants, are indeed but the slaves of the Almighty.

Section 57

I believe many are saved who to man seem reprobated, and many are reprobated who in the opinion and sentence of man stand elected. There will appear at the last day strange and unexpected example both of His justice and His mercy, and therefore to define either is folly in man and insolency even in the devils. Those acute and subtile spirits in all their sagacity can hardly divine who shall be saved, which if they could prognostic,[38] their labor were at an end; nor need they compass the earth seeking whom they may devour. Those who upon a rigid application of the law sentence Solomon unto damnation condemn not only him, but themselves and the whole world; for by the letter and written word of God we are without exception in the state of death; but there is a prerogative of God, and an arbitrary pleasure above the letter of His own law, by which alone we can pretend unto salvation, and through which Solomon might be as easily saved as those who condemn him.

Section 58

The number of those who pretend unto salvation, and those infinite swarms who think to pass through the eye of this needle,[39] have much amazed me. That name and compellation of "little flock"[40] doth not comfort but deject my devotion, especially when I reflect upon mine own unworthiness, wherein, according to my humble apprehensions, I am below them all. I believe there shall never be an anarchy in heaven, but as there are hierarchies amongst the angels,[41] so shall there be degrees of priority amongst the saints. Yet is it (I protest) beyond my ambition to aspire unto the first ranks; my desires only are, and I shall be happy therein, to be but the last man, and bring up the rear in heaven.

[29]Demonstrable and statutory insanity.
[30]According to Talmudic tradition, the world would last 2,000 years under vanity, 2,000 years under the Mosaic law, and 2,000 years under Christ. For a similarly periodic Christian scheme see Matthew 1.17 and St. Augustine, *The City of God*, XXII.30.
[31]The oracle at the shrine of Apollo at Delphi, noted for cryptic and ambiguous utterances. [32]Ambiguity. [33]Matthew 24.6.
[34]Luke 21.25. [35]1 Thessalonians 5.2. [36]Intimation.
[37]Revelation 6.9–10. [38]Foretell. [39]Matthew 19.24.
[40]Luke 12.32. [41]Seraphim, cherubim, thrones, etc.

Section 60

Insolent zeals that do decry good works, and rely only upon faith,[42] take not away merit; for depending upon the efficacy of their faith, they enforce the condition of God, and in a more sophistical way do seem to challenge heaven. It was decreed by God that only those that lapped in the water like dogs should have the honor to destroy the Midianites;[43] yet could none of those justly challenge, or imagine he deserved that honor thereupon. I do not deny but that true faith, and such as God requires, is not only a mark or token but also a means of our salvation; but where to find this is as obscure to me as my last end. And if our Saviour could object[44] unto His own disciples and favorites a faith that, to the quantity of a grain of mustard seed, is able to remove mountains,[45] surely that which we boast of is not anything, or at the most but a remove from nothing. This is the tenor of my belief, wherein, though there be many things singular, and to the humor of my irregular self, yet if they square not with maturer judgements I disclaim them, and do no further father[46] them than the learned and best judgements shall authorize them.

THE SECOND PART

Section 1

Now for that other virtue of charity, without which faith is a mere notion, and of no existence, I have ever endeavored to nourish the merciful disposition and humane inclination I borrowed from my parents, and regulate it to the written and prescribed laws of charity; and if I hold the true anatomy of myself,[47] I am delineated and naturally framed to such a piece of virtue. For I am of a constitution so general that it comforts and sympathizeth with all things; I have no antipathy, or rather idiosyncrasy, in diet, humor, air, anything. I wonder not at the French for their dishes of frogs, snails, and toadstools, nor at the Jews for locusts and grasshoppers; but being amongst them, make them my common viands, and I find they agree with my stomach as well as theirs. I could digest a salad gathered in a churchyard as well as in a garden. I cannot start at the presence of a serpent, scorpion, lizard, or salamander, at the sight of a toad or viper I find in me no desire to take up a stone to destroy them. I feel not in myself those common antipathies that I can discover in others: those national repugnances do not touch me, nor do I behold with prejudice the French, Italian, Spaniard, or Dutch; but where I find their actions in balance with my countrymen's, I honor, love and embrace them in the same degree. I was born in the eighth climate,[48] but seem for to be framed and constellated unto all. I am no plant that will not prosper out of a garden. All places, all airs make unto me one country; I am in England everywhere and under any meridian. I have been shipwrackt,[49] yet am not enemy with the sea or winds; I can study, play, or sleep in a tempest. In brief, I am averse from nothing; my conscience would give me the lie if I should say I absolutely detest or hate any essence but the devil, or so at least abhor anything but that we might come to composition.[50] If there be any among

those common objects of hatred I do contemn and laugh at, it is that great enemy of reason, virtue, and religion, the multitude—that numerous piece of monstrosity which, taken asunder, seem men and the reasonable creatures of God, but confused together make but one great beast, and a monstrosity more prodigious than Hydra.[51] It is no breach of charity to call these fools; it is the style all holy writers have afforded them, set down by Solomon in canonical Scripture, and a point of our faith to believe so. Neither in the name of multitude do I only include the base and minor sort of people; there is a rabble even amongst the gentry, a sort of plebeian heads whose fancy moves with the same wheel as these; men in the same level with mechanics, though their fortunes do somewhat guild their infirmities, and their purses compound for their follies. But as in casting account, three or four men together come short in account of one man placed by himself below them,[52] so neither are a troop of these ignorant dorados[53] of that true esteem and value as many a forlorn person whose condition doth place him below their feet. Let us speak like politicians, there is a nobility without heraldry, a natural dignity whereby one man is ranked with another, another filed before him, according to the quality of his desert, and preeminence of his good parts. Though the corruption of these times and the bias of present practice wheel another way, thus it was in the first and primitive commonwealths, and is yet in the integrity and cradle of well-ordered polities, till corruption getteth ground, ruder desires laboring after that which wiser considerations contemn, everyone having a liberty to amass and heap up riches, and they a license or faculty to do or purchase anything.

Section 7

To do no injury, nor take none, was a principle which to my former years and impatient affections seemed to contain enough of morality; but my more settled years and Christian constitution have fallen upon severer resolutions. I can hold there is no such thing as injury; that if there be, there is no such injury as revenge, and no such revenge as the contempt of an injury; that to hate another is to malign himself; that the truest way to love another is to despise ourselves. I were unjust unto mine own conscience if I should say I am at variance with anything like myself. I find there are many pieces in this one fabric of man; this frame is raised upon a mass of antipathies. I am one, methinks, but as the world, wherein notwithstanding there are a swarm of distinct essences, and in them another world of contrarieties; we carry

[42]Calvinists who put "faith" above "works."   [43]Judges 7.5–7.
[44]Propose.   [45]Matthew 17.20.   [46]Acknowledge.
[47]*If I hold...myself:* if I understand myself aright.
[48]In the eighth of the twenty-four regions between the equator and the poles.
[49]Browne was shipwrecked in returning to England from Ireland in 1630.   [50]Reach an agreement.
[51]In Greek mythology, a nine-headed serpent that grew two heads for each one that was cut off.
[52]Thus in the number 2789 the first digit represents more than the three larger ones that follow.   [53]Wealthy persons.

private and domestic enemies within, public and more hostile adversaries without. The devil, that did but buffet St. Paul, plays, methinks, at sharp[54] with me. Let me be nothing if within the compass of myself I do not find the battle of Lepanto,[55] passion against reason, reason against faith, faith against the devil, and my conscience against all. There is another man within me that's angry with me, rebukes, commands, and dastards[56] me. I have no conscience of marble to resist the hammer of more heavy offences, nor yet too soft and waxen as to take the impression of each single peccadillo or scape of infirmity. I am of a strange belief that it is as easy to be forgiven some sins as to commit some others. For my original sin, I hold it to be washed away in my baptism, for my actual transgressions I compute and reckon with God but from my last repentance, sacrament, or absolution; and therefore am not terrified with the sins or madness of my youth. I thank the goodness of God I have no sins that want a name; I am not singular in offences; my transgressions are epidemical, and from the common breath of our corruption. For there are certain tempers of body which, matched with an humorous depravity of mind, do hatch and produce viciosities[57] whose newness and monstrosity of nature admits no name; this was the temper of that lecher that carnaled with a statua,[58] and constitution of Nero in his spintrian recreations.[59] For the heavens are not only fruitful in new and unheard-of stars, the earth in plants and animals, but men's minds also in villainy and vices. Now the dullness of my reason and the vulgarity of my disposition never prompted my invention, nor solicited my affection unto any of these; yet even those common and quotidian infirmities that so necessarily attend me, and do seem to be my very nature, have so dejected me, so broken the estimation that I should have otherwise of myself, that I repute myself the most abjectest piece of mortality. Divines prescribe a fit of sorrow to repentance; there goes indignation, anger, sorrow, hatred into mine, passions of a contrary nature which neither seem to suit with this action nor my proper constitution. It is no breach of charity to ourselves to be at variance with our vices, nor to abhor that part of us which is an enemy to the ground of charity, our God; wherein we do but imitate our great selves, the world,[60] whose divided antipathies and contrary faces do yet carry a charitable regard unto the whole by their particular discords, preserving the common harmony, and keeping in fetters those powers whose rebellions, once masters, might be the ruin of all.

Section 9

I was never yet once, and commend their resolutions who never marry twice. Not that I disallow of second marriage, as neither, in all cases, of polygamy, which, considering some times and the unequal number of both sexes, may be also necessary. The whole world was made for man, but the twelfth part of man for woman. Man is the whole world, and the breath of God; woman the rib and crooked piece of man.[61] I could be content that we might procreate like trees, without conjunction, or that there were any way to perpetuate the world without this trivial and vulgar way

of coition;[62] it is the foolishest act a wise man commits in all his life; nor is there anything that will more deject his cooled imagination when he shall consider what an odd and unworthy piece of folly he hath committed. I speak not in prejudice, nor am averse from that sweet sex, but naturally amorous of all that is beautiful; I can look a whole day with delight upon a handsome picture, though it be but of an horse. It is my temper, and I like it the better, to affect all harmony; and sure there is music even in the beauty and the silent note which Cupid strikes far sweeter than the sound of an instrument. For there is a music wherever there is a harmony, order, or proportion; and thus far we may maintain the music of the spheres; for those well-ordered motions and regular paces, though they give no sound unto the ear, yet to the understanding they strike a note most full of harmony. Whosoever is harmonically composed delights in harmony, which makes me much distrust the symmetry of those heads which declaim against all church music.[63] For myself, not only from my obedience but my particular genius, I do embrace it; for even that vulgar and tavern music, which makes one man merry, another mad, strikes in me a deep fit of devotion, and a profound contemplation of the first composer. There is something in it of divinity more than the ear discovers: it is an hieroglyphical and shadowed lesson of the whole world and creatures of God; such a melody to the ear as the whole world, well understood, would afford the understanding. In brief, it is a sensible fit of that harmony which intellectually sounds in the ears of God. I will not say, with Plato, the soul is an harmony, but harmonical, and hath its nearest sympathy unto music: thus some whose temper of body agrees, and humors the constitution of their souls, are born poets, though indeed all are naturally inclined unto rhythm. This made Tacitus in the very first line of his story fall upon a verse; and Cicero, the worst of poets but declaiming for a poet, falls in the very first sentence upon a perfect hexameter.[64] I feel not in me those sordid and unchristian desires of my profession; I do not secretly implore and wish for plagues, rejoice at famines, revolve ephemerides and almanacs in expectation of malignant aspects, fatal conjunctions, and eclipses. I rejoice not at unwholesome springs nor unseasonable winters; my prayer goes with the husbandman's; I desire every thing in its proper season, that

[54]With pointed sword, thus, in earnest.
[55]A great naval encounter in the Gulf of Corinth (1571) at which a Christian fleet repulsed the Turkish threat to western Europe.
[56]Terrifies.   [57]Vicious acts.
[58]Had sexual relations with a statue. The allusion is probably to Pygmalion, a sculptor who so ardently loved his statue of Galatea that Aphrodite brought the marble to life.
[59]Sexual perversions.   [60]Macrocosm.   [61]Genesis 2.22.
[62]In 1641 Browne married a woman seventeen years his junior, who presented him with twelve children in eighteen years.
[63]The Puritans, who opposed instrumental music in churches on the ground that it was not authorized by the Scriptures.
[64]The two prose passages that may be scanned as poetry are the opening sentence of Tacitus' *Annals* (*Urbem Romam a principio reges habuere*) and Cicero's *Pro Archia* (*In que me non inficior mediocriter esse*).

neither men nor the times be put out of temper. Let me be sick myself if sometimes the malady of my patient be not a disease unto me; I desire rather to cure his infirmities than my own necessities; where I do him no good, methinks it is scarce honest gain, though I confess 'tis but the worthy salary of our well-intended endeavors. I am not only a-shamed but heartily sorry that besides death there are diseases incurable, yet not for my own sake, or that they be beyond my art, but for the general cause and sake of humanity, whose common cause I apprehend as mine own. And to speak more generally, those three noble professions[65] which all civil commonwealths do honor are raised upon the fall of Adam, and are not exempt from their infirmities; there are not only diseases incurable in physic, but cases indissoluble in laws, vices incorrigible in divinity. If general councils may err, I do not see why particular courts should be infallible; their perfectest rules are raised upon the erroneous reasons of man; and the laws of one do but condemn the rules of another, as Aristotle ofttimes the opinions of his predecessors because though agreeable to reason yet were not consonant to his own rules and the logic of his proper principles. Again, to speak nothing of the sin against the Holy Ghost, whose cure not only but whose nature is unknown, I can cure the gout or stone in some sooner than divinity pride or avarice in others. I can cure vices by physic when they remain incurable by divinity; and shall obey my pills when they contemn their precepts. I boast nothing, but plainly say we all labor against our own cure, for death is the cure of all diseases. There is no catholicon[66] or universal remedy I know but this, which, though nauseous to queasy stomachs, yet to prepared appetites is nectar, and a pleasant potion of immortality.

SECTION 11[67]

Now for my life, it is a miracle of thirty years, which to relate were not a history but a piece of poetry, and would sound to common ears like a fable. For the world, I count it not an inn but an hospital, and a place not to live but to die in. The world that I regard is myself; it is the microcosm of my own frame that I cast mine eye on; for the other, I use it but like my globe, and turn it round sometimes for my recreation. Men that look upon my outside, perusing only my condition and fortunes, do err in my altitude, for I am above Atlas[68] his shoulders. The earth is a point not only in respect of the heavens above us but of that heavenly and celestial part within us. That mass of flesh that circumscribes me limits not my mind. That surface that tells the heavens it hath an end cannot persuade me I have any. I take my circle to be above three hundred and sixty;[69] though the number of the ark do measure my body, it comprehendeth not my mind: whilst I study to find how I am a microcosm, or little world, I find myself something more than the great. There is surely a piece of divinity in us, something that was before the elements, and owes no homage unto the sun. Nature tells me I am the image of God, as well as Scripture: he that understands not thus much hath not his introduction or first lesson, and is yet to begin the alphabet of man. Let me not injure the felicity of others if

I say I am as happy as any: *Ruat coelum, fiat voluntas tua*[70] salveth all; so that whatsoever happens, it is but what our daily prayers desire. In brief, I am content, and what should providence add more? Surely this is it we call happiness, and this do I enjoy; with this I am happy in a dream, and as content to enjoy a happiness in a fancy as others in a more apparent truth and reality. There is surely a nearer apprehension of anything that delights us in our dreams than in our waked senses; without this I were unhappy, for my awaked judgment discontents me, ever whispering unto me that I am from my friend; but my friendly dreams in night requite me, and make me think I am within his arms. I thank God for my happy dreams as I do for my good rest, for there is a satisfaction in them unto reasonable desires, and such as can be content with a fit of happiness. And surely it is not a melancholy conceit to think we are all asleep in this world, and that the conceits of this life are as mere dreams to those of the next, as the phantasms of the night to the conceits of the day. There is an equal delusion in both, and the one doth but seem to be the emblem or picture of the other; we are somewhat more than ourselves in our sleeps, and the slumber of the body seems to be but the waking of the soul. It is the ligation[71] of sense but the liberty of reason, and our waking conceptions do not match the fancies of our sleeps. At my nativity my ascendant was the watery[72] sign of Scorpius; I was born in the planetary hour of Saturn, and I think I have a piece of that leaden planet in me.[73] I am no way facetious, nor disposed for the mirth and galliardize[74] of company; yet in one dream I can compose a whole comedy, behold the action, apprehend the jests, and laugh myself awake at the conceits thereof. Were my memory as faithful as my reason is then fruitful, I would never study but in my dreams, and this time also would I choose for my devotions; but our grosser memories have then so little hold of our abstracted[75] understanding that they forget the story, and can only relate to our awaked souls a confused and broken tale of that that hath passed. Aristotle, who hath written a singular tract of sleep, hath not methinks thoroughly defined it; nor yet Galen, though he seem to have corrected it; for those noctambulos and night-walkers, though in their sleep, do yet enjoy the action of their senses. We must therefore say that there is something in us that is not in the jurisdiction of Morpheus,[76] and that those abstracted and ecstatic souls do walk about in their own corps, as spirits with the bodies they assume, wherein they seem to hear and feel, though indeed the organs are destitute of sense, and their natures of those faculties that should inform them. Thus it is observed that men sometimes upon the hour of their departure do

[65]Law, medicine, and divinity. [66]Panacea. [67]Text *12.*
[68]In Greek mythology, a Titan who supported the world on his shoulders. [69]Degrees.
[70]"May your will be done though the heavens fall." [71]Binding.
[72]Text *earthly,* corrected in "Errata."
[73]Browne's birthday (October 19) fell in the zodiacal sign of Scorpio and under the planetary influence of Saturn. [74]Gaiety.
[75]Withdrawn, removed. Later in the paragraph Browne couples this Latinism with its Greek synonym *ecstatic.*
[76]The god of sleep.

speak and reason above themselves, for then the soul begins to be freed from the ligaments of the body, begins to reason like herself, and to discourse in a strain above mortality.

SECTION 15

I conclude therefore and say there is no happiness under (or as Copernicus will have it, above) the sun, nor any crambe[77] in that repeated verity and burden of all the wisdom of Solomon, "All is vanity and vexation of spirit."[78] There is no felicity in that the world adores. Aristotle, whilst he labors to refute the ideas of Plato, falls upon one himself, for his *summum bonum* is a chimera, and there is no such thing as his felicity.[79] That wherein God himself is happy, the holy angels are happy, in whose defect the devils are unhappy, that dare I call happiness; whatsoever conduceth unto this

may with an easy metaphor deserve that name; whatsoever else the world terms happiness is to me a story out of Pliny,[80] an apparition or neat delusion wherein there is no more of happiness than the name. Bless me in this life with but peace of my conscience, command of my affections, the love of Thyself and my dearest friends, and I shall be happy enough to pity Caesar. These are, O Lord, the humble desires of my most reasonable ambition, and all I dare call happiness on earth, wherein I set no rule or limit to Thy hand or providence. Dispose of me according to the wisdom of Thy pleasure. Thy will be done, though in my own undoing.

[77]Distasteful repetition. [78]Ecclesiastes 2.11.
[79]Aristotle's notion of man's greatest good as rational behavior is as unsatisfactory as Plato's of the contemplation of ideas.
[80]An implausible tale.

from Pseudodoxia Epidemica (1650)

TO THE READER

Would Truth dispense, we could be content, with Plato, that knowledge were but remembrance,[1] that intellectual acquisition were but reminiscential evocation, and new impressions but the colorishing[2] of old stamps which stood pale in the soul before. For—what is worse—knowledge is made by oblivion, and to purchase a clear and warrantable body of truth we must forget and part with much we know. Our tender inquiries taking up learning at large, and together with true and assured notions receiving many wherein our reviewing judgments do find no satisfaction, and therefore in this encyclopedy[3] and round of knowledge, like the great and exemplary wheels of heaven,[4] we must observe two circles: that while we are daily carried about and whirled on by the swinge and rapt[5] of the one we may maintain a natural and proper course in the slow and sober wheel of the other. And this we shall more readily perform if we timely survey our knowledge, impartially singling out those encroachments which junior[6] compliance and popular credulity hath admitted. Whereof at present we have endeavored a long and serious *adviso*,[7] proposing not only a large and copious list, but from experience and reason attempting their decisions.[8]

And first we crave exceeding pardon in the audacity of the attempt, humbly acknowledging a work of such concernment unto truth and difficulty in itself did well deserve the conjunction of many heads. And surely more advantageous had it been unto truth to have fallen into the endeavors of some cooperating advancers[9] that might have performed it to the life and added authority thereto, which the privacy of our condition and unequal[10] abilities cannot expect. Whereby notwithstanding we have not been diverted, nor have our solitary attempts been so discouraged as to despair the favorable look of learning upon our single and unsupported endeavors.

Nor have we let fall our pen upon discouragement of

contradiction, unbelief, and difficulty of dissuasion from radicated beliefs and points of high prescription,[11] although we are very sensible how hardly[12] teaching years do learn, what roots old age contracteth into errors, and how such as are but acorns in our younger brows grow oaks in our elder heads and become inflexible unto the powerfullest arm of reason. Although we have also beheld what cold requitals others have found in their several redemptions of truth, and how their ingenuous inquiries have been dismissed with censure and obliquy of singularities.

Some consideration we hope from the course of our profession,[13] which though it leadeth us into many truths that pass undiscerned by others, yet doth it disturb their communications and much interrupt the office of our pens in their well intended transmissions; and therefore surely in this work attempts will exceed performances, it being composed by snatches of time, as medical vacations and the fruitless importunity of uroscopy[14] would permit us. And therefore also perhaps it hath not found that regular and constant style, those infallible experiments, and those assured determinations which the subject sometime requireth, and might be expected from others whose quiet doors and unmolested hours afford no such distractions. Although who shall in-

PSEUDODOXIA EPIDEMICA [1]A striking demonstration of this notion is in Plato's *Meno* (Sect. 82 ff.), where Socrates elicits abstruse mathematical theorems from an ignorant slave boy. [2]Coloring. [3]Encyclopedia (which etymologically means a "circle" or a "round" of knowledge). [4]See *sphere* in the Glossary. [5]Impetus and force. [6]Youthful. [7]Canvass. [8]Testing their conclusions. [9]A syndicate of investigators (like the Royal Society, which was founded in 1645, a year before the first edition of Browne's work appeared). [10]Inadequate. [11]*Radicated...prescription:* rooted beliefs reinforced by long-continued custom. [12]Painfully. [13]Medicine. [14]"Inspection of urines" (Browne's gloss).

differently perpend[15] the exceeding difficulty which either the obscurity of the subject or unavoidable paradoxology[16] must often put upon the attempter will easily discern a work of this nature is not to be performed upon one leg,[17] and should smell of oil[18] if duly and deservedly handled.

Our first intentions, considering the common interest of truth, resolved to propose it unto the Latin republic and equal judges of Europe,[19] but owing in the first place this service unto our country, and therein especially unto its ingenuous gentry, we have declared ourself in a language best conceived.[20] Although I confess the quality of the subject will sometimes carry us into expressions beyond mere English apprehensions; and indeed if elegancy still proceedeth, and English pens maintain that stream we have of late observed to flow from many, we shall within few years be fain to learn Latin to understand English, and a work will prove of equal facility in either. Nor have we addressed our pen or style unto the people whom books do not redress[21] and are this way incapable of reduction,[22] but unto the knowing and leading part of learning, as well understanding (at least probably hoping) except they be watered from higher regions and fructifying meteors of knowledge, these weeds must lose their alimental sap and wither of themselves; whose conserving influence could our endeavors prevent, we should trust the rest unto the scythe of Time and hopeful dominion of Truth.

We hope it will not be unconsidered that we find no open tract or constant manuduction[23] in this labyrinth, but are ofttimes fain to wander in the America and untraveled parts of Truth. . . . And therefore we are often constrained to stand alone against the strength of opinion, and to meet the Goliah[24] and giant of authority with contemptible pebbles and feeble arguments drawn from the scrip[25] and slender stock of ourselves. Nor have we indeed scarce named any author whose name we do not honor; and if detraction could invite us, discretion surely would contain us from any derogatory intention where highest pens and friendliest eloquence must fail in commendation.

And therefore also we cannot but hope the equitable considerations and candor of reasonable minds. We cannot expect the frown of theology herein, nor can they which behold the present state of things, and controversy of points so long received in divinity, condemn our sober inquiries in the doubtful appurtenancies of arts and receptaries[26] of philosophy. Surely, philologers[27] and critical discoursers, who look beyond the shell and obvious exteriors of things, will not be angry with our narrower explorations. And we cannot doubt our brothers in physic[28] (whose knowledge in naturals[29] will lead them into a nearer apprehension of many things delivered) will friendly accept, if not countenance, our endeavors. Nor can we conceive it may be unwelcome unto those honored worthies who endeavor the advancement of learning, as being likely to find a clearer progression when so many rubs are leveled and many untruths taken off, which, passing as principles with common beliefs, disturb the tranquility of axioms, which otherwise might be raised. And wise men cannot but know that arts and learning want this expurgation; and if the course of truth be permitted unto itself, like that of time and uncorrected computations, it cannot escape many errors which duration still enlargeth.

Lastly, we are not magisterial in opinions, nor have we dictator-like obtruded our conceptions; but in the humility of inquiries or disquisitions have only proposed them unto more ocular discerners. And therefore opinions are free, and open it is for any to think or declare the contrary. And we shall so far encourage contradiction as to promise no disturbance or reoppose any pen that shall fallaciously refute us, that shall only lay hold of our lapses, single out digressions, corollaries, or ornamental conceptions to evidence his own in as indifferent truths. And shall only take notice of such whose experimental and judicious knowledge shall solemnly look upon it, not only to destroy of ours but to establish of his own, not to traduce or extenuate but to explain and dilucidate,[30] to add and ampliate[31] according to the laudable custom of the ancients in their sober promotions of learning. Unto whom, notwithstanding, we shall not contentiously rejoin or only to justify our own, but to applaud or confirm his maturer assertions, and shall confer[32] what is in us unto his name and honor, ready to be swallowed in any worthy enlarger as having acquired our end if any way, or under any name, we may obtain a work so much desired and yet desiderated of truth.

Thomas Browne

THE FIRST BOOK, OR GENERAL PART

CHAPTER 1
OF THE CAUSES OF COMMON ERRORS

The first and father cause of common error is the common infirmity of human nature, of whose deceptible[33] condition, although perhaps there should not need any other eviction[34] than the frequent errors we shall ourselves commit even in the express declarement hereof, yet shall we illustrate the same from more infallible constitutions, and persons presumed as far from us in condition as time, that is, our first and ingenerated forefathers.[35] From whom as we derive our being and the several wounds of constitution, so may we in some manner excuse our infirmities in the depravity of those parts whose traductions[36] were pure in them and their originals but once removed from God. Who notwithstanding— if posterity may take leave to judge of the fact, as they are assured to suffer in the punishment—were grossly deceived in their perfection, and so weakly deluded in the clarity of their understanding that it hath left no small obscurity in ours, how error should gain upon them.

[15]Ponder. [16]Self-contradiction.
[17]Without effort, extemporaneously (Horace, *Satires*, I.iv.10).
[18]Appear to be done laboriously.
[19]*Latin...Europe:* international community of learned men. *Equal:* impartial. [20]Understood. [21]Correct, reform.
[22]Correction, i.e. instruction. [23]Guidance.
[24]Goliath, the giant slain by the shepherd boy David (1 Samuel 17).
[25]Wallet. [26]Received opinions. [27]Scholars. [28]Medicine.
[29]Natural objects. [30]Illuminate. [31]Amplify. [32]Contribute.
[33]Prone to be deceived. [34]Demonstration, proof.
[35]Adam and Eve. *Ingenerate:* not conceived and born as other people. [36]Derivations, descents.

For first they were deceived by Satan, and that not in an invisible insinuation but an open and discoverable apparition, that is, in the form of a serpent, whereby although there were many occasions of suspicion, and such as could not easily escape a weaker circumspection, yet did the unwary apprehension of Eve take no advantage thereof. . . .

They were deceived by one another, and in the greatest disadvantage of delusion, that is, the stronger by the weaker: for Eve presented the fruit, and Adam received it from her. Thus the serpent was cunning enough to begin the deceit in the weaker, and the weaker of strength sufficient to consummate the fraud in the stronger. Art and fallacy was used unto her, a naked offer proved sufficient unto him: so his superstructure was his ruin, the fertility of his sleep[37] an issue of death unto him. And although the condition of sex and posteriority of creation might somewhat extenuate the error of the woman, yet it was very strange and inexcusable in the man, especially if, as some affirm, he was the wisest of all men since, or if, as others have conceived, he was not ignorant of the fall of the angels and had thereby example and punishment to deter him.

They were deceived from themselves, and their own apprehensions, for Eve either mistook or traduced the commandment of God. . . .

They were deceived through the conduct of their senses, and by temptations from the object itself, whereby although their intellectuals[38] had not failed in the theory of truth, yet did the inservient[39] and brutal faculties control the suggestion of reason, pleasure and profit already overswaying the instructions of honesty, and sensuality perturbing the reasonable commands of virtue. . . .

Lastly, man was not only deceivable in his integrity, but the angels of light in all their clarity. He that said he would be like the highest[40] did err if in some way he conceived not himself so already, but in attempting so high an effect from himself he misunderstood the nature of God and held a false apprehension of his own, whereby vainly attempting not only insolencies but impossibilities, he deceived himself as low as hell. In brief, there is nothing infallible but God, who cannot possibly err. For things are really true as they correspond unto His conception, and have so much of verity as they hold of conformity unto that intellect in whose idea they had their first determinations. And therefore being the rule, He cannot be irregular; nor being truth itself, conceivably admit the impossible society of error.

> Expanding his discussion, Browne turns to the problems of cognition, the discrimination of truth and error, and the tonic force of skepticism. It is here, where he juxtaposes conventional pieties with secular and Baconian explanations of man's infirmities, that he most clearly shows the complexity and diversity of his own allegiances.

CHAPTER 3

OF THE SECOND CAUSE OF COMMON ERRORS, THE ERRONEOUS DISPOSITION OF PEOPLE

Having thus declared the fallible nature of man even from his first production, we have beheld the general cause of error. But as for popular errors, they are more nearly founded upon an erroneous inclination of the people, as being the most deceptible part of mankind, and ready with open arms to receive the encroachments of error. Which condition of theirs, although deducible from many grounds, yet shall we evidence it but from a few, and such as most nearly and undeniably declare their natures.

How unequal discerners of truth they are, and openly exposed unto error, will first appear from their unqualified intellectuals, unable to umpire the difficulty of its dissensions. For error, to speak strictly, is a firm assent unto falsity. Now, whether the object whereunto they deliver up their assent be true or false, they are incompetent judges.

For the assured truth of things is derived from the principles of knowledge and causes which determine their verities. Whereof their uncultivated understanding scarce holding any theory, they are but bad discerners of verity, and in the numerous track[41] of error but casually[42] do hit the point and unity of truth.

Their understanding is so feeble in the discernment of falsities and averting the errors of reason that it submitteth unto the fallacies of sense, and is unable to rectify the error of its sensations. Thus the greater part of mankind, having but one eye of sense and reason, conceive the earth far bigger than the sun, the fixed stars lesser than the moon, their figures plain, and their spaces equidistant. For thus their sense informeth them, and herein their reason cannot rectify them; and, therefore, hopelessly continuing in their mistakes, they live and die in their absurdities, passing their days in perverted apprehensions and conceptions of the world, derogatory unto God and the wisdom of the creation.

Again, being so illiterate in the point of intellect, and their sense so incorrected, they are further indisposed ever to attain unto truth, as commonly proceeding in those ways which have most reference unto sense and wherein there lieth most notable and popular delusion.

For being unable to wield the intellectual arms of reason, they are fain to betake themselves unto wasters[43] and the blunter weapons of truth, affecting the gross and sensible ways of doctrine, and such as will not consist with strict and subtile reason. Thus unto them a piece of rhetoric is a sufficient argument of logic, an apologue of Aesop beyond a syllogism in barbara,[44] parables than propositions, and proverbs more powerful than demonstrations. And therefore are they led rather by example than precept, receiving persuasions from visible inducements before intellectual

[37]Eve, whom God created from one of Adam's ribs when he was in a "deep sleep" (Genesis 2.21). [38]Intellects. [39]Subordinate, serving. [40]*He...highest:* Lucifer, leader of the rebel angels. [41]Thronged path. [42]Accidentally. [43]Wooden foils. [44]*An apologue . . . barbara:* a fable of Aesop is more convincing than irrefutable logic. *Barbara:* a mnemonic term designating a kind of syllogism in which both premises and the conclusion are universal affirmations, and in which the middle term serves both as subject of the first proposition and attribute of the second:
bar Every wicked man is miserable;
ba all tyrants are wicked men;
ra therefore all tyrants are miserable.

instructions. And therefore also they judge of human actions by the event;[45] for, being uncapable of operable circumstances,[46] or rightly to judge the prudentiality of affairs, they only gaze upon the visible success, and thereafter condemn or cry up the whole progression. And so, from this ground, in the lecture[47] of holy Scripture their apprehensions are commonly confined unto the literal sense of the text, from whence have ensued the gross and duller sort of heresies. For not attaining the deuteroscopy[48] and second intention of the words, they are fain to omit their super-consequences, coherences, figures, or tropologies[49] and are not sometime persuaded by fire beyond their literalities.[50] And therefore also things invisible but unto intellectual discernments, to humor the grossness of their comprehensions have been degraded from their proper forms, and God himself dishonored into manual[51] expressions. And so likewise being unprovided or unsufficient for higher speculations, they will always betake themselves unto sensible representations, and can hardly be restrained the dullness of idolatry. A sin or folly not only derogatory unto God but men, overthrowing their reason as well as His divinity. In brief, a reciprocation or rather an inversion of the creation, making God one way, as He made us another; that is, after our image, as he made us after His.

Moreover, their understanding, thus weak in itself, and perverted by sensible delusions, is yet farther impaired by the dominion of their appetite; that is, the irrational and brutal part of the soul, which, lording it over the sovereign faculty, interrupts the actions of that noble part, and chokes those tender sparks which Adam hath left them of reason. And therefore they do not only swarm with errors, but vices depending thereon. Thus they commonly affect no man any farther than he deserts his reason, or complies with their aberrancies. Hence they embrace not virtue for itself, but its reward; and the argument from pleasure or utility is far more powerful than that from virtuous honesty, which Mahomet and his contrivers well understood when he set out the felicity of his heaven by the contentments of flesh and the delight of sense, slightly passing over the accomplishment of the soul and the beatitude of that part which earth and visibilities too weakly affect. But the wisdom of our Saviour and the simplicity of His truth proceeded another way, defying the popular provisions of happiness from sensible expectations, placing His felicity in things removed from sense, and [in] the intellectual enjoyment of God. And therefore the doctrine of the one was never afraid of universities or endeavored the banishment of learning, like the other. And though Galen doth sometimes nibble at Moses, and, beside the apostate Christian,[52] some heathens have questioned his philosophical part, or treaty[53] of the creation, yet is there surely no reasonable pagan that will not admire the rational and well grounded precepts of Christ, whose life, as it was conformable unto His doctrine, so was that unto the highest rules of reason, and must therefore flourish in the advancement of learning, and the perfection of parts best able to comprehend it. . . .

Lastly, being thus divided from truth in themselves, they are yet farther removed by advenient[54] deception. For true it is (and I hope I shall not offend their vulgarities if I say) they are daily mocked into error by subtiler devisors, and have been expressly deluded by all professions and ages. Thus the priests of elder time have put upon them many incredible conceits, not only deluding their apprehensions with ariolation,[55] soothsaying, and such oblique idolatries, but winning their credulities unto the literal and downright adorement of cats, lizards, and beetles. And thus also in some Christian churches (wherein is presumed an irreprovable truth) if all be true that is suspected, or half what is related, there have not wanted many strange deceptions, and some thereof are still confessed by the name of pious frauds. Thus Theudas, an impostor, was able to lead away four thousand into the wilderness,[56] and the delusions of Mahomet almost the fourth part of mankind. Thus all heresies, how gross soever, have found a welcome with the people. . . .

Having thus laid the basis for his analysis of man's regretable proclivity for error, Browne proceeds to analyze the "immediate causes." One of these he ascribes (Chapter IV) to "a mistake or a misconception of things, either in their first apprehension or secondary relations," and another (Chapter V) to our "credulity and supinity." But more important, and more damaging, is our habit of deferring to authority (Chapter VI).

CHAPTER 6
OF ADHERENCE UNTO ANTIQUITY

But the mortalest enemy unto knowledge, and that which hath done the greatest execution upon truth, hath been a peremptory adhesion unto authority, and more especially the establishing of our belief upon the dictates of antiquity. For (as every capacity may observe) most men of ages present so superstitiously do look upon ages past that the authorities of the one exceed the reasons of the other. Whose persons indeed being far removed from our times, their works, which seldom with us pass uncontrolled, either by contemporaries or immediate successors, are now become out of the distance of envies, and, the farther removed from present times, are conceived to approach the nearer unto truth itself. Now hereby methinks we manifestly delude ourselves, and widely walk out of the track of truth.

For, first, men hereby impose a thraldom on their times, which the ingenuity of no age should endure, or indeed the presumption of any did ever yet enjoin. Thus Hippocrates, about two thousand years ago, conceived it no injustice either to examine or refute the doctrines of his predecessors; Galen the like, and Aristotle the most of any. Yet did not any of these conceive themselves infallible, or set down their dictates as verities irrefragable, but when they either deliver their

[45]Outcome
[46]Incapable of judging what is to be done under any given circumstance. [47]Reading. [48]Inward or allegorical meaning.
[49]Metaphors.
[50]*Are not . . . literalities:* even torture cannot make them recant their crudely literal interpretations.
[51]Furnished with hands, i.e., anthropomorphic.
[52]Julian the Apostate, Roman emperor (361–363) who publicly announced his conversion to paganism in 361. [53]Treatise.
[54]Adventitious. [55]Prophesying, foretelling. [56]Acts 5.36.

own inventions or reject other men's opinions, they proceed with judgment and ingenuity, establishing their assertions not only with great solidity, but submitting them also unto the correction of future discovery.

Secondly, men that adore times past consider not that those times were once present, that is, as our own are at this instant; and we ourselves unto those to come, as they unto us at present: as we rely on them, even so will those on us, and magnify us hereafter, who at present condemn ourselves. Which very absurdity is daily committed amongst us, even in the esteem and censure of our own times. And, to speak impartially, old men, from whom we should expect the greatest example of wisdom, do most exceed in this point of folly, commending the days of their youth, which they scarce remember, at least well understood not, extolling those times their younger years have heard their fathers condemn, and condemning those times the gray heads of their posterity shall commend. And thus is it the humor of many heads to extol the days of their forefathers and declaim against the wickedness of times present. Which notwithstanding they cannot handsomely do without the borrowed help and satires of times past, condemning the vices of their own times by the expressions of vices in times which they commend, which cannot but argue the community of vice in both. Horace, therefore, Juvenal, and Persius[57] were no prophets, although their lines did seem to indigitate[58] and point at our times. There is a certain list of vices committed in all ages, and declaimed against by all authors, which will last as long as human nature, or, digested into commonplaces, may serve for any theme and never be out of date until doomsday.

Thirdly, the testimonies of antiquity, and such as pass oraculously amongst us, were not, if we consider them, always so exact as to examine the doctrine they delivered. For some, and those the acutest of them, have left unto us many things of falsity, controllable not only by critical and collective reason but common and country[59] observation. . . .

Fourthly, while we so eagerly adhere unto antiquity and the accounts of elder times, we are to consider the fabulous condition thereof. And that we shall not deny if we call to mind the mendacity of Greece, from whom we have received most relations, and that a considerable part of ancient times was by the Greeks themselves termed μυθικόν, that is, made up or stuffed out with fables. And surely the fabulous inclination of those days was greater than any since, which swarmed so with fables, and from such slender grounds took hints for fictions, poisoning the world ever after. . . .

Fifthly, we applaud many things delivered by the ancients which are in themselves but ordinary, and come short of our conceptions. Thus we usually extol, and our orations cannot escape, the sayings of the wise men of Greece. *Nosce teipsum* of Thales; *Nosce tempus* of Pittacus; *Nihil nimis*[60] of Cleobulus; which, notwithstanding, to speak indifferently, are but vulgar precepts in morality, carrying with them nothing above the line, or beyond the extemporary sententiosity of common conceits with us. Thus we magnify the apothegms or reputed replies of wisdom, whereof many are to be seen in Laertius, more in Lycosthenes, not a few in the second book of Macrobius,[61] in the salts[62] of Cicero, Augustus, and the comical wits of those times: in most whereof there is not much to admire, and are, methinks, exceeded not only in the replies of wise men, but the passages[63] of society and urbanities of our times. And thus we extol their adages or proverbs, and Erasmus hath taken great pains to make collections of them,[64] whereof, notwithstanding, the greater part will, I believe, unto indifferent judges be esteemed no extraordinaries, and may be paralleled if not exceeded by those of more unlearned nations, and many of our own.

Sixthly, We urge authorities in points that need not, and introduce the testimony of ancient writers to confirm things evidently believed, and whereto no reasonable hearer but would assent without them; such as are: *Nemo mortalium omnibus horis sapit; virtute nil praestantius, nil pulchrius; omnia vincit amor; praeclarum quiddam veritas.*[65] All which, although known and vulgar, are frequently urged by many men; and though trivial verities in our mouths, yet noted from Plato, Ovid, and Cicero, they become reputed elegancies. For many hundred to instance in one we meet with while we are writing, Antonius Guevara,[66] that elegant Spaniard, in his book entituled, *The Dial of Princes,* beginneth his epistle thus: "Apollonius Thyaneus, disputing with the scholars of Hiarchas, said that among all the affections of nature, nothing was more natural than the desire all have to preserve life." Which, being a confessed truth and a verity acknowledged by all, it was a superfluous affectation to derive its authority from Apollonius, or seek a confirmation thereof as far as India, and the learned scholars of Hiarchas. Which, whether it be not all one as to strengthen common dignities and principles, known by themselves, with the authority of mathematicians; or [to] think a man should believe the whole is greater than its parts rather upon the authority of Euclid than if it were propounded alone, I leave unto the second and wiser cogitations of all men. 'Tis sure a practice that savors much of pedantry, a reserve of puerility we have not shaken off from school; where, being seasoned with

[57]Roman writers who ridiculed contemporary vices and follies.
[58]Point with a finger, indicate.   [59]Native, untutored.
[60]*Nosce . . . nimis:* "Know thyself," "Know the right time," "nothing in excess"—gnomic tags worn thin by repetition.
[61]Writers who retailed the gossip, witticisms, and miscellaneous lore of the ancients. Diogenes Laertius (ca. 200–250) wrote *Lives and Opinions of Eminent Philosophers;* "Lycosthenes" was the German scholar Conrad Wolffhart (1518–61), who compiled a volume of *Apothegmata* as well as a curious work called *Prodigorum chronicon;* Macrobius (fl. ca. 400) was a distinguished grammarian whose *Saturnalia* Browne himself was to draw on heavily in writing *Urn Burial* (see p. 481, n. 35).
[62]Pungent witticisms.   [63]Conversational exchanges.
[64]Erasmus' *Collectanea adagiorum* (or *Adagia*), which he expanded repeatedly after its first edition in 1500, was one of the most popular books of the 16th century.
[65]"No mortal man is wise at all hours." "Nothing is more excellent or more beautiful than virtue." "Love conquers all." "Truth has a certain splendor."
[66]Spanish ecclesiastic and writer (1480?–1555) whose widely admired *Relox de principes* was an idealized portrait of the perfect prince as exemplified by the Emperor Marcus Aurelius.

minor sentences, by a neglect of higher inquiries they pre-scribe[67] upon our riper ears, and are never worn out but with our memories.

Lastly, while we so devoutly adhere unto antiquity in some things, we do not consider we have deserted them in several others. For they, indeed, have not only been imperfect in the conceit of some things, but either ignorant or erroneous in many more. They understood not the motion of the eighth sphere from west to east, and so conceived the longitude of the stars invariable. They conceived the torrid zone un-habitable, and so made frustrate the goodliest part of the earth. But we now know 'tis very well empeopled, and the habitation thereof esteemed so happy that some have made it the proper seat of paradise, and been so far from judging it unhabitable that they have made it the first habitation of all. Many of the ancients denied the antipodes, and some unto the penalty of contrary affirmations; but the experience of our enlarged navigations can now assert them beyond all dubita-tion.[68] Having thus totally relinquished them in some things, it may not be presumptuous to examine them in others; but surely most unreasonable to adhere to them in all, as though they were infallible, or could not err in any.

> For several chapters Browne lavishes his erudition and his wit upon a display of ancient frauds and modern credulity, but as he nears the end of Book I he reassumes the theo-logian's stance.

CHAPTER 10

OF THE LAST AND GREAT PROMOTER OF FALSE OPINIONS, THE ENDEAVORS OF SATAN

But beside the infirmities of human nature, the seed of error within ourselves, and the several ways of delusion from each other, there is an invisible agent, the secret promoter without us, whose activity is undiscerned, and plays in the dark upon us; and that is the first contriver of error, and professed opposer of truth, the devil. For though, permitted unto his proper principles, Adam perhaps would have sinned without the suggestion of Satan, and from the transgressive infirmities of himself might have erred alone, as well as the angels before him; and although were there no devil at all, yet there is now in our natures a confessed sufficiency unto corruption, and the frailty of our own economy[69] were able to betray us out of truth; yet wants there not another agent, who, taking advantage hereof, proceedeth to obscure the diviner part and efface all tract of its traduction.[70] To attempt a particular[71] of all his wiles is too bold an arithmetic for man: what most considerably concerneth his popular and practised ways of delusion, he first deceiveth mankind in five main points concerning God and himself.

And first, his endeavors have ever been, and they cease not yet, to instill a belief in the mind of man, there is no God at all. And this he specially labors to establish in a direct and literal apprehension; that is, that there is no such reality existent, that the necessity of His entity dependeth upon ours, and is but a political chimera; that the natural truth of God is an artificial erection of man, the Creator himself but a subtile invention of the creature. Where he succeeds not thus high,

he labors to introduce a secondary and deductive atheism, that although men concede there is a God, yet should they deny His providence. And therefore assertions have flown about that He intendeth only the care of the species or common natures, but letteth loose the guard of individuals and single existencies therein; that He looks not below the moon,[72] but hath designed the regiment of sublunary affairs unto inferior deputations. To promote which apprehensions, or empuzzle their due conceptions, he casteth in the notions of fate, destiny, fortune, chance, and necessity, terms com-monly misconceived by vulgar heads, and their propriety[73] sometime perverted by the wisest. Whereby extinguishing in minds the compensation of virtue and vice, the hope and fear of heaven and hell, they comply in their actions unto the drift of his delusions, and live like creatures below the ca-pacity of either.

Now hereby he not only undermineth the base of religion, and destroyeth the principle preambulous[74] unto all belief, but puts upon us the remotest error from truth. For atheism is the greatest falsity, and to affirm there is no God, the highest lie in nature. And therefore strictly taken, some men will say his labor is in vain; for many there are who cannot conceive there was ever any absolute atheist, or such as could determine there was no God, without all check from him-self or contradiction from his other opinions. And therefore those few so called by elder times might be the best of pagans, suffering that name rather in relation to the gods of the gentiles than the true Creator of all. A conceit that cannot befall his greatest enemy, or him that would induce the same in us, who hath a sensible apprehension hereof, for he believeth with trembling. To speak yet more strictly and conformably unto some opinions, no creature can wish thus much, nor can the will which hath a power to run into vel-leities,[75] and wishes of impossibilities, have any *utinam*[76] of this. For to desire there were no God were plainly to unwish their own being, which must needs be annihilated in the substraction[77] of that essence which substantially supporteth them, and restrains them from regression into nothing. And if, as some contend, no creature can desire his own annihilation, that nothing is not appetible,[78] and not to be at all is worse than to be in the miserablest condi-tion of something; the devil himself could not embrace that motion, nor would the enemy of God be freed by such a redemption.

But coldly thriving in this design, as being repulsed by the principles of humanity and the dictates of that production which cannot deny its original, he fetcheth a wider circle; and when he cannot make men conceive there is no God at all, he endeavors to make them believe there is not one, but many, wherein he hath been so successful with common

---

[67]Assert a claim. [68]Doubt. [69]Organization, nature. [70]Trace of its descent. [71]Itemization. [72]In the realm of change and death (the sphere of the moon being supposed to mark the boundary between the incorruptible heavens and variable nature). [73]Property, particular character. [74]Prefatory. [75]Wishes. [76]"Would that!" [77]Subtraction, withdrawal. [78]Desirable.

heads that he hath led their belief through all the works of nature. . . .

Thus he endeavors to entangle truths, and when he cannot possibly destroy its substance he cunningly confounds its apprehensions—that from the inconsistent and contrary determinations thereof, consectary[79] impieties and hopeful conclusions may arise, there's no such thing at all.

THE THIRD BOOK

OF DIVERS POPULAR AND RECEIVED TENETS CONCERNING ANIMALS, WHICH EXAMINED PROVE EITHER FALSE OR DUBIOUS

CHAPTER 5

OF THE BADGER

That a brock or badger hath the legs on one side shorter than of the other, though an opinion perhaps not very ancient, is yet very general, received not only by theorists and unexperienced believers but assented unto by most who have the opportunity to behold and hunt them daily. Which, notwithstanding, upon inquiry, I find repugnant unto the three determinators of truth—authority, sense, and reason. For first, Albertus Magnus[80] speaks dubiously, confessing he could not confirm the verity hereof; but Aldrovand[81] affirmeth plainly there can be no such inequality observed. And for my own part, upon indifferent inquiry I cannot discover this difference, although the regardable side be defined, and the brevity by most imputed unto the left.

Again, it seems no easy affront unto reason, and generally repugnant unto the course of nature; for if we survey the total set of animals, we may, in their legs or organs of progression, observe an equality of length and parity of numeration: that is, not any to have an odd leg, or the supporters and movers of one side not exactly answered by the other. Although the hinder may be unequal unto the fore and middle legs, as in frogs, locusts, and grasshoppers; or both unto the middle, as in some beetles and spiders, as is determined by Aristotle, *De incessu animalium*. Perfect and viviparous quadrupeds, so standing in their position of proneness that the opposite joints of neighbor legs consist in the same plane, and a line descending from their navel intersects at right angles the axis of the earth. It happeneth often, I confess, that a lobster hath the chely or great claw of one side longer than the other, but this is not properly their leg, but a part of apprehension,[82] and whereby they hold or seize upon their prey; for the legs and proper parts of progression are inverted backward, and stand in a position opposite unto these.

Lastly, the monstrosity is ill contrived, and with some disadvantage, the shortness being affixed unto the legs of one side which might have been more tolerably placed upon the thwart or diagonal[83] movers. For the progression of quadrupeds being performed *per diametrum*, that is, the cross legs moving or resting together so that two are always in motion, and two in station at the same time, the brevity had been more tolerable in the cross legs. For then the motion and station had been performed by equal legs, whereas herein they are both performed by unequal organs, and the imperfection becomes discoverable at every hand.

THE SEVENTH BOOK

CONCERNING MANY HISTORICAL TENETS GENERALLY RECEIVED, AND SOME DEDUCED FROM THE HISTORY OF HOLY SCRIPTURE

CHAPTER 2

THAT A MAN HATH ONE RIB LESS THAN A WOMAN

That a man hath one rib less than a woman is a common conceit derived from the history of Genesis, wherein it stands delivered that Eve was framed out of a rib of Adam,[84] whence 'tis concluded the sex of men still wants that rib our father lost in Eve. And this is not only passant[85] with the many, but was urged against Columbus[86] in an anatomy of his at Pisa, where, having prepared the skeleton of a woman that chanced to have thirteen ribs on one side, there arose a party that cried him down, and even unto oaths affirmed, this was the rib wherein a woman exceeded. Were this true, it would autoptically[87] silence that dispute out of which side Eve was framed; it would determine the opinion of Oleaster[88] that she was made out of the ribs of both sides, or such as from the expression of the text maintain there was a plurality required; and might indeed decry the parabolical[89] exposition of Origen, Cajetan,[90] and such as fearing to concede a monstrosity, or mutilate the integrity of Adam, preventively conceive the creation of thirteen ribs.

But this will not consist with reason or inspection. For if we survey the skeleton of both sexes, and therein the compage[91] of bones, we shall readily discover that men and women have four and twenty ribs; that is, twelve on each side, seven greater, annexed unto the *sternon*,[92] and five lesser which come short thereof. Wherein if it sometimes happen that either sex exceed, the conformation is irregular, deflecting from the common rate or number, and no more inferrible[93] upon mankind than the monstrosity of the son of Rapha,[94] or the vicious excess in the number of fingers and toes. And although some difference there be in figure, and the female *os innominatum*[95] be somewhat more protuberant

[79]Following.
[80]German scholastic philosopher (d. 1280) known as the Universal Doctor for his erudition. One of his works is a natural history entitled *Summa de creaturis*.
[81]Ulisse Aldrovandi (1522–1605), Italian naturalist.   [82]Seizing.
[83]Diagonal.   [84]Genesis 2.21–22.   [85]Current.
[86]Realdo Colombo (1544–76), distinguished Italian anatomist, whose *De re anatomica* (1559) was a major contribution to his subject.
[87]With the force of eyewitness evidence.
[88]Jerome Oleaster (d. 1563), a learned Portuguese monk who wrote a commentary on Isaiah.   [89]Metaphorical.
[90]Respectively, an Alexandrian father (d. 254?) who wrote commentaries on both the Old and New Testament, and Gaetano Cardinal Cajetan (1470–1534), a learned Dominican noted as much for his theological and philosophical works as for his stalwart opposition to the Lutheran reformation.
[91]Compages, i.e., complex structure.   [92]Sternum, breastbone.
[93]Deducible.
[94]Sippai, a Philistine giant slain by the Israelites (1 Chronicles 20.4)?
[95]"The nameless bone," i.e., a bone forming one side of the pelvis.

to make a fairer cavity for the infant, the coccyx sometime more reflected to give the easier delivery, and the ribs themselves seem a little flatter, yet are they equal in number. And therefore, while Aristotle doubteth the relations made of nations which had but seven ribs on a side, and yet delivereth that men have generally no more than eight, as he rejecteth their history, so can we not accept of his anatomy.

Again, although we concede there wanted one rib in the skeleton of Adam, yet were it repugnant unto reason and common observation that his posterity should want the same. For we observe that mutilations are not transmitted from father unto son; the blind begetting such as can see, men with one eye children with two, and cripples mutilate[96] in their own persons do come out perfect in their generations. For the seed conveyeth with it not only the extract and single idea of every part, whereby it transmits their perfections or infirmities, but double and over again, whereby sometimes it multipliciously delineates the same, as in twins, in mixed and numerous generations. And to speak more strictly, parts of the seed do seem to contain the idea and power of the whole; so parents deprived of hands beget manual issues, and the defect of those parts is supplied by the idea[97] of others.

So in one grain of corn appearing similarly and insufficient for a plural germination, there lieth dormant the virtuality of many other; and from thence sometimes proceed above an hundred ears. And thus may be made out the cause of multiparous[98] productions; for though the seminal materials disperse and separate in the matrix, the formative operator will not delineate a part, but endeavor the formation of the whole, effecting the same as far as the matter will permit, and from divided materials attempt entire formations. And therefore, though wondrous strange, it may not be impossible what is confirmed at Lausdun concerning the Countess of Holland;[99] nor what Albertus reports of the birth of an hundred and fifty. And if we consider the magnalities[1] of generation in some things, we shall not controvert its possibilities in others, nor easily question that great work whose wonders are only second unto those of the creation; and a close apprehension of the one might perhaps afford a glimmering light and crepusculous[2] glance of the other.

[96]Mutilated. [97]Genetic pattern.
[98]Bringing forth many young at a birth. [99]Unidentified.
[1]Wonders. [2]Crepuscular, dim.

from Hydriotaphia, Urn Burial (1658)

TO MY WORTHY AND HONORED FRIEND, THOMAS LE GROS OF CROSTWICK,[1] ESQUIRE

When the funeral pyre was out, and the last valediction over, men took a lasting adieu of their interred friends, little expecting the curiosity of future ages should comment upon their ashes, and, having no old experience of the duration of their relics, held no opinion of such after considerations.

But who knows the fate of his bones, or how often he is to be buried? Who hath the oracle of his ashes, or whether they are to be scattered? The relics of many lie, like the ruins of Pompey's, in all parts of the earth;[2] and when they arrive at your hands, these may seem to have wandered far, who in a direct and meridian travel have but few miles of known earth between yourself and the pole.[3]

That the bones of Theseus should be seen again in Athens[4] was not beyond conjecture and hopeful expectation, but that these should arise so opportunely to serve yourself was an hit of fate and honor beyond prediction.

We cannot but wish these urns might have the effect of theatrical vessels and great Hippodrome urns in Rome,[5] to resound the acclamations and honor due unto you. But these are sad and sepulchral pitchers which have no joyful voices, silently expressing old mortality, the ruins of forgotten times, and can only speak with life how long in this corruptible frame some parts may be uncorrupted, yet able to outlast bones long unborn, and noblest pile among us.

We present not these as any strange sight or spectacle unknown to your eyes, who have beheld the best of urns and noblest variety of ashes; who are yourself no slender master of antiquities, and can daily command the view of so many imperial faces,[6] which raiseth your thoughts unto old things and consideration of times before you, when even living men were antiquities; when the living might exceed the dead, and to depart this world could not be properly said to go unto the greater number;[7] and so run up your thoughts upon the Ancient of Days,[8] the antiquary's truest object, unto whom the eldest parcels are young, and earth itself an infant; and, without Egyptian account,[9] makes but small noise in thousands.

We were hinted by the occasion, not catched the opportunity,[10] to write of old things, or intrude upon the anti-

HYDRIOTAPHIA [1]Crostwick Hall, a country seat near Norwich.
[2]Following his murder at the command of Ptolemy after his defeat at the battle of Pharsalia (48 B.C.), Pompey's head was taken to Caesar and his body was buried on the coast of Egypt.
[3]Since Crostwick Hall was not far inland there was nothing but open sea between it and the North Pole.
[4]"Brought back by Cimon. Plutarch" (Browne's gloss).
[5]"Conceived to resound the voices of people at their shows" (Browne's gloss). [6]On ancient coins.
[7]Go...number: "Abiit ad plures" (Browne's gloss, from Petronius, Satyricon, xlii.5). [8]God (Daniel 7.9).
[9]"Which makes the world so many years old" (Browne's gloss).
[10]We were hinted...opportunity: we did not seek the opportunity but were prompted by the occasion.

quary. We are coldly drawn unto discourses of antiquities, who have scarce time before us to comprehend new things, or make out learned novelties; but seeing they arose as they lay, almost in silence among us, at least in short account suddenly passed over, we were very unwilling they should die again, and be buried twice among us.

Beside, to preserve the living, and make the dead to live, to keep men out of their urns, and discourse of human fragments in them is not impertinent unto our profession, whose study is life and death, who daily behold examples of 10 mortality, and of all men least need artificial mementos, or coffins, by our bedside to mind us of our graves.

'Tis time to observe occurrences, and let nothing remarkable escape us; the supinity of elder days hath left so much in silence, or time hath so martyred the records, that the most industrious heads do find no easy work to erect a new *Britannia*.[11]

'Tis opportune to look back upon old times and contemplate our forefathers. Great examples grow thin, and to be fetched from the past world. Simplicity flies away, and 20 iniquity comes at long strides upon us. We have enough to do to make up ourselves from present and past times, and the whole stage of things scarce serveth for our instruction. A complete piece of virtue must be made up from the centos[12] of all ages, as all the beauties of Greece could make but one handsome Venus.

When the bones of King Arthur were digged up,[13] the old race might think they beheld therein some originals of themselves. Unto these of our urns none here can pretend relation, and can only behold the relics of those persons, 30 who in their life giving the laws unto their predecessors, after long obscurity, now lie at their mercies. But remembering the early civility they brought upon these countries, and forgetting long-passed mischiefs, we mercifully preserve their bones and piss not upon their ashes.[14]

In the offer of these antiquities we drive not at ancient families, so long outlasted by them. We are far from erecting your worth upon the pillars of your forefathers, whose merits you illustrate. We honor your old virtues, conformable unto times before you, which are the noblest armory. 40 And having long experience of your friendly conversation, void of empty formality, full of freedom, constant and generous honesty, I look upon you as a gem of the old rock,[15] and must profess myself, even to urn and ashes,

Your ever faithful friend and servant,
Thomas Browne

Norwich
May 1
[1658]

CHAPTER 1

In the deep discovery of the subterranean world a shallow part would satisfy some inquirers, who, if two or three yards were open about the surface, would not care to rake the bowels of Potosi[16] and regions towards the center. Nature 50 hath furnished one part of the earth, and man another. The treasures of time lie high, in urns, coins, and monuments, scarce below the roots of some vegetables. Time hath endless

rarities, and shows of all varieties, which reveals old things in heaven, makes new discoveries in earth, and even earth itself a discovery. That great antiquity, America, lay buried for a thousand years, and a large part of the earth is still in the urn unto us.

Though if Adam were made out of an extract of the earth,[17] all parts might challenge a restitution, yet few have returned their bones far lower than they might receive them, not affecting the graves of giants under hilly and heavy coverings, but content with less 'than their own depth have wished their bones might lie soft, and the earth be light upon them; even such as hope to rise again would not be content with central[18] interment, or so desperately to place their relics as to lie beyond discovery, and in no way to be seen again; which happy contrivance hath made communication with our forefathers, and left unto our view some parts which they never beheld themselves.

Though earth hath engrossed the name yet water hath proved the smartest[19] grave, which in forty days swallowed almost all mankind and the living creation, fishes not wholly escaping except the salt ocean were handsomely contempered by a mixture[20] of the fresh element.

Many have taken voluminous pains to determine the state of the soul upon disunion, but men have been most fantastical in the singular contrivances of their corporeal dissolution, whilst the soberest nations have rested in two ways—of simple inhumation and burning.

That carnal interment, or burying, was of the elder date, the old examples of Abraham and the patriarchs are sufficient to illustrate; and were without competition if it could be made out that Adam was buried near Damascus or Mount Calvary, according to some tradition. God himself, that buried but one,[21] was pleased to make choice of this way, collectible from Scripture expression and the hot contest between Satan and the archangel about discovering the body of Moses.[22] But the practice of burning was also of a great antiquity and of no slender extent. For (not to derive the same from Hercules)[23] noble descriptions there are hereof in the Grecian funerals of Homer, in the formal obsequies of Patroclus and Achilles,[24] and somewhat elder in the Theban war and solemn combustion of Meneceus and Archemorus, contemporary unto Jair, the eighth judge of Israel. Confirmable also among the Trojans from the funeral pyre of Hector,[25] burnt before the gates of Troy, and the burning of Penthesilea, the Amazonean queen, and long continuance

[11]A work comparable to William Camden's famous book that appeared in 1586 (see p. 816). [12]Scraps. [13]See p. 813.
[14]*Minxerit in patrios cineres* (Horace, *Ars poetica*, l. 471).
[15]Of exceptional quality.
[16]"The rich mountain of Peru" (Browne's gloss). [17]Genesis 2.7.
[18]Deep in the earth (the "center" of the Ptolemaic universe).
[19]Widest and deepest.
[20]In at least one surviving copy of his book Browne himself changed *a mixture* to *admixture*. [21]Moses (Deuteronomy 34.6).
[22]"Yet Michael, the archangel, when contending with the devil when he disputed about the body of Moses, etc." (Jude, v. 9).
[23]When the dying Hercules was about to fling himself upon a funeral pyre that he himself had built, he was caught up into a cloud and transported to Olympus.
[24]*Iliad*, XXIII.127 ff.; *Odyssey*, XXIV.57 ff. [25]*Iliad*, XXIV.777 ff.

of that practice in the inward countries of Asia; while as low[26] as the reign of Julian we find that the king of Chionia burnt the body of his son and interred the ashes in a silver urn.

The same practice extended also far west, and besides Herulians, Getes, and Thracians, was in use with most of the Celtae, Sarmatians, Germans, Gauls, Danes, Swedes, Norwegians, not to omit some use thereof among Carthaginians and Americans, of great antiquity among the Romans than most opinion or Pliny seems to allow. For (beside the old Table Laws[27] of burning or burying within the city, of making the funeral fire with planed wood, or quenching the fire with wine) Manlius, the consul, burnt the body of his son. Numa, by special clause of his will, was not burnt, but buried; and Remus was solemnly buried, according to the description of Ovid.[28] . . .

[In the rest of Chapter I Browne canvasses the burial customs of ancient India, Persia, Egypt, and Israel, concluding with a comment on the early Christians (who "even in times of subjection and hottest use . . . conformed not unto the Roman practice of burning").]

CHAPTER 2

The solemnities, ceremonies, rites of their cremation or interment, so solemnly delivered by authors, we shall not disparage our reader to repeat. Only the last and lasting part in their urns, collected bones and ashes, we cannot wholly omit or decline that subject, which occasion lately presented in some discovered among us.

In a field of Old Walsingham, not many months past, were digged up between forty and fifty urns, deposited in a dry and sandy soil, not a yard deep, not far from one another. Not all strictly of one figure,[29] but most answering these described; some containing two pounds of bones, distinguishable in skulls, ribs, jaws, thighbones, and teeth, with fresh impressions of their combustion. Besides the extraneous substances, like pieces of small boxes, or combs handsomely wrought, handles of small brass instruments, brazen nippers, and in one some kind of opal.

Near the same plot of ground for about six yards compass were digged up coals and incinerated substances, which begat conjecture that this was the *ustrina* or place of burning their bodies, or some sacrificing place unto the *manes*,[30] which was properly below the surface of the ground, as the *arae*[31] and altars unto the gods and heroes above it.

That these were the urns of Romans, from the common costume and place where they were found, is no obscure conjecture, not far from a Roman garrison, and but five miles from Brancaster, set down by ancient record under the name of Brannodunum. And where the adjoining town, containing seven parishes, in no very different sound, but Saxon termination, still retains the name of Burnham, which being an early station, it is not improbable the neighbor parts were filled with habitations, either of Romans themselves or Britons Romanized, which observed the Roman customs. . . .

Than the time of these urns deposited, of the precise antiquity of these relics, nothing of more uncertainty; for since the lieutenant of Claudius seems to have made the first

progress into these parts since Boadicea was overthrown by the forces of Nero, and Agricola put a full end to these conquests, it is not probable the country was fully garrisoned or planted before; and therefore, however these urns might be of later date, not likely of higher antiquity.[32]

And the succeeding emperors desisted not from their conquests in these and other parts, as testified by history and medal inscription yet extant. The province of Britain, in so divided a distance from Rome, beholding the faces of many imperial persons, and in large account no fewer than Caesar, Claudius, Britannicus, Vespasian, Titus, Adrian, Severus, Commodus, Geta, and Caracalla.

A great obscurity herein, because no medal or emperor's coin enclosed, which might denote the date of their interments; observable in many urns, and found in those of Spitalfields[33] by London, which contained the coins of Claudius, Vespasian, Commodus, Antoninus, attended with lachrymatories,[34] lamps, bottles of liquor, and other appurtenances of affectionate superstition, which in these rural interments were wanting.

Some uncertainty there is from the period or term of burning, or the cessation of that practice. Macrobius affirmeth it was disused in his days;[35] but most agree, though without authentic record, that it ceased with the Antonini—most safely to be understood after the reign of those emperors, which assumed the name of Antoninus, extending unto Heliogabalus. Not strictly after Marcus, for about fifty years later we find the magnificent burning, and consecration of Severus;[36] and if we so fix this period or cessation, these urns will challenge above thirteen hundred years. . . .

[Continuing his far-ranging account of mortuary customs, Browne sweeps through a dozen civilizations and two thousand years of history, but finally, toward the end of Chapter 4, he moves majestically toward his mighty peroration.]

CHAPTER 4

. . . Were the happiness of the next world as closely apprehended as the felicities of this, it were a martyrdom to

[26]Late.
[27]The Twelve Tables, an ancient Roman legal code devised about 450 B.C. [28]*Fasti,* IV.850 ff.
[29]Shape. The text contains a frontispiece depicting four of the burial urns. [30]"Spirit." [31]"Altars."
[32]*Than the time . . . antiquity:* the date of the urns could scarcely be earlier than A.D. 78, when, following the first Roman excursions (50) into Suffolk and Norfolk by Publius Ostorius Scapula (*the lieutenant of Claudius*) and the suppression of native uprisings led by Queen Boadicea (d. 62), Gnaeus Julius Agricola began the systematic pacification of all Britain.
[33]A district of London north of the Tower.
[34]Phials of glass, alabaster, etc., found in Roman tombs and presumably intended to hold tears.
[35]The late 4th and early 5th centuries. For much of his information about Roman mortuary customs, Browne drew heavily on Ambrosius Theodosius Macrobius' *Saturnalia,* a series of dissertations on history and mythology.
[36]The opening of the 3d century. Marcus Aurelius, last of the Antonines, died in 180, and the magnificent obsequies for Lucius Septimius Severus occurred in 211.

live; and unto such as consider none hereafter it must be more than death to die, which makes us amazed at those audacities that durst be nothing and return into their chaos again. Certainly such spirits as could contemn death, when they expected no better being after, would have scorned to live had they known any. And therefore we applaud not the judgment of Machiavel that Christianity makes men cowards,[37] or that with the confidence of but half dying, the despised virtues of patience and humility have abased the spirits of men which pagan principles exalted, but rather regulated the wildness of audacities in the attempts, grounds, and eternal sequels of death, wherein men of the boldest spirits are often prodigiously temerarious. Nor can we extenuate the valor of ancient martyrs, who contemned death in the uncomfortable scene of their lives, and in their decrepit martyrdoms did probably lose not many months of their days, or parted with life when it was scarce worth the living. For (beside that long time past holds no consideration unto a slender time to come) they had no small disadvantage from the constitution of old age, which naturally makes men fearful and complexionally superannuated from the bold and courageous thoughts of youth and fervent years. But the contempt of death from corporeal animosity promoteth not our felicity. They may sit in the orchestra and noblest seats of heaven who have held up shaking hands in the fire and humanly contended for glory.

Meanwhile Epicurus lies deep in Dante's hell,[38] wherein we meet with tombs inclosing souls which denied their immortalities. But whether the virtuous heathen, who lived better than he spake, or, erring in the principles of himself, yet lived above philosophers of more specious maxims, lie so deep as he is placed, at least so low as not to rise against Christians, who, believing or knowing that truth, have lastingly denied it in their practice and conversation, were a query too sad to insist on.

But all or most apprehensions rested in opinions of some future being, which, ignorantly or coldly believed, begat those perverted conceptions, ceremonies, sayings which Christians pity or laugh at. Happy are they which live not in that disadvantage of time when men could say little for futurity but from reason, whereby the noblest minds fell often upon doubtful deaths and melancholy dissolutions. With these hopes Socrates warmed his doubtful spirits against that cold potion;[39] and Cato, before he durst give the fatal stroke, spent part of the night in reading the immortality of Plato,[40] thereby confirming his wavering hand unto the animosity[41] of that attempt.

It is the heaviest stone that melancholy can throw at a man to tell him he is at the end of his nature, or that there is no further state to come, unto which this seems progressional, and otherwise made in vain. Without this accomplishment the natural expectation and desire of such a state were but a fallacy in nature; unsatisfied considerators would quarrel with the justice of their constitutions, and rest content that Adam had fallen lower; whereby by knowing no other original and deeper ignorance of themselves, they might have enjoyed the happiness of inferior creatures, who in tranquillity possess their constitutions as having not the

apprehension to deplore their own natures. And being framed below the circumference of these hopes or cognition of better being, the wisdom of God hath necessitated their contentment. But the superior ingredient and obscured part of ourselves, whereto all present felicities afford no resting contentment, will be able at last to tell us we are more than our present selves, and evacuate[42] such hopes in the fruition of their own accomplishments.

CHAPTER 5

Now since these dead bones have already outlasted the living ones of Methuselah,[43] and in a yard under ground, and thin walls of clay, outworn all the strong and spacious buildings above it, and quietly rested under the drums and tramplings of three conquests,[44] what prince can promise such diuturnity[45] unto his relics, or might not gladly say,

Sic ego componi versus in ossa velim?[46]

Time, which antiquates antiquities, and hath an art to make dust of all things, hath yet spared these minor monuments. In vain we hope to be known by open and visible conservatories,[47] when to be unknown was the means of their continuation, and obscurity their protection. If they died by violent hands, and were thrust into their urns, these bones become considerable, and some old philosophers would honor them, whose souls they conceived most pure, which were thus snatched from their bodies, and to retain a stronger[48] propension[49] unto them, whereas they weariedly left a languishing corpse, and with faint desires of reunion. If they fell by long and aged decay, yet wrapt up in the bundle of time, they fall into indistinction, and make but one blot with infants. If we begin to die when we live, and long life be but a prolongation of death, our life is a sad composition; we live with death, and die not in a moment. How many pulses made up the life of Methuselah were work for Archimedes;[50] common counters sum up the life of Moses his man.[51] Our days become considerable, like petty sums, by minute accumulations, where numerous fractions make up but small round numbers, and our days of a span long make not one little finger.[52]

[37] *Discorsi*, II.2.
[38] Dante puts Epicurus and his followers "who make the soul die with the body" in the dreadful sixth circle of hell (*Inferno*, X.13–15).
[39] Plato, *Phaedo*, Sect. 107, where Socrates' death (from the *cold potion* of hemlock) is movingly described.
[40] According to Plutarch, Cato the Younger (d. 46 B.C.) prepared for his suicide by reading the *Phaedo*. [41] Courage. [42] Nullify.
[43] The oldest of men, a patriarch who lived 969 years (Genesis 5.27).
[44] Saxon, Danish, and Norman. [45] Long duration.
[46] "So I would wish to be laid to rest when I am nothing but bones" (Tibullus, *Elegies*, III.ii.26). [47] Public buildings. [48] Text *stranger*.
[49] Propensity. [50] Greek mathematician (d. 212 B.C.)
[51] "In the Psalm of Moses" (Browne's gloss), i.e., Psalm 90 (subtitled "A Prayer of Moses the Man of God"), where a man's normal longevity is set (v. 10) as "threescore and ten."
[52] "According to the ancient arithmetic of the hand wherein the little finger of the right hand contracted signified an hundred" (Browne's gloss).

If the nearness of our last necessity brought a nearer conformity unto it, there were a happiness in hoary hairs, and no calamity in half senses. But the long habit of living indisposeth us for dying, when avarice makes us the sport of death, when even David grew politically cruel,[53] and Solomon could hardly be said to be the wisest of men. But many are too early old, and before the date of age. Adversity stretcheth our days, misery makes Alcmena's nights,[54] and time hath no wings unto it. But the most tedious being is that which can unwish itself, content to be nothing, or never to have been, which was beyond the malcontent of Job, who cursed not the day of his life, but his nativity;[55] content to have so far been as to have a title to future being, although he had lived here but in an hidden state of life, and as it were an abortion.

What song the sirens sang, or what name Achilles assumed when he hid himself among women,[56] though puzzling questions, are not beyond all conjecture. What time the persons of these ossuaries [57]entered the famous nations of the dead, and slept with princes and counsellors, might admit a wide solution. But who were the proprietaries[58] of these bones, or what bodies these ashes made up, were a question above antiquarism,[59] not to be resolved by man, nor easily perhaps by spirits, except we consult the provincial guardians or tutelary observators.[60] Had they made as good provision for their names as they have done for their relics they had not so grossly erred in the art of perpetuation. But to subsist in bones, and be but pyramidally extant, is a fallacy in duration. Vain ashes, which in the oblivion of names, persons, times, and sexes, have found unto themselves a fruitless continuation, and only arise unto late posterity as emblems of mortal vanities, antidotes against pride, vainglory, and madding vices. Pagan vainglories, which thought the world might last for ever, had encouragement for ambition, and finding no Atropos[61] unto the immortality of their names, were never damped with the necessity of oblivion. Even old ambitions had the advantage of ours in the attempts of their vainglories, who, acting early and before the probable meridian of time, have by this time found great accomplishment of their designs, whereby the ancient heroes have already outlasted their monuments, and mechanical preservations. But in this latter scene of time we cannot expect such mummies unto our memories, when ambition may fear the prophecy of Elias,[62] and Charles the Fifth can never hope to live within two Methuselahs of Hector.[63]

And therefore restless inquietude for the diuturnity of our memories unto present considerations seems a vanity almost out of date, and superannuated piece of folly. We cannot hope to live so long in our names as some have done in their persons. One face of Janus holds no proportion unto the other. 'Tis too late to be ambitious. The great mutations of the world are acted, or time may be too short for our designs. To extend our memories by monuments, whose death we daily pray for, and whose duration we cannot hope without injury to our expectations in the advent of the last day, were a contradiction to our beliefs. We, whose generations are ordained in this setting part of time, are providentially taken off from such imaginations; and, being necessitated to eye the remaining particle of futurity, are naturally constituted unto thoughts of the next world, and cannot excusably decline the consideration of that duration which maketh pyramids pillars of snow, and all that's past a moment.

Circles and right lines limit and close all bodies, and the mortal right-lined circle[64] must conclude and shut up all. There is no antidote against the opium of time, which temporally considereth all things. Our fathers find their graves in our short memories, and sadly tell us how we may be buried in our survivors. Gravestones tell truth scarce forty years. Generations pass while some trees stand, and old families last not three oaks. To be read by bare inscriptions like many in Gruter,[65] to hope for eternity by enigmatical epithets, or first letters of our names, to be studied by antiquaries who we were, and have new names given us like many of the mummies, are cold consolations unto the students of perpetuity, even by everlasting languages.

To be content that times to come should only know there was such a man, not caring whether they knew more of him, was a frigid ambition in Cardan,[66] disparaging his horoscopal inclination and judgment of himself. Who cares to subsist, like Hippocrates' patients, or Achilles' horses in Homer,[67] under naked nominations, without deserts and noble acts, which are the balsam of our memories, the *entelechia*[68] and soul of our subsistences? To be nameless in worthy deeds exceeds an infamous history. The Canaanitish woman lives more happily without a name than Herodias with one. And who had not rather have been the good thief than Pilate?[69]

[53]1 Kings 11.4.
[54]"One night as long as three" (Browne's gloss, referring to the conception of Hercules by Zeus and Alcmena). [55]Job 3.11.
[56]In his life of Tiberius (Sect. lxx), Suetonius cites as an example of the old emperor's silly interest in mythology the posing of such questions as the name of Hecuba's mother, the name that Achilles took when disguised as a maiden, and the song the Sirens sang.
[57]Urns for holding bones. [58]Proprietors. [59]Antiquarianism.
[60]*Provincial...observators:* guardian spirits over certain places or persons.
[61]The third of the three Fates or Moirae, who cuts the thread of life.
[62]"That the world may last but six thousand years" (Browne's gloss). For Browne's fuller speculation on this question see p. 462.
[63]"Hector's fame lasting above two lives of Methuselah before that famous prince [i.e., the Emperor Charles V] was extant" (Browne's gloss).
[64]"Θ, the letter of death" (Browne's gloss), i.e., the first letter of θάνατος, "death."
[65]*Inscriptiones antiquae totius orbis Romanorum* (1602?) by the eminent Dutch scholar Jan Gruter (1560–1627).
[66]In a gloss Browne cites a passage in the autobiography (*De propria vita,* 1576) of the Italian mathematician and physician Geronimo Cardano (1501–76).
[67]Homer (*Iliad,* XVI.149) names Achilles' horses as Xanthus and Balius.
[68]In Aristotelian philosophy, defining characteristic, that by virtue of which a thing is what it is.
[69]*The Canaanitish woman ... Pilate:* posterity has honored the nameless woman who gave water to Jesus (Matthew 15.22–28) more than the evil daughter of King Herod who asked for the head of John the Baptist on a platter (Matthew 14.8), the good

But the iniquity[70] of oblivion blindly scattereth her poppy,[71] and deals with the memory of men without distinction to merit of perpetuity. Who can but pity the founder of the pyramids? Herostratus lives that burnt the temple of Diana;[72] he is almost lost that built it. Time hath spared the epitaph of Adrian's horse, confounded that of himself.[73] In vain we compute our felicities by the advantage of our good names, since bad have equal durations; and Thersites is like to live as long as Agamemnon.[74] Who knows whether the best of men be known, or whether there be not more remarkable persons forgot than any that stand remembered in the known account of time? Without the favor of the everlasting register[75] the first man had been as unknown as the last, and Methuselah's long life had been his only chronicle.

Oblivion is not to be hired: the greater part must be content to be as though they had not been, to be found in the register of God, not in the record of man. Twenty-seven names make up the first story,[76] and the recorded names ever since contain not one living century.[77] The number of the dead long exceedeth all that shall live. The night of time far surpasseth the day, and who knows when was the equinox? Every hour adds unto that current arithmetic, which scarce stands one moment. And since death must be the Lucina[78] of life, and even pagans could doubt whether thus to live were to die; since our longest sun sets at right descensions, and makes but winter arches,[79] and therefore it cannot be long before we lie down in darkness, and have our light in ashes;[80] since the brother of death daily haunts us with dying mementos, and time, that grows old itself, bids us hope no long duration, diuturnity is a dream and folly of expectation.

Darkness and light divide the course of time, and oblivion shares with memory a great part even of our living beings; we slightly remember our felicities, and the smartest strokes of affliction leave but short smart upon us. Sense endureth no extremities, and sorrows destroy us or themselves. To weep into stones are fables.[81] Afflictions induce callosities, miseries are slippery, or fall like snow upon us, which, notwithstanding, is no unhappy stupidity. To be ignorant of evils to come, and forgetful of evils past, is a merciful provision in nature, whereby we digest the mixture of our few and evil days, and our delivered senses not relapsing into cutting remembrances, our sorrows are not kept raw by the edge of repetitions. A great part of antiquity contented their hopes of subsistency with a transmigration of their souls. A good way to continue their memories, while, having the advantage of plural successions, they could not but act something remarkable in such variety of beings, and, enjoying the fame of their passed selves, make accumulation of glory unto their last durations. Others, rather than be lost in the uncomfortable night of nothing, were content to recede into the common being, and make one particle of the public soul of all things, which was no more than to return into their unknown and divine original again. Egyptian ingenuity was more unsatisfied, contriving[82] their bodies in sweet consistences to attend the return of their souls. But all was vanity, feeding the wind, and folly. The Egyptian mummies, which Cambyses[83] or time hath spared, avarice now consumeth. Mummy[84] is become merchandise, Mizraim[85] cures wounds, and Pharaoh is sold for balsams.

In vain do individuals hope for immortality or any patent from oblivion in preservations below the moon; men have been deceived even in their flatteries above the sun, and studied conceits to perpetuate their names in heaven. The various cosmography of that part hath already varied the names of contrived constellations: Nimrod is lost in Orion, and Osiris in the Dog Star.[86] While we look for incorruption in the heavens, we find they are but like the earth: durable in their main bodies, alterable in their parts; whereof, beside comets and new stars, perspectives[87] begin to tell tales, and the spots that wander about the sun, with Phaeton's[88] favor, would make clear conviction.

There is nothing strictly immortal but immortality. Whatever hath no beginning may be confident of no end—all others have a dependent being, and within the reach of destruction—which is the peculiar of that necessary essence that cannot destroy itself, and the highest strain of omnipotency, to be so powerfully constituted as not to suffer even from the power of itself.[89] But the sufficiency of Christian

thief who was crucified with Jesus (Mark 23.40–43) more than the Roman proconsul who presided at his trial.
[70]Inequity, unfairness. [71]Opiate.
[72]The famous temple of Diana at Ephesus, one of the Seven Wonders of the World, was burned by Herostratus on the night of Alexander's birth (356 B.C.).
[73]The Emperor Hadrian erected an inscribed monument to his horse Borysthenes.
[74]Respectively, an evil railer and the leader of the Greeks in Homer's *Iliad*.
[75]*Without...register:* In the text this apparently misplaced phrase is put earlier to follow "Thersites is like to live as long as Agamemnon." [76]"Before the flood" (Browne's gloss in later editions).
[77]One hundred living at one time.
[78]Since death must preside at our entrance into eternity. Lucina was the goddess of childbirth.
[79]Even the longest human life is like the short sunlight of a winter's day.
[80]"According to the custom of the Jews, who place a lighted wax candle in a pot of ashes by the corpse" (Browne's gloss in later editions).
[81]When Niobe boasted of her many children, the gods struck down all but one of them and turned her into a stone, but still she wept for all her losses. Inevitably, statues of her were often used in ornamental fountains.
[82]Some editors have emended to *continuing*.
[83]Persian king who invaded Egypt in 525 B.C.
[84]A medicinal preparation for embalming cadavers, long regarded as a universal panacea.
[85]A son of Ham and grandson of Noah (Genesis 10.6), the supposed ancestor of Egyptians.
[86]*Nimrod...Dog Star:* even the eternal stars have acquired new names. [87]Telescopes.
[88]In Greek mythology, the son of Helios, who drove his father's chariot of the sun so recklessly that Zeus destroyed him with a thunderbolt. For Robert Burton's much fuller discussion of the disquieting implications of astronomical discoveries following Galileo's invention of the telescope (1609) see pp. 450 ff.
[89]It is the unique distinction (*peculiar*) of God to have the power of destroying everything except himself.

immortality frustrates all earthly glory, and the quality of either state[90] after death makes a folly of posthumous memory. God, who can only[91] destroy our souls, and hath assured our resurrection, either of our bodies or names, hath directly promised no duration. Wherein there is so much of chance that the boldest expectants have found unhappy frustration; and to hold long subsistence seems but a scape[92] in oblivion. But man is a noble animal, splendid in ashes and pompous[93] in the grave, solemnizing nativities and deaths with equal luster, nor omitting ceremonies of bravery in the infamy of his nature.

Life is a pure flame, and we live by an invisible sun within us. A small fire sufficeth for life; great flames seemed too little after death, while men vainly affected precious pyres, and to burn like Sardanapalus;[94] but the wisdom of funeral laws found the folly of prodigal blazes, and reduced undoing fires unto the rule of sober obsequies, wherein few could be so mean as not to provide wood, pitch, a mourner, and an urn.

Five languages secured not the epitaph of Gordianus.[95] The man of God[96] lives longer without a tomb than any by one, invisibly interred by angels, and adjudged to obscurity, though not without some marks directing human discovery. Enoch and Elias, without either tomb or burial, in an anomalous state of being, are the great examples of perpetuity in their long and living memory, in strict account being still on this side death, and having a late part yet to act upon this stage of earth.[97] If in the decretory[98] term of the world we shall not all die but be changed, according to received translation,[99] the last day will make but few graves; at least quick resurrections will anticipate lasting sepultures.[1] Some graves will be opened before they be quite closed, and Lazarus[2] be no wonder. When many that feared to die shall groan that they can die but once, the dismal state is the second and living death, when life puts despair on the damned, when men shall wish the coverings of mountains, not of monuments, and annihilation shall be courted.

While some have studied monuments, others have studiously declined them; and some have been so vainly boisterous that they durst not acknowledge their graves, wherein Alaricus[3] seems most subtle, who had a river turned to hide his bones at the bottom. Even Sylla,[4] that thought himself safe in his urn, could not prevent revenging tongues, and stones thrown at his monument. Happy are they whom privacy makes innocent, who deal so with men in this world that they are not afraid to meet them in the next, who, when they die, make no commotion among the dead, and are not touched with that poetical taunt of Isaiah.[5]

Pyramids, arches, obelisks were but the irregularities of vainglory and wild enormities of ancient magnanimity. But the most magnanimous resolution rests in the Christian religion, which trampleth upon pride and sits on the neck of ambition, humbly pursuing that infallible perpetuity unto which all others must diminish their diameters, and be poorly seen in angles of contingency.[6]

Pious spirits who passed their days in raptures of futurity made little more of this world than the world that was before it, while they lay obscure in the chaos of preordination and night of their forebeings. And if any have been so happy as truly to understand Christian annihilation, extasis, exolution, liquefaction, transformation, the kiss of the spouse, gustation of God, and ingression into the divine shadow,[7] they have already had a handsome anticipation of heaven; the glory of the world is surely over, and the earth in ashes unto them.

To subsist in lasting monuments, to live in their productions, to exist in their names, and predicament of chimeras[8] was large satisfaction unto old expectations, and made one part of their elysiums. But all this is nothing in the metaphysics of true belief. To live indeed is to be again ourselves, which being not only an hope but an evidence in noble believers, it is all one to lie in St. Innocent's churchyard[9] as in the sands of Egypt: ready to be anything in the ecstasy of being ever, and as content with six foot as the *moles* of Adrianus.[10]

Lucan

Tabesne cadavera solvat
An rogus haud refert.[11]

[90]Heaven or hell.
[91]Some editors have plausibly emended to *only can.*
[92]Escape, i.e., inadvertence, lucky accident.   [93]Splendid.
[94]Assyrian king (ca. 822 B.C.) who, when his capital Nineveh was threatened, destroyed himself, his many wives, and his palace in a holocaust.
[95]"The epitaph of Gordianus in Greek, Latin, Hebrew, Egyptian, Arabic, defaced by Licinius the Emperor" (Browne's gloss in later editions). Marcus Antonius Gordianus was a Roman emperor who committed suicide (238) after reigning only a few weeks.
[96]Moses.
[97]*Enoch . . . earth:* Enoch was the patriarch "who walked with God, and he was not, for God took him" (Genesis 5.24); Elijah (*Elias*) was transported to heaven in a chariot of fire (2 Kings 2.11).
[98]Decreed.
[99]"Behold, I show you a mystery: we shall not all sleep, but we shall all be changed" (1 Corinthians 15.51).
[1]Sepulchers.
[2]The brother of Mary and Martha whom Jesus raised from the dead (John 11.43–44).
[3]Alaric, king of the Goths who captured Rome in 410.
[4]Lucius Cornelius Sulla (d. 78 B.C.), Roman dictator.
[5]Isaiah 14.4–17.
[6]"*Angulus contingentiae,* the least of angles" (Browne's gloss).
[7]*Annihilation . . . shadow:* theological terms expressing the mystical union of the worshiper with God. *Extasis:* ecstasy. *Exolution:* setting free. *Gustation:* taste.
[8]In the category of wild fancies.
[9]"In Paris, where bodies soon consume" (Browne's gloss).
[10]"A stately mausoleum or sepulchral pile built by Adrianus [the Emperor Hadrian] in Rome where now standeth the Castle of St. Angelo" (Browne's gloss).
[11]"It is unimportant whether bodies are burned on a pyre or simply decompose" (*Pharsalia,* VII.809–810).

Sir Kenelm Digby [1603-1665]

Sir Kenelm Digby's life was so eventful, not to say bizarre, that he could have been a hero of romance. John Aubrey, who had an eye for special men, thought that "he was such a goodly, handsome person, gigantic and great voice, and had so graceful elocution and noble address, etc., that had he been dropped out of the clouds in any part of the world he would have made himself respected." As the son of one of the Gunpowder Plot conspirators and himself an ardent Roman Catholic, he had to make his way by luck and pluck and cunning—all of which he had. Aided by a small inheritance (which had to be secured by litigation because his father died a felon's death), he attended Oxford, traveled widely on the Continent, and achieved a knighthood by the age of twenty. Thereafter, in a swashbuckling career that ranged across the face of Europe, he lived a dozen lives—routing a French and Venetian fleet off the coast of Syria, churning out Catholic propaganda, going over briefly to the Protestants, wooing and at long last winning the celebrated beauty Venetia Stanley, killing his man in a duel to protect the honor of his king, writing almost twenty books (including a treatise on the soul and some *Observations* on *The Faerie Queene*), editing the second folio of Jonson's works, serving as Charles' emissary to the Holy See and as Cromwell's agent on the Continent, helping found the Royal Society, and so on. In short, he was, as Clarendon concluded, "a person very eminent and notorious throughout the whole course of his life, from his cradle to his grave" (p. 796).

It was in 1642, while he was in prison by order of the House of Commons, that at the urging of his friend the earl of Dorset he secured a copy of Browne's newly published *Religio Medici*, read it almost at a sitting, and at once proceeded "to blot a sheet or so of paper" with his comments on the book. When Browne, busy with the forthcoming authorized edition of his work (see p. 796), learned that Digby was about to publish his "animadversions," he wrote to him in great civility (3 March 1643), disowning the "broken and imperfect" 1642 edition and requesting that he withhold his *Observations* until the new and better version of Browne's own work appeared. On March 20 Digby replied that he had vainly tried to stop the printing of his manuscript, which in any event was hardly fit for publication, being "notes hastily set down" solely for the earl of Dorset's use. Besides, he added debonairely, any contest with a man like Browne was bound to be uneven.

> I pretend not to learning; those slender notions I have are but disjointed pieces I have by chance gleaned up here and there; to encounter such a sinewy opposite or make animadversions upon so smart a piece as yours is requireth a solid stock and exercise in school learning. My superficial besprinkling will serve only for a private letter or a familiar discourse with lady-auditors. With longing I expect the coming abroad of the true copy of that book whose false and stolen one hath already given me so much delight.

And so, preceded by such persiflage, Digby's little book appeared. Although Johnson thought that this exchange of letters showed "the reciprocal civility of authors" to be "one of the most risible scenes in the farce of life," Browne must have viewed the matter gravely. Prefixed to his new edition of *Religio Medici* was a note of warning (signed "A. B.") about Sir Kenelm's *Observations* as a hasty, careless piece of work quite unworthy of its author. "But I leave him to repentance," A. B. informed the reader, "and thee to thy satisfaction. Farewell."

I have based my text on the second (1644) edition of Digby's *Observations* (Wing D-1443), the Harvard copy of which is, appropriately enough, bound in with the 1643 edition of Browne's

Religio Medici. Biographies of Digby by E. W. Bligh (1932) and J. F. Fulton (1937) have been superseded by Robert T. Petersson's careful study of Digby's life and works (1956).

from Observations upon Religio Medici (1644)

To the Right Honorable Edward, Earl of Dorset, Baron of Buckhurst, etc.[1]

My Lord,

I received yesternight Your Lordship's of the nineteenth current, wherein you are pleased to oblige me not only by extreme gallant expressions of favor and kindness but likewise by taking so far into your care the expending of my time, during the tediousness of my restraint, as to recommend to my reading a book that had received the honor and safeguard of your approbation; for both which I most humbly thank Your Lordship. And since I cannot in the way of gratefulness express unto Your Lordship, as I would, those 10 hearty sentiments I have of your goodness to me, I will at the least endeavor, in the way of duty and observance, to let you see how the little needle of my soul is thoroughly touched at the great loadstone of yours, and followeth suddenly and strongly which way soever you beckon it. In this occasion, the magnetic motion was impatience to have the book in my hands that Your Lordship gave so advantageous a character of; whereupon I sent presently (as late as it was) to Paul's churchyard, for this favorite of yours, *Religio Medici,* which after a while found me in a condition fit to 20 receive a blessing by a visit from any of such masterpieces as you look upon with gracious eyes—for I was newly gotten into bed. This good natured creature I could easily persuade to be my bedfellow, and to wake with me as long as I had any edge[2] to entertain myself with the delights I sucked from so noble a conversation. And truly, my Lord, I closed not my eyes till I had enriched myself with (or at least exactly surveyed) all the treasures that are lapped up in the folds of those few sheets. To return only a general commendation of this curious piece, or at large to admire the author's spirit and 30 smartness, were too perfunctory an account, and too slight an one, to so discerning and steady an eye as yours after so particular and encharged a summons to read heedfully this discourse. I will therefore presume to blot a sheet or two of paper with my reflections upon sundry passages through the whole context of it as they shall occur to my remembrance. Which now Your Lordship knoweth this packet is not so happy as to carry with it any other expression of my obsequiousness[3] to you, it will be but reasonable you should even here give over your further trouble of reading what my 40 respect engageth me to the writing of.

Whose first step is ingenuity and a well natured evenness of judgment shall be sure of applause and fair hopes in all men for the rest of his journey. And indeed, my Lord, methinketh this gentleman setteth out excellently poised with that happy temper, and showeth a great deal of judicious piety in making a right use of the blind zeal that bigots lose themselves in. Yet I cannot satisfy my doubts throughly[4] how he maketh good his professing to follow the great wheel of the church in matters of divinity,[5] which surely is the solid basis of true religion. For to do so without jarring against the conduct of that first mover by eccentrical and irregular motions obligeth one to yield a very dutiful obedience to the determinations of it, without arrogating to one's self a controlling ability in liking or misliking the faith, doctrine, and constitutions of that church which one looketh upon as their north-star, whereas, if I mistake not, this author approveth the Church of England not absolutely, but comparatively with other reformed churches. . . .

I am extremely pleased with him, when he saith "there are not impossibilities enough in religion for an active faith."[6] And no whit less, when in philosophy he will not be satisfied with such naked terms as in schools use to be obtruded upon easy minds, when the masters' fingers are not strong enough to untie the knots proposed unto them. I confess, when I inquire what light (to use our author's example) is, I should be as well contented with his silence as with his telling me it is *actus perspicui,*[7] unless he explicate clearly to me what those words mean, which I find very few go about to do. Such meat they swallow whole, and eject it as entire. But were such things scientifically and methodically declared they would be of extreme satisfaction and delight. And that work taketh up the greatest part of my formerly mentioned treatise.[8] For I endeavor to show by a continued progress, and

OBSERVATIONS UPON RELIGIO MEDICI [1]Sir Edward Sackville (1591–1652), fourth earl of Dorset, a devoted royalist who had served the House of Stuart in various high offices for many years, was at the time of Digby's writing (1642) in attendance on the beleaguered Charles I at Oxford, where he then held his court. [2]*Keenness* (of desire). [3]*Sense of duty and obligation.* [4]*Thoroughly.* [5]*Matters of divinity:* see *Religio Medici,* I.6 (p. 460). [6]*Active faith:* see *Religio Medici,* I.9 (p. 461). [7]"An act of clarity." See *Religio Medici,* I.10 (p. 461). [8]Earlier, in a section omitted from these excerpts, Digby explained that he himself had required "near two hundred sheets of paper" to "explicate" his analysis of the human soul. This work was subsequently published as *Two Treatises Concerning the Soul and Body of Man* (Paris, 1644).

not by leaps, all the motions of nature, and unto them to fit intelligibly the terms used by her best secretaries, whereby all wild fantastic qualities and moods (introduced for refuges of ignorance) are banished from my commerce.

In the next place, my Lord, I shall suspect that our author hath not penetrated into the bottom of those conceptions that deep scholars have taught us of eternity.[9] Methinketh he taketh it for an infinite extension of time and a never ending revolution of continual succession, which is no more like eternity than a gross body is like to a pure spirit. Nay, such an infinity of revolutions is demonstrable to be a contradiction, and impossible. In the state of eternity there is no succession, no change, no variety. Souls or angels, in that condition, do not so much as change a thought. All things, notions, and actions that ever were, are, or shall be in any creature are actually present to such an intellect. And this, my Lord, I aver not as deriving it from theology, and having recourse to beatific vision to make good my tenet (for so, only glorified creatures should enjoy such immense knowledge), but out of the principles of nature and reason, and from thence shall demonstrate it to belong to the lowest soul of the ignorantest wretch whiles he lived in this world, since damned in hell. A bold undertaking, you will say. But I confidently engage myself to it. Upon this occasion occurreth also a great deal to be said of the nature of predestination (which, by the short touches our author giveth of it, I doubt[10] he quite mistakes) and how it is an unalterable series and chain of causes, producing infallible (and, in respect of them, necessary) effects. But that is too large a theme to unfold here, too vast an ocean to describe in the scant map of a letter. And therefore I will refer that to a fitter opportunity, fearing I have already too much trespassed upon Your Lordship's patience, but that indeed, I hope, you have not had enough to read thus far.

I am sure, my Lord, that you (who never forgot anything which deserved a room in your memory) do remember how we are told that *abyssus abyssum invocat.*[11] So here our author, from the abyss of predestination, falleth into that of the trinity of persons consistent with the indivisibility of the divine nature;[12] and out of that (if I be not exceedingly deceived) into a third, of mistaking when he goeth about to illustrate this admirable mystery by a wild discourse of a trinity in our souls. The dint of wit is not forcible enough to dissect such tough matter, wherein all the obscure glimmering we gain of that inaccessible light cometh to us clothed in the dark weeds of negations, and therefore little can we hope to meet with any positive examples to parallel it withal.

I doubt he also mistaketh, and imposeth upon the severer schools, when he intimateth that they gainsay this visible world's being but a picture or shadow of the invisible and intellectual, which manner of philosophizing he attributeth to Hermes Trismegistus,[13] but is everywhere to be met with in Plato, and is raised since to a greater height in the Christian schools. . . .

I go on with our physician's contemplations. Upon every occasion, he showeth strong parts and a vigorous brain. His wishes and aims, and what he pointeth at speak[14] him

owner of a noble and a generous heart. He hath reason to wish that Aristotle had been as accurate in examining the causes, nature, and affections of the great universe he busied himself about as his patriarch Galen hath been in the like considerations upon his little world, man's body, in that admirable work of his *De usu partium.*[15] But no great human thing was ever born and perfected at once. It may satisfy us if one in our age buildeth that magnificent structure upon the other's foundations, and especially if where he findeth any of them unsound he eradicateth those, and fixeth new unquestionable ones in their room; but so, as they still engross,[16] keep a proportion, and bear a harmony with the other's great work. This hath now (even now) our learned countryman done, the knowing Master White, (whose name, I believe, Your Lordship hath met withal) in his excellent book, *De mundo,* newly printed at Paris, where he now resideth, and is admired by the world of lettered men there as the prodigy of these latter times.[17] Indeed, his three dialogues upon that subject (if I am able to judge anything) are full of the profoundest learning I ever yet met withal. And I believe who hath well read and digested them will persuade himself there is no truth so abstruse, nor hitherto conceived out of our reach, but man's wit may raise engines to scale and conquer. I assure myself when our author hath studied him thoroughly he will not lament so loud for Aristotle's mutilated and defective philosophy. . . .

I acknowledge ingenuously our physician's experience hath the advantage of my philosophy in knowing there are witches.[18] Yet I am sure I have no temptation to doubt of the Deity, nor have any unsatisfaction in believing there are spirits. I do not see such a necessary conjunction between them as that the supposition of the one must needs infer the other. Neither do I deny there are no witches. I only reserve my assent till I meet with stronger motives to carry it. . . .

I must acknowledge that where he balanceth life and death against one another and considereth that the latter is to be a king of nothing for a moment, to become a pure spirit within one instant, and what followeth of this strong thought is extreme handsomely said, and argueth very gallant and generous resolutions in him.[19]

[9]See *Religio Medici,* I.11 (p. 461). It should be noted that Digby seriously misrepresents Browne's own views of the subject. [10]Fear. [11]"Deep calleth unto deep" (Psalm 42.7).
[12]*Divine nature:* See *Religio Medici,* I.12 (p. 462).
[13]See *Religio Medici,* I.12 (p. 462). [14]Show.
[15]Of the scores of extant medical and anatomical treatises by Claudius Galenus (ca. 129–199), the most celebrated physician of antiquity, that "On the Uses of Parts of the Body of Man" had the most lasting influence. [16]Include, i.e., accommodate.
[17]Thomas White (1593–1676), an English Catholic and controversialist who taught at St. Omer, Douay, and elsewhere, wrote many books on theology and philosophy under various pseudonyms. A friend and coreligionist of Digby, he also knew Descartes and Hobbes. His *De mundo dialogi tres,* which reflects some of Digby's own Aristotelianism, was published at Paris in 1642.
[18]See *Religio Medici,* I.30 (p. 464).
[19]*Resolutions in him:* See *Religio Medici,* I.38 (p. 466).

To exemplify the immortality of the soul he needeth not have recourse to the philosopher's stone.[20] His own store furnisheth him with a most pregnant one of reviving a plant (the same numerical[21] plant) out of his own ashes. But, under his favor, I believe his experiment will fail if, under the notion of the same, he comprehendeth all the accidents that first accompanied that plant; for since in the ashes there remaineth only the fixed salt, I am very confident that all the color, and much of the odor and taste of it, is flown away with the volatile salt.

What should I say of his making so particular a narration of personal things and private thoughts of his own, the knowledge whereof cannot much conduce to any man's betterment, which I make account is the chief end of his writing this discourse? As where he speaketh of the soundness of his body, of the course of his diet, of the coolness of his blood at the summer solstice of his age, of his neglect of an epitaph, how long he hath lived or may live, what popes, emperors, kings, grand signiors he hath been contemporary unto, and the like.[22] Would it not be thought that he hath a special good opinion of himself—and indeed he hath reason—when he maketh such great princes the landmarks in the chronology of himself? Surely if he were to write by retail[23] the particulars of his own story and life, it would be a notable romance, since he telleth us in one total sum it is a continued miracle of thirty years.[24] Though he creepeth gently upon us at the first, yet he groweth a giant, an Atlas (to use his own expression) at the last. . . .

[Following a long and digressive excursion into ethical theory Digby returns to Browne.]

But to come back to our physician: truly, my Lord, I must needs pay him, as a due, the acknowledging his pious discourses to be excellent and pathetical[25] ones, containing worthy motives to incite one to virtue and to deter one from vice, thereby to gain heaven and to avoid hell. Assuredly he is owner of a solid head and of a strong, generous heart. Where he employeth his thoughts upon such things as resort to no higher or more abstruse principles than such as occur in ordinary conversation with the world, or in the common track of study and learning, I know no man would say better. But when he meeteth with such difficulties as his next, concerning the resurrection of the body[26] (wherein after deep meditation upon the most abstracted principles and speculations of the metaphysics, one hath much ado to solve the appearing contradictions in nature) there I do not at all wonder he should tread a little awry, and go astray in the dark, for I conceive his course of life hath not permitted him to allow much time unto the unwinding of such entangled and abstracted subtilties. But if it had, I believe his natural parts are such as he might have kept the chair[27] from most men I know; for even where he roveth widest, it is with so much wit and sharpness as putteth me in mind of a great man's censure upon Joseph Scaliger's *Cyclometrica* (a matter he was not well versed in), that he had rather err so ingeniously as he did than hit upon truth in that heavy manner as the Jesuit his antagonist stuffeth his books.[28] Most assuredly his

wit and smartness in this discourse is of the finest standard; and his insight into severer learning will appear as piercing unto such as use not strictly the touchstone and the test, to examine every piece of the glittering coin he payeth his reader with. But to come to the resurrection. Methinks it is but a gross conception to think that every atom of the present individual matter of a body, every grain of ashes of a burned cadaver, scattered by the wind throughout the world, and, after numerous variations, changed paradventure into the body of another man, should at the sounding of the last trumpet be raked together again from all the corners of the earth, and be made up anew into the same body it was before of the first man. Yet if we will be Christians and rely upon God's promises, we must believe that we shall rise again with the same body that walked about, did eat, drink, and live, here on earth; and that we shall see our Savior and Redeemer with the same, the very same eyes, wherewith we now look upon the fading glories of this contemptible world.

How shall these seeming contrarieties be reconciled? If the latter be true, why should not the former be admitted? . . . In such abstracted speculations [as those concerning the relation of form and matter], where we must consider matter without form (which hath no actual being), we must not expect adequated[29] examples in nature. But enough is said to make a speculative man see that if God should join the soul of a lately dead man (even whiles his dead corpse should lie entire in his winding sheet here) unto a body made of earth taken from some mountain in America, it were most true and certain that the body he should then live by were the same identical body he lived with before his death and late resurrection. It is evident that sameness, thisness, and thatness belongeth not to matter by itself (for a general indifference runneth through all) but only as it is distinguished and individuated by the form. Which in our case, whensoever the same soul doth, it must be understood always to be the same matter and body. . . .

But were it not time that I made an end? Yes, it is more

20In *Religio Medici,* I.39, Browne, arguing for the continuing identity of the soul through prenatal existence, through life "upon the scene of this world," and after death, says that "the smattering I have of the philosopher's stone (which is something more than the perfect exaltation of gold) hath taught me a great deal of divinity, and instructed my belief how that immortal spirit and incorruptible substance of my soul may lie obscure and sleep a while within this house of flesh."
21Particular, individual. Text *unmericall.*
22See *Religio Medici,* I.41 (p. 467).   23In detail.
24See *Religio Medici,* II.11 (p. 471).   25Moving, affecting.
26"How shall the dead arise," Browne says (*Religio Medici,* I.48), "is no question of my faith; to believe only possibilities is not faith, but mere philosophy; many things are true in divinity which are neither inducible by reason nor confirmable by sense, and many things in philosophy confirmable by sense yet not inducible by reason."   27Taken precedence.
28The last years of Joseph Justus Scaliger (1540–1609), universally recognized as one of the most learned man of his time, were disturbed by the relentless attacks of the Jesuits and notably of one Kaspar Scioppius. Scaliger's *Cyclometrica elementa duo* appeared in 1594.   29Proved sufficient.

than time. And therefore having once passed the limit that confined what was becoming, the next step carried me into the ocean of error, which being infinite, and therefore more or less bearing no proportion in it, I will proceed a little further to take a short survey of his Second Part, and hope for as easy pardon after this addition to my sudden and indigested remarks as if I had inclosed them up now.

Methinks he beginneth with somewhat an affected discourse to prove his natural inclination to charity, which virtue is the intended theme of all the remainder of his discourse. And I doubt he mistaketh the lowest orb or limb of that high seraphic virtue for the top and perfection of it, and maketh a kind of human compassion to be divine charity. He will have it to be a general way of doing good. It is true he addeth then, for God's sake, but he allayeth that again with saying he will have that good done as by obedience, and to accomplish God's will; and looketh at the effects it worketh upon our souls, but in a narrow compass, like one in the vulgar throng that considereth God as a judge and as a rewarder or a punisher. Whereas perfect charity is that vehement love of God for His own sake, for His goodness, for His beauty, for His excellency that carrieth all the motions of our soul directly and violently to Him, and maketh a man disdain or rather hate all obstacles that may retard his journey to Him. And that face of it that looketh toward mankind, with whom we live, and warmeth us to do others good is but like the overflowing of the main stream that, swelling above its banks, runneth over in a multitude of little channels. . . .

I cannot agree to his resolution of shutting his books and giving over the search of knowledge, and resigning himself up to ignorance upon the reason that moveth him, as though it were extreme vanity to waste our days in the pursuit of that which by attending but a little longer (till death hath closed the eyes of the body to open those of our soul) we shall gain with ease, we shall enjoy by infusion and as an accessory of our glorification.[30] It is true, as soon as death hath played the midwife to our second birth, our soul shall then see all truths more freely than our corporal eyes at our first birth see all bodies and colors. . . . Yet far be it from us to think that time lost which in the mean season we shall laboriously employ to warm ourselves with blowing a few little sparks of that glorious fire which we shall afterwards in one instant leap into the middle of without danger of scorching. And that for two important reasons (besides several others too long to mention here): the one, for the great advantage we have by learning in this life; the other, for the huge contentment that the acquisition of it here (which implieth a strong affection to it) will be unto us in the next life. . . . I do not mean such study as armeth wrangling champions for clamorous schools, where the ability of subtile disputing to and fro is more prized than the retrieving of truth, but such as filleth the mind with solid and useful notions, and doth not endanger the swelling it up with windy vanities. Besides, the sweetest companion and entertainment of a well-tempered mind is to converse familiarly with the naked and bewitching beauties of those mistresses, those verities and sciences, which by fair courting of them they gain and enjoy, and

every day bring new fresh ones to their seraglio, where the ancientest never grow old or stale. Is there anything so pleasing or so profitable as this? . . .

I believe Your Lordship will scarcely join with him in his wish that we might procreate and beget children without the help of women or without any conjunction or commerce with that sweet and bewitching sex.[31] Plato taxeth his fellow philosopher (though otherwise a learned and brave man) for not sacrificing to the Graces, those gentle female goddesses. What thinketh Your Lordship of our physician's bitter censure of that action which Mahomet maketh the essence of his paradise? Indeed, besides those his unkindnesses, or rather forwardnesses, at that tender-hearted sex (which must needs take it ill at his hands), methinketh he setteth marriage at too low a rate, which is assuredly the highest and divinest link of human society. And where he speaketh of Cupid and of beauty it is in such a praise as putteth me in mind of the learned Greek reader in Cambridge, his courting of his mistress out of Stephens his *Thesaurus*. . . .[32]

In his concluding prayer,[33] wherein he summeth up all he wisheth, methinketh his arrow is not winged with that fire which I should have expected from him upon this occasion; for it is not the peace of conscience nor the bridling up of one's affections that expresseth the highest delightfulness and happiest state of a perfect Christian. It is love only that can give us heaven upon earth as well as in heaven, and bringeth us thither too, so that the Tuscan Vergil[34] had reason to say,

In alte dolcezze
Non si puo gioir, se non amando.[35]

And this love must be employed upon the noblest and highest object, not terminated in our friends. But of this transcendent and divine part of charity, that looketh directly and immediately upon God himself, and that is the intrinsical form, the utmost perfection, the scope and final period of true religion (this gentleman's intended theme, as I conceive) I have no occasion to speak anything, since my author

[30]Terming pride the "mortal enemy to charity, the first and father sin," Browne (*Religio Medici*, II.8) vigorously attacks those who vaunt themselves on their learning. "Solomon, that complained of ignorance in the height of knowledge, hath not only humbled my conceits but discouraged my endeavors. There is yet another conceit that hath sometimes made me shut my books, which tells me it is a vanity to waste our days in the blind pursuit of knowledge; it is but attending a little longer, and we shall enjoy that by instinct and infusion which we endeavor at here by labor and inquisition. It is better to sit down in a modest ignorance and rest contented with the natural blessing of our own reason than buy the uncertain knowledge of this life with sweat and vexation, which death gives every fool gratis and is an accessory of our glorification." [31]See *Religio Medici*, II.9 (p. 470).
[32]Digby is probably alluding to the great *Thesaurus linguae Graecae* (1572) by Henri Estienne (Stephanus), a member of the notable French family of scholars and printers. Henri's father Robert had published a very influential *Thesaurus linguae Latinae* in 1532.
[33]See *Religio Medici*, II.15 (p. 472).
[34]Presumably Petrarch, whose most ambitious work was an unfinished epic, *Africa*, modeled on Vergil's *Aeneid*.
[35]"Without love one is unable to enjoy the highest pleasures."

doth but transiently mention it, and that too in such a phrase as ordinary catechisms speak of it to vulgar capacities.

Thus, my Lord, having run though the book (God knows how slightly, upon so great a sudden) which Your Lordship commanded me to give you an account of, there remaineth yet a weightier task upon me to perform, which is to excuse myself of presumption for daring to consider any moles in that face which you had marked for a beauty. But who shall well consider my manner of proceeding in these remarks will free me from that censure. I offer not at judging [10] the prudence and wisdom of this discourse: those are fit inquiries for Your Lordship's court of highest appeal; in my inferior one I meddle only with little knotty pieces of particular sciences (*Matinae apis instar, operosa parvus carmina fingo*)[36] in which it were peradventure a fault for Your Lordship to be too well versed; your employments are of a higher and nobler strain, and that concerns the welfare of millions of men:

> *Tu regere imperio populos (Sackville) memento*
> *(Hae tibi erunt artes) pacisque imponere morem.*[37]   [20]

Such little studies as these belong only to those persons that are low in the rank they hold in the commonwealth, low in their conceptions, and low in a languishing and rusting leisure, such an one as Vergil calleth *ignobile otium,*[38] and such an one as I am now dulled withal. If Alexander or Caesar should have commended a tract of land as fit to fight a battle in for the empire of the world or to build a city upon, to be the magazine and staple[39] of all the adjacent countries, nobody could justly condemn that husbandman who, according to his own narrow art and rules, should censure [30] the plains of Arbela or Pharsalia[40] for being in some places sterile, or the meadows about Alexandria for being sometimes subject to be overflown, or could tax aught he should say in that kind for a contradiction unto the other's com-

mendations of those places, which are built upon higher and larger principles.

So, my Lord, I am confident I shall not be reproached of unmannerliness for putting in a demurrer unto a few little particularities in that noble discourse, which Your Lordship gave a general applause unto; and by doing so, I have given Your Lordship the best account I can of myself, as well as of your commands. You hereby see what my entertainments are, and how I play away my time,

> *Dorset dum magnus ad altum*
> *Fulminat Oxonium bello, victorque volentes*
> *Per populos dat jura; viamque affectat Olympo.*[41]

May your counsels there be happy and successful ones to bring about that peace which, if we be not quickly blessed withal, a general ruin threateneth the whole kingdom.

From Winchester House,[42] the 22 (I think I may say the 23, for I am sure it is morning, and I think it is day) of December 1642.

> *Your Lordship's most humble*
> *and obedient servant,*
> *Kenelm Digby*

[36]"Like the Matinian bee I insignificantly and laboriously fashion my verses" (a garbled version of Horace, *Odes,* IV.ii.27–32).
[37]"Remember, Sackville, to rule the people with imperial sway— these will be your arts—and to impose law on peace" (adapted from Vergil, *Aeneid,* VI.851–852).   [38]"Ignoble leisure."
[39]Commercial center.
[40]Respectively, sites of famous battles between Alexander the Great and Darius, Caesar and Pompey.
[41]"While great Dorset thundered in war at Oxford, as victor gave laws to willing people, and tried the way to heaven" (adapted from Vergil, *Georgics,* IV.560–562).
[42]Ancient seat of the bishops of Winchester in Southwark which in 1642 Parliament converted into a prison.

Thomas Hobbes[1] [1588–1679]

Although Hobbes vehemently disapproved of Greek and Latin learning as an engine of sedition and told John Aubrey he "repented" the two years that he, when young, had wasted poring over plays and fiction, he nonetheless belongs to literature, both as a massive figure in the thought and culture of his time and as the master of a style as swift and strong and pure as any of the age. Actually, his notorious aversion to humanistic learning is not in keeping with the facts of his career: he started Greek and Latin at the age of six, made a Latin version of Euripides' *Medea* when he was in his early teens, became a published author with a translation of Thucydides (see pp. 904 ff.), was the cherished friend of Jonson and many other men of letters, produced one of the most important critical treatises of the period in his exchange with Davenant (see pp. 780 ff.), and closed his long career (when he was almost ninety) by writing his own life in Latin verses and turning Homer into

[1]For other works of Hobbes, see Books and Men, pp. 784 ff., and History and Historiography pp. 904 ff.

English. Despite all this the old man persisted in his strenuous disregard for literature. "Why did I write it?" he asked in the preface to his Homer. "Because I had nothing else to do. Why publish it? Because I thought it might take off my adversaries from showing their folly upon my more serious writings and set them upon my verses to show their wisdom."

In explanation of his "extraordinary timorousness," Hobbes said that his birth was premature because his mother had been frightened by news of the Armada. After a sound classical education (provided by an uncle) at the grammar school in Malmesbury, Wiltshire, and then at Magdalen College, Oxford (B.A. 1608), he was appointed tutor to the son of William Cavendish, later second earl of Devonshire, and to this distinguished family he continued more or less attached for the remainder of his life. One consequence of this attachment may have been his Thucydides (which was designed, as he explained, to show the folly of democracy), but others were the knowledge of foreign tongues and manners and the acquaintance with such European thinkers as Galileo, Gassendi, and Marsenne that he acquired during three extended visits to the Continent (1610, 1629–30, 1634–36) as tutor and companion to young Cavendish and to his former pupils's son.

Hobbes was middle-aged and England was on the verge of civil war before he turned to philosophic speculation with a projected three-part work involving physics ("De corpore"), psychology ("De homine"), and politics ("De cive"); but the mounting pressure of events led him to interrupt this major undertaking with *The Elements of Law, Natural and Politic,* a "little treatise in English" that by 1640 was circulating in manuscript as separate studies of "Human Nature" and "De corpore politico." Although they brought him into notice as a thinker, he, with characteristic timidity, thought they put him in "danger of his life" and so he fled to Paris.

His next eleven years abroad were filled with this and that: disputing with Descartes, developing his political convictions in *De cive* (1642), consorting with other exiled royalists, serving as tutor to the Prince of Wales, and getting *Human Nature* and *De corpore politico* into print (1650); but by far the most important product of his long exile was *Leviathan*. It had been presented to King Charles (in a handsome vellum manuscript), but when important persons saw in it an artful plea for atheism and sedition Hobbes was barred from court. Thus endangered, as he thought, both by English royalists and by vindictive French divines, he took flight again—this time back to England just before his controversial book appeared in 1651.

His travels now were ended. Like his patron, he submitted to the Council of State and was allowed to live in peace until the Restoration, when Charles characteristically forgot whatever grievance he had held against the author of *Leviathan*, welcomed him at court, and even promised him a pension. And so Hobbes passed into his later years, which if not serene were at any rate secure. Among the more important products of this final phase of his career were *De corpore* (1655), which had been begun about 1642, *De homine* (1658), and *Behemoth*, a "history of the causes of the civil wars in England" that was finished about 1668, suppressed at the king's request, printed surreptitiously in 1679, and published posthumously in the *Tracts* of 1682. He expounded and defended his opinions against a host of adversaries, engaged in rancorous quarrels with Bishop Bramhall and other theologians about the smell of atheism in his work, disputed interminably with such eminent mathematicians as Seth Ward and Robert Boyle (who routinely bested him), and beguiled his leisure time by turning Homer's hexameters into heroic quatrains because he "had nothing else to do." His extreme old age, says Aubrey, was spent in "contemplation and study" at Chatsworth and Hardwick, where the earl of Devonshire protected him until he died at ninety-one, still possessed of that "brisk fervor and vigor of his mind" that energize every page he wrote.

To represent adequately this great man's large production (which runs to sixteen volumes) is not easy. From the four books of *Leviathan*, 1651 (Wing H-2246)—the first on the nature of man, the second on the state as an "artificial" creation of human will, the third on the proper subordination of the church to the sovereign power of the state, and the fourth on the "kingdom of darkness" or the Roman Catholic Church—I have chosen some of the more assertive statements of the materialism, mechanism, and nominalism that dismayed his orthodox contemporaries. My text for his translation of Thucydides (pp. 904 ff.) is based upon *Eight Books of the Peloponnesian War*, 1629 (STC 24058), and for his famous epistolary exchange on literary theory with Sir William Davenant (pp. 780 ff.)—the circumstances of which are summarized on pp. 252 ff.—on *A Discourse upon Gondibert . . . with an Answer to it by Mr. Hobbs*, 1650 (Wing D-322). As noted earlier, *Behemoth* (pp. 906 ff.) had a complicated history, but the authority of the posthumous *Tracts* of 1682 (Wing H-2265, on which my text is based) seems to rest securely on its printer's attestation:

> I am compelled by the force of Truth to declare how much both the world and the name of Mr. Hobbes have been abused by the several spurious editions of *The History of the Civil Wars*, wherein by various and unskillful transcriptions are committed above a thousand faults, and in above a hundred places whole lines left out, as I can make appear.
>
> I must confess Mr. Hobbes, upon some considerations, was averse to the publishing thereof, but since it is impossible to suppress it—no book being more commonly sold by all booksellers —I hope I need not fear the offense of any man by doing right to the world and this work, which I now publish from the original manuscript done by his own amanuensis and given me by himself above twelve years since.

Apart from Sir William Molesworth's standard edition of the works in Latin and English (16 vols., 1839–45), there are editions of *Leviathan* by A. R. Waller (1904), W. G. P. Smith (1909), and Michael Oakeshott (1946); of the translation of Thucydides by David Grene (2 vols., 1959); of the exchange between Davenant and Hobbes in J. E. Spingarn's *Critical Essays of the Seventeenth Century* (3 vols., 1908–09); and of *Behemoth* by Ferdinand Tönnies (2d ed., 1969). E. H. Sneath (1898), M. W. Calkins (1905), and F. J. E. Woodbridge (1930) have edited useful selections from the principal works.

Hobbes of course occupies a large place in many of the works on philosophy cited in the General Bibliography, Section II. There are separate biographical or interpretative studies by G. C. Robertson (1886), Sir Leslie Stephen (1904), G. E. C. Catlin (1922), Tönnies (3d ed., 1925), John Laird (1934), Richard Peters (1956), and Howard Warrender (*The Political Philosophy of Hobbes*, 1957). Of special interest to literary students are Spingarn's introduction, C. M. Dowling's study of the exchange with Davenant (1934), C. D. Thorpe's *Aesthetic Theory of Thomas Hobbes* (1940), D. G. James' *Life of Reason: Hobbes, Locke, Bolingbroke* (1949), S. I. Mintz's *Hunting of Leviathan* (1962), and T. E. Jessop's *Thomas Hobbes* (1960). R. B. Schlatter has written informatively on Hobbes and Thucydides (*JHI*, VI, 1945), and there is an exhaustive bibliography by Hugh Macdonald and Mary Hargreaves (1952).

from Leviathan (1651)

THE INTRODUCTION

Nature, the art whereby God hath made and governs the world, is by the art of man, as in many other things, so in this also imitated, that it can make an artificial[1] animal. For seeing life is but a motion of limbs, the beginning whereof is in some principal part within, why may we not say that all *automata* (engines that move themselves by springs and wheels as doth a watch) have an artificial life? For what is the heart but a spring; and the nerves but so many strings; and the joints but so many wheels, giving motion to the whole body, such as was intended by the artificer? Art goes yet further, imitating that rational and most excellent work of nature, man. For by art is created that great Leviathan called a commonwealth or state, in Latin *civitas*, which is but an artificial man; though of greater stature and strength than the natural, for whose protection and defense it was intended; and in which the sovereignty is an artificial soul, as giving life and motion to the whole body; the magistrates and other officers of judicature and execution, artificial joints; reward and punishment, by which fastened to the seat of the sovereignty every joint and member is moved to perform his duty,

LEVIATHAN [1]Made by or resulting from art or artifice (as in Sir Thomas Browne's comment [p. 463] that "nature is the art of God").

are the nerves, that do the same in the body natural; the wealth and riches of all the particular members are the strength; *salus populi*, the people's safety, its business; counselors, by whom all things needful for it to know are suggested unto it, are the memory; equity and laws, an artificial reason and will; concord, health; sedition, sickness; and civil war, death. Lastly, the pacts and covenants, by which the parts of this body politic were at first made, set together and united, resemble that *fiat*, or the first "Let us make man," pronounced by God in the creation.[2]

To describe the nature of this artificial man, I will consider:

First, the matter thereof and the artificer, both which is man.

Secondly, how and by what covenants it is made, what are the rights and just power or authority of a sovereign, and what it is that preserveth and dissolveth it.

Thirdly, what is a Christian commonwealth.

Lastly, what is the kingdom of darkness.

Concerning the first, there is a saying much usurped of late that wisdom is acquired not by reading of books, but of men. Consequently whereunto, those persons that for the most part can give no other proof of being wise take great delight to show what they think they have read in men by uncharitable censures of one another behind their backs. But there is another saying not of late understood, by which they might learn truly to read one another if they would take the pains; that is, *Nosce teipsum*, read thyself: which was not meant, as it is now used, to countenance either the barbarous state of men in power towards their inferiors, or to encourage men of low degree to a saucy behavior towards their betters; but to teach us that for the similitude of the thoughts and passions of one man to the thoughts and passions of another, whosoever looketh into himself, and considereth what he doth when he does think, opine, reason, hope, fear, etc., and upon what grounds, he shall thereby read and know what are the thoughts and passions of all other men upon like occasions. I say the similitude of passions, which are the same in all men (desire, fear, hope, etc.,) not the similitude of the objects of the passions, which are the things desired, feared, hoped, etc.; for these the constitution individual and particular education do so vary, and they are so easy to be kept from our knowledge, that the characters of man's heart, blotted and confounded as they are with dissembling, lying, counterfeiting, and erroneous doctrines, are legible only to Him that searcheth hearts. And though by men's actions we do discover their design sometimes, yet to do it without comparing them with our own and distinguishing all circumstances by which the case may come to be altered is to decipher without a key, and be for the most part deceived by too much trust or too much diffidence, as he that reads is himself a good or evil man.

But let one man read another by his actions never so perfectly, it serves him only with his acquaintance, which are but few. He that is to govern a whole nation must read in himself not this or that particular man, but mankind; which, though it be hard to do, harder than to learn any language or science, yet when I shall have set down my own reading orderly and perspicuously, the pains left another will be only to consider if he also find not the same in himself. For this kind of doctrine admitteth no other demonstration.

Beginning with the blunt assertion that "there is no conception in a man's mind which hath not at first, totally or by parts, been begotten upon the organs of sense," Hobbes proceeds implacably with his analysis of man's mental operations. Imagination and memory are the same, he says, one being "decaying sense" and the other our recollection of what is "fading, old, and past." One sort of understanding, which Hobbes identifies as prudence, is a natural wisdom based upon experience and shared by man and beast, but there is another kind of understanding that is man's alone, for it relies upon his unique gift of language. "For a dog by custom will understand the call or the rating[3] of his master, and so will many other beasts. That understanding which is peculiar to man is the understanding not only his will, but his conceptions and thoughts by the sequel and contexture of the names of things into affirmations, negations, and other forms of speech; and of this kind of understanding I shall speak hereafter." And so Hobbes comes to talk of speech and language.

PART I.   OF MAN

CHAPTER 4
OF SPEECH

The invention of printing, though ingenious, compared with the invention of letters is no great matter. But who was the first that found the use of letters is not known. He that first brought them into Greece, men say, was Cadmus, the son of Agenor, King of Phoenicia.[4] A profitable invention for continuing the memory of time past and the conjunction[5] of mankind, dispersed into so many and distant regions of the earth, and withal difficult, as proceeding from a watchful observation of the divers motions of the tongue, palate, lips, and other organs of speech, whereby to make as many differences of characters as to remember them. But the most noble and profitable invention of all other was that of speech, consisting of names or appellations and their connection, whereby men register their thoughts, recall them when they are past, and also declare them one to another for mutual utility and conversation; without which there had been amongst men neither commonwealth nor society nor contract nor peace no more than amongst lions, bears, and wolves. The first author of speech was God himself, that instructed Adam how to name such creatures as He presented to his sight,[6] for the Scripture goeth no further in this matter. . . .

The general use of speech is to transfer our mental discourse into verbal, or the train of our thoughts into a train of words; and that for two commodities, whereof one is the registering of the consequences of our thoughts, which, being apt to slip out of our memory and put us to a new labor, may again be recalled by such words as they were

[2]Genesis 1.26.   [3]Scolding.
[4]The mythical Cadmus was said to have introduced into Greece from Phoenicia or Egypt an alphabet of sixteen letters.
[5]Social cohesion.   [6]Genesis 2.20.

marked by. So that the first use of names is to serve for marks or notes of remembrance. Another is, when many use the same words to signify by their connection and order one to another what they conceive or think of each matter, and also what they desire, fear, or have any other passion for. And for this use they are called signs. Special uses of speech are these: first, to register what by cogitation we find to be the cause of anything, present or past, and what we find things present or past may produce or effect; which, in sum, is acquiring of arts. Secondly, to show to others that knowledge which we have attained, which is to counsel and teach one another. Thirdly, to make known to others our wills and purposes that we may have the mutual help of one another. Fourthly, to please and delight ourselves and others by playing with our words for pleasure or ornament, innocently.

To these uses there are also four correspondent abuses. First, when men register their thoughts wrong by the inconstancy of the signification of their worlds, by which they register for their conception that which they never conceived, and so deceive themselves. Secondly, when they use words metaphorically, that is, in other sense than that they are ordained for, and thereby deceive others. Thirdly, by words, when they declare that to be their will which is not. Fourthly, when they use them to grieve one another; for seeing nature hath armed living creatures—some with teeth, some with horns, and some with hands—to grieve an enemy, it is but an abuse of speech to grieve him with the tongue, unless it be one whom we are obliged to govern, and then it is not to grieve, but to correct and amend.

The manner how speech serveth to the remembrance of the consequences of causes and effects consisteth in the imposing of names, and the connection of them. . . . When two names are joined together into a consequence or affirmation, as thus, "A man is a living creature," or thus, "If he be a man, he is a living creature," if the latter name *living creature* signify all that the former name *man* signifieth, then the affirmation or consequence is true; otherwise false. For *true* and *false* are attributes of speech, not of things. And where speech is not, there is neither truth nor falsehood; error there may be, as when we expect that which shall not be, or suspect what has not been; but in neither case can a man be charged with untruth.

Seeing then that truth consisteth in the right ordering of names in our affirmations, a man that seeketh precise truth had need to remember what every name he uses stands for and to place it accordingly, or else he will find himself entangled in words as a bird in lime twigs—the more he struggles the more belimed. And therefore in geometry, which is the only science[7] that it hath pleased God hitherto to bestow on mankind, men begin at settling the significations of their words; which settling of significations they call definitions, and place them in the beginning of their reckoning.

By this, it appears how necessary it is for any man that aspires to true knowledge to examine the definitions of former authors; and either to correct them where they are negligently set down, or to make them himself. For the errors of definitions multiply themselves according as the reckoning proceeds, and lead men into absurdities which at last they see but cannot avoid without reckoning anew from the beginning, in which lies the foundation of their errors. From whence it happens that they which trust to books do as they that cast up many little sums into a greater, without considering whether those little sums were rightly cast up or not; and at last, finding the error visible and not mistrusting their first grounds, know not which way to clear themselves, but spend time in fluttering over their books, as birds that, entering by the chimney and finding themselves inclosed in a chamber, flutter at the false light of a glass window for want of wit to consider which way they came in. So that in the right definition of names lies the first use of speech, which is the acquisition of science; and in wrong or no definitions lies the first abuse; from which proceed all false and senseless tenets, which make those men that take their instruction from the authority of books, and not from their own meditation, to be as much below the condition of ignorant men as men endued with true science are above it. For between true science and erroneous doctrines, ignorance is in the middle. Natural sense and imagination are not subject to absurdity. Nature itself cannot err, and as men abound in copiousness of language, so they become more wise or more mad than ordinary. Nor is it possible without letters for any man to become either excellently wise, or, unless his memory be hurt by disease or ill constitution of organs, excellently foolish. For words are wise men's counters—they do but reckon by them; but they are the money of fools, that value them by the authority of an Aristotle, a Cicero, or a Thomas,[8] or any other doctor whatsoever, if but a man. . . .

CHAPTER 5
OF REASON AND SCIENCE

> Speech, then, is essential to specifically human intellection, for what we call reason is "nothing but reckoning, that is, adding and subtracting of the consequences of general names agreed upon for the marking and signifying of our thoughts."

. . . By this it appears that reason is not, as sense and memory, born with us, nor gotten by experience only, as prudence is, but attained by industry: first in apt imposing of names and secondly by getting a good and orderly method in proceeding from the elements, which are names, to assertions made by connection of one of them to another, and so to syllogisms, which are the connections of one assertion to another, till we come to a knowledge of all the consequences of names appertaining to the subject in hand; and that is it men call science. And whereas sense and memory are but knowledge of fact, which is a thing past and irrevocable, science is the knowledge of consequences, and dependence of one fact upon another; by which, out of that we can presently do we know how to do something else when we will, or the like another time, because when we see how anything comes about, upon

---

[7] In Chapter V, Hobbes defines science as "the knowledge of consequences, and dependence of one fact upon another."
[8] St. Thomas Aquinas (1225?–74), Italian Dominican monk and theologian.

what causes and by what manner, when the like causes come into our power we see how to make it produce like effects.

Children, therefore, are not endued with reason at all till they have attained the use of speech, but are called reasonable creatures for the possibility apparent of having the use of reason in time to come. And the most part of men, though they have the use of reasoning a little way (as in numbering, to some degree), yet it serves them to little use in common life, in which they govern themselves—some better, some worse—according to their differences of experience, quickness of memory, and inclinations to several ends; but specially according to good or evil fortune, and the errors of one another. For as for science, or certain rules of their actions, they are so far from it that they know not what it is. Geometry they have thought conjuring; but for other sciences, they who have not been taught the beginnings and some progress in them, that they may see how they be acquired and generated, are in this point like children that, having no thought of generation, are made believe by the women that their brothers and sisters are not born, but found in the garden.

But yet they that have no science are in better and nobler condition with their natural prudence than men that, by misreasoning or by trusting them that reason wrong, fall upon false and absurd general rules. For ignorance of causes and of rules does not set men so far out of their way as relying on false rules and taking for causes of what they aspire to those that are not so, but rather causes of the contrary.

To conclude: the light of human minds is perspicuous words, but by exact definitions first snuffed[9] and purged from ambiguity. Reason is the pace, increase of science the way, and the benefit of mankind the end. And on the contrary, metaphors and senseless and ambiguous words are like *ignes fatui*[10] and reasoning upon them is wandering amongst innumerable absurdities; and their end, contention and sedition, or contempt. . . .

> It is man's reason, then, that enables him precariously (if at all) to regulate his "passions"—those aversions and desires, based ultimately on "sense," which inexorably motivate his actions. Since in man's "natural" state there are no moral absolutes, "good" is anything he seeks, "evil" is anything he flees, and "felicity" is simply his "continuing success" in getting what he wants. Therefore the acquired or "intellectual" virtues by which he checks and curbs his natural, feral instincts are essential to any kind of civilized behavior. In his discussion of these intellectual virtues Hobbes formulates the famous distinction between "wit" (or "fancy") and "judgment" that he himself applied to literature in his correspondence with Sir William Davenant (pp. 784 ff.) and that was to be endlessly reiterated by theorists of succeeding generations.

Chapter 8. Of The Virtues Commonly Called Intellectual; and Their Contrary Defects

Virtue generally, in all sorts of subjects, is somewhat that is valued for eminence and consisteth in comparison. For if all things were equal in all men, nothing would be prized. And by virtues intellectual are always understood such abilities of the mind as men praise, value, and desire should be in themselves; and go commonly under the name of a *good*

wit, though the same word *wit* be used also to distinguish one certain ability from the rest.

These virtues are of two sorts, natural and acquired. By natural, I mean not that which a man hath from his birth, for that is nothing else but sense, wherein men differ so little one from another and from brute beasts as it is not to be reckoned amongst virtues. But I mean that wit which is gotten by use only and experience, without method, culture, or instruction. This natural wit consisteth principally in two things: celerity of imagining, that is, swift succession of one thought to another, and steady direction to some approved end. On the contrary, a slow imagination maketh that defect, or fault of the mind, which is commonly called dullness, stupidity, and sometimes by other names that signify slowness of motion or difficulty to be moved.

And this difference of quickness is caused by the difference of men's passions, that love and dislike, some one thing, some another, and therefore some men's thoughts run one way, some another, and are held to and observe differently the things that pass through their imagination. And whereas in this succession of men's thoughts there is nothing to observe in the things they think on but either in what they be like one another or in what they be unlike, or what they serve for, or how they serve to such a purpose, those that observe their similitudes, in case they be such as are but rarely observed by others, are said to have a good wit; by which, in this occasion, is meant a good fancy. But they that observe their differences and dissimilitudes, which is called distinguishing and discerning, and judging between thing and thing, in case such discerning be not easy are said to have a good judgment; and particularly in matter of conversation and business, wherein times, places, and persons are to be discerned, this virtue is called discretion. The former, that is, fancy, without the help of judgment, is not commended as a virtue; but the latter, which is judgment and discretion, is commended for itself, without the help of fancy. Besides the discretion of times, places, and persons necessary to a good fancy, there is required also an often application of his thoughts to their end; that is to say, to some use to be made of them. This done, he that hath this virtue will be easily fitted with similitudes that will please not only by illustrations of his discourse and adorning it with new and apt metaphors, but also, by the rarity of their invention. But without steadiness and direction to some end a great fancy is one kind of madness; such as they have that, entering into any discourse are snatched from their purpose by everything that comes in their thought into so many and so long digressions and parentheses that they utterly lose themselves: which kind of folly I know no particular name for; but the cause of it is sometimes want of experience, whereby that seemeth to a man new and rare which doth not so to others; sometimes pusillanimity, by which that seems great to him which other men think a trifle: and whatsoever is new or great, and therefore thought fit to be told, withdraws a man by degrees from the intended way of his discourse.

[9]Made clearer and brighter.
[10]Will-of-the-wisps, i.e., deceptive appearances.

In a good poem, whether it be epic or dramatic (as also in sonnets, epigrams, and other pieces) both judgment and fancy are required; but the fancy must be more eminent because they please for the extravagancy but ought not to displease by indiscretion.

In a good history the judgment must be eminent because the goodness consisteth in the method, in the truth, and in the choice of the actions that are most profitable to be known. Fancy has no place but only in adorning the style.

In orations of praise and in invectives the fancy is predominant because the design is not truth, but to honor or dishonour, which is done by noble or by vile comparisons. The judgment does but suggest what circumstances make an action laudable or culpable.

In hortatives[11] and pleadings, as truth or disguise serveth best to the design in hand, so is the judgment or the fancy most required.

In demonstration, in counsel, and all rigorous search of truth, judgment does all, except sometimes the understanding have need to be opened by some apt similitude, and then there is so much use of fancy. But for metaphors, they are in this case utterly excluded. For seeing they openly profess deceit, to admit them into counsel or reasoning were manifest folly.

And in any discourse whatsoever, if the defect of discretion be apparent, how extravagant soever the fancy be, the whole discourse will be taken for a sign of want of wit; and so will it never when the discretion is manifest, though the fancy be never so ordinary. . . .

CHAPTER 12
OF RELIGION

Seeing there are no signs, nor fruit of religion, but in man only, there is no cause to doubt but that the seed of religion is also only in man; and consisteth in some peculiar quality, or at least in some eminent degree thereof, not to be found in any other living creatures.

And first, it is peculiar to the nature of man to be inquisitive into the causes of the events they see, some more, some less; but all men so much as to be curious in the search of the causes of their own good and evil fortune.

Secondly, upon the sight of anything that hath a beginning, to think also it had a cause which determined the same to begin then when it did rather than sooner or later.

Thirdly, whereas there is no other felicity of beasts but the enjoying of their quotidian food, ease, and lusts, as having little or no foresight of the time to come, for want of observation and memory of the order, consequence, and dependence of the things they see, man observeth how one event hath been produced by another; and remembereth in them antecedence and consequence; and when he cannot assure himself of the true causes of things (for the causes of good and evil fortune for the most part are invisible) he supposes causes of them either such as his own fancy suggesteth or trusteth the authority of other men such as he thinks to be his friends, and wiser than himself.

The two first make anxiety. For being assured that there be causes of all things that have arrived hitherto or shall arrive hereafter, it is impossible for a man who continually endeavoreth to secure himself against the evil he fears and procure the good he desireth not to be in a perpetual solicitude of the time to come; so that every man, especially those that are overprovident, are in a state like to that of Prometheus.[12] For as Prometheus, which interpreted is the prudent man, was bound to the hill Caucasus, a place of large prospect where an eagle, feeding on his liver, devoured in the day as much as was repaired in the night: so that man which looks too far before him in the care of future time hath his heart all the day long gnawed on by fear of death, poverty, or other calamity; and has no repose, nor pause of his anxiety, but in sleep.

This perpetual fear, always accompanying mankind in the ignorance of causes, as it were in the dark, must needs have for object something. And therefore when there is nothing to be seen, there is nothing to accuse, either of their good or evil fortune, but some power, or agent invisible: in which sense perhaps it was that some of the old poets said that the gods were at first created by human fear:[13] which spoken of the gods, that is to say, of the many gods of the gentiles,[14] is very true. But the acknowledging of one God, eternal, infinite, and omnipotent, may more easily be derived from the desire men have to know the causes of natural bodies, and their several virtues and operations, than from the fear of what was to befall them in time to come. For he that from any effect he seeth come to pass should reason to the next and immediate cause thereof, and from thence to the cause of that cause, and plunge himself profoundly in the pursuit of causes, shall at last come to this, that there must be, as even the heathen philosophers confessed, one first mover; that is, a first and an eternal cause of all things, which is that which men mean by the name of God: and all this without thought of their fortune, the solicitude whereof both inclines to fear and hinders them from the search of the causes of other things; and thereby gives occasion of feigning of as many gods as there be men that feign them.

And for the matter or substance of the invisible agents so fancied, they could not by natural cogitation fall upon any other conceit but that it was the same with that of the soul of man; and that the soul of man was of the same substance with that which appeareth in a dream to one that sleepeth or in a looking glass to one that is awake; which men, not knowing that such apparitions are nothing else but creatures of the fancy, think to be real and external substances, and therefore call them ghosts, as the Latins called them *imagines* and *umbrae*;[15] and thought them spirits, that is, thin aerial bodies; and those invisible agents, which they feared, to be like them, save that they appear and vanish when they please. But the opinion that such spirits were incorporeal

---

[11]Hortatory or inspirational speeches.
[12]In Greek mythology, a Titan who stole fire from heaven for the benefit of mankind, for which offense he was chained to a rock where he was daily gnawed by an eagle until Hercules freed him.
[13]*Primus in orbe deos fecit timor* ("fear first created gods in the world"), a remark borrowed from Petronius Arbiter by Statius, *Thebiad*, III.661. [14]Pagans. [15]"Apparitions" and "spirits."

or immaterial could never enter into the mind of any man by nature; because, though men may put together words of contradictory signification, as *spirit* and *incorporeal,* yet they can never have the imagination of anything answering to them: and therefore men that by their own meditation arrive to the acknowledgment of one infinite, omnipotent, and eternal God chose rather to confess He is incomprehensible, and above their understanding, than to define His nature by *spirit incorporeal,* and then confess their definition to be unintelligible: or if they give Him such a title, it is not dogmatically, with intention to make the divine nature understood, but piously, to honor Him with attributes of significations as remote as they can from the grossness of bodies visible. . . .

Thirdly, for the worship which naturally men exhibit to powers invisible, it can be no other but such expressions of their reverence as they would use towards men: gifts, petitions, thanks, submission of body, considerate addresses, sober behavior, premeditated words, swearing, that is, assuring one another of their promises by invoking them. Beyond that, reason suggesteth nothing, but leaves them either to rest there or for further ceremonies to rely on those they believe to be wiser than themselves.

Lastly, concerning how these invisible powers declare to men the things which shall hereafter come to pass, especially concerning their good or evil fortune in general, or good or ill success in any particular undertaking, men are naturally at a stand; save that using to conjecture of the time to come by the time past, they are very apt not only to take casual things, after one or two encounters, for prognostics of the like encounter ever after, but also to believe the like prognostics from other men, of whom they have once conceived a good opinion.

And in these four things—opinion of ghosts, ignorance of second causes, devotion towards what men fear, and taking of things casual for prognostics—consisteth the natural seed of religion, which by reason of the different fancies, judgments, and passions of several men hath grown up into ceremonies so different that those which are used by one man are for the most part ridiculous to another. . . .

CHAPTER 13
OF THE NATURAL CONDITION OF MANKIND AS CONCERNING THEIR FELICITY AND MISERY

Nature hath made men so equal in the faculties of body and mind as that though there be found one man sometimes manifestly stronger in body or of quicker mind than another, yet when all is reckoned together, the difference between man and man is not so considerable as that one man can thereupon claim to himself any benefit to which another may not pretend as well as he. For as to the strength of body, the weakest has strength enough to kill the strongest, either by secret machination or by confederacy with others that are in the same danger with himself.

And as to the faculties of the mind, setting aside the arts grounded upon words, and especially that skill of proceeding upon general and infallible rules, called science, which very few have and but in few things, as being not a native faculty born with us nor attained as prudence, while we look after somewhat else, I find yet a greater equality amongst men than that of strength. For prudence is but experience, which equal time equally bestows on all men in those things they equally apply themselves unto. That which may perhaps make such equality incredible is but a vain conceit of one's own wisdom, which almost all men think they have in a greater degree than the vulgar; that is, than all men but themselves and a few others, whom by fame or for concurring with themselves they approve. For such is the nature of men that howsoever they may acknowledge many others to be more witty or more eloquent or more learned, yet they will hardly believe there be many so wise as themselves. For they see their own wit at hand, and other men's at a distance. But this proveth rather that men are in that point equal, than unequal. For there is not ordinarily a greater sign of the equal distribution of anything than that every man is contented with his share.

From this equality of ability ariseth equality of hope in the attaining of our ends. And therefore if any two men desire the same thing, which nevertheless they cannot both enjoy, they become enemies; and in the way to their end (which is principally their own conservation, and sometimes their delectation only), endeavor to destroy or subdue one another. And from hence it comes to pass that where an invader hath no more to fear than another man's single power, if one plant, sow, build, or possess a convenient seat, others may probably be expected to come prepared with forces united to dispossess and deprive him not only of the fruit of his labor, but also of his life or liberty. And the invader again is in the like danger of another.

And from this diffidence of one another there is no way for any man to secure himself so reasonable as anticipation; that is, by force or wiles to master the persons of all men he can, so long till he see no other power great enough to endanger him; and this is no more than his own conservation requireth, and is generally allowed. Also because there be some, that taking pleasure in contemplating their own power in the acts of conquest, which they pursue farther than their security requires; if others, that otherwise would be glad to be at ease within modest bounds, should not by invasion increase their power, they would not be able, long time, by standing only on their defense, to subsist. And by consequence, such augmentation of dominion over men, being necessary to a man's conservation, it ought to be allowed him.

Again, men have no pleasure, but on the contrary a great deal of grief, in keeping company where there is no power able to overawe them all. For every man looketh that his companion should value him at the same rate he sets upon himself; and upon all signs of contempt or undervaluing naturally endeavors, as far as he dares (which amongst them that have no common power to keep them in quiet is far enough to make them destroy each other), to extort a greater value from his contemners by damage, and from others by the example.

So that in the nature of man we find three principal causes of quarrel. First, competition; secondly, diffidence; thirdly, glory.

The first maketh men invade for gain; the second, for safety; and the third, for reputation. The first use violence to make themselves masters of other men's persons, wives, children, and cattle; the second, to defend them; the third, for trifles, as a word, a smile, a different opinion, and any other sign of undervalue, either direct in their persons or by reflection in their kindred, their friends, their nation, their profession, or their name.

Hereby it is manifest that during the time men live without a common power to keep them all in awe they are in that condition which is called war; and such a war as is of every man against every man. For war consisteth not in battle only or the act of fighting, but in a tract of time wherein the will to contend by battle is sufficiently known; and therefore the notion of time is to be considered in the nature of war, as it is in the nature of weather. For as the nature of foul weather lieth not in a shower or two of rain, but in an inclination thereto of many days together; so the nature of war consisteth not in actual fighting, but in the known disposition thereto during all the time there is no assurance to the contrary. All other time is peace.

Whatsoever, therefore, is consequent to a time of war, where every man is enemy to every man, the same is consequent to the time wherein men live without other security than what their own strength and their own invention shall furnish them withal. In such condition there is no place for industry because the fruit thereof is uncertain, and consequently no culture of the earth, no navigation nor use of the commodities that may be imported by sea, no commodious building, no instruments of moving and removing such things as require much force, no knowledge of the face of the earth, no account of time, no arts, no letters, no society, and, which is worst of all, continual fear and danger of violent death; and the life of man, solitary, poor, nasty, brutish, and short.

It may seem strange to some man that has not well weighed these things that nature should thus dissociate and render men apt to invade and destroy one another; and he may therefore, not trusting to this inference made from the passions, desire perhaps to have the same confirmed by experience. Let him therefore consider with himself: when taking a journey, he arms himself and seeks to go well accompanied; when going to sleep, he locks his doors; when even in his house he locks his chests, and this when he knows there be laws and public officers, armed, to revenge all injuries shall be done him; what opinion he has of his fellow subjects, when he rides armed of his fellow citizens when he locks his doors, and of his children and servants when he locks his chests. Does he not there as much accuse mankind by his actions as I do by my words? But neither of us accuse man's nature in it. The desires and other passions of man are in themselves no sin. No more are the actions that proceed from those passions till they know a law that forbids them; which till laws be made they cannot know; nor can any law be made till they have agreed upon the person that shall make it.

It may peradventure be thought there was never such a time nor condition of war as this; and I believe it was never generally so over all the world; but there are many places where they live so now. For the savage people in many places of America, except the government of small families, the concord whereof dependeth on natural lust, have no government at all, and live at this day in that brutish manner as I said before. Howsoever, it may be perceived what manner of life there would be where there were no common power to fear, by the manner of life which men that have formerly lived under a peaceful government use to degenerate into in a civil war.

But though there had never been any time wherein particular men were in a condition of war one against another, yet in all times, kings and persons of sovereign authority, because of their independency, are in continual jealousies, and in the state and posture of gladiators; having their weapons pointing, and their eyes fixed on one another; that is, their forts, garrisons, and guns upon the frontiers of their kingdoms and continual spies upon their neighbors, which is a posture of war. But because they uphold thereby the industry of their subjects, there does not follow from it that misery which accompanies the liberty of particular men.

To this war of every man against every man, this also is consequent, that nothing can be unjust. The notions of right and wrong, justice and injustice, have there no place. Where there is no common power, there is no law; where no law, no injustice. Force and fraud are in war the two cardinal virtues. Justice and injustice are none of the faculties neither of the body nor mind. If they were, they might be in a man that were alone in the world, as well as his senses and passions. They are qualities that relate to men in society, not in solitude. It is consequent also to the same condition that there be no propriety,[16] no dominion, no "mine" and "thine" distinct; but only that to be every man's that he can get, and for so long as he can keep it. And thus much for the ill condition which every man by mere nature is actually placed in; though with a possibility to come out of it, consisting partly in the passions, partly in his reason.

The passions that incline men to peace are fear of death, desire of such things as are necessary to commodious living, and a hope by their industry to obtain them. And reason suggesteth convenient articles of peace, upon which men may be drawn to agreement. These articles are they which otherwise are called the laws of nature. . . .

PART II. OF COMMONWEALTH

CHAPTER 17

OF THE CAUSES, GENERATION, AND DEFINITION OF A COMMONWEALTH

The final cause, end, or design of men, who naturally love liberty and dominion over others, in the introduction of that restraint upon themselves in which we see them live in commonwealths is the foresight of their own preservation, and of a more contented life thereby; that is to say, of getting themselves out from that miserable condition of war, which

[16]Property.

is necessarily consequent, as hath been shown, to the natural passions of men when there is no visible power to keep them in awe, and tie them by fear of punishment to the performance of their covenants, and observation of those laws of nature set down in the fourteenth and fifteenth chapters.

For the laws of nature (as justice, equity, modesty, mercy, and, in sum, doing to others as we would be done to) of themselves, without the terror of some power to cause them to be observed, are contrary to our natural passions, that carry us to partiality, pride, revenge, and the like. And covenants without the sword are but words, and of no strength to secure a man at all. Therefore notwithstanding the laws of nature (which everyone hath then kept when he has the will to keep them, when he can do it safely) if there be no power erected, or not great enough for our security, every man will and may lawfully rely on his own strength and art for caution against all other men. And in all places where men have lived by small families, to rob and spoil one another has been a trade, and so far from being reputed against the law of nature that the greater spoils they gained, the greater was their honor; and men observed no other laws therein but the laws of honor, that is, to abstain from cruelty, leaving to men their lives and instruments of husbandry. And as small families did then, so now do cities and kingdoms, which are but greater families, for their own security enlarge their dominions upon all pretences of danger and fear of invasion, or assistance that may be given to invaders, endeavor as much as they can to subdue or weaken their neighbors by open force and secret arts for want of other caution, justly; and are remembered for it in after ages with honor.

Nor is it the joining together of a small number of men that gives them this security, because in small numbers small additions on the one side or the other make the advantage of strength so great as is sufficient to carry the victory, and therefore gives encouragement to an invasion. The multitude sufficient to confide in for our security is not determined by any certain number, but by comparison with the enemy we fear; and is then sufficient when the odds of the enemy is not of so visible and conspicuous moment to determine the event of war, as to move him to attempt.

And be there never so great a multitude, yet if their actions be directed according to their particular judgments and particular appetites, they can expect thereby no defense nor protection, neither against a common enemy, nor against the injuries of one another. For being distracted in opinions concerning the best use and application of their strength, they do not help, but hinder one another; and reduce their strength by mutual opposition to nothing; whereby they are easily not only subdued by a very few that agree together, but also when there is no common enemy they make war upon each other for their particular interests. For if we could suppose a great multitude of men to consent in the observation of justice, and other laws of nature, without a common power to keep them all in awe, we might as well suppose all mankind to do the same; and then there neither would be, nor need to be, any civil government or commonwealth at all because there would be peace without subjection.

Nor is it enough for the security which men desire should last all the time of their life that they be governed and directed by one judgment for a limited time, as in one battle or one war. For though they obtain a victory by their unanimous endeavor against a foreign enemy, yet afterwards, when either they have no common enemy, or he that by one part is held for an enemy, is by another part held for a friend, they must needs by the difference of their interests dissolve and fall again into a war amongst themselves.

It is true that certain living creatures, as bees and ants, live sociably one with another, which are therefore by Aristotle numbered amongst political creatures and yet have no other direction than their particular judgments and appetites; nor speech, whereby one of them can signify to another what he thinks expedient for the common benefit; and therefore some man may perhaps desire to know why mankind cannot do the same.[17] To which I answer:

First, that men are continually in competition for honor and dignity, which these creatures are not; and consequently amongst men there ariseth on that ground envy and hatred and finally war, but amongst these not so.

Secondly, that amongst these creatures the common good differeth not from the private; and being by nature inclined to their private, they procure thereby the common benefit. But man, whose joy consisteth in comparing himself with other men, can relish nothing but what is eminent.

Thirdly, that these creatures, having not (as man) the use of reason, do not see nor think they see any fault in the administration of their common business; whereas amongst men there are very many that think themselves wiser and abler to govern the public better than the rest; and these strive to reform and innovate, one this way, another that way; and thereby bring it into distraction and civil war.

Fourthly, that these creatures, though they have some use of voice in making known to one another their desires and other affections, yet they want that art of words by which some men can represent to others that which is good in the likeness of evil, and evil in the likeness of good; and augment or diminish the apparent greatness of good and evil, discontenting men, and troubling their peace at their pleasure.

Fifthly, irrational creatures cannot distinguish between *injury* and *damage*, and therefore as long as they be at ease they are not offended with their fellows; whereas man is then most troublesome when he is most at ease, for then it is that he loves to show his wisdom, and control the actions of them that govern the commonwealth.

Lastly, the agreement of these creatures is natural, that of men is by covenant only, which is artificial; and therefore it is no wonder if there be somewhat else required (besides covenant) to make their agreement constant and lasting; which is a common power to keep them in awe and to direct their actions to the common benefit.

The only way to erect such a common power as may be able to defend them from the invasion of foreigners and the injuries of one another, and thereby to secure them in such sort as that by their own industry and by the fruits of the

[17]*It is true...same*: Perhaps Hobbes is thinking of Aristotle's *Politics*, Sect. 1253.

earth they may nourish themselves and live contentedly, is to confer all their power and strength upon one man, or upon one assembly of men, that may reduce all their wills by plurality of voices unto one will; which is as much as to say, to appoint one man or assembly of men to bear their person; and everyone to own and acknowledge himself to be author of whatsoever he that so beareth their person shall act, or cause to be acted, in those things which concern the common peace and safety; and therein to submit their wills, everyone to his will, and their judgments to his judgment. This is more than consent or concord; it is a real unity of them all, in one and the same person, made by covenant of every man with every man in such manner as if every man should say to every man, "I authorize and give up my right of governing myself to this man, or to this assembly of men, on this condition, that thou give up thy right to him, and authorize all his actions in like manner." This done, the multitude so united in one person is called a commonwealth, in Latin, *civitas*. This is the generation of that great Leviathan, or rather, to speak more reverently, of that mortal god to which we owe, under the immortal God, our peace and defense. For by this authority, given him by every particular man in the commonwealth, he hath the use of so much power and strength conferred on him that by terror thereof he is enabled to form the wills of them all to peace at home and mutual aid against their enemies abroad. And in him consisteth the essence of the commonwealth, which, to define it, is "One person, of whose acts a great multitude, by mutual covenants one with another, have made themselves everyone the author, to the end he may use the strength and means of them all as he shall think expedient for their peace and common defense."

And he that carrieth this person is called sovereign, and said to have sovereign power; and everyone besides, his subject.

The attaining to this sovereign power is by two ways. One, by natural force, as when a man maketh his children to submit themselves and their children to his government, as being able to destroy them if they refuse; or by war subdueth his enemies to his will, giving them their lives on that condition. The other is when men agree amongst themselves to submit to some man or assembly of men voluntarily, on confidence to be protected by him against all others. This latter may be called a political commonwealth, or commonwealth by instutition, and the former a commonwealth by acquisition. . . .

Alexander Ross [1591-1654]

Hobbes inspired in so many able men such a wide response, ranging from disagreement to rage and even terror, that it may seem perverse to let Alexander Ross represent his host of adversaries. *Leviathan Drawn Out with a Hook* deserves to be remembered, however, because its very crudity enables us to feel the first tremor of alarm at the specter Hobbes had raised. Although more illustrious opponents like Descartes, Seth Ward, Clarendon, Cudworth, and More—to name only a few—registered their objections to Hobbes' mathematics, metaphysics, politics, or ethics with more knowledge and authority, few succeed so well as Ross in saying what many common readers must have thought about the "giant Goliah."

> For do we not see how atheism strives to justle out religion, how ignorance is crawling up into the chair of learning, how piety is affronted by profaneness and devotion by irreverence, how divinity is assaulted by heretical opinions and solid philosophy by dreams and fanatical whimsies?

Following his education at King's College, Aberdeen, Ross enjoyed what Johnson later called the noblest prospect that a Scotchman ever sees, the highroad to England. He thrived in his adopted country, becoming master of the Free School at Southampton about 1616 and then chaplain to King Charles, who, in 1642, bestowed on him the vicarage of Carisbrooke on the Isle of Wight (where that unhappy monarch would one day be imprisoned). Somehow Ross managed to accumulate a fortune large enough to supply substantial legacies not only to a nephew and a flock of nieces but also to Southampton and Carisbrooke, to the libraries of Oxford and Cambridge, and to his own university. His executor was reported to have found a thousand pounds in gold, mostly tucked away between the pages of his books.

Although he produced so many works—"in Latin and English, and in prose and verse"—that Anthony Wood declined to make a list of them, it is hard to believe that Ross had made his money by his writing. A few of his many publications are remembered, if no longer read, because he was so much given to jousting with his betters. In *The Philosophical Touchstone* (1645), for instance, he expressed his stern opinion of Sir Kenelm Digby; in *Medicus Medicatus* (1645) he gave instruction and reproof to Thomas Browne, whose vulgar errors (together with those of Bacon and William Harvey) he again explored in *Arcana Microcosmi* (1651, 1652); and in addition to his book on Hobbes (1653) he was disburdened of *Animadversions* (1653) on Sir Walter Raleigh's *History of the World* (for which he himself had supplied a six-book continuation in 1652). All these works—plus more than twenty others like *Three Decades of Divine Meditations* (1630), *Mel Heliconium, or Poetical Honey Gathered Out of the Weeds of Parnassus, with Meditations in Verse* (1642), *Mystagogus Poeticus, or the Muses' Interpreter* (1647), and *Pansebeia, or a View of All Religions in the World* (1653)—give point to Samuel Butler's famous quip in *Hudibras*:

> There was an ancient sage philosopher
> That had read Alexander Ross over.

My text for *Leviathan Drawn Out with a Hook* is based upon its first and last edition in 1653 (Wing R-1960). Not surprisingly, Ross' works have never been collected, but he has been discussed by scholars interested in some of his illustrious victims, and so receives attention in Grant McColley's articles on John Wilkins (*Annals of Science*, I, III, IV, 1936–39; *PMLA*, LII, 1937; *SP*, XXXV, 1938), and Joan Bennett's on Browne (*Studies in the Renaissance*, III, 1956), as well as in John Bowle's *Hobbes and His Critics* (1951).

from Leviathan Drawn Out with a Hook[1] (1653)

TO THE RIGHT WORSHIPFUL FRANCIS LUCY, ESQUIRE

Sir,

The giant Goliah[2] so affrighted the whole host of Israel by the vast bulk of his body, the weight and large dimensions of his spear and armor, with his defying and bragging words that none of all that army durst encounter him. Only David, a shepherd by profession, in stature low, in years young, the least of all his brethren, and of meanest account among the people took the boldness to enter the lists with that uncircumcised Philistine. So I, a spiritual shepherd by profession, the least of the Tribe of Levi,[3] little in my own eyes, and of small account in the world, observing how all the host of learned men in this land look upon but adventure not to buckle with Mr. Hobbes his Leviathan, *nec quisquam ex agmine tanto audet adire virum manibusque inducere caestus.*[4] I say, being animated by some lovers of the truth, have this summer set aside for a while my other studies to peruse this book and to detect some of his chief tenets, which though erroneous and dangerous, are swallowed down by some young sciolists without nauseating, which to me is an argument of great distemper in the minds and affections of men, who with the Israelites loathing the manna of true philosophy and divinity, covet after the quails of new errors, or rather old in a new guise, which in the end will poison them. Methinks I see religion

and learning, divinity and true philosophy, devotion and piety, for which this island hath been glorious for many generations saying, as the voice that the Christians heard in Jerusalem immediately before the destruction thereof, *Migremus hinc.*[5] These are the *palladia* and, as it were, the tutelar gods by which this British Empire hath so long stood, which if they forsake us, what are we else but a prey to our enemies? God grant we may not complain of their departure, as Aeneas did of his Trojan gods, *Excessere omnes adytis, arisque relictis Di quibus imperium hoc steterat.*[6]

For do we not see how atheism strives to justle out religion, how ignorance is crawling up into the chair of learning, how piety is affronted by profaneness and devotion by irrever-

LEVIATHAN DRAWN OUT WITH A HOOK   [1]"Canst thou draw Leviathan with an hook, or his tongue with a cord which thou lettst down?" (Job 41.1).
[2]Goliath, a Philistine giant of Gath whose fatal encounter with the shepherd boy David is related in 1 Samuel 17.
[3]Descendants of Levi, a son of Jacob and Leah, from whom were traditionally chosen those who assisted the priest in the temple.
[4]"But none of all that throng dared face him or draw the gloves onto his hands" (Vergil, *Aeneid,* V.578–79).
[5]"Let us leave this place."
[6]"All the gods on whom this empire stood have departed, leaving shrine and alter" (Vergil, *Aeneid,* II.352–53).

ence, how divinity is assaulted by heretical opinions and solid philosophy by dreams and fanatical whimsies? I doubt not but I shall be blamed by some for encountering this champion of Malmesbury,[7] as David was for venturing upon that champion of Gath, but I will answer them in David's words (1 Samuel 17.29): "What have I now done? Is there not a cause?" Goliah defied the whole host of Israel and Mr. Hobbes defieth the whole host of learned men, esteeming his Leviathan as formidable and unconquerable as that in Job 41.16, of whose majesty the mighty are afraid, and for fear they faint in themselves. But this Leviathan is not so, for a hook may be cast into his nose, and his jaws may be pierced with an angle (Job 40.21).[8]

Sir, this piece (which makes its addresses to you as to one truly judicious, pious, and a lover of solid learning) is but small; so was David, who notwithstanding foiled Goliah; the ichneumon is but a small rat, yet it can kill the great crocodile; *in est sua gratia parvis*, small things have their magnitude, though not of bulk yet of virtue; there is more nourishment in a small lark than in a great kite or raven; and so there is more luster in a small diamond than a whole quarry of other stones; as in a little bee, so in this little book there may be much spirit; *ingentes animos angusto in corpore gestat*. But how small soever it be, it hath drawn out Leviathan with an hook, which it presents to you; and so do I, by it, my thankful acknowledgments for all your favors, praying for an increase of all happiness on yourself, your religious lady, and your hopeful son, my scholar, with the rest of your family. Which is the hearty desire of

Your most humble servant,
Alex. Ross

To the Reader

Good reader, David encountered with a lion and a bear; Daniel conversed among lions; Paul fought with beasts at Ephesus; Hercules skirmished with an Erymanthian bear, a Nemean lion, a Lernean hydra; Aeneas drew his sword against the shadows of centaurs, harpies, gorgons, and chimeras; but I have to do with a strange monster called Leviathan, which some (out of David, Psalm 104) think to be a whale; the prophet Isaiah calls him a piercing and crooked serpent;[9] Job saith he is a beast with fearful teeth, with scales strong as shields, with a heart as strong as the nether millstone, out of his mouth leap sparks of fire, and smoke out of his nostrils.[10] Lastly, some there are that take him for the devil, and indeed it may be so; for he is said in Job to be a king over all the children of pride.[11]

I hope Mr. Hobbes is none of his subjects, and yet his book is much inflated with pride against learning and learned men. But in my opinion this paper Leviathan is like that beast in the Revelation, which opened his mouth into blasphemy against God and His tabernacle, and against them that dwell in heaven (Revelation 13.6). Against God in saying He made the world by nature and by consequence of necessity, whereas He made it indeed voluntarily and freely. 2. In making the three persons of the Trinity rather names than substances. 3. In making Christ only to personate God the Son. 4. In making God the author of sin. 5. In making

Him corporeal and part of the universe. Against His tabernacle, that is, against His church, in laboring to overthrow her faith, knowledge, miracles, and ordinances. Against them that dwell in heaven, that is, the angels and separated souls, in making the one but fancies and dreams and the others mortal, and not capable hereafter of any other happiness than earthly. He tells us besides that faith is not by inspiration or infusion, but by study and industry; that to believe in God is not to trust in His person but to confess the doctrine. That our belief is in the church; that they were not devils but madmen which confessed Christ; that covetousness and ambition and injustice with power are honorable; that tyrants and good princes are all one; that a man may sin against his conscience; that men should not render a reason or account of their faith; that princes are not subject to their own laws; that private men have no property in their goods; that our natural reason is the word of God; that divine dreams cannot win belief; that it was a wind, not the Holy Spirit, which in the creation moved on the waters; that the dove and fiery tongues may be called angels; that Christ hath no spiritual kingdom here on earth; that He did not cast out devils, but only cured madness; that Satan did not enter into Judas; that we may dissemble in matter of religion; that we may disobey Christ and His apostles without sin.

Such and much more like stuff and smoke doth this Leviathan send out of his nostrils, as out of a boiling pot or cauldron (Job 41.20). This is the *sperma caete*[12] or spawn which this whale casteth out; a whale, I say, that hath not swallowed up Jonah the prophet but Cerinthus[13] the heretic, and vomited up the condemned opinions of the old heretics, and chiefly the Anthropomorphites, Sabellians, Nestorians, Saduceans, Arabeans, Tacians or Eucratites, Manichees, Mahumetans, and others.[14] For in holding life eternal to be only on earth he is a Cerinthian and Mahumetan; in giving to God corporiety he is an Anthropomorphite, Manichean, Tertullianist, and Audean; in holding the three persons to be distinct names and essences represented by Moses, Christ, and the apostles he is a Sabellian, Montanist, Aetian, and Priscillianist; in saying that Christ personated God the Son he is a Nestorian giving him two personalities, for no person can personate himself; in denying spirits he is a Saducean; in making the soul to rest with the body till the resurrection he is an Arabean; in making the soul of man corporeal he is an Luciferian; by putting a period to hell torments he is a Originist; by teaching dissimulation in religion he is a Tacian or Eucratite; in making God the cause of injustice or sin he is a Manichee; in slighting Christ's miracles he is a Jew; and in making our natural reason the word of God he is Socinian.

---

[7]Town in Wiltshire near which Hobbes was born.   [8]Fish hook.
[9]Isaiah 27.1.   [10]A loose paraphrase of Job 41.12–20.   [11]Job 41.34.
[12]Spermaceti, a white, waxy substance found in the head of the sperm whale.
[13]First-century Gnostic of Jewish descent who heretically tried to combine Christianity with Judaism and various oriental religions.
[14]The heresies in this formidable catalogue are perhaps sufficiently explained in the paragraph that follows.

In discovering[15] of these errors I quarrel not with Mr. Hobbes, but with his book, which not only I but many more who are both learned and judicious men look upon as a piece dangerous both to government and religion. All the hurt I wish him is true illumination, a sanctified heart, and Christian sobriety, that he may retract what is amiss. And so I bid him and thee farewell.

A. R.

In his introduction he calls nature "the art whereby God hath made and governs the world."[16] God made not the world by nature, for nature had no being till God made it; and when He made it it was neither the exemplary nor adjuvant[17] cause of the creation. The world could not be made by that which had no being till it was made, and when it was made it was nothing else but the form and matter of things; the one being the active, the other the passive nature, and both but parts of the universe. If again by "nature" (that we may make a favorable construction of his phrase) he meaneth the ordinary power of God, the world was not made thus. By His ordinary power He governs it, but by His extraordinary power He made it, which power is never called natural, but miraculous. Neither again is nature "art," as he calls it, though both be principles, because nature is an internal, art an external principle; I say external in respect of essence, though it may be internal in regard of site, albeit art, as it is an habit and in the mind of the artificer is altogether external, but take it for the effect of art, it may be internal in the thing made by art, as may be seen in the motions of a watch. . . .

"Imagination," saith he, "is nothing but decaying sense,"[18] and the sense fading is called memory, so that imagination and memory are but one thing. This is a riddle which Oedipus himself cannot unriddle. Doth the strength of imagination consist in decaying of sense? It must follow that dying men must have strongest fancies, for then sense decays. But if sense be the generical essence of imagination how can the one increase upon the other's decay? Doubtless they, like Hippocrates' twins,[19] live and die together, so that if sense decay, imagination must needs decay, for as he confesseth (Cap. I), "There is no conception in the mind which was not at first begotten upon the organs of sense."[20] Now that imagination and memory are not the same thing is apparent by their different organs and operations: the one is in the fore part, the other in the back part of the head, and for the most part where the imagination is strongest, the memory is weakest; and where this is strongest, that is weakest. . . .

When he distingisheth religion from superstitition I hear the voice of Leviathan, not of a Christian. For, saith he, fear of power invisible, feigned by the mind or from tales publicly allowed, is religion: not allowed, superstition; and when the power imagined is truly such as we imagine, true religion.[21] It seems, then, both religion and superstition are grounded upon tales and imagination, only they differ in this; that tales publicly allowed beget religion, not allowed, superstition. But what will he say of the gentiles?[22] Among them tales were publicly allowed. Were they therefore religious and not superstitious? And is religion grounded upon fiction or imagination, even true religion? I thought that faith and not imagination had been the substance and ground of things not seen; that the just live by faith, not by imagination; that by faith we are saved; by faith we are justified, by faith we overcome the world, not by fancy, fiction, or imagination. We must mend the Creed if Mr. Hobbes his religion be true, and instead of saying "I believe in God" we must say "I imagine or feign in my mind an invisible power." In this also he contradicts himself, for if the power be invisible how can it be imagined, seeing (as he saith before) imagination "is only of things perceived by the sense, and it is so called from the image made in seeing." . . .

When he saith that "whatsoever the prince doth can be no injury to the subject, nor ought he to be accused by any of them of injustice, for he that doth anything by authority from another doth therein no injury to him by whose authority he acteth."[23] This doctrine will hardly down with freeborn people who choose to themselves princes not to tyrannize over them, but like good shepherds or fathers of their country to rule them. The people were not mad to give their power so to princes as to be their slaves, or to think that tyrannical cruelties and oppressions are not injuries to the subject, or that tyrants must not be accused of injustice; for although the prince acteth by the people's authority in things lawful, yet in his lawless exorbitancies he acteth by his own tyrannizing power, not by the peoples' authority. . . .

In his third part and Chapter I he saith "that our natural reason is the undoubted word of God." But I doubt Leviathan himself for all his great strength and power cannot make this good; for God's word is infallible; so is not our natural reason, which faileth in many things. God's word saith that a virgin did conceive and bear a son; that God became man; that our bodies shall rise again out of the dust; but our natural reason saith this is impossible; therefore when St. Paul preached the resurrection to the Athenians (who wanted not natural reason enough) they thought he had been mad.[24] How comes it that the apostle saith, "The natural man understandeth not the things of God's spirit"?[25] And Christ tells Peter that flesh and blood—that is, natural reason—had not revealed the mystery of His divinity to Him, but His Father in heaven.[26] And St. Paul saith that he received not the gospel of man, nor was he taught it but by the revelation of Jesus Christ (Galatians 1.12). And that he was not taught by man's wisdom, but by the Holy Ghost (1 Corinthians 2.13). How comes it, I say, that the Scripture speaks thus in vilifying natural reason if it be the infallible word of God? Yea, what need was there of any written word at all if our natural reason be that infallible word? . . .

---

[15]Revealing. [16]See p. 493. [17]Assisting.
[18]*Leviathan*, I.iii. For a similar statement of the same proposition see Hobbes' *Letter* to Davenant, p. 786.
[19]Unidentified. Hippocrates (b. ca. 460 B.C.) was the most celebrated physician of antiquity. [20]See p. 494.
[21]See p. 501. Here as elsewhere Ross seems to be paraphrasing Hobbes rather than quoting him directly. [22]Pagans.
[23]See p. 497. [24]Acts 17.22–33. [25]1 Corinthians 2.14.
[26]Matthew 16.17.

In his forty-sixth chapter he spurns at all learning except his own, and that with such a magisterial spirit and so supercilious scorn as if Aristotle, Plato, Zeno, the Peripatetics, Academics, Stoics, colleges, schools, universities, synagogues, and all the wise men of Europe, Asia, and Africa hitherto were scarce worth to carry his books. With him logic is but "captions of words," Aristotle's metaphysics are "absurd," his politics "repugnant to government," his ethics "ignorant," the natural philosophy of the schools is a "dream rather than a science, set forth in senseless and insignificant language," Aristotle's philosophy is "vain," and many such like expressions which shows how little he hath of the spirit of humility and modesty. I find not too much learning, but too much pride makes some men mad.

True learning is always joined with humility. The deepest rivers, saith Seneca, make the least sound; the cypress tree is tall but fruitless; the apple tree is low but fruitful; and the more it's laden the more it stoops. . . .

To conclude: I would have Mr. Hobbes take notice that I have no quarrel against him, but against his tenets. I honor his worth and learning, but dislike his opinions. I know not his person, but I know and respect his parts. If there be anything amiss in these my animadversions (for we are all apt to mistake) I shall thank him if he will set me right and inform me better; for I never had so great an opinion of myself as not to yield to reason, and such as are able to convince my understanding. The God of truth direct us all into the way of truth. Amen.

Joseph Glanvill [1636-1680]

It is appropriate that this section of this book, which began with *The Advancement of Learning*, should end with *The Vanity of Dogmatizing,* for chronologically, thematically, and otherwise Bacon and Glanvill mark the limits of our period. The propriety reveals itself in another way: just as Bacon bridged the Elizabethan and Jacobean periods, Glanvill, who was born before the Civil War, lived long enough into the Restoration to celebrate the triumph of the intellectual revolution that Bacon had proclaimed.

A Devonian who took two degrees at Oxford (B.A. 1655, M.A. 1656) and served as chaplain to Francis Rous (1579–1659), provost of Eton and one of Cromwell's stalwarts in the Council of State, young Glanvill wrote *The Vanity of Dogmatizing* in the interval between his patron's death and his appointment (as an Anglican, of course) to the rectory of Wimbish, Essex, in 1660. Although he had thus far made his way among Cromwellians and had sought Richard Baxter's friendship and support, at the Restoration, said one of his admirers later, he

> showed great readiness in conforming, as other eminent and learned persons who had been educated in those unhappy times also did without deserving in the least to be reproached for turning about, because in all probability they followed the light of reason and their own consciences.

Thereafter his career, both literary and ecclesiastic, was a series of successes: as a rising cleric he attained the rectorship of the Abbey Church at Bath (1666), a chaplaincy with the king (1672), and a prebend's stall at Worcester (1678); as a writer—and, after 1664, as a fellow of the Royal Society—he neglected scarcely any of the avant-garde opinions of the age, to most of which he gave his warm support. Among his more than twenty books were *Lux Orientalis* (1662), a defense of his friend Henry More's doctrine of the pre-existence of souls, *Scepsis Scientifica* (1665), a reworking of *The Vanity of Dogmatizing, Philosophical Considerations Touching Witches and Witchcraft* (1666), a defense of spiritual phenomena not unlike Sir Thomas Browne's (see p. 465), *Plus Ultra* (1668), an account of "the progress and advancement of knowledge since the days of Aristotle" that was presented to the Royal Society, a catena of objections and rebuttals to the cantankerous Henry Stubbe, and several collections of essays and sermons.

In both style and content *The Vanity of Dogmatizing* fairly represents Glanvill's blend of conventional piety with innovative thinking, and if it does not quite resolve "the old antipathy/ 'Tween rhetoric and philosophy" (as one of its admirers claimed), it does succeed in showing how adroitly the Christian view of fallen man could be accommodated to the anti-authoritarianism, empiricism, and optimism that Bacon and Descartes had made the slogans of the age. With his "quick, warm, spruce, and gay fancy" he may have been, as Anthony Wood remarked, luckier in his "first hints and thoughts of things than in his after-notions," but in his skeptical reassessment of the basis for man's pride and of his present state of knowledge, his attack on the "empty loquacities" and "nugacious disputations" of scholastic and other kinds of dogmatism, his naive confidence in the gains to be expected from "neoteric endeavors," and his Baconian segregation of "natural" and "religious" knowledge, Glanvill was a graceful, somewhat facile spokesman for the neo-orthodoxy of the Restoration.

I have based my text upon the first (1661) edition of *The Vanity of Dogmatizing* (Wing G-834), which has been edited by John Owen (1885) and reproduced in facsimile by M. E. Prior (1931). Glanvill is discussed by several of the scholars cited in the General Bibliography, Section I, and is the subject of substantial monographs by Ferris Greenslet (1900) and J. I. Cope (1956). M. E. Prior has written of his belief in witches in *MP*, XXX (1932), R. H. Popkin on the growth of his reputation as a philosopher in *JHI*, XV (1954), and Dorothea Krook on the Baconian elements in his (and Robert Boyle's) thought in *HLQ*, XVIII (1955).

from The Vanity of Dogmatizing (1661)

THE PREFACE

. . . For the design of this discourse, the title speaks it. It is levied against dogmatizing, and attempts upon a daring enemy: confidence[1] in opinions. The knowledge I teach is ignorance, and methinks the theory of our own natures should be enough to learn it us. We came into the world, and we know not how; we live in't in a self-nescience,[2] and go hence again and are as ignorant of our recess.[3] We grow, we live, we move at first in a microcosm, and can give no more scientifical account of the state of our three quarters' confinement[4] than if we had never been extant in the greater world, but had expired in an abortion. We are enlarged from the prison of the womb, we live, we grow, and give being to our like; we see, we hear, and outward objects affect our other senses; we understand, we will, we imagine and remember; and yet know no more of the immediate reasons of most of these common functions than those little embryo anchorites. We breathe, we talk, we move while we are ignorant of the manner of these vital performances.

The dogmatist knows not how he moves his finger, nor by what art or method he turns his tongue in his vocal expressions. New parts are added to our substance to supply our continual decayings, and as we die we are born daily; nor can we give a certain account how the aliment is so prepared for nutrition or by what mechanism it is so regularly distributed. The turning of it into chyle by the stomach's heat is a general and unsatisfying solution. We love, we hate, we joy, we grieve: passions annoy us, and our minds are disturbed by those corporal estuations.[5] Nor yet can we tell how these should reach our unbodied selves, or how the soul should be affected by these heterogeneous agitations. We lay us down to sleep away our diurnal cares; night shuts up the senses' windows; the mind contracts into the brain's center. We live in death and lie as in the grave. Now we know nothing, nor can our waking thoughts inform us who is Morpheus[6] and what that leaden key that locks us up within our senseless cells.

There's a difficulty that pincheth, nor will it easily be resolved. The soul is awake and solicited by external motions, for some of them reach the perceptive region in the most silent repose and obscurity of night. What is't, then, that prevents our sensations, or if we do perceive, how is't that we know it not? But we dream, see visions, converse with chimeras: the one half of our lives is a romance, a fiction. We retain a catch[7] of those pretty stories, and our awakened imagination smiles in the recollection. Nor yet can our most severe inquiries find what did so abuse us, or show the nature and manner of these nocturnal illusions. When we puzzle ourselves in the disquisition we do but dream, and every hypothesis is a fancy. Our most industrious conceits are but like their object, and as uncertain as those of midnight. Thus when some days and nights have gone over us, the stroke of fate concludes the number of our pulses; we take our leave of the sun and moon, and bid mortality adieu.

THE VANITY OF DOGMATIZING [1]Arrogance.
[2]Ignorance of ourselves. [3]Departing.
[4]Nine-month prenatal existence. [5]Feverish disturbances.
[6]The god of sleep. [7]Fragment, snatch.

The vital flame is extinct, the soul retires into another world, and the body to dwell with dust. Nor doth the last scene yield us any more satisfaction in our autography,[8] for we are as ignorant how the soul leaves the light as how it first came into it: we know as little how the union is dissolved—that is, the chain of the so differing subsistencies that compound us—as how it first commenced.

This, then, is the creature that so pretends to knowledge, and that makes such a noise and bustle for opinions. The instruction of Delphos[9] may shame such confidents[10] into modesty, and till we have learnt that honest *adviso* (though from hell), Γνῶθι σεατόν. Confidence is arrogance, and dogmatizing unreasonable presuming. I doubt not but the opinionative resolver thinks all these easy knowables, and the theory here accounted mysteries are to him revelations. But let him suspend that conclusion till he hath weighed the considerations hereof, which the discourse itself will present him with. And if he can untie those knots, he is able to teach all humanity, and will do well to oblige mankind by his informations. . . .

CHAPTER 17

That this philosophy [i.e. Aristotelianism] is litigious, the very spawn of disputations and controversies as undecisive as needless, is the natural result of the former:[11] storms are the products of vapors. For where words are imposed arbitrariously, having no stated real meaning or else distorted from their common use and known significations, the mind must needs be led into confusion and misprision,[12] and so things plain and easy in their naked natures made full of intricacy and disputable uncertainty. For we cannot conclude with assurance but from clearly apprehended premises, and these cannot be so conceived but by a distinct comprehension of the words out of which they are elemented.[13] So that where they are unfixed or ambiguous, our propositions must be so, and our deductions can be no better. One reason, therefore, of the uncontroverted certainty of mathematical science is because 'tis built upon clear and settled significations of names which admit no ambiguity or insignificant obscurity.

But in the Aristotelian philosophy it's quite otherwise. Words being here carelessly and abusively admitted, and as inconstantly retained, it must needs come to pass that they will be diversely apprehended by contenders, and so made the subject of controversies that are endless both for use and number. And thus being at their first step out of the way to science, by mistaking in simple terms, in the progress of their inquiries they must needs lose both themselves and the truth in a verbal labyrinth. And now the entangled disputants, as Master Hobbes ingeniously observeth,[14] like birds that came down the chimney, betake them to the false light, seldom suspecting the way they entered; but attempting by vain, impertinent, and coincident distinctions to escape the absurdity that pursues them, do but weary themselves with as little success as the silly bird attempts the window. The misstated words are the original mistake, and every other essay is a new one. Now these canting contests, the usual entertainment of the *Peripatum*,[15] are not only the accidental

vitiosities[16] of the philosophers but the genuine issues of the philosophy itself. And Aristotle seems purposely to intend the cherishing of controversial digladiations[17] by his own affectation of an intricate obscurity. Himself acknowledged it when he said his *Physics* were published, and not so; and by that double advice in his *Topics* 'tis as clear as light. In one place he adviseth his sectators[18] in disputations to be ambiguous, and in another to bring forth anything that occurs rather than give way to their adversary—counsel very well becoming an inquirer after verity! Nor did he here advise them to anything but what he followeth himself and exactly copies out in his practice. The multitudes of his lame, abrupt, equivocal, self-contradicting expressions will evidence it as to the first part, which who considers may be satisfied in this: that if Aristotle found nature's face under covert of a veil, he hath not removed the old, but made her a new one. And for the latter, his frequent slightness[19] in arguing doth abundantly make it good. . . .

Now this disputing way of inquiry is so far from advancing science that 'tis no inconsiderable retarder; for in scientifical discoveries many things must be considered which the hurry of a dispute indisposeth for, and there is no way to truth but by the most clear comprehension of simple notions, and as wary an accuracy in deductions. If the fountain be disturbed, there's no seeing to the bottom; and here's an exception to the proverb, " 'Tis no good fishing for verity in troubled waters." One mistake of either simple apprehension or connection[20] makes an erroneous conclusion. So that the precipitancy of disputation and the stir and noise of passions that usually attend it must needs be prejudicial to verity: its calm insinuations can no more be heard in such a bustle than a whisper among a crowd of contending sailors in a storm. Nor do the eager clamors of contending disputants yield any more relief to eclipsed truth than did the sounding brass of old to the laboring moon. When it's under question, 'twere as good flip cross and pile[21] as to dispute for 't, and to play a game at chess for an opinion in philosophy (as myself and an ingenious friend have sometime sported)[22] is as likely a way to determine.

Thus the Peripatetic procedure is inept for philosophical solutions: the lot[23] were as equitable a decision as their empty loquacities. 'Tis these nugacious disputations that have been the great hindrance to the more improvable parts of learning,

[8]Autobiography.
[9]In antiquity, the site of a famous shrine to Apollo, whose priestesses, famed for their cryptic oracles, took as their motto Γνῶθι σεατόν ("know thyself"). [10]Overconfident persons?
[11]The previous chapter, in which Glanvill had developed the proposition that Aristotelianism "is an huddle of words and terms insignificant." [12]Misunderstanding. [13]Compounded.
[4]*Hobbes...observeth: Leviathan,* I.iv.
[15]*Peripatus,* the walk in the Lyceum where Aristotle lectured while strolling, hence Aristotelian or Peripatetic philosophy. [16]Faults.
[17]Literally, sword fights; here, verbal encounters.
[18]Follows, partisans. [19]Weakness. [20]Inference.
[21]*Flip...pile:* toss a coin for heads or tails. Coins stamped with a cross on one side normally showed a *pile* or mint mark on the reverse. [22]Done in sport. [23]Drawing by lot.

and the modern retainers to the Stagirite[24] have spent their sweat and pains upon the most litigious parts of his philosophy while those that find less play for the contending genius are incultivate.[25] Thus logic, physics, metaphysics are the burden of volumes and the daily entertainment of the disputing schools, while the more profitable doctrines of the heavens, meteors, minerals, animals—as also the more practical ones of politics and economics—are scarce so much as glanced at. And the indisputable mathematics—the only science heaven hath yet vouchsafed humanity—have but few votaries among the slaves of the Stagirite. What the late promoters of the Aristotelian philosophy have writ on all these so fertile subjects can scarce compare with the single[26] disputes about *materia prima*.[27]

Nor hath human science monopolized the damage that hath sprung from this root of evils: theology hath been as deep a sharer. The volumes of the Schoolmen are deplorable evidence of Peripatetic depravations, and Luther's censure of that divinity—*Quam primum apparuit theologia scholastica, evanuit theologia crucis*[28]—is neither uncharitable nor unjust. This hath mudded the fountain of certainty with notional and ethnic admixtions,[29] and platted[30] the head of evangelical truth (as the Jews did its author's) with a crown of thorns. Here, the most obvious verity is subtilized into niceties and spun into a thread indiscernible by common optics but through the spectacles of the adored heathen. This hath robbed the Christian world of its unity and peace, and made the church the stage of everlasting contentions; and while Aristotle is made the center of truth and unity, what hope of reconciling? And yet most of these scholastic controversies are ultimately resolved into the subtleties of his philosophy. And methinks an Athenian should not be the best guide to the Θεὸς ἄγνωστος,[31] nor an idolater to that God he neither knew nor owned. When I read the eager contests of these notional theologies about things that are not, I cannot but think of that pair of wise ones[32] that fought for the middle; and methinks many their controversies are such as if we and our antipodes should strive who were uppermost: their title to truth is equal. He that divided his text into one part did but imitate the Schoolmen in their coincident distinctions; and the best of their curiosities are but like paint on glass, which intercepts and dyes the light the more desirable splendor. I cannot look upon their elaborate trifles but with a sad reflection on the degenerate state of our lapsed intellects, and as deep a resentment of the mischiefs of this school philosophy.

CHAPTER 19

The Aristotelian philosophy is inept for new discoveries, and therefore of no accommodation to the use of life. That all arts and professions are capable of maturer improvements cannot be doubted by those who know the least of any. And that there is an America of secrets, an unknown Peru of nature, whose discovery would richly advance them is more than conjecture. Now while we either sail by the land of gross and vulgar doctrines or direct our inquiries by the cynosure of mere abstract notions we are not likely to reach the treasures on the other side the Atlantic, the directing of

the world the way to which is the noble end of true philosophy.

That the Aristotelian physiology cannot boast itself the proper author of any one invention is pregnant evidence of its infecundous[33] deficiency; and 'twould puzzle the schools to point at any considerable discovery made by the direct, sole manuduction[34] of Peripatetic principles. Most of our rarities have been found out by casual emergency, and have been the works of time and chance rather than of philosophy. What Aristotle hath of experimental knowledge in his books *Of Animals* or elsewhere is not much transcending vulgar observation; and yet what he hath of this was never learnt from his hypotheses, but forcibly fetched into suffrage[35] to them. And 'tis the observation of the noble St. Alban[36] that that philosophy is built on a few vulgar experiments, and if upon further inquiry any were found to refragate they were to be discharged by a distinction.[37] Now what is founded on and made up but of vulgarities cannot make known anything beyond them. For nature is set agoing by the most subtle and hidden instruments, which it may be have nothing obvious which resembles them. Hence judging by visible appearances, we are discouraged by supposed impossibilities which to nature are none, but within her sphere of action. And therefore what shows only the outside and sensible structure of nature is not likely to help us in finding out the *magnalia*.[38] 'Twere next to impossible for one who never saw the inward wheels and motions to make a watch upon the bare view of the circle of hours and index;[39] and 'tis as difficult to trace natural operations to any practical advantage by the sight of the cortex[40] of sensible appearances. He were a poor physician that had no more anatomy than were to be gathered from the physomy.[41] Yea, the most common phenomena can be neither known nor improved without insight into the more hidden frame. For nature works by an invisible hand in all things, and till Peripateticism can show us further than those gross solutions of qualities and elements, 'twill never make us benefactors to the world, nor considerable discovers.

But its experienced sterility through so many hundred years drives hope to desperation. We expect greater things from neoteric[42] endeavors. The Cartesian philosophy[43] in this regard hath shown the world the way to be happy.

[24]Aristotle (from his birthplace Stagira in Macedonia). [25]Uncultivated. [26]Trivial. [27]"First matter," the unformed and inderminate substance postulated by the Aristotelians. [28]When scholastic disputation appears the Cross vanishes. [29]*Notional...admixtions*: speculative and pagan admixtures. [30]Interweaved. [31]"The unknown God." [32]Unidentified. [33]Barren, unproductive. [34]Guidance. [35]As support. [36]Sir Francis Bacon, who was created Viscount St. Albans in 1621. [37]*If upon...distinction*: incompatible data were glibly rationalized. *Refragate*: oppose, controvert. [38]"Wonders." [39]*Circle...index*: i.e., the face and hands of a watch. [40]Rind, bark; i.e., externals. [41]Physiognomy, face. [42]Modern. [43]The "new philosophy" of René Descartes (1596–1650), whose *Discourse on Method* (1637), *Meditations* (1641), and *Principles of Philosophy* (1644) had brilliantly exemplifed the use of mathematics as an instrument of knowledge.

Methinks this age seems resolved to bequeath posterity somewhat to remember it, and the glorious undertakers[44] wherewith heaven hath blest our days will leave the world better provided than they found it. And whereas in former times such generous free-spirited worthies were as the rare, newly observed stars—a single one the wonder of an age—in ours they are like the lights of the greater size that twinkle in the starry firmament; and this last century can glory in numerous constellations.[45] Should those heroes go on as they have happily begun they'll fill the world with wonders. And I doubt not but posterity will find many things that are now but rumors verified into practical realities. It may be some ages hence a voyage to the southern unknown tracts, yea possibly the moon, will not be more strange than one to America. To them that come after us it may be as ordinary to buy a pair of wings to fly into remotest regions as now a pair of boots to ride a journey. And to confer at the distance of the Indies by sympathetic conveyances may be as usual to future times as to us in a literary correspondence. The restoration of gray hairs to juvenility and renewing the exhausted marrow may at length be effected without a miracle; and the turning of the now comparatively desert world into a paradise may not improbably be expected from late[46] agriculture.

Now those that judge by the narrowness of former principles will smile at these paradoxical expectations. But questionless those great inventions that have in these later ages altered the face of all things in their naked proposals and mere suppositions were to former times as ridiculous. To have talked of a new earth to have been discovered had been a romance to antiquity, and to sail without sight of stars or shores by the guidance of a mineral, a story more absurd than the flight of Daedalus.[47] That men should speak after their tongues were ashes, or communicate with each other in differing hemispheres, before the invention of letters could not but have been thought a fiction. Antiquity would not have believed the almost incredible force of our cannons, and would as coldly have entertained the wonders of the telescope. In these, we all condemn antique credulity, and 'tis likely posterity will have as much cause to pity ours. But yet notwithstanding this straightness[48] of shallow observers, there are a set of enlarged souls that are more judiciously credulous; and those who are acquainted with the fecundity of Cartesian principles and the diligent and ingenuous endeavors of so many true philosophers will despair of nothing.

But again, the Aristotelian philosophy is in some things impious and inconsistent with divinity, and in many more inconsistent with itself. That the Resurrection is impossible, that God understands not all things, that the world was from eternity, that there's no substantial form but moves some orb, that the first mover moves by an eternal, immutable necessity, that if the world and motion were not from eternity then God was idle were all the assertions of Aristotle, which theology pronounceth impieties. Which yet we need not strange[49] at from one of whom a father saith, *Nec Deum coluit nec curavit*,[50] especially if it be as Philoponus[51] affirms, that he philosophized by command from the oracle. Of the Aristotelian contradictions Gassendus[52] hath presented

us with a catalogue; we'll instance in a few of them. In one place he saith the planets' scintillation is not seen because of their propinquity, but that of the rising and setting sun is because of its distance; and yet in another place he makes the sun nearer us than they are. He saith that the elements are not eternal, and seeks to prove it; and yet he makes the world so, and the elements its parts. In his *Meteors* he sayeth no dew is produced in the wind, and yet afterwards admits it under the south, and none under the north. In one place he defines a vapor humid and cold, and in another humid and hot. He sayeth the faculty of speaking is a sense, and yet before he allowed but five. In one place, that nature doth all things best, and in another that it makes more evil than good. And somewhere he contradicts himself within a line, saying that an immoveable mover hath no principle of motion. 'Twould be tedious to mention more, and the quality of a digression will not allow it.

Thus we have, as briefly as the subject would bear, animadverted on the so much admired philosophy of Aristotle. The nobler spirits of the age are disengaged from those detected vanities, and the now adorers of that philosophy are few, but such narrow souls that know no other; or if any of them look beyond the leaves of their master, yet they try other principles by a jury of his, and scan Cartes with "genus" and "species."[53] From the former sort I may hope they'll pardon this attempt, and for the latter, I value not their censure.

Thus we may conclude upon the whole that the stamp of authority can make leather as current as gold, and that there's nothing so contemptible but antiquity can render it august and excellent. But because the fooleries of some affected novelists have discredited new discoveries,[54] and rendered the very mention suspected of vanity at least, and in points divine of heresy, it will be necessary to add that I intend not the former discourse in favor of any new-broached conceit in divinity; for I own no opinion there which cannot plead the prescription of above sixteen hundred. There's nothing I have more sadly resented than the frenetic whimsies with which our age abounds, and therefore am not likely to patron[55] them. In theology I put as great a difference between our new lights and ancient truths as between the sun and an unconcocted, evanid meteor.[56] Though I confess that in philosophy I'm

[44]Innovators.
[45]Following Galileo's construction of a telescope in 1609, the science of astronomy had made dizzying advances. [46]Advanced.
[47]In Greek mythology, an Athenian architect who escaped from Crete with artificial wings. [48]Narrowness, i.e., intellectual rigidity.
[49]Wonder. [50]He neither cares for nor reverences God.
[51]Joannes Philoponus (7th cent.), an Alexandrian scholar and grammarian whose many works include a set of commentaries on Aristotle.
[52]Pierre Gassendi (1592–1655), French empiricist who strenuously opposed Aristotelianism.
[53]*Scan...*"*species*": evaluate Descartes' work in terms of obsolete Aristotelian jargon.
[54]*Fooleries...discoveries*: Glanvill is perhaps thinking of such early examples of science fiction as John Wilkins' *Discovery of a World in the Moon* (1638) and Savinien Cyrano de Bergerac's *L'histoire comique des états de la lune* (1656?). [55]Champion, defend.
[56]An insubstantial, evanescent shooting star.

a seeker, yet cannot believe that a skeptic in philosophy must be one in divinity. Gospel light began in its zenith, and, as some say, the sun was created in its meridian strength and luster. But the beginnings of philosophy were in a crepusculous obscurity, and it's yet scarce past the dawn. Divine truths were most pure in their source, and time could not perfect what eternity began. Our divinity, like the grand father of humanity,[57] was born in the fulness of time and in the strength of its manly vigor. But philosophy and arts commenced embryos, and are completed by time's gradual accomplishments. And therefore what I cannot find in the leaves of former inquisitors I seek in the modern attempts of nearer authors. I cannot receive Aristotle's πιστόταιοι παλαιοί[58] in so extensive an interpretation as some would enlarge it to; and that discouraging maxim *Nil dictum quod non dictum prius*[59] hath little room in my estimation. Nor can I tie up my belief to the letter of Solomon:[60] except Copernicus be in the right, there hath been something "new under the sun." I'm sure later times have seen novelties in the heavens above it. I do not think that all science is tautology. The last ages have shown us what antiquity never saw—no, not in a dream.

CHAPTER 20

Confidence of science is one great reason we miss it,[61] whereby presuming we have it everywhere, we seek it not where it is and therefore fall short of the object of our inquiry. Now to give further check to dogmatical pretensions, and to discover the vanity of assuming[62] ignorance, we'll make a short inquiry whether there be any such thing as science in the sense of its assertors. In their notion, then, it is the knowledge of things in their true, immediate, necessary causes, upon which I'll advance the following observations.

All knowledge of causes is deductive, for we know none by simple intuition, but through the mediation of its effects. Now we cannot conclude anything to be the cause of another but from its continual accompanying it, for the causality itself is insensible.[63] Thus we gather fire to be the cause of heat and the sun of daylight because wherever fire is we find there's heat, and wherever the sun is, light attends it, and *e contra.*[64] But now to argue from a concomitancy to a causality is not infallibly conclusive; yea, in this way lies notorious delusion. Is 't not possible—and how know we the contrary?—but that something which alway attends the grosser flame may be the cause of heat? And may not it and its supposed cause be only parallel effects? Suppose the fire had never appeared, but had been still hid in smoke, and that heat did always proportionably increase and diminish with the greater or less quantity of that fuliginous[65] exhalation, should we ever have doubted that smoke was the cause on 't? Suppose we had never seen more sun than in a cloudy day, and that the lesser lights had ne'er shown us their lucid substance. Let us suppose the day had always broke with a wind, and had proportionably varied as that did, had not he been a notorious skeptic that should question the causality? . . .

We hold no demonstration in the notion of the dogmatist but where the contrary is impossible, for necessary is that which cannot be otherwise. Now whether the acquisitions of any on this side perfection can make good the pretensions to so high-strained an infallibility will be worth a reflection. And, methinks, did we but compare the miserable scantness of our capacities with the vast profundity of things, both truth and modesty would teach us a dialect more becoming short-sighted mortality. Can nothing be otherwise which we conceive impossible to be so? Is our knowledge and things so adequately commensurate as to justify the affirming that that cannot be which we comprehend not? Our demonstrations are levied upon principles of our own, not universal nature; and as my Lord Bacon notes, we judge from the analogy of ourselves, not the universe. Now are not many things certain by the principles of one which are impossible to the apprehensions of another? Thus some things our juvenile reasons tenaciously adhere to which yet our maturer judgments disallow of; many things to mere sensible discerners are impossible which to the enlarged principles of more advanced intellects are easy verities; yea, that's absurd in one philosophy which is a worthy truth in another; and that's a demonstration to Aristotle which is none to Descartes: that every fixed star is a sun, and that they are as distant from each other as we from some of them; that the sun which lights us is in the center of our world, and our earth a planet that wheels about it; that this globe is a star only crusted over with the grosser element, and that its center is of the same nature with the sun; that it may recover its light again and shine amids the other luminaries; that our sun may be swallowed up of another and become a planet.

All these, if we judge by common principles of the rules of vulgar philosophy, are prodigious impossibilities, and their contradictories[66] as good as demonstrable; but yet to a reason informed by Cartesianism these have their probability. Thus, it may be, the grossest absurdities to the philosophies of Europe may be justifiable assertions to that of China; and 'tis not unlikely but what's impossible to all humanity may be possible in the metaphysics and physiology of angels. Now the best principles, excepting divine and mathematical, are by hypotheses, within the circle of which we may indeed conclude many things with security from error; but yet the greatest certainty, advanced from supposal, is still but hypothetical. So that we may affirm things are thus and thus according to the principles we have espoused, but we strangely forget ourselves when we plead a necessity of their being so in nature, and an impossibility of their being otherwise.

That one man should be able to bind the thoughts of another and determine them to their particular objects will be reckoned in the first rank of impossibles, yet by the power of advanced imagination it may very probably be effected, and story abounds with instances. I'll trouble the reader but

---

[57]Adam.　[58]Former reputation and prestige.
[59]"Nothing is said that has not been said before."
[60]"There is no new thing under the sun" (Ecclesiastes 1.9).
[61]*Confidence . . . it*: reliance upon obsolete dogmatisms prevents our advances in true knowledge.　[62]Pretentious.
[63]Not apprehended by the senses.　[64]Vice versa.　[65]Smoky.
[66]Contraries.

with one, and the hands from which I had it make me secure of the truth on 't.

There was very lately a lad in the University of Oxford who, being of very pregnant and ready parts and yet wanting the encouragement of preferment, was by his poverty forced to leave his studies there and to cast himself upon the wide world for a livelihood. Now his necessities growing daily on him, and wanting the help of friends to relieve him, he was at last forced to join himself to a company of vagabond gypsies whom occasionally he met with, and to follow their trade for a maintenance. Among these extravagant[67] people, by the insinuating subtilty of his carriage[68] he quickly got so much of their love and esteem as that they discovered to him their mystery,[69] in the practice of which, by the pregnancy of his wit and parts he soon grew so good a proficient as to be able to outdo his instructors. After he had been a pretty while well exercised in the trade there chanced to ride by a couple of scholars who had formerly been of his acquaintance. The scholars had quickly spied out their old friend among the gypsies, and their amazement to see him among such society had well nigh discovered him; but by a sign he prevented their owning him before that crew, and taking one of them aside privately, desired him with his friend to go to an inn not far distant thence, promising there to come to them.

They accordingly went thither, and he follows. After their first salutations his friends inquire how he came to lead so odd a life as that was, and to join himself with such a cheating, beggarly company. The scholar-gypsy, having given them an account of the necessity which drove him to that kind of life, told them that the people he went with were not such impostors as they were taken for, but that they had a traditional kind of learning among them, and could do wonders by the power of imagination, and that himself had learnt much of their art and improved it further than themselves could. And to evince the truth of what he told them he said he'd remove into another room, leaving them to discourse together; and upon his return tell them the sum of what they had talked of, which accordingly he performed, giving them a full account of what had passed between them in his absence. The scholars, being amazed at so unexpected a discovery, earnestly desired him to unriddle the mystery. In which he gave them satisfaction by telling them that what he did was by the power of imagination, his fancy binding theirs, and that himself had dictated to them the discourse they held together while he was from them; that there were warrantable ways of heightening the imagination to that pitch as to bind another's; and that when he had compassed the whole secret, some parts of which he said he was yet ignorant of, he intended to leave their company and give the world an account of what he had learned. . . .

CHAPTER 24

AN APOLOGY FOR PHILOSOPHY

> Glanvill closes his attack on the obsolete "dogmatism" of the Aristotelians with a spirited defense of true "philosophy," by which he means empiricism. Significantly, his terminal paragraphs assert the incompatibility of irreligion and philosophy.

I think I may conclude the charge which hot-brained folly lays in against philosophy—that it leads to irreligion—frivolous and vain. I dare say, next after the divine Word it's one of the best friends to piety. Neither is it any more justly accountable for the impious irregularities of some that have paid homage to its shrine than religion itself for the sinful extravagances both opinionative and practical of high pretenders to it. It is a vulgar conceit that philosophy holds a confederacy with atheism itself, but most injurious, for nothing can better antidote[70] us against it, and they may as well say that physicians are the only murderers. A philosophic atheist is as good sense as a divine one, and I dare say the proverb *ubi tres medici, duo athei*[71] is a scandal. I think the original of this conceit might be that the students of nature, conscious to her more cryptic ways of working, resolve many strange effects into the nearer efficiency of second causes,[72] which common ignorance and superstition attribute to the immediate causality of the first, thinking it to derogate from the divine power that anything which is above their apprehensions should not be reckoned above nature's activity, though it be but His instrument and works nothing but as impowered from Him. Hence they violently declaim against all that will not acknowledge a miracle in every extraordinary effect, as setting nature in the throne of God, and so it's an easy step to say they deny Him. Whenas indeed nature is but the chain of second causes, and to suppose second causes without a first is beneath the logic of Gotham.[73] Neither can they—who, to make their reproach of philosophy more authentic, allege the authority of an apostle to conclude it vain—upon any whit more reasonable terms make good their charge, since this allegation stands in force but against its abuse, corrupt sophistry or traditionary impositions which lurked under the mask of so serious a name. At the worst the text will never warrant an universal conclusion any more than that other, where the apostle[74] speaks of "silly women" (who yet are the most rigid urgers of this), can justly blot the sex with an unexceptionable note of infamy.

Now what I have said here in this short "Apology for Philosophy" is not so strictly verifiable of any that I know as the Cartesian, the entertainment of which among truly ingenuous, unpossessed[75] spirits renders an after-commendation superfluous and impertinent. It would require a wit like its author's to do it right in an encomium. The strict rationality of the hypothesis in the main and the critical coherence of its parts I doubt not but will bear it down to posterity with a glory that shall know no term[76] but the universal ruins. Neither can the pedantry or prejudice of the present age any more obstruct its motion in that supreme sphere wherein its desert hath placed it than can the howling wolves

---

[67]Wandering, vagrant. [68]Behavior. [69]Craft, calling. [70]Fortify.
[71]Among three medical men there will be two atheists.
[72]Causes caused by something else, specifically by God, who is the first cause or prime mover.
[73]A village in Nottinghamshire, England, proverbial for the folly of its inhabitants.
[74]"For of this sort are they who creep into houses, and lead captive silly women laden with sins, led away with divers lusts, ever learning, and never able to come to the knowledge of the truth" (2 Timothy 3.6–7). [75]Unbiased, impartial. [76]End, terminus.

pluck Cynthia[77] from her orb, who, regardless of their noise, securely glides through the indisturbed ether. Censure here will disparage itself, not it. He that accuseth the sun of darkness shames his own blind eyes, not its light. The barking of cynics at that hero's chariot wheels will not sully the glory of his triumph. But I shall supersede this endless attempt: sunbeams best commend themselves.

[77]The moon goddess.

RELIGION AND POLITICS

Lewis Bayly [1565-1631]

In a famous passage of *Grace Abounding to the Chief of Sinners* (1666), John Bunyan relates that although he and his young wife began their married life "as poor as poor might be, not having so much household stuff as a dish or a spoon betwixt us both," they did possess two treasures that had come to them from Mrs. Bunyan's "godly" father. One was Arthur Dent's *Plain Man's Pathway to Heaven*, the other Lewis Bayly's *Practice of Piety*; and it was through these books, said Bunyan, that even in his "sad and sinful state" he for the first time felt the stirrings of religion. There were many men of Bunyan's sort who shared his admiration, for *The Practice of Piety*, though written by an Anglican divine and dedicated to the Prince of Wales, was so much venerated by the Puritans that certain envious clergymen asserted its authority was for its admirers equal to the Bible.

Its author, who made his reputation as a preacher and served as chaplain to Prince Henry before his appointment (1616) to the See of Bangor, was not himself a mild and Christlike man. Repeatedly in trouble for his attacks upon the papists, for "disputing malapertly" with King James, for the loose administration of his see, even for alleged sexual improprieties, he was on one occasion reprimanded by the Privy Council and on another imprisoned in the Fleet (perhaps because he disapproved of Prince Charles' projected Spanish marriage); but somehow, though embattled to the end, he fended off his adversaries and retained his office and its functions until his death in 1631.

The work that made him famous was contrived, he told Prince Charles, "to extract out of the chaos of endless controversies the old practice of true piety." Consisting of forty-four meditations, discourses, and prayers, it is both a handbook of Calvinistic theology and a manual of devotion, unambiguous in its doctrine, unadorned in style, and blunt in its prescriptions of man's religious duties. Thus it moves from "a plain description of God" to "the miseries of a man's life and death that is not reconciled to God in Christ," and it goes on to expound, in terms that anyone could understand, the things that God requires of Adam's sinful heirs. In Section 5, for instance, we are told "how to begin the morning with pious meditations and prayers," in Section 6 "how to read the Bible with profit and ease once over every year," in Section 17 how to observe the sabbath, in Section 27 how to pray "when one begins to be sick," in Section 28 how to make a will, in Section 29 how to pray "before taking of physic." It closes, appropriately, with a flurry of mortuary injunctions that leads into a coda on the passion of our Lord.

Published anonymously in the first years of the century, *The Practice of Piety* was such a perennial success that by 1613 it had reached a third edition, by 1619 an eleventh, by 1633 a thirty-first, and by 1735 a fifty-ninth. Its fame, moreover, was not confined to England. By 1647 it had been translated into French, German, Welsh, and Polish; and in 1665 an enterprising Cambridge printer published an edition for the sinful Massachusetts Indians. The rumor that the work was not of Bayly's composition was dismissed by Anthony Wood as "a lying Puritan story, invented by that proud pharisaical faction, who were not willing a book so well esteemed should be writ by a bishop."

Since the earliest editions of *The Practice of Piety* have not survived—no doubt because they were literally read to pieces—I have based my text on what purports to be the thirty-first (STC 1611), which, "amplified by the author," appeared two years after Bayly's death in 1631. The work receives attention from McAdoo and others cited in the General Bibliography, Section III, and is analyzed in some detail by C. J. Stranks in *Anglican Devotion* (1961).

from The Practice of Piety

TO THE HIGH AND MIGHTY PRINCE
CHARLES, PRINCE OF WALES

Christ Jesus, the Prince of Princes, bless Your Highness with length of days and an increase of all graces which may make you truly prosperous in this life and eternally happy in that which is to come.

Jonathan shot three arrows to drive David further off from Saul's fury,[1] and this is the third epistle which I have written to draw Your Highness nearer to God's favor by directing your heart to begin (like Josiah) in your youth to seek after the God of David (and of Jacob, your father).[2] Not but that I know that Your Highness doth this without mine admonition, but because I would, with the apostle,[3] have you abound in every grace, in faith and knowledge, and in all diligence, and in your love to God's service and true religion. Never was there more need of plain and unfeigned admonition, for the comic, in that saying, seems but to have prophesied of our times: *Obsequim amicos, veritas odium parit.*[4] And no marvel, seeing that we are fallen into the dregs of time, which being the last must needs be the worst days. And how can there be worse, seeing vanity knows not how to be vainer, nor wickedness how to be more wicked? And whereas heretofore those have been counted most holy who have showed themselves most zealous in their religion, they are not reputed most discreet who can make the least profession of their faith. And that these are the last days appears evidently, because the security of men's eternal state hath so overwhelmed (as Christ foretold it should)[5] all sorts, that most who now live are become lovers of pleasures more than lovers of God. And of those who pretend to love God, O God! what sanctified heart can but bleed to behold how seldom they come to prayers, how irreverently they hear God's word, what strangers they are at the Lord's table, what assiduous spectators they are at stage plays—where, being Christians, they can sport themselves to hear the vassals of the devil scoffing religion, and blasphemously abusing phrases of holy Scripture on their stages as familiarly as they use their tobacco pipes in their bibbing-houses.[6] So that he who would nowadays seek in most Christians for the power shall scarce almost find the very show of godliness. Never was there more sinning, never less remorse for sin. Never was the Judge nearer to come, never was there so little preparation for His coming; and if the bridegroom should now come, how many (who think themselves wise enough, and full of all knowledge) would be found foolish virgins without one drop of the oil of saving faith in their lamps?[7] For the greatest wisdom of most men in this age consists in being wise first to deceive others and in the end to deceive themselves. . . .

In my desire, therefore, of the common salvation, but especially of Your Highness' everlasting welfare, I have endeavored to extract out of the chaos of endless controversies the old practice of true piety, which flourished before these controversies were hatched, which my poor labors (in a short while) come now forth again the twenty-fourth time under the gracious protection of Your Highness' favor, and by their entertainment seem not to be altogether unwelcome to the Church of Christ. If to be pious hath in all ages been held the truest honor, how much more honorable is it in so impious an age to be the true patron and pattern of piety? Piety made David, Solomon, Jehoshaphat, Ezekias, Josias, Zerubabel, Constantine, Theodosius, Edward the Sixt, Queen Elizabeth, Prince Henry,[8] and other religious princes to be so honored that their names (since their deaths) smell in the Church of God like a precious ointment, and their remembrances sweet as honey in all mouths, and as music at a banquet of wine; whenas the lips of others, who have been godless and irreligious princes, do rot and stink in the memory of God's people. And what honor is it for great men to have great titles on earth when God counts their names unworthy to be written in His book of life in heaven?. . .

To help you the better to seek and serve this God Almighty who must be your chief protector in life and only comfort in death I here once again, on my bended knees, offer my old mite, new stamped, into Your Highness' hands, daily for Your Highness offering up unto the Most High my humblest prayers that as you grow in age and stature, so you may (like your master Christ) increase in wisdom and favor with God and all good men. This suit will I never cease; in all other matters I will ever rest

Your Highness' humble servant,
during life to be commanded,
Lewis Bayly

TO THE DEVOUT READER

I had not purposed to enlarge the last edition save that the importunity of many devoutly disposed prevailed with me to add some points and to amplify others. To satisfy whose godly requests I have done my best endeavor, and withal finished all that I intend in this argument. If thou shalt hereby reap any more profit, give God the more praise, and remember him in thy prayers who hath vowed both his life and his labors to further thy salvation as his own.

Farewell in the Lord Jesus

MEDITATIONS ON[9] THE MISERY OF A MAN NOT RECONCILED TO GOD IN CHRIST

O wretched man! Where shall I begin to describe thine endless misery, who art condemned as soon as conceived and adjudged to eternal death before thou wast born to a temporal life? A beginning indeed I find, but no end of thy

THE PRACTICE OF PIETY   [1]1 Samuel 20.20.
[2]2 Chronicles 34.3. Bayly here permits himself a gentle play on words, Jacob (us) being both David's ancestor and Prince Charles' father.   [3]2 Corinthians 8.7.
[4]"Flattery gains friends; truth makes enemies" (Terence, *Andria,* line 67).   [5]2 Timothy 3.1–6.   [6]Tippling houses, i.e., taverns.
[7]Matthew 25.1–13.
[8]Henry, Prince of Wales (d. 1612), the eldest son of James I, to whom the early editions of Bayly's treatise were dedicated.
[9]Text *of.*

miseries, for when Adam and Eve being created after God's own image and placed in paradise that they and their posterity might live in a blessed state of life immortal, having dominion of all earthly creatures and only restrained from the fruit of one tree as a sign of their subjection to the almighty Creator, though God forbade them this one small thing under the penalty of eternal death, yet they believed the devil's word before the word of God, making God, as much as in them lay, a liar; and so, being unthankful for all the benefits which God bestowed on them, they became malcontented with their present state, as if God had dealt enviously or niggardly with them, and believed that the devil would make them partakers of far more glorious things than ever God had bestowed upon them; and in their pride they fell into high treason against the Most High, and, disdaining to be God's subjects, they affected blasphemously to be gods themselves, equals unto God. Hence till they repented, losing God's image, they became like unto the devil; and so all their posterity, as a traitorous brood, whilst they remain impenitent like thee, are subject in this life to all cursed miseries, and in the life to come to the everlasting fire prepared for the devil and his angels.

Lay, then, aside for a while thy doting vanities and take the view with me of thy doleful miseries, which, duly surveyed, I doubt not but that thou wilt conclude that it is far better never to have nature's being than not to be by grace a practitioner of religious piety.

Consider, therefore, thy misery (1) in thy life, (2) in thy death, (3) after death. In thy life (1) the miseries accompanying thy body, (2) the miseries which deform thy soul. In thy death, the miseries which shall oppress thy body and soul. After death, the miseries which overwhelm both body and soul together in hell. And first let us take a view of those miseries which accompany thy body according to the four ages of thy life: (1) infancy, (2) youth, (3) manhood, (4) old age.

MEDITATIONS ON THE MISERIES OF INFANCY

What wast thou, being an infant, but a brute having the shape of a man? Was not thy body conceived in the heat of lust, the secret of shame, and stain of original sin? And thus was thou cast naked upon the earth, all imbrued in the blood of filthiness. (Filthy indeed! when the Son of God, who disdained not to take on him man's nature and the infirmities thereof, yet thought it unbeseseming His holiness to be conceived after the sinful manner of man's conception). So that thy mother was ashamed to let thee know the manner thereof. What cause, then, hast thou to boast of thy birth, which was a cursed pain to thy mother and to thyself the entrance into a troublesome life, the greatness of which miseries, because thou couldest not utter in words, thou diddest express, as well as thou couldest, in weeping tears?

MEDITATIONS ON THE MISERIES OF YOUTH

What is youth but an untamed beast, all whose actions are rash and rude, not capable of good counsel when it is given and apelike delighting in nothing but in toys and babies?[10]

Therefore thou no sooner beganst to have a little strength and discretion but forthwith thou wast kept under the rod and fear of parents and masters, as if thou hadst been born to live under the discipline of others rather than at the disposition of thine own will. No tired horse was ever more willing to be rid of his burthen than thou was to get out of the servile state of this bondage, a state not worthy the description.

MEDITATIONS ON THE MISERIES OF MANHOOD

What is man's state but a sea wherein, as waves, one trouble ariseth in the neck of another, the latter worse than the former? No sooner diddest thou enter into the affairs of this world but thou wast enwrapped about with a cloud of miseries. Thy flesh provokes thee to lust, the world allures thee to pleasures, and the devil tempts thee to all kind of sins; fears of enemies affright thee, suits in law do vex thee, wrongs of ill neighbors do oppress thee, cares for wife and children do consume thee, and disquietness twixt open foes and false friends do in a manner confound thee. Sin stings thee within, Satan lays snares before thee, conscience of sins past doggeth behind thee. Now adversity on the left hand frets thee; anon prosperity on thy right hand flatters thee; over thy head God's vengeance, due to thy sin, is ready to fall upon thee; and under thy feet hell mouth is ready to swallow thee up. And in this miserable estate whither wilt thou go for rest and comfort? The house is full of cares, the field full of toil, the country of rudeness, the city of factions, the court of envy, the church of sects, the sea of pirates, the land of robbers. Or in what state wilt thou live, seeing wealth is envied and poverty contemned, wit is distrusted and simplicity is derided; superstition is mocked and religion is suspected; vice is advanced and virtue is disgraced? O with what a body of sin art thou compassed about in a world of wickedness! What are thine eyes but windows to behold vanities? What are thine ears but floodgates to let in the streams of iniquity? What are thy senses but matches to give fire to thy lusts? What is thine heart but the anvil whereon Satan hath forged the ugly shape of all lewd affections? Art thou nobly descended? Thou must put thyself in peril of foreign wars to get the reputation of earthly honor, ofttimes hazard thy life in a desperate combat to avoid the aspersion of a coward. Art thou born in mean estate? Lord! what pains and drudgery must thou endure at home and abroad to get maintenance, and all perhaps scarce sufficient to serve thy necessity? And when, after much service and labor, a man hath got something, how little certainty is there in that which is gotten, seeing thou seest by daily experience that he who was rich yesterday is today a beggar, he that yesterday was in health today is sick, he that yesterday was merry and laughed has cause today to mourn and weep, he that yesterday was in favor today is in disgrace, and he who yesterday was alive today is dead—and thou knowest not how soon, nor in what manner, thou shalt die thyself. And who can enumerate the losses, crosses, griefs, disgraces, sicknesses, and calamities which are incident to sinful man? To speak nothing of the death of friends and

[10]Dolls.

children, which ofttimes seems to be unto us far more bitter than present death itself.

MEDITATIONS ON THE MISERIES OF OLD AGE

What is old age but the receptacle of all maladies? For if thy lot be to draw thy days to a long date, in comes old, bald-headed age stooping under dotage with his wrinkled face, rotten teeth, and stinking breath, testy with choler, withered with dryness, dimmed with blindness, absurded with deafness, overwhelmed with sickness, and bowed together with weakness, having no use of any sense but of the sense of pain, which so racketh every member of his body that it never 10 easeth him of grief till he hath thrown him down to his grave.

Thus far of the miseries which accompany the body; now of the miseries which accompany chiefly the soul in this life.

. . . . . .

THINGS TO BE MEDITATED UPON AS THOU ART PUTTING OFF THY CLOTHES

1. That the day is coming when thou must be as barely unstript of all that thou hast in the world as thou art now of thy clothes; thou hast therefore here but the use of all things as a steward for a time, and that upon accounts; whilst, therefore, thou art trusted with this stewardship be wise 20 and faithful.

2. When thou seest thy bed let it put thee in mind of thy grave, which is now the bed of Christ; for Christ, by laying His holy body to rest three days and three nights in the grave[11] hath sanctified and, as it were, warmed it for the bodies of His saints to rest and sleep in till the morning of the resurrection; so that now unto the faithful death is but a sweet sleep, and the grave but Christ's bed where their bodies rest and sleep in peace until the joyful morning of the resurrection day shall dawn unto them.

Let therefore thy bedclothes represent unto thee the mold of the earth that shall cover thee, thy sheets thy winding-sheet, thy sleep thy death, thy waking thy resurrection; and being laid down in thy bed, when thou perceivest sleep to approach say, "I will lay me down and sleep in peace, for Thou, Lord, only makest me dwell in safety."[12]

Thus religiously opening every morning thy heart and shutting it up again every evening with the word of God and prayer, as it were with a lock and key, and so beginning the day with God's worship, continuing it in His fear, and ending it in His favor, thou shalt be sure to find the blessing of God upon all thy days' labors and good endeavors, and at night thou mayst assure thyself thou shalt sleep safely and sweetly in the arms of thy heavenly Father's providence.

Thus far of the piety which every Christian in private ought to practice every day; now followeth that which he, being a householder, must practice publicly with his family.

[11]Matthew 12.40.   [12]Psalm 4.8.

Lancelot Andrewes [1555-1626]

When young John Milton, then a Cambridge undergraduate, eulogized the late bishop of Winchester as an adornment of the human race (*generis humani decus*), he expressed a widely shared conviction, for in his later years Lancelot Andrewes enjoyed a fame unmatched by any other churchman of his day. Like Spenser a student of the renowned Richard Mulcaster at the Merchant Taylors' School, he, like Spenser, went on to Pembroke Hall, Cambridge, where, following his B.A. (1575), he stayed and climbed through various posts until he was elected master in 1589. Meanwhile he had been ordained (1580), and he rose so quickly in the church—as a preacher at St. Giles, Cripplegate, a prebendary of St. Paul's, a chaplain of the queen's, and dean of Westminster— that he twice refused Elizabeth's offer of a bishopric before accepting his appointment to the See of Chichester from James in 1605.

Under the new king Andrewes' honors mounted. Combining unassailable piety with massive erudition and marked administrative skill, he became the very model of the model "court divine." He served his monarch as a member of the abortive Hampton Court conference (1604), as almoner (1605), as one of that remarkable committee of divines who produced the Authorized Version of the Bible (1611), as the king's collaborator in his controversy with the formidable Cardinal Bellarmine over the oath of allegiance, as bishop successively of Ely (1609) and Winchester (1619), and as a member of the Privy Council (1619). If we may believe Clarendon, had Andrewes been promoted to the See of Canterbury in 1611 (when he almost got the post), the "infection" of dissent would perhaps have been relieved, and England spared the wounds of civil war. It is unlikely, however, that such a champion of the Anglican status quo could have pacified the angry Presbyterians, who distrusted his theology and abhorred his politics.

Throughout his glittering career Andrewes was, as he himself asserted, most concerned with preaching, and it was as a preacher that he was most renowned. He was so "diligent and painful" in the preparation of his sermons, the speaker at his funeral said, that he revised them thrice before delivery; and he left a "world of sermon notes" so "perfect" and "complete" that his editors—one of whom was William Laud—could send them to the press without additions or deletions. The result was *XCVI Sermons*, a splendid folio that, published "by His Majesty's special command" three years after Andrewes' death, reached a fourth edition by 1641 "See here a shadow from that setting sun," young Richard Crashaw wrote (p. 312) of Andrewes' portrait that served as frontispiece for these collected sermons,

> Whose glorious course, through this horizon run,
> Left the dim face of our dull hemisphere
> All one great eye, all drown'd in one great tear.

These sermons are, with Donne's, our best memorials of that dense and "witty" style of Jacobean pulpit oratory that did not long survive the triumph of plain prose later in the century. Despite the range of his allusions and his jolting juxtapositions, Andrewes' wit does not consist in surprise or innovation. For the most part his sermons stick to major themes. The Incarnation, the Resurrection, and the workings of the Holy Spirit held for him an endless fascination; and year by year, at the great feasts of the church that he adorned, he progressively explored their meaning and their mystery. Thus in *XCVI Sermons* there are seventeen on Christmas, eighteen on Easter, and fifteen on Whitsuntide (i.e., Pentecost)—as well as eight on the Gowrie conspiracy and ten on the Gunpowder Plot, in compliance with the necessities of Jacobean politics.

The outstanding feature of these sermons is not their style (which is terse and supple and colloquial), but their immense display of mind. Andrewes' intellect reveals itself not only in the unhurried and inexorable deployment of his notions but also in his enormous range of knowledge. As one who mastered fifteen languages, he was noted for his learning in an age when learning was esteemed, and the heavy freight of erudition in his sermons, which baffles or repels most modern readers, must have been a main attraction for his sophisticated listeners in the court of James I—a king whose learning earned for him such sobriquets as the British Solomon and the wisest fool in Christendom. As Andrewes kneads and probes and wrings a text we come to recognize his erudition for what it is: a tool of exegesis, and thus of comprehension. History, philosophy, pagan literature, patristic lore, comparative religions, etymology, grammar—all are brought to bear upon the meaning of the words that constitute the text, and this, as his coreligionist T. S. Eliot said, was the greatest of the bishop's many triumphs—for when Andrewes leads us to the meaning he tries to lead us also to assent.

Following the posthumous publication of *XCVI Sermons* by Bishops Laud and John Buckeridge in 1629 (STC 606, on which my text is based), there appeared such lesser works as *Opuscula quaedam posthuma* (1629), *Institutiones piae*, or *Instructions to Pray* (1630), *A Pattern of Catechistical Doctrine* (1630), the "long expected" *Moral Law Expounded* (1642), the famous *Private Devotions* (1647), and *A Collection of Posthumous and Orphan Lectures* (1657) of questionable authenticity. In 1692 there were added to the canon seventeen sermons that Laud and Buckeridge had excluded, and two more in 1711. The complete works were reprinted in the Library of Anglo-Catholic Theology (11 vols., 1841–54), and there is a convenient selection from the sermons by G. M. Story (1967). *Private Devotions* (i.e., *Preces privatae*, which was translated as early as 1648) has had many editors, among them John Henry Newman (1840) and F. E. Brightman (1903). There are lives by Florence Higham (1952) and P. A. Welsby (1958), and studies of Andrewes' thought by W. H. Frere (1898) and M. R.

Reidy, S.J. (1955). T. S. Eliot's famous essay first appeared in 1928 and was subsequently included in his *Selected Essays* (1932).

from XCVI Sermons (1629)

A Sermon Preached before the King's Majesty at Whitehall on Wednesday, the Twenty-fifth of December, A.D. 1622, Being Christmas Day

Matthew 2, Verses 1–2
Behold, there came Wise Men from the east to Jerusalem saying, Where is the king of the Jews that is born? For we have seen His star in the east, and are come to worship Him.

[*Ecce Magi ab oriente venerunt Jerosolyman dicentes, Ubi est qui natus est rex Judaeorum? Vidimus enim stellam ejus in oriente, et venimus adorare eum.*][1]

There be in these two verses two principal points (as was observed when time was): (1) the persons that arrived at Jerusalem (2) and their errand. The persons in the former verse, whereof hath been treated heretofore;[2] their errand in the latter, wherewith we are now to deal.

Their errand we may best learn from themselves out of their *dicentes*[3] etc., which, in a word, is "to worship him." Their errand, our errand, and the errand of this day.

This text may seem to come a little too soon before the time, and should have stayed till the day it was spoken on rather than on this day.[4] But if you mark them well there are in the verse four words that be *verba diei hujus,* proper and peculiar to this very day. (1) For first, *natus est* is most proper to this day of all days, the day of His nativity. (2) Secondly, *vidimus stellam,* for this day it was first seen, appeared first. (3) Thirdly, *venimus,* for this day they set forth, began their journey. (4) And last, *adorare eum,*[5] for when "He brought His only begotten Son into the world He gave in charge, Let all the angels of God worship Him."[6] And when the angels to do it, no time more proper for us to do it as then. So these four appropriate it to this day, and none but this.

The main heads of their errand are (1) *vidimus stellam,* the occasion; (2) and *venimus adorare,* the end of their coming. But for the better conceiving it I will take another course to set forth these points to be handled.

I. Their faith first: faith in that they never ask whether He be but where He is born, for that born He is, that they steadfastly believe.

II. Then the work, or service of this faith, as St. Paul calleth it;[7] the touch or trial (δοκίμιον), as St. Peter;[8] the *ostende mihi,* as St. James,[9] of this their faith in these five. (1) Their confessing of it in *venerunt dicentes. Venerunt,* they

were no sooner come but *dicentes,* they tell it out: confess Him and His birth to be the cause of their coming. (2) Secondly, as confess their faith, so the ground of their faith: *vidimus enim,* for they had "seen His star," and His star being risen, by it they knew He must be risen too. (3) Thirdly, as St. Paul calls them,[10] in Abraham's *vestigia fidei,* (the steps of their faith), in *venimus,* their coming—coming such a journey, at such a time, with such speed. (4) Fourthly, when they were come their diligent inquiring Him out by *Ubi est?*[11] For here is the place of it, asking after Him to find where He was. (5) And last, when they had found Him, the end of their seeing, coming, seeking, and all for no other end but to worship Him. Here they say it; at the eleventh verse they do it in these two acts: (1) *procidentes,* their falling down, (2) and *obtulerunt,* their offering to Him:[12] worship Him with their bodies, worship Him with their goods—their worship and ours, the true worship of Christ.

The text is of a star; and we may make all run on a star that so the text and day may be suitable, and heaven and earth hold a correspondence. St. Peter calls faith "the daystar rising in our hearts,"[13] which sorts well with the star in the text, rising in the sky: that, in the sky, manifesting itself from above to them; this, in their hearts, manifesting itself from below to Him, to Christ. Manifesting itself by these five: (1) by *ore fit confessio,*[14] the confessing of it; (2) by *fides est substantia,*[15] the ground of it; (3) by *vestigia fidei,* the steps of it in their painful coming; (4) by their *ubi est,* careful

SERMON . . . CHRISTMAS DAY [1]Although Andrewes does not announce the text in Latin he cites it constantly throughout his sermon.
[2]Two years before, in 1620, Andrewes had preached his Christmas sermon on the same text. [3]"Saying."
[4]The text might be more appropriate for Epiphany (January 6), the feast day commemorating the coming of the Magi, than for Christmas.
[5]The Latin phrases mean respectively "He is born," "we have seen the star," "we have come," and "to worship Him."
[6]Hebrews 1.6. [7]Philippians 2.17. [8]1 Peter 1.7.
[9]"Show me" (James 2.18). [10]Romans 4.12. [11]"Where is he?"
[12]The Vulgate (*et procidentes adoraverunt eum; et apertis thesauris suis obtulerunt ei munera*) is rendered in the Authorized Version thus: "and fell down and worshiped Him; and when they had opened their treasures they presented unto Him gifts" (Matthew 2.11). [13]2 Peter 1.19.
[14]"With the mouth confession is made" (Romans 10.10). In citing the Vulgate (no doubt usually from memory), Andrewes is frequently imprecise.
[15]"Now faith is the substance of things hoped for, the evidence of things not seen" (Hebrews 11.1).

inquiring; (5) and last by *adorare eum*, their devout worship-ing. These five as so many beams of faith, the daystar risen in their hearts. To take notice of them: for everyone of them is of the nature of a condition, so as if we fail in them *non lucet nobis stella haec*,[16] we have no part in the light or conduct of this star—neither in *stellam*, the star itself; nor in *ejus*, in Him whose the star is, that is nor in Christ neither.

We have now got us a star on earth for that in heaven, and these both lead us to a third. So as, upon the matter, three stars we have, and each His proper manifestation. (1) The first, in the firmament: that appeared unto them, and in them to us: a figure of St. Paul's Ἐπεφάνη χάρις "the grace of God appearing, and bringing salvation to all men,"[17] Jews and Gentiles and all. (2) The second, here on earth, is St. Peter's *lucifer in cordibus*,[18] and this appeared in them and so must in us. Appeared (1) in their eyes, *vidimus*; (2) in their feet, *venimus*; (3) in their lips, *dicentes, ubi est*; (4) in their knees, *procidentes*, falling down; (5) in their hands, *obtulerunt*, by offering. These five, every one a beam of this star. (3) The third is Christ himself, St. John's star, "the generation and root of David, the bright morning star"[19] Christ. And He, His double appearing: (1) one at this time, now, when He appeared in great humility, and we see and come to Him by faith; (2) the other, which we wait for, even "the blessed hope, and appearing of the great God and our Saviour"[20] in the majesty of His glory.

These three: (1) the first that manifested Christ to them; (2) the second that manifested them to Christ; (3) the third, Christ himself, in whom both these were (as it were) in conjunction:[21] Christ the bright morning star of that day which shall have no night, the *beatifica visio*, the blessed sight of which day is the *consummatum est*[22] of our hope and happi-ness forever.

Of these three stars the first is gone, the third yet to come, the second only is present. We to look to that, and to the five beams of it. That is it must do us all the good, and bring us to the third.

I. Their Faith

St. Luke calleth faith "the door of faith";[23] at this door let us enter. Here is a coming, and he that cometh to God (and so he that to Christ) must believe that Christ is. So do these. They never ask *an sit* but *ubi sit*: not whether but where He is born. They that ask *ubi, qui natus* take *natus* for granted, presuppose that born He is. Herein is faith, faith of Christ's being born, the third article of the Christian creed.[24]

And what believe they of Him? Out of their own words here: (1) first, that *natus*, that born He is, and so man He is: His human nature. (2) And as His nature, so His office: in *natus est rex*, born a king. They believe that too. (3) But *Judaeorum* may seem to be a bar, for then what have they to do with the king of the Jews? They be Gentiles, none of His lieges, no relation to Him at all. What do they seeking or worshiping Him? But weigh it well, and it is no bar. For this they seem to believe: He is so *rex Judaeorum*, king of the Jews, as He is *adorandus a Gentibus*, the Gentiles to adore Him. And though born in Jewry, yet whose birth concerned them though Gentiles. though born far off in the mountains of the

east: they to have some benefit by Him and His birth and for that to do him worship, seeing *officium fundatur in beneficio*[25] ever. (4) As thus born in earth, so a star He hath in heaven of His own, *stellam ejus*, His star, He the owner of it. Now we know the stars are the stars of heaven, and He that Lord of them, Lord of heaven too, and so to be adored of them, of us, and of all. St. John puts them together: "the root and generation of David, His earthly and the bright morning star," His heavenly or divine generation. *Haec est fides Magorum*,[26] this is the mystery of their faith: in *natus est*, man; in *stellam ejus*, God; in *rex*, a king, though of the Jews yet the good of whose kingdom should extend and stretch itself far and wide to Gentiles and all, and He of all to be adored. This for *corde creditur*,[27] the daystar itself in their hearts. Now to the beams of this star.

II. The Work of Their Faith

1. Their Confession: Dicentes

Next to *corde creditur* is *ore fit confessio*, the confession of this faith. It is in *venerunt dicentes*, they came with it in their mouths. *Venerunt*, they were no sooner come but they spake of it so freely to so many as it came to Herod's ear and troubled him not a little that any king of the Jews should be worshiped beside himself. So then their faith is no bosom-faith, kept to themselves without ever a *dicentes*, without saying anything of it to anybody. No: *credidi propter quod locutus sum*, "they believed and therefore they spake."[28] The star in their hearts cast one beam out at their mouths. And though Herod, who was but *rex factus*,[29] could evil brook[30] to hear of *rex natus*,[31] must needs be offended at it, yet they were not afraid to say it. And though they came from the east (those parts to whom and their king the Jews had long time been captives and underlings),[32] they were not ashamed neither to tell that one of the Jews' race they came to seek and to seek Him to the end to worship Him. So neither afraid of Herod nor ashamed of Christ, but professed their errand

[16]"This star does not shine for us."
[17]Titus 2.11. Here and elsewhere Andrewes does not follow the Authorized Version exactly. Oddly enough, for a bishop of the Church of England and as one of the translators of the Authorized Version, he seems customarily to have used the so-called Geneva Bible (1560), which was favored by generations of Puritans.
[18]*Et dies elucescat, et lucifer oriatur in cordibus vestris*: "until the day dawn, and the daystar arise in your hearts" (2 Peter 1.19).
[19]Revelation 22.16.   [20]Titus 2.13.
[21]In astronomy, the position of two heavenly bodies in the same longitude or right ascension.   [22]"It is accomplished."
[23]Acts 14.27.
[24]The Apostles' Creed, whose third article asserts that Christ was "born of the Holy Spirit and the Virgin Mary."
[25]"Favor is found in service."
[26]"This is the faith of the Magi."
[27]"Believed in the heart."   [28]Psalm 116.10.
[29]"Made a king." Herod the Great (73?–4 B.C.), king of Judea at the time of Christ's birth, had been given his office by Antony, Octavius, and the Roman Senate.   [30]Scarcely endure.
[31]"Born a king."
[32]During the Babylonian captivity (597 ff.), when, following the destruction of Jerusalem, the Jews were driven into exile.

and cared not who knew it. This for their confessing Him boldly.

2. THEIR GROUND: VIDIMUS ENIM

But faith is said by the apostle to be ὑπόστασις, and so there is a good ground; and ἔλεγχος, and so hath a good reason for it.[33] This puts the difference between *fidelis* and *credulus*,[34] or (as Solomon terms Him) *fatuus qui credit omni verbo*:[35] between faith and lightness of belief. Faith hath ever a ground—*vidimus enim*, an *enim*,[36] a reason for it—and is ready to render it. How came you to believe? *Audivimus enim*, for we have heard an angel, say the shepherds;[37] *vidimus enim*, for we have seen a star, say the Magi. And this is a well grounded faith. We came not of our own heads;[38] we came not before we saw some reason for it, saw that which set us on coming. *Vidimus enim stellam ejus.*

Vidimus stellam: we can well conceive that any that will but look up may see a star. But how could they see the *ejus* of it, that it was His? Either that it belonged to any or that He it was it belonged to. This passeth all perspective.[39] No astronomy could show them this. What, by course of nature, the stars can produce that they, by course of art or observation, may discover. But this birth was above nature. No trigon, triplicity, exaltation[40] could bring it forth. They are but idle that set figures[41] for it. The star should not have been His, but He the star's, if it had gone that way. Some other light, then, they saw this *ejus* by.

Now with us in divinity there be but two in all: (1) *vespertina* and (2) *matutina lux.*[42] *Vespertina,* the owl-light of our reason or skill is too dim to see it by. No remedy, then, but it must be (as Esai calls it) *matutina lux.* The morning light, the light of God's laws must certify them of the *ejus* of it: there or not at all to be had whom this star did portend.

And in the Law[43] there we find it in the twenty-fourth of Numbers.[44] One of their own prophets that came (from whence they came) from the mountains of the east was ravished in spirit, fell in a trance, had "his eyes opened," and saw the *ejus* of it many an hundred years before it rose. Saw *orietur* in Jacob, that there it should rise, which is as much as *natus est* here. Saw *stella,* that He should be the bright morning star, and so might well have a star to represent Him. Saw *sceptrum* in Israel (which is just as much as *rex Judaeorum*), that it should portend a king there, such a king as should not only "smite the corners of Moab" (that is, Balak their enemy for the present) but should reduce and "bring under Him all the sons of Seth," that is all the world. For all are now Sheth's sons; Cain's were all drowned in the flood. Here now is the *ejus* of it clear. A prophet's eye might discern this; never a Chaldean of them all could take it with his astrolabe. Balaam's eyes were opened to see it, and he helped to open their eyes by leaving behind him this prophecy, to direct them how to apply it (when it should arise) to the right *ejus* of it.

But these had not the Law. It is hard to say that the Chaldee paraphrase[45] was extant long before this. They might have had it. Say they had it not: if Moses were so careful to record this prophecy in his book it may well be thought that some memory of this so memorable a prediction was left remaining among them of the east, his[46] own country where he was born and brought up. And some help they might have from Daniel too, who lived all his time in Chaldea and Persia, and prophesied among them of such a king, and set the just time of it.[47]

And this, as it is conceived, put the difference between the east and the west. For I ask, was it *vidimus in oriente* with them? Was it not *vidimus in occidente?*[48] In the west such a star, it or the fellow of it, was seen nigh about that time, or the Roman stories deceive us. Toward the end of Augustus' reign such a star was seen, and much scanning there was about it. Pliny saith it was generally holden that star to be *faustum sidus,* a lucky comet, and portended good to the world, which few or no comets do.[49] And Vergil (who then lived) would needs take upon him to set down the *ejus* of it; *ecce Dionaei*, etc., entitled Caesar to it.[50] And verily there is no man that can (without admiration) read his fourth[51] eglogue of a birth that time expected, that should be the offspring of the gods, and that should "take away their sins." Whereupon it hath gone for current, the east and west *vidimus*, both.

But by the light of their prophecy, the east, they went straight to the right *ejus*. And for want of this light the west wandered and gave it a wrong *ejus:* as Vergil, applying it to little Salonine, and (as evil hap was) while he was making his verses the poor child died, and so his star shot, vanished, and came to nothing. Their *vidimus* never came to a *veni-*

---

[33]Andrewes refers to Hebrews 11.1, which he had earlier (p. 520) cited in Latin. The Greek words mean respectively "foundation" and "proof."   [34]"Faith and credulity."
[35]"The simple believeth every word" (Proverbs 14.15).
[36]"For," "because."   [37]Luke 2.20.   [38]On our own initiative.
[39]Laws of optics.
[40]*Trigon...exaltation:* astrological jargon. The first two terms (which are synonymous) mean a set of three signs of the zodiac in the shape of an equilateral triangle, and the third refers to that place in the zodiac in which a planet was supposed to exert its greatest influence.   [41]Draw diagrams.   [42]Dusk and daybreak.
[43]The Mosaic code (as distinguished from the Gospel).
[44]The following passage—a typical exercise in typology, whereby the Old Testament is construed as symbolizing, prophesying, or prefiguring events and characters in the New—is based on Numbers 22–24, where it is recorded that the pagan prophet Balaam, sent by Balak, king of Moab, to curse the Israelite invaders, was warned by God not to molest His chosen people, whereupon (much to Balak's irritation) he bestowed a blessing on the Israelites. When the angry king reproved him, Balaam prophesied (Numbers 24.17) that "there shall come a Star out of Jacob, and a scepter shall rise out of Israel, and shall smite the corners of Moab, and destroy all the children of Sheth."
[45]The ancient legend of Balaam's prophecy that was subsequently recorded in the Bible. In biblical times, Chaldea—which was synonymous with the mysterious east—comprised the Tigris and the Euphrates Valley and sometimes Babylonia.   [46]Balaam's.
[47]Andrewes is probably thinking of the apocalyptic vision in Daniel 7.9–14.
[48]"We have seen in the east," "we have seen in the west."
[49]*Natural History,* II.xxiii.
[50]"See! The star of Caesar, descendant of Dione, etc." (Vergil, *Eclogues,* ix.47–49).
[51]Text *sixt*. The allusion is to *Eclogues,* iv.13–14, the so-called Messianic eclogue that, for obvious reasons, was frequently cited by Christian apologists.

mus:[52] they neither went nor worshiped Him, as these here did.

But by this we see, when all is done, hither we must come for our morning light to this book, to the Word of Prophecy. All our *vidimus stellam* is as good as nothing without it. That star is past and gone long since: "heaven and earth shall pass, but this Word shall not pass."[53] Here, on this, we to fix our eye and to ground our faith. Having this, though we neither hear angel nor see star, we may, by the grace of God, do full well. For even they that have had both those have been fain to resolve into this as their last, best, and chiefest point of all. Witness St. Peter: he saith he (and they with him) "saw Christ's glory and heard the voice from heaven in the Holy Mount."[54] What then? After both these—*audivimus* and *vidimus,* both senses—he comes to this: *habemus autem firmiorem,* etc., "we have a more sure Word of Prophecy"[55] than both these; *firmiorum,* a more sure, a more clear than them both. And *si hic legimus* (for *legimus* is *vidimus*), if here we read it written, it is enough to ground our faith and let the star go.

And yet (to end this point) both these, the star and the prophecy, they are but *circumfusa lux:*[56] without, both. Besides these there must be a light within, in the eye; else, we know, for all them nothing will be seen. And that must come from Him and the enlightening of His Spirit. Take this for a rule: no knowing of *ejus absque eo,* of His without Him whose it is. Neither of the star without Him that created it, nor of the prophecy with Him that inspired it. But this third coming too, He sending the light of His Spirit within, into their minds, they then saw clearly this the star, now the time, He the child that this day was born.

He that sent these two without sent also this third within, and then it was *vidimus* indeed. The light of the star in their eyes, the Word of Prophecy in their ears, the beam of His Spirit in their hearts: these three made up a full *vidimus.* And so much for *vidimus stellam ejus,* the occasion of their coming.

3. THEIR COMING: VENIMUS

Now to *venimus,* their coming itself. And it follows well, for it is not a star only but a lodestar. And whither should *stella ejus ducere* but *ad eum?* Whither lead us but to Him whose the star is? The star to the star's master.

All this while we have been at *dicentes,* saying and seeing; now we shall come to *facientes,*[57] see them do somewhat upon it. It is not saying nor seeing will serve St. James: he will call and be still calling for *ostende mihi,* show me thy faith by some work.[58] And well may he be allowed to call for it this day. It is the day of *vidimus,* appearing, being seen. You have seen His star, let Him now see your star another while; and so they do. Make your faith to be seen; so it is: their faith in the steps of their faith. And so was Abraham's first by coming forth of his country. As these here do, and so "walk in the steps of the faith of Abraham,"[59] do his first work.

It is not commended to stand "gazing up into heaven"[60] too long, not on Christ himself ascending, much less on His star. For they sat not still gazing on the star. Their *vidimus* begat *venimus:* their seeing made them come, come a great

journey. *Venimus* is soon said, but a short word, but many a wide and weary step they made before they could come to say *venimus,* Lo here we are come; come, and at our journey's end. To look a little on it. In this their coming we consider: (1) first, the distance of the place they came from. It was not hard by, as the shepherds' (but a step to Bethlehem, over the fields). This was riding many a hundred miles, and cost them many a day's journey. (2) Secondly, we consider the way that they came, if it be pleasant or plain and easy. For if it be, it is so much the better. (1) This was nothing pleasant, for, through deserts, all the way waste and desolate. (2) Nor, secondly, easy neither, for over the rocks and crags of both Arabies[61] (specially Petraea) their journey lay. (3) Yet if safe, but it was not, but exceeding dangerous, as lying through the middest of the Black Tents of Kedar,[62] a nation of thieves and cutthroats; to pass over the hills of robbers infamous then and infamous to this day: no passing without great troop or convoy. (4) Last, we consider the time of their coming, the season of the year. It was no summer progress. A cold coming they had of it at this time of the year, just the worst time of the year to take a journey, and specially a long journey, in. The ways deep, the weather sharp, the days short, the sun farthest off in *solstitio brumali,* the very dead of winter.[63] *Venimus,* we are come, if that be one; *venimus,* we are now come, come at this time: that, sure, is another.

All these difficulties they overcame of a wearisome, irksome, troublesome, dangerous, unseasonable journey; and for all this they came, and came it cheerfully and quickly, as appeareth by the speed they made. It was but *vidimus, venimus* with them: they saw and they came, no sooner saw but they set out presently. So as upon the first appearing of the star (as it might be, last night) they knew it was Balaam's star, it called them away, they made ready straight to begin their journey this morning. A sign, they were highly conceited[64] of His birth, believed some great matter of it that they took all these pains, made all this haste that they might be there to worship Him with all the possible speed they could. Sorry for nothing so much as that they could not be there soon enough, with the very first, to do it even this day, the day of His birth. All considered, there is more in *venimus* than shows at the first sight. It was not for nothing; it was said, in the first verse, *ecce venerunt;* their coming hath an *ecce*[65] on it; it well deserves it.

---

[52]Among the many suggestions concerning the identity of the marvelous child destined to inaugurate the new golden age, whose birth is predicted in Vergil's fourth eclogue, was Saloninus, son of the consul Caius Asinius Pollio, to whom the poem was dedicated.
[53]Luke 21.33.
[54]2 Peter 1.17. The episode that Peter recalls is recorded in Matthew 17.1–8. [55]2 Peter 1.19. [56]"Surrounding light." [57]"Doing."
[58]James 2.18. [59]Romans 4.12. [60]Acts 1.11.
[61]Arabia Felix (the fertile region of the Arabian peninsula) and Arabia Petraea (the rocky, arid region including the wilderness around Mt. Sinai).
[62]The dangerous region inhabited by nomads descended from Kedar, a son of Ishmael (Genesis 25.13).
[63]*A cold coming...winter:* This passage was adapted by T. S. Eliot in his "Journey of the Magi." *Solstitio brumali:* the winter solstice, i.e., December 21. [64]Keenly aware of. [65]"Behold!"

And we, what should we have done? Sure, these men of the east shall "rise in judgment against the men of the west,"[66] that is, us, and their faith against ours in this point. With them it was but *vidimus, venimus;* with us it would have been but *veniemus*[67] at most. Our fashion is to see and see again before we stir a foot, specially if it be to the worship of Christ. Come such a journey at such a time? No, but fairly have put it off to the spring of the year, till the days longer and the ways fairer and the weather warmer, till better traveling to Christ. Our Epiphany[68] would sure have fallen in Easter week at the soonest.

But then for the distance, desolateness, tediousness, and the rest, any of them were enough to mar our *venimus* quite. It must be no great way, first, we must come: we love not that. Well fare the shepherds yet, they came but hard by; rather like them than the Magi. Nay, not like them neither, for with us, the nearer (lightly), the further off. Our proverb is, you know, the nearer the church, the further from God.

Nor it must not be through no desert, over no Petraea. If rugged or uneven the way, if the weather ill disposed, if any never so little danger, it is enough to stay us. To Christ we cannot travel but weather and way and all must be fair. If not, no journey, but sit still and see further. As indeed all our religion is rather *vidimus,* a contemplation, than *venimus,* a motion or stirring to do aught.

But when we do it we must be allowed leisure. Ever *veniemus,* never *venimus;* ever coming, never come. We love to make no very great haste. To other things, perhaps, not to *adorare,* the place of the worship of God. Why should we? Christ is no wild cat. What talk you of twelve days?[69] And it be forty days hence, ye shall be sure to find His mother and Him; she cannot be churched[70] till then. What needs such haste? The truth is, we conceit[71] Him and His birth but slenderly, and our haste is even thereafter. But if we be at that point we must be out of this *venimus:* they like enough to leave us behind. Best, get us a new Christmas in September. We are not like to come to Christ at this feast. Enough for *venimus.*

4. THEIR INQUIRY: UBI EST?

But what is *venimus* with *invenimus?*[72] And when they came they hit not on Him at first. No more must we think, as soon as ever we be come, to find Him straight. They are fain to come to their *ubi est.* We must now look back to that, for though it stand before in the verse, here is the right place of it. They saw before they came, and came before they asked, asked before they found, and found before they worshiped. Between *venimus* (their coming) and *adorare* (their worshiping), there is the true place of *dicentes, ubi est?*

Where, first, we note a double use of their *dicentes* these Wise Men had: (1) As to manifest what they knew, *natus est,* that He is born, so to confess and ask what they knew not, the place, where. We to have the like. (2) Secondly, set down this: that to find where He is we must learn of these to ask where He is, which we full little set ourselves to do. If we stumble on Him, so it is; but for any asking we trouble not ourselves, but sit still (as we say) and let nature work; and so let grace too, and so, for us, it shall. I wot well it is said (in a

place of Esai), He was found *a non quaerentibus,* of some that "sought Him not,"[73] never asked *ubi est?* But it is no good holding by that place. It was their good hap that so did, but trust not to it: it is not everybody's case, that. It is better advice you shall read in the Psalm, *Haec est generatio quaerentium,* "there is a generation of them that seek Him."[74] Of which these were, and of that generation let us be. Regularly, there is no promise of *invenietis,* but to *quaerite;* of finding, but to such as seek. It is not safe to presume to find Him otherwise.

I thought there had been small use, now, of *ubi est,* yet there is, except we hold the ubiquity that Christ is *ubi non,* anywhere. But He is not so. Christ hath His *ubi,* His proper place where He is to be found; and if you miss of that you miss of Him. And well may we miss, saith Christ himself, there are so many will take upon them to tell us where, and tell us of so many *ubi*'s: *ecce hic,* look you, here He is; *ecce illic,* nay then, there; *in deserto,* in the desert; nay, *in penetralibus,*[75] in such a privy conventicle you shall be sure of Him. And yet, He (saith He himself) in none of them all. There is, then, yet place for *ubi est.* I speak not of His natural body, but of His mystical.[76] That is Christ too.

How shall we then do? Where shall we get this *where* resolved? Where these did. They said it to many, and oft, but gat no answer till they had got together a convocation of Scribes,[77] and they resolved them of Christ's *ubi.* For they in the east were nothing so wise or well seen[78] as we in the west are now grown. We need call no Scribes together and get them tell us where. Every artizan hath a whole synod of Scribes in his brain, and can tell where Christ is better than any learned man of them all. Yet these were Wise Men; best learn where they did.

And how did the Scribes resolve it them? Out of Micah.[79] As before, to the star they join Balaam's prophecy, so now again to his *orietur* (that such a one shall be born) they had put Micah's *et tu Bethlehem,* the place of His birth. Still helping and giving light, as it were, to the light of heaven by a more clear light, the light of the sanctuary.

Thus then to do. And to do it ourselves, and not seek Christ *per alium,*[80] set others about it (as Herod did these)[81] and sit still ourselves; for so we may hap never find Him, no more than he did.

5. THEIR END: ADORARE EUM

And now we have found *where,* what then? It is neither in seeking nor finding, *venimus* nor *invenimus,* the end of all.

[66]Matthew 8.11. [67]"We are going to come."
[68]The feast day (January 6) commemorating the manifestation of Christ to the Gentiles as represented by the Magi.
[69]The twelve days between Christmas (the birth of Christ) and the coming of the Magi (Epiphany).
[70]Received and blessed in the church following childbirth.
[71]Esteem. [72]"We find." [73]Isaiah 65.1. [74]Psalm 24.6.
[75]"In inner chambers," i.e., among small and exclusive sects.
[76]Symbolical. Andrewes is referring to the church itself, conceived of as the mystical body of Christ.
[77]Teachers and interpreters of the Mosaic Law, unillumined by the Gospel. [78]Versed, instructed. [79]Micah 5.2.
[80]"Through another." [81]Matthew 2.8.

The cause of all is in the last words, *adorare eum*, to worship Him. That is all in all; and without it all our seeing, coming, seeking, and finding is to no purpose. The Scribes, they could tell, and did tell, *where* He was, but were never the nearer for it, for they worshiped Him not. For this end, to seek Him.

This is acknowledged; Herod, in effect, said as much. He would know where He were, fain, and if they will bring him word where, he will come too and worship Him, that he will. None of that worship: if he find Him, his worship- [10] ing will prove worrying,[82] as did appear by a sort of seely poor lambs[83] that he worried when he could not have his will on Christ. Thus he, at His birth.

And at His death the other Herod, he sought Him too, but it was that he and his soldiers might "make themselves sport" with Him.[84] Such seeking there is otherwhile; and such worshiping, as they in the judgment hall worshiped Him with *Ave Rex*[85] and then gave Him a bob[86] blindfold— the world's worship of Him, for the most part.

But we may be bold to say, "Herod was a fox."[87] These [20] mean as they say: to worship Him they come, and worship Him they will. Will they so? Be they well advised what they promise, before they know whether they shall find Him in a worshipful taking[88] or no? For full little know they where and in what case they shall find Him. What if in a stable, laid there in a manger, and the rest suitable to it, in as poor and pitiful a plight as ever was any, more like to be abhorred than adored of such persons? Will they be as good as their word, trow? Will they not step back at the sight, repent themselves of their journey, and wish themselves at home [30] again? But so find Him, and so finding Him, worship Him for all that? If they will, verily, then, great is their faith. This the clearest beam of all.

The Queen of the South[89] (who was a figure[90] of these kings of the east), she came as great a journey as these, but when she came she found a king indeed, King Solomon in all his royalty. Saw a glorious king and a glorious court about him; saw him and heard him; tried him with many hard questions, received satisfaction of them all. This was worth her coming. Weigh what she found, and what these here: [40] as poor and unlikely a birth as could be ever to prove a king, or any great matter; no sight to comfort them, nor a word for which they any whit the wiser, nothing worth their travel. Weigh these together, and great odds will be found between her faith and theirs. Theirs, the greater far.

Well, they will take Him as they find Him, and all this notwithstanding worship Him for all that. The star shall make amends for the manger, and for *stella ejus* they will dispense with *eum*.

And what is it to worship? Some great matter, sure, it is [50] that heaven and earth, the stars and the prophets thus do but serve to lead them, and conduct us, too. For all, we see, ends in *adorare*. *Scriptura et mundus ad hoc sunt, ut colatur qui creavit, et adoretur qui inspiravit*: the Scripture and world are but to this end, that He that created the one and inspired the other, might be but worshiped. Such reckoning did these seem to make of it here; and such, the Great Treasurer of the Queen Candace.[91] These came from the mountains in the east;

he from the uttermost part of Ethiopia came, and came for no other end but only this, to worship; and when they had done that, home again. *Tanti est adorare.*[92] Worth the while, worth our coming if, coming, we do but that: but worship and nothing else. And so I would have men accompt of it.

To tell you what it is in particular I must put you over to the eleventh verse, where it is set down what they did when they worshiped. It is set down in two acts: $\pi\rho o\sigma\kappa\upsilon\nu\epsilon\hat{\iota}\nu$ and $\pi\rho o\sigma\phi\acute{\epsilon}\rho\epsilon\iota\nu$, falling down and offering. Thus did they; thus we to do: we to do the like when we will worship. These two are all, and more than these we find not.

We can worship God but three ways: we have but three things to worship Him withal: (1) the soul He hath inspired, (2) the body He hath ordained us, (3) and the worldly goods He hath vouchsafed to bless us withal. We to worship Him with all, seeing there is but one reason for all.

If He breathed into[93] us our soul but framed not our body (but some other did that), neither bow your knee nor uncover your head, but keep on your hats and sit even as you do hardly.[94] But if He have framed that body of yours and every member of it, let Him have the honor both of head and knee and every member else.

Again, if it be not He that gave us our worldly goods, but somebody else, what He gave not, that withhold from Him and spare not. But if all come from Him, all to return to Him: if He sent all, to be worshiped with all. And this, in good sooth, is but *rationabile obsequium*,[95] as the apostle calleth it. No more than reason would, we should worship Him withal.

Else if all our worship be inward only, with our hearts and not our hats (as some[96] fondly imagine), we give Him but one of three: we put Him to his thirds,[97] bid Him be content with that, He gets no more but inward worship. That is out of the text quite; for though I doubt not but these here performed that also, yet here it is not. St. Matthew mentions it not; it is not to be seen; no *vidimus* on it. And the text is a *vidimus*, and of a star, that is, of an outward visible worship to be seen of all. There is a *vidimus* upon the worship of the body; it may be seen. *Procidentes*: let us see you fall down. So is there upon the worship with our worldly goods, that may be seen and felt. *Offerentes*: let us see whether and what you offer. With both which, no less than with the soul, God is to be worshiped. "Glorify God with your

[82]Harassing, destroying. The allusion is to Herod's slaughter of the innocents (Matthew 2.16).
[83]*Sort...lambs*: group of helpless babes.
[84]Luke 23.11. The "other Herod" was Herod Antipas, son of Herod the Great and ruler of Judea at the time of Christ's death.
[85]"Hail, king!" [86]Blow with the fist. [87]Luke 13.32.
[88]Condition, plight.
[89]Matthew 12.42, referring to the Queen of Sheba, whose journey to Solomon's court is recorded in 2 Chronicles 12.1–12.
[90]Emblem, type. [91]Acts 8.27.
[92]"Of such importance it is to worship." [93]Literally "inspired."
[94]Hardily, boldly. [95]"Reasonable service" (Romans 12.1).
[96]The Puritans, who objected to the liturgy and formality of the Anglican church.
[97]Restricted Him to only a third part of what is owed.

bodies, for they are God's," saith the apostle.[98] "Honor God with your substance, for He hath blessed your store," saith Solomon.[99] It is the precept of a wise king, of one, there; it is the practice of more than one, of these three, here. Specially now, for Christ hath now a body, for which to do Him worship with our bodies. And now He was made poor to make us rich, and so *offerentes* will do well, comes very fit.

To enter further into these two would be too long, and indeed they be not in our verse here, and so for some other treatise at some other time.

There now remains nothing but to include ourselves, and bear our part with them and with the angels and all who this day adored Him.

THE APPLICATION

This was the lodestar of the Magi, and what were they? Gentiles; so are we. But if it must be ours, then we are to go with them: *vade et fac similiter,* "go and do likewise."[1] It is *stella gentium* but *idem agentium:*[2] the Gentiles' star, but such Gentiles as overtake these and keep company with them. In their *dicentes* confessing their faith freely; in their *vidimus* grounding it thoroughly, in their *venimus* hasting to come to Him speedily, in their *ubi est* inquiring Him out diligently, and in their *adorare eum* worshiping Him devoutly: *per omnia* doing as these did—worshiping and thus worshiping, celebrating and thus celebrating the feast of His birth.

We cannot say *vidimus stellam.* The star is gone long since, not now to be seen. Yet I hope for all that that *venimus adorare,* we be come hither to worship. It will be the more acceptable if, not seeing it, we worship though. It is enough we read of it in the text; we see it there; and indeed, as I said, it skills not for the star in the firmament if the same daystar be risen in our hearts that was in theirs, and the same beams of it to be seen, all five. For then we have our part in it no less—nay, full out as much as they. And it will bring us whither it brought them, to Christ, who at His second appearing in glory shall call forth these Wise Men and all those that have ensued[3] the steps of their faith, and that upon the reason specified in the text. For I have seen their star shining and showing forth itself by the like beams, and as they came to worship me, so am I come to do them worship. A *venite*[4] then for a *venimus* now. Their star I have seen, and give them a place above, among the stars. They fell down; I will lift them up and exalt them. And as they offered to me, so am I come to bestow on them, and to reward them with the endless joy and bliss of my heavenly kingdom. To which, etc.

[98]1 Corinthians 6.20. [99]Proverbs 3.9.
[1]Luke 10.37.
[2]It is the star of the Gentiles, but only of such Gentiles as emulate the Magi. [3]Followed in.
[4]"Come!" (the first word of Psalm 95: *Venite, exsultemus Domino:* "O come, let us sing unto the Lord").

Joseph Hall[1] [1574-1656]

Thomas Fuller's swift assessment of Joseph Hall's immense production—"not unhappy at controversies, more happy at comments, very good in his characters, better in his sermons, best of all in his meditations"—suggests something his range and versatility, and also of his service to the Church of England in its most embattled period. The son of a formidably pious mother who, as he recalled, was "oft" afflicted with a "wounded spirit," Hall was also a product of Emmanuel College, Cambridge (B.A. 1592, M.A. 1596, B.D. 1603, D.D. 1612), a fertile seedbed of dissent, and therefore he might have been expected to turn into a Puritan. Instead, he became an adornment of the Jacobean church, and in the course of a long and active life wrote so many works in verse and prose that *The British Museum Catalogue of Printed Books* requires six double-column pages just to list their titles.

As a young man with an eye for human foibles he—like Marston, Donne, and others—progressed from verse satire (*Virgidemiarum,* 1597–98) to holy orders, but his priestly duties, first in Suffolk and then at Waltham Holy Cross in Essex, did not prevent his writing. As a consequence he soon was in a small way famous for his prose, which in its jerky wit and terseness—to say nothing of its Christian Stoicism—earned for him the sobriquet of the "English Seneca." By 1606 he

[1]For other work of Joseph Hall, see Books and Men, pp. 711 ff.

had published *Mundus alter et idem* (a utopian prose satire in Latin), three "centuries" of moral aphorisms called *Meditations and Vows* (pp. 528 ff.), and the devotional *Heaven upon Earth*. These were followed two years later by the first of several volumes of *Epistles* and by the famous *Characters of Virtues and Vices* (pp. 713 ff.), a depiction of contrasting ethical types (the wise man and the malcontent, the honest man and the flatterer, and so on) inspired by Theophrastus. Meanwhile he was also thriving in the church. His appointment (1608) as chaplain to the Prince of Wales led to other things, including several foreign missions and appointment (1616) as the dean of Worcester. In 1618 James sent him as his representative to the Synod of Dort, where he scored a marked success, and for almost forty years thereafter—as preacher, controversialist, and ecclesiastical politician—he followed the great wheel of his church with indefatigable devotion.

In the welter of official duties as troubleshooter for two Stuart monarchs and as bishop of Exeter (1627) and Norwich (1641), his prose poured forth in torrents. Among many other works he produced eight volumes of *Contemplations* on the Bible (1612–26), *An Explication by Way of Paraphrase of All the Hard Texts in the Old and New Testaments* (1633), several dozen published sermons, and enough disputatious prose about Catholics, Puritans, and other adversaries of his church to fatigue the most devoted Anglican. Skirting the vast expanse of his meditative, exegetical, and homiletic writings, the modern reader may glimpse the veteran controversialist in his *Humble Remonstrance* (1640). It is important not only as a careful statement of the Anglican position just before the civil war but also as the work that stirred young Milton's wrath and prompted a rebuttal (p. 258).

Like many of his generation, Hall lived to see his cause defeated and himself go down in ruin. In December 1641 he, together with eleven of his brethren, was charged with treason and committed to the Tower, but he could and would not change his views. "I have unpartially ransacked this fag-end of my life and curiously examined every step of my ways," he told a sympathetic friend, "and I cannot, by the most exact scrutiny of my saddest thoughts, find what it is that I have done to forfeit that good estimation wherewith you say I was once blessed." Following his conviction of a charge of praemunire and the forfeiture of his estate he made his way to Norwich, but there more trouble waited: the spoliation of his household goods, the sack of his cathedral, and his own ejection from the bishop's palace. After these tumultuous events, which he himself recorded in a pamphlet called *Hard Measure* (1647), he and his family finally found repose in Higham, a village west of Norwich. There, though stripped of all his functions, he could not be kept from writing, and he wrote until he died (attended by his friend and townsman Thomas Browne) at eighty-two. "Few men of his age have ascended so high upon Jacob's ladder as he did," the preacher at his funeral said; "he was one that, with Israel, lived and died in a Goshen of light in the midst of Egyptian darkness."

My texts are based upon *Meditations and Vowes Diuine and Morall. Serving For direction in Christian and Ciuill practice. Diuided into two Bookes: By Jos. Hall*, 1606 (STC 12680), and *An Humble Remonstrance*, 1640 (STC 12675). Despite its title page, *Meditations and Vows* contains three books or "centuries" of meditations. Hall's voluminous works were edited by Phillip Wynter (10 vols., 1863), the poems alone by A. B. Grosart (1879) and Arnold Davenport (1959). There is an old biography by George Lewis (1886) and an unsatisfactory newer one by T. F. Kinloch (1951). Hall the ecclesiastical politician is treated by many of the writers cited in the General Bibliography, Section III; his sermons and theology have been discussed by Mitchell and McAdoo (as listed in the General Bibliography, Section III), and the innovations of his prose by George Williamson (*The Senecan Amble*, 1951), R. F. Jones, and others. Inevitably, he receives a good deal of attention in W. R. Parker's *Milton's Contemporary Reputation* (1940) and in such books as Barker's and Wolfe's (General Bibliography, Section III) on Milton as a controversialist. For works about his characters and essays see p. 711.

from Meditations and Vows, Divine and Moral (1606)

TO THE RIGHT WORSHIPFUL SIR ROBERT DRURY,[1]
KNIGHT, MY SINGULAR GOOD PATRON, ALL
INCREASE OF TRUE HONOR AND VIRTUE

Sir, that I have made these my homely aphorisms public needs no other reason but that though the world is furnished with other writings even to satiety and surfeit, yet of those which reduce[2] Christianity to practice there is at least scarcity enough; wherein yet, I must needs confess, I had some eye to myself, for having after a sort vowed this austere course of judgment and practice to myself, I thought it best to acquaint the world with it, that it may either witness my answerable proceeding[3] or check me in my straying therefrom. By which means, so many men as I live amongst, so many monitors I shall have, which shall point me to my own rules and upbraid me with my aberrations. Why I have dedicated them to your name cannot be strange to any that knows you my patron and me your pastor. The regard of which bond easily drew me on to consider that whereas my body, which was ever weak, began of late to languish more, it would be not inexpedient, at the worst, to leave behind me this little monument of that great respect which I deservedly bear you. And if it shall please God to reprieve me until a longer day,[4] yet it shall not repent me to have sent this unworthy scroll to wait upon you in your necessary absence. Neither shall it be, I hope, bootless for you to adjoin these my mean speculations unto those grounds of virtue you have so happily laid, to which if they shall add but one scruple[5] it shall be to me sufficient joy, content, recompense. From your Halsted, Decemb[er] 4, [1605?].

> *Your Worship's humbly devoted*
> *Jos. Hall*

THE FIRST BOOK, CONTAINING A FULL CENTURY OF MEDITATIONS AND VOWS, BOTH DIVINE AND MORAL

1

In meditation, those which begin heavenly thoughts and prosecute them not are like those which kindle a fire under green wood and leave it so soon as it but begins to flame, losing the hope of a good beginning for want of seconding it with a suitable proceeding. When I set myself to meditate I will not give over till I come to an issue. It hath been said by some that the beginning is as much as the midst, yea, more than all; but I say the ending is more than the beginning.

14

I am a stranger even at home; therefore if the dogs of the world bark at me I neither care nor wonder.

19

I will not care what I have, whether much or little. If little, my account shall be the less; if more, I shall do the more good and receive the more glory.

100

Many vegetable and many brute creatures exceed man in length of age, which hath opened the mouths of heathen philosophers to accuse Nature as a step-mother to man, who hath given him the least time to live that only could make use of his time in getting knowledge. But herein religion doth most magnify God in His wisdom and justice, teaching us that other creatures live long and perish to nothing; only man recompenses the shortness of his life with eternity after it, that the sooner he dies well, the sooner he comes to perfection of knowledge, which he might in vain seek below; the sooner he dies ill, the less hurt he doth with his knowledge. There is great reason, then, why man should live long, greater why he should die early. I will never blame God for making me too soon happy, for changing my ignorance for knowledge, my corruption for immortality, my infirmities for perfection. Come, Lord Jesus, come quickly.

THE SECOND BOOK

30

The world is a stage; every man an actor, and plays his part here either in a comedy or tragedy. The good man is a comedian, which, however he begins, ends merrily; but the wicked man acts a tragedy, and therefore even ends in horror. Thou seest a wicked man vaunt himself on his stage; stay till the last act and look to his end, as David did,[6] and see whether that be peace. Thou wouldst make strange tragedies if thou wouldst have but one act. Who sees an ox, grazing in a fat[7] and rank pasture, and thinks not that he is near to the slaughter? Whereas the lean beast that toils under the yoke is far enough from the shambles. The best wicked man

---

MEDITATIONS [1]Sir Robert Drury (d. 1615)—who survives in literary history mainly through his friendship with Donne (see p. 75) —had at his wife's instigation appointed Hall to the somewhat meager living at Halsted (or Hawstead) Place, his family's ancient seat in Suffolk, in 1601. Despite the warmth of this dedication, relations between the two men subsequently became strained as a consequence of Sir Robert's parsimony.
[2]Lead back (a Latinism).
[3]My behavior in the light of these precepts.
[4]Hall survived the writing of this book by some fifty years.
[5]Minute quantity. [6]Psalms 37.37–38. [7]Fertile.

cannot be so envied in his first shows as he is pitiable in the conclusion.

76[8]

I have wondered oft, and blushed for shame, to read in mere philosophers, which had no other mistress but Nature, such strange resolution in the contempt of both fortunes,[9] as they call them; such notable precepts for a constant settledness and tranquillity of mind; and to compare it with my own disposition and practice, whom I have found too much drooping and dejected under small crosses, and easily again carried away with little prosperity: to see such courage and strength to contemn death in those which thought they wholly perished in death, and to find such faintheartedness in myself at the first conceit of death, who yet am thoroughly persuaded of the future happiness of my soul. I have the benefit of Nature as well as they, besides infinite more helps that they wanted. O the dulness and blindness of us unworthy Christians that suffer heathens, by the dim candlelight of Nature, to go further than we by the clear sun of the Gospel, that an indifferent man could not tell by our practice whether[10] were the pagan! Let me never, for shame, account myself a Christian unless my art of Christianity have imitated and gone beyond Nature so far that I can find the best heathen as far below me in true resolution as the vulgar sort were below them. Else I may shame religion; it can neither honest[11] nor help me.

82

A faithful man hath three eyes: the first of sense, common to him with brute creatures; the second of reason, common to all men; the third of faith, proper to his profession; whereof each looketh beyond other, and none of them meddleth with others' objects. For neither doth the eye of sense reach to intelligible things and matters of discourse, nor the eye of reason to those things which are supernatural and spiritual; neither doth faith look down to things that may be sensibly seen. If thou discourse to a brute beast of the depths of philosophy never so plainly, he understands not, because they are beyond the view of his eye, which is only of sense; if to a mere carnal man of divine things, he perceiveth not the things of God, neither indeed can do, because they are spiritually discerned; and therefore no wonder if those things seem unlikely, incredible, impossible to him which the faithful man, having a proportionable means of apprehension, doth as plainly see as his eye doth any sensible thing. Tell a plain countryman that the sun, or some higher or lesser star, is much bigger than his cartwheel, or at least so many scores bigger than the whole earth, he laughs thee to scorn as affecting admiration with a learned untruth. Yet the scholar, by the eye of reason, doth as plainly see and acknowledge this truth as that his hand is bigger than his pen. What a thick mist, yea what a palpable and more than Egyptian darkness,[12] doth the natural man live in! What a world is there that he doth not see at all! And how little doth he see in this which is his proper element! There is no bodily thing but the brute creatures see as well as he, and

some of them better. As for his eye of reason, how dim is it in those things which are best fitted to it! What one thing is there in nature which he doth perfectly know? What herb, or flower, or worm that he treads on is there whose true essence he knoweth? No, not so much as what is in his own bosom, what it is, where it is, or whence it is that gives being to himself. But for those things which concern the best world, he doth not so much as confusedly see them, neither knoweth whether they be. He sees no whit into the great and awful majesty of God. He discerns Him not in all His creatures, filling the world with His infinite and glorious presence. He sees not His wise providence overruling all things, disposing all casual events, ordering all sinful actions of men to His own glory. He comprehends nothing of the beauty, majesty, power, and mercy of the Saviour of the world, sitting in His humanity at His Father's right hand. He sees not the unspeakable happiness of the glorified souls of the saints. He sees not the whole heavenly commonwealth of angels, ascending and descending to the behoof of God's children, waiting upon Him at all times invisibly, not excluded with that closeness[13] of prisons nor desolateness of wildernesses; and the multitude of evil spirits passing and standing by him to tempt him unto evil; but like unto the foolish bird when he hath hid his head that he sees nobody, he thinks himself altogether unseen, and then counts himself solitary when his eye can meet with no companion. It was not without cause that we call a mere fool a natural, for however worldlings have still thought Christians God's fools, we know them the fools of the world. The deepest philosopher that ever was (saving the reverence of the schools) is but an ignorant sot to the simplest Christian; for the weakest Christian may, by plain information, see somewhat into the greatest mysteries of Nature, because he hath the eye of reason common with the best; but the best philosopher, by all the demonstration in the world, can conceive nothing of the mysteries of godliness, because he utterly wants the eye of faith. Though my insight into matters of the world be so shallow that my simplicity moveth pity, or maketh sport unto others, it shall be my contentment and happiness that I see further into better matters. That which I see not is worthless, and deserves little better than contempt; that which I see is unspeakable, inestimable, for comfort, for glory.

A THIRD CENTURY

10

The eldest of our forefathers lived not so much as a day to[14] God, to whom a thousand years is as no more; we live but as an hour to the day of our forefathers, for if nine hundreth and sixty were but their day,[15] our fourscore is but as the

---

[8]Text *79.* [9]Good and bad. [10]Which. [11]Excuse, justify.
[12]Exodus 10.21–23. [13]Confinement. [14]Compared to.
[15]Hall is apparently generalizing on the vital statistics of the patriarchs (Genesis 5), of whom Methuselah, at 969, was the longest lived. *Hundreth*: hundred.

twelfth part of it. And yet of this our hour we live scarce a minute to God; for take away all that time that is consumed in sleeping, dressing, feeding, talking, sporting; of that little time there can remain not much more than nothing; yet the most seek pastimes to hasten it. Those which seek to mend the pace of time spur a running horse. I had more need to redeem it with double care and labor than to seek how to sell it for nothing.

14

Our infancy is full of folly, youth of disorder and toil, age of infirmity. Each time hath his burden, and that which may justly work our weariness; yet infancy longeth after youth, and youth after more age; and he that is very old, as he is a child for simplicity, so he would be for years. I account old age the best of three,[16] partly for that it hath passed through the folly and disorder of the other, partly for that the inconveniences of this are but bodily, with a bettered estate of the mind, and partly for that it is nearest to dissolution. There is nothing more miserable than an old man that would be young again. It was an answer worthy the commendations of Petrarch,[17] and that which argued a mind truly philosophical of him, who, when his friend bemoaned his age appearing in his white temples, telling him he was sorry to see him look so old, replied, "Nay, be sorry rather that ever I was young, to be a fool."

56

He can never wonder enough at God's workmanship that knows not the frame of the world, for he can never else conceive of the hugeness and strange proportion of the creatures. And he that knows this can never wonder more at anything else. I will learn to know that I may admire, and by that little I know I will more wonder at that I know not.

57

There is nothing below but toiling, grieving, wishing, hoping, fearing—and weariness in all these. What fools are we to be besotted with the love of our own trouble, and to hate our liberty and rest! The love of misery is much worse than misery itself. We must first pray that God would make us wise before we can wish He would make us happy.

98[18]

Earth, which is the basest element, is both our mother that brought us forth, our stage that bears us alive, and our grave wherein at last we are entombed; giving to us both our original, our harbor, our sepulcher. She hath yielded her back to bear thousands of generations, and at last opened her womb to receive them, so swallowing them up that she still both beareth more and looks for more, not bewraying any change in herself while she so oft hath changed her brood and her burden. It is a wonder we can be proud of our parentage or of ourselves while we see both the baseness and stability of the earth whence we came. What difference is there? Living earth treads upon the dead earth, which afterwards descends into the grave as senseless and dead as the earth that receives it. Not many are proud of their souls, and none but fools can be proud of their bodies. While we walk and look upon the earth we cannot but acknowledge sensible admonitions of humility, and while we remember them, we cannot forget ourselves. It is a motherlike favor of the earth that she bears and nourishes me, and at the last entertains my dead carcass; but it is a greater pleasure that she teacheth me my vileness by her own, and sends me to heaven for what she wants.

An Humble Remonstrance to the High Court of Parliament by a Dutiful Son of the Church (1640)

Most Honorable Lords; and ye, the Knights, Citizens, and Burgesses of the Honorable House of Commons

Lest the world should think the press had of late forgot to speak any language other than libelous, this honest paper hath broken through the throng, and prostrates itself before you. How meanly soever and unattended it presents itself to your view, yet it comes to you on a great errand, as the faithful messenger of all the peaceable and right affected sons of the Church of England, and in their names humbly craves a gracious admittance. Had it regarded the pomp and ostentation of names, it might have gloried in a train past number. It is but a poor stock that may be counted. Millions of hands, if that tumultuary and underhand way of procured subscriptions could have reason to hope for favor in your eyes, shall at your least command give attestation to that which this scroll doth in their names humbly tender unto you.

Ye are now happily, through God's blessing, met in a much longed-for Parliament.[1] It were but a narrow word, to say that the eyes of all us, the good subjects of the whole realm, are fixed upon your success. Certainly there are not more eyes in these three interested kingdoms than are now bent upon you: yea, all the neighbour churches and kingdoms, if I may not say the whole Christian world, and no small part beyond it, look wishly[2] upon your faces, and with stretched-out necks gaze at the issue of your great meeting. Neither doubt we, but since sovereign authority hath for this purpose both summoned and actuated you, you will not fail to produce something worthy of so high an expectation.

Ye are the sanctuary whereto now every man flees, whether really or pretendedly distressed. Even a Joab or Adonijah will be also taking hold of the horns of the altar.[3] Your

---

[16]Hall himself was 31 at the time.

[17]Italian poet and humanist (1304–74).

[18]Actually 99, the printer having used 86 for two adjacent paragraphs. The third "century" actually contains 101 items.

AN HUMBLE REMONSTRANCE [1]Eleven years after proroguing his third Parliament in 1629, Charles reluctantly convened the so-called Long Parliament in November 1640. [2]Wishfully.

[3]When King David's treacherous sons Joab and Adonijah were exposed as political conspirators and sought refuge by grasping the horns of the altar in the sanctuary, the former was slain, whereas the latter was spared. See 1 Kings 1.50–53, 2.28–34.

noble wisdoms know how to distinguish of men and actions; and your inviolable justice knows to award each his own.

Many things there are doubtless which you find worthy of a seasonable reformation, both in church and state. Neither can it be otherwise, but that in a pampered full body diseases will grow through rest. Ponds that are seldom scoured will easily gather mud; metals rust; and those patients that have inured themselves to a set course of medicinal evacuations, if they intermit their springs and falls, fall into feverous distempers.

Not that supreme and immediately subordinate authority hath in the meantime been wanting to its charge. Surely, unless we would suppose princes to be gods, we cannot think they can know all things. Of necessity they must look with others' eyes, and hear with others' ears, and be informed by others' tongues, and act by others' hands; and when all is done, even the most regular and carefully inquisitive state is not like the sun, from whose light and heat nothing is hid.

It cannot be expected that those constellations which attend the southern pole should take view of our hemisphere, or intermix their influences with those above our heads. Every agent is required and allowed to work within the compass of its own activity. Ye therefore who, by the benefit of your dispersed habitations, enjoy the advantage of having the whole kingdom and all the corners of it within your eyes, may both clearly see all those enormities wherewith any part is infested, unknown to remoter intelligence, and can best judge to apply meet remedies thereunto. Neither can it be but that those eyes of yours, which have been privately vigilant within the places of your several abodes, must needs, not without much regret, in this your public meeting take notice of the miserable disorders of so many vicious and misaffected persons as have thrust themselves upon your cognizance.

Whiles the orthodox part in this whole realm hath, to the praise of their patience, been quietly silent, as securely conscious of their own right and innocence, how many furious and malignant spirits everywhere have burst forth into sclanderous libels, bitter pasquins, railing pamphlets under which more presses than one have groaned, wherein they have endeavoured, through the sides of some misliked persons, to wound that sacred government which by the joint confession of all reformed divines derives itself from the times of the blessed apostles without any interruption, without the contradiction of any one congregation in the Christian world, unto this present age.

Wherein, as no doubt their lewd boldness hath been extremely offensive to your wisdoms and piety, so may it please you to check this daring and misgrounded insolence of these libelers, and by some speedy declaration to let the world know how much you detest this their malicious or ignorant presumption, and by some needful act to put a present restraint upon the wild and lawless courses of all their factious combinations abroad and enterprises of this kind.

And if you find it pass for one of the main accusations against some great persons now questioned before you that they endeavored to alter the form of the established government of the commonwealth, how can these pamphleteers seem worthy of but an easy censure, which combine their counsels and practices for the changing of the settled form of the government of the church? Since, if antiquity may be the rule, the civil polity hath sometimes varied; the sacred, never. And if original authority may carry it, that came from arbitrary imposers; this from men inspired, and from them in an unquestionable clearness derived to us. And if those be branded for incendiaries which are taxed of attempting to introduce new forms of administration and rules of divine worship into our neighbour church, how shall those *boutefeux*[4] of ours escape, that offer to do these offices to our own? The several and daily variable projects whereof are not worthy of your knowledge or our confutation.

Let me have leave to instance in two, the prime subjects of their quarrel and contradiction: liturgy and episcopacy.

The liturgy of the Church of England hath been hitherto esteemed sacred, reverently used by holy martyrs, daily frequented by devout Protestants, as that which more than once hath been allowed and confirmed by the edicts of religious princes, and by your own parliamentary acts, and but lately being translated into other languages, hath been entertained abroad with the great applause of foreign divines and churches; yet now begins to complain of scorn at home.

The matter is quarreled[5] by some, the form by others, the use of it by both.

That which was never before heard of in the church of God, whether Jewish or Christian, the very prescription of the most holy devotion offendeth. Surely our blessed Saviour and his gracious forerunner[6] were so far from this new divinity as that they plainly taught that which these men gainsay, a direct form of prayer, and such as that part of the frame prescribed by our Saviour was composed of the forms of devotion then formerly usual. And God's people, ever since Moses his days, constantly practised it, and put it over unto the times of the Gospel under which, whiles it is said that Peter and John went up to the temple at the ninth hour of prayer,[7] we know the prayer wherewith they joined was not of an extemporary and sudden conception, but of a regular prescription, the forms whereof are yet extant and ready to be produced. And the evangelical church ever since thought it could never better improve her peace and happiness than in composing those religious models of invocation and thanksgiving which they have traduced[8] unto us.

And can ye then with patience think that any ingenuous Christian should be so far mistransported as to condemn a good prayer because as it is in his heart, so it is in his book too?

Far be it from me to dishearten any good Christian from the use of conceived prayer in his private devotions, and upon occasion also in the public. I would hate to be guilty of pouring so much water upon the Spirit, to which I shall gladly add oil rather. No, let the full soul freely pour out itself in gracious expressions of its holy thoughts into the bosom of the Almighty. Let both the sudden flashes of our quick ejaculations and the constant flames of our more fixed con-

---

[4]"Firebrands." [5]Contested. [6]John the Baptist. [7]Acts 3.1. [8]Transmitted.

ceptions mount up from the altar of a zealous heart unto the throne of grace; and if there be some stops or solecisms in the fervent utterance of our private wants, these are so far from being offensive that they are the most pleasing music to the ears of that God unto whom our prayers come. Let them be broken off with sobs and sighs and incongruities of our delivery, our good God is no otherwise affected to this imperfect elocution than an indulgent parent is to the clipped and broken language of his dear child, which is more delightful to him than any other's smooth oratory. This is not to be opposed in another, by any man that hath found the true operation of this grace in himself.

But in the meantime let the public forms of the sacred church liturgy have its due honour. Let this by the power of your authority be reinforced, as that which, being selected out of ancient models (not Roman, but Christian) and contrived by the holy martyrs and confessors of the blessed reformation of religion, hath received abundant supply of strength, both from the zealous recommendation of four most religious princes[9] and your own most firm and peremptory establishment.[10]

Amongst which powerful inducements that is worthy of no slight consideration which I humbly tender unto you from the judgment of the learnedest king that ever sat upon this throne, or, as I verily think, since Solomon's time, upon any other: King James of blessed memory, who, however misalleged[11] by some as letting fall disgraceful speeches concerning this subject, after a solemn hearing of those exceptions which were taken by some against this open form of common prayer (as it is called in Queen Elizabeth's act for uniformity),[12] shuts up in his proclamation, given at Westminster the fifth of March, in the first year of his reign, with these words: "And last of all, we admonish all men that hereafter they shall not expect or attempt any farther alteration in the common and public form of God's service from this which is now established; for that neither will we give way to any to presume that our own judgment, having determined in a matter of this weight, shall be swayed to alteration by the frivolous suggestion of any light spirit, neither are we ignorant of the inconveniences that do arise in government by admitting innovation in things once settled by mature deliberation and how necessary it is to use constancy in the upholding of the public determinations of states; for that such is the unquietness and unsteadfastness of some dispositions, affecting every year new forms of things, as if they should be followed in their inconstancy would make all actions of state ridiculous and contemptible; whereas the steadfast maintaining of things by good advice established is the weal of all commonwealths."[13]

Thus that great oracle of wisdom and learning, whom, I beseech you, suppose that you still hear directing this prudent and religious advice to your present ears; and consider how requisite it is for you, out of the reason both of state[14] and piety, to rest in that his sound and exquisite judgment.

As for those particularities of exceptions which have been taken by some at certain passages of that book,[15] they have more than once received full satisfaction by other pens. Let me only say thus much, that were the readers but as charitable

as the contrivers were religiously devout, those quarrels had either never been raised or had soon died alone.

O suffer not then, I beseech you, this holy form of God's service to be exposed to the proud contempt of ignorant and ill affected persons. Maintain and bear up the pious acts of your godly predecessors; yea, make good your own. And if our holy martyrs heretofore went to heaven with a litany in their mouth, let not an ill advised new-fangledness be suffered to put scorn upon that wherein they thought themselves happy.

As for that form of episcopal government which hath hitherto obtained in the church of God, I confess I am confounded in myself to hear with what unjust clamors it is cried down abroad by either weak or factious persons, of either or both which I may well take up that word of our Saviour, "Father forgive them, for they know not what they do."[16] Surely could those look with my eyes, they would see cause to be thoroughly ashamed of this their injurious misconceit,[17] and should be forced to confess that never any good cause had more reason to complain of a wrongful prosecution.

Were this ordinance merely human and ecclesiastical if there could no more be said for it but that it is exceeding ancient, of more than fifteen hundred years standing, and that it hath continued in this island since the first plantation of the Gospel to this present day without contradiction, a man would think this were enough plea to challenge a reverent respect, and an immunity from all thoughts of alteration; for even nature itself teaches us to rise up before the hoar head, and hath wrought in us a secret honor even to the very outward gravity of age; and just policy teaches us not easily to give way to the change of those things which long use and many laws have firmly established as necessary or beneficial.

Yea, the wisdom of the ancient Grecians went so far as to forbid the removal of a well settled evil. But if religion teach us better things, and tell us that nothing morally evil can be settled well, and being however settled had the more need to be after too long delay removed, yet right reason and sound experience inform us that things indifferent[18] or good,

[9]Edward VI (who sponsored the first version of the Book of Common Prayer in 1549), Elizabeth, James I, and Charles I.
[10]Decisive legislation.   [11]Falsely cited.
[12]Elizabeth's first Parliament (1559) passed the so-called Act of Uniformity, prescribing compulsory use of the Book of Common Prayer that had been promulgated by Edward VI and suppressed by Mary.
[13]At a conference at Hampton Court James and some of his bishops met with spokesmen for the Puritans to discuss the demands set forth in the so-called Millenary Petition that had been presented to the new king on his progress from Edinburgh to London. The abortive conference, which prompted James' famous maxim "No bishop, no king," resulted only in a strong assertion of compulsory conformity to the prayerbook and subscription to the Thirty-nine Articles, and thus was galling to the Puritans.
[14]Political necessity.   [15]The Book of Common Prayer.
[16]Luke 23.34.   [17]Misconception.
[18]Liturgical, vestiarian, and disciplinary practices that, though not prescribed by Scripture and therefore not essential for salvation,

having been by continuance and general approbation well rooted in church or state, may not upon light grounds be pulled up.

But this holy calling fetches its pedigree higher, even from no less than apostolical (and therefore in that right divine) institution. For although those things which the founders and prime governors of the evangelical church did as men went no farther than their own persons, yet what they did as apostles is of an higher and more sacred consideration; and if, as apostolic men, they did upon occasion enact some temporary things which were to die with or before them; yet those things which they ordained for the succeeding administration of the church which they should leave behind them, in all essential matters, can be no otherwise construed than as exemplary and perpetual.

Now if to this text we shall add the undoubted commentary of the apostles' own practices, and to this commentary we shall superadd the unquestionable gloss of the clear practice of their immediate successors in this administration continued in Christ's church to this very day, what scruple can remain in any ingenuous heart?

But if any one resolve to continue unsatisfied in spite of reason and all evidence of history, and will wilfully shut his eyes with a purpose not to see the light, that man is past my cure, and almost my pity. The good God of heaven be merciful to such a miszealous obstinacy!

Certainly, except all histories, all authors, fail us, nothing can be more plain than this truth. Out of them we can and do show on whom the apostles of Christ laid their hands, with an acknowledgment and conveyance of imparity[19] and jurisdiction; we show what bishops so ordained lived in the times of the apostles, and succeeded each other in their several charges under the eyes and hands of the then living apostles; we show who immediately succeeded those immediate successors in their several sees throughout all the regions of the Christian church, and deduce their uninterrupted line through all the following ages to this present day. And if there can be better evidence under heaven for any matter of fact (and in this cause matter of fact so derived evinceth matter of right) let episcopacy be for ever abandoned out of God's church. But if these be, as they are, certain and irrefragable, alas, what strange fury possesseth the minds of ignorant, unstable men, that they should thus headily desire and sue to shake off so sacred and well grounded an institution?

But I hear what they say. It is not the office of episcopacy that displeases, but the quality. The Apostles' bishops and ours were two. Theirs was no other than a parochial pastor, a preaching presbyter, without inequality, without any rule over his brethren: ours claims an eminent superiority, whether in a distinct order or degree, and a power of ordination, jurisdiction, unknown to the primitive times.

Alas, alas, how good people may be abused by misinformation! Hear, I beseech you, the words of truth and confidence. If our bishops challenge any other spiritual power than was by apostolic authority delegated unto and required of Timothy and Titus,[20] and the angels of the seven Asian churches[21] (some whereof are known to us by name),

let them be disclaimed as usurpers; and if we do not show out of the genuine and undeniable writings of those holy men, which lived both in the times of the apostles and some years after them, and conversed with them as their blessed fellow-laborers, a clear and received distinction both of the names and offices of the bishops, presbyters, and deacons as three distinct subordinate callings in God's church with an evident specification of the duty and charge belonging to each of them, let this claimed hierarchy be for ever hooted out of the church. And if the bounty of religious princes have thought meet to grace this sacred function with some accession of titles and maintenance, far be it from us to think that the substance and essential parts of that calling is aught impaired or altered by such gracious munificence. And although, as the world goes, these honors cannot balance the contempt of those eminent places, and that portion which is now made hereditary to the church cannot in the most of these dignities, after all deductions, boast of any superfluity, yet such as they are, if any man have so little grace and power of self-government as to be puffed up with pride, or transported to an immoderation in the use of these adventitious favours, the sin is personal, the calling free; which may be and is managed by others with all humble sociableness, hospital[22] frugality, conscionable improvement of all means and opportunities to the good of God's church.

I may not yet dissemble that whiles we plead the divine right of episcopacy, a double scandal is taken by men otherwise not injudicious and cast upon us from the usual suggestions of some late pamphleteers.[23]

The one, that we have deserted our former tenet, not without the great prejudice of sovereignty; for whereas we were wont to acknowledge the deriving of our tenure as in fee from the beneficent hand of kings and princes, now, as either proudly or ungratefully casting off that just dependence and beholdingness, we stand upon the claim of our episcopacy from a divine original. The other, that whiles we labor to defend the divine right of our episcopacy we seem to cast a dangerous imputation upon those reformed churches which want that government. Both which must be shortly cleared.

---

were defended by the Anglicans on the grounds of precedent and expediency. Richard Hooker's defense of *things indifferent* in *Of the Laws of Ecclesiastical Polity* (1594 ff.), the crowning work of Anglican apologetics, was frequently cited by Stuart divines.
[19]Disparity.
[20]Two of Paul's converts to whom he addressed the so-called "pastoral epistles" wherein he explained the office and duties of a bishop (for example, 1 Timothy 3.1–9 and Titus 1.6.16).
[21]Churches in Asia Minor (at Ephesus, Smyrna, Pergamum, Thyatira, Sardis, Philadelphia, and Laodicea) addressed by St. John in Revelation 1.4.
[22]Hospitable.
[23]Among the flood of pamphlets denouncing the Anglican claims that Hall (with Laud's close supervision) had defended in *Episcopacy by Divine Right* (1640) were Robert Baillie's *Ladensium . . . The Canterburian's Self-Conviction*, William Prynne's *Lord Bishops, None of the Lord Bishops*, and Alexander Henderson's *Unlawfulness and Danger of Limited Prelacy*.

The former had never been found worth objecting if men had wisely learned to consider how little incompatibleness there is in this case of God's act and the king's. Both of them have their proper object and extent. The office is from God; the place and station and power wherein that office is exercised is from the king. It is the king that gives the bishopric; it is God that makes the bishop. Where was it ever heard of that a sovereign prince claimed the power of ordaining a pastor in the church? This is derived from none but spiritual hands. On the other side, who but princes can take upon them to have power to erect and dispose of episcopal sees within their own dominions? It is with a king and a bishop as with the patron and the incumbent: the patron gives the benefice to his clerk, but pretends not to give him orders: that this man is a minister he hath from his diocesan; that he is beneficed he hath from his patron: whiles he acknowledgeth his orders from the reverend hands of his bishop, doth he derogate aught from the bounty of a patron's free presentation? No otherwise is it with episcopacy, which thankfully professes to hold at once from God and the king: its calling of God, its place and exercise of jurisdiction of the king. And if it be objected that both some former and modern divines both abroad and at home, borrowing St. Jerome's phrase,[24] have held the superiority of bishops over presbyters to be grounded rather upon the custom of the church than any appointment of Christ, I must answer, first, that we cannot prescribe to other men's thoughts: when all is said, men will take liberty (and who can hinder it?) to abound in their own sense; but, secondly, if they shall grant, as they shall be forced, that this custom was of the church apostolical, and had its rise with the knowledge, approbation, practice of those inspired legates of Christ, and was from their very hands recommended to the then present and subsequent church for continuance, there is no such great dissonance in the opinions as may be worthy of a quarrel.

The second is intended to raise envy against us, as the uncharitable censurers and condemners of those reformed churches abroad which differ from our government. Wherein we do justly complain of a sclanderous aspersion cast upon us. We love and honor those sister churches as the dear spouse of Christ. We bless God for them; and we do heartily wish unto them that happiness in the partnership of our administration which I doubt not but they do no less heartily wish unto themselves.

Good words! you will perhaps say; but what is all this fair compliment if our act condemn them, if our very tenet exclude them? For if episcopacy stand by divine right, what becomes of those churches that want it?

Malice and ignorance are met together in this unjust aggravation.

First, our position is only affirmative, implying the justifiableness and holiness of an episcopal calling, whitout any further implication.

Next, when we speak of divine right we mean not an express law of God, requiring it upon the absolute necessity of the being of a church, what hindrances soever may interpose, but a divine institution, warranting it where it is, and requiring it where it may be had.

Every church, therefore, which is capable of this form of government both may and ought to affect it, as that which is with so much authority derived from the apostles to the whole body of the church upon earth; but those particular churches to whom this power and faculty is denied lose nothing of the true essence of a church, though they miss something of their glory and perfection, whereof they are barred by the necessity of their condition; neither are liable to any more imputation in their credit and esteem than an honest, frugal, officious[25] tenant, who, notwithstanding the proffer of all obsequious services, is tied to the limitations and terms of an hard landlord.

But so much we have reason to know of the judgment of the neighbor churches and their famous divines that if they might hope to live so long as to see a full freedom of option tendered unto them by sovereign authority, with all suitable conditions, they would most gladly embrace this our form of government, which differs little from their own, save in the perpetuity of their προστασία or moderatorship, and the exclusion of that lay presbytery which never till this age had footing in the Christian church.

Neither would we desire to choose any other judges of our calling and the glorious eminence of our church so governed, than the famous professors of Geneva itself: learned Lectius for a civilian,[26] and for a divine Fredericus Spanhemius,[27] the now renowned pastor and reader of divinity in Geneva; who in his dedicatory epistle before the third part of his *Dubia evangelica* to the incomparable lord primate of Ireland,[28] doth zealously applaud and congratulate unto us the happy and, as he conceiveth, flourishing estate of our church under this government, magnifying the graces of God in the bishops thereof, and shuts up with fervent prayers to God for the continuance of the authority of the prelates of these churches. O then, whiles Geneva itself praiseth our government, and God for it, and prays for the happy perpetuation of it, let it not be suffered that any ignorant or spiteful sectaries should openly in their libels curse it, and maliciously brand it with the terms of unlawful and antichristian.

Your wisdoms cannot but have found abundant reason to hate and scorn this base and unreasonable suggestion, which would necessarily infer that not Christ but Antichrist hath had the full sway of all God's church upon earth for these whole sixteen hundred years: a blasphemy which any Christian heart must needs abhor.

And who that hath ever looked into either books or men knows not that the religious bishops of all times are and have been they which have strongly held up the kingdom of

---

[24]In *Episcopacy by Divine Right* Hall had rested heavily on St. Jerome's explanation (Letter CXLVI) of a bishop's function and prerogatives.   [25]Dutiful.

[26]One learned in civil law.

[27]*Lectius...Spanhemius*: Jacques Lect (1560–1611), Swiss jurisconsulist whose works include an edition of Greek poets (1606) as well as many treatises on law, and Friedrich Spanheim (1600–49), a Bavarian theologian and professor of theology at Leiden whose *Dubia evangelica* appeared in 1639.

[28]James Ussher (1581–1656), archbishop of Armagh, one of the ablest and most erudite defenders of episcopacy.

Christ, and the sincere truth of the Gospel, against all the wicked machinations of Satan and his Antichrist? And even amongst our own, how many of the reverend and learned fathers of the church now living have spent their spirits and worn out their lives in the powerful opposition of that "man of sin!"[29] Consider then, I beseech you, what a shameful injustice it is in these bold sclanderers to cast upon these zealously religious prelates, famous for their works (against Rome) in foreign parts, the guilt of that which they have so meritoriously and convincingly opposed. If this most just defence may satisfy them, I shall for their sakes rejoice; but if they shall either with the wilfully deaf adder stop their ears, or against the light of their own consciences, out of private respects, bear up a known error of uncharitableness, this very paper shall one day be an evidence against them before the dreadful tribunal of the Almighty.

What should I urge in some others the careful, peaceable, painful, conscionable managing of their charges to the great glory of God and comfort of his faithful people? And if, whiles these challenge a due respect from all well-minded Christians, some others hear ill (how deservedly God knows, and will in due time manifest), yet why should an holy calling suffer? why should the faults, if such be, of some diffuse their blame to all? Far, far we know is this from the approved integrity of your noble justice; whiles in the meantime, unless your just check do seasonably remedy it, the impetuous and undistinguishing vulgar are ready so to involve all as to make innocence itself a sin; and which, I am amazed to think of, dare say and write, "The better man, the worse bishop."

And now, since I am fallen upon this sad subject, give me leave, I beseech you, to profess with how bleeding an heart I hear of the manifold scandals of some of the inferior clergy presented to your view from all parts. It is the misery and shame of this church if they be so foul as they are suggested; but if I durst presume so far, I should in the bowels of Christ beseech you upon the finding of so hateful enormities to give me leave to put you in mind of the charitable example of our religious Constantine in the like case.[30] You cannot dislike so gracious a pattern. I plead not for their impunity: let them within the sphere of their offence bear their own sin. But O forbid to have it told in Gath, or published in the streets of Ashkelon.[31] Your wisdoms well see under what malignant eyes we are of opposite[32] spectators. What a death it is to think of the sport and advantage these watchful enemies will be sure to make of our sins and shame! What exprobrations,[33] what triumphs of their will hence ensue! These and all other our cares are now securely cast upon your exquisite prudence and goodness. The very mention of our fears, whiles ye sit, had need to crave pardon of presumption. But withal to take down the insolence of those envious insulters, it may please you to give me leave to tell them that however in so numerous a multitude there be found some foully vicious, as there is no pomegranate wherein some grains are not rotten; and even in twelve there is one Judas; yet upon a just survey it will be found that no one clergy in the whole Christian world yields so many eminent scholars, learned preachers, grave, holy, and accomplished divines as this Church of England doth at this day. And long and ever may it thus flourish, as it surely shall, through God's blessing, whiles the bountiful encouragements of learning and ingenuous education are happily continued to it. And the more when those luxuriant boughs of disorder and debauchedness are, through just censures, seasonably lopped off.

But stay. Where are we, or what is this we speak of, or to whom? Whiles I mention the Church of England, as thinking it your honor and my own to be the professed sons of such a mother, I am now taught a new divinity, and bidden to ask which church we mean. My simplicity never thought of any more churches of England but one. Now this very day's wiser discovery tells us of more. There is a prelatical church, they say, for one; and which is the other? Surely it is so young that as yet it hath no name, except we shall call it indefinitely,[34] as the Jews were wont to style the creature they could not abide to mention, "that other thing." And what thing shall that be, think we? Let it be called, if you please, the church antiprelatical, but leave England out of the style.[35] Let it take a larger denomination, and extend to our friends at Amsterdam and elsewhere, and not be confined to our England. Withal, let them be put in mind that they must yet think of another subdivision of this division. Some there are, they know, which can be content to admit of an orderly subordination of several parishes to presbyteries, and those again to synods; others are all for a parochial absoluteness and independence. Yea, and of these there will be a division, in *semper divisibilia*,[36] till they come to very atoms; for to which of those scores of separated[37] congregations, known to be within and about these walls, will they be joined? and how long without a further scissure?[38] O God, where do men stay when they are once past the true bounds!

But if it be so that the prelatical part must needs make up one divident[39] member of this English church, tell me, brethren, I beseech you, what are the bounders[40] of this church? what the distinction of the professors and religion? and if the clients of the prelacy and their adherents, whose several thousands are punctually calculated, be they who make up this prelatical church, what grounds of faith, what new creed do they hold, different from their neighbors? what scriptures, what baptism, what eucharist, what Christ, what heaven, what means of salvation, other than the rest?

Alas! my brethren, whiles we do fully agree in all these, and all other doctrinal and practical points of religion, why will ye be so uncharitable as by these frivolous and causeless divisions to rend the seamless coat of Christ? Is it a title, or a retinue, or a ceremony, a garment, or a color, or an organ-pipe, that can make us a different church, whiles we preach

[29]2 Thessalonians 2.3.
[30]Hall is presumably alluding to Constantine the Great (280?–337), who as *pontifex maximus* following his conversion to Christianity in 313 strove for uniformity of creed and worship throughout his far-flung empire.
[31]"Tell it not in Gath, publish it not in the streets of Ashkelon; lest the daughters of the Philistines rejoice, lest the daughters of the uncircumcised triumph" (2 Samuel 1.20). [32]Hostile. [33]Upbraidings, reproaches. [34]Ambiguously. [35]Title. [36]Continuing differences. [37]Independent, autonomous, sectarian. [38]Division, schism. [39]Separate. [40]Boundaries.

and profess the same saving truth? whiles we desire, as you profess to do, to walk conscionably with our God, according to that one rule of the royal law of our Maker? whiles we oppose one and the same common enemy? whiles we unfeignedly endeavor to "hold the unity of the Spirit in the bond of peace"?[41] O consider, I beseech you in the fear of God, consider whether these be the thoughts of the sons of peace, and such as are suitable to the charge and legacy of our dear Saviour; and think seriously from what spirit they proceed.

For us, we make no difference at all in the right and interest of the church betwixt clergy and laity, betwixt the clergy and laity of one part and another. We are all your true brethren. We are one with you both in heart and brain, and hope to meet you in the same heaven; but if ye will needs be otherwise minded, we can but bewail the church's misery and your sin, and shall beseech God to be merciful to your willing and uncharitable separation. Howsoever, I have freed my soul before my God in the conscience of this just expostulation and faithful advice.

What remains, but that I pour out my heart in my fervent and daily prayers to the Father of all mercies, that it would please him to inspire this great council with all wisdom from above and crown this great meeting with the blessing of all happy success, so as it may produce much glory to His own name, much complacency[42] and contentment to His dear Anointed, comfort to all good hearts, terror to His enemies, seasonable restraint to all insolence and faction, prevention of all innovations, and lastly a firm peace and settlement to this church and commonwealth and to all other His Majesty's dominions? Which God grant for the sake of the Son of His love, Jesus Christ the righteous. Amen. Amen.

Finis

[41]Ephesians 4.3. [42]Delight, satisfaction.

Thomas Adams [ca.1583-ca.1655]

Of the five sermons included in this book, those by Andrewes, Donne, and Taylor may be said to exemplify the intellectual and stylistic resources of the Anglican establishment at or near its summit, that by young Ralph Cudworth before the House of Commons the moral energy of the Cambridge Platonists in a time of social peril, and that by Thomas Adams the fervor and the terror of Puritan devotion as expounded by a gifted City preacher.

In the reigns of James and Charles, when to be a grandee of the Church of England was to be Erastian, Arminian, and royalist, Adams, who held the line of rigid Calvinism, could not aspire to high position. It was well for him, therefore, that he quickly found his true vocation as a preacher, for the pulpit was for him a bishop's throne and miter. Neither a politician nor a speculative thinker, he merely preached his creed, and the components of his creed were simple: the majesty of God, the sinfulness of man, and an incandescent hope of heaven. On these he built his vivid sermons, and as he inflamed, inspired, bullied, and cajoled his listeners to purify their lives before they had to meet their God, he seemed to make the ancient themes of sin and retribution come alive. Not much concerned with doctrinal and liturgical complexities, or—despite his knowledge of the ancients whom he often quotes—with the sort of erudition whereby polymaths like Andrewes overwhelm the modern reader, this "prose Shakespeare of Puritan theologians," as Southey called him, was preeminently a moralist who deployed the arts and even artifices of language to achieve a moral purpose. He was gifted with a writer's eye and ear, and an uncanny sense of style. His prose reveals a bravura play of wit and metaphor, a juxtaposition of grand sonorities with pert colloquialisms, a knack for rapid change of pace (for example, from euphuistic balance to the jerky, asymmetric rhythms of a newer Senecanism), a brilliant use of interpolated characters and dramatic interludes, a jolting oscillation between the full-breathed, rolling exhortation and the whiplash epigram, a jaunty ease in doing anything he wished with words. But these and other tricks of style, as he himself explained, were purely instrumental: "all our preaching is but to beget your praying."

Apart from what this remarkable writer says or implies about himself in the dedicatory epistles before his published sermons, we know little of his life. Two degrees from Cambridge (B.A. 1602, M.A. 1606) presumably fitted him for the clerical career that led from Willington in Bedfordshire (1612–14) and Wingrave in Buckinghamshire (1614–15) to the pulpit of St. George's under St. Paul's in London, where he preached from 1618 to 1623. Despite his plaintive comments about the painful work of preaching in that wicked city—"we may say of it in another sense what Christ said of Jerusalem, 'O thou that killest the prophets!'"—Adams clearly had a marked success in London. In various dedications he himself attests to the friendship and support of such dignitaries as Lord Chancellor Ellesmere (who, as Sir Thomas Egerton, had befriended Donne and Bacon), William Herbert, third earl of Pembroke (who may have been the youth for whom Shakespeare wrote his sonnets and was certainly the benefactor of Jonson and many other men of letters), and Henry Montagu, first earl of Manchester (at whose "command" Adams, his "observant chaplain," preached and published many of his sermons). By 1629, when the majestic folio of Adams' works appeared, he had moved to St. Benet's at Paul's Wharf, but he could rise no higher in the church that Laud had come to dominate. Indeed, despite the appearance (1633) of a gigantic *Commentary*, in folio, on Second Peter, his fortunes seemed to sink. He had prophesied, perhaps, his own decline in dedicating the folio of 1629 to his parishioners at St. Benet's. "Many a minister comes to a parish with his veins full of blood, his bones of marrow," he had said,

> but how soon doth he exhaust his spirits, waste his vigor! And albeit there are many good souls for whose sake he is content to make himself a sacrifice, yet there are some so unmerciful that after all his labor would send him a beggar to his grave.

Although his later years are mainly unrecorded, his comments in what appears to be his final published sermon in 1652 about his "necessitous and decrepit old age" suggests that they were very bleak. Even the date and circumstances of his death are matters of conjecture.

In the pith and puissance of his youth, however, Adams must have been a virtuoso preacher. *The Gallant's Burden*, a sermon preached at Paul's Cross in March 1612, was so successful that it was promptly printed and went through three editions. Others, whose arresting titles still rivet our attention, swelled into a stream of prose: *The White Devil or the Hypocrite Uncased* (which achieved five editions between 1613 and 1617), a set of six discourses called *The Devil's Banquet* (1614), *The Sinner's Passing Bell* (1614), *The Black Devil or the Apostate, with the Wolf Worrying the Lambs and the Spiritual Navigator* (1615), double sermons on *England's Sickness* and *Mystical Bedlam* (1615), *A Divine Herbal together with a Forest of Thorns* (1616), and *The Sacrifice of Thankfulness . . . whereunto Are Annexed Five Other Sermons* (1616). Even in London, where his pastoral duties must have been demanding, Adams did not slacken his production. *The Barren Tree* (1623) was followed by a set of three new sermons in 1625, and then by two gatherings of five sermons each in 1626 and 1629 before all of these and others were brought together as "one entire volume, with the addition of some new and emendations of the old," in the folio of 1629. In presenting this collection—whose sixty-four sermons, filling almost eleven hundred pages, are eked out with some copious *Meditations* on the Creed—Adams was at pains to justify the undertaking. "I hear of some idle drones," he told "the candid and ingenious reader,"

> humming out their dry derisions that we, forsooth, affect to be men in print, as if that were the only end of these publications. But let the communication of goodness stop their mouths. Speech is only for presence; writings have their use in absence. *Quo liceat libris non licet ire mihi*: our books may come to be seen where our selves shall never be heard. These may preach when the author cannot, and—which is more—when he is not.

As noted earlier, on its initial publication in 1615 *Mystical Bedlam* was printed as a double sermon. My text is based upon the *Workes* of 1629 (STC 104), whose confusing, overlapping flights of Arabic numbers have been replaced with Roman numerals and capital letters (in square brackets) to mark the main divisions of the text. Despite his great contemporary reputation, Adams quickly fell into neglect. More than two centuries separate the second printing of the folio in 1630 and W. H. Stowell's edition of several of his sermons as *The Three Divine Sisters* in 1847. Thomas Smith published two volumes of his *Works* in 1861–62, but a promised third (with a life by J. Angus) apparently died aborning. John Brown issued a dozen of his sermons in 1909, H. H. Henson included one of them in his *Selected English Sermons* in 1939, and Gwendolen Murphy excerpted some half a dozen characters from his works for her *Cabinet of Characters* in 1925. The massive *Commentary* on Second Peter was "revised and corrected" by James Sherman in 1848. Adams of course receives attention in W. F. Mitchell's *English Pulpit Oratory from Andrewes to Tillotson* (1932) and in Millar Maclure's *Paul's Cross Sermons* (1958), and there is a perceptive essay on his merits as a writer by William Mulder in the *Harvard Theological Review*, XLVIII (1955). A good edition of his sermons —or of some of them, at least—remains a great desideratum.

from The Works (1629)

MYSTICAL BEDLAM, OR THE WORLD OF MADMEN

Ecclesiastes, Chapter 9, Verse 3. "The heart of the sons of men is full of evil, and madness is in their heart while they live; and after that, they go to the dead."

[GENERAL INTRODUCTION]

The subject of the discourse is man, and the speech of him hath three points in the text: (1) his comma, (2) his colon, (3) his period. (1) Men's hearts are full of evil: there's the comma. (2) Madness is in their hearts whiles they live: there's the colon. (3) Whereat not staying, after that they go down to the dead: and there's their period. The first begins, the second continues, the third concludes their [10] sentence. Here is man's setting forth, his peregrination, and his journey's end. (1) At first putting out his heart is full of evil. (2) Madness is in his heart all his peregrination whiles they live. (3) His journey's end is the grave; he goes to the dead. First, man is born from the womb as an arrow shot from the bow. (2) His flight through this air is wild and full of madness, of indirect courses. (3) The center where he lights is the grave. First, his comma begins so harshly that it promiseth no good consequence in the colon. (2) The colon is so mad and inordinate that there is small hope of the period. [20] (3) When both the premises are so faulty, the conclusion can never be handsome. Wickedness in the first proposition, madness in the second; the *ergo*[1] is fearful, the conclusion of all is death. So then, (1) the beginning of man's race is full of evil, as if he stumbled at the threshold. (2) The further he goes, the worse: madness is joined tenant in his heart with life. (3) At last, in his frantic flight, not looking to his feet, he drops into the pit, goes down to the dead.

[PART I. THE COMMA]

To begin at the uppermost stair of this gradual descent, the comma of this tripartite sentence gives man's heart for a [30] vessel. Wherein observe (1) the owners of this vessel, men, and derivatively the sons of men. (2) The vessel itself is earthen, a pot of God's making and man's marring, the heart. (3) The liquor it holds is evil, a defective, privative, abortive thing, not instituted but destituted by the absence of original goodness. (4) The measure of this vessel's pollution with evil

liquor. It is not said *sprinkled*, not seasoned with a moderate and sparing quantity. It hath not an aspersion nor imbution, but impletion;[2] it is filled to the brim, full of evil. Thus at first putting forth we have man in his best member corrupted.

A.[3] THE OWNER OR POSSESSORS, SONS OF MEN

Adam was called the son of God (Luke 3). Enos was the son of Seth, Seth the son of Adam, Adam the son of God.[4] But all his posterity the sons of men, we receiving from him both flesh and the corruption of flesh, yea, and of soul too, though the substance thereof be inspired of God, not traduced[5] from man, for the purest soul becomes stained and corrupt when it once toucheth the body.

The sons of men: this is a derivative and diminutive speech whereby man's conceit of himself is lessened, and himself lessoned to humility. Man, as God's creation left him, was a goodly creature, an abridgment of heaven and earth, an epitome of God and the world: resembling God, who is a spirit, in his soul, and the world, which is a body, in the composition of his. *Deus maximus invisibilium, mundus maximus visibilium*: God the greatest of invisible natures, the world the greatest of visible creatures: both brought into the little compass of man. Now man is grown less; and as his body in size, his soul in vigor, so himself in all virtue[6] is abated; so that the son of man is a phrase of diminution, a bar in the arms[7] of his ancient glory, a mark of his derogate[8] and degenerate worth.

Two instructions may the sons of men learn in being called so: (1) their spiritual corruption; (2) their natural corruptibleness.

[1. THEIR SPIRITUAL CORRUPTION]

(1) That corruption and original pravity[9] which we have derived from our parents. Psalm 51: "Behold," saith David, "I was shapen in iniquity, and in sin did my mother conceive me."[10] The original word is "warm" me, as if the first heat derived to him were not without contamination. I was born a sinner, saith a saint.

MYSTICAL BEDLAM　[1]Consequence.
[2]Not a sprinkling or a soaking, but a filling.　[3]Text 1.
[4]*Enos...son of God*: See Luke 3.38.　[5]Transmitted.
[6]1) power; 2) goodness.
[7]In heraldry, a fess or band drawn horizontally across the center of an escutcheon. Adams is perhaps thinking of the bar sinister, popularly (but incorrectly) used as a mark of illegitimacy.　[8]Debased.
[9]Depravity.　[10]Psalm 51.3.

It is said (Genesis 5) that "Adam begat a son in his own likeness after his image, and called his name Seth."[11] This image and likeness cannot be understood of the soul, for this Adam begat not. Nor properly and merely of the body's shape; so was Cain as like to Adam as Seth, of whom it is spoken. Nor did that image consist in the piety and purity of Seth: Adam could not propagate that to his son which he had not in himself; virtues are not given by birth, nor doth grace follow generation, but regeneration. Neither is Seth said to be begotten in the image of Adam because mankind was continued and preserved in him. But it intends[12] that corruption which descended to Adam's posterity by natural propagation. The Pelagian error[13] was *Peccatum primae transgressionis in alios homines, non propagatione sed imitatione transisse*: that the guilt of the first sin was derived to other men not by propagation but by imitation. But then could not Adam be said to beget a son in his own image; neither could death have seized on infants who had not then sinned. But all have sinned (Romans 5): "As by one man sin entered into the world, and death by sin; so death passed upon all men for that all have sinned."[14]

This title, then, "the sons of men" put us in mind of our original contamination whereby we stand guilty before God, and liable to present and eternal judgments. *Dura tremenda refers*, you will say with the disciple[15] (John 6): "This is an hard saying. Who can hear it?"[16] Bear it? Nay, be ready to conclude with a sadder inference, as the same disciple, after a particular instance (Matthew 19): "Who then can be saved?"[17] I answer, we derive from the first Adam sin and death, but from the second Adam grace and life. . . . It is our happiness not to be born, but to be new-born. The first birth kills, the second gives life. It is not the seed of man in the womb of our mother, but the seed of grace in the womb of the church that makes us blessed. Generation lost us; it must be regeneration that recovers us. As the tree falls, so it lies; and lightly it falls to that side which is most loden[18] with fruits and branches. If we abound most with the fruits of obedience, we shall fall to the right hand, life; if with wicked actions, affections, to the left side, death. . . .

[2. THEIR "NATURAL CORRUPTIBLENESS"]

(2) Our corruptibleness is here also demonstrated. A mortal father cannot beget an immortal son. If they that brought us into the world have gone out of the world themselves, we may infallibly conclude our own following. He that may say, "I have a man to my father, a woman to my mother" in his life may in death, with Job, say to corruption, "Thou art my father; to the worm, thou art my mother and my sister."[19] It hath been excepted[20] against the justice of God that the sin of one man is devolved to his posterity, and that for the father's eating sour grapes the children's teeth are set on edge, according to the Jewish proverb (Jeremiah 31.29). As if we might say to every son of man as Horace sung to his friend: *Delicta maiorum immeritus lues*:[21] thou, being innocent, dost suffer for thy nocent[22] superiors. This a philosopher objected against the gods, strangely conferring[23] it as if for the father's disease physic should be ministered to the son.

I answer, Adam is considered as the root of mankind: that corrupt mass whence can be deduced no pure thing. Can we be born Morians[24] without their black skins? Is it possible to have an Amorite to our father and an Hittite to our mother without participation of our corrupted natures?[25] If a man slip a science[26] from a hawthorne, he will not look to gather from it grapes. There is not, then, a son of man in the cluster of mankind but—*eodem modo et nodo, vinctus et victus*[27]—it is liable to that common and equal law of death,

Unde superbus homo, natus, satus, ortus ab humo?

Proud man forgets earth was his native womb
Whence he was born; and dead, the earth's his tomb.

Morieris, non quia aegrotas, sed quia vivis, saith the philosopher: thou shalt die, O son of man, not because thou art sick, but because the son of man. *Cui nasci contigit, mori restat*: who happened to come into the world must upon necessity go out of the world. It is no new thing to die, since life itself is nothing else but a journey to death. *Quicquid ad summum pervenit, ad exitum properat*: he that hath climbed to his highest is descending to his lowest. All the sons of men die not one death, for time and manner; for the matter and end, one death is infallible to all the sons of men. The corn is sometimes bitten in the spring, often trode[28] down in the blade, never fails to be cut up in the ear when ripe. *Quisquis queritur hominem mortuum esse, queritur hominum fuisse*: who laments that a man is dead laments that he was a man. . . .

B.[29] THE VESSEL ITSELF IS THE HEART

The heart is man's principal vessel. We desire to have all the implements in our house good, but the vessel of chiefest honor, principally good. *Quam male de te ipse meruisti* etc., saith St. Augustine: how mad is that man that would have all his vessels good but his own heart! We would have a strong nerve, a clear vein, a moderate pulse, a good arm, a good face, a good stomach; only we care not how evil the heart is, the principal of all the rest. For howsoever the head be called the tower of the mind, the throne of reason, the house of wisdom, the treasure of memory, the capitol of judgment, the shop of affections, yet is the heart the receptacle of life. And *spiritus*, which, they say, is *copula animae et corporis*, a virtue uniting the soul and the body, if it be in the liver natural, in the head animal, yet is in the heart vital.[30] It is the member that hath first life in man and is the last that dies in man, and to all the other members give vivification.

[11]Genesis 5.3.   [12]Means.
[13]The doctrine—advanced by the monk Pelagius (d. 420?), declared heretical by the Roman Catholic Church, and denied by the Calvinists—that there is no hereditary taint of Adam's sin.
[14]Romans 5.12.   [15]Text *Disciples* (and also later in the paragraph).
[16]John 6.60.   [17]Matthew 19.25.   [18]Loaded.   [19]Job 17.14.
[20]Objected.   [21]Horace, *Odes*, III.vi.1.   [22]Guilty.   [23]Comparing.
[24]Moors.
[25]*Is it possible . . . corrupted natures*: The Amorites, a powerful tribe in Canaan before the Israelite conquest, and the Hittites, whose sway extended from Armenia westward into Asia Minor, were regarded as symbols of evil by Adams (and also by the writers of the Old Testament) because of their hostility to the Jews.
[26]Graft a cutting. *Science*: scion.
[27]In the same manner fettered and subdued.   [28]Trodden.
[29]Text *2*.   [30]See *spirits* in the Glossary.

As man is *microcosmus*, an abridgment of the world, he hath heaven resembling his soul; earth his heart, placed in the midst as a center; the liver is like the sea, whence flow the lively springs of blood; the brain, like the sun, gives the light of understanding; and the senses are set round about like the stars. The heart in man is like the root in a tree; the organ or lung-pipe that comes of the left cell of the heart is like the stock of the tree, which divides itself into two parts and thence spreads abroad (as it were) sprays and boughs into all the body, even to the arteries of the head. . . . It is a vessel properly because hollow: hollow to keep heat and for the more facile closing and opening. It is a spiritual vessel, made to contain the holy dews of grace which "make glad the City of God."[31] It is ever full, either with that precious juice or with the pernicious liquor of sin. As our Saviour saith (Matthew 15), "Out of the heart proceed evil thoughts, murders, adulteries, fornications, thefts, false witness, blasphemies."[32] "Know you not," saith His Apostle, "that you are the temple of God, and that the spirit of God dwelleth in you?"[33] . . . The good heart is a receptacle for the whole Trinity, and therefore it hath three angles, as if the three Persons of that one Deity would inhabit there. The Father made it, the Son bought it, the Holy Ghost sanctifies it; therefore they all three claim a right in the heart. It hath three cells for the three Persons, and is but one heart for one God. The world cannot satisfy it: a globe cannot fill a triangle. Only God can sufficiently content the heart. . . .

> The heart is plagued and endangered by "four busy requirers": the Pope, who begs it, the Devil, who tries to buy it, the Flesh, who borrows it, and the World, who steals it.

Therefore lock up this vessel with the key of faith, bar it with resolution against sin, guard it with supervisiting[34] diligence, and repose it in the bosom of thy Saviour. There it is safe from all obsidious or insidious oppugnations,[35] from the reach of fraud or violence. Let it not stray from this home, lest like Dinah[36] it be deflowered. If we keep this vessel ourselves, we endanger the loss. Jacob bought Esau's birthright[37] and Sathan stole Adam's paradise whiles the tenure was in their own hands. An apple beguiled the one, a mess of pottage the other. Trust not thy heart in thine own custody, but lay it up in heaven with thy treasure. Commit it to Him that is the maker and preserver of men, who will lap it up with peace and lay it in a bed of joy where no adversary power can invade it, nor thief break through to steal it.

C.[38] The Liquor This Vessel Holds Is Evil

. . . God created this vessel good; man poisoned it in the seasoning. And being thus distained[39] in the tender newness, *servat odorem testa diu*: it smells of the old infection till a new juice be put into it, or rather itself made new. As David prays, "Create in me, O Lord, a clean heart, and renew a right spirit within me."[40] God made us good; we have marred ourselves; and behold, we call on Him to make us good again. Yea, even the vessel thus recreated is not without a tang of the former corruption. . . . O ingrate, inconsiderate man! To whom God hath given so good a vessel, and he fills it with so evil sap. "In a great house there be vessels of honor and vessels of dishonor,"[41] some for better, some for baser uses. The heart is a vessel of honor, sealed, consecrated for a receptacle, for an habitacle[42] of the graces of God. Shall we take the member of Christ and make it an harlot's? The vessel of God, and make it Satan's? Did God infuse into us so noble a part, and shall we infuse into it such ignoble stuff? Was fraud, falsehood, malice, mischief, adultery, idolatry, variance, variableness ordained for the heart, or the heart for them? When the seat of holiness is become the seat of hollowness, the house of innocence the house of impudence, the place of love the place of lust, the vessel of piety the vessel of uncleanness, the throne of God the court of Satan, the heart is become rather a jelly than an heart. Wherein there is a tumultuous, promiscuous, turbulent throng, heaped and amassed together like a wine-drawer's stomach full of Dutch, French, Spanish, Greek, and many country wines; envy, lust, treason, ambition, avarice, fraud, hypocrisy obsessing it, and by long tenure pleading prescription:[43] that custom, being a second nature, the heart hath lost the name of heart and is become the nature of that it holds, a lump of evil. . . .

D.[44] The Measure of This Vessel's Infection: Full

It hath not aspersion nor imbution, but impletion. It is not a moderate contamination, which, admitted into comparison with other turpitudes, might be exceeded; but a transcendent, egregious, superlative matter to which there can be no accession: the vessel is full and more than full, what can be? One vessel may hold more than another, but when all are filled, the least is as full as the greatest. . . . Whiles the heart, like a cistern, stands perpetually open, and the devil, like a tankard-bearer, never rests fetching water from the conduit of hell to fill it, and there is no vent of repentance to empty it, how can it choose but be full of evil? The heart is but a little thing; one would therefore think it might soon be full; but the heart holds much; therefore is not soon filled. It is a little morsel, not able to give a kite her breakfast, yet it contains as much in desires as the world doth in her integral parts. Neither if the whole world were given to the Pellaean monarch[45] would he yet say, "My heart is full, my mind is satisfied." . . . This is the precipitation[46] of sin, if God doth not prevent, as Sathan doth provoke it: it rests not till it be full. Sinful man is evermore carrying a stick to his pile, a talent to his burden, more foul water to his cistern, more torments to be laid up in his hell: he ceaseth not, without a supernatural interruption and gracious revocation, till his measure be full.

Thus I have run through these four circumstances of the comma or first point of man, observing (A) from the owners, their corruptible fragility; (B) from the vessel, the heart's

---

[31]Psalm 46.4.   [32]Matthew 15.19   [33]1 Corinthians 3.16.
[34]Supervising.
[35]*Obsidious . . . oppugnations*: attacks from either without or within.
[36]A daughter of Jacob who was raped by Shechem, son of Hamor the Hivite (Genesis 34.2).   [37]Genesis 27.   [38]Text *3*.
[39]Discolored.   [40]Psalm 51.10.   [41]Adapted from 2 Timothy 2.20.
[42]Dwelling place.
[43]In law, a title to property based on long possession.   [44]Text *4*.
[45]Alexander the Great, who was born at Pella in Macedonia.
[46]Headlong rush.

excellency; (C) from the liquor contained in it, the pollution of our natures; (D) and lastly, from the plenitude, the strength and height of sin. The summe is: (1) the heart (2) of man (3) is full (4) of evil.

> This first section of his sermon ended, Adams says he should now leave his listeners to their own disquieting meditations. Instead, in a brief coda to Part I he, like a good physician, prescribes remedies for the "malady" that he has diagnosed: "(1) Seeing this vessel is full, to empty it. (2) Seeing it is foul, to wash it. (3) Since it hath caught an ill tang, to sweeten it. (4) And when it is well, so to preserve it. With these four uses, go in peace."[47]

[PART II. THE COLON]

[INTRODUCTION]

Man's sentence is yet but begun, and you will say, a comma doth not make a perfect sense. We are now got to his colon, having left his heart full of evil, we come to his madness. No marvel if, when the stomach is full of strong wines, the head grow drunken. The heart being so filled with that pernicious liquor, evil, becomes drunk with it. Sobriety, a moral daughter, nay, Reason the mother, is lost; he runs mad, stark mad. This frenzy possessing not some out-room, but the principal seat, the heart. Neither is it a short madness, that we may say of it as the poet of anger, *furor brevis est*; but of long continuance, even during life, whiles they live. Other drunkenness is by sleep expelled, but this is a perpetual lunacy. Considerable, then, is (A) the matter, (B) the men, (C) the time. *Quid, in quo, quamdiu*: what, in whom, and how long. Madness is the matter. (B) The place, the heart. (C) The time, whiles they live. The colon or medium of man's sentence spends itself in the description of [the] tenant: madness; tenement: the heart; tenure: whiles they live. (A) Madness (B) holds the heart (C) during life. It is pity (A) so bad a tenant (B) hath so long time (C) in so good a house.

A.[48] THE TENANT: MADNESS

There is a double madness, corporal and spiritual. The object of the former is reason, of the latter, religion. That obsesseth the brain, this the heart. That expects the help of the natural physician, this of the mystical. The difference is, this spiritual madness may *insanire cum ratione, cum religione nunquam*: the morally frantic[49] may be mad with reason, never with religion. Physicians have put a difference betwixt frenzy and madness, imagining madness to be only an infection and perturbation of the foremost cell of the head, whereby imagination is hurt; but the frenzy to extend further, even to offend the reason and memory, and is never without a fever. Galen calls it an inflammation of the brains, or films thereof, mixed with a sharp fever. My purpose needs not to be curious of this distinction.

To understand the force of madness we must conceive in the brain three ventricles, as houses assigned by physicians for three dwellers: imagination, reason, and memory. According to these three internal senses of faculties, there be three kinds of frenzies or madness. (1) There are some mad that can rightly judge of the things they see, as touching imagination and fantasy; but for cogitation and reason, they swarve[50] from natural judgment. (2) Some, being mad, are not deceived so much in common cogitation and reason, but they err in fantasy and imagination. (3) There are some that be hurt in both imagination and reason, and they necessarily therewithal do lose their memories. That whereas in perfect, sober, and well-composed men imagination first conceives the forms of things and presents them to the reason to judge, and reason, discerning them, commits them to memory to retain, in mad men nothing is conceived aright, therefore nothing derived, nothing retained.

For spiritual relation,[51] we may conceive in the soul understanding, reason, will. (1) The understanding apprehendeth things according to their right natures. (2) The reason discusseth them, arguing their fitness or inconvenience, validity or vanity, and examines their desert of probation or disallowance, their worthiness either to be received or rejected. (3) Will hath her particular working, and embraceth or refuseth the objects which the understanding hath propounded and the reason discoursed.

Spiritual madness is a depravation or almost deprivation[52] of all these faculties *quoad coelestia*: so far as they extend to heavenly things. (1) For understanding, the apostle saith, "the natural man perceives not spiritual things, because they are spiritually discerned."[53] And the very "minds of unbelievers are blinded by the god of this world."[54] (2) For reason: it judgeth vanities more worthy of prosecution when they are absent, of embracing when they salute us. "It is in vain to serve the Lord; and what profit is it that we have kept His ordinance and walked mournfully before Him?"[55] This is the voice of distracted cogitation, and of reason out of the wits. "We call the proud happy; and the workers of wickedness are set up: yea, they that tempt God are delivered."[56] (3) For will, it hath lost the propenseness to good, and freedom of disposing itself to well doing; neither hath it any power of its[57] own to stop and retard the precipitation to evil. . . .

As corporal madness draws a thick obfuscation over these lights [of *ratio*, whereby the soul "judgeth between good and evil, truth and falsehood," and of *intellectus*, "whereby she comprehends things not only visible but intelligible, as God, angels, etc."], so spiritual corrupts and perverts them, that as they are strangers to heaven, *quoad intellectum*, so at last they become fools in natural things, *quoad rationem*. As the apostle plainly [saith], "even as they did not like to retain God in their knowledge, so God gave them over to a reprobate mind, to do those things that are not convenient."[58] They that forget God shall forget nature. Hence ensue both these frenzies, and with them a dissimilitude to men, to Christian men. It is reckoned up among the curses that wait on the heels of disobedience (Deuteronomy 28): "The Lord shall smite thee with madness, blindness, and astonishment of heart."[59] But it is a fearful accumulation of

[47]In the 1615 edition of *Mystical Bedlam*, which there was printed as two sermons, this (with a slightly different peroration, marks the ending of the first. [48]Text *1*. [49]Madman. [50]Swerve. [51]Correspondingly for man's spiritual constitution. [52]Impairment or almost total loss. [53]1 Corinthians 2.14. [54]2 Corinthians 4.4. [55]Malachi 3.14. [56]Malachi 3.15. [57]Text *it*. [58]Romans 1.28. [59]Deuteronomy 28.28.

God's judgments and our miseries when spiritual frenzy shall possess the soul and scatter the powers of the inner man: evacuating not only imagination, but knowledge; not reason, but faith; not sense, but conscience. When the opinion of the world shall repute men sober and wise, and the scrutiny of God shall find them madmen.

To draw yet nearer to the point of our compass and to discover this spiritual madness, let us conceive in man's heart (for therein this frenzy consists) in answerable reference to those three faculties in the brain and powers of the soul before manifested these three virtues: knowledge, faith, affections. The defect of grace and destitution of integrity to the corrupting of these three cause madness. We will not inquire further into the causes of corporal frenzy; the madness which I would minister to is thus caused: a defective knowledge, a faith not well informed, affections not well reformed. Ignorance, unfaithfulness, and refractory desires make a man mad. . . .

> Passing rather briskly over ignorance and unfaithfulness as motives to spiritual madness, Adams comes to those "refractory and perverse affections" which, with Burtonian zest and amplitude, he illustrates in a "mad morisco"[60] of nineteen vivid characters. "I promised to particularize and set open the gates of Bedlam,"[61] he explains, "to leave madness as naked as ever sin left the first propagators of it and mankind. The Epicure shall lead the ring, as the foreman of this mad morisco."

1. THE EPICURE

I would fain speak not only of him but with him. Can you tend it, Belly God? The first question of my catechism shall be, "What is your name?" "Epicure." "Epicure? What's that? Speak not so philosophically, but tell us in plain dealing what are you." "A lover of pleasure more than of God. One that makes much of myself, born to live, and living to take mine ease. One that would make my belly my executor, and bequeath all my goods to consumption for the consummation of my own delights." "Ho, a good fellow, a merry man, a madman! What is your *summum bonum?*" "Pleasure." "Wherein consists it? Rehearse the articles of your belief." "I believe that delicacies, junkets, quotidian feasts, suckets,[62] and marmalades are very delectable. I believe that sweet wines and strong drinks, the best blood of the grape or sweat of the corn, is fittest for the belly. I believe that midnight revels, perfumed chambers, soft beds, close curtains, and a Dalilah in mine arms are very comfortable. I believe that glistering silks and sparkling jewels, a purse full of golden charms, a house neatly decked, gardens, orchards, fish ponds, parks, warrens, and whatsoever may yield pleasurable stuffing to the corps is a very heaven upon earth. I believe that to sleep till dinner and play till supper and quaff till midnight and to dally till morning—except there be some intermission to toss some painted papers or to whirl about squared bones[63] with as many oaths and curses, vomited out in an hour as would serve the devil himself for a legacy or stock to bequeath to any of his children—this is the most absolute and perfect end of man's life."

"Now, a deft creed, fit to stand in the devil's catechism! Is not this madness, stark and staring madness! What is the

flesh which thou pamperest with such indulgence? As thou feedest beasts to feed on them, dost thou not fat thy flesh to fat the worms? Go, Heliogabalus,[64] to thy prepared muniments,[65] the monuments of thy folly and madness. Thy tower is polished with precious stones and gold but to break thy neck from the top of it, if need be; thy halters enwoven with pearl but to hang thyself, if need be; thy sword enameled, hatched with gold, and embossed with margarites[66] but to kill thyself, if need be. Yet, for all this, death prevents[67] thy preparation, and thou must fall into thine enemies' hands."

. . . How many of these madmen ramble about this city! That lavish out their short times in this confused distribution of playing, dicing, drinking, feasting, beasting.[68] A cupping-house,[69] a vaulting-house,[70] a gaming-house share their means, lives, souls. They watch, but they pray not; they fast when they have no money and steal when they have no credit; and reveling the whole week, day and night, only the Sunday is reserved for sleep, and for no other cause respected. Be not mad, as the apostle saith: "Be not deceived, for because of these things cometh the wrath of God on the children of disobedience."[71] Are not these madmen that buy the merry madness of an hour with the eternal agonies of a tormented conscience? . . .

> In Adams' gallery of moral monsters the Epicure is followed by the Proud Man, the Lustful Man, the Hypocrite, the "Avarous," the Usurer, the Ambitious Man, and the Drunkard before the Idle Man appears.

9. THE IDLE MAN,

you will say, is not mad, for madmen can hardly be kept in, and he can hardly be got out. You need not bind him to a post of patience; the love of ease is strong fetters to him. Perhaps he knows his own madness and keeps his chamber, both that sleep may quiet his frenzy and that the light may not distract him. He lives by the sweat of other men's brows, and will not disquiet the temples of his head. If this be his wit, it is madness; for by this means his field is covered with nettles and thorns, his body overgrown with infirmities, his soul with vices, his conscience shall want a good witness to itself, and his heart be destitute of that hope which in the time of calamity might have rejoiced it.

Seneca could say, *Malo mihi male esse, quam molliter*: I had rather be sick than idle. And indeed to the slothful ease is a disease, but these men had rather be sick than work. These are mad, for they would not be poor nor want means to give allowance to their sluggishness, yet by their refusal of pains they call on themselves a voluntary and inevitable want. O that the want of grace thus procured were not more heavy to their souls than the other to their carcasses! Complain they of want? Justly may they, should they, shall they;

[60]Morris dance.
[61]The Hospital of St. Mary of Bethlehem for the insane in Bishopsgate, London; hence, a madhouse.   [62]Succades, candied fruits.
[63]*Toss some...bones*: play cards or throw dice.
[64]Marcus Aurelius Antoninus (218–22), Roman emperor notorious for his dissipations. [65]Defenses, protections. [66]Pearls.
[67]Anticipates. [68]Acting bestially. [69]Tavern. [70]Brothel.
[71]Ephesians 5.6.

for the want of diligence hath brought them to the want of sustenance. Thus their quiet is frenzy, their idleness madness.

16. THE ENVIOUS MAN

is more closely but more dangerously mad. "Envy is the consumption of the bones," saith Solomon:[72] he doth make much of that which will make nothing of him; he whets a knife to cut his own throat. The Glutton feeds beasts to feed on, but the Envious, like a witch, nourisheth a devil with his own blood. He keeps a disease fat which will ever keep him lean, and is indulgent to a serpent that gnaws his entrails. He punisheth and revengeth the wrongs on himself 10 which his adversary doth him. Is not this a madman? Others strike him; and like a strangely penitential monk, as if their blows were not sufficient, he strikes himself. That physicians may not beg him when he's dead; he makes himself an anatomy[73] living. Sure, he gives cause to think that all the old fables of walking ghosts were meant of him, and but for a little starved flesh he demonstratively expounds them. If it were not for his soul the devil could scarce tell what to do with his body. He would do much mischief if he lives to 't; but there is great hope that he will kill himself beforehand. 20 If you miss him in a stationer's shop jeering at books, or at a sermon caviling at doctrines, or amongst his neighbors' cattle grudging at their full udders, or in the shambles[74] plotting massacres, yet thou shalt be sure to find him in Bedlam.

19. THE VAINGLORIOUS

is a mere madman whether he boast of his good deeds or his ill. If of his virtues, they are generally more suspicable;[75] if of his vices, he is the more despicable; if of his wealth, his hearers the less trust him (this noise prevents him from being a debtor); if of his valor, he is the more infallibly held a 30 coward. In what strain soever his mountebank ostentation insults he loseth that he would find by seeking it the wrong way. He is mad, for when he would be accounted virtuous, honorable, rich, valiant, in favor with greatness, and the world takes not ample notice of it, he sounds it with his own trumpet; then at once they hear it, and deride it. By seeking fame he loseth it, and runs made upon 't. Put him into Bedlam!

20. LASTLY;

to omit our schismatics and separatists, who are truly called Protestants out of their wits, liable to the imputation of 40 frenzy, the papists are certainly madmen, dangerous mad-men, mad in themselves, dangerous to us, and would happily be confined to some local Bedlam lest their spiritual lunacy do us some hurt.

Mad in themselves, for who but madmen would forsake the fountain of living water, the word of truth, and pin their faith and salvation on the pope's sleeve—a prelate, a Pilate, that mingles their own blood with their sacrifices. Think how that enchanting cup of fornication prevails over their besotted souls, and you will say they are not less than 50 mad. Come you into their temples and behold their pageants and histrionical gestures, bowings, mowings,[76] windings, and turnings, together with their service in an unknown language, and (like a deaf man that sees men dancing when

he hears no music) you would judge them mad. Behold the mass-priest with his baked god,[77] towzing,[78] tossing, and dandling it to and fro, upward and downward, backward and forward, till at last, the jest turning into earnest, he chops it into his mouth at one bit whiles all stand gaping with admiration. *Spectatum admissi, risum teneatis amici?* Would you not think them ridiculously mad? But no wonder if they run mad that have drunk that poison. Many volumes have been spent in the discovery of their madness; I do but touch it, lest I seem to write Iliads after our learned Homer's.

Surely madmen are dangerous without restraint. Papists are ready instruments of commotion, perversion, treason. These are a sickness,

> *immedicabile vulnus*
> *Ense recidendum, ne pars sincera trahatur.*[79]

Our land cannot be at ease so long as these lie on her stomach. They prick and wound her sides not with praying against her (for their imprecations, we hope, are *irrita vota*)[80] but with preying upon her; and when all stratagems fail they are ready to fetch arguments from the shambles and conclude *inferio*.[81] Whose religion is politic,[82] learning bloody, affections malicious, ambitious, devilish. The Inquisition is their grammar, fire and faggot their rhetoric, fleet[83] and fetters their logic, the cannon's roar their music, and poisoning is their physic.[84] Whose priests have such almighty power that they can make their Maker, that whereas in their sacrament of order[85] (as they term it) God makes an impotent creature a priest, now in their sacrament of the altar the priest shall make almighty God. Yea, as He made them with a word and put them in their mother's womb, so they can make Him with a word and put Him in a box.[86] They that thus blaspheme their Creator, shall we trust them with their fellow-creature?

. . . There are many other madmen whom, though I particularly name not in this catalogue you shall find in Bedlam. I desire not to say all, but enough. All are not taken into that taming-house[87] in a day; it is filled at times. If this muster can work any reformation on these frantic patients, another discovery will not be lost labor. . . .

> Presumably exhausted by his "catalogue" of madmen, Adams quickly disposes of the final topics in Part II—(B) the heart as the "tenement" of madness and (C) man's whole life as the term or "tenure" of his aberrations. And so, after thirty-five folio pages, he almost rushes through Part III.

[72]Proverbs 14.30. [73]Skeleton. [74]Slaughterhouse.
[75]Open to suspicion. [76]Grimacings.
[77]The bread of the Eucharist. [78]Tousing, handling roughly.
[79]"An incurable wound that must be cut away with a knife lest the sound part also draw infection" (Ovid, *Metamorphoses*, I.190–191). [80]"Ineffectual vows." [81]"Further down" (i.e., in hell).
[82]Crafty.
[83]Adams is probably thinking of the Armada, with which Catholic Spain tried and failed to conquer England in 1588. [84]Medicine.
[85]Ordination, one of the seven sacraments of the Roman Catholic Church.
[86]The pyx, a box or casket wherein the Host is preserved.
[87]House of correction.

[PART III.] THE PERIOD

We have ended man's comma and his colon, but not his sentence: the period continues and concludes it. We (1) found his heart full of evil. (2) We left it full of madness. (3) Let us observe at the shutting up what will become of it. "After that, they go to the dead." Here's the end of man's progress: now he betakes himself to his standing-house, his grave. The period is delivered

consequently, "After that"
discessively,[88] "they go"
descensively,[89] "down to the dead."   10

The sum is, "Death is the wages of sin."[90] (1) "After that" they have nourished evil and madness in their hearts this is the successive (not successful) event[91] and consequence. (2) "They go": they shall travel a new journey, take an unwilling walk, not to their meadows, gardens, taverns, banketing-houses[92] but (3) "to the dead," a dismal place, the habitation of darkness and discontent, where fineness shall be turned to filthiness, luster to obscurity,[93] beauty and strength to putre-faction and rottenness.

If a man looks into what life itself is he cannot but find both   20
by experience of the past and proof of the present age that he must die. "As soon as we are born we begin to draw to our end."[94] Life itself is nothing but a journey to death. There is no day but hath his night, no sentence but hath his period, no life on earth but hath the death. Examine the scope of thy desires and thou shalt perceive how they hasten to the grave, as if death were the goal, prize, or principal end which the vanity of human endeavors runs at. Be a man in honor, in wealth, in government, he still, ambitiously blind, languisheth for the time to come: the one   30 in hope to enlarge his greatness, the other his riches, the last his dominions. Thus they covet the running-on of time and age, and rest not till they have concluded their sentence and attained their period, "gone to the dead."

All men, yea all inferior things, must be freed by an end; and as the philosopher answered to the news of his son's death, *"Scio me genuisse mortalem,"* so God the Father of all may say of every man living, *"Scio me creasse mortalem"*:[95] I have made a man that hath made himself mortal. Man is a little world, the world a great man; if the great man   40

must die, how shall the little one scape? He is made of more brittle and fragile matter than the sun and stars—of a less substance than the earth, water, etc. Let him make what show he can with his glorious adornments;[96] let rich apparel disguise him living; cerecloths,[97] spices, balms enwrap him, lead and stone immure him, dead: his original mother will at last own him again for her natural child and triumph over him with this insultation,[98] "He is in my bowels." (Psalm 146) "He returneth to his earth."[99] His body returneth not immediately to heaven, but to earth, nor to earth as a stranger to him, or an unknown place, but to his earth as one of his most familiar friends, and of oldest acquaintance.

To conclude: if we be sinful we must die; if we be full of evil and cherish madness in our hearts we must to the dead. We have sins enough to bring us all to the grave. God grant they be not so violent, and full of ominous precipitation, that they portend our more sudden ruin. Yea, they do portend it, but *O nullum sit in omine pondus.*[1]

But I have been so prolix in the former parts of the sentence that I must not dwell upon the period. He needs not be tedious that reads a lecture of mortality. How many in the world, since this sermon begun, have made an experimental proof of this truth! This sentence is but the moral of those spectacles, and those spectacles the examples of this sentence. They are come to their period before my speech; my speech, myself, and all that hear me, all that breathe this air, must follow them. It hath been said, "We live to die." Let me a little invert it, "Let us live to live." Live the life of grace that we may live the life of glory. Then though we must go to the dead, we shall rise from the dead, and live with our God out of the reach of death forever. Amen.

[88]With reference to departing. The word is not recorded in the *Oxford English Dictionary*.   [89]Descendingly.   [90]Romans 6.23.   [91]Outcome.   [92]Banqueting houses.   [93]Light to darkness.   [94]The Apocryphal Wisdom of Solomon 5.13.   [95]According to Diogenes Laertius (*Lives of Eminent Philosophers*, II.13), when Anaxagoras (d. 428 B.C.), following his trial for impiety, was told that he had been condemned to death and that his sons were already dead, he remarked merely that Nature had long before sentenced both him and his judges and that of course he knew his sons were born to die. Similarly, says Adams, God knows that men were created to die.   [96]Adornments.   [97]Winding sheets.   [98]Insult.   [99]Psalm 146.4.   [1]"O may the portents prove to be untrue!"

John Donne[1] [1572-1631]

from Essays in Divinity (1651)

TO THE READER

It is thought fit to let thee know that these *Essays* were printed from an exact copy under the author's own hand, and that they were the voluntary sacrifices of several hours

when he had many debates betwixt God and himself whether he were worthy and competently learned to enter into Holy

[1]For a commentary on Donne and other excerpts from his work, see Poetry, pp. 56 ff., and Books and Men, pp. 680 ff., 717 f.

Orders. They are now published both to testify his modest valuation of himself and to show his great abilities, and they may serve to inform thee in many holy curiosities.

Farewell

[BOOK I]

Of the Bible

God hath two books of life: that in the Revelation and elsewhere, which is an eternal register of His elect, and this Bible. For of this it is therefore said, "Search the Scriptures, because in them ye hope to have eternal life." And more plainly when, in the 24th of Ecclesiasticus,[1] Wisdom hath said in the first verse, "Wisdom shall praise herself," saying, "He created me from the beginning, and I shall never fail." Verse 12: "I give eternal things to all my children, and in me is all grace of life and truth." Verse 21: "They that eat me shall have the more hunger, and they that drink me shall thirst the more." Verse 24, at last in Verse 26: "All these things are the book of life and the covenants of the most high God and the law of Moses."

And as our orderly love to the understanding this Book of Life testifies to us that our names are in the other, so there is another book subordinate to this, which is *liber creaturarum*.[2] Of the first book we may use the words of Esay, "It is a book that is sealed up, and if it be delivered to one (*scienti literas*) that can read, he shall say, I cannot, for it is sealed."[3] So far removed from the search of learning are those eternal decrees and rolls of God, which are never certainly and infallibly produced and exemplified *in foro exteriori*,[4] but only insinuated and whispered to our hearts, *ad informandum conscientiam judicis*,[5] which is the conscience itself.

Of the second book, which is the Bible, we may use the next verse:[6] "The book shall be given"—as interpreters agree, "open"—"*nescienti literas*, to one which cannot read; and he shall be bid read, and shall say, I cannot read." By which we learn that as all mankind is naturally one flock feeding upon one common, and yet for society and peace, propriety,[7] magistracy, and distinct functions are reasonably induced, so though all our souls have interest in this their common pasture, the Book of Life (for even the ignorant are bid to read), yet the church hath wisely hedged us in so far that all men may know and cultivate and manure their own part, and not adventure upon great reserved mysteries, nor trespass upon this book without inward humility and outward interpretations. For it is not enough to have objects and eyes to see, but you must have light too. The first book is, then, impossible; the second difficult; but of the third book, the Book of Creatures, we will say the 18th verse: "The deaf shall hear the word of this book, and the eyes of the blind shall see out of obscurity."

And so much is this book available to the other that Sebund,[8] when he had digested this book into a written book, durst pronounce that it was an art which teaches all things, presupposes no other, is soon learned, cannot be forgotten, requires no books, needs no witnesses, and in this is safer than the Bible itself, that it cannot be falsified by heretics. And ventures further after to say that because his book is made according to the order of creatures, which express fully the will of God, whosoever doth according to his book fulfills the will of God. Howsoever, he may be too abundant in affirming that *in libro creaturarum* there is enough to teach us all particularities of Christian religion; for Trismegistus,[9] going far, extends not his proofs to particulars; yet St. Paul clears it thus far, that there is enough to make us inexcusable if we search not further.[10]

And that first step is the knowledge of this Bible, which only, after philosophy hath evicted[11] and taught us an unity in the Godhead, shows also a Trinity. As, then, this life compared to blessed eternity is but a death, so the books of philosophers, which only instruct this life, have but such a proportion[12] to this book. Which hath in it certainty, for no man assigns to it other beginning[13] than we do, though all allow not ours; dignity, for what author proceeds so *sine teste* (and he that requires a witness believes not the thing, but the witness); and a *non notis* (for he which requires reason believes himself and his own approbation and allowance of the reason);[14] and it hath sufficiency, for it either rejecteth or judgeth all traditions. It exceeds all others in the object (for it considers the next life), in the way (for it is written by revelation—yea, the first piece of it which ever was written, which is the Decalogue, by God's own finger). And as Lyra[15] notes, being perchance too allegorical and typic[16] in this, it hath this common with all other books, that the words signify things; but hath this particular, that all the things signify other things.

There are but two other books (within our knowledge) by which great nations or troops are governed in matter of religion, the Alcoran and Talmud,[17] of which the first is esteemed only where ours is not read. And besides the com-

---

ESSAYS IN DIVINITY [1]Donne here quotes the Apocryphal Ecclesiasticus, or the Wisdom of Jesus the Son of Sirach, from the Geneva Bible (1560), which varies from the Authorized Version in both language and verse numbers.
[2]"The book of creatures" or of nature, which Sir Thomas Browne (*Religio Medici*, I.16) calls "that universal and public manuscript that lies expansed unto the eyes of all." [3]Isaiah 29.11. [4]Publicly.
[5]"To inform the conscience of the wise." [6]Isaiah 29.12.
[7]Property.
[8]Raimundo (or Raymond) of Sabunde (d.? 1437), a Spanish philosopher whose ardent exposition of natural religion in *Liber naturae sive creaturarum* prompted the longest and most famous of Montaigne's essays—the ironical "Apology for Raymond Sebond," a devastating attack on facile optimism.
[9]Hermes Trismegistus ("Hermes the Thrice Greatest"), supposed author of a group of neoplatonic and Hermetic writings of the third or fourth century. [10]Romans 2. [11]Proved. [12]Relation.
[13]Divine inspiration.
[14]*Dignity...reason*: Whatever the convolutions of his syntax, Donne's meaning is that since the Bible has inherent authority (*dignity*), it requires neither the evidence of witnesses nor the support of human reason.
[15]Nicholas de Lyra (d. 1340), a French theologian whose *Postillae perpetuae* was an influential commentary on the Bible.
[16]Symbolic, emblematic.
[17]Respectively, the Koran, the sacred book of Moslems, and the

mon infirmity of all weak and suspicious and crazy[18] reli-
gions, that it affords salvation to all good men in any re-
ligion—yea, to devils also—with our singular Origen[19]
is so obnoxious and self-accusing that to confute it all
Christian churches have ever thought it the readiest and
presentest[20] way to divulge it. And therefore Luther, after
it had received *cribrationem* (a "sifting" by Cusanus),[21] per-
suades[22] an edition of the very text because he thinks the
Roman Church can no way be shaked more than thus to let
the world see how sister-like those two churches are. But
that man of infinite undertaking and industry and zeal and
blessings from the Highest had not seen the Alcoran when
he writ this, though he mention it, nor Cusanus his book
certainly, for else he could not have said that the cardinal
had only excerpted and exhibited to the world the infamous
and ridiculous parts of it, and slipt[23] the substantial; for he
hath deduced an harmony and conformity of Christianity
out of that book. Melanchthon also counsels this edition
ut sciamus quale poema sit.[24] And Bibliander[25] observes that
it is not only too late to suppress it now, but that the church
never thought it fit to suppress it, because, sayeth he, there
is nothing impious in it but is formerly reprehensively
registered[26] in the fathers.

As Cusanus hath done from the Alcoran, Galantinus[27]
hath from the Talmud deduced[28] all Christianity and more.
For he hath proved all Roman traditions from thence.
We grudge them not those victories, but this flexibility and
appliableness to a contrary religion shows perfectly how
leaden a rule those laws are. Without doubt their books
would have been received with much more hunger than
they are if the Emperor Maximilian, by Reuchlin's counsel,
had not allowed them free and open passage.[29] If there
were not some compassion belonged to them who are
seduced by them, I should profess that I never read merrier
books than those two.

Ours, therefore, begun not only in the first stone but in
the entire foundation by God's own finger and pursued by
His spirit, is the only legible Book of Life, and is without
doubt devolved[30] from those to our times. For God—who
first writ His law in the tables of our hearts, and when our
corruption had defaced them writ it again in stone tables,[31]
and when Moses' zealous anger had broken them writ
them again in other tables[32]—leaves not us worse provided
whom He loves more, both because He ever in His prov-
idence foresaw the Jews' defection and because in a natural
fatherly affection He is delighted with His Son's purchases.[33]
For that interruption which the course of this book is im-
agined by great authors to have had by the perishing in
the captivity[34] cannot possibly be allowed if either God's
promise or that history be considered; nor, if that were
possible, is it the less the work of God if Esdras refreshed and
recompiled it by the same spirit which was in the first
author;[35] nor is it the less ancient, no more than a man is
the less old for having slept, then walked out a day.

Our age therefore hath it, and our church, in our language;
for since the Jesuit Sacroboscus[36] and more late interpreters of
the Trent Council[37] have abandoned their old station and
defense of the letter of the canon, pronouncing the Vulgate
edition to be authentic (which they heretofore assumed for

the controverted point), and now say that that canon doth
only prefer it before all Latin translations, and that not
absolute (so to avoid barbarisms) but *in ordine ad fidem et
mores,*[38] and have given us limits and rules of allowable
infirmities in a translation as corruptions not offensive to
faith, observing the meaning though not the words if the
Hebrew text may bear that reading, and much more, we
might—if we had not better assurances—rely upon their
words that we have the Scripture, and nearer perfection,
than they.

PART i

⎡ Having thus established the significance of the Bible as the
  indispensable base of Christian devotion, Donne con-
  tinues with a series of meditations on the opening verse
  of Genesis, which at length brings him to the date of the
  creation and the problem of time. Unlike most of his
  knotty treatise, the peroration of this section anticipates
⎣ some of the splendors of his later prose.

Truly, the creation and the last judgment are the *diluculum*
and *crepusculum,* the morning and the evening twilights of
the long day of this world. Which times, though they be
not utterly dark, yet they are but of uncertain, doubtful,

body of Jewish civil and religious law not included in the Pen-
tateuch (the first five books of the Old Testament).
[18]Questionable and flawed.
[19]An influential Greek father of the church (d. 254?), author
of many commentaries and homilies.   [20]Quickest.
[21]Nicholas Cardinal de Cusa (d. 1464), a German mathematician
and philosopher who wrote a *sifting* or analysis of the Koran
entitled *Cribratio Alcorani.* [22]Urges. [23]Slighted.
[24]That we may know how fanciful it is.
[25]Theodore Buchman (1504–64), Swiss theologian and orientalist
who collaborated with Melanchthon in publishing an edition of
the Koran. [26]Noted with opprobrium.
[27]Peter Galatin, a Jew who became a Franciscan friar and wrote
De arcanis Catholicae veritatis (1572), wherein he tried to show that
many of the doctrines and sacraments of the Roman Catholic
Church had been anticipated in the Talmud. [28]Derived.
[29]In 1511 the great Hebraist Johann Reuchlin urged Emperor
Maximilian I to ignore the advice of the reactionary Dominicans
of Cologne that he confiscate and burn Jewish books.
[30]Descended. [31]Exodus 31.18. [32]Exodus 34.1.
[33]Acquisitions through suffering (i.e., the salvation of humanity
through Christ's death on the cross).
[34]*Interruption...captivity*: the break in the writing of the Scriptures
resulting from the Babylonian captivity of the Jews by Nebu-
chadnezzar in 597 B.C.
[35]Ezra (or Esdras), a Hebrew scribe of the fifth century B.C., is
the supposed author of the biblical account of postexilic history in
Ezra and Nehemiah as well as of two Apocryphal books bearing
his name.
[36]Christopherus Sacrobosco published a defense of the Council
of Trent (*Defensio decreti Tridenti...*) in 1604.
[37]The Council of Trent, a general council of the Roman Catholic
Church at Trent, in Northern Italy (1545–63), which decreed
(among many other matters of doctrine and organization) that
only St. Jerome's Latin version of the Scriptures known as the
Vulgate was to be regarded as "sacred and canonical."
[38]*Not absolute...mores*: not merely for determining controverted
points of theology but for regulating faith and morals.

and conjectual light. Yet not equally, for the break of the day, because it hath a succession of more and more light, is clearer than the shutting in, which is overtaken with more and more darkness; so is the birth of the world more discernible than the death because upon this God hath cast more clouds, yet since the world in her first infancy did not speak to us at all (by any authors), and when she began to speak by Moses she spake not plain, but diversely to divers understandings, we must return again to our stronghold, faith, and end with this: that this beginning was, and before it, nothing. It is elder than darkness, which is elder than light; and was before confusion, which is elder than order by how much the universal chaos preceded forms and distinctions. A beginning so near eternity that there was no *then*, nor a minute of time between them. Of which, eternity could never say "tomorrow," nor speak as of a future thing because this beginning was the first point of time, before which, whatsoever God did He did it uncessantly[39] and unintermittingly, which was but the generation of the Son and procession of the Spirit and enjoying one another— things which if ever they had ended, had begun, and those be terms incompatible with eternity. And therefore St. Augustine says religiously and exemplarily, "If one ask me what God did before this beginning I will not answer as another did merrily, 'He made hell for such busy inquirers.' But I will sooner say I know not when I know not than answer that by which he shall be deluded which asked too high a mystery, and he be praised which answered a lie."[40]

Part ii
Of God

Men which seek God by reason and natural strength (though we do not deny common notions and general impressions of a sovereign power) are like mariners which voyaged before the invention of the compass, which were but coasters,[41] and unwillingly left the sight of the land. Such are they which would arrive at God by this world, and contemplate him only in His creatures and seeming demonstration. Certainly, every creature shows God as a glass,[42] but glimmeringly and transitorily, by the frailty both of the receiver[43] and beholder. Ourselves have His image, as medals, permanently and preciously delivered.[44] But by these meditations we get no further than to know what He *doth*, not what He *is*. But as by the use of the compass men safely dispatch Ulysses' dangerous ten years' travel in so many days, and have found out a new world richer than the old, so doth faith, as soon as our hearts are touched with it, direct and inform it in that great search of the discovery of God's essence and the New Hierusalem,[45] which reason durst not attempt. And though the faithfullest heart is not ever directly and constantly upon God but that it sometimes descends also to reason, yet it is [not] thereby so departed from Him but that it still looks towards Him, though not fully to Him: as the compass is ever northward, though it decline and have often variations towards east and west. By this faith, as by reason, I know that God is all that which all men can say of all good; I believe He is somewhat which no man can say nor know. For *si scirem quid Deus esset, Deus essem*.[46] For all acquired knowledge is by degrees, and

successive; but God is impartible,[47] and only faith, which can receive it all at once, can comprehend Him.

BOOK II

Part ii
[Concerning Miracles]

Nature is the common law by which God governs us, and miracle is His prerogative. For miracles are but so many *non obstantes*[48] upon nature. And miracle is not like prerogative in anything more than in this, that nobody can tell what it is.[49] For first, creation and such as that are not miracles because they are not (to speak in that language) *nata fieri per alium modum*.[50] And so only that is a miracle which might be done naturally and is not so done. And then, lest we allow the devil a power to do miracles, we must say that miracle is *contra totam naturam*, against the whole order and disposition of nature. For as in cities a father governs his family by a certain order which yet the magistrate of the city may change for the city's good, and a higher officer may change the city's order, but none, all, except the king; so I can change some natural things (as I can make a stone fly upward), a physician more, and the devil more than he, but only God can change all. And after that is out of necessity established —that miracle is against the whole order of nature I see not how there is left in God a power of miracles. For the miracles which are produced today were determined and inserted into the body of the whole history of nature (though they seem to us to be but interlineary and marginal) at the beginning, and are as infallible and certain as the most ordinary and customary things. Which is evicted and approved by that which Lactantius[51] says and particularly proves, that all Christ's miracles were long before prophesied. So that truly nothing can be done against the order of nature. For St. Augustine says truly, that is natural to each thing which God doth, from whom proceeds all fashion, number, and order of nature, for that God, whose

[39]Incessantly.
[40]*Confessions*, XI.xii. Throughout this section of the *Essays*, Donne draws heavily on the twelfth book of St. Augustine's *Confessions*.
[41]Mariners who sail along the coast. [42]Mirror.
[43]The imperfect mirror.
[44]"And God said, Let us make man in our image, after our likeness" (Genesis 1.26).
[45]The New Jerusalem, i.e., the City of God, heaven.
[46]"If I knew what God is, I myself would be God."
[47]Indivisible.
[48]In English law, a royal dispensation to do a thing notwithstanding any statute to the contrary. This prerogative was abolished by the Bill of Rights in 1689.
[49]In the developing struggle between crown and Parliament that was to eventuate in the civil war, one of the most controversial questions was that of defining and limiting the royal prerogative, which had been traditionally regarded by the crown as a right or privilege exercised without accountability.
[50]Designed to operate in any other way.
[51]An eminent rhetorician (d. ca. 320) who, though born a pagan, gained such renown as a Christian apologist that he was appointed tutor to the son of Constantine the Great.

decree is the nature of everything, should do against His own decree if He should do against nature. As therefore if we understood all created nature, nothing would be *mirum* to us; so if we knew God's purpose, nothing would be *miraculum*.[52] . . .

But because the danger of believing false miracles is extremely great, and the essential differences of false and true very few and very obscure—for what human understanding can discern whether they be wrought immediately or by second causes? and then for the end to which they are addressed, what sect of Christians or what sect departed from all Christians will refuse to stand to that law? "If there arise a prophet, and he give a wonder, and the wonder come to pass, saying, Let us go after other gods, that prophet shall be slain"[53]—I incline to think that God for the most part works His miracles rather to show His power than mercy, and to terrify enemies rather than comfort His children. For miracles lessen the merit of faith. . . . I speak not thus to cherish their opinion who think God doth no miracle now—that were to shorten His power or to understand His counsels—but to resist theirs who make miracles ordinary. For besides that it contradicts and destroys the nature of miracle to be frequent, God at first possessed His church *fortiter*[54] (by conquest of miracles), but He governs it now *suaviter*[55] (like an indulgent king by a law which he hath let us know). God forbid I should discredit or diminish the great works that He hath done at the tombs of His martyrs or at the pious and devout commemoration of the sanctity and compassion of His most Blessed Mother. But to set her up a bank[56] almost in every good town and make her keep a shop of miracles greater than her Son's—for is it not so to raise a child which was born dead and had been buried seventeen days to so small end, for it died again as soon as it was carried from her sight[57]—is fearful and dangerous to admit. . . .

For excepting the staying of the sun and carrying it back[58] (if it be clear that the body of the sun was carried back, and not the shadow only) and a very few more, it appears enough that the devil hath done oftener greater miracles than the children of God, for God delights not so much in the exercise of His power as of His mercy and justice, which partakes of both the other. For mercy is His paradise and garden in which He descends to walk and converse with man, power His army and arsenal by which he protects and overthrows, justice His exchequer where He preserves His own dignity and exacts our forfeitures.

PRAYERS

> In addition to a prayer dividing the two main sections of the *Essays* (that is, the meditations on Genesis and on Exodus) there are four terminal prayers wherein Donne seems to express something of the hope and faith toward which he had slowly made his way. The last one is especially moving.

O eternal and most merciful God, against whom, as we know and acknowledge that we have multiplied contemptuous and rebellious sins, so we know and acknowledge too that it were a more sinful contempt and rebellion than all those to doubt of Thy mercy for them, have mercy upon us! In the merits and mediation of Thy Son, our Saviour Christ Jesus, be merciful unto us! Suffer not, O Lord, so great a waste as the effusion of His blood without any return to Thee; suffer not the expense of so rich a treasure as the spending of His life without any purchase to Thee; but as Thou didst empty and evacuate His glory here upon earth, glorify us with that glory which His humiliation purchased for us in the kingdom of heaven. And as Thou didst empty that kingdom of thine, in a great part, by the banishment of those angels whose pride threw them into everlasting ruin, be pleased to repair that kingdom which their fall did so far depopulate by assuming us into their places and making us rich with their confiscations. And to that purpose, O Lord, make us capable of that succession to thine angels there. Begin in us here in this life an angelical purity, an angelical chastity, an angelical integrity to Thy service, an angelical acknowledgment that we always stand in Thy presence and should direct our actions to Thy glory. Rebuke us not, O Lord, in Thine anger, that we have not done so till now, but enable us now to begin that great work; and imprint in us an assurance that Thou receivest us now graciously as reconciled, though enemies, and fatherly as children, though prodigals, and powerfully as the God of our salvation, though our own consciences testify against us. Continue and enlarge Thy blessings upon the whole church, etc.

[52]*Mirum, Miraculum*: "astonishing," "miraculous."
[53]Adapted from Deuteronomy 13.1–5.   [54]"Strongly."
[55]"Gently."   [56]Bench (for selling merchandise).
[57]In a marginal gloss Donne cites a recently published (1606) collection of miracles of the Virgin.
[58]God stopped the sun to aid the Israelites against their enemies (Joshua 10.13) and, at Isaiah's request, turned it back in order to strengthen King Hezekiah's faith (2 Kings 20.11).

from Devotions upon Emergent Occasions (1624)

To the Most Excellent Prince, Prince Charles[1]

Most Excellent Prince,
I have had three births: one natural when I came into the world, one supernatural when I entered into the ministry,

and now a preternatural birth in returning to life from this sickness. In my second birth Your Highness' royal father

DEVOTIONS   [1]Charles, second son of James I, became Prince of Wales on the death of his elder brother Henry in 1612.

vouchsafed me his hand, not only to sustain me in it but to lead me to it.[2] In this last birth I myself am born a father: this child of mine, this book, comes into the world from me and with me. And therefore I presume (as I did the father to the father) to present the son to the son, this image of my humiliation[3] to the lively image of His Majesty, Your Highness. It might be enough that God hath seen my devotions, but examples of good kings are commandments, and Ezekiah writ the meditations of his sickness after his sickness.[4] Besides, as I have lived to see (not as a witness only, but as a 10 partaker) the happiness of a part of your royal father's time, so shall I live (in my way) to see the happiness of the times of Your Highness too if this child of mine, inanimated by your gracious acceptation, may so long preserve alive the memory of Your Highness'

humblest and devotedest
John Donne

I. INSULTUS MORBI PRIMUS

THE FIRST ALTERATION, THE FIRST
GRUDGING, OF THE SICKNESS

i. Meditation

Variable and therefore miserable condition of man! this minute I was well, and am ill this minute. I am surprised with 20 a sudden change, and alteration to worse, and can impute it to no cause nor call it by any name. We study health, and we deliberate upon our meats and drink and air, and exercises, and we hew and we polish every stone that goes to that building; and so our health is a long and a regular work. But in a minute a cannon batters all, overthrows all, demolishes all, a sickness unprevented for all our diligence, unsuspected for all our curiosity; nay, undeserved, if we consider only disorder, summons us, seizes us, possesses us, destroys us in an instant. O miserable condition of man! 30 which was not imprinted by God, who, as He is immortal himself, had put a coal, a beam of immortality into us, which we might have blown into a flame, but blew it out by our first sin; we beggared ourselves by hearkening after false riches, and infatuated ourselves by hearkening after false knowledge. So that now we do not only die, but die upon the rack, die by the torment of sickness; nor that only, but are pre-afflicted, super-afflicted with these jealousies and suspicions and apprehensions of sickness before we can call it a sickness. We are not sure we are ill; one hand asks the 40 other by the pulse, and our eye asks our own urine how we do. O multiplied misery! we die, and cannot enjoy death because we die in this torment of sickness; we are tormented with sickness, and cannot stay till the torment come, but pre-apprehensions and presages prophesy those torments which induce that death before either come; and our dissolution is conceived in these first changes, quickened in the sickness itself, and born in death, which bears date from these first changes. Is this the honor which man hath by being a little world, that he hath these earthquakes in himself, sudden 50 shakings; these lightnings, sudden flashes; these thunders, sudden noises; these eclipses, sudden offuscations[5] and darkenings of his senses; these blazing stars, sudden fiery exhalations;[6] these rivers of blood, sudden red waters? Is he a

world to himself only, therefore, that he hath enough in himself not only to destroy and execute himself, but to presage that execution upon himself; to assist the sickness, to antedate the sickness, to make the sickness the more irremediable by sad apprehensions, and, as if he would make a fire the more vehement by sprinkling water upon the coals, so to wrap a hot fever in cold melancholy lest the fever alone should not destroy fast enough without this contribution, nor perfect the work (which is destruction) except we joined an artificial sickness of our own melancholy to our natural, our unnatural fever. O perplexed discomposition. O riddling distemper, O miserable condition of man!

i. Expostulation

If I were but mere dust and ashes I might speak unto the Lord, for the Lord's hand made me of this dust, and the Lord's hand shall re-collect these ashes; the Lord's hand was the wheel upon which this vessel of clay was framed, and the Lord's hand is the urn in which these ashes shall be preserved. I am the dust and the ashes of the temple of the Holy Ghost, and what marble is so precious? But I am more than dust and ashes: I am my best part, I am my soul. And being so, the breath of God, I may breathe back these pious expostulations to my God: My God, my God, why is not my soul as sensible as my body? Why hath not my soul these apprehensions, these presages, these changes, those antidotes, those jealousies, those suspicions of a sin, as well as my body of a sickness? Why is there not always a pulse in my soul to beat at the approach of a tentation[7] to sin? Why are there not always waters in mine eyes to testify my spiritual sickness? I stand in the way of tentations, naturally, necessarily; all men do so; for there is a snake in every path, tentations in every vocation; but I go, I run, I fly into the ways of tentation which I might shun; nay, I break into houses where the plague is; I press into places of tentation, and tempt the devil himself, and solicit and importune them who had rather be left unsolicited by me. I fall sick of sin, and am bedded and bedrid, buried and putrified in the practice of sin, and all this while have no presage, no pulse, no sense of my sickness. O height, O depth of misery, where the first symptom of the sickness is hell, and where I never see the fever of lust, of envy, of ambition by any other light than the darkness and horror of hell itself, and where the first messenger that speaks to me doth not say, "Thou mayest die," no, nor "Thou must die," but "Thou art dead"; and where the first notice that my soul hath of her sickness is irrecoverableness, irremediableness; but, O my God, Job did not charge Thee foolishly in his temporal afflictions, nor may I in my spiritual. Thou hast imprinted a pulse in our soul, but we do not examine it; a voice in our conscience, but we do not hearken unto it. We talk it out, we jest it out, we drink it out, we sleep it out; and when we wake, we do not say with Jacob, "Surely the Lord is in this place, and I knew it not." But

[2]For Izaak Walton's account of James I's part in Donne's ordination see p. 761. [3]Account of my illness.
[4]When King Hezekiah (*Ezekiah*) was "sick unto death" he was restored through the good offices of the prophet Isaiah (2 Kings 20.1–11). [5]Obfuscations, stupefactions.
[6]Vapors emitted by heavenly bodies and taking the form of meteors, comets, and other ill omens. [7]Temptation.

though we might know it, we do not, we will not.[8] But will God pretend to make a watch and leave out the spring? to make so many various wheels in the faculties of the soul and in the organs of the body and leave out grace, that should move them? or will God make a spring and not wind it up? Infuse His first grace[9] and not second it with more, without which we can no more use his first grace when we have it than we could dispose ourselves by nature to have it? But alas, that is not our case; we are all prodigal sons and not disinherited; we have received our portion and misspent it, not been denied it. We are God's tenants here, and yet here, He, our landlord, pays us rents, not yearly nor quarterly but hourly and quarterly; every minute He renews His mercy, but we "will not understand lest that we should be converted, and He should heal us.[10]

i. Prayer

O eternal and most gracious God, who, considered in thyself, art a circle, first and last and altogether, but, considered in Thy working upon us, art a direct line, and leadest us from our beginning through all our ways to our end, enable me by Thy grace to look forward to mine end, and to look backward too, to the considerations of Thy mercies afforded me from the beginning, that so by that practice of considering Thy mercy in my beginning in this world, when Thou plantedst me in the Christian Church, and Thy mercy in the beginning in the other world, when thou writest me in the book of life, in my election, I may come to a holy consideration of Thy mercy in the beginning of all my actions here: that in all the beginnings, in all the accesses and approaches, of spiritual sicknesses of sin I may hear and hearken to that voice, "O thou man of God, there is death in the pot,"[11] and so refrain from that which I was so hungerly, so greedily flying to. "A faithful ambassador is health,"[12] says Thy wise servant Solomon. Thy voice received in the beginning of a sickness, of a sin, is true health. If I can see that light betimes and hear that voice early, "Then shall my light break forth as the morning, and my health shall spring forth speedily."[13] Deliver me, therefore, O my God, from these vain imaginations that it is an overcurious thing, a dangerous thing, to come to that tenderness, that rawness, that scrupulousness, to fear every concupiscence, every offer of sin, that this suspicious and jealous diligence will turn to an inordinate dejection of spirit and a diffidence[14] in Thy care and providence; but keep me still established both in a constant assurance that Thou wilt speak to me at the beginning of every such sickness, at the approach of every such sin, and that if I take knowledge of that voice then and fly to Thee, Thou wilt preserve me from falling, or raise me again when by natural infirmity I am fallen. Do this, O Lord, for His sake who knows our natural infirmities, for He had them; and knows the weight of our sins, for He paid a dear price for them—Thy Son, our Saviour, Christ Jesus. Amen.

IV. MEDICUSQUE VOCATUR

THE PHYSICIAN IS SENT FOR

iv. Meditation

It is too little to call man a little world; except God, man is a diminutive to nothing. Man consists of more pieces, more parts, than the world; than the world doth, nay, than the world is. And if those pieces were extended and stretched out in man as they are in the world, man would be the giant and the world the dwarf, the world but the map and the man the world. If all the veins in our bodies were extended to rivers, and all the sinews to veins of mines, and all the muscles that lie upon one another to hills, and all the bones to quarries of stones, and all the other pieces to the proportion of those which correspond to them in the world, the air would be too little for this orb of man to move in, the firmament would be but enough for this star; for as the whole world hath nothing to which something in man doth not answer, so hath man many pieces of which the whole world hath no representation. Enlarge this meditation upon this great world, man, so far as to consider the immensity of the creatures this world produces; our creatures are our thoughts, creatures that are born giants; that reach from east to west, from earth to heaven; that do not only bestride all the sea and land, but span the sun and firmament at once; my thoughts reach all, comprehend all. Inexplicable mystery! I their creator am in a close prison, in a sick bed, anywhere, and any one of my creatures, my thoughts, is with the sun, and beyond the sun, overtakes the sun, and overgoes the sun in one pace, one step, everywhere. And then, as the other world produces serpents and vipers, malignant and venomous creatures, and worms and caterpillars that endeavor to devour that world which produces them, and monsters compiled and complicated[15] of divers parents and kinds; so this world, ourselves, produces all these in us in producing diseases and sicknesses of all those sorts: venomous and infectious diseases, feeding and consuming diseases, and manifold and entangled diseases made up of many several ones. And can the other world name so many venomous, so many consuming, so many monstrous creatures as we can diseases of all these kinds? O miserable abundance, O beggarly riches, how much do we lack of having remedies for every disease, when as yet we have not names for them? But we have a Hercules against these giants,[16] these monsters, that is the physician; he musters up all the forces of the other world to succor this, all nature to relieve man. We have the physician, but we are not the physician. Here we shrink in our proportion, sink in our dignity, in respect of very mean creatures who are physicians to themselves. The hart that is pursued and wounded, they say, knows an herb which, being eaten, throws off the arrow: a strange kind of vomit. The dog that pursues it, though he be subject to sickness, even proverbially, knows his grass that recovers him. And it may be true that the drugger[17] is as near to man as to other

[8]Genesis 28.16.

[9]Prevenient grace, which precedes repentance and conversion and enables fallen man to seek God. Thus Milton's God, predicting the regeneration of humanity (*Paradise Lost*, III.188–190), declares:
    I will clear their senses dark,
    What may suffice, and soft'n stony hearts
    To pray, repent, and bring obedience due.

[10]Matthew 13.15.   [11]2 Kings 4.40.   [12]Proverbs 13.17.
[13]Isaiah 58.8.   [14]Doubt, mistrust.
[15]Folded or twisted together.
[16]One of the fabled twelve labors of Hercules was to destroy the nine-headed hydra of Lerna.   [17]Means of relief.

creatures; it may be that obvious and present simples,[18] easy to be had, would cure him; but the apothecary is not so near him, nor the physician so near him, as they two are to other creatures; man hath not that innate instinct to apply those natural medicines to his present danger as those inferior creatures have; he is not his own apothecary, his own physician, as they are. Call back, therefore, thy meditation again, and bring it down:[19] what's become of man's great extent and proportion when himself shrinks himself and consumes himself to a handful of dust; what's become of his soaring thoughts, his compassing thoughts, when himself brings himself to the ignorance, to the thoughtlessness, of the grave? His diseases are his own, but the physician is not; he hath them at home, but he must send for the physician.

X. LENTE ET SERPENTI SATAGUNT OCCURRERE MORBO

THEY FIND THE DISEASE TO STEAL ON
INSENSIBLY AND ENDEAVOR TO MEET WITH IT SO

x. *Meditation*

This is nature's nest of boxes: the heavens contain the earth; the earth, cities; cities, men. And all these are concentric; the common center[20] to them all is decay, ruin; only that is eccentric which was never made; only that place, or garment rather, which we can imagine but not demonstrate. That light, which is the very emanation of the light of God, in which the saints shall dwell, with which the saints shall be apparelled, only that bends not to this center, to ruin; that which was not made of nothing is not threatened with this annihilation. All other things are, even angels, even our souls; they move upon the same poles, they bend to the same center; and if they were not made immortal by preservation, their nature could not keep them from sinking to this center, annihilation. In all these (the frame of the heavens, the states upon earth, and men in them comprehend all) those are the greatest mischiefs which are least discerned; the most insensible[21] in their ways come to be the most sensible[22] in their ends. The heavens have had their dropsy, they drowned the world; and they shall have their fever, and burn the world. Of the dropsy, the flood, the world had a foreknowledge 120 years before it came;[23] and so some made provision against it, and were saved; the fever shall break out in an instant and consume all; the dropsy did no harm to the heavens from whence it fell, it did not put out those lights, it did not quench those heats; but the fever, the fire, shall burn the furnace itself, annihilate those heavens that breathe it out. Though the Dog Star[24] have a pestilent breath, an infectious exhalation, yet because we know when it will rise, we clothe ourselves, and we diet ourselves, and we shadow ourselves to a sufficient prevention; but comets and blazing stars, whose effects or significations no man can interrupt or frustrate, no man foresaw: no almanac tells us when a blazing star will break out, the matter is carried up in secret; no astrologer tells us when the effects will be accomplished, for that's a secret of a higher sphere than the other; and that which is most secret is most dangerous. It is so also here in the societies of men, in states and common-wealths. Twenty rebellious drums make not so dangerous a noise as a few whisperers and secret plotters in corners. The cannon doth not so much hurt against a wall as a mine under the wall, nor a thousand enemies that threaten so much as a few that take an oath to say nothing. God knew many heavy sins of the people, in the wilderness, and after, but still He charges them with that one, with murmuring, murmuring in their hearts, secret disobediences, secret repugnances against His declared will;[25] and these are the most deadly, the most pernicious. And it is so too with the diseases of the body; and that is my case. The pulse, the urine, the sweat, all have sworn to say nothing, to give no indication of any dangerous sickness. My forces are not enfeebled, I find no decay in my strength; my provisions are not cut off, I find no abhorring[26] in mine appetite; my counsels are not corrupted nor infatuated, I find no false apprehensions to work upon mine understanding; and yet they see that invisibly, and I feel that insensibly, the disease prevails. The disease hath established a kingdom, an empire in me, and will have certain *arcana imperii,* secrets of state, by which it will proceed and not be bound to declare them. But yet against those secret conspiracies in the state, the magistrate hath the rack; and against these insensible diseases physicians have their examiners; and those these employ now.

XIV. IDQUE NOTANT CRITICIS MEDICI EVENISSE DIEBUS

THE PHYSICIANS OBSERVE THESE ACCIDENTS
TO HAVE FALLEN UPON THE CRITICAL DAYS

xiv. *Meditation*

I would not make man worse than he is, nor his condition more miserable than it is. But could I though I would? As a man cannot flatter God nor overpraise him, so a man cannot injure man nor undervalue him. Thus much must necessarily be presented to his remembrance, that those false happinesses which he hath in this world have their times and their seasons and their critical days, and they are judged and denominated according to the times when they befall us. What poor elements are our happinesses made of if time, time which we can scarce consider to be anything, be an essential part of our happiness! All things are done in some place; but if we consider place to be no more but the next hollow superficies of the air, alas! how thin and fluid a thing

[18]Medicinal herbs.
[19]*Call back...down:* check your far-ranging speculations and apply them to the present situation. *Meditation:* text *meditations.*
[20]The imagery of this passage is built on that of the geocentric universe described by Ptolemy, which, it was thought, would eventually be destroyed by fire.   [21]Imperceptible.
[22]Keenly felt.
[23]According to Genesis 6.3, God had planned the flood 120 years before the inundation of the earth.
[24]Sirius, whose period of helical rising (July 3–August 11), marked by hot, sultry weather, was traditionally associated with pestilence.
[25]Donne is perhaps thinking of Numbers 11.1, where God's wrath at the incessant complaints of the Israelites during their wandering in the desert led Him to consume some of them with fire.
[26]Shrinking with horror, i.e., diminution.

is air, and how thin a film is a superficies, and a superficies of air! All things are done in time too, but if we consider time to be but the measure of motion, and howsoever it may seem to have three stations, past, present, and future, yet the first and last of these are not (one is not now, and the other is not yet), and that which you call present is not now the same that it was when you began to call it so in this line (before you sound that word *present*, or that monosyllable *now*, the present and the now is past). If this imaginary, half-nothing time be of the essence of our happinesses, how can they be 10 thought durable? Time is not so; how can they be thought to be? Time is not so, not so considered in any of the parts thereof. If we consider eternity, into that time never entered; eternity is not an everlasting flux of time, but time is as a short parenthesis in a long period; and eternity had been the same as it is though time had never been. If we consider not eternity but perpetuity, not that which had no time to begin in, but which shall outlive time, and be when time shall be no more, what a minute is the life of the durablest creature compared to that! and what a minute is man's life in respect 20 of the sun's, or of a tree! And yet how little of our life is occasion, opportunity to receive good in; and how little of that occasion do we apprehend and lay hold of? How busy and perplexed a cobweb is the happiness of man here, that must be made up with a watchfulness to lay hold upon occasion, which is but a little piece of that which is nothing, time? And yet the best things are nothing without that. Honors, pleasures, possessions presented to us out of time, in our decrepit and distasted and unapprehensive age, lose their office and lose their name; they are not honors to us 30 that shall never appear nor come abroad into the eyes of the people, to receive honor from them who give it; nor pleasures to us who have lost our sense to taste them; nor possessions to us who are departing from the possession of them. Youth is their critical day that judges them, that denominates them, that inanimates and informs them and makes them honors and pleasures and possessions; and when they come in an unapprehensive age they come as a cordial when the bell rings out, as a pardon when the head is off. We rejoice in the comfort of fire, but does any man cleave to 40 it at midsummer? We are glad of the freshness and coolness of a vault, but does any man keep his Christmas there? Or are the pleasures of the spring acceptable in autumn? If happiness be in the season or in the climate, how much happier, then, are birds than men, who can change the climate, and accompany and enjoy the same season ever.

XVII. NUNC LENTO SONITU DICUNT, MORIERIS

NOW THIS BELL TOLLING SOFTLY FOR ANOTHER
SAYS TO ME, THOU MUST DIE

xvii. Meditation

Perchance he for whom this bell tolls may be so ill as that he knows not it tolls for him; and perchance I may think myself so much better than I am as that they who are about me and 50 see my state may have caused it to toll for me, and I know not that. The church is catholic, universal; so are all her actions;

all that she does belongs to all. When she baptizes a child, that action concerns me, for that child is thereby connected to that head which is my head too, and ingrafted into that body whereof I am a member. And when she buries a man, that action concerns me: all mankind is of one author, and is one volume; when one man dies, one chapter is not torn out of the book, but translated into a better language; and every chapter must be so translated; God employs several translators; some pieces are translated by age, some by sickness, some by war, some by justice; but God's hand is in every translation, and His hand shall bind up all our scattered leaves again for that library where every book shall lie open to one another. As therefore the bell that rings to a sermon calls not upon the preacher only, but upon the congregation to come, so this bell calls us all; but how much more me, who am brought so near the door by this sickness. There was a contention as far as a suit[27] (in which both piety and dignity, religion and estimation, were mingled), which of the religious orders should ring to prayers first in the morning; and it was determined that they should ring first that rose earliest. If we understand aright the dignity of this bell that tolls for our evening prayer, we would be glad to make it ours by rising early, in that application that it might be ours as well as his whose indeed it is. The bell doth toll for him that thinks it doth; and though it intermit again, yet from that minute that that occasion wrought upon him, he is united to God. Who casts not up his eye to the sun when it rises? but who takes off his eye from a comet when that breaks out? Who bends not his ear to any bell which upon any occasion rings? but who can remove it from that bell which is passing a piece of himself out of this world? No man is an island, entire of itself; every man is a piece of the continent, a part of the main.[28] If a clod be washed away by the sea, Europe is the less, as well as if a promontory were, as well as if a manor of thy friend's or of thine own were; any man's death diminishes me because I am involved in mankind, and therefore never send to know for whom the bell tolls; it tolls for thee. Neither can we call this a begging of misery or a borrowing of misery, as though we were not miserable enough of ourselves, but must fetch in more from the next house in taking upon us the misery of our neighbors. Truly it were an excusable covetousness if we did, for affliction is a treasure, and scarce any man hath enough of it. No man hath affliction enough that is not matured and ripened by it, and made fit for God by that affliction. If a man carry treasure in bullion, or in a wedge of gold, and have none coined into current moneys, his treasure will not defray[29] him as he travels. Tribulation is treasure in the nature of it, but it is not current money in the use of it, except we get nearer and nearer our home, heaven, by it. Another man may be sick too, and sick to death, and this affliction may lie in his bowels, as gold in a mine, and be of no use to him; but this bell that tells me of his affliction digs out and applies that gold to me: if by this consideration of another's danger I take mine own into contemplation, and so secure myself by making my recourse to my God, who is our only security.

[27]Formal litigation.   [28]Mainland.   [29]Suffice to support.

from LXXX Sermons (1640)

SERMON LXVI

THE SECOND OF MY PREBEND SERMONS UPON MY FIVE
PSALMS. PREACHED AT ST. PAUL'S, JANUARY 29, 1625.[1]
*Psalms 63.7. "Because Thou hast been my help, therefore in
the shadow of Thy wings will I rejoice."*

The Psalms are the manna of the church. As manna tasted to
every man like that that he liked best,[2] so do the Psalms
minister instruction and satisfaction to every man in every
emergency and occasion. David was not only a clear prophet
of Christ himself, but a prophet of every particular Christian;
he foretells what I, what any, shall do and suffer and say. [10]
And as the whole Book of Psalms is *oleum effusum* (as the
spouse speaks of the name of Christ),[3] an ointment poured
out upon all sorts of sores, a cerecloth that supples[4] all bruises,
a balm that searches all wounds, so are there some certain
Psalms that are imperial Psalms, that command over all
affections and spread themselves over all occasions—catholic,
universal Psalms that apply themselves to all necessities.
This is one of those, for of those constitutions which are
called apostolical[5] one is that the church should meet every
day to sing this Psalm. And acccordingly St. Chrysostom[6] [20]
testifies that it was decreed and ordained by the primitive
fathers that no day should pass without the public singing of
this Psalm. Under both these obligations (those ancient
constitutions called the apostle's and those ancient decrees
made by the primitive fathers) belongs to me, who have my
part in the service of God's church, the especial meditation
and recommendation of this Psalm. And under a third
obligation too, that it is one of those five Psalms, the daily
rehearsing whereof is enjoined to me by the constitutions
of this church, as five other are to every other person of our [30]
body.[7] As the whole book is manna, so these five Psalms are
my gomer, which I am to fill and empty every day of this
manna.

DIVISIO[8]

Now as the spirit and soul of the whole Book of Psalms is
contracted into this Psalm, so is the spirit and soul of this
whole Psalm contracted into this verse. The key of the Psalm
(as St. Hierome calls the titles of the Psalms) tells us that
David uttered this Psalm "when he was in the wilderness
of Judah"; there we see the present occasion that moved [40]
him; and we see what was passed between God and him
before, in the first clause of our text ("Because thou hast
been my help"), and then we see what was to come by the
rest ("Therefore in the shadow of thy wings will I rejoice").
So that we have here the whole compass of time—past,
present, and future; and these three parts of time shall be
at this time the three parts of this exercise: first, what David's
distress put him upon for the present, and that lies in the
context; secondly, how David built his assurance upon
that which was past ("Because thou hast been my help"); [50]
and thirdly, what he established to himself for the future

("Therefore in the shadow of thy wings will I rejoice").
First, his distress in the wilderness, his present estate carried
him upon the memory of that which God had done for him
before, and the remembrance of that carried him upon that
of which he assured himself after. Fix upon God anywhere,
and you shall find Him a circle; He is with you now, when
you fix upon Him; He was with you before, for He brought
you out to this fixation; and He will be with you hereafter,
for "He is yesterday, and today, and the same for ever."[9]

For David's present condition, who was now in a banish-
ment,[10] in a persecution in the wilderness of Judah (which is
our first part) we shall only insist upon that (which is indeed
spread over all the Psalm to the text, and ratified in the text)
that in all those temporal calamities David was only sensible
of his spiritual loss; it grieved him not that he was kept from
Saul's court, but that he was kept from God's church. For
when he says, by way of lamentation, "that he was in a dry
and thirsty land, where no water was," he expresses what
penury, what barrenness, what drought, and what thirst he
meant; "to see Thy power, and thy glory, so as I have seen
Thee in the sanctuary." For there "my soul shall be satisfied
as with marrow, and with fatness" and there "my mouth
shall praise thee with joyful lips." And in some few considera-
tions conducing to this, that spiritual losses are incom-
parably heavier than temporal, and that therefore the restitu-
tion to our spiritual happiness, or the continuation of it, is
rather to be made the subject of our prayers to God, in all
pressures and distresses, than of temporal, we shall determine
that first part. And for the particular branches of both the
other parts (the remembering of God's benefits past and the
building of an assurance for the future upon that remem-
brance) it may be fitter to open them to you anon, when we
come to handle them, than now. Proceed we now to our
first part, the comparing of temporal and spiritual afflictions.

LXXX SERMONS [1]The date is given in Old Style; the year in New
Style is 1626. [2]The Apocryphal Wisdom of Solomon 16.20.
[3]Song of Solomon 1.3. [4]A bandage that relieves.
[5]*Constitutions...apostolical*: a collection of injunctions of the 2d or
3d century concerning the duties of Christians. Except for the so-
called Apostolic Canons (a set of eighty-five rules concerning
ceremonies and discipline), they have never been accepted as au-
thoritative by the western church.
[6] St. John Chrysostom (i.e. "Golden Mouthed," 345?–407), a
father of the Greek church noted for the eloquence of his
homilies and letters.
[7]As one of the thirty prebendaries of St. Paul's (i.e., members of
the chapter receiving special stipends), Donne, whose prebend was
Chiswick, was required to recite five psalms (Nos. 62–66), each
day and to make them subjects of special meditations. The first
of his so-called Prebend Sermons (on Psalm 62) had been delivered
on 8 May 1625, and the third (5 November 1626) followed the
second by almost a year.
[8]"Division," i.e., the analysis of the text. [9]Hebrews 13.8.
[10]Following his anointment by Samuel as King Saul's successor
and his subsequent military successes, David was exiled by the
jealous Saul and fled into the desert (1 Samuel 18–19).

FIRST PART. AFFLICTIO UNIVERSALIS[11]

In the way of this comparison falls first the consideration of the universality of afflictions in general and the inevitableness thereof. It is a blessed metaphor that the Holy Ghost hath put into the mouth of the apostle, *"pondus gloriae,"* that our *"afflictiones"* are but "light" because there is an "exceeding" and an "eternal weight of glory" attending them.[12] If it were not for that exceeding weight of glory, no other weight in this world could turn the scale, or weigh down those infinite weights of afflictions that oppress us here. There is not only *"pestis valde gravis"* ("the pestilence grows heavy upon the land")[13] but there is *"musca valde gravis,"* God calls in but the fly to vex Egypt, and even the fly is a heavy burden unto them.[14] It is not only Job that complains "that he was a burden to himself"[15] but even Absalom's hair was a burden to him till it was polled.[16] It is not only Jeremy that complains, *"aggravavit compedes,"* that God had made their fetters and their chains heavy to them,[17] but the workmen in harvest complain that God had made a fair day heavy unto them ("we have borne the heat, and the burden of the day").[18] "Sand is heavy," says Solomon;[19] and how many suffer so under a sandhill of crosses, daily, hourly afflictions, that are heavy by their number if not by their single weight? And "a stone is heavy" (says he in the same place), and how many suffer so? How many, without any former preparatory cross, or comminatory or commonitory[20] cross, even in the midst of prosperity and security, fall under some one stone, some grindstone, some millstone, some one insupportable cross that ruins them? But then (says Solomon there) "a fool's anger is heavier than both";[21] and how many children and servants and wives suffer under the anger and morosity and peevishness and jealousy of foolish masters and parents and husbands, though they must not say so? David and Solomon have cried out that all this world is "vanity" and "levity"; and (God knows) all is weight and burden and heaviness and oppression; and if there were not a weight of future glory to counterpoise it, we should all sink into nothing.

I ask not Mary Magdalen whether lightness were not a burden (for sin is certainly, sensibly a burden) but I ask Susanna whether even chaste beauty were not a burden to her; and I ask Joseph whether personal comeliness were not a burden to him. I ask not Dives,[22] who perished in the next world, the question; but I ask them who are made examples of Solomon's rule, of that "sore evil," (as he calls it), "riches kept to the owners thereof for their hurt,"[23] whether riches be not a burden.

All our life is a continual burden, yet we must not groan; a continual squeezing, yet we must not pant; and as in the tenderness of our childhood we suffer, and yet are whipped if we cry, so we are complained of, if we complain, and made delinquents if we call the times ill. And that which adds weight to weight, and multiplies the sadness of this consideration, is this, that still the best men have had most laid upon them. As soon as I hear God say that He hath found "an upright man, that fears God and eschews evil,"[24] in the next lines I find a commission to Satan to bring in Sabeans and Chaldeans upon his cattle and servants, and fire and tempest upon his children, and loathsome diseases upon himself. As soon as I hear God say that He hath found "a man according to His own heart,"[25] I see his sons ravish his daughters, and then murder one another, and then rebel against the father, and put him into straits for his life. As soon as I hear God testify of Christ at His baptism, "This is my beloved Son in whom I am well pleased,"[26] I find that Son of His "led up by the Spirit to be tempted of the devil."[27] And after I hear God ratify the same testimony again at His transfiguration ("This is my beloved Son, in whom I am well pleased") I find that beloved Son of His deserted, abandoned, and given over to scribes and Pharisees and publicans and Herodians[28] and priests and soldiers and people and judges and witnesses and executioners, and He that was called the beloved Son of God and made partaker of the glory of heaven, in this world, in His transfiguration, is made now the sewer of all the corruption, of all the sins of this world, as no Son of God, but a mere man, as no man, but a contemptible worm. As though the greatest weakness in this world were man, and the greatest fault in man were to be good, man is more miserable than other creatures, and good men more miserable than any other men.

Afflictio Spiritualis[29]

But then there is *"pondus gloriae,"* "an exceeding weight of eternal glory," and that turns the scale; for as it makes all worldly prosperity as dung, so it makes all worldly adversity as feathers. And so it had need, for in the scale against it there are not only put temporal afflictions, but spiritual too; and to these two kinds we may accommodate those words, "he that falls upon this stone" (upon temporal afflictions) may be bruised, broken, "but he upon whom that stone falls" (spiritual afflictions) "is in danger to be ground to powder."[30] And then the great and yet ordinary danger is that these spiritual afflictions grow out of temporal; murmuring and diffidence in God and obduration out of worldly calamities; and so against nature, the fruit is greater and heavier than the tree, spiritual heavier than temporal afflictions.

[11]"Universal affliction." [12]2 Corinthians 2.17.
[13]Exodus 9.3. In 1625 there had been a particularly severe epidemic of the plague in London. [14]Exodus 8.24. [15]Job 7.20.
[16]2 Samuel 14.26. *Polled*: cut. [17]Lamentations 3.7.
[18]Matthew 20.12. [19]Proverbs 27.3.
[20]Denunciatory or admonitory. [21]Proverbs 27.3.
[22]*Magdalen...Dives*: Mary Magdalen, a woman out of whom Jesus cast seven devils (Luke 8.2), has often been identified as the penitent sinner of Luke 7.36–50. Susanna, a Jewish captive in Babylon whose story is told in the Apocryphal book bearing her name, was saved by Daniel when falsely accused of adultery. Joseph, the youngest of Jacob's sons, incurred his brothers' jealousy because he was his father's favorite (Genesis 37). Dives was the "certain rich man" who, from his torments in hell, saw the beggar Lazarus rejoicing "in Abraham's bosom" (Luke 16.19–31).
[23]Ecclesiastes 5.13. [24]Job 1.1. [25]1 Samuel 13.14.
[26]Matthew 3.17. [27]Matthew 4.1.
[28]Followers of Herod, King of Judea. [29]"Spiritual affliction."
[30]Matthew 21.44.

They who write of natural story propose that plant[31] for the greatest wonder in nature, which, being no firmer than a bulrush or a reed, produces and bears for the fruit thereof no other but an entire and very hard stone. That temporal affliction should produce spiritual stoniness and obduration is unnatural, yet ordinary. Therefore doth God propose it as one of those greatest blessings which He multiplies upon His people: "I will take away your stony hearts, and give you hearts of flesh";[32] and, Lord, let me have a fleshly heart in any sense, rather than a stony heart. We find mention amongst the observers of rarities in nature of hairy hearts, hearts of men, that have been overgrown with hair; but of petrified hearts, hearts of men grown into stone, we read not; for this petrifaction of the heart, this stupefaction of a man, is the last blow of God's hand upon the heart of man in this world. Those great afflictions which are poured out of the vials of the seven angels upon the world[33] are still accompanied with that heavy effect, that that affliction hardened them. "They were scorched with heats and plagues" by the fourth angel, and it follows, they blasphemed the name of God, and repented not, to give Him glory." Darkness was induced upon them by the fifth angel, and it follows, "they blasphemed the God of heaven, and repented not of their deeds." And from the seventh angel there fell hailstones of the weight of talents[34] (perchance four pound weight) upon men; and yet these men had so much life left as to "blaspheme God" out of that respect, which alone should have brought them to glorify God "because the plague thereof was exceeding great." And when a great plague brings them to blaspheme, how great shall that second plague be that comes upon them for blaspheming?

Let me wither and wear out mine age in a discomfortable, in an unwholesome, in a penurious prison, and so pay my debts with my bones, and recompense the wastefulness of my youth with the beggary of mine age; let me wither in a spital under sharp and foul and infamous diseases, and so recompense the wantonness of my youth with that loathsomeness in mine age; yet if God withdraw not His spiritual blessings, His grace, His patience, if I can call my suffering His doing, my passion[35] His action, all this that is temporal is but a caterpillar got into one corner of my garden, but a mildew fallen upon one acre of my corn; the body of all, the substance of all is safe as long as the soul is safe. But when I shall trust to that which we call a good spirit, and God shall deject and impoverish and evacuate that spirit, when I shall rely upon a moral constancy, and God shall shake and enfeeble and enervate, destroy, and demolish that constancy; when I shall think to refresh myself in the serenity and sweet air of a good conscience, and God shall call up the damps and vapors of hell itself, and spread a cloud of diffidence and an impenetrable crust of desperation upon my conscience; when health shall fly from me, and I shall lay hold upon riches to succor me and comfort me in my sickness, and riches shall fly from me, and I shall snatch after favor and good opinion to comfort me in my poverty; when even this good opinion shall leave me, and calumnies and misinformations shall prevail against me;

when I shall need peace, because there is none but Thou, O Lord, that should stand for me, and then shall find that all the wounds that I have come from Thy hand, all the arrows that stick in me from Thy quiver; when I shall see, that because I have given myself to my corrupt nature, Thou hast changed Thine; and because I am all evil towards Thee, therefore Thou hast given over being good towards me; when it comes to this height, that the fever is not in the humors but in the spirits, that mine enemy is not an imaginary enemy, fortune, nor a transitory enemy, malice in great persons, but a real and an irresistible and an inexorable and an everlasting enemy, the Lord of hosts himself, the Almighty God himself, the Almighty God himself only knows the weight of this affliction, and except He put in that *pondus gloriae,* that exceeding weight of an eternal glory, with His own hand into the other scale, we are weighed down, we are swallowed up irreparably, irrevocably, irrecoverably, irremediably.

This is the fearful depth, this is spiritual misery, to be thus fallen from God. But was this David's case? Was he fallen thus far, into a diffidence in God? No. But the danger, the precipice, the slippery sliding into that bottomless depth is to be excluded from the means of coming to God or staying with God; and this is that that David laments here, that by being banished and driven into the wilderness of Judah, he had not access to the sanctuary of the Lord, to sacrifice his part in the praise and to receive his part in the prayers of the congregation; for angels pass not to ends but by ways and means, nor men to the glory of the triumphant church but by participation of the communion of the militant.[36] To this note David sets his harp in many, many Psalms: sometimes, that God had suffered His enemies to possess His tabernacle ("he forsook the tabernacle of Shiloh, he delivered his strength into captivity, and his glory into the enemies' hands"),[37] but most commonly he complains that God disabled him from coming to the sanctuary. In which one thing he had summed up all his desires, all his prayers ("One thing have I desired of the Lord, that will I look after; that I may dwell in the house of the Lord, all the days of my life, to behold the beauty of the Lord, and to inquire in His temple");[38] his vehement desire of this he expresses again: "My soul thirsteth for God, for the living God; when shall I come and appear before God?"[39] He expresses a holy jealousy, a religious envy, even to the sparrows and swallows, yea, "the sparrow hath found a house, and the swallow a nest for herself, and where she may lay her young, even thine altars, O Lord of hosts, my King and my God."[40] Thou art my King and my God, and yet

[31]Pliny (*Natural History,* XXVII.1xxiv) describes the plant lithospermum as famous for its fruit that looks like "little stones, white and round as pearls." [32]Ezekiel 11.19.
[33]Revelation 16, which is paraphrased and cited throughout the rest of the paragraph. [34]Ancient denominations of weight.
[35]Suffering.
[36]The Church Militant, the body of the faithful on earth warring against the powers of evil (as distinguished from the Church Triumphant, the saved in heaven). [37]Psalm 78.60–61.
[38]Psalm 27.4. [39]Psalm 42.2. [40]Psalm 84.3.

excludest me from that which thou affordest to sparrows, "And are not we of more value than many sparrows?"[41]

And as though David felt some false ease, some half-tentation,[42] some whispering that way, that God is "in the wilderness of Judah," in every place, as well as in his "Sanctuary," there is in the original in that place a pathetical, a vehement, a broken expressing expressed: "O thine altars."[43] It is true (says David) Thou art here in the wilderness, and I may see Thee here, and serve Thee here, but "O Thine altars, O Lord of hosts, my King and my God." When David could not come in person to that place, yet he bent towards the temple ("In Thy fear will I worship towards Thy holy temple").[44] Which was also Daniel's devotion when he prayed "his chamber windows were open towards Jerusalem";[45] and so is Hezekiah's turning to the wall to weep, and to pray in his sickbed,[46] understood to be to that purpose, to conform and compose himself towards the temple. In the place consecrated for that use, God by Moses fixes the service and fixes the reward;[47] and towards that place (when they could not come to it) doth Solomon direct their devotion in the consecration of the temple ("When they are in the wars, when they are in captivity, and pray towards this house, do thou hear them").[48] For as in private prayer when (according to Christ's command) we are shut in our chamber, there is exercised *modestia fidei,* the modesty and bashfulness of our faith, not pressing upon God in His house: so in the public prayers of the congregation there is exercised the fervor and holy courage of our faith, for *agmine facto obsidemus Deum,* it is a mustering of our forces and a besieging of God. Therefore does David so much magnify their blessedness that are in this house of God ("Blessed are they that dwell in thy house, for they will be still praising thee"); those that look towards it may praise Thee sometimes, but those men who dwell in the church, and whose whole service lies in the church, have certainly an advantage of all other men (who are necessarily withdrawn by worldly businesses) in making themselves acceptable to Almighty God if they do their duties and observe their church services aright.

Excommunicatio[49]

Man being therefore thus subject naturally to manifold calamities, and spiritual calamities being incomparably heavier than temporal, and the greatest danger of falling into such spiritual calamities being in our absence from God's church, where only the outward means of happiness are ministered unto us, certainly there is much tenderness and deliberation to be used before the church doors be shut against any man. If I would not direct a prayer to God to excommunicate any man from the triumphant church (which were to damn him) I would not oil the key, I would not make the way too slippery for excommunications in the militant church; for that is to endanger him. I know how distasteful a sin to God contumacy and contempt and disobedience to order and authority is; and I know (and all men, that choose not ignorance, may know) that our excommunications (though calumniators impute them to small things because, many times, the first complaint is of

some small matter) never issue but upon contumacies, contempts, disobediences to the church. But they are real contumacies, not interpretative, apparent contumacies, not presumptive, that excommunicate a man in heaven; and much circumspection is required, and (I am far from doubting it) exercised in those cases upon earth; for though every excommunication upon earth be not sealed in heaven, though it damn not the man, yet it dams up that man's way by shutting him out of that church through which he must go to the other; which being so great a danger, let every man take heed of excommunicating himself. The impersuasible recusant does so; the negligent libertine does so; the fantastic separatist does so; the half-present man, he, whose body is here and mind away, does so; and he, whose body is but half here, his limbs are here upon a cushion, but his eyes, his ears are not here, does so: all these are[50] self-excommunicators, and keep themselves from hence. Only he enjoys that blessing, the want whereof David deplores, that is here entirely, and is glad he is here, and glad to find this kind of service here that he does, and wishes no other.

And so we have done with our first part, David's aspect, his present condition, and his danger of falling into spiritual miseries, because his persecution and banishment amounted to an excommunication, to an excluding of him from the service of God, in the church. And we pass, in our order proposed at first, to the second, his retrospect, the consideration what God had done for him before, "because Thou hast been my help."

SECOND PART

Through this second part we shall pass by these three steps. First, that it behoves us in all our purposes and actions to propose to ourselves a copy to write by, a pattern to work by, a rule or an example to proceed by; because it hath been thus heretofore, says David, I will resolve upon this course for the future. And secondly, that the copy, the pattern, the precedent which we are to propose to ourselves is the observation of God's former ways and proceedings upon us; because God hath already gone this way, this way I will await His going still. And then, thirdly and lastly, in this second part, the way that God had formerly gone with David, which was that He had been his help ("because Thou hast been my help").

Ideae[51]

First, then, from the meanest artificer through the wisest philosopher to God himself, all that is well done or wisely undertaken is undertaken and done according to preconceptions, fore-imaginations, designs, and patterns proposed to ourselves beforehand. A carpenter builds not a house, but that he first sets up a frame in his own mind, what kind of

---

[41]Luke 12.7. [42]Temptation. [43]Psalm 84.3. [44]Psalm 5.7.
[45]Daniel 6.10.
[46]Isaiah 38.2. Donne cites the same passage in dedicating his *Devotions* to Prince Charles (see p. 549). [47]Deuteronomy 31.11.
[48]1 Kings 8.44. [49]"Excommunication." [50]Text *all these are.*
[51]"Ideas," i.e., preconceptions, patterns.

house he will build. The little great philosopher Epictetus[52] would undertake no action, but he would first propose to himself what Socrates or Plato, what a wise man would do in that case, and according to that he would proceed. Of God himself it is safely resolved in the school that He never did anything in any part of time of which He had not an eternal preconception, an eternal Idea, in himself before. Of which Ideas, that is, preconceptions, predeterminations in God, St. Augustine pronounces, *"Tanta vis in ideis constituitur."* There is so much truth and so much power in these Ideas as that without acknowledging them no man can acknowledge God, for he does not allow God counsel and wisdom and deliberation in His actions, but sets God on work before He have thought what He will do. And therefore he and others of the fathers read that place (which we read otherwise), *"Quod factum est, in ipso vita erat"*;[53] that is, in all their expositions, whatsoever is made in time was alive in God before it was made, that is, in that eternal Idea and pattern which was in Him. So also do divers of those fathers read those words to the Hebrews[54] (which we read, "the things that are seen are not made of things that do appear"), *ex invisibilibus visibilia facta sunt,* "things formerly invisible were made visible"; that is, we see them not till now, till they are made, but they had an invisible being in that Idea, in that pre-notion, in that purpose of God before, forever before. Of all things in heaven and earth but of himself, God had an Idea, a pattern in himself, before He made it.

And therefore let Him be our pattern for that, to work after patterns; to propose to ourselves rules and examples for all our actions; and the more, the more immediately, the more directly our actions concern the service of God. If I ask God by what Idea he made me, God produces his *"faciamus hominem ad imaginem nostram,"*[55] that there was a concurrence of the whole Trinity to make me in Adam according to that image which they were, and according to that Idea which they had predetermined. If I pretend to serve God, and He ask me for my Idea, how I mean to serve him, shall I be able to produce none? If he ask me an Idea of my religion, and my opinions, shall I not be able to say, "It is that which Thy word, and Thy catholic church hath imprinted in me?" If He ask me an Idea of my prayers, shall I not be able to say, "It is that which my particular necessities, that which the form prescribed by Thy Son, that which the care and piety of the church, in conceiving fit prayers, hath imprinted in me?" If He ask me an Idea of my sermons, shall I not be able to say, "It is that which the a- nalogy of faith, the edification of the congregation, the zeal of Thy work, the meditations of my heart hath imprinted in me?" But if I come to pray or to preach without this kind of Idea, if I come to extemporal prayer and extemporal preaching, I shall come to an extemporal faith and extem- poral religion; and then I must look for an extemporal heaven, a heaven to be made for me; for to that heaven which belongs to the catholic church I shall never come except I go by the way of the catholic church, by former Ideas, former examples, former patterns, to believe ac- cording to ancient beliefs, to pray according to ancient forms, to preach according to former meditations. God does

nothing, man does nothing well, without these Ideas, these retrospects, this recourse to pre-conceptions, pre-delibera- tions.

Via Domini[56]

Something, then, I must propose to myself to be the rule and the reason of my present and future actions, which was our first branch in this second part; and then the second is that I can propose nothing more availably than the con- templation of the history of God's former proceeding with me; which is David's way here, because this was God's way before, I will look for God in this way still. That language in which God spake to man, the Hebrew, hath no present tense; they form not their verbs as our western lan- guages do, in the present, "I hear" or "I see" or "I read"; but they begin at that which is past, "I have seen" and "heard" and "read." God carries us in His language, in His speaking, upon that which is past, upon that which He hath done already; I cannot have better security for present nor future than God's former mercies exhibited to me. *"Quis non gaudeat,"* says St. Augustine: who does not triumph with joy when he considers what God hath done? *"Quis non et ea, quae nondum venerunt, ventura sperat, propter illa, quae jam tanta impleta sunt?"* Who can doubt of the performance of all that sees the greatest part of a prophesy performed? If I have found that true that God hath said of the person of Antichrist, why should I doubt of that which He says of the ruin of Antichrist? *"Credamus modicum quod restat,"* says the same father, it is much that we have seen done, and it is but little that God hath reserved to our faith, to believe that it shall be done.

There is no state, no church, no man that hath not this tie upon God, that hath not God in these bands, that God by having done much for them already hath bound himself to do more. Men proceed in their former ways, sometimes, lest they should confess an error, and acknowledge that they had been in a wrong way. God is obnoxious[57] to no error, and therefore He does still as He did before. Every one of you can say now to God, "Lord, Thou broughtest me hither, therefore enable me to hear; Lord, Thou doest that, therefore make me understand; and that, therefore let me believe; and that too, therefore strengthen me to the practice; and all that, therefore continue me to a perseverance." Carry it up to the first sense and apprehension that ever thou hadst of God's working upon thee, either in thyself, when thou camest first to the use of reason, or in others in thy behalf, in thy baptism, yet when thou thinkest thou art at the first, God had done something for thee before all that; before that, he had elected thee, in that election which St. Augus- tine speaks of, *"Habet electos, quos creaturus est eligendos,"* God hath elected certain men, whom He intends to create that He may elect them; that is, that He may declare His election upon them. God had thee before He made thee;

[52]Greek Stoic philosopher (60?–?120) who taught mainly in Rome.
[53]John 1.3–4. [54]Hebrews 11.3.
[55]"Let us make man in our image" (Genesis 1.26).
[56]"The way of the master." [57]Liable, exposed.

He loved thee first, and then created thee, that thou loving Him, He might continue His love to thee. The surest way, and the nearest way to lay hold upon God is the consideration of that which He had done already. So David does; and that which he takes knowledge of, in particular, in God's former proceedings towards him, is because God had been his help, which is our last branch in this part, "Because thou hast been my help."

Quia Auxilium[58]

From this one word, that God hath been my "help," I make account that we have both these notions: first, that God hath not left me to myself, He hath come to my succor, He hath helped me; and then, that God hath not left out myself; He hath been my help, but He hath left something for me to do with Him, and by His help. My security for the future, in this consideration of that which is past, lies not only in this, that God hath delivered me, but in this also, that He hath delivered me by way of a help, and help always presumes an endeavour and cooperation in him that is helped. God did not elect me as a helper, nor create me, nor redeem me, nor convert me by way of helping me; for He alone did all, and He had no use at all of me. God infuses His first grace,[59] the first way, merely as a giver, entirely, all himself; but His subsequent graces as a helper; therefore we call them auxiliant graces, helping graces; and we always receive them when we endeavour to make use of His former grace. "Lord, I believe" (says the man in the Gospel to Christ), "help mine unbelief."[60] If there had not been unbelief, weakness, unperfectness in that faith, there had needed no help; but if there had not been a belief, a faith, it had not been capable of help and assistance, but it must have been an entire act, without any concurrence on the man's part.

So that if I have truly the testimony of a rectified conscience that God hath helped me, it is in both respects: first, that He hath never forsaken me, and then that He hath never suffered me to forsake myself; He hath blessed me with that grace, that I trust in no help but His, and with this grace too, that I cannot look for His help except I help myself also. God did not help heaven and earth to proceed out of nothing in the creation,[61] for they had no possibility of any disposition towards it, for they had no being: but God did help the earth to produce grass and herbs; for, for that, God had infused a seminal disposition into the earth which, for all that, it could not have perfected without His farther help. As in making of woman, there is the very word of our text, *gnazar*, God made him a "helper," one that was to do much for him, but not without him. So that, then, if I will make God's former working upon me an argument of His future gracious purposes, as I must acknowledge that God hath done much for me, so I must find that I have done what I could by the benefit of that grace with Him; for God promises to be but a helper. "Lord, open thou my lips," says David;[62] that is God's work entirely; and then, "My mouth, my mouth shall show forth thy praise"; there enters David into the work with God. And then, says God to him, "*Dilata os tuum,* Open thy mouth" (it is now made "thy mouth," and therefore do thou open it), "and I will

fill it";[63] all inchoations and consummations, beginnings and perfectings, are of God, of God alone; but in the way there is a concurrence on our part (by a successive continuation of God's grace) in which God proceeds as a helper; and I put Him to more than that if I do nothing. But if I pray for His help, and apprehend and husband His graces well when they come, then He is truly, properly my helper; and upon that security, that testimony of a rectified conscience, I can proceed to David's confidence for the future, "Because thou hast been my help, therefore in the shadow of thy wings will I rejoice"; which is our third and last general part.

DIVISIO. THIRD PART

In this last part, which is (after David's aspect[64] and consideration of his present condition, which was, in the effect, an exclusion from God's temple, and his retrospect, his consideration of God's former mercies to him, that He had been his help) his prospect, his confidence for the future, we shall stay a little upon these two steps; first, that that which he promises himself is not an immunity from all powerful enemies, nor a sword of revenge upon those enemies; it is not that he shall have no adversary, nor that that adversary shall be able to do him no harm, but that he should have a refreshing, a respiration *in velamento alarum,* under the shadow of God's wings. And then (in the second place), that this way which God shall be pleased to take, this manner, this measure of refreshing which God shall vouchsafe to afford (though it amount not to a full deliverance) must produce a joy, a rejoicing in us; we must not only not decline to a murmuring that we have no more, no, nor rest upon a patience for that which remains, but we must ascend to a holy joy, as if all were done and accomplished, "In the shadow of Thy wings will I rejoice."

Umbra Alarum[65]

First, then, lest any man in his dejection of spirit or of fortune should stray into a jealousy or suspicion of God's power to deliver him, as God hath spangled the firmament with stars, so hath He his Scriptures with names and metaphors and denotations of power. Sometimes he shines out in the name of a sword and of a target and of a wall and of a tower and of a rock and of a hill; and sometimes in that glorious and manifold constellation of all together, *"Dominus exercituum,* the Lord of hosts." God, as God, is never represented to us with defensive arms; He needs them not. When the poets present their great heroes and their worthies, they always insist upon their arms, they spend much of their invention upon the description of their arms, both because the greatest valor and strength needs arms (Goliah[66] himself was

[58]"Because [Thou hast been my] help" (the opening words of Donne's text, Psalm 63.7).
[59]Prevenient grace, which works upon the human will antecedent to its turning to God.   [60]Mark 9.24.
[61]For Sir Walter Raleigh's discussion of the widely held doctrine of creation *ex nihilo*, see p. 871.   [62]Psalm 51.15.   [63]Psalm 81.10.
[64]Contemplation.
[65]"[Therefore in] the shadow of Thy wings [will I rejoice,]" the concluding words of Donne's text.
[66]Goliath, the giant Philistine slain by David with a sling (1 Samuel

armed) and because to expose one's self to danger unarmed is not valor but rashness. But God is invulnerable in himself, and is never represented armed; you find no shirts of mail, no helmets, no cuirasses in God's armory. In that one place of Esay where it may seem to be otherwise, where God is said "to have put on righteousness as a breastplate, and a helmet of salvation upon His head"[67]in that prophecy God is Christ, and is therefore in that place called "the Redeemer." Christ needed defensive arms, God does not. God's word does; his Scriptures do; and therefore St. Hierome hath armed them, and set before every book his *prologum galeatum,*[68] that prologue that arms and defends every book from calumny. But though God need not nor receive not defensive arms for himself, yet God is to us a helmet, a breastplate, a strong tower, a rock, everything that may give us assurance and defence; and as often as He will, He can refresh that proclamation, *"Nolite tangere Christos meos,"* our enemies shall not so much as touch us.[69]

But here, by occasion of His metaphor in this text (*"Sub umbra alarum,* In the shadow of thy wings") we do not so much consider an absolute immunity, that we shall not be touched, as a refreshing and consolation, when we are touched, though we be pinched and wounded. The names of God which are most frequent in the Scriptures are these three: Elohim and Adonai and Jehovah; and to assure us of his power to deliver us, two of these three are names of power. Elohim is *Deus fortis,* the mighty, the powerful God; and (which deserves a particular consideration) Elohim is a plural name; it is not *Deus fortis,* but *Dii fortes,* powerful gods. God is all kind of gods; all kinds which either idolators and Gentiles can imagine (as riches or justice or wisdom or valor or such) and all kinds which God himself hath called gods (as princes and magistrates and prelates and all that assist and help one another). God is Elohim, all these gods, and all these in their height and best of their power, for Elohim is *Dii fortes,* gods in the plural, and those plural gods in their exaltation.

The second name of God is a name of power too, Adonai. For, Adonai is *Dominus,* the Lord, such a lord as is lord and proprietary of all his creatures, and all creatures are his creatures; and then, *"Dominium est potestas tum utendi, tum abutendi."* says the law; to be absolute lord of anything gives that lord a power to do what he will with that thing. God, as he is Adonai, the Lord, may give and take, quicken[70] and kill, build and throw down where and whom He will. So, then, two of God's three names are names of absolute power, to imprint and reimprint an assurance in us that He can absolutely deliver us, and fully revenge us, if He will. But, then, His third name, and that name which He chooses to himself, and in the signification of which name He employs Moses for the relief of His people under Pharaoh, that name Jehovah, is not a name of power, but only of essence, of being, of subsistence, and yet in the virtue of that name God relieved His people. And if in my afflictions God vouchsafe to visit me in that name, to preserve me in my being, in my subsistence in Him, that I be not shaked out of Him, disinherited in Him, excommunicate from Him, divested of Him, annihilated towards Him, let Him, at His good pleasure, re-

serve his Elohim and His Adonai, the exercises and declarations of His mighty power, to those great public[71] causes that more concern His glory than anything that can befall me; but if He impart His Jehovah, enlarge himself so far towards me as that I may live and move and have my being in Him, though I be not instantly delivered, nor mine enemies absolutely destroyed, yet this is as much as I should promise myself, this is as much as the Holy Ghost intends in this metaphor, *"Sub umbra alarum,* Under the shadow of thy wings," that is a refreshing, a respiration, a conservation, a consolation in all afflictions that are inflicted upon me.

Yet is not this metaphor of wings without a denotation of power. As no act of God's, though it seem to imply but spiritual comfort, is without a denotation of power (for it is the power of God that comforts me; to overcome that sadness of soul and that dejection of spirit which the adversary by temporal afflictions would induce upon me is an act of His power), so this metaphor "the shadow of His wings" (which in this place expresses no more than consolation and refreshing in misery, and not a powerful deliverance out of it) is so often in the Scriptures made a denotation of power too as that we can doubt of no act of power if we have this shadow of His wings. For in this metaphor of wings doth the Holy Ghost express the maritime power, the power of some nations at sea, in navies ("Woe to the land shadowing with wings");[72] that is, that hovers over the world and intimidates it with her sails and ships. In this metaphor doth God remember His people of His powerful deliverance of them ("You have seen what I did unto the Egyptians, and how I bare you on eagles' wings, and brought you to myself.")[73] In this metaphor doth God threaten His and their enemies what He can do ("The noise of the wings of His cherubims are as the noise of great waters, and of an army").[74] So also what he will do ("He shall spread his wings over Bozrah, and at that day shall the hearts of the mighty men of Edom be as the heart of a woman in her pangs").[75] So that if I have the shadow of His wings, I have the earnest[76] of the power of them too; if I have refreshing and respiration from them, I am able to say, as those three confessors did to Nebuchadnezzar, "My God is able to deliver me," I am sure He hath power; "and my God will deliver me" when it conduces to His glory, I know He will; "but if He do not, be it known unto thee, O King, we will not serve thy gods";[77] be it known unto thee, O Satan, how long soever God defer my deliverance, I will not seek false comforts, the miserable comforts of this world. I will not, for I need not; for I can subsist under this shadow of these wings, though I have no more.

The mercy seat itself was covered with the cherubim's wings,[78] and who would have more than mercy and a mercy seat; that is, established, resident mercy, permanent and perpetual mercy, present and familiar mercy, a mercy seat. Our Saviour Christ intends as much as would have

---

17). [67]Isaiah 59.17.
[68]*Prologus galeatus,* i.e., helmeted or defensive prologue.
[69]Psalm 105.15. [70]Give life to. [71]Text *puklike.* [72]Isaiah 18.1.
[73]Exodus 19.4. [74]Ezekiel 1.24. [75]Jeremiah 49.22.
[76]Foretaste, pledge. [77]Daniel 3.17. [78]Exodus 25.20.

served their turn, if they had laid hold upon it, when He says "that He would have gathered Jerusalem, as a hen gathers her chickens under her wings."[79] And though the other prophets do (as ye have heard) mingle the signification of power and actual deliverance in this metaphor of wings, yet our prophet, whom we have now in especial consideration, David, never doth so; but in every place where he uses this metaphor of wings (which are in five or six several Psalms) still he rests and determines in that sense which is his meaning here; that though God do not actually deliver us, nor actually destroy our enemies, yet if He refresh us in the shadow of His wings, if He maintain our subsistence (which is a religious constancy) in Him, this should not only establish our patience (for that is but half the work) but it should also produce a joy and rise to an exultation, which is our last circumstance: "Therefore in the shadow of thy wings I will rejoice."

Gaudium[80]

I would always raise your hearts and dilate your hearts to a holy joy, to a joy in the Holy Ghost. There may be a just fear that men do not grieve enough for their sins; but there may be a just jealousy, and suspicion too, that they may fall into inordinate grief, and diffidence[81] of God's mercy; and God hath reserved us to such times as, being the later times, give us even the dregs and lees of misery to drink. For God hath not only let loose into the world a new spiritual disease, which is an equality and an indifferency, which religion our children or our servants or our companions profess (I would not keep company with a man that thought me a knave or a traitor; with him that thought I loved not my prince, or were a faithless man, not to be believed, I would not associate myself; and yet I will make him my bosom companion that thinks I do not love God, that thinks I cannot be saved), but God hath accompanied and complicated almost all our bodily diseases of these times with an extraordinary sadness, a predominant melancholy, a faintness of heart, a cheerlessness, a joylessness of spirit, and therefore I return often to this endeavor of raising your hearts, dilating your hearts with a holy joy, joy in the Holy Ghost, for "under the shadow of His wings" you may, you should "rejoice."

If you look upon this world in a map you find two hemispheres, two half worlds. If you crush heaven into a map you may find two hemispheres too, two half heavens; half will be joy, and half will be glory; for in these two, the joy of heaven and the glory of heaven is all heaven often represented unto us. And as of those two hemispheres of the world the first hath been known long before, but the other (that of America, which is the richer in treasure) God reserved for later discoveries; so though He reserve that hemisphere of heaven, which is the glory thereof, to the resurrection, yet the other hemisphere, the joy of heaven, God opens to our discovery and delivers for our habitation even whilst we dwell in this world. As God hath cast upon the unrepentant sinner two deaths, a temporal and a spiritual death, so hath He breathed into us two lives; for so, as the word for death is doubled, *"Morte morieris,* Thou shalt die the death,"[82] so is the word for life expressed in the plural, *"Chaiim, vitarum,* God breathed into

his nostrils the breath of lives," of divers lives. Though our natural life were no life, but rather a continual dying, yet we have two lives besides that, an eternal life reserved for heaven, but yet a heavenly life too, a spiritual life, even in this world; and as God doth thus inflict two deaths and infuse two lives, so doth He also pass two judgments upon man, or rather repeats the same judgment twice. For that which Christ shall say to thy soul then at the last judgment, "Enter into thy Master's joy,"[83] He says to thy conscience now, "Enter into thy Master's joy." The everlastingness of the joy is the blessedness of the next life, but the entering, the inchoation, is afforded here. For that which Christ shall say then to us, *"Venite benedicti,* Come ye blessed,"[84] are words intended to persons that are coming, that are upon the way, though not at home; here in this world he bids us "come," there in the next he shall bid us "welcome." The angels of heaven have joy in thy conversion, and canst thou be without that joy in thyself? If thou desire revenge upon thine enemies, as they are God's enemies, that God would be pleased to remove and root out all such as oppose him, that affection appertains to glory; let that alone till thou come to the hemisphere of glory; there join with those martyrs under the altar, *"Usquequo Domine,"* How long, O Lord, dost thou defer judgment?[85] and thou shalt have thine answer there for that. Whilst thou art here, here join with David and the other saints of God in that holy increpation[86] of a dangerous sadness, "Why art thou cast down, O my soul? why art thou disquieted in me?"[87] That soul that is dissected and anatomized to God in a sincere confession, washed in the tears of true contrition, embalmed in the blood of reconciliation, the blood of Christ Jesus, can assign no reason, can give no just answer that interrogatory, "Why art thou cast down, O my soul? why art thou disquieted in me?" No man is so little as that he can be lost under these wings, no man so great as that they cannot reach to him; *"Semper ille major est, quantumcumque creverimus,"*[88] To what temporal, to what spiritual greatness soever we grow, still pray we Him to shadow us under His wings; for the poor need those wings against oppression, and the rich against envy. The Holy Ghost, who is a dove, shadowed the whole world under his wings; *Incubabat aquis,* He hovered over the waters,[89] He sat upon the waters, and He hatched all that was produced, and all that was produced so was good. Be thou a mother where the Holy Ghost would be a father, conceive by Him, and be content that He produce joy in thy heart here. First think that as a man must have some land or else he cannot be in wardship,[90] so a man must have some of the love of God or else he could not fall under God's correction; God would not give him his physic, God would not study his cure, if He cared not for him. And then think also that if God afford thee the shadow of His wings, that is, consolation, respiration, refreshing, though not a

[79]Matthew 23.37. [80]"Rejoicing." [81]Mistrust, doubt.
[82]Genesis 2.17. [83]Matthew 25.23. [84]Matthew 25.34.
[85]Revelation 6.10. [86]Reproof, rebuke. [87]Psalm 42.5.
[88]"No matter how great we become, He is always greater."
[89]Genesis 1.2.
[90]Serve as guardian for the person or property of a minor.

present and plenary deliverance in thy afflictions, not to thank God is a murmuring, and not to rejoice in God's ways is an unthankfulness. Howling is the noise of hell, singing, the voice of heaven; sadness the damp of hell, rejoicing, the serenity of heaven. And he that hath not this joy here, lacks one of the best pieces of his evidence for the joys of heaven; and hath neglected or refused that earnest by which God uses to bind His bargain, that true joy in this world shall flow into the joy of heaven as a river flows into the sea; this joy shall not be put out in death, and a new joy kindled in me in heaven; but as my soul, as soon as it is out of my body, is in heaven and does not stay for the possession of heaven nor for the fruition of the sight of God till it be ascended through air and fire and moon and sun and planets and firmament to that place which we conceive to be heaven, but without the thousandth part of a minute's stop, as soon as it issues is in a glorious light, which is heaven (for all the way to heaven is heaven; and as those angels, which came from heaven hither, bring heaven with them and are in heaven here, so that soul that goes to heaven meets heaven here; and as those angels do not divest heaven by coming, so these souls invest heaven in their going). As my soul shall not go towards heaven, but go by heaven to heaven, to the heaven of heavens, so the true joy of a good soul in this world is the very joy of heaven; and we go thither, not that, being without joy, we might have joy infused into us, but that as Christ says, "our joy might be full," perfected, sealed with an everlastingness; for as He promises "that no man shall take our joy from us,"[91] so neither shall death itself take it away, nor so much as interrupt it or discontinue it, but as in the face of death, when he lays hold upon me, and in the face of the devil, when he attempts me, I shall see the face of God (for everything shall be a glass, to reflect God upon me) so in the agonies of death, in the anguish of that dissolution, in the sorrows of that valediction, in the irreversibleness of that transmigration I shall have a joy which shall no more evaporate than my soul shall evaporate, a joy that shall pass up, and put on a more glorious garment above, and be joy superinvested in glory. Amen.

[91]John 16.24, 22.

William Chillingworth [1602-1644]

William Chillingworth, whose career epitomized the restless search for truth amid the controversies of his troubled age, turned disputation into art and then into a way of life. As the son of a prosperous Oxford citizen and the godson of William Laud (already on the winding stair to power), he was so bright and well connected that when his brilliant career at Trinity College, Oxford (B.A. 1620), was climaxed by a fellowship in 1628 his future seemed to be secure. Already, however, he was in a small way famous for his love of disputation. "He would often walk in the college grove and contemplate," Anthony Wood reported,

> but when he met with any scholar there he would enter into discourse and dispute with him, purposely to facilitate and make the way of wrangling common with him, which was the fashion used in those days, especially among the disputing theologists or among those that set themselves apart purposely for divinity.

It was his fatal passion for controversy, said Clarendon, that got him into trouble. His many Oxford friends were not surprised when this fastidious young Anglican exercised his "rare facility" in contention against a Jesuit who called himself John Fisher, but they were stunned when he declared himself persuaded by his adversary's arguments and become a convert of the Church of Rome. Although his apostasy created a sensation both in the little world of Oxford and in higher quarters too, he was soon to veer a second time: commissioned by the Jesuits at Douai, where he went in 1630, to justify his own conversion, he started shifting once again when Laud, in earnest correspondence, persuaded him to re-examine his position. Upon "better consideration," therefore, he became a "doubting papist"; by 1631 he was back at Oxford among such liberal and accommodating friends as Sir Lucius Cary, John Hales, and Gilbert Sheldon; and two years later he announced that he had left the Roman Catholic Church.

Such vacillation would in most men be condemned, said the sympathetic Clarendon, but Chillingworth was safe from blame:

> The sincerity of his heart was so conspicuous, and without the least temptation of any corrupt end, and the innocence and candor in his nature so evident and without any perverseness that all who knew him clearly discerned that all those restless motions and fluctuations proceeded only from the warmth and jealousy of his own thoughts in a too nice inquisition for truth.

But if he was once again a Protestant, he was not a member of the Church of England. His scruples concerning the Thirty-nine Articles (which he regarded as an "imposition on men's consciences") did not deter a sharp exchange of views with his former co-religionists (who were savage in reproaching him), but they did preclude a prompt return to the Anglican communion, and—more important—they forced on him a fundamental reassessment not merely of the infallibility claimed by Rome but of the authority claimed by any other church. And so, to clarify his own position and to secure, if possible, the basis of belief, he wrote *The Religion of Protestants a Safe Way to Salvation* (1638), a masterpiece of latitudinarian apologetics.

Apart from Chillingworth's own emotional and intellectual perplexities, this great work was complicated by the circumstances of its composition. In a sense it had its origin in the publication (1630) of *Charity Mistaken*, a strong defense of Roman Cathólic claims of universality and infallibility by an English Jesuit known as Edward Knott. This closely argued book provoked a rebuttal by Barnaby Potter, provost of Queen's College, Oxford, and bishop of Carlisle, with the unwieldy title *Want of Charity Justly Charged on All Such Romanists as Dare (without Truth or Modesty) Affirm that Protestancy Destroyeth Salvation* (1633), and Knott at once replied to Potter with *Mercy and Truth, or Charity Maintained by Catholics* (1634). It was then that Chillingworth was drawn into the fray, partly to defend his old friend Potter, partly to expound his own hard-earned conviction that the basis of belief was free inquiry and personal commitment, not dogmatic and compulsory formulations. Moreover, when news of Chillingworth's projected book stirred Knott to discredit his intentions in *A Direction to Be Observed by N. N. if He Mean to Proceed in Answering the Book Entitled Mercy and Truth* (1636), he was forced to answer this attack and so to complicate his work still more. •

As a result, *The Religion of Protestants* offers many problems to the modern reader. To reach the body of the work he must surmount (1) a dedication to King Charles, (2) an imprimatur by three Oxford dignitaries (for Laud, as Chillingworth explained, insisted that the book "pass through the fiery trial of the exact censures of many understanding judges"), (3) "The Preface to the Author of *Charity Maintained*, with an Answer to His Pamphlet Entitled *A Direction to N. N.*," (4) Knott's own preface to *Charity Maintained*, and (5) Chillingworth's reply. Even after all these hurdles one still must toil to get at Chillingworth's own views in the body of the work. Like many controversialists of the period, he develops his positions by citing long excerpts from his adversary's book and then replying to them point by point. Thus through seven chapters he gives us Knott's opinion and then his own rejoinder on such controverted questions as the means whereby truths are conveyed to the believer's understanding (Chapter II), the procedures for distinguishing "fundamental" truths (Chapter III), and the nature of the great reformers' "heresies" (Chapter VI). My excerpts represent the spacious general preface and also Chapter VI, which is built upon the strong but simple notion that "God does not and therefore . . . men ought not to require any more of a man than this, to believe the Scripture to be God's word, to endeavor to find the true sense of it, and to live according to it."

In an age of clashing dogmatisms such libertarian views were bound to give offense to bigots of all creeds. The indefatigable Knott promptly answered them with *Christianity Maintained* (1638); stalwart Presbyterians were alarmed; there were at least two strenuous rebuttals emanating from Douai in 1639; and in 1652, almost a decade after Chillingworth had died, Knott struck a final blow with *Infidelity Unmasked*. As for Chillingworth himself, when he finally overcame his scruples and subscribed to the Articles of the Church of England, he was at once made welcome and appointed chancellor of the See of Salisbury (1638). Inevitably, he sided with the king as England moved toward civil war, and when the fighting started he joined the royal forces. It is ironical that this man of peace and moderation apparently became a kind of army engineer who devised (on ancient models) a *testudo*, or engine of assault, for the seige of Gloucester in August 1643. Soon thereafter he fell ill at Arundel Castle and was taken captive by the parliamentary forces, whereupon the ghastly farce of his last phase began. As he lay dying in the bishop's palace at Chichester, where he had been permitted to retire, he was so incessantly plagued by the exhortations and recriminations of one Francis Cheynell, a Presbyterian fanatic, that death, which came to him on 30 January 1644, must have been a sweet release. Cheynell's own account of the dying man's last days and of his final rites in Chichester Cathedral (pp. 570 ff.) luridly exemplifies the rancor and the bigotry that Chillingworth had tried in vain to moderate. "He was a man of little stature but of great soul," said Wood in retrospect, "which, if times had been serene and life spared, might have done incomparable service to the Church of England."

My text is based upon the first (1638) edition of *The Religion of Protestants* (STC 5138). This and lesser things—for Chillingworth was in fact a one-book man—were included in the *Works* (3 vols., 1820). There are biographies of a sort by Pierre des Maizeaux (1725) and E. H. Plumptre (in *Masters in English Theology*, ed. Alfred Barry, 1877), and Chillingworth, not unnaturally, turns up in most accounts of seventeenth-century Anglicanism, some of which are cited in the General Bibliography, Section III.

from The Religion of Protestants a Safe Way to Salvation (1638)

THE PREFACE TO THE AUTHOR OF "CHARITY MAINTAINED," WITH AN ANSWER TO HIS PAMPHLET ENTITLED "A DIRECTION TO N. N."

Sir,

Upon the first news of the publication of your book, I used all diligence with speed to procure it, and came with such a mind to the reading of it as St. Austin, before he was a settled Catholic, brought to his conference with Faustus the Manichee.[1] For as he thought that if anything more than ordinary might be said in defence of the Manichean doctrine, Faustus was the man from whom it was to be expected, so my persuasion concerning you was, *Si Pergama dextra defendi possunt, certe hac defensa videbo.*[2] For I conceived that among the champions of the Roman Church the English in reason must be the best, or equal to the best, as being by most expert masters trained up purposely for this war, and perpetually practiced in it. Among the English, I saw the Jesuits would yield the first place to none; and men so wise in their generation as the Jesuits were, if they had any Achilles among them, I presumed, would make choice of him for this service. And besides, I had good assurance that in the framing of this building, though you were the only architect, yet you wanted not the assistance of many diligent hands to bring you in choice materials towards it, nor of many careful and watchful eyes to correct the errors of your work, if any should chance to escape you. Great reason, therefore, had I to expect great matters from you, and that your book should have in it the spirit and elixir of all that can be said in defence of your church and doctrine; and to assure myself that if my resolution not to believe it were not built upon the rock of evident grounds and reasons, but only upon some sandy and deceitful appearances, now the wind and storm and floods were coming, which would undoubtedly overthrow it.

2. Neither, truly, were you more willing to effect such an alteration in me than I was to have it effected. For my desire is to go the right way to eternal happiness. But whether this way lie on the right hand, or the left, or straight forwards; whether it be by following a living guide, or by seeking my direction in a book, or by hearkening to the secret whisper of some private spirit, to me it is indifferent. And he that is otherwise affected, and has not a traveler's indifference, which Epictetus requires in all that would find the truth, but much desires, in respect of his ease, or pleasure, or profit, or advancement, or satisfaction of friends, or any human

THE RELIGION OF PROTESTANTS [1]In his *Confessions* (V.iii), St. Augustine (*Austin*) tells that when, as a young man, he was strongly attracted to the Manichean heresy, God sent to Carthage the highly touted Faustus ("a great snare of the devil"), who had only to be heard to be rejected.
[2]If Troy can be defended strongly, then surely I shall see you do it.

consideration that one way should be true rather than another it is odds but he will take his desire that it should be so for an assurance that it is so. But I, for my part, unless I deceive myself, was, and still am so affected as I have made profession, not willing, I confess, to take anything upon trust, and to believe it without asking myself why; no, nor able to command myself (were I never so willing) to follow, like a sheep, every sheepherd that should take upon him to guide me, or every flock that should chance to go before me; but most apt and most willing to be led by reason to any way, or 10 from it, and always submitting all other reasons to this one: God hath said so, therefore it is true. Nor yet was I so unreasonable as to expect mathematical demonstrations from you in matters plainly incapable of them, such as are to be believed, and, if we speak properly, cannot be known; such, therefore, I expected not. For as he is an unreasonable master who requires a stronger assent to his conclusions than his arguments deserve, so I conceive him a froward and undisciplined scholar who desires stronger arguments for a conclusion than the matter will bear. But had you represented 20 to my understanding such reasons of your doctrine as, being weighed in an even balance, held by an even hand with those on the other side, would have turned the scale, and have made your religion more credible than the contrary, certainly I should have despised the shame of one more alteration,³ and with both mine arms and all my heart, most readily have embraced it. Such was my expectation from you, and such my preparation, which I brought with me to the reading of your book.

3. Would you know now what the event was, what 30 effect was wrought in me, by the perusal and consideration of it? To deal truly and ingenuously with you, I fell somewhat in my good opinion both of your sufficiency and sincerity, but was exceedingly confirmed in my ill opinion of the cause maintained by you. I found everywhere snares that might entrap and colors that might deceive the simple, but nothing that might persuade, and very little that might move, an understanding man, and one that can discern between discourse and sophistry: in short, I was verily persuaded that I plainly saw, and could 40 make it appear to all dispassionate and unprejudicate⁴ judges, that a vein of sophistry and calumny did run clean through it from the beginning to the end. And letting some friends understand so much, I suffered myself to be persuaded by them that it would not be either unproper for me, nor unacceptable to God, nor peradventure altogether unserviceable to His church, nor justly offensive to you (if you indeed were a lover of truth, and not a maintainer of a faction) if setting aside the second part, which was in a manner wholly employed in particular disputes, repetitions, and references, 50 and in wranglings with Dr. Potter about the sense of some supernumerary quotations, and whereon the main question no way depends, I would make a fair and ingenuous answer to the first, wherein the substance of the present controversy is confessedly contained; and which if it were clearly answered, no man would desire any other answer to the second. This, therefore, I undertook with a full resolution to be an adversary to your errors, but a friend and servant to your

person, and so much the more a friend to your person by how much the severer and more rigid adversary I was to your errors.

4. In this work my conscience bears me witness that I have, according to your advice, "proceeded always with this consideration, that I am to give a most strict account of every line and word that passeth under my pen," and therefore have been precisely careful, for the matter of my book, to defend truth only, and only by truth, and then scrupulously fearful of scandalizing you or any man with the manner of handling it. From this rule, sure I am, I have not willingly swerved in either part of it; and that I might not do it ignorantly, I have not only myself examined mine own work (perhaps with more severity than I have done yours, as conceiving it a base and unchristian thing to go about to satisfy others with what I myself am not fully satisfied) but have also made it pass the fiery trial of the exact censures of many understanding judges, always heartily wishing that you yourself had been of the quorum. But they who did undergo this burden, as they wanted not sufficiency to discover any heterodox doctrine, so I am sure they have been very careful to let nothing slip dissonant from truth or from the authorized doctrine of the Church of England; and therefore whatsoever causeless and groundless jealousy any man may entertain concerning my person, yet my book, I presume, in reason and common equity, should be free from them; wherein I hope that little or nothing hath escaped so many eyes, which being weighed in the balance of the sanctuary will be found too light; and in this hope I am much confirmed by your strange carriage of yourself in this whole business. For though by some crooked and sinister arts you have got my answer into your hands, now a year since and upwards, as I have been assured by some that know it and those of your own party, though you could not want every day fair opportunities of sending to me and acquainting me with any exceptions which you conceived might be justly taken to it, or any part of it (than which nothing could have been more welcome to me) yet hitherto you have not been pleased to acquaint me with any one; nay more, though you have been at sundry times, and by several ways, entreated and solicited, nay pressed and importuned by me, to join with me in a private discussion of the controversy between us before the publication of my answer (because I was extremely unwilling to publish anything which had not passed all manner of trials, as desiring not that I or my side but that truth might overcome, on which side soever it was) though I have protested to you, and set it under my hand (which protestation by God's help I would have made good) if you, or any other would undertake your cause, would give me a fair meeting, and choose out of your whole book any one argument whereof you were most confident, and by which you would be content the rest should be judged of, and make it appear that I had not or could not answer it, that I would desist from the work which I had undertaken,

³In his search for religious truth Chillingworth had gone from Anglicanism to Roman Catholicism and then back to Anglicanism. See headnote. ⁴Unprejudiced.

and answer none at all; though by all the arts which possibly I could devise I have provoked you to such a trial, in particular by assuring you that if you refused it the world should be informed of your tergiversation. Notwithstanding all this, you have perpetually and obstinately declined it, which to my understanding is a very evident sign that there is not any truth in your cause nor (which is impossible there should be) strength in your arguments, especially considering what our Saviour hath told us, "Everyone that doth evil hateth the light, neither cometh to the light, lest his deeds should be [10] reproved; but he that doth truth cometh to the light, that his deeds may be made manifest, that they are wrought in God."[5]

5. In the meanwhile, though you despaired of compassing your desire this honest way, yet you have not omitted to tempt me by base and unworthy considerations to desert the cause which I had undertaken, letting me understand from you, by an acquaintance common to us both, how that "in case my work should come to light, my inconstancy in religion" (so you miscall my constancy in following that way [20] to heaven which for the present seems to me the most probable) "should be to my great shame painted to the life"; that "my own writings should be produced against myself; that I should be urged to answer my own motives against Protestantism; and that such things should be published to the world touching my belief (for my painter, I must expect, should have great skill in perspective) "of the doctrine of the Trinity, the Deity of our Saviour, and all supernatural verities as should endanger all my benefices, present [and] future"; that "this warning was given me not out of fear of [30] what I could say (for that Catholics, if they might wish any ill, would beg the publication of my book, for respects[6] obvious enough), but out of a mere charitable desire of my good and reputation"; and that "all this was said upon a supposition that I was answering or had a mind to answer *Charity Maintained*; if not, no harm was done." To which courteous premonition, as I remember, I desired the gentleman who dealt between us to return this answer, or to this effect: that I believed the doctrine of the Trinity, the Deity of our Saviour, and all other supernatural verities revealed in [40] Scripture as truly and as heartily as yourself or any man, and therefore herein your charity was very much mistaken; but much more, and more uncharitably, in conceiving me a man that was to be wrought upon with these *terribiles visu formae*,[7] those carnal and base fears which you presented to me; which were very proper motives for the devil and his instruments to tempt poor-spirited men out of the way of conscience and honesty, but very incongruous either for teachers of truth to make use of or for lovers of truth (in which company I had been long ago matriculated) to hearken [50] to with any regard. But if you were indeed desirous that I should not answer *Charity Maintained*, one way there was, and but one, whereby you might obtain your desire; and that was by letting me know when and where I might attend you and by a fair conference, to be written down on both sides, convincing mine understanding (who was resolved not to be a recusant if I were convicted) that any one part of it, any one argument in it, which was of moment and

consequence, and whereon the cause depends, was indeed unanswerable. This was the effect of my answer, which I am well assured was delivered; but reply from you I received none but this, that you would have no conference with me but in print; and soon after finding me of proof[8] against all these batteries, and thereby, I fear, very much enraged, you took up the resolution of the furious goddess in the poet, madded with the unsuccessfulness of her malice,

Flectere si nequeo superos, Acheronta movebo![9]

6. For certainly those indign[10] contumelies, that mass of portentous and execrable calumnies, wherewith in your pamphlet of *Directions to N.N.* you have loaded not only my person in particular, but all the learned and moderate divines of the Church of England, and all Protestants in general, nay, all wise men of all religions but your own, could not proceed from any other fountain.

> There follows a long list of Knott's offenses. You have, Chillingworth told his adversary, fastened "the imputation of atheism and irreligion upon all wise and gallant men that are not of your own religion," declared that the denial of Rome's infallibility "is the mother-heresy from which all other must follow at ease," impugned the intellect and morals of the English clergy, and sneered that "Protestantism waxeth weary of itself." Chillingworth retorts to these and other calumnies before turning finally to his own defense against the charges of cynical self-interest, false doctrine, and hypocrisy.

27. And thus my friends, I suppose, are clearly vindicated from your scandals and calumnies. It remains now that in the last place I bring myself fairly off from your foul aspersions, that so my person may not be (as indeed howsoever it should not be) any disadvantage or disparagement to the cause, nor any scandal to weak Christians.

28. Your injuries, then, to me (no way deserved by me but by differing in opinion from you, wherein yet you surely differ from me as much as I from you) are especially three: for first, upon hearsay, and refusing to give me opportunity of begetting in you a better understanding of me, you charge me with a great number of false and impious doctrines, which I will not name in particular because I will not assist you so far in the spreading of my own undeserved defamation—but whosoever teaches or holds them, let him be anathema! The sum of them all, cast up by yourself in your first chapter, is this: "Nothing ought or can be certainly believed, farther than it may be proved by evidence of natural reason" (where, I conceive, natural reason is opposed to supernatural revelation)—and whosoever holds so, let him be anathema! And moreover, to clear myself once for all from all imputations of this nature, which charge me injuriously with denial of supernatural verities, I profess sincerely that I believe all those books of Scripture which the Church of England accounts canonical to be the infallible

[5]John 3.20–21. [6]Reasons. [7]"Specters of terrifying shapes."
[8]Invulnerable.
[9]"If I cannot bend heaven, then I shall stir up hell (Vergil, *Aeneid*, VII.312). The *furious goddess* is Hera, enraged at the sight of Aeneas in apparent safety. [10]Unworthy.

word of God. I believe all things evidently contained in them, all things evidently, or even probably, deducible from them. I acknowledge all that to be heresy which by the act of Parliament *primo* of Queen Elizabeth is declared to be so,[11] and only to be so, and though in such points which may be held diversely of divers men *salva fidei compage*[12] I would not take any man's liberty from him, and humbly beseech all men that they would not take mine from me; yet thus much I can say (which I hope will satisfy any man of reason), that whatsoever hath been held necessary to salvation, either by the catholic church of all ages, or by the consent of fathers, measured by Vincentius Lyrinensis' his rule,[13] or is held necessary either by the catholic church of this age or by the consent of Protestants, or even by the Church of England, that, against the Socinians and all others whatsoever, I do verily believe and embrace.[14]

29. Another great and manifest injury you have done me in charging me to have forsaken your religion "because it conduced not to my temporal ends" and suited not with my desires and designs, which certainly is a horrible crime, and whereof if you could convince me by just and strong presumptions, I should then acknowledge myself to deserve that opinion which you would fain induce your credents[15] unto, that I changed not your religion for any other, but for none at all. But of this great fault my conscience acquits me, and God, who only knows the hearts of all men, knows that I am innocent. Neither doubt I but all they who know me, and amongst them many persons of place and quality, will say they have reason in this matter to be my compurgators.[16] And for you, though you are very affirmative in your accusation, yet you neither do nor can produce any proof or presumption for it; but forgetting yourself (as it is God's will ofttimes that slanderers should do), have let fall some passages which, being well weighed, will make considering men apt to believe that you did not believe yourself. For how is it possible you should believe that I deserted your religion for ends, and against the light of my conscience, out of a desire of preferment; and yet, out of scruple of conscience, should refuse (which also you impute to me) to subscribe the Thirty-nine Articles, that is, refuse to enter at the only common door which here in England leads to preferment?[17] Again, how incredible is it that you should believe that I forsook the profession of your religion as not suiting with my desires and designs, which yet reconciles the enjoying of the pleasures and profits of sin here with the hope of happiness hereafter, and proposes as great hope of great temporal advancements to the capable servants of it as any, nay more than any, religion in the world; and, instead of this, should choose Socinianism, a doctrine, which, howsoever erroneous in explicating the mysteries of religion, and allowing greater liberty of opinion in speculative matters than any other company of Christians doth, or they should do, yet certainly, which you, I am sure, will pretend and maintain to explicate the laws of Christ with more rigor, and less indulgence and condescendence[18] to the desires of flesh and blood, than your doctrine doth. And besides, such a doctrine, by which no man in his right mind can hope for any honor or preferment either in this church or state or any

other! All which clearly demonstrates that this foul and false aspersion which you have cast upon me proceeds from no other fountain but a heart abounding with the gall and bitterness of uncharitableness, and even blinded with malice towards me, or else from a perverse zeal to your superstition, which secretly suggests this persuasion to you: that for the Catholic cause nothing is unlawful, but that you may make use of such indirect and crooked arts as these to blast my reputation and to possess men's minds with disaffection to my person, lest otherwise, peradventure, they might with some indifference hear reason from me. God, I hope, which bringeth light out of darkness, will turn your counsels to foolishness, and give all good men grace to perceive how weak and ruinous that religion must be which needs supportance from such tricks and devices: so I call them, because they deserve no better name. For what are all these personal matters, which hitherto you have spoke of, to the business in hand? If it could be proved that Cardinal Bellarmine was indeed a Jew, or that Cardinal Perron was an atheist,[19] yet I presume you would not accept of this for an answer to all their writings in defence of your religion. Let then my actions and intentions and opinions be what they will, yet I hope truth is nevertheless truth, nor reason ever the less reason because I speak it. And therefore the Christian reader, knowing that his salvation or damnation depends upon his impartial and sincere judgment of these things, will guard himself, I hope, from these impostures, and regard not the person, but the cause and the reasons of it; not who speaks, but what is spoken; which is all the favor I desire of him, as knowing that I am desirous not to persuade him unless it be truth whereunto I persuade him. . . .

> Toward the end of his "Answer to the Sixth Chapter" (on the affinity of Protestantism and heresy), Chillingworth goes beyond his point-by-point refutation of Knott's charges to formulate his conception of essential Protestantism.

THE ANSWER TO THE SIXTH CHAPTER, THAT PROTESTANTS ARE NOT HERETICS

56. It remains now that I should show that many reasons of moment may be alleged for the justification of Protestants,

[11]I accept the doctrinal and ecclesiastical decrees of Elizabeth's first (1559) Parliament, which passed the Acts of Supremacy and of Uniformity, thereby establishing the Church of England.
[12]"For securing sound faith."
[13]*Commonitorium pro catholicae fidei antiquitate et universitate*, a codification of orthodox doctrine by Vincent of Lérins in 434.
[14]In Chillingworth's view, one of Knott's grossest calumnies was that "the very doctrine of Protestants, if it be followed closely and with coherence to itself, must of necessity induce Socinianism."
[15]Believers.   [16]Character witnesses.
[17]Even after he had formally renounced his brief conversion to Roman Catholicism, Chillingworth for a period declined to take orders in the Church of England because he was not satisfied that all of its Thirty-nine Articles could be proved from Scripture.
[18]Complaisance, concession.
[19]Robert Cardinal Bellarmine (1542–1621) and Jacques Cardinal Du Perron (1556–1618) were two of the most formidable Jesuit controversialists of the age.

which are dissembled by you and not put into the balance. Know then, Sir, that when I say the religion of Protestants is in prudence to be preferred before yours, as, on the one side, I do not understand by your religion the doctrine of Bellarmine or Baronius or any other private man amongst you, nor the doctrine of the Sorbonne, or of the Jesuits, or of the Dominicans,[20] or of any other particular company among you, but that wherein you all agree, or profess to agree, "the doctrine of the Council of Trent";[21] so accordingly on the other side by the "religion of Protestants" I do not understand the doctrine of Luther, or Calvin, or Melancthon, nor the Confession of Augusta or Geneva, nor the catechism of Heidelberg, nor the articles of the Church of England,[22] no, nor the harmony of Protestant confessions; but that wherein they all agree, and which they all subscribe with a greater harmony as a perfect rule of their faith and actions: that is, the Bible. The Bible, I say, the Bible only is the religion of Protestants! Whatsoever else they believe besides it and the plain, irrefragable, indubitable consequences of it, well may they hold it as a matter of opinion; but as matter of faith and religion, neither can they with coherence to their own grounds believe it themselves, nor require the belief of it of others without most high and most schismatical presumption. I for my part, after a long and (as I verily believe and hope) impartial search of "the true way to eternal happiness," do profess plainly that I cannot find any rest for the sole of my foot but upon this rock only. I see plainly and with mine own eyes that there are popes against popes, councils against councils, some fathers against others, the same fathers against themselves, a consent of fathers of one age against a consent of fathers of another age, the church of one age against the church of another age. Traditive[23] interpretations of Scripture are pretended, but there are few or none to be found. No tradition but only of Scripture can derive itself from the fountain but may be plainly proved either to have been brought in, in such an age after Christ, or that in such an age it was not in. In a word, there is no sufficient certainty but of Scripture only for any considering man to build upon. This therefore, and this only, I have reason to believe. This I will profess, according to this I will live, and for this, if there be occasion, I will not only willingly but even gladly lose my life, though I should be sorry that Christians should take it from me. Propose me anything out of this book and require whether I believe it or no, and seem it never so incomprehensible to human reason, I will subscribe it with hand and heart as knowing no demonstration can be stronger than this: God hath said so, therefore it is true. In other things I will take no man's liberty of judgment from him; neither shall any man take mine from me. I will think no man the worse man nor the worse Christian, I will love no man the less, for differing in opinion from me. And what measure I mete to others, I expect from them again. I am fully assured that God does not and therefore that men ought not to require any more of any man than this, to believe the Scripture to be God's word, to endeavor to find the true sense of it, and to live according to it.

57. This is the religion which I have chosen after a long deliberation, and I am verily persuaded that I have chosen wisely, much more wisely than if I had guided myself according to your church's authority. For the Scripture being all true, I am secured by believing nothing else, that I shall believe no falsehood as matter of faith. And if I mistake the sense of Scripture, and so fall into error, yet I am secure from any danger thereby if but your grounds be true; because endeavoring to find the true sense of Scripture, I cannot but hold my error without pertinacy,[24] and be ready to forsake it when a more true and a more probable sense shall appear unto me. And, then, all necessary truth being, as I have proved, plainly set down in Scripture, I am certain by believing Scripture to believe all necessary truth; and he that does so, if his life be answerable to his faith, how is it possible he should fail of salvation?

58. Besides, whatsoever may be pretended to gain to your church the credit of a guide, all that, and much more, may be said for the Scripture. Hath your church been ancient? The Scripture is more ancient. Is your church a means to keep men at unity? So is the Scripture to keep those that believe it and will obey it in unity of belief in matters necessary or very profitable, and in unity of charity in points unnecessary. Is your church universal for time or place? Certainly the Scripture is more universal, for all the Christians in the world (those, I mean, that in truth deserve this name) do now and always have believed the Scripture to be the word of God, whereas only you say that you only are the church of God, and all Christians besides you deny it.

59. Thirdly, following the Scripture I follow that whereby you prove your church's infallibility (whereof were it not for Scripture, what pretence could you have, or what notion could we have?) and by so doing tacitly confess that yourselves are surer of the truth of the Scripture than of your church's authority. For we must be surer of the proof than of the thing proved; otherwise it is no proof.

60. Fourthly, following the Scripture I follow that which must be true if your church be true, for your church gives attestation to it. Whereas if I follow your church I must follow that which, though Scripture be true, may be false; nay, which, if Scripture be true, must be false, because the Scripture testifies against it.

61. Fifthly, to follow the Scripture I have God's express warrant and command, and no color of any prohibition; but to believe your church infallible I have no command at all, much less an express command. Nay, I have reason to fear that I am prohibited to do so in these words: "Call no man master on earth. They fell by infidelity, thou standest by

[20]Chillingworth refers to some of the most authoritative sources of contemporary Roman Catholic doctrine: the two mighty apologists Cardinal Bellarmine and Caesar Cardinal Baronius (1538–1607), the notoriously conservative theologians of the Sorbonne, the fairly recently established (1534) Society of Jesus, and the ancient and scholarly order that had produced St. Thomas Aquinas.
[21]The famous general council (1545–63) that, in response to the Reformation, redefined the doctrine and reformed some of the abuses of the Roman Catholic Church.
[22]Spokesmen and codifications of various doctrinal and credal positions of reformed theology. [23]Traditional. [24]Pertinacity.

faith. Be not highminded, but fear. The Spirit of truth the world cannot receive."[25]

62. Following your church I must hold many things not only above reason, but against it, if anything be against it; whereas following the Scripture I shall believe many mysteries, but no impossibilities; many things above reason, but nothing against it; many things which, had they not been revealed, reason could never have discovered, but nothing which by true reason may be confuted; many things which reason cannot comprehend how they can be, but nothing which reason can comprehend that it cannot be. Nay, I shall believe nothing which reason will not convince that I ought to believe it, for reason will convince any man, unless he be of a perverse mind, that the Scripture is the word of God. And then no reason can be greater than this: God says so, therefore it is true.

63. Following your church I must hold many things, which to any man's judgment, that will give himself the liberty of judgment, will seem much more plainly contradicted by Scripture than the infallibility of your church appears to be confirmed by it; and consequently must be so foolish as to believe your church exempted from error upon less evidence, rather than subject to the common condition of mankind upon greater evidence. Now if I take the Scripture only for my guide, I shall not need to do anything so unreasonable.

64. If I will follow your church I must believe impossibilities, and that with an absolute certainty, upon motives which are confessed to be but only prudential and probable; that is, with a weak foundation I must firmly support a heavy, a monstrous heavy building: now following the Scripture I shall have no necessity to undergo any such difficulties.

65. Following your church I must be servant of Christ and a subject of the king, but only *ad placitum papae*.[26] I must be prepared in mind to renounce my allegiance to the king when the pope shall declare him an heretic and command me not to obey him;[27] and I must be prepared in mind "to esteem virtue vice and vice virtue, if the pope shall so determine." Indeed, you say it is impossible he should do the latter; but that, you know, is a great question, neither is it fit my obedience to God and the king should depend upon a questionable foundation. And, howsoever, you must grant that if by an impossible supposition the pope's commands should be contrary to the law of Christ, that they of your religion must resolve to obey rather the commands of the pope than the law of Christ; whereas if I follow the Scripture I may, nay I must, obey my sovereign in lawful things, though an heretic, though a tyrant; and though, I do not say the pope, but the apostles themselves, nay, an angel from heaven, should teach any thing against the gospel of Christ, I may, nay I must, denounce anathema to him.

66. Following the Scripture I shall believe a religion which, being contrary to flesh and blood, without any assistance from worldly power, wit, or policy, nay, against all the power and policy of the world, prevailed and enlarged itself in a very short time all the world over; whereas it is too too apparent that your church hath got, and still maintains, her authority over men's consciences by counterfeiting false miracles, forging false stories, by obtruding on the world supposititious writings, by corrupting the monuments of former times, and defacing out of them all which any way makes against you, by wars, by persecutions, by massacres, by treasons, by rebellions; in short, by all manner of carnal means, whether violent or fraudulent.

67. Following the Scripture I shall believe a religion the first preachers and professors whereof, it is most certain, they could have no worldly ends upon the world; that they could not project to themselves by it any of the profits, or honors, or pleasures of this world; but rather were to expect the contrary, even all the miseries which the world could lay upon them. On the other side, the head of your church, the pretended successor of the apostles and guide of faith, it is even palpable that he makes your religion the instrument of his ambition, and by it seeks to entitle himself directly or indirectly to the monarchy of the world. And besides it is evident to any man that has but half an eye that most of those doctrines which you add to the Scripture do make, one way or other, for the honor or temporal profit of the teachers of them.

68. Following the Scripture only I shall embrace a religion of admirable simplicity, consisting in a manner wholly in the worship of God in spirit and truth, whereas your church and doctrine is even loaded with an infinity of weak, childish, ridiculous, unsavory superstitions and ceremonies, and full of that righteousness for which Christ shall judge the world.

69. Following the Scripture I shall believe that which universal, never failing tradition assures me, that it was by the admirable supernatural work of God confirmed to be the word of God; whereas never any miracle was wrought, never so much as a lame horse cured, in confirmation of your church's authority and infallibility. And if any strange things have been done which may seem to give attestation to some parts of your doctrine, yet this proves nothing but the truth of the Scripture, which foretold that (God's providence permitting it, and the wickedness of the world deserving it) "strange signs and wonders should be wrought to confirm false doctrine, that they which love not the truth may be given over to strange delusions."[28] Neither does it seem to me any strange thing that God should permit some true wonders to be done to delude them who have forged so many to deceive the world.

70. If I follow the Scripture I must not promise myself salvation without effectual dereliction[29] and mortification of

[25]A conflation of Matthew 29.9, Romans 11.20, and John 14.17.
[26]"At the pope's pleasure."
[27]In 1570 Pius V had excommunicated Queen Elizabeth and released her Roman Catholic subjects from allegiance to their sovereign.
[28]A paraphrase of 2 Thessalonians 2.9–11. Here Chillingworth misquotes (perhaps from memory) *strong* as *strange*. Below (p. 569) he gets it right.   [29]Forsaking.

all vices, and the effectual practice of all Christian virtues. But your church opens an easier and a broader way to heaven, and though I continue all my life long in a course of sin, and without the practice of any virtue, yet gives me assurance that I may be let into heaven at a postern gate, even by any act of attrition[30] at the hour of death if it be joined with confession, or by an act of contrition without confession.

71. Admirable are the precepts of piety and humility, of innocence and patience, of liberality, frugality, temperance, sobriety, justice, meekness, fortitude, constancy and gravity, contempt of the world, love of God, and the love of mankind, in a word, of all virtues, and against all vice, which the Scriptures impose upon us, to be obeyed under pain of damnation, the sum whereof is in manner comprised in our Saviour's sermon upon the mount, recorded in the fifth, sixth, and seventh of St. Matthew, which if they were generally obeyed could not but make the world generally happy and the goodness of them alone were sufficient to make any wise and good man believe that this religion, rather than any other, came from God the fountain of all goodness. And that they may be generally obeyed, our Saviour hath ratified them all in the close of his sermon with these universal sanctions: "Not every one that saith, Lord, Lord, shall enter into the kingdom, but he that doth the will of my Father which is in heaven." And again: "Whosoever heareth these sayings of mine, and doth them not, shall be likened unto a foolish man, which built his house upon the sand: and the rain descended, and the flood came, and the winds blew, and it fell, and great was the fall thereof."[31] Now your church, notwithstanding all this, enervates and in a manner dissolves and abrogates many of these precepts, teaching men that they are not laws for all Christians, but counsels of perfection and matters of supererogation; that a man shall do well if he do observe them, but he shall not sin if he observe them not; that they are for them who aim at high places in heaven, who aspire with the two sons of Zebedee[32] to the right hand or to the left hand of Christ; but if a man will be content barely to go to heaven, and to be a doorkeeper in the house of God, especially if he will be content to taste of purgatory in the way, he may attain it at any easier purchase. Therefore the religion of your church is not so holy nor so good as the doctrine of Christ delivered in Scripture, and therefore not so likely to come from the fountain of holiness and goodness.

72. Lastly, if I follow your church for my guide I shall do all one as if I should follow a company of blind men in a judgment of colors or in the choice of a way. For every unconsidering man is blind in that which he does not consider. Now what is your church but a company of unconsidering men who comfort themselves because they are a great company together? But all of them either out of idleness refuse the trouble of a severe trial of their religion (as if heaven were not worth it) or out of superstition fear the event of such a trial, that they may be scrupled[33] and staggered and disquieted by it; and therefore, for the most part, do it not at all. Or if they do it, they do it negligently

and hypocritically and perfunctorily, rather for the satisfaction of others than themselves; but certainly without indifference, without liberty of judgment, without a resolution to doubt of it if upon examination the grounds of it prove uncertain, or to leave it if they prove apparently false. My own experience assures me that in this imputation I do you no injury, but it is very apparent to all men from your ranking "doubting of any part of your doctrine" among mortal sins. For from hence it follows that seeing every man must resolve that he will never commit mortal sin, that he must never examine the grounds of it at all for fear he should be moved to doubt; or if he do, he must resolve that no motives, be they never so strong, shall move him to doubt, but that with his will and resolution he will uphold himself in a firm belief of your religion, though his reason and his understanding fail him. And seeing this is the condition of all those whom you esteem good Catholics, who can deny but you are a company of men unwilling and afraid to understand, lest you should do good that have eyes to see and will not see, that "have not the love of truth" (which is only to be known by an indifferent trial) and therefore deserve to be "given over to strong delusions";[34] men that "love darkness more than light"; in a word, that you are "the blind leading the blind"; and what prudence there can be in following such guides our Saviour hath taught us in saying, "If the blind lead the blind, both shall fall into the ditch."[35]

73. There remains unspoken to in this section some places out of St. Austin and some sayings of Luther, wherein he confesses that in the papacy are many good things. But the former I have already considered, and returned the argument grounded on them. As for Luther's speeches, I told you, not long since, that we follow no private men, and regard not much what he says either against the church of Rome or for it, but what he proves. He was a man of a vehement spirit, and very often what he took in hand he did not do it, but overdo it. He that will justify all his speeches, especially such as he wrote in heat of opposition, I believe will have work enough. Yet in these sentences, though he overreach in the particulars, yet what he says in general we confess true, and confess with him, "that in the papacy are many good things" which have come from them to us, but withal we say there are many bad; neither do we think ourselves bound in prudence either to reject the good with the bad, or to retain the bad with the good, but rather conceive it a high point of wisdom to separate between the precious and the vile, to sever the good from the bad, and to put the good in vessels to be kept, and to cast the bad away; to try all things, and that to hold which is good.[36]

[30]In scholastic theology, an imperfect remorse for sin having as its motive not love of God but fear of punishment (as distinguished from contrition, which is an utterly crushing consciousness of sin).
[31]Matthew 7.21, 24–27.
[32]The disciples James and John, who told Christ that they aspired to sit on either side of Him in His glory (Mark 10.37).
[33]Made to feel scruples. [34]2 Thessalonians 2.11.
[35]Matthew 15.14. [36]See Matthew 13.48, Philippians 1.10.

Francis Cheynell [1608-1665]

Although Francis Cheynell was, as Johnson said, "turbulent, obstinate, and petulant," his account of William Chillingworth's last days deserves inclusion in this book as a hostile comment on a great and greatly influential work (pp. 563 ff.), as an indication of the depths to which religious controversy sank in Milton's time, and as a sample of the angry rhetoric with which bigots waged their savage wars of truth. As he himself makes clear, Cheynell was an educated, strong-willed man whose Presbyterian convictions, feeding on his sense of injured merit, turned a commonplace divine into a self-appointed agent of destruction. Such a man could well have been Scott's model, one supposes, for the fanatical Habakkuk Mucklewrath in *Old Mortality*. Trained at Merton College, Oxford, where he became a fellow (1629) before his ordination in the Church of England, he was denied his B.D. degree when he would not relax his stubborn Calvinistic views on predestination, and this injustice, as he himself regarded it, together with such "injuries" as the "plundering" of his house and books, made him writhe in indignation. Despite some unspecified dispute with Laud, he remained an Anglican divine throughout the 1630's, but in 1641 he declared himself a Presbyterian, took the Covenant, and prepared to smite the bishops hip and thigh. Soon thereafter a second plundering of his house by a band of cavaliers confirmed his fiery zeal against Episcopalians.

As the pressures of the forties mounted he was busy in the parliamentary cause—as a preacher for the House of Commons, a chaplain in the army (in which capacity he hectored the dying Chillingworth and then consigned him to "corruption"), a member of the Westminster Assembly, a ruthless "visitor" to Oxford University (where he caused many academic heads to roll), the incumbent of a valuable living at Petworth in Sussex, the president of St. John's College (where he replaced an ejected Anglican), and the Lady Margaret Professor of Divinity. When, for reasons not entirely clear (although madness was alleged), his career declined throughout the 1650's, he retired to an estate in Sussex, and there, "little better than distracted," he died in 1665. In addition to the notorious *Chillingworthi Novissima* he wrote some dozen books, among them *The Rise, Growth, and Danger of Socinianism* (1643), an account of his strenuous Oxford visitation (1647), and *The Divine Triunity of the Father, Son, and Holy Spirit . . . Declared* (1650). According to Anthony Wood, "he was accounted by many, especially by those of his party (who had him always in great veneration) a good disputant and preacher, and better he might have been, and of a more sober temper, had he not been troubled with a weakness in his head, which some in his time called craziness."

My text is based upon (to use only a portion of the title) *Chillingworthi Novissima. Or, The Sicknesse, Heresy, Death, and Buriall of William Chillingworth. (In his own phrase) Clerk of Oxford, and in the conceit of his fellow Souldiers, the Queens Arch-Engineer, and Grand-Intelligencer . . . By Francis Cheynell, late Fellow of Merton Colledge,* 1644 (Wing C-3810). It is not surprising that Cheynell still languishes for his biographer.

from Chillingworthi Novissima[1] (1644)

TO THE LEARNED AND EMINENT FRIENDS
OF MASTER CHILLINGWORTH . . .

Your deceased friend is not yet speechless: he calls upon you to beware and repent. Some preach more, at least more practically, when they are dead than ever they did whilst they were alive. You that were his patrons and encouragers, as he acknowledged ever when he was in the heighth of his rebellion, do you beware lest a worse thing come unto you. You that were the licensers of his subtile atheism,[2] repent, repent, for he was so hardened by your flattery that (for aught the most charitable man can judge) he perished by your approbation. He ever appealed to his works even to [10] his very dying day, and what was it which made him dote upon them but your license and approbation? . . .

Sirs, the following history will testify my compassion towards your deceased friend, whom I ever opposed in a charitable and friendly way. I do not account it any glory to trample upon the carcass of Hector, or to pluck a dead lion by the beard. Should I misquote his book and make that error mine own by a false citation, which I pretend to be his in an accusation, you that were the unhappy licensers of his book would soon take me tripping. If you conceive that he [20] deserved a more honorable burial, be pleased to answer my reasons and patronize[3] his errors with all the learning Bodley's library[4] can afford, or else study his catechism. Pardon my boldness. Some courtiers never learned, and some doctors have forgot, their catechism, or else this man we speak of had never been so much admired, his book extolled, or these antichristian wars fomented by such great clerks and busy wits.

I looked upon Mr. Chillingworth as one who had his head as full of scruples as it was of engines,[5] and therefore dealt [30] as tenderly with him as I use to do with men of the most nice and tender consciences; for I considered that though beef must be preserved with salt, yet plums must be preserved with sugar. I can assure you I stooped as low to him as I could without falling, and you know he is not a wise man, in the judgment of the philosopher, who stoops so low to another man's weakness that he himself falls into weakness; and it is a rule with us at Westminster that he falls into weakness who falls into sin.[6]

Do not conceive that I snatched up my pen in an angry [40] mood, that I might vent my dangerous wit and ease my overburdened spleen. No, no, I have almost forgot the visitation at Merton College, the denial of my grace, the plundering of my house and little library.[7] I know when and where and of whom to demand satisfaction for all these injuries and indignities. . . .

I remember an old story of King Canutus,[8] who (as the chronicler relates) took off the crown from his own head and set it upon the crucifix at Westminster. But tell me, you that have read some Italian Jesuit more subtile than the [50] politicians' saint, St. Machiavel, do you conceive that you can persuade our king to take off his crown from his own head and place it upon your idol, the queen,[9] or her idol, the crucifix at Oxford? We have none at Westminster. Well, plot on, my masters, and walk in the light and warmth of that fire which you have kindled. But hear what the prophet saith: "Behold, all you that kindle a fire and compass about yourselves with sparks, walk in the light of your fire and in the sparks which ye have kindled. This shall ye have of mine hand; ye shall lay down in sorrow."[10] Pardon our just fear if we dare not say a confederacy to[11] all those Welsh atheists, Irish rebels, bloody papists of the French or Spanish faction to whom you say a confederacy. Associate yourselves together (you know what follows), take counsel together (in your pretended Parliament), and it will be brought to nought; enact and pronounce a decree, imagine mischief as a law, yet you shall not prosper, for God is with us. I know you urge the thirteenth to the Romans[12] to justify your royal cruelty, but you know what Chrysostom[13] and many others have said upon that place. But I shall only ask you one question (with which I stopped your friend Chillingworth's mouth). Be pleased to answer it. Do you believe that tyranny is God's ordinance? I ever held it a violation of God's ordinance, and whether the supreme judicatory[14] of the kingdom may not repel that force with force which would violate God's ordinance, judge ye. For it is absurd to talk, as Doctor Ferne[15] doth, of a moral restraint in such a case.

CHILLINGWORTHI NOVISSIMA. 1"The latest news of Chillingworth."
2Chillingworth's *Religion of Protestants* had been published (1638) with formal imprimatur by the vice-chancellor of Oxford and two professors of divinity. 3Defend.
4The great Bodleian Library at Oxford had been founded by Sir Thomas Bodley in 1602.
5Plots, wiles, perhaps referring to the *testudo*, or engine of assault, that Chillingworth designed for the seige of Gloucester in 1643 (see p. 563).
6See Milton, *Samson Agonistes*, l. 834: "All wickedness is weakness."
7Owing to his heated advocacy of extreme Calvinist doctrines in defiance of the king's injunction to the contrary, Cheynell, though a fellow of Merton College, Oxford, had been denied the necessary grace (or formal approval) for his degree of B.D. Other acts of harassment (which he perhaps exaggerated) were probably related to a later dispute with Laud, the details of which are lacking.
8Canute, or Cnut, the last Danish king of England (1016–35).
9Henrietta Maria, long unpopular with the Puritans because of her Roman Catholicism, became an object of special vituperation through her efforts to enlist papal support for her beleaguered husband. She herself had been impeached by Parliament in 1643.
10Isaiah 50.11. 11Come to terms with.
12Romans 13.1–7 ("Let every soul be subject unto the higher powers," etc.), long one of the favorite texts of Anglican divines supporting the divine right of kings.
13Greek father (345?–407) noted for his fiery attacks on vices of the imperial court. 14Parliament.
15Henry Ferne (1602–62), chaplain to Charles I and a strenuous

Sure I am the Parliament hath power to raise an army to preserve God's ordinance inviolable when it cannot be preserved by any other means. They do certainly resist God's ordinance who seek to violate it. You endeavor to violate it, we to preserve it. Who is in the fault? . . .

I will not hold you any longer upon the rack. Learn the first lesson of Christianity, self-denial. Deny your own will and submit yourselves to God's; deny your reason and submit to faith. Reason tells you that there are some things above reason, and you cannot be so unreasonable as to make 10 reason judge of those things which are above reason. Remember that Master Chillingworth, your friend, did run mad with reason, and so lost his reason and religion both at once. He thought he might trust his reason in the highest points; his reason was to be judge whether or no there be a God, whether that God wrote any book, whether the books usually received as canonical be the books, the Scriptures of God, what is the sense of those books, what religion is best, what church purest. Come, do not wrangle, but believe and obey your God, and then I shall be encouraged to subscribe 20 myself

> *Your friend and servant,*
> *Francis Cheynell*

A BRIEF AND PLAIN RELATION OF MASTER CHILLINGWORTH'S SICKNESS, DEATH, AND BURIAL, TOGETHER WITH A JUST CENSURE OF HIS WORKS BY A DISCOVERY OF HIS ERRORS COLLECTED OUT OF HIS BOOK AND FRAMED INTO A KIND OF ATHEISTICAL CATECHISM . . .

I am very religious in observing that old proverb (if it be taken in its right sense), "Nothing is to be spoken of the dead but good." If that be true which Quintilian saith, *adversus miseros* (I may better say *adversus mortuos*) *inhumanus est jocus*: that man is void of humanity who makes sport with the dead. Mr. Chillingworth was looked upon by me at the first sight as a conquered man, and therefore I was not only civil but 30 (as he confessed) charitable unto him; and now he is dead, I cannot deal with him as Asinius Pollio did with Plancus,[16] set forth an oration to which no answer is to be expected unless (according to the desire of Saul or Dives)[17] a messenger should arise from the dead to give me an answer as full of terror as satisfaction. It is no glory to triumph over one that is conquered, nay dead, for that of the poet is true:

> *Nullum cum victis certamen et aethere cassis.*[18]

But I consider that Master Chillingworth's party is alive though he be dead; and though one of his books is buried, 40 there are many hundred copies divulged, and therefore though I speak not of his human frailties or personal infirmities and imperfections which died with him, yet I may speak of his heretical book and of some destructive policies he used, which do yet survive in their sad and lamentable effects. Judge what I say, put the case a man commits notorious crimes scandalously, because publicly, and doth not only

hold but vent damnable heresies, and vent them not only in the pulpit but in the press. Shall not his damnable heresies and printed heresies be confuted after his death? Shall thousands be seduced and perish, and all orthodox divines silenced, with that one proverb, "Nothing is to be spoken of the dead but good"? Nay, put the case further yet: suppose a man hath had his head full of powder-plots[19] and his heart full of bloody desires, nay, hath been a ringleader and encourager of others to bloody practices against the very light of nature as well as Scripture. Must nothing be said of such a man when he is gone, but good?

Master Chillingworth and I met in Sussex by an unexpected providence. I was driven from my own house by force of arms, only (as the Cavaliers confessed) because I was nominated to be a member of the Assembly;[20] and when I heard that my living[21] was bestowed upon a doctor (who, if some Cambridge men deceive me not, became the stage far better than he doth the pulpit) I resolved to exercise my ministry in Sussex amongst my friends in a place where there hath been little of the power of religion either known or practiced. About the latter end of November [1643] I traveled from London to Chichester, according to my usual custom, to observe the monthly fast;[22] and in my passage—with a thankful heart I shall ever acknowledge it—I was guarded by a convoy of sixteen soldiers who faced about two hundred of the enemy's forces and put them all to flight. . . . Master Chillingworth was at that time in Arundel Castle,[23] which was surrendered to the much renowned commander, Sir William Waller, Sergeant-Major-General of all the associated counties in the east and west, upon the sixt of January. As soon as the castle was surrendered I represented Master Chillingworth's condition to Sir William Waller, who commended him to the care of his worthy chaplain, and

---

advocate of the royalist cause. His *Resolving of Conscience upon This Question: Whether…Subjects May Take Arms and Resist* (1642) was the first pamphlet to support openly the king's defiance of Parliament.

[16]According to Pliny (*Natural History*, Preface, Sect. 31), when Plancus learned that Asinius Pollio was composing defamatory orations about him for use after Plancus' death, he remarked that "only phantoms fight with the dead."

[17]King Saul commanded the Witch of Endor to summon the prophet Samuel from the dead (1 Samuel 28.7–21), and Dives looked up from hell to see the beggar Lazarus in Abraham's bosom (Luke 16.19–31).

[18]"No war is fought with conquered men, deprived of the air of heaven" (Vergil, *Aeneid*, XI.104).

[19]Cheynell alludes, of course, to the infamous Gunpowder Plot (1605) that had been fomented by certain English Catholics.

[20]The Westminster Assembly of Divines (1643–49), commissioned by Parliament to prescribe theological and liturgical reforms, was dominated by the Presbyterians.

[21]Early in the war Cheynell's living at Banbury, near Oxford, had been plundered by royalist troops and he himself had been ejected.

[22]A designated "Day of Humiliation" set aside by Parliament for fasts, sermons, and prayer.

[23]Ancient seat of the dukes of Norfolk near Chicester in Sussex.

his chaplain showed so much charity and respect towards him that he laid him upon his own bed and supplied him with all necessaries which the place did afford. When the rest of the prisoners were sent up to London, Master Chillingworth made it evident to me that he was not able to endure so long a journey, and if he had been put to it he had certainly died by the way. I desired, therefore, that his journey might be shortened, and upon my humble motion he was sent to Chichester, where I intreated the governor that he might be secured by some officer of his acquaintance, and not put into the hands of the marshall. The governor gave order that Lieutenant Golledge should take charge of him and placed him in the bishop of Chichester's palace, where he had very courteous usage and all accommodations which were requisite for a sick man. . . .

I took all the care I could of his body whilst he was sick, and will (as far as he was innocent [of meddling in military affairs]) take care of his fame and reputation now he is dead. Nay, whilst he was alive I took care of something more precious than his health or reputation, to wit, his precious and beloved soul; for in compassion to his soul I dealt freely and plainly with him, and told him that he had been very active in fomenting these bloody wars against the Parliament and commonwealth of England, his natural country, and by consequent against the very light of nature. "I acknowledge," saith he, "that I have been active in these wars, but I have ever followed the dictates of my conscience, and if you convince me that I am in an error, you shall not find me obstinate." I told him I conceived that he might want sleep, being at that time newly come out of the castle, and therefore I gave him time to refresh himself; and when I came to him again I asked him whether he was fit for discourse. He told me yes, but somewhat faintly. . . .

⌐ And so the ghastly farce began, with Cheynell hectoring ⌐
the dying Chillingworth about his royalist politics and
Anglican theology. As Cheynell tells the story, he had
an easy triumph in their first "discourse" about the "great
controversy" between king and Parliament, and he left his
⌐ victim "somewhat puzzled." ⌐

I desired to know whether the saints were not to make war against the whore and the beast,[24] whether it be not an act of charity for Protestants to lay down their lives for their brethren, whether it be not an act of faith to wax valiant in fight for the defense of that faith which was once delivered to the saints. I perceived my gentleman somewhat puzzled, and I took my leave that he might take his rest.

My heart was moved with compassion towards him, and I gave him many visits after this first visit, but I seldom found him in fit case to discourse because his disease grew stronger and stronger, and he weaker and weaker. I desired to know his opinion concerning that liturgy which hath been formerly so much extolled and even idolized amongst the people,[25] but all the answer that I could get was to this purpose, that "there were some truths which the ministers of the gospel are not bound upon pain of damnation to publish to the people." And indeed he conceived it very unfit to publish anything concerning the Common Prayer Book or the Book of

Ordination, etc., "for fear of scandal." I was sorry to hear such an answer drop from a dying man, and I conceived it could not but be much more scandalous to seduce or hoodwink the people than to instruct and edify them in a point which did directly concern the public worship of God in this land.

When I found him pretty hearty one day I desired him to tell me whether he conceived that a man living and dying a Turk, papist, or Socinian could be saved. All the answer that I could gain from him was that "he did not absolve them, and would not condemn them." I was much displeased with the answer upon divers reasons: first, because the question was put home of a man living and dying, so or so; secondly, it was frivolous to talk of absolution, for it was out of question that he could not absolve them; thirdly, it showed that he was too well persuaded of Turcism and Socinianism, which run exactly parallel in too many points; fourthly, he seems to anathematize the Socinians in "The Preface to the Author of *Charity Maintained*" [at the beginning of *The Religion of Protestants*].[26] . . . When Mr. Chillingworth saw himself entangled in disputes he desired me that I would deal charitably with him, for, saith he, I was ever a charitable man. My answer was somewhat tart, and therefore the more charitable, considering his condition and the counsel of the apostle (Titus 1.13): "Rebuke them sharply"—or as Beza[27] hath it, "precisely"—"that they may be sound in the faith." And I desire not to conceal my tartness. It was to this effect: "Sir, it is confessed that you have been very excessive in your charity. You have lavished out so much charity upon Turks, Socinians, papists that I am afraid you have very little to spare for a truly reformed Protestant. Sure I am the zealous Protestants find very little charity at Oxford."

The last time I visited him was on the Lord's Day, for I thought it a sabbath duty; and then he began to speak of some questions which I formerly propounded to him, whereof this was one: whether tyranny was God's ordinance. I presently took him off from that discourse because I knew he had been laid up fast by that argument before, for it is impossible that any man should ever prove that tyranny is not to be resisted upon this ground (because we must not resist God's ordinance) unless they could prove that which is blasphemy to mention, viz. that tyranny is God's ordinance. I desired him that he would now take off his thoughts from all matters of speculation, and fix upon some practical point which might make for his edification. He thanked me, as I hope, very heartily, and told me that in all points of religion

[24]The Roman Catholic Church, conceived of as the whore of Babylon, and the seven-headed beast described by St. John (Revelation 13.1).
[25]The liturgical rites prescribed by the Anglican Book of Common Prayer, which in 1644 was declared illegal and replaced with a Presbyterian *Directory for Public Worship.* [26]See p. 562.
[27]The edition of the New Testament by Calvin's associate Théodore de Bèze (1519–1605) had markedly influenced the so-called Geneva translation of the Bible (1560), itself the work of English refugees.

he was settled, and had fully expressed himself for the satisfaction of others in his book. . . .

> Mercifully, Chillingworth's release was not far off, but though death soon freed him (on January 30) from his physical afflictions, it could not save him from Cheynell's irritable busyness about the condition of his soul. Overriding those who held that as a heretic and rebel Chillingworth deserved no burial rites at all, Cheynell consented to his interment in the cloisters of the cathedral "amongst the old shavelings, monks, and priests of whom he had so good an opinion all his life," but he refused to read the Anglican burial service on the ground that "it was favor enough" to permit the "malignants" of Chillingworth's persuasion to indulge in such idolatry. He took care, however, to have the final word.

When the malignants brought his hearse to the burial I met them at the grave with Master Chillingworth's book in my hand, at the burial of which book I conceived it fit to make this little speech following.

A Speech Made at the Funeral of Mr. Chillingworth's Mortal Book

Brethren, it was the earnest desire of that eminent scholar whose body lies here before you that his corpse might be interred according to the rites and customs approved in the English liturgy, and in most places of this kingdom heretofore received. But his second request (in case that were denied him) was that he might be buried in this city after such a manner as might be obtained in these times of unhappy difference and bloody wars. His first request is denied for many reasons of which you cannot be ignorant. It is too well known that he was once a professed papist and a grand seducer; he perverted divers persons of considerable rank and quality, and I have good cause to believe that his return to England, commonly called his conversion, was but a false and pretended conversion. And for my own part I am fully convinced that he did not live or die a genuine son of the Church of England (I retain the usual phrase that you may know what I mean). I mean he was not of that faith or religion which is established by law in England. He hath left that fantasy which he called his religion upon record in this subtile book. He was not ashamed to print and publish this destructive tenet, "that there is no necessity of Church or Scripture to make men faithful men" (in the 100 page of this unhappy book), and therefore I refuse to bury him myself, yet let his friends and followers who have attended his hearse to this Golgotha know that they are permitted, out of mere humanity, to bury their dead out of our sight. If they please to undertake the burial of his corpse, I shall undertake to bury his errors which are published in this so much admired yet unworthy book; and happy would it be for this kingdom if this book and all its fellows could be so buried that they might never rise more, unless it were for a confutation. And happy would it have been for the author if he had repented of those errors, that they might never rise for his condemnation. Happy, thrice happy will he be if his works do not follow him, if they do never rise with him—nor against him.

Get thee gone, then, thou cursed book, which hast seduced so many precious souls! Get thee gone, thou corrupt,

rotten book, earth to earth and dust to dust! Get thee gone into the place of rottenness, that thou mayest rot with thy author and see corruption!

So much for the burial of his errors. Touching the burial of his corpse I need say no more than this: it will be most proper for the men of his persuasion to commit the body of their deceased friend, brother, master to the dust; and it will be most proper for me to hearken to that counsel of my Savior, Luke 9.60. "Let the dead bury their dead, but go thou and preach the kingdom of God." And so I went from the grave to the pulpit, and preached on that text to the congregation. . . .

I dare boldly say that I have been more sorrowful for Mr. Chillingworth, and merciful to him, than his friends at Oxford. His sickness and obstinacy cost me many a prayer and many a tear. I did heartily bewail the loss of such strong parts and eminent gifts, the loss of so much learning and diligence. Never did I observe more acuteness and eloquence so exactly tempered in the same person. *Dialobus ab illo ornari cupiebat,*[28] for he had eloquence enough to set a fair varnish upon the foulest design. He was a master of his learning: he had all his arguments *in procinctu*[29] and all his notions *in numerato.*[30]

"Howl, ye fir tree, for a cedar is fallen!"[31] Lament, ye sophisters, for the master of sentences[32] (shall I say?) or fallacies is vanished! Wring your hands and beat your breasts, ye antichristian engineers,[33] for your arch-engineer is dead, and all his engines buried with him. Ye daughters of Oxford, weep over Chillingworth, for he had a considerable and hopeful project how to clothe you and himself in scarlet, and other delights.[34] "I am distressed for thee, my brother Chillingworth," may his executrix say. "Very pleasant hast thou been unto me. Thy love to me was wonderful, passing the love of father, husband, brother." O how are the mighty fallen, and the weapons, nay engines, of war perished! O tell it not in Gath[35] that he who raised a battery against the pope's chair,[36] that he might place reason in the chair instead of antichrist, is dead and gone. Publish it not in the streets of Askelon that he who did at once batter Rome and undermine England—the reforming church of England, that he might prevent a reformation—is dead, lest if you publish it you puzzle all the conclave, and put them to consider whether they should mourn or triumph.

> Cheynell closes his work with a "Profane Catechism" of alleged heresies culled from *The Religion of Protestants.* Although compiled, with artful malice, to show the full enormity of Chillingworth's latitudinarian theology, it shows instead the depth of Cheynell's rancor.

[28]The devil himself would be glad to use his tricks.
[29]"Ready for action." [30]"Sorted out." [31]Zechariah 11.2.
[32]Passages of Scripture. [33]Plotters.
[34]1 Samuel 1.24. Chillingworth's *hopeful project,* Cheynell implies, was to return England to Roman Catholicism.
[35]"Tell it not in Gath, publish it not in the streets of Ashkelon" (1 Samuel 1.20). [36]Throne.

Thomas Fuller[1] [1608-1661]

It is regrettable that so fine a writer as Fuller should so often be dismissed as merely "quaint." Coleridge—who, with Lamb, revived his reputation—ranked him with Shakespeare, Milton, Defoe, and Hogarth as one of the "uniques" among the "mighty host of our great men," and although that ranking may be open to objection, it does suggest the stature of Pepys' "great Tom Fuller."

The son of a clergyman and nephew (as well as godson) of a future bishop, Fuller, "a boy of pregnant wit," of course was destined for the church, and at thirteen he duly entered Cambridge. Unlike his contemporary Jeremy Taylor, he was not catapulted into early fame. When, following the customary degrees (B.A. 1625, M.A. 1628), he failed to get a fellowship at Queens', he transferred to Sidney Sussex College, and thus, assisted by his uncle, inched onward and upward as curate of St. Benet's, Cambridge (1630), as holder of a prebend's stall in Salisbury Cathedral (1631), and as rector of Broadwindsor, Dorsetshire (1634), where his preaching gained attention. Although he had lugubriously versified *David's Heinous Sin, Hearty Repentance, Heavy Punishment* as early as 1631, it was not until 1639 that he ventured into print again with *The History of the Holy War*. This lively account of the crusades was followed in 1640 by *Joseph's Parti-colored Coat* (a collection of sermons whose "witty" style is suggested by the title) and in 1642 by the most perennially successful of all his many books, *The Holy State and the Profane State*.

A sort of prose miscellany combining the character with the essay and biography, this resolutely didactic work devotes its first, second, and fourth books to expounding such types of domestic and professional virtue as the good husband, the good sea captain, the good herald, the wise statesman, and the good bishop, and then illustrating most of them with *exempla* based upon the lives of actual persons (respectively, Abraham, Sir Francis Drake, William Camden, Lord Burleigh, and St. Augustine). Book V similarly reports on the "profane state" through such aberrant types as the harlot (Queen Joan of Naples), the atheist (Cesare Borgia), and the tyrant (the duke of Alva). Under the rubric "General Rules," Book III presents some twenty-five disquisitions on hospitality, apparel, recreation, marriage, and the like, which, eked out with anecdotes and maxims, constitute a kind of manual of behavior for the godly citizen.

The war—which in his gentle, even genial, fashion he of course opposed—turned Fuller from a country parson into an itinerant scholar-preacher. Leaving Broadwindsor for London after his wife's death in 1641, he was so successful in the pulpit at the Savoy that those flocking to his "mellifluous discourse" were compared to swarming bees. Fuller showed no trace of bigotry, but he was nonetheless devoted to the crown and church, and when life in London got too hard he joined the king at Oxford (1643), then marched with Hopton's troops as chaplain (1643–44), served the little household of the infant Princess Henrietta at Exeter, and finally, when that city fell to Fairfax in 1646, turned up again in London. His subsequent scramblings and uncertainties ended in 1649, when the Roundhead earl of Carlisle presented him the curacy of Waltham Abbey in Essex, where he finally found a measure of repose.

Through all these troubled years he had continued writing. Although a history of the British church announced in the preface to *The Holy State* in 1642 had had to wait, as he predicted, until he could "enjoy the benefit of walking and standing libraries, without which advantages the best

[1]For other works of Fuller see Books and Men, pp. 741 ff.

vigilancy doth but vainly dream to undertake such a task," he tossed off several smaller things even in the tumult of the forties. At Exeter, in the "dangerous days" of 1645, appeared a collection of "Personal Meditations," "Scripture Observations," "Historical Applications," and "Mixed Contemplations" entitled *Good Thoughts in Bad Times*. Like its two sequels—*Good Thoughts in Worse Times* (1647) and *Mixed Contemplations in Better Times* (1660)—this valiant little book provides a wry and often witty comment on what Fuller called "the distractions of our age." Much more learned, but still potboilers of a sort, were *A Pisgah-Sight of Palestine*, an irresistibly readable account of the Holy Land that appeared in 1650, and *Abel Redivivus* (1651), a collection of clerical biographies for which Fuller wrote the preface and several of the lives (including those of such eminent Englishmen as Cranmer and Fox the martyrologist).

Fuller in his last decade was active as a preacher (at St. Clement's, St. Bride's, and other London churches) and prolific as a writer of many published sermons, commentaries on the Bible, and substantial histories of Cambridge University and of Waltham Abbey (1655). His chief concern, however, was the completion of two major works that had been long deferred—the promised *Church History of Britain* (1655) and *The History of the Worthies of England* (1662), an encyclopedic account (like Camden's *Britannia* and Drayton's *Poly-Olbion*) of the geography, physical resources, proverbs, history, sheriffs and gentry, and distinguished sons of all the English counties. Into these two massive undertakings he poured enough antiquarian zeal, piety, patriotism, erudition, and witty common sense to supply a dozen lesser men. As his first, anonymous biographer observed in 1661, Fuller's later life was "a kind of errantry," with the object of his quest the history of his native land. Wherever he went, jogging through the English countryside,

> he spent frequently most of his time in views and researches of their antiquities and church-monuments, insinuating himself into the acquaintance (which frequently ended in a lasting friendship) of the learnedst and gravest persons residing in the place, thereby to inform himself fully of those things he thought worthy the commendation of his labors.

He himself records that he wrote the first three books of *The Church History of Britain* (from the birth of Christ to the later fourteenth century) before 1649 and the other nine (which end with Charles' execution) after "monarchy was turned into a state." Despite "much difficulty" in completing this gigantic labor, the twelve books, each provided with a lavish dedication, appeared in 1655.

As a graceful footnote to this ambitious work, Fuller in 1659 published *An Appeal of Injured Innocence*, wherein he gracefully and wittily responded to the strictures of *Examen Historicum* (1659) by Peter Heylyn, a former royal chaplain, the future biographer of Laud, and a notoriously irascible custodian of Anglican proprieties. "Indeed, Sir," Fuller told his angry critic,

> I conceive our time, pains, and parts may be better expended to God's glory and the church's good than in these needless contentions. Why should Peter fall out with Thomas, both being disciples of the same Lord and Master? I assure you, Sir, whatever you conceive to the contrary, I am cordial to the cause of the English church, and my hoary hairs will go down to the grave in sorrow for her sufferings.

Although Fuller lived long enough to accompany his last patron, Lord Berkeley, to the Hague to prepare for Charles' restoration, to celebrate that glad event in a poetical *Panegyric*, and to rejoice in his appointment as "chaplain in extraordinary" to the king, his "well grounded expectation" of future royal favors was disappointed when, on 16 August 1661, "Death stepped in and drew the curtain betwixt him and his succeeding ecclesiastical dignities." In view of his disordered middle years his enormous production seems scarcely possible for a man of only fifty-five, but there was more to come: shortly after his death *The History of the Worthies of England* (1662) was published in an enormous folio with a dedication to the king by the author's eldest son.

My texts are based upon *The Holy State* and (bound together with a separate title page) *The Profane State*, 1642 (Wing F-2443), *Good Thoughts in Bad Times*, 1645 (Wing F-2425), *Good Thoughts in Worse Times*, 1647 (Wing F-2436), *Mixt Contemplations in Better Times*, 1660 (Wing

F-2451), *The Church-History of Britain; From the Birth of Jesus Christ, Untill the Year M.D.C.XLVIII*, 1665 (Wing F-2416), and *The History of the Worthies of England*, 1662 (Wing F-2440).

Although Fuller's massive corpus has never been collected, there are more or less modern editions of his verse by A. B. Grosart (1868), *The Holy War* (1840), *The Holy State* (ed. James Nichols, 1841; ed. in facsimile by M. G. Walten, 2 vols., 1938), *Abel Redivivus* (ed. W. Nichols, 2 vols., 1867), *The Church History of Britain* (ed. J. S. Brewer, 6 vols., 1845), *The History of the Worthies of England* (ed. P. A. Nuttall, 3 vols., 1840; abridged by J. Freeman, 1952), and *The Collected Sermons* (ed. J. E. Bailey and W. E. A. Axon, 2 vols., 1891). There are volumes of selections by Augustus Jessopp (1892), A. R. Waller (1902), and E. K. Broadus (1928).

The anonymous biographer (1661) cited above is included in Brewer's edition of *The Church History* and in Broadus, and there are more modern lives by J. E. Bailey (1874), D. B. Lyman (1935), and William Addison (1951). Walter Houghton's *Formation of Thomas Fuller's Holy and Profane State* (1938) is illuminating and judicious on Fuller as a man of letters; in his capacity as essayist, biographer, and Anglican divine he has been handled by Benjamin Boyce and other students of the character cited in the General Bibliography, Section IV, Donald Stauffer (*English Biography before 1700*, 1930), W. Fraser Mitchell (*English Pulpit Oratory from Andrewes to Tillotson*, 1932), and W. K. Jordan (*The Development of Religious Toleration in England*, 4 vols., 1932–40). Strickland Gibson has tackled the formidable task of providing a bibliography in *Oxford Bibliographical Society Proceedings & Papers*, IV (1936) and New Series I (1948).

from The Church History of Britain (1655)

To the Reader

An ingenious gentleman some moneths since in jest-earnest advised me to make haste with my history of the Church of England for fear, said he, lest the Church of England be ended before the history thereof.

This history is now, though late (all church-work is slow), brought with much difficulty to an end. And blessed be God, the Church of England is still (and long may it be) in being, though disturbed, distempered, distracted. God help and heal her most sad condition!

The three first books of this volume were for the main written in the reign of the late king, as appeareth by the passages then proper for the government. The other nine books we made since monarchy was turned into a state.[1]

May God alone have the glory and the ingenuous reader the benefit of my endeavors, which is the hearty desire of

Thy servant in Jesus Christ,
Thomas Fuller

From my chamber in
Sion College[2]

THE ELEVENTH BOOK, CONTAINING THE REIGN OF KING CHARLES

⌈ In Book XI Fuller traces the mounting hostility between
Archbishop Laud, intent upon the strictest conformity, and
his increasingly vocal adversaries. One of the most notorious
episodes in this continuing struggle was the trial of three
⌊ unruly Presbyterians before the Star Chamber in 1637. ⌋

. . . Dr. Laud, formerly archbishop in power, now so in place after the decease of Bishop Abbot,[3] this year [1635] kept his metropolitical[4] visitation, and henceforward conformity was more vigorously pressed than before. Insomuch that a minister was censured in the High Commission[5] for this expression in a sermon: "that it was suspicious that now the night did approach, because the shadows were so much longer than the body, and ceremonies more in force than the power of godliness." And now many differences about di-

THE CHURCH HISTORY [1]The first three books of Fuller's *Church History* trace the progress of Christianity in England from the "doleful state of the pagan Britons" at the birth of Christ to the later years of Edward III (i.e., about 1370). The last nine books, which are much more detailed, go from "the first appearing of Wycliffe" to the death and burial of Charles I in 1649. The change of government during the composition of the work occurred formally on 19 May 1649, when Parliament proclaimed England to be a commonwealth.

[2]A college and almshouse (the latter subsequently abandoned) that was founded in 1623 near Blackfriars Bridge for the benefit of Anglican clergymen. Fuller had chambers there for several years, attracted no doubt in part by the library for which the establishment had long been notable.

[3]For the circumstances of Laud's translation to the see of Canterbury, see pp. 917,930. The numbering of the paragraphs in the text has been omitted in these excerpts.   [4]Archiepiscopal.

[5]The Court of High Commission, a court erected by Queen Elizabeth in 1559 to try offenses against the church or the crown's supremacy therein. Its use by Laud (1634–37) as an instrument for enforcing the strictest conformity made it odious to the Puritans, and therefore it and the equally detested Court of Star Chamber were abolished by the Long Parliament in 1641.

vine worship began to arise, whereof many books were written *pro* and *con*. So common in all hands, that my pains may be well spared in rendering a particular account of what is so universally known. So that a word or two will suffice.

One controversy was about the holiness of our churches, some maintaining that they succeed to the same degree of sanctity with the tabernacle of Moses and temple of Solomon, which others flatly denied. First, because the tabernacle and temple were and might be but one at a time, whilst our churches (without fault) may be multiplied without any set number. They both for their fashion, fabric, and utensils were *jure divino*,[6] their architects being inspired, whilst our churches are the product of human fancy. Thirdly, God gloriously appeared both in the tabernacle and temple, only graciously present[7] in our churches. Fourthly, the temple was a type[8] of Christ's body, which ours are not. More true it is, our churches are heirs to the holiness of the Jewish synagogues, which were many, and to whom a reverence was due as publicly destined to divine service.

Not less the difference about the manner of adoration to be used in God's house, which some would have done towards the communion table as the most remarkable place of God's presence. Those used a distinction between bowing *ad altare* ("towards the altar") as directing their adoration that way, and *ad altare* ("to the altar") as terminating their worship therein. The latter they detested as idolatrous, the former they defended as lawful and necessary; such a slovenly unmannerliness had lately possessed many people in their approaches to God's house that it was high time to reform.

But such as disliked the gesture could not or would not understand the distinction, as in the suburbs of superstition. These allowing some corporal adoration lawful, yea necessary, seeing no reason the moiety of man, yea the total sun of him which is visible, his body, should be exempted from God's service, except such a writ of ease could be produced and proved from Scripture. But they were displeased with this adoration because such as enjoin it maintain one kind of reverence due to the very place, another to the elements of the sacraments (if on the table), a third to God himself: these several degrees of reverence ought to be railed about as well as the communion table and clearly distinguished, lest that be given to the creature which belongs to the Creator, and such as shun profanation run into idolatry.

A controversy was also started about the posture[9] of the Lord's board, communion table, or altar, the last name beginning now in many men's mouths to out the two former. Some would have it constantly fixed with the sides east and west, ends north and south, on a graduated advance next the east wall of the chancel, citing a canon and the practice in the King's Chapel for the same. Others pressed the queen's injunctions that, allowing it at other times to stand, but not altarwise in the chancel, it ought to be set in the body of the church when the sacrament is celebrated thereon.

Such the heat about this altar till both sides had almost sacrificed up their mutual charity thereon, and this controversy was prosecuted with much needless animosity. This mindeth me of a passage in Cambridge when King James was there present, to whom a great person complained

of the inverted situation of a college chapel, north and south, out of design to put the house to the cost of new building the same. To whom the King answered, "It matters not how the chapel stands, so their hearts who go thither be set aright in God's service." Indeed, if moderate men had had the managing of these matters, the accommodation had been easy with a little condescension[10] on both sides. But as a small accidental heat or cold (such as a healthful body would not be sensible of) is enough to put him into a fit who was formerly *in latitudine febris*,[11] so men's minds, distempered in this age with what I may call a mutinous tendency, were exasperated with such small occasions which otherwise might have been passed over, and no notice taken thereof.

For now came the censure of Master Prynne, Dr. Bastwick, and Master Burton, and we must go a little backwards to take notice of the nature of their offences. Master William Prynne, born [1600] about Bath in Gloucestershire, bred some time in Oxford, afterwards utter barrister of Lincoln's Inn, began with the writing of some useful and orthodox books. I have heard some of his detractors account him as only the hand of a better head, setting forth at first the endeavors of others. Afterwards he delighted more to be numerous with many than ponderous with select quotations, which maketh his books to swell, with the loss ofttimes of the reader, sometimes of the printer; and his pen, generally querulous, hath more of the plaintiff than of the defendant therein.[12]

Some three years [i.e., 1632] since he set forth a book called *Histriomastix,* or "the whip of stage-players." Whip so held and used by his hand that some conceived the lashes thereof flew into the face of the Queen herself, as much delighted in masques. For which he was severely censured [1634] to lose his ears on the pillory, and for a long time (after two removals to the Fleet)[13] imprisoned in the Tower. Where he wrote and whence he dispersed new pamphlets which were interpreted to be libels against the established discipline of the Church of England,[14] for which he was indicted in the Star Chamber.

Dr. John Bastwick (by vulgar error generally mistaken to be a Scotchman) was born [1593] at Writtle in Essex, bred a short time in Emmanuel College, then traveled nine years beyond the seas, made Doctor of Physic at Padua. Returning home [1623], he practiced it at Colchester and set forth a book in Latin (wherein his pen commanded a pure and fluent style) entitled *Flagellum pontificis et episcoporum Latialium.* But it seems he confined not his character so to the Latian[15] bishops beyond the Alps but that our English prelates counted

---

[6]"By divine law." [7]Present through the efficacy of divine grace. [8]Model. [9]Text *pasture.* [10]Concession [11]Feverish. [12]The nature of Prynne's early work may be inferred from some of the titles: *The Perpetuity of a Regenerate Man's Estate* (1627), *The Unloveliness of Lovelocks* (1628), *Health's Sickness, or a Compendious Discourse Proving the Drinking of Healths to Be Sinful* (1628). [13]An ancient London prison near Fleet Street, at this period commonly used for persons condemned by the Star Chamber. [14]For example, *A Looking-Glass for All Lordly Prelates* (1636) and *News from Ipswich: Discovering Practices of Domineering Lordly Prelates* (1636?). [15]Latin, i.e. Roman.

themselves touched therein. Hereupon he was accused in the High Commission, committed to the Gatehouse[16] where he wrote a second book[17] taxing the injustice of the proceedings of the High Commission, for which he was indicted in the Star Chamber.

Master Henry Burton, minister, rather took a snap than made a meal in any university; was first schoolmaster to the sons of the Lord Carey (afterwards earl of Monmouth), whose lady was governess to King Charles when Prince. And this opportunity, say some, more than his own deserts preferred him to the service of Prince Charles,[18] being designed (as I have heard) to wait on him in Spain[19] but afterwards (when part of his goods were shipped for the voyage) excluded the attendance. Whether because his parts and learning were conceived not such as to credit our English Church in foreign countries, or because his principles were accounted uncomplying with[20] that employment.

The crudity of this affront lay long on his mind, hot stomachs (contrary to corporal concoction) being in this kind the slowest of digestion. After the venting of many mediate discontents, on the last fifth of November [1636] he took for his text Proverbs 24.21: "My son, fear thou the Lord and the king; and meddle not with them that are given to change." This sermon was afterwards printed, charging the prelates for introducing of several innovations into divine worship, for which, as a libel, he was indicted in the Star Chamber.

But the fault general, which at this day was charged on these three prisoners at the bar in the Star Chamber, was this; that they had not put in their effectual answer into that court wherein they were accused, though sufficient notice and competent time was allowed them for the performance thereof. The Lord Keeper Coventry[21] minded them that for such neglect they had a precedent, wherein the court after six days had taken a cause *pro confesso*,[22] whereas the favor of six weeks was allowed unto them, and now leave given them to render reason why the court should not proceed to present censure.

Hereat Master Prynne first moved that they would be pleased to accept a cross bill (which he there tendered) against the prelates. This the Lord Keeper refused to accept of at the present, as not being the business of the day. Then he moved that the prelates might be dismissed the court, it being agreeable neither to nature, reason, nor justice that those who were their adversaries should be their judges. This also was rejected by the Lord Keeper because by the same proportion, had he libeled against the temporal lords, judges, and Privy Councillors in the place, by this plea none should pass censure upon them because all were made parties.

Master Prynne proceeded to show he had done his endeavor to prepare his answer, being hindered first by his close imprisonment, denied pen, ink, and paper; and by the imprisonment also of his servant, who was to solicit his business. That the counsel assigned him came very late, and though twice payed for their pains deferred the drawing up of his answer, and durst not set their hands unto it. Master Holt,[23] one of his counsel, being present, confessed that he found his answer would be very long, and of such a nature as he durst not subscribe it, fearing to give their lordships distaste.

Dr. Bastwick, being spoken to to speak for himself why he brought not in his answer before, laid the blame on the cowardice of his counsel, that durst not sign if for fear of the prelates. He there tendered his answer on oath with his own hand, which would not be accepted. He spake much of his own abilities, that he had been a soldier able to lead an army of men into the field, and now was a physician able to cure kings, princes, and emperors; and therefore how unworthy it was to curtailize[24] his ears, generally given out by the bishops' servants as a punishment intended unto him. He minded them of the mutability of all earthly things, and chiefly of the changes in the court, where he lately the chief judge therein was the next day to have his own cause censured;[25] wishing them seriously to consider that some who now sat there on the bench might stand prisoners at the bar another day, and need the favor which now they denied.

Master Burton, being asked what he could allege why the court should not take his fault *pro confesso*, pleaded that he had put in his answer, drawn up with great pains and cost, signed by his counsel, and received into the court. The Lord Keeper rejoined that the judges had cast his answer out as imperfect, Judge Finch[26] affirming that they did him a good

[16]A prison over the gate of the palace at Westminster.
[17]Πράξεις τῶν ἐπισκόπων, *sive apologeticus ad praesules Anglicanos* (1636). It was apparently for writing *The Litany of J. Bastwick* (1637), wherein Bastwick resorted to English to smite the bishops, that he was summoned before the Star Chamber.
[18]Burton (b. 1578) was educated at St. John's College, Cambridge (M.A. 1602), and it was through his services as tutor to Sir Robert Carey that he was named clerk of the closet to Prince Henry shortly before the heir-apparent's death in 1612. Thereafter he served in the same capacity for Prince Charles until shortly after his accession to the throne in 1625, when he was dismissed for his attacks upon the bishops. Undeterred, he increased the violence of these attacks from the pulpit of St. Matthew's, Friday Street, until he reached the bad eminence of his summons before the Star Chamber in 1637.
[19]King James, eager to cement the unpopular Spanish alliance that lay at the heart of his foreign policy, sent Prince Charles (accompanied by the hated Buckingham) to Madrid in 1623 to woo the Infanta. Much to the delight of most Englishmen, who feared that the price of such a match would be concessions to the Catholics, the undertaking failed. [20]Unsuitable for.
[21]The distinguished lawyer Thomas Coventry, first Baron Coventry (1578–1640) was appointed lord keeper in 1625. In an age of violent partisanship he was generally regarded as one of the ablest and most moderate of the men around King Charles.
[22]"As if admitted." [23]Text *Hole*. [24]Shorten, i.e., crop.
[25]John Williams (1582–1650), bishop of Lincoln and a powerful ecclesiastical politician during Buckingham's heyday, was charged in the Star Chamber with betraying secrets of the Privy Council (1628) and later (1635) with subornation of perjury. Although fined, suspended from the exercise of his episcopal functions, and imprisoned in the Tower (1637–40), he landed on his feet, and died as archbishop of York (1641–50).
[26]Sir John Finch, Baron Finch of Fordwich (1584–1660), though named lord keeper in April 1640, was impeached by the Long Parliament a few months later and promptly fled to Holland. He lived just long enough to see the Restoration.

turn in making it imperfect, being otherwise as libelous as his book, and deserving a censure alone.

Here the prisoners, desiring to speak, were commanded silence, and the premises notwithstanding, the court proceeded to censure [14 June 1637]: namely, that they should lose their ears in the Palace Yard at Westminster, fining them also five thousand pound a man to His Majesty, perpetual imprisonment in three remote places. The Lord Finch added to Master Prynne's censure that he should be branded in each cheek with "S. L." for "slanderous libeler," to which the whole court agreed. The Archbishop of Canterbury made a long speech, since printed,[27] to excuse himself from the introducing of any innovations in the church, concluding it that he left the prisoners to God's mercy and the King's justice.

It will be lawful and safe to report the discourse of several persons hereon. This censure fell out scarce adequate to any judgment, as conceiving it either too low or too high for their offence. High conformists counted it too low, and that it had been better if the pillory had been changed into a gallows. They esteemed it improvident—but, by their leaves, more of Machiavel than of Christ in such counsel—to kindle revenge, and not to quench life in such turbulent spirits. The only way with them had been to rid them out of the way.

Most moderate men thought the censure too sharp, too base and ignominious for gentlemen of their ingenuous[28] vocation. Besides, though it be easy in the notion, it is hard in the action to fix shame on the professors and sever it from the professions of divinity, law, and physic. As for the former, though Burton was first degraded, yet such who maintain an indelible character of priesthood hold that degradation cannot delete what ordination hath impressed; and grant the censure pronounced *ad terrorem*,[29] it might have become the bishops to mediate for a mitigation thereof. Let canvas be rough and rugged, lawn[30] ought to be soft and smooth, meekness, mildness, and mercy being more proper for men of the episcopal function.

Two days after,[31] three pillories were set up in the Palace Yard, or one double one and a single one at some distance for Master Prynne as the chief offender. Master Burton first suffered, making a long speech in the pillory, not entire and continued but interrupted with occasional expressions. But the main intent thereof was to parallel his sufferings with our Saviour's. For at the first sight of the pillory, "Methinks," said he, "I see Mount Calvary, whereon the three crosses were erected. If Christ was numbered amongst thieves, shall a Christian think much for His sake to be numbered amongst rogues?" And whereas one told an halberteer[32] standing by, who had an old rusty halbert (the iron whereof was tacked to the staff with an old crooked nail), "What an old rusty weapon is this!" Master Burton overhearing them answered, "It seems to be one of those halberts which accompanied Judas when Christ was betrayed and apprehended."

His ears were cut off very close, so that the temporal or head artery being cut, the blood in abundance streamed down upon the scaffold, all which he manfully endured without manifesting the least shrinking thereat. Indeed, of such who

measured his mind by his words some conceived his carriage far above; others, though using the same scale, suspected the same to be somewhat beside himself. But let such who desire more of his character consult with his printed life, written with his own hand,[33] though it be hard for the most excellent artist truly to draw his own picture.

Dr. Bastwick succeeded him, making a speech to this effect: "Here are many spectators of us who stand here as delinquents, yet am I not conscious to myself of the least trespass wherein I have deserved this outward shame. Indeed, I wrote a book against Antichrist the Pope, and the Pope of Canterbury said it was written against him. But were the press open unto us, we would scatter his kingdom and fight courageously against Gog and Magog.[34] There be many here that have set many days apart on our behalf—let the prelates take notice thereof—and have sent up strong prayers to God for us, the strength and fruit whereof we have felt all along in this cause. In a word, so far am I from fear or care that had I as much blood as would swell the Thames"—then visible unto him, his face respecting[35] the south—"I would lose every drop thereof in this cause."

His friends much admired and highly commended the erection of his mind triumphing over pain and shame, making the one easy, the other honorable, and imputed the same to an immediate spiritual support.[36] Others conceived that anger in him acted the part of patience as to the stout undergoing of his sufferings. And that in a Christian there lieth a real distinction betwixt spirit and stomach, valor and stubbornness.

Master Prynne concluded the sad sight of that day, and spake to this purpose: "The cause of my standing here is for not bringing in my answer. God knoweth, my conscience beareth witness, and my counsel can tell, for I paid them twice, though to no purpose. But their cowardice stands upon record. And that's the reason why they did proceed, and take the cause *pro confesso* against me. But rather than I would have my cause a leading cause to the depriving of the subject's liberties, which I seek to maintain, I choose to suffer my body to become an example of this punishment."

The censure was with all rigor executed on him, and he who felt the most fretted the least, commended for more kindly patience than either of his predecessors in that place. So various were men's fancies in reading the same letters

[27] *A Speech Delivered in the Star Chamber at the Censure of J. Bastwick* (1637).
[28] Noble, high-minded.
[29] To inspire terror (as a deterrent to others).
[30] Fine linen or cotton fabric used in clerical vestments.
[31] Actually, the savage sentences were carried out on 30 June 1637.
[32] Halberdier, i.e., a soldier armed with a halberd, a weapon combining the functions of an ax and spear.
[33] *A Narration of the Life of Mr. H. B. . . . According to a Copy Written with His Own Hand* (1643).
[34] The nations foretold in Revelation 20.8 that, led by Satan, would wage war against the kingdom of God.   [35] Looking toward.
[36] According to one eyewitness of the bloody scene in Palace Yard, Bastwick's wife was so much pleased by her husband's behavior that she thriftily gathered up his severed ears, wrapped them in a "clean handkerchief," and took them home with her.

imprinted in his face that some made them to spell the guiltiness of the sufferer, but others the cruelty of the imposer. Of the latter sort many for the cause, more for the man, most for humanity sake bestowed pity upon him. And now all three were remanded to their former prisons; and Master Prynne, as he returned by water to the Tower, made this distich upon his own stigmatizing:

S.L.

Stigmata maxillis referens, insignia Laudis,
Exultans remeo, victima grata Deo.[37]

Not long after they were removed, Master Prynne to Car- [10] narvon Castle in Wales, Dr. Bastwick and Master Burton the one to Lancaster Castle, the other to Launceston in Cornwall.

But it seems these places were conceived to have either too little of privacy or too much of pleasure. The two latter therefore were removed again, one to the Isle of Scilly, the other to the Isle of Guernsey, and Master Prynne to Mount Orgueil Castle in Jersey.[38] This in vulgar apprehensions added breadth to the former depth of their sufferings, scattering the same over all the English dominions, making the islands thereof as well as the continent partake of their [20] patience. And here we leave them all in their prisons, and particularly Master Prynne, improving the rocks and the seas (good spiritual husbandry) with pious meditations.[39] But we shall hear more of them hereafter at the beginning of the Parliament. . . .

> When Charles was finally forced to call the Long Parliament, in November 1640, the Puritan opposition that the King and Archbishop Laud had so ruthlessly suppressed was quick to make its power felt.

About this time [November 1640] Master Prynne, Dr. [30] Bastwick, and Master Burton were brought out of durance

and exile with great triumph into London, it not sufficing their friends to welcome them peaceably, but victoriously, with bays and rosemary in their hands and hats. Wise men conceived that their private returning to the town had signified as much gratitude to God, and less affront to authority; but some wildness of the looks must be pardoned in such who came suddenly into the light out of long darkness.

> To complete the story it should be added that after their hour of martyrdom and triumph, the three victims of Laud's terror continued indefatigably to share their views of church and state with anyone who listened. Prynne became so warm against Cromwell and the Independents that in 1649 he was imprisoned (without trial) for three years, but he was resilient, and so gladly hailed the Restoration that he was thanked by Charles II and appointed keeper of the records in the Tower. Scribbling to the end, he died in 1669, the author of some two hundred books and pamphlets. Bastwick, who served as a captain in the parliamentary army, was captured and released by the royalists in 1642, and thereafter, until his death twelve years later, occupied himself mainly by pointing out the errors of the Independents. Burton returned to his pulpit at St. Matthews, wrote avidly in support of Independency, and died in 1648.

[37]"The brands on my jaw being marks of honor [literally, the signs of Laud], I return rejoicing, a sacrifice to God's grace."
[38]*Isle of Scilly...Jersey*: respectively, islands off the coast of Cornwall and in the English Channel.
[39]Barred from controversial subjects, Prynne beguiled the time in prison by writing, in lamentable verse, *Mount Orgueil, or Divine and Profitable Meditations Raised from the Contemplation of These Three Leaves of Nature's Volume: 1. Rocks, 2. Seas, 3. Gardens, Digested into Three Distinct Poems. To Which Is Prefixed a Poetical Description of Mount Orgueil Castle in the Isle of Jersey...* (1641).

Agitation for Reform

The mounting political and religious pressures of the reign of Charles I are recorded elsewhere in this book, and from various points of view, by such notable participants and observers as the King himself, Clarendon, Hobbes, Milton, Fuller, Hall, and May. With the possible exception of the last (who was famous in his day), the reputations of these men have been secured against devouring Time by virtue of their rank or genius, but the quartet here assembled under the rubric "Agitation for Reform" may be said to owe their presence in this book to their involvement in the controversies of the period. All of them were able writers who used their writing to effect reform, but there resemblance ends. Lilburne was an apprentice to a London merchant, Parker a lawyer, Goodwin an Independent minister, and Walwyn a member of the Merchant Adventurers' Company who had prospered in the trade of silk before drifting into politics. One tried to gain his goal by civil disobedience, one by parliamentary action, one by incendiary preaching, and one by disputation; but in their different aims and methods they provide a sample of the enormous and ephemeral literature of discontent with which the presses groaned as England braced itself for civil war and then was forced to reconstruct its state and church.

Aligned with other writers in this book, the reformers represented here may be said to constitute a sort of spectrum that runs from Stuart royalism to political and economic egalitarianism. From right to left this spectrum would include such royalists and Anglicans as the author of *Eikon Basilike*, Clarendon, Hobbes, Hall, Fuller, and maybe Chillingworth; such Parliamentarians as Thomas May and Henry Parker, together with young Milton (in *Of Reformation*) and the dreadful Francis Cheynell; such Independents in the center as John Goodwin and the slightly older Milton of *Areopagitica*; and, on the radical left, a wide variety of Levelers and Sectarians who are represented here by John Lilburne and William Walwyn. When one recalls that between 1641 and 1662 the bookseller George Thomason (d. 1666) collected some 23,000 books, pamphlets, and broadsides on contemporary affairs, and that Thomas Edwards, the virulent custodian of Presbyterian orthodoxy, exposed hundreds of "errors, heresies, blasphemies, and pernicious practices of the Sectaries of this time" in his *Gangraena* (1646–47), it is clear that no four, or even forty, men could fairly represent the shifting winds of doctrine as royalist and Parliamentarian, Anglican and Presbyterian, Presbyterian and Independent, Independent and Sectarian waged what Milton called the wars of truth. Nonetheless, our four pamphleteers enable us to understand something of the passion and the knotty issues of the unprecedented public debate on religion and politics that was conducted in the press while the English made their revolution.

Certain facts about this revolution should be kept in mind as the reader first confronts the issues, personalities, and topicalities with which these pamphlets swarm. Despite the harsh controls whereby Charles and Laud had tried to crush dissent during the 1630's—a reign of terror vividly described by John Lilburne in *A Work of the Beast*—the Parliament that the king reluctantly convened in November 1640 (see *Eikon Basilike*, pp. 615 f.) was anything but docile. It quickly made its old resentments felt by a series of impeachments (including those of Laud and the hated earl of Strafford), by revoking the Anglican canons of 1640 that had asserted the divine right of bishops, by freeing from prison some of Laud's illustrious victims, by passing the revolutionary Triennial Act that required the summoning of Parliament every three years even without the initiative of the crown, by introducing the Root and Branch bill designed to extirpate episcopacy, and by abolishing the courts of Star Chamber and High Commission, the King's chief instruments of repression. With these extraordinary actions England plunged toward civil war. When the hapless Charles, having virtually surrendered Scotland to the Presbyterians, was confronted with the Grand Remonstrance (November 1641), wherein Parliament obligingly listed all his faults and errors (see Milton, *Eikonoklastes*, pp. 611 ff.), he made an abortive effort to arrest five members of the House of Commons (January 1642) and six days later left London for the North of England. In June he indignantly rejected some nineteen parliamentary propositions that would have formalized his fall from kingly power, and when Parliament thereupon began amassing troops he himself proclaimed a state of war when he raised his royal standard at Nottingham on August 22. It was to justify this unprecedented show of parliamentary power, whereby a legislative body made a revolution, that Henry Parker wrote his *Observations*.

Apart from the one dramatic moment in November 1642 when Charles almost regained his capital (a crisis that prompted Goodwin's *Anti-Cavalierism*), the actual conduct of the fighting was of less compelling interest to the pamphleteers than were the theological and political problems engendered by the war. Inevitably, these problems were exacerbated by divisions among the dissidents themselves, who found it easier to unite against the king and prelates than to harmonize their conflicting programs for reform. With episcopacy abolished and the excesses of the king curtailed, the Presbyterians in Parliament—the right wing of Puritanism—would have been content with a constitutional monarchy and a national church "reformed" along the lines that Calvin had prescribed. But as influential men like Goodwin and nobodies like Milton soon discovered, these zealots, more intolerant of dissent than Laud himself had been, could find no place within their scheme of things for Independents, whose central demand for congregational autonomy (or the so-called "gathered churches") was based upon a principle of toleration abhorrent to the Presbyterians. "New Presbyter is but Old Priest writ large," Milton soon concluded (p. 287), and in his stirring *Areopagitica* (pp. 603 ff.)—one of the few enduring monuments of these forgotten quarrels—he transformed his disenchantment with the Presbyterians into a splendid work of art.

Finally, and well to the left of the Independents of the center, were a bewildering variety of Sectarians, who, prompted by the Holy Ghost, found any sort of corporate or congregational religious experience irrelevant and any sort of Erastian or legislated conformity intolerable. Such intense religious individualism produced its share of freaks and fools, of course, but its implications, as developed by such Levelers as William Walwyn, John Overton, and Lilburne (in his middle phase), take us far beyond the limits of this troubled period. To trace the evolution and the eventual consequences of the sort of freedom that Walwyn advocates in *The Good Samaritan* would be to show how the great Protestant principle of Christian liberty was used to justify freedom of conscience, then at least some sort of toleration, then the separation of church and state, and then—vaulting from theology to politics—the claim, as "natural rights," of such inadmissible ideals as political and economic egalitarianism, with its vision of a real democracy.

To take our pamphleteers up in order, John Lilburne (1615–57) appeared, or rather leapt, upon the stage of history during one of the most brutal episodes in Laud's campaign against dissent—the trial of those stalwart Presbyterians William Prynne, John Bastwick, and Henry Burton for publishing unlicensed pamphlets against episcopacy in 1637. According to Thomas Fuller (for whose account of the background and the actual conduct of this famous trial see pp. 577 ff.), even loyal subjects of the king had mixed reactions to the savage sentences meted out by the Star Chamber, "high conformists" thinking them too mild and "most moderate men" thinking them too "sharp"; but nonconformists were agreed that for pious, learned citizens to be fined, pilloried, shorn of their ears, and perpetually imprisoned in an effort to maintain a wicked status quo was a pure abomination.

One young firebrand who made his disapproval known was Lilburne. The son of a litigious citizen of Durham, this apprentice to a London clothier was, according to Anthony Wood, a bright and very forward youth, but so much "addicted to contention, novelties, opposition of government, and to violent and bitter expressions" that his later stormy life could have been predicted. Already inclined toward Puritanism, he became a friend of Bastwick, visited him in prison, and even had a hand in printing his inflammatory *Litany* in 1637 (see p. 379, n. 17). Following his mentor's trial, which he must have heard with mounting indignation, it seems he went to Holland in hope of setting up in trade. Instead, he was soon involved in printing and exporting the *Litany* and similarly seditious works, for which offense he was arrested on his return to England in December 1637. Before his release from the Fleet three years later (on Cromwell's instigation), he poured forth at least seven fiery pamphlets and petitions, one of them (*A Christian Man's Trial*) describing his arraignment and conviction and another (*A Work of the Beast*) the execution of his savage sentence.

With these two pamphlets—the first of dozens that he wrote—he was embarked upon the windy seas of controversy. His later life as a soldier in the parliamentary forces (which was rewarded with a lieutenant-colonelcy) and then—"the boiling of his conscience swelling now as high against the convenanted Presbytery as they had formerly done against the prerogative and episcopacy"—as a critic of the army's high command, a leader of the Levelers, an opponent of Cromwell's coup d'état, and as an adversary of nearly any form of constituted power, led him at various times to prison, to a trial (1648) for seditious and scandalous practices against the state which ended with acquittal, to a fine of £7,000 and exile overseas (1652) for his attacks on powerful men whom he thought had wronged his uncle, to a long incarceration on his return to England, and finally to an implausible association with the Quakers, for whom he sometimes preached before his death in 1657. Appropriately, his funeral in Moorfields, where 4,000 noisy people gathered, was enlivened by a riot. "If the world were emptied of all but John Lilburne," someone said of this extraordinary man, "Lilburne would quarrel with John, and John with Lilburne."

Whereas Lilburne was a nondescript apprentice when he defied the Star Chamber in 1637, John

Goodwin (1594?–1665) had long been an influential London preacher and a leader of the Independents when he rang the tocsin of alarm against the king's advancing hosts in 1642. A fellow of Queens' College, Cambridge (M.A. 1617), and then a rising preacher in the East of England, in 1633 he was called to London to become the vicar of St. Stephen's, Coleman Street, and there—"as a Republican, an Independent, and a thorough Arminian"—he soon attracted much attention. When Milton, in *The Reason of Church Government* (1642), spoke about "the power of the pulpit" in arousing and sustaining civil spirit, he might well have thought of Goodwin, who for various reasons, theological and other, had disagreed with Laud and sided with the liberal Puritans long before the war had sharpened party lines and stiffened his convictions. The same convictions, which inspired his stirring plea for toleration in *Imputatio Fidei* (1642), inflamed his *Anti-Cavalierism* (October 1642) as he sought to rouse his fellow Londoners against the threat of royal power.

Goodwin's call to arms appeared at a most uneasy time, just before the first (and indecisive) meeting of the royalist and parliamentary forces at Edgehill on 23 October 1642. Soon thereafter, Charles, hoping to end the war with one decisive stroke, began to march on London. To the consternation of his foes he had taken Brentford by November 12, and then pushed on to Turnham Green, in the very outskirts of the capital; but there, finding his way barred by some 24,000 parliamentary troops and ragged trained bands from the City, he paused and then drew back to Oxford (November 13). Never again would he come so close to regaining the heart and symbol of his realm. One wonders how many of the Londoners who streamed along the western road to check their king's advance had Goodwin's exhortations ringing in their ears:

> Give me leave in that which remains to excite and stir you up, from the greatest to the least, both young and old, rich and poor, men and women, to quit yourselves like men—yea, and if it be possible above the line of men—in this great exigency and stress of imminent danger that hangs over your heads and threatens you every hour. O let it be as abomination unto us—as the very shadow of death to every man, woman, and child of us—not to be active, not to lie out and strain ourselves to the utmost of our strength and power in every kind, as far as the law of God and nature will suffer us, to resist that high hand of iniquity and blood that is stretched out against us; to make our lives, and our liberties, and our religion good against that accursed generation that now magnifieth themselves, to make a prey and spoil of them, to make havoc and desolation of them all at once if the Lord shall yet please to deliver us out of their hands.

Having helped avert one real and present danger, Goodwin, "the great red dragon of Coleman Street," promptly turned to others. In *Os Ossorianum* (1643) he denounced the royalists and Presbyterians; in *Theomachi* (1644) he wrote a stirring plea for Independency; and by 1645 his assertive liberalism led to his ejection from the pulpit that had served him as a barricade for more than twenty years. When he retaliated by organizing a congregation of his own in Coleman Street, it was clear, as one of his detractors said, that he had become little better than "a monstrous Sectary, a compound of Socinianism, Arminianism, antinomianism, Independency, popery, yea, and of skepticism." With the passing years Goodwin grew no gentler with bigots, royalists, and Presbyterians; instead, he defended Cromwell against his parliamentary opposition, supported Charles' execution, urged an expanded toleration, and in a string of publications took the liberal side of almost every question. Like Milton, he was endangered at the Restoration by his defense of regicide, but he soon was preaching once again in Coleman Street, where he died, a victim of the plague, in 1665. As the author of some fifty books and pamphlets, almost all on controversial subjects, he was, said Edmund Calamy, "a man by himself," but once, and at a crucial hour, he seemed to speak for all.

Though just as dangerous to the Caroline establishment as Lilburne and Goodwin, Henry Parker (1604–52) was cut from very different cloth. Well born and conventionally educated at St. Edmund's Hall, Oxford (B.A. 1625, M.A. 1628), he was called to the bar at Lincoln's Inn in 1637, and soon thereafter he was speaking boldly on the urgent problems of the time. But whereas Lilburne raged against the indignities that he himself had borne and Goodwin wrote with zeal and passion and great forensic skill to rouse his coreligionists against the foes of freedom, Parker, always crisp and cool, argued his opinions like a lawyer at the bar. The very titles of his pamphlets reveal the workings of his legalistic mind and make his parliamentary leanings clear: *The Case of Ship Money* (1640), *A Discourse Concerning Puritans* (1641), and *The Question Concerning the Divine Right of Episcopacy Truly Stated* (1641). It was in 1642, just before Charles flung down the gauntlet to his foes, that the ominous "contestation between royal and Parliamentary power" moved Parker to write his most influential book. First published in May as *Some Few Observations upon His Majesty's Late Answers* and then in July expanded as *Observations upon Some of His Majesty's Late Answers and Expresses*, it was one of the ablest attacks on royalism yet produced in England. Building his case on the proposition that power was "originally inherent in the people" and by a social contract merely delegated to the sovereign, Parker has no trouble showing that a sovereign forfeits his "prerogative" when he violates the contract by abuse of power, whereupon this power reverts to Parliament, the "essence" of the people. "The name of a king is great, I confess," he concedes

> and worthy of great honor, but is not the name of people greater? Let not mere terms deceive us; let us weigh names and things together, admit that God sheds here some rays of majesty upon His viceregents on earth, yet except we think He doth this out of particular love to princes themselves, and not to communities of men, we must not hence invert the course of nature and make nations subordinate in end to princes.

Parker's pamphlet stirred a great debate, which Professor Haller sees as leading ultimately to. such important counterstatements as *Eikon Basilike* (see pp. 615f.), Hobbes' *Leviathan* (see pp. 493 ff.), and Sir Robert Filmer's *Partiarcha* (1680). Throughout the forties Parker himself continued to reassert and amplify his view of parliamentary power, and so, following a period as secretary to the Merchant Adventurers' Company at Hamburg, he was at last rewarded with the lucrative registership of the Prerogative Office (1449) and then with various posts in Ireland, still reeling from the shock of Cromwell's subjugation. Anthony Wood said that when he died there in 1652 Parker was "distracted," and he implied that such an end was fitting for a man so faithless to his king.

William Walwyn (1600–80), the last of our four pamphleteers, is in some respects the most engaging of them all. Born in Worcestershire as a younger son (and as the grandson of a bishop), he, like Lilburne, was apprenticed to a London tradesman, prospered in a business of his own, and began the heroic work of siring twenty children before he turned to politics and agitation in the 1640's. Both his theology (which was antinomian) and his reading (which included, in addition to the Bible, Seneca, Plutarch, Lucian, Hooker, Montaigne, and Pierre Charron) suggest his liberal cast of mind, but they do not explain how this solid, solvent London burgher became an innovative thinker and a member of the avant-garde. Apart from a few autobiographical allusions in his later pamphlets, Walwyn himself does little to dispel our ignorance, and since the few tracts that he wrote were usually published anonymously it is hard to reconstruct the progress of his thinking.

However, on the basis of two early pamphlets that have been ascribed to him—*Some Considerations Tending to the Undeceiving Those Whose Judgments Are Misinformed by Politic Protestations, Declarations, &c.* (1642) and *The Power of Love* (1643)—it appears that he was stirred to pamphleteering by his dismay at the savage opposition, Anglican as well as Presbyterian, to despised Sectarians. Since the apostle (1 Thessalonians 5.19–21) advises us "to try all things, and to hold fast that which is good, to prove the spirits whether they be of God or not," Walwyn reminds the reader in the preface to *The Power of Love*, toleration should be regarded not as a reluctant and enforced concession but as a Christian duty.

> Let brotherly love continue, and let everyone freely speak his mind without molestation; and so there may be hope that truth may come to light, that otherwise may be obscured for particular ends, plain truth will prove all, sufficient for vanquishing of the most artificial, sophistical error that ever was in the world. Give her but due and patient audience, and her persuasions are ten thousand times more powerful to work upon the most dull, refractory mind than all the adulterate allurements and deceivings of art.

The same persuasive theme informs *The Good Samaritan* as Walwyn, addressing the "chosen men" in the House of Commons in 1644, repudiates all kinds of persecution—"papistical, prelatical, and regal"—and attacks the evil done by Presbyterian censors.

> 'Tis common freedom every man ought to aim at, which is every man's peculiar right so far as 'tis not prejudicial to the common. Now because little can be done in their behalf unless liberty of conscience be allowed for every man or sort of men to worship God in that way and perform Christ's ordinances in that manner as shall appear to them most agreeable to God's word, and no man be punished or discountenanced by authority for his opinion unless it be dangerous to the state, I have endeavored in this discourse to make appear by the best reason I have that every man ought to have liberty of conscience of what opinion soever.

It is not surprising that Milton's *Areopagitica* shows the influence of *The Good Samaritan*, or that the revised edition of Walwyn's little tract (1645) reveals his knowledge of his great contemporary's newly published work.

Walwyn's subsequent career as a Leveler, when he broadened his demands for toleration from theology to politics, earned for him not only Thomas Edwards' condemnation as "a seeker, a dangerous man, a stronghead," but also strict confinement in the Tower (1649) along with Lilburne and others charged with inciting parliamentary troops to insurrection. About 1651 he seems to have retreated to the silence that engulfed his later years.

My texts are based upon the facsimile reprints of the four tracts in William Haller's edition of *Tracts on Liberty in the Puritan Revolution 1638–1647* (3 vols., 1933–34) as follow: [John Lilburne], *A Worke of the Beast or a Relation of a most unchristian Censure, Executed upon John Lilburne . . . Very usefull for these times both for the encouragement of the Godly to suffer, And for the terrour and shame of the Lords Adversaries*, 1638 (STC 15599); John Goodwin, *Anti-Cavalierisme, or, Truth Pleading As well the Necessity, as the Lawfulness of this present War*, [1642] (Wing G–1146); [Henry Parker], *Observations upon some of his Majesties late Answers and Expresses. The second Edition corrected from some grosse errors in the Presse*, [1642] (Wing P–413); and [William Walwyn], *The Compassionate Samaritane Vnbinding The Conscience, and powring Oyle into the wounds which have been made upon the Separation . . . The Second Edition, corrected and enlarged*, 1644 (Wing W–681A).

In addition to discussions of the Levelers in Haller's introduction, T. C. Pease's *Leveller Movement* (1916), W. Schenk's *Concern for Social Justice in the Puritan Revolution* (1948), Joseph Frank's *The Levellers* (1955), L. F. Scott's *Saints in Arms: Puritanism and Democracy in Cromwell's Army* (1959), and H. N. Brailsford's *The Levellers and the English Revolution* (ed. Christopher Hill, 1961) there are biographies of Lilburne by M. A. Gibbs (1947) and Pauline Gregg (1961), an old and unsatisfactory life of Goodwin by Thomas Jackson (1822, rev. 1872), and a useful account of Parker by W. K. Jordan in his *Men of Substance* (1942). Although Walwyn still lacks a biographer, he is treated incidentally in almost all the works cited above. Other titles and collections of Leveler tracts are listed in the General Bibliography, Section III.

John Lilburne [1615-1657]

from A Work of the Beast (1638)

THE PUBLISHER TO THE READER

Tender-hearted Reader:
Of the wicked it is truly said in Job, their light shall be put out.[1] Now we see in a candle, being almost extinguished, that after it hath glimmered a while it raiseth some few blazing flashes and so suddenly vanisheth.

A WORK OF THE BEAST   [1] Job 18.5.

To speak what I think, my mind gives me that the Lord is now upon extinguishing the bloody prelates out of our land. For whereas they have not in some late years showed the cruelty which they did before, but now increase in persecution, methinks this is a clear foregoing sign that, like a snuff[2] in the socket, their end and ruin is at hand.

I write this to have thee the more patient, contented, and comforted when thou either hearest, seest, or readest of their barbarous cruelty. Be sure their condemnation sleepeth not, but when their wickedness is full—I say, when they have once filled up the measure of their iniquity, the which I trust they have almost done—then will the Lord send back these locusts to the bottomless pit from whence they came.[3]

In the meantime fear not their faces, but stand in the truth and let God's house and His ordinances be dear to thy soul. And know that as the Lord gave strength to this His servant[4] to suffer joyfully for Christ's cause, so He will to thee and me and all others of His saints if He count us worthy to be called thereto.

> *Thine if thou be Christ's, and a hater of the*
> *English popish prelates,*
> *F. R.*[5]

> When young John Lilburne, just returned from Holland, was arrested and brought before the Star Chamber on a turncoat informer's charge of printing and circulating unlicensed books, he at once enlivened the proceedings by refusing to take the oath on grounds of self-incrimination. Such a challenge to the jurisdiction of the court could not be tolerated, and after a noisy interrogation Lilburne was sentenced to pay a fine of £500 and to be whipped, pilloried, and imprisoned in the Fleet until such time as he was willing to submit. Told on April 18 that his suffering was at hand, he fortified himself by meditating on what the Bible has to say about unjust persecution, and as he descended to the porter's lodge he felt, as he reported later, like a bridegroom on his wedding day. What lay in store for him, however, was designed to test his resolution.

"Mr. Lilburne, I am very sorry for your punishment you are now to undergo: you must strip you and be whipped from hence to Westminster." I replied, "The will of my God be done, for I know He will carry me through it with an undaunted spirit." But I must confess it seemed at the first a little strange to me in regard[6] I had no more notice given me for my preparation for so sore a punishment. For I thought I should not have been whipped through the street, but only at the pillory. And so, passing along the lane, being attended with many staves and halberds,[7] as Christ was when he was apprehended by His enemies and led to the high priest's hall (Matthew 26), we came to Fleet Bridge,[8] where was a cart standing ready for me. And I being commanded to strip me, I did it with all willingness and cheerfulness, whereupon the executioner took out a cord and tied my hands to the cart's arse, which caused me to utter these words: "Welcome be the cross of Christ!"

With that there drew near a young man of my acquaintance, and bid me put on a courageous resolution to suffer cheerfully and not to dishonor my cause, "For you suffer," said he, "for a good cause." I gave him thanks for his Christian encouragement, replying,[9] "I know the cause is good, for it is God's cause; and for my own part I am cheerful and merry in the Lord, and am as well contented with this my present portion as if I were to receive my present liberty. For I know my God, that hath gone along with me hitherto, will carry me through[10] to the end. And for the affliction itself, though it be the punishment inflicted upon rogues, yet I esteem it not the least disgrace, but the greatest honor that can be done unto me that the Lord counts me worthy to suffer anything for His great name. And you, my brethren, that do now here behold my present condition this day, be not discouraged, be not discouraged at the ways of godlinesse by reason of the cross which accompanies it, for it is the lot and portion of all which will live godly in Christ Jesus to suffer persecution."

The cart being ready to go forward, I spake to the executioner (when I saw him pull out his corded whip out of his pocket) after this manner: Well, my friend, do thy office." To which he replied, "I have whipped many a rogue, but now I shall whip an honest man. But be not discouraged," said he; "it will be soon over." To which I replied: "I know my God hath not only enabled me to believe in His name but also to suffer for His sake." So the carman drove forward his cart, and I labored with my God for strength to submit my back with cheerfulness unto the smiter. And he heard my desire and granted my request, for when the first stripe was given I felt not the least pain, but said, "Blessed be Thy name, O Lord my God, that hast counted me worthy to suffer for Thy glorious name's sake." And at the giving of the second I cried out with a loud voice, "Hallelujah, hallelujah! Glory, honor, and praise be given to Thee, O Lord, forever, and to the Lamb that sits upon the throne!" So we went up Fleet Street, the Lord enabling me to endure the stripes with such patience and cheerfulness that I did not in the least manner show the least discontent at them, for my God hardened my back and steeled my reins,[11] and took away the smart and pain of the stripes from me. But I must confess if I had had no more but my own natural strength I had sunk under the burden of my punishment, for to the flesh the pain was very grievous[12] and heavy. . . .

And as we went along the Strand many friends spoke to me and asked how I did and bid me be cheerful, to whom I replied I was merry and cheerful, and was upheld with a divine and heavenly supportation, comforted with the sweet consolations of God's spirit. And about the middle of the Strand there came a friend and bid me speak with boldness, to whom I replied, "When the time comes, so I will." For then if I should have spoken and spent my strength it would

[2]Burned wick in a candle.
[3]*Locusts . . . came*: See Revelation 9.3 (a text repeatedly applied by Lilburne to the Anglican hierarchy).   [4]Lilburne.
[5]The publisher of Lilburne's unlicensed pamphlet is unknown.
[6]In view of the fact that, because.   [7]Pikemen and halberdiers.
[8]The bridge over Fleet Brook, a small stream (and open sewer) that flowed from Hampstead Heath past St. Paul's Cathedral to join the Thames at Blackfriars Bridge. On its east bank stood the ancient and infamous Fleet Prison, and leading westward to the Strand was Fleet Street, then as now one of the main thoroughfares of London.   [9]Text *I replying*.   [10]Text *though*.   [11]Kidneys.
[12]Grievous.

have been but as water spilt on the ground in regard of the noise and press of people. And also at that time I was not in a fit temper to speak because the dust much troubled me and the sun shined very hot upon me. And the tipstaff man at the first would not let me have my hat to keep the vehement heat of the sun from my head. Also he many times spoke to the cartman to drive softly,[13] so that the heat of the sun exceedingly pierced my head and made me somewhat faint. But yet my God upheld me with courage, and made me undergo it with a joyful heart. And when I came to Charing 10 Cross some Christian spake to me and bid me be of good cheer. . . .

And as we went through King Street[14] many encouraged me and bid me be cheerful. Others whose faces (to my knowledge) I never saw before, and who, I verily think, knew not the cause of my suffering, but seeing my cheerfulness under it, beseeched the Lord to bless me and strengthen me. At the last we came to the pillory, where I was unloosed from the cart, and having put on some of my clothes, we went to the tavern, where I stayed a pretty while 20 waiting for my surgeon (who was not yet come to dress me), where were many of my friends who exceedingly rejoiced to see my courage, that the Lord had enabled me to undergo my punishment so willingly, who asked me how I did. I told them, as well as ever I was in my life, I bless my God for it, for I felt such inward joy and comfort, cheering up my soul, that I lightly esteemed my sufferings. And this I counted my wedding-day in which I was married to the Lord Jesus Christ, for now I know He loves me in that He hath bestowed so rich apparel this day upon me, and counted me worthy to 30 suffer for His sake.

I having a desire to retire into a private room from the multitude of people that were about me, which made me like to faint, I had not been there long but Mr. Lightburne, the tipstaff[15] of the Star Chamber, came to me saying the lords sent him to me to know if I would acknowledge myself to be in a fault, and then he knew what to say unto me. To whom I replied: "Have Their Honors caused me to be whipped from the Fleet to Westminster, and do they now send to know if I will acknowledge a fault? They should have 40 done this before I had been whipped, for now, seeing I have undergone the greatest part of my punishment, I hope the Lord will assist me to go through it all; and besides, if I would have done this at the first I needed not to have come to this, but as I told the lords when I was before them at the bar, so I desire you to tell them again: that I am not conscious to myself of doing anything that deserves a submission, but yet I do willingly submit to Their Lordships' pleasures in my censure." He told me if I would confess a fault, it would save me a standing on the pillory; otherwise I must undergo 50 the burden of it. "Well, Sir," said I, "I regard not a little outward disgrace for the cause of my God. . . ." And so he went away, and I prepared myself for the pillory, to which I went with a joyful courage. And when I was upon it I made obeisance to the lords, some of them (as I suppose) looking out at the Star Chamber window towards me. And so I put my neck into the hole, which being a great deal too

low for me, it was very painful to me in regard of the continuance of time that I stood on the pillory, which was about two hours, my back also being very sore and the sun shining exceeding hot. . . .

> As the Star Chamber no doubt had feared, and as Lilburne himself clearly had foreseen in his painful progress down the Strand, the pillory provided both an audience and a rostrum, and no sooner had the culprit been installed in that "place of ignominy and shame" than he embarked upon a full account of his misfortunes. His accuser was a perjured knave, he said, his interrogation was illegal, and his punishment was an act of savage persecution that the prelates had decreed. A part of his excoriation of the Anglican hierarchy will supply a sample of his fervor and his style.

"Now I will here maintain it before them all that their calling is so far from being *jure divino* (as they say they are) that they are rather *jure diabolico*,[16] which if I be not able to prove, let me be hanged up at the Hall gate.[17] But, my brethren, for your better satisfaction read the ninth and thirteenth chapters of the Revelation, and there you shall see that there came locusts out of the bottomless pit, part of whom they are, and they are there lively described. Also you shall there find that the beast (which is the pope, or Roman state and government) hath given to him by the dragon (the devil) his power and seat and great authority. So that the pope's authority comes from the devil, and the prelates and their creatures in their printed books do challenge[18] their authority, jurisdiction, and power (that they exercise over all sorts of people) is from Rome.

"And for proving of the Church of England to be a true church, their best and strongest argument is that the bishops are lineally descended from His Holiness (or impiousness) of Rome, as you may read in Pocklington's book called *Sunday No Sabbath*.[19] So that by their own confession they stand by that same power and authority that they have received from the pope. So that their calling is not from God, but from the devil, for the pope cannot give a better authority or calling to them than he himself hath. But his authority and calling is from the devil; therefore the prelates' calling and authority is from the devil also. Revelation 9.3: "And there came out of the smoke locusts upon the earth, and unto them was given power as the scorpions of the earth have power to hurt"—and undo men, as the prelates daily do. And also Revelation 13.2: "And the beast which I saw," sayeth St. John, "was like unto a leopard, and his feet were as the feet of a bear, and his mouth as the mouth of a lion, and the dragon"—that is to say, the devil—"gave him his power, his seat, and great authority." And verses fifteen, sixteen, seven-

[13]Slowly (in order to prolong the punishment).
[14]Text *Kings Street*.   [15]Text *Tibstaffe*.
[16]*Jure . . . diabolico*: "by divine right . . . by Satanic right."
[17]The portal to Westminster Hall, before which stood the pillory.
[18]Claim, assert.
[19]As chaplain to King Charles and thus a vehement apologist for the Anglican establishment, John Pocklington (d. 1642) was so offensive to the Puritans that his anti-sabbatarian book was ordered burned in 1641.

teen. And whether the prelates as well as the pope do not daily the same things, let every man that hath but common reason judge.

"For do not their daily practises and cruel burdens—imposed on all sorts of people, high and low, rich and poor—witness that their descent is from the beast, part of his state and kingdom? See also Revelation sixteen, thirteen, fourteen, all which places do declare that their power and authority being from the pope (as they themselves confess); therefore it must needs originally come from the devil. . . . For in their [10] sermons that they preach before His Majesty, how do they incense the king and nobles against the people of God, laboring to make them odious in his sight, and stirring him up to execute vengeance upon them, though they be the most harmless generation of all others. . . .

"And thus the holiness of the minister is a cloak to cover the unlawfulness of his calling and make the people continue rebels against Christ His scepter and kingdom, which is an aggravation of his sin; for by this means the people are kept off from receiving the whole truth into their souls, and rest [20] in being but almost Christians, or but Christians in part. But O, my brethren, it behooves all you that fear God and tender the salvation of your own souls to look about you and to shake off that long security and formality in religion that you have lain in. For God of all things cannot endure lukewarmness (Revelation 3.16). And search out diligently the truth of things, and try them in the balance of the sanctuary. I beseech you, take things no more upon trust, as hitherto you have done, but take pains to search and find out those spiritual and hidden truths that God hath enwrapped in His sacred book, [30] and find out a bottom for your own souls. For if you will have the comforts of them you must bestow some labor for the getting of them, and you must search diligently before you find them (Proverbs 2). Labor also to withdraw your necks from under that spiritual and antichristian bondage unto which you have for a long time subjected your souls, lest the Lord cause His plagues and the fierceness of His wrath to seize both upon your bodies and souls, seeing you are now warned of the danger of these things. . . .

"It is true I am a young man and no scholar, according to [40] that which the world counts scholarship, yet I have obtained mercy of the Lord to be faithful, and He by a divine providence hath brought me hither this day, and I speak to you in the name of the Lord, being assisted with the spirit and power of the God of heaven and earth; and I speak not the words of rashness or inconsiderateness, but the words of soberness and mature deliberation; for I did consult with my God before I came hither, and desired Him that He would direct and enable me to speak that which might be for His glory and the good of His people. And as I am a soldier fighting under the [50] banner of the great and mighty captain, the Lord Jesus Christ, and as I look for that crown of immortality which one day I know shall be set upon my temples, being in the condition that I am in, I dare not hold my peace, but speak unto you with boldness, in the might and strength of my God, the things which the Lord in mercy hath made known unto my soul, come life, come death."

When I was hereabout there came a fat lawyer—I do not know his name—and commanded me to hold my peace and eave my preaching. To whom I replied and said, "Sir, I will not hold my peace, but speak my mind freely though I be hanged at Tyburn for my pains." It seems he himself was galled and touched as the lawyers were in Christ's time when He spake against the scribes and pharisees, which made them say, "Master, in saying thus thou revilest us also."[20] So he went away and, I think, complained to the lords, but I went on with my speech and said:

"My brethren, be not discouraged at the ways of God for the affliction and cross that doth accompany them, for it is sweet and comfortable drawing in the yoke of Christ for all that, and I have found it so by experience, for my soul is filled so full of spiritual and heavenly joy that with my tongue I am not able to express it, neither are any capable, I think, to partake of so great a degree of consolation but only those upon whom the Lord's gracious afflicting hand is. And for mine own part I stand this day in the place of an evildoer, but my conscience witnesseth that I am not sot.' And hereabout I put my hand in my pocket and pulled out three of worthy Dr. Bastwick's books[21] and threw them among the people and said: "There is part of the books for which I suffer. Take them among you and read them, and see if you find anything in them against the law of God, the law of the land, the glory of God, the honor of the king or state. . . .

Having proceeded in a manner thus far by the strength of my God, with boldness and courage in my speech, the warden of the Fleet came with the fat lawyer and commanded me to hold my peace, to whom I replied I would speak and declare my cause and mind though I were to be hanged at the gate for my speaking. And he caused proclamation to be made upon the pillory for bringing to him the books.[22] So then he commanded me to be gagged, and if I spake any more that then I should be whipped again upon the pillory. So I remained about an hour and a half gagged, being intercepted of much matter which, by God's assistance, I intended to have spoken. But yet with their cruelty I was nothing at all daunted, for I was full of comfort and courage, being mightily strengthened with the power of the Almighty, which made me with cheerfulness triumph over all my sufferings, not showing one sad countenance or a disconted heart. And when I was to come down, having taken out my head out of the pillory, I looked about me upon the people and said, "I am more than a conqueror through[23] Him that loved me. *Vivat Rex!* Let the king live forever!" And so I came down. . . .

[20]Luke 11.45.
[21]In a later section of his pamphlet omitted here, Lilburne identified these books as Bastwick's *Answer* to Sir John Banks, an *Answer to the Exceptions against His Litany*, and *Flagellum pontificis* (an attack on the Roman Catholic Church). On Bastwick himself (1593–1654) and his notorious persecution at the hands of Archbishop Laud, see p. 579.
[22]Bastwick's books that Lilburne had thrown among the crowd.
[23]Text *though*.

Enraged by such defiance, the Star Chamber resolved to make life very hard for Lilburne. Shortly after he had been returned to the Fleet and had been denied all but the most cursory medical attention, he learned from the "porter" in his cell that new oppressions were decreed.

"What is it," said I. "I hear," said he, "that the lords have ordered that you must be put into the wards and kept close prisoner there, and lie in irons, and none must be suffered to come at you to bring you anything, but you must live upon the poor man's box."[24] "Sir, that's very hard," said I, "but 10 the will of God be done. For mine own part, it nothing at all troubles me, for I know in whom I have believed, and I know not one hair of my head shall fall to the ground without His providence. . . ."

Afterwards the woman [who "looked to" that section of the prison] telling me she hoped I should not have so sore a punishment laid on me, but that I might have things brought me from my friends, I told her I did not much care how it went with me, for Jeremiah's dungeon or Daniel's den or the three children's furnace[25] is as pleasant and welcome to 20 me as a palace; for wheresoever I am I shall find God there, and if I have Him, that is enough to me. And for victuals, I told her I did not doubt but that God that fed the Prophet Eliah by a raven[26] would preserve me and fill me to the full by the way of His providence; and if no meat should be brought me, I knew, if they take away my meat, God would take away my stomach. Therefore I weighed not their cruelty, and thereupon uttered to her these four verses:

I do not fear nor dread the face
   Of any mortal man,
Let him against me bend his power
   And do the worst he can;
For my whole trust, strength, confidence,
   My hope and all my aid,
Is in the Lord Jehovah's fence,
   Which heaven and earth hath made.

The rest that I intended by the strength of my God to have spoken (if I had not been prevented by the gag) I now forbear to set down in regard I hear I am to come into the field again to fight a second battle, unto which time I reserve it if the Lord so order it that I may have liberty to speak. I doubt not but by the might and power of my God, in whom I rest and trust, valiantly to display the weapons of a good soldier of Jesus Christ, come life, come death. And in the meantime to what I have here said and written I set to my name, by me, John Lilburne, being written with part of my own blood. The rest of which by the Lord's assistance I will willingly shed if He call for it in the maintaining of His truth and glory, and that which I have here said and written by me,

John Lilburne

[24]*You must be put...box*: you must be placed in solitary confinement and rely upon charitable donations for your food.
[25]*Jeremiah's...furnace*: See Jeremiah 32.2; Daniel 3.12–25, 6.16.
[26]See 1 Kings 17.5–6. *Eliah*: Elijah.

John Goodwin [1594?-1665]

from Anti-Cavalierism (1642)

. . . What shall we think of that legion of devils (I had almost called them) who now possess the land, and after the 30 manner of devils indeed seek all to rent and tear it in pieces? I mean that colluvies,[1] that heap or gathering together of the scum and dross and garbage of the land, that most accursed confederacy made up of Gebal and Ammon and Amaleck, Philistims with the inhabitants of Tyre,[2] of Jesuits and papists and atheists, of stigmatical[3] and infamous persons in all kinds, with that bloody and butcherly generation commonly known by the name of cavaliers. Have they not through some black art or other gotten the chief treasure of the land, the king, into their possession, setting him still 40 in the front of all their desperate designs, which are these and their fellows: 1) To pull those stars out of the firmament of the land, to dissolve and ruin that assembly[4] which is by interpretation or representation (which you will) the whole nation. 2) When they have opened this door of hope unto themselves, to turn the laws and present frame of government upside down. 3) To make havoc and desolation, to root out the generation of the saints rush and branch, men and women, young and old fearing God out of the land. 4) To make rapine and spoil of all the goods and possessions, at least of all those that withstand them and are not brethren in iniquity with them. 5) To build up the walls of Jericho, to put Lucifer again into heaven; I mean, to advance the tyrannical thrones of the hierarchy to their former heighth or higher, if they know how. 6) By their authority and power to excommunicate and cast out all the pure and precious

ANTI-CAVALIERISM [1]Ulcerous discharges, i.e., rabble.
[2]*Most accursed...Tyre*: "For they have consulted together with one consent; they are confederate against thee...Gebal, and Ammon, and Amalek; the Philistines with the inhabitants of Tyre" (Psalm 83.5–7). *Philistims*: Philistines.
[3]Ignominious. [4]Parliament.

ordinances of God out of His house, and to supply this defect with antichristian and spurious institutions. 7) To spread that veil or covering of antichristian darkness again over the face of the land, which God by a most gracious hand of providence had rent and taken off many years since; to leaven the whole lump of the land the second time with the sour leaven of Romish error and superstition. 8) And lastly, as is much to be feared, when they have served their turns with and upon the king, and used him as an engine to get all the stones together for their building, then to make rubbidge[5] of him, as if they had honored him sufficiently to cause such sacred designs as these to pass through his hands, and made him instrumental or any ways accessory in such angelical achievements.

Do we think that the light of the knowledge of God shines in the hearts and consciences of these men? Have these men the mind of Christ amongst them? Do they know who is the Lord? Or do they not think rather that Baal or Belial[6] is He? "Have all the workers of iniquity," sayeth David; "no knowledge that they eat up my people as they eat bread" (Psalms 14.4), i.e. that they injure, vex, and consume them with no more remorse, regret, or touch of conscience than they eat and drink to preserve their natural lives, as if such men as these, the people of God, were made for the same end and purpose to them that bread is, viz. to be eaten up and devoured by them? Have they no knowledge (sayeth the Prophet)[7] that they dare attempt such a thing as this, implying (as it should seem) that to vex, molest, persecute, and destroy the people of God argues the most profound ignorance and thickest darkness in the minds and understandings of men that can likely be found there, and that the weakest impressions or glimmerings of any true light of knowledge would keep men from dashing their foot against this stone howsoever?

If men had but as much knowledge of God as Pilate's wife had in a dream[8] they would take heed of having anything to do with just men. And these things (sayeth our Saviour to His disciples concerning those that should kill them and think they did God service therein), these things (sayeth He) they shall do unto you because they have not known the Father nor me (John 16.3). If men had the least degree of the true knowledge of God in Christ they must needs have some knowledge of His people and children also; and if they know these, this knowledge would be as a hook in their nose or a bridle in their lips to keep them from falling foul upon them, as the knowledge of Christ, the Lord of Glory, would have kept the princes of this world from crucifying Him, had it been in them.

And since we are fallen upon the mention of those men who are ready in a posture of hatred and malice and revenge, with other preparations answerable hereunto, to fall upon us and our lives and liberties, both spiritual and civil, upon our estates, our gospel and religion, and all that is or ought to be dear and precious unto us, and in our miseries and ruins to render our posterities more miserable than we, and have advanced their design this way to that maturity and heighth which we all know and tremble to think of: give me leave in that which remains to excite and stir you up, from the greatest to the least, both young and old, rich and poor, men and women, to quit yourselves like men, yea, and (if it be possible) above the line of men in this great exigency and stress of imminent danger that hangs over your heads and threatens you every hour.[9] O let it be as abomination unto us, as the very shadow of death to every man, woman, and child of us, not to be active, not to lie out, and strain ourselves to the utmost of our strength and power in every kind, as far as the law of God and nature will suffer us, to resist that high hand of iniquity and blood that is stretched out against us; to make our lives and our liberties and our religion good against that accursed generation that now magnifieth themselves, to make a prey and spoil of them, to make havoc and desolation of them all at once, if the Lord shall yet please to deliver us out of their hands.

Let not our lives, our liberties, our estates be at all precious or dear unto us in this behalf to expose them, be it unto the greatest danger to prevent the certain and most unquestionable ruin of them otherwise. Let us resolve to put all into the hands of God to prevent the falling of all, or anything, into the hands of these men. There is neither man nor woman of us, neither young nor old, but hath somewhat or other, more or less, a mite or two at least, to cast into the treasury of the public safety. Men that have strength of body for the war and fingers that know how to fight, let them to the battle and not fear to look the enemy in the face. Men and women that have only purses and estates, let them turn them into men and swords for the battle. Men that have heads but want arms and hands for outward execution, let these study and contrive methods and ways of proceedings: head-work is every whit as necessary in such a time, and exigent, as hand-work is. They that have neither hands nor heads nor estates, let them find hearts to keep the mountain of God, to pray the enemies down and the armies of the Lord up: let them find tongues to whet up the courage and resolutions of others. This is a service wherein women also may quit themselves like men, whose prayers commonly are as masculine, and do as great and severe execution, as the prayers of men. As for little children that know not the right hand from the left, and so are incapable of exhortation or putting on this way by their weakness and innocency (innocency, I mean, as concerning the enemies, and giving them the least cause or color of their bloody intendments,[10] as likewise in respect of the crying sins and horrid provocations of other men), they do every whit as much towards the furtherance of the service as men do by their strength, by their wisdom, by their estates, or otherwise, as we see in the case of God's sparing Nineveh.[11] The sixscore thousand children that

[5]Rubbish. [6]Heathen gods.
[7]Perhaps Goodwin is thinking of Isaiah 45.20.
[8]*Pilate's...dream*: Before Pilate condemned Christ to death "his wife sent unto him, saying, Have thou nothing to do with that just man; for I have suffered many things this day in a dream because of him" (Matthew 27.19).
[9]For the nature of this crisis see the headnote to this section, p. 584. Milton's eighth sonnet, "When the Assault Was Intended to the City," was also prompted by this dangerous situation.
[10]Intentions.
[11]When Jonah warned the sinful inhabitants of Nineveh that after

knew not their right hand from the left were the great intercessors and chief mediators in the behalf of the city with Him.[12] Yea, the brute beasts themselves, the cattle, their case and condition working upon the goodness and graciousness of God, were contributors too in their nature towards this service, as is to be seen in the last clause of the place cited from the prophet Jonah: "And should not I spare Nineveh, etc.—and also much cattle?"

Therefore now I beseech you that are capable of the great evils and dangers that threaten you, and are even at your door, be not you wanting and backward in anything that is in your hand to do: if it be possible, and as far as in you lieth, redeem your lives with your lives, your estates with your estates, your religion with your religion out of the hands of those men; set them all to work for their own maintenance and preservation; yea, if you know how to create more strength than you have, or to improve yourselves seventy times seven fold above the proportion of any your present abilities, I beseech you do it; at least "be willing" (as the apostle bears the Corinthians witness they were in a case not altogether unlike) "above that you are able,"[13] that so you may be sure to give out yourselves to the utmost of your ability the more freely. . . .

Now then, inasmuch as God hath set you this day as the sun in the firmament of heaven, from whence he hath an opportunity and advantage to send forth his beams and to furnish and fill the world with his light and influence round about him, since you have the commodiousness of such a standing, that you may do good to all that is God's, I mean to all the saints in all their dispersions and quarters throughout so many kingdoms and such a considerable part of the world as hath been mentioned, so that you may cause them to rise up before you and call you blessed, I beseech you do not betray this first-born opportunity of heaven: look upon it as a great and solemn invitation from God himself unto you to do greater things for the world, at least for the Christian world, than ever you did unto this day, or than ever you are like to do the second time, yea than any particular Christian state ever did or is like to do while the world stands. God hath prepared and fitted a table for you large enough, if you will but spread and furnish it with such provisions as are under your hand, that you may feast and give royal entertainment to the whole household of faith almost throughout the whole world at once. And shall it now seem any great thing in our ages, or be in the least measure grievous unto any man or woman of you, even to lavish his gold out of bags, to bestow his whole substance, to divest himself of all he possesseth in the world, even to his shoe latchet, to furnish and set out such an occasion as this is, like itself? Shall not the very conscience and comfortable remembrance of such a thing as this, done with uprightness and simplicity of heart by you, be a thousand times better than any superfluities of silver or of gold or of meats or of drinks or of houses or of jewels or apparel whatsoever? Nay, if we shall bring poverty and nakedness and hunger and thirst upon ourselves to purchase and procure it, will it not be better than an estate, than clothing, than meats and drinks unto us? Will it not take out the burning and allay the bitterness of all these? Doubtless the honor and conscience of the fact will bear all the charges and answer all the expense of it to the full. The opportunity and occasion is so rich and glorious that it calls to remembrance (as sometimes the shadow doth the substance) the great opportunity that was before the Lord Jesus Christ for the salvation of the world: we know that He, being rich, became poor, that the world through His poverty might be made rich. You have the pattern in the mount before you. See that according to your line and measure you make all things like to it!

forty days the city would be destroyed there was such a prompt and general reformation that God withheld His threatened doom (Jonah 3).
[12] *The sixscore . . . Him*: "And should not I spare Nineveh, that great city, in which are more than sixscore thousand persons that cannot discern between their right hand and their left hand; and also much cattle" (Jonah 4.11)?
[13] 2 Corinthians 8.3.

Henry Parker [1604-1652]

from Observations upon Some of His Majesty's Late Answers and Expresses[1] (1642)

In this contestation[2] between regal and Parliamentary power, for method's sake it is requisite to consider first of regal,

OBSERVATIONS   [1] Assertions.
[2] Contest. Following a series of exchanges between Charles and the

then of Parliamentary power, and in both to consider the efficient and final causes, and the means by which they are supported. The king attributeth the original[3] of his royalty to God and the law, making no mention of the grant, consent, or trust of man therein; but the truth is, God is no more the author of regal than of aristocratical power, nor of supreme than of subordinate command; nay, that dominion which is usurped and not just, yet whilst it remains dominion and till it be legally again divested, refers to God as to its author and donor, as much as that which is hereditary. And that law which the king mentioneth is not to be understood to be any special ordinance sent from heaven by the ministry of angels or prophets (as amongst the Jews it sometimes was). It can be nothing else amongst Christians but the pactions[4] and agreements of such and such politic corporations.[5] Power is originally inherent in the people, and it is nothing else but that might and vigor which such or such a society of men contains in itself; and when by such or such a law of common consent and agreement it is derived into such and such hands, God confirms that law, and so man is the free and voluntary author; the law is the instrument, and God is the establisher of both. And we see, not that prince which is the most potent over his subjects but that prince which is most potent in his subjects is indeed most truly potent, for a king of one small city, if he be intrusted with a large prerogative,[6] may be said to be more potent over his subjects than a king of many great regions whose prerogative is more limited; and yet in true reality of power that king is most great and glorious which hath the most and strongest subjects, and not he which tramples upon the most contemptible vassals. This is, therefore, a great and fond[7] error in some princes to strive more to be great over their people than in their people, and to eclipse themselves by impoverishing rather than to magnify themselves by infranchising their subjects. . . .

To be *deliciae humani generis*[8] is grown sordid with princes; to be public torments and carnificines[9] and to plot against those subjects whom by nature they ought to protect is held Caesar-like, and therefore bloody Borgias,[10] by mere cruelty and treachery, hath gotten room in the calendar of witty and of spirited heroes. And our English court of late years hath drunk too much of this state poison, for either we have seen favorites raised to poll[11] the people and razed again to pacify the people, or else (which is worse for king and people too) we have seen engines of mischief preserved against the people and upheld against law, merely that mischief might not want encouragement. But our king here doth acknowledge it the great business of his coronation oath to protect us, and I hope under this word *protect* he intends not only to shield us from all kind of evil, but to promote us also to all kind of political happiness according to his utmost devoir,[12] and I hope he holds himself bound thereunto not only by his oath but also by his very office and by the end of his sovereign dignity. . . .

The word *grace* sounds better in the people's mouths than in his; his dignity was erected to preserve the commonalty; the commonalty was not created for his service; and that which is the end is far more honorable and valuable

in nature and policy than that which is the means. This directs us, then, to the transcendent ἀχμή)[13] of all politics, to the paramount law that shall give law to all human laws whatsoever, and that is *salus populi*.[14] The law of prerogative itself, it is subservient to this law; and were it not conducing thereunto it were not necessary nor expedient. Neither can the right of conquest be pleaded to acquit princes of that which is due to the people as the authors or ends of all power, for mere force cannot alter the course of nature or frustrate the tenor of law; and if it could, there were more reason why the people might justify force to regain due liberty than the prince might to subvert the same. And 'tis a shameful stupidity in any man to think that our ancestors did not fight more nobly for their free customs and laws, of which the Conqueror[15] and his successors had in part disinherited them by violence and perjury, than they which put them to such conflicts, for it seems unnatural to me that any nation should be bound to contribute its own inherent puissance merely to abet tyranny and support slavery, and to make that which is more excellent a prey to that which is of less worth. . . .

The name of a king is great, I confess, and worthy of great honor, but is not the name of people greater? Let not mere terms deceive us; let us weigh names and things together, admit that God sheds here some rays of majesty upon His viceregents on earth, yet except we think He doth this out of particular love to princes themselves, and not to communities of men, we must not hence invert the course of nature and make nations subordinate in end to princes. My Lord of Strafford says that the law of prerogative is like that of the first Table,[16] but the law of common safety and utility

Parliament—the most notable of which was the nineteen propositions (2 June 1642) which virtually required that the king abdicate his supremacy—on June 15 one Denzil Holles, on behalf of Commons, brought an impeachment of certain peers wherein he made the revolutionary assertion that "the Parliament is the foundation and basis of government. . . . It creates the law." It was in support of this position that Parker wrote his influential *Observations*. [3]Origin. [4]Pacts. [5]Corporate political bodies.
[6]In English law, the privileges and powers claimed by or arrogated to the sovereign. The actual extent of the royal prerogative (which the early Stuart kings had steadily expanded) was a hotly argued question in the reign of Charles I. [7]Foolish.
[8]Suetonius (*Divus Titus*, Sect. i) remarked of the Emperor Titus that he was *amor et deliciae generis humani* ("the delight and darling of the human race"). Parker is alleging that monarchs have come to regard mere popularity as ignoble (*sordid*). [9]Executioners.
[10]Parker is probably thinking of Cesare Borgia (d. 1507), one of the most ruthless of a family of Italian politicians notorious for their cruelty.
[11]Plunder (by excessive taxation). Parker is perhaps thinking of the hated Thomas Wentworth, earl of Strafford, to whose execution (1641) Charles I had reluctantly assented in dread of mob violence. Later in the pamphlet Strafford is arraigned as an evil counselor of the king's. [12]Duty. [13]Acme, final end.
[14]"The public good."
[15]William the Conqueror (d. 1087), the first Norman king of England and founder of a dynasty notable for its depredations on the liberties and property of the native Britons.
[16]Fundamental law, referring to the so-called Twelve Tables, an ancient code of Roman law promulgated in 451–450 B.C.

like that of the second, and hence concludes that precedence is to be given to that which is more sacred, that is, regal prerogative. Upon this ground all parasites build when they seek to hoodwink princes for their own advantages, and when they assay to draw that esteem to themselves which they withdraw from the people, and this doctrine is common because 'tis so acceptable; for as nothing is more pleasant to princes than to be so deified, so nothing is more gainful to courtiers than so to please.

But to look into terms a little more narrower, and dispel umbrages,[17] princes are called gods, fathers, husbands, lords, heads, etc., and this implies them to be of more worth and more unsubordinate in end than their subjects are, who by the same relation must stand as creatures, children, wives, servants, members, etc. I answer: these terms do illustrate some excellency in princes by way of similitude, but must not in all things be applied, and they are most truly applied to subjects, taken *divisim* but not *conjunctim*.[18] Kings are gods to particular men, *secundum quid*,[19] and are sanctified with some of God's royalty; but it is not for themselves: it is for an extrinsical end, and that is the prosperity of God's people; and that end is more sacred than the means, as to themselves they are most unlike God; for God cannot be obliged by anything extrinsical; no created thing whatsoever can be of sufficient value or excellency to impose any duty or tie upon God, as subjects upon princes. Therefore granting prerogative to be but mediate and the weal public to be final, we must rank the laws of liberty in the first Table and prerogative in the second, as nature doth require; and not after a kind of blasphemy ascribe that unsubordination to princes which is only due to God. So the king is a father to his people, taken singly but not universally; for the father is more worthy than the son in nature, and the son is wholly a debtor to the father, and can by no merit transcend his duty nor challenge anything as due from his father; for the father doth all his offices meritoriously, freely, and unexactedly. Yet this holds not in the relation betwixt king and subject, for it's more due in policy and more strictly to be challenged that the king should make happy the people than the people make glorious the king. This same reason is also in relation of husband, lord, etc., for the wife is inferior in nature, and was created for the assistance of man, and servants are hired for their lords' mere attendance; but it is otherwise in the state betwixt man and man, for that civil difference which is for civil ends, and those ends are that wrong and violence may be repressed by one for the good of all, not that servility and drudgery may be imposed upon all for the pomp of one. So the head naturally doth not more depend upon the body than that does upon the head; both head and members must live and die together. But it is otherwise with the head political, for that receives more subsistence from the body than it gives, and being subservient to that, it has no being when that is dissolved, and that may be preserved after its dissolution.

And hence it appears that the very order of princes binds them not to be insolent, but lowly; and not to aim at their own good but secondarily, contrary to the Florentine's[20] wretched politics. And it follows that such princes, as contrary to the end of government, effect evil instead of good, insulting[21] in common servility rather than promoting common security, and placing their chiefest pomp in the sufferance of their subjects, commit such sins as God will never countenance; nay, such as the unnatural father, the tyrannous husband, the merciless master is not capable of committing; nay, we must conceive that treason in subjects against their prince, so far only as it concerns the prince, is not so horrid in nature as oppression in the prince exercised violently upon subjects. God commands princes to study His law day and night, and not to amass great treasures, or to increase their cavaliers, or to lift up their hearts above their brethren, nor to waste their own demesnes lest necessity should tempt them to rapine. But on the contrary, Machiaveli's instructions puff up princes, "That they may treat subjects not as brethren, but as beasts, as the basest beasts of drudgery, teaching them by subtility and by the strength of their militia to uphold their own will and to make mere sponges of the public coffers." And sure if that cursed heretic in policy could have invented anything more repugnant to God's commands and nature's intention he had been held a deeper statesman than he is; but I conceive it is now sufficiently cleared that all rule is but fiduciary,[22] and that this and that prince is more or less absolute as he is more or less trusted, and that all trusts differ not in nature or intent, but in degree only and extent; and therefore since it is unnatural for any nation to give away its own propriety[23] in itself absolutely and to subject itself to a condition of servility below men, because this is contrary to the supreme of all laws, we must not think that it can stand with the intent of any trust that necessary defense should be barred and natural preservation denied to any people. No man will deny but that the people may use means of defense where princes are more conditionate[24] and have a sovereignty more limited; and yet these being only less trusted than absolute monarchs, and no trust being without an intent of preservation, it is no more intended that the people shall be remedilessly oppressed in a monarchy than in a republic. But tracing this no further, I will now rest upon this: that whatsoever the king has alleged against raising of arms and publishing of orders indefinitely is of no force to make Sir John Hotham[25] or those by whose authority he acted traitors unless it fall out that there was no ground nor necessity of such defense. So much of danger certain.

---

[17]Shadows, i.e., confusion.
[18]*Divisim...conjunctim*: separately, not collectively.
[19]"In accordance with which" (i.e., the principle of "similitude" announced above).
[20]Niccoló Machiavelli (1469–1527), a Florentine politician whose absolutist prescriptions were anathema to Parliamentarians like Parker. [21]Glorying. [22]Held in trust. [23]Property. [24]Limited.
[25]Sir John Hotham, parliamentary commander at Hull, whose refusal to admit Charles to that city on 23 April 1642 was decried by royalists and applauded by their adversaries.

I come now to those seven doctrines and positions which the king, by way of recapitulation, lays open as so offensive, and they run thus:

1. "That the Parliament has an absolute, indisputable power of declaring law, so that all the right of the king and people depends upon their pleasure." It has been answered that this power must rest in them, or in the king, or in some inferior court, or else all suits must be endless; and it can nowhere rest more safely than in Parliament.

2. "That Parliaments are bound to no precedents." ¹⁰ Statutes are not binding to them, why then should precedents? Yet there is no obligation stronger than the justice and honor of a Parliament.

3. "That they are Parliaments and may judge of public necessity without the king, and dispose of anything." They may not desert the king, but being deserted by the king when the kingdom is in distress, they may judge of that distress and relieve it, and are to be accounted by the virtue of representation as the whole body of the state.

4. "That no member of Parliaments ought to be troubled ²⁰ for treason, etc. without leave." This is intended of suspicions only, and when leave may be seasonably had, and when competent accusers appear not in the impeachment.

5. "That the sovereign power resides in both houses of Parliament, the king having no negative voice." This power is not claimed as ordinary, nor to any purpose but to save the kingdom from ruin; and in case where the king is so seduced as that he prefers dangerous men and prosecutes his loyal subjects.

6. "That levying forces against the personal commands of ³⁰ the king (though accompanied with his presence) is not levying war against the king; but war against his authority, though not person, is war against the king." If this were not so, the Parliament, seeing a seduced king ruining himself and the kingdom, could not save both, but must stand and look on.

7. "That according to some Parliaments, they may depose the king." 'Tis denied that any king was deposed by a free Parliament fairly elected.

To stand in comparison with these I shall recite some such ⁴⁰ positions as the king's papers offer to us, and they follow thus:

1. "That regal power is so derived from God and the law as that it has no dependence upon the trust and consent of man; and the king is accountable therefore to God and his other kingdoms, not to this; and it is above the determination of Parliaments and by consequence boundless."

2. "That the king is supreme indefinitely, viz. as well *universis* as *singulis*."²⁶

3. "That the king has such a propriety in his subjects, ⁵⁰ towns, forts, etc. as is above the propriety of the state, and not to be seized by the Parliament, though for the public safety."

4. "That so far as the king is trusted he is not accountable how he performs," so that in all cases the subject is remediless.

5. "That the being of Parliaments is merely of grace, so that the king might justly have discontinued them, and being summoned, they are limited by the writ,²⁷ and that *ad consilium* only, and that but *in quibusdam arduis*,²⁸ and if they pass the limits of the writ they may be imprisoned. That if the king desert them, they are a void assembly, and no honor due to them, nor power to save the kingdom. That Parliamentary privileges are nowhere to be read of, and so their representation of this whole kingdom is no privilege, nor adds no majesty nor authority to them. That the major part in Parliament is not considerable when so many are absent or dissent. That the major part is no major part because the fraud and force of some few overrules them. That Parliaments may do dishonorable things, nay treasonable; nay, that this hath been so blinded by some few malignants that they have abetted treason in Sir John Hotham, trampled upon all law and the king's prerogative, and sought to induce the whole kingdom under the tyranny of some few, and sought the betraying of church and state, and to effect the same erected an upstart authority in the new militia and levied war upon the king under pretense that he levies war upon them. That Parliaments cannot declare law but in such and such particular cases legally brought before them. That Parliaments are questionable and tryable elsewhere."

These things, we all see, tend not only to the desolation of this Parliament but to the confusion of all other, and to the advancing of the king to a higher power over Parliaments than ever he had before over inferior courts. Parliaments have hitherto been sanctuaries to the people and banks against arbitrary tyranny, but now the mere breath of the king blasts them in an instant; and how shall they hereafter secure us when they cannot now secure themselves? Or how can we expect justice when the mere imputation of treason—without hearing, trial, or judgment—shall sweep away a whole Parliament, nay, all Parliaments forever? And yet this is not yet the depth of our misery, for that private council which the king now adheres to, and prefers before Parliaments, will still inforce upon our understandings that all these doctrines and positions tend to the perfection of Parliaments, and all the king's forces in the North²⁹ to the protection of law and liberty. I find my reason already captivated. I cannot further—.

²⁶Over the whole state as well as over individual citizens.
²⁷Formal summons.
²⁸*Ad consilium...arduis*: for purpose of consultation only, and that on certain urgent matters.
²⁹Following Charles' declaration of war at Nottingham on 22 August 1642, his strength lay mainly in the North of England, the southern and eastern counties being strongly sympathetic to Parliament.

William Walwyn [1600-1680]

from The Compassionate Samaritan (1644)

To The Commons of England

To you whom the people have chosen for the managing
of their affairs I present this necessary treatise without
boldness and without fear, for I am well assured that as it
is mine and every man's duty to furnish you with what we
conceive will advance the common good or bring ease or
comfort to any sort of men that deserve well of their country
—as you cannot but know the Separation[1] do, if you con-
sider with what charge and hazard, with what willingness
and activity they have furthered the reformation so happily
begun—so likewise it is your duty to hear and put in ex- 10
ecution whatsoever to your judgments shall appear conduc-
ing to those good ends and purposes. I recommend here to
your view the oppressed Conscience and the despised
Separation. They have been much wounded—I believe
everybody can say by whom—and the people have passed
by without compassion or regard, though they themselves
must necessarily partake in their sufferings. There are none
left to play the good Samaritan's part[2] but yourselves, who
as you have power will, I make no question, be willing too
when you have once well considered the matter which this 20
small treatise will put you in mind to do. It is not to be
supposed that you (who have so long spent your time in
recovering the common liberties of England) should in
conclusion turn the common into particular.[3] Let the in-
sinuations and suggestions[4] of some in the synod[5] be what
they will, I make no question but you will see both through
and beyond them, and will never be swayed from a good
conscience to maintain particular men's interests.

In the beginning of your session, when our divines (as
they would have us call them) wrote freely against the 30
bishops and the bishops made complaint to you for redress,[6]
some of you made answer that there was no remedy, foras-
much as the press was to be open and free for all in time of
Parliament, I shall make bold as a common[7] of England to
lay claim to that privilege, being assured that I write nothing
scandalous or dangerous to the state (which is justly and
upon good grounds prohibited by your ordinance to that
effect).[8] Only I humbly desire you to consider whether more
was not got from you by that ordinance than you intended,
and that though it was purposed by you to restrain the 40
venting[9] and dispersing of the king's writings and his agents,
yet it hath by reason of the qualifications of the licensers

wrought[10] a wrong way, and stopped the mouths of good
men who must either not write at all or no more than is
suitable to the judgments and interests of the licensers. The
Separation (I guess) would have took it for better dealing
if the divines had in express terms obtained of you an ordi-
nance for suppression of all Anabaptistical, Brownistical, or
Independent writings, than to[11] have their mouths stopped
so subtlely, so insensibly, and their just liberty in time of
Parliament taken from them unawares. There can be no
greater argument that the divines intend not well than their
taking uncouth[12] and mysterious, subtle ways to effect their
ends, even such as far better become politicians than min-
isters.

It is high time, O Commons of England, to put an end to
the sufferings of the Separation, who have for many years
been the object of all kind of tyranny—papistical, prelatical,

COMPASSIONATE SAMARITAN [1]The body of left-wing Protestants
or Sectarians ("Anabaptistical, Brownistical, or Independent," as
Walwyn later itemizes them) who, in opposition to the Pres-
byterians dominating Parliament and the Westminster Assembly,
advocated such libertarian ideals as freedom of conscience and the
separation of church and state. In the next sentence Walwyn
personifies these Sectarians as "the oppressed Conscience" of
England.
[2]In one of the most moving of Christ's parables (Luke 10.30–37),
only a despised Samaritan, of several passers-by, showed com-
passion for a traveler who had been robbed and beaten.
[3]*Turn...particular*: convert a tract of land regarded as the property
of the community into private property.   [4]Incitements to evil.
[5]The Westminster Assembly of Divines (1643–49) that Parliament
had empowered to investigate the practice of religion.
[6]A notable specimen of such a petition for redress of Anglican
grievances was Joseph Hall's *Humble Remonstrance* (1640). See pp.
530ff.   [7]Commoner.
[8]For several years after the rigid censorship decreed by the Star
Chamber in 1637 was lifted with the abolition of that hated body
in 1641, Englishmen had enjoyed an unprecedented freedom of
expression. However, the Presbyterian majority in Parliament,
alarmed by the spread of ideas that they considered dangerous
(both Sectarian and royalist) on 14 August 1644 passed an
ordinance re-establishing the licensing of the press. It was to protest
this retrogressive legislation that Milton wrote *Areopagitica* (see
pp. 603ff.) and Walwyn *The Compassionate Samaritan*.
[9]Spreading abroad.   [10]Worked.   [11]*Than to*: text *hento*.
[12]Unfamiliar. Text *uncough*.

and regal. The first foundation of honor and respect was certainly from public service and protection of the distressed. Make it your work, and assure yourselves you will find not only the universal love of all good men accompanying you but a quiet and cheerful conscience, which is above all honor and riches. Others may weary themselves in plots and contrivances to advance self-ends and interests to the people's damage and molestations; sadness and distraction will be their companions for it. But make it your business, ye chosen men of England, according to the trust reposed in you to [10] protect the innocent, to judge their cause impartially, to circumvent men in their wicked endeavors, and so you will become the beloved of God, the beloved of good men.

LIBERTY OF CONSCIENCE ASSERTED AND

THE SEPARATIST VINDICATED

The publication in early January 1644 of *An Apologetical Narration* by Thomas Goodwin and four other "dissenting brethren" of the Westminster Assembly was an event of great importance in the tumultuous history of the period. In resisting the stiff requirements of the Presbyterian majority for a national church on the Genevan model, these Independent ministers appealed to the public (rather [20] than to the Assembly or the Parliament) for the principle of congregational autonomy and at least partial freedom of worship. It was, said Walwyn, with "gladness of heart" that he began to read their plea, but to his "heart's grief" he found the five brethren's neglect of the legitimate demands of left-wing Separatists and Sectarians to be as illiberal as the Presbyterians'.

. . . Methinks every man is bound in conscience to speak and do what he can in the behalf of such a harmless people as these. What though you are no Separatist (as I myself am [30] none), the love of God appears most in doing good for others: that love which aims only at itself, those endeavors which would procure liberty only to themselves, can at best be called but self-love and self-respect. 'Tis common freedom every man ought to aim at, which is every man's peculiar right so far as 'tis not prejudicial to the common.[13] Now because little can be done in their behalf unless liberty of conscience be allowed for every man or sort of men to worship God in that way and perform Christ's ordinances in that manner as shall appear to them most agreeable [40] to God's word, and no man be punished or discountenanced by authority for his opinion unless it be dangerous to the state, I have endeavored in this discourse to make appear by the best reason I have that every man ought to have liberty of conscience of what opinion soever, with the caution above named; in doing whereof I have upon occasion removed all prejudices that the people have concerning the Separatist and vindicated them from those false aspersions[14] that are usually cast upon them to make them odious, wherein my end, I make account, will evidently appear to be the peace [50] and union of all, and to beget this judgment in the people and Parliament that 'tis the principal interest of the commonwealth that authority should have equal respect and afford protection to all peaceable good men alike, notwith-

standing their difference of opinion that all men may be encouraged to be alike serviceable thereunto.

Liberty of conscience is to be allowed every man for these following reasons:

1. Reason. Because of what judgment soever a man is, he cannot choose but be of that judgment, that is so evident in itself that I suppose it will be granted by all: whatsoever a man's reason doth conclude, or be true or false, to be agreeable or disagreeable to God's word, that same to that man is his opinion or judgment, and so man is by his own reason necessitated to be of that mind he is. Now where there is a necessity there ought to be no punishment, for punishment is the recompense of voluntary actions; therefore no man ought to be punished for his judgment.

Objection. But it will be objected that the Separatists are a rash, heady people, and not so much concluded[15] by their reason as their fancy; that they have their *enthusiasm*[16] and revelations which nobody knows what to make of, and that if they were a people that examined things rationally, the argument would hold good for them.

Answer. That I suppose this to be the argument not of the present but of the loose-witted times before the Parliament, where some politic bishop or Dr. Ignorant University Man or knave poet would endeavor by such a suggestion to the people to misguide their credulous hearts into hatred of those good men who they knew to be the constant enemies to their delusions. But let all men now have other thoughts, and assure themselves that the Brownist and Anabaptist are rational examiners of those things they hold for truth, mild discoursers, and able to give an account of what they believe. They who are unsatisfied in that particular may, if they please to visit their private congregations which are open to all comers, have further satisfaction. Perhaps here and there amongst them may be a man that out of his zeal and earnestness for that which he esteems truth may outrun his understanding and show many weaknesses in his discourse—I would the like frailty and inabilities were not to be found in many of us—but if the slips and wanderings of a few, and those the weakest, be an argument sufficient to discountenance the Separation and work them out of the world's favor, I pray God the same argument may never be made use of against us, amongst whom many—and they not esteemed the weakest neither—would give great advantages that way. In the meantime I wish with all my heart we could all put on the spirit of meekness, and rather endeavor to rectify by argument and persuasion one another's infirmities than upbraid the owners of them with a visible rejoicing that such things are slipped from them to their disadvantage. . . .

2. Reason. The uncertainty of knowledge in this life. No man nor no sort of men can presume of an unerring spirit. 'Tis known that the fathers, general councils, national assemblies, synods, and Parliaments in their times have been most grossly mistaken; and though the present times be wiser than the former, being much freed from superstition

[13]Commonwealth. [14]Text *aspertious.* [15]Convinced. [16]Enthusiasms.

and taking a larger liberty to themselves of examining all things, yet since there remains a possibility of error, notwithstanding never so great presumptions of the contrary, one sort of men are not to compel another, since this hazard is run thereby, that he who is in an error may be the constrainer of him who is in the truth.

Objection. But unity and uniformity in religion is to be aimed at, and confusion above all things to be avoided. By toleration, new opinions will every day break forth, and to the scandal of the nation we shall become a very monster in matters of religion, one part being Presbyter, another Anabaptist, Brownist another, and a fourth an Independent, and so divers according to the diversity of opinions that are already or may be broached hereafter.

Answer. I answer that in truth this objection appears specious at the first gloss, and therefore is very moving upon the people, which the bishops well knew whose it was, and taken up as the fairest pretense for the suppression of those who (it is to be feared) will prove the suppressors. For answer whereunto I aver that a compulsion is of all ways the most unlikely to beget unity of mind and uniformity in practice, which experience will make evident. For the fines, imprisonments, pillories, etc. used by the bishops as means to unite rather confirmed men in their judgments, and begot the abomination and odium which these times have cast upon the hierarchy, being in the worst kind tyrannical as endeavoring by the punishment of the person the bowing and subjecting of the conscience. And if it be instanced[17] that some there were that turned with the wind and were terrified by fear of punishment into a compliance, I answer that such men are so far from being examples to be followed that they may more justly be condemned for weather-cocks, fit to be set up for men to know which way blows the wind of favor, delicacy, ease, and preferment.

Secondly, the conscience being subject only to reason (either that which is indeed, or seems to him which hears it to be so) can only be convinced or persuaded thereby. Force makes it run back and struggle; it is the nature of every man to be of any judgment rather than his that forces. 'Tis to be presumed that 'tis upon some good grounds of reason that a man is of that judgment whereof he is. Wouldest thou have him be of thine? Show him thy grounds, and let them both work, and see which will get the victory in his understanding. Thus possibly he may change his mind and be of one judgment with thee; but if you will use club law, instead of convincing and uniting you arm men with prejudice against you to conclude that you have no assurance of truth in you, for then you would make use of that and presume of the efficacy thereof, and not fight with weapons which you do or at least should know not to be the weapons of truth. . . .

Since, as Walwyn thinks, the Presbyterians in Parliament and Assembly have themselves become a persecuting body, it is necessary to examine—and of course refute—their arguments for compulsory conformity. Quickly disposing of the alleged necessity for preserving a distinction between church and state, clergy and laity (which would maintain by law the privileges and sanctions of a priestly class), he

turns to the more important question of each believer's right to read the Bible for himself. "How presumptious and confident the learned scribes, priests, and doctors of the law were that they best understood the Scriptures! How the poor and unlearned fishermen and tent-makers were made choice of for Christ's disciples and apostles before any of them! How in process of time they that took upon them to be ministers, when they had acquired to themselves the mystery of arts and learning, and confounded thereby the clear streams of the Scripture, and perverted the true gospel of Jesus Christ, and by politic glosses and comments introduced another gospel suitable to the covetous, ambitious, and persecuting spirit of the clergy!. . ." And so as Walwyn winds his way through the Presbyterians' "objections" and his own rebuttals his theme emerges clear: "All times have produced men of several ways, and I believe no man thinks there will be an agreement of judgment as long as this world lasts. If ever there be, in all probability it must proceed from the power and efficacy of truth, not from constraint." In the final section of his little book he deals with constraints upon the Anabaptists and the Brownists, the *bêtes noires* of Presbyterian orthodoxy.

I will add one thing more to the Brownists' and Anabaptists' glory: that in the times of the bishops' domineering, when many of the Presbyterians complied (some to the very top of Wren's conformity),[18] and preached for those things they now pretend[19] chiefly to reform, and the Independents fled to places where they might live at ease and enjoy their hundred pounds a year without danger, the Brownist and Anabaptist endured the heat and brunt of persecution, and notwithstanding the several ways of vexing them continued doing their duties, counting it the glory of a Christian to endure tribulation for the name of Christ.

And the times altering, the Presbyterian soon comes about, and the Independent comes over to be leaders of the reformation, when, forgetting the constancy and integrity of those who bore the heat and burden of the day, they hold the same heavy hand over them that their fathers the bishops did. And as the Brownists' and Anabaptists' affection to the common good of all was then firm and able to endure the trial of persecution, so hath it in these present searching times continued constant and unshaken, notwithstanding the many almost unsufferable injuries and provocations of the divines on the one side and the fair promises and frequent invitations of the king on the other, so that had any ends of their own been aimed at, they could not have continued such resolved and immovable enemies of tyranny and friends to their country.

I believe if we would suppose other men to be in their condition we could hardly expect the like even and upright carriage from them amidst so many storms and temptations surrounding them. I hope all good men will take all that hath been said into consideration, especially the Parliament who, I presume, are most ingenuous and impartial of all others and whom it chiefly concerns, they being called and

[17]Text *if it be it instanced.*
[18]Matthew Wren (1585–1667), who held successively the bishoprics of Hereford (1634), Norwich (1635), and Ely (1638), was so notorious for persecuting nonconformists that he was imprisoned in the Tower from 1642 to 1660.   [19]Text *prerend.*

trusted to vindicate and preserve the people's liberties in general, and not to enthrall the consciences, persons, or estates of any of them into a pragmatical,[20] pretended clergy, whether Episcopal, Presbyterial, or any other whatsoever.

The greatest glory of authority is to protect the distressed; and for those that are judges in other men's causes to bear themselves as if the afflicted men's cases were their own, observing that divine rule of our Saviour, "Whatsoever ye would that men should do unto you, even so do ye to them."[21] And if to the Parliament it shall appear for the reasons given or other better reasons they can suggest to themselves that it is most unjust—and much more, unchristian—that any man should be compelled against his conscience to a way he approves not of, I doubt not but they will be pleased for God's glory and union sake and likewise for these good men's sake (which for the present it principally concerns), at least for their own sakes (for who knows how soon this may be his own case) speedily to stop all proceedings that tends thereunto; and for the future provide that as well particular or private congregations as public may have public protection, so that upon a penalty no injury or offence be offered either to them from others or by them to others. That all statutes against the Separatists be reviewed and repealed (especially that of the 35 of Elizabeth).[22] That the press may be free for any man that writes nothing scandalous or dangerous to the state. That so this Parliament may prove themselves loving fathers to all sorts of good men, bearing equal respect to all according to the trust reposed in them, and so inviting an equal affection and assistance from all, that after ages may report of them they did all these things not because of the importunity of the people or to please a party, but from the reason and justness of them, which did more sway with them than a petition subscribed with twenty thousand hands could have done.

[20]Dogmatic, doctrinaire. [21]Matthew 7.12.
[22]A parliamentary statute of 1583 prescribing rigid penalties for nonconformity.

John Milton[1] [1608-1674]

OF REFORMATION TOUCHING CHURCH DISCIPLINE IN ENGLAND (1641)

Of Reformation, the first of the five so-called anti-prelatical pamphlets that Milton wrote in 1641–42, analyzes the forces that tend to block reform and then attacks the political bishops of the Anglican Church. Although generally temperate in its tone and style, it ends with a tumultuous prayer and curse in which young Milton's puritanism, patriotism, and utopianism find dithyrambic statement.

O, Sir,[1] I do now feel myself inwrapped on the sudden into those mazes and labyrinths of dreadful and hideous thoughts, that which way to get out, or which way to end, I know not, unless I turn mine eyes, and with your help lift up my hands to that eternal and propitious throne, where nothing is readier than grace and refuge to the distresses of mortal suppliants: and it were a shame to leave these serious thoughts less piously than the heathen were wont to conclude their graver discourses.

Thou, therefore, that sittest in light and glory unapproachable, parent of angels and men! next, Thee I implore, omnipotent King, Redeemer of that lost remnant whose nature Thou didst assume, ineffable and everlasting Love! and Thou, the third subsistence of divine infinitude, illumining Spirit, the joy and solace ef created things! one Tripersonal godhead! look upon this Thy poor and almost spent and expiring church, leave her not thus a prey to these importunate wolves, that wait and think long till they devour Thy tender flock; these wild boars that have broke into Thy vineyard, and left the print of their polluting hoofs on the souls of Thy servants. O let them not bring about their damned designs, that stand now at the entrance of the bottomless pit, expecting the watchword to open and let out those dreadful locusts and scorpions, to reinvolve us in that pitchy cloud of infernal darkness, where we shall never more see the sun of Thy truth again, never hope for the cheerful dawn, never more hear the bird of morning sing. Be moved with pity at the afflicted state of this our shaken monarchy, that now lies laboring under her throes, and struggling against the grudges of more dreaded calamities.

O Thou, that, after the impetuous rage of five bloody inundations,[2] and the succeeding sword of intestine war, soaking the land in her own gore, didst pity the sad and ceaseless revolution of our swift and thick-coming sorrows; when we were quite breathless, of Thy free grace didst motion peace and terms of covenant with us; and having first well nigh freed us from antichristian thraldom, didst build up this Britannic empire to a glorious and enviable height, with all her daughter-islands about her; stay us in this felicity, let not the obstinacy of our half-obedience

[1]For a commentary on Milton and for other excerpts from his work see Poetry, pp. 256 ff., Books and Men, pp. 769 ff., and History and Historiography, pp. 921 ff.
OF REFORMATION [1]Unlike most of Milton's early pamphlets (which are addressed to Parliament), the first one was "Written to a Friend," as the title page declares.
[2]The invasions of the Romans, the Picts and Scots, the Saxons, the Danes, and the Normans.

and will-worship bring forth that viper of sedition, that for these fourscore years[3] hath been breeding to eat through the entrails of our peace; but let her cast her abortive spawn without the danger of this travailing and throbbing kingdom: that we may still remember in our solemn thanksgivings, how for us, the northern ocean even to the frozen Thule[4] was scattered with the proud shipwrecks of the Spanish Armada, and the very maw of hell ransacked, and made to give up her concealed destruction, ere she could vent it in that horrible and damned blast.

O how much more glorious will those former deliverances appear, when we shall know them not only to have saved us from greatest miseries past, but to have reserved us for greatest happiness to come! Hitherto Thou hast but freed us, and that not fully, from the unjust and tyrannous claim of Thy foes; now unite us entirely, and appropriate us to thyself, tie us everlastingly in willing homage to the prerogative of Thy eternal throne.

And now we know, O thou our most certain hope and defence, that Thine enemies have been consulting all the sorceries of the great whore,[5] and have joined their plots with that sad intelligencing tyrant[6] that mischiefs the world with his mines of Ophir, and lies thirsting to revenge his naval ruins that have larded our seas: but let them all take counsel together, and let it come to nought; let them decree, and do Thou cancel it; let them gather themselves, and be scattered; let them embattle themselves, and be broken; let them embattle, and be broken, for Thou art with us.

Then, amidst the hymns and hallelujahs of saints, some one may perhaps be heard offering at high strains in new and lofty measures to sing and celebrate Thy divine mercies and marvelous judgments in this land throughout all ages; whereby this great and warlike nation, instructed and inured to the fervent and continual practice of truth and righteousness, and casting far from her the rags of her old vices, may press on hard to that high and happy emulation to be found the soberest, wisest, and most Christian people at that day, when Thou, the eternal and shortly expected King, shalt open the clouds to judge the several kingdoms of the world,[7] and distributing national honors and rewards to religious and just commonwealths, shalt put an end to all earthly tyrannies, proclaiming Thy universal and mild monarchy through heaven and earth; where they undoubtedly, that by their labors, counsels, and prayers, have been earnest for the common good of religion and their country, shall receive above the inferior orders of the blessed, the regal addition of principalities, legions, and thrones into their glorious titles, and in supereminence of beatific vision, progressing the dateless and irrevoluble circle of eternity, shall clasp inseparable hands with joy and bliss, in overmeasure for ever.

But they contrary, that by the impairing and diminution of the true faith, the distresses and servitude of their country, aspire to high dignity, rule, and promotion here, after a shameful end in this life (which God grant them), shall be thrown down eternally into the darkest and deepest gulf of hell, where, under the despiteful control, the trample and spurn of all the other damned, that in the anguish of

their torture shall have no other ease than to exercise a raving and bestial tyranny over them as their slaves and Negroes, they shall remain in that plight for ever, the basest, the lowermost, the most dejected, most underfoot, and downtrodden vassals of perdition.

THE REASON OF CHURCH GOVERNMENT URGED AGAINST PRELATY (1642)

The fourth, longest, and most interesting of Milton's five anti-prelatical pamphlets (and the only one published over his name), *The Reason of Church Government* elaborately develops some of its author's most characteristic and persistent convictions. The two following excerpts concern, respectively, the source and nature of religious truth and the moral utility for the true wayfaring Christian of search and trial and struggle. The famous digression in Book II, where Milton speculates about his own career in literature, will be found on pp. 769–72.

[THE FIRST BOOK]

CHAPTER I

THAT CHURCH GOVERNMENT IS PRESCRIBED IN THE GOSPEL, AND THAT TO SAY OTHERWISE IS UNSOUND

The first and greatest reason of church government we may securely, with the assent of many on the adverse part, affirm to be, because we find it so ordained and set out to us by the appointment of God in the Scriptures; but whether this be presbyterial or prelatical,[1] it cannot be brought to

[3]Since the so-called Elizabethan Settlement (1559–60), by which was created the Anglican church that Milton is here attacking as a barrier to the continuation and completion of the reformation begun by Henry VIII, suppressed by the Catholic Mary, and only partially restored by Elizabeth.
[4]Generally a vague term for the Arctic, but Milton is perhaps thinking of the Shetland Islands and Norway, where parts of the Spanish Armada had been driven by storms in 1588. England's "deliverance" from this powerful threat of Catholic Spain was widely regarded (by Protestants) as an act of providential intervention.
[5]The Roman Catholic Church, commonly identified as the "Whore of Babylon" in the light of Revelation 17.1 and 19.2.
[6]The Catholic king of Spain, whose possessions, though rich in minerals, did not include the legendary gold mines of Ophir, an ancient country of unknown location, perhaps in Arabia.
[7]Milton's millennarian expectations are based on Matthew 24.30 and John 1.51.

REASON OF CHURCH GOVERNMENT [1]In 1642 the basic question about church government or "discipline" (which Milton expansively defines as "the practice work of preaching, directed and applied") was whether the national church should be organized and administered along Anglican lines as prescribed by the Thirty-nine Articles or along Genevan (i.e., Presbyterian) lines as expounded by Calvin in his *Institutes*. The former (which allowed for a hierarchy of archbishops, bishops, priests, and deacons) was attacked by its Puritan adversaries as preserving many relics of papistry; the latter (which allowed for presbyters, deacons, and preachers) was defended by its partisans as sanctioned by the Bible and as restoring the purity of the early church. Milton's own

the scanning[2] until I have said what is meet to some who do not think it for the ease of their inconsequent opinions to grant that church discipline is platformed in the Bible but that it is left to the discretion of men. To this conceit of theirs I answer that it is both unsound and untrue, for there is not that thing in the world of more grave and urgent importance throughout the whole life of man than is discipline. What need I instance! He that hath read with judgment of nations and commonwealths, of cities and camps, of peace and war, sea and land, will readily agree that the flourishing 10 and decaying of all civil societies, all the moments[3] and turnings of human occasions are moved to and fro as upon the axle of discipline. So that whatsoever power or sway in mortal things weaker men have attributed to Fortune, I durst with more confidence (the honor of divine providence ever saved) ascribe either to the vigor or the slackness of discipline. Nor is there any sociable perfection in this life, civil or sacred, that can be above discipline; but she is that which with her musical chords preserves and holds all the parts thereof together. Hence in those perfect armies of 20 Cyrus in Xenophon, and Scipio in the Roman stories,[4] the excellence of military skill was esteemed not by the not needing, but by the readiest submitting to the edicts of their commander. And certainly discipline is not only the removal of disorder; but if any visible shape can be given to divine things, the very visible shape and image of virtue, whereby she is not only seen in the regular gestures and motions of her heavenly paces as she walks, but also makes the harmony of her voice audible to mortal ears. Yea, the angels themselves, in whom no disorder is feared, as the apostle 30 that saw them in his rapture describes,[5] are distinguished and quaternioned[6] into their celestial princedoms and satrapies, according as God himself hath writ His imperial decrees through the great provinces of heaven. The state also of the blessed in paradise, though never so perfect, is not therefore left without discipline, whose golden surveying reed marks out and measures every quarter and circuit of New Jerusalem.[7] Yet is it not to be conceived, that those eternal effluences[8] of sanctity and love in the glorified saints should by this means be confined and cloyed with repetition of that 40 which is prescribed, but that our happiness may orb itself into a thousand vagancies[9] of glory and delight, and with a kind of eccentrical equation be, as it were, an invariable planet of joy and felicity; how much less can we believe that God would leave his frail and feeble, though not less beloved, church here below to the perpetual stumble of conjecture and disturbance in this our dark voyage, without the card[10] and compass of discipline? Which is so hard to be of man's making that we may see even in the guidance of a civil state to worldly happiness, it is not for every learned or every wise 50 man, though many of them consult in common to invent or frame a discipline: but if it be at all the work of man, it must be of such a one as is a true knower of himself, and himself in whom contemplation and practice, wit, prudence, fortitude, and eloquence must be rarely met, both to comprehend the hidden causes of things and span in his thoughts all the various effects that passion or complexion[11] can work in man's nature; and hereto must his hand be at defiance with

gain, and his heart in all virtues heroic, so far is it from the ken of these wretched projectors[12] of ours that bescrawl their pamphlets every day with new forms of government for our church. And therefore all the ancient lawgivers were either truly inspired, as Moses, or were such men as with authority enough might give it out to be so, as Minos, Lycurgus, Numa,[13] because they wisely forethought that men would never quietly submit to such a discipline as had not more of God's hand in it than man's. To come within the narrowness of household government, observation will show us many deep counsellors of state and judges to demean themselves incorruptly in the settled course of affairs, and many worthy preachers upright in their lives, powerful in their audience: but look upon either of these men where they are left to their own disciplining at home, and you shall soon perceive, for all their single[14] knowledge and uprightness, how deficient they are in the regulating of their own family; not only in what may concern the virtuous and decent composure of their minds in their several places, but, that which is of a lower and easier performance, the right possessing of the outward vessel, their body, in health or sickness, rest or labor, diet or abstinence, whereby to render it more pliant to the soul, and useful to the commonwealth: which if men were but as good to discipline themselves, as some are to tutor their horses and hawks, it could not be so gross in most households. If, then, it appear so hard and so little known how to govern a house well, which is thought of so easy discharge, and for every man's undertaking, what skill of man, what wisdom, what parts can be sufficient to give laws and ordinances to the elect household of God? If we could imagine that He had left it at random without His provident and gracious ordering, who is he so arrogant, so presumptuous, that durst dispose and guide the living ark of the Holy Ghost, though he should find it wandering in the field of Bethshemesh,[15] without the conscious warrant of some high calling? But no profane insolence can parallel that which our prelates dare avouch, to drive outrageously,

---

intemperate zeal against the "prelates" is an index of the passions that this conflict generated. For a sober statement of the Anglican position see Bishop Joseph Hall's *Humble Remonstrance,* pp. 530–36. [2]Close examination. [3]Movements.
[4]Histories. The military career of Cyrus the Great is treated by the Greek historian Xenophon in his *Cyropaedia,* that of Scipio Africanus, the conqueror of Carthage, by Livy.
[5]"I saw four angels standing on the four corners of the earth" (Revelation 7.1). [6]Arranged in fours. [7]Revelation 21.10–17. [8]Outflows.
[9]Although the *Century Dictionary,* citing this very passage, defines *vagancy* as "extravagance," perhaps Milton intends something like "wandering" or "deviation," which by the complex *eccentrical equation* of Ptolemaic astronomy could be explained as regular orbital movement. [10]Map, chart. [11]Temperament. [12]Schemers.
[13]*Minos . . . Numa:* respectively, a son of Europa and Zeus who ruled so wisely in Crete that he became a judge in Hades, a Spartan lawgiver of the ninth century B.C., and the legendary second king of Rome. [14]Honest.
[15]A place where God destroyed fifty thousand, threescore, and ten Philistines because they had peered into the Ark (1 Samuel 6.19).

and shatter the holy ark of the church, not borne upon their shoulders with pains and labor in the word, but drawn with rude oxen, their officials, and their own brute inventions. Let them make shows of reforming while they will, so long as the church is mounted upon the prelatical cart, and not, as it ought, between the hands of the ministers, it will but shake and totter; and he that sets to his hand, though with a good intent to hinder the shogging of it, in this unlawful waggonry wherein it rides, let him beware it be not fatal to him, as it was to Uzzah.[16] Certainly if God be the father of His family the church, wherein could He express that name more than in training it up under His own all-wise and dear economy, not turning it loose to the havoc of strangers and wolves, that would ask no better plea than this, to do in the church of Christ whatever humor, faction, policy, or licentious will would prompt them to? Again, if Christ be the church's husband, expecting her to be presented before Him a pure unspotted virgin, in what could He show His tender love to her more than in prescribing His own ways, which He best knew would be to the improvement of her health and beauty, with much greater care doubtless than the Persian king could appoint for his queen Esther those maiden dietings and set prescriptions of baths and odors, which may render her at last the more amiable to his eye?[17] For of any age or sex, most unfitly may a virgin be left to an uncertain and arbitrary education. Yea, though she be well instructed, yet is she still under a more strait tuition, especially if betrothed. In like manner the church bearing the same resemblance, it were not reason to think she should be left destitute of that care which is as necessary and proper to her as instruction. For public preaching indeed is the gift of the Spirit, working as best seems to His secret will; but discipline is the practice work of preaching directed and applied, as is most requisite, to particular duty; without which it were all one to the benefit of souls, as it would be to the cure of bodies if all the physicians in London should get into the several pulpits of the city and, assembling all the diseased in every parish, should begin a learned lecture of pleurisies, palsies, lethargies, to which perhaps none there present were inclined; and so, without so much as feeling one pulse, or giving the least order to any skilful apothecary, should dismiss them from time to time, some groaning, some languishing, some expiring, with this only charge, to look well to themselves, and do as they hear. Of what excellence and necessity then church-discipline is, how beyond the faculty of man to frame, and how dangerous to be left to man's invention, who would be every foot turning it to sinister ends; how properly also it is the work of God as father, and of Christ as husband, of the church, we have by thus much heard.

CHAPTER VII

THAT THOSE MANY SECTS AND SCHISMS BY SOME SUPPOSED TO BE AMONG US . . . OUGHT NOT TO BE A HINDRANCE BUT A HASTENING OF REFORMATION

As for those many sects and divisions rumored abroad to be amongst us, it is not hard to perceive that they are partly the mere fictions and false alarms of the prelates, thereby to cast amazements and panic terrors into the hearts of weaker Christians, that they should not venture to change the present deformity of the church for fear of I know not what worse inconveniences. With the same objected[18] fears and suspicions, we know that subtle prelate Gardner[19] sought to divert the first reformation.[20] It may suffice us to be taught by St. Paul that there must be sects for the manifesting of those that are sound-hearted.[21] These are but winds and flaws[22] to try the floating vessel of our faith, whether it be stanch and sail well, whether our ballast be just, our anchorage and cable strong. By this is seen who lives by faith and certain knowledge, and who by credulity and the prevailing opinion of the age; whose virtue is of an unchangeable grain,[23] and whose of a slight wash. If God come to try our constancy, we ought not to shrink or stand the less firmly for that, but pass on with more steadfast resolution to establish the truth, though it were through a lane of sects and heresies on each side. Other things men do to the glory of God: but sects and errors, it seems, God suffers to be for the glory of good men, that the world may know and reverence their true fortitude and undaunted constancy in the truth. Let us not therefore make these things an incumbrance, or an excuse of our delay in reforming, which God sends us as an incitement to proceed with more honor and alacrity: for if there were no opposition, where were the trial of an unfeigned goodness and magnanimity? Virtue that wavers is not virtue, but vice revolted from itself, and after a while returning. The actions of just and pious men do not darken in their middle course; but Solomon tells us they are as the shining light, that shineth more and more unto the perfect day.[24] But if we shall suffer the trifling doubts and jealousies of future sects to overcloud the fair beginnings of purposed reformation, let us rather fear that another proverb of the same wise man be not upbraided to us, that "the way of the wicked is as darkness; they stumble at they know not what."[25] If sects and schisms be turbulent in the unsettled estate of a church while it lies under the amending hand, it best beseems our Christian courage to think they are but as the throes and pangs that go before the birth of reformation, and that the work itself is now in doing. For if we look but on the nature of elemental[26] and mixed things, we know they cannot suffer any change of one kind or quality into another without the struggle of contrarieties. And in things artificial,[27] seldom my elegance is wrought without a superfluous waste and refuse in the transaction. No marble

[16]An Israelite who put his hand upon the Ark to steady it while it was being moved by oxen and was promptly destroyed for his impiety (2 Samuel 6.7).
[17]Esther's beautification for her appearance before King Ahasuerus is described in Esther 2.12. [18]Alleged, advanced.
[19]Stephen Gardiner (d. 1555), bishop of Winchester, who as Queen Mary's Lord Chancellor was relentless in persecuting Protestants. [20]The reformation inaugurated by Henry VIII.
[21]"For there must be also heresies among you, that they who are approved may be made manifest among you" (1 Corinthians 11.19). [22]Gusts. [23]Dye. [24]Proverbs 4.18. [25]Proverbs 4.19.
[26]Referring to the four elements—earth, air, fire, and water.
[27]Made by art, manufactured (as opposed to natural).

statue can be politely[28] carved, no fair edifice built, without almost as much rubbish and sweeping. Insomuch that even in the spiritual conflict of St. Paul's conversion, there fell scales from his eyes, that were not perceived before.[29] No wonder then in the reforming of a church, which is never brought to effect without the fierce encounter of truth and falsehood together, if, as it were, the splinters and shares[30] of so violent a jousting, there fall from between the shock many fond errors and fanatic opinions, which, when truth has the upper hand, and the reformation shall be 10 perfected, will easily be rid out of the way, or kept so low, as that they shall be only the exercise of our knowledge, not the disturbance or interruption of our faith. . . .

AREOPAGITICA,[1] A SPEECH . . .
FOR THE LIBERTY OF
UNLICENSED PRINTING (1644)

They, who to states[2] and governors of the Commonwealth direct their speech, High Court of Parliament, or, wanting such access in a private condition, write that which they foresee may advance the public good, I suppose them, as at the beginning of no mean endeavor, not a little altered and moved inwardly in their minds: some with doubt of what will be the success, others with fear of what will be the 20 censure; some with hope, others with confidence of what they have to speak. And me perhaps each of these dispositions, as the subject was whereon I entered, may have at other times variously affected; and likely might in these foremost expressions now also disclose which of them swayed most, but that the very attempt of this address thus made, and the thought of whom it hath recourse to, hath got the power within me to a passion,[3] far more welcome than incidental to a preface.

Which though I stay not to confess ere any ask, I shall be 30 blameless, if it be no other than the joy and gratulation which it brings to all who wish and promote their country's liberty; whereof this whole discourse proposed will be a certain testimony, if not a trophy. For this is not the liberty which we can hope, that no grievance ever should arise in the Commonwealth—that let no man in this world expect; but when complaints are freely heard, deeply considered and speedily reformed, then is the utmost bound of civil liberty attained that wise men look for. To which if I now manifest by the very sound of this which I shall utter, that we are 40 already in good part arrived, and yet from such a steep disadvantage of tyranny and superstition grounded into our principles as was beyond the manhood of a Roman recovery,[4] it will be attributed first, as is most due, to the strong assistance of God our deliverer, next to your faithful guidance and undaunted wisdom, Lords and Commons of England. Neither is it in God's esteem the diminution of His glory, when honourable things are spoken of good men and worthy magistrates; which if I now first should begin to do, after so fair a progress of your laudable deeds, and such a 50 long obligement upon the whole realm to your indefati-

gable virtues,[5] I might be justly reckoned among the tardiest, and the unwillingest of them that praise ye.

Nevertheless there being three principal things without which all praising is but courtship and flattery: first, when that only is praised which is solidly worth praise; next, when greatest likelihoods are brought that such things are truly and really in those persons to whom they are ascribed; the other, when he who praises, by showing that such his actual persuasion is of whom he writes, can demonstrate that he flatters not. The former two of these I have heretofore endeavored, rescuing the employment from him who went about to impair your merits with a trivial and malignant encomium;[6] the latter as belonging chiefly to mine own acquittal, that whom I so extolled I did not flatter, hath been reserved opportunely to this occasion.

For he who freely magnifies what hath been nobly done, and fears not to declare as freely what might be done better, gives ye the best covenant of his fidelity; and that his loyalist affection and his hope waits on your proceedings. His highest praising is not flattery, and his plainest advice is a kind of praising. For though I should affirm and hold by argument that it would fare better with truth, with learning and the Commonwealth if one of your published orders,[7] which I should name, were called in: yet at the same time it could not but much redound to the luster of your mild and equal[8] government, whenas private persons are hereby animated to think ye better pleased with public advice than other statists[9] have been delighted heretofore with public flattery. And men will then see what difference there is between the magnanimity of a triennial Parliament,[10] and that jealous haughtiness of prelates and cabin counsellors[11] that usurped of late, whenas they shall observe ye in the midst of your victories and successes more gently brooking written

[28]Smoothly.   [29]Acts 9.18.   [30]Pieces cut or torn away.

AREOPAGITICA   [1]Milton probably found his title in the *Areopagitic Discourse* (or *Areopagiticus*) of Isocrates (d. 338 B.C.), head of a famous school of oratory in Athens. The Court of the Areopagus (so called from the hill west of the Acropolis where it held its sessions), was originally empowered to legislate on moral and educational questions. [2]Heads of states. [3]Enthusiasm.
[4]*Beyond . . . recovery*: beyond the capacity of the Romans to free themselves from papal tyranny.
[5]*After so fair . . . virtues*: This flattering assessment of the Long Parliament may be compared with that of Clarendon (p. 929) and Thomas May (p. 914) and also with Milton's own radically different opinion in *The History of Britain* (p. 925).
[6]Milton is alluding to Bishop Joseph Hall's *Modest Confutation of a Slanderous and Scurrilous Libel* (1642), wherein Hall had strenuously attacked his Presbyterian adversaries while praising the Parliament that they controlled. For Milton's own part in this controversy see p. 258.
[7]The parliamentary ordinance of 14 June 1643 for licensing the press. [8]Impartial. [9]Politicians, statesmen.
[10]Mindful of the eleven years (1629–40) when Charles had ruled alone, the Long Parliament promptly took two measures to protect itself: by the Triennial Parliaments Act of 16 February 1641 it provided for an automatic convening of the body within three years of its dissolution, and on the following May 10 Parliament forbade its dissolution without its own consent.
[11]Intimate advisers.

exceptions against a voted order than other courts, which had produced nothing worth memory but the weak ostentation of wealth, would have endured the least signified dislike at any sudden proclamation. . . .

[The exordium concluded, Milton opens his defense of freedom by tracing the odious history of censorship.]

I deny not but that it is of greatest concernment in the church and Commonwealth to have a vigilant eye how books demean themselves as well as men; and thereafter to confine, imprison, and do sharpest justice on them as male- factors. For books are not absolutely dead things, but do contain a potency of life in them to be as active as that soul was whose progeny they are; nay, they do preserve as in a vial the purest efficacy and extraction of that living intellect that bred them. I know they are as lively, and as vigorously productive, as those fabulous dragon's teeth; and being sown up and down, may chance to spring up armed men.[12] And yet, on the other hand, unless wariness be used, as good almost kill a man as kill a good book. Who kills a man kills a resonable creature, God's image; but he who destroys a good book, kills reason itself, kills the image of God, as it were, in the eye. Many a man lives a burden to the earth; but a good book is the precious life-blood of a master spirit, embalmed and treasured up on purpose to a life beyond life. 'Tis true, no age can restore a life, whereof perhaps there is no great loss; and revolutions of ages do not oft recover the loss of a rejected truth, for the want of which whole nations fare the worse.

We should be wary therefore what persecutions we raise against the living labors of public men, how we spill[13] that seasoned life of man, preserved and stored up in books; since we see a kind of homicide may be thus committed, sometimes a martyrdom, and if it extend to the whole impression, a kind of massacre; whereof the execution ends not in the slaying of an elemental life, but strikes at that ethereal and fifth essence,[14] the breath of reason itself, slays an immor- tality rather than a life. But lest I should be condemned of introducing licence while I oppose licensing, I refuse not the pains to be so much historical as will serve to show what hath been done by ancient and famous commonwealths against this disorder, till the very time that this project of licensing crept out of the Inquisition,[15] was catched up by our prelates, and hath caught some of our presbyters. . . .

[With easy erudition Milton surveys the attempts at sporadic censorship among the Greeks and Romans and in the early church, and then the massive assaults on liberty by the Inquisition and the Council of Trent. "And thus ye have the inventors and the original of book-licensing ripped up and drawn as lineally as any pedigree." He then moves on to a couple of related questions: "what is to be thought in general of reading books, whatever sort they be, and whether be more the benefit or the harm that thence proceeds?" The answer to such queries may be found, he says, in St. Paul's remark to Titus: "To the pure, all things are pure" (Titus 1.15).]

For books are as meats and viands are—some of good, some of evil substance; and yet God, in that unapocryphal vision,[16] said without exception, "Rise, Peter, kill and eat,"

leaving the choice to each man's discretion. Wholesome meats to a vitiated stomach differ little or nothing from unwholesome; and best books to a naughty mind are not unappliable to occasions of evil. Bad meats will scarce breed good nourishment in the healthiest concoction;[17] but herein the difference is of bad books, that they to a discreet and judicious reader serve in many respects to discover, to confute, to forewarn, and to illustrate. Whereof what better witness can ye expect I should produce than one of your own now sitting in Parliament, the chief of learned men reputed in this land, Mr. Selden;[18] whose volume of natural and national laws proves, not only by great authorities brought together, but by exquisite reasons and theorems almost mathematically demonstrative, that all opinions, yea errors, known, read, and collated, are of main service and assistance toward the speedy attainment of what is truest. I conceive, therefore, that when God did enlarge the universal diet of man's body, saving ever the rules of temperance, He then also, as before, left arbitrary the dieting and re- pasting[19] of our minds; as wherein every mature man might have to exercise his own leading capacity.

How great a virtue is temperance, how much of moment through the whole life of man! Yet God commits the managing so great a trust without particular law or pre- scription, wholly to the demeanor of every grown man. And therefore when He himself tabled the Jews from heaven,[20] that omer,[21] which was every man's daily portion of manna, is computed to have been more than might have well sufficed the heartiest feeder thrice as many meals. For those actions which enter into a man, rather than issue out of him and therefore defile not, God uses not to captivate under a perpetual childhood of prescription, but trusts him in with the gift of reason to be his own chooser; there were but little work left for preaching if law and compulsion should grow so fast upon those things which heretofore were governed only by exhortation. Solomon informs us that much read- ing is a weariness to the flesh;[22] but neither he nor other inspired author tells us that such or such reading is unlawful: yet certainly had God thought good to limit us herein, it had been much more expedient to have told us what was unlawful than what was wearisome. As for the burning of those Ephesian books by St Paul's converts; 'tis replied the

[12]According to Ovid (*Metamorphoses*, III.95–126), when Cadmus, king of Boeotia, sowed the teeth of a dragon he had slain, armed men sprang up from them and promptly fought with one another. [13]Destroy. [14]*Slaying . . . essence*: slaying not only the physical man (composed of the elements of air, earth, fire, and water) but also his spiritual or *ethereal* part, which is his *fifth essence*. [15]The "Holy Office," the notorious ecclesiastical tribunal charged with suppressing heresy that, though sporadically active since 1231, had been revived and strengthened in 1480 by Ferdinand and Is- abella of Spain. [16]Acts 10.9–16, where Peter dreams that he had been released from the dietary strictures of the Law.   [17]Digestion. [18]For the eminent scholar and Parliamentarian John Selden (whom Milton praises on several occasions), see p. 852. Selden's *De jure naturalia et gentium* had appeared in 1640.   [19]Feeding. [20]Exodus 16.   [21]Measurement.   [22]Ecclesiastes 12.12.

books were magic, the Syriac so renders them.[23] It was a private act, a voluntary act, and leaves us to a voluntary imitation: the men in remorse burn those books which were their own; the magistrate by this example is not appointed; these men practised the books, another might perhaps have read them in some sort usefully.

Good and evil we know in the field of this world grow up together almost inseparably; and the knowledge of good is so involved and interwoven with the knowledge of evil, and in so many cunning resemblances hardly to be discerned, that those confused seeds which were imposed on Psyche as an incessant labor to cull out, and sort asunder,[24] were not more intermixed. It was from out the rind of one apple tasted that the knowledge of good and evil, as two twins cleaving together, leaped forth into the world. And perhaps this is that doom which Adam fell into of knowing good and evil, that is to say of knowing good by evil. As therefore the state of man now is, what wisdom can there be to choose, what continence to forbear without the knowledge of evil? He that can apprehend and consider vice with all her baits and seeming pleasures, and yet abstain, and yet distinguish, and yet prefer that which is truly better, he is the true wayfaring[25] Christian.

I cannot praise a fugitive and cloistered virtue, unexercised and unbreathed, that never sallies out and sees her adversary, but slinks out of the race, where that immortal garland is to be run for, not without dust and heat. Assuredly we bring not innocence into the world, we bring impurity much rather; that which purifies us is trial, and trial is by what is contrary. That virtue therefore which is but a youngling[26] in the contemplation of evil, and knows not the utmost that vice promises to her followers, and rejects it, is but a blank virtue, not a pure; her whiteness is but an excremental whiteness. Which was the reason why our sage and serious poet Spenser, whom I dare be known to think a better teacher than Scotus or Aquinas, describing true temperance under the person of Guyon, brings him in with his Palmer through the cave of Mammon, and the bower of earthly bliss, that he might see and know, and yet abstain.[27] Since therefore the knowledge and survey of vice is in this world so necessary to the constituting of human virtue, and the scanning of error to the confirmation of truth, how can we more safely, and with less danger, scout into the regions of sin and falsity than by reading all manner of tractates and hearing all manner of reason? And this is the benefit which may be had of books promiscuously read. . . .

One by one, three major counterarguments are examined and rejected: that the "infection" of bad or "dangerous" books will spread, that "we must not expose ourselves to temptations without necessity," and that (as Plato realized) men should be forbidden to indulge in "vain" pursuits. Milton replies that whatever safety censorship provides is not really safe at all, that it costs too high a price, and that in any event men cannot be legislated into virtue. "If we think to regulate printing, thereby to rectify manners, we must regulate all recreations and pastimes, all that is delightful to man. . . . It will ask more than the work of twenty licensers to examine all the lutes, the violins, and the guitars in every house; they must not be suffered to prattle as they do, but must be licensed what they may say. And who shall silence all the airs and madrigals that whisper softness in chambers?"

If every action, which is good or evil in man at ripe years, were to be under pittance and prescription and compulsion, what were virtue but a name, what praise could be then due to well-doing, what gramercy[28] to be sober, just, or continent? Many there be that complain of divine providence for suffering Adam to transgress; foolish tongues! When God gave him reason He gave him freedom to choose, for reason is but choosing; he had been else a mere artificial Adam, such an Adam as he is in the motions.[29] We ourselves esteem not of that obedience, or love, or gift, which is of force: God therefore left him free, set before him a provoking object, ever almost in his eyes; herein consisted his merit, herein the right of his reward, the praise of his abstinence. Wherefore did He create passions within us, pleasures round about us, but that these rightly tempered are the very ingredients of virtue?

They are not skilful considerers of human things who imagine to remove sin by removing the matter of sin; for besides that it is a huge heap increasing under the very act of diminishing, though some part of it may for a time be withdrawn from some persons, it cannot from all, in such a universal thing as books are; and when this is done, yet the sin remains entire. Though ye take from a covetous man all his treasure, he has yet one jewel left: ye cannot bereave him of his covetousness. Banish all objects of lust, shut up all youth into the severest discipline that can be exercised in any hermitage, ye cannot make them chaste that came not thither so: such great care and wisdom is required to the right managing of this point. Suppose we could expel sin by this means, look how much we thus expel of sin, so much we expel of virtue; for the matter of them both is the same: remove that, and ye remove them both alike. This justifies the high providence of God, who, though He commands us temperance, justice, continence, yet pours out before us, even to a profuseness, all desirable things, and gives us minds that can wander beyond all limit and satiety. Why should we then affect a rigor contrary to the manner of God and of nature by abridging or scanting those means, which books freely permitted are, both to the trial of virtue and the exercise of truth? It would be better done to learn that the law must needs be frivolous which goes to restrain things, uncertainly and yet equally[30] working to good and to evil.

[23]Acts 19.19.
[24]Having angered Venus by winning Cupid's love, Psyche was doomed to sort out the different kinds of grain in a huge, mixed heap. Happily, some helpful ants came to her assistance.
[25]In four presentation copies of *Areopagitica* this word has been changed in ink—presumably by Milton or with his consent—to *warfaring.* [26]Novice.
[27]*Which was...abstain:* Milton is inaccurately remembering *The Faerie Queene,* II.xii, where Guyon resists the witch Acrasia and destroys her Bower of Bliss without the assistance of his Palmer. The great scholastic philosophers St. Thomas Aquinas and Duns Scotus are cited as exemplars of philosophical theology. [28]Thanks.
[29]Puppet shows. [30]Impartially.

And were I the chooser, a dram of well-doing should be preferred before many times as much the forcible hindrance of evil-doing. For God sure esteems the growth and completing of one virtuous person more than the restraint of ten vicious. . . .

I lastly proceed from the no good it can do to the manifest hurt it causes in being first the greatest discouragement and affront that can be offered to learning and to learned men.

It was the complaint and lamentation of prelates, upon every least breath of a motion to remove pluralities and distribute more equally Church revenues, that then all learning would be for ever dashed and discouraged. But as for that opinion, I never found cause to think that the tenth part of learning stood or fell with the clergy: nor could I ever but hold it for a sordid and unworthy speech of any churchman who had a competency left him. If therefore ye be loth to dishearten utterly and discontent, not the mercenary crew of false pretenders to learning, but the free and ingenuous sort of such as evidently were born to study and love learning for itself, not for lucre or any other end but the service of God and of truth, and perhaps that lasting fame and perpetuity of praise which God and good men have consented shall be the reward of those whose published labors advance the good of mankind, then know that, so far to distrust the judgment and the honesty of one who hath but a common repute in learning, and never yet offended, as not to count him fit to print his mind without a tutor and examiner, lest he should drop a schism, or something of corruption, is the greatest displeasure and indignity to a free and knowing spirit that can be put upon him.

What advantage is it to be a man over it is to be a boy at school if we have only escaped the ferular[31] to come under the fescue[32] of an Imprimatur, if serious and elaborate writings, as if they were no more than the theme of a grammar-lad under his pedagogue, must not be uttered[33] without the cursory eyes of a temporizing and extemporizing licenser? He who is not trusted with his own actions, his drift not being known to be evil, and standing to the hazard of law and penalty, has no great argument to think himself reputed in the Commonwealth wherein he was born for other than a fool or a foreigner. When a man writes to the world, he summons up all his reason and deliberation to assist him; he searches, meditates, is industrious, and likely consults and confers with his judicious friends; after all which done he takes himself to be informed in what he writes, as well as any that writ before him. If, in this the most consummate act of his fidelity and ripeness, no years, no industry, no former proof of his abilities can bring him to that state of maturity as not to be still mistrusted and suspected unless he carry all his considerate diligence, all his midnight watchings and expense of Palladian[34] oil, to the hasty view of an unleisured licenser, perhaps much his younger, perhaps far his inferior in judgment, perhaps one who never knew the labor of book-writing, and if he be not repulsed or slighted, must appear in print like a puny[35] with his guardian, and his censor's hand on the back of his title to be his bail and surety that he is no idiot or seducer, it cannot be but a dishonor and derogation to the author, to the book, to the privilege and dignity of learning. . . .

> Just as faith and knowledge, through trial and "exercise," advance indefinitely toward truth, so truth itself (which the Bible likens to a streaming fountain) must flow in a "perpetual progression" or else "sicken into a muddy pool of conformity and tradition." The calamitous results of compulsion and prescription are apparent: in the individual, spiritual and intellectual torpor; in the church, "laziness"; in the nation, an embargo on "our richest merchandise, truth."

Trust indeed came once into the world with her divine Master, and was a perfect shape most glorious to look on: but when He ascended, and His apostles after Him were laid asleep, then straight arose a wicked race of deceivers, who, as that story goes of the Egyptian Typhon[36] with his conspirators, how they dealt with the good Osiris, took the virgin Truth, hewed her lovely form into a thousand pieces, and scattered them to the four winds. From that time ever since, the sad friends of Truth, such as durst appear, imitating the careful search that Isis made for the mangled body of Osiris, went up and down gathering up limb by limb, still as they could find them. We have not yet found them all, Lords and Commons, nor ever shall do, till her Master's second coming; He shall bring together every joint and member, and shall mold them into an immortal feature[37] of loveliness and perfection. Suffer not these licensing prohibitions to stand at every place of opportunity, forbidding and disturbing them that continue seeking, that continue to do our obsequies to the torn body of our martyred saint.

We boast our light, but if we look not wisely on the sun itself, it smites us into darkness. Who can discern those planets that are oft combust,[38] and those stars of brightest magnitude that rise and set with the sun until the opposite motion of their orbs bring them to such a place in the firmament where they may be seen evening or morning? The light which we have gained was given us, not to be ever staring on, but by it to discover onward things more remote from our knowledge. It is not the unfrocking of a priest, the unmitering of a bishop, and the removing him from off the presbyterian shoulders that will make us a happy nation. No, if other things as great in the church, and in the rule of life both economical[39] and political, be not looked into and reformed, we have looked so long upon the blaze that Zuinglius and Calvin[40] hath beaconed up to us that we are stark blind. There be who perpetually complain of schisms and sects, and make it such a calamity that any man dissents from their maxims. 'Tis their own pride and ignorance which causes the disturbing, who neither will hear with meekness,

[31]Ferula, i.e., cane, rod (for punishment of schoolboys).
[32]Twig, straw. [33]Published.
[34]Referring to Pallas Athene, goddess of wisdom. [35]Minor.
[36]The Greek name of the Egyptian Set, god of evil, who killed and dismembered his brother (or father) Osiris. [37]Shape.
[38]Burned (by the near conjunction of the sun). [39]Domestic.
[40]Ulrich Zwingli (1484–1531) and John Calvin (1509–64), leaders of the Protestant Reformation.

nor can convince: yet all must be suppressed which is not found in their syntagma.[41] They are the troublers, they are the dividers of unity, who neglect and permit not others to unite those dissevered pieces which are yet wanting to the body of Truth. To be still searching what we know not by what we know, still closing up truth to Truth as we find it (for all her body is homogeneal and proportional), this is the golden rule in theology as well as in arithmetic, and makes up the best harmony in a church: not the forced and outward union of cold and neutral, and inwardly divided minds.

Lords and Commons of England, consider what nation it is whereof ye are, and whereof ye are the governors: a nation not slow and dull, but of a quick, ingenious and piercing spirit, acute to invent, subtle and sinewy to discourse, not beneath the reach of any point, the highest that human capacity can soar to. Therefore the studies of learning in her deepest sciences have been so ancient and so eminent among us that writers of good antiquity and ablest judgment have been persuaded that even the school of Pythagoras and the Persian wisdom took beginning from the old philosophy of this island[42] And that wise and civil Roman, Julius Agricola,[43] who governed once here for Caesar, preferred the natural wits of Britain before the labored studies of the French. Nor is it for nothing that the grave and frugal Transylvanian sends out yearly from as far as the mountainous borders of Russia, and beyond the Hercynian[44] wilderness, not their youth, but their staid men, to learn our language and our theologic arts.

Yet that which is above all this, the favor and the love of Heaven, we have great argument to think in a peculiar manner propitious and propending towards us. Why else was this nation chosen before any other, that out of her, as out of Sion, should be proclaimed and sounded forth the first tidings and trumpet of Reformation to all Europe? And had it not been the obstinate perverseness of our prelates against the divine and admirable spirit of Wyclif, to suppress him as a schismatic and innovator, perhaps neither the Bohemian Huss and Jerome,[45] no nor the name of Luther or of Calvin, had been ever known: the glory of reforming all our neighbours had been completely ours. But now, as our obdurate clergy have with violence demeaned the matter, we are become hitherto the latest and the backwardest scholars, of whom God offered to have made us the teachers. Now once again by all concurrence of signs, and by the general instinct of holy and devout men, as they daily and solemnly express their thoughts, God is decreeing to begin some new and great period in His church, even to the reforming of reformation itself: what does He then but reveal Himself to His servants, and as His manner is, first to His Englishmen? I say, as His manner is, first to us, though we mark not the method of His counsels, and are unworthy.

Behold now this vast city: a city of refuge, the mansion house of liberty, encompassed and surrounded with His protection; the shop of war hath not there more anvils and hammers waking to fashion out the plates and instruments of armed Justice in defence of beleaguered Truth than there be pens and heads there, sitting by their studious lamps,

musing, searching, revolving new notions and ideas wherewith to present, as with their homage and their fealty, the approaching reformation: others as fast reading, trying all things, assenting to the force of reason and convincement. What could a man require more from a nation so pliant and so prone to seek after knowledge? What wants there to such a towardly and pregnant soil but wise and faithful laborers to make a knowing people, a nation of prophets, of sages, and of worthies? We reckon more than five months yet to harvest; there need not be five weeks; had we but eyes to lift up, the fields are white already.[46]

Where there is much desire to learn, there of necessity will be much arguing, much writing, many opinions; for opinion in good men is but knowledge in the making. . . .

Methinks I see in my mind a noble and puissant nation rousing herself like a strong man after sleep, and shaking her invincible locks.[47] Methinks I see her as an eagle mewing[48] her mighty youth and kindling her undazzled eyes at the full midday beam, purging and unscaling her long-abused sight at the fountain itself of heavenly radiance while the whole noise of timorous and flocking birds, with those also that love the twilight, flutter about, amazed at what she means, and in their envious gabble would prognosticate a year of sects and schisms.

What should ye do then? should ye suppress all this flowery crop of knowledge and new light sprung up and yet springing daily in this city? should ye set an oligarchy of twenty engrossers over it, to bring a famine upon our minds again, when we shall know nothing but what is measured to us by their bushel? Believe it, Lords and Commons, they who counsel ye to such a suppressing do as good as bid ye suppress yourselves; and I will soon show how. If it be desired to know the immediate cause of all this free writing and free speaking, there cannot be assigned a truer than your own mild and free and humane government. It is the liberty, Lords and Commons, which your own valorous and happy counsels have purchased us, liberty which is the nurse of all great wits; this is that which hath rarefied and enlightened our spirits like the influence of heaven; this is that which hath

[41]Treatise.

[42]Milton is perhaps thinking of the legend that the ancient Druids transmitted to Pythagoras and other sages the doctrine of metempsychosis. [43]A Roman proconsul in Britain from 78 to 85.

[44]Referring to Hyrcania Silva, Julius Caesar's name for the mountains and forests of central and southern Germany.

[45]*Wyclif. . .Jerome*: Respectively, the Englishman John Wyclif (d. 1384) and the Bohemians John Hus (d. 1415) and Jerome of Prague (d. 1416), all commonly regarded as harbingers of the Protestant Reformation that Martin Luther launched in 1517.

[46]"Say not ye, There are yet four months, and then cometh harvest? Behold, I say unto you, Lift up your eyes, and look on the fields; for they are white already to harvest" (John 4.35).

[47]Milton is thinking of Samson's initial resistance to Delilah and the Philistines in refusing to reveal that his strength lay in his unshorn locks (Judges 16.6–14).

[48]Molting (a term from falconry). Text *muing,* which some editors regard as a misprint for "newing" or "renewing."

enfranchised, enlarged and lifted up our apprehensions degrees above themselves.

Ye cannot make us now less capable, less knowing, less eagerly pursuing of the truth unless ye first make yourselves, that made us so, less the lovers, less the founders of our true liberty. We can grow ignorant again, brutish, formal, and slavish, as ye found us; but you then must first become that which ye cannot be, oppressive, arbitrary and tyrannous, as they were from whom ye have freed us. That our hearts are now more capacious, our thoughts more erected to the search and expectation of greatest and exactest things, is the issue of your own virtue propagated in us; ye cannot suppress that, unless ye reinforce an abrogated and merciless law, that fathers may dispatch at will their own children. And who shall then stick closest to ye, and excite others? not he who takes up arms for coat and conduct, and his four nobles of Danegelt.[49] Although I dispraise not the defence of just immunities, yet love my peace better, if that were all. Give me the liberty to know, to utter, and to argue freely according to conscience, above all liberties.

What would be best advised, then, if it be found so hurtful and so unequal to suppress opinions for the newness or the unsuitableness to a customary acceptance, will not be my task to say. I only shall repeat what I have learned from one of your own honorable number, a right noble and pious lord, who, had he not sacrificed his life and fortunes to the church and Commonwealth, we had not now missed and bewailed a worthy and undoubted patron of this argument. Ye know him, I am sure; yet I for honor's sake, and may it be eternal to him, shall name him, the Lord Brooke.[50] He writing of episcopacy, and by the way treating of sects and schisms, left ye his vote, or rather now the last words of his dying charge, which I know will ever be of dear and honored regard with ye, so full of meekness and breathing charity, that next to His last testament, who bequeathed love and peace to His disciples,[51] I cannot call to mind where I have read or heard words more mild and peaceful. He there exhorts us to hear with patience and humility those, however they be miscalled, that desire to live purely, in such a use of God's ordinances as the best guidance of their conscience gives them, and to tolerate them, though in some disconformity to ourselves. The book itself will tell us more at large, being published to the world, and dedicated to the Parliament by him who, both for his life and for his death, deserves that what advice he left be not laid by without perusal.

And now the time in special is by privilege to write and speak what may help to the further discussing of matters in agitation. The temple of Janus[52] with his two controversial faces might now not unsignificantly be set open. And though all the winds of doctrine[53] were let loose to play upon the earth, so Truth be in the field, we do injuriously, by licensing and prohibiting, to misdoubt her strength. Let her and Falsehood grapple; who ever knew Truth put to the worse, in a free and open encounter? Her confuting is the best and surest suppressing. He who hears what praying there is for light and clearer knowledge to be sent down among us would think of other matters to be constituted beyond the discipline of Geneva,[54] framed and fabricked already to our

hands. Yet when the new light which we beg for shines in upon us, there be who envy and oppose, if it come not first in at their casements. What a collusion is this whenas we are exhorted by the wise man to use diligence, to seek for wisdom as for hidden treasures early and late, that another order shall enjoin us to know nothing but by statute? When a man hath been laboring the hardest labour in the deep mines of knowledge; hath furnished out his findings in all their equipage; drawn forth his reasons as it were a battle ranged; scattered and defeated all objections in his way; calls out his adversary into the plain, offers him the advantage of wind and sun, if he please, only that he may try the matter by dint of argument; for his opponents then to skulk, to lay ambushments, to keep a narrow bridge of licensing where the challenger should pass, though it be valor enough in soldiership, is but weakness and cowardice in the wars of Truth. . . .

I fear yet this iron yoke of outward conformity hath left a slavish print upon our necks; the ghost of a linen decency[55] yet haunts us. We stumble and are impatient at the least dividing of one visible congregation from another, though it be not in fundamentals; and through our forwardness to suppress, and our backwardness to recover any enthralled piece of truth out of the gripe of custom, we care not to keep truth separated from truth, which is the fiercest rent and disunion of all. We do not see that, while we still affect by all means a rigid external formality we may as soon fall again into a gross conforming stupidity, a stark and dead congealment of wood and hay and stubble, forced and frozen together, which is more to the sudden degenerating of a church than many subdichotomies of petty schisms.

Not that I can think well of every light separation, or that all in a church is to be expected gold and silver and precious stones: it is not possible for man to sever the wheat from the tares, the good fish from the other fry; that must be the angels' ministry at the end of mortal things.[56] Yet if all cannot be of one mind—as who looks they should be?— this doubtless is more wholesome, more prudent, and more

---

[49]*Coat...Danegelt*: offensive forms of taxation. For Charles I's attempts to levy taxes (without the consent of Parliament) for the outfitting and transporting (*coat and conduct*) of his troops, see p. 915. *Danegelt* was originally a tax for means to resist or bribe the marauding Danes. *Noble*: a coin worth 6*s.* 8*d.*

[50]Robert Greville, (1608–43), second Lord Brooke, a leading Parliamentarian and general who died in an assault on Lichfield. His *Discourse Opening the Nature of That Episcopacie Which Is Exercised in England* (1641; 2d ed., "Corrected and Enlarged," 1642) was an influential plea for enlightened reformation.

[51]John 14.15–31.

[52]The Roman god of beginnings (hence our "January"), depicted as having two faces that looked before and behind. In time of war the doors of his temple in the Forum were *set open*, but they were closed in time of peace.

[53]"That we henceforth be no more children, tossed to and fro, and carried about with every wind of doctrine...." (Ephesians 4.14).

[54]Presbyterianism.

[55]Referring to Archbishop Laud's efforts to compel conformity (in vestments and ceremonies) on the ground of *decency*.

[56]See Matthew 13.24–30, 36–43.

Christian that many be tolerated rather than all compelled. I mean not tolerated popery, and open superstition, which, as it extirpates all religions and civil supremacies, so itself should be extirpate, provided first that all charitable and compassionate means be used to win and regain the weak and the misled: that also which is impious or evil absolutely either against faith or manners no law can possibly permit that intends not to unlaw itself: but those neighboring differences, or rather indifferences, are what I speak of, whether in some point of doctrine or of discipline, which, though they [10] may be many, yet need not interrupt the unity of Spirit, if we could but find among us the bond of peace.

In the meanwhile if any one would write, and bring his helpful hand to the slow-moving reformation which we labor under, if Truth have spoken to him before others, or but seemed at least to speak, who hath so bejesuited us that we should trouble that man with asking licence to do so worthy a deed? and not consider this, that if it come to prohibiting, there is not aught more likely to be prohibited than truth itself; whose first appearance to our eyes, bleared and [20] dimmed with prejudice and custom, is more unsightly and unplausible than many errors, even as the person is of many a great man slight and contemptible to see to. And what do they tell us vainly of new opinions, when this very opinion of theirs that none must be heard but whom they like, is the worst and newest opinion of all others; and is the chief cause why sects and schisms do so much abound, and true knowledge is kept at distance from us; besides yet a greater danger which is in it?

For when God shakes a kingdom with strong and healthful [30] commotions to a general reforming, 'tis not untrue that many sectaries and false teachers are then busiest in seducing; but yet more true it is, that God then raises to His own work men of rare abilities, and more than common industry, not only to look back and revise what hath been taught heretofore, but to gain further and go on some new enlightened steps in the discovery of truth. For such is the order of God's enlightening His Church, to dispense and deal out by degrees His beam, so as our earthly eyes may best sustain it. . . .

This I know, that errors in a good government and in [40] a bad are equally almost incident; for what magistrate may not be misinformed, and much the sooner, if liberty of printing be reduced into the power of a few? But to redress willingly and speedily what hath been erred, and in highest authority to esteem a plain advertisement more than others have done a sumptuous bribe, is a virtue, honored Lords and Commons, answerable to your highest actions, and whereof none can participate but greatest and wisest men.

EIKONOKLASTES, IN ANSWER TO A BOOK ENTITLED *Eikon Basilike* (1650)

[INTRODUCTION]

To descant on the misfortunes of a person fallen from so high a dignity, who hath also paid his final debt both to [50] nature and his faults, is neither of itself a thing commend-

able nor the intention of this discourse. Neither was it fond ambition, or the vanity to get a name, present or with posterity, by writing against a king. I never was so thirsty after fame nor so destitute of other hopes and means better and more certain to attain it. For kings have gained glorious titles from their favorers by writing against private men (as Henry VIII did against Luther),[1] but no man ever gained much honor by writing against a king, as not usually meeting with that force of argument in such courtly antagonists, which to convince might add to his reputation. Kings most commonly, though strong in legions, are but weak at arguments; as they who ever have accustomed from the cradle to use their will only as their right hand, their reason always as their left. Whence unexpectedly constrained to that kind of combat, they prove but weak and puny adversaries; nevertheless, for their sakes who through custom, simplicity, or want of better teaching have not more seriously considered kings than in the gaudy name of majesty, and admire them and their doings as if they breathed not the same breath with other mortal men, I shall make no scruple to take up (for it seems to be the challenge both of him[2] and all his party) to take up this gauntlet, though a king's, in the behalf of liberty and the Commonwealth.

And further, since it appears manifestly the cunning drift of a factious and defeated party to make the same advantage of his book which they did before of his regal name and authority, and intend it not so much the defence of his former actions as the promoting of their own future designs (making thereby the book their own rather than the king's, as the benefit now must be their own more than his), now the third time[3] to corrupt and disorder the minds of weaker men by new suggestions and narrations, either falsely or fallaciously representing the state of things to the dishonor of this present government and the retarding of a general peace, so needful to this afflicted nation and so nigh obtained; I suppose it no injury to the dead, but a good deed rather to the living, if by better information given them, or, which is enough, by only remembering[4] them the truth of what they themselves know to be here[5] misaffirmed, they may be kept from entering the third time unadvisedly into war and bloodshed. For as to any moment[6] of solidity in the book itself (save only that a king is said to be the author, a name than which there needs no more among the blockish vulgar to make it wise and excellent and admired, nay to set it next the Bible, though otherwise containing little else but the common grounds of tyranny and popery, dressed up the better to deceive in a new Protestant guise, and trimly garnished over) or as to any need of answering, in

EIKONOKLASTES [1]For writing *Assertio septem sacramentorum adversus Martinum Lutherum* (1521)—in which he had much help—Henry VIII was given the title *Defensor Fidei* ("Defender of the Faith") by Leo X.
[2]Charles I, the reputed author of *Eikon Basilike* ("The royal image") whose errors and deceits Milton undertakes to expose in *Eikonoklastes* ("The image-breaker").
[3]Milton implies that the royalists—already defeated in two wars (1642–47, April–May 1648)—were preparing to disturb the peace again. [4]Reminding. [5]In *Eikon Basilike*. [6]Fragment.

respect of staid and well-principled men, I take it on me as a work assigned rather than by me chosen or affected: which was the cause both of beginning it so late, and finishing it so leisurely in the midst of other employments and diversions.[7]

And though well it might have seemed in vain to write at all, considering the envy and almost infinite prejudice likely to be stirred up among the common sort against whatever can be written or gainsaid to the King's Book, so advantageous to a book it is only to be a king's; and though it be an irksome labor to write with industry and judicious pains that which, neither weighed nor well read, shall be judged without industry or the pains of well judging, by faction and the easy literature of custom and opinion; it shall be ventured yet, and the truth not smothered, but sent abroad in the native confidence of her single self to earn, how she can, her entertainment in the world, and to find out her own readers: few perhaps, but those few such of value and substantial worth as truth and wisdom, not respecting numbers and big names, have been ever wont in all ages to be contented with.

And if the late king had thought sufficient those answers and defences made for him in his lifetime, they who on the other side accused his evil government, judging that on their behalf enough also hath been replied, the heat of this controversy was in likelihood drawing to an end; and the further mention of his deeds, not so much unfortunate as faulty, had in tenderness to his late sufferings been willingly forborne; and perhaps for the present age might have slept with him unrepeated, while his adversaries, calmed and assuaged with the success of their cause, had been the less unfavorable to his memory. But since he himself, making new appeal to truth and the world, hath left behind him this book as the best advocate and interpreter of his own actions, and that his friends, by publishing, dispersing, commending, and almost adoring it, seem to place therein the chief strength and nerves of their cause, it would argue doubtless in the other party great deficience and distrust of themselves not to meet the force of his reason in any field whatsoever, the force and equipage of whose arms they have so often met victoriously. And he who at the bar stood excepting against the form and manner of his judicature, and complained that he was not heard,[8] neither he nor his friends shall have that cause now to find fault, being met and debated with in this open and monumental court of his own erecting; and not only heard uttering his whole mind at large, but answered, which to do effectually, if it be necessary, that to his book nothing the more respect be had for being his, they of his own party can have no just reason to exclaim.

For it were too unreasonable that he, because dead, should have the liberty in his book to speak all evil of the Parliament; and they, because living, should be expected to have less freedom, or any for them,[9] to speak home the plain truth of a full and pertinent reply. As he, to acquit himself, hath not spared his adversaries to load them with all sorts of blame and accusation, so to him, as in his book alive, there will be used no more courtship[10] than he uses; but what is properly his own guilt, not imputed any more to his evil counsellors,[11]

(a ceremony used longer by the Parliament than he himself desired) shall be laid here without circumlocutions at his own door. That they who from the first beginning, or but now of late, by what unhappiness I know not, are so much affatuated[12] not with his person only but with his palpable faults, and dote upon his deformities, may have none to blame but their own folly if they live and die in such a stricken blindness as next to that of Sodom[13] hath not happened to any sort of men more gross or more misleading. Yet neither let his enemies expect to find recorded here all that hath been whispered in the court or alleged openly of the king's bad actions, it being the proper scope of this work in hand not to rip up and relate the misdoings of his whole life, but to answer only and refute the missayings of his book. . . . This however would be remembered and well noted, that while the king, instead of that repentance which was in reason and in conscience to be expected from him, without which we could not lawfully readmit him, persists here to maintain and justify the most apparent of his evil doings, and washes over with a court-fucus[14] the worst and foulest of his actions, disables and uncreates the Parliament itself, with all our laws and native liberties that ask not his leave, dishonors and attaints[15] all Protestant churches not prelatical and what they piously reformed with the slander of rebellion, sacrilege, and hypocrisy; they, who seemed of late to stand up hottest for the covenant,[16] can now sit mute and much pleased to hear all these opprobrious things uttered against their faith, their freedom, and themselves in their own doings made traitors to boot. The divines, also, their wizards,[17] can be so brazen as to cry Hosanna to this his book, which cries louder against them for[18] no disciples of Christ, but of Iscariot; and to seem now convinced with these withered arguments and reasons here, the same which in some other writings of that party and in his own former declarations and expresses,[19] they have so often heretofore endeavored to confute and to explode, none appearing all this while to vindicate church or state from these calumnies and reproaches

---

[7]For Milton's later account of the circumstances under which he wrote *Eikonoklastes* see p. 779.
[8]For Clarendon's account of this celebrated episode see p. 934.
[9]Any of their spokesmen. [10]Courtesy.
[11]In the early stages of their quarrel with the king, the parliamentary leaders charitably attributed Charles' misbehavior to bad advice. [12]Infatuated.
[13]An ancient city that, persisting in its evil ways despite repeated warnings, was finally destroyed by God. See Genesis 19.
[14]Cosmetics fashionable at court (with satirists a common symbol for evasion and deceit). [15]Convicts.
[16]*They . . . covenant*: One of Milton's many blasts against the Presbyterians, whose blind adherence to the Solemn League and Covenant made them, as he came to think, self-serving bigots, and whose fear of Cromwell and the Independents in the army led them to oppose Charles' trial and execution. See p. 937, n. 46.
[17]The reactionary Presbyterian ministers in the Westminster Assembly, a body authorized by Parliament in 1643 to reform the established church. For Milton's low opinion of their accomplishments see p. 926. [18]As being. [19]Communications.

but a small handful of men, whom they defame and spit at with all the odious names of schism and sectarism. I never knew that time in England when men of truest religion were not counted sectaries; but wisdom now, valor, justice, constancy, prudence united and embodied to defend religion and our liberties, both by word and deed against tyranny, is counted schism and faction.

Thus in a graceless age things of highest praise and imitation under a right name, to make them infamous and hateful to the people are miscalled. Certainly, if ignorance and per- [10] verseness will needs be national and universal, then they who adhere to wisdom and to truth are not therefore to be blamed for being so few as to seem a sect or faction. But in my opinion it goes not ill with that people where these virtues grow so numerous and well joined together as to resist and make head against the rage and torrent of that boisterous folly and superstition that possesses and hurries on the vulgar sort. This therefore we may conclude to be a high honor done us from God, and a special mark of His favour, whom He hath selected as the sole remainder, after all these [20] changes and commotions, to stand upright and steadfast in His cause; dignified with the defence of truth and public liberty while others, who aspired to be the top of zealots and had almost brought religion to a kind of trading monopoly, have not only by their late silence and neutrality belied their profession, but foundered themselves and their consciences to comply with enemies in that wicked cause and interest, which they have too often cursed in others to prosper now in the same themselves.

CHAPTER I.

Upon the King's Calling This Last Parliament

That which the King lays down here as his first foundation, [30] and as it were the headstone of his whole structure, that "he called this last Parliament, not more by others' advice, and the necessity of his affairs, than by his own choice and inclination," is to all knowing men so apparently not true that a more unlucky and inauspicious sentence, and more betokening the downfall of his whole fabric, hardly could have come into his mind. For who knows not that the inclination of a prince is best known either by those next about him, and most in favour with him, or by the current of his own actions? Those nearest to this king, and most his favorites, [40] were courtiers and prelates, men whose chief study was to find out which way the king inclined, and to imitate him exactly: how these men stood affected to Parliaments cannot be forgotten. No man but may remember it was their continual exercise to dispute and preach against them; and in their common discourse nothing was more frequent than that "they hoped the king should now have no need of Parliaments any more." And this was but the copy which his parasites had industriously taken from his own words and actions, who never called a Parliament but to supply his [50] necessities; and having supplied those, as suddenly and ignominiously dissolved it without redressing any one grievance of the people, sometimes choosing rather to miss

of his subsidies, or to raise them by illegal courses, than that the people should not still miss of their hopes to be relieved by Parliaments.

The first he broke off at his coming to the crown, for no other cause than to protect the duke of Buckingham[20] against them who had accused him, besides other heinous crimes, of no less than poisoning the deceased king, his father; concerning which matter the declaration of "No more addresses" hath sufficiently informed us.[21] And still the latter breaking was with more affront and indignity put upon the House and her worthiest members than the former.[22] Insomuch that in the fifth year of his reign, in a proclamation, he seems offended at the very rumor of a Parliament divulged among the people,[23] as if he had taken it for a kind of slander that men should think him that way exorable,[24] much less inclined; and forbids it as a presumption to prescribe him any time for Parliaments, that is to say, either by persuasion or petition, or so much as the reporting of such a rumor: for other manner of prescribing was at that time not suspected. By which fierce edict, the people, forbidden to complain, as well as forced to suffer, began from thenceforth to despair of Parliaments. Whereupon such illegal actions, and especially to get vast sums of money, were put in practice by the king and his new officers as monopolies, compulsive knighthoods, coat, conduct, and ship-money,[25] the seizing not of one Naboth's vineyard[26] but of whole inheritances, under the pretence of forest or crown-lands; corruption and bribery compounded for, with impunities granted for the future, as gave evident proof, that the king never meant, nor could it stand with the reason of his affairs, ever to recall Parliaments: having brought by these irregular courses the people's interest and his own to so direct an opposition that he might foresee plainly, it nothing

[20]Despite his political and military bungling, George Villiers (1592–1628), duke of Buckingham, who had been loaded with honors by James I, increased his power and his unpopularity after Charles' accession to the throne. Saved from impeachment only by the young King's dissolution of his first Parliament in 1625, he was not so lucky in the following year; and when, in August 1628, he was finally struck down by an assassin (see p.791) the act was viewed in certain quarters as a proof of providential intervention.

[21]A parliamentary *Declaration* of 17 January 1648 (explaining the decision to make "no more addresses to the King") revived many of the charges that had been brought against Buckingham in the early years of Charles' reign.

[22]The dissolution (*breaking*) of Charles' third—and, for eleven years, last—Parliament was prompted by unprecedented hostility between the crown and House of Commons.

[23]Following the dissolution of his second and third Parliaments, Charles issued declarations highly critical of what he regarded as invasions of his royal prerogatives.

[24]Capable of being moved by entreaty.

[25]For a somewhat fuller statement of these grievances against Charles during the years (1629–1640) when he dispensed with Parliament, see pp. 914 ff.

[26]When Naboth the Jezreelite refused to give his vineyard to King Ahab, Queen Jezebel contrived the good man's judicial murder and then the seizure of his property. See 1 Kings 21.1–16.

but a Parliament could save the people, it must necessarily be his undoing.

Till eight or nine years after, proceeding with a high hand in these enormities, and having the second time levied an injurious war against his native country, Scotland, and finding all those other shifts of raising money, which bore out his first expedition, now to fail him, not "of his own choice and inclination," as any child may see, but urged by strong necessities, and the very pangs of state, which his own violent proceedings had brought him to, he calls a Parliament: first in Ireland, which only was to give him four subsidies, and so to expire;[27] then in England, where his first demand was but twelve subsidies to maintain a Scotch war,[28] condemned and abominated by the whole kingdom, promising their grievances should be considered afterward. Which when the Parliament, who judged that war itself one of their main grievances, made no haste to grant, not enduring the delay of his impatient will, or else fearing the conditions of their grant, he breaks off the whole session, and dismisses them and their grievances with scorn and frustration.[29]

Much less therefore did he call this last Parliament[30] by his own choice and inclination; but having first tried in vain all undue ways to procure money, his army of their own accord being beaten in the north, the lords petitioning, and the general voice of the people almost hissing him and his ill-acted regality off the stage, compelled at length both by his wants and by his fears, upon mere extremity he summoned this last Parliament. And how is it possible that he should willingly incline to Parliaments who never was perceived to call them but for the greedy hope of a whole national bribe, his subsidies; and never loved, never fulfilled, never promoted the true end of Parliaments, the redress of grievances; but still put them off, and prolonged[31] them, whether gratified or not gratified; and was indeed the author of all those grievances? To say, therefore, that he called this Parliament of his own choice and inclination argues how little truth we can expect from the sequel[32] of this book, which ventures in the very first period to affront more than one nation with an untruth so remarkable; and presumes a more implicit faith in the people of England than the pope ever commanded from the Romish laity, or else a natural sottishness fit to be abused and ridden. While in the judgment of wise men, by laying the foundation of his defence on the avouchment of that which is so manifestly untrue he hath given a worse foil[33] to his own cause than when his whole forces were at any time overthrown. They, therefore, who think such great service done to the king's affairs in publishing this book, will find themselves in the end mistaken, if sense and right mind, or but any mediocrity of knowledge and remembrance, hath not quite forsaken men. . . .

[Proceeding relentlessly—almost clause by clause—through the first chapter of *Eikon Basilike* in order to expose its errors and deceits, Milton finally comes to "A Prayer in Time of Captivity," with which the king was alleged to have solaced his afflictions.]

And this is the substance of his first section, till we come to the devout[34] of it, modeled into the form of a private

psalter. Which they who so much admire, either for the matter or the manner, may as well admire the archbishop's late breviary,[35] and many other as good manuals and handmaids of devotion, the lip-work of every prelatical liturgist, clapped together and quilted out of Scripture phrase with as much ease and as little need of Christian diligence or judgment as belongs to the compiling of any ordinary and saleable piece of English divinity[36] that the shops value. But he who from such a kind of psalmistry, or any other verbal devotion, without the pledge and earnest of suitable deeds, can be persuaded of a zeal and true righteousness in the person, hath much yet to learn, and knows not that the deepest policy of a tyrant hath been ever to counterfeit religious. And Aristotle, in his *Politics*,[37] hath mentioned that special craft among twelve other tyrannical sophisms. Neither want we examples: Andronicus Comnenus,[38] the Byzantine emperor, though a most cruel tyrant, is reported by Nicetas[39] to have been a constant reader of Saint Paul's Epistles, and by continual study had so incorporated the phrase and style of that transcendent apostle into all his familiar letters that the imitation seemed to vie with the original. Yet this availed not to deceive the people of that empire, who, notwithstanding his saint's vizard, tore him to pieces for his tyranny.

From stories of this nature both ancient and modern which abound, the poets also, and some English, have been in this point so mindful of decorum as to put never more pious words in the mouth of any person than of a tyrant. I shall not instance an abstruse author wherein the king might be less conversant, but one whom we well know was the closest companion of these his solitudes, William Shakespeare, who introduces the person of Richard III speaking in as high a strain of piety and mortification as is uttered in any passage of this book, and sometimes to the same sense and purpose with some words in this place: "I intended," saith he, "not only to oblige my friends but mine enemies." The like saith Richard (Act II, Scene i):

> I do not know that Englishman alive
> With whom my soul is any jot at odds
> More than the infant that is born tonight.
> I thank my God for my humility.

[27]At the urging of the earl of Strafford in his capacity of lord-lieutenant, the Irish Parliament in 1640 voted Charles four subsidies of £45,000 each.
[28]The so-called Short Parliament (13 April–5 May 1640), which Charles reluctantly called only in order to get money for his war against the Scots.
[29]For another account by Milton of the tumultuous events of 1639–40 see p. 778.
[30]The so-called Long Parliament (3 November 1640–16 March 1660). [31]Adjourned. [32]Remainder. [33]Injury.
[34]Devotional part.
[35]In 1637, when Charles and Archbishop Laud ordered the Scots to replace John Knox's Book of Common Order with the Anglican Prayer Book, the response was so violent that the king at last revoked the order (September 1638). [36]Theology. [37]V.ix.15.
[38]An eastern emperor who, after a licentious and disordered reign, was killed by a mob in 1185.
[39]Nicetas Acominatus (d. ca. 1215), Byzantine historian.

Other stuff of this sort may be read throughout the whole tragedy, wherein the poet used not much license in departing from the truth of history, which delivers[40] him a deep dissembler not of his affections only but of religion.

In praying, therefore, and in the outward work of devotion, this king, we see, hath not at all exceeded the worst of kings before him. But herein the worst of kings, professing Christianism, have by far exceeded him. They, for aught we know, have still prayed their own, or at least borrowed from fit authors. But this king, not content with that which, although in a thing holy, is no holy theft, to attribute to his own making other men's whole prayers hath, as it were, unhallowed and unchristened the very duty of prayer itself by borrowing to a Christian use prayers offered to a heathen god. Who would have imagined so little fear in him of the true, all-seeing Deity, so little reverence of the Holy Ghost, whose office is to dictate and present our Christian prayers, so little care of truth in his last words or honor to himself or to his friends, or sense of his afflictions or of that sad hour which was upon him, as immediately before his death to pop into the hand of that grave bishop[41] who attended him, for a special relic of his saintly exercises, a prayer stolen word for word from the mouth of a heathen fiction praying to a heathen god, and that in no serious book, but the vain amatorious poem of Sir Philip Sidney's *Arcadia*—a book in that kind full of worth and wit, but among religious thoughts and duties not worthy to be named, nor to be read at any time without good caution, much less in time of trouble and affliction to be a Christian's prayer book?[42]

They who are yet incredulous of what I tell them for a truth, that this philippic[43] prayer is no part of the king's goods, may satisfy their own eyes at leisure in the third book of Sir Philip's *Arcadia*, page 248, comparing Pamela's prayer with the first prayer of His Majesty, delivered to Dr. Juxon immediately before his death and entitled "A Prayer in Time of Captivity," printed in all the best editions of his book. . . .

Certainly they that will may now see at length how much they were deceived in him and were ever like to be hereafter, who cared not, so near the minute of his death, to deceive his best and dearest friends with the trumpery of such a prayer, not more secretly than shamefully purloined, yet given them as the royal issue of his own proper zeal. And sure it was the hand of God to let them fall and be taken in such a foolish trap as hath exposed them to all derision, if for nothing else to throw contempt and disgrace in the sight of all men upon this his idolized book and the whole rosary of his prayers, thereby testifying how little he accepted them from those who thought no better of the living God than of a buzzard[44] idol, fit to be so served and worshipped in reversion[45] with the polluted orts[46] and refuse of Arcadias and romances, without being able to discern the affront rather than the worship of such an ethnic[47] prayer. . . .

Thus much be said in general to his prayers, and in special to that Arcadian prayer used in his captivity, enough to undeceive us what esteem we are to set upon the rest. For he certainly, whose mind could serve him to seek a Christian prayer out of a pagan legend and assume it for his own, might gather up the rest God knows from whence—one perhaps out of the French *Astraea*, another out of the Spanish *Diana*; *Amadis* and *Palmerin*[48] could hardly scape him. Such a person, we may be sure, had it not in him to make a prayer of his own, or at least would excuse himself the pains and cost of his invention so long as such sweet rhapsodies of heathenism and knight-errantry could yield him prayers. How dishonorable then, and how unworthy of a Christian king, were these ignoble shifts to seem holy and to get a saintship among the ignorant and wretched people, to draw them by this deception, worse than all his former injuries, to go awhoring after him! And how unhappy, how forsook of grace and unbeloved of God that people who resolve to know no more of piety or of goodness than to account him their chief saint and martyr whose bankrupt devotion came not honestly by his very prayers, but having sharked them from the mouth of a heathen worshipper (detestable to teach him prayers) sold them to those that stood and honored him next to the Messiah as his own heavenly compositions in adversity, for hopes no less vain and presumptuous—and death at that time so imminent upon him—than by these goodly relics to be held a saint and martyr in opinion with the cheated people.

And thus far in the whole chapter we have seen and considered, and it cannot but be clear to all men, how and for what ends, what concernments and necessities, the late king was no way induced but every way constrained to call this last Parliament. Yet here in his first prayer he trembles not to avouch, as in the ears of God, "That he did it with an upright intention, to his glory, and his people's good." Of which dreadful attestation, how sincerely meant, God, to whom it was avowed, can only judge; and He hath judged already, and hath written His impartial sentence in characters legible to all Christendom, and besides hath taught us that there be some whom He hath given over to delusion, whose very mind and conscience is defiled—of whom Saint Paul to Titus makes mention.[49]

[40]Declares.
[41]William Juxon (1582–1663), bishop of London. For his services to the king during his imprisonment, trial, and execution, Juxon was rewarded by Charles II with the archbishopric of Canterbury in 1660. See p. 917
[42]On Sidney's *Arcadia* as the source of Charles' "Prayer in Time of Captivity" see p. 616.
[43]Pertaining to (Sir) Philip (Sidney).   [44]Senseless.
[45]In law, reversion is the right of succeeding to an estate after the previous occupant's death or forfeiture. Milton thus implies that Charles had resorted to plagiarism in order to appear devout.
[46]Scraps. [47]Pagan.
[48]Of these immensely popular works of fiction Honoré d'Urfé's *L'Astrée* (1610–27) was a series of dialogues between two courtly lovers, Celadon and Astrée; Jorge Montemayor's *Diana Enamorada* (ca. 1559) was one of Sidney's models for the *Arcadia*; the 14th-century *Amadis of Gaul* and the 16th-century *Palmerin of England* had been translated and adapted through all of western Europe.
[49]Titus 1.15.

John Gauden [1605-1662]

Whatever its literary attractions, *Eikon Basilike* was one of the most successful books of the seventeenth or any other century. As the "portraiture" of Charles I "in his solitudes and sufferings" the work was allegedly from the martyred king's own hand but most likely put together from Charles' drafts and memoranda by John Gauden, a royalist divine who was subsequently rewarded with the sees of Exeter and Worcester. It is a series of twenty-seven essays or meditations, each followed by a prayer, on some of the principal events of the troubled years between the convening of the Long Parliament in 1640 and the king's imprisonment in Carisbrooke Castle in 1647. In an epistle "To the Prince of Wales" (Chapter XXVII), the author said he hoped to be instructive:

> Son, if these papers with some others, wherein I have set down the private reflections of my conscience and my most impartial thoughts touching the chief passages which have been most remarkable or disputed in my late troubles, come to your hands, to whom they are chiefly designed, they may be so far useful to you as to state your judgment aright in what hath passed, whereof a pious is the best use can be made; and may they also give you some directions how to remedy the present distempers and prevent, if God will, the like for time to come.

And so as the writer remembers and explains such crises as the earl of Strafford's execution in 1641 (Chapter II), the king's departure from London in 1642 (Chapter VI), the outbreak of hostilities (Chapter IX), the abortive negotiations at Uxbridge in 1645 (Chapter XVIII), the king's surrender to the Scots in 1646 (Chapter XXII), and the closing scenes of this great drama (Chapter XXVIII), his intentions are apparent: to trace the history of a crucial time, to vindicate a fallen cause, and to reassert the claims of royal power.

His success was so prompt and overwhelming that *Eikon Basilike* must be regarded as one of the most triumphant works of propaganda ever written. Copies were in print, it seems, when Charles, in his finest and most regal hour, died a felon's death at Whitehall on 30 January 1649, and a few weeks later some two thousand had been sold by furtive hawkers at the exorbitant sum of fifteen shillings each. The demand continued so insatiable that there were thirty-five editions within a year of Charles' execution; and after the printer William Dugard published (15 March 1649) such addenda as four new royal prayers (one of which was plagiarized from Sir Philip Sidney's *Arcadia*), a letter from the Prince of Wales to his beleaguered father, and various "relations" of the king's last words to members of his family, the work became, if possible, still more poignant and appealing. Charles himself had prudently commissioned a Latin translation by John Earle—as a young man noted for his brilliant characters (see pp. 722 ff.) but now a royal chaplain—and this, together with others based upon it, so well assured the work its European reputation that at least twenty versions (in Dutch, French, German, and Danish) appeared before the Restoration.

Since, as Gauden boasted later, the "King's Book" became "an army, and did vanquish more than any sword could," the regicides were obliged to discredit it by any means at their disposal. When efforts to prevent its publication and then to stop its many new editions failed, another tack was tried with counterpropaganda. An anonymous rebuttal entitled *Eikon Alethine* (ca. August 1649) was quickly followed (October 1649) by Milton's *Eikonoklastes* (see pp. 609 ff.). Milton, who had been named secretary for foreign tongues to the Council of State the March before, says that he did not propose to "descant on the misfortunes" of a fallen foe who had "paid his final debt both to nature and his faults," but he concedes that his task had been "assigned," not "chosen or affected." His chapter-by-chapter refutation is notable not only for its laborious demonstration of the errors and "missayings" of the King, but also for its startling revelation that the source of Charles' alleged "Prayer in Time of Captivity" was "stolen word for word from the mouth of a heathen fiction praying to a heathen god, and that in no serious work, but the vain amatorious poem of Sir Philip Sidney's *Arcadia*." Milton may have scored a telling point, but nonetheless he lived to see, deplore, and suffer from the triumph of King Charles' son.

I have based my text on Εἰκὼν Βασιλική. *The Portraicture of His Sacred Maiestie in His Solitudes and Sufferings. Whereunto Are annexed His Praiers and Apophthegms, &c.,* [1649] (Wing E-269). Although F. F. Madan's view, in his exhaustive and authoritative *New Bibliography of the Eikon Basilike of King Charles the First* (1950), that Gauden was the author has not gone uncontested, it is now generally accepted. For a discussion of S. B. Lilegren's charge that Milton and John Bradshaw, the regicide, arranged the plagiarism from Sidney in order to jeopardize the mounting reputation of the book, see Merritt Hughes' introduction to *Eikonoklastes* in the Yale edition of Milton's *Complete Prose Works*, III (1962), 147–67. There is a modern edition of *Eikon Basilike* by Philip A. Knachel (1966), who in his introduction conveniently summarizes Madan's labyrinthine data.

from Eikon Basilike:[1] The Portraiture of His Sacred Majesty in His Solitudes and Sufferings (1649)

I. UPON HIS MAJESTY'S CALLING THIS LAST PARLIAMENT

This last Parliament[2] I called, not more by others' advice and necessity of my affairs than by my own choice and inclination, who have always thought the right way of Parliaments most safe for my crown and best pleasing to my people. And although I was not forgetful of those sparks which some men's distempers formerly studied to kindle in Parliaments (which by forbearing to convene for some years I hoped to have extinguished),[3] yet resolving with myself to give all just satisfaction to modest and sober desires, and to redress all public grievances in church and state, I hoped, by my freedom and their moderation, to prevent all misunderstandings and miscarriages in this; in which, as I feared affairs would meet with some passion and prejudice in other men, so I resolved they should find least of them in myself, not doubting but by the weight of reason I should counterpoise the overbalancings of any factions.

I was indeed sorry to hear with what partiality and popular heat elections were carried in many places, yet, hoping that the gravity and discretion of other gentlemen would allay and fix the Commons to a due temperament, guiding some men's well-meaning zeal by such rules of moderation as are best both to preserve and restore the health of all states and kingdoms, no man was better pleased with the convening of this Parliament than myself; who, knowing best the largeness of my own heart toward my people's good and just contentment, pleased myself most in that good and firm understanding which would hence grow between me and my people.

All jealousies being laid aside, my own and my children's interests gave me many obligations to seek and preserve the love and welfare of my subjects, the only temporal blessing that is left to the ambition of just monarchs, as their greatest honor and safety next God's protection. I cared not to lessen myself in some things of my wonted prerogative, since I knew I could be no loser if I might gain but a recompense in my subjects' affections.

I intended not only to oblige my friends, but mine enemies also, exceeding even the desires of those that were factiously discontented if they did but pretend to any modest and sober sense.

The odium and offenses which some men's rigor or remissness in church and state had contracted upon my government I resolved to have expiated by such laws and regulations for the future as might not only rectify what was amiss in practice but supply what was defective in the constitution, no man having a greater zeal to see religion settled and preserved in truth, unity, and order than myself, whom it most concerns both in piety and policy, as knowing that

EIKON BASILIKE [1]"The royal image."
[2]The so-called Long Parliament (1640–60), which Charles convened with great reluctance and during whose protracted sittings he was ultimately deposed and executed (1649).
[3]Outraged by what he regarded as parliamentary attacks on his royal prerogative, Charles had ruled without Parliament for eleven years (1629–40).

no flames of civil dissensions are more dangerous than those which make religious pretensions the grounds of factions.

I resolved to reform what I should, by free and full advice in Parliament, be convinced to be amiss, and to grant whatever my reason and conscience told me was fit to be desired. I wish I had kept myself within those bounds and not suffered my own judgment to have been overborne in some things, more by others' importunities than their arguments. My confidence had less betrayed myself and my kingdoms to those advantages which some men sought for who wanted nothing but power and occasion to do mischief.

But our sins being ripe, there was no preventing of God's justice from reaping that glory in our calamities which we robbed Him of in our prosperity.

For Thou, O Lord, hast made us see that resolutions of future reforming do not always satisfy Thy justice, nor prevent Thy vengeance for former miscarriages.
Our sins have overlaid our hopes; Thou hast taught us to depend on Thy mercies to forgive, not on our purpose to amend. . . .
O Thou Sovereign Goodness and Wisdom, who overrulest all our counsels, overrule also all our hearts, that the worse things we suffer by Thy justice, the better may be by Thy mercy.
As our sins have turned our antidotes into poison, so let Thy grace turn our poisons into antidotes.
As the sins of our peace disposed us to this unhappy war, so let this war prepare us for Thy blessed peace.
That although I have but troublesome kingdoms here, yet I may attain to that kingdom of peace in my heart and in Thy heaven which Christ hath purchased and Thou wilt give to Thy servant, though a sinner, for my Saviour's sake. Amen.

. . . . . .

PRAYERS USED BY HIS MAJESTY IN THE TIME OF HIS SUFFERINGS, DELIVERED TO DOCTOR JUXON, BISHOP OF LONDON, IMMEDIATELY BEFORE HIS DEATH . . . 4

A PRAYER IN TIME OF CAPTIVITY

O powerful and eternal God, to whom nothing is so great that it may resist, or so small that it is contemned, look upon my misery with Thine eye of mercy and let Thine infinite power vouchsafe to limit out some proportion of

deliverance unto me as to Thee shall seem most convenient. Let not injury, O Lord, triumph over me, and let my faults by Thy hand be corrected, and make not my unjust enemies the ministers of Thy justice. But yet, my God, if in Thy wisdom this be the aptest chastisement for my unexcusable transgressions, if this ungrateful bondage be fittest for my overhigh desires, if the pride of my not enough humble heart be thus to be broken, O Lord, I yield unto Thy will and cheerfully embrace what sorrow Thou wilt have me suffer. Only thus much let me crave of Thee (let my craving, O Lord, be accepted of, since it even proceeds from Thee), that by Thy goodness, which is Thyself, Thou wilt suffer some beam of Thy Majesty so to shine in my mind that I, who acknowledge it my noblest title to be Thy creature, may still in my greatest afflictions depend confidently on Thee. Let calamity be the exercise but not the overthrow of my virtue. O let not their prevailing power be to my destruction. And if it be Thy will that they more and more vex me with punishment, yet, O Lord, never let their wickedness have such a hand but that I may still carry a pure mind and steadfast resolution ever to serve Thee without fear or presumption, yet with that humble confidence which may best please Thee, so that at the last I may come to Thy eternal kingdom through the merits of Thy Son, our alone Saviour, Jesus Christ. Amen.[5]

[4]This section—together with such additional material as a letter from the Prince of Wales to his father, several anecdotes of Charles' last days, and some apothegms culled from the text of *Eikon Basilike*—was added to an edition of *Eikon Basilike* printed by William Dugard on 15 March 1649. This material was so popular that it was not only included in most subsequent editions of the work but also added to unsold copies of the earlier editions.
[5]Although Milton charged (p. 613) that this famous passage was "stolen word for word" from Pamela's prayer in the 1590 edition of Sir Philip Sidney's *Arcadia* (III.vi), there are several minor verbal changes and one important alteration at the end, when Pamela's plea for the safety of her lover Musidorus is replaced by Charles' for his own salvation. In Sidney, the conclusion is as follows: " 'Let calamity be the exercise but not the overthrow of my virtue. Let their power prevail, but prevail not to destruction. Let my greatness be their prey; let my pain be the sweetness of their revenge; let them, if so it seem good unto Thee, vex me with more and more punishment. But, O Lord, let never their wickedness have such a hand but that I may carry a pure mind in a pure body.' And pausing a while, 'And, O most gracious Lord,' said she, 'whatever become of me, preserve the virtuous Musidorus!' " See *The Countesse of Pembrokes Arcadia* (ed. Albert Feuillerat, 1922), pp. 282–283.

The Cambridge Platonists

The so-called Cambridge Platonists did not constitute a school or sect or even cult, but as a group of like-minded academics who shared—sometimes very loosely—certain aversions and attachments they made their presence felt. These men, almost all of them from Emmanuel College, Cambridge, were idealists who found, or thought they found, a primal unity and radiance of spirit beneath and beyond such distractions as sectarian controversy and sensory illusion, and so they recoiled from both Puritan dogmatism and Hobbesian or Cartesian materialism to embrace those "intelligible forms" of goodness, truth, and beauty that they believed to be implanted as "truths of first inscription" in the human soul and to define the moral structure of the universe.

Not that they were all alike: Benjamin Whichcote and his students John Smith and Nathanael Culverwel spent their lives in teaching, preaching, and research, and had published nothing when they died, whereas Henry More (from Christ's) was regrettably indefatigable in both prose and verse while Ralph Cudworth was toiling for thirty years or more on *The True Intellectual System of the Universe*, a gigantic and encyclopedic answer to the atheists and materialists. With his homely common sense, Whichcote thought that all eccentric, "enthusiastic" doctrines were "good things strained out of their wits," but his disciple Smith (whose *Discourses* swarm with erudite allusions) urged the "knitting" of the soul to God in mystic rapture as the highest stage of knowledge. Nonetheless, their ideological and personal affinities enable us to treat them as a group, with Whichcote as their animating source. It was his profound conviction that " 'the spirit of a man is the candle of the Lord,' lighted by God and lighting us to God, *res illuminata, illuminans*," and this text from Proverbs (20.27) serves as well as any to adumbrate the theology, ethics, and even metaphysics to which these learned, pious men subscribed.

Whichcote (1609–83) must have had uncommon power and charm and candor, for following his A.B. at Emmanuel (1629–30) he became and long remained a vital force at Cambridge, first as a fellow of his college and after 1636 as a lecturer at Trinity Church. Since he refused to take the Covenant so dear to triumphant and dogmatic Puritans, his appointment by Parliament as provost of King's College, where he succeeded an ejected royalist in 1644, must be regarded as a tribute to the man rather than as a guerdon to the politician. Through all these troubled years—and despite a controversy in the early fifties with his former tutor Anthony Tuckney, then master of Emmanuel—he remained a tonic, civilizing figure on the Cambridge scene until the Restoration. Although then stripped of his appointments, he complied with the Act of Uniformity, and so continued his benign and influential ministry at St. Anne's, Blackfriars, then (after the Great Fire) at Milton in Cambridgeshire, and finally St. Lawrence Jewry, where John Tillotson preached his funeral sermon in 1683. "Never passionate, never peremptory," according to his eulogist, Whichcote was

> so far from imposing upon others that he was rather apt to yield. And though he had a most profound and well-poised judgment, yet was he of all men I ever knew the most patient to hear others differ from him, and the most easy to be convinced when good reason was offered; and, which is seldom seen, more apt to be favorable to another man's reason than his own.

Although Whichcote published nothing, certain of his works were eventually stitched together and issued as *Select Sermons* (1698) and *Several Discourses* (4 vols., 1701–07). According to Samuel Salter, his eighteenth-century editor, some five thousand of his famous aphorisms, "whether digested or loose and imperfect," were collected by his friend John Jeffery, who arranged to have a thousand of them printed at Norwich in 1703. In 1753 Salter himself, working with the "transcripts" made by Jeffery, reordered and expanded this material into twelve hundred *Moral and Religious Aphorisms*, together with eight letters wherein Whichcote and Tuckney had explored their disagreements over rigid Calvinism a hundred years before.

Ralph Cudworth (1617–88) arrived at Cambridge two years after Whichcote took his first degree, and there he stayed until he died. Combining uncommon erudition (especially in Hebrew) with marked administrative skill, he progressed in 1645 from a fellowship at Emmanuel to the mastership of Clare Hall (where he, like Whichcote, supplanted an ejected royalist), and thereafter, as Regius Professor of Hebrew (1645) and master of Christ's (1654), he adorned his university for almost forty years. Although his two great monuments—*The True Intellectual System of the Universe* (1678) and the posthumous *Treatise Concerning Eternal and Immutable Morality* (1731)—are among the most imposing products of the period, it is as a Christian moralist rather than as a polymath that he is represented here. Indeed, in his famous sermon preached before the House of Commons in 1647—when he was only thirty—a certain kind of acrid scholarship is shown to be a peril to the Christian. In the preface to his sermon Cudworth, perhaps anticipating a misconstruction of his views, calls "ingenuous learning" to the bulwark of religion, but the sermon itself is not a work of learning or a defense of erudition. It is, rather, a stirring plea for goodness and compassion and conciliation at a time when the heat and smoke of disputation—both political and theological—seemed to suffocate the simple Christian virtues. Cudworth tells the politicians that controversy, however craftily reinforced by learning, is bound to be the bane of Christian living, for it is not "wrangling disputes and syllogistical reasons" that certify the conquering force of truth, but "the holiness of our hearts and lives."

> Ink and paper can never make us Christians, can never beget a new nature, a living principle in us, can never form Christ or any true notions of spiritual things in our hearts. The gospel, that new law which Christ delivered to the world, is not merely a letter without us, but a quickening spirit within us. Cold theorems and maxims, dry and jejune disputes, lean syllogistical reasons could never yet of themselves beget the least glimpse of true heavenly light, the least sap of saving knowledge in any heart.

Although John Smith (1618–52) died young and published nothing, he, like his master Whichcote, seemed to galvanize his students and his friends. As one of his admirers said, "I never got so much good among all my books by a whole day's plodding in a study as by an hour's discourse I have got with him." First at Emmanuel (A.B. 1640) and then at Queen's (where he became a fellow in 1644), he was so famous for his goodness and his erudition that when he died, a "living library" of only thirty-four, the sense of shock and grief was numbing. "It grieved me in my thoughts," said Simon Patrick at his funeral in the college chapel, "that there should be so many orphans left without a father, a society left naked without one of her best guardians and chieftains, her very chariot and horsemen."

Smith, like Whichcote, cared so little for his own renown that it remained the kindly office of his friends to prepare his work for publication. According to John Worthington, editor of the ten *Select Discourses* that appeared in 1660, the assignment posed real problems. Smith's papers were so "loose and scattered" and his mind was such "a bountiful and ever-bubbling fountain" that the manuscripts could scarcely be reduced to order. We may therefore assume that considerable editorial discretion (and even carpentry) was needed to achieve the shapely essays on superstition, atheism, the immortality of the soul, the existence and nature of God, prophecy, and similarly edifying subjects in the 1660 volume.

My texts are based upon *Moral and Religious Aphorisms. Collected from the Manuscript Papers of The Reverend and Learned Doctor Whichcote; and Published in MDCCIII, By Dr. Jeffery. Now republished, with very large Additions, from the Transcripts of the latter, By Samuel Salter, D. D., 1753;* Ralph Cudworth, *A Sermon Preached before the Honourable House of Commons, At Westminster, March 31. 1647*, 1647 (Wing C-7469); *Select Discourses . . . By John Smith, late Fellow of Queen's College in Cambridge*, 1660 (Wing S-4117).

Whichcote's other posthumously published works—some put together from the author's and his listeners' notes—include the *Select Sermons* (1698, 1742), *Several Discourses* (ed. J. Jeffery, 4 vols., 1701–07), and a collection of his *Works* (4 vols., 1751). Cudworth's *True Intellectual System of the Universe* (1678) has been edited by Thomas Birch (2 vols., 1743) and J. Harrison (3 vols., 1845), and his *Treatise Concerning Eternal and Immutable Morality* was published posthumously in 1731. His career has been thoroughly treated by J. A. Passmore (1951). Following Worthington's compilation, Smith's *Select Discourses* were republished in 1673, 1821, and 1859 (ed. H. G. Williams).

There are anthologies of the Cambridge Platonists by E. T. Campagnac (1901), Gerald Cragg (1968), and C. A. Patrides (1969), the last with excellent notes and apparatus. In addition to works about these thinkers by F. J. Powicke (1926), G. P. H. Pawson (1930), W. C. de Pauley (*The Candle of the Lord*, 1937), J. J. de Boer (*The Theory of Knowledge of the Cambridge Platonists*, 1931), and E. M. Austin (*Ethics of the Cambridge Platonists,* 1935), they come in for serious attention from Cassirer, Cragg (*From Puritanism to the Age of Reason*), and Tulloch, as cited in the General Bibliography, Section III. Nathanael Culverwel's *Discourse of the Light of the Light of Nature* (1652)—one of the important monuments to the thinking of the Cambridge Platonists—has been edited (1971) by Robert A. Greene and Hugh MacCallum.

Benjamin Whichcote [1609-1683]

from Moral and Religious Aphorisms (1753)

CENTURY I

4. If there be no knowledge, there is no beginning of religion; if there be no goodness, there is no sincerity of religion, but a contradiction to it by "holding the truth in unrighteousness."[1]

8. God made man intelligent and voluntary, and the law of his nature and the reason of his mind God intended for the great rule of his life to take place in all particulars where God did not think good farther to express His will and declare His pleasure.

24. There is a natural propension[2] in everything to return to its true state if by violence it has been disturbed: should it not be so in Grace, in the divine life? Virtue is the health, true state, natural complexion of the soul; he that is vicious in his practice is diseased in his mind.

35. Everyone that is honestly disposed may find direction for what he is to do from right reason and plain Scripture: the only ways by which men are taught of God, nor is there any other teaching necessary.

42. Man, as man, is averse to what is evil and wicked, for evil is unnatural and good is connatural to man.

58. Those that differ upon reason may come together by reason.

68. It had been better for the Christian church if that which calls itself Catholic had been less employed in creating pretended faith and more employed in maintaining universal charity.

76. To go against reason is to go against God. It is the selfsame thing to do that which the reason of the case doth require and that which God himself doth appoint. Reason is the divine governor of man's life; it is the very voice of God.

99. Reason discovers what is natural, and reason receives what is supernatural.

CENTURY II

109. God hath set up two lights to enlighten us in our way: the light of reason, which is the light of His creation, and the light of Scripture, which is after-revelation from Him. Let us make use of these two lights and suffer neither to be put out.

114. Nothing spoils human nature more than false zeal. The good nature of an heathen is more godlike than the furious zeal of a Christian.

116. Good and evil are not by positive institution, are not things arbitrary or during any pleasure whatsoever; but just, right, and holy, wicked, impious, and profane are so by their own nature and quality. If we understand this as we ought, we abide in the truth; if not, we are self-flatterers, and life in a lie. Things are as they are, whether we think so or not; and we shall be judged by things as they be, not by our own presumptuous imaginations.

121. In the use of reason and the exercise of virtue we enjoy God.

130. Our fallibility and the shortness of our knowledge should make us peaceable and gentle. Because I *may* be mistaken I *must* not be dogmatical and confident, peremptory and imperious. I will not break the certain laws of charity for a doubtful doctrine or of uncertain truth.

168. If there be anything monstrous or prodigious in nature it is a proud creature and an insolent sinner.

APHORISMS [1]Romans 1.18. [2]Propensity.

169. Religion begins in knowledge, proceeds in practice, and ends in happiness.

178. Govern thyself from within.

CENTURY III

212. Vice is contrary to the nature of man, as man, for it is contrary to the order of reason, the peculiar and highest principle in man; nor is anything in itself more unnatural or of greater deformity in the whole world than that an intelligent agent should have the truth of things in his mind and that it should not give law and rule to his temper, life, and actions.

221. The moral part of religion never alters. Moral laws are laws of themselves, without sanction by will; and the necessity of them arises from the things themselves. All other things in religion are in order to these. The moral part of religion does sanctify the soul, and is final both to what is instrumental and instituted.

236. Truth is connatural to a man's soul, and in conjunction with it becomes the mind's temper and complexion and constitution.

248. We worship God best when we resemble Him most.

253. Whosoever doth commit sin departeth from the natural use of himself, his powers and faculties; he sinks below his own nature, for there is no natural action so mean as every sinful action is. Sin is below any man; sin is every man's dishonor.

290. We must *now* naturalize ourselves to the employment of eternity.

291. Religion doth not destroy nature, but is built upon it.

298. In morality we are sure as in mathematics.

CENTURY IV

339. If you would be religious, be rational in your religion.

349. Enthusiasm is the confounder both of reason and religion; therefore nothing is more necessary to the interest of religion than the prevention of enthusiasm.

367. Good men study to spiritualize their bodies; bad men do incarnate their souls.[3]

377. He that is conceited of his wisdom is readier to impose error than to receive truth.

379. None are known to be good till they have opportunity to be bad.

393. I have always found that such preaching of others hath most commanded my heart which hath most illuminated my head.

CENTURY V

444. The truths of God are connatural to the soul of man, and the soul of man makes no more resistance to them than the air does to light.

457. There is nothing so intrinsically rational as religion is, nothing that can so justify itself, nothing that hath so pure reason to recommend itself as religion hath.

460. Reason is not a shallow thing; it is the first participation from God; therefore he that observes reason observes God.

464. Heaven is *first* a temper and *then* a place.

479. The government of man should be the monarchy of reason; it is too often a democracy of passions or anarchy of humors.

500. The longest sword, the strongest lungs, the most voices are false measures of truth.

CENTURY VI

523. Nothing is more unnatural to men than wickedness, for wickedness is contrary to the reason of the mind and to the reason of things: contrary to the reason of the mind, which is our governor, and contrary to the reason of things, which is our law.

530. We are no more than second causes, and our sufficiency is only in God, who is the First. A second cause is no cause, divided from the First.

561. The law of nature is that which is reason, which is right and fit. Will stands for nothing in disjunction from reason and right, and our apprehensions of right are regulated by the nature of things. To give will or power for reason is contrary to reason. Will is no rule, no justification of anything.

590. Morality is the congruity and proportion that is between the actions of rational beings and the objects of those actions.

598. We ought to *be* such as we intend to *appear*.

CENTURY VII

625. The spirit of God in us is a living law informing the soul, not constrained by a law without, that enlivens not; but we act in the power of an inward principle of life which enables, inclines, facilitates, determines. Our nature is reconciled to the law of heaven, the rule of everlasting righteousness, goodness, and truth.

644. True reason is so far from being an enemy to any matter of faith that a man is disposed and qualified by reason for the entertaining those matters of faith that are proposed by God.

679. Universal charity is a thing final in religion.

682. Sin is an attempt to control the immutable and unalterable laws of everlasting righteousness, goodness, and truth, upon which the universe depends.

CENTURY VIII

712. Religion, which is a bond of union, ought not to be a ground of division, but it is in an unnatural use when it doth

---

[3]Milton expresses the same idea in *Comus* (11. 467–69):
> The soul grows clotted by contagion,
> Imbodies and imbrutes, till she quite lose
> The divine property of her first being.

disunite. Men cannot differ by true religion because it is true religion to agree. The spirit of religion is a reconciling spirit.

726. There is a malignity in sin that poisons the nature of man, and through sin one man is formidable to another.

732. Mind and understanding were made for God and for eternity. Sense holds a proportion to worldly things and time.

734. Man, that is a moral agent, must be morally dealt withal.

737. Natural truths are truths of God's creation; supernatural truths are truths of God's revelation. Nothing is more knowable than natural truth; nothing is more credible than revealed truth.

743. Morality is not a means to anything but to happiness; everything else is a means to morality.

756. There is nothing more unnatural to religion than contentions about it.

783. Knowledge in the understanding is truth; in practice, is goodness.

CENTURY IX

811. Do not think God has done anything concerning thee before thou camest into being whereby thou art determined either to sin or misery. This is a falsehood, and they that entertain such thoughts live in a lie.

822. There must be great perfections than we are invested with, and man is an argument to himself that there is a God.

839. It is no less a divine work to restore the lapsed creation of God than it was to raise that creation out of nothing.

869. There is nothing in religion necessary which is uncertain.

880. Nothing without reason is to be proposed; nothing against reason is to be believed: Scripture is to be taken in a rational sense.

881. There is more solid satisfaction in good self-government than in all the forced jollities and pleasures of the world.

889. Christian religion is not mystical, symbolical, enigmatical, emblematical; but unclothed, unbodied, intellectual, rational, spiritual.

CENTURY X

916. "The spirit of a man is the candle of the Lord,"[4] lighted by God and lighting us to God, *res illuminata, illuminans.*[5]

917. Men are not so far to press the principles of God's creation as to neglect the grace of God, nor so far to depend upon the grace of God as to neglect the principles of God's creation.

925. He knows most who does best.

931. Truth is not only a man's ornament, but his instrument; it is the great man's glory and the poor man's stock. A man's truth is his livelihood, his recommendation, his letters of credit.

943. A man's reason is nowhere so much satisfied as in matters of faith.

947. The religious represent God to themselves as amiable; the superstitious represent God to themselves as formidable.

956. Religion doth possess and affect the whole man. In the understanding it is knowledge; in the life it is obedience; in the affections it is delight in God; in our carriage and behavior it is modesty, calmness, gentleness, quietness, candor, ingenuity. In our dealing it is uprightness, integrity, correspondence with the rule of righteousness. Religion makes men virtuous in all instances.

974. There is no fate, but on our part reason and prudence, on God's part providence; and this providence and all necessary help are as sure and certain as the existence and perfections of God.

990. Religion begets in us rational confidence and a transcendent pleasure.

CENTURY XI

1007. Religion is not a hearsay, a presumption, a supposition; is not a customary pretension and profession; is not an affectation of any mode; is not a piety or particular fancy, consisting in some pathetic devotions, vehement expressions, bodily severities, affected anomalies and aversions from the innocent usages of others, but consisteth in a profound humility and an universal charity.

1014. The more mysterious, the more imperfect. That which is mystically spoken is but half spoken. As darkness is in compare with light, so is mystery in comparison with knowledge.

1021. Reason is the foundation of nature; learning is the superstructure of art.

1030. How much easier is it quietly to enjoy than eagerly to contest! How vastly wiser!

1036. To multiply questions is not the way to improve religion: the zeal of man should be turned from curiosity of speculation to honesty of practice.

1082. Embodied acts, such as the sacramental are, are beneath acts purely mental and spiritual, such as prayer is. It is not for the credit of religion to lay all the stress upon one motion in religion and to be remiss in others, not to advance a temporary act, accommodate[6] to the state of imperfection, above acts purely spiritual, which are to continue to eternity.

1097. *Fear* is the denomination of the Old Testament; *believe* is the denomination of the New.

CENTURY XII

1104. The great excellence of Christ's sacrifice did consist in the moral considerations belonging to it.

1113. A good man's life is all of a piece.

1127. Religion is not a system of doctrines, an observance of modes, a heat of affections, a form of words, a spirit of censoriousness.

[4]Proverbs 20.27.
[5]Something lighted from within and also shedding light.
[6]Suitable.

1182. Enthusiastic doctrines—good things strained out of their wits. Among Christians, those that pretend to be inspired seem to be mad; among the Turks, those that are mad are thought to be inspired.

1186. It is not good to live in jest, since we must die in earnest.

1188. Where the doctrine is necessary and important, the Scripture is clear and full; but where the Scripture is not clear and full, the doctrine is not necessary or important.

1200. A rectified understanding that hath a settled judgment of truth, a sanctified nature reconciled to goodness, a pacified conscience discharged of guilt: these things are contained in a state of religion.

Ralph Cudworth [1617-1688]

A Sermon Preached Before the Honorable House of Commons at Westminster, March 31, 1647

1 John 2.3–4. "And hereby we do know that we know Him if we keep His commandments. He that saith, I know Him, and keepeth not His commandments, is a liar, and the truth is not in him."

We have much inquiry concerning knowledge in these latter times.[1] The sons of Adam are now as busy as ever himself was about the Tree of Knowledge of good and evil, shaking the boughs of it and scrambling for the fruit, whilst, I fear, many are too unmindful of the Tree of Life. And though there be now no cherubims with their flaming swords to fright men off from it, yet the way that leads to it seems to be solitary and untrodden, as if there were but few that had any mind to taste of the fruit of it. There be many that speak of new glimpses and discoveries of truth, of dawnings of gospel light; and no question but God hath reserved much of this for the very evening and sunset of the world, for in the latter days "knowledge shall be increased."[2] But yet I wish we could in the meantime see that day to dawn which the apostle speaks of, and that "daystar to arise in men's hearts."[3] I wish whilst we talk of light and dispute about truth we could walk more as "children of the light." Whereas if St. John's rule be good here in the text, that no man truly knows Christ but he that keepeth His commandments, it is much to be suspected that many of us which pretend to light have a thick and gloomy darkness within overspreading our souls.

There be now many large volumes and discourses written concerning Christ, thousands of controversies discussed, infinite problems determined concerning His divinity, humanity, union of both together, and what not, so that our bookish Christians, that have all their religion in writings and papers, think they are now completely furnished with all kind of knowledge concerning Christ; and when they see all their leaves lying about them they think they have a goodly stock of knowledge and truth, and cannot possibly miss of the way to heaven—as if religion were nothing but a little book-craft, a mere paper-skill. But if St. John's rule here be good, we must not judge of our knowing of Christ by our skill in books and papers, but by our keeping His commandments. And that, I fear, will discover many of us (notwithstanding all this light which we boast of round about us) to have nothing but Egyptian darkness within upon our hearts.

The vulgar sort think that they know Christ enough out of their creeds and catechisms and confessions of faith; and if they have but a little acquainted themselves with these, and like parrots conned the words of them, they doubt not but that they are sufficiently instructed in all the mysteries of the Kingdom of Heaven. Many of the more learned, if they can but wrangle and dispute about Christ, imagine themselves to be grown great proficients in the school of Christ. The greatest part of the world, whether learned or unlearned, think that there is no need of purging and purifying of their hearts for the right knowledge of Christ and His gospel; but though their lives be never so wicked, their hearts never so foul within, yet they may know Christ sufficiently out of their treatises and discourses, out of their mere systems and bodies of divinity; which I deny not to be useful in a subordinate way, although our Saviour prescribeth His disciples another method: to come to the right knowledge of divine truths by doing of God's will. "He that will do my Father's will," saith he, "shall know of the doctrine whether it be of God."[4] He is a true Christian indeed, not he that is only book-taught but he that is God-taught, he that hath an "unction from the Holy One"[5] (as our apostle calleth it) that teacheth him all things, he that hath the spirit of Christ within him, that searcheth out the deep things of God. "For as no man knoweth the things of a man save the spirit of man which is in him, even so the things of God knoweth no man but the spirit of God."[6]

Ink and paper can never make us Christians, can never beget a new nature, a living principle in us, can never form Christ or any true notions of spiritual things in our hearts.

SERMON PREACHED AT WESTMINSTER [1]For other statements of this popular notion of progressive deterioration see pp. 415 ff., 483, 871 ff. [2]Daniel 12.4. [3]2 Peter 1.19. [4]John 7.17. [5]1 John 2.20. [6]1 Corinthians 2.11.

The gospel, that new law which Christ delivered to the world, is not merely a letter without us, but a quickening spirit within us. Cold theorems and maxims, dry and jejune disputes, lean syllogistical reasons could never yet of themselves beget the least glimpse of true heavenly light, the least sap of saving knowledge in any heart. All this is but the groping of the poor, dark spirit of man after truth, to find it out with his own endeavors and feel it with his own cold and benumbed hands. Words and syllables, which are but dead things, cannot possibly convey the living notions of heavenly truths to us. The secret mysteries of a divine life, of a new nature, of Christ formed in our hearts, they cannot be written or spoken; language and expressions cannot reach them, neither can they ever be truly understood except the soul itself be kindled from within and awakened into the life of them. A painter that would draw a rose, though he may flourish some likeness of it in figure and color, yet he can never paint the scent and fragrancy; or if he would draw a flame, he cannot put a constant heat into his colors. He cannot make his pencil drop a sound, as the echo in the epigram mocks at him: *si vis similem pingere, pinge sonum.*[7] All the skill of cunning artisans and mechanics[8] cannot put a principle of life into a statue of their own making. Neither are we able to enclose in words and letters the life, soul, and essence of any spiritual truths, and as it were to incorporate it in them. Some philosophers have determined that ἀρετὴ is not διδακτὸν: virtue cannot be taught by any certain rules or precepts. Men and books may propound some directions to us that may set us in such a way of life and practice as in which we shall at last find it within ourselves, and be experimentally acquainted with it; but they cannot teach it us like a mechanic art or trade. No, surely, there is a spirit in man, and "the inspiration of the Almighty giveth this understanding."[9] But we shall not meet with this spirit anywhere but in the way of obedience: the knowledge of Christ and the keeping of His commandments must always go together, and be mutual causes of one another.

"Hereby we know that we know Him if we keep His commandments. He that saith, I know Him, and keepeth not His commandments, is a liar, and the truth is not in him."

I come now unto these words themselves, which are so pregnant that I shall not need to force out anything at all from them. I shall therefore only take notice of some few observations which drop from them of their own accord, and then conclude with some application of them to ourselves.

First, then, if this be the right way and method of discovering our knowledge of Christ by our keeping of His commandments, then we may safely draw conclusions concerning our state and condition from the conformity of our lives to the will of Christ. Would we know whether we know Christ aright, let us consider whether the life of Christ be in us. *Qui non habet vitam Christi, Christum non habet:* he that hath not the life of Christ in him, he hath nothing but the name, nothing but a fancy of Christ; he hath not the substance of Him. He that builds his house upon this foundation

—not an airy notion of Christ swimming in his brain, but Christ really dwelling and living in his heart—as our Saviour himself witnesseth, he "buildeth his house upon a rock";[10] and when the floods come, and the winds blow, and the rain descends and beats upon it, it shall stand impregnably. But he that builds all his comfort upon an ungrounded persuasion that God from all eternity hath loved him and absolutely decreed him to life and happiness, and seeketh not for God really dwelling in his soul, he builds his house upon a quicksand, and it shall suddenly sink and be swallowed up: "his hope shall be cut off, and his trust shall be a spider's web; he shall lean upon his house, but it shall not stand; he shall hold it fast, but it shall not endure."[11]

We are nowhere commanded to pry into these secrets, but the wholesome counsel and advice given us is this: to make our calling and election sure. We have no warrant in Scripture to peep into these hidden rolls and volumes of eternity, and to make it our first thing that we do when we come to Christ to spell out our names in the stars, and to persuade ourselves that we are certainly elected to everlasting happiness before we see the image of God in righteousness and true holiness shaped in our hearts. God's everlasting decree is too dazzling and bright an object for us at first to set our eye upon. It is far easier and safer for us to look upon the rays of His goodness and holiness as they are reflected in our own hearts, and there to read the mild and gentle characters of God's love to us in our love to Him and our hearty compliance with His heavenly will, as it is safer for us if we would see the sun to look upon it here below in a pail of water than to cast up our daring eyes upon the body of the sun itself, which is too radiant and scorching for us. The best assurance that anyone can have of his interest in God is doubtless the conformity of his soul to Him. Those divine purposes, whatsoever they be, are altogether unsearchable and unknowable by us; they lie wrapped up in everlasting darkness, and covered in a deep abyss. Who is able to fathom the bottom of them?

Let us not, therefore, make this our first attempt towards God and religion, to persuade ourselves strongly of these everlasting decrees; for if at our first flight we aim so high, we shall happily[12] but scorch our wings and be struck back with lightning, as those giants of old were that would needs attempt to invade and assault heaven.[13] And it is indeed a most gigantical essay to thrust ourselves so boldly into the lap of heaven. It is the prank of a Nimrod,[14] of a mighty hunter, thus rudely to deal with God, and to force heaven and happiness before His face whether He will or no. The

---

[7]"If you wish to paint a true likeness, paint a sound." [8]Craftsmen. [9]Job 32.8. [10]Matthew 7.24. [11]Job 8.14–15. [12]Haply.
[13]In Greek mythology, the race of giants sprung from the blood of Uranus as it dropped upon Ge (the earth) vainly assaulted heaven, whereupon the gods, with the aid of Hercules, imprisoned them under Etna and other volcanos. Cudworth may also be remembering the giants mentioned in Genesis 6.4 ff.
[14]A "mighty hunter before the Lord" mentioned in Genesis 10.8–9. Milton (*Paradise Lost*, XII.24–37) depicts him as a man "of proud ambitious heart" who savagely disrupted the era of pastoral serenity.

way to obtain a good assurance indeed of our title to heaven is not to clamber up to it by a ladder of our own ungrounded persuasions, but to dig as low as hell by humility and self-denial in our own hearts; and though this may seem to be the furthest way about, yet it is indeed the nearest and safest way to it. . . .

Secondly, if hereby only we know that we know Christ by our keeping His commandments, then the knowledge of Christ doth not consist merely in a few barren notions, in a form of certain dry and sapless opinions. Christ came not [10] into the world to fill our heads with mere speculations, to kindle a fire of wrangling and contentious dispute amongst us, and to warm our spirits against one another with nothing but angry and peevish debates, whilst in the meantime our hearts remain all ice within towards God, and have not the least spark of true heavenly fire to melt and thaw them. Christ came not to possess our brains only with some cold opinions that send down nothing but a freezing and benumbing influence upon our hearts. Christ was *vitae magister*, not *scholae*;[15] and he is the best Christian whose heart beats [20] with the truest pulse towards heaven, not he whose head spinneth out the finest cobwebs. He that endeavors really to mortify his lusts and to comply with that truth in his life which his conscience is convinced of is nearer a Christian, though he never heard of Christ, than he that believes all the vulgar articles of the Christian faith and plainly denieth Christ in his life. Surely, the way to heaven that Christ hath taught us is plain and easy if we have but honest hearts. We need not many criticisms, many school-distinctions, to come to a right understanding of it. Surely, Christ came not to [30] ensnare us and entangle us with captious niceties, or to pulse[16] our heads with deep speculations and lead us through hard and craggy notions into the kingdom of heaven. I persuade myself that no man shall ever be kept out of heaven for not comprehending mysteries that were beyond the reach of his shallow understanding, if he had but an honest and good heart that was ready to comply with Christ's commandments. . . .

Do we not nowadays open and lock up heaven with the private key of this and that opinion of our own according [40] to our several fancies as we please? And if anyone observe Christ's commandments never so sincerely, and serve God with faith and a pure conscience, that yet happily skills not of some contended-for opinions,[17] some darling notions: he hath not the right shibboleth; he hath not the true watchword; he must not pass the guards into heaven. Do we not make this and that opinion, this and that outward form, to be the wedding garment, and boldly sentence those to outer darkness that are not invested therewith? Whereas every true Christian finds the least dram of hearty affection [50] towards God to be more cordial and sovereign to his soul than all the speculative notions and opinions in the world; and though he study also to inform his understanding aright, and free his mind from all error and misapprehensions, yet it is nothing but the life of Christ deeply rooted in his heart which is the chemical elixir that he feeds upon. . . .

Thirdly, if hereby we are to judge whether we truly know Christ by our keeping of His commandments, so that he

that saith he knoweth him, and keepeth not his commandments, is a liar, then this was not the plot[18] and design of the gospel, to give the world an indulgence to sin upon what pretense soever. Though we are too prone to make such misconstructions of it, as if God had intended nothing else in it but to dandle our corrupt nature, and contrive a smooth and easy way for us to come to happiness without the toilsome labor of subduing our lusts and sinful affections. Or as if the gospel were nothing else but a declaration to the world of God's engaging His affections from all eternity on some particular persons in such a manner as that He would resolve to love them and dearly embrace them though He never made them partakers of His image in righteousness and true holiness; and though they should remain under the power of all their lusts, yet they should still continue His beloved ones, and He would notwithstanding at last bring them undoubtedly into heaven. Which is nothing else but to make the God that we worship, the God of the New Testament, a προσωπολήπτης, an accepter of persons, and one that should encourage that in the world which is diametrally[19] opposite to God's own life and being. And indeed nothing is more ordinary than for us to shape out such monstrous and deformed notions of God unto ourselves by looking upon Him through the colored medium of our own corrupt hearts, and having the eye of our soul tinctured by the suffusions of our own lusts. . . .

That I may therefore come nearer to the thing in hand: God, who is absolute goodness, cannot love any of His creatures and take pleasure in them without bestowing a communication of His goodness and likeness upon them. God cannot make a gospel to promise men life and happiness hereafter without being regenerated, and made partakers of His holiness. As soon may heaven and hell be reconciled together, and lovingly shake hands with one another, as God can be fondly indulgent to any sin, in whomsoever it be. As soon may light and darkness be espoused together, and midnight be married to the noonday, as God can be joined in a league of friendship to any wicked soul. The great design of God in the gospel is to clear up this mist of sin and corruption which we are here surrounded with, and to bring up his creatures out of the shadow of death to the region of light above, the land of truth and holiness. The great mystery[20] of the gospel is to establish a godlike frame and disposition of spirit, which consists in righteousness and true holiness, in the hearts of men. And Christ, who is the great and mighty Saviour, He came on purpose into the world not only to save us from fire and brimstone but also to save us from our sins. . . . Christ, that was nothing but divinity dwelling in a tabernacle of flesh, and God himself immediately acting a human nature, He came into the world to kindle here that divine life amongst men, which is certainly dearer unto God than anything else whatsoever in the world, and to propagate this celestial fire from one heart still unto another until the

---

15"The master of life, not of schools." 16Beat. Text *pusle*.
17*That yet . . . opinions;* that is perhaps regarded as less important than arguable points of theology. 18Plan. 19Diametrically.
20Service, function.

end of the world. Neither is He, or was He, ever absent from this spark of His divinity kindled amongst men, wheresoever it be, though He seem bodily to be withdrawn from us. He is the standing, constant, inexhausted fountain of this divine light and heat that still toucheth every soul that is enlivened by it with an outstretched ray, and freely lends His beams and disperseth His influence to all from the beginning of the world to the end of it. "We all receive of His fulness, grace for grace,"[21] as all the stars in heaven are said to light their candles at the sun's flame. For though His body be withdrawn from us, yet by the lively and virtual contact of His spirit He is always kindling, cheering, quickening, warming, enlivening hearts. Nay, this divine life begun and kindled in any heart, wheresoever it be, is something of God in flesh, and, in a sober and qualified sense, divinity incarnate, and all particular Christians that are really possessed of it so many mystical Christs. . . .

I have now done with the first part of my discourse concerning those observations which arise naturally from the words and offer themselves to us; I shall in the next place proceed to make some general application of them altogether.

Now therefore, I beseech you, let us consider whether or no we know Christ indeed—not by our acquaintance with systems and models of divinity, not by our skill in books and papers, but by our keeping of Christ's commandments. All the books and writings which we converse with, they can but represent spiritual objects to our understandings, which yet we can never see in their own true figure, color, and proportion until we have a divine light within to irradiate and shine upon them. . . . The great mystery of the gospel, it doth not lie only in Christ without us (though we must know also what He hath done for us), but the very pith and kernel of it consists in Christ inwardly formed in our hearts. Nothing is truly ours but what lives in our spirits. . . .

I mean by holiness nothing else but God stamped and printed upon the soul. And we may please ourselves with what conceits we will, but so long as we are void of this, we do but dream of heaven and I know not what fond paradise; we do but blow up and down an airy bubble of our own fancies, which riseth out of the froth of our vain hearts; we do but court a painted heaven and woo happiness in a picture, whilst in the meantime a true and real hell will suck in our souls into it and soon make us sensible of a solid woe and substantial misery. . . . Nay, we do but deceive ourselves with names: hell is nothing but the orb of sin and wickedness, or else that hemisphere of darkness in which all evil moves; and heaven is the opposite hemisphere of light, or else, if you please, the bright orb of truth, holiness, and goodness; and we do actually in this life instate ourselves in the possession of one or other of them. Take sin and disobedience out of hell, and it will presently clear up unto light, tranquillity, serenity, and shine out into a heaven. Every true saint carrieth his heaven about with him in his own heart, and hell—that is without him—can have no power over him. . . .

I am sure there be many of us that are perpetual dwarfs in our spiritual stature, like those "silly women" that St. Paul speaks of, "laden with sins and led away with divers lusts," that are "ever learning and never able to come to the knowledge of the truth";[22] that are not now one jot taller in Christianity than we were many years ago, but have still as sickly, crazy, and unsound a temper of soul as we had long before. Indeed, we seem to do something: we are always moving and lifting at the stone of corruption that lies upon our hearts, but yet we never stir it notwithstanding, or at least never roll it off from us. . . . We have the same water to pump out in every prayer, and still we let the same leak in again upon us. We make a great deal of noise and raise a great deal of dust with our feet, but we do not move from off the ground on which we stood, we do not go forward at all; or if we do sometimes make a little progress, we quickly lose again the ground which we had gained, like those upper planets in the heaven which (as the astronomers tell us) sometimes move forwards, sometimes quite backwards, and sometimes perfectly stand still: have their stations and retrogradations as well as their direct motions. As if religion were nothing else but a dancing up and down upon the same piece of ground and making several motions and friskings on it, and not a sober journeying and traveling onwards toward some certain place. . . .

When we would convince men of any error by the strength of truth, let us withal pour the sweet balm of love upon their heads. Truth and love are two of the most powerful things in the world, and when they both go together they cannot easily be withstood. The golden beams of truth and the silken cords of love, twisted together, will draw men on with a sweet violence whether they will or no. Let us take heed we do not sometimes call that zeal for God and His gospel which is nothing else but our own tempestuous and stormy passion. True zeal is a sweet, heavenly, and gentle flame which maketh us active for God, but always within the sphere of love. It never calls for fire from heaven to consume those that differ a little from us in their apprehensions. It is like that kind of lightning (which the philosophers speak of) that melts the sword within but singeth not the scabbard. It strives to save the soul, but hurteth not the body. True zeal is a loving thing, and makes us always active to edification and not to destruction. If we keep the fire of zeal within the chimney, in its own proper place, it never doth any hurt: it only warmeth, quickeneth, and enliventh us; but if we let it break out, and catch hold of the thatch of our flesh, and kindle our corrupt nature, and set the house of our body on fire, it is no longer zeal; it is no heavenly fire; it is a most destructive and devouring thing. . . .

Let nothing be esteemed of greater consequence and concernment to thee than what thou doest and actest, how thou livest. Nothing without us can make us either happy or miserable, nothing can either defile us or hurt us but what goeth out from us, what springeth and bubbleth up out of our own hearts. We have dreadful apprehensions of the flames of hell without us; we tremble and are afraid when we hear of fire and brimstone, whilst in the meantime we securely nourish within our own hearts a true and living hell, *et caeco carpimur igni:*[23] the dark fire of our lusts consumeth

---

[21]John 1.16. [22]2 Timothy 3.6–7.
[23]"Wasting with a hidden fire" (Vergil, *Aeneid*, IV.2).

our bowels within and miserably scorcheth our souls, and we are not troubled at it. We do not perceive how hell steals upon us whilst we live here. And as for heaven, we only gaze abroad, expecting that it should come in to us from without, but never look for the beginnings of it to arise within, in our own hearts. . . .

I will now shut up all with one or two considerations to persuade you further to the keeping of Christ's commandments. First, from the desire which we all have of knowledge: if we would indeed know divine truths, the only way to come to this is by keeping of Christ's commandments. The grossness of our apprehensions in spiritual things, and our many mistakes that we have about them, proceed from nothing but those dull and foggy steams which rise up from our foul hearts and becloud our understandings. If we did but heartily comply with Christ's commandments, and purge our hearts from all gross and sensual affections, we should not then look about for truth wholly without ourselves, and enslave ourselves to the dictates of this and that teacher, and hang upon the lips of man; but we should find the great eternal God, inwardly teaching our souls and continually instructing us more and more in the mysteries of His will; and "out of our bellies should flow rivers of living waters."[24] Nothing puts a stop and hindrance to the passage of truth in the world but the carnality of our hearts, the corruption of our lives. 'Tis not wrangling disputes and syllogistical reasons that are the mighty pillars that underprop truth in the world: if we would but underset it with the holiness of our hearts and lives, it should never fail. Truth is a prevailing and conquering thing, and would quickly overcome the world, did not the earthiness of our dispositions and the darkness of our false hearts hinder it. Our Saviour Christ bids the blind man wash off the clay that was upon his eyes in the pool of Siloam, and then he should see clearly;[25] intimating this to us, that it is the earthiness of men's affections that darkens the eye of the understandings in spiritual things. Truth is always ready and near at hand if our eyes were not closed up with mud. That we could but open them to look upon it! Truth always waits upon our souls and offers itself freely to us, as the sun offers its beams to every eye that will but open and let them shine in upon it. If we could but purge our hearts from that filth and defilement which hangeth about them, there would be no doubt at all of truth's prevailing in the world. For truth is great, and stronger than all things; all the earth calleth upon truth, and the heaven blesseth it; all works shake and tremble at it. The truth endureth and is always strong; it liveth and conquereth forevermore. She is the strength, kingdom, power, and majesty of all ages. Blessed be the God of truth!

Last of all, if we desire a true reformation, as we seem to do, let us begin here in reforming our hearts and lives, in keeping of Christ's commandments. All outward forms and models of reformation, though they be never so good in their kind, yet they are of little worth to us without this inward reformation of the heart. Tin or lead or any other baser metal, if it be cast into never so good a mold and made up into never so elegant a figure, yet it is but tin or lead still; it is the same metal that it was before. And if we be molded into never so good a form of outward government, unless we new mold our hearts within too, we are but little better than we were before. If adulterate silver, that hath much allay or dross in it, have never so current a stamp put upon it, yet it will not pass notwithstanding, when the touchstone trieth it. We must be reformed within with a spirit of fire and a spirit of burning to purge us from the dross and corruption of our hearts, and refine us as gold and silver; and then we shall be reformed truly, and not before. When this once comes to pass, then shall Christ be set upon His throne indeed; then the glory of the Lord shall overflow the land; then we shall be a people acceptable unto Him, and as Mount Sion, which He dearly loved.

[24]John 7.38   [25]John 9.1–7.

John Smith [1616-1652]

from Select Discourses (1660)

A PREFATORY DISCOURSE
CONCERNING THE TRUE WAY OR
METHOD OF ATTAINING TO DIVINE
KNOWLEDGE

SECTION I

That divine things are to be understood rather by a spiritual sensation than a verbal description or mere speculation. Sin and wickedness prejudicial to true knowledge. That purity of heart and life, as also an ingenuous freedom of judgment, are the best grounds and preparations for the entertainment of truth.

It hath been long since well observed that every art and science hath some certain principles upon which the whole frame and body of it must depend, and he that will fully acquaint himself with the mysteries thereof must come furnished with some *praecognita*[1] or προλήψεις, that I may

A PREFATORY DISCOURSE [1]Preconception, anticipation.

speak in the language of the Stoics. Were I indeed to define divinity I should rather call it a divine life than a divine science, it being something rather to be understood by a spiritual sensation than by any verbal description, as all things of sense and life are best known by sentient and vital faculties; γνῶσις ἑκάστων δι᾿ ὁμοιότητος γίνεται, as the Greek philosopher[2] hath well observed: everything is best known by that which bears a just resemblance and analogy with it; and therefore the Scripture is wont to set forth a good life as the prolepsis and fundamental principle of divine science. "Wisdom hath built her an house, and hewn out her seven pillars," but "the fear of the Lord is . . . the beginning of wisdom"[3]—the foundation of the whole fabric.

We shall therefore, as a prolegomenon or preface to what we shall afterward discourse upon the heads of divinity speak something of this true method of knowing, which is not so much by notions as actions, as religion itself consists not so much in words as things. They are not always the best skilled in divinity that are the most studied in those pandects[4] which it is sometimes digested into, or that have erected the greatest monopolies of art and science. He that is most practical in divine things hath the purest and sincerest knowledge of them, and not he that is most dogmatical. Divinity indeed is a true efflux from the eternal light, which, like the sunbeams, does not only enlighten, but heat and enliven; and therefore our Saviour hath, in His beatitudes, connext purity of heart with the beatifical vision. And as the eye cannot behold the sun, ἡλιοειδὴς μὴ γινόμενος, unless it be sunlike and hath the form and resemblance of the sun drawn in it, so neither can the soul of man behold God, θεοειδὴς μὴ γινομένη, unless it be godlike, hath God formed in it, and be made partaker of the divine nature. And the apostle St. Paul, when he would lay open the right way of attaining to divine truth, he saith that "knowledge puffeth up," but it is "love that edifieth."[5] The knowledge of divinity that appears in systems and models is but a poor, wan light, but the powerful energy of divine knowledge displays itself in purified souls: here we shall find the true πεδίον ἀληθείας, as the ancient philosophy speaks, "the land of truth."

To seek our divinity merely in books and writings is to seek the living among the dead: we do but in vain seek God many times in these, where His truth too often is not so much enshrined as entombed. No, *intra te quaere Deum*, seek for God within thine own soul; He is best discerned νοερᾷ ἐπαφῇ, as Plotinus phraseth it, by an intellectual touch of Him; we must "see with our eyes, and hear with our ears, and our hands must handle the word of life,"[6] that I may express it in St. John's words. Ἔστι καὶ ψυχῆς αἴσθησίς τις—the soul itself hath its sense as well as the body, and therefore David, when he would teach us how to know what the divine goodness is, calls not for speculation but sensation: "Taste and see how good the Lord is."[7] This is not the best and truest knowledge of God which is wrought out by the labor and sweat of the brain, but that which is kindled within us by an heavenly warmth in our hearts. As in the natural body it is the heart that sends up good blood and warm spirits into the head, whereby it is best enabled to its several

functions, so that which enables us to know and understand aright in the things of God must be a living principle of holiness within us. When the tree of knowledge is not planted by the tree of life, and sucks not up sap from thence, it may be as well it fruitful with evil as with good, and bring forth bitter fruit as well as sweet. If we would indeed have our knowledge thrive and flourish we must water the tender plants of it with holiness. When Zoroaster's scholars[8] asked him what they should do to get winged souls, such as might soar aloft in the bright beams of divine truth, he bids them bathe themselves in the waters of life; they asking what they were, he tells them, the four cardinal virtues, which are the four rivers of paradise.[9] It is but a thin, airy knowledge that is got by mere speculation, which is ushered in by syllogisms and demonstrations; but that which springs forth from true goodness is θειότερόν τι πάσης ἀποδείξεως, as Origen[10] speaks: it brings such a divine light into the soul as is more clear and convincing than any demonstration. The reason why, notwithstanding all our acute reasons and subtile disputes, truth prevails no more in the world is, we so often disjoin truth and true goodness, which in themselves can never be disunited; they grow both from the same root, and live in one another. We may, like those in Plato's deep pit,[11] with their faces bended downwards, converse with sounds and shadows but not with the life and substance of truth while our souls remain defiled with any vice or lusts. These are the black Lethe[12] lake which drench the souls of men; he that wants true virtue, in heaven's logic "is blind, and cannot see afar off."[13] Those filthy mists that arise from impure and terrene minds, like an atmosphere, perpetually encompass them that they cannot see that sun of divine truth that shines about them, but never shines into any unpurged souls; the darkness comprehends it not, the foolish man understands it not. All the light and knowledge that may seem sometimes to rise up in unhallowed minds is but like those fuliginous[14] flames that arise up from our culinary fire, that are soon quenched in their own smoke; or like those foolish fires that fetch their birth from terrene exudations, that do but hop up and down, and flit to and fro upon the surface of this

[2]Plotinus (205?–270), most influential of neoplatonic philosophers, whose works, as arranged by his disciple Porphyry in six books of nine chapters each (hence called the *Enneads*), were the favorite text of Smith and the other Cambridge Platonists. Most of the many Greek tags in Smith's discourse, which will not be specifically identified and located, are drawn or adapted from the *Enneads*. [3]Proverbs 9.1, 10. [4]Codes. [5]1 Corinthians 8.1. [6]1 John 1.1. [7]Psalm 34.8.
[8]Zoroaster (perhaps of the early 6th century B.C.) was the supposed founder of the ancient Persian religion recorded in the Zend-Avesta.
[9]*Four cardinal virtues . . . paradise*: As defined by Plato, the four cardinal virtues are wisdom, courage, temperance, and justice. The four rivers of paradise are named in Genesis 2.10–14.
[10]A father of the Greek church (185?–254) notable for his efforts to reconcile paganism and Christianity.
[11]Plato's famous parable of the cave is expounded in the seventh book of the *Republic* (Sect. 514 ff.).
[12]In Greek mythology, a river in Hades whose waters caused forgetfulness. [13]2 Peter 1.9. [14]Smoky.

earth, where they were first brought forth, and serve not so much to enlighten as to delude us; not[15] to direct the wandering traveler into his way, but to lead him farther out of it. While we lodge any filthy vice in us this will be perpetually twisting up itself into the thread of our finest-spun speculations; it will be continually climbing up into the τὸ Πγεμον-ικόν—the hegemonical[16] powers of the soul, into the bed of reason, and defile it: like the wanton ivy twisting itself about the oak, it will twine about our judgments and understandings till it hath sucked out the life and spirit of them. I cannot think such black oblivion should possess the minds of some as to make them question that truth which to good men shines as bright as the sun at noonday, had they not foully defiled their own souls with some hellish vice or other, how fairly soever it may be they may dissemble it. There is a benumbing spirit, a congealing vapor that ariseth from sin and vice, that will stupify the senses of the soul, as the naturalists say there is from the torpedo,[17] that smites the senses of those that approach to it. This is that venomous *Solanum*—that deadly nightshade[18] that derives its cold poison into the understandings of men.

Such as men themselves are, such will God himself seem to be. It is the maxim of most wicked men that the deity is some way or other like themselves; their souls do more than whisper it, though their lips speak it not; and though their tongues are silent, yet their lives cry it upon the housetops and in the public streets. That idea which men generally have of God is nothing else but the picture of their own complexion: that archetypal notion of Him which hath the supremacy in their minds is none else but such an one as hath been shaped out according to some pattern of themselves, though they may so clothe and disguise this idol of their own, when they carry it about in a pompous procession to expose it to the view of the world, that it may seem very beautiful, and indeed anything else rather than what it is. Most men (though it may be they themselves take no great notice of it), like that dissembling monk,[19] do *aliter sentire in scholis, aliter in musaeis*, are of a different judgment in the schools from what they are in the retirements of their private closets. There is a double head as well as a double heart. Men's corrupt hearts will not suffer their notions and conceptions of divine things to be cast into that form that an higher reason, which may sometime work within them, would put them into.

I would not be thought, all this while, to banish the belief of all innate notions of divine truth, but these are too often smothered or tainted with a deep dye of men's filthy lusts. It is but *lux sepulta in opaca materia*—light buried and stifled in some dark body, from whence all those colored, or rather discolored, notions and apprehensions of divine things are begotten. Though these common notions may be very busy sometimes in the vegetation[20] of divine knowledge, yet the corrupt vices of men may so clog, disturb, and overrule them (as the naturalists say this unruly and masterless matter doth the natural forms in the formation of living creatures) that they may produce nothing but monsters, miserably distorted and misshapen. This kind of science, as Plotinus speaks, "companying too familiarly with matter, and re-

ceiving and imbibing it into itself, changeth its shape by this incestuous mixture." At best, while any inward lust is harbored in the minds of men, it will so weaken them that they can never bring forth any masculine or generous knowledge; as Aelian[21] observes of the stork, that if the night owl chanceth to sit upon her eggs they become presently as it were ὑπηνέμια[22] and all incubation rendered impotent and ineffectual. Sin and lust are alway of an hungry nature, and suck up all those vital affections of men's souls which should feed and nourish their understandings.

What are all our most sublime speculations of the deity, that are not impregnated with true goodness, but insipid things that have no taste nor life in them, that do but swell, like empty froth, in the souls of men! They do not feed men's souls, but only puff them up and fill them with pride, arrogance, and contempt, and tyranny towards those that cannot well ken their subtile curiosities, as those philosophers that Tully complains of in his times *qui disciplinam suam ostentationem scientiae, non legem vitae, putabant*[23]—which made their knowledge only matter of ostentation, to venditate[24] and set off themselves, but never caring to square and govern their lives by it. Such as these do but, spider-like, take a great deal of pains to spin a worthless web out of their own bowels, which will not keep them warm. These indeed are those silly souls that are "ever learning, but never come to the knowledge of the truth."[25] They may, with Pharaoh's lean kine,[26] eat up and devour all tongues and sciences, and yet, when they have done, still remain lean and ill-favored as they were at first. Jejune and barren speculations may be hovering and fluttering up and down about divinity, but they cannot settle or fix themselves upon it; they unfold the plicatures[27] of Truth's garment, but they cannot behold the lovely face of it. There are hidden mysteries in divine truth, wrapt up one within another, which cannot be discerned but only by divine epoptists.[28]

We must not think we have then attained to the right knowledge of truth when we have broke through the outward shell of words and phrases that house it up; or when, by a logical analysis, we have found out the dependencies and coherencies of them one with another; or when, like stout champions of it, having well guarded it with the invincible strength of our demonstration, we dare stand out in the face of the world and challenge the field of all those that would pretend to be our rivals.

[15]Text *nor.*   [16]Ruling.   [17]A fish that emits electrical discharges.
[18]A reputedly poisonous plant of the genus *Solanum.*
[19]Unidentified, but in the copious anti-clerical literature of the Renaissance there were many monks of the sort that Smith describes.
[20]*Busy...vegetation*: allegedly important in the cultivation.
[21]Claudius Aelianus, (3d cent.), Roman rhetorician who wrote (in Greek) various works on natural history.
[22]"Full of wind," i.e., an egg which produces no chicken.
[23]Adapted from Cicero's *Tusculan Disputations*, II.iv.11.
[24]Exhibit ostentatiously.   [25]2 Timothy 3.7.   [26]Genesis 41.1–4.
[27]Folds.
[28]In ancient Greece, initiates of the Eleusinian mysteries and therefore beholders of the sacred, secret rites.

We have many grave and reverend idolaters that worship truth only in the image of their own wits; that could never adore it so much as they may seem to do, were it anything else but such a form of belief as their own wandering speculations had at last met together in, were it not that they find their own image and superscription upon it.

There is a knowing of the truth as it is in Jesus—as it is in a Christlike nature, as it is in that sweet, mild, humble, and loving spirit of Jesus which spreads itself, like a morning sun, upon the souls of good men, full of light and life. It profits little to know Christ himself after the flesh, but He gives His spirit to good men that searcheth the deep things of God. There is an inward beauty, life, and loveliness in divine truth which cannot be known but only then when it is digested into life and practice. The Greek philosopher could tell those high-soaring Gnostics[29] that thought themselves no less than *Jovis alites*;[30] that could (as he speaks in the comedy) ἀεροβατεῖν καὶ περιφρονεῖν τὸν ἥλιον,[31] and cried out so much, "Look upon God!" that "without virtue and real goodness God is but a name," a dry and empty notion. The profane sort of men, like those old gentile[32] Greeks, may make many ruptures in the walls of God's temple and break into the holy ground, but yet may find God no more there than they did.

Divine truth is better understood as it unfolds itself in the purity of men's hearts and lives than in all those subtile niceties into which curious wits may lay it forth. And therefore our Saviour, who is the great master of it, would not, while He was here on earth, draw it up into any system or body, nor would His disciples after Him; He would not lay it out to us in any canons or articles of belief, not being indeed so careful to stock and enrich the world with opinions and notions as with true piety and a godlike pattern of purity as the best way to thrive in all spiritual understanding. His main scope was to promote an holy life as the best and most compendious way to a right belief. He hangs all true acquaintance with divinity upon the doing God's will: "If any man will do His will, he shall know of the doctrine, whether it be of God."[33] This is that alone which will make us, as St. Peter tells us, "that we shall not be barren nor unfruitful in the knowledge of our Lord and Saviour."[34] There is an inward sweetness and deliciousness in divine truth which no sensual mind can taste or relish: this is that ψυχικὸς ἀνήρ—that natural man that savors not the things of God. Corrupt passions and terrene affections are apt, of their own nature, to disturb all serene thoughts, to precipitate our judgments, and warp our understandings. It was a good maxim of the old Jewish writers: "the Holy Spirit dwells not in terrene and earthly passions." Divinity is not so well perceived by a subtile wit, ὥσπερ αἰσθήσει κεκα θμρμένη, "as by a purified sense," as Plotinus phraseth it.

Neither was the ancient philosophy unacquainted with this way and method of attaining to the knowledge of divine things, and therefore Aristotle himself thought a young man unfit to meddle with the grave precepts of morality till the heat and violent precipitancy of his youthful affections was cooled and moderated.[35] And it is observed of Pythago-ras[36] that he had several ways to try the capacity of his scholars and to prove the sedateness and moral temper of their minds before he would entrust them with the sublimer mysteries of his philosophy. The Platonists were herein so wary and solicitous that they thought the minds of men could never be purged enough from those earthly dregs of sense and passion, in which they were so much steeped, before they could be capable of their divine metaphysics; and therefore they so much solicit a χωρισμὸς ἀπὸ τοῦ σώματος, as they are wont to phrase it, "a separation from the body" in all those that would καθαρῶς φιλοσοφεῖν, as Socrates speaks, that is, indeed "sincerely understand divine truth," for that was the scope of their philosophy. This was also intimated by them in their defining philosophy to be μελέτη θανάτου— "a meditation of death," aiming herein at only a moral way of dying by loosening the soul from the body and this sensitive life, which they thought was necessary to a right contemplation of intelligible things; and therefore, besides those ἀρεταὶ καθαρτικαί[37] by which the souls of men were to be separated from sensuality and purged from fleshly filth, they devised a further way of separation more accommodated to the condition of philosophers, which was their *mathemata* or mathematical contemplations, whereby the souls of men might farther shake off their dependency upon sense, and learn to go as it were alone, without the crutch of any sensible or material thing to support them; and so be a little inured, being once got up above the body, to converse freely with immaterial natures without looking down again and falling back into sense. Besides, many other ways they had whereby to rise out of this dark body—ἀναβάσεις ἐκ τοῦ σπηλαίου, as they are wont to call them—several steps and ascents out of this miry cave of mortality before they could set any sure footing with their intellectual part in the land of light and immortal being.

And thus we should pass from this topic of our discourse, upon which we have dwelt too long already, but that before we quite let it go I hope we may fairly make this use of it farther (besides what we have openly driven at all this while), which is to learn not to devote or give up ourselves to any private opinions or dictates of men in matters of religion, nor too zealously to propugn the *dogmata*[38] of any sect. As we should not, like rigid censurers, arraign and condemn the creeds of other men which we comply not with before a full and mature understanding of them, ripened not only by the natural sagacity of our own reasons but by the benign influence of holy and mortified affection, so neither should we overhastily *credere in fidem alienam*—subscribe to the symbols and articles of other men. They are not always the best men that blot most paper: truth is not, I fear, so volumi-

[29]In the early centuries of the church, followers of a hybrid system of Greek and oriental philosophy combined with Christian doctrine. [30]God's winged prophets.
[31]"Walk on air and contemplate the sun" (adapted from Aristophanes, *The Clouds*, 1. 225). [32]Pagan. [33]John 7.17.
[34]2 Peter 1.8. [35]*Nicomachean Ethics*, I.iii.
[36]Greek philosopher and mathematician (6th cent. B.C.).
[37]"Cleansing virtues." [38]Defend the doctrines.

nous, nor swells into such a mighty bulk as our books do. Those minds are not always the most chaste that are most parturient[30] with these learned discourses, which too often bear upon them a foul stain of their unlawful propagation. A bitter juice of corrupt affections may sometimes be strained into the ink of our greatest clerks; their doctrines may taste too sour of the cask they come through. We are not always happy in meeting with that wholesome food (as some are wont to call the doctrinal part of religion) which hath been dressed out by the cleanest hands. Some men have too bad hearts to have good heads: they cannot be good at theory who have been so bad at the practice, as we may justly fear too many of those, from whom we are apt to take the articles of our belief, have been. Whilst we plead so much our right to the patrimony of our fathers, we may take too fast a possession of their errors, as well as of their sober opinions. There are *idola specus*—innate prejudices and deceitful hypotheses that many times wander up and down in the minds of good men, that may fly out from them with their graver determinations. We can never be well assured what our traditional divinity is, nor can we securely enough addict ourselves to any sect of men. That which was the philosopher's motto, Ἐλεύθερον εἶναι δεῖ τῇ γνώμῃ τὸν μέλλοντα φιλοσοφεῖν, we may a little enlarge, and so fit it for an ingenuous pursuer after divine truth: "he that will find truth must seek it with a free judgment and a sanctified mind." He that thus seeks shall find; he shall live in truth, and that shall live in him; it shall be like a stream of living waters issuing out of his own soul; he shall drink of the waters of his own cistern and be satisfied; he shall every morning find this heavenly manna lying upon the top of his own soul and be fed with it to eternal life; he will find satisfaction within, feeling himself in conjunction with truth, though all the world should dispute against him.

SECTION II

An objection against the method of knowing laid down in the former section, answered. That men generally, notwithstanding their apostasy, are furnished with the radical principles of true knowledge. Men want not so much means of knowing what they ought to do as wills to do what they know. Practical knowledge differs from all other knowledge, and excels it.

And thus I should again leave this argument but that perhaps we may, all this while, have seemed to undermine what we intend to build up. For if divine truth spring only up from the root of true goodness, how shall we ever endeavor to be good before we know what it is to be so? Or how shall we convince the gainsaying world of truth unless we could also inspire virtue into it?

To both which we shall make this reply: that there are some radical principles of knowledge that are so deeply sunk into the souls of men as that the impression cannot easily be obliterated, though it may be much darkened. Sensual baseness doth not so grossly sully and bemire the souls of all wicked men at first as to make them, with Diagoras,[40] to deny the deity, or, with Protagoras,[41] to doubt of, or, with Diodorus,[42] to question the immortality of rational souls. Neither are the common principles of virtue so pulled up by the roots in all as to make them so dubious in stating the bounds of virtue and vice as Epicurus was, though he could not but sometime take notice of them. Neither is the retentive power of truth so weak and loose in all skeptics as it was in him, who, being well scourged in the streets till the blood ran about him, questioned, when he came home, whether he had been beaten or not. Arrianus[43] hath well observed that the common notions of God and virtue impressed upon the souls of men are more clear and perspicuous than any else; and that if they have not more certainty, more yet have they evidence, and display themselves with less difficulty to our reflexive faculty than any geometrical demonstrations; and these are both available to prescribe out ways of virtue to men's own souls and to force an acknowledgment of truth from those that oppose, when they are well guided by a skillful hand. Truth needs not any time fly from reason, there being an eternal amity between them. They are only some private *dogmata* that may well be suspected as spurious and adulterate,[44] that dare not abide the trial thereof. And this reason is not everywhere so extinguished as that we may not, by that, enter into the souls of men. What the magnetical virtue is in these earthly bodies, that reason is in men's minds which, when it is put forth, draws them one to another. Besides, in wicked men there are sometimes distastes of vice and flashes of love to virtue, which are the motions which spring from a true intellect, and the faint strugglings of an higher life within them, which they crucify again by their wicked sensuality. As truth doth not always act in good men, so neither doth sense always act in wicked men; they may sometimes have their *lucida intervalla*—their sober fits; and a divine spirit blowing and breathing upon them may then blow up some live sparks of true understanding within them, though they may soon endeavor to quench them again and to rake them up in the ashes of their own earthly thoughts.

All this and more that might be said upon this argument may serve to point out the way of virtue. We want not so much means of knowing what we ought to do as wills to do that which we may know. But yet all that knowledge which is separated from an inward acquaintance with virtue and goodness is of a far different nature from that which ariseth out of a true living sense of them, which is the best discerner thereof, and by which alone we know the true

[39]About to give birth.

[40]Greek sophist and poet (5th cent. B.C.) whom the Athenians condemned to death for atheism and impiety.

[41]Greek philosopher (5th cent. B.C.) whom the Athenians banished because he questioned the existence of the gods.

[42]Presumably Diodorus Cronus (4th cent. B.C.), Greek philosopher noted for his skill in dialectic.

[43]Greek historian (2d cent.) who wrote on the Stoic philosophy of his friend and teacher Epictetus. [44]Mixed, impure.

perfection, sweetness, energy, and loveliness of them, and all that which is οὔτε ῥητὸν, οὔτε γραπτόν[45]—that which can no more be known by a naked demonstration than colors can be perceived of a blind man by any definition or description which he can hear of them.

And further, the clearest and most distinct notions of truth that shine in the souls of the common sort of men may be extremely clouded if they be not accompanied with that answerable practice that might preserve their integrity; these tender plants may soon be spoiled by the continual droppings of our corrupt affections upon them; they are but of a weak and feminine nature, and so may be sooner deceived by that wily serpent of sensuality that harbors within us.

While the soul is πλήρης τοῦ σώματος—"full of the body" —while we suffer those notions and common principles of religion to lie asleep within us, that γενεσιουργὸς δύναμις— "the power of an animal life"—will be apt to incorporate and mingle itself with them; and that reason that is within us, as Plotinus hath well expressed it, becomes more and more σύμφυτος κακαῖς ταῖς ἐπιγινομέναις δόξαις—it will be infected with those evil opinions that arise from our corporal life. The more deeply our souls dive into our bodies, the more will reason and sensuality run one into another and make up a most dilute, unsavory, and muddy kind of knowledge. We must therefore endeavor more and more to withdraw ourselves from these bodily things, to set our soul as free as may be from its miserable slavery to this base flesh; we must shut the eyes of sense and open that brighter eye of our understandings, that other eye of the soul (as the philosopher calls our intellectual faculty) ἣν ἔχει μὲν πᾶς, χρῶνται δὲ ὀλίγοι—"which indeed all have, but few make use of it." This is the way to see clearly; the light of the divine world will then begin to fall upon us, and those sacred ἐλλάμψεις—those pure coruscations of immortal and everliving truth will shine out into us, and in God's own light shall we behold Him. The fruit of this knowledge will be sweet to our taste and pleasant to our palates, "sweeter than the honey or the honeycomb."[46] The priests of Mercury, as Plutarch tells us, in the eating of their holy things, were wont to cry out γλυκὺ ἡ ἀλήθεια—"sweet is truth." But how sweet and delicious that truth is which holy and heaven-born souls feed upon in their mysterious converses with the deity, who can tell but they that taste it? When reason once is raised by the mighty force of the divine Spirit into a converse with God, it is turned into sense: that which before was only faith well built upon sure principles (for such our science may be) now becomes vision. We shall then converse with God τῷ νῷ, whereas before we conversed with Him only τῇ διανοίᾳ—with our discursive faculty—as the Platonists were wont to distinguish. Before, we laid hold on Him only λόγῳ ἀποδεικτικῷ—with a struggling, agonistical, and contentious reason, hotly combating with difficulties and sharp contests of diverse opinions, and laboring in itself, in its deductions of one thing from another; we shall then fasten our minds upon Him λόγῳ ἀποφαντικῷ, with such a "serene understanding," γαλήνῃ νοερᾷ, such an intellectual calmness and serenity as will present us with a blissful, steady, and invariable sight of Him.

Section III

Men may be considered in a fourfold capacity in order to the perception of divine things. That the best and most excellent knowledge of divine things belongs only to the true and sober Christian; and that it is but in its infancy while he is in this earthly body.

And now, if you please, setting aside the Epicurean herd of brutish men who have drowned all their own sober reason in the deepest Lethe of sensuality, we shall divide the rest of men into these four ranks, according to that method which Simplicius[47] upon Epictetus hath already laid out to us, with respect to a fourfold kind of knowledge, which we have all this while glanced at.

The first whereof is ἄνθρωπος συμπεφυρμένος τῇ γενέσει, or, if you will, ἄνθρωπος ὁ πολύς—"that complex and multifarious man that is made up of soul and body," as it were by a just equality and arithmetical proportion of parts and powers in each of them. The knowledge of these men I should call ἀμυδρὸν δόξαν in Plutarch's phrase: "a knowledge wherein sense and reason are so twisted up together" that it cannot easily be unravelled and laid out into its first principles. Their highest reason is ὁμόδοξος ταῖς αἰσθήσεσι —"complying with their senses"—and both conspire together in vulgar opinion. To these that motto which the Stoics have made for them may very well agree, βίος ὑπόληψις, their life being steered by nothing else but opinion and imagination. Their higher notions of God and religion are so entangled with the birdlime of fleshly passions and mundane vanity that they cannot rise up above the surface of this dark earth, or easily entertain any but earthly conceptions of heavenly things. Such souls as are here lodged, as Plato speaks, are ὀπισθοβαρεῖς, "heavy behind", and are continually pressing down to this world's center; and though, like the spider, they may appear sometime moving up and down aloft in the air, yet they do but sit in the loom and move in that web of their own gross fancies, which they fasten and pin to some earthly thing or other.

The second is ἄνθρωπος κατὰ τὴν λογικὴν ζωὴν οὐσιωμένος—the man that looks at himself as being what he is rather by his soul than by his body; that thinks not fit to view his own face in any other glass but that of reason and understanding; that reckons upon his soul as that which was made to rule, his body as that which was born to obey, and like

[45]"Neither spoken nor written."
[46]Psalm 19.10.
[47]Neoplatonist (6th cent.) who wrote an influential commentary on the *Enchiridion* of Epictetus.

an handmaid perpetually to wait upon his higher and nobler part. And in such an one the *communes notitiae*, or common principles of virtue and goodness, are more clear and steady. To such an one we may allow τρανεστέραν καὶ ἐμφανεστέραν δόξαν—"more clear and distinct opinions," as being already ἐν καθάρσει—"in a method or course of purgation," or, at least, fit to be initiated into the *mysteria minora*—"the lesser mysteries of religion." For though these innate notions of truth may be but poor, empty, and hungry things of themselves, before they be fed and filled with the practice of true virtue, yet they are capable of being impregnated and exalted with the rules and precepts of it. And therefore the Stoic supposed ὅτι τοιούτῳ προσήκουσιν αἱ ἠθικαὶ καὶ πολιτικαὶ ἀρεταί—that the doctrine of political and moral virtues was fit to be delivered to such as these; and though they may not be so well prepared for divine virtue (which is of an higher emanation), yet they are not immature for human, as having the seeds of it already within themselves, which, being watered by answerable practice, may sprout up within them.

The third is ἄνθρωπος ἤδη κεκαθαρμένος—he whose soul is already purged by this lower sort of virtue, and so is continually flying off from the body and bodily passion, and returning into himself. Such, in St. Peter's language, are those "who have escaped the pollutions which are in the world through lust."[48] To these we may attribute a νόθη ἐπιστήμη—a lower degree of science, their inward sense of virtue and moral goodness being far transcendent to all mere speculative opinions of it. But if this knowledge settle here, it may be quickly apt to corrupt. Many of our most refined moralists may be, in a worse sense than Plotinus means, πληρωθέντες τῇ ἑαυτῶν φύσει—"full with their own pregnancy"; their souls may too much heave and swell with the sense of their own virtue and knowledge; there may be an ill ferment of self-love lying at the bottom, which may puff it up the more with pride, arrogance and self-conceit. These forces with which the divine bounty supplies us to keep a stronger guard against the evil spirit may be abused by our own rebellious pride, enticing of them from their allegiance to heaven to strengthen itself in our souls and fortify them against heaven: like that supercilious Stoic who, when he thought his mind well armed and appointed with wisdom and virtue, cried out, *Sapiens contendet cum ipso Jove de felicitate*.[49] They may make an airy heaven of these, and wall it about with their own self-flattery, and then sit in it as gods, as Cosroes the Persian king was sometime laughed at for enshrining himself in a temple of his own. And therefore if this knowledge be not attended with humility and a deep sense of self-penury and self-emptiness, we may easily fall short of that true knowledge of God which we seem to aspire after. We may carry such an image and species of ourselves constantly before us as will make us lose the clear sight of the divinity, and be too apt to rest in a mere "logical life" (it's Simplicius his expression) without any true participation of the divine life, if we do not (as many do, if not all, who rise no higher) relapse and slide back by vainglory, popularity, or such like vices into some mundane and external vanity or other.

The fourth is ἄνθρωπος θεωρητικός—the true metaphysical and contemplative man, ὃς τὴν ἑαυτοῦ λογικὴν ζωὴν ὑπερτρέχων, ὅλως εἶναι βούλεται τῶν κρειττόνων—who, running and shooting up above his own logical or self-rational life, pierceth into the highest life; such a one who, by universal love and holy affection, abstracting himself from himself, endeavors the nearest union with the divine essence that may be, κέντρον κέντρῳ συνάψας, as Plotinus speaks, knitting his own center, if he have any, unto the center of divine being. To such an one the Platonists are wont to attribute θεῖαν ἐπιστήμην—"a true divine wisdom," powerfully displaying itself ἐν νοερᾷ ζωῇ—"in an intellectual life," as they phrase it. Such a knowledge, they say, is always pregnant with divine virtue, which ariseth out of an happy union of souls with God, and is nothing else but a living imitation of a godlike perfection drawn out by a strong, fervent love of it. This divine knowledge καλοὺς καὶ ἐραστοὺς ποιεῖ, etc., as Plotinus speaks, makes us amorous of divine beauty, beautiful and lovely; and this divine love and purity reciprocally exalts divine knowledge, both of them growing up together like that Ἔρως and Ἀντέρως that Pausanias sometimes speaks of.[50] Though by the Platonists' leave such a life and knowledge as this is peculiarly belongs to the true and sober Christian, who lives in Him who is life itself, and is enlightened by Him who is the truth itself, and is made partaker of the divine unction, "and knoweth all things," as St. John speaks.[51] This life is nothing else but God's own breath within him, and an infant Christ (if I may use the expression) formed in his soul, who is in a sense ἀπαύγασμα τῆς δόξης, "the shining forth of the Father's glory." But yet we must not mistake; this knowledge is but here in its infancy; there is an higher knowledge, or an higher degree of this knowledge, that doth not, that cannot, descend upon us in these earthly habitations. We cannot here see . . . *in speculo lucido*;[52] here we can see but in a glass, and that darkly too. Our own imaginative powers, which are perpetually attending the highest acts of our souls, will be breathing a gross dew upon the pure glass of our understandings, and so sully and besmear it that we cannot see the image of the divinity sincerely in it. But yet this knowledge, being a true, heavenly fire kindled from God's own altar, begets an undaunted courage in the souls of good men, and enables them to cast a holy scorn upon the poor, petty trash of this life in comparison with divine things, and to pity those poor brutish Epicureans that have nothing but the mere husks of fleshly pleasure to feed themselves with. This sight of God makes pious souls breathe after that blessed time when mortality shall be swallowed up of life, when they shall no more behold the divinity through those dark mediums that eclipse the blessed sight of it.

---

[48]2 Peter 2.20.
[49]"A wise man can challenge the happiness of Jove himself" (adapted from Seneca, *Epistulae morales*, XXV.4).
[50]In his account of Athens, Pausanias (*Description of Greece*, I.xxx.1) tells of one altar to Eros (love) and another to Anteros (rejected love), the latter in memory of one Timagoras, who had killed himself at the cruel command of his love Meles. [51]John 3.20.
[52]"In a shining mirror."

Jeremy Taylor [1613-1667]

Anthony Wood was exaggerating only slightly when he said that Taylor "tumbled out of his mother's womb into the lap of the Muses at Cambridge." The son of a barber who "grounded him in grammar and mathematics," he was so precocious that between the age of thirteen (when he was admitted as a sizar to Gonville and Caius College) and twenty-one he earned two degrees, was made a fellow of his college, and had taken holy orders. "Had he lived among the ancient pagans," George Rust, the preacher at his funeral said, "he had been ushered into the world with a miracle, and swans must have danced and sung at his birth; and he must have been a great hero, and no less than the son of Apollo, the god of wisdom and eloquence." A few sermons delivered at the invitation of a lecturer at St. Paul's who had roomed with him in college brought this dazzling youth to Laud's attention, and that canny prelate at once arranged for his removal to University College, Oxford (M.A. 1635), and then, in 1636, for a perpetual fellowship at All Soul's. Thereafter his advance was very rapid—as a brilliant Oxford preacher, as chaplain to both his powerful patron and the king, and as rector successively of Uppingham in Rutland and at Overstone in Northamptonshire (1643).

But then his troubles started, for to Taylor, as to his powerful patrons, the war brought sharp reverses. Following his capture with a group of Charles' troops at Cardigan Castle and a brief incarceration in 1645, he found a post as teacher in a school near Golden Grove, Carmarthenshire. Again his talent, looks, and charm brought him to the notice of a patron, and he was soon appointed chaplain to the local squire and magnate Richard Vaughan, second earl of Carbery, whose friendship and protection provided him a haven in the wilds of western Wales. Although there were sometimes trips to London (on one of which King Charles, just before his execution, presented him his watch), for the next decade Taylor mainly stayed at Golden Grove, where "this great storm which hath dashed the vessel of the church all in pieces" had cast him in his hour of need.

He had, of course, begun to write and publish in the later thirties—a famous sermon on the Gunpowder Plot (1638), a Laudian defense of the Anglican establishment (1642), and so on—but the years at Golden Grove brought him to the fullness of his power. He was, he said, a stricken man, but despite—or perhaps because of—his dismay at the bleak condition of the church and his grief when both his wife and Lady Carbery died, he soon produced a string of major books. The *Liberty of Prophesying* (1647), the first great product of this middle phase of his career, was written, Taylor said, at the nadir of his fortunes. Seeking to relieve his "perpetual meditation" on his private sorrow and the public woe, fearing that he should "live unprofitably, and die obscurely, and be forgotten," and finding it impossible, even in his isolation, to exempt himself from "the participation of the common calamity," he resolved to write about the troubles of the church. The result was a spacious plea for reason, love, and toleration as correctives for those discords of religion "which this day, and for some years past, have exercised and disquieted Christendom."

The Rule and Exercises of Holy Living (1650) was also rooted in the troubles of the time. In an age when most men "are apt to prefer a prosperous error before an afflicted truth," he told Lord Carbery, "those few good people who have no other plot in their religion but to serve God and save their souls" are denied the "ghostly counsel" that they need, and therefore Taylor undertook, through written discourse, to serve the pastoral function of solace and instruction. "I have told what men ought to do," he said, "and by what means they may be assisted; and in most cases I have also told them why." Under more than twenty rubrics on such basic themes as sobriety, modesty, faith, prayer, alms, and repentance, Taylor tried to show how Christian faith and morals could be applied to daily living. Resolutely practical, rather plain in style, and uncluttered with the erudition that he usually lavished on his work, the book was so successful that by 1703 it had reached nineteen editions. Its great companion piece, *The Rule and Exercises of Holy Dying* (1651)— which was prompted by Lady Carbery's death following her tenth delivery in thirteen years—is more ornate and inward and allusive. Here, as Taylor weaves his meditations on a universal theme, his prose reveals the weight and pattern of a rich brocade, and its majestic erudition gives the work a richness not to be confused with ostentation. "He who wrote in this manner also wore a miter," Hazlitt said, "and is now a heap of dust; but when the name of Jeremy Taylor is no longer remembered with reverence, genius will have become a mockery, and virtue an empty shade." Other products of this period—in addition to an endless stream of sermons—are a defiant *Apology* for the Anglican liturgy (1649), a life of Christ called *The Great Exemplar* (1649), *Two Discourses* on baptism and prayer (1653), and the important *Unum Necessarium* (1655), whose liberal views on original sin greatly vexed the Presbyterians and led to much dispute.

In about 1655—and for reasons not altogether clear—Taylor took his leave of Golden Grove, and what remained of his career exemplified the "heights and declensions" that he had said described the life of man. As the torrent of his prose poured forth—*A Discourse of . . . Friendship* (1657), a set of *Polemical and Moral Discourses* (1657), *The Worthy Communicant* (1660), and the gigantic *Ductor Dubitantium* (1660), a treatise on casuistry dedicated to Charles II—his troubles came not as single spies, but in battalions. He suffered two brief stays in prison (perhaps for debt or perhaps for his libertarian views), the deaths of several of his children, and the attritions of incessant controversy in defense of his opinions. However, his appointment (1558) to a lectureship at Lisburn in County Antrim, Ireland, enabled him to teach and preach and write until the Restoration, when his long fidelity to the House of Stuart was rewarded with the bishopric of Down and Connor. Although his new dignity led to such collateral distinctions as membership in the Irish privy council and the vice-chancellorship of the University of Dublin, it was made so turbulent by the opposition of the embattled local clergy that his death at fifty-four could be regarded as a boon. Rust's great sermon at his funeral in Dromore Cathedral (which he himself had reconstructed) is no doubt overwrought, but its praise imparts conviction:

> This great prelate had the good humor of a gentleman, the eloquence of an orator, the fancy of a poet, the acuteness of a schoolman, the profoundness of a philosopher, the wisdom of a counsellor, the sagacity of a prophet, the reason of an angel, and the piety of a saint; he had devotion enough for a cloister, learning enough for a university, and wit enough for a college of virtuosi.

My texts are based upon the only contemporary edition (1647) of θεολογια εκλεκτικη. *A Discourse of the Liberty of Prophesying* (Wing T–400), the first (1650) edition of *The Rule and Exercises of Holy Living* (Wing T–371), the only edition (1650) of Lady Carbery's funeral sermon (Wing T–335), and the first (1651) edition of *The Rule and Exercises of Holy Dying* (Wing T–361).

Richard Heber's edition (15 vols., 1822) of Taylor's immense production has been revised by C. P. Eden (10 vols., 1847–54). Things like *Ductor Dubitantium* have few readers nowadays, but certain of his books—notably *Holy Living* and *Holy Dying* have survived more than three centuries of almost steady publication, and in our own time at least three anthologists—M. Armstrong (1923), L. P. Smith (*The Golden Grove*, 1930), and Margaret Gest (*The House of Understanding*, 1954)—have kept his name and gorgeous style alive. Edmund Gosse's life of Taylor (1903), like his lives of Donne and Browne, has been superseded, for C. J. Stranks' biography (1952), together with his chapter on Taylor in *Anglican Devotion* (1961), firmly puts the cleric and the preacher in his age. Taylor finds a place in most of the books on church history, prose style, and preaching in the General Bibliography, Sections III and IV. In addition, his performance as a rhetorician has been studied by Sister M. S. Antoine (1946), his contributions to the controversies of his troubled age by F. L. Huntley (*Jeremy Taylor and the Great Rebellion: A Study of His Mind and Temper in Controversy*, 1970), and his importance as a theologian by W. J. Brown (1925), H. R. Williamson (1952), Thomas Wood (1952), and H. T. Hughes (1960). Robert Gathorne-Hardy and William P. Williams have supplied a useful *Bibliography* (1972).

from The Liberty of Prophesying (1647)

To the Right Honorable Christopher Lord Hatton, Baron Hatton of Kirby, Comptroller of His Majesty's Household and One of His Majesty's Most Honorable Privy Council.[1]

My Lord,

In this great storm which hath dashed the vessel of the church all in pieces I have been cast upon the coast of Wales, and, in a little boat, thought to have enjoyed that rest and quietness which, in England, in a greater, I could not hope for. Here I cast anchor, and thinking to ride safely, the storm followed me with so impetuous violence that it broke a cable, and I lost my anchor: and here again I was exposed to the mercy of the sea and the gentleness of an element that could neither distinguish things nor persons. And but that He [10] who stilleth the raging of the sea, and the noise of his waves, and the madness of his people had provided a plank for me, I had been lost to all the opportunities of content or study. . . . And now since I have come ashore, I have been gathering a few sticks to warm me, a few books to entertain my thoughts and divert them from the perpetual meditation of my private troubles and the public dyscrasy[2]; but those which I could obtain were so few, and so impertinent and unuseful to any great purposes, that I began to be sad upon a new stock,[3] and full of apprehension that I should live [20] unprofitably, and die obscurely, and be forgotten, and my bones thrown into some common charnel house without any name or note to distinguish me from those who only served their generation by filling the number of citizens, and who could pretend to no thanks or reward from the public beyond a *jus trium liberorum*.[4] While I was troubled with these thoughts, and busy to find out an opportunity of doing some good in my small proportion, still the cares of the public did so intervene that it was as impossible to separate my design from relating to the present as to ex-[30]empt myself from the participation of the common calamity; still half my thoughts was, in despite of all my diversions and arts of avocations, fixed upon and mingled with the present concernments; so that besides them I could not go. Now because the great question is concerning religion, and in that also my scene lies, I resolved here to fix my considerations; especially when I observed the ways of promoting the several opinions, which now are busy, to be such as besides that they were most troublesome to me and such as I could, by no means, be friends withal, they were also such [40]

as to my understanding did the most apparently disserve their ends, whose design in advancing their own opinions was pretended for religion. For as contrary as cruelty is to mercy, as tyranny to charity, so is war and bloodshed to the meekness and gentleness of Christian religion. . . .

[Convinced, however, that Christians are, or ought to be, amenable to the persuasions of "peace and charity, and forgiveness and permissions mutual,"] I resolved to encounter with all objections, and to do something to which I should be determined by the consideration of the present distemperatures and necessities, by my own thoughts, by the questions and scruples, the sects and names, the interests and animosities which at this day, and for some years past, have exercised and disquieted Christendom.

Thus far I discoursed myself into employment, and having come thus far I knew not how to get farther; for I had heard of a great experience how difficult it was to make brick without straw, and here I had even seen my design blasted in the bud, and I despaired, in the calends, of doing what I purposed in the ides before.[5] For I had no books of my own here nor any in the voisinage;[6] and but that I remembered the result of some of those excellent discourses I had heard Your Lordship make when I was so happy as, in private, to gather up what your temperance and modesty forbids to be public, I had come in *proelia inermis*,[7] and, like enough, might have fared accordingly. I had this only advantage besides, that I have chosen a subject in which, if my own reason does not abuse me, I needed no other books or aids than what a man carries with him on horseback, I mean, the common principles of Christianity and those $\dot{\alpha}\xi\iota\dot{\omega}\mu\alpha\tau\alpha$[8] which men

To Lord Hatton [1]Although Clarendon called Christopher Hatton (1605?–70) "a person of great reputation, which in a few years he found a way utterly to lose," he was honored by two Stuart kings. Following service as a member of the Privy Council and as master of the King's Household (1642–46) he lived for several years abroad, but in 1662 Charles II reappointed the old courtier to the Privy Council.
[2]Disordered condition of the body politic. [3]For another reason.
[4]A Roman law, sponsored by Julius Caesar, whereby the father of three legitimate children was granted certain privileges and exemptions.
[5]What I intended doing one week I relinquished in despair a week or so thereafter. *Calends*: the first day of the Roman month. *Ides*: the middle of the Roman month. [6]Neighborhood, vicinity.
[7]"Unarmed for battle." [8]"Axioms."

use in the transactions of the ordinary occurrences of civil society; and upon the strength of them, and some other collateral assistances, I have run through it *utcunque*;[9] and the sum of the following discourses is nothing but the sense of these words of Scripture, that since "we know in part, and prophesy in part, and that now we see through a glass darkly,"[10] we should not despise or contemn persons not so knowing as ourselves, but "him that is weak in the faith, we should receive, but not to doubtful disputations";[11] therefore, certainly to charity and not to vexations, not to those which are the idle effects of impertinent wranglings. And provided they keep close to the foundation, which is faith and obedience, let them build upon this foundation matter more or less precious, yet if the foundation be entire they shall be saved with or without loss. And since we profess ourselves servants of so meek a Master, and disciples of so charitable an institute, "Let us walk worthy of the vocation wherewith we are called, with all lowliness and meekness, with long-suffering, forbearing one another in love";[12] for this is the best endeavoring to keep the unity of the Spirit when it is fast tied in the bond of peace. And although it be a duty of Christianity that "we all speak the same thing, that there be no divisions among us, but that we be perfectly joined together in the same mind, and in the same judgment";[13] yet this unity is to be estimated according to the unity of faith in things necessary, in matters of creed, and articles fundamental; for as for other things, it is more to be wished than to be hoped for. There are some "doubtful disputations," and in such the scribe, the wise, the disputer of this world[14] are, most commonly, very far from certainty, and many times from truth. There are diversity of persuasions in matters adiaphorous,[15] as meats, and drinks, and holy days, etc.; and both parties, the affirmative and the negative, affirm and deny with innocence enough, for the observer and he that observes not intend both to God, and God is our common Master: we all fellow-servants, and not the judge of each other in matters of conscience or doubtful disputation; and every man that hath faith, must have it to himself before God, but no man must either in such matters judge his brother or set him at nought but let us follow after the things which make for peace and things wherewith one may edify another.[16] And the way to do that is not by knowledge but by charity, for "knowledge puffeth up, but charity edifieth."[17] And since there is not in "every man the same knowledge, but the conscience of some are weak,"[18] as "my liberty must not be judged of another man's weak conscience,"[19] so must not I please myself so much in my right opinion, but I must also take order that his weak conscience be not offended or despised; for no man must "seek his own, but every man another's wealth."[20] And although we must contend earnestly for the faith, yet, "above all things, we must put on charity, which is the bond of perfectness."[21] And therefore this contention must be with arms fit for the Christian warfare, "the sword of the Spirit, and the shield of faith, and preparation of the gospel of peace, instead of shoes, and a helmet of salvation."[22] But not with other arms, for a churchman must not be πληκτικὸς, "a striker"; for "the weapons of our warfare are not carnal, but spiritual,"[23] and

the persons that use them ought to be "gentle, and easy to be entreated";[24] and we "must give an account of our faith to them that ask us, with meekness and humility, for so is the will of God, that with welldoing ye may put to silence the ignorance of foolish men."[25]

These, and thousands more to the same purpose, are the doctrines of Christianity, whose sense and intendment I have prosecuted in the following discourse, being very much displeased that so many opinions and new doctrines are commenced among us; but more troubled that every man that hath an opinion thinks his own and other men's salvation is concerned in its maintenance; but most of all that men should be persecuted and afflicted for disagreeing in such opinions, which they cannot, with sufficient grounds, obtrude upon others necessarily because they cannot propound them infallibly, and because they have no warrant from Scripture so to do. For if I shall tie other men to believe my opinion, because I think I have a place of Scripture which seems to warrant it to my understanding, why may he not serve up another dish to me in the same dress, and exact the same task of me to believe the contradictory? And then, since all the heretics in the world have offered to prove their articles by the same means by which true believers propound theirs, it is necessary that some separation, either of doctrine or of persons, be clearly made, that all pretences may not be admitted, nor any just allegations be rejected; and yet that in some other questions, whether they be truly or falsely pretended, if not evidently or demonstratively, there may be considerations had to the persons of men and to the laws of charity more than to the triumphing in any opinion or doctrine not simply necessary. Now, because some doctrines are clearly not necessary, and some are absolutely necessary, why may not the first separation be made upon this difference, and articles necessary be only urged as necessary, and the rest left to men indifferently, as they were by the Scripture indeterminately? And it were well if men would as much consider themselves as the doctrines, and think that they may as well be deceived by their own weakness as persuaded by the arguments of a doctrine, which other men, as wise, call inevident.[26] For it is a hard case that we shall think all Papists, and Anabaptists,[27] and Sacramentaries[28] to be fools and wicked persons: certainly, among all these sects there are very many wise men and good men, as well as erring. And although some zeals are so hot, and their eyes so inflamed with their ardors, that they do not think their

[9]"In whatever way." [10]1 Corinthians 13.9, 12.
[11]Romans 14.1. [12]Ephesians 4.1–2. [13]I Corinthians 1.10.
[14]*The scribe...this world*: a paraphrase of I Corinthians 1.20.
[15]Indifferent, neutral.
[16]*Every man...edify another*: a paraphrase of Romans 14.22, 10, 19.
[17]1 Corinthians 8.1. [18]1 Corinthians 8.7. [19]1 Corinthians 10.29.
[20]1 Corinthians 10.24. [21]Colossians 3.14. [22]Ephesians 6.14–17.
[23]2 Corinthians 10.4. [24]James 3.17. [25]1 Peter 3.15.
[26]Not evident, obscure.
[27]Followers of various Protestant reformers—most notoriously John of Leiden (d. 1536)—who denied the validity of infant baptism and advocated the separation of church and state.
[28]Protestant sectarians who regarded the bread and wine of the Eucharist as merely symbolic of the body and the blood of Christ.

adversaries look like other men, yet certainly we find by the result's of their discourses, and the transactions of their affairs of civil society, that they are men that speak and make syllogisms, and use reason, and read Scripture; and although they do no more understand all of it than we do, yet they endeavor to understand as much as concerns them, even all that they can, even all that concerns repentance from dead works and faith in our Lord Jesus Christ. And, therefore, methinks this also should be another consideration distinguishing the persons: for, if the persons be Christians in [10] their lives and Christians in their profession, if they acknowledge the eternal Son of God for their Master and their Lord and live in all relations as becomes persons making such professions, why then should I hate such persons whom God loves, and who love God, who are partakers of Christ, and Christ hath a title to them, who dwell in Christ, and Christ in them, because their understandings have not been brought up like mine, have not had the same masters, they have not met with the same books, nor the same company, or have not the same interest, or are not so wise, or else are wiser; [20] that is, for some reason or other, which I neither do understand nor ought to blame, have not the same opinions that I have, and do not determine their school questions[29] to the sense of my sect or interest?

But now, I know beforehand, that those men who will endure none but their own sect will make all manner of attempts against these purposes of charity and compliance, and, say I or do I what I can, will tell all their proselytes that I preach indifferency of religion; that I say it is no matter how we believe, nor what they profess, but that they may [30] comply with all sects and do violence to their own consciences; that they may be saved in all religions, and so make way for a *colluvies*[30] of heresies, and, by consequence, destroy all religion. Nay, they will say worse than all this; and, but that I am not used to their phrases and forms of declamation, I am persuaded I might represent fine tragedies beforehand. And this will be such an objection that although I am most confident I shall make apparent to be as false and scandalous as the objectors themselves are zealous and impatient, yet, besides that I believe the objection will come where my [40] answers will not come or not be understood, I am also confident that in defiance and incuriousness of all that I shall say, some men will persist pertinaciously in the accusation and deny my conclusion in despite of me. Well, but however, I will try. . . .

In the following section Taylor tries to make his own position clear. Sharply defining the limits of his own toleration, he insists that he would "allow no indifferency nor any countenance to those religions whose principles destroy government, nor to those religions (if there be any such) [50] that teach ill life." The sole "intendment" of his discourse is to show the value of an open mind in "questions speculative, indeterminable, curious, and unnecessary," and on the assumption that "no man, or company of men, can judge or punish our thoughts or secret purposes, whilst they so remain," he asserts that "God alone is judge of erring persons." Because opinion hardens into dogma, and compulsion leads so quickly to hypocrisy, men should be wary of calling their own fragile notions "by the name of religion,

and superstructures by the name of fundamental articles, and all fancies by the glorious appellative of faith." We must bear with one another's frailties because "no man is bound to have an excellent understanding, or to be infallible, or to be wiser than he can; for these are things that are not in his choice, and therefore not a matter of law, nor subject to reward and punishment." As the long and bloody record of religious persecution shows, "restraint of prophesying, imposing upon other men's understanding, being masters of their consciences, and lording it over their faith came in with the retinue and train of Antichrist," and there is little reason to expect that we ourselves shall win a certain hold on truth.

If we look abroad and consider how there is scarce any church but is highly charged by many adversaries in many things, possibly we may see a reason to charge every one of them in some things, and what shall we do then? The Church of Rome hath spots enough, and all the world is inquisitive enough to find out more, and to represent these to her greatest disadvantage. The Greek Church denies the procession[31] of the Holy Ghost from the Son. If that be false doctrine, she is highly to blame; if it be not, then all the western churches are to blame for saying the contrary. And there is no church that is in prosperity but alters her doctrine every age, either by bringing in new doctrines, or by contradicting her old; which shows that none are satisfied with themselves or with their own confessions. And since all churches believe themselves fallible, that only excepted which all other churches say is most of all deceived, it were strange if in so many articles, which make up their several bodies of confessions, they had not mistaken, every one of them, in some thing or other. The Lutheran churches maintain consubstantiation, the Zwinglians[32] are Sacramentaries, the Calvinists are fierce in the matters of absolute predetermination, and all these reject episcopacy, which the primitive church would have made no doubt to have called heresy. The Socinians[33] profess a portentous number of strange opinions: they deny the holy Trinity and the satisfaction[34] of our blessed Saviour. The Anabaptists laugh at paedobaptism;[35] the Ethiopian churches are Nestorian.[36] Where then shall we fix our confidence, or join communion? To pitch upon any one of these is to throw the dice if salvation be to be had only in one of them, and that every error that by chance hath made a sect and is distinguished by a name be damnable.

If this consideration does not deceive me, we have no other help in the midst of these distractions and disunions but all of us to be united in that common term, which as it does

[29]Trivial points of theology (such as those argued by the Schoolmen). [30]"Collection of filth." [31]Issuing forth.
[32]Followers of Ulrich Zwingli (1484–1531), Swiss reformer who denied the doctrine of the Real Presence in the Eucharist.
[33]Followers of Faustus Socinus and Laelius Socinus, sixteenth-century Italian theologians who rejected the Trinity, the divinity of Christ, and the doctrine of original sin. [34]Atonement.
[35]Infant baptism.
[36]Ancient Christian sect founded by the Syrian ecclesiastic Nestorius (d. 431?), who maintained that the human and divine natures were not merged in Christ.

constitute the church in its being such, so it is the medium
of the communion of saints; and that is the Creed of the
Apostles; and, in all other things, an honest endeavor to
find out what truths we can and a charitable and mutual
permission to others that disagree from us and our opinions.
I am sure this may satisfy us, for it will secure us; but I
know not any thing else that will; and no man can be rea-
sonably persuaded or satisfied in anything else unless he
throws himself upon chance, or absolute predestination, or
his own confidence; in every one of which it is two to one,
at least, but he may miscarry.

Thus far, I thought I had reason on my side, and I sup-
pose I have made it good, upon its proper grounds, in the
pages following, But, then, if the result be that men must be
permitted in their opinions, and that Christians must not
persecute Christians, I have also as much reason to reprove
all those oblique arts which are not direct persecutions of
men's persons, but they are indirect proceedings, ungentle
and unchristian, servants of faction and interest, provocations
to zeal and animosities, and destructive of learning and ingen-
uity. And these are, suppressing all the monuments of their
adversaries, forcing them to recant, and burning their
books. [Such "ungentle" procedures, as Taylor thinks, are
wrong as well as foolish, for they are always self-defeating.]
. . . It is but an illiterate policy to think that such indirect
and uningenuous proceedings can, amongst wise and free
men, disgrace the authors and disrepute their discourses.
And I have seen that the price hath been trebled upon a
forbidden or a condemned book; and some men in policy
have got a prohibition, that their impression might be the
more certainly vendible and the author himself thought con-
siderable.

The best way is to leave tricks and devices, and to fall
upon that way which the best ages of the church did use.
With the strength of argument, and allegations of Scripture,
and modesty of deportment, and meekness and charity to the
persons of men they converted misbelievers, stopped the
mouths of adversaries, asserted truth, and discountenanced
error; and those other stratagems and arts of support and
maintenance to doctrines were the issues of heretical brains.
. . . To my understanding it is a plain art and design of the
devil to make us so in love with our own opinions as to call
them faith and religion, that we may be proud in our un-
derstanding; and besides that, by our zeal in our opinions
we grow cool in our piety and practical duties; he also by
this earnest contention does directly destroy good life by
engagement of zealots to do anything rather than be over-
come and lose their beloved propositions. But I would fain
know why is not any vicious habit as bad or worse than a
false opinion. Why are we so zealous against those we call
heretics, and yet great friends with drunkards and fornica-
tors and swearers and intemperate and idle persons? . . .
I am certain that a drunkard is as contrary to God, and lives
as contrary to the laws of Christianity, as a heretic; and I
am also sure that I know what drunkenness is, but I am not
sure that such an opinion is heresy; neither would other men
be so sure as they think for if they did consider it aright and
observe the infinite deceptions and causes of deceptions in

wise men, and in most things, and in all doubtful questions,
and that they did not mistake confidence for certainty. . . .

But now if men would a little turn the tables and be as
zealous for a good life and all the strictest precepts of Christ-
ianity (which is a religion the most holy, the most reasonable,
and the most consummate that ever was taught to man) as
they are for such propositions in which neither the life nor
the ornament of Christianity is concerned, we should find
that as a consequent of this piety men would be as careful
as they could to find out all truths, and the sense of all rev-
elations which may concern their duty; and where men
were miserable and could not, yet others that lived good lives
too would also be so charitable as not to add affliction to
this misery; and both of them are parts of good life. To be
compassionate and to help to bear one another's burdens,
not to destroy the weak but to entertain him meekly, that's
a precept of charity; and to endeavor to find out the whole
will of God, that also is a part of the obedience, the choice,
and the excellency of faith; and he lives not a good life that
does not do both these. . . .

If we consider that sects are made, and opinions are called
heresies upon interest and the grounds of emolument, we
shall see that a good life would cure much of this mischief.
For first, the Church of Rome, which is the great dictatrix[37]
of dogmatical resolutions, and the declarer of heresy, and
calls heretic more than all the world besides, hath made that
the rule of heresy, which is the conservator of interest and
the ends of men. For to recede from the doctrine of the
church, with them, makes heresy; that is, to disrepute their
authority, and not to obey them, not to be their subjects,
not to give them the empire of our conscience is the great
κριτήριον[38] of heresy.

So that, with them, heresy is to be esteemed clearly by
human ends, not by divine rules; that is formal heresy
which does materially disserve them. And it would make a
suspicious man a little inquisitive into their particular
doctrines; and when he finds that indulgencies and jubilees
and purgatories and masses and offices for the dead are very
profitable—that the doctrine of primacy, of infallibility, of
superiority over councils, of indirect power in temporals
are great instruments of secular honor—he would be apt
enough to think that if the Church of Rome would learn to
lay her honor at the feet of the crucifix, and despise the
world, and prefer Jerusalem before Rome, and heaven above
the Lateran[39] that these opinions would not have in them
any native strength to support them against the perpetual
assaults of their adversaries, that speak so much reason and
Scripture against them. I have instanced in the Roman re-
ligion, but I wish it may be considered also how far men's
doctrines in other sects serve men's temporal ends; so far
that it would not be unreasonable or unnecessary to attempt
to cure some of their distemperatures or mispersuasions by
the salutary precepts of sanctity and holy life. Sure enough,
if it did not more concern their reputation and their lasting

[37]Dictator. Taylor playfully uses the Latin feminine suffix, which
survives in such words as *aviatrix*. [38]"Criterion."
[39]St. John Lateran, the ancient Roman church of the pope in his
capacity as bishop of Rome.

interest to be counted true believers rather than good livers, they would rather endeavor to live well than to be accounted of a right opinion in things beside the Creed.

For my own particular, I cannot but expect that God, in His justice, should enlarge the bounds of the Turkish empire, or some other way punish Christians, by reason of their pertinacious disputing about things unnecessary, undeterminable, and unprofitable, and for their hating and persecuting their brethren, which should be as dear to them as their own lives, for not consenting to one another's follies [10] and senseless vanities. How many volumes have been written about angels, about immaculate conception, about original sin, when that all that is solid reason or clear revelation in all these three articles may be reasonably enough comprised in forty lines? And in these trifles and impertinencies men are curiously busy while they neglect those glorious precepts of Christianity and holy life, which are the glories of our religon and would enable us to a happy eternity.

My Lord, thus far my thoughts have carried me, and then [20] I thought I had reason to go further and to examine the proper grounds upon which these persuasions might rely and stand firm, in case anybody should contest against them. For, possibly, men may be angry at me and my design, for I do all them great displeasure who think no end is then well served when their interest is disserved; and but that I have writ so untowardly and heavily that I am not worth a confutation, possibly some or other might be writing against me. But then I must tell them I am prepared of an answer beforehand, for I think I have spoken reason in my book, [30] and examined it with all the severity I have; and if after all this I be deceived, this confirms me in my first opinion, and becomes a new argument to me that I have spoken reason; for it furnishes me with a new instance that it is necessary there should be a mutual compliance and toleration, because even then when a man thinks he hath most reason to be confident he may easily be deceived.

For I am sure I have no other design but the prosecution and advantage of truth, and I may truly use the words of Gregory Nazianzen:[40] *Non studemus paci in detrimentum verae* [40] *doctrinae—ut facilitatis et mansuetudinis famam colligamus.*[41] But I have writ this because I thought it was necessary, and

seasonable, and charitable, and agreeable to the great precepts and design of Christianity, consonant to the practice of the apostles and of the best ages of the church, most agreeable to Scripture and reason, to revelation and the nature of the thing; and it is such a doctrine that if there be variety in human affairs, if the event[42] of things be not settled in a durable consistence but is changeable, everyone of us all may have need of it. I shall only, therefore, desire that they who will read it may come to the reading it with as much simplicity of purposes and unmixed desires of truth as I did to the writing it, and that no man trouble himself with me or my discourse that thinks beforehand that his opinion cannot be reasonably altered. If he thinks me to be mistaken before he tries, let him also think that he may be mistaken too—and that he who judges before he hears is mistaken though he gives a right sentence. . . .

And now, my Lord, that I have inscribed this book to Your Lordship although it be a design of doing honor to myself, that I have marked it with so honored and beloved a name might possibly need as much excuse as it does pardon but that Your Lordship knows your own; for out of your mines I have digged the mineral; only I have stamped it with my own image, as you may perceive by the deformities which are in it. But your great name in letters will add so much value to it as to make it obtain its pardon amongst all them that know how to value you, and all your relatives and dependents by the proportion of relation. For others I shall be incurious, because the number of them that honor you is the same with them that honor learning and piety, and they are the best theater and the best judges; amongst which the world must needs take notice of my ambition to be ascribed by my public pretence to be what I am in all heartiness of devotion, and for all the reason of the world,

my honored Lord,
Your Lordship's most faithful
and most affectionate servant,
J. Taylor.

[40]Gregory of Nazianzus (329?–?389), one of the fathers of the Eastern Church.
[41]We do not seek peace at the expense of true doctrine, but we do value a reputation for courtesy and compassion.
[42]Outcome.

from The Rule and Exercises of Holy Living (1650)

CHAPTER II

OF CHRISTIAN SOBRIETY

SECTION VI

OF CONTENTEDNESS IN ALL ESTATES AND ACCIDENTS[1]

Virtues and discourses are, like friends, necessary in all fortunes; but those are the best which are friends in our sadnesses and support us in our sorrows and sad accidents; and

in this sense, no man that is virtuous can be friendless; nor hath any man reason to complain of the divine providence, or accuse the public disorder of things, or his own in felicity, since God hath appointed one remedy for all the evils in the world, and that is a contented spirit: for this alone makes a man pass through fire, and not be scorched; through seas,

HOLY LIVING   [1]Happenings (fortunate or unfortunate).

and not be drowned; through hunger and nakedness, and want nothing. For since all the evil in the world consists in the disagreeing between the object and the appetite, as when a man hath what he desires not, or desires what he hath not, or desires amiss, he that composes his spirit to the present accident hath variety of instances for his virtue, but none to trouble him, because his desires enlarge not beyond his present fortune; and a wise man is placed in the variety of chances, like the nave or center of a wheel in the midst of all the circumvolutions and changes of posture, without violence or change save that it turns gently in compliance with its changed parts, and is indifferent which part is up and which is down; for there is some virtue or other to be exercised whatever happens, either patience or thanksgiving, love or fear, moderation or humility, charity or contentedness, and they are every one of them equally in order to his great end, an immortal felicity; and beauty is not made by white or red, by black eyes and a round face, by a straight body and a smooth skin, but by a proportion to the fancy. No rules can make amiability: our minds and apprehensions make that, and so is our felicity, and we may be reconciled to poverty and a low fortune if we suffer contentedness and the grace of God to make the proportions. For no man is poor that does not think himself so; but if, in a full fortune, with impatience he desires more, he proclaims his wants and his beggarly condition. But because this grace of contentedness was the sum of all the old moral philosophy, and a great duty in Christianity, and of most universal use in the whole course of our lives, and the only instrument to ease the burdens of the world and the enmities of sad chances, it will not be amiss to press it by the proper arguments, by which God hath bound it upon our spirits, it being fastened by reason and religion, by duty and interest, by necessity and convenience, by example, and by the proposition of excellent rewards no less than peace and felicity.

1. Contentedness in all estates is a duty of religion; it is the great reasonableness of complying with the divine providence, which governs all the world and hath so ordered us in the administration of his great family. He were a strange fool that should be angry because dogs and sheep need no shoes, and yet himself is full of care to get some. God hath supplied those needs to them by natural provisions, and to thee by an artificial; for He hath given thee reason to learn a trade, or some means to make or buy them, so that it only differs in the manner of our provision; and which had you rather want, shoes or reason? And my patron, that hath given me a farm, is freer to me than if he gives a loaf ready baked. But, however, all these gifts come from Him, and therefore it is fit He should dispense them as He pleases; and if we murmur here, we may, at the next melancholy, be troubled that God did not make us to be angels or stars. For if that which we are or have do not content us, we may be troubled for everything in the world which is besides our being or our possessions.

God is the master of the scenes: we must not choose which part we shall act; it concerns us only to be careful that we do it well, always saying, "If this please God, let it be as it is": and we who pray that God's will may be done in earth as it is in heaven must remember that the angels do whatsoever is commanded them, and go wherever they are sent, and refuse no circumstances: and if their employment be crossed by a higher decree, they sit down in peace and rejoice in the event; and when the angel of Judea could not prevail in behalf of the people committed to his charge because the angel of Persia opposed it, he only told the story at the command of God, and was as content, and worshipped with as great an ecstasy in his proportion as the prevailing spirit.[2] Do thou so likewise; keep the station where God hath placed you, and you shall never long for things without, but sit at home feasting upon the divine providence and thy own reason, by which we are taught that it is necessary and reasonable to submit to God.

For is not all the world God's family? Are not we his creatures? Are we not as clay in the hand of the potter? Do we not live upon his meat, and move by his strength, and do our work by his light? Are we any thing but what we are from him? And shall there be a mutiny among the flocks and herds because their lord or their shepherd chooses their pastures, and suffers them not to wander into deserts and unknown ways? If we choose, we do it so foolishly that we cannot like it long, and most commonly not at all; but God, who can do what He please, is wise to choose safely for us, affectionate to comply with our needs, and powerful to execute all His wise decrees. Here, therefore, is the wisdom of the contented man, to let God choose for him; for when we have given up our wills to Him, and stand in that station of the battle where our great general hath placed us, our spirits must needs rest while our conditions have for their security the power, the wisdom, and the charity of God.

2. Contentedness in all accidents brings great peace of spirit, and is the great and only instrument of temporal felicity. It removes the sting from the accident, and makes a man not to depend upon chance and the uncertain dispositions of men for his well-being, but only on God and his own spirit. We ourselves make our fortunes good or bad, and when God lets loose a tyrant upon us, or a sickness, or scorn, or a lessened fortune, if we fear to die, or know not to be patient, or are proud, or covetous, then the calamity sits heavy on us. But if we know how to manage a noble principle, and fear not death so much as a dishonest action, and think impatience a worse evil than a fever, and pride to be the biggest disgrace, and poverty to be infinitely desirable before the torments of covetousness; then we, who now think vice to be so easy, and make it so familiar, and think the cure so impossible, shall quickly be of another mind, and reckon these accidents amongst things eligible.

But no man can be happy that hath great hopes and great fears of things without, and events depending upon other men, or upon the chances of fortune. The rewards of virtue are certain, and our provisions for our natural support are certain; or if we want meat till we die, then we die of that disease, and there are many worse than to die with an atrophy or consumption, or unapt and coarser nourishment. But he that suffers a transporting passion concerning things within the power of others is free from sorrow and amazement no

[2]Daniel 10.10–21.

longer than his enemy shall give him leave; and it is ten to one but he shall be smitten then and there, where it shall most trouble him: for so the adder teaches us where to strike. by her curious and fearful defending of her head. The old Stoics, when you told them of a sad story, would still answer τί πρὸς μέ, "What is that to me?"—"Yes, for the tyrant hath sentenced you also to prison"—"Well, what is that? He will put a chain upon my leg, but he cannot bind my soul."— "No, but he will kill you."—"Then I'll die. If presently, let me go, that I may presently be freer than himself: but if not till anon or to-morrow, I will dine first, or sleep, or do what reason and nature calls for, as at other times." This, in gentile[3] philosophy, is the same with the discourse of St. Paul, "I have learned in whatsoever state I am, therewith to be content. I know both how to be abased, and I know how to abound; everywhere and in all things I am instructed, both how to be full and to be hungry, both to abound and suffer need."[4]

We are in the world like men playing at tables:[5] the chance is not in our power, but to play it is; and when it is fallen, we must manage it as we can, and let nothing trouble us but when we do a base action, or speak like a fool, or think wickedly; these things God hath put into our powers, but concerning those things which are wholly in the choice of another, they cannot fall under our deliberation, and therefore neither are they fit for our passions. My fear may make me miserable, but it cannot prevent what another hath in his power and purpose; and prosperities can only be enjoyed by them who fear not at all to lose them, since the amazement and passion concerning the future takes off all the pleasure of the present possession. Therefore if thou hast lost thy land do not also lose thy constancy; and if thou must die a little sooner, yet do not die impatiently. For no chance is evil to him that is content, and to a man nothing is miserable unless it be unreasonable. No man can make another man to be his slave unless he hath first enslaved himself to life and death, to pleasure or pain, to hope or fear. Command these passions, and you are freer than the Parthian kings.

A Funeral Sermon Preached at the Obsequies of the Right Honorable and Most Virtuous Lady, the Lady Frances, Countess of Carbery (1650)[1]

. . . I have now done with my text, but yet am to make you another sermon. I have told you the necessity and the state of death, it may be, too largely for such a sad story; I shall, therefore, now with a better compendium[2] teach you how to live by telling you a plain narrative of a life, which if you imitate, and write after the copy, it will make that death shall not be an evil, but a thing to be desired, and to be reckoned amongst the purchases[3] and advantages of your fortune. When Martha and Mary went to weep over the grave of their brother, Christ met them there and preached a funeral sermon, discoursing of the resurrection, and applying to

the purposes of faith, and confession of Christ, and glorification of God.[4] We have no other, we can have no better precedent to follow; and now that we are come to weep over the grave of our dear sister, this rare personage, we cannot choose but have many virtues to learn, many to imitate, and some to exercise.

1. I chose not to declare her extraction and genealogy; it was indeed fair and honorable; but having the blessing to be descended from worthy and honored ancestors, and herself to be adopted and ingrafted into a more noble family; yet she felt such outward appendages to be none of hers because not of her choice, but the purchase of the virtues of others, which although they did engage her to do noble things, yet they would upbraid all degenerate and less honorable lives than were those which began and increased the honor of the families. She did not love her fortune for making her noble, but thought it would be a dishonor to her if she did not continue a nobleness and excellency of virtue fit to be owned by persons relating to such ancestors. It is fit for all of us to honor the nobleness of a family; but it is also fit for them that are noble to despise it, and to establish their honor upon the foundation of doing excellent things, and suffering in good causes, and despising dishonorable actions, and in communicating good things to others; for this is the rule in nature: those creatures are most honorable which have the greatest power and do the greatest good; and accordingly myself have been a witness of it, how this excellent lady would, by an act of humility and Christian abstraction, strip herself of all that fair appendage of exterior honor which decked her person and her fortune, and desired to be owned by nothing but what was her own, that she might only be esteemed honorable according to that which is the honor of a Christian and a wise person.

2. She had a strict and severe education, and it was one of God's graces and favors to her: for being the heiress of a great fortune, and living amongst the throng of persons, in the sight of vanities and empty temptations, that is, in that part of the kingdom where greatness is too often expressed in great follies and great vices, God had provided a severe and angry[5] education to chastise the forwardnesses of a young spirit and a fair fortune, that she might

---

[3]Pagan. [4]Philippians 4.11–12.
[5]Games of chance, like draughts or backgammon.
A funeral sermon [1]Taking as his text 2 Samuel 14.14 ("For we must needs die, etc."), Taylor conventionally devotes the first part of this funeral sermon to a sonorous treatment of "the necessity and the state of death." The concluding section, which is given here, is at once a threnody for his departed friend and patroness, a sort of saint's life, and a character. Its subject, a daughter of Sir John Altham of Oxfordshire, became Lord Carbery's second wife in 1637 and died in 1650 following the birth of her tenth child. Incidentally, she was succeeded (1652) by Lady Alice Egerton, daughter of the earl of Bridgewater, who in 1634 had represented the role of the Lady in the first production of Milton's *Comus* at Ludlow Castle. See p. 272, n. 1.
[2]More briefly and effectively (by relating the life of Lady Carbery).
[3]Benefits, advantages.
[4]*When Martha...glorification of God*: John 11.
[5]Trying, demanding.

for ever be so far distant from a vice that she might only see it and loathe it, but never taste of it, so much as to be put to her choice whether she would be virtuous or no. God, intending to secure this soul to himself, would not suffer the follies of the world to seize upon her by way of too near a trial or busy temptation.

3. She was married young; and besides her businesses of religion seemed to be ordained in the providence of God to bring to this honorable family a part of a fair fortune, and to leave behind her a fairer issue, worth ten thousand times her portion: and as if this had been all the public business of her life, when he had so far served God's ends, God in mercy would also serve hers, and take her to an early blessedness.

4. In passing through which line of providence she had the art to secure her eternal interest by turning her condition into duty, and expressing her duty in the greatest eminency of a virtuous, prudent, and rare affection that hath been known in any example. I will not give her so low a testimony as to say only that she was chaste; she was a person of that severity, modesty, and close[6] religion (as to that particular) that she was not capable of uncivil temptation; and you might as well have suspected the sun to smell of the poppy that he looks on as that she could have been a person apt to be sullied by the breath of a foul question.

5. But that which I shall note in her is that which I would have exemplar to all ladies, and to all women: she had a love so great for her lord, so entirely given up to a dear affection, that she thought the same things and loved the same loves, and hated according to the same enmities, and breathed in his soul, and lived in his presence, and languished in his absence; and all that she was or did was only for and to her dearest lord:

> *Si gaudet, si flet, si tacet, hunc loquitur;*
> *Cenat, propinat, poscit, negat innuit: unus*
> *Naevius est.*[7]

And although this was a great enamel to the beauty of her soul, yet it might in some degrees be also a reward to the virtue of her lord: for she would often discourse it to them that conversed with her, that he would improve that interest which he had in her affection to the advantages of God and of religion; and she would delight to say that he called her to her devotions, he encouraged her good inclinations, he directed her piety, he invited her with good books; and then she loved religion, which she saw was not only pleasing to God, and an act or state of duty, but pleasing to her lord, and an act also of affection and conjugal obedience; and what at first she loved the more forwardly for his sake, in the using of religion left such relishes upon her spirit that she found in it amiability[8] enough to make her love it for its own. So God usually brings us to Him by instruments of nature and affections, and then incorporates us into His inheritance by the more immediate relishes of heaven and the secret things of the Spirit. He only was (under God) the light of her eyes, and the cordial of her spirits, and the guide of her actions, and the measure of her affections, till her affections swelled up into a religion, and then it could go no higher, but was confederate with those other duties which made her dear to God:

which rare combination of duty and religion I choose to express in the words of Solomon: "She forsook not the guide of her youth, nor brake the covenant of her God."[9]

6. As she was a rare wife, so she was an excellent mother; for in so tender a constitution of spirit as hers was, and in so great a kindness towards her children, there hath seldom been seen a stricter and more curious[10] care of their persons, their deportment, their nature, their disposition, their learning, and their customs; and if ever kindness and care did contest and make parties in her, yet her care and her severity was ever victorious; and she knew not how to do an ill turn to their severer part by her more tender and forward kindness. And as her custom was, she turned this also into love to her lord; for she was not only diligent to have them bred nobly and religiously, but also was careful and solicitous that they should be taught to observe all the circumstances and inclinations, the desires and wishes of their father, as thinking that virtue to have no good circumstances which was not dressed by his copy, and ruled by his lines and his affections; and her prudence in the managing her children was so singular and rare that whenever you mean to bless this family, and pray a hearty and a profitable prayer for it, beg of God that the children may have those excellent things which she designed to them, and provided for them in her heart and wishes; that they may live by her purposes, and may grow thither whither she would fain have brought them. All these were great parts of an excellent religion as they concerned her greatest temporal relations.

7. But if we examine how she demeaned herself towards God, there also you will find her not of a common but of an exemplar piety. She was a great reader of Scripture, confining herself to great portions every day; which she read, not to the purposes of vanity and impertinent curiosities, not to seem knowing, or to become talking, not to expound and rule; but to teach her all her duty, to instruct her in the knowledge and love of God and of her neighbors; to make her more humble, and, to teach her to despise the world and all its gilded vanities; and that she might entertain passions wholly in design and order to heaven. I have seen female religion that wholly dwelt upon the face and tongue; that like a wanton and an undressed[11] tree spends all its juice in suckers and irregular branches, in leaves and gum, and after all such goodly outsides, you should never eat an apple, or be delighted with the beauties or the perfumes of a hopeful blossom. But the religion of this excellent lady was of another constitution: it took root downward in humility, and brought forth fruit upward in the substantial graces of a Christian, in charity and justice, in chastity and modesty, in fair friendships and sweetness of society: she had not very much of the forms and outsides of godliness, but she was hugely careful for the power of it, for the moral, essential, and useful parts; such which would make her be, not seem to be, religious.

[6]Reserved, private.
[7]"If joyful, if sad, if quiet, she speaks of him. He dines, toasts, requests, denies, or nods: Naevius is everything to her" (adapted from Martial, *Epigrams*, I.68). [8]Lovableness. [9]Proverbs 2.17.
[10]Solicitous [11]Untrained and unpruned.

8. She was a very constant person at her prayers, and spent all her time which nature did permit to her choice in her devotions, and reading, and meditating, and the necessary offices of household government; every one of which is an action of religion, some by nature, some by adoption. To these, also, God gave her a very great love to hear the word of God preached; in which, because I had sometimes the honor to minister to her, I can give this certain testimony, that she was a diligent, watchful, and attentive hearer; and to this, had so excellent a judgment that if ever I saw a woman whose judgment was to be revered, it was hers alone; and I have sometimes thought that the eminency of her discerning faculties did reward a pious discourse, and placed it in the regions of honor and usefulness, and gathered it up from the ground, where commonly such homilies are spilt, or scattered in neglect and inconsideration. But her appetite was not soon satisfied with what was useful to her soul: she was also a constant reader of sermons, and seldom missed to read one every day; and that she might be full of instruction and holy principles, she had lately designed to have a large book in which she purposed to have a stock of religion transcribed in such assistances as she would choose, that she might be "readily furnished and instructed to every good work." But God prevented that, and hath filled her desires, not out of cisterns and little aqueducts, but hath carried her to the fountain, where "she drinks of the pleasures of the river,"[12] and is full of God.

9. She always lived a life of much innocence, free from the violences of great sins; her person, her breeding, her modesty, her honor, her religion, her early marriage, the guide of her soul, and the guide of her youth were as so many fountains of restraining grace to her, to keep her from the dishonors of a crime. *Bonum est portare jugum ab adolescentia:* "it is good to bear the yoke of the Lord from our youth"; and though she did so, being guarded by a mighty providence, and a great favor and grace of God, from staining her fair soul with the spots of hell, yet she had strange fears and early cares upon her; but these were not only for herself, but in order to others, to her nearest relatives: for she was so great a lover of this honorable family, of which now she was a mother, that she desired to become a channel of great blessings to it unto future ages, and was extremely jealous lest anything should be done, or lest anything had been done, though an age or two since, which should entail a curse upon the innocent posterity; and, therefore (although I do not know that ever she was tempted with an offer of the crime) yet she did infinitely remove all sacrilege from her thoughts, and delighted to see her estate of a clear and disentangled interest: she would have no mingled rights with it; she would not receive anything from the church but religion and a blessing; and she never thought a curse and a sin far enough off, but would desire it to be infinitely distant; and that as to this family God had given much honor, and a wise head to govern it, so He would also forever give many more blessings: and because she knew that the sins of parents descend upon children, she endeavored, by justice and religion, by charity and honor, to secure that her channel should convey nothing but health, and a fair example, and a blessing.

10. And though her accounts to God was made up of nothing but small parcels, little passions, and angry words, and trifling discontents, which are the allays of the piety of the most holy persons, yet she was early at her repentance; and toward the latter end of her days grew so fast in religion as if she had had a revelation of her approaching end, and therefore that she must go a great way in a little time: her discourses more full of religion, her prayers more frequent, her charity increasing, her forgiveness more forward, her friendships more communicative, her passion more under discipline; and so she trimmed her lamp, not thinking her night was so near, but that it might shine also in the daytime, in the temple and before the altar of incense.

But in this course of hers there were some circumstances, and some appendages of substance, which were highly remarkable.

1. In all her religion, and in all her actions of relation towards God, she had a strange evenness and untroubled passage, sliding toward her ocean of God and of infinity with a certain and silent motion. So have I seen a river, deep and smooth, passing with a still foot and a sober face, and paying to the *fiscus,* the great "exchequer" of the sea, the prince of all the watery bodies, a tribute large and full; and hard by it, a little book skipping and making a noise upon its unequal and neighbor bottom; and after all its talking and bragged motion, it paid to its common audit no more than the revenues of a little cloud or a contemptible vessel: so have I sometimes compared the issues of her religion to the solemnities and famed outsides of another's piety. It dwelt upon her spirit, and was incorporated with the periodical work of every day: she did not believe that religion was intended to minister to fame and reputation, but to pardon of sins, to the pleasure of God, and the salvation of souls. For religion is like the breath of heaven: if it goes abroad into the open air, it scatters and dissolves like camphire;[13] but if it enters into a secret hollowness, into a close conveyance, it is strong and mighty, and comes forth with vigor and great effect at the other end, at the other side of this life, in the days of death and judgment.

2. The other appendage of her religion, which also was a great ornament to all the parts of her life, was a rare modesty and humility of spirit, a confident despising and undervaluing of herself. For though she had the greatest judgment, and the greatest experience of things and persons, that I ever yet knew in a person of her youth, and sex, and circumstances; yet, as if she knew nothing of it, she had the meanest opinion of herself; and like a fair taper, when she shined to all the room, yet round about her own station, she had cast a shadow and a cloud, and she shined to everybody but herself. But the perfectness of her prudence and excellent parts could not be hid; and all her humility, and arts of concealment, made the virtues more amiable and illustrious. For as pride sullies the beauty of the fairest virtues, and makes our understanding but like the craft and learning of a devil, so humility is the greatest eminency and art of publication in the whole world; and she, in all her arts of secrecy and hiding

[12]Psalm 36.8.   [13]Camphor.

her worthy things, was but "like one that hideth the wind, and covers the ointment of her right hand."[14]

I know not by what instrument it happened, but when death drew near, before it made any show upon her body or revealed itself by a natural signification, it was conveyed to her spirit: she had a strange secret persuasion that the bringing this child should be her last scene of life; and we have known that the soul, when she is about to disrobe herself of her upper garment, sometimes speaks rarely, "*Magnifica verba mors prope admota excutit*";[15] sometimes it is prophetical; sometimes God, by a superinduced persuasion wrought by instruments or accidents of His own, serves the ends of His own providence, and the salvation of the soul; but so it was that the thought of death dwelt long with her, and grew from the first steps of fancy and fear to a consent, from thence to a strange credulity and expectation of it; and without the violence of sickness she died as if she had done it voluntarily, and by design, and for fear her expectation should have been deceived; or that she should seem to have had an unreasonable fear or apprehension; or rather, as one said of Cato, *Sic abiit e vita, ut causam moriendi nactam se esse gauderet*:[16] "she died as if she had been glad of the opportunity."

And in this I cannot but adore the providence and admire the wisdom and infinite mercies of God; for having a tender and soft, a delicate, and fine constitution and breeding, she was tender to pain, and apprehensive of it as a child's shoulder is of a load and burden: *Grave est tenerae cervici jugum:* and in her often discourses of death, which she would renew willingly and frequently, she would tell that "she feared not death, but she feared the sharp pains of death": *Emori nolo, me esse mortuam non curo.* The being dead, and being freed from the troubles and dangers of this world, she hoped would be for her advantage, and therefore that was no part of her fear; but she, believing the pangs of death were great, and the use and aids of reason little, had reason to fear lest they should do violence to her spirit, and the decency of her resolution. But God, that knew her fears and her jealousy concerning herself, fitted her with a death so easy, so harmless, so painless that it did not put her patience to a severe trial. It was not (in all appearance) of so much trouble as two fits of a common ague, so careful was God to remonstrate to all that stood in that sad attendance that this soul was dear to Him, and that since she had done so much of her duty towards it, He that began would also finish her redemption by an act of a rare providence and a singular mercy. Blessed be that goodness of God, who does so careful actions of mercy for the ease and security of his servants! But this one instance was a great demonstration that the apprehension of death is worse than the pains of death; and that God loves to reprove the unreasonableness of our fears by the mightiness and by the arts of His mercy.

She had in her sickness, if I may so call it—or rather in the solemnities and graver preparations towards death—some curious and well-becoming fears concerning the final state of her soul; but from thence she passed into a *deliquium,* or a kind of trance; and as soon as she came forth of it, as if it had been a vision, or that she had conversed with an angel, and from his hand had received a label or scroll of the Book of Life, and there seen her name enrolled, she cried out aloud, "Glory be to God on high! now I am sure I shall be saved." Concerning which manner of discoursing we are wholly ignorant what judgment can be made; but certainly there are strange things in the other world, and so there are in all the immediate preparations to it; and a little glimpse of heaven, a minute's conversing with an angel, any ray of God, any communication extraordinary from the spirit of comfort which God gives to his servants in strange and unknown manners, are infinitely far from illusions, and they shall then be understood by us when we feel them, and when our new and strange needs shall be refreshed by such unusual visitations.

But I must be forced to use summaries and arts of abbreviature in the enumerating those things, in which this rare personage was dear to God and to all her relatives.

If we consider her person, she was in the flower of her age, *jucundum cum aetas florida ver ageret;*[17] of a temperate, plain, and natural diet, without curiosity or an intemperate palate; she spent less time in dressing than many servants; her recreations were little and seldom, her prayers often, her reading much; she was of a most noble and charitable soul, a great lover of honorable actions, and as great a despiser of base things; hugely loving to oblige others, and very unwilling to be in arrear to any upon the stock of courtesies and liberality; so free in all acts of favor that she would not stay to hear herself thanked, as being unwilling that what good went from her to a needful or an obliged person should ever return to her again. She was an excellent friend, and hugely dear to very many, especially to the best and most discerning persons, to all that conversed with her, and could understand her great worth and sweetness. She was of an honourable, a nice and tender reputation; and of the pleasures of this world, which were laid before her in heaps, she took a very small and inconsiderable share, as not loving to glut herself with vanity or to take her portion of good things here below.

If we look on her as a wife, she was chaste and loving, fruitful and discreet, humble and pleasant, witty and compliant, rich and fair; and wanted nothing to the making her a principal and a precedent to the best wives of the world but a long life and a full age.

If we remember her as a mother, she was kind and severe, careful and prudent, very tender and not at all fond;[18] a greater lover of her children's souls than of their bodies, and one that would value them more by the strict rules of honor and proper worth than by their relation to herself.

Her servants found her prudent and fit to govern, and yet open-handed and apt to reward; a just exacter of their duty, and a great rewarder of their diligence.

---

[14]Proverbs 27.16.

[15]"When death comes near it drives out boastful words" (Seneca, *Troades,* l. 575).

[16]"He left life rejoicing that he had found a reason for death" (Cicero, *Tusculan Disputations*, I.xxx.74).

[17]"When my youth in its flower was keeping happy springtime" (Catullus, lxvii.16).   [18]Foolish, doting.

She was in her house a comfort to her dearest lord, a guide to her children, a rule to her servants, an example to all.

But as she related to God in the offices of religion, she was even and constant, silent and devout, prudent and material; she loved what she now enjoys, and she feared what she never felt, and God did for her what she never did expect; her fears went beyond all her evil; and yet the good which she hath received, was, and is, and ever shall be beyond all her hopes.

She lived as we all should live, and she died as I fain would 10 die:

> *Et cum supremos Lachesis perneverit annos,*
> *Non aliter cineres mando jacere meos.*[19]

I pray God I may feel those mercies on my deathbed that she felt, and that I may feel the same effect of my repentance which she feels of the many degrees of her innocence. Such was her death that she did not die too soon; and " her life was so useful and so excellent that she could not have lived too long": *Nemo parum diu vixit, qui virtutis perfectae perfecto funetus est munere.* And as now in the grave it shall not be 20 inquired concerning her how long she lived, but how well;

so to us who live after her to suffer a longer calamity, it may be some ease to our sorrows, and some guide to our lives, and some security to our conditions to consider that God hath brought the piety of a young lady to the early rewards of a never-ceasing and never-dying eternity of glory. And we also if we live as she did, shall partake of the same glories; not only having the honor of a good name and a dear and honored memory, but the glories of these glories, the end of all excellent labors, and all prudent counsels, and all holy religion, even the salvation of our souls in that day when all the saints, and amongst them this excellent woman, shall be shown to all the world to have done more, and more excellent things than we know of or can describe. *Mors illos consecrat, quorum exitum, et qui timent, laudant:*[20] "death consecrates and makes sacred that person whose excellency was such that they that are not displeased at the death cannot dispraise the life, but they that mourn sadly think they can never commend sufficiently."

[19]"When Lachesis shall have spun my final years I command that my ashes be distributed no differently" (adapted from Martial, *Epigrams,* I.88).   [20]Seneca, *De provedentia,* II.12.

from The Rule and Exercises of Holy Dying (1651)

To the Right Honorable and Most Truly Noble Richard, Lord Vaughan, Earl of Carbery, Baron of Emlin and Molingar . . .

My Lord,
I am treating Your Lordship as a Roman gentleman did St. Augustine and his mother: I shall entertain you in a charnel-house and carry your meditations awhile into the chambers of death, where you shall find the rooms dressed up with melancholy arts and fit to converse with your most retired thoughts, which begin with a sigh, and proceed in deep consideration, and end in a holy resolution. The sight that St. Augustine most noted in that house of sorrow was the body of Caesar, clothed with all the dishonors of corruption that you can suppose in a six moneths' burial.[1] But I know that, without pointing, your first thoughts will remember the change of a greater beauty,[2] which is now dressing for the brightest immortality, and from her bed of darkness calls to you to dress your soul for that change which shall mingle your bones with that beloved dust and carry your soul to the same choir, where you may both sit and sing forever. My Lord, it is your dear lady's anniversary, and she deserved the biggest honor, and the longest memory, and the fairest monument, and the most solemn mourning; and in order to it, give me leave, my Lord, to cover her hearse with these following sheets. This book was intended first to minister to her piety, and she desired all good people

should partake of the advantages which are here recorded: she knew how to live rarely well, and she desired to know how to die, and God taught her by an experiment. But since her work is done, and God supplied her with provisions of His own before I could minister to her and perfect what she desired, it is necessary to present to Your Lordship those bundles of cypress which were intended to dress her closet but come now to dress her hearse. My Lord, both Your Lordship and myself have lately seen and felt such sorrows of death, and such sad departure of dearest friends, that it is more than high time we should think ourselves nearly concerned in the accidents. Death hath come so near to you as to fetch a portion from your very heart; and now you cannot choose but dig your own grave and place your coffin in your eye, when the angel hath dressed your scene of sorrow and meditation with so particular and so near an object; and therefore, as it is my duty, I am come to minister to your pious thoughts and to direct your sorrows that they may turn into virtue and advantages.

And since I know Your Lordship to be so constant and

HOLY DYING   [1]In his *Life of Christ* (I.ix.36), Taylor again alludes to this episode and even translates some of Augustine's lurid Latin from *Ad fratres in eremo,* Sermon 48.
[2]Frances, Lady Carbery, who, having borne ten children in thirteen years, died on 9 October 1650, only a few months before Taylor's own wife Phoebe.

regular in your devotions and so tender in the matter of justice, so ready in the expressions of charity, and so apprehensive of religion; and that you are a person whose work of gracc is apt, and must every day grow towards those degrees where, when you arrive, you shall triumph over imperfection and choose nothing but what may please God, I could not by any compendium conduct and assist your pious purposes so well as by that which is the great argument and the great instrument of *Holy Living,* the consideration and exercises of death. . . .

> Explaining that his book is designed to make men live so that they will be prepared to die, Taylor discusses and rejects the Roman Catholic practices of extreme unction and prayers for the dead. "To be erring and innocent is hugely pitiable, and incident to mortality: that we cannot help; but to deceive or to destroy so great an interest as is that of a soul, or to lessen its advantages by giving it trifling and false confidences is injurious andintolerable. . . . For it is a sad thing to see our dead go forth of our hands; they live incuriously and die without regard; and the last scene of their life, which should be dressed with all spiritual advantages, is abused by flattery and easy propositions, and let go with carelessness and folly."

My Lord, I have endeavored to cure some part of the evil as well as I could, being willing to relieve the needs of indigent people in such ways as I can; and therefore have described the duties which every sick man may do alone, and such in which he can be assisted by the minister; and am the more confident that these my endeavors will be the better entertained because they are the first entire body of directions for sick and dying people that I remember to have been published in the Church of England. In the Church of Rome there have been many, but they are dressed with such doctrines which are sometimes useless, sometimes hurtful, and their whole design of assistance which they commonly yield is at the best imperfect, and the representment is too careless and loose for so severe an employment. So that in this affair I was almost forced to walk alone, only that I drew the rules and advices from the fountains of Scripture and the purest channels of the primitive church, and was helped by some experience in the cure[3] of souls. I shall measure the success of my labors not by popular noises or the sentences of curious persons, but by the advantage which good people may receive. My work here is not to please the speculative part of men, but to minister to practice, to preach to the weary, to comfort the sick, to assist the penitent, to reprove the confident, to strengthen weak hands and feeble knees, having scarce any other possibilities left me of doing alms or exercising that charity by which we shall be judged at doomsday. It is enough for me to be an under-builder in the house of God, and I glory in the employment; I labor in the foundations, and therefore the work needs no apology for being plain, so it be strong and well laid. But, my Lord, as mean as it is I must give God thanks for the desires and the strength, and next to Him to you for that opportunity and little portion of leisure which I had to do it in; for I must acknowledge it publicly (and, besides my prayers, it is all the recompense I can make you): my being quiet I owe to

your interest, much of my support to your bounty, and many other collateral comforts I derive from your favor and nobleness. My Lord, because I much honor you, and because I would do honor to myself, I have written your name in the entrance of my book. I am sure you will entertain it because the design related to your dear lady, and because it may minister to your spirit in the day of visitation, when God shall call for you to receive your reward for your charity and your noble piety, by which you have not only endeared very many persons but in great degrees have obliged me to be,

> *my noblest Lord,*
> *Your Lordship's most thankful*
> *and most humble servant,*
> *Taylor.*

CHAPTER I
A General Preparation towards a Holy and Blessed Death, by Way of Consideration

SECTION i.
Consideration of the Vanity and Shortness of Man's Life

"A man is a bubble," said the Greek proverb, which Lucian[4] represents with advantages and its proper circumstances to this purpose, saying that all the world is a storm, and men rise up in their several generations like bubbles descending *a Jove pluvio,*[5] from God and the dew of heaven, from a tear and drop of rain,[6] from nature and providence: and some of these instantly sink into the deluge of their first parent, and are hidden in a sheet of water, having had no other business in the world but to be born that they might be able to die; others float up and down two or three turns, and suddenly disappear, and give their place to others; and they that live longest upon the face of the water are in perpetual motion, restless, and uneasy; and, being crushed with the great drop of a cloud, sink into flatness and a froth; the change not being great, it being hardly possible it should be more a nothing than it was before. So is every man: he is born in vanity and sin; he comes into the world like morning mushrooms, soon thrusting up their heads into the air, and conversing with their kindred of the same production, and as soon they turn into dust and forgetfulness; some of them without any other interest in the affairs of the world but that they made their parents a little glad, and very sorrowful; others ride longer in the storm, it may be until seven years of vanity be expired, and then, peradventure, the sun shines hot upon their heads, and they fall into the shades below, into the cover of death and darkness of the grave to hide them. But if the bubble stands the shock of a bigger drop, and outlives the chances of a child, of a careless nurse, of drowning in a pail of water, of being overlaid by a sleepy servant, or such little accidents, then the young man dances like a bubble, empty and gay, and shines like a dove's neck,

[3]Care (Latin *cura*).
[4]Greek satirist (2d cent.). Taylor is perhaps remembering his "Charon, or the Inspectors," Sect. 3.
[5]Like rain from heaven. [6]Text *Man*.

or the image of a rainbow, which hath no substance, and whose very imagery and colors are fantastical; and so he dances out the gaiety of his youth, and is all the while in a storm, and endures only because he is not knocked on the head by a drop of bigger rain, or crushed by the pressure of a load of indigested meat, or quenched by the disorder of an ill-placed humor; and to preserve a man alive in the midst of so many chances and hostilities is as great a miracle as to create him; to preserve him from rushing into nothing and at first to draw him up from nothing were equally the issues of an almighty power. And therefore the wise men of the world have contended who shall best fit man's condition with words signifying his vanity and short abode. Homer calls a man "a leaf,"[7] the smallest, the weakest piece of a short-lived, unsteady plant. Pindar calls him "the dream of a shadow."[8] Another, "the dream of the shadow of smoke." But St. James spake by a more excellent Spirit, saying, "Our life is but a vapor,"[9] viz. drawn from the earth by a celestial influence, made of smoke or the lighter parts of water, tossed with every wind, moved by the motion of a superior body, without virtue in itself, lifted up on high or left below according as it pleases the sun its foster-father. But it is lighter yet. It is but appearing; a fantastic vapor, an apparition, nothing real: it is not so much as a mist, not the matter of a shower, nor substantial enough to make a cloud; but it is like Cassiopeia's chair, or Pelops' shoulder, or the circles of heaven, φαινόμενα,[10] for which you cannot have a word that can signify a verier nothing. And yet the expression is one degree more made diminutive: a *vapor,* and *fantastical,* or *a mere appearance,* and this but for a little while neither; the very dream, the phantasm disappears in a small time "like the shadow that departeth, or like a tale that is told, or as a dream when one awaketh." A man is so vain, so unfixed, so perishing a creature that he cannot long last in the scene of fancy; a man goes off, and is forgotten like the dream of a distracted person. The sum of all is this: that thou art a man, than whom there is not in the world any greater instance of heights and declensions, of lights and shadows, of misery and folly, of laughter and tears, of groans and death.

And because this consideration is of great usefulness and great necessity to many purposes of wisdom and the spirit, all the succession of time, all the changes in nature, all the varieties of light and darkness, the thousand thousands of accidents in the world, and every contingency to every man and to every creature does preach our funeral sermon, and calls us to look and see how the old sexton Time throws up the earth and digs a grave where we must lay our sins or our sorrows, and sow our bodies, till they rise again in a fair or in an intolerable eternity. Every revolution which the sun makes about the world divides between life and death; and death possesses both those portions by the next morrow; and we are dead to all those moneths which we have already lived, and we shall never live them over again; and still God makes little periods of our age. First we change our world when we come from the womb to feel the warmth of the sun. Then we sleep and enter into the image of death, in which state we are unconcerned in all the changes of the world;

and if our mothers or our nurses die, or a wild boar destroy our vineyards, or our king be sick, we regard it not, but during that state are as disinterested as if our eyes were closed with the clay that weeps in the bowels of the earth. At the end of seven years our teeth fall and die before us, representing a formal prologue to the tragedy; and still, every seven year, it is odds but we shall finish the last scene: and when nature, or chance, or vice, takes our body in pieces, weakening some parts and loosing others, we taste the grave and the solemnities of our own funerals, first in those parts that ministered to vice, and next in them that served for ornament; and in a short time even they that served for necessity become useless, and entangled like the wheels of a broken clock. Baldness is but a dressing to our funerals, the proper ornament of mourning, and of a person entered very far into the regions and possession of death, and we have many more of the same signification: gray hairs, rotten teeth, dim eyes, trembling joints, short breath, stiff limbs, wrinkled skin, short memory, decayed appetite. Every day's necessity calls for a reparation of that portion which death fed on all night, when we lay in his lap and slept in his outer chambers. The very spirits of a man prey upon the daily portion of bread and flesh, and every meal is a rescue from one death, and lays up for another; and while we think a thought, we die; and the clock strikes, and reckons on our portion of eternity: we form our words with the breath of our nostrils, we have the less to live upon for every word we speak.

Thus nature calls us to meditate of death by those things which are the instruments of acting it; and God, by all the variety of His providence, makes us see death everywhere, in all variety of circumstances, and dressed up for all the fancies, and the expectation of every single person. Nature hath given us one harvest every year, but death hath two: and the spring and the autumn send throngs of men and women to charnel houses; and all the summer long men are recovering from their evils of the spring, till the dog days come, and then the Sirian star[11] makes the summer deadly; and the fruits of autumn are laid up for all the year's provision, and the man that gathers them, eats and surfeits, and dies and needs them not, and himself is laid up for eternity; and he that escapes till winter only stays for another opportunity, which the distempers of that quarter minister to him with great variety. Thus death reigns in all the portions of our time. The autumn with its fruits provides disorders for us, and the winter's cold turns them into sharp diseases, and the spring brings flowers to strew our hearse, and the summer gives green turf and brambles to bind upon our graves. Calentures[12] and surfeit, cold and agues, are the four quarters of the year, and all minister to death; and you can go no whither but you tread upon a dead man's bones.

[7] *Iliad,* VI.146.   [8] *Pythian Odes,* VIII.135.   [9] James 4.14.
[10] "Phenomena," i.e., implausible things such as the constellation shaped like a chair, the ivory shoulder allegedly given to Pelops after he had been dismembered by his father Tantalus, and the spheres (*circles*) thought to contain the heavenly bodies.
[11] Sirius, the Dog Star that reaches its ascendancy in July and August.   [12] Fevers caused by extreme heat.

The wild fellow in Petronius,[13] that escaped upon a broken table from the furies of a shipwreck, as he was sunning himself upon the rocky shore espied a man rolled upon his floating bed of waves, ballasted with sand in the folds of his garment, and carried by his civil enemy, the sea, towards the shore to find a grave, and it cast him into some sad thoughts: that peradventure this man's wife in some part of the continent, safe and warm, looks next moneth for the good man's return; or, it may be, his son knows nothing of the tempest; or his father thinks of that affectionate kiss which still is warm upon the good old man's cheek ever since he took a kind farewell; and he weeps with joy to think how blessed he shall be when his beloved boy returns into the circle of his father's arms. These are the thoughts of mortals, this is the end and sum of all their designs: a dark night and an ill guide, a boisterous sea and a broken cable, a hard rock and a rough wind dashed in pieces the fortune of a whole family, and they that shall weep loudest for the accident are not yet entered into the storm, and yet have suffered shipwreck. Then looking upon the carcass, he knew it, and found it to be the master of the ship, who, the day before, cast up the accounts of his patrimony and his trade, and named the day when he thought to be at home. See how the man swims who was so angry two days since: his passions are becalmed with the storm, his accounts cast up, his cares at an end, his voyage done, and his gains are the strange events of death, which whether they be good or evil, the men that are alive seldom trouble themselves concerning the interest of the dead.

But seas alone do not break our vessel in pieces: everywhere we may be shipwrecked. A valiant general, when he is to reap the harvest of his crowns and triumphs, fights unprosperously, or falls into a fever with joy and wine, and changes his laurel into cypress,[14] his triumphal chariot to an hearse; dying, the night before he was appointed to perish, in the drunkenness of his festival joys. It was a sad arrest of the loosenesses and wilder feasts of the French court, when their king (Henry II) was killed really by the sportive image of a fight.[15] And many brides have died under the hands of paranymphs[16] and maidens dressing them for uneasy joy, the new and undiscerned chains of marriage, according to the saying of Ben Sira,[17] the wise Jew, "The bride went into her chamber, and knew not what should befall her there." Some have been paying their vows, and giving thanks for a prosperous return to their own house, and the roof hath descended upon their heads, and turned their loud religion into the deeper silence of a grave. And how many teeming mothers have rejoiced over their swelling wombs, and pleased themselves in becoming the channels of blessing to a family; and the midwife hath quickly bound their heads and feet, and carried them forth to burial! Or else the birthday of an heir hath seen the coffin of the father brought into the house, and the divided mother hath been forced to travail twice, with a painful birth and a sadder death.

There is no state, no accident, no circumstance of our life but it hath been soured by some sad instance of a dying friend; a friendly meeting often ends in some sad mischance, and makes an eternal parting; and when the poet Aeschylus

was sitting under the walls of his house an eagle hovering over his bald head mistook it for a stone and let fall his oyster, hoping there to break the shell, but pierced the poor man's skull.

Death meets us everywhere and is procured by every instrument, and in all chances, and enters in at many doors: by violence and secret influence, by the aspect of a star and the stink of a mist, by the emissions of a cloud and the meeting of a vapor, by the fall of a chariot and the stumbling at a stone, by a full meal or an empty stomach, by watching at the wine or by watching at prayers, by the sun or the moon, by a heat or a cold, by sleepless nights or sleeping days, by water frozen into the hardness and sharpness of a dagger, or water thawed into the floods of a river, by a hair or a raisin, by violent motion or sitting still, by severity or dissolution, by God's mercy or God's anger, by everything in providence and everything in manners, by everything in nature and everything in chance. We take pains to heap up things useful to our life, and get our death in the purchase; and the person is snatched away, and the goods remain. And all this is the law and constitution of nature; it is a punishment to our sins, the unalterable event of Providence, and the decree of Heaven. The chains that confine us to this condition are strong as destiny, and immutable as the eternal laws of God.

I have conversed with some men who rejoiced in the death or calamity upon others, and accounted it as a judgment upon them for being on the other side, and against them in the contention; but within the revolution of a few moneths, the same man met with a more uneasy and unhandsome death, which when I saw, I wept, and was afraid; for I knew that it must be so with all men; for we also shall die, and end our quarrels and contentions by passing to a final sentence.

SECTION ii
The Consideration Reduced to Practice

It will be very material to our best and noblest purposes if we represent this scene of change and sorrow a little more dressed up in circumstances, for so we shall be more apt to practise those rules, the doctrine of which is consequent to this consideration. It is a mighty change that is made by the death of every person, and it is visible to us who are alive. Reckon but from the sprightfulness of youth, and the fair cheeks and full eyes of childhood, from the vigorousness and strong flexure of the joints of five-and-twenty to the hollowness and dead paleness, to the loathsomeness and horror of a three days' burial, and we shall perceive the distance to be very great and very strange. But so have I seen a rose newly springing from the clefts of its hood, and, at first, it was fair

[13] *The Satyricon*, Ch. CXV.
[14] Trees associated respectively with triumph and with death.
[15] Henry II, king of France (1547–59), died of a wound received in a joust.
[16] Bridesmaids.
[17] Taylor is perhaps alluding to the pseudonymous author of *Proverbia Ben-Sirae, autoris antiquissimi, qui creditur fuisse nepos Jeremiae prophetae,* a collection of Jewish lore published in 1597.

as the morning, and full with the dew of heaven as a lamb's fleece; but when a ruder breath had forced open its virgin modesty, and dismantled its too youthful and unripe retirements, it began to put on darkness, and to decline to softness and the symptoms of a sickly age: it bowed the head, and broke its stalk, and, at night, having lost some of its leaves and all its beauty, it fell into the portion of weeds and outworn faces. The same is the portion of every man and every woman: the heritage of worms and serpents, rottenness and cold dishonor, and our beauty so changed that our acquaintance quickly knew us not; and that change mingled with so much horror, or else meets so with our fears and weak discoursings, that they who, six hours ago, tended upon us either with charitable or ambitious services cannot, without some regret, stay in the room alone where the body lies stripped of its life and honor. I have read of a fair young German gentleman, who, living, often refused to be pictured, but put off the importunity of his friends' desire by giving way that after a few days' burial they might send a painter to his vault, and, if they saw cause for it, draw the image of his death unto the life. They did so, and found his face half eaten, and his midriff and backbone full of serpents; and so he stands pictured among his armed ancestors. So does the fairest beauty change, and it will be as bad with you and me; and then what servants shall we have to wait upon us in the grave? what friends to visit us? what officious people to cleanse away the moist and unwholesome cloud reflected upon our faces from the sides of the weeping vaults, which are the longest weepers for our funeral?

This discourse will be useful if we consider and practise by the following rules and considerations respectively.

1. All the rich and all the covetous men in the world will perceive, and all the world will perceive for them, that it is but an ill recompense for all their cares that, by this time, all that shall be left will be this, that the neighbours shall say, "He died a rich man." And yet his wealth will not profit him in the grave, but hugely swell the sad accounts of doomsday. And he that kills the Lord's people with unjust or ambitious wars for an unrewarding interest shall have this character, that he threw away all the days of his life that one year might be reckoned with his name, and computed by his reign or consulship; and many men, by great labors and affronts, many indignities and crimes, labor only for a pompous epitaph and a loud title upon their marble; whilst those, into whose possessions their heirs or kindred are entered, are forgotten, and lie unregarded as their ashes, and without concernment or relation, as the turf upon the face of their grave. A man may read a sermon, the best and most passionate that ever man preached, if he shall but enter into the sepulchers of kings. In the same Escurial[18] where the Spanish princes live in greatness and power, and decree war or peace, they have wisely placed a cemetery, where their ashes and their glories shall sleep till time shall be no more; and where[19] our kings have been crowned, their ancestor lay interred, and they must walk over their grandsire's head to take his crown. There is an acre sown with royal seed, the copy of the greatest change, from rich to naked, from ceiled roofs to arched coffins, from living like gods to die like men. There is enough to cool the flames of lust, to abate the heights of pride, to appease the itch of covetous desires, to sully and dash out the dissembling colors of a lustful, artificial, and imaginary beauty. There the warlike and the peaceful, the fortunate and the miserable, the beloved and the despised princes mingle their dust, and pay down their symbol of mortality, and tell all the world that when we die our ashes shall be equal to kings', and our accounts easier, and our pains or our crowns shall be less. To my apprehension it is a sad record which is left by Athenaeus[20] concerning Minus, the great Assyrian monarch, whose life and death is summed up in these words: "Ninus, the Assyrian, had an ocean of gold, and other riches more than the sand in the Caspian Sea; he never saw the stars, and perhaps he never desired it; he never stirred up the holy fire among the Magi,[21] nor touched his god with the sacred rod according to the laws; he never offered sacrifice, nor worshipped the deity, nor administered justice, nor spake to his people, nor numbered them; but he was most valiant to eat and drink, and having mingled his wines, he threw the rest upon the stones. This man is dead: behold his sepulcher; and now hear where Ninus is. Sometimes I was Ninus, and drew the breath of a living man; but now am nothing but clay. I have nothing but what I did eat, and what I served to myself in lust, that was and is all my portion. The wealth with which I was esteemed blessed, my enemies, meeting together, shall bear away, as the mad Thyades[22] carry a raw goat. I am gone to hell; and when I went thither, I neither carried gold, nor horse, nor silver chariot. I that wore a miter am now a little heap of dust." I know not any thing that can better represent the evil condition of a wicked man, or a changing greatness. From the greatest secular dignity to dust and ashes his nature bears him, and from thence to hell his sins carry him, and there he shall be forever under the dominion of chains and devils, wrath and an intolerable calamity. This is the reward of an unsanctified condition, and a greatness ill gotten or ill administered.

2. Let no man extend his thoughts, or let his hopes wander towards future and far distant events and accidental contingencies. This day is mine and yours, but ye know not what shall be on the morrow: and every morning creeps out of a dark cloud, leaving behind it an ignorance and silence deep as midnight, and undiscerned as are the phantasms that make a chrisom child[23] to smile; so that we cannot discern what comes hereafter unless we had a light from heaven brighter than the vision of an angel, even the spirit of prophecy. Without revelation, we cannot tell whether we

---

[18]Escorial, an immense palace built by Philip II of Spain near Madrid. [19]Westminster Abbey.
[20]Greek scholar (2d cent. B.C.) whose *Deipnosophists* is a compendium of information and gossip on many subjects.
[21]Priestly class of ancient Persia.
[22]Bacchantes, female votaries of Dionysius.
[23]Innocent babe. A *chrisom* was the white robe put on a child at baptism.

shall eat tomorrow, or whether a squinzy[24] shall choke us; and it is written in the unrevealed folds of divine predestination that many who are this day alive shall tomorrow be laid upon the cold earth, and the women shall weep over their shroud, and dress them for their funeral. St. James, in his epistle,[25] notes the folly of some men, his contemporaries, who were so impatient of the event of tomorrow, or the accidents of next year, or the good or evils of old age that they would consult astrologers and witches, oracles and devils, what should befall them the next calends;[26] what should be the event of such a voyage; what God had written in His book concerning the success of battles, the election of emperors, the heir of families, the price of merchandise, the return of the Tyrian fleet, the rate of Sidonian carpets; and as they were taught by the crafty and lying demons, so they would expect the issue; and oftentimes by disposing their affairs in order toward such events really did produce some little accidents according to their expectation; and that made them trust the oracles in greater things, and in all. Against this He opposes his counsel, that we should not search after forbidden records, much less by uncertain significations; for whatsoever is disposed to happen by the order of natural causes or civil counsels may be rescinded by a peculiar decree of providence, or be prevented by the death of the interested persons; who, while their hopes are full, and their causes conjoined, and the work brought forward, and the sickle put into the harvest, and the first fruits offered and ready to be eaten, even then, if they put forth their hand to an event that stands but at the door, at that door their body may be carried forth to burial before the expectation shall enter into fruition. When Richilda, the widow of Albert, earl of Ebersberg, had feasted the Emperor Henry III,[27] and petitioned in behalf of her nephew Welpho for some lands formerly possessed by the earl, her husband, just as the emperor held out his hand to signify his consent the chamber floor suddenly fell under them, and Richilda, falling upon the edge of a bathing vessel, was bruised to death, and stayed not to see her nephew sleep in those hands which the emperor was reaching forth to her, and placed at the door of restitution.

3. As our hopes must be confined, so must our designs: let us not project long designs, crafty plots, and diggings so deep that the intrigues of a design shall never be unfolded till our grandchildren have forgotten our virtues or our vices. The work of our soul is cut short, facile, sweet, and plain, and fitted to the small portions of our shorter life; and as we must not trouble our inquiry, so neither must we intricate[28] our labour and purposes with what we shall never enjoy. This rule does not forbid us to plant orchards which shall feed our nephews with their fruit, for by such provisions they do something towards an imaginary immortality, and do charity to their relatives; but such projects are reproved which discompose our present duty by long and future designs: such which, by casting our labors to events at distance, make us less to remember our death standing at the door. It is fit for a man to work for his day's wages, or to contrive for the hire of a week, or to lay a train[29] to make provisions for such a time as is within our eye, and in our duty, and within the usual periods of man's

life; for whatsoever is made necessary is also made prudent; but while we plot and busy ourselves in the toils of an ambitious war, or the levies of a great estate, night enters in upon us, and tells all the world how like fools we lived, and how deceived and miserably we died. Seneca[30] tells of Senecio Cornelius, a man crafty in getting and tenacious in holding a great estate, and one who was as diligent in the care of his body as of his money, curious of his health as of his possessions, that he all day long attended upon his sick and dying friend; but, when he went away, was quickly comforted, supped merrily, went to bed cheerfully, and on a sudden, being surprised by a squinzy, scarce drew his breath until the morning, but by that time died, being snatched from the torrent of his fortune, and the swelling tide of wealth, and a likely hope bigger than the necessities of ten men. This accident was much noted then in Rome because it happened in so great a fortune, and in the midst of wealthy designs; and presently it made wise men to consider how imprudent a person he is who disposes of ten years to come when he is not lord of tomorrow.

4. Though we must not look so far off, and prey abroad, yet we must be busy near at hand; we must, with all arts of the spirit, seize upon the present because it passes from us while we speak, and because in it all our certainty does consist. We must take our waters as out of a torrent and sudden shower, which will quickly cease dropping from above, and quickly cease running in our channels here below; this instant will never return again, and yet, it may be, this instant will declare or secure the fortune of a whole eternity. The old Greeks and Romans taught us the prudence of this rule, but Christianity teaches us the religion of it. They so seized upon the present that they would lose nothing of the day's pleasure. "Let us eat and drink, for tomorrow we shall die": that was their philosophy, and at their solemn feasts they would talk of death to heighten the present drinking, and that they might warm their veins with a fuller chalice, as knowing the drink that was poured upon their graves would be cold and without relish. "Break the beds, drink your wine, crown your heads with roses, and besmear your curled locks with nard, for God bids you to remember death": so the epigrammatist speaks the sense of their drunken principles.[31] Something towards this signification is that of Solomon, "There is nothing better for a man than that he should eat and drink, and that he should make his soul enjoy good in his labor, for that is his portion: for who shall bring him to see that which shall be after him?"[32] But although he concludes all this to be vanity, yet, because it was the best thing that was then commonly known, that they should seize upon the present with a temperate use of permitted pleasures, I had reason to say that Christianity taught us to turn this into religion. For he that by a present

[24]Squinancy, quinsy, inflammation of the tonsils.
[25]Perhaps Taylor is thinking of James 5.13–14.
[26]The first day of the Roman month.
[27]Turbulent Holy Roman emperor (1039–56) who subdued the Bohemians and Hungarians and deposed three rival popes to make way for his appointment of Clement II.　[28]Complicate.
[29]Make plans.　[30]*Epistulae Morales*, CI.1–4.
[31]Martial, *Epigrams*, II.59.　[32]Ecclesiastes 2.24, 3.22.

and a constant holiness secures the present, and makes it useful to his noblest purposes, he turns his condition into his best advantage by making his unavoidable fate become his necessary religion.

To the purpose of this rule is that collect[33] of Tuscan hieroglyphics, which we have from Gabriel Simeon.[34] "Our life is very short, beauty is a cozenage, money is false and fugitive; empire is odious, and hated by them that have it not, and uneasy to them that have; victory is always uncertain, and peace, most commonly, is but a fraudulent bargain; old age is miserable, death is the period, and is a happy one if it be not sorrowed[35] by the sins of our life; but nothing continues but the effects of that wisdom which employs the present time in the acts of a holy religion and a peaceable conscience." For they make us to live even beyond our funerals, embalmed in the spices and odors of a good name, and entombed in the grave of the holy Jesus, where we shall be dressed for a blessed resurrection to the state of angels and beatified spirits.

5. Since we stay not here, being people but of a day's abode, and our age is like that of a fly, and contemporary with a gourd, we must look somewhere else for an abiding city, a place in another country to fix our house in, whose walls and foundation is God, where we must find rest, or else be restless for ever. For whatsoever ease we can have or fancy here is shortly to be changed into sadness or tediousness: it goes away too soon, like the periods of our life; or stays too long, like the sorrows of a sinner; its own weariness, or a contrary disturbance, is its load; or it is eased by its revolution into vanity and forgetfulness; and where either there is sorrow or an end of joy, there can be no true felicity; which, because it must be had by some instrument, and in some period of our duration, we must carry up our affections to the mansions prepared for us above, where eternity is the measure, felicity is their state, angels are the company, the Lamb is the light, and God is the portion and inheritance.

[33]Collection.
[34]Gabrielle Simeoni (1509–75), Italian antiquarian and writer on emblems and hieroglyphics. His *Interpretatione greca, latina, toscana & franzese del monstro, o enigma d'Italia* was published in 1555. [35]Text *sowred*. Perhaps Taylor means *soured*.

Richard Baxter [1615-1691]

It is ironical that Richard Baxter, near the start of his career, should have said that he had no intention of "burdening the world" with any of his writings, for in the course of forty years this great father of English nonconformity produced so many works of "controversial, casuitical, positive, and practical divinity"—in folios, quartos, duodecimos, pamphlets, sheets, and even broadsides—that they total more than one hundred sixty items. Apart from the very early *Saints' Everlasting Rest* (1650), to which he devoted four months of "vacancy . . . in the midst of continual languishing and medicine," all of them, he said, were tossed off in a hurry.

> I wrote them in the crowd of all my other employments, which would allow me no great leisure for polishing and exactness, or any ornament; so that I scarce ever wrote one sheet twice over, nor stayed to make any blots or interlinings, but was fain to let it go as it was first conceived.

Ranging from the stirring evangelism of *A Call to the Unconverted* (1658) to the relentless didacticism of *The Christian Directory* (1673) and the elegiac sweetness of the *Breviate* (1681) in memory of his wife, Baxter's output was immense in range as well as size, but since most of this production lies beyond the limits of our period it need not be rehearsed. However, to the generalization of an eighteenth-century writer that Baxter's books would likely share their author's fate of being "mightily esteemed by some and mightily condemned by others," one exception must be made. The enormously successful *Saints' Everlasting Rest* still deserves to be remembered not only for its style and passion, but also as a tribute to the lasting strength of nonconformist piety.

Although Baxter, by his own account, was pious almost from his cradle, there was nothing in his early life and rather skimpy schooling to suggest that he would be among the leaders of his age. His father was the well-intentioned ne'er-do-well of an ancient Shropshire family, and his native village gave so little in the way of education that it supplied four teachers "successively in six years'

time, ignorant men, and two of them immoral in their lives, who were all my schoolmasters."
Although the little boy "delighted" in the Bible, he suffered great remorse of sin for such transgres-
sions as "the excessive, gluttonous eating of apples and pears" (to which he attributed the "imbecil-
ity and flatulency" of stomach that plagued him through his life), an addiction to the "romances,
fables, and old tales" that "corrupted" his affections, and the "idle, foolish chat" that led to "scur-
rilous, foolish words and actions." Through God's providential grace, however, he survived the
consequences of his sin, as well as several years of country schooling. There followed some wide but
desultory reading in the library of Ludlow Castle under the casual supervision of the chaplain to
the council there, a brief exposure to the court at Whitehall (which disgusted him), much soul-
searching and reading in theology back in Shropshire, and at last his ordination (1638) in the Church
of England.

His subsequent preaching and teaching at Dudley and Bridgnorth by no means made him fa-
mous, but in 1641 they earned for him a call to Kidderminster in Worcestershire, and there, in a town
notorious for ignorance and corruption, he came into his own. As the minute and even tortuous
record of his spiritual struggles in *Reliquiae Baxterianae* (1696) shows, by this time he had made a
significant advance from Anglican orthodoxy to some sort of Presbyterianism, and his historic
ministry at Kidderminster (which, with interruptions caused by war and illness, lasted almost
twenty years) made him a leader of the nonconformists.

A true warfaring Christian, he became an army chaplain in the troubles of the forties, and his
firsthand knowledge of the horrors of a civil war confirmed his trust in reason as a guide to human
action. It was as a consequence of his pastoral duties in the war that he fell ill and almost died in
1647, and as the title page of *The Saint's Everlasting Rest* records, it was "in the time of his languish-
ing, when God took him off from his public employment," that he wrote his famous book as a
sort of funeral sermon for his own instruction. He survived, however, and returned to Kidder-
minster to resume his influential preaching, become a spokesman for the nonconformists, and
assist in the negotiations that resulted in the king's return. Although Baxter welcomed this event
and even served as one of Charles' royal chaplains, he declined the offer of a bishopric; and when
the failure of the ecumenical Savoy Conference (1661), which he had helped to organize, and the
triumph of the restrictive Act of Uniformity (1662) blasted all his hopes for toleration, he assumed
that characteristic posture of defiance and defense that made a hero of the preacher and the politi-
cian. As the years went by his lot was very hard. Mounting harassment, the malice and brutality
of Justice Jeffreys, and even imprisonment (1685–86) under the Catholic James II could not silence
him or stop his flood of prose, but he no doubt thought his struggles vindicated by the Glorious
Revolution and the Toleration Act of 1689. In contrast to the tumult of his middle years, his ending
was serene. Asked how he did as he lay dying, "I have pain," the old man said; "there is no arguing
against sense. But I have peace, I have peace."

My text is based upon the second (1651) edition, "corrected and enlarged," of *The Saints' Ever-
lasting Rest: or, a Treatise of the Blessed State of the Saints in their enjoyment of God in Glory* (Wing
B–1384). Of its innumerable subsequent editions the most important is that edited by William
Young (1907). J. T. Wilkinson (1928) has edited the *Breviat*, Baxter's tender memoir of his wife,
Jeannette Tawney (1925) *Chapters from Baxter's Christian Directory*, and R. B. Schlatter (1959) a
generous selection of his political writings. Baxter's vivid autobiography, abridged from the
trackless expanse of *Reliquiae Baxterianae* (1696) by Edmund Calamy (1702, 1713), has been edited
by J. M. Lloyd-Thomas (1925) and conveniently reprinted in Everyman's Library (1931). F. J.
Powicke has written an ample biography (2 vols., 1924–27), and there are shorter studies of his
life and works by Invonwy Morgan (1946), Hugh Martin (1954), Margaret Bottrall (*Every Man a
Phoenix: Studies in Seventeenth-Century Autobiography*, 1958), and G. F. Nuttall (1966). A. B.
Grosart's bibliography (1868), though still useful, should be checked against A. G. Matthews'
(1933).

from The Saints' Everlasting Rest (1651)

To My Dearly Beloved Friends, the Inhabitants of
the Borough and Foreign of Kederminster,[1]
Both Magistrates and People

My dear Friends,
If either I or my labors have anything of public use or worth, it is wholly, though not only, yours; and I am convinced, by providence, that it is the will of God it should be so. This I clearly discerned in my first coming to you, in my former abode with you, and in the time of my forced absence from you. When I was separated by the miseries of the late unhappy war, I durst not fix in any other congregation, but lived in a military, unpleasing state, lest I should forestall my return to you, for whom I took myself reserved. The offers [10] of greater worldly accommodations, with five times the means which I receive with you, was no temptation to me once to question whether I should leave you: your free invitation of my return, your obedience to my doctrine, the strong affection which I have yet towards you above all people, and the general, hearty return of love which I find from you do all persuade me that I was sent into this world especially for the service of your souls. And that even when I am dead I might yet be a help to your salvation, the Lord hath forced me, quite beside[2] my own resolution, to write this [20] treatise and leave it in your hands. It was far from my thoughts ever to have become thus public, and burdened the world with any writings of mine; therefore have I oft resisted the requests of my reverend brethren, and some superiors, who might else have commanded much more at my hands. But see how God overruleth and crosseth[3] our resolutions!

Being in my quarters, far from home, cast into extreme languishing by the sudden loss of about a gallon of blood, after many years' foregoing weaknesses, and having no [30] acquaintance about me, nor any books but my Bible, and living in continual expectation of death, I bent my thoughts on my "Everlasting Rest"; and because my memory, through extreme weakness, was imperfect, I took my pen and began to draw up my own funeral sermon, or some helps for my own meditations of heaven, to sweeten both the rest of my life and my death. In this condition God was pleased to continue me about five moneths from home, where, being able for nothing else, I went on with this work, which so lengthened to this which here you see.[4] It is no wonder, therefore, [40] if I be too abrupt in the beginning, seeing I then intended but the length of a sermon or two; much less may you wonder if the whole be very imperfect, seeing it was written, as it were, with one foot in the grave, by a man that was betwixt living and dead, that wanted strength of nature to quicken invention or affection, and had no book but his Bible while the chief part was finished, nor had any mind of human ornaments if he had been furnished. But O how sweet is this providence now to my review, which so happily forced me to that work of meditation which I had formerly [50] found so profitable to my soul, and showed me more mercy

in depriving me of other helps than I was aware of, and hath caused my thoughts to feed on this heavenly subject, which hath more benefited me than all the studies of my life!

And now, dear friends, such as it is I here offer it you; and upon the bended knees of my soul I offer up my thanks to the merciful God who hath fetched up both me and it, as from the grave, for your service; who reversed the sentence of present death, which, by the ablest physicians, was passed upon me; who interrupted my public labors for a time that He might force me to do you a more lasting service, which else I had never been like to have attempted. That God do I heartily bless and magnify, who hath rescued me from the many dangers of four years' war, and after so many tedious nights and days, and so many doleful sights and tidings, hath returned me, and many of yourselves, and reprieved us till now to serve him in peace; and though men be ungrateful, and my body ruined beyond hope of recovery, yet He hath made up all in the comforts I have in you. To the God of mercy do I here offer my most hearty thanks, and pay the vows of acknowledgment which I oft made in my distress, who hath not rejected my prayers, which in my dolor I put up, but hath, by a wonder, delivered me in the midst of my duties; and hath supported me this fourteen years in a languishing state, wherein I have scarce had a waking hour free from pain; who hath, above[5] twenty several times, delivered me when I was near to death. And though He hath made me spend my days in groans and tears, and in a constant expectation of my change, yet hath He not wholly disabled me to His service; and hereby hath more effectually subdued my pride, and made this world contemptible to me, and forced my dull heart to more importunate requests, and occasioned more rare discoveries of His mercy than ever I could have expected in a prosperous state. Forever blessed be the Lord, that hath not only honored me to be a minister of His Gospel, but hath also set me over a people so willing to obey, and given me that success of my labors which He hath denied to many more able and faithful; who hath kept you in the zealous practice of godliness when so many grow negligent or despise the ordinances of God; who hath kept you stable in His truth, and saved you from the spirit of

SAINTS' EVERLASTING REST   [1]The town and environs of Kidderminster in Worcestershire, where in 1641 Baxter had been appointed a lecturer (i.e., preacher and spiritual leader), and where, following service as a chaplain in the parliamentary forces, he lived and worked from 1647 until 1660. [2]In addition to. [3]Thwarts.
[4]In the huge gathering of autobiographical and historical recollections published posthumously (1696) as *Reliquiae Baxterianae,* Baxter records that he spent much of his convalescence in the home of Sir Thomas Rous in Worcestershire, where Lady Rous—"a godly, grave, understanding woman"—nursed him back to health "with the greatest care and tenderness." In an epistle (here omitted) at the end of this dedication, Baxter writes warmly of the Rous' hospitable establishment where "the first part of this treatise was written."   [5]More than.

giddiness, levity, and apostasy of this age; who hath pre-
served you from those scandals whereby others have so
heinously wounded their profession,[6] and hath given you to
see the mischief of separation and divisions, and made you
eminent for unity and peace when almost all the land is in a
flame of contention, and so many that we thought godly are
busily demolishing the church and striving in a zealous
ignorance against the Lord. Beloved, though few of you are
rich or great in the world, yet for this riches of mercy to-
wards you I must say, ye are my glory, my crown, and my
joy; and for all these rare favors to myself and you, as I have
oft promised to publish the praises of our Lord, so do I
here set up this stone of remembrance, and write upon it,
"Glory to God in the highest: hitherto hath the Lord helped
us: my flesh and my heart failed, but God is the strength of
my heart, and my portion forever."[7]

But have all these deliverances brought us to our rest?
No; we are as far yet from it as we are from heaven. You
are yet under oppression and troubles, and I am yet under
consuming sickness; and feeling that I am like to be among
you but a little while, and that my pained body is hastening
to the dust, I shall here leave you my best advice for your
immortal souls and bequeath you this counsel as the legacy of
a dying man, that you may here read it and practice it when
I am taken from you; and I beseech you receive it as from one
that you know doth unfeignedly love you, and that re-
gardeth no honors or happiness in this world in comparison
of the welfare and salvation of your souls; yea, receive it from
me as if I offered it you upon my knees, beseeching you, for
your souls' sake, that you would not reject it, and beseech-
ing the Lord to bless it to you. . . .

Practice that great duty of daily watching; pray earnestly
that you be not led into temptation. Fear the beginnings and
appearances of sin. Beware lest conscience once lose its
tenderness. Make up every breach between God and your
consciences betime. Learn how to live the life of faith and
keep fresh the sense of the love of Christ and of your con-
tinual need of His blood, spirit, and intercession, and how
much you are beholden and engaged to him. Live in a con-
stant readiness and expectation of death, and be sure to get
acquainted with this heavenly conversation, which this book
is written to direct you in, which I commend to your use,
hoping you will be at the pains to read it, as for your sakes
I have been to write it; and I shall beg for you of the Lord,
while I live on this earth, that He will persuade your souls
to this blessed work, and that when death comes it may find
you so employed that I may see your faces with joy at the
bar of Christ, and we may enter together into the everlasting
rest. Amen.

Your most affectionate though unworthy
teacher,
Richard Baxter

Kederminster, January 15, 1649

A PREMONITION

. . . Concerning the book itself, let me advertize[8] you that
the first and last part were all that I intended when I begun it,
which I fitted merely to my own use; and therefore if you
find some strains of self-application, you may excuse them.
And for the second part, it fell from my pen besides my first
intention, but was occasioned partly by assaults that I had
oft suffered in that point, and partly by my apprehensions of
the exceeding necessity of it, and that to the main end which
I intended in this book.[9] Who will set his heart on the good-
ness of a thing that is not certain of the truth, or part with
all his present delights till he is sure he may have better? And
because I have only in brief given you these reasons which
most prevailed with myself, having then no authors by me,
I wish you would read Grotius, and the Lord Du Plessis "Of
the Verity of Christian Religion," (specially Chap. 25, 26,
and last,) both which are translated into English.[10] The third
part I last added: the four first chapters for the use of secure
and sensual sinners, if any of them should happen to read this
book; the three last for the godly, to direct and comfort them
in affliction, and specially to persuade them to the great duty
of helping to save their brethren's souls; the seven middle
chapters for the use both of the godly and the ungodly, as
being of unspeakable concernment to all. So that all parts of
this book are not fitted to the same persons.

Some, I hear, blame me for being so tedious, and say all
this might have been in a lesser room. Such I would inform
that in thus doing I have more crossed myself than them,
having naturally such a style as, because of brevity, is accused
of obscurity; and had much ado to bring myself to this which
they blame; and did obey my reason in it against my dis-
position. For as I thought my views of this glory should not
be short, nor my speeches too contracted, so I considered that
I speak to plain, unlearned men that cannot find our meaning
in too narrow a room, and that use to overlook the fullness
of significant words. As they must be long in thinking, so we
must be long in speaking, or else our words fall short of the
mark, and die before they can produce the desired effect, so
great is the distance betwixt these men's ears and their brains.
Besides, I knew I am to speak to men's affections, which yet
lie deep and far more remote. How guilty I am myself, let
others judge; but surely I approve not tautologies, or a
tedious style, or the heaping up of useless matter or words;
nor can I choose but judge those Tostatuses[11] impudently

[6]Profession of faith as Christians.   [7]Psalm 73.26.   [8]Inform.
[9]Of the four main parts of Baxter's treatise the first expounds the
text (Hebrews 4.9), "There remaineth, therefore, a rest for the
people of God"; the second, addressed to "unbelievers and anti-
scripturalists," develops "the proofs of the truth and certain
futurity of our rest"; the third luridly depicts the torments of the
damned; and the fourth—a sort of Puritan manual of spiritual
exercises represented here by excerpts from Chapter XIV—pro-
vides instruction in those Christian duties "which are necessary
to raise the heart to God and to a heavenly and comfortable life
on earth."
[10]Hugo Grotius' *De veritate religionis Christianae* (1627) appeared in
English as *True Religion Explained and Defended* in 1632. Philippe
de Mornay, Seigneur du Plessis-Marly (1549–1623) was a prom-
inent Huguenot whose *De la verité de la religion Chréstienne*
was translated in part by Sir Philip Sidney, completed by Arthur
Golding, and published in 1587.
[11]Perhaps an allusion to Alonso Tostado (1400–45), bishop of

proud who think the world should read nobody's works but theirs. Yet if the length of my discourse do but occasion the reader's longer thoughts on this so sweet and needful a subject, I shall scarce repent of my reprehended tediousness. And I confess I never loved affectation, or too much industry about words, nor like the temper of them that do. May I speak pertinently, plainly, piercingly, and somewhat properly, I have enough. I judge, as judicious Dr. Stoughton,[12] that "he is the best preacher that feels what he speaks, and then speaks what he feels." I confess also that I had made the first and fourth parts of this book much longer, but that upon my return home (to my books) I found in Mr. Burrough's *Moses' Choice*[13] and others the same things already abroad which I intended. And had I been at home when I begun this, or read so much on the like subjects as I have since done, I think I should have left out all or most that I have written; yet do I not repent it, for God, that compelled me to it, knows how to make use of it. If this apology satisfy not, I offer the plaintiff these three motions to take his choice: (1) either let it alone, and then it will do you no harm; (2) or if you will needs read it, blame the author and spare him not, so you will but entertain the truth and obey what you are convinced to be your duty; (3) or set on the work and do it better, that God's church may yet have more help in so needful a business. But no more of this. Were not the success of my labor more desirable to me than the maintenance of my esteem, I should think three lines long enough for apology. . . .

The living God, who is the portion and rest of His saints, make these, our carnal minds, so spiritual and our earthly hearts so heavenly that loving Him and delighting in Him may be the work of our lives; and that neither I that write nor you that read this book may ever be turned from this path of life, lest a promise being left us of entering into rest, we should come short of it through our own unbelief or negligence.

May 17, 1651

THE FOURTH PART

Containing a Directory for the Getting and Keeping of the Heart in Heaven by the Diligent Practice of That Excellent Unknown Duty of Heavenly Meditation, Being the Main Thing Intended by the Author in the Writing of This Book, and to Which All the Rest Is but Subservient

CHAPTER XIV
An Example of This Heavenly Contemplation for the Help of the Unskillful

There Remaineth a Rest to the People of God

SECTION 2

Rest! How sweet a word is this to mine ears! Methinks the sound doth turn to substance, and having entered at the ear doth possess my brain, and thence descendeth down to my very heart: methinks I feel it stir and work, and that through all my parts and powers, but with a various work

upon my various parts. To my wearied senses and languid spirits it seems a quieting, powerful opiate; to my dulled powers it is spirit and life; to my dark eyes it is both eye-salve and a prospective;[14] to my taste it is sweetness; to mine ears it is melody; to my hands and feet it is strength and nimbleness. Methinks I feel it digest as it proceeds, and increase my native heat and moisture; and, lying as a reviving cordial at my heart, from thence doth send forth lively spirits, which beat through all the pulses of my soul. Rest—not as the stone that rests on the earth, nor as these clods of flesh shall rest in the grave; so our beast must rest as well as we. Nor is it the satisfying of our fleshly lusts, nor such a rest as the carnal world desireth: no, no; we have another kind of rest than these. Rest we shall from all our labors, which were but the way and means to rest, but yet that is the smallest part. O blessed rest, where we shall never rest day or night crying "Holy, holy, holy, Lord God of sabbaths!" When we shall rest from sin, but not from worship; from suffering and sorrow, but not from solace! O blessed day, when I shall rest with God; when I shall rest in the arms and bosom of my Lord; when I shall rest in knowing, loving, rejoicing, and praising; when my perfect soul and body together shall in these perfect actings perfectly enjoy the most perfect God; when God also, who is love itself, shall perfectly love me; yea, and rest in His love to me as I shall rest in my love to Him, and rejoice over me with joy and singing as I shall rejoice in him! How near is that most blessed, joyful day! It comes apace; even He that comes will come, and will not tarry. Though my Lord do seem to delay His coming, yet a little while and He will be here. What is a few hundred years when they are over! How surely will His sign appear, and how suddenly will He seize upon the careless world! Even as the lightning that shines from east to west in a moment, He who is gone hence will even so return. Methinks I even hear the voice of His foregoers; methinks I see Him coming in the clouds, with the attendants of His angels, in majesty and in glory. O poor, secure sinners, what will you now do? Where will you hide yourselves, or what shall cover you? Mountains are gone; the earth and heavens that were are passed away; the devouring fire hath consumed all except yourselves, who must be the fuel forever. O that you could consume as soon as the earth, and melt away as did the heavens! Ah, these wishes are now but vain; the Lamb himself would have been your friend; He would have loved you, and ruled you, and now have saved you; but you would not then, and now too late. Never cry, "Lord, Lord!" Too late, too late, man. Why dost thou look about? Can any save thee? Whither dost thou run? Can any hide thee?

Avila, an indefatigable Spanish theologian whose commentaries on the Bible run to thirteen volumes.
[12]John Stoughton (d. 1639) was a prolific preacher, several collections of whose *Choice Sermons* were published the year after his death.
[13]Jeremiah Burroughs (1599–1646), a leading Congregational minister and member of the Westminster Assembly, presumably wrote *Moses His Choice* (a treatise on Hebrews 11.24) in 1641, but the work remained unpublished until 1650.
[14]Prospective glass, i.e., telescope.

O wretch, that hast brought thyself to this! Now blessed saints that have believed and obeyed, this is the end of faith and patience; this is it for which you prayed and waited; do you now repent your sufferings and sorrows, your self denying and holy walking? Are your tears of repentance now bitter or sweet? O see how the Judge doth smile upon you; there's love in His looks; the titles of Redeemer, Husband, Head are written in His amiable, shining face. Hark, doth He not call you? He bids you stand here on His right hand; fear not, for there He sets His sheep. O joyful sentence pronounced by that blessed mouth: "Come, ye blessed of my Father, inherit the kingdom prepared for you from the foundations of the world." See how your Saviour takes you by the hand; go along you must, the door is open, the kingdom's His, and therefore yours. There's your place before His throne; the Father receiveth you as the spouse of His Son; He bids you welcome to the crown of glory: never so unworthy, crowned you must be. This was the project of free redeeming grace, and this was the purpose of eternal love. O blessed grace! O blessed love! Oh, the frame that my soul will then be in! Oh, how love and joy will stir! But I cannot express it; I cannot conceive it. . . .

Awake, then, O my drowsy soul! Who but an owl or mole would love this world's uncomfortable darkness, when they are called forth to live in light? To sleep under the light of grace is unreasonable, much more in the approach of the light of glory. The night of thy ignorance and misery is past, the day of glorious light is at hand; this is the daybreak betwixt them both. Though thou see not yet the sun itself appear, methinks the twilight of a promise should revive thee. Come forth, then, O my dull, congealed spirits, and leave these earthly cells of dumpish sadness, and hear thy Lord that bids thee rejoice, and again rejoice! Thou hast lain here long enough in thy prison of flesh, where Satan hath been thy jailer, and the things of this world have been the stocks for the feet of thy affections; where cares have been thy irons, and fears thy scourge, and the bread and water of affliction thy food; where sorrows have been thy lodging, and thy sins and foes have made the bed; and a carnal, hard, unbelieving heart have been the iron gates and bars that have kept thee in, that thou couldst scarce have leave to look through the lattices, and see one glimpse of the immortal light. The angel of the covenant now calls thee, and strikes thee, and bids thee arise and follow him. Up, O my soul, and cheerfully obey, and thy bolts and bars shall all fly open. Do thou obey, and all will obey; follow the Lamb which way ever He leads thee. Art thou afraid because thou knowest not whither? Can the place be worse than where thou art? Shouldst thou fear to follow such a guide? Can the sun lead thee to a state of darkness; or can He mislead thee, that is the light of every man that cometh into the world? Will He lead thee to death, who died to save thee from it; or can He do thee any hurt, who for thy sake did suffer so much? Follow Him, and He will show thee the paradise of God; He will give thee a sight of the New Jerusalem; He will give thee a taste of the tree of life. Sit no longer, then, by the fire of earthly, common comforts, whither the cold of carnal fears and sorrows did drive thee; thy winter is past, and wilt thou house thyself still in earthly thoughts, and confine thyself to drooping and dullness? Even the silly flies will leave their holes when the winter is over, and the sun draws near them; the ants will stir, the fishes rise, the birds will sing, the earth look green, and all with joyful note will tell thee the spring is come. Come forth, then, O my drooping soul, and lay aside thy winter mourning robes. Let it be seen in thy believing joys and praise that the day is appearing and the spring is come, and as now thou seest thy comforts green, thou shalt shortly see them white and ripe for harvest; and then thou who art now called forth to see and taste shalt be called forth to reap and gather and take possession. Shall I suspend and delay my joys till then? Should not the joys of the spring go before the joys of harvest? Is title nothing before possession? Is the heir in no better a state than the slave? My Lord hath taught me to rejoice in hope of His glory, and to see it through the bars of a prison; and even when I am "persecuted for righteousness' sake," when I am "reviled and all manner of evil sayings are said against me falsely for His sake,"[15] then hath He commanded me to "rejoice, and be exceeding glad," because of this my "great reward in heaven." How justly is an unbelieving heart possessed by sorrow, and made a prey to cares and fears when itself doth create them, and thrust away its offered peace and joy! I know it is the pleasure of my bounteous Lord that none of His family should want for comfort, nor live such a poor and miserable life, nor look with such a famished, dejected face. I know He would have my joys exceed my sorrows; and as much as He delighteth in the humble and contrite, yet doth He more delight in the soul as it delighteth in Him. I know He taketh no pleasure in my self-procured sadness; nor would He call on me to weep or mourn but that it is the only way to these delights. Would I spread the table before my guest, and bring him forth my best provision, and bid him sit down and eat and welcome if I did not unfeignedly desire he should do so? Hath my Lord spread me a table in this wilderness, and furnished it with the promises of everlasting glory, and set before me angels' food, and broached for me the side of His beloved Son that I might have a better wine than the blood of the grape? Doth He so frequently and importunately invite me to sit down, and draw forth my faith, and feed, and spare not; nay, hath He furnished me to that end with reason and faith and a rejoicing disposition; and yet is it possible that He should be unwilling of my joys? Never think it, O my unbelieving soul, nor dare to charge Him with thy uncomfortable heaviness, who offereth thee the foretaste of the highest delights that heaven doth afford, and God bestow. Doth He not bid thee "delight thyself in the Lord," and promise to give thee then "the desires of thy heart"?[16] Hath he not charged thee to "rejoice evermore",[17] yea, "to sing aloud and shout for joy"?[18] Why should I then draw back discouraged? My

[15]Matthew 5.10–12. [16]Psalm 37.4. [17]2 Thessalonians 5.16. [18]Psalm 32.11.

God is willing, if I were but willing. He is delighted in my delights. He would fain have it my constant frame and daily business to be near to him in my believing meditations, and to live in the sweetest thoughts of His goodness, and to be always delighting my soul in himself. O blessed work; employment fit for the sons of God! . . .

BOOKS AND MEN IV

Francis Bacon[1] [1561-1626]

from The Essays or Counsels, Civil and Moral

To The Right Honorable My Very Good Lord the Duke of Buckingham, His Grace, Lord High Admiral of England[1]

Excellent Lord,

Solomon says a good name is as a precious ointment,[2] and I assure myself such will Your Grace's name be with posterity. For your fortune and merit both have been eminent, and you have planted things that are like to last. I do now publish my *Essays*, which of all my other works have been most current, for that, as it seems, they come home to men's business and bosoms. I have enlarged them both in number and weight, so that they are indeed a new work. I thought it therefore agreeable to my affection and obligation to Your [10] Grace to prefix your name before them, both in English and in Latin.[3] For I do conceive that the Latin volume of them, being in the universal language, may last as long as books last. My *Instauration* I dedicated to the king,[4] my *History of Henry the Seventh* (which I have now also translated into Latin) and my portions of *Natural History* to the prince.[5] And these I dedicate to Your Grace, being of the best fruits that by the good increase which God gives to my pen and labors I could yield. God lead Your Grace by the hand.

Your Grace's most obliged and [20]
faithful servant,
Francis, St. Albans

1. OF TRUTH[6]

"What is truth?" said jesting Pilate,[7] and would not stay for an answer. Certainly there be that delight in giddiness, and count it a bondage to fix a belief, affecting free-will in thinking as well as in acting. And though the sects of philosophers of that kind[8] be gone, yet there remain certain discoursing wits which are of the same veins, though there be not so much blood in them as was in those of the ancients. But it is not only the difficulty and labor which men take in [30] finding out of truth; nor again, that when it is found, it imposeth upon men's thoughts, that doth bring lies in favor; but a natural though corrupt love of the lie itself. One of the later schools[9] of the Grecians examineth the matter,[10] and is at a stand to think what should be in it, that men should love lies; where neither they make for pleasure, as with poets, nor for advantage, as with the merchant, but for the lie's sake. But

I cannot tell: this same truth is a naked and open daylight, that doth not show the masks and mummeries and triumphs of the world half so stately and daintily as candle-lights. Truth may perhaps come to the price of a pearl, that showeth best by day, but it will not rise to the price of a diamond or carbuncle,[11] that showeth best in varied lights. A mixture of a lie doth ever add pleasure. Doth any man doubt that if there were taken out of men's minds vain opinions, flattering hopes, false valuations, imaginations as one would, and the like but it would leave the minds of a number of men poor shrunken things, full of melancholy and indisposition, and unpleasing to themselves? One of the fathers, in great severity, called poesy *vinum daemonum*[12] because it filleth the imagination, and yet it is but with the shadow of a lie. But it is not the lie that passeth through the mind, but the lie that sinketh in, and settleth in it, that doth the hurt, such as we spake of before. But howsoever these things are thus in men's depraved judgments and affections, yet truth, which only doth judge itself, teacheth that the inquiry of truth, which is the love-making or wooing of it, the knowledge of truth, which is the presence of it, and the belief of truth, which is the enjoying of it is the sovereign good of human nature. The first creature[13] of God, in the works of the days, was the light of the sense;[14] the last was the light of reason;[15] and His sabbath work ever

---

[1]For a commentary on Bacon and for other excerpts from his work, see Philosophy and Speculation, pp. 397 ff., and History and Historiography, pp. 878 ff.

ESSAYS OR COUNSELS [1]For Thomas Fuller's character of George Villiers (1592–1628), first duke of Buckingham, see p. 754; for James Howell's account of his violent death, see pp. 791–92. [2]Ecclesiastes 7.1.

[3]The Latin translation of his *Essays* that Bacon superintended in the last months of his life was published by his "learned chaplain" William Rawley (see p. 669) in 1638, but with a dedication to Charles I.   [4]For this dedication see p. 407.

[5]For the dedication of Bacon's life of Henry VII see p. 882. *Historia naturalis et experimentalis ad condendam philosophiam*—the third part of *The Great Instauration* (see p. 406 ff.)—appeared with a dedication to Prince Charles in 1622.

[6]First published in the 1625 edition. In the text the title of each essay precedes its number.   [7]John 18.38.

[8]The ancient Skeptics, whose philosophical school was founded by Pyrrho of Elis (ca. 340–300 B.C.).   [9]Text *schoole*.

[10]Lucian, *Philopseudes*, Sect. 1.   [11]Garnet.   [12]"The wine of devils."

[13]Created thing.   [14]Genesis 1.3.   [15]Genesis 1.26–27.

since is the illumination of His spirit. First, He breathed light upon the face of the matter, or chaos; then He breathed light into the face of man; and still He breathed and inspireth light into the face of His chosen. The poet that beautified the sect, that was otherwise inferior to the rest,[16] saith yet excellently well: "It is a pleasure to stand upon the shore and to see ships tossed upon the sea, a pleasure to stand in the window of a castle and to see a battle and the adventures thereof below, but no pleasure is comparable to the standing upon the vantage ground of truth" (a hill not to be commanded,[17] and where the air is always clear and serene), "and to see the errors and wanderings and mists and tempests in the vale below:"[18] so[19] always that this prospect be with pity, and not with swelling or pride. Certainly, it is heaven upon earth, to have a man's mind move in charity, rest in providence, and turn upon the poles of truth.

To pass from theological and philosophical truth to the truth of civil business: it will be acknowledged even by those that practise it not that clear and round[20] dealing is the honor of man's nature, and that mixture of falsehood is like alloy in coin of gold and silver, which may make the metal work the better, but it embaseth[21] it. For these winding and crooked courses are the goings of the serpent, which goeth basely upon the belly, and not upon the feet. There is no vice that doth so cover a man with shame as to be found false and perfidious; and therefore Mountaigny saith prettily, when he inquired the reason why the word of the lie should be such a disgrace and such an odious charge, saith he, "If it be well weighed, to say that man lieth is as much to say as that he is brave towards God and a coward towards men. For a lie faces God, and shrinks from man."[22] Surely the wickedness of falsehood and breach of faith cannot possibly be so highly expressed as in that it shall be the last peal to call the judgments of God upon the generations of men, it being foretold that when Christ cometh, He shall not find faith upon the earth.[23]

2.   OF DEATH[24]

Men fear death as children fear to go in the dark, and as that natural fear in children is increased with tales, so is the other. Certainly, the contemplation of death as the wages of sin[25] and passage to another world is holy and religious; but the fear of it as a tribute due unto nature is weak. Yet in religious meditations there is sometimes mixture of vanity and of superstition. You shall read in some of the friars' books of mortification[26] that a man should think with himself what the pain is if he have but his finger's end pressed or tortured, and thereby imagine what the pains of death are when the whole body is corrupted and dissolved; when[27] many times death passeth with less pain than the torture of a limb, for the most vital parts are not the quickest of sense. And by him that spake only as a philosopher, and natural man, it was well said, *"Pompa mortis magis terret quam mors ipsa."*[28] Groans and convulsions, and a discolored face, and friends weeping, and blacks[29] and obsequies, and the like show death terrible. It is worthy the observing that there is no passion in the mind of man so weak but it mates[30] and masters the fear of death,

and therefore death is no such terrible enemy when a man hath so many attendants about him that can win the combat of him.[31] Revenge triumphs over death; love slights it; honor aspireth to it; grief flieth to it; fear preoccupateth[32] it; nay, we read, after Otho the emperor had slain himself, pity (which is the tenderest of affections) provoked many to die out of mere compassion to their sovereign,[33] and as the truest sort of followers. Nay, Seneca adds niceness and society:[34] *"Cogita quam diu eadem feceris; mori velle, non tantum fortis, aut miser, sed etiam fastidiosus potest."*[35] A man would die, though he were neither valiant nor miserable, only upon a weariness to do the same thing so oft over and over. It is no less worthy to observe how little alteration in good spirits the approaches of death make, for they appear to be the same men till the last instant. Augustus Caesar died in a compliment, *"Livia, conjugii nostri memor, vive et vale."*[36] Tiberius in dissimulation, as Tacitus saith of him *"Jam Tiberium vires et corpus, non dissimulatio, deserebant."*[37] Vespasian in a jest, sitting upon the stool, *"Ut puto deus fio."*[38] Galba with a sentence *"Feri, si ex re sit populi Romani"*[39] holding forth his neck. Septimus Severus in dispatch, *"Adeste si quid mihi restat agendum,"*[40] and the like. Certainly the Stoics bestowed too much cost upon death, and by their great preparations made it appear more fearful. Better saith he, *"Qui finem vitae extremum inter munera ponat naturae."*[41] It is as natural to die as to be born, and to a little infant, perhaps, the one is as painful as the other. He that dies in an earnest pursuit is like one that is wounded in hot blood; who, for the time, scarce feels the hurt; and therefore a mind fixed and bent upon somewhat that is good doth avert the dolors of death;

[16]Titus Lucretius Carus (96?–55 B.C.), Roman poet whose *De rerum natura*, a philosophical work in six books, is the greatest literary monument of Epicurean doctrine.
[17]Overlooked by another height.
[18]A paraphrase of *De rerum natura*, II.1–10.   [19]Provided that.
[20]Plain, straightforward.   [21]Debases.
[22]Michel Eyquem de Montaigne, *Essays*, II.18. The passage attributed to Montaigne is in fact cited by him from Plutarch's "Life of Lysander."   [23]Adapted from Luke 18.8.
[24]First printed in the 1612 edition.
[25]"For the wages of sin is death" (Romans 6.23.)
[26]Humiliation, penance.   [27]Whereas.
[28]"The trappings of death are more terrifying than death itself" (perhaps adapted from Seneca, *Epistulae morales*, No. XXIV, Sect. 14).   [29]Mourning garments.   [30]Overpowers.
[31]From death itself.   [32]Anticipates.
[33]The story is told of the Emperor Otho (32–69) by Tacitus, *The Histories*, II.49.   [34]Fastidiousness and satiety.
[35]"Think how long you have been doing the same things. Not only the valiant or the wretched may wish to die, but also the man who is tired of living" (adapted from Seneca, *Epistulae morales*, No. LXXVII, Sect. 6, where the remark is attributed to "a Stoic friend" of the author).
[36]"Farewell, Livia, remember our marriage and live on."
[37]"His strength and vigor now deserted Tiberius, but not his duplicity."   [38]"I suppose I am about to become a god."
[39]"Strike, if it is for the good of Rome."
[40]"Hurry, if there is anything left for me to do."
[41]"Who accounts the end of life a natural boon" (adapted from Juvenal, *Satires*, X.358–359).

but, above all, believe it, the sweetest canticle is *Nunc dimittis,*[42] when a man hath obtained worthy ends and expectations. Death hath this also, that it openeth the gate to good fame, and extinguisheth envy: *Extinctus amabitur idem.*[43]

4. OF REVENGE[44]

Revenge is a kind of wild justice, which the more man's nature runs to, the more ought law to weed it out; for as for the first wrong, it doth but offend the law, but the revenge of that wrong putteth the law out of office. Certainly, in taking revenge a man is but even with his enemy, but in passing it over he is superior; for it is a prince's part to pardon, and Solomon, I am sure, saith, "It is the glory of a man to pass by an offence."[45] That which is past is gone and irrevocable, and wise men have enough to do with things present and to come; therefore they do but trifle with themselves that labor in past matters. There is no man doth a wrong for the wrong's sake, but thereby to purchase himself profit, or pleasure, or honor, or the like; therefore why should I be angry with a man for loving himself better than me? And if any man should do wrong merely out of ill-nature, why, yet it is but like the thorn or briar, which prick and scratch because they can do no other. The most tolerable sort of revenge is for those wrongs which there is no law to remedy; but then, let a man take heed the revenge be such as there is no law to punish, else a man's enemy is still beforehand, and it is two for one. Some when they take revenge are desirous the party should know whence it cometh: this is the more generous, for the delight seemeth to be not so much in doing the hurt as in making the party repent; but base and crafty cowards are like the arrow that flieth in the dark. Cosmus, Duke of Florence,[46] had a desperate saying against perfidious or neglecting friends, as if those wrongs were unpardonable. "You shall read" (saith he) "that we are commanded to forgive our enemies, but you never read that we are commanded to forgive our friends." But yet the spirit of Job was in a better tune: "Shall we" (saith he) "take good at God's hands, and not be content to take evil also?"[47] And so of friends in a proportion. This is certain, that a man that studieth revenge keeps his own wounds green, which otherwise would heal and do well. Public revenges are for the most part fortunate; as that for the death of Caesar, for the death of Pertinax, for the death of Henry the Third of France,[48] and many more. But in private revenges it is not so; nay, rather vindictive persons live the life of witches, who, as they are mischievous, so end they infortunate.[49]

5. OF ADVERSITY[50]

It was an high speech of Seneca (after the manner of the Stoics) that the good things which belong to prosperity are to be wished, but the good things that belong to adversity are to be admired. ("*Bona rerum secundarum optabilia, adversarum mirabilia.*")[51] Certainly, if miracles be the command over nature, they appear most in adversity. It is yet a higher speech of his than the other (much too high for a heathen), it is true greatness to have in one the frailty of a man and the security of a god. (*"Vere magnum habere fragilitatem hominis, securitatem dei."*)[52] This would have done better in poesy, where transcendencies[53] are more allowed; and the poets, indeed, have been busy with it; for it is in effect the thing which is figured in that strange fiction of the ancient poets, which seemeth not to be without mystery,[54] nay, and to have some approach to the state of a Christian, that Hercules, when he went to unbind Prometheus (by whom human nature is represented), sailed the length of the great ocean in an earthen pot or pitcher,[55] lively describing Christian resolution that saileth in the frail bark of the flesh through the waves of the world. But to speak in a mean,[56] the virtue of prosperity is temperance, the virtue of adversity is fortitude, which in morals is the more heroical virtue. Prosperity is the blessing of the Old Testament, adversity is the blessing of the New, which carrieth the greater benediction and the clearer revelation of God's favor. Yet even in the Old Testament, if you listen to David's harp, you shall hear as many hearse-like airs as carols; and the pencil of the Holy Ghost hath labored more in describing the afflictions of Job than the felicities of Solomon. Prosperity is not without many fears and distastes,[57] and adversity is not without comforts and hopes. We see in needleworks and embroideries it is more pleasing to have a lively work upon a sad[58] and solemn ground than to have a dark and melancholy work upon a lightsome ground: judge, therefore, of the pleasure of the heart by the pleasure of the eye. Certainly virtue is like precious odors, most fragrant when they are incensed[59] or crushed: for prosperity doth best discover vice, but adversity doth best discover virtue.

8. OF MARRIAGE AND SINGLE LIFE[60]

He that hath wife and children hath given hostages to fortune, for they are impediments to great enterprises, either of virtue or mischief. Certainly the best works,

[42]*Nunc dimittis servum tuum, Domine, secundum verbum tuum in pace:* "Lord, now lettest Thou Thy servant depart in peace, according to Thy word" (Luke 2.29), a *canticle* for evening prayer in the Anglican Book of Common Prayer.
[43]He who was reviled in life will be beloved in death (Horace, *Epistles,* II.i.14).   [44]First printed in the 1625 edition.
[45]Proverbs 19.11.   [46]Cosimo de' Medici (1389–1464).   [47]Job 2.10.
[48]*Public . . . France:* illustrious victims of assassination whose *revenges,* Bacon enigmatically implies, were for the public good. Julius Caesar's assassination (44 B.C.) led to the extinction of the Roman Republic and the establishment of the Empire under his great-nephew Augustus; the murder of the Emperor Pertinax by the Praetorian Guard (193) was avenged by Septimius Severus; the assassin of Henry III was summarily put to death (1589).   [49]Unfortunate.   [50]First printed in the 1625 edition.
[51]Adapted from Seneca, *Epistulae morales,* No. LXVI, Sect. 29.
[52]Adapted from Seneca, *Epistulae morales,* No. LIII, Sect. 12.
[53]Lofty assertions, exaggerations.   [54]Hidden meaning.
[55]Although the fable of Hercules' unbinding Prometheus was widely reported by the ancients, Bacon's allusion to his sailing in *an earthen pot or pitcher* has not been traced.
[56]With moderation.   [57]Annoyances.   [58]Dark.
[59]Burned.   [60]First printed in the 1612 edition.

and of greatest merit for the public, have proceeded from the unmarried or childless men, which both in affection and means have married and endowed the public. Yet it were great reason that those that have children should have greatest care of future times, unto which they know they must transmit their dearest pledges. Some there are who, though they lead a single life, yet their thoughts do end with themselves, and account future times impertinences. Nay, there are some other that account wife and children but as bills of charges; nay more, there are some foolish, rich, covetous men that take a pride in having no children because[61] they may be thought so much the richer; for perhaps they have heard some talk, "Such an one is a great rich man," and another except[62] to it, "Yea, but he hath a great charge of children," as if it were an abatement to his riches. But the most ordinary cause of a single life is liberty, especially in certain self-pleasing and humorous minds, which are so sensible of every restraint as they will go near to think their girdles and garters to be bonds and shackles. Unmarried men are best friends, best masters, best servants; but not always best subjects, for they are light[63] to run away, and almost all fugitives are of that condition. A single life doth well with churchmen, for charity will hardly water the ground where it must first fill a pool. It is indifferent for judges and magistrates, for if they be facile and corrupt you shall have a servant five times worse than a wife. For soldiers, I find the generals commonly, in their hortatives,[64] put men in mind of their wives and children; and I think the despising of marriage amongst the Turks maketh the vulgar soldier more base. Certainly, wife and children are a kind of discipline of humanity; and single men, though they be many times more charitable because their means are less exhaust,[65] yet, on the other side, they are more cruel and hard-hearted (good to make severe inquisitors) because their tenderness is not so oft called upon. Grave natures, led by custom and therefore constant are commonly loving husbands, as was said of Ulysses, *"Vetulam suam praetulit immortalitati."*[66] Chaste women are often proud and froward, as presuming upon the merit of their chastity. It is one of the best bonds both of chastity and obedience in the wife if she think her husband wise, which she will never do if she find him jealous. Wives are young men's mistresses, companions for middle age, and old men's nurses, so as a man may have a quarrel[67] to marry when he will: but yet he was reputed one of the wise men[68] that made answer to the question when a man should marry: "A young man not yet, an elder man not at all." It is often seen that bad husbands have very good wives; whether it be that it raiseth the price of their husbands' kindness when it comes, or that the wives take a pride in their patience; but this[69] never fails if the bad husbands were of their own choosing, against their friends' consent, for then they will be sure to make good their own folly.

14   OF NOBILITY[70]

We will speak of nobility first as a portion of an estate,[71] then as a condition of particular persons. A monarchy, where there is no nobility at all, is ever a pure and absolute tyranny, as that of the Turks; for nobility attempers[72] sovereignty, and draws the eyes of the people somewhat aside from the line royal. But for democracies they need it not, and they are commonly more quiet and less subject to sedition than where there are stirps[73] of nobles; for men's eyes are upon the business and not upon the persons; or if upon the persons, it is for the business sake, as fittest, and not for flags[74] and pedigree. We see the Switzers last well, notwithstanding their diversity of religion and of cantons, for utility is their bond, and not respects.[75] The united provinces of the Low Countries in their government excel, for where there is an equality the consultations are more indifferent, and the payments and tributes more cheerful. A great and potent nobility addeth majesty to a monarch, but diminisheth power, and putteth life and spirit into the people, but presseth[76] their fortune. It is well when nobles are not too great for sovereignty nor for justice, and yet maintained in that height as the insolency of inferiors may be broken upon them before it come on too fast upon the majesty of kings. A numerous nobility causeth poverty and inconvenience in a state, for it is a surcharge of expense; and besides, it being of necessity that many of the nobility fall in time to be weak in fortune, it maketh a kind of disproportion between honor and means.

As for nobility in particular persons, it is a reverend thing to see an ancient castle or building not in decay, or to see a fair timber tree sound and perfect; how much more to behold an ancient noble family which hath stood against the waves and weathers of time! For new nobility is but the act of power, but ancient nobility is the act of time. Those that are first raised to nobility are commonly more virtuous,[77] but less innocent, than their descendants; for there is rarely any rising but by a commixture of good and evil arts; but it is reason[78] the memory of their virtues remain to their posterity, and their faults die with themselves. Nobility of birth commonly abateth industry, and he that is not industrious envieth him that is. Besides, noble persons cannot go much higher, and he that standeth at a stay when others rise can hardly avoid motions of envy.[79] On the other side, nobility extinguisheth the passive envy from others towards them, because they are in possession of honor. Certainly, kings that have able men of their nobility shall find ease in employing them, and a better slide into their business;[80]

[61]In order that.   [62]Take exception.   [63]Apt?   [64]Exhortations.
[65]Exhausted.
[66]"He preferred his old wife to immortality" (perhaps adapted from Cicero, *De oratore*, I.xliv). Ulysses rejected the goddess Calypso in order to return to his wife Penelope in Ithaca.
[67]Pretext, reason.
[68]Thales (640?–546 B.C.), a Greek philosopher and mathematician, one of the Seven Wise Men of antiquity.
[69]The pride of wives in their patience.
[70]First printed in the 1612 edition, greatly altered and enlarged in 1625.   [71]State.   [72]Tempers, moderates.
[73]Families, stock (a Latinism).   [74]Armorial bearings.
[75]Considerations of rank.   [76]Oppresses.
[77]Endowed with manly qualities (a Latinism).   [78]Reasonable.
[79]Feelings of malice.
[80]*Better slide . . . business*: more ease in conducting their affairs?

for people naturally bend to them as born in some sort to command.

17 OF SUPERSTITION[81]

It were better to have no opinion of God at all than such an opinion as is unworthy of him, for the one is unbelief, the other is contumely: and certainly superstition is the reproach of the deity. Plutarch saith well to that purpose: "Surely" (saith he) "I had rather a great deal men should say there was no such man at all as Plutarch than that they should say that there was one Plutarch that would eat his children as soon as they were born,"[82] as the poets speak of Saturn: and as the contumely is greater towards God, so the danger is greater towards men. Atheism leaves a man to sense,[83] to philosophy, to natural piety, to laws, to reputation: all which may be guides to an outward moral virtue, though religion were not; but superstition dismounts all these, and erecteth an absolute monarchy in the minds of men; therefore atheism did never perturb states, for it makes men wary of themselves, as looking no further, and we see the times inclined to atheism (as the time of Augustus Caesar) were civil[84] times; but superstition hath been the confusion of many states, and bringeth in a new *primum mobile* that ravisheth all the spheres of government.[85] The master of superstition is the people, and in all superstition wise men follow fools: and arguments are fitted to practice in a reversed order. It was gravely said by some of the prelates in the Council of Trent,[86] where the doctrine of the Schoolmen bare great sway, that the Schoolmen were like astronomers, which did feign eccentrics and epicycles, and such engines of orbs to save the phenomena,[87] though they knew there were no such things; and, in like manner, that the Schoolmen had framed a number of subtile and intricate axioms and theorems to save the practice of the church. The causes of superstition are pleasing and sensual[88] rites and ceremonies; excess of outward and pharisaical holiness; overgreat reverence of traditions, which cannot but load the church; the stratagems of prelates for their own ambition and lucer; the favoring too much of good intentions, which openeth the gate to conceits and novelties; the taking an aim at divine matters by human, which cannot but breed mixture of imaginations: and, lastly, barbarous times, especially joined with calamities and disasters. Superstition, without a veil, is a deformed thing; for as it addeth deformity to an ape to be so like a man, so the similitude of superstition to religion makes it the more deformed. And as wholesome meat corrupteth to little worms, so good forms and orders corrupt into a number of petty observances. There is a superstition in avoiding superstition, when men think to do best if they go furthest from the superstition formerly received; therefore care would be had that (as it fareth in ill purgings) the good be not taken away with the bad, which commonly is done when the people is the reformer.

18 OF TRAVAIL[89]

Travail, in the younger sort, is a part of education; in the elder, a part of experience. He that travaileth into a country before he hath some entrance into the language, goeth to school, and not to travail. That young men travail under some tutor or grave servant I allow well,[90] so that he be such a one that hath the language and hath been in the country before; whereby he may be able to tell them what things are worthy to be seen in the country where they go, what acquaintances they are to seek, what exercises or discipline the place yieldeth; for else young men shall go hooded,[91] and look abroad little. It is a strange thing that in sea voyages, where there is nothing to be seen but sky and sea, men should makes diaries; but in land travel, wherein so much is to be observed, for the most part they omit it, as if chance were fitter to be registered than observation. Let diaries therefore be brought in use. The things to be seen and observed are the courts of princes, especially when they give audience to ambassadors; the courts of justice, while they sit and hear causes; and so of consistories ecclesiastic; the churches and monasteries, with the monuments which are therein extant; the walls and fortifications of cities and towns; and so the havens and harbors, antiquities and ruins, libraries, colleges, disputations, and lectures, where any are; shipping and navies; houses and gardens of state and pleasure near great cities; armories, arsenals, magazines, exchanges, burses,[92] warehouses, exercises of horsemanship, fencing, training of soldiers, and the like; comedies, such whereunto the better sort of persons do resort; treasuries of jewels and robes; cabinets and rarities; and, to conclude, whatsoever is memorable in the places where they go, after all which the tutors or servants ought to make diligent inquiry. As for triumphs,[93] masks, feasts, weddings, funerals, capital executions, and such shows, men need not to be put in mind of them, yet are they not to be neglected. If you will have a young man to put his travail into a little room, and in short time to gather much, this you must do: first, as was said, he must have some entrance into the language before he goeth; then he must have such a servant or tutor as knoweth the country, as was likewise said; let him carry with him also some card[94] or book describing the country where he travaileth, which will be a good key to his inquiry; let him keep also a diary; let him not stay long in one city or town, more or less as the place deserveth, but not long; nay, when he stayeth in one city or town, let him change his lodging from one end and part of the town to another, which is a great adamant[95] of acquaintance; let him sequester himself from the company of his countrymen, and diet[96] in such

[81]First printed in the 1612 edition, enlarged in 1625.
[82]"Of Superstition or Indiscreet Devotion," Sect. 10.
[83]Empirical knowledge. [84]Peaceful, orderly.
[85]*New primum . . . government*: a new alignment of power that sweeps away the government. See *sphere* in the Glossary.
[86]A general council (1545–63) called to define doctrine and effect reforms in the Roman Catholic Church.
[87]*Feign . . . phenomena*: contrive spurious explanations in order to preserve appearances. In Ptolemaic astronomy *epicycles* were planetary orbits regarded as *eccentrics* because their centers did not coincide with the earth. [88]Appealing to the senses.
[89]First printed in the 1625 edition. [90]Entirely approve.
[91]Blindfold (a term from falconry). [92]Exchanges. [93]Pageants.
[94]Map. [95]Lodestone, magnet. [96]Board.

places where there is good company of the nation where he travaileth; let him, upon his removes from one place to another, procure recommendation to some person of quality residing in the place whither he removeth, that he may use his favor in those things he desireth to see or know; thus he may abridge his travail with much profit. As for the acquaintance which is to be sought in travail, that which is most of all profitable is acquaintance with the secretaries and employed men of ambassadors, for so in travailing in one country he shall suck the experience of many. Let him also see and visit 10 eminent persons in all kinds which are of great name abroad, that he may be able to tell how the life agreeth with the fame. For quarrels, they are with care and discretion to be avoided; they are commonly for mistresses, healths,[97] place, and words; and let a man beware how he keepeth company with choleric and quarrelsome persons, for they will engage him into their own quarrels. When a travailer returneth home, let him not leave the countries where he hath travailed altogether behind him, but maintain a correspondence by letters with those of his acquaintance which are of most 20 worth. And let his travail appear rather in his discourse than in his apparel or gesture; and in his discourse let him be rather advised[98] in his answers than forwards to tell stories; and let it appear that he doth not change his country[99] manners for those of foreign parts, but only prick in[1] some flowers of that he hath learned abroad into the customs of his own country.

36   OF AMBITION[2]

Ambition is like choler, which is an humor that maketh men active, earnest, full of alacrity, and stirring if it be not stopped; but if it be stopped, and cannot have his way, 30 it becometh adust,[3] and thereby malign and venomous. So ambitious men, if they find the way open for their rising, and still get forward, they are rather busy than dangerous; but if they be checked in their desires they become secretly discontent, and look upon men and matters with an evil eye, and are best pleased when things go backward, which is the worst property in a servant of a prince or state. Therefore it is good for princes if they use ambitious men to handle it so as they be still progressive, and not retrograde;[4] which, because it cannot be without inconvenience, it is 40 good not to use such natures at all; for if they rise not with their service they will take order[5] to make their service fall with them. But since we have said it were good not to use men of ambitious natures except it be upon necessity, it is fit we speak in what cases they are of necessity. Good commanders in the wars must be taken, be they never so ambitious, for the use of their service dispenseth with[6] the rest, and to take a soldier without ambition is to pull off his spurs. There is also great use of ambitious men in being screens to princes in matters of danger and envy; for no man 50 will take that part except he be like a seeled[7] dove, that mounts and mounts because he cannot see about him. There is use also of ambitious men in pulling down the greatness of any subject that overtops, as Tiberius used Macro in the pulling down of Sejanus.[8] Since, therefore, they must be used in such cases there resteth[9] to speak how they are to be

bridled, that they may be less dangerous. There is less danger of them if they be of mean birth than if they be noble, and if they be rather harsh of nature than gracious and popular, and if they be rather new raised than grown cunning and fortified in their greatness. It is counted by some a weakness in princes to have favorites; but it is, of all others, the best remedy against ambitious great ones; for when the way of pleasuring and displeasuring[10] lieth by the favorite, it is impossible any other should be overgreat. Another means to curb them is to balance them by others as proud as they, but then there must be some middle counselors to keep things steady, for without that ballast the ship will roll too much. At the least, a prince may animate and inure[11] some meaner persons to be, as it were, scourges to ambitious men. As for the having of them obnoxious[12] to ruin, if they be of fearful natures it may do well, but if they be stout and daring it may precipitate their designs, and prove dangerous. As for the pulling of them down, if the affairs require it, and that it may not be done with safety suddenly, the only way is the interchange continually of favors and disgraces,[13] whereby they may not know what to expect, and be, as it were, in a wood, Of ambitions, it is less harmful the ambition to prevail in great things than that other to appear in everything, for that breeds confusion and mars business. But yet it is less danger to have an ambitious man stirring in business than great in dependencies.[14] He that seeketh to be eminent amongst able men hath a great task, but that is ever good for the public. But he that plots to be the only figure amongst ciphers is the decay[15] of an whole age. Honor hath three things in it: the vantage ground to do good, the approach to kings and principal persons, and the raising of a man's own fortunes. He that hath the best of these intentions, when he aspireth, is an honest man; and that prince that can discern of these intentions in another that aspireth is a wise prince. Generally, let princes and states choose such ministers as are more sensible of duty than of rising,[16] and such as love business rather upon conscience than upon bravery; and let them discern a busy nature from a willing mind.

50   OF STUDIES[17]

Studies serve for delight, for ornament, and for ability. Their chief use for delight is in privateness and retiring,

[97]Drinking bouts. [98]Deliberate. [99]Native. [1]Implant.
[2]First printed in the 1612 edition and greatly enlarged in the 1625 edition. [3]Burned, scorched (a medical term).
[4]They are steadily advanced and not demoted. [5]Arrange.
[6]Compensate for.
[7]With eyelids sewn together (a term from falconry).
[8]The Emperor Tiberius used his cruel favorite Naevius Sertorious Macro to arrest the ambitious Sejanus when the latter tried to usurp imperial power. This situation provided the plot for Ben Jonson's tragedy *Sejanus, His Fall* (1603). [9]It remains.
[10]Pleasing and displeasing. [11]Make use of. [12]Exposed.
[13]Affronts, repulses. [14]Followers. [15]Ruin.
[16]*More sensible . . . rising:* more intent on serving the sovereign than on promoting their own interests.
[17]First printed in the 1597 edition, greatly enlarged in 1612 and again in 1625.

for ornament is in discourse, and for ability is in the judgment and disposition of business; for expert men can execute and perhaps judge of particulars one by one, but the general counsels and the plots and marshaling of affairs come best from those that are learned. To spend too much time in studies is sloth; to use them too much for ornament is affectation; to make judgment wholly by their rules is the humor of a scholar. They perfect nature and are perfected by experience, for natural abilities are like natural plants that need proyning[18] by study; and studies themselves do give forth directions too much at large except they be bounded in by experience. Crafty men contemn studies, simple men admire them, and wise men use[19] them; for they teach not their own use, but that is a wisdom without them and above them, won by observation. Read not to contradict and confute, nor to believe and take for granted, nor to find talk and discourse, but to weigh and consider. Some books are to be tasted, others to be swallowed, and some few to be chewed and digested. That is, some books are to be read only in parts, others to be read but not curiously,[20] and some few to be read wholly and with diligence and attention. Some books also may be read by deputy, and extracts made of them by others; but that would be only in the less important arguments and the meaner sort of books; else distilled books are, like common distilled waters, flashy[21] things. Reading maketh a full man, conference[22] a ready man, and writing an exact man; and therefore if a man write little, he had need have a great memory; if he confer little, he had need have a present[23] wit; and if he read little, he had need have much cunning, to seem to know that he doth not. Histories make men wise; poets, witty; the mathematics, subtile; natural philosophy, deep; moral, grave; logic and rhetoric, able to contend: *Abeunt studia in mores*.[24] Nay, there is no stond[25] or impediment in the wit but may be wrought out[26] by fit studies. Like as diseases of the body may have appropriate exercises—bowling is good for the stone and reins,[27] shooting for the lungs and breast, gentle walking for the stomach, riding for the head, and the like—so if a man's wit be wandering, let him study the mathematics, for in demonstrations if his wit be called away never so little, he must begin again. If his wit be not apt to distinguish or find difference, let him study the Schoolmen, for they are *cymini sectores*.[28] If he be not apt to beat over matters and to call up one thing to prove and illustrate another, let him study the lawyer's cases. So every defect of the mind may have a special receipt.[29]

[18]Pruning, cultivating. [19]Apply. [20]Attentively. [21]Insipid.
[22]Conversation. [23]Ready.
[24]"Studies develop into manners" (Ovid, *Heroides*, XV.83).
[25]Obstacle. [26]Worked out, i.e., removed. [27]Kidneys.
[28]"Carvers of cumin seed." Here and elsewhere Bacon uses the phrase to mean "splitters of hairs" instead of "niggards."
[29]Prescriptions.

from Of the Proficience and Advancement of Learning, Divine and Human (1605)

THE SECOND BOOK

[POETRY]

Poesy is a part of learning in measure of words for the most part restrained, but in all other points extremely licensed, and doth truly refer to the imagination; which, being not tied to the laws of matter, may at pleasure join that which nature hath severed, and sever that which nature hath joined; and so make unlawful matches and divorces of things; *Pictoribus atque poetis,* etc.[1] It is taken in two senses in respect of words or matter. In the first sense it is but a character of style, and belongeth to arts of speech, and is not pertinent for the present. In the latter it is (as hath been said) one of the principal portions of learning, and is nothing else but feigned history, which may be styled as well in prose as in verse.[2]

The use of this feigned history hath been to give some shadow of satisfaction to the mind of man in those points wherein the nature of things doth deny it, the world being in proportion inferior to the soul; by reason whereof there is, agreeable to the spirit of man, a more ample greatness, a more exact goodness, and a more absolute variety, than can be found in the nature of things. Therefore, because the acts or events of true history have not that magnitude which satisfieth the mind of man, poesy feigneth acts and events greater and more heroical. Because true history propoundeth the successes and issues of actions not so agreeable to the merits of virtue and vice, therefore poesy feigns them more just in retribution, and more according to revealed providence. Because true history representeth actions and events more ordinary and less interchanged, therefore poesy endueth them with more rareness, and more unexpected and alterna-

OF THE PROFICIENCE [1]" 'But surely,' you will say, 'painters and poets have always enjoyed equal freedom to attempt anything' " (Horace, *Ars poetica,* ll. 9–10).
[2]*Which may ... verse:* which may be described as *feigned history* whether cast as prose or verse. Bacon, like Sir Philip Sidney, broadens the term *poesy* to include all imaginative literature.

tive variations. So as it appeareth that poesy serveth and conferreth[3] to magnanimity, morality, and to delectation. And therefore it was ever thought to have some participation of divineness, because it doth raise and erect the mind by submitting the shows of things to the desires of the mind, whereas reason doth buckle and bow the mind unto the nature of things. And we see that by these insinuations[4] and congruities with man's nature and pleasure, joined also with the agreement and consort it hath with music, it hath had access[5] and estimation in rude times and barbarous regions, where other learning stood excluded.

The division of poesy which is aptest in the propriety thereof (besides those divisions which are common unto it with history, as feigned chronicles, feigned lives, and the appendices of history, as feigned epistles, feigned orations, and the rest) is into poesy narrative, representative, and allusive. The narrative is a mere imitation of history, with the excesses before remembered; choosing for subject commonly wars and love, rarely state,[6] and sometimes pleasure or mirth. Representative is as a visible history, and is an image of actions as if they were present, as history is of actions in nature as they are (that is) past. Allusive or parabolical[7] is a narration applied only to express some special purpose or conceit. Which latter kind of parabolical wisdom was much more in use in the ancient times, as by the fables of Aesop, and the brief sentences of the Seven,[8] and the use of hieroglyphics may appear. And the cause was for that it was then of necessity to express any point of reason which was more sharp or subtle than the vulgar in that manner, because men in those times wanted both variety of examples and subtlety of conceit. And as hieroglyphics were before letters, so parables were before arguments; and nevertheless now and at all times they do retain much life and vigor, because reason cannot be so sensible,[9] nor examples so fit.

But there remaineth yet another use of poesy parabolical opposite to that which we last mentioned, for that tendeth to demonstrate and illustrate that which is taught or delivered, and this other to retire and obscure it: that is, when the secrets and mysteries of religion, policy, or philosophy are involved in fables or parables. Of this in divine poesy we see the use is authorized. In heathen poesy we see the exposition of fables doth fall out sometimes with great felicity, as in the fable that the Giants being overthrown in their war against the gods, the Earth their mother in revenge thereof brought forth Fame:

Illam Terra parens, ira inritata deorum,
Extremam, ut perhibent, Coeo Enceladoque sororem
Progenuit.[10]

Expounded, that when princes and monarchs have suppressed actual and open rebels, then the malignity of people (which is the mother of rebellion) doth bring forth libels and slanders and taxations[11] of the states, which is of the same kind with rebellion, but more feminine. So in the fable that the rest of the gods having conspired to bind Jupiter, Pallas[12] called

Briareus with his hundred hands to his aid: expounded, that monarchies need not fear any curbing of their absoluteness by mighty subjects as long as by wisdom they keep the hearts of the people, who will be sure to come in on their side. So in the fable that Achilles was brought up under Chiron the centaur,[13] who was part a man and part a beast, expounded ingeniously but corruptly by Machiavel,[14] that it belongeth to the education and discipline of princes to know as well how to play the part of the lion in violence and the fox in guile as of the man in virtue and justice. Nevertheless, in many the like encounters, I do rather think that the fable was first, and the exposition devised, than that the moral was first, and thereupon the fable framed. For I find it was an ancient vanity in Chrysippus, that troubled himself with great contention to fasten the assertions of the Stoics upon fictions of the ancient poets;[15] but yet that all the fables and fictions of the poets were but pleasure and not figure,[16] I interpose no opinion. Surely of those poets which are now extant, even Homer himself (notwithstanding he was made a kind of scripture by the later schools of the Grecians), yet I should without any difficulty pronounce that his fables had no such inwardness in his own meaning. But what they might have upon a more original tradition[17] is not easy to affirm, for he was not the inventor of many of them.

In this third[18] part of learning, which is poesy, I can report no deficience. For being as a plant that cometh of the lust[19] of the earth, without a formal[20] seed, it hath sprung up and spread abroad more than any other kind. But to ascribe unto it that which is due for the expressing of affections, passions, corruptions, and customs we are beholding to poets more than to the philosophers' works; and for wit and eloquence, not much less than to orators' harangues. But it is not good to stay too long in the theatre. Let us now pass on to the judicial place or palace of the mind,[21] which we are to approach and view with more reverence and attention.

[3]Contributes. [4]Intimate connections. [5]Accessibility.
[6]Politics. [7]Like a parable, i.e., figurative.
[8]The gnomic utterances (*sententiae*) attributed to the Seven Wise Men of antiquity (Thales, Solon, *et al.*).
[9]Evident to the senses.
[10]"It is said that the Earth, roused to anger against the gods, at last brought her forth as sister to Caeus and Enceladus" (Vergil, *Aeneid*, IV.178–180). [11]Censures.
[12]A mistake for *Thetis*. The story is told by Homer, *Iliad*, I.399–404.
[13]See Homer, *Iliad*, XI.830–831.
[14]Niccolò Machiavelli, *The Prince*, Ch. XVIII.
[15]Bacon paraphrases the account of Chrysippus, a Greek Stoic philosopher of the third century B.C., in Cicero, *De natura deorum*, I.xv.38–41.
[16]Designed for entertainment and not instruction (through their figurative or *parabolical* implications).
[17]In an older and more primitive form.
[18]A mistake for *second*. Earlier, Bacon had named the three parts of learning as history, poesy, and philosophy. [19]Fertility.
[20]Determining its form or structure.
[21]Philosophy, the third part of learning, which is discussed in the following section of *The Advancement of Learning*.

William Rawley [1588?-1667]

Like George Cavendish, Cardinal Wolsey's humble usher, William Rawley has a small but tidy niche in English literature for his memorial to a great but fallen man. A graduate of Corpus Christi College, Cambridge, who served as a fellow of his college and then as rector of Landbeach, a village north of Cambridge, in 1618 he was named by Bacon, in his new dignity as Lord Chancellor, to be his chaplain and amanuensis, and from then until his own death almost half a century later he served his master and preserved his reputation with uncommon knowledge and devotion. Following his disgrace and financial difficulties in 1621 (which Rawley makes no mention of), Bacon of course no longer kept a chaplain, but Rawley continued as his confidant and scribe. Thus it fell to him to supervise the publication of *De augmentis scientiarum* in 1623 and *Sylva sylvarum* four years later. On Bacon's death in 1626 it was he who edited *Memoriae honoratissimi domini Francisci*, thirty-two elegies by the great man's academic friends (including George Herbert and Thomas Randolph), and it was he who set about assembling his master's hitherto unpublished writings. In 1629 appeared *Certain Miscellany Works*, in 1638 *Operum moralium et civilium tomus* (which contained Rawley's Latin version of the *Essays*), in 1657 *Resuscitatio, or Bringing into Public Light Several Pieces of the Works . . . Hitherto Sleeping of . . . Francis Bacon . . . together with His Lordship's Life*, and in 1658 *Opuscula varia posthume* (with a Latin version of the life). Rawley's long editorial labors, like his memoir of the man whom he was proud to serve, show him to have been a loyal, learned friend, and his moving tribute to "the glory of his age and nation" became the basis of all subsequent biographies.

My text is based on *Resuscitatio . . . The Second Edition, some-what Enlarged. By William Rawley, Doctor in Divinity, His Lordships First, and Last, Chaplein and now His Majesties Chuplein, In Ordinary,* 1661 (Wing B-320).

from The Life of the Honorable Author [Francis Bacon] (1661)

Francis Bacon, the glory of his age and nation, the adorner and ornament of learning, was born in York House, or York Place, in the Strand,[1] on the two and twentieth day of January in the year of our Lord 1560[2]. His father was that famous counsellor to Queen Elizabeth, the second prop of the kingdom in his time, Sir Nicholas Bacon, Knight, Lord Keeper of the Great Seal of England; a lord of known prudence, sufficiency, moderation, and integrity. His mother was Ann, one of the daughters of Sir Anthony Cooke, unto whom the erudition of King Edward the Sixth had been committed;[3] [10] a choice lady, and eminent for piety, virtue, and learning, being exquisitely skilled, for a woman, in the Greek and Latin tongues.[4] These being the parents, you may easily imagine what the issue was like to be, having had whatsoever nature or breeding could put into him.

His first and childish years were not without some mark of eminency, at which time he was endued with that preg-

LIFE OF THE AUTHOR [1]Former London residence of Nicholas Heath, archbishop of York and Lord Chancellor (1556–58), near Charing Cross. [2]1561 New Style.
[3]At his coronation Edward VI made Cooke, his former tutor, a Knight of the Bath in recognition of his services.
[4]The formidable Lady Bacon (1528–1610) was so learned that as a girl she assisted her father in Prince Edward's education and as a woman she translated (from the Latin) Bishop John Jewel's *Apology for the Church of England* (1564).

nancy and towardness of wit as they were presages of that deep and universal apprehension which was manifest in him afterward, and caused him to be taken notice of by several persons of worth and place, and especially by the queen, who (as I have been informed) delighted much then to confer with him and to prove him with questions; unto whom he delivered himself with that gravity and maturity above his years that Her Majesty would often term him "the young Lord Keeper." Being asked by the queen how old he was, he answered with much discretion, being then but a boy, "That he was two years younger than Her Majesty's happy reign," with which answer the queen was much taken.

At the ordinary years of ripeness for the university, or rather something earlier, he was sent by his father to Trinity College in Cambridge to be educated and bred under the tuition of Doctor John Whitgift, then Master of the college, afterwards the renowned archbishop of Canterbury; a prelate of the first magnitude for sanctity, learning, patience, and humility, under whom he was observed to have been more than an ordinary proficient in the several arts and sciences.[5] Whilst he was commorant[6] in the university, about sixteen years of age (as His Lordship hath been pleased to impart unto myself), he first fell into the dislike of the philosophy of Aristotle, not for the worthlessness of the author, to whom he would ever ascribe all high attributes, but for the unfruitfulness of the way, being a philosophy (as His Lordship used to say) only strong for disputations and contentions, but barren of the production of works for the benefit of the life of man, in which mind he continued to his dying day.

After he had passed the circle of the liberal arts, his father thought fit to frame and mold him for the arts of state, and for that end sent him over into France with Sir Amias Paulet, then employed ambassador lieger into France,[7] by whom he was after a while held fit to be entrusted with some message or advertisement to the Queen; which having performed with great approbation, he returned back into France again with intention to continue for some years there. In his absence in France his father the Lord Keeper died,[8] having collected (as I have heard of knowing persons) a considerable sum of money, which he had separated with intention to have made a competent purchase of land for the livelihood of this his youngest son (who was only unprovided for, and though he was the youngest in years, yet he was not the lowest in his father's affection); but the said purchase being unaccomplished at his father's death, there came no greater share to him than his single part and portion of the money dividable amongst five brethren; by which means he lived in some straits and necessities in his younger years. For as for that pleasant site and manor of Gorhambury,[9] he came not to it till many years after, by the death of his dearest brother, Master Anthony Bacon,[10] a gentleman equal to him in height of wit, though inferior to him in the endowments of learning and knowledge; unto whom he was most nearly conjoined in affection, they two being the sole male issue of a second venter.[11]

Being returned from travel, he applied himself to the study

of the common law, which he took upon him to be his profession; in which he obtained to great excellency,[12] though he made that (as himself said) but as an accessary, and not as his principal study. He wrote several tractates upon that subject, wherein, though some great masters of the law did outgo him in bulk and particularities of cases, yet in the science of the grounds and mysteries of the law he was exceeded by none. In this way he was after a while sworn of the Queen's Counsel Learned Extraordinary, a grace (if I err not) scarce known before.[13] He seated himself, for the commodity of his studies and practice, amongst the Honourable Society of Gray's Inn, of which house he was a member; where he erected that elegant pile or structure commonly known by the name of the Lord Bacon's Lodgings, which he inhabited by turns the most part of his life (some few years only excepted) unto his dying day. In which house he carried himself with such sweetness, comity,[14] and generosity that he was much revered and loved by the readers and gentlemen of the house.

Notwithstanding that he professed the law for his livelihood and subsistence, yet his heart and affection was more carried after the affairs and places of estate, for which, if the Majesty Royal then had been pleased, he was most fit. In his younger years he studied the service and fortunes (as they call them) of that noble but unfortunate earl, the earl of Essex, unto whom he was, in a sort, a private and free counselor and gave him safe and honorable advice till in the end the Earl inclined too much to the violent and precipitate counsel of others his adherents and followers, which was his fate and ruin.[15]

[5]Bacon's brief university career—from 1573 to 1575, and with a long absence owing to the plague—ended before he turned sixteen. John Whitgift, who served as master of Trinity from 1567 to 1577, was Elizabeth's great archbishop of Canterbury for the last twenty years of her reign (1583–1603).   [6]Resident.

[7]Paulet was resident ambassador (*lieger*) in France from 1576 to 1579.   [8]February 1579.

[9]Sir Nicholas Bacon's sumptuous house near St. Albans, Hertfordshire.

[10]It was to his rather feckless elder brother (1558–1601) that Bacon affectionately dedicated the first edition of his *Essays* (1597).

[11]Womb, i.e., mother. By his first marriage (to Jane Fernley) Sir Nicholas Bacon had three sons and three daughters, by his second (to Ann Cooke) two sons—Anthony and Francis.

[12]Entering Gray's Inn in 1579, Bacon rose steadily through the ranks of utter barrister (1582), bencher (1586), reader (1588), and double reader (1600).

[13]Rawley is in error here. Although Bacon sat in successive Parliaments after 1584, his opposition to certain subsidies requested by the queen so much offended her that despite Essex' powerful and generous support he was denied the post of attorney-general in 1594 and that of solicitor-general a year later. It was not until 1596 that Elizabeth relented sufficiently to name the needy son of her former Lord Keeper one of her Counsel Learned. *Extraordinary*: by special commandment, as opposed to an ordinary (i.e., permanent and regularly paid) appointment.   [14]Courtesy.

[15]Although Bacon, like his brother Anthony, was a friend and protégé of the powerful Robert Devereux, earl of Essex, throughout the nineties he took an active—and some thought savage—part in the prosecution of his former benefactor after his abortive uprising of 1601 (on which see pp. 843 ff.).

His birth and other capacities qualified him above others of his profession to have ordinary accesses at court, and to come frequently into the Queen's eye, who would often grace him with private and free communication, not only about matters of his profession or business in law, but also about the arduous affairs of estate, from whom she received from time to time great satisfaction. Nevertheless, though she cheered him much with the bounty of her countenance, yet she never cheered him with the bounty of her hand, having never conferred upon him any ordinary place or means of honor or profit, save only one dry reversion of the Register's Office in the Star Chamber, worth about £1,600 per annum, for which he waited in expectation either fully or near twenty years,[16] of which His Lordship would say in Queen Elizabeth's time, "That it was like another man's ground buttalling[17] upon his house, which might mend his prospect, but it did not fill his barn." Nevertheless, in the time of King James it fell unto him, which might be imputed not so much to Her Majesty's averseness or disaffection towards him as to the arts and policy of a great statesman then, who labored by all industrious and secret means to suppress and keep him down, lest if he had risen he might have obscured his glory.[18]

But though he stood long at a stay in the days of his mistress Queen Elizabeth, yet after the change and coming in of his new master King James, he made a great progress; by whom he was much comforted in places of trust, honor, and revenue. I have seen a letter of His lordship's to King James wherein he makes acknowledgment "that he was that master to him that had raised and advanced him nine times thrice in dignity, and six times in office." His offices (as I conceive) were Counsel Learned Extraordinary[19] to His Majesty, as he had been to Queen Elizabeth; King's Solicitor-General; His Majesty's Attorney-General; Counselor of Estate, being yet but Attorney; Lord Keeper of the Great Seal of England; lastly, Lord Chancellor;[20] which two last places, though they be the same in authority and power, yet they differ in patent,[21] height, and favor of the prince, since whose time none of his successors, until this present honourable lord,[22] did ever bear the title of Lord Chancellor. His dignities were first Knight, then Baron of Verulam, lastly Viscount St. Alban;[23] besides other good gifts and bounties of the hand which His Majesty gave him, both out of the Broad Seal and out of the Alienation Office[24] to the value in both of £1,800 per annum; which, with his manor of Gorhambury and other lands and possessions near thereunto adjoining, amounting to a third part more, he retained to his dying day.

Towards his rising years, not before, he entered into a married estate,[25] and took to wife Alice, one of the daughters and coheirs of Benedict Barnham, Esquire and Alderman of London, with whom he received a sufficiently ample and liberal portion in marriage. Children he had none; which, though they be the means to perpetuate our names after our deaths, yet he had other issues to perpetuate his name, the issues of his brain, in which he was ever happy and admired, as Jupiter was in the production of Pallas.[26] Neither did the want of children detract from his good usage of his consort during the intermarriage, whom he prosecuted with much conjugal love and respect, with many rich gifts and endowments, besides a robe of honor[27] which he invested her withal, which she wore until her dying day, being twenty years and more after his death.

The last five years of his life, being withdrawn from civil affairs[28] and from an active life, he employed wholly in contemplation and studies—a thing whereof His Lordship would often speak during his active life, as if he affected to die in the shadow and not in the light, which also may be found in several passages of his works. In which time he composed the greatest part of his books and writings, both in English and Latin, which I will enumerate (as near as I can) in the just order wherein they were written. . . .

[There follows a somewhat casual list of Bacon's published works and unpublished fragments, some of which have not survived.]

There is a commemoration due as well to his abilities and virtues as to the course of his life. Those abilities which commonly go single in other men, though of prime and observable parts, were all conjoined and met in him. Those are sharpness of wit, memory, judgment, and elocution. For the former three his books do abundantly speak them, which with what sufficiency he wrote, let the world judge; but with what celerity he wrote them, I can best testify. But for the fourth, his elocution, I will only set down what I heard Sir Walter Raleigh once speak of him by way of comparison (whose judgment may well be trusted,) "that the earl of Salisbury was an excellent speaker, but no good penman; that the earl of Northampton (the Lord Henry Howard) was an excellent penman, but no good speaker; but that Sir Francis Bacon was eminent in both."

I have been induced to think that if there were a beam of

---

[16]This reversion (which Bacon himself attributed to the intervention of his powerful uncle, Lord Burghley) was granted in 1589.

[17]Bordering, abutting.

[18]Rawley is presumably alluding to the powerful Robert Cecil (1563?–1612), earl of Salisbury and secretary of state (1596–1612), who, though Bacon's cousin, was notably indifferent to advancing his kinsman's political fortunes.

[19]A slip of the pen, for James promoted Bacon from an *extraordinary* to an *ordinary* counsel. See n. 13 above.

[20]Bacon's appointments were as follows: Solicitor-General 1607, Attorney-General 1613, Counsellor of State 1616, Lord Keeper 1617, Lord Chancellor 1618. [21]Authority.

[22]Edward Hyde, earl of Clarendon (see pp. 794 f.).

[23]Bacon was knighted in 1603, raised to the peerage as Baron Verulam in 1618, and created Viscount St. Albans in 1621.

[24]From properties in the king's own disposition under the Great (*Broad*) Seal and from properties forfeited through legal action.

[25]May 1606.

[26]In ancient mythology *Pallas* Athene (called Minerva by the Romans) was said to have sprung fully armed from the forehead of her father Zeus (*Jupiter*). [27]The title of viscountess?

[28]Rawley discreetly omits any mention of Bacon's fall in 1621, when, having pleaded guilty of corruption, he was fined £40,000, imprisoned in the Tower (from which the king released him in a few days), barred from Parliament or from any office under the crown, and forbidden to come within the verge (i.e., twelve miles) of the court.

knowledge derived from God upon any man in these modern times, it was upon him. For though he was a great reader of books, yet he had not his knowledge from books but from some grounds and notions from within himself, which, notwithstanding, he vented with great caution and circumspection. His book of *Instauratio Magna*[29] (which in his own account was the chiefest of his works) was no slight imagination or fancy of his brain, but a settled and concocted notion, the production of many years' labor and travel. I myself have seen at the least twelve copies of the *Instauration,* revised year by year one after another, and every year altered and amended in the frame thereof till at last it came to that model in which it was committed to the press, as many living creatures do lick their young ones till they bring them to their strength of limbs.

In the composing of his books he did rather drive at a masculine and clear expression than at any fineness or affectation of phrases, and would often ask if the meaning were expressed plainly enough, as being one that accounted words to be but subservient or ministerial to matter, and not the principal. And if his style were polite it was because he could do no otherwise. Neither was he given to any light conceits, or descanting upon words, but did ever purposely and industriously avoid them; for he held such things to be but digressions or diversions from the scope intended, and to derogate from the weight and dignity of the style.

He was no plodder upon books, though he read much, and that with great judgment and rejection of impertinences incident to many authors; for he would ever interlace a moderate relaxation of his mind with his studies, as walking or taking the air abroad in his coach or some other befitting recreation; and yet he would lose no time, inasmuch as upon his first and immediate return he would fall to reading again, and so suffer no moment of time to slip from him without some present improvement.

His meals were reflections of the ear as well as of the stomach, like the *Noctes Atticae* or *Convivia Deipnosophistarum,*[30] wherein a man might be refreshed in his mind and understanding no less than in his body. And I have known some, of no mean parts, that have professed to make use of their notebooks when they have risen from his table. In which conversations, and otherwise, he was no dashing[31] man, as some men are, but ever a countenancer and fosterer of another man's parts.[32] Neither was he one that would appropriate the speech wholly to himself, or delight to outvie others, but leave a liberty to the coassessors to take their turns. Wherein he would draw a man on and allure him to speak upon such a subject as wherein he was peculiarly skilful, and would delight to speak. And for himself, he contemned no man's observations, but would light his torch at every man's candle.

His opinions and assertions were for the most part binding, and not contradicted by any, rather like oracles than discourses; which may be imputed either to the well weighing of his sentence by the scales of truth and reason, or else to the reverence and estimation wherein he was commonly had, that no man would contest with him; so that there was no argumentation, or *pro* and *con* (as they term it), at his table,

or if there chanced to be any, it was carried with much submission and moderation.

I have often observed, and so have other men of great account, that if he had occasion to repeat another man's words after him, he had an use and faculty to dress them in better vestments and apparel than they had before, so that the author should find his own speech much amended, and yet the substance of it still retained, as if it had been natural to him to use good forms, as Ovid spake of his faculty of versifying,

Et quod temptabam scribere, versus erat.[33]

When his office called him, as he was of the King's Counsel Learned, to charge any offenders, either in criminals or capitals,[34] he was never of an insulting or domineering nature over them, but always tenderhearted, and carrying himself decently towards the parties (though it was his duty to charge them home),[35] but yet as one that looked upon the example with the eye of severity, but upon the person with the eye of pity and compassion. And in civil business, as he was Counselor of Estate, he had the best way of advising, not engaging his master in any precipitate or grievous courses, but in moderate and fair proceedings, the King whom he served giving him this testimony, "that he ever dealt in business *suavibus modis,*[36] which was the way that was most according to his own heart."

Neither was he in his time less gracious with the subject than with his sovereign. He was ever acceptable to the House of Commons when he was a member thereof. Being the King's Attorney, and chosen to a place in Parliament, he was allowed and dispensed with to sit in the House, which was not permitted to other attorneys.

And as he was a good servant to his master, being never in nineteen years' service (as himself averred) rebuked by the King for anything relating to His Majesty, so he was a good master to his servants, and rewarded their long attendance with good places freely when they fell into his power; which was the cause that so many young gentlemen of blood and quality sought to list themselves in his retinue. And if he were abused by any of them in their places, it was only the error of the goodness of his nature, but the badges of their indiscretions and intemperances.

This lord was religious, for though the world be apt to

[29]By this (and by "the *Instauration*" a few lines later), Rawley presumably means the *Novum organum*, Bacon's discourse on method that was published in a volume called *Instauratio Magna* (1620), containing several of his earlier works. See pp. 407 ff.
[30]Convivial, urbane, and far-ranging discussions of various subjects. *Noctes Atticae* ("Attic Nights") by Aulus Gellius (ca. 132–ca. 165) and *Deipnosophistae* ("The Learned Banquet") by Athenaeus (fl. ca. 200) are symposiums about law, philosophy, literature, history, and other topics.
[31]Censorious, wittily destructive. [32]Talents, abilities.
[33]"Whatever I tried to write was verse" (Ovid, *Tristia*, IV.x.26). *Temptabam*: text *tentabam*.
[34]*Offenders...capitals:* those charged with minor offences or with crimes punishable by death.
[35]Prosecute them to the limit of the law.
[36]"In a gentle manner."

suspect and prejudge great wits and politics to have some-what of the atheist, yet he was conversant with God, as appeareth by several passages throughout the whole current of his writings. Otherwise he should have crossed his own principles, which were "that a little philosophy maketh men apt to forget God, as attributing too much to second causes; but depth of philosophy bringeth a man back to God again." Now I am sure there is no man that will deny him, or ac-count otherwise of him, but to have been a deep philosopher. And not only so, but he was able "to render a reason of the hope which was in him,"[37] which that writing of his of the *Confession of the Faith*[38] doth abundantly testify. He repaired frequently, when his health would permit him, to the service of the church, to hear sermons, to the administra-tion of the Sacrament of the Blessed Body and Blood of Christ; and died in the true faith, established in the Church of England.

This is most true—he was free from malice, which (as he said himself) "he never bred nor fed." He was no revenger of injuries, which if he had minded he had both opportunity and place high enough to have done it. He was no heaver of men out of their places, as delighting in their ruin and undoing. He was no defamer of any man to his prince. One day, when a great statesman was newly dead that had not been his friend, the King asked him "what he thought of that lord which was gone?" He answered "that he would never have made His Majesty's estate better, but he was sure he would have kept it from being worse." Which was the worst he would say of him, which I reckon not amongst his moral but his Christian virtues.

His fame is greater and sounds louder in foreign parts abroad than at home in his own nation, thereby verifying that divine sentence, "A prophet is not without honor, save in his own country, and in his own house."[39] Concerning which I will give you a taste only, out of a letter written from Italy (the storehouse of refined wits) to the late Earl of Devonshire, then the Lord Candish: "I will expect the new *Essays* of my Lord Chancellor Bacon, as also his *History,* with a great deal of desire, and whatsoever else he shall compose. But in particular of his *History* I promise myself a thing perfect and singular, especially in Henry the Seventh, where he may exercise the talent of his divine understanding.[40] This lord is more and more known, and his books here more and more delighted in; and those men that have more than ordinary knowledge in human affairs esteem him one of the most capable spirits of this age; and he is truly such." Now his fame doth not decrease with days since, but rather increase. Divers of his works have been anciently and yet lately translated into other tongues, both learned and modern, by foreign pens. Several persons of quality, during His Lordship's life crossed the seas on purpose to gain an opportunity of seeing him and discoursing with him, whereof one carried His Lordship's picture from head to foot over with him into France, as a thing which he foresaw would be much desired there, that so they might enjoy the image of his person as well as the images of his brain, his books. Amongst the rest, Marquis Fiat, a French nobleman who came ambassador into England in the beginning of Queen Mary, wife to King Charles,[41] was taken with an extraordinary desire of seeing him; for which he made way by a friend; and when he came to him, being then through weakness confined to his bed, the marquis saluted him with this high expression, "that his lordship had been ever to him like the angels, of whom he had often heard, and read much of them in books, but he never saw them." After which they contracted an intimate acquaintance, and the marquis did so much revere him that besides his frequent visits they wrote letters one to the other under the titles and appellations of father and son. As for his many salutations by letters from foreign worthies devoted to learning, I forbear to mention them because that is a thing common to other men of learning or note, together with him.

But yet, in this matter of his fame, I speak in the com-parative only, and not in the exclusive. For his reputation is great in his own nation also, especially amongst those that are of a more acute and sharper judgment, which I will exemplify but with two testimonies and no more. The former, when his *History of King Henry the Seventh* was to come forth it was delivered to the old Lord Brooke, to be perused by him; when he had dispatched it, returned it to the author with this eulogy, "Commend me to my lord, and bid him take care to get good paper and ink, for the work is excellent." The other shall be that of Doctor Samuel Collins, late Provost of King's College in Cambridge, a man of no vulgar wit, who affirmed unto me "that when he had read the book of *The Advancement of Learning*,[42] he found himself in a case to begin his studies anew, and that he had lost all the time of his studying before."

It hath been desired that something should be signified touching his diet, and the regimen of his health, of which, in regard of his universal insight into nature, he may perhaps be to some an example. For his diet, it was rather a plentiful and liberal diet, as his stomach would bear it, than a restrained; which he also commended in his book of the *History of Life and Death*.[43] In his younger years he was much given to the finer and lighter sort of meats, as of fowls, and such like; but afterward, when he grew more judicious he preferred the stronger meats, such as the shambles[44] afforded, as those meats which bred the more firm and substantial juices of the

[37]A paraphrase of 1 Peter 3.15.
[38]A statement of Bacon's religious beliefs that was written before 1603 and first published in 1648 in a volume called *The Remains of Francis, Lord Verulam.* [39]Matthew 13.57.
[40]The famous *Essays* (see pp. 661 ff.), first published in 1597, were re-issued with additions in 1612 and 1625. *The History of the Reign of King Henry the Seventh* (see pp. 883 ff.) was published in 1622, not long after Bacon's fall from power.
[41]Prince Charles was betrothed to Henrietta Maria of France in December 1624; having succeeded to the throne the following March and married her by proxy two months later, he received his bride at Canterbury in June 1625.
[42]Bacon's first important statement of his philosophical system (1605). See pp. 399 ff., 667 ff., 878 ff.
[43]*Historia vitae et mortis*, a work designed for *The Great Instauration*, Part III (wherein natural phenomena were to be compiled and arranged as suitable data for induction), but published separately in 1623. [44]Slaughterhouse.

body, and less dissipable;[45] upon which he would often make his meal, though he had other meats upon the table. You may be sure he would not neglect that himself which he so much extolled in his writings, and that was the use of niter, whereof he took in the quantity of about three grains in thin warm broth every morning for thirty years together next before his death. And for physic,[46] he did indeed live physically, but not miserably; for he took only a maceration of rhubarb,[47] infused into a draught of white wine and beer mingled together for the space of half an hour, once in six or seven days, immediately before his meal (whether dinner or supper), that it might dry the body less; which (as he said) did carry away frequently the grosser humors of the body, and not diminish or carry away any of the spirits, as sweating doth. And this was no grievous thing to take. As for other physic, in an ordinary way (whatsoever hath been vulgarly spoken) he took not. His receipt for the gout, which did constantly ease him of his pain within two hours, is already set down in the end of the *Natural History*.

It may seem the moon had some principal place in the figure of his nativity, for the moon was never in her passion, or eclipsed, but he was surprised with a sudden fit of fainting, and that though he observed not nor took any previous knowledge of the eclipse thereof; and as soon as the eclipse ceased, he was restored to his former strength again.

He died on the ninth day of April in the year 1626, in the early morning of the day then celebrated for our Saviour's resurrection, in the sixty-sixth year of his age, at the earl of Arundel's house in Highgate, near London, to which place he casually repaired about a week before; God so ordaining that he should die there of a gentle fever, accidentally ac-

companied with a great cold, whereby the defluxion of rheum fell so plentifully upon his breast that he died by suffocation; and was buried in St. Michael's Church at St. Albans, being the place designed for his burial by his last will and testament, both because the body of his mother was interred there and because it was the only church then remaining within the precincts of old Verulam;[48] where he hath a monument erected for him of white marble by the care and gratitude of Sir Thomas Meautys,[49] Knight, formerly His Lordship's secretary, afterwards clerk of the king's honorable Privy Council under two kings; representing his full portraiture in the posture of studying, with an inscription composed by that accomplished gentleman and rare wit, Sir Henry Wotton.

But howsoever his body was mortal, yet no doubt his memory and works will live, and will in all probability last as long as the world lasteth. In order to which I have endeavored, after my poor ability, to do this honor to His Lordship by way of conducing to the same.

[45]Capable of being dissipated and therefore less strengthening.
[46]*And for physic:* with the aid of medicine (*physic*).
[47]Stewed rhubarb?
[48]Site of the ancient Roman town (Verulamium), adjacent to the modern St. Albans. Bacon's titles as baron and viscount suggest his deep attachment to the region.
[49]Civil servant and Parliamentarian (ca. 1592–1649). Entering Bacon's service as secretary about 1616, he was so unswervingly loyal that when his master died he left to Meautys' use (under trustees) his beloved estate at Gorhambury. Meautys was buried in Bacon's vault in St. Michael's Church.

John Hoskins [1566-1638]

Fortune seemed to smile on Hoskins. A product of such civilizing institutions as Westminster, Winchester, New College, Oxford (B.A. 1588, M.A. 1592), and the Middle Temple, he became the friend of Raleigh, Camden, Jonson, Donne, Daniel—indeed, said Aubrey, of "all ingeniose persons" in an age that glittered with such men. His marriage (1601) to a wealthy widow freed him from the scramble to survive, but not from the honorific burdens of a member of Parliament, a stockholder in the Virginia Company, a reader in the Middle Temple, a judge in Wales, and a member of the Council of the Marches. Even a period of incarceration in the Tower (1614–15)—for speaking freely of the Scottish favorites of the king—was not without its compensations, for Hoskins beguiled the time by helping his friend and fellow-prisoner Raleigh "polish" and refine his style. It was ironical that this witty and accomplished man should die of gangrene that set in when "a massive country-fellow" stepped upon his toe.

Although Hoskins published little, he wrote, among other things, a Greek dictionary (up to the letter *mu*), a fragmentary "method of law," enough poetry to fill a volume "bigger than Dr. Donne's" (which someone borrowed from his son and neglected to return), a fragmentary autobiography, a group of Latin elegies in memory of Sir Philip Sidney, various epigrams and epitaphs, and—most important—a rhetorical treatise now known as *Directions for Speech and Style*. The survival, in manuscript, of this engaging little work has secured his reputation, for there is perhaps no better barometer of the literary climate at the turn of the seventeenth century than these unpretentious comments on good writing. Cast in the form of an epistle, it reveals a man of learning, taste, and wit who was both attracted by what was then the avant-garde and also committed to the ancient craft of letters. Hoskins wore his learning lightly, but he was steeped in literature; and if his *Directions* lack Sidney's stately charm and Jonson's burly strength it nonetheless conveys the thinking of a highly cultivated man about the disciplines and amenities of an art that he admired. Language, he reminds us, is not merely decoration; it is the means whereby we represent "the right proportion and coherence of things," and therefore we must learn to use it with discrimination based on knowledge. "Careless speech doth not only discredit the personage of the speaker, but it doth discredit the opinion of his reason and judgment; it discrediteth the truth, force, and uniformity of the matter and substance."

Jonson thought so well of these and similar remarks that he included them (without acknowledgment) in his own *Discoveries* (p. 706); Thomas Blount transferred most of the *Directions* (with only minor changes and again without acknowledgment) to his very popular *Academy of Eloquence* (1654); and in *The Mystery of Rhetoric Unveiled* (1657)—which by 1709 had reached a ninth edition— John Smith calmly appropriated most of what Blount himself had filched from Hoskins.

The object of these flattering if illicit borrowings is a letter, addressed to "a gentleman of the Temple," on the proper modes of speech and writing, accompanied by a marked copy of the 1590 edition of Sidney's *Arcadia* to illustrate the precepts of the author. An allusion (p. 678) to the Earl of Essex' Irish expedition suggests a date of 1599 or shortly later. In his graceful, offhand fashion Hoskins cites an imposing list of sources (from Aristotle to the contemporary Talon), and he might have added more. Nonetheless, the *Directions* is his own. Instead of rehearsing the five canonical constituents of rhetorical theory—*inventio* (choosing or "finding" a subject), *dispositio* (arrangement), *elocutio* (style), *memoria* (memorizing), and *pronuntiatio* (delivery)—he concentrates on only speech and style, but since his discussion of speech has not survived, the *Directions* is in fact concerned with only style, or, as Hoskins says, with how to "pen letters, vary, amplify, and illustrate." In treating these four topics (to each of which a separate section of the treatise is devoted) Hoskins makes no innovations, but he is always brisk and witty, even in his pedagogic function, and his allusions to contemporary writers, and notably to Sir Philip Sidney, are frequent, pointed, and revealing.

Although the *Directions* must have circulated widely in manuscripts, only three of them survive: British Museum Harleian MSS 4604 and 850 (which is incomplete) and Bodleian Ashmole Mus. d. 1. My text is based on Louise Brown Osborn's transcription of Harleian 4604 in *The Life, Letters, and Writings of John Hoskyns 1566–1638* (1937), pp. 114–166. The same manuscript has been modernized and edited by Hoyt H. Hudson (1935).

from Directions for Speech and Style (1599?)

TO PRONOUNCE, PEN LETTERS, VARY, AMPLIFY, ILLUSTRATE OTHERWISE THAN EVER ANY PRECEPTS HAVE TAUGHT.

CONTAINING ALL THE FIGURES OF RHETORIC AND THE ART OF THE BEST ENGLISH, EXEMPLIFIED EITHER ALL OUT OF ARCADIA, WHICH IT CENSURETH,[1] OR BY INSTANCES, THE MATTER WHEREOF MAY BENEFIT CONVERSATION, THE QUOTATIONS BEING TAKEN OUT OF SIR PHILIP SIDNEY'S ARCADIA, THE FIRST EDITION IN QUARTO WITHOUT SAMFORD'S ADDITIONS.[2]

DIRECTIONS [1]Assesses, evaluates.
[2]Hoskins is specifying that his reader use the first (1590) edition of the *Arcadia*, whose publication was supervised by Sidney's friend Fulke Greville (pp. 4f.). The "additions" in the second (1593) edition, which was prepared by Sidney's sister Mary, countess of Pembroke, with the assistance of Hugh Sanford (or Sandford), a tutor and secretary in the Pembroke household, consist of Books III–V of the novel and some poems.

To the Forwardness of Many Virtuous Hopes in a Gentleman of the Temple by the Author[3]

The conceits[4] of the mind are pictures of things, and the tongue is interpreter of those pictures. The order of God's creatures in themselves is not only admirable and glorious, but eloquent; then he that could apprehend the consequence of things in their truth and utter his apprehensions as truly were a right orator. Therefore Cicero said much when he said, *Dicere recte nemo potest nisi qui prudenter intelligit.*[5]

The shame of speaking unskilfully were small if the tongue were only disgraced by it, but as the image of the king in a seal of wax ill represented is not so much a blemish to the wax or the signet that sealeth it as to the king whom it resembleth, so disordered speech is not so much injury to the lips which give it forth, or the thoughts which put it forth, as to the right proportion and coherence of things in themselves so wrongfully expressed. Yet cannot his mind be thought in tune whose words do jar, nor his reason in frame whose sentences are preposterous, nor his fancy clear and perfect whose utterance breaks itself into fragments and uncertainties. Were it an honor to a prince to have the majesty of his embassage spoiled by a careless ambassador? And is it not as great an indignity that an excellent conceit and capacity by the indiligence[6] of an idle tongue should be defaced? Careless speech doth not only discredit the personage of the speaker, but it doth discredit the opinion of his reason and judgment; it discrediteth the truth, force, and uniformity of the matter and substance. If it be so then in words which fly and escape censure, and where one good phrase begs pardon for many incongruities and faults, how shall it be thought wise whose penning is thin and shallow? How shall you look for wit from him whose leisure and whose head (assisted with the examination of his eyes) could yield you no life and sharpness in his writing? I never flattered you, and now methinks I terrify and threaten you, for you see my opinion of you if you should not write well. Nay, you were happy if I should think so favorably of you. I know how far you are stepped into the judgment, skill, and practice of a good style. You cannot but make a most shameful retreat to the ordinary fashion of penning. If I were not bound to your father's love and yours, if I saw not in him most kind providence[7] and in you most willing endeavor to make somewhat more of you than one of my young masters of the Temple, I should think it ill manners to trouble myself and you with a great deal of instruction taken out of Aristotle, Hermogenes, Quintilian, Demosthenes, Cicero,[8] and some latter (as Sturmius and Talaeus[9] and such honest men), who, but for your sake, had never renewed their acquaintance with me nor had not become clients to any student of Her Majesty's laws. Well, what I have done, he that reads must know (if he hath read much) I did it most willingly, and I dedicate it to your future discretion.

> *The dearest lover of your well-doings,*
> John Hoskins

[Of the five topics announced in the title of this treatise—pronunciation, letter-writing, varying, amplifying, and illustrating—the first appears in none of the three extant manuscripts.]

[II] FOR PENNING OF LETTERS

In writing of letters there is to be regarded the invention[10] and the fashion, for the invention that ariseth upon your business whereof there can be no rules of more certainty or precepts of better direction given you than conjecture can lay down of all the several occasions of all particular men's lives and vocations. . . .

Now for *fashion*, it consisteth in four things or qualities of your style. The first is *brevity*, for letters must not be treatises or discoursings except it be among learned men, and even amongst them there is a kind of thrift or saving of words. Therefore are you to examine the clearest passages of your understanding, and through them to convey your sweetest and most significant English words that you can devise, that you may the easier teach them the readiest way to another man's conceit and to pen it fully, roundly, and distinctly, so as the reader may not think a second view cast away upon your letter. . . . Brevity is attained, by the matter, in avoiding idle compliments, places,[11] protestations, parenthesis, superfluous and wanton circuits of figures, and digressions; by the composition, omitting conjunctions—"not only but also," "both one and the other," "whereby it cometh to pass"—and such idle particularities that have no great business in a serious letter; by breaking of sentences, as oftentimes a long journey is made shorter by many baits. But, as Quintilian saith, there is a briefness or parts sometimes that make the whole long, as:

> I came to the stairs; I took a pair of oars. They
> launched out, rowed apace; I landed at the Court-gate;
> I paid my fare, went up to the presence, asked for
> My Lord. I was admitted.[12]

[3]This introduction and the following section entitled "For Penning of Letters" reveal an interesting aspect of literary imitation in the Renaissance. For the introduction on the relation of thought and speech (down to "I never flattered you"), Hoskins drew heavily on Pierre de la Primaudaye's *L'Académie Françoise* (1577–1594), the first two books of which had been Englished by Thomas Bowes in 1586 and 1594; for the section on letters he was largely indebted to the *Epistolica institutio* (1591) of Justus Lipsius (1547–1606), the eminent Dutch humanist and editor of Tacitus and Seneca. The borrowing was continued, moreover, by Ben Jonson, who included virtually all of Hoskins' introduction and discussion of letter-writing in his *Discoveries* (1641). See p. 706. *Forwardness:* fulfillment. [4]Conceptions.
[5]"No one speaks well who does not think intelligently" (altered from Marcus Tullius Cicero, *Brutus*, vi.23). [6]Lack of diligence.
[7]Foresight.
[8]Influential theorists or practitioners of classical rhetoric and oratory.
[9]Johannes Sturm (1507–89) and Omer Talon (1510?–62), authors respectively of the widely used *De universa ratione elocutionis rhetoricae libri IIII* and *Institutiones oratoriae*, the latter based upon the system of Talon's friend and associate Peter Ramus.
[10]In rhetorical theory, the selection (literally the "finding") of topics and arguments for development.
[11]In rhetorical theory, subjects, topics. In his *Discoveries*, Jonson renders this word as "prefaces."
[12]*Quintilian . . . admitted:* adapted from Marcus Fabius Quintilianus, *Institutio oratoria*, IV.ii.4.

All this is but "I went to the Court and spake with My Lord." This is the fault of some Latin writers (within this last hundred years) of my reading; and perhaps Seneca[13] may be appeached of[14] it. I accuse him not.

The next good property of epistolary style is *perspicuity*, and is oftentimes endangered by the former quality (brevity), oftentimes by affection[15] of some wit ill angled for or ostentation of some hidden terms of art. Few words they darken the speech and so do too many, as well too much light hurts the eyes as too little, and a long bill of Chancery[16] confounds the understanding as much as the shortest note. Therefore let not your letter be penned like an English statute. This is obtained, and their vices eschewed, by pondering your business well and distinctly conceiving of[17] yourself, which is much furthered by uttering your thoughts and letting them as well come forth to light and judgment of your own outward senses as to the censure of other men's ears. That is the reason why many good scholars speak but stumblingly, like a rich man that for want of particular note and difference can bring you no certain ware readily out of his shop. For this reason talkative, shallow men do often content the hearers more than the wise. But this may find a speedier redress in writing, where all comes under the last examination of the eyes. First mind it well, then pen it, then examine it, then amend it, and you may be in the better hope of doing reasonable well.

Under this virtue may come *plainness*, which is not to be curious in the order, as to answer a letter as if you were to answer interrogatories ("to the first, second," etc.), but both in method and word to use, as ladies use in their attire, a kind of diligent negligence. And though with some men you are not to jest or practise tricks, yet the delivery of most weighty and important things may be carried with such a grace as that it may yield a pleasure to the conceit of the reader. There must be store, though not excess, of terms; as if you are to name *store*, sometimes you may call it *choice*, sometimes *plenty*, sometimes *copiousness*, or *variety*; and so that the word which comes in lieu have not such difference of meaning as that it may put the sense in hazard to be mistaken. You are not to cast a ring for the perfumed terms of the time, as *apprehensiveness, compliments, spirit, accommodate*,[18] etc., but use them properly in their places, as others.

Thereof followeth life, which is the very strength and sinews, as it were, of your penning, made up by pithy sayings, similitudes, conceits, allusions to some known history, or some other commonplace, such as are in *The Courtier* and the second book of Cicero *De oratore*.[19]

Last is *respect*, to discern what fits yourself, him to whom you write, and that which you handle; which is a quality fit to include the rest. And that must proceed from ripeness of judgment, which, as another truly saith, is given by four means: God, nature, diligence, and conversation. Serve the first well and the rest will serve you.

[III] FOR VARYING

A *metaphor* or translation is the friendly and neighborly borrowing of one word to express a thing with more light and better note, though not so directly and properly as the natural name of the thing meant would signify. As "feigned sighs":[20] the nearest to feigning is teaching[21] an imitation of truth by art and endeavor; therefore Sir Philip Sidney would not say "unfeigned sighs," but "untaught sighs."[22] "Desirous": now desire is a kind of thirst, and not much different from thirst is hunger, and therefore for "swords desirous of blood" he saith "hungry of blood," where you may note three degrees of metaphors in the understanding: first that the fitness of bloodshed in a weapon usurps the name "desirous," which is proper to a living creature, and then that it proceedeth to "thirst," and then to "hunger." The rule of a metaphor is that it be not too bold nor too farfetched. And though all metaphors go beyond the signification of things, yet are they requisite to match the compassing sweetness of men's minds, that are not content to fix themselves upon one thing but they must wander into the confines; like the eye, that can not choose but view the whole knot[23] when it beholds but one flower in a garden of purpose;[24] or like an archer that, knowing his bow will overcast or carry too short, takes an aim on this side or beyond his mark.

Besides, a metaphor is pleasant because it enricheth our knowledge with two things at once, with the truth and with similitude, as this: "heads disinherited of their natural seigniories," whereby we understand both beheading and the government of the head over the body as the heir hath over the lordship which he inheriteth. Of the same matter in another place: "to divorce the fair marriage of the head and the body," where besides the cutting off the head we understand the conjunction of head and body to resemble marriage. The like in "concealing love," uttered by these words: "to keep love close prisoner"; and in number of places in your book, which are all noted with this letter *M*[25] in the margent.[26] "There came along the streets a whole fleet of coaches" for "a great number."

[13]Lucius Annaeus Seneca (4? B.C.–65), Roman statesman and philosopher, whose terse, asymmetrical, and somewhat jerky style (in marked contrast to the orotundity and balance of Cicero's) was increasingly popular in the late 16th and 17th century.
[14]Blamed for.   [15]Jonson renders this word as "affectation."
[16]Petition presented to the court presided over by the Lord Chancellor, i.e., a heavy legal document.   [17]Understanding.
[18]Most of these words, which have long since become thoroughly established, were neologisms in the later 16th century. For Shakespeare's comments on the then new word *accommodate* see *2 Henry IV*, III.ii.72 ff.
[19]Baldassare Castiglione's *Libro de Cortegiano* (1528), which in Sir Thomas Hoby's translation (1561) was widely read in England, and Cicero's *De oratore* (55 B.C.), an influential treatise (in three books) on rhetoric. Excerpts from both works were included in *Civil and Uncivil Life* (1579), a dialogue containing many anecdotes and allusions that was reissued as *The English Courtier and the Country Gentleman* in 1586.   [20]Text *sights*.   [21]Text *streching*.
[22]Here and elsewhere—and especially in Part V—Hoskins inserts in parentheses page references to the 1590 edition of Sidney's *Arcadia*, a marked copy of which he had sent to his young correspondent as the source of most of his examples. These references have been omitted from the present text.
[23]Intricately arranged flower bed.   [24]Planned, designed.
[25]Hoskins' abbreviation for *metaphor*.   [26]Margin.

An *allegory* is the continual following of a metaphor (which before I defined to be the translation of one word) and proportionable through the sentence or through many sentences. As "Philoclea was so environed with sweet rivers of virtue as that she could neither be battered nor undermined," where Philoclea is expressed by the similitude of a castle, her nature (defense) by the natural fortification of a river about a castle, and the metaphor continues in the tempting her by force or craft expressed by battering and undermining. . . . As I said before that a metaphor might be too bold or too far-fetched, so I now remember that it may be too base. As "the tempest of judgment had broken the mainmast of his will," "a goodly audience of sheep," "shoulders of friendship," and suchlike too base; as in that speech, "fritter of fraud and seething-pot of iniquity," and they that say "a red herring is a shoeing-horn to a pot of ale."[27] But they that speak of a scornful[28] thing speak grossly. Therefore to delight generally, take those terms from ingenious and several professions: from ingenious arts[29] to please the learned, and from several arts to please the learned of all sorts; as from the meteors, planets, and beasts in natural philosophy; from the stars, spheres, and their motions in astronomy; from the better part of husbandry; from the politic government of cities; from navigation, from military profession, from physic, but not out of the depth of these mysteries. But ever—unless your purpose be to disgrace—let the world be taken from a thing of equal or greater dignity, as, speaking of virtue, "the sky of perfect virtue ever clouded with sorrow," where he thought it unfit to stoop to any metaphor lower than heaven. You may assure yourself of this observation, and all the rest, if you but compare those places in your book noted with this note *M*; and in truth it is the best flower, growing most plentifully, in all *Arcadia*. . . .

Metonymia[30] is an exchange of a name when one word comes in lieu of another, not for similitude but for other natural affinity and coherence; as when the matter is used for that which thereof consisteth, as "I want silver" for "money"; when the efficient[31] or author is used for the thing made, as "my blade is a right Sebastian"[32] for "of Sebastian's making"; the thing containing for the thing or person contained, as "the City met the Queen" for "the citizens"; the adjunct, property, quality, or badge for the subject of it, as "deserts are preferred" for "men deserving"; give "room to the coif"[33] for "the sergeant." No doubt better examples of this sort are in *Arcadia*, if I had leisure to look so low as where they are.

Synecdoche is an exchange of the name of the part for the whole or of the name of the whole for the part. As "Aye, my name is toss'd and censured by many tongues" for "many men," where the part of an entire body goes for the whole. Contrariwise, "he carries a goldsmith's shop on his fingers" for "rings"; "he fell into the water and swallowed the Thames" for "the water." So the general name for the special ("put up your weapon" for "your dagger"), and the special for the particular (as "the Earl is gone into Ireland" for "[the] E[arl of] E[ssex]"),[34] the particular for the special (as "I would willingly make you a Sir Philip Sidney" for "an eloquent, learned, valiant gentleman"), one for many (as "the Spaniard, they say, comes against us" for "the

Spaniards"), and suchlike, which because they are easy I have exemplified familiarly. Both these figures serve well when you have mentioned a thing before, for variety in repetition; and you may well observe better instances in your reading than my interrupted thought can now meet with. . . .

[Hoskins similarly runs through and illustrates the other figures of "varying": catachresis ("the expressing of one matter by the name of another which is incompatible with it, and sometimes clean contrary"), anadiplosis ("a repetition in the end of a former sentence and beginning of the next"), climax ("a kind of anadiplosis leading by degrees and making the last word a step to the further meaning"), anaphora ("when many clauses have the like beginning"), etc.]

Paranomasia is a pleasant touch of the same letter, syllable, or word with a different meaning, as for the running upon the word *more*: "This very little is more than too much." Sir Philip Sidney, in *Astrophil and Stella*, calls [it] the "dictionary method," and the verses so made "rhymes running in rattling rows,"[35] which is an example of it. There is a swinish poem made thereof in Latin, called *Pugna Porcorum*,[36] and L[odowick] Lloyd[37] in his youth tickled [it] in fashion of a poet's dictionary:

Hector, Hamo, Hannibal, dead Pompey, Pyrrhus spill'd,
Cyrus, Scipio, Caesar slain, and Alexander kill'd.

The author of *Albion's England*[38] hath set forth good invention too often in this attire. In those days, Lyly, the author of *Euphues*,[39] seeing the dotage of the time upon this small ornament, invented varieties of it, for he disposed the agnominations[40] in as many fashions as repetitions are distinguished by the author's rhetoric. Sometimes the first word and the

[27]Of Hoskins' five examples of "base" metaphor, the first, third, and fourth are from Sidney's *Arcadia*, the second is from Thomas Wilson's *Art of Rhetoric* (1560), and the fifth is apparently proverbial. [28]Contemptible. [29]Text *Acts*. [30]Metonymy.
[31]Efficient cause, in this case the author.
[32]Name of a famous family of swordmakers in Toledo.
[33]White cap worn by a sergeant-at-law as part of his official dress.
[34]For the disastrous Irish misadventure of Robert Devereux (1566–1601), second earl of Essex, in the summer of 1599 see pp. 843–846. This is one of the topical allusions that suggest 1599 as the date of Hoskins' little treatise.
[35]The allusion is to the fifteenth sonnet in Sidney's *Astrophil and Stella* (1591), the sonnet sequence published five years after his death:
You that do Dictionarie's methode bring
Into your rimes, running in ratling rowes.
[36]Latin poem (1530?) of some 250 lines, every word of which begins with the letter *p*, by Joannes Leo Placentius, a Flemish friar.
[37]Literary man and minor civil servant (fl. 1573–1610) whose "Epitaph upon the Death of Sir Edward Saunders" (from which Hoskins quotes) was printed as a broadside in 1570 and reprinted in the second (1578) and subsequent editions of *The Paradise of Dainty Devices*, a popular miscellany.
[38]William Warner (1558?–1609), whose enormously popular metrical history of England (1586) went through many editions and expansions.
[39]Hoskins' condescending remarks on the intricate stylistic devices of John Lyly (1554?–1606) suggest how far the vast popularity of *Euphues, the Anatomy of Wit* (1578) and its sequel *Euphues and His England* (1580) had slipped by the end of the century. [40]Puns.

middle harped one upon another, sometimes the first and last, sometimes in several sentences, sometimes in one—and this with a measure, *compar*:[41] a change of contention, or contraries, and a device of a similitude, in those days made a gallant show. But Lyly himself hath outlived this style and breaks well from it. . . .

[IV] TO AMPLIFY

To *amplify* and *illustrate* are two the chiefest ornaments of eloquence, and gain of men's minds two the chiefest advantages, admiration and belief; for how can you commend a thing more acceptably to our attention than by telling us it is extraordinary and by showing us that it is evident? There is no looking at a comet if it be either little or obscure, and we love and look on the sun above all stars for these two excellencies: his greatness, his clearness. Such in speech is amplification and illustration.

> Hoskins' treatment of the five "ways" of amplifying—comparison, division, accumulation, intimation, and progression—may be sampled in his comments on the second and third.

Division, the second way of amplification, which Bacon in his fifth color[42] took out of the rhetoricians: "a way to amplify anything," quoth he, "is to break it and make an anatomy of it into several parts, and to examine it according to several circumstances." He said true. It is like the show which peddlers make of their packs, when they display them; contrary to the German magnificence that serves in all the good meat in one dish. But whereas he says that this art of amplifying will betray itself in method and order, I think that it rather adorneth itself. For instead of saying "he put the whole town to the sword," let men reckon all ages and sorts, and say:

> He neither saved the young men, as pitying the unripe flower of their youth, nor the aged men, as respecting their gravity, nor children, as pardoning their weakness, nor women, as having compassion upon their sex: soldier, clergyman, citizen, armed or unarmed, resisting or submitting—all within the town destroyed with the fury of that bloody execution.

Note that your divisions here are taken from age, profession, sex, habit, or behavior, and so may be from all circumstances. This only trick made up J[ohn] D[avies'] poem of dancing:[43] all danceth, the heavens, the elements, men's minds, commonwealths, and so by parts all danceth. Another example varied, "he apparelleth himself with great discretion," thus amplified by circumstances:

> For the stuff, his clothes were more rich than glittering; as for the fashion, rather usual for his sort than fantastical for his invention; for color, more grave and uniform than wild and light; for fitness, made as well for ease of exercise as to set forth to the eye those parts which in him had most excellency. . . .

The third kind of amplification is *accumulation*, which is heaping up of many terms of praise or accusing, importing but the same matter without descending to any part, and hath his due season after some argument or proof. Otherwise it is like a schoolmaster foaming out synonymies, or

words of one meaning, and will sooner yield a conjecture of superfluity of words than of sufficiency of matter. But let us give some example. To amplify "a sedition":

> Tumults, mutinies, uproars, desperate conspiracies, wicked confederacies, furious commotions, traitorous rebellions, associations in villainy, distractions from allegiance, bloody garboils, and intestine massacres of the citizens.

But this example is somewhat too swelling. Now to talk of one "with mild looks" you may say: "he hath a sweet countenance, a most pleasant eye, a most amiable presence, a cheerful aspect; he is a most delectable object, etc." You will be well stored for this purpose when you have made up your *synonyma* book after my direction. . . .

> Following a long discussion of "figures serving for amplification"—for example, hyperbole, *correctio*, *ironia*, interrogation, exclamation, etc.—Hoskins comes to the final section of his work, which is concerned with illustration.

[V] TO ILLUSTRATE

Illustration consists in things or words in the description of things living or dead: of living things, either reasonable (as of men and of personages and qualities), or unreasonable (as of horses, ships, islands, castles, and suchlike).

Men are described most excellent in *Arcadia*: Basilius, Plexirtus, Pyrocles, Musidorus, Anaxius, etc.; but he that will truly set down a man in a figured[44] story must first learn truly to set down an humor, a passion, a virtue, a vice, and therein keeping decent proportion add but names and knit together the accidents and encounters. The perfect expressing of all qualities is learned out of Aristotle's ten books of moral philosophy,[45] but because (as Machiavelli saith)[46] perfect virtue or perfect vice is not seen in our time, which altogether is humorous and spiriting,[47] therefore the understanding of Aristotle's *Rhetoric* is the directest means of skill to describe, to move, to appease, or to prevent any motion whatsoever; whereunto whosoever can fit his speech shall be truly eloquent. This was my opinion ever, and Sir Philip

[41]Perhaps a synonym (of Hoskins' own invention) for the *measure* or stylistic device of parison, i.e., a balancing of corresponding elements in a sentence or a group of sentences. An example of Lyly's fondness for such balance (and also for alliteration) is seen in this sentence from his first novel: "Here, yea, here, Euphues, mayst thou see not the carved visard of a lewd woman, but the incarnate visage of a lascivious wanton, not the shadow of love, but the substance of lust."

[42]*Fifth color*: text *first colonie*. Hoskins refers to Section V of Francis Bacon's *Colors of God and Evil*, a fragmentary collection of "colors"—that is, rhetorical modes or figures—whereby moral questions may be argued. One of Bacon's earliest works, it was printed in the same volume with his *Essays* (1597) and many years later expanded in *De augmentis scientiarum* (1623), VI.iii.

[43]In *Orchestra, or a Poem of Dancing* (1595), John Davies fancifully explores the significance of measured motion throughout the universe. [44]Adorned with rhetorical figures.

[45]The *Nicomachean Ethics*.

[46]Hoskins is perhaps thinking of Niccolò Machiavelli's *Discorsi sopra la prima deca de Tito Livio*, I.xxvi, which he could have known through the hostile paraphrase of Innocent Gentillet's *Contre Nicol. Machiavel* (1576).

[47]Moody and volatile.

Sidney betrayed his knowledge in this book of Aristotle to me before ever I knew that he had translated any part of it, for I found the two first books Englished by him in the hands of that noble, studious Henry Wotton.[48] But lately I think also he had much help out of *Theophrasti Imagines*.[49] For the web, as it were, of his story he followed three: Heliodorus in Greek, Sannazarus' *Arcadia* in Italian, and *Diana* by [50] Montemayor in Spanish.[51]

But to our purpose: what personages and affections are set forth in Arcadia for men? For men: pleasant, idle retiredness in King Basilius, and the dangerous end of it; unfortunate valor in Plangus: courteous valor in Amphialus; proud valor in Anaxius; hospitality in Kalander; the mirrow of true courage and friendship in Pyrocles and Musidorus; miserableness and ingratitude in Chremes; fear and fatal subtility in Clinias; fear and rudeness, with ill-affected civility, in Dametas. And through the story, mutual virtuous love: in marriage in Argalus and Parthenia; out of marriage in Pyrocles and Philoclea, Musidorus and Pamela; true constant love unrespected in Plangus and Helena in the true Zelmane, inconstancy and envy; suspicion and tyranny in a king and his counselors: generally false love in Pamphilus; and light courage and credulity in Chremes' daughter; base dotage on a wife in Plangus' father. But in women: a mischievous, seditious stomach[52] in Cecropia; wise courage in Pamela; mild discretion in Philoclea; Pamela's prayer;[53] her discourse; squeamish, cunning unworthiness in Artesia; respective and restless dotage in Gynecia's love; proud, ill-favored, sluttish simplicity in Mopsa. Now in these persons is ever a steadfast decency and uniform difference of manners observed, wherever you find them and howsoever each interrupt the other's story and actions.

And for actions of persons, there are many rarely described: as a mutiny and fire in a ship, causes of an uproar, the garboil,[54] an armed skirmish, policy[55] and preparation—but policy generally in all particular actions is noted in your

book &c.[56]—managing a horse is described, tilting shows.[57] Many other notable and lively portraits are, which I will not lay down to save you so sweet a labor as the reading of that which may make you eloquent and wise. For Philip Sidney's course was—besides reading Aristotle and Theophrastus—to imagine the thing present in his own brain that his[58] pen might the better present it to you. Whose example I would you durst follow till I pulled you back. . . .

> Hoskins ends his work by discussing such specific "figures" of illustration as distinction, definition, division, periphrasis, and apostrophe.

[48]*The two first books...Wotton:* this translation has not survived. On Sir Henry Wotton (1568–1638) see p. 54
[49]The *Characters* of Theophrastus (d. ca. 287 B.C.), a series of thirty sketches of such types as the flatterer, the loquacious man, the grumbler, etc. See p. 711 f. [50]Text *de*.
[51]*Heliodorus...Spanish:* Heliodorus (A.D. 4th cent.?), author of the so-called Greek romance *Ethiopia*, a work widely read in England in the translation (1569?) of Thomas Underdowne; Jacopo Sannazaro (1458–1530), author of the Italian prose pastoral *Arcadia* (1504); Jorge de Montemayor (1521?–61), Portuguese author of the Spanish *Diana Enamorada*, an unfinished pastoral romance in both prose and verse that was Englished by Bartholomew Young in 1598. [52]Disposition.
[53]This famous passage, in which the heroine Pamela asks mercy for her lover Musidorus (*Arcadia*, III.vi), was subsequently incorporated into *Eikon Basilike* (1649), purportedly Charles I's own account of his meditations and prayers as he was awaiting execution. In *Eikonoklastes* (1649), which was written to discredit this enormously popular piece of royalist propaganda, John Milton gleefully pointed out that this moving prayer, allegedly Charles' own effusion, was in fact "stolen word for word from the mouth of a heathen fiction praying to a heathen god; and that in no serious book, but the vain and amatorious poem of Sir Philip Sidney's *Arcadia*." See pp. 612 f. [54]Uproar. [55]Political cunning.
[56]Perhaps a scribal error for some such abbreviation as "pol" to stand for "policy." [57]Jousts, chivalric games. [58]Text *is*.

John Donne[1] [1572-1631]

from Juvenilia, or Certain Paradoxes and Problems (1633)

PARADOXES

II. THAT WOMEN OUGHT TO PAINT

Foulness is loathsome: can that be so which helps it? Who forbids his beloved to gird in her waist? to mend by shoeing

her uneven lameness? to burnish her teeth? or to perfume her breath? Yet that the face be more precisely regarded, it

[1]For a commentary on Donne and for other excerpts from his work, see Poetry, pp. 56 ff. and Religion and Politics, pp. 544 ff.
JUVENILIA [1]*Yet that...more:* because the face is more noticed it is more important.

concerns more;[1] for as open confessing sinners are always punished, but the wary and concealing offenders without witness do it also without punishment, so the secret parts needs the less respect; but of the face, discovered to all examinations and surveys, there is not too nice a jealousy.[2] Nor doth it only draw the busy eyes, but it is subject to the divinest touch of all, to kissing, the strange and mystical union of souls. If she should prostitute herself to a more unworthy man than thyself, how earnestly and justly wouldst thou exclaim that for want of this easier and ready way of repairing,[3] to betray her body to ruin and deformity (the tyrannous ravishers, and sudden deflowerers of all women) what a heinous adultery is it! What thou lovest in her face is color, and painting gives that, but thou hatest it, not because it is, but because thou knowest it. Fool, whom ignorance makes happy, the stars, the sun, the sky whom thou admirest alas have no color, but are fair because they seem to be colored. If this seeming will not satisfy thee in her, thou hast good assurance of her color when thou seest her lay it on. If her face be painted on a board or wall, thou wilt love it, and the board, and the wall. Canst thou loathe it, then, when it speaks, smiles, and kisses, because it is painted? Are we not more delighted with seeing birds, fruits, and beasts painted than we are with naturals?[4] And do we not with pleasure behold the painted shape of monsters and devils, whom true we durst not regard! We repair the ruins of our houses, but first cold tempests warns us of it, and bites us through it; we mend the wrack and stains of our apparel, but first our eyes and other bodies are offended; but by this providence of women this is prevented. If in kissing or breathing upon her the painting fall off, thou art angry; wilt thou be so if it stick on? Thou didst love her; if thou beginnest to hate her, then 'tis because she is not painted. If thou wilt say now thou didst hate her before, thou didst hate her and love her together. Be constant in something, and love her who shows her great love to thee, in taking this pains to seem lovely to thee.

IV. THAT GOOD IS MORE COMMON THAN EVIL

I have not been so pitifully tired with any vanity as with silly old men's exclaiming against these times and extolling their own. Alas! they betray themselves, for if the times be changed, their manners have changed them. But their senses are to pleasures as sick men's tastes are to liquors,[5] for indeed no new thing is done in the world: all things are what and as they were, and good is as ever it was, more plenteous, and must of necessity be more common than evil, because it hath this for nature and perfection to be common. It makes love to all natures: all, all affect it. So that in the world's early infancy there was a time when nothing was evil, but if this world shall suffer dotage, in the extremest crookedness[6] thereof there shall be no time when nothing shall be good. It dares appear and spread and glister in the world, but evil buries itself in night and darkness, and is chastised and suppressed when good is cherished and rewarded. And as embroiderers, lapidaries, and other artisans can by all things

adorn their works—for by adding better things, the better they show in luster[7] and in eminency—so good doth not only prostrate her amiableness[8] to all, but refuses no end (no, not of her utter contrary evil) that she may be the more common to us. For evill manners are parents of good laws; and in every evil there is an excellency which (in common speech) we call good. For the fashions of habits, for our moving in gestures, for phrases in our speech, we say they were good as long as they were used, that is, as long as they were common; and we eat, we walk only when it is or seems good to do so. All fair, all profitable, all virtuous is good, and these three things, I think, embrace all things but their utter contraries; of which also fair may be rich and virtuous, poor may be virtuous and fair, vicious may be fair and rich; so that good hath this good means to be common, that some subjects she can possess entirely; and in subjects poisoned with evil she can humbly stoop to accompany the evil. And of indifferent things many things are become perfectly good by being common, as customs by use are made binding lawes. But I remember nothing that is therefore ill because it is common[9] but women, of whom also they that are most common are the best of that occupation[10] they profess.

VIII. THAT NATURE IS OUR WORST GUIDE

Shall she be guide to all creatures which is herself one? Or if she also have a guide, shall any creature have a better guide than we? The affections of lust and anger yea, even to err is natural. Shall we follow these? Can she be a good guide to us which hath corrupted not us only but herself? Was not the first man, by the desire of knowledge, corrupted even in the whitest integrity of nature? And did not nature (if nature did anything) infuse into him this desire of knowledge, and so this corruption in him, into us? If by nature we shall understand our essence, our definition or reason, nobleness, then this being alike common to all (the idiot and the wizard being equally reasonable) why should not all men, having equally all one nature, follow one course? Or if we shall understand our inclinations, alas, how unable a guide is that which follows the temperature[11] of our slimy bodies! For we cannot say that we derive our inclinations, our minds, or souls, from our parents by any way: to say that it is all from all is error in reason, for then with the first nothing remains; or is a part from all is error in experience, for then this part, equally imparted to many children, would like gavelkind[12] lands in few generations become nothing; or to say it by communication is error in divinity, for to communicate the ability of communicating whole essence with any but God is utterly blasphemy. And if thou hit thy father's nature and

[2]Too fastidious a concern.   [3]The use of cosmetics.
[4]Vegetation and creatures in their natural state.
[5]They are as much repelled by pleasure as sick men are by liquors.
[6]Advanced senility.   [7]Text *lush*.   [8]Make herself attractive.
[9]1) generally accessible; 2) promiscuous.   [10]Prostitution.
[11]Temperament.
[12]In English law, the custom of dividing a tenant's lands at his death equally among his direct or collateral male heirs.

inclination, he also had his fathers, and so, climbing up, all comes of one man, all have one nature, all shall embrace one course—but that cannot be; therefore our complexions[13] and whole bodies we inherit from parents; our inclinations and minds follow that. For our mind is heavy in our bodies' afflictions, and rejoyceth in our bodies' pleasure: how, then, shall this nature govern us that is governed by the worst part of us? "Nature though oft chased away, it will return";[14] 'tis true, but those good motions and inspirations which be our guides must be wooed, courted, and welcomed, or else they abandon us. And that old axiom, *nihil invita, etc.*[15] must not be said "thou shalt," but "thou wilt" do nothing against nature; so unwilling he notes us to curb our naturall appetites. We call our bastards always our "natural issue," and we define a fool by nothing so ordinary as by the name of "natural." And that poor knowledge whereby we conceive what rain is, what wind, what thunder, we call metaphysic, supernatural; such small things, such nothings do we allow to our pliant nature's apprehension. Lastly, by following her we lose the pleasant and lawful commodities of this life, for we shall drink water and eat roots, and those not sweet and delicate, as now by man's art and industry they are made. We shall lose all the necessities of societies, laws, arts, and sciences, which are all the workmanship of man. Yea, we shall lack the last best refuge of misery, death, because no death is natural, for if ye will not dare to call all death violent (though I see not why sicknesses be not violences), yet causes of all deaths proceed of the defect of that which nature made perfect, and would preserve, and therefore all against nature.

PROBLEMS

II. WHY PURITANS MAKE LONG SERMONS

It needs not for perspicuousness, for God knows they are plain enough; nor do all of them use sem-brief accents, for some of them have crotchets enough.[16] It may be they intend not to rise like glorious tapers and torches, but like thin-wretched sick-watching candles, which languish and are in a divine consumption from the first minute, yea in their snuff[17] and stink, when others are in their more profitable glory. I have thought sometimes that out of conscience they allow long measure to coarse ware.[18] And sometimes that usurping in that place a liberty to speak freely of kings, they would reign as long as they could. But now I think they do it out of a zealous imagination that it is their duty to preach on till their auditory wake.

III. WHY DID THE DEVIL RESERVE JESUITS TILL THESE LATTER DAYS?

Did he know that our age would deny the devil's possessing,[19] and therefore provided by these to possess men and kingdoms? Or to end the disputation of Schoolmen why the devil could not make lice in Egypt,[20] and whether those things he presented there might be true, hath he sent us a true and real plague, worse than those ten? Or in ostentation of the greatness of his kingdom, which even division[21] cannot shake, doth he send us these which disagree with all the rest? Or knowing that our times should discover the Indies and abolish their idolatry, doth he send these to give them another for it? Or peradventure they have been in the Roman Church these thousand years, though we have called them by other names.

V. WHY DO YOUNG LAYMEN SO MUCH STUDY DIVINITY?

Is it because others, tending busily church's preferment, neglect study? Or had the Church of Rome shut up all our ways till the Lutherans broke down their uttermost stubborn doors and the Calvinists picked their inwardest and subtlest locks? Surely the devil cannot be such a fool to hope that he shall make this study contemptible by making it common. Nor that as the dwellers by the River Origus[22] are said by drawing infinite ditches to sprinkle their barren country to have exhausted and intercepted their main channel and so lost their more profitable course to the sea, so we, by providing everyone's self divinity enough for his own use, should neglect our teachers and fathers. He cannot hope for better heresies than he hath had, nor was his kingdom ever so much advanced by debating religion (though with some aspersions[23] of error) as by a dull and stupid security in which many gross things are swallowed. Possibly[24] out of such an ambition as we have now to speak plainly and fellow-like with lords and kings we think also to acquaint ourselves with God's secrets. Or perchance when we study it by mingling human respects, it is not divinity.

[13]Temperaments.
[14]*Naturam expelles furca, tamen usque recurret* (Horace, *Epistles*, I.x.24).
[15]Based on Cicero, *De officiis*, I.xxxi.110: *nihil decet invita Minerva, ut aiunt, id est adversante et repugnante natura* ("nothing is proper that 'goes against the grain,' as they say—that is, if it runs directly counter to one's natural inclination").
[16]*Nor do all...crotchets enough*: an elaborate and only moderately successful play on words from musical notation: not all long-winded Puritan preachers talk at length (i.e., in semibreves or whole notes, the longest notes in music), for some of them exhibit many crotchets (i.e., quarter notes, with a pun on *crotchet* as perverse notion or eccentricity). [17]The burned wick of a candle.
[18]They preach overlong sermons because their material is so shoddy. [19]Discredit the ancient belief in demonic seizure.
[20]After Moses had plagued the Egyptians by turning dust into lice, the magicians at Pharaoh's court tried "with their enchantments to bring forth lice, but they could not" (Exodus 8.16–18). Donne himself later wrote a long and murky discussion of this passage for his *Essays in Divinity* (ed. Evelyn M. Simpson, 1952, pp. 82 ff.). [21]Dissension.
[22]Probably the Orague, a river in Estremadura, the arid western region of Spain. [23]Sprinklings, scatterings. [24]Text *possible*.

Samuel Daniel[1] [1563?-1619]

from A Defence of Rhyme (1603)

To All the Worthy Lovers and Learned
Professors of Rhyme within His Majesty's
Dominions, Samuel Daniel

Worthy gentlemen, about a year since, upon the great re-proach[1] given to the professors of rhyme and the use thereof, I wrote a private letter as a defense of mine own undertakings in that kind to a learned gentleman, a great friend[2] of mine then in court. Which I did rather to confirm myself in mine own courses, and to hold him from being won from us, than with any desire to publish the same to the world.

But now, seeing the times to promise a more regard to the present condition of our writings in respect of our sovereign's happy inclination this way,[3] whereby we are rather to expect an encouragement to go on with what we do than that any innovation should check us with a show of what it would do in another kind (and yet do nothing but deprave), I have now given a greater body to the same argument and here present it to your view under the patronage of a noble earl, who in blood and nature[4] is interested to take our part in this cause with others, who cannot, I know, but hold dear the monuments that have been left unto the world in this manner of composition,[5] and who, I trust, will take in good part this my *Defense,* if not as it is my particular yet in respect of the cause I undertake,[6] which I here invoke you all to protect.

S. D.

To William Herbert, Earl of Pembroke

The general custom and use of rhyme in this kingdom,[7] Noble Lord, having been so long (as if from a grant of nature) held unquestionable, made me to imagine that it lay alto-gether out of the way of contradiction, and was become so natural as we should never have had a thought to cast it off into reproach or be made to think that it ill became our language. But now I see, when there is opposition made to all things in the world by words, we must now at length likewise fall to contend for words themselves and make a question whether they be right or not. For we are told how that our measures go wrong, all rhyming is gross, vulgar, barbarous; which, if it be so, we have lost much labor to no purpose; and, for mine own particular, I cannot but blame the fortune of the times and mine own genius that cast me upon so wrong a course, drawn with the current of custom and an unexamined example. Having been first encouraged or framed thereunto by your most worthy and honorable

mother,[8] receiving the first notion for the formal ordering of those compositions at Wilton (which I must ever acknowl-edge to have been my best school, and thereof always am to hold a feeling and grateful memory), afterward drawn farther on by the well-liking and approbation of my worthy lord, the fosterer of me and my Muse, I adventured to bestow all my whole powers therein, perceiving it agreed so well

[1]For a commentary on Daniel and for other excerpts from his work, see Poetry, pp. 24 ff. and History and Historiography, pp. 847 ff
DEFENSE OF RHYME [1]By Campion's *Observations.* See headnote, p. 24
[2]Perhaps Fulke Greville, first Baron Brooke (1554–1628), the schoolmate, intimate friend, and biographer of Sir Philip Sidney, who himself combined an interest in literature with a distinguished career in politics (pp. 4 f.) As a member of the literary circle at Wilton House over which Sidney and his sister the countess of Pembroke presided, he would of course have known young Samuel Daniel in his capacity as tutor to William Herbert, the countess' eldest son.
[3]*Sovereign's...way:* James I, who had just succeeded to the throne, prided himself on his erudition and his literary accomplishments. In addition to the famous *Basilikon Doron* (1599), a treatise on politics written for his heir, they included *The Essays of a Prentice in the Divine Art of Poesy* (1584), *His Majesty's Poetical Exercises* (1591), and a treatise on witchcraft called *Demonology* (1598).
[4]Because of heredity and temperament. William Herbert (1580–1630), third earl of Pembroke, whose tutor Daniel had been and to whom he *addressed* his *Defence,* was the nephew of Sir Philip Sidney, perhaps the young man who figures largely in Shake-speare's *Sonnets* (1609), and certainly a notable patron of such writers as Jonson, Massinger, and William Browne. Twenty years later the editors of the first Folio of Shakespeare's plays dedicated that great book to him and his brother Philip, earl of Montgomery.
[5]In rhyme.
[6]*If not...undertake:* if not for my sake, then for the justice of the cause that I espouse.
[7]Since Campion had attributed the popularity of rhyme to a servile and uncritical respect for established practice, the word *custom* serves almost as a refrain in Daniel's little treatise of rebuttal. "For custom," Campion had said, "I allege that ill uses are to be abol-ished, and that things naturally imperfect can not be perfected by use. Old customs, if they be better, why should they not be recalled, as the yet flourishing custom of numerous poesy used among the Romans and Grecians?"
[8]Mary Herbert (1561–1621), countess of Pembroke who as col-laborator and literary executor of her famous brother Sir Philip Sidney presided over a literary circle at Wilton House, her great home near Salisbury, where Daniel lived in the early 1590's as tutor to her eldest son.

both with the complexion of the times and mine own constitution as I found not wherein I might better employ me. But yet now, upon the great discovery of these new measures,[9] threatening to overthrow the whole state of rhyme in this kingdom, I must either stand out to defend or else be forced to forsake myself and give over all. And though irresolution and a self-distrust be the most apparent faults of my nature—and that the least check of reprehension,[10] if it savor of reason, will as easily shake my resolution as any man's living—yet in this case I know not how I am grown more resolved and, before I sink, willing to examine what those powers of judgment are that must bear me down and beat me off from the station of my profession, which by the law of nature I am set to defend; and the rather for that this detractor (whose commendable rhymes, albeit now himself an enemy to rhyme, have given heretofore to the world the best notice of his worth) is a man of fair parts[11] and good reputation; and therefore the reproach forcibly cast from such a hand may throw down more at once than the labors of many shall in long time build up again, specially upon the slippery foundation of opinion and the world's inconstancy, which knows not well what it would have, and

> Discit enim citius meminitque libentius illud
> Quod quis deridet, quam quod probat et veneratur.[12]

And he who is thus become our unkind adversary must pardon us if we be as jealous of our fame and reputation as he is desirous of credit by his new-old art,[13] and must consider that we cannot, in a thing that concerns us so near, but have a feeling of the wrong done, wherein every rhymer in this universal island, as well as myself, stands interested. So that if his charity had equally drawn with his learning he would have forborne to procure the envy of so powerful a number upon him, from whom he cannot but expect the return of a like measure of blame, and only have made way to his own grace by the proof of his ability without the disparaging of us, who would have been glad to have stood quietly by him and perhaps commended his adventure, seeing that evermore of one science another may be born, and that these sallies made out of the quarter of our set knowledges are the gallant proffers only of attemptive spirits, and commendable though they work no other effect than make a bravado.[14] And I know it were *indecens et morosum nimis, alienae industriae, modum ponere.*[15] We could well have allowed of his numbers had he not disgraced our rhyme. which both custom and nature doth most powerfully defend—custom that is before all law, nature that is above all art. Every language hath her proper number or measure fitted to use and delight, which custom, entertaining by the allowance of the ear, doth endenize[16] and make natural. All verse is but a frame of words confined within certain measure, differing from the ordinary speech and introduced, the better to express men's conceits, both for delight and memory. Which frame of words consisting of *rithmus* or *metrum*, number or measure, are disposed into divers fashions according to the humor of the composer and the set of the time. And these *rhythmi*, as Aristotle saith,[17] are familiar amongst all nations and *e naturali et sponte fusa compositione*;[18] and they fall as naturally already in our language as ever art can make them, being such as the ear of itself doth marshal in their proper rooms; and they of themselves will not willingly be put out of their rank, and that in such a verse as best comports with the nature of our language. And for our rhyme (which is an excellency added to this work of measure, and a harmony far happier than any proportion antiquity could ever shew us) doth add more grace and hath more of delight than ever bare numbers, howsoever they can be forced to run in our slow language, can possibly yield. Which, whether it be derived of *rhythmus* or of *romance*, which were songs the bards and Druids about rhymes used, and thereof were called *Remensi*, as some Italians hold, or howsoever, it is likewise number and harmony of words, consisting of an agreeing sound in the last syllables of several verses, giving both to the ear an echo of a delightful report and to the memory a deeper impression of what is delivered therein. For as Greek and Latin verse consists of the number and quantity of syllables, so doth the English verse of measure and accent. And though it doth not strictly observe long and short syllables, yet it most religiously respects the accent; and as the short and the long make number, so the acute and grave accent yield harmony. And harmony is likewise number, so that the English verse, then, hath number, measure, and harmony in the best proportion of music. Which, being more certain and more resounding, works that effect of motion with as happy success as either the Greek or Latin. And so natural a melody is it, and so universal, as it seems to be generally borne with all the nations of the world as an hereditary eloquence proper to all mankind. The universality argues the general power of it: for if the barbarian use it, then it shows that it sways th' affection of the barbarian; if civil nations practice it, it proves that it works upon the hearts of civil nations; if all, then that it hath a power in nature on all. . . .

"Ill customs are to be left." I grant it, but I see not how that can be taken for an ill custom which nature hath thus ratified, all nations received, time so long confirmed, the effects such as it performs those offices of motion for which it is employed; delighting the ear, stirring the heart, and satisfying the judgment in such sort as I doubt whether ever single numbers will do in our climate if they show no more work of wonder than yet we see. And if ever they prove to become anything, it must be by the approbation of many ages that must give them their strength for any operation, or before the world will feel where the pulse, life, and energy lies; which now we are sure where to have in our rhymes, whose known frame hath those due stays for the mind,

---

[9]The quantitative meters advocated by Campion.

[10]Reproof, i.e., opposition.   [11]Notable talents.

[12]"For men more quickly learn and more gladly recall what they deride than what they approve and esteem" (Horace, *Epistles*, II.i.262–263).

[13]The art of quantitative verse, which had been practiced by the ancients and was being urged upon the moderns.

[14]Ostentatious show.

[15]"It is indecorous, ill natured, and alien to the discipline of art to make rules for others."   [16]Naturalize.   [17]*Poetics* 1447b.

[18]"Produced by natural and spontaneous composition."

those encounters of touch, as makes the motion certain though the variety be infinite. Nor will the general sort for whom we write (the wise being above books) taste these labored measures but as an orderly prose when we have all done. For this kind acquaintance and continual familiarity ever had betwixt our ear and this cadence is grown to so intimate a friendship as it will now hardly ever be brought to miss it. For be the verse never so good, never so full, it seems not to satisfy nor breed that delight as when it is met and combined with alike-sounding accents; which seems as 10 the jointure without which it hangs loose and cannot subsist, but runs wildly on like a tedious fancy without a close. Suffer, then, the world to enjoy that which it knows and what it likes. Seeing that whatsoever force of words doth move, delight, and sway the affections of men—in what Scythian[19] sort soever it be disposed or uttered—that is true number, measure, eloquence, and the perfection of speech; which, I said, hath as many shapes as there be tongues or nations in the world, nor can with all the tyrannical rules of idle rhetoric be governed otherwise than custom and 20 present observation will allow. And being now the trim[20] and fashion of the times to suit a man otherwise cannot but give a touch of singularity, for when he hath all done, he hath but found other clothes to the same body, and peradventure not so fitting as the former. . . .

For seeing it is matter that satisfies the judicial, appear it in what habit it will, all these pretended proportions of words, howsoever placed, can be but words, and peradventure serve but to embroil our understanding; whilst seeking to please our ear we enthrall our judgment; to delight an 30 exterior sense we smooth up a weak, confused sense, affecting sound to be unsound—and all to seem *servum pecus*,[21] only to imitate the Greeks and Latins, whose felicity in this kind might be something to themselves, to whom their own *idioma*[22] was natural, but to us it can yield no other commodity than a sound. We admire them not for their smooth-gliding words nor their measures, but for their inventions; which treasure, if it were to be found in Welsh and Irish, we should hold those languages in the same estimation; and they may thank their sword that made their tongues so 40 famous and universal as they are. For to say truth, their verse is many times but a confused deliverer of their excellent conceits, whose scattered limbs we are fain to look out and join together to discern the image of what they represent unto us. And even the Latins, who profess not to be so licentious[23] as the Greeks, show us many times examples but of strange cruelty in torturing and dismembering of words in the middest or disjoining such as naturally should be married and march together, by setting them as far asunder as they can possibly stand; that sometimes, unless 50 the kind reader, out of his own good nature, will stay them up by their measure, they will fall down into flat prose, and sometimes are no other indeed in their natural sound; and then again, when you find them disobedient to their own laws you must hold it to be *licentia poetica*,[24] and so dispensable. The striving to show their changeable measures in the variety of their odes have been very painful, no doubt, unto them, and forced them thus to disturb the quiet stream of their words, which by a natural succession otherwise desire to follow in their due course.

But such affliction doth laborsome curiosity still lay upon our best delights (which ever must be made strange and variable) as if art were ordained to afflict nature, and that we could not go but in fetters. Every science, every profession, must be so wrapped up in unnecessary intrications[25] as if it were not to fashion but to confound the understanding, which makes me much to distrust man and fear that our presumption goes beyond our ability, and our curiosity is more than our judgment, laboring ever to seem to be more than we are, or laying greater burthens upon our minds than they are well able to bear, because we would not appear like other men.

And indeed I have wished there were not that multiplicity of rhymes as is used by many in sonnets, which yet we see in some so happily to succeed, and hath been so far from hindering their inventions as it hath begot conceit beyond expectation and comparable to the best inventions of the world; for sure in an eminent spirit, whom nature hath fitted for that mystery, rhyme is no impediment to his conceit but rather gives him wings to mount and carries him, not out of his course, but, as it were, beyond his power to a far happier flight. All excellencies being sold us at the hard price of labor, it follows where we bestow most thereof we buy the best success; and rhyme, being far more laborious than loose measures (whatsoever is objected), must needs, meeting with wit and industry, breed greater and worthier effects in our language. So that if our labors have wrought out a manumission from bondage, and that we go at liberty notwithstanding these ties, we are no longer the slaves of rhyme, but we make it a most excellent instrument to serve us. . . .

Methinks we should not so soon yield our consents captive to the authority of antiquity unless we saw more reason; all our understandings are not to be built by the square of Greece and Italy. We are the children of Nature as well as they; we are not so placed out of the way of judgment but that the same sun of discretion shineth upon us; we have our portion of the same virtues as well as of the same vices. *Et Catilinam quocunque in populo videas, quocunque sub axe.*[26] Time and the turn of things bring about these faculties according to the present estimation; and *res temporibus, non tempora rebus, servire oportet.*[27] So that we must never rebel against use, *quem penes arbitrium est et vis et normal loquendi.*[28] It is not the observing of trochaics nor their iambics that will make our writings ought the wiser. All their poesy, all their philosophy, is nothing unless we bring the discerning light of conceit with us to apply it to use. It is not books but only

[19]Barbaric, undisciplined. [20]Manner, style. [21]"A slavish herd."
[22]"Idiom." [23]Metrically irregular. [24]"Poetic license."
[25]Complications, entanglements.
[26]"You may see a Catiline [i.e., a moral monster] among any people under the sky" (Juvenal, *Satires*, XIV.41–42).
[27]"It is necessary to fit the thing to the times, not the times to the thing."
[28]"Which governs both the force and the form of speech" (adapted from Horace, *Ars poetica*, l. 72).

that great book of the world and the all-overspreading grace of heaven that makes men truly judicial. Nor can it be but a touch of arrogant ignorance to hold this or that nation barbarous, these or those times gross, considering how this manifold creature man, wheresoever he stand in the world, hath always some disposition of worth, entertains the order of society, affects that which is most in use, and is eminent in some one thing or other that fits his humor and the times. The Grecians held all other nations barbarous but themselves, yet Pyrrhus,[29] when he saw the well-ordered marching of the Romans, which made them see their presumptuous error, could say it was no barbarous manner of proceeding. The Goths, Vandals, and Longobards,[30] whose coming down like an inundation overwhelmed, as they say, all the glory of learning in Europe, have yet left us still their laws and customs as the originals of most of the provincial constitutions of Christendom, which, well considered with their other courses of government, may serve to clear them from this imputation of ignorance. And though the vanquished never yet spake well of the conqueror, yet even through the unsound coverings of malediction appear those monuments of truth as argue well their worth and proves them not without judgment, though without Greek and Latin.

Will not experience confute us if we should say the state of China, which never heard of anapestics, trochees, and tribrachs, were gross, barbarous, and uncivil? And is it not a most apparent ignorance, both of the succession of learning in Europe and the general course of things, to say "that all lay pitifully deformed in those lack-learning times from the declining of the Roman empire till the light of the Latin tongue was revived by Reuchlin, Erasmus, and More" when for three hundred years before them, about the coming-down of Tamburlaine[31] into Europe, Franciscus Petrarca (who then, no doubt, likewise found whom to imitate) showed all the best notions of learning in that degree of excellency both in Latin, prose and verse, and in the vulgar Italian as all the wits of posterity have not yet much overmatched him in all kinds to this day? His great volumes written in moral philosophy show his infinite reading and most happy power of disposition: his twelve *Eglogues*, his *Africa* (containing nine books of the last Punic war) with his three books of *Epistles* in Latin verse show all the transformations of wit and invention that a spirit naturally born to the inheritance of poetry and judicial knowledge could express; all which, notwithstanding, wrought him not that glory and fame with his own nation as did his poems in Italian, which they esteem above all whatsoever wit could have invented in any other form than wherein it is, which questionless they will not change with the best measures Greeks or Latins can show them, howsoever our adversary imagines. . . . Hereupon [after the revival of Greek studies and the spread of printing] came that mighty confluence of learning in these parts which, returning as it were *per postliminium*[32] and here meeting then with the new-invented stamp of printing, spread itself indeed in a more universal sort than the world ever heretofore had it; when Pomponius Laetus, Aeneas Sylvius, Angelus Politianus, Hermolaus Barbarus, Johannes Picus de Mirandula[33]

(the miracle and phoenix of the world) adorned Italy and wakened up other nations likewise with this desire of glory long before it brought forth Reuchlin, Erasmus, and More— worthy men, I confess, and the last a great ornament to this land, and a rhymer. . . .

We must not look upon the immense course of times past as men overlook spacious and wide countries from off high mountains, and are never the near to judge of the true nature of the soil or the particular site and face of those territories they see. Nor must we think, viewing the superficial figure of a region in a map, that we know straight the fashion and place as it is. Or reading an history (which is but a map of men, and doth no otherwise acquaint us with the true substance of circumstances than a superficial card[34] doth the seaman with a coast never seen, which always proves other to the eye than the imagination forecast it), that presently we know all the world and can distinctly judge of times, men, and manners just as they were; when the best measure of man is to be taken by his own foot, bearing ever the nearest proportion to himself, and is never so far different and unequal in his powers that he hath all in perfection at one time and nothing at another. The distribution of gifts are universal, and all seasons hath them in some sort. We must not think but that there were Scipios. Caesars, Catos, and Pompeys[35] born elsewhere than at Rome; the rest of the world hath ever had them in the same degree of nature, though not of state. And it is our weakness that makes us mistake or misconceive in these delineations of men the true figure of their worth. And our passion and belief is so apt to lead us beyond truth that unless we try them by the just compass of humanity, and as they were men, we shall cast their figures in the air when we should make their models upon earth. . . . There is but one learning, which *omnes gentes habent scriptum in cordibus suis*, one and the selfsame spirit that worketh in all. We have but one body of justice, one body of wisdom, throughout the whole world, which is but appareled according to the fashion of every nation.

Eloquence and gay words are not of the substance of wit; it is but the garnish of a nice time, the ornaments that do but deck the house of a state *et imitatur publicos mores*. Hunger is as well satisfied with meat served in pewter as silver. Discretion is the best measure, the rightest foot in what habit soever it run. Erasmus, Reuchlin, and More brought no more wisdom into the world with all their new revived words than we find was before: it bred not a profounder divine than Saint Thomas, a greater lawyer than

[29]King of Epirus (ca. 318–272 B.C.), who, after a string of victories over Rome, was defeated at Beneventum, a city in southern Italy, in 275.   [30]Lombards.

[31]Tamerlane, i.e., Timur Lenk ("Timur the Lame," 1336?–1405), Mongol conqueror who overran most of southern and western Asia, and even penetrated Russia as far as Moscow.

[32]"By the threshold," i.e., by restoring former rights and privileges (a term from Roman law).

[33]Notable Italian humanists of the fifteenth century.

[34]Map, chart.

[35]Types of military and political grandeur as exemplified by the ancient Romans.

Bartolus, a more acute logician than Scotus;[36] nor are the effects of all this great amass of eloquence so admirable or of that consequence but that *impexa illa antiquitas*[37] can yet compare with them.

Let us go no further but look upon the wonderful architecture of this state of England, and see whether they were deformed times that could give it such a form: where there is no one the least pillar of majesty but was set with most profound judgment and borne up with the just conveniency of prince and people; no court of justice but laid by the rule and square of nature, and the best of the best commonwealths that ever were in the world; so strong and substantial as it hath stood against all the storms of factions, both of belief and ambition, which so powerfully beat upon it, and all the tempestuous alterations of humorous[38] times whatsoever, being continually in all ages furnished with spirits fit to maintain the majesty of her own greatness and to match in an equal concurrency all other kingdoms round about her with whom it had to encounter.

But this innovation, like a viper, must ever make way into the world's opinion through the bowels of her own breeding, and is always borne with reproach in her mouth; the disgracing others is the best grace it can put on to win reputation of wit; and yet is it never so wise as it would seem, nor doth the world ever get so much by it as it imagineth, which, being so often deceived and seeing it never performs so much as it promises, methinks men should never give more credit unto it. For let us change never so often, we cannot change man; our imperfections must still run on with us. . . . But shall we not tend to perfection? Yes, and that ever best by going on in the course we are in, where we have advantage, being so far onward of him that is but now setting forth. For we shall never proceed if we be ever beginning, nor arrive at any certain port, sailing with all winds that blow—*non convalescit planta quae saepius transfertur*[39]—and therefore let us hold on in the course we have undertaken and not still be wandering. Perfection is not the portion of man, and, if it were, why may we not as well get to it this way as another, and suspect these great undertakers lest they have conspired with envy to betray our proceedings and put us by the honor of our attempts with casting us back upon another course, of purpose to overthrow the whole action of glory when we lay the fairest for it and were so near our hopes? I thank God that I am none of these great scholars if thus their high knowledges do but give them more eyes to look out into uncertainty and confusion, accounting myself rather beholding to my ignorance that hath set me in so low an under-room of conceit with other men and hath given me as much distrust as it hath done hope, daring not adventure to go alone but plodding on the plain tract I find beaten by custom and the time, contenting me with what I see in use. . . .

Were it not far better to hold us fast to our old custom than to stand thus distracted with uncertain laws wherein right shall have as many faces as it pleases passion to make it, that wheresoever men's affections stand, it shall still look that way? What trifles doth our unconstant curiosity call up to contend for? What colors are there laid upon indifferent things to make them seem other than they are, as if it were but only to entertain contestation amongst men who, standing according to the prospective of their own humor,[40] seem to see the selfsame things to appear otherwise to them than either they do to other or are indeed in themselves, being but all one in nature?

For what ado have we here?[41] What strange precepts of art about the framing of an iambic verse in our language? Which, when all is done, reaches not by a foot,[42] but falleth out to be the plain ancient verse consisting of ten syllables or five feet, which hath ever been used amongst us, time out of mind, and, for all this cunning and counterfeit name, can or will [not] be any other in nature than it hath been ever heretofore. And this new dimeter is but the half of this verse divided in two, and no other than the caesura or breathing-place in the middest thereof, and therefore it had been as good to have put two lines in one but only to make them seem diverse. Nay, it had been much better for the true English reading and pronouncing thereof, without violating the accent, which now our adversary hath herein most unkindly done; for, being as we are to sound it according to our English march, we must make a rest and raise the last syllable, which falls out very unnatural in *desolate, funeral, Elizabeth, prodigal,* and in all the rest, saving the monosyllables. Then follows the English trochaic, which is said to be a simple verse, and so indeed it is, being without rime, having here no other grace than that in sound it runs like the known measure of our former ancient verse ending (as we term it according to the French) in a feminine foot, saving that it is shorter by one syllable at the beginning, which is not much missed by reason it falls full at the last. Next comes the elegiac, being the fourth kind, and that likewise is no other than our old accustomed measure of five feet; if there be any difference it must be made in the reading, and therein we must stand bound to stay where often we would not and sometimes either break the accent or the due course of the word. And now for the other four kinds of numbers, which are to be employed for odes, they are either of the same measure or such as have ever been familiarly used amongst us.

So that of all these eight several kinds of new-promised numbers, you see what we have: only what was our own before, and the same but appareled in foreign titles, which,

[36]*Thomas...Scotus*: St. Thomas Aquinas (1225?–74), greatest of scholastic philosophers; Bartolus (1314–57), noted jurist and professor of civil law at Perugia; Duns Scotus (1265?–?1308), Franciscan theologian. [37]"The uncombed ancients." [38]Fantastic.
[39]"No plant grows strong which is too often moved."
[40]*Standing...humor*: governed by their whims and fads.
[41]In this paragraph Daniel addresses himself to Campion's main contention: that "our kind of rhyming" requires so much wrenching of the language it results only in a "confused inequality of syllables" offensive to the ear. In order to correct this situation Campion had proposed replacing rhyme with eight meters (based on classical prototypes) that he termed iambic, dimeter, trochaic, elegiac, three varieties of Sapphic, and Anacreontic (the last four being especially "fit for ditties or odes"). Daniel discusses and rejects these one by one.
[42]Is a foot shorter than the classical hexameter.

had they come in their kind and natural attire of rhyme, we should never have suspected that they had affected to be other or sought to degenerate into strange manners, which now we see was the cause why they were turned out of their proper habit and brought in as aliens, only to induce men to admire them as far-comers. But see the power of nature! It is not all the artificial coverings of wit that can hide their native and original condition, which breaks out through the strongest bands of affectation and will be itself, do singularity what it can. And as for those imagined quantities of [10] syllables, which have been ever held free and indifferent in our language, who can inforce us to take knowledge of them, being *in nullius verba jurati*[43] and owing fealty to no foreign invention? Especially in such a case where there is no necessity in nature, or that it imports either the matter or form, whether it be so or otherwise. But every versifier that well observes his work finds in our language, without all these unnecessary precepts, what numbers best fit the nature of her idiom, and the proper places destined to such accents as she will not let into any other rooms than into [20] those for which they were born. . . .

But now for whom hath our adversary taken all this pains? For the learned, or for the ignorant, or for himself to show his own skill? If for the learned, it was to no purpose, for every grammarian in this land hath learned his *prosodia*[44] and already knows all this art of numbers; if for the ignorant, it was vain, for if they become versifiers we are like to have lean numbers instead of fat rime. And if Tully would have his orator skilled in all the knowledges appertaining to God and man, what should they have who would be a degree [30] above orators? Why, then, it was to show his own skill, and what himself had observed; so he might well have done without doing wrong to the fame of the living and wrong to England in seeking to lay reproach upon her native ornaments and to turn the fair stream and full course of her accents into the shallow current of a less uncertainty, clean out of the way of her known delight. And I had thought it could never have proceeded from the pen of a scholar (who sees no profession free from the impure mouth of the scorner) to say the reproach of others' idle tongues is the curse of [40] nature upon us, when it is rather her curse upon him that knows not how to use his tongue. What? Doth he think himself is now gotten so far out of the way of contempt that his numbers are gone beyond the reach of obloquy and that, how frivolous or idle soever they shall run, they shall be protected from disgrace—as though that light rhymes and light numbers did not weigh all alike in the grave opinion of the wise? . . .

Here I stand forth only to make good the place we have thus taken up and to defend the sacred monuments erected [50] therein, which contain the honor of the dead, the fame of the living, the glory of peace, and the best power of our speech, and wherein so many honorable spirits have sacrificed to memory their dearest passions, showing by what divine influence they have been moved and under what stars they lived.

But yet notwithstanding all this which I have here delivered in the defense of rhyme I am not so far in love with mine own mystery,[45] or will seem so froward, as to be against the reformation and the better settling these measures of ours. Wherein there be many things I could wish were more certain and better ordered, though myself dare not take upon me to be a teacher therein, having so much need to learn of others. And I must confess that to mine own ear those continual cadences of couplets used in long and continued poems are very tiresome and unpleasing by reason that still, methinks, they run on with a sound of one nature and a kind of certainty which stuffs the delight rather then entertains it. But yet, notwithstanding, I must not out of mine own daintiness[46] condemn this kind of writing which peradventure to another may seem most delightful; and many worthy compositions we see to have passed with commendation in that kind. Besides, methinks, sometimes to beguile the ear with a running out and passing over the rhyme, as no bound to stay us in the line where the violence of the matter will break through, is rather graceful than otherwise. Wherein I find my Homer-Lucan, as if he gloried to seem to have no bounds, albeit he were confined within his measures, to be, in my conceit, most happy.[47] For so thereby they who care not for verse or rhyme may pass it over without taking notice thereof and please themselves with a well-measured prose. And I must confess my adversary hath wrought this much upon me, that I think a tragedy would indeed best comport with a blank verse and dispense with rhyme, saving in the chorus or where a sentence shall require a couplet. And to avoid this overglutting the ear with that always certain and full encounter of rhyme I have assayed in some of my *Epistles* to alter the usual place of meeting and to set it further off by one verse, to try how I could disuse my own ear and to ease it of this continual burthen which indeed seems to surcharge it a little too much; but as yet I cannot come to please myself therein, this alternate or cross rhyme holding still the best place in my affection.[48]

Besides, to me this change of number in a poem of one nature fits not so well, as to mix uncertainly feminine rhymes with masculine, which, ever since I was warned of that deformity by my kind friend and countryman Master Hugh Samford,[49] I have always so avoided it as there are not above two couplets in that kind in all my poem of the *Civil Wars*;[50]

[43]"Sworn to no prescribed oath," i.e., not bound to follow any one formula (perhaps adapted from Horace, *Epistles*, I.i.14).
[44]Rules of classical prosody.
[45]Profession, calling (i.e., poetry).   [46]Fastidiousness.
[47]Any English poet who, emulating the Homeric epics or Lucan's *Pharsalia*, tries to achieve the effect of the classical hexameter by using blank verse. Such a writer, though not shackled by the *bounds* of rhyme, would nonetheless be *confined within his measures* of iambic pentameter.
[48]Daniel experimented with a variety of meters in his verse epistles: for example, *ottava rima* (abababcc) in "To Sir Thomas Egerton," abcabcdd in "To the Lady Margaret, Countess of Cumberland," and abcabc in "To the Lady Ann Clifford."
[49]Hugh (or Henry) Sanford, Daniel's predecessor as William Herbert's tutor. As a member of the literary coterie at Wilton House, he was apparently commissioned by the Countess of Pembroke to act as editor of the 1593 edition of her brother's *Arcadia*. See p. 675, n.2.   [50]See pp. 28 ff.

and I would willingly, if I could, have altered it in all the rest, holding feminine rhymes to be fittest for ditties, and either to be set certain or else by themselves. But in these things, I say, I dare not take upon me to teach that they ought to be so, in respect myself holds them to be so, or that I think it right, for indeed there is no right in these things that are continually in a wandering motion, carried with the violence of our uncertain likings, being but only the time that gives them their power. For if this right or truth should be no other thing than that we make it, we shall shape it into a thousand figures, seeing this excellent painter, man, can so well lay the colors which himself grinds in his own affections as that he will make them serve for any shadow and any counterfeit. But the greatest hinderer to our proceedings and the reformation of our errors is this self-love whereunto we versifiers are ever noted to be especially subject—a disease of all other the most dangerous and incurable, being once seated in the spirits, for which there is no cure but only by a spiritual remedy. *Multos puto ad sapientiam potuisse pervenire, nisi putassent se pervenisse.*[51] And this opinion of our sufficiency makes so great a crack in our judgment as it will hardly ever hold anything of worth. *Caecus amor sui;*[52] and though it would seem to see all without it, yet certainly it discerns but little within. For there is not the simplest writer that will ever tell himself he doth ill, but, as if he were the parasite only to soothe his own doings, persuades him that

his lines cannot but please others which so much delight himself. . . .

Next to this deformity stands our affectation wherein we always bewray ourselves to be both unkind and unnatural to our own native language in disguising or forging strange or unusual words as if it were to make our verse seem another kind of speech out of the course of our usual practice, displacing our words or investing new only upon a singularity, when our own accustomed phrase, set in the due place, would express us more familiarly and to better delight than all this idle affectation of antiquity or novelty can ever do. And I cannot but wonder at the strange presumption of some men that dare so audaciously adventure to introduce any whatsoever foreign words, be they never so strange, and of themselves, as it were, without a Parliament, without any consent or allowance, establish them as free denizens in our language. But this is but a character of that perpetual revolution which we see to be in all things that never remain the same, and we must herein be content to submit ourselves to the law of time, which in few years will make all that for which we now contend *nothing.*

Finis

[51]"I think that many could have attained wisdom if they had not thought they had already attained it."
[52]"Self-love is blind" (Horace, *Odes,* I.xviii.14).

Fulke Greville, Baron Brooke[1] [1554-1628]

from The Life of the Renowned Sir Philip Sidney (1652)

CHAPTER I

The difference which I have found between times, and consequently the changes of life into which their natural vicissitudes do violently carry men, as they have made deep furrows of impressions into my heart, so the same heavy wheels cause me to retire my thoughts from free traffic with the world, and rather seek comfortable ease or employment in the safe memory of dead men than disquiet in a doubtful conversation amongst the living. Which I ingenuously confess to be one chief motive of dedicating these exercises of my youth to that worthy Sir Philip Sidney, so long since departed. For had I grounded my ends upon active wisdoms of the present, or sought patronage out of hope or fear in the future, who knows not that there are some noble friends of mine, and many honorable magistrates yet living, unto whom both my fortune and reputation were and are far more subject? But besides this self-respect of

dedication, the debt I acknowledge to that gentleman is far greater, as with whom I shall ever account it honor to have been brought up, and in whom the life itself of true worth did (by way of example) far exceed the pictures of it in any moral precepts. So that (if my creation had been equal) it would have proved as easy for me to have followed his pattern in the practice of real virtue as to engage myself into this characteristical kind of poesy, in defense whereof he hath written so much as I shall not need to say anything.[1] For that this representing of virtues, vices, humors, counsels,

[1]For a commentary on Greville and for other excerpts from his work, see Poetry, pp. 4 ff.
LIFE OF SIDNEY [1]*So that. . . anything:* Sidney's life being such a model of virtue, this symbolic (*characteristical*) reconstruction of it will perhaps exemplify the principles that he himself had enunciated about the moral function of literature. Sidney's literary theory was splendidly expounded in his *Defense of Poesy,* a treatise written in the early 1580's and published posthumously in 1595.

and actions of men unfeigned, and unscandalous images, is an enabling of free-born spirits to the greatest affairs of states he himself hath left such an instance in the too short scene of his life as I fear many ages will not draw a line out of any other man's sphere to parallel with it.

For my own part, I observed, honored, and loved him so much as with what caution soever I have passed through my days hitherto among the living, yet in him I challenge a kind of freedom even among the dead. So that although with Socrates I profess to know nothing for the present, yet with Nestor I am delighted in repeating old news of the ages past, and will therefore stir up my drooping memory touching this man's worth, powers, ways, and designs to the end that in the tribute I owe him our nation may see a seamark raised upon their native coast above the level of any private pharos[2] abroad, and so by a right meridian line of their own learn to sail through the straits of true virtue into a calm and spacious ocean of human honor.

It is ordinary among men to observe the races of horses and breeds of other cattle. But few consider that as divers humors mixed in men's bodies make different complexions, so every family hath, as it were, divers predominant qualities in it, which as they are tempered together in marriage give a certain tincture to all the descent. In my time I have observed it in many houses, especially in this. Sir Henry Sidney,[3] his father, was a man of excellent natural wit, large heart, sweet conversation; and such a governor as sought not to make an end of the state in himself but to plant his own ends in the prosperity of his country. Witness his sound establishments both in Wales and Ireland, where his memory is worthily grateful unto this day, how unequal and bitter soever the censure of provincials is usually against sincere monarchal governors, especially such as, though in worth and place superior, are yet in their own degrees of heraldry inferior to them.

On the other side, his mother,[4] as she was a woman by descent of great nobility, so was she by nature of a large, ingenuous spirit. Whence, as it were even racked with native strengths, she chose rather to hide herself from the curious eyes of a delicate time than come upon the stage of the world with any manner of disparagement, the mischance of sickness having cast such a kind of veil over her excellent beauty as the modesty of that sex doth many times upon their native and heroical spirits.

So that it may probably be gathered that this clearness of his father's judgment and ingenious sensibleness of his mother's brought forth so happy a temper in this well-mixed offspring of theirs as—without envy be it spoken— Sir Philip deserves to be accompted amongst those eminent plants of our soil which blast or bite not, but rather statuminate[5] and refresh the vines, corn, fruits, or whatsoever groweth under their shadows. And as he was their first born, so was he not the contraction but the extension of their strength and the very aim[6] and perfect type of it.

Of whose youth I will report no other wonder but this: that though I lived with him and knew him from a child, yet I never knew him other than a man—with such staidness of mind, lovely and familiar gravity as carried grace and reverence above greater years. His talk ever of knowledge and his very play tending to enrich his mind, so as even

his teachers found something in him to observe and learn above that which they had usually read or taught. Which eminence by nature and industry made his worthy father style Sir Philip in my hearing (though I unseen) *lumen familiae suae*.[7] But why do I mention this relative harmony of worth between father and son? Did not his country soon after take knowledge of him as a light, or leading star, to every degree within her? Are not the arts and languages which enabled him to travail[8] at fourteen years old,[9] and in his travail to win reverence amongst the chief learned men abroad, witnesses beyond exception that there was great inequality of worth and goodness in him? . . .

Now from these particular testimonies to go on with Sir Philip's life: though he purposed no monuments of books to the world out of this great harvest of knowledge, yet do not his Arcadian romanties[10] live after him, admired by our four-eyed critics? Who, howsoever their common end upon common arts be to affect reputation by depraving[11] censure, yet where nature placeth excellency above envy, there (it seemeth) she subjecteth these carping eyes to wander, and shows the judicious reader how he may be nourished in the delicacy of his own judgment.

For instance, may not the most refined spirits in the scope of these dead images (even as they are now) find that when sovereign princes, to play with their own visions, will put off public action, which is the splendor of majesty, and unactively charge the managing of their greatest affairs upon the second-hand faith and diligence of deputies, may they not, I say, understand that even then they bury themselves and their estates in a cloud of contempt, and under it both encourage and shadow the conspiracies of ambitious subalterns to their false ends, I mean the ruin of states and princes?[12]

Again, where kingly parents will suffer or rather force their wives and daughters to descend from inequality and reservedness of princely education into the contemptible familiarity and popular freedom of shepherds, may we not

[2]Lighthouse, beacon.
[3]Though not of particularly high birth, Sir Henry Sidney (1529–86) served the Tudors in a variety of important posts, notably as president of Wales and as lord deputy of Ireland.
[4]As daughter of John Dudley, duke of Northumberland, and sister of Robert, earl of Leicester, Lady Mary Sidney belonged to one of the greatest families of Tudor England. As a consequence of nursing the young Queen Elizabeth during a virulent attack of smallpox in 1562, she herself contracted the disease, which so sadly marred her beauty that in her rare public appearances thereafter she always wore a mask.　[5]Support.　[6]Design, intention.
[7]"The light of his family."　[8]Travel.
[9]In 1572 (when Sidney was eighteen, not fourteen) he secured the queen's permission for a visit to the Continent "for his attaining the knowledge of foreign languages." His travels, in the course of which he met and charmed many important persons, took him as far east as Hungary and as far south as Italy before he returned to England in 1575.　[10]Romances?　[11]Disparaging.
[12]The main plot of *Arcadia*—which Greville interprets as a vehicle of moral and political instruction—turns on the voluntary retirement of King Basilius, accompanied by his queen and two daughters, to a pastoral retreat where also come Pyrocles and Musidorus, two princes traveling incognito. The resulting complications lead almost to domestic and political disaster.

discern that even therein they give those royal births warrant or opportunity to break over all circles of honor, safeguards to the modesty of that sex, and withal make them fraily apt to change the commanding manners of princely birth into the degrading images of servile baseness? Lastly, where humor takes away this pomp and apparatus from king, crown, and scepter, to make fear a counselor and obscurity a wisdom, be that king at home what the current or credit of his former government for a while may keep him, yet he is sure among foreign princes to be justly censured as a princely shepherd or shepherdish king, which creatures of scorn seldom fail to become fit sacrifices for home-born discontentments or ambitious foreign spirits to undertake and offer up. . . .

To be short, the like and finer moralities offer themselves throughout that various and dainty[13] work of his for sounder judgments to exercise their spirits in; so that if the infancy of these ideas, determining in the first generation, yield the ingenuous reader such pleasant and profitable diversity both of flowers and fruits, let him conceive if this excellent image-make had lived to finish and bring to perfection this extraordinary frame of his own commonwealth.[14] . . .
I say, what a large field an active, able spirit should have had to walk in, let the advised reader conceive with grief. Especially if he please to take knowledge that in all these creatures of his making, his intent and scope was to turn the barren philosophy precepts into pregnant images of life; and in them, first on the monarch's part, lively to represent the growth, state, and declination of princes, change of government and laws, vicissitudes of sedition, faction, succession, confederacies, plantations[15] with all other errors or alterations in public affairs. Then again in the subject's case: the state of favor, disfavor, prosperity, adversity, emulation, quarrel, undertaking, retiring, hospitality, travail, and all other moods of private fortunes or misfortunes. In which traverses,[16] I know, his purpose was to limn out such exact pictures of every posture in the mind that any man being forced, in the strains of this life, to pass through any straits or latitudes of good or ill fortune might (as in a glass)[17] see how to set a good countenance upon all the discountenances of adversity and a stay upon the exorbitant smiling of chance.

Now as I know this was the first project[18] of these works, rich (like his youth) in the freedom of affections, wit, learning, style, form, and facility to please others, so must I again as ingenuously confess that when his body declined and his piercing inward powers were lifted up to a purer horizon, he then discovered not only the imperfection but vanity of these shadows, how daintily soever limned: as seeing that even beauty itself in all earthly complexions was more apt to allure men to evil than to fashion any goodness in them. And from this ground, in that memorable testament of his he bequeathed no other legacy but the fire to this unpolished embryo.[19] From which fate it is only reserved until the world hath purged away all her more gross corruptions.

Again, they that knew him well will truly confess this *Arcadia* of his to be, both in form and matter, as much inferior to that unbounded spirit of his as the industry and images of other men's works are many times raised above the writers' capacities; and besides acknowledge that how-

soever he could not choose but give them many aspersions[20] of spirit and learning from the father, yet that they were scribbled rather as pamphlets for entertainment of time and friends than any accompt of himself to the world.[21] Because if his purpose had been to leave his memory in books, I am confident in the right use of logic, philosophy, history, and poesy—nay, even in the most ingenuous of mechanical arts— he would have showed such tracts of a searching and judicious spirit as the professors of every faculty would have striven no less for him than the seven cities did to have Homer of their sept.[22] But the truth is, his end was not writing, even while he wrote, nor his knowledge molded for tables[23] or schools; but both his wit and understanding bent upon his heart to make himself and others, not in words or opinion but in life and action, good and great.

In which architectional art he was such a master, with so commending and yet equal[24] ways amongst men, that wheresoever he went he was beloved and obeyed; yea, into what action soever he came last at the first he became first at the last, the whole managing of the business not by usurpation or violence but (as it were) by right and acknowledgment falling into his hands as into a natural center.
` By which only commendable monopoly of alluring and improving men, how the same draws all winds after it in fair weather, so did the influence of this spirit draw men's affections and undertakings to depend upon him.

CHAPTER III

. . . Indeed, he was a true model of worth: a man fit for conquest, plantation, reformation, or what action soever is greatest and hardest amongst men; withal such a lover of mankind and goodness that whosoever had any real parts in him found comfort, participation, and protection to the uttermost of his power, like Zephyrus[25] he giving life where

---

[13]Varied and delightful.
[14]Greville seems to be saying that since Sidney's early draft (*first generation*) of *Arcadia* was so delightful and instructive, its revision, which was not completed, would have been even more impressive. See n. 19 below.   [15]Colonial enterprises.   [16]Mishaps, adversities.
[17]Mirror.   [18]Purpose, intention.
[19]Sidney's dying request that his unpublished *Arcadia* be destroyed was, of course, ignored. In 1590 the printer William Ponsonby, almost surely with Greville's knowledge and assistance (not to say collusion), published an unauthorized edition of the fragmentary "New" *Arcadia*, consisting of some two and a half books that Sidney had completed the revision of before his death in 1586. In 1593 this fragment, after considerable editorial tinkering, was eked out with the last half of the "Old" *Arcadia* that Sidney had not had time to alter. In 1598 Sidney's sister, the formidable countess of Pembroke, presided over a presumably authorized edition of her famous brother's work. Not until 1926, however, did Albert Feuillerat publish the complete "Old" *Arcadia* as Sidney wrote it in his youth.   [20]Sprinklings.
[21]In the dedicatory epistle to the "Old" *Arcadia*, addressed to the countess of Pembroke, Sidney urbanely deprecated his "idle work" as "but a trifle, and that triflingly handled."
[22]Tribe, clan. Since even in antiquity the facts of Homer's life were uncertain, many cities claimed the honor of his birth.
[23]Writing tablets.   [24]*Commending. . . equal*: graceful and yet impartial.   [25]In Greek mythology, the west wind.

he blew. The universities abroad and at home accompted him a general Maecenas[26] of learning, dedicated their books to him, and communicated every invention or improvement of knowledge with him. Soldiers honored him and were so honored by him as no man thought he marched under the true banner of Mars that had not obtained Sir Philip Sidney's approbation. Men of affairs in most parts of christendom entertained correspondency[27] with him. But what speak I of these with whom his own ways and ends did concur, since (to descend) his heart and capacity were 10 so large that there was not a cunning painter, a skillful engenier,[28] an excellent musician, or any other artificer of extraordinary fame that made not himself known to this famous spirit and found him his true friend without hire and the common rendezvous of worth in his time.

Now let princes vouchsafe to consider of what importance it is to the honor of themselves and their estates to have one man of such eminence, not only as a nourisher of virtue in their courts or service but besides for a reformed standard by which even the most humorous persons could not but have a 20 reverend ambition to be tried and approved current. This I do the more confidently affirm because it will be confessed by all men that this one man's example and personal respect did not only encourage learning and honor in the schools, but brought the affection and true use thereof both into the court and camp. Nay more, even many gentlemen excellently learned amongst us will not deny but that they affected to row and steer their course in his wake. Besides which honor of unequal nature and education, his very ways in the world did generally add reputation to his prince and 30 country by restoring amongst us the ancient majesty of noble and true dealing: as a manly wisdom that can no more be weighed down by any effeminate craft than Hercules could be overcome by that contemptible army of dwarfs. This was it which, I profess, I loved dearly in him, and still shall be glad to honor in the great men of this time: I mean that his heart and tongue went both one way, and so with everyone that went with the truth, as knowing no other kindred, party, or end.

Above all, he made the religion he professed the firm basis 40 of his life. For this was his judgment (as he often told me), that our true-heartedness to the reformed religion in the beginning brought peace, safety, and freedom to us, concluding that the wisest and best way was that of the famous William, Prince of Orange,[29] who never divided the consideration of estate[30] from the cause of religion, nor gave that sound party occasion to be jealous or distracted upon any appearance of safety whatsoever; prudently resolving that to temporize with the enemies of our faith was but (as among sea gulls) a strife not to keep upright but aloft upon 50 the top of every billow: which false-heartedness to God and man would in the end find itself forsaken of both, as Sir Philip conceived. For to this active spirit of his all depths of the devil proved but shallow fords, he piercing into men's counsels and ends not by their words, oaths, or compliments (all barren in that age), but by fathoming their hearts and powers by their deeds, and found no wisdom where he found no courage, nor courage without wisdom, nor either without honesty and truth. With which solid and active reaches of his, I am persuaded, he would have found or made a

way through all the traverses even of the most weak and irregular times. But it pleased God in this decrepit age of the world not to restore the image of her ancient vigor in him, otherwise than as in a lightning before death. . . .

CHAPTER XII

Thus shall it suffice me to have trod out some steps of this Britain Scipio,[31] thereby to give the learned a scantling[32] for drawing out the rest of his dimensions by proportion. And to the end the abruptness of this treatise may suit more equally with his fortune I will cut off his actions as God did his life, in the midst, and so conclude with his death. . . .

> After characteristic delay and equivocation Elizabeth, in June 1585, decided to send military aid in support of the Protestant Dutch in their rebellion against Catholic Spain, and the following November Sidney, bearing his commission as governor of Flushing, set forth to join his uncle, the earl of Leicester, who had been named commander-in-chief of the English forces. Almost a year later (September 1586) he met his untimely death in an abortive cavalry charge at Zutphen. For once, Greville's narrative descends to particulars.

Thus they go on, every man in the head of his own troop, and the weather being misty, fell unawares upon the enemy, who had made a strong stand to receive them near to the very walls of Zutphen; by reason of which accident their troops fell not only unexpectedly to be engaged within the level of the great shot that played from the rampiers,[33] but more fatally within shot of their muskets, which were laid in ambush within their own trenches.

Now whether this were a desperate cure in our leaders for a desperate disease, or whether misprision,[34] neglect, audacity, or what else induced it, it is no part of my office to determine, but only to make the narration clear, and deliver rumor—as it passed then—without any stain or enamel.

Howsoever, by this stand an unfortunate hand out of those forespoken trenches brake the bone of Sir Philip's thigh with a musket shot. The horse he rode upon was rather furiously choleric than bravely proud, and so forced him to forsake the field but not his back, as the noblest and fittest bier to carry a martial commander to his grave. In which sad progress, passing along by the rest of the army where his uncle, the general, was, and being thirsty with excess of bleeding, he called for drink, which was presently brought him; but as he was putting the bottle to his mouth he saw a poor soldier carried along who had eaten his last at the same feast ghastly casting up his eyes at the bottle. Which Sir

[26]Gaius Cilnius Maecenas (d. 8 B.C.), a Roman statesman who was such a generous benefactor of Horace and Vergil that his name has become synonymous with "patron."
[27]Welcomed correspondence. [28]Engineer, designer.
[29]William the Silent (1533–84), who, as head of the great Protestant House of Orange and founder of the Dutch Republic, was one of the most influential Protestant statesmen of his age.
[30]Political question.
[31]Scipio the Elder (or Africanus), the general who defeated Hannibal (202 B.C.) and became the very symbol of Roman piety and patriotism. [32]Rough draft, outline. [33]Ramparts. [34]Mistake.

Philip perceiving, took it from his head before he drank and delivered it to the poor man with these words, "Thy necessity is yet greater than mine." And when he had pledged this poor soldier he was presently carried to Arnhem. . . .

CHAPTER XIII

After almost a month of pain and medical bungling Sidney realized that his wound was fatal, and so prepared himself for easeful death.

First, he called the ministers unto him, who were all excellent men of divers nations, and before them made such a confession of Christian faith as no book but the heart can truly and feelingly deliver. Then desired them to accompany him in prayer, wherein he besought leave to lead the assembly in respect, as he said, that[35] the secret sins of his own heart were best known to himself, and out of that true sense he more properly instructed to apply the eternal sacrifice of our Saviour's passion and merits to him. His religious zeal prevailed with this humbly devout and afflicted company, in which well chosen progress of his—howsoever they were all moved, and those sweet motions witnessed by sighs and tears, even interrupting their common devotion—yet could no man judge in himself, much less in others, whether this rake[36] of heavenly agony whereupon they all stood were forced by sorrow for him or admiration of him, the fire of this Phoenix hardly being able out of any ashes to produce his equal, as they conceived. . . .

The next change used was the calling for his will, which though at first sight it may seem a descent from heaven to earth again, yet he that observes the distinction of those offices[37] which he practiced in bestowing his own shall discern that as the soul of man is all in all, and all in every part, so was the goodness of his nature equally dispersed into the greatest and least actions of his too short life. Which will of his will ever remain for a witness to the world that those sweet and large—even dying—affections in him could no more be contracted with the narrowness of pain, grief, or sickness than any sparkle of our immortality can be privately buried in the shadow of death.[38]

Here again this restless soul of his, changing only the air and not the chords of her harmony, calls for music, especially that song which himself had entitled "La Cuisse Rompue,"[39] partly (as I conceive by the name) to show that the glory of mortal flesh was shaken in him, and by that music itself to fashion and enfranchise his heavenly soul into that everlasting harmony of angels whereof these concords were a kind of terrestrial echo. And in this supreme or middle orb of contemplations he blessedly went on, within a circular motion, to the end of all flesh.

The last scene of this tragedy was the parting between the two brothers, the weaker showing infinite strength in suppressing sorrow and the stronger [i.e., Robert Sidney] infinite weakness in expressing of it. So far did invaluable worthiness in the dying brother enforce the living to descend beneath his own worth, and by abundance of childish tears bewail the public in his particular loss. Yea, so far was his true remission of mind transformed into ejulation[40] that Sir Philip (in whom all early passion did even as it were flash like lights ready to burn out) recalls those spirits together with a strong virtue but weak voice, mildly blaming him for relaxing the frail strengths left to support him in his final combat of separation at hand. And to stop this natural torrent of affection in both, took his leave with these admonishing words: "Love my memory, cherish my friends: their faith to me may assure you they are honest. But above all govern your will and affections by the will and word of your Creator, in me beholding the end of this world with all her vanities."

And with this farewell desired the company to lead him away. Here this noble gentleman ended the too short scene, his life, in which path whosoever is not confident that he walked the next[41] way to eternal rest will be found to judge uncharitably.

[35]*In respect...that*: because. [36]Path, course.
[37]Duties, moral obligations.
[38]In his will Sidney was principally concerned with bequests for his friends and dependents.
[39]"The Broken Leg." This song has not survived. [40]Lamentation.
[41]Nearest.

Ben Jonson [1572/3-1637]

from Conversations with Drummond[1]

INFORMATIONS BY BEN JONSON TO WILLIAM DRUMMOND WHEN HE CAME TO SCOTLAND UPON FOOT 1619

Certain Informations and Manners of Ben Jonson's to William Drummond

1

That he had an intention to perfect an epic poem entitled *Heroölogia*[2] of the worthies of his country roused by fame, and was to dedicate it to his country. It is all in couplets, for he detesteth all other rhymes. Said he had written a discourse of poesy both against Campion and Daniel, especially this last; where he proves couplets to be the bravest sort of verses, especially when they are broken, like hexameters; and that cross-rhymes and stanzas (because the purpose would lead him beyond eight lines to conclude) were all forced.[3]

2

He recommended to my reading Quintilian (who, he said, would tell me the faults of my verses as if he had lived with me) and Horace, Plinius Secundus' epistles, Tacitus, Juvenal, Martial, whose epigram, "*Vitam quae faciunt beatiorem, etc.*" he hath translated.[4]

3

His censure of the English poets was this:

That Sidney did not keep a decorum in making everyone speak as well as himself.[5] Spenser's stanzas pleased him not, nor his matter; the meaning of which allegory he had delivered in papers to Sir Walter Raleigh.[6]

Samuel Daniel was a good, honest man; had no children; but no poet.

That Michael Drayton's *Poly-Olbion*[7] if [he] had performed what he promised (to write the deeds of all the worthies) had been excellent. His long verses pleased him not.[8]

That Sylvester's translation of Du Bartas was not well done, and that he wrote his verses before it, ere he understood to confer.[9] Nor that of Fairfax his.[10]

That the translations of Homer and Virgil in long alexandrines were but prose.[11]

That John Harington's Ariosto, under all translations, was the worst.[12]

That when Sir John Harington desired him to tell the truth of his epigrams, he answered him that he loved not the truth, for they were narrations and not epigrams.[13]

That Warner, since the King's coming to England, had marred all his *Albion's England*.[14]

That Donne's *Anniversary* was profane and full of blasphemies. That he told Master Donne if it had been written of the Virgin Mary, it had been something; to which he answered that he described the idea of a woman, and not as she was.[15]

That Donne, for not keeping of accent, deserved hanging.

That Shakespeare wanted art. . . .[16]

7

He esteemeth John Donne the first poet in the world in some things. His verses of the lost chain[17] he hath by heart, and that passage of "The Calm," that dust and feathers do not stir, all was so quiet.[18] Affirmeth Donne to have written all his best pieces ere he was twenty-five years old.

Sir Henry[19] Wotton's verses of a happy life[20] he hath by heart, and a piece of Chapman's translation of the thirteenth[21] of the *Iliads*, which he thinketh well done.

That Donne said to him he wrote the epitaph on Prince Henry, "Look to me, Faith,"[22] to match Sir Edward Herbert in obscureness.[23]

[1]For a commentary on Jonson and for other excerpts from his work see Poetry, pp. 86 ff.

CONVERSATIONS WITH DRUMMOND   [1]Although a garbled version of Drummond's manuscript (which subsequently disappeared) was prepared for the folio edition of his collected *Works* in 1711, fortunately a much more careful version had been made by the Edinburgh physician and antiquarian Sir Robert Sibbald (1641–1722). This transcription, now preserved in the National Library of Scotland, was reproduced by C. H. Herford and Percy Simpson in the first volume (1925) of their great edition of Jonson's works, and forms the basis of my text. For comment on the *Conversations* see pp. 87, 142 f.

[2]Heroic tales. Jonson did not fulfill this plan.

[3]See p. 688, for Daniel's comments on the couplet.

[4]That these were among Jonson's favorite classical authors is shown by his use of them (and especially of Quintilian) in his *Discoveries* (pp. 698 ff.). The tag from Martial (*Epigrams*, X.47) means "the things that make life happier."

[5]Jonson's criticism is directed to *Arcadia*, Sir Philip Sidney's great romance that was published in an unauthorized edition in 1590 and in a more reliable version in 1593. See p. 691, n.19.

[6]Although Jonson is perhaps alluding to "A Letter of the Author's" that Spenser addressed to Raleigh and printed as a sort of preface to the first (1590) installment of *The Faerie Queene*, Bks. I–III, the remarks on Spenser's allegory in Section 12 below (p. 695) suggest that he had access to another document that has not survived.

[7]Text *Polyobion*.

[8]The first eighteen "Songs" of Drayton's massive *Poly-Olbion* (see pp. 33 ff.) appeared in 1612, the last twelve in 1622, all in the *long verses* of hexameter couplets.

[9]*That Sylvester's . . . confer*: Jonson's commendatory sonnet to Joshua Sylvester (see p. 92)—which was included in the 1605 edition of *Divine Weeks and Works*—was written before he knew enough French (*ere he understood to confer*) to assess the merits of the translation.

[10]Edward Fairfax's notable translation (in *ottava rima*) of Tasso's *Gerusalemme Liberata* was published as *Godfrey of Bulloigne* in 1600.

[11]There had been two English versions of Homer in septenary couplets (which is apparently what Jonson means by "long alexandrines"): Arthur Hall's clumsy rendition (of the French of Hagues Salel) as *Ten Books of Homer's Iliads* (1581) and George Chapman's vigorous *Iliads of Homer, Prince of Poets* (1598–1611). For his *Odyssey* (1614–16), however, Chapman used heroic couplets. An earlier translation of Vergil's *Aeneid*—begun by Thomas Phaer (1558) and completed by Thomas Twyne (1584)—had lumbered along in fourteeners.

[12]Like Fairfax later, Sir John Harington used *ottava rima* for his *Orlando Furioso in English Heroical Verse* (1591). Here, as in Milton's description of the meter of *Paradise Lost* as "English heroic verse," the term *heroical* means merely iambic pentameter.

[13]*Narrations . . . epigrams*: harmless fictions without the sting of truth. Harington's *Epigrams Both Pleasant and Serious* had appeared in 1615.

[14]The first of many installments of William Warner's popular versified history of England (in septenary couplets) had appeared in 1586. By 1606 he had brought the story down to the "happy reign" of James I, who succeeded to the throne in 1603.

[15]Donne's two *Anniversaries*—*An Anatomy of the World* (1611) and *The Progress of the Soul* (1612)—were written as annual commemorations of young Elizabeth Drury (d. 1610). See pp. 75 ff.

[16]See *Discoveries*, p. 700.   [17]"The Bracelet" (Elegy xi).

[18]"No use of lanthorns, and in one place lay/Feathers and dust, today and yesterday" (ll.17 f.).   [19]Text *Edward*.

[20]"The Character of a Happy Life" (p. 719). Jonson's own manuscript copy of this poem (which differs slightly from the printed text) survives at Dulwich.   [21]The thirteenth book.

[22]*Poems*, ed. Grierson, I, 267–70. For other comments on Henry, Prince of Wales (d. 1612), one of the most generous literary patrons of the age, see pp. 833, 874.

[23]For Edward, Lord Herbert, see pp. 114 ff.

He hath by heart some verses of Spenser's *Calender* about wine, between Cuddie[24] and Percie.

8

The conceit of Donne's transformation, or μετεμψύχωσις was that he sought the soul of that apple which Eva pulled, and thereafter made it the soul of a bitch, then of a she-wolf, and so of a woman. His general purpose was to have brought in all the bodies of the heretics from the soul of Cain, and at last left it in the body of Calvin.[25] Of this he never wrote but one sheet, and now, since he was made Doctor, repenteth highly and seeketh to destroy all his poems.[26]

10

For a heroic poem, he said, there was no such ground as King Arthur's fiction, and that Sir P. Sidney had an intention to have transformed all his *Arcadia* to the stories of King Arthur.[27]

11

His acquaintance and behavior with poets living with him:
    Daniel was at jealousies with him.
    Drayton feared him, and he esteemed not of him. . . .
    He beat Marston and took his pistol from him. . . .[28]
    That Chapman and Fletcher[29] were loved of him.
    Overbury was first his friend, then turned his mortal enemy.[30]

12

Particulars of the actions of other poets, and apothegms:
    That the Irish having robbed Spenser's goods and burnt his house, and a little child new born, he and his wife escaped; and after, he died for lack of bread in King Street, and refused twenty pieces sent to him by my Lord of Essex, and said he was sorry he had no time to spend them.[31]
    That in that paper Sir W. Raleigh had of the allegories of his *Faerie Queene*, by the Blatant Beast the Puritans were understood; by the false Duessa, the Queen of Scots.[32]
    That Southwell was hanged, yet, so he had written that piece of his, "The Burning Babe," he would have been content to destroy many of his. . . .[33]
    Donne's grandfather on the mother side was Heywood the Epigrammist.[34]
    That Donne himself, for not being understood, would perish.
    That Sir W. Raleigh esteemed more of fame than conscience.
    The best wits of England were employed for making of his *History*. Ben himself had written a piece to him of the Punic War, which he altered and set in his book. Sir W[alter] hath written the life of Queen Elizabeth, of which there is copies extant.[35]
    Sir P. Sidney had translated some of the Psalms, which went abroad under the name of the Countess of Pembroke. . . .[36]
    Shakespeare, in a play, brought in a number of men saying they had suffered shipwrack in Bohemia, where there is no sea near by some one hundred miles.[37]
    Daniel wrote *Civil Wars* and yet hath not one battle in all his book. . . .[38]

Sir P. Sidney was no pleasant man in countenance, his face being spoiled with pimples, and of high blood, and long.

[24]Text *Coline*. The passage that Jonson memorized is from the "October" eclogue of *The Shepherdes Calender* (1579).
[25]As printed in the *Poems* of 1633, Donne's "Infinitati Sacrum, 16 Augusti 1601. Metempsychosis" (*Poems*, ed. Grierson, I, 293–316), an obscure and cynical work on transmigration, reveals significant differences from the work that Jonson described to Drummond. Among others, it has the "deathless soul" of heresy reach its final residence not in Calvin, but in Queen Elizabeth, "the great soul which here amongst us now/Doth dwell."
[26]After a long period of hardship and indecision, Donne, who was born a Roman Catholic, was ordained a minister of the Anglican Church in 1615, and thereafter his success as a preacher was such that in only six years he had risen to be dean of St. Paul's. Izaak Walton reports that in his "penitential years" he wished that his poems—"most of them being written before the twentieth year of his age"—had been "abortive or so short-lived that his own eyes had witnessed their funerals."
[27]Although the so-called "New" *Arcadia* (1590)—Sidney's uncompleted revision of the original "Old" *Arcadia*—shows no trace of this design, both Milton and Dryden later considered writing an Arthuriad.
[28]John Marston (1575?–1634), poet and playwright whose extravagances in style and plotting were ridiculed by Jonson in *Poetaster* (1601). Marston's retaliation in *Satiromastix* (1602) kept alive the so-called War of the Theaters that Jonson alludes to in Section 13 below.
[29]John Fletcher (1579–1625), one of the ablest and most prolific playwrights of the period. In addition to the dozen or so plays that he wrote (between about 1606 and 1616) in collaboration with Francis Beaumont (1584–1616), he also worked with such dramatists as Philip Massinger and William Rowley—and perhaps even Shakespeare (on *Henry VIII* and *The Two Noble Kinsmen*).
[30]Although Jonson had addressed an epigram to Sir Thomas Overbury (See pp. 715 f.), they quarreled, as reported elsewhere in the *Conversations*, over the poet's refusal to act as go-between in his friend's intrigue with the countess of Rutland.
[31]Although it is reliably reported (by William Camden) that Spenser was buried "at the charges of the earl of Essex," Jonson's lurid account of the poet's final months has been generally rejected by modern scholars.
[32]*The Blatant Beast* (*The Faerie Queene*, Bk. VI) is a foul monster with many tongues (usually thought to personify slander) that is captured by and then escapes from Sir Calidore. *Duessa* is a loathsome old woman who, disguised as young and beautiful, personifies duplicity and evil. Although apparently personifying the Roman Catholic Church in Book I, in Book V she clearly stands for Mary Queen of Scots.
[33]On Southwell see p. 895. "The Burning Babe," one of the most famous nativity poems in the language, begins, "As I in hoary winter's night stood shivering in the snow."
[34]John Heywood (1497?–?1580), author of *The Spider and the Fly* (1556) and of various interludes including *The Four P's*.
[35]On Jonson's contributions to Raleigh's *History of the World* (1614) see p. 861. The life of Queen Elizabeth has not survived.
[36]The metrical version of the Psalms by Sidney and his sister (to which Sidney contributed Nos. 1–43) remained in manuscript until 1823, when they were published as *The Psalmes of David Translated into Divers and Sundry Kindes of Verse*.
[37]Shakespeare took the quaint geography of *The Winter's Tale* III.iii from Robert Greene's *Pandosto* (1588), his principal source for the play.
[38]Jonson's complaint about *The Civil Wars* (see pp. 28 ff.) is without foundation, for the work is thickly strewn with scenes of battle.

That my Lord Lisle, now earl of Leicester,[39] his eldest son, resembleth him.

13

Of his own life, education, birth, actions:

His grandfather came from Carlisle, and he thought from Annandale to it; he served King Henry VIII, and was a gentleman. His father losed all his estate under Queen Mary, having been cast in prison and forefeited, at last turned minister; so he was a minister's son. He himself was posthumous born a month after his father's decease, brought up poorly, put to school by a friend (his master, Camden);[40] after, taken from it and put to another craft (I think was to be a wright or bricklayer), which he could not endure. Then went he to the Low Countries, but, returning soon, he betook himself to his wonted studies. In his service in the Low Countries, he had, in the face of both the camps, killed an enemy and taken *opima spolia*[41] from him; and since his coming to England, being appealed to the fields,[42] he had killed his adversary, which had hurt him in the arm, and whose sword was ten inches longer than his; for the which he was imprisoned, and almost at the gallows. Then took he his religion by trust, of a priest who visited him in prison. Thereafter he was twelve years a papist.

He was Master of Arts in both the universities by their favor, not his study.[43]

He married a wife who was a shrew, yet honest. Five years he had not bedded with her, but remained with my Lord Aubigny.[44]

In the time of his close imprisonment under Queen Elizabeth, his judges could get nothing of him, to all their demands, but ay and no. They placed two damned villains, to catch advantage of him, with him; but he was advertised by his keeper. Of the spies he hath an epigram.[45]

When the King came in England, at that time the pest was in London, he being in the country at Sir Robert Cotton's house[46] with old Camden, he saw in a vision his eldest son (then a child and at London) appear to him with the mark of a bloody cross on his forehead, as if it had been cutted with a sword; at which, amazed, he prayed unto God, and in the morning he came to Master Camden's chamber to tell him, who persuaded him it was but an apprehension of his fantasy, at which he should not be disjected. In the meantime comes there letters from his wife, of the death of that boy in the plague. He appeared to him, he said, of a manly shape, and of that growth that he thinks he shall be at the resurrection.[47]

He was delated[48] by Sir James Murray to the King for writing something against the Scots in a play, *Eastward Ho*, and voluntarily imprisoned himself with Chapman and Marston, who had written it amongst them. The report was that they should then had their ears cut, and noses. After their delivery, he banqueted all his friends; there was Camden, Selden,[49] and others. At the midst of the feast, his old mother drank to him, and shew him a paper which she had (if the sentence had taken execution) to have mixed in the prison among his drink, which was full of lusty,

strong poison. And that she was not churl,[50] she told, she minded first to have drunk of it herself.

He had many quarrels with Marston, beat him and took his pistol from him, wrote his *Poetaster* on him. The beginning of them were that Marston represented him in the stage.

In his youth, given to venery. He thought the use of a maid nothing in comparison to the wantonness of a wife, and would never have another mistress. He said two accidents strange befell him: one, that a man made his own wife to court him, whom he enjoyed two years ere he knew of it, and one day finding them by chance, was passingly delighted with it; one other, lay divers times with a woman who shew him all that he wished, except the last act, which she would never agree unto.

Sir W. Raleigh sent him governor with his son,[51] *Anno* 1613, to France. This youth, being knavishly inclined, among other pastimes (as the setting of the favor of damosels on a codpiece) caused him to be drunken and dead drunk, so that he knew not where he was; thereafter laid him on a car, which he made to be drawn by pioneers[52] through the streets, at every corner showing his governor stretched out, and telling them that was a more lively image of the crucifix than any they had. At which sport young Raleigh's mother delighted much, saying his father young was so inclined, though the father abhorred it.[53]

He can set horoscopes, but trusts not in them. He, with the consent of a friend, cozened a lady with whom he had made

[39]Text *Worster* (i.e., Worcester). The sentence refers to the eldest son (i.e., Robert Sidney) of Sir Philip's brother Robert (1563–1626), Viscount Lisle and earl of Leicester. Sir Philip had no sons.

[40]For Jonson's poetical tribute to the great antiquarian, his master at Westminster School, see p. 89.

[41]The arms taken by one general from another.

[42]Challenged to a duel. As recorded in Jonson's subsequent indictment for murder (October 1598), the place of the encounter was Hoxton Fields beyond Shoreditch (a district of London) and the victim was one Gabriel Spencer, an actor of Philip Henslowe's company. Although branded on the thumb as a felon, Jonson escaped execution by pleading benefit of clergy (at that time a legal measure available to laymen).

[43]Although Oxford conferred on Jonson an honorary degree in 1619 (following his trip to Scotland) there is no record of Cambridge doing likewise.

[44]Text *Aulbanie*. Esmé Stuart (1579–1624), seigneur of Aubigny and duke of Lennox, a naturalized Englishman and leading Catholic propagandist, was the generous patron to whom Jonson dedicated *Sejanus* in the Folio of 1616.   [45]No. 59.

[46]Conington in Huntingdonshire. See p. 753.

[47]Jonson movingly commemorated the death of his son in Epigram 45 (pp. 89 f.).

[48]Reported, accused. The hurly-burly resulting from the alleged slurs on the Scots in *Eastward Ho* (III.ii) occurred in 1605.

[49]See pp. 852 ff.   [50]Baseborn.

[51]Walter Raleigh the younger, who was killed in his father's disastrous expedition to New Guiana in 1618.

[52]In military usage, soldiers who dig trenches and otherwise prepare the way for the troops who follow them.

[53]*His father young . . . abhorred it*: Sir Walter Raleigh when young and when middle-aged.

an appointment to meet an old astrologer in the suburbs; which she kept, and it was himself disguised in a long gown and a white beard, at the light of [a][54] dim-burning candle, up in a little cabinet reached unto by a ladder.

Every first day of the new year, he had twenty pounds sent him from the earl of Pembroke[55] to buy books.

After he was reconciled with the church and left off to be a recusant, at his first communion, in token of true reconciliation, he drank out all the full cup of wine.[56]

Being at the end of my Lord Salisbury's table with Inigo Jones, and demanded by my Lord why he was not glad, "My Lord," said he, "you promised I should dine with you, but I do not." For he had none of his meat; he esteemed only that his meat which was of his own dish.[57]

He hath consumed a whole night in lying looking to his toe, about which he hath seen Tartars and Turks, Romans and Carthaginians, fight in his imagination.

Northampton was his mortal enemy for brawling,[58] on a Saint George's day,[59] one of his attenders. He was called before the Council for his *Sejanus*, and accused both of popery and treason by him.[60]

Sundry times he hath devoured his books, i.e. sold them all for necessity.

He hath a mind to be a churchman, and so he might have favor to make one sermon to the King, he careth not what thereafter should befall him; for he would not flatter, though he saw Death. . . .

14

His narrations of great ones:

He never esteemed of a man for the name of a Lord. . . .

Sir P. Sidney's mother, Leicester's sister,[61] after she had the little pox never shew herself in court thereafter but masked.

The Earl of Leicester gave a bottle of liquor to his lady which he willed her to use in any faintness, which she, after his return from court, not knowing it was poison, gave him, and so he died. . . . [62]

The King said Sir P. Sidney was no poet; neither did he see ever any verses in England to the Sculler's.[63]

It were good that the half of the preachers of England were plain ignorants[64] for that either in their sermons they flatter or strive to show their own eloquence.

15

His opinion of verses:

That he wrote all his first in prose, for so his master Camden had learned him.

That verses stood by sense, without either colors or accent;[65] which yet other times he denied.

A great many epigrams were ill because they expressed in the end what should have been understood by what was said. . . . .

18

Miscellanies:

John Stow[66] had monstrous observations in his *Chronicle*, and was of craft a tailor.

He and I[67] walking alone, he asked two cripples what they would have to take him to their order.

In his *Sejanus* he hath translated a whole oration of Tacitus.[68]

The first four books of Tacitus ignorantly done in English. . . . [69]

He dissuaded me from poetry, for that she had beggared him when he might have been a rich lawyer, physician, or merchant. . . .

He was better versed, and knew more in Greek and Latin,

---

[54]Not in text.

[55]Jonson dedicated his *Catiline* (1611) and *Epigrams* (1616) to this great patron of letters, and celebrated him in Epigram 102. See pp. 88 f., 683.

[56]To show that he was once again a Protestant (the sacramental wine not being extended to the laity in the Catholic Eucharist). As he told Drummond (Sect. 13 above), Jonson became a Catholic during his imprisonment in 1598 and returned to the Church of England twelve years later.

[57]The incident perhaps occurred in 1607, when Robert Cecil (1563?–1612), earl of Salisbury and secretary of state, turned over his great mansion at Theobalds Park just north of London for the production of *An Entertainment of King James and Queen Anne*, the collaboration of Jonson and the scenic designer Inigo Jones (1573–1652). Despite their close association, these two artists were notoriously antagonistic. As the leading architect of the period, Jones numbered among his triumphs such buildings as the Queen's House at Greenwich and the Banqueting House at Whitehall, from which Charles I stepped to his execution in 1649.

[58]Scolding, reviling. [59]April 23.

[60]For Henry Howard, earl of Northampton and son of the famous earl of Surrey who had contributed to *Tottel's Miscellany*, see p. 896. Although perhaps a Spanish agent and certainly (as Bacon's mother said) "a subtle papist inwardly," Northampton was showered with honors by James, and it was as a member of the Privy Council—and in the anomalous role of Protestant watchdog —that he interrogated Jonson about his *Sejanus* (acted 1603, printed 1605).

[61]Mary Dudley (d. 1586), daughter of the powerful John Dudley, duke of Northumberland, sister of the earl of Leicester who was the favorite of young Queen Elizabeth, and mother of Sir Philip Sidney and Mary, countess of Pembroke. Having nursed the queen through the smallpox in 1562, she herself contracted the disease, which left her badly scarred. See p. 690, n.4.

[62]The marital career of Robert Dudley (1532?–1586), earl of Leicester, was sensational. Widely thought to have contrived the murder of his first wife, Amye, in order to become the consort of the queen herself, in 1573, two days before the birth of their son he secretly married Lady Sheffield, whose husband he was rumored to have poisoned. Following the death of his second wife (perhaps by poison), in 1578 he married the widowed countess of Essex whose son, the second earl of Essex, was to dominate and darken the aging queen's last years. Whatever the circumstances of Leicester's death, his countess was known to be infatuated with Christopher Blount, whom she married (ca. 1589) as soon as she was free. [63]See p. 699, n. 27 [64]Dunces.

[65]Stylistic embellishment or meter. [66]See pp. 807 ff.

[67]Stow and Jonson. Stow's poverty was notorious.

[68]The speech of Cremutius Cordus (see p. 893, n. 11) in *Sejanus*, Act III, lls. 407–60, based upon *The Annals*, IV. 34–35.

[69]Jonson is referring to Richard Greneway's translation of 1598, not to Sir Henry Savile's of 1591 (on which see p. 894, n. 16).

than all the poets in England, and quintessenceth[70] their brains. . . .

19

. . . He is a great lover and praiser of himself, a contemner and scorner of others; given rather to lose a friend than a jest, jealous of every word and action of those about him (especially after drink, which is one of the elements in which he liveth). A dissembler of ill parts which reign in him, a bragger of some good that he wanteth; thinketh nothing well but what either he himself, or some of his friends and countrymen, hath said or done. He is passionately kind and angry, careless either to gain or keep: vindictive, but—if he be well answered—at himself.

For any religion, as being versed in both.

Interpreteth best sayings and deeds often to the worst.

Oppressed with fantasy, which hath ever mastered his reason, a general disease in many poets. His inventions are smooth and easy, but above all he excelleth in a translation.

When his play of a silent woman was first acted there was found verses after on the stage against him, concluding that that play was well named *The Silent Woman*; there was never one man to say *plaudite*[71] to it.

Finis

[70]Text *quintessence*. The word means to extract the quintessence of.
[71]"Applaud!" *Epicoene, or the Silent Woman* was acted in 1609 and apparently first printed in the 1616 Folio.

from Timber or Discoveries (1641)

Fortuna[1]

Ill fortune never crushed that man whom good fortune deceived not. I therefore have counseled my friends never to trust to her fairer side though she seemed to make peace with them, but to place all things she gave them so as she might ask them again without their trouble. She might take them from them, not pull them, to keep always a distance between her and themselves. He knows not his own strength that hath not met adversity. Heaven prepares good men with crosses, but no ill can happen to a good man. Contraries are not mixed. Yet that which happens to any man may to every man. But it is in his reason what he accounts it and will make it.

Applausus[2]

We praise the things we hear with much more willingness than those we see because we envy the present and reverence the past, thinking ourselves instructed by the one and overlaid by the other.

Opinio[3]

Opinion[4] is a light, vain, crude, and imperfect thing, settled in the imagination, but never arriving at the understanding, there to obtain the tincture of reason. We labour with it more than truth. There is much more holds us than presseth us. An ill fact is one thing, an ill fortune is another. Yet both oftentimes sway us alike by the error of our thinking.

Impostura[5]

Many men believe not themselves what they would persuade others; and less, do the things which they would impose on others; but least of all, know what they themselves most confidently boast. Only they set the sign of the cross over their outer doors, and sacrifice to their gut and their groin in their inner closets.

Iactura vitae[6]

What a deal of cold business doth a man misspend the better part of life in! in scattering compliments, tendering visits, gathering and venting news, following feasts and plays, making a little winter love in a dark corner.

Vita recta[7]

Wisdom without honesty is mere craft and cozenage. And therefore the reputation of honesty must first be gotten, which cannot be but by living well. A good life is a main argument.

Perspicuitas[8]

A man should so deliver himself to the nature of the subject whereof he speaks that his hearer may take knowledge of his discipline with some delight; and so apparel fair and good matter that the studious of elegancy be not defrauded. Redeem arts from their rough and braky[9] seats, where they lay hid and overgrown with thorns, to a pure, open, and

TIMBER OR DISCOVERIES [1]Such sectional titles (which in the 1641 Folio are indicated in the margins) and the Latin tags throughout the text are translated in the notes only when Jonson himself does not provide a gloss. This section is based on Seneca, *Consolatio ad Helviam*, v.4, and *De tranquillitate*, xi.8.
[2]Based on Velleius Paterculus, *Historia Romana*, ii.92.
[3]Based in part on Seneca, *Epistulae morales*, xiii.4. [4]Reputation.
[5]"Imposture."
[6]"Waste of life." Based on Pliny, *Epistolae*, I.ix, and Quintilian, *Institutio oratoria*, XII.xi.18.
[7]"An upright life." This section, as well as several preceding and following it in the 1641 Folio, is based on *De consultatione* by Juan Luis Vives (1492–1540), the great Spanish humanist who, after Sir Thomas More had introduced him to the English court, lectured at Oxford and served as tutor to Princess Mary.
[8]"Perspicuity." This section and the three following are based on Vives, *In libros de disciplinis praefatio.* [9]Brambly.

flowery light, where they may take the eye and be taken by the hand.

Natura non effoeta[10]

I cannot think Nature is so spent and decayed that she can bring forth nothing worth her former years. She is always the same, like herself; and when she collects her strength is abler still. Men are decayed, and studies; she is not.

Non nimium credendum antiquitati[11]

I know nothing can conduce more to letters than to examine the writings of the ancients, and not to rest in their sole authority or take all upon trust from them, provided the plagues of judging and pronouncing against them be away, such as are envy, bitterness, precipitation,[12] impudence, and scurrile[13] scoffing. For to all the observations of the ancients we have our own experience, which, if we will use and apply, we have better means to pronounce. It is true they opened the gates and made the way that went before us, but as guides, not commanders: *non domini nostri, sed duces fuere.* Truth lies open to all; it is no man's several.[14] *Patet omnibus veritas, nondum est occupata. Multum ex illa etiam futuris relictum[15] est.*

Dissentire licet sed cum ratione[16]

If in some things I dissent from others whose wit, industry, diligence, and judgment I look up at and admire, let me not therefore hear presently of ingratitude and rashness. For I thank those that have taught me, and will ever, but yet dare not think the scope of their labor and inquiry was to envy their posterity what they also could add and find out.

Bellum scribentium[17]

What a sight it is to see writers committed together by the ears for ceremonies, syllables, points, colons, commas, hyphens, and the like, fighting as for their fires and their altars, and angry that none are frighted at their noises and loud brayings under the asses' skins.

Vulgi expectatio[18]

Expectation of the vulgar is more drawn and held with newness than goodness. We see it in fencers, in players, in poets, in preachers, in all where Fame promiseth anything. So it be new, though never so naught[19] and depraved, they run to it and are taken, which shows that the only decay or hurt of the best men's reputation with the people is their wits have outlived the people's palates. They have been too much or too long a feast.

Veritas proprium hominis[20]

Truth is man's proper good, and the only immortal thing was given our mortality to use. No good Christian or ethnic,[21] if he be honest, can miss it; no statesman or patriot should. For without truth all the actions of mankind are craft, malice, or what you will, rather than wisdom. Homer[22] says he hates him worse than hell-mouth that utters one thing with his tongue and keeps another in his breast. Which high expression was grounded on divine reason, for a lying mouth is a stinking pit, and murthers with the contagion it venteth. Beside, nothing is lasting that is feigned; it will have another face than it had ere long. As Euripides saith, "No lie ever grows old."[23]

Censura de poetis[24]

Nothing in our age, I have observed, is more preposterous than the running judgments upon poetry and poets, when we shall hear those things commended, and cried up for the best writings, which a man would scarce vouchsafe to wrap any wholesome drug in; he would never light his tobacco with them. And those men almost named for miracles who yet are so vile that if man should go about to examine and correct them he must make all they have done but one blot. Their good is so entangled with their bad as forcibly one must draw on the other's death with it. A sponge, dipped in ink, will do all:

> comitetur Punica librum
> spongea.
> *Et paulo post:*
>
> Non possunt . . . multae, . . . una litura potest.[25]

Yet their vices have not hurt them. Nay, a great many they have profited, for they have been loved for nothing else. And this false opinion grows strong against the best men, if once it take root with the ignorant. Cestius, in his time, was preferred to Cicero,[26] so far as the ignorant durst. They learned him without book, and had him often in their mouths. But a man cannot imagine that thing so foolish or rude but will find and enjoy an admirer, at least a reader or spectator. The puppets are seen now in despite of the players. Heath's epigrams and the Sculler's poems[27] have their applause. There are never wanting that dare prefer the worst preachers, the worst pleaders, the worst poets; not that the better have left to write or speak better, but that they that hear them judge worse. *Non illi peius dicunt, sed hi corruptius iudicant.* Nay, if it were put to the question of the Water-Rhymer's works against Spenser's, I doubt not but they

[10]"Nature not decayed."
[11]"Antiquity not to be too much relied on."
[12]Inconsiderate haste. [13]Scurrilous. [14]Private possession.
[15]Text *relicta.*
[16]"It is permissible to dissent, but with reason."
[17]"War of writers."
[18]Based on Marcus Annaeus Seneca, *Controversiae,* Bk. IV, preface. [19]Wicked. [20]Based on Justus Lipsius, *Politica,* I.i.
[21]Pagan. [22]*Iliad,* IX. 312–13.
[23]Apparently a fragment of Sophocles' lost *Acrisius,* conventionally but mistakenly attributed to Euripides.
[24]"Judgments upon poetry."
[25]" 'Let a Punic sponge accompany the book.' And shortly later: 'Many corrections cannot suffice, but one sponging [i.e., erasure] could' " (Martial, *Epigrams,* IV.x).
[26]Lucius Cestius Pius, orator and teacher of the Augustan age, was noted for his dislike of his great predecessor Cicero.
[27]The poetaster John Heath (fl. 1615) published *Two Centuries of Epigrams* (1610); John Taylor (1580–1653), a prolific writer of doggerel known as the "Water-Poet" or "Sculler" from his occupation as a Thames waterman, published his *Works* in 1630.

would find more suffrages;[28] because the most favor common vices, out of a prerogative the vulgar have to lose their judgments and like that which is naught.

Poetry, in this latter age, hath proved but a mean mistress to such as have wholly addicted themselves to her or given their names up to her family. They who have but saluted her on the by,[29] and now and then tendered their visits, she hath done much for, and advanced in the way of their own professions (both the law and the gospel) beyond all they could have hoped, or done for themselves, without her favor. Wherein she doth emulate the judicious but preposterous bounty of the time's grandees, who accumulate all they can upon the parasite or freshman[30] in their friendship, but think an old client or honest servant bound, by his place, to write and starve.

Indeed, the multitude commend writers as they do fencers or wrastlers, who, if they come in robustiously and put for it with a deal of violence, are received for the braver fellows, when many times their own rudeness is a cause of their disgrace, and a slight touch of their adversary gives all that boisterous force the foil. But in these things the unskilful are naturally deceived, and, judging wholly by the bulk, think rude things greater than polished, and scattered more numerous than composed.[31] Nor think this only to be true in the sordid multitude, but the neater sort of our gallants; for all are the multitude, only they differ in clothes, not in judgment or understanding.

De Shakespeare nostrati[32]

I remember, the players have often mentioned it as an honor to Shakespeare that in his writing, whatsoever he penned, he never blotted out line. My answer hath been, "Would he had blotted a thousand!" Which they thought a malevolent speech. I had not told posterity this but for their ignorance who choose that circumstance to commend their friend by wherein he most faulted; and to justify mine own candor, for I loved the man, and do honor his memory (on this side idolatry) as much as any. He was, indeed, honest and of an open and free nature; had an excellent fancy, brave notions, and gentle expressions; wherein he flowed with that facility that sometime it was necessary he should be stopped. *Sufflaminandus erat*, as Augustus said of Haterius.[33] His wit was in his own power; would the rule of it had been so too. Many times he fell into those things could not escape laughter: as when he said in the person of Caesar, one speaking to him, "Caesar, thou dost me wrong," he replied, "Caesar did never wrong, but with just cause";[34] and suchlike, which were ridiculous. But he redeemed his vices with his virtues. There was ever more in him to be praised than to be pardoned.

Ingeniorum discrimina[35]

In the difference of wits, I have observed, there are many notes. And it is a little mastery to know them, to discern what every nature, every disposition, will bear. For before we sow our land we should plough it. There are no fewer forms of minds than of bodies amongst us. The variety is incredible, and therefore we must search. Some are fit to make divines, some poets, some lawyers, some physicians; some to be sent to the plow and trades.

There is no doctrine will do good where nature is wanting. Some wits are swelling and high, others low and still; some hot and fiery, others cold and dull. One must have a bridle, the other a spur.

There be some that are forward and bold, and these will do every little thing easily—I mean that is hard by, and next them; which they will utter unretarded, without any shamefastness. These never perform much, but quickly. They are what they are on the sudden. They show presently like grain that, scattered on the top of the ground, shoots up but takes no root; has a yellow blade, but the ear empty. They are wits of good promise at first, but there is an *ingenistitium*;[36] they stand still at sixteen, they get no higher.

You have others that labor only to ostentation, and are ever more busy about the colors and surface of a work than in the matter and foundation. For that is hid, the other is seen.

Others that in composition are nothing but what is rough and broken. *Quae per salebras altaque saxa cadunt.*[37] And if it would come gently, they trouble it of purpose. They would not have it run without rubs,[38] as if that style were more strong and manly that stroke [39] the ear with a kind of unevenness. These men err not by chance, but knowingly and willingly. They are like men that affect a fashion by themselves; have some singularity in a ruff, cloak, or hat-band; or their beards specially cut to provoke beholders and set a mark upon themselves. They would be reprehended while they are looked on. And this vice, one that is in authority with the rest, loving, delivers over to them to be imitated, so that ofttimes the faults which he fell into, the others seek for. This is the danger when vice becomes a precedent.[40]

Others there are that have no composition[41] at all, but a

[28]Votes. [29]Casually, as amateurs. [30]Newcomer.

[31]*Indeed . . . composed*: This passage and the paragraph beginning "But the wretcheder" on p. 701—both of which Jonson used in a slightly altered form in the address "To the Reader" prefixed to *The Alchemist* (1612)—are based on Quintilian, *Institutio oratoria*, II.xii.1–3. [32]"Concerning our countryman Shakespeare."

[33]According to Marcus Annaeus Seneca, *Oratorum et rhetorum* (ed. H. S. Müller, 1887, p. 227), the Emperor Augustus found the oratory of the senator Quintus Haterius so fluent and facile that he said, "He ought to be clogged."

[34]The fact that this passage and a similar one in the introduction to Jonson's play *The Staple of News* (1626)—"Cry you mercy, you never did wrong but with just cause"—both slightly misquote *Julius Caesar*, III.i. 47–48 ("Know, Caesar doth not wrong, nor without cause/Will he be satisfied") suggests that Shakespeare's lines were perhaps altered from their original form when reprinted in the Folio of 1623.

[35]The first two paragraphs of this section are based on Quintilian, *Institutio oratoria*, II.viii.1–11, the third on I.iii.3.

[36]"A wit-stand" (Jonson's marginal gloss).

[37]"Which tumble over rough places and high rocks" (Martial, *Epigrams*, XI. xci). Jonson quotes the line in two other places in his *Discoveries*. [38]Impediments, deflections (a term from bowling). [39]Struck.

[40]*Others that in composition . . . precedent*: this paragraph is based on Seneca, *Epistulae morales*, cxiv.15, 21, 18. [41]Style.

kind of tuning and rhyming fall in what they write. It runs and slides and only makes a sound. Women's poets they are called, as you have women's tailors.

> They write a verse as smooth, as soft as cream,
> In which there is no torrent, nor scarce stream.[42]

You may sound these wits and find the depth of them with your middle finger. They are cream-bowl, or but puddle-deep.

Some that turn over all books and are equally searching in all papers; that write out of what they presently find or meet, without choice; by which means it happens that what they have discredited and impugned in one work, they have before or after extolled the same in another. Such are all the essayists, even their master, Montaigne.[43] These, in all they write, confess still what books they have read last, and therein their own folly, so much that they bring it to the stake raw and undigested; not that the place did need it neither, but that they thought themselves furnished, and would vent it.

Some again who—after they have got authority or (which is less) opinion by their writings to have read much—dare presently to feign whole books and authors, and lie safely. For what never was will not easily be found, not by the most curious.

And some, by a cunning protestation against all reading, and false vendition of their own naturals,[44] think to divert the sagacity of their readers from themselves and cool the scent of their own fox-like thefts, when yet they are so rank[45] as a man may find whole passages together usurped from one author. Their necessities compelling them to read for present use, which could not be in many books; and so come forth more ridiculously and palpably guilty than those who, because they cannot trace, they yet would slander their industry.

But the wretcheder are the obstinate contemners of all helps and arts, such as, presuming on their own naturals (which, perhaps, are excellent), dare deride all diligence and seem to mock at the terms when they understand not the things, thinking that way to get off wittily with their ignorance. These are imitated often by such as are their peers in negligence, though they cannot be in nature. And they utter all they can think with a kind of violence and indisposition, unexamined, without relation either to person, place, or any fitness else. And the more wilful and stubborn they are in it, the more learned they are esteemed of the multitude through their excellent vice of judgment, who think those things the stronger that have no art, as if to break were better than to open, or to rent asunder gentler than to loose.

It cannot but come to pass that these men who commonly seek to do more than enough may sometimes happen on something that is good and great, but very seldom. And when it comes, it doth not recompense the rest of their ill. For their jests and their sentences (which they only and ambitiously seek for) stick out and are more eminent because all is sordid and vile about them, as lights are more discerned in a thick darkness than a faint shadow. Now, because they speak all they can, however unfitly, they are thought to have the greater copy. Where the learned use ever election[46]

and a mean, they look back to what they intended at first, and make all an even and proportioned body. The true artificer will not run away from Nature as if he were afraid of her, or depart from life and the likeness of truth, but speak to the capacity of his hearers. And though his language differ from the vulgar somewhat, it shall not fly from all humanity with the Tamerlanes and Tamar Chams of the late age,[47] which had nothing in them but the scenical strutting and furious vociferation to warrant them to the ignorant gapers. He knows it is his only art so to carry it as none but artificers perceive it. In the meantime, perhaps, he is called barren, dull, lean, a poor writer, or by what contumelious word can come in their cheeks, by these men who, without labor, judgment, knowledge, or almost sense, are received or preferred before him. He gratulates[48] them and their fortune. Another age or juster men will acknowledge the virtues of his studies: his wisdom in dividing, his subtlety in arguing; with what strength he doth inspire his readers, with what sweetness he strokes them; in inveighing, what sharpness, in jest what urbanity he uses; how he doth reign in men's affections, how invade and break in upon them, and makes their minds like the thing he writes. Then in his elocution[49] to behold what word is proper; which hath ornament, which height; what is beautifully translated;[50] where figures are fit—which gentle, which strong—to show the composition manly. And how he hath avoided faint, obscure, obscene, sordid, humble, improper, or effeminate phrase; which is not only praised of the most, but commended, which is worse, especially for that it is naught.[51]

Ignorantia Animae[52]

I know no disease of the soul but ignorance, not of the arts and sciences but of itself; yet relating to those it is a pernicious evil, the darkener of man's life, the disturber of his reason, and common confounder of truth, with which a man goes groping in the dark no otherwise than if he were blind. Great understandings are most wracked and troubled with it; nay, sometimes they will rather choose to die than not to know the things they study for. Think, then, what an evil it is, and what good the contrary.

Scientia

Knowledge is the action of the soul, and is perfect without the senses, as having the seeds of all science and virtue in

[42]Jonson uses the same couplet in his masque *News from the New World* (1621), ll. 164–65. The allusion is perhaps to Samuel Daniel.
[43]Michel Eyquem de Montaigne (1533–92), whose *Essais* (1580, 1595) became widely known in England through John Florio's famous translation (1603). [44]Display of their own talents.
[45]Strong in odor (a term from hunting). [46]Selection.
[47]Jonson is alluding contemptuously to such old-fashioned, swashbuckling plays as Christopher Marlowe's immensely popular *Tamburlaine* (1587?) and, presumably, the lost *Tamar Cham*, which the theater manager Philip Henslowe mentions in his diary.
[48]Congratulates. [49]Eloquence. [50]Figuratively expressed.
[51]Based on Quintilian, *Institutio oratoria*, II.xi.5–7; II.xii.11,12.
[52]"Ignorance of the soul."

itself, but not without the service of the senses: by those organs the soul works; she is a perpetual agent, prompt and subtle, but often flexible and erring, entangling herself like a silkworm; but her reason is a weapon with two edges, and cuts through. In her indagations[53] ofttimes new scents put her by, and she takes in errors into her by the same conduits she doth truths.

Dominus Verulanus[54]

One, though he be excellent and the chief, is not to be imitated alone, for never no imitator ever grew up to his author: likeness is always on this side truth. Yet there happened in my time one noble speaker who was full of gravity in his speaking. His language (where he could spare, or pass by a jest) was nobly censorious.[55] No man ever spake more neatly, more pressly,[56] more weightily, or suffered less emptiness, less idleness in what he uttered. No member of his speech but consisted of his own graces. His hearers could not cough or look aside from him without loss. He commanded where he spoke, and had his judges angry and pleased at his devotion. No man had their affections more in his power. The fear of every man that heard him was lest he should make an end.

Scriptorum catalogus[57]

Cicero is said to be the only wit that the people of Rome had equalled to their empire. *Ingenium par imperio*.[58] We have had many, and in their several ages—to take in but the former *seculum*[59]—Sir Thomas More, the elder Wyatt, Henry, earl of Surrey, Chaloner, Smith, Elyot, Bishop Gardiner[60] were, for their times, admirable; and the more because they began eloquence with us. Sir Nicholas Bacon[61] was singular and almost alone at the beginning of Queen Elizabeth's times. Sir Philip Sidney[62] and Master Hooker,[63] in different matter, grew great masters of wit and language, and in whom all vigor of invention and strength of judgment met. The earl of Essex,[64] noble and high; and Sir Walter Raleigh,[65] not to be contemned either for judgment or style. Sir Henry Savile,[66] grave and truly lettered; Sir Edwin Sandys,[67] excellent in both; Lord Egerton,[68] the Chancellor, a grave and great orator, and best when he was provoked. But his learned and able, though unfortunate, successor is he who hath filled up all numbers, and performed that in our tongue which may be compared, or preferred, either to insolent Greece or haughty Rome. In short, within his view and about his times were all the wits born that could honor a language or help study. Now things daily fall, wits grow downward, and eloquence grows backward; so that he may be named, and stand, as the mark and ἀκμή[69] of our language.

De augmentis scientiarum[70]

I have ever observed it to have been the office of a wise patriot, among the greatest affairs of the state to take care of the commonwealth of learning. For schools, they are the seminaries of state; and nothing is worthier the study of a statesman than that part of the republic which we call the advancement of letters. Witness the care of Julius Caesar, who, in the heat of the Civil War, writ his books of analogy,[71] and dedicated them to Tully. This made the late Lord Saint Albans entitle his work *Novum Organum*.[72] Which though by the most of superficial men, who cannot get beyond the title of nominals,[73] it is not penetrated nor understood, it really openeth all defects of learning whatsoever, and is a book

Que longum noto scriptori prorogat aevum.[74]

My conceit of his person was never increased toward him by his place or honors. But I have and do reverence him for the greatness that was only proper to himself, in that he seemed to me ever, by his work, one of the greatest men, and most worthy of admiration, that had been in many ages. In his adversity,[75] I ever prayed that God would give him strength, for greatness he could not want. Neither could I condole, in a word or syllable, for him, as knowing no accident could do harm to virtue, but rather help to make it manifest.

Controversiales scriptores[76]

Some controverters in divinity are like swaggerers in a

[53]Investigations.
[54]"Master Verulam," i.e., Francis Bacon (1561–1626), First Baron Verulam and Viscount St. Albans. This passage on Bacon is virtually paraphrased from Marcus Annaeus Seneca's on Cassius Severus, *Contraversiae*, Bk. III, preface. [55]Grave, severe.
[56]Precisely. [57]"List of writers."
[58]"His intelligence [was] equal to the Empire." [59]"Age."
[60]Noted writers and public personages of the early Tudor period: Sir Thomas More (1480–1534), author of *Utopia* and Lord Chancellor; Sir Thomas Wyatt (1516–42) and Henry, earl of Surrey (1516–47), courtiers and poets, some of whose works were collected in *Tottel's Miscellany* (1557); Sir Thomas Chaloner (1521–65), diplomat and translator (1549) of Erasmus' *Praise of Folly*; Sir Thomas Smith (1513–77), eminent statesman and scholar whose important treatise on the Tudor constitution, *De republica Anglorum*, was published (in English) in 1583; Sir Thomas Elyot (1490–1546), author of *The Book Named the Governor* (1531) and of a Latin-English dictionary (1538); Stephen Gardiner (1483?–1555), bishop of Winchester and Lord Chancellor under Queen Mary.
[61]Tudor statesman (1509–79), father of Sir Francis Bacon.
[62]Elizabethan courtier, novelist, and poet (1554–86).
[63]Richard Hooker (1553–1600), divine and author of the most majestic statement of Anglican theology, *Of the Laws of Ecclesiastical Polity* (1594 ff.). [64]See pp. 843 ff. [65]See p. 860 f. [66]See p. 894, n.16.
[67]Statesman (1561–1629), colonial entrepreneur and writer on public affairs.
[68]Thomas Egerton (1540–1617), Baron Ellesmere and Viscount Brackley, noted jurist and Lord Chancellor.
[69]Acme. The reference is, of course, to Bacon.
[70]"Concerning the advancement of learning," title of the Latin translation and expansion (1623) of Francis Bacon's *Advancement of Learning* (1605).
[71]*De analogia* (or *De ratione Latine loquendi*), a lost work that Cicero (*Tully*) says Caesar wrote while crossing the Alps and dedicated to him.
[72]Bacon's discourse (1620) on his empirical and inductive methodology. [73]Mere names of things.
[74]"Which extends the author's fame throughout the ages" (Horace, *Ars poetica*, l. 346).
[75]In 1621 Bacon, found guilty by his peers in the House of Lords of bribery and corruption as Lord Chancellor, was deprived of his office, fined, and imprisoned in the Tower. See p. 671, n.28.
[76]"Argumentative writers."

tavern that catch that which stands next them, the candlestick or pots; turn everything into a weapon, Ofttimes they fight blindfold, and both beat the air. The one milks a he-goat, the other holds under a sieve. Their arguments are as fluxive as liquor spilt upon a table, which with your finger you may drain as you will. Such controversies or disputations, carried with more labor than profit, are odious; where most times the truth is lost in the midst or left untouched. And the fruit of their fight is that they spit one upon another and are both defiled. These fencers in religion I like not.   10

De piis et probis[77]

Good men are the stars, the planets of the ages wherein they live, and illustrate the times. God did never let them be wanting to the world: as Abel, for an example of innocency; Enoch of purity, Noah of trust in God's mercies, Abraham of faith, and so of the rest. These, sensual men thought mad because they would not be partakers or practicers of their madness; but they, placed high on the top of all virtue, looked down on the stage of the world and contemned the play of Fortune. For though the most be players, some must be spectators.   20

De stultitia[78]

What petty things they are we wonder at, like children that esteem every trifle, and prefer a fairing[79] before their fathers! What difference is between us and them, but that we are dearer fools, coxcombs at a higher rate? They are pleased with cockle-shells, whistles, hobby-horses and such-like; we, with statues, marble pillars, pictures, gilded roofs where underneath is lath and lime, perhaps loam. Yet we take pleasure in the lie, and are glad we can cozen ourselves. Nor is it only in our walls and ceilings, but all that we call happiness is mere painting and gilt, and all for money. What   30 a thin membrane of honor that is! And how hath all true reputation fallen since money began to have any! Yet the great herd, the multitude, that in all other things are divided, in this alone conspire and agree: to love money. They wish for it, they embrace it, they adore it; while yet it is possessed with greater stir and torment than it is gotten.

Poesis et pictura[80]

Poetry and picture are arts of a like nature, and both are busy about imitation. It was excellently said of Plutarch,[81] poetry was a speaking picture, and picture a mute poesy. For they both invent, feign, and devise many things, and   40 accommodate all they invent to the use and service of nature. Yet of the two the pen is more noble than the pencil. For that can speak to the understanding, the other but to the sense. They both behold pleasure and profit as their common object, but should abstain from all base pleasures lest they should err from their end, and while they seek to better men's minds destroy their manners. They both are born artificers, not made. Nature is more powerful in them than study.

De stilo et optimo scribendi genere[82]

For a man to write well there are required three necessaries: 50

to read the best authors, observe the best speakers, and much exercise his own style. In style, to consider what ought to be written, and after what manner, he must first think and excogitate the matter, then choose his words, and examine the weight of either. Then take care in placing and ranking both matter and words that the composition be comely; and to do this with diligence, and often. No matter how slow the style be at first, so it be labored[83] and accurate; seek the best and be not glad of the forward conceits[84] or first words that offer themselves to us, but judge of what we invent and order what we approve. Repeat often what we have formerly written, which beside that it helps the consequence and makes the juncture better, it quickens the heat of imagination (that often cools in the time of setting down) and gives it new strength, as if it grew lustier by the going back. As we see in the contention of leaping, they jump farthest that fetch their race largest; or, as in throwing a dart or javelin, we force back our arms to make our loose[85] the stronger. Yet if we have a fair gale of wind I forbid not the steering out of our sail, so the favor of the gale deceive us not. For all that we invent doth please us in the conception or birth, else we would never set it down. But the safest is to return to our judgment and handle over again those things, the easiness of which might make them justly suspected. So did the best writers in their beginnings: they imposed upon themselves care and industry; they did nothing rashly; they obtained[86] first to write well, and then custom made it easy, and a habit. By little and little their matter show'd itself to 'em more plentifully; their words answered, their composition followed, and all (as in a well ordered family) presented itself in the place. So that the sum of all is: ready writing makes not good writing, but good writing brings on ready writing. Yet when we think we have got the faculty it is even then good to resist it, as to give a horse a check sometimes with a bit, which doth not so much stop his course as stir his mettle. Again, whether[87] a man's genius is best able to reach, thither it should more and more contend, lift, and dilate itself, as men of low stature raise themselves on their toes, and so ofttimes get even if not eminent. Besides, as it is fit for grown and able writers to stand of themselves and work with their own strength, to trust and endeavor by their own faculties, so it is fit for the beginner and learner to study others, and the best. For the mind and memory are more sharply exercised in comprehending another man's things than our own; and such as accustom themselves and are familiar with the best authors shall ever and anon find somewhat of them in themselves; and in the expression of their minds, even when they feel it not, be able to utter something like theirs which hath an authority above their own. Nay, sometimes it is the reward of a man's

[77]"Concerning good and upright men."   [78]"Concerning folly."
[79]Small gift bought at a fair.   [80]"Poetry and picture."
[81]"How the Young Man Should Study Poetry," *Moralia*. Sect. xvii.
[82]"Concerning style and the best kind of writing." This and the following section are pieced together almost entirely from widely separated precepts in the tenth and second books of Quintilian's *Institutio oratoria*.   [83]Careful.   [84]First and most forcible ideas.
[85]Hurl.   [86]Undertook by endeavor.   [87]Whither.

study, the praise of quoting another man fitly; and though a man be more prone and able for one kind of writing than another, yet he must exercise all. For as in an instrument, so in style: there must be a harmony and consent of parts.

Praecipiendi modi[88]

I take this labor in teaching others that they should not be always to be taught, and I would bring my precepts into practice. For rules are ever of less force and value than experiments. Yet with this purpose: rather to show the right way to those that come after than to detect any that have slipped before, by error; and I hope it will be more profitable. For men do more willingly listen, and with more favor, for precept than reprehension. Among diverse opinions of an art, and most of them contrary in themselves, it is hard to make election; and therefore, though a man cannot invent new things after so many, he may do a welcome work yet to help posterity to judge rightly of the old. But arts and precepts avail nothing except nature be beneficial and aiding. And therefore these things are no more written to a dull disposition than rules of husbandry to a barren soil. No precepts will profit a fool, no more than beauty will the blind, or music the deaf. As we should take care that our style in writing be neither dry nor empty, we should look again it be not winding or wanton with far-fetched descriptions. Either is a vice, but that is worse which proceeds out of want than that which riots out of plenty. The remedy of fruitfulness is easy, but no labor will help the contrary. I will like and praise some things in a young writer which yet if he continue in I cannot but justly hate him for the same. There is a time to be given all things for maturity; and that even your country husbandman can teach, who to a young plant will not put the pruning-knife because it seems to fear the iron, as not able to admit the scar. No more would I tell a green writer all his faults, lest I should make him grieve and faint, and at last despair. For nothing doth more hurt than to make him so afraid of all things as he can endeavor nothing. Therefore youth ought to be instructed betimes, and in the best things; for we hold those longest we take soonest, as the first scent of a vessel lasts, and that tint the wool first receives. Therefore a master should temper his own powers and descend to the other's infirmity. If you pour a glut of water upon a bottle, it receives little of it; but with a funnel, and by degrees, you shall fill many of them, and spill little of your own; to their capacity they will all receive and be full. And as it is fit to read the best authors to youth first, so let them be of the openest and clearest. As Livy before Sallust, Sidney before Donne;[89] and beware of letting them taste Gower or Chaucer[90] at first lest, falling too much in love with antiquity, and not apprehending the weight, they grow rough and barren in language only. When their judgments are firm, and out of danger, let them read both, the old and the new. But no less take heed that their new flowers and sweetness do not as much corrupt as the others' dryness and squalor, if they choose not carefully. Spenser, in affecting the ancients, writ no language. Yet I would have him read for his matter, but as Vergil read Ennius.[91] The reading of Homer and Vergil is counseled by

Quintilian[92] as the best way of informing youth and confirming man. For besides that the mind is raised with the height and sublimity of such a verse, it takes spirit from the greatness of the matter, and is tincted with the best things. Tragic and lyric poetry is good too, and comic with the best, if the manners of the reader be once in safety. In the Greek poets, as also in Plautus, we shall see the economy and disposition of poems better observed than in Terence[93] and the later, who thought the sole grace and virtue of their fable the sticking in of sentences,[94] as ours do the forcing in of jests.

Praecepta elementa[95]

It is not the passing through these learnings that hurts us, but the dwelling and sticking about them. To descend to those extreme anxieties and foolish cavils of grammarians is able to break a wit in pieces, being a work of manifold misery and vainness to be *elementarii senes*.[96] Yet even letters are, as it were, the bank of words, and restore themselves to an author as the pawns of language. But talking and eloquence are not the same: to speak and to speak well are two things. A fool may talk, but a wise man speaks, and out of the observation, knowledge, and use of things. Many writers perplex their readers and hearers with mere nonsense. Their writings need sunshine. Pure and neat language I love, yet plain and customary. A barbarous phrase hath often made me out of love with a good sense, and doubtful[97] writing hath wracked me beyond my patience. The reason why a poet is said that he ought[98] to have all knowledges is that he should not be ignorant of the most, especially of those he will handle. And indeed, when the attaining of them is possible, it were a sluggish and base thing to despair. For frequent imitation of anything becomes a habit quickly. If a man should prosecute as much as could be said of everything, his work would find no end.

Consuetudo[99]

Custom is the most certain mistress of language, as the public stamp makes the current money. But we must not be too frequent with the mint, every day coining. Nor fetch

[88]"Methods of teaching."
[89]The prose style of the Latin historian Titus Livius (59 B.C.–A.D. 17) was notably fluent and lucid, that of Gaius Sallustius Crispus (86–34 B.C.) knotty and obscure. Jonson implies that the poems of Sir Philip Sidney and John Donne reveal a similar contrast.
[90]Two fourteenth-century writers whose Middle English would pose problems for the young reader.
[91]Quintus Ennius (239?–169 B.C.), whose epic poem *Annales* survives only in fragments.
[92]Marcus Fabius Quintilianus (ca. 35–ca. 95), author of *Institutio oratoria*, an influential treatise on classical rhetoric. As we have seen, he was one of Jonson's principal sources for the *Discoveries*.
[93]Titus Maccius Plautus (254–184 B.C.) and Publius Terentius Aper (195–159 B.C.), the two most noted writers of Latin comedy.
[94]Moral reflections.   [95]"Elementary rules."
[96]Old men too much concerned with rudiments.
[97]Ambiguous, obscure.
[98]*The reason . . . ought*: the reason it is said that a poet ought.
[99]"Custom." The beginning of this section (down to the comments

words from the extreme and utmost ages, since the chief virtue of a style is perspicuity, and nothing so vicious in it as to need an interpreter. Words borrowed of antiquity do lend a kind of majesty to style, and are not without their delight sometimes. For they have the authority of years, and, out of their intermission, do win to themselves a kind of grace-like newness. But the eldest of the present and newest of the past language is the best. For what was the ancient language, which some men so dote upon, but the ancient custom? Yet when I name custom I understand not the vulgar custom—for that were a precept no less dangerous to language than life, if we should speak or live after the manners of the vulgar—but that I call custom of speech which is the consent of the learned, as custom of life which is the consent of the good. Vergil was most loving of antiquity; yet how rarely doth he insert *aquai* and *pictai*![1] Lucretius[2] is scabrous and rough in these; he seeks 'em, as some do Chaucerisms with us, which were better expunged and banished. Some words are to be culled out for ornament and color, as we gather flowers to straw[3] houses or make garlands; but they are better when they grow to our style, as in a meadow where, though the mere grass and greenness delights, yet the variety of flowers doth heighten and beautify. Marry, we must not play or riot too much with them, as in paranomosies,[4] nor use too swelling or ill-sounding words, *quae per salebras altaque saxa cadunt*.[5] It is true there is no sound but shall find some lovers, as the bitterest confections are grateful to some palates. Our composition must be more accurate in the beginning and end than in the midst, and in the end more than in the beginning; for through the midst the stream bears us. And this is attained by custom, more than care and diligence. We must express readily and fully, not profusely. There is a difference between a liberal and a prodigal hand. As it is a great point of art, when our matter require it, to enlarge and veer out all sail, so to take it in and contract it is of no less praise when the argument doth ask it. Either of them hath their fitness in the place. A good man always profits by his endeavor, by his help—yea, when he is absent; nay, when he is dead, by his example and memory: so good authors in their style. A strict and succinct style is that where you can take away nothing without loss, and that loss to be manifest. The brief style is that which expresseth much in little. The concise style, which expresseth not enough, but leaves somewhat to be understood. The abrupt style, which hath many breaches, and doth not seem to end, but fall. The congruent and harmonious sitting of parts in a sentence hath almost the fastening and force of knitting and connection, as in stones well squared, which will rise strong a great way without mortar. Periods[6] are beautiful when they are not too long, for so they have their strength too, as in a pike or javelin. As we must take the care that our words and sense be clear, so if the obscurity happen through the hearer's or reader's want of understanding, I am not to answer for them, no more than for their not listening or marking. I must neither find them ears nor mind. . . .

Oratio imago animi[7]

Language most shows a man: speak, that I may see thee. It springs out of the most retired and inmost parts of us, and is the image of the parent of it, the mind. No glass renders a man's form or likeness so true as his speech. Nay, it is likened to a man; and as we consider feature and composition in a man, so words in language, in the greatness, aptness, sound, structure, and harmony of it. Some men are tall and big; so some language is high and great. Then the words are chosen, their sound ample, the composition full, the absolution plenteous and poured out, all grave, sinewy, and strong. Some are little, and dwarfs; so of speech it is humble and low, the words poor and flat, the members and periods thin and weak, without knitting or number. The middle are of a just stature. There the language is plain and pleasing; even without stopping, round without swelling; all well torned,[8] composed, elegant, and accurate. The vicious language is vast and gaping, swelling and irregular; when it contends to be high, full of rock, mountain, and pointedness; as it affects to be low, it is abject, and creeps, full of bogs and holes. And according to their subject, these styles vary and lose their names. For that which is high and lofty, declaring excellent matter, becomes vast and tumorous,[9] speaking of petty and inferior things. So that which was even and apt in a mean and plain subject will appear most poor and humble in a high argument. Would you not laugh to meet a great counselor of state in a flat cap, with his trunk hose and a hobby-horse cloak, his gloves under his girdle; and yon haberdasher in a velvet gown, furred with sables? There is a certain latitude in these things by which we find the degrees. The next thing to the stature is the figure and feature in language: that is, whether it be round and straight, which consists of short and succinct periods, numerous and polished; or square and firm, which is to have equal and strong parts, everywhere answerable and weighed. The third is the skin and coat, which rests in the well joining, cementing, and coagmentation[10] of words whenas it is smooth, gentle, and sweet—like a table upon which you may run your finger without rubs, and your nail cannot find a joint—not horrid,[11] rough, wrinkled, gaping, or chapped. After these, the flesh, blood, and bones come in question. We say it is a fleshy style when there is much periphrasis and circuit of words, and when, with more than enough, it grows fat and corpulent: *arvina orationis*,[12] full of suet and tallow. It hath blood and juice when the words are proper and apt, their sound sweet, and the phrase neat and picked. *Oratio uncta te bene pasta*.[13] But where there is redundancy, both the blood and juice are faulty and vicious. *Redundat sanguine, quae multo plus dicit quam necesse est*.[14]

---

on Vergil's archaisms) is based on Quintilian's *Institutio oratoria*, I.vi-vii; the remainder and also all of the following section on language is paraphrased from Vives' *De ratione dicendi*.
[1] Archaic forms of the genitive case (for *aquae* and *pictae*).
[2] Titus Lucretius Carus (96?–55 B.C.), author of the great philosophical poem *De rerum natura*. [3] Strew. [4] Paronomasies, i.e., puns. [5] See p. 700, n. 37. [6] Sentences.
[7] "Speech is the image of the mind." [8] Turned. [9] Tumid.
[10] Joining. [11] Rough, bristling (a Latinism).
[12] "The fat of language."
[13] "The language sumptuous and well nourished."
[14] "It has excessive blood, by which it says more than is necessary."

Juice, in language, is somewhat less than blood; for if the words be but becoming and signifying, and the sense gentle, there is juice. But where that wanteth, the language is thin, flagging, poor, starved, scarce covering the bone; and shows like stones in a sack. Some men, to avoid redundancy, run into that; and while they strive to have no ill blood, or juice, they lose their good. There are some styles again that have not less blood, but less flesh and corpulence. These are bony any sinewy: *ossa habent et nervos.*[15]

De optimo scriptore[16]

Now that I have informed you in the knowing these things,   10
let me lead you by the hand a little farther in the direction of the use, and make you an able writer by practice. The conceits of the mind are pictures of things, and the tongue is the interpreter of those pictures. The order of God's creatures in themselves is not only admirable and glorious, but eloquent. Then he who could apprehend the consequence of things in their truth, and utter his apprehensions as truly, were the best writer or speaker. . . .

WHAT IS A POET?

A poet is that which by the Greeks is called κατ᾽ ἐξοχὴν, ὁ ποιητής,[17] a maker or a feigner; his art, an art of imitation   20
or feigning, expressing the life of man in fit measure, numbers, and harmony, according to Aristotle;[18] from the word ποιειν, which signifies to make or feign. Hence he is called a poet, not he which writeth in measure only, but that feigneth and formeth a fable,[19] and writes things like the truth. For the fable and fiction is, as it were, the form and soul of any poetical work or poem.

WHAT MEAN YOU BY A POEM?

A poem is not alone any work or composition of the poet's in many or few verses, but even one alone verse sometimes makes a perfect poem. As when Aeneas hangs up and con-   30
secrates the arms of Abas with this inscription:

> *Aeneas haec de Danais victoribus arma,*[20]

and calls it a poem or *carmen.* Such are those in Martial,

> *Omnia, Castor, emis: sic fiet, ut omnia vendas,*[21]

and

> *Pauper videri Cinna vult, et est pauper.*[22]

So were Horace his odes called *carmina,* his lyric songs. And Lucretius designs[23] a whole book in his sixt,

> *Quod in primo quoque carmine claret.*[24]

And anciently all the oracles were called *carmina,* or what-   40
ever sentence[25] was expressed (were it much or little) it was called an epic, dramatic, lyric, elegiac, or epigrammatic poem.

BUT HOW DIFFERS A POEM FROM WHAT WE CALL POESY?

A poem, as I have told you, is the work of the poet, the end and fruit of his labor and study. Poesy is his skill or craft of making: the very fiction itself, the reason or form of the

work. And these three voices differ as the thing done, the doing, and the doer; the thing feigned, the feigning, and the feigner; so the poem, the poesy, and the poet. Now, the poesy is the habit or the art—nay, rather the Queen of Arts, which had her original from heaven, received thence from the Ebrews,[26] and had in prime estimation with the Greeks, transmitted to the Latins and all nations that professed civility.[27] The study of it, if we will trust Aristotle,[28] offers to mankind a certain rule and pattern of living well and happily, disposing to us all civil offices of society. If we will believe Tully,[29] it nourisheth and instructeth our youth, delights our age, adorns our prosperity, comforts our adversity, entertains us at home, keeps us company abroad, travels with us, watches, divides the times of our earnest and sports, shares in our country recesses and recreations, insomuch as the wisest and best learned have thought her the absolute mistress of manners, and nearest of kin to virtue. And, whereas they entitle philosophy to be a rigid and austere poesy, they have, on the contrary, styled poesy a dulcet and gentle philosophy, which leads on and guides us by the hand to action with a ravishing delight and incredible sweetness. But before we handle the kinds of poems, with their special differences, or make court to the art itself, as a mistress, I would lead you to the knowledge of our poet by a perfect information, what he is, or should be, by nature, by exercise, by imitation, by study; and so bring him down through the disciplines of grammar, logic, rhetoric, and the ethics, adding somewhat, out of all, peculiar to himself and worthy of your admittance or reception.

First, we require in our poet, or maker (for that title our language affords him elegantly with the Greek) a goodness of natural wit. For, whereas all other arts consist of doctrine and precepts, the poet must be able, by nature and instinct, to pour out the treasure of his mind, and, as Seneca saith,

---

[15]"They have bones and sinews."
[16]"Concerning the best writer." This section (only part of which is given here) as well as the following sections (from "De stylo epistolari" through "Discretio") are taken almost verbatim from John Hoskins' *Directions for Speech and Style.* See p. 676, n. 3.
[17]"Preeminently a maker."   [18]*Poetics,* Ch. I.
[19]Lat. *fabula,* i.e., plot.
[20]"Aeneas here sets the arms won from Danaan conquerors" (*Aeneid,* III.288).
[21]"You buy everything, Castor; it may come to pass that you will sell everything" (Martial, *Epigrams,* VII.98).
[22]"Cinna wishes to seem poor—and is" (*Epigrams,* VIII.19).
[23]Designates.
[24]"Which is set forth in my first song" (*De rerum natura,* VI.937).
[25]Opinion, reflection.   [26]Hebrews.   [27]Civilization.
[28]In his edition (1906) of the *Discoveries,* Maurice Castelain traces this allusion to Aristotle to Julius Caesar Scaliger's famous commentary on the *Poetics* (1561).
[29]Marcus Tullius Cicero (106–43 B.C.), *Pro Archia poeta,* Sect. 7. This famous passage—a favorite text of literary theorists in the Renaissance—perhaps lies behind Sir Philip Sidney's comment in his *Defense of Poesy* that the poet comes "with a tale which holdeth children from play and old men from the chimney corner."

Aliquando secundum Anacreontem insanire iucundum esse: by which he understands the poetical rapture. And according to that of Plato, *Frustra poeticas fores sui compos pulsavit*. And of Aristotle, *Nullum magnum ingenium sine mixtura dementiae fuit. Nec potest grande aliquid et supra ceteros loqui, nisi mota mens*.[30] Then it riseth higher, as by a divine instinct, when it contemns common and known conceptions. It utters somewhat above a mortal mouth. Then it gets aloft and flies away with his rider whither before it was doubtful to ascend. This the poets understood by their Helicon, Pegasus, or Parnassus;[31] and this made Ovid to boast,

> *Est deus in nobis; agtante calescimus illo;*
> *Sedibus aethereis spiritus ille venit.*[32]

And Lipsius to affirm, *Scio poetam neminem praestantem fuisse sine parte quadam uberiore divinae aurae*.[33] And hence it is that the coming up of good poets (for I mind not *mediocres* or *imos*)[34] is so thin and rare among us. Every beggarly corporation affords the state a major,[35] or two bailiffs, yearly; but *solus rex aut poeta non quotannis nascitur*.[36]

To this perfection of nature in our poet we require exercise of those parts, and frequent. If his wit will not arrive soddenly at the dignity of the ancients, let him not yet fall out with it, quarrel, or be overhastily angry, offer to turn it away from study in a humor; but come to it again upon better cogitation, try another time, with labor. If then it succeed not, cast not away the quills yet, nor scratch the wainscot, beat not the poor desk; but bring all to the forge and file again, tourn[37] it anew. There is no statute law of the kingdom bids you be a poet against your will, or the first quarter. If it come in a year or two, it is well. The common rhymers pour forth verses, such as they are, extempore, but there never come from them one sense worth the life of a day. A rhymer and a poet are two things. It is said of the incomparable Vergil that he brought forth his verses like a bear, and after formed them with licking. Scaliger the Father[38] writes it of him that he made a quantity of verses in the morning, which afore night he reduced to a less number. But that which Valerius Maximus[39] hath left recorded of Euripides, the tragic poet, his answer to Alcestis, another poet, is as memorable as modest; who—when it was told to Alcestis that Euripides had in three days brought forth but three verses, and those with some difficulty and throes, Alcestis glorying he could with ease have sent forth a hundred in the space—Euripides roundly replied. "Like enough, but here is the difference: thy verses will not last those three days; mine will to all time." Which was as to tell him he could not write a verse. I have met many of these rattles that made a noise and buzzed. They had their hum, and no more. Indeed, things wrote with labor deserve to be so read, and will last their age.

The third requisite in our poet, or maker, is imitation: to be able to convert the substance or riches of another poet to his own use. To make choice of one excellent man above the rest, and so to follow him till he grow very he,[40] or so like him as the copy may be mistaken for the principal. Not

as a creature that swallows what it takes in, crude, raw, or undigested; but that feeds with an appetite, and hath a stomach to concoct,[41] divide, and turn all into nourishment. Not to imitate servilely, as Horace[42] saith, and catch at vices for virtue, but to draw forth out of the best and choicest flowers, with the bee, and turn all into honey; work it into one relish and savor; make our imitation sweet; observe how the best writers have imitated, and follow them. How Vergil and Statius have imitated Homer; how Horace, Archilochus; how Alcaeus and the other lyrics;[43] and so of the rest.

But that which we especially require in him is an exactness of study and multiplicity of reading, which maketh a full man, not alone enabling him how to know the history or argument of a poem and to report it, but so to master the matter and style as to show he knows how to handle, place, or dispose of either with elegancy when need shall be. And not think he can leap forth suddainly a poet by dreaming he hath been in Parnassus, or having washed his lips—as they say—in Helicon. There goes more to his making than so. For to nature, exercise, imitation, and study art must be added, to make all these perfect. And though these challenge to themselves much in the making up of our maker, it is art only can lead him to perfection, and leave him there in possession, as planted by her hand. . . .

[30]*Aliquando . . . mens*: This passage, which seems to comprise a catena of quotations from Seneca, Plato, and Aristotle, is in fact based entirely on Seneca's *De tranquillitate animi*, Sect. 17 (with the substitution of "Anacreon" for Seneca's "the Greek poet"): "sometimes, according to Anacreon, it is pleasant to be mad"; "the sane mind knocks in vain at the door of poetry"; "no remarkable intelligence has been without a touch of madness." The final sentence, which Jonson cites as Aristotle's, is adapted from Seneca: "nor is it possible to speak imposingly, and above the style of others, unless the mind is moved."
[31]In Greek myth, symbols of poetic inspiration. Pegasus was the winged horse, a blow of whose hoof caused Hippocrene, the fountain of poetic inspiration, to gush from Mt. Helicon. Parnassus was a lofty mountain sacred to Apollo and the Muses.
[32]"There is a god in us who warms us by his motions; from his heavenly seat this spirit comes to us" (a conflation of Ovid's *Fasti*, vi.5, and *Ars amatoria*, iii.549-50).
[33]"I know there has never been a remarkable poet without an uncommon share of divine inspiration."
[34]"Mediocre or worse." [35]Mayor.
[36]"Only a king or a poet is not born every year." [37]Turn.
[38]Julius Caesar Scaliger (1484–1558) famous Italian physician and scholar (see note 28 above), as distinguished from his equally famous son Joseph Justus Scaliger (1540–1609), one of the most learned men of his time.
[39]First-century anecdotist, author of *De factis dictisque memorabilis*, which records the anecdote about Euripides at III.vii.11.
[40]A man in his own right. [41]Digest. [42]*Ars poetica*, ll.131-35.
[43]How such eminent Latin writers of epic poetry as Vergil and Statius (author of the *Thebiad*) have imitated Homer, how Horace has imitated the Greek lyric poets Archilochus, Alcaeus, and others.

from Dedications and Addresses

EVERY MAN IN HIS HUMOR (1616)

TO THE MOST LEARNED, AND MY HONORED FRIEND, MASTER CAMDEN, CLARENTIAUX[1]

There are, no doubt, a supercilious race in the world who will esteem all office done you in this kind[2] an injury, so solemn a vice it is with them to use the authority of their ignorance to the crying down of poetry or the professors. But my gratitude must not leave to correct their error, since I am none of those that can suffer the benefits conferred upon my youth to perish with my age. It is a frail memory that remembers but present things, and had the favor of the times so conspired with my disposition as it could have brought forth other or better, you had had the same proportion and [10] number of fruits: the first. Now I pray you to accept this, such wherein neither the confession of my manners shall make you blush nor of my studies repent you to have been the instructor. And for the profession of my thankfulness, I am sure, it will with good men find either praise or excuse.

Your true lover,
Ben Jonson

EVERY MAN OUT OF HIS HUMOR (1616)

TO THE NOBLEST NOURCERIES[3] OF HUMANITY AND LIBERTY IN THE KINGDOM, THE INNS OF COURT

I understand you, gentlemen, not your houses, and a worthy succession of you, to all time, as being born the judges of these studies.[4] When I wrote this poem I had friendship [20] with divers[5] in your societies, who as they were great names in learning so they were no less examples of living. Of them and then—that I say no more—it was not despised. Now that the printer, by a doubled charge, thinks it worthy a longer life than commonly the air of such things doth promise,[6] I am careful to put it a servant to their pleasures, who are the inheritors of the first favor borne it. Yet I command it lie not in the way of your more noble and useful studies to the public, for so I shall suffer for it. But when the gown and cap is off, and the Lord of Liberty[7] reigns, then to take it in your [30] hands perhaps may make some bencher,[8] tincted with humanity, read and not repent him.

By your honorer,
Ben Jonson

CYNTHIA'S REVELS, OR THE FOUNTAIN OF SELF-LOVE (1616)

TO THE SPECIAL FOUNTAIN OF MANNERS, THE COURT

Thou art a bountiful and grave spring, and waterest all the noble plants of this island. In thee the whole kingdom dresseth itself, and is ambitious to use thee as her glass. Beware, then, thou render men's figures truly and teach them no less to hate their deformities than to love their forms. For to grace there should come reverence, and no man can call that lovely which is not also venerable. It is not pouldering,[9] perfuming, and everyday smelling of the tailor that converteth to a beautiful object, but a mind, shining through any suit, which needs no false light either or riches or honors to help it. Such shalt thou find some here, even in the reign of Cynthia (a Crites and an Arete).[10] Now, under thy Phoebus,[11] it will be thy province to make more, except thou desirest to have thy source mix with the spring of self-love, and so wilt draw upon thee as welcome a discovery of thy days as was then made of her nights.

Thy servant but not slave,
Ben Jonson

SEJANUS HIS FALL (1605)

TO THE READERS

The following and voluntary labors[12] of my friends prefixed to my book have relieved me in much whereat, without them, I should necessarily have touched. Now I will only use three or four short and needful notes, and so rest.

First, if it be objected that what I publish is no true poem in the strict laws of time, I confess it, as also in the want of a proper chorus, whose habit and modes are such and so difficult as not any whom I have seen since the ancients— no, not they who have most presently affected laws[13]—have

---

DEDICATIONS AND ADDRESSES [1]Clarenceux King-of-Arms in the Heralds' College, to which William Camden was named in 1597 over the strenuous protest of his rival Ralph Brooke (pp. 821 ff.). For Jonson's poetical tribute to his former master at Westminster see p. 89.
[2]*Office . . . kind*: the civility of dedicating a play to you.
[3]Nurseries.
[4]Although a layman unacquainted with the intricacies of the Inns of Court (see Glossary), I know something of your taste and interest in literature.
[5]For example, John Hoskins (pp. 674 f.) and Donne (pp. 56 ff.).
[6]First printed in 1600, *Every Man Out of His Humor* was republished in the 1616 folio edition of Jonson's *Works*.
[7]The Lord of Misrule, one chosen to preside over the Christmas games and revels at the Inns of Court. Shakespeare's *Twelfth Night* was performed at the Christmas festivities at the Middle Temple in 1601.
[8]A senior member of one of the Inns of Court. [9]Powdering.
[10]In *Cynthia's Revels*, an allegorical and "comical satire" first printed in 1601, the scholarly Crites (who perhaps represents Jonson himself) and the judicious Arete (which means "excellence" in Greek) are contrasted with the knaves and fools at the court of Cynthia (Queen Elizabeth).
[11]Phoebus Apollo, the sun god, i.e., James I.
[12]Commendatory verses by George Chapman, John Marston, and others that were printed in the 1605 quarto edition of *Sejanus*.
[13]*They . . . laws*: contemporary playwrights who have most recently (*presently*) tried to emulate the chorus in classical drama.

yet come in the way off. Nor is it needful, or almost possible, in these our times (and to such auditors as commonly things are presented) to observe the old state and splendor of dramatic poems with preservation of any popular delight. But of this I shall take more seasonable cause to speak in my observations upon Horace his *Art of Poetry,* which (with the text translated) I intend shortly to publish.[14] In the meantime, if in truth of argument, dignity of persons, gravity and height of elocution, fullness and frequency of sentence[15] I have discharged the other offices of a tragic writer, let not the absence of these forms be imputed to me, wherein I shall give you occasion hereafter—and without my boast—to think I could better prescribe than omit the due use for want of a convenient knowledge.

The next is lest in some nice nostril the quotations[16] might savor affected I do let you know that I abhor nothing more, and have only done it to show my integrity in the story and save myself in those common torturers that bring all wit to the rack, whose noses are ever like swine spoiling and rooting up the Muse's gardens, and their whole bodies like moles, as blindly working under earth to cast any—the least —hills upon virtue.

Whereas they are in Latin and the work in English, it was presupposed none but the learned would take the pains to confer[17] them, the authors themselves being all in the learned tongues save one,[18] with whose English side I have had little to do. To which it may be required, since I have quoted the page, to name what edition I followed. . . .

[Jonson then proceeds to specify his sources in Tacitus, Dio Cassius, Suetonius, and Seneca.]

Lastly, I would inform you that this book in all numbers is not the same with that which was acted on the public stage, wherein a second pen[19] had good share; in place of which I have rather chosen to put weaker—and no doubt less pleasing—of mine own than to defraud so happy a genius of his right by my loathed usurpation.

Fare you well, and if you read farder of me and like, I shall not be afraid of it though you praise me out.

Neque enim mihi cornea fibra est.[20]

But that I should plant my felicity in your general saying "Good" or "Well," etc. were a weakness which the better sort of you might worthily contemn, if not absolutely hate me for.

Ben Jonson, and no such
Quem palma negata macrum, donata reducit optimum.[21]

VOLPONE, OR THE FOX (1607)

TO THE MOST NOBLE AND MOST EQUAL SISTERS, THE TWO FAMOUS UNIVERSITIES, FOR THEIR LOVE AND ACCEPTANCE SHOWN TO HIS POEM IN THE PRESENTATION, BEN JONSON, THE GRATEFUL ACKNOWLEDGER, DEDICATES BOTH IT AND HIMSELF[22]

Never, most equal sisters, had any man a wit so presently excellent as that it could raise itself but there must come both matter, occasion, commenders, and favorers to it. If this be true—and that the fortune of all writers doth daily prove it—it behooves the careful to provide well toward these accidents, and having acquired them to preserve that part of reputation most tenderly wherein the benefit of a friend is also defended. Hence is it that I now render myself grateful, and am studious to justify the bounty of your act; to which, though your mere authority were satisfying, yet it being an age wherein poetry and the professors of it hear so ill on all sides, there will a reason be looked for in the subject. It is certain, nor can it with any forehead[23] be opposed, that the too much license of poetasters in this time hath much deformed their mistress, that every day their manifold and manifest ignorance doth stick unnatural reproaches upon her. But for their petulancy it were an act of the greatest injustice either to let the learned suffer or so divine a skill (which, indeed, should not be attempted with unclean hands) to fall under the least contempt.

For if men will impartially, and not asquint, look toward the offices and function of a poet, they will easily conclude to themselves the impossibility of any man's being the good poet without first being a good man. He that is said to be able to inform[24] young men to all good disciplines, inflame grown men to all great virtues, keep old men in their best and supreme state (or, as they decline to childhood, recover them to their first strength), that comes forth the interpreter and arbiter of nature, a teacher of things divine no less than human, a master in manners, and can alone (or with a few) effect the business of mankind—this, I take him, is no subject for pride and ignorance to exercise their railing rhetoric upon.

But it will here by hastily answered that the writers of these days are other things; that not only their manners but their natures are inverted, and nothing remaining with them of

[14]Despite this announcement of its imminent appearance, Jonson's infelicitous translation of the *Ars poetica,* which was probably made about 1604 and subsequently revised, did not appear until 1640, when both versions were printed posthumously. His commentary on this famous text was lost in the fire (1623) that destroyed many of his books and papers.
[15]*Sententia,* i.e., sententious utterance.
[16]*Sejanus* is notable for its use of direct citation from Latin writers.
[17]Compare.
[18]Richard Greneway's translation of *The Annales of Corn. Tacitus* (1598), whose inadequacy Jonson later spoke about to Drummond (p. 697).
[19]Perhaps George Chapman, who may have contributed certain passages to *Sejanus* that were omitted or modified when the play was printed. For Jonson's own account of his interrogation by the Privy Council about the alleged "popery and treason" in the work, see p. 697.
[20]"My heart is not made of horn," i.e., I am not impervious to praise (Persius, *Satires,* I.47).
[21]"Whom disapproval makes lean and applause makes fat" (Horace, *Epistles,* II.i.181).
[22]Although Thomas Fuller (p. 754) said that Jonson had been a member of St. John's College, Cambridge, he himself told Drummond (p. 696) that he held degrees from both Cambridge and Oxford "by their favor, not his study." See p. 696, n.43.
[23]Modesty. [24]Shape, mold.

the dignity of poet but the abused name, which every scribe usurps; that now, especially in dramatic or (as they term it) stage poetry, nothing but ribaldry, profanation, blasphemy, all license of offence to God and man is practiced. I dare not deny a great part of this (and am sorry I dare not), because in some men's abortive features—and would they had never boasted the light—it is overtrue; but that all are embarked in this bold adventure for hell is a most uncharitable thought and, uttered, a more malicious slander.

For my particular[25] I can (and from a most clear conscience) affirm that I have ever trembled to think toward the least profaneness, have loathed the use of such foul and unwashed bawdry as is now made the food of the scene. And howsoever I cannot escape from some the imputation of sharpness, but that they will say I have taken a pride or lust to be bitter, and not my youngest infant[26] but hath come into the world with all his teeth, I would ask of these supercilious politiques[27] what nation, society, or general order or state I have provoked. What public person? Whether I have not, in all these, preserved their dignity, as mine own person, safe? My works are read, allowed (I speak of those that are entirely mine);[28] look into them. What broad reproofs have I used? Where have I been particular? Where personal, except to a mimic, cheater, bawd, or buffoon—creatures, for their insolencies, worthy to be taxed? Yet to which of these so pointingly as he might not either ingenuously have confessed or wisely dissembled his disease?

But it is not rumor can make men guilty, much less entitle me to other men's crimes. I know that nothing can be so innocently writ or carried but may be made obnoxious to construction.[29] Marry, whilst I bear mine innocence about me, I fear it not. Application[30] is now grown a trade with many, and there are that profess to have a key for the deciphering of everything; but let wise and noble persons take heed how they be too credulous, or give leave to these invading interpreters to be overfamiliar with their fames, who cunningly and often utter their own virulent malice under other men's simplest meanings.

As for those that will—by faults which charity hath raked up or common honesty concealed—make themselves a name with the multitude, or (to draw their rude and beastly claps) care not whose living faces they intrench with their petulant styles,[31] may they do it without a rival for me. I choose rather to live graved in obscurity than share with them in so preposterous a fame. Nor can I blame the wishes of those severe and wiser patriots who, providing[32] the hurts these licentious spirits may do in a state, desire rather to see fools and devils and those antique relics of barbarism retrieved, with all other ridiculous and exploded follies, than behold the wounds of private men, of princes, and nations. For as Horace makes Trebatius speak, among these

sibi quisque timet, quamquam est intactus, et odit.[33]

And men may justly impute such rages, if continued, to the writer as his sports.

The increase of which lust in liberty, together with the present trade of the stage in all their misc'line[34] interludes, what learned or liberal soul doth not already abhor? Where

nothing but the filth of the time is uttered, and that with such impropriety of phrase, such plenty of solecisms, such dearth of sense, so bold prolepses,[35] so racked metaphors, with brothelry[36] able to violate the ear of a pagan and blasphemy to turn the blood of a Christian to water. I cannot but be serious in a cause of this nature, wherein my fame and the reputations of divers honest and learned are the question; when a name so full of authority, antiquity, and all great mark is (through their insolence) become the lowest scorn of the age; and those men subject to the petulancy of every vernaculous[37] orator that were wont to be the care of kings and happiest monarchs.

This it is that hath not only rapt[38] me to present indignation, but made me studious heretofore and by all my actions to stand off from them, which may most appear in this my latest work which you (most learned arbitresses) have seen, judged, and to my crown approved; wherein I have labored, for their instruction and amendment, to reduce[39] not only the ancient forms but manners of the scene, the easiness, the propriety, the innocence, and last the doctrine which is the principal end of poesy: to inform men in the best reason of living. And though my catastrophe[40] may, in the strict rigor of comic law, meet with censure as turning back to my promise, I desire the learned and charitable critic to have so much faith in me to think it was done of industry.[41] For with what ease I could have varied it nearer his scale (but that I fear to boast my own faculty) I could here insert. But my special aim being to put the snaffle in their mouths that cry out we never punish vice in our interludes, etc., I took the more liberty, though not without some lines of example drawn even in the ancients themselves, the goings-out of whose comedies are not always joyful, but ofttimes the bawds, the servants, the rivals, yea and the masters are mulcted; and fitly, it being the office of a comic poet to imitate justice and instruct to life, as well as purity of language or stir up gentle affections. To which I shall take the occasion elsewhere[42] to speak.

For the present, most reverenced sisters, as I have cared to be thankful for your affections past and here made the understanding acquainted with some ground of your favors, let me not despair their continuance to the maturing of some worthier fruits, wherein, if my Muses be true to me, I shall raise the despised head of poetry again and, stripping her

---

[25]As for myself.   [26]*Sejanus.*   [27]Temporizers.
[28]Jonson had twice been in trouble with plays which were collaborations. For his difficulties with *Sejanus* see n. 19 above, and with *Eastward Ho* (for which he went to jail) p. 696.
[29]Liable to misinterpretation.
[30]Finding personal (and offensive) allusions in works of art.
[31]Pens (Latin *stylus*).   [32]Anticipating.
[33]"Each man fears for himself and, though untouched, hates you" (Horace, *Satires*, II.i.23).
[34]Misceline, a variant form of *maslin*, i.e., mixed, mingled.
[35]Representations of future events as already accomplished, hence anachronisms.   [36]Lewdness.   [37]Scurrilous   [38]Transported.
[39]Bring back (a Latinism).   [40]Conclusion (of a play).
[41]Intentionally.
[42]In a lost commentary on Horace's *Ars poetica*. See n. 14 above.

out of those rotten and base rags wherewith the times have adulterated her form, restore her to her primitive habit, feature, and majesty, and render her worthy to be embraced and kissed of all the great and master-spirits of our world. As for the vile and slothful who never affected an act worthy of celebration, or are so inward with their own vicious natures as they worthily fear her and think it a high point of policy to keep her in contempt with their declamatory and windy invectives, she shall out of just rage incite her servants (who are *genus irritabile*)[43] to spout ink in their faces that shall eat farder than their marrow into their fames, and not Cinnamus the barber,[44] with his art, shall be able to take out the brands; but they shall live and be read till the wretches die as things worst deserving of themselves in chief, and then of all mankind.

[43]An irritable race.

[44]Martial (*Epigrams*, VI.lxiv) told his detractors that he would brand them so deeply that not even Cinnamus, apparently a well-known barber-surgeon of the time, would be able to efface the scars.

Joseph Hall[1] [1574-1656]

When the character and the essay were described by those who wrote them as, respectively, "wit's descant on any plain song" and as that sort of prose "nearest to a running discourse," the mere anthologist may be forgiven his reluctance to indulge in rigid definitions. Indeed, in the seventeenth century the essay so often merges with the character—to say nothing of the moral treatise, the aphorism, and the epistle—that the rubrics cease to have much meaning. Almost any kind of prose not novelistic or dramatic could be assigned to one or several of these forms. Thus, to take a random sampling of the authors represented in this book, the very title of one of Breton's later works (*Characters upon Essays*) suggests the fusion of these two kinds of writing; Browne's *Religio Medici* could be regarded as a group of moral essays strung upon a common theme; many parts of Burton's multitudinous *Anatomy of Melancholy* exhibit all the features of the character; the biographies in Fuller's *Holy State* and *Profane State* are almost as much concerned with generic moral types as Hall's *Characters of Virtues and Vices*, whereas his *Good Thoughts in Bad Times* like Peacham's *Truth of Our Time*—are essays on matters of contemporary concern; Hall's *Meditations and Vows* and Whichcote's *Aphorisms* have obvious affinities with the gnomic tags of Bacon's first *Essays*; the most memorable parts of Clarendon's great attempt to explain his life and times are the trenchant characters of the men whom he had hated or esteemed; Howell's letters (especially the later ones) are often little essays with a salutation and a signature; and Jonson's *Timber*, which is made up mainly of excerpts from his reading, is in fact a string of little essays on literature and morals.

Whatever their affinities, however, the essay and the character flowed from different sources and were at the start distinct. It is possible to find classical analogues and maybe even sources for the essay in Plutarch, Cicero, and Seneca, but it was Montaigne who served as Bacon's model, and it was Bacon who set the vogue for such smaller fry as Sir William Cornwallis (*Essays*, 1601), John Stephens (*Satirical Essays, Characters, and Others*, 1615), and Geffray Minshull (*Certain Characters and Essays of a Prison and Prisoners*, 1618). Concurrently the impulse toward a candid reappraisal of man's behavior as a social creature found expression in the so-called Theophrastan character. The portrayal of character was, of course, almost as old as literature, but the scholars of the Renaissance evolved for it a jargon and technique, as exemplified by the *descriptio* that had long been taught in rhetoric and the *exemplum* that was standard in the sermon. Chaucer's Canterbury pilgrims and Jonson's gallery of rogues and fools in the dramatis personae of *Every Man Out of His Humor* exhibit other aspects of the long tradition, but it was the Greek philosopher and moralist Theophrastus (ca. 371–ca. 287 B.C.) who inspired the flood of formal characters in early Stuart England. In 1592 the French humanist Isaac Casaubon (whose later years in England earned for him a funeral in the

[1]For a commentary on Hall and other excerpts from his work see Religion and Politics, pp. 526 ff.

Abbey) published at Lyons the Greek text of twenty-three of Theophrastus' thirty extant *Characters*, together with a Latin translation, an important introduction, and a set of annotations. In 1599 he added five more pieces, and by 1616 a translation by John Healy (who had also Englished Augustine's *City of God*) put these witty, caustic sketches within the reach of everyone.

If it was Casaubon who resurrected Theophrastus, it was Joseph Hall who showed how he could be adopted and adapted, and therefore the publication of this young clergyman's *Characters of Virtues and Vices* in 1608 may be regarded as an event of some importance. Like his model, who addressed himself to such perennial misfits as the miser and the misanthrope, Hall's concern is with the type and not the individual, with delineating generic characteristics rather than with portraying certain special persons. He differs from his predecessors, though, in treating good as well as evil, so that exemplars of wisdom, prudence, and fidelity might be juxtaposed and counterpointed with deviants from the norm of social virtue. Employing a resolutely "Senecan" and even colloquial style that is clipped and terse and pointed, and adroitly fitted to his purpose, Hall makes his own intentions clear. His nine virtuous and fifteen vicious characters are designed, he says, as a set of "speaking pictures, or living images, whereby the ruder multitude might even by their senses learn to know virtue and discern what to detest. . . . More might be said, I deny not, of every virtue, or every vice; I desired not to say all, but enough." If the number of his imitators may be taken as a gauge, Hall said enough to win a great success.

M y text is based on *Characters of Vertues and Vices*, 1608 (STC 12648). Hall's importance in the history of the character is treated by W. J. Paylor in his edition of *The Overburian Characters* (1936), Benjamin Boyce in *The Theophrastan Character in England to 1642* (1947), and Rudolf Kirk in his edition of *Heaven upon Earth and Characters* (1948). There are bibliographies of the character by Gwendolen Murphy in the *Transactions* of the Bibliographical Society, No. 4 (1925), and by C. N. Greenough (1947).

from Characters of Virtues and Vices (1608)

A PREMONITION[1] OF THE TITLE AND USE OF CHARACTERS

Reader, the divines of the old heathens were their moral philosophers. These received the acts of an inbred law in the Sinai of nature and delivered them with many expositions to the multitude.[2] These were the overseers of manners, correctors of vices, directors of lives, doctors of virtue, which yet taught their people the body of their natural divinity not after one manner: while some spent themselves in deep discourses of human felicity and the way to it in common, others thought best to apply the general precepts of goodness or decency to particular conditions and persons. A third sort in a mean course betwixt the two other, and compounded of them both, bestowed their time in drawing out the true lineaments of every virtue and vice so lively that who saw the medals might know the face, which art they significantly termed charactery. Their papers were so many tables,[3] their writings so many speaking pictures, or living images, whereby the ruder multitude might even by their sense[4] learn to know virtue and discern what to detest. I am deceived if any course could be more likely to prevail, for herein the gross conceit is led on with pleasure, and informed while it feels nothing but delight; and if pictures have been accounted the books of idiots, behold here the benefit of an image without the offence. It is no shame for us to learn wit of heathens, neither is it material in whose school we take out a good lesson. Yea, it is more shame not to follow their good than not to lead them better. As one, therefore, that in worthy examples hold imitation better than invention, I have trod in their paths, but with an higher and wider step,

CHARACTERS   [1]Preliminary comment.
[2]The figure is based on Exodus 19–20, where Moses receives the Ten Commandments on Mt. Sinai.
[3]Slabs or tablets for writing or drawing on.
[4]Senses (of sight, sound, etc.).

and out of their tablets have drawn these larger portraitures of both sorts. More might be said, I deny not, of every virtue, of every vice; I desired not to say all, but enough. If thou do but read or like these I have spent good hours ill; but if thou shalt hence abjure those vices which before thou thoughtest not ill-favoured, or fall in love with any of these goodly faces of virtue, or shalt hence find where thou hast any little touch of these evils, to clear thyself, or where any defect in these graces to supply it, neither of us shall need to repent of our labor.

THE FIRST BOOK

Characterisms[5] of Virtue

THE PROEM

Virtue is not loved enough because she is not seen, and vice loseth much detestation because her ugliness is secret. Certainly, my Lords, there are so many beauties and so many graces in the face of goodness that no eye can possibly see it without affection, without ravishment; and the visage of evil is so monstrous, through loathsome deformities, that if her lovers were not ignorant they would be mad with disdain and astonishment. What need we more than to discover these two to the world? This work shall save the labor of exhorting and dissuasion. I have here done it as I could, following that ancient master[6] of morality who thought this the fittest task for the ninety and ninth year of his age, and the profitablest monument that he could leave for a farewell to his Grecians. Lo here, then, virtue and vice stripped naked to the open view and despoiled, one of her rags, the other of her ornaments, and nothing left them but bare presence to plead for affection: see now whether[7] shall find more suitors. And if still the vain minds of lewd men shall dote upon their old mistress, it will appear to be not because she is not foul, but for that they are blind and bewitched. And first behold the goodly features of wisdom, an amiable virtue, and worthy to lead this stage; which as she extends herself to all the following graces, so amongst the rest is for her largeness most conspicuous.

CHARACTER OF THE WISE MAN

There is nothing that he desires not to know, but most and first himself, and not so much his own strength as his weaknesses; neither is his knowledge reduced to discourse, but practice. He is a skilful logician, not by nature so much as use; his working mind doth nothing all his time but make syllogisms and draw out conclusions; everything that he sees and hears serves for one of the premises; with these he cares first to inform himself, then to direct others. Both his eyes are never at once from home, but one keeps house while the other roves abroad for intelligence.[8] In material and weighty points he abides not his mind suspended in uncertainties, but hates doubting where he may, where he should, be resolute: and first he makes sure work for his soul, accounting it no safety to be unsettled in the foreknowledge of his final estate. The best is first regarded, and vain is that regard which endeth not in security. Every care hath his just order, neither is there any one either neglected or misplaced. He is seldom overseen[9] with credulity; for, knowing the falseness of the world, he hath learned to trust himself always, others so far as he may not be damaged by their disappointment. He seeks his quietness in secrecy, and is wont both to hide himself in retiredness and his tongue in himself. He loves to be guessed at, not known; and to see the world unseen; and when he is forced into the light, shows by his actions that his obscurity was neither from affectation nor weakness. His purposes are neither so variable as may argue inconstancy, nor obstinately unchangeable, but framed according to his after-wits, or the strength of new occasions. He is both an apt scholar and an excellent master; for both everything he sees informs him, and his mind, enriched with plentiful observation, can give the best precepts. His free discourse runs back to the ages past, and recovers events out of memory, and then preventeth time in flying forward to future things; and comparing one with the other, can give a verdict well near prophetical, wherein his conjectures are better than another's judgments. His passions are so many good servants, which stand in a diligent attendance ready to be commanded by reason, by religion; and if at any time forgetting their duty, they be miscarried to rebel, he can first conceal their mutiny, then suppress it. In all his just and worthy designs he is never at a loss, but hath so projected all his courses that a second begins where the first failed, and fetcheth strength from that which succeeded not. There be wrongs which he will not see, neither doth he always look that way which he meaneth, nor take notice of his secret smarts when they come from great ones. In good turns he loves not to owe more than he must; in evil, to owe and not pay. Just censures he deserves not, for he lives without the compass[10] of an adversary; unjust he contemneth, and had rather suffer false infamy to die alone than lay hands upon it in an open violence. He confineth himself in the circle of his own affairs, and lists not to thrust his finger into a needless fire. He stands like a center unmoved while the circumference of his estate is drawn above, beneath, about him. Finally, his wit hath cost him much, and he can both keep and value and employ it. He is his own lawyer, the treasury of knowledge, the oracle of counsel; blind in no man's cause, best sighted in his own.

THE SECOND BOOK

Characterisms of Vices

THE PROEM

I have showed you many fair virtues: I speak not for them; if their sight cannot command affection, let them lose it.

[5]Characterizations.
[6]Theophrastus (d. 287 B.C.), Greek philosopher who succeeded Aristotle as head of the Academy in Athens, wrote his thirty character sketches in his extreme old age.   [7]Which.
[8]Knowledge based on observation.   [9]Deluded.
[10]Beyond the reach.

They shall please yet better after you have troubled your eyes a little with the view of deformities; and by how much more they please, so much more odious and like themselves shall these deformities appear. This light contraries give to each other in the midst of their enmity, that one makes the other seem more good or ill. Perhaps in some of these (which thing I do at once fear and hate) my style shall seem to some less grave, more satirical: if you find me, not without cause, jealous,[11] let it please you to impute it to the nature of those vices which will not be otherwise handled. The fashions of some evils are, besides the odiousness, ridiculous, which to repeat is to seem bitterly merry. I abhor to make sport with wickedness, and forbid any laughter here but of disdain. Hypocrisy shall lead this ring worthily, I think, because both she cometh nearest to virtue and is the worst of vices.

THE HYPOCRITE

An hypocrite is the worst kind of player by so much as he acts the better part, which hath always two faces, ofttimes two hearts: that can compose his forehead to sadness and gravity, while he bids his heart be wanton and careless within, and in the meantime laughs within himself to think how smoothly he hath cozened the beholder. In whose silent face are written the characters of religion, which his tongue and gestures pronounce but his hands recant. That hath a clean face and garment with a foul soul, whose mouth belies his heart, and his fingers belie his mouth. Walking early up into the City, he turns into the great church,[12] and salutes one of the pillars on one knee, worshipping that God which at home he cares not for, while his eye is fixed on some window, on some passenger,[13] and his heart knows not whither his lips go. He rises, and looking about with admiration, complains of our frozen charity, commends the ancient. At church he will ever sit where he may be seen best, and in the midst of the sermon pulls out his tables in haste, as if he feared to lose that note—when he writes either his forgotten errand or nothing. Then he turns his Bible with a noise to seek an omitted quotation, and folds the leaf as if he had found it, and asks aloud the name of the preacher, and repeats it, whom he publicly salutes, thanks, praises, invites, entertains with tedious good counsel, with good discourse, if it had come from an honester mouth. He can command tears when he speaks of his youth, indeed because it is past, not because it was sinful; himself is now better, but the times are worse. All other sins he reckons up with detestation, while he loves and hides his darling in his bosom. All his speech returns to himself, and every occurrence draws in a story to his own praise. When he should give, he looks about him and says, "Who sees me?": No alms, no prayers fall from him without a witness, belike lest God should deny that He hath received them; and when he hath done (lest the world should not know it) his own mouth is his trumpet to proclaim it. With the superfluity of his usury he builds an hospital, and harbors them whom his extortion hath spoiled; so while he makes many beggars he keeps some. He turneth all gnats into camels,[14] and cares not to undo the world for a circumstance. Flesh on a Friday is more abomination to him than his neigh-

bor's bed: he not abhors more to uncover at the name of Jesus than to swear by the name of God. When a rhymer reads his poem to him he begs a copy, and persuades the press[15] there is nothing that he dislikes in presence that in absence he censures not. He comes to the sickbed of his stepmother and weeps, when he secretly fears her recovery. He greets his friend in the street with so clear a countenance, so fast a closure,[16] that the other thinks he reads his heart in his face, and shakes hands with an indefinite invitation of "When will you come?" and when his back is turned joys that he is so well rid of a guest. Yet if that guest visit him unfeared he counterfeits a smiling welcome and excuses his cheer, when closely he frowns on his wife for too much. He shows well and says well, and himself is the worst thing he hath. In brief, he is the stranger's saint, the neighbor's disease, the blot of goodness, a rotten stick in a dark night, a poppy in a cornfield, an ill-tempered candle with a great snuff that in going out smells ill, an angel abroad, a devil at home—and worse when an angel than when a devil.

THE VAINGLORIOUS

All his humor rises up into the froth of ostentation, which if it once settle falls down into a narrow room. If the excess be in the understanding part, all his wit is in print; the press hath left his head empty, yea, not only what he had, but what he could borrow without leave. If his glory be in his devotion, he gives not an alms but on record; and if he have once done well, God hears of it often, for upon every unkindness he is ready to upbraid Him with His merits. Over and above his own discharge, he hath some satisfactions to spare for the common treasure. He can fulfil the law with ease, and earn God with superfluity. If he hath bestowed but a little sum in the glazing, paving, parieting[17] of God's house, you shall find it in the church window. Or if a more gallant humor possess him, he wears all his land on his back, and walking high, looks over his left shoulder, to see if the point of his rapier follow him with a grace. He is proud of another man's horse, and well mounted, thinks every man wrongs him that looks not at him. A bare head in the street doth him more good than a meal's meat. He swears big at an ordinary,[18] and talks of the court with a sharp accent; neither vouchsafes to name any not honorable, nor those without some term of familiarity, and likes well to see the hearer look upon him amazedly, as if he said, "How happy is this man that is so great with great ones!" Under pretence of seeking for a scroll of news, he draws out an handful of letters endorsed with his own style to the height, and half reading every title, passes over the latter part with a murmur, not without signifying what lord sent this, what great lady the other, and for what suits; the last paper (as it happens) is his news from his honorable friend in the French court. In the midst of dinner, his lackey comes sweating in with a sealed note from his creditor, who now threatens a speedy arrest, and whispers

[11]Suspicious, apprehensive of evil. [12]St. Paul's. [13]Passer-by. [14]See Matthew 23.24: "Ye blind guides, which strain at a gnat, and swallow a camel." [15]Crowd. [16]Such a hearty embrace. [17]Pargeting, plastering. [18]Tavern.

the ill news in his master's ear, when he aloud names a counselor of state, and professes to know the employment. The same messenger he calls with an imperious nod, and after expostulation, where he hath left his fellows, in his ear, sends him for some new spur-leathers or stockings by this time footed; and when he is gone half the room, recalls him, and sayeth aloud, "It is no matter, let the greater bag alone till I come." And yet again calling him closer, whispers (so that all the table may hear), "that if his crimson suit be ready against the day, the rest need no haste." He picks his teeth when his 10 stomach is empty, and calls for pheasants at a common inn. You shall find him prizing the richest jewels and fairest horses when his purse yields not money enough for earnest.[19] He thrusts himself into the press before some great ladies, and loves to be seen near the head of a great train. His talk is how many mourners he furnished with gowns at his father's funerals, how many messes,[20] how rich his coat is, and how

ancient, how great his alliance; what challenges he hath made and answered; what exploits he did at Cales or Nieuport;[21] and when he hath commended others' buildings, furnitures, suits, compares them with his own. When he hath undertaken to be the broker for some rich diamond, he wears it, and pulling off his glove to stroke up his hair, thinks no eye should have any other object. Entertaining his friend, he chides his cook for no better cheer, and names the dishes he meant and wants. To conclude, he is ever on the stage, and acts still a glorious part abroad, when no man carries a baser heart, no man is more sordid and careless at home. He is a Spanish soldier on an Italian theater,[22] a bladder full of wind, a skinful of words, a fool's wonder and a wise man's fool.

[19]Down payment. [20]Servings of food.
[21]Scenes of military action between the Spanish and the Flemish in the 1590's. *Cales*: Calais. [22]Stage, platform.

The Overburian Character

Although Joseph Hall's imitation of Theophrastus (see pp. 711 ff.) has pride of place among the many seventeenth-century collections of characters, the big gathering associated with Sir Thomas Overbury (1581–1613) marks a real advance in the history of the form. Ironically, Overbury himself played a minor role in this successful undertaking. A product of Queen's College, Oxford, and of the Middle Temple, he had the good luck—or perhaps misfortune—to attach himself to Robert Carr, an impecunious young Scot who jockeyed his friendship with King James into an earldom and a position of unrivaled power at court. As Carr—successively Sir Robert, then Viscount Rochester, and finally earl of Somerset—gathered titles and prestige, Overbury improved his fortunes too. The friend of many writers (including Jonson for a while), he was sly and able and ambitious, and following his knighthood and his appointment as sewer (i.e., server) to the king in 1608 his future seemed to be secure—until he crossed his patron. It appears that Overbury was willing to abet Carr's liaison with the profligate Frances Howard, countess of Essex, but he opposed their marriage; and after he declined the diplomatic post in Russia with which the king had tried to purchase his assent (and also his silence about Carr's doings and misdoings), he was imprisoned in the Tower (April 1613), where he died of poison five months later. The circumstances of his death, which were (and are) obscure, were for a time suppressed, and following the countess' divorce and Carr's creation as the earl of Somerset, the wedding—which was lavishly commemorated by Donne and Chapman and other hopeful poets —was a national event (December 1613). But the scandal would not die, and after Somerset was dislodged as favorite by George Villiers, later duke of Buckingham, he and his wife, together with their alleged accomplices, were finally charged with murder. A lurid trial in which Bacon, as attorney-general, led the prosecution, resulted in the execution of four of the defendants, but the two principals escaped more lightly: although condemned to death, they were pardoned by the king, the countess in 1616 and Somerset six years later, when both were freed from prison.

A few months after Overbury's death his poem called *A Wife*—on, of all subjects, ideal marriage—was published in a commemorative volume to which some twenty men of letters contributed elegiac pieces. Owing more to the bad eminence of the honoré than to the merits of his work, this book was so successful that it went through five editions within its year of publication (1614). Although *A Wife* had little claim upon posterity, it was buttressed, in the second edition, with twenty-two characters allegedly by Overbury himself, and it was these that turned the sober little book into a continuing success. Although apparently very few of the twenty-two characters were of Overbury's composition, the rest (which on the title page were attributed to "other learned gentlemen his friends") were good enough to keep the work alive. New editions and additions followed almost every year until 1622, when the eleventh reprinting supplied a total of eighty-two characters by various anonymous contributors. Despite the anonymity, however, certain attributions have been made, and some of them seem sure. Thirty-two "new characters (drawn to the life) of several persons in several qualities" that were added (with a special title page) to the sixth (1615) edition have been ascribed to the playwright John Webster; Thomas Dekker, writing out of hard-bought knowledge, probably contributed the set of six characters on debtors and prisons to the ninth (1616) edition; and Donne, according to his son, wrote "The True Character of a Dunce" that was printed in the eleventh (1622) edition. After 1622 no new characters were added to the canon, but the work continued popular enough to reach a seventeenth edition in 1664.

I have based my text on *Sir Thomas Ouerbury His Wife. With Additions of New Characters, and many other Wittie Conceits Neuer before Printed. The eleuenth Impression,* 1622 (STC 18913). W. J. Paylor's *Overburian Characters* (1936) is important for our understanding not only of the growth of *Sir Thomas Overbury His Wife* but also of the history of the form. Paylor carried his researches further in the *Library*, XVII (1936–37), and other items are cited in the note on Joseph Hall, p. 712. Charles R. Forker has investigated John Webster's contributions to the Overburian canon (*MLQ*, XXX, 1969), which have been included in F. L. Lucas' edition of the playwright's works (1927).

from Sir Thomas Overbury His Wife. With Additions of New Characters and Many Other Witty Conceits Never Before Printed (1622)

A COURTIER[1]

To all men's thinking is a man, and to most men the finest. All things else are defined by the understanding, but this by the senses; but his surest mark is that he is to be found only about princes. He smells, and putteth away[2] much of his judgment about the situation of his clothes. He knows no man that is not generally known. His wit, like the marigold, openeth with the sun, and therefore he riseth not before ten of the clock. He puts more confidence in his words than meaning, and more in his pronunciation than his words. Occasion[3] is his Cupid, and he hath but one receipt of making love. He follows nothing but inconstancy, admires nothing but beauty, honors nothing but fortune; loves nothing. The sustenance of his discourse is news, and his censure, like a shot, depends upon the charging. He is not if he be out of court, but fishlike breathes destruction if out of his own element. Neither his motion or aspect are regular, but he moves by the upper spheres, and is the reflection of higher substances.[4] If you find him not here you shall in Paul's, with a picktooth[5] in his hat, capecloak, and a long stocking.

AN AFFECTATE TRAVELER[6]

Is a speaking fashion. He hath taken pains to be ridiculous, and hath seen more than he hath perceived. His attire speaks

SIR THOMAS OVERBURY HIS WIFE [1]First printed in the second (1614) edition. [2]Wastes. [3]Opportunity.
[4]*Neither . . . substances*: like a planet, his behavior (*motion*) and appearance (*aspect*) are determined by superiors (*higher substances*).
[5]Toothpick.
[6]First printed in the second (1614) edition. *Affectate*: affected.

French or Italian, and his gait cries, "Behold me!" He censures all things by countenances,[7] and shrugs and speaks his own language with shame and lisping. He will choke rather than confess beer good drink, and his picktooth is a main part of his behavior. He chooseth rather to be counted a spy than not a politician, and maintains his reputation by naming great men familiarly. He chooseth rather to tell lies than not wonders, and talks with men singly; his discourse sounds big but means nothing; and his boy[8] is bound to admire him howsoever. He comes still from great personages, but goes with mean. He takes occasion to show jewels, given him in regard of his virtue, that were bought in St. Martin's,[9] and not long after having with a mountbank's[10] method pronounced them worth thousands, impawneth them for a few shillings. Upon festival days he goes to court and salutes without resaluting;[11] at night in an ordinary[12] he canvasseth the business in hand and seems as conversant with all intents and plots as if he begot them. His extraordinary account of men is first to tell them the ends of all matters of consequence, and then to borrow money of them. He offereth courtesies to show them, rather than himself, humble. He disdains all things above his reach, and preferreth all countries before his own. He imputeth his want and poverty to the ignorance of the time, not his own unworthiness; and concludes his discourse with half a period or a word, and leaves the rest to imagination. In a word, his religion is fashion, and both body and soul are governed by fame: he loves most voices above truth.

A BRAGGADOCIO WELSHMAN[13]

Is the oyster that the pearl is in, for a man may be picked out of him. He hath the abilities of the mind in *potentia*, and *actu*[14] nothing but boldness. His clothes are in fashion before his body, and he accounts boldness the chiefest virtue. Above all men he loves a herald,[15] and speaks pedigrees naturally. He accounts none well descended that call him not cousin, and prefers Owen Glendower before any of the Nine Worthies.[16] The first note of his familiarity is the confession of his valor, and so he prevents quarrels. He voucheth Welsh a pure and unconquered language, and courts ladies with the story of their chronicle. To conclude, he is precious in his own conceit, and upon St. Davy's Day[17] without comparison.

A PEDANT[18]

He treads in a rule,[19] and one hand scans verses and the other holds his scepter.[20] He dares not think a thought that the nominative case governs not the verb; and he never had meaning in his life, for he traveled only for words. His ambition is criticism, and his example Tully. He values phrases and elects them by the sound, and the eight parts of speech are his servants. To be brief, he is a heteroclite,[21] for he wants the plural number, having only the single quality of words.

THE TRUE CHARACTER OF A DUNCE[22]

[*By John Donne*]

He hath a soul drowned in a lump of flesh, or is a piece of earth that Prometheus[23] put not half his proportion of fire into. A thing that hath neither edge of desire nor feeling of affection in it; the most dangerous creature for confirming an atheist, who would swear his soul were nothing but the bare temperature of his body. He sleeps as he goes,[24] and his thoughts seldom reach an inch further than his eyes. The most part of the faculties of his soul lie fallow, or are like the restive jades that no spur can drive forwards towards the pursuit of any worthy designs. One of the most unprofitable of God's creatures, being as he is a thing put clean beside[25] the right use, made fit only for the cart and the flail, and by mischance entangled amongst books and papers. A man cannot tell possibly what he is now good for save to move up and down and fill room, or to serve as *animatum instrumentum*[26] for others to work withal in base employments, or to be foil for better wits, or to serve (as they say monsters do) to set out the variety of nature and ornament of the universe. He is mere nothing of himself: neither eats, nor drinks, nor goes, nor spits but by imitation, for all which he hath set forms and fashions which he never varies, but sticks to with the like plodding constancy that a millhorse follows his trace. But the Muses and the Graces are his hard mistresses; though he daily invocate them, though he sacrifice hecatombs, they still look asquint. You shall note him—besides his dull eye and louting[27] head, and a certain clammy benumbed pace—by a fair displayed beard, a nightcap, and a gown whose very wrinkles proclaim him the true genius of formality. But of all others his discourse and compositions best speak him, both of them are much of one stuff and fash-

[7]Appearances, i.e., superficially. [8]Page, servant.
[9]St. Martin's Lane, a disreputable London street (now St. Martin's le Grand) noted as a market for cheap jewelry. [10]Mountebank's.
[11]His greetings are not returned. [12]Inn, tavern.
[13]First printed in the second (1614) edition.
[14]*Potentia . . . actu*: potentially and actually. [15]Genealogist.
[16]He esteems the Welsh rebel Glendower (whom Shakespeare had depicted as a verbose braggart in *1 Henry IV*) more highly than such authentic heroes as Hector, Alexander the Great, Caesar, *et al.*
[17]March 1, the feast day of St. David, the patron saint of Wales, whom tradition held to be the founder of the ancient bishopric of St. David's and a relation of King Arthur.
[18]First printed in the second (1614) edition.
[19](1) he follows a strict routine (*regula*); (2) he enforces rules of grammar.
[20]Ferrule, ruler (with which the schoolmaster strikes his pupils).
[21]In Latin grammar, a word of irregular declension, i.e., a freak.
[22]First printed in the eleventh (1622) edition. The younger John Donne included this character in an edition of his father's early prose entitled *Paradoxes, Problems, Essays, Characters* (1652). See p. 57.
[23]In Greek myth, a Titan who stole fire from heaven for the use of men. [24]Walks. [25]Wholly outside. [26]"Living tool."
[27]Bowed.

ion. He speaks just what his books or last company said unto him without varying one whit, and very seldom understands himself. You may know by his discourse where he was last, for what he heard or read yesterday he now dischargeth his memory or notebook of—not his understanding, for it never came there. What he hath he flings abroad at all adventures,[28] without accommodating it to time, place, persons, or occasions. He commonly loseth himself in his tale, and flutters up and down windless[29] without recovery; and whatsoever next presents itself, his heavy conceit seizeth upon and goeth along with, however heterogeneal[30] to his matter in hand. His jests are either old fled[31] proverbs, or lean-starved hackney apothegms,[32] or poor verbal quips outworn by servingmen, tapsters, and milkmaids—even laid aside by balladers. He assents to all men that bring any shadow of reason, and you may make him, when he speaks most dogmatically, even with one breath to aver poor contradictions. His compositions differ only *terminorum positione*[33] from dreams: nothing but rude heaps of immaterial, incoherent, drossy, rubbish stuff promiscuously thrust up together. Enough to infuse dullness and barrenness of conceit into him that is so prodigal of his ears as to give the hearing; enough to make a man's memory ache with suffering such dirty stuff cast into it. As unwelcome to any true conceit as sluttish morsels or wallowish[34] potions to a nice stomach, which whiles he empties himself of it sticks in his teeth, nor can he be delivered without sweat and sighs and hems and coughs enough to shake his grandam's teeth out her head. He spits and scratches and sprawls and turns like sick men from one elbow to another, and deserves as much pity during his torture as men in fits of tertian[35] fevers or self-lashing penitentiaries. In a word, rip him quite asunder and examine every shred of him, you shall find him to be just nothing but the subject of nothing—the object of contempt; yet such as he is you must take him, for there is no hope he should ever become better.

A PRECISIAN[36]

[By John Webster?]

To speak no otherwise of this varnished rottenness than in truth and verity he is, I must define him to be a demure creature, full of oral sanctity and mental impiety; a fair object to the eye, but stark naught for the understanding, or else a violent thing much given to contradiction. He will be sure to be in opposition with the papist, though it be sometimes accompanied with an absurdity, like the islanders near adjoining unto China who salute by putting off their shoes because the men of China do it by their hats. If at any time he fast, it is upon Sunday, and he is sure to feast upon Friday.[37] He can better afford you ten lies than one oath, and dare commit any sin gilded with a pretence of sanctity. He will not stick to commit fornication or adultery so it be done in the fear of God and for the propagation of the godly, and can find in his heart to lie with any whore save the Whore of Babylon.[38] To steal he holds it lawful so it be from the wicked and Egyptians.[39] He had rather see Antichrist than a picture in the church window, and chooseth

sooner to be half hanged than see a leg[40] at the name of Jesus or one stand at the Creed. He conceives his prayer in the kitchen rather than in the church, and is of so good discourse that he dares challenge the Almighty to talk with him extempore. He thinks every organist is in the state of damnation, and had rather hear one of Robert Wisdom's Psalms[41] than the best hymn a cherubim can sing. He will not break wind without an apology or asking forgiveness, nor kiss a gentlewoman for fear of lusting after her. He hath nicknamed all the prophets and apostles with his sons, and begets nothing but virtues for daughters.[42] Finally, he is so sure of his salvation that he will not change places in heaven with the Virgin Mary without boot.

A JESUIT[43]

[By John Webster?]

Is a larger spoon for a traitor to feed with the devil than any other order.[44] Unclasp him, and he's a gray wolf with a golden star in the forehead; so superstitiously he follows the pope that he forsakes Christ in not giving Caesar his due.[45] His vows seem heavenly, but in meddling with state business he seems to mix heaven and earth together. His best elements are confession and penance: by the first he finds out men's inclinations, and by the latter heaps wealth to his seminary. He sprang from Ignatius Loyola,[46] a Spanish soldier; and though he were found out long since the invention of the cannon, 'tis thought he hath not done less mischief. He is a half-key to open princes' cabinets and pry in their councils, and where the pope's excommunication thunders he holds it no more sin the decrowning of kings than our Puritans do the suppression of bishops. His order is full of irregularity and disobedience, ambitious above all measure; for of late days, in Portugal and the Indies, he rejected the name of Jesuit and would be called "disciple." In Rome and other countries that give him freedom he wears a mask upon his heart; in England he shifts it, and puts it upon his face. No

---

[28]By chance, thoughtlessly. [29]Breathless.
[30]Heterogeneous, unsuitable. [31]Vanished, i.e., obsolete.
[32]Worn-out maxims. [33]In respect to their endings.
[34]Nauseous. [35]Recurring every other day.
[36]First printed in the sixth (1615) edition. *Precisian*: Puritan.
[37]Because Friday is a day of fasting for Roman Catholics.
[38]The Roman Catholic Church (in allusion to Revelation 17.1, 5).
[39]Gypsies. [40]Genuflection.
[41]Metrical versions of the Psalms (a form popular with Puritans for congregational singing) by a Tudor divine and Reformer (d. 1568) who was forced into exile during the reign of Queen Mary, a Roman Catholic. [42]*He hath . . . daughters*: his sons are named for biblical characters and his daughters for the Christian virtues (Faith, Hope, and Charity).
[43]First printed in the sixth (1615) edition.
[44]The allusion is to the proverb that Shakespeare (*Comedy of Errors*, IV.iii.64) renders as "Marry, he must have a long spoon that must eat with the devil." [45]See Matthew 22.21.
[46]Spanish soldier and ecclesiastic (1491–1556) who obtained papal sanction for the Society of Jesus (i.e., the Jesuit order) in 1540 and thereafter served as its "general" or superior until his death. He was canonized in 1622.

place in our climate hides him so securely as a lady's chamber; the modesty of the pursevant[47] hath only forborne the bed, and so missed him. There is no disease in Christendom that may so properly be called the king's evil.[48] To conclude, would you know him beyond sea? In his seminary he's a fox, but in the Inquisition a lion rampant.[49]

A COMMON CRUEL JAILER[50]

[By Thomas Dekker?]

Is a creature mistaken in the making, for he should be a tiger; but the shape being thought too terrible, it is covered, and he wears the vizor of a man, yet retains the qualities of his former fierceness, currishness, and ravening. Of that red earth of which man was fashioned[51] this piece was the basest; of the rubbish which was left and thrown by, came this jailer; his descent is, then, more ancient but more ignoble, for he comes of the race of those angels that fell with Lucifer from heaven, whither he never (or very hardly)[52] returns. Of all his bunches of keys, not one hath wards to open that door, for this jailer's soul stands not upon those two pillars that support heaven—justice and mercy; it rather sits upon those two footstools of hell—wrong and cruelty. He is a judge's slave, and a prisoner's his. In this they differ: he is a voluntary one, the other compelled. He is the hangman of the law with a lame hand, and if the law gave him all his limbs perfect he would strike those on whom he is glad to fawn. In fighting against a debtor he is a creditor's second, but observes not the laws of the *duello*, for his play is foul, and on all base advantages.[53] His conscience and his shackles hang up together, and are made very near of the same metal, saving that the one is harder than the other and hath one property above iron, for that never melts. He distills money out of the poor men's tears and grows fat by their curses. No man coming to the practical part of hell can discharge it better, because here he does nothing but study the theoric[54] of it. His house is the picture of hell in little, and the original of the letters patent[55] of his office stands exemplified there. A chamber of lousy beds is better worth to him than the best acre of corn land in England. Two things are hard to him, nay, almost impossible, viz., to save all his prisoners that none ever escape, and to be saved himself. His ears are stopped to the cries of others, and God's to his; and good reason, for lay the life of a man in one scale and his fees on the other, he will lose the first to find the second. He must look for no mercy if he desires justice to be done to him, for he shows none; and I think he cares the less because he knows heaven hath no need of such tenants: the doors there want no porters, for they stand ever open. If it were possible for all creatures in the world to sleep every night, he only and a tyrant cannot. That blessing is taken from them, and this curse comes in the stead: to be ever in fear and ever hated. What estate can be worse?

WHAT A CHARACTER IS[56]

If I must speak the schoolmaster's language I will confess that *character* comes of this infinitive mood χαράσσειν,[57]

which signifies "to engrave or make a deep impression." And for that cause a letter (as *A, B*) is called a character: those elements which we learn first, leaving a strong seal in our memories.

Character is also taken for an Egyptian hieroglyphic, for an impress[58] or short emblem, in little comprehending much.

To square out a character by our English level, it is a picture (real or personal) quaintly drawn in various colors, all of them heightened by one shadowing.

It is a quick and soft touch of many strings, all shutting up in one musical close;[59] it is wit's descant on any plain song.

THE CHARACTER OF A HAPPY LIFE[60]

By Sir H[enry] W[otton]

How happy is he born or taught
That serveth not another's will;
Whose armor is his honest thought,
And silly[61] truth his highest skill!

Whose passions not his masters are,
Whose soul is still prepared for death,
Untied unto the world with care
Of princely love or vulgar breath.

Who hath his life from rumors freed,
Whose conscience is his strong retreat;
Whose state can neither flatterers feed,
Nor ruin make accusers great.

Who envieth none whom chance doth raise
Or vice, who never understood
How deepest wounds are given with praise,
Not rules of state, but rules of good.

Who God doth late and early pray
More of His grace than gifts to lend;
Who entertains the harmless day
With a well-chosen book or friend.
This man is free from servile bands,
Of hope to rise or fear to fall;
Lord of himself though not of lands,
And having nothing, he hath all.

[47]Pursuivant, i.e., messenger, attendant.
[48]Normally, scrofula, which was thought to be curable by the monarch's touch.
[49]Rearing with the forepaws in the air (a term from heraldry).
[50]First printed in the ninth (1616) edition.
[51]It was an ancient Christian tradition (apparently deriving from *adom*, the Hebrew word for "red") that God created Adam from red earth. Thus Donne prays ("A Litany," Stanza 1), "From this red earth, O Father, purge away/All vicious tinctures."
[52]Scarcely ever.
[53]*Observes not . . . advantages*: flouting the punctilious code of the duelist, he fights unfairly and takes advantage of his reprehensible position. [54]Theory. [55]License.
[56]First printed in the ninth (1616) edition. [57]Text χαράξω.
[58]Ital. *impresa*, "emblem," device (usually with a motto).
[59]Concluding in a single cadence.
[60]First printed in the fourth (1614) edition. [61]Innocent.

Nicholas Breton [1555?-?1626]

Like many better writers of his generation, Nicholas Breton was an Elizabethan who perforce became a Jacobean. Little of his early life is known. He may have been at Oxford and he may have soldiered on the Continent, but as the stepson of that stalwart man of letters George Gascoigne (d. 1577), he naturally drifted or was pushed into the trade of letters. Although he may have made his first attempt as early as 1575 with a little book of poems entitled *A Small Handful of Fragrant Flowers*, it is certain that the equally conventional *Flourish upon Fancy* (1577) must be assigned to him, and that for almost fifty years thereafter his pen was rarely idle. Patronized by the countess of Pembroke (for whom he wrote several of his early works), represented in such splendid miscellanies as *The Phoenix Nest* (1593) and *England's Helicon* (1600), highly praised by Jonson, and ranked by Francis Meres (in *Palladis Tamia*, 1598) with Spenser, Daniel, Drayton, and Shakespeare among the best of "lyric poets," Breton soon became and long remained a prolific and successful minor writer. Since he had to write to make a living, his large production, in both prose and verse, provides a kind of index to the reading public's taste. It was no doubt the success of Bacon's *Essays* (see pp. 661 ff.) and Hall's *Characters* (see pp. 711 ff.) that prompted—"inspired" would be too strong a word—the old Elizabethan to emulate these modish works. He had written prose before, of course—notably the pastoral dialogue *Wit's Trenchmour* (1597), *Melancholic Humours* (1600), the satirical *A Mad World, My Masters* (1603), and the "characters" of the seasons, months, and even hours in *Fantastics* (1604?)—but as he seems to imply in dedicating *Characters upon Essays* to Bacon, in this book he was attempting a new amalgamation. However, his ponderous effort to personify such abstractions of Learning, Patience, Love, and Valor underscores his own assertion that "characters are not every man's construction."

I have based my text on *Characters vpon Essaies Morall, and Diuine, Written For those good Spirits, that will take them in good part, And Make vse of them to good purpose*, 1615 (STC 3635). A. B. Grosart's edition of Breton's *Works in Verse and Prose* (2 vols., 1879), which is not complete, has been supplemented by Jean Robertson's of the poetry "not hitherto reprinted" (1952); her authoritative discussion of the complicated canon supersedes the *Concise Bibliography* by S. A. and D. R. Tannenbaum (1947). Among other modern editions are G. B. Harrison's of *Melancholic Humors* (1929), Ursula Kentish-Wright's of *A Mad World My Masters* (2 vols., 1929), and Arnold Davenport's of *The Whipper Pamphlets* (1951). The fullest study of the prose is N. E. Monroe's *Nicholas Breton as a Pamphleteer* (1929), but Breton is treated by Benjamin Boyce and other students of the character listed in the General Bibliography, Section IV.

from Characters upon Essays, Moral and Divine (1615)

To the Honorable and My Much Worthy Honored, Truly Learned, and Judicious Knight, Sir Francis Bacon, His Majesty's Attorney-General, Increase of Honor, Health, and Eternal Happiness

Worthy knight, I have read of many essays and a kind of charactering of them by such, as when I looked into the form or nature of their writing, I have been of the conceit that they were but imitators of your breaking the ice to their inventions, which how short they fall of your worth I had rather think than speak, though truth need not blush at her blame. Now for myself, unworthy to touch near the rock of those diamonds, or to speak in their praise who so far exceed the power of my capacity, vouchsafe me leave yet, I beseech you, among those apes that would counterfeit the actions of men to play the like part with learning, and as a monkey that would make a face like a man and cannot, so to write like a scholar and am not. And thus, not daring to adventure the print under your patronage without your favorable al- 10 lowance in the devoted service of my bounden duty, I leave these poor travels[1] of my spirit to the perusing of your pleasing leisure, with the further fruits of my humble affection, to the happy employment of your honorable pleasure.

> *At your service in all humbleness,*
> *Nicholas Breton*

To the Reader

Read what you list and understand what you can. Characters are not every man's construction, though they be writ in our mother tongue; and what I have written, being of no other 20 nature, if they fit not your humor they may please a better. I make no comparison because I know you not, but if you will vouchsafe to look into them, it may be you may find something in them. Their natures are diverse, as you may see if your eyes be open; and if you can make use of them to good purpose, your wits may prove the better. In brief, fearing the fool will be put upon me for being too busy with matters too far above my understanding, I will leave my imperfection to pardon or correction and my labor to their liking that will not think ill of a well-meaning, and so 30 rest

> *Your well-willing friend,*
> *N. B.*

Who reads this book with a judicious eye
Will in true judgment true discretion try,
Where words and matter—close and sweetly couch'd—
Do show how truth, wit, art, and nature touch'd.
What need more words these characters to praise?
They are the true charactering of essays.

> *I. R.*[2]   40

LEARNING

Learning is the life of reason and the light of nature, where time, order, and measure square out the true course of knowledge; where discretion in the temper of passion brings experience to the best fruit of affection; while both the theoric and practic[3] labor in the life of judgment, till the perfection of art show the honor of understanding. She is the key of 50 knowledge that unlocketh the cabinet of conceit, wherein are laid up the labors of virtue for the use of the scholars of wisdom; where every gracious spirit may find matter enough worthy of the record of the best memory. She is the nurse of nature, with that milk of reason that would make a child of grace never lie from the dug. She is the schoolmistress of wit

and the gentle governor of will, when the delight of understanding gives the comfort of study. She is unpleasing to none that knows her, and unprofitable to none that loves her. She fears not to wet her feet, to wade through the waters of comfort, but comes not near the seas of iniquity, where folly drowns affection in the delight of vanity. She opens her treasures to the travaillers in virtue, but keeps them close from the eyes of idleness. She makes the king gracious and his council judicious, his clergy devout and his kingdom prosperous. She gives honor to virtue, grace to honor, reward to labor, and love to truth. She is the messenger of wisdom to the minds of the virtuous, and the way to honor in the spirits of the gracious. She is the storehouse of understanding, where the affection of grace cannot want instruction of goodness, while, in the rules of her directions, reason is never out of square. She is the exercise of wit in the application of knowledge, and the preserver of the understanding in the practice of memory. In brief, she makes age honorable and youth admirable, the virtuous wise and the wise gracious. Her libraries are infinite, her lessons without number, her instruction without comparison, and her scholars without equality. In brief, finding it a labyrinth to go through the grounds of her praise, let this suffice, that in all ages she hath been and ever will be the darling of wisdom, the delight of wit, the study of virtue, and the stay of knowledge.

KNOWLEDGE

Knowledge is a collection of understanding gathered in the grounds of learning by the instruction of wisdom. She is the exercise of memory in the actions of the mind, and the employer of the senses in the will of the spirit: she is the notary of time and the trier of truth, and the labor of the spirit in the love of virtue: she is the pleasure of wit and the paradise of reason, where conceit gathereth the sweet of understanding. She is the king's counselor and the council's grace, youth's guard and age's glory. It is free from doubts and fears no danger, while the care of providence cuts off the cause of repentance. She is the enemy of idleness and the maintainer of labor in the care of credit and pleasure of profit: she needs no advice in the resolution of action, while experience in observation finds perfection infallible. It clears errors and cannot be deceived, corrects impurity and will not be corrupted. She hath a wide ear and a close mouth, a pure eye and a perfect heart. It is begotten by grace, bred by virtue, brought up by learning, and maintained by love. She converseth with the best capacities and communicates with the soundest judgments, dwells with the divinest natures and loves the most patient dispositions. Her hope is a kind of assurance, her faith a continual expectation, her love an apprehension of joy, and her life the light of eternity. Her labors are infinite, her ways are unsearchable, her graces incomparable, and her excellencies inexplicable; and therefore, being so little acquainted with her worth as makes me blush at my unworthiness to speak in the least of her praise,

CHARACTERS   [1]Travails.   [2]Unidentified.   [3]Theory and practice.

I will only leave her advancement to virtue, her honor to wisdom, her grace to truth, and to eternity her glory.

TRUTH

Truth is the glory of time and the daughter of eternity, a title of the highest grace, and a note of a divine nature. She is the life of religion, the light of love, the grace of wit, and the crown of wisdom: she is the beauty of valor, the brightness of honor, the blessing of reason, and the joy of faith. Her truth is pure gold, her time is right precious, her word is most gracious, and her will is most glorious. Her essence is in God and her dwelling with His servants, her will in His wisdom and her work to His glory. She is honored in love and graced in constancy, in patience admired and in charity beloved. She is the angel's worship, the virgin's fame, the saint's bliss, and the martyr's crown: she is the king's greatness and his counsel's goodness, his subject's peace and his kingdom's praise; she is the life of learning and the light of law, the honor of trade and the grace of labor. She hath a pure eye, a plain hand, a piercing wit, and a perfect heart. She is wisdom's walk in the way of holiness, and takes up her rest but in the resolution of goodness. Her tongue never trips, her heart never faints, her hand never fails, and her faith never fears. Her church is without schism, her city without fraud, her court without vanity, and her kingdom without villainy. In sum, so infinite is her excellence in the construction of all sense, that I will thus only conclude in the wonder of her worth: she is the nature of perfection in the perfection of nature, where God in Christ shows the glory of Christianity.

TIME

Time is a continual motion, which from the highest Mover hath his operation in all the subjects of nature, according to their quality or disposition. He is in proportion like a circle, wherein he walketh with an even passage to the point of his prefixed place. He attendeth none, and yet is a servant to all; he is best employed by wisdom, and most abused by folly. He carrieth both the sword and the sceptre, for the use both of justice and mercy. He is present in all invention, and cannot be spared from action. He is the treasury of graces in the memory of the wise, and brings them forth to the world upon necessity of their use. He openeth the windows of heaven to give light unto the earth, and spreads the cloak of the night to cover the rest of labor. He closeth the eye of nature and waketh the spirit of reason; he traveleth through the mind, and is visible but to the eye of understanding. He is swifter than the wind, and yet is still as a stone; precious in his right use, but perilous in the contrary. He is soon found of the careful soul, and quickly missed in the want of his comfort: he is soon lost in the lack of employment, and not to be recovered without a world of endeavor. He is the true man's peace and the thief's perdition, the good man's blessing and the wicked man's curse. He is known to be, but his being unknown, but only in his being in a Being above knowledge. He is a riddle not to be read but in the circumstance of description, his name better known than his nature, and he that maketh best use of him hath the best understanding of him. He is like the study of the philosopher's stone, where a man may see wonders and yet short of his expectation. He is at the invention of war, arms the soldier, maintains the quarrel, and makes the peace. He is the courtier's playfellow and the soldier's schoolmaster, the lawyer's gain and the merchants' hope. His life is motion and his love action, his honour patience and his glory perfection. He masketh modesty and blusheth[4] virginity, honoreth humility and graceth charity. In sum, finding it a world to walk through the wonder of his worth, I will thus briefly deliver what I find truly of him: he is the agent of the living and the register of the dead, the direction of God and a great work-master in the world.

[4]Expresses, exhibits. Cf. Shakespeare, *The Winter's Tale*, IV.iv.584: "I'll blush you thanks."

John Earle   [1601?-1665]

John Earle was a prelate famous for his piety, charm, and learning who by chance secured his place in English literature with a youthful *jeu d'esprit*. A Yorkshireman who, according to Anthony Wood, was noted at Oxford for "oratory, poetry, and witty fancies," he apparently wrote his famous characters with no thought of publication. At any rate, Edward Blount, who issued fifty-four of them anonymously as *Microcosmography* in 1628, said that he had to serve as "midwife" to these "infants" whom their father would have "smothered" had not the "forcible request" of friends led to their brisk but private circulation and finally to their appearance in a book. The ill-printed little volume enjoyed a prompt success. Although the record of its early issues is obscure, by 1629 it had reached a so-called fifth edition "much enlarged" by twenty-three new pieces; a sixth, "augmented" to a total of seventy-eight, appeared in 1633; and others duly followed in the middle of the century until the eleventh was attained in 1669.

By 1630 Earle had been appointed chaplain to Philip, fourth earl of Pembroke and chancelor of Oxford University, but the success of *Microcosmography*, says Clarendon, reinforced his rising reputation:

> he grew suddenly into a very general esteem with all men, being a man of great piety and devotion, a most eloquent and powerful preacher, and of a conversation so pleasant and delightful, so very innocent and so very facetious, that no man's company was more desired and more loved.

A devout Anglican and sturdy royalist, Earle, like most successful men, had the knack of making useful friends. During the thirties he adorned Lord Falkland's circle at Great Tew; in 1639 the earl of Pembroke named him to William Chillingworth's former post as rector of Bishopston in Wiltshire; and two years later he became the tutor to the harum-scarum Prince of Wales. Thereafter his fortunes, good and bad, hinged upon the House of Stuart, which he served with true devotion. When, after many hardships in England and in exile with his royal master, he returned to England at the Restoration, it was to gather the rewards that he had earned, first as dean of Westminster (1660) and then as bishop of Worcester (1662) and Salisbury (1663).

In this final phase of his career Earle was universally esteemed, even by the flinty Presbyterians. Izaak Walton thought that not since Richard Hooker had there been a man of "more innocent wisdom, more sanctified learning, or a more pious, peaceable, primitive temper"; and Clarendon— an experienced judge of men—numbered him among those happy few "who never had nor ever could have an enemy but such a one who was an enemy to all learning and virtue, and therefore would never make himself known." His literary career, such as it was, had long since ended, for apart from the famous *Microcosmography* his books, though much admired by fellow Anglicans, did not amount to much: a few occasional poems in English and Latin, a Latin translation of *Eikon Basilike* (see p. 614) that appeared in 1649, and a Latin version of Hooker's *Laws of Ecclesiastical Polity* that he presumably wrote to solace his exile. Although this translation of Hooker was asserted as early as 1703 to have been "utterly destroyed by prodigious heedlessness and carelessness," a manuscript (in a contemporary hand) of Books I–V has recently been acquired by the Folger Shakespeare Library.

I have based my text on *Micro-cosmographie. Or, A Peece of the World Discovered; in Essayes and Characters*, 2d ed., 1628 (STC 7440). There have been editions by Philip Bliss (1811), Gwendolen Murphy (1928), Harold Osborne (1933), and A. S. West (1951), and Earle of course has had a place of honor in all the studies of the character listed in the General Bibliography, Section IV. The discovery of the long-lost Hooker was reported in the *Folger Library Newsletter* for December 1971.

from Microcosmography, or a Piece of the World Discovered in Essays and Characters (1628)

To the Reader, Gentile or Gentle

I have for once adventured to play the midwife's part, helping to bring forth these infants into the world which the father would have smothered, who, having left them lapped up in loose sheets, as soon as his fancy was delivered of them, written especially for his private recreation to pass away the time in the country, and by the forcible request of friends drawn from him, yet passing severally from hand to hand in written copies grew at length to be a pretty number in a little volume; and among so many sundry dispersed transcripts some very imperfect and surreptitious had like to have passed the press if the author had not used speedy means to prevention, when, perceiving the hazard he ran to be wronged, was unwillingly willing to let them pass as now they appear to the world. If any faults have escaped the press —as few books can be printed without—impose them not on the author, I intreat thee, but rather impute them to mine and the printer's oversight, who seriously promise on the re-impression hereof by greater care and diligence for this our former default to make thee ample satisfaction. In the meantime I remain

Thine
Ed. Blount[1]

3. A GRAVE DIVINE

Is one that knows the burden of his calling, and hath studied to make his shoulders sufficient; for which he hath not been hasty to launch forth of his port, the university, but expected the ballast of learning, and the wind of opportunity. Divinity is not the beginning but the end of his studies, to which he takes the ordinary stair and makes the arts his way. He counts it not profaneness to be polished with humane reading, or to smooth his way by Aristotle to School divinity. He has sounded both religions,[2] and anchored in the best, and is a Protestant out of judgment, not faction; not because his country, but his reason is on this side. The ministry is his choice, not refuge, and yet the pulpit not his itch, but fear. His discourse there is substance, not all rhetoric, and he utters more things than words. His speech is not helped with enforced action, but the matter acts itself. He shoots all his meditations at one butt; and beats upon his text, not the cushion; making his hearers, not the pulpit, groan. In citing of popish errors, he cuts them with arguments, not cudgels them with barren invectives; and labours more to show the truth of his cause than the spleen. His sermon is limited by the method, not the hourglass;[3] and his devotion goes along with him out of the pulpit. He comes not up thrice a week, because he would not be idle; nor talks three hours together, because he would not talk nothing; but his tongue preaches at fit times, and his conversation is the every day's exercise. In matters of ceremony, he is not ceremonious, but thinks he owes that reverence to the church to bow his judgment to it, and make more conscience of schism than a surplice. He esteems the church hierarchy as the church's glory, and however we jar with Rome, would not have our confusion distinguish us. In simoniacal purchases[4] he thinks his soul goes in the bargain, and is loath to come by promotion so dear: yet his worth at length advances him, and the price of his own merit buys him a living. He is no base grater of his tithes, and will not wrangle for the odd egg.[5] The lawyer is the only man he hinders, [by whom][6] he is spited for taking up quarrels. He is a main pillar of our church, though not yet dean nor canon, and his life our religion's best apology. His death is his last sermon, where, in the pulpit of his bed, he instructs men to die by his example.

6. A DISCONTENTED MAN

Is one that is fallen out with the world and will be revenged on himself. Fortune has denied him in something, and he now takes pet,[7] and will be miserable in spite. The root of his disease is a self-humoring pride and an accustomed tender-

ness not to be crossed in his fancy; and the occasion[8] commonly of one of these three: a hard father, a peevish wench, or his ambition thwarted. He considered not the nature of the world till he felt it, and all blows fall on him heavier because they light not first on his expectation. He has now forgone all but his pride, and is yet vainglorious in the ostentation of his melancholy. His composure of himself is a studied carelessness, with his arms across and a neglected hanging of his head and cloak; and he is as great an enemy to an hatband as fortune.[9] He quarrels at the time and upstarts, and sighs at the neglect of men of parts, that is, such as himself. His life is a perpetual satire, and he is still girding the age's vanity when this very anger shows he too much esteems it. He is much displeased to see men merry, and wonders what they can find to laugh at. He never draws his own lips higher than a smile, and frowns wrinkle him before forty. He at the last falls into that deadly melancholy to be a bitter hater of men, and is the most apt companion for any mischief. He is the spark that kindles the commonwealth and the bellows himself to blow it, and if he turn any thing it is commonly one of these: either friar, traitor, or madman.

7. AN ANTIQUARY

He is a man strangely thrifty of time past, and an enemy indeed to his maw, whence he fetches out many things when they are now all rotten and stinking. He is one that hath that unnatural disease to be enamored of old age and wrinkles, and loves all things (as Dutchmen do cheese) the better for being moldy and worm-eaten. He is of our religion because we say it is most ancient, and yet a broken statue would almost make him an idolater. A great admirer he is of the rust of old monuments, and reads only those characters where time hath eaten out the letters. He will go you forty miles to see a saint's well or ruined abbey; and there be but a cross or stone footstool in the way, he'll be considering it so long till he forget his journey. His estate consists much in shekels and Roman coins, and he hath more pictures of

MICROCOSMOGRAPHY [1]Famous London bookseller who published, among many other things, the plays of his friend Christopher Marlowe, John Florio's translation of Montaigne (1603), and (as one of a syndicate) the First Folio (1623) of Shakespeare.
[2]*Sounded both religions:* thoroughly investigated Roman Catholic and Protestant theology.
[3]*Method . . . hourglass:* systematic arrangement and development of topics rather than by the conventional length as marked by the running of sand through an hourglass on the pulpit.
[4]Jockeying for ecclesiastical benefices or emoluments.
[5]*He is . . . egg:* in collecting the tithe (the tenth part of one's income required as a tribute to the church), he does not dun his parishioners or resort to barter. Tithing, against which John Selden wrote a notorious treatise (pp. 857 ff), was a common source of complaint in this age of mounting hostility to the Anglican Church.
[6]Supplied from "the sixth edition, augmented," 1633.
[7]Becomes sulky.   [8]Text *occasions.*
[9]*He is . . . fortune:* he rails against conventional attire as much as against his bad luck.

Caesar than James or Elizabeth. Beggars cozen him with musty things which they have raked from dunghills, and he preserves their rags for precious relics. He loves no library but where there are more spiders' volumes than authors', and looks with great admiration on the antique work of cobwebs. Printed books he contemns as a novelty of this latter age, but a manuscript he pores on everlastingly, especially if the cover be all moth-eaten and the dust make a parenthesis between every syllable. He would give all the books in his study (which are rarities all) for one of the old Roman bind- 10 ing, or six lines of Tully in his own hand. His chamber is hung commonly with strange beasts' skins, and is a kind of charnel house of bones extraordinary; and his discourse upon them, if you will hear him, shall last longer. His very attire is that which is the eldest out of fashion, and you may pick a criticism out of his breeches. He never looks upon himself till he is gray haired, and then he is pleased with his own antiquity. His grave does not fright him, for he has been used to sepulchers, and he likes death the better because it gathers him to his fathers. 20

41. A PLAUSIBLE MAN

Is one that would fain run an even path in the world and jut[10] against no man. His endeavor is not to offend, and his aim the general opinion. His conversation is a kind of continued compliment and his life a practice of manners. The relation he bears to others, a kind of fashionable respect, and his kindnesses seldom exceed courtesies. He loves not deeper mutualities because he would not take sides nor hazard himself on displeasures, which he principally avoids. At your first acquaintance with him he is exceeding kind and friendly, and at your twentieth meeting after but 30 friendly still. He has an excellent command over his patience and tongue, especially the last, which he accommodates always to the times and persons, and speaks seldom what is sincere, but what is civil. He is one that uses all companies, drinks all healths, and is reasonable cool in all religions. He can listen to a foolish discourse with applausive attention and conceal his laughter at nonsense. Silly men much honor and esteem him because by his fair reasoning with them as with men of understanding he puts them into an erroneous opinion of themselves and makes them forwarder here- 40 after to their own discovery. He is one rather well thought on than beloved, and that love he has is more of whole companies together than anyone in particular. Men gratify him, notwithstanding, with a good report, and whatever vices he has besides, yet having no enemies he is sure to be an honest fellow.

45. A SHE PRECISE HYPOCRITE

Is one in whom good women suffer and have their truth misinterpreted by her folly. She is one she knows not what herself if you ask her, but she is indeed one that has taken a toy at the fashion of religion, and is enamored of the new 50 fangle. She is a nonconformist in a close stomacher and ruff of Geneva print,[11] and her purity consists much in her linen.

She has heard of the rag of Rome, and thinks it a very sluttish religion, and rails at the Whore of Babylon[12] for a very naughty woman. She has left her virginity as a relic of popery, and marries in her tribe without a ring. Her devotion at the church is much in the turning up of her eye and turning down the leaf in her book when she hears named chapter and verse. When she comes home she commends the sermon for the Scripture, and two hours. She loves preaching better than praying, and of preachers, lecturers;[13] and thinks the weekday's exercise far more edifying than the Sunday's. Her oftest gossipings[14] are Sabbath-day's journeys, where (though an enemy to superstition), she will go in pilgrimage five mile to a silenced minister[15] when there is a better sermon in her own parish. She doubts of the Virgin Marie's salvation, and dare not saint her, but knows her own place in heaven as perfectly as the pew she has a key to. She is so taken up with faith she has no room for charity, and understands no good works but what are wrought on the sampler.[16] She accounts nothing vices but superstition and an oath, and thinks adultery a less sin than to swear "by my truly." She rails at other women by the names of Jezebel and Dalilah;[17] and calls her own daughters Rebecca and Abigail, and not Ann but Hannah.[18] She suffers them not to learn on the virginals because of their affinity with organs, but is reconciled to the bells for the chimes' sake, since they were reformed to the tune of a psalm. She overflows so with the Bible that she spills it upon every occasion, and will not cudgel her maids without Scripture. It is a question whether she is more troubled with the devil, or the devil with her: she is always challenging and daring him, and her weapons are spells no less potent than different, as being the sage sentences of some of her own sectaries.[19] Nothing angers her so much as that women cannot preach, and in this point only thinks the Brownist[20] erroneous; but what she cannot at the church she does at the table, where she prattles more than any against sense and Antichrist, till a capon wing silence her. She expounds the priests of Baal, reading minis-

[10]Push, shove.

[11]A kind of pleated linen worn by Puritan women (in jocular allusion to the print used in the Geneva Bible, which was much favored by Puritans). [12]The Roman Catholic Church.

[13]Divines not holding regular livings but appointed to give special evening sermons or to provide religious instructions for corporate bodies like guilds or trade associations. Such lecturers were often noted for their rigid Puritanism.

[14]Most frequent topics of conversation.

[15]A clergyman disciplined for insubordination, an unyielding Puritan. [16]A piece of canvas for embroidery.

[17]Vicious or voluptuous women. Jezebel was the evil wife of Ahab (1 King 16.31) and Delilah (*Dalilah*) the mistress and betrayer of Samson (Judges 16.4–20).

[18]In calling her daughters after biblical heroines she uses strictly Protestant forms of the names. In the Douay or Catholic version of the Bible, Hannah, mother of the prophet Samuel, was called Anna.

[19]Members of dissenting sects, i.e., zealous Puritans.

[20]A follower of the Puritan Robert Browne (1550?–?1633), one of the founders of Congregationalism, who was opposed to women preachers.

ters,[21] and thinks the salvation of that parish as desperate as the Turk's. She is a main derider to her capacity of those that are not her preachers, and censures all sermons but bad ones. If her husband be a tradesman she helps him to customers, howsoever to good cheer, and they are a most faithful couple at these meetings, for they never fail. Her conscience is like others' lust, never satisfied, and you might better answer Scotus[22] than her scruples. She is one that thinks she performs all her duties to God in hearing, and shows the fruits of it in talking. She is more fiery against the maypole than her husband, and thinks she might do a Phinehas his act to break the pate of the fiddler.[23] She is an everlasting argument, but I am weary of her.

53. PAUL'S WALK

Is the land's epitome, or you may call it the lesser isle of Great Britain. It is more than this: the whole world's map, which you may here discern in its perfectest motion, jostling and turning. It is a heap of stones and men, with a vast confusion of languages; and were the steeple not sanctified, nothing liker Babel. The noise in it is like that of bees, a strange humming or buzz mixed of walking tongues and feet: it is a kind of still roar or loud whisper. It is the great exchange of all discourse, and no business whatsoever but is here stirring and afoot. It is the synod of all pates politic, jointed and laid together in most serious posture, and they are not half so busy at the Parliament. It is the antic of tails to tails and backs to backs,[24] and for vizards you need go no farther than faces. It is the market of young lecturers, whom you may cheapen[25] here at all rates and sizes. It is the general mint of all famous lies, which are here, like the legends of popery, first coined and stamped in the church. All inventions are emptied here and not few pockets. The best signs of a temple in it is that it is the thieves' sanctuary, which rob more safely in the crowd than a wilderness, whilst every searcher is a bush to hide them. It is the other expense of the day, after plays, tavern, and a bawdy-house, and men have still some oaths left to swear here: it is the ear's brothel, and satisfies their lust and itch. The visitants are all men without exceptions, but the principal inhabitants and possessors are stale knights and captains out of service: men of long rapiers and breeches, which after all turn merchants here and traffic for news. Some make it a preface to their dinner, and travel for a stomach;[26] but thriftier men make it their ordinary,[27] and board here very cheap. Of all such places it is least haunted with hobgoblins, for if a ghost would walk more he could not.[28]

---

[21]Clergymen who merely read the lessons or the service without preaching.
[22]John Duns Scotus (1265?–1308), Franciscan scholastic known as the Subtle Doctor for his skill in dialectics.
[23]*Thinks . . . fiddler*: she thinks violence is justified against licentious people like fiddlers. When an Israelite brazenly took a Midianite woman to his tent, Phinehas, a grandson of the High Priest Aaron, seized a spear, "went after the man of Israel into the tent, and thrust both of them through, the man of Israel, and the woman through her belly. So the plague was stayed from the children of Israel" (Numbers 25.7–8).
[24]*Antic . . . backs*: it is like the grotesque anti-masque, a representation of fantastic and monstrous characters in the masques at the Jacobean court. [25]Buy. [26]Appetite.
[27]A public meal at a fixed price in a tavern; i.e., an inexpensive repast. [28]Because it is so crowded.

Owen Felltham [1602?-1668]

Felltham's *Resolves* is a pleasant little book with useful indications of what happened to the essay after Bacon, but it hardly merits Thomas Randolph's praise as "th' *Iliads* in a nutshell." Felltham's own characteristically modest assessment is less flattering but more accurate: it was written "to the middle sort of people," he explained, being too humble for the wisest kind of reader and yet not so "flat and low as to be only fit for fools." The circumstances of its composition, like the meager facts about its author, can be quickly stated. The first edition, which appeared perhaps in 1623, when Felltham, as he remarked in his old age, was "but eighteen," contained a hundred essays. By 1628, when this first installment was reprinted, he was ready with a second century that was issued separately, and the two were promptly brought together as a "duple century" (but in inverted order) in 1628–29. The work was so successful that it had reached a sixth edition by 1636; a seventh came in 1647; and in 1661, as a sort of valedictory gesture, Felltham issued a thoroughly revised edition of *Resolves* together with a pair of weighty essays on the Bible, forty-one poems, "A Brief Character of the Low Countries" (which had already appeared in unauthorized editions in 1648 and 1652), and a substantial group of letters. These "Lusoria, or Occasional Pieces" were merely "sports," he said, that he looked upon as "recreations." Although well enough known in London literary circles to write an answer to Jonson's "Come Leave the Loathed Stage" (p. 103), to be overpraised by Thomas Randolph, and to contribute to *Jonsonus Virbius* (a memorial volume published in honor of the laureate in 1638), Felltham passed almost all his adult life in devoted service to the earls of Thomond at their seat in Northamptonshire, and it was at the London residence of the countess dowager of this illustrious family that the old retainer died in 1668. When the jewel is gone we use not to be solicitous about the case," he had noted in his will, and therefore if the countess (to whom he had affectionately dedicated the 1661 *Resolves*) gave him the sort of funeral that he said he wanted, the services at St. Martin's in the Fields were simple.

My text is based on *Resolves A Duple Century ye 3d edition*, 1628 (STC 10758). Having reached a twelfth edition by 1709, the collection slumbered through the eighteenth century before it was edited by James Cumming in 1806, after which it slumbered once again until Oliver Smeaton resuscitated it in 1904. Smeaton's is the last edition, but E. N. S. Thompson has included Felltham in his *Seventeenth-Century English Essay* (1926), McD. Hazlett has discussed his merits as a writer (*MP*, LI, 1953–54), and Jean Robertson has worked upon his bibliography (*MLN*, LVIII, 1943).

from Resolves (1628-29)

TO THE READERS

I am to answer two objections, one, that I have made use of story, yet not quoted my authorities; and this I have purposely done. It had been all one labor, inserting the matter, to give them both the author and place. But while I am not controversial, I should only have troubled the text or spotted a margent,[1] which I always wish to leave free for the comments of the man that reads. Besides, I do not profess myself a scholar, and for a gentleman I hold it a little pedantical. He should use them rather as brought in my memory— *raptim*[2] and occasional—than by study, search, or strict collection, especially in essay, which of all writing is the nearest to a running discourse. I have so used them as you may see I do not steal, but borrow. If I do, let the reader trace me, and if he will, or can, to my shame discover. There is no cheating like the felony of wit; he which thieves that robs the owners and cozens those that hear him.

The next is for the poetry, wherein, indeed, I have been strict yet would be full. In my opinion they disgrace our language that will not give a Latin verse his English under two for one.[3] I confess, the Latin (besides the curiousness of the tongue) hath in every verse the advantage of three or four syllables, yet if a man will labor for 't he may turn it as short and, I believe, as full. And for this some late translations are my proof. What you find here, if you please, like; but remember always, to censure a resolve in the middle is to give your judgment a possibility of erring. If you ask why I writ them, 'twas because I loved my study; if why I publish them, know that having no other means to show myself to the world so well, I chose this—not to boast, but because I would not deceive.

5. OF PURITANS

I find many that are called Puritans, yet few or none that will own the name. Whereof the reason sure is this, that 'tis for the most part held a name of infamy, and is so new that it hath scarcely yet obtained a definition, nor is it an appellation derived from one man's name whose tenents[4] we may find digested into a volume, whereby we do much err in the application. It imports a kind of excellency above another, which man (being conscious of his own frail bendings) is ashamed to assume to himself. So that I believe there are men which would be Puritans, but indeed not any that are. One will have him one that lives religiously, and will not revel it[5] in a shoreless excess. Another, him that separates from our divine assemblies. Another, him that in some tenets only is peculiar. Another, him that will not swear. Absolutely to define him is a work, I think, of difficulty; some I know that rejoice in the name, but sure they be such as least understand it. As he is more generally in these times taken, I suppose we may call him a church-rebel, or one that would exclude order,[6] that his brain might rule. To decline offenses, to be careful and conscionable in our several actions, is a purity that every man ought to labour for, which we may well do without a sullen segregation from all society. If there be any privileges, they are surely granted to the children of the King,[7] which are those that are the children of heaven.

RESOLVES [1]Margin. [2]"Impetuously."
[3]*The next . . . for one*: although some translations from Latin to English double the number of words, Felltham has tried to be both literal and concise. [4]Tenets. [5]Misbehave.
[6]Anglican liturgy and organization. [7]God.

If mirth and recreations be lawful, sure such a one may lawfully use it. If wine were given to cheer the heart, why should I fear to use it for that end? Surely, the merry soul is freer from intended mischief than the thoughtful man. A bounded mirth is a patent, adding time and happiness to the crazed life of man. Yet if Laertius[8] reports him rightly, Plato deserves a censure for allowing drunkenness at festivals because, says he, as then the gods themselves reach wines to present men.[9] God delights in nothing more than in a cheerful heart, careful to perform Him service. What parent is it that rejoiceth not to see his child pleasant, in the limits of filial duty? I know we read of Christ's weeping,[10] not of His laughter, yet we see He graceth a feast with His first miracle,[11] and that a feast of joy: and can we think that such a meeting could pass without the noise of laughter? What a lump of quickened care is the melancholic man! Change anger into mirth, and the precept will hold good still: be merry but sin not. As there be many that in their life assume too great a liberty, so I believe there are some that abridge themselves of what they might lawfully use. Ignorance is an ill steward to provide for either soul or body. A man that submits to reverent order, that sometimes unbends himself in a moderate relaxation and in all, labors to approve himself in the sereneness of a healthful conscience, such a Puritan I will love immutably. But when a man, in things but ceremonial, shall spurn at the grave authority of the church, and out of a needless nicety be a thief to himself of those benefits which God hath allowed him or out of a blind and uncharitable pride censure and scorn others, as reprobates, or out of obstinacy fill the world with brawls about undeterminable tenents: I shall think him one of those whose opinion hath fevered his zeal to madness and distraction. I have more faith in one Solomon than in a thousand Dutch parlors[12] of such opinionists. "Behold then, what I have seen good! That it is comely to eat, and to drink, and to take pleasure in all his labor wherein he travaileth under the sun, the whole number of the days of his life which God giveth him. For this is his portion. Nay, there is no profit to man but that he eat, and drink, and delight his soul with the profit of his labor."[13] For he that saw other things but vanity, saw this also, that it was the hand of God. Methinks the reading of Ecclesiastes should make a Puritan undress his brain, and lay off all those fanatic toys that jingle about his understanding. For my own part, I think the world hath not better men than some that suffer under that name, nor withal more scelestic[14] villanies. For when they are once elated with that pride, they so contemn others that they infringe the laws of all human society.

20. OF PREACHING

The excess which is in the defect of preaching has made the pulpit slighted: I mean the much bad oratory we find it guilty of. 'Tis wonder to me how men can preach so little, and so long; so long a time, and so little matter: as if they thought to please by the inculcation of their vain tautologies. I see no reason that so high a princess as divinity is should be presented to the people in the sordid rags of the tongue, nor that he which speaks from the Father of languages should

deliver his embassage in an ill one. A man can never speak too well where he speaks not too obscure. Long and distended clauses are both tedious to the ear and difficult for their retaining. A sentence well couched takes both the sense and the understanding. I love not those cart-rope speeches that are longer than the memory of man can fathom. I see not but that divinity, put into apt significants, might ravish as well as poetry. The weighty lines men find upon the stage I am persuaded, have been the lures to draw away the pulpit-followers. We complain of drowsiness at a sermon, when a play of a doubled length leads us on still with alacrity. But the fault is not all in ourselves. If we saw divinity acted, the gesture and variety would as much invigilate.[15] But it is too high to be personated[16] by humanity. The stage feeds both the ear and the eye, and through this latter sense the soul drinks deeper draughts. Things acted possess us more, and are, too, more retainable than the passable tones of the tongue. Besides, here we meet with more compassed language: the *dulcia sermonis*,[17] molded into curious phrase. Though 'tis to be lamented, such wits are not set to the right tune, and consorted to divinity, who without doubt, well decked, will cast a far more radiant luster than those obscene scurrilities that the stage presents us with, though oe'd and spangled in their gaudiest tire.[18] At a sermon well dressed, what understander can have a motion to sleep? Divinity well ordered casts forth a bait which angles the soul into the ear, and can that close when such a guest sits in it? They are sermons but of baser metal which lead the eyes to slumber. And should we hear a continued oration upon such a subject as the stage treats on, in such words as we hear some sermons, I am confident it would not only be far more tedious, but nauseous and contemptful.[19] The most advantage they have of other places is in their good lines and action, for 'tis certain Cicero and Roscius are most complete when they both make but one man.[20] He answered well that after often asking said still that action was the chiefest part of an orator. Surely, the oration is most powerful where the tongue is diffusive, and speaks in a native decency, even in every limb. A good orator should pierce the ear, allure the eye, and invade the mind of his hearer. And this is Seneca's opinion: fit words are better than fine ones. I like not those that are injudiciously made, but such as be expressively significant, that lead the mind to something besides the naked term. And he that speaks thus must not look to speak thus every day. A kembed [21]oration will cost both sweat and the rubbing of

[8]Diogenes Laertius (ca. 200–50), author of *Lives and Opinions of Eminent Philosophers*, a set of gossipy biographies in Greek.
[9]Present wines to living men. [10]Luke 19.41, John 11.35.
[11]The turning of water into wine at the marriage feast at Cana (John 2.1–10).
[12]Felltham is no doubt thinking of Holland as the refuge of disaffected Puritans (like those who emigrated to Leden in 1608 before going on the *Mayflower* to New England).
[13]A paraphrase of Ecclesiastes 2.10, whose author concluded (2.11) that "all was vanity and vexation of spirit." [14]Wicked.
[15]Arouse. [16]Impersonated. [17]"Graceful language."
[18]Attire. [19]Contemptible.
[20]Cicero, the famous orator, and Roscius, the famous actor, would each benefit by pooling their talents. [21]Combed.

the brain: and kembed I wish it, not frizzled nor curled. Divinity should not lasciviate.[22] Unwormwooded[23] jests I like well; but they are fitter for the tavern than the majesty of a temple. Christ taught the people with authority— gravity becomes the pulpit. Demosthenes[24] confessed he became an orator by spending more oil than wine. This is too fluid an element to beget substantials.[25] Wit, procured by wine, is for the most part like the sparklings in the cup when it is filling; they brisk it for a moment, but die immediately. I admire the valor of some men that before their studies dare ascend the pulpit, and do there take more pains than they have done in their library; but having done this, I wonder not that they there spend sometimes three hours but to weary the people into sleep. And this makes some such fugitive divines that, like cowards, they run away from their text. Words are not all, nor matter is not all, nor gesture; yet together they are. 'Tis much moving in an orator when the soul seems to speak as well as the tongue. Saint Augustine says Tully was admired more for his tongue than his mind, Aristotle more for his mind than his tongue, but Plato for both. And surely, nothing decks an oration more than a judgment able well to conceive and utter. I know God hath chosen by weak things to confound the wise, yet I see not but in all times a washed language hath much prevailed. And even the Scriptures (though I know not the Hebrew), yet I believe they are penned in a tongue of deep expression, wherein almost every word hath a metaphorical sense which does illustrate by some allusion. How political is Moses in his Pentateuch! How philosophical is Job! How massy and sententious is Solomon in his Proverbs! how quaint and flamingly amorous in the Canticles![26] how grave and solemn in his Ecclesiastes! that in the world there is not such another dissection of the world as it. How were the Jews astonished at Christ's doctrine! How eloquent a pleader is Paul at the bar; in disputation how subtile! And he that reads the fathers shall find them as if written with a crisped pen. Nor is it such a fault as some would make it, now and then, to let a philosopher or a poet come in and wait, and give a trencher at this banquet. Saint Paul is precedent for it.[27] I wish no man to be too dark and full of shadow. There is a way to be pleasingly plain, and some have found it. Nor wish I any man to a total neglect of his hearers. Some stomachs rise at sweetmeats. He prodigals[28] a mine of excellency that lavishes a terse oration to an aproned auditory.[29] Mercury[30] himself may move his tongue in vain if he has none to hear him but a non-intelligent. They that speak to children assume a pretty lisping. Birds are caught by the counterfeit of their own shrill notes. There is a magic in the tongue can charm the wild man's motions. Eloquence is a bridle wherewith a wise man rides the monster of the world—the people. He that hears has only those affections that thy tongue will give him.

> Thou mayest give smiles or tears, which joys do blot;
> Or wrath to judges, which themselves have not.

You may see it in Lucan's words:

> *Flet, si flere jubes; gaudet, gaudere coactus:*
> *Et te dante, capit judex quam non habet iram.*

I grieve that any thing so excellent as divinity is should fall into a sluttish handling. Sure, though other interposures[31] do eclipse her, yet this is a principal. I never yet knew a good tongue that wanted ears to hear it. I will honor her in her plain trim, but I will wish to meet her in her graceful jewels, not that they give addition to her goodness but that she is more persuasive in working on the soul it meets with. When I meet with worth which I cannot overlove, I can well endure that art which is a means to heighten liking. Confections that are cordial[32] are not the worse but the better for being gilded.

49. THAT ALL THINGS HAVE A LIKE PROGRESSION AND FALL

There is the same method through all the world in general. All things come to their height by degrees; there they stay the least of time; then they decline as they rose. Only mischief, being more importunate, ruins at once what nature hath been long arearing. Thus the poet[33] sung the fall:

> *Omnia sunt hominum tenui pendentia filo,*
> *Et subito casu quae valuere, ruunt.*

> All that man holds hangs but by slender twine;
> By sudden chance the strongest things decline.

Man may be killed in an instant; he cannot be made to live, but by space of time, in conception. We are curdled to the fashion of a life by time and set successions, when all again is lost and in the moment of a minute gone. Plants, fishes, beasts, birds, men all grow up by leisurely progressions; so families, provinces, states, kingdoms, empires have the same way of rise—by steps. About the height they must stay awhile because there is a nearness to the middle on both sides as they rise and as they fall; otherwise, their continuance in that top is but the very point of time, the present *now*, which *now* again is gone. Then they, at best, descend, but, for the most part tumble. And that which is true in the smallest particulars is, by taking a larger view, the same in the distended bulk. There were first men, then families, then tribes, then commonwealths, then kingdoms, monarchies, empires; which, we find, have been the height of all worldly dignities; and, as we find those monarchies did rise by degrees, so we find they have slid again to decay. There was the Assyrian, the Persian, the Grecian, the Roman.[34] And sure, the height of the world's glory was in the days of the Roman Empire; and the height of that Empire in the days of Augustus.[35] Peace then gently breathed through the universal[36]

[22]Sport wantonly. [23]Not bitter.
[24]Famous Athenian orator and statesman (385?–322 B.C.).
[25]Substantial things. [26]The Song of Solomon.
[27]See Acts 17.28. [28]Spends profusely.
[29]Illiterate audience (aprons being the habitual garments of shopkeepers, laborers, and mechanics).
[30]In Roman mythology, the messenger of the gods, noted for his eloquence. [31]Rivals. [32]Invigorating.
[33]Ovid (*Ex Ponto*, IV.iii.35–36).
[34]Felltham is paraphrasing the famous vision of the four empires in Daniel 7.3–8.
[35]Gaius Octavius, adopted son of Julius Caesar and first Roman emperor (27 B.C.–14). [36]Universe.

—learning was then in her fullest flourish: no age, either before or since, could present us with so many towering ingenuities. And then, when the whole world was most like unto God, in the sway of one monarch, when they saluted him by the title of Augustus, and they then, like God, began in rule to be called imperators[37]—this, I take it, was the fulness of time, wherein GOD, the Saviour of the World, vouchsafed, by taking human nature upon Him, to descend into the world. And surely, the consideration of such things as these are not unworthy our thoughts. Though our faith be not bred, yet it is much confirmed by observing such like circumstances. But then, we may think, how small a time this empire continued in this flourish. Even the next emperor, Tiberius, began to degenerate, Caligula more, Nero yet more than he, till it came to be embroiled and dismembered to an absolute division. Since, how has the Turk seized one in the east, and the other in the west! how much is it subdivided by the deduction[38] of France, Britain, Spain! Some have also observed the site of these empires, how the first was nearest the east; the next, a degree further off; and so on, in distant removals, following the course of the sun, as if, beginning in the morning of the world, they would make a larger day by declining towards the west, where the sun goes down after his rising in the east. This may stand to the southern and western inhabitants of the world, but I know not how to the northern: for else, how can that be said to rise anywhere which resteth nowhere, but is perpetually in the speed of a circular motion? For the time, it was when the world was within a very little[39] aged 4000 years,[40] which, I believe, was much about the middle age of the world: though, seeing there are promises that the latter days shall be shortened, we cannot expect the like extent of time after it which we find did go before it. Nor can we think but that decay, which hastens in the ruin of all lesser things, will likewise be more speedy in this. If all things in the world decline faster by far than they do ascend, why should we not believe the world to do so too? I do not know what certain grounds they have that dare assume to foretell the particular time of the world's conflagration; but surely, in reason and nature, the end cannot be mightily distant. We have seen the infancy, the youth, the virility all past. Nay, we have seen it well stept into years and declination, the most infallible premonitors of a dissolution. Some can believe it within less than this nine and twenty years, because as the flood destroyed the former world one thousand six hundred fifty and six years after the first destroying Adam, so the latter world shall be consumed by fire one thousand six hundred fifty and six years after the second saving Adam, which is Christ. But I dare not fix a certainty where God hath left the world in ignorance. The exact knowledge of all things is in God only. But, surely, by collections from nature and reason man may much help himself in likelihood and probabilities. Why hath man an arguing and premeditating soul if not to think on the course and causes of things, thereby to magnify his Creator in them? I will often muse in such like themes, for besides the pleasure I shall meet in knowing further, I shall find my soul, by admiration of these wonders, to love both reason and the Deity better. As our admiring of things evil guides us to a

secret hate and decession,[41] so whatsoever we applaud for goodness cannot but cause some raise[42] in our affections.

THE SECOND CENTURY

TO THE PERUSER

To begin with apologies and entreat a kind censure were to disparage the work and beg partiality: equal with ostentation I rank them both. . . . I writ it without encouragement from another, and as I writ it I send it abroad. Rare, I know it is not; honest, I am sure it is. Though thou findest not to admire, thou mayest to like. What I aim at in it, I confess, hath most respect to myself, that I might out of my own school take a lesson and should serve me for my whole pilgrimage, and if I should wander from these rests that my own items might set me in heaven's direct way again. We do not so readily run into crimes that from our own mouth have had sentence of condemnation. Yet as no physician can be so abstemious as to follow strictly all his own prescriptions, so I think there is no Christian so much his mind's master as to keep precisely all his resolutions. They may better show what he would be than what he is. Nature hath too slow a foot to follow religion close at the heel. Who can expect our dull flesh should wing it with the flights of the soul? He is not a good man that lives perfect, but he that lives as well as he can, and as human frailties will let him. He that thus far strives not, never began to be virtuous, nor knows he those transcending joys that continually feast in the noble-minded man. All the external pleasures that mortality is capable of can never enkindle a flame that shall so bravely warm the soul as the love of virtue, and the certain knowledge of the rule we have over our own wild passions. That I might curb those, I have writ these, and if in them thou find'st a line may mend thee, I shall think I have divulged it to purpose. Read all, and use thy mind's liberty. How thy suffrage falls I weigh not, for it was not so much to please others as to profit myself. Farewell.

16. DEATH IS THE BEGINNING OF A GODLY MAN'S JOY

Death to a righteous man, whether it cometh soon or late, is the beginning of joy and the end of sorrow. I will not much care whether my life be long or short. If short, the fewer my days be, the less shall be my misery, the sooner shall I be happy. But if my years to many, that my head wax gray, even the long expectation of my happiness shall make my joy more welcome.

68. THE THREE BOOKS IN WHICH GOD MAY BE EASILY FOUND

God hath left three books to the world, in each of which He

[37]Emperors. [38]Taking away.
[39]*Within . . . little*: approximately.
[40]Most chronologers in Felltham's time agreed that the creation of the world occurred about 4000 B.C. [41]Diminution. [42]Rise.

may easily be found: the book of the creatures, the book of conscience, and His written word. The first shows His omnipotency, the second His justice, the third His mercy and goodness. So though there be none of them so barren of the rudiments of knowledge but is sufficient to leave all without excuse, apologies, yet in them all I find all the good that ever either the heathen or the Christian hath published abroad. In the first is all natural philosophy, in the second all moral philosophy, in the third all true divinity. To those admirable pillars of all human learning, the philosophers, 10 God showed himself in His omnipotence and justice, but seemed, as it were, to conceal His mercy. To us Christians

He shines in that which outshines all His works, His mercy. Oh, how should we regratulate[43] His favors for so immense a benefit, wherein, secluding himself from others, He hath wholly imparted himself to us! In the first of these I will admire His works by a serious meditation of the wonders in the creatures. In the second I will reverence His justice by the secret and inmost checks of the conscience. In the third embrace His love by laying hold of those promises wherein He hath not only left me means to know Him, but to love Him, rest in Him, and enjoy Him forever.

[43]Make return for, repay.

Henry Peacham [1578?-?1642]

When, at the start of *The Complete Gentleman*, Peacham aligns himself with a tradition that runs from Plutarch to Roger Ascham, he certifies a major impulse in his work, which is the pedagogic. Although he knew from hard experience that teaching is a form of drudgery—"one of the most laborious callings in the world," as he said in his old age—he was a natural pedagogue, one for whom the acquisition and the sharing of knowledge were essential and reciprocal functions. Neither a pedant nor a polymath, he had a very lively interest in poetry, heraldry, mathematics, painting, music, geography, and many other things; and since he would just as gladly teach as learn, his books, whatever their ostensible subject, are all directed to what he succinctly calls "the culture of the mind."

It is regrettable that in an age that valued learning this very able man—so honest, so open to experience, and so disarming in his candor—should have lived and died a kind of hack. The son and namesake of the author of *The Garden of Eloquence* (1577), one of the most useful of Elizabethan books on rhetoric, the younger Peacham had earned two degrees from Trinity College, Cambridge (B.A. 1595, M.A. 1598), when, as he himself explained, he was "left young to the wide world" to survive as best he could. Thereafter the story of his life is anything but clear: he may (or may not) have been ordained a deacon at Lincoln in 1606; he certainly sought preferment in the household of Henry, Prince of Wales, before that young Maecenas' death in 1612 blasted many hopes; he traveled on the Continent for a year or so (1613–14); around 1618 he served as master of a grammar school near Norwich; even toward the end, when he had to scribble for a living, his mind and style were firm. "I have seen and known much, as well in England as somewhere else abroad," he wrote in 1638,

> and have had much acquaintance (and which hath been my happiness, if it be an happiness) with the most famous men of our time in all excellent professions, whence I am not altogether ignorant in the noble sciences, as well the theoric as practic; but, to say the truth, I have ever found multiplicity of knowledge in many things to have been rather an hindrance than ever any way tending to advancement.

Peacham's first book—and allegedly the first of its kind in English—was *The Art of Drawing With the Pen and Limning in Water Colors* (1606); perhaps his last (for the order of his latest works is hard to ascertain) was a wittily instructive little treatise on *The Art of Living in London* (1642). In the four decades between these termini he turned his hand to many things: a Latin verse translation (1610) of King James' *Basilikon Doron* that he presented to the Prince of Wales, an elaborate book of emblems entitled *Minerva Britanna* (1612), much commendatory and elegiac verse, a

Most True Relation (1615) of contemporary events in Holland, a volume of poetical epigrams called *Thalia's Banquet* (1620), and (in his last impoverished years) various tracts and essays on politics, economics, and contemporary affairs.

But by far his most important and influential work was *The Complete Gentleman*, which, following its publication in 1622, was reissued and enlarged three times by 1661. This famous little book, which undertook to discuss "the most necessary and commendable qualities concerning mind or body that may be required in a noble gentleman," was dedicated to young William Howard, the third son of Thomas, earl of Arundel and Surrey; but unlike such aristocratic predecessors as Castiglione's *Courtier* and Sir Thomas Elyot's *Governor* it was really written for the middle classes, whose political and cultural values it embodied and expounded. "Since the fountain of all counsel and instruction, next to the fear of God," Peacham told the little peer,

> is the knowledge and good learning whereby our affections are persuaded and our ill manners mollified, I here present you with the first and plainest directions (though but as so many keys to lead you into far fairer rooms) and the readiest method I know for your studies in general and to the attaining of the most commendable qualities that are requisite in every noble or gentleman.

After an introductory discussion of active virtue as the defining characteristic of true nobility and of the means whereby it is attained, Peacham proceeds to canvass, chapter by chapter, those disciplines and pursuits—history, cosmography, mathematics, poetry, music, antiquities, pictorial art, heraldry, exercise, and travel—of which he himself had firsthand knowledge and which, as he informed young Howard, would "recover" him "from the tyranny of these ignorant times and from the common education, which is to wear the best clothes, eat, sleep, drink much, and to know nothing." Taken altogether, it enables us to gauge the impact of the Renaissance upon the Stuart middle class, and so it still has value.

Combining, in a sort, the essay and the character, *The Truth of Our Times* fairly represents the later work of Peacham. The astringency of its fourteen little pieces perhaps betrays a man of learning whom learning had not saved from want, but at least the wit and supple style and wisdom exemplify that "culture of the mind" to which Peacham, first and last, had always been committed. The book provides a pleasant valediction for a most engaging writer.

M y texts are based on *The Compleat Gentleman. Fashioning him absolut, in the most necessary and commendable Qualities concerning Minde or Body, that may be required in a Noble Gentleman*, 1634 (STC 19504) and *The Truth of our Times: Revealed out one Man's Experience, by way of Essay*, 1638 (STC 19517). To judge by posthumous editions of his work, Peacham has had more attention dead than he ever had when living. There are editions of *The Complete Gentleman* by G. S. Gordon (1906), of *The Truth of Our Times* by R. R. Cawley (Facsimile Text Society, 1942), of *The Worth of a Peny* (1641?) by Edward Arber (*An English Garner*, VI, 1883), of *The Art of Living in London* (1642) by Thomas Park (*Harleian Miscellany*, IX, 1812), and of a volume of selections (from *The Complete Gentleman, The Truth of Our Times*, and *The Art of Living in London*) by Virgil B. Heltzel (1962), the last with a useful introduction. M. C. Pitman has discussed his life and work in the *Institute of Historical Research*, XI (1934), and J. E. Mason his importance in the history of the courtesy book in *Gentlefolk in the Making* (1935).

from The Complete Gentleman (1634)

To My Reader

I am not ignorant, judicious reader, how many pieces of the most curious masters have been uttered to the world of this subject, as Plutarch, Erasmus, Vives, Sadolet, Sturmius, Osorius, Sir Thomas Elyot, Master Ascham, with sundry others,[1] so that my small taper among so many torches were as good out as seeming to give no light at all. I confess it true. But as rare and curious stamps upon coins for their variety and strangeness are daily inquired after and bought up, though the silver be all one and common with ours, so fares it with books which as medals bear the pictures and devices of our various invention. Though the matter be the same, yet for variety sake they shall be read, yea, and, as the same dishes dressed after a new fashion, perhaps please the tastes of many better. But this regard neither moved me. When I was beyond the seas and in a part of France adjoining upon Artois, I was invited oftentimes to the house of a noble personage who was both a great soldier and an excellent scholar. And one day above the rest, as we sat in an open and goodly gallery at dinner, a young English gentleman, who, desirous to travel, had been in Italy and many other places, fortuned[2] to come to his house, and not so well furnished for his return home as was fitting, desired entertainment into his service. My Lord, who could speak as little English as my countryman French, bade him welcome and demanded by me of him what he could do. "For I keep none," quoth he, "but such as are commended for some good quality or other, and I give them good allowance—some an hundred, some sixty, some fifty crowns by the year." And calling some about him, very gentlemanlike, as well in their behavior as apparel. "This," sayeth he, "rideth and breaketh my great horses; this is an excellent lutenist; this, a good painter and surveyor of land; this, a passing linguist and scholar who instructeth my sons," etc. "Sir," quoth this young man, "I am a gentleman born and can only attend you in your chamber or wait upon Your Lordship abroad." "See," quoth Monsieur de Ligny, for so was his name, "how your gentry of England are bred, that when they are distressed or want means in a strange country, they are brought up neither to any quality to prefer them, nor have they so much as the Latin tongue to help themselves withal." I knew it generally to be true, but for the time and upon occasion excused it as I could. Yet he was received and after returned to his friends in good fashion.

Hereby I only give to know that there is nothing more deplorable than the breeding in general of our gentlemen, none any more miserable than one of them if he fall into misery in a strange country. Which I can impute to no other thing than the remissness of parents and negligence of masters in their youth. Wherefore, at my coming over, considering the great forwardness and proficience of children in other countries, the backwardness and rawness of ours; the industry of masters there, the ignorance and idleness of most of ours; the exceeding care of parents in their children's education, the negligence of ours; being taken through change of air with a quartan fever, that leisure I had ἀπὸ παροξυσμοῦ,[3] as I may truly say, by fits I employed upon this discourse for the private use of a noble young gentleman,[4] my friend, not intending it should ever see light, as you may perceive by the plain and shallow current of the discourse, fitted to a young and tender capacity. Howsoever, I have done it, and if thou shalt find herein any thing that may content, at the least not distaste, thee, I shall be glad and encouraged to a more

serious piece; if neither, but out of a malignant humor disdain what I have done, I care not. I have pleased myself, and long since learned Envy, together with her sister Ignorance, to harbor only in the basest and most degenerate breast.

CHAPTER VI

Of Style in Speaking and Writing, and of History

Since speech is the character of a man and the interpreter of his mind, and writing the image of that, that so often as we speak or write, so oft we undergo censure and judgment of ourselves, labor first by all means to get the habit of a good style in speaking and writing, as well English as Latin. I call with Tully that a good and eloquent style of speaking "where there is a judicious fitting of choice words, apt and grave sentences, unto matter well disposed, the same being uttered with a comely moderation of the voice, countenance, and gesture."[5] Not that same ampullous[6] and scenical pomp, with empty furniture of phrase, wherewith the stage and our petty poetic pamphlets sound so big, which like a net in the water, though it feeleth weighty, yet it yieldeth nothing, since our speech ought to resemble plate, wherein neither the curiousness of the picture or fair proportion of letters but the weight is to be regarded; and, as Plutarch sayeth, when our thirst is quenched with the drink, then we look upon the enameling and workmanship of the bowl; so first your hearer coveteth to have his desire satisfied with matter ere he looketh upon the form or vinetry[7] of words, which many times fall in of themselves to matter well contrived, according to Horace:

COMPLETE GENTLEMAN [1]*Plutarch . . . others*: some of the principal contributors to the big literature of courtesy books. Plutarch's "Of the Education of Children" (in the collection of ethical treatises known as the *Moralia*) was a perennial favorite throughout the Renaissance; Erasmus—an incorrigible pedagogue—wrote his *Institutio principis Christiani* (1516) for the edification of the future Emperor Charles V; the great Spanish humanist Juan Luis Vives' *De tradendis disciplinis* (1523) was a highly influential treatise; Jacopo Cardinal Sadoleto interrupted his busy ecclesiastical career to write *De liberis recte instituendis* (1533); Johann Sturm ("the German Cicero") wrote *De literarum ludis recte aperiendis* (1538), a work that no doubt influenced his friend Roger Ascham's famous *Schoolmaster* (1570); the "Portuguese Cicero" Jeronymo Osorio (1506–80) was a learned bishop whose *De regis institutione et disciplina* was notable for its supple Latin prose; Elyot's *The Governor* (1531), dedicated to Henry VIII, was mainly concerned with the proper education of the ruling class of Tudor England. [2]Happened. [3]"From irritation."
[4]William Howard, son of Thomas, earl of Arundel and Surrey, to whom Peacham dedicated *The Complete Gentleman*. It is by no means certain that, as formerly believed, Peacham in 1613 was appointed tutor to Arundel's older sons and traveled with them on the Continent.
[5]Perhaps a loose paraphrase of *Rhetorica ad Herennium*, I.ii, but the notion is common in all of Cicero's works on rhetoric (for example, *De oratore*, I.v.). [6]Inflated, turgid. [7]Ornament.

Rem bene dispositam vel verba invita sequuntur.[8]

To matter well disposed words of themselves do fall.

Let your style therefore be furnished with solid matter, and compact of the best, choice, and most familiar words, taking heed of speaking or writing such words as men shall rather admire than understand (herein were Tiberius, M. Antony, and Maecenas much blamed and jested at by Augustus, himself using ever a plain and most familiar style, and, as it is said of him, *verbum insolens tanquam scopulum effugiens*);[9] then, sententious, yea, better furnished with sentences than words, and, as Tully willeth, without affectation (for, as a king said, *Dum tersiori studemus eloquendi formulae, subterfugit nos clanculum apertus ille et familiaris dicendi modus*);[10] flowing at one and the selfsame height, neither taken in and knit up too short, that like rich hangings of arras or tapestry thereby lose their grace and beauty, as Themistocles[11] was wont to say, nor suffered to spread so far, like soft music in an open field, whose delicious sweetness vanisheth and is lost in the air, not being contained within the walls of a room. In speaking rather lay down your words one by one than pour them forth together. This hath made many men, naturally slow of speech, to seem wisely judicious and be judiciously wise, for, beside the grace it giveth to the speaker, it much helpeth the memory of the hearer and is a good remedy against impediment of speech. Sir Nicholas Bacon, sometime Lord Chancellor of England and father to my Lord of St. Albans,[12] a most eloquent man and of as sound learning and wisdom as England bred in many ages, with the old Lord William Burghley, Lord Treasurer of England, have above others herein been admired and commended in their public speeches in the Parliament House and Star Chamber. For nothing draws our attention more than good matter eloquently digested and uttered with a graceful, clear, and distinct pronunciation.

But to be sure your style may pass for current, as of the richest alloy, imitate the best authors as well in oratory as history, beside the exercise of your own invention, with much conference with those who can speak well. Nor be so foolish precise as a number are who make it religion to speak otherwise than this or that author. As Longolius[13] was laughed at by the learned for his so apish and superstitious imitation of Tully, insomuch as he would have thought a whole volume quite marred if the word *possibile* had passed his pen, because it is not to be found in all Tully, or every sentence had not sunk with *esse posse videatur*,[14] like a peal ending with a chime or an *amen* upon the organs in Paul's.[15] For, as the young virgin to make her fairest garlands gathereth not altogether one kind of flower, and the cunning painter to make a delicate beauty is forced to mix his complexion[16] and compound it of many colors, the arras worker to please the eyes of princes to be acquainted with many histories; so are you to gather this honey of eloquence, a gift of heaven, out of many fields, making it your own by diligence in collection, care in expression, and skill in digestion. But let me lead you forth into these all-flowery and verdant fields where so much sweet variety will amaze and make you doubtful where to gather first.

First, Tully, in whose bosom the treasure of eloquence seemeth to have been locked up and with him to have perished, offereth himself as *pater Romani eloquii*,[17] whose words and style, that you may not be held an heretic of all the world, you must prefer above all other, as well for the sweetness, gravity, richness, and unimitable[18] texture thereof as that his works are throughout seasoned with all kind of learning and relish of a singular and Christianlike honesty. "There wanted not in him" saith Tacitus, "knowledge of geometry, of music, of no manner of art that was commendable and honest. He knew the subtlety of logic, each part of moral philosophy," and so forth.[19] How well he was seen[20] in the civil laws his books *De legibus* and the actions[21] *In Verrem* will show you; which are the rather worthy your reading because you shall there see the grounds of many of our laws here in England. For the integrity of his mind, though his *Offices*[22] had lain suppressed, let this one saying among many thousands persuade you to a charitable opinion of the same: *A recta conscientia transversum unguem non oportet quenquam in omni sua vita discedere.*[23] Whereto I might add that tale of Gyges' ring in his *Offices*,[24] which book, let it not seem contemptible unto you because it lieth tossed and torn in every school, but be precious, as it was sometime unto the old Lord Burghley, Lord High Treasurer of England, before named, who to his dying day would always carry it about him, either in his bosom or pocket, being sufficient, as one said of Aristotle's *Rhetorics*, to make both a scholar and an honest man. Imitate Tully for his phrase and style, especially in his epistles *Ad Atticum*, his books *De oratore*, among his orations those *Pro M. Marcello, Pro Archia poeta, T. Annio Milone, Sext. Rosc. Amerino, Pub. Quinctio*, the first two

---

[8]A garbled version, no doubt from memory, of *Ars poetica*, l. 311: *Verbaque provisam rem non invita sequentur* ("when the subject is prepared the words will quickly follow").

[9]Avoiding the unusual word as if it were a rock at sea.

[10]"While we seek neater rules of eloquence the lucid and familiar way of speaking secretly eludes us." In a marginal gloss Peacham identifies the source as a letter from Henry VIII to Erasmus.

[11]Athenian statesman and general (527?–?460 B.C.).

[12]Sir Francis Bacon.

[13]Christophe de Longueil (1507–43), Belgian scholar who published *Lexicon Graeco-Latinum auctum* (1533).   [14]"It might appear to be."

[15]St. Paul's Cathedral in London.   [16]Combination.

[17]"The father of Roman eloquence."   [18]Inimitable.

[19]Tacitus, *Dialogus de oratoribus*, Sect. 22.   [20]Versed.

[21]Legal proceedings. *In Verrem*, together with some of Cicero's pleadings cited later in the paragraph, were widely studied in the Renaissance as triumphs of forensic oratory.

[22]Cicero's *De officiis* (44 B.C.), a treatise "on duties" in the form of a letter to his son, was both a standard school text and an immensely influential treatise on moral philosophy throughout the Renaissance.

[23]"In a man's whole life he ought not to depart by a finger's breadth from the straight path of conscience" (adapted from *Letters to Atticus*, XIII.xx).

[24]The tale—which passed from Herodotus to Plato to Cicero (*De officiis*, III.ix)—concerns a shepherd who took a golden ring from a corpse in a cave. Learning that the ring made him invisible, he contrived with its aid to debauch the queen, murder the king, and usurp the crown.

against Catiline and the third action against Verres.[25] These in my opinion are fullest of life, but you may use your discretion; you cannot make your choice amiss. . . .

[Ignoring the poets, Peacham continues his guided tour through the "all-flowery and verdant" fields of classical literature with eulogistic treatments of Julius Caesar, Tacitus ("the prince of historians"), Livy (who, "like a milky fountain," flows with "elegant sweetness"), Quintus Curtius, Sallust, and Xenophon. Thus he comes to a general discussion of historiography.]

All history divideth itself into four branches. The first spreadeth itself into and over all places, as geography; the second groweth and gathereth strength with tract of time, as chronology; the third is laden with descents, as genealogy; the fourth and last, like the golden bough Proserpina gave Aeneas,[26] is that truly called by Cicero *lux veritatis*,[27] which telleth us of things as they were done, and of all other most properly is called history. For all history in times past, saith Tully, was none other than *annalium confectio*,[28] the making of *annales*, that is, recording of what was done from year to year. But while I wander in foreign history, let me warn you *ne sis peregrinus domi*, that you be not a stranger in the history of your own country, which is a common fault imputed to our English travelers in foreign countries, who, curious in the observation and search of the most memorable things and monuments of other places, can say, as a great peer of France told me, nothing of their own, our country of England being no whit inferior to any other in the world for matter of antiquity and rarities of every kind worthy remark and admiration. Herein I must worthily and only prefer unto you the glory of our nation, Master Camden,[29] as well for his judgment and diligence as the purity and sweet fluence of the Latin style; and with him the rising star of good letters and antiquity, Master John Selden[30] of the Inner Temple. As for Giraldus, Geoffrey, Higden, Ranulph of Chester, Walsingham, a monk of St. Albans,[31] with the rest, they did *cum saeculo caecutire*,[32] and took upon credit many a time more than they could well answer; that I may omit Polydore Vergil, an Italian, who did our nation that deplorable injury in the time of King Henry the Eighth for that his own history might pass for current he burned and embezzled the best and most ancient records and monuments of our abbeys, priories, and cathedral churches under color (having a large commission under the Great Seal) of making search for all such monuments, manuscript records, ledger books, etc., as might make for his purpose; yet for all this he hath the ill luck to write nothing well, save the life of Henry the Seventh, wherein he had reason to take a little more pains than ordinary, the book being dedicated to Henry the Eighth, his son.

No subject affecteth us with more delight than history, imprinting a thousand forms upon our imaginations from the circumstances of place, person, time, matter, manner, and the like. And what can be more profitable, sayeth an ancient historian,[33] than sitting on the stage of human life, to be made wise by their example who have trod the path of error and danger before us? Bodin[34] tells us of some who

have recovered their healths by reading of history; and it is credibly affirmed of King Alphonsus that the only reading of Quintus Curtius cured him of a very dangerous fever. If I could have been so rid of my late quartan ague, I would have said with the same good king: *Valeat Avicenna, vivat Curtius*,[35] and have done him as much honor as ever the Chians their Hippocrates, or the sunburned Egyptians their Aesculapius.[36]

For morality and rules of well-living, delivered with such sententious gravity, weight of reason, so sweetened with lively and apt similitudes, entertain Plutarch, whom, according to the opinion of Gaza,[37] the world would preserve should it be put to the choice to receive one only author (the sacred Scriptures excepted) and to burn all the rest, especially his *Lives* and *Morals*. After him, the virtuous and divine Seneca, who, for that he lived so near the times of the apostles and had familiar acquaintance with St. Paul (as it is supposed by those epistles that pass under either [of their] names) is thought in heart to have been a Christian; and certes so it seemeth to me, by that spirit wherewith so many rules of patience, humility, contempt of the world are refined and exempt from the degrees of paganism.[38] Some say that about the beginning of Nero's reign he came over hither into Britain, but most certain it is he had divers lands bestowed on him here in England, and those supposed to have lain in Essex near to Camalodunum, now Maldon.

Again, while you are intent to foreign authors and languages, forget not to speak and write your own properly and eloquently, whereof, to say truth, you shall have the greatest

[25]The first two of Cicero's four orations against the conspirator Catiline and the third of his five against the extortioner Verres.
[26]Vergil, *Aeneid*, VI.142 ff.
[27]"The light of truth" (*De oratore*, II.ix). For the rest of this famous definition of history see p. 828.
[28]"A compilation of annals" (*De oratore*, II.xii). [29]See pp. 856 f.
[30]See pp. 852 ff.
[31]*Giraldus . . . St. Albans*: Geraldus Cambrensis, Geoffrey of Monmouth, Ranulf Higden, and Thomas of Walsingham were medieval (or, as Milton contemptuously called them, "monkish") chroniclers who by the 17th century had become objects of derision. [32]"Become blind with age."
[33]Identified by Peacham in a marginal gloss as Diodorus Siculus, a Greek historian of the first century B.C.
[34]Jean Bodin (1530–96), eminent French historian and political economist, whose *Methodus ad facilem historiarum cognitionem* (1566) is one of the most notable works of historiography of the 16th century.
[35]"Farewell, Avicenna [an Arabian writer on medical subjects]! Long live Curtius!"
[36]*Chians . . . Aesculapius*: The great Greek physician Hippocrates was born (ca. 460 B.C.) on the Aegean island of Cos, not Chios. The mythical Aesculapius, god of medical science, was worshiped all over the Hellenic world.
[37]Theodore Gaza, 15th-century Greek scholar who emigrated to Italy and thereafter translated many Greek classics into Latin.
[38]Seneca's moral treatises (for example, *De providentia, De vita beata, De clementia*) were so widely admired by early Christian writers that St. Jerome and others believed him to have been a Christian and a correspondent of the Apostle Paul.

use, since you are like to live an eminent person in your country and mean to make no profession of scholarship. I have known even excellent scholars so defective this way that, when they had been beating their brains twenty or four-and-twenty years about Greek etymologies or the Hebrew roots and rabbins, could neither write true English nor true orthography. And to have heard them discourse in public or privately at a table, you would have thought you had heard Loy talking to his pigs or John de Indagine declaiming in the praise of wild geese;[39] otherwise for their [10] judgment in the arts and other tongues very sufficient.

To help yourself herein, make choice of those authors in prose who speak the best and purest English. I would commend unto you, though from more antiquity, the life of Richard the Third written by Sir Thomas More, the *Arcadia* of the noble Sir Philip Sidney, whom Du Bartas makes one of the four columns of our language, the *Essays* and other pieces of the excellent master of eloquence, my Lord of St. Albans, who possesseth not only eloquence but all good learning, as hereditary both by father and mother. You [20] have, then, Master Hooker his *Policy*; *Henry the Fourth*, well written by Sir John Hayward; that first part of our English kings by Master Samuel Daniel.[40] There are many others, I know, but these will taste[41] you best, as proceeding from no vulgar judgment. The last Earl of Northampton[42] in his ordinary style of writing was not to be mended. Procure, then, if you may, the speeches made in Parliament, frequent learned sermons; in term time resort to the Star Chamber, and be present at the pleadings in other public courts, whereby you shall better your speech, enrich your [30] understanding, and get more experience in one month than in other four by keeping your melancholy study and by solitary meditation. Imagine not that hereby I would bind you from reading all other books, since there is no book so bad, even *Sir Bevis* himself, *Owlglass*, or Nashe's *Herring*,[43] but some commodity[44] may be gotten by it. For as in the same pasture the ox findeth fodder, the hound a hare, the stork a lizard, the fair maid flowers, so we cannot, except we list[45] ourselves, sayeth Seneca, but depart the better from any book whatsoever. [40]

And ere you begin a book, forget not to read the epistle,[46] for commonly they are best labored and penned. For as in a garment, whatsoever the stuff[47] be, the owner for the most part affecteth a costly and extraordinary facing; and in the house of a country gentleman, the porch of a citizen, the carved gate and painted posts carry away the glory from the rest; so is it with our common authors. If they have any wit at all, they set it like velvet before, though the back, like a bankrupt's doublet, be but of poldavy[48] or buckram.

Affect not, as some do, that bookish ambition to be stored [50] with books and have well-furnished libraries yet keep their heads empty of knowledge. To desire to have many books and never to use them is like a child that will have a candle burning by him all the while he is sleeping.

Lastly, have a care of keeping your books handsome and well bound, not casting away overmuch in their gilding or stringing[49] for ostentation sake, like the prayer books of girls

and gallants, which are carried to church but for their outsides. Yet for your own use spare them not for noting or interlining, if they be printed, for it is not likely you mean to be a gainer by them when you have done with them; neither suffer them through negligence to mold and be moth-eaten or want their strings and covers.

King Alphonsus, about to lay the foundation of a castle at Naples, called for Vitruvius his book of architecture.[50] The book was brought in very bad case, all dusty and without covers, which the king observing said, "He that must cover us all must not go uncovered himself," then commanded the book to be fairly bound and brought unto him. So say I. Suffer them not to lie neglected who must make you regarded, and go in torn coats who must apparel your mind with the ornaments of knowledge above the robes and riches of the most magnificent princes.

To avoid the inconvenience of moths and moldiness, let your study be placed and your windows open, if it may be, toward the east, for where it looketh south or west, the air being ever subject to moisture, moths are bred and darkishness increased, whereby your maps and pictures will quickly become pale, losing their life and colors or, rotting upon their cloth or paper, decay past all help and recovery.

[39]*Loy . . . geese*: talking gibberish. The allusion to Loy and John de Indagine presumably derives from Thomas Nashe's epistle dedicatory to his *Lenten Stuff* (*Works*, ed. Ronald B. McKerrow, III, 148 f.), although the point of the allusion is by no means clear. St. Loy (or Elois or Eligius)—whose name was the "gretteste ooth" of Chaucer's Prioress—was the patron saint of goldsmiths and horse-keepers, and *John de Indagine* was probably the Johannes de Indagines who, as a Carthusian monk of the fifteenth century, wrote on theology and church history.
[40]*The life . . . Daniel*: The recommended works are More's famous *History of King Richard the Third*, which was written probably about 1513 and survives in both a Latin and an English version; Sidney's *Arcadia*, on the complex history of whose publication see p. 691, n. 19; Bacon's *Essays*, on which see p. 397; Richard Hooker's *Of the Laws of Ecclesiastical Polity* (1594 ff.), the most enduring monument of Anglican theology; Hayward's *First Part of the Life and Reign of King Henry the Fourth*, for which see p. 827; and Daniel's *Civil Wars*, a versified account of fifteenth-century English history that was published in installments between 1595 and 1609 (see p. 24). [41]Please.
[42]Henry Howard, first earl of Northampton (1540–1614), a son of Henry Howard, earl of Surrey (the Tudor poet and translator), who became one of the most powerful figures at the court of James I.
[43]*Sir Bevis . . . Herring*: trashy popular literature. *Bevis of Hampton* was a 14th-century verse romance; *Owlglass* was William Copland's *Howleglass*, a translation (ca. 1560) of German tales about the roguish Till Eulenspiegel; *Herring* was Thomas Nashe's *Lenten Stuff* (1599), a burlesque panegyric of red herring.
[44]Benefit. [45]Please. [46]Dedicatory epistle, preface. [47]Fabric. [48]Coarse canvas.
[49]Ties (of cord, ribbon, or leather) attached in pairs to the edges of book covers.
[50]*De architectura* by Pollio Vitruvius (first century B.C.), the most authoritative and influential treatise on classical architecture.

from The Truth of Our Times (1638)

To the Reader

It fareth with me now, honest reader, as with a travailer[1] in winter, who, having foolishly ventured over some dangerous river or passage quite frozen with ice, stands on the other side pointing with his finger and showing his following friends where it cracked. In the same manner I have ventured before, tried the coldness of these frozen and hard times together with the slippery ways of this deceitful and trustless world. Standing, I hope, now at the last safe on this other side, I show those that are to follow me where the danger is. I have seen and known much, as well in England as some- [10] where else abroad, and have had much acquaintance (and which hath been my happiness, if it be an happiness) with the most famous men of our time in all excellent professions, whence I am not altogether ignorant in the noble sciences, as well the theoric as practic,[2] but, to say the truth, I have ever found multiplicity of knowledge in many things to have been rather an hindrance than ever any way tending to advancement. Having hereby found much employment to no purpose, but as we see a carrier's horse when he is heavily loaden hath bells hung about his neck to give him some [20] content on the way and to allay the pain of his burthen, so have I taken pains and deserve well at the hands of many of good rank, yet got I never anything hereby save the horse-bells of praise, thanks, and fruitless promises, which, like the carriers, they can put on and take off at their pleasure. *Vix vivitur gratiis,*[3] sayeth Plautus. The peacock, as Mantuan[4] hath it, was admired for his plumes, which every beholder would be ready to snatch off, but in the meantime there was none of them all would give him so much as a grain to fill his belly. In a word, the main and most material of my [30] observations, and which the nearest concerned myself, reader, I present thee withal; the less will fall in of themselves, and are obvious. But fearing thou shouldst give me such a jeer as Diogenes did unto those of Myndum,[5] I make my gate but little lest the whole city should run out. Thus leaving what I have known by mine own experience to be certain unto thy friendly censure, I rest thine

H. P.

OF OPINION

Opinion is a monster of more heads than Hercules his Hydra.[6] And if one happily one be cut off, another ariseth forthwith in the room. One day when I [was] walking in Breda in Brabant [40] not far from the market place, I passed by a gentleman or merchant's house, over whose great gates was written in letters of gold upon a blue ground, *Totus mundus regitur opinione.*[7] I stood still and, pondering upon it, I found [it] witty and weighty, to concern the whole world and everyone in particular, and myself especially at that time, since I thought it to be the best that I had seen, which perhaps another would have disliked.

And I have often wondered why the ancient pagans, in their deifying so many, passed by opinion, bearing far greater sway than dogs, onions, and leeks in Egypt, *cui numen crescebat in hortis.*[8] Yet it is no great wonder. Since deifying was wont to be done with a general consent, Opinion was never to expect it, every man where she reigns being of a several mind. It was but opinion that caused Count Martinengo of Italy, of a noble house and of an exceeding great estate, to marry a common laundress. Whereupon, within two or three days following, Pasquin[9] in Rome had a foul shirt upon his back and underneath this in Italian: *Perche Pasquino,* etc. "Pasquin, how haps it thou hast a foul shirt on upon a Sunday morning?" *Riposto.*[10] "Because my laundress is made a countess."

It is but opinion that makes all the marriages in the world. For there is no beauty, favor, or complexion but is loved and liked of by one or other, nature so providing that none might be lost for having.

It is but opinion that great ladies many times marry their grooms, refusing great men and of great means.

It is but opinion that one goes to Rome, another to New England, and a third to Amsterdam. It is also but opinion that a proud coxcomb in the fashion, wearing taffeta and an ill-favored lock on his shoulder, thinks all that wear cloth and are out of fashion to be clowns, base and unworthy of his acquaintance.

So that opinion is the compass the fool only saileth by in the vast ocean of ignorance. For hereby vices are taken for virtues, and so the contrary. And all the errors that men commit in their whole lives is for want of the line and level of an even and true judgment. And it is the very rock whereat many, yea, the most, make shipwrack[11] of their credits, estates, and lives.

That emblem was a pretty one which was an old woman who, having gathered up into her apron many dead men's skulls which she found scattered upon the ground, with an intent to lay them up in a charnel house, but her apron slipping upon a hill where she stood, some ran one way and some another; which the old woman seeing, "Nay," quoth she, "go your ways, for thus ye differed in your opinion when ye had life, everyone taking his several way as he

TRUTH OF OUR TIMES [1]Traveler.
[2]Theoretical . . . practical.
[3]"One can hardly live on thanks."
[4]Johannes Baptista Spagnola (1448–1516), a Carmelite friar of Mantua who wrote (in Latin) ten influential eclogues.
[5]See p. 829, n. 10. *Myndum:* Myndus, a seaport in Asia Minor.
[6]In Greek myth, a nine-headed monster that grew two new heads for each one that was cut off. Hercules killed her with a firebrand. [7]"The whole world is ruled by opinion."
[8]"Whose god was growing in gardens." *Numen:* text *nomen.*
[9]A mutilated statue disinterred in Rome (1501) and set up near the Piazza Navona. On it were pasted satirical verses and lampoons (i.e., pasquinades). [10]"Answer." [11]Shipwreck.

fancied." There is no writer, none of public or private employment in the commonwealth, but passeth in danger by the den of this one-eyed Polyphemus.[12] And while I write, by how many opinions am I censured, one saying one thing and another another! But I am not so unhappy as to fear or care for them. I hold on a direct course and will never strike sail to rovers.[13]

OF FOLLOWING THE FASHION

Ecclesiasticus saith that "by gait, laughter, and apparel a man is known what he is."[14] Truly nothing more discovereth the gravity or levity of the mind than apparel. I never knew a solid or wise man to affect this popular vanity, which caused Henry the Fourth of France to say usually of his counselors and learneder sort of his courtiers that they had so much within them that they never cared to beg regard from feathers and gold lace. And himself would commonly go as plain as an ordinary gentleman or citizen, only in black, sometime in a suit no better than buckram. The Emperor Charles the Fifth seldom or never wore any gold or silver about him save his Order of the Fleece.[15] And the plainness of our English kings in former times hath been very remarkable. King Henry the Eighth was the first that ever ware[16] a band about his neck, and that very plain, without lace, and about an inch or two in depth. We may see how the case is altered. He is not a gentleman, nor in the fashion, whose band of Italian cutwork now standeth[17] him not at the least in three or four pounds. Yea, a seamster in Holborn[18] told me that there are of threescore pound price a piece, and shoeties that go under the name of roses, from thirty shillings to three, four, and five pounds the pair. Yea, a gallant of the time not long since paid thirty pound for a pair. I would have had him by himself to have eaten that dish of buttered eggs prepared with musk and ambergris, which cost thirty and five pounds, and when his belly had been full, to have laid him to sleep upon my Lady N[—'s] bed, whose furniture cost her ladyship five hundred and threescore pounds.

I never knew any wholly affected to follow fashions to have been any way useful or profitable to the commonwealth, except that way Aristotle affirmeth the prodigal man to be, by scattering his money about to the benefit of many—tailors, seamsters, silkmen, etc. Neither ever knew I any man esteemed the better or the wiser for his bravery but among simple people. Now this thing we call the fashion [is] so much hunted and pursued after, like a thief with an hue and cry, that our tailors dog it into France even to the very door. It reigns commonly like an epidemical disease, first infecting the court, then the City, after the country, from the countess to the *chambrière*,[19] who rather than she will want her curled locks will turn them up with a hot pair of tongs instead of the irons. The fashion, like an higher orb, hath the revolution commonly every hundred year, when the same comes into request again; which I saw once in Antwerp handsomely described by an he- and she-fool turning a wheel about, with hats, hose, and doublets in the fashion fastened round about it, which, when they were below, began to mount up again, as we see them. For example, in the time of King Henry the Seventh the slashed[20]

doublets now used were in request. Only the coats of the king's guard[21] keep the same form they did since they were first given them by the said King, who was the first king of England that had a guard about his person, and that by the advice of Sir William Stanley, who was shortly after beheaded for treason, albeit he set the crown, found thrown in a hawthorn bush, upon the King's head in the field.[22] After that the Flemish fashion in the time of King Henry the Eighth came in request—of straight doublets, huge breeches let out with puffs and codpieces. In Queen Mary's time the Spanish was much in use.[23] In Queen Elizabeth's time were the great-bellied doublets, wide saucy sleeves that would be in every dish before their master, and buttons as big as tablemen[24] or the lesser sort of Sandwich turnips, with huge ruffs that stood like cartwheels about their necks, and round breeches not much unlike St. Omer's onions, whereto the long stocking without garters was joined; which then was the earl of Leicester's fashion, and theirs who had the handsomest leg.[25] The women wore straight-bodied gowns with narrow sleeves drawn out with lawn or fine cambric in puff, with highbolstered wings, little ruffs edged with gold or black silk. And maids wore cauls[26] of gold, now quite out of use. Chains of gold were then of lords, knights and gentlemen commonly worn, but a chain of gold now (to so high a rate is gold raised) is as much as some of them are worth.

The like variety hath been in hats, which have been but of late years. Henry the Fourth is commonly portrayed with a hood on his head such as the liveries of the City[27] wear on their shoulders. Henry the Sixth, the Seventh, and Eighth wore only caps. King Philip[28] in England wore commonly a somewhat high velvet cap with a white feather. After came in hats of all fashions, some with crowns so high that, beholding them far off, you would have thought you had discovered the Tenerife.[29] Those close to the head like bar-

---

[12]In the *Odyssey*, a one-eyed Cyclops who imprisoned Odysseus and his companions in a cave. [13]Pirates.

[14]The Apocryphal Ecclesiasticus or the Wisdom of Jesus the Son of Sirach 19.30.

[15]The prestigious Order of the Golden Fleece was founded by Philip the Good of Burgundy in 1429. [16]Wore. [17]Costs.

[18]A commercial district in London. [19]"Chambermaid."

[20]Having vertical slits to show a contrasting lining.

[21]The Yeomen of the Guard, the personal bodyguard for the sovereign instituted by Henry VII in 1485, who even today retain their original uniforms on duty in the Tower of London.

[22]The famous scene occurred at the battle of Bosworth Field (September 1485) when the usurper Henry, earl of Richmond, defeated Richard III to become Henry VII, the first Tudor king of England.

[23]The Catholic Mary took as her consort Philip II of Spain.

[24]Pieces used for a game played upon a board, like chess.

[25]Robert Dudley, earl of Leicester (1532?–88) was Elizabeth's favorite and therefore most powerful courtier in her early reign. [26]Netted caps.

[27]Freemen of the City of London were entitled to wear the liveries of their companies or guilds.

[28]Philip II of Spain lived in England only briefly following his marriage with Queen Mary in 1554.

[29]The largest of the Canary Islands, the chief feature of which is a

er's basins, with narrow brims, we were at that time beholden to Cadiz in Spain for. After them came up those with square crowns and brims almost as broad as a brewer's mash-fat[30] or a reasonable upper stone of a mustard quern,[31] which among my other epigrams gave me occasion of this:

> Soranzo's broad-brimmed hat I oft compare
> To the vast compass of the heavenly sphere:
> His head, the earth's globe fixed under it,
> Whose center is his wondrous little wit.

No less variety hath been in hatbands, the cypress[32] being now quite out of use save among some few of the graver sort.

Wherefore the Spaniard and Dutch are much to be commended, who for some hundreds of years never altered their fashion, but have kept always one and the same.

The Switzers, ever since the fatal and final overthrow which they gave to the Duke of Burgundy at Nancy in Lorraine,[33] have worn their parti-colored doublets, breeches, and codpieces, drawn out with huge puffs of taffeta or linen, and their stockings, like the knave of our cards, parti-colored of red and yellow or other colors. I remember at the taking in of the town of Rees in Cleveland between Wesel and Embrick[34] upon the river of Rhine (I being there at the same time), when a part of the Swiss quarter, being before the town, was by accident burned. I demanded of a Swiss captain the reason of their so much affecting colors above other nations. He told me the occasion was honorable, which was this. At what time the Duke of Burgundy received his overthrow and the Swiss recovering their liberty, he entered the field in all the state and pomp he could possible[35] devise. He brought with him all his plate and jewels; all his tents were of silk of several colors, which, the battle being ended, being torn all to pieces by the Swiss soldiers, of a part of one color they made them doublets, of the rest of other colors breeches, stockings, and caps, returning home in that habit. So ever since, in remembrance of that famous victory by them achieved and their liberty recovered, even to this day they go still in their parti-colors. Let me not forget to tell you the occasion of this mortal war. It was only, as Guicciardini[36] tells us, but for the toll of a load of calves' skins coming over a bridge, which toll the Duke claimed as his right and the Swiss theirs. But this by the way.

I have much wondered why our English above other nations should so much dote upon new fashions, but more I wonder at our want of wit that we cannot invent them ourselves, but, when one is grown stale, run presently over into France to seek a new, making that noble and flourishing kingdom the magazine of our fooleries. And for this purpose many of our tailors lie leger[37] there and ladies post over their gentlemen-ushers to accouter them and themselves as you see. Hence came your slashed doublets (as if the wearers were cut out to be carbonadoed[38] upon the coals) and your half shirts; piccadillies,[39] now out of request; your long breeches, narrow toward the knees like a pair of smith's bellows; the spangled garters pendant to the shoe; your perfumed perukes or periwigs to show us that lost hair may be had again for money; with a thousand such fooleries unknown to our manly forefathers.

It was a saying of that noble Roman Cato, *Cui corporis*

summa cura, ei virtutis maxima incuria.[40] And most true it is, since on the contrary we daily find by experience our greatest scholars and statists[41] to offend on the contrary part, being careless and sometime slovenly in their apparel that many times—their thoughts being taken up with studious and profound meditations—they forget to button or to truss themselves. They love their old clothes better than new; they care not for curious setting their ruff, wearing cuffs, etc.

Erasmus in *Epistolis*, I remember, reporteth of Sir Thomas More that *a puero in vestitu semper fuit negligentissimus.*[42] And I believe it to be most true that God hath said by the mouth of his prophet, that "He will visit or send his plague among such as are clothed with strange apparel."[43]

A RELIGIOUS HONEST MAN

I never knew any man of sound judgment and fit for employment either in church or commonwealth but he endeavored to be religious. For *virtutem vel optimarum actionum basis religio,*[44] and there are many who, though they make no outward show thereof by those actions and gestures which may also be common to hypocrites, yet the bias of the life of an honest man would ever lean, for doing and discourse, to a serious service of God. Hence such men keep their church together with their families constantly, there carrying himself with the greatest reverence and humility.

You shall know a religious honest man by humility, charity, or love of hospitality. Hence he is discreet in his discourse, affable, pleasant, and peaceable among his neighbors, loving, and beloved.

He backbiteth and traduceth none, meddleth not with matters and affairs of state, well knowing, like those builders of the Tower of Babel, that a rash affection of things too high bringeth discord and confusion. And if any controversy shall arise among his neighbors, he commonly hath compounded the strife ere the la[w]yer can finger his fee.

His tithes he payeth cheerfully and with the most, well knowing that God by Malachi hath promised a blessing by

---

dormant volcano more than 12,200 feet high.
[30]Mash-vat.
[31]A small handmill for grinding pepper, mustard, etc.
[32]A fabric brought originally from the island of Cyprus.
[33]Their great victory over Charles the Bold of Burgundy on 5 January 1477 established the military reputation of the Swiss, who were thereafter in great demand as mercenaries.
[34]The town of Rees in the Duchy of Cleves between Wesel and Emmerich on the lower Rhine. [35]Possibly.
[36]Franceso Guicciardini (1483–1540), Florentine historian whose *Storia d'Italia* (1561–64) is one of the monuments of Renaissance historiography. [37]Ledger, i.e., resident, permanent.
[38]Scored across and broiled.
[39]Expansive collars with laced or perforated borders.
[40]He who is chiefly concerned with the health of his body neglects his soul. [41]Statesmen.
[42]"From childhood he was always supremely indifferent to his dress." [43]Zephaniah 1.8.
[44]"Religion is the foundation of virtue and of our best actions." *Virtutem*: text *virtutum*.

the opening of the windows of heaven upon such as pay their tithes truly and with alacrity.[45]

He is versed and very ready in the Holy Scriptures and their orthodox exposition, never wresting or misapplying them, as sectaries[46] do to serve their purposes and suit with their fantastical or willful opinions.

As Mahomet and his followers affirmed that place of St. John, where our Saviour saith, "I will send you a comforter,"[47] to be meant of himself, or in that place something to be written of Mahomet which the Christians have scraped or blotted out.

So not long since a false prophet affirmed that himself was one of those two witnesses St. John speaketh of in the eleventh of the Revelation.[48]

The like examples may be produced from David-George, Knipperdolling, Hacket,[49] and others, which we pass.

Again, the moderate religious man forbears with open mouth to rail against the pope, but speaks of him in a modest reverence as of a great bishop and a temporal prince.

He is also to his power a benefactor to poor scholars, and though not learned himself, he is a prompter[50] of learning. So was Wykeham, Bishop of Winchester,[51] who, being no great scholar himself, said, to make amends he would make scholars, and soon after he founded Winchester School and New College in Oxford.

He loveth unity and praiseth it as well in church or commonwealth as his own parish and family. Hence is he opposite *ex diametro*[52] to separatists and schismatics, who, since they fall in my way, let me tell you what out of my own experience I have known and found by them, having remained a good time at Leyden in Holland and other places where they have their congregations and conventicles. There are about thirty-two several sects, among some whereof are called *huiskoopers*, other *huisverkoopers*, i.[e.], housebuyers and housesellers, and such enmity there is among them that the pride of their heads or ringleaders will never [allow] an unity one with another.

Now why our sectaries should single out themselves after[53] this manner I confess I know not; perhaps not without the divine providence, and for that very same reason Joseph Acosta[54] giveth of beasts and birds of prey, whom God as pernicious and hurtful to mankind hath set at odds and at enmity one with the other. For if they should accompany together in herds and flocks, they would overrun and devour a whole country, as among beasts, lions, bears, wolves, foxes, badgers, polecats, etc.; and among birds, eagles, hawks, kites, ravens, vultures, buzzards, etc., when nature for the behoof of man hath set others which are most profitable unto him at unity among themselves and to live peacefully one with the other, as kine, horses, deer, sheep, goats, conies, etc.; of birds, pigeons, geese, ducks, partridges, the most of the daintiest of sea birds, with sundry others.

I have heard some of their sermons and been present at their private ordinary discourse, and somewhat alway seasoned the same that savored either pride or malice or both, especially against our church and the happy and well-settled estate of the same.

We must make a difference between our stricter people in England, whom your profaner sort call Precisians, and those who are superintendents over a few buttonmakers and weavers at Amsterdam. For of ours we have many conformable to His Majesty's laws and the ceremonies of the church, carrying themselves very honestly and consconably; among which I reckon not the professed Puritan, of whom I know many who gladly take that name and profession upon them, being tradesmen in cities and market towns, only to get custom to their shops. And working themselves into the opinion of the world to be honest, religious, and upright-dealing men, they procure to themselves many salutations—like the Pharisees—in the market place, and hence they become the prime men at feasts and meetings, and are trusted with the estates and education of men's children at the death of the parents, out of the opinion of their zeal and honesty, whereby they become marvelous rich and by consequent so proud that, as St. Augustine saith of the Donatists,[55] *ne nostri cuiquam dicant Ave*, they will not bid a conformist good morrow or good even, and, sitting in their fur- or velvet-faced gowns, with their neat-set double ruffs, they tax, with Augustus, all the world.[56] But some of these men have not many years since reformed themselves.

There is yet another sort amongst us worse than these, who like double-faced Janus one way look to their own parish church and the other eastward toward St. Peter's in Rome. These indeed are *filii huius seculi*,[57] and here only have their reward, making religion only as a cloak or waistcoat to be worn both sides alike. Some profess themselves Roman Catholics that their families might keep Lent, all the saints' eves, Ember,[58] and all other fasting days, whereby their masters save in their victuals their whole year's wages. Another while they are Protestants and will monthly visit the church to avoid the penalty of the law[59] or to insinuate

---

[45]Malachi 3.10.

[46]Sectarians, i.e., members of the various schismatical or heretical offshoots of the major reformed churches.

[47]"And I will pray the Father, and he shall give you another Comforter, that he may abide with you forever" (John 14.16).

[48]Revelation 11.3.

[49]Respectively, the founder of a sect called Davidists and a self-proclaimed Messiah, a notorious leader of the Anabaptists at Munster, and an English fanatic who (with his associate Edward Coppinger) was executed for alleged plots against the queen (1591).

[50]Promoter.

[51]William of Wykeham (1324–1404), an ecclesiastical politician whose notable contributions to English civilization included Winchester School (1378) and New College, Oxford (1379).

[52]"Diametrically."   [53]Text *aftes*.

[54]José de Acosta, a Spanish missionary whose *Historia Natural y Moral de las Indias* appeared in 1590.

[55]Members of a 4th-century Christian schismatic sect in North Africa that was strenuously denounced by Augustine, bishop of Hippo.

[56]A pun upon *tax*-accuse and *tax*-impose a tax upon (after the manner of the Emperor Augustus, who ruled the whole known world).   [57]"Sons of this age."

[58]Ember days, when fasting and prayers are observed at certain times in the ecclesiastical calendar of the Roman Catholic and other Christian churches.

[59]Under the Act of Uniformity passed by Elisabeth's first

themselves into some gainful employment or other in the commonwealth. These be those lukewarm Laodiceans[60] whom God cannot digest and whom I have known both Protestant and papist alike to have discarded. There, I remember, is a country, whether Utopia or no, where those who side equally with contrary factions wear parti-colored coats and stockings. Besides, they are great rackers[61] of their tenants, backward and resty[62] in all levies and payments for the common good, seldom charitable to the poor, and the

worst payers of their tithes and duties to the church and minister that may be.

Parliament (1559), persons absenting themselves from Anglican services were liable to progressively severe penalties.
[60]According to St. John (Revelation 3.15), the members of the church at Laodicea were "neither cold nor hot."
[61]Landlords who charge excessive rents.   [62]Sluggish.

Thomas Fuller[1] [1608-1661]

from The Holy State *and* The Profane State (1642)

THE HOLY STATE

TO THE READER

Who is not sensible with sorrow[1] of the distractions of this age? To write books, therefore, may seem unseasonable, especially in a time wherein the press, like an unruly horse, hath cast off his bridle of being licensed, and some serious books which dare fly abroad are hooted at by a flock of pamphlets.[2]

But be pleased to know that when I left my home it was fair weather, and my journey was half past before I discovered the tempest and had gone so far in this work that I could neither go backward with credit nor forward with comfort.

As for the matter of this book, therein I am resident in my profession, holiness in the latitude thereof falling under the cognizance[3] of a divine. For curious method, expect none, essays for the most part not being placed as at a feast, but placing themselves as at an ordinary.[4]

The characters I have conformed to the then standing laws of the realm. A twelvemonth ago were they sent to the press, since which time the wisdom of the king and state hath thought fitting to alter many things, and I expect the discretion of the reader should make his alterations accordingly. And I conjure thee, by all Christian ingenuity, that if lighting here on some passages rather harsh-sounding than ill-intended to construe the same by the general drift and main scope which is aimed at.

Nor let it render the modesty of this book suspected because it presumes to appear in company unmanned by any patron. If right, it will defend itself; if wrong, none can defend it. Truth needs not, falsehood deserves not a supporter. And indeed the matter of this work is too high for a subject's, the workmanship thereof too low for a prince's, patronage.

And now I will turn my pen into prayer that God would be pleased to discloud these gloomy days with the beams of His mercy, which if I may be so happy as to see it will then encourage me to count it freedom to serve two apprenticeships[5] (God spinning out the thick thread of my life so long) in writing the ecclesiastical history from Christ's time to our days,[6] if I shall from remoter parts be so planted as to enjoy the benefit of walking and standing libraries,[7] without which advantages the best vigilancy doth but vainly dream to undertake such a task.

Meantime I will stop the leakage of my soul, and what heretofore hath run out in writing shall hereafter, God willing, be improved in constant preaching in what place soever God's providence, with friends' good will, shall fix.

Thine in all Christian offices,
Thomas Fuller

THE SECOND BOOK

CHAPTER IV. THE CONTROVERSIAL DIVINE

He is truth's champion to defend her against all adversaries, atheists, heretics, schismatics, and erroneous persons whatso-

---

[1]For a commentary on Fuller and other excerpts from his work see Religion and Politics, pp.575 ff.
HOLY...PROFANE STATE   [1]Sorrowfully aware.
[2]When the Long Parliament, in 1640, eased the rigid censorship that had been decreed by Charles I and enforced by the hated Court of the Star Chamber, a flood of pamphlets (most of them by disaffected Puritans) poured from the presses.   [3]Crest, badge.
[4]A public meal for a fixed price in an inn or tavern.
[5]As preacher and writer.
[6]For Fuller's *Church History of Britain*, which finally appeared in 1655, see pp. 577 ff.
[7]Gather data from both learned persons and from books. Fuller himself was subsequently described by an anonymous biographer

ever. His sufficiency appears in opposing, answering, moderating, and writing.

Maxim 1. *He engageth both his judgment and affections in opposing all falsehood.* Not like country fencers who play only to make sport, but like duelers indeed, at it for life and limb, chiefly if the question be of large prospect and great concernings, he is zealous in the quarrel. Yet some, though their judgment weigh down on one side, the beam of their affections stands so even they care not which part prevails.

2. *In opposing a truth, he dissembles himself her foe, to be her better friend.* Wherefore he counts himself the greatest conqueror when truth hath taken him captive. With Joseph, having sufficiently sifted the matter in a disguise, he discovereth himself: "I am Joseph, your brother,"[8] and then throws away his vizard. Dishonest they, who, though the debt be satisfied, will never give up the bond, but continue wrangling when the objection is answered.

3. *He abstains from all foul and railing language.* What! make the Muses, yea, the Graces, scolds? Such purulent[9] spittle argues exulcerated lungs. Why should there be so much railing about the body of Christ, when there was none about the body of Moses in the act kept betwixt the devil and Michael the Archangel?[10]

4. *He tyrannizeth not over a weak and undermatched adversary,* but seeks rather to cover his weakness, if he be a modest man. When a professor pressed an answerer[11] (a better Christian than a clerk) with an hard argument, "*Reverende Professor,*" said he, "*ingenue confiteor me non posse respondere huic argumento.*" To whom the professor, "*Rectè respondes.*"[12]

5. *In answering, he states the question, and expoundeth the terms thereof.* Otherwise the disputants shall end, where they ought to have begun, in differences about words; and be barbarians each to other, speaking in a language neither understand. If the question also be of historical cognizance, he shows the pedigree thereof—who first brewed it, who first broached it—and sends the wandering error, with a passport, home to the place of its birth.

6. *In taking away an objection, he not only puts by the thrust, but breaks the weapon.* Some rather escape than defeat an argument; and though by such an evasion they may shut the mouth of the opponent, yet may they open the difficulty wider in the hearts of the hearers. But our answerer either fairly resolves the doubt, or else shows the falseness of the argument by beggaring the opponent to maintain such a fruitful generation of absurdities as his argument hath begotten, or, lastly, returns and retorts it back upon him again. The first way unties the knot, the second cuts it asunder, the third whips the opponent with the knot himself tied. Sure, 'tis more honor to be a clear answerer than a cunning opposer, because the latter takes advantage of man's ignorance, which is ten times more than his knowledge.

7. *What his answers want in suddenness, they have in solidity.* Indeed, the speedy answer adds luster to the disputation and honor to the disputant; yet he makes good payment who, though he cannot presently throw the money out of his pocket, yet will pay it, if but going home to unlock his chest. Some that are not for *speedy* may be for *sounder* performance. When Melancthon, at the disputation of Ratisbon,

was pressed with a shrewd argument by Eckius, "I will answer thee," said he, "tomorrow." "Nay," said Eckius, "do it now, or it's nothing worth." "Yea," said Melancthon, "I seek the truth, and not mine own credit; and therefore it will be as good if I answer thee tomorrow by God's assistance."[13]

8. *In moderating, he sides with the answerer if the answerer sides with the truth.* But if he be conceited, and opinioned of his own sufficiency, he lets him swound[14] before he gives him any hot water. If a paradox-monger, loving to hold strange, yea, dangerous, opinions, he counts it charity to suffer such a one to be beaten without mercy, that he may be weaned from his wilfulness. For the main, he is so a staff to the answerer that he makes him stand on his own legs.

9. *In writing, his Latin is pure, so far as the subject will allow.* For, those who are to climb the Alps are not to expect a smooth and even way. True it is that Schoolmen, perceiving that fallacy had too much covert under the nap of flourishing language, used threadbare Latin on purpose, and cared not to trespass on grammar and tread down the fences thereof to avoid the circuit of words and to go the nearest way to express their conceits. But our divine, though he useth barbarous school-terms, which, like standers,[15] are fixed to the controversy, yet in his movable Latin passages and digressions his style is pure and elegant.

10. *He affects clearness and plainness in all his writings.* Some men's heads are like the world before God said unto it, *Fiat lux!*[16] These dark-lanterns may shine to themselves, and understand their own conceits, but nobody else can have light from them. Thus Matthias Farinator, Professor at Vienna, assisted with some other learned men, as the times then went, was thirty years making a book of applying Plato's, Aristotle's, and Galen's rules in philosophy to Christ and His prophets; and 'tis called *Lumen Animae; quo tamen nihil est caliginosius, labore magno, sed ridiculo et inani.*[17] But this obscurity is worst when affected; when they do as Persius, of whom one saith, *Legi voluit quae scripsit, intelligi noluit quae legerentur.*[18] Some affect this darkness that they may be accounted profound, whereas one is not bound to believe that all the water is deep that is muddy.

11. *He is not curious in searching matters of no moment.* Captain

(*The Life of That Divine and Learned Historian, Dr. Thomas Fuller*, 1661), as "a perfect walking library."

[8]Genesis 45.4.   [9]Corrupt, festering.

[10]When the Archangel Michael contended with the devil for the body of Moses, he "durst not bring against him a railing accusation, but said, the Lord rebuke thee" (Jude, Verse 9). *Act*: transaction, contention.   [11]Adversary in a dispute.

[12]"Honored Professor, I candidly admit that I am unable to answer your argument." "You answer correctly."

[13]At the Conference of Ratisbon (1541) the Lutheran reformer Philip Melanchthon skillfully defended his views against the Roman Catholic Johann Eck (or Eckius), a formidable theological adversary.   [14]Swoon.   [15]Fixtures.

[16]"Let there be light" (Genesis 1.3).

[17]*The Light of the Soul*, a work of great labor which, however, is ridiculous and useless."

[18]"He wished readers for what he wrote, but he did not care whether they understood what they read."

Martin Frobisher[19] fetched from the farthest northern countries a ship's lading of mineral stones (as he thought) which afterwards were cast out to mend the highways. Thus are they served, and miss their hopes, who, long seeking to extract hidden mysteries out of nice questions, leave them off as useless at last. Antoninus Pius,[20] for his desire to search to the least differences, was called *cumini sector,* "the carver of cumin seed." One need not be so accurate, for as soon shall one scour the spots out of the moon as all ignorance out of man. When Eunomius the heretic vaunted that he knew God and His divinity, St. Basil[21] gravels[22] him in twenty-one questions about the body of an ant or pismire: so dark is man's understanding! I wonder, therefore, at the boldness of some, who, as if they were lord-marshals of the angels, place them in ranks and files. Let us not believe them here, but rather go to heaven to confute them.

12. *He neither multiplies needless, nor compounds necessary, controversies.* Sure, they light on a labor in vain who seek to make a bridge of reconciliation over the μέγα χάσμα[23] betwixt papists and Protestants; for though we go ninety-nine steps, they (I mean their church) will not come one to give us a meeting. And as for the offers of Clara's[24] and private men (besides that they seem to be more of the nature of baits than gifts), they may make large proffers without any commission to treat, and so the Romish church not bound to pay their promises. In Merionethshire, in Wales, there are high mountains, whose hanging tops come so close together that shepherds on the tops of several hills may audibly talk together, yet will it be a day's journey for their bodies to meet, so vast is the hollowness of the valleys betwixt them! Thus, upon sound search, shall we find a grand distance and remoteness betwixt popish and Protestant tenents[25] to reconcile them, which, at the first view, may seem near, and tending to an accommodation.

13. *He is resolute and stable in fundamental points of religion.* These are his fixed poles and axletree about which he moves whilst they stand unmovable. Some sail so long on the sea of controversies, tossed up and down, to and fro, *pro and con,* that the very ground to them seems to move, and their judgments grow sceptical and unstable in the most settled points of divinity. When he cometh to preach, especially if to a plain auditory, with the Paracelsians[26] he extracts an oil out of the driest and hardest bodies; and, knowing that knotty timber is unfit to build with, he edifies people with easy and profitable matter.

CHAPTER VII. THE GENERAL ARTIST[27]

I know the general cavil against general learning is this: that *aliquis in omnibus est nullus in singulis.* "He that sips of many arts, drinks of none." However, we must know that all learning, which is but one grand science, hath so homogeneal a body that the parts thereof do with a mutual service relate to and communicate strength and luster each to other. Our artist, knowing language to be the key of learning, thus begins.

Maxim 1. *His tongue being but one by nature, he gets cloven by art and industry.* Before the confusion of Babel[28] all the world was one continent in language, since divided into several tongues as several islands. Grammar is the ship by benefit whereof we pass from one to another in the learned languages generally spoken in no country. His mother tongue was like the dull music of a monochord, which, by study, he turns into the harmony of several instruments.

2. *He first gaineth skill in the Latin and Greek tongues.* On the credit of the former alone he may trade in discourse over all Christendom. But the Greek, though not so generally spoken, is known with no less profit, and more pleasure. The joints of her compounded words are so naturally oiled that they run nimbly on the tongue, which makes them, though long, never tedious because significant. Besides, it is full and stately in sound: only it pities our artist to see the vowels therein racked in pronouncing them, hanging oftentimes one way by their native force, and haled another by their accents which countermand them.

3. *Hence he proceeds to the Hebrew, the mother tongue of the world.* More pains than quickness of wit is required to get it, and with daily exercise he continues it. Apostasy herein is usual, to fall totally from the language by a little neglect. As for the Arabic and other oriental languages, he rather makes sallies and incursions into them than any solemn sitting down before them.

4. *Then he applies his study to logic and ethics.* The latter makes a man's soul mannerly and wise; but as for logic, that is the armory of reason, furnished with all offensive and defensive weapons. There are syllogisms, long swords; enthymemes,[29] short daggers; dilemmas, two-edged swords that cut on both sides; sorites,[30] chain-shot:[31] and, for the defensive, distinctions, which are shields; retortions,[32] which are targets with a pike in the midst of them, both to defend and oppose. From hence he raiseth his studies to the knowledge of physics, the great hall of nature, and metaphysics, the closet thereof; and is careful not to wade therein so far till, by subtle distinguishing of notions, he confounds himself.

[19]Sir Martin Frobisher (1535?–94), English mariner who sought (but failed to find) the Northwest Passage, served under Sir Francis Drake in the West Indies, and commanded a ship against the Spanish Armada in 1588.
[20]Roman emperor (138–61) whose reign was notably serene.
[21]*Eunomius...Basil:* respectively, a Roman Catholic bishop (d. ca. 393) deposed for his adherence to the Arian heresy, and a bishop of Caesarea (330?–79) famed for his unyielding orthodoxy.
[22]Perplexes. [23]"Great chasm."
[24]Christopher Davenport (1598–1680), one of Queen Henrietta Maria's chaplains and a friend of Archbishop Laud who, under the soubriquet Franciscus a Santa Clara, tried to effect a reconciliation between the Roman Catholic and Anglican churches. His principal work was *Deus, natura, gratia* (1634). [25]Tenets.
[26]Followers of Philippus Aureolus Paracelsus (1493?–1541), an alchemist and physician notorious for his unorthodox opinions and daring experiments. [27]One trained in the liberal arts.
[28]See Genesis 11.1–9.
[29]In logic, defective arguments in which the conclusion or one of the premises is not stated.
[30]In logic, compound syllogisms made of successive coordinate members. For example: Spot is a dog, a dog is a quadruped, a quadruped is an animal, therefore Spot is an animal.
[31]Cannonballs linked together. [32]Retorts, counter-arguments.

5. *He is skilful in rhetoric, which gives a speech color, as logic doth favor, and both together beauty.* Though some condemn rhetoric as the mother of lies, speaking more than the truth in hyperboles, less in her meiosis,[33] otherwise in her metaphors, contrary in her ironies; yet is there excellent use of all these when disposed of with judgment. Nor is he a stranger to poetry, which is music in words; nor to music, which is poetry in sound; both excellent sauce, but they have lived and died poor that made them their meat.

6. *Mathematics he moderately studieth, to his great contentment.* 10 Using it as ballast for his soul, yet to fix it, not to stall it; nor suffers he it to be so unmannerly as to justle out other arts. As for judicial astrology (which hath the least judgment in it) this vagrant hath been whipped out of all learned corporations. If our artist lodgeth her in the outrooms of his soul for a night or two, it is rather to hear than believe her relations.

7. *Hence he makes his progress into the study of history.* Nestor, who lived three ages, was accounted the wisest man in the world. But the historian may make himself wise 20 by living as many ages as have passed since the beginning of the world. His books enable him to maintain discourse, who, besides the stock of his own experience, may spend on the common purse of his reading. This directs him in his life so that he makes the shipwracks of others seamarks to himself; yea, accidents which others start from for their strangeness, he welcomes as his wonted acquaintance, having found precedents for them formerly. Without history a man's soul is purblind, seeing only the things which almost touch his eyes.

8. *He is well seen*[34] *in chronology, without which history is but* 30 *a heap of tales.* If, by the laws of the land, he is counted a natural who hath not wit enough to tell twenty, or to tell his age, he shall not pass with me for wise in learning who cannot tell the age of the world, and count hundreds of years: I mean not so critically as to solve all doubts arising thence, but that he may be able to give some tolerable account thereof. He is also acquainted with cosmography, treating of the world in whole joints; with chorography,[35] shredding it into countries; and with topography, mincing it into particular places. 40

Thus, taking these sciences in their general latitude, he hath finished the round circle, or golden ring, of the arts; only he keeps a place for the diamond to be set in; I mean for that predominant profession of law, physic, divinity, or state-policy, which he intends for his principal calling hereafter.

Chapter XXIV. The Life of Master William Camden

William Camden was born *anno* 1550[36] in Old Bailey in the City of London. His father, Samson Camden, was descended of honest parentage in Staffordshire, but by his mother's side he was extracted from the worshipful family of the Cur- 50 wens in Cumberland.

He was brought up first in Christ Church, then in Paul's School,[37] in London; and at fifteen years of age went to Magdalen College in Oxford, and thence to Broadgates Hall where he first made those short Latin graces which the

servitors still use. From hence he was removed, and made student of Christ Church where he profited to such eminency that he was preferred to be Master of Westminster School,[38] a most famous seminary of learning.

For whereas before, of the two grand schools of England[39] one sent all her foundation scholars[40] to Cambridge, the other all to Oxford, the good queen (as the head equally favoring both breasts of learning and religion) divided her scholars here betwixt both universities, which were enriched with many hopeful plants sent from hence, through Camden's learning, diligence, and clemency.[41] Sure, none need pity the beating of that scholar who would not learn without it under so meek a master.

His deserts called him hence to higher employments. The queen first made him Richmond Herald, and then Clarencieux King of Arms.[42] We read how Dionysius, first king of Sicily, turned afterwards a schoolmaster in his old age. Behold here Dionysius inverted, one that was a schoolmaster in his youth become a King (of Arms) in his riper years, which place none ever did or shall discharge with more integrity.[43] He was a most exact antiquary: witness his worthy work, which is a comment on three kingdoms, and never was so large a text more briefly—so dark a text more plainly—expounded.[44] Yea, what a fair garment hath been made out of the very shreds and remains of that greater work![45]

[33]In rhetoric, the use of understatement, with the suggestion that something is less in size or significance than in fact it is.
[34]Versed.
[35]The art of describing or mapping particular regions. Michael Drayton described his *Poly-Olbion* (1612, 1622) as a "chorographical description" of Great Britain.
[36]Camden was born 2 May 1551.
[37]Christ's Hospital, a school for poor children founded under a charter of Edward VI, and St. Paul's School, which had been established (1512) by John Colet (with the assistance of Erasmus). Coleridge and Lamb would one day attend the former, Milton and Pepys the latter.
[38]Another distinguished Tudor foundation, established by Queen Elizabeth in 1560, whose students were to include Jonson, George Herbert, Locke, Dryden, and many other famous Englishmen. Camden served as its usher (or submaster) from 1575 to 1593, and thereafter as its headmaster until 1597, when he was appointed Clarencieux King-of-Arms.
[39]St. Paul's, whose students generally went to Cambridge, and Winchester, whose students generally went to New College, Oxford (which, like Winchester, had been founded in the later 14th century by William of Wykeham, bishop of Winchester and chancellor of England).   [40]Scholarship students.
[41]Mildness of manner.
[42]Offices in the Heralds' College, the body entrusted by the crown with authenticating armorial bearings and genealogies.
[43]For a different opinion of Camden's qualifications for his high office see pp. 822 ff.
[44]Fuller alludes, of course, to Camden's famous *Britannia* (1586), for which see pp. 817 ff.
[45]*Remains of a Greater Work Concerning Britain* (1605), a book that Camden himself called "the rude rubble and outcast rubbish of a great and more serious work."

It is most worthy observation with what diligence he inquired after ancient places, making hue and cry after many a city which was run away, and, by certain marks and tokens, pursuing to find it, as by the situation on the Roman highways, by just distance from other ancient cities, by some affinity of name, by tradition of the inhabitants, by Roman coins digged up, and by some appearance of ruins. A broken urn is a whole evidence, or an old gate still surviving, out of which the city is run out. Besides, commonly some new, spruce town, not far off, is grown out of the ashes thereof, which yet hath so much natural affection as dutifully to own those reverend ruins for her mother.

By these and other means, he arrived at admirable knowledge, and restored Britain to herself. And let none tax him for presumption in conjectures where the matter was doubtful, for many probable conjectures have stricken the fire out of which truth's candle hath been lighted afterwards. Besides, conjectures, like parcels of unknown ore, are sold but at low rates: if they prove some rich metal, the buyer is a great gainer; if base, no loser, for he pays for it accordingly.

His candor and sweet temper were highly to be commended, gratefully acknowledging those by whom he was assisted in the work (in such a case, confession puts the difference betwixt stealing and borrowing), and surely so heavy a log needed more levers than one. He honorably mentioneth such as differ from him in opinion; not like those antiquaries who are so snarling, one had as good dissent a mile as a hair's breadth from them.

Most of the English ancient nobility and gentry he hath unpartially[46] observed. Some indeed object that he claws and flatters the grandees of his own age, extolling some families rather great than ancient, making them to flow from a far fountain because they had a great channel, especially if his private friends. But this cavil hath more of malice than truth: indeed, 'tis pity he should have a tongue that hath not a word for a friend on just occasion, and justly might the stream of his commendations run broader where meeting with a confluence of desert and friendship in the same party. For the main, his pen is sincere and unpartial, and they who complain that Grantham steeple stands awry will not set a straighter by it.[47]

Some say that in silencing many genteel families he makes balks[48] of as good ground as any he plougheth up. But these again acquit him when they consider that it is not only difficult but impossible to anatomize the English gentry so exactly as to show where every smallest vein thereof runs. Besides, many houses, conceived to be by him omitted, are rather rightly placed by him not where they live, but whence they came. Lastly, we may perceive that he prepared another work[49] on purpose for the English gentry.

I say nothing of his learned *Annals of Queen Elizabeth*,[50] industriously performed. His very enemies (if any) cannot but commend him. Sure, he was as far from loving popery as from hating learning, though that aspersion be general on antiquaries, as if they could not honor hoary hairs but presently themselves must dote.

His liberality to learning is sufficiently witnessed in his founding of a history professor in Oxford,[51] to which he gave the manor of Bexley in Kent, worth in present a hundred and forty pounds, but (some years expired) four hundred pounds *per annum*: so that he merited that distich,

> *Est tibi pro tumulo, Camdene, Britannia tota;*
> *Oxonium vivens est epigramma tibi.*[52]

The military part of his office he had no need to employ, passing it most under a peaceable prince. But now, having lived many years in honor and esteem, death at last, even contrary to *jus gentiun*,[53] killed this worthy herald; so that it seems mortality, the law of nature, is above the law of arms. He died *anno* 1623, the ninth of November, in the seventy-fourth[54] year of his age.

THE THIRD BOOK, CONTAINING GENERAL RULES

CHAPTER XIV. OF TOMBS

Tombs are the clothes of the dead. A grave is but a plain suit, and a rich monument is one embroidered. Most moderate men have been careful for the decent interment of their corpse. Few of the fond[55] mind of Arbogastus, an Irish saint and Bishop of Spires in Germany, who would be buried near the gallows, in imitation of our Saviour, whose grave was in Mount Calvary, near the place of execution.

Maxim 1. *'Tis a provident way to make one's tomb in one's lifetime*, both hereby to prevent the negligence of heirs and to mind him of his mortality. Vergil tells us[56] that when bees swarm in the air, and two armies, meeting together, fight as it were a set battle with great violence, cast but a little dust upon them, and they will be quiet:

> *Hi motus animorum, atque haec certamina tanta,*
> *Pulveris exigui jactu compressa quiescunt.*

> These stirrings of their minds and strivings vast,
> If but a little dust on them be cast,
> Are straightways stinted, and quite overpast.

Thus the most ambitious motions and thoughts of man's mind are quickly qualled when dust is thrown on him, whereof his foreprepared sepulcher is an excellent remembrancer.

2. *Yet some seem to have built their tombs, therein to bury their thoughts of dying*, never thinking thereof, but embracing the world with greater greediness. A gentleman made choice of a fair stone, and, intending the same for his gravestone,

---

[46]Impartially.
[47]The spire of St. Wulfram's in Grantham, Lincolnshire, is famous for its height and grace. [48]Unplowed ridges.
[49]Fuller presumably means the *Remains*, a smaller and less expensive work than *Britannia*. See p. 744, n. 44
[50]*Annales rerum Anglicarum et Hibernicarum regnante Elizabetha* (1615), Camden's great memorial to the queen whom he revered.
[51]The first appointment to the professorship founded by Camden in 1622 was his friend Degory Wheare, for whose own work on history see pp. 897 ff.
[52]"Camden, all Britain is your tomb, and Oxford is your living epitaph." [53]"The law of nations." [54]Actually, seventy-third.
[55]Foolish. [56]*Georgics*, IV. 86–87.

caused it to be pitched up in a field a pretty distance from his house, and used often to shoot at it for his exercise. "Yea, but," said a wag that stood by, "you would be loath, Sir, to hit the mark." And so are many unwilling to die, who, notwithstanding, have erected their monuments.

3. *Tombs ought, in some sort, to be proportioned not to the wealth, but deserts, of the party interred.* Yet may we see some rich man of mean worth loaden under a tomb big enough for a prince to bear. There were officers appointed in the Grecian games who always by public authority did pluck down the statues erected to the victors if they exceeded the true symmetry and proportion of their bodies. We need such nowadays to order monuments to men's merits, chiefly to reform such depopulating tombs as have no good fellowship with them, but engross all the room, leaving neither seats for the living nor graves for the dead. It was a wise and thrifty law which Reutha, King of Scotland, made: that noblemen should have so many pillars or long pointed stones set on their sepulchers as they had slain enemies in the wars. If this order were also enlarged to those who in peace had excellently deserved of the church or commonwealth, it might well be revived.

4. *Overcostly tombs are only baits for sacrilege.* Thus sacrilege hath beheaded that peerless prince, King Henry V, the body of whose statue on his tomb in Westminster was covered over with silver plate gilded, and his head of massy silver, both which now are stolen away. Yea, hungry palates will feed on coarser meat. I had rather Master Stow than I should tell you of a nobleman who sold the monuments of noblemen in St. Augustine's church in Broad Street for a hundred pounds, which cost many thousands, and in the place thereof made fair stabling for horses,[57] as if Christ, who was born in a stable, should be brought into it the second time. It was not without cause, in the civil law, that a wife might be divorced from her husband if she could prove him to be one that had broken the sepulchers of the dead, for it was presumed he must needs be a tyrannical husband to his wife who had not so much mercy as to spare the ashes of the departed.

5. *The shortest, plainest, and truest epitaphs are best.* I say "the shortest," for when a passenger sees a chronicle written on a tomb, he takes it on trust, some great man lies there buried, without taking pains to examine who he is. Master Camden in his *Remains* presents us with examples of great men that had little epitaphs. And when once I asked a witty gentleman, an honored friend of mine, what epitaph was fittest to be written on Master Camden's tomb, "Let it be," said he, "Camden's Remains."

I say also "the plainest," for except the sense lie above ground, few will trouble themselves to dig for it. Lastly, it must be "true," not, as in some monuments, where the red veins in the marble may seem to blush at the falsehoods written on it. He was a witty man that first taught a stone to speak, but he was a wicked man that taught it first to lie.

6. *To want a grave is the cruelty of the living, not the misery of the dead.* An English gentleman, not long since, did lie on his deathbed in Spain, and the Jesuits did flock about him to pervert him to their religion. All was in vain. Their last argument was, "If you will not turn Roman Catholic, then

your body shall be unburied." "Then," answered he, "I will stink" and so turned his head, and died. Thus love, if not to the dead to the living, will make him, if not a grave, a hole: and it was the beggar's epitaph:—

Nudus eram vivus, mortuus ecce tegor.

Naked I lived, but, being dead,
Now, behold, I'm covered.

7. *A good memory is the best monument.* Others are subject to casualty and time, and we know that the pyramids themselves, doting with age, have forgotten the names of their founders. To conclude: let us be careful to provide rest for our souls, and our bodies will provide rest for themselves. And let us not be herein like unto gentlewomen, which care not to keep the inside of the orange, but candy and preserve only the outside thereof.

THE PROFANE STATE

THE FIFTH BOOK

CHAPTER III. THE WITCH

Before we come to describe her we must premise and prove certain propositions whose truth may otherwise be doubted of.

1. *Formerly there were witches.* Otherwise God's law had fought against a shadow: "Thou shalt not suffer a witch to live."[58] Yea, we read how King Saul, who had formerly scoured witches out of all Israel, afterwards drank a draught of that puddle himself.[59]

2. *There are witches for the present, though those night-birds fly not so frequently in flocks since the light of the gospel.* Some ancient arts and mysteries are said to be lost, but, sure, the devil will not wholly let down any of his gainful trades. There be many witches at this day in Lapland who sell winds to mariners for money, (and must they not needs go whom the devil drives?), though we are not bound to believe the old story of Ericus, King of Swedeland, who had a cap, and, as he turned it, the wind he wished for would blow on that side.

3. *It is very hard to prove a witch.* Infernal contracts are made without witnesses. She that in presence of others will compact with the devil deserves to be hanged for her folly as well as impiety.

4. *Many are unjustly accused for witches.* Sometimes out of ignorance of natural—and misapplying of supernatural—causes, sometimes out of their neighbors' mere malice, and the suspicion is increased if the party accused be notoriously ill-favored, whereas deformity alone is no more argument to make her a witch than handsomeness had been evidence to prove her a harlot, sometimes out of their own causeless confession: being brought before a magistrate, they acknowledge themselves to be witches, being themselves

[57]The anecdote, in a rather different form, appears in John Stow's *Survey of London* (Everyman's Library, p. 159). [58]Exodus 22.18. [59]King Saul himself commanded the Witch of Endor to summon up the ghost of Samuel (1 Samuel 28.7–25).

rather bewitched with fear, or deluded with fancy. But the self-accusing of some is as little to be credited as the self-praising of others, if alone, without other evidence.

5. *Witches are commonly of the feminine sex.* Ever since Satan tempted our grandmother Eve, he knows that that sex is most liquorish[60] to taste, and most careless to swallow, his baits. *Nescio quod habet muliebre nomen semper cum sacris.* If they light well, they are inferior to few men in piety; if ill, superior to all in superstition.

6. *They are commonly distinguished into white and black witches.* White—I dare not say *good* witches (for "woe be to him that calleth evil good")—heal those that are hurt, and help them to lost goods. But better it is to lap one's pottage like a dog than to eat it mannerly[61] with a spoon of the devil's giving. Black witches hurt and do mischief. But in deeds of darkness there is no difference of colors: the white and the black are both guilty alike in compounding with the devil. And now we come to see by what degrees people arrive at this height of profaneness.

Maxim 1. *At the first she is only ignorant, and very malicious.* She hath usually a bad face and a worse tongue, given to railing and cursing, as if constantly bred on Mount Ebal;[62] yet speaking, perchance, worse than she means, though meaning worse than she should. And as the harmless wapping[63] of a cursed cur may stir up a fierce mastiff to the worrying of sheep, so on her cursing the devil may take occasion by God's permission to do mischief without her knowledge, and perchance against her will.

2. *Some have been made witches by endeavoring to defend themselves against witchcraft,* for fearing some suspected witch should hurt them, they fence themselves with the devil's shield against the devil's sword, put on his "whole armor,"[64] beginning to use spells and charms to safeguard themselves. The art is quickly learnt to which nothing but credulity and practice is required; and they often fall from defending themselves to offending of others, especially the devil not being dainty of his company where he finds welcome; and being invited once, he haunts ever after.

3. *She begins at first with doing tricks rather strange than hurtful.* Yea, some of them are pretty and pleasing. But it is dangerous to gather flowers that grow on the banks of the pit of hell, for fear of falling in; yea, they which play with the devil's rattles will be brought by degrees to wield his sword, and from making of sport they come to doing of mischief.

4. *At last she indents[65] downright with the devil.* He is to find her some toys for a time, and to have her soul in exchange. At the first (to give the devil his due) he observes the agreement to keep up his credit, else none would trade with him; though at last he either deceives her with an equivocation, or at some other small hole this serpent winds out himself, and breaks the covenants. And where shall she, poor wretch, sue the forfeited band?[66] In heaven she neither can nor dare appear; on earth she is hanged, if the contract be proved; in hell her adversary is judge, and it is woful to appeal from the devil to the devil. But for a while let us behold her in her supposed felicity.

5. *She taketh her free progress from one place to another.*

Sometimes the devil doth locally transport her; but he will not be her constant hackney, to carry such luggage about, but oftentimes, to save portage, deludes her brains in her sleep, so that they brag of long journeys whose heads never traveled from their bolsters. These, with Drake,[67] sail about the world; but it is on an ocean of their own fancies, and in a ship of the same. They boast of brave banquets they have been at, but they would be very lean should they eat no other meat. Others will persuade, if any list to believe, that by a witch-bridle they can make a fair of horses of an acre of besom weed.[68] O silly souls! O subtle Satan, that deceived them!

6. *With strange figures and words she summons the devils to attend her,* using a language which God never made at the confusion of tongues, and an interpreter must be fetched from hell to expound it. With these, or Scripture abused, the devil is ready at her service. Who would suppose that roaring lion could so finely act the spaniel? One would think he were too old to suck, and yet he will do that also for advantage.

7. *Sometimes she enjoins him to do more for her than he is able,* as to wound those whom God's providence doth arm, or to break through the tents of blessed angels to hurt one of God's saints. Here Satan is put to his shifts, and his wit must help him where his power fails: he either excuseth it, or seemingly performs it, lengthening his own arm by the dimness of her eye, and presenting the seeming bark of that tree which he cannot bring.

8. *She lives commonly but very poor.* Methinks she should bewitch to herself a golden mine, at least good meat and whole clothes. But it is as rare to see one of her profession as a hangman in a whole suit. Is the possession of the devil's favor here no better? Lord! what is the reversion[69] of it hereafter?

9. *When arraigned for her life, the devil leaves her to the law to shift for herself.* He hath worn out all his shoes in her former service, and will not now go barefoot to help her; and the circle of the halter is found to be too strong for all her spirits. Yea, Zoroastes[70] himself, the first inventor of magic (though he laughed at his birth) led a miserable life and died a woful death in banishment. We will give a double example of a witch: first of a real one out of the Scripture, because it shall be above all exception; and then of one deeply suspected, out of our own chronicles.[71]

[60]Lickerous, i.e., eager. [61]Politely.
[62]"And these shall stand upon Mount Ebal to curse" (Deuteronomy 27.13). [63]Yelping.
[64]"Wherefore, take unto you the whole armor of God," etc. (Ephesians 6.13). [65]Covenants, enters into agreement. [66]Bond.
[67]Sir Francis Drake (1545?–96), English mariner who completed a circumnavigation of the globe in 1580. [68]Broom plant.
[69]In law, the return of an estate to the grantor after the expiration of the grant.
[70]Zoroaster (or Zarathustra), ancient Persian magi who founded Zoroastrianism.
[71]Fuller illustrates witchcraft with biographies (V.iv-v) of the Witch of Endor and Joan of Arc, the former certified a witch in the Bible (1 Samuel 28) and the latter at least "deeply suspected" by English historians. Drawing upon the chronicles that Fuller had in mind, Shakespeare conventionally vilifies Joan as a witch in *1 Henry VI* (especially V.iii).

from Good Thoughts in Bad Times (1645)

To the Right Honorable the Lady Dalkeith, Lady Governess to Her Highness the Princess Henrietta[1]

Madam,

It is unsafe in these dangerous days for any to go abroad without a convoy or, at the least, a pass; my book hath both in being dedicated to Your Honor. The apostle saith, "Who planteth a vineyard, and eateth not of the fruit thereof?"[2] I am one of Your Honor's planting, and could heartily wish that the fruit I bring forth were worthy to be tasted by your judicious palate. However, accept these grapes, if not for their goodness, for their novelty: though not sweetest relished, they are soonest ripe, being the first fruits of Exeter press,[3] presented unto you. And if ever my ingratitude should forget my obligations to Your Honor, these black lines will turn red, and blush his unworthiness that wrote them. In this pamphlet Your Ladyship shall praise whatsoever you are pleased but to pardon. But I am tedious, for Your Honor can spare no more minutes from looking on a better book, her infant Highness committed to your charge. Was ever more hope of worth in a less volume? But O, how excellently will the same in due time be set forth, seeing the paper is so pure, and Your Ladyship the overseer to correct the press! The continuance and increase of whose happiness here and hereafter is desired in his daily devotions, who resteth

Your Honor's in all Christian service,
Tho. Fuller

PERSONAL MEDITATIONS

1

Lord, how near was I to danger, yet escaped! I was upon the brink of the brink of it, yet fell not in: they are well kept who are kept by Thee. Excellent archer! Thou didst hit thy mark in missing it, as meaning to fright, not hurt, me. Let me not now be such a fool as to pay my thanks to blind Fortune for a favor which the eye of Providence hath bestowed upon me. Rather let the narrowness of my escape make my thankfulness to Thy goodness the larger, lest my ingratitude justly cause that whereas this arrow but hit my hat, the next pierce my head.

4

Lord, since these woful wars began, one, formerly mine intimate acquaintance, is now turned a stranger, yea, an enemy. Teach me how to behave myself towards him. Must the new foe quite justle[4] out the old friend? May I not with him continue some commerce of kindness? Though the amity be broken on his side, may not I preserve my counterpart entire? Yet how can I be kind to him without being cruel to myself and Thy cause? O guide my shaking hand to draw so small a line straight; or rather, because I know not how to carry myself towards him in this controversy, even

be pleased to take away the subject of the question, and speedily to reconcile these unnatural differences.

5

Lord, my voice by nature is harsh and untunable, and it is vain to lavish any art to better it. Can my singing of psalms be pleasing to thy ears, which is unpleasant to my own? Yet though I cannot chant with the nightingale or chirp with the blackbird, I had rather chatter with the swallow,[5] yea, rather croak with the raven, than be altogether silent. Hadst Thou given me a better voice I would have praised Thee with a better voice. Now what my music wants in sweetness let it have in sense, singing praises with understanding.[6] Yea, Lord, create in me a new heart (therein to make melody)[7] and I will be contented with my old voice until in Thy due time, being admitted into the choir of heaven, I have another, more harmonious, bestowed upon me.

12

Lord, what faults I correct in my son, I commit myself: I beat him for dabbling in the dirt, whilst my own soul doth wallow in sin; I beat him for crying to cut his own meat, yet am not myself contented with that state Thy providence hath carved unto me; I beat him for crying when he is to go to sleep, and yet I fear myself shall cry when Thou callest me to sleep with my fathers. Alas, I am more childish than my child, and what I inflict on him I justly deserve to receive from Thee. Only here is the difference: I pray and desire that my correction on my child may do him good; it is in Thy power, Lord, to effect that Thy correction on me shall do me good.

25

Lord, be pleased to shake my clay cottage before Thou throwest it down. May it totter awhile before it doth tumble. Let me be summoned before I am surprised.[8] Deliver me from sudden death. Not from sudden death in respect of itself, for I care not how short my passage be, so it be safe. Never any weary traveler complained that he came too soon to his journey's end. But let it not be sudden in respect of

IN BAD TIMES [1]Henrietta Anne (1644–70), the fifth daughter of Charles and his queen, was born at Exeter (16 June 1644) because the king thought that royalist stronghold safer for his pregnant consort than Oxford, where he then held court. Having confided the infant to the care of Sir John Berkeley and Lady Dalkeith, the queen set sail for France about two weeks after her delivery, but when Charles visited Exeter for several days the following September he established a household for the little princess and named Fuller as her chaplain. [2]1 Corinthians 9.7. [3]Fuller's book was published at Exeter by one Thomas Hunt, who seems to have operated as a bookseller and printer there between 1640 and 1648. [4]Jostle. [5]Isaiah 38.14. [6]Psalm 47.7. [7]Ephesians 5.19. [8]Seized unexpectedly.

me. Make me always ready to receive death. Thus no guest comes unawares to him who keeps a constant table.

SCRIPTURE OBSERVATIONS

1

Lord, in the parable of the four sorts of ground whereon the seed was sown, the last alone proved fruitful. There the bad were more than the good; but amongst the servants, two improved their talents or pounds, and one only buried them.[9] There the good were more than the bad. Again, amongst the ten virgins, five were wise and five foolish;[10] there the good and bad were equal. I see that concerning the number of the saints in comparison to the reprobates no certainty can be collected from these parables. Good reason, for it is not their principal purpose to meddle with that point. Grant that I may never rack a Scripture simile beyond the true intent thereof, lest, instead of sucking milk, I squeeze blood out of it.

18

Lord, I read that Thou didst make grass, herbs, and trees the third day. As for the sun, moon, and stars, Thou madest them on the fourth day of the Creation.[11] Thus at first Thou didst confute the folly of such who maintain that all vegetables, in their growth, are enslaved to a necessary and unavoidable dependence on the influence of the stars. Whereas plants were even when planets were not. It is false that the marigold follows the sun, whereas rather the sun follows the marigold, as made the day before him. Hereafter I will admire Thee more and fear astrologers less, not affrighted with their doleful predictions of dearth and drought collected from the complexions of the planets. Must the earth of necessity be sad because some ill-natured star is sullen, as if the grass could not grow without asking it leave? Whereas Thy power, which made herbs before the stars, can preserve them without their propitious, yea, against their malignant, aspects.

HISTORICAL APPLICATIONS

3

In Merionethshire in Wales there be many mountains whose hanging tops come so close together that shepherds sitting on several mountains may audibly discourse one with another. And yet they must go many miles before their bodies can meet together, by the reason of the vast hollow valleys which are betwixt them. Our sovereign and the members of his Parliament at London seem very near agreed in their general and public professions: both are for the Protestant religion; can they draw nearer? Both are for the privileges of Parliament; can they come closer? Both are for the liberty of the subject; can they meet evener? And yet, alas, there is a great gulf and vast distance betwixt them which our sins have

made, and God grant that our sorrow may seasonably make it up again.

18[12]

I have heard that the brook near Lutterworth, in Leicestershire, into which the ashes of the burnt bones of Wycliffe were cast,[13] never since doth drown the meadow about it. Papists expound this to be because God was well pleased with the sacrifice of the ashes of such a heretic. Protestants ascribe it rather to proceed from the virtue of the dust of such a reverend martyr. I see 'tis a case for friend.[14] Such accidents signify nothing in themselves, but according to the pleasure of interpreters. Give me such solid reasons whereon I may rest and rely. Solomon saith, "The words of the wise are like nails, fastened by the masters of the assembly."[15] A nail is firm, and will hold driving in, and will hold driven in. Send me such arguments. As for these waxen topical devices,[16] I shall never think worse or better of any religion for their sake.

MIXED CONTEMPLATIONS

6

Looking on the Chapel of King Henry the Seventh in Westminster—God grant I may once again see it with the saint who belongs to it, our sovereign,[17] there in a well-conditioned peace!—I say, looking on the outside of the Chapel I have much admired the curious workmanship thereof. It added to the wonder that it is so shadowed with mean houses well-nigh on all sides that one may almost touch it as soon as see it. Such a structure needed no base buildings about it as foils to set it off. Rather, this Chapel may pass for the emblem of a great worth living in a private way. How is he pleased with his own obscurity whilst others of less desert make greater show, and whilst proud people stretch out their plumes in ostentation he useth their vanity for his shelter, more pleased to have worth than to have others take notice of it.

21

When a child I loved to look on the pictures in the *Book of Martyrs*.[18] I thought that there the martyrs at the stake seemed

[9]Matthew 13.3–8, 25.14–18; Luke 19.11–27.
[10]Matthew 25.2. [11]Genesis 1.11, 16. [12]Text *xiii*.
[13]In 1428, forty-four years after his burial at Lutterworth, the body of the proto-reformer John Wycliffe was, at the command of the Council of Constance, disinterred, burned, and cast into the River Swift. [14]Unexplained. [15]Ecclesiastes 12.11.
[16]Unstable general principles of explanation based on a priori notions rather than on facts.
[17]Charles I. Although the chapel was planned by Henry VII as a shrine for Henry VI—who was venerated as a saint and martyr, and whose canonization had been proposed—it became the tomb, and took the name, of its builder.
[18]John Foxe's *Acts and Monuments* (1563), the immensely popular Protestant martyrology.

like the three children in the fiery furnace;[19] ever since I had known them there, not one hair more of their head was burnt, nor any smell of the fire singeing of their clothes. This made me think martyrdom was nothing. But O, though the lion be painted fiercer than he is, the fire is far fiercer than it is painted. Thus it is easy for one to endure an affliction as he limns[20] it out in his own fancy, and represents it to himself but in a bare speculation. But when it is brought indeed, and

laid home to us, there must be the man, yea there must be more than the man, yea there must be God to assist the man to undergo it.

[19]Daniel 3.27. Fuller's *three children* were, of course, Shadrach, Meshach, and Abednego, whom the author of Daniel describes as adult Jewish magistrates (3.12).
[20]Paints.

from Good Thoughts in Worse Times (1647)

To the Christian Reader

When I read the description of the tumult in Ephesus, Acts 9.32 (wherein they would have their Diana to be *jure divino*,[1] that it fell down from Jupiter), it appears to me the too methodical character[2] of our present confusions. Some therefore cried one thing and some another, for the assembly was confused, and the more[3] part knew not wherefore they were come together. O the distractions of our age! And how many thousand know as little why the sword was drawn as when it will be sheathed. Indeed, thanks be to God, we have no more house-burnings, but many heart-burnings; and though outward bleeding be stanched, it is to be feared that the broken vein bleeds inwards, which is more dangerous.

This being our sad condition, I perceive controversial writing (sounding somewhat of drums and trumpets) do but make the wound the wider. Meditations are like the minstrel the prophet called for to pacify his mind discomposed with passion[4] which moved me to adventure on this treatise as the most innocent and inoffensive manner of writing.

I confess, a volume of another subject and larger size[5] is expected from me. But in London I have learnt the difference betwixt downright breaking[6] and craving time of their creditors. Many sufficient merchants, though not solvable from the present, make use of the latter,[7] whose example I follow. And though I cannot pay the principal, yet I desire such small treatises may be accepted from me as interest, or consideration money, until I shall, God willing, be enabled to discharge the whole debt.

If any wonder that this treatise comes patronless into the world, let such know that dedications begin nowadays to grow out of fashion. His policy was commended by many (and proved profitable unto himself) who instead of select godfathers made all the congregation witnesses to his child, as I invite the world to this my book, requesting each one would patronize therein such parts and passages thereof as please them, so hoping that by several persons the whole will be protected.

I have, Christian reader (so far I dare go, not inquiring into the surname of thy side or sect) nothing more to burden thy patience with. Only I will add that I find our Saviour

in Tertullian[8] and ancient Latin fathers constantly styled a sequestrator,[9] in the proper notion of the word. For God and man being at odds, the difference was sequestered or referred into Christ's his hand to end and umpire it. How it fareth with thine estate on earth I know not, but I earnestly desire that in heaven both thou and I may ever be under sequestration in that Mediator for God's glory and our good, to whose protection thou art committed by

Thy brother in all Christian offices,
Thomas Fuller

PERSONAL MEDITATIONS

3. Nor Full nor Fasting

Living in a country village where a burial was a rarity, I never thought of death, it was so seldom presented unto me. Coming to London, where there is plenty of funerals (so that coffins crowd one another, and corps[10] in the grave justle for elbow-room), I slight and neglect death, because grown an object so constant and common.

How foul is my stomach to turn all food into bad humors? Funerals neither few nor frequent work effectually upon me. London is a library of mortality. Volumes of all sorts and sizes, rich, poor, infants, children, youth, men, old men daily die; I see there is more required to make a good scholar than only the having of many books. Lord, be thou my schoolmaster and teach me to number my days that I may apply my heart unto wisdom.

IN WORSE TIMES [1]"By divine decree." [2]Apt description.
[3]Larger. [4]2 Kings 3.15.
[5]Fuller is probably alluding to *The History of the Worthies of England,* which, though under way in the mid-forties, did not appear until 1662, a year after its author's death. [6]Becoming bankrupt.
[7]Although in fact not solvent, maintain themselves on credit.
[8]Quintus Septeimus Florens Tertullianus (160?–?230), Carthaginian convert to Christianity who became one of the most prolific and influential apologists for his adopted religion.
[9]Sequester, i.e., mediator. [10]Corpses.

MEDITATIONS ON THE TIMES

11. THE USE OF THE ALPHABET

There was not long since a devout but ignorant papist dwelling in Spain. He perceived a necessity of his own private prayers to God besides the Pater Nosters, Ave Marias, etc. used of course in the Romish Church. But so simple was he that how to pray he knew not. Only every morning, humbly bending his knees and lifting up his eyes and hands to heaven, he would deliberately repeat the alphabet. "And now," said he, "O good God, put these letters together to spell syllables, to spell words, to make such sense as may be most to Thy glory and my good."

In these distracted times I know what generals[11] to pray for: God's glory, truth and peace, His Majesty's honor, privileges of Parliament, liberty of subjects, etc. But when I descend to particulars—when, how, by whom I should desire these things to be effected—I may fall to that poor pious man's A, B, C, D, E, etc.

14. WORSE BEFORE BETTER

Strange was the behavior of our Saviour toward his beloved Lazarus: informed by a messenger of his sickness, He abode two days still in the place where He was.[12] Why so slow? Bad sending Him, or to Him, on a dying man's errands. But the cause was because Lazarus was not bad enough for Christ to cure, intending not to recover him from sickness but revive him from death, to make the glory of the miracle greater.

England doth lie desperately sick of a violent disease in the bowels thereof. Many messengers we dispatch—monthly fasts, weekly sermons, daily prayers—to inform God of our sad condition. He still stays in the same place; yea, which is worse, seems to go backward, for every day less likelihood, less hope of help. May not this be the reason that our land must yet be reduced to more extremity, that God may have the higher honor of our deliverance?

[11]General benefits, public goods.   [12]John 11.6. Text *I was.*

from Mixed Contemplations in Better Times (1660)

6. DOWN YET UP

Hypocrite, in the native etymology of the word as it is used by ancient Greek authors, signifieth such a one *qui alienae personae in commoedia aut tragoedia est effector et repraesentator,* "who in comedy or tragedy doth feign and represent the person of another." In plain English, hypocrite is neither more nor less than a stage-player.

We all know that stage-players some years since were put down by public authority,[1] and though something may be said for them, more may be brought against them, who are rather in an employment than a vocation.

But let me safely utter my too just fears: I suspect the fire was quenched in the chimney, and in another respect scattered about the house. Never more strange stage-players than now who wear the vizards of piety and holiness that under that covert they may more securely commit sacrilege, oppression, and what not.

In the days of Queen Elizabeth, a person of honor or worship would as patiently have digested the lie[2] as to have been told that they did wear false pendants or any counterfeit pearl or jewels about them, so usual in our age; yet would it were the worst piece of hypocrisy in fashion. O, let us all labor for integrity of heart, and either appear what we are or be what we appear!

43. IN THE MIDDLE

God in His providence fixed my nativity in a remarkable place. I was born at Aldwinkle in Northamptonshire, where my father was the painful[3] preacher of St. Peter's. This village was distanced one good mile west from Achurch, where Master Brown,[4] founder of the Brownists, did dwell, whom, out of curiosity, when a youth I often visited. It was likewise a mile and a half distant east from Lavenden, where Francis Tresham,[5] Esquire, so active in the Gunpowder Treason, had a large demesne and ancient habitation.

My nativity may mind me of moderation, whose cradle was rocked betwixt two rocks. Now, seeing I was never such a churl as to desire to eat my morsel alone, let such who like my prayer join with me therein: God grant we may hit the golden mean and endeavor to avoid all extremes—the fanatic Anabaptist on the one side and the fiery zeal of the Jesuit on the other—that so we may be true Protestants, or, which is a far better name, real Christians indeed.

IN BETTER TIMES [1]On 2 September 1642 there was published a parliamentary ordinance commanding that "while these sad causes and set times of humiliation do continue, public stage-plays shall cease and be forborne." With some evasions and exceptions this so-called dramatic interregnum lasted until the Restoration of Charles II in 1660.   [2]Submitted to the charge of lying.
[3]Painstaking.
[4]Robert Brown (1550?–1633), notorious nonconformist divine who formulated the principles of Congregationalism and urged the separation of church and state.
[5]A fomenter of the Gunpowder Plot (1605) who betrayed his co-conspirators and thus brought about their execution. Tresham himself died before being brought to trial.

from The History of the Worthies of England (1662)

THE DESIGN OF THE ENSUING WORK

England may not unfitly be compared to an house, not very great, but convenient; and the several shires may properly be resembled to the *rooms* thereof. Now, as learned Master Camden and painful Master Speed,[1] with others, have described the rooms themselves, so is it our intention, God willing, to describe the *furniture* of those rooms, such eminent commodities which every country doth produce, with the persons of quality bred therein, and some other observables[2] coincident with the same subject.

Cato,[3] that great and grave philosopher, did commonly demand, when any new project was propounded unto him, *Cui bono?* What good would ensue, in case the same was effected? A question more fit to be asked than facile to be answered in all undertakings, especially in the setting forth of new books, insomuch that they themselves who complain that they are too many already help daily to make them more.

Know, then, I propound five ends to myself in this book: first, to gain some glory to God: secondly, to preserve the memories of the dead; thirdly, to present examples to the living; fourthly, to entertain the reader with delight; and lastly (which I am not ashamed publicly to profess) to procure some honest profit to myself. If not so happy to obtain all, I will be joyful to attain some; yea, contented and thankful too, if gaining any (especially the first) of these ends, the motives of my endeavours.

First, glory to God, which ought to be the aim of all our actions, though too often our bow starts, our hand shakes, and so our arrow misseth the mark. Yet I hope that our describing so good a land, with the various fruits and fruitful varieties therein, will engage both writer and reader in gratitude to that God who hath been so bountiful to our nation. In order whereunto, I have not only always taken, but often sought, occasions to exhort to thankfulness, hoping the same will be interpreted no straggling from my subject, but a closing with my calling.[4]

Secondly, to preserve the memories of the dead. A good name is an ointment poured out, smelt where it is not seen. It hath been the lawful desire of men in all ages to perpetuate their memories, thereby in some sort revenging themselves of mortality, though few have found out effectual means to perform it. For monuments made of wood are subject to be burnt; of glass, to be broken; of soft stone, to molder; of marble and metal (if escaping the teeth of time) to be demolished by the hand of covetousness; so that, in my apprehension, the safest way to secure a memory from oblivion is (next his own virtues) by committing the same in writing to posterity.

Thirdly, to present examples to the living, having here precedents of all sorts and sizes of men famous for valor, wealth, wisdom, learning, religion, and bounty to the public, on which last we most largely insist. The scholar,

being taxed by his writing master for idleness in his absence, made a fair defense when pleading that his master had neither left him paper whereon or copy[5] whereby to write. But rich men will be without excuse if not expressing their bounty in some proportion, God having provided them paper enough ("the poor you have always with you")[6] and set them signal examples, as in our ensuing work will plainly appear.

Fourthly, to entertain the reader with delight. I confess, the subject is but dull in itself, to tell the time and place of men's birth and deaths, their names, with the names and number of their books; and therefore this bare skeleton of time, place, and person must be fleshed with some pleasant passages. To this intent I have purposely interlaced (not as meat, but as condiment) many delightful stories, that so the reader, if he do not arise, which I hope and desire, *religiosior* or *doctior*, with more piety or learning, at least he may depart *jocundior*, with more pleasure and lawful delight.

Lastly, to procure moderate profit to myself in compensation of my pains. It was a proper question which plain-dealing Jacob pertinently propounded to Laban his father-in-law: "And now when shall I provide for mine house also?"[7] Hitherto no stationer hath lost by me; hereafter it will be high time for me (all things considered) to save for myself.

The matter following may be divided into real and personal, though not according to the legal acception of the words. By *real,* I understand the commodities and observables[8] of every county; by *personal,* the characters of those worthy men who were natives thereof.

. . . . . .

GLOUCESTERSHIRE

[*Sir Thomas Overbury*][9]

Sir Thomas Overbury, Knight, son to Sir Nicholas Overbury, one of the judges of the Marches, was born at Bourton on the Hill in this country, bred[10] in Oxford, and attained to be a most accomplished gentleman, which the happiness of his pen, both in poetry and prose, doth declare. In the latter he was the first writer of "characters" of our nation, so far as I have observed.

HISTORY OF THE WORTHIES [1]William Camden's *Britannia* (1586) and John Speed's *History of Great Britain* (1611), for which see pp. 817 ff and 842 ff. *Painful*: painstaking. [2]Noteworthy facts. [3]Marcus Porcius Cato (234–149 B.C.), Roman statesman noted for his rugged honesty and austerity. [4]*Closing. . .calling*: a proper exercise of my function as a divine. [5]Something to be copied. [6]Matthew 21.11. [7]Genesis 30.30. [8]Natural resources and physical characteristics. [9]See p. 715. [10]Educated.

But if the great parts of this gentleman were guilty of insolency and petulancy, which some since have charged on his memory, we may charitably presume that his reduced age[11] would have corrected such juvenile extravagancies.

It is questionable whether Robert Carr, earl of Somerset, were more in the favor of King James or this Sir Thomas Overbury in the favor of the earl of Somerset until he lost it by dissuading that lord from keeping company with a lady (the wife of another person of honor) as neither for his credit here or comfort hereafter.

Soon after Sir Thomas was by King James designed ambassador for Russia. His false friends persuaded him to decline the employment as no better than an honorable grave. Better lie some days in the Tower than more months in a worse prison—a ship by sea and a barbarous cold country by land. Besides they possessed[12] him that within a small time the king should be wrought to a good opinion of him. But he who willingly goes into a prison out of hope to come easily out of it may stay therein so long till he be too late convinced of another judgment. Whilst Sir Thomas was in the Tower, his refusal was represented to the king as an act of high contempt, as if he valued himself more than the king's service. His strict restraint gave the greater liberty to his enemies to practice[13] his death, which was by poison performed.

Yet was his blood legally revenged, which cost some a violent and others a civil death, as deprived of their offices. The earl was soon abated in King James' affection—oh, the short distance betwixt the cooling and quenching of a favorite!—being condemned and banished the court. The death of this worthy knight did happen *Anno Domini* 1613.[14]

HUNTINGDONSHIRE

[*Sir Robert Cotton*][15]

Sir Robert Cotton, Knight and Baronet, son to John Cotton, Esquire, was born at Conington in this county, descended by the Bruces from the blood royal of Scotland.[16] He was bred in Jesus[17] College in Cambridge, where, when a youth, he discovered his inclination to the study of antiquity (they must spring early who would sprout high in that knowledge) and afterwards attained to such eminency that sure I am he had no superior, if any his equal, in the skill thereof.

But that which rendered him deservedly to the praise of present and future times, yea the wonder of our own and foreign nations, was his collection of his library in Westminster, equally famous for 1. *Rarity*: having so many manuscript originals, or else copies so exactly transcribed, that, reader, I must confess he must have more skill than I have to distinguish them. 2. *Variety*: he that beholdeth their number would admire they should be rare, and he that considereth their rarity will more admire at their number. 3. *Method*: some libraries are labyrinths not for the multitude but confusion of volumes, where a stranger seeking for a book may quickly lose himself; whereas these are so exactly methodized (under the heads of the twelve Roman emperors)[18] that it is harder for one to miss than to hit any author he desireth.

But what addeth a luster to all the rest is the favorable access thereunto, for such as bring any competency of skill with them, and leave thankfulness behind them. Some antiquaries are so jealous of their books as if every hand which toucheth would ravish them, whereas here no such suspicion of ingenious persons. And here give me leave to register myself amongst the meanest of those who through the favor of Sir Thomas Cotton[19] (inheriting as well the courtesy as estate of his father Sir Robert) have had admittance into that worthy treasure.

Yea, most true it is what one saith, that the grandest antiquaries have here fetched their materials:

Omnis ab illo
Et Camdene tua, et Seldini gloria crevit.

Camden to him, to him doth Selden owe
Their glory: what they got from him did grow.

I have heard that there was a design driven on in the pope's conclave, after the death of Sir Robert, to compass this library to be added to that in Rome, which, if so, what a Vatican had there been within the Vatican by the accession thereof! But, blessed be God, the project did miscarry, to the honor of our nation and advantage of the Protestant religion.[20] For therein are contained many privities of princes and transactions of state, insomuch that I have been informed that the fountains have been fain to fetch water from the stream; and the Secretaries of State, and Clerks of the Council, glad from hence to borrow back again many originals, which, being lost by casualty or negligence of officers, have here been recovered and preserved. He was a man of a public spirit, it being his principal endeavor in all Parliaments (wherein he served so often) that the prerogative and privilege might run in their due channel; and in truth he did cleave the pin[21] betwixt the sovereign and the subject. He was wont to say "that he himself had the least share in himself," whilst his country and friends had the greatest interest in him. He died at his house in Westminster, May the 6, *Anno Domini* 1631, in the sixty-first year of his age—though one may truly say his age was adequate to the con-

---

[11]Later years. [12]Informed.
[13]Bring about. [14]Text 1615.
[15]Antiquary (1571–1631) whose remarkable library and collection of antiquities (now in the British Museum) were among the marvels of the age. The friend and benefactor of many learned men, most of whom paid equal tribute to his treasures and his liberality, Cotton was also sporadically a member of Parliament, and his support of parliamentary opposition to the crown so deeply offended Charles I that this headstrong monarch put the famous library under seal (1629).
[16]Cotton was so proud of his descent from the Scottish royal house that he took Bruce as his second name. [17]Text *Trinity*.
[18]Cotton shelved his holdings in cases identified by the busts of the Roman emperors decorating them. Thus the unique manuscript of the *Beowulf* is still known as Cotton Vitellius A-XV.
[19]Sir Robert's son (1594–1662), who with some difficulty reclaimed, preserved, and added to his father's library.
[20]Sir John Cotton (1621–1701) presented his grandfather's library to the nation in 1700. Although damaged by fire in 1731 while temporarily housed in Ashburnham House, the great collection was finally transferred to the British Museum in 1753.
[21]Split the peg or stud fixed in the center of a target, i.e., aim precisely.

tinuance of the creation, such was his exact skill in all antiquity. . . . The *opera posthuma* of this worthy Knight are lately set forth in one volume,[22] to the great profit of posterity.

LEICESTERSHIRE

[George Villiers, Duke of Buckingham][23]

George Villiers was born at Brooksby in this county, fourth son to his father Sir George Villiers, and second son to his mother Mary Beaumont. Being debarred (by his late nativity) from his father's lands, he was happy in his mother's love, maintaining him in France till he returned one of the completest courtiers in Christendom, his body and behavior mutually gracing one another.

Sir Tho[mas] Lake may be said to have ushered him to the English court, whilst the Lady Lucy, countess of Bedford, led him by the one hand, and William, earl of Pembroke by the other, supplying him with a support far above his patrimonial income. The truth is, Somerset's growing daily more wearisome made Villiers hourly more welcome to King James.

Soon after, he was knighted, created successively baron, Viscount Villiers, earl, marquess, duke of Buckingham; and to bind all his honors the better together, the noble Garter was bestowed upon him. And now offices at court (not being already void) were voided for him. The earl of Worcester was persuaded to part with his place of Master of the Horse, as the earl of Nottingham with his office of Admiral, and both conferred on the Duke.

He had a numerous and beautiful female kindred, so that there was hardly a noble stock in England into which one of these his cients[24] was not grafted. Most of his nieces were matched with little more portion than their uncle's smiles, the forerunner of some good office or honor to follow on their husbands. Thus with the same act did he both gratify his kindred and fortify himself with noble alliance.

It is seldom seen that two kings (father and son) tread successively in the same tract as to a favorite, but here King Charles had as high a kindness for the duke as King James. Thenceforward he became the plenipotentiary in the English court, some of the Scottish nobility making room for him by their seasonable departure out of this life. The earl of Bristol was justled[25] out, the bishop of Lincoln cast flat on the floor, the earls of Pembroke and Carlisle content to shine beneath him, Holland behind him, none even with, much less before, him.

But it is generally given to him who is the little god at the court to be the great devil in the country. The commonalty hated him with a perfect hatred, and all miscarriages in church and state at home, abroad, at sea and land were charged on his want of wisdom, valor, or loyalty.

John Felton, a melancholy, malcontented gentleman and a sullen soldier, apprehending himself injured, could find no other way to revenge his conceived wrongs than by writing them with a point of a knife in the heart of the duke, whom he stabbed at Portsmouth, *Anno Domini* 1628.[26] It is hard to say how many of this nation were guilty of this murther, either by public praising or private approving thereof.

His person from head to foot could not be charged with any blemish, save that some hypercritics conceived his brows somewhat overpendulous, a cloud which in the judgment of others was by the beams of his eyes sufficiently dispelled. The reader is remitted for the rest of his character to the exquisite epitaph on his magnificent monument in the Chapel of Henry the Seventh.[27]

WESTMINSTER

[Ben Jonson]

Benjamin Jonson was born in this city. Though I cannot, with all my industrious inquiry, find him in his cradle, I can fetch him from his longcoats.[28] When a little child, he lived in Hartshorn Lane near Charing Cross, where his mother married a bricklayer for her second husband.

He was first bred in a private school in Saint Martin's Church, then in Westminster school, witness his own epigram:

> Camden, most reverend head, to whom I owe
> All that I am in arts, all that I know;
> How nothing's that to whom my country owes
> The great renown and name wherewith she goes, etc.[29]

He was statutably admitted into Saint John's College in Cambridge[30] (as many years after incorporated a honorary member of Christ Church in Oxford) where he continued but few weeks for want of further maintenance, being fain to return to the trade of his father-in-law. And let not them blush that have, but those that have not, a lawful calling. He helped in the building of the new structure of Lincoln's Inn, when, having a trowel in his hand, he had a book in his pocket.

Some gentlemen, pitying that his parts should be buried

---

[22]*Cottoni Posthuma* (1657), edited by James Howell (pp. 789 f.), which contains some fourteen tracts on parliamentary and political questions as well as Cotton's *Short View of the Long Life and Reign of Henry III* (1627).
[23]George Villiers (1592–1628), one of the most powerful and detested men of the age, enjoyed the adulation of both James and Charles. One measure of his extraordinary success was the ease with which he replaced Robert Carr, earl of Somerset, as James' favorite soon after his introduction at court in 1614; others were the honors and the powers that two doting kings bestowed upon him. By 1620 he was virtually the executive head of the government, and despite the hostility engendered by his arrogance, venality, and incompetence he never lost his royal masters' favor. His military ventures against the Palatinate, France, and Spain were so disastrous and unpopular that it was only by twice dissolving Parliament (1626, 1627) that Charles withstood his foes, and his assassination at the hands of John Felton, a discharged officer, was in many quarters greeted with immense relief. [24]Scions.
[25]Jostled. [26]Text *1620*.
[27]The elaborate monument over Buckingham's grave in the Henry VII Chapel at Westminster Abbey was erected by his widow, a daughter of the Roman Catholic earl of Rutland, whom he married in 1620. [28]Baby clothes. [29]Epigram 14. See p. 89.
[30]Fuller's comment on Jonson's education, which is supported by no collateral evidence, seems to be contradicted by Jonson's statement to Drummond (p. 696) that he was a Master of Arts in both the universities "by their favor, not his study." See p. 696, n. 43.

under the rubbish of so mean a calling, did by their bounty manumise[31] him freely to follow his own ingenuous[32] inclinations. Indeed, his parts[33] were not so ready to run of themselves as able to answer the spur, so that it may be truly said of him that he had an elaborate wit wrought out by his own industry. He would sit silent in learned company, and suck in (besides wine) their several humors into his observation. What was *ore* in others, he was able to refine to himself.

He was paramount in the dramatic part of poetry, and taught the stage an exact conformity to the laws of comedians. His comedies were above the *volge*[34] (which are only tickled with downright obscenity) and took not so well at the first stroke as at the rebound, when beheld the second time; yea, they will endure reading, and that with due commendation, so long as either ingenuity or learning are fashionable in our nation. If his later be not so spriteful[35] and vigorous as his first pieces, all that are old will, and all that desire to be old should, excuse him therein.

He was not very happy in his children, and most happy in those which died first, though none lived to survive him. This he bestowed as part of an epitaph on his eldest son, dying in infancy:

> Rest in soft peace, and, ask'd, say here doth lie
> Ben Jonson his best piece of poetry.[36]

He died *Anno Domini* 1637,[37] and was buried about the belfry in the Abbey Church at Westminster.

THE PRINCIPALITY OF WALES, MONTGOMERYSHIRE

[George Herbert]

George Herbert was born at Montgomery Castle, younger brother to Edward Lord Herbert (of whom immediately), bred fellow of Trinity College in Cambridge and orator of the university, where he made a speech, no less learned than the occasion was welcome, of the return of Prince Charles out of Spain.[38]

He was none of the nobles of Tekoa, who, at the building of Jerusalem, "put not their necks to the work of the Lord,"[39] but waiving worldly preferment chose serving at God's altar before state employment. So pious his life that as he was a copy of primitive,[40] he might be a pattern of sanctity to posterity. To testify his independency on all others he never mentioned the name of Jesus Christ but with this addition, "My Master." Next God the Word he loved the Word of God,[41] being heard often to protest that he "would not part with one leaf thereof for the whole world."

Remarkable his conformity to church discipline, whereby he drew the greater part of his parishioners to accompany him daily in the public celebration of divine service. Yet had he (because not desiring) no higher preferment than the benefice of Bemerton nigh Salisbury, where he built a fair house for his successor, and the prebend of Leighton (founded in the cathedral of Lincoln), where he built a fair church with the assistance of some few friends' free offerings. When a friend on his deathbed went about to comfort him with the remembrance thereof, as an especial good work, he returned, "It is a good work if sprinkled with the blood of Christ." But his *Church*[42]—that inimitable piece of poetry —may outlast this in structure. His death happened *Anno Domini* 1633.[43]

---

[31]Manumit, liberate.   [32]High-minded, i.e., literary.
[33]Talents, native abilities.
[34]The vulgar (i.e., common) playgoer.   [35]Spirited.
[36]Epigram 45. See p. 89.   [37]Text *1638*.
[38]For Prince Charles' unsuccessful wooing of the Spanish Infanta in 1623 see p. 579, n.19.   [39]Nehemiah 3.5.   [40]Primitive piety.
[41]*Next . . . God:* next to Christ as the Logos or the Word of God he loved the Bible.   [42]*The Temple.* See pp. 201 ff.   [43]Text *163-*.

Izaak Walton [1593-1683]

Izaak Walton, who was born a subject of Elizabeth and died, almost a century later, near the end of Charles II's reign, professed to be a simple, artless writer, but his *Compleat Angler*—which went through 164 editions in the nineteenth century alone—has been second only to the Bible in terms of publication, and his famous lives of Hooker, Donne, and others have continued to attract and charm successive generations. So diffident about his meager education and his "mean abilities" that he wondered how he ever stumbled into print, he has nonetheless achieved a kind of extraliterary renown unmatched by that of any other writer of his splendid century.

Humbly born at Stafford and apprenticed to a London kinsman who prepared him for his trade of haberdashery (or, as some think, ironmongery), by 1614 he was established in "half a shop" in Chancery Lane, just around the corner from St. Dunstan's in the West. As a parishioner (and eventually a vestryman) of this ancient, famous church, he must have been elated when, in

1624, John Donne became its vicar, for Walton was a connoisseur of high-placed clergymen. His first wife, who at her death had survived all seven of her children, was a collateral descendant of Archbishop Cranmer; her successor, who died in 1662, was a half-sister of the famous Bishop Thomas Ken; Walton himself, whose favorite subject as a writer was the lives of noted Anglicans, spent his ripe old age in Bishop Morley's palace; and his sole surviving son was a protégé successively of Seth Ward and Gilbert Burnet, two Restoration magnates of the Church of England.

Though only a tradesman, Walton enjoyed the acquaintance of Jonson and Drayton and other men of letters, and was even guilty of a few commendatory and elegiac verses; but it was not until his middle age that he found his metier when he wrote his vivid life of Donne. This came about by accident, as he says, when Sir Henry Wotton (p. 54) died before completing—indeed, almost before beginning—the life of Donne that he had promised for the forthcoming *LXXX Sermons* (1640). Since Walton had agreed to gather notes for Wotton, when he learned that

> these sermons were to be printed and want the author's life, which I thought to be very remarkable, indignation or grief—indeed I know not which—transported me so far that I reviewed my forsaken collections, and resolved the world should see the best plain picture of the author's life that my artless pencil, guided by the hand of truth, could present to it.

The result was one of the first authentic masterpieces of English biography, and for the rest of his long life—which had more than forty years to run—Walton was off and on a writer. In the absence of almost any factual data one might guess that the forties and the fifties were for such a devoted Anglican and royalist a time of grief and trouble, and so, according to the old man's recollections in his life of Sanderson (1678), they proved to be. "This I saw, and suffered by it," he says about the uproar at the beginning of the civil war;

> but when I looked back upon the ruin of families, the bloodshed, the decay of common honesty, and how the former piety and plain dealing of this now sinful nation is turned into cruelty and cunning, I praise God that He prevented me from being of that part which helped to bring in this covenant, and those sad confusions that have followed it.

Our ignorance of Walton's middle years is relieved by little but the record of his publications. In 1651 he performed the office of a friend by bringing together Wotton's literary remains as *Reliquiae Wottonianae*, for which he wrote the second of his lives. This was followed two years later by that perenniel best seller, *The Compleat Angler*, which was significantly altered and enlarged in 1655. In 1658—"in an age, too, in which Truth and Innocence have not been able to defend them selves from worse than severe censures"—he enlarged his life of Donne and printed it without the sermons.

For the aging Walton and his coreligionists, the Restoration was of course a time of grateful jubilation. Among "the suffering clergy freed from their sequestration, restored to their revenues and to a liberty to adore, praise, and pray in such order as their consciences and oaths had formerly obliged them" was George Morley, a priest whose loyalty to the exiled Stuarts was to be rewarded with the deanery of Christ Church, Oxford, the honor of delivering Charles' coronation sermon, and the bishoprics of Worcester (1660) and Winchester (1662). It was in this great prelate's household that Walton passed his peaceful later years. In 1665 he dedicated to his host and benefactor the life of Richard Hooker that he had undertaken at the request of Gilbert Sheldon, Archbishop of Canterbury, in an effort to correct the "many dangerous mistakes" in Bishop Gauden's recent treatment of the subject. His life of George Herbert—"so far a free-will offering that it was writ chiefly to please myself"—appeared in 1670, and in the same year it and its three companion pieces (on Donne, Wotton, and Hooker) were printed in a single volume (which, rather confusingly, was reissued as a "fourth edition" in 1675). Walton's final effort of this kind—a life of Robert Sanderson (1587–1663), bishop of Lincoln—appeared in 1678, five years before the old man's death in the house of his clerical son-in-law at Winchester. It was fitting that this gentle champion of the Church of England be buried in the great cathedral there.

Although the *Lives* cannot approach the phenomenally successful record of *The Compleat Angler*, it also has a very complicated history. *Donne* first appeared in *LXXX Sermons* in 1640 and (much expanded) separately in 1658, *Wotten* in *Reliquiae Wottonianae* in 1651, 1654, and 1672, *Hooker* separately in 1665 and with the *Works* in 1666, *Herbert* separately in 1670 as well as in the collected *Lives* of 1670 and in the tenth edition of the *Temple* in 1674, and *Sanderson* with that cleric's tracts in 1678 and with his sermons in 1681 and 1686. The first four lives were brought together in 1670 and reissued (in the so-called fourth edition) in 1675 (Wing W–672, on which my text is based). Sanderson joined his brethren in Thomas Zouch's edition of the *Lives* in 1796. Among the many subsequent editions are those of John Major (1825), W. Nicol (1847), Henry Morley (1888), Austin Dobson (1898), George Saintsbury (1927), and Sir Geoffrey Keynes (*The Compleat Walton*, 1929). The standard biography of the great biographer is Stapleton Martin's (2d ed., 1904). Donald Stauffer has discussed his methods (*English Biography before 1700*, 1930), as has John Butt (*Essays and Studies by Members of the English Association*, XIX, 1934), and David Novarr's *Making of Walton's "Lives"* (1958) provides a fascinating study of the construction of the famous book.

from The Lives of Dr. John Donne, Sir Henry Wotton, Mr. Richard Hooker, Mr. George Herbert (1675)

TO THE READER

Though the several introductions to these several lives have partly declared the reasons how and why I undertook them, yet since they are come to be reviewed and augmented and reprinted, and the four are now become one book, I desire leave to inform you that shall become my reader that when I sometime look back upon my education and mean abilities, 'tis not without some little wonder at myself that I am come to be publicly in print. And though I have in those introductions declared some of the accidental reasons that occasioned me to be so, yet let me add this to what is there said, that by my undertaking to collect some notes for Sir Henry Wotton's writing the life of Dr. Donne, and by Sir Henry's dying before he performed it,[1] I became like those men that enter easily into a lawsuit or a quarrel, and having begun, cannot make a fair retreat and be quiet when they desire it. And really, after such a manner I became engaged into a necessity of writing the life of Dr. Donne, contrary to my first intentions, and that begot a like necessity of writing the life of his and my ever-honored friend, Sir Henry Wotton.

And having writ these two lives, I lay quiet twenty years without a thought of either troubling myself or others by any new engagement in this kind, for I thought I knew my unfitness. But about that time Dr. Gauden[2] (then Lord Bishop of Exeter) published the life of Master Richard Hooker (as he called it) with so many dangerous mistakes, both of him and his books, that discoursing of them with His Grace Gilbert, that now is lord archbishop of Canterbury,[3] he

enjoined me to examine some circumstances and then rectify the bishop's mistakes by giving the world a fuller and a truer account of Mr. Hooker and his books than that bishop had done, and I know I have done so. And let me tell the reader that till His Grace had laid this injunction upon me I could not admit a thought of any fitness in me to undertake it; but when he had twice enjoined me to it, I then declined my own and trusted his judgment, and submitted to his commands, concluding that if I did not I could not forbear accusing myself of disobedience and indeed of ingratitude for his many favors. Thus I became engaged into the third life.

For the life of that great example of holiness, Mr. George Herbert, I profess it to be so far a free-will offering that it was writ chiefly to please myself, but yet not without some respect to posterity; for though he was not a man that the next age can forget, yet many of his particular acts and virtues might have been neglected or lost if I had not collected and presented them to the imitation of those that shall succeed us. For I humbly conceive writing to be both a safer and

THE LIVES [1]Sir Henry Wotton (1568–1639), diplomat and minor man of letters, had been Donne's friend since the mid-nineties, when both were at the Inns of Court. After many years in ambassadorial service (mainly at Venice), he returned to England to end his career as provost of Eton College (1624–39). See p. 54.
[2]See p. 614. Gauden's life of Hooker was written for the edition (1662) that first printed all eight books of the *Laws of Ecclesiastical Polity*.
[3]Gilbert Sheldon (1598–1677) became archbishop of Canterbury in 1663. As chancellor of the university he built at his own expense the famous Sheldonian Theater at Oxford (1669).

truer preserver of men's virtuous actions than tradition, especially as 'tis managed in this age. And I am also to tell the reader that though this life of Mr. Herbert was not by me writ in haste, yet I intended it a review before it should be made public; but that was not allowed me by reason of my absence from London when 'twas printing, so that the reader may find in it some mistakes, some double expressions, and some not very proper, and some that might have been contracted, and some faults that are not justly chargeable upon me, but the printer; and yet I hope none so great as may not, by this confession, purchase pardon from a good-natured reader.

And now I wish that as that learned Jew Josephus[4] and others, so these men had also writ their own lives, but since 'tis not the fashion of these times, I wish their relations or friends would do it for them before delays make it too difficult. And I desire this the more because 'tis an honor due to the dead, and a generous debt due to those that shall live and succeed us, and would to them prove both a content and satisfaction. For when the next age shall (as this does) admire the learning and clear reason which that excellent causist Dr. Sanderson,[5] the late bishop of Lincoln, hath demonstrated in his sermons and other writings, who, if they love virtue, would not rejoice to know that this good man was as remarkable for the meekness and innocence of his life as for his great and useful learning, and indeed as remarkable for his fortitude in his long and patient suffering (under them that then called themselves the godly party) for that doctrine which he had preached and printed in the happy days of the nation's and the church's peace? And who would not be content to have the like account of Dr. Field,[6] that great schoolman, and others of noted learning? And though I cannot hope that my example or reason can persuade to this undertaking, yet I please myself that I shall conclude my preface with wishing that it were so.

I.W.

The Life of Dr. John Donne, Late Dean of St. Paul's Church, London

The Introduction

If that great master of language and art Sir Henry Wotton, the late provost of Eton College, had lived to see the publication of these sermons, he had presented the world with the author's life exactly written; and 'twas pity he did not, for it was a work worthy his undertaking, and he fit to undertake it, betwixt whom and the author there was so mutual a knowledge and such a friendship contracted in their youth as nothing but death could force a separation. And though their bodies were divided, their affections were not, for that learned knight's love followed his friend's fame beyond death and the forgetful grave; which he testified by entreating me, whom he acquainted with his design, to inquire of some particulars that concerned it, not doubting but my knowledge of the author and love to his memory might

make my diligence useful. I did most gladly undertake the employment, and continued it with great content till I had made my collection ready to be augmented and completed by his matchless pen, but then death prevented his intentions.

When I heard that sad news, and heard also that these sermons were to be printed and want the author's life, which I thought to be very remarkable, indignation or grief—indeed I know not which—transported me so far that I reviewed my forsaken collections, and resolved the world should see the best plain picture of the author's life that my artless pencil, guided by the hand of truth, could present to it.

And if I shall now be demanded, as once Pompey's poor bondsman was,—"the grateful wretch had been left alone on the seashore with the forsaken dead body of his once glorious lord and master, and was then gathering the scattered pieces of an old broken boat to make a funeral pile to burn it, which was the custom of the Romans—'Who art thou, that alone hast the honor to bury the body of Pompey the Great?' "[7]—so who am I that do thus officiously set the author's memory on fire? I hope the question will prove to have in it more of wonder than disdain, but wonder indeed the reader may that I, who profess myself artless, should presume with my faint light to show forth his life whose very name makes it illustrious! But be this to the disadvantage of the person represented, certain I am it is to the advantage of the beholder, who shall here see the author's picture in a natural dress, which ought to beget faith in what is spoken, for he that wants skill to deceive may safely be trusted.

And if the author's glorious spirit, which now is in heaven, can have the leisure to look down and see me, the poorest, the meanest of all his friends, in the midst of his officious duty, confident I am that he will not disdain this well-meant sacrifice to his memory; for whilst his conversation made me and many others happy below, I know his humility and gentleness was then eminent; and I have heard divines say those virtues that were but sparks upon earth become great and glorious flames in heaven.

Before I proceed further I am to intreat the reader to take notice that when Dr. Donne's sermons were first printed[8] this was then my excuse for daring to write his life, and I dare not now appear without it.

THE LIFE

Master John Donne was born in London in the year 1573,[9] of good and virtuous parents; and though his own learning

---

[4]The eminent Jewish historian Flavius Josephus (37?–100) wrote his autobiography about 97.
[5]Walton himself wrote a life of Robert Sanderson (1587–1663), Anglican divine and noted causist (i.e., one who resolves ethical problems or "cases of conscience") for an edition of that prelate's tracts in 1678.
[6]Richard Field (1561–1616), an erudite divine whose *Of the Church* (1606) ranks with his friend Hooker's *Laws* as one of the monuments of Anglican theology. Field's second wife was Walton's aunt.   [7]Plutarch, "Pompey," Sect. lxxx.
[8]*LXXX Sermons* (1640).
[9]Donne was born in Bread Street, London, between 24 January

and other multiplied merits may justly appear sufficiently to dignify both himself and his posterity, yet the reader may be pleased to know that his father was masculinely and lineally descended from a very ancient family in Wales, where many of his name now live that deserve and have great reputation in that country.

By his mother he was descended of the family of the famous and learned Sir Thomas More, sometime Lord Chancellor of England, as also from that worthy and laborious Judge Rastall, who left posterity the vast statutes of the law of this nation most exactly abridged.[10]

He had his first breeding in his father's house, where a private tutor had the care of him until the tenth year of his age; and in his eleventh year was sent to the University of Oxford,[11] having at that time a good command both of the French and Latin tongue. This and some other of his remarkable abilities made one then give this censure of him: "That this age had brought forth another Picus Mirandula,"[12] of whom story says, "That he was rather born, than made wise by study."

There he remained for some years in Hart Hall,[13] having for the advancement of his studies tutors of several sciences to attend and instruct him, till time made him capable and his learning expressed in public exercises declared him worthy to receive his first degree in the schools; which he forbore by advice from his friends, who being for their religion of the Romish persuasion were consciferably averse to some parts of the oath that is always tendered at those times and not to be refused by those that expect the titulary honor of their studies.[14]

About the fourteenth year of his age he was transplanted from Oxford to Cambridge; where, that he might receive nourishment from both soils, he stayed till his seventeenth year; all which time he was a most laborious student, often changing his studies but endeavoring to take no degree for the reasons formerly mentioned.

About the seventeenth year of his age he was removed to London and then admitted into Lincoln's Inn[15] with an intent to study the law; where he gave great testimonies of his wit, his learning, and of his improvement in that profession which never served him for other use than an ornament and self-satisfaction.

His father died [1578] before his admission into this society and being a merchant left him his portion in money (it was £3000). His mother and those to whose care he was committed were watchful to improve his knowledge and to that end appointed him tutors both in the mathematics and in all the other liberal sciences to attend him. But with these arts they were advised to instill into him particular principles of the Romish Church; of which those tutors professed (though secretly) themselves to be members.

They had almost obliged him to their faith, having for their advantage, besides many opportunities, the example of his dear and pious parents, which was a most powerful persuasion and did work much upon him, as he professeth in his preface to his *Pseudo-Martyr*,[16] a book of which the reader shall have some account in what follows.

He was now entered into the eighteenth year of his age;

and at that time had betrothed himself to no religion that might give him any other denomination than a Christian. And reason and piety had both persuaded him that there could be no such sin as schism if an adherence to some visible church were not necessary.

About the nineteenth year of his age he, being then unresolved what religion to adhere to and considering how much it concerned his soul to choose the most orthodox, did therefore, though his youth and health promised him a long life, to rectify all scruples that might concern that, presently lay aside all study of the law and of all other sciences that might give him a denomination; and begun seriously to survey, and consider the body of divinity as it was then controverted betwixt the Reformed and the Roman Church. And as "God's blessed Spirit did then awaken him to the search and in that industry did never forsake him"—they be his own words—"so he calls the same Holy Spirit to witness this protestation: that in that disquisition and search he proceeded with humility and diffidence in himself, and by that which he took to be the safest way, namely, frequent prayers and an indifferent affection to both parties";[17] and indeed, truth had too much light about her to be hid from so sharp an inquirer; and he had too much ingenuity not to acknowledge he had found her.

Being to undertake this search, he believed the Cardinal Bellarmine[18] to be the best defender of the Roman cause and therefore betook himself to the examination of his reasons. The cause was weighty, and willful delays had been inexcusable both towards God and his own conscience; he therefore proceeded in this search with all moderate haste, and about the twentieth year of his age did show the then Dean of Gloucester[19] (whose name my memory hath now lost) all the cardinal's works marked with many weighty

and 19 June 1572.

[10]Donne's mother was the granddaughter of More's sister Elizabeth Rastell and the daughter of John Heywood (1497?–?1580), the epigrammist and writer of interludes.

[11]Donne and his brother Henry matriculated from Hart Hall, Oxford, 23 October 1584, when they were eleven and ten respectively.

[12]Pico della Mirandola (1463–94), fabulously precocious Italian humanist.

[13]Ancient Oxford foundation formerly attached to Exeter College and in 1710 chartered as the now defunct Hertford College.

[14]In Donne's time—and for centuries thereafter—all degree candidates were required to subscribe to the Thirty-nine Articles of the Anglican Church.

[15]Following a brief period at Thavies Inn, Donne read law at Lincoln's Inn from 1592 to 1595.

[16]The first (and dullest) of Donne's published prose (1610), in which he attacks the Jesuit position that English Catholics refusing allegiance to the king (because he was a heretic) would gain their martyrs' crowns through execution. To die in such a foolish cause, Donne argued, was not martyrdom but suicide.

[17]Paraphrased from "A Preface to the Priests and Jesuits and to Their Disciples in This Kingdom," Paragraph 4, *Pseudo-Martyr* (1610).

[18]Roberto Bellarmino (1542–1621), renowned Jesuit controversialist and cardinal.

[19]Anthony Rudd (1549?–1615), dean of Gloucester 1584–94 and bishop of St. David's 1594–1615.

observations under his own hand; which works were bequeathed by him at his death as a legacy to a most dear friend.[20]

About a year following he resolved to travel; and the earl of Essex going first the Cales[21] and after the Island voyages, the first *anno* 1596, the second 1597, he took the advantage of those opportunities, waited upon his lordship, and was an eye-witness of those happy and unhappy employments.[22]

But he returned not back into England till he had stayed some years first in Italy and then in Spain, where he made many useful observations of those countries, their laws and manner of government, and returned perfect in their languages.[23]

The time that he spent in Spain was at his first going into Italy designed for traveling to the Holy Land and for viewing Jerusalem and the sepulcher of our Saviour. But at his being in the furthest parts of Italy, the disappointment of company or of a safe convoy or the uncertainty of returns of money into those remote parts denied him that happiness; which he did often occasionally mention with a deploration.[24]

Not long after his return into England, that exemplary pattern of gravity and wisdom, the Lord Ellesmere, then Keeper of the Great Seal and Lord Chancellor of England, taking notice of his learning, languages, and other abilities and much affecting his person and behavior, took him to be his chief secretary, supposing and intending it to be an introduction to some more weighty employment in the state; for which, His Lordship did often protest, he thought him very fit.[25]

Nor did His Lordship in this time of Master Donne's attendance upon him account him to be so much his servant as to forget he was his friend; and to testify it did always use him with much courtesy, appointing him a place at his own table, to which he esteemed his company and discourse to be a great ornament.

He continued that employment for the space of five years, being daily useful and not mercenary to his friends. During which time he—I dare not say unhappily—fell into such a liking as, with her approbation, increased into a love with a young gentlewoman that lived in that family who was niece to the Lady Ellesmere, and daughter to Sir George More, then Chancellor of the Garter and Lieutenant of the Tower.

Sir George had some intimation of it and, knowing prevention to be a great part of wisdom, did therefore remove her with much haste from that to his own house at Lothesley, in the County of Surrey, but too late by reason of some faithful promises which were so interchangeably passed as never to be violated by either party.

These promises were only known to themselves, and the friends of both parties used much diligence and many arguments to kill or cool their affections to each other. But in vain, for love is a flattering mischief that hath denied aged and wise men a foresight of those evils that too often prove to be the children of that blind father, a passion, that carries us to commit errors with as much ease as whirlwinds remove feathers and begets in us an unwearied industry to the attainment of what we desire. And such an industry did, notwithstanding much watchfulness against it, bring them secretly together—I forbear to tell the manner how—and at last to a marriage too without the allowance of those friends whose approbation always was and ever will be necessary to make even a virtuous love become lawful.

And that the knowledge of their marriage might not fall like an unexpected tempest on those that were unwilling to have it so and that preapprehensions might make it the less enormous when it was known, it was purposely whispered into the ears of many that it was so, yet by none that could affirm it. But to put a period to the jealousies of Sir George—doubt often begetting more restless thoughts than the certain knowledge of what we fear—the news was in favor to Master Donne and with his allowance made known to Sir George by his honorable friend and neighbor Henry, earl of Northumberland. But it was to Sir George so immeasurably unwelcome and so transported him that as though his passion of anger and inconsideration might exceed theirs of love and error he presently engaged his sister, the Lady Ellesmere, to join with him to procure her lord to discharge Master Donne of the place he held under His Lordship. This request was followed with violence; and though Sir George were remembered that errors might be overpunished and desired therefore to forbear till second considerations might clear some scruples, yet he became restless until his suit was granted and the punishment executed. And though the Lord Chancellor did not at Master Donne's dismission give him such a commendation as the great Emperor Charles the Fifth did of his secretary Eraso, when he presented him to his son and successor, Philip the Second, saying, "That in his Eraso he gave to him a greater gift than all his estate and all the kingdoms which he then resigned to him"; yet the Lord Chancellor said, "He parted with a friend and such a secretary as was fitter to serve a king than a subject."

Immediately after his dismission from his service, he

[20]In a letter of 17 November 1664 from Henry King, bishop of Chicester, to "Honest Izaak" about the publication of his *Lives*, the bishop recalled that three days before his death Donne, in Walton's presence, handed to King as one of his executors a great many sermons ready for the press and also "all his sermon-notes and his other papers containing an extract of near fifteen hundred authors. How these were got out of my hands," King adds cryptically, "you, who were the messenger for them, and how lost both to me and yourself, is not now seasonable to complain" (*Lives*, 4th ed., 1675, p. 2). It is possible that the manuscripts and papers had been purloined by Donne's disreputable son, John Donne the younger (1604–62). [21]Cadiz.

[22]Of Donne's two naval expeditions, the first—under the command of Raleigh, Lord Howard, and Essex—took and sacked Cadiz, but the second—an indecisive attempt to intercept a fleet of Spanish treasure-ships off the Azores—was a failure.

[23]*But he returned not...languages*: There is no record of Donne's alleged travels to the Continent at this time. [24]Lamentation.

[25]Donne became secretary to Sir Thomas Egerton (1540?–1617), later Baron Ellesmere and Viscount Brackley, about 1597–98. The imprudent secret marriage that ended the appointment occurred in December 1601, when Donne was about thirty and his bride seventeen.

sent a sad letter to his wife to acquaint her with it; and after the subscription of his name writ

John Donne, Anne Donne, Undone,

and God knows it proved too true.

For this bitter physic of Master Donne's dismission was not strong enough to purge out all Sir George's choler; for he was not satisfied till Master Donne and his sometime compupil[26] in Cambridge that married him, namely, Samuel Brooke, who was after Doctor of Divinity, and master of Trinity College, and his brother Master Christopher Brooke, sometime Master Donne's chamber-fellow in Lincoln's Inn, who gave Master Donne his wife and witnessed the marriage, were all committed to three several prisons.[27]

Master Donne was first enlarged, who neither gave rest to his body or brain nor to any friend in whom he might hope to have an interest until he had procured an enlargement for his two imprisoned friends. . . .

> Although Donne had made a happy (and uncommonly productive) marriage, he had also blasted his career, and for almost a decade his life was one of poverty, fitful literary activity, and galling dependence upon relatives and patrons. Finally, however, Sir George More relented sufficiently to begin paying his daughter's dowry, and thereafter the tide of fortune slowly turned. It was about 1612, after Donne had returned with his great friend and benefactor Sir Robert Drury from a "glorious embassy" to France, that "many of the nobility and others that were powerful at Court" began to stir in his behalf.

The king had formerly both known and put a value upon his company and had also given him some hopes of a state-employment, being always much pleased when Master Donne attended him, especially at his meals, where there were usually many deep discourses of general learning and very often friendly disputes or debates of religion betwixt His Majesty and those divines whose places required their attendance on him at those times, particularly the Dean of the Chapel, who then was Bishop Montagu,[28] the publisher of the learned and eloquent works of His Majesty, and the most reverend Doctor Andrewes, the late learned Bishop of Winchester, who then was the king's almoner.[29]

About this time there grew many disputes that concerned the oath of supremacy and allegiance in which the king had appeared and engaged himself by his public writings now extant. And His Majesty discoursing with Master Donne concerning many of the reasons which are usually urged against the taking of those oaths, apprehended such a validity and clearness in his stating the questions and his answers to them that His Majesty commanded him to bestow some time in drawing the arguments into a method and then to write his answers to them, and having done that not to send but be his own messenger and bring them to him. To this he presently and diligently applied himself and within six weeks brought them to him under his own handwriting as they be now printed, the book bearing the name of *Pseudo-Martyr*, printed *anno* 1610.[30]

When the king had read and considered that book he persuaded Master Donne to enter into the ministry;[31] to which at that time he was, and appeared, very unwilling, apprehending it (such was his mistaking modesty) to be too weighty for his abilities; and though His Majesty had promised him a favor and many persons of worth mediated with His Majesty for some secular employment for him, to which his education had apted him, and particularly the earl of Somerset[32] when in his greatest height of favor; who being then at Theobalds[33] with the king, where one of the clerks of the Council died that night, the earl posted a messenger for Master Donne to come to him immediately and at Master Donne's coming said, "Master Donne, to testify the reality of my affection and my purpose to prefer you, stay in this garden till I go up to the king and bring you word that you are clerk of the Council. Doubt not my doing this, for I know the king loves you, and know the king will not deny me." But the king gave a positive denial to all requests and, having a discerning spirit, replied, "I know Master Donne is a learned man, has the abilities of a learned divine, and will prove a powerful preacher. And my desire is to prefer him that way, and in that way I will deny you nothing for him." After that time, as he professeth, "The king descended to a persuasion, almost to a solicitation of him to enter into sacred orders."[34] Which though he then denied not, yet he deferred it for almost three years. All which time he applied himself to an incessant study of textual divinity and to the attainment of a greater perfection in the learned languages, Greek and Hebrew.[35]

In the first and most blessed times of Christianity, when the clergy were looked upon with reverence and deserved

[26]Fellow student.

[27]Samuel Brooke (d. 1631) ended his distinguished clerical career as master of Trinity College, Cambridge. His brother Christopher (d. 1628)—a bencher at Lincoln's Inn, an occasional poet, and a friend of many men of letters—was the recipient of Donne's two verse epistles about his naval expeditions, "The Storm" (p. 72) and "The Calm." Concerning Christopher's part in Donne's wedding, it was remarked by Edmund Gosse that in giving away the bride he made a gift "which he was certainly in no way competent to bestow." [28]See p. 895, n.33.

[29]Lancelot Andrewes (1555–1626), one of the most erudite and distinguished divines of his age, headed the commission to prepare the so-called King James translation of the Bible (1611). See p. 518.

[30]*Pseudo-Martyr* was printed with a fulsome preface wherein James is told that the influence of his own theological works, like the sun, "hath wrought upon me, and is drawn up, and exhaled from my poor meditations these discourses."

[31]Here as elsewhere Walton's chronology is uncertain. It was in 1615, five years after the publication of *Pseudo-Martyr*, that Donne was ordained a priest in the Anglican Church.

[32]Robert Carr (d. 1645), an impecunious Scot who accompanied James to England in 1603 and became the most powerful of his favorites until he was dislodged by George Villiers, later duke of Buckingham, in 1614. For his part in the murder of Sir Thomas Overbury, one of the greatest scandals of the age, see p. 715.

[33]A favorite hunting lodge of James' at Cheshunt, Hertfordshire. James died there in 1625.

[34]Based on *Devotions*, Expostulation 8 (1624 ed., pp. 192–93).

[35]It was about this time, while wrestling with the question of his ordination, that Donne wrote the knotty *Essays in Divinity* which his son exhumed and published in 1651. See pp. 544 ff.

it, when they overcame their opposers by high examples of virtue, by a blessed patience and long suffering, those only were then judged worthy the ministry whose quiet and meek spirits did make them look upon that sacred calling with an humble adoration and fear to undertake it; which indeed requires such great degrees of humility and labor and care that none but such were then thought worthy of that celestial dignity. And such only were then sought out and solicited to undertake it. This I have mentioned because forwardness and inconsideration[36] could not in Master Donne, as in many others, be an argument of insufficiency or unfitness; for he had considered long and had many strifes within himself concerning the strictness of life and competency of learning required in such as enter into sacred orders; and doubtless, considering his own demerits, did humbly ask God with St. Paul, "Lord, who is sufficient for these things?"[37] and with meek Moses, "Lord, who am I?"[38] And sure if he had consulted with flesh and blood, he had not for these reasons put his hand to that holy plow. But God, who is able to prevail, wrestled with him, as the angel did with Jacob,[39] and marked him, marked him for His own, marked him with a blessing, a blessing of obedience to the motions of His blessed Spirit. And then—as he had formerly asked God with Moses, "Who am I?"—so now, being inspired with an apprehension of God's particular mercy to him in the king's and others' solicitations of him, he came to ask King David's thankful question, "Lord, who am I that thou art so mindful of me?"[40] So mindful of me as to lead me for more than forty years through this wilderness of the many temptations and various turnings of a dangerous life, so merciful to me as to move the learnedest of kings to descend to move me to serve at the altar, so merciful to me as at last to move my heart to embrace this holy motion. Thy motions I will and do embrace. And I now say with the blessed Virgin, "Be it with thy servant as seemeth best in Thy sight."[41] And so, blessed Jesus, I do take the cup of salvation and will call upon Thy name and will preach Thy gospel.

Such strifes as these St. Austin had when St. Ambrose endeavored his conversion to Christianity, with which he confesseth he acquainted his friend Alypius.[42] Our learned author, a man fit to write after no mean copy, did the like. And declaring his intentions to his dear friend Dr. King,[43] then bishop of London, a man famous in his generation and no stranger to Master Donne's abilities, for he had been chaplain to the Lord Chancellor at the time of Master Donne's being His Lordship's secretary, that reverend man did receive the news with much gladness; and after some expressions of joy and a persuasion to be constant in his pious purpose, he proceeded with all convenient speed to ordain him first deacon and then priest not long after.

Now the English Church had gained a second St. Austin, for I think none was so like him before his conversion, none so like St. Ambrose after it. And if his youth had the infirmities of the one, his age had the excellencies of the other, the learning and holiness of both.

And now all his studies, which had been occasionally diffused, were all concentered in divinity. Now he had a new calling, new thoughts, and a new employment for his wit and eloquence. Now all his earthly affections were changed into divine love, and all the faculties of his own soul were engaged in the conversion of others, in preaching the glad tidings of remission to repenting sinners and peace to each troubled soul. To these he applied himself with all care and diligence. And now such a change was wrought in him that he could say with David, "Oh how amiable are Thy tabernacles. O Lord God of Hosts!"[44] Now he declared openly "that when he required a temporal, God gave him a spiritual blessing." And that "he was now gladder to be a door-keeper in the house of God than he could be to enjoy the noblest of all temporal employments."

Presently after he entered into his holy profession, the king sent for him and made him his Chaplain in Ordinary and promised to take a particular care for his preferment.[45]

And though his long familiarity with scholars and persons of greatest quality was such as might have given some men boldness enough to have preached to any eminent auditory, yet his modesty in this employment was such that he could not be persuaded to it but went, usually accompanied with some one friend, to preach privately in some village not far from London, his first sermon being preached at Paddington.[46] This he did till His Majesty sent and appointed him a day to preach to him at Whitehall, and, though much were expected from him both by His Majesty and others, yet he was so happy (which few are) as to satisfy and exceed their expectations, preaching the word so as showed his own heart was possessed with those very thoughts and joys that he labored to distill into others. A preacher in earnest, weeping sometimes for his auditory, sometimes with them, always preaching to himself like an angel from a cloud, but in none, carrying some, as St. Paul was, to heaven in holy raptures and enticing others by a sacred art and courtship to amend their lives, here picturing a vice so as to make it ugly to those that practiced it and a virtue so as to make it be beloved even by those that loved it not; and all this with a most particular grace and an unexpressible addition of comeliness.

There may be some that may incline to think—such indeed as have not heard him—that my affection to my

---

[36]Lack of consideration.   [37]2 Corinthians 2.16.   [38]Exodus 3.11.
[39]Genesis 32.24–30.   [40]Based on Psalm 8.4.
[41]Based on Luke 1.38.
[42]In his *Confessions*, Bk. VIII, St. Augustine (354–430) tells how, after a sinful youth, he passed through a spiritual crisis, came under the influence of the great Ambrose, bishop of Milan, and was at last converted with the aid of his mother Monica and his friend Alypius.
[43]John King (1559?–1621), bishop of London, was the father of Henry King (1592–1669), bishop of Chichester. A prebendary of St. Paul's (1616), a friend of many men of letters, and a poet, the younger King was one of Donne's closest friends, and finally served as his executor. See pp. 188 ff.   [44]Psalm 84.1.
[45]In 1616 Donne was presented with the living of Keyston, a village in Huntingdonshire, and in the same year he became rector of Sevenoaks in Kent (which was in the gift of the crown). A pluralist like so many of his brethren, he lived in neither place, but left his pastoral duties to his curates because, as Walton said, "he could not leave his beloved London."
[46]In the 17th century a village to the west of London.

friend hath transported me to an immoderate commendation of his preaching, If this meets with any such, let me entreat, though I will omit many, yet that they will receive a double witness for what I say, it being attested by a gentleman of worth, Master Chidley,[47] a frequent hearer of his sermons, in part of a funeral elegy writ by him on Dr. Donne, and is a known truth, though it be in verse:

> Each altar had his fire—
> He kept his love but not his object; wit
> He did not banish, but transplanted it,
> Taught it both time and place, and brought it home
> To piety, which it doth best become.
> For say, had ever pleasure such a dress?
> Have you seen crimes so shaped? or loveliness
> Such as his lips did clothe religion in?
> Had not reproof a beauty passing sin?
> Corrupted nature sorrowed that she stood
> So near the danger of becoming good.
> And when he preached she wished her ears exempt
> From piety that had such power to tempt.
> How did his sacred flattery beguile
> Men to amend!

More of this and more witnesses might be brought, but I forbear and return.

That summer, in the very same month in which he entered into sacred orders and was made the king's chaplain, His Majesty then going his progress,[48] was entreated to receive an entertainment in the University of Cambridge. And Master Donne attending His Majesty at that time, His Majesty was pleased to recommend him to the university, to be made Doctor in Divinity; Dr. Harsnett,[49] after archbishop of York, was then vice-chancellor, who, knowing him to be the author of that learned book the *Pseudo-Martyr*, required no other proof of his abilities but proposed it to the university, who presently assented and expressed a gladness that they had such an occasion to entitle him to be theirs.[50]

His abilities and industry in his profession were so eminent and he so known and so beloved by persons of quality that within the first year of his entering into sacred orders he had fourteen advowsons[51] of several benefices presented to him. But they were in the country, and he could not leave his beloved London, to which place he had a natural inclination, having received both his birth and education in it and there contracted a friendship with many whose conversation multiplied the joys of his life. But an employment that might affix him to that place would be welcome, for he needed it.

Immediately after his return from Cambridge, his wife died,[52] leaving him a man of a narrow unsettled estate and, having buried five, the careful father of seven children then living, to whom he gave a voluntary assurance never to bring them under the subjection of a step-mother; which promise he kept most faithfully, burying with his tears all his earthly joys in his most dear and deserving wive's grave, and betook himself to a most retired and solitary life.

In this retiredness, which was often from the sight of his dearest friends, he became crucified to the world and all those vanities, those imaginary pleasures that are daily acted on that restless stage; and they were as perfectly crucified to him. Nor is it hard to think, being passions may be both changed and heightened by accidents, but that that abundant affection which once was betwixt him and her who had long been the delight of his eyes and the companion of his youth, her with whom he had divided so many pleasant sorrows and contented fears as common people are not capable of—not hard to think but that she being now removed by death, a commeasurable grief took as full a possession of him as joy had done. And so indeed it did, for now his very soul was elemented of nothing but sadness; now grief took so full a possession of his heart as to leave no place for joy. If it did, it was a joy to be alone where like a pelican in the wilderness he might bemoan himself without witness or restraint and pour forth his passions like Job in the days of his affliction, "Oh, that I might have the desire of my heart! Oh that God would grant the thing that I long for!"[53] For then, "as the grave is become her house, so I would hasten to make it mine also, that we two might there make our beds together in the dark!" Thus as the Israelites sate mourning by the rivers of Babylon when they remembered Sion,[54] so he gave some ease to his oppressed heart by thus venting his sorrows. Thus he began the day and ended the night, ended the restless night and began the weary day in lamentations. And thus he continued till a consideration of his new engagements to God and St. Paul's "Woe is me, if I preach not the Gospel"[55] dispersed those sad clouds that had then benighted his hopes and now forced him to behold the light.

His first motion from his house was to preach where his beloved wife lay buried in St. Clement's Church, near Temple Bar, London, and his text was a part of the Prophet Jeremy's lamentation, "Lo, I am the man that have seen affliction."[56]

And indeed, his very words and looks testified him to be truly such a man; and they with the addition of his sighs

[47]John Chudleigh, a part of whose elegy Walton quotes (in a sadly garbled form) from the 1635 edition of Donne's *Poems*.
[48]Making a series of royal visits to various provincial towns and country houses.
[49]Samuel Harsnett (1561–1631), although forced to resign as vice-chancellor of Cambridge in 1616 under a barrage of charges including popery, excessive absences, and fiscal irregularities, went on to become archbishop of York in 1629. From his *Declaration of Egregious Popish Impostures* (1603) Shakespeare took the names of some of the evil spirits that Edgar mentions in *King Lear*.
[50]According to the letter writer John Chamberlain (1553–1627), a far more trustworthy reporter than Walton, Donne's Cambridge degree was reluctantly conferred (March 1615) only after the king had threatened the university with a "mandate" that could not be ignored.
[51]Rights of presentation of vacant clerical benefices. One of Donne's subsequent appointments (in 1624) was the vicarage of St. Dunstan's in the West, and thus it was that Izaak Walton, who lived in Chancery Lane, just around the corner from that famous church in Fleet Street, became one of his parishioners.
[52]Anne Donne died at the age of thirty-three on 15 August 1617, a few days after the birth of her twelfth child. [53]Job 6.8.
[54]Psalm 137.1. [55]1 Corinthians 9.16. [56]Lamentations 3.1.

and tears expressed in his sermon did so work upon the affections of his hearers as melted and molded them into a companionable sadness; and so they left the congregation; but then their houses presented them with objects of diversion; and his presented him with nothing but fresh objects of sorrow in beholding many helpless children, a narrow fortune, and a consideration of the many cares and casualties that attend their education. . . .

> Despite his grief, Donne enjoyed glittering success as a preacher. Only a year after his ordination he was named to the prestigious post of reader in divinity to the benchers at Lincoln's Inn, where he himself had once read law; in 1619 he returned to the Continent as part of the earl of Doncaster's embassy to Germany; and in 1621 he reached the summit of his career when the king nominated him dean of St. Paul's. Two years later (not four, as Walton says) he underwent a serious illness that had important consequences for English literature.

Within a few days his distempers abated; and as his strength increased so did his thankfulness to Almighty God, testified in his most excellent book of *Devotions*,[57] which he published at his recovery. In which the reader may see the most secret thoughts that then possessed his soul paraphrased and made public, a book that may not unfitly be called a sacred picture of spiritual ecstasies occasioned and appliable to the emergencies of that sickness; which book, being a composition of meditations, disquisitions, and prayers, he writ on his sickbed, herein imitating the holy patriarchs who were wont to build their altars in that place where they had received their blessings.

This sickness brought him so near to the gates of death and he saw the grave so ready to devour him that he would often say his recovery was supernatural. But that God that then restored his health continued it to him till the fifty-ninth year of his life. And then in August 1630, being with his eldest daughter, Mistress Harvey, at Abury Hatch in Essex,[58] he there fell into a fever, which with the help of his constant infirmity (vapors[59] from the spleen) hastened him into so visible a consumption that his beholders might say, as St. Paul of himself, "He dies daily";[60] and he might say with Job, "My welfare passeth away as a cloud, the days of my affliction have taken hold of me, and weary nights are appointed for me."[61]

Reader, this sickness continued long, not only weakening but wearying him so much that my desire is he may now take some rest and that before I speak of his death thou wilt not think it an impertinent digression to look back with me upon some observations of his life, which, whilst a gentle slumber gives rest to his spirits, may, I hope, not unfitly exercise thy consideration.

His marriage was the remarkable error of his life; an error which, though he had a wit able and very apt to maintain paradoxes, yet he was very far from justifying it. And though his wive's competent[62] years and other reasons might be justly urged to moderate severe censures, yet he would occasionally condemn himself for it. And doubtless it had been attended with an heavy repentance, if God had not blest them with so mutual and cordial affections as in the

midst of their sufferings made their bread of sorrow taste more pleasantly than the banquets of dull and low-spirited people.

The recreations of his youth were poetry, in which he was so happy as if nature and all her varieties had been made only to exercise his sharp wit and high fancy; and in those pieces which were facetiously composed and carelessly scattered (most of them being written before the twentieth year of his age) it may appear by his choice metaphors that both nature and all the arts joined to assist him with their utmost skill.

It is a truth that in his penitential years, viewing some of those pieces that had been loosely (God knows too loosely) scattered in his youth,[63] he wished they had been abortive or so short-lived that his own eyes had witnessed their funerals. But though he was no friend to them, he was not so fallen out with heavenly poetry as to forsake that. No, not in his declining age, witnessed then by many divine sonnets and other high, holy, and harmonious composures.[64] Yea, even on his former sickbed he wrote this heavenly hymn expressing the great joy that then possessed his soul in the assurance of God's favor to him when he composed it:

> Walton then gives the text of "A Hymn to God the Father." See p. 86.

. . . Before I proceed further, I think fit to inform the reader that not long before his death he caused to be drawn a figure of the body of Christ extended upon an anchor, like those which painters draw when they would present us with the picture of Christ crucified on the cross, his varying no otherwise than to affix him not to a cross but to an anchor, the emblem of hope. This he caused to be drawn in little,[65] and then many of those figures thus drawn to be engraven very small in helitropian stones[66] and set in gold, and of these he sent to many of his dearest friends to be used as seals or rings and kept as memorials of him and of his affection to them.

His dear friends and benefactors, Sir Henry Goodyer and Sir Robert Drury, could not be of that number, nor could the Lady Magdalen Herbert, the mother of George Herbert, for they had put off mortality and taken possession of the

[57]*Devotions upon Emergent Occasions* (1624). See pp. 548 ff.
[58]Aldborough Hatch, near Barking, Essex. Following the death of her aging husband Edward Alleyn (1566–1626) after only three years of marriage, Donne's daughter Constance became the wife of Samuel Harvey in June 1630. Alleyn, the famous Elizabethan actor who had created most of Marlowe's heroic roles, had married (1592) the stepdaughter of the theatrical manager Philip Henslowe, made a fortune in real estate and other ventures, and founded (1619) Dulwich College.
[59]Exhalations thought to cause a morbid condition.
[60]1 Corinthians 15.31: "I protest by your rejoicing which I have in Jesus Christ our Lord, I die daily."
[61]A conflation of Job 30.15 and 7.3.
[62]Suitable, legally sufficient.
[63]Donne's poetry, though for the most part unpublished in his lifetime, was widely read in manuscript. See p. 56.
[64]Compositions. Probably most of Donne's "Holy Sonnets" were written in 1609–10.   [65]As a miniature.   [66]Bloodstones.

grave before him. But Sir Henry Wotton and Dr. Hall, the then late deceased Bishop of Norwich, were; and so were Dr. Duppa, Bishop of Salisbury, and Dr. Henry King, Bishop of Chichester, lately deceased,[67] men in whom there was such a commixture of general learning, of natural eloquence, and Christian humility that they deserve a commemoration by a pen equal to their own, which none have exceeded.

And in this enumeration of his friends, though many must be omitted, yet that man of primitive piety, Master [10] George Herbert may not; I mean that George Herbert who was the author of *The Temple, or Sacred Poems and Ejaculations*,[68] a book in which by declaring his own spiritual conflicts he hath comforted and raised many a dejected and discomposed soul and charmed them into sweet and quiet thoughts, a book by the frequent reading whereof and the assistance of that Spirit that seemed to inspire the author the reader may attain habits of peace and piety and all the gifts of the Holy Ghost and heaven, and may by still reading still keep those sacred fires burning upon the altar of so pure a [20] heart as shall free it from the anxieties of this world and keep it fixed upon things that are above. Betwixt this George Herbert and Dr. Donne there was a long and dear friendship made up by such a sympathy of inclinations that they coveted and joyed to be in each other's company; and this happy friendship was still maintained by many sacred endearments. . . .

The latter part of his life may be said to be a continued study; for as he usually preached once a week, if not oftener, so after his sermon he never gave his eyes rest till he had [30] chosen out a new text, and that night cast his sermon into a form and his text into divisions;[69] and the next day betook himself to consult the fathers,[70] and so commit his meditations to his memory, which was excellent. But upon Saturday he usually gave himself and his mind a rest from the weary burthen of his week's meditations and usually spent that day in visitation of friends or some other diversions of his thoughts and would say, "that he gave both his body and mind that refreshment that he might be enabled to do the work of the day following, not faintly, but with courage [40] and cheerfulness."

Nor was his age only so industrious, but in the most unsettled days of his youth his bed was not able to detain him beyond the hour of four in a morning; and it was no common business that drew him out of his chamber till past ten. All which time was employed in study, though he took great liberty after it; and if this seem strange, it may gain a belief by the visible fruits of his labors, some of which remain as testimonies of what is here written, for he left the [50] resultance of 1400 authors, most of them abridged and analyzed with his own hand; he left also six score of his sermons, all written with his own hand, also an exact and laborious treatise concerning self-murther, called *Biathanatos*,[71] wherein all the laws violated by that act are diligently surveyed and judiciously censured, a treatise written in his younger days which alone might declare him then not only perfect in the civil and canon law but in many other such studies and arguments as enter not into the consideration of

many that labor to be thought great clerks and pretend to know all things.

Nor were these only found in his study, but all businesses that passed of any public consequence, either in this or any of our neighbor nations, he abbreviated either in Latin or in the language of that nation and kept them by him for useful memorials. So did he the copies of divers letters and cases of conscience[72] that had concerned his friends, with his observations and solutions of them, and divers other businesses of importance, all particularly and methodically digested by himself. . . .

[On 13 December 1630 Donne wrote a will—rather tediously discussed by Walton—with many specific bequests for his old friends.]

Nor was this blessed sacrifice of charity expressed only at his death but in his life also by a cheerful and frequent visitation of any friend whose mind was dejected or his fortune necessitous. He was inquisitive after the wants of prisoners and redeemed many from thence that lay for their fees or small debts;[73] he was a continual giver to poor scholars, both of this and foreign nations. Besides what he gave with his own hand, he usually sent a servant or a discreet and trusty friend to distribute his charity to all the prisons in London at all the festival times of the year, especially at the birth and resurrection of our Saviour. He gave an hundred pounds at one time to an old friend whom he had known live plentifully and by a too liberal heart and carelessness became decayed in his estate. And when the receiving of it was denied by the gentleman's saying, "He wanted not" —for the reader may note that as there be some spirits so generous as

67Walton's syntax is confusing. He presumably means that whereas such old friends and patrons as Goodyer, Drury, and Lady Herbert predeceased Donne, others who survived him had subsequently died.

67*His dear . . . deceased:* Sir Henry Goodyer (d. 1627) and Sir Robert Drury (d. 1615) were friends with whom Donne, in his letters, shared all his sorrows and his triumphs. Lady Magdalen Herbert (d. 1627) inspired not only Donne's "Autumnal" (see p. 70) but also one of his most moving funeral sermons. In 1608, as a widow of forty with ten children, she married the much younger Sir John Danvers, who subsequently became one of Charles I's regicides and thus the object of Clarendon's withering contempt (p. 935). Of the other friends whom Walton names, Wotton and King have been noted earlier; Joseph Hall (1574–1656) was an eminent divine and also a prolific writer and controversialist who lived to stir the wrath of young John Milton (see p. 258); Brian Duppa (1588–1662) survived the Commonwealth to become bishop of Winchester in 1660.

68*The Temple. Sacred Poems and Private Ejaculations* (1633). See pp. 201 ff.

69He blocked out the main structure of his sermon and arranged its biblical text into sections for discussion.

70Patristic commentators. Donne's favorite theologian was St. Augustine, whom he cites incessantly in his sermons.

71A treatise, written probably about 1608 but not published until 1646, in which Donne learnedly tries to justify suicide under certain conditions.

72Ethical and moral problems (like the question of suicide that is treated in *Biathanatos*).

73Secured the release of many persons from debtor's prison.

to labor to conceal and endure a sad poverty rather than expose themselves to those blushes that attend the confession of it, so there be others to whom nature and grace have afforded such sweet and compassionate souls as to pity and prevent the distresses of mankind—which I have mentioned because of Mr. Donne's reply, whose answer was, "I know you want not what will sustain nature, for a little will do that; but my desire is that you who in the days of your plenty have cheered and raised the hearts of so many of your dejected friends would now receive this from me and use it as a cordial for the cheering of your own." And upon these terms it was received. He was an happy reconciler of many differences in the families of his friends and kindred—which he never undertook faintly, for such undertakings have usually faint effects—and they had such a faith in his judgment and impartiality that he never advised them to anything in vain. He was even to her death a most dutiful son to his mother, careful to provide for her supportation, of which she had been destitute but that God raised him up to prevent her necessities; who having sucked in the religion of the Roman Church with her mother's milk spent her estate in foreign countries to enjoy a liberty in it and died in his house but three months before him.

And to the end it may appear how just a steward he was of his Lord and Master's revenue I have thought fit to let the reader know that after his entrance into his deanery, as he numbered his years, he—at the foot of a private account to which God and His angels were only witnesses with him—computed first his revenue, then what was given to the poor and other pious uses, and lastly what rested for him and his; and having done that, he then blest each year's poor remainder with a thankful prayer. . . .

But I return from my long digression. We left the author sick in Essex, where he was forced to spend much of that winter by reason of his disability to remove from that place. And having never for almost twenty years omitted his personal attendance on His Majesty in that month in which he was to attend and preach to him nor having ever been left out of the roll and number of Lent preachers, and there being then (in January 1630)[74] a report brought to London or raised there that Dr. Donne was dead, that report gave him occasion to write this following letter to a dear friend:

Sir,

This advantage you and my other friends have by my frequent fevers, that I am so much the oftener at the gates of heaven, and this advantage by the solitude and close imprisonment that they reduce me to after, that I am so much the oftener at my prayers, in which I shall never leave out your happiness; and I doubt not among His other blessings, God will add some one to you for my prayers. A man would almost be content to die (if there were no other benefit in death) to hear of so much sorrow and so much good testimony from good men as I (God be blessed for it) did upon the report of my death; yet I perceive it went not through all; for one writ to me that some (and he said of my friends) conceived I was not so ill as I pretended, but withdrew myself to live at ease, discharged of preaching. It is an unfriendly and, God knows, an ill-grounded interpretation; for I have always been sorrier when I could not

preach than any could be they could not hear me. It hath been my desire, and God may be pleased to grant it, that I might die in the pulpit; if not that, yet that I might take my death in the pulpit, that is, die the sooner by occasion of those labors. Sir, I hope to see you presently after Candlemass,[75] about which time will fall my Lent sermon at court, except my Lord Chamberlain believe me to be dead and so leave me out of the roll; but as long as I live and am not speechless, I would not willingly decline that service, I have better leisure to write than you to read; yet I would not willingly oppress you with too much letter. God so bless you and your son as I wish to

> *Your poor friend and servant*
> *in Christ Jesus,*
> J. Donne

Before that month ended, he was appointed to preach upon his old constant[76] day, the first Friday in Lent; he had notice of it and had in his sickness so prepared for that employment that as he had long thirsted for it so he resolved his weakness should not hinder his journey; he came therefore to London some few days before his appointed day of preaching. At his coming thither many of his friends—who with sorrow saw his sickness had left him but so much flesh as did only cover his bones—doubted his strength to perform that task and did therefore dissuade him from undertaking it, assuring him, however, it was like to shorten his life; but he passionately denied their requests, saying, "he would not doubt that that God who in so many weaknesses had assisted him with an unexpected strength would now withdraw it in his last employment," professing an holy ambition to perform that sacred work. And when to the amazement of some beholders he appeared in the pulpit, many of them thought he presented himself not to preach mortification by a living voice but mortality by a decayed body and a dying face. And doubtless many did secretly ask that question in Ezekiel: "Do these bones live?[77] or can that soul organize that tongue to speak so long time as the sand in that glass will move towards its center and measure out an hour of this dying man's unspent life? Doubtless it cannot"; and yet, after some faint pauses in his zealous prayer, his strong desires enabled his weak body to discharge his memory of his preconceived meditations, which were of dying, the text being, "To God the Lord belong the issues from death." Many that then saw his tears and heard his faint and hollow voice professing they thought the text prophetically chosen and that Dr. Donne "had preached his own funeral sermon."[78]

Being full of joy that God had enabled him to perform this desired duty, he hastened to his house; out of which he never moved till, like St. Stephen, he was carried by devout men to his grave.[79]

[74]1631 by the New Style calendar.   [75]February 2.   [76]Regular.   [77]Ezekiel 27.3.

[78]In view of Walton's somewhat confused and confusing presentation of events it may be useful to set the record straight. Donne fell ill while visiting the Samuel Harveys, his son-in-law and daughter, at Aldborough Hatch in Essex in the autumn of 1630. On 13 December he signed his will; on 25 February 1631 he gave his final sermon (the famous *Death's Duel*, which appeared in print in 1632); he died on 31 March and was buried in St. Paul's on 3 April.   [79]Acts 8.2.

The next day after his sermon, his strength being much wasted and his spirits so spent as indisposed him to business or to talk, a friend that had often been a witness of his free and facetious discourse asked him, "Why are you sad?" To whom he replied with a countenance so full of cheerful gravity as gave testimony of an inward tranquillity of mind and of a soul willing to take a farewell of this world, and said:

"I am not sad, but most of the night past I have entertained myself with many thoughts of several friends that have left 10 me here and are gone to that place from which they shall not return, and that within a few days I also shall go hence and be no more seen. And my preparation for this change is become my nightly meditation upon my bed, which my infirmities have now made restless to me. But at this present time I was in a serious contemplation of the providence and goodness of God to me, to me who am less than the least of his mercies; and looking back upon my life past, I now plainly see it was His hand that prevented me from all temporal employment and that it was His will I should never settle 20 nor thrive till I entered into the ministry; in which I have now lived almost twenty years (I hope to his glory) and by which, I most humbly thank Him, I have been enabled to requite most of those friends which showed me kindness when my fortune was very low, as God knows it was; and as it hath occasioned the expression of my gratitude, I thank God most of them stood in need of my requital. I have lived to be useful and comfortable to my good father-in-law, Sir George More,[80] whose patience God hath been pleased to exercise with many temporal crosses; I have maintained 30 my own mother, whom it hath pleased God after a plentiful fortune in her younger days to bring to a great decay in her very old age. I have quieted the consciences of many that have groaned under the burthen of a wounded spirit, whose prayers I hope are available for me. I cannot plead innocency of life, especially of my youth. But I am to be judged by a merciful God who is not willing to see what I have done amiss. And, though of myself I have nothing to present to him but sins and misery, yet I know He looks not upon me now as I am of myself but as I am in my 40 Saviour and hath given me even at this present time some testimonies by His holy Spirit that I am of the number of His elect. I am therefore full of unexpressible joy and shall die in peace."

I must here look so far back as to tell the reader that at his first return out of Essex to preach his last sermon, his old friend and physician, Dr. Foxe[81] a man of great worth, came to him to consult his health, and that after a sight of him and some queries concerning his distempers he told him, "That by cordials and drinking milk twenty days 50 together there was a probability of his restoration to health"; but he passionately denied to drink it. Nevertheless, Dr. Foxe, who loved him most entirely, wearied him with solicitations till he yielded to take it for ten days; at the end of which time he told Dr. Foxe, "he had drunk it more to satisfy him than to recover his health and that he would not drink it ten days longer upon the best moral assurance of having twenty years added to his life, for he loved it not,

and was so far from fearing death, which to others is the King of Terrors, that he longed for the day of his dissolution."

It is observed that a desire of glory or commendation is rooted in the very nature of man and that those of the severest and most mortified[82] lives, though they may become so humble as to banish self-flattery and such weeds as naturally grow there, yet they have not been able to kill this desire of glory, but that, like our radical[83] heat, it will both live and die with us; and many think it should do so; and we want not sacred examples to justify the desire of having our memory to outlive our lives. Which I mention, because Dr. Donne, by the persuasion of Dr. Foxe, easily yielded at this very time to have a monument made for him; but Dr. Foxe undertook not to persuade him how or what monument it should be; that was left to Dr. Donne himself.

A monument being resolved upon, Dr. Donne sent for a carver to make for him in wood the figure of an urn, giving him directions for the compass and height of it, and to bring with it a board of the just height of his body. These being got, then without delay a choice painter was got to be in a readiness to draw his picture, which was taken as followeth: several charcoal fires being first made in his large study, he brought with him into that place his winding-sheet in his hand and, having put off all his clothes, had this sheet put on him and so tied with knots at his head and feet and his hands so placed as dead bodies are usually fitted to be shrouded and put into their coffin or grave. Upon this urn he thus stood with his eyes shut and with so much of the sheet turned aside as might show his lean, pale, and deathlike face, which was purposely turned toward the east, from whence he expected the second coming of his and our Saviour, Jesus. In this posture he was drawn at his just[84] height; and when the picture was fully finished, he caused it to be set by his bedside, where it continued and became his hourly object till his death and was then given to his dearest friend and executor, Dr. Henry King, then chief residentiary of St. Paul's, who caused him to be thus carved in one entire piece of white marble, as it now stands in that church. . . .[85]

And now, having brought him through the many labyrinths and perplexities of a various life, even to the gates of death and the grave, my desire is he may rest till I have told my reader that I have seen many pictures of him in several habits and at several ages and in several postures. And I now mention this because I have seen one picture[86] of him,

[80]Sir George survived his son-in-law, with whom he had long been reconciled, by only a year.
[81]Simeon Foxe (1568–1642), president of the College of Surgeons.
[82]Most austere and self-denying.   [83]Essential to life.
[84]Proper, correct.
[85]Donne's monument, which had been executed by the well-known sculptor Nicholas Stone (1586–1647), somehow survived the fire of 1666 that destroyed old St. Paul's and was eventually re-erected in the present building. A similar, though half-length, statue of the same period is in Chelsea Old Church.
[86]This picture, which was used as a frontispiece in the second (1635) edition of Donne's *Poems*, bears in a cartouche the Spanish

drawn by a curious hand at his age of eighteen, with his sword and what other adornments might then suit with the present fashions of youth and the giddy gaieties of that age; and his motto then was,

> How much shall I be changed
> Before I am changed!

And if that young and his now dying picture were at this time set together, every beholder might say, "Lord! how much is Dr. Donne already changed, before he is changed!" And the view of them might give my reader occasion to ask himself with some amazement, "Lord! how much may I also that am now in health be changed, before I am changed! before this vile, this changeable body shall put off mortality!" and therefore to prepare for it.—But this is not writ so much for my reader's *memento*[87] as to tell him that Dr. Donne would often in his private discourses and often publicly in his sermons mention the many changes both of his body and mind, especially of his mind from a vertiginous giddiness, and would as often say his great and most blessed change was from a temporal to a spiritual employment. In which he was so happy that he accounted the former part of his life to be lost and the beginning of it to be from his first entering into sacred orders and serving his most merciful God at His altar.

Upon Monday after the drawing this picture he took his last leave of his beloved study, and being sensible of his hourly decay, retired himself to his bedchamber; and that week sent at several times for many of his most considerable friends, with whom he took a solemn and deliberate farewell, commending to their considerations some sentences useful for the regulation of their lives, and then dismissed them, as good Jacob did his sons,[88] with a spiritual benediction. The Sunday following he appointed his servants, that if there were any business yet undone that concerned him or themselves, it should be prepared against Saturday next; for after that day he would not mix his thoughts with anything that concerned this world; nor ever did, but, as Job, so he waited for the appointed day of his dissolution.[89]

And now he was so happy as to have nothing to do but to die; to do which he stood in need of no longer time, for he had studied it long and to so happy a perfection that in a former sickness he called God to witness, "He was that minute ready to deliver his soul into his hands if that minute God would determine his dissolution."[90] In that sickness he begged of God the constancy to be preserved in that estate forever; and his patient expectation to have his immortal soul disrobed from her garment of mortality makes me confident he now had a modest assurance that his prayers were then heard and his petition granted. He lay fifteen days earnestly expecting his hourly change; and in the last hour of his last day, as his body melted away and vapored into spirit, his soul having, I verily believe, some revelation of the beatifical vision, he said, "I were miserable if I might not die"; and after those words, closed many periods of his faint breath by saying often, "Thy kingdom come, thy will be done." His speech, which had long been his ready and faithful servant, left him not till the last minute of his life, and then

forsook him not to serve another master (for who speaks like him!) but died before him for that it was then become useless to him that now conversed with God on earth as angels are said to do in heaven, only by thoughts and looks. Being speechless and seeing heaven by that illumination by which he saw it, he did, as St. Stephen,[91] look steadfastly into it, till he saw the Son of Man, standing at the right hand of God, His Father; and being satisfied with this blessed sight, as his soul ascended and his last breath departed from him, he closed his own eyes; and then disposed his hands and body into such a posture as required not the least alteration by those that came to shroud him.

Thus variable, thus virtuous was the life; thus excellent, thus exemplary was the death of this memorable man.

He was buried in that place of St. Paul's Church which he had appointed for that use some years before his death and by which he passed daily to pay his public devotions to Almighty God (who was then served twice a day by a public form of prayer and praises in that place). But he was not buried privately, though he desired it; for, beside an unnumbered number of others, many persons of nobility and of eminency for learning, who did love and honor him in his life, did show it at his death by a voluntary and sad attendance of his body to the grave, where nothing was so remarkable as a public sorrow.

To which place of his burial some mournful friend repaired, and as Alexander the Great did to the grave of the famous Achilles,[92] so they strewed his with an abundance of curious and costly flowers, which course they (who were never yet known) continued morning and evening for many days, not ceasing till the stones that were taken up in that church to give his body admission into the cold earth (now his bed of rest) were again by the mason's art so leveled and firmed as they had been formerly and his place of burial undistinguishable to common view.

The next day after his burial some unknown friend, some one of the many lovers and admirers of his virtue and learning, writ this epitaph with a coal on the wall, over his grave.

> Reader! I am to let thee know,
> Donne's body only lies below;
> For, could the grave his soul comprise,
> Earth would be richer than the skies.

Nor was this all the honor done to his reverend ashes; for as there be some persons that will not receive a reward for that for which God accounts himself a debtor, persons that dare trust God with their charity, and without a witness, so there was by some grateful unknown friend, that thought Dr. Donne's memory ought to be perpetuated, an hundred marks[93] sent to his two faithful friends and executors[94]

---

motto *Antes muerto que mudado* ("rather dead than changed," i.e., constant until death), which Walton mistranslates below.
[87] Reminder. [88] Genesis 49.28. [89] Job 14.14.
[90] Based on *Devotions*, Prayer 23 (1624 ed., pp. 627–28).
[91] Acts 7.55. [92] Plutarch, "Alexander," Sect. xv.
[93] Denomination of money equivalent to two-thirds of a pound sterling.
[94] Henry King, later bishop of Chichester, and Dr. John Montford.

towards the making of his monument.[95] It was not for many years known by whom, but after the death of Dr. Foxe, it was known that 'twas he that sent it; and he lived to see as lively a representation of his dead friend as marble can express, a statue indeed so like Dr. Donne that, as his friend Sir Henry Wotton hath expressed himself, it seems to breathe faintly; and posterity shall look upon it as a kind of artificial miracle.

He was of stature moderately tall, of a straight and equally proportioned body, to which all his words and actions gave 10 an unexpressible addition of comeliness.

The melancholy and pleasant humor were in him so contempered that each gave advantage to the other and made his company one of the delights of mankind.

His fancy was unimitably high, equalled only by his great wit; both being made useful by a commanding judgment.

His aspect was cheerful and such as gave a silent testimony of a clear-knowing soul and of a conscience at peace with itself.

His melting eye showed that he had a soft heart, full of 20 noble compassion, of too brave a soul to offer injuries and too much a Christian not to pardon them in others.

He did much contemplate—especially after he entered into his sacred calling—the mercies of Almighty God, the immortality of the soul, and the joys of heaven, and would often say, in a kind of sacred ecstasy, "Blessed be God that he is God only and divinely like himself."

He was by nature highly passionate but more apt to reluct[96] at the excesses of it. A great lover of the offices of humanity and of so merciful a spirit that he never beheld the miseries of mankind without pity and relief.

He was earnest and unwearied in the search of knowledge, with which his vigorous soul is now satisfied and employed in a continual praise of that God that first breathed it into his active body, that body which once was a temple of the Holy Ghost and is now become a small quantity of Christian dust.

But I shall see it reanimated.

I.W.
Feb. 15, 1639

[95]In his account book Nicholas Stone, the sculptor, recorded that he had received £120, half of which he took "in plate." For the more elaborate monument to Donne's friend and patron Sir Robert Drury (d. 1615) in Hawstead Church, Suffolk, he had been paid £140.   [96]Struggle, strive against.

John Milton[1] [1608-1674]

THE REASON OF CHURCH GOVERNMENT URGED AGAINST PRELATY (1642)

THE SECOND BOOK

[Milton's Literary Intentions]

. . . For me, I have determined to lay up as the best treasure and solace of a good old age, if God vouchsafe it me, the honest liberty of free speech from my youth, where I shall think it available in so dear a concernment as the church's good. For if I be, either by disposition or what other cause, too inquisitive or suspicious of myself and mine own doings, who can help it? But this I foresee, that should the church 30 be brought under heavy oppression, and God have given me ability the while to reason against that man that should be the author of so foul a deed, or should she, by blessing from above on the industry and courage of faithful men, change this her distracted estate into better days without the least furtherance or contribution of those few talents which God at that present had lent me, I foresee what stories I should hear within myself, all my life after, of discourage and reproach. . . .

But now by this little diligence, mark what a privilege 40 I have gained: with good men and saints to claim my right of lamenting the tribulations of the church, if she should

suffer, when others that have ventured nothing for her sake have not the honor to be admitted mourners. But if she lift up her drooping head and prosper, among those that have something more than wished her welfare I have my charter and freehold[1] of rejoicing to me and my heirs. Concerning therefore this wayward[2] subject against prelaty, the touching whereof is so distasteful and disquietous to a number of men, as by what hath been said I may deserve of charitable readers to be credited that neither envy nor gall hath entered me upon this controversy, but the enforcement of conscience only and a preventive fear lest the omitting of this duty should be against me when I would store up to myself the good provision of peaceful hours; so, lest it should be still imputed to me, as I have found it hath been, that some self-pleasing humor of vainglory hath incited me to contest with men of high estimation,[3] now while green years are upon my head, from this needless surmisal I shall hope to dissuade the intelligent and equal[4] auditor if I can but say successfully

[1]For a commentary on Milton and for other excepts from his work see Poetry pp. 256 ff, Religion and Politics, pp. 599 ff, and History and Historiography, pp. 921 ff.
REASON OF CHURCH GOVERNMENT [1]Life tenure of an estate or office.
[2]Refractory, vexatious.
[3]With such distinguished divines as Bishops Joseph Hall and James Ussher, whose defense of the Anglican status quo young Milton was attacking. See p. 258.   [4]Impartial (a Latinism.)

that which in this exigent[5] behoves me; although I would be heard only, if it might be, by the elegant and learned reader, to whom principally for a while I shall beg leave I may address myself. To him it will be no new thing though I tell him that if I hunted after praise by the ostentation of wit and learning, I should not write thus out of mine own season, when I have neither yet completed to my mind the full circle of my private studies (although I complain not of any insufficiency to the matter in hand); or, were I ready to my wishes, it were a folly to commit anything elaborately composed to the careless and interrupted listening of these tumultuous times. Next, if I were wise only to mine own ends, I would certainly take such a subject as of itself might catch applause, whereas this hath all the disadvantages on the contrary, and such a subject as the publishing whereof might be delayed at pleasure, and time enough to pencil it over[6] with all the curious touches of art, even to the perfection of a faultless picture; whenas in this argument the not deferring is of great moment to the good speeding,[7] that if solidity have leisure to do her office, art cannot have much.

Lastly, I should not choose this manner of writing, wherein, knowing myself inferior to myself, led by the genial[8] power of nature to another task, I have the use, as I may account it, but of my left hand. And though I shall be foolish in saying more to this purpose, yet, since it will be such a folly as wisest men going about to commit have only confessed and so committed, I may trust with more reason, because with more folly, to have courteous pardon. For although a poet, soaring in the high region of his fancies with his garland and singing robes about him, might without apology speak more of himself than I mean to do, yet for me, sitting here below in the cool element of prose, a mortal thing among many readers of no empyreal conceit,[9] to venture and divulge unusual things of myself, I shall petition to the gentler sort, it may not be envy[10] to me.

I must say, therefore, that after I had from my first years, by the ceaseless diligence and care of my father (whom God recompense), been exercised to the tongues and some sciences,[11] as my age would suffer, by sundry masters and teachers both at home and at the schools,[12] it was found that whether aught was imposed me by them that had the overlooking, or betaken to of mine own choice in English or other tongue, prosing or versing, but chiefly this latter, the style, by certain vital signs it had, was likely to live. But much latelier, in the private academies of Italy, whither I was favored to resort—perceiving that some trifles which I had in memory, composed at under twenty or thereabout (for the manner is that everyone must give some proof of his wit and reading there), met with acceptance above what was looked for, and other things which I had shifted[13] in scarcity of books and conveniences to patch up amongst them, were received with written encomiums,[14] which the Italian is not forward to bestow on men of this side the Alps—I began thus far to assent both to them and divers of my friends here at home, and not less to an inward prompting which now grew daily upon me, that by labor and intent study (which I take to be my portion in this life) joined with the strong propensity of nature, I might perhaps leave something so written to aftertimes as they should not willingly let it die.

These thoughts at once possessed me, and these other: that if I were certain to write as men buy leases, for three lives and downward,[15] there ought no regard be sooner had than to God's glory by the honor and instruction of my country. For which cause, and not only for that I knew it would be hard to arrive at the second rank among the Latins, I applied myself to that resolution which Ariosto followed against the persuasions of Bembo,[16] to fix all the industry and art I could unite to the adorning of my native tongue; not to make verbal curiosities the end (that were a toilsome vanity), but to be an interpreter and relater of the best and sagest things among mine own citizens throughout this island in the mother dialect. That what the greatest and choicest wits of Athens, Rome, or modern Italy, and those Hebrews of old did for their country, I, in my proportion, with this over and above of being a Christian, might do for mine; not caring to be once named abroad, though perhaps I could attain to that, but content with these British islands as my world; whose fortune hath hitherto been that, if the Athenians, as some say, made their small deeds great and renowned by their eloquent writers, England hath had her noble achievements made small by the unskillful handling of monks and mechanics.[17]

Time serves not now, and perhaps I might seem too profuse to give any certain account of what the mind at home, in the spacious circuits of her musing, hath liberty to propose to herself, though of highest hope and hardest attempting: whether that epic form whereof the two poems of Homer and those other two of Vergil and Tasso are a diffuse, and the book of Job a brief, model; or whether the rules of Aristotle herein are strictly to be kept, or nature to be followed,[18] which, in them that know art and use judgment, is no transgression but an enriching of art; and lastly, what king or knight before the conquest might be chosen in whom to lay

[5]Urgent state of affairs. [6]Touch up its style. [7]Success.
[8]Pertaining to genius or natural disposition.
[9]Heavenly imagination. [10]Odium. [11]Practical subjects.
[12]See Milton's later and fuller account of his education in the autobiography in his *Second Defence of the English People* (1654), pp. 776 ff. [13]Contrived.
[14]A few years later Milton included some of these encomiums in the first collected edition of his *Poems* (1645).
[15]A lease remaining in force during the life of the longest liver of three specified persons.
[16]When Pietro Cardinal Bembo, one of the most fastidious humanists of the age, warned Ludovico Ariosto (1474–1533) against writing in Italian, the author of *Orlando Furioso* replied that he would rather be preeminent in his own language than second-rate in Latin.
[17]Illiterates. Milton is referring to the medieval monastic chroniclers whom he later denigrated in his *History of Britain* (pp. 921 ff)
[18]Milton is weighing the alternatives of a *diffuse* (i.e., long) epic after the example of the *Iliad*, the *Odyssey*, the *Aeneid*, and *Gerusalemme Liberata* or the *brief* epic as exemplified by the Book of Job. Put in other terms, the choice is between a "regular" epic written in conformity with the principles laid down by Aristotle in his *Poetics*, Sect. xxvi, or the sprawling, episodic, and romantic epic represented by Ariosto's *Orlando Furioso*.

the pattern of a Christian hero.[19] And as Tasso gave to a prince of Italy his choice whether he would command him to write of Godfrey's expedition against the infidels, or Belisarius against the Goths, or Charlemagne against the Lombards;[20] if to the instinct of nature and the emboldening of art aught may be trusted, and that there be nothing adverse in our climate or the fate of this age, it haply would be no rashness, from an equal diligence and inclination, to present the like offer in our own ancient stories; or whether those dramatic constitutions,[21] wherein Sophocles and Euripides reign, shall be found more doctrinal and exemplary to a nation. The Scripture also affords us a divine pastoral drama in the Song of Solomon, consisting of two persons and a double chorus, as Origen[22] rightly judges. And the Apocalypse of St. John[23] is the majestic image of a high and stately tragedy, shutting up and intermingling her solemn scenes and acts with a sevenfold chorus of halleluiahs and harping symphonies: and this my opinion the grave authority of Pareus,[24] commenting that book, is sufficient to confirm. Or if occasion shall lead, to imitate those magnific odes and hymns, wherein Pindarus and Callimachus[25] are in most things worthy, some others in their frame judicious, in their matter most an end[26] faulty. But those frequent songs throughout the Law and Prophets beyond all these, not in their divine argument alone, but in the very critical art of composition, may be easily made appear over all the kinds of lyric poesy to be incomparable.[27]

These abilities, wheresoever they be found, are the inspired gift of God, rarely bestowed, but yet to some (though most abuse) in every nation; and are of power, beside the office of a pulpit, to inbreed and cherish in a great people the seeds of virtue and public civility, to allay the perturbations of the mind, and set the affections in right tune; to celebrate in glorious and lofty hymns the throne and equipage of God's almightiness, and what He works and what He suffers to be wrought with high providence in His church; to sing the victorious agonies of martyrs and saints, the deeds and triumphs of just and pious nations doing valiantly through faith against the enemies of Christ; to deplore the general relapses of kingdoms and states from justice and God's true worship. Lastly, whatsoever in religion is holy and sublime, in virtue amiable[28] or grave, whatsoever hath passion or admiration[29] in all the changes of that which is called fortune from without, or the wily subtleties and refluxes of man's thoughts from within, all these things with a solid and treatable smoothness to paint out and describe. Teaching over the whole book of sanctity and virtue through all the instances of example, with such delight to those especially of soft and delicious[30] temper, who will not so much as look upon truth herself unless they see her elegantly dressed, that whereas the paths of honesty and good life appear now rugged and difficult, though they be indeed easy and pleasant, they would then appear to all men both easy and pleasant, though they were rugged and difficult indeed. And what a benefit this would be to our youth and gentry may be soon guessed by what we know of the corruption and bane which they suck in daily from the writings and interludes of libidinous and ignorant poetasters, who, having scarce ever

heard of that which is the main consistence of a true poem, the choice of such persons as they ought to introduce, and what is moral and decent to each one, do for the most part lap up vicious principles in sweet pills to be swallowed down, and make the taste of virtuous documents harsh and sour.

But because the spirit of man cannot demean itself lively[31] in this body without some recreating intermission of labor and serious things, it were happy for the commonwealth if our magistrates, as in those famous governments of old,[32] would take into their care not only the deciding of our contentious law-cases and brawls, but the managing of our public sports and festival pastimes; that they might be, not such as were authorized a while since,[33] the provocations of drunkenness and lust, but such as may inure and harden our bodies by martial exercises to all warlike skill and performance; and may civilize, adorn, and make discreet our minds by the learned and affable meeting of frequent academies, and the procurement of wise and artful recitations sweetened with eloquent and graceful enticements to the love and practice of justice, temperance, and fortitude, instructing and bettering the nation at all opportunities, that the call of wisdom and virtue may be heard everywhere, as Solomon saith: "She crieth without, she uttereth her voice in the streets, in the top of high places, in the chief concourse, and in the openings of the gates."[34] Whether this may not be, not only in pulpits but after another persuasive method, at set and solemn panegyrics,[35] in theatres, porches,[36] or what other place or way may win most upon the people to receive at once both recreation and instruction, let them in authority consult.

The thing which I had to say, and those intentions which

[19]In the Latin poems *Mansus* (1639) and *Epitaphium Damonis* (1640) Milton had expressed his hope to write a Christian epic about King Arthur, and in some jottings in his poetical workbook he had mentioned Alfred the Great's struggle with the Danes as a possible subject for a "heroical poem."
[20]Tasso is reported to have offered Alfonso II, duke of Ferrara, a choice of epics on Godfrey of Bouillon and the First Crusade, the wars in Italy between Belisarius and the Ostrogoths, and Charlemagne's campaign (771–74) against the Lombards.
[21]Dramas serving as vehicles of moral instruction.
[22]One of the Greek fathers of the church (185?–?254) renowned for his classical erudition. [23]The Book of Revelation.
[24]David Pareus (1548–1622), professor of theology at Heidelberg, whose *In Apocalypsin Johannis commentarius* was Englished by Elias Arnold in 1644.
[25]The odes of Pindar (522?–443 B.C.) and the hymns of Callimachus (b. 310 B.C.). [26]Generally.
[27]For Milton's high opinion of biblical poetry see *Paradise Regained*, IV.331–64. [28]Worthy of being loved. [29]Ardor or wonder.
[30]Sensuous. [31]Conduct itself actively.
[32]In ancient Greece, where the Olympian and the Nemean games were quasi-religious festivals.
[33]Milton is contemptuously referring to James' and Charles I's so-called *Book of Sports* (first issued in 1618 and republished in 1633), which the Puritans thought encouraged profanation of the Sabbath. See p. 917.
[34]A conflation of Proverbs 1.20–21 and 8.2–3.
[35]Solemn religious assemblies. [36]Church porticos.

have lived within me ever since I could conceive myself anything worth to my country, I return to crave excuse that urgent reason hath plucked from me by an abortive and foredated discovery. And the accomplishment of them lies not but in a power above man's to promise; but that none hath by more studious ways endeavored, and with more unwearied spirit that none shall, that I dare almost aver of myself, as far as life and free leisure will extend; and that the land had once enfranchised herself from this impertinent yoke of prelaty, under whose inquisitorious and tyrannical duncery no free and splendid wit can flourish. Neither do I think it shame to covenant with any knowing reader, that for some few years yet I may go on trust with him toward the payment of what I am now indebted, as being a work not to be raised from the heat of youth or the vapors of wine, like that which flows at waste from the pen of some vulgar amorist or the trencher fury of a rhyming parasite; nor to be obtained by the invocation of Dame Memory and her siren daughters,[37] but by devout prayer to that eternal Spirit who can enrich with all utterance and knowledge, and sends out his seraphim with the hallowed fire of his altar to touch and purify the lips of whom he pleases:[38] to this must be added industrious and select reading, steady observation, insight into all seemly and generous arts and affairs; till which in some measure be compassed, at mine own peril and cost I refuse not to sustain this expectation from as many as are not loth to hazard so much credulity upon the best pledges that I can give them.

Although it nothing content me to have disclosed thus much beforehand but that I trust hereby to make it manifest with what small willingness I endure to interrupt the pursuit of no less hopes than these, and leave a calm and pleasing solitariness, fed with cheerful and confident thoughts, to embark in a troubled sea of noises and hoarse disputes, put from beholding the bright countenance of truth in the quiet and still air of delightful studies, to come into the dim reflection of hollow antiquities sold by the seeming bulk,[39] and there be fain to club quotations with men whose learning and belief lies in marginal stuffings, who, when they have like good sumpters[40] laid ye down their horse-load of citations and fathers at your door, with a rhapsody of who and who were bishops here or there, ye may take off their packsaddles, their day's work is done, and episcopacy, as they think, stoutly vindicated. Let any gentle apprehension that can distinguish learned pains from unlearned drudgery imagine what pleasure or profoundness can be in this, or what honor to deal against such adversaries. But were it the meanest underservice, if God by His secretary Conscience enjoin it, it were sad for me if I should draw back; for me especially, now when all men offer their aid to help ease and lighten the difficult labors of the church, to whose service, by the intentions of my parents and friends, I was destined of a child, and in mine own resolutions, till coming to some maturity of years, and perceiving what tyranny had invaded the church—that he who would take orders must subscribe slave and take an oath withal,[41] which, unless he took with a conscience that would retch, he must either straight perjure or split his faith—I thought it better to prefer a blameless

silence before the sacred office of speaking, bought and begun with servitude and forswearing. Howsoever thus church-outed by the prelates, hence may appear the right I have to meddle in these matters, as before the necessity and constraint appeared.

An Apology against a Pamphlet Called a Modest Confutation (1642)

(An Apology for Smectymnuus)

. . . But because as well by this upbraiding to me the bordellos as by other suspicious glancings[1] in his book he[2] would seem privily to point me out to his readers as one whose custom of life were not honest but licentious, I shall entreat to be borne with though I digress; and in a way not often trod acquaint ye with the sum of my thoughts in this matter through the course of my years and studies. . . . With me it fares now as with him whose outward garment hath been injured and ill bedighted;[3] for, having no other shift, what help but to turn the inside outwards, especially if the lining be of the same or, as it is sometimes, much better? So if my name and outward demeanor be not evident enough to defend me I must make trial if the discovery of my inmost thoughts can, wherein of two purposes, both honest and both sincere, the one perhaps I shall not miss: although I fail to gain belief with others of being such as my perpetual thoughts shall here disclose me, I may yet not fail of success in persuading some to be such really themselves as they cannot believe me to be more than what I feign.

I had my time, readers, as others have who have good learning bestowed upon them, to be sent to those places where, the opinion was, it might be soonest attained; and, as the manner is, was not unstudied in those authors which are most commended. Whereof some were grave orators and historians, whose matter methought I loved indeed, but as my age then was, so I understood them; others were the smooth elegiac poets,[4] whereof the schools are not scarce,

---

[37]The Muses. [38]See Isaiah 6.1–2, 6.
[39]One of the Anglicans' favorite defences of their position was an appeal to precedent and antiquity. [40]Drivers of pack animals.
[41]Like all other degree candidates, Milton had to subscribe to the Thirty-nine Articles when he proceeded B.A. (1629) and M.A. (1632) at Cambridge. But perhaps he is referring to the notorious "Et Cetera Oath" of *Constitutions and Canons Ecclesiastical* of 1640, which required that a candidate for holy orders swear to resist any alteration in the government of the Anglican church by "archbishops, bishops, deans, and archdeacons, etc."
AN APOLOGY [1]Sly insinuations of misbehavior.
[2]The unknown author of *A Modest Confutation*, who had charged Milton with intellectual and moral turpitude. Elsewhere in the *Apology* Milton implies that this offensive pamphlet was the work of Bishop Hall, or perhaps of Hall and one of his sons.
[3]Bedecked.
[4]Poets who wrote in the classical elegiac meter of alternate hexameters and pentameters, i.e., Ovid, Tibullus, and Propertius.

whom both for the pleasing sound of their numerous[5] writing, which in imitation I found most easy and most agreeable to nature's part in me, and for their matter, which what it is, there be few who know not, I was so allured to read that no recreation came to me better welcome. For that it was then those years with me which are excused, though they be least severe, I may be saved the labor to remember[6] ye. Whence having observed them to account it the chief glory of their wit, in that they were ablest to judge, to praise, and by that could esteem themselves worthi- est to love those high perfections which under one or other name they took to celebrate, I thought with myself by every instinct and presage of nature, which is not wont to be false, that what emboldened them to this task might, with such diligence as they used, embolden me; and that what judgment, wit, or elegance was my share would herein best appear, and best value itself, by how much more wisely and with more love of virtue I should choose (let rude ears be absent) the object of not unlike praises. For albeit these thoughts to some will seem virtuous and commendable, to others only pardonable, to a third sort perhaps idle, yet the mentioning of them now will end in serious.[7]

Nor blame it, readers, in those years to propose to them- selves such a reward as the noblest dispositions above other things in this life have sometimes preferred: whereof not to be sensible when good and fair in one person meet, argues both a gross and shallow judgment and withal an ungentle and swainish breast. For by the firm settling of these persua- sions I became, to my best memory, so much a proficient that, if I found those authors[8] anywhere speaking unworthy things of themselves, or unchaste of those names which before they had extolled, this effect it wrought with me; from that time forward their art I still applauded, but the men I deplored, and above them all preferred the two famous renowners of Beatrice and Laura[9] who never write but honor of them to whom they devote their verse, dis- playing sublime and pure thoughts, without transgression. And long it was not after when I was confirmed in this opinion, that he who would not be frustrate of his hope to write well hereafter in laudable things ought himself to be a true poem, that is, a composition and pattern of the best and honorablest things—not presuming to sing high praises of heroic men or famous cities unless he have in himself the experience and the practice of all that which is praise- worthy. These reasonings, together with a certain niceness[10] of nature, an honest haughtiness, and self-esteem either of what I was or what I might be (which let envy call pride), and lastly that modesty, whereof, though not in the title- page,[11] yet here I may be excused to make some beseeming profession; all these, uniting the supply of their natural aid together, kept me still above those low descents of mind beneath which he must deject[12] and plunge himself that can agree to saleable and unlawful prostitutions.

Next (for hear me out now, readers) that I may tell ye whither my younger feet wandered, I betook me among those lofty fables and romances which recount in solemn cantos the deeds of knighthood founded by our victorious kings, and from hence had in renown over all Christendom.

There I read it in the oath of every knight, that he should defend to the expense of his best blood, or of his life if it so befell him, the honor and chastity of virgin or matron, from whence even then I learned what a noble virtue chastity sure must be, to the defense of which so many worthies, by such a dear adventure[13] of themselves, had sworn. And if I found in the story afterward, any of them, by word or deed, breaking that oath, I judged it the same fault of the poet as that which is attributed to Homer,[14] to have written in- decent things of the gods. Only this my mind gave me, that every free and gentle spirit, without that oath, ought to be born a knight, nor needed to expect the gilt spur, or the laying of a sword upon his shoulder, to stir him up both by his counsel and his arm to secure and protect the weakness of any attempted[15] chastity. So that even those books which to many others have been the fuel of wantonness and loose living, I cannot think how, unless by divine indulgence, proved to me so many incitements, as you have heard, to the love and steadfast observation of that virtue which abhors the society of bordellos.

Thus, from the laureate fraternity of poets, riper years and the ceaseless round of study and reading led me to the shady spaces of philosophy, but chiefly to the divine volumes of Plato and his equal,[16] Xenophon:[17] where, if I should tell ye what I learnt of chastity and love, I mean that which is truly so, whose charming cup is only virtue, which she bears in her hand to those who are worthy (the rest are cheated with a thick intoxicating potion which a certain sorceress,[18] the abuser of love's name, carries about), and how the first and chiefest office of love begins and ends in the soul, producing those happy twins of her divine generation, knowledge and virtue—with such abstracted sublimities as these, it might be worth your listening, readers, as I may one day hope to have ye in a still time, when there shall be no chiding; not in these noises, the adversary, as ye know, barking at the door or searching for me at the bordellos, where it may be he has lost himself and raps up without pity the sage and rheumatic old prelatess with all her young Corinthian laity,[19] to inquire for such a one.

Last of all, not in time, but as perfection is last, that care was ever had of me, with my earliest capacity, not to be negligently trained in the precepts of Christian religion. This that I have hitherto related hath been to show that though Christianity had been but slightly taught me, yet a

---

[5]Metrical. [6]Remind, recall. [7]Seriously.
[8]The elegiac poets referred to earlier.
[9]Dante had celebrated Beatrice in his *Vita Nuova* and *Paradiso*, and Petrarch Laura in his *Canzoniere*. [10]Nicety.
[11]Milton's *Apology* was published anonymously. [12]Debase. [13]Severe trial.
[14]Milton is thinking of Plato's criticism of Homer in the *Republic*, Sect. 377e. [15]Threatened. [16]Contemporary.
[17]Greek historian and essayist (434?–?355 B.C.), whose *Memorabilia* and *Symposium* are largely concerned with Socrates. [18]Circe, an enchantress of the island of Aeaea with whom Ulysses (*Odyssey*, Bk. X) lingered for a whole year after she had turned his men into swine with her spells.
[19]Prostitutes (from ancient Corinth, which was notorious for its profligacy).

certain reservedness of natural disposition, and moral discipline learnt out of the noblest philosophy, was enough to keep me in disdain of far less incontinences than this of the bordello. But having had the doctrine of Holy Scripture unfolding those chaste and high mysteries with timeliest care infused, that "the body is for the Lord, and the Lord for the body,"[20] thus also I argued to myself: that if unchastity in a woman, whom St. Paul terms the glory of man,[21] be such a scandal and dishonor, then certainly in a man, who is both the image and glory of God, it must, though commonly not so thought, be much more deflowering and dishonorable in that he sins both against his own body, which is the perfecter sex, and his own glory, which is in the woman, and—that which is worst—against the image and glory of God which is in himself. Nor did I slumber over that place[22] expressing such high rewards of ever accompanying the Lamb with those celestial songs to others inapprehensible, but not to those who were not defiled with women, which doubtless means fornication, for marriage must not be called a defilement.

Thus large I have purposely been, that if I have been justly taxed with this crime, it may come upon me, after all this my confession, with a tenfold shame.

Of Education (1644)

. . . Brief I shall endeavor to be, for that which I have to say, assuredly this nation hath extreme need should be done sooner than spoken. To tell you, therefore, what I have benefited herein among old renowned authors I shall spare; and to search what many modern Januas and Didactics[1] (more than ever I shall read) have projected, my inclination leads me not. But if you can accept of these few observations which have flowered off, and are as it were the burnishing of many studious and contemplative years altogether spent in the search of religious and civil knowledge, and such as pleased you so well in the relating, I here give you them to dispose of.

The end, then, of learning is to repair the ruins of our first parents by regaining to know God aright, and out of that knowledge to love him, to imitate him, to be like him, as we may the nearest by possessing our souls of true virtue, which being united to the heavenly grace of faith makes up the highest perfection. But because our understanding cannot in this body found itself but on sensible things, nor arrive so clearly to the knowledge of God and things invisible as by orderly conning over the visible and inferior creature, the same method is necessarily to be followed in all discreet teaching. And seeing every nation affords not experience and tradition enough for all kind of learning, therefore we are chiefly taught the languages of those people who have at any time been most industrious after wisdom; so that language is but the instrument conveying to us things useful to be known. And though a linguist should pride himself to have all the tongues that Babel[2] cleft the world into, yet, if he have not studied the solid things in them as well as the words and lexicons, he were nothing so much

to be esteemed a learned man, as any yeoman or tradesman competently wise in his mother[3] dialect only. Hence appear the many mistakes which have made learning generally so unpleasing and so unsuccessful; first we do amiss to spend seven or eight years merely in scraping together so much miserable Latin and Greek as might be learned otherwise easily and delightfully in one year. And that which casts our proficiency therein so much behind is our time lost partly in too oft idle vacancies[4] given both to schools and universities, partly in a preposterous[5] exaction, forcing the empty wits of children to compose themes, verses, and orations, which are the acts of ripest judgment and the final work of a head filled by long reading, and observing, with elegant maxims and copious invention.[6] These are not matters to be wrung from poor striplings, like blood out of the nose, or the plucking of untimely fruit: besides the ill habit which they get of wretched barbarizing against the Latin and Greek idiom, with their untutored Anglicisms, odious to be read, yet not to be avoided without a well continued and judicious conversing[7] among pure authors digested, which they scarce taste, whereas, if after some preparatory grounds of speech by their certain forms got into memory, they were led to the praxis[8] thereof in some chosen short book lessoned thoroughly to them, they might then forthwith proceed to learn the substance of good things, and arts in due order, which would bring the whole language quickly into their power. This I take to be the most rational and most profitable way of learning languages, and whereby we may best hope to give account to God of our youth spent herein. And for the usual method of teaching arts, I deem it to be an old error of universities not yet well recovered from the scholastic grossness of barbarous ages, that instead of beginning with arts most easy, and those be such as are most obvious to the sense, they present their young unmatriculated[9] novices at first coming with the most intellective abstractions of logic and metaphysics, so that they having but newly left those grammatic flats and shallows where they stuck unreasonably to learn a few words with lamentable construction, and now on the sudden transported under another climate to be tossed and turmoiled with their unballasted wits in fathomless and unquiet deeps of con-

---

[20] 1 Corinthians 6.13.　[21] I Corinthians 11.7.
[22] Passage in the Bible (i.e., Revelation 14.1–5).
OF EDUCATION [1] Pedagogical manuals like *Janua linguarum resertata* and *Didactica magna* by the Moravian philosopher John Amos Comenius (Jan Amos Komensky, 1592–1670). After its appearance in England as *Porta linguarum trilinguis. The Gate of Tongues Unlocked* (1631) the *Janua* had gone through five editions by 1640, and although the *Didactica* was not published until 1657, parts of it had been widely publicized in various works of Samuel Hartlib. (d. 1670?), a Polish immigrant and writer on educational reform to whom Milton addressed the present treatise.
[2] See Genesis 11.1–9.　[3] Native.　[4] Vacations.
[5] In reversed order, with the last part first (a Latinism).
[6] *Inventio*, that part of rhetoric devoted to the "discovery" of material suitable for use in writing and speaking.
[7] Association.　[8] Practice.
[9] Not yet enrolled at a university.

troversy, do for the most part grow into hatred and contempt of learning, mocked and deluded all this while with ragged notions and babblements, while they expected worthy and delightful knowledge; till poverty or youthful years call them importunately their several ways, and hasten them with the sway of friends either to an ambitious and mercenary or ignorantly zealous divinity:[10] some allured to the trade of law, grounding their purposes not on the prudent and heavenly contemplation of justice and equity which was never taught them, but on the promising and pleasing thoughts of litigious terms,[11] fat contentions, and flowing fees; others betake them to state affairs with souls so un-principled in virtue and true generous breeding that flattery and court-shifts and tyrannous aphorisms appear to them the highest points of wisdom, instilling their barren hearts with a conscientious slavery, if, as I rather think, it be not feigned. Others, lastly, of a more delicious[12] and airy spirit retire themselves, knowing no better, to the enjoyments of ease and luxury, living out their days in feast and jollity; which indeed is the wisest and safest course of all these, unless they were with more integrity undertaken. And these are the errors, and these are the fruits of misspending our prime youth at the schools and universities as we do, either in learning mere words or such things chiefly, as were better unlearned.

I shall detain you now no longer in the demonstration of what we should not do, but straight conduct ye to a hillside, where I will point ye out the right path of a virtuous and noble education; laborious indeed at the first ascent, but else so smooth, so green, so full of goodly prospect and melodious sounds on every side that the harp of Orpheus[13] was not more charming. I doubt not but ye shall have more ado to drive our dullest and laziest youth, our stocks and stubs, from the infinite desire of such a happy nurture than we have now to hale and drag our choicest and hopefullest wits to that asinine feast of sowthistles and brambles which is commonly set before them, as all the food and enter-tainment of their tenderest and most docible[14] age. I call therefore a complete and generous[15] education that which fits a man to perform justly, skilfully and magnanimously all the offices both private and public of peace and war. And how all this may be done between twelve and one-and-twenty, less time than is now bestowed in pure trifling at grammar and sophistry, is to be thus ordered. . . .

> Milton's formidable program for educating boys from twelve to twenty-one begins with a quick but thorough grounding in Latin grammar followed by some "easy and delightful book of education" like Plutarch's *Moralia*, together with arithmetic and geometry. The curriculum, based on progressively difficult reading, then spreads to agriculture, cartography, biblical history, Greek, geography, botany, anatomy, medicine, and to such poets as Hesiod, Theocritus, Lucretius, and "the rural part of Vergil" (i.e., the *Georgics* and *Eclogues*). Thus prepared, by the age of fifteen or so the students are ready to move onward and upward.

By this time, years and good general precepts will have furnished them more distinctly with that act of reason which in ethics is call proairesis[16], that they may with some judgment contemplate upon moral good and evil. Then will be required a special reinforcement of constant and sound indoctrinating to set them right and firm, instructing them more amply in the knowledge of virtue and the hatred of vice; while their young and pliant affections are led through all the moral works of Plato, Xenophon, Cicero, Plutarch, Laertius, and those Locrian remnants;[17] but still to be re-duced[18] in their nightward studies wherewith they close the day's work, under the determinate[19] sentence of David, or Solomon, or the Evangels and apostolic Scriptures. Being perfit in the knowledge of personal duty, they may then begin the study of economics.[20] And either now, or before this, they may have easily learned at any odd hour the Italian tongue. And soon after, but with wariness, and good antidote, it would be wholesome enough to let them taste some choice comedies, Greek, Latin, or Italian; those trag-edies also that treat of household matters, as *Trachiniae, Alcestis,*[21] and the like. The next remove must be to the study of politics; to know the beginning, end, and reasons of political societies, that they may not in a dangerous fit of the commonwealth be such poor, shaken, uncertain reeds, of such a tottering conscience, as many of our great counselors have lately shewn themselves, but steadfast pillars of the state. After this they are to dive into the grounds of law, and legal justice; delivered first, and with best warrant by Moses; and as far as human prudence can be trusted, in those extolled remains of Grecian lawgivers, Lycurgus, Solon, Zaleucus, Charondas, and thence to all the Roman edicts and tables with their Justinian; and so down to the Saxon and common laws of England, and the statutes.[22]

[10]Clerical career.
[11]Periods appointed for the sitting of certain courts of law.
[12]Sensuous.
[13]In Greek myth, a musician who charmed birds, rocks, and trees with his art. [14]Teachable.
[15]Suitable for one of noble birth or spirit (a Latinism).
[16]Choice.
[17]Milton is probably thinking of such famous *moral works* as Plato's ethical dialogues (for example, *Crito* and *Phaedo*), Xeno-phon's *Memorabilia* and *Cyropaedia*, Cicero's *De officiis*, and Plu-tarch's *Moralia*. Diogenes Laertius was the 2d- or 3d-century author of the gossipy *Lives and Opinions of Eminent Philosophers*, and the *Locrian remnants* is Milton's name for a dialogue *On the Soul of the World and Nature* formerly attributed to Timaeus of Locri (the principal speaker in Plato's *Timaeus*) but now regarded as a late forgery. [18]Brought back (a Latinism).
[19]Authoritative because inspired by God.
[20]Text *Economies.* For Milton the word retained its original meaning of household management.
[21]Dramas by Sophocles and Euripides respectively, both con-cerned with marriage and portraying devoted wives.
[22]In this one compendious sentence Milton adumbrates the history of some three thousand years of jurisprudence: the Mosaic code, such scrappy *remains* of legendary Greek lawgivers (including *Zaleucus* and *Charondas* who lived in southern Italy and Sicily respectively) as are preserved by ancient commentators, the primitive Twelve *Tables* of republican Rome and the *edicts*

Sundays also and every evening may be now understandingly spent in the highest matters of theology and church history ancient and modern; and ere this time the Hebrew tongue at a set hour might have been gained, that the Scriptures may be now read in their own original; whereto it would be no impossibility to add the Chaldee and the Syrian dialect.[23] When all these employments are well conquered, then will the choice histories, heroic poems, and Attic tragedies of stateliest and most regal argument, with all the famous political orations, offer themselves; which if they were not only read, but some of them go by memory, and solemnly pronounced with right accent and grace, as might be taught, would endue them even with the spirit and vigor of Demosthenes or Cicero, Euripides or Sophocles.

And now lastly[24] will be the time to read with them those organic arts[25] which enable men to discourse and write perspicuously, elegantly, and according to the fitted[26] style of lofty, mean, or lowly.[27] Logic therefore, so much as is useful, is to be referred to this due place with all her well-couched heads and topics, until it be time to open her contracted palm[28] into a graceful and ornate rhetoric taught out of the rule of Plato, Aristotle, Phalereus, Cicero, Hermogenes, Longinus.[29] To which poetry would be made subsequent, or indeed rather precedent,[30] as being less subtle and fine, but more simple, sensuous and passionate.[31] I mean not here the prosody of a verse, which they could not but have hit on before among the rudiments of grammar; but that sublime art which in Aristotle's *Poetics*, in Horace, and the Italian commentaries of Castelvetro, Tasso, Mazzoni,[32] and others, teaches what the laws are of a true epic poem, what of a dramatic, what of a lyric, what decorum is, which is the grand masterpiece to observe. This would make them soon perceive what despicable creatures our common rhymers and playwrites[33] be, and show them what religious, what glorious and magnificent, use might be made of poetry both in divine and human things.

From hence and not till now will be the right season of forming them to be able writers and composers in every excellent matter, when they shall be thus fraught with an universal insight into things. Or whether they be to speak in Parliament or council, honor and attention would be waiting on their lips. There would then also appear in pulpits other visages, other gestures, and stuff otherwise wrought than what we now sit under, ofttimes to as great a trial of our patience as any other that they preach to us. These are the studies wherein our noble and our gentle youth ought to bestow their time in a disciplinary way from twelve to one-and-twenty; unless they rely more upon their ancestors dead than upon themselves living. In which methodical course it is so supposed they must proceed by the steady pace of learning onward, as at convenient times for memory's sake to retire back into the middle ward, and sometimes into the rear of what they have been taught, until they have confirmed, and solidly united the whole body of their perfeted knowledge, like the last embattling of a Roman legion. . . .

In the final section of his treatise, headed "Their Exercise," Milton turns to the less bookish part of his program. It includes, in addition to hearing a great deal of music, swordsmanship, wrestling, military maneuvers, and field trips in a variety of subjects.

THE SECOND DEFENCE OF THE PEOPLE OF ENGLAND (1654)

. . . I will now mention who and whence I am. I was born at London,[1] of an honest family; my father was distinguished by the undeviating integrity of his life, my mother by the esteem in which she was held and the alms which she

of a later period that were codified in the *Institutes* and *Digests* of the Eastern Emperor Justinian (527–65), and finally the *common* and statute law of England.
[23]Respectively, the Old Testament and New Testament forms of Aramaic, the prevailing language of ancient Babylonia and Syria. Parts of the Book of Daniel are preserved in Chaldee, and much of the Gospels in Syriac (*Syrian*).
[24]At the end of a boy's schooling, when he would presumably be capable of writing the *themes, verses, and orations* that Milton, contrary to contemporary procedures, excluded from the earlier parts of the curriculum (p. 774).
[25]Arts like playwriting and poetical composition that require a capacity for organization and structure.
[26]Appropriate (to speaker, subject, and audience).
[27]This distinction between the three levels of style had been a commonplace in rhetoric since Cicero. Milton alludes to it at the start of *Paradise Lost* (I.14) when he announces that he intends to soar "with no middle flight."
[28]According to Cicero (*De finibus*, II.6), it was Zeno, the founder of Stoicism, who first compared logic to a closed fist and rhetoric to an open hand.
[29]Plato dealt with rhetoric in *Gorgias* and *Phaedrus*; Aristotle's *Rhetoric* was one of the most influential ancient works upon the subject; Demetrius Phalereus (345?–283 B.C.) was an Athenian orator and statesman to whom is attributed (perhaps wrongly) a treatise *On Style*; Cicero's *De oratore* and the dialogue *Orator* were the most widely read of his many works on rhetoric; Hermogenes of Tarsus (b. about 150), a rhetorician who taught in Rome, was the author of five treatises on rhetoric long used as textbooks; Longinus is the name commonly ascribed to the unknown author of *On the Sublime*, one of the most distinguished works of ancient criticism.
[30]Subsequent in Milton's program but precedent in importance.
[31]This famous comment seems to mean that as compared with rhetoric, poetry appeals more directly to the senses.
[32]In addition to Aristotle and Horace, whose *Poetics* and *Ars poetica* are works of perennial significance, Milton alludes to Ludovico Castelvetro (1505–71), the Italian translator of the *Poetics*; Torquato Tasso (1544–95), author of the epic *Gerusalemme Liberata* as well as three *Discourses on the Art of Poetry*; and Giacomo Mazzoni (1548–98), who defended Dante against the strictures of Aristotelian purists. [33]Playwrights.
THE SECOND DEFENCE [1]Milton was born 9 December 1608, the son of John 1563–1647) and Sarah Jeffrey Milton (1572?–1637), at their home in Bread Street, Cheapside. The elder Milton was a prosperous scrivener (i.e., notary and conveyancer) with an almost professional interest and competence in musical composition.

bestowed. My father destined me from a child to the pursuits of literature, and my appetite for knowledge was so voracious that from twelve years of age I hardly ever left my studies or went to bed before midnight. This primarily led to my loss of sight.[2] My eyes were naturally weak, and I was subject to frequent head-aches, which, however, could not chill the ardour of my curiosity or retard the progress of my improvement. My father had me daily instructed in the grammar school and by other masters at home.[3] He then, after I had acquired a proficiency in various languages, and had made a considerable progress in philosophy, sent me to the University of Cambridge. Here I passed seven years in the usual course of instruction and study, with the approbation of the good, and without any stain upon my character, till I took the degree of Master of Arts.[4]

After this I did not, as this miscreant[5] feigns, run away into Italy, but of my own accord retired to my father's house, whither I was accompanied by the regrets of most of the fellows of the college, who showed me no common marks of friendship and esteem. On my father's estate, where he had determined to pass the remainder of his days, I enjoyed an interval of uninterrupted leisure which I entirely devoted to the perusal of the Greek and Latin classics, though I occasionally visited the metropolis either for the sake of purchasing books or of learning something new in mathematics or in music, in which I, at that time, found a source of pleasure and amusement. In this manner I spent five years till my mother's death.

I then became anxious to visit foreign parts, and particularly Italy.[6] My father gave me his permission, and I left home with one servant. On my departure, the celebrated Henry Wotton,[7] who had long been King James' ambassador at Venice, gave me a signal proof of his regard in an elegant letter which he wrote, breathing not only the warmest friendship but containing some maxims of conduct which I found very useful in my travels. The noble Thomas Scudamore,[8] King Charles' ambassador, to whom I carried letters of recommendation, received me most courteously at Paris. His Lordship gave me a card of introduction to the learned Hugo Grotius,[9] at that time ambassador from the queen of Sweden to the French court, whose acquaintance I anxiously desired, and to whose house I was accompanied by some of His Lordship's friends. A few days after, when I set out for Italy, he gave me letters to the English merchants on my route, that they might show me any civilities in their power. Taking ship at Nice, I arrived at Genoa, and afterwards visited Leghorn, Pisa, and Florence. In the latter city, which I have always more particularly esteemed for the elegance of its dialect, its genius, and its taste, I stopped about two months, when I contracted an intimacy with many persons of rank and learning and was a constant attendant at their literary parties; a practice which prevails there, and tends so much to the diffusion of knowledge and the preservation of friendship. No time will ever abolish the agreeable recollections which I cherish of Jacob Gaddi, Carolo Dati, Frescobaldo, Cultellero, Bonomatthai, Clementillo, Francisco, and many others.

From Florence I went to Siena, thence to Rome, where, after I had spent about two months in viewing the antiquities of that renowned city, where I experienced the most friendly attentions from Lucas Holstein, and other learned and ingenious men, I continued my route to Naples. There I was introduced by a certain recluse, with whom I had traveled from Rome, to John Baptista Manso, Marquis of Villa, a nobleman of distinguished rank and authority, to whom Torquato Tasso, the illustrious poet, inscribed his book on friendship.[10] During my stay he gave me singular proofs of his regard: he himself conducted me round the city and to the palace of the viceroy, and more than once paid me a visit at my lodgings. On my departure he gravely apologized for not having shown me more civility, which he said he had been restrained from doing because I had spoken with so little reserve on matters of religion.

When I was preparing to pass over into Sicily and Greece, the melancholy intelligence which I received of the civil commotions in England made me alter my purpose; for I thought it base to be travelling for amusement abroad while my fellow-citizens were fighting for liberty at home. While I

---

[2]After almost a decade of failing vision, Milton became totally blind in the winter of 1651–52, when he was forty-three.

[3]One of these tutors was Thomas Young (1587?–1655), a Scottish Presbyterian divine to whom Milton, as an undergraduate at Cambridge, addressed an affectionate verse epistle in Latin and who participated in the pamphlet controversies of the early forties as one of the Smectymnuans (see p. 258).

[4]About his education, as about certain other topics, Milton is sparing of details. At some time between 1615 and 1620 he was enrolled at the famous St. Paul's School, where he presumably stayed until matriculating at Christ's College, Cambridge, in 1625. Although briefly rusticated because of some difficulty with his tutor in the spring of 1626, he soon returned, proceeded B.A. in 1629 and M.A. in 1632.

[5]Alexander More (1616–70), a Scottish Presbyterian divine whom Milton thought to be the author of *Regii sanguinis clamor* (1552), a savage reply to Milton's own *Defensio* (1651) justifying the recent revolution and regicide. It was in part to answer the vituperative personal attack on himself in the *Clamor*—which was actually the work of one Peter du Moulin—that Milton inserted this autobiography in his *Defensio secunda*.

[6]Following six years of rustication and study at his father's houses at Hammersmith (a suburb of London) and Horton (a Buckinghamshire village near Windsor), Milton set out for the Continent in the spring of 1638. He returned to England some fifteen months later, in the late summer of 1639.

[7]After many years in diplomatic service, Sir Henry Wotton (see p. 54) was ending his career as provost of Eton College (1624–39). In reprinting *A Mask* (i.e., *Comus*) in his 1645 *Poems*, Milton included a highly commendatory letter about the work from Wotton. See p. 261, n.3

[8]John Scudamore (1601–71), first Viscount Scudamore, served in Paris between 1635 and 1639.

[9]The celebrated Dutch jurist and statesman (1583–1645) whose play *Adamus Exul* (1601) may have contributed something to *Paradise Lost*.

[10]Manso (1561–1647) was the recipient of the Latin verse epistle *Mansus*, which Milton included in the 1645 *Poems*. Tasso's tribute to his benefactor was a dialogue entitled *Il Manso*.

was on my way back to Rome, some merchants informed me that the English Jesuits had formed a plot against me if I returned to Rome, because I had spoken too freely on religion; for it was a rule which I laid down to myself in those places never to be the first to begin any conversation on religion, but if any questions were put to me concerning my faith, to declare it without any reserve or fear. I nevertheless returned to Rome. I took no steps to conceal either my person or my character, and for about the space of two months I again openly defended, as I had done before, the reformed religion in the very metropolis of popery.

By the favor of God, I got safe back to Florence, where I was received with as much affection as if I had returned to my native country. There I stopped as many months as I had done before, except that I made an excursion for a few days to Lucca; and, crossing the Apennines, passed through Bologna and Ferrara to Venice. After I had spent a month in surveying the curiosities of this city, and had put on board a ship the books which I had collected in Italy, I proceeded through Verona and Milan, and along the Leman lake to Geneva. The mention of this city brings to my recollection the slandering More,[11] and makes me again call the Deity to witness, that in all those places in which vice meets with so little discouragement, and is practised with so little shame, I never once deviated from the paths of integrity and virtue, and perpetually reflected that though my conduct might escape the notice of men, it could not elude the inspection of God. At Geneva I held daily conferences with John Diodati,[12] the learned professor of theology.

Then pursuing my former route through France, I returned to my native country, after an absence of one year and about three months, at the time when Charles, having broken the peace, was renewing what is called the episcopal war with the Scots, in which the royalists being routed in the first encounter and the English being universally and justly disaffected, the necessity of his affairs at last obliged him to convene a Parliament.[13] As soon as I was able, I hired a spacious house in the City for myself and my books, where I again with rapture renewed my literary pursuits, and where I calmly awaited the issue of the contest, which I trusted to the wise conduct of providence and to the courage of the people.

The vigor of the Parliament had begun to humble the pride of the bishops. As long as the liberty of speech was no longer subject to control, all mouths began to be opened against the bishops; some complained of the vices of the individuals, others of those of the order. They said that it was unjust that they alone should differ from the model of other reformed churches; that the government of the church should be according to the pattern of other churches, and particularly the word of God. This awakened all my attention and my zeal. I saw that a way was opening for the establishment of real liberty, that the foundation was laying for the deliverance of man from the yoke of slavery and superstition, that the principles of religion, which were the first objects of our care, would exert a salutary influence on the manners and constitution of the republic; and as I had from my

youth studied the distinctions between religious and civil rights, I perceived that if I ever wished to be of use, I ought at least not to be wanting to my country, to the church, and to so many of my fellow-Christians in a crisis of so much danger. I therefore determined to relinquish the other pursuits in which I was engaged, and to transfer the whole force of my talents and my industry to this one important object.

I accordingly wrote two books to a friend concerning the reformation of the Church of England. Afterwards, when two bishops of superior distinction vindicated their privileges against some principal ministers, I thought that on those topics, to the consideration of which I was led solely by my love of truth and my reverence for Christianity, I should not probably write worse than those who were contending only for their own emoluments and usurpations. I therefore answered the one in two books, of which the first is inscribed *Concerning Prelatical Episcopacy,* and the other *Concerning the Mode of Ecclesiastical Government;* and I replied to the other in some *Animadversions,* and soon after in an Apology. On this occasion it was supposed that I brought a timely succor to the ministers, who were hardly a match for the eloquence of their opponents; and from that time I was actively employed in refuting any answers that appeared.[14]

When the bishops could no longer resist the multitude of their assailants I had leisure to turn my thoughts to other subjects to the promotion of real and substantial liberty, which is rather to be sought from within than from without, and whose existence depends not so much on the terror of the sword as on sobriety of conduct and integrity of life. When, therefore, I perceived that there were three species of liberty which are essential to the happiness of social life—religious, domestic, and civil; and as I had already written concerning the first, and the magistrates were strenuously active in obtaining the third, I determined to turn my attention to the second or the domestic species.[15] As this seemed to involve three material questions—the conditions of the conjugal tie, the education of the children, and the free publi-

[11]Alexander More had lived several years in Geneva as professor of Greek and theology.

[12]An uncle of Charles Diodati (1608?–38), Milton's most intimate friend since their schooldays at St. Paul's. His untimely death prompted Milton's *Epitaphium Damonis,* one of his most important Latin poems.

[13]Having ruled without Parliament since 1629, Charles, in an abortive effort to force Anglicanism on the Scots, sent an army as far as Berwick, where he signed a humiliating peace in June 1639. Still intent on war with Scotland but without the funds to wage it, the king convened the so-called Short Parliament in the spring of 1640, but when the Scots responded by invading England he was forced to call the famous Long Parliament (1640–60), thus setting in motion the events that led to revolution.

[14]For comment on Milton's five anti-prelatical pamphlets of 1641–42 see p. 258.

[15]For comment on Milton's four divorce tracts of 1643–45 see p. 258. It is odd that he says nothing about his marriage to Mary Powell in the summer of 1642, for their long separation (from a few weeks after the wedding until perhaps the summer of 1645) wasu srely foremost in his mind in these unhappy years.

cation of the thoughts—I made them objects of distinct consideration. I explained my sentiments not only concerning the solemnization of the marriage but the dissolution, if circumstances rendered it necessary; and I drew my arguments from the divine law, which Christ did not abolish, or publish another more grievous than that of Moses. I stated my own opinions, and those of others, concerning the exclusive exception of fornication, which our illustrious Selden has since, in his *Hebrew Wife*,[16] more copiously discussed; for he in vain makes a vaunt of liberty in the senate or in the forum who languishes under the vilest servitude to an inferior at home. On this subject, therefore, I published some books which were more particularly necessary at that time, when man and wife were often the most inveterate foes, when the man often stayed to take care of his children at home while the mother of the family was seen in the camp of the enemy, threatening death and destruction to her husband.

I then discussed the principles of education[17] in a summary manner, but sufficiently copious for those who attend seriously to the subject; than which nothing can be more necessary to principle[18] the minds of men in virtue, the only genuine source of political and individual liberty, the only true safeguard of states, the bulwark of their prosperity and renown. Lastly, I wrote my *Areopagitica*[19] in order to deliver the press from the restraints with which it was encumbered, that the power of determining what was true and what was false, what ought to be published and what to be suppressed, might no longer be entrusted to a few illiterate and illiberal individuals, who refused their sanction to any work which contained views or sentiments at all above the level of the vulgar superstition.[20]

On the last species of civil liberty I said nothing because I saw that sufficient attention was paid to it by the magistrates; nor did I write anything on the prerogative of the crown till the king, voted an enemy by the Parliament and vanquished in the field, was summoned before the tribunal which condemned him to lose his head. But when, at length, some Presbyterian ministers, who had formerly been the most bitter enemies to Charles, became jealous of the growth of the Independents,[21] and of their ascendancy in the Parliament, most tumultuously clamoured against the sentence, and did all in their power to prevent the execution, though they were not angry so much on account of the act itself as because it was not the act of their party, and when they dared to affirm that the doctrine of the Protestants and of all the reformed churches was abhorrent to such an atrocious proceeding against kings, I thought that it became me to oppose such a glaring falsehood; and accordingly, without any immediate or personal application to Charles, I showed, in an abstract consideration of the question, what might lawfully be done against tyrants; and in support of what I advanced produced the opinions of the most celebrated divines, while I vehemently inveighed against the egregious ignorance or effrontery of men who professed better things, and from whom better things might have been expected. That book[22] did not make its appearance till

after the death of Charles, and was written rather to reconcile the minds of the people to the event than to discuss the legitimacy of that particular sentence which concerned the magistrates, and which was already executed.

Such were the fruits of my private studies, which I gratuitously presented to the church and to the state and for which I was recompensed by nothing but impunity, though the actions themselves procured me peace of conscience and the approbation of the good, while I exercised that freedom of discussion which I loved. Others, without labour or desert, got possession of honors and emoluments, but no one ever knew me either soliciting anything myself or through the medium of my friends, ever beheld me in a supplicating posture at the doors of the senate or the levees of the great. I usually kept myself secluded at home, where my own property, part of which had been withheld during the civil commotions and part of which had been absorbed in the oppressive contributions which I had to sustain, afforded me a scanty subsistence. When I was released from these engagements, and thought that I was about to enjoy an interval of uninterrupted ease, I turned my thoughts to a continued history of my country, from the earliest times to the present period.[23] I had already finished four books, when, after the subversion of the monarchy, and the establishment of a republic, I was surprised by an invitation from the Council of State, who desired my services in the office for foreign affairs. A book appeared soon after, which was ascribed to the king and contained the most invidious charges against the Parliament. I was ordered to answer it; and opposed the *Iconoclast* to his *Icon*.[24] I did not insult over fallen majesty, as is pretended;[25] I only preferred Queen Truth to King Charles. The charge of insult, which I saw that the malevolent would urge, I was at some pains to remove in the beginning of the work, and as often as possible in other

[16]*Uxor Ebraica* (1646). For Selden see pp. 852 ff.

[17]For *Of Education* (June 1644) see pp. 744 ff. [18]Ground.

[19]For this, Milton's most enduring piece of prose, (November 1644), see pp. 603 ff.

[20]In June 1643 the Presbyterian majority in Parliament, alarmed by the rising flood of such unorthodox (and therefore, as they thought, dangerous) publications as those by Milton on divorce, re-imposed the rigid censorship that they themselves had abolished in 1641.

[21]Those Puritans, very numerous in the army, who urged that all religious discipline and administration be vested in local congregations of believers (instead of in a national church demanded by the Presbyterians who dominated Parliament). Milton's growing disaffection with the Presbyterians, matched by his growing admiration for the Independents, is one of the major themes of his prose after the early forties.

[22]*The Tenure of Kings and Magistrates* (February 1649). For Charles' trial and execution (30 January 1649) see pp. 933 ff.

[23]For Milton's *History of Britain*, which was not published until 1670, see pp. 921 ff.

[24]Milton was named secretary of foreign tongues to the Council of State on 15 March 1649, a few weeks after the appearance of *The Tenure of Kings and Magistrates* and about seven months before that of *Eikonklastes*, the official reply to the alarmingly popular *Eikon Basilike* (see pp. 609 ff). [25]Alleged.

places. Salmasius then appeared, to whom they[26] were not, as More says, long in looking about for an opponent, but immediately appointed me, who happened at the time to be present in the Council.[27] I have thus, Sir, given some account of myself in order to stop your mouth and to remove any prejudices which your falsehoods and misrepresentations might cause even good men to entertain against me.

[26]The Council of State.

[27]Claudius Salmasius (i.e., Claude de Saumaise, 1588–1653), a noted French scholar whom Charles II commissioned to defend his father's reign, published his *Defensio regia pro Carlo I* in May 1649, some four months after the king's execution. Milton answered it with *Pro populo Anglicano defensio* (1651), which, together with its sequel *Defensio secunda* (1654), he regarded as his most important contributions to the cause of English liberty.

Sir William Davenant [1606-1668] and Thomas Hobbes[1] [1588-1679]

from A Discourse upon *Gondibert*, an Heroic Poem Written by Sir William Davenant. With an Answer to It by Master Hobbes (1650)

The Author's Preface to His Much Honored Friend Master Hobbes

Sir,

Since you have done me the honor to allow this poem a daily examination as it was writing, I will presume, now it hath attained more length, to give you a longer trouble, that you may yield me as great advantages by censuring the method as by judging the numbers and the matter.[1] And because you shall pass through this new building with more ease to your disquisition, I will acquaint you what care I took of my materials ere I began to work. . . .

> Davenant first surveys the line of "heroic" (i.e., epic) poets from Homer to Spenser, and in each of them, as he concedes, critics have found something to deplore. Homer, although "standing upon the poets' famous hill like the eminent seamark by which they have in former ages steered," intrudes too many "fables" into the tale of human actions; Vergil's force "hath more of strength than quickness, and of patience than activity"; Lucan's subject was more suitable for a historian than a poet; Tasso, though esteemed "both in time and merit the first of the moderns," was too imitative of his ancient models; Spenser's archaic language and his complex stanza, together with his studious allegory, have obscured his other merits. Taken altogether, they show the strength and weakness of tradition, "such limits to the progress of everything, even of worthiness as well as defect, doth imitation give."

But I feel, Sir, that I am falling into the dangerous fit of a hot writer, for instead of performing the promise which

begins this preface, and doth oblige me, after I had given you the judgment of some upon others, to present myself to your censure, I am wandering after new thoughts; but I shall ask your pardon, and return to my undertaking.

My argument I resolved should consist of Christian persons; for since religion doth generally beget and govern manners, I thought the example of their actions would prevail most upon our own by being derived from the same doctrine and authority, as the particular sects educated by philosophers were diligent and pliant to the dictates and fashions of such as derived themselves from the same master, but lazy and froward[2] to those who conversed in other schools. Yet all these sects pretended to the same beauty, virtue, though each did court her more fondly when she was dressed at their own homes by the hands of their acquaintance; and so subjects bred under the laws of a prince—though laws differ not much in morality or privilege throughout the civil world, being everywhere made for direction of life more than for sentences of death—will rather die near that prince, defending those they have been taught than live by taking new from another.

These were partly the reasons why I chose a story of such persons as professed Christian religion; but I ought to have been most inclined to it because the principles of our re-

[1]For a commentary on Davenant and excerpts from his work see Poetry, pp. 251 ff.; for a commentary on Hobbes and excerpts from his other work see Philosophy and Speculation, pp. 491 ff., History and Historiography, pp. 904 ff.

THE AUTHOR'S PREFACE [1]The versification and the subject. *And:* text *in.* [2]Refractory.

ligion conduce more to explicable virtue, to plain demonstrative justice, and even to honor (if virtue, the mother of honor, be voluntary and active in the dark, so as she need not laws to compel her, nor look for witnesses to proclaim her) than any other religion that ever assembled men to divine worship. . . .

When I considered the actions which I meant to describe (those inferring[3] the persons), I was again persuaded rather to choose those of a former age than the present, and in a century so far removed as might preserve me from their improper examinations who know not the requisites of a poem, nor how much pleasure they lose—and even the pleasures of heroic poesy are not unprofitable—who take away the liberty of a poet and fetter his feet in the shackles of an historian. For why should a poet doubt in story to mend the intrigues of fortune by more delightful conveyances of probable fiction because austere historians have entered into bond to truth—an obligation which were in poets as foolish and unnecessary as is the bondage of false martyrs who lie in chains for a mistaken opinion? But by this I would imply that truth narrative and past is the idol of historians, who worship a dead thing; and truth operative and by effects continually alive is the mistress of poets, who hath not her existence in matter but in reason.[4]

I was likewise more willing to derive my theme from elder times, as thinking it no little mark of skillfulness to comply with the common infirmity; for men, even of the best education, discover their eyes to be weak when they look upon the glory of virtue, which is great actions, and rather endure it at distance than near, being more apt to believe and love the renown of predecessors than of contemporaries, whose deeds, excelling theirs in their own sight, seem to upbraid them, and are not reverenced as examples of virtue but envied as the favors of fortune. But to make great actions credible is the principal art of poets, who, though they avouch the utility of fictions, should not, by altering and subliming[5] story, make use of their privilege to the detriment of the reader, whose incredulity, when things are not represented in proportion, doth much allay as the relish of his pity, hope, joy, and other passions. For we may descend to compare the deceptions in poesy to those of them that profess dexterity of hand which resembles conjuring, and to such we come not with the intention of lawyers to examine the evidence of facts, but are content, if we like the carriage of their feigned motion, to pay for being well deceived.

As in the choice of time, so of place I have complied with the weakness of the generality of men, who think the best objects of their own country so little to the size of those abroad as if they were showed them by the wrong end of a prospective;[6] for man, continuing the appetites of his first childhood till he arrive at his second, which is more froward, must be quieted with something that he thinks excellent which he may call his own, but when he sees the like in other places, not staying to compare them, wrangles at all he hath. This leads us to observe the craftiness of the comics, who are only willing when they describe humor (and humor is the drunkenness of a nation, which no sleep can cure), to lay

the scene in their own country, as knowing we are, like the son of Noah,[7] so little distasted to behold each other's shame that we delight to see even that of a father; yet when they would set forth greatness and excellent virtue, which is the theme of tragedy, publicly to the people, they wisely, to avoid the quarrels of neighborly envy, remove the scene from home. And by their example I traveled too, and Italy, which was once the stage of the world, I have made the theater where I show in either sex some patterns of human life that are perhaps fit to be followed.

Having told you why I took the actions that should be my argument from men of our own religion and given you reasons for the choice of the time and place designed for those actions, I must next acquaint you with the schools where they were bred, not meaning the schools where they took their religion, but morality; for I know religion is universally rather inherited than taught, and the most effectual schools of morality are courts and camps; yet towards the first the people are unquiet through envy, and towards the other through fear, and always jealous of both for injustice, which is the natural scandal cast upon authority and great force. They look upon the outward glory or blaze of courts as wild beasts in dark nights stare on their hunters' torches; but though the expenses of courts, whereby they shine, is that consuming glory in which the people think their liberty is wasted—for wealth is their liberty, and loved by them even to jealousy, being themselves a coarser sort of princes, apter to take than to pay—yet courts (I mean all abstracts of the multitude, either by king or assemblies) are not the schools where men are bred to oppression but the temples where sometimes oppressors take sanctuary, a safety which our reason must allow them. For the ancient laws of sanctuary, derived from God, provided chiefly for actions that proceeded from necessity; and who can imagine less than a necessity of oppressing the people, since they are never willing either to buy their peace or to pay for war?
. . .

I may now believe I have usefully taken from courts and camps the patterns of such as will be fit to be imitated by the most necessary men, and the most necessary men are those who become principal by prerogative of blood, which is seldom unassisted with education or by greatness of mind, which in exact definition is virtue. The common crowd, of whom we are hopeless,[8] we desert, being rather to be corrected by laws, where precept is accompanied with punishment, than to be taught by poesy. For few have arrived at the skill of Orpheus[9] or at his good fortune, whom we may suppose to have met with extraordinary Grecian

---

[3]Implying.
[4]This distinction, a commonplace in Renaissance criticism, derives ultimately from Aristotle's assertion (*Poetics*, Sect. ix) that poetry is more "philosophical and serious than history, for poetry deals more with things in a universal way, but history with each thing for itself." [5]Elevating, exalting. [6]Telescope.
[7]For the story of Ham, one of Noah's sons who looked upon his drunken father's nakedness, see Genesis 9.22. [8]Despairing.
[9]In Greek myth, a musician who charmed birds and beasts and even stones with his art.

beasts when so successfully he reclaimed them with his harp. Nor is it needful that heroic poesy should be leveled to the reach of common men; for if the examples it presents prevail upon their chiefs, the delight of imitation (which we hope we have proved to be as effectual to good as to evil) will rectify, by the rules which those chiefs establish of their own lives, the lives of all that behold them; for the example of life doth as much surpass the force of precept as life doth exceed death.

In the choice of these objects which are as seamarks to direct the dangerous voyage of life I thought fit to follow the rule of coasting maps, where the shelves and rocks are described as well as the safe channel, the care being equal how to avoid as to proceed; and the characters of men whose passions are to be eschewed I have derived from the distempers of love or ambition, for love and ambition are too often the raging fevers of great minds. . . .

I have now given you the accompt of such provisions as I made for this new building, and you may next please, having examined the substance, to take a view of the form, and observe if I have methodically and with discretion disposed of the materials which with some curiosity I had collected. I cannot discern by any help from reading or learned men, who have been to me the best and briefest indexes of books, that any nation hath in representment of great actions, either by heroics or dramatics,[10] digested story into so pleasant and instructive a method as the English by their drama; and by that regular species, though narratively and not in dialogue, I have drawn the body of an heroic poem. In which I did not only observe the symmetry— proportioning five books to five acts, and cantos to scenes, the scenes having their number ever governed by occasion— but all the shadowings, happy strokes, secret graces, and even the drapery, which together make the second beauty I have, I hope, exactly followed; and those compositions of second beauty I observe in the drama to be the underwalks, interweaving, or correspondence of lesser design in scenes, not the great motion of the main plot and coherence of the acts.[11] . . .

I shall say a little why I have chosen my interwoven stanza of four,[12] though I am not obliged to excuse the choice; for numbers in verse must, like distinct kinds of music, be exposed to the uncertain and different taste of several ears. Yet I may declare that I believed it would be more pleasant to the reader, in a work of length, to give this respite or pause between every stanza, having endeavored that each should contain a period, than to run him out of breath with continued couplets. Nor does alternate rhyme by any lowliness of cadence make the sound less heroic, but rather adapt it to a plain and stately composing of music; and the brevity of the stanza renders it less subtle to the composer and more easy to the singer, which in *stilo recitativo*,[13] when the story is long, is chiefly requisite. And this was, indeed, if I shall not betray vanity in my confession, the reason that prevailed most towards my choice of this stanza and my division of the main work into cantos, every canto including a sufficient accomplishment of some worthy design or action; for I had so much heat

(which you, Sir, may call pride, since pride may be allowed in Pegasus[14] if it be a praise to other horses) as to presume they might, like the works of Homer ere they were joined together and made a volume by the Athenian king,[15] be sung at village feasts, though not to monarchs after victory nor to armies before battle. For so as an inspiration of glory into the one and of valor into the other did Homer's spirit, long after his body's rest, wander in music about Greece.

Thus you have the model of what I have already built, or shall hereafter join to the same frame. If I be accused of innovation, or to have transgressed against the method of the ancients, I shall think myself secure in believing that a poet who hath wrought with his own instruments at a new design is no more answerable for disobedience to predecessors than lawmakers are liable to those old laws which themselves have repealed.

Having described the outward frame, the large rooms within, the lesser conveyances, and now the furniture, it were orderly to let you examine the matter of which that furniture is made. But though every owner who hath the vanity to show his ornaments or hangings must endure the curiosity and censure of him that beholds them, yet I shall not give you the trouble of inquiring what is, but tell you of what I designed, their substance, which is wit. And wit is the laborious and the lucky resultances of thought, having towards its excellence, as we say of the strokes of painting, as well a happiness as care. It is a web consisting of the subtlest threads, and like that of the spider is considerately woven out of ourselves; for a spider may be said to consider not only respecting his solemness and tacit posture (like a grave scout in ambush for his enemy), but because all things done are either from consideration or chance, and the works of chance are accomplishments of an instant having commonly a dissimilitude, but hers[16] are the works of time, and have their contextures alike.

Wit is not only the luck and labor but also the dexterity of the thought, rounding the world like the sun with unimaginable motion, and bringing swiftly home to the memory universal surveys. It is the soul's powder, which when suppressed, as forbidden from flying upward, blows up the restraint and loseth all force in a farther ascension towards heaven (the region of God), and yet by nature is much less able to make any inquisition downward towards hell, the cell of the devil; but breaks through all about it as far as the utmost it can reach, removes, uncovers, makes way for light where darkness was inclosed, till great bodies are more examinable by being scattered into parcels and

[10]Epic poetry or drama.
[11]Davenant implies that the *great motion* (or first beauty) of literary art is structural organization, to which the *second beauty* of variety and embellishment is of course subordinate.
[12]Quatrain (of iambic pentameter) rhyming abab.
[13]In a manner resembling declamation, a musical term that Davenant adapts to the requirements of narrative poetry.
[14]In Greek myth, a winged horse regarded as the symbol of poetic inspiration.
[15]Pisistratus (d. 527 B.C.), Athenian tyrant believed to have assembled in written form the poems ascribed to Homer.
[16]The works of *consideration*.

till all that find its strength (but most of mankind are strangers to wit, as Indians are to powder) worship it for the effects as derived from the Deity. It is in divines humility, exemplariness, and moderation; in statesmen gravity, vigilance, benign complacency, secrecy, patience, and dispatch; in leaders of armies valor, painfulness, temperance, bounty, dexterity in punishing and rewarding, and a sacred certitude of promise. It is in poets a full comprehension of all recited in all these, and an ability to bring those comprehensions into action, when they shall so far forget the true measure of what is of greatest consequence to humanity (which are things righteous, pleasant, and useful) as to think the delights of greatness equal to that of poesy, or the chiefs of any profession more necessary to the world than excellent poets. Lastly, though wit be not the envy of ignorant men, 'tis often of evil statesmen, and of all such imperfect great spirits as have it in a less degree than poets; for though no man envies the excellence of that which in no proportion he ever tasted, as men cannot be said to envy the condition of angels, yet we may say the devil envies the supremacy of God because he was in some degree partaker of His glory.

That which is not, yet is accompted, wit I will but slightly remember,[17] which seems very incident to imperfect youth and sickly age. Young men, as if they were not quite delivered from childhood, whose first exercise is language, imagine it consists in the music of words, and believe they are made wise by refining their speech above the vulgar dialect, which is a mistake almost as great as that of the people who think orators (which is a title that crowns at riper years those that have practiced the dexterity of tongue) the ablest men, who are indeed so much more unapt for governing as they are more fit for sedition; and it may be said of them as of the witches of Norway who can sell a storm for a dollar, which for ten thousand they cannot allay. From the esteem of speaking they proceed to the admiration of what are commonly called conceits, things that sound like the knacks or toys of ordinary epigrammists, and from thence, after more conversation and variety of objects, grow up to some force of fancy. Yet even then, like young hawks, they stray and fly far off, using their liberty as if they would ne'er return to the lure, and often go at check[18] ere they can make a steady view and know their game.

Old men, that have forgot their first childhood and are returning to their second, think it lies in agnominations,[19] and in a kind of an alike tinkling of words, or else in a grave telling of wonderful things, or in comparing of times without a discovered partiality; which they perform so ill by favoring the past that, as 'tis observed, if the bodies of men should grow less though but an unmeasurable proportion in seven years, yet, reckoning from the flood, they would not remain in the stature of frogs: so if states and particular persons had impaired[20] in government and increased in wickedness proportionably to what old men affirm they have done from their own infancy to their age, all public policy had been long since confusion, and the congregated world would not suffice not to people a village.

The last thing they suppose to be wit is their bitter morals when they almost declare themselves enemies to youth and beauty, by which severity they seem cruel as Herod when he surprised the sleeping children of Bethleem.[21] For youth is so far from wanting enemies that it is mortally its own, so unpracticed that it is everywhere cozened more than a stranger among Jews, and hath an infirmity of sight more hurtful than blindness to blind men, for though it cannot choose the way, it scorns to be led. And beauty, though many call themselves her friends, hath few but such as are false to her. Though the world sets her in a throne, yet all about her, even her gravest counselors, are traitors, though not in conspiracy yet in their distinct designs; and to make her certain not only of distress but ruin she is ever pursued by her most cruel enemy, the great destroyer Time. But I will proceed no farther upon old men, nor in recording mistakes, lest finding so many more than there be verities, we might believe we walk in as great obscurity as the Egyptians when darkness was their plague.[22] Nor will I presume to call the matter of which the ornaments or substantial parts of this poem are composed wit, but only tell you my endeavor was in bringing truth, too often absent, home to men's bosoms to lead her through unfrequented and new ways, and from the most remote shades, by representing nature though not in an affected yet in an unusual dress.

'Tis now fit, after I have given you so long a survey of the building, to render you some accompt of the builder, that you may know by what time, pains, and assistance I have already proceeded or may hereafter finish my work; and in this I shall take occasion to accuse and condemn, as papers unworthy of light, all those hasty digestions of thought which were published in my youth[23]—a sentence not pronounced out of melancholy rigor but from a cheerful obedience to the just authority of experience. For that grave mistress of the world, experience—in whose profitable school those before the flood stayed long,[24] but we like wanton children come thither late, yet too soon are called out of it and fetched home by death—hath taught me that the engenderings of unripe age become abortive and deformed, and that after obtaining more years, those must needs prophesy with ill success who make use of their visions in wine; that when the ancient poets were valued as prophets they were long and painful in watching the correspondence of causes ere they presumed to foretell effects, and that 'tis a high presumption to entertain a nation (who are a poet's standing guests, and require monarchical respect) with hasty provisions; as if a poet might imitate the familiar dispatch of falconers, mount his Pegasus, unhood his Muse,

[17]Recall.

[18]In hawking, a false stoop, when a hawk forsakes her prey for lesser game. [19]Puns. [20]Deteriorated.

[21]Bethlehem, where all male children under two were ordered slaughtered by King Herod after Joseph and Mary had fled with the infant Jesus to Egypt (Matthew 2.16–19).

[22]Exodus 10.21–23.

[23]Such early publications as *The Tragedy of Albovine, King of the Lombards* (1629), *The Temple of Love*, a masque (1634), *The Platonic Lovers*, a tragi-comedy (1636), and *The Wits*, a comedy (1636). Davenant's later works may be said to show no marked advance on the ones he here repudiates.

[24]Because, like Methuselah, they lived to be so old.

and with a few flights boast he hath provided a feast for a prince. Such posting upon Pegasus I have long since forborne, and during my journey in this work have moved with a slow pace,[25] that I might make my surveys as one that traveled not to bring home the names but the proportion and nature of things; and in this I am made wise by two great examples: for the friends of Vergil acknowledge he was many years in doing honor to Aeneas, still contracting at night into a closer force the abundance of his morning strengths; and Statius rather seems to boast than blush when he confesses he was twice seven years in renowning the war between Argos and Thebes.[26] . . . For a wise poet, like a wise general, will not show his strengths till they are in exact government and order, which are not the postures of chance, but proceed from vigilance and labor.

Yet to such painful poets some upbraid the want of extemporary fury, or rather inspiration—a dangerous word which many have of late successfully used. And inspiration is a spiritual fit, derived from the ancient ethnic[27] poets, who then as they were priests were statesmen too, and probably loved dominion, and as their well dissembling of inspiration begot them reverence then equal to that which was paid to laws, so these who now profess the same fury may perhaps by such authentic example pretend authority over the people, it being not unreasonable to imagine they rather imitate the Greek poets than the Hebrew prophets, since the latter were inspired for the use of others, and these, like the former,[28] prophesy for themselves. But though the ancient poets are excused as knowing the weak constitution of those deities from whom they took their priesthood and the frequent necessity of dissembling for the ease of government, yet these, who also from the chief to the meanest are statesmen and priests but have not the luck to be poets, should not assume such saucy familiarity with a true God. . . .

[Following a very long discussion of poetry as a vehicle of instruction, Davenant prepares to end his preface.]

Thus having taken measure, though hastily, of the extent of those great professions that in government contribute to the necessities, ease, and lawful pleasures of men, and finding poesy as useful now as the ancients found it towards perfection and happiness, I will, Sir, unless with these two books you return me a discouragement, cheerfully proceed; and though a little time would perfect the third and make it fit for the press, I am resolved rather to hazard the inconvenience which expectation breeds—for divers with no ill satisfaction have had a taste of *Gondibert*—than endure that violent envy which assaults all writers whilst they live, though their papers be but filled with very negligent and ordinary thoughts; and therefore I delay the publication of any part of the poem till I can send it you from America, whither I now speedily prepare,[29] having the folly to hope that when I am in another world (though not in the common sense of dying) I shall find my readers, even the poets of the present age, as temperate and benign as we are all to the dead, whose remote excellence cannot hinder our reputation. And now Sir, to end with the allegory which I have so long continued,

I shall, after all my busy vanity in showing and describing my new building, with great quietness (being almost as weary as yourself) bring you to the back door, that you may make no review but in my absence, and steal hastily from you as one who is ashamed of all the trouble you have received from, *Sir,*

> *Your most humble and most affectionate servant,*
> *Wil. Davenant*

From the Louvre in Paris,[30]
January 2, 1650

THE ANSWER OF MASTER HOBBES TO SIR WILLIAM DAVENANT'S PREFACE BEFORE *Gondibert*

Sir,

If to commend your poem I should only say (in general terms) that in the choice of your argument, the disposition of the parts, the maintenance of the characters of your persons, the dignity and vigor of your expression you have performed all the parts of various experience, ready memory, clear judgment, swift and well governed fancy, though it were enough for the truth, it were too little for the weight and credit of my testimony. For I lie open to two exceptions, one of an incompetent, the other of a corrupted witness. Incompetent because I am not a poet, and corrupted with the honor done me by your preface. The former obliges me to say something (by the way) of the nature and differences of poesy.

As philosophers have divided the universe (their subject) into three regions, celestial, aerial, and terrestrial; so the poets (whose work it is by imitating human life, in delightful and measured lines, to avert men from vice and incline them to virtuous and honorable actions) have lodged themselves in the three regions of mankind, court, city, and country correspondent in some proportion to those three regions of the world. For there is in princes and men of conspicuous power (anciently called heroes) a luster and influence upon the rest of men resembling that of the heavens; and an insincereness, inconstancy, and troublesome

[25]*Have . . . Pace*: text *hath . . . place.*
[26]Although Vergil probably began the *Aeneid* about 27 B.C., he was so much dissatisfied with it that on his deathbed eight years later he ordered it to be destroyed; happily the order was countermanded by the Emperor Augustus himself. At the conclusion of his *Thebaid* (XII.811), Statius says that the poem had required twelve years (*bissenos annos*) of heavy work.　[27]Pagan.
[28]Modern writers professing inspiration like the *ancient ethnic* (i.e., pagan) poet-priests.
[29]Ordered by Queen Henrietta Maria to escort a group of royalist refugees to Virginia, Davenant was captured (1650) by a parliamentary ship in the English Channel and for two years was imprisoned under peril of execution. It was during his involuntary stay in the Tower that he completed *Gondibert*, which was published in three books in 1651. See pp. 252 ff.
[30]Davenant was living in the Louvre as the guest of Henry Jermyn, Queen Henrietta Maria's secretary and commander of her bodyguard.

humor of those that dwell in populous cities like the mobility, blustering, and impurity of the air; and a plainness and (though dull) yet a nutritive faculty in rural people that endures a comparison with the earth they labor.

From hence have proceeded three sorts of poesy, heroic, scommatic[1] and pastoral. Every one of these is distinguished again in the manner of representation, which sometimes is narrative, wherein the poet himself relateth, and sometimes dramatic, as when the persons are every one adorned and brought upon the theater to speak and act their own parts. There is therefore neither more nor less than six sorts of poesy. For the heroic poem narrative (such as is yours) is called an epic poem; the heroic poem dramatic is tragedy. The scommatic narrative is satire; dramatic is comedy. The pastoral narrative, is called simply pastoral (anciently bucolic), the same dramatic, pastoral comedy. The figure therefore of an epic poem and of a tragedy ought to be the same, for they differ no more but in that they are pronounced by one or many persons. Which I insert to justify the figure[2] of yours, consisting of five books divided into songs or cantos, as five acts divided into scenes has ever been the approved figure of a tragedy.

They that take for poesy whatsoever is writ in verse will think this division imperfect, and call in sonnets, epigrams, eclogues, and the like pieces (which are but essays, and parts of an entire poem) and reckon Empedocles and Lucretius (natural philosophers) for poets, and the moral precepts of Phocylides, Theognis, and the quatrains of Pibrac, and the history of Lucan,[3] and others of that kind amongst poems; bestowing on such writers for honor the name of poets rather than of historians or philosophers. But the subject of a poem is the manners of men, not natural causes; manners presented, not dictated; and manners feigned (as the name of poesy imports), not found in men. They that give entrance to fictions writ in prose err not so much, but they err. For poesy requireth delightfulness not only of fiction but of style, in which if prose contend with verse, it is with disadvantage (as it were) on foot against the strength and wings of Pegasus.

For verse amongst the Greeks was appropriated anciently to the service of their gods, and was the holy style: the style of the oracles, the style of the laws, and the style of men that publicly recommended to their gods the vows and thanks of the people; which was done in their holy songs called hymns, and the composers of them were called prophets and priests before the name of poet was known. When afterwards the majesty of that style was observed, the poets chose it as best becoming their high invention. And for the antiquity of verse it is greater than the antiquity of letters. For it is certain Cadmus[4] was the first that (from Phoenicia, a country that neighboreth Judea) brought the use of letters into Greece. But the service of the gods and the laws (which by measured sounds were easily committed to the memory) had been long time in use before the arrival of Cadmus there.

There is besides the grace of style another cause why the ancient poets chose to write in measured language, which is this. Their poems were made at first with intention to have them sung, as well epic as dramatic (which custom hath been long time laid aside, but began to be revived, in part, of late years in Italy) and could not be made commensurable to the voice or instruments in prose, the ways and motions whereof are so uncertain and undistinguished (like the way and motion of a ship in the sea) as not only to discompose the best composers, but also to disappoint sometimes the most attentive reader, and put him to hunt counter for the sense. It was therefore necessary for poets in those times to write in verse.

The verse which the Greeks and Latins (considering the nature of their own languages) found by experience most grave, and for an epic poem most decent, was their hexameter, a verse limited not only in the length of the line but also in the quantity of the syllables. Instead of which we use the line of ten syllables, recompensing the neglect of their quantity with the diligence of rhyme. And this measure is so proper for an heroic poem as without some loss of gravity and dignity it was never changed. A longer is not far from ill prose, and a shorter is a kind of whisking (you know) like the unlacing rather than the singing of a Muse. In an epigram or a sonnet a man may vary his measures and seek glory from a needless difficulty, as he that contrived verses into the forms of an organ, a hatchet, an egg, an altar, and a pair of wings; but in so great and noble a work as is an epic poem, for a man to obstruct his own way with unprofitable difficulties is great imprudence. So likewise to choose a needless and difficult correspondence of rhyme is but a difficult toy, and forces a man sometimes for the stopping of a chink to say somewhat he did never think. I cannot therefore but very much approve your stanza, wherein the syllables in every verse are ten, and the rhyme alternate.

For the choice of your subject you have sufficiently justified yourself in your preface. But because I have observed in Vergil that the honor done to Aeneas and his companions has so bright a reflection upon Augustus Caesar, and other great Romans of that time, as a man may suspect him not constantly possessed with the noble spirit of those his heroes, and believe you are not acquainted with any great man of the race of Gondibert, I add to your justification the purity of your purpose, in having no other motive of your labor but to adorn virtue, and procure her

THE ANSWER [1]Scoffing, mocking. [2]Form, structure.
[3]*Empedocles . . . Lucan*: writers who used poetry as a vehicle of instruction. Most of the extant philosophical fragments of Empedocles (5th cent. B.C.) are in verse, as is the great *De rerum natura* of Titus Lucretius Carus (96?–55 B.C.). Phocylides and Theognis were Greek gnomic poets of the 6th century B.C. Gui du Faur, Seigneur de Pibrac (1529–84) was a French statesman whose *Cinquante quatrains, contenans preceptes & enseignemens utiles pour la vie de l'homme* (1574) was Englished by Joshua Sylvester in 1605. Marcus Annaeus Lucanus (39–65) was the author of the *Pharsalia*, an epic treatment of the civil war between Caesar and Pompey.
[4]In Greek legend, the son of Agenor, king of Phoenicia, who founded Thebes and introduced the so-called Phoenician letters in his adopted country, i.e., brought writing to the Greeks.

lovers, than which there cannot be a worthier design and more becoming noble poesy.

In that you make so small account of the example of almost all the approved poets, ancient and modern, who thought fit in the beginning, and sometimes also in the progress of their poems, to invoke a Muse or some other deity that should dictate to them, or assist them in their writings, they that take not the laws of art from any reason of their own, but from the fashion of precedent times, will perhaps accuse your singularity. For my part, I neither subscribe to their accusation nor yet condemn that heathen custom otherwise than as necessary to their false religion. For their poets were their divines, had the name of prophets, exercised amongst the people a kind of spiritual authority, would be thought to speak by a divine spirit, have their works which they writ in verse (the divine style) pass for the word of God, and not of man, and to be harkened to with reverence. Do not our divines (excepting the style) do the same, and by us that are of the same religion cannot justly be reprehended for it? Besides, in the use of the spiritual calling of divines there is danger sometimes to be feared from want of skill, such as is reported of unskillful conjurers that, mistaking the rites and ceremonious points of their art, call up such spirits as they cannot at their pleasure allay again; by whom storms are raised that overthrow buildings, and are the cause of miserable wracks at sea. Unskillful divines do oftentimes the like, for when they call unseasonably for zeal, there appears a spirit of cruelty; and by the like error instead of truth they raise discord; instead of wisdom, fraud; instead of reformation, tumult; and controversy instead of religion.[5] Whereas in the heathen poets, at least in those whose works have lasted to the time we are in, there are none of those indiscretions to be found that tended to subversion or disturbance of the commonwealths wherein they lived. But why a Christian should think it an ornament to his poem either to profane the true God or invoke a false one, I can imagine no cause but a reasonless imitation of custom, of a foolish custom; by which a man, enabled to speak wisely from the principles of nature and his own meditation, loves rather to be thought to speak by inspiration, like a bagpipe.

Time and education begets experience; experience begets memory; memory beget[s] judgment and fancy: judgment begets the strength and structure, and fancy begets the ornaments of a poem. The ancients therefore fabled not absurdly in making memory the mother of the Muses. For memory is the world (though not really, yet so as in a looking glass) in which the judgment (the severer sister) busieth herself in a grave and rigid examination of all the parts of nature, and in registering by letters their order, causes, uses, differences, and resemblances; whereby the fancy, when any work of art is to be performed, findeth her materials at hand and prepared for use, and needs no more than a swift motion over them, that what she wants, and is there to be had, may not lie too long unespied. So that when she seemeth to fly from one Indies to the other,[6] and from heaven to earth, and to penetrate into the hardest matter

and obscurest places, into the future and into herself, and all this in a point of time; the voyage is not very great, herself being all she seeks; and her wonderful celerity consisteth not so much in motion as in copious imagery discreetly ordered and perfectly registered in the memory; which most men under the name of philosophy have a glimpse of, and is pretended to by many that, grossly mistaking her, embrace contention in her place. But so far forth as the fancy of man has traced the ways of true philosophy, so far it hath produced very marvelous effects to the benefit of mankind. All that is beautiful or defensible in building, or marvelous in engines and instruments of motion; whatsoever commodity men receive from the observation of the heavens, from the description of the earth, from the account of time, from walking on the seas; and whatsoever distinguisheth the civility of Europe from the barbarity of the American savages is the workmanship of fancy, but guided by the precepts of true philosophy. But where these precepts fail, as they have hitherto failed in the doctrine of moral virtue, there the architect (fancy) must take the philosopher's part upon herself. He therefore that undertakes an heroic poem (which is to exhibit a venerable and amiable image of heroic virtue) must not only be the poet, to place and connect,[7] but also the philosopher, to furnish and square his matter, that is, to make both body and soul, color and shadow of his poem out of his own store: which how well you have performed I am now considering.

Observing how few the persons be you introduce in the beginning, and how in the course of the actions of these (the number increasing) after several confluences they run all at last into the two principal streams of your poem, Gondibert and Oswald,[8] methinks the fable is not much unlike the theater. For so, from several and far distant sources, do the lesser brooks of Lombardy, flowing into one another, fall all at last into the two main rivers, the Po and the Adige.[9] It hath the same resemblance also with a man's veins, which proceeding from different parts, after the like concourse, insert themselves at last into the two principal veins of the body. But when I considered that also the actions of men, which singly are inconsiderable, after many conjectures grow at last either into one great protecting power or into two destroying factions, I could not but approve the structure of your poem, which ought to be no other than such as an imitation of human life requireth.

In the streams themselves I find nothing but settled valor, clean honor, calm counsel, learned diversion, and pure love, save only a torrent or two of ambition, which (though a fault) hath somewhat heroic in it, and therefore must have place in an heroic poem. To show the reader in what place he shall find every excellent picture of virtue you have drawn

[5]The *unskillful divines* whom Hobbes deprecates are, of course, Puritan ministers preaching sedition masked as piety.
[6]The East and West Indies, which Donne, in "The Sun Rising" (p. 62), calls "th' Indias of spice and mine."   [7]Text *connex*.
[8]The principal male characters of Davenant's *Gondibert*, of whom one rejects and the other seeks the love of Rhodalind, daughter of King Aribert.   [9]Text *Adice*.

is too long. And to show him one is to prejudice the rest; yet I cannot forbear to point him to the description of love in the person of Birtha, in the seventh canto of the second book.[10] There hath nothing been said of that subject neither by the ancient nor modern poets comparable to it. Poets are painters: I would fain see another painter draw so true, perfect, and natural a love to the life, and make use of nothing but pure lines, without the help of any the least uncomely shadow, as you have done. But let it be read as a piece by itself, for in the almost equal heighth of the whole the eminence of parts is lost.

There are some that are not pleased with fiction unless it be bold not only to exceed the work but also the possibility of nature; they would have impenetrable armors, enchanted castles, invulnerable bodies, iron men, flying horses, and a thousand other such things which are easily feigned by them that dare. Against such I defend you (without assenting to those that condemn either Homer or Vergil by dissenting only from those that think the beauty of a poem consisteth in the exorbitancy of the fiction. For as truth is the bound of historical, so the resemblance of truth is the utmost limit of poetical liberty. In old time amongst the heathens, such strange fictions and metamorphoses were not so remote from the articles of their faith as they are now from ours, and therefore were[11] not so unpleasant. Beyond the actual works of nature a poet may now go, but beyond the conceived possibility of nature, never. I can allow a geographer to make in the sea a fish or a ship which by the scale of his map would be two or three hundred miles long, and think it done for ornament because it is done without the precincts of his undertaking; but when he paints an elephant so, I presently apprehend it as ignorance, and a plain confession of *terra incognita*.[12]

As the description of great men and great actions is the constant design of a poet, so the descriptions of worthy circumstances are necessary accessions to a poem, and being well performed are the jewels and most precious ornaments of poesy. Such in Vergil are the funeral games of Anchises, the duel of Aeneas and Turnus, etc. And such in yours are the Hunting, the Battle, the City Mourning, the Funeral, the House of Astragon, the Library, and the Temples[13] equal to his, or those of Homer whom he imitated.

There remains now no more to be considered but the expression, in which consisteth the countenance and color of a beautiful Muse, and is given her by the poet out of his own provision or is borrowed from others. That which he hath of his own is nothing but experience and knowledge of nature, and specially human nature, and is the true and natural color. But that which is taken out of books (the ordinary boxes of counterfeit complexion) shows well or ill as it hath more or less resemblance with the natural, and are not to be used (without examination) unadvisedly. For in him that professes the imitation of nature (as all poets do) what greater fault can there be than to bewray an ignorance of nature in his poem, especially having a liberty allowed him, if he meet with any thing he cannot master, to leave it out?

That which giveth a poem the true and natural color consisteth in two things, which are to know well—that is, to have images of nature in the memory distinct and clear—and to know much. A sign of the first is perspicuity, property,[14] and decency, which delight all sorts of men, either by instructing the ignorant or soothing the learned in their knowledge. A sign of the latter is novelty of expression, and pleaseth by excitation of the mind; for novelty causeth admiration; and admiration, curiosity; which is a delightful appetite of knowledge.

There be so many words in use at this day in the English tongue that, though of magnific sound, yet (like the windy blisters of a troubled water) have no sense at all, and so many others that lose their meaning by being ill coupled, that it is a hard matter to avoid them; for having been obtruded upon youth in the schools by such as make it, I think, their business there, as 'tis expressed by the best poet,

*With terms to charm the weak and
pose the wise,*[15]

they grow up with them, and gaining reputation with the ignorant, are not easily shaken off.

To this palpable darkness, I may also add the ambitious obscurity of expressing more than is perfectly conceived, or perfect conception in fewer words than it requires. Which expressions, though they have had the honor to be called strong lines,[16] are indeed no better than riddles, and not only to the reader but also (after a little time) to the writer himself dark and troublesome.

To the property of expression I refer that clearness of memory by which a poet when he hath once introduced any person whatsoever, speaking in his poem, maintaineth in him, to the end, the same character he gave to him in the beginning. The variation whereof is a change of pace that argues the poet tired.

Of the indecencies of an heroic poem the most remarkable are those that show disproportion either between the persons and their actions, or between the manners of the poet and the poem. Of the first kind is the uncomeliness of representing in great persons the inhumane vice of cruelty or the sordid vices of lust and drunkenness. To such parts as those, the ancient approved poets thought it fit to suborn not the

---

[10]*Description of love . . . second book*: For an excerpt from this passage so highly praised by Hobbes see pp. 254 ff.
[11]Text *we are.*
[12]"Unknown country."
[13]*The duel . . . Temples*: The funeral games of Anchises and the duel between Aeneas and Turnus are described in the *Aeneid* in Books V and XII respectively. The comparable episodes in *Gondibert* are at I.v, II.i, II.iv, II.v, and II.vi. [14]Propriety.
[15]*Gondibert*, I.v.
[16]Lines marked by terse and striking—even jolting—use of the conceit. Although Thomas Carew praised Donne for such "masculine expression" (p. 230), Dr. Johnson, in his life of Cowley (which is in fact a critique of metaphysical poetry) found much to deplore in an obscure and mannered style where "the most heterogeneous ideas are yoked by violence together."

persons of men but of monsters and beastly giants, such as Polyphemus, Cacus, and the centaurs.[17] For it is supposed a Muse, when she is invoked to sing a song of that nature, should maidenly advise the poet to set such persons to sing their own vices upon the stage, for it is not so unseemly in a tragedy. Of the same kind it is to represent scurrility, or any action or language that moveth much laughter. The delight of an epic poem consisteth not in mirth but in admiration. Mirth and laughter is proper to comedy and satire. Great persons that have their minds employed on great designs have not leisure enough to laugh, and are pleased with the contemplation of their own power and virtues, so as they need not the infirmities and vices of other men to recommend themselves to their own favor by comparison, as all men do when they laugh. Of the second kind, where the disproportion is between the poet and the persons of his poem, one is in the dialect of the inferior sort of people which is always different from the language of the court. Another is to derive the illustration of anything from such metaphors or comparisons as cannot come into men's thoughts but by mean conversation and experience of humble or evil arts, which the persons of an epic poem cannot be thought acquainted with.

From knowing much proceedeth the admirable variety and novelty of metaphors and similitudes, which are not possibly to be lighted on in the compass of a narrow knowledge. And the want whereof compelleth a writer to expressions that are either defaced by time or sullied with vulgar or long use. For the phrases of poesy, as the airs of music, with often hearing become insipid, the reader having no more sense of their force than our flesh is sensible of the bones that sustain it. As the sense we have of bodies consisteth in change and variety of impression, so also does the sense of language in the variety and changeable use of words. I mean not in the affectation of words newly brought home from travel, but in new (and withal significant) translation to our purposes of those that be already received, and in far-fetched (but withal apt, instructive, and comely) similitudes.

Having thus (I hope) avoided the first exception, against the incompetency of my judgment, I am but little moved with the second, which is of being bribed by the honor you have done me by attributing in your preface somewhat to my judgment. For I have used your judgment no less in many things of mine, which coming to light will thereby appear the better. And so you have your bribe again.

Having thus made way for the admission of my testimony, I give it briefly thus: I never yet saw poem that had so much shape of art, health of morality, and vigor and beauty of expression as this of yours. And but for the clamor of the multitude that hide their envy of the present under a reverence of antiquity, I should say further that it would last as long as either the *Aeneid* or *Iliad* but for one disadvantage. And the disadvantage is this: The languages of the Greeks and Romans (by their colonies and conquest) have put off flesh and blood and are become immutable, which none of the modern tongues are like to be. I honor antiquity, but

that which is commonly called old time is young time. The glory of antiquity is due not to the dead, but to the aged.

And now, whilst I think on't, give me leave with a short discord to sweeten the harmony of the approaching close. I have nothing to object against your poem, but dissent only from something in your preface, sounding to the prejudice of age.[18] 'Tis commonly said, that old age is a return to childhood. Which methinks you insist on so long as if you desired it should be believed. That's the note I mean to shake a little. That saying, meant only of the weakness of body, was wrested to the weakness of mind by froward children weary of the controlment of their parents, masters, and other admonitors. Secondly, the dotage and childishness they ascribe to age is never the effect of time, but sometimes of the excesses of youth, and not a returning to but a continual stay with childhood. For they that wanting the curiosity of furnishing their memories with the rarities of nature in their youth, and pass their time in making provision only for their ease and sensual delight, are children still, at what years soever; as they that coming into a populous city never go out of their own inn are strangers still, how long soever they have been there. Thirdly, there is no reason for any man to think himself wiser today than yesterday, which doth not equally convince he shall be wiser tomorrow than today. Fourthly, you will be forced to change your opinion hereafter when you are old, and in the meantime you discredit all I have said before in your commendation, because I am old already.[19] But no more of this.

I believe, Sir, you have seen a curious kind of perspective, where he that looks through a short hollow pipe upon a picture containing diverse figures sees none of those that are there painted, but some one person made up of their parts, conveyed to the eye by the artificial cutting of a glass. I find in my imagination an effect not unlike it from your poem. The virtues you distribute there amongst so many noble persons represent (in the reading) the image but of one man's virtue to my fancy, which is your own; and that so deeply imprinted as to stay forever there, and govern all the rest of my thoughts and affections in the way of honoring and serving you to the utmost of my power, that am

> Sir,
> *Your most humble,*
> *and obedient Servant,*
> *Thomas Hobbes*

January 10, 1650

---

[17]Unnatural creatures such as the one-eyed Cyclops in Homer's *Odyssey*, the giant of Roman legend whom Hercules slew for stealing the oxen of three-headed Geryon, and the monsters of Greek myth having the head and torso of a man united to the body and legs of a horse.
[18]Hobbes is thinking of the passage beginning "Old men, that have forgot their first childhood" (p. 783).
[19]Although Hobbes and Davenant were respectively sixty-two and forty-four at the time of this exchange, the older man survived the younger by eleven years, dying in 1679 at the age of ninety-one.

James Howell   [1593/4-1666]

Although tediously assertive of his descent from an ancient Welsh family, James Howell conceded that he "came tumbling out into the world a pure cadet, a true cosmopolite, not born to land, lease, house, or office." Compelled therefore to make a living, after taking a degree (1613) from Jesus College, Oxford, he began his checkered career by becoming superintendent of a glass manufactory in London. It was in this unliterary capacity that he went in 1617 to search for workmen and materials on the Continent, where his subsequent travels through Holland, France, Spain, and Italy enabled him to learn the foreign ways and languages that enrich his later work. "Venice the Rich, Padua the Learned, Bologna the Fat, Rome the Holy, Naples the Gentle, Genoa the Proud, Florence the Fair, and Milan the Great"—to say nothing of many other cities— were not merely names for him, but places he had seen and known.

Back in London by 1620, he used his skills in many ways, serving successively as a tutor and traveling companion, as a commercial agent at the Spanish court (during Prince Charles' abortive wooing of the Infanta in 1623), and as secretary to Lord Scrope (whose influence led to his election to Parliament in 1627). For ten years or more after his patron's death in 1630 the record is so blank that his most authoritative biographer thinks he may have lived the furtive life of a Royalist "intelligencer" or spy. This conjecture is supported by the fact that shortly after his appointment as clerk of the Council by King Charles in 1642 he was arrested on parliamentary order. As Howell related the event, one morning after he had "lately" come to London

> there rushed into my chamber five armed men with swords, pistols, and bills, and told me that they had a warrant from the Parliament for me. . . . So they rushed presently into my closet and seized on all my papers and letters, and anything that was manuscript . . . and hurled all into a great hair trunk, which they carried away with them.

His papers, which upon examination did not prove to be incriminating, were returned to him, but not before he himself had been committed to the Fleet, where he languished seven years (1643-50).

"Languished" is perhaps not quite the proper word, for in the depth of his misfortune this obscure cavalier of fifty finally stumbled, or was forced, into his true vocation. He had already published a popular historical allegory called *Dodona's Grove* (1640), as well as *The Vote, or a Poem Royal Presented to His Majesty for a New Year's Gift* (1642) and *Instructions for Foreign Travel* (1642), but during his imprisonment and after his release he turned out books and pamphlets in such profusion that they total half a hundred. This remarkable production includes all kinds of things: political tracts (*The Pre-eminence and Pedigree of Parliament*, 1644), historical treatises (*An Exact History of the Late Revolutions in Naples*, 1650), antiquarian collections (*Cottoni Posthuma: Divers Choice Pieces of That Renown Antiquary Sir Robert Cotton* (1651), books of travel (*A Survey of the Signory of Venice*, 1651), moral and philosophical speculations (*The Vision, or a Dialogue between the Soul and Body*, 1652), translations (Josephus' *Wonderful and Most Deplorable History of the Latter Times of the Jews*, 1652), poetry (*Ah Ha, Tumulus, Thalamus*, 1653), topographical descriptions (*Londinopolis, an Historical Discourse or Perlustration of the City of London*, 1657), dictionaries (*A Particular Vocabulary or Nomenclature in English, Italian, French, and Spanish*, 1659), and philological works (*A New English Grammar*, 1662).

But by far the most lasting and important of his many books is the famous *Epistolae Ho-Elianae*. First published in 1645 by Humphrey Moseley (who in the same year brought out Milton's *Poems*), this collection of more than two hundred "familiar letters, domestic and foreign" was so successful that a second volume followed two years later. In 1650, when Howell was still in prison, Volumes I and II were bound together and reprinted (with a few new letters) almost simultaneously with a genuine "second edition, enlarged with divers supplements, and the dates annexed which were wanting in the first, with an addition of a third volume of new letters." Although the third edition of 1655, which added a fourth volume of hitherto unpublished items, was the last that Howell supervised, it by no means closed the record, for nine editions followed between 1673 and 1754, as well as others later.

It is still not certain whether Howell worked up the contents of the *Epistolae* from his travel notes and diaries or thriftily used the "papers and letters" that had been seized and then returned to him in 1643. Whereas the letters of the first volume (1645), even with the wildly inaccurate dates that were subsequently "annexed," reveal a freshness, immediacy, and sequence that seem to reflect the writer's own experience, the successive additions often read like essays, or pieces written on assignment. When, in the early letters, we follow the impecunious young Welshman as he goes out into the world, embarks upon his travels, observes Prince Charles' wooing, or records the shock of Buckingham's assassination, we feel the presence of a man; but the subsequent additions—although full of lore about things like language, history, and religion—seem to come from study, not from wide-eyed observation. In a rough table of contents (or "Extracts of the Heads") in the 1655 edition, "the faithful relation of the privatest passages" of the courts of James and Charles I is listed as the "principal subject," but many other things are promised too: comments on the military situation in Germany, on Dutch commercial enterprise, on "the extent of Christianity and of other religions upon earth," on the comparative study of foreign tongues, and on "divers new opinions in philosophy." Howell is rarely dull, but often relentlessly instructive.

Following his release from the Fleet in a general amnesty of 1650, he continued his incessant scribbling, but it was not until the Restoration that the aging cavalier finally gained some recognition for his old devotion to the king. Even after his appointment (1661) as Historiographer Royal, however, he did not slacken his production. *A New English Grammar* appeared in 1662, a volume of collected poems in 1663, and in 1664 an ambitious *Discourse Concerning the Precedency of Kings*, a stately folio tracing the history of royal prerogatives in England, France, and Spain. He would have written more, no doubt, had death not kindly intervened.

My text is based on *Epistolae Ho-Elianae. Familiar Letters Domestic and Forren. Divided into sundry Sections, Partly Historicall, Politicall, Philosophicall . . . The Third Edition. With a Fourth Volume of New Letters Never Publish'd before*, 1655 (Wing H–3073). The title page, lacking in the Harvard copy, is supplied by W. H. Vann, *Notes on the Writings of James Howell* (1924), p. 54. Oddly, the first modern edition of the *Epistolae*—that by J. Jacobs (2 vols., 1890–92)—is still authoritative, and remains unthreatened by W. H. Bennett's (2 vols., 1890), Agnes Repplier's (2 vols., 1907), and Oliver Smeaton's (3 vols., 1903). Vann's *Notes*, cited just above, must be regarded as an unsung triumph of patient bibliography.

from Epistolae Ho-Elianae (1655)

VOLUME I. SECTION IV.

[LETTER] 8

TO DR. PRITCHARD[1]

Sir,

Since I was beholden to you for your many favors in Oxford, I have not heard from you (*ne γρὺ quidem*);[2] I pray let the wonted correspondence be now revived and receive new vigor between us.

EPISTOLAE HO-ELIANAE [1]In 1621 Thomas Pritchard was appointed vice-principal of Jesus College, Oxford, where Howell had been an undergraduate, and where he himself became a fellow in 1623. [2]"Not worth a grain."

My Lord Chancellor Bacon is lately dead of a long languishing weakness;[3] he died so poor so that he scarce left money to bury him, which, though he had a great wit, did argue no great wisdom, it being one of the essential properties of a wise man to provide for the main chance. I have read that it hath been the fortunes of all poets commonly to die beggars; but for an orator, a lawyer, and philosopher, as he was, to die so, 'tis rare. It seems the same fate befell him that attended Demosthenes, Seneca, and Cicero (all great men), of whom the two first fell by corruption.[4] The fairest diamond may have a flaw in it, but I believe he died poor out of a contempt of the pelf of fortune, as also out of an excess of generosity; which appeared, as in divers other passages, so once when the king had sent him a stag, he sent up for the underkeeper, and having drunk the king's health unto him in a great silver-gilt bowl, he gave it him for his fee.

He wrote a pitiful letter to King James not long before his death, and concludes, "Help me, dear sovereign lord and master, and pity me so far that I who have been born to a bag be not now in my age forced in effect to bear a wallet; nor I that desire to live to study may be driven to study to live." Which words, in my opinion, argued a little abjection[5] of spirit, as his former letter to the prince did of profaneness; wherein he hoped that as the father was his creator the son will be his redeemer.[6] I write not this to derogate from the noble worth of the Lord Viscount Verulam, who was a rare man, a man *reconditae scientiae et ad salutem literarum natus*,[7] and I think the eloquentest that was born in this isle. They say he shall be the last Lord Chancellor, as Sir Edward Coke[8] was the last Lord Chief Justice of England; for ever since they have been termed Lord Chief Justices of the King's Bench: so hereafter there shall be only Keepers of the Great Seal, which for title and office are deposable; but they say the Lord Chancellor's title is indelible.

I was lately at Gray's Inn with Sir Eubule, and he desired me to remember him unto you, as I do also salute *meum Prichardum ex imis praecordiis, Vale. Κεφαλή μοι προσφιλεσάτη.*[9]

Yours most affectionately, while

J.H.

London, Jan. 6, 1625[10]

Volume I. Section v.

[Letter] 7

To the Right Honorable the Lady Scrope, Countess of Sunderland,[11] from Stamford[12]

Madam,
I lay yesternight at the post-house at Stilton, and this morning betimes the postmaster came to my bed's head and told me the duke of Buckingham was slain; my faith was not then strong enough to believe it, till an hour ago I met in the way with my Lord of Rutland (your brother) riding post towards London; it pleased him to alight and show me a letter, wherein there was an exact relation of all the circumstances of this sad tragedy.[13]

Upon Saturday last,[14] which was but next before yesterday, being Bartholomew eve, the Duke did rise up in a well-disposed humor out of his bed, and cut a caper or two; and being ready, and having been under the barber's hands (where the murderer had thought to have done the deed, for he was leaning upon the window all the while), he went to breakfast, attended by a great company of commanders, where Monsieur Soubize came unto him and whispered him in the ear that Rochelle was relieved;[15] the duke seemed to slight the news, which made some think that Soubize went away discontented. After breakfast, the duke going out, Colonel Fryer stepped before him, and, stopping him upon some business, one Lieutenant Felton, being behind, made a thrust with a common tenpenny knife over Fryer's arm at the duke, which lighted so fatally that he slit his heart in two, leaving the knife sticking in the body. The duke took out the knife and threw it away, and laying his hand on his sword, and drawing[16] it half out, said, "The villain hath killed me," meaning, as some think, Colonel Fryer, for there had been some difference 'twixt them; so reeling against a chimney, he fell down dead. The duchess, being with child, hearing the noise below, came in her night-gears from her bedchamber, which was in an upper room, to a kind of rail, and thence beheld him weltering in his own blood. Felton had lost his hat in the crowd, wherein there was a paper sewed, wherein he declared that the reason which moved him to this act was no grudge of his own, though he had

[3]Bacon died 9 April 1626.
[4]Near the end of his life Demosthenes, the famous Athenian orator, was imprisoned on a charge of bribery. Lucius Annaeus Seneca, the Stoic philosopher, committed suicide at the command of the Emperor Nero, whose tutor he had been.   [5]Dejection.
[6]Although vastly successful under James I, following his disgrace in 1621 Bacon never regained the favor of either the old king or of his son, Charles I, who succeeded to the throne in 1625.
[7]A man of the profoundest erudition, born for the advancement of learning.
[8]Bacon's inveterate enemy, Sir Edward Coke (1552–1634), was dismissed as chief justice of the King's Bench in 1616 because of his incorruptible zeal in investigating the murder of Sir Thomas Overbury (see p. 715).
[9]Pritchard, my beloved friend, I bid you farewell from the bottom of my heart.
[10]Like most of the dates on Howell's letters, this one raises questions. Even though we can shift the year to 1626 (by the New Style calendar) it is hard to explain Howell's account of Bacon's death three months before it occurred.
[11]Lady Scrope, the wife of Howell's patron between 1626 and 1630, was a sister of Francis Manners, sixth earl of Rutland, whose daughter Katherine was duchess of Buckingham.
[12]Like Stilton (mentioned in the first sentence of this letter), a town in Huntingdonshire in east central England, far from the scene of Buckingham's assassination in Portsmouth.
[13]For Thomas Fuller's account of the dazzling career of George Villiers (1592–1628), first duke of Buckingham, see p. 754.
[14]23 August 1628.
[15]The report was of course erroneous. Although Buckingham had made strenuous efforts to lift Cardinal Richelieu's siege of the Huguenots at La Rochelle, the city surrendered 28 October 1628 after a heroic resistance of fourteen months.
[16]Text *drawn*.

been far behind for his pay, and had been put by his captain's place twice, but in regard he thought the duke an enemy to the state because he was branded in Parliament;[17] therefore what he did was for the public good of his country. Yet he got clearly down, and so might have gone to his horse, which, was tied to a hedge hard by; but he was so amazed that he missed his way, and so struck into the pastry,[18] where, though the cry went that some Frenchman had done it, he thinking the word was Felton, he boldly confessed 'twas he that had done the deed, and so he was in their hands. Jack Stamford[19] would have run at him, but he was kept off by Mr. Nicholas;[20] so being carried up to a tower, Captain Mince tore off his spurs, and asking how he durst attempt such an act, making him believe the duke was not dead, he answered boldly that he knew he was dispatched, for 'twas not he but the hand of heaven that gave the stroke, and though his whole body had been covered over with armor of proof, he could not have avoided it. Captain Charles Price went post presently to the king four miles off, who being at prayers on his knees when it was told him, yet he never stirred, nor was he disturbed a whit till all divine service was done. This was the relation, as far as my memory could bear, in my Lord of Rutland's letter, who willed me to remember him unto Your Ladyship, and tell you that he was going to comfort your niece (the duchess) as fast as he could. And so I have sent the truth of this sad story to Your Ladyship as fast as I could by this post because I cannot make that speed myself, in regard of some business I have to dispatch for my lord in the way. So I humbly take my leave, and rest

Your Ladyship's most dutiful servant,
J.H.

Stamford, Aug. 5, 1628

A New Volume of Familiar Letters

[LETTER] 79

To Sir Kenelm Digby at Rome[21]

Sir,

Though you know well that in the carriage and course of my rambling life I had occasion to be, as the Dutchman sayeth, a landloper,[22] and to see much of the world abroad, yet methinks I have traveled more since I have been immured and martyred 'twixt these walls than ever I did before;[23] for I have traveled the Isle of Man, I mean this little world, which I have carried about me and within me so many years, for, as the wisest of pagan philosophers[24] said, that the greatest learning was the knowledge of one's self, to be his own geometrician. If one do so he need not gad abroad to see fashions; he shall find enough at home; he shall hourly meet with new fancies, new humors, new passions within doors.

This traveling o'er of one's self is one of the paths that lead a man to paradise. It is true that 'tis a dirty and a dangerous one, for it is thick set with extravagant desires, irregular affections, and concupiscences, which are but odd comrades,

and oftentimes do lie in ambush to cut our throats; there are also some melancholy companions in the way, which are our thoughts, but they turn many times to be good fellows and the best company; which makes me that among these disconsolate walls I am never less alone than when I am alone; I am ofttimes sole, but seldom solitary; some there are who are overpestered with these companions, and have too much mind for their bodies, but I am none of those.

There have been (since you shook hands with England) many strange things happened here, which posterity must have a strong faith to believe; but for my part I wonder not at anything, I have seen such monstrous things. You know there is nothing that can be casual;[25] there is no success, good or bad, but is contingent to man sometimes or other, nor are there any contingencies, present or future, but they have their parallels from times passed; for the great wheel of fortune, upon whose rim (as the twelve signs upon the zodiac) all worldly chances are embossed, turns round perpetually, and the spokes of that wheel, which points at all human actions, return exactly to the same place after such a time of revolution, which makes me little marvel at any of the strange traverses of these distracted times, in regard there hath been the like, or suchlike, formerly. If the liturgy is now suppressed,[26] the missal and Roman breviary was used some hundred years since; if crosses, church windows, organs, and fonts are now battered down I little wonder at it, for chapels, monasteries, hermitages, nunneries, and other religious houses, were used so in the time of old King Henry; if bishops and deans are now in danger to be demolished I little wonder at it, for abbots, priors, and the pope himself had that fortune here an age since. That our king is reduced to this pass I do not much wonder at it, for the first time I traveled France, Louis the Thirteenth (afterwards a most triumphant king as ever that country had) in a dangerous civil war was brought to such straits, for he was brought to dispense with part of his coronation oath, to remove from his court of justice, from the council table, from his very bedchamber his greatest favorites. He was driven to be content to pay the expense of the war, to reward those that took arms against him, and publish a declaration that the ground of their quarrel was good, which was the same in effect with ours, viz., a discontinuance of the assembly of the three

---

[17]Following Buckingham's impeachment by the Commons in 1626 King Charles dissolved the parliamentary session.
[18]A place where pastry is made. [19]A servant of the duke.
[20]Edward Nicholas, secretary to the duke and later (1641) secretary of state to Charles I.
[21]For Clarendon's character of Sir Kenelm Digby (p. 486) see p. 796. In 1645–46 Digby, himself a Roman Catholic, was in Rome trying to raise money for the royalist cause in his capacity as Queen Henrietta Maria's chancelor. The mission ended in failure when, characteristically, he quarreled violently with the pope. [22]Vagabond, adventurer.
[23]Howell was imprisoned in the Fleet between 1643 and 1650 because of his royalist sympathies and connections. [24]Plato?
[25]Occurring without design.
[26]In 1644 Parliament declared the Anglican Book of Common Prayer illegal and replaced it with the Presbyterian *Directory of Public Worship.*

estates,[27] and that Spanish counsels did predominate in France.

You know better than I that all events, good or bad, come from the all-disposing high Deity of heaven: if good, He produceth them; if bad, He permits them. He is the pilot that sits at the stern and steers the great vessel of the world, and we must not presume to direct Him in His course, for He understands the use of the compass better than we. He commands also the winds and the weather, and after a storm He never fails to send us a calm, and to recompense ill times with better, if we can live to see them—which I pray you may do, whatsoever becomes of your still most faithful, humble servitor,

J.H.

From the Fleet, London,
3 March 1646

A Third Volume of Familiar Letters of a Fresher Date

[LETTER] 14

To Master W.B.

How glad was I, my choice and precious nephew,[28] to receive yours of the 24 current, wherein I was sorry, though satisfied in point of belief, to find the ill fortune of interception[29] which befell my last unto you.

Touching the condition of things here, you shall understand that our miseries lengthen with our days; for though the sun and the spring advance nearer us, yet our times are not grown a whit the more comfortable. I am afraid this city hath fooled herself into a slavery. The army, though forbidden to come within ten miles of her by order of Parliament, quarters now in the bowels of her. They threaten to break her percullies,[30] posts, and chains, to make her pervious[31] upon all occasions. They have secured also the Tower, with addition of strength for themselves. Besides, a famine doth insensibly creep upon us, and the mint is starved for want of bullion. Trade, which was ever the sinew of this island, doth visibly decay, and the insurance of ships is risen from two to ten in the hundred. Our gold is engrossed in private hands or gone beyond sea to travel without licence, and much, I believe, of it is returned to the earth (whence it first came) to be buried where our late nephews[32] may chance to find it a thousand years hence, if the world lasts so long, so that the exchanging of white earth into red (I mean silver into gold) is now above six in the hundred; and all these, with many more, are the dismal effects and concomitants of a civil war. 'Tis true we have had many such black days in England in former ages, but those paralleled to the present are as the shadow of a mountain compared to the eclipse of the moon. My prayers, early and late, are that God Almighty would please not to turn away His face quite, but cheer us again with the light of His countenance. And I am well assured you will join with me in the same orison to heaven's gate, in

which confidence I rest yours most affectionately to serve you,

J.H.

From the Fleet, 10 of December 1647[33]

[LETTER] 15

To Sir Kenelm Digby at Paris

Sir,
Now that you are returned and fixed a while in France, an old servant of yours takes leave to kiss your hands and salute you in an intense degree of heat and height of passion. 'Tis well you shook hands with this infortunate[34] isle when you did, and got your liberty by such a royal mediation as the Queen Regent's,[35] for had you stayed you would have taken but little comfort in your life, in regard that ever since there have been the fearfullest distractions here that ever happened upon any part of the earth. A beluin[36] kind of immanity[37] never raged so among men, insomuch that the whole country might have taken its appellation from the smallest part thereof and be called the Isle of Dogs;[38] for all humanity, common honesty, and that mansuetude[39] with other moral civilities which should distinguish the rational creature from other animals have been lost here a good while. Nay, besides this cynical, there is a kind of wolfish humor hath seized upon most of this people, a true lycanthropy.[40] They so worry and seek to devour one another, so that the wild Arab and fiercest Tartar may be called civil men in comparison of us; therefore he is happiest who is furthest off from this woeful island. The king is straitened of that liberty he formerly had in the Isle of Wight, and as far as I see, may make up the number of Nebuchadnezzar's[41] years before he be restored. The Parliament persists in their first propositions and will go nothing less. This is all I have to send at this time, only I will adjoin the true respects of your most faithful, humble servitor,

J.H.

From the Fleet, this 5 of May 1647[42]

[27]Nobles, clergy, and commons.
[28]Kinsman? The "W. B." to whom this letter is addressed was perhaps one William Blois, whose precise relation to Howell is unknown.
[29]Because of the military and political disorders of the time.
[30]Portcullises. [31]Open, accessible. [32]Remote descendants.
[33]An error for 1648. [34]Unfortunate. [35]See p. 486.
[36]Brutal. [37]Inhuman cruelty.
[38]A disreputable district of London on the lower Thames opposite Greenwich. [39]Gentleness. [40]The condition of a werewolf.
[41]*Make up . . . Nebuchadnezzar*: become like the king of Babylonia who heard a voice from heaven announcing that "the kingdom is departed from thee" (Daniel 4.31). Following his capture by parliamentary forces in June 1647, King Charles escaped to the Isle of Wight, where was again kept in custody until December 1648, when he was taken to Windsor and from there to London for his trial and execution (30 January 1649). For Clarendon's famous account of these matters see pp. 933 ff.
[42]An obvious error for the late fall of 1648.

Edward Hyde, Earl of Clarendon[1]   [1609-1674]

Like Sir Walter Raleigh, Clarendon started writing history only when he could no longer make it; but whereas Raleigh, convinced that "whosoever, in writing a modern history, shall follow truth too near the heels, it may haply strike out his teeth," got no closer to the present than 168 B.C., Clarendon wrote of things that he himself had known and done. At the start of his career there was nothing to suggest that Edward Hyde, a convivial young barrister of middle-class beginnings, would become the mighty earl of Clarendon, the confidant of kings, and the father of a royal duchess, two of whose descendants would sit upon the throne of England. However Clarendon may have viewed the strange eventful history of his own career, his readers should be duly grateful for the political reverses that twice forced him from the scene of action into authorship; for in his "full and clear narration of the grounds, circumstances, and artifices" of the rebellion that convulsed his age we have the sort of record that only he could write. From 1642, when he joined King Charles at York, until 1667, when, deserted by another Charles, he fled before the wrath of Parliament into exile and neglect, he served the House of Stuart with wisdom, valor, and devotion; and if his account of the fall and restoration of that House reflects his own commitment to the crown and church that he revered, it also shows a matchless firsthand knowledge of the things and men whereof he wrote.

The actual composition of *The History of the Rebellion* was almost as fitful and distracted as the times with which it deals. It was begun in 1646 in the Scilly Islands, where Clarendon—or Edward Hyde, as he then was—had withdrawn with Prince Charles following royalist reverses in the west of England. The next two years of enforced leisure, mainly on the Isle of Jersey, enabled Hyde to record the progress of events from the accession of King Charles in 1625 to the spring of 1644, but he had just begun Book VIII when the rumblings of the second civil war in 1648 recalled him to another kind of action. When he took up the work again, in 1668, he was writing as a broken man and he had a different motive: not to vindicate his party by tracing "the total and prodigious alteration and confusion of the whole kingdom," but to tell the story of his life and thus to vindicate his own career. Since he had lived so near the center of events, however, the change meant not that he abandoned history for autobiography, but that in the autumn of his life he wrote history from a more supple and subjective point of view. Thus the *Life*, far more than the *History*, reveals his remarkable capacity for friendship, and his ability to define, with candor and precision, the characters of those whom he had known. Writing mainly from the reservoir of memory (and without the documents that sometimes make the *History* so austere and circumstantial), within a couple of years he brought the record of his own career from his birth in 1609 to the proudest moment of his life—his monarch's restoration, in which he himself had played a major role.

The possibility of combining the old, unfinished *History* with the newly written *Life* became a reality in 1671, when Clarendon's son, at last allowed to see his father, brought with him from England the manuscript that had been laid aside in 1648. Although Sir Charles Firth, the most authoritative student of the problem, has called the mechanics of this merger "very simple," the consequences are from time to time confusing. In Clarendon's effort to telescope, consolidate, and supplement the two narrations he often merely lifted excerpts from the *Life* and put them in

[1]For other work of Clarendon, see History and Historiography, pp. 929 ff.

the framework of the *History*; for the period between 1644 and 1660 he mainly used the *Life*; and he occasionally tried to bridge the gaps and heal the sutures by supplying new material. The result of all this carpentry is a somewhat ragged piece of work, but it has the contour of a great design, with a beginning, a middle, and an end, and it remains a massive contribution to our knowledge of a crucial phase of English history. A generation after Clarendon's death in exile at Rouen this conflation was finally published in three fine folios as *The History of the Rebellion and the Civil Wars in England* (1702–04). The unused portions of the *Life*, together with a "continuation" that brought the record down to 1668, appeared in 1759.

It is pleasant to recall that Clarendon's manuscripts (and the proceeds of their publication) finally found their way to Oxford, which was his own university (B.A. 1626) and which he had served as chancelor in his days of glory (1660–67). There his name and memory were preserved in the Clarendon Building that, erected in 1713 largely from the profits of his *History*, gave its name to the press so long and intimately associated with the literature of England.

My texts are based upon *The History of the Rebellion and Civil Wars in England, Begun in the Year 1641 . . . Written by the Right Honourable Edward Earl of Clarendon, Late Lord High Chancellor of England, Privy Counsellor in the Reigns of King Charles the First and the Second* (3 vols., 1702–04) and *The Life of Edward Earl of Clarendon, Lord High Chancellor of England, and Chancellor of the University of Oxford . . . Written by Himself. Printed from his Original Manuscripts, given to the University of Oxford, by the Heirs of the late Earl of Clarendon* (1759). In his copy of the *History* now at Harvard Thomas Hollis wrote the following note:

> Edward Hyde, at length Earl of Clarendon, in the opinion of the Writer, so far as he can judge, a hack Lawyer of *commendam*, of working, but not first-rate abilities; a wordy, partial Historian. See the Prose-works of his opposite, the man, who in no respect, would subscribe SLAVE, the matchless John Milton.
>
> T. H. Aug. 7, 1767.

The standard edition of the *History* is that of W. D. Macray (6 vols., 1888), but G. Huehns has edited a useful volume of selections from both the *History* and the *Life* (1955). T. H. Lister's old biography (3 vols., 1838) has been supplanted by Sir Henry Craik's (2 vols., 1911), D. II. G. Wormald has written brilliantly on Clarendon's middle years (1951), as has Robert S. Bosher (*The Making of the Restoration Settlement*, 1951). There are studies of Clarendon as a man of letters by Sir James Stephen (*Horae Sabbaticae*, Series I, 1892), Sir Charles Firth (*Essays Historical and Literary*, 1938), A. L. Rouse (*The English Spirit*, 1944), L. C. Knights (*Further Explorations*, 1965), and H. R. Trevor-Roper (*Milton and Clarendon*, 1965).

from The Life of Edward, Earl of Clarendon (1759)

Whilst he was only a student of the law, and stood at gaze,[1] and irresolute what course of life to take, his chief acquaintance were Ben Jonson, John Selden, Charles Cotton, John Vaughan, Sir Kenelm Digby, Thomas May, and Thomas Carew,[2] and some others of eminent faculties in their several ways.

[BEN JONSON]

Ben Jonson's name can never be forgotten, having by his

THE LIFE [1] *Stood at gaze*: was bewildered and uncertain.
[2] *Ben Jonson . . . Carew*: Charles Cotton. whose son of the same name (1630–87) is remembered for his translation of Montaigne (1685), was esteemed by Jonson, Donne, Selden, and other men of letters. Addressing him as "his honored and most ingenious friend" in *Hesperides*, Herrick said "it is my pride to be/Not so much known, as to be lov'd of thee." Sir John Vaughan, who, despite their early friendship, was one of the most ardent movers of Clarendon's impeachment in 1667, ended his career as chief justice of the Court of Common Pleas. Clarendon's characters of

very good learning and the severity of his nature and man-
ners very much reformed the stage and indeed the English
poetry itself. His natural advantages were judgment to order
and govern fancy rather than excess of fancy, his produc-
tions being slow and upon deliberation, yet then abounding
with great wit and fancy, and will live accordingly; and
surely as he did exceedingly exalt the English language in
eloquence, propriety, and masculine expressions, so he was
the best judge of and fittest to prescribe rules to poetry and
poets of any man who had lived with or before him—or 10
since, if Mr. Cowley had not made a flight beyond all men
with that modesty yet to ascribe much of this to the example
and learning of Ben Jonson. His conversation was very good,
and with the men of most note, and he had for many years
an extraordinary kindness for Mr. Hyde till he found he
betook himself to business, which he believe ought never to
be preferred before his company. He lived to be very old,
and till the palsy made a deep impression upon his body and
his mind.

[John Selden]

Mr. Selden was a person whom no character can flatter or 20
transmit in any expressions equal to his merit and virtue.
He was of so stupendous learning in all kinds and in all
languages (as may appear in his excellent and transcendent
writings) that a man would have thought he had been en-
tirely conversant amongst books, and had never spent an
hour but in reading and writing; yet his humanity, courtesy,
and affability was such that he would have been thought to
have been bred in the best courts but that his good nature,
charity, and delight in doing good, and in communicating
all he knew, exceeded that breeding. His style in all his 30
writings seems harsh and sometimes obscure, which is not
wholly to be imputed to the abstruse subjects of which he
commonly treated, out of the paths trod by other men, but
to a little undervaluing the beauty of a style and too much
propensity to the language of antiquity; but in his conver-
sation he was the most clear discourser, and had the best
faculty in making hard things easy and presenting them to
the understanding, of any man that hath been known. Mr.
Hyde was wont to say that he valued himself upon nothing
more than upon having had Mr. Selden's acquaintance 40
from the time he was very young, and held it with great
delight as long as they were suffered to continue together in
London;[3] and he was very much troubled always when he
heard him blamed, censured, and reproached for staying in
London, and in the Parliament after they were in rebellion,
and in the worst times, which his age obliged him to do;
and how wicked soever the actions were which were every
day done, he was confident he had not given his consent to
them, but would have hindered them if he could with his
own safety, to which he was always enough indulgent. If 50
he had some infirmities with other men they were weighed
down with wonderful and prodigious abilities and excel-
lencies in the other scale. . . .

[Following his characters of Cotton and Vaughan, Clarendon]
[turns to Sir Kenelm Digby.]

[Sir Kenelm Digby]

Sir Kenelm Digby was a person very eminent and notorious
throughout the whole course of his life, from his cradle to
his grave, of an ancient family and noble extraction, and
inherited a fair and plentiful fortune notwithstanding the
attainder of his father. He was a man of a very extraordinary
person and presence which drew the eyes of all men upon
him, which were more fixed by a wonderful graceful be-
havior, a flowing courtesy and civility, and such a volubility
of language as surprised and delighted; and though in an-
other man it might have appeared to have somewhat of
affectation, it was marvelous graceful in him and seemed
natural to his size and mold of his person, to the gravity of
his motion, and the tune of his voice and delivery. He had a
fair reputation in arms, of which he gave an early testimony in
his youth in some encounters in Spain and Italy, and after-
wards in an action in the Mediterranean Sea, where he had
the command of a squadron of ships of war set out at his own
charge under the King's commission; with which, upon an
injury received or apprehended[4] from the Venetians, he
encountered their whole fleet, killed many of their men, and
sunk one of their galleasses,[5] which in that drowsy and un-
active time was looked upon with a general estimation,
though the Crown disavowed it. In a word, he had all the
advantages that nature and art and an excellent education
could give him, which, with a great confidence and pres-
entness of mind, buoyed him up against all those prejudices
and disadvantages (as the attainder and execution of his
father for a crime of the highest nature, his own marriage
with a lady though of an extraordinary beauty of as ex-
traordinary fame, his changing and rechanging his religion,[6]
and some personal vices and licenses in his life) which would
have suppressed and sunk any other man, but never clouded
or eclipsed him from appearing in the best places and the
best company, and with the best estimation and satisfaction.

[Thomas May]

Thomas May was the eldest son of his father, a knight, and
born to a fortune if his father had not spent it, so that he had
only an annuity left him not proportionable to a liberal
education; yet since his fortune could not raise his mind, he
brought his mind down to his fortune by a great modesty
and humility in his nature, which was not affected but very

Digby, May, and Carew are included in the following excerpts
from his *Life*.
[3]*From the Time . . . London*: from the mid-twenties, when
Clarendon became a member of the Middle Temple, until 1642,
when he joined the king at York just before the outbreak of
hostilities. [4]Anticipated.
[5]Heavy vessels impelled by both sail and oars. The exploit that
Clarendon relates occurred off Scanderoon (now Alexandretta),
Syria, in June 1628.
[6]Digby's father, Sir Everard Digby, was executed (1606) for com-
plicity in the Gunpowder Plot. After a long and uncommonly
strenuous courtship the younger Digby secretly married the
beautiful Venetia, daughter of Sir Edward Stanley, in 1625.
Reared as a Catholic, he embraced Protestantism about 1630
but soon reverted to his early faith. See pp. 486 f.

well became an imperfection in his speech, which was a great mortification to him and kept him from entering upon any discourse but in the company of his very friends. His parts of nature and art were very good, as appears by his translation of Lucan (none of the easiest work of that kind) and more by his supplement to Lucan, which, being entirely his own, for the learning, the wit, and the language may be well looked upon as one of the best epic poems in the English language. He writ some other commendable pieces of the reign of some of our kings; he was cherished by many [10] persons of honor, and very acceptable in all places; yet (to show that pride and envy have their influences upon the narrowest minds, and which have the greatest semblance of humility) though he had received much countenance and a very considerable donative[7] from the King, upon His Majesty's refusing to give him a small pension (which he had designed and promised to another very ingenious person whose qualities he thought inferior to his own), he fell from his duty and all his former friends, and prostituted himself to the vile office of celebrating the infamous acts of those who [20] were in rebellion against the King;[8] which he did so meanly that he seemed to all men to have lost his wits when he left his honesty; and so shortly after died miserable and neglected, and deserves to be forgotten.

[THOMAS CAREW]

Thomas Carew was a younger brother of a good family and of excellent parts, and had spent many years of his youth in France and Italy; and returning from travel followed the Court, which the modesty of that time disposed men to do some time before they pretended to be of it; and he was very [30] much esteemed by the most eminent persons in the Court and well looked upon by the King himself some years before he could obtain to be sewer[9] to the King; and when the King conferred that place upon him it was not without the regret even of the whole Scotch nation, which united themselves in recommending another gentleman to it; of so great value were those relations held in that age when Majesty was beheld with the reverence it ought to be. He was a person of a pleasant and facetious wit, and made many poems (especially in the amorous way) which for the sharpness of the fancy and the elegancy of the language in which [40] that fancy was spread, were at least equal if not superior to any of that time. But his glory was that after fifty years of his life, spent with less severity or exactness than it ought to have been, he died with the greatest remorse for that license and with the greatest manifestation of Christianity that his best friends could desire.

Among these persons Mr. Hyde's usual time of conversation was spent till he grew more retired to his more serious studies, and never discontinued his acquaintance with any of them though he spent less time in their company; only upon [50] Mr. Selden he looked with so much affection and reverence that he always thought himself best when he was with him; but he had then another conjunction and communication[10] that he took so much delight in that he embraced it in the time of his greatest business and practice,[11] and would suffer no

other pretence or obligation to withdraw him from that familiarity and friendship; and took frequent occasions to mention their names with great pleasure, being often heard to say "that if he had anything good in him, in his humor or in his manners, he owed it to the example and the information he had received in and from that company, with most of whom he had an entire friendship." And they were, in truth, in their several qualifications men of more than ordinary eminence before they attained the great preferments many of them lived to enjoy. The persons were Sir Lucius Cary (eldest son to the Lord Viscount Falkland, Lord Deputy of Ireland), Sir Francis Wenman of Oxfordshire, Sidney Godolphin of Godolphin in Cornwall, Edmund Waller of Beaconsfield, Dr. Gilbert Sheldon, Dr. George Morley, Dr. John Earles, Mr. John Hales of Eton, and Mr. William Chillingworth.[12]

[LUCIUS CARY, SECOND VISCOUNT FALKLAND]

With Sir Lucius Cary he had a most entire friendship without reserve from his age of twenty years to the hour of his

[7]Gift.
[8]In *The History of the Parliament of England* (1642). See pp. 912 ff.
[9]A ceremonial attendant at meals.
[10]*Conjunction and communication*: group of friends.
[11]Legal practice in the Court of Requests, where Clarendon was a rising young lawyer during the 1630's.
[12]*Cary . . . Chillingworth*: This group of liberal Anglicans and royalists who found a social and intellectual center at Great Tew, the Oxfordshire seat of Lucius Cary, second Viscount Falkland (1610?–43), would have been notable at any time, but in their advocacy of moderation, reason, and tolerance they were especially so in the tumultuous 1630's. The son of a lord deputy of Ireland and an ardent Catholic mother, Falkland succeeded to his title in 1633 and retired to Great Tew the following year, but at length the mounting pressures of the age brought him forth to take part in the Bishops' War (1639), enter Parliament, and accept appointment (1642) as Charles I's secretary of state. Dismayed by the misery of war and despairing of the peace for which he longed, according to Clarendon he sought and found a welcome death at the battle of Newbury, but John Aubrey tells a different story: "I have been well informed by those who best knew him and knew intrigues behind the curtain (as they say) that it was the grief of the death of Mistress Moray, a handsome lady at court who was his mistress and whom he loved above all creatures, was the true cause of his being so madly guilty of his own death." In any event there is no reason to think that Clarendon's famous valediction to his friend (*History*, Bk. VII) was undeserved: "Thus fell that incomparable young man in the four-and-thirtieth year of his age, having so much dispatched the business of life that the oldest rarely attain to that immense knowledge, and the youngest enter not into the world with more innocence; and whoever leads such a life need not care upon how short warning it be taken from him." A similar tribute is in Jonson's famous ode to Cary and Morison, pp. 99 ff. Of the other habitués of Great Tew, Godolphin (1610–43) was a minor poet who also died in battle; Sheldon (1598–1677) lived to become chancellor of the University of Oxford (like Clarendon) and archbishop of Canterbury; and Morley (1597–1684) ended his distinguished career as bishop of Winchester. Clarendon's characters of Earle, Hales, and Chillingworth are included in the excerpts that follow; for a sketch of Waller's life see pp. 244 ff.

death near twenty years after, upon which there will be occasion to enlarge when we come to speak of that time,[13] and often before; and therefore we shall say no more of him in this place than to show his condition and qualifications, which were the first ingredients into that friendship which was afterwards cultivated and improved by a constant conversation and familiarity and by many accidents which contributed thereunto.

He had the advantage of a noble extraction and of being born his father's eldest son, when there was a greater fortune in prospect to be inherited (besides what he might reasonably expect by his mother) than came afterwards to his possession. His education was equal to his birth, at least in the care if not in the climate, for his father, being Deputy of Ireland, before he was of age fit to be sent abroad, his breeding was in the Court and in the University of Dublin, but under the care, vigilance, and direction of such governors and tutors that he learned all those exercises and languages better than most men do in more celebrated places, insomuch as when he came into England, which was when he was about the age of eighteen years, he was not only master of the Latin tongue (and had read all the poets and other of the best authors with notable judgment for that age), but he understood and spake and writ French as if he had spent many years in France.

He had another advantage which was a great ornament to the rest: that was a good, a plentiful estate, of which he had the early possession. His mother was the sole daughter and heir of the Lord Chief Baron Tanfield, who, having given a fair portion with his daughter in marriage, had kept himself free to dispose of his land and his other estate in such manner as he should think fit; and he settled it in such manner upon his grandson Sir Lucius Cary, without taking notice of his father or mother, that upon his grandmother's death (which fell out about the time that he was nineteen years of age) all the land with two very good houses[14]—very well furnished, worth above £2,000 per annum, in a most pleasant country, and the two most pleasant places in that country, with a very plentiful personal estate—fell into his hands and possession, and to his entire disposal.

With these advantages he had one great disadvantage, which in the first entrance into the world is attended with too much prejudice: in his person and presence, which was in no degree attractive or promising. His stature was low and smaller than most men, his motion not graceful, and his aspect so far from inviting that it had somewhat in it of simplicity; and his voice the worst of the three, and so untuned that instead of reconciling, it offended the ear, that nobody would have expected music from that tongue, and sure no man was less beholden to nature for its recommendation into the world. But then no man sooner or more disappointed this general and customary prejudice: that little person and small stature was quickly found to contain a great heart, a courage so keen, and a nature so fearless that no composition of the strongest limbs and most harmonious and proportioned presence and strength ever more disposed any man to the greatest enterprise, it being his greatest weakness to be solicitous for such adventures; and that untuned

tongue and voice easily discovered itself to be supplied and governed by a mind and understanding so excellent that the wit and weight of all he said carried another kind of luster and admiration in it, and even another kind of acceptation from the persons present, than any ornament of delivery could reasonably promise itself or is usually attended with. And his disposition and nature was so gentle and obliging—so much delighted in courtesy, kindness, and generosity—that all mankind could not but admire and love him.

In a short time after he had possession of the estate his grandfather had left him, and before he was of age, he committed a fault against his father in marrying a young lady[15] whom he passionate loved, without any considerable portion, which exceedingly offended him and disappointed all his reasonable hopes and expectation of redeeming and repairing his own broken fortune and desperate hopes in Court by some advantageous marriage of his son, about which he had then some probable treaty. Sir Lucius Cary was very conscious to himself of his offence and transgression and the consequence of it, which though he could not repent, having married a lady of a most extraordinary wit and judgment and of the most signal virtue and exemplary life that the age produced, and who brought him many hopeful children in which he took great delight, yet he confessed it with the most sincere and dutiful applications to his father for his pardon that could be made, and for the prejudice he had brought upon his fortune by bringing no portion to him he offered to repair it by resigning his whole estate to his disposal, and to rely wholly upon his kindness for his own maintenance and support; and to that purpose he had caused conveyances to be drawn by counsel, which he brought ready engrossed to his father, and was willing to seal and execute them that they might be valid. But his father's passion and indignation so far transported him (though he was a gentleman of excellent parts) that he refused any reconciliation and rejected all the offers that were made him of the estate, so that his son remained still in the possession of his estate against his will, of which he found great reason afterwards to rejoice; but he was for the present so much afflicted with his father's displeasure that he transported himself and his wife into Holland, resolving to buy some military command and to spend the remainder of his life in that profession, but being disappointed in the treaty[16] he expected and finding no opportunity to accommodate himself with such a command, he returned again into England, resolving to retire to a country life and to his books, that since he was not like to improve himself in arms he might advance in letters.

[13]Clarendon included another character of Falkland in his *History* (Bk. VII), where he dealt at length with his friend's public career toward the end of his life.

[14]Great Tew and Burford, Oxfordshire. To settle his financial problems Falkland in 1634 sold his life interest in the Burford estate to William Lenthall, who was subsequently speaker of the Long Parliament.

[15]Lettice, daughter of Sir Richard Morison of Tooley Park, Leicestershire. Falkland's friendship with her brother is celebrated in Jonson's famous ode pp. 99 ff.

[16]Negotiations leading to a compact.

In this resolution he was so severe (as he was always naturally very intent upon what he was inclined to) that he declared he would not see London in many years (which was the place he loved of all the world) and that in his studies he would first apply himself to the Greek and pursue it without intermission till he should attain to the full understanding of that tongue; and it is hardly to be credited what industry he used and what success attended that industry, for though his father's death [1633], by an unhappy accident, made his repair to London absolutely necessary in fewer years than he had proposed for his absence, yet he had first made himself master of the Greek tongue—in the Latin he was very well versed before—and had read not only all the Greek historians, but Homer likewise and such of the poets as were worthy to be perused.

Though his father's death brought no other convenience to him but a title to redeem an estate mortgaged for as much as it was worth and for which he was compelled to sell a finer seat of his own, yet it imposed a burthen upon him of the title of a viscount and an increase of expence, in which he was not in his nature too provident or restrained, having naturally such a generosity and bounty in him that he seemed to have his estate in trust for all worthy persons who stood in want of supplies and encouragement, as Ben Jonson and many others of that time whose fortunes required and whose spirits made them superior to ordinary obligations; which yet they were contented to receive from because his bounties were so generously distributed and so much without vanity and ostentation that except from those few persons from whom he sometimes received the characters of fit objects for his benefits,[17] or whom he intrusted for the more secret deriving to them, he did all he could that the persons themselves who received them should not know from what fountain they flowed; and when that could not be concealed he sustained any acknowledgment from the persons obliged with so much trouble and bashfulness that they might well perceive that he was even ashamed of the little he had given, and to receive so large a recompense for it.

As soon as he had finished all those transactions which the death of his father had made necessary to be done he retired again to his country life and to his severe course of study, which was very delightful to him as soon as he was engaged in it; but he was wont to say that he never found reluctancy in anything he resolved to do but in his quitting London and departing from the conversation of those he enjoyed there, which was in some degree preserved and continued by frequent letters and often visits which were made by his friends from thence whilst he continued wedded to the country, and which were so grateful to him that during their stay with him he looked upon no book except their very conversation made an appeal to some book; and truly his whole conversation was one continued *convivium philosophicum* or *convivium theologicum*,[18] enlivened and refreshed with all the facetiousness[19] of wit and good humor and pleasantness of discourse which made the gravity of the argument itself, whatever it was, very delectable.

His house where he usually resided—Tew or Burford in Oxfordshire—being within ten or twelve miles of the university, looked like the university itself by the company that was always found there. There were Dr. Sheldon, Dr. Morley, Dr. Hammond,[20] Dr. Earles, Mr. Chillingworth, and indeed all men of eminent parts and faculties in Oxford, besides those who resorted thither from London, who all found their lodgings there as ready as in their colleges; nor did the lord of the house know of their coming or going, nor who were in his house, till he came to dinner or supper where all still met; otherwise there was no troublesome ceremony or constraint to forbid men to come to the house or to make them weary of staying there; so that many came thither to study in a better air, finding all the book they could desire in his library and all the persons together whose company they could wish and not find in any other society. Here Mr. Chillingworth wrote and formed and modeled his excellent book[21] against the learned Jesuit Mr. Knott after frequent debates upon the most important particulars, in many of which he suffered himself to be overruled by the judgment of his friends, though in others he still adhered to his own fancy, which was skeptical enough even in the highest points.

In this happy and delightful conversation and restraint he remained in the country many years, and until he had made so prodigious a progress in learning that there were very few classic authors in the Greek or Latin tongue that he had not read with great exactness. He had read all the Greek and Latin Fathers, all the most allowed and authentic ecclesiastical writers, and all the Councils[22] with wonderful care and observation, for in religion he thought too carefull and too curious an inquiry could not be made amongst those whose purity was not questioned and whose authority was constantly and confidently urged by men who were furthest from being of one mind amongst themselves and for the mutual support of their several opinions in which they most contradicted each other; and in all those controversies he had so dispassioned[23] a consideration, such a candor in his nature, and so profound a charity in his conscience that in those points in which he was in his own judgment most clear he never thought the worse, or in any degree declined the familiarity of those who were of another mind, which without question is an excellent temper for the propagation and advancement of Christianity. With these great advantages of industry he had a memory retentive of all that he had ever read and an understanding and judgment to apply it seasonably and appositely with the most dexterity and address, and the least pedantry and affectation, that ever man who knew so much was possessed with of what quality soever. It is not a trivial evidence of his learning, his wit,

17 *Those . . . benefits*: those who recommended persons eligible for his assistance.
18"Philosophical or theological banquet." 19Urbanity.
20Henry Hammond (1605–60), a fellow of Magdalen College, Oxford, who subsequently served as chaplain to Charles I and who wrote largely on theological subjects.
21 *The Religion of Protestants* (1638). See pp. 561 ff.
22The creeds and directives promulgated by such general councils as the Nicene, Lateran, etc. 23Dispassionate, impartial.

and his candor that may be found in that discourse of his against the infallibility of the Church of Rome,[24] published since his death and from a copy under his own hand, though not prepared and digested by him for the press, and to which he would have given some castigations.

But all his parts, abilities, and faculties by art and industry were not to be valued or mentioned in comparison of his most accomplished mind and manners. His gentleness and affability was so transcendent and obliging that it drew reverence and some kind of compliance from the roughest 10 and most unpolished and stubborn constitutions, and made them of another temper in debate in his presence than they were in other places. He was in his nature so severe a lover of justice and so precise a lover of truth that he was superior to all possible temptations for the violation of either; indeed, so rigid an exacter of perfection in all those things which seemed but to border upon either of them, and by the common practice of men were not thought to border upon either, that many who knew him very well, and loved and admired his virtue (as all who did know him must love and 20 admire it), did believe that he was of a temper and composition fitter to live in *republica Platonis* than in *faece Romuli*.[25] But this rigidness was only exercised towards himself; towards his friends' infirmities no man was more indulgent. In his conversation, which was the most cheerful and pleasant that can be imagined, though he was young (for all I have yet spoken of him doth not exceed his age of twenty-five or twenty-six years) and of great gaiety in his humor, with a flowing delightfulness of language, he had so chaste a tongue and ear that there was never known a profane or loose word 30 to fall from him, nor in truth in his company, the integrity and cleanliness of the wit of that time not exercising itself in that license before persons for whom they had any esteem. . . .

[JOHN EARLE]

Dr. Earles was at that time chaplain in the house of the Earl of Pembroke, Lord Chamberlain of His Majesty's household, and had a lodging in the Court under that relation. He was a person very notable for his elegance in the Greek and Latin tongues, and being Fellow of Merton College in Oxford, and having been Proctor of the university, and some very witty and sharp discourses[26] being published in print 40 without his consent, though known to be his, he grew suddenly into a very general esteem with all men, being a man of great piety and devotion, a most eloquent and powerful preacher, and of a conversation so pleasant and delightful, so very innocent and so very facetious, that no man's company was more desired and more loved. No man was more negligent in his dress and habit and mien, no man more wary and cultivated in his behavior and discourse, insomuch as he had the greater advantage when he was known by promising so little before he was known. He was an excellent 50 poet both in Latin, Greek, and English, as appears by many pieces yet abroad, though he suppressed many more himself, especially of English, incomparably good, out of an austerity[27] to those sallies of his youth. He was very dear to the Lord Falkland, with whom he spent as much time as he could make his own; and as that lord would impute the

speedy progress he made in the Greek tongue to the information and assistance he had from Mr. Earles, so Mr. Earles would frequently profess that he had got more useful learning from his conversation at Tew (the Lord Falkland's house) than he had at Oxford. In the first settling of the Prince his family he was made one of his chaplains, and attended on him when he was forced to leave the kingdom.[28] He was amongst the few excellent men who never had nor ever could have an enemy but such a one who was an enemy to all learning and virtue, and therefore would never make himself known.

[JOHN HALES]

Mr. John Hales[29] had been Greek professor in the University of Oxford and had borne the greatest part of the labor of that excellent edition and impression of St. Chrysostom's works set out by Sir Harry Savile, who was then Warden of Merton College, when the other was fellow of that house.[30] He was chaplain in the house with Sir Dudley Carleton, ambassador at the Hague in Holland at the time when the Synod of Dort[31] was held, and so had liberty to be present at the consultations in that assembly, and hath left the best memorial behind him of the ignorance and passion and animosity and injustice of that convention, of which he often made very pleasant relations, though at that time it received too much countenance from England. Being a person of the greatest eminency for learning and other

[24]*Sir L. Cary, Late Lord Viscount Falkland, His Discourse of Infallibility* (1651).
[25]In Plato's ideal republic than in the sewers of Rome.
[26]*Microcosmography* (1628). See pp. 722 ff. [27]Judicial severity.
[28]Earle, who was appointed tutor to Prince Charles (later Charles II) in 1641, followed his former pupil into exile in 1646.
[29]The "ever memorable" Hales (1584–1656), a man vastly admired by many of his illustrious contemporaries, was a graduate of Christ College, Oxford, and a fellow of Merton (1605) before becoming Regius Professor of Greek and fellow of Eton (1613–49). The most stirring events of his uneventful life—his attendance at the Synod of Dort and his encounter with Laud—are duly noted by Clarendon, and some of his rather scrappy literary remains (none of them apparently designed for publication) were brought together posthumously in his *Golden Remains* (1659).
[30]For Savile's contributions to historical research see p. 894, n.16.
[31]An assembly called by the States General at Dordrecht (1618–19) to resolve the differences between the liberal Arminians or Remonstrants and the orthodox Calvinists. The issue was decided in favor of the Calvinists with the reaffirmation of the so-called five points of Calvinism: predestination, limited atonement, total depravity, irresistibility of grace, and perseverance of the saints. Conversely, the five opposing points of Arminianism were repudiated: conditional rather than absolute predestination, universal redemption, the necessity of regeneration through the operation of the Holy Spirit, the possibility of resistance to divine grace, and the possibility of relapse from grace.
Hales, then serving in Holland as chaplain to Sir Dudley Carleton, Viscount Dorchester (1573–1632), one of the most accomplished diplomats of the age, was an observer at the synod for almost a year, and his reports to his chief, some of which were eventually printed in *Golden Remains*, astutely record the rancors of theological controversy in that troubled age.

abilities, from which he might have promised himself any preferment in the Church, he withdrew himself from all pursuits of that kind into a private fellowship at the College of Eton, where his friend Sir Harry Savile was Provost, where he lived amongst his books, and the most separated from the world of any man then living, though he was not in the least degree inclined to melancholy, but on the contrary of a very open and pleasant conversation, and therefore was very well pleased with the resort of his friends to him, who were such as he had chosen, and in whose company he delighted, and for whose sake he would sometimes (once in a year) resort to London only to enjoy their cheerful conversation.

He would never take any cure of souls, and was so great a contemner of money that he was wont to say that his fellowship and the bursar's place which for the good of the college he held many years was worth him fifty pounds a year more than he could spend, and yet besides his being very charitable to all poor people, even to liberality, he had made a greater and better collection of books than were to be found in any other private library that I have seen, as he had sure read more and carried more about him in his excellent memory than any man I ever knew, my Lord Falkland only excepted, who, I think, sided[32] him. He had, whether from his natural temper and constitution or from his long retirement from all crowds or from his profound judgment and discerning spirit, contracted some opinions which were not received, nor by him published[33] except in private discourses, and then rather upon occasion of dispute than of positive opinion; and he would often say his opinions he was sure did him no harm, but he was far from being confident that they might not do others harm who entertained them, and might entertain other results from them than he did, and therefore he was very reserved in communicating what he thought himself in those points in which he differed from what was received.

Nothing troubled him more than the brawls which were grown from religion, and he therefore exceedingly detested the tyranny of the Church of Rome, more for their imposing uncharitably upon the consciences of other men than for their errors in their own opinions; and would often say that he would renounce the religion of the Church of England tomorrow if it obliged him to believe that any other Christians should be damned, and that nobody would conclude another man to be damned who did not wish him so. No man more strict and severe to himself, to other men so charitable as to their opinions, that he thought that other men were more in fault for their carriage towards them than the men themselves were who erred; and he thought that pride and passion, more than conscience, were the cause of all separation from each other's communion; and he frequently said that that only kept the world from agreeing upon such a liturgy as might bring them into one communion, all doctrinal points upon which men differed in their opinions being to have no place in any liturgy. Upon an occasional discourse with a friend of the frequent and uncharitable reproaches of heretic and schismatic too lightly thrown at each other amongst men who differ in their judg-

ment, he writ a little discourse of schism[34] contained in less than two sheets of paper, which being transmitted from friend to friend in writing was at last without any malice brought to the view of the Archbishop of Canterbury, Dr. Laud, who was a very rigid surveyor of all things which never so little bordered upon schism, and thought the Church could not be too vigilant against and jealous of such incursions.

He sent for Mr. Hales, whom when they had both lived in the University of Oxford he had known well, and told him that he had in truth believed him to be long since dead, and chid him very kindly for having never come to him, having been of his old acquaintance; then asked him whether he had lately writ a short discourse of schism and whether he was of that opinion that the discourse implied. He told him that he had, for the satisfaction of a private friend (who was not of his mind), a year or two before writ such a small tract without any imagination that it would be communicated, and that he believed it did not contain anything that was not agreeable to the judgment of the primitive Fathers; upon which the Archbishop debated with him upon some expressions of Irenaeus[35] and the most ancient Fathers, and concluded with saying that the time was very apt to set new doctrines on foot, of which the wits of the age were too susceptible, and that there could not be too much care taken to preserve the peace and unity of the Church; and from thence asked him of his condition, and whether he wanted anything, and the other answering that he had enough and wanted or desired no addition; so dismissed him with great courtesy, and shortly after sent for him again when there was a prebendary of Windsor fallen, and told him the King had given him that preferment because it lay so convenient to his Fellowship of Eton, which (though indeed the most convenient preferment that could be thought of for him) the Archbishop could not without great difficulty persuade him to accept; and he did accept it rather to please him than himself, because he really believed he had enough before.[36] He was one of the least men in the kingdom, and one of the greatest scholars in Europe.

[WILLIAM CHILLINGWORTH]

Mr. Chillingworth was of a stature little superior to Mr. Hales—and it was an age in which there were many great and wonderful men of that size—and a man of so great a subtlety of understanding and so rare a temper in debate that as it was impossible to provoke him into any passion, so it was very difficult to keep a man's self from being a little discomposed by his sharpness and quickness of argument and instances, in which he had a rare facility and a great ad-

[32]Equaled. [33]Shared with others, made accessible.
[34]*Schism and Schismatics*, a treatise written about 1636 (perhaps for the use of Chillingworth, who was then at work on his *Religion of Protestants*) and published without Hales' name or permission in 1642.
[35]A father of the Greek church (ca. 130–ca. 200), notable for his efforts to reconcile paganism and Christianity.
[36]In addition to naming Hales to a canonry at Windsor (1639), Laud also appointed him one of his chaplains.

vantage over all the men I ever knew. He had spent all his younger time in disputation, and had arrived to so great a mastery as he was inferior to no man in those skirmishes; but he had with his notable perfection in this exercise contracted such an irresolution and habit of doubting that by degrees he grew confident of nothing and a skeptic, at least in the greatest mysteries of faith.

This made him from first wavering in religion and indulging to scruples to reconcile himself too soon and too easily to the Church of Rome, and carrying still his own inquisitiveness about him, without any resignation to their authority (which is the only temper can make that Church sure of its proselytes), having made a journey to Saint-Omer[37] purely to perfect his conversion by the conversation of those who had the greatest name, he found as little satisfaction there, and returned with as much haste from them, with a belief that an entire exemption from error was neither inherent in nor necessary to any Church; which occasioned that war which was carried on by the Jesuits with so great asperity and reproaches against him, and in which he defended himself by such an admirable eloquence of language and the clear and incomparable power of reason that he not only made them appear unequal adversaries but carried the war into their own quarters, and made the Pope's infallibility to be as much shaken and declined by their own doctors and as great an acrimony amongst themselves upon that subject, and to be at least as much doubted as in the schools of the Reformed or Protestant, and forced them since to defend and maintain those unhappy controversies in religion with arms and weapons of another nature than were used or known in the Church of Rome when Bellarmine[38] died, and which probably will in time undermine the very foundation that supports it.

Such a levity and propensity to change is commonly attended with great infirmities in, and no less reproach and prejudice to, the person; but the sincerity of his heart was so conspicuous, and without the least temptation of any corrupt end, and the innocence and candor in his nature so evident and without any perverseness that all who knew him clearly discerned that all those restless motions and fluctuations proceeded only from the warmth and jealousy of his own thoughts in a too nice inquisition for truth. Neither the books of the adversary nor any of their persons, though he was acquainted with the best of both, had ever made great impression upon him; all his doubts grew out of himself when he assisted his scruples with all the strength of his own reason, and was then too hard for himself; but finding as little quiet and repose in those victories, he quickly recovered by a new appeal to his own judgment, so that he was in truth upon the matter in all his sallies and retreats his own convert, though he was not so totally divested of all thoughts of this world but that when he was ready for it he admitted some great and considerable churchmen to be sharers with him in his public conversion.

Whilst he was in perplexity, or rather some passionate disinclination to the religion he had been educated in, he had the misfortune to have much acquaintance with one Mr. Lewgar,[39] a minister of that Church, a man of a competency of learning in those points most controverted with the Romanists but of no acute parts of wit or judgment, and wrought so far upon him by weakening and enervating those arguments by which he found he was governed (as he had all the logic and all the rhetoric that was necessary to persuade very powerfully men of the greatest talents) that the poor man, not able to live long in doubt, too hastily deserted his own Church and betook himself to the Roman, nor could all the arguments and reasons of Mr. Chillingworth make him pause in the expedition he was using or reduce[40] him from that Church after he had given himself to it; but he had always a great animosity against him for having (as he said) unkindly betrayed him and carried him into another religion and there left him: so unfit are some constitutions to be troubled with doubts after they are once fixed.

He did really believe all war to be unlawful, and did not think that the Parliament (whose proceedings he perfectly abhorred) did in truth intend to involve the nation in a civil war till after the battle of Edgehill,[41] and then he thought any expedient or stratagem that was like to put a speedy end to it to be the most commendable; and so having too mathematically conceived an engine[42] that should move so lightly as to be a breastwork in all encounters and assaults in the field, he carried it, to make the experiment, into that part of His Majesty's army which was only in that winter season in the field under the command of the Lord Hopton in Hampshire upon the borders of Sussex, where he was shut up in the Castle of Arundel, which was forced after a short, sharp seige to yield for want of victual; and poor Mr. Chillingworth with it falling into the rebels' hands and being most barbarously treated by them, especially by that clergy which followed them, and being broken with sickness contracted by the ill accommodation and want of meat and fire during the seige (which was in a terrible season of frost and snow), he died shortly after in prison.[43] He was a man of

[37]Text *St. Omers*, a town in northern France where a college founded by the Jesuits in 1592 long served as a training ground for English Catholics.
[38]Roberto Bellarmino (1542–1621), Jesuit cardinal noted for his skill in disputation.
[39]Text *Lugar*. John Lewgar (1602–65), a Catholic controversialist and associate of Lord Baltimore in settling Maryland, whose grievances were at long last aired in *A Conference between John Lewgar and Mr. Chillingworth* (1687).   [40]Lead back (a Latinism).
[41]23 October 1642, the first important battle of the Civil War.
[42]Apparently a contrivance inspired by the Roman *testudo* ("tortoise"), a kind of portable shed for besiegers.
[43]Too ill to be sent to London with the other prisoners taken at the fall of Arundel Castle on 9 December 1643, Chillingworth was given permission to go to Chichester, where he died (30 January 1644) in the bishop's palace and was buried in the cathedral. His last days were enlivened or made miserable by the incessant recriminations of Francis Cheynell, a Puritan divine who flung into his grave a copy of *The Religion of Protestants* with the hope that it might "rot with its author and see corruption." Subsequently Cheynell's savage piety found fuller expression in *Chillingworthi Novissima, or the Sickness, Heresy, Death, and Burial of W. Chillingworth* (1644), excerpts from which may be found on pp. 571 ff.

excellent parts and of a cheerful disposition, void of all kind of vice and endued with many notable virtues, of a very public heart and an indefatigable desire to do good. His only unhappiness proceeded from his sleeping too little and thinking too much, which sometimes threw him into violent fevers.

This was Mr. Hyde's company and conversation, to which he dedicated his vacant times and all that time which he could make vacant from the business of his profession, which he indulged with no more passion than was necessary to keep up the reputation of a man that had no purpose to be idle, which indeed he perfectly abhorred; and he took always occasion to celebrate the time he had spent in that conversation with great satisfaction and delight. . . .

HISTORY AND HISTORIOGRAPHY V

John Stow [1525?-1605] and Edmund Howes [d.1631]

Although the "painful" John Stow was born in the middle of Henry VIII's reign and died (at eighty) when James was scarcely settled on the throne of England, he deserves a place in this anthology because his work, however burly and old-fashioned, continued to appeal to readers, and thus to merit new editions, well into the age of Milton. Speaking for the later generations the fastidious Edmund Bolton (p. 893) might disparage books like Stow's as "vast vulgar tomes procured for the most part by the husbandry of printers"; but Thomas Fuller, while deprecating the old chronicler's naïveté and lack of style, shrewdly pointed out that his more "elegant" successors, "though throwing away the basket, have taken the fruit; though not mentioning his name, making use of his endeavors." However badly Stow "kept tune," concluded Fuller, "he kept time very well, no author being more accurate in the notation thereof."

Like his fellow-chronicler John Speed, a tailor by trade, Stow was almost forty before he found his true vocation editing the works of Chaucer in 1561. Thereafter his production was immense. Stirred by the deficiencies of Richard Grafton's *Abridgment of the Chronicles of England* (1562) to attempt a better work, he published his own *Summary of English Chronicles* in 1565 and its abridgment one year later. Although these books provoked a sputtering quarrel with Grafton (who sneered at the "memories of superstitious foundations, fables, and lies foolishly *Stowed* together"), Stow's handbooks achieved so many reprintings and expansions that the *Summary* reached a sixth edition in 1590 and the abridgment a ninth as late as 1618.

Not even the harassment (and, of course, the danger) resulting from an apparently baseless charge of popish sympathies and an ugly family quarrel with his elder brother could stem Stow's tide of publication. With the encouragement and subvention of Archbishop Parker, himself a notable antiquarian, he edited Matthew of Westminster's *Flores historiarum* (1567) and the chronicles of Matthew Paris (1571) and Walsingham (1574); but his major undertaking in his middle years was *The Chronicles of England from Brut until This Present Year*, which was published (with a dedication to the earl of Leicester) in 1580. After its appearance as *The Annals of England* in 1592 there were two new editions and expansions (1601, 1605) before the old man died, and two others (under the direction of Edmund Howes) in 1615 and 1631. Apart from his contributions to the second (1585–87) edition of Holinshed's influential *Chronicles,* Stow's final years were given mainly to the most famous and perennially useful of all his many works, the matchless *Survey of London* (1598, 1603), a lovingly detailed description of his native city. Despite poverty and the afflictions of age, he continued scribbling to the end, both on new editions of the *Annals* and the *Survey* and on what he hoped would be his magnum opus—a "history of this island" that, according to Howes, he began and finished at Archbishop Whitgift's instigation. Though "ready for the press" at his death in 1605, the work has disappeared.

Edmund Howes seems to have begun his long career as Stow's successor by supervising an edition of *The Summary of English Chronicles* in 1607, but in an epistle "To the King's Most Excellent Majesty" in the 1631 *Annals* he says that "these my thirty years' labors of impartial truth" in carrying on that massive work had been in fulfillment of his "oath and promise" to Whitgift, by whose "especial instruction and encouragement" he was moved to undertake the task. That it was both massive and continuous is indicated by new editions (and expansions) in 1615, 1618, and 1631. Howes implies that his intention was to carry on his predecessor's style and method with no modish innovations. "Expect no filed phrases, inkhorn terms, unquoth words," he tells the "honest and understanding" reader, "nor fantastic speeches, but good plain English without affectation, rightly befitting chronology." In an "Epistle Dedicatory" to the Lord Mayor and aldermen of London (oddly placed at the end of the volume), he adds that he had entered on the "troublesome business of chronology" because others, presumably better qualified than he, had been deterred by sloth or envy or the expenses of research. But having given thirty years to a project that at the start he thought would take no more than one—all the while being "intolerably abused and scandalized" by "precurrent vipers, lurking adders, and venomous tongues"—Howes declared that he would do no more. "I here proclaim a cessation from any further observation or practice in the premises or continuation of the English chronicle." It was just as well perhaps, for his own death coincided with the last edition of the *Annals* in 1631.

Following Howes' long "Historical Preface" (which illustrates his own conception of his function as "chronologer" and his elephantine scheme of periodic history), a "short note" on Britain's first inhabitants, "A Brief Proof of Brut" (which may also have been supplied by Howes for its first appearance in the 1615 edition), and a long account of Brut and his successors (with a digression of ancient history, sacred and profane), the *Annals* proper opens with the birth of Christ and then proceeds relentlessly, year by year, to the date of publication. Inevitably, the work gets fuller as Stow approaches modern times. Whereas ten pages suffice for Henry II's reign, forty-six are needed for that of Richard II, more than twice that number for Henry VIII's, and almost two hundred for Elizabeth's. The annals of the first two Stuart kings are, of course, the work of Howes, whose additions, though the "lively emblem" of the times, said Fuller, were "as far short of Master Stow in goodness as our age is of the integrity and charity of those which went before it." Apart from Howes' "Historical Preface" and "An Appendix" on the educational institutions of England (part of it by James I's master of the revels, Sir George Buc), the *Annals* runs to almost eleven hundred double-column pages of small black letter type.

My text is based upon *Annales, or A Generall Chronicle of England. Begun by Iohn Stow: Continued and Augmented with matters Forraigne and Domestique, Ancient and Moderne, vnto the end of this present year, 1631. By Edmund Howes, Gent.,* 1631 (STC 23340). Although the *Annals* have slumbered undisturbed since 1631, Stow's life and works have been learnedly explored by C. L. Kingsford (*A Survey of London,* 2 vols., 1908) and discussed by Kendrick and other students of historiography cited in the General Bibliography, Section V. There is a useful note by J. A. Bryant on the Stow-Howes collaboration in *MLR,* XLV (1950).

from Annals (1631)

AN HISTORICAL PREFACE TO THIS BOOK

The law of God forbiddeth us to receive a false report, and the law of histories is that we ought to publish no falsehood nor dissemble any truth. If in anything this should be observed it ought to be in the preservation of those monuments which do set forth the memory of our ancestors, the honor of our ancient fathers, the mercies of God upon our country, and His judgments warning us what to follow and avoid. This excellent use of aged stories we are deprived of by those who, when they have laid hold upon some one or two mistakings[1] in the life of some one man, do by and by not only deny that there was any such man, but dash and cashier[2] a whole succession of princes and the consenting testimonies

of many learned and worthy historians. The example hereof is in Brut,[3] the first king of this monarchy, who in that age when almost all the world, especially Europe, ran doting in desire of the Trojan or Italian ancestors, some writers fabled to be the son of Silvius, descended of Aeneas, and that he killed his father and came by oracle into Britain. . . .

[Despite his own rejection of the more fabulous "mistakings" concerning Trojan Brut, Howes excoriates those who disbelieve, and even write against, the historicity of such a man as founder of an ancient race of British kings.]

ANNALS [1]Errors. [2]Depose.
[3]The mythological founder of Britain. According to the legend

Those that prefer the conjectures of a few incompetent witnesses before the gravity and authority of so many ancient authors, whereof most are very learned and sincere, and by all likelihood had seen divers ancient writings and monuments[4] which are now utterly unknown and extinct, do violate both the rules of wisdom and of justice. Of wisdom, first in preferring incompetent witnesses before competent, strangers before native[s], few before many, arguments before testimonies; secondly, in not discerning betwixt fables and truth, between that which may stand with other histories 10 and that which cannot, but for some aspersions of fiction rejecting altogether. Of justice, towards their country in depriving it of the glory of so many ancient kings, and towards God in suppressing many examples of His divine justice, whose judgments as upon other sins so especially upon idolatry, heresy, cruelty, dissensions, rebellions, murders, and confused lusts registered in our records ought now to be so many trumpets to summon us to repentance. . . .

Beginning his panoramic view of English history, therefore, with the conquest of the island by Brut, Howes sees the 20 subsequent course of events as marked by six major "alterations," which he explains as follows.

About a thousand years before the birth of our Saviour Christ, Brut, of the race of Trojans, with his company possessed this whole island of Great Britain containing England, Scotland, and Wales. He left one part thereof to his son Locrine and so founded the kingdom, since which foundation there hath happened in the same (the last only excepted) sundry strange alterations of kings, princes, and religion, people, and nations. The first alterations have been 30 most great and universal about the shifting of the period or revolutions of five hundred years, somewhat more or less, but always after the fourth hundred years and before the sixt.

The alteration of this kingdom upon the revolution of the first five hundred years after the foundation thereof was presently upon the death of Gorboduc. After he had reigned sixty and three years he would needs ordain and cause his youngest son Porrex to be crowned king jointly with his eldest son Ferrex, who within five years' reign fell at mortal hatred for sovereignty, and entered furiously and unreconcil- 40 ably into arms one against another. Porrex slew his elder brother, then came his mother unto him under color of kindness to congratulate her younger son's victory; she murthered him treacherously in his chamber; her most affection was to her eldest son and was wholy against their joint government. When the multitude understood her unkind bloody act, they fell into an uproar and slew her, whereupon the crown became vacant and the land fell into extreme misery and confusion.[5] The civil wars continued fifty-four years and ceased not until Don Wallo Mol- 50 mutius,[6] after infinite battles and bloodshed, had subdued all other competitors, and then from him began a new line.

The causes of this ruin of the realm was the folly of Gorboduc, to join his youngest son with his eldest, the devilish malice of the old queen to butcher her youngest son, having then no issue to succeed, and the people's wantonness and security after long peace. The effects of this alteration was the laying open of the crown to be as a prey

for him that could win it, and the change of the government into another line. . . .

In terms of this crude cyclic and periodic scheme, Howes identifies the second "alteration" with the Roman invasion of Britain by Julius Caesar (55, 54 B.C.), the third with the Saxon invasion some five hundred years later, the fourth ("a double blow, as it were, in the neck one of another") with the Danish incursions followed by the Norman Conquest (1066), the fifth with the Henrician reformation of the early sixteenth century, and the sixth with the accession of James I (1603).

This last alteration upon the revolution, which by God's divine providence was far more admirable, mild, gracious, and propitious to this kingdom than ever happened since it first was inhabited, came in the height of period or fullness of time when the hearts of the English were big swoln with grief and overgrown with fear, and the eyes of foreign neighbors fixed upon this land, expecting more strange and terrible events to have suddenly ensued upon the queen's [i.e., Elizabeth's] death than at any of the former alterations upon the revolutions; because by them, all the forenamed

---

accepted as sober fact by generations of patriotic chroniclers like Stow, Brut was a Trojan refugee (the son of Silvius, grandson of Ascanius, and great-grandson of Aeneas) who, having accidentally killed his father, wandered until at last, about eleven centuries before Christ, he came to the island to which he later gave his name, conquered the race of giants already in possession, and (as predicted by a riddling oracle) founded a line of kings that included Gorboduc, Ferrex and Porrex, Cymbeline, Lear, the celebrated Arthur, Cadwallader, and the Tudor-Stuart dynasties. This so-called British history—a charming blend of myth, folklore, and fiction—derives mainly from the *Historia regum Britanniae* that Geoffrey of Monmouth or Geoffrey ap Arthur (1100?–54), bishop of St. Asaph, constructed on some slender hints in Bede and Nennius and on the authority of "a very ancient book written in the British [i.e., Welsh] language" that had been given him by one Walter (or Galfridius), archdeacon of Oxford. Although Geoffrey's principal source was apparently unknown to any of his contemporary chroniclers—some of whom, indeed, like William of Newburgh and Ranulf Higden, doubted its existence—his work became so popular that it survives in more than two hundred manuscripts. It was translated into Anglo-Norman by Geoffrey Gaimar (whose version is lost) and by Wace as *Roman de Brut* (1155). Wace in turn inspired the splendid Middle English of Layamon's *Brut* (ca. 1205), whose vigorous embellishments of the Arthurian material stocked dozens of metrical romances and prose chronicles. Despite its great appeal for such old-fashioned historians as Stow—to say nothing of poets like Spenser, Drayton, and the younger Milton—the British history could not long survive the critical scrutiny of such scholars as William Camden (pp. 816 ff.) and John Selden (pp. 852 ff.), and by the middle of the 17th century it had been generally rejected as a fraud.
[4]Documents, records.
[5]*After . . . confusion*: This legend supplied the plot for Thomas Sackville and Thomas Norton's *Gorboduc* (acted 1561), one of the earliest English tragedies employing blank verse and a five-act structure.
[6]Dunvalla Molmutius, according to Geoffrey of Monmouth a son of Cloten, king of Cornwall, who gained the throne of Britain and established a legal code (the "Molmutine Laws") that he enforced throughout his realm.

time, policies, and practices were more observed abroad than noted or known at home, being free from the danger of laws which with great penalty (no less than high treason) forbade the English either to dispute or determine any person in the right of succession. When the queen, according to the course of nature, was past childbearing, she was often very importunately urged by Parliament with many humble petitions for the universal and everlasting safety of her kingdom and subjects that she would vouchsafe to appoint and declare her successor, but she would never 10 consent thereunto by any means, whereat the subjects' fear hourly increased, and the more because no care could cure their long-feared misery.

Then the rich began to hoard up money for a rainy day, and a general proverb passed current among all men that the time would come, which could not be far off, that a hundred pound of ready money should be better than an hundred pound of yearly revenues, and in that terror divers times there were more that offered land to sell than men to buy. Thus were the hearts of young and old perplexed, for 20 such as had fair possessions were at their wit's ends in devising which way they might leave the same in good estate in time to come without hope or means for their redress, but only humble prayers to the King of Kings, whose arm in mercy, as in justice, is never shortened, nor His hand wearied, inspired the forenamed nobility and Privy Councilors of estate,[7] uniting their hearts with due acknowledgment of our sovereign's [i.e., James'] right, and he as graciously approved their actions and desires in due obedience to his sovereignty, whose long patience in digesting 30 wrongs of sundry kinds offered to him and his without the least disturbance or impeach[8] of any practice or proceedings which were used to impair his right, and without all attempts of interruption to his land or state or will[9] to show his strength to take revenge, being daily thereunto provoked, and most strongly allied and backed by all Christian princes besides his proper[10] power and assured friends within this land who were always prest[11] to lay down their lives and goods in his true service and defense; all which laid together, with his said admired patience and free spirit duly consid- 40 ered, he hath given to all posterity a lasting precedent worth his honor and the greatness of so gentle and speedy an alteration.

The queen being but six hours dead, his right and dignity was straightway proclaimed and received with the greatest joy and peace that man's heart could wish, without any sign of faction or interruption, being universally glad to have a king of chastity, patience, piety, mercy, and judgment, wisdom, learning, bounty, peace, and munificence, having a hopeful issue and healthful race descended from the most 50 ancient kings of Europe, and from his infancy had continued in perfect amity with all Christian princes to the general good of all Christendom and weakening of the common enemy, the Turk.[12]

The effects of this alteration were in all respects clean different from all former changes and was no less wonderful to all other regions than beneficial to the English nation, who in a moment had their kingdom settled, the crown rightly established, the clergy cherished, the nobility ad-

vanced, their common laws continued, and the people resting in all tranquility, enjoying their ancient customs, laws, and liberties in as good and as ample manner as either their heart could wish or is enjoyed by any other nation; who were no sooner sensible of what high blessings they possessed but were instantly lulled in security and became senseless, forgetful, and unthankful of God's aboundant grace and mercy and of the unspeakable benefit of the unity and concord of king and peers of both kingdoms, being absolute instruments and good means that brought this wondrous work unto desired effect to the utter daunting[13] of all adversaries and endless admiration of all posterities.

And thus much briefly touching the law of history, the authority and proof of Brut and Troy, and the five[14] several changes and alterations, or revolutions, since the first habitation of this most famous and renowned island of Great Britain; and also of the effects and observations of every of those several changes, alterations, and revolutions.

All which, both generally and particularly, though here but briefly mentioned, yet their extremities, alterations, and effects worthily deserve judicious observation and lasting memory, especially by the rusty minds of this iron age, whose extreme willful forgetfulness and ingratitude for infinite benefits and boundless blessings received have compelled me in discharge of my duty diligently to search into the depth of our ancient English chronicles and others to place before their eyes a mirror of the miseries of former times. In setting down whereof I have used all diligence and laid away partiality with both my hands: I was bred and born free from schism and faction, hate contention.

The original and true purpose of chronology, as I said before, was to show successors the actions good and bad of their ancestors, and to remain as documents[15] to pursue the good and eschew the bad, and not to fill up great volumes with superfluous curiosity, lofty style, and needless eloquence, such as our forefathers never knew or heard of.

Plain truth was the ark I aimed at in the beginning, midst, and end; and in that simplicity of solid truth I end, leaving this short discourse as a token and remembrance to after ages but chiefly to those to whom it shall please Almighty God to give understanding of His divine mercy and judgments, hoping it will be as kindly accepted as it is freely offered. *Vale.*[16]

Edmund Howes

OF THE FIRST HABITATION OF THIS ISLAND

A SHORT NOTE TO THE READER

Where it is recorded by the sacred and most ancient history that after the universal flood the isles of the gentiles were divided by the posterity of Japheth, the son of Noah,[17] we

---

[7]State.   [8]Impediment.
[9]Any disruption in the normal functions of government?
[10]Own.   [11]Ready.
[12]For a contemporary's estimate of the Turkish peril see Richard Knolles' *General History of the Turks* (1603), pp. 836 ff.
[13]Intimidation.   [14]A mistake for *six*? See p. 809.
[15]Admonitions, warnings.   [16]"Farewell."
[17]*Where . . . Noah*: According to ancient legend, after the flood

doubt not but this isle of Britain was also then peopled by
his progeny, the history of whom, as it is to be wished, and
appertinent to this purpose, so sith[18] it is irrecoverable not
only unto us but also to other nations, I think it better to say
nothing therein than to set down here Samothes, Magus,
Sarron, Druys, and Bardus for his successors, which are
upholden and bolstered only by the credit and authority of
a new small pamphlet[19] falsely forged and thrust into the
world under the title of the ancient historian Berosus.[20]
For that is the censure of all the best learned as concerning 10
our common[21] Berosus, which at his first appearing about
one hundred years since was partly suspected by Lodovicus
Vives, afterward convinced to be fabulous by the learned
Gasparus Varrerius in a several treatise, and now universally
rejected of all skillful antiquaries as a mere fable unworthy
the name of Berosus. Therefore I dare not ground the begin-
ning of our history upon the credit thereof unless I would be
prejudicial to the truth, whereunto I level all my endeavor.
I hope it shall be sufficient in this history for the Britons'
time to follow the authority of the received *British History* 20
which Geoffrey, archdeacon of Monmouth, translated out
of the British tongue about four hundred years since, begin-
ning with Brut, who, after the progeny of Japheth, seemeth
to be first namer and ruler of this land. Yet before we enter
into the history of Brut it shall not be impertinent to note
here that whereas Pomponius Mela[22] mentioneth that one
Hercules killed Albion, a giant, about the mouth of Rhosne[23]
in France, many learned men have judged the said Albion
to have ruled here (sith the Greek monuments do alway call
this isle Albion); and after his death that Hercules came 30
hither, Lilius Giraldus[24] writeth. An ancient altar also con-
taining the inscription of a vow, found in the uttermost
north part of Britain fifteen hundred years since, as Solinus[25]
reporteth, plainly proved that Ulysses, the renowned
Grecian, in his ten years' travels after the sacking of Troy,
arrived in this our country. And thus much is found only in
approved histories as concerning Britain before the time
of Brutus.[26]

A BRIEF PROOF OF BRUT

The history of this Brut is affirmed by very many ancient
and learned historians, upon whose uniform consent, al- 40
though I dare not precisely defend that he was descended of
Aeneas of Silvius, or came hither by oracle accompanied
with Trojans, yet I dare boldly say that near the time here-
after mentioned there was one Brut or Brito, king of this
realm, which left it to his posterity. And the impugners of
this ancient history must not with so light a breath as they
do seem to blow away the authority of so many grave testi-
monies, the succession of so many princes, the founders of
so many monuments and laws, and the ancient honors of
the nations that first with public authority received Chris- 50
tianity. The names of the learned men that affirm this history,
or so many as are come to my knowledge, are these:

Stow then offers an imposing list of English historians
starting with Gildas and Nennius "before the Conquest,"
going on to Henry of Huntington, Matthew of Paris, Mat-
thew of Westminster, and Giraldus Cambrensis (as well as

"an ancient chronicle in French verse" that he had seen in the
library of Sir Robert Cotton, "a most diligent antiquary"),
and ending with such recent annalists as Robert Fabian,
Richard Grafton, Thomas Lanquet, and Thomas Cooper.

Against these so many, so ancient, so learned and judicious
authors (who had more books to inform them than we have,
and took more pains to be informed both by foreign and
domestical monuments than we can) are produced some
five or six strangers that either could not or would not look
into British antiquities, and not above one or two of our own
nation. Of these the chief is Johannes de Whethampsted,[27]
admitted to be an Englishman, yet not two hundred years
ago, who rather oppugneth the process and circumstances
of the narration than the person of Brut, saying that no such
thing is found in the Roman histories, nor any mention
made of any such Brut. To him Sir John Price, Master
Lambert, and Doctor Powell[28] shortly answer that an
argument negative *ab authoritate humana*[29] is not good, and
much worse it is to say that it is incredible that Brut should
kill his father and so come hither; therefore no such Brut
was. For by such inferences not only our own antiquities
but the Roman and all other ancient chronicles shall be
rejected, seeing not one of them is free from such imputa-
tions. And again, though many things be objected against
this Trojan pedigree, yet neither he nor any other objecteth
anything against the British pedigree set forth by Floriligus,[30]

the earth was repeopled by the three sons of Noah named in
Genesis 5.32, Shem being the progenitor of the Semitic races,
Ham of the Negro, and Japheth of the Aryan. [18]Since.
[19]Pamphlet.
[20]Babylonian priest of the 3d century B.C. who wrote, in Greek,
a history of the world allegedly tracing the 36,000 years from
Adam to Alexander the Great's conquest of Babylon. Parts of this
fanciful narrative were incorporated into the works of the Jewish
historian Flavius Josephus (37?–100) and of Eusebius of Caesarea
(260?–?330). The "new small pamphlet" to which Stow alludes so
disrespectfully was perhaps *Berosus Babylonicus. De his quae praeces-
serunt inundationem terrarum* (1498), a collection of forgeries at-
tacked by the eminent Spanish humanist Juan Luis Vives (1492–
1540) and exposed as fradulent by Garpar Barreiros (*Gasparus
Varrerius*), the Portuguese geographer (d. 1574), in his *Censura
in quendam auctorem qui sub falsa inscriptione Berosi Chaldaei. cir-
cumfertur* (1565). [21]Generally known.
[22]First-century geographer whose *De situ orbis* is the earliest Latin
description of the ancient world. [23]The River Rhone.
[24]Giglio Gregorio Giraldi (1479–1552), Italian poet and humanist
noted for his erudition.
[25]Gaius Julius Solinus (3d cent.?), author of a geographical com-
pendium (known variously as *Collectanea rerum memorabilium* or
Polyhistor) on the origin and history of various peoples. [26]Brut.
[27]John Whethamstede (d. 1485), abbot of St. Albans and author
of *Granarium de viris illustribus*.
[28]*Price . . . Powell*: Sir John Price (d. 1573?) was a Welsh antiquar-
ian who challenged Polydore Vergil's aspersions on the legendary
British history in *Historiae Britannicae defensio* and *Fides historiae
Britannicae*; William Lambarde (1536–1601) was the author of the
notable *Perambulation of Kent* (1570), the first history of an English
county; David Powell (1532?–98) was a Welsh historian whose
History of Cambria (1584) defended the authenticity of British
history. [29]"From human authority."
[30]Unidentified. Perhaps Stow had in mind the *Flores historiarum*,

Gildas,[31] and other British authors, as Sir John Price affirmeth. The next therefore is William Petit,[32] a Frenchman born, as his name importeth, who most sharply inveigheth not against Brut but against Galfridus Monmouthensis,[33] calling him the forger of the *British History*. This man lived in the time when Wales, not wholly subdued, stirred up wars against the English, and therefore not only speaketh of ignorance, being a stranger, but of spleen, to disgrace the Britains. And himself hath some things not very credible, as the tale of the green children caught in the sea, and such like. The last, Polidore, an Italian, though learned yet with a vainglorious envy to advance his own country will not endure that any other country shall have monuments of antiquity. And whereas the rest only except against[34] Brut, this man with one dash of a pen cashiereth threescore princes together, with all their histories and historians, yea, and some ancient laws also: a judgment so inconsiderate as of itself deserveth a censure, besides the manifold gross errors by every man now discovered in the rest of his story. To these are added Boccas, Vives, Junius, Buchanan, Bodin,[35] although learned yet strangers, like *pedarii senatores*[36] to fill up the number, and unfit to be witnesses in this case, seeing it cannot be presumed they had any understanding of the English tongue and much less of the Welsh. Wherefore there is no reason that such weak testimonies and arguments should remove the settled and approved authority of our ancient histories, whereof who desireth to be better informed let him read Sir John Price, John Leland,[37] Mr. Lambert, and other authors who have defended it more copiously.

THE RACE OF THE KINGS OF BRITAIN AFTER
THE COMMON RECEIVED OPINION
SINCE BRUT, ETC. . . .

[BRUT]

[Although many Tudor chroniclers—Raphael Holinshed, for instance—begin at the beginning with the creation of the world, Stow, following an introduction on the geography of the British Isles, more modestly starts with Trojan Brut.]

Brut therefore, according to the common opinion the son of Silvius, the son of Ascanius, the son of Aeneas, after the death of his father being banished into Greece, delivered there the remnant of the Trojans from their long captivity wherein they were detained under the Grecians, with whom he departed thence for to seek some habitation; and associating to himself Corineus with his Trojans (whom he found in the way), after a long and weary journey and many notable acts achieved in Aquitaine,[38] he arrived in this island (which was called Albion) at a place now called Totnes in Devonshire, the year of the world 2855, the year before Christ's nativity 1108. Wherein he first began to reign, and named it Britain (as some write), or rather after his own name Brutain. . . . Brut builded the city of New Troy, now called London; he established therein the Trojan laws and gave the uttermost western part of the realm to his companion Cor-

ineus, of whose name it was called Corinea, and to this day Cornwall. . . . And now, following the common opinion after Geoffrey Monmouth: Brut divided the whole island among his three sons which he had by Innogen, his wife: Locrine, Camber, and Albanact. Unto Locrine he gave the middle part between Humber and Severn, which of him was called Loegria. To Camber he gave all the region beyond Severn, which of him took the name of Cambria, and is now called Wales. To Albanact he gave all the lands beyond Humber, which of his name was called Albania. After which partition he deceased when he had reigned twenty-four years, and was buried at New Troy.

Locrine, the eldest son of Brut, reigned twenty years. He chased the Huns which invaded this realm and pursued them so sharply that many of them with their king were drowned in a river which then parted England and Scotland. And for so much as the king of Huns, named Humber, was there drowned, the river is till this day named Humber. This King Locrine had to wife Gwendoline, daughter of Corineus, Duke of Cornwell, by whom he had a son named Madan. He also kept as paramour the beautiful Lady Estrild, by whom he had a daughter named Sabrine. And after the death of Corineus he put from him the said Gwendoline and wedded Estrild; but Gwendoline repaired to Cornwall, where she gathered a great power and fought with King Locrine and slew him. He was buried at New Troy. She drowned the Lady Estrild with her daughter Sabrine in a river that after the young maiden's name is called Severn. . . .[39]

---

an immensely popular 16th-century compilation (long attributed to a nonexistent "Matthew of Westminster") that contained a long account of Brut. See p. 855, n.4.

[31]British historian of the sixth century whose *De excidio Britanniae* supplies a history of Britain from the earliest times. See p. 820 n.52.

[32]William of Newburgh (1136–98?), whose estimable *Historia rerum Anglicorum* denounces British history as a fabrication. A native of Yorkshire (and therefore not, as Stow infers from his name, a Frenchman born), he received his soubriquet Gulielmus Parvus (i.e., William the Little) from the Tudor antiquarian John Leland (on whom see note 37 below).

[33]Geoffrey of Monmouth.   [34]Reject.

[35]*Boccas . . . Bodin*: Giovanni Boccaccio, Juan Luis Vives, Franciscus Junius, George Buchanan, and Jean Bodin, eminent humanists and scholars between the 14th and 16th centuries (representing respectively Italy, Spain, France, Scotland, and France) who wrote on history and antiquities.

[36]"Inferior senators."

[37]English antiquarian (1506?–52) who vigorously defended the British history against Polydore Vergil in *Assertio inclytissimi Arturii, regis Britanniae* (1544). For his famous *New Year's Gift*, a report of his indefatigable researches presented to Henry VIII in 1545 and a kind of Magna Carta of Tudor chroniclers, see pp. 825 ff.

[38]A region of southwest France (ancient Aquitania).

[39]For a fuller account of the career of Trojan Brut and his descendants—including the parts that Stow rejects as merely fabulous—see Geoffrey of Monmouth, *The History of the Kings of Britain* (trans. Lewis Thorpe, The Penguin Classics, 1966), pp. 53–77.

[ARTHUR]⁴⁰

> Having traced the line of British kings from Brut to Cas-
> sibelanus, whose fate it was to lose his realm to Julius Caesar,
> Stow then inserts a long account ("painfully and carefully
> abstracted out of many grave and authentic authors") of
> Greek and Roman history, finally returning to his proper
> subject with a treatment of the long and "doubtful war"
> between the British and the "Saxon" Picts and Scots. It is
> here that he writes of Arthur as one of the last and greatest
> leaders of the ancient British race.

Arthur having abated the rage of the Saxons, as is afore- 10
showed, and reduced his country to quietness, he constituted
the Order of the Round Table, into the which order he only
retained such of his nobility as were most renowned for
virtue and chivalry. This Round Table he kept in divers
places, especially at Carleon, Winchester, and Camelet⁴¹
in Somersetshire. This Camalet, sometimes a famous town
or castle, standeth at the south end of the church of South
Cadbury;⁴² the same is situate on a very tor or hill, wonder-
fully strengthened by nature, to the which be two enterings
up by very steep way, one by north, another by southwest. 20
The very root of the hill whereon this fortress stood is more
than a mile in compass. . . .

There was found in memory of men a horseshoe of silver
at Camalet. The people can tell nothing there but that they
have heard say that Arthur much resorted to Camolet. . . .

There is yet to be seen in Denbighshire,⁴³ in the parish of
Lansanan, in the side of a stony hill, a place compassed,
wherein be the four and twenty seats for men to sit in, some
less and some bigger, cut out of the main⁴⁴ rock by man's
hand, where children and young men, coming to seek their 30
cattle, use to sit and play. They commonly call it Arthur's
Round Table.

While Arthur was valiantly occupied in his wars beyond
the seas (where he wrought many wonders, as some have
written, but far unlike to be true), Mordred, to whom he
had committed the government of Britain, confederating
himself with Cerdicus, first king of the West Saxons,
traitorously usurped the kingdom, of which treason when
relation came to Arthur, he speedily returned into Britain,
and at Richborough near to Sandwich⁴⁵ gave battle to him 40
and won the field. Anguisel of Scotland,⁴⁶ Gawain, and
Cador were there slain. Then pursuing him into Cornwall
gave him battle there again by the River of Alanne, of some
histories called Cablan,⁴⁷ where Mordred was slain. And
Arthur, being deadly wounded, was conveyed to Glaston-
bury,⁴⁸ where he died on the twenty-first day of May in
the year of Christ 542, and was there buried after he had
victoriously governed this realm twenty-six years. . . .
More than six hundred years after his death, to wit, about
the year of Christ 1189, which was the last year of the reign 50
of King Henry the Second, his body was found buried in
the churchyard betwixt two pillars, sixteen foot deep
underground; but those that digged the ground there to
find his body, after they had entered about seven foot deep
into the earth, they found a mighty broad stone with a leaden

cross fastened to that part which lay downwards towards
the corpse, containing this inscription:

> *Hic jacet sepultum inclitus Rex Arturius*
> *in insula Avalonia.*⁴⁹

This inscription was graven on that side of the cross which
was next to the stone, so that till the cross was taken from the
stone it was not seen. His body was found not enclosed
within a tomb of stone but within a great tree made hollow
like a trough, the which being digged upon and opened,
therein were found the bones of Arthur, which were of a
marvelous bigness, as Giraldus Cambrensis,⁵⁰ a learned man
that then lived, reporteth to have heard of the abbot of
Glastonbury. . . . The cross of lead with the inscription,
as it was found and taken off the stone, was kept in the
treasury or revester⁵¹ of Glastonbury church till the sup-
pression thereof in the reign of King Henry the Eight.

THE LIFE AND REIGN OF QUEEN ELIZABETH 1579

> As Stow, relentlessly canvassing the monarchs of the British
> Isles, approaches his own time, his data of course become
> more ample and precise, and in presenting them he eventu-
> ally acquires a kind of journalistic force. Some specimen
> entries from 1579—when he himself was in his fifties, and
> his queen was almost at the midpoint of her reign—may
> serve to represent his artless, annalistic method.

The four-and-twentieth of April fell such a snow betwixt the
hours of four of the clock in the morning and nine of the
clock before noon that at London some was found to lie
almost one foot deep.

The twenty-fifth of April Sir Thomas Bromley,⁵² knight,
was made Lord Chancellor of England.

The twenty-sixth of April William Kimpton, alderman
of London, was by the Lord Chancellor sent to the Fleet⁵³

---

⁴⁰For a more imaginative account of Arthur see Drayton's *Poly-
Olbion*, pp. 34 ff.

⁴¹Caerleon, a town on the River Usk in Monmouthshire; Win-
chester, ancient Celtic and Roman settlement in Hampshire, later
the seat of Alfred the Great; Camelot, alleged capital of King
Arthur, located variously in Hampshire, Somerset, and Wales.

⁴²Village in eastern Somerset containing ruins of unknown origin
still associated with King Arthur. ⁴³County in north Wales.

⁴⁴Solid. ⁴⁵Town in Kent, one of the ancient Cinque Ports.

⁴⁶In Geoffrey of Monmouth (trans. Thorpe, p. 258), "Auguselus,
the King of Albany."

⁴⁷The River Cablam (the modern Camel) in eastern Cornwall.

⁴⁸Ancient town in Somerset where, among the ruins of the
famous Benedictine abbey demolished (1539) by Henry VIII,
the so-called grave of Arthur is still to be seen.

⁴⁹"Here lies buried the renowned King Arthur [who is] in the
Isle of Avalon."

⁵⁰Giraldus de Barri (1146?–1220), Welsh cleric and historian,
author of *Itinerarium Cambriae*. ⁵¹Vestry.

⁵²Prominent Tudor statesman and jurist (1530–87), one of whose
last services for the crown was to preside over the trial of Mary
Queen of Scots (1586). ⁵³Ancient London prison.

about a letter late by him received from the vicar of Hadley in Middlesex beside Barnet.[54] This letter amongst other matters mentioned of a pale[55] pulled down at Northall by the commons there, etc., for concealing of which letter the said alderman was committed as aforesaid. And on the fifteenth of May was in the Starred Chamber[56] condemned to pay five hundred marks[57] fine and to remain prisoner at the pleasure of Her Majesty.

The fourth of May were arraigned at Barnet, in Hertfordshire, certain men of Northall, Mimms, and the parts near adjoining for pulling down a pale at Northall late set up on the common ground by the earl of Warwick; eight of them were condemned, two were burned in the hand, two were hanged betwixt Barnet and Whetstone; the other four condemned remained prisoners in Hartford gaol long after; many were bound[58] to appear at the next size,[59] and such as could not put in bail for their appearing were committed, etc. Matthew Hamont of Hethersett, by his trade a plowwright[60] three miles from Norwich, was convented[61] before the Bishop of Norwich[62] for that he denied Christ to be our Saviour. At the time of his appearance it was objected that he had published these heresies following: that the New Testament and Gospel of Christ are but mere foolishness, a story of men or rather a mere fable: *item*,[63] that man is restored to grace by the mere mercy of God without the mean of Christ's blood, death, and passion; *item*, that Christ is not God nor the Saviour of the world, but a mere man, a sinful man, and an abominable idol. . . . For the which heresies he was condemned in the consistory and sentence was read against him by the Bishop of Norwich the fourteenth of April, and thereupon delivered to the sheriffs of Norwich, and because he spake words of blasphemy against the Queen's Majesty and others of her Council he was by the recorder, Master Sergeant Windham, and the mayor, Sir Robert Wood of Norwich, condemned to lose both his ears, which were cut off the thirteenth of May in the marketplace of Norwich, where he confirmed his blasphemous speeches against our Saviour, Jesus Christ, for which on the twentieth of May he was burned in the castle ditch of Norwich.

The first of June deceased Robert Horne,[64] Doctor of Divinity, bishop of Winchester, at Winchester Place in Southwark,[65] and was buried at Winchester.

The seventeenth of July the Queen's Majesty, being on the River of Thames betwixt Her Highness' manor of Greenwich and Deptford[66] in her privy barge, accompanied with the French ambassador, the earl of Lincoln, and Master Vice-Chamberlain, etc., with whom she entered discourse about weighty affairs, it chanced that one Thomas Appletree, a young man and servant to Master Henry Cary, with two or three children of Her Majesty's Chapel[67] and one other, being in a boat on the Thames rowing up and down betwixt the places aforenamed, the aforesaid Thomas Appletree had a caliver or harquebus[68] which he had three or four times discharged with bullet, shooting at randon[69] very rashly, who by great misfortune shot one of the watermen, being the second man next unto the bales of the said

barge, laboring with his oar, which sat within six foot of Her Highness, clean through both his arms. The blow was so great and grievous that it moved him out of his place and forced him to cry and scritch[70] out piteously, supposing himself to be slain, and saying he was shot through the body. The man bleeding aboundantly, the Queen's Majesty showed such noble courage as is most wonderful to be heard and spoken of, for beholding him so maimed, she never bashed[71] threat but bade him be of good cheer, and said he should want nothing that might be for his ease, etc. For the which fact the said Thomas, being apprehended and condemned to death, was on the twenty-first of July brought to the waterside where was a gibbet set up, directly placed between Deptford and Greenwich, and when the hangman had put the rope about his neck he was by the queen's most gracious pardon delivered from execution. . . .

In September and October fell great winds and raging floods in sundry places of this realm, wherethrough many men, cattle, and houses were drowned. . . .

On Saturday, the twenty-first of November, Sir Thomas Gresham,[72] Knight, agent to the Queen's Highness, who had in his lifetime builded the Royal Exchange in London, as is aforeshowed, deceased at his house in Bishopsgate Street of London and was buried in the parish church of Saint Ellen there. By his last will and testament, dated *Anno* 1579, he gave to one hundred poor men so many black gowns of six shillings eight pence the yard; to one hundred poor women the like gowns at the day of his burial. . . .

Henry Fitzalan,[73] the last of that name, [twelfth] earl of

[54]Near Barnet, a town north of London in Hertfordshire.
[55]Fence.
[56]The Court of the Star Chamber, so called because its judges, most of whom were members of the Privy Council, met in an apartment of Westminster Palace whose roof was adorned with gilt stars. Noted for its severity in protecting the monarch's prerogatives, it became almost an instrument of terror under the Stuarts and was abolished by Parliament in 1641.
[57]Sums of money, each equivalent to two-thirds of a pound sterling.   [58]Put under legal obligation.
[59]Assize, stated meeting of a court.   [60]Maker of plows.
[61]Summoned.
[62]Edmund Freake (1516?–91), whose diocese was much plagued by Puritan dissidents.   [63]Also.
[64]Tudor cleric (1519?–80) notable for his zeal in harassing Catholics and demolishing their shrines and relics.
[65]Section of London on the south bank of the Thames, site of the bishop of Winchester's palace.
[66]Stretch of the Thames below the Tower and between the royal palace at Greenwich and the docks at Deptford.
[67]Boys recruited from the choristers of the Chapel Royal who performed both plays and music before the court.
[68]Kind of portable firearm.   [69]Random.   [70]Shriek.
[71]Was undaunted.
[72]Noted entrepreneur (1519?–79), financial agent for the crown, founder of the *Royal Exchange* and of Gresham College (to which he left his famous mansion in *Bishopsgate Street*, a principal thoroughfare of the City). His funeral in St. Helen's (*Ellen*) Church was one of the most elaborate of the century.
[73]Tudor statesman (1511?–80) whose later years were devoted

Arundel, deceased on the twenty-fourth of February and was buried at Arundel[74] on the twenty-second of March.

[When Stow died it fell to Howes, as his successor, to include the aged annalist in the work that he himself had carried on for almost half a century.]

Master John Stow of London, merchant tailor, a painful writer of the English chronicle for the space of forty-and-seven years, who purposed if he had lived but one year longer to have put in print Reyne Wolf's *Chronicle*,[75] which chronicle he began and finished at the request of Dr. 10 Whitgift,[76] late lord archbishop of Canterbury, but being prevented by death left the same in his study orderly written, ready for the press; but it came to nothing. He wrote also *The Survey of London*.[77]

He was tall of stature, lean of body and face, his eyes small and crystalline, of a pleasant and cheerful countenance, his sight and memory very good, very sober, mild, and courteous to any that required his instructions, and retained the true use of all his senses unto the day of his death, being of an excellent memory. He always protested never to have 20 written anything either for malice, fear, or favor, nor to seek his own particular gain or vainglory, and that his only pains and care was to write truth. He could never ride, but traveled on foot unto divers cathedral churches and other chief places of the land to search records. He was very careless of scoffers, backbiters, and detractors; he lived peacefully and died of the stone colic, being fourscore years of age, and was buried the eighth of April, 1605, in his parish church of Saint Andrew's Undershaft,[78] whose mural monument near unto his grave was there set up at the charges 30 of Elizabeth his wife.

THE LIFE AND REIGN OF KING JAMES 1618

[SIR WALTER RALEIGH'S EXECUTION]

About two years past, Sir Walter Raleigh[79] obtained his liberty and was discharged out of the Tower, and within a while after he built a goodly ship of war for a voyage to Guiana to gain possession of a rich mine which himself and one Captain Keymish[80] had formerly discovered by the information of the Indians inhabiting in that country; and for the furtherance of this voyage divers knights and gentlemen of quality furnished divers ships and went in consort with him. And whereas it was by them generally intended to 40 have been at Guiana in the moneth of April, they lingered so long that it was August before they set sail clear from the coast of England, by which tract of time all Christian nations understood the purpose of his voyage; and being come to Guiana could make no manner of discovery of any mine but found many new fortifications which were not formerly; and there they assaulted the new city of Saint Thome, and at the taking thereof his son, Master Walter Raleigh, was slain; and having sacked the city and taken the full spoil thereof, they burned it and four churches in it. 50

Then Sir Walter Raleigh with his ship returned for England, against whom the Spanish ambassador[81] had made divers complaints of damages, slaughters, and spoils done against the king of Spain and his people. Whereupon Sir Walter Raleigh was again committed to the Tower, for he never had his pardon for his former treason. And upon Wednesday the eight and twenty of October, viz. the Feast of Simon and Jude, Sir Walter Raleigh was brought from the Tower to the king's Bench bar, and by the Lord Chief Justice[82] was asked what he could say for himself, why he should not suffer execution of death according to the judgment of death for his treason in the first year of the king; whereupon he could not make any sufficient answer. And from thence he was carried to the Gatehouse, and the next morning about eight a clock he was brought upon a scaffold in the Parliament Yard, where for more than an hour's space he made sundry speeches as apologies to sundry imputations formerly laid upon him; and about nine of the clock his head was struck off. He died very resolutely; his head and body were buried at the discretion of his wife.[83]

---

largely to plots for replacing Elizabeth with her cousin Mary Queen of Scots.

[74]Ancient castle in Sussex, seat of the dukes of Norfolk.

[75]Presumably a continuation of the famous *Chronicles of England, Scotland, and Ireland* (1577) that the printer Renier (or Reginald) Wolfe (d. 1573) hired Raphael Holinshed (d. 1580?) to compile and that Stow himself had already seen through a second edition in 1587.

[76]John Whitgift (1530?–1604), primate for the last twenty years of Elizabeth's reign, who lived to celebrate the coronation of her successor James I in 1603.

[77]Perhaps Stow's most memorable work, a description of the capital first published in 1598 and still in print today.

[78]Early 16th-century church in Leadenhall Street, so called, according to Stow's *Survey of London*, because on May Day "an high or long shaft or May-pole was set up there, in the midst of the street" that was higher than the steeple.

[79]Famous Elizabethan explorer, courtier, and writer (1552?–1618). Tried and condemned (1603) on a trumped-up charge of treason against James I, he was reprieved and imprisoned in the Tower until 1616, when he was permitted to lead an expedition to Guiana (modern Venezuela) in search of the gold that had prompted an earlier voyage in 1595. The failure of the expedition, together with the destruction by Raleigh's lieutenant of the Spanish settlement of San Tomás on the Orinoco River (despite James' orders for a peaceful expedition), brought Raleigh home to certain death.

[80]Lawrence Kemys, (d. 1618), sea captain and adventurer. Long a friend and associate of Raleigh, when he realized that through his blunder in razing San Tomás his master was destroyed, he killed himself aboard his ship.

[81]Gondomar, count of Diego Sarmiento de Acuña (1567–1626), an inveterate foe of Raleigh and of his anti-Spanish policy.

[82]Sir Henry Montagu (1563?–1642), later earl of Manchester.

[83]The former Elizabeth Throgmorton, whom Raleigh had seduced and married about 1592, when she was one of Queen Elizabeth's maids of honor. Although she buried her husband's body in St. Margaret's Church, Westminster, she retained possession of his head which she kept by her in a velvet bag—perhaps as a memento—until she died.

William Camden [1551-1623]

Although Camden's erudition became a treasure of the nation, he, like many British worthies, had a slow beginning. The son of an artisan, he progressed from Christ's Hospital (where he may have been admitted as an orphan) to St. Paul's School and then (1566) to Oxford. There, after what may have been an unhappy start at Magdalen, he followed his new patron Thomas Thornton from Broadgates Hall to Christ Church; but when he failed to get a fellowship at All Souls he left the university (1571), apparently without even taking a degree. For several years thereafter (and with the financial support of Gabriel Goodman, dean of Westminster and uncle of Godfrey Goodman, who wrote the famous *Fall of Man*) he traveled up and down the realm, searching out antiquities, transcribing inscriptions, and preparing for the work that he was clearly born to do. Although an appointment (1575) to the second mastership in Westminster School—where Jonson, among others, came to venerate his learning (see p. 89)—must have interfered with his researches, it did not stifle his resolve to "renew ancientry, enlighten obscurity, clear doubts, and recall home verity." His efforts were crowned by the publication of the great *Britannia* in 1586, when he himself was only thirty-five. As Thomas Fuller said, this majestic work (which was dedicated to Lord Burleigh) "restored Britain to herself." Following an account of ancient Britain and of the invasions—Roman, Saxon, Danish, and Norman—that were the birth pangs of the modern nation, Camden at last arrived at his great task: a detailed description of the geography, resources, monuments, and antiquities of every country in England, Wales, Scotland, and Ireland (with "the smaller islands in the British Ocean"). It was a daring enterprise for one man to undertake, and in its range and size and erudition it reveals a kind of Renaissance exuberance. The work at once achieved the fame that it has never lost. By 1607 it had gone through six editions and expansions, and then in 1610 Philemon Holland—the Coventry physician whose versions of Livy, Pliny, Plutarch, and others qualified him as "the translator general in his age"—turned it into splendid English.

Although *Britannia* would have been enough to secure a dozen reputations it was just the start of Camden's great career. "Nothing remaineth now," he said in winding up the work,

> seeing my pen hath with much labor struggled and sailed at length out of so many blind shelves and shallows of the ocean and craggy rocks of Antiquity, save only this: that as seamen were wont in old time to present Neptune with their torn sails or some saved planks, according to their vow, so I also should consecrate some monument unto the Almighty and most gracious God, and to venerable Antiquity, which now right willingly and of duty I vow, and, God willing, in convenient time I will perform and make good my vow.

Camden kept his word. Two years after succeeding to the mastership of Westminster in 1593, he published a Greek grammar that stayed in use for many generations. In 1597 he was named (at Fulke Greville's instigation) Clarenceux King-of-Arms—a prestigious appointment that provoked a rancorous attack from one Ralph Brooke (pp. 821 ff.), his disappointed rival for the post. "An exact critic and philologist, an excellent Grecian, Latinist, and historian, and above all a profound antiquary," as John Aubrey later said, Camden had already gained a European reputation that he sustained and strengthened by steady publication. In addition to the progressive expansions of *Britannia* (which attained the dignity of a folio in 1607) his books included an account of the epitaphs and monuments in Westminster Abbey (1600); an edition (dedicated to Fulke Greville) of Asser, Walsingham, and other chroniclers (1603); the famous *Remains of a Greater Work Concerning*

Britain (1605), an antiquarian collection, dedicated to Sir Robert Cotton, that Camden himself described as "the rude rubble and outcast rubbish of a greater and more serious work"; and a history of the Gunpowder Plot (1607). But his second major undertaking, and the only rival to *Britannia*, was the splendid *Annales rerum Anglicarum et Hibernicarum regnante Elizabethae*, a book proposed to him by Burleigh in the old queen's later reign, whose first installment (1615) Camden said, took "eighteen years and more" to finish. In accordance with the author's wishes the second part was published posthumously in 1625. In introducing this great paean to the queen and to the country that he loved, Camden shows something of the modesty, the candor, and the high resolve that distinguish all his scholarship:

> What the loftiness of the argument requires, I confess, and am sorry I have not come up with; yet what pains I was able I have willingly bestowed. Myself I have not in the least satisfied, either in this or my other writings; yet shall I think myself well rewarded for my labor if by my ready willingness to preserve the memory of things, to relate the truth, and to train up the minds of men to honesty and wisdom I may thereby find a place amongst the petty writers of great matters. What it be, to God, my country, and posterity at the altar of Truth I dedicate and consecrate it.

In 1622, not long before his death, he established a professorship of history at Oxford (whose belated offer of a degree he had declined nine years before), and he had the satisfaction, as donor, of naming as its first incumbent his old friend Degory Wheare (for whose inaugural lecture see pp. 897 ff.). But "now having lived many years in honor and esteem," said Thomas Fuller, "death at last, even contrary to *jus gentium*, killed this worthy herald, so that it seems Mortality, the Law of Nature, is above the Law of Arms." His burial in Westminster Abbey was an honor richly earned.

My text is based on *Britain, or a Chorographicall Description of the Most flourishing Kingdomes, England, Scotland, and Ireland, and the Ilands adioyning, out of the depth of Antiquitie . . . Written first in Latine by William Camden Clarenceus K. of A. Translated newly into English by Philémon Holland Doctour in Physick: Finally, revised, amended, and enlarged with sundry Additions by the said Author*, 1610 (STC 4509). Even after Henry Holland published a new edition of his father's great translation in 1637, the year the old man died, Camden's masterpiece lived on for many generations. At the end of the century it began a new career in Edmund Gibson's enlarged translation, which went through four editions (1695, 1722, 1753, 1772) before a new version by Richard Gough supplanted it (1789, 1806). The *Remains* survived into Victoria's reign, the *Annales* into Anne's. Camden finds respectful mention, and often full discussion, in Kendrick, Wright, Fussner, and other writers on historiography in the General Bibliography, Section V, and there are assessments of his work by Sir Maurice Powicke (*Essays and Studies by Members of the English Association*, New Series, I, 1948), Stuart Piggott (*Proceedings of the British Academy*, XXXVII, 1951), and Hugh Trevor-Roper (*Queen Elizabeth's First Historian: William Camden and the Beginnings of English "Civil History,"* 1971). Wallace MacCaffrey has edited selections from the *Annals* with a useful introduction (1970).

from Britain (1610)

THE AUTHOR TO THE READER

I hope it shall be to no discredit if I now use again by way of preface the same words (with a few more) that I used twenty-four years since in the first edition of this work.[1] Abraham

BRITAIN [1]*Britannia* was first published (in Latin) in 1586.

Ortelius,[2] the worthy restorer of ancient geography, arriving here in England about thirty-four years past, dealt earnestly with me that I would illustrate this isle of Britain, or (as he said) that I would restore antiquity to Britain and Britain to his[3] antiquity; which was, as I understood, that I would renew ancientry,[4] enlighten obscurity, clear doubts, and recall home verity by way of recovery, which the negligence of writers and credulity of the common sort had in a manner proscribed and utterly banished from amongst us. A painful matter, I assure you, and more than difficult, wherein what toil is to be taken, as no man thinketh, so no man believeth but he that hath made the trial. Nevertheless, how much the difficulty discouraged me from it, so much the glory of my country encouraged me to undertake it. So while at one and the same time I was fearful to undergo the burden and yet desirous to do some service to my country, I found two different affections, fear and boldness, I know not how, conjoined in me. Notwithstanding, by the most gracious direction of the Almighty, taking industry for my consort, I adventured upon it; and with all my study, care, cogitation, continual meditation, pain, and travail I employed myself thereunto when I had any spare time. I made search after the etymology of *Britain* and the first inhabitants timorously, neither in so doubtful a matter have I affirmed aught confidently. For I am not ignorant that the first originals of nations are obscure by reason of their profound antiquity, as things which are seen very deep and far remote; like as the courses, the reaches, the confluence, and the outlets of great rivers are well known, yet their first fountains and heads lie commonly unknown. I have succinctly run over the Romans' government in Britain and the inundation of foreign people thereinto, what they were and from whence they came. I have traced out the ancient divisions of these kingdoms. I have summarily specified the states[5] and judicial courts of the same.

In the several counties I have compendiously set down the limits (and yet not exactly by perch and pole[6] to breed questions), what is the nature of the soil, which were the places of greatest antiquity, who have been the dukes, marquesses, earls, viscounts, barons, and some of the most signal and ancient families therein—for who can particulate[7] all? What I have performed I leave to men of judgment. But Time, the most sound and sincere witness, will give the truest information when Envy, which persecuteth the living, shall have her mouth stopped. Thus much give me leave to say: that I have in no wise neglected such things as are most material to search and sift out the truth. I have attained so some skill of the most ancient British and English-Saxon tongues; I have travailed[8] over all England for the most part; I have conferred with most skillful observers in each country; I have studiously read over our own country writers, old and new, all Greek and Latin authors which have once made mention of Britain; I have had conference with learned men in other parts of Christendom; I have been diligent in the records of this realm; I have looked into most libraries, registers, and memorials of churches, cities, and corporations; I have pored upon many an old roll[9] and evidence,[10] and produced their testimony (as beyond all exception), when the cause required, in their very own

words (although barbarous they be), that the honor of verity might in no wise be impeached.

For all this I may be censured unadvised and scant modest, who, being but of the lowest form in the school of antiquity, where I might well have lurked in obscurity have adventured as a scribbler upon the stage in this learned age amidst the diversities of relishes[11] both in wit and judgment. But to tell the truth unfeignedly, the love of my country (which compriseth all love in it and hath endeared me unto it), the glory of the British name, the advice of some judicious friends hath overmastered my modesty, and (willed I, nilled I)[12] hath enforced me against my own judgment to undergo this burden too heavy for me, and so thrust me forth into the world's view. For I see judgments, prejudices, censures, reprehensions, obtrectations,[13] detractions, affronts, and confronts[14] as it were in battail-array to environ me on every side: some there are which wholly contemn and avile[15] this study of antiquity as a back-looking curiosity; whose authority as I do not utterly vilify so I do not overprize or admire their judgment. Neither am I destitute of reasons whereby I might approve this my purpose to well-bred and well-meaning men which tender the glory of their native country; and moreover could give them to understand that in the studies of antiquity (which is always accompanied with dignity, and hath a certain resemblance with eternity) there is a sweet food of the mind well befitting such as are of honest and noble disposition. If any there be which are desirous to be strangers in their own soil and foreigners in their own city, they may so continue and therein flatter themselves. For suchlike I have not written these lines nor taken these pains. Some there be who may object the silly web of my style and rough-hewed form of my writing. Verily, I acknowledge it, neither have I weighed every word in goldmiths' scales, as Varro[16] commanded, neither purposed I to pick flowers out of the gardens of eloquence. . . .

To accomplish this work the whole main[17] of my industry hath been employed for many years with a firm settled study of the truth and sincere antique[18] faithfulness to the glory of God and my country. I have done dishonor to no nation, have descanted upon no man's name; I have impaired no man's reputation; I have impeached no man's credit, no not Geoffrey of Monmouth,[19] whose history (which I would gladly support) is held suspected amongst the judicious. Neither have I assumed upon myself any persuasion of knowledge but only that I have been desirous to know much. And so I right willingly acknowledge that I may err much, neither will I soothe and smooth my errors. Who,

[2]Abraham Ortelius (1527–98), Dutch geographer who visited England the year (1577) that his famous atlas *Theatrum orbis terrarum* was published. [3]Its. [4]Bring the past to life.
[5]Forms of government.
[6]By measuring rods, i.e., precisely. [7]Particularize.
[8]Traveled. [9]Register (of names, deeds, etc.).
[10]Piece of evidence. [11]Tastes. [12]Willy-nilly.
[13]Disparagements, slanders. [14]Confrontations.
[15]Deprecate, degrade.
[16]Publius Terentius Varro (116–27 B.C.), Roman scholar and historian of great erudition, most of whose voluminous works are lost. [17]Force. [18]Old-fashioned. [19]See p. 808, n.3.

shooting all day long, doth always hit the mark? Many matters in these studies are raked under deceitful ashes. There may be some escapes from memory, for who doth so comprehend particularities in the treasury of his memory that he can utter them at his pleasure? There may be mistakings in regard of my unskillfulness, for who is so skillful that, struggling with Time in the foggy dark sea of antiquity, may not run upon rocks? It may be that I have been misled by the credit of authors and others whom I took to be most true and worthy of credit. "Neither is there, verily," as Pliny saith, "any easier slipping from truth than when a grave author warranteth an untruth."[20] Others may be more skillful and more exactly observe the particularities of the places where they are conversant. If they, or any other whosoever, will advertise[21] me wherein I am mistaken, I will amend it with manifold thanks; if I have unwitting omitted aught, I will supply it; if I have not fully explicated any point, upon their better information I will more clear it, if it proceed from good meaning and not from a spirit of contradiction and quarreling, which do not befit such as are well bred and affect the truth. Meanwhile let your kind courtesy, my industry, the common love of our common mother our native country, the ancient honor of the British name obtain so much upon their entreaty that I may utter my judgment without prejudice to others, that I may proceed in that course that others have formerly done in the like argument, and that you would pardon my errors upon my acknowledgment, which may be as well hoped as requested from good, indifferent, and reasonable men. . . .

[THE LEGEND OF TROJAN BRUT]

One Geoffrey ap Arthur[22] of Monmouth, among us (whom I would not pronounce in this behalf liable to this suspicion),[23] in the reign of King Henry the Second[24] published an *History of Britain,* and that out of the British tongue, as he saith himself; wherein he writeth that Brutus, a Trojan born, the son of Sylvius, nephew[25] of Ascanius, and in a third degree nephew to that great Aeneas descended from supreme Jupiter (for the goddess Venus bare him), whose birth cost his mother her life and who by chance slew his own father in hunting (a thing that the wise magi had foretold), fled his country and went into Greece; where he delivered out of thraldom[26] the progeny of Helenus, King Priam's son, vanquished King Pandrasus, wedded his daughter, and accompanied with a remnant of Trojans fell upon the island Leogetia, where by the oracle of Diana he was advised to go unto this western isle. From thence through the Straits of Gibraltar, where he escaped the mermaids and afterward through the Tuscan Sea he came as far as to Aquitaine,[27] in a pight[28] battle defeated Golfarius the Pict, King of Aquitaine, together with twelve princes of Gaul; and after he had built the city Tours (as witnesseth Homer)[29] and made spoil of Gaul, passed oversea into this island inhabited of giants, whom when he had conquered together with Gogmagog, the hugest of them all, according to his own name he called it Britain, in the year of the world 2855, before the first Olympiad[30] 334 years and before the nativity of Christ 1108.

Thus far Geoffrey of Monmouth. Yet others there be that fetch the name of Britain from some other causes. Sir Thomas Elyot,[31] by degree a worshipful[32] knight and a man of singular learning, draweth it from the Greek "fountain," to wit πρυτανεία, a term that the Athenians gave to their public finances or revenues.[33] Humphrey Lhuyd,[34] reputed by our countrymen for knowledge of antiquity to carry, after a sort, with him all the credit and authority, referreth it confidently to the British word *prid-cain,* that is to say "a pure white form." Pomponius Laetus[35] reporteth that the Britons out of Armorica[36] in France gave it that name. Goropius Becanus saith[37] that the Danes sought here to plant themselves, and so named it Bridania, that is "Free Dania." Others derive it from Prutenia, a region in Germany. Bodin[38] supposeth that it took the name of[39] *bretta,* the Spanish word which signifieth "earth"; and Forcatulus,[40] of *brithin,* which, as we read in Athenaeus,[41] the Greeks used for "drink." Others bring it from the Brutii[42] in Italy, whom the Grecians

[20]Gaius Plinius Secundus, "the Elder" (23–79), *Historia naturalis,* V.i.12.   [21]Inform.

[22]Geoffrey son of Arthur, i.e., Geoffrey of Monmouth, whose father, according to Welsh legend, was one Arthur, a family priest of William, earl of Gloucester.

[23]The suspicion of having fabricated "facts" in the absence of reliable data (a practice that Camden had denounced in the previous paragraph).   [24]King of England (1154–89).

[25]Descendant (here, son).   [26]Bondage, captivity.

[27]*From thence . . . Aquitaine:* Apparently Camden errs. Brut, sailing westward from Greece, could hardly have entered the *Tuscan Sea* (i.e., the western Mediterranean) after passing Gibraltar on his way to *Aquitaine,* a region in southwestern France.

[28]Pitched, i.e., formally arranged.

[29]Camden is ironically quoting Geoffrey of Monmouth's own preposterous assertion. *Venit ad locum ubi nunc sita est civitas Turonorum: quam ut Homerus testatur, ipse postmodum construxit.*

[30]In antiquity, a method of computing time by the four-year intervals between successive Olympic games. Although the first Olympiad is normally reckoned as 776 B.C., Camden himself later (p. 820) dates it 770.

[31]Early Tudor humanist and statesman (1490?–1546), author of *The Book Named the Governor* (1531) and of a Latin-English dictionary (1538).

[32]Distinguished in respect of rank or character.

[33]Actually, the *prytaneia* ("presidency") was the term of office (some thirty-five days) of the leaders in the Council of Five Hundred in ancient Athens.

[34]Humphrey Llwyd (1527–68), Welsh antiquarian, author of *The Breviary of Britain* (1573).

[35]Julio Pomponio Leto (1425–98), Italian humanist who wrote on Roman antiquities and literature.

[36]Ancient name for Brittany.

[37]Joannes Goropius (1518–72), Flemish antiquarian whose works included a commentary on Tacitus' *Germania* called *Notationes de origine et antiquitate gentis et linguae Cimbricae seu Germanicae* (1580).

[38]Jean Bodin (1530–96), eminent French historian and political economist, author of *Methodus ad facilem historiarum cognitionem* (1566).   [39]From.

[40]Etienne Forcadel (d. 1573), French jurist and humanist.

[41]Greek grammarian (fl. ca. 200) whose only extant work, *The Deipnosophists,* describes contemporary social behavior and customs.   [42]Ancient inhabitants of southern Italy.

called βρεττιοι. As for those smatterers in grammar who keep a babbling and prating that Britain should carry that name of brutish manners, let them be packing.

These are all the opinions (to my knowledge) that have been received touching the name of Britain. But herein as we cannot but smile at the fictions of strangers, so the devices coined by our own countrymen pass not current with general allowance. And verily in these and suchlike cases an easier matter it is to impeach the false than to teach and maintain a truth. For besides this, that it were an absurdity to seek the reason of this name in a foreign language, the general consent of all historiographers of better note doth confute Laetus, who with one accord deliver unto us that those Armorican Britons departed hence and so from us carried the name with them. Again, Britain flourished under this name many hundred years before the names of Dania and Prutenia came up. But what hath the word *Britannia* to do with the Spaniards' *bretta,* which I doubt whether it be Spanish or no? And why should this island be so termed rather than any other land? That the drink called *brithin* was ever in use among our countrymen can hardly be proved, and to give name to our nation of the Greeks' drink were ridiculous. As for those Brutii in Italy, whom, as Strabo[43] witnesseth, the Luccans called βρεττιοι, as one would say "traitorous fugitives," it can never be proved that they like runagates[44] ran hither into Britain. But to come now to our own countrymen's conjectures; Elyot's πρυτανεια seemeth not probable, seeing that word was proper to the Athenians, and considering the Greeks called this isle βρετανιαν, not πρυτανειαν, Lhuyd's *prid-cain* for *Britain* seemeth not only too far-fetched but also overhardly strained—to say nothing how that word *cain* came from the Latins' *candidum,* and so crept into the provincial language of the Britains.

But as touching those reports of Brutus: were they true, certain, and undoubted, there is no cause why any man should bestow farther study and labor in searching out the beginning of the Britains; the thing is dispatched to our hand, and the searchers of antiquity are eased of their troublesome and painful travel. For mine own part, it is not my intent, I assure you, to discredit and confute that story which goes of him, for the upholding whereof (I call Truth to record) I have from time to time strained to the height[45] all that little wit of mine. For that were to strive with[46] the stream and current of time, and to struggle against an opinion commonly and long since received. How, then, may I, a man of so mean parts and small reckoning, be so bold as to sit in examination of a matter so important and thereof definitively to determine? Well, I refer the matter full and whole to the senate of antiquarians for to be decided. Let every man, for me, judge as it pleaseth him; and of what opinion soever the reader shall be of, verily I will not make it a point much material.

And yet I see—that I may tell you so much aforehand, being, as I am, a plain, honest, and diligent searcher after the truth—how men most judicious and passing well learned go about divers ways to extenuate[47] the credit of this narration, and so often as I stand in defense thereof to come upon me fiercely with these and suchlike arguments. First, grounding their reason upon the time, they protest and say that all is but fabulous (with reservation only of the sacred history)[48] whatsoever is reported to have been done before the first Olympias,[49] to wit the year 770 before the birth of Christ, like as these reports of Brutus, which are before the said time 300 years and more. . . . Then they allege that for the confirmation of this matter in question the authority of sufficient writers (which to the knowledge of things past maketh most, and is all in all) is altogether defective. Now, those they call sufficient writers, whose antiquity and learning the greater it is so is their credit the better accepted, who all of them (like as the ancient Britains themselves, by their saying) knew not so much as the name of Brutus. Caesar, say they, sixteen hundred years since, as he testifieth himself, "by all the inquiry that he could make found no more but this, that the inland part of Britain was inhabited by those who, they said, were born in the very island, and the maritime coasts by such as from out of Belgium passed over thither."[50] Tacitus also, a thousand and four hundred years ago, who searched diligently into these particulars, wrote thus: "What manner of men the first inhabitants of Britain were, born in the land or brought in, as among barbarous people it is not certainly known."[51] Gildas,[52] being himself a wise and learned Britain who lived a thousand years since, hath not one word of this Brutus, and doubteth whether the old Britains had any records or writings whereby they might convey unto posterity their own beginning and history. . . . Nennius[53] also, a disciple of Elvodugus,[54] taking in hand to write a chronicle eight hundred years ago, complaineth that "the great masters and doctors of Britain had no skill and left no memorial in writing," confessing "that himself gathered whatsoever he wrote out of the annals and chronicles of the holy fathers." To these they adjoin Beda,[55] William of Malmesbury,[56] and as many as wrote eleven hundred and threescore years since, who seem not once to have heard of Brutus his name, so silent are they of him in all their own writings.

[43]Greek geographer (63 B.C.–24), whose *Geography* describes most of the known world of his time, discusses the *Brutii* at VI.i.4. Camden's *Luccans* are the Leucani, a tribe of southern Italy who lived adjacent to the Brutii. [44]Renegades. [45]Height.
[46]Swim against. [47]Disparage.
[48]History recorded in the Bible, which was generally thought to be of unimpeachable authority and veracity. See p. 901.
[49]Olympiad. [50]*De bello Gallico,* V.xii.
[51]*De vita Iulii Agricolae,* Sect. 10.
[52]British historian (516?–?570) whose *De excidio Britanniae,* a history of Britain from the earliest times, makes no mention of Brut or King Arthur but does record the great battle of Mt. Badon with which Arthur was later associated.
[53]Welsh historian of the late eighth century whose *Historia Britonum* is a compilation based upon (and formerly identified with) Gildas' *De excidio Britanniae.* The quotation is from the "Prologus" to his works (trans. A.W. Wade-Evans, 1938, p. 35).
[54]Elbodugus, bishop of Bangor (d. 809), whose *"discipulus"* Nennius (*Historia Britonum,* "Prologus") claimed to be.
[55]The so-called "Venerable" Bede (673–735), eminent English scholar and churchman, abbot of Jarrow, of whose many works the *Historia ecclesiastica gentis Anglorum* is most notable.
[56]Historian (d. 1143?) who compiled *Gesta regum Anglorum* and its sequel *Historia novella.*

Hereupon they have noted that the name of that Brutus was never heard of in the world before that in a barbarous age, and amid the thickest clouds of ignorance, one Hunibald,[57] a bald[58] writer, fabled and feigned that Francio, a Trojan, King Priam's son, was the founder of the French nation. Hence they collect that when our countrymen heard once how the Frenchmen, their neighbors, drew their line from the Trojans, they thought it a foul dishonor that those should outgo them in nobility of stock whom they matched every way in manhood and prowess. Therefore that Geoffrey ap Arthur of Monmouth, four hundred years ago, was the first, as they think, that to gratify our Britains produced unto them this Brutus, descended from the gods, by birth also a Trojan, to be the author of the British nation. And before that time, verily, not one man, as they say, made any mention at all of the said Brutus. . . .

As for these observations and judgments of other men which I have recited, I beseech you let no man commence action against me, a plain-meaning man and an ingenuous student of the truth, as though I impeached that narration of Brutus; forasmuch as it hath been always, I hope, lawful for every man in suchlike matters both to think what he will and also to relate what others have thought. For mine own part, let Brutus be taken for the father and founder of the British nation, I will not be of a contrary mind. Let the Britains resolve still of their original to have proceeded from the Trojans (into which stock, as I will hereafter prove, they may truly ingraff[59] themselves), I will not gainstand it. I wot full well that nations in old time for their original had recourse unto Hercules and in later ages to the Trojans. Let antiquity herein be pardoned if by intermingling falsities and truths, human matters and divine together, it make the first beginnings of nations and cities more noble, sacred, and of greater majesty; seeing that, as Pliny writeth, "even falsely to claim and challenge descents from famous personages implieth in some sort a love of virtue."[60] As for myself, I willingly acknowledge with Varro, the best-learned of all Romans, such originals as these, fetched from the gods, "to be profitable that valorous men may believe, although untruly, that they are descended from the gods and thereby the mind of man, assuredly persuaded of some divine race, may presume to enterprise great matters more boldly, act the same more resolutely, and upon the very security thereof perform all more happily."[61] By which words, nevertheless, St. Augustine gathereth that the said most learned Varro confesseth (although not stoutly nor confidently, yet covertly) that these opinions are altogether truthless. . . .

[57]Perhaps an allusion to a treatise entitled *De origine gentis Francorum compendium . . . ex duodecim ultimis Hunibaldi libris quorum sex primos Wasthaldus conscripsit* that the German jurist Simon Schard (1535–73) included, with many similar texts, in his compilation *Historicum Opus, in quatuor tomos divisum* (1574).
[58]Devoid of ornament or grace.   [59]Engraft.
[60]*Historia naturalis*, XXXV.ii.8.
[61]Quoted from Varro (see n.16 pp. 818) by St. Augustine (354–430), greatest of the early fathers of the church, in *De civitate Dei*, III.iv.

Ralph Brooke [1553-1625]

Ralph Brooke would scarcely earn a place in this anthology for the vigor of his style and sweetness of his character, but as party to a once famous literary squabble he not only illustrates a seamy side of Jacobean scholarship but also, in his forlorn attempt to mortify a better man, enables us to catch a glimpse of John Leland, the early Tudor antiquary who proclaimed the need for such a mighty work as William Camden finally wrote in his *Britannia* (pp. 817 ff.). Brooke's attack on Camden was no doubt prompted more by envy and a sense of injured merit than by his adversary's errors. Humbly born like many scholars, he had been a student at the Merchant Taylors' School and then a member of the Painter Stainers' Company before his appointment (1580) as Rouge Croix Pursuivant in the Heralds' College, a post in which he labored thirteen years before his first and last promotion (to York Herald). An able genealogist, he was also known to be an angry and embittered man, and he may have planned his exposé of *Britannia* in 1594, when that enormously successful book attained its fourth edition. His anger must have been inflamed anew, however, when his upstart rival—not even a member of the Heralds' College—was irregularly named Richmond Herald on 23 October 1597 and the next day advanced to Clarenceux King-of-Arms. Nothing could justify such favoritism except Camden's reputation and distinction, but one of these Brooke thought overblown and the other he denied. Thus it was that in 1599 he published his *Discovery of Certain Errors Published in Print in the Much Commended Britannia.*

Although Camden replied temperately to Brooke's virulence and arrogance in the preface to the fifth (1600) edition of *Britannia*, he also, like a wise and generous man, accepted some of Brooke's corrections. There he let the matter rest; but the irascible Brooke continued his attack in *A Second Discovery* (which remained in manuscript until 1723), and then, having nursed his rancor for almost twenty years, renewed his charges in 1619 in *A Catalogue and Succession of the Kings, Princes, Dukes, Marquisses and Viscounts of the Realm of England* (which he expanded and reprinted in 1622). This long, unseemly controversy was finally laid to rest in 1622 when Augustine Vincent (1584?–1626), a protégé of Camden who subsequently became Windsor Herald, published his *Discovery* of the errors in Brooke's own *Catalogue*. Vincent said that he approached Brooke's disclosures with a certain apprehension, but as he went farther in the book and saw its author "grow from vinegar to gall and from gall to venom against so renowned and revered a man, and the same mixed with pride, arrogancy, and admiration of himself," he began to look for Brooke's own faults, which he found and itemized in great abundance. In the 1622 edition of his *Catalogue,* Brooke, still smarting at the "calumniations" of such "envious detractors," blamed his lapses on the printer—but what answer could be made to the charge that his "tongue glided over no man's name but that it left a slime behind it"? When Brooke died in 1625 he had at least outlived his ancient foe. It was a meager triumph, to be sure, but no doubt one that gave him angry satisfaction.

Whereas Brooke, in eking out his *Discovery* with Leland's *New Year's Gift,* sought to show how Camden had plagiarized his predecessor's work, he showed instead how a vision was fulfilled. After almost a decade of traveling the length and breadth of England to gather data for a massive history and description of the realm, John Leland (1506?–52)—whom Henry VIII had named his "antiquary" in 1533—made a preliminary report of his researches and intentions to the king in 1545. Spurred by patriotic zeal (which was reinforced by a savage disesteem of his Roman Catholic rivals) and well equipped by learning, Leland might have hoped to write the book that Camden later wrote; instead, he died insane, having published almost nothing. His enormous labor was not wholly lost, however, for eight volumes of his *Itinerary* and five of his disordered *Collectanea* survived in manuscript to be quarried by generations of English scholars (including Camden) before Thomas Hearne at long last prepared them for the press in the early eighteenth century. *A New Year's Gift* was published (with extensive annotations) by Leland's friend and fellow-antiquary John Bale in 1549 and first reprinted by Brooke in his *Discovery* half a century later.

My text is based on *A Discoverie of Certaine Errours Published in Print in the much commended Britannia,* 1599 (misdated 1596 in STC 3834). There is a full account of the Brooke-Camden imbroglio by Sir Nicholas Harris Nicolas, *Memoir of Augustine Vincent, Windsor Herald* (1827).

from A Discovery of Certain Errors ... (1599)

To the Right Honorable Robert Earl of Essex, Earl Marshal of England[1]...

Right Honorable, having upon diligent search apprehended within the compass of my profession and science of heraldry certain errors in descents and successions[2] such as may be scandalous to the gray hears[3] of Antiquity and prejudicial to the branches of our nobility, I thought it my duty to present them as captives at Your Honor's feet, being the undoubted champion of Truth and the worthy marshal of all heroic magnanimity and honor, unto whom I humble

myself for a favorable censure and protection of this my poor service. As no child is so deformed but the father commonly hath a natural affection towards it, so these erors will

DISCOVERY OF CERTAIN ERRORS [1]Robert Devereux (1566–1601), second earl of Essex, Elizabeth's favorite courtier in her later years, who as Earl Marshal (1597) was *ex officio* head of the Heralds' College and thus the proper person with whom to register complaints about Camden's faulty genealogies. For John Speed's account of Essex' rebellion and execution see pp. 843 ff. [2]Genealogies and transmission of hereditary titles. [3]Hairs.

no doubt be both fathered and favored of the author, whose reputation for learning is so great, and beard of Antiquity lately grown so long, that the goodly Britannia, mother of us all, is become his daughter, trained up and taught to speak Latin in his school—only she lisps, and makes no good congruity in these principles of heraldry. For which I challenge him, not that my exception and challenge is about the words and terms of our art—that is the least—but touching the falsifying of noble descents, depriving some nobles of issue to succeed them, who had issue of whom are descended 10 many worthy families; naming others to have but one sole daughter and heir when they had divers sons and daughters; denying barons and earls that were and making barons and earls of others that were not; mistaking the father for the son and the son for the father; affirming legitimate children to be illegitimate and illegitimate to be legitimate; those to be basely born who were indeed descended of very honorable parentage; assigning arms and ensigns of honor to others not their own; lastly, the framing incestious[4] and unnatural marriages, making the father to marry his son's wife and the 20 son his own mother. These and suchlike matters of importance are the errors that I have examined and attached,[5] to abide Your Honor's censure and reformation, for whom, with bowed heart and knee, I pray to God for all increase of honor, heart's contentment, and happy victory.

Your Honor's in all duty,

Ra. Brooke,

York Herald-at-Arms

To Master Camden

Whereas you expect thanks at the hands of Her Majesty's heralds for intermeddling so "sparingly" and "gently" with 30 that which appertaineth to their profession, contrary to your expectation and answerable to your deserts myself (being the most unable) have undertaken to answer your unkind speeches, as also your untrue and erroneous writing touching matters of our profession and science published in your *Britannia.* Indeed, you dealt but "sparingly" and after a sort "gently," as you say, in the handling of our mysteries[6] at the first, but in your fourth and last edition,[7] though your "Preface" spake as it did, "sparingly still," yet your book hath swelled with large additions of heraldry, in which you 40 have (by your patience) been too busy and venterous[8] except your proceedings in those points had been more firmly grounded upon experience. And I doubt not but the growth and increase of your book hath sprung from some of those heralds' labors which you so much hold in scorn. Nay, it cannot be denied but since the death of Glover,[9] late Somerset Herald, 1588, you have gleaned not only handfuls but whole sheaves out of his industrious collections, being reserved in the library of that Honorable Lord Treasurer deceased[10] and by that means incommoned[11] to your use 50 and free recourse. I would his gloves might have fitted your hands in such sort as you might have smoothly carried them away: his notes, I mean, I wish you had neither misunderstood nor misreported, as contrariwise you have, in such palpable manner that, methinks, ever hereafter you should distrust yourself in the search of such mystical points without the advice of an herald better experimented[12] than yourself.

I prognosticate already what entertainment in these mine advertisements[13] I shall have. It will be objected from yourself that I understand not your book. I confess mine intelligence not so great, but my fear is the greater, and my care the more, to understand you by helps, so that the trust in myself is the less. And this suspicion, I hope, will force me to make sure work in that I undertake. Valure,[14] they say, may be too bold, and learning too full of quillities,[15] the one standing more upon the bravery of his fight than the goodness of the quarrel, the other more upon the generality of his knowledge than the truth of his cause. The mother tongue of every nation, as you affirm, is the best conserver of original names, and yourself endeavor to get a more ample credit in history by avouching that you have read over many homebred historians. By your example, therefore, I am induced to believe that English authors and English heralds (though they have concealed their travails from the world, and not published a *rapiamus*[16] general upon every light occasion) are to be credited for the truth of English successions, descents, and reports of all honorable designments.[17]

Again, who is more unfit to describe the truth of actions in their proper nature than such affectate[18] novices as have their mouths and pens running over with the foaming must[19] of unrefined eloquence, who choose rather to let the truth of the matter slip than to abate one title of their self-pleasing phrase? Therefore, I have heard many great statesmen affirm that the court hath afforded more absolute wisemen for any active employment in the commonwealth than the schools, which falleth out especially because to these proceedings of the one in art there hath not been added some lecture of discretion to qualify the same withal, which is to be had daily by examples and practice in the other.[20] And doubtless for a mere scholar to be an historian, that must take up all by hearsay and uncertain rumors, not being acquainted with the secrets and occurrences of state matters, I take it—as many others affirm with me—very unfit and

---

[4]Incestuous. [5]Attacked.
[6]The complex technical problems of genealogical research.
[7]Following its first appearance in 1586, Camden's *Britannia* went through new and enlarged editions in 1587, 1590, 1594, 1600, and 1607. Philemon Holland's English version appeared in 1610. See p. 816. [8]Venturous.
[9]Robert Glover (1544–88), Portcullis Pursuivant (1567) and Somerset Herald (1571) in the Heralds' College, a famed genealogist who assisted Camden in his *Britannia* (1586), and whose *industrious collections*—an enormous mass of manuscript material on genealogy and topography—have been drawn upon by antiquarians until almost the present day.
[10]William Cecil, Baron Burghley (1520-98), Lord High Treasurer (1572-98) and chief minister of Elizabeth, who purchased part of Glover's voluminous manuscript collections. [11]Made accessible.
[12]Experienced. [13]Admonitions, instructions. [14]Valor.
[15]Quibbles. [16]"Let us plunder." [17]Heraldic designations.
[18]Affected. [19]Unfermented wine or liquor.
[20]*Which falleth . . . other:* mere book learning must be reinforced by practical experience.

dangerous. I hope you will, in some sort, acknowledge this to be true if indifferently you take a view of these errors by yourself committed, a man of so rare knowledge and singular industry. Yet no one man so generally well seen[21] in all things but an inferior person in some one special matter may go beyond him. In regard whereof, contemn not these few collections of mine (wherein I have not vaunted my learning, but cleared the truth according to the oath and profession of an herald) unless learnedly with truth you confute the same. Until then, I bid you farewell.

A Discovery of Divers Errors...

> In the body of his work Brooke sallies forth to meet the foe. His procedure—to quote a passage from *Britannia* and then to expose and ridicule its errors—is effective, for despite his tedious irony and vituperation he usually has his facts secure. A few examples will suffice.

Widehay was the ancient seat of the Barons St. Amand, whose inheritance and dignity came to Gerald Braybroke in right of his wife; and Elizabeth, his grandchild by Gerald his son, transported the same to William de Beauchamp, who left issue but one only son, which was a bastard.

[*Britannia*,] *pagina*[22] 207.

What an ungodly course is this you take to deprive noblemen both of their honor and honesty, framing to some unnatural marriages, falsifying the descents of others, and making legitimate heirs illegitimate! Which abuses, by reason of my oath taken at my creation,[23] I may not let pass without telling you thereof. Understand therefore that where you affirm William Beauchamp, Lord St. Amand (who married Elizabeth, grandchild to Gerald Braybroke) to have issue one only son, and he a bastard, therein do you greatly both wrong and scandalize him, for he had in lawful matrimony by his said wife Richard Beauchamp, Lord St. Amand, his legitimate son that succeeded him in the dignity of St. Amand and married Anne, the daughter of Sir Walter Wrotesley, Knight. And therefore very untruly have you charged the said William to have had any such bastard.[24]

> "Now let us come to the Earls of Warwick. And to let pass Guare, Morindus, Guy that bare the bell of England,[25] and others of like account whom the fruitful wits of our Heralds were brought abed with all at one birth &c."
> [*Britannia*,] *pagina* 438.

By this may all men evidently see your malicious and disdainful humor against Her Majesty's Heralds of Arms, in that you cannot be contented in many other places of your book to make doubt and question of their reports and doings, whether the same may be credited, yea or no, but here most injuriously and falsely you charge them to have brought forth for earls of Warwick Guare, Morindus, Guy the Bell-ringer, and many others of that rank, of which, though Rous of Warwick and others have written of Guy, yet are not you able to justify that the heralds were authors of any such suspected chieftains. And in that you make Your Worship merry with "the fruitful wits of our heralds," supposed by you "to have been brought abed with those imagined earls all at one birth," I wonder that so cunning a

midwife should make us the reputed fathers of those which we never wrapped up within the sheets or leaves of our records. But such a midwife, such a nurse are you, as have not only changed other men's children in the cradle and sophisticated the reports of worthy authors, but also most ungratefully have charged the parents and first collectors of many sound notes—helpful to your credit and labors—as the inventors of your misreports, whereby you have not only falsified in your book many things concerning the descents of noble families, imagining of your own brain, divers nobles to have been that never were, and extinguishing the memorial of others that were, but also most untruly have made Her Majesty's heralds the authors of feigned stories and legends of lies, when beside concealment of many favors received from the heralds you cease not to carp at them from whose works you have borrowed the substance of your heraldy[26] and the grounds of your skill in descents; therefore owe them good words at the least for your own credit, lest they should call for their lent feathers again and leave you naked of your armory as Aesop's crow.[27]

> "The first lord of Coventry was Leofric, from whom by Luce, his niece (daughter of Algar, his son), it passed to the earls of Chester; for she married the first Ranulph of Chester, &c."
> [*Britannia*,] *pagina* 434.

From Lincoln to Coventry is a long and wearisome journey, especially when the traveler is ignorant of the way and

[21]Versed.   [22]Page.
[23]Appointment as an officer in the Heralds' College.
[24]For an authoritative account of this complex genealogy see *The Complete Peerage* (ed. Geoffrey H. White), XI (1949), 301 f.
[25]*Guare...England: The Rows Rol*, a eulogistic and lavishly illustrated history of the earls of Warwick by John Rous (1411?–91), chaplain of the chantry at Guy's Cliff, near Warwick, describes Gwayr (*Guare*) as a "noble prince" of the ancient Britons, a "nigh cousin" of King Arthur, and an earl of Warwick who, by withstanding the attack of a giant armed with a branch torn from a tree, bequeathed to his descendants their famous insignia of a ragged staff. *Morindus* is probably the Morvidius mentioned by Rous as another earl of Caerware (i.e., Warwick). *Guy* is a famous legendary hero of French and English romance, a son of the earl of Warwick's steward whose exploits (long accepted as true by chroniclers) included combats with the Saracens, a pilgrimage to the Holy Land, marriage with Felice, daughter of Earl Roalt, a famous victory over the Danish giant Colbrand, and a tranquil old age as a holy hermit at Guy's Cliff (where, in 1423, Richard de Beauchamp, earl of Warwick, built a chantry to celebrate his memory). Among Guy's alleged relics in Warwick Castle is his so-called porridge pot, a large vessel made of bell-metal. The continuing popularity of his story is attested by two French and four Middle English romances, John Lydgate's mid-fifteenth-century poem based on the Latin of Girardus Cornubiensis, various chapbooks and ballads, Samuel Rowlands' *Famous History of Guy, earl of Warwick* (1607 ff.), a lost play (1618–19) by John Day and Thomas Dekker, the thirteenth "Song" (or canto) of Michael Drayton's *Poly-Olbion* (1612), and many other works.   [26]Heraldry.
[27]According to a fable traditionally ascribed to Aesop, when a crow disguised himself in the plumage of the peacock and tried to pass as a handsome bird, he was stripped of his borrowed finery and exposed as a fraud.

wanteth a guide, as here, it seemeth, you did when you passed
from the one to the other; and setting down the successions
of the earls of Lincoln and lords of Coventry, where in the
first you have made Luce (daughter of Algar the Saxon) to
be wife to Ranulph, the second earl of Chester, and after in
the other (not far distant) to be wife to Ranulph, the first
earl of Chester, the one being the father and the other his
son. But how lawful a thing it is for the father to marry his
son's wife, or the son his own mother (as your words in
these two places import), I refer myself to the judgment of ₁₀
the indifferent readers.

An Enforced Conclusion

Whenas I had collected ready for the press so many of
your defects and errors (published in your so highly com-
mended *Britannia*) as might well have satisfied the world
that I undertook not this work in vain, nor yet without
good cause me moving thereunto, then was I stayed in the
printing thereof by the disturbance and indirect dealing of
your friends the stationers (who heretofore have made no
small gain of your four former impressions) and thereby
constrained abruptly here to make an end, suppressing a ₂₀
great part of my first pretended purpose; yet before I do end
I think it my duty here to put the nobility in mind that your
book now going in hand may be both seen and allowed,
before it go to the press, by such as have both skill and
authority so to do—I mean the Earl Marshal—and not to
pass as before it hath done, to the prejudice of so many
honorable families.

And to the end the world may know with whose plumes
you have heretofore feathered your nest (besides the heralds')
I have hereunto annexed *A New Year's Gift* dedicated to ₃₀
King Henry the Eight in the thirty-seventh year of his reign
by that worthy and learned English antiquary Master John
Leland, concerning his six years' travail and laborious journey
for the search of England's antiquities upon the said king's
commission and charges; by which it may appear unto the
indifferent reader who was the first author and contriver of
this late born *Britannia*, either he whose name is clean razed
and blotted out or you that have both taken the title and
whole credit thereof to yourself. Also, I may not here let
pass the words of Master John Bale[28] in his declarations upon ₄₀
the same work, dedicated to King Edward the Sixt, which
are these following: "Blessed be the man which shall set
this worthy work abroad, and contrariwise cursed be he
forever and ever that shall in spite of his nation seek thereof
the destruction."

John Leland's New Year's Gift, given of him to King Henry the VIII in the 37 year of his reign, concerning his laborious journey and search for England's antiquities

Whereas it pleased Your Highness, upon very just considera-
tions, to encourage me by the authority of your most
gracious commission, in the thirty-fifth year of your pros-
perous reign, to peruse and diligently to search all the

libraries of monasteries and colleges of this your noble realm
to the intent that the monuments of ancient writers, as well
of other nations as of your own province, might be brought
out of deadly darkness to lively light and to receive like
thanks of their posterity as they hoped for at such time as
they employed their long and great studies to the public
wealth; yea, and furthermore that the Holy Scripture of
God might both be sincerely taught and learned, all manner
of superstition and crafty colored doctrine of a rout of Roman
bishops totally expelled out of this your most Catholic
realm; I think it now no less than my very duty briefly to
declare to Your Majesty what fruit have sprung of my la-
borious journey and costly enterprise, both rooted upon
your infinite goodness and liberality, qualities right highly
to be esteemed in all princes and most specially in you, as
naturally your own well known proprieties.[29]

First, I have conserved many good authors, the which
otherwise had been like to have perished to no small in-
commodity of good letters. Of the which, part remain in
the most magnificent libraries of your royal palaces. Part also
remain in my custody, whereby I trust right shortly so to
describe your most noble realm and to publish the majesty
of the excellent acts of your progenitors, hitherto sore
obscured both for lack of imprinting of such works as lay
secretly in corners and also because men of eloquence hath
not enterprised to set them forth in a flourishing style, in
some times past not commonly used in England of writers
otherwise well learned, and now in such estimation that
except truth be delicately clothed in purpure,[30] her written
verities can scant find a reader. That all the world shall
evidently perceive that no particular region may justly be
more extolled than yours for true nobility and virtues at
all points renowmed. . . .[31]

That profit hath risen by the aforesaid journey in bringing
full many things to light as concerning the usurped authority
of the bishop of Rome and his complices[32] to the manifest
and violent derogation of kingly dignity. I refer myself most
humbly to your most prudent, learned, and high judgment
to discern my diligence in the long volume[33] wherein I
have made answer for the defense of your supreme dignity,
alonely[34] leaning to the strong pillar of Holy Scripture
against the whole college of the Romanists, cloaking their
crafty assertions and arguments under the name of one poor
Pighius of Ultraiect in Germany, and standing to them as
to their only anchor-hold against tempests that they know
will arise if truth may be by license let in to have a voice in
the general counsel.

Yet herein only I have not pitched the supreme work of
my labor, whereunto Your Grace, most like a kingly patron

[28]English clergyman and antiquary (1495–1563) who first pub-
lished Leland's *New Year's Gift* in 1549.
[29]Properties, qualities.
[30]Lavishly adorned in style. *Purpure:* purple. [31]Renowned.
[32]Accomplices.
[33]Presumably a manuscript treatise entitled "Antiphilarchia" that
was dedicated to Henry VIII and directed against Albert Pighius
(ca. 1490–1542), a Dutch Catholic theologian of Utrecht who had
attacked the Henrician reformation in *Hierarchiae ecclesiasticae
assertio* (1538). [34]Only, solely.

of all good learning, did animate me; but also considering and expending[35] with myself how great a number of excellent godly wits and writers, learned with the best as the times served, hath been in this your region, not only at such times as the Roman emperors had recourse to it but also in those days that the Saxons prevailed of the Britains, and the Normans of the Saxons, could not but with a fervent zeal and an honest courage commend them to memory. Else, alas, like to have been perpetually obscured, or to have been lightly remembered as uncertain shadows.

Wherefore I, knowing by infinite varity of books and assiduous reading of them who hath been learned and who hath written from time to time in this realm, have digested into four books the names of them, with their lives and monuments of learning. . . . The first book, beginning at the Druids, is deducted[36] unto the time of the coming of St. Augustine into England. The second is from the time of Augustine unto the advent of the Normans. The third from the Normans to the end of the most honorable reign of the mighty, famous, and prudent prince, Henry the VII, your father.[37] The fourth beginneth with the name of Your Majesty, whose glory in learning is to the world so clearly known that though among the lives of other learned men I have accurately celebrated the names of Bladudus, Molmutius, Constantinus Magnus, Sigeberius, Alfridus, Alfridus Magnus, Athelstan, and Henry the First, kings and your progenitors;[38] and also Ethelward, second son to Alfred the Great, Humphrey,[39] duke of Gloucester, and Tiptoft,[40] earl of Worcester; yet conferred[41] with Your Grace they seem as small lights—if I may freely say my judgment, your high modesty not offended—in respect of the daystar. . . .

And as touching historical knowledge, there hath been to the number of a full hundreth or moe[42] that from time to time hath with great diligence and no less faith (would to God with like eloquence) perscribed[43] the acts of your most noble predecessors and the fortunes of this your realm, so incredibly great, that he that hath not seen and throughly[44] read their works can little pronounce in this part.

Wherefore, after that I had perpended[45] the honest and profitable studies of these historiographers I was totally inflamed with a love to see throughly all those parts of this your opulent and ample realm that I had read of in the aforesaid writers. In so much that, all my other occupations intermitted, I have so traveled in your dominions both by the seacoasts and the middle parts, sparing neither labor nor costs, by the space of these six years past that there is almost neither cape nor bay, haven, creek or pier, river or confluence of rivers, breaches,[46] washes,[47] lakes, meres, fenny waters, mountains, valleys, moors, heaths, forests, woods, cities, burgs, castles, principal manor places, monasteries, and colleges but I have seen them and noted in so doing a whole world of things very memorable. . . .

And because that it may be more permanent and farther known than to have it engraved in silver or brass, I intend, by the leave of God, within the space of twelve moneths following, such a description to make of your realm in writing that it shall be no mastery after for the graver or

painter to make the like by a perfect example. Yea, and to wade further in this matter, whereas now almost no man can well guess at the shadow of the ancient names of havens, rivers, promontories, hills, woods, cities, towns, castles, and variety of kinds of people that Caesar, Livy, Strabo, Diodorus, Fabius Pictor, Pomponius Mela, Plinius, Cornelius Tacitus, Ptolomeus, Sextus Rufus, Ammianus, Marcellinus, Solinus, Antoninus,[48] and divers other make mention of, I trust so to open this window that the light shall be seen so long, that is to say by the space of a whole thousand years stopped up, and the old glory of your renowned Britain to reflourish through the world.

This done, I have matter at plenty already prepared to this purpose: that is to say, to write an history to the which I intend to adscribe[49] this title, *De antiquitate Britannica,* or else, *Civilis historia.*[50] And this work I intend to divide into so many books as there be shires in England and shires and great dominions in Wales, so that I esteem that this volume will include a fifty books, whereof each one severally shall contain the beginnings, increases, and memorable acts of the chief towns and castles of the province allotted to it.

Then I intend to distribute into six books such matter as I have already collected concerning the isles adjacent to your noble realm and under your subjection; whereof three shall be of these isles, Vecta, Mona, and Menavia,[51] sometime kingdoms.

And to superadd a work as an ornament and a right comely garland to the enterprises aforesaid, I have selected stuff to be distributed into three books, the which I purpose thus to entitle *De nobilitate Britannica,*[52] whereof the first shall declare the names of kings and queens with their children, dukes, earls, lords, captains, and rulers in this realm to the

[35]Weighing mentally. [36]Brought, traced.
[37]*The first book . . . father:* Leland blocks out his history in customary periodic segments: from the prehistoric Celtic *Druids* to the arrival of *St. Augustine* (who was sent by Pope Gregory I as missionary to England in 596), from Augustine to the Norman Conquest (1066), from the Conquest to the death of Henry VII (1509), and from the accession of Henry VIII to the 1540's.
[38]*Bladudus. . .progenitors:* kings of England, some (from Bladud to Alfrid) drawn from British legend as recorded by Geoffrey of Monmouth (see p. 808, n.3) and the rest historical. *Alfridus Magnus* is Alfred the Great (849–901), famous king of the West Saxons who led his people against the invading Danes; Athelstan (895–940) united virtually all the English under West Saxon supremacy; Henry I (1068–1135), fourth son of William the Conqueror, succeeded his brother William II and ruled England from 1100 to 1135.
[39]Text *Hunfryde.* Humphrey (1391–1447), youngest son of Henry IV, was noted as a patron of learned men and a collector of manuscripts.
[40]Text *Tipetote.* John, earl of Worcester (1427?–70), Yorkist stalwart famous for his learning (and also for his brutality against the Lancastrians). [41]Compared. [42]Hundred or more.
[43]Fully recorded. [44]Thoroughly. [45]Pondered.
[46]Bays, harbors. [47]Tidal flats.
[48]Greek and Roman historians and geographers. [49]Affix.
[50]*Concerning British Antiquity* or *Civil History.*
[51]The isles of Wight, Anglesey, and Man.
[52]*Concerning the Nobility of Britain.*

coming of the Saxons and their conquest. The second shall be of the Saxons and Danes to the victory of King William the Great. The third from the Normans to the reign of your most noble Grace, descending lineally of the Britain, Saxon, and Norman kings. So that all noblemen shall clearly perceive their lineal parentele.[53]

Now if it shall be the pleasure of Almighty God that I may live to perform these things that be already begun and in a great forwardness, I trust that this your realm shall so well be known, once painted with his native colors, that 10 the renown thereof shall give place to the glory of no other region. And my great labors and costs, proceeding from the most abundant fountain of your infinite goodness towards me, your poor scholar and most humble servant, shall be evidently seen to have not only pleased but also profited the studious, gentle, and equal readers. This is the brief

declaration of my laborious journey, taken by motion of Your Highness so much studying at all hours about the fruitful preferment of good letters and ancient virtues.

Christ continue your most royal estate and the prosperity, with succession in kingly dignity, of your dear and worthily beloved son, Prince Edward,[54] granting you a number of princely sons by the most gracious, benign, and modest lady, your Queen Catherine.[55]

Joannes Leylandus Antiquarius

[53]Derivation, hereditary descent.
[54]Only legitimate son (1537–53) of Henry VIII (by Jane Seymour), who succeeded his father as Edward VI in 1547.
[55]Catherine Parr (1512–48), sixth and last wife of Henry VIII, who married her (1542) following the execution of her predecessor, Catherine Howard.

Sir John Hayward [1564?-1627]

Although it had been routine for Elizabethan chroniclers like Stow and Holinshed to make a virtue of their studiously simple prose, Hayward thought that history should be belletristic. Is it not an "error" to let any clumsy hack record the country's glory, he reports Prince Henry asking. "Shall every filthy finger defile our reputation? Shall our honor be basely buried in the dross of rude and absurd writings?" When, in 1599, Hayward put his theory into practice with an elaborate account of Richard II's deposition—a topic that had just been treated by Daniel and Shakespeare in quasi-epic and dramatic form—he used such art (and even artifice) in contriving fabricated speeches, complex play of character, and stylistic exhibitions that he achieved a kind of novel of romance. Moreover, he got in serious trouble. His little book—rather misleadingly entitled *The First Part of the Life and Reign of King Henry the Fourth*—had been buttressed with a fulsome dedication (in Latin) to Robert, earl of Essex, and when, a few months later, that impetuous peer launched the series of events that led to his abortive insurrection (for John Speed's account of which see pp. 843 ff.), the book became a *cause célèbre* and its author was endangered. The queen herself, who did not relish works about the deposition of a monarch, even one so weak as Richard, smelled treason in the book. "I am Richard II, know ye not that?" she is reported to have said. Although Bacon, trying to allay her fear, wittily pointed out that Hayward was guilty of nothing more than felony for having rifled Tacitus, the unhappy and no doubt innocent historian was haled before the Star Chamber and then imprisoned in the Tower, where, it seems, he stayed until the old queen died. He was clearly speaking from experience when he later told Prince Henry that writing history was a dangerous line of work.

Thereafter Hayward was careful not to give offense, either as a busy and successful lawyer or as a writer. Although two books early in the new king's reign—one defending James' title to the throne (1603) and the other advocating the union of England and Scotland (1604)—had made him *persona grata* to the crown, when, a decade after his debacle, he returned to writing history it was only at the urging of the Prince of Wales. In addition to *The Lives of the Three Normans, Kings of England* (1613) he also undertook *The Life and Reign of King Edward the Sixth* (which was published three years after he had died) and a number of devotional works on such edifying themes as *David's Tears* (1622) and *Christ's Prayer upon the Cross* (1623).

By far the most successful of his books, however, was *The Sanctuary of a Troubled Soul*. Begun perhaps as early as 1600, in Hayward's time of trouble, it went through at least eight editions between 1604 and 1636. Despite various honors and emoluments that later came his way—including his appointment (with the illustrious William Camden) as one of the two historiographers of Chelsea College in 1610, membership in the College of Advocates in 1616, and a knighthood three years later—Hayward continued to embellish and expand this treatise on the moral benefits of self-denial; and it is possible that when, in his last recension of the work in 1623, he spoke of "being grieved with indignities or neglect from great persons, against which civility and reason forbade me to oppose," he was thinking of his own misfortunes in the Tower.

My texts are based on *The First Part of The Life and raigne of King Henrie the IIII. Extending to the end of the first year of his raigne,* 1599 (STC 12995) and *The Lives of the III. Normans, Kings of England: William the first. William the second. Henrie the first,* 1613 (STC 13000). Hayward's troublesome little book on Henry IV was reprinted (with Sir Robert Cotton's *Henry III,* 1627, which had also been in trouble) in 1642, when kings began to lose their luster, and again in 1706 in White Kennett's *Complete History of England,* and his *Lives of the Three Normans* in the *Harleian Miscellany* (ed. Thomas Park, II, 1809, and IX, 1812). An interesting statement of the aging Hayward's view of history is provided in his preface to Sir Roger Williams' *Actions of the Low Countries* (1618). The fullest account of his troubles at the start of his career is Margaret Dowling's in the *Library,* 4th Series, XI (1930–31); S. L. Goldberg has assessed his merits as a historian (RES, VI, 1955); W. A. Jackson has traced the complex history of the publication of his book on Henry IV in "Counterfeit Printing in Jacobean Times," *Library,* 4th Series, XV (1934); and there are discussions of his work by Fussner, Tillyard, and Levy as listed in the General Bibliography, Section V.

from The First Part of the Life and Reign of King Henry the Fourth (1599)

A. P. TO THE READER[1]

Among all sorts of human writers there is none that have done more profit or deserved greater praise than they who have committed to faithful records of histories either the government of mighty states or the lives and acts of famous men, for by describing the order and passages of these two, and what events hath followed what counsails, they have set forth unto us not only precepts but lively patterns both for private directions and for affairs of state, whereby in short time young men may be instructed and old men more fully furnished with experience than the longest age of man can afford. . . . 10

Cicero doth rightly call history "the witness of times, the light of truth, the life of memory, and the messenger of antiquity."[2] Hereby we are armed against all the rage and rashness of Fortune, and hereby we may seem—in regard of the knowledge of things—to have traveled in all countries, to have lived in all ages, and to have been conversant in all affairs. Neither is that the least benefit of history that it preserveth eternally both the glory of good men and shame of evil. Some philosophers do deny that glory is to be desired, for virtue (say they) is a reward unto itself and must 20

not be respected for the vain and titular blasts of glory; yet in writing these things they affect that especially which they especially deprave.[3] And indeed there is no man hath so horny heartstrings, as Persius[4] speaketh, who is not tickled with some pleasure of praise; again, there is no man of so flinty a forehead who is not touched with some fear of infamy and shame. Do we think that the valiant soldier thinketh no toil too tough, but boldly adventureth the hazard of all haps because he is weary of his life? Death cometh by nature

FIRST PART   [1]When, during his examination in the Tower, Hayward himself was asked about this puzzling dedication, he explained (*Calendar of State Papers, Domestic Series . . . 1598–1601,* p. 539) that "the preface to the reader was of his own inditing; entitled it under the letters A.P., as other writers have done. Spoke in it generally of histories, and intended no particular application to present history."
[2]A slightly garbled version of the favorite text of Renaissance historiographers: *Historia vero testis temporum, lux veritatis, vita memoriae, magistra vitae, nuntia vetustatis* (*De oratore,* II.ix).
[3]Disparage.
[4]Perhaps an allusion to *Satires,* I.41 of Aulus Persius Flaccus (34–62).

to all men alike, only with difference of memory with posterity.

And I would think that cities at the first were builded, laws made, and many thing invented for the use of men chiefly for desire of glory; which humor except the old governors of commonwealths had thought necessary, they would never have fostered it as they did with garlands, statues, trophies, and triumphs,[5] in which notwithstanding it is but temporary and short, but in histories of worth it is only perpetual. This Cicero perceiving, he dealt with Luc-ceius[6] to commit his actions to the monuments of his writings, and Pliny the Younger[7] did wish that he might be mentioned in the histories of Cornelius Tacitus because he did foresee that they should never decay.

But these are such as are not led away with a lust either to flatter or to deface, whereby the credit of history is quite overthrown. Yet the endeavor to curry favor is more easily disliked, as bearing with it an open note of servility, and therefore Alexander, when he heard Aristobulus read many things that he had written of him far above truth, as he was sailing the flood Hydaspes he threw the book into the river and said that he was almost moved to send Aristobulus after for his servile dealing.[8] But envious carping carrieth a counterfeit show of liberty and thereby findeth the better acceptance.

And since I am entered into this point, it may seem not impertinent to write of the style of a history, what beginning, what continuance, and what mean is to be used in all matter; what things are to be suppressed, what lightly touched, and what to be treated at large; how credit may be won and suspicion avoided; what is to be observed in the order of times and description of places and other such circumstances of weight; what liberty a writer may use in framing speeches and in declaring the causes, counsails, and events of things done; how far he must bend himself to profit,[9] and when and how he may play upon pleasure. But this were too large a field to enter into; therefore lest I should run into the fault of the Myndians, who made their gates wider than their town,[10] I will here close up, only wishing that all our English histories were drawn out of the dross of rude and barbarous English, that by pleasure in reading them the profit in knowing them might more easily be attained.

[RICHARD II'S DEPOSITION][11]

When all were set in their places, King Richard was brought forth apparelled in his royal robe, the diadem on his head, and the scepter in his hand, and was placed amongst them in a chair of estate.[12] Never was prince so gorgeous, with less glory and greater grief, to whom it was not disgrace sufficient to lose both the honor and ornaments of a king, but he must openly to his greater scorn renounce the one and deliver the other. After a little pause and expectation, the king arose from his seat and spake to the assembly these words, or the very like in effect:

"I assure myself that some at this present, and many hereafter, will accompt my case lamentable, either that I have deserved this dejection[13] if it be just, or if it be wrongful that I could not avoid it. Indeed, I do confess that many times I

have showed myself both less provident and less painful for the benefit of the commonwealth than I should, or might, or intended to do hereafter; and have in many actions more respected the satisfying of my own particular humor than either justice to some private persons or the common good of all. Yet I did not at any time either omit duty or commit grievance upon natural dullness or set[14] malice, but partly by abuse of corrupt counselors, partly by error of my youthful judgment. And now the remembrance of these oversights is so unpleasant to no man as to myself, and the rather because I have no means left either to recompense the injuries which I have done or to testify to the world my reformed affections, which experience and staidness of years had already corrected and would daily have framed to more perfection. But whether all the imputations wherewith I am charged be true either in substance or in such quality as they are laid,[15] or whether, being true, they be so heinous as to inforce these extremities, or whether any other prince, expecially in the heat of youth and in the space of two and twenty years (the time of my unfortunate reign),[16] doth not sometimes either for advantage or upon displeasure in as deep manner grieve some particular subject, I will not now examine. It helpeth not to use defense, neither booteth it to make complaint; there is left no place for the one nor pity for the other, and therefore I refer it to the judgment of God and your less distempered considerations.

"I accuse no man, I blame no fortune, I complain of nothing; I have no pleasure in such vain and needless comforts, and if I listed to have stood upon terms,[17] I know I have great favorers abroad and some friends (I hope) at home who would have been ready, yea forward, on my behalf to set up a bloody and doubtful war. But I esteem not my

[5]Triumphal processions.
[6]Lucius Lucceius, Roman senator and historian whom his friend and neighbor Cicero urged (*Epistolae ad familiares*, V.xii) to write a full account of Catiline's conspiracy.
[7]Gaius Plinius Caecilius Secundus (62–113), *Epistolae*, VII.xxxiii. In another letter (VI.xvi) Pliny asked Tacitus to record and so immortalize the career of his uncle, Pliny the Elder.
[8]*Alexander...dealing*: anecdote told by the Greek satirist Lucian (ca. 115–200) in "How To Write History," Sect. 12, of Aristobulus of Cassandrea, a historian who accompanied Alexander the Great and recorded his exploits. *Hydaspes*: river in northern India.
[9]Instruction.
[10]*Myndians . . . town*: Diogenes Laertius (*Lives of Eminent Philosophers*, "Diogenes," Sect. 57) relates that when Diogenes, the Greek Cynic, came to Myndus and found very large gates leading to a very small town, he exclaimed, "Men of Myndus, bar your gates lest the city should run away." See p. 737.
[11]Richard's downfall was precipitated by his own cousin, the powerful and ambitious Henry Bolingbroke, earl of Lancaster, who, though exiled in 1398, invaded England in July 1399 and so quickly gathered strength that when the king returned from Ireland a few weeks later he was captured, taken to London, and forced to abdicate. These events are treated in Shakespeare's *Richard II*. [12]Throne. [13]Abasement, humiliation.
[14]Deliberate. [15]*In such . . . laid*: in the way alleged.
[16]Richard succeeded his grandfather Edward III in 1377 and was deposed in 1399. See the genealogical chart inside front and back covers of this text.
[17]If I wanted to stand on my legal rights.

dignity at so high a price as the hazard of so great valure,[18] the spilling of so much English blood, and the spoil and waste of so flourishing a realm as thereby might have been occasioned. Therefore, that the commonwealth may rather rise by my fall than I stand by the ruin thereof, I willingly yield to your desires and am here come to dispossess myself of all public authority and title, and to make it free and lawful for you to create for your king Henry, duke of Lancaster, my cousin-german,[19] whom I know to be as worthy to take that place as I see you willing to give it to him."

Then he read openly and distinctly the form of his cession,[20] wherein he did declare that he had discharged his subjects from their oaths of fealty and homage and all other oaths whatsoever, and of his own will and free motion did abdicate the title, dignity, and aucthority of a king; and rendered up the possession of the realm with the use and title thereof and all the rights thereunto appertaining. To this the king subscribed and was sworn, and then he delivered with his own hands the crown, the scepter, and the robe to the duke of Lancaster, wishing unto him more happiness therewith than had ever happened unto himself. Then he did constitute the archbishop of York and the bishop of Hereford his procurators,[21] to intimate and declare this his resignation to all the states[22] of the realm which should be assembled together in Parliament. Lastly, he gave all his riches and goods, to the sum of three hundred thousand pounds in coin, besides his jewels and plate, for satisfaction of the injuries that he had done, desiring the duke and all the rest that were present severally by their names not altogether to forget that he had been their king, nor yet too much to think upon the same, but to retain of him a moderate remembrance; and in recompense of the ease that he had done them by his voluntary yielding, to permit him to live safely in a private and obscure life, with the sweetness whereof he was so possessed that from thenceforth he would prefer it before any preferment in the world. All this was delivered and done by the king with voice and countenance so agreeable to his present heaviness that there was no man so[23] unmindful of human instability which was not in some measure moved thereat, insomuch as a few secret tears melted from the eyes of many that were present, in whose minds a confessed and obscure alteration already gan[24] to begin. So prone and inclinable are men to pity misery although they have procured it, and to envy prosperity, even that which they have raised.

[A few days later, after Parliament had drawn up and voted a staggering indictment of Richard's follies and misdeeds and then had listened to Lancaster's formal claim to the throne, the drama moved to its conclusion.]

After these words [of Lancaster] it was demanded[25] in both houses, of the nobility and of the commons which were assembled, whether they did consent that the duke should reign. Who, all with one voice, acknowledged and accepted him for their king. Then the archbishop of Canterbury took him by the hand and placed him in the throne of estate, the archbishop of York assisting him and all the assembly testifying their own joy and wishing his. Then the arch-

bishop made an oration, and took for his theme this place of Scripture: "See, this is the man whom I spake to thee of, this same shall reign over my people."[26]. . . After all this he was proclaimed king of England and of France and lord of Ireland, and the common people, which is void of cares, not searching into sequels, but without difference of right or wrong inclinable to follow those that are mighty, with shouts and clamors gave their applause, not all upon judgment or faithful meaning, but most only upon a received custom to flatter the prince whatsoever he be. Yet lest the heat of this humor should allay by delay, it was forthwith proclaimed in the great hall[27] that upon the thirtieth[28] day of September next ensuing, the coronation of the king should be celebrated at Westminster. These matters being thus dispatched, the king proclaimed arose from his seat and went to Whitehall,[29] where he spent the rest of the day in royal feasting and all other complements of joy, notwithstanding there appeared in him no token of stateliness or pride, nor any change in so great a change.

Upon Wednesday next following, the procurators, before mentioned, went to the presence of King Richard, being within the Tower,[30] and declared unto him the admission of his resignation and also the order and form of his deposition, and in the name of all the states of the realm[31] did surrender the homage and fealty which had been due unto him, so that no man from thenceforth would bear to him faith and obedience as to their king. The king answered that he nothing regarded these titular circumstances, but contented himself with hope that his cousin would be gracious lord and good friend unto him.

So upon the thirteenth day of October, which was the day of the translation of Edward the Confessor,[32] the duke was with all accustomed solemnities by the archbishop of Canterbury sacred,[33] anointed, and crowned king at Westminster by the name of King Henry the Fourth, upon the very same day wherein the year before he had been banished the realm.

[Although the new king moved quickly to invest his eldest son as Prince of Wales and name him heir-apparent, he had still to deal with Richard.]

The inheritance of the kingdom being in this sort settled in King Henry and in his line, it was moved in the Parliament what should be done with King Richard. The bishop of

---

[18]Value.
[19]First cousin. Henry Bolingbroke was the son of Richard's uncle John, duke of Lancaster (John of Gaunt).
[20]Ceding, surrender (of his title). [21]Agents, representatives.
[22]Ranks (i.e., both Lords and Commons). [23]Text *to*. [24]Began.
[25]Asked, as a point of law. [26]1 Samuel 9.17.
[27]Westminster Hall, the eleventh-century edifice that, rebuilt by Richard II, served as the principal seat of justice until the nineteenth century. [28]Text *thirteenth*.
[29]Formerly a royal palace in Westminster.
[30]The Tower of London, formerly used as a prison.
[31]Clergy, nobles, and commons, the traditional "three estates" in England.
[32]Edward I (d. 1066), the last Saxon king of England, who was canonized in 1161. [33]Consecrated.

Caerliel,[34] who was a man learned and wise, and one that always used both liberty and constancy in a good cause, in his secret judgment did never give allowance to these proceedings, yet dissembled his dislike until he might to some purpose declare it; therefore now being in place to be heard of all, and by order of the House to be interrupted by none, he rose up and with a bold and present[35] spirit uttered his mind as followeth:

"This question, Right Honorable Lords, concerneth a matter of great consequence and weight, the determining whereof will assuredly procure either safe quiet or dangerous disturbance both to our particular consciences and also to the common state. Therefore before you resolve upon it I pray you call to your considerations these two things: first, whether King Richard be sufficiently[36] deposed or no; secondly, whether King Henry be with good judgment or justice chosen in his place. For the first point we are first to examine whether a king, being lawfully and fully instituted by any just title, may upon imputation either of negligence or of tyranny be deposed by his subjects; secondly, what King Richard hath omitted in the one or committed in the other for which he should deserve so heavy judgment. I will not speak what may be done in a popular state or in a consular,[37] in which, although one beareth the name and honor of a prince, yet he hath not supreme power of majesty; but in the one, the people have the highest empire, in the other, the nobility and chief men of estate; in neither, the prince....

"In these and suchlike governments the prince hath not regal rights, but is himself subject to that power which is greater than his, whether it be in the nobility or in the common people. But if the sovereign majesty be in the prince, as it was in the three first empires[38] and in the kingdoms of Judea and Israel, and is now in the kingdoms of England, France, Spain, Scotland, Muscovia,[39] Turkey, Tartaria,[40] Persia, Ethiopia, and almost all the kingdoms of Asia and Africa, although for his vices he be unprofitable to the subjects, yea hurtful, yea intolerable, yet can they lawfully neither harm his person nor hazard[41] his power, whether by judgment or else by force; for neither one nor all magistrates have any authority over the prince, from whom all authority is derived, and whose only presence doth silence and suspend all inferior jurisdiction and power. As for force, what subject can attempt, or assist, or counsail, or violence[42] against his prince and not incur the high and heinous crime of treason?

"It is a common saying, thought is free: free indeed from punishment of secular laws except by word or deed it break forth into action. Yet the secret thoughts against the sacred majesty of a prince, without attempt, without endeavor, have been adjudged worthy of death; and some who in auricular confession have discovered their treacherous devices[43] against the person of their prince have afterwards been executed for the same. All laws do exempt a mad man from punishment, because their actions are not governed by their will and purpose, and the will of man being set aside, all his doings are indifferent; neither can the body offend without a corrupt or erroneous mind; yet if a mad man draw his sword upon his king, it hath been adjudged to

deserve death. And lest any man should surmise that princes, for the maintenance of their own safety and sovereignty, are the only authors of these judgments, let us a little consider the patterns and precepts of Holy Scripture. Nebuchadnezzar, king of Assyria, wasted all Palestine with fire and sword, oppugned Jerusalem a long time, and at the last expunged it: slew the king, burnt the temple, took away the holy vessels and treasure; the rest he permitted to the cruelty and spoil of his unmerciful soldiers, who defiled all places with rape and slaughter and ruinated to the ground that flourishing city. After the glut of this bloody butchery, the people which remained he led captive into Chaldea, and there erected his golden image, and commanded that they which refused to worship it should be cast into a fiery furnace.[44]

"What cruelty, what injustice, what impiety is comparable to this? And yet God calleth Nebuchadnezzar his servant, and promiseth him hire and wages for his service; and the prophets Jeremiah and Baruch did write unto the Jews to pray for the life of him and of Balthasar his son, that their days might be upon earth as the days of heaven; and Ezekiel with bitter terms abhorreth the disloyalty of Zedekiah because he revolted from Nebuchadnezzar, whose homager and tributary he was.[45] What shall we say of Saul?[46] Did he not put all the priests to execution because one of them did relieve holy and harmless David? Did he not violently persecute that his most faithful servant and dutiful son-in-law, during which pursuit he fell twice into the power of David, who did not only spare but also protect the king and reproved the praetorian soldiers[47] for their negligent watch, and was touched in heart for cutting away the lap of his garment, and afterwards caused the messenger to be slain who upon request and for pity had lent his hand (as he said) to help forward the voluntary death of that

[34]Thomas Merke, bishop of Carlisle (d. 1409). Although deprived of his bishopric and imprisoned for his opposition to Henry's usurpation, he was subsequently released and restored, at least in part, to his episcopal functions. In Shakespeare's *Richard II* (IV.i. 114–49) he eloquently denounces Henry's impious seizure of the throne and predicts disaster for the realm.
[35]Collected, self-possessed. [36]Effectively, i.e., legally.
[37]*In a popular . . . consular*: in a direct democracy or in a limited monarchy where the people delegate their power to a *prince*.
[38]Babylon (or Assyria), Persia, and Greece, which (with Rome) constituted the four monarchies whose rise and fall the prophet Daniel envisioned (Daniel 7.4–7).
[39]Russia.
[40]Tartary (the Mongol empire of Asia and eastern Europe).
[41]Jeopardize. [42]Do violence to, violate.
[43]*Discovered . . . devices*: revealed their treasonous plots.
[44]*Nebuchadnezzar . . . furnace*: The depredations of Nebuchadnezzar, king of Babylon (d. 562 B.C.), against Judea are related in 2 Kings 24–25.
[45]*And yet God . . . he was*: some of the Old Testament and Apocryphal passages behind this paragraph are Jeremiah 25.9, 29.18, Baruch 1.11, and Ezekiel 29.18. *Homager and tributary*: one who owes fealty and pays tribute.
[46]First king of Israel, patron and later rival of his successor David. See 1 Samuel 10–31. [47]Bodyguard.

sacred king? As for the contrary examples, as that of Jehu[48] who slew Jehoram and Ahaziah, kings of Israel and Judah, they were done by express oracle and revelation from God, and are no more set down for our imitation than the robbing of the Egyptians or any other particular and privileged commandment, but in the general precept, which all men must ordinarily follow. Not only our actions but our speeches also and our very thoughts are strictly charged with duty and obedience unto princes, whether they be good or evil: the law of God ordaineth that he which doth presumptuously 10 against the ruler of the people shall die. And the prophet David forbiddeth[49] to touch the Lord's anointed. "Thou shalt not," saith the Lord, "rail upon the judges, neither speak evil against the ruler of the people."[50] And the apostles[51] do demand further that even our thoughts and souls be obedient to higher powers. And lest any should imagine that they meant of good princes only, they speak generally of all, and further to take away all doubt they make express mention of the evil. For the power and authority of wicked princes is the ordinance of God. . . . 20

"We must neither wholly obey nor violently resist, but with a constant courage submit ourselves to all manner of punishment, and show our subjection by enduring and not performing. Yea, the church hath declared it to be an heresy to hold that a prince may be slain or deposed by his subjects for any disorder or default, either in life or else in government. There will be faults so long as there are men, and as we endure with patience a barren year if it happpen, and unseasonable weather, and such other defects of nature, so 30 must we tolerate the imperfections of rulers, and quietly expect either reformation or else a change.

"But alas good King Richard, what such cruelty? what such impiety hath he ever committed? Examine rightly those imputations which are laid against him, without any false circumstance of aggravation, and you shall find nothing objected either of any truth or of great moment. It may be that many errors and oversights have escaped him, yet none so grievous to be termed tyranny, as proceeding rather from unexperienced ignorance or corrupt counsail than from 40 any natural and willful malice. . . .

"O Englishmen, worse bewitched than the foolish Galatians![52] Our unstayed minds and restless resolutions do nothing else but hunt after our own harms. No people have more hatred abroad and none less quiet at home. In other countries the sword of invasion hath been shaken against us, in our own land the fire of insurrection hath been kindled amongs us. And what are these innovations but whetstones to sharpen the one and bellows to blow up the other? . . .

"And thus have I declared my mind concerning this question in more words than your wisdom yet fewer than 50 the weight of the cause doth require, and do boldly conclude that we have neither power nor policy[53] either to depose King Richard or to elect Duke Henry in his place; that King Richard remaineth still our sovereign prince, and therefore it is not lawful for us to give judgment upon him; that the duke whom you call king hath more offended against the king and the realm than the king hath done, either against him or us, for being banished the realm for ten years by the

king and his counsail (amongst whom his own father was chief)[54] and sworn not to return again without special license, he hath not only violated his oath but with impious arms disturbed the quiet of the land and dispossessed the king from his royal estate, and now demandeth judgment against his person without offense proved or defense heard. If this injury and this perjury doth nothing move us, yet let both our private and common dangers somewhat withdraw us from these violent proceedings."

This speech was diversely taken, as men were diversely affected between fear, hope, and shame; yet the most part did make show for King Henry, and thereupon the bishop was presently attached[55] by the Earl Marshal and committed to prison in the Abbey of St. Albones.[56] Whose counsail and conjecture then contemned was afterwards better thought upon, partly in the lifetime of King Henry, during whose reign almost no year passed without great slaughters and executions, but more especially in the times succeeding, when within the space of thirty-six years twelve set battails upon this quarrel were fought within the realm by Englishmen only, and more than four score princes of the royal blood slain one by another.[57]

[THE DEATH OF RICHARD II][58]

The most current report at that time went that he was princely served every day at the table with aboundance of costly meats, according to the order prescribed by Parliament, but was not suffered to taste or touch any one of them, and so perished of famine, being tormented with the presence of that whereof he died for want. But such horrible and unnatural cruelty, both against a king and a kinsman, should not proceed from King Henry (methink), a man of a moderate and mild disposition, nor yet from any other mind which is not altogether both savage in humanity and in religion profane. One writer[59] who would seem to have the

[48]King of Israel whose killing of Jehoram and Ahaziah is related in 2 Kings 9.
[49]Psalm 105.15.   [50]Exodus 22.28.
[51]Romans 13.1, Titus 3.1.
[52]When the new converts at Galatia, in Asia Minor, seemed to be wavering in their faith, Paul reproved and instructed them in one of his most emphatic epistles.   [53]Right, warrant.
[54]As a member of King Richard's council, John of Gaunt concurred in the judgment on his son. See Shakespeare, *Richard II*, I.iv.233–34.   [55]Immediately taken into custody.
[56]St. Albans, an ancient monastic establishment north of London.
[57]*During whose reign . . . another*: the dynastic struggles of the 15th century—the Wars of Roses, so called from the white and red roses taken as badges respectively by the great ducal houses of York and Lancaster—were often cited as a demonstration of the moral consequences of insubordination.
[58]Following his forced abdication in late September 1399, Richard was taken first to Kent and then to Yorkshire, where he died—probably of starvation and neglect—at Pontefract (*Pomfret*) Castle about mid-February 1400.
[59]Presumably the anonymous author of *Chronicque de la traïson et mort de Richart Deux roy Dengleterre*, the sole contemporary authority for the account of Richard's death that Hayward fol-

perfect intelligence of these affairs maketh report that King Henry, sitting at his table, sad and pensive, with a deep sigh brake forth into these words: "Have I no faithful friend that will deliver me of him whose life will breed destruction to me and disturbance to the realm, and whose death will be a safety and quiet to both? For how can I be free from fear so long as the cause of my danger doth continue? And what security, what hope, shall we have of peace, unless the seed of sedition be utterly rooted out?"

Upon this speech a certain knight called Sir Pierce of 10 Exton presently departed from the court, accompanied with eight tall men, and came to Pomfret, and there commanded that the esquire who was accustomed to sew and take the assay[60] before King Richard should no more use that manner of service. "And let him," quoth he, "now eat well, for he shall not eat long." King Richard sat down to dinner and was served without courtesy or assay, whereat he marveled and demanded of the esquire why he did not his duty? The esquire answered that he was otherwise commanded by Sir Pierce of Exton, who was lately come from King Henry. 20 The king, being somewhat moved at this act and answer, took the carving knife in his hand and struck the esquire therewith lightly on the head, saying, "The devil take Henry of Lancaster and thee together." With that, Sir Pierce entered the chamber with eight men in harness,[61] every one having a bill[62] in his hand; whereupon King Richard, perceiving their drift and his own danger, put the table from him and stepping stoutly to the foremost man, wrested the bill out of his hand, wherewith (although unarmed and alone) he manfully defended himself a good 30 space and slew four of his assailants. Sir Pierce leapt to the chair where King Richard was wont to sit, whilst the rest chased him about the chamber. At the last, being forced towards the place where Sir Pierce was, he with a stroke of his pollax[63] felled him to the ground, and forthwith he was miserably rid out of his miserable life. It is said that at the point of his death he gathered some spirit and with a faint and feeble voice groaned forth these words:

"My great-grandfather King Edward the Second[64] was in this manner deposed, imprisoned, and murthered, by which means my grandfather King Edward the Third obtained possession of the crown; and now is the punishment of that injury poured upon his next successor. Well, this is right for me to suffer, but not for you to do. Your king for a time may joy at my death and enjoy his desire, but let him qualify his pleasures with expectation of the like justice, for God who measureth all our actions by the malice of our minds will not suffer this violence unrevenged."

. . . . . .

And thus was King Richard brought to his death by violence and force, as all writers agree, although all agree not upon the manner of the violence. He was a man of personage rather well proportioned than tall, of great beauty and grace and comeliness in presence; he was of a good strength, and no abject spirit, but the one by ease, the other by flattery, were much abased. He deserved many friends but found few because he sought them more by liberality than virtuous dealing. He was marvelous infortunate in all his actions, which may very well be imputed to his negligence and sloth, for he that is not provident can seldom prosper, but by his looseness will lose whatsoever fortune or other men's labors do cast upon him. At the last he was driven to such distress that he accompted it as a benefit to be disburdened of his royal dignity, for which other men will not stick to put their goods and lives and souls in hazard.

---

lowed. Generally Hayward seems to have used the second (1587) edition of Holinshed's *Chronicles*, the ultimate source of which was Thomas Walsingham (d. 1422), precentor of the great monastic scriptorium at St. Albans.
[60]*Sew . . . assay:* serve and taste (the food).
[61]Armor [62]Weapon with a hook-shaped blade, halberd.
[63]Poleax, battle-ax.
[64]The murder of Edward II (1384–27) at the instigation of Queen Isabella and her lover, Roger de Mortimer, brought his son to the throne at the age of thirteen.

from The Lives of the Three Normans, Kings of England (1613)

To the High and Mighty Prince Charles, Prince of Wales[1]

Our late, too late born or too soon dying, Prince Henry[2] of 40 famous memory, your deceased brother, sent for me a few moneths before his death. And at my second coming to his presence, among some other speeches he complained much of our histories of England, and that the English nation, which is inferior to none in honorable actions, should be surpassed by all in leaving the memory of them to posterity.

For this cause he blamed the negligence of former ages, as if they were ignorant of their own deservings, as if they esteemed themselves unworthy of their worth.

I answered that I conceived these causes hereof: one, that

THE LIVES [1]Second son (1600–49) of James I, who succeeded his brother Henry as Prince of Wales at Henry's untimely death in 1612, and his father as Charles I in 1625.
[2]Henry Frederick, Prince of Wales (1594–1612), eldest son of James I and a notable patron of literary men.

men of sufficiency were otherwise employed, either in public affairs or in wrestling with the world, for maintenance or increase of their private estates. Another is for that men might safely write of others in manner of a tale but in manner of a history safely they could not because, albeit they should write of men long since dead, and whose posterity is clean worn out, yet some alive, finding themselves foul in those vices which they see observed, reproved, and condemned in others, their guiltiness maketh them apt to conceive that whatsoever the words are, the finger pointeth only at them. The last is for that the argument of our English history hath been so foiled heretofore by some unworthy writers that men of quality may esteem themselves discredited by dealing in it.

"And is not this," said he, "an error in us, to permit every man to be a writer of history? Is it not an error to be so curious in other matters and so careless in this? We make choice of the most skillful workmen to draw or carve the portraiture of our faces, and shall every artless pencil delineate the disposition of our minds? Our apparel must be wrought by the best artificers and no soil must be suffered to fall upon it, and shall our actions, shall our conditions, be described by every bungling hand? Shall every filthy finger defile our reputation? Shall our honor be basely buried in the dross of rude and absurd writings? We are careful to provide costly sepulchers to preserve our dead lives, to preserve some memory what we have been; but there is no monument either so durable or so largely extending, or so lively and fair, as that which is framed by a fortunate pen. The memory of the greatest monuments had long since perished had it not been preserved by this means."

To this I added that I did always conceive that we should make our reckoning of three sorts of life: the short life of nature, the long life of fame, and the eternal life of glory. The life of glory is so far esteemed before the other two, as grace is predominant in us; the life of fame before our natural life is so far esteemed, as a generous spirit surmounteth sensuality, as human nature overruleth brutish disposition. So far as the noble nature of man hath dominion in our minds, so far do we contemn either the incommodities or dangers or life of our body in regard of our reputation and fame. Now seeing this life of fame is both preserved and enlarged chiefly by history, there is no man (I suppose) that will either resist or not assist the commendable or at least tolerable writing thereof but such as are conscious to themselves either that no good or that nothing but ill can be reported of them; in whom notwithstanding it is an error to think that any power of the present time can either extinguish or obscure the memory of times succeeding. Posterity will give to every man his due. Some ages hereafter will afford those who will report unpartially of all.

Then he questioned whether I had wrote any part of our English history other than that which had been published,[3] which at that time he had in his hands. I answered that I had wrote of certain of our English kings by way of a brief description of their lives; but for history I did principally bend and bind myself to the times wherein I should live, in which my own observations might somewhat direct me, but

as well in the one as in the other I had at that time perfected nothing.

To this he said that in regard of the honor of the time he liked well of the last, but for his own instruction he more desired the first; that he desired nothing more than to know the actions of his ancestors because he did so far esteem his descent from them as he approached near them in honorable endeavors. Hereupon, beautifying his face with a sober smile, he desired me that against his return from the progress[4] then at hand I would perfect somewhat of both sorts for him, which he promised amply to requite; and was well known to be one who esteemed his word above ordinary respects. This stirred in me not only a will but power to perform; so as, engaging my duty far above the measure either of my leisure or of my strength, I finished the lives of these three kings of Norman race and certain years of Queen Elizabeth's reign.[5]

At his return from the progress to his house at St. James[6] these pieces were delivered unto him, which he did not only courteously but joyfully accept. And because this seemed a perfect work, he expressed a desire that it should be published. Not long after he died, and with him died both my endeavors and my hopes. . . .

Whatsoever this is, I have presumed to present it to Your Highness for these causes following: first, for that it received this being from him who was most dearly esteemed by you, who may be justly proposed as an example of virtue, as a guide to glory and fame. Secondly, for that the persons of whom it treateth are those most worthy ancestors of yours, who laid the foundation of this English empire, who were eminent among all the princes of their times and happily for many ages after as well in actions of peace as of war. Lastly, for that I esteem histories the fittest subject for Your Highness' reading, for by diligent perusing the acts of great men, by considering all the circumstances of them, by comparing counsails and means with events, a man may seem to have lived in all ages, to have been present at all enterprises, to be more strongly confirmed in judgment, to have attained a greater experience than the longest life can possibly afford.

But because many errors do usually arise by ignorance of the state wherein we live, because it is dangerous to frame rules of policy out of countries differing from us both in nature and custom of life and form of government, no histories are so profitable as our own. In these Your Highness may see the noble disposition and delights of your ancestors, what were their sweet walks, what their pleasant chases,[7] how far they preferred glory before either pleasure or safety, how by the brave behavior of their sword they hewed honor out of the sides of their enemies. In these you may see the largeness, commodities, and strength of this country, the nature of the people, their wealth, pleasure, exercise and

---

[3] *The First Part of the Life and Reign of King Henry IV* (1599). See pp. 828 ff.   [4] State journey.
[5] *Certain . . . reign: The Beginning of the Reign of Queen Elizabeth,* a fragmentary manuscript first printed (by the Camden Society) in 1840.
[6] St. James' Palace, a royal residence in London.
[7] Hunting preserves.

trade of life, and what else is worthy of observation. Generally, by these you may so furnish yourself as not easily to be abused either by weak or deceitful advice.

The Most High preserve and prosper Your Highness that as you succeed many excellent ancestors in blood, so you may exceed them all in honorable atchievements.

Your Highness' most devoted
J. Hayward

Richard Knolles   [1550?-1610]

As befits a country schoolmaster, Knolles' life was so uneventful that much of it remains a blank. Although his birth is unrecorded, we know that in 1565 he was admitted Bachelor of Arts by Lincoln College, Oxford, the kindly "nursing mother house," as he called it with affection, where he stayed on as fellow for perhaps half a dozen years. This phase of his sedate career ended about 1572, when he was appointed master of the grammar school at Sandwich, Kent, which, following its suppression in 1547, had recently been refunded by the notable jurist Sir Roger Manwood. Once proudly eminent as one of the Cinque Ports, Sandwich had become a sleepy country town, and here, as Knolles himself said later, "in a world of troubles and cares, in a place that afforded no means of comfort" to proceed in mighty works, he labored in obscurity for two decades or more. Sometime in the 1590's—perhaps after young Sir Peter Manwood succeeded to his formidable father's estate and functions in 1592—he must have started his great work. Given "the sea and world of matter I was to pass through (requiring both great labor and time)," it was, said Knolles in retrospect, a task "almost impossible." We know nothing of its progress, but when *The General History of the Turks* appeared as a folio of almost twelve hundred pages in 1603, the grateful author took occasion (in his dedication to King James) to explain that Sir Peter had been not only the "first mover" of the massive undertaking but also his "continual and only helper therein."

Compared with most specimens of contemporary historiography, Knolles' book is a marvel of disciplined narration. As he traces the history of the Turks ("the present terror of the world") from their dim beginnings in Troy or Persia or Arabia or even Palestine (as one of the lost tribes of Israel) down to 1603, when they had overrun the Balkans and stood poised before Vienna, he never lets the interest flag. Even big set pieces like the fall of Constantinople and the battle of Lepanto do not interrupt the steady flow, and when the reader finally leaves the book it is with the hovering expectation that something is about to happen—it being "the time of the year that the Turks use commonly to set forth with their great armies and to undertake their greatest exploits in."

Measured by the record of its publication, Knolles' *History* must have been a great success. A second edition, which brought the story down to 1610, appeared in the year its author died; there were three reprintings (with continuations by other hands, of course) between 1621 and 1638; and the sixth and last edition, which was published in three stately folios between 1687 and 1700, spawned a two-volume abridgment that appeared in 1701. With his poignant sense of mutability, Knolles himself would not have been surprised, perhaps, that he finally fell into neglect; but Johnson—who took the plot of his ill-starred tragedy *Irene* from Knolles and who rated him above such mighty opposites as Raleigh and Clarendon—attributed his eventual "obscurity" to the "remoteness and barbarity of the people whose story he relates." It was probably those very qualities, however, that attracted the Romantics to this almost forgotten book. For example, Byron, not long before his death, said that the pleasure "old Knolles" had given him, when he was but a boy, had not only fired his hope to see the Middle East, but also supplied him with the "oriental coloring" that suffused his early work.

Only three years after *The General History of the Turks* appeared Knolles ventured into print again, this time as the translator of Jean Bodin's *Six Books of a Commonweal*. In dedicating it to Manwood he implied that although he would have preferred to press forward with the "Saracen history," the problem and expense of gathering information—"besides the difficulty of the labor to so weak a body, apace declining, wanting all comfort and help but your own"—had forced him to a lesser undertaking. As noted earlier, however, these deterrents did not prevent a new edition of his *History*, which must have kept him busy to the end. A translation of William Camden's *Britannia* (see p. 816), which was presumably made for Sir Peter Manwood's use, was found in Camden's library at his death in 1623. It still remains unpublished.

Μy text is based upon *The Generall Historie of the Turkes, from The first beginning of that Nation to the rising of the Othoman Familie . . . Faithfullie collected out of the best Histories, both auntient and moderne, and digested into one continuat Historie untill this present yeare 1603: By Richard Knolles*, 1603 (STC 15051). In addition to an account of Knolles' life and works in Kenneth D. McRae's edition of *The Six Bookes of the Commonweale* (1962) there is an assessment of his work in S. C. Chew's *Crescent and the Rose* (1937). Johnson's accolade first appeared in the *Rambler*, No. 122 (18 May (1751).

from The General History of the Turks (1603)

The Author's Induction to the Christian Reader unto the History of the Turks Following

The long and still declining state of the Christian commonweal, with the utter ruin and subversion of the Empire of the East[1] and many other most glorious kingdoms and provinces of the Christians never to be sufficiently lamented, might with the due consideration thereof worthily move even a right stony heart to ruth; but therewith also to call to remembrance the dishonor done unto the blessed name of our Saviour Christ Jesus, the desolation of His church here militant upon earth, the dreadful danger daily threatened unto the poor remainder thereof, the millions of souls cast headlong [10] into eternal destruction, the infinite numbers of woeful Christians (whose grievous groanings under the heavy yoke of infidelity no tongue is able to express), with the carelessness of the great for the redress thereof, might give just cause unto any good Christian to sit down and with the heavy prophet[2] to say, as he did of Jerusalem, "O how hath the Lord darkened the daughter of Sion in His wrath? And cast down from heaven unto the earth the beauty of Israel and remembered not His footstool in the day of His wrath?"[3]

All which miseries (with many others so great as greater [20] there can none be) the Prince of Darkness and author of all mischief hath, by the persecuting princes of all ages and ancient heretics, his ministers, labored from time to time to bring upon the church of God to the obscuring of His blessed name and utter subversion of His most sacred word; but yet by none—no, not by them all together—so much prevailed

as by the false prophet Mahomet,[4] born in an unhappy hour to the great destruction of mankind, whose most gross and blasphemous doctrine,[5] first phantasied by himself in Arabia and so by him obtruded unto the world, and afterwards by the Saracen caliphs[6] (his seduced successors) with greater forces maintained, was by them together with their empire dispersed over a great part of the face of the earth, to the unspeakable ruin and destruction of the Christian religion and state, especially in Asia and Afric, with some good part of Europe also. But the unity of this great Mahometan monarchy being once dissolved, and it divided into many kingdoms and so after the manner of worldly things drawing unto the fatal period[7] of itself, in process of time became of far less force than before, and so less dreadful unto the Christian princes of the West, by whom these Saracens were again expulsed out of all the parts of Europe excepting one corner of Spain which they yet held within the remembrance of

GENERAL HISTORY [1]The Byzantine or eastern part of the Roman Empire, which separated from Rome on the death of Theodosius in 395 and ended with the fall of Constantinople in 1453.
[2]Jeremiah, who specialized in denunciation and warning.
[3]Lamentations 2.1.
[4]Mohammed (570?–632), founder of Islam.
[5]The teachings of Mohammed as formulated in the Koran, believed by Moslems to be the revelations of Allah.
[6]Dynasty of Islamic rulers that after 634 conquered the Middle East, North Africa, and Spain and remained unchecked until the battle of Poitiers in 732. [7]Conclusion, end.

our fathers until that by their victorious forces they were thence at length happily removed also after that they had possessed the same about the space of seven hundred years.[8]

In this declination of the Saracens (the first champions of the Mahometan superstition, who though they had lost much yet held many great kingdoms both in Asia and Afric, taken for the most part from the Christians) arise the Turks, an obscure and base people before scarce known unto the world, yet fierce and courageous, who by their valor first aspired unto the kingdom of Persia with divers other large provinces, from whence they were about an hundred threescore and ten years after again expulsed by the Tartars and enforced to retire themselves into the Lesser Asia, where, taking the benefit of the discord of the Christian princes of the East and the carelessness of the Christians in general, they in some good measure repaired their former losses again and maintained the state of a kingdom at Iconium[9] in Cilicia (now of them called Caramania), holding in their subjection the greater part of that fruitful country, still seeking to gain from the Christians what they had before lost unto the Tartars.

But this kingdom of the Turks declining also by the dismembering of the same, there stepped up among the Turks in Bithynia[10] one Osman[11] or Othoman of the Oguzian tribe or family, a man of great spirit and valor who, by little and little growing up amongst the rest of his countrymen and other the effeminate Christians on that side of Asia, at last like another Romulus[12] took upon him the name of a sultan or king, and is right worthily accounted the first founder of the mighty Empire of the Turks. Which, continued by many descents directly in the line of himself even unto Mahomet the third of that name[13] who now reigneth, is from a small beginning become the greatest terror of the world, and, holding in subjection many great and mighty kingdoms in Asia, Europe, and Afric, is grown to that height of pride as that it threateneth destruction unto the rest of the kingdoms of the earth, laboring with nothing more than with the weight of itself. In the greatness whereof is swallowed up both the name and empire of the Saracens, the glorious empire of the Greeks, the renowned kingdoms of Macedonia, Peloponnesus, Epirus, Bulgaria, Servia, Bosnia, Armenia, Cyprus, Syria, Egypt, India, Tunis, Algiers, Media, Mesopotamia, with a great part of Hungary as also of the Persian kingdom and all those churches and places so much spoken of in Holy Scripture (the Romans only excepted); and in brief so much of Christendom as far exceedeth that which is thereof at this day left.

So that at this present, if you consider the beginning, progress, and perpetual felicity of this the Othoman Empire, there is in this world nothing more admirable or strange; if the greatness and luster thereof, nothing more magnificent or glorious; if the power and strength thereof, nothing more dreadful or dangerous. Which, wondering at nothing but at the beauty of itself, and drunk with the pleasant wine of perpetual felicity, holdeth all the rest of the world in scorn, thundering out nothing but still blood and war, with a full persuasion in time to rule over all, prefining[14] unto itself no other limits than the uttermost bounds of the earth, from the rising of the sun unto the going down of the same.

The causes whereof are many and right lamentable, but for the most part so shut up in the counsels of the great as that for me to seek after them were great folly; yet amongst the rest some others there be so pregnant and manifest as that the blind world taketh thereof, as it were, a general knowledge, and may therefore without offense of the wiser sort (as I hope) even in these our nice days be lightly touched. Whereof the first and greatest is the just and secret judgment of the Almighty, who in justice delivereth into the hands of these merciless miscreants nation after nation and kingdom upon kingdom as unto the most terrible executioners of His dreadful wrath, to be punished for their sins, others, in the meanwhile, no less sinful than they, in His mercy enjoying the benefit of a longer time, calling them unto repentance.

Then, the uncertainty of worldly things, which, subject to perpetual change, cannot long stay in one state, but as the sea is with the wind so are they in like sort tossed up and down with the continual surges and waves of alteration and change. So that being once grown to their height, they there stay not long, but fall again as fast as ever they rise, and so in time come to nothing. As we see the greatest monarchies that ever yet were upon earth have done, their course being run: over whom Time now triumpheth as no doubt at length it shall over this so great a monarchy also, when it shall but then live by fame, as the others now do.

Next to these causes from above (without offence be it said) is the small care of the Christian princes, especially those that dwelt further off, have had of the common state of the Christian commonweal, whereof even the very greatest are to account themselves but as the principal members of one and the same body, and have or ought to have as sharp a feeling one of another's harms as hath the head of the wrongs done unto the feet, or rather as if it were done unto themselves. Instead of which Christian compassion and unity they have ever and even at this time are so divided among themselves with endless quarrels, partly for questions of religion (never by the sword to be determined), partly for matters touching their own proper state and sovereignty, and that with such distrust and implacable hatred, that they never could as yet (although it have been long wished) join their common forces against the common enemy. . . .

Unto which so great a cause of the common decay may be added the evil choice of our soldiers employed in those wars, who, taken up hand over head out of the promiscuous

---

[8]The Saracens controlled Granada from 711 until 1492, when they were expelled by Ferdinand and Isabella.

[9]Having held Persia from about 635 until they themselves were conquered by the Tartars from eastern Asia in 1097, the Saracens established a sultanate at Iconium (modern Knoieh) in southeastern Asia Minor (*the Lesser Asia*).

[10]Ancient province in northwestern Asia Minor.

[11]Founder of the Ottoman empire (1259–1326), who assumed the title of sultan in 1299.

[12]Legendary founder (with his brother Remus) and first king of Rome.

[13]Mohammed III, sultan of Turkey, 1595–1603.

[14]Predetermining, prescribing.

vulgar people,[15] are for most part untrained men serving rather for show and the filling up of number than for use, and in no respect to be compared with the Turk's janizaries[16] and other his most expert soldiers continually, even from their youth, exercised in feats of arms. Not to speak in the meantime of the want of the ancient martial discipline, the wholesome preservative of most puissant armies, which breedeth in the proud enemy a contempt of the Christian forces with a full persuasion of himself that he is not by such disordered and weak means to be withstood. . . .

[Deeply concerned with these and other aspects of the Turkish peril, Knolles explains that he] had with long search and much labor, mixed with some pleasure and mine own reasonable contentment, passed through the whole melancholy course of their tragical history, yet without purpose ever to have commended the same or any part thereof unto the remembrance of posterity, as deeming it an argument of too high a reach and fitter for some more happy wit, better furnished with such helps both of nature and art as are of necessity requisite for the undertaking of so great a charge than was myself, of many thousands the meanest. . . . Besides that so many difficulties even at the first presented themselves unto my view as that to overcome the same, if I should take the labor in hand, seemed to me almost impossible; for beside the sea and world of matter I was to pass through (requiring both great labor and time), full of the most rare example both of the better and worse fortune in men of all sort and condition, yielding more pleasure unto the reader than facility to the writer, I saw not any among so many as had taken this argument in hand whom I might as a sure guide or loadstar long follow in the course of this so great an history. . . .

[Finally convinced, despite the formidable difficulties, that he should undertake the job, Knolles set to work.] Now what I for my part have in this my long travel performed I leave it to thy good discretion to consider, contenting myself in so great a matter to have been willing to have done something, wishing no longer to live than in some measure to be profitable to the Christian commonweal, which long since, in my nursing mother house, Lincoln College in Oxford,[17] where I was sometime fellow, I did purpose to perform, as it should please God in time to give me means and occasion; in which mind I hope by the goodness and mercy of Christ so long as I live to continue. Only this favor, to conclude with, I request of thee: that if in this so long and perplexed an history (by piecemeal of so many diversely handled) written by me in a world of troubles and cares, in a place[18] that afforded no means or comfort to proceed in so great a work, thou chance to light upon some things otherwise reported than thou hast elsewhere read them (as I doubt not but thou mayst) not therefore forthwith to condemn what thou here findest, being happily taken from a more certain reporter than was that whereunto thou givest more credit, or at leastwise not written by me as meaning in anything to prejudice thy better judgment, but to leave it to thy good choice in such diversity of reports to follow that which may seem unto thee most true. By which courtesy thou mayst hereafter encourage me to perform some

other work[19] to thy no less contentment. So wishing thee all happiness, I bid thee farewell. From Sandwich the last of September, 1603.

Thine in all dutiful kindness,
R. Knolles

The Rising of the Great and Mighty Empire of the Turks under Othoman, First Founder thereof, with His Life and Doings

[Knolles begins the second major section of his work with a deep-toned meditation on mutability.]

What small assurance there is in men's affairs, and how subject unto change even those things are wherein we for the most part repose our greatest felicity and bliss (beside that the whole course of man's frail life by many notable examples well declare), nothing doth more plainly manifest the same than the heavy events and woeful destructions of the greatest kingdoms and empires; which, founded upon great fortunes, increased with perpetual success, exalted by exceeding power, established with most puissant armies, wholesome laws, and deep counsels, have yet grown old and in time come to naught. So that even as men, all things else belonging unto man are subject unto the inevitable course of destiny, or, more truly to say, unto the fatal doom of the Most Highest, prefining unto everything that in time begun a time also wherein to take end, being himself without time the great Commander thereof and of all things else done therein.

The fame of the first Assyrian monarchy[20] is very ancient, and was no doubt both great and long, yet hath it nevertheless found an end; and, the more to put us in remembrance of our infirmity, was never with so much glory and valor by Ninus erected as it was with shame and cowardice by Sardanapalus[21] subverted. With like necessity fell the great empire of the Medes and Persians, the time thereof being come. And after them the Macedonians also. Neither hath the great Roman empire, or the proud city of Rome itself (sometimes the mistress of the world), herein found any exemption, but run the same course with the rest; which, grown great with continual triumphs and so strong as that it was not with foreign power to be shaken, converted the

---

[15]*Promiscuous. . . people:* those of the lower classes confusedly mingled.

[16]After about 1300, the Sultan's most formidable military force (composed originally of slaves and prisoners).

[17]Knolles proceeded B.A. in 1564–65, M.A. 1570.

[18]Sandwich, Kent, where Knolles was master of the grammar school.

[19]Probably the translation of Jean Bodin's *Six Books of a Commonweal* that Knolles published in 1606.

[20]Knolles' analysis is based upon the vision of the four monarchies in Daniel 7.4–7. See pp. 831, n.38. [Hayward, Henry IV, p. 8].

[21]*Ninus . . . Sardanapalus:* respectively the legendary founder of Nineveh and a notoriously profligate king of Assyria (ca. 822 B.C.).

forces of itself upon itself to the overthrow of the ancient liberty thereof, together with the utter subversion of the state. After which time that mighty monarchy (of all that every yet were the greatest) under the Roman emperors felt many an hard and perilous storm, and by little and little still declining (though sometime like a sick, aged body, by the valor or virtue of some one or other her worthy emperors a little relieved, and by and by again cast down by the folly or negligence of some others succeeding), it became at length a prey unto a foolish, rude, and barbarous nation 10 which it had before oftentimes overcome, and over which many the Roman captains had triumphed, and thereof taken their glorious surnames;[22] which now again without compassion, burning and sacking it, caused it to stoop and to yield unto the servile yoke which it had in former time proudly imposed upon the necks of others; wherein if anything be to be blamed it is not the fortune or folly of this or that man then sitting at the helm (although that may also much help the matter as a mean), but the instability of worldly things, never permanent but always changeable, 20 and the sooner for their heighth, and that so forcibly as that no man knoweth how to remedy the same, either if he did were he able to perform it; the greatest means that men could possibly devise for the stay thereof being oftentimes by a greater power from above converted unto the more speedy effecting of that against the which they were by man's wisdom provided. The like might be said of the Athenians, the Lacedaemonians, the Thebans, and of whom not?

What marvel, then, if the ancient kingdoms of the Turks 30 likewise in Persia and the lesser Asia, in Syria, Palestina, and Egypt, having run their appointed times, mightily impugned by the Christians, oppressed on the one side by the Tartars and on the other by the Mamalukes,[23] and at length by themselves rent in sunder (their destiny so requiring), lost at last their wonted majesty and so fell into a mere anarchy, as is in the former part of this history at large declared? Yet in this far more than any other people fortunate, that after the ruin of their former kingdoms, straightway out of themselves arise another, namely this Othoman monarchy, 40 the chief object of this history. . . .

THE LIFE OF MAHOMET... FIRST EMPEROR OF THE TURKS, AND FOR HIS MANY VICTORIES SURNAMED THE GREAT

[THE FALL OF CONSTANTINOPLE]

[On 29 May 1453, after a siege of fifty-three days, Mahomet II mounted his final assault upon the greatest prize of all, the capital of the Eastern empire.]

A little before day the Turks approached the walls and begun the assault, where shot and stones were delived upon them from walls as thick as hail, whereof little fell in vain by reason of the multitude of the Turks, who, pressing fast unto the walls, could not see in the dark how to defend themselves, but were without number wounded or slain. But these were of the common and worst soldiers, of whom the Turkish king made no more reckoning than to abate the first force of the defendants. Upon the first appearance of the day, Mahomet gave the sign appointed for the general assault, whereupon the city was in a moment and at one instant on every side most furiously assaulted by the Turks; for Mahomet, the more to distress the defendants and the better to see the forwardness of the soldiers, had before apppointed which part of the city every colonel with his regiment should assail. Which they valiantly performed, delivering their arrows and shot upon the defendants so thick that the light of the day was therewith darkened; others in the meantime courageously mounting the scaling ladders and coming even to handy[24] strokes with the defendants upon the wall, where the foremost were for most part violently borne forward by them which followed after. On the other side the Christians with no less courage withstood the Turkish fury, beating them down again with great stones and weighty pieces of timber, and so overwhelmed them with shot, darts, and arrows, and other hurtful and deadly devices from above that the Turks, dismayed with the terror thereof, were ready to retire.

Mahomet, seeing the great slaughter and discomfiture of his men, sent in fresh supplies of his janizaries and best men of war, whom he had for that purpose reserved as his last hope and refuge; by whose coming on, his fainting soldiers were again encouraged, and the terrible assault begun afresh. At which time the barbarous king ceased not to use all possible means to maintain the assault, by name calling upon this and that captain, promising unto some whom he saw forward golden mountains, and unto others in whom he saw any sign of cowardice threatening most terrible death; by which means the assault became most dreadful, death there raging in the middest of many thousands. And albeit that the Turks lay dead by heaps upon the ground, yet other fresh men pressed on still in their places over their dead bodies, and with divers event either slew or were slain by their enemies.

In this so terrible a conflict it chanced that Justinianus,[25] the general, to be wounded in the arm, who, losing much blood, cowardly withdrew himself from the place of his charge, not leaving any to supply his room, and so got into the city by the gate called Romana,[26] which he had caused to be opened in the inner wall, pretending the cause of his

[22]Additional names (*agnomina*) by which the Romans honored a man for some quality or achievement. Thus Publius Cornelius Scipio was given the *agnomen* "Africanus" in recognition of his victory over Carthage, in northern Africa.
[23]Members of a military caste (originally a body of fighting slaves sold by Genghis Khan to the sultan of Egypt in the 13th century) that dominated their adopted country for hundreds of years.
[24]Manual, hand-to-hand.
[25]John Justiniani (or Giustiniani), a Genoese who assumed command of the imperial troops several months before the final siege.
[26]Porta Romani (or St. Romanus), one of the principal gates in the wall bounding Constantinople on the west.

departure to be for the binding up of his wound but being indeed a man now altogether discouraged.

The soldiers there present, dismayed with the departure of their general and sore charged by the janizaries, forsook their stations and in haste fled to the same gate whereby Justinianus was entered; with the sight whereof the other soldiers, dismayed, ran thither by heaps also. But whilest they violently strive all together to get in at once, they so wedged one another in the entrance of the gate that few of so great a multitude got in; in which so great a press and confusion of minds eight hundred persons were there by them that followed trodden underfoot or thrust to death. The emperor[27] himself, for safeguard of his life flying with the rest, in that press as a man not regarded, miserably ended his days, together with the Greek empire. His dead body was shortly after found by the Turks amongst the slain, and known by his rich apparel; whose head, being cut off, was forthwith presented to the Turkish tyrant, by whose commandment it was afterward thrust upon the point of a lance and in great derision carried about as a trophy of his victory, first in the camp and afterwards up and down the city.

The Turks, encouraged with the flight of the Christians, presently advanced their ensigns upon the top of the uttermost wall crying victory; and by the breach entered as if it had been a great flood, which, having once found a breach in the bank, overfloweth and beareth down all before it; so the Turks, when they had won the utter[28] wall, entered the city by the same gate that was opened for Justinianus, and by a breach which they had before made with their great artillery; and without mercy cutting in pieces all that came in their way, without further resistance became lords of that most famous and imperial city. Some few there were of the Christians who, preferring death before the Turkish slavery, with their swords in their hands sold their lives dear unto their enemies; amongst whom, the two brethren Paulus and Troilus Bochiardi, Italians, with Theophilus Palaeologus, a Greek, and Joannus Stiauus, a Dalmatian, for their great valor and courage deserve to be had in eternal remembrance; who, after they had like lions made slaughter of their enemies, died in the midst of them embrued with their blood, rather oppressed by multitude than by true valor overcome. In this fury of the barbarians perished many thousands of men, women, and children without respect of age, sex, or condition. Many for safeguard of their lives fled into the temple of Sophia,[29] where they were all without pity slain except some few reserved by the barbarous victors to purposes more grievous than death itself. The rich and beautiful ornaments and jewels of that most sumptuous and magnificent church (the stately building of Justinianus the Emperor) were in the turning of a hand plucked down and carried away by the Turks, and the church itself, built for God to be honored in, for the present converted into a stable for their horses or a place for the execution of their abhominable and unspeakable filthiness. The image of the crucifix was also by them taken down and a Turk's cap put upon the head thereof, and so set up and shot at with their arrows, and afterwards in great derision carried about in their camp as it had been in procession, with drums playing before it, railing, and spitting at it, and calling it the god of the Christians. Which I note not so much done in contempt of the image as in the despite of Christ and the Christian religion.

But whilest some were thus spoiling of the churches, others were as busy in ransacking of private houses, where the miserable Christians were enforced to endure in their persons whatsoever pleased the insolent victors, unto whom all things were now lawful that stood with their lust, every common soldier having power of life and death, at his pleasure to spare or spill.[30] At which time riches were no better than poverty, and beauty worse than deformity. What tongue were able to express the misery of that time, or the proud insolence of those barbarous conquerors? Whereof so many thousands, every man with greediness fitted his own unreasonable desire, all which the poor Christians were enforced to endure. But to speak of the hidden treasure, money, plate, jewels, and other riches there found passeth credit. The Turks themselves wondered thereat, and were therewith so enriched that it is a proverb amongst them at this day if any of them grow suddenly rich to say, "He hath been at the sacking of Constantinople"; whereof if some reasonable part had in time been bestowed upon defence of the city, the Turkish king had not so easily taken both it and the city. . . .

The soldiers being all retired into the camp [after the three-day sack], Mahomet as a proud conqueror with great triumph entered into the city of Constantinople, then desolate and void of all Christian inhabitants; and there, after the manner of the Turkish kings, made a sumptuous and royal feast unto his bassas and other great captains, where, after he had surcharged himself with excess of meat and drink, he caused divers of the chief Christian captives, both men and women (of whom many were of the late emperor's line and race), to be in his presence put to death as he with his Turks sat banqueting, deeming his feast much more stately by such effusion of Christian blood. . . .

The glory of this famous city of Constantinople continued many hundred years, commanding a great part of the world until that by civil discord and private gain it was by little and little so weakened that the emperors of later times, for the maintenance of their estate, were glad to rely sometime upon one and sometime upon another,[31] yet still holding the title and state of an empire by the space of 1,121 years, whenas (God His judgment set apart, wonderful and shameful it is to consider how) it was by this Turkish king Mahomet so quickly taken and the Christian Empire of the East there utterly overthrown; which happened in the nine and twentieth day of May in the year of our Lord 1453,

[27]Constantine XI, last of the Palaeologus dynasty that ruled the Eastern empire from 1259 until 1453.   [28]Outer.
[29]Santa Sophia, famous church built in the 6th century by Justinian(us) the Great (d. 565), most notable of the emperors of the Eastern empire.   [30]Kill.
[31]*For the maintenance . . . another*: in order to survive had to rely upon first one ally and then another.

Constantinus Paleologus, the son of Helena and last Christian emperor, being then slain when he had reigned about eight years. Since which time it hath continued the imperial seat of the Turkish emperors, and so remaineth at this day.

John Speed [1552?-1629]

Despite a trace of condescension in Sir Henry Spelman's witticism (as reported by the gossipy John Aubrey) that Stow and Speed, both of whom were tailors, had stitched up English history, these two doughty chroniclers had served their new vocation well. With his plain, blunt style—and despite his occasional credulities—Stow at least had tried to ascertain and state the facts; and Speed, as Edmund Bolton pointed out (p. 894), was, though not elegantly learned, "without many fellows in Europe" in gathering and arranging data.

The son of a member of the Merchant Tailors' Company, Speed himself was admitted to the freedom of that guild in 1580 and thereafter plied his trade with some success. In part through thrift and work, no doubt, but mainly through the generous patronage of Fulke Greville, as Speed himself acknowledged, he was finally able to relinquish "the daily employments of a manual trade" for the ardors of research, whereby he could "express the inclination" of his mind. Parlaying an interest in cartography into a sound commercial venture, between 1608 and 1610 he published a series of fifty-four county maps (the work of John Norden and Christopher Saxton), and in 1611 he brought them all together (accompanied by his own descriptions) as *The Theater of the Empire of Great Britain*. In a prefatory epistle "To the Well-Affected and Favorable Reader," Speed, in apologizing for the use that he had made of others' work, shows something of his florid, fluent style:

> Applying myself wholly to the frame of this most goodly building, [I] have, as a poor laborer, carried the carved stones and polished pillars from the hands of the more skilled architects to be set in their fit places, which here I offer upon the altar of love to my country, and wherein I have held it no sacrilege to rob others of their richest jewels to adorn this my most beautiful nurse, whose womb was my conception, whose breasts were my nourishment, whose bosom my cradle, and lap (I doubt not) shall be my bed of rest, till Christ by His trumpet raise me thence.

It was as a sort of massive supplement (and with continuous pagination) to the *Theater* that Speed, in the same year, produced *The History of Great Britain*. For this ambitious undertaking he had, as he acknowledged, the help of many men, "so plenteous is our story, and largely requires it to be writ." But the work remains his own in structure and in its highly colored prose. With the obvious intention of improving on the clumsy annalistic method that Stow and even Camden (in the *Annales*) had employed, Speed divides the history of the realm into books, which, despite their disparities in length, detail, and quality, present a sequential, panoramic view of England's long travail with her invaders and her emergence as a nation. Thus the seven chapters of the first book (to which Speed assigns the number five, as a continuation of the *Theater*) deal with prehistoric Britain before the advent of the Romans. It is significant that the cherished myth of Trojan Brut, which Stow and Howes had vehemently asserted and which even Camden held in some affection, is rejected as a fraud. Whoever ruled the island before the Romans came, says Speed, it is no honor to derive them "from the scum of such conquered people as the Trojans were," for Brut "cloudeth" England's glory by the murder of his parents and "embaseth" the modern Englishman "as sprung from Venus, that lascivious adulteress."

Whereas Speed requires fifty-four chapters in Book VI to deal with Roman Britain and forty-four in Book VII to relate the history of the Saxons, in Book VIII he devotes only seven chapters to the Danes. But the gigantic summit of the work is Book IX, entitled "The Succession of England's Monarchs" from William the Conqueror to Elizabeth. Its twenty-four chapters and almost five hundred pages make the eleven pages of Book X, on the reign of James I, appear to be a tiny coda. The "Summary Conclusion of the Whole" is a "scanted epitome" where, as Speed explains, the reader may "ascend these five national stories already finished" and thus be led into the sixth "now most happily begun."

As Degory Wheare's encomium shows (p. 903), Speed's works enjoyed a great success. The *Theater* was promptly published in a Latin version (1616) and reprinted twice in English (1627, 1631), while the first edition of the *History* was reissued in 1614 and successively enlarged in 1623, 1632, and 1650 before attaining an epitome in 1676. Meanwhile the "venerable author," as Wheare referred to him, was adding to his fame with other publications. In 1610 he had secured an exclusive right for ten years to print and insert into the Holy Bible his *Genealogies Recorded in the Sacred Scriptures*, and the work became so popular that by 1640 it had gone through more than thirty printings. *A Cloud of Witnesses . . . Confirming unto Us the Truth of the Histories in God's Most Holy Work*, which achieved three editions between 1616 and 1628, no doubt added to his wealth and reputation. He died at seventy-seven, having produced not only these weighty and successful books but also twelve sons and six daughters.

My text is based upon *The History of Great Britaine Under the Conquests of yᵉ Romans, Saxons, Danes and Normans. Their Originals, Manners, Warres, Coines & Seales: with yᵉ Successions, Lives, acts & Issues of the English Monarchs from Iulius Caesar, to our most gracious Soueraigne King Iames. By Iohn Speed*, 1611 (STC 23045). Speed receives at least incidental mention from most students of historiography listed in the General Bibliography, Section V. J. Arlott has edited *John Speed's England. A Coloured Facsimile of the Maps and Text* (4 parts, 1953–54), and E. G. Taylor has edited *An Atlas of Tudor England and Wales: Forty Plates from John Speed's Pocket Atlas of 1627* (1951).

from The History of Great Britain (1611)

THE PROEME. TO THE LEARNED AND LOVERS
OF GREAT BRITAIN'S GLORY.

Having thus far traveled in the protract and description of this famous Empire of Great Britain,[1] I might here have rested and claimed the privilege that years and imbecility have brought me unto, had not a further desire in others urged it a matter incident[2] historically to lay down the originals of those nations and successions of those monarchs which either by birth or conquest have aspired to the imperial crown. And albeit I find myself both tired in the former and most unfit to prosecute this latter, yet will I endeavor to give herein my best assays,[3] though as my [10] labors, so my wants also, thereby will be made more vulgar to the world. . . .

But by what fate I am enforced still to go forward I know not, unless it be the ardent affection and love to my native country, wherein I must confess that nature in those gifts hath been both liberal, yea, and prodigal, though Fortune as sparing and fast-handed[4] against me, ever checking the bit with the reins of necessity, and curbing the means that should illustrate my labors. Which moves me sometimes to think that if the great philosopher Theophrastus[5] had cause on his deathbed to accuse nature for giving man so long a lesson and so short a life, then I against fortune may as justly exclaim, that hath assigned me so great a labor and so little

HISTORY OF GREAT BRITAIN   [1]Speed's *History* developed from and is a continuation of his *Theater of the Empire of Great Britain* (1611), a sumptuous collection of maps by such eminent cartographers as Christopher Saxton and John Norden for which he supplied descriptions. *Protract*: delineation.   [2]Pertinent.   [3]Endeavors.
[4]Stingy, tight-fisted.
[5]Greek philosopher and scientist (d. ca. 287 B.C.) who succeeded Aristotle as head of the Peripatetic school. The anecdote about his death seems to be based on Diogenes Laertius, *Lives of Eminent Philosophers*, V.40–41.

means. And therefore let it not seem offensive that I draw my waters from the cisterns of others, who am not able to fetch them at the springhead myself; neither that I strike upon the same anvil unto their sound, though nothing so loud nor with the like strength, wherein yet this fruit at least will (I hope) redound of my endeavors that I shall incite the more learned—if not otherwise, yet in emulation of me—to free the face drawn by Apelles[6] from the censure of the fault or defect in the foot, and not only to amend but even to new-mold the whole. Which thing, though my days are near spent, and with Barzillai I may say that "music to me is now unpleasing,"[7] yet doth my ear thirst after the set of that strain, as Socrates' thoughts ran ever on his book, who, the night before he was to suffer death, was desirous to learn music because "he would die learning still something." . . .[8]

Although our many records are perished by the invasions of strangers, through their covetous conquest of so fair a land, or in the civil dissensions of homebred aspirers that have sought the possession of so rich a crown, yet Truth hath left us no less beholding unto her than mightier nations, and them that would be far more famous. Neither is it to be wondered at that the records of Great Britain are eaten up with Time's teeth, as Ovid speaks,[9] whenas in Time's ruins lie buried their registers that have been kept with a stronger guard, as Titus Livy in the entrance of his *History* affirmeth of the Romans. "As for those things," saith he, "as are reported either before or at the foundation of the City more beautified and set out with poets' fables than grounded upon pure and faithful reports, I mean neither to aver nor disprove."[10] Of whose uncertainties let us a while hear the reporters themselves speak before we proceed to the certain successions of our British monarchs; until which time the credit of our history may well be said to weigh with (if not down peise)[11] many others. . . . [Since the Greeks and Romans supplied the deficiencies of their early records with fabulous and sometimes fanciful reconstructions, we too must sometimes be content with less than sober facts.]

These things thus standing, let us give leave to Antiquity, who sometimes mingleth falsehoods with truth to make the beginnings of policies seem more honorable, and whose power is far screwed into the world's conceit that with Jerome we may say "Antiquity is allowed with such general applause that known untruths many times are pleasing unto many."[12] Yet with better regard to reverend Antiquity, whom Job's opposer wills us inquire after,[13] and to our own relations in delivering their censures, let this be considered: that more things are let slip than are comprehended in any man's writings, and yet more therein written than any man's life (though it be long) will admit him to read. Neither let us be forestalled with any prejudicate[14] opinions of the reporters that in some things may justly be suspected, or in affection which by nature we owe to our natural country; nor consent, as Livy speaketh, to stand to the ancientness of reports when it seemeth to take away the certainty of truth.[15] To keep a mean betwixt both, myself with Bildad do confess that "I am but of yesterday, and know nothing,"[16] and therefore will relate the original names and

nations of this famous island, with the successions of her monarchs and historical actions, so far only as is most approved by the best writers, and will leave other clouds of obscurity to be cleared by the labors of a more learned pen.

BOOK IX, CHAPTER 24

[THE ESSEX REBELLION]

The fall of Robert Devereux, second earl of Essex, constituted a lurid finale to the splendors of Elizabethan England. When this dazzling but hot-headed young favorite of the queen set forth from London in March 1599 as the newly appointed governor-general of Ireland, the enthusiasm was so high that Shakespeare, writing in the summer of that year, could compare his anticipated victory over the rebellious Irish to the triumph of a "conqu'ring Caesar":

> Were now the general of our gracious empress,
> As in good time he may, from Ireland coming,
> Bringing rebellion broached on his sword,
> How many would the peaceful city quit,
> To welcome him!

But when Essex, after an abortive campaign, made a dishonorable treaty with Tyrone, the Irish leader, and, without permission, slunk back to London in September, the queen and her Privy Council were both angry and dismayed. Despite her own affection (or perhaps infatuation) for Essex, the queen resolved to take decisive action: "first," as Speed says, "to remit his durance to his own house and then—loth to look into his faults but with her princely eye of favor—to proceed unto some moderate censure of his actions, to the end he might see his own errors, and she so limit his power as her own might be secured."

To which end she assigned certain of her Privy Council to convent[17] him concerning the breaking of his former instructions for the North-Irish prosecution and the manner of his treating with Tyrone,[18] his coming from Ireland and leaving that kingdom contrary to Her Majesty's express commandment signed under the royal hand and signet.[19] Whereunto his answer was that the state of war held it a maxim to make good the stand before the remove, and that

[6]Most celebrated painter of antiquity (fourth cent. B.C.), none of whose works survive. [7]2 Samuel 19.35.
[8]Speed is perhaps thinking of Plato's *Apology*, 60–61.
[9]*Metamorphoses*, XV.234–36.
[10]Titus Livius (59 B.C.–17 A.D.), Roman historian whose *Annals* (some of which are lost) trace the history of Rome from its legendary beginnings to his own day. Speed quotes from Bk. I, "Praefatio." [11]Weigh down.
[12]Jerome or Eusebius Hieronymus (340?–420), great father of the church, whose Latin version of the Bible, known as the Vulgate, is still in use. Speed is quoting from "In Librum Iob praefatio," *Opera* (ed. Desiderius Erasmus, 1565), III, 24.
[13]Job 8.8. [14]Prejudiced, biased. [15]*Annals*, VIII.xl.3–5.
[16]Job 8.9. [17]Summon.
[18]Hugh O'Neill, third baron of Dungannon and third earl of Tyrone (1540?–1616), Irish rebel whom Essex had been instructed to subdue. [19]Seal.

it was one thing at table to direct but another thing in field to effect, especially in Ireland, whose war was with bogs and woods as well as with men. And to the rest of the objections he answered with such obedient discretion and loyal submission as he well satisfied the honorable presence: only a suspension from the exercise of some of his offices was decreed until Her Majesty's pleasure should otherwise order it. Shortly after, he was set at full liberty, the queen sending him word that she well hoped his surest guard would now be his own discretion.

But seeing his wonted greatness restrained though the scope of his liberty was thus far enlarged, he presently mounted higher with the wings of discontent; for deprived of offices, neglected in court, and all his foreign services poured into Her Majesty's lap, was now (as he imagined) there wrapped up and laid in oblivion. Neither were these his grievances lessened by his military followers, who daily watered these ill-set plants with their exasperated complaints till they were sprung to some height; and still to nourish their sap, many projects were cast and conferences held how to lop off other branches which, as they feared, would hinder their growth; till lastly, at Drury House,[20] they agreed on the manner—O had it withered before it had blowmed,[21] or died in the graffing[22] before it took sap!— which was by violent hand to bring the earl into Her Majesty's presence and to remove from her such as they deemed his opposites.

The frequent assembly unto Essex House[23] by noblemen, knights, captains, and others was presently observed by the statists[24] in court, to stop the current of which confluence before it grew to a flood Secretary Herbert[25] was sent from Her Majesty to require him to repair before the Lords of her Council, then assembled at Salisbury Court,[26] which he, excusing with sickness, neglected to do; and the same night, upon some sinister reports, set a double watch about him, pretending some danger to be meant to his person. For whose defense, the next morning (being Sunday) many repaired unto his house, among whom as chief were the Earls of Rutland and Southampton, the Lords Sands and Monteagle, accompanied with a troop of gallant gentlemen, their followers.[27]

Her Majesty, hearing of these disorderly proceedings, in her princely wisdom thought to cast water upon this begun fire before it brake forth into flame, and thereupon sent four men of much honor unto his place to offer him justice for any griefs and to command the assembly to depart. The persons sent were the Lord Keeper of the Great Seal, the earl of Worcester, Sir Francis Knollys, his [i.e., Essex'] uncle, and the Lord Chief Justice of England, all of them in high honor and favour with the earl himself.[28]

These, coming to his house without Temple Bar,[29] were received in themselves, but scarce any of their servants suffered to follow excepting the Bearer of the Purse and Seal, where, finding the court full of those his followers, the Lord Keeper, putting off his hat, told them that "they were sent by Her Majesty to understand the cause of this their assembly and to let them know that if they had any particular cause of grief against any person whatsoever they

should have hearing and justice." The earl of Essex answered that his life was sought after, and that he had been perfidiously dealt withal. To which the Lord Chief Justice replied that if any such matter was attempted, it was fit for him to declare it, assuring him of a faithful relation, and that Her Majesty would do him justice. Which promises the Lord Keeper seconded and desired the earl to declare his griefs, if not openly yet in private, and he doubted not but to procure him full satisfaction; and then turning towards the multitude with a louder voice said: "I do command you all upon your allegiance to lay down your weapons and to depart." Whereupon the earl himself went into his bookchamber, these four councilors following him in hope of private conference; but so far off was he from hearing them further, or answering to their demands, that leaving them there under sure custody he returned to his other attendants.

With whom in tumultuous manner he made into London;[30] his followers crying that the earl of Essex should

[20]Town house of Henry Wriothesley, third earl of Southampton (1573–1624), Essex's intimate friend and aide-de-camp, to whom Shakespeare had dedicated *Venus and Adonis* (1593) and *Lucrece* (1594) and whom some scholars identify with the young man of the *Sonnets* (1609). It was Southampton who on the very eve of Essex's rebellion on Sunday, 8 February 1601, arranged and paid for a revival of Shakespeare's *Richard II* at the Globe, presumably in an effort to prepare the public for a coup d'état. Though brought to trial with Essex as a principal party to the alleged conspiracy and condemned to execution, his punishment was commuted to life imprisonment. Following his release by James I in 1603 he rose to new and higher honors.   [21]Bloomed.
[22]Grafting.
[23]Princely residence of the earl of Essex between the Strand and the River Thames, formerly occupied by Robert Dudley, earl of Leicester, and therefore known as Leicester House.
[24]Politicians.
[25]Dr. John Herbert, recently appointed second secretary to the Privy Council.
[26]Former London residence of the bishops of Salisbury in Fleet Street that, according to John Stow's *Survey of London* (1598), had recently been acquired by Sir Thomas Sackville, the Lord Treasurer, and "enlarged" with "stately buildings."
[27]In addition to Southampton, some of the principal figures in the Essex coterie were Roger Manners (1576–1612), fifth earl of Rutland, William Parker (d. 1618), fourth earl of Monteagle (later famous for his part in exposing the Gunpowder Plot), and Charles Blount (1563–1606), earl of Devonshire, long the lover and finally the husband of Essex' sister Penelope. Although these magnates, despite their deep involvement in the plot, survived, some of Essex' humbler followers were less lucky. Sir Christopher Blount, Sir Charles Danvers, and Sir John Davies—three professional soldiers who had served with him in Ireland—were all condemned to death (although Davies was reprieved). Two others who met their master's fate were his learned secretary Henry Cuff, a former professor of Greek at Oxford, and Sir Gelly (or Gilliam) Merrick, his steward.
[28]Sir Thomas Egerton, Edward Somerset, Sir William (not Francis) Knollys, and Sir Edward Popham.
[29]A gateway separating the Strand from Fleet Street, and thus Westminster from the City of London.
[30]The geography of the situation is important. Leaving Essex House in the Strand, the earl and his followers went down Fleet

have been murthered by Cobham, Cecil, and Raleigh,[31] all men amazed what this did mean. Thus passed he from Ludgate through Cheapside into Fenchurch Street, where he entered the house of a supposed friend[32] (then one of the sheriffs), who, seeing the multitude, avoided himself out at a back door; when presently in divers parts of the City Essex was proclaimed a traitor to the no less grief of the citizens than fears of his followers; and thence returning with a halberd in his hand and a table napkin about his neck, came into Gracious Street, where a while he made his stand (the Lord Mayor and others being assembled at the upper end towards Leadenhall), no one citizen or servant showing him any sign of assistance. The case so desperate, one of the principal offenders contrived how by redeeming his fault to save his own life; who, hastening into the Strand to Essex House and coming to Sir John Davies as being sent from the earl, gat release of the four councilors, under whose guard they had been hitherto kept.

Essex, now despairing of all succors in London, saw it was bootless there to make his abode and therefore retired again towards Paul's, meaning to pass Ludgate the way that he came; but being resisted by a company of pikemen and other forces, made by that stout and noble prelate the then lord bishop of London,[33] he was put back, Sir Christopher Blount sore hurt, and young Tracy slain, besides some others on the queen's part, himself narrowly escaping, being thrust through the hat with a pike. So hence again returning, at Queen Hive he took boat, bidding the City and his fortunes adieu.

His enterprise thus frustrate, with a mind distracted he rowed up the river and landed at the water gate of his own house, which he presently fortified; and the Lord Admiral assaulted, suffering notwithstanding the countess of Essex,[34] the Lady Rich,[35] and their gentlewomen to depart, which done, he forced the garden even to the walls of the house. Some resistance was made and some persons slain upon either part, which the earl perceiving presently yielded, desiring only that he might be civilly used and that he might have an honorable trial; and so being first brought to Lambeth House,[36] where an hour or two he remained with the lord archbishop (his ever most loving but then most mournful friend), was thence with some other lords and gentlemen conveyed by water to the Tower about ten of the clock the same night; having then experience that vain is the love of the commons to a subject (how great soever) when it is counterbalanced with the dutiful obedience unto their prince.

Upon the nineteenth of the same moneth the earl of Essex and Southampton were arraigned at Westminster, the Lord Buckhurst,[37] Lord High Treasurer of England, being made Lord Steward for the day, where the great resolution of the one contemning death and the sweet temper of the other well deserving life did breed most compassionate affections in all men, hearing the sentence of law to pass upon them.[38] The one of them remained prisoner in the Tower during the reign of the queen, and by the gracious clemency of our sovereign lord King James at his coming to the crown had pardon of life and restauration[39]

of blood; the other (Essex) the five-and-twentith of February, being Ash Wednesday, suffered upon the green within the Tower, rendering his soul to God with a most penitent and Christian constancy, whose last speeches were to this effect:

"My lords and Christian brethren who are present witnesses of my just punishment, I confess (to God's glory) myself a most wretched sinner, and that my sins in number exceed the hairs of my head; that good which I would have done, that did I not, and the evil which I would not, that did I. For all which I beseech my Saviour Christ to be a mediator to His Father my God, especially for this my last sin, this great, this crying, this bloody, this infectious sin wherein, through love of me, so many have been drawn to offend God, their sovereign, and the world. I beseech God, Her Majesty, and the state, to forgive us. And I beseech Him to bless her with a prosperous reign, with a wise and understanding heart, to bless the nobles and ministers of the church and state. I likewise beseech you and all the world to hold a charitable opinion of me for my intention towards Her Majesty, whose death (I protest) I never meant, nor any violence towards her person. I thank God I never was atheist in not believing the Scriptures; neither papist, trusting in my own merits; but am assured to be saved by the mercies and merits of Christ Jesus my Saviour. This faith I was brought up in, and herein I am now ready to die, beseeching you all to join your souls with me in prayer that

---

Street past Ludgate and St. Paul's into the heart of the City, where they spread along such principal thoroughfares as Cheapside, Fenchurch Street, Gracechurch (*Gracious*) Street, and Leadenhall Street in a futile effort to arouse the citizenry. Retracing their route, they were blocked by troops at Ludgate, whereupon the earl made his way to the dock at Queen Hythe (*Queen Hive*) and ignominiously returned to Essex House by water.

[31]Sir Henry Cobham, Sir Robert Cecil (Lord Burghley's brother), and Sir Walter Raleigh, leaders of the court faction hostile to Essex.

[32]Sir Thomas Smith or Smythe (1558?–1625), wealthy merchant and entrepreneur who was subsequently acquitted of the charge of complicity in Essex' rebellion.

[33]Actually, the file of City soldiers who drew a chain across Ludgate and thus blocked Essex' retreat along the Strand had been stationed on orders of the queen.

[34]The former Frances Walsingham, daughter of Elizabeth's secretary of state and widow of Sir Philip Sidney (d. 1586), who married Essex four years after her first husband's death.

[35]Essex' sister Penelope (1562?–1607), allegedly the inspiration of Sir Philip Sidney's *Astrophil and Stella*, who married Robert Rich, third Baron Rich, in 1581 and was divorced by him, after a long estrangement, in 1605.

[36]Palace of Thomas Whitgift, archbishop of Canterbury, at Lambeth on the south bank of the Thames.

[37]Thomas Sackville (1536–1608), one of the most distinguished of Elizabeth's advisers, who in his youth had contributed notably to *A Mirror for Magistrates* (1563) and had collaborated with Thomas Norton in writing *Gorboduc* (1561), the first English tragedy in blank verse.

[38]One of the conspicuous omissions in Speed's skimpy account of Essex' trial is the part played in it by Francis Bacon, who turned bitterly upon his former benefactor and taunted him with treason.

[39]Restoration.

my soul may be lifted up by faith above all earthly things; and first I desire forgiveness of all the world, even as freely as from my heart I forgive all the world."

And then kneeling down said, "I have been divers times in places of danger, where death was neither so present nor so certain; and yet even then I felt the weakness of my flesh; and therefore now in this last and great conflict I desire God's assistance by His preserving spirit." And so with a most heavenly prayer and faithful constancy (as if his soul were then already in heavenly fruition) he humbled himself to the block, and spreading abroad his arms (the sign that he had given to his headsman), his head was with three strokes of the ax severed from his body; the great heaviness of all men appearing as well by their countenances as spleen[40] against his executioner, who was in danger of his life at his return had not the sheriffs assisted him to his home.

For accessories and chief counselors in this offence died at Tyburn[41] Sir Gilliam Merrick, knight, and Henry Cuff (for his exquisite learning much bewailed of all men); and five days after them, upon the scaffold on Tower Hill, were beheaded Sir Charles Danvers and Sir Christopher Blount, knights. And before any of these, Thomas Lee,[42] a captain, was executed for words spoken touching the earl of Essex his deliverance, to move or rather to enforce the queen thereunto, as his words were construed; who nevertheless confidently took his death that he never had thought of any violent attempt.

As the death of this nobleman was much lamented by the subjects (whose love towards him was so ingrafted as I think I may well say never subject had more), so Her Majesty likewise, having such a star fallen from her firmament, was inwardly moved and outwardly oftentimes would show passions of her grief, even till the time of her approaching end, when two years after she laid down her head in the grave as the most resplendent sun setteth at last in a western could.

A SUMMARY CONCLUSION OF THE WHOLE

[Having brought his history down to the accession of James I and the auspicious beginning of a new reign and a new dynasty, Speed casts a backward glance at the terrain he had traversed and makes his formal valediction.]

These then, worthy reader, are the heads whence have issued such plentiful springs, that now, met together in one body, the stream is grown very big, which thing I ever feared but could never prevent, offending rather with the niggard who thinketh every mite too much than sinning with the prodigal in superfluous excess: so plenteous is our story, and so largely requires it to be writ. Through all which my weak body with many years' labor hath alone traveled, as well in the reviewing of the geographical parts of the land as in the compiling of the succeeding history, though far unable to perfect either according to their own worths.

But lest the weight of the whole should rest upon so slender a prop as myself, I have laid my buildings upon far stronger arches, as by the many alleged[43] authorities may appear. For first, the charts[44] for the most part traced by others[45] and most of them divulged unto view were the foundations of my begun pains in supplying their wants with my many additions and dimensions of the shire-towns and cities' true platforms.[46] The further descriptions of sundry provinces I have gleaned from the famous works of the most worthy and learned Camden,[47] whose often sowed seeds in that soil hath lastly brought forth a most plenteous harvest. For the body of the history many were the manuscripts, notes, and records wherewith my honored and learned friends supplied me; but none more, or so many, as did the worthy repairer of eating Time's ruins, the learned Sir Robert Cotton, knight baronet, another Philadelphus[48] in preserving old monuments and ancient records: whose cabinets were unlocked and library continually set open to my free access, and from whence the chiefest garnishments of this work have been enlarged and brought—such as are the antique altars and trophies in stone by him preserved from perishing oblivion; the coins of gold, silver, alcumy, and copper of the Britons, Romans, Saxons, Danes, and English, with the broad seals of those kings since the same were in use; all of them so followed from the original models and moneys by the most exquisite and curious hand[49] of our age, as any eye may witness they are the true prints from those stamps. The like most acceptable helps, both of books and collections (especially in matters remoter from our times), I continually received from that worthy divine, Master John Barkham,[50] a gentleman composed of learning, virtue, and courtesy as being no less ingenuously willing than learnedly able to advance and forward all virtuous endeavors. Besides these some other supply I have had, for my disease grown dangerous, and life held in suspense, it behooved him who had towards the

[40]Anger.

[41]Principal place of execution of malefactors until 1783, near the present site of the Marble Arch.

[42]Valued associate of Essex in Ireland who, following his master's arrest, was detected in a crazy plan to break in upon the queen at dinner and compel from her a royal pardon.

[43]Cited. [44]Maps. Text *chards*.

[45]In a marginal gloss Speed specifies, among others to whom he was indebted for the *charts* (in *The Theater of the Empire of Great Britain*, the companion volume to his *History*), Christopher Saxton, whose handsome maps of English and Welsh counties were published in 1579, and John Norden (1548–1625?), author of such immensely popular books of devotion as *A Pensive Man's Practice* (1584) and *A Pensive Soul's Delight* (1603), compiler of an incomplete series of county histories called *Speculum Britanniae* (1593 ff.), and engraver of a famous map of contemporary London. [46]Ground plans. [47]See pp. 816 ff.

[48]Surname of Ptolemy II (309–246 B.C.), king of Egypt, noted for his patronage of the library at Alexandria.

[49]The draftsman responsible for the illustrations of coins and seals (a feature of Speed's *History*) is identified in a marginal gloss as "Christ. Swifter."

[50]Antiquary and divine (1572?–1642) who contributed to Speed's *History* the sections on King John and Henry II. The extensive collection of coins that he presented to Archbishop Laud was deposited by that prelate in the Bodleian Library at Oxford.

publishing bestowed so great cost to forward the finishing;[51] and to that end he procured me to his further charges an assistant[52] in the lives of our middle English kings, whose stories and reigns by the judicious may by their styles be known to be written with another pen. Lastly for the matters of heraldry, the willing and ready pains of Master William Smith,[53] Rouge Dragon (an officer-at-arms) was ever at hand. And by these hands this building is mounted to such an height as thou seest, which thus now finished, this scanted epitome may well serve thy footsteps as stairs to ascend these [10] five national stories already finished and lead thee into the sixth[54] now most happily begun.

Where from those mounted heights thou mayst behold how Time hath squared the stones of these buildings, how Fortune hath varied in contriving the work, and how the Fates have erected, polished, and pulled down the supporting pillars of Great Britain's Theater. From whose terrace with David cast not thy lusting eye upon unlawful delights,[55] nor with Babel's king boast that this was built by thy own might;[56] but with Moses confess that from a small stock [20] (as a graft of the Lord's planting) thou art now grown into a great nation, mighty and full of people.[57] And with Solomon make supplication unto thy great Jehovah that the ark of His strength may ever rest in this house, and His eyes be ever open thereon day and night.[58] With the prophet pray that this building may be as beauteous as his, the foundations laid with sapphires, her windows with the emeralds, and her gates with the carbuncles;[59] that the deserts of this

chosen Zion may be as Eden, and her wilderness like the garden of God;[60] her government peace, her people the saints of salvation, and her kings the signets on God's right hand, successively to sit on this royal throne till Christ, the King of Kings, shall come in the clouds and from the rainbow, the throne of His majesty, pronounce us blessed and make us heirs with himself of that kingdom which never shall have end. Unto which, Christ with His Father and Holy Spirit, three in persons but one God eternal, undividable in deity, be ascribed all praise, honor, glory, wisdom, power, and might for evermore. Amen.

[51]*Him . . . finishing*: presumably George Humble (fl. 1611–32), a London printer and bookseller in Pope's Head Alley at the sign of the White Horse, who had secured the rights to Speed's *Theater of the Empire of Great Britain* on 29 April 1608, and who (with his partner John Sudbury) brought out the *History* "cum privilegio."
[52]Identified in a marginal gloss as "M[aster] Ed[mund] Bol[ton]," for whom see pp. 891 ff.
[53]Noted authority on heraldry (1550?–1618) who was created Rouge Dragon (that is, a pursuivant in the College of Arms) in 1597.
[54]*Five . . . sixth*: the British, Roman, Saxon, Danish, and Norman eras, leading to the happy reign of James I with which Speed closes. [55]2 Samuel 11.2–3.
[56]Daniel 4.30. *Babel's king*: Nebuchadnezzar, king of Babylon (d. 562 B.C.). [57]*Moses . . . people*: Deuteronomy 26.
[58]*Solomon . . . night*: 2 Chronicles 6.20.
[59]*Prophet . . . carbuncles*: Isaiah 54.11–12. [60]Isaiah 51.3.

Samuel Daniel[1] [1563?-1619]

from The First Part of the History of England (1613)

I. EPISTLE DEDICATORY

TO THE RIGHT HONORABLE SIR ROBERT CARR,[1] VISCOUNT ROCHESTER, KNIGHT OF THE MOST NOBLE ORDER OF THE GARTER, AND ONE OF HIS MAJESTY'S MOST HONORABLE PRIVY COUNCIL

To give a reason of my work is in my part as well as to do it. And therefore, my noble Lord, why I undertook to write [30] this history of England, I allege, that having spent much time of my best understanding in this part of human learning, history, both in foreign countries[2] where especially I took those notions as made most for the conduct of business in this kind, and also at home, where it hath been in my fortune (besides conference with men of good experience)

to have seen many of the best discourses, negotiations,

[1]For a commentary on Daniel, and for other excerpts from his work, see Poetry, pp. 24 ff. and Books and Men, pp. 683 ff.
THE FIRST PART [1]An impecunious but handsome Scot (d. 1645) who accompanied James I to England in 1603 and, until dislodged by George Villiers, later duke of Buckingham, in 1614 (see p. 754), was the most powerful of the king's favorites. Created Viscount Rochester in 1611 and earl of Somerset three years later, he was finally brought down by his notorious marriage to the divorced countess of Essex and by his complicity in the murder of Sir Thomas Overbury in 1613 (see p. 715).
[2]Daniel apparently visited Italy in the late 1580's, just before becoming tutor to William Herbert, son of the second earl of Pembroke and his countess, herself the famous sister of Sir Philip Sidney.

instructions, and relations of the general affairs of the world, I resolved to make trial of my forces in the contexture[3] of our own history, which for that it lay dispersed in confused pieces hath been much desired of many; and held to be some blemish to the honor of our country to come behind other nations in this kind, when neither in magnificence of state, glory of action, or abilities of nature we are any way inferior to them. Nor is there any nation whose ancestors have done more worthy things, both at home and abroad, especially for matter of war. For since the Romans no one people hath fought so many battails prosperously. And therefore out of the tender remorse to see these men much defrauded of their glory so dearly bought, and their affairs confusedly delivered, I was drawn (though the lest able for such a work) to make this adventure; which howsoever it prove will yet show the willingness I have to do my country the best service I could; and perhaps, by my example, induce others of better abilities to undergo the same. In the meantime, to draw out a small substance of so huge a mass, as might have something of the virtue of the whole, could not be but an extraction worthy the pains, seeing it concerns them most to know the general affairs of England who have least leisure to read them.

And the better to fit their use, I have made choice to deliver only those affairs of action that most concern the government, dividing my work into three sections according to the periods of those ages that brought forth the most remarkable changes; and every section into three books. Whereof the first briefly relates the various mutations of state, plantation, and supplantation of the inhabitants in the chiefest part of this isle before the coming of the Norman. The second book contains the life and reign of William the First. The third, the succession of William the Second, Henry the First, and Stephen. And this part I have here done.[4]

The second section begins with Henry the Second, the first of the royal family of Plantagenet,[5] contains the lives of fourteen princes of that line, and takes up 339 years. A space of time that yields us a view of a wider extent of dominion by the accession[6] of a third part of France to the crown of England; more matter of action, with a greater magnificence and glory of state than ever, intermixed with strange varieties and turns of fortune; the inflammation of three civil wars, besides popular insurrections; the deposing of four kings; and five usurpations, which, in the end, so rent the state as all the glory of foreign greatness which that line brought expired with itself.

The third section contains the succession of five sovereign princes of the line of Tudor, and the space of 129 years.[7] A time not of that virility as the former, but more subtle, and let out into wider notions, and bolder discoveries of what lay hidden before. A time wherein began a greater improvement of the sovereignty, and more came to be effected by wit than the sword: equal and just encounters of state and state in forces, and of prince and prince in sufficiency. The opening of a new world which strangely altered the manner of this, enhancing both the rate of all things by the induction[8] of infinite treasure, and opened a wider way to corruption, whereby princes got much without their swords. Protections and confederations to counterpoise and prevent overgrowing powers came to be maintained with larger pensions; ledger[9] ambassadors first employed abroad for intelligences; common banks erected to return and furnish moneys for these businesses; besides strange alterations in the state ecclesiastical; religion brought forth to be an actor in the greatest designs of ambition and faction. To conclude, a time stored with all variety of accidents fit for example and instruction. This is the scope of my design.

And this I address to you, my noble Lord, not only as a testimony of my gratitude for the honorable regard you have taken of me but also in respect you being now a public person, and thereby engaged in the state of England, as well as incorporated into the body thereof, may here learn by the observance of affairs past (for that reason is strengthened by the success of example) to judge the righter of things present; and withal that herein you, seeing many precedents of such as have run even and direct courses like your own (howsoever the success was) never wanted glory, may thereby be comforted to continue this way of integrity, and of being a just servant both to the king and the kingdom. Nor can there be a better testimony to the world of your own worth than that you love and cherish the same (wheresoever you find it) in others.

And if by your hand it may come to the sight of His Royal Majesty, whose abilities of nature are such as whatsoever comes within his knowledge is presently under the dominion of his judgment, I shall think it happy; and though in itself it shall not be worthy his leisure, yet will it be much to the glory of his reign that in his days there was a true history written—a liberty proper only to commonwealths, and never permitted to kingdoms but under good princes. Upon which liberty notwithstanding I will not usurp, but tread as tenderly on the graves of his magnificent progenitors as possibly I can, knowing there may, in a kind, be *laesa maiestas*[10] even against dead princes. And as in reverence to them I will deliver nothing but what is fit for the world to know, so through the whole work I will make conscience that it shall know nothing but (as faithfully as I can gather it) truth, protesting herein to have no other passion than the zeal thereof, nor to hold any stubborn opinion, but liable to submission and better information.

Your Lordship's to command,
Samuel Daniel

[3]Weaving together.
[4]*And . . . done*: in *The First Part of the History of England* (1612).
[5]The dynasty (sometimes called Anjou or Angevin) founded by Geoffrey, count of Anjou (1113–51) and his wife Matilda, daughter of Henry I of England, that occupied the English throne from the accession of Henry II (1154) to the deposition of Richard II (1399) and that survived in its collateral branches of York and Lancaster until the advent of Henry VII (1485). Although Daniel is accurate in assigning to this royal line the *fourteen princes* from Henry II to Richard III, his arithmetic is faulty: they ruled for 331 years.
[6]Acquisition, addition.
[7]Henry VII, his son Henry VIII, and his grandchildren Edward VI, Mary, and Elizabeth ruled England from 1485 to 1603.
[8]Introduction.   [9]Resident.
[10]*Lèse majesté*, affront to royalty.

from The Collection of the History of England (1618)

CERTAIN ADVERTISEMENTS TO THE READER[1]

This piece of our history, which here I divulge[2] not but impart privately to such worthy persons as have favored my endeavors therein, should long since have been much more, and come abroad with dedication, preface, and all the complements of a book, had my health and means been answerable to my desire; but being otherwise, I must entreat my friends to be content to be paid by pieces, as I may, and accept my willingness to yield as much as mine ability can perform. It is more than the work of one man (were he of never so strong forces) to compose a passable contexture of the whole history of England. For although the inquisition of ancient times, written by others, be prepared, yet the collection and disposition I find most laborious. And I know *quam sit magnum dare aliquid in manus hominum*,[3] especially in this kind, wherein more is expected than hath been delivered before. Curiosity will not be content with ordinaries.[4] For mine own part, I am so greedy of doing well as nothing suffices the appetite of my care herein. I had rather be master of a small piece handsomely contrived than of vast rooms ill proportioned and unfurnished, and I know many others are of my mind.

> Daniel then proceeds to name his principal sources, or, as he says, "to render an account whence I had my furniture." They include most of the standard chroniclers from William of Malmesbury and Ingulf in the twelfth century to such "diligent and famous travailers in the search of our history" as Polydore Vergil, Richard Grafton, Edward Hall, Raphael Holinshed, John Stow, and John Speed.

And where otherwise I have had any supplies extraordinary, either out of record or such instruments of state as I could procure, I have given a true account of them in the margin. So that the reader shall be sure to be paid with no counterfeit coin, but such as shall have the stamp of antiquity, the approbation[5] of testimony, and the allowance of authority, so far as I shall proceed herein.

And for that I would have this breviary[6] to pass with an uninterrupted delivery of the especial affairs of the kingdom (without embroiling the memory of the reader), I have in a body apart, under the title of an appendix, collected all treaties, letters, articles, charters, ordinances, entertainments, provisions of armies, businesses of commerce, with other passages of state appertaining to our history,[7] which as soon as I have means to print shall, for the better satisfying of such worthy persons as may make use of such materials, accompany this collection; and to this appendix I have made references in the margin as occasion requires.

For the work itself, I can challenge[8] nothing therein but only the sewing it together and the observation of those necessary circumstances and inferences which the history naturally ministers, desirous to deliver things done in as even and quiet an order as such a heap will permit without quarreling with the belief of antiquity, depraving[9] the actions of other nations to advance our own, or keeping back those reasons of state they had for what they did in those times; holding it fittest and best agreeing with integrity (the chiefest duty of a writer) to leave things to their own fame and the censure thereof to the reader as being his part rather than mine, who am only to recite things done, not to rule them. . . .

[AUTHORIAL INTENTIONS]

Undertaking to collect the principal affairs of this kingdom, I had a desire to have deduced the same from the beginning of the first British kings as they are registered in their catalogue, but finding no authentical warrant how they came there, I did put off that desire with these considerations: that a lesser part of time, and better known (which was from William the First, surnamed the Bastard),[10] was more than enough for my ability; and how it was but our curiosity to search further back into times past than we might well discern, and whereof we could neither have proof nor profit. How the beginnings of all people and states were as uncertain as the heads of great rivers, and could not add to our virtue, and peradventure little to our reputation, to know them. Considering how commonly they rise from the springs of poverty, piracy, robbery, and violence, howsoever fabulous writers (to glorify their nations) strive to abuse the credulity of after ages with heroical or miraculous beginnings. For states, as men, are ever best seen when they are up, and as they are, not as they were. Besides, it seems, God in His providence, to check our presumptuous inquisitions, wraps up all things in uncertainty, bars us out from long antiquity, and bounds our searches within the compass of a few ages, as if the same were sufficient both for example and instruction to the government of men. For had we the particular occurrents[11] of all ages and all nations, it might more stuff but not better our understanding. We shall find still the same correspondencies to hold in the actions of men: virtues and vices the same, though rising and falling according to the worth or weakness of governors, the causes of the ruins and mutations of states to be alike, and the train of affairs

THE COLLECTION [1]This preface was added to the 1618 edition, which, despite Daniel's bold intention to bring his history down through the reign of Elizabeth, stops with the death of Edward III in 1377. [2]Impart generally.
[3]"How great a thing it is to surrender something into men's hands." [4]Common fare. [5]Proof.
[6]Brief statement, epitome.
[7]*I have . . . history*: regrettably, this appendix was not printed.
[8]Lay claim to. [9]Disparaging.
[10]William the Conqueror, king of England (1066–87), was the illegitimate son of Robert the Devil, duke of Normandy.
[11]Occurrences.

carried by precedent in a course of succession under like colors.

[THE MURDER OF THOMAS BECKET]

When the ecclesiastical politician Thomas Becket was named chancelor by Henry II (1155), it was to be expected that as a crony of the king he would continue to support his master's anti-papal policies, but on becoming archbishop of Canterbury (1162) he at once began to side with Rome on such questions as royal jurisdiction over clergy charged with crime and royal control of episcopal appointments. Although forced to flee to France in 1164, he returned to Canterbury six years later, and there, at Henry's instigation, he was murdered at the altar of his own cathedral just after Christmas 1170.

And whilst he [Henry] remained there [in France], means was made that the archbishop of Canterbury (who had been now six years in exile) was brought to have conference with the king by the mediation of the king of France, Theobald, earl of Blois, and divers great bishops; which the king of England was the more willing to accept in regard he saw this breach with the church might much prejudice his temporal businesses, whensoever they should break out. And how the archbishop continually was working the pope and all the great prelates of the Christian world against him, which "How much such a party as swayed the empire of souls might do in a time of zeal against a ruler of bodies" was to be considered. And therefore descends he from the height of his will to his necessity, and they meet at Montmirial[12] before the king of France, where the archbishop, kneeling at the feet of his sovereign lord the king of England, said, "He would commit the whole cause in controversy to his royal order, God's honor only reserved."

The king (who had been often used to that reservation) grew into some choler and said to the king of France and the rest: "Whatsoever displeaseth this man, he would have to be against God's honor, and so by that shift will challenge to himself all that belongs to me. But because you shall not think me to go about to resist God's honor and him, in what shall be fit, look what the greatest and most holy of all his predecessors have done to the meanest of mine, let him do the same to me, and it shall suffice." Which answer, being beyond expectation so reasonable, turned the opinion of all the company to the king's cause, insomuch as the King of France said to the archbishop: "Will you be greater than saints? Better than Saint Peter? What can you stand upon? I see it is your fault if your peace be not made." The archbishop replied to this effect: "That as the authority of kings had their beginning by degrees, so had that of the church, which being now by the providence of God come to that estate it was, they were not to follow the example of any that had been faint or yielding in their places. The church had risen and increased out of many violent oppressions, and they were now to hold what it had gotten. Our fathers," said he, "suffered all manner of afflictions because they would not forsake the name of Christ, and shall I, to be reconciled to any man's favor living, derogate anything from His honor?"

This haughty reply of a subject to so yielding an offer of his sovereign so much distasted[13] the hearers as they held the maintenance of his cause rather to proceed from obstinacy than zeal, and with that impression the conference for that time brake up. But after this were many other meetings and much debate about the business. And the king of France (at whose charge lay[14] the archbishop all this while) came to another conference with them upon the confines of Normandy,[15] where the king of England took the archbishop apart and had long speech with him: twice they alighted from their horses, twice remounted, and twice the king held the Archbishop's bridle, and so again they part, prepared for an atonement but not concluding any. In the end, by mediation of the archbishop of Rouen, the matter is quietly ended before the earl of Blois at Amboise.[16] And thereupon Henry the father writes to Henry the son,[17] being then in England, in this wise: "Know ye that Thomas, archbishop of Canterbury, hath made peace with me to my will, and therefore I charge you that he and all his have peace; and that you cause to be restored unto him, and to all such as for him went out of England, all their substances in as full and honorable manner as they held it three moneths before their going, etc." And thus by this letter we see in which king the command lay.

The archbishop returning into England (not as one who had sought his peace but enforced it) with larger power to his resolution than before suspends by the pope's bull the archbishop of York from all episcopal office for crowning the young king within the province of Canterbury without his leave and against the pope's commandment, and without taking (according to the custom) the cautionary oath for conservation of the liberties of the church. He brought also other letters to suspend in like manner the bishops of London, Salisbury, Oxford, Chester, Rochester, St. Asaph, and Llandaff for doing service at the coronation and upholding the king's cause against him. And by these letters were they all to remain suspended till they had satisfied the Archbishop insomuch as he thought fit.

Thus to return home showed that he had the better of the time and came all untied, which so terrified the bishops that presently (having no other refuge) they repair to the king in Normandy and show him this violent proceeding of the archbishop, how since his return he was grown so imperious as there was no living under him. Wherewith the king was so much moved as he is said in extreme passion to have uttered these words: "In what a miserable state am I, that cannot be quiet in mine own kingdom for one only priest! Is there no man will rid me of this trouble?" Where-

[12]Montmirail, a town some fifty miles east of Paris.
[13]Disgusted.   [14]To whom fell the expense of.
[15]This famous meeting between Henry and Becket occurred at Fréteval, a little town on the River Loir west of Orléans.
[16]Town on the River Loire in central France.
[17]Henry "the Young King" (1155–83), eldest son of Henry II and Eleanor of Aquitaine, whom Henry, disregarding Becket's strong protest, had ordered crowned (1170) by Roger of Pont l'Eveque, archbishop of York, in an effort to secure an orderly succession.

upon, they report, four knights—Sir Hugh Morville, Sir William Tracy, Sir Richard Breton, and Sir Reginald[18] Fitzurse—then attending upon the king, and guessing his desire by his words, depart presently into England to be the unfortunate executioners of the same; but by some it seems rather these four gentlemen were sent with commission from the king to deal with the archbishop in another manner, and first to wish him to take his oath of fealty to the young king, then to restore these bishops to the execution of their function, and thirdly to bear himself with moderation in his place, whereby the church might have comfort upon his return, and the kingdom quietness.

But they, finding the archbishop not answering their humor,[19] but peremptory and untractable, without regarding their master's message, grew into rage, and first from threatening force fell to commit it, and that in an execrable manner. Putting on their armor (to make the matter more hideous), they entered into the church whither the archbishop was withdrawn, the monks at divine service, and there calling him traitor and furiously reviling him gave him many wounds, and at length strake[20] out his brains that with his blood besprinkled the altar. His behavior in this act of death, his courage to take it, his passionate committing the cause of the church, with his soul, to God and His saints, the place, the time, the manner, and all aggravates the hatred of the deed and makes compassion and opinion to be on his side.

The unfortunate gentlemen, having effected this great service, rifled the archbishop's house, and after weighing the foulness of what they had committed, and doubtful whether the king, though they had done him a great pleasure, would seem so to acknowledge it, withdrew themselves into the north parts; and from thence pursued fled into several countries, where they all within four years after (as is reported) died miserable fugitives.[21]

[THE DEATH OF EDWARD III]

The king[22] was desirous to have reconciled them to his son [i.e., a group of disaffected London citizens to John of Gaunt, duke of Lancaster], but sickness having now vanquished him, he is forced to give over the world, as the same did him, before his breath left him. And first his concubine,[23] packing away what she could snatch, even to the rings of his fingers, left him; then his other attendants, by her example, seizing on what they could fasten, shift away; and all his counselors and others forsook him in his last agony when most he needed them, leaving his chamber quite empty; which a poor priest in the house, seeing by chance as he passed, approaches to the king's bedside, and finding him yet breathing, calls upon him to remember his Saviour and to ask mercy for his offenses, which none before about him would do, but everyone putting him still in hope of life, though they knew death was upon him (a misery fatal to princes and great persons, whom flattery will never suffer to know themselves, nor their own state either in health or sickness), made him neglective of those spiritual cogitations fit for a dying Christian. But now stirred up by the voice of

this priest, he shows all signs of contrition, and his last breath expresses the name of Jesu. Thus died this mighty and victorious king at his manor of Sheen[24] (now Richmond) the twenty-first day of June, *Anno Domini* 1377, in the sixty-fourth year of his age, having reigned fifty years, four moneths, and odd days. . . .

Provident he was in all his actions, never undertaking anything before he had first furnished himself with means to perform it. And therein his subjects allowed him more with less ado than ever any of his predecessors had; and he as fairly issued what he received from them, having none other private vent of profusion than his enterprises for advancing the state and honor of the kingdom. True it is that most attent[25] and careful he was to get moneys, but yet it was without the sackage[26] of any man, such as his grandfather[27] made upon the officers of justice, the Jews, and others. . . .

His magnificence was showed in his triumphs and feasts, which were sumptuously celebrated with all due rites and ceremonies, the preservers of reverence and majesty. To conclude, he was a prince whose nature agreed with his office as only made for it. Those defaillances[28] we find in him at last we must not attribute to him but his age, wherein we never yet saw prince happy. When their vigor fails them (which is commonly about sixty), their fortune doth. Whilest this prince held together he was indissoluble, and as he was then, we take his figure.

Fortunate he was also in his wife,[29] a lady of excellent virtue who, though she brought him little or none estate, she brought him much content, some benefit by alliance, and a fair issue. She drew evenly with him in all the courses of honor that appertained to her side, and seems a piece so just cut for him as answered him rightly in every joint.

[10]Text *Raynold.*
[19]*Not answering. . . humor:* unresponsive to their mood. [20]Struck.
[21]Daniel's moralistic inference is not supported by the facts. Although Richard le Breton's death is unrecorded, Hugh de Morville, after doing penance in the Holy Land, was restored to the king's favor and lived another thirty years. William de Tracy died in 1173 while on a pilgrimage to Jerusalem. By one account Reginald Fitzurse died in Palestine, but by another he went to Ireland and there thrived mightily.
[22]Edward III, King of England (1327–77), whose long reign was marked by famous victories over the French at Crécy (1346) and Poitiers (1356). The death of his heir, Edward the Black Prince, who predeceased his father by a year, led to the accession of the old king's grandson as Richard II.
[23]Alice Perrers (d. 1400), whose ascendancy over her aging lover became a matter of public concern after the death of Queen Philippa in 1369.
[24]Formerly a royal palace on the Surrey side of the Thames west of London, a favorite resort of English monarchs from Edward II to Elizabeth. [25]Intent. [26]Financial ruin.
[27]Edward I, king of England (1272–1307), was noted for such stern measures as banishing the Jews from his realm in 1290.
[28]Failures.
[29]Philippa of Hainault (1314?–69), daughter of William the Good, count of Holland and Hainault, who married Edward in 1328 and bore him twelve children, including the seven sons whom Shakespeare's Richard II called the "seven vials" of Edward's "sacred blood."

Gracious and loving she ever showed herself to this nation, and did many works of piety, amongst which Queen's College[30] in Oxford remains especially, a monument of her name and renown. And it is worthy the mark that this king and his grandfather Edward the First, the best of our kings, had the two best wives.[31] Which shows that worthiness is such an elixir as by contaction (if there be any disposition of goodness in the metal) it will render it of the same property, so that these queens could be no otherwise than they were, having so excellent husbands.

She bare unto him seven sons, whereof five lived to have issue: Edward, prince of Wales, Lionel, duke of Clarence, John, duke of Lancaster, Edmund, earl of Cambridge (after duke of York), and Thomas of Woodstock, which became duke of Gloucester. Four daughters (of five she bare) lived to be married: Isabel the eldest to Ingelram, lord of Couci, earl of Soissons and Bedford; Joan to Alphonso II, king of Castile, but she died before she lay with him; Mary to John Montfort, duke of Britain; Margaret to John Hastings, earl of Pembroke, and she also died without issue.

Thus have we seen the end of this great king, who, how he came to the crown we know, and now how he left it we see. In both are considerations of importance. His stepping over his father's head[32] to come to his throne, though it were not his fault, yet had it a punishment, and that in a most high kind; for, having so plentiful and so able an issue male, he had not yet a son of his own to sit on his seat, but left the same (worse than he found it) to a child of eleven years of age,[33] exposed to the ambition of uncles which overweighed him, to a factious and discontented state at home, to broken and distracted inheritances abroad, himself having seen all his great gettings, purchased with so much expense, travail, and bloodshed, rent clean from him, and nothing remaining but only the poor town of Calais.[34] To show that our

bounds are prescribed us, and a pillar set by Him who bears up the heavens, which we are not to transpass.

.   .   .   .   .   .

Thus far[35] have I brought this *Collection* of our history and am now come to the highest exaltation of this kingdom, to a state full built, to a government reared up with all those main complements of form and order as have held it together ever since, notwithstanding those dilapidations made by our civil discord,[36] by the nonage or negligence of princes, by the alterations of religion, by all those corruptions which Time hath brought forth to fret and canker-eat the same. And here I leave, unless by this which is done I find encouragement to go on.

[30]Actually founded (1340) by Robert of Eglesfield, Philippa's confessor, who named it for his royal mistress.
[31]Edward I's queen, the famous Eleanor of Castile, accompanied him on a crusade in 1270.
[32]When Edward II was imprisoned, forced to abdicate, and then murdered by Queen Isabella and her lover Roger de Mortimer, his son and heir, a boy of fourteen, was proclaimed guardian of the kingdom (1326).
[33]Richard II, king of England (1377–99).
[34]Daniel rather overstates the situation. Although Edward III had lost most of Aquitaine by 1374, he retained possession of Cherbourg, Brest, Bayonne, and Bordeaux, in addition to Calais.
[35]To the death of Edward III in 1377.
[36]The deposition of Richard II (1399) and the resulting struggle between the great ducal houses of York and Lancaster for the throne of England. These *dilapidations*, which were ended only by the accession of Henry VII in 1485, had provided the subject for Daniel's long poem called *The Civil Wars* (1595–1609) and also for eight of Shakespeare's ten history plays. See pp. 28 ff.

John Selden [1584-1654]

Like Camden, Selden was a polymath whose learning was the treasure of his age and nation. Now perhaps best known for the incisive *Table-Talk* that his former secretary put together in 1689, in his own day he was esteemed—and by his adversaries feared—for what Clarendon called his "stupendous" erudition in the common law, history, Oriental languages, and comparative religions; and since he mainly used his learning to ascertain and state the facts of controverted public questions—or, as he himself explained, to use his knowledge of the past in order "to give other light to the practice and doubts of the present"—he was the erudite par excellence in an age when scholarship and literature and even politics were often coextensive. "His learning did not live in a lane," said Thomas Fuller, "but traced all the latitude of arts and languages." As early as 1614 Jonson, who described Selden to Drummond as "the law book of the judges of England, the bravest man in all languages," hailed him in a stirring verse epistle as a "monarch in letters" whose command of "general knowledge" was, like a circle, flawless and complete. Writing as an old man, Clarendon extolled the Selden of the 1630's as "a person whom no character can flatter or transmit in an expression equal to his merit or virtue" (see p. 796), and Milton, in his *Areopagitica* (see p. 604), compendiously described an even older Selden as "the chief of learned men reputed in this land."

Born the son of a "sufficient plebeian" in Sussex, this prodigy of learning went from the free school at Chichester to Hart Hall, Oxford, which (like Camden) he left (1602) without taking a degree. Already, however, he was attracted to the law, and he promptly entered Clifford's Inn to launch himself upon the course that he would follow to the end. Although he was admitted to the Inner Temple in 1604 and called to the bar eight years later, his real career was scholarship, for even at the Temple, said Anthony Wood, he had "not only run through the whole body of the law but became a prodigy in most parts of learning, especially in those which were not common." A widening acquaintance with such men as Jonson, Camden, and Sir Robert Cotton (whose great library was put at his disposal) no doubt spurred him in those studies that led to *Analecton Anglo-Britannicon* (a history of early Britain that was finished as early as 1607 and published eight years later), a study of ancient British law called *Jani Anglorum facies altera* (1610), and a treatise on *The Duello, or Single Combat* (1610).

Rather less austere but just as bristling in their erudition were the notes or "Illustrations" with which, at the poet's invitation, he fortified the first eighteen cantos of Michael Drayton's *Poly-Olbion* in 1612. These notes, as conspicuous for their knotty style as for their far-flung learning, sometimes do great violence to the ancient myths and legends that Drayton wove throughout his massive work (see pp. 33 ff.), but the annotator's duty, Selden said, was to distinguish fact from fiction and then to trace the fiction to its source.

> I justify all by the self authors cited, crediting no transcribers but when of necessity I must. My thirst compelled me always seek the fountains, and by that, if means grant it, judge the river's nature. Nor can any conversant in letters be ignorant what error is ofttimes fallen into by trusting authorities at second hand, and rash collecting (as it were) from visual beams refracted through another's eye.

These and other early works like *Titles of Honor* (1614) and an edition of Sir John Fortescue's *De laudibus legum Angliae* (1616) were dwarfed by the publication of a pair of major books that secured the scholar's rising reputation: *De diis Syris* (1617), the first of his many Oriental studies (which young Milton may have tapped for the arcane lore in his hymn "On the Morning of Christ's Nativity") and *The History of Tithes* (1618), which traced the use of tithing from the ancient Herbrews through the Romans to the Christians, with very pointed reference toward the practice of the Church of England. Selden himself asserted that he did not write this famous book "to prove that tithes are not due by the law of God" (as the angry prelates charged) but by impartial scholarship to clarify a murky question.

> For as on the one side it cannot be doubted but that the too studious affectation of bare and sterile antiquity—which is nothing else but to be exceeding busy about nothing—may soon descend to a dotage, so on the other the neglect or only vulgar regard of the fruitful and precious part of it—which gives necessary light to the present in matter of state, law, history, and the understanding of good autors—is but preferring that kind of ignorant infancy which our short life alone allows us before the many ages of former experience and observation, which may so accumulate years to us if we had lived even from the beginning of time.

Despite such disclaimers, *The History of Tithes* gave such deep offense to the clergy and King James that the Court of High Commission arranged to have the book suppressed and compelled its haughty author to submit a statement of regret for having published it.

This experience may have been decisive in bringing Selden from the study to the stage of public action. After 1621, when he (though not yet a member of the House) helped prepare the great protest of Commons in defense of "the liberties, franchises, privileges, and jurisdictions of Parliament," he was busy as a member of the opposition for more than three decades. Although steady in his parliamentary loyalties, he must have been a terror to zealots of all parties. Tall and witty and sardonic, he used his matchless erudition like a sword. Neither the overweening prelates nor the self-intoxicated Puritans were safe against his learning. Aubrey reports that as a member of the Westminster Assembly in 1643 he was "like a thorn" in the sides of the more pious, ignorant brethren. "He was wont to mock the Assembly-men about their little gilt Bibles, and would baffle and vex them sadly. Said he, 'I do consider the original,' for he was able to run them all down with his Greek and antiquities."

Although Selden's years of public service included several terms (1623–28) as a member of the House of Commons (where his knowledge of the common law made him feared by church and crown), a period of incarceration (1629–31) for his opposition to what he regarded as the king's illegal actions, election to the Long Parliament in 1640, assignment to the Westminster Assembly three years later, and appointment as keeper of the records in the Tower (1643), his main work was scholarship, and his production as a scholar was immense. In addition to many lesser things he published an exhaustive account of the antiquities collected by the earl of Arundel (*Marmora Arundelliana*, 1628), an answer to the great Hugo Grotius' defense of freedom of the seas (*Mare clausum*, 1635), many works on English law, and even more on Jewish history and religion.

Owing to his attachment—nominally as a steward—to the earl of Kent and, after the earl's death in 1639, his notorious intimacy with his patron's widow, Selden came to be a very wealthy man, but he never lost his thirst for knowledge. Wood reports that at his splendid funeral in the Temple Church Archbishop Ussher "did not, or could not, say much of his sound principles in religion," but the master of the Temple, speaking on a different topic, did not need to guard his language: "if learning could have kept a man alive," he said, "our brother had not died."

My texts are based upon *Poly-Olbion. Or A Chorographicall Description of Tracts, Rivers, Mountaines, Forests, and other Parts of this renowned Isle of Great Britaine . . . Digested in a Poem*, 1612 (STC 7226) and *The Historie of Tithes That is, The Practice of Payment of them. The Positive Laws made for them. The Opinions touching the Right of them. A Review of it Is also annext, which both Confirmes it and directs in the Vse of it. By I. Selden*, 1618 (STC 22172). Since most scholarship on Selden has been directed toward his legal works it lies beyond the limits of this book; however, he comes into many of the general histories of the period listed in the General Bibliography, Section II; his *Table-Talk* was edited by Edward Arber (1868), Sir Frederick Pollack (1927), and others before it finally gained admittance to Everyman's Library (1934); and the "Illustrations" to *Poly-Olbion* have been expertly handled in the great edition of Drayton by J. W. Hebel, Kathleen Tillotson, and B. H. Newdigate (5 vols., 1931–41). David Wilke edited the weighty *Opera omnia* (6 vols., 1726), and there are old biographies by John Aikin (1812) and G. W. Johnson (1835), and a recent lecture (1969) by Sir Eric G. M. Fletcher.

from The "Illustrations" to Michael Drayton's *Poly-Olbion* (1613)

FROM THE AUTHOR OF THE ILLUSTRATIONS

Permit me thus much of these notes to my friend. What the verse oft with allusion, as supposing a full knowing reader, lets slip, or in winding steps of personating fictions (as sometimes) so infolds that suddain conceit cannot abstract a form of the clothed truth, I have, as I might, illustrated. Brevity and plainness (as the one endured the other) I have joined, purposely avoiding frequent commixture of different language, and whensoever it happens either the page or margin (specially for gentlewomen's sake) summarily[1]

ILLUSTRATIONS   [1] Briefly.

interprets it, except where interpretation aids not. Being not very prodigal of my historical faith, after explanation I oft adventure on examination and censure. The author in passages of first inhabitants, name, state and monarchic succession in this isle follows Geoffrey ap Arthur,[2] *Polychronicon*,[3] Matthew of Westminster,[4] and such more. Of their traditions, for that one so much controverted,[5] and by Cambro-Britons[6] still maintained, touching the Trojan Brut, I have but as an advocate for the Muse argued, disclaiming in[7] it if alleged for my own opinion. In most of the rest, upon weighing the reporter's credit, comparison with more persuading authority, and synchronism (the best touchstone in this kind of trial), I leave note of suspicion or add conjectural amendment. . . .

And indeed, my jealousy[8] hath oft vexed me with particular inquisition of whatsoever occurs bearing not a mark of most apparent truth ever since I found so intolerable antichronism,[9] incredible reports, and bardish impostures as well from ignorance as assumed liberty of invention in some of our ancients; and read also such palpable fauxeties[10] of our nation thrust into the world by later time as (to give a taste) that of Randall Higden[11] affirming the beginning of Wards[12] in 6 Henry III,[13] Polydore's[14] assertion (upon mistaking of the statute of 1 Henry VII) that it was death by the English laws for any man to wear a vizard, with many like errors in his history. . . .

[Such errors, presented as "history," are bizarre, says Selden, but even worse are legends like those of Trojan Brut]

which are even equally warrantable as Ariosto's narrations of persons and places in his Rolands,[15] Spenser's elfin story,[16] or Rabelais his strange discoveries.[17] Yet the capricious faction will, I know, never quit their belief of wrong, although some Elias[18] or Delian diver[19] should make open what is so inquired after. Briefly, until Polybius,[20] who wrote near eighteen hundred [years] since—for Aristotle περὶ κόσμου is clearly counterfeited in title[21]—no Greek mentions the isle; until Lucretius,[22] some one hundred years later, no Roman hath expressed a thought of us; until Caesar's *Commentaries*[23] no piece of its description was known that is now left to posterity. For time, therefore, preceding Caesar I dare trust none, but with others adhere to conjecture. In ancient matter since, I rely on Tacitus and Dio especially; Vopiscus, Capitolin, Spartian for so much as they have; and the rest of the Augustan story; afterward Gildas, Nennius (but little is left of them, and that of the last very imperfect), Bede, Asserio, Ethelward (near of blood to King Alfred), William of Malmesbury, Marian, Florence of Worcester, . . . and the numerous rest of our monkish and succeeding chronographers.[24] In all, I believe him most which, freest from affection and hate (causes of corruption), might best know, and hath with most likely assertion delivered his report. Yet so that to explain the author, carrying himself in this part an historical as in the other a chorographical poet,[25] I insert oft, out of the British story,[26] what I importune you not to credit. Of that kind are those prophecies out of Merlin[27] sometime interwoven; I discharge

[2]Geoffrey of Monmouth. See p. 808, n.3.
[3]Widely popular universal history by Ranulf Higden (d. 1364), a Benedictine monk of Chester.
[4]Alleged author of a fifteenth-century chronicle called *Flores historiarum* that was actually the compilation of various writers at St. Albans and Westminster. See p. 811, n.30.
[5]Disputed. The allusion is, of course, to Trojan Brut, the legendary founder of Britain.
[6]Welsh (from Cambria, the ancient name for Wales).
[7]Disavowing, dissenting from.   [8]Eagerness, solicitude.
[9]Anachronism.   [10]Falsities, deceits.   [11]Ranulf Higden.
[12]The Court of Wards, a court established by Henry VIII for adjudicating cases relating to wardships.
[13]The sixth year of the reign of Henry III (1213).
[14]Polydore Vergil. See Glossary.
[15]The fabulous stories in Ludovico Ariosto's *Orlando Furioso* (1516, 1532), which concerns the madness of Roland, Charlemagne's chief paladin, when disappointed in his love for Angelica.
[16]*The Faerie Queene* (1590, 1596).
[17]In *Pantagruel* (1532) by François Rabelais (1494?–1553) there are various *discoveries*, including Panurge's remarkable voyage to Utopia around the Cape of Good Hope and Ephistemon's to the underworld.
[18]Elijah, Hebrew prophet who raised the dead, did various other miraculous things, and was carried to heaven in a chariot of fire. See 1 Kings 17 ff.
[19]One who penetrates mysteries, from Delos, an Aegean island sacred to the worship of Apollo and Artemis.
[20]Greek historian (250?–125 B.C.) who wrote a history (now mostly lost) of Rome and surrounding countries, alludes cryptically to Britain in his *Histories*, xxxiv.5.
[21]In *De mundo*, a geographical treatise (first published in 1497) that was widely but erroneously attributed to Aristotle, the unknown author speaks of "two very large islands"—Albion and Ierne—in the wide ocean beyond the Pillars of Hercules.
[22]Titus Lucretius Carus (96?–55 B.C.), author of the great philosophical poem *De rerum natura*, mentions Britain at VI.1106.
[23]*De bello Gallico*, which relates the two invasions of Britain by Gaius Julius Caesar in 55 and 54 B.C.
[24]*In ancient . . . chronographers*: Selden's thumbnail bibliography of British history following its first authentic notice in Caesar's *Commentaries*. For Tacitus see p. 820 [Camden]; Diodorus Siculus ("Dio"), a Greek historian of the late 1st century B.C., composed a universal history in forty books that survives only in fragments; Flavius Vopiscus, Julius Capitolinus, and Aelius Spartianus were three of the six so-called *Scriptores historiae Augustae* of the 3d century who wrote lives of the Roman emperors—what Selden calls the *Augustan story*. On the early English historians Gildas, Nennius, Bede, and William of Malmesbury see p. 820 Asserio or Asser, bishop of Sherborne (d. 909?), wrote a life of Alfred the Great; Ethelwerd or Aethelward (d. 998?) traced the history of the world from its creation to 973; Marian or Marianus Scotus (1028–1082?) was another universal chronicler whose work was continued by Florence of Worcester (d. 1118) in *Chronicon ex chronicis*.
[25]*Yet so . . . poet*: i.e., in order to explain Drayton's work in its allegedly historical as well as in its geographical and descriptive sections. *Chorographical*: pertaining to the art of describing or delineating particular regions or districts.
[26]The legendary history of Britain compiled and invented by Geoffrey of Monmouth.
[27]Legendary bard and magician, one of whose alleged accomplishments was the miraculous construction of Stonehenge.

myself, nor impute you to me any serious respect of them.
. . .

From vain loading my margin with books, chapters, folios, or names of our historians, I abstain: course of time as readily directs to them. But where the place might not so easily occur (chiefly in matter of philology) there only, for view of them which shall examine me, I have added assisting references. For most of what I use of chorography, join with me in thanks to that most learned nourice[28] of antiquity . . . my instructing friend, Mr. Camden, Clarenceux.[29] From him and Girald of Cambria[30] also comes most of my British.[31] And then may Mercury and all the Muses deadly hate me when, in permitting occasion, I profess not by whom I learn! Let them vent judgment on me which understand. I justify all by the self authors cited, crediting no transcribers but when of necessity I must. My thirst compelled me always seek the fountains, and by that, if means grant it, judge the river's nature. Nor can any conversant in letters be ignorant what error is ofttimes fallen into by trusting authorities at second hand, and rash collecting (as it were) from visual beams refracted through another's eye. In performance of this charge undertaken at request of my kind friend, the author, brevity of time—which was but little more than since the poem first went to the press—and that daily discontinued both by my other most different studies seriously attended and interrupting business, as enough can witness, might excuse great faults, especially of omission. But I take not thence advantage to desire more than common courtesy in censure. . . .

Ingenuous readers, to you I wish your best desires. Grant me too, I pray, this one, that you read me not without comparing the "Faults Escaped"; I have collected them for you. Compelled absence, endeavored dispatch, and want of revises soon bred them. To the author I wish (as an old cosmographical poet did long since to himself)

’Αλλά σοι ὕμνων

’Αυτῶν ἐκ μακάρων ἀντάξιος ἐίν ἀμουβή.[32]

To gentlewomen and their loves is consecrated all the wooing language, allusions to love-passions, and sweet embracements feigned by the Muse mongst hills and rivers. Whatsoever tastes of description, battle, story, abstruse antiquity, and (which my particular study caused me sometime remember) law of the kingdom, to the more severe reader. To the one be contenting enjoyments of their auspicious desires; to the other, happy attendance of their chosen Muses.

From the Inner Temple,[33]
May 9, 1612

THE FIRST SONG

[In the First Song of *Poly-Olbion* Drayton elaborately rehearses the story of Trojan Brut, "Which now," as he explains, "the envious world doth slander for a dream." Selden's "Illustrations" of this passage follow.]

I should the sooner have been of the author's opinion, in more than poetical form standing for Brut, if in any Greek or Latin story authentic, speaking of Aeneas and his planting in Latium,[34] were mention made of any suchlike thing. To reckon the learned men which deny him, or at least permit him not in conjecture, were too long a catalogue; and indeed this critic age scarce any longer endures any nation their first supposed author's name: not Italus to the Italian, not Hispalus to the Spaniard, Bato to the Hollander, Brabo to the Brabantine, Francio to the French, Celtes to the Celt, Galathes to the Gaul, Scota to the Scot—no, nor scarce Romulus to his Rome[35]—because of their unlikely and fictitious mixtures. Especially this of Brut, supposed long before the beginning of the Olympiads[36] (whence all time backward is justly called by Varro[37] unknown or fabulous) some twenty-seven hundred and more years since, about Samuel's[38] time, is most of all doubted. But, reserving my censure, I thus maintain the author: although nor Greek nor Latin nor our country[39] stories of Bede and Malmesbury especially nor that fragment yet remaining of Gildas speak of him, and that his name were not published until Geoffrey of Monmouth's edition of the British story (which grew and continues much suspected, in much rejected), yet observe that Taliesin,[40] a great bard more than one thousand years since, affirms it, Nennius (in some copies he is under name of Gildas) above eight hundred years past and the gloss of Samuel Beaulan[41] (or some other crept into his text) mention both the common report and descent from Aeneas, and withal . . . continuing a pedigree to Adam, joining these words: "This genealogy I found by tradition of the ancients which were first inhabitants of Britain." In a manuscript epistle of Henry of Huntingdon[42]

[28]Nurse.

[29]The great antiquarian William Camden (see p. 816) served as Clarenceux King-of-Arms (with jurisdiction over heraldic questions south of the River Trent) in the Heralds' College from 1597 until his death in 1623.

[30]Giraldus Cambrensis (1146?–?1220). See p. 813, n.50.

[31]Knowledge of British antiquity?

[32]As promised for "gentlewomen's sake," Selden "summarily" translates this unidentified *old cosmographical poet* in a marginal gloss: "That the godlike sort of men may worthily guerdon his labors."

[33]One of the four Inns of Court—domiciles for legal instruction and practice—which Selden entered as a student in 1604 and of which he became a barrister in 1612.

[34]*Aeneas . . . Latium*: the story of Vergil's *Aeneid*.

[35]*Italus . . . Rome*: legendary and eponymous heroes of various countries (like Trojan Brut of Britain). Hispalus' and Bato's association with their respective countries is clearer in the Latin names *Hispania* (Spain) and *Batavia* (Holland).

[36]See p. 819, n.30. [37]See p. 818, n.16.

[38]Hebrew judge and prophet (ca. 1160–1065 B.C.) whose career is related in 1 Samuel 1–25. [39]Native, i.e., English.

[40]Quasi-legendary British bard (sixth cent.) to whom was attributed much popular poetry and prophecy.

[41]Beulan, a priest named in one manuscript of Nennius' *Historia Britonum* as the author's master.

[42]Chronicler (1084?–1155) whose *Historia Anglorum* comes down to 1154.

to one Warin I read the Latin of this English: "You ask me, Sir, why, omitting the succeeding reigns from Brut to Julius Caesar, I begin my story at Caesar. I answer you that neither by word nor writing could I find any certainty of those times, although with diligent search I oft inquired it; yet this year in my journey towards Rome, in the Abbey of Beccensam,[43] even with amazement I found the story of Brut." And in his own printed book he affirms that what Bede had in this part omitted was supplied to him by other authors, of which Girald seems to have had use. The British story of Monmouth was a translation, but with much liberty and no exact faithfulness, of a Welsh book delivered to Geoffrey by one Walter, Archdeacon of Oxford, and hath been followed (the translator being a man of some credit, and Bishop of St. Asaph's[44] under King Stephen)[45] by Ponticus Virunnius[46] (an Italian), most of our country historians of middle times,[47] and this age. . . .

Arguments are there also drawn from some affinity of the Greek tongue, and much of Trojan and Greek names with the British. These things are the more enforced by Cambro-Britons through that universal desire, bewitching our Europe, to derive their blood from Trojans, which for them might as well be by supposition of their ancestors' marriages with the hither deduced Roman colonies, who by

original were certainly Trojan, if their antiquities deceive not. . . .

Briefly, seeing no national story except such as Thucydides, Xenophon, Polybius, Caesar, Tacitus, Procopius, Cantacuzen, the late Guicciardin, Commines, Macchiavel,[48] and their like, which were employed in the state of their times, can justify themselves but by tradition, and that many of the fathers and ecclesiastical historians, especially the Jewish rabbins (taking their highest learning of Cabala,[49] but from antique and successive report), have inserted upon tradition many relations current enough, where Holy Writ crosses them not, you shall enough please Saturn and Mercury, presidents of antiquity and learning, if with the author you foster this belief.

[43]Le Bec-Hellouin, site of a Benedictine abbey in northern France.
[44]Bishopric in northern Wales.   [45]King of England (1135-54).
[46]Lodovico da Ponte (1467-1520), Italian historian.
[47]English medieval chroniclers.
[48]Eminent Greek, Roman, Byzantine, French, and Italian historians who recorded the events of their own times.
[49]Traditional Jewish mystical interpretations of the Scriptures formulated between the ninth and thirteenth centuries in the *Sepher Yezirah* and *Zohar*.

from The History of Tithes (1618)

TO THE MOST HONORED SIR ROBERT COTTON[1]
OF CONNINGTON, KNIGHT AND BARONET

Noble Sir:

Justice no less than observance urges me to inscribe this *History of Tithes* to your name. So great a part of it was let me by your most ready courtesy and able direction that I restore it rather than give it you. And it cannot but receive an increase of estimation from your interest thus seen in it. For to have borrowed your help, or used that your inestimable library (which lives in you), assures a curious diligence in search after the inmost, least known, and most useful parts of historical truth both of past and present ages. For such is that truth which your humanity liberally dispenses, and such is that which by conference is learned from you: such indeed, as if it were, by your example more sought after. So much headlong error, so many ridiculous impostures would not be thrust on the too credulous by those which stumble on in the road, but never with any care look on each side or behind them; that is, those which keep their understandings always in a weak minority that ever wants the autority and admonition of a tutor. For as on the one side it cannot be doubted but that the too studious affectation of bare and sterile antiquity—which is nothing else but to be exceeding busy about nothing—may soon

descend to a dotage, so on the other the neglect or only vulgar regard of the fruitful and precious part of it—which gives necessary light to the present in matter of state, law, history, and the understanding of good autors—is but preferring that kind of ignorant infancy which our short life alone allows us before the many ages of former experience and observation, which may so accumulate years to us as if we had lived even from the beginning of Time. But you best know this, in whom that useful part is so fully eminent that the most learned through Europe willingly acknowledge it; and so open hath your courtesy ever made the plenteous store of it to me that I could not but thus offer you whatsoever is in this of mine own also as a symbol of some thankfulness. It was at first destined to you, and however through the hasty fortune that (I know not why) it suffered at the press, some pieces of it have been dispersed without the honor that your name might add to them,[2]

HISTORY OF TITHES [1]Antiquarian and statesman (1571-1631), friend and indefatigable benefactor of many men of learning (among them Jonson, Camden, Speed, and Bacon), whose notable collection of books, manuscripts, and coins is now in the British Museum. See p. 753 f.
[2]*It was . . . them:* None of the more than fifty copies of the four known editions of the book lacks the dedication to Cotton.

I shall be yet ever so ambitious of that honor that the whole shall never (for so much as I can prevent) be communicated without this prefixed testimony of duty to you. Receive it favorably, noble Sir, and continue to me that happiness which I enjoy in that you neither repute me unworthy of your love nor permit me in ignorance when I come to learn of you.

From the Inner Temple
April 4, 1618

The Preface

It hath even so happened with not a few of the malicious— what through lazy ignorance, what through peevish jealousy —at their sight or hearing of the name of this *History of Tithes* as it was wont with those raw novices that, upon their first admission to the sacred mysteries of the gentiles,[3] troubled and frighted themselves with a world of false apparitions while they thought of what they should see in the inmost sanctuary at the unknown presence of their deity. And doubtless the priest had not a little work to persuade them that what they should there meet with was not an unlucky Empusa, not a formidable Mormo, not a wanton Cobalus, not a mischievous Fury,[4] not indeed anything that their idle brains, being such mere strangers to the abstrusest parts of truth, had fashioned out. The many fancies that Malice, Ignorance, and Jealousy have framed to themselves touching this of mine have been no less ridiculous, and some equally fearful but equally false. And I must here first play the priest also, and so clear, if it were possible, those fancies by protesting that it is not written to prove that tithes are not due by the law of God, not written to prove that the laity may detain them, not to prove that lay hands may still enjoy appropriations:[5] in sum, not at all against the maintenance of the clergy. Neither is it anything else but itself, that is, a mere narration and the history of tithes. Nor is the law of God, whence tithes are commonly derived, more disputed of in it than the divine law, whence all creatures have their continuing subsistence, is inquired after in Aristotle's *History of Living Creatures,* in Pliny's *Natural History,* or in Theophrastus his *History of Plants;*[6] or than the justice of the old courts of Rome is examined in Brodaeus[7] his history of them, or the convenience of the civil and canon laws in that of Rivallius.[8] Nor was anything that belonged to the title purposely omitted. Nor was any piece of it stolen from any other man's notes. . . .

[If any man disbelieves these assertions, says Selden, let him read the book.] He may be there further satisfied and shall then see also that it is not of the pitch of the doctrine of the breviary[9] or within the compass of pocket-learning. Nor will it, I think, look like what were patched up out of postils, polyantheas,[10] commonplace books, or any of the rest of such excellent instruments for the advancement of ignorance and laziness. Nor is any end in it to teach any innovation by an imperfit pattern had from the musty relics of former time. Neither is antiquity related in it to show barely what hath been—for the sterile part of antiquity, which shows that only and to no further purpose, I value

even as slightly as dull ignorance doth the most precious and useful part of it—but to give other light to the practice and doubts of the present. . . .

But we leave this preposterous admonition in negatives— yet by reason of the headlong importunity of such as have in great number already misconceived it, they were necessary and could not elsewhere have had so fit place—and shortly thus delineate what it is by the end and purpose of writing it, by the argument of it, by the course of composing it, and by the sum of performance in it in behalf of the clergy.

For the first, we find that in the frequent disputations about tithes not only arguments out of Holy Writ for proof of a divine right to them, but matter also of fact—that is, practice and story—is very often used: as the kinds of payment of them among the Ebrews, among the Gentiles, the maintenance of the church in the primitive times, the arbitrary consecrations, appropriations, and infeodations[11] of them in the middle times,[12] the payment of them at this day in the several states of Christendom, together with the various opinions and positive laws[13] touching them. For opinions and laws, as they are related only and fall under the question of what and whence they were, are merely of fact, and proofs are hence often drawn to confirm sundry occurrences in inquiry for the truth on either side. That of the divine right of them is so wholly a point of divinity and handled so fully by divers Schoolmen, so imperiously by most of the canonists, and so confidently by some of our late divines that whatever could be said touching that only by inference out of the Holy Text (which must be the sole trial of it) would but seem taken from some of them which have so purposely disputed it. Neither were that so fit to be meddled with by any as by a professed divine. But for that other part which falls under history, there is not one of them all which, having boldness enough to adventure on it (while he disputes withal

---

[3]The initiatory rites of the Eleusinian and Orphic cults of ancient Greece, notable for their terror and exhilaration.
[4]*Empusa . . . Fury*: hobgoblins of classical mythology, Empusa being a spectral monster attendant on Hecate, Mormo a female demon, Cobalus apparently a name of Selden's own invention, and the Furies (or Eumenides) avenging deities who torture the guilty.
[5]In ecclesiastical law, transference of the spiritual or temporal interests of a benefice (usually to a spiritual corporation). Although forbidden by the Lateran Council of 1179, such appropriations, which were often very profitable, became common after the dissolution of the monasteries under Henry VIII.
[6]Three notable ancient works of natural history, without theological implications.   [7]Unidentified.
[8]Aymar Rivault, French jurist who wrote *Historia juris civilis* (1527).
[9]In the Roman Catholic Church, a book of daily offices and prayers for the canonical hours.
[10]Books of homilies on set texts, anthologies.
[11]Infeudations, the granting of tithes to laymen.
[12]The Middle Ages.
[13]Laws formally imposed by legislative action (as opposed to "natural" laws).

of the divine right), shows not also too much either igno-
rance or negligence in talking of it, being usually deceived
and deceiving in it those most of readers that give their
historical faith captive to bare names and common repu-
tation. . . . Which of them relates towards what is fit
to be known touching the payment [of tithes] among the
Ebrews? Among the Gentiles? Among Christians of former
time? Nay, which of them seem to know or to have heard
of the chief human positive laws made for tithes? Yet would
they gladly use them if they had them. Where is there among
them an ingenuous discovery of the various opinions of past
ages that belong hither? Who of them once touches the
right ancient course of settling tithes at first in monasteries,
colleges, or other such corporations by appropriations and con-
secrations of them? Who of them tells us other than mere
fables while he talks of the original of infeodations . . . ?

[Promising to repair the gross deficiencies of his pred-
ecessors, Selden asserts that his chief end is to ascertain the
truth about an important subject that had been lamentably
mishandled.] Neither at all wish I that this of mine should
gain any strength of truth from my name alone, but from
those authorities which I have designed and brought both
for elder, late, and present times out of such both printed and
manuscript annals, histories, counsels, chartularies,[14] laws,
lawyers, and records only as were to be used in the most
accurate way of search that might furnish for the subject
Yet also I have not neglected the able judgments of such of
the learned of later time as give light to former ages. But
I so preferred the choicest and most able that I have wholly
abstained from any mention or use here of those many
ignorants that while they write rather instruct us in their
own wants of ability than direct to anything that may
satisfy. If through ignorance I have omitted anything in the
history or the review that deserved place in them, whoever
shall admonish me of it shall have a most willing acknowledg-
ment of his learning and courtesy. But all the bad titles that
are ever due to abuse of the holiest obtestation[15] be always
my companions if I have purposely omitted any good au-
tority of ancient or late time that I saw necessary or could
think might give further or other light to any position or
part of it!

For I sought only truth, and was never so far engaged in
this or aught else as to torture my brains or venture my
credit to make or create premises for a chosen conclusion
that I rather would than could prove. My premises made
what conclusions or conjectures I have, and were not bred
by them; and although both of them here not a little some-
times vary from what is vulgarly received, yet that happened
not at all from any desire to differ from common opinion,
but from another course of disquisition than is commonly
used: that is, by examination of the truth of those supposi-
tions which patient idleness too easily takes for clear and
granted. For the old Skeptics,[16] that never would profess
that they had found a truth, showed yet the best way to
search for any when they doubted as well of what those of
the dogmatical sects too credulously received for infallible
principles as they did of the newest conclusions. They were

indeed questionless too nice, and deceived themselves with
the nimbleness of their own sophisms, that permitted no
kind of established truth; but plainly he that avoids their
disputing levity, yet, being able, takes to himself their liberty
of inquiry, is in the only way that in all kinds of studies
leads and lies open even to the sanctuary of Truth, while
others, that are servile to common opinion and vulgar
suppositions, can rarely hope to be admitted nearer than into
the base-court[17] of her temple, which too speciously often
counterfaits[18] her inmost sanctuary. And to this purpose also
is that of Quintilian most worthy of memory: *Optimus
est in discendo patronus incredulus.*[19]

. . . Let not, then, either the purpose or convenience of
this history be valued from what distempered Malice,
Ignorance, or Jealousy have cried it down with in corners.
The learned Friar Bacon's[20] most noble studies, being out
of the road of the lazy clergy of his time, were vehemently
at first suspected for such as might prejudice the church.
Reuchlin[21] and Budé,[22] the one for his Ebrew, the other for
his Greek, were exceedingly hated because they learned and
taught what the friars and monks were mere strangers to.
Others about their time had like fortune. Neither was any
one thing in the beginning of the Reformation so unwillingly
received or more opposed by such as labored that Ignorance
might still continue in her triumph than that singular light
to the clearing of error, the Greek text of the New Testament,
first published in print by Erasmus.[23] And it was ordained,
as he says, under great penalty in I know not what college of
Cambridge that no fellow of the house should be so impious
as bring it within the gates. For the world hath never wanted
store of such blocks laid in the way of learning, as willingly
endure not any part of curious diligence that seeks or
teaches whatsoever is beyond their commonly received
nihil ultra.[24] But there are others that both can judge and do
wish for all light to truth. Such they were that even while
Ignorance yet held her declining empire defended those
worthies, Bacon, Budé, Reuchlin, Erasmus, and the rest that
so suffered; and to doubt whether this of mine shall find such
also were but to question whether every man were yet a

[14]Cartularies, records or registers of a monastery.
[15]Supplication.
[16]Philosophic sect founded by Sextus Empiricus (2d cent.) that
taught the relativity of sensory knowledge and of beliefs.
[17]The lower or outer court of a castle, occupied by servants.
[18]Counterfeits.
[19]"In arguing a case a skeptical advocate is best" (*Institutes*, XII.
viii.11).
[20]Roger Bacon (1214?–94), English Franciscan whose unorthodox
speculations on science and philosophy led to his imprisonment.
[21]Johann Reuchlin (1455–1522), German humanist whose philo-
logical studies, especially in Hebrew, led to controversy with the
powerful and reactionary Dominicans.
[22]Guillaume Budé (1468–1540), French scholar eminent for his
Hellenic studies.
[23]Desiderius Erasmus (1466?–1536), Dutch scholar, the most
influential humanist of his time, whose edition of the Greek New
Testament with a Latin translation (1516) is a landmark in biblical
scholarship.
[24]Nothing more, i.e., this far and no farther.

malicious rebel to Truth, and wholly without ingenuity, that performs even as much in fostering her as Time doth in breeding her.

   . . . But I stay you too long here, reader. Try now how I have performed my promise; spare not to try with your most censorious examination;

> *sed magis acri*
> *Iudicio perpende, et, si tibi vera videntur,*
> *Dede manus, aut, si falsum est, accingere contra.*[25]

[25]"Rather ponder it with keen judgment; and if it seems to be true, then yield assent, or if it be false, gird up your loins to challenge it" (Lucretius, *De rerum natura*, II.1041–43).

Sir Walter Raleigh   [1552?-1618]

As one of that remarkable generation of Englishmen which included Camden, Sidney, Spenser, Hooker, and Andrewes, Raleigh in his first five decades lived so many lives with such bravado —as soldier, seaman, courtier, poet, explorer, colonial entrepreneur, and politician—that when, in 1603, his old enemy and new king arranged for his conviction on an unproved charge of treason, there seemed nothing left for him but death. Reprieved the night before his scheduled execution, he still had many things to do and suffer: before him lay a long incarceration in the Tower (1603–16), an abortive effort to retrieve his reputation in Guiana, and, as the last forlorn adventure, the judicial murder of his execution (see p. 815). To this final phase of his career belongs also *The History of the World*.

   As his recently discovered notebook shows, he had started making notes for this gigantic enterprise in the 1590's, but it was apparently not until about 1607 that the aging prisoner set to work in earnest. Spurred by the encouragement of Henry, Prince of Wales ("who, had he survived his father," John Aubrey said, "would quickly have enlarged him with rewards of honor"), Raleigh planned a massive and audacious undertaking: a history of the world that would record the progress of events, both sacred and profane, from the creation to the Roman conquest of Britain as a background for the body of the work, which would be a history of the British people.

   Like Spenser's vast intentions for *The Faerie Queene* (which might have been four times its present size), Raleigh's plan was not to be completed. Although Part I, devoted mainly to the history of the Jews, was entered in the Stationers' Register in 1611 (when, presumably, it was ready for the press), "the inestimable Prince Henry" seems to have objected to "the unsuitable division of the books" on the ground that a fuller treatment of the Persians, Greeks, and Romans was required. Raleigh undertook the alterations and expansions, but before they were complete the prince to whom they were "directed" died (November 1612), and with him died the author's inspiration. The revised Part I was duly published two years later (by which time Parts II and III had already been "hewn out"), but as Raleigh said in valediction, he lacked the heart to carry out his grandiose intentions.

   The book remains a fragment, then, but its dimensions are imposing. Following the long preface—a monument of Jacobean prose that expresses, along with other things, its author's view of providential history, his low assessment of many English kings, and his fatigue and desolation— the history proper starts at the beginning, with the creation, and ends five books, sixty-five chapters, 576 sections, and a million words later with the Roman subjugation of Greece in 168 B.C. Since Raleigh looked on history as the progressive revelation of divine intentions to the end that we may learn by its examples "such wisdom as may guide our desires and actions," he could find a place for almost anything. Thus his account of Jewish history is counterpointed by the rise and fall of three great empires—Babylon, Assyria, and Greece—that the prophet Daniel had foretold (7.4–8), and this capacious record is often deadened or enlivened with digressions on theology, metaphysics, geography, comparative religion, mythology, astronomy, astrology, politics, military tactics, moral philosophy, and many other kinds of lore. Such digressions were essential, Raleigh said, to clothe the "nakedness" of a strict narration. "For seeing we digress in all the ways of our lives, yea, seeing the life of man is nothing else but digression, I may the better be excused in writing their lives and actions. I am not altogether ignorant in the laws of history, and of the kinds."

However, he was ignorant of Hebrew, as he himself conceded, and very shaky in his Greek. Raleigh clearly lacked the learning required for such a spacious undertaking, but as he wryly pointed out, eleven years of "leisure" had enabled him to read a lot of books, and he often cites his sources in detail. Moreover he, like many lesser men before and since, did not hesitate to call upon his learned friends for aid. If we may believe the bibulous Jonson, "the best wits of England" (including, of course, the playwright himself) assisted in the enterprise. Robert Burhill, an erudite divine, helped Raleigh with the Greek and Hebrew; Sir Robert Cotton lent him books; and old friends like John Hoskins and the mathematician Thomas Harriot supplied what aid they could. But Raleigh's "waking spirit" is everywhere apparent, and there can be no doubt that the book, as authenticated by its breadth and style, was mainly his creation.

As might have been predicted, King James was not amused or edified. He objected to the work on "divers" grounds, John Chamberlain reported, but especially because its author—a convicted traitor in the Tower—was "too saucy in censuring princes." As a consequence, in December 1614 the archbishop of Canterbury informed the Stationers' Company that he had received "express directions from his Majesty" that the book "should be suppressed, and not suffered for hereafter to be sold." After the handsome title page with Raleigh's name and portrait was removed, however, the work was issued once again, and it at once achieved a fame, ratified by a stream of new editions, that lasted through the century. Partly because of Raleigh's view of providential history and partly (as Sir Charles Firth observed) because the author, as a victim of the Stuarts, became a hero to the opposition, *The History of the World* was especially liked by Puritans. In a more enlightened era Matthew Arnold called it obsolete and ridiculed its superstition, but in both its strength and weakness it retains a great importance for any serious student of the age.

My text is based upon *The Historie of the World,* 1628 (STC 20640). Although the so-called *Remains of Sir Walter Raleigh* appeared in 1651, and the "political, commercial, and philosophical" *Works* (with a life by Thomas Birch) just a century later, the first and last collected edition of the works was that published at Oxford in eight volumes in 1829 (which reprinted Birch's life and added one by William Oldys). The poems have been edited by Sir Egerton Brydges (1813), John Hannah (1845), and Agnes M. C. Latham (rev. 1951), and there are selections from the works by F. W. C. Hersey (1909), G. E. Hadow (1917), W. R. Macklin (1926), and Miss Latham (1965); as well as a serviceable abridgment of *The History of the World* by C. A. Patrides (1971). Of the many biographies—apart from those by Birch and Oldys—one might mention the important works by Edward Edwards (2 vols., 1868), William Stebbing (2d ed., 1899), W. M. Wallace (1959), and (as challenging newcomers), Jack Adamson and Harold Folland (*The Shepherd of the Ocean,* 1969), Stephen J. Greenblatt (1973), and Robert Lacey (1974). E. A. Strathman's study of Raleigh's thought (1951) is valuable, as is Sir Charles Firth's British Academy Lecture (1918) on his *History of the World* (*Essays Literary and Historical,* 1938). M. C. Bradbrook has written on Raleigh's relation to the so-called School of Night (1936), W. F. Oakeshott on the notebook (the London *Times,* 29 November 1952), Philip Edwards on Raleigh as a man of letters (1953), and Miss Latham on his achievements in politics and art (1964). The fullest bibliography is T. N. Brushfield's (2d ed., 1908), but John Racin, Jr., has recently sorted out the early editions of *The History of the World* in *Studies in Bibliography,* XVII (1964).

from The History of the World (1614)

THE PREFACE

How unfit and how unworthy a choice I have made of myself, to undertake a work of this mixture, mine own reason, though exceeding weak, hath sufficiently resolved me. For had it been begotten then with my first dawn of day, when the light of common knowledge began to open itself to my younger years, and before any wound received either from fortune or time, I might yet well have doubted that the darkness of age and death would have covered over both it and me long before the performance. For, beginning with the creation, I have proceeded with the history of the world; and lastly purposed (some few sallies excepted) to confine my discourse within[1] this our renowned island of Great Britain. I confess that it had better sorted with my disability, the better part of whose times are run out in other travails, to have set together (as I could) the unjointed and scattered frame of our English affairs than of the universal: in whom had there been no other defect (who am all defect) than the time of the day, it were enough; the day of a tempestuous life, drawn on to the very evening ere I began. But those inmost and soul-piercing wounds, which are ever aching while uncured, with the desire to satisfy those few friends which I have tried by the fire of adversity, the former enforcing, the latter persuading, have caused me to make my thoughts legible, and myself the subject of every opinion, wise or weak.

To the world I present them, to which I am nothing indebted: neither have others that were (fortune changing) sped much better in any age. For prosperity and adversity have evermore tied and untied vulgar affections. And as we see it in experience that dogs do always bark at those they know not and that it is their nature to accompany one another in those clamors, so is it with the inconsiderate multitude: who, wanting that virtue which we call honesty in all men, and that especial gift of God which we call charity in Christian men, condemn without hearing, and wound without offence given; led thereunto by uncertain report only, which His Majesty truly acknowledgeth for the author of all lies.[2] "Blame no man" (saith Siracides) "before thou have inquired the matter; understand first, and then reform righteously."[3] *Rumor, res sine teste, sine judice, maligna, fallax:* "Rumor is without witness, without judge, malicious and deceivable." This vanity of vulgar opinion it was that gave St. Augustine argument to affirm that he feared the praise of good men, and detested that of the evil. And herein no man hath given a better rule than this of Seneca: *Conscientiae satisfaciamus: nihil in famam laboremus; sequatur vel mala, dum bene merearis:* "Let us satisfy our own consciences, and not trouble ourselves with fame: be it never so ill, it is to be despised, so we deserve well."

For myself, if I have in anything served my country, and prized it before my private,[4] the general acceptation can yield me no other profit at this time than doth a fair sunshine day to a seaman after shipwreck; and the contrary, no other harm than an outrageous tempest after the port attained. I know that I lost the love of many for my fidelity towards her[5] whom I must still honor in the dust; though further than the defence of her excellent person I never persecuted any man. Of those that did it, and by what device they did it, He that is the supreme judge of all the world hath taken the accompt: so as for this kind of suffering I must say with Seneca, *Mala opinio, bene parta, delectat.*[6]

As for other men, if there be any that have made themselves fathers of that fame which hath been begotten for them, I can neither envy at such their purchased glory nor much lament mine own mishap in that kind, but content myself to say with Vergil, *Sic vos non vobis,*[7] in many particulars. To labor other satisfaction were an effect of frenzy not of hope, seeing it is not truth, but opinion, that can travel the world without a passport. For were it otherwise, and were there not as many internal forms of the mind as there are external figures of men, there were then some possibility to persuade by the mouth of one advocate, even equity[8] alone.

But such is the multiplying and extensive virtue of dead earth, and of that breath-giving life which God hath cast upon slime and dust, as that among those that were, of whom we read and hear, and among those that are, whom we see and converse with, every one hath received a several picture of face, and every one a diverse picture of mind; every one a form apart, every one a fancy and cogitation differing, there being nothing wherein nature so much triumpheth as in dissimilitude. From whence it cometh that there is found so great diversity of opinions, so strong a contrariety of inclinations, so many natural and unnatural, wise, foolish, manly and childish affections and passions in mortal men. For it is not the visible fashion and shape of plants, and of reasonable creatures, that makes the difference of working in the one and of condition in the other, but the form internal.

And though it hath pleased God to reserve the art of reading men's thoughts to himself, yet as the fruit tells the name of the tree, so do the outward works of men (so far as their

THE PREFACE   [1]Text *with.*
[2]James I, *Demonologie* (1597), III.i (ed. G. B. Harrison, 1924, p. 62).
[3]The Apocryphal Ecclesiasticus or the Wisdom of Jesus the Son of Sirach 11.7.   [4]Personal affairs.
[5]Queen Elizabeth, for whom Raleigh's loyalty and affection never failed.
[6]"It is a pleasure to be ill esteemed in a good cause."
[7]When Bathyllus, a poetaster, challenged Vergil by posting in a public place four incomplete lines beginning *Sic vos non vobis,* Vergil completed each of them in a different and masterly fashion. Thus the phrase (which means "you labor, but not for yourselves") became proverbial for one who does the work while another gets the credit.   [8]Justice.

cogitations are acted) give us whereof to guess at the rest. Nay, it were not hard to express the one by the other, very near the life, did not craft in many, fear in the most, and the world's love in all teach every capacity, according to the compass it hath, to qualify and mask over their inward deformities for a time. Though it be also true, *Nemo potest diu personam ferre fictam: cito in naturam suam residunt, quibus veritas non subest:* "No man can long continue masked in a counterfeit behavior: the things that are forced for pretences, having no ground of truth, cannot long dissemble their own natures." Neither can any man (saith Plutarch)[9] so change himself but that his heart may be sometimes seen at his tongue's end.

In this great discord and dissimilitude of reasonable creatures, if we direct ourselves to the multitude, *omnis honestae rei malus judex est vulgus:* "the common people are evil judges of honest things," and whose wisdom (saith Ecclesiastes) is to be despised;[10] if to the better sort, every understanding hath a peculiar judgment by which it both censureth other men and valueth itself. And therefore unto me it will not seem strange though I find these my worthless papers torn with rats: seeing the slothful censurers of all ages have not spared to tax the reverend fathers of the church with ambition, the severest men to themselves with hypocrisy, the greatest lovers of justice with popularity, and those of the truest valor and fortitude with vainglory. But of these natures which lie in wait to find fault, and to turn good into evil, seeing Solomon complained long since,[11] and that the very age of the world renders it every day after other more malicious, I must leave the professors to their easy ways of reprehension, than which there is nothing of more facility.

To me it belongs in the first part of this preface, following the common and approved custom of those who have left the memories of time past to after-ages, to give, as near as I can, the same right to history which they have done. Yet seeing therein I should but borrow other men's words, I will not trouble the reader with the repetition. True it is that among many other benefits for which it hath been honored, in this one it triumpheth over all human knowledge, that it hath given us life in our understanding, since the world itself had life and beginning, even to this day: yea, it hath triumphed over time, which, besides it, nothing but eternity hath triumphed over: for it hath carried our knowledge over the vast and devouring space of many thousands of years, and given so fair and piercing eyes to our mind, that we plainly behold living now, as if we had lived then, that great world, *magni Dei sapiens opus,* "the wise work," saith Hermes,[12] "of a great God," as it was then when but new to itself. By it, I say, it is that we live in the very time when it was created; we behold how it was governed; how it was covered with waters, and again repeopled; how kings and kingdoms have flourished and fallen; and for what virtue and piety God made prosperous, and for what vice and deformity he made wretched, both the one and the other. And it is not the least debt which we owe unto history that it hath made us acquainted with our dead ancestors; and, out of the depth and darkness of the earth, delivered us their memory

and fame. In a word, we may gather out of history a policy no less wise than eternal, by the comparison and application of other men's forepassed miseries with our own like errors and ill deservings.

But it is neither of examples the most lively instruction, nor the words of the wisest men, nor the terror of future torments that hath yet so wrought in our blind and stupefied minds as to make us remember that the infinite eye and wisdom of God doth pierce through all our pretences; as to make us remember that the justice of God doth require none other accuser than our own consciences: which neither the false beauty of our apparent actions, nor all the formality which (to pacify the opinions of men) we put on, can in any or the least kind cover from his knowledge. And so much did that heathen wisdom confess, no way as yet qualified by the knowledge of a true God. If any (saith Euripides),[13] having in his life committed wickedness, think he can hide it from the everlasting gods, he thinks not well.

To repeat God's judgments in particular upon those of all degrees which have played with His mercies would require a volume apart, for the sea of examples hath no bottom. The marks set on private men are with their bodies cast into the earth, and their fortunes written only in the memories of those that lived with them: so as they who succeed, and have not seen the fall of others, do not fear their own faults. God's judgments upon the greater and greatest have been left to posterity, first by those happy hands which the Holy Ghost hath guided, and secondly by their virtue who have gathered the acts and ends of men mighty and remarkable in the world. Now to point far off, and to speak of the conversion of angels into devils for ambition; or of the greatest and most glorious kings, who have gnawn the grass of the earth with beasts for pride and ingratitude towards God;[14] or of that wise working of Pharaoh when he slew the infants of Israel ere they had recovered their cradles;[15] or of the policy of Jezebel in covering the murder of Naboth by a trial of the elders, according to the law;[16] with many thousands of the like: what were it other than to make an hopeless proof that far-off examples would not be left to the same far-off respects as heretofore? For who hath not observed what labor, practice, peril, bloodshed, and cruelty the kings and princes of the world have undergone, exercised, taken on them, and committed, to make themselves and

---

[9]Greek biographer and moralist (46?–120), author of the *Parallel Lives* of eminent Greeks and Romans, an immensely influential work in the English Renaissance in Sir Thomas North's translation (1579). [10]Ecclesiastes 9.16.
[11]*Solomon . . . since:* Ecclesiastes 2.
[12]Hermes Trismegistus ("Hermes the thrice greatest"), the Greek name of the Egyptian god Thoth, reputed author of various mystical, theosophical, occult, and neoplatonic writings constituting the so-called "Hermetic books." Actually a sort of encyclopedia based on Egyptian mythology, the work (which survives only in fragments) dealt with art, sciences, geometry, astronomy, medicine, ceremonial hymns, and the like.
[13]Greek playwright (5th cent. B.C.), eighteen of whose works survive. [14]Daniel 4.28–34. [15]Exodus 1.15–22. [16]1 Kings 21.

their issues masters of the world? And yet hath Babylon, Persia, Egypt, Syria, Macedon, Carthage, Rome, and the rest no fruit, flower, grass, nor leaf springing upon the face of the earth of those seeds. No, their very roots and ruins do hardly remain. *Omnia quae manu hominum facta sunt, vel manu hominum evertuntur, vel stando et durando deficiunt:* "All that the hand of man can make is either overturned by the hand of man, or at length by standing and continuing consumed." The reasons of whose ruins are diversely given by those that ground their opinions on second causes.[17] All kingdoms and states have fallen (say the politicians) by outward and foreign force, or by inward negligence and dissension, or by a third cause arising from both. Others observe that the greatest have sunk down under their own weight, of which Livy hath a touch: *Eo crevit, ut magnitudine laboret sua.*[18] Others, that the divine providence (which Cratippus objected to Pompey)[19] hath set down the date and period of every estate before their first foundation and erection. But hereof I will give myself a day over to resolve.

For seeing the first books of the following story have undertaken the discourse of the first kings and kingdoms, and that it is impossible for the short life of a preface to travel after and overtake far-off antiquity and to judge of it, I will for the present examine what profit hath been gathered by our own kings and their neighbor princes, who having beheld, both in divine and human letters, the success of infidelity, injustice, and cruelty, have (notwithstanding) planted after the same pattern.

True it is that the judgments of all men are not agreeable, nor (which is more strange) the affection of any one man stirred up alike with examples of like nature; but every one is touched most with that which most nearly seemeth to touch his own private, or otherwise best suiteth with his apprehension. But the judgments of God are forever unchangeable; neither is He wearied by the long process of time, and won to give His blessing in one age to that which He hath cursed in another. Wherefore those that are wise, or whose wisdom, if it be not great, yet is true and well grounded, will be able to discern the bitter fruits of irreligious policy as well among those examples that are found in ages removed far from the present as in those of latter times. And that it may no less appear by evident proof than by asseveration that ill doing hath always been attended with ill success, I will here, by way of preface, run over some examples, which the work ensuing hath not reached.

Among our kings of the Norman race, we have no sooner passed over the violence of the Norman Conquest than we encounter with a singular and most remarkable example of God's justice upon the children of Henry the First.[20] For that King, when both by force, craft, and cruelty he had dispossessed, overreached, and lastly made blind and destroyed his elder brother Robert, duke of Normandy, to make his own sons lords of this land, God cast them all, male and female, nephews and nieces (Maud excepted), into the bottom of the sea, with above a hundred and fifty others that attended them; whereof a great many were noble, and of the King dearly beloved.

To pass over the rest, till we come to Edward the Second.[21]

It is certain that after the murder of that King, the issue of blood then made, though it had some times of stay and stopping, did again break out; and that so often, and in such abundance, as all our princes of the masculine race (very few excepted) died of the same disease. And although the young years of Edward the Third made his knowledge of that horrible fact no more than suspicious, yet in that he afterwards caused his own uncle the earl of Kent to die, for no other offence than the desire of his brother's redemption, whom the earl as then supposed to be living, the king making that to be treason in his uncle which was indeed treason in himself, had his uncle's intelligence been true, this, I say, made it manifest that he was not ignorant of what had passed, nor greatly desirous to have had it otherwise, though he caused Mortimer to die for the same.

This cruelty the secret and unsearchable judgment of God revenged on the grandchild of Edward the Third,[22] and so it fell out, even to the last of that line, that in the second or third descent they were all buried under the ruins of those buildings of which the mortar had been tempered with innocent blood. For Richard the Second, who saw both his treasurers, his chancellor, and his steward, with divers others of his counsailors, some of them slaughtered by the people, others in his absence executed by his enemies, yet he always took himself for overwise to be taught by examples. The earls of Huntington and Kent, Montague and Spencer, who thought themselves as great politicians in those days as others

---

[17]God's instruments or agents (which permit a "natural" explanation) rather than God himself.

[18]"It grew until it collapsed under its own weight."

[19]According to Plutarch's life of Pompey (Sect. lxxv), when that great Roman statesman questioned the providence that led to his defeat by Caesar at Pharsalia (48 B.C.), Cratippus, a philosopher of Mytilene, refrained from asking him why he supposed that he would have made a better use of success than his adversary. *Objected*: presented for consideration, adduced.

[20]King of England (1100–35). When Henry heard of the foundering of the so-called White Ship (1120)—in which were destroyed William, his only legitimate son, as well as William's half-brother and sister and many of the younger nobility—he fell senseless to the ground.

[21]King of England (1307–27). Forced to abdicate and then murdered by Queen Isabella and her lover Roger de Mortimer, Edward was succeeded by his fifteen-year-old son as Edward III (1327–77), who subsequently imprisoned his mother and executed her accomplice. The execution of the young king's uncle, Edmund of Woodstock, earl of Kent (1330), upon a trumped-up charge of treason contrived by Isabella and Mortimer was probably effected without Edward's knowledge or permission. For Samuel Daniel's assessment of Edward III see p. 851 f.

[22]The disorder and savage political jockeying in the early reign of Richard II, king of England (1377–99), culminated in the death, under suspicious circumstances, of his uncle Thomas of Woodstock, duke of Gloucester, at Calais in 1397. The next year the banishment of his cousin Henry of Lancaster, son of John of Gaunt, led to Henry's insurrection and to Richard's abdication and murder, and ultimately to the long dynastic struggles of the fifteenth century between the Lancastrians and Yorkists. For Sir John Hayward's more sympathetic account of Richard II see pp. 828 ff.

have done in these, hoping to please the King and to secure themselves by the murder of Gloucester, died soon after, with many other their adherents, by the like violent hands, and far more shamefully than did that duke. And as for the king himself (who in regard of many deeds unworthy of his greatness cannot be excused, as the disavowing himself by breach of faith, charters, pardons, and patents), he was in the prime of his youth deposed, and murdered by his cousin-german[23] and vassal, Henry of Lancaster, afterwards Henry the Fourth.

This king, whose title was weak and his obtaining the crown traitorous, who brake faith with the lords at his landing, protesting to intend only the recovery of his proper inheritance, brake faith with Richard himself, and brake faith with all the kingdom in Parliament, to whom he swore that the deposed king should live. After that he had enjoyed this realm some few years, and in that time had been set upon on all sides by his subjects, and never free from conspiracies and rebellions, he saw (if souls immortal see and discern any things after the body's death) his grandchild Henry the Sixth and his son the prince suddenly and without mercy murdered; the possession of the crown (for which he had caused so much blood to be poured out) transferred from his race, and by the issues[24] of his enemies worn and enjoyed—enemies whom by his own practice he supposed that he had left no less powerless than the succession of the kingdom questionless, by entailing the same upon his own issues by Parliament. And out of doubt, human reason could have judged no otherwise, but that these cautious provisions of the father, seconded by the valor and signal victories of his son Henry the Fifth, had buried the hopes of every competitor under the despair of all reconquest and recovery.[25] I say that human reason might so have judged, were not this passage of Casaubon[26] also true: *Dies, hora, momentum, evertendis dominationibus sufficit, quae adamantinis credebantur radicibus esse fundatae:* "A day, an hour, a moment is enough to overturn the things that seemed to have been founded and rooted in adamant."[27]

Now for Henry the Sixth, upon whom the great storm of his grandfather's grievous faults fell, as it formerly had done upon Richard, the grandchild of Edward: although he was generally esteemed for a gentle and innocent prince, yet as he refused the daughter of Armagnac, of the house of Navarre, the greatest of the princes of France, to whom he was affianced (by which match he might have defended his inheritance in France), and married the daughter of Anjou[28] (by which he lost all that he had in France), so as in condescending[29] to the unworthy death of his uncle of Gloucester,[30] the main and strong pillar of the house of Lancaster, he drew on himself and this kingdom the greatest joint-loss[31] and dishonor that ever it sustained since the Norman conquest. Of whom it may truly be said, which a counselor of his own spake of Henry the Third of France, *Qu'il estoit un fort gentil prince; mais son reigne est advenu en un fort mauvais temps:* "That he was a very gentle prince, but his reign happened in a very unfortunate season."

It is true that Buckingham and Suffolk[32] were the practisers[33] and contrivers of the duke's death: Buckingham and

Suffolk, because the Duke gave instructions to[34] their authority, which otherwise under the queen had been absolute; the queen, in respect of her personal wound, *spretaeque injuria formae,*[35] because Gloucester dissuaded[36] her marriage. But the fruit was answerable to the seed, the success to the counsail. For after the cutting down of Gloucester, York[37] grew up so fast as he dared to dispute his right, both by arguments and arms, in which quarrel Suffolk and Buckingham, with the greatest number of their adherents, were dissolved. And although, for his breach of oath by sacrament, it pleased God to strike down York, yet his son the earl of March, following the plain path which his father had trodden out, despoiled Henry the father and Edward the son both of their lives and kingdom. And what was the end now of that politic lady the queen other than this, that she lived to behold the wretched ends of all her partakers;[38] that she lived to look on while her husband the king, and her only son the prince, were hewn in sunder, while the crown was set on his head that did it. She lived to see herself despoiled of her estate and of her movables, and lastly her father, by rendering up to the crown of France the earldom of Provence and other places, for the payment of fifty thousand crowns for her ransom, to become a stark beggar. And this was the end of that sub-

[23]First cousin. [24]Descendants.
[25]Despite the insurrection that placed Henry IV on the throne and the incessant troubles of his reign (1399–1413), the Lancastrian line that he founded seemed to be secured by the military successes of his son Henry V (1413–22). However, the ineffectual Henry VI (1422–61, 1470–71) was no match for the ambitious Yorkists, who, after murdering him and his young son, came to power in the person of Edward IV (1461–70, 1471–83).
[26]Isaac Casaubon (1559–1614), eminent French humanist and Protestant theologian who settled in England in 1610.
[27]Diamond, i.e., something very hard.
[28]Margaret (1430–82), daughter of René of Anjou, at whose marriage (1445) to Henry VI the English ceded to the French the rich provinces of Anjou and Maine, and subsequently Normandy. The queen's savage and relentless hostility to the Yorkists is one of the main themes of Shakespeare's *Henry VI* plays.
[29]Descending, stooping.
[30]Humphrey, duke of Gloucester (1391–1447), whose persistent opposition to his nephew's disastrous French policy and to his marriage with Margaret of Anjou led to his downfall. Although he died in custody, the suspicions of his murder (which Shakespeare depicts as a fact in *2 Henry VI,* III.ii) were probably groundless.
[31]Dangerous or destructive circumstance?
[32]Humphrey Stafford (1402–60), first duke of Buckingham, and William de la Pole (1396–1450), fourth earl and first duke of Suffolk, allies of Queen Margaret against the duke of Gloucester.
[33]Plotters. [34]Curbed.
[35]"The offense of despising her beauty" (Vergil, *Aeneid,* I.27).
[36]Advised against, opposed.
[37]Richard, third duke of York (1411–60), grandson of Edward III and thus leader of the Yorkists in their long attempt to wrest the crown from their Lancastrian cousins. Although he was killed by Queen Margaret's troops, his son succeeded Henry VI in the latter's insanity between 1461 and 1470 and again, after the final defeat of the Lancastrians at the battle of Tewkesbury, in 1471.
[38]Accomplices.

tilty which Siracides calleth *fine* but *unrighteous*,[39] for other fruit hath it never yielded since the world was.

And now came it to Edward the Fourth's turn (though after many difficulties) to triumph. For all the plants of Lancaster were rooted up, one only earl of Richmond[40] excepted, whom also he had once bought of the duke of Britain, but could not hold him. And yet was not this of Edward such a plantation as could any way promise itself stability. For this Edward the king (to omit more than many of his other cruelties) beheld and allowed the slaughter which Gloucester, Dorset, Hastings, and others made of Edward the Prince[41] in his own presence, of which tragical actors there was not one that escaped the judgment of God in the same kind. And he which (besides the execution of his brother of Clarence,[42] for none other offence than he himself had formed in his own imagination) instructed Gloucester to kill Henry the Sixth, his predecessor, taught him also by the same art to kill his own sons and successors, Edward and Richard.[43] For those kings which have sold the blood of others at a low rate have but made the market for their own enemies to buy of theirs at the same price.

To Edward the Fourth succeeded Richard the Third, the greatest master in mischief of all that forewent him, who, although for the necessity of his tragedy he had more parts to play, and more to perform in his own person, than all the rest, yet he so well fitted every affection that played with him as if each of them had but acted his own interest.[44] For he wrought so cunningly upon the affections of Hastings and Buckingham, enemies to the queen and to all her kindred, as he easily allured them to condescend that Rivers and Grey, the king's maternal uncle and half-brother, should (for the first) be severed from him; secondly, he wrought their consent to have them imprisoned; and lastly (for the avoiding of future inconvenience), to have their heads severed from their bodies. And having now brought those his chief instruments to exercise that common precept which the devil hath written on every post, namely, to depress those whom they had grieved and to destroy those whom they had depressed,[45] he urged that argument so far and so forcibly as nothing but the death of the young king himself and of his brother could fashion the conclusion. For he caused it to be hammered into Buckingham's head that whensoever the king or his brother should have able years to exercise their power, they would take a most severe revenge of that cureless wrong offered to their uncle and brother, Rivers and Grey.

But this was not his manner of reasoning with Hastings, whose fidelity to his master's sons was without suspect;[46] and yet the devil, who never dissuades by impossibility, taught him to try him, and so he did. But when he found by Catesby, who sounded[47] him, that he was not fordable, he first resolved to kill him sitting in council; wherein having failed with his sword, he set the hangman upon him with a weapon of more weight. And because nothing else could move his appetite, he caused his head to be stricken off before he eat his dinner. A greater judgment of God than this upon Hastings I have never observed in any story. For the selfsame day that the Earl Rivers, Grey, and others were (without trial of law or offence given) by Hastings' advice executed at Pomfret[48]—I say, Hastings himself in the same day, and (as I take it) in the same hour, in the same lawless manner, had his head stricken off in the Tower of London. But Buckingham lived a while longer, and with an eloquent oration persuaded the Londoners to elect Richard for their king. And having received the earldom of Hereford for reward, besides the high hope of marrying his daughter to the king's only son, after many grievous vexations of mind and unfortunate attempts, being in the end betrayed and delivered up by his trustiest servant, he had his head severed from his body at Salisbury without the trouble of any of his peers.[49] And what success had Richard himself, after all these mischiefs and murders, policies and counter-policies to Christian religion, and after such time as with a most merciless hand he had pressed out the breath of his nephews and natural lords, other than the prosperity of so short a life as it took end ere himself could well look over and discern it? The great outcry of innocent blood obtained at God's hands the effusion of his, who became a spectacle of shame and dishonor both to his friends and enemies.

This cruel King Henry the Seventh cut off,[50] and was therein (no doubt) the immediate instrument of God's justice. A politic prince he was, if ever there were any, who by the engine of his wisdom beat down and overturned as many strong oppositions, both before and after he wore the crown, as ever king of England did. I say by his wisdom because as he ever left the reins of his affections in the hands of his profit, so he always weighed his undertakings by his abilities, leaving nothing more to hazard than so much as cannot be denied it

---

[39]*Siracides . . . unrighteous*: In the Apocryphal Eccelesiasticus or the Wisdom of Jesus the Son of Sirach (19.25) the passage reads, "There is a cleverness which is scrupulous but unjust."

[40]Henry Tudor (1457–1509), later Henry VII, king of England (1485–1509), who claimed the crown through his maternal descent from John of Gaunt and finally won it by defeating Richard III at the battle of Bosworth, thus bringing the long Plantagenet rule to an end and inaugurating the Tudor dynasty.

[41]Edward, Prince of Wales (1453–71), only son of Henry VI and Margaret of Anjou, was barbarously killed by the victorious Yorkists at the battle of Tewkesbury.

[42]George, duke of Clarence (1449–78), charged with plotting Edward IV's death through necromancy, was secretly executed in the Tower, allegedly by drowning in a butt of malmsey (as in Shakespeare's *Richard III*, I.iv) at the command of their brother Richard, duke of Gloucester, later Richard III (1483–85).

[43]The boy-king Edward V and his brother Richard, duke of York, sons of Edward IV, allegedly murdered in the Tower on orders of their uncle Richard, duke of Gloucester, in his bloody progress to the throne as Richard III.

[44]Most of the enormous crimes of Richard III that Raleigh cites—both the real ones and those alleged by Sir Thomas More and other Tudor historians—are depicted in Shakespeare's lurid play.

[45]To humble those whom they had wronged and to destroy those whom they had humbled.   [46]Suspicion.

[47]Tested his depth, i.e., explored his mind.

[48]Pontefract, Yorkshire, site of an ancient castle where Richard II had been murdered.   [49]Without a proper trial.

[50]After his bloody two-year reign, Richard III was killed at the battle of Bosworth in 1485.

in all human actions. He had well observed the proceedings of Louis the Eleventh,[51] whom he followed in all that was royal or royal-like, but he was far more just, and begun not their processes[52] whom he hated or feared by the execution, as Louis did.

He could never endure any mediation in rewarding his servants, and therein exceeding wise; for whatsoever himself gave, he himself received back the thanks and the love, knowing it well that the affections of men (purchased by nothing so readily as by benefits) were trains[53] that better became great kings than great subjects. On the contrary, in whatsoever he grieved his subjects, he wisely put it off on those that he found fit ministers for such actions. Howsoever, the taking off of Stanley's head, who set the crown on his, and the death of the young earl of Warwick, son to George, duke of Clarence,[54] shows, as the success also did, that he held somewhat of the errors of his ancestors; for his possession in the first line ended in his grandchildren,[55] as that of Edward the Third and Henry the Fourth had done.

Now for King Henry the Eighth. If all the pictures and patterns of a merciless prince were lost in the world, they might all again be painted to the life out of the story of this king. For how many servants did he advance in haste (but for what virtue no man could suspect) and with the change of his fancy ruined again, no man knowing for what offense! To how many others of more desert gave he aboundant flowers from whence to gather honey, and in the end of harvest burnt them in the hive! How many wives did he cut off and cast off, as his fancy and affection changed![56] How many princes of the blood (whereof some of them for age could hardly crawl towards the block), with a world of others of all degrees (of whom our common chronicles have kept the accompt), did he execute![57] Yea, in his very deathbed, and when he was at the point to have given his accompt to God for the aboundance of blood already spilt, he imprisoned the duke of Norfolk the father, and executed the earl of Surrey the son:[58] the one, whose deservings he knew not how to value, having never omitted anything that concerned his own honor and the king's service; the other, never having committed anything worthy of his least displeasure: the one exceeding valiant and advised;[59] the other no less valiant than learned, and of excellent hope. But besides the sorrows which he heaped upon the fatherless and widows at home, and besides the vain enterprises abroad wherein it is thought that he consumed more treasure than all our victorious kings did in their several conquests, what causeless and cruel wars did he make upon his own nephew King James the Fifth![60] What laws and wills did he devise, to establish this kingdom in his own issues, using his sharpest weapons to cut off and cut down those branches which sprang from the same root that himself did. And in the end (notwithstanding these his so many irreligious provisions) it pleased God to take away all his own without increase, though, for themselves in their several kinds, all princes of eminent virtue. For these words of Samuel to Agag, king of the Amalekites, have been verified upon many others: "As thy sword hath made other women childless, so shall thy mother be childless among other women."[61]

And that blood which the same King Henry affirmed that the cold air of Scotland had frozen up in the north, God hath diffused by the sunshine of His grace, from whence His Majesty now living,[62] and long to live, is descended. Of whom I may say it truly that if all the malice of the world were infused into one eye, yet could it not discern in his life, even to this day, any one of those foul spots by which the consciences of all the forenamed princes (in effect) have been defiled, nor any drop of that innocent blood on the sword of his justice with which the most that forewent him have stained both their hands and fame. And for this crown of England, it may truly be avowed that he hath received it even from the hand of God, and hath stayed the time of putting it on, howsoever he were provoked to hasten it; that he never took revenge of any man that sought to put him beside it; that he refused the assistance of her enemies that wore it long[63] with as great glory as ever princess did; that His Majesty entered not by a breach nor by blood, but by the ordinary gate which his own right set open, and into which, by a general love and obedience, he was received. And howsoever His Majesty's preceding title to this kingdom was preferred by many princes (witness the treaty at Cambray[64] in the year 1559), yet he never pleased to

[51]King of France (1461–83) notorious for his perfidy and cunning. [52]Legal proceedings against them. [53]Attendants.
[54]Henry executed William Stanley (1495), who had played a decisive role at Bosworth, for alleged treason, and Edward, earl of Warwick (1499), on a spurious charge of conspiracy.
[55]The Tudors were a short-lived dynasty, comprising only Henry VII, his son Henry VIII (1509–47), and his three grandchildren—Edward VI (1547–53), Mary (1553–58), and the great Elizabeth (1558–1603).
[56]Of Henry's six wives two (Catherine of Aragon and Anne of Cleves) were divorced, two (Anne Boleyn and Catherine Howard) were executed, one (Jane Seymour) died in childbed, and one (Catherine Parr) survived her husband.
[57]Because the Tudors had such a shaky claim upon the throne, Henry VIII, like his father, ruthlessly destroyed—usually through judicial murder—every potential rival who fell into his hands. One of his most pitiable victims was the aged Margaret, countess of Salisbury, a daughter of George, duke of Clarence (see n. 42 above), who was dragged to the block in 1541, three years after her son, Baron Montague, had met the same fate.
[58]Henry Howard (1517?–47), earl of Surrey, with Sir Thomas Wyatt a notable contributor to the important collection of early Tudor poetry known as *Tottel's Miscellany* (1557). He was executed on a flimsy charge of treason in the last months of Henry VIII's reign. [59]Deliberate, judicious.
[60]King of Scotland (1513–42), son of James IV (who died in battle with the English at Flodden Field in 1513) and of Henry's sister Margaret, father of Mary Queen of Scots, and grandfather of James VI of Scotland and I of England. [61]1 Samuel 15.32.
[62]James VI of Scotland (1567–1625) and I of England (1603–25), an inveterate enemy of Raleigh.
[63]Elizabeth I, whose cousin Mary Queen of Scots, James' mother, was her most dangerous rival to the throne until her execution in 1587.
[64]The treaty of Cateau-Cambrésis, by which England, France, and Spain sought to resolve some of their territorial and political disputes. In one of its articles Philip II of Spain agreed to relinquish his matrimonial designs upon Elizabeth, half-sister of his deceased

dispute it during the life of that renowned lady, his predecessor, no, notwithstanding the injury of not being declared heir in all the time of her long reign.

Neither ought we to forget or neglect our thankfulness to God for the uniting of the northern parts of Britany to the south, to wit of Scotland to England, which, though they were severed but by small brooks and banks, yet by reason of the long continued war and the cruelties exercised upon each other, in the affection of the nations they were infinitely severed.[65] This, I say, is not the least of God's blessings which His Majesty hath brought with him unto this land: no, put all our petty grievances together and heap them up to their height, they will appear but as a molehill, compared with the mountain of this concord. And if all the historians since then have acknowledged the uniting of the red rose and the white[66] for the greatest happiness (Christian religion excepted) that ever this kingdom received from God, certainly the peace between the two lions of gold and gules,[67] and the making them one, doth by many degrees exceed the former; for by it, besides the sparing of our British blood, heretofore and during the difference so often and abundantly shed, the state of England is more assured, the kingdom more enabled to recover her ancient honor and rights, and by it made more invincible, than by all our former alliances, practices, policies, and conquests. It is true that hereof we do not yet find the effect. But had the duke of Parma, in the year 1588, joined the army which he commanded with that of Spain and landed it on the south coast, and had His Majesty at the same time declared himself against us in the north, it is easy to divine what had become of the liberty of England; certainly we would then without murmur have bought this union at a far greater price[68] than it hath since cost us.[69]

It is true that there was never any commonweal or kingdom in the world wherein no man had cause to lament. Kings live in the world, and not above it. They are not infinite to examine every man's cause, or to relieve every man's wants. And yet in the latter (though to his own prejudice) His Majesty hath had more compassion of other men's necessities than of his own coffers. Of whom it may be said, as of Solomon, *Dedit Deus Salomoni latitudinem cordis;*[70] which if other men do not understand with Pineda[71] to be meant by *liberality,* but by *latitude of knowledge,* yet may it be better spoken of His Majesty than of any king that ever England had; who as well in divine as human understanding hath exceeded all that forewent him by many degrees. . . .

Oh, by what plots, by what forswearings, betrayings, oppressions, imprisonments, tortures, poisonings, and under what reasons of state and politic subtlety, have these forenamed kings, both strangers and of our own nation, pulled the vengeance of God upon themselves, upon theirs, and upon their prudent ministers! And in the end have brought those things to pass for their enemies, and seen an effect so directly contrary to all their own counsails and cruelties, as the one could never have hoped for themselves, and the other never have succeeded, if no such opposition had ever been made. God hath said it, and performed it ever: *Perdam*

sapientiam spaientum, "I will destroy the wisdom of the wise."[72]

But what of all this? and to what end do we lay before the eyes of the living the fall and fortunes of the dead, seeing the world is the same that it hath been, and the children of the present time will still obey their parents? It is in the present time that all the wits of the world are exercised. To hold the times we have, we hold all things lawful; and either we hope to hold them for ever, or at least we hope that there is nothing after them to be hoped for. For as we are content to forget our own experience, and to counterfeit the ignorance of our own knowledge, in all things that concern ourselves, or persuade ourselves that God hath given us letters patents[73] to pursue all our irreligious affections with a *non obstante:*[74] so we neither look behind us what hath been nor before us what shall be. It is true that the quantity which we have is of the body: we are by it joined to the earth; we are compounded of earth; and we inhabit it. The heavens are high, far off, and unsearchable; we have sense and feeling of corporal things, and of eternal grace but by revelation. No marvel, then, that our thoughts are also earthy: and it is less to be wondered at that the words of worthless men cannot cleanse them, seeing their doctrine and instruction, whose understanding the Holy Ghost vouchsafed to inhabit, have not performed it. For as the prophet Esay cried out long agone, "Lord, who hath believed our reports?"[75] And out of doubt, as Esay complained then for himself and others, so are they less believed every day after other. For although religion, and the truth thereof, be in every man's mouth, yea, in the discourse of every woman, who, for the greatest number, are but idols of vanity, what is it other than an universal dissimulation?

---

wife, Queen Mary of England.
[65]Although James was of course king of both England and Scotland after 1603, Parliament rejected a bill for the formal union of the two countries in 1607, and it was not until a century later that union was achieved. See p. 882, n.1.
[66]The accession of Henry VII (1485), which ended the Wars of the Roses between the houses of Lancaster and York.
[67]The heraldic emblems of the royal houses of England and Scotland. *Gules* is the heraldic term for red.
[68]Text *brought this union a far greater praise.*
[69]Raleigh speculates upon the disastrous consequences of young James VI of Scotland having joined in a three-pronged invasion with the duke of Parma's troops in the Low Countries and the so-called invincible Armada sent against the southern coast of England in 1588. It was the execution (1587) of James' mother, Mary Queen of Scots, that led Philip II of Spain to launch his assault on England.
[70]1 Kings 4.29: "And God gave Solomon wisdom and understanding beyond measure, and largeness of mind [*latitudinem cordis*] like the sand on the seashore."
[71]Juan de Pineda (1557–1637), Spanish theologian who (like Raleigh) wrote a universal history and also commentaries on the Bible.   [72]1 Corinthians 1.19.
[73]In English law, documents authorizing special rights or privileges.
[74]In old English statutes and letters patent, the phrase *non obstante aliquo statuo contrarium* ("any other statute to the contrary notwithstanding") granted dispensation from the legal penalty of a thing done despite statutory prohibition.   [75]Isaiah 53.1.

We profess that we know God, but by works we deny him. For beatitude doth not consist in the knowledge of divine things, but in a divine life; for the divels know them better than men. *Beatitudo non est divinorum cognitio, sed vita divina.* And certainly there is nothing more to be admired, and more to be lamented, than the private contention, the passionate dispute, the personal hatred, and the perpetual war, massacres, and murders for religion among Christians, the discourse whereof hath so occupied the world as it hath well near driven the practice thereof out of the world. Who would not soon resolve, that took knowledge but of the religious disputations among men, and not of their lives which dispute, that there were no other thing in their desires than the purchase of heaven, and that the world itself were but used as it ought, and as an inn or place wherein to repose ourselves in passing on towards our celestial habitation? When, on the contrary, besides the discourse and outward profession, the soul hath nothing but hypocrisy. We are all (in effect) become comedians in religion; and while we act in gesture and voice divine virtues, in all the course of our lives we renounce our persons and the parts we play. For charity, justice, and truth have but their being in terms, like the philosopher's *materia prima.*[76]

Neither is it that wisdom which Solomon defineth to be the "Schoolmistress of the knowledge of God"[77] that hath valuation in the world—it is enough that we give it our good word—but the same which is altogether exercised in the service of the world, as the gathering of riches chiefly, by which we purchase and obtain honor, with the many respects which attend it. These indeed be the marks which (when we have bent our consciences to the highest) we all shoot at. For the obtaining whereof it is true that the care is our own; the care our own in this life, the peril our own in the future, and yet when we have gathered the greatest aboundance, we ourselves enjoy no more thereof than so much as belongs to one man. For the rest, he that had the greatest wisdom and the greatest ability that ever man had hath told us that this is the use: "When goods increase," saith Solomon, "they also increase that eat them: and what good cometh to the owners but the beholding thereof with their eyes?"[78] As for those that devour the rest, and follow us in fair weather, they again forsake us in the first tempest of misfortune, and steer away before the sea and wind, leaving us to the malice of our destinies. Of these, among a thousand examples, I will take but one out of Master Danett,[79] and use his own words: "Whilst the Emperor Charles the Fifth,[80] after the resignation of his estates, stayed at Flushing[81] for wind to carry him his last journey into Spain, he conferred on a time with Seldius, his brother Ferdinand's ambassador, till the deep of the night. And when Seldius should depart, the Emperor calling for some of his servants, and nobody answering him (for those that attended upon him were some gone to their lodgings, and all the rest asleep), the Emperor took up the candle himself and went before Seldius to light him down the stairs; and so did, notwithstanding all the resistance that Seldius could make. And when he was come to the stairs foot, he said thus unto him: 'Seldius, remember this of Charles the Emperor when he shall be dead and gone, that him

whom thou hast known in thy time environed with so many mighty armies and guards of soldiers, thou hast also seen alone, abandoned and forsaken, yea even of his own domestical servants, etc. I acknowledge this change of fortune to proceed from the mighty hand of God, which I will by no means go about to withstand.' "

But you will say that there are some things else, and of greater regard than the former. The first is the reverend respect that is held of great men, and the honor done unto them by all sorts of people. And it is true indeed, provided that an inward love for their justice and piety accompany the outward worship given to their places and power, without which what is the applause of the multitude but as the outcry of an herd of animals, who, without the knowledge of any true cause, please themselves with the noise they make? For seeing it is a thing exceeding rare to distinguish virtue and fortune, the most impious, if prosperous, have ever been applauded; the most virtuous, if unprosperous, have ever been despised. For as fortune's man rides the horse, so fortune herself rides the man: who when he is descended and on foot, the man taken from his beast, and fortune from the man, a base groom beats the one, and a bitter contempt spurns at the other with equal liberty. . . .

Shall we therefore value honor and riches at nothing, and neglect them as unnecessary and vain? Certainly no, for that infinite wisdom of God, which hath distinguished His angels by degrees, which hath given greater and less light and beauty to heavenly bodies, which hath made differences between beasts and birds, created the eagle and the fly, the cedar and the shrub, and among stones given the fairest tincture to the ruby and the quickest light to the diamond, hath also ordained kings, dukes, or leaders of the people, magistrates, judges, and other degrees among men. And as honor is left to posterity for a mark and ensign of the virtue and understanding of their ancestors, so, seeing Siracides preferreth death before beggary,[82] and that titles without proportionable estates fall under the miserable succor of other men's pity, I accompt it foolishness to condemn such a care, provided that worldly goods be well gotten and that we raise not our own buildings out of other men's ruins. For as Plato doth first prefer the perfection of bodily health, secondly the form and beauty, and thirdly *divitias nulla fraude quaesitas,*[83] so Jeremy cries, "Woe unto them that erect

[76]"First matter," i.e., the original and irreducible substance from which everything is made.
[77]Raleigh is perhaps thinking of Proverbs 15.33: "the fear of the Lord is instruction in wisdom."   [78]Ecclesiastes 5.11.
[79]Thomas Danett (fl. 1566–1601), whose *History of Philip de Commines* (1596), a translation of Philippe de Commines' *Mémoires,* was followed by *A Continuation of the History of France* (1600), from which Raleigh loosely quotes, p. 131.
[80]Holy Roman Emperor (1519–56), who relinquished his vast powers as king of Spain to his son Philip II and as emperor to his brother Ferdinand in 1556, retiring to a Spanish monastery where he died two years later.
[81]Vlissingen, a seaport in the Netherlands.
[82]The Apocryphal Sirach 40.28.
[83]"Wealth acquired without dishonesty." The notion is a com-

their houses by unrighteousness, and their chambers without equity";[84] and Esay the same, "Woe to those that spoil, and were not spoiled."[85] And it was out of the true wisdom of Solomon that he commandeth us "not to drink the wine of violence, not to lie in wait for blood, and not to swallow them up alive whose riches we covet, for such are the ways," saith he, "of everyone that is greedy of gain."[86]

And if we could afford ourselves but so much leisure as to consider that he which hath most in the world hath, in respect of the world, nothing in it; and that he which hath the longest time lent him to live in it hath yet no proportion[87] at all therein, setting it either by that which is past when we were not, or by that time which is to come in which we shall abide forever; I say, if both, to wit, our proportion in the world and our time in the world, differ not much from that which is nothing, it is not out of any excellency of understanding that we so much prize the one, which hath (in effect) no being, and so much neglect the other, which hath no ending, coveting those mortal things of the world as if our souls were therein immortal, and neglecting those things which are immortal as if ourselves after the world were but mortal. . . .

For myself, this is my consolation, and all that I can offer to others, that the sorrows of this life are but of two sorts, whereof the one hath respect to God, the other to the world. In the first we complain to God against ourselves for our offences against Him, and confess, *Et tu justus es in omnibus quae venerunt super nos:* "And thou, O Lord, art just in all that hath befallen us."[88] In the second, we complain to ourselves against God, as if He had done us wrong, either in not giving us worldly goods and honors answering our appetites, or for taking them again from us, having had them, forgetting that humble and just acknowledgment of Job, "The Lord hath given, and the Lord hath taken."[89] To the first of which St. Paul hath promised blessedness; to the second, death. And out of doubt he is either a fool or ungrateful to God, or both, that doth not acknowledge, how mean soever his estate be, that the same is yet far greater than that which God oweth him; or doth not acknowledge, how sharp soever his afflictions be, that the same are yet far less than those which are due unto him. And if an heathen wise man call the adversities of the world but *tributa vivendi*, "the tributes of living,"[90] a wise Christian man ought to know them and bear them but as the tributes of offending; he ought to bear them manlike and resolvedly, and not as those whining soldiers do, *qui gementes sequuntur imperatorem.*[91]

For seeing God, who is the author of all our tragedies, hath written out for us and appointed us all the parts we are to play, and hath not, in their distribution, been partial to the most mighty princes of the world; that gave unto Darius the part of the greatest emperor and the part of the most miserable beggar, a beggar begging water of an enemy, to quench the great drought of death; that appointed Bajazet to play the grand signior of the Turks in the morning, and in the same day the footstool of Tamerlane (both which parts Valerian had also played, being taken by Sapores);[92] that made Belisarius play the most victorious captain and lastly the part of a blind beggar; of which examples many thousands may be produced: why should other men, who are but as the least worms, complain of wrongs? Certainly there is no other account to be made of this ridiculous world than to resolve that the change of fortune on the great theater is but as the change of garments on the less, for when, on the one and the other, every man wears but his own skin, the players are all alike. Now if any man, out of weakness, prize the passages of this world otherwise (for, saith Petrarch, *Magni ingenii est revocare mentem a sensibus*),[93] it is by reason of that unhappy fantasy of ours which forgeth in the brains of man all the miseries (the corporal excepted) whereunto he is subject: therein it is that misfortune and adversity work all that they work. For seeing death, in the end of the play, takes from all whatsoever fortune or force takes from anyone, it were a foolish madness, in the shipwrack of worldly things, where all sinks but the sorrow, to save it. That were, as Seneca saith, *fortunae succumbere, quod tristius est omni fato:* "to fall under fortune, of all other the most miserable destiny."

But it is now time to sound a retreat, and to desire to be excused of this long pursuit, and withal that the good intent which hath moved me to draw the picture of time past (which we call history) in so large a table may also be accepted in place of a better reason.

The examples of divine Providence everywhere found (the first divine histories being nothing else but a continuation of such examples) have persuaded me to fetch my beginning from the beginning of all things, to wit, creation. For though these two glorious actions of the Almighty be so near, and, as it were, linked together, that the one necessarily implieth the other: creation inferring[94] providence (for what father forsaketh the child that he hath begotten?) and providence presupposing creation; yet many of those that have seemed to excel in worldly wisdom have gone about to disjoin this coherence: the Epicure[95] denying both creation and providence, but granting that the world had a

monplace in Plato, for example *Laws*, III.697, V.743, IX.870.
[84]Jeremiah 22.13.   [85]Isaiah 33.1.
[86]Raleigh makes a pastiche from several passages of Proverbs (4.17, 1.11, etc.).   [87]Portion, share.   [88]Nehemiah 9.33.
[89]Job 1.21.
[90]Lucius Annaeus Seneca (4 B.C.?–65), *De remediis fortuitorum*, xvi.9 (*Opera quae supersunt*, "Supplementum," ed. Fr. Hasse, 1902, p. 55): *Mors, exilium, luctus, dolor non sunt supplicia sed tributa vivendi* ("Death, exile, suffering, and sorrow are not punishments but the allotted payments of living").
[91]"Who follow their leader mourning."
[92]*Darius . . . Belisarius*: notable victims of misfortune. Darius III, king of Persia, was conquered by Alexander the Great in 331 B.C.; Bajazet I, sultan of the Ottoman empire, was taken captive by the Scythian tyrant Tamerlane in 1402; Valerian, emperor of Rome, was imprisoned by Shapur (*Sapores*), king of Persia, in 260; Belisarius, a general of the Eastern empire who captured Rome for Emperor Justinian in 536, died in disgrace and poverty.
[93]It requires remarkable gifts to be able to withdraw the mind from objects of sense.   [94]Implying.
[95]Epicurean, a follower of Epicurus (342?–270 B.C.), Greek philosopher who taught that matter, made up of atoms, is eternal.

beginning; the Aristotelian granting providence, but denying both the creation and the beginning.[96]

Now although this doctrine of faith, touching the creation in time (for "by faith we understand that the world was made by the word of God"),[97] be too weighty a work for Aristotle's rotten ground to bear up, upon which he hath (notwithstanding) founded the defences and fortresses of all his verbal doctrine; yet that the necessity of infinite power, and the world's beginning, and the impossibility of the contrary, even in the judgment of natural reason, wherein he believed, had not better informed him, it is greatly to be marvailed at. And it is no less strange that those men which are desirous of knowledge (seeing Aristotle hath failed in this main point, and taught little other than terms[98] in the rest) have so retrenched their minds from the following and overtaking of truth, and so absolutely subjected themselves to the law of those philosophical principles, as all contrary kind of teaching, in the search of causes, they have condemned either for fantastical or curious. But doth it follow that the positions of heathen philosophers are undoubted grounds and principles indeed, because so called? or that *ipsi dixerunt*[99] doth make them to be such? Certainly no. But this is true, that where natural reason hath built anything so strong against itself as the same reason can hardly assail it, much less batter it down, the same, in every question of nature and finite power, may be approved for a fundamental law of human knowledge. . . .

But for myself, I shall never be persuaded that God hath shut up all light of learning within the lantern of Aristotle's brains; or that it was ever said unto him, as unto Esdras, *Accendam in corde tuo lucernam intellectus;*[1] that God hath given invention but to the heathen, and that they only invaded nature and found the strength and bottom thereof, the same nature having consumed all her store and left nothing of price to after-ages. That these and these be the causes of these and these effects time hath taught us, and not reason; and so hath experience, without art. The cheese-wife knoweth it as well as the philosopher that sour rennet[2] doth coagulate her milk into a curd. But if we ask a reason of this cause—why the sourness doth it? whereby it doth it? and the manner how? I think that there is nothing to be found in vulgar philosophy to satisfy this and many other like vulgar questions. But man, to cover his ignorance in the least things, who cannot give a true reason for the grass under his feet, why it should be green rather than red or of any other color; that could never yet discover the way and reason of nature's working in those which are far less noble creatures than himself, who is far more noble than the heavens themselves; "Man," saith Solomon, "that can hardly discern the things that a e upon the earth, and with great labor find out the things that are before us";[3] that hath so short a time in the world as he no sooner begins to learn than to die; that hath in his memory but borrowed knowledge, in his understanding nothing truly; that is ignorant of the essence of his own soul, and which the wisest of the naturalists (if Aristotle be he) could never so much as define but by the action and effect, telling us what it works (which all men know as well as he) but not what it

is, which neither he nor any else doth know, but God that created it ("For though I were perfect, yet I know not my soul," saith Job):[4] man, I say, that is but an idiot in the next[5] cause of his own life, and in the cause of all actions of his life, will, notwithstanding, examine the art of God in creating the world; of God, "who," saith Job, "is so excellent as we know him not";[6] and examine the beginning of the work which had end before mankind had a beginning of being. He will disable God's power to make a world without matter to make it of. He will rather give the moths of the air for a cause; cast the work on necessity or chance; bestow the honor thereof on nature; make two powers, the one to be the author of the matter, the other of the form; and lastly, for want of a workman, have it eternal: which latter opinion Aristotle, to make himself the author of a new doctrine, brought into the world, and his sectators[7] have maintained it. . . .

Touching those which conceive the matter of the world to have been eternal, and that God did not create the world *ex nihilo* but *ex materia prae-existente,*[8] the supposition is so weak as is hardly worth the answering. For, saith Eusebius,[9] *Mihi videntur qui hoc dicunt, fortunam quoque Deo annectere:* "They seem unto me, which affirm this, to give part of the work to God and part to fortune." Insomuch as if God had not found this "first matter" by chance, He had neither been author, nor father, nor creator, nor lord of the universal. For were the "matter" or "chaos" eternal, it then follows that either this supposed "matter" did fit itself to God, or God accommodate himself to the "matter." For the first, it is impossible that things without sense could proportion themselves to the workman's will; for the second, it were horrible to conceive of God that as an artificer He applied himself according to the proportion of "matter" which he lighted upon. . . . Those that feign this matter to be eternal must of necessity confess that infinite cannot be separate from eternity, and then had "infinite matter" left no place for "infinite form"; but that the "first matter" was finite, the form which it received proves it. For conclusion of this part, whosoever will make choice rather to believe in eternal deformity, or in eternal dead matter, than in eternal light and eternal life, let eternal death be his reward. For it is a madness of that kind as wanteth terms to express it. . . .

[96]Aristotle's conviction that matter is eternal was of course incompatible with the Christian doctrine that God created the world *ex nihilo* ("out of nothing").   [97]Hebrews 11.3.
[98]Philosophical jargon such as the "categories" and "predicaments" that were commonly derided by anti-Aristotelians like Raleigh.
[99]"They themselves have said it" (and therefore it is true); i.e. unproved or dogmatic assertions.
[1]The Apocryphal 2 Esdras 14.25 :"I will light in your heart the lamp of understanding."
[2]The contents of the stomach of an unweaned calf used for curdling milk.   [3]Perhaps a paraphrase of Ecclesiastes 10.14.
[4]Job 9.21.   [5]Nearest, i.e., least remote.   [6]Job 37.23.
[7]Followers
[8]Not out of nothing but out of pre-existing matter.
[9]Eusebius of Caesarea (260?–?340), theologian and historian

Raleigh nonetheless finds many "terms" to expose the
error and impiety of those who maintain that matter is
eternal, and that God and nature are the same. In his
generally orthodox and linear view of history the world
which God created *ex nihilo,* and which He sustains through
His inscrutable providence, will end when He decrees its
final conflagration. Indeed, as Raleigh and many of his
generation thought, there was reason to believe that the
world was growing old, and that the end was not far off.

The sun, by whose help all creatures are generate,[10] doth
not in these latter ages assist nature as heretofore. We have
neither giants such as the eldest world had, nor mighty men
such as the elder world had; but all things in general are
reputed of less virtue which from the heavens receive virtue.
Whence, if the nature of a preface would permit a larger
discourse, we might easily fetch store of prove[11] as that this
world shall at length have end, as that once it had beginning.
And I see no good answer that can be made to this objection:
if the world were eternal, why not all things in the world
eternal? If there were no first, no cause, no father, no creator,
no incomprehensible wisdom, but that every nature had
been alike eternal and man more rational than every other
nature, why had not the eternal reason of man provided for
his eternal being in the world? For if all were equal, why not
equal conditions to all? Why should heavenly bodies live
forever, and the bodies of men rot and die?

Again, who was it that appointed the earth to keep the
center, and gave order that it should hang in the air; that
the sun should travel between the tropics and never exceed
those bounds, nor fail to perform that progress once in
every year; the moon to live by borrowed light; the fixed
stars[12] (according to common opinion) to be fastened like
nails in a cartwheel and the planets to wander at their
pleasure? Or if none of these had power over other, was it
out of charity and love that the sun, by his perpetual travel
within those two circles, hath visited, given light unto, and
relieved all parts of the earth and the creatures therein by
turns and times? Out of doubt, if the sun have of his own
accord kept this course in all eternity he may justly be called
eternal charity and everlasting love. The same may be said
of all the stars, who, being all of them most large and clear
fountains of virtue and operation, may also be called eternal
virtues; the earth may be called eternal patience; the moon
an eternal borrower and beggar; and man, of all other the
most miserable, eternally mortal. And what were this but to
believe again in the old play of the gods, yea in more gods by
millions than ever Hesiodus[13] dreamt of? But instead of this
mad folly we see it well enough with our feeble and mortal
eyes, and the eyes of our reason discern it better, that the
sun, moon, stars and the earth are limited, bounded, and
constrained: themselves they have not constrained, nor could.
*Omne determinatum causam habet aliquam efficientem, quae
illud determinaverit:* "Everything bounded hath some efficient
cause by which it is bounded."

. . . For the rest, I do also account it not the meanest,
but an impiety monstrous, to confound God and nature, be
it but in terms. For it is God that only disposeth of all things
according to His own will, and maketh of one earth "vessels

of honor and dishonor";[14] it is nature that can dispose of
nothing but according to the will of the matter wherein it
worketh. It is God that commandeth all; it is nature that is
obedient to all. It is God that doth good unto all, knowing
and loving the good He doth; it is nature that secondarily
doth also good, but it neither knoweth nor loveth the good
it doth. It is God that hath all things in Himself, nature
nothing in itself. It is God which is the Father, and hath
begotten all things; it is nature which is begotten by all
things, in which it liveth and laboreth, for by itself it existeth
not. For shall we say that it is out of affection to the earth
that heavy things fall towards it? Shall we call it reason
which doth conduct every river into the salt sea? Shall we
term it knowledge in fire that makes it to consume combus-
tible matter? If it be affection, reason, and knowledge in
these, by the same affection, reason, and knowledge it is
that nature worketh.

And therefore, seeing all things work as they do—call it by
form, by nature, or by what you please—yet because they
work by an impulsion[15] which they cannot resist, or by a
faculty infused by the supremest power, we are neither to
wonder at nor to worship the faculty that worketh, nor the
creature wherein it worketh.

But herein lies the wonder, and to Him is the worship
due who hath created such a nature in things, and such a
faculty as, neither knowing itself, the matter wherein it
worketh, nor the virtue and power which it hath, do yet
work all things to their last and uttermost perfection. And
therefore every reasonable man, taking to himself for a
ground that which is granted by all antiquity, and by all
men truly learned that ever the world had, to wit, that there
is a power infinite and eternal—which also necessity doth
prove unto us without the help of faith, and reason without
the force of authority—all things do as easily follow which
have been delivered by divine letters as the waters of a run-
ning river do successively pursue each other from the first
fountains. . . . For seeing both reason and necessity teach
us—reason, which is *pars divini spiritus in corpus humanum
mersi*[16]—that the world was made by a power infinite, and
yet how it was made it cannot teach us; and seeing the same
reason and necessity make us know that the same infinite
power is everywhere in the world, and yet how everywhere
it cannot inform us; our believe[17] hereof is not weakened,
but greatly strengthened, by our ignorance, because it is the
same reason that tells us that such a nature cannot be said to
be God that can be in all conceived by man.

I have been already overlong to make any large discourse
either of the parts of the following story, or in mine own
excuse, especially in the excuse of this or that passage, seeing

who wrote a history of the Christian church and also a universal
history to 325. [10]Generated. [11]Proof.
[12]Text *first stars.* See *sphere* in the Glossary.
[13]Hesiod (8th cent. B.C.), Greek poet whose *Theogony* relates the
beginning of the world and the birth of the gods. [14]Romans 9.21.
[15]Impulse.
[16]"A part of the Divine Spirit thrust into the human body."
[17]Belief.

the whole is exceeding weak and defective. Among the grossest, the unsuitable division of the books I could not know how to excuse had I not been directed to enlarge the building after the foundation was laid and the first part finished. All men know that there is no great art in the dividing evenly of those things which are subject to number and measure. For the rest, it suits well enough with a great many books of this age, which speak too much and yet say little. *Ipsi nobis furto subducimur:* "We are stolen away from ourselves," setting a high price on all that is our own. But hereof though a late good writer make complaint, yet shall it not lay hold on me, because I believe as he doth that whoso thinks himself the wisest man is but a poor and miserable ignorant. Those that are the best men of war against all the vanities and fooleries of the world do always keep the strongest guards against themselves, to defend them from themselves, from self-love, self-estimation, and self-opinion.

Generally concerning the order of the work, I have only taken counsail from the argument.[18] For of the Assyrians, which, after the downfall of Babel,[19] take up the first part, and were the first great kings of the world, there came little to the view of posterity, some few enterprises, greater in fame than faith,[20] of Ninus and Semiramis[21] excepted.

It was the story of the Hebrews, of all before the Olympiads,[22] that overcame the consuming disease of time and preserved itself from the very cradle and beginning to this day, and yet not so entire but that the large discourses thereof (to which in many scriptures we are referred) are nowhere found. The fragments of other stories, with the actions of those kings and princes which shot up here and there in the same time, I am driven to relate by way of digression, of which we may say with Vergil, *Apparent rari nantes in gurgite vasto:*[23] "They appear here and there floating in the great gulf of time."

To the same first ages do belong the report of many inventions therein found, and from them derived to us, though most of the authors' names have perished in so long a navigation. For those ages had their laws; they had diversity of government; they had kingly rule, nobility, policy in war, navigation, and all or the most of needful trades. To speak therefore of these (seeing in a general history we should have left a great deal of nakedness by their omission), it cannot properly be called a digression. True it is that I have made also many others, which, if they shall be laid to my charge, I must cast the fault into the great heap of human error. For seeing we digress in all the ways of our lives, yea, seeing the life of man is nothing else but digression, I may the better be excused in writing their lives and actions. I am not altogether ignorant in the laws of history, and of the kinds.[24]

The same hath been taught by many, but by no man better, and with greater brevity, than by that excellent learned gentleman Sir Francis Bacon.[25] Christian laws are also taught us by the Prophets and Apostles, and every day preached unto us. But we still make large digressions; yea, the teachers themselves do not (in all) keep the path which they point out to others.

For the rest, after such time as the Persians had wrested the empire from the Chaldeans, and had raised a great monarchy, producing actions of more importance than were elsewhere to be found, it was agreeable to the order of story to attend this empire whilst it so flourished that the affairs of the nations adjoining had reference thereunto. The like observance was to be used towards the fortunes of Greece when they again[26] began to get ground upon the Persians, as also towards the affairs of Rome when the Romans grew more mighty than the Greeks.

As for the Medes, the Macedonians, the Sicilians, the Carthaginians, and other nations who resisted the beginnings of the former empires and afterwards became but parts of their composition and enlargement, it seemed best to remember[27] what was known of them from their several beginnings in such times and places as they in their flourishing estates opposed those monarchies which in the end swallowed them up. And herein I have followed the best geographers, who seldom give names to those small brooks, whereof many, joined together, make great rivers, till such time as they become united and run in main stream to the ocean sea. If the phrase be weak, and the style not everywhere like itself,[28] the first shows their legitimation and true parent; the second will excuse itself upon the variety of matter. For Vergil, who wrote his Eclogues *gracili avena*,[29] used stronger pipes when he sounded the wars of Aeneas. It may also be laid to my charge that I use divers Hebrew words in my first book and elsewhere, in which language others may think, and I myself acknowledge it, that I am altogether ignorant; but it is true that some of them I find in Montanus,[30] others in Latin character in S. Senensis,[31] and of the rest I have borrowed the interpretation of some of my friends. But say I had been beholden to neither, yet were it not to be wondered at, having had a eleven years' leisure[32] to attain the knowledge of that or of any other tongue; howsoever, I know that it will be said by many that I might have been more pleasing to the reader if I had written the story of mine own times, having been permitted to draw

---

[18]*Taken . . . argument:* let the structure of the work be governed by the narrative. [19]Babylon, ancient city on the Euphrates.
[20]Better known than authenticated.
[21]Legendary founder of Nineveh and his wife.
[22]See p. 819, n.30 [23]*Aeneid*, I.118.
[24]Classes (e.g., universal, ecclesiastical, civil, etc.).
[25]Raleigh no doubt has in mind Bacon's discussion of history in *The Advancement of Learning* (1605), for which see pp. 878 ff.
[26]Similarly, in turn. [27]Relate. [28]Uniform.
[29]*Ille ego, qui quondam gracili modulatus avena/Carmen:* "I am he who formerly tuned my song on a slender reed," Vergil's introduction to the *Aeneid* in which he announces his progress from pastoral to epic poetry.
[30]Arias Montano (1527–98), Spanish theologian and linguist who edited a famous polyglot Bible (1572).
[31]Sixtus Senensis or Sisto da Sienna (1520–69), Italian monk whose *Bibliotheca Sancta* went through several editions in the later 16th century.
[32]Following his conviction for conspiring against James I, Raleigh was imprisoned in the Tower from 1603 until 1616, when he was released to make his last disastrous voyage to South America.

water as near the well-head as another. To this I answer that whosoever, in writing a modern history, shall follow truth too near the heels, it may haply strike out his teeth. There is no mistress or guide that hath led her followers and servants into greater miseries. He that goes after her too far off loseth her sight, and loseth himself; and he that walks after her at a middle distance, I know not whether I should call that kind of course temper or baseness.[33] It is true that I never traveled after men's opinions when I might have made the best use of them; and I have now too few days remaining to imitate those that, either out of extreme ambition or extreme cowardice, or both, do yet (when death hath them on his shoulders) flatter the world between the bed and the grave. It is enough for me (being in that state I am) to write of the eldest times, wherein also why may it not be said that in speaking of the past I point at the present, and tax the vices of those that are yet living in their persons that are long since dead, and have it laid to my charge? But this I cannot help, though innocent. And certainly if there be any that, finding themselves spotted like the tigers of old time, shall find fault with me for painting them over anew, they shall therein accuse themselves justly and me falsely.

For I protest before the majesty of God that I malice[34] no man under the sun. Impossible I know it is to please all, seeing few or none are so pleased with themselves, or so assured of themselves, by reason of their subjection to their private passions, but that they seem divers person in one and the same day. Seneca hath said it, and so do I: *Unus mihi pro populo erat;*[35] and to the same effect Epicurus, *Hoc ego non multis, sed tibi;*[36] or (as it hath since lamentably fallen out) I may borrow the resolution of an ancient philosopher, *Satis est unus, satis est nullus.*[37] For it was for the service of that inestimable Prince Henry,[38] the successive hope, and one of the greatest of the Christian world, that I undertook this work. It pleased him to peruse some part thereof, and to pardon what was amiss. It is now left to the world without a master, from which all that is presented hath received both blows and thanks. *Eadem probamus, eadem reprehendimus: hic exitus est omnis judicii, in quo lis secundum plures datur.*[39] But these discourses are idle. I know that as the charitable will judge charitably, so against those *qui gloriantur in malitia*[40] my present adversity hath disarmed me. I am on the ground already, and therefore have not far to fall; and for rising again, as in the natural privation there is no recession to habit, so it is seldom seen in the privation politic.[41] I do therefore forbear to style my readers "gentle," "courteous," and "friendly," thereby to beg their good opinions, or to promise a second and third volume (which I also intend) if the first receive grace and good acceptance. For that which is already done may be thought enough, and too much; and it is certain, let us claw[42] the reader with never so many courteous phrases, yet shall we evermore be thought fools that write foolishly. For conclusion, all the hope I have lies in this, that I have already found more ungentle and uncourteous readers of my love towards them, and well-deserving of them, than ever I shall do again. For had it been otherwise, I should hardly have had this leisure to have made myself a fool in print.

THE FIRST PART OF THE HISTORY OF THE WORLD

THE SECOND BOOK

CHAPTER V

SECTION 10. OBSERVATIONS OUT OF THE STORY OF MOSES, HOW GOD DISPOSETH BOTH THE SMALLEST OCCASIONS AND THE GREATEST RESISTANCES TO THE EFFECTING OF HIS PURPOSE

Now let us a little, for instruction, look back to the occasions of sundry of the great events which have been mentioned in this story of the life of Moses,[1] for—excepting God's miracles, His promise, and fore-choice of this people—he wrought in all things else by the medium of men's affections and natural appetites. And so we shall find that the fear which Pharaoh had of the increase of the Hebrews, multiplied by God to exceeding great numbers, was the next[2] natural cause of the sorrows and loss which befell himself and the Egyptian nation; which numbers when he sought, by cruel and ungodly policies, to cut off and lessen, as when he commanded all the male children of the Hebrews to be slain, God (whose providence cannot be resisted, nor His purposes prevented by all the foolish and salvage[3] craft of mortal men) moved compassion in the heart of Pharaoh's own daughter to preserve that child which afterward became the most wise, and of all men the most gentle and mild, the most excellently learned in all divine and human knowledge, to be the conductor and deliverer of his oppressed brethren, and the overthrow of Pharaoh and all the flower of his nation, even then when he sought by the strength of his men of war, of his horse and chariots, to tread them under and bury them in the dust. The grief which Moses conceived of the injuries and of the violence offered to one of the Hebrews in his own presence moved him to take revenge of the Egyptian that offered it; the ingratitude of one of his own nation, by threatening him to discover the slaughter of the Egyptian, moved him to fly into Midian; the contention between the shepherds of that place and Jethro's daughters made him known to their father, who not only entertained him but married him to one of those sisters; and in that solitary life of keeping of his father-in-law's sheep, far from the press of the world, contenting himself (though bred as a king's son) with the lot of a poor

[33]Moderation or cowardice.   [34]Entertain malice against.
[35]One person took the place of everybody.
[36]I intend this for you alone, not for the multitude.
[37]"One is enough, none is enough."
[38]See p. 860.
[39]When a question is referred to many men it always happens that one admires what another dislikes.
[40]"Who delight in malice."
[41]*As in . . . politic:* there is as little hope of retrieving political disaster as of restoring our decayed natural faculties.   [42]Flatter.
HISTORY OF THE WORLD   [1]The events to which Raleigh alludes are related in Exodus 1–4.
[2]Nearest.   [3]Savage.

herdsman, God found him out in that desert, wherein He first suffered him to live many years, the better to know the ways and passages through which He purposed that he should conduct His people toward the land promised; and therein appearing unto him, He made him know His will and divine pleasure for his return into Egypt. The like may be said of all things else which Moses afterward by God's direction performed in the story of Israel before remembered. There is not therefore the smallest accident which may seem unto men as falling out by chance, and of no conse- [10] quence, but that the same is caused by God to effect somewhat else by, yea, and oftentimes to effect things of the greatest worldly importance, either presently or in many years after, when the occasions are either not considered or forgotten.

Chapter XXI

SECTION 6. A DIGRESSION WHEREIN IS MAINTAINED THE LIBERTY OF USING CONJECTURE IN HISTORIES

Thus much concerning the person of Joas,[4] from whom, as from a new root, the tree of David was propagated into many branches. In handling of which matter, the more I consider the nature of this history, and the diversity between it and others, the less, methinks, I need to suspect mine own [20] presumption as deserving blame for curiosity in matter of doubt, or boldness in liberty of conjecture. For all histories do give us information of human counsails and events as farforth as the knowledge and faith of the writers can afford; but of God's will, by which all things are ordered, they speak only at random, and many times falsely. This we often find in profane writers, who ascribe the ill success of great undertakings to the neglect of some impious rites, whereof indeed God abhorred the performance as vehemently as they thought Him to be highly offended with the [30] omission. Hereat we may the less wonder if we consider the answer made by the Jews in Egypt unto Jeremy the prophet reprehending their idolatry.[5] For howsoever the written law of God was known unto the people, and His punishments laid upon them for contempt thereof were very terrible, and even then but newly executed, yet were they so obstinately bent unto their wills that they would not by any means be drawn to acknowledge the true cause of their affliction; but they told the prophet roundly that they would worship the Queen of Heaven[6] as they and their [40] fathers, their kings and their princes, had used to do. "For then," said they, "had we plenty of victuals, and were well, and felt no evil," adding that all manner of miseries were befallen them since they left off that service of the Queen of Heaven. So blind is the wisdom of man in looking into the counsail of God, which to find out there is no better nor other guide than His own written will not perverted by vain additions.

But this history of the kings of Israel and Judah hath herein a singular prerogative above all that have been writ- [50] ten by the most sufficient of merely human authors: it setteth down expressly the true and first causes of all that happened; not in imputing the death of Ahab to his overforwardness in battail,[7] the ruin of his family to the security

of Jeroboam in Izreel,[8] nor the victories of Hazael to the great commotions raised in Israel by the coming of Jehu,[9] but referring all unto the will of God, I mean, to His revealed will, from which that His hidden purposes do not vary, this story, by many great examples, gives most notable proof. True it is that the concurrence of second causes with their effects is in these books nothing largely described, nor perhaps exactly in any of those histories that are in these points most copious. For it was well noted by that worthy gentleman Sir Philip Sidney that historians do borrow of poets not only much of their ornament but somewhat of their substance.[10] Informations are often false, records not always true, and notorious actions commonly insufficient to discover the passions which do set them first on foot. Wherefore they are fain (I speak of the best, and in that which is allowed for to take out of Livy every one circumstance of Claudius' his journey against Asdrubal in Italy,[11] fitting all to another business, or any practice of that kind, is neither historical nor poetical) to search into the particular humor of princes, and of those which have governed their affections, or the instruments by which they wrought, from whence they do collect the most likely motives or impediments of every business, and so, figuring as near to the life as they can imagine the matter in hand, they judiciously consider the defects in council or obliquity in proceeding.

Yet all this, for the most part, is not enough to give assurance, howsoever it may give satisfaction. For the heart of man is unsearchable; and princes, howsoever their intents be seldom hidden from some of those many eyes which pry both into them and into such as live about them, yet sometimes, either by their own close temper,[12] or by subtle close mist, they conceal the truth from all reports. Yea, many times the affections themselves lie dead and buried in oblivion when the preparations which they begat are converted to another use. The industry of an historian, having so many things to weary it, may well be excused when, finding apparent cause enough of things done, it forbeareth to make further search; though it often fall out, where sundry occasions work to the same end, that one small matter in a weak mind is more effectual than many that seems far greater. So comes it many times to pass that great

---

[4]Joash, king of Israel. This *Digression* follows Raleigh's tortuous effort, in the preceding sections of Book II, Chapter xxi, to unravel some of the intricacies of Old Testament genealogy from the murky data in 2 Kings 13–14 and 2 Chronicles 22–24.
[5]Jeremiah 44.15–30.
[6]The Babylonian-Assyrian goddess Ishtar, who corresponded to the Canaanite Astarte, the Greek Aphrodite, and the Roman Venus.
[7]2 Chronicles 18.
[8]Jezreel, a town in Samaria. See 1 Kings 18.45.   [9]2 Kings 9.
[10]*Sidney...substance:* see Sir Philip Sidney, *An Apology for Poetry* in *Elizabethan Critical Essays* (ed. G. Gregory Smith, 1904), I, 152–53.
[11]*Livy...Italy:* according to Titus Livius (59 B.C.–17), when Hannibal's brother Hasdrubal (*Asdrubal*) led his Carthaginian troops and burst upon the terrified Romans in 207 B.C. the consul Claudius met and defeated him in a brilliantly conducted battle (*journey*).   [12]Habit of evasion and concealment.

fires, which consume whole houses or towns, begin with a few straws that are wasted or not seen when the flame is discovered, having fastened upon some woodpile that catcheth all about it. Questionless it is that the war commenced by Darius and pursued by Xerxes against the Greeks proceeded from desire of the Persians to enlarge their empire, howsoever the enterprise of the Athenians upon Sardes was noised abroad as the ground of that quarrel; yet Herodotus telleth us that the wanton desire of queen Atossa to have the Grecian dames her bondwomen did first move Darius to prepare for this war,[13] before he had received any injury, and when he did not yet so much desire to get more as to enjoy what was already gotten.

I will not here stand to argue whether Herodotus be more justly reprehended by some, or defended by others, for alleging the vain appetite and secret speech of the queen in bed with her husband as the cause of those great evils following; this I may boldly affirm (having, I think, in every estate some sufficient witness), that matters of much consequence, founded in all seeming upon substantial reasons, have issued indeed from such petty trifles as no historian would either think upon or could well search out.

Therefore it was a good answer that Sixtus Quintus the Pope[14] made to a certain friar coming to visit him in his popedom, as having long before in his meaner estate been his familiar friend. This poor friar, being emboldened by the Pope to use his old liberty of speech, adventured to tell him that he very much wondered how it was possible for His Holiness, whom he rather took for a direct honest man than any cunning politician, to attain unto the papacy, in compassing of which, "all the subtlety," said he, "of the most crafty brains finds[15] work enough, and therefore the more I think upon the art of the conclave, and your unaptness thereto, the more I needs must wonder." Pope Sixtus, to satisfy the plain-dealing friar, dealt with him again as plainly, saying, "Hadst thou lived abroad as I have done, and seen by what folly this world is governed, thou wouldest wonder at nothing."

Surely, if this be referred unto those exorbitant engines by which the course of affairs is moved, the Pope said true; for the wisest of men are not without their vanities, which, requiring and finding mutual toleration, work more closely and earnestly than right reason either needs or can. But if we lift up our thoughts to that supreme Governor of whose empire all that is true which by the poet was said of Jupiter,

> *Qui terram inertem, qui mare temperat*
> *Ventosum, et urbes regnaque tristia*
> *Divosque mortalesque turbas,*
> *Imperio regit unus aequo:*[16]

Who rules the duller earth, the wind-swoln streams,
The civil cities, and th' infernal realms,
Who th' host of heaven and the mortal band
Alone doth govern by his just command,

then shall we find the quite contrary. In Him there is no uncertainty nor change; He foreseeth all things, and all things disposeth to His own honor: He neither deceiveth nor can be deceived; but continuing one and the same forever, doth constantly govern all creatures by that law which He hath prescribed, and will never alter. The vanities of men beguile their vain contrivers, and the prosperity of the wicked is the way leading to their destruction; yea, this broad and headlong passage to hell is not so delightful as it seems at the first entrance, but hath growing in it, besides the poisons which infect the soul, many cruel thorns deeply wounding the body; all which, if any few escape, they have only this miserable advantage of others, that their descent was the more swift and expedite.[17] But the service of God is the path guiding us to perfect happiness, and hath in it a true, though not complete, felicity, yielding such abundance of joy to the conscience as doth easily countervail all afflictions whatsoever: though indeed those brambles that sometimes tear the skin of such as walk in this blessed way do commonly lay hold upon them at such time as they sit down to take their ease, and make them wish themselves at their journey's end, in the presence of their Lord, whom they faithfully serve, in whose "presence is the fullness of joy, and at whose right hand are pleasures for evermore."[18]

Wherefore it being the end and scope of all history to teach by example of times past such wisdom as may guide our desires and actions, we should not marvail though the chronicles of the kings of Judah and Israel, being written by men inspired with the Spirit of God, instruct us chiefly in that which is most requisite for us to know as the means to attain unto true felicity both here and hereafter, propounding examples which illustrate this infallible rule, "The fear of the Lord is the beginning of wisdom,"[19] Had the expedition of Xerxes (as it was foretold by Daniel)[20] been written by some prophet after the captivity,[21] we may well believe that the counsail of God therein, and the executioners of His righteous will, should have occupied either the whole or the principal room in that narration. Yet had not the purpose of Darius, the desire of his wife, and the business at Sardes, with other occurrents,[22] been the less true, though they might have been omitted as the less material; but these things it had been lawful for any man to gather out of profane histories or out of circumstances otherwise appearing, wherein he should not have done injury to the sacred writings as long as he had forborne to derogate from the first causes by ascribing to the second more than was due.

Such, or little different, is the business that I have now in hand, wherein I cannot believe that any man of judgment will tax me as either fabulous or presumptuous. For he doth not feign that rehearseth probabilities as bare conjectures; neither doth he deprave the text that seeketh to illustrate and make good in human reason those things which authority alone, without further circumstance, ought to have confirmed in every man's belief. And this may

[13]*Herodotus...war:* Herodotus, *The Persian Wars*, III.134.
[14]Sixtus V (1585–90), a pope notable for his administrative reforms.
[15]Text *find.*
[16]Quintus Horatius Flaccus (65–8 B.C.), *Odes*, III.iv.45–48.
[17]Expeditious. [18]Psalm 16.11. [19]Proverbs 1.7. [20]Daniel 2.31–46
[21]The Babylonian captivity of the Jews (597–537 B.C.).
[22]Occurrences.

suffice in defence of the liberty which I have used in conjectures, and may hereafter use when occasion shall require, as neither unlawful nor misbeseeming an historian.

THE FIFTH BOOK

CHAPTER VI

SECTION 12 . . . THE CONCLUSION OF THE WORK

. . . By this which we have already set down is seen the beginning and end of the three first monarchies of the world,[23] whereof the founders and erectors thought that they could never have ended. That of Rome, which made the fourth, was also at this time almost at the highest. We have left it flourishing in the middle of the field, having rooted up or cut down all that kept it from the eyes and admiration of the world. But after some continuance it shall begin to lose the beauty it had; the storms of ambition shall beat her great boughs and branches one against another, her leaves shall fall off, her limbs wither, and a rabble of barbarous nations enter the field and cut her down.

Now these great kings and conquering nations have been the subject of those ancient histories which have been preserved and yet remain among us, and withal of so many tragical poets as in the persons of powerful princes and other mighty men have complained against infidelity, time, destiny, and most of all against the variable success of worldly things, and instability of fortune. To these undertakings these great lords of the world have been stirred up rather by the desire of fame, which ploweth up the air and soweth in the wind, than by the affection of bearing rule, which draweth after it so much vexation and so many cares. And that this is true, the good advice of Cineas to Pyrrhus proves.[24] And certainly, as fame hath often been dangerous to the living, so is it to the dead of no use at all, because separate from knowledge. Which were it otherwise, and the extreme ill bargain of buying this lasting discourse understood by them which are dissolved, they themselves would then rather have wished to have stolen out of the world without noise than to be put in mind that they have purchased the report of their actions in the world by rapine, oppression, and cruelty, by giving in spoil the innocent and laboring soul to the idle and insolent, and by having emptied the cities of the world of their ancient inhabitants and filled them again with so many and so variable sorts of sorrows.

Since the fall of the Roman Empire (omitting that of the Germans, which had neither greatness nor continuance) there hath been no state fearful[25] in the east but that of the Turk; nor in the west any prince that hath spread his wings far over his nest but the Spaniard, who, since the time that Ferdinand expelled the Moors out of Granado,[26] have made many attempts to make themselves masters of all Europe. And it is true that by the treasures of both Indies,[27] and by the many kingdoms which they possess in Europe, they are at this day the most powerful. But as the Turk is now counterpoised by the Persian, so instead of so many millions as have been spent by the English, French, and Netherlands

in a defensive war, and in diversions against them,[28] it is easy to demonstrate that with the charge of two hundred thousand pound continued but for two years, or three at the most, they may not only be persuaded to live in peace, but all their swelling and overflowing streams may be brought back into their natural channels and old banks. These two nations, I say, are at this day the most eminent, and to be regarded; the one seeking to root out the Christian religion altogether, the other the truth and sincere profession thereof; the one to join all Europe to Asia, the other the rest of all Europe to Spain.

For the rest, if we seek a reason of the succession and continuance of this boundless ambition in mortal men, we may add to that which hath been already said that the kings and princes of the world have always laid before them the actions, but not the ends, of those great ones which preceded them. They are always transported with the glory of the one, but they never mind the misery of the other till they find the experience in themselves. They neglect the advice of God while they enjoy life or hope it, but they follow the counsel of Death upon his first approach. It is he that puts into man all the wisdom of the world, without speaking a word, which God, with all the words of His law, promises, or threats doth infuse. Death, which hateth and destroyeth man, is believed; God, which hath made him and loves him, is always deferred. "I have considered," saith Solomon, "all the works that are under the sun, and, behold, all is vanity and vexation of spirit";[29] but who believes it till Death tells it us? It was Death which, opening the conscience of Charles the Fift, made him enjoin his son Philip to restore Navarre;[30] and King Francis the First of France to command that justice should be done upon the murderers of the Protestants in Mérindol and Cabrières,[31] which till then he neglected. It is therefore Death alone that can suddenly make man to know himself. He tells the proud and insolent that they are but abjects, and humbles them at the instant, makes them cry, complain, and repent, yea, even to hate their forepassed happiness.

---

[23]The monarchies of Babylon, Assyria, and Greece allegedly foretold by Daniel 7.4–7.

[24]According to Plutarch's life of Pyrrhus, king of Epirus (318?–272 B.C.), that ambitious conqueror was gently urged by Cineas (Sect. xiv) to reconsider his intention of subduing southern Italy, then Rome, and at length the world: "My lord, what letteth [prevents] us now to be quiet and merry together, sith we enjoy that presently without farther travel and trouble, which we will now go seek for abroad with such shedding of blood and so manifest danger; and yet we know not whether ever we shall attain unto it after we have both suffered and caused others to suffer infinite sorrows and troubles." [25]To be feared.

[26]Ferdinand and Isabella expelled the Moors from Granada (*Granado*), their last stronghold in Spain, in 1492.

[27]East and West, modern India and the Caribbean.

[28]"The Spaniard." [29]Ecclesiastes 1.14.

[30]Although part of the ancient kingdom of Navarre had been conquered by Ferdinand II of Aragon in 1515 and annexed to Spain, the dying Charles V's advice to his son Philip II was ignored.

[31]Towns in Provence, the scene of savage persecution of Protestants in 1545 during the reign of Francis I.

He takes the account of the rich, and proves him a beggar, a naked beggar, which hath interest in nothing but in the gravel that fills his mouth. He holds a glass before the eyes of the most beautiful, and makes them see therein their deformity and rottenness, and they acknowledge it.

O eloquent, just, and mighty Death! whom none could advise, thou hast persuaded; what none hath dared, thou hast done; and whom all the world hath flattered, thou only hast cast out of the world and despised. Thou hast drawn together all the far-stretched greatness, all the pride, cruelty, and ambition of man, and covered it all over with these two narrow words, *Hic jacet!*[32]

Lastly, whereas this book, by the title it hath, calls itself

The First Part of the General History of the World, implying a second and third volume, which I also intended, and have hewn out: besides many other discouragements persuading my silence, it hath pleased God to take that glorious prince[33] out of the world to whom they were directed, whose unspeakable and never enough lamented loss hath taught me to say with Job, *Versa est in luctum cithara mea, et organum meum in vocem flentium.*[34]

[32]"Here lies."
[33]Prince Henry, eldest son of James I.
[34]"My harp also is turned to mourning, and my organ into the voice of them that weep" (Job 30.31).

Francis Bacon[1] [1561-1626]

from Of the Proficience and Advancement of Learning, Divine and Human (1605)

THE SECOND BOOK

[History and Historiography]

The parts of human learning have reference to the three parts of man's understanding, which is the seat of learning: history to his memory, poesy to his imagination, and philosophy to his reason. Divine learning receiveth the same distribution, for the spirit of man is the same, though the revelation of oracle and sense be diverse. So as theology consisteth also of history of the church; of parables, which is divine poesy; and of holy doctrine or precept. For as for that part which seemeth supernumerary, which is prophecy, it is but divine history, which hath that prerogative over human as the narration may be before the fact as well as after.

History is natural, civil, ecclesiastical, and literary, whereof the three first I allow as extant, the fourth I note as deficient. For no man hath propounded to himself the general state of learning to be described and represented from age to age, as many have done the works of nature and the state civil and ecclesiastical, without which the history of the world seemeth to me to be as the statua[1] of Polyphemus[2] with his eye out, that part being wanting which doth most show the spirit and life of the person. And yet I am not ignorant that in divers particular sciences, as of the jurisconsults, the mathematicians, the rhetoricians, the philosophers, there are set down some small memorials of the schools, authors, and books; and so likewise some barren relations touching the invention of arts or usages. But a just story[3] of learning, containing the antiquities and originals of knowledges and their

sects, their inventions, their traditions, their diverse administrations and managings, their flourishings, their oppositions, decays, depressions, oblivions, removes,[4] with the causes and occasions of them, and all other events concerning learning throughout the ages of the world, I may truly affirm to be wanting. The use and end of which work I do not so much design for curiosity or satisfaction of those that are the lovers of learning, but chiefly for a more serious and grave purpose, which is this in few words: that it will make learned men wise in the use and administration of learning. For it is not Saint Augustine's nor Saint Ambrose' works[5] that will make so wise a divine as ecclesiastical history, throughly read and observed; and the same reason is of learning. . . .

[Following a brief discussion of "natural" history—which is analyzed as the "history of creatures," the "history of marvels" (that is, "of nature erring or varying"), and the "history of arts"—Bacon proceeds to civil history, which he clearly thinks to be of great importance.]

[1]For a commentary on Bacon and for other excerpts from his work, see Philosophy and Speculation, pp. 397 ff., and Books and Men, pp. 661 ff.

OF THE PROFICIENCE   [1]Statue.
[2]One of the Cyclopes, a race of one-eyed giants sired by Poseidon. Homer relates (*Odyssey*, IX.106 ff.) how Ulysses escaped from him by putting out his eye with a firebrand.   [3]Adequate history.
[4]Changes (from power to weakness and oblivion).
[5]Those by the bishop of Hippo (396–430) and the bishop of Milan (374–97) respectively, two of the most influential fathers of the early church.

For civil history, it is of three kinds not, unfitly to be compared with the three kinds of pictures or images. For of pictures or images we see some are unfinished, some are parfit,[6] and some are defaced. So of histories we may find three kinds: memorials, parfit histories, and antiquities; for memorials are history unfinished, or the first or rough draughts of history; and antiquities are history defaced, or some remnants of history which have casually[7] escaped the shipwreck of time.

Memorials, or preparatory history, are of two sorts, whereof the one may be termed commentaries and the other registers. Commentaries are they which set down a continuance of the naked events and actions, without the motives or designs, the counsels, the speeches, the pretexts, the occasions and other passages of action: for this is the true nature of a commentary (though Caesar, in modesty mixed with greatness, did for his pleasure apply the name of a commentary to the best history of the world).[8] Registers are collections of public acts, as decrees of council, judicial proceedings, declarations and letters of estate, orations and the like, without a perfect continuance or contexture of the thread of the narration.

Antiquities, or remnants of history, are, as was said, *tanquam tabula naufragii*:[9] when industrious persons, by an exact and scrupulous diligence and observation, out of monuments, names, words, proverbs, traditions, private records and evidences, fragments of stories, passages of books that concern not story, and the like, do save and recover somewhat from the deluge of time.

In these kinds of unperfect histories I do assign no deficience, for they are *tanquam imperfecte mista*;[10] and therefore any deficience in them is but their nature. As for the corruptions and moths of history, which are epitomes, the use of them deserveth to be banished, as all men of sound judgment have confessed, as those that have fretted and corroded the sound bodies of many excellent histories, and wrought them into base and unprofitable dregs.

History, which may be called just and parfit history, is of three kinds, according to the object which it propoundeth or pretendeth to represent: for it either representeth a time, or a person, or an action. The first we call chronicles, the second lives, and the third narrations or relations. Of these, although the first be the most complete and absolute kind of history, and hath most estimation and glory, yet the second excelleth it in profit and use, and the third in verity and sincerity. For history of times representeth the magnitude of actions and the public faces and deportments of persons, and passeth over in silence the smaller passages and motions of men and matters. But such being the workmanship of God, as he doth hang the greatest weight upon the smallest wires, *maxima è minimis suspendens*, it comes therefore to pass that such histories do rather set forth the pomp of business than the true and inward resorts thereof. But lives, if they be well written, propounding to themselves a person to represent in whom actions both greater and smaller, public and private, have a commixture, must of necessity contain a more true, native, and lively representation. So again narrations and relations of actions, as the war

of Peloponnesus, the expedition of Cyrus Minor, the conspiracy of Catiline,[11] cannot but be more purely and exactly true than histories of times, because they may choose an argument comprehensible within the notice and instructions of the writer: whereas he that undertaketh the story of a time, specially of any length, cannot but meet with many blanks and spaces which he must be forced to fill up out of his own wit and conjecture.

For the history of times (I mean of civil history), the providence of God hath made the distribution. For it hath pleased God to ordain and illustrate two exemplar[12] states of the world for arms, learning, moral virtue, policy, and laws: the state of Grecia and the state of Rome, the histories whereof, occupying the middle part of time, have more ancient to them histories which may by one common name be termed the antiquities of the world, and after them, histories which may be likewise called by the name of modern history.

Now to speak of the deficiencies. As to the heathen antiquities of the world, it is in vain to note them for deficient. Deficient they are, no doubt, consisting most of fables and fragments; but the deficience cannot be holpen,[13] for antiquity is like fame: *caput inter nubila condit,* her head is muffled from our sight. For the history of the exemplar states it is extant in good perfection. Not but I could wish there were a perfect course of history for Grecia from Theseus to Philopoemen (what time the affairs of Grecia drowned and extinguished in the affairs of Rome), and for Rome from Romulus to Justinianus, who may be truly said to be *ultimus Romanorum*.[14] In which sequences of story the text of Thucydides and Xenophon in the one, and the texts of Livius, Polybius, Sallustius, Caesar, Appianus, Tacitus, Herodianus[15] in the other to be kept entire without any diminution at all, and only to be supplied and continued. But this is matter of magnificence, rather to be commended than required, and we speak now of parts of learning supplemental and not of supererogation.

But for modern histories, whereof there are some few very worthy, but the greater part beneath mediocrity, leaving the care of foreign stories to foreign states because I will not be *curiosus in aliena republica*,[16] I cannot fail to represent to Your Majesty[17] the unworthiness of the history of England in the main continuance thereof, and the partiality

[6]Perfect, i.e., finished, complete. [7]Accidentally, by chance.
[8]The *Commentaries—De bello Gallico* and *De bello civili*—of Gaius Julius Caesar (110–44 B.C.). [9]"Like planks from a shipwreck."
[10]"Like imperfect mixtures."
[11]The allusion is to famous historical works by Thucydides, Xenophon (*Anabasis*), and Sallust (*Bellum Catilinae*) respectively.
[12]Exemplary. [13]Helped.
[14]*Theseus. . . Romanorum*: in Grecian history from the legendary hero of Attica to the general (d. 183 B.C.) known as "the last of the Greeks"; in Roman history from the legendary founder of Rome to Justinian the Great (483–565), "the last of the Romans."
[15]Famous historians of antiquity between the 5th century B.C. and the 3d century A.D.
[16]"Inquisitive about foreign states."
[17]Bacon dedicated his book to, and wrote it for the instruction of, James I. See p. 399.

and obliquity[18] of that of Scotland in the latest and largest author[19] that I have seen; supposing that it would be honor for Your Majesty, and a work very memorable, if this island of Great Brittany,[20] as it is now joined in monarchy[21] for the ages to come, so were joined in one history for the times passed, after the manner of the sacred history, which draweth down the story of the ten tribes and of the two tribes[22] as twins together. And if it shall seem that the greatness of this work may make it less exactly performed, there is an excellent period of a much smaller compass of time as to the story of England; that is to say, from the uniting of the Roses to the uniting of the kingdoms,[23] a portion of time wherein, to my understanding, there hath been the rarest varieties that in like number of successions of any hereditary monarchy hath been known. For it beginneth with the mixed adeption[24] of a crown by arms and title, an entry by battail,[25] an establishment by marriage; and therefore times answerable, like waters after a tempest, full of working and swelling, though without extremity of storm; but well passed through by the wisdom of the pilot, being one of the most sufficient kings of all the number. Then followeth the reign of a king whose actions, howsoever conducted, had much intermixture with the affairs of Europe, balancing and inclining them variably; in whose time also began that great alteration in the state ecclesiastical, an action which seldom cometh upon the stage. Then the reign of a minor, then an offer of an usurpation (though it was but as *febris ephemera*),[26] then the reign of a queen matched with a foreigner, then of a queen that lived solitary and unmarried, and yet her government so masculine as it had greater impression and operation upon the states abroad than it any ways received from thence. And now last, this most happy and glorious event, that this island of Brittany, divided from all the world, should be united in itself: and that oracle of rest given to Aeneas, *antiquam enquirite matrem*,[27] should now be performed and fulfilled upon the nations of England and Scotland, being now reunited in the ancient mother name of Brittany as a full period[28] of all instability and peregrinations. So that as it cometh to pass in massive bodies that they have certain trepidations and waverings before they fix and settle, so it seemeth that by the providence of God this monarchy, before it was to settle in Your Majesty and your generations (in which I hope it is now established forever), it had these prelusive[29] changes and varieties.

For lives, I do find strange that these times have so little esteemed the virtues of the times as that the writings of lives should be no more frequent. For although there be not many sovereign princes or absolute commanders, and that states are most collected into monarchies, yet are there many worthy personages that deserve better than dispersed report or barren elogies.[30] For herein the invention of one of the late poets[31] is proper, and doth well enrich the ancient fiction. For he feigneth that at the end of the thread or web of every man's life there was a little medal containing the person's name, and that Time waited upon the shears, and as soon as the thread was cut, caught the medals and carried them to the river of Lethe;[32] and about the bank there were many birds flying up and down that would get the medals

and carry them in their beak a little while, and then let them fall into the river. Only there were a few swans, which if they got a name would carry it to a temple where it was consecrate. And although many men, more mortal in their affections than in their bodies, do esteem desire of name and memory but as a vanity and ventosity,[33]

Animi nil magnae laudis egentes,[34]

which opinion cometh from that root, *Non prius laudes contempsimus, quam laudanda facere desivimus:*[35] yet that will not alter Solomon's judgment, *Memoria justi cum laudibus, at impiorum nomen putrescet:*[36] the one flourisheth, the other either consumeth to present oblivion or turneth to an ill odor. And therefore in that style or addition,[37] which is and hath been long well received and brought in use, *felicis memoriae, piae memoriae, bonae memoriae,*[38] we do acknowledge that which Cicero saith, borrowing it from Demosthenes, that *bona fama propria possessio defunctorum:*[39] which possession I cannot but note that in our times it lieth much waste, and that therein there is a deficience.

For narrations and relations of particular actions, there were also to be wished a greater diligence therein, for there

---

[18]Deviation from objective truth, bias.
[19]*Largest author:* most copious writer, i.e., George Buchanan (1506–82), whose *Rerum Scoticarum historia* (1582) offended James I by its defense of popular rights.   [20]Britain.
[21]When James VI of Scotland became James I of England (1603), the royal houses of the two countries were *joined*. See pp. 882 f.
[22]The so-called "ten lost tribes" of Israel that were deported following the Assyrian conquest in 721 B.C., as distinguished from the two tribes of Judah.
[23]From the accession of Henry VII in 1485 to that of James I in 1603. In the following passage Bacon alludes to such pivotal events of Tudor history as Henry VII's victory over Richard III, his marriage to Elizabeth of York, Henry VIII's direction of the English Reformation, the brief reign of the boy-king Edward VI, the earl of Northumberland's abortive effort to put his daughter-in-law Lady Jane Grey on the throne, the reigns of Queen Mary (whose unpopular consort was Philip II of Spain) and of her half-sister Elizabeth, and finally the providential accession of James I. Bacon himself subsequently treated some of these events in his life of Henry VII (see pp. 882 ff.) and in various fragments on sixteenth-century history.   [24]Attainment.   [25]Battle.   [26]"Brief fever."
[27]"Seek out your ancient mother" (Vergil, *Aeneid*, III.96).
[28]End.   [29]Preliminary.   [30]Eulogies.
[31]Ludovico Ariosto (1474–1533), *Orlando Furioso*, Cantos xxxiv-xxxv.
[32]In classical mythology, the river of forgetfulness in Hades.
[33]Windiness.
[34]"Souls not craving high renown" (Vergil, *Aeneid*, V.751). The original reads *animos*.
[35]"Men hardly despise praise till they have ceased to deserve it" (adapted from Pliny, *Epistles*, III. xxi).
[36]"The memory of the just is blessed: but the name of the wicked shall rot" (Proverbs 10.7).   [37]Title.
[38]"Of happy memory, of pious memory, of good memory."
[39]"A good name is all that the dead possess," perhaps based on Cicero's remark (*Philippicae*, ix.5)—itself derived from Demosthenes—*vita enim mortuorum in memoria vivorum est posita:* "the life of the dead rests in the memory of the living."

is no great action but hath some good pen which attends it. And because it is an ability not common to write a good history, as may well appear by the small number of them, yet if particularity of actions memorable were but tolerably reported as they pass, the compiling of a complete history of times mought[40] be the better expected when a writer should arise that were fit for it for the collection of such relations mought be as a nursery garden whereby to plant a fair and stately garden when time should serve.

There is yet another partition[41] of history which Cornelius Tacitus maketh, which is not to be forgotten, specially with that application which he accoupleth it withal, annals and journals:[42] appropriating to the former matters of estate,[43] and to the latter acts and accidents of a meaner nature. For giving but a touch of[44] certain magnificent buildings, he addeth, *Cum ex dignitate populi Romani repertum sit, res illustres annalibus, talia diurnis urbis actis mandare.*[45] So as there is a kind of contemplative[46] heraldry as well as civil. And as nothing doth derogate from the dignity of a state more than confusion of degrees, so it doth not a little imbase[47] the authority of an history to intermingle matters of triumph, or matters of ceremony, or matters of novelty, with matters of state. But the use of a journal hath not only been in the history of time, but likewise in the history of persons, and chiefly of actions; for princes in ancient time had, upon point of honor and policy both, journals kept, what passed day by day. For we see the chronicle which was read before Ahasuerus when he could not take rest contained matter of affairs indeed, but such as had passed in his own time and very lately before.[48] But the journal of Alexander's house expressed every small particularity, even concerning his person and court;[49] and it is yet an use well received in enterprises memorable, as expeditions of war, navigations, and the like, to keep diaries of that which passeth continually.

I cannot likewise be ignorant of a form of writing which some grave and wise men have used, containing a scattered history of those actions which they have thought worthy of memory, with politic[50] discourse and observation thereupon: not incorporate into the history, but separately, and as the more principal in their intention; which kind of ruminated history[51] I think more fit to place amongst books of policy, whereof we shall hereafter speak, than amongst books of history. For it is the true office of history to represent the events themselves together with the counsels, and to leave the observations and conclusions thereupon to the liberty and faculty of every man's judgment. But mixtures[52] are things irregular, whereof no man can define.

So also is there another kind of history manifoldly mixed, and that is history of cosmography, being compounded of natural history in respect of the regions themselves; of history civil in respect of the habitations, regiments,[53] and manners of the people; and the mathematics in respect of the climates and configurations towards the heavens, which part of learning of all others in this latter time hath obtained most proficience. For it may be truly affirmed to the honor of these times, and in a virtuous emulation with antiquity, that this great building of the world had never through-lights made in it till the age of us and our fathers. For although they had knowledge of the antipodes,

Nosque ubi primus equis Oriens adflavit anhelis,
Illic sera rubens accendit lumina Vesper,[54]

yet that mought be by demonstration, and not in fact; and if by travel, it requireth the voyage but of half the globe. But to circle the earth as the heavenly bodies do was not done nor enterprised till these later times, and therefore these times may justly bear in their word not only *plus ultra,* in precedence of the ancient *non ultra,* and *imitabile fulmen,* in precedence of the ancient *non imitabile fulmen,*

Demens qui nimbos et non imitabile fulmen, etc.

but likewise *imitabile caelum* in respect of the many memorable voyages after the manner of heaven about the globe of the earth.[55]

And this proficience in navigation and discoveries may plant also an expectation of the furder[56] proficience and augmentation of all sciences because it may seem they are ordained by God to be coevals, that is, to meet in one age. For so the prophet Daniel speaking of the latter times foretelleth, *Plurini pertransibunt, et multiplex erit scientia,*[57] as if the openness and through-passage of the world and the increase of knowledge were appointed to be in the same ages; as we see it is already performed in great part, the learning of these later times not much giving place to the former two periods or returns of learning, the one of the Grecians, the other of the Romans.

History ecclesiastical receiveth the same divisions with history civil: but furder in the propriety[58] thereof may be divided into history of the church (by a general name), history of prophecy, and history of providence. The first describeth the times of the militant church, whether it be fluctuant,[59] as the ark of Noah, or movable, as the ark in the

---

[40]Might [41]Text *portion.* [42]Yearly and daily records. [43]State.
[44]Alluding to.
[45]"Such trivial matters may be left to journals, it being beneath the dignity of the Roman people that any but great events be recorded in their annals" (Tacitus, *Annals,* XIII.31).
[46]The discrimination and ranking of notable (as opposed to insignificant) events. [47]Debase.
[48]*For...before:* Esther vi.1: "On that night could not the king [Ahasuerus] sleep, and he commanded to bring the book of records of the chronicles; and they were read before the king."
[49]*Alexander's...court:* Bacon is perhaps thinking of Plutarch's "small particularities" about Alexander like those in *Moralia,* Sections 127, 180, and in his life of the conqueror, Ch. XXII.
[50]Sagacious.
[51]Perhaps works like Machiavelli's *Discorsi* on Livy, in which the historical data support speculations about man's political behavior.
[52]Text *mixture.* [53]Methods of governing.
[54]"When for us the sun first breathes with panting steeds, for them the shining Vesper lights the evening star" (Vergil, *Georgics,* I.250–51).
[55]*Therefore...earth:* despite Vergil's warning (*Aeneid,* VI.590) that "he is mad who challenges the clouds and thunder," the moderns may take as their motto (*bear in their word*) "yet further" instead of the ancients' "no further," imitate Jove's awful lightning (*fulmen*) with their gunpowder, and even match the heavenly bodies by making complete circuits of the earth.
[56]Further.
[57]"Many shall run to and fro, and knowledge shall be increased" (Daniel 12.4). [58]Property, characteristic. [59]Floating.

wilderness, or at rest, as the ark in the temple: that is, the state of the church in persecution, in remove,[60] and in peace. This part I ought in no sort to note as deficient; only I would the virtue and sincerity of it were according to the mass and quantity. But I am not now in hand[61] with censures, but with omissions.

The second, which is history of prophecy, consisteth of two relatives, the prophecy and the accomplishment; and therefore the nature of such a work ought to be that every prophecy of the Scripture be sorted[62] with the event fulfilling the same throughout the ages of the world, both for the better confirmation of faith and for the better illumination of the church touching those parts of prophecies which are yet unfulfilled: allowing nevertheless that latitude which is agreeable and familiar unto divine prophecies, being of the nature of their Author, with whom a thousand years are but as one day, and therefore are not fulfilled punctually at once, but have springing and germinant[63] accomplishment throughout many ages, though the height or fullness of them may refer to some one age. This is a work which I find deficient; but is to be done with wisdom, sobriety, and reverence, or not at all.

The third, which is history of providence, containeth that excellent correspondence which is between God's revealed will and his secret will, which though it be so obscure as for the most part it is not legible to the natural man—no, nor many times to those that behold it from the tabernacle—yet at some times it pleaseth God, for our better establishment and the confuting of those which are as without God in the world, to write it in such text and capital letters that, as the prophet saith, "He that runneth by may read it;"[64] that is, mere sensual persons, which hasten by God's judgments, and never bend or fix their cogitations upon them, are nevertheless in their passage and race urged to discern it. Such are the notable events and examples of God's judgments, chastisements, deliverances, and blessings; and this is a work which hath passed through the labor of many, and therefore I cannot present as omitted.

There are also other parts of learning which are appendices to history. For all the exterior proceedings of man consist of words and deeds, whereof history doth properly receive and retain in memory the deeds, and if words, yet but as inducements and passages to deeds; so are there other books and writings which are appropriate to the custody and receipt of words only, which likewise are of three sorts: orations, letters, and brief speeches or sayings. Orations are pleadings, speeches of counsel, laudatives, invectives, apologies, reprehensions, orations of formality or ceremony, and the like. Letters are according to all the variety of occasions, advertisements,[65] advices, directions, propositions, petitions, commendatory, expostulatory, satisfactory,[66] of compliment, of pleasure, of discourse, and all other passages of action. And such as are written from wise men are of all the words of man, in my judgment, the best, for they are more natural than orations and public speeches, and more advised than conferences or present speeches.[67] So again letters of affairs from such as manage them, or are privy to them, are of all others the best instructions for history, and to a diligent reader the best histories in themselves. For apophthegms, it is a great loss of that book of Caesar's;[68] for as his history, and those few letters of his which we have, and those apophthegms which were of his own, excel all men's else, so I suppose would his collection of apophthegms have done. For as for those which are collected by others, either I have no taste in such matters, or else their choice hath not been happy. But upon these three kinds of writings I do not insist because I have no deficiencies to propound concerning them.

Thus much, therefore, concerning history, which is that part of learning which answereth to one of the cells, domiciles, or offices of the mind of man, which is that of the memory.

---

[60]Alteration, i.e., transition. [61]Concerned. [62]*Be sorted*: agree. [63]Germinating.
[64]Habakkuk 2.2. In the King James version the passage reads, "that he may run that readeth it."
[65]Information, admonition, instruction.
[66]Serving to make plausible.
[67]*More advised...speeches*: more carefully considered than conversation or impromptu speeches.
[68]*Apophthegmata* or *Dicta collectanea*, which has not survived.

from The History of the Reign of King Henry the Seventh (1622)

To the Most Illustrious and Most Excellent
Prince Charles, Prince of Wales, Duke of
Cornwall, Earl of Chester, etc.

It may please Your Highness:
In part of my acknowledgment to Your Highness I have endeavored to do honor to the memory of the last king of England that was ancestor to the king your father and yourself and was that king to whom both unions may in a sort refer: that of the roses being in him consummate, and that of the kingdoms by him begun.[1] Besides, his times deserve it. For he was a wise man and an excellent king; and yet the

history of the reign [1]Henry effected "both unions"—i.e., of Lancaster and York and of Scotland and England—by marrying (1486) Elizabeth, daughter of Edward IV, and by subsequently siring the child (Margaret) upon whom the House of Stuart based its title to the English throne. See inside front and back covers.

times were rough, and full of mutations and rare accidents.[2] And it is with times as it is with ways. Some are more uphill and downhill, and some are more flat and plain; and the one is better for the liver, and the other for the writer. I have not flattered him, but took him to life[3] as well as I could, sitting so far off and having no better light. It is true, Your Highness hath a living pattern, incomparable, of[4] the king your father. But it is not amiss for you also to see one of these ancient pieces.[5] God preserve Your Highness.

> *Your Highness' most humble and* 10
> *devoted servant,*
> *Francis St. Alban*[6]

After that Richard, the third of that name, king in fact only, but tyrant both in title and regiment,[7] and so commonly termed and reputed in all times since, was by the divine revenge, favoring the design of an exiled man, overthrown and slain at Bosworth Field,[8] there succeeded in the kingdom the earl of Richmond, thenceforth styled Henry the Seventh. The king immediately after the victory, as one that had been bred under a devout mother,[9] and was in his nature a 20 great observer of religious forms, caused *Te deum laudamus*[10] to be solemnly sung in the presence of the whole army upon the place, and was himself with general applause and great cries of joy, in a kind of militar[11] election or recognition, saluted king. Meanwhile the body of Richard after many indignities and reproaches (the dirigies[12] and obsequies of the common people towards tyrants) was obscurely buried. For though the king of his nobleness gave charge unto the friars of Leicester[13] to see an honorable interment to be given to it, yet the religious people themselves (being not free from 30 the humors of the vulgar) neglected it, wherein nevertheless they did not then incur any man's blame or censure. No man thinking any ignominy or contumely unworthy of him that had been the executioner of King Henry the Sixth (that innocent prince) with his own hands; the contriver of the death of the Duke of Clarence, his brother; the murderer of his two nephews (one of them his lawful king in the present, and the other in the future, failing of him);[14] and vehemently suspected to have been the impoisoner of his wife, thereby to make vacant his bed for a marriage within 40 the degrees forbidden.[15] And although he were a prince in militar virtue approved, jealous of the honor of the English nation, and likewise a good law-maker for the ease and solace of the common people, yet his cruelties and parricides[16] in the opinion of all men weighed down his virtues and merits; and in the opinion of wise men, even those virtues themselves were conceived to be rather feigned and affected things to serve his ambition than true qualities ingenerate[17] in his judgment or nature. And therefore it was noted by men of great understanding (who seeing his after-acts looked 50 back upon his former proceedings) that even in the time of King Edward his brother he was not without secret trains and mines[18] to turn envy and hatred upon his brother's government, as having an expectation and a kind of divination that the king, by reason of his many disorders, could not be of long life, but was like to leave his sons of tender

years; and then he knew well how easy a step it was from the place of a protector and first prince of the blood to the crown. And that out of this deep root of ambition it sprang that as well at the treaty of peace that passed between Edward the Fourth and Lewis the Eleventh of France, concluded by interview of both kings at Piqueny,[19] as upon all other occasions, Richard, then duke of Gloucester, stood ever upon the side of honor, raising his own reputation to the disadvantage of the king his brother, and drawing the eyes of all (especially of the nobles and soldiers) upon himself; as if the king by his voluptuous life and mean marriage[20] were become effeminate, and less sensible of honor and reason of state than was fit for a king. And as for the politic and wholesome laws which were enacted in his time, they were interpreted to be but the brocage[21] of an usurper, thereby to woo and win the hearts of the people, as being conscious to himself that the true obligations of sovereignty in him failed and were wanting.

But King Henry, in the very entrance of his reign and the instant of time when the kingdom was cast into his arms, met with a point of great difficulty and knotty to solve, able to trouble and confound the wisest king in the newness of his estate; and so much the more because it could not endure a deliberation, but must be at once deliberated and determined. There were fallen to his lot, and concurrent in his person, three several titles to the imperial crown. The first, the title of the Lady Elizabeth, with whom, by precedent pact[22] with the party that brought him in, he was to marry.

---

[2]Unusual events. [3]Portrayed him accurately. [4]In the person of. [5]Masterpieces.

[6]Bacon was raised to the peerage as Baron Verulam in 1618 and created Viscount St. Albans three years later. [7]Government.

[8]Site of the battle (September 1485) in Leicestershire where the usurper Henry, earl of Richmond, defeated Richard III, the last Yorkist king of England.

[9]Margaret Beaufort (1441–1509), through whom, as a descendant of John of Gaunt, duke of Lancaster, Henry derived his Lancastrian claim to the throne. See inside front and back covers.

[10]"We praise thee, O God," opening words of an ancient hymn sung at a thanksgiving service. [11]Military. [12]Funeral hymns.

[13]Important town near Bosworth Field.

[14]If he (the elder brother) should die without issue.

[15]Degrees of consanguinity, or closeness of kinship, within which marriage was forbidden by the church. For a fuller catalogue of Richard's crimes—which became articles of faith for Tudor historians, and for Shakespeare too—see Raleigh's account, pp. 866.

[16]Homicides. [17]Congenital. [18]*Trains and mines*: schemes and plots. [19]Picquigny, town in northern France where, in a treaty signed (1475) with Louis XI, Edward IV committed himself not to press his claims for the French throne.

[20]Edward IV's secret marriage (1464) with the commoner Elizabeth, daughter of Sir Richard Woodville and widow of Sir John Grey, gave great offense, especially to his family.

[21]Brokage, i.e., base or petty trafficking for profit.

[22]The abortive uprising of Henry Stafford, second duke of Buckingham (1454?–83), had been prompted by Henry's agreement to marry Elizabeth of York and thus to unite the titles of Lancaster and York. When the duke's forces from Brittany were prevented by a storm at sea from joining his allies in England, the enterprise collapsed and he was captured and summarily executed.

The second, the ancient and long disputed title (both by plea[23] and arms) of the House of Lancaster, to which he was inheritor in his own person. The third, the title of the sword or conquest, for that he came in by victory of battail, and that the king in possession was slain in the field. The first of these was fairest, and most like to give contentment to the people, who by two-and-twenty years' reign of King Edward the Fourth had been fully made capable[24] of the clearness of the title of the White Rose or House of York; and by the mild and plausible[25] reign of the same king toward his latter time were become affectionate to that line. But then it lay plain before his eyes that if he relied upon that title, he could be but a king at courtesy, and have rather a matrimonial than a regal power, the right remaining in his queen, upon whose decease, either with issue or without issue, he was to give place and be removed. And though he should obtain by Parliament to be continued, yet he knew there was a very great difference between a king that holdeth his crown by a civil[26] act of estates[27] and one that holdeth it originally by the law of nature and descent of blood. Neither wanted there even at that time secret rumors and whisperings (which afterwards gathered strength and turned to great troubles) that the two young sons of King Edward the Fourth, or one of them (which were said to be destroyed in the Tower), were not indeed murthered but conveyed secretly away, and were yet living: which, if it had been true, had prevented the title of the Lady Elizabeth. On the other side, if he stood upon his own title of the House of Lancaster, inherent in his person, he knew it was a title condemned by Parliament,[28] and generally prejudged in the common opinion of the realm, and that it tended directly to the disinherison[29] of the line of York, held then the indubitate[30] heirs of the crown. So that if he should have no issue by the Lady Elizabeth, which should be descendants of the double line, then the ancient flames of discord and intestine wars, upon the competition of both Houses, would again return and revive.

As for conquest, notwithstanding Sir William Stanley,[31] after some acclamations of the soldiers in the field, had put a crown of ornament (which Richard wore in the battail and was found amongst the spoils) upon King Henry's head, as if there were his chief title, yet he remembered well upon what conditions and agreements he was brought in; and that to claim as conqueror was to put as well his own party as the rest into terror and fear, as that which gave him power of disannulling of laws, and disposing of men's fortunes and estates, and the like points of absolute power, being in themselves so harsh and odious as that William himself, commonly called the Conqueror, howsoever he used and exercised the power of a conqueror to reward his Normans, yet he forbare to use that claim in the beginning, but mixed it with a titulary pretence[32] grounded upon the will and designation of Edward the Confessor.[33]

But the king, out of the greatness of his own mind, presently cast the die; and the inconveniences appearing unto him on all parts, and knowing there could not be any interreign[34] or suspension of title, and preferring his affection to his own line and blood, and liking that title best which

made him independent, and being in his nature and constitution of mind not very apprehensive or forecasting of future events afar off, but an entertainer of fortune by the day, resolved to rest upon the title of Lancaster as the main, and to use the other two, that of marriage and that of battail, but as supporters, the one to appease secret discontents and the other to beat down open murmur and dispute; not forgetting that the same title of Lancaster had formerly maintained a possession of three descents in the crown and might have proved a perpetuity had it not ended in the weakness and inability of the last prince.[35] Whereupon the king presently that very day, being the two-and-twentieth of August, assumed the style of king in his own name, without mention of the Lady Elizabeth at all, or any relation thereunto. In which course he ever after persisted, which did spin him a thread of many seditions and troubles. The king, full of these thoughts, before his departure from Leicester despatched Sir Robert Willoughby to the castle of Sheriff-Hutton, in Yorkshire, where were kept in safe custody, by King Richard's commandment, both the Lady Elizabeth, daughter of King Edward, and Edward Plantagenet,[36] son and heir to George, duke of Clarence. This Edward was by the king's warrant delivered from the constable of the castle to the hand of Sir Robert Willoughby, and by him with all safety and diligence conveyed to the Tower of London, where he was shut up close prisoner. Which act of the king's (being an act merely of policy and power) proceeded not so much from any apprehension he had of Dr. Shaw's tale at Paul's Cross for the bastarding of Edward the Fourth's issues,[37] in which case this young gentleman was

[23]The spurious Lancastrian contention that their line deriving from Edmund, earl of Lancaster (1245–96) was entitled to the throne because Edmund, allegedly the eldest son of Henry III, had been illegally set aside as heir because of his deformities.   [24]Aware.
[25]Praiseworthy.   [26]Text *will*.
[27]Parliamentary action. The so-called three estates composing Parliament were Lords, Commons, and Convocation.
[28]The first Parliament of Edward IV had formally declared (1461) that Henry IV, Henry V, and Henry VI (the Lancastrian kings of England) were traitors and usurpers.   [29]Disinheritance.
[30]Undoubted.
[31]A Lancastrian stalwart (d. 1495) who had saved the day for Henry at Bosworth by bringing 3,000 men in action at the climax of the battle. Although rewarded with lucrative posts and with the ribbon of the Garter, he was subsequently implicated in the rebellion of Perkin Warbeck and executed as a traitor.
[32]Claim to the title.   [33]See pp. 927 f.
[34]Interregnum.
[35]Henry VI, whose insanity led to the accession of his Yorkist rival Edward IV (1461), thus ending the Lancastrian line begun by his grandfather Henry IV and maintained by his father Henry V.
[36]Edward, earl of Warwick (1475–99), eldest son of George, duke of Clarence, and heir of Edward IV, was Henry's most dangerous Yorkist rival. After long imprisonment he was executed in 1499, and with his death the male line of the House of York became extinct.
[37]*Dr. Shaw's...issues:* One of Richard, duke of Gloucester's ruses (as protector) to secure the throne was to arrange for Ralph Shaw, prebendary of London, to preach at Paul's Cross a sermon against bastardy, with the obvious implication that because the marriage

to succeed (for that fable was ever[38] exploded), but upon a settled disposition to depress[39] all eminent persons of the line of York. Wherein still the king, out of strength of will or weakness of judgment, did use to show a little more of the party than of the king.[40]

For the Lady Elizabeth, she received also a direction to repair with all convenient speed to London, and there to remain with the queen dowager her mother, which accordingly she soon after did, accompanied with many noblemen and ladies of honor. In the mean season the king set forwards by easy journeys to the City of London, receiving the acclamations and applauses of the people as he went, which indeed were true and unfeigned, as might well appear in the very demonstrations and fullness of the cry. For they thought generally that he was a prince as ordained and sent down from heaven to unite and put to an end the long dissensions of the two Houses;[41] which although they had had, in the times of Henry the Fourth, Henry the Fifth, and a part of Henry the Sixth on the one side, and the times of Edward the Fourth on the other, lucid intervals and happy pauses, yet they did ever hang over the kingdom, ready to break forth into new perturbations and calamities. And as his victory gave him the knee, so his purpose of marriage with the Lady Elizabeth gave him the heart, so that both knee and heart did truly bow before him. He on the other side with great wisdom (not ignorant of the affections and fears of the people), to disperse the conceit and terror[42] of a conquest, had given order that there should be nothing in his journey like unto a warlike march or manner, but rather like unto the progress of a king in full peace and assurance.

He entered the City upon a Saturday, as he had also obtained the victory upon a Saturday; which day of the week, first upon an observation,[43] and after upon memory and fancy, he accounted and chose as a day prosperous unto him. The major[44] and companies of the City received him at Shoreditch,[45] whence with great and honorable attendance, and troops of noblemen and persons of quality, he entered the City, himself not being on horseback, or in any open chair or throne, but in a close[46] chariot, as one that having been sometimes an enemy to the whole state, and a proscribed person, chose rather to keep state[47] and strike a reverence into the people than to fawn upon them.

He went first into St. Paul's Church, where, not meaning that the people should forget too soon that he came in by battail, he made offertory of his standards,[48] and had orisons[49] and *Te Deum* again sung; and went to his lodging prepared in the bishop of London's palace,[50] where he stayed for a time.

During his abode there he assembled his council and other principal persons, in presence of whom he did renew again his promise to marry with the Lady Elizabeth. This he did the rather because having at his coming out of Brittain[51] given artificially[52] for serving of his own turn some hopes, in case he obtained the kingdom, to marry Anne, inheritress to the duchy of Brittain, whom Charles the Eight of France soon after married, it bred some doubt and suspicion amongst divers that he was not sincere, or at least not fixed, in going on with the match of England so much desired:

which conceit also, though it were but talk and discourse, did much afflict the poor Lady Elizabeth herself. But howsoever he both truly intended it and desired also it should be so believed (the better to extinguish envy and contradiction to his other purposes), yet was he resolved in himself not to proceed to the consummation thereof till his coronation and a Parliament were past. The one, lest a joint coronation of himself and his queen might give any countenance of participation of title; the other, lest in the entailing[53] of the crown to himself, which he hoped to obtain by Parliament, the votes of the Parliament might any ways reflect upon her.

About this time in autumn, towards the end of September, there began and reigned in the city and other parts of the kingdom a disease then new, which of the accidents and manner thereof they called "sweating sickness." This desease had a swift course, both in the sick body and in the time and period of the lasting thereof. For they that were taken with it, upon four-and-twenty hours escaping were thought almost assured. And as to the time of the malice and reign of the disease ere it ceased, it began about the one-and-twentieth of September and cleared up before the end of October, insomuch as it was no hinderance to the king's coronation, which was the last of October; nor (which was more) to the holding of the Parliament, which began but seven days after. It was a pestilent fever, but (as it seemeth) not seated in the veins or humors,[54] for that there followed no carbuncle, no purple or livid spots, or the like, the mass of the body being not tainted; only a malign vapor flew to the heart and seized the vital spirits, which stirred nature to strive to send it forth by an extreme sweat. And it appeared by experience that this disease was rather a surprise of nature[55] than obstinate to remedies, if it were in time looked unto. For if the patient were kept in an equal temper,[56] both for clothes, fire, and drink moderately warm, with temperate cordials, whereby nature's work were neither irritated by heat nor turned back by cold, he commonly recovered. But infinite persons died sudainly of it before the manner of the cure and attendance was known. It was conceived not to be an epidemic disease, but to proceed from a malignity in the constitution of the air, gathered by the predispositions of seasons, and the speedy cessation declared as much.

---

of Edward IV and Elizabeth was bigamous, their issue could not claim the crown. [38]Utterly. [39]Put down.
[40]*The party. . . King:* more of partisan politics than of royalty.
[41]Lancaster and York. [42]Terrifying idea.
[43]Because he himself had noticed it. [44]Mayor.
[45]District north of the City of London.
[46]Enclosed, i.e., curtained. [47]Maintain regal dignity.
[48]Banners. [49]Prayers.
[50]The episcopal residence at Fulham, a town on the Thames above Westminster.
[51]Brittany, where Henry, as earl of Richmond, had plotted his invasion during his years of exile in the reigns of Edward IV and Richard III (1471 ff.). [52]Deceitfully.
[53]Transmitting as an inalienable inheritance.
[54]The circulatory system (*humors* being the four chief fluids of the body—blood, phlegm, choler, and black choler—whose relative proportion determined one's temperament or disposition).
[55]Sudden conquest. [56]Temperature.

On Simon and Jude's Even[57] the king dined with Thomas Bourchier,[58] archbishop of Canterbury and cardinal, and from Lambeth[59] went by land over the bridge to the Tower, where the morrow after he made twelve knights-bannerets.[60] But for creations,[61] he dispensed them with a sparing hand. For notwithstanding a field so lately fought and a coronation so near at hand, he only created three: Jasper, earl of Pembroke (the King's uncle), was created duke of Bedford; Thomas the Lord Stanley (the King's father-in-law), earl of Derby; and Edward Courtenay, earl of Devon;[62] though the king had then nevertheless a purpose in himself to make more in time of Parliament, bearing a wise and decent respect to distribute his creations, some to honor his coronation and some his Parliament.

The coronation followed two days after, upon the thirtieth day of October in the year of our Lord 1485. At which time Innocent the Eight was pope of Rome; Frederick the Third, emperor of Almain;[63] and Maximilian his son, newly chosen king of the Romans;[64] Charles the Eight, king of France; Ferdinando and Isabella, kings of Spain; and James the Third, king of Scotland: with all which kings and states the king was at that time in good peace and amity. At which day also (as if the crown upon his head had put perils into his thoughts) he did institute for the better security of his person a band of fifty archers under a captain to attend him, by the name of Yeomen of His Guard; and yet that it might be thought to be rather a matter of dignity, after the imitation of that he had known abroad, than any matter of diffidence appropriate to his own case, he made it to be understood for an ordinance not temporary, but to hold in succession forever after.

The seventh of November the king held his Parliament at Westminster, which he had summoned immediately after his coming to London. His ends in calling a Parliament (and that so speedily) were chiefly three. First, to procure the crown to be entailed upon himself. Next, to have the attainders[65] of all of his party (which were in no small number) reversed, and all acts of hostility by them done in his quarrel remitted and discharged; and on the other side, to attaint[66] by Parliament the heads and principals of his enemies. The third, to calm and quiet the fears of the rest of that party by a general pardon, not being ignorant in how great danger a king stands from his subjects when most of his subjects are conscious in themselves that they stand in his danger.[67] Unto these three special motives of a Parliament was added that he as a prudent and moderate prince made this judgment that it was fit for him to hasten to let his people see that he meant to govern by law, howsoever he came in by the sword; and fit also to reclaim[68] them to know him for their king, whom they had so lately talked of as an enemy or banished man. For that which concerned the entailing of the crown (more than that he was true to his own will that he would not endure any mention of the Lady Elizabeth, no not in the nature of special entail), he carried it otherwise with great wisdom and measure. For he did not press to have the act penned by way of declaration or recognition of right, as on the other side he avoided to have it by new law or ordinance; but chose rather a kind of middle way, by way of establish-

ment, and that under covert and indifferent[69] words, "that the inheritance of the crown should rest, remain, and abide in the king, etc." which words might equally be applied that the crown should continue to him, but whether as having former right to it (which was doubtful) or having it then in fact and possession (which no man denied) was left fair[70] to interpretation either way. And again for the limitation of the entail, he did not press it to go further than to himself and to the heirs of his body, not speaking of his right[71] heirs but leaving that to the law to decide, so as the entail might seem rather a personal favor to him and his children than a total disinherison to the House of York. And in this form was the law drawn and passed. Which statute he procured to be confirmed by the pope's bull[72] the year following, with mention nevertheless (by way of recital) of his other titles both of descent and conquest. So as now the wreath of three was made a wreath of five, for to the three first titles, of the two houses or lines and conquest, were added two more, the authorities Parliamentary and papal.

The king likewise in the reversal of the attainders of his partakers,[73] and discharging them of all offences incident to his service and succor, had his will, and acts did pass accordingly. In the passage whereof, exception was taken to divers persons in the House of Commons for that they were attainted, and thereby not legal nor habilitate[74] to serve in Parliament, being disabled[75] in the highest degree and that it should be a great incongruity to have them to make laws who themselves were not inlawed.[76] The truth was that divers of those which had in the time of King Richard been strongest and most declared for the king's party were returned knights and burgesses for the Parliament, whether by care or recommendation from the state or the voluntary inclination of the people, many of which had been by Richard the Third attainted by outlawries,[77] or otherwise. The king was somewhat troubled with this, for though it had a grave and specious show, yet it reflected upon his party. But wisely not showing himself at all moved therewith, he would not understand it but as a case in law, and wished the

[57]*Simon...Even*: October 27.

[58]Noted ecclesiastical statesman—successively bishop of Worcester and Ely, archbishop of Canterbury (1454), and cardinal—who worked for a lasting peace following the Wars of the Roses.

[59]Site of the archbishop of Canterbury's palace on the Thames opposite Westminster.

[60]Originally, persons knighted on the field of battle by the king himself in the presence of the royal *banner.*

[61]Investitures of a title, function, or office.

[62]Respectively, Henry's uncle, his mother's third husband, and a descendant of Edward I.   [63]Germany.   [64]I.e., heir-apparent.

[65]Judgments of death or outlawry for treason or felony, with forfeiture of property, disqualification of inheriting or transmitting by descent, and extinction of civil rights and capacities.

[66]Pass acts of attainder against.   [67]At his mercy.

[68]Subdue, make gentle (a term from falconry).

[69]Ambiguous and unspecific.   [70]Open.   [71]Legitimate.

[72]Innocent VIII's bull of 27 March 1486 recognizing Henry's title to the throne and threatening excommunication for all dissidents.

[73]Supporters.   [74]Qualified.   [75]Disqualified.

[76]Within the authority and protection of the law.

[77]Actions of putting a person beyond protection of the law.

judges to be advised thereupon, who for that purpose were forthwith assembled in the Exchequer Chamber (which is the council-chamber of the judges), and upon deliberation they gave a grave and safe opinion and advice, mixed with law and convenience; which was that the knights and burgesses attainted by the course of law should forbear to come into the House till a law were passed for the reversal of their attainders.

It was at that time incidentally moved amongst the judges in their consultation what should be done for the king himself, who likewise was attainted, but it was with unanimous consent resolved that the crown takes away all defects and stops in blood;[78] and that from the time the king did assume the crown, the fountain was cleared, and all attainders and corruption of blood discharged. But nevertheless, for honor's sake, it was ordained by Parliament that all records wherein there was any memory or mention of the king's attainder should be defaced, canceled, and taken off the file.

But on the part of the king's enemies there were by Parliament attainted the late duke of Gloucester, calling himself Richard the Third, the duke of Norfolk, the earl of Surrey, Viscount Lovell, the Lord Ferrers, the Lord Zouch, Richard Ratcliffe, William Catesby, and many others of degree[79] and quality. In which bills of attainders nevertheless there were contained many just and temperate clauses, savings, and provisos well showing and foretokening the wisdom, stay,[80] and moderation of the king's spirit of government. And for the pardon of the rest that had stood against the king, the king upon a second advice thought it not fit it should pass by Parliament, the better (being matter of grace) to impropriate[81] the thanks to himself, using only the opportunity of a Parliament time the better to disperse it into the veins of the kingdom. Therefore during the Parliament he published his royal proclamation, offering pardon and grace of restitution[82] to all such as had taken arms or been participant of any attempts against him, so as they submitted themselves to his mercy by a day, and took the oath of allegiance and fidelity to him, whereupon many came out of sanctuary, and many more came out of fear, no less guilty than those that had taken sanctuary.

As for money or treasure, the king thought it not seasonable or fit to demand any of his subjects at this Parliament, both because he had received satisfaction from them in matters of so great importance and because he could not remunerate them with any general pardon (being prevented therein by the coronation pardon passed immediately before); but chiefly for that it was in every man's eye what great forfeitures and confiscations he had at that present to help himself; whereby those casualties[83] of the crown might in reason spare the purses of the subject, especially in a time when he was in peace with all his neighbors. Some few laws passed at that Parliament almost for form sake: amongst which there was one, to reduce aliens being made denizens to pay strangers' customs;[84] and another, to draw to himself the seizures and compositions of Italians' goods for not employment;[85] being points of profit to his coffers, whereof from the very beginning he was not forgetful; and had been more happy at the latter end if his early providence, which

kept him from all necessity of exacting upon his people, could likewise have attempered his nature therein. He added during Parliament to his former creations the ennoblement or advancement in nobility of a few others. The Lord Chandos of Brittain was made earl of Bath; Sir Giles Dawbeney was made Lord Dawbeney, and Sir Robert Willoughby, Lord Brooke.

The king did also with great nobleness and bounty (which virtues at that time had their turns in his nature) restore Edward Stafford (eldest son to Henry, duke of Buckingham, attainted in the time of King Richard) not only to his dignities but to his fortunes and possessions, which were great; to which he was moved also by a kind of gratitude for that the duke was the man that moved the first stone against the tyranny of King Richard, and indeed made the king a bridge to the crown upon his own ruins.[86] Thus the Parliament brake up.

The Parliament being dissolved, the king sent forthwith money to redeem the Marquis Dorset and Sir John Bourchier, whom he had left as his pledges at Paris for money which he had borrowed when he made his expedition for England; and thereupon he took a fit occasion to send the Lord Treasurer and Master Bray[87] (whom he used as counselor) to the lord major of London, requiring of the City a prest[88] of six thousand marks.[89] But after many parleys he could obtain but two thousand pounds, which nevertheless the king took in good part, as men use to do that practise to borrow money when they have no need.

About this time the king called unto his Privy Counsel John Morton and Richard Foxe, the one bishop of Ely, the other bishop of Exeter;[90] vigilant men and secret,[91] and such

[78]Prohibitions on attainted persons against inheriting, retaining, or transmitting property. [79]Noble rank. [80]Restraint. [81]Appropriate.

[82]Opportunity to regain titles and properties through submission. [83]Fortunate (and unexpected) acquisitions.

[84]To require foreign-born persons who had been naturalized as citizens (*denizens*) to pay the same customs as aliens (*strangers*).

[85]To confiscate the holdings of Italian merchants who tried to take out of England moneys they had received in exchange for merchandise.

[86]The younger Stafford, third duke of Buckingham, thus restored to his *dignities* and vast possessions, eventually met the same fate as his father, being executed on a trumped-up charge of treason by Henry VIII in 1521. See p. 883, n.22.

[87]Sir Reginald (or Reignold) Bray (d. 1503), factotum in the household of Sir Henry Stafford, second husband of Lady Margaret, Henry's mother, who served the king in a variety of financial and political matters. It was probably he who designed the Henry VII Chapel in Westminster Abbey (see p. 891, n.28.). [88]Loan.

[89]Moneys of account, each representing two-thirds of a pound sterling (i.e., 13*s.* 4*d.*). Thus the sum demanded was 4,000 pounds.

[90]Two powerful Tudor politicians whose fortunes rose with their king's. John Morton (1420?–1500) succeeded (1486) Bourchier as archbishop of Canterbury, became a cardinal in 1493, and served Henry in many ways. It was probably he who wrote the Latin version of the hostile life of Richard III usually ascribed to Thomas More (whose patron he was). Richard Foxe (1448?–1528) was a loyal, ruthless servant to Henry and his son in various high offices, political and ecclesiastical. [91]Uncommunicative, i.e., trustworthy.

as kept watch with him almost upon all men else. They had been both versed in his affairs before he came to the crown, and were partakers of his adverse fortune. This Morton soon after, upon the death of Bourchier, he made archbishop of Canterbury. And for Foxe, he made him Lord Keeper of his Privy Seal; and afterwards advanced him by degrees, from Exeter to Bath and Wells, thence to Durham, and last to Winchester. For although the king loved to employ and advance bishops, because having rich bishoprics they carried their reward upon themselves, yet he did use to raise them 10 by steps that he might not lose the profit of the first fruits,[92] which by that course of gradation was multiplied.

At last, upon the eighteenth of January was solemnized the so long expected and so much desired marriage between the king and the Lady Elizabeth, which day of marriage was celebrated with greater triumph and demonstrations (especially on the people's part) of joy and gladness than the days either of his entry or coronation, which the king rather noted than liked. And it is true that all his lifetime, while the Lady Elizabeth lived with him (for she died before him), 20 he showed himself no very indulgent husband towards her though she was beautiful, gentle, and fruitful. But his aversion towards the House of York was so predominant in him as it found place not only in his wars and counsels, but in his chamber and bed. . . .

[BACON'S FINAL ESTIMATE OF HENRY VII]

And thus this Solomon of England (for Solomon also was too heavy upon his people in exactions), having lived two-and-fifty years and thereof reigned three-and-twenty years and eight moneths, being in perfect memory and in a most blessed mind, in a great calm of a consuming sickness, passed 30 to a better world, the two-and-twentieth of April 1508,[93] at his palace of Richmond[94] which himself had built.

This king (to speak of him in terms equal to his deserving) was one of the best sort of wonders: a wonder for wise men. He had parts (both in his virtues and his fortune) not so fit for a commonplace as for observation.[95] Certainly he was religious, both in his affection and observance. But as he could see clear (for those times) through superstition, so he would be blinded now and then by human policy. He advanced churchmen. He was tender in the privilege of 40 sanctuaries, though they wrought him much mischief. He built and endowed many religious foundations besides his memorable hospital of the Savoy,[96] and yet was he a great alms-giver in secret, which showed that his works in public were dedicated rather to God's glory than his own. He professed always to love and seek peace; and it was his usual preface in his treaties that when Christ came into the world peace was sung, and when He went out of the world peace was bequeathed. And this virtue could not proceed out of fear or softness, for he was valiant and active; and therefore 50 no doubt it was truly Christian and moral. Yet he knew the way to peace was not to seem to be desirous to avoid wars. Therefore would he make offers and fames[97] of wars till he had mended the conditions of peace. It was also much that

one that was so great a lover of peace should be so happy in war. For his arms, either in foreign or civil wars, were never infortunate, neither did he know what a disaster meant. The war of his coming in, and the rebellions of the earl of Lincoln and the Lord Audley, were ended by victory. The wars of France and Scotland, by peaces sought at his hands. That of Brittain, by accident of the duke's death. The insurrection of the Lord Lovell, and that of Perkin at Exeter and in Kent, by flight of the rebels before they came to blows.[98] So that his fortune of arms was still inviolate. The rather sure, for that in the quenching of the commotions of his subjects he ever went in person, sometimes reserving himself to back and second his lieutenants, but ever in action; and yet that was not merely forwardness, but partly distrust of others.

He did much maintain and countenance his laws, which (nevertheless) was no impediment to him to work his will. For it was so handled that neither prerogative nor profit went to diminution. And yet as he would sometimes strain up his laws to his prerogative, so would he also let down his prerogative to his Parliament. For mint and wars and martial discipline (things of absolute power) he would nevertheless bring to Parliament. Justice was well administered in his time, save where the king was party; save also that the counsel table intermeddled too much with *meum* and *tuum*.[99] For it was a very court of justice during his time, especially in the beginning. But in that part both of justice and policy which is the durable part, and cut as it were in brass or marble, which is the making of good laws, he did excel. And with his justice he was also a merciful prince, as in whose time there were but three of the nobility that suffered:[1] the earl of Warwick, the Lord Chamberlain, and the

[92]Annates, i.e., first year's revenues of bishops customarily paid to the pope. [93]A mistake (perhaps copied from John Speed) for 1509. [94]The ancient palace of Sheen (see p. 851), which Henry restored after a fire in 1498 and renamed Richmond.
[95]*Not so fit. . . observation*: not a subject for routine comment but for scrutiny and analysis.
[96]Ancient palace in the Strand which Henry rebuilt and endowed (1505) as a Hospital of St. John the Baptist for the relief of one hundred poor people. [97]Feints and rumors.
[98]*Rebellions. . .blows*: a roster of the principal disturbances of Henry's reign. John de la Pole, earl of Lincoln (1464?–87), a nephew of Edward IV, promoted the Yorkist plot of Lambert Simnel, an impostor posing as Edward, earl of Warwick, and thereby pretender to the throne; he was killed at the battle of Stoke (1487), where Simnel's ragged forces were dispersed. James Touchet, seventh Baron Audley (1465?–97), was one of the leaders of the rebellious Cornishmen who, marching on London in 1497, were turned back at Blackheath; he was captured and beheaded. Henry's foreign wars were ended by treaties with France (1492) and Scotland (1497), and his difficulties in Brittany were resolved—somewhat more dubiously—by the death of Duke Francis II (1488). Francis Lovell, first Viscount Lovell (1454–87?), a Yorkist who fought for Simnel at Stoke, disappeared after the battle and presumably died of starvation. Perkin Warbeck (1474–99), a pretender accepted in Scotland and Ireland as a son of Edward IV, invaded Cornwall in 1497, but was quickly captured at Exeter and, after long imprisonment, hanged. [99]"Mine" and "yours." [1]Were executed.

Lord Audley[2] (though the first two were instead of numbers in the dislike and obloquy of the people). But there were never so great rebellions expiated with so little blood drawn by the hand of justice as the two rebellions of Blackheath and Exeter.[3] As for the severity used upon those which were taken in Kent, it was but upon a scum of people.[4] His pardons went ever both before and after his sword. But then he had withal a strange kind of interchanging of large and inexpected[5] pardons with severe executions, which (his wisdom considered) could not be imputed to any incon- stancy or inequality, but either to some reason which we do not now know, or to a principle he had set unto himself that he would vary and try both ways in turn.

But the less blood he drew, the more he took of treasure; and as some construed it, he was the more sparing in the one that he might be the more pressing in the other, for both would have been intolerable. Of nature assuredly he coveted to accumulate treasure, and was a little poor in admiring riches. The people (into whom there is infused for the preservation of monarchies a natural desire to discharge[6] their princes, though it be with the unjust charge of their counselors and ministers) did impute this unto Cardinal Morton and Sir Reginald Bray; who (as it after appeared) as counselors of ancient authority with him did so second his humors as nevertheless they did temper them. Whereas Empson and Dudley[7] that followed, being persons that had no reputation with him otherwise than by the servile following of his bent, did not give way only (as the first did) but shape him way[8] to those extremities, for which himself was touched with remorse at his death, and which his successor renounced and sought to purge. This excess of his had at that time many glosses and interpretations. Some thought the continual rebellions wherewith he had been vexed had made him grow to hate his people; some thought it was done to pull down their stomachs[9] and to keep them low; some, for that he would leave his son a Golden Fleece; some suspected he had some high design upon foreign parts. But those perhaps shall come nearest the truth that fetch not their reasons so far off, but rather impute it to nature, age, peace, and a mind fixed upon no other ambition or pursuit: whereunto I should add that having every day occasion to take notice of the necessities and shifts for money of other great princes abroad, it did the better by comparison set off to him the felicity of full coffers. As to his expending of treasure, he never spared charge which his affairs required, and in his buildings was magnificent; but his rewards were very limited. So that his liberality was rather upon his own state and memory than upon the deserts of others.

He was of an high mind, and loved his own will and his own way, as one that revered himself, and would reign indeed. Had he been a private man he would have been termed proud, but in a wise prince it was but keeping of distance, which indeed he did towards all, not admitting any near or full approach either to his power or to his secrets. For he was governed by none. His queen (notwithstanding she had presented him with divers children, and with a crown also, though he would not acknowledge it) could

do nothing with him. His mother he reverenced much, heard little. For any person agreeable to him for society (such as was Hastings to King Edward the Fourth, or Charles Brandon after to King Henry the Eighth),[10] he had none, except we should account for such persons Foxe and Bray and Empson because they were so much with him. But it was but as the instrument is much with the workman. He had nothing in him of vainglory, but yet kept state and majesty to the height, being sensible that majesty maketh the people bow, but vainglory boweth to them.

To his confederates abroad he was constant and just, but not open. But rather such was his inquiry and such his closeness as they stood in the light towards him, and he stood in the dark to them, yet without strangeness,[11] but with a semblance of mutual communication of affairs. As for little envies or emulations upon foreign princes (which are frequent with many kings), he had never any, but went substantially to his own business. Certain it is that though his reputation was great at home, yet it was greater abroad. For foreigners that could not see the passages of affairs, but made their judgments upon the issues of them, noted that he was ever in strife and ever aloft. It grew also from the airs which the princes and states abroad received from their ambassadors and agents here, which were attending the court in great number; whom he did not only content with courtesy, reward, and privateness, but (upon such conferences as passed with them) put them in admiration to find his universal insight into the affairs of the world; which though he did suck chiefly from themselves, yet that which he had gathered from them all seemed admirable to every one. So that they did write ever to their superiors in high terms concerning his wisdom and art of rule. Nay, when they were returned they did commonly maintain intelligence with him, such a dexterity he had to impropriate to himself all foreign instruments.

He was careful and liberal to obtain good intelligence from

[2]See notes 31, 36 and 98.
[3]The unsuccessful Cornish rebellion and Warbeck's invasion, both in 1597. [4]The lowest classes. [5]Unexpected. [6]Exonerate.
[7]Sir Richard Empson (d. 1510) and Edmund Dudley (1462?–1510), Henry's notorious instruments for extorting taxes and fees, whom "the people," Bacon said, "esteemed as his horseleeches and shearers, bold men and careless of fame, and that took toll of their master's grist." Although both were promptly executed by Henry VIII following his accession, the Dudleys, an ambitious and tenacious tribe, added to their wealth and power throughout the 16th century. Edmund's son John, earl of Warwick and duke of Northumberland under Edward VI, almost succeeded in putting his son Lord Guildford Dudley, husband of Lady Jane Grey, upon the throne. Another of John's many children was Mary, who became the mother of Sir Philip Sidney; and her famous brother Robert, earl of Leicester, was Queen Elizabeth's favorite courtier in her early reign. [8]Prepare the way for him. [9]High spirits.
[10]William, Baron Hastings (1430?–83), a favorite of Edward IV whom Richard, duke of Gloucester (later Richard III) executed early in his protectorate; Charles Brandon, first duke of Suffolk (d. 1545), a favorite of Henry VIII who bigamously married Henry's sister Mary. [11]Reserve, coldness.

all parts abroad, wherein he did not only use his interest in the liegers[12] here and his pensioners which he had both in the court of Rome and other the courts of Christendom, but the industry and vigilancy of his own ambassadors in foreign parts. For which purpose his instructions were ever extreme curious and articulate, and in them more articles touching inquisition than touching negotiation, requiring likewise from his ambassadors an answer, in particular distinct articles, respectively to his questions.

As for his secret spials which he did employ both at home and abroad, by them to discover what practices and conspiracies were against him, surely his case required it; he had such moles perpetually working and casting to undermine him. Neither can it be reprehended; for if spials be lawful against lawful enemies, much more against conspirators and traitors. But indeed to give them credence by oaths or curses,[13] that cannot be well maintained, for those are too holy vestments for a disguise. Yet surely there was this further good in his employing of these flies and familiars: that as the use of them was cause that many conspiracies were revealed, so the fame and suspicion of them kept (no doubt) many conspiracies from being attempted.

Towards his queen he was nothing uxorious, nor scarce indulgent; but companiable and respective[14] and without jealousy. Towards his children he was full of paternal affection, careful of their education, aspiring to their high advancement, regular to see that they should not want of any due honor and respect, but not greatly willing to cast any popular luster upon them.

To his Council he did refer much, and sat oft in person, knowing it to be the way to assist his power and inform his judgment: in which respect also he was fairly patient of liberty both of advice and of vote, till himself were declared.[15]

He kept a strait hand on his nobility, and chose rather to advance clergymen and lawyers, which were more obsequious to him, but had less interest in the people; which made for his absoluteness but not for his safety. Insomuch as I am persuaded it was one of the causes of his troublesome reign for that his nobles, though they were loyal and obedient, yet did not cooperate with him, but let every man go his own way. He was not afraid of an able man, as Lewis the Eleventh was. But contrariwise he was served by the ablest men that then were to be found, without which his affairs could not have prospered as they did. . . . Neither did he care how cunning they were that he did employ, for he thought himself to have the master-reach. And as he chose well, so he held them up well. For it is a strange thing that though he were a dark prince, and infinitely suspicious, and his times full of secret conspiracies and troubles, yet in twenty-four years reign he never put down or discomposed counselor or near servant, save only Stanley the Lord Chamberlain. As for the disposition of his subjects in general towards him, it stood thus with him: that of the three affections which naturally tie the hearts of the subjects to their sovereigns—love, fear, and reverence—he had the last in height, the second in good measure, and so little of the first as he was beholding to the other two.

He was a prince sad, serious, and full of thoughts and secret observations; and full of notes and memorials of his own hand, especially touching persons: as whom to employ, whom to reward, whom to inquire of, whom to beware of, what were the dependencies, what were the factions, and the like; keeping (as it were) a journal of his thoughts. There is to this day a merry tale, that his monkey (set on, as it was thought, by one of his chamber) tore his principal notebook all to pieces when by chance it lay forth; whereat the court, which liked not those pensive accompts,[16] was almost tickled with sport.

He was indeed full of apprehensions and suspicions. But as he did easily take them, so he did easily check them and master them, whereby they were not dangerous, but troubled himself more than others. It is true, his thoughts were so many as they could not well always stand together; but that which did good one way did hurt another. Neither did he at some times weigh them aright in their proportions. Certainly that rumor which did him so much mischief (that the duke of York should be saved and alive) was (at the first) of his own nourishing, because he would have more reason not to reign in the right of his wife. He was affable, and both well and fair spoken; and would use strange sweetness and blandishments of words where he desired to effect or persuade anything that he took to heart. He was rather studious than learned, reading most books that were of any worth in the French tongue. Yet he understood the Latin, as appeareth in that Cardinal Hadrian[17] and others, who could very well have written French, did use to write to him in Latin.

For his pleasures, there is no news[18] of them. And yet by his instructions to Marsin and Stile[19] touching the queen of Naples, it seemeth he could interrogate well touching beauty. He did by pleasures as great princes do by banquets: come and look a little upon them, and turn way. For never prince was more wholly given to his affairs, nor in them more of himself: insomuch as in triumphs of justs and tourneys and balls and masques (which they then called disguises) he was rather a princely and gentle spectator than seemed much to be delighted.

No doubt, in him as in all men (and most of all in kings), his fortune wrought upon his nature, and his nature upon his fortune. He attained to the crown not only from a private fortune, which might endow him with moderation, but also from the fortune of an eviled man, which had quickened in him all seeds of observation and industry. And his times, being rather prosperous than calm, had raised his confidence by success, but almost marred his nature by troubles. His wisdom, by often evading from perils, was turned rather

[12]Resident ambassadors.
[13]To reinforce his spies' charges by pronouncing solemn curses on their victims.   [14]Attentive.
[15]Until his decision was made and announced.
[16]Gloomy accounts.
[17]Adrian de Castello (1460?–1521?), Italian humanist and scholar, papal nuncio to Scotland who rose high in Henry's favor and served as his ambassador to Rome.   [18]Information.
[19]Unidentified.

into a dexterity to deliver himself from dangers when they pressed him than into a providence to prevent and remove them afar off. And even in nature, the sight of his mind was like some sights of eyes: rather strong at hand than to carry afar off. For his wit increased upon the occasion, and so much the more if the occasion were sharpened by danger. Again, whether it were the shortness of his foresight, or the strength of his will, or the dazeling[20] of his suspicions, or what it was, certain it is that the perpetual troubles of his fortunes (there being no more matter out of which they grew) could not 10 have been without some great defects and main errors in his nature, customs, and proceedings, which he had enough to do to save and help with a thousand little industries and watches. But those do best appear in the story itself. Yet take him with all his defects, if a man should compare him with the kings his concurrents[21] in France and Spain, he shall find him more politic than Lewis the Twelfth of France and more entire and sincere than Ferdinando of Spain. But if you shall change Lewis the Twelfth for Lewis the Eleventh, who lived a little before, then the consort[22] is more perfect. For that Lewis the 20 Eleventh, Ferdinando, and Henry may be esteemed for the *tres magi*[23] of kings of those ages. To conclude, if this king did no greater matters, it was long of[24] himself, for what he minded he compassed.

He was a comely personage, a little above just[25] stature, well and straight limbed, but slender. His countenance was reverend, and a little like a churchman; and as it was not strange or dark, so neither was it winning or pleasing, but as the face of one well disposed. But it was to the disadvantage of the painter, for it was best when he spake. 30

His worth may bear a tale or two that may put upon him somewhat that may seem divine. When the Lady Margaret his mother had divers great suitors for marriage, she dreamed one night that one in the likeness of a bishop in pontifical habit did tender her Edmund, earl of Richmond (the king's father), for her husband. Neither had she ever any child but the king, though she had three husbands. One day when King Henry the Sixth (whose innocency gave him holiness) was washing his hands at a great feast, and cast his eye upon King Henry, then a young youth, he said; "This is the lad that shall possess quietly that that we now strive for."[26] But that that was truly divine in him was that he had the fortune of a true Christian as well as of a great king, in living exercised and dying repentant. So as he had an happy warfare in both conflicts, both of sin and the Cross.

He was born at Pembroke Castle, and lieth buried at Westminster in one of the stateliest and daintiest[27] monuments of Europe, both for the chapel and for the sepulcher.[28] So that he dwelleth more richly dead, in the monument of his tomb, than he did alive in Richmond or any of his palaces. I could wish he did the like in this monument of his fame.

[20]Dazzling, i.e., overpowering.   [21]Contemporaries.
[22]Resemblance.   [23]The Three Wise Men.   [24]Owing to.
[25]Average.
[26]See Shakespeare, *3 Henry VI*, IV.vi.67–76.   [27]Handsomest.
[28]The famous Henry VII Chapel in Westminster Abbey, which contains the tombs of Henry and his queen (the work of the Florentine Pietro Torregiano) and also those of his granddaughters Mary and Elizabeth, his great-granddaughter Mary Queen of Scots, and other royal persons. See p. 749.

Edmund Bolton [1575?–?1633]

Bolton's life is a forlorn story of lost causes and grandiose but uncompleted schemes. He spent some time at Cambridge and also at the Inner Temple, but as a devout Roman Catholic he was barred from the career in church or state for which his learning fitted him. Some of his poems found a place in *England's Helicon* (1600), perhaps the most brilliant of Elizabethan miscellanies, but in the galaxy of Sidney, Spenser, Drayton, Marlowe, and Shakespeare his light shone very dim. Deeply read in history and antiquities, he wrote a piece on Henry II for Speed's *History of Great Britain* (p. 847). but because it showed Becket in too good a light it had to be rejected. He promoted an elaborate scheme for a sort of royal academy or senate of honor whose members (drawn from the Knights of the Garter, certain members of the nobility, and eminent commoners) would be protected by a royal charter, distinguished by their own insignia, and endowed with certain privileges (including censorship of books) whereby they might sustain and elevate the intellectual life of England. King James, who gloried in his learning, expressed some interest in the undertaking, and so did the all-powerful duke of Buckingham, but the years went by and nothing was accomplished before the scheme collapsed with James' death in 1625. Of the some dozen works that Bolton wrote—most of them on historical and antiquarian subjects—only four were printed in his own lifetime: a dialogue on heraldry called *The Elements of Armories* (1610), a translation of the minor Roman historian Lucius Annaeus Florus (1619), a life of Nero (1624), and *The City's Advocate* (1629), which was another book on heraldry.

It is appropriately ironical that Bolton's modest reputation rests upon a little book that had to wait a hundred years for publication. Although not printed until 1722 (when the antiquarian Anthony Hall included it in his edition of Nicholas Trivet's chronicle), *Hypercritica* was apparently intended as a kind of puff or prologue for a much more massive book that Bolton planned but failed to write—a history of the realm (*corpus rerum Anglicarum*) that the esteemed Sir Henry Savile, master of Merton and provost of Eton, had called for in 1596 (see p. 894, n.16.) and that in the conclusion of his little treatise Bolton seems to be announcing as his own forthcoming publication. Despite a certain elephantine stance and a characteristic pomposity of style, Bolton was a thoughtful, learned man, and his four "addresses" on historiography help us understand the prestige of that kind of writing in the age of Camden, Speed, and Raleigh. The fourth "Address," on style, provides a contemporary response to what we regard as some of the monuments of Elizabethan and Jacobean literature, and so it helps us chart the shifting tides of taste.

As noted earlier, *Hypercritica* was first printed by Anthony Hall in his edition of *Nicolai Trivete annalium continuatio* (1722). My text is based upon Joseph Haslewood's *Ancient Critical Essays upon English Poets and Poësy* (2 vols., 1811–15). Excerpts from the work are included in J. E. Spingarn's *Critical Essays of the Seventeenth Century* (3 vols., 1908–9), and Thomas H. Blackburn has edited the text of Bolton's proposals for an "Academ Roial" in *Studies in the Renaissance*, XIV (1967). These proposals have been discussed by E. M. Portal (*Proceedings of the British Academy*, VII, 1915–16) and by Joan Evans (*History of the Society of Antiquaries*, 1956). Richard L. Dowling's unpublished Harvard dissertation (2 vols., 1954) supplies a full account of Bolton and his feckless undertakings.

from Hypercritica, or A Rule of Judgment for Writing or Reading Our Histories (1618?)

The Chief Points or Sums of the Addresses

I.
Concerning the historical use of the old book of Brut, dedicated to Robert, earl of Gloucester, brother of the Empress Maud.[1]

II.
The religious necessity of impartiality in historiographers and of abstinence in general from censure.

III.
The historical states of times among us from Julius Caesar till King Henry the Seventh, with discoveries of our chief historical dangers.[2]

IV.
Prime gardens for gathering English, according to the true gauge or standard of the tongue about fifteen or sixteen years ago.

ADDRESS THE FIRST

Section II

Among the greatest wants in our ancient authors are the wants of art and style, which as they add to the luster of the

HYPERCRITICA   [1]In some of the surviving manuscripts of Geoffrey of Monmouth's *Historia regum Britanniae* (see p. 808, n.3.) there is a double dedication: one to Waleran, Count of Mellent or Melun (1104–66), the other to Robert, an illegitimate son (d. 1147) of Henry I and an ally of his half-sister Matilda (*Maud*) in the dynastic struggles of the 12th century. Following the death (1125) of her first husband, Henry V of Germany, Maud married (1128) Geoffrey of Anjou, and their son Henry II became the first of the Plantagenet kings of England. See inside front and back covers.
[2]In this section, most of which has been omitted in these excerpts, Bolton conventionally outlines the history of his country as a periodic and linear progression from the Romans, British, Anglo-Saxons, and Danes to the Normans, who inaugurated the "Revolution" triumphantly completed by James I at his accession in

works and delights of the reader yet add they nothing to the truth, which they so esteemed as they seem to have regarded nothing else. For without truth, art and style come into the nature of crimes by imposture. It is an act of high wisdom, and not of eloquence only, to write the history of so great and noble a people as the English. For the causes of things are not only wonderfully wrapped one within the other, but placed oftentimes far above the ordinary reaches of human wit; and he who relates events without their premises and circumstances deserves not the name of an historian, as being like to him who numbers the bones of a man anatomized,[3] or presenteth unto us the bare skeleton without declaring the nature of the fabric or teaching the use of parts.

SECTION V

There is a great complaint among some of the most learned against Galfridus, Arthurius, or Galfridus Monumenthensis[4] for want of truth and modesty as creating a Brut unto us for the founder of our Britain. But who is he that, proving it to be a fiction, can prove it withal to be his? If that work be quite abolished there is a vast blank upon the times of our country from the creation of the world till the coming of Julius Caesar, not *terra incognita*[5] itself being less to be known than ours. The things of which ages as we understand not the more for Monmouth's history unless the same be true, so neither seem they (as being those times which our critics mark with their "Ἀδελον and their Μύθικον, their *ignotum* and *fabulosum*)[6] much to be stood[7] upon. Nevertheless, out of that very story—let it be what it will—have titles been framed in open Parliament, both in England and Ireland, for the rights of the crown of England, even to entire kingdoms. And though no Parliament can make that to be a truth which is not such in the proper nature thereof, nor that much authority is added thereby to that traditional monument, because Parliament men are not always antiquaries, yet are we somewhat the more—and rather tied—to look with favor on the case. Therefore it pleased me well what once I did read in a great divine, that *in Apocryphis non omnia esse apocrypha.*[8] And that very much of Monmouth's book or pretended translation *de origine et gestis Britannorum*[9] be granted to be fabulous, yet many truths are mixed.

ADDRESS THE SECOND

In Section i of the second Address Bolton shows how Bede's *Historia Ecclesiastica* exemplifies the "indifferency and even dealing" that are "the glory of historians," and in Section ii he derives the precept from example: "an history ought to be nothing else but an image of truth, and as it were a table of things done, permitting the judgment of all to the competent reader, which judgment we ought not forestall, howsoever in some rare cases it may be lawful to lead the same."

SECTION III

This steel rule whosoever honestly follows may perhaps write incommodiously for some momentary purposes but shall thereby, both in present and to posterity, live with honor through the justice of his monuments.[10] And if for them he should suffer death, as brave Cremutius Cordus did, yet other historians shall eternize his sufferings and that prince's great disgrace, under whom that tragedy was committed.[11] Nor in so sacred a business as the putting into books, for immortal remembrance, the acts of famous men need, I fear, to call it a canonical and inviolable aphorism of historiography, because it is absurd in the historical volumes of Holy Scripture, whose majesty no Attic nor Tullian[12] eloquence can express, nor to whose entireness of verity any human wit or diligence can come near. For in those divine records, facts[13] (whether good or bad) and their circumstances are simply and clearly related without (for the more part) any manner of censure or judgment upon the facts as in the writer's person. On the contrary, let those other writings which abound in the different humor be stripped by readers who have discretion unto the bare matter which they profess to handle, so that all their authors' commentations, conjectures, notes, passions, and censures—which they utter as in their proper persons—be diligently marked, abstracted, and laid apart; and then the things which they write may be received without danger, or certainly with little. . . .

SECTION V

An historiographer's office therefore abhorreth all sorts of abuse and deceit as impiety or sacrilege, and so our writer must if he will live indeed, and live with love and glory.

ADDRESS THE THIRD

SECTION III

The vast vulgar tomes[14] procured for the most part by the husbandry of printers, and not by appointment of the prince or authority of the commonweal, in their tumultuary and centonical[15] writings do seem to resemble some huge disproportionable temple whose architect was not his art's master, but in which store of rich marble and many most

---

1603. Bolton's list of the *chief historical dangers*—that is, occupational hazards of historians—include partisanship, mendacity, and the like. [3]Dissected.
[4]Walter, archdeacon of Oxford, (whose "ancient book" was said by Geoffrey to be the prime source of his history of the British kings), King Arthur, and Geoffrey of Monmouth himself.
[5]"Unknown country."
[6]The Latin words ("unknown" and "fabulous") translate the Greek.
[7]Relied.
[8]"Not everything in the Apocrypha is apocryphal."
[9]"Concerning the origin and the deeds of the Britons."
[10]Records.
[11]When Cremutius Cordus, a Roman historian of the later Augustan age, was challenged by the agents of the Emperor Tiberius for having eulogized Brutus and Cassius, leaders of the conspiracy against Julius Caesar, he starved himself to death.
[12]Ciceronian (from Marcus Tullius Cicero). [13]Acts, deeds.
[14]The huge and shapeless chronicles of such Tudor historians as Richard Grafton, Raphael Holinshed, and John Stow.
[15]Confused and thrown together.

goodly statues, columns, arks, and antique pieces recovered from out of innumerable ruins, are here and there in greater number than commendable order erected—with no dispraise to their excellency, however they were not happy in the restorer. In Master Speed's stories published since that knight's epistle,[16] besides all common helps there are for the later times the collections, notes, and extracts out of the compositions of Lord Viscount St. Alban, of the Lord Carew, of Sir Robert Cotton, of Sir Henry Spelman, of Dr. Barkham, of Master Edmund Bolton, etc.[17] Speed's own part is such therein for style and industry that for one who (as Martial speaks)[18] hath neither a Grecian Χαῖρε nor an *Ave Latinum*[19] is perhaps without many fellows in Europe. So much also have I understood of him, by sure information, that he had no meaning in that labor to prevent great practic learnedness,[20] but to furnish it for the common service of England's glory.

ADDRESS THE FOURTH

SECTION I

As for language and style, the coat and apparel of matter, he who would pen our affairs in English and compose unto us an entire body of them ought to have a singular care thereof. For our tongue, though it have no noted dialects nor accentual notes, as the Greeks, nor any received or enacted certainty of grammar or orthography, is very copious, and few there be who have the best and most proper graces thereof. In which the rule cannot but be variable, because the people's judgments are uncertain. The books also out of which we gather the most warrantable English are not many, to my remembrance. The principal which I have seen, and can in present call to mind, either for prose or verse are these whose names do follow.

SECTION II

The histories written by Sir Thomas More[21] (some few antiquated words excepted) contain a clear and proper phrase.

The *Arcadia* of Sir Philip Sidney[22] is most famous for rich conceits and splendor of courtly expressions, warily to be used by an historian whose style should have gloss and luster but otherwise rather solidity and fluency than singularity of oratorial or poetical notions. Such things as I have read of Queen Elizabeth's own doing carry in them a most princely and vital character, not without singular energy and force of sought elegancy.[23] . . . Perhaps the world never saw a lady in whose person more greatness of parts met than in hers, unless it were in that most noble princess and heroine Mary Queen of Scots, inferior to her only in her outward fortunes, in all other respects and abilities at least her equal.[24] A princely, grave, and flourishing piece of natural and exquisite English is Cardinal Allen's *Apology* said to be, and many have commended the style and phrase of Father Robert Parsons highly.[25] *The End of Nero and Beginning of Galba*, prefixed to the translated *Histories* of Tacitus and thought to be Sir Henry Savile's own[26]—as whose

else should so rare a piece be?—is the work of a very great master indeed, both in our tongue and in that story. That tractate which goeth under the name of the earl of Essex his *Apology* was thought by some to be Master Anthony Bacon's, but as it bears that earl's name so do I also think that it was the earl's own,[27] as also his advices for travel to

[16]In John Speed's *History of Great Britain* (see pp. 841 ff.), which appeared after Sir Henry Savile (1549–1622), master of Merton College, Oxford, provost of Eton, translator of Tacitus (*The End of Nero and Beginning of Galba*, 1591), and editor of a notable edition of Chrysostom (1610–13), had called for "an universal history of England" that would exemplify the learning, veracity, and art so regrettably lacking in the Tudor chroniclers. Savile's program for the reform of English historiography as outlined in the preface of his *Rerum Anglicarum scriptores post Bedam praecipui* (1596)—a massive collection of the chronicles of William of Malmsbury, Henry of Huntingdon, Roger of Hovenden, and others—was hailed by Bolton as a kind of Magna Carta. Something of Savile's manner may be gained from a section of this preface paraphrased by Bolton in his third Address: "Our historians (saith the Knight) being of the dregs of the common people, while they have endeavoured to adorn the majesty of so great a work [as the history of England] have stained and defiled it with most fusty fooleries. Whereby, through I wot not by what hard fortune of this island, it is come to pass that your ancestors, most gracious Queen, most puissant princes, who, embracing a great part of this our world within their empire, did easily overgo all the kings of their times in the glory of great achievements, now destitute of, as it were, the light of brave wits, do lie unknown and unregarded."
[17]Of the only two persons not named by Speed himself among his benefactors (see. p. 846 f.), the Viscount St. Albans was the celebrated Francis Bacon (for whose theory and practice of history see pp. 878 ff.), and Sir Henry Spelman (1564?–1641), one of the foremost antiquarians of the age, was the author of *Concilia, decreta, leges, constitutiones* (1639–64).   [18]*Satires*, V.li.
[19]*One who. . . Latinum*: who does not know enough Greek or Latin to say hello in either language.
[20]*No meaning. . . learnedness*: no intention of forestalling the advance of practical knowledge.
[21]The most important essay in historical writing by Sir Thomas More (1478–1535) was his famous life of Richard III, which was first printed in Richard Grafton's *Chronicle* (1543). A Latin version, perhaps like the English a collaboration or perhaps the independent work of More's early patron, John Cardinal Morton (1420?–1500), also survives. See p. 887, n.90.
[22]For the complicated history of the publication of Sidney's influential novel see p. 641, n.19.
[23]Queen Elizabeth's slender literary production included some schoolgirl translations (from Seneca and Petrarch), a few infelicitous lyrics, and versions (undertaken in her later years) of Boethius' *Consolation of Philosophy* as well as scraps from Plutarch's *Moralia* and Horace's *Ars poetica*.
[24]Among Mary Queen of Scots' literary remains, nearly all of them in French or Latin, are some verses on the death of her husband Francis II, some sonnets (to her cousin Queen Elizabeth and others), and a few works on the comforts of religion.
[25]William Cardinal Allen (1532–94) and Robert Parsons (1546–1610) worked and wrote tirelessly in the Jesuit attempt to reclaim England for the Roman Catholic Church.
[26]See n.16 above.
[27]In 1603, two years after the execution of Robert Devereux, earl of Essex (see pp. 843 ff.), there appeared an account of his

Roger, earl of Rutland,[28] than which nothing almost can be more honorably uttered nor more to the writer's praise, so far as belongs to a noble English orator. Master Hooker's preface to his books of ecclesiastical policy[29] is a singular and choice parcel of our vulgar language. Dr. Hayward's phrase and words are very good, only some have wished that in his *Henry the Fourth* he had not called Sir Hugh Linn by so light a word as *madcap* (though he were such), and that he had not changed his historical state into a dramatical, where he induceth a mother uttering a woman's passion in the case of her son.[30] Sir Walter Raleigh's *Guiana* and his prefatory epistle before his mighty undertaking in *The History of the World* are full of proper, clear, and courtly graces of speech.[31] Most of all, Sir Francis Bacon's writings, which have the freshest and most savory form and aptest utterances that, as I suppose, our tongue can bear.[32]

These, next to His Majesty's own most royal style, are the principal prose writers whom out of my present memory I dare commend for the best garden-plots out of which to gather English language.[33]

SECTION III

In verse there are Edmund Spenser's *Hymns*. I cannot advise the allowance of other his poems as for practic English, no more than I can do Geoffrey Chaucer, Lydgate, *Piers Plowman*, or Laureate Skelton.[34] It was laid as a fault to the charge of Sallust that he used some old outworn words, stolen out of Cato his books *De originibus*.[35] And for an historian in our tongue to affect the like out of those our poets would be accounted a foul oversight. That therefore must not be unless perhaps we cite the words of some old monument, as Livy cites *Carmen Martium*[36] or as other Latins might allege Pacuvius, Andronicus, or Laws of the Twelve Tables,[37] or what else soever of the ancients. My judgment is nothing at all in poems or poesy, and therefore I dare not go far, but will simply deliver my mind concerning those authors among us whose English hath in my conceit most propriety, and is nearest to the phrase of court and to the speech used among the noble and among the better sort in London, the two sovereign seats and, as it were, Parliament tribunals to try the question in. Brave language are Chapman's *Iliads*,[38] those, I mean, which are translated into tessara-decasyllabons, or lines of fourteen syllables. The works of Samuel Daniel contained somewhat aflat,[39] but yet withal a very pure and copious English and words as warrantable as any man's, and fitter perhaps for prose than measure.[40] Michael Drayton's *Heroical Epistles* are well worth the reading also for the purpose of our subject, which is to furnish an English historian with choice and copy of tongue.[41] Queen Elizabeth's verses, those which I have seen and read, some extant in the elegant, witty, and artificial book of *The Art of English Poetry*—the work (as the fame is) of one of her Gentlemen Pensioners, Puttenham—are princely as her prose.[42]

Never must be forgotten *St. Peter's Complaint* and those other serious poems said to be Father Southwell's, the English whereof as it is most proper, so the sharpness and light of wit is very rare in them.[43]

Noble Henry Constable was a great master in English tongue, nor had any gentleman of our nation a more pure, quick, or higher delivery of conceit; witness, among all

brilliant and disastrous career entitled *An Apology of the Earl of Essex.*
[28]"The Late E. of E. His Advice to the E. of R. in His Travels" was included in *Profitable Instructions... by the Three Much Admired, Robert, Late Earl of Essex. Sir Philip Sidney. And Secretary Davison* (1633). Bolton must have known the work in manuscript.
[29]*Of the Laws of Ecclesiastical Polity* by Richard Hooker (1554?–1600), of which the first four books appeared in 1594, the fifth in 1597, the sixth and eighth in 1648, and the seventh in 1662, is, despite the questionable authenticity of the later books, the noblest work of Anglican apologetics in the language.
[30]For Sir John Hayward's *First Part of the Life and Reign of King Henry the Fourth* (1599), see pp. 828 ff.
[31]Raleigh's *Discovery of the Large, Rich, and Beautiful Empire of Guiana* was published in 1595 to further his scheme for colonizing that country. For the preface to his *History of the World* see pp. 862 ff.
[32]Bacon's merits as a stylist had been most clearly shown in his *Essays* (1597, 1612) and *Advancement of Learning* (1605), the latter containing a notable discussion of historiography (see pp. 878 ff.).
[33]For King James' literary accomplishments see p. 683, n.3. His collected *Works* were edited by James Montagu, bishop of Winchester, in 1616.
[34]Although Bolton could endorse Edmund Spenser's *Four Hymns* (1596), the archaisms in *The Faerie Queene* and those in the works of his illustrious predecessors disqualified such writers as models of usable (*practic*) English.
[35]*Origines*, by Porcius Cato or Cato the Censor (274–149 B.C.), a history of Rome (surviving only in fragments) that exemplified the moral austerity and simplicity of the early Romans.
[36]*Carmen Marciana* ("the song of Marcius"), oracular utterances of a supposed early Roman seer whose crude hexameters were cited admiringly by Livy (XXV. 12).
[37]Respectively an early Roman tragedian (d. 132 B.C.), an epic poet (fl. third century B.C.), and an ancient legal code drawn up about 450 B.C.
[38]George Chapman (1559?–1634) published his famous translation of the *Iliad* in septenary couplets between 1598 and 1611. See p. 11.
[39]*Contained. . . aflat*: included some rather uninteresting material.
[40]Bolton is perhaps alluding to *The Civil Wars* (pp. 28 ff.), a long poem (in *ottava rima*) on 15th-century English history that Samuel Daniel (1562–1619) published between 1595 and 1609. This work prompted Ben Jonson's famous remark that Daniel was "a good, honest man . . . but no poet" (694).
[41]*England's Heroical Epistles* by Michael Drayton (1563–1631)—a series of versified letters between such famous lovers as Henry II and Rosamond, Edward IV and Jane Shore, *et al.*—began to appear in 1597.
[42]Although George Puttenham (d. 1590) probably wrote his graceful and accomplished (*artificial*) treatise on English poetry in the late 1560's, it was not revised and published (anonymously) until 1589. In Book III ("Of Ornament"), Chapter xx, the author quotes a "ditty of Her Majesty's own making" to illustrate the rhetorical figure *exargasia* ("the gorgeous").
[43]*St. Peter's Complaint* (1595)—a long narrative and meditative poem about Christ's passion and Peter's remorse that appeared in the same year as Robert Southwell's death as a Jesuit martyr—was so popular that it was reprinted (with additions) thirteen times by 1638.

other, that sonnet of his before his Majesty's *Lepanto*.[44] I have not seen much of Sir Edward Dyer's poetry.[45] Among the lesser late poets George Gascoigne's works may be endured.[46] But the best of those times—if *Albion's England*[47] be not preferred—for our business is *The Mirror of Magistrates*, and in that *Mirror* Sackville's "Induction," the work of Thomas, afterward earl of Dorset and Lord Treasurer of England, whose also the famous tragedy of *Gorboduc* was the best of that time, even in Sir Philip Sidney's judgment, and all skillful Englishmen cannot but ascribe as much thereto for his phrase and eloquence therein.[48] But before in age, if not also in noble, courtly, and lustrous English, is that of the *Songs and Sonnets* of Henry Howard, earl of Surrey (son of that victorious prince, the duke of Norfolk, and father of that learned Howard, his most lively image, Henry, earl of Northampton) written chiefly by him and by Sir Thomas Wyatt, not the dangerous commotioner but his worthy father. Nevertheless they who most commend those poems and exercises of honorable wit, if they have seen that incomparable earl of Surrey his English translation of Vergil's *Aeneids*, which for a book or two he admirably rendereth almost line for line, will bear me witness that those other were foils and sportives.[49]

The English poems of Sir Walter Raleigh, of John Donne, of Hugh Holland, but especially of Sir Fulke Greville in his matchless *Mustapha* are not easily to be mended.[50] I dare not presume to speak of His Majesty's exercises in this heroic kind because I see them all left out in that edition which Montagu, Lord Bishop of Winchester, hath given us of his royal writings.[51] But if I should declare mine own rudeness rudely I should then confess that I never tasted English more to my liking, nor more smart and put to the height of use in poetry, than in that vital, judicious, and most practicable language of Benjamin Jonson's poems.[52]

SECTION VII

God Almighty, I hope, hath now graciously brought me to the conclusion of this high and hypercritical[53] argument, which to His glory I close up with this final admonition to myself or to whosoever else doth meditate the herculean and truly noble labor of composing an entire and compleat body of English affairs, a *corpus rerum Anglicarum*, a general history of England, to which not only the exquisite knowledge of our own matters is altogether necessary but of all other our neighbors' whatsoever, yea of all the world; for where our arms and armies have not been, our arts and navies have. Know, therefore, whosoever art in love with glory for good and heroic deserts, that in writing an history thou bearest a fourfold person, and in regard of that impersonation thou standest charged with a fourfold duty.

1. As a Christian cosmopolite to discover God's assistances, disappointments, and overruling in human affairs, as He is sensibly conversant in the actions of men; to establish the just fear of His celestial majesty against atheists and voluptuaries for the general good of mankind and the world.

2. As a Christian patriot to disclose the causes and authors of thy country's good or evil, to establish thereby the lawful liberty of nations.

3. As a Christian subject to observe to thy reader the benefit of obedience and damage of rebellions, to establish thereby the regular authority of monarchs and people's safety.

[44]Like Bolton himself, as well as several writers mentioned in this section, Henry Constable (1562–1613) was a Roman Catholic whose *Diana* (1592) was one of the many sonnet sequences inspired by the posthumous appearance of Sir Philip Sidney's *Astrophil and Stella* (1591). His fulsome sonnet prefixed to James I's *Poetical Exercise at Vacant Hours* (1591) begins thus:

> Where others, hooded with blind love, do fly
> Low on the ground with buzzard Cupid's wings,
> A heavenly love from love of love thee brings,
> And makes thy Muse to mount above the sky.

[45]Sir Edward Dyer (d. 1607) was a courtier and minor poet whose friends included Sidney and Fulke Greville.

[46]George Gascoigne (1525?–77), one of the most productive writers of his time in both prose and verse, published prose fiction and masques as well as his *Posies* (1575) and *The Steel Glass* (1576), a long verse-satire.

[47]*Albion's England*, a versified history of England by William Warner (1558?–1609), went through many editions and expansions after it appeared in 1586.

[48]*A Mirror for Magistrates* (1559 ff.), one of the most popular and influential works of the later sixteeth century, was a series of exemplary "tragedies" (in rime royal) on such notable unfortunates as Richard II, Thomas of Woodstock, *et al.* The "Induction" to the tragedy of Henry, duke of Buckingham, which has been called the greatest English poem between Chaucer and Spenser, was contributed to the second (1563) edition by Thomas Sackville (1536–1608), later earl of Dorset and Baron Buckhurst, and co-author (with Thomas Norton) of *Gorboduc* (acted 1561). If only it had observed the unities of time and place, said Sir Philip Sidney in *The Defence of Poesy* (1595), *Gorboduc* could serve "as an exact model of all tragedies."

[49]The two chief contributors to *Songs and Sonnets* (1557)—a collection of early Tudor verse commonly called *Tottel's Miscellany* after its compiler and publisher—were as notable for their political activity as for their poetry. Henry Howard (1517–47), the so-called earl of Surrey and a scion of one of the great families of Tudor England, was the son of the third duke of Norfolk (1473–1554), an immensely powerful figure at the court of Henry VIII, and the father of the first earl of Northampton (1540–1614), who was equally influential under James I. Surrey himself was executed, when only thirty, on a flimsy charge of treasonable ambition. His blank verse translation of the *Aeneid*, Books II and IV—to which his other works, says Bolton, were but a trifling backdrop (*foils and sportives*)—was published in 1554. His elder contemporary Sir Thomas Wyatt (1503?–42) had a busy if rather jagged career as a diplomat, in the course of which he wrote or translated the songs, sonnets, psalms, and satires that make him the most interesting poet of his generation. His son, also Sir Thomas (1521?–54), was a political malcontent (*commotioner*) who was executed for high treason following his abortive attempt to block the marriage of Queen Mary and Philip of Spain.

[50]Raleigh's poems, most of which were unpublished in his lifetime, have been brought together by Agnes Latham (1951); for Donne see pp. 56 ff.; Hugh Holland (d. 1633), a convert to Romanism and author of *Pancharis* (1603), was a member of the coterie around Ben Jonson at the Mermaid Tavern who contributed a prefatory sonnet to Shakespeare's first Folio (1623); Fulke Greville's closet-drama *Mustapha* appeared in 1609.   [51]See n.33 above.

[52]See pp. 86 ff.   [53]Minutely critical.

4. As a Christian *paterfamilias*[54] so to order thy studies that thou neglect not thy private,[55] because the public hath few real friends, and labors of this noble nature are fitter to get renown than riches, which they will need, not amplify.

SECTION VIII

Of such writings thou needest not feign with Dio,[56] the consul of Rome, any promise in vision that thy name and praise shall be immortal by means of them. For they will outlast the nations themselves whose acts in competent style they memorize.[57] And of such works the late earl of Essex under the letters "A.B." (for fame[58] gives it him) in an epistle before the translated Tacitus of his friend Sir Henry Savile it is as probably pronounced for true as if an oracle had uttered it: "that there is no treasure so much enriches the mind of man as learning, there is no learning so proper for the direction of the life of man as history, there is no history so well worth reading"—I say not with him—"as Tacitus," but as that of thine whosoever.[59]

Deo gloria et honor[60]

[54]"Head of a family." [55]Personal concerns, self-interest.
[56]Dio (or Dion) Cassius (d. after 230), Roman statesman who wrote (in Greek) a history of Rome in eighty volumes, only parts of which survive. [57]Memorialize. [58]Rumor. Text *Fames*.
[59]The preface by "A.B." in Sir Henry Savile's translation of Tacitus (see p. 894, n.16) is also attributed to Essex by Jonson in the *Conversations with Drummond* (*Ben Jonson*, ed. C. H. Herford and Percy Simpson, I, 1925, 142).
[60]"Glory and honor be to God."

Degory Wheare [1573-1647]

Wheare was not a great historian—indeed, he was a mere professor—but his once famous lectures on historiography deserve to be retrieved because they neatly summarized the received opinion of his time and transmitted it to later generations. He thought he knew what history was ("the register and explication of particular affairs") and he was certain of its function (to preserve the memory of events so that we may thereby be instructed); and since he was widely read in all the proper texts, from Herodotus to Speed and Raleigh, he was able to assess and classify the various kinds of records, both sacred and profane, and adjudicate the merits of their authors. As his translator said in 1685, Wheare was so systematic, well informed, and lucid in his explanations that his work was "the best, in its kind, that ever was yet printed."

A Cornishman who once had held a fellowship at Exeter College, Oxford (1603–8) and then stayed on for many years at Gloucester Hall, Wheare had a sort of greatness thrust upon him in October 1622 when he was named by William Camden to the chair of modern history which that great man had newly founded. *De ratione et methodo legendi historias dissertatio*, Wheare's inaugural lecture on 12 July 1623, at once established his credentials. It was printed, with a proper dedication to the donor of the chair, later in that year and again in 1625; and because by 1637 these editions had been "many years since sold off, and yet most eagerly sought after by many," Wheare reworked his lectures for the "younger students" and published them as *Relectiones hyemales* ("wintry reperusals"). This book was twice reissued, with "additions" and corrections by one Nicholas Horsman (1662–84), and in 1685 Edmund Bohun produced an English version based mainly, it would seem, upon the third (1637) edition but including Horsman's contributions. The treatise had in fact become so standard that it enjoyed the status of a text at Cambridge until the early eighteenth century.

In 1626, three years after he first gave his famous lecture, Wheare was named principal of Gloucester Hall, where he had long maintained his residence. According to Anthony Wood, the foundation prospered greatly under his administration, but he, like other men, was not without detractors: "he was esteemed by some a learned and genteel man, and by others a Calvinist." Although it was his "great calamity," said the translator of his book, to live in times of trouble and confusion, yet God was pleased to let him depart in peace before the execrable murther of his sovereign, and before the rebels had purged that University of whatever was loyal and constant.

After his death in 1647 his family fell on evil times, Wood reported cryptically, "and whether the females lived honestly, 'tis not for me to dispute it."

My text is based on *The Method and Order of Reading Both Civil and Ecclesiastical Histories . . . To which is Added, An Appendix . . . By Nicholas Horseman. Made English, and Enlarged, By Edmund Bohun, Esq.,* 1685 (Wing W-1592). Wheare himself has received but scant attention from modern scholars, but the Camden professorship that he held has been investigated by William H. Allison (*American Historical Review,* XXVII, 1922) and H. Stuart Jones (*Oxoniensia,* VIII-IX, 1943–44).

from De ratione et methodo legendi historias dissertatio (1623) *as translated by Edmund Bohun in* The Method and Order of Reading Both Civil and Ecclesiastical Histories (1685)

THE PREFACE TO THE READER [BY EDMUND BOHUN]

The great number both of Greek and Latin historians which have, within the course of a few years, been most accurately and elegantly turned into English by persons of great learning and of, perhaps, as flourishing styles as any age has produced may justly seem to claim a piece of the same nature with that I here present the reader with, which, though it has been attempted by several in Latin, has not, to my knowledge, been done by any one pen in English.

And indeed, till that great number of excellent versions[1] had made way for it, it would have been of no use, for those who could have then read the authors, are here mentioned, would not have needed a translation of this, and the rest would only have been tantalized by it, and a mighty thirst have been raised without any possibility of satisfying it in any tolerable degree.

But now that so many of these excellent historians have been taught so rarely well to speak our language, which is now too become so copious, elegant, and smooth that it is capable of expressing all the treasures and beauties, and almost all the idioms and varieties, of those too rich and valued languages, what greater service can be done to our English nobility and gentry than to show them how to marshal these authors into their proper places in ranks and files to extend or enlarge the history of any age or people, as any man's leisure or curiosity leads or invites him?

And as to those historians which have not yet been published in our language, the very representing them here

with all their beauties and rare perfections may perhaps work upon some of our great men and invite them to give encouragement to learned men to translate them too, till our language become as rich in books as it is in words and polite expressions; and as this will increase at once their knowledge and delight, so it will contribute to their glories too, not only in this age and nation but in following times and neighbor countries, who will value our tongue according to the number of those excellent pieces they find in it. At least I am persuaded nothing else has perpetuated to this day the Greek and Latin tongues (now no nation speaks either of them) but the great variety of excellent books which were originally written in or translated into those two tongues. And I am confident the French tongue is at this day as much esteemed for the sake of their delicate versions as for any of their original pieces. . . .

[Following a heavily ironical attack on those "morose gentlemen of the world who, having at the price of many a sore lashment possessed themselves of the Greek and Latin tongues, would now very fain monopolize all the learning in them" and consequently deprecate all translations as an

DE RATIONE [1]Among the many Renaissance translations of classical historians were Sir Thomas North's Plutarch (1579), Arthur Golding's Pompeius Trogus (1564), Caesar (1565), and Pomponius Mela (1585), B[arnabe?] R[ich?]'s Herodotus (1584), Sir Henry Savile's Tacitus (1591), Philemon Holland's Livy (1600) and Suetonius (1606), Thomas Heywood's Sallust (1608), and Thomas Hobbes' Thucydides (1629).

["invasion of their privileges," Bohun proceeds to describe and assess the work at hand.]

Having premised[2] this short apology for versions in general, I come in the next place to that piece I here present the reader with, which I take to be the best, in its kind, that ever was yet printed, because the author has not only furnished the reader with an exact series and method of reading all the Greek and Latin historians, whether civil or ecclesiastical, in their proper order and places (which has, in part, been done by Vossius,[3] Lipsius,[4] and some others), but has also taken a great deal of pains to invite the reader to peruse them too.

First, by giving short but very beautiful schemes or plans of all their several works, which is the most winning way of engaging a reader to undertake that task, such plans being a kind of pictures or landscapes to show the reader what pleasing objects he may expect to meet with if he have the courage to proceed. And if the reader please but to peruse the eighth section of the first part, where he gives an account of Herodotus his history,[5] he will then be able to judge for himself without taking my word for it.

Secondly, by informing his reader where every history begins and where it ends, which has been done by few others, and by nobody with more exactness. This too is a great invitation to a reader to know in what age of the world he is and how far his author will conduct him, before he reads one word in him.

Thirdly, he has acquainted his reader with how much remains now extant, and how much is lost, of any history which hath not come down perfect and entire to us, as very few of the more ancient have done.

Fourthly, he has told us when each historian wrote or lived, of what country and interest he was, which are things of great use as to the advancing or abating the credit of any writer.

Fifthly, he has represented the styles, characters, virtues, and vices of each historian, which are notices of the greatest use and advantage to a reader that is possible, and of the greatest pleasure and delight.

Lastly, he has not given us his own thoughts in all these only, but has taken the pains to search out and transcribe the very words and censures of the more ancient and latter critics of greatest fame and reputation, which was a work of great labor and difficulty. . . .

As to the version, I have done the best I could to make it true and smooth, which was not so easy as at first I thought it would have been, by reason of the great number of quotations out of other authors, many of which are so very short and dark in their expressions that I could scarce, if at all, tell how to find English words that would represent their notions truly. And besides this, it is uneasy for a man to accommodate himself so suddenly to such a variety of styles as here occur in almost every page, and therefore it is not improbable I may have committed many errors and mistakes.

I have also presumed in some places to make additions too when I thought it necessary, but then I have given the reader notice of them, that he may know what is added, and what is the author's.

THE ANTELOGIUM, OR THE INTRODUCTORY ORATION, MADE BY THE AUTHOR THE SEVENTEENTH OF OCTOBER, 1635 . . .

It is now about ten years and some months, if my calculation deceive me not, most honorable academics, since I made some discourses in this very place, in the presence of a great assembly, concerning the order and method of reading histories.[6] Whereupon some of my then hearers prevailed upon me by their importunity so far as to publish from the press, and bring into the light, those meditations, such as they were. Of late some of my learned friends have solicited me with the same vigor and irresistible earnestness that I would bring these lectures the second time to the anvil, and still insist, urge, and inculcate these reasons for it, that they may surmount my reluctance. The former impression is many years since sold off, and yet most eagerly sought after by many, that therefore a new edition would be very acceptable, and very useful too, to the younger students without doubt. And there are some also of my present hearers whom I have heard wish, very passionately, that I would read again upon that subject, and afterwards, if I thought fit, communicate my lectures to the learned and publish them to the world. At length I yielded to the desires of both, as far as I am capable, though at the same time I cannot with the same facility satisfy my own private humor by it, and much less my judgment. My design, then, is (with the favorable assistance of God) to represent to you, my hearers, those former meditations, with additions and amendments in some places, in my next lectures, and that so carefully improved and corrected as none of you may justly retort upon me the satirist's proverb,

Occidit miseros crambe repetita magistros.

The oft repeated crambe kills the wretched master.[7]

. . . Things standing thus, my hearers, what hinderance remains that we may not cheerfully prepare ourselves for the designed work, which, having thus bespoke your affections, we will begin forthwith in the next lecture, and

---

[2]Stated by way of introduction.

[3]Gerhard Johannes Vossius or Voss (1577–1649), Dutch scholar and theologian whose *De historicis Graecis* (1623–24) was followed by *De historicis Latinis* (1626).

[4]Justus Lipsius or Joest Lips (1547–1606), Flemish scholar noted for his translations of Tacitus, Seneca, and others.

[5]Wheare's discussion of Herodotus, which as Bohun says is a good example of his *method*, is reprinted below, pp. 901 f.

[6]*It is...histories*: Following his appointment (October 1622) to the Oxford chair of modern history recently founded by William Camden, Wheare gave his inaugural lecture a year later as *De ratione et methodo legendi historias*. Promptly printed with a dedication to Camden, it reached a third edition in 1637, and after the Restoration was reprinted (with additions) in 1662 and 1684. Bohun translated from the 1637 edition (*Relectiones hyemales de ratione et methodo legendi historias civiles et ecclesiasticas*).

[7]Decimus Junius Juvenalis (60?–?140), *Satires*, VII.154. *Crambe*: cabbage.

in the meantime, lest whilst we are to discourse concerning the order and method of reading histories we should break the rules of method, if our younger hearers (for whose sake this task is undertaken) be not told what histories we mean, we think it now worth our while to premise first the definition and then the division of histories, and then briefly to explain them, that by this means we may open a more clear passage to the bringing our designed undertaking to its end. The definition, then, which we formerly made, and which I will still stand by, is this: history is the register and explication of particular affairs, undertaken to the end that the memory of them may be preserved, and so universals may be the more evidently confirmed by which we may be instructed how to live well and happily. I say first, then, that it is a register and explication because we are to discourse of it as it may be read, so that recording and explaining are the genus; for the object or matter I put particular affairs, that is, public or private actions worthy of the memory of men. I assign a manifold end that the memory of particular actions may be preserved and also that out of particulars general precepts may be deduced and confirmed; and lastly that by these we may be the more instructed how to live well and happily, for this was the reason why M. Tully[8] styled history the "mistress of life," and to this relate those excellent words of Livy in the preface to his history: "this is the most healthful and profitable attendant of the knowledge of history, that you may contemplate the instructions of variety of examples united in one illustrious monument, and from thence take out such things as are useful to thee or to thy country, and that thou mayst wisely consider that what has an ill beginning will have an ill end, and so avoid it."[9]

According to this our definition we subjoin our divisions, which are not subtle and exquisite (for such would be of no use here) but popular and common. I know that history has been divided both by the ancients and some of the modern writers into divine (which treats of God and divine things), natural (which treats of naturals[10] and their causes), and human history (which relates the actions of man as living in society); and our definition has respect only to the latter; and this again we subdivide into political or civil and ecclesiastical history, and again both these into general and particular histories.[11] The political or civil history is that which explains the rise or beginning, constitutions, increases, changes, and affairs of empires, commonwealths, and cities. Ecclesiastical history is that which principally describes the affairs of the church, though at the same time the transactions of monarchs and kingdoms are also inserted. Universal —either civil or ecclesiastical history—is that which contains the actions of all or at least many, and those the most considerable, commonwealths or churches for many ages; the particular history is that which comprehends the affairs of any one people, city, or commonwealth, or of one particular church.

This our method is intended to describe the distinct and regular way of reading all these in their due order. There is another division of history which offers itself to our consideration and is especially worth the observation of youths,

which is taken from the circumstances and modes of relating or explaining things: as of histories some are called chronicles, which are those that chiefly take notice of the times in which actions are done; others are called lives, which describe the persons of particular men, and their actions and manners; others are called relations or narratives, whose chief business is to relate faithfully and clearly the memorable actions of particular men or any particular affairs of communities. As to the first of these heads, all histories do, or at least ought to, note the times in which actions happen, for every relation is obscure, and like a fable without the addition of the time in which it falls; and yet all do not observe the same intervals of time nor keep the same order in relating, and this produces variety of chronicles, from whence has sprung the various denominations of annals, fasts, ephemerides or diaries, menologies, bimestrias, trimestrias, semestrias, decades, and centuries,[12] of all which we have largely discoursed in our preliminaries of history.

PART THE FIRST

SECTION VI
How the Reading of History Is to Be Begun. Good Epitomes Not to Be Condemned . . .

Wherefore if any man desires to run over with advantage the history of these monarchies or empires,[13] and in them the history of the world, I would advise him to begin with some short compendium, chronology, or synopsis before he enter that vast ocean, because he may by that means learn at once the series of times and ages, the successions of empires, and the greatest changes which have happened amongst mankind; and so he may, if he please, draw in his mind an exemplar or idea of the whole body of the universal history, which he may contemplate with ease, as it were, at once. . . . . [Having run through, and commended, an imposing list of universal historians from Herodotus to Johannes Sleidanus (who died in 1556), Wheare suggests that] after these some of the modern writers may be read, amongst which Sir Walter Raleigh,[14] our countryman, deserves the first place, a man of great fame, and for his great both valor and prudence worthy of a better fate. He has built up an universal history from the creation of the world to the fall of the Macedonian, or third, monarchy out of the most approved authors, which is written in English with very great judgment

---

[8]Marcus Tullius Cicero (106–43 B.C.), whose definition of history (*De oratore*, II.ix.36), part of which Wheare quotes, was a favorite text of Renaissance historiographers. See p. 828 for a more extended citation of the same famous passage.

[9]"*This . . . avoid it*": Titus Livius (59 B.C.–A.D. 17), *Annals*, I.10.

[10]Natural things or actions.

[11]For Bacon's similar analysis see pp. 878 ff.

[12]Various ways of recording events chronologically (by years, regular religious observances, days, months, two- or three- or six-month intervals, decades, and centuries).

[13]The Assyrian, Persian, Greek, and Roman empires whose rise and fall were thought to be prophesied by Daniel (7.4ff.) in a text often cited and embellished by Renaissance historians.

[14]See pp. 860 ff.

in a perspicuous method and an elegant and masculine style. And the incomparable Gerardus Joannes Vossius some years since began an universal history of all the foregoing ages and nations; I heartily wish, my hearers, that I may once see that noble work and enjoy it with you. For what can be expected from so great a treasure of antiquity and history but what is most excellent, and above the reach of the wits not only of this but of many of the better ages?

But, however, let the history of the Bible lead the way, which is incontestably not only the most ancient but the truest of all histories, and to this tends the grave reprehension of Carolus Sigonius[15] of the common way of instituting or entering upon the study of antiquity:

> In laying the foundations of the knowledge of ancient times and things, as also in the beginning of almost all other studies, I know not how we are carried away with the impetuous torrent of an ill custom, and generally commit a very great error by beginning with those monuments[16] in which the acute Grecians, who were totally ignorant of the truth, have comprehended their traditions of the false gods and the fictitious actions of their feigned heroes, which we can neither make any good use of nor improve ourselves thereby in the least in piety; when, if there were any sense, that I may not say prudence, in us, we ought rather to begin with what is contained in the holy writings of the Hebrews. For if we search for the origin of things we can begin no higher than the creation of the world and the formation of man, which is there treated of. If we seek truth, there is nowhere so much of it as here, where it is proclaimed by the mouth of the living God. If we seek grave things, what is more magnificent than these illustrious monuments in which the holy commands of God, the saving promises, the certain oracles, and other helps to our salvation are comprehended? From whence can we derive more excellent examples of virtue, or sharper detestations of vices, or actions worthy of memory than from these monuments of the Hebrews? In which only is apparently discovered how much mankind has been relieved by the powerful and present assistance of God Almighty in the exercise of true religion, or in the neglect of it have been trodden down and ruined by His anger.

SECTION XVIII

Where Herodotus Began His History,
and Where He Ended It. . .

Herodotus, the father of the heathen history, begins where the prophetic history[17] ends, which is owing to the goodness and providence of God, that, as it were, in the selfsame moment where the history of the Bible concludes, Herodotus Halicarnassensis should begin his. For when the prophets of the Holy Scriptures had related what seemed more worthy of the care of the Holy Ghost from the beginning of the world to Cyrus, Herodotus, beginning with Gyges, King of Lydia, contemporary with Hezekias and Manasseh, kings of Judah, about the year of the world 3238, about 150 years before Cyrus his reign in Persia, immediately descends to Cyrus the Great, founder of the Medio-Persian empire, and so deduceth[18] the history of the Medes and Persians in a smooth style, which flows like a quiet and pleasant river (as Cicero in his *Orator*[19] expresses it well) to

the time of the wretched flight of Xerxes out of Greece. Which happened in the second year of the seventy-fifth Olympiad, in the year of the world 3471, in which time Herodotus flourished, and lived to the beginning of the Peloponnesian war. . . .[20]

He has contained in nine books, which he distinguished by the names of the nine Muses, a continued history of 234 years. Will you have the contents of his several books? I will give you them shortly. In his first book, besides what he relates of Gyges and the succeeding kings of Lydia to Croesus, of the ancient Jonia, of the manners of the Persians, Babylonians, and some others, he gives an elegant account of the birth of Cyrus, the author of the Medio-Persian monarchy, and then of his miraculous preservation, of his education and actions. In his second book he describes all Egypt to the life, declares the customs of the Egyptians, and commemorates the succession of their kings. In his third book he weaves the history of Cambyses and of Smerdis the Mage, which simulated[21] Cyrus and so reigned seven months, and explicates the fraud and the discovery. Then he subjoins the election of Darius Hystaspis, and then enumerates the provinces of the Persian empire, and gives an account of the taking of Babylon by the faithful industry of Zopyrus, in the praises of whom he ends it. In his fourth book he presents us with an exact description of Scythia, to which he adds the unfortunate expedition of Darius against the Scythians, and there we read the history of the Mynians, and the city of Cyrene[22] built by them in Libya, and the description of the people of those countries. The fifth book contains the Persian embassy to Amyntas, King of Macedonia, and also the just punishment of Sisamnes,[23]

[15]Carlo Sigonio (1524–84), eminent Italian humanist whose many works include histories of Roman law (1560), of the Athenian republic (1564), and of the kingdom of Italy (1580), as well as an uncompleted history of the Christian church undertaken at the request of Pope Gregory XIII. [16]Records.

[17]The so-called sacred history as recorded by the Hebrew prophets and by certain uncanonical writers like Flavius Josephus (37–?100).

[18]Traces [19]*Orator*, Sect. 39.

[20]Since Wheare, like most of his contemporaries, based his chronology on the doctrine of creation *ex nihilo* (on which see Raleigh, pp. 871 f.), he dates all events from the moment of creation, which was generally computed as about 4000 B.C. In his compendious view the prophetic history, from the creation until the reign of Cyrus the Great (550–529 B.C.), leads smoothly into—and indeed slightly overlaps—the history of Herodotus, which begins about where the other stops. On the ancient system of reckoning time by *Olympiads* see p. 819, n.30.

[21]Impersonated. Gaumata, a Magian priest known as "the False Smerdis" because he usurped (552 B.C.) the throne of Persia after the murder of Smerdis, younger son of Cyrus the Great, was quickly exposed and killed by Darius.

[22]City in North Africa founded by Greeks about 630 B.C.

[23]According to Herodotus (V.25), when Sisamnes, a royal judge, was detected taking a bribe, Cambyses "slew and flayed Sisamnes, and cutting his skin into strips, stretched them across the seat of the throne whereon he had sat when he heard cases. Having so done, Cambyses appointed the son of Sisamnes to be judge in his father's place, and bade him never forget in what way his seat was cushioned."

an unjust judge; the sedition of Aristagoras the Milesian, and his end; and then he shows what was the state of the cities of Athens, Lacedemonium, and Corinth in the time of Darius Hystaspis. The sixth book describes the ruin of the seditious Histiaeus,[24] and then shows the origin of the kings of Sparta, and the preparations of war made by Darius against the Grecians, and the fight at Marathon in which Miltiades bravely defeated the Persians. The seventh contains a most excellent consultation concerning the war with Greece held by Xerxes, and then represents his famous expedition into Greece, and the battle of Thermopilas.[25] The eighth describes the sea fight at the island of Salamine.[26] The ninth, besides the punishment of one Lycidas,[27] gives an account of two great battles fought in one day: the one at Plateas[28] in the dawn of the morning and the other at Mycalen,[29] a promontory of Asia, in the evening, in both which the Persians were beaten and at last totally expelled out of Greece.

And in these nine books you will find, besides the history of the Medes and Persians, the histories also of the Lydians, Ionians, Lycians, Egyptians, Mynians, Grecians, and Macedonians, and of some other nations. Their manners and religions are also intermixed, and delivered with that purity, elegance, and sweetness of style that the Muses were by the ancient feigned to have spoken by the mouth of Herodotus, and for this cause the names of the Muses were put before these books, not by the author but by some other persons, as some think. . . .[30]

Though Herodotus inserts some narratives that are not much unlike fables, yet the body of his history is compiled with a rare fidelity and a diligent care of truth. Concerning his other narratives, he for the most part premiseth that he recites them not because he thought them true, but as he had received them from others. "I ought," saith he, "to unfold in my history what I have heard from others, but there is not the same necessity I should believe all relations alike, which I desire the reader would once for all take notice of, and remember throughout my history."[31] And we may enlarge and confirm the history of these times of which Herodotus writ by reading the second, third, and seventh books of Justin,[32] and by reading the lives of those famous generals Aristides, Themistocles, Cimon, Miltiades, and Pausanias, written both by Plutarch and Cornelius Nepos;[33] and to these may be added the lives of the philosophers of those times written by Laertius,[34] viz. Anaximander, Zenon,[35] Empedocles, Heraclitus, Democritus, and others of that age.

SECTION XXVII

A Transition to the British History: How the Reader Ought to Prepare Himself for the Reading of It; in What Order He Shall Go On . . .

But that we may not be thought wholly ignorant and negligent of our own history whilst we search into that of other nations, it is convenient to give some account of the British writers, and to annex it by way of supplement to the former catalogue, and to point out at the same time in what order they are to be read; for I have no small confidence I shall thereby more oblige our university youth than by the

other, that is, by showing a more certain and shorter way to the knowledge of our British history, as you see I have already done in relation to the universal history; for who is there that doth not esteem it a shameful thing to be thought a stranger in his own city, a foreigner in his own country? As for me, what M. Cicero said once of the Latin poets to the Romans I should with much greater confidence apply to Englishmen as to the histories of Britain: "none can seem learned to me who is ignorant of what is our own."[36]

In truth, to search out the great actions of other countries and in the mean time despise our own is a certain sign either of a most lazy inactivity or of a soft and unmanly delicacy; for though that which Sir Henry Savile,[37] the great and eternally to be remembered ornament of our university, saith is most certainly true, and confirmed not only by his but by the testimony also of Mr. John Selden, the lawyer, a man not only excellently versed in history but in all sorts of

[24]Histiaeus (d. 494 B.C.), a tyrant of Miletus under Darius who, dispatched to suppress a rebellion in Ionia, established himself in power at Byzantium and was subsequently captured and crucified.
[25]Thermopylae, mountain pass in eastern Greece where the Greeks and their allies under Leonidas of Sparta checked the invading Persians in 480 B.C. Although the pass was held, Leonidas and all his forces were destroyed.
[26]Salamis, island off the western coast of Attica, scene of the famous naval battle in which the Greeks defeated the Persian fleet of Xerxes in 480 B.C.
[27]Herodotus tells (IX.5) that when the Athenian counselor Lycidas advised his countrymen to accept the insulting peace proposals of the Persian general Mardonius, the Greeks "were full of wrath, and forthwith surrounded Lycidas, and stoned him to death."
[28]Plataea, Boeotian city where the Greeks under Pausanias decisively defeated the Persians in 479 B.C., thus assuring the independence of their country.
[29]Mycale, promontory in southern Ionia, scene of a notable Greek victory over the Persians in 479 B.C.
[30]In marginal glosses Wheare supplies the name of the Muse (Clio, Euterpe, Thalia, etc.) traditionally assigned to each of Herodotus' nine books.
[31]Wheare's marginal gloss to this passage (VII.152) reads: "I heartily wish we might once have a good version of Herodotus, which though in French was never yet made English." Although one "B. R."—perhaps Barnabe Rich—had published his version of the first two books of Herodotus in 1584, the first scholarly (and still the standard) translation was George Rawlinson's in 1858.
[32]Marcus Junianus Justinus, 3d-century historian who composed an epitome of a lost history by Gnaeus Pompeius Trogus.
[33]Notable Grecian leaders in the Persian wars whose careers were treated by Plutarch (46?–?120) in his *Parallel Lives* and by Cornelius Nepos (fl. 1st cent. B.C.) in his *Vitae excellentium imperatorum*.
[34]Diogenes Laertius, 2d-century Greek scholar whose gossipy *Lives of the Philosophers* contains accounts of the early thinkers mentioned by Wheare.
[35]Zeno, founder of the Stoic school of philosophy.
[36]*De finibus bonorum et malorum*, I.5.
[37]English classical scholar (1549–1622) who translated four books of Tacitus (1591), assisted in the preparation of the King James version of the Bible, and edited the works of St. Chrysostum (1610–13). A long-time (1585–1622) warden of Merton College, Oxford, he died in the year of Wheare's appointment to the Camden professorship. See p. 894, n.16.

ancient learning, that "there was never yet any man who hath written an entire body of our history with that fidelity and dignity as became the greatness of the subject," yet the former of these confesseth that we have some particular parts of our history which are not ill written in former ages, and the latter (Mr. Selden) acknowledgeth and commendeth some others[38] as written exceedingly well in this last age. But be this as it will, I shall with the greatest confidence assert that there are many noble actions, and things that are worthy of our contemplation and observation, which will never occur in the reading of the greatest part of our histories. This, then, is the order which I should recommend for the reading of our British history to the studious in it.

First, let our student begin with the famous Sir William Camden's *Britannia*,[39] in which, besides a most accurate description of the whole island, he will find briefly represented the history of the first inhabitants and an account given of the origin of the name, the manners of the Britons, the history of the Romans in Britain, and many other things infinitely worth our knowledge, collected not out "of mere fictions and fables, which none but a vain man would write, nor any but an ignorant man believe" (as he expresseth himself), but out of the most sincere and uncorrupted monuments of antiquity. My advice, therefore, is that this book, or rather treasury, should in the very first place be most diligently perused, nor will it be amiss here to call in the assistance of Mr. Selden's two books of collections[40] of the antiquities of the Britons and English, either of which books consists of eight chapters in which he has collected what doth most properly belong to the ancient civil administration of that part of Great Britain which is now called England, and in which he has most excellently described both from ancient and modern writers our public transactions both civil and sacred, and our state catastrophes to William the Conqueror. And then, according to the method proposed by us in the beginning of our course of history, the reader may be pleased to read over George Lily's *Chronicle*[41] (or short enumeration) of the kings and princes who by the changes of fortune in diverse and succeeding times have been possessed of the empire of Britain, or those commentaries which J. Theodorus Clain[42] printed of the affairs of Great Britain in the year 1603 under the title of *A Compendium of the British History*, which is elegantly formed and written.

SECTION XXXI

. . . *John Speed His* Theater of the British Empire . . .

[Following a survey and assessment of English historians, from the "monkish" chronicles of William of Malmesbury and Geoffrey of Monmouth in the twelfth century to Bacon's life of Henry VII (which appeared in 1622), Wheare ends with hearty praise of John Speed's recent work in English history.]

But now, if any of our countrymen who are desirous to read the history of England be so delicate that he thinks it a task of too much labor and trouble to undertake the reading of so many authors, and therefore would rather choose from one historian who may serve instead of all the rest, and stick

to and pursue him alone, he must remember, as I said before, that there is no such Latin historian extant who hath well described the affairs of Britain from its first inhabiting to our times; but yet there are some who, in English, have commendably attempted to do this. Amongst whom I shall not fear to commend in the first place that famous man John Speed.[43] He, having traveled over all Great Britain, read diligently all our own historians and those of our neighbor nations, together with a diligent search in the public offices, rolls, monuments, and ancient writings or charters, built up a splendid and admired *Theater of the British Empire* which, with great expedition and labor, he perfected in fourteen years in ten scenes or books in this order: In his first scene he hath most excellently represented the image of this kingdom with its distinct counties and principal cities and towns. In his second he exhibits all the provinces of Wales. In the third he gives a description of the whole kingdom of Scotland. In the fourth he shows the kingdom of Ireland and all the several parts of it. Nor has he only proposed to our view the naked images and bare maps—though he has done that too with great exactness and beauty—in these four first scenes, but he hath also, by short narratives adjoined to his maps, discovered whatever in each part is memorable and worthy to be seen or taken notice of. If from thence the reader turns his eyes upon the fifth scene he will see the situation and greatness of the British Islands: the ancient names, first inhabitants, manners, polities,[44] with the most ancient kings and governors. When he comes to the sixth scene he will find there the successions and actions of those monarchs and presidents[45] who flourished during the times in which the Romans were masters of Britain. In the seventh scene the author doth express the history of the Saxon and English monarchs and the times of their reigns. In the eighth scene he commemorates the origin of the Danes, their expeditions and incursions into England, and all their actions here which are worth the taking notice of. In the ninth he describes the invasion of the Normans, their conquest, and the history of William the Conqueror and all his successors. And lastly, in the tenth scene, he hath contained the joyful entrance of James the First, the most happy union of the two kingdoms, and the peace established by King James with all the neighbor kings and princes. And then, as a corollary, the venerable author doth, with a vivid and unaffected style

[38]The works of William Camden and Francis Bacon. See the present editor's *Race of Time* (1967), p. 77. [39]See pp. 816 ff.
[40]*Analecton Anglo-Britannicon* (1615), an attempt to summarize the history of the inhabitants of the British Isles down to the Norman invasion.
[41]*Anglorum regum chronices epitome*, an account (later extended) of English monarchs through 1547 by George Lily (d. 1559), Roman Catholic divine and author of various historical and genealogical works. George was the son of William Lily, highmaster of St. Paul's School (1512–22) and author of a famous Latin grammar used by generations of Tudor schoolboys.
[42]Johann Theodor Clain, author of *Historia Britannica . . . quibus accesserunt praeter Angliae descriptionem marginalia et index* (1603).
[43]See pp. 841 ff. [44]Administrations, governments.
[45]Appointed governors or lieutenants of a province.

which runs through his whole work, most clearly show that horrible, black, and never before heard-of design of the Gunpowder Plot,[46] which was by God miraculously discovered and prevented.

[46]Abortive plot by a group of disaffected Roman Catholics to blow up the Houses of Parliament on 5 November 1605 and thus destroy the king, Lords, and Commons assembled there. The discovery of the plot and the capture of the conspirators were often cited as a sign of God's providential care of England.

Thomas Hobbes[1]   [1588-1679]

from Eight Books of the Peloponnesian War (1629)

To the Readers

Though this translation have already passed the censure of some whose judgments I very much esteem, yet because there is something—I know not what—in the censure of a multitude more terrible than any single judgment, how severe or exact soever, I have thought it discretion in all men that have to do with so many, and to me in my want of perfection necessary, to bespeak your candor. Which that I may upon the better reason hope for, I am willing to acquaint you briefly upon what grounds I undertook this work at first, and have since by publishing it put myself upon the hazard of your censure with so small hope of glory as from a thing of this nature can be expected. For I know that mere translations have in them this property, that they may much disgrace if not well done, but if well, not much commend the doer.

It hath been noted by divers that Homer in poesy, Aristotle in philosophy, Demosthenes in eloquence, and others of the ancients in other knowledge do still maintain their primacy, none of them exceeded, some not approached by any in these later ages. And in the number of these is justly ranked also our Thucydides, a workman no less perfect in his work than any of the former, and in whom (I believe with many others) the faculty of writing history is at the highest. For the principal and proper work of history being to instruct and enable men, by the knowledge of actions past, to bear themselves prudently in the present and providently towards the future, there is not extant any other (merely human) that doth more fully and naturally perform it than this of my author. It is true that there be many excellent and profitable histories written since, and in some of them there be inserted very wise discourses both of manners and policy. But being discourses inserted, and not of the contexture of the narration, they indeed commend the knowledge of the writer but not the history itself, the nature whereof is merely narrative. In others there be subtle conjectures at the secret aims and inward cogitations of such as fall under their pen, which is also none of the least virtues in a history where the conjecture is throughly[1] grounded, not forced to serve the purpose of the writer in adorning his style or manifesting

his subtlety in conjecturing. But these conjectures cannot often be certain unless withal so evident that the narration itself may be sufficient to suggest the same also to the reader. But Thucydides is one who, though he never digress to read a lecture, moral or political, upon his own text, nor enter into men's hearts further than the actions themselves evidently guide him, is yet accounted the most politic[2] historiographer that ever writ. The reason whereof I take to be this: he filleth his narrations with that choice of matter, and ordereth them with that judgment, and with such perspicuity and efficacy expresseth himself, that, as Plutarch saith,[3] he maketh his auditor a spectator. For he setteth his reader in the assemblies of the people and in the senates at their debating, in the streets at their seditions, and in the field at their battles. So that look how much[4] a man of understanding might have added to his experience if he had then lived a beholder of their proceedings and familiar with the men and business of the time, so much almost may he profit now by attentive reading of the same here written. He may from the narrations draw out lessons to himself, and of himself be able to trace the drifts and counsails of the actors to their seat. . . .

⎡ Pointing out that earlier versions in Latin, Italian, French, and very faulty English (by Thomas Nichols "in the time of King Edward the Sixth")[5] mainly reproduced and multiplied each other's errors, Hobbes asserts that Thucydides had hitherto been not translated but traduced. ⎤

Hereupon I resolved to take him immediately from the Greek according to the edition of Aemilius Porta,[6] not re-

[1]For a commentary on Hobbes and for other excerpts from his work, see Philosophy and Speculation, pp. 491 ff., and Books and Men, pp. 784 ff.
EIGHT BOOKS [1]Thoroughly. [2]Sagacious.
[3]"Were the Athenians More Famous in War or in Wisdom," *Moralia*, Sect. 347. [4]However much.
[5]Thomas Nichols, a goldsmith, translated Thucydides from the French version by Claude de Seyssel (1527) as *The History Written by Thucydides the Athenian* in 1550. It was the only English translation before Hobbes'.
[6]Aemilius Portus (1550–1610), Italian scholar and professor of

fusing or neglecting any version, comment, or other help I could come by, knowing that when with diligence and leisure I should have done it, though some error might remain, yet they would be errors but of one descent; of which nevertheless I can discover none, and hope they be not many. After I had finished it, it lay long by me,[7] and other reasons taking place, my desire to communicate it ceased. . . .

[Finally, however, Hobbes decided to publish his translation, to which end he had provided such editorial apparatus as maps and glosses.] With these maps and those few brief notes in the margin upon such passages as I thought most required them, I supposed the history might be read with very much benefit by all men of good judgment and education (for whom also it was intended from the beginning by Thucydides), and have therefore at length made my labor public, not without hope to have it accepted. Which if I obtain, though no otherwise than in virtue of the author's excellent matter, it is sufficient.

T. H.

OF THE LIFE AND HISTORY OF THUCYDIDES

. . . For his opinion touching the government of the state, it is manifest that he least of all liked the democracy. And upon divers occasions he noteth the emulation and contention of the demagogues for reputation and glory of wit with their crossing of each other's counsels to the damage of the public; the inconstancy of resolutions caused by the diversity of ends and power of rhetoric in the orators; and the desperate actions undertaken upon the flattering advice of such as desired to attain or to hold what they had attained of authority and sway amongst the common people. Nor doth it appear that he magnifieth anywhere the authority of the few, amongst whom he saith everyone desireth to be chief, and they that are undervalued bear it with less patience than in a democracy, whereupon sedition followeth, and dissolution of the government. He praiseth the government of Athens when it was mixed of the few and the many, but more he commendeth it both when Pisistratus[8] reigned (saving that it was an usurped power) and when, in the beginning of this war,[9] it was democratical in name but in effect monarchical under Pericles.[10] So that it seemeth that as he was of regal descent,[11] so he best approved of the regal government. It is therefore no marvel if he meddled as little as he could in the business of the commonwealth, but gave himself rather to the observation and recording of what was done by those that had the managing thereof. Which also he was no less prompt, diligent, and faithful by the disposition of his mind than by his fortune, dignity, and wisdom able to accomplish. How he was disposed to a work of this nature may be understood by this, that when, being a young man, he heard Herodotus[12] the historiographer reciting his history in public (for such was the fashion both of that and many ages after), he felt so great a sting of emulation that it drew tears from him, insomuch as Herodotus himself took notice how violently his mind was set on letters, and told his father Olorus. When the Peloponnesian war began to break out he conjectured truly that it would prove an argument[13] worthy his labor, and no sooner it began than he began his history; pursuing the same not in that perfect manner in which we see it now but by way of commentary, or plain register of the actions and passages thereof, as from time to time they fell out and came to his knowledge. But such a commentary it was as might perhaps deserve to be preferred before a history written by another. For it is very probable that the eighth book is left the same it was when he first writ it, neither beautified with orations nor so well cemented at the transitions as the former seven books are. And though he began to write as soon as ever the war was on foot, yet began he not to perfect and polish his history till after he was banished.[14] . . .

Now for his writings, two things are to be considered in them: truth and elocution. For in truth consisteth the soul and in elocution the body of history. The latter without the former is but a picture of history, and the former without the latter unapt to instruct. But let us see how our author hath acquitted himself in both. For the faith of this history, I shall have the less to say in respect that no man hath ever yet called it into question. Nor indeed could any man justly doubt of the truth of that writer in whom they had nothing at all to suspect of those things that could have caused him either voluntarily to lie or ignorantly to deliver an untruth. He overtasked not himself by undertaking an history of things done long before his time, and of which he was not able to inform himself. He was a man that had as much means, in regard both of his dignity and wealth, to find the truth of what he relateth as was needful for a man to have. He used as much diligence in search of the truth (noting everything whilst it was fresh in memory, and laying out his wealth upon intelligence)[15] as was possible for a man to use. He affected least of any man the acclamations of popular

---

Greek at Heidelberg, who edited and supplied Latin translations for Thucydides (1594), Euripides, Aristotle's *Rhetoric*, Xenophon, and others. His important Greek-Latin dictionary appeared in 1603.
[7]Hobbes' translation was undertaken following his graduation from Oxford in 1608, when he became tutor and traveling companion to William Cavendish, later second earl of Devonshire.
[8]Tyrant of Athens (d. 527 B.C.) whose power was built upon his popularity with the lower classes.
[9]The Peloponnesian War (431–404 B.C.) between Sparta and Athens, the subject of Thucydides' history.
[10]Athenian statesman and leader of the democratic faction, who died in 429 B.C., early in the Peloponnesian War. Thucydides' report (II.35 ff.) of his funeral oration on the Athenians who had fallen in the war—a majestic tribute to Athens and indeed to Hellenism—is one of the enduring splendors of historiography.
[11]Thucydides' father was a man of great wealth and his mother allegedly a descendant of Miltiades, the conqueror of Marathon, and Hegesipyle, daughter of a Thracian king.
[12]Modern scholars have rejected the ancient legend that Thucydides as a boy was moved to tears of emulation on hearing Herodotus, the great fifth-century historian of the Persian wars, read from his work at the Olympic games.   [13]Theme, subject.
[14]Following the failure of an expedition that he led in the Peloponnesian war, Thucydides went into exile—perhaps voluntarily—from 423 to 403, during which time he wrote his famous history.
[15]Information.

auditories, and wrote not his history to win present applause, as was the use of that age, but for a monument to instruct the ages to come. . . . In sum, if the truth of a history did ever appear by the manner of relating, it doth so in this history, so coherent, perspicuous, and persuasive is the whole narration and every part thereof.

In the elocution also two things are considerable: disposition (or method) and style. Of the disposition here used by Thucydides it will be sufficient in this place briefly to observe only this: that in his first book, first he hath by way of exordium derived the state of Greece from the cradle to the vigorous stature it then was at when he began to write; and next declared the causes, both real and pretended, of the war he was to write of. In the rest, in which he handleth the war itself, he followeth distinctly and purely the order of time throughout, relating what came to pass from year to year, and subdividing each year into a summer and winter. The grounds and motives of every action he setteth down before the action itself, either narratively or else contriveth them into the form of deliberative orations[16] in the persons of such as from time to time bare sway in the commonwealth. After the actions, when there is just occasion he giveth his judgment of them, showing by what means the success came either to be furthered or hindered. Digresssions for instruction's cause and other such open conveyances of precepts (which is the philosopher's part) he never useth, as having so clearly set before men's eyes the ways and events of good and evil counsels that the narration itself doth secretly instruct the reader, and more effectually than possibly can be done by precept.

For his style, I refer it to the judgment of divers ancient and competent judges. [Hobbes then canvasses, at considerable length, the big body of ancient and modern commentary on Thucydides.] Lucian in his book entitled "How a History Ought To Be Written" doth continually exemplify the virtues which he requires in an historiographer by Thucydides. And if a man consider well that whole discourse of his he shall plainly perceive that the image of this present history, preconceived in Lucian's mind, suggested unto him all the precepts he there delivereth. Lastly, hear the most true and proper commendation of him from Justus Lipsius in his notes to his book *De doctrina civili*,[17] in these words: "Thucydides, who hath written not many nor very great matters, hath perhaps yet won the garland from all that have written of matters both many and great. Everywhere for elocution grave, short and thick with sense, sound in his judgments, everywhere secretly instructing and directing a man's life and actions. In his orations and excursions almost divine. Whom the oftener you read, the more you shall carry away, yet never be dismissed without appetite. Next to him is Polybius,[18] etc." And thus much concerning the life and history of Thucydides.

[16]Interpolated speeches (of persuasion or dissuasion) that are perhaps the most notable stylistic feature of Thucydides' history. The other two types of orations recognized by classical rhetoricians are the demonstrative (whose function is to praise or blame) and the judicial (whose function is to accuse or defend).
[17]*Politicorum sive civilis doctrinae libri sex* (1589) by the eminent Flemish scholar Joest Lips or Justus Lipsius (1547–1606), noted mainly for his editions of Tacitus and Seneca. The work from which Hobbes quotes, which went through many editions in various languages, was translated in English by W. Jones as *Six Books of Politics or Civil Doctrine* (1594).
[18]Greek historian (205?–125 B.C.) whose history of Rome and nearby countries in forty books is extant only in part.

from Behemoth, the History of the Causes of the Civil Wars of England (1682)

PART I[1]

A. If in time, as in place, there were degrees of high and low, I verily believe that the highest of time would be that which passed between 1640 and 1660. For he that thence, as from the devil's mountain,[2] should have looked upon the world and observed the actions of men, especially in England, might have had a prospect of all kinds of injustice and of all kinds of folly that the world could afford, and how they were produced by their hypocrisy and self-conceit, whereof the one is double iniquity and the other double folly.

B. I should be glad to behold that prospect. You that have lived in that time and in that part of your age, wherein men used to see best into good and evil, I pray you to set me (that

BEHEMOTH [1]*Behemoth* consists of four dialogues between *A* (an elderly man who has lived through the civil wars) and his young friend *B* (who seeks to be informed about the causes and the progress of that cataclysm). In the dedication (to Sir Henry Bennet, baron of Arlington) prefixed to a scribal manuscript now in the library of St. John's College, Oxford, Hobbes explains that the first dialogue concerns "certain opinions in divinity and politics" which were the "seeds" of the conflict. "The second," he continues, "hath the growth of it in declarations, remonstrances, and other writings between the king and Parliament published. The last two are a very short epitome of the war itself, drawn out of Mr. Heath's chronicle" (i.e., James Heath's assertively royalist *Brief Chronicle of the Late Intestine War*, which appeared in 1663). Variants between this scribal copy and the *Tracts* of 1682 are supplied by Fendinand Tönnies in his edition of *Behemoth* (1969).
[2]Presumably an allusion to the "exceedingly high mountain" from

could not see so well) upon the same mountain, by the relation of the actions you then saw, and of their causes, pretensions, justice, order, artifice, and event.[3]

A. In the year 1640 the government of England was monarchical; and the king that reigned, Charles, the first of that name, holding the sovereignty by right of a descent continued above six hundred years, and from a much longer descent king of Scotland, and from the time of his ancestor[4] Henry II, king of Ireland;[5] a man that wanted[6] no virtue, either of body or mind, nor endeavoured anything more [10] than to discharge his duty towards God in the well governing of his subjects.

B. How could he then miscarry, having in every county so many trained soldiers as would, put together, have made an army of 60,000 men, and divers magazines of ammunition in places fortified?

A. If those soldiers had been, as they and all other of his subjects ought to have been, at His Majesty's command, the peace and happiness of the three kingdoms[7] had continued as it was left by King James. But the people were [20] corrupted generally, and disobedient persons esteemed the best patriots.

B. But sure there were men enough, besides those that were ill-affected, to have made an army sufficient to have kept the people from uniting into a body able to oppose him.

A. Truly, I think, if the king had had money, he might have had soldiers enough in England. For there were very few of the common people that cared much for either of the causes, but would have taken any side for pay or plunder. [30] But the king's treasury was very low, and his enemies, that pretended the people's ease from taxes, and other specious things, had the command of the purses of the City of London, and of most cities and corporate towns in England, and of many particular persons besides.

B. But how came the people to be so corrupted? And what kind of people were they that did so seduce them?

A. The seducers were of divers sorts. One sort were ministers; ministers, as they called themselves, of Christ; and sometimes, in their sermons to the people, God's ambas- [40] sadors; pretending to have a right from God to govern every one his parish and their assembly the whole nation.

Secondly, there were a very great number, though not comparable to the other, which, notwithstanding that the pope's power in England, both temporal and ecclesiastical, had been by act of Parliament abolished,[8] did still retain a belief that we ought to be governed by the pope, whom they pretended to be the vicar of Christ, and, in the right of Christ, to be the governor of all Christian people. And these were known by the name of papists, as the ministers [50] I mentioned before were commonly called Presbyterians.

Thirdly, there were not a few who in the beginning of the troubles were not discovered, but shortly after declared themselves for a liberty in religion, and those of different opinions one from another. Some of them, because they would have all congregations free and independent upon one another, were called Independents. Others that held baptism to infants, and such as understood not into what

they are baptized, to be ineffectual, were called therefore Anabaptists. Others that held that Christ's kingdom was at this time to begin upon the earth, were called Fifth Monarchy men;[9] besides divers other sects, as Quakers, Adamites,[10] &c., whose names and peculiar doctrines I do not well remember. And these were the enemies which arose against His Majesty from the private interpretation of the Scripture, exposed to every man's scanning in his mother tongue.

Fourthly, there were an exceeding great number of men of the better sort that had been so educated as that in their youth having read the books written by famous men of the ancient Grecian and Roman commonwealths concerning their polity and great actions, in which books the popular government was extolled by that glorious name of liberty and monarchy disgraced by the name of tyranny, they became thereby in love with their forms of government. And out of these men were chosen the greatest part of the House of Commons, or if they were not the greatest part, yet, by advantage of their eloquence, were always able to sway the rest.

Fifthly, the city of London and other great towns of trade, having in admiration the great prosperity of the Low Countries after they had revolted from their monarch, the king of Spain, were inclined to think that the like change of government here would to them produce the like prosperity.[11]

Sixthly, there were a very great number that had either wasted their fortunes, or thought them too mean for the good parts[12] they thought were in themselves; and more there were that had able bodies but saw no means how honestly to get their bread. These longed for a war, and hoped to maintain themselves hereafter by the lucky choosing of a party to side with, and consequently did for the most part serve under them that had greatest plenty of money.

---

whose peak Satan showed Jesus "all the kingdoms of the world, and the glory of them" (Matthew 4.8). [3]Outcome.
[4]Text *ancestors.*
[5]Charles I, king of England (1625–49), inherited the throne of Scotland from his father James I of England (1603–25) and VI of Scotland (1567–1625) and his title to the throne of Ireland from Henry II (1154–89), on whom the English Pope Adrain IV had bestowed it in 1154. [6]Lacked.
[7]England, Scotland, and Ireland.
[8]*Pope's power...abolished*: Papal power in England had finally been destroyed by the Act of Supremacy that Henry VIII's so-called "Reformation Parliament" (1529–36) passed in 1535.
[9]A fanatical English sect whose members thought that the Assyrian, Persian, Greco-Macedonian, and Roman empires prophesied in Daniel 2 would be succeeded by the thousand-year reign of Christ on earth. Their abortive uprisings in 1657 and 1661 were easily suppressed.
[10]Members of a fanatical sect who allegedly practiced nudity in their religious rites.
[11]The long revolt of the Netherlands against their Hapsburg rulers (1568–1648) led to the establishment of the Republic of the United Provinces, which enjoyed great financial power in the 17th century.
[12]Native capabilities.

Lastly, the people in general were so ignorant of their duty as that not one perhaps of ten thousand knew what right any man had to command him, or what necessity there was of king or commonwealth for which he was to part with his money against his will; but thought himself to be so much master of whatsoever he possessed that it could not be taken from him upon any pretence of common safety without his own consent. King, they thought, was but a title of the highest honor, which gentleman, knight, baron, earl, duke were but steps to ascend to with the help of riches; and had no rule of equity but precedents and custom; and he was thought wisest and fittest to be chosen for a Parliament that was most averse to the granting of subsidies or other public payments.

B. In such a constitution of people, methinks, the King is already outed of his government, so as they needed[13] not have taken arms for it. For I cannot imagine how the King should come by any means to resist them.

A. There was indeed very great difficulty in the business. But of that point you will be better informed in the pursuit of this narration. . . .

> Following a discussion of the papacy's long and unsuccessful attempt to retain its power in England, the talk turns to the rise of a more recent and more formidable threat from the Presbyterians.

A. This controversy between the Papist and the Reformed Churches could not choose but make every man, to the best of his power, examine by the Scriptures which of them was in the right; and to that end they were translated into vulgar tongues, whereas before, the translation of them was not allowed, nor any man to read them but such as had express license so to do. For the pope did concerning the Scriptures the same that Moses did concerning Mount Sinai. Moses suffered no man to go up to it to hear God speak or gaze upon him but such as he himself took with him; and the pope suffered none to speak with God in the Scriptures that had not some part of the pope's spirit in him, for which he might be trusted.

B. Certainly Moses did therein very wisely, and according to God's own commandment.[14]

A. No doubt of it, and the event itself hath made it since appear so. For after the Bible was translated into English, every man, nay, every boy and wench, that could read English thought they spoke with God Almighty, and understood what He said, when by a certain number of chapters a day they had read the Scriptures once or twice over. The reverence and obedience due to the reformed church here, and to the bishops and pastors therein, was cast off; and every man became a judge of religion, and an interpreter of the Scriptures to himself.

B. Did not the Church of England intend it should be so? What other end could they have in recommending the Bible to me if they did not mean I should make it the rule of my actions? Else they might have kept it, though open to themselves, to me sealed up in Hebrew, Greek, and Latin, and fed me out of it in such measure as had been requisite for the salvation of my soul and the church's peace.

A. I confess this licence of interpreting the Scripture was the cause of so many several sects, as having lain hid till the beginning of the late king's reign, and did then appear to the disturbance of the commonwealth. But to return to the story. Those persons that fled for religion in the time of Queen Mary,[15] resided, for the most part, in places where the reformed religion was professed and governed by an assembly of ministers; who also were not a little made use of (for want of better statesmen), in points of civil government. Which pleased so much the English and Scotch Protestants that lived amongst them that at their return they wished there were the same honor and reverence given to the ministry in their own countries. In Scotland (King James being then young) soon (with the help of some of the powerful nobility) they brought it to pass. Also they that returned into England in the beginning of the reign of Queen Elizabeth endeavored the same here, but could never effect it till this last rebellion, nor without the help of the Scots. And it was no sooner effected but they were defeated again by the other sects, which, by the preaching of the Presbyterians and private interpretation of Scripture, were grown numerous.

B. I know indeed that in the beginning of the late war the power of the Presbyterians was so very great that not only the citizens of London were almost all of them at their devotion, but also the greatest part of all other cities and market towns of England. But you have not yet told me by what art and what degrees they became so strong.

A. It was not their own art alone that did it, but they had the concurrence of a great many gentlemen that did no less desire a popular government in the civil state than these ministers did in the church. And as these did in the pulpit draw the people to their opinions and to a dislike of the church-government, canons, and Common Prayer Book, so did the other make them in love with democracy by their harangues in the Parliament, and by their discourses and communication with people in the country, continually extolling of liberty and inveighing against tyranny, leaving the people to collect of themselves[16] that this tyranny was the present government of the state. And as the Presbyterians brought with them into their churches their divinity from the universities, so did many of the gentlemen bring their politics from thence into the Parliament, but neither of them did this very boldly during the time of Queen Elizabeth. And though it be not likely that all of them did it out of malice, but many of them out of error, yet certainly the chief leaders were ambitious ministers and ambitious gentlemen; the ministers envying the authority of bishops, whom they thought less learned, and the gentlemen envying the Privy Council whom they thought less wise than themselves. For 'tis a hard matter for men who do all think highly of their own wits, when they have also acquired the learning

---

[13]Text *need.*   [14]Exodus 19.12.

[15]The persecutions of the intensely Catholic Mary (1553–58) drove many English Protestants to the Continent. The return of these "democratical" Marian exiles at Elizabeth's accession in 1558 was, in Hobbes' view, the beginning of the troubles that eventuated in civil war almost a century later.   [16]Infer.

of the university, to be persuaded that they want any ability requisite for the government of a commonwealth, especially having read the glorious histories and the sententious politics of the ancient popular governments of the Greeks and Romans, amongst whom kings were hated and branded with the name of tyrants, and popular government (though no tyrant was ever so cruel as a popular assembly) passed by the name of liberty. The Presbyterian ministers, in the beginning of the reign of Queen Elizabeth, did not (because they durst not) publicly preach against the discipline of the church. But not long after, by the favor perhaps of some great courtier, they went abroad preaching in most of the market towns of England, as the preaching friars had former-ly done, upon working-days in the morning; in which sermons these and others of the same tenets, that had charge of souls, both by the manner and matter of their preaching applied themselves wholly to the winning of the people to a liking of their doctrines and good opinion of their persons.

And first for the manner of their preaching, they so framed their countenance and gesture at their entrance into the pulpit, and their pronunciation both in their prayer and sermon, and used the Scripture phrase (whether understood by the people or not) as that no tragedian in the world could have acted the part of a right godly man better than these did; insomuch as a man unacquainted with such art could never suspect any ambitious plot in them to raise sedition against the state (as they then had designed) or doubt that the vehemence of their voice (for the same words with the usual pronunciation had been of little force) and forcedness of their gesture and looks could arise from any-thing else but zeal to the service of God. And by this art they came into such credit that numbers of men used to go forth of their own parishes and towns on workingdays, leaving their calling, and on Sundays leaving their own churches, to hear them preach in other places, and to despise their own and all other preachers that acted not so well as they. And as for those ministers that did not usually preach, but in-stead of sermons did read to the people such homilies[17] as the church had appointed, they esteemed and called them *dumb dogs.*

Secondly, for the matter of their sermons, because the anger of the people in the late Roman usurpation was then fresh, they saw there could be nothing more gracious with them than to preach against such other points of the Romish religion as the bishops had not yet condemned, that so receding further from popery than they did, they might with glory to themselves leave a suspicion on the bishops as men not yet well purged from idolatry.

Thirdly, before their sermons, their prayer was or seemed to be *extempore,* which they pretended to be dictated by the Spirit of God within them, and many of the people believed or seemed to believe it. For any man might see, that had judgment, that they did not take care beforehand what they should say in their prayers. And from hence came a dislike of the Common Prayer Book, which is a set form, premeditated, that men might see to what they were to say *Amen.*

Fourthly, they did never in their sermons, or but lightly, inveigh against the lucrative vices of men of trade or handi-craft, such as are feigning, lying, cozening, hypocrisy, or other uncharitableness, except want of charity to their pastors and to the faithful: which was a great ease to the generality of citizens and the inhabitants of market towns, and no little profit to themselves.

Fifthly, by preaching up an opinion that men were to be assured of their salvation by the testimony of their own private spirit, meaning the Holy Ghost dwelling within them. And from this opinion the people that found in themselves a sufficient hatred towards the papists, and an ability to repeat the sermons of these men at their coming home, made no doubt but that they had all that was neces-sary, how fraudulently and spitefully soever they behaved themselves to their neighbours that were not reckoned amongst the saints, and sometimes to those also.

Sixthly, they did, indeed, with great earnestness and severity, inveigh often against two sins, carnal lusts and vain swearing, which, without question, was very well done. But the common people were thereby inclined to believe that nothing else was sin but that which was forbidden in the third and seventh commandments[18] (for few men do understand by the name of lust any other concupiscence than that which is forbidden in that seventh commandment, for men are not ordinarily said to lust after another man's cattle, or other goods or possessions): and therefore never made much scruple of the acts of fraud and malice, but endeavored to keep themselves from uncleanness only, or at least from the scandal of it. And whereas they did, both in their sermons and writings, maintain and inculcate that the very first motions of the mind, that is to say, the delight men and women took in the sight of one another's form, though they checked the proceeding thereof so that it never grew up to be a design,[19] was nevertheless a sin, they brought young men into desperation and to think themselves damned because they could not (which no man can, and is contrary to the constitution of nature) behold a delightful object without delight. And by this means they became confessors to such as were thus troubled in conscience, and were obeyed by them as their spiritual doctors in all cases of conscience.

B. Yet divers of them did preach frequently against oppression.

A. It is true, I had forgot that; but it was before such as were free enough from it; I mean the common people, who would easily believe themselves oppressed, but never op-pressors. And therefore you may reckon this among their artifices, to make the people believe they were oppressed by the king, or perhaps by the bishops, or both; and incline the meaner sort to their party afterwards, when there should be occasion. But this was but sparingly done in the time of

[17]The sermons written for the books of homilies that were pub-lished by the government in 1547 and 1563 and appointed to be read annually in all Anglican churches were intensely disliked by Puritans, whose worship required extemporary preaching.
[18]The commandments prohibiting violation of the sabbath and adultery (Exodus 20.8, 14).
[19]*Grew. . . design:* expressed itself in open sexuality.

Queen Elizabeth, whose fear and jealousy they were afraid of. Nor had they as yet any great power in the Parliament House whereby to call in question her prerogative by petitions of right and other devices, as they did afterwards, when democratical gentlemen had received them into their counsels for the design of changing the government from monarchical to popular, which they called liberty.

B. Who would think that such horrible designs as these could so easily and so long remain covered with the cloak of godliness? For that they were most impious hypocrites is manifest enough by the war their proceedings ended in, and by the impious acts in that war committed. But when began first to appear in Parliament the attempt of popular government, and by whom?

A. As to the time of attempting the change of government from monarchical to democratical, we must distinguish. They did not challenge the sovereignty in plain terms, and by that name, till they had slain the king; nor the rights thereof altogether by particular heads till the king was driven from London by tumults raised in that city against him, and retired for the security of his person to York;[20] where he had not been many days, when they sent unto him nineteen propositions, whereof above a dozen were demands of several powers, essential parts of the power sovereign.[21] But before that time they had demanded some of them in a petition which they called a Petition of Right;[22] which nevertheless the king had granted them in a former Parliament, though he deprived himself thereby not only of the power to levy money without their consent, but also of his ordinary revenue by custom of tonnage and poundage, and of the liberty to put into custody such men as he thought likely to disturb the peace and raise sedition in the kingdom. As for the men that did this, it is enough to say they were members of the last Parliament, and of some other Parliaments in the beginning of King Charles and the end of King James his reign; to name them all is not necessary, further than the story[23] shall require. Most of them were members of the House of Commons; some few also, of the Lords; but all such as had a great opinion of their sufficiency in politics, which they thought was not sufficiently taken notice of by the king.

B. How could the Parliament, when the king had a great navy, and a great number of trained soldiers, and all the magazines of ammunition in his power, be able to begin the war?

A. The king had these things indeed in his right; but that signifies little when they that had the custody of the navy and magazines, and with them all the trained soldiers, and in a manner all his subjects, were by the preaching of Presbyterian ministers and the seditious whisperings of false and ignorant politicians made his enemies; and when the king could have no money but what the Parliament should give him, which you may be sure should not be enough to maintain his regal power, which they intended to take from him. And yet, I think, they never would have ventured into the field but for that unlucky business of imposing upon the Scots, who were all Presbyterians, our Book of Common Prayer. For I believe the English would never have taken well that the Parliament should make war

upon the king, upon any provocation, unless it were in their own defence, in case the king should first make war upon them; and therefore it behoved them to provoke the king, that he might do something that might look like hostility.

It happened in the year 1637[24] that the King, by the advice, as it was thought, of the archbishop of Canterbury, sent down a Book of Common Prayer into Scotland, not differing in substance from ours, nor much in words besides the putting of the word *presbyter* for that of *minister*, commanding it to be used (for conformity with this kingdom) by the ministers there for an ordinary form of divine service. This being read in the church at Edinburgh caused such a tumult there that he that read it had much ado to escape with his life; and gave occasion to the greatest part of the nobility and others to enter, by their own authority, into a covenant amongst themselves, which impudently they called a *Covenant with God*, to put down episcopacy without consulting with the king: which they presently did, animated thereto by their own confidence, or by assurance from some of the democratical Englishmen that in former Parliaments had been the greatest opposers of the king's interests, that the king would not be able to raise an army to chastise them

[20]Goaded by such parliamentary thrusts as the impeachment of the earl of Strafford and Archbishop Laud (November 1640), the abolition of the courts of Star Chamber and High Commission (July 1641), and the airing of a formidable list of grievances in the Grand Remonstrance (December 1641), on 4 January 1642 Charles invaded the House of Commons with a troop of soldiers in an abortive attempt to arrest five of its leaders. Six days later he left London for the North of England, not to return until he was brought back for his trial and execution in 1649.
[21]Parliament's submitting to the king (July 1642) nineteen propositions—including a restructuring of the Church of England and assigning to Parliament the power to appoint and dismiss all royal ministers—marked its final overture to Charles before the outbreak of hostilities in August 1642. See pp. 592 ff.
[22]In 1628 Charles had reluctantly assented to the Petition of Rights whereby were prohibited all forms of taxation without consent of Parliament, the billeting of soldiers in private houses, imprisonment of citizens on unspecified charges, etc.   [23]History.
[24]Although the events that Hobbes here glances at are treated elsewhere in this book more fully (pp. 609 ff., 915 ff., 929 ff.) a summary might be useful. Charles' attempt to impose the Anglican Prayer Book on the Scottish Presbyterians led to disturbances in Edinburgh (July 1637) that led in turn to the promulgation of the Solemn League and Covenant (February 1638) for the defense of reformed religion (or, as Hobbes says bitterly, for the suppression of episcopacy "without consulting the king"). Stung to action, in 1639 Charles led an army as far as Berwick, where after a bloodless confrontation with the Scots he signed a "pacification" providing for further deliberations on the devisive issue of conformity. When these deliberations by the Scottish Parliament and clerical assembly at Edinburgh merely stiffened their resistance, Charles, despite the failure of the so-called Short Parliament (13 April–5 May 1640) to vote money until its grievances were settled, resolved on war again. After the abortive Second Bishops' War proved to be a military humiliation and a financial disaster for the king he at last convened the famous Long Parliament (November 1640–March 1660) that pushed through a series of reforms, waged and won a war against the king himself, and brought him to the block in 1649.

without° calling a Parliament which would be sure to favor them. For the thing which those democraticals chiefly then aimed at was to force the king to call a Parliament, which he had not done for[25] ten years before, as having found no help, but hindrance to his designs in the Parliaments he had formerly called. Howsoever, contrary to their expectation, by the help of his better-affected subjects of the nobility and gentry he made a shift to raise a sufficient army to have reduced the Scots to their former obedience if it had proceeded to battle. And with this army he marched himself into Scot- 10 land, where the Scotch army was also brought into the field against him, as if they meant to fight. But then the Scotch sent to the king for leave to treat by commissioners on both sides; and the king, willing to avoid the destruction of his own subjects, condescended to it. The issue[26] was peace; and the king thereupon went to Edinburgh, and passed an Act of Parliament there to their satisfaction.

B. Did he not then confirm episcopacy?

A. No, but yielded to the abolishing of it, but by this means the English were crossed in their hope of a Parlia- 20 ment. But the said democraticals, formerly opposers of the king's interest, ceased not to endeavor still to put the two nations into a war to the end the king might buy the Parliament's help at no less a price than sovereignty itself.

B. But what was the cause that the gentry and nobility of Scotland were so averse from the episcopacy? For I can hardly believe that their consciences were extraordinarily tender, nor that they were so very great divines, as to know what was the true church-discipline established by our Saviour and his apostles, nor yet so much in love with 30 their ministers as to be overruled by them in the government either ecclesiastical or civil. For in their lives they were just as other men are, pursuers of their own interests and preferments, wherein they were not more opposed by the bishops than by their Presbyterian ministers.

A. Truly I do not know; I cannot enter into other men's thoughts farther than I am led by the consideration of human nature in general. But upon this consideration I see, first, that men of ancient wealth and nobility are not apt to brook that poor scholars should (as they must when 40 they are made bishops) be their fellows. Secondly, that from the emulation of glory between the nations they might be willing to see this nation afflicted by civil war, and might hope, by aiding the rebels here, to acquire some power over the English, at least so far as to establish here the Presbyterian discipline; which was also one of the points they afterwards openly demanded. Lastly, they might hope for, in the war, some great sum of money as a reward of their assistance. besides great booty, which they afterwards obtained. But whatsoever was the cause of their 50 hatred to bishops, the pulling of them down was not all they aimed at: if it had, now that episcopacy was abolished by act of Parliament, they would have rested satisfied, which they did not. For after the king was returned to London, the English Presbyterians and democraticals, by whose favor they had put down bishops in Scotland, thought it reason to have the assistance of the Scotch for the pulling down of bishops in England. And in order thereunto they might perhaps deal with the Scots secretly, to rest unsatisfied

with that pacification which they were before contented with. Howsoever it was, not long after the king was returned to London they sent up to some of their friends at court a certain paper containing, as they pretended, the articles of the said pacification; a false and scandalous paper, which was by the king's command burnt, as I have heard, publicly. And so both parties returned to the same condition they were in, when the king went down with his army.

B. And so there was a great deal of money cast away to no purpose. . . .

PART III

⌈ Tracing the events of 1648, Hobbes shows how Cromwell and the army, having seized control of Parliament, pushed on inexorably to Charles' execution. His account of this great drama may be compared with that of Clarendon (pp. 933 ff.) and Marvell (pp. 365 f.). ⌉

. . . At the same time, with the like violence, they took the king from Newport in the Isle of Wight to Hurst Castle till things were ready for his trial.[27] The Parliament in the meantime (to avoid perjury) by an ordinance declared void the oaths of supremacy and allegiance, and presently after made another to bring the king to his trial.

B. This is a piece of law I understood not before, that when many men swear singly, they may, when they are assembled, if they please, absolve themselves.

A. The ordinance being drawn up was brought into the House, where after three several[28] readings it was voted "that the Lords and Commons of England, assembled in Parliament, do declare that by the fundamental laws of the realm, it is treason in the king of England to levy war against the Parliament." And this vote was sent up to the Lords; and they denying their consent, the Commons in anger made another vote: "That all members of committees should proceed and act in any ordinance whether the Lords concurred or no; and that the people, under God, are the original[29] of all just power; and that the House of Commons have the supreme power of the nation; and that whatsoever the House of Commons enacteth is law." All this passed *nemine contradicente*.[30]

B. These propositions fight not only against the king of England but against all the kings of the world. It were good they thought on't. But yet, I believe that under God the original of all laws was in the people.

A. But the people, for them and their heirs, by consent and oaths, have long ago put the supreme power of the

---

[25]Text *of.* [26]Outcome.
[27]Following the decisive royalist defeat at Naseby (June 1645), the desperate Charles at last surrendered to the Scots (May 1646), who in January 1647 turned him over to the English. In June 1647 he was seized by the army (then at odds with Parliament) and lodged at Hampton Court before he himself at last took refuge on the Isle of Wight (November 1647). When the subsequent negotiations between the king and his captors collapsed, Cromwell and the army summarily expelled the Presbyterian majority in the House of Commons (December 1648) and then proceeded quickly to Charles' trial and execution (January 1649). [28]Different.
[29]Source. [30]"No one speaking in opposition."

nation into the hands of their kings, for them and their heirs; and consequently into the hands of this king, their known and lawful sovereign.[31]

B. But does not the Parliament represent the people?

A. Yes, to some purposes; as to put up petitions to the king, when they have leave, and are grieved; but not to make a grievance of the king's power. Besides, the Parliament never represents the people but when the king calls them; nor is it to be imagined that he calls a Parliament to depose himself. Put the case, every county and borough 10 should have given this Parliament for a benevolence a sum of money; and that every county, meeting in their county-court or elsewhere, and every borough in their town hall, should have chosen certain men to carry their several sums respectively to the Parliament. Had not these men represented the whole nation?

B. Yes, no doubt.

A. Do you think the Parliament would have thought it reasonable to be called to account by this representative?

B. No, sure; and yet I must confess the case is the same. 20

A. This ordinance contained, first, a summary of the charge against the king, in substance this: that not content with the encroachments of his predecessors upon the freedom of the people, he had designed to set up a tyrannical government; and to that end, had raised and maintained in the land a civil war against the Parliament, whereby the country hath been miserably wasted, the public treasure exhausted, thousands of people murdered, and infinite other mischiefs committed. Secondly, a constitution passed of a high court of justice, that is, of a certain number of com- 30 missioners, of whom any twenty had power to try the King, and to proceed to sentence according to the merit of the cause, and see it speedily executed.

The commissioners met on Saturday, January 20, in Westminster Hall, and the king was brought before them; where, sitting in a chair, he heard the charge read, but denied to plead to it either guilty or not guilty, till he should know by what lawful authority he was brought thither. The president told him that the Parliament affirmed their own authority, and the king persevered in his refusal to plead. 40

Though many words passed between him and the president, yet this was the substance of it all.

On Monday, January 22, the court met again; and then the solicitor moved that if the king persisted in denying the authority of the court, the charge might be taken *pro confesso*:[32] but the king still denied their authority.

They met again January the 23, and then the solicitor moved the court for judgment, whereupon the king was required to give his final answer, which was again a denial of their authority.

Lastly, they met again January 27, where the king desired to be heard before the Lords and Commons in the Painted Chamber, and promising after that to abide the judgment of the court. The commissioners retired for half an hour to consider of it, and then returning caused the king to be brought again to the bar, and told him that what he proposed was but another denial of the court's jurisdiction; and that if he had no more to say, they would proceed. Then the king answering that he had no more to say, the president began a long speech in justification of the Parliament's proceedings, producing the examples of many kings killed or deposed by wicked Parliaments, ancient and modern, in England, Scotland, and other parts of the world. All which he endeavored to justify from this only principle: that the people have the supreme power, and the Parliament is the people. This speech ended, the sentence of death was read; and the same upon Tuesday after, January 30, executed at the gate of his own palace of Whitehall. He that can delight in reading how villainously he was used by the soldiers between the sentence and execution may go to the chronicle itself,[33] in which he shall see what courage, patience, wisdom, and goodness was in this prince, whom in their charge the members of that wicked Parliament styled tyrant, traitor, and murderer. . . .

[31]*Sovereign*: text *heir*. The emendation is supplied by the scribal copy (with Hobbes' own corrections) now at St. John's College, Oxford.

[32]"As if admitted."

[33]James Heath's *Brief Chronicle of the Late Intestine War* (1663), for which see n.1. p. 906.

Thomas May [1595–1650]

May's diverse effect on his contemporaries may be gauged by Clarendon's praise of the man who wrote "one of the best epic poems in the English language" and (in the same paragraph) his denunciation of the turncoat who "lost his wits when he left his honesty . . . and deserves to be forgotten" (pp. 796 f.). Thomas Carew protested that May's enormous talent as a playwright made any panegyric futile; Jonson, writing as his "true friend in judgment and choice," asserted that his translation of the *Pharsalia* matched Lucan's in its art and splendor; but Marvell celebrated the death of the "malignant" poet and historian by calling him a "most servile wit and mercenary pen." The subject of this immoderate praise and blame was the product of "a worshipful but decayed family" who attended Sidney Sussex College, Cambridge (B.A. 1612), and then Gray's Inn before a mortifying speech impediment turned him from the law to literature. Although he wrote some half a dozen plays—notably the energetic *Heir* (1620), which prompted Carew's accolade—it was his knowledge of the classics that brought him into notice. His versions of Vergil's *Georgics* (1628), Martial (1629), and other works displayed his erudition, but his translation of Lucan (1626–27) secured his reputation. The king himself was so much taken by the work that May inscribed to him its *Continuation* (1630), and it was at Charles' own suggestion that May tapped the lode of English history with long narrative poems on Henry II (1633) and Edward III (1635).

Perhaps, as Aubrey said, because his work on Lucan had made him partial to republics ("which tang stuck by him") or perhaps in his resentment at losing out to Davenant for the laureateship on Jonson's death in 1637, he "fell from his duty and all his former friends" to become an ardent anti-royalist in the troubles of the forties. As a "secretary" to Parliament with lodgings in the House of Commons, he supplied his party with such works as *A Discourse Concerning the Success of Former Parliaments* (1642) and *The Character of a Right Malignant* (1644); but he said he wrote his famous *History of the Parliament of England* (1647) not as propaganda but as a "plain and naked discourse" of the events that led to civil war.

> If in this discourse more particulars are set down concerning the actions of those men who defended the Parliament than of them that warred against it, it was because my conversation gave me more light on that side; to whom as I have endeavored to give no more than what is due, so I have cast no blemishes on the other, nor bestowed any more characters than what the truth of story must require. If those that write on the other side will use the same candor, there is no fear but that posterity may receive a full information concerning the unhappy distractions of these kingdoms.

Although royalists, not unnaturally, ridiculed the "candor" that May exhibits in his *History*, Milton, who shared his politics, drew upon him heavily in his own *Eikonoklastes* (pp. 609 ff.). *A Breviary of the History of the Parliament of England* appeared in both English and Latin not long before its author's death. According to Aubrey's terse report, this event occurred untimely "after drinking with his chin tied with his cap (being fat): suffocated." By order of the Council of State May was buried in the Abbey, but at the Restoration his body was exhumed and cast into a pit in the yard of St. Margaret's Church, Westminster. Since he was not a man of action, the barbaric retribution may be regarded as a sort of tribute to the writer.

M y text is based upon *The History of the Parliament of England: Which began November the third, M.DC.XL. With a short and necessary view of some precedent years. Written by Thomas May Esquire, Secretary for the Parliament*, 1647 (Wing M-1410). Whereas the *History* was not reprinted until the nineteenth century, *Historiae Parliamenti Angliae breviarium* appeared in 1650 and 1651, and as *A Breviary of the History of the Parliament of England* in 1650, 1655, 1680, and 1689. They were edited by Francis Maseres in 1812 and 1815 respectively. The standard account of May's life and works is that by A. G. Chester (1932).

from The History of the Parliament of England (1647)

THE PREFACE

The use of history and the just rules for composure[1] of it have been so well and fully described heretofore by judicious writers that it were lost labor, and a needless extension of the present work, to insist by way of introduction upon either of them. I could rather wish my abilities were such as that the reader, to whose judgment it is left, might find those

HISTORY OF PARLIAMENT [1] Composition.

rules observed in the narration itself than told him in the preface by a vain anticipation.

I will only profess to follow that one rule, truth, to which all the rest (like the rest of moral virtues to that of justice) may be reduced, against which there are many ways, besides plain falsehood, whereby a writer may offend. Some historians, who seem to abhor direct falsehood, have notwithstanding dressed truth in such improper vestments as if they brought her forth to act the same part that falsehood would; and taught her by rhetorical disguises, partial concealments, and invective[2] expressions instead of informing to seduce a reader and carry the judgment of posterity after that bias which themselves have made. It was the opinion of a learned bishop of England, not long ago deceased, that Cardinal Baronius his *Annals*[3] did more wound the Protestant cause than the controversies of Bellarmine;[4] and it may well be true. For against the unexpected stroke of partial history the ward[5] is not so ready as against that polemic writing where hostility is professed with open face.

This fault I have endeavored to avoid, but it is my misfortune to undertake such a subject in which to avoid partiality is not very easy. But to escape the suspicion or censure of it is almost impossible for the clearest integrity that ever wrote. Others, I suppose, will handle this theme; and because that none, perchance, may perfectly please, I shall, in the behalf of all, entreat a reader that in his censure he would deal with the writings of men as with mankind itself: to call that the best which is least bad.

The subject of this work is a civil war, a war indeed as much more than civil and as full of miracle, both in the causes and effects of it, as was ever observed in any age; a war as cruel as unnatural, that has produced as much rage of swords, as much bitterness of pens both public and private as was ever known; and divided the understandings of men, as well as their affections, in so high a degree that scarce could any virtue gain due applause, any reason give satisfaction, or any relation obtain credit unless amongst men of the same side. It were therefore a presumptuous madness to think that this poor and weak discourse, which can deserve no applause from either side, should obtain from both so much as pardon, or that they should here meet in censure[6] which in nothing else have concurred. . . .

For the truth of this plain and naked discourse which is here presented to the public view, containing a brief narration of those distractions which have fallen amongst us during the sitting of this present Parliament,[7] as also some passages[8] and visible actions of the former government (whether probably conducing to these present calamities or not, of which let the reader judge), I appeal only to the memory of any Englishman whose years have been enow[9] to make him know the actions that were done, and whose conversation[10] has been enough public to let him hear the common voice and discourses of people upon those actions. To his memory, I say, do I appeal, whether such actions were not done and such judgments made upon them as are here related. In which, perchance, some readers may be put in mind of their own thoughts heretofore, which thoughts have since, like Nebuchadnezzar's dream,[11] departed from them. An English gentleman who went to travel when this Parliament was called and returned when these differences were grown among us, hearing what discourses were daily made, affirmed that the Parliament of England (in his opinion) was more misunderstood in England than at Rome; and that there was greater need to remember our own countrymen[12] than to inform strangers of what was past. "So much," said he, "have they seemed to forget the things themselves, and their own notions[13] concerning them."

But where war continues, people are enforced to make their residence in several quarters; and therefore several, according to the places where they converse, must their information be concerning the condition and state of things. From whence arises not only a variety but a great discrepancy for the most part in the writings of those who record the passages of such times. And therefore it has seldom happened but that in such times of calamity and war historians have much dissented from each other. . . .

[Although striving to be candid and objective, May explains that because his residence "hath been, during these wars, in the quarters and under the protection of the Parliament,"[14] he can report more fully of that side.]

If in this discourse more particulars are set down concerning the actions of those men who defended the Parliament than of them that warred against it, it was because my conversation gave me more light on that side; to whom as I have endeavored to give no more than what is due, so I have cast no blemishes on the other, nor bestowed any more characters than what the truth of story must require. If those that write on the other side will use the same candor, there is no fear but that posterity may receive a full information concerning the unhappy distractions of these kingdoms.

CHAPTER II

A Brief Relation of Some Grievances of the Kingdom . . .

It cannot but be thought by all wise and honest men that the sins of England were at a great height, that the injustice of governors and vices of private men were very great, which have since called down from Almighty God so sharp a

[2]Abusive.
[3]Caesar Baronius (1538–1607), ecclesiastical historian and Vatican librarian whose *Annales* (1588–1607), tracing the history of Christianity from the birth of Christ until 1198, constituted a defense of the Roman Catholic Church against its Protestant adversaries.
[4]Roberto Bellarmino (1542–1621), Jesuit cardinal and controversialist famed for his skill and erudition in theological disputation.
[5]Guard. [6]*Meet in censure*: concur in judgment (of my book).
[7]The so-called Long Parliament (1640–60). [8]Transactions.
[9]Enough. [10]Manner of life.
[11]According to Daniel 2.5, when Nebuchadnezzar, king of Babylon, had a terrifying dream, he summoned his Chaldean soothsayers to interpret it but first called upon them to recover its details, explaining that "the thing is gone from me."
[12]*Remember . . . countrymen*: recall and record for the benefit of Englishmen. [13]Text *Nations*.
[14]In January 1645 May was appointed secretary to the Parliament, a post which provided him a salary and also lodging in parliamentary quarters.

judgment, and drawn on by degrees so calamitous and consuming a war. Those particular crimes an English historian can take no pleasure to relate, but might rather desire to be silent in, and say with Statius:

Nos certe taceamus, et obruta multa
Nocte tegi nostrae patiamur crimina gentis.

Let us be silent, and from after times
Conceal our own unhappy nation's crimes.

But to be silent in that were great injustice and impiety toward God; to relate His judgments upon a kingdom and [10] forget the sins of that kingdom which were the cause of them. The heathen historians do well instruct us in that point of piety, who never almost describe any civil war or public affliction without relating at the beginning how vicious and corrupted their state was at that time grown; how faulty both the rulers and people were, and how fit to be punished either by themselves or others. Nor do any of the Roman poets undertake to write of that great and miserable civil war[15] which destroyed the present state and enslaved posterity without first making a large enumeration of such [20] causes: how wicked the manners of Rome were grown, how the chief rulers were given to avarice and oppression, and the whole state drowned in luxury, lusts, and riot, as you may see upon that subject in two the most elegant of them.[16] And shall we Christians, who adore the true God and live under the gospel light, not be sensible under so heavy a judgment of our own offences?

To begin with the faults of the higher powers and their illegal oppression of the people during these eight or nine years in which Parliaments were denied to England,[17] [30] which I briefly touch, referring the reader to a more full narration in the *Remonstrance*:[18] multitudes of monopolies[19] were granted by the king and laid upon all things of most common and necessary use, such as soap, salt, wine, leather, sea coal, and many other of that kind.

Regia privatis crescunt aeraria damnis. Claudius.

By loss of private men th' exchequer grows.

Large sums of money were exacted through the whole kingdom for default of knighthood under the shadow of an obsolete law.[20] Tonnage and poundage[21] were received [40] without the ordinary course of law; and though they were taken under pretense of guarding the seas, yet that great tax of ship-money[22] was set on foot under the same color, by both which there was charged upon the people some years near 700,000 pounds though the seas at that time were not well guarded.

These things were accompanied with an enlargement of forests contrary to Magna Charta, the forcing of coat- and conduct-money, taking away the arms of trained bands in divers counties, disarming the people by engrossing of [50] gunpowder,[23] keeping it in the Tower of London, and setting so high a rate upon it that the poorer sort were not able to buy it; nor could any have it without license, whereby several parts of the kingdom were left destitute of their necessary defence.

No courts of judicature could give redress to the people for these illegal sufferings whilst judges were displaced by the king for not complying with his will, and so awed that they durst not do their duties. For to hold a rod over them the clause *quamdiu se bene gesserint* was left out of their patents and a new clause, *durante bene placito*,[24] inserted.

New, illegal oaths were enforced upon the subjects and new judicatories erected without law; and when commissions were granted for examining the excess of fees and great exactions discovered, the delinquents were compounded with not only for the time past but immunity to offend for the time to come; which instead of redressing did confirm and increase the grievance of the subjects.

By this time, all thoughts of ever having a Parliament again were quite banished. So many oppressions had been set on foot, so many illegal actions done, that the only way to justify the mischiefs already done was to do that one greater: to take away the means which was ordained to redress them, the lawful government of England by Parliaments.

Whilst the kingdom was in this condition the serious and just men of England, who were no way interested[25] in the emolument of these oppressions, could not but entertain sad thoughts and presages of what mischief must needs follow so great an injustice; that things carried so far on in a wrong way must needs either enslave themselves

---

[15]The savage struggle between Caesar and Pompey (49–48 B.C.) that led to Caesar's dictatorship and thus ultimately to his assassination.

[16]May is thinking of perhaps Horace (65–8 B.C.) and Ovid (43 B.C.–A.D. 17), the former a reluctant participant in the civil war and both, as poets, much concerned with the *luxury, lusts, and riot* of Augustan Rome. The most important literary treatment of the civil war was the *Pharsalia* of Marcus Annaeus Lucanus (39–65), which May translated in 1627 and sebsequently expanded in a *Continuation* (English 1630, Latin 1640). See p. 797.

[17]From the dissolution of Charles I's third Parliament in 1629 until the calling of the so-called Short Parliament in 1640.

[18]The Grand Remonstrance, a statement of Charles I's offenses against Parliament that was drawn up by Commons, adopted after a stormy debate, and printed in 1641.

[19]In Tudor and Stuart England, exclusive economic privileges granted by the crown for the control of basic commodities and essential services, and therefore the subject of wide complaint. In 1621 Parliament took positive measures against some of the monopolists, and Sir Giles Mompesson, the most notorious of them all, was forced to flee the kingdom.

[20]*Default... law*: The hard-pressed Charles exacted heavy fines (or "knighthood-money") from persons who declined the empty honor of a knighthood.

[21]Customs duties normally voted by Parliament to a new king for life. Charles I's levying these duties without Parliamentary sanction became a major subject of contention between him and his third Parliament in 1629.

[22]A tax levied by the crown against seaports for building and maintaining the Royal Navy. Charles' extension of this levy to inland towns in 1635 was deeply resented.

[23]*Enlargement...gunpowder*: respectively, enclosing lands for royal use in violation of the basic charter of English liberties wrested from King John in 1215; levying taxes on the pretext of providing clothing and traveling expenses for Charles' troops; depriving local militia of arms; monopolizing the entire supply of gunpowder. [24]"During good behavior...during the pleasure of."
[25]Interested.

and posterity forever, or require a vindication so sharp and smarting as that the nation would groan under it; and though the times were jolly for the present, yet having observed the judgment of God upon other secure nations they could not choose but fear the sequel. Another sort of men, and especially lords and gentlemen by whom the pressures of the government were not much felt, who enjoyed their own plentiful fortunes with little or insensible[26] detriment, looking no farther than their present safety and prosperity, and the yet undisturbed peace of the nation whilst other kingdoms were embroiled in calamities, and Germany sadly wasted by a sharp war,[27] did nothing but applaud the happiness of England and called those ingrateful and factious spirits who complained of the breach of laws and liberties; that the kingdom abounded with wealth, plenty, and all kind of elegancies more than ever; that it was for the honor of a people that the monarch should live splendidly and not be curbed at all in his prerogative, which would bring him into the greater esteem with other princes and more enable him to prevail in treaties; that what they suffered by monopolies was insensible and not grievous if compared with other states; that the Duke of Tuscancy[28] sat heavier upon his people in that very kind;[29] that the French king[30] had made himself an absolute lord and quite depressed the power of parliaments, which had been there as great as in any kingdom, and yet that France flourished and the gentry lived well; that the Austrian princes, especially in Spain,[31] laid heavy burdens upon their subjects.

Thus did many of the English gentry, by way of comparison in ordinary discourse, plead for their own servitude. . . .

The queen[32] was fruitful, and now grown of such an age as might seem to give her privilege of a farther society with the king than bed and board, and make her a partner of his affairs and business, which his extreme affection did more encourage her to challenge:[33] that conjugal love, as an extraordinary virtue of a king in midst of so many temptations, the people did admire and honor.

But the queen's power did by degrees give privilege to papists, and among them the most witty and Jesuited, to converse, under the name of civility and courtship, not only with inferior courtiers but the king himself, and to sow their seed in what ground they thought best; and by degrees, as in compliment to the queen, nuntios[34] from the pope were received in the court of England—Panzani, Con, and Rosetti[35]—the king himself maintaining in discourse that he saw no reason why he might not receive an ambassador from the pope, being a temporal prince. But those nuntios were not entertained with public ceremony, so that the people in general took no great notice of them, and the courtiers were confident of the king's religion by his due frequenting prayers and sermons.

The clergy, whose dependence was merely upon the king, were wholly taken up in admiration of his happy government, which they never concealed from himself as often as the pulpit gave them access to his ear; and not only there, but at all meetings, they discoursed with joy upon that theme, affirming confidently that no prince in Europe was so great a friend to the church as King Charles, that religion flourished nowhere but in England, and no reformed church retained the face and dignity of a church but that.

Many of them used to deliver their opinion that God had therefore so severely punished the Palatinate because their sacrilege had been so great in taking away the endowments of bishoprics.[36]

Queen Elizabeth herself, who had reformed religion, was but coldly praised, and all her virtues forgotten when they remembered how she cut short the bishopric of Ely.[37]

Henry the Eight was much condemned by them for seizing upon the abbeys and taking so much out of the several bishoprics as he did in the thirty-seven years of his reign.[38] To maintain, therefore, that splendor of a church which so much pleased them was become their highest endeavor, especially after they had gotten in the year 1633 an archbishop after their own heart, Dr. Laud,[39] who had before for divers years ruled the clergy in the secession of Archbishop Abbot, a man of better temper and discretion. Which discretion or virtue to conceal would be an injury to that archbishop: he was a man who wholly followed the true interest of England and that of the reformed churches in Europe, so far as that in his time the clergy was not much envied here in England, nor the government of episcopacy much disfavored by Protestants beyond the seas. Not only the pomp of ceremonies were daily increased, and innovations of great scandal brought into the church; but in

[26]Imperceptible.
[27]The Thirty Years' War (1618–48) between Protestants and Catholics.
[28]Ferdinand II (ruled 1620–70), whose reign was much disturbed by wars. [29]*Sat...kind*: was even more oppressive in these matters.
[30]Louis XIII (1601–43), whose great minister Cardinal Richelieu did much to consolidate and extend royal power.
[31]*Austrian...Spain*: the Hapsburgs, who ruled Spain from 1516 to 1700.
[32]Henrietta Maria (1600–69), daughter of Henri IV and Marie de Médicis, who married Charles I just after his accession in 1625. Her Catholicism and her political activities gave great concern, especially to the Puritans. [33]Claim. [34]Nuncios, papal envoys.
[35]Gregorio Panzani, an Oratorian who, sent to England in 1634 to obtain alleviation for the Catholics, enjoyed a success terrifying to the Puritans; George Con, a Scotch Catholic who, as the pope's representative at the court of Queen Henrietta Maria after 1635, powerfully encouraged her efforts in behalf of her coreligionists; Count Rosetti, an Italian prelate who, as Con's successor, remained in England until 1641.
[36]*Palatinate...bishoprics*: The aggressive Protestantism of Frederick V (1596–1632), elector of the Palatinate (a German state on the Rhine), son-in-law of James I of England, and briefly (1619–20) king of Bohemia, led to his own downfall and exile and to the ravage of his electorate in the Thirty Years' War.
[37]When Thomas Thirlby (1506?–70), bishop of Ely under Queen Mary and an unyielding foe of Protestantism, refused to take the oath of supremacy for Queen Elizabeth, she deposed and imprisoned him.
[38]Henry VIII's spoliation of the monasteries and confiscation of their immense wealth occurred mainly in 1537–38, the twenty-eighth year of his reign.
[39]William Laud (1573–1645), chief architect of Charles I's ecclesiastical policy, who, following his appointment as bishop of London (1628) and then, upon the death of the temperate George Abbot, as archbishop of Canterbury (1633), ruthlessly suppressed religious and political dissent. Impeached by the Long Parliament in 1640, he was executed five years later. For a different assessment of Laud see pp. 930 ff.

point of doctrine many fair approaches made towards Rome, as he that pleaseth to search may find in the books of Bishop Laud, Montague, Heylyn, Pocklington,[40] and the rest, or in brief collected by a Scottish minister, Master Bailey.[41] And as their friendship to Rome increased, so did their scorn to the reformed churches beyond the seas, whom, instead of lending that relief and succor to them which God had enabled this rich island to do, they failed in their greatest extremities, and instead of harbors became rocks to split them.

Archbishop Laud, who was now grown into great favor with the king, made use of it especially to advance the pomp and temporal honor of the clergy, procuring the Lord Treasurer's place for Dr. Juxon,[42] bishop of London, and endeavoring, as the general report went, to fix the greatest temporal preferments upon others of that coat,[43] insomuch as the people merrily, when they saw that treasurer with the other bishops riding to Westminster, called it "the Church Triumphant."[44] Doctors and parsons of parishes were made everywhere justices of peace, to the great grievance of the country in civil affairs, and depriving them of their spiritual edification.

The archbishop by the same means which he used to preserve his clergy from contempt exposed them to envy, and as the wisest could then prophesy, to a more than probability of losing all; as we read of some men who, being foredoomed by an oracle to a bad fortune, have run into it by the same means they used to prevent it. The like unhappy course did the clergy then take to depress[45] Puritanism, which was to set up irreligion itself against it, the worst weapon which they could have chosen to beat it down, which appeared especially in point of keeping the Lord's day; when not only books were written to shake the morality of it, as that of *Sunday No Sabbath*, but sports and pastimes of jollity and lightness permitted to the country people upon that day by public authority, and the warrant commanded to be read in churches; which, instead of producing the intended effect, may credibly be thought to have been one motive to a stricter observance of that day in that part of the kingdom which before had been well devoted; and many men who had before been loose and careless began upon that occasion to enter into a more serious consideration of it,

and were ashamed to be invited by the authority of churchmen to that which themselves, at the best, could but have pardoned in themselves as a thing of infirmity.[46]

The example of the court, where plays were usually presented on Sundays, did not so much draw the country to imitation as reflect with disadvantage upon the court itself, and sour those other court pastimes and jollities which would have relished better without that, in the eyes of all the people, as things ever allowed to the delights of great princes.

The countenancing of looseness and irreligion was no doubt a good preparative to the introducing of another religion, and the power of godliness being beaten down, popery might more easily by degrees enter. Men quickly leave that of which they never took fast hold; and though it were questionable whether the bishops and great clergy of England aimed at popery, it is too apparent such was the design of Romish agents; and the English clergy, if they did not their own work, did theirs.

[40]In addition to Archbishop Laud, some of the most notable Anglican spokesmen were James Montagu (1568?–1618), bishop of Winchester; Peter Heylyn (1600–62), author of many works including a history of the Reformation and a life of Laud; and John Pocklington (d. 1642), chaplain of Charles I who was deprived of his various preferments by Parliament in 1641.
[41]Robert Baillie (1559–1662), learned Scottish Presbyterian who exhaustively exposed the errors of his Anglican adversaries in such books as *Antidote against Arminianism* (1641) and *The Canterburian's Self-Conviction* (1641). He later attacked Independents and Sectarians with undiminished zeal.
[42]William Juxon (1582–1663), notable royalist divine who succeeded Laud as bishop of London, served as lord high treasurer (1636–41), attended Charles I on the scaffold, and survived the Commonwealth to become archbishop of Canterbury in 1660.
[43]Others . . . coat: Others holding the same royalist opinions.
[44]In normal usage, the collective body of victorious saints when glorified in heaven (as opposed to the Church Militant, the church on earth in struggle with the sins of the world).   [45]Suppress.
[46]Puritan restrictions of popular amusements on Sunday, which seemed to challenge the right of the established church to regulate its festivals and holy days, were countered by James I (1618) and Charles I (1633) in the so-called *Book of Sports*, a work abominated by Puritans because it permitted and even advocated maypoles, morris dances, and Whitsun games on the sabbath.

Edward, Lord Herbert of Cherbury[1]   [1582-1648]

from The Life and Reign of King Henry the Eighth (1649)

TO THE KING'S MOST EXCELLENT MAJESTY[1]

Most excellent and most gracious sovereign, I present here in all humble manner unto Your Majesty a work, the

[1]For a commentary on Lord Herbert, and for other excerpts from his work, see Poetry, pp. 114 ff.
LIFE OF HENRY   [1]Charles I, who was executed (30 January 1649) not long after Herbert's book appeared.

authority whereof is solely yours, not yet so much because it took its first beginning from Your Majesty's particular and (I may say) unexpected commands, but that the parts thereof, as fast as I could finish them, were lustrated[2] by your gracious eye and consummated by your judicious animadversions;[3] besides, the substance thereof in all home[4] affairs hath been drawn chiefly out of your majesty's records. So that by more than one title it craves Your Majesty's protection.

As for the defects, I no way presume to interess Your Majesty in them: let them all fall on myself. Though as I have endeavored to set down the truth impartially I hope they will not be so great or many as to exauctorate[5] the rest. I am not yet ignorant that the king whose history I write is subject to more obloquies than any since the worst Roman emperors' times. But I shall little care for censure as long as the testimonies I use do assure and warrant me, since I intend not to describe him otherwise, either good or bad, but as he really was. Only where he holds any doubtful part, I conceive it will be but just to give a favorable construction. For if even private men will expect the like in their own case, it will be much more due to princes, both as a reverence belongs to their persons and that they above all others must be thought to endeavor the common good, who will suffer more than any else in a general calamity. How far yet I make use hereof to assert[6] this king my free pen doth everywhere declare, since I give not this interpretation where arguments to the contrary convince me. Nevertheless, as many things will be required to an entire narration of public actions in difficult times, I cannot affirm them beyond those memorials[7] which have been delivered to posterity. And if thus they may be obscure, so again where they sufficiently appear in their causes their nature yet is often found so perplexed and intricate as it will not be easy for aftertimes to define their qualities, few of this sort being so sincere as to employ no inconvenience,[8] while the advantage of many is seldom obtained without the detriment of some. Neither ought this to seem strange if in the present constitution of the affairs no better expedient could be offered, reason of state[9] pretending no farther than to procure the greater good.

So that if some mixture of ill be discovered therein, it might yet conduce to the general[10] by the same reason that certain noxious ingredients, being put into antidotes, make their operation more powerful. Which yet my reader, I hope, will not so understand as if I thought any rude hand could temper them, every ill being not proper for this composition in this kind, but that only which is opposite to the malady; not everyone a fit patient, but those only who are of infirm and crazy[11] constitutions. So that it will be needful that a careful and able person both dispense and exhibit[12] it. I wish yet that good princes may seldom use this maxim, it being (at best) but a dangerous suspected wisdom. Since state government, where it is well administered, will rarely need such helps, no otherwise than extreme and last remedies, therefore in my opinion recourse should not be had to them but where other means fail. The practice of virtue and piety being alone a just exercise for a healthful and well-constituted commonwealth, neither will there be any danger this way of distraction, those causes which make men good

uniting them best. Only I hold it requisite that a due disposition and order be observed, no virtue being proper but in its place.

Therefore though some one or other be still so pertinent as there is no occasion totally to recede from them, yet experience teacheth that neither fortitude hath been always successful, nor temperance safe, nor justice itself opportune, the fury and insolence of outrageous people having in some insurrections grown to that excess that it hath been more wisdom to pass by a while than to punish them. So that until a due election and choice be had, even virtue itself will be obnoxious. For which purpose, therefore, each of them hath its station[13] or orb assigned, that so whilst some descend, others arising in the horizon of government may maintain a perpetual vicissitude and revolution. There being (I dare say) no reason for any to decline to ill acts or vices if they comply with the right virtue, their harmonic system[14] being so admirably framed that some one or other will eternally bear a concordant part.

Of all which Your Majesty being so great a master and example that you had rather merit than hear a due commendation, I shall only pray that the virtues which are eminent in your person may be so visible and exalted in your happy and long government that to all ages you may be renowned and glorious. Thus in all true devotion resteth

Your Majesty's most faithful subject and servant,
Ed. Herbert

THE LIFE AND REIGN OF KING HENRY THE EIGHTH. TOGETHER WITH WHICH IS BRIEFLY REPRESENTED A GENERAL HISTORY OF THE TIMES

[HENRY'S COMPLEX CHARACTER]

It is not easy to write that prince's history of whom no one thing may constantly be affirmed. Changing of manners and condition alters the coherence of parts which should give an uniform description. Nor is it probable that contradictories should agree to the same person; so that nothing can shake the credit of a narration more than if it grow unlike itself, when yet it may be not the author but the argument caused the variation. It is unpossible to draw his picture well who hath several countenances.

I shall labor with this difficulty in King Henry the Eighth, not yet so much for the general observation (among *poli-*

---

[2]Viewed.

[3]*Consummated . . . animadversions*: perfected through: your discerning criticism.

[4]Domestic (as opposed to foreign).   [5]Jeopardize.   [6]Vindicate.

[7]Records.

[8]*Few. . . inconvenience*: few public actions being so straightforward (*sincere*) as to involve no dissimulation or inconsistency.

[9]Concealment or evasion on grounds of political necessity.

[10]*So that . . . general*: even evil deeds might contribute to the general good.   [11]Impaired.   [12]Administer.

[13]Fixed place, sphere (a term from astronomy, on which the imagery of the following passage is based).

[14]Alluding to the so-called music of the spheres resulting from the synchronous revolution of the planets in their respective orbits. See *sphere* in Glossary.

tiques)[15] that the government of princes rarely grows milder towards their latter end, but that this king in particular (being about his declining age so diverse in many of his desires as he knew not well how either to command or obey them) interverted[16] all, falling at last into such violent courses as in common opinion derogated not a little from those virtues which at first made him one of the most renowned princes of Christendom.

[THE CHARACTER OF CARDINAL WOLSEY]

And thus concluded that great cardinal, a man in whom ability of parts[17] and industry were equally eminent, though, for being employed wholly in ambitious ways, they became dangerous instruments of power in active and mutable times. By these arts yet he found means to govern not only the chief affairs of this kingdom but of Europe, there being no potentate which, in his turn, did not seek to him. And as this procured him divers pensions, so, when he acquainted the king therewith, his manner was so cunningly to disoblige that prince who did see him last as he made way thereby oftentimes to receive as much on the other side. But not of secular princes alone but even of the pope and clergy of Rome he was no little courted; of which therefore he made especial use while he drew them to second him on most occasions. His birth being otherwise so obscure and mean[18] as no man had ever stood so single,[19] for which reason also his chief endeavor was not to displease any great person, which yet could not secure him against the divers pretenders of that time. For as all things passed through his hands, so they who failed in their suits generally hated him; all which, though it did but exasperate his ill nature, yet this good resultance followed: that it made him take the more care to be just. Whereof also he obtained the reputation in his public hearing of causes, for as he loved nobody, so his reason carried him.

And thus he was an useful minister of his king in all points where there was no question of deserving[20] the Roman Church; of which (at what price soever) I find he was a zealous servant as hoping thereby to aspire to the papacy, whereof (as the factious times then were) he seemed more capable than any had he not so immoderately affected[21] it. Whereby also it was not hard to judge of his inclinations, that prince who was ablest to help him to this dignity being ever preferred by him; which therefore was the ordinary bait by which the emperor and French king, one after the other, did catch him.[22] And upon these terms he doubted not to convey vast treasures out of this kingdom, especially unto Rome, where he had not a few cardinals at his devotion. By whose help, though he could not obtain that supreme dignity[23] he so passionately desired, yet he prevailed himself so much of their favor as he got a kind of absolute power in spiritual matters at home. Wherewith again he so served the king's turn as it made him think the less of using his own authority. One error seemed common to both, which was that such a multiplicity of offices and places were invested in him, for as it drew much envy upon the cardinal in particular, so it derogated no little from the regal authority while one man alone seemed to exhaust all. Since it becometh princes to do like good husbandmen when they sow their grounds, which is to scatter and not to throw all in one

place. He was no great dissembler for so qualified a person, as ordering his businesses (for the most part) so cautiously as he got more by keeping his word than by breaking it.

As for his learning (which was far from exact), it consisted chiefly in the subtleties of the Thomists,[24] wherewith the king and himself did more often weary than satisfy each other. His style in missives was rather copious than eloquent, yet ever tending to the point. Briefly, if it be true (as Polydore observes) that no man ever did rise with fewer virtues, it is true that few that ever fell from so high a place had lesser crimes objected against him. Though yet Polydore (for being at his first coming into England committed to prison by him,[25] as we have said) may be suspected as a partial author. So that in all probability he might have subsisted longer when either his pride and immense wealth had not made him obnoxious and suspected to the king, or that other than women[26] had opposed him; who as they are vigilant and close enemies, so for the most part they carry their businesses in that manner as they leave fewer advantages against themselves than men do. In conclusion, as I cannot assent to those who thought him happy for enjoying the untimely compassion of the people a little before his end, so I cannot but account it a principal felicity that during his favor with the king all things succeeded better than afterwards, though yet it may be doubted whether the impressions he gave did not occasion divers irregularities which were observed to follow.

[LORD HERBERT'S FINAL ESTIMATE OF KING HENRY]

And now if the reader (according to my manner in other great personages) do expect some character of this prince, I must affirm (as in the beginning) that the course of his life being commonly held various and diverse from itself, he will hardly suffer any,[27] and that his history will be his best character and description. Howbeit, since others have so much defamed him . . . I shall strive to rectify their understandings who are impartial lovers of truth, without either presuming audaciously to condemn a prince, heretofore sovereign of our kingdom, or omitting the just freedom of an historian.

And because his most bitter censures agree that he had all manner of perfection either of nature or education, and that

---

[15]Objective observers of political behavior.
[16]Misused, misapplied. [17]Talents.
[18]*Birth . . . mean*: Wolsey's father was allegedly a butcher at Ipswich.
[19]Unaided by family connections.
[20]Serving, being serviceable to. [21]Desired and sought.
[22]*Emperor . . . him*: It was charged by Wolsey's enemies that in order to advance his papal ambitions he curried favor with Emperor Charles V and Francis I of France by neglecting or betraying Henry's interests. [23]The papacy.
[24]Scholastic theologians who embraced the theology of St. Thomas Aquinas (1225?–74). After the Reformation their *subtleties* became the object of derision, much of it ill-informed and partisan.
[25]*For being . . . him*: In 1515 Polydore Vergil (see Glossary) was imprisoned briefly on the charge of having vilified Wolsey during a recent visit to Italy (his first since arriving in England in 1501).
[26]Catherine of Aragon, Henry's first wife whose divorce Wolsey bungled, and her successor Anne Boleyn.
[27]Allow of any summing up.

he was besides of a most deep judgment in all affairs to which he applied himself; a prince not only liberal and indulgent to his family and court and even to strangers (whom he willingly saw), and one that made choice both of able and good men for the clergy and of wise and grave counselors for his state affairs, and above all a prince of a royal courage, I shall not controvert these points, but come to my particular observations. According to which I find him to have been ever most zealous of his honor and dignity, insomuch that his most questioned passages[28] were countenanced either with home or foreign authority: so many universities of Italy and France maintaining his repudiating of Queen Catherine of Spain,[29] and his Parliament (for the rest) authorizing the divorces and decapitations of his following wives,[30] the dissolutions of the monasteries,[31] and divers others of his most branded actions. So that by his Parliaments in public and juries in private affairs he at least wanted not color and pretext to make them specious[32] to the world. . . .

As for matter of state, I dare say never prince went upon a truer maxim for this kingdom, which was to make himself arbiter of Christendom. And had it not cost him so much, none had ever proceeded more wisely. But as he would be an actor (for the most part) where he needed only be a spectator, he both engaged himself beyond what was requisite, and by calling in the money he lent his confederates and allies did often disoblige them when he had most need of their friendship. Yet thus he was the most active prince of his time. The examples whereof are so frequent in his history that there was no treaty, or almost conventicle,[33] in Christendom wherein he had not his particular agent and interest; which together with his intelligence in all countries and concerning all affairs, and the pensions given for that purpose, was one of his vast ways for spending of money. . . .

At home it was his manner to treat much with his Parliaments, where, if gentle means served not, he came to some degrees of the rough, though more sparingly that he knew his people did but too much fear him. Besides, he understood well that foul ways[34] are not always passable, nor to be used (especially in suspected and dangerous times) but where others fail. However, it may be noted that none of his predecessors understood the temper of Parliaments better than himself, or that prevailed[35] himself more dexterously[36] of them. . . .

As for his faults, I find that of opiniate[37] and willful much objected,[38] insomuch that the impressions privately given him by any court-whisperer were hardly or never to be effaced. And herein the persons near him had a singular ability: while beginning with the commendations of those they would disgrace, their manner was to insinuate such exceptions as they would discommend a man more in few words than commend him in many. Doing therein like cunning wrestlers, who, to throw one down, first take him up. Besides, this willfulness had a most dangerous quality annexed to it (especially towards his later end), being an intense jealousy almost of all persons and affairs, which disposed him easily to think the worst, whereas it is a greater part of wisdom to prevent than to suspect. These conditions again, being armed with power, produced such terrible

effects as styled him both at home and abroad by the name of Cruel. . . .

[Having conceded and discussed Henry's alleged faults of covetousness and prodigality, Lord Herbert proceeds to the conclusion of his character of the king.]

As for the third vice wherewith he was justly charged, being lust and wantonness, there is little to answer more than that it was rather a personal fault than damageable to the public. Howbeit, they who reprove it ought not only to examine circumstances (which much aggravate or extenuate the fact) but even the complexions of men. That concupiscence which in some is a vice, being in others a disease of repletion, in others a necessity of nature. It doth not yet appear that this fault did hasten the death of his queens, he being noted more for practising of private pleasures than secret mischiefs, so that if any undue motive did cooperate herein it may be thought an inordinate desire to have posterity (especially masculine) which might be the undoubted heirs of him and the kingdom, rather than anything else.

With all his crimes[39] yet he was one of the most glorious princes of his time, insomuch that not only the chief potentates of Christendom did court him but his subjects in general did highly reverence him, as the many trials he put them to sufficiently testify; which yet expired so quickly that it may be truly said all his pomp died with him, his memory being now exposed to obloquy, as his accusers will neither admit reason of state to cover anywhere or necessity to excuse his actions. For as they were either discontented clergymen (for his relinquishing the papal authority and overthrowing the monasteries) or offended women (for divers severe examples against their sex) that first opposed and cried him down, the clamor hath been the greater. So that although one William Thomas,[40] a clerk to the Council to Edward the Sixth, and living about the later times of Henry the Eighth's reign, did in great part defend him in an Italian book printed *anno* 1552, it hath not availed.

But what this prince was and whether and how farforth excusable in point of state, conscience, or honor, a diligent observation of his actions, together with a conjuncture of the times, will, I conceive, better declare to the judicious reader than any factious relation on what side whatsoever. To conclude, I wish I could leave him in his grave.

[28]Actions, escapades.
[29]Catherine of Aragon (1485–1536), Henry's first wife whom he divorced (1533) on the alleged grounds of incest, she being the widow of his elder brother Prince Arthur (1486–1502).
[30]See p. 867, n.56.
[31]Following his break with Rome over the divorce of Catherine of Aragon, Henry suppressed the English monasteries and confiscated their immense wealth. [32]Plausible. [33]Clandestine meeting. [34]Muddy roads. [35]Availed. [36]Dexterously. [37]Opinionated. [38]Brought forward, adduced.
[39]The many savage executions—some of them judicial murders—that disfigured Henry's later years?
[40]Scholar and civil servant (d. 1534), tutor of Edward VI and later clerk of his Council, whose defense of Henry VIII, though published in Italian in 1552, never appeared in English. He was executed for his complicity in the abortive efforts to prevent Queen Mary's accession in 1553.

John Milton[1] [1608-1674]

from The History of Britain (1670)

THE FIRST BOOK

The beginning of nations, those excepted of whom sacred books have spoken, is to this day unknown. Nor only the beginning but the deeds also of many succeeding ages, yea, periods of ages, either wholly unknown, or obscured and blemisht with fables. Whether it were that the use of letters came in long after, or were it the violence of barbarous inundations, or they themselves, at certain revolutions of time, fatally decaying and degenerating into sloth and ignorance, whereby the monuments of more ancient civility have been some destroyed, some lost. Perhaps disesteem and contempt [10] of the public affairs then present, as not worth recording, might partly be in cause. Certainly ofttimes we see that wise men, and of best ability, have forborne to write the acts of their own days, while they beheld with a just loathing and disdain not only how unworthy, how perverse, how corrupt, but often how ignoble, how petty, how below all history the persons and their actions were, who either by fortune or some rude election had attained, as a sore judgment and ignominy upon the land, to have chief sway in managing the commonwealth. But that any law or super- [20] stition of our philosophers, the Druids, forbade the Britons to write their memorable deeds, I know not why any out of Caesar[1] should allege. He indeed saith that their doctrine they thought not lawful to commit to letters; but in most matters else, both private and public, among which well may history be reckoned, they used the Greek tongue; and that the British Druids, who taught those in Gaul, would be ignorant of any language known and used by their disciples, or, so frequently writing other things, and so inquisitive into highest, would for want of recording be ever children in [30] the knowledge of times and ages, is not likely. Whatever might be the reason, this we find: that of British affairs, from the first peopling of the island to the coming of Julius Caesar, nothing certain, either by tradition, history, or ancient fame, hath hitherto been left us. That which we have of oldest seeming hath by the greater part of judicious antiquaries been long rejected for a modern fable.

Nevertheless there being others, besides the first supposed author, men not unread nor unlearned in antiquity, who admit that for approved story which the former explode for [40] fiction; and seeing that ofttimes relations heretofore accounted fabulous have been after found to contain in them many footsteps and reliques of something true, as what we read in poets of the flood and giants, little believed till undoubted witnesses[2] taught us that all was not feigned; I have therefore determined to bestow the telling over even of these reputed tales, be it for nothing else but in favor of our English poets and rhetoricians, who by their art will know how to use them judiciously.

I might also produce example, as Diodorus among the Greeks, Livy and others of the Latins, Polydore and Virunius accounted among our own writers.[3] But I intend not with controversies and quotations to delay or interrupt the smooth course of history, much less to argue and debate long who were the first inhabitants, with what probabilities, what authorities, each opinion hath been upheld; but shall endeavor that which hitherto hath been needed most: with plain and lightsome brevity to relate well and orderly things worth the noting, so as may best instruct and benefit them that read. Which, imploring divine assistance, that it may redound to His glory and the good of the British nation, I now begin.

That the whole earth was inhabited before the flood, and to the utmost point of habitable ground, from those effectual words of God in the creation may be more than conjectured.[4] Hence that this island also had her dwellers, her affairs, and perhaps her stories, even in that old world those many hundred years, with much reason we may infer. After the flood and the dispersing of nations, as they journeyed leisurely from the east, Gomer, the eldest son of Japhet,[5] and his

[1]For a commentary on Milton and for other excerpts from his work, see Poetry, pp. 256 ff. Religion and Politics, pp. 599 ff., and Books and Men, pp. 769 ff.
HISTORY OF BRITAIN [1]Gaius Julius Caesar (100–44 B.C.), Roman general whose invasion of Britain (55, 54 B.C.) was related in his *Commentaries* (i.e., *De bello Gallico*). Like most of his contemporaries, Milton regarded Caesar's account of the ancient Britons (V. 8 ff., VI.13 ff.) as the first authentic record of those mysterious people. [2]Those recorded in the Bible.
[3]Reputable historians who did not scruple to record (with varying degrees of skepticism) fabulous accounts of national origins: Diodorus Siculus (first cent. B.C.), author of a *Historical Library* in forty books, most of which are lost; Titus Livius (59 B.C.–17 A.D.), author of *The Annals of the Roman People* in 142 books that survive only in part; Polydore Vergil (1470?–1555), Italian humanist whose notable history of England was commissioned by Henry VII; Ludovicus Ponticus Virunius (1467–1520), Italian historian who edited an abridgment (1508 ff.) of Geoffrey of Monmouth's *Historia Britonum* (on which see p. 808. n.3.)
[4]Genesis 1–10. [5]Genesis 10.1–3.

offspring, as by authorities, arguments, and affinity of divers names is generally believed, were the first that peopled all these west and northern climes. But they of our own writers, who thought they had done nothing unless with all circumstance they tell us when and who first set foot upon this island, presume to name out of fabulous and counterfeit authors a certain Samothes or Dis, a fourth or sixt son of Japhet (whom they make, about two hundred years after the flood, to have planted with colonies first the continent of Celtica or Gaul, and next this island, thence to have named it Samothea), to have reigned here, and after him lineally four kings, Magus, Saron, Druis, and Bardus. But the forged Berosus,[6] whom only they have to cite, nowhere mentions that either he or any of those whom they bring did ever pass into Britain, or send their people hither. So that this outlandish figment may easily excuse our not allowing it the room here so much as of a British fable.

That which follows, perhaps as wide from truth though seeming less impertinent, is that these Samotheans under the reign of Bardus were subdued by Albion, a giant, son of Neptune, who called the island after his own name and ruled it forty-four years. Till at length passing over into Gaul in aid of his brother Lestrygon, against whom Hercules was hasting out of Spain into Italy, he was there slain in fight, and Bergion, also his brother.

Sure enough[7] we are that Britain hath been anciently termed Albion, both by the Greeks and Romans. And Mela,[8] the geographer, makes mention of a stony shore in Languedoc,[9] where by report such a battle was fought. The rest, as his[10] giving name to the isle, or even landing here, depends altogether upon late surmises. But too absurd and too unconscionably gross is that fond invention that wafted hither the fifty daughters of a strange Dioclesian, King of Syria, brought in, doubtless, by some illiterate pretender to something mistaken in the common poetical story of Danaus, king of Argos, while his vanity, not pleased with the obscure beginning which truest antiquity affords the nation, labored to contrive us a pedigree, as he thought, more noble. These daughters, by appointment of Danaus on the marriage-night having murdered all their husbands except Linceus, whom his wive's loyalty saved, were by him, at the suit of his wife, their sister, not put to death, but turned out to sea in a ship unmanned, of which whole sex they had incurred the hate, and as the tale goes were driven on this island. Where the inhabitants, none but devils, as some write, or as others, a lawless crew left here by Albion, without head or governor, both entertained them and had issue by them a second breed of giants, who tyrannized the isle till Brutus came.

The eldest of these dames in their legend they call Albina; and from thence, for which cause the whole scene was framed, will have the name Albion derived.[11] Incredible it may seem so sluggish a conceit should prove so ancient as to be authorized by the elder Nennius,[12] reputed to have lived above a thousand years ago. This I find not in him, but that Histion, sprung of Japhet, had four sons: Francus, Romanus, Alemannus, and Britto, of whom the Britons; as true, I believe, as that those other nations whose names are resembled came

of the other three; if these dreams give not just occasion to call in doubt the book itself which bears that title.

Hitherto the things themselves have given us a warrantable dispatch to run them soon over. But now of Brutus and his line, with the whole progeny of kings, to the entrance[13] of Julius Caesar, we cannot so easily be discharged: descents of ancestry long continued, laws and exploits not plainly seeming to be borrowed or devised, which on the common belief have wrought no small impression; defended by many, denied utterly by few. For what though Brutus and the whole Trojan pretence were yielded up (seeing they who first devised to bring us from some noble ancestor were content at first with Brutus the Consul,[14] till better invention, although not willing to forego the name, taught them to remove it higher into a more fabulous age, and by the same remove lighting on the Trojan tales in affectation to make the Briton of one original with the Roman, pitched there; yet those old and inborn names of successive kings never any to have been real persons or done in their lives at least some part of what so long hath been remembered cannot be thought without too strict an incredulity.

For these and those causes above mentioned, that which hath received approbation from so many I have chosen not to omit. Certain or uncertain, be that upon the credit of those whom I must follow: so far as keeps aloof from impossible and absurd, attested by ancient writers from books more ancient, I refuse not, as the due and proper subject of story. The principal author is well known to be Geoffrey of Monmouth; what he was and whence his authority, who in his age or before him have deliver'd the same matter, and suchlike general discourses will better stand in a treatise by themselves.

> With this careful disclaimer, Milton proceeds to devote the remainder of Book I to the so-called British history. His account of King Leir (which he no doubt knew in Shakespeare's version too) may serve to represent his attitude and method.

Hitherto from father to son the direct line [of Brut's descendants] hath run on; but Leir, who next reigned, had only three daughters and no male issue; governed laudably, and built Caerlier, now Leicester, on the bank of Sora.[15] But at last, failing through age, he determines to bestow[16] his daughters, and so among them to divide his kingdom. Yet first to try which of them loved him best—a trial that might

---

[6]See p. 811, n.20. William Camden (*Britannia*, trans. Philemon Holland, 1611, p. 10) regarded Berosus as "nothing else but a ridiculous figment of some crafty foister and juggling deceiver."
[7]Enough.
[8]Pomponius Mela, 1st-century geographer whose *De situ orbis* is the earliest Latin description of the ancient world.
[9]Region in southern France.   [10]The giant Albion's.
[11]As for "that pretty tale" of Albina, asked Camden contemptuously (*Britannia*, p. 24), "who can abide to hear it without indignation, as the most loud lie of some lewd losel?"
[12]See p. 820, n.53.   [13]Invasion.
[14]Lucius Junius Brutus, one of the first two consuls in Roman history (509 B.C.), legendarily famed for his patriotism.
[15]The River Soar.   [16]In marriage.

have made him, had he known as wisely how to try as he seemed to know how much the trying behooved him—he resolves a simple resolution, to ask them solemnly in order; and which of them should profess largest, her to believe. Gonorill, th' eldest, apprehending too well her father's weakness, makes answer, invoking Heaven, "That she loved him above her soul." "Therefore," quoth the old man, overjoyed, "since thou so honorest my declined age, to thee and the husband whom thou shalt choose I give the third part of my realm." So fair a speeding[17] for a few words soon uttered was to Regan, the second, ample instruction what to say. She, on the same demand, spares no protesting; and the gods must witness that otherwise to express her thoughts she knew not but that "She loved him above all creatures"; and so receives an equal reward with her sister. But Cordeilla, the youngest, though hitherto best beloved, and now before her eyes the rich and present hire of a little easy soothing,[18] the danger also and the loss likely to betide plain dealing, yet moves not from the solid purpose of a sincere and virtuous answer. "Father," saith she, "my love towards you is as my duty bids: what should a father seek, what can a child promise more? They who pretend beyond this, flatter." When the old man, sorry to hear this, and wishing her to recall those words, persisted asking; with a loyal sadness at her father's infirmity, but something, on the sudden, harsh, and glancing rather at her sisters than speaking her own mind, "Two ways only," saith she, "I have to answer what you require me: the former, your command is, I should recant; accept then this other which is left me; look how much you have, so much is your value, and so much I love you." "Then hear thou," quoth Leir, now all in passion, "what thy ingratitude hath gained thee: because thou hast not reverenced thy aged father equal to thy sisters, part in my kingdom, or what else is mine, reckon to have none." And, without delay, gives in marriage his other daughters, Gonorill to Maglaunus, Duke of Albania, Regan to Henninus, Duke of Cornwall; with them in present half his kingdom, the rest to follow at his death.

In the meanwhile, fame was not sparing to divulge the wisdom and other graces of Cordeilla, insomuch that Aganippus, a great king in Gaul (however he came by his Greek name), seeks her to wife; and, nothing altered at the loss of her dowry, receives her gladly in such manner as she was sent him. After this King Leir, more and more drooping with years, became an easy prey to his daughters and their husbands, who now, by daily encroachment, had seized the whole kingdom into their hands; and the old king is put to sojourn with his eldest daughter, attended only by threescore knights. But they in a short while grudged at, as too numerous and disorderly for continual guests, are reduced to thirty. Not brooking that affront, the old king betakes him to his second daughter; but there also, discord soon arising between the servants of differing masters in one family, five only are suffered to attend him. Then back again he returns to the other, hoping that she his eldest could not but have more pity on his gray hairs; but she now refuses to admit him unless he be content with one only of his followers. At last the remembrance of his youngest, Cordeilla, comes to

his thoughts; and now acknowledging how true her words had been, though with little hope from whom he had so injured, be it but to pay her the last recompense she can have from him, his confession of her wise forewarning, that so perhaps his misery, the proof and experiment[19] of her wisdom, might something soften her, he takes his journey into France.

Now might be seen a difference between the silent or downright spoken affection of some children to their parents and the talkative obsequiousness of others while the hope of inheritance overacts[20] them and on the tongue's end enlarges their duty. Cordeilla, out of mere love, without the suspicion of expected reward, at the message only of her father in distress, pours forth true filial tears. And not enduring either that her own or any other eye should see him in such forlorn condition as his messenger declared, discreetly appoints one of her trusted servants first to convey him privately towards some good sea-town, there to array him, bathe him, cherish him, furnish him with such attendance and state as beseemed his dignity; that then, as from his first landing, he might send word of his arrival to her husband Aganippus. Which done with all mature and requisite contrivance, Cordeilla, with the king her husband and all the barony of his realm, who then first had news of his passing the sea, go out to meet him; and after all honorable and joyful entertainment, Aganippus, as to his wive's father and his royal guest, surrenders him, during his abode there, the power and disposal of his whole dominion, permitting his wife Cordeilla to go with an army and set her father upon his throne. Wherein her piety so prospered as that she vanquished her impious sisters with those dukes, and Leir again, as saith the story, three years obtained the crown. To whom, dying, Cordelia with all regal solemnities gave burial in the town of Leicester, and then, as right heir succeeding, and her husband dead, ruled the land five years in peace, until Marganus and Cunedagius, her two sisters' sons, not bearing that a kingdom should be governed by a woman in the unseasonablest time to raise that quarrel against a woman so worthy make war against her, depose her, and imprison her; of which impatient, and now long unexercised to suffer, she there, as is related, killed herself.

Coming to the end of his account of legendary British history, Milton expresses mingled nostalgia and relief: nostalgia for the fables that, despite their strong attraction, he cannot accept, and relief that he at last can work with data that command his grudging admiration and respect.

Thus far, though leaning only on the credit of Geoffrey Monmouth and his assertors,[21] I yet, for the specified causes, have thought it not beneath my purpose to relate what I found. Whereto I neither oblige the belief of other person nor overhastily subscribe mine own. Nor have I stood with others computing or collating years and chronologies, lest I should be vainly curious about the time and circumstance of things whereof the substance is so much in doubt. By this time, like one who had set out on his way by night, and

---

[17]So successful an outcome. [18]*Hire . . . soothing:* reward for cajolery. [19]Instance. [20]Overcomes. [21]Advocates.

travailed through a region of smooth or idle dreams, our history now arrives on the confines, where daylight and truth meet us with a clear dawn, representing to our view, though at a far distance, true colors and shapes. For albeit Caesar, whose authority we are now first to follow, wanted not who taxed him of misreporting in his *Commentaries*, yea in his civil wars against Pompey, much more, may we think, in the British affairs, of whose little skill in writing he did not easily hope to be contradicted; yet now in such variety of good authors we hardly can miss, from one hand or other, to be sufficiently informed as of things past so long ago. But this will better be referred to a second discourse.

THE SECOND BOOK

I am now to write of what befell the Britons from fifty-and-three years before the birth of our Saviour, when first the Romans came in,[22] till the decay and ceasing of that empire; a story of much truth, and for the first hundred years and somewhat more, collected without much labor: so many and so prudent were the writers which those two, the civilest and the wisest of European nations, both Italy and Greece, afforded to the actions of that puissant city.[23] For worthy deeds are not often destitute of worthy relaters, as by a certain fate great acts and great eloquence have most commonly gone hand in hand, equaling and honoring each other in the same ages. 'Tis true that in obscurest times, by shallow and unskilful writers, the indistinct noise of many battles and devastations of many kingdoms overrun and lost hath come to our ears. For what wonder, if in all ages ambition and the love of rapine hath stirred up greedy and violent men to bold attempts in wasting and ruining wars, which to posterity have left the work of wild beasts and destroyers rather than the deeds and monuments of men and conquerors? But he whose just and true valor uses the necessity of war and dominion not to destroy but to prevent destruction, to bring in liberty against tyrants, law and civility among barbarous nations, knowing that when he conquers all things else he cannot conquer Time or Detraction, wisely conscious of this his want as well as of his worth not to be forgotten or concealed, honors and hath recourse to the aid of eloquence, his friendliest[24] and best supply; by whose immortal record his noble deeds, which else were transitory, becoming fixed and durable against the force of years and generations, he fails not to continue through all posterity, over Envy, Death, and Time also victorious.

Therefore when the esteem of science and liberal study waxes low in the commonwealth, we may presume that also there all civil virtue and worthy action is grown as low to a decline, and then eloquence, as it were consorted in the same destiny, with the decrease and fall of virtue corrupts also and fades; at least resigns her office of relating to illiterate and frivolous historians such as the persons themselves both deserve and are best pleased with, whilst they want either the understanding to choose better or the innocence to dare invite the examining and searching style of an intelligent and faithful writer to the survey of their unsound[25] exploits, better befriended by obscurity than fame.

As for these, the only authors we have of British matters while the power of Rome reached hither—for Gildas[26] affirms that of the Roman times no British writer was in his days extant, or if any ever were, either burned by enemies or transported with such as fled the Pictish and Saxon invasions—these therefore, only Roman authors, there be who in the English tongue have laid together as much, and perhaps more, than was requisite to a history of Britain. So that were it not for leaving an unsightly gap so near to the beginning I should have judged this labor wherein so little seems to be required above transcription almost superfluous. Notwithstanding, since I must through it, if aught by diligence may be added or omitted, or by other disposing may be more explained or more expressed, I shall assay.

[THE FALL OF ROMAN BRITAIN]

[Having told of the decline of Rome before the mounting force of the Saxon barbarians, Milton ends Book II with an elegiac comment on the cyclic change of cultures.]

Thus expired this great empire of the Romans, first in Britain, soon after in Italy itself, having borne chief sway in this island—though never throughly subdued or all at once in subjection, if we reckon from the coming in of Julius to the taking of Rome by Alaric, in which year Honorius[27] wrote those letters of discharge into Britain—the space of 462 years. And with the empire fell also what before in this western world was chiefly Roman: learning, valor, eloquence, history, civility, and even language itself, all these together, as it were, with equal pace diminishing and decaying. Henceforth we are to steer by another sort of authors [that is, "monkish" chroniclers], near enough to the things they write as in their own country (if that would serve), in time not much belated, some of equal age, in expression barbarous, and to say how judicious I suspend a while. This we must expect: in civil[28] matters to find them dubious relaters, and still to the best advantage of what they term "Holy Church," meaning indeed themselves; in most other matters of religion blind, astonished,[29] and strook[30] with superstition as with a planet—in one word, monks. Yet these guides, where can be had no better, must be followed. In gross it may be true enough; in circumstance[31] each man, as his judgment gives him, may reserve his faith, or bestow it. But so different a state of things requires a several relation.

THE THIRD BOOK

This third book, having to tell of accidents as various and exemplary as the intermission or change of government

---

[22]By modern reckoning, Caesar's first invasion of Britain is dated 55 B.C., the second a year later.   [23]Rome.   [24]Most propitious.   [25]Wicked.   [26]See p. 820, n.52.   [27]Flavius Honorius (384–423) Roman emperor of the West during whose inglorious reign (395–423) the Visigoths under Alaric twice invaded Italy and finally took and plundered Rome itself in the same year (410) so that the emperor, from his imperial court in Ravenna, released the Britons from their allegiance.   [28]Political and domestic.   [29]Bewildered, i.e., stupid.   [30]Struck.   [31]Matters of detail.

hath anywhere brought forth, may deserve attention more than common and repay it with like benefit to them who can judiciously read, considering especially that the late civil broils[32] had cast us into a condition not much unlike to what the Britons then were in when the imperial jurisdiction departing hence left them to the sway of their own councils; which times by comparing seriously with these later, and that confused anarchy with this interreign,[33] we may be able from two such remarkable turns of state, producing like events among us, to raise a knowledge of ourselves both great and weighty by judging hence what kind of men the Britons generally are in matters of so high enterprise, how by nature, industry, or custom fitted to attempt or undergo matters of so main consequence; for if it be a high point of wisdom in every private man, much more is it in a nation to know itself, rather than puffed up with vulgar flatteries and encomiums, for want of self-knowledge, to enterprise rashly and come off miserably in great undertakings.

THE DIGRESSION IN MILTON'S HISTORY OF ENGLAND . . .[34]

[A COMPARISON OF ANCIENT AND CONTEMPORARY ENGLAND]

But because the gaining or losing of liberty is the greatest change to better or to worse that may befall a nation under civil government, and so discovers, as nothing more, what degree of understanding or capacity, what disposition to justice and civility, there is among them, I suppose it will be many ways profitable to resume a while the whole discourse of what happened in this island soon after the Romans, going out; and to consider what might be the reason why, seeing other nations both ancient and modern with extreme hazard and danger have strove for liberty as a thing invaluable, and by the purchase thereof have so ennobled their spirits as from obscure and small to grow eminent and glorious commonwealths, why the Britons, having such a smooth occasion given them to free themselves as ages have not afforded, such a manumission as never subjects had a fairer, should let it pass through them as a cordial medicine through a dying man without the least effect of sense or natural vigor. And no less to purpose if not more usefully to us it may withal be enquired, since God after twelve ages and more had drawn so near a parallel between their state and ours in the late commotions, why they who had the chief management therein having attained, though not so easily, to a condition which had set before them civil government in all her forms and given them to be masters of their own choice, were not found able after so many years doing and undoing to hit so much as into any good and laudable way that might show us hopes of a just and well amended commonwealth to come.

For these our ancestors it is alleged that their youth and chief strength was carried oversea to serve the Empire, that the Scots and Picts and Saxons lay sore upon them without respite. And yet we hear the Romans telling them that their

enemies were not stronger than they, whenas one legion drove them twice out of the isle at first encounter. Nor could the Britons be so ignorant of war, whom the Romans had then newly instructed, or if they were to seek, alike were their enemies rude and naked barbarians. But that they were so timorous and without heart as Gildas reports them is no way credible, for the same he reports of those whom the Romans testify to have found valiant. Whereof those also gave not the least proof when a few of them, and these in their greatest weakness taking courage, not defended themselves only against the Scots and Picts, but repulsed them well beaten home.

Of these who swayed most in the late troubles [i.e., the Civil War in England], few words as to this point may suffice. They had armies, leaders, and successes to their wish, but to make use of so great advantages was not their skill. To other causes, therefore, and not to want of force or warlike manhood in the Britons, both those and these lately, we must impute the ill husbanding of those fair opportunities which might seem to have put liberty, so long desired, like a bird into their hands. Of which other causes equally belonging both to ruler, priest, and people above hath been related, which as they brought those ancient natives to misery and ruin by liberty, which rightly used might have made them happy, so brought they these of late after many labors, much bloodshed, and vast expense to ridiculous frustration. In whom the like defects the like miscarriages notoriously appeared with vices not less hateful or inexcusable; nor less enforcing, whosoever shall write their story, to revive those ancient complaints of Gildas as deservedly on these lately as on those his times.

For a Parliament being called[35] and, as was thought, many things to redress, the people with great courage and expectation to be now eased of what discontented them chose to their behoof[36] in Parliament such as they thought best affected[37] to the public good, and some indeed men of wisdom and integrity. The rest, and to be sure the greatest part, whom wealth and ample possessions or bold and active am-

---

[32]The disturbances of the 1630's and 1640's leading to the civil war between Charles I and the Long Parliament. [33]Interregnum.
[34]This section is based upon a twelve-page manuscript in a contemporary hand, not Milton's, now in the Houghton Library at Harvard University. Presumably written about 1648 and omitted (perhaps at Milton's own request) from the first edition of *The History of Britain* (1670), it was first published in a shorter version in 1681 by Henry Brome as *Mr. John Miltons Character of the Long Parliament and Assembly of Divines. In MDCXLI. Omitted in his other Works, and never before Printed, And very seasonable for these times.* How Brome obtained the manuscript is unknown, but he himself explained its belated publication on the ground that "out of tenderness to a party (whom neither this nor much more lenity has had the luck to oblige) it was struck out for some harshness, being only such a digression as the *History* itself would not be discomposed by its omission. . . ." Certain inaccuracies in the transcription of the Harvard manuscript as reprinted in the Columbia edition of Milton's *Works* (Vol. X) are recorded in the notes that follow.
[35]The so-called Long Parliament, which began its twenty-year session on 3 November 1640. [36]Behalf. [37]Most devoted.

bition rather than merit had commended to the same place, when once the superficial zeal and popular fumes that acted[38] their new magistracy were cooled and spent in them, straight everyone betook himself, setting the commonwealth behind and his private ends before, to do as his own profit or ambition led him. Then was justice delayed and soon after denied; spite and favor determined all: hence faction, then treachery both at home and in the field, everywhere wrong and oppression, foul and dishonest things committed daily or maintained in secret or in open.

Some who had been called from shops and warehouses without other merit to sit in supreme counsels and committees, as their breeding was, fell to huckster the commonwealth; others did thereafter as men could soothe and humor them best, so that he only who could give most, or under covert of hypocritical zeal insinuate basest, enjoyed unworthily the rewards of learning and fidelity, or escaped the punishment of his crimes and misdeeds. Their votes and ordinances, which men looked should have contained the repealing of bad laws and the immediate constitution of better, resounded with nothing else but new impositions, taxes, excises—yearly, monthly, weekly—not to reckon the offices, gifts, and preferments bestowed and shared among themselves.

They in the meanwhile who were ever faithfulest to their cause and freely aided them in person or with their substance when they durst not compel either, slighted soon after and quite bereaved of their just debts by greedy sequestration,[39] were tossed up and down after miserable attendance from one committee to another with petitions in their hands, yet either missed the obtaining of their suit or if it were at length granted by their orders, mere shame and reason ofttimes extorting from them at least a show of justice, yet by their sequestrators and subcommittees abroad, men for the most part of insatiable hands and noted disloyalty, those orders were commonly disobeyed, which for certain durst not have been without secret compliance, if not compact, with some superiors able to bear them out.

Thus were their friends confiscate[40] in their enemies while they forfeited their debtors to the state (as they called it), but indeed to the ravening seizure of innumerable thieves in office, yet were withal no less burdened in all extraordinary assessments and oppressions than whom they took to be disaffected. Nor were we happier creditors to the state than to them who were sequestered as the state's enemies, for that faith which ought to be kept as sacred and inviolable as anything holy, the public faith, after infinite sums received and all the wealth of the church not better employed but swallowed up into a private gulf, was not ere long ashamed to confess bankrupt. And now besides the sweetness of bribery and other gain with the love of rule, their own guiltiness and the dreaded name of just account (which the people had long called for) discovered plainly that there were of their own number who secretly contrived and fomented those troubles and combustions in the land which openly they sat to remedy, and would continually find such work as should keep them from ever being brought to the terrible stand of laying down their authority for lack of new

business, or not drawing it out to any length of time though upon the necessary ruin of a whole nation.

And if the state were in this plight, religion was not in much better, to reform which a certain number of divines were called,[41] neither chosen by any rule or custom ecclesiastical nor eminent for either piety or knowledge above others left out; only as each member of Parliament in his private fancy thought fit, so elected one by one. The most of them were such as had preached and cried down with great show of zeal the avarice and pluralities of bishops and prelates: that one cure of souls[42] was a full employment for one spiritual pastor how able so ever, if not a charge rather above human strength. Yet these conscientious men, ere any part of the work for which they came together (and that on the public salary), wanted not impudence, to the ignominy and scandal of their pastorlike profession and especially of their boasted reformation, to seize into their hands or not unwillingly to accept (besides one, sometimes two or more, of the best livings) collegiate masterships in the university, rich lectures in the City,[43] setting sail to all winds that might blow gain into their covetous bosoms. By which means these[44] great rebukers of nonresidence among so many distant cures were not ashamed to be seem so quickly pluralists and nonresidents themselves, to a fearful condemnation, doubtless, by their own mouths.

And yet the main doctrine for which they took such pay, and insisted upon with more vehemence than gospel, was but to tell us in effect that their doctrine was worth nothing and the spiritual power of their ministry less available than bodily compulsion, persuading the magistrate to use it as a stronger means to subdue and bring in conscience than evangelic persuasion. But while they taught compulsion without convincement[45]—which not long before they so much complained of as executed unchristianly against themselves— their intents were clear to be no other than to have set up a spiritual tyranny by a secular power to the advancing of their own authority above the magistrate. And well did their disciples manifest themselves to be no better principled than their teachers, trusted with committeeships and other gainful offices upon their commendations for zealous and (as they sticked not to term them) godly men, but executing their places more like children of the devil, unfaithfully, unjustly, unmercifully, and (where not corruptly) stupidly. So that between them the teachers and these the disciples there

[38]Animated.
[39]Diversion or confiscation of the income of a property or ecclesiastical benefice.   [40]Forfeited.
[41]The Westminster Assembly, which began its meetings on 1 July 1643 for the purpose of reforming the doctrine and discipline of the Church of England, consisted of ten peers, twenty members of Commons, 126 Presbyterian and Independent (but no Baptist) divines, and six Scottish deputies. Its sessions, which were increasingly dominated by the reactionary Presbyterians, continued until 1649.   [42]Spiritual charge of parishioners.
[43]Lectureships endowed by merchants or Puritan sympathizers in the City of London, a center of Presbyterian strength.
[44]The Columbia edition (X, 322) reads *those*.
[45]Conviction.

hath not been a more ignominious and mortal wound to faith, to piety, nor more cause of blaspheming given to the enemies of God and of truth since the first preaching of reformation, which needed most to have begun in the forwardest reformers themselves.

The people, therefore, looking one while[46] on the statists,[47] whom they beheld without constancy or firmness laboring doubtfully beneath the weight of their own too-high undertakings, busiest in petty things, trifling in the main, deluded and quite alienated, expressed divers ways their disaffection, some despising whom before they honored, some deserting, some inveighing, some conspiring against them. Then looking on the churchmen, most of whom they saw now to have preached their own bellies rather than the gospel, many illiterate, persecutors more than lovers of the truth, covetous, worldly, to whom not godliness with contentment seemed great gain, but godliness with gain seemed great contentment, like in many things whereof they had accused their predecessors. Looking on all these, the people, who had been kept warm a while by the affected zeal of their pulpits, after a false heat became more cold and obdurate than before, some turning to lewdness, some to flat atheism, put beside[48] their old religion, and foully[49] scandalized in what they expected should be new. Thus they who but of late were extolled as great deliverers, and had a people wholly at their devotion, by so discharging their trust as we see did not only weaken and unfit themselves to be dispensers of what liberty they pretended, but unfitted also the people, now grown worse and more disordinate, to receive or to digest any liberty at all.

For stories teach us that liberty sought out of season in a corrupt and degenerate age brought Rome itself into further slavery. For liberty hath a sharp and double edge fit only to be handled by just and virtuous men; to bad and dissolute it becomes a mischief unwieldy in their own hands. Neither is it completely given but by them who have the happy skill to know what is grievance and unjust to a people, and how to remove it wisely, that good men may enjoy the freedom which they merit and the bad the curb which they need. But to do this and to know these exquisite proportions, the heroic wisdom which is required surmounted far the principles of narrow politicians. What wonder, then, if they sunk as those unfortunate Britons before them, entangled and oppressed with things too hard and generous[50] above their strain and temper? For Britain—to speak a truth not oft spoken—as it is a land fruitful enough of men stout and courageous in war, so is it naturally not overfertile of men able to govern justly and prudently in peace; trusting only on their mother wit, as most do, and consider not that civility, prudence, love of the public more than of money or vain honor are to this soil in a manner outlandish;[51] grow not here but in minds well implanted with solid and elaborate breeding; too impolitic else and too crude, if not headstrong and intractable to the industry and virtue either of executing or understanding true civil government. Valiant indeed and prosperous to win a field, but to know the end and reason of winning, unjudicious and unwise, in good or bad success alike unteachable.

For the sun, which we want, ripens wits as well as fruits; and as wine and oil are imported to us from abroad, so must ripe understanding and many civil virtues be imported into our minds from foreign writings and examples of best ages. We shall else miscarry still and come short in the attempt of any great enterprise. Hence did their victories prove as fruitless as their losses dangerous, and left them still conquering under the same grievances that men suffer conquered, which was indeed unlikely to go otherwise unless men more than vulgar, bred up (as few of them were) in the knowledge of ancient and illustrious deeds, invincible against money and vain titles, impartial to friendships and relations, had conducted their affairs. But then from the chapman[52] to the retailer many, whose ignorance was more audacious than the rest, were admitted with all their sordid rudiments to bear no mean sway among them both in church and state. From the confluence of all these errors, mischiefs, and misdemeanors, what in the eyes of man could be expected but what befell those ancient inhabitants whom they so much resembled, confusion in the end? But on these things and this parallel having enough insisted, I return back to the story which gave matter to this digression.

THE SIXTH BOOK

[The End of Saxon England]

When Harold, son of Godwin, earl of Wessex, was chosen to rule a divided and distracted England on the death of Edward the Confessor in January 1066, he knew he had a potent rival in William, duke of Normandy, who promptly claimed the throne through his descent from Edward's mother Emma. During the spring and summer William assembled his forces and prepared his fleet along the Norman coast, and in the early fall he led his troops ashore in Sussex and set up camp at Hastings. Rushing from the north of England, Harold encountered him near Hastings, and there, on October 14, the fate of England was determined.

Harold . . . sitting jollily at dinner, news is brought him that Duke William of Normandy, with a great multitude of horse and foot, slingers and archers, besides other choice auxiliaries which he had hired in France, was arrived at Pevensey.[53] Harold, who had expected him all the summer, but not so late in the year as now it was, for it was October, with his forces much diminished after two sore conflicts,[54] and the departing of many others from him discontented, in great haste marches to London. Thence, not tarrying for supplies, which were on their way towards him, hurries into Sussex (for he was always in haste since the day of his coronation), and ere the third part of his army could be well put in order, finds the duke about nine miles from Hastings,[55]

[46]At one time, sometimes. [47]Politicians. [48]Alienated from.
[49]The Columbia edition (X, 323) omits this word.
[50]Magnanimous. [51]Alien. [52]Merchant.
[53]Town in East Sussex about twelve miles southwest of Hastings.
[54]Before moving south to meet the Norman threat, Harold had subdued a coalition of Danes and disaffected Englishmen (including his own brother, Tostig).
[55]The actual scene of the battle was Senlac, a ridge upon which

and now drawing nigh, sent spies before him to survey the strength and number of his enemies: them, discovered such, the duke causing to be led about, and after well filled with meat and drink, sent back. They, not overwise, brought word that the duke's army were most of them priests, for they saw their faces all over shaven, the English then using to let grow on their upper lip large mustachios, as did anciently the Britons. The king laughing answered that they were not priests, but valiant and hardy soldiers. Therefore said Girtha his brother, a youth of noble courage and understanding above his age, "Forbear thou thyself to fight, who art obnoxious to Duke William by oath;[56] let us unsworn undergo the hazard of battle, who may justly fight in the defence of our country; thou, reserved to fitter time, maist either reunite us flying or revenge us dead." The king, not hearkening to this lest it might seem to argue fear in him or a bad cause, with like resolution rejected the offers of Duke William sent to him by a monk before the battle, with this only answer hastily delivered, "Let God judge between us." The offers were these: that Harold would either lay down the scepter, or hold it of him,[57] or try his title with him by single combat in sight of both armies, or refer it to the pope. These rejected, both sides prepared to fight the next morning, the English from singing and drinking all night, the Normans from confession of their sins, and communion of the Host.

The English were in a strait disadvantageous place, so that many, discouraged with their ill ordering, scarce having room where to stand, slipped away before the onset; the rest in close order, with their battleaxes and shields, made an impenetrable squadron: the king himself with his brothers on foot stood by the royal standard, wherein the figure of a man fighting was inwoven with gold and precious stones. The Norman foot, most bowmen, made the foremost front, on either side wings of horse somewhat behind. The duke arming, and his corslet given him on the wrong side, said pleasantly, "The strength of my dukedom will be turned now into a kingdom." Then the whole army singing the song of Roland,[58] the remembrance of whose exploits might hearten them, imploring lastly divine help, the battle began, and was fought sorely on either side; but the main body of English foot by no means would be broken till the duke, causing his men to feign flight, drew them out with desire of pursuit into open disorder, then turned suddenly upon them so routed by themselves, which wrought their overthrow; yet so they died not unmanfully, but turning oft upon their enemies, by the advantage of an upper ground, beat them down by heaps, and filled up a great ditch with their carcasses. Thus hung the victory wavering on either side from the third hour of day to evening, when Harold, having maintained the fight with unspeakable courage and personal valor, shot into the head with an arrow, fell at length, and left his soldiers without heart longer to withstand the unwearied enemy. With Harold fell also his two brothers, Leofwin and Girtha, with them greatest part of the English nobility. His body lying dead a knight or soldier wounding on the thigh was by the duke presently turned out of military service. Of Normans and French were slain no small number; the duke himself also that day not a little hazarded

his person, having had three choice horses killed under him.

Victory obtained, and his dead carefully buried, the English also by permission, he sent the body of Harold to his mother without ransom, though she offered very much to redeem it; which having received she buried at Waltham,[59] in a church built there by Harold. In the meanwhile, Edwin and Morcar[60] who had withdrawn themselves from Harold, hearing of his death, came to London, sending Aldgith the queen, their sister, with all speed to Westchester. Aldred, Archbishop of York, and many of the nobles, with the Londoners, would have set up Edgar[61] the right heir, and prepared themselves to fight for him; but Morcar and Edwin, not liking the choice, who each of them expected to have been chosen before him, withdrew their forces and returned home. Duke William, contrary to his former resolution (if Florent of Worcester[62] and they who follow him say true), wasting, burning, and slaying all in his way; or rather, as saith Malmesbury,[63] not in hostile but in regal manner came up to London, met at Barcham[64] by Edgar, with the nobles, bishops, citizens, and at length Edwin and Morcar, who all submitted to him, gave hostages, and swore fidelity; he to them promised peace and defense, yet permitted his men the while to burn and make prey. Coming to London with all his army, he was on Christmas day solemnly crowned in the great church at Westminster by Aldred, archbishop of York, having first given his oath at the altar, in presence of all the people, to defend the church, well govern the people, maintain right law, prohibit rapine and unjust judgment.

Thus the English, while they agreed not about the choice of their native king, were constrained to take the yoke of an outlandish conqueror. With what minds and by what course of life they had fitted themselves for this servitude, William of Malmesbury spares not to lay open. Not a few years before the Normans came, the clergy, though in Edward the Confessor's days,[65] had lost all good literature and religion,

---

William subsequently erected Battle Abbey to commemorate his victory.

[56]Earlier, when Harold had fallen into William's hands after being shipwrecked on the French coast, he had sworn some sort of oath which, as William charged, he thereafter violated.

[57]As his vassal.

[58]A lay (perhaps an early version of the twelfth-century *Chanson de Roland*) about the most famous of Charlemagne's paladins, who, returning through the Pyrenees from an expedition into Spain, died (778) in a rearguard action at Roncevaux.

[59]Waltham Holy Cross or Waltham Abbey, formerly a town in Essex, now a part of greater London.

[60]Harold's brothers-in-law, Eadwine, earl of Mercia, and Morkere, earl of Northumberland, to whose assistance he had gone the previous summer when they were threatened by the Danes.

[61]Eadgar the Atheling (fl. 1066–1106), grandson of King Eadmund Ironside (d. 1016), who had been forced to yield most of northern England to the Danes.

[62]Florence of Worcester (d. 1118), author of a *Chronicon ex Chronicis* that extends to 1117.

[63]William of Malmesbury (see p. 820, n.56).

[64]Barking, formerly a town in Essex, now a suburb of London.

[65]*Though . . . days*: despite the fact that the king at the time was the saintly Edward the Confessor, who ruled from 1042 to 1066.

scarce able to read and understand their Latin service: he was a miracle to others who knew his grammar. The monks went clad in fine stuffs, and made no difference what they eat, which though in itself no fault, yet to their consciences was irreligious. The great men, given to gluttony and dissolute life, made a prey of the common people, abusing their daughters whom they had in service, then turning them off to the stews;[66] the meaner sort, tippling together night and day, spent all they had in drunkenness, attended with other vices which effeminate[67] men's minds. Whence it [10] came to pass that, carried on with fury and rashness more than any true fortitude or skill of war, they gave to William their conqueror so easy a conquest. Not but that some few of all sorts were much better among them, but such was the generality. And as the long suffering of God permits bad men to enjoy prosperous days with the good, so His severity ofttimes exempts not good men from their share in evil times with the bad.

If these were the causes of such misery and thralldom to those our ancestors, with what better close can be concluded than here in fit season to remember[68] this age in the midst of her security to fear from like vices, without amendment, the revolutions[69] of like calamities?

[66]Brothels.   [67]Make unmanly, enervate.   [68]Remind.
[69]Repetition, recurrence.

Edward Hyde, Earl of Clarendon[1]   [1609-1674]

from The History of the Rebellion and Civil Wars in England (1702-04)

BOOK I . . .

[INTRODUCTION]

That posterity may not be deceived by the prosperous wickedness of those times of which I write into an opinoin that nothing less than a general combination and universal apostasy in the whole nation from their religion and allegiance could, in so short a time, have produced such a total and prodigious alteration and confusion over the whole [20] kingdom; and that the memory of those who, out of duty and conscience, have opposed that torrent which did overwhelm them may not lose the recompense due to their virtue, but having undergone the injuries and reproaches of this may find a vindication in a better age; it will not be unuseful, for the information of the judgment and conscience of men, to present to the world a full and clear narration of the grounds, circumstances, and artifices of this rebellion, not only from the time since the flame hath been visible in a civil war, but, looking farther back, from those former passages and [30] accidents[1] by which the seedplots were made and framed from whence those mischiefs have successively grown to the height they have since arrived at.

And in this ensuing history, though the hand and judgment of God will be very visible in infatuating a people (as ripe and prepared for destruction) into all the perverse actions of folly and madness, making the weak to contribute to the designs of the wicked, and suffering even those by degrees, out of a conscience of their guilt, to grow more wicked than they intended to be, letting the wise to be [40] imposed upon by men of small understanding, and permitting the innocent to be possessed with laziness and sleep in the most visible article of danger, uniting the ill, though of the most different opinions, opposite interests, and distant affections, in a firm and constant league of mischiefs, and dividing those whose opinions and interests are the same into faction and emulation, more pernicious to the public than the treason of the others, whilst the poor people, under pretence of zeal to religion, law, liberty, and Parliaments—words of precious esteem in their just signification—are furiously hurried into actions introducing atheism, and dissolving all the elements of Christian religion, canceling all obligations and destroying all foundations of law and liberty, and rendering not only the privileges but the very being of Parliaments desperate and impracticable: I say, though the immediate finger and wrath of God must be acknowledged in these perplexities and distractions, yet he who shall diligently observe the distempers and conjunctures of time, the ambition, pride, and folly of persons, and the suddain growth of wickedness, from want of care and circumspection in the first impressions, will find all these miseries to have proceeded and to have been brought upon us from the same natural causes and means which have usually attended kingdoms swoln with long plenty, pride, and excess, towards some signal mortification and castigation of heaven. And it may

[1]For a commentary on Clarendon and for another excerpt from his works see Books and Men, pp. 795 ff.
HISTORY OF THE REBELLION   [1]*Passages and accidents*: circumstances and events.

be, upon the consideration how impossible it was to foresee many things that have happened, and of the necessity of overlooking many other things, we may not yet find the cure so desperate but that, by God's mercy, the wounds may be again bound up; and then this prospect may not make the future peace less pleasant and durable.

I have the more willingly induced myself to this unequal task[2] out of the hope of contributing somewhat to that blessed end; and though a piece of this nature (wherein the infirmities of some and the malice of others must be boldly 10 looked upon and mentioned) is not likely to be published in the age in which it is writ, yet it may serve to inform myself, and some others, what we ought to do as well as to comfort us in what we have done. For which work, as I may not be thought altogether an incompetent person, having been present as a member of Parliament in those councils before and till the breaking out of the rebellion, and having since had the honor to be near two great kings in some trust, so I shall perform the same with all faithfulness and ingenuity,[3] with an equal observation of the faults and infirmities of 20 both sides, with their defects and oversights in pursuing their own ends; and shall no otherwise mention small and light occurrences than as they have been introductions to matters of the greatest moment; nor speak of persons otherwise than as the mention of their virtues or vices is essential to the work in hand: in which I shall with truth preserve myself from the least sharpness that may proceed from private provocation, and in the whole observe the rules that a man should who deserves to be believed.

I shall not, then, lead any man farther back in this journey, 30 for the discovery of the entrance into these dark ways, than the beginning of this king's reign.[4] For I am not so sharp-sighted as those who have discerned this rebellion contriving from (if not before) the death of Queen Elizabeth, and fomented by several princes and great ministers of state in Christendom, to the time that it brake out. Neither do I look so far back as I do because I believe the design to have been so long since formed, but that, by viewing the temper, disposition, and habit at that time of the court and of the country, we may discern the minds of men prepared of some 40 to act and of others to suffer all that hath since happened: the pride of this man and the popularity of that, the levity of one and the morosity of another, the excess of the court in the greatest want and the parsimony and retention[5] of the country in the greatest plenty, the spirit of craft and subtlety in some and the unpolished integrity of others too much despising craft or art—all contributing jointly to this mass of confusion now before us. . . .

[LAUD'S RISE TO POWER]

It was within one week after the king's return from Scotland that Abbot died at his house at Lambeth.[6] The king 50 took very little time to consider who should be his successor, but the very next time the bishop of London[7] (who was longer on his way home than the king had been) came to him, His Majesty entertained him very cheerfully with this compellation,[8] "My Lord's Grace of Canterbury, you are very welcome"; and gave order the same day for the dis-

patch of all the necessary forms for the translation, so that within a month or thereabouts after the death of the other archbishop he was completely invested in that high dignity, and settled in his palace at Lambeth. This great prelate had been before in great favor with the duke of Buckingham,[9] whose chief confidant he was, and by him recommended to the king as fittest to be trusted in the conferring all ecclesiastical preferments when he was but bishop of St. David's, or newly preferred to Bath and Wells; and from that time he entirely governed that province without a rival, so that his promotion to Canterbury was long foreseen and expected, nor was it attended with any increase of envy or dislike.

He was a man of great parts and very exemplary virtues, allayed and discredited by some unpopular natural infirmities, the greatest of which was (besides a hasty, sharp way of expressing himself) that he believed innocence of heart and integrity of manners was a guard strong enough to secure any man in his voyage through this world, in what company soever he traveled and through what ways soever he was to pass; and sure never any man was better supplied with that provision. He was born of honest parents who were well able to provide for his education in the schools of learning, from whence they sent him to St. John's College in Oxford, the worst endowed at that time of any in that famous university. From a scholar he became a fellow, and then the president of the college,[10] after he had received all the graces and degrees (the proctorship and the doctorship) could be obtained there. He was always maligned and persecuted by those who were of the Calvinian faction, which was then very powerful, and who, according to their usual maxim and practice, call every man they do not love "papist"; and under this senseless appellation they created him many troubles and vexations, and so far suppressed him that though he was the king's chaplain, and taken notice of for an excellent preacher and a scholar of the most sublime parts, he had not any preferment to invite him to leave his poor college, which only gave him bread, till the vigor of his age was past; and when he was promoted by King James, it was but to a poor bishopric in Wales, which

[2]Task to which the writer was unequal.   [3]Candor.
[4]The reign of Charles I, who succeeded his father James I in 1625.
[5]Illiberality?
[6]George Abbot (1562–1633), whom James I had named archbishop of Canterbury in 1611, had long offended Charles by his Puritan sympathies. Following a virtually enforced sequestration he died at his archiepiscopal palace at Lambeth on 4 August 1633.
[7]William Laud (1573–1645), who had risen so rapidly in the English hierarchy that in only twelve years he was advanced from the obscure Welsh bishopric of St. David's (1621) through Bath and Wells (1626) and London (1628) to Canterbury (1633). As primate he became one of the chief instruments of Charles' unyielding opposition to Parliament and Puritans.
[8]*Entertained . . . compellation*: greeted him with this salutation.
[9]George Villiers (1592–1628), after about 1615 the immensely powerful favorite of James I and then of Charles I. His assassination in 1628 was regarded by many of the Puritans as providential.
[10]Laud entered St. John's in 1589, became a fellow in 1593, and president in 1611.

was not so good a support for a bishop as his college was for a private scholar, though a doctor.

Parliaments in that time were frequent, and grew very busy; and the party under which he had suffered a continual persecution appeared very powerful and full of design, and they who had the courage to oppose them began to be taken notice of with approbation and countenance; under this style he came to be first cherished by the duke of Buckingham, who had made some experiments of the temper and spirit of the other people, nothing to his satisfaction. From this time he prospered at the rate of his own wishes, and being transplanted out of his cold, barren diocese of St. David's into a warmer climate, he was left, as was said before, by that great favorite in that great trust with the king, who was sufficiently indisposed towards the persons or the principles of Calvin's disciples.

When he came into great authority, it may be, he retained too keen a memory of those who had so unjustly and uncharitably persecuted him before, and, I doubt, was so far transported with the same passions he had reason to complain of in his adversaries that, as they accused him of popery because he had some doctrinal opinions which they liked not, though they were nothing allied to popery, so he entertained too much prejudice to some persons, as if they were enemies to the discipline of the church because they concurred with Calvin in some doctrinal points, when they abhorred his discipline, and reverenced the government of the church, and prayed for the peace of it with as much zeal and fervency as any in the kingdom; as they made manifest in their lives and in their sufferings with it and for it. He had, from his first entrance into the world, without any disguise or dissimulation declared his own opinion of that classis[11] of men; and as soon as it was in his power he did all he could to hinder the growth and increase of that faction, and to restrain those who were inclined to it from doing the mischief they desired to do. But his power at court could not enough qualify him to go through with that difficult reformation whilst he had a superior[12] in the church, who, having the reins in his hand, could slacken them according to his own humor and indiscretion, and was thought to be the more remiss to irritate his choleric disposition. But when he had now the primacy in his own hand, the king being inspired with the same zeal, he thought he should be to blame, and have much to answer for, if he did not make haste to apply remedies to those diseases which he saw would grow apace.

In the end of September of the year 1633 he was invested in the title, power, and jurisdiction of archbishop of Canterbury, and entirely in possession of the revenue thereof, without a rival in church or state; that is, no man professed to oppose his greatness, and he had never interposed or appeared in matters of state to this time. His first care was that the place he was removed from might be supplied with a man who would be vigilant to pull up those weeds which the London soil was too apt to nourish, and so he drew his old friend and companion Dr. Juxon[13] as near to him as he could. They had been fellows together in one college in Oxford, and when he was first made bishop of St. David's he made him president of that college; when he could no longer keep the

deanery of the Chapel Royal he made him his successor in that near attendance upon the king; and now he was raised to be archbishop, he easily prevailed with the king to make the other bishop of London before, or very soon after, he had been consecrated bishop of Hereford, if he were more than elect of that church.[14] . . .

BOOK VIII

[LAUD'S TRIAL AND EXECUTION][15]

It was . . . a very sad omen to the treaty that, after they had received the king's message by those noble lords, and before they returned any answer to it, they proceeded in the trial of the archbishop of Canterbury, who had lain prisoner in the Tower, from the beginning of the Parliament, about four years, without any prosecution till this time. Now they brought him to the bars of both Houses, charging him with several articles of high treason, which, if all that was alleged against him had been true, could not have made him guilty of treason. They accused him "of a design to bring in popery, and of having correspondence with the pope," and suchlike particulars as the consciences of his greatest enemies absolved him from. No man was a greater or abler enemy to popery, no man a more resolute and devout son of the Church of England. He was prosecuted by lawyers, assigned to that purpose, out of those who, from their own antipathy to the church and bishops or from some disobligations[16] received from him, were sure to bring passion, animosity, and malice enough of their own, what evidence soever they had from others. And they did treat him with all the rudeness, reproach and barbarity imaginable, with which his judges were not displeased.

He defended himself with great and undaunted courage, and less passion than was expected from his constitution; answered all their objections with clearness and irresistible reason, and convinced all impartial men of his integrity and his detestation of all treasonable intentions. So that though few excellent men have ever had fewer friends to their persons, yet all reasonable men absolved him from any foul

[11]Presbytery, in the Presbyterian church a court composed of the ministers and one or two presbyters of each church in a district. Clarendon is punning on the word. [12]Archbishop Abbot. [13]See p. 917, n.42 [14]Juxon was named bishop of Hereford in late September 1633 and bishop of London, succeeding Laud, the next month. [15]Although Laud had been impeached of treason and imprisoned in the Tower in December 1640, a month after the Long Parliament assembled, it was not until March 1644 that he was brought to trial, and not until the following winter that his fate was finally settled. The previous six months, a particularly uneasy stage of the war, had seen Cromwell's victory at Marston Moor (July 2) and Charles' indecisive encounter with the parliamentary forces at Newbury (October 27), which led to abortive negotiations at Uxbridge in January and February 1645. It was at this moment that Laud's trial, a travesty of judicial procedure, was forced to its conclusion by an extralegal "ordinance" sent up from Commons on November 22, tentatively accepted by Lords on December 17, and finally voted on January 4. Laud's execution on Tower Hill followed six days later. [16]Affronts, annoyances.

crime that the law could take notice of and punish. However, when they had said all they could against him, and he all for himself that need to be said, and no such crime appearing as the Lords, as the supreme court of judicatory, would take upon them to judge him to be worthy of death, they resorted to their legislative power, and by ordinance of Parliament, as they called it—that is, by a determination of those members who sat in the Houses (whereof in the House of Peers there were not above twelve)—they appointed him to be put to death as guilty of high treason. The first time that two Houses of Parliament had ever assumed that jurisdiction, or that ever ordinance had been made to such a purpose, nor could any rebellion be more against the law than that murtherous act.

When the first mention was made of their monstrous purpose of bringing the archbishop to a trial for his life, the Chancelor of the Exchequer, who had always a great reverence and affection for him, had spoken to the king of it, and proposed to him "that in all events there might be a pardon prepared and sent to him under the Great Seal of England to the end if they proceeded against him in any form of law, he might plead the king's pardon, which must be allowed by all who pretended to be governed by the law; but if they proceeded in a martial or any other extraordinary way, without any form of law, His Majesty should declare his justice and affection to an old, faithful servant whom he much esteemed in having done all towards his preservation that was in his power to do." The king was wonderfuly pleased with the proposition, and took from thence occasion to commend the piety and virtue of the archbishop with extraordinary affection, and commanded the Chancelor of the Exchequer to cause the pardon to be prepared, and His Majesty would sign and seal it with all possible secrecy, which at that time was necessary. Whereupon the chancelor sent for Sir Thomas Gardiner, the King's Solicitor, and told him the king's pleasure, upon which he presently drew the pardon, which was signed and sealed[17] with the Great Seal of England, and carefully sent, and delivered into the archbishop's own hand before he was brought to his trial; who received it with great joy, as it was a testimony of the king's gracious affection to him and care of him, without any opinion that they who endeavored to take away the king's life would preserve his by His Majesty's authority.

When the archbishop's counsel had perused the pardon, and considered that all possible exceptions would be taken to it, though they should not reject it, they found that the impeachment was not so distinctly set down in the pardon as it ought to be; which could not be helped at Oxford because they had no copy of it, and therefore had supplied it with all those general expressions as, in any court of law, would make the pardon valid against any exceptions the king's own counsel could make against it. Hereupon the archbishop had, by the same messenger, returned the pardon again to the chancelor with such directions and copies as were necessary, upon which it was perfected accordingly, and delivered safely again to him, and was in his hands during the whole time of his trial. So when his trial was over,

and the ordinance passed for his execution, and he called and asked, according to custom in criminal proceedings, "what he could say more, why he should not suffer death," he told them "that he had the king's gracious pardon, which he pleaded, and tendered to them, and desired that it might be allowed." Whereupon he was sent to the Tower, and the pardon read in both Houses, where without any long debate it was declared "to be of no effect, and that the king could not pardon a judgment of Parliament." And so without troubling themselves farther they gave order for his beheading, which he underwent with all Christian courage and magnanimity, to the admiration of the beholders and confusion of his enemies. Much hath been said of the person of this great prelate before, of his great endowments and natural infirmities, to which shall be added no more in this place (his memory deserving a particular celebration) than that his learning, piety, and virtue have been attained by very few, and the greatest of his infirmities are common to all, even to the best men. . . .

BOOK X . . .

[OLIVER CROMWELL][18]

Cromwell, though the greatest dissembler living, always made his hypocrisy of singular use and benefit to him, and never did anything, how ungracious or imprudent soever it seemed to be, but what was necessary to the design; even his roughness and unpolishedness, which, in the beginning of the Parliament, he affected contrary to the smoothness and complacency which his cousin and bosom friend Mr. Hampden[19] practised towards all men, was necessary; and his first public declaration, in the beginning of the war, to his troop when it was first mustered, "that he would not deceive or couzen[20] them by the perplexed and involved expressions in his commission to fight for king and Parliament"; and therefore told them "that if the king chanced to be in the body of the enemy that he was to charge, he would as soon discharge his pistol upon him as any other private person, and if their conscience would not permit them to do the like, he advised

[17]12 April 1644.
[18]Oliver Cromwell (1599–1658), the villain of Clarendon's *History*, entered Parliament as an obscure country squire in 1628, but it was not until the forties that he began his dizzy rise to fame and power. He quickly exhibited his military genius in the war that he so ardently supported, and after a series of stunning successes emerged as a leader of the Independents (who controlled the army) against the reactionary Presbyterians in Parliament. Influential in reorganizing the New Model Army (1645) to supplant the aristocratic and ineffectual parliamentary generals, he helped bring the war to a successful conclusion, pressed for the trial and execution of Charles (1649), and was instrumental in abolishing the monarchy. Thereafter he became commander-in-chief, and ended his career as lord protector (1653–58).
[19]John Hampden (1594–1643), politician long notable for his opposition to Charles during the thirties and a powerful parliamentary leader after 1640. His death in action, says Clarendon elsewhere, caused as much consternation among the Puritans as if their whole army had been defeated.   [20]Cozen, cheat, impose upon.

them not to list themselves in his troop or under his command"; which was generally looked upon as imprudent and malicious, and might, by the professions the Parliament then made, have proved dangerous to him, yet served his turn, and severed from others and united among themselves all the furious and incensed men against the government, whether ecclesiastical or civil, to look upon him as a man for their turn, upon whom they might depend as one who would go through his work that he undertook. And his strict and unsociable humor in not keeping company with the other [10] officers of the army in their jollities and excesses, to which most of the superior officers under the earl of Essex[21] were inclined, and by which he often made himself ridiculous or contemptible, drew all those of the like sour or reserved natures to his society and conversation, and gave him opportunity to form their understandings, inclinations, and resolutions to his own model. By this he grew to have a wonderful interest in the common soldiers, out of which, as his authority increased, he made all his officers well instructed how to live in the same manner with their soldiers, [20] that they might be able to apply them to their own purposes. Whilst he looked upon the Presbyterian humor as the best incentive to rebellion, no man more a Presbyterian: he sang all psalms with them to their tunes, and loved the longest sermons as much as they; but when he discovered that they would prescribe some limits and bounds to their rebellion, that it was not well breathed, and would expire as soon as some few particulars were granted to them in religion (which he cared not for), and then that the government must run still in the same channel, it concerned him to make [30] it believed "that the state had been more delinquent than the church, and that the people suffered more by the civil than by the ecclesiastical power, and therefore that the change of one would give them little ease if there were not as great an alteration in the other, and if the whole government in both were not reformed and altered"; which though it made him generally odious at first, and irreconciled many of his old friends to him, yet it made those who remained more cordial and firm: he could better compute his own strength, and upon whom he might depend. This discovery made him [40] contrive the New Model[22] of the army, which was the most unpopular act, and disobliged all those who first contrived the rebellion, and who were the very soul of it; and yet if he had not brought that to pass, and changed a general who, though not very sharpsighted, would never be governed nor applied to anything he did not like, for another who had no eyes and so would be willing to be led, all his designs must have come to nothing, and he remained a private colonel of horse, not considerable enough to be in any figure upon an advantageous composition. . . . [50]

BOOK XI . . .

[THE TRIAL AND EXECUTION OF CHARLES I]

When he was first brought to Westminster Hall, which was upon the twentieth of January, [1649,] before their High Court of Justice, he looked upon them and sat down without any manifestation of trouble, never stirring his hat, all the impudent judges sitting covered, and fixing their eyes upon him without the least show of respect. The odious libel, which they called a charge and impeachment, was then read by the clerk, which in effect contained "that he had been admitted king of England and trusted with a limited power to govern according to law, and by his oath and office was obliged to use the power committed to him for the good and benefit of the people; but that he had, out of a wicked design to erect to himself an illimited[23] and tyrannical power and to overthrow the rights and liberties of the people, traitorously levied war against the present Parliament and the people therein represented." And then it mentioned his first appearance at York with a guard, then his being at Beverly, then his setting up his standard at Nottingham,[24] the day of the month and the year in which the battle had been at Edgehill,[25] and all the other several battles which had been fought in his presence; "in which," it said, "he had caused and procured many thousands of the freeborn people of the nation to be slain; that, after all his forces had been defeated and himself become a prisoner, he had in that very year caused many insurrections to be made in England, and given a commission to the prince his son to raise a new war against the Parliament, whereby many who were in their service, and trusted by them, had revolted, broken their trust, and betook themselves to the service of the prince against the Parliament and the people; that he had been the author and contriver of the unnatural, cruel, and bloody wars and was therein guilty of all the treasons, murthers, rapines, burnings, spoils, desolations, damage, and mischief to the nation which had been committed in the said war or been occasioned thereby; and that he was therefore impeached for the said treasons and crimes on the behalf of the people of England as a tyrant, traitor, and murtherer, and a public, implacable enemy to the commonwealth of England." And it was prayed "that he might be put to answer to all the particulars, to the end that such an examination, trial, and judgment might be had thereupon as should be agreeable to justice."

Which being read, their president Bradshaw,[26] after he had

[21]Robert Devereux (1591–1646), son of Elizabeth's favorite (see pp. 843 ff.), third earl of Essex, general of the parliamentary army from 1642 until his resignation (prompted by Cromwell's growing power) in 1645.
[22]Reorganized parliamentary army (1645) that, led by Sir Thomas Fairfax and dominated by Cromwell and his following of Independent officers, secured victory in the civil war and brought Charles to his trial and execution. [23]Unlimited.
[24]*York...Nottingham*: Charles' mounting conflicts with the Long Parliament, climaxed by his abortive attempt (4 January 1642) to arrest five of its leaders on the floor of Commons, led to his leaving London for the north of England, where he began assembling troops and money preparatory to raising his standard (and thus declaring war) at Nottingham on 22 August 1642.
[25]Ridge in Warwickshire, site of the first important—but indecisive—battle of the civil war (23 October 1642).
[26]John Bradshaw (1602–59), jurist who, as "Lord President" of the parliamentary commission to try Charles, pronounced sentence of death upon the king. Although buried in Westminster Abbey,

insolently reprehended the king "for not having showed more respect to that high tribunal," told him "that the Parliament of England had appointed that court to try him for the several treasons and misdemeanors which he had committed against the kingdom during the evil administration of his government, and that, upon the examination thereof, justice might be done." And after a great sauciness and impudence of talk he asked the king "what answer he had to make to that impeachment?"

The king, without any alteration in his countenance by all that insolent provocation, told them "he would first know of them by what authority they presumed by force to bring him before them, and who gave them power to judge of his actions, for which he was accountable to none but God, though they had been always such as he need not be ashamed to own them before all the world." He told them "that he was their king, they his subjects who owed him duty and obedience, that no Parliament had authority to call him before them, but that they were not the Parliament, nor had any authority from the Parliament to sit in that manner; that of all the persons who sat there and took upon them to judge him, except those persons who, being officers of the army, he could not but know whilst he was forced to be amongst them, there were only two faces which he had ever seen before, or whose names were known to him," and after urging "their duty that was due to him and his superiority over them" by such lively reasons and arguments as were not capable of any answer, he concluded "that he would not so much betray himself and his royal dignity as to answer anything they objected against him, which were to acknowledge their authority; though he believed that every one of themselves, as well as the spectators, did, in their own consciences, absolve him from all the material things which were objected against him."

Bradshaw advised him, in a very arrogant manner, "not to deceive himself with an opinion that anything he had said would do him any good; that the Parliament knew their own authority, and would not suffer it to be called in question or debated"; therefore required him "to think better of it, against he should be next brought thither, and that he would answer directly to his charge; otherwise he could not be so ignorant as not to know what judgment the law pronounced against those who stood mute, and obstinately refused to plead." So the guard carried His Majesty back to St. James',[27] where they treated him as before.

There was an accident happened that first day which may be fit to be remembered. When all those who were commissioners had taken their places, and the king was brought in, the first ceremony was to read their commission, which was the ordinance of Parliament for the trial; and then the judges were all called, every man answering to his name as he was called, and the president being first called and making answer, the next who was called being the general, Lord Fairfax,[28] and no answer being made, the officer called him the second time, when there was a voice heard that said "he had more wit than to be there," which put the court into some disorder, and somebody asking who it was, there was no other answer but a little murmuring. But presently, when

the impeachment was read, and that expression used of "all the good people of England," the same voice in a louder tone answered, "No, nor the hundreth part of them," upon which one of the officers bid the soldiers give fire into that box whence those presumptuous words were uttered. But it was quickly discerned that it was the general's wife, the Lady Fairfax, who had uttered both those sharp sayings, who was presently persuaded or forced to leave the place to prevent any new disorder. She was of a very noble extraction, one of the daughters and heirs of Horace, Lord Vere of Tilbury,[29] who, having been bred in Holland, had not that reverence for the Church of England as she ought to have had, and so had unhappily concurred in her husband's entering into rebellion, never imagining what misery it would bring upon the kingdom; and now abhorred the work in hand as much as anybody could do, and did all she could to hinder her husband from acting any part in it. Nor did he ever sit in that bloody court, though he was throughout overwitted by Cromwell, and made a property[30] to bring that to pass which could very hardly have been otherwise effected.

As there was in many persons present at that woeful spectacle a real duty and compassion for the king, so there was in others so barbarous and brutal a behavior towards him that they called him tyrant and murtherer; and one spit in his face, which His Majesty, without expressing any trouble, wiped off with his handkerchief.

The two men who were only known to the king before the troubles were Sir Harry Mildmay,[31] Master of the King's Jewel House, who had been bred up in the court, being younger brother of a good family in Essex, and who had been prosecuted with so great favors and bounties by King James and by His Majesty that he was raised by them to a great estate, and preferred to that office in his House which is the best under those which entitle the officers to be of the Privy Council. No man more obsequious to the court than he whilst it flourished: a great flatterer of all

after the Restoration his body—together with those of Cromwell and other regicides—was exhumed, hanged, and reburied at Tyburn.
[27]Royal palace near the scene of Charles' trial in Westminster Hall.
[28]Thomas Fairfax (1612–71), third Baron Fairfax of Cameron, commander-in-chief of the parliamentary forces after 1645. Although he opposed Charles' execution and resigned his command in 1650, he remained in public life and even headed the commission sent to negotiate with Charles II about his return in 1660. It was Fairfax whom Milton extolled (in Sonnet XV) as one "whose name in arms through Europe rings" and whose services to the state were celebrated by Andrew Marvell (at one point the tutor of his daughter) in "Upon Appleton House" (see pp. 361 ff.).
[29]Anne, Lady Fairfax, was the daughter of Sir Horace Vere (1565–1635), Baron Vere of Tilbury, one of the most distinguished military leaders of his generation.   [30]Used as an instrument.
[31]Sir Henry Mildmay (d. 1664?), who, although long favored by the House of Stuart—he was made master of the Jewel House by James I in 1620—deserted the king in 1641 and thereafter was prominent in parliamentary affairs until 1660, when he attempted escape on being ordered to account for the royal jewels, was apprehended, and sentenced to life imprisonment.

persons in authority, and a spy in all places for them. From the beginning of the Parliament he concurred with those who were most violent against the court and most like to prevail against it, and being thereupon branded with ingratitude, as that brand commonly makes men most impudent, he continued his desperate pace with them till he became one of the murtherers of his master. The other was Sir John Danvers,[32] the younger brother and heir of the earl of Danby, who was a gentleman of the Privy Chamber to the king, and being neglected by his brother, and having, by a vain expense in his way of living, contracted a vast debt which he knew not how to pay, and being a proud, formal, weak man, between being seduced and a seducer became so far involved in their counsels that he suffered himself to be applied to their worst offices, taking it to be a high honor to sit upon the same bench with Cromwell, who employed and contemned him at once; nor did that party of miscreants look upon any two men in the kingdom with that scorn and detestation as they did upon Danvers and Mildmay.

The several unheard-of insolencies which this excellent prince was forced to submit to at the other times he was brought before that odious judicatory, his majestic behavior and resolute insisting upon his own dignity and defending it by manifest authorities in the law as well as by the clearest deductions from reason, the pronouncing that horrible sentence upon the most innocent person in the world, the execution of that sentence by the most execrable murther that was ever committed since that of our blessed Saviour, and the circumstances thereof; the application and interposition that was used by some noble persons to prevent that woeful murther and the hypocrisy with which that interposition was eluded; the saintlike behavior of that blessed martyr and his Christian courage and patience at his death, are all particulars so well known, and have been so much enlarged upon in a treatise[33] peculiarly writ to that purpose, that the farther mentioning it in this place would but afflict and grieve the reader, and make the relation itself odious as well as needless, and therefore no more shall be said here of that deplorable tragedy so much to the dishonor of the nation and the religion professed by it, though undeservedly.

But it will not be unnecessary to add a short character of his person, that posterity may know the inestimable loss which the nation then underwent in being deprived of a prince whose example would have had a greater influence upon the manners and piety of the nation than the most strict laws can have. To speak first of his private qualifications as a man, before the mention of his princely and royal virtues, he was, if ever any, the most worthy of the title of an honest man: so great a lover of justice that no temptation could dispose him to a wrongful action, except it was so disguised to him that he believed it to be just. He had a tenderness and compassion of nature which restrained him from ever doing a hardhearted thing, and therefore he was so apt to grant pardon to malefactors that the judges of the land represented to him the damage and insecurity to the public that flowed from such his indulgence; and then he restrained himself from pardoning either murthers or high-

way robberies, and quickly discerned the fruits of his severity by a wonderful reformation of those enormities. He was very punctual and regular in his devotions; he was never known to enter upon his recreations or sports, though never so early in the morning, before he had been at public prayers, so that on hunting days his chaplains were bound to a very early attendance. He was likewise very strict in observing the hours of his private cabinet devotions, and was so severe an exactor of gravity and reverence in all mention of religion that he could never endure any light or profane word, with what sharpness of wit soever it was covered; and though he was well pleased and delighted with reading verses made upon any occasion, no man durst bring before him anything that was profane or unclean. That kind of wit had never any countenance then. He was so great an example of conjugal affection that they who did not imitate him in that particular durst not brag of their liberty; and he did not only permit but direct his bishops to prosecute those scandalous vices in the ecclesiastical courts against persons of eminence and near relation to his service.

His kingly virtues had some mixture and allay that hindered them from shining in full luster and from producing those fruits they should have been attended with. He was not in his nature very bountiful, though he gave very much. This appeared more after the duke of Buckingham's death, after which those showers fell very rarely; and he paused too long in giving, which made those to whom he gave less sensible of the benefit. He kept state to the full,[34] which made his court very orderly, no man presuming to be seen in a place where he had no pretence[35] to be. He saw and observed men long before he received them about his person, and did not love strangers nor very confident men. He was a patient hearer of causes, which he frequently accustomed himself to at the Council board; and judged very well, and was dextrous in the mediating part, so that he often put an end to causes by persuasion which the stubbornness of men's humors made dilatory in courts of justice.

He was very fearless in his person, but in his riper years not very enterprising. He had an excellent understanding, but was not confident enough of it, which made him oftentimes change his own opinion for a worse, and follow the advice of men that did not judge so well as himself.

[32]Sir John Danvers (1588?–1655), scion of a distinguished family who, as second husband of the much older Magdalen Herbert, became father-in-law of Lord Herbert of Cherbury, the philosopher, and of George Herbert, the poet. Following service as a colonel in the parliamentary army, he subsequently (1649–53) served on the Council of State under Cromwell.

[33]Perhaps George Bate's *Elenchus motuum nuperorum in Anglia* (Frankfurt-am-Main, 1650), which was published in England in 1660, 1663, 1676, and (translated and enlarged) 1685—a work apparently related to Bate's *Royall Apology* (1648) and *Short Narrative of the Late Troubles in England* (1649). Another possibility is *England's Black Tribunall. Set forth in the Trial of K. Charles, I. at the Pretended Court of Justice at Westminster Hall, Jan. 20. 1648,* which appeared belatedly in 1660 and again in 1673, 1680, 1703, 1720, and ("very much enlarged") 1737.

[34]*He kept . . . full:* maintained the protocol and splendor of royalty.

[35]Reason, pretext.

This made him more irresolute than the conjuncture of his affairs would admit: if he had been of a rougher and more imperious nature he would have found more respect and duty. And his not applying some severe cures to approaching evils proceeded from the lenity of his nature and the tenderness of his conscience, which, in all cases of blood, made him choose the softer way and not hearken to severe counsels, how reasonably soever urged. This only restrained him from pursuing his advantage in the first Scottish expedition,[36] when, humanly speaking, he might have reduced that nation to the most entire obedience that could have been wished. But no man can say he had then many who advised him to it, but the contrary, by a wonderful indisposition all his Council had to the war or any other fatigue. He was always a great lover of the Scottish nation, having not only been born there but educated by that people, and besieged by them always, having few English about him till he was king; and the major number of his servants being still of that nation, who he thought could never fail him. And among these no man had such an ascendant over him, by the humblest insinuations, as Duke Hamilton[37] had.

As he excelled in all other virtues, so in temperance he was so strict that he abhorred all debauchery to that degree that at a great festival solemnity where he once was, when very many of the nobility of the English and Scots were entertained, being told by one who withdrew from thence what vast draughts of wine they drank and "that there was one earl who had drank most of the rest down, and was not himself moved or altered," the king said "that he deserved to be hanged"; and that earl coming shortly after into the room where His Majesty was, in some gaiety, to show how unhurt he was from that battle, the king sent one to bid him withdraw from His Majesty's presence, nor did he in some days after appear before him.

So many miraculous circumstances contributed to his ruin that men might well think that heaven and earth conspired it. Though he was, from the first declension of his power, so much betrayed by his own servants that there were very few who remained faithful to him, yet that treachery proceeded not always from any treasonable purpose to do him any harm, but from particular and personal animosities against other men. And afterwards the terror all men were under of the Parliament, and the guilt they were conscious of themselves, made them watch all opportunities to make themselves gracious to those who could do them good; and so they became spies upon their master, and from one piece of knavery were hardened and confirmed to undertake another, till at last they had no hope of preservation but by the destruction of their master. And after all this, when a man might reasonably believe that less than a universal defection of three nations could not have reduced a great king to so ugly a fate, it is most certain that in that very hour when he was thus wickedly murthered in the sight of the sun, he had as great a share in the hearts and affections of his subjects in general, was as much beloved, esteemed, and longed for by the people in general of the three nations as any of his predecessors had ever been. To conclude: he was the worthiest gentleman, the best master, the best friend, the best husband, the best father, and the best Christian that the age in which he lived produced. And if he were not the greatest king, if he were without some parts and qualities which have made some kings great and happy, no other prince was ever unhappy who was possessed of half his virtues and endowments, and so much without any kind of vice.

This unparalleled murther and parricide was committed upon the thirtieth of January in the year, according to the account used in England,[38] 1648, in the forty and ninth year of his age, and when he had such excellent health and so great vigor of body that when his murtherers caused him to be opened (which they did, and were some of them present at it with great curiosity), they confessed and declared "that no man had ever all his vital parts so perfect and unhurt, and that he seemed to be of so admirable a composition and constitution that he would probably have lived as long as nature could subsist." His body was immediately carried into a room at Whitehall where he was exposed for many days to the public view, that all men might know that he was not alive. And he was then embalmed, and put into a coffin, and so carried to St. James', where he likewise remained several days. They who were qualified to order his funeral declared "that he should be buried at Windsor[39] in a decent manner, provided that the whole expense should not exceed five hundred pounds." The duke of Richmond, the marquis of Hertford, the earls of Southampton and Lindsey,[40] who had been of his bedchamber and always very faithful to him, desired those who governed "that they might have leave to perform the last duty to their dead master, and to wait upon him to his grave"; which, after some pauses, they were permitted to do, with this: "that they

[36] In 1639, in an ill-managed and futile attempt to impose episcopacy on the stubbornly Presbyterian Kirk, Charles invaded the borders of Scotland but was promptly forced to sign a treaty that signalized the failure of his plan for compulsory conformity. See p. 910, n.24.
[37] James Hamilton (1606–49), third marquis and first duke of Hamilton in the Scottish peerage, second earl of Cambridge in the English peerage, one of Charles' most trusted advisers and a principal architect of his disastrous Scottish policy. Following the defeat of his army at Preston (1648), he was condemned and executed in the same year as his royal master.
[38] The Old Style (or Julian) calendar—used in England until 1752—began the year on March 25 instead of the previous January 1. By modern reckoning Charles' execution occurred 30 January 1649.
[39] Ancient royal castle and fortress on the Thames a few miles west of London. Its St. George's Chapel serves as both the seat of the Order of the Garter and also the burial place of many English kings.
[40] James Stuart (1612–55), fourth duke of Lennox and first duke of Richmond; William Seymour (1588–1660), first marquis and second earl of Hertford and duke of Somerset; Thomas Wriothesley (1607–67), fourth earl of Southampton; Montague Bertie (1608?–66), second earl of Lindsey. It is to Southampton that we owe the famous story of a muffled man who, in the middle of the night, came to Charles' bier in the Banqueting House at Whitehall, stared at the mutilated body, sighed out the words "Cruel necessity," and then stalked away into the night. By the mysterious intruder's gait and voice, said Southampton, he knew him to be Cromwell.

should not attend the corpse out of the town, since they resolved it should be privately carried to Windsor without pomp or noise, and then they should have timely notice, that, if they pleased, they might be at his interment." And accordingly it was committed to four of those servants who had been by them appointed to wait upon him during his imprisonment that they should convey the body to Windsor, which they did.[41] And it was that night placed in that chamber which had usually been his bedchamber; the next morning it was carried into the great hall, where it remained till the lords came, who arrived there in the afternoon and immediately went to Colonel Whitchcot, the governor of the castle, and showed the order they had from the Parliament to be present at the burial; which he admitted, but when they desired that His Majesty might be buried according to the form of the Common Prayer Book, the bishop of London[42] being present with them to officiate, he positively and roughly refused to consent to it, and said "it was not lawful: that the Common Prayer Book was put down,[43] and he would not suffer it to be used in that garrison where he commanded"; nor could all the reasons, persuasions, and entreaties prevail with him to suffer it. Then they went into the church, to make choice of a place for burial. But when they entered into it, which they had been so well acquainted with, they found it so altered and transformed, all inscriptions and those landmarks pulled down by which all men knew every particular place in that church, and such a dismal mutation over the whole, that they knew not where they were; nor was there one old officer that had belonged to it, or knew where our princes had used to be interred. At last there was a fellow of the town who undertook to tell them the place, where, he said, "there was a vault in which King Harry the Eighth and Queen Jane Seymour were interred." As near that place as could conveniently be they caused the grave to be made. There the king's body was laid without any words or other ceremonies than the tears and sighs of the few beholders. Upon the coffin was a plate of silver fixed with these words only: "King Charles 1648." When the coffin was put in, the black velvet pall that had covered it was thrown over it, and then the earth thrown in; which the governor stayed to see perfectly done, and then took the keys of the church. . . .

BOOK XVI . . .

[THE RESTORATION OF CHARLES II][44]

With these commissioners from the Parliament and from the City there came a company of their clergymen, to the number of eight or ten, who would not be looked upon as chaplains to the rest, but being the popular preachers of the City—Reynolds, Calamy, Case, Manton,[45] and others the most eminent of the Presbyterians—desired to be thought to represent that party. They entreated to be admitted all together to have a formal audience of His Majesty, where they presented their duties and magnified the affections of themselves and their friends, who, they said, "had always, according to the obligation of their Covenant,[46] wished His

Majesty very well; and had lately, upon the opportunity that God had put into their hands, informed the people of their duty; which, they presumed, His Majesty had heard had proved effectual, and been of great use to him." They thanked God "for his constancy to the Protestant religion" and professed "that they were no enemies to moderate episcopacy; only desired that such things might not be pressed upon them in God's worship which in their judgment who used them were acknowledged to be matters indifferent, and by others were held unlawful."

The king spoke very kindly to them, and said "that he had heard of their good behavior towards him, and that he had no purpose to impose hard conditions upon them with reference to their consciences; that they well knew he had referred the settling all differences of that nature to the wisdom of the Parliament, which best knew what indulgence and toleration was necessary for the peace and quiet of the kingdom." But His Majesty could not be so rid of them; they desired several private audiences of him which he never denied, wherein they told him "the Book of Common Prayer had been long discontinued in England, and the people having been disused to it, and many of them having never heard it in their lives, it would be much wondered at if His Majesty should, at his first landing in the kingdom, revive the use of it in his own chapel, whither all persons would resort; and therefore they besought him that he would not use it entirely and formally, but have only some parts of it read, with mixture of other good prayers which his chaplains might use."

The king told them with some warmth "that whilst he

[41] February 1649.
[42] William Juxon (see p. 917, n.2, who had also attended Charles on the scaffold.
[43] *Common...down*: on 4 January 1645 Parliament outlawed the use of the Anglican Book of Common Prayer and replaced it with a Presbyterian Directory of Worship.
[44] Following Oliver Cromwell's death (1658), the inept rule of his son and successor Richard made England ripe for the Stuart Restoration. After General George Monck (1608–70), commander of the army in Scotland, led his troops across the border and down to London in January 1660, events moved quickly toward the dissolution of the Long Parliament (March 16) and to negotiations with Charles in Holland. The so-called Declaration of Breda (April 4), in which Charles set forth the conditions of his return, was eagerly accepted by the new Parliament, and thus by May everything was ready for the king's trip across the Channel to reclaim his throne.
[45] Although Reynolds seems to have sunk with a trace, the other three clergymen named by Clarendon were famous in their day. Edmund Calamy (1600–66), one of the Smectymnuans whom young Milton had defended in the early forties, was, like Thomas Case (1598–1682), a member of the Westminster Assembly, for which body Thomas Manton (1620–77) served as scribe. Each was noted as a preacher, and each was active in the complex Presbyterian maneuvering that ushered in the Restoration.
[46] The Solemn League and Covenant, a treaty (1643) between Scotland and the English Parliament by which the English bound themselves to "the reformation of religion in the Church of England according to the example of the best reformed [i.e., Presbyterian] churches" and "according to the word of God."

gave them liberty, he would not have his own táken from him: that he had always used that form of service, which he thought the best in the world, and had never discontinued it in places where it was more disliked than he hoped it was by them; that when he came into England he would not severely inquire how it was used in other churches, though he doubted not he should find it used in many; but he was sure he would have no other used in his own chapel." Then they besought him with more importunity "that the use of the surplice might be discontinued by his chaplains 10 because the sight of it would give great offence and scandal to the people." They found the king as inexorable in that point as in the other. He told them plainly "that he would not be restrained himself when he gave others so much liberty; that it had been always held a decent habit in the church, constantly practised in England till these late ill times; that it had been still retained by him, and though he was bound for the present to tolerate much disorder and undecency in the exercise of God's worship, he would never in the least degree by his own practice discountenance the 20 good old order of the church in which he had been bred." Though they were very much unsatisfied with him, whom they thought to have found more flexible, yet they ceased farther troubling him, in hope and presumption that they should find their importunity in England more effectual.

After eight or ten days spent at the Hague in triumphs and festivals, which could not have been more splendid if all the monarchs of Europe had met there, and which were concluded with several rich presents made to His Majesty, the king took his leave of the States[47] with all the professions 30 of amity their civilities deserved and embarked himself on the *Royal Charles*, which had been before called the *Naseby*, but had been new christened the day before, as many others had been, in the presence, and by the order, of His Royal Highness the Admiral.[48] Upon the four-and-twentieth day of May the fleet set sail; and in one continued thunder of cannon arrived near Dover so early on the six-and-twentieth that His Majesty disembarked;[49] and being received by the general[50] at the brink of the sea (whom he met and embraced with great demonstrations of affection), he presently took 40 coach, and came that night to Canterbury, where he stayed the next day, being Sunday, and went to his devotions to the cathedral, which he found very much dilapidated and out of repair, yet the people seemed glad to hear the Common Prayer again. Thither came very many of the nobility and other persons of quality to present themselves to the king, and there His Majesty assembled his Council, and swore the general of the Council, and Mr. Morice,[51] whom he there knighted, and gave him the signet, and swore him Secretary of State. That day His Majesty gave the Garter to the 50 general and likewise to the marquis of Hertford and the earl of Southampton (who had been elected many years before), and sent it likewise by Garter, Herald, and King-at-Arms to Admiral Mountagu,[52] who remained in the Downs.[53]

On Monday he went to Rochester;[54] and the next day, being the nine-and-twentieth of May and his birthday, he entered London, all the ways thither being so full of people and acclamations as if the whole kingdom had been gathered there. Between Deptford and Southwark[55] the lord mayor and aldermen met him with all such protestations of joy as can hardly be imagined. The concourse was so great that the king rode in a crowd from the Bridge[56] to Whitehall, all the companies of the City standing in order on both sides and giving loud thanks to God for His Majesty's presence. He no sooner came to Whitehall but the two Houses of Parliament solemnly cast themselves at his feet with all vows of affection and fidelity to the world's end. In a word, the joy was so unexpressible and so universal that His Majesty said smilingly to some about him "he doubted it had been his own fault he had been absent so long, for he saw nobody that did not protest he had ever wished for his return."

In this wonderful manner, and with this incredible expedition, did God put an end to a rebellion that had raged near twenty years, and been carried on with all the horrid circumstances of murther, devastation, and parricide that fire and sword, in the hands of the most wicked men in the world, could be instruments of, almost to the desolation of two kingdoms and the exceeding defacing and deforming the third. . . .

By these remarkable steps, among others, did the merciful hand of God, in this short space of time, not only bind up and heal all those wounds, but even make the scars as undiscernible as, in respect of the deepness, was possible, which was a glorious addition to the deliverance. And after this miraculous restoration of the crown and the church and the just rights of Parliaments, no nation under heaven can ever be more happy, if God shall be pleased to add establishment and perpetuity to the blessings He then restored.

The End of the Last Book

[47]The States General, the Netherlands.
[48]James, duke of York (later James II), Charles' younger brother.
[49]Actually, Charles sailed on May 23 and landed at Dover on May 25.
[50]General George Monck, whom Charles created first duke of Albemarle in gratitude for his good offices at the Restoration.
[51]William Morice (1602–76), politician and former Parliamentarian whose effective work for Charles' restoration led to a knighthood and membership on the Privy Council.
[52]Edward Montagu (1625–72), first earl of Sandwich, noted military and naval leader who commanded the flotilla that accompanied Charles to England. Young Samuel Pepys, at the start of his career, was his secretary.
[53]Roadstead off the Kentish coast.
[54]Town in Kent between Canterbury and London.
[55]London suburbs on the south bank of the Thames.
[56]London Bridge, a massive 12th-century structure that for centuries was the only bridge across the Thames.

Glossary

ABROAD out of one's own house or country

ABSOLUTE finished, entire, perfect

ABUSE imposture, deceit

ACCIDENT happening (fortunate or unfortunate)

ACCOMPT account

ADMIRABLE to be wondered at

ADMIRE wonder (at)

ADVANCE raise, lift up

AENEAS in Vergil's *Aeneid*, son of Anchises and Venus who survived the fall of Troy to found the Roman empire

AEOLUS god of the winds

AFFECT(ION) *n.*, desire, passion; *v.*, love, desire. AFFECTIONS, inclinations, likes and dislikes

AFTER in accordance with

AGAINST in preparation for

AGANIPPE see HELICON

ALBION England

ALCIDES see HERCULES

AMAZE confuse, dismay

AMPHION legendary Greek musician who with the music of his magic lyre caused the walls of Thebes to rise

AMPHITRITE wife of Poseidon, god of the sea

ANGEL gold coin with the Archangel Michael shown on it

ANGELS see HIERARCHY, THE CELESTIAL

APPEAL accuse, impeach

APOLLO god of music and poetry, often identified with the sun

APPROVE prove, test

ARGUMENT theme, subject

ARIOSTO, LUDOVICO (1474–1533) author of the chivalric epic poem *Orlando Furioso* (1516–32)

ARMINIAN follower of Jacobus Arminius (1560–1609), Dutch Protestant theologian who opposed Calvin's rigorous doctrine of predestination

ARTHUR legendary sixth-century King of Britain. See p. 813 n.

AS as if

ASPECT in astrology, the relative position of the planets at a given time, thought to have an influence (benign or malign) on earthly creatures. See INFLUENCE.

ASTRAEA goddess of justice who left the earth at the end of the Golden Age and was subsequently stellified in the constellation Virgo

ATHENE Minerva, goddess of wisdom

ATTACH arrest

AURORA goddess of the dawn

AVERNUS a crater near Naples, Italy, anciently regarded as the entrance to Hades or the underworld

AVOID leave, be gone

BACCHUS god of wine and revelry

BANK bench

BARTAS, SEIGNEUR DU Guillaume de Salluste (1544–90), French religious poet. See pp. 50–53.

BASILISK a fabled reptile whose look was thought to kill.

BEDLAM the hospital of St. Mary of Bethlehem in London for the insane; a madhouse

BILL spear or ax with a concave blade

BLOWN blossomed

BOCCACCIO (BOCCACE), GIOVANNI (1313–75) Italian humanist, author of the *Decameron* (1353) and other works in Latin and Italian

BOREAS the north wind

BRAKE broke

BRAVE showy, handsome

BRAVERY display, show, splendor

BRUT legendary founder of Britain and progenitor of a line of kings. See p. 812 n.

BUCKINGHAM, DUKE OF George Villiers (1592–1628), powerful favorite of James I and Charles I. See p. 754.

BURTHEN burden

BUSY officious

CABINET private room

CALVIN, JOHN (1509–64) French religious reformer

CARD map

CAREFUL full of grief, anxious

CARR, ROBERT see SOMERSER, EARL OF

CASTALIAN referring to a spring, sacred to Apollo and the Muses, on Mt. Parnassus

CASUAL subject to chance or accident

CENSURE *n.*, judgment, opinion; *v.*, judge, evaluate

CENTER in Ptolemaic astronomy, the earth, thought to occupy the middle point of the concentric spheres of the planets and the fixed stars. See SPHERE.

CICERO, MARCUS TULLIUS or TULLY (106–43 B.C.) Roman statesman, orator, and writer.

CLINCHES puns

CLIP hug, embrace

CLOSE *n.*, musical cadence; *adj.*, secret, enclosed; *v.*, come together, unite

COLOR pretext

COMPETENT suitable, sufficient

COMPLAIN lament

COMPLETE perfect, accomplished

COMPLEXION the combination of elemental qualities (hot, cold, moist, dry) or of humors (*q.v.*) believed to determine the nature of things; thus, temperament, defining characteristic. See ELEMENT.

COMPOUND come to terms with

CONCEIT conception, thought, idea, opinion

CONCEITED ingenious, witty, fanciful

CONCOCT(ION) digest(ion)

CONDITION rank, status

CONFER compare

CONFERENCE comparison

CONFOUND overthrow, defeat

CONFUSION discomfiture, ruin

CONSORT harmony

CONSTANT loyal

CONTROL overpower

CONVENIENT fit, proper

CONVERSATION social behavior

COPERNICUS, NICHOLAS (1473–1543), Polish astronomer whose epoch-making *De revolutionibus orbium coelestium* (1543), advancing the theory that the earth rotates daily on its axis and that planets revolve in orbits around the sun, gradually replaced the ancient geocentric system ascribed to Ptolemy, an Alexandrian astronomer of the second century A.D.

COTTON, SIR ROBERT (1571–1631) antiquarian and statesman, friend and benefactor of many men of learning (among them Jonson, Camden, Speed, and Bacon), whose notable collection of books, manuscripts, and coins is now in the British Museum. For Thomas Fuller's account of his career see pp. 752–755.

COVENANT, THE SOLEMN LEAGUE AND a treaty (1645) between Scotland and the English Parliament by which the English bound themselves to "the reformation of religion in the Church of England according to the example of the best reformed [i.e. Presbyterian] churches" and "according to the word of God."

COY shy

CROWN coin, stamped with a crown or a crowned head, worth five shillings.

CRUDE undigested, unripe

CUPID son of Venus and lover of Psyche, the god of love whose golden shafts inflamed desire, whereas the leaden ones repelled it

CURIOUS careful, solicitous, artful, elaborate

CURIOSITY, CURIOUSNESS carefulness, elaborate workmanship

CYNTHIA Diana, goddess of the moon

DEAR glorious, grievous

DEFEND forbid

DELIVER report, relate

DELPHI Delphos, site of a shrine on Mt. Parnassus sacred to Apollo

DESCANT discussion; varied melody or song

DESERT solitary, unpeopled

DIAN(A) goddess of the hunt, virginity, and the moon

DIE consummate sexual intercourse

DINT blow

DISCOVER exhibit, reveal, explore, gain information of

DISCOVERY revelation

DISHONEST shameful, unchaste

DISMAL ill-fated, calamitous

DOOM statute, judgment, sentence

DORT, SYNOD OF a synod (1618–19) of the Reformed Church of the Netherlands at Dort (Dordrect), where, with certain foreign visitors in attendance, controversial issues between the Arminians (*q.v.*) and the Calvinists were resolved in favor of the latter.

DOUBT fear

DU BARTAS, SEIGNEUR see BARTAS

EAT ate

EIGHT eighth

ELEMENT natural habitation; the sky; one of the four fundamental ingredients of all created things: air (which is hot and moist), fire (hot and dry), water (cold and moist), and earth (cold and dry). These elements were thought to be continually in strife until order was imposed on them. See COMPLEXION, HUMOR.

ELIXIR the quintessence (*q.v.*); in alchemy, a preparation which it was thought could prolong life and change baser matter into gold

ENTERTAIN receive, take into service

ENTERTAINMENT reception

ENVIOUS malicious, grudging

ENVY malice, enmity

EPICYCLE in Ptolemaic astronomy, an orbit whose center follows the circumference of a larger orbit concentric with the earth

EQUAL impartial; contemporary

ERASMUS, DESIDERIUS (1466?–1536) Dutch scholar and humanist

ERRING straying

ERROR wandering, deviation

ESAY Isaiah

ESSENCE, FIFTH the quintessence (*q.v.*)

EURYDICE wife of Orpheus (*q.v.*)

EVEN equal

EVENT outcome, issue, consequence

EXHALATION vapor

EXPECT await

EXPEDITION speedy progress

EXQUISITE elaborate, far-fetched

EY(E)N eyes

FACT act, feat, crime

FAME rumor

FANTASTIC imaginary, unreal, quaint, eccentric

FARDER further

FATES, THE the Moirai or Parcae, goddesses thought to

determine the course of human life. They were usually represented as three old women spinning, Clotho holding the distaff, Lachesis drawing off the thread, and Atropos cutting it.

FLACCUS Horace (*q.v.*)

FLOWN flushed, swollen

FOND foolish, doting

FREE FROM away from, remote from

FREQUENT *v.*, crowd, fill; *adj.*, crowded, full

FRONT forehead, brow

FURIES, THE the Dirae or Eumenides, goddesses of vengeance usually identified as Tisiphone, Megaera, and Alecto

FURNITURE equipment

GALEN (2d century A.D.) Greek physician whose many medical and anatomical treatises were influential in the Renaissance

GANYMEDE a Trojan youth whom the infatuated Jove made cupbearer of the gods

GAT got

GENIUS local divinity or tutelary deity

GENTILE pagan

GENTLE of high birth, noble

GEOFFREY OF MONMOUTH (1100?–54) English ecclesiastic and chronicler whose *Historia Britonum* (or *Historia regum Britanniae*) was a source of the so-called British history. See p. 000 n.

GRACES, THE Euphrosyne (mirth), Aglaia (splendor), and Thalia (abundance), three sisters (of disputed parentage) who were thought to confer grace and joy on human beings

GRAIN color, dye

GRAY'S INN, see INNS OF COURT

GROTIUS, HUGO (1583–1645) Dutch scholar, jurist, and statesman

HABIT attire

HALBERD a combination of spear and battle-ax mounted on a long shaft; a soldier armed with such a weapon

HALCYON a legendary bird thought to charm the winds and seas at the winter solstice so that it might breed in a nest on the water

HAPPILY haply, perhaps

HAPPY fortunate

HARDLY with difficulty

HATEFUL full of hatred, hostile

HEAVINESS grief

HEAVY sorrowful

HENRY, PRINCE (1594–1612) Henry Frederick, Prince of Wales, eldest son of James I, a friend and patron of Raleigh, Chapman, and many other men of letters

HEBE goddess of youth and cupbearer of the gods

HEIGHTH height

HELICON a mountain range in Boeotia, legendary home of the Muses (*q.v.*) and site of the fountains of Aganippe and Hippocrene, associated with poetic inspiration

HERCULES (often called Alcides because he was descended through his step-father from the legendary Alcaeus, son of Perseus), a son of Alcmene and Zeus, noted for his strength and endurance. He was often regarded as a type (*q.v.*) of Christ.

HERMES son of Zeus and Maia, messenger of the gods

HERMES TRISMEGISTHUS alleged author of a group of mystical and Neoplatonic treatises by various Alexandrian writers of the third century A.D.

HESPERIDES daughters of Hesperus, the evening star, who guarded the golden apples given to Hera by Gaia; the garden where these apples grew

HESPERUS Venus, the evening star

HIERARCHY, THE CELESTIAL in Christian tradition, the nine orders of angels: seraphim, cherubim, thrones, dominations, virtues, powers, principalities, archangels, angels

HIEROME Jerome (*q.v.*)

HINDERANCE hindrance

HIPPOCRENE, see HELICON

HIS its

HONEST chaste, decent; worthy, honorable

HONESTY respectability, chastity

HORACE (65–8 B.C.) Quintus Horatius Flaccus, Roman poet

HORRID rough, bristling (a Latinism)

HUMOR whim, mood; temperament, habitual cast of mind; a fluid, distilled from one of the four elements (*q.v.*), that was thought to determine temperament. An excess of blood was thought to make one sanguine; of choler, choleric; of phlegm, phlegmatic; of melancholy, morose. See COMPLEXION.

HUNDERD hundred

IMP *n.*, child; *v.*, replace a falcon's damaged feather

IMPUDENT shameless

INCESTIOUS incestuous

INCONSIDERATE rash, thoughtless

INDEPENDENT a member of one of the various unrelated Protestant churches conducted on the principle of congregational autonomy, as opposed to the Presbyterians who subscribed to the ecclesiastical organization and discipline prescribed in Calvin's *Institutes*.

INDIFFERENT impartial; morally neutral, neither good nor bad

INDIVIDUAL undividable, thus eternal

INFLUENCE an ethereal fluid or secret force supposedly emitted by the stars to affect man's destiny

INGRAFF ingraft

INNS OF COURT Lincoln's Inn, the Inner Temple, the Middle Temple, and Gray's Inn, corporate societies, each with its own buildings near the Strand in London, that admitted students of the law

INSENSIBLE imperceptible to the senses

INSTANT urgent

INSTINCT impelled, inspired

INSULT exult

INTELLIGENCE news, tidings; espionage

INTEND consider

INTERESS interest, implicate in
INVENTION finding, discovery; the fresh and imaginative treatment of a literary subject

JEREMY Jeremiah
JEROME Eusebius Hieronymus (340?–420), one of the four Doctors of the Roman Catholic Church, author of many works of biblical exegesis and of the Latin version of the Bible known as the Vulgate
JOVE Jupiter, Zeus, son of Saturn and Rhea, ruler of the gods
JUNO wife of Jove, queen of the gods

KIND nature
KINDLY naturally

LANTHERN, LANTHORN lantern
LATINS writers of Latin
LAUD, WILLIAM (1573–1645) English prelate, Archbishop of Canterbury 1633–45
LAWES, HENRY (1596–1662) musician and composer who set many lyrics to music and presumably suggested to Milton the composition of *Comus* (1634)
LET hindrance
LEAVE cease
LIGHT(NESS) wanton(ness)
LINCOLN'S INN, see INNS OF COURT
LIQUID clear
LIST *n.*, pleasure; *v.*, please
LUST pleasure, desire
LUTHER, MARTIN (1483–1546) German religious reformer
LUXURY lust, lasciviousness
LUXURIOUS lascivious, unchaste

MACHIAVEL(LI), NICCOLO (1469–1527) Italian politician, author of *Il Principe* and other works on statecraft
MARRY by (the Virgin) Mary
MEAN humble, inferior; intermediate
MEASURE Stately dance; moderation
MELANCHTHON, PHILIPP SCHWARZERT (1497–1560), German scholar and religious reformer, a colleague of Martin Luther
MERCURY see HERMES
MERE pure, unmixed, out and out
MERELY purely, absolutely
MID(D)EST midst
MIDDLE AIR the cold and misty middle layer of the atmosphere, thought to be the seat of storms
MIND consider, remember
MINERVA Athene, goddess of wisdom, the arts, and war
MONTAIGNE, MICHEL EYQUEM DE (1533–92) French essayist
MORE, SIR THOMAS (1478–1535) English humanist and statesman, author of *Utopia*
MORNING STAR Lucifer, Venus
MORPHEUS god of sleep and dreams

MOSELEY, HUMPHREY (d. 1661) bookseller and publisher of many poets and playwrights including Beaumont and Fletcher, Suckling, Waller, Crashaw, Cowley, Quarles, Davenant, and Milton
MOTION cause, movement
MURTHER murder
MUSES The nine daughters of Mnemosyne (memory) and Zeus, worshiped at Pieria near the Thessalian Olympus and at Mt. Helicon in Boeotia as goddesses of the arts and literature (Calliope of epic poetry, Clio of history, Melpomene of tragedy, Erato of the lyre, Polyhymnia of sacred song, etc.).
MYSTERY religious mystery; trade, craft
MYSTIC, MYSTICAL mythical, mysterious

NARCISSUS a youth whose indifference caused the death of the nymph Echo, following which he fell in love with his own image in the water, pined for it until he died, and then was turned into the flower that bears his name
NASO see OVID
NERVE sinew
NEXT nearest
NICE fastidious, foolish
NOURICE nurse
NUMBERS verses
NUMEROUS measured, rhythmical

OBNOXIOUS liable to censure or injury
OBSEQUIOUS obedient
OBVIOUS open, exposed, bold
OFFICE duty, function
OFFICIOUS eager, dutiful
ORB circle, sphere (*q.v.*), earth, heavenly body; eye-ball
ORDINARY a public meal regularly provided at a fixed price in an eating-house or tavern, hence available to anybody
ORIENT shining, radiant
ORPHEUS a Greek singer of extraordinary renown who by the beauty of his music persuaded Pluto to release his wife Eurydice from Hades, lost her again when, contrary to his promise, he looked back to her as they were climbing to the surface of the earth. For Ovid's version of this famous myth, as translated by George Sandys, see pp. 104–111.
OUTLANDISH alien, foreign
OVERBURY, SIR THOMAS (1581–1613) minor poet and courtier whose murder in the Tower led to the fall of his former patron, the powerful Earl of Somerset. See p. 715.
OVERLOOK survey
OVID Publius Ovidius Naso (43 B.C.–?17), Roman poet whose *Metamorphoses* (see pp. 106–110) was one of the most popular and influential poems in the Renaissance.

PAINFUL assiduous, painstaking
PARFAIT perfect (*q.v.*)
PARTS qualities, endowments
PEGASUS the winged steed of poetic inspiration

PERFECT finished, complete

PERFET, PERFIT perfect (*q.v.*)

PERIOD sentence

PERSPECTIVE GLASS telescope

PETRARCH, FRANCESCO (1304–74) Italian humanist and poet

PHOENIX a unique mythical bird which died every five hundred years and was reborn of its own ashes

PITCH highest point of a falcon's flight

PLEASANT jocose, joking

POLICY crafty device, stratagem, cunning

POLITICIAN crafty intriguer

POLYDORE, see VERGIL, POLYDORE

POMP procession

POMPOUS magnificent, splendid, processional

PORT bearing, demeanor

PORTER, ENDYMION (1587–1649) courtier and minor poet who befriended many men of letters

PORTLY stately

POSSESS inform

POWER armed force

PRACTICE treachery, artifice, plot

PREFER advance, promote

PRESBYTER Presbyterian, especially a minister or elder of the church

PRESENT(LY) immediate(ly), prompt(ly)

PRETEND profess, claim; present

PRETENSE claim

PREVENT anticipate, act in preparation for

PRIDE height, prime

PRIME early morning

PRIMUM MOBILE "the first mover" in Ptolemaic astronomy; see SPHERE.

PROMETHEUS a Titan who stole fire from heaven for the benefit of mankind and was punished by being chained to a rock in the Caucasus. There an eagle fed daily on his liver, which was restored again each succeeding night until, after ages of torment, he was released by Hercules.

PROPRIETY property

PROPER own

PROUD splendid, lavish

PROVE try

QUAINT elaborate, odd, dainty

QUICK living

QUINTESSENCE the fifth and ethereal essence or power (sometimes called the elixir) that with the four elements (*q.v.*) constituted all created things

QUIRE choir

RAMUS, PETRUS (1515–72) Pierre la Ramée, French philosopher and mathematician, noted for his opposition to Aristotle

REMEMBER remind, recall

RESPECT consider, heed

REUCHLIN, JOHANN (1455–1522) German humanist whose philological studies, especially in Hebrew, led to controversy with the powerful and reactionary Dominicans

RIOT dissipation

RUIN fall

SAD sober, serious, steadfast

ST. ALBAN(s), VISCOUNT Francis Bacon

SALVAGE savage

SATURN Cronus, ruler of gods and men in the Golden Age who was overthrown by his son Zeus (Jove)

SAVILE, SIR HENRY (1549–1622) Warden of Merton College, Oxford (1585–1622) and Provost of Eton (1596–1622), secretary of Latin tongues to Queen Elizabeth, editor of St. Chrysostom (1610–13), and translator of Tacitus (1591)

SCENE stage

SCIENCE knowledge, trade, profession. In medieval theory the so-called liberal sciences were grammar, logic, rhetoric, arithmetic, geometry, astronomy, and music.

SECULAR lasting for ages

SECURE careless, overconfident

SECURITY carelessness, overconfidence

SENECA, LUCIUS ANNAEUS (ca. 4 B.C.–A.D. 65), Roman moralist and tragedian

SENSE sense perception, the five senses

SENSIBLE conscious of, sensitive to

SENTENCE aphorism, saying (Latin *sententia*); thought, meaning

SEVERAL different, separate

SILLY helpless, simple, humble, innocent

SINGLE complete, mere

SITH since

SIXT sixth

SO AS so that

SOCINIAN a follower of Faustus Socinus (1539–1604) and his uncle Laelius Socinus (1525–62), Italian theologians who denied the Trinity, the natural depravity of man, and the efficacy of sacraments

SOLEMN LEAGUE AND COVENANT, THE, see COVENANT

SOMERSET, EARL OF Robert Carr (d. 1645), Viscount Rochester (1611) and Earl of Somerset (1613), powerful favorite of James I whose marriage to the divorced Countess of Essex (1613) was quickly followed by the revelation of his complicity in the murder of Sir Thomas Overbury (*q.v.*) and his fall from power See p. 715.

SOMETHING somewhat, a little

SOMETIMES formerly

SPEED *n.*, success, prosperity; *v.*, succeed

SPHERE in Ptolemaic astronomy, one of the concentric and transparent globes that contained a heavenly body and revolved around the earth (or center) to produce the celestial harmony known as the music of the spheres. The seven spheres nearest the earth contained the seven "planets" (the moon, Mercury, Venus, the sun, Mars, Jupiter, and Saturn), the eighth contained the fixed stars, the ninth was the crystalline sphere, and the tenth was the *primum mobile* ("first mover") that imparted motion to all the bodies within the hard outer shell of the universe.

SPIRITS in Galenic physiology, highly refined substances or fluids thought to permeate the blood and chief organs of the body. The natural spirits, converted from the blood by the liver, were thought to control nutrition, growth, and generation; the vital spirits, converted from the natural spirits by the heart, were thought to convey heat and life through the arteries; and the animal spirits, converted from the vital spirits by the brain, were thought to distribute the power of motion and feeling through the nerves.

STAGIRITE   Aristotle (from his birthplace Stagira, a city of ancient Macedonia)

STAR CHAMBER, THE   a secret court, much employed by Charles I, consisting of members of the Privy Council and two judges of the courts of common law but not a jury, that was abolished by Parliament in 1641

STATE   majesty; stately procession; canopy

STILL   constantly, always

STORE   plenty, abundance

STORY   history, narration

STOUT   brave, proud

STRANGER   foreigner

SUCCESS   result, outcome (good or bad)

SUGGEST   tempt

SUGGESTION   prompting or incitement to evil, temptation

TAKE   charm, captivate

TALL   brave, stately

TASSO, TORQUATO (1544–95)   Italian poet, author of the epic *Gerusalemme Liberata* (1575), various poems and plays, and three *Discorsi dell'Arte Poetica*

TELL   count

TEMPLE, THE, see INNS OF COURT

TENDER   esteem

THAN   then

THOROUGH   through

THROUGH(LY)   thorough(ly)

TIMELESS   untimely

TOWER   *v.*, soar; *n.*, lofty flight (terms from falconry)

TULLY, see CICERO

TWENTITH   twentieth

TYPE   in theology, that by which something or someone is anticipated or prefigured. Thus Joshua was regarded as a type of Christ (as was Hercules) and the Jewish sacrifice of the paschal lamb as a type of the Christian Eucharist, etc.

UNCOUTH   unfamiliar, unknown; rustic

UNKIND(LY)   unnatural(ly)

URANIA   the Muse of astronomy, often associated with religious inspiration

USE   be accustomed

UTTER   outer

VALURE   valor

VERGIL   Publius Vergilius Maro (70–19 B.C.), Roman poet, author of the *Aeneid*

VERGIL, POLYDORE (1470?–?1555)   emigrated Italian humanist and ecclesiastic whose *Anglicae historiae* (1534, 1555), undertaken with the patronage of Henry VII, was both a major source of later Tudor chronicles and a common object of vituperation because of its aspersions on Geoffrey of Monmouth (*q.v.*) and the legendary history of Britain

VILLIERS, GEORGE, see BUCKINGHAM, DUKE OF

VIRTUE   strength, natural power

VIVES, JUAN LUIS (1492–1540)   Spanish humanist and philosopher

VULGAR   popular, common, widely known

WANT   lack

WEED   garment

WESTMINSTER ASSEMBLY, THE   an "Assembly of Divines" that, by Parliamentary statute, met from 1643 to 1649 to debate religious and theological questions. Under the domination of the Presbyterians it became, as Milton and other Independents (*q.v.*) thought, a reactionary body.

WHAN   when

WHENAS   when

WHICH   who

WILL   intention, desire

WINK   close both eyes

WIT   intelligence, native ability

WITHAL   moreover, nevertheless

WOOD   mad

WORSHIP   honor

WRACK   wreck

General Bibliography

The titles in the following bibliography are arranged alphabetically by authors to correspond to the five principal rubrics whereby the texts are organized:

I. Poetry
II. Philosophy and Speculation
III. Religion and Politics
IV. Books and Men
V. History and Historiography

Regrettably, the revision now in progress of *The Cambridge Bibliography of English Literature* (ed. F. W. Bateson, 4 vols., 1940) has not yet reached our period, but Volume I of that great work is still essential, as are its *Supplement* (ed. George Watson, 1957) and the bibliographies in Douglas Bush's *English Literature of the Earlier Seventeenth Century* (2d ed., 1962). Among annual publications are *The Year's Work in English Studies* (English Association, 1919–), *Annual Bibliography of English Language and Literature* (Modern Humanities Research Association, 1920–), and the bibliographies in *PMLA* (1922) and *Studies in Philology* (1922–). Other listings or reviews of books within our period may be found in *Bibliothèque d'humanisme et renaissance, Seventeenth-Century News,* and *Renaissance Quarterly.* The following abbreviations have been used throughout the introductions:

ELH *English Literary History*
ELR *English Literary Renaissance*
HLQ *Huntington Library Quarterly*
JEGP *Journal of English and Germanic Philology*
JHI *Journal of the History of Ideas*
MLQ *Modern Language Quarterly*
MP *Modern Philology*
PQ *Philological Quarterly*
RES *Review of English Studies*
SP *Studies in Philology*

I. POETRY

Allen, Don Cameron. *Image and Meaning: Metaphoric Traditions in Renaissance Poetry.* Rev. ed., 1968.

Alvarez, Alfred. *The School of Donne.* 1961.

Bennett, Joan. *Five Metaphysical Poets: Donne, Herbert, Vaughan, Crashaw, Marvell.* 1964.

Berry, Lloyd E. *Bibliography of Studies in Metaphysical Poetry.* 1964.

Bradbury, Malcolm and David Palmer (eds.). *Metaphysical Poetry.* 1969. A collection of essays.

Bush, Douglas. *Mythology and the Renaissance Tradition in English Poetry.* 1932.

Cruttwell, Patrick. *The Shakespearean Moment and Its Place in the Poetry of the 17th Century.* 1954.

Doughty, William L. *Studies in the Religous Poetry of the Seventeenth Century.* 1947.

Duncan, J. E. *The Revival of Metaphysical Poetry: The History of a Style.* 1959.

Eliot, T. S. *Selected Essays.* 1932.

Ellrodt, Robert. *Les Poètes métaphysiques anglais.* 2 vols., 1960.

Ford, Boris (ed.). *From Donne to Marvell.* 1956. Essays on literary history.

Freeman, Rosemary. *English Emblem Books.* 1947.

Giamatti, A. Bartlett. *The Earthly Paradise and the Renaissance Epic.* 1966.

Greg, W. W. *Pastoral Poetry and Pastoral Drama.* 1906.

Grierson, H. J. C. *Cross Currents in English Literature of the Seventeenth Century.* 1929.

Grundy, Joan. *The Spenserian Poets: A Study in Elizabethan and Jacobean Poetry.* 1969.

Halewood, William H. *The Poetry of Grace: Reformation Themes and Structures in Seventeenth-Century English Verse.* 1970.

Howarth, R. G. (ed.). *Minor Poets of the 17th Century.* Everyman's Library, rev. 1953. Substantial selections from Lord Herbert, Carew, Suckling, and Lovelace.

Hunter, J. M. *The Metaphysical Poets.* 1965.

Jonas, Leah. *The Divine Science: The Aesthetics of Some Representative Seventeenth-Century English Poets.* 1940.

Keast, William R. (ed.). *Seventeenth-Century Poetry: Modern Essays in Criticism.* 1962.

Kermode, Frank (ed.). *The Metaphysical Poets.* 1969. A collection of essays.

——— (ed.). *English Pastoral Poetry: From the Beginnings to Marvell.* 1952.

Kurth, B. O. *Milton and Christian Heroism: Biblical Epic Themes and Forms in Seventeenth-Century England.* 1959.

Lanham, Richard A. *A Handlist of Rhetorical Terms.* 1968.

Leishman, J. B. *The Metaphysical Poets: Donne, Herbert, Vaughan, Traherne.* 1934.

Mahood, Molly M. *Poetry and Humanism.* 1950.

Martz, Louis L. *The Paradise Within: Studies in Vaughan, Traherne, and Milton.* 1964.

———. *The Poetry of Meditation: A Study in English Religious Literature of the Seventeenth Century.* 1954.

————. *The Wit of Love: Donne, Carew, Crashaw, Marvell.* 1970.

McEuen, K. A. *Classical Influence upon the Tribe of Ben.* 1939.

Miner, Earl. *The Cavalier Mode from Jonson to Cotton.* 1971.

————. *The Metaphysical Mode from Donne to Cowley.* 1969.

Partridge, A. C. (ed.). *The Tribe of Ben: Pre-Augustan Classical Verse in English.* 1970. An anthology.

Piper, William B. *The Heroic Couplet.* 1969.

Praz, Mario. *Studies in Seventeenth-Century Imagery.* 2d ed., 1964.

Ross, M. M. *Poetry & Dogma: The Transfiguration of Eucharistic Symbols in Seventeenth-Century English Poetry.* 1954.

Sharp, Robert L. *From Donne to Dryden: The Revolt against Metaphysical Poetry.* 1940.

Skelton, Robin. *Cavalier Poets.* 1960. Carew, Suckling, Lovelace, Waller.

Sonnino, Lee Ann. *A Handbook of Sixteenth-Century Rhetoric.* 1968.

Spencer, Theodore, and Mark Van Doren. *Studies in Metaphysical Poetry: Two Essays and a Bibliography.* 1939.

Stewart, Stanley. *The Enclosed Garden: The Tradition and the Image in Seventeenth-Century Poetry.* 1966.

Summers, Joseph H. *The Heirs of Donne and Jonson.* 1970.

Swardson, Harold R. *Poetry and the Fountain of Light: Observations on the Conflict between Christian and Classical Traditions in Seventeenth-Century Poetry.* 1962.

Tillyard, E. M. W. *The English Epic and Its Background.* 1954.

————. *The Metaphysicals and Milton.* 1956.

Trimpi, Wesley. *Ben Jonson's Poems: A Study of the Plain Style.* 1962.

Tuve, Rosemond. *Elizabethan and Metaphysical Imagery.* 1947.

Wallerstein, Ruth C. *Studies in Seventeenth-Century Poetic.* 1950.

Walton, Geoffrey. *Metaphysical to Augustan: Studies in Tone and Sensibility in the Seventeenth Century.* 1955.

Wedgwood, Cicely V. *Poetry and Politics under the Stuarts.* 1960.

White, Helen C. *The Metaphysical Poets: A Study in Religious Experience.* 1936.

Willey, Margaret. *Three Metaphysical Poets.* 1961. Crashaw, Vaughan, Traherne.

Williamson, George. *The Donne Tradition.* 1930.

————. *The Proper Wit of Poetry.* 1961.

————. *Seventeenth Century Contexts.* Rev. 1969.

————. *Six Metaphysical Poets: A Reader's Guide.* 1967.

II. PHILOSOPHY AND SPECULATION

Babb, Lawrence. *The Elizabethan Malady: A Study of Melancholia in English Literature from 1580 to 1642.* 1951.

Baker, Herschel. *The Wars of Truth: Studies in the Decay of Christian Humanism in the Earlier Seventeenth Century.* 1952.

Bethell, S. L. *The Cultural Revolution of the Seventeenth Century.* 1951.

Burtt, E. A. *Metaphysical Foundations of Modern Physical Sciences.* Rev. 1932.

Bush, Douglas. *Science and English Poetry.* 1950.

Cassirer, Ernst. *The Platonic Renaissance in England.* Trans. J. P. Pettigrove, 1953.

Colie, Rosalie L. *Paradoxia Epidemica: The Renaissance Tradition of Paradox.* 1966.

Collingwood, R. G. *The Idea of Nature.* 1945.

Craig, Hardin. *The Enchanted Glass: The Elizabethan Mind in Literature.* 1936.

Crombie, A. G. *Augustine to Galileo: The History of Science A.D. 400–1650.* 2d ed., 2 vols., 1954.

Hall, A. R. *The Scientific Revolution 1500–1800: The Foundation of the Modern Scientific Attitude.* 1954.

Harrison, John. *Platonism in English Poetry of the Sixteenth and Seventeenth Centuries.* 1903.

Jones, Richard Foster. *Ancients and Moderns: A Study of the Rise of the Scientific Movement in Seventeenth-Century England.* 2d ed., 1961.

———— et al. *The Seventeenth Century: Studies in the History of English Thought and Literature from Bacon to Pope.* 1969.

Mazzeo, Joseph Anthony. *Renaissance and Revolution: Backgrounds to Seventeenth-Century English Literature.* 1967.

Nicolson, Marjorie H. *The Breaking of the Circle: Studies in the Effect of the "New Science" upon Seventeenth-Century Poetry.* Rev. 1960.

————. *Science and Imagination.* 1956.

Sorley, W. R. *History of English Philosophy.* 1920.

Westfall, R. S. *Science and Religion in Seventeenth-Century England.* 1958.

Whitehead, Alfred North. *Science and the Modern World.* 1925.

Wiley, Margaret L. *The Subtle Knot: Creative Scepticism in Seventeenth-Century England.* 1952.

Willey, Basil. *The English Moralists.* 1964. Chapters on Bacon, Hobbes, the Cambridge Platonists, and Browne.

————. *The Seventeenth Century Background: Studies in the Thought of the Age in Relation to Poetry and Religion.* 1934.

Williamson, George. "Mutability, Decay, and Seventeenth-Century Melancholy," *ELH,* II (1935).

III. RELIGION AND POLITICS

Allen, J. W. *English Political Thought 1603–1660. Vol. I, 1603–44.* 1938.

Barclay, Robert. *The Inner Life of the Religious Societies of the Commonwealth.* 1876.

Barker, Arthur. *Milton and the Puritan Dilemma.* 1942.

Barry, Alfred (ed.). *Masters in English Theology.* 1877.

Bourne, E. C. E. *The Anglicanism of William Laud.* 1947.

Burrage, Champlin. *The Early English Dissenters . . . (1550–1641).* 2 vols., 1912.

Campagnac, E. T. (ed.). *The Cambridge Platonists.* 1901. Selections from Whichcote, Smith, Culverwel.

Clark, Sir G. N. *The Seventeenth Century.* Rev. 1947.

Collinson, Patrick. *The Elizabethan Puritan Movement.* 1967.

Cragg, Gerald R. (ed.). *The Cambridge Platonists.* 1968. Generous selections from all the leading figures.

————. *From Puritanism to the Age of Reason.* 1950.

Davies, Godfrey. *The Early Stuarts, 1603–1660.* Rev. 1959.

Davies, Horton. *The Worship of the English Puritans.* 1948.

Dowden, Edward. *Puritan and Anglican: Studies in Literature.* 1900.

Emerson, Everett H. (ed.). *English Puritanism from John Hooper to John Milton.* 1968. An anthology.

Fink, Zera S. *The Classical Republicans: An Essay in the Recovery of a Pattern of Thought in Seventeenth-Century England.* 2d ed., 1962.

Frank, Joseph. *The Levellers: A History of the Writings of Three Seventeenth-Century Social Democrats: John Lilburne, Richard Overton, William Walwyn.* 1955.

Friedrich, Carl J. *The Age of the Baroque, 1610–1660.* 1952.

Gardiner, S. R. *History of England from the Accession of James I to the Outbreak of the Civil War.* 10 vols., 1863–82.

———. *History of the Great Civil War.* 3 vols., 1886–91; 4 vols., 1893.

———. *History of the Commonwealth and Protectorate.* Rev. ed., 4 vols., 1903.

George, Charles H. and Katherine. *The Protestant Mind of the English Reformation 1570–1640.* 1961.

Gooch, G. P. *English Democratic Ideas in the Seventeenth Century.* Rev. H. J. Laski, 1927.

———. *Political Thought in England from Bacon to Halifax.* 1915.

Haller, William. *Liberty and Reformation in the Puritan Revolution.* 1955.

———. *The Rise of Puritanism.* 1938.

——— (ed.). *Tracts on Liberty in the Puritan Revolution 1638–1647.* 3 vols., 1933–34.

——— and Godfrey Davies (eds.). *The Leveller Tracts 1647–1653.* 1944.

Henson, H. H. *Puritanism in England.* 1912.

———. *Studies in English Religion in the Seventeenth Century.* 1903.

Hill, Christopher. *The English Revolution, 1640.* 2d ed., 1949.

———. *God's Englishman: Oliver Cromwell and the English Revolution.* 1970.

———. *Intellectual Origins of the English Revolution.* 1965.

———. *Puritanism and Revolution: Studies in Interpretation of the English Revolution of the 17th Century.* 1958.

———. *Society and Puritanism in Pre-Revolutionary England.* 1964.

Hughes, Phillip. *Rome and the Counter-Reformation in England.* 1942.

Jones. I. D. *The English Revolution 1603–1714.* 1931.

Jordan, W. K. *The Development of Religious Toleration in England.* 4 vols., 1932–40.

———. *Philanthropy in England 1480–1660.* 3 vols., 1959–61.

Knappen, M. M. *Tudor Puritanism.* 1939.

Knights, L. C. *Drama & Society in the Age of Jonson.* 1937.

Mackie, John Duncan. *Cavalier and Puritan.* Rev. 1936.

Maclure, Millar. *The Paul's Cross Sermons 1534–1642.* 1958.

Mason, J. E. *Gentlefolk in the Making: Studies in the History of English Courtesy Literature and Related Topics from 1531 to 1774.* 1935.

Mathew, David. *The Social Structure in Caroline England.* 1948.

Mazzeo, Joseph. *Renaissance and Seventeenth-Century Studies.* 1964.

McAdoo, Henry R. *The Spirit of Anglicanism: A Survey of Anglican Theological Method in the Seventeenth Century.* 1965.

———. *The Structure of Caroline Moral Theology.* 1949.

McIlwain, C. H. (ed.). *The Political Works of James I.* 1918.

Miller, P. G. E. *The New England Mind: The Seventeenth Century.* 1939.

——— and T. H. Johnson (eds.). *The Puritans.* 1938. An anthology.

Mitchell, W. Fraser. *English Pulpit Oratory from Andrewes to Tillotson.* 1932.

More, Paul Elmer, and F. L. Cross (eds.). *Anglicanism: The Thought and Practice of the Church of England, Illustrated from the Religious Literature of the Seventeenth Century.* 1935.

Muirhead, J. H. *The Platonic Tradition in Anglo-Saxon Philosophy.* 1931.

Murdock, Kenneth B. *The Sun at Noon: Three Biographical Sketches.* 1939. Elizabeth Cary, Viscountess Falkland; Lucius Cary, Viscount Falkland; John Wilmot, Earl of Rochester.

Nuttall, Geoffrey. *Visible Saints: The Congregational Way, 1640–1660.* 1957.

Patrides, C. A. (ed.). *The Cambridge Platonists.* 1969. Selections from Whichcote, Smith, More, Cudworth.

Pease, T. C. *The Leveller Movement.* 1916.

Sasek, L. A. *The Literary Temper of the English Puritans.* 1961.

Stone, Lawrence. *The Crisis of the Aristocracy, 1558–1641.* 1965.

Stranks, Charles J. *Anglican Devotion: Studies in the Spiritual Life of the Church of England between the Reformation and the Oxford Movement.* 1961.

Tatham, G. B. *The Puritans in Power: A Study in the History of the English Church from 1640 to 1660.* 1913.

Trevelyan, G. M. *England under the Stuarts.* 21st ed., 1949.

Trevor-Roper, H. R. *Archbishop Laud, 1573–1645.* 1940.

———. *The Crisis of the Seventeenth Century: Religion, the Reformation, and Social Change.* 1967.

Tulloch, John. *Rational Theology and Christian Philosophy in England in the Seventeenth Century.* Rev. ed., 2 vols., 1874.

Usher, Ronald G. *Reconstruction of the English Church.* 2 vols., 1910.

Wakefield, Gordon S. *Puritan Devotion.* 1957.

Wedgwood, Cicily V. *A Coffin for King Charles.* 1964.

———. *The Great Rebellion: The King's Peace, 1637–1641: The King's War, 1641–1647.* 2 vols., 1955–59.

Wilson, John F. *Pulpit in Parliament: Puritanism during the English Civil War, 1640–1648.* 1969.

Wolfe, D. M. *Milton in the Puritan Revolution.* 1941.

Woodhouse, A. S. P. (ed.). *Puritanism and Liberty: Being the Army Debates (1647–9) from the Clarke Manuscripts with Supplementary Documents.* 1938.

Yale, George. *The Independents in the English Civil War.* 1958.

IV. BOOKS AND MEN

Adolph, Robert. *The Rise of Modern Prose Style.* 1968.

Atkins, J. W. H. *English Literary Criticism: 17th and 18th Centuries.* 1951.

Bennett, H. S. *English Books and Readers: 1603 to 1640.* 1970.

Boyce, Benjamin. *The Polemic Character 1640–1661.* 1955.

———. *The Theophrastan Character in England to 1642.* 1947.

Clark, Donald L. *John Milton at St. Paul's School: A Study of Ancient Rhetoric in English Renaissance Education.* 1948.

———. *Rhetoric and Poetry in the Renaissance.* 1922.

Croll, Morris W. *"Attic" and Baroque Prose Style.* Ed. J. Max Patrick *et al.,* 1969.

Fisch, Harold. "The Puritans and the Reform of Prose-style." *ELH,* XIX (1952).

Fish, Stanley E. (ed.). *Seventeenth Century Prose: Modern Essays in Criticism.* 1971.

Gilbert, A. H. (ed.). *Literary Criticism: Plato to Dryden.* 1940.

Greenough, C. N., and J. M. French. *Bibliography of the Theophrastan Character in English.* 1947.

Howell, W. S. *Logic and Rhetoric in England, 1500–1700.* 1956.

Jones, Richard Foster. *The Triumph of the English Language: A Survey of Opinions Concerning the Vernacular from the Introduction of Printing to the Restoration.* 1953.

Krapp, G. P. *The Rise of English Literary Prose.* 1915.

MacDonald, Hugh (ed.). *Portraits in Prose: A Collection of Characters.* 1947.

MacDonald, W. L. *Beginnings of the English Essay.* 1914.

Morley, Henry (ed.). *Character Writings of the Seventeenth Century.* 1891.

Mulder, John R. *The Temple of the Mind: Education and Literary Taste in Seventeenth-Century England.* 1969.

Noyes, G. E. *Bibilography of Courtesy and Conduct Books in Seventeenth-Century England.* 1937.

Paylor, W. J. (ed.). *The Overburian Characters.* 1936.

Saintsbury, George. *History of English Criticism.* 1911.

———. *History of English Prose Ryhthm.* 1912.

Smith, D. Nichol (ed.). *Characters from the Histories and Memoirs of the Seventeenth Century.* 1918.

Spingarn, J. E. (ed.). *Critical Essays of the Seventeenth Century.* 3 vols., 1908–09.

———. *Literary Criticism in the Renaissance.* 2d ed., 1908.

Stauffer, Donald A. *English Biography before 1700.* 1930.

Sypher, Wylie. *Four Stages of Renaissance Style.* 1955.

Thompson, Elbert N. S. *Literary Bypaths of the Renaissance.* 1924. Essays on the character, emblem books, war journalism of the seventeenth century, familiar letters, courtesy books, Thomas Fuller.

———. *The Seventeenth-Century English Essay.* 1924.

Vickers, Brian. *Francis Bacon and Renaissance Prose.* 1968.

Wallace, K. R. *Francis Bacon on Communication and Rhetoric.* 1943.

Webber, Joan. *The Eloquent "I": Style and Self in Seventeenth-Century Prose.* 1968.

Williamson, George. *The Senecan Amble: A Study in Prose Form from Bacon to Collier.* 1951.

Wilson, F. P. *Elizabethan and Jacobean.* 1946.

———. *Seventeenth Century Prose.* 1960.

V. HISTORY AND HISTORIOGRAPHY

Baker, Herschel. *The Race of Time: Three Lectures on Historiography.* 1967.

Brinkley, Roberta Florence. *Arthurian Legend in the Seventeenth Century.* 1932.

Butt, John. "Facilities for Antiquarian Study in the Seventeenth Century," *Essays and Studies of the English Association,* XXIV (1939).

Butterfield, Herbert. *The Englishman and His History.* 1944.

Collingwood, R. G. *The Idea of History.* 1946.

Colson, F. J. "Some Considerations as to the Influence of Rhetoric upon History," *Proceedings of the Classical Association,* XIV (1917).

Davies, Godfrey. *Bibliography of British History: Stuart Period, 1603–1704.* 1928.

Douglas, D. C. *English Scholars 1660–1730.* Rev. 1951.

Evans, Joan. *History of the Society of Antiquaries.* 1956.

Firth, Sir Charles. *Essays Historical and Literary.* 1938.

Fox, Levi (ed.). *English Historical Scholarship in the Sixteenth and Seventeenth Centuries.* 1956.

Friedlaender, Marc. *Growth in the Resources for Studies in Earlier English History, 1534–1625.* 1943.

Fussner, Frank Smith. *The Historical Revolution: English Historical Writing and Thought, 1580–1640.* 1962.

Hanning, Robert W. *The Vision of History in Early Britian: From Gildas to Geoffrey of Monmouth.* 1966.

Kendrick, Sir T. D. *British Antiquity.* 1950.

Kennett, White (ed.). *The Complete History of England.* 3 vols., 1706. Reprints of the histories of Milton, Daniel, Bacon, Lord Herbert, Hayward, Camden, and others.

Levy, F. J. *Tudor Historical Thought.* 1967.

McKisack, May. *Medieval History in the Tudor Age.* 1971.

Nearing, Homer, Jr. *English Historical Poetry 1599–1641.* 1945.

Patrides, C. A. *The Grand Design of God: The Literary Form of the Christian View of History.* 1972.

Pocock, J. G. A. *The Ancient Constitution and the Feudal Law: A Study of English Historical Thought in the Seventeenth Century.* 1957.

Ribner, Irving. *The English History Play in the Age of Shakespeare.* 1957.

Tillyard, E. M. W. *Shakespeare's History Plays.* 1947.

Wright, Louis B. *Middle-Class Culture in Elizabethan England.* 1935.

Index

Authors' names appear in capital letters; titles are in *italics*; and first lines are in roman.

949